THE RIVERSIDE SHAKESPEARE

THE RIVERSIDE

Shakespeare

VOLUME I

TEXTUAL EDITOR

G. Blakemore Evans *Harvard University*

GENERAL INTRODUCTION

Harry Levin *Harvard University*

Herschel Baker *Harvard University*

Anne Barton *Bedford College, London*

Frank Kermode *University College, London*

Hallett Smith *California Institute of Technology*

Marie Edel *Houghton Mifflin Company*

WITH AN ESSAY ON STAGE HISTORY BY

Charles H. Shattuck *University of Illinois*

HOUGHTON MIFFLIN COMPANY BOSTON

Library of Congress Cataloging in Publication Data

Shakespeare, William, 1564-1616.
  The Riverside Shakespeare.

  Issued in a case.
  Bibliography: p.
  I. Evans, Gwynne Blakemore, ed.   II. Title.
PR2754.E9   822.3'3   74-2007
ISBN 0-395-17226-8

The "Through Line Numbers" as established by Charlton Hinman in *The Norton
Facsimile: The First Folio of Shakespeare* and in the forthcoming *Norton Shakespeare*
are copyright © 1968 by W. W. Norton & Company, Inc., and used in this
volume with their permission.

The poem on page 1852 is copyright © 1972 by the University of Chicago.
All rights reserved.

Reproductions of Crown-copyright records in the Public Record Office, London,
appear by permission of H. M. Stationery Office.

Printed in the United States of America

H 10 9 8 7 6 5

Publisher's Preface

In the words of the First Folio of 1623, *The Riverside Shakespeare* is addressed "To the great Variety of Readers. From the most able, to him that can but spell." In the plainer language of our day, this means that the book has been designed with the general reader, the student, and the scholar equally in mind.

The plan of the volume was ambitious from the start. The central spire of its accomplishment is a completely re-edited text, generally modern in spelling and punctuation, yet sensitively reflecting the rhythms and modulations of the Elizabethan voice. This text and its appurtenances, including full textual notes and a history of Shakespeare textual scholarship and editing, is the sole work of G. Blakemore Evans of Harvard University, and will, we believe, stand as a model for generations to come.

In somewhat the manner of Dr. Johnson's preface of 1765, the volume is introduced by a classic statement of the known facts of Shakespeare's life and work, together with the major critical opinions and salient existing problems. This statement, by Harry Levin of Harvard University, will generously reward repeated reading as the reader's knowledge and appreciation grow; it is compact of thought and learning which will yield up their fullest savor with experience and time.

Introductions and explanatory notes to the plays and poems record existing scholarship and criticism, and are rich in original insights. These were provided by a panel of distinguished editors: Herschel Baker of Harvard University for the history plays; Frank Kermode of University College, London, for the tragedies; Hallett Smith of the California Institute of Technology for the romances and the poems; and Anne Barton of Bedford College, London, for the introductions to the comedies. Notes to the comedies, begun by Lloyd E. Berry of the University of Missouri, were completed by Professor Evans and Marie Edel of Houghton Mifflin Company. Professor Evans has also supplied a fully edited and annotated text of those additions to *The Booke of Sir Thomas Moore* which are thought by many to be Shakespeare's and partly written in his hand.

An afterpiece by Charles H. Shattuck of the University of Illinois reviews and assesses the staging and acting of Shakespeare's plays from the Restoration to the present, and ends with a section on Shakespeare in film. Two appendixes by Professor Evans, "Annals, 1552–1616" and "Records, Documents, and Allusions," provide unusually full historical setting and references for the main events of Shakespeare's life and career, and for the main political, literary, and cultural events of Tudor and Jacobean England. And a body of contemporary illustration, provided largely through the researches of Professors Evans and Baker, sheds light on Elizabethan life and thought and will greatly help the student and the general reader to understand and visualize what he reads, over a range from costume to cosmology, from the life of street and tavern to the panoply of place and state.

Over ten years in the making, the project developed a life of its own, with its own vital statistics. The undertaking was jointly conceived and launched by Gordon N. Ray of the John Simon Guggenheim Foundation and Henry F. Thoma of Houghton Mifflin Company. Without the learning and long devotion of Marie Edel, who tirelessly enspirited and oversaw the whole development of the book, the volume could never have seen the light of day. Each of our editors has served beyond the requirements of his task. And each has stood as a model not only of erudition but of grace under pressure and comfort in crisis.

The Riverside Shakespeare began to spread its influence some years before its publication. Its text is the basis for Professor Marvin Spevack's computer-generated *Complete and Systematic Concordance to the Works of Shakespeare*, and for the one-volume *Harvard Concordance to Shakespeare* based on this longer work.

It is with a sense of making a contribution to the culture of this generation, as well as of offering an exemplum of dedication and unselfish accomplishment by our distinguished editors, that Houghton Mifflin Company presents *The Riverside Shakespeare*.

Harold T. Miller, President
Houghton Mifflin Company

Textual Editor's Acknowledgments

The Textual Editor has received, over the years, much special help and advice from friends and colleagues which it is now his happy privilege to acknowledge. Dr. Marie Edel, apart from her own share in this edition, has served throughout as an unofficial general editor, and her learning, critical insight, and infallible eye for detail have placed me, *sine spe*, profoundly in her debt. Our long association has been a continuing source of pleasure to me. Professor Marvin Spevack, who used the present text as the basis for his *Complete and Systematic Concordance to the Works of Shakespeare* (6 vols., 1968–70), has been more than helpful in a variety of ways, particularly in rechecking the accuracy of the text and Textual Notes. To both these friends my gratitude goes far beyond anything I can possibly express. I am further greatly indebted to the unfailing kindness and patience of the staffs of the Houghton Library and the Harvard Theatre Collection, especially to my old friend Dr. William Bond, Director of the Houghton Library, Miss Carolyn Jakeman, Miss Katherine Pantzer, Miss Marte Shaw, and Dr. Jeanne Newlin. Miss Eva Faye Benton, English Librarian at the University of Illinois, also has my special thanks, as do Professors Michael T. Kiernan, Frederick Kiefer, and David George, each of whom in different ways assisted me at need. Finally, to my wife, who with truly Spartan endurance read aloud to me the complete text (including all the punctuation marks!), I offer once again my wondering and loving thanks for her continual support in this and all other things.

G. Blakemore Evans

Contents

Volume I

COMEDIES

HISTORIES

Volume II

TRAGEDIES

ROMANCES

POEMS

List of Illustrations

Volume I

MAPS

Volume II

BLACK-AND-WHITE PLATES

ILLUSTRATIONS IN THE TEXT

Abbreviations

F1, F2, etc. First Folio, Second Folio, etc.

O1, O2, etc. First Octavo, Second Octavo, etc.

Q1, Q2, etc. First Quarto, Second Quarto, etc.

(c) corrected state

(u) uncorrected state

conj. conjecture

om. omit(s), omitted

o.s.d. opening stage direction

s.d(d). stage direction(s)

s.p(p). speech-prefix(es)

subs. substantially

Key to Works Cited

Reference in explanatory and textual notes is in general by last name of editor or author. Not included in the following list of works so cited are editions of individual plays or special studies referred to in the selected bibliographies appended to the "Note on the Text" following each of the plays and poems.

ALEXANDER, Peter, ed., *Works*, 1951

BELL, Robert, ed., Shakespeare's *Poems*, 1855

BENSON, John, *Poems: Written by Wil. Shake-speare. Gent.*, 1640

BOSWELL, James, ed., *Works*, 1821 (21 vols.)

BROOKE, Tucker, ed., *Much Ado about Nothing* (Yale), 1917

BULLEN, Arthur H., ed., *Works*, 1904–7 (10 vols.)

BULLOCH, John, *Studies on the Text of Shakespeare*, 1878

BULLOUGH, Geoffrey, *Narrative and Dramatic Sources of Shakespeare*, 1957–73 (7 vols.)

BUTLER, Samuel, ed., *Shakespeare's Sonnets*, 1899

CAMBRIDGE, *Works*, ed. W. G. Clark and W. A. Wright, 1863–66 (9 vols.); ed. W. A. Wright, 1891–93 (9 vols.)

CAPELL, Edward, ed., *Works*, [1768] (10 vols.)

CAPELL MS, Edward Capell's marked copy of Lintott's edition of Shakespeare's *Poems* (Trinity College, Cambridge)

COLLIER, John P., ed., *Works*, 1842–44 (8 vols.); 1853; 1858 (6 vols.)

COLLIER MS, Perkins' Second Folio, 1632 (Huntington Library)

COLMAN, George, ed., *Dramatick Works of Beaumont and Fletcher*, 1778 (vol. X)

COWDEN CLARKE, Charles and Mary, eds., *Works*, 1864–68 (3 vols.)

COWL, R. P. (with A. E. Morgan), *1 Henry IV* (Arden), 1939

CRAIG, William J., ed., *Works*, 1891

CRAIK, George L., *The English of Shakespeare*, 1857

CROW, John, "Editing and Emending," *Essays and Studies*, n.s., VII (1955), 1–20

DANIEL, P. A., *Notes and Conjectural Emendations*, 1870

DAVENANT, William, *The Rivals*, 1668 (adaptation of *The Two Noble Kinsmen*)
      Macbeth, 1674
      The Law against Lovers (combination of *Measure for Measure*
      and *Much Ado about Nothing*)

DAVENANT-DRYDEN, John Dryden and William Davenant, *The Tempest: or the Enchanted Island*, 1669

DAVENPORT, A., "Notes on *King Lear*," *N & Q*, n.s., CXCVIII (1953), 20–22

DEIGHTON, K., ed., *Timon of Athens* (Arden), 1905

DELIUS, Nicolaus, ed., *Works*, 1854–60 (7 vols.); 1872 (2 vols.)

DERING MS, Sir Edward Dering, *Henry IV* (two parts combined) (Folger MS. V. b. 34), ed. G. W. Williams and G. B. Evans, 1973

DOUAI MS (*Twelfth Night*, *As You Like It*, *Comedy of Errors*, *Romeo and Juliet*, *Julius Caesar*, *Macbeth*), Douai MS. 7.87, in the Douai Public Library (see G. B. Evans, *PQ*, XLI [1962], 158–72).

DREW, Philip, "A Suggested Reading in *Measure for Measure*," *SQ*, IX (1958), 202–4

DYCE, Alexander, ed., *Works*, 1857 (6 vols.); 1864–67 (9 vols.); 1875–76 (9 vols.)
      Works of Beaumont and Fletcher, 1843–46 (11 vols.)

EDWARDS, Thomas, *The Canons of Criticism*, 1748

ELN, *English Language Notes*

EVANS, Thomas, ed., Shakespeare's *Poems*, [1775]

EWING, Thomas, ed., Shakespeare's *Poems*, 1771

FARMER, Richard, in *Works* (Johnson-Steevens), 1773

FOLGER MS: (*Julius Caesar*) Folger Shakespeare Library, MS. V. a. 85 (see G. B. Evans, *JEGP*, XLI [1942], 401–17); (*Merry Wives of Windsor*) MS. V. a. 73

FURNESS, H. H., ed., *New Variorum Edition*, 1871–1928 (vols. 1–15; vols. 16–21 by H. H. Furness, Jr.)

GENTLEMEN, Francis, ed., *Poems Written by Shakespeare*, 1774

GILDON, Charles, ed., Shakespeare's *Poems*, 1710; 1714

GLOBE, ed. William G. Clark and W. A. Wright, *Works*, 1864

HALLIWELL, James O., ed., *Works*, 1853–65 (16 vols.)

HANMER, Thomas, ed., *Works*, 1743–44 (6 vols.); 1745; 1770–71 (6 vols.)

HARNESS, William, ed., *Works*, 1825 (8 vols.)

HARRISON, G. B., ed., *Works* (Penguin), 1937–56 (37 vols.)

HART, H. C., ed., *Love's Labour's Lost* (Arden), 1906

HEATH, Benjamin, *Revisal of Shakespeare's Text*, 1765

HERFORD, Charles H., ed., *Works*, 1899 (10 vols.)
      The Two Noble Kinsmen (Temple), 1897

HINMAN, Charlton, *The Printing and Proof-Reading of the First Folio of Shakespeare*, 1963 (2 vols.)

HOPKINSON, A. F., ed., *The Two Noble Kinsmen*, 1894

HOUSMAN, R. F., *A Collection of English Sonnets*, [1835]

HUDSON, Henry N., ed., *Works*, 1851–56 (11 vols.); 1880–81 (20 vols.)

HUNTER, John, ed., *Macbeth*, 1870

JEGP, *Journal of English and Germanic Philology*

JENNENS, Charles, ed., *Hamlet* (1773), *Julius Caesar* (1773, 1774), *King Lear* (1770), *Macbeth* (1773), *Othello* (1773)

JOHNSON, Samuel, ed., *Works*, 1765 (2 eds., 8 vols.); 1768 (8 vols.)

KEIGHTLEY, Thomas, ed., *Works*, 1864 (6 vols.)

KELLNER, Leon, *Restoring Shakespeare*, 1925

KITTREDGE, George L., ed., *Works*, 1936

KNIGHT, Charles, ed., *Works*, 1838–43 (8 vols.); 1842–44 (12 vols.)

LANSDOWNE, George Granville, Lord Lansdowne, *The Jew of Venice* (adaptation of *The Merchant of Venice*); 1701

LEISI, Ernst, ed., *Measure for Measure*, 1964

Lintott, Bernard, ed., Shakespeare's *Poems*, [1709] (2 vols.); [1711] (2 vols.)

Littledale, Harold, ed., *The Two Noble Kinsmen* (New Shakespeare Society), 1876, 1885

Macmillan, Michael, ed., *Julius Caesar* (Arden), 1942

Malone, Edmond, ed., *Works*, 1790 (10 vols.)

Mason, John Monck, *Comments on . . . Shakespeare's Plays*, 1785

MLR, *Modern Language Review*

Munro, John, ed., *Works* (The London Shakespeare), 1958 (6 vols.)

Murden, A. (R. Newton et al.), *Poems* [Shakespeare's] *on Several Occasions*, [1760?]

Neilson, William A., ed., *Works*, 1906

Neilson-Hill, *Works*, ed. W. A. Neilson and C. J. Hill, 1942

N & Q, *Notes and Queries*

O.E.D., *Oxford English Dictionary*

Onions, C. T., *A Shakespeare Glossary* (2nd ed. revised), 1953

Oulton, W. C., ed., Shakespeare's *Poems*, 1804 (2 vols.)

Padua prompt-book (*Macbeth, Measure for Measure, The Winter's Tale*) in *Shakespearean Prompt-Books of the Seventeenth Century*, ed. G. B. Evans, 1960–63 (vols. I and II)

PBSA, Papers of the Bibliographical Society of America

Pelican, *Works*, general ed. Alfred Harbage (rev. 1-vol. ed.), 1969

PQ, *Philological Quarterly*

Pope, Alexander, ed., *Works*, 1723–25 (6 vols.); 1728 (8 vols.)

Rann, Joseph, ed., *Works*, 1786–[94] (6 vols.)

Reed, Edward B., ed., *Shakespeare's Sonnets* (Yale), 1923

Reed, Isaac, ed., *Works*, 1803 (21 vols.); 1813 (21 vols.)

RES, *Review of English Studies*

Ridley, M. R., ed., *Works* (New Temple), 1935–36 (40 vols.)

Ringler, William, "Exit Kent," *SQ*, XI (1960), 311–17

Ritson, Joseph, *Remarks, Critical and Illustrative . . . on the Last Edition of Shakespeare*, 1778

Roderick, Richard, *Remarks on Shakespear* (in Thomas Edwards, *Canons of Criticism*, 6th ed.), 1758

Rolfe, W. J., ed., *The Two Noble Kinsmen*, 1883

Rowe, Nicholas, ed., *Works*, 1709 (2 eds., 6 vol.); 1714 (8 vols.)

SB, *Studies in Bibliography*

Schmidt, Alexander, *Shakespeare-Lexicon* (2 vols., 4th ed., rev. G. Sarrazin), 1923

Seward, Thomas (see Theobald, *Works of Beaumont and Fletcher*, 1750)

Sewell, George, ed., Shakespeare's *Poems*, 1725; 1728

Seymour, E. H., *Remarks . . . upon the Plays of Shakespeare*, 1805 (2 vols.)

Singer, S. W., ed., *Works*, 1826 (10 vols.); 1855–56 (10 vols.)

Sisson, Charles, ed., *Works*, 1954

Skeat, Walter W., ed., *The Two Noble Kinsmen*, 1875

Smock Alley prompt-book (*Hamlet, Macbeth, Othello, King Lear, Twelfth Night, A Midsummer Night's Dream, Henry VIII, 1 Henry IV, The Comedy of Errors, The Merry Wives of Windsor, The Winter's Tale*), Smock Alley Theatre, Dublin (see G. B. Evans, ed., *Shakespearean Prompt-Books of the Seventeenth Century*, 1960–70 [vols. I, IV, V]

SP, *Studies in Philology*

SQ, *Shakespeare Quarterly*

State Poems, *Poems on Affairs of State*, 1707

Staunton, Howard, ed., *Works*, 1858–60 (3 vols.)

Steevens, George, ed., *Works*, 1773 (with Samuel Johnson, 10 vols.); 1778 (10 vols.); 1793 (15 vols.)

Sympson, J. (see Theobald, *Works of Beaumont and Fletcher*, 1750)

Theobald, Lewis, ed., *Works*, 1733 (7 vols.); 1740 (8 vols.); 1757 (8 vols.)
> (with Thomas Seward and J. Sympson), *Works of Beaumont and Fletcher*, 1750 (vol. X: *The Two Noble Kinsmen*)

THIRLBY, Styan (see THEOBALD, *Works*, 1733)

TLS, (London) *Times Literary Supplement*

TONSON, J., *The Works of Mr. Francis Beaumont and Mr. John Fletcher*, 1711 (vol. VII)

TYRRELL, Henry, ed., *Works*, 1850–53 (4 vols.)

TYRWHITT, Thomas, *Observations and Conjectures upon Some Passages of Shakespeare*, 1766

UPTON, John, *Critical Observations on Shakespeare*, 1747

VAUGHAN, Henry B., *New Readings . . . of Shakespeare's Tragedies*, 1878–86 (3 vols.)

WALKER, William S., *Critical Examination of the Text of Shakespeare*, 1860 (3 vols.)

WARBURTON, William, ed., *Works*, 1747 (8 vols.)

WHITE, Richard Grant, ed., *Works*, 1857–66 (12 vols.); 1883 (6 vols.)

WILSON, John Dover (with A. Quiller-Couch et al.), ed., *Works* (New Cambridge), 1921–66 (39 vols.)

THE RIVERSIDE SHAKESPEARE

General Introduction

Harry Levin

I. THE SHAKESPEAREAN HERITAGE

Now and again the observation is offered about a great writer that he has created a world of his own. Such artificial worlds are necessarily smaller than the one we live in; otherwise they would not help us much to understand it; like a map, they locate situations by reducing them to a comprehensible scale. Lifelike and large as these representations of truth may seem to us, they are limited nonetheless by the means and motives of their creation. Yet the writers whom we regard as the very greatest have a way of surpassing limitations by convincing us that their range of perception is just as wide, and their sense of reality just as authentic, as anything that we are ever likely to encounter during the course of our own experience. So the ancients placed Homer in a unique position because his epic outlook seemed to be coextensive with the breadth and depth of the world they knew. Similarly, for the Middle Ages, all the circumstances of human existence were summed up in the luminous vision of Dante. Since then man's horizons have so enlarged and his problems have so complicated themselves that, although he still can find much beauty and significance in the poetry of Homer and Dante, they have long since ceased to serve as his active guides. Indeed, if it were not for Shakespeare, we might well doubt whether any single creative genius could have encompassed so much of the variety, the profundity, and the abundance of life as it has been lived in the modern era of civilization.

Shakespeare's works have therefore been accorded a place in our culture above and beyond their topmost place in our literature. They have been virtually canonized as humanistic scriptures, the tested residue of pragmatic wisdom, a general collection of quotable texts and usable examples. Reprinted, reedited, commented upon, and translated into most languages, they have preempted more space on the library shelves than the books of—or about—any other author. Meanwhile they have become a staple of the school and college curricula, as well as the happiest of hunting-grounds for scholars and critics. As plays they continue to meet the one decisive criterion by maintaining their importance in the dramatic repertory, all the way from Harlem to Uzbekistan, and to provide the roles that leading actors compete in when they seek to demonstrate their talents. Ever since David Garrick staged his Stratford Jubilee of 1769, Shakespeare's native town has been a shrine for literary pilgrims; more recently its festival has come to set a standard for Shakespearean productions; and now the cult has spread to transatlantic Stratfords in Ontario and Connecticut, not to mention regular performance at innumerable theatres elsewhere. If all this seems to smack too uncritically of ritual observance and traditional piety, we should be reminded that Shakespearean drama has continually renewed itself through adaptation to changing times. It has adapted not only to contemporary dress but to current issues; thus the conflicts of the Roman plays have been sharpened by the political pressures of the twentieth century.

Shakespeare showed prophetic insight into his own future when, looking back to Rome in *Julius Caesar*, he allowed his Cassius to look ahead down the centuries to come:

How many ages hence
Shall this our lofty scene be acted over
In states unborn and accents yet unknown!

(III.i.113–15)   1

The leading spirit among his fellow dramatists, Ben Jonson, also foresaw that triumphant survival when he prefaced Shakespeare's First Folio with the poetic tribute: "He was not of an age, but for all time!" But Jonson, who was well aware that such universality must have its basis in a firm grasp of immediacy, had begun his poem by hailing Shakespeare as the major voice of his time: "Soul of the Age!" Few of his contemporaries had been quite so magnanimous or far-seeing. The earliest critical recognition of his career had been a truculent outburst from Robert Greene, hack-writing upon his very deathbed in 1592, and denouncing Shakespeare as a young upstart for his presumption in vying with those already established playwrights whom we call the University Wits. That outburst was countered soon enough by a handsome retraction from Greene's editor, Henry Chettle, and the subsequent testimonials from Shakespeare's colleagues suggest their personal affection and professional esteem.[1] In those days, however, merely to be recognized as a playwright was to be rather an artisan than an artist; it did not carry with it any particular standing as a man of letters. His more serious literary pretensions were declared when he brought out his two narrative poems in the classical erotic vein, and when he privately circulated his sonnets, which would be published belatedly under other auspices.

As for the plays, they were the property of the producing company, which had commissioned and bought them outright at ten pounds or so apiece. So long as they were popular on the stage, it would not have been in the company's interest for them to be printed. Sooner or later slightly more than half of them found their way into print, many of these pirated and garbled, through the separate editions known as quartos. Subject to such hazards of publication and to the rigors of censorship, Shakespeare's hand was obscured by anonymity while he was young and unknown, and credited apocryphally with plays by other hands when he was older and famous. On the whole, it is surprising and fortunate that the corpus of his writing has mainly come down to us through so authoritative an edition as the First Folio. Seven years before that landmark appeared, Jonson had braved the scorn of critics for gathering up the plays he had written to date and bringing them out in folio as *Works*—a format and a title which then seemed much too pretentious for mere stage-pieces. Shakespeare's collected volume, edited by two of his fellow actors and theatrical partners, John Heminge and Henry Condell, bore a title simply indicating the disposition of its contents: *Comedies, Histories, and Tragedies.* From its appearance in 1623, seven years after his death, Shakespeare stood among England's principal authors; but through the seventeenth century he shared equal applause with the scholarly Jonson and the courtly John Fletcher; he did not emerge into the light of preeminence until Dryden signalized him

as that writer who possessed "the most comprehensive soul."

The neo-classicists of the eighteenth century, emphasizing that opposition between nature and art which Shakespeare had done so much to reconcile, thought of him as a wholly natural genius who was consequently lacking in conscious artistry. The turning point in the history of his reputation came with the preface to Samuel Johnson's edition of 1765. It was Dr. Johnson who, rescuing Shakespeare from the indignity of being harshly judged by neo-classical rules, insisted on granting him the status of a classic. If his plays followed certain laws of their own, henceforth the path lay open to the discovery of those laws. But the Romantics were as eager to associate him with nature itself as their predecessors had been to distinguish his endeavors from their notions of art. Even Ben Jonson's eulogy had been, as he dryly put it, "on this side idolatry." During the later eighteenth and most of the nineteenth century, Shakespeare's interpreters practiced what Bernard Shaw liked to call "Bardolatry." They all but deified the Bard of Avon because he was the creator of so many characters who could be treated as if they were human beings—could be identified with, psychologized over, arraigned for moral judgment. Shakespeare's full-bodied realism, as opposed to the more formal characterization of continental drama, meanwhile triumphed over the barriers of verse translation. His name became a rallying cry in the campaigns for Romanticism, and his influence contributed to the self-realization of the various national literatures of Europe.

Our century, which has latterly celebrated the four-hundredth anniversary of his birth, has brought him the twelfth generation of his continuing audience. Yet, despite the ever-widening time-span, we may approach him somewhat more closely today than we could have done at intervals in the past. Historical knowledge of his period has helped to bridge the gap, while a comparative view of the drama is helping us to see his work in more extended and clarifying perspective. So much interpretation has surrounded it that we sometimes barely glimpse the forest because of the many screeds which the commentators, like his Orlando, have hung upon the trees. But commentary is useful in alerting us to assumptions or implications we might have missed, and editorial scholarship has learned to correct distortions by removing encrustations. It is the purpose of this introduction, and of the comments that herewith introduce and accompany Shakespeare's texts, to set them into their most meaningful contexts. Universal as his attraction has been, it is best understood through particulars. Though—to our advantage—his creations are relatively timeless, they would not mean so much to us if they had not been timely in their day. Nor would they have made their lasting impact, if their author had not been past master of his exacting and exciting medium, linguistic, poetic, dramatic. Since that mastery was the ripe attainment of an individual mind, we owe some attention to the man in his time before turning to the materials and techniques of his art.

[1] The passages from Greene and Chettle, together with various other biographical and critical documents referred to in this essay, are reprinted in Appendix B below.

II. THE BIOGRAPHICAL RECORD

Contrary to a fairly widespread impression, there is no special mystery about his life. Indeed it is unusually well documented, for a commoner's of his period. Unfortunately for our personal curiosity, most of this documentation takes the colorless form of entries in parish registers or municipal archives, legal instruments involving property, all too fragmentary theatrical records, and a few business letters to or about him. The biographical outline provided by more than a hundred such documents is filled in by well over fifty literary allusions to Shakespeare and his works in the published writings of contemporaries. But these details, even when they have been eked out by traditions and conjectures, scarcely combine to portray a vivid personality. Modern readers, accustomed by the Romantics to poets who lived their poems and dramatized their lives, have felt somewhat put off by the undramatic nature of the dramatist's private career. The figure of Shakespeare as a practical man of affairs, although well attested by the evidence, seemed rather too modest to occupy the lofty pedestal reared by the Bardolaters. Hence the strange proliferation of irresponsible theories proposing rival candidates for the authorship of Shakespeare's work, most of them titled and all of them colorful but none of them circumstanced to have done the job—as William Shakespeare indubitably was. His existence should not seem uneventful if we consider that its main events were the thirty-eight plays created, in rapid succession and brilliant diversity, within a span of less than twenty-five years.

The first recorded fact under the family name at Stratford-on-Avon is neither inspiring nor revealing: it is the imposition of a fine upon the poet's father for countenancing a dunghill too near the house and shop on Henley Street that would be pointed out as Shakespeare's birthplace. What would be truly significant was the son's lifelong connection with the prosperous and picturesque market town in the rich heart of rural England. He was a country boy, and he kept returning to the Warwickshire countryside, like the fabled giant who renewed his energies by touching his native soil. North of the winding Avon lay the Forest of Arden, which must have cast some shade on the woodland scenes of *As You Like It*, even though the play introduces tropical flora and fauna, and is linked by verbal associations with the Franco-Belgian Ardennes. The association that means most here, however, is the fact that Shakespeare's mother had been Mary Arden, and that her yeoman family was related to those Ardens who held large estates nearby. Her husband, John Shakespeare, son of a local tenant farmer, was by trade a glover or leatherworker. He became one of Stratford's leading citizens, was elected a burgess or member of the town council, acted as magistrate and in various civic capacities, and served a brief term as bailiff or mayor during William's infancy. Though John's fortunes declined before his death in 1601, about the time when *Hamlet* was being completed, he lived to be granted the arms and style of a gentleman, probably through the endeavors and the successes of his son.

Thus, like many good English families, the Shakespeares made the transition from the status of tradesman to that of esquire during the reign of Queen Elizabeth. The name of their eldest son William appears first on record under the date of his baptism, April 26, 1564, at the Church of the Holy Trinity, where he was to be buried just fifty-two years afterward. Since the day of his death in 1616 was (if the inscription on his monument in the church can be trusted) April 23, which is also the holiday of England's patron Saint George, it is coincidentally celebrated as Shakespeare's birthday. Because the sons of burgesses were specifically entitled to free tuition at the local grammar school, it seems most probable that he studied there, absorbing a curriculum strongly based on rhetoric, Christian ethics, and classical literature. He did not go on to attend a university; and, understandably, he would not be regarded as a man of learning by such consciously erudite humanists as Jonson and Milton. But our age is so much less devoted than theirs to the cultivation of the classics that what looked to Jonson like "small Latin and less Greek" might well strike us as a respectable grounding in the humanities. His plays show amply that he was conversant with Latin and French, plus a smattering of other foreign languages, history both ancient (notably Plutarch) and modern (the British chronicles), philosophic speculation (Montaigne), continental fiction such as Boccaccio's, earlier English poets like Chaucer and Gower—not to mention fellow Elizabethans, from the high-minded Sidney to the abusive Greene.

A writer's reading tends to reveal itself most directly through his earliest efforts, and Shakespeare's smell somewhat of the Greco-Roman lamp in their use of quotation and mythological ornament. The prototypes for academic drama, as Polonius would duly observe, were Seneca for tragedy and Plautus for comedy. It is no accident that the apprentice Shakespeare, while feeling his way toward popular dramatic forms of his own, was to experiment with the Senecan *Titus Andronicus* and the Plautine *Comedy of Errors*; and it is noteworthy that Francis Meres, when he attempted a survey of English writers in his *Palladis Tamia* of 1598, cited Shakespeare as the versatile counterpart of both Roman playwrights—also mentioning Ovid as his forerunner in the field of amorous poetry. One of the better-grounded Shakespearean rumors, coming down to us from an actor in his troupe, tells us that he taught Latin for a while as a country schoolmaster. But he has expressed his opinion of pedantry in Holofernes and *Love's Labor's Lost*. The book-learning that Shakespeare displays here and there is far less impressive, in the long run, than his fund of general information. His frame of reference is so far-ranging, and he is so concretely versed in the tricks of so many trades, that lawyers have written to prove he was trained in the law, sailors about his expert seamanship, naturalists upon his botanizing, and so on through the professions. If

3

this be paradox, it is resolved by Fielding's remark that Shakespeare was "learned in human nature." So far as education has genuine meaning, he must be viewed as a genuinely educated man.

Some confusion seems to attend the facts regarding his marriage, but these are too meagre to encourage surmises. We know that a license was obtained on November 27, 1582, that the former Anne Hathaway was eight years his senior, and that their elder daughter Susanna was born six months later and christened on May 26, 1583. But, since the betrothal might have taken place at some previous point, we may allow the couple the benefit of ceremonies timed more casually in their day than in ours. Nor should we infer any reservations about his wife from the one bequest to her in his will: that "second-best bed" may have been hallowed by conjugal sentiments, and she was provided for otherwise through her dower rights. Given the circumstances of his calling, which inevitably centred on London and occasionally branched out into provincial tours, it could be said that he was at some pains to keep up his domestic ties with Stratford. Twin children, Hamnet and Judith, were born there in 1585; Hamnet, his only son, was to die eleven years later. Biography loses sight of Shakespeare during the interval between the birth of the twins and Greene's attack in 1592, but the latter makes it quite explicit that Shakespeare had meanwhile become a player and was already emerging as a playwright. Retrospectively it would seem clear that those crucial seven years had been fully occupied, not to say well spent, in preparing to meet the demands of the theatrical profession and to endow it with a steady sequence of its finest vehicles.

Though he is listed as having appeared in his own plays and Jonson's, we have no account of his acting. The two roles that tradition has assigned to him are secondary, though not uncongenial: the Ghost in *Hamlet* and the old servitor Adam in *As You Like It*. In any case, the fundamental certainty about Shakespeare is that he was a man of the theatre to his fingertips. No titled amateur could have conceivably handled, with such practiced and inventive skill, all the available resources of his professional medium. His craftsmanship as a dramatist was solidly backed, like Molière's, by long experience as an actor-manager—by the manager's sense of the public, as well as the actor's talent for projecting himself into other selves. During the seasons of 1592–3 the plague was making its terrible visitations; and while the London theatres were closed, Shakespeare seems to have been composing his non-dramatic Ovidian poems, *Venus and Adonis* and *The Rape of Lucrece*. When the theatres reopened, he was one of the sharers or partners in a newly organized company under the sponsorship of the Lord Chamberlain, head of the royal household. This company was to dominate the Elizabethan and the Jacobean stage (in the later period under the sponsorship of King James himself), performing publicly at the famous Globe playhouse and for smaller audiences at the Blackfriars. Along with its best-known actors,

Richard Burbage and William Kemp, he received payment for presenting two plays before the Queen at court during the Christmas festivities of 1594.

The Chamberlain's Men had not infrequent occasion to offer such command performances; and after 1603, when the troupe became His Majesty's Servants, its sharers were officially treated as members of the royal household. Shakespeare made other connections with courtly circles, principally through the patronage of the dashing young Earl of Southampton, to whom he had dedicated both of his printed poems. Southampton is one of those actual personages who have been identified with the noble youth addressed in Shakespeare's sonnets. On that theme there has been—in Falstaffian disproportion—an intolerable deal of conjecture to one halfpennyworth of fact. If the sonnets constitute the key with which Shakespeare "unlocked his heart," in Wordsworth's unguarded phrase, then they have opened no secret doors; if they had done so, as Browning retorted, "the less Shakespeare he." To reread them as if they were confessions is to beg a moot question, since there is just as little external support for attempts at other identifications: the Dark Lady, the rival poet. Doubtless Shakespeare could not have dealt so movingly with love and friendship and with literary and sexual rivalry if he had not experienced them in some intimate guise. But his sonnets would differ unbelievably from his plays, and would come suspiciously close to the effusions of more subjective writers, if he had not again been exercising his gift for dramatic projection. The sonneteer's involvement, within his formal genre, is that of the dramatist with his *dramatis personae*. After all, it is he himself who assumes the identities of his characters:

> my nature is subdu'd
> To what it works in, like the dyer's hand.
>
> (Sonnet 111.6–7)

The advance in Shakespeare's worldly fortunes is evident from a number of business transactions. In 1597 he acquired New Place, one of the most substantial residences in Stratford. Gradually he had given up acting for writing; and by his late forties, several years before his relatively early death, he was living in retirement there. His meticulous testament, which remembers his colleagues, seems designed to perpetuate his estate through his elder daughter's progeny. But his line did not survive his grandchildren; for his many living descendants we must look to the drama. His monument, the bust in the chancel of Holy Trinity Church, is thought to be a true—if stylized—portrait. The same benignant features greet the reader from the frontispiece to the Folio. The recurrent word in the testimonials of Shakespeare's friends and acquaintances is "gentle." It characterizes an engaging but self-effacing person who, while remaining impersonal, could penetrate the minds of multitudinous personalities. Coleridge described him as "myriad-minded." Keats suggested how those many aspects must have been integrated when he spoke of "Negative Capability," that quality of sympathetic imagination, that unexampled gift of insight which enabled Shakespeare to empathize with all sorts and conditions of men. It was Keats again who threw light on the symbolic relation between an artist's *modus vivendi* and his artistic achievement, when he succinctly noted: "Shakespeare lived a life of Allegory. His works are the comments on it."

All lives are more or less allegorical, insofar as they relive the cycle of Everyman. Shakespeare's uniqueness lies in his commentary, his memorable power of individualizing those common experiences. The course of his worldly career has sometimes been subdivided into four periods, which were neatly but problematically formulated by Edward Dowden. To label the first period "In the Workshop" and the second "In the World" is cogent enough, since it merely implies an objective development from apprenticeship to maturity through the mastery of a craft. But to call the third phase "Out of the Depths" and the fourth "On the Heights" is to misread the plays by presuming that Shakespeare intended them as successive chapters in a kind of spiritual autobiography. We are less well acquainted with what went into his work than with what came out of it. That there are emotions of despair in *Hamlet* and attitudes of serenity in *The Tempest* we cannot doubt; yet he could not simply have chosen to write tragedies while he was feeling depressed and comedies when a mellower mood came upon him; there were more determining factors, as we shall see. Clearly the man who wrote *Romeo and Juliet* knew what it felt like to be in love. It may be that the author of *King Lear* had known sufferings that brought him near to madness. But, by following that line of rationalization, we reduce it to the absurd presumption that the author of *Macbeth* had committed murder. Whereas the play is an imaginative exercise, a psychological discipline which we undergo with the playwright, who—by conveying what it might feel like to be a murderer—ends by enlarging our consciousness.

III. THE HISTORICAL BACKGROUND

We can follow the development of Shakespeare's work in greater clarity if we view it as a response to, and an expression of, the proud and eventful period in which he lived and for which he constructed the principal monument. To recollect that the year of his birth marked the deaths of both Michelangelo and Calvin is to set him at the zenith of the two great formative movements in the arts and religion that they personify, the Renaissance and the Reformation. The year of his own death also bore witness to Harvey's first lectures on physiology, heralding a momentous succession of new achievements for scientific method. Putting Shakespeare beside his immediate contemporaries, we may note that he was born in the same year as Galileo and died in the same year as Cervantes. Cervantes is said to have written an epitaph for the Middle Ages by demonstrating, through the very first of modern novels, that the invention of gunpowder had exploded the institution

of chivalry. Yet Shakespeare seems to have anticipated that point in *1 Henry IV*, where the antagonistic conceptions of honor advanced by Hotspur and Falstaff run parallel to the ideological argument between Don Quixote and Sancho Panza. And Shakespeare seems to have anticipated Galileo's demonstration that the earth revolves around the sun, which supported the astronomical challenge to the anthropocentric conception of the universe, when Hamlet wrote in his little metaphysical poem addressed to Ophelia:

> Doubt thou the stars are fire,
> Doubt that the sun doth move. . . . (II.ii.116–17)

But heretical doubts were still counterweighed by an orthodox belief that the human race played the central role in a cosmic spectacle, whose interpretation might be sought in the antiquated pseudo-science of astrology, as Sonnet 15 affirms in a characteristically theatrical metaphor:

> That this huge stage presenteth nought but shows
> Whereon the stars in secret influence comment.

The drama is the most social of literary forms, since it stands in so direct a relationship to its audience. Hence it presupposes certain fostering conditions, and its golden ages have been sporadic in finding their conjunctions of time and place: ancient Athens, classical France, baroque Spain, Zen Buddhist Japan, and Shakespeare's lifetime in England. We like to look back on his age as "the spacious times of great Elizabeth." The nostalgic phrase of Queen Victoria's poet laureate, Tennyson, conjures up the national cult of the Virgin Queen, with its emanations of courtly compliment and magnificent pageantry. Elizabethan men of letters vied with courtiers in paying their elaborate respects to the royal coquette, most elaborately in Spenser's *Faerie Queene*. Shakespeare was not remiss in declaring his homage, gallantly alluding to "a fair vestal throned by the west" in *A Midsummer Night's Dream* (II.i.158) and retroactively prophesying blessings for the reign of the newly christened Princess Elizabeth in *Henry VIII* (V.v). But the spaciousness of the times found surer justification in its discoveries, conquests, and hitherto unparalleled geographical expansion. "This England," of which the Bastard Faulconbridge boasts in *King John* (V.vii.112–18) and for which John of Gaunt voices his fears in *Richard II* (II.i.40 ff.), was breathlessly transforming itself from an island off the coast of Europe into a dominant sea power and an emergent colonial empire. Shakespeare was well abreast what was happening; *The Tempest* reenacts a shipwreck encountered by the Virginia Company's fleet; conversely, *Hamlet* and *Richard II* were performed on the East India Company's flagship off the coast of Sierra Leone in 1607.

The imperial trend, which had its prose epic in the voyages chronicled by Hakluyt and Purchas, brought commercial affluence in its wake. But rapidly accumulating wealth, inequitably distributed at best, was by no means a guarantee of widespread economic security; the discontented populace of Shakespeare's Roman plays and the hungry followers of Jack Cade in *2 Henry VI* lend a prefiguring voice to protests against the enclosure of common lands and other social grievances of the sixteenth century. England's main international effort, during the late Middle Ages and the early Renaissance, had been to disentangle the ties that had bound her to France since the Norman Conquest. The rhythm of Shakespeare's history plays, which is agitated by the battles of the Hundred Years' War, accelerates to its patriotic climax with the triumph of Henry V at Agincourt. The long-drawn-out civil conflict, the struggle among the barons over the kingship, had led on through the Wars of the Roses to the attrition of feudal power and the establishment of a more centralized monarchy under the house of Tudor—a consummation which Shakespeare hails at the end of *Richard III*. For him— as for the chroniclers he rather freely followed, the compendious Holinshed and especially the apologist Edward Hall—the Tudors had conjointly inherited the strongest claims of their warring predecessors, the houses of York and Lancaster. Their enthronement seemed to have been providentially ordained to foster the restoration of peace, with the attendant cultural benefits that distinguish a glorious epoch.

Loyal subjects were bound to see the whole historical sequence as the consummation of a legendary design. Shakespeare even envisages a laying-on-of-hands between the last of the Lancastrian kings, the ill-fated Henry VI, and the founder of the Tudor line, the young Earl of Richmond, later to be crowned as Henry VII. Yet the claim of the Lancasters was itself open to question, since their crown had been wrenched away from Richard II by Henry IV, practicing an admixture of force and "policy" (a word which always connotes the intrigues of Machiavellian statecraft). The situation, as Shakespeare has treated it, illustrates the division of loyalties that intensified the complications of king-making and -unmaking. Ideally, God's ruler can do no wrong; he rules by divine right, as the legitimate Richard ineffectually reminds his refractory peers. The blame for his mistakes is largely placed upon his parasitical favorites, those "caterpillars of the commonwealth" (II.iii.166). At all events, there is nothing that could morally justify his dethronement; and the scene of Richard's deposition was considered such political tinder that it was omitted from the earlier quartos of the play. Consequently Henry's rule is regarded by his enemies as a usurpation, though he is much abler than his deposed cousin, and the curse of the Plantagenets hangs heavy over the destinies of the Lancastrians. In their turn the latter yield to the brief and violent Yorkist dynasty, culminating in the nightmarish regime of the arch-usurper Richard III, from which the Tudors bring about England's happy deliverance.

Their strategy was that of the popular monarch, firmly controlling baronial factions, while commanding enthusiastic loyalty from the common people. Shakespeare's commoners are as likely to be misled by demagogues as his kings are by self-serving councillors; but when king and people strive together in mutual confidence, then they fulfill the basic Tudor principle of "commonweal." Unhappily, the ensuing era of stability and prosperity was menaced and riven by religious dissension. The English Reformation, made official at the personal behest of the sovereign, Henry VIII, broke politically with the Roman Catholic Church but did not embrace the theological doctrines of the extreme Puritans. During the short reigns of Henry's son and elder daughter, Edward VI and "Bloody Mary," Catholics and Protestants were successively persecuted, the Queen having married the King of Spain and attempted to revive Catholicism in England. The accession of Henry's younger daughter Elizabeth in 1558 reaffirmed and established the Anglican compromise, while the Tudor dynasty was guided to its culmination through her fortunate gifts, which included longevity. Thus the intellectual climate surrounding Shakespeare was one in which inherited dogmas had been forcibly questioned and strategically modified. Like all Elizabethans, he was —at least nominally—an Anglican whose forebears had been brought up in the Catholic confession. Unlike the majority of contemporary believers, he was tolerant enough to enter into the spirit of both faiths with that "wonderful philosophic impartiality" which Coleridge has discerned in his politics.

The tone of his comedies is sometimes affected by the bustle of current mercantile enterprise; even their foreign settings seem to reflect an increasingly cosmopolitan outlook. Through the resounding series of explorations, exploitations, and naval campaigns against Spain, with the western hemisphere as the grand prize, England was achieving its leadership among nations. The climactic decade of Elizabeth's reign occurred between the defeat of the Spanish Armada in 1588 (*Love's Labor's Lost* jibes at its fallen vainglory in the mock-heroic person of Don Armado) and the return of the Essex expedition from Ireland in 1599 (welcomed in triumphal expectation by the Chorus in the fifth act of *Henry V*). Shakespeare, who was even then moving through the dramatic workshop into a wider world, expressed the upsurging nationalism of those fervent years through his cycle of history plays; all but the belated *Henry VIII* were produced during that decade. But the Irish expedition proved a failure; the brilliant Earl of Essex, long the Queen's favorite, was precipitated from her favor; and, after an abortive conspiracy against her, he was beheaded in 1601. Confronted with an aging Queen, the unsettled problem of her succession, and the mounting unrest at the turn of the century, many anxious and thoughtful Englishmen had pinned their hopes upon him. Possibly Shakespeare had done so; we know that his company's revival of *Richard II*, as a possible incitement to treason, topically figured in Essex's trial. His downfall heralded the approaching transition, as did the concurrent appearance of *Hamlet*.

A modulation, deeper perhaps and sadder and wiser

than the conventionally mellow Elizabethan note, could be heard in the literature of the later fifteen-nineties, as writers turned away from sonnets to satires, cultivated their melancholia, and began to sound the depths of tragedy. It may be symptomatic, if not prophetic, that the typical protagonist of Jacobean drama is rather a disinherited prince than a self-crowned king. James I, who finally succeeded Elizabeth upon her demise in 1603, never approached her in popularity; yet, since he was already King James VI of Scotland, his accession united the crowns of both kingdoms; and, being a conscientious patron of letters, he accorded royal sponsorship to the Shakespearean troupe, as well as to the standard English Bible that perpetuates his name. Shakespeare, for his part, paid homage to the new king with *Macbeth*, not only by choosing a Scottish theme, but more specifically by recalling the legend that traced the Stuart line back to Banquo. Shakespeare's Witches predict a brighter future for the Stuarts than they were to have, and James himself stored up trouble for his successors by promoting a courtly aristocracy and alienating a more and more Puritanical middle class. But the most salient characteristic of Jacobean culture was its devotion to the pursuit of knowledge, which involved the most searching introspection and the most fanciful speculation, along with the ambitious program for science that Bacon outlined in his *Advancement of Learning*. "And New Philosophy," as Donne lamented, "calls all in doubt."

Shakespeare, of course, was a playwright and not a philosopher. Yet drama is dialectic in concrete form; the attitudes and actions of its characters would have little value or meaning if they were not based on certain philosophical premises. Shakespeare's plays are very richly charged with implicit ideas, some of which are made memorably explicit by sententious remarks or purple passages, whose purpose is to keep us well aware of the larger issues and moral implications. One of his fullest statements in this vein, the monologue of Ulysses on "degree" in *Troilus and Cressida* (I.iii.85 ff.), frames his weary Greek heroes against a backdrop as wide as the universe. But this particular universe is the traditional cosmos of Ptolemaic astronomy, where the planets revolve around the earth in concentric orbits, influencing human destiny in ways that the astrologers claimed to interpret. This macrocosm centres upon that microcosm which is man, in whose person the elements are mixed, the humors disposed, and the faculties governed to accord with a similar pattern. Hence King Lear, within his "little world of man" (III.i.10), reproduces the storm that rages upon the heath. His psychological breakdown has its external counterpart in the disintegration of his kingdom. The body politic resembles the human body; the order of physical nature is a visible mirror of the divine order. The age-old conception of a "great chain of being," extending from God through the angels toward mankind and downward to beasts, plants, and inanimate matter, links together all created things. Prospero, through his natural magic, is served by the ethereal Ariel from on high and by the bestial Caliban at the subhuman level.

Given this all-embracing continuity, every creature must adhere to its hierarchic position in order to discharge its preordained function—must, in Ulysses' words, "observe degree, priority, and place." The stars set the universal example, and it is their harmonious functioning that generates the music of the spheres. All is well with societies, families, and individuals when they do their duties and know their places. But when they stray out of orbit, Ulysses warns of disastrous consequences, shifting his comparison from the planetary to the musical plane:

> Take but degree away, untune that string,
> And hark what discord follows. Each thing meets
> In mere oppugnancy: the bounded waters
> Should lift their bosoms higher than the shores,
> And make a sop of all this solid globe. . . .

It seems unlikely that so word-conscious a writer could have penned that last line without a side-glance at the theatre where his plays were being performed; for the Globe was truly a microcosm or little world of man, an artistic replica of the whole human condition. As for its solidity, we are told in *The Tempest* (IV.i.148–58) that Prospero's pageant and "the great globe itself" have been compounded of the same insubstantial fabric, the stuff of dreams. Ulysses, having sketched his ideal world-order, visualizes its impending dissolution, and opens up a harrowing prospect of chaos and anarchy. Similarly, a number of Shakespeare's histories and his tragedies take place in a "time misord'red" (*2 Henry IV*, IV.ii.33) which the hero is called upon to set right, while his comedies revel in timeless disorder until the norms of society are restored by the happy ending. Now, as between a set of professed ideals and the observed realities of experience, there is usually some sort of gap or lag, which tends to widen during critical periods such as the Renaissance, thereby amplifying the dimensions of the tragic or the comic point of view. And if the accepted world view was founded upon an obsolete cosmology, as the scientists were impressively showing, then scholastic traditions could be undermined by experimental approaches and monarchic authority itself would soon be challenged by more democratic ideologies.

The humanism of the Renaissance, with its consciousness of historic renewal, its revivals of the classics and the fine arts, its confidence in the mind, and its embellishment of its material surroundings, was a flowering of plenitude, to be sure; but it was likewise a crisis of uncertainty. It balanced the immediacies of this world against otherworldly values; its enjoyment of the senses quickened the lively spirits of comedy; but its fullness of life was deeply grounded in the inevitability of death, which is the precondition of tragedy. The medieval vision, with its tangible hopes for an afterlife in the next world, found its fulfillment in a *Divine Comedy*. In the Middle Ages tragedies were falls of princes, like Richard II's "sad stories of the death of kings" (III.ii.156). Men's decline from prosperity to adversity taught a moral lesson by manifesting the power of providence and the transience of mere earthly glory. The fickle bitch-goddess Fortune determined the fates of captains and kings, alike with beggars and clowns, through the revolutions of her allegorical wheel. To suffer her slings and arrows had been the sanctioned course; to take arms against them was a novel and tempting alternative. To become the captain of one's fate, to make one's own fortune, to rise in the world by exerting one's will—it is through this dynamic choice that the self-reliant protagonists of Marlowe's plays attain their heroic stature. The individualism of Dr. Faustus, exploring all the available possibilities, recognizes no limits. Shakespeare reveals a more comprehensive awareness of the opposing forces that take the measure of the individual, and of the resulting interplay between character and destiny.

The exclamation of Hamlet, "What a piece of work is a man!" (II.ii.303), carries an ironic reverberation. His melancholy gaze looks up and down: skyward toward "this brave o'erhanging firmament" and earthward toward the grave. Those two portraits which he shows to the Queen illustrate man's potentialities for good and for evil. The scale ascends or descends with the spiritual and carnal aspects of his dual nature; he can aspire to be a godlike Hyperion or else can grovel like a brutal satyr. Hamlet's existential dilemma echoes the self-interrogations of Montaigne, not merely through the language of John Florio's translation but in its ambiguous balance between scepticism and faith. Though the supernatural is invoked and evoked throughout Shakespeare's work, it remains—as it doubtless should—an ultimate mystery. We are mystified with Hamlet over questions which were highly problematic in Shakespeare's day; we share the suspense over whether the Ghost is real or false, and whether it has been sent from heaven, purgatory, or hell. With Lady Macbeth we suspect that the apparition of Banquo may be a subjective phenomenon, while the "dagger of the mind" (II.i.38) might conceivably be the playwright's expressionistic device for conveying Macbeth's remorse of conscience. As for the Witches, though they foretell the outcome, they do not control it, since their prophecies are equivocations and Macbeth is free to choose at every stage. Omens and dreams portending catastrophes, though they are often greeted with disbelief, charge the air with fatality when they come true.

Most of the plays, unfolding within a Biblical frame of reference, broadly conform to the tenets of Christianity: witness the enforced conversion of Shylock the Jew. Yet *King Lear* deliberately reverts to a pre-Christian Britain, where the gods are pluralized and supplicated by pagan names, and where the enigma of their relation to men is argued back and forth: is it supernal grace or naturalistic indifference, poetic justice or cosmic irony? Moreover, the characters in the Roman plays are measured by the ethics of Stoicism. Suicide is denounced in the tragedies subject to Christian doctrine; Hamlet resists it because God's ethical canon is set against self-slaughter; and Ophelia's funeral rites are abridged because "her death was doubtful" (V.i.227). Whereas, in the environment of Rome and under the danger of humiliation, self-inflicted death can be an act of greatness, ennobling the final moments of both Cleopatra and Brutus. An anachronistic clock is mentioned in *Julius Caesar* (II.i.192), and it has been charged that Shakespeare's Romans are Elizabethans thinly disguised. Yet, in our single drawing of a contemporaneous Shakespearean production, the cast of *Titus Andronicus* is depicted in something like Roman dress. What is more important, Shakespeare has used his imagination to catch the moral atmosphere breathed by his ancient heroes. His recreation of a vital past is animated by the sense of living in a time of greatness, which is so energetically affirmed by King Henry V in his speech on Saint Crispin's Day. As the Earl of Warwick tells Henry IV, "There is a history in all men's lives" (*2 Henry IV*, III.i.80).

IV. THE LINGUISTIC MEDIUM

Among the various circumstances that made his moment so opportune for Shakespeare, the fundamental one was the state of the language, which was just ripe for his formative use of it. Language, as a means of communication, is always the key to other human relationships; as a mode of expression, it has been more incisive and effective at certain times than at others. "Words, words, words," as Hamlet wearily intimates to Polonius (II.ii.192), lose their significance when they are divorced from actuality. The increased diffusion of the printed word, during the centuries since Shakespeare wrote, has led toward inflation and devaluation. More recently, the audio-visual revolution of our time seems to be restoring the impact of the spoken word. But, though it is our great good fortune to have inherited the tongue of Shakespeare, we cannot claim that this is the dialect we speak and hear. If we are Americans, approaching him from some remove in culture as well as history, we must traverse a longer distance; yet American speech has occasionally preserved spellings, pronunciations, or turns of phrase which have not survived in British English. In any case, the primary source of confusion for the modern reader is not the rare or archaic term, which can be looked up as readily as the learned allusion, but terms which look familiar and sound strange because their meanings have shifted. Thus, when Shakespeare speaks of "conceit," he does not mean vanity, as we might; adhering to etymology more closely than we do, he means a conception or notion, or possibly the imagination itself.

To understand the difference between Shakespeare's English and ours, we must allow for the process of semantic change, which has been continually eroding or encrusting his original meaning. For example, he uses the old word *anon* for "right away," whereas in our minds it has slowed down to mean "by and by."

We miss the joke played by the Prince on Francis, in the first tavern scene of *1 Henry IV*, unless we catch the full force of that locution. The passage of time, which has weakened some expressions, has had a strengthening influence upon others. The epithet *villain*, which originally signified a member of a lower class, has acquired an undertone of hostility and immorality. On the other hand, *fellow*, which has friendly overtones for us, was insulting in Shakespeare's day. Phrases that were metaphors to him have often lost their coloring with us: since we seldom play the game of bowls, we overlook the concrete implications of "There's the rub" (an impediment on the green) or "assays of bias" (a weight on the ball). When the Germans possessively refer to *unser* (our) Shakespeare, they have at least one point in favor of their claim. The text through which they usually approach him was translated, largely by A. W. Schlegel, into the standard literary German of not much more than 150 years ago. The text of Shakespeare, as we come to know him, is separated from us by an interval of some 350 years. Linguistically, their Shakespeare is as accessible to them as, let us say, the poems of Wordsworth are to us.

To commune directly with our Shakespeare is a more demanding and more rewarding task of elucidation. His language is neither Old nor Middle English; yet it obviously differs from the current vernacular; it is what the linguists describe as Early New English. Its heyday coincided with many other creative activities of the Renaissance. The Elizabethans shared the grandiose humanistic confidence in the power of the word as an instrument of the reason. Logic and grammar stood squarely behind rhetoric, and rhetoric was the art of persuasion by words. Witness the reactions of the crowd in *Julius Caesar* to the respective speeches of Brutus and Antony: Brutus persuades them at first, but in the long run Antony proves the more persuasive. Since the stage is an unavoidably limited arena for the display of heroic action, words must be accepted as deeds, and heroes confound one another by declamation rather than by prowess. The warrior must "play the orator." Hotspur disclaims eloquence and despises poetry; yet he outtalks nearly everyone else in the play, and turns out to be its most poetical character. Comparably another valiant soldier, Othello, deprecates himself as rude in speech. His address to the Senate in Act I is not only eloquent in itself, but evocative of the verbal magic by which he has won Desdemona. He rises to epic pitch again with his monologues in Acts III and V, when he is driven by jealousy to take leave of military glory, and when on the brink of suicide he recaptures a victory out of his past.

Even Shakespeare's fools are dialecticians, like Feste in *Twelfth Night*; while it is Costard, the clown of *Love's Labor's Lost*, who enunciates the longest word in the Shakespearean glossary: *honorificabilitudinitatibus* (V.i.41). *Love's Labor's Lost* may be viewed as a virtual war of words, a campaign by the women—who habitually stand closer to nature— against the bookishness of the men, who are finally (V.ii.402 ff.) compelled to give up their cult of preciosity,

> Taffata phrases, silken terms precise,
> Three-pil'd hyperboles, spruce affection,
> Figures pedantical,

and to express their courtship in plain-spoken homespun: "In russet yeas and honest kersey noes." Accordingly, their spokesman Berowne completes his renunciation of literary artifice by protesting:

> And to begin, wench, so God help me law!
> My love to thee is sound, sans crack or flaw.

But his Rosaline, still detecting a note of courtly affectation, manages to have the last word by mockingly asking him to dispense with the French preposition:

> Sans "sans," I pray you.

The tables are turned in *Henry V*, when an English king courts a French princess by teaching her to speak plainly. There too the humorous dialects of the three captains, the Welsh Fluellen, the Scottish Jamie, and the Irish McMorris, all of them fighting together under the crown of England, resound with a patriotic zeal which is linguistic as well as political. And when the Duke of Norfolk is condemned to lifelong banishment in *Richard II*, his lament at being cut off from his native English (I.iii.159–73) gives Shakespeare a chance to salute his cherished medium.

Many languages have their valid claims to poetic euphony. However, if the criterion be expressiveness, then English has two incomparable advantages, its rich vocabulary and its flexible syntax. These it owes to the intermingling of the cultures that contributed to it, Roman and Celtic, Anglo-Saxon and Norman French. The high proportion of loan-words and phrases has endowed it, to a unique degree, with what the rhetoricians called "copiousness": a multiplicity of words to choose from, a variety of ways for saying the same thing. But if you say the same thing another way, what you are actually saying is somewhat different; you are shading it differently, so that your capacity for precise and perceptive description has been increased. Working with about 2,000 words, Racine could employ the same word for different things, and so could Shakespeare on occasion. Berowne's single line,

> Light, seeking light, doth light of light beguile,
> (*Love's Labor's Lost*, I.i.77)

uses "light" in four significations: *intellect*, seeking *wisdom*, cheats *eyesight* out of *daylight*. The paraphrase should help to explain how, with *Love's Labor's Lost*, Shakespeare freed himself from his early virtuosity. Ultimately he drew upon well over 21,000 words, probably a wider range than any other writer, which opened up immense potentialities for obtaining the right nuance, the *mot juste* in any particular situation. Now you can get along on as few as 850 words in a synthetic language, notably Basic English, where the aim is straightforward denotation, flat statement. But poetry depends on connotation, shaded suggestion, and Shakespeare's verbal shadings reflect the subtlety and the penetration of his insights.

We could illustrate the kind of resources available for his diction by citing a common instance, the official adjective *royal* deriving historically from the French through the Normans. It has not one but two synonyms: the Latin *regal*, which now and then adds weight, and the Saxon *kingly*, most emphatic of the three, since it goes beyond the Romance and the Latinate versions to the underlying Germanic substructure. English poetry borrows its strength from the Saxon, and its color from the other sources. Hopkins and Milton represent those extremes among the poets; Shakespeare so combines the elements as to produce a dramatic conflict at the stylistic level. When Horatio is admonished by Hamlet,

> Absent thee from felicity a while,
> And in this harsh world draw thy breath in pain,
>
> (V.ii.347–48)

the Latinate abstraction for heaven remains mysterious, opaque, and far away, while the Germanic monosyllables of the next line emphasize the grim immediacy of the present world. They also tend to retard the speed of the verse, as Pope observed and exemplified: "And ten low words oft creep in one dull line." Whereas the effect of polysyllables, as Marlowe discovered with his mouth-filling proper names ("Usumcasane and Theridamas"), is to accelerate the rhythm. Hence, in the echoing heart-cry of Macbeth, the pace adjusts itself to the mood:

> No; this my hand will rather
> The multitudinous seas incarnadine,
> Making the green one red.   (II.ii.58–60)

The sentence begins in immediate circumstance, when Macbeth looks down at his bloody hand; then the guilty vision of the second line swells up hyperbolically like an advancing wave, which recedes as the third line tapers off.

If vocabulary can be endlessly elaborated, syntax has been relatively simplified. Since English is not a highly inflected language, it is easy to transpose parts of speech. When Prospero refers to "the dark backward and abysm of time" (*The Tempest*, I.ii.50), he makes a substantive out of the Anglo-Saxon adverb "backward," characteristically pairing it off in a doublet with the Greco-Roman "abysm" (or abyss). Inversions of word-order, adapting to the metrical framework, occur so freely that they end by increasing the complexity and formality of the sentence-structure. Elisions like *'tis* and contractions like *o'er* may strike us as rather stilted today, and ethical datives (Hotspur's "See how this river comes *me* cranking in" [*1 Henry IV*, III.i.97]) as positively Chaucerian, but they still had a colloquial ring for Shakespeare's contemporaries. The intimate singular form of the personal pronoun (*thou* and *thee*) had not yet given way to the indiscriminate plural *you*. The present tense of the verb could still command the

suffixes *-est* and *-eth* in prose, though in verse these were tending to drop out. The King James Bible, which has subsequently done so much to stabilize and standardize English usage, did not appear until late in Shakespeare's career. During his lifetime there were no English grammars to lay down rules or dictionaries to restrict word-formation. This was an immeasurable boon for writers, though it has augmented the problems of their editors, particularly in the field of orthography. Shakespeare was free to experiment with the language, stimulated by its intermixture of archaisms and neologisms, at the point when it had reached its maximum of structural plasticity.

His idiom is differentiated from ours, not only by grammar and semantics, but by phonetic changes. What is known as the Great Vowel Shift, intervening a century before, had given rise to some of the existing disparities between English and continental pronunciation. The capital letter *I* had come to stand for the same typical diphthong as the interjection *ay*. The dropping of the final *-e*, which went out in the wake of Middle English, was more than the loss of an extra syllable; it left behind it a terminal stress which confirmed the iambic tendencies of English versification and brought about a shortage of unaccented feminine endings. The preterite and participial ending *-ed* is sounded at times and slurred at others by Shakespeare, according to the beat of his blank verse, as in this clause of Romeo's:

> Which the | dark night | hath so | discov | ered.

Nouns that terminate in *-tion* are normally prolonged by two syllables, as in this line from *A Midsummer Night's Dream*:

> Such tricks | hath strong | imag | ina | tion.

But certain words that have two syllables for us, notably *heaven* and *spirit*, are generally monosyllabic with Shakespeare. Others that are monosyllabic for us, conversely, may be disyllabic for him: *fire*, *hour*. Word-accent, which was not so rigidly fixed in his day, may vary with the verse-accent; simply reading the verse aloud should teach one how to pronounce *perséver* or *revénue*. Some of the rhymes may point back to the older pronunciations. If *join* accords with *line* or *sea* with *way*, then it is not difficult to imagine a contemporaneous performance of Shakespeare sounding as though it were acted in the brogue at the Abbey Theatre. In general, the vowels seem to have been purer, the gutturals firmer than in later practice.

In reading and studying Shakespeare, at best we merely approximate the actual conditions of his art. All too frequently we forget that it was designed to be projected vocally and taken in by ear, or else we find that our auditory responses are insufficiently trained or experienced. Here we find ourselves facing a matter of taste upon which criticism has been most severe, Shakespeare's puns. "A quibble," in the dictum of Dr. Johnson, "was to him the fatal Cleopatra for which he lost the world and was content to lose it." We can scarcely believe that, just because Shakespeare was fond of wordplay, he could ever have played for such high stakes. Here it seems to be Johnson who has staked too much in order to make a sweeping epigram. When Prince Hal is challenging Falstaff's tall tale, he insists: "Come, your reason, Jack, your reason." And Falstaff evades the Prince by standing upon his mock-dignity: "If reasons were as plentiful as blackberries, I would give no man a reason upon compulsion, I" (*1 Henry IV*, II.iv.205 ff.). The Elizabethan pronunciation of *reason* as *raisin* improves the joke; but it does not, in our reaction, make it funny. A pun consists, by Addison's definition, of two words that agree in sound while differing in sense. Consequently, for serious-minded men, it is a distraction. Yet Falstaff is the incarnation of frivolous-minded man, and poets put the sound before the sense whenever they search for a rhyme. For the Elizabethans, wit was a precondition of poetry, not less so when the two were brought together on a verbal plane. In the playhouse especially, the poet's aptness must have called forth a matching alertness on the part of the spectators.

Punning was not invariably comic, in the facetious sense; it could even have a tragic reverberation, as when John of Gaunt plays with his name on his deathbed. The dirge in *Cymbeline* becomes a dance of death, levelling young lovers with kings and beggars, when the refrain of the first stanza closes with a domestic pun:

> Golden lads and girls all must,
> As chimney-sweepers, come to dust.

> (IV.ii.262–63)

An audience which could feel and absorb that shock must have had both sharp hearing and mental agility. It must have been keenly aware of the uses of words in order to gain enjoyment from their calculated abuses. Shakespeare was more than a master at putting the proper word in the proper place; he could inspire some of his slower-witted characters with a gift for putting the improper word in the proper place. This device for promulgating the *mal à propos* has been named the malapropism, after the garrulous dowager in Sheridan's *Rivals*, Mrs. Malaprop. But Shakespeare seems to have inspired her too; for, as a past mistress at "abusing God's patience and the Queen's English," she was long preceded by Mistress Quickly. In such nonsense, as in Shakespeare's puns, there is unexpected pith. Dogberry, the constable of *Much Ado about Nothing*, personifies the self-importance of the petty official. When insulted, he rises to the heights of bumbling indignation: "Dost thou not suspect my place? Dost thou not suspect my years?" (IV.ii.74–75). Striving to command respect, he unwittingly reverses himself and concurs with his detractors. It is an application of the same principle when Mistress Quickly, seeking to attest her own respectability, casts suspicion on herself with an unconscious double-entendre: "Thou or any man knows where to have me, thou knave, thou!" (*1 Henry IV*, III.iii.129–30).

A Shakespearean phrase, like a musical theme, is subject to orchestration. Developed through a sequence of repetitions and variations, modulated into changing harmonies, and counterpointed with other themes, it can set forth a distinguishing pattern of thought. Sometimes a key-word, which invites careful scrutiny, illuminates the basic idea of a play: consider the preoccupation with "grief" in *Richard II*, the emphasis on "blood" in *Macbeth*, the scrutiny of "nature" in *King Lear*, the irony of "honest" in *Othello*, the amplification of "space" in *Antony and Cleopatra*, or the ambiguities of "art" in *The Tempest*. Concordances may prove useful, not merely for locating passages, but for bringing out thematic significances. In browsing through the *Oxford English Dictionary*, one is struck by the number of quotations indicating Shakespeare as the first user of a given word. It was he who introduced such ordinary words as *lonely* and *laughable*, invented such onomatopoetic vocables as *bump*, borrowed from their classical cognates *monumental* and *aerial*—not to mention *critic* and *pedant*, without which his students would be at a loss. Some of our idioms started out as his coinages: to fall to blows, to breathe one's last, to drink someone's health, to see something in the mind's eye. Unconsciously we quote *2 Henry IV* (IV.v.92) when we affirm that a wish is father to a thought. Shakespearean aphorisms have turned into proverbs: "The devil can quote scripture" and "Misery makes strange bedfellows" come, with slight modification, from *The Merchant of Venice* (I.iii.98) and *The Tempest* (II.ii.40) respectively. When we state that a boy is poor but honest or a girl fancy-free, we never give the author due credit for coining those epithets; and if we swear a mild oath by the dickens, we are likely to think of another writer than Shakespeare.

V. THE STYLISTIC TECHNIQUE

Style could be envisaged as the difference between the linguistic materials available to a writer and the individual use to which he puts them, but the line would not be easy to draw in the case of Shakespeare because he did so much to shape and extend them. We seldom refer to a Shakespearean style because, whenever the protean dramatist speaks, it is through the distinctive voices of more than a thousand characters. Every voice is so individualized—according to Pope—that, even if the speech-prefixes were removed, we should have little difficulty in identifying the speaker. Shakespeare characterizes his *dramatis personae* fully as much by their words as by their actions, yet many of their finest lines bear a family resemblance which distinguishes them further as the utterance of our greatest poet. Poetry, of course, is not necessarily delimited by metre. Shakespeare often turns to prose, with brilliant effectiveness and always for a definite reason—if only to fulfill the pedestrian function of reading a letter or interposing some document. Though there is no invariable rule, the comic scenes are frequently in prose, whereas the tragic scenes are usually in verse. Yet some of the most tragic, notably

Ophelia's mad scenes and the sleep-walking scene of Lady Macbeth, are in that special kind of distracted prose which Shakespeare reserved for moments of mental distraction, when the fragments of suppressed emotion well up from the unconscious. The Falstaffian comedy of *The Merry Wives of Windsor* is mostly prose; such histories as *King John* and *Richard II* are wholly verse.

Moreover, Shakespeare utilizes a good deal of rhyme, particularly in his earlier works; nearly half of *Love's Labor's Lost* is rhymed, in accordance with its interplay of stylistic awareness. The habit of rhyming is sloughed off more and more by the later plays: if we exclude the incidental songs and the interpolated masque, there is scarcely more than a single couplet to interrupt the blank verse of *The Tempest*. Shakespeare's lyrics, many of them set to music by such gifted Elizabethan composers as Thomas Morley, are among the most melodious outpourings of a golden age of song. They are also designed to fit succinctly into their dramatic contexts. For the most part, they add to the entertainment of the comedies; but on occasion, as with Ophelia or the Fool in *King Lear*, the pathos of the tragedies is enhanced by snatches from ballads or popular airs. The plays written in the mid-fifteen-nineties belong to what is termed Shakespeare's lyrical period. Stylistically, they employ the mellifluous rhythms, the witty conceits, and the courtly conventions that—through his two epyllia (*Venus and Adonis* and *Lucrece*) and his 154 sonnets—gained him his repute as the singer of love. Typical of their *cantabile* manner, as W. H. Auden would describe it with an apt musical term, is the set-piece of Oberon in *A Midsummer Night's Dream*: "I know a bank where the wild thyme blows . . ." (II.i.249 ff.). The dialogue that introduces Romeo to Juliet forms a sonnet and coincides with the movement of a dance. The farewell of Richard II to his queen, like the introduction of Berowne to Rosaline, is presented in stichomythy, repartee which alternates lines between two speakers:

> *Queen.* And must we be divided? must we part?
> *Richard.* Ay, hand from hand, my love, and heart
>   from heart.   (V.i.81–82)

How consciously Shakespeare handled his verbal vehicles may be inferred from a brief interchange in *As You Like It.* Rosalind and Jaques are talking, in the elegant prose that composes so much of the comedy, when Orlando enters and salutes her:

> Good day and happiness, dear Rosalind!

Whereupon Jaques makes his exit brusquely and prosaically:

> Nay then God buy you, and [i.e. if] you talk in
> blank verse.   (IV.i.30–32)

Iambic pentameter, the Shakespearean measure, is a compromise between the strict formality of verse and the apparent formlessness of prose. It came into existence as a rough vernacular equivalent for the classical hexameter. Though it retained the traditional English stress, it abandoned rhyme; it organized and regulated the flow of natural speech within the rhythmic structure of poetry; its metrical recurrences allowed for unlimited variety in the phrasing. Shakespeare's meteoric contemporary Marlowe first established control over his medium, after a generation of awkward experiments. He developed the verse-paragraph, which was actually a periodic sentence wherein each clause corresponded with a line, building up to a rhetorical climax. "Marlowe's mighty line," as Ben Jonson labelled it, owed its sweep and resonance to its strategic deployment of polysyllables, with colorful and euphonious names to round out a terminal flourish: "And ride in triumph through Persepolis!" The declamatory rhetoric of the stentorian *Tamburlaine* is imitated in Shakespeare's histories and parodied, through Ancient Pistol, in *2 Henry IV*. Once the five-foot cadence became the regular pattern, in a succession of steady beats following unstressed syllables, it could be varied and modified. When the underlying beat was fixed in the mind, extra syllables could be accommodated or shorts and longs shifted, substituting trochees or spondees for iambs. An ever-changing syncopation could be set up between the speech rhythm and the prosodic scheme.

Shakespeare's developing mastery of his technique is graphically revealed in his treatment of the blank-verse line. The apprentice plays depend on set speeches, beginning and ending squarely with the beginning and ending of a line; subsequently these are broken up, so that speeches may end and begin again in the middle of a line. Only one percent of the lines in *The Comedy of Errors* are divided in this way; in *The Tempest* the proportion is eighty-five percent. The caesura, that traditional breathing-space within the line, falls regularly in the third foot with the early Shakespeare, but later tends to fall back farther or else to move about. Most of the early lines are end-stopped, with a pause which is generally marked by the punctuation; but the later ones tend increasingly to run over; and these enjambments range from an earlier twelve percent to a late forty-one percent. The resulting effect of limpidity, in Shakespeare's final phase, is reinforced by a tendency to use feminine endings, thereby converting the pentameter into an eleven-syllable line which terminates on the off-beat. (Wolsey's "Farewell, a long farewell to all my greatness" is not less typical for having been frequently attributed to the collaboration of Fletcher.) Here the figures are five percent at the earliest and thirty-five percent at the latest. English heroic verse was thus carried along, through the course of Shakespeare's twenty-five-year development, from its first Marlovian fluency toward its culminating Miltonic elaboration. Illustrations, however, are more convincing than either generalizations or statistics. We can follow that evolution more clearly by contrasting a pair of passages from his earliest and his latest writing. This is Joan La Pucelle, Shakespeare's disparaging characterization of Joan of Arc, introducing herself to Charles the Dauphin in *1 Henry VI*:

Lo, whilest I waited on my tender lambs,
And to sun's parching heat display'd my cheeks,
God's Mother deigned to appear to me,
And in a vision full of majesty
Will'd me to leave my base vocation
And free my country from calamity. . . .
Resolve on this: thou shalt be fortunate
If thou receive me for thy warlike mate.

(I.ii.76 ff.)

The regularity is absolute to the point of monotony, though it has not been achieved without certain procrustean tricks of stretching out and slurring over: the definite article is omitted from the second line, and in the fifth "vocation" must be pronounced with four syllables. The verse-paragraph is built up through a sequence of lines corresponding to its component clauses, and the passage is rounded out with a sententious couplet. Note also the archaic alliterations: "whilest / waited," "country / calamity." Here, by way of comparison, is the valedictory speech of the dying Katherine of Aragon, spoken to her gentlewoman Patience in *Henry VIII*:

When I am dead, good wench,
Let me be us'd with honor. Strew me over
With maiden flowers, that all the world may know
I was a chaste wife to my grave. Embalm me,
Then lay me forth. Although unqueen'd, yet like
A queen, and daughter to a king, inter me.
I can no more. (IV.ii.167–73)

These seven lines contain five short sentences, four of them commencing and four of them concluding somewhere within the pentameter. There are three feminine endings and three enjambments—a high percentage even for a late work. The abrupt breaks and the breathless run-overs seem to echo the feelings they convey. The context lends a poignant modesty to the personal pronoun, when it becomes the unaccented eleventh syllable: "Embalm me," "inter me." The contrast between the pomposity of artificial diction and the simplicity of genuine anguish is as striking as the improvement in Shakespeare's portraiture between La Pucelle and Katherine.

Whether it be as loud as a public proclamation or as muted as a breaking heart, Shakespeare's discourse is intended to be spoken. But its appeal is visual as well as vocal, proceeding directly through the ear to the eye; hence it enables us, by listening closely, to visualize the scene. Every word is a picture, Thomas Gray suggested, exaggerating somewhat in order to make an important point. The verbal sound is completed by the pictorial image. When Berowne says,

Light, seeking light, doth light of light beguile,

his ingenuity calls our attention to the words themselves, obscuring the realities beyond them. But when Othello, approaching Desdemona's bed in V.ii, says,

Put out the light, and then put out the light,

his thought moves from the plane of words to the plane of deeds and their consequences. The actual candle, which is being extinguished, becomes a symbol of Desdemona's fated life. Othello, like Hotspur, "apprehends a world of figures," a whole new dimension of experience which Shakespeare reveals through his imagery. Like all great poets, he views the world metaphorically—or, as Hamlet would put it, "tropically." The basic trope, or figure of speech, can be illustrated by an obvious example from the Old English. Literally, we say that a ship *sails* the sea. But figuratively, speaking the language of connotation rather than denotation, we may say that the ship *ploughs* the sea. This implies a correspondence which can be stated logically:

$$\frac{\text{SHIP}}{\text{SEA}} = \frac{\text{PLOUGH}}{\text{(LAND)}}$$

The literal reality is the first term of the equation; the figurative extension is the second; and "land" is in parentheses because it is out of sight.

When the relationship is made explicit, it becomes a simile: "Even as a plough is to the land, so is a ship to the sea." Shakespeare makes frequent use of this more formal device. The messenger in the second scene of *Macbeth* reports that the opposing armies are

As two spent swimmers that do cling together
And choke their art.

But metaphor is so inherent a mode of apprehension that it has no need for the guideposts of *like* or *as*; the relationship it expresses is implicit. Rhetoricians term it the figure of transport, and indeed Shakespeare uses it to transport us from the events on the stage to a wider universe of discourse. To be sure, all language is metaphorical. We could hardly enunciate a sentence without making use of fossilized metaphors. We use *bias* as a synonym for prejudice, without remembering the weighted bowl; and when we speak of spurring someone on, we seldom think in terms of horsemanship. Yet Macbeth, who is never far from the battlefield, brings out the original force of the phrase when he soliloquizes:

I have no spur
To prick the sides of my intent, but only
Vaulting ambition, which o'erleaps itself,
And falls on th' other. (I.vii.25–28)

Here the literal meaning is an abstraction, the description of a psychological process, which is made concrete by the equestrian analogy. To sum it up in another paradigm:

$$\frac{\text{AMBITION}}{\text{INTENTION}} = \frac{\text{SPUR}}{\text{(HORSE)}}$$

But the analogy is a negative one, to which Macbeth does not adhere consistently. Ambition, instead of acting as a spur, seems to become a horse itself—or perhaps its rider—and to run away with the situation. The metaphor becomes a hyperbole, and the leap that fails by its very excess of energy becomes a portent of Macbeth's fall.

Shakespeare's vision of things is at times so vivid that it seems to leave his expression turgid, and he falls into what the classical-minded critics deplored as mixed metaphor. When Hamlet proposes "to take arms against a sea of troubles" (III.i.58), Pope replaced *sea* with the emendation *siege* to preserve the military tone. Yet the bold image of a warrior stalking, sword in hand, into the sea is not uncharacteristic of the Anglo-Saxon imagination. Since the Elizabethan poets worked from a repertory of conventionalized tropes and stock comparisons, which they adapted and recombined, they ran the continual risk of standardization. We are not altogether surprised when, at the first sight of Juliet, Romeo muses:

> It seems she hangs upon the cheek of night
> As a rich jewel in an Ethiop's ear.   (I.v.45–46)

Juliet is to night, in other words, what the jewel is to its Ethiopian wearer. The conceit is a static one which, while personifying the night, turns Juliet into an inanimate object, an earring, a mere decoration. Like so much of the diction in the first act, this is surface embellishment, reminding us of the comedies or of the sonneteers. Yet the fundamental antithesis between light and darkness pervades the tragedy like a motif in music, and calls forth such numerous and intricate variations that the reader can best be referred to Caroline Spurgeon's essay on the subject. A simpler instance, which suggests how the same pair of opposites can be tensely dramatic rather than dazzlingly poetic, is Macbeth's invocation:

> Stars, hide your fires,
> Let not light see my black and deep desires.
>   (I.iv.50–51)

The broken couplet does nothing to decorate surfaces; momentarily it peers into depths; it psychologizes Macbeth's resolve by framing it within a moral perspective. It extends the imaginative focus from what is being enacted before us to the more speculative drama that takes place in the mind's eye.

The sphere of Shakespeare's images is so vast and rich in itself that it has been investigated and charted for clues to his personal temperament. But though we can follow up associations of thought through his image-clusters, these are subordinated to his controlling purposes as a playwright. The imagery fulfills a structural and a thematic function, linking together a train of ideas or projecting a scheme of values. It enhances the strain of melancholy in *Hamlet* by dwelling on sickness and decay, and sharpens the ethical choices in *King Lear* through its emphasis on sight and blindness. The sun, a traditional emblem of kingship from the time of the Pharaohs, sheds its light on Shakespeare's procession of English kings, detaching itself from Richard II after his downfall to shine on the erstwhile Bullingbrook, now King Henry IV. Above all, the man from Stratford keeps returning to the theme of a garden; it is the norm of all that is soundest and happiest within his frame of reference. The moral of *Richard II* is pronounced by a gardener, who compares his well-tended plot with the commonwealth gone to seed (III.iv.29 ff.). The war of *Henry V* is ended when the King conquers France, "this best garden of the world" (V.ii.36). The Wars of the Roses start with a confrontation in the Temple Garden (*1 Henry VI*, II.iv), and the rebellious Cade is run to earth in a quiet Kentish garden (*2 Henry VI*, IV.x). A charming garden in Belmont resolves the urban tensions of *The Merchant of Venice*. Hamlet's blighted world is "an unweeded garden" (I.ii.135). Iago affirms the freedom of the will, and draws a microcosmic parallel, when he tells Roderigo: "Our bodies are our gardens" (*Othello*, I.iii.320).

The allegory is applied by Friar Lawrence, in *Romeo and Juliet*, when he discusses the benign and malignant properties of plants. It is acted out when Perdita in *The Winter's Tale*—or, with a pathetic difference, Ophelia—distributes flowers, or when the madness of Lear is crowned with weeds. Images are suited to the styles of the characters: Othello's parlance is full of martial pomp and circumstance. When Iago vilifies him as an old black ram (I.i.88), Iago's string of beastly epithets serves to characterize himself. With Macbeth the characteristic gesture is dressing or undressing, arming or disarming. Its significance is made clear by his preliminary question:

> The Thane of Cawdor lives; why do you dress me
> In borrowed robes?   (I.iii.108–9)

After he has seized the crown, his disaffected thanes look upon the ensuing disorder as an almost Falstaffian spectacle:

> He cannot buckle his distemper'd cause
> Within the belt of rule.   (V.ii.15–16)

The same note of carnal grossness—perhaps foreshadowing the drunken grooms— is intermixed with the clothing metaphor, when Lady Macbeth is urging him not to let his resolution bog down in an anticlimax:

> Was the hope drunk
> Wherein you dress'd yourself? Hath it slept since?
> And wakes it now to look so green and pale
> At what it did so freely?   (I.vii.35–38)

Macbeth has felt himself restrained by a surge of pity, symbolized in the person of "a naked new-born babe" (I.vii.21)—a symbol which unites the related themes of his childlessness, Banquo's progeny, and the doomed children of Macduff. Recent critics have traced these configurations in such fascinating detail that we are sometimes tempted to read the plays as if they were metaphysical poems. But though we cannot overrate the importance of the poetry, its function is to orchestrate the drama, to integrate the words at every turn with the actions and the ideas.

VI. THE THEATRICAL SETTING

To take full advantage of reading Shakespeare, we must cultivate both the mind's ear and the mind's eye; we must learn to hear the verse spoken aloud as we read it, and also to see the drama enacted in an imaginary theatre. Experienced musicians are able to read score, to glance at the notes on a sheet of paper and know how the music will sound. Similarly, theatrical experience can teach one to look at a script and imagine what the rendition would be like. Shakespeare's plays, though they have meant so many things to so many men, are primarily scripts. The fact that they are so commonly apprehended through the printed page has caused a certain amount of misapprehension among his readers, including his critics. But with Shakespearean criticism there has been a growing effort to understand his work in its own terms, to reconstruct the means by which he gained his effects: such was the approach of Granville-Barker, who himself had been a successful actor-manager-playwright. When we open an edition of *Hamlet* at Act I, Scene 1, we are usually confronted with the designation: "Elsinore. A platform before the castle." This was supplied for the reader's convenience by eighteenth-century editors, along with such standard rubrics as "A room in the palace" for tragedy, "A battlefield" for history, or "Another part of the forest" for comedy. With few exceptions, designations of place do not appear in the quartos and folios, and many of the earliest texts make no designation of act and scene.

Shakespeare's stage itself was basically a platform. That of the Globe (as we infer from the extant specifications of a rival playhouse modelled on it, the Fortune) measured $27\frac{1}{2}$ feet deep by 43 feet wide. The editions of the eighteenth century presupposed a theatre of their own time, with its proscenium framing a picture of the play's visual background, a landscape or an edifice painted in perspective on shutters or drop-curtains and wings. The theatre of the ancient Greeks had embraced two concentric circles, an orchestra (originally meaning a dancing-place) all but surrounded by an embankment of seats. Circular arrangements of this kind existed in England when the strolling players acted out their moralities and interludes upon the village green. The emphasis was horizontal, bringing the actors and the spectators together in a vital interrelationship. Modern theatres tend, by contrast, to be vertical in their thrust. The orchestra has shrunk to a pit for musicians, dividing the actors within their lighted picture-frame from the passive spectators in the darkened auditorium. The Elizabethan theatre had a horizontal basis, which it happily combined with certain vertical features. Its platform-stage was encircled on three sides by the standing spectators or groundlings (who paid a penny for admittance), so that the production—if not quite in the round—employed what today we call arena staging. The surrounding amphitheatre (apparently polygonal at the Globe) consisted of three stories, each with its gallery, like those old-fashioned inn-yards used on occasion for theatres. Admission to the galleries cost an additional penny and entitled the spectator to a seat.

Just beyond the stage rose the tiring-house, containing—as the name (attiring-house) implies—the actors' dressing rooms, and providing a conventionalized background which adapted itself to their histrionic requirements. Most of the acting had to take place downstage; but upstage there was a curtained area which could be used for discoveries, could be opened up to disclose—we can readily imagine—Ferdinand and Miranda playing at chess. Behind its curtain or arras, which was black for tragedy and particolored for comedy (a painted cloth or imitation tapestry), would be discovered the body of the slain Polonius or the sleeping Falstaff, "snorting like a horse." In back at a higher level, there was a specialized playing space indicated in the Shakespearean directions as "above" or "aloft." Thence the invisible Prospero looked down on the lovers and the conspirators; this was a battlement ("on the walls") for the history plays; from it Richard II made his punning descent, a symbolic come-down, to the "base court." There seem to have been practical upper windows, at one of which Juliet first made her most celebrated appearance, in what later came to be known as the balcony scene. Somewhere beneath the windows, to the left and right of the mainstage, were the doors for major exits and entrances. Housed at the highest level were the musicians and the instruments for other sound effects that punctuated the dramatic rhythm. Cannonades and fireworks won even more applause than the familiar hautboys (oboes) or rebecks (fiddles), and started the fire that burned down the Globe during a representation of *Henry VIII* in 1613.

The tiring-house was crowned with a small hut or turret, whence a flag and a trumpeter announced the day's performance. Though the large pit was open to the sky, most of the stage was covered by a projecting roof called the shadow or heavens, whose underside was illuminated with signs of the zodiac. The posts or pillars that supported this projection could lend themselves to the play at hand; they might have been the trees in the Forest of Arden on which Orlando hangs his verses. The stage, which stood about five feet from the ground, could be entered from underneath by a trap or traps, whose most famous use was to serve as a grave for Ophelia. Actors could be lowered from above, like the supernatural personages in *The Tempest*, or pulled upward, as when the dying Antony is lifted into Cleopatra's monument, by some sort of machine. Plays had to be performed in broad daylight, of course, between the hours of two and four or five in the afternoon. Open-air performances must have fostered a more exaggerated style of acting than that to which we have become accustomed, more dependent on sonorous elocution and stylized gesture, although it is significant that Hamlet cautions the Players against overacting. In an age when both men and women prided themselves on the extravagant design and flamboyant color of their garments, it was the actors who cut the most gorgeous figures. Appearing in the dress of their day, with certain exotic or historical touches relating to their roles, they set a modish standard: "The glass of fashion and the mould of form."

Most of the attempted reconstructions err by making the Shakespearean playhouse look like a quaint little Tudor cottage, thatched and half-timbered. Actually, we gather from the Fortune contract that the Globe may have had arches, pilasters, and other details of baroque architecture. When these were further embellished with bright hangings, costumed actors, and all the trappings of pageantry, the impression must have been spectacular. Thomas Coryat, the Jacobean traveller, found the theatres of Venice less stately than those of London, and he is corroborated by foreign observers who were impressed by English playhouses. Though their average size has been variously computed, they would seem to have held an audience of between 2,000 and 3,000. Nonetheless, the prologue to *Henry V* is somewhat apologetic:

> Can this cockpit hold
> The vasty fields of France? Or may we cram
> Within this wooden O the very casques
> That did affright the air at Agincourt?

But this was a request for "that willing suspension of disbelief, which," as Coleridge would argue, "constitutes poetic faith." As the Chorus intimates, the theatres were in the sporting districts near the cock-fighting arenas and the bear-baiting pits, not to mention the stews or houses of prostitution. The Globe was located in Southwark on the Bankside, south of the river Thames and out of the city of London, where public plays were officially frowned upon. Shakespeare and his colleagues were to acquire a private playhouse indoors at Blackfriars, north of London Bridge, in 1608; and they would frequently perform before the court at Whitehall Palace and on tour elsewhere. However, their greatest successes were inalterably associated with that wooden O which lived up to so proud a title as the Globe, *theatrum mundi*. Its sign is referred to in *Hamlet* (II.ii.362) when Rosencrantz speaks of "Hercules and his load" (i.e. the world on his shoulders), and tradition recounts that its motto was *Totus mundus agit histrionem* (literally, "All the world plays the actor"). Shakespeare's rendering, "All the world's a stage," furnishes the theme for the set-piece of the melancholy Jaques in *As You Like It*, and the première of that comedy may well have marked the opening of the Globe in 1599.

Though there was no scenery, there were a good many properties: a throne or bed, for example, or a conventional hedge. Romeo evidently jumps over an "orchard wall" to hide in the Capulets' garden, and the departing Benvolio concludes that scene (II.i) by saying:

> Go then, for 'tis in vain
> To seek him here that means not to be found.

And the next scene—the balcony scene—begins, in the modernized text, with Romeo coming forward to say:

> They jest at scars that never felt a wound.

Here the change of pronunciation obscures a rhyme which shows that the action has been continuous.

Scenes do not need to be localized unless the locality forms a meaningful aspect of the situation, and then Shakespeare tells us whatever we need to know by merely dropping an appropriate word. "This is Illyria, lady," Viola is told on her first entrance in *Twelfth Night*. On the other hand, when Bullingbrook asks, "How far is it, my lord, to Berkeley now?", the reply is:

> Believe me, noble lord,
> I am a stranger here in Gloucestershire.
> (*Richard II*, II.iii.1–3)

Shakespeare does his own scene-painting through speeches. It is King Duncan himself who sets the stage, when he arrives at Inverness as Macbeth's guest (I.vi):

> This castle hath a pleasant seat, the air
> Nimbly and sweetly recommends itself
> Unto our gentle senses.

The picture, reflecting his own serene nobility of character, is thereupon filled in by the noble Banquo, who is likewise destined to be a victim of their host:

> This guest of summer,
> The temple-haunting marlet, does approve,
> By his loved mansionry, that the heaven's breath
> Smells wooingly here.

Banquo's delicate evocation of the swift, building its lofty nest in churches, is at odds with the omens hinted by other birds, the croaking raven and the fatal owl. It has a special effect which Sir Joshua Reynolds would compare with "repose" in painting. Repose indeed! It is there at Macbeth's castle that Duncan is to take his last repose. That temple-haunting marlet proves to be another omen of death, and we are nearer to hell's breath than to heaven's, as the clownish Porter will bring home to us in his drunken monologue next morning.

Shakespeare's numerous shifts of scene were made possible by this technique of verbal description. *Antony and Cleopatra* has no less than forty-two scenes, as it has been editorially subdivided, fifteen of them in the fourth act alone. A play which keeps shuttling back and forth between Rome and Alexandria, moving on to Athens and even to Asia Minor at one point, is far too immense to be produced with the pictorial scenery of latter-day stagecraft. But poetry can take continents in its stride, as Donne reminds us in "A Valediction: Of Weeping":

> On a round ball
> A workman that hath copies by, can lay
> An Europe, Afric, and an Asia,
> And quickly make that which was nothing all.

Time proves to be no more of an obstacle than space is for Shakespeare. In *The Winter's Tale* it is Father Time himself who offers an apologia for skipping over sixteen years, allowing the hero and heroine to grow up between the third and fourth acts. Dr. Johnson defended Shakespeare against those neoclassical critics who could not forgive him for neglecting their dogmatic unities of time and place, and the romantic Coleridge would declare that Shakespeare's plays observe the one important unity, that of feeling. Yet, as if to confound his detractors by showing them that he could solve any technical problem they put to him, he pays strict attention to all the unities in the academic *Comedy of Errors* and in the courtly *Tempest*. His dramaturgy was broad enough to comprehend both of the extremes that Polonius holds up: "scene individable, or poem unlimited; . . . the law of writ and the liberty" (II.ii.399–401).

Ben Jonson, as a professing classicist, disapproved of such liberties, believed in a more rigorous verisimilitude, and thought it implausible that a history play could

> with three rusty swords,
> And help of some few foot-and-half-foot words,
> Fight over York and Lancaster's long jars,
> And in the tiring-house bring wounds to scars.
> (*Every Man in His Humor*, Prologue)

From a realistic standpoint, it is perfectly true that all theatrical illusion hinges upon a series of makeshifts: "In little room confining mighty men" (*Henry V*, Epilogue). Since there could be no question of staging a military campaign within the confines of the theatre, it had to be suggested by alarums and excursions: by ringing the bell that called men forth to arms and by sending small parties of supernumeraries across the stage, wearing counterfeit armor, bloody make-up, and the heraldic escutcheons of Lancaster or York. Trumpets and banners would help; but it was oratory that had to do the rest, with vaunts before the battle and parleys afterward, volleys of sesquipedalian verbiage. This required some cooperation on the part of the audience, a meeting of minds which the Chorus bespeaks in the Prologue to *Henry V*:

> Piece out our imperfections with your thoughts.

Shakespeare seems to be reaching the limits of the dramatic medium and to be striking out toward the epic—or, more prophetically, the cinema—when his self-conscious Chorus interlinks the episodes with narrative exposition and makes his repeated appeals to the hearers' imagination:

> Still be kind,
> And eche [i.e. eke] out our performance with
> your mind.   (III.Cho.34–35)

Through the choruses of *Henry V*, Shakespeare manifests his own awareness of convention, that body of unspoken assumptions without which the theatre could not exist. Convention may be defined as a gentlemen's agreement between the actor and the spectator to take the word for the deed, to accept the symbol as the reality, and thereby to gain impressive effects with limited means. Though the Elizabethans did not follow the classical rules, it would be a serious mistake to conclude that their drama was amorphous. On the contrary, they worked with an elaborate set of conventions, which Shakespeare followed conscientiously.

French classicism, which forbade a tragic protagonist to think out loud, supplied him with a confidant invariably at hand to draw out his thoughts through conversation. This device would seem to be no less conventional—and scarcely more natural—than the Shakespearean soliloquy, which enables us to overhear a character's innermost stream of consciousness, or its briefer version, the aside. Simply to speak in verse is an artifice, after all, comparatively more artificial with rhyme than with blank verse. Shakespeare ordinarily utilizes a rhyming couplet to close a blank-verse scene. Tragedies conventionally terminate with didactic couplets pronounced by the highest-ranking figure among the survivors. It is the Prince of Verona who makes the concluding pronouncement:

> For never was a story of more woe
> Than this of Juliet and her Romeo.

Marked by their terminal rhymes, which were less of an interruption than a falling curtain would have been, scenes succeeded one another as actors walked on and off the Elizabethan stage. Acts were more perceptibly divided, most appropriately by music, which could be harmonized with the stage business. Act III of *A Midsummer Night's Dream* ends with the stage direction "*They sleep all the act.*" That is to say, the enchanted lovers remain in sleeping postures through the musical *entr'acte* to wake up disenchanted in Act IV. There was some danger that, without a clear-cut interval, the audience might not realize when one scene was ending and the next one beginning. Hence an actor who left the stage at the end of one scene could not immediately reappear in the next. In *Richard II* a dramatically unmotivated exit is made by John of Gaunt a few lines before the end of the first scene for no other reason than that he must be onstage at the beginning of the second scene. Scholars have retroactively named this practice the law of re-entry, though it had no such name for the playwrights who practiced it. It is the intrinsic nature of conventions that they be taken for granted, without being made too explicit or codified. We can attend a film and grasp the temporal significance of a flashback or slow dissolve without giving them names.

Given the vast potentialities and the adaptable mechanisms of the Shakespearean theatre, everything hinged upon the contribution of those human beings who brought it to life. Shakespeare's career was paralleled—and fulfilled—by the development of the profession or "quality" of acting. That had been a precarious way of life, since stage-players were "glorious vagabonds," who would have been arrested as vagrants if they had not been taken into the service of some highly placed protector. Consequently, Shakespeare's troupe enjoyed the distinction of being patronized by the Lord Chamberlain, the traditional arbiter of English entertainment, and subsequently by the King himself. Inasmuch as it was a stock company, Shakespeare must have owed something to the talents of the fellow actors for whom he wrote. His leading actor, Richard Burbage (whose more flexible style superseded the popular ranting of Marlowe's tragedian, Edward Alleyn), was able to create the successive roles of Romeo, Hamlet, and Lear within the decade of their composition. Hamlet, keenly interested in matters theatrical, gives us a glimpse of a typical cast when the Players come to Elsinore:

> He that plays the king shall be welcome—his Majesty shall have tribute on me, the adventerous knight shall use his foil and target, the lover shall not sigh gratis, the humorous man shall end his part in peace, the clown shall make those laugh whose lungs are tickle a' th' sere, and the lady shall say her mind freely, or the blank verse shall halt for't. (II.ii.319–25)

The Shakespearean repertory is not so easily reduced to types as the Savoy Operas, yet Shakespeare must have had certain actors in mind for certain parts, and his characterizations may have been influenced by their personal traits. Hamlet looks askance at the improvised gags of the clown; Shakespeare took pains to write lines that suited the styles of his comedians. The principal comedian of earlier years, Will Kemp, seems to have specialized in not-so-clever servants like Peter in *Romeo and Juliet*. Presumably, he was Launce in *The Two Gentlemen of Verona* and the closely related Launcelot Gobbo in *The Merchant of Venice*, both of whom engage in dialogues with themselves (a gag which Shakespeare elaborated for Falstaff and the Porter). He was succeeded by Robert Armin, whose specialty was fools, which may explain the remarkable exfoliation of such jesters from *As You Like It* through *King Lear*. The most difficult part, from our point of view, would have been the lady, since she had to be impersonated by a boy. That may help to account for the number of shrews and viragoes in the early plays, or the fondness of heroines in the comedies for assuming—or resuming—masculine garb. The boy-actor needed the utmost that blank verse could offer, by way of feminine aura, to catch the adolescent charms of Juliet, let alone the mature seductions of Cleopatra.

Among the factors converging toward the inspiration for Shakespeare, we should not overlook that presence which has left the least record. To have great poets, said Whitman, you must have great audiences. Shakespeare's work was predicated, to a considerable degree, upon the imaginative collaboration of his Elizabethan-Jacobean audience. Doubtless it was easily amused by the slapstick of the clowns; but it must also have relished the blandishments of the lovers and subtleties of the humorous men. A large middle-class public at the Globe, a select circle in the private house at Blackfriars, and finally the court itself—all could react with enthusiasm to the same playwright. But they reacted according to their "divers capacities," as Heminge and Condell noted, in addressing the First Folio "to the great variety of readers, from the most able to him that can but spell."

Shakespeare's universality—his ability to please every taste, to win "all men's suffrage," in Ben Jonson's phrase—was compounded out of his very heterogeneity, his appeal to individuals through a concrete understanding of their concerns. Normally, about half a dozen theatres were functioning in his London. At the other end of the seventeenth century, when the size of the city had doubled and was tripling, there would be no more than two or three. Already during his lifetime, as his company's acquisition of the Blackfriars portended, the democratic base for the drama was dwindling. Cut off altogether by the Puritans during the Commonwealth, and partially revived by the Restoration as an upper-class amusement, it never again came so close to so large a proportion of the people.

VII. THE ARTISTIC DEVELOPMENT

Socrates is said to have reconciled the idea of tragedy with that of comedy, and to have predicted that the two ideas would some day be realized by the same genius. But that was in the small hours of Plato's *Symposium*, when the listeners were overcome by wine or sleep, and the argument has been lost to posterity. Two thousand years afterward, when the Elizabethans blended both modes into what they called a gallimaufry or hodgepodge, they were attacked by traditionalists for juxtaposing—in Sidney's phrase—"hornpipes and funerals." Dr. Johnson would defend Shakespeare by arguing that, although his plays were neither tragedies nor comedies in the strictly classical sense, they came closer to life than either through their variety; and Victor Hugo would maintain that they distilled the very essence of modern drama by intermixing the grotesque and the sublime. The combination, by whatever name it be invoked, is an organic feature of English dramaturgy. It goes back at least as far as *The Second Shepherds' Play* of Wakefield, where the ritual of the babe in the manger is parodied by the farce of the stolen sheep. Thus the drunken Porter of *Macbeth* is no mere vulgar interpolation to tickle the groundlings; he is a quizzical commentator upon the serious action, like the Gravedigger in *Hamlet*. The clown, who enhances the merriment of *As You Like It* or *Twelfth Night* by opposing the cult of melancholy personified in Jaques or Malvolio, does not proffer comic relief in *King Lear*; he brings out the pathos by making the King "taste his folly," by joking with ill-timed persistence about Lear's fatal mistake.

The Shakespearean practice of complementing and contrasting the main plot with a secondary plot reaches its fullest development in *King Lear*. The Celtic tale about a father with kind and unkind daughters is deliberately paralleled by the episode—drawn from Sidney's *Arcadia*—of another father with kind and unkind sons, and the physical blinding of Gloucester is a commentary upon the moral blindness of Lear. Such underplots are often romantic, and always parodic, in their relation to the central theme. The underplot of *Hamlet* focuses on Laertes, another son avenging his father, after mischances brought about through Hamlet's love for Ophelia. But there is also an overplot which involves still another son avenging his father, through the military campaign of Fortinbras and the power struggle between Denmark and Norway. Such overplots are enveloping actions which frame the personal issue at a dynastic or a national level. The title-page of the Folio indicates Shakespeare's versatility by naming the principal genres of Elizabethan drama: comedy, history, tragedy. Polonius, who shares Hamlet's interest in theatrical criticism, recognizes categories as hybrid as "tragical-comical-historical-pastoral," and it would be easy to extend his list of the permutations made possible by the multiple plot. "Seneca cannot be too heavy, nor Plautus too light," continues Polonius (II.ii.396–402). We have already noted how the apprentice playwright took those Latin models in his stride and encompassed their extremes with *Titus Andronicus* and *The Comedy of Errors*.

The evolution of the English drama is deeply rooted in the liturgy of the medieval church and, beyond it, in the substratum of folklore. The hobby-horse of the primitive May-games was not altogether forgotten by Shakespeare. Certainly in his youth he must have visited the neighboring cathedral town of Coventry, still a centre for the street performance of Biblical cycles, and watched the pageant representing the Slaughter of the Innocents, where Herod rants in the manner that Hamlet describes. The scene where Lady Macduff and her children are slaughtered is more understandable, though not less terrible, in the light of that popular precedent. The members of the local gilds that put on those mysteries could not have been too unlike Bottom the Weaver and his fellow tradesmen. Shakespeare is recalling the morality plays, as they were performed by strolling actors, when he alludes to the mischief-making Vice, who marshalled the Deadly Sins with his dagger of lath (*Twelfth Night*, IV.ii.124 ff.). Falstaff is likened to that prototype for leading Prince Hal astray (*1 Henry IV*, II.iv.453), while the latter—like the prodigal hero of the moralities—is beguiled by temptation in tavern scenes. During the Tudor period these native strains converged with more self-consciously literary influences—in the Senecan tragedy of the Inns of Court and the Plautine comedy of the colleges—and were augmented by tournaments, processions, and other quasi-dramatic manifestations. By the time England's first playhouse (expressly named the Theatre) was erected in 1576, the outstanding need was for young talents who would take up playwriting as a career.

Gradually and brilliantly, during the fifteen-eighties, that requirement was met. John Lyly, adapting his ornate prose to the clever badinage of the child-actors, charmed a patrician audience with his brittle "court comedies"; Falstaff mocks at their euphuistic style in his play-acting scene (*1 Henry IV*, II.iv.398 ff.). Christopher Marlowe, at the forefront of the University Wits, caught the collective voice of the Armada decade in his tragedies of overreaching ambition; Shakespeare (who was born in the same year

as Marlowe and lived twenty-three years longer) was indebted to him not only for his pioneering in blank verse but for his characterization of hero-villains like Richard III. Thomas Kyd set his stamp on the tragedy of revenge with the play that probably enjoyed the longest run and the widest influence of its author's generation; *The Spanish Tragedy*, with its father avenging a son, its play within the play, its introductory ghost, and its heroine's madness, prepared the way for *Hamlet*. Insofar as these Shakespearean prototypes had their own forerunners among the classics, they conformed roughly to the traditional five-act scheme. But the internal structure of a play, as it was analyzed by Renaissance critics, counted no more than four stages: *protasis* (introduction), *epitasis* (development), *catastasis* (crisis), and *catastrophe* (final overturn). Modern handbooks of dramatic technique, such as that of Gustav Freytag, reduce the sequence to three: exposition, climax, dénouement. This gives the Shakespearean play a pyramidal shape, which rises from Act I to Act III and falls thence to Act V. Sometimes one of the intervening acts, especially the fourth, may seem thin or else padded.

The average number in the cast of a Shakespearean comedy is eighteen, just about half as many as the thirty-five in a history, with tragedy in between at twenty-seven. It follows that comedy is constructed most tightly and history most loosely, since the one contrives and controls its *dramatis personae* while the other must take them as they emerge (and ask the players to double in lesser roles). The histories were bound to be more or less episodic, since they were expected to stick fairly close to the annals of England, as chronicled by Holinshed and others, reign by reign and year by year. Shakespeare first achieved and asserted his mastery through his cycle of plays in this genre. If we regard *King John* as its prologue and *Henry VIII* as its epilogue, it comprises further two tetralogies mainly covering the fifteenth century. The earlier and cruder tetralogy deals with the later reigns: the three parts of *Henry VI* and *Richard III*. The four remaining plays, composed later but dealing with the earlier chronology, stand together as a culmination: *Richard II*, the two parts of *Henry IV*, and *Henry V*. "All is true," the name by which Sir Henry Wotton knew *Henry VIII*, is the implicit claim of each history, even though it be colored by Tudor propaganda. Its pedagogical tendencies are underlined by its catalogues of heraldry and genealogy. Above all, like the well-known Elizabethan collection of didactic monologues in verse, it is a *Mirror for Magistrates*. Richard II proposes himself as an object lesson in how not to govern, when he enjoins his queen: "Tell thou the lamentable tale of me" (V.i.44). The delinquent Prince Hal becomes the exemplary Henry V, having learned to rule by fraternizing with his future subjects and having thereby acted out his allegorical education.

The line between the histories and the tragedies need not be quite so sharply drawn as it is by the classifications of the Folio. *Richard II* and *Richard III*

19

could qualify as tragedies, insofar as they are unified through the persons of their weak or wicked protagonists. *King Lear* and *Macbeth* might almost be reckoned with the histories, since they somewhat marginally stem from the historical—or legendary—matter of Britain, if not of England. Shakespeare was freer to face some of the ethical issues raised in the history plays, with less political constraint and more dramatic artistry, by turning in mid-career to the matter of Rome. For the good European, the Englishman whose myth traced his cultural heritage from the line of its founder Brutus (and ultimately, through Aeneas, back to Troy), all roads—if pursued far enough—led in that direction. Rome's original Forum provided the best sounding-board for civic debate and ideological rhetoric, Plutarch's *Parallel Lives of the Noble Greeks and Romans*, was the great casebook for studies in heroic virtue; Plutarch, though writing in Greek, cites the Latin *virtus*, which is rendered as "valiantness" by the translator Shakespeare depended upon, Sir Thomas North; and the concept has its Renaissance counterpart in Machiavelli's *virtù*, which in turn approximates our notions of self-reliance or individualism. In transferring his venue from the English monarchy to the Roman republic, Shakespeare shifted his emphasis from kingship to citizenship, and from the duties of the subject to the rights of the citizen.

Julius Caesar, Shakespeare's most forensic play, shows the state in danger of domination by an individual, with consequences that lead from forum to battlefield and look ahead from republican ideals toward the corruptions of empire. *Coriolanus*, set in a prior age, pits an individual against the state—so vigorously that twentieth-century audiences, protesting as loudly as the Roman populace, have rioted against its authoritarian hero. *Antony and Cleopatra*, by presenting a pair of individuals abandoning their public responsibilities in favor of their private relationship, weighs the claims of state against a love magnified to a corresponding grandeur. *Titus Andronicus* is merely a pseudo-Roman play, really an immature tragedy of revenge; and perhaps *Timon of Athens* belongs on the opposite edge of this group, for its Plutarchan origin, if not for its stark reduction of magnanimity to misanthropy. But *Antony and Cleopatra*, in its expansiveness, transcends the sphere of the Roman plays to embrace that of Shakespeare's romantic tragedies. It is not less poignant than *Romeo and Juliet* because its concern is with last love rather than first love. However, the very notion that love could be tragic material was something of an innovation with Shakespeare; the subject had been conventionally viewed as the peculiar domain of comedy. Since *Romeo and Juliet* marks a strategic turning-point in this regard, we should not be surprised that its formal and stylistic features are reminiscent of Shakespeare's early comedies, or that it is characterized in the First Quarto by the paradoxical phrase, "conceited tragedy."

If *Antony and Cleopatra* magnifies a passion to the scale of imperial war, *Troilus and Cressida* belittles the Trojan war by reducing it to the plane of cynical intrigue. A double plot, not balanced but precariously loaded on both sides, contributes to the general feeling of irresolution and disintegration. *Othello* has more in common with its Italianate predecessor, *Romeo and Juliet*, though the youthful lovers were the victims of fatality, whereas the Moor is victimized by malign human agency. The element of contrivance, of sheer stage-management on the part of Iago, is not without its faintly comic overtone. Othello lives in a world of human relations, good or bad, unlike the three tragic protagonists with whom he is commonly grouped, whose existence is a confrontation with the universe at large. Lear and Macbeth share with Hamlet, albeit to a less explicit degree, the ambivalent preoccupation with man in his pride and shame, his angelic possibilities and animal limitations. Hamlet's plight is a paradigm of man's divided condition: his personal gifts, his cosmic doubts, his oppressive mandate, his interrupted quest. Lear's downfall is all the more tragic for having been self-decreed. Blindly he must condemn himself to suffer before he can understand the sufferings of others; he must put off the trappings of majesty, submit to the rigors of nature, and be abased to the level of "unaccommodated man," a mad and naked beggar like Tom o' Bedlam. His questioning becomes a theodicy, an inquiry into the justice of God or the gods, providence or chance.

Macbeth is less reflective, a diametrical contrast with *Hamlet*, which is nearly twice as long. Yet the hero, degenerating so rapidly into a villain before our eyes, offers himself as a test case in ironic support of his declaration: "I dare do all that may become a man" (I.vii.46). Indeed he is daring enough to attempt any action. As for his conception of what is becoming to human nature, it has been fatally confused by his encounter with the Weird Sisters:

Fair is foul, and foul is fair,
Hover through the fog and filthy air. (I.i.11–12)

If fair looked fair and foul looked foul, if the good were always attractive and the bad as black as the devil, then there would be no serious problem of evil. But moral choice is difficult precisely because of the murky atmosphere through which men walk at the crises of their lives. Shakespeare's crudest villain happens to be a black man, Aaron the Moor in *Titus Andronicus*. It required the growth of psychological insight to portray the inherent nobility of Othello, the Moor of Venice—or, for that matter, the latent depravity of his white friend who is known as "honest Iago." The casket scene in *The Merchant of Venice* acts out the parable: "All that glisters is not gold." Again and again, in comedy as well as tragedy, the cry of disillusionment goes up, when it is discovered that the beautiful appearances have been masking the ugly realities. Such a recognition, which Aristotle termed *anagnorisis*, brings with it the special illumination that tragedy casts. The protagonist, forced to see through and look beyond the entrammelling circumstances of his life heretofore, seems to gain a momentary glimpse into the ultimate nature of things. The disparity between his expectations and what has happened to him is what we term dramatic irony.

The protagonist is not only the leading character, but (as the derivation of the word *agony* suggests) he is engaged in an *agon* or conflict. His conflict is not simply with recognizable antagonists, but with an inner self on the one hand and with the outermost forces that shape events on the other. When those events come to pass, his part in the total pattern—looking back upon it—we view as his destiny. Meanwhile speculation has been rife as to whether it could be foreseen, and here is where all the oracles come in. But though the Witches have access to foreknowledge by virtue of being supernatural creatures, this cannot help mere humans; it can only mislead Macbeth. Macbeth's position is that of the sleepless sailor, harassed by the First Witch because his wife has flouted her:

> Though his bark cannot be lost,
> Yet it shall be tempest-toss'd.   (I.iii.24–25)

Though the Witches can conjure up a storm, it is the captain who steers the ship and who would be responsible for its loss. So it is with Macbeth, whose course through the dangerous seas of necessity must be charted by his own free will. Soliloquizing over each step he takes, he is fully aware of the moral implications of his own misdeeds. Since the social and natural order was conceived as so rigid a set of structures, it had to be the villain who would take the initiative of breaking through them. Both Iago and Edmund challenge man's superstitious habit of blaming the fates and affirm both his freedom and his responsibility, just as Cassius did in *Julius Caesar*:

> The fault, dear Brutus, is not in our stars,
> But in ourselves, that we are underlings.
>   (I.ii.140–41)

The individualist who adopts such an attitude is willing to risk the immediate outcome. His challenge to the powers that be is bound to fail, and the mundane pattern is completed when the corpses are borne off the stage. The rest, the initiation into the last mystery, must perforce be silence. But with Richard II, whose posture of dying is so much nobler than the postures he has assumed in his heyday, we welcome the termination of our vicarious sufferings:

> Cry woe, destruction, ruin, and decay:
> The worst is death, and death will have his day.
>   (III.ii.102–3)

The last act is death's day; and, both for the moribund and the survivors, the moment of leaving this world is the supreme occasion. Othello rises to a farewell gesture by reenacting one of his braver deeds. A patriarch like John of Gaunt may be visited on his deathbed with the gift of prophecy (*Richard II*, II.i.31 ff.). A thorough scoundrel, like the former Thane of Cawdor, may display redeeming qualities in the manner of his death:

> Nothing in his life
> Became him like the leaving it. He died
> As one that had been studied in his death. . . .
>   (*Macbeth*, I.iv.7–9)

For a better man there would have been a fuller report, and the normal conclusion of a tragedy strikes the note of eulogy.

Tragedy is based on the stuff of history or legend—at any rate, on matters of public importance. Comedy is concerned with private matters, and derives from fiction rather than fact. Of course, the comic in Shakespeare is by no means limited to plays that have been labelled comedies. His unclassical habit of allowing clowns to associate with kings, which led to some of the most touching moments in *King Lear*, created the greatest clown of all as a boon companion for the playboy prince in *Henry IV*; and Falstaff is all the more of a creation for having had so little warrant as a historic personage. As a master of the revels, his office is highly unofficial; whereas the fool is a licensed purveyor of high spirits, the court or household jester in the plays where he appears. Given his motley garb, his cap and bells, and the bauble with which he pretends to converse, it is remarkable how many variations Shakespeare can impose on so conventionalized a role. Fools, like Feste, are obliged to be festive; but, like the equally well named Touchstone, they may also serve to authenticate or to discredit the intelligence and good will of the others. Such buffoons are shrewd professional entertainers.

> This fellow is wise enough to play the fool,
> And to do that well craves a kind of wit,

so Viola comments in *Twelfth Night* (III.i.60–61). Yet the nameless Fool of *King Lear* is a natural, a half-witted mascot, a simpleton inspired with the intuitive wisdom of nature. The fool's stock joke is to engage another character in a dialectical exchange which demonstrates that the other, though he wears no coxcomb, is no less given to folly. The classic retort is some version of *tu quoque* (you too, you're another). That demonstration comprises the gambit of Feste, when his syllogisms prove that Olivia is a greater fool than he (I.iv.66–72). He is incidentally doing his duty by chasing gloom, by persuading his mistress not to mourn. In *Hamlet* the fool is conspicuously dead; he is represented by the skull of Yorick, who was the King's jester some twenty-three years before. Though the unspoken catchword is still *tu quoque*, its exuberant cry has darkly altered into *memento mori*: you too will come to this one day.

It is not for nothing that the word *play* has the double meaning of drama and game. Comedy reverts to the playful origins of the theatre by celebrating a festival of some sort. Two of Shakespeare's titles commemorate such seasonal occasions: *A Midsummer Night's Dream* and *Twelfth Night, or What You Will*. Twelfth Night (the Feast of the Epiphany) was the high season for the presentation of plays at court, while the subtitle expresses the same desire to please the public that is advertised in the title of *As You*

Like It. In that play (IV.i) the disguised Rosalind encourages Orlando by inviting him to rehearse his suit: "Come, woo me, woo me; for now I am in a holiday humor and like enough to consent." It is this holiday humor that sets the mood and pace for Shakespearean comedy. When Orlando's protestations wax too warm, Rosalind cools them by comparing him with a clutch of unhappy lovers out of mythology, concluding with an astringent generalization: "Men have died from time to time, and worms have eaten them, but not for love." Where a tragic situation seems absolutely unique, a comic one keeps reminding us of others, referring us back from the individual to the standards and usages of society. Comedy gains its effects through the intellectual detachment of the spectator, tragedy through his emotional involvement. Empathizing with Romeo and Juliet, we may well agree with the Prince that there never was a story of more woe. Looking down with Berowne from his hiding-place aloft, we can take a detached overview of his fellow suitors as, one by one, they go through parallel speeches and motions (and of him too, shortly, when he reveals identical frailties):

> Like a demigod here sit I in the sky,
> And wretched fools' secrets heedfully o'er-eye.
> *(Love's Labor's Lost,* IV.iii.77–78)

The heroes and heroines of *Love's Labor's Lost,* having forgathered "to parley, to court, and dance" (V.ii.122), are fairly typical in their behavior. Dancing is a stylization of courtship; and, even when they are not paired off in a galliard or a coranto, the movement of the plot is a choreography. Inevitably, its resolution is marriage; in technical terms, "the catastrophe is a nuptial." Yet the happy ending of this particular play must be grimly postponed, while *The Taming of the Shrew* and *All's Well That Ends Well* are largely devoted to post-marital problems. Sooner or later Jack is bound to get Jill; but if the course of true love ran too smoothly there would be no drama. The obstacles placed in its way take the form of "errors" or "supposes," crisscrosses or mistaken identities, tangled and disentangled either by accident or by mischief, usually by an engaging combination of both. Comedy inclines toward the farcical, to the extent that it is propelled by manipulations of this kind. Puck's love-potion makes a mockery out of the convention of love at first sight. But there can be no doubt that Dan Cupid holds sway over the motivation of the comedies, even more than Machiavelli does with the histories and tragedies. Hence the heroines offer a clinching illustration for Meredith's theory of the comic spirit, whose prerequisite is the civilizing presence of womanhood. Shakespeare's women are not content to be mere cynosures; they are the pursuers of the men, as Bernard Shaw pointed out in a characteristic overstatement. The battle of the sexes becomes a banter of wits. It is a tennis game between Berowne and Rosaline, "a set of wit well played" (V.ii.29). Definitively, it is the "merry war" between Beatrice and Benedick in *Much Ado.*

Falstaff surpasses other comic figures because, in his own analysis, he is both witty in himself and the cause that wit is in other men (*2 Henry IV,* I.ii.9–10). He is not only a laughingstock but a laugher, who can enjoy the laugh on himself and turn it against the scoffers. Ben Jonson peopled his stage with laughingstocks, who thereupon became the obvious targets for his own sardonic wit. Shakespeare greeted the Jonsonian Comedy of Humors through Corporal Nym in *Henry V* and his catchphrase, "That's the humor of it." But Shakespeare's *dramatis personae* are characteristically the laughers, the wits who can poke fun and bandy it back when it is directed against them. Jonson's setting is that of New Comedy, the realistic middle-class milieu of shops and city streets. Shakespeare solves his characters' dilemmas by wafting them away from town or court into the romantic woods—another part of some forest or the enchanted island of *The Tempest.* Yet he was not unaffected by the new tendency toward satire that was in the air at the turn of the century. It invaded his artistic province with the War of the Theatres, the controversy to which Rosencrantz alludes and which has sent the Players abroad to Elsinore (*Hamlet,* II.ii.329 ff.). Hamlet himself is, among innumerable other things, a malcontent or—as Shakespeare would put it—a humorous man, like Jaques and so many of Jonson's spokesmen. The "late innovation" may have intensified the satiric thrust and the disillusioned tone of Shakespeare's so-called problem plays or bitter comedies: the mock-heroic and mock-romantic ironies of *Troilus and Cressida,* the fleshly revulsions and repressive countermeasures of *Measure for Measure.*

But even Shakespeare's sunniest comedies have some shadow hanging over them; the cakes and ale of Illyria are consumed in a house of mourning; and if the heroine does not die in *Much Ado about Nothing,* that is not the hero's fault. It seems a natural development, after Shakespeare's major tragedies, that his latest work should mark a reversion to comedy with a note of thoughtful speculation and imaginative surprise. We classify these final plays under the subspecies of Shakespearean romance, not only because their plots are traceable to continental fictions and treat of love like most of the other comedies, but because they exude a sense of strangeness; they reflect the exploratory impulse of their day in sea voyages and fabulous adventures; they invite

> a wild dedication of yourselves
> To unpath'd waters, undream'd shores.
> *(The Winter's Tale,* IV.iv.566–67)

The freshness of the experience is conveyed through the innocent eyes of the heroines, and indeed by their very names: Marina (daughter of the sea) in *Pericles,* Perdita (lost child) in *The Winter's Tale,* and Miranda (wonder) in *The Tempest.* The romances might also be classed as tragicomedies (*Cymbeline* is actually printed with the tragedies in the Folio). A tragicomedy, as distinguished from a tragedy with comic episodes, is more like a melodrama; it has its serious entanglements and its threatened deaths, particularly in its opening phase; but calamities are averted by happy endings, after stretching the long arm of coincidence. John Fletcher, presumably Shakespeare's junior collaborator in *The Two Noble Kinsmen* and his heir presumptive as chief playwright for the King's Men, won his facile success in this vein. There are signs in the romances—their increasing use of music, dance, and the spectacular devices of Stuart masques— that the drama was drawing closer to the private theatre and its courtly audience. Structurally, in registering the passage of time, the succession of generations, the recapitulation of the past, they tend toward narrative and verge upon the novelistic. Thematically much preoccupied with reconciliation, exile and return, mock-death and revival, they abound in recognition scenes. If the harvest masque in *The Tempest* is autumnal, *The Winter's Tale* is redeemed by a sheep-shearing festival in the spring. Shakespeare's playwriting career was rounded out in the mellow ripeness of craft and thought.

VIII. THE CONTINUING IMPACT

Like most tragedies, Shakespeare's are named for their heroes (when the major theme is love, the heroine is accorded a double billing). In the histories, too, the title centres on the name of the protagonist (or, at all events, the reigning monarch). Comedies, on the other hand, are titled with a proverbial expression or a generalizing phrase (*Troilus and Cressida* and *Cymbeline* are polymorphous in this respect, as in others). Comedy thus follows its traditional function of subordinating individuals to a social pattern, whereas they are dominant in tragedy. Yet that comic individualist, Falstaff, makes so large a place for himself that he plays hob with the historical values of *2 Henry IV*. From the lifetime of Shakespeare, it was recognized that the breadth and depth of his appeal were based upon his prolific capacities for the discernment and the depiction of character. His characterization was so dynamic that, by the later years of the eighteenth century, it was looked upon— almost religiously—as an act of creation. His nine-teenth-century critics, whose approach was moralistic and psychological rather than theatrical, concentrated on his characters to the virtual exclusion of everything else, treating them as if they were actual people and speculating on what they did offstage. That process of introspective and rationalistic scrutiny reached its high point with the influential study of A. C. Bradley, *Shakespearean Tragedy*, published in the earliest years of the present century. More recently, a fuller understanding of Shakespeare's background and medium has prompted the ironic query of L. C. Knights's challenging pamphlet, *How Many Children Had Lady Macbeth?* Character remains the central factor in our apprehension of Shakespeare. However, we have come to regard his characters less as independent personalities than as actors' roles, less as old friends than as second selves. The Latin plural noun used by his editors in listing them, *personae*, which is the source of our word "persons," signified masks. This was derived, in turn, from the verb *personare*, meaning "to impersonate"; originally it had meant "to sound through," with reference to the mouthpiece that amplified the actor's voice within the classical mask. A theatre of masks, such as the Commedia dell'Arte, tends to stylize personality and to depend on recurrent types. Shakespeare, in his versatility, uses this un-Shakespearean method on rare occasions, notably in the underplot of *Love's Labor's Lost*. Don Armado and Holofernes are even designated by the generic names of Braggart and Pedant in the speech-prefixes of the quarto text. When they join the low comedians in the rustic pageant of the Nine Worthies, they are treated like Ben Jonson's laughingstocks and hooted off the stage. But few of Shakespeare's comic figures are such humorless butts or one-track minds. When the laughing courtiers make cruel fun of the play within the play in *A Midsummer Night's Dream*, Theseus—who has just uttered his eloquent speech on the power of imagination—offers a defense of amateur actors which is essentially a plea to all spectators: "The best in this kind are but shadows; and the worst are no worse, if imagination amend them" (V.i.211–12).

In the Jonsonian world, human nature is masked by caricatures which, through their emphasis on typical traits, exhibit *Every Man in His Humor*. In the Shakespearean world every man is individualized, compounded of many humors, richly endowed with unsuspected qualities which are unmasked by the intervention of circumstance. Prince Hal, who has been masquerading as a prodigal son, approaches his exposure of Falstaff's cowardice with this high-spirited affirmation:

I am now of all humors that have show'd themselves humors since the old days of goodman Adam to the pupil age of this present twelve a' clock at midnight.
(*1 Henry IV*, II.iv.92–95)

He is conscious of flouting the laws of decorum, both dramatic and political, which require that princes shall act and talk like nobody else except princes. Yet the raffish company he consorts with is ennobling to Falstaff, just as the humbling of Lear proves to be the apotheosis of the Fool. Hal's irregular apprenticeship will make it possible for Henry V, moving incognito among his common soldiers on the eve of Agincourt, to tell them: "I think the King is but a man, as I am" (IV.i.101–2). Villains are humanized as much as heroes. The case that Cassius makes against Julius Caesar is one that is likely to touch our ideological sympathies. Richard III can blame his misshapen body, Edmund his illegitimacy, as a reason for taking so resentful and aggressive an attitude toward society. Iago likewise searches his mind for motives, though they remain so inscrutable that Coleridge has accused him of "a motiveless malignity." It has remained for our epoch to demonstrate that there can be such things as gratuitous crimes, that malignity can be a

23

motive unto itself. Shylock is not, strictly speaking, a villain; he is a serio-comic intriguer who will justly be hoisted with his own petard. Yet his pound of flesh is a legalistic and ineffectual attempt to compensate for racial indignities which, like the prejudices against Othello, have provoked his grim revenge and do something to extenuate it.

In the mythology of popular allusion, where Romeo has become a synonym for any youthful lover and *Falstaffian* is an epithet for corpulent conviviality, Shylock has persisted more as a stereotype of the extortionate miser than an archetype of the eternal Jew. Benedick seems to have bequeathed his name— usually normalized into Benedict—to all men who have ever accepted the married condition, in spite of his own reluctance to abandon that militant bachelorhood which constitutes his characteristic stance. If an individual had not been characterized with such memorable complexity, in each of these instances, posterity might not have cared enough to simplify him into a stock type. Othello has become a byword for jealousy, popularly identified with the green-eyed monster itself. Yet everything we see and hear bears out his own description of himself as "one not easily jealous" (V.ii.345). His noble-minded lack of suspicion, as a senior officer placing trust in his subalterns and somewhat out of his element in a domestic situation, inclines him to believe Iago and therefore to feel that his love has been betrayed by Desdemona. His main fault, as Dostoevsky perceived, was to be overtrustful rather than jealous. Comparably, Hamlet has been taken to task—or, perhaps more often, sentimentalized—for an alleged inability to make up his mind. Actually, both the testimony about him and his ultimate heroism show that his hesitations are uncharacteristic. It is a measure of the baffling predicament in which he finds himself that

the native hue of resolution
Is sicklied o'er with the pale cast of thought.
(III.i.84)

If Hamlet's personality seems peculiarly elusive, if his different interpreters can endow him with such widely differing characteristics, it is because his part is presented subjectively, much of it confided to us through soliloquies. His dilemmas, for the moment, seem our very own. Confronted with the suspense he faces, we cannot but share his doubts and deliberations. The example of Laertes, seeking revenge for the death of Polonius, enables Hamlet to take a more objective view of his own situation by recognizing that it is not unique:

For by the image of my cause I see
The portraiture of his. (V.ii.77–78)

Through some such chain of empathy, we can also put ourselves in Hamlet's place and learn to know ourselves from his experience. Our identification with Macbeth is not likely to be so complete; it would be quite impossible, if we thought of him from the outside as the hardened criminal he becomes. But no man is created a criminal type; even the hired murderers, when Macbeth compares them to dogs, respond with dignity: "We are men, my liege" (III.i.90). A man becomes whatever he decides; and, from the inside, while Macbeth takes one wrong turn after another, we share with him the anguish of every decision. Lady Macbeth seems monolithic by contrast, seemingly untouched by the moral compunctions that make his path to power so thorny. Yet her latent sense of guilt betrays itself by making her a somnambulist, condemned to recapitulate the episode of Duncan's murder over and over again. And though she gives the dire command that her husband executes, her suppressed compassion rises to the surface ambivalently at the doomed king's bedside:

Had he not resembled
My father as he slept, I had done't. (II.ii.12–13)

Though the absence of actresses may have limited the number and the length of feminine parts, it did not inhibit Shakespeare's gifts for feminine characterization. Witness the "infinite variety" of Cleopatra in her moods and changes, ranging from a spoiled child to an oriental despot, from a lustful gipsy to a goddess of love.

Just as these characters ask for our participation in their emotions, so they exist by virtue of Shakespeare's. Having presumably lived and felt for them all, he should not be linked with any single one of them to the exclusion of others. Yet there are certain personages who play the theatrical role of the *raisonneur*, who are spokesmen not so much for the playwright himself as for the scheme of values that frames the play. Such a personage is Menenius Agrippa, genial and tart by turns as he moderates between the plebeians and Coriolanus. Such are the royal uncles— John of Gaunt and, after his demise, Edmund of York —serving as an ethical weathervane for the rights and wrongs of Richard II. Through their comments we gain a longer and clearer perspective on the fortunes of the protagonists, who—as they recede into the middle distance—stay with us as patterns of behavior or cases of conscience, case histories or secular rituals. Their precepts have taken flight and become *geflügelte Worte*, winged words which have left the playhouse to enter into the contexts of our lives. Though we laugh at the old lady who enjoyed *Hamlet* because it contained so many familiar quotations, she was simply paying an artless tribute to Shakespeare's skill in providing human problems with usable formulations. This is reflected among the titles of modern writers, who very frequently take Shakespearean echoes as their points of departure. Aldous Huxley's satirical utopia, *Brave New World*, harks back to the last act of *The Tempest*:

O brave new world
That has such people in't! (V.i.183–84)

Huxley's echo is an irony; but so is Miranda's naive exclamation, which the experienced Prospero intercepts at once with the dry retort: "'Tis new to thee."

Macbeth's revulsive summary of life itself as

a tale
Told by an idiot, full of sound and fury,
Signifying nothing,   (V.v.26–28)

has its all too literal exemplification by William Faulkner, with Benjy's narrative in *The Sound and the Fury*. But though existence has become meaningless for Macbeth, it is replete with endless meaning for Shakespeare. In his *Pale Fire* Vladimir Nabokov goes out of his way not to quote from *Timon of Athens*;

and the passage that he pointedly avoids,

The moon's an arrant thief,
And her pale fire she snatches from the sun,
                                    (IV.iii.437–38)

becomes a generalization about the literary indebtedness of lesser luminaries to Shakespeare. That he stands among our most valued possessions would go without saying, if it were not that, the more we reflect on the matter, the more we realize the large extent to which we are possessed by him.

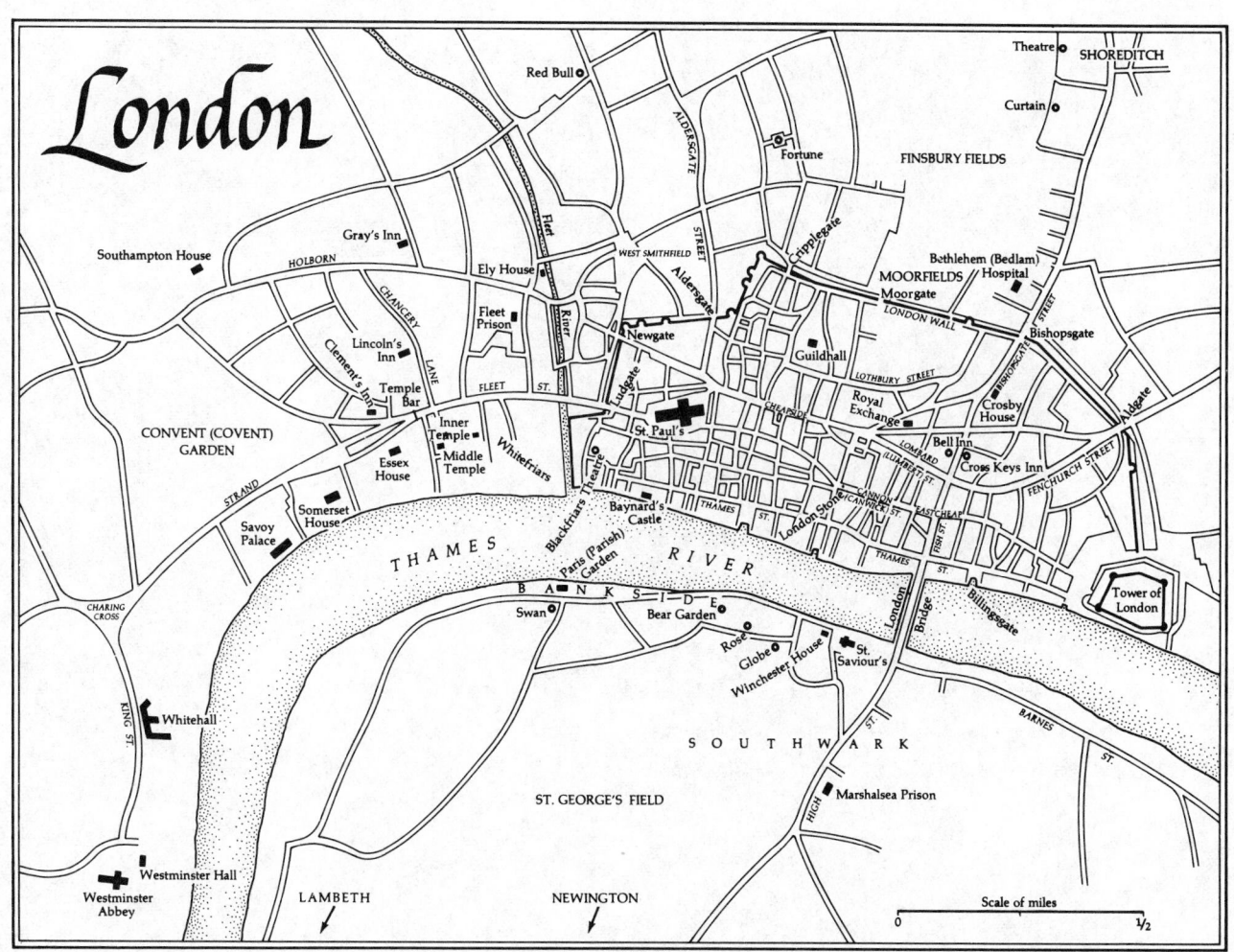

Shakespeare's Text

G. Blakemore Evans

Most readers of Shakespeare know that Macbeth, reproached by Lady Macbeth for seeming cowardice, asserts, "I dare do all that may become a man; / Who dares do more is none" (I.vii.46–47); that Richard III, frightened by a threatening dream, insists defensively, "Richard loves Richard, that is, I am I" (V.iii.183); that Romeo in despair after receiving word of Juliet's supposed death cries out, "Is it e'en so? Then I defy you stars!" (V.i.24); that the villain-bastard Edmund convinces himself that "Edmund the base / Shall top th' legitimate" Edgar (I.ii.20–21); and that as Falstaff lay dying, about to be transported straight to Arthur's bosom, "'a babbl'd of green fields" (Henry V, II.iii.16–17). What most readers are not aware of, however, is that none of these familiar lines appears in the original, basic texts in exactly the form here quoted; that, in fact, each contains one or more emended words designed to restore meaning to an otherwise corrupt passage.[1] And these are but five out of hundreds of passages in Shakespeare's plays that require some sort of editorial intervention. The different kinds and several sources of textual corruption and what such corruption may imply for the general authority of a particular text, together with an examination of the various bibliographical techniques and approaches that have been devised to recover what may be called the "true text"—these, the disease, its causes, and the proposed remedies, are among the principal subjects of the following essay.

Before we turn, however, to a consideration of the various problems involved in establishing Shakespeare's

text, it will be useful to give a brief statement of what is meant when we speak of the Shakespeare canon, that is, the body of writing (plays and poems) which by general consensus is now accepted as constituting Shakespeare's "works."

So far as the plays are concerned, the bounds of the canon are, with three exceptions, laid down by the contents of the first collected edition of Shakespeare's dramatic works, published by William Jaggard in 1623 and now universally referred to as the First Folio (F1). This collection contains thirty-six plays and forms the central core of the canon. Eighteen of these plays had been published earlier in separate quarto (Q) editions of different degrees of authority, ranging in date from 1594 (Titus Andronicus) to 1622 (Othello). The remaining eighteen plays were here printed for the first time, and for these plays the First Folio is our sole authority. Since 1623 only two other plays, and two passages from a third, have been generally admitted to the canon: Pericles, The Two Noble Kinsmen, and Sir Thomas More (two passages only).[2] The first was attributed to Shakespeare on the title-page of the first quarto (Q1) in 1609; the second to John Fletcher and Shakespeare on the title-page of the only quarto edition in 1634. The two passages from the manuscript play Sir Thomas More (first printed in 1844) are now widely accepted as by Shakespeare. Indeed, one of the passages, a substantial scene of 147 lines, is believed by many to be written in Shakespeare's autograph (Hand

---

[1] The original, unemended readings for these passages may be consulted in the Textual Notes following each play. The passage from King Lear is discussed later in this essay (page 38).

[2] Although a number of critics, since Capell (1760) first claimed the play for him, have identified Shakespeare's hand in parts (particularly the "Countess scenes") of the anonymous Edward III (c. 1590–95), the play has not been included in the present edition. See Kenneth Muir, Shakespeare as Collaborator (London, 1960).

D in the manuscript).[3] It should be observed that the inclusion of a play in the canon does not necessarily imply that it is wholly the work of Shakespeare. The questions of Shakespeare's revision of older plays by other hands or his collaboration with other writers are a source of endless disagreement among scholars. Discussion of such matters will be found in the separate critical introductions and, to some extent, in the "Note on the Text" to each play.

The canon of the poems includes *Venus and Adonis*, *The Rape of Lucrece*, the sonnets, "The Phoenix and Turtle," and, in the view of some, "A Lover's Complaint." Five poems that appear elsewhere in Shakespeare's work are included in *The Passionate Pilgrim*; whether any of the unattributed poems in that collection are his is uncertain.

I. THE MANUSCRIPTS, OR
WHAT LIES BEHIND THE PRINTED TEXTS

The extent of corruption or uncertain authority in Shakespeare's texts will appear strange to most present-day readers, who are accustomed to accept any book they may read as reproducing exactly what the author wrote. Although their faith is in fact not always fully justified, their general assumption is relatively sound. Today there is ordinarily a direct link between the author and the published text, and the line of authority is thus continuous from author to reader. But for Elizabethan-Jacobean printed drama, with rare exceptions (especially the plays of Ben Jonson), the line from author to reader was much more tortuous, even broken. This relative dissociation of author and printed text gives rise to a basic question. What was the source, or sources, of the manuscripts from which Shakespeare's plays were set up by the printer, both the separately published plays (the quartos) and those in the First Folio (1623) collection? Until about sixty years ago no one seems to have given much serious consideration to this question, and yet the answer can tell us a great deal about a number of the problems that plague Shakespeare's text.

Unfortunately, no substantive manuscripts, either authorial or scribal, have survived for the main body of the Shakespeare canon,[4] but it is nevertheless possible from what we know of extant contemporary manuscripts of plays by other writers, and with some aid from the scene in *Sir Thomas More* generally believed to be in Shakespeare's hand, to sketch with some degree of accuracy what may be called the "fortunes" of a dramatic manuscript in the Elizabethan-Jacobean

period. After an author had completed his working draft, known then as "foul papers," either he prepared a "fair copy" of it himself, presumably making last-minute changes and adjustments as he copied, or he (or his acting company) hired a professional scribe to make a clean transcript of the "foul papers," which, depending upon opportunity or the author's literary conscience, he might or might not read over to catch errors or make improvements. From what we believe we know of Shakespeare's "foul papers," learned from a study of a number of his plays thought to have been printed from such copy (e.g. *Hamlet*, Q2; *Romeo and Juliet*, Q2; and *Antony and Cleopatra*, F1)[5] and the evidence of the scene from *Sir Thomas More* (see the "Note on the Text" to that play), it is clear that his working drafts presented considerable difficulties for scribes (as later for compositors) and that the resulting text could in many significant details be inaccurate or confused. Moreover, there is essentially no evidence that Shakespeare was himself at all concerned with preserving an authoritative text of his plays for future readers. Although he may possibly have seen his two major poems, *Venus and Adonis* and *Lucrece*, through the press personally, visiting the printing-house daily to correct, forme by forme, the sheets as they were printed off,[6] there is no evidence to suggest that he interested himself in the publication of a single one of his plays. If he had, we may ask, why did he, after the appearance, for example, of corrupt pirated texts of *Romeo and Juliet* (Q1, 1597) and *Hamlet* (Q1, 1603), permit the so-called "good" quartos of these two plays (Q2, 1599 and 1604) to be printed from his "foul papers" instead of seeing to it that "fair copies" were provided? Or, again, why did he do nothing to see that the pirated texts of *Henry V* (Q1, 1600) and *The Merry Wives of Windsor* (Q1, 1602) were replaced by the publication of sound editions during his lifetime? Relevant here also is the question as to why he allowed so many of his plays to remain unpublished. It is true that, generally speaking, once a dramatist had completed a play and sold it to an acting company, he ceased to have any personal rights in it, the play becoming the property of the company, which thus controlled the uses to which the play could be put, including its publication. But even if this impediment was not (as some would argue) more apparent than real, it seems reasonable, considering Shakespeare's eminence in his company and hence his presumed authority, to conclude that his attitude toward his plays, once the immediate excitement of creation had worn off, was more that of a practical man of the theatre, interested in performance and the box-office, than that of a man with deeply-felt literary pretensions, like Jonson, bent on preserving his works in authoritative texts for posterity.

[3] See the discussion of Shakespeare's involvement in *Sir Thomas More* in the introduction to the specially prepared texts of these two passages included in the present edition. These texts are accompanied by photographic reproductions of the three pages believed to be in Shakespeare's autograph.

[4] The earliest extant manuscript of one of Shakespeare's canonical plays is a telescoped version of *1* and *2 Henry IV*, prepared by Sir Edward Dering about 1623 and based on the earlier quartos. See G. W. Williams and G. B. Evans, eds., *William Shakespeare, "The History of King Henry the Fourth," As Revised by Sir Edward Dering, Bart.* (Folger Facsimiles, 1974).

[5] Q2 = Second Quarto; F1 = First Folio. For definitions of "quarto" (Q) and "folio" (F) and other technical bibliographical terms used in this introduction and in the separate "Note on the Text" prefixed to the Textual Notes for each play, see the "Glossary of Selected Bibliographical Terms" (hereafter referred to as "Glossary") following the introduction.

[6] See the Glossary, under *Sheet* and *Forme*.

THE MOST LA
mentable Romaine
Tragedie of Titus Andronicus:

As it was Plaide by the Right Honourable the Earle of *Darbie*, Earle of *Pembrooke*, and Earle of *Sussex* their Seruants.

LONDON,
Printed by Iohn Danter, and are
to be sold by *Edward White* & *Thomas Millington*,
at the little North doore of Paules at the
signe of the Gunne,
1594.

The earliest known "good" quarto of a Shakespearean play: title-page of the First Quarto of *Titus Andronicus* (1594), from the unique copy discovered in Sweden in 1904 and now in the Folger Shakespeare Library

After the manuscript of a play became the property of an acting company, several things could (and did) happen to it. If still in author's draft form ("foul papers"), it might be annotated by the company's official book-keeper in preparation for the transcription of a "fair copy" intended for use as the company's prompt-book. If already a "fair copy" when it came into the book-keeper's hands, it would undergo a similar process. In either case, the book-keeper's attentions might include regularizing speech-prefixes, adding missing stage directions (both matters about which Shakespeare seems to have been careless, as the first *More* passage and some of the quarto and First Folio texts show), indicating properties and sound effects needed at certain points, and marking cuts in the full text (Shakespeare's plays, for example, were generally over the average length required) either to improve the pace of scenes or simply to reduce the text to actable proportions within what Shakespeare loosely called the "two hours' traffic" of the stage. Once transcribed as "fair copy" the "foul papers" seem to have been retained in the company's archives. After the "book of the play" (that is, the official prompt-book) had been prepared, it had to be licensed by the Master of the Revels before it could be publicly acted—a step which in itself often necessitated changes to meet official demands. It could then be subjected to further alterations as various matters of detail came to be ironed out in rehearsal and performance, obviously a continuing process. Later still, in an attempt to give an older play a new look, the same manuscript (or even the "foul papers") might undergo drastic and far-reaching revisions, with additions, perhaps by another hand. Thus several different manuscript versions of the same play (including possible private transcripts made at any point in the stages described above) might be simultaneously in existence and hence more or less available to serve as copy for a printed edition.

Investigation, under the leadership of A. W. Pollard, J. Dover Wilson, W. W. Greg, Fredson Bowers, and Alice Walker, has been able to distinguish five general categories of manuscripts which, it is believed, may be shown to underlie Shakespeare's printed texts. First, author's manuscript, either his final carefully prepared "fair copy" or some stage of his working draft or "foul papers." Second, a scribal transcript of either the author's "fair copy" or his "foul papers." Third, the official theatre prompt-book (itself based on a manuscript falling under one of the two preceding heads), or a scribal copy based on it. Fourth, a manuscript, probably prepared for provincial touring by an unauthorized company and representing a reconstruction from memory by one or more actors who had at some earlier time taken part in an authorized production of the play. Fifth, in the case of a number of the First Folio texts, a kind of mixed copy, partly printed and partly manuscript, in which the printer employed an earlier printed edition (one or more quartos) that had been corrected and in some cases augmented by collation with a presumably authoritative manuscript. Further comment on these categories will be made in the following section.

II. THE EARLY PRINTED TEXTS

(1) *The quarto editions.* Nineteen[7] of Shakespeare's plays were published individually in quarto format before the appearance of his collected plays in the First Folio (1623). Among these quarto editions it is necessary to distinguish two main classes: the "good" quartos and the "bad" quartos. A "good" quarto is one printed from an authoritative manuscript, most often some form of the author's manuscript; in Shakespeare's case, most frequently the "foul papers." There are twelve "good" quartos: *Titus Andronicus* (1594), *Richard II* (1597), *1 Henry IV* (1598),[8] *Love's Labor's Lost* (1598), *Romeo and Juliet* (Q2, 1599), *2 Henry IV* (1600), *The Merchant of Venice* (1600),

[7] Twenty-one, if the quarto editions of *The Troublesome Reign of John, King of England* (1591) and *The Taming of a Shrew* (1594) are considered as "bad" quartos of *King John* and *The Taming of the Shrew*. The present discussion does not treat them as such, although the view that *A Shrew* is a "bad" quarto of *The Shrew* has recently met with wider acceptance.
[8] An earlier edition, probably also 1598, survives in a single sheet. This edition is discussed in the "Note on the Text" to *1 Henry IV*.

A Midsummer Night's Dream (1600), *Much Ado about Nothing* (1600), *Hamlet* (Q2, 1604/5), *Troilus and Cressida* (1609), and *Othello* (1622).[9] Each of these (except *Troilus and Cressida* and *Othello* and perhaps *1 Henry IV*) is believed to have been printed from Shakespeare's "foul papers," and each (except *Othello*) is now generally accepted as furnishing the basic text of the play. To this official list of twelve "good" quartos must here be added the quarto edition of *The Two Noble Kinsmen* (1634), a play generally accepted as a collaboration between Shakespeare and John Fletcher, and probably printed in those parts now assigned to Shakespeare from his "foul papers."[10]

The class of "bad" quartos represents a very different kind of textual authority, or lack of authority. According to the most widely accepted theory,[11] what lies behind a "bad" quarto text is a manuscript based on "memorial reconstruction." For most "bad" quarto texts this theory postulates an actor (or actors) who has taken some part (usually minor) in a performance of the play, most often a provincial performance, and who attempts to reconstruct the play from memory in order to produce a version of the text for some unauthorized acting group or to sell to a not too scrupulous printer. The resulting text is, thus, at several removes from any authoritative manuscript and suffers from the characteristic weaknesses of its memorially contaminated source: misplaced scenes or groups of lines (technically called anticipations and recollections), assimilations, garbled and farced-out speeches, amateurish and frequently unmetrical verse, commonplace word substitutions and flat prosaic paraphrases, actors' expletives, and bits and pieces from analogous scenes and situations in other plays. Such texts tend to be much shortened (the "bad" quarto of *Hamlet* is about half as long as the "good" quarto), not only because of failure of memory on the part of the reporter(s) but also as a result of original cutting in the performance from which the reported text was reconstructed. Despite these shortcomings the "bad" quartos are of special value for three reasons: they sometimes preserve the correct reading at points where the "good" text has been garbled in printing (notably in *Romeo and Juliet*); they occasionally contain lines which appear to be authorial but which are wanting in the "good" text either through compositorial carelessness or because they represent

THE
First part of the Con-
tention betwixt the two famous Houses of Yorke and Lancaster, with the death of the good Duke Humphrey:

And the banishment and death of the Duke of Suffolke, and the Tragicall end of the proud Cardinall of VVinchester, vvith the notable Rebellion of Iacke Cade:

And the Duke of Yorkes first claime vnto the Crowne.

LONDON.
Printed by Thomas Creed, for Thomas Millington, and are to be sold at his shop vnder Saint Peters Church in Cornwall.
1594.

The "bad" quarto of the play known in the received text as *Henry VI, Part 2*: title-page of a copy of the First Quarto (1594) in the Folger Shakespeare Library

later additions by the author; and they afford a number of lively descriptive stage directions which record an eyewitness view of what took place during actual performance. There are "bad" quartos of nine plays: *2* and *3 Henry VI* (called *The First Part of the Contention betwixt the Two Famous Houses of York and Lancaster*, 1594, and *The True Tragedy of Richard Duke of York*, 1595), *Richard III* (1597), *Romeo and Juliet* (1597), *Henry V* (1600), *The Merry Wives of Windsor* (1602), *Hamlet* (1603), *King Lear* (1608), and *Pericles* (1609).[12] There was also almost certainly a "bad" quarto of *Love's Labor's Lost*, but no copy of this edition has survived. The "bad" quartos of *Richard III* and *King Lear*, both of which present comparatively superior texts, pose special problems of provenience; they are, nevertheless, here included in the "bad" quarto category as showing evidence of some form of memorial contamination.[13]

---

[9] For a complete list of the several editions through which a number of the quarto texts ("good" and "bad") passed, see the "Note on the Text" for each play.

[10] Paul Bertram (*Shakespeare and "The Two Noble Kinsmen*," New Brunswick, New Jersey, 1965) has gone so far as to claim the whole play as Shakespeare's. His arguments have not been generally accepted.

[11] Two other theories have been advanced to account for the generally inferior texts found in the "bad" quartos: (1) the revision theory, which explained these texts as early versions, either by the author himself or by some other writer, of the final form of the play as it appeared in a "good" text; (2) the stenographic theory, which accounted for the badness of the "bad" quartos by postulating a shorthand report taken down in the theatre during performance. Neither theory is now generally accepted, although the revision theory has had a few unsuccessful recent proponents.

[12] *Pericles* was not included in either the First Folio (1623) or the Second Folio (1632); it was first added to the so-called Folio canon in the second issue of the Third Folio (1664), in a text derived from one of the later editions (Q6) of the "bad" quarto. *Pericles* is the only play in the Shakespeare canon that is entirely dependent for its text on a "bad" quarto.

[13] For a discussion of the special problems here involved, see the "Note on the Text" to *Richard III* and to *King Lear*.

One other quarto edition should be mentioned. When, in his *Palladis Tamia* (1598), Francis Meres published a list of six "tragedies" and six comedies by Shakespeare, he included a comedy called "Loue labours wonne." No such play, at least under that name, has come down to us, but we now know, since T. W. Baldwin's discovery in 1957, that a quarto edition of a play with that name was included in a bookseller's stock in 1603.[14]

(2) *The First Folio.* Seven years after Shakespeare's death, the printer and publisher William Jaggard and his son Isaac, in association with three other booksellers and publishers, William Aspley, John Smethwick, and Edward Blount, produced the volume now regularly called the First Folio (1623), the first collected edition of Shakespeare's plays.[15] This collection seems to have been undertaken with the advice and aid of Shakespeare's company, the King's Men, and was prefaced with a dedication to the Earls of Pembroke and Montgomery and an address "To the great Variety of Readers," both signed by two of Shakespeare's oldest acting colleagues, John Heminge and Henry Condell. It contains thirty-six plays, eighteen here printed for the first time in any form: *The Tempest, The Two Gentlemen of Verona, Measure for Measure, The Comedy of Errors, As You Like It, The Taming of the Shrew, All's Well That Ends Well, Twelfth Night, The Winter's Tale, King John, 1 Henry VI, Henry VIII, Coriolanus, Timon of Athens, Julius Caesar, Macbeth, Antony and Cleopatra,* and *Cymbeline.* For these eighteen plays the First Folio is our sole authority. For *Othello,* and for six plays which had appeared earlier only in "bad" quarto texts (*The Merry Wives of Windsor, Henry V, 2* and *3 Henry VI, Richard III,* and *King Lear*), it also gives us our most authoritative texts.

Although the several kinds of printer's copy that

Jaggard, presumably with the cooperation of Heminge and Condell, assembled for the texts of the First Folio have been touched on occasionally in the preceding section, the matter of printer's copy as it applies specifically to the Folio may be briefly outlined here. For more finely drawn distinctions and the expression of conflicting opinions the reader must consult the fuller discussions in the "Note on the Text" to each of the plays.

Half the plays included in the First Folio had already been printed in some form in separate quarto editions (i.e. the "good" and "bad" quartos). Those responsible for the Folio collection made use of these earlier printed texts in roughly two ways. In some cases, they reprinted the quarto text (not necessarily from the first edition), sometimes introducing a few new readings of uncertain authority and making occasional modifications in stage directions and some more or less obvious corrections (for example, *Titus Andronicus* [with one new scene from manuscript], *1 Henry IV, Love's Labor's Lost, Romeo and Juliet, A Midsummer Night's Dream, The Merchant of Venice,* and *Much Ado about Nothing,* all from "good" quartos). As copy for other plays, they arranged for a revision and correction of a quarto text by collation with a presumably authoritative manuscript (perhaps the official prompt-book), thus producing copy for the printer that was a combination of printed and manuscript material (*Richard III* and *King Lear* [from "bad" quartos], *Richard II, 1 Henry IV,* and *Troilus and Cressida* [from "good" quartos], and, in the view of many, *2 Henry IV, Hamlet,* and *Othello* [from "good" quartos]).[16] Partial use of this sort seems also to have been made of the "bad" quarto texts of *2* and *3 Henry VI* and *Henry V.* These three plays, however, are basically dependent on manuscript copy, probably "foul papers." Alone among the already published plays included in the First Folio, *The Merry Wives of Windsor* seems totally uninfluenced by its earlier ("bad") quarto edition.[17] It was printed from a transcript, based perhaps on the official prompt-book, and specially prepared for the Folio by a scrivener named Ralph Crane.

The eighteen plays now first printed were based upon various types of manuscript copy. For some plays Shakespeare's own manuscripts were drawn upon, either the "foul papers" (*The Comedy of Errors, The Taming of the Shrew, All's Well That Ends Well, King John, 1 Henry VI, Timon of Athens* [in good part at least], and *Antony and Cleopatra*), or "fair copy" (*Coriolanus*). The remaining plays in this group show evidence of having been set from some form of scribal copy: some from specially prepared transcripts by

---

[14] Apart from "Loue labours wonne," a number of other "lost" plays have been attributed to Shakespeare. On September 9, 1653, Humphrey Moseley entered on the Stationers' Register "The History of Cardenio, by Mᵣ Fletcher & Shakespeare." and "Henry yᵉ first, & Hen: the 2ᵈ. by Shakespeare, & Davenport."; and on June 28, 1660, "The History of King Stephen.", "Duke Humphrey, a Tragedy.", and "Iphis and Iantha or a marriage without a man, a Comedy.", all three being attributed to "Will: Shakespeare." Two of these plays (*Henry the First* and *Duke Humphrey*) also appear with the same attributions in John Warburton's eighteenth-century holograph list of manuscript plays, all but a very few of which (including the two above) were accidentally destroyed by his servant. Except for *Cardenio*, nothing further is known about these plays that connects them with Shakespeare, and Moseley's attributions are often of uncertain authority. In the case of *Cardenio*, we possess a drastic revision of the play published by Lewis Theobald in 1728 under the title *The Double Falsehood, or The Distress'd Lovers,* but the three manuscripts of *Cardenio* that he claimed to have owned have disappeared.

[15] The nine so-called "Pavier" quartos, printed in 1619, though with various dates, are sometimes thought of as the first attempt at a selected collection of the plays. The nine include: *The Whole Contention* (i.e. the "bad" quarto versions of *2* and *3 Henry VI*), *The Merry Wives of Windsor, Henry V, King Lear, Pericles* (all "bad" quartos), *The Merchant of Venice, A Midsummer Night's Dream,* and two apocryphal plays, *A Yorkshire Tragedy* and *Sir John Oldcastle.*

[16] The most recent study of the F1 copy for *2 Henry IV, Hamlet,* and *Othello* (J. K. Walton, *The Quarto Copy for the First Folio of Shakespeare,* Dublin, 1971) declares in favor of manuscript copy for these three plays. Unfortunately Mr. Walton's study appeared too late for use in the present edition.

[17] Unless we include as "bad" quartos *The Taming of a Shrew* and *The Troublesome Reign of John, King of England,* which had no influence upon the Folio texts of *The Shrew* and *King John* respectively.

Ralph Crane (*The Tempest* [perhaps transcribed from Shakespeare's "fair copy"], *The Two Gentlemen of Verona* [perhaps from "foul papers"], *Measure for Measure* [from "foul papers"], *The Winter's Tale* [probably from "foul papers"], and perhaps *Cymbeline* [probably from "foul papers"] and parts of *Timon of Athens* [from "foul papers"]); [18] others, from the official prompt-books, either directly or through a prepared scribal transcript (*Twelfth Night, Julius Caesar,* and *Macbeth*). *As You Like It* is thought to have been set from a transcript of some form of Shakespeare's autograph, perhaps his "fair copy," and *Henry VIII* from clean scribal copy based probably on the "foul papers."

Although the several procedures described above may fail to inspire, and rightly, great confidence in the integrity of the Folio texts, they do suggest some degree of discrimination and sense of responsibility on the part of those concerned with the First Folio collection. Even so we are scarcely able to endorse Heminge and Condell's claim (in "To the great Variety of Readers") that the texts as they are printed in the First Folio are "cur'd, and perfect of their limbes [referring to those plays earlier published in what are now considered to be "bad" quarto editions]; and all the rest, absolute in their numbers, as he [Shakespeare] conceiued them."

The textual history of Shakespeare's plays from 1623 to the end of the seventeenth century may be shortly dealt with. A second folio appeared in 1632, a third in 1663/4,[19] and a fourth in 1685, each printed from the one immediately preceding. They show a progressive modernizing and regularizing of the text, affecting not only punctuation and spelling but language and syntax as well. None of the changes so made, not even the occasional verbal corrections or additions in the Second Folio (1632), has any independent manuscript authority. Such quarto editions as appeared after 1623 were either reprints of the earlier quartos or texts derived from the First Folio, including several Restoration acting versions (*Othello, Hamlet, Julius Caesar*) which show evidence of contemporary stage practice.

(3) *The Poems. Venus and Adonis,* the first of Shakespeare's works to appear in print, was printed and published by Richard Field, in quarto, in 1593. The first quarto edition of *The Rape of Lucrece* followed in the next year (1594), again printed by Field but published by John Harrison. Both poems were printed with Shakespeare's authorization and each contains a short prose dedication to his patron, Henry Wriothes-

ley, the young Earl of Southampton. The volume entitled *Shakespeare's Sonnets* (1609), which contains also the questionably Shakespearean "A Lover's Complaint," was, on the other hand, almost certainly unauthorized. So was the small earlier miscellany of short poems by Shakespeare and others (all, however, attributed to Shakespeare) called *The Passionate Pilgrim* and published in 1599 (enlarged with more non-Shakespearean materials in 1612) by William Jaggard. The only other poem generally accepted as Shakespeare's, "The Phoenix and Turtle," was first printed among a group of commendatory verses appended to Robert Chester's *Love's Martyr* in 1601.

None of the poems appeared in the First Folio, except for three set-pieces in *Love's Labor's Lost* that were later printed as separate poems in *The Passionate Pilgrim.* The nearest thing to a collected edition before the eighteenth century was *Poems: Written by Wil. Shake-speare. Gent.* published by John Benson in 1640. It included all but eight of the sonnets (misleadingly rearranged, grouped, and titled), "A Lover's Complaint," "The Phoenix and Turtle," and the complete contents of the 1612 *Passionate Pilgrim,* together with other non-Shakespearean poems, but not *Venus and Adonis* and *Lucrece.*

III. THE HISTORY OF THE TEXT, 1700–1900

In considering the later history of Shakespeare's text it is important to draw a general distinction between the textual approach taken by editors and critics before roughly 1909, the date of A. W. Pollard's important *Shakespeare Folios and Quartos,* and the approach, based on a growing knowledge of kinds of manuscript copy and analytical bibliographical techniques, since adopted by most scholars. Valuable contributions to the better understanding of the text of individual plays had, of course, been made before Pollard's study, particularly those of P. A. Daniel, but the larger principles of textual criticism, particularly of what lay behind the printed text, were for the most part unformed. As a result, a more or less ungoverned eclecticism prevailed. To say this is not to discount the value and importance of the work done by the small army of editors who, from the time of Nicholas Rowe's edition (1709) to the great Cambridge edition of 1863–66, exercised their critical ingenuity in improving the text—as a glance at the Textual Notes to any of the plays and poems in this volume will immediately show. But their work was largely concerned with the details of emendation, made for the most part without any very clear understanding of the special conditions which had governed the production of the early printed texts.

The eighteenth century marks the beginning of what may be called the scholarly or academic approach to Shakespeare. In 1709 Nicholas Rowe produced the first edited text of the plays. Rowe was himself a dramatist and had connections with the theatre, and his edition reflects these professional interests. Unfortunately, Rowe chose to base his text on the Fourth Folio (1685), with very occasional consultation of one of the earlier folios or quartos. The result was a

---

[18] For a discussion of Crane's scribal characteristics, see the "Note on the Text" to *The Tempest* and to *The Two Gentlemen of Verona.*

[19] Six plays in addition to *Pericles* (*The London Prodigal, The Life and Death of Thomas Lord Cromwell, The History of Sir John Oldcastle, The Puritan, or The Widow of Watling Street, A Yorkshire Tragedy,* and *The Tragedy of Locrine*) were added in the second issue of the Third Folio (and reprinted in the Fourth) and are now commonly referred to as the "Shakespeare Apocrypha." None of the six is now accepted as Shakespeare's.

generally inferior text that seriously vitiated later editions for the next sixty years and more. Nevertheless, Rowe made some substantial contributions. To him as the first official editor of the plays we owe a large number of corrections and emendations that continue as part of any modern edition.[20] He also undertook a more or less systematic division of all the plays into acts and scenes and was the first, except for some sporadic instances in the Restoration actors' quartos, to indicate a localized setting for many of the individual scenes. Further, his edition contains the first serious attempt at a biography of Shakespeare, still an important source on certain matters, and illustrations that tell us a good deal about early eighteenth-century staging.

Shakespeare's second editor was Alexander Pope. When Pope produced his edition in 1723, he was already established as England's leading poet and *arbiter elegantiarum*. These roles he exercised much too freely to qualify in any sense as a serious editor. He pontificated on what was good or bad in the plays, marking the "good" or "moral" with inverted commas and relegating the "bad" to the bottom of the page as the illiterate interpolations of the ignorant actors and unworthy of a place in the text proper. If he did not understand a word or construction, he often changed it, and he worked assiduously to regularize Shakespeare's metre. He did, however, recover passages and scenes from some of the quartos ignored by Rowe (that is, he undertook some limited collation of the quarto texts), and he also restored to verse many passages that had been misprinted in the early editions as prose, and to prose many that had been misprinted as verse. It has been said—if unkindly, nevertheless with considerable truth—that it took over a hundred years for Shakespeare's text to recover from the well-meant but misguided ministrations of both Pope and Rowe.

In 1733 Lewis Theobald published his first edition of the plays, but before doing so he had dared to cross swords with Pope. His attack on Pope's edition, which appeared in 1726, he called *Shakespeare Restor'd* and in it he showed in unflattering detail how basically bad Pope's edition was. Pope's answer, apart from incorporating a number of Theobald's readings in the text of his second edition (1728) and including others in a sneering appendix, was to make Theobald the hero of his first *Dunciad* (1728) as the pre-eminent type and prince of dullness and to nickname him "piddling Tibbald." From that day to this, Pope's attack has done much to obscure Theobald's remarkable capabilities as an editor, which were of a sort that Pope, as poet and critic, tended by nature to despise. Indeed, Theobald may fairly be considered the first of Shakespeare's major editors, and his contributions, particularly in felicitous emendations, are to be found everywhere in any modern text. But beyond this, he approached the editor's task with a much clearer

notion than his predecessors had of what such duties entailed, and with a much wider acquaintance with other Elizabethan drama and non-dramatic literature. He also had a greater respect for his author's language and syntax and a scholarly perspective foreign to Rowe and Pope.

The next three editors, Sir Thomas Hanmer (1744), William Warburton (1747), and Samuel Johnson (1765), may, so far as the history of the text is concerned, be passed over quickly. Each made occasional brilliant emendations, although Warburton is principally famous as a warning example of the danger of overingenuity in emendation and of emending where no emendation is needed. Johnson, who knew and outlined (in his "Proposals," 1756) the proper method by which a relatively sound text might be achieved, did only a bare minimum of what he rightly said should no longer be stigmatized as, in Pope's words, the "dull duty of an editor" (namely, collation and evaluation of the various early editions), instead concerning himself largely with explanatory annotation and general criticism, both of which he was especially well qualified to perform and for both of which he is still recognized as one of the great Shakespearean critics.

In 1768, quietly and pretty much unnoticed, Edward Capell brought out his text of the plays. None of his important contemporaries had a kind word to say about Capell's edition, and his two principal successors, George Steevens and Edmond Malone, denigrated it at every opportunity—and stole from it unblushingly. Later opinion, however, has more and more seen Capell as the first so-called modern editor, and his edition as an important landmark. Capell deserves the title of the first modern for a number of reasons. He was the first to put into practice, though perhaps not the first to understand, the principle of copy-text, that is, the need for choosing, in the light of the evidence, a basic substantive text and for adhering faithfully to that text. In his search for such basic texts, Capell also for the first time recognized the usual superiority of the earliest printed texts (the "good" quartos) as opposed to those texts as they appeared in the First Folio. Thus he began the trend away from the eclecticism of the earlier editors, who, failing to take a definite stand on a particular copy-text, allowed themselves considerable liberty in adopting readings from any text, early or late, that happened to appeal to their esthetic sensibilities. Succeeding editors learned something of this cardinal rule from Capell, but in the case of a textually complex play like *Hamlet*, for example, which Capell for the first time based directly on Q2 (1604/5), no later influential text comparably faithful to Q2 was produced until Dover Wilson's edition in 1934.[21]

In a special sense Capell's was the first "pure" edited text. His predecessors, and most of his successors, employed as printer's copy some other more or

---

[20] Reference to the Textual Notes following each play will reveal the extent to which Rowe and his many successors have influenced the text of the present edition.

[21] Some details in the discussion of Capell I owe to an unpublished doctoral dissertation by my friend, Hymen H. Hart.

less recent edition into which they inserted their manuscript corrections.[22] This method almost inevitably perpetuated and gave a specious authority to readings from the Fourth Folio, on which Rowe, the first link in the chain, had based his 1709 edition. Capell, on the other hand, prepared a wholly new text for the printer, meticulously copied out by himself (reputedly ten times!), based on his own thorough collation of all the obtainable sixteenth- and seventeenth-century editions (quarto and folio). To Capell also belongs the credit of being the first to print a systematic textual apparatus—a remarkably full one—recording the variants from the early editions and the readings of the first five of his eighteenth-century predecessors. Nothing comparable was attempted until the Cambridge edition of 1863–66, nearly a hundred years later. The problem of chronology, an important approach to an understanding of Shakespeare's development, was first attacked by Capell, though the credit is usually given to Malone, and he was the first to attempt a serious treatment of Shakespeare's metrics. His official position as deputy-inspector of plays brought Capell into close contact with the theatre and goes far to explain his special sensitivity, continually reflected in his text, to stage business and movement. It may also explain why he was the first to understand fully the concept of the "cleared stage" as the limiting principle of Elizabethan scene division. A measure of Capell's importance may perhaps be seen in the fact that his name appears more frequently in the Textual Notes to the present edition than that of any later editor.

Capell's immediate followers, George Steevens and Edmond Malone, both produced major editions (Steevens, 1787, 1793; Malone, 1790), but textually they leaned heavily on Capell—at the same time affecting to despise him. It is, indeed, scarcely an exaggeration to say that by the end of the eighteenth century the texts of Shakespeare that went under the names of Steevens and Malone were, with some refinements in specific readings, in basic essentials the text of Edward Capell. To assert this is not to deny the importance of the work done by Steevens and Malone, especially Malone. Like Capell, who had published in what he called *The School of Shakespeare* the results of his combing of Elizabethan and Jacobean literature for Shakespeare's sources and other material that might be used to illustrate and throw new light on the plays, both men were what the wits called "black-letter editors"—that is, editors who drew on a wide reading in the popular literature of Shakespeare's time, some of which was even then still printed in the so-called gothic black-letter typeface. Unlike Capell, both Steevens and Malone wrote polished and untortured English, and their commentaries, though often owing much to Capell's notes, became widely known and were reprinted in edition

after edition, culminating in the so-called First Variorum, the Boswell-Malone edition of 1821.[23] Malone, moreover, was the first to demonstrate through a careful analytical study the sole authority of the First Folio (1623) in relation to the later folios, showing that even the variant readings of the Second Folio (1632) were entirely without independent manuscript authority. He also deserves special praise for his scholarly researches into the early history of the English stage and for his careful transcriptions of early manuscript materials, some of which have since disappeared. He was also the first to publish a scholarly edition of Shakespeare's *Poems* and *Pericles* (1780), though in the *Poems* he again had Capell as his guide since he made essentially unacknowledged use of a marked copy of Lintott's 1709 edition of the *Poems* prepared by Capell for an edition of his own which he did not live to publish.

With Capell, Steevens, and Malone the text of Shakespeare had been brought about as far as the limited textual approach employed by these men could bring it, and the nineteenth century, although it produced many new editions under highly competent and learned editors (Charles Knight, J. P. Collier, Alexander Dyce, and R. G. White, especially), brought very little advance in new theory or basic techniques. The culmination of the line initiated by Capell is the great Cambridge *Shakespeare* edited by W. G. Clark and W. A. Wright, which appeared between 1863 and 1866 (with its important revision by Wright in 1891–93), a text that was to remain, especially in its one-volume Globe edition (1864), the standard for the next fifty years.

IV. SHAKESPEARE'S TEXT AND THE "NEW BIBLIOGRAPHY"

The first decade of the twentieth century marked the beginnings of what has been called the "New Bibliography." Spearheaded by men like R. B. McKerrow, A. W. Pollard, W. W. Greg, and J. Dover Wilson, a fresh and comparatively "scientific" approach to the problems presented by the text was undertaken. An important forward step was made in 1909 by Pollard, who clarified the whole problem of the quarto texts by recognizing that, when Heminge and Condell in their address "To the great Variety of Readers" in the First Folio criticized earlier printed texts of the plays as "stolne, and surreptitious copies, maimed, and deformed by the frauds and stealthes of iniurious imposters, that expos'd them," they were not

---

[22] Thus Pope's edition was printed from Rowe's third (1714), Theobald's and Hanmer's from Pope's second (1728), Warburton's from Theobald's second (1740), and Johnson's partly from Warburton's (1747) and partly from Theobald's 1757 edition.

[23] As here used, the term "Variorum" means that the edition reprints all the prefaces of the earlier editors, selected studies and essays by various hands, and a great part of the annotation from Pope through Reed. Actually, all major editions had been "Variorums" in this sense since the 1773 Johnson-Steevens edition, so that the traditional term "First Variorum" as applied to the Boswell-Malone 1821 edition is a misnomer. As used today, with reference to the *New Variorum Shakespeare*, the idea of a "Variorum" has been enlarged to include an exhaustive record of all significant textual variants, emendations, source materials, and selected criticism.

thereby condemning, as had usually been supposed, all the earlier quartos, but only certain piratically published or "expos'd" quartos. These Pollard designated the "bad" quartos to distinguish them from the "good" quartos, or texts published, usually with the company's permission, from authoritative manuscripts. Pollard's distinction stimulated investigation in two fruitful directions. It was supported by W. W. Greg's analysis (1910) of the quarto of *The Merry Wives of Windsor*, in which he outlined the basic essentials of the theory of "memorial reconstruction," a theory which he was able to confirm and extend in his famous monograph on Greene's *Orlando Furioso* and Peele's *Battle of Alcazar* (1923). From these beginnings rose the widespread application of the "memorial reconstruction" theory to the whole class of "bad" quartos (see, particularly, the studies of Peter Alexander, Madeleine Doran, D. L. Patrick, G. I. Duthie, and H. R. Hoppe) and a sounder understanding of the extent to which these "bad" quarto texts might be of value to an editor.

The "good" quartos, given an improved status by Pollard's distinction, came under new scrutiny with the pioneer work of Dover Wilson, both in his essay on Shakespeare's spelling forms in *Shakespeare's Hand in "Sir Thomas More"* (1923) and in his later important study *The Manuscript of Shakespeare's "Hamlet"* (1934). Thus the first serious attempts to learn exactly what kinds of manuscripts lay behind the texts of the "good" quartos and the First Folio got under way. Other important studies followed, most notably W. W. Greg's *The Editorial Problem in Shakespeare* (1942, revised 1951) and *The Shakespeare First Folio* (1955), Alice Walker's *Textual Problems of the First Folio* (1953), and Fredson Bowers' *On Editing Shakespeare and the Elizabethan Dramatists* (1955) and *Bibliography and Textual Criticism* (1964), each probing, synthesizing, and correcting earlier work and adding valuable new techniques and further detailed information.[24]

Another aspect of textual study has received a good deal of attention in more recent years: the analysis of printing-house procedures and the way in which these procedures and the habits of individual compositors may have influenced the printed text. Aside from the interest in analytical bibliography that had been increasing steadily since R. B. McKerrow's edition of Thomas Nashe (1904–10), part of the impetus for this kind of study may be said to stem from Thomas Satchell's suggestion (*The Times Literary Supplement*, 1920) that two compositors can be distinguished, through certain spelling preferences, at work on the text of the First Folio *Macbeth*. Out of this combined interest in printing-house practice and compositor study grew E. E. Willoughby's important monograph, *The Printing of the First Folio of Shakespeare* (1932),

which was to remain the standard work for the next twenty-five years. Willoughby substantiated Satchell's suggestion by showing the presence of two main compositors (usually called A and B) at work throughout the First Folio, and he placed renewed emphasis on the already recognized but still largely unexplored problem of stop-press correction, those changes made in the printed text, through proof-reader and compositor, during the process of printing. This latter problem, for the quarto texts, was pursued further by Dover Wilson in his work on *Hamlet* (1934) and W. W. Greg in his monograph *The Variants in the First Quarto of "King Lear"* (1940).

In 1963 Charlton Hinman, after twenty years of unremitting work, published his monumental two-volume study, *The Printing and Proof-Reading of the First Folio of Shakespeare*. Hinman, correcting a number of serious misconceptions and errors in Willoughby's pioneer study, demonstrated by a variety of new techniques exactly how (by the method known as cast-off copy)[25] and in what order the plays in the First Folio were printed. He also established the presence of five compositors (two main compositors, A and B, and three others, C and D, who set largely in the Comedies, and E, apparently an apprentice, who worked in the Tragedies), distinguishing their work partly through an analysis of type-fonts, a technique which greatly strengthened and refined the older results arrived at through spelling tests alone.[26] In addition, Hinman was able to place the texts of all plays that depend on the First Folio for their basic copy-text (twenty-five) on a much firmer basis by offering the results of a thorough machine collation of some fifty copies of the First Folio. Allowing for the possibility of earlier proof correction of the standing type, the comparatively small number of significant press-corrections which were revealed demonstrates to what a slight extent, except in the work of Compositor E, any serious effort was made to ensure a sound text. Indeed, much of the press-correction seems to have been more concerned with the appearance of the page than with the accuracy of the text, and such substantive press-correction as was undertaken appears most frequently to have been made without consultation of the printer's copy.[27]

As a result of the impetus given by the "New Bibliography" a number of important editions of Shakespeare have appeared during the last fifty years. Among the most significant are J. Dover Wilson's New Cambridge (1921–66), G. L. Kittredge's (1936; revised by Irving Ribner, 1971), W. A. Neilson and C. J. Hill's (1942), Peter Alexander's (1951), Hardin

[24] E. K. Chambers' *William Shakespeare: A Study of Facts and Problems* (2 vols., Oxford, 1930) surveys and assesses textual theory up to within a year or so of its publication. An important work, always worth consulting. The most significant studies devoted to the textual problems of the individual plays may be found listed following the "Note on the Text" to each play.

[25] For a discussion of cast-off copy, see the Glossary under *Casting off*.
[26] Since Hinman's study, T. H. Howard-Hill has identified a sixth compositor (F), who replaces Hinman's Compositor A so far as the Comedies are concerned ("The Compositors of Shakespeare's Folio Comedies," *SB*, XXVI (1973), 61–106); and A. S. Cairncross ("Compositors C and D of the Shakespeare First Folio," *PBSA*, LXV (1971), 41–52) has studied and extended the scope of Compositor C's work.
[27] See the Glossary under *Proof correction* and *Stop-press correction*.

Craig's (1951; revised by David Bevington, 1973), C. J. Sisson's (1953), John Munro's (The London Shakespeare, 1958), and the individually edited volumes of the New Variorum (beginning with S. B. Hemingway's *1 Henry IV*, 1936), the New Arden (1951– , uncompleted), the revised New Yale (1954– , uncompleted), the Pelican (1956–68; re-issued in one volume, under the general editorship of Alfred Harbage, 1969), and the Signet (1963–68; reissued in one volume, under the general editorship of Sylvan Barnet, 1972).

V. THE EDITING OF
A SHAKESPEAREAN PLAY

Some of the matters discussed in the foregoing sections may be clarified if we examine in some small detail the various steps in the editorial process as it applies to a single play: *King Lear*. *King Lear* affords an unusually complicated set of textual problems, a discussion of which will illustrate a variety of similar problems encountered individually and in varying degrees in other plays.

Let us suppose, for the sake of the present discussion, that an editor is undertaking a critical edition of *King Lear* for the first time and that he does not have ready to hand a body of earlier scholarly research on which to draw in formulating his premises. There are three early printed texts of *Lear*: Q1 (1608), Q2 (1619), and F1 (1623). Pursuing the principle of copy-text selection (i.e. choosing as the basic text that edition or manuscript which appears most nearly to represent an author's final intention), the editor must first analyze each of these editions to determine which of them best fulfills this criterion. After a complete collation and analysis of the three texts, he will find that Q2 is essentially a reprint, without independent authority, of Q1 and may thus, for the moment, be dismissed. Comparison of Q1 and F1 will reveal that these texts differ in several hundred readings and that each contains words, lines, and longer passages (Q1 a whole scene) not present in the other. Given this sort of situation, the editor must now try to determine which of these texts offers the best authority for what Shakespeare wrote. Upon careful examination, he will discover, first, that, although Q1 exhibits many of the characteristics that are associated with the "bad" quartos or memorially reported texts, other aspects of Q1 suggest direct contact at places with an authoritative manuscript, probably Shakespeare's "foul papers." Second, he will find that F1 presents a text printed from copies of both Q1 and Q2 that have been corrected and amplified by collation with an apparently authoritative manuscript, probably the official prompt-book of the King's Men.[28] The editor must now decide which of these two texts to select as the copy-text. Since Q1 gives evidence of considerable memorial

contamination, he is forced to turn to F1 as the basic copy-text. But he does so without any great assurance of the ultimate authority of that text in the matter of individual readings, since the quality of the F1 text, so far as it differs from the Q1–2 text, depends upon the care and accuracy of the collator who was responsible for the preparation of the printer's copy. (A similar situation exists in *Richard III*.)

Other complicating factors remain to be considered, however. First, the question of the authority of the manuscript used by the collator from which corrections, additions, even deletions were made in preparing the Q1–2 copy for the Folio text. If, as seems likely, this manuscript was the official prompt-book, a certain caution must be exercised, because such a manuscript is almost sure to contain theatrical cuts and sophisticated readings. The matter of theatrical cuts will be discussed later in more detail. Here we may simply notice two examples of sophisticated readings. When F1 in III.vii.58 and 63 reads "sticke boarish phangs" and "that sterne time" for the Q1–2 readings "rash borish phangs" and "that dearne time", most editors now feel justified in adopting the Q1–2 readings, believing, according to the principle of *lectio difficilior*, that the more commonplace F1 readings reflect a vulgarizing of Shakespeare's idiom by stage performance. In other words, although F1 offers a generally sounder text than Q1–2, its readings, where they differ from Q1–2, may arise through several agencies, only the first of which carries any authority: (1) genuine corrections made by the collator from manuscript authority, including possible revisions made by Shakespeare himself; (2) changes made by some other person (the book-keeper or the actors); (3) errors committed by the collator; (4) errors or sophistications introduced by the compositor(s) or proof-reader in the printshop.

Second, since the F1 text was, we now believe, set up from corrected and augmented printed copy (Q1 and, to a lesser degree, Q2), it is necessary to know whether the particular copies of Q1 and Q2 used by the collator were made up of corrected or uncorrected sheets. Thus at IV.ii.28, where F1 reads "My Foole vsurps my body", Q1 in the corrected state of the sheet reads "A foole vsurps my bed". In the uncorrected state, however, Q1 reads "My foote vsurps my body" and is followed in part by Q2, which reads in turn "My foote vsurps my head". A comparison of these several readings makes it clear that in this section F1 was printed from an uncorrected state of Q1, retaining "my" and "body", and that the collator caught the error in "foote" (probably from the manuscript) but either decided to allow "My" and "body" to stand (as making sufficient sense) or failed to notice them. Since the extent and kind of correction of the line in Q1 strongly suggest that the proof-corrector consulted his manuscript copy, its reading, even allowing for the ambiguous authority of that manuscript, must be accorded considerable weight. Hence, because the F1 line seems to be a combination of correction and the following of uncorrected printed copy, most modern editors choose to read the line as in Q1: "A fool usurps my bed". This is a particularly reveal-

---

[28] For a discussion of the problems presented by the F1 and Q1 texts, see the "Note on the Text." The most recent discussion of the F1 copy for *King Lear* (J. K. Walton, *The Quarto Copy for the First Folio of Shakespeare*, Dublin, 1971) argues against any use of Q2 in the production of the F1 text.

ing example and illustrates how textual corruption can happen, and how difficult, without the kind of bibliographical evidence here fortunately present, it may be to detect it. Who, for instance, would seriously challenge the F1 reading or even that of Q2 (an obvious compositorial fudge to make better sense of "foote" by contrasting it with "head" instead of "body") were no other texts available—if, in other words, either only the text of F1 or the text of Q2 were now extant? Such a consideration should make an editor especially wary in dealing with those plays of which only one basic text has survived, such as the eighteen plays printed for the first time in F1.

This example also raises a question of the relative validity of bibliographical method. The principle here followed assumes that where the F1 text was printed from an uncorrected state of Q1 (or Q2) an editor is justified in restoring the reading of the corrected state of Q1 as more likely to represent what he believes Shakespeare wrote. Such an assumption is based upon a number of factors that make it a probable method of approaching the textual situation here involved, but obviously it cannot claim to be based on certainty. Textual analysis is not in any real sense a scientific discipline, because the essentially human element (stupidity, error, inconsistency, and simple laziness) must always be allowed for and can so easily upset the nicest calculations. It deals for the most part, aside from its most mechanical aspects, in approaches and principles based on a weighing of a variety of kinds of evidence and often reaches conclusions that allow only a measure of greater or lesser probability. Thus when an editor in the instances discussed above chooses to desert his copy-text (here F1) and read with the corrected state of Q1, he is making an editorial decision that is based not on unassailable evidence or certainty but on a method of approach that, given the evidence available, seems to him most likely to restore the author's original language. No one, it should be stressed, is more painfully conscious than the editor how often the "principles" that he seems to lay down with an inevitable appearance of dogma, particularly in textually difficult plays like *Lear*, *Hamlet*, *Richard III*, *Othello*, and *Troilus and Cressida*, are indeed only working hypotheses and hence open to challenge on a different interpretation of the same evidence.

Another related aspect of the F1 text must be considered: the use of corrected Q2 copy for parts of the F1 text. Since Q2 is essentially a reprint of Q1, with one or two slight additions (III.vi.47, IV.vi.197), and its variants cannot lay claim to manuscript authority, where F1 reproduces a reading from its Q2 copy that differs from the reading of Q1, it may be fairly argued that the collator in preparing his Q2 copy failed to make the proper correction from the manuscript and that the Q1 reading, which has at least some manuscript authority, should be restored (see the Textual Notes at I.iv.22, 31, II.ii.65, 100, 151, etc.). Again the principle employed must be recognized as one involving only a measure of probability.

Speaking generally, an editor today, having chosen for what he considers sound reasons a particular copy-text, will adhere to that copy-text unless he sees substantial grounds for departing from it. Several examples of deliberate departure from the copy-text readings have already been cited in the preceding discussion, involving F1 sophistication or vulgarization, press variants, and faulty printer's copy. But these are all matters of substituting one early reading for another early reading that the evidence suggests has superior authority. What, however, guides the editor when he has to determine whether a passage unique to a text of such uneven authority as Q1 is indeed Shakespeare's and not rather the work of some alien hand? He may find, for instance, that the passage fits naturally into the context of surrounding lines or that it contains actual verbal links which show that at one time it was part of the original, cut in the printer's copy or accidentally (even intentionally) omitted by the compositor. For example, in I.ii, lines 95–97 are found only in Q1–2. Where F1 reads "*Glou.* He cannot bee such a Monster. *Edmond* seeke him out:", Q1–2 reads "*Glost.* He cannot be such a monster. / *Bast.* Nor is not sure. / *Glost.* To his father, that so tenderly and intirely loues him, heauen and earth! *Edmund* seeke him out,". The tone of Edmund's "Nor is not sure." is perfectly in keeping with his pretended defense of Edgar in lines 85–88 ("I dare pawne downe my life for him, that he hath writ this to feele my affection to your Honor, & to no other pretence of danger." [F1]), and an editor is justified in feeling that the F1 omission is most probably the result of a theatrical cut. Even more clearly the result of an intentional cut in the prompt-book, however, is the omission in F1 of lines 16–20 toward the end of I.iii, where the first half of the additional Q1–2 line 16 ("Not to be ouerrul'd.") completes the full sense of lines 14–15, common to both F1 and Q1–2. One more example may be noted in I.iv, where, at line 137, both F1 and Q1–2 make the Fool say "Do'st thou know the difference my Boy, betweene a bitter Foole, and a sweet one." and Lear answers "No Lad, teach me." At this point F1 omits lines 140–155 found in Q1–2 ("*Foole.* That Lord . . . they'l be snatching;"), in the first part of which lines the Fool gives in detail the answer to the question he had posed in lines 137–38. The omission of this passage makes relative nonsense of the F1 text, and it is difficult to believe that such an omission represents an intentional theatrical cut reflecting the collator's use of a prompt-book manuscript, but it is also difficult to explain how a passage of this length could be accidentally omitted by the F1 compositor.

One substantial passage, a whole scene (IV.iii), occurs only in Q1–2, and in such a case the editor is forced to judge its authenticity on its own merits, without the aid of immediate context. The poetic quality and general context of the scene are such, however, that no editor, since Pope first included it in an edited text, has seriously questioned its Shakespearean origin. It is, moreover, the kind of scene that can be deleted without any dislocation of the plot-line, hence a natural prey for a book-keeper intent on shortening an overlong play.

Occasionally, however, an editor rejects Q1–2 additions. Such rejected readings tend to be extra-metrical single words or phrases, which, given the postulated memorial contamination of the Q1 text, are looked upon as the work of either the reporters or the actors. For instance, in I.i.45, Q1–2 read "The two great Princes *France* and *Burgundy*", where F1 reads "The Princes, *France* & *Burgundy*". To include "two great" would make the F1 line, already extra-metrical ("May be preuented now. The Princes, *France* & *Burgundy*"), completely unmanageable as a single line and necessitate its being broken into a half-line plus a full line, the half-line being left uncompleted in the middle of a speech. It is clear, moreover, that the additional Q1–2 words are in fact mere padding to substitute metrically for the omission of lines 40–45 in Q1–2. (An analogous example of F1 padding, to accommodate a cut of some lines occurring in Q1–2, may be studied in the Textual Notes to II.ii.145.) Again, in line 90 of the opening scene, the Q1–2 reading "How, nothing can come of nothing, speake againe." offers a good instance of the extra-metrical expletive common in reported texts and usually considered as an actor's trick for false emphasis. F1 reads "Nothing will come of nothing, speake againe."—a stronger and metrically better balanced line. (Compare the Q1–2 addition of "Goe to, goe to" in line 233 of this same scene.)

At this point, an editor, having determined that a critically edited text of *Lear* should, on the evidence sketched above, be based on F1 but admit a substantial number of lines found only in Q1–2, still has to face the problem of necessary emendation. In a number of instances, even with the aid of Q1–2, individual readings require editorial emendation to bring meaning to an otherwise corrupt passage. Significant emendation is made on two levels: (1) substantive (i.e. corrections concerned with the verbal texture of a passage, including also stage directions and speech-prefixes); and (2) semi-substantive (i.e. corrections concerned with punctuation, the so-called accidentals, that may be said to affect the meaning of a passage). Examples of semi-substantive emendation occur frequently in *Lear*, particularly in passages dependent on the lightly and erratically punctuated Q1 text, and may be readily studied by turning to the Textual Notes (see, for example, I.i.20–21, 127, I.iv.92, 204, II.i.14, II.ii.45–46, 51, II.iv.102, III.iv.117, III.vi.68–69, III.vii.46–47, IV.i.2, IV.ii.66, IV.iii.17–18, 19, 51, IV.vi.265–66, V.iii.51–52, 121–22). Substantive emendation is generally speaking a more complicated matter and is worth illustration here.

In I.ii.20–21, where Edmund says in F1, "*Edmond* the base / Shall to'th' Legitimate:", Q1–2 read: "*Edmund* the base shall tooth' legitimate:". Several emendations have been suggested ("Shall be the" [Pope], "Shall toe the" [Hanmer]) and a few editors have defended the F1 reading (Sisson most recently) on the grounds that it might be interpreted to mean "shall fight against" or "shall turn into"—both strained interpretations. But most editors accept, as does the present editor, Edwards' conjecture, "Shall top the legitimate"—a reading that on both graphic ("to" or "too" to "top") and associative terms (with "I grow" [line 21] and by contrast with the repeated burden of "base" that informs much of the soliloquy) fulfills the demands of the context perfectly.

Again, in II.ii.143 (a passage found only in Q1–2) the uncorrected state of Q1 reads "as basest and contaned wretches". In the corrected state "contaned" is altered to "temnest", a reading followed by Q2. The puzzling "temnest" is a nonce-word of at best questionable meaning; moreover, it is metrically unsatisfactory. Pope emended it to "the meanest" and was followed in desperation by several of his successors. Capell was the first to see that the true reading was a combination of the corrected and uncorrected states: "contemned'st". It is possible, in this case, to reconstruct how the corrected state of Q1 came to read "temnest". The proof-corrector wrote "temnest" in the margin of his proof-sheet and crossed through "taned" in the uncorrected reading "contaned"; the compositor, however, in making the correction, thought "contaned" as a whole was marked for deletion and hence did not retain the necessary "con". One further point. The form "contemnest" which the proof-corrector intended is a possible Elizabethan past participial superlative, but it does not take account of the "d" in "contaned", the presence of which in the uncorrected reading, however badly garbled that reading may be, probably reflects a "d" form in the manuscript.

A final example: in IV.vi.165–67 (part of a passage found only in F1) F1 reads "Place sinnes with Gold . . . Arme it in ragges". Pope was the first to suggest reading "Plate sins with gold". He was probably led to his emendation by "Arme", since the meaning of "plate" was in Shakespeare's time "to cover with metal plates for ornament or protection," but he may also have recognized how easily a carelessly formed "t" in the English secretary hand could be misread as a secretary "c". A little later Theobald (in his second edition, 1740), adopting Pope's "Plate", emended "sinnes" to "sin", making clear for the first time the antecedent of "it" in line 167. Both Pope's and Theobald's emendations illustrate what is called the principle of *ductus literarum* (i.e. the guidance, through form or shape and number, of the letters in a word requiring emendation). Thus a compositor would be much more likely to misread "Plate" as "Place" than to misread "Plate" as "Disguise" or "Cover", either word in itself possible, though metrically awkward, if only the context of the passage is considered. Theobald, on the other hand, instead of emending "sinnes" to "sin", might have emended "it" (line 167) to "them" to make it agree with "sinnes". But it is obviously much more probable that a compositor would misread "sinne" as "sinnes" (the misreading of a singular as a plural is not uncommon in F1 and other contemporary printed texts) than that he would misread "them" as "it."

The three examples just discussed illustrate most of the approaches that may, with some degree of safety, be taken to the problem of emendation, always allowing, of course, for sheer inspiration, which, though most often highly dangerous, may be on properly rare occasions the "very opening of the mouth of nature." To sum up, these approaches are: (1) through the immediate or larger context; (2) through contributory bibliographical evidence, when any is available; (3) through metrical considerations; (4) through recognizing possible compositorial misreading of the various kinds of hands practiced in the period; and (5) through the *ductus literarum*, an approach closely associated with (4).

We have now followed an editor through the principal steps he must take before he can begin to produce a critical text, modernized or old-spelling, of *King Lear*. Enough has been said to make it clear that, even when all the procedures outlined above have been conscientiously applied, much remains uncertain and problematical. That no two editors, given the diversity and complicated nature of the textual situation and the considerable element of personal editorial decision involved, would ever produce identical critical texts of *Lear* need not be a matter for surprise or alarm. It is indeed the very presence of the human element, the possibility for the exercise of individual taste and critical acumen, that has made the editing of Shakespeare such a challenge to so many scholars for the last two hundred and fifty years.

VI. THE PRESENT EDITION

The present text is based on a new collation and study of the early substantive editions and consultation of all the major edited texts from Rowe's (1709) onward. Every effort consistent with critical sense has been made to adhere to the declared copy-text (see the "Note on the Text" following each of the plays and poems), and unnecessary emendation, that pricking devil, has been carefully eschewed. When the copy-text, however, resisted all reasonable attempts to make sense of it, readings from another early printed text or from other editions have, of course, been admitted, but in all such cases the emendation has been placed in square brackets to warn the reader that the text at this point is open to question. The original reading, and the source of the emended reading, will be found recorded in the Textual Notes. Obvious compositorial errors, unless the error produces a new word, are corrected without employing square brackets, but the original reading is nevertheless recorded in the Textual Notes. Square brackets have also been used to alert the reader to all added or altered material in stage directions and to distinguish words or passages that have been inserted into the basic copy-text from some other early edition which there is reason to believe preserves Shakespearean words or lines missing for one reason or another from the copy-text. The source of all such additional bracketed material is indicated in the Textual Notes, except for certain supplementary character identifications that are plain from the context, e.g. "*Enter* DUKE [FREDERICK] *with* LORDS.", "*Enter* CLOWN, *Old Lady* [COUNTESS], *and* LAFEW." When the speech-prefixes for a character show more than one

form in the copy-text, they have been regularized to a single form throughout; altered forms are not enclosed in square brackets, but the copy-text variations, where they seem of textual or bibliographical interest, are recorded in the Textual Notes. When a speech is assigned to a speaker different from the one designated in the copy-text, the speech-prefix is of course treated like any other emendation.

Although the present text is basically a modern-spelling text, an attempt has been made to preserve a selection of Elizabethan spelling forms that reflect, or may reflect, a distinctive contemporary pronunciation, both those that are invariant in the early printed texts and those that appear beside the spellings familiar today and so suggest possible variant pronunciations of single words. In the first category, examples may be found in such forms (including also proper names) as haberdepois (avoirdupois), fift or sixt (fifth or sixth), wrack (wreck); Birnan (Birnam), Bullingbrook (Bolingbroke), Callice (Calais), Dolphin (Dauphin), Roan (Rouen). In the second category: bankrout–bankrupt, conster–construe, embassador–ambassador, fadom–fathom, incestious–incestuous, renowm–renown, vild–vile. For words in this second category the present text, following the example of Kittredge, adopts on each occurrence the variant form that appears in the copy-text. Although the forms preserved may in many cases represent scribal or compositorial choices rather than Shakespeare's own preferences, such an approach nevertheless suggests the kind of linguistic climate in which he wrote and avoids the unhistorical and sometimes insensitive levelling that full-scale modernization (never consistent itself) imposes. It was believed, in short, that something valuable was to be gained by allowing, within limits, some of the variety and color of the originals to survive the process of modernization.

The punctuation of a modernized text presents serious problems. A frequent practice is to impose a single modern standard throughout, but this leads almost inevitably to a heavy use of semicolons and periods. The punctuation in the early texts is comparatively light, especially in the earlier quartos, and creates occasional difficulties for the modern reader, but an editor who feels, as Dr. Johnson did, that punctuation is entirely in his power, and who ignores the punctuation of the copy-text, does so at the risk of continual damage to the movement and frequently to the meaning of the lines, either verse or prose. Judging from the evidence of the insurrection scene in *Sir Thomas More* (accepted in this edition as almost certainly in Shakespeare's autograph), Shakespeare employed a punctuation so light as to be almost nonexistent. This single example need not, of course, mean that he always did so, but the supposition that he favored a light and running punctuation receives considerable support from the quarto texts believed to have been set from some form of his autograph. Thus, though the punctuation in the early texts may be in good part the work of someone in the printing-house, or of a scribe, it is probably nearer to Shakespeare's intentions and nearer to the speech rhythms of the period than any later and more tightly logical system can pretend to be. In the present edition, therefore, the punctuation of the different copy-texts has been followed as closely as is consistent with clarity. In many plays this means a frequent use of the comma where modern punctuation would employ either a semicolon or a period, but the resulting freedom in the flow of the verse and the immediacy with which sentences and sentence elements are related justify such an approach. Where, however, there is danger of misreading or ambiguity in the original pointing, the punctuation has been adjusted; but all changes that seem to involve a shift in meaning are recorded in the Textual Notes.

In writing verse, Elizabethan poets made a regular distinction, usually carefully preserved in printed texts, between final -*ed* (syllabic) and -'*d* (non-syllabic) in words to which it is phonetically possible to attach both forms of the suffix. This useful distinction has been retained in verse passages, and all departures from the copy-text form are recorded in the Textual Notes. In prose, however, the two forms appear to have been used indiscriminately, the choice being governed sometimes merely by the compositor's need to justify his lines. For this reason the present text has levelled all such forms in prose passages to -'*d*, except (a) in certain words where the form in -*ed* seems to have been commonly employed in colloquial usage, and (b) in the speeches of a very few characters, such as Don Armado or Fluellen, who are presented to us as affected or "outlandish" speakers.

The act and scene designations in the present text generally agree with those found in the Globe edition (1864). Where such designations are additions to the copy-text, or alterations of it, they are here enclosed in square brackets and their sources are recorded in the Textual Notes. In addition, a summary statement of the act-scene arrangement in the copy-text will be found at the beginning of the Textual Notes to each play. The scene-by-scene line-numbering is based on the lineation of verse and prose as that appears in the present text; hence it will often differ, especially in prose passages, from that found in other texts, but usually by not more than a few lines either way. Recently, a system of what is called through-line-numbering (TLN) has been introduced by Charlton Hinman in his facsimile of the First Folio published in 1968. The basis of his system, which numbers the lines of each play consecutively, ignoring scene breaks, from beginning to end, is the text as it is printed in the First Folio. Thus line numbers are assigned to whatever act and scene designations occur, to stage directions, and to every line and part line (including verse run-overs but excluding turn-overs and turn-unders) that takes up what might be considered a line space in the First Folio. Where additional lines, not in the Folio, appear in a modern text edited from quarto copy-text, these additional lines are indicated by placing after the last numbered folio line a plus sign followed by the number of added lines. For example, "2225+10" indicates that, following line 2225 in the Folio numeration, the text contains ten lines found only in the quarto text. A system of block TLN notation, based on Hinman's facsimile, has been devised for the present edition. At the top of each column of the text (the first page of a play excepted) may be found the numbers of the first and last lines in that column (e.g. 2403–2455). Thus a reference to line 2425 of *Hamlet* may be readily located with something approaching accuracy. Two special points need to be noticed. First, frequently in prose passages (and occasionally in verse passages) the second number in a block reappears as the first number in the next block because a prose line (or mislined verse line) in the Folio numeration has necessarily been divided between two lines in the present text. Second, where a series of lines that do not appear in F1 (and hence have no Folio line numbers) are divided between the end of one column and the beginning of the next, the lines are described thus: "1065+9(1–3)" and "1065+9(4–9)", indicating that a total of nine lines are involved in the non-F1 lines and that individual lines in this group may be distinguished as "1065+1", "1065+2", etc. TLN numbering for *Pericles* and *The Two Noble Kinsmen* is based on the first quarto of *Pericles* (1609) and the quarto of *The Two Noble Kinsmen* (1634). The reader should be warned that the total number of lines recorded for a play by the TLN method does not at all accurately indicate the actual number of lines of dialogue contained in the play, since such numeration includes F1 act-scene divisions and stage directions, verse run-overs, and part lines, and on the other hand does not include in the final figure all the additional lines not present in the F1 text.

The Textual Notes, which follow the individual plays, are intended to serve two principal functions. First, as has already been pointed out, they are intended to document the texts in the present edition by recording the source of all emendations and additions, i.e. the authority (other early printed texts or later editions) on which the emendation or addition has been adopted. They include also a record of all changes in the punctuation of the copy-text that may be said to affect meaning significantly. New readings introduced by the present editor are designated "*ed*." Second, the Textual Notes have been so constructed as to offer a reader all the essential information he may need to study in depth the whole textual situation as it has been outlined for him in the "Note on the Text" prefixed to the Textual Notes for each play. Thus for what may be called two-text plays (i.e. plays published first in quarto from an authoritative manuscript and later in F1 in a substantially different text) the Textual Notes record the more significant variations between the version here chosen as copy-text and the other substantive version, and for *Richard III*, *Hamlet*, *Troilus and Cressida*, *King Lear*, and *Othello*, where the choice of copy-text is more complicated than in other plays, they record all substantive variants of the second text.

Five qualifications on the inclusiveness of the Textual Notes should be pointed out here. (1) Although substantial passages of special interest are quoted from each of the "bad" quartos at appropriate places in the Textual Notes, no systematic attempt could be made to record the great mass of individual textual variants in these quartos (apart from those for *Richard III* and *Lear*, both special cases) except where such variants are cited as part of an entry concerned with a particular reading in the substantive texts. (2) Where there is more than a single edition of a quarto published before the appearance of F1 in 1623, the numerous errors or unauthoritative compositorial variants introduced into the second and all succeeding editions are in general not recorded unless they figure as part of the presentation of the development of the substantive texts. (3) The variant readings of the later folios (1632, 1663, 1685) and of those quartos published after F1 (1623), since they possess no independent or manuscript authority, are included only when they seem to be of special significance in the later history of the text. (4) No attempt has been made to record the many hundreds of textual emendations offered by editors and critics during the past two hundred and fifty years unless (a) one of these emendations has been adopted in the present text or (b) the textual situation was desperate enough to warrant a selection of the proposed readings. In particular cases, some of the suggested emendations are noticed in the glossarial notes. (5) Adjustments in verse alignment are not recorded unless they affect the passage in some significant way. Although in one sense these partial exclusions in the Textual Notes constitute a limitation, in another they greatly sharpen the focus on significant readings and serve to winnow out a great deal of meaningless chaff. The reader who desires additional details may refer to the collations in the revised Cambridge *Shakespeare* (1891–93) or to the more recent volumes of the *New Variorum Shakespeare*.

The text of the present edition has been used by Professor Marvin Spevack as the basis of his recently published *Complete and Systematic Concordance to the Works of Shakespeare* (6 vols., 1968–70). This invaluable concordance is the first that in any definitive sense deserves the term "complete." It lists, with context, arranged alphabetically for the works as a whole (Vols. IV–VI) and individually, without context, for each work (Vols. I–III), *all* uses of *all* words occurring in the present text of the plays and poems. It also presents, as part of Vols. I–III, separate character concordances to each play, and includes in Vol. VI a number of extremely useful appendices: a Word-Frequency Index, a Reverse-Word Index, a list of Hyphenated Words alphabetized by first, second, and third elements, a list of Homographs, and a Conversion Table for through-line-numbering. Professor Spevack's concordance completely supersedes the old John Bartlett *Concordance* (1894), which is far from complete; and it serves a large variety of interests (including inclusiveness) not covered by the old-spelling concordances now being published, a separate volume to each play, by T. H. Howard-Hill. In fairness to Professor Spevack, it should here be noted that the very occasional discrepancies between his concordance and the texts as now published must be laid to the present editor's belated change of mind. In Vol. VI (pp. 4341–42) Professor Spevack has included a list of substantive changes; some adjustments in punctuation do not in any way affect the use of the concordance. A one-volume concordance based on Vols. IV–VI, *The Harvard Concordance to Shakespeare*, has been published by Harvard University Press (1973).

Glossary of Selected Bibliographical Terms

The following definitions are intended for use with the foregoing essay and with the bibliographical "Note on the Text" preceding the Textual Notes to each play. They should be considered as general working definitions, aimed primarily at the non-specialist. For further information the reader may consult: Fredson Bowers, *Principles of Bibliographical Description* (Princeton, 1949); Philip Gaskell, *A New Introduction to Bibliography* (Oxford, 1972); Charlton Hinman, *The Printing and Proof-Reading of the First Folio of Shakespeare*, 2 vols. (Oxford, 1963); Joseph Moxon, *Mechanick Exercises on the Whole Art of Printing* (1683–84), ed. Herbert Davis and Harry Carter (London, 1958); and R. B. McKerrow, *An Introduction to Bibliography for Literary Students* (Oxford, rev. ed., 1928).

Analytical bibliography (sometimes referred to as the "New Bibliography"). Analytical bibliography (as distinguished from descriptive or merely enumerative bibliography) is concerned with the printing process (i.e. the various steps through which printer's copy passes on its way to becoming a book) and seeks to establish, so far as possible, (a) the kind and authority (source), usually manuscript (except in reprints), of the printer's copy; and (b) the extent to which the composition and printing processes may have affected the quality of the printed text. The principal matters with which an analytical bibliographer concerns himself are: (a) the method employed in composition (whether seriatim or by casting off); (b) compositor determination (i.e. determining the identity and the characteristics of the compositor or compositors responsible for setting the type); (c) analysis of the amount and accuracy of press-correction through the collation of multiple copies of the same edition; (d) analysis of the running-titles, rules, etc. to establish the possible order of imposition within the sheet, or of sheets within the book; and (e) the detection and interpretation of cancels. Most of the bibliographical terms employed above are separately defined elsewhere in the Glossary.

Broadside: usually, a single folio leaf (half the size of the basic sheet), printed on one side only, used for the publication of proclamations, ballads, and ephemera generally. Occasionally the full, unfolded sheet was used.

Cancel: a term used to describe newly set printed matter substituted for some part of the contents of a work as originally set and printed off. The leaf (or leaves) that is replaced is known as the *cancellandum* (plural *cancellanda*); the leaf (or leaves) that is substituted (necessarily reset recto and verso), as the *cancellans* (plural *cancellantes*). Very occasionally a short passage may be found cancelled by a newly set printed slip pasted over the original setting of type; thus the necessity of resetting a whole leaf is avoided.

Casting off and cast-off copy. To cast off or count off printer's copy is (a) to estimate in advance as nearly as possible how many sheets a given amount of manuscript or printed copy will require to produce a book in a chosen type-size and format (folio, quarto, octavo, or other); (b) to estimate, even more exactly, the amount of copy, page by page, that may be contained in a sheet (or sheets), inner and outer forme, thus permitting copy to be divided among two or more printing shops, or two compositors within a single shop working simultaneously, either together on the setting of one sheet or independently on different sheets, with the necessary assurance, not always justified in actual practice, that one will end where the other began. The Shakespeare First Folio (a folio-in-sixes) used setting by cast-off copy generally throughout. For a large book like the First Folio, in which each page contains two long columns of relatively small type, this method had certain definite advantages. First, it allowed two compositors to work simultaneously on each six-leaf quire (see *Folio-in-sixes*). Assuming a six-leaf quire with the pages numbered consecutively 1 through 12, one compositor could, after the copy had been cast off, begin setting page 6, working back from page 6 to page 5, from 5 to 4, finally ending by setting page 1. The second compositor could at the same time begin setting page 7, working forward to page 8 and so seriatim through page 12. Such a procedure essentially halved the time it would have taken a single compositor working serially from page 1 through 12 on the same amount of copy, and thus balanced the differential in time between the comparatively slower process of composition (type-setting) and the faster mechanical process of impression (printing off), by permitting printing to begin as soon as pages 6 and 7 (constituting the inner forme of the innermost of the three sheets employed in the quire and the first to be set up by the two compositors working simultaneously) were in type, to be followed in sequence by pages 5 and

8, 4 and 9, etc. In contrast, if the six-leaf quire were set seriatim (i.e. pages 1 through 12), printing could not begin until page 7 had been set, completing the first printable forme. Second, the technique of setting from cast-off copy considerably reduced the amount of type locked up in type-pages at any one time, since once pages 6 and 7, 5 and 8, etc. had been printed off, the type could at once be redistributed in the type cases and become available for use in setting later pages of the same quire. In the seriatim method a much larger amount of type was out of circulation for a considerably longer period. Since the quantity of a particular type-face was necessarily limited, the comparatively speedier freeing of that type for further setting was an important consideration. The use of cast-off copy was not, however, without some attendant dangers. If, in a folio-in-sixes for example, the copy had been inaccurately cast off, the compositor who was working back from page 6 to page 1 of a given quire might discover when he came to set page 1 that he had either too little or too much copy to fit the regular format of the page. Since he had no place to go, the last page of the preceding quire and the following page of the present quire being either already printed off or in the process of being so, he had to solve his problem within the limits of page 1. If his copy had been overestimated, he could employ more white space in setting up the page (allowing some extra space between speeches, setting with extra space for entries and exits, turning over verse lines, etc.). If his copy had been underestimated, he might be in deeper trouble. If by the utmost squeezing and crowding he could not accommodate his remaining material, "judicious" omission was his only recourse. How often this desperate situation arose, we do not know, but Charlton Hinman (*The Printing and Proof-Reading of the First Folio of Shakespeare*, II, 507–8) suggests such an explanation to account for the omission of an important stage direction in *Antony and Cleopatra* at V.ii.34, where the folio page, significantly the first page of quire 2z, shows other obvious evidence of crowding.

Catchword: a printer's device, derived from earlier manuscript practice, to link page to page, both within the quire and from quire to quire. It consists of setting the first word of the following page (or the beginning of the word if it is of several syllables) at the foot of the preceding page, below the text and as far to the right as the line-measure (see *Line-measure*) being employed will allow. Catchwords were considered useful both in imposition and binding procedures. A lack of agreement between the catchword and the first word on the following page is a warning signal of possible textual difficulties, involving perhaps the omission of one or more words. Abbreviated as "cw."

Collation: (a) A formula for describing the make-up of a printed book (or manuscript); for example, 4to A–H⁴ (i.e. a quarto, with quires signed A through H, each quire containing four leaves).

(b) The word-for-word and point-for-point comparison of two texts of the same work (either printed or manuscript) made with the intention of correcting one text by reference to the other or of recording differences between the two texts.

Composition: the setting of type from printer's copy.

Compositor: one who composes or sets type from printer's copy.

Copy: see *Printer's copy*.

Copy-text: the printed edition or manuscript upon which an editor bases his text.

Edition: all copies of a book printed from the same setting of type (allowing for the differences between copies resulting from press-correction). See *State*; *Issue*; *Stop-press correction*.

Folio: (a) A printer's designation for the format of a book (applied also to the bound volume) in which the individual sheets have been folded once, across the middle of the longer side (i.e. parallel with the shorter side), thus producing two leaves for every sheet (see *Sheet*). The measurements of each leaf, depending on the size of the sheet employed, vary from approximately 15″ by 10″ (large folio) to 12″ by 8″ (small folio), with many intermediate sizes. Abbreviated as "2°" and in non-collational reference as "F". Folio volumes in Elizabethan-Jacobean times (and later) were usually gathered in fours, sixes, or eights (see *Folio-in-sixes*). Bound copies of the same book will differ in leaf measurements depending on the amount of trimming the sheets were subjected to in the process of binding (true also, of course, of bound copies in quarto, octavo, and other formats). (b) Used also (derived from manuscript terminology and abbreviated as "fol." or "f.") to designate a single leaf (as distinguished from a page) in a quire (even in books of other than folio format).

Folio-in-sixes: a book (like the Shakespeare First Folio) in folio format in which each quire is made up of three folded sheets placed one inside another at the fold so as to produce a quire of six leaves (twelve pages). In such a folio quire, leaves 1 and 6, 2 and 5, 3 and 4 will be what are called conjugate leaves, i.e. leaves which are part of the same sheet and joined at the fold. This method of production facilitated both the sewing and binding process, reducing the bulk of a folio volume's spine. The same process was used to produce a folio-in-fours (two sheets) and a folio-in-eights (four sheets).

Format: see *Folio*; *Quarto*; *Octavo*.

Forme: a term applied to type-pages once they have been imposed (see *Imposition*) and firmly locked in the "chase" (the metal rectangular frame surrounding the imposed type-pages). A forme is described as "outer" or "inner," the outer forme always containing the first page of a quire (i.e. the recto of the first leaf) in all formats (folio, quarto, octavo, etc.)

Gathering: used as synonymous with "quire" (see *Quire*).

Imposition: the correct placement of the type-pages in the forme (outer and inner). See *Forme*. In quarto format, pages 1, 4, 5, 8 would thus be imposed in the outer forme and pages 2, 3, 6, 7 in the inner forme, each set so arranged in its forme that when the sheet is correctly folded the pages will appear in the sequence 1 through 8.

Impression: any continuous press-run from one setting of type. In Elizabethan-Jacobean times an ordinance of the Stationers' Company issued in 1587 made it illegal (with rare exceptions, specially authorized) to print off more than 1250 to 1500 copies of a work from the same setting of type. The rule (not always observed) was aimed at protecting the compositors from exploitation by the master printers. Since type was regularly redistributed to the type-cases as soon as the press-run had been completed for each forme, the same type being employed in setting other parts of the same book, what we would call a new impression (or reimpression) from the original setting of type very rarely occurred at this period.

Issue: a term used to designate the republication (second issue) of what are basically the original sheets of a book, but with the addition or substitution of newly set matter (usually a cancel title-page, more rarely other reset material supplied by a cancel leaf or cancel quire). See *Cancel*.

Justifying: the process by which a compositor in setting prose (occasionally verse) might adjust his line length to fit the adopted line-measure (see *Line-measure*), thus producing an even right type-page margin. The compositor could "justify" his line by altering the amount of space between words and by variations in spelling forms (e.g. "do" or "doe", "sin" or "sinne", "felicity" or "felicitie").

Line-measure: the chosen width of a type-page, or of a column in a two-column page (hence controlling the capacity of the individual type-line), determined in advance according to book format and page design, and controlled, from page to page, by the setting on the compositor's composing-stick. See *Justifying*.

Octavo: a printer's designation for the format of a book (applied also to the bound volume) in which the individual sheets have been folded three times, the direction of all three folds repeating that used in folio and quarto format, thus producing eight leaves (sixteen pages) to a quire. Abbreviated as "8°" or "8vo" and in non-collational reference as "O". The measurements of an octavo may be taken as roughly half those of a quarto, with the proviso noted under *Folio*.

Perfecting: the impression or printing off of the second side (either outer or inner forme) of a sheet that has already been printed off on one side.

Press-correction: see *Stop-press correction*.

Printer's copy: the manuscript or printed material from which the compositor set his type-pages. When the compositor used an earlier edition of a work as copy for a new edition in the same format, he usually

hould my performance perish.

Rom. Thou haſt *Ventidius* that, without the which a
Souldier and his Sword grauuts ſcarce diſtinction : thou
wilt write to *Anthony.*

Ven. Ile humbly ſignifie what in his name,
That magicall word of Warre we haue effected,
How with his Banners,and his well paid ranks,
The nere-yet beaten Horſe of Parthia,
We haue iaded out o'th Field.

Rom. Where is he now?

Ven. He purpoſeth to Athens, whither with what haſt
The waight we muſt conuay with's,will permit :
We ſhall appeare before him. On there, paſſe along.

Exeunt.

Enter Agrippa at one doore, Enobarbus at another.

Agri. What are the Brothers parted?

Eno. They haue diſpatcht with *Pompey*,he is gone,
The other three are Sealing. *Octauia* weepes
To part from Rome: *Caſar* is ſad,and *Lepidus*
Since *Pompey's* feaſt, as *Menas* ſaies,is troubled
With the Greene-Sickneſſe.

Agri. 'Tis a Noble *Lepidus.*

Eno. A very fine one : oh, how he loues *Caſar.*

Agri. Nay but how deerely he adores *Mark Anthony.*

Eno. *Caſar* ? why he's the Iupiter of men.

Ant. What's *Anthony*,the God of Iupiter ?

Eno. Spake you of *Caſar* ? How, the non-pareill ?

Agri. Oh *Anthony*,oh thou Arabian Bird !

Eno. Would you praiſe *Caſar*,ſay *Caſar* go no further.

Agr. Indeed he plied them both with excellent praiſes.

Eno. But he loues *Caſar* beſt,yet he loues *Anthony* :
Hoo Hearts,Tongues,Figure,
Scribes,Bards,Poets,cannot
Thinke ſpeake, caſt,write,ſing,number: hoo,
His loue to *Anthony.* But as for *Caſar,*
Kneele downe,kneele downe,and wonder.

Agri. Both he loues.

Eno. They are his Shards,and he their Beetle,ſo:
This is to horſe : Adieu,Noble *Agrippa.*

Agri. Good Fortune worthy Souldier,and farewell.

Enter Caſar, Anthony, Lepidus, and Octauia.

Antho. No further Sir.

Caſar. You take from me a great part of my ſelfe:
Vſe me well in't. Siſter,proue ſuch a wife
As my thoughts make thee,and as my fartheſt Band
Shall paſſe on thy approoſe : moſt Noble *Anthony,*
Let not the peece of Vertue which is ſet
Betwixt vs,as the Cyment of our loue
To keepe it builded,be the Ramme to batter
The Fortreſſe of it:for better might we
Haue lou'd without this meane,if on both parts
This be not cheriſht.

Ant. Make me not offended,in your diſtruſt.

Caſar, I haue ſaid.

Ant. You ſhall not finde,
Though you be therein curious,the leſt cauſe
For what you ſeeme to feare,ſo the Gods keepe you,
And make the hearts of Romaines ſerue your ends :
We will heere part.

Caſar. Farewell my deereſt Siſter,fare thee well,
The Elements be kind to thee,and make
Thy ſpirits all of comfort : fare thee well.

Octa. My Noble Brother.

Anth. The Aprill's in her eyes, it is Loues ſpring,
And theſe the ſhowers to bring it on : be cheerfull.

Octa. Sir,looke well to my Husbands houſe : and

Caſar. What *Octauia* ?

Octa. Ile tell you in your eare.

Ant. Her tongue will not obey her heart,nor can
Her heart informe her tougue.
The Swannes downe feather
That ſtands vpon the Swell at the of full Tide :
And neither way inclines.

Eno. Will *Caſar* weepe?

Agr. He ha's a cloud in's face.

Eno. He were the worſe for that were he a Horſe,ſo is
he being a man.

Agri. Why *Enobarbus* :
When *Anthony* found *Iulius Caſar* dead,
He cried almoſt to roaring : And he wept,
When at Phillippi he found *Brutus* ſlaine.

Eno. That yeare indeed,he was troubled with a rume,
What willingly he did confound,he wail'd,
Beleeu't till I weepe too.

Caſar. No ſweet *Octauia,*
You ſhall heare from me ſtill : the time ſhall not
Out-go my thinking on you.

Ant. Come Sir,come,
Ile wraſtle with you in my ſtrength of loue,
Looke heere I haue you,thus I let you go,
And giue you to the Gods.

Caſar. Adieu,be happy.

Lep. Let all the number of the Starres giue light
To thy faire way.

Caſar. Farewell,farewell. Kiſſes Octauia.

Ant. Farewell. Trumpets ſound. Exeunt.

Enter Cleopatra,Charmian,Iras,and Alexas.

Cleo. Where is the Fellow ?

Alex. Halfe afeard to come.

Cleo. Go too,go too. Con e hither Sir.

Enter the Meſſenger as before.

Alex. Good Maieſtie: *Herod* of Iury dare not looke
vpon you,but when you are well pleaſ'd.

Cleo. That *Herods* head,Ile haue : but how? When
Anthony is gone,through whom I might commaund it:
Come thou neere.

Meſ. Moſt gratious Maieſtie.

Cleo. Did'ſt thou behold *Octauia* ?

Meſ. I dread Queene.

Cleo. Where ?

Meſ. Madam in Rome, I lookt her in the face: and
ſaw her led betweene her Brother,and *Marke Anthony.*

Cleo. Is ſhe as tall as me ?

Meſ. She is not Madam.

Cleo. Didſt heare her ſpeake ?
Is ſhe ſhrill tongu'd or low ?

Meſ. Madam,I heard her ſpeake ſhe is low voic'd.

Cleo. That's not ſo good : he cannot like her long.

Char. Like her ? Oh *Iſis* : 'tis impoſſible.

Cleo. I thinke ſo *Charmian*: dull of tongue, & dwarfiſh
What Maieſtie is in her gate,remember
If ere thou look'ſt on Maieſtie.

Meſ. She creepes:her motion,& her ſtation are as one.
She ſhewes a body,rather then a life,
A Statue,then a Breather.

Cleo. Is this certaine ?

Meſ. Or I haue no obſeruance.

Cha. Three in Egypt cannot make better note.

Cleo. He's very knowing,I do perceiu't,
There's nothing in her yet.

The

Proof-page of *Antony and Cleopatra* from the First Folio (1623), sig. xx6ᵛ. It
represents the uncorrected state of the page and shows the proof-reader's marks
indicating corrections. All but two of the corrections here marked were duly
made in the corrected state. (*The Folger Shakespeare Library*)

set it page for page (a paginary reprint). A revised edition of a work was often set from mixed copy, an earlier edition with manuscript insertions.

Proof correction (see also *Stop-press correction*). The extent and kind of correction in the Elizabethan-Jacobean printing-house is at present a matter of some dispute. The older orthodox view was that what is usually called stop-press correction or simply press-correction (i.e. corrections to the forme, the imposed type-pages, made in the process of printing off) represented essentially all the correction to which a book at this time was subjected. Recently, however, it has been suggested that stop-press correction is only the last step of several stages of correction, the earlier stages of which were conducted before the forme ever reached the press—in other words, that stop-press correction represents only the final tidying up of errors that had evaded correction in the rough proofs taken directly from the standing type (see *Standing type*) prior to its bedding in the press. This newer view has the support of Joseph Moxon's discussion of proof correction in his *Mechanick Exercises* (1683–84), a discussion that the proponents of the older view deny has any necessary bearing on the practices of the early part of the century. The truth probably lies somewhere in the middle. Under certain circumstances some books may have been corrected only after presswork began; others (possibly including the First Folio of Shakespeare) underwent proof correction in several stages, press-correction being the final step.

Quarto: a printer's designation for the format of a book (applied also to the bound volume) in which the individual sheets have been folded twice, the direction of both folds repeating that used for folio format, thus producing four leaves (eight pages). Abbreviated as "4°" or "4to" and in non-collational references as "Q". Quartos were sometimes gathered in eights, producing a quire of eight leaves (sixteen pages). The measurements of a quarto, though it gives a squarer appearance, are roughly half those of a folio, with the proviso noted under *Folio*.

Quire: (a) The sheet as folded to produce a book in folio format (two leaves, four pages), quarto format (four leaves, eight pages), etc. (b) Two or more sheets gathered one within another and so arranged as to form a bibliographical unit (e.g. quarto-in-eights, folio-in-sixes).

Recto: the front of a leaf; in an opened book (or manuscript) always the right-hand page. Abbreviated as superscript "r" following the leaf number. See *Verso*.

Running-title: a line of type, placed at the top of each page, containing the title of the work or distinguishing different sections of the work. Also called "running-head." Running-titles were not composed as part of the type-page, but inserted at the top of each type-page at the time of imposition. In this way the same set (or sets) of running-titles might

be used throughout a book without the necessity of resetting.

Sheet: the basic component of a book. In Elizabethan-Jacobean times the size of the sheet varied considerably, measuring approximately from 20″ by 15″ (large folio) to 16″ by 12″ (small folio). The size of the sheets used in the Shakespeare First Folio falls between these limits, the largest known copy, after being trimmed in the process of binding, measuring 17″ by $13\frac{3}{8}$″ (McKerrow).

Signature: (a) A printer's device for indicating the correct order of quires in a book and of the individual pages in a particular quire. The "signature," which is placed below the text at the foot of a recto page, is usually made up of (1) a symbol (usually a letter of the alphabet) which implies definite sequence and serves as an aid to the binder and (2) a numeral which indicates the exact position of that leaf within the quire and serves as an aid to the correct imposition of the type-pages in the outer and inner formes (see *Forme*) and as a guide to the folding of the printed sheet. Thus in a book printed in quarto format (having four leaves, eight pages, to a quire) the recto of the first leaf of the first quire (not including preliminary matter, which is often signed with an arbitrary symbol to distinguish it and is frequently the last part of a book to be printed) may be signed A1, the second leaf A2, and the third A3, the fourth leaf being, as a rule, unsigned. (b) Also used (abbreviated as "sig.") to refer, especially in unfoliated or unpaged books, to an individual page of a particular quire, as, for example, sig. A3^v, referring to the verso of the third leaf in quire A. The word will also, unfortunately, be found used in earlier bibliographical work as a synonym for "quire" or "gathering."

Standing type: (a) Type-pages before final imposition and bedding on the press. (b) Type-pages preserved as originally set after a completed press-run.

State: (a) A term used to distinguish different copies of the same edition some of which (second state) contain cancels inserted before first publication or reset material introduced in the course of the original press-run. (b) Also used to describe the corrected and uncorrected stages resulting from proof correction of the outer and inner formes of individual sheets. In sense (a) the terms "state" and "issue" are often difficult, sometimes impossible, to distinguish.

Stop-press correction (see also *Proof correction*). Although it now seems probable that, in the production of a number of books, one or more proofs were taken from the standing type and corrections made before the type-pages were locked up in the chase and placed on the press, the only corrected proofs, with the exception of two or three non-Shakespearean examples, that have survived seem to represent proofs taken at the beginning of a press-run. While such press-proofs were being read and marked by the proof-corrector, the printing process was continued, something around an average of ten percent of the total number of sheets in the press-run being printed off (either outer or inner forme) before the corrected press-proof was returned; printing was then stopped, and corrections were made by a compositor, either with the forme still in the press or, if the required corrections were substantial enough to warrant it, by removing the forme from the press bed to the correcting stone. Once the corrections had been made, printing was resumed, but those sheets printed off while the press-proof was being corrected were not discarded. If further errors in the printed sheets were observed, the press might be stopped a second, even a third, time and the correction process repeated, thus producing a second or third state of correction in a certain number of sheets. When it came to the point of assembling copies of the book from the separate quire piles of printed sheets, corrected (abbreviated as "c") and uncorrected (abbreviated as "u") sheets were treated indiscriminately, different copies of the bound volume being made up of different chance assortments of the corrected and uncorrected states. Accidents damaging or disarranging (i.e. pieing) the type during a press-run might also result in stop-press corrections.

Verso: the back of a leaf; in an opened book (or manuscript) always the left-hand page. Abbreviated as superscript "v" following the leaf number. See *Recto*.

A sixteenth-century printing shop. From Stephen Batman, *The Doom Warning All Men to the Judgment* (1581). The printing press here shown, in all essentials typical of presses used down to the end of the eighteenth century, is being worked at "full press" (i.e. with two men), one man (right) removing from the tympan a sheet just printed off, the other inking the type-bed with the ink-balls, preparatory to the next "pull." Note (left) the "platen" (half the size of a sheet), fastened flexibly at the lower end of the large screw spindle, which, when the carriage was slid back under it, was brought down evenly and firmly on the type-bed by a strong pull of the "bar" to make the impression. In the foreground are two "piles," one of sheets already printed off in the press-run, the other of sheets still waiting to be "impressed." In the rear of the shop a compositor (right), sitting before a "case" of type, is seen setting from "copy," which is held in a copy-holder to his left. Opposite him, another compositor is either making press-corrections or setting type. (*By permission of the Harvard College Library*)

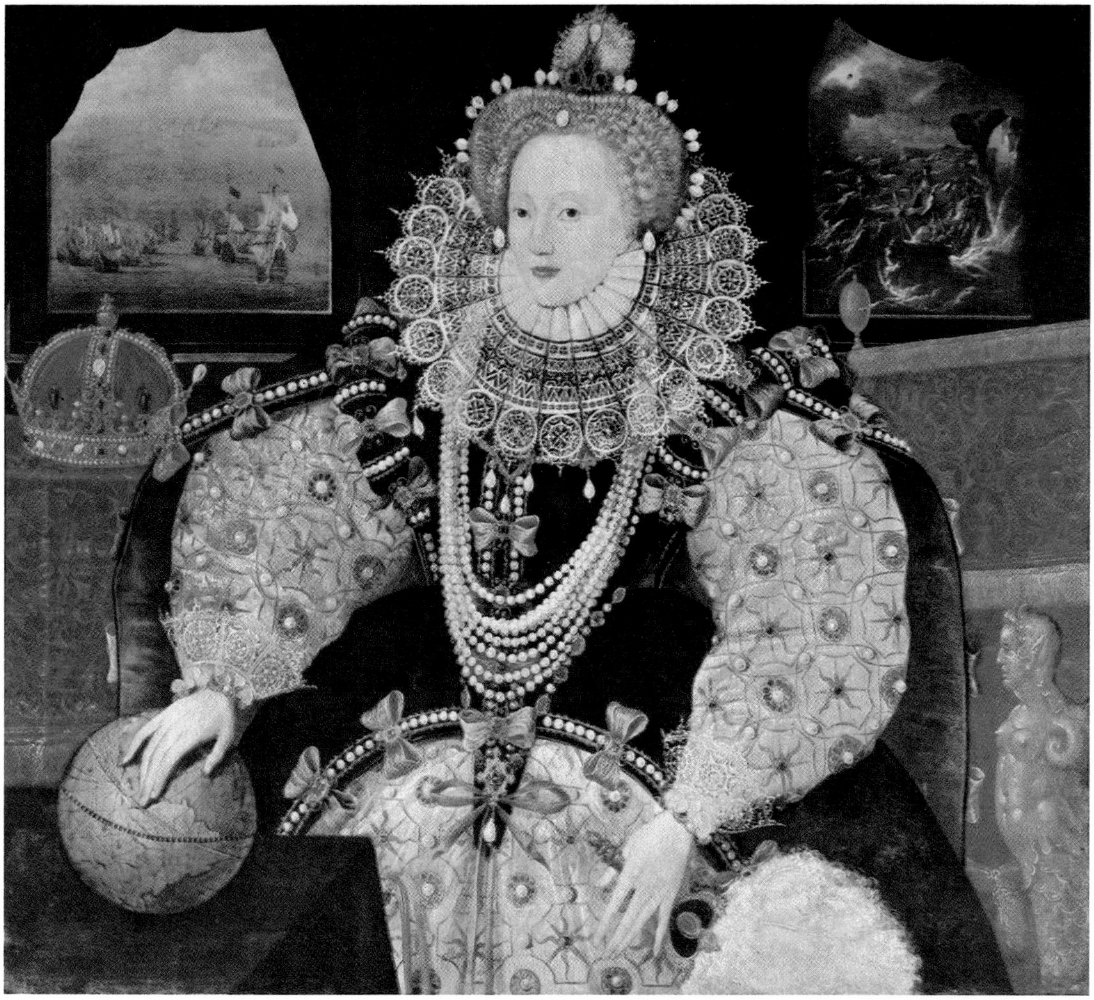

Elizabeth Tudor dominated her age in symbol and in fact, a dominance celebrated in the portrait above (by an unknown artist) commemorating the defeat of the Spanish Armada in 1588. Through the left window are seen English ships arrayed against the Spanish fleet; through the right, a storm taking savage toll of the Armada. The magnificence of the Queen's highly stylized gem-encrusted costume befits the proud occasion here signalized.

The portrait of James I, her successor, is related to a different aspect of English foreign policy. It is a detail from a larger painting, by the Indian artist Bichitr, in which James, together with the Ottoman sultan, is represented as paying homage to the Mogul emperor Jahāngīr at his court in Delhi. The likeness of James was almost certainly copied from a miniature carried to India by Sir Thomas Roe on his embassy of 1615–18 to negotiate commercial privileges for the East India Company. The figure at the bottom is a court official holding a picture of an elephant and two horses—presumably the gifts which James is imagined as offering.

PLATE I

Many of Elizabeth's courtiers patronized the arts, and both Henry Wriothesley, third Earl of Southampton (facing page) and William Herbert, third Earl of Pembroke (left) were Shakespeare's patrons. *Venus and Adonis* and *The Rape of Lucrece* are dedicated to Southampton, and he is the man most often conjectured to be the fair youth addressed in many of Shakespeare's sonnets. Heminge and Condell dedicated the First Folio (1623) to Pembroke and his brother the Earl of Montgomery and described them as having "prosequuted both [the plays], and their Authour liuing, with so much fauour." The portrait of Southampton was painted to commemorate his imprisonment in the Tower for his part in the ill-fated Essex rebellion of 1601. Both Southampton and Robert Devereux, second Earl of Essex (above left) were condemned to death, but only Essex was executed. On the eve of the attempted rebellion the conspirators subsidized a special performance of *Richard II* (with its dangerous precedent of a king's deposition) by Shakespeare's company, the Chamberlain's Men; an investigation evidently cleared them of complicity, for no charges were brought against them.

At the upper right is a portrait of William Cecil, Baron Burghley, Elizabeth's Principal Secretary (later Lord High Treasurer) and her most trusted adviser from the beginning of her reign until his death in 1598, five years before her own.

PLATE 2

IN VINCVLIS
INVICTVS

FEBRVA: 8: 1600
602: 603: AP

PLATE 3

The subject of this curious birth-to-death painting was
Sir Henry Unton (1557?–1596), diplomatist and soldier,
whose family seat, at Wadley, near Faringdon, in
Berkshire, is shown in parts of the picture. In a
general right-to-left direction, the scenes depict his
birth, his· student years at Oxford, his wedding feast
and masque (1580), and (above the feast) the activities
of his maturity as a traveller in Italy, a general in the
Netherlands, and an ambassador in France (where he
died), before ending with his funeral. His typically

ostentatious tomb in the church at Faringdon is shown
in the lower left corner. Of particular interest is the
wedding masque. In the hall, below the banqueting
chamber, is placed a consort of six musicians. The
masquers, in costume, preceded by a taborer and a
"truchman" (an interpreter or presenter) with a paper
in his hand, represent Mercury, Diana, and six Nymphs,
all in red masks, with ten Cupids (five white and five
black, perhaps representing day and night) who act
as torchbearers to the principals.

PLATE 4

The artifacts pictured on this page and the next, all of them from the end of the sixteenth century or the beginning of the next, reflect the widespread taste for elegance and the high refinement achieved in the arts and crafts. The exceptionally fine miniature above, by Nicholas Hilliard, shows an unknown young man holding his locket (doubtless containing a portrait of his beloved) over his heart, against a background of gold flames symbolizing the ardor of his passion. The tankard to the right is of faience with English silver mounts. Below, the wool and silk tent-stitched panel depicts French styles of dress which had become highly fashionable in England.

PLATE 5

Museum of Fine Arts, Boston

Museum of Fine Arts, Boston

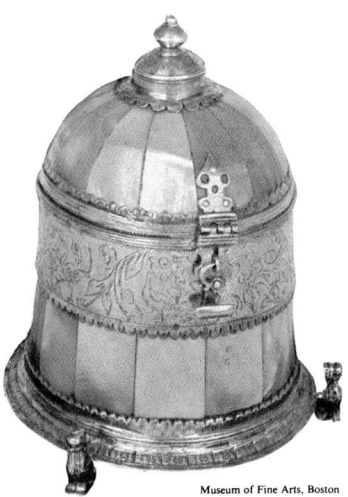

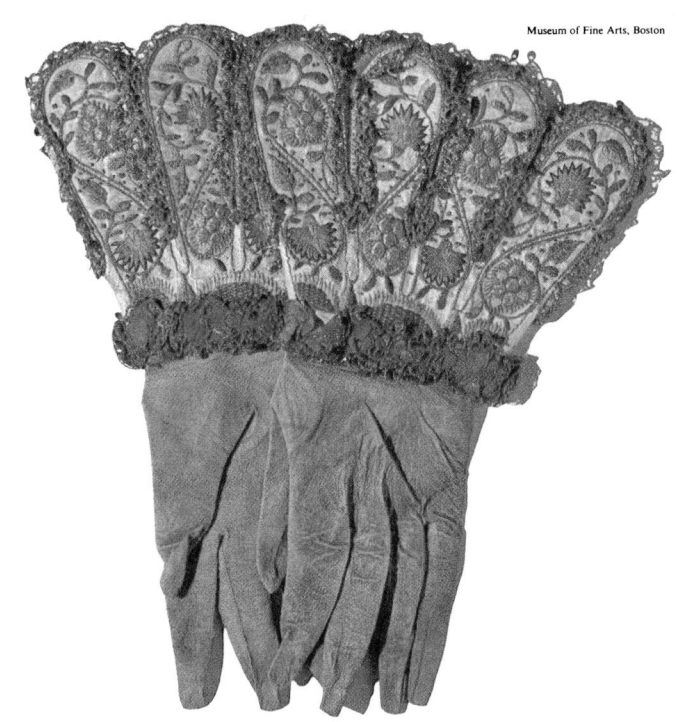

The casket above is fashioned of silver-mounted mother-of-pearl; its height is nearly six inches. The buff leather gloves at the right have white satin tabbed cuffs embroidered with silk and metal threads and trimmed with metal lace and spangles. In the mural below (part of the frieze in the Great Chamber of Gilling Castle, Yorkshire), the musicians play tenor violin, cittern, treble violin, and pandore; the woodwork visible below the frieze is also Elizabethan.

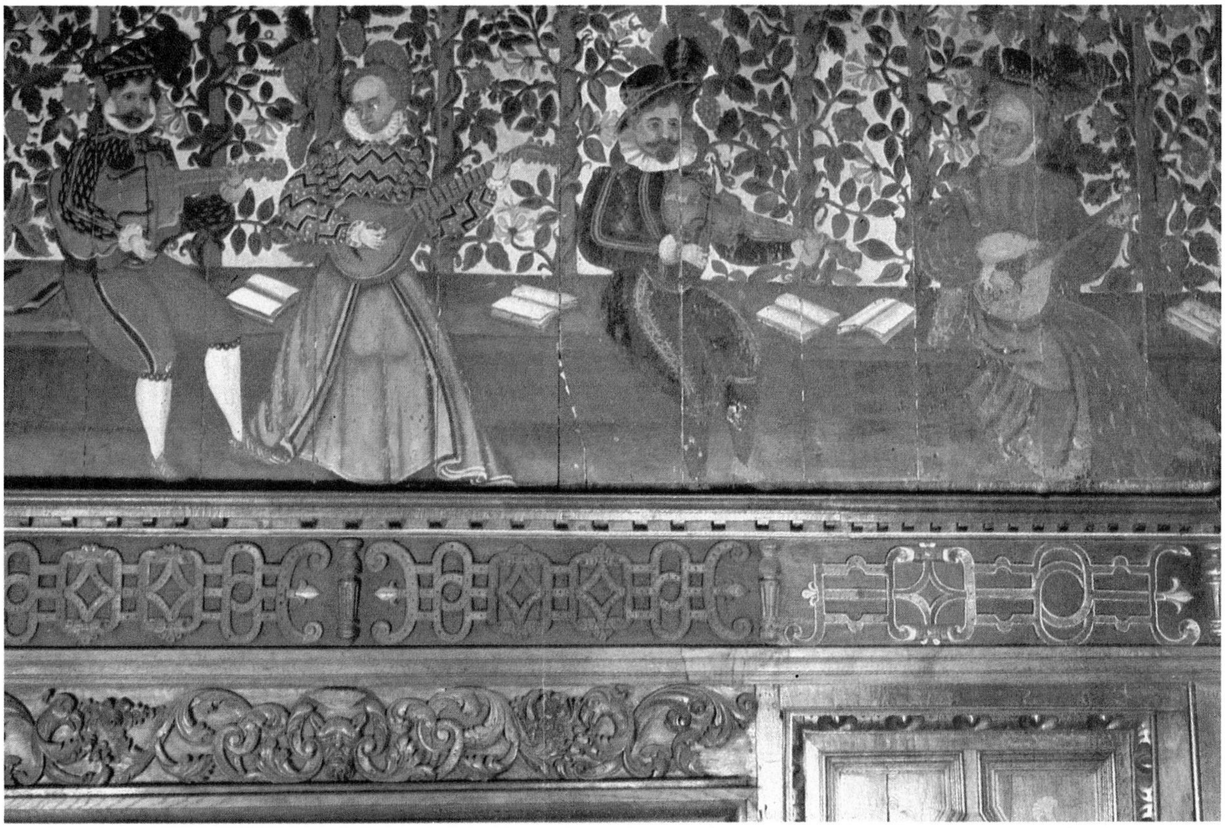

Courtesy of the Abbot of Ampleforth

Yeomen *Of the Conninghouse* *of the Spicery* *of the Chamber* *Robes and Standish* *Earles and Cominesses* *Servants* *foure Trompetters* *Samuell Thomson Portcullis* *Officer of Armes* *A Sergeant of Armes* *The Standerd of* *the lyon borne by* *M.r Thomas Sameos*

The Charret drawne by foure Horses upon which Charret *stood the Coffin covered with purple Veluet and upon* *that the representation. The Canopy borne by six Knights* *footemen*

The Sergeant of *the wostne* *Children of the Chappell* *Gentlemen of the* *Chappell*

Queen Elizabeth died on March 24, 1603, and her funeral, conducted with great magnificence, took place on April 28. The Lords and Ladies of the Realm and their servants, ambassadors, members of the Council, the Lord Mayor of London, the Heralds of the College of Arms, the Master of the Revels, and all the many members of the Queen's houschold, high and low, were in dutiful attendance, dressed in decent black. The pictures here shown are from a contemporary watercolor sketch of the whole procession, possibly by William Camden. The lower section includes some of the Children of the Chapel (the "little eyases" of *Hamlet*, II.ii.339), who had been acting with great success at the Second Blackfriars Theatre since 1600.

PLATE 7

Chronology and Sources

G. Blakemore Evans

The following table attempts to arrange Shakespeare's plays and poems in the order of their composition, to present the evidence for the proposed order, and, because dating sometimes depends upon the time when particular sources became available, to list the source materials for each work.

Any attempt to arrange the plays chronologically is beset with hazards and uncertainties, and, as the information in the table will make clear, the undertaking has given rise to differences of opinion among a long line of editors and critics. The first to attack the problem was Edward Capell, although the credit as pioneer is usually assigned to Edmond Malone, whose "An Attempt to Ascertain the Order in Which the Plays Attributed to Shakspeare Were Written" was published in 1778, two years before Capell's earlier chronology appeared in print. Since the time of Capell and Malone, many of whose proposed dates are no longer acceptable, other scholars have addressed themselves to the problem of chronology, and the results of their labors may be found authoritatively brought together by Sir Edmund Chambers in the first volume of his *William Shakespeare: A Study of Facts and Problems* (Oxford, 1930). The most recent general review of the evidence for dating is James G. McManaway's "Recent Studies in Shakespeare's Chronology" in Volume III of *Shakespeare Survey* (1950).

Evidence for dating may be distinguished as of two kinds: internal evidence and external evidence. Internal evidence, as the term suggests, is drawn from the texts of the plays and poems and deals for the most part in topical allusions (which if dateable can establish a *terminus a quo*, i.e. a date before which the work cannot have been written), metrical development, kinds and handling of imagery, incidence of rhyme, and vocabulary. External evidence is concerned with rather more concrete matters: dates of actual publication; entry on the Stationers' Register (cited below

as *S.R.*), Henslowe's *Diary*, Francis Meres's *Palladis Tamia* (1598), Revels accounts, etc.; allusions to, or imitations of, Shakespeare's plays or poems by contemporary writers whose work can be dated.

Even with the aid of all the known evidence it is frequently impossible to narrow the date of a play to the limits even of a particular year, although it will be noticed that the dating set forth below becomes somewhat firmer beginning with *Richard II* (1595). External evidence can generally establish a *terminus ad quem*, i.e. the date after which the work cannot have been written, but it tells us nothing definite about how long before this terminal date the work was in fact composed. It is at this point that internal evidence must be brought to bear, but internal evidence is slippery in the extreme and often susceptible of more than one interpretation. The problem is further complicated by two other factors: the possibility that Shakespeare reworked an earlier play by another writer (mixed authorship) and the possibility that a play as we now have it represents Shakespeare's reworking of his original version (revision). The claims of both mixed authorship and revision have given rise to much disagreement among critics, and consequently to further uncertainty in establishing a chronology.

The table, which for the chronology is based in great part on the work of Chambers and McManaway and more recent investigations of particular plays, is arranged, following the name of the play or poem, to give, in the first column, the most commonly accepted date or dates for that play or poem (where more than one title is assigned to the same year or years the order of listing represents the probable order of composition) and, where indicated, the date of suggested revision; in the second column, the basic evidence for the dating, followed by a list of the proposed sources, arranged under the categories employed by Geoffrey Bullough in *Narrative and Dramatic Sources of Shakespeare* (7 vols., London, 1957–73).

	TITLE	PROPOSED DATE	EVIDENCE FOR DATING; SOURCES
	1 Henry VI	1589–90 (revised 1594–95)	Published in F1 (1623). Performed March 3, 1592 (marked "ne," i.e. new, by Henslowe, *Diary*). Alluded to by Nashe (*Pierce Penniless*, August 8, 1592; see Appendix B, Number 12). Rival theories of authorship: (1) wholly by Shakespeare and revised after *2* and *3 Henry VI*; (2) reworking of an earlier play by another hand or hands (Greene, Peele, Nashe the strongest candidates). Some would place the play in any form later than *2* and *3 Henry VI*. No definite proof that the F1 text represents the play in essentially the same form as performed for Henslowe or referred to by Nashe.
			SOURCES: (1) Hall, *The Union of the Two Noble and Illustre Families of Lancaster and York* (1548). (2) Holinshed, *Chronicles* (2nd ed., 1587). (3) Fabyan, *Chronicle* (1559 ed.; first English version 1533). (4) Geoffrey of Monmouth, *Historia Regum Britanniae*. PROBABLE SOURCE: Sir Thomas Coningsby, *Journal of the Siege of Rouen* (MS; published 1847).
	2 Henry VI	1590–91	"Bad" quarto (*The First Part of the Contention betwixt the Two Famous Houses of York and Lancaster*) entered on *S.R.* March 12, 1594; published 1594. Received text published in F1 (1623). The plague closed the theatres in London for three months in 1592, the whole of 1593, and the first half of 1594. The "bad" quarto version presumably resulted from forced provincial tours and implies a date not later than the beginning of 1592 for the original play. Greene parodied a line in *3 Henry VI* (I.iv.137) before his death on September 3, 1592 (*Groatsworth of Wit*; see Appendix B, Number 8), which seems to require a still earlier date for *2 Henry VI*. As for *1 Henry VI*, authorship problems raise further difficulties, but it seems relatively sure that the F1 texts of *2* and *3 Henry VI* are essentially the plays as performed around 1590–91.
			SOURCES: (1) Hall, *The Union of . . . Lancaster and York* (1548). (2) Fabyan, *Chronicle* (1559 ed.). PROBABLE SOURCES: (1) Holinshed, *Chronicles* (2nd ed., 1587). (2) Foxe, *Acts and Monuments* (1570 ed.). (3) Grafton, *Chronicle at Large* (1569).
	3 Henry VI	1590–91	"Bad" quarto (*The True Tragedy of Richard Duke of York*) published 1595. Received text published in F1 (1623). See Greene's allusion (1592) under *2 Henry VI* above. The two parts are closely connected (both "bad" quartos were published by the same publisher) and present essentially the same problems.
			SOURCES: (1) Hall, *The Union of . . . Lancaster and York* (1548). (2) Holinshed, *Chronicles* (2nd ed., 1587). POSSIBLE SOURCE: Baldwin, ed., *A Mirror for Magistrates* (1559).
	Richard III	1592–93	"Bad" quarto entered on *S.R.* October 20, 1597; published 1597. Somewhat enlarged and revised text published in F1 (1623). Close links with *3 Henry VI* suggest that it was composed immediately after that play.
			SOURCES: (1) Hall, *The Union of . . . Lancaster and York* (1548). (2) Holinshed, *Chronicles* (2nd ed., 1587). PROBABLE SOURCES: (1) Baldwin, ed., *A Mirror for Magistrates* (1559). (2) Anon., *The True Tragedy of Richard III* (c. 1591). (3) Stow, *The Chronicles of England* (1580).
	Venus and Adonis	1592–93	Entered on *S.R.* April 18, 1593; published 1593. Generally thought of as being composed in 1592–93 because of the enforced suspension of theatrical performances in London as a result of the plague. A minority interpret Shakespeare's reference to the poem as "the first heire of my inuention" as implying that it predates any of his work in the drama, thus throwing the date of composition back into the late 1580's.
			SOURCE: Ovid, *Metamorphoses* (tr. Golding, 1565, 1567), Bks. III, IV, X.
	The Comedy of Errors	1592–94	Published in F1 (1623). Performed at Gray's Inn December 28, 1594 (see Appendix B, Number 14). The allusion to France "arm'd and reverted, making war against her heir" (III.ii.123–24) has generally been taken to date the play before July 9, 1593, when a truce was declared between Henry IV and the League, but it has recently been shown that comments on

The Comedy of Errors (cont.)

the struggle as still in progress appeared for several years after 1593. It is therefore possible that the Gray's Inn performance was the first (1594) and that the play with its classical source and unusual amount of legal terminology was written for that occasion.

SOURCES: Plautus, (1) *Menaechmi* (English tr. by William Warner, 1595) and (2) *Amphitruo*. (3) Lyly, *Midas* (c. 1589). (4) Gascoigne, *Supposes* (1566). PROBABLE SOURCE: Gower, *Confessio Amantis* (1554 ed.), Bk. VIII.

Sonnets 1593–99

Entered on *S.R.* May 20, 1609; published 1609. The date span here suggested is a kind of average of critical opinion (Rollins, *New Variorum*, II, 73). Minority views would either push the dating back into the middle 1580's for some sonnets or see other sonnets as late as 1609. There are one or two facts and one interesting implication. Meres (before September 7, 1598) refers to Shakespeare's "sugred Sonnets among his priuate friends" (see Appendix B, Number 22), and William Jaggard printed two of the sonnets (138, 144) in the 1599 *Passionate Pilgrim*. Some of the sonnets, therefore, were in existence by 1598, a conclusion that helps not at all, since all dating theories allow this premise. More significant, perhaps, is the large number of verbal and thematic parallels that can be established between the sonnets and the earlier plays (through *King John*, 1594–96), the only later plays to show such parallels being *As You Like It* (1599) and *Troilus and Cressida* (1601–2).

SOURCES: None specific; probable influence of Daniel's *Delia* (1592) and Sidney's *Astrophel and Stella* (1591).

The Rape of Lucrece 1593–94

Published 1594. Many verbal links have been pointed out between *Lucrece* and *Titus Andronicus* (some, though fewer, between that play and *Venus and Adonis*).

SOURCES: (1) Ovid, *Fasti*, Bk. II. (2) Livy, *Historia*, Bk. I (with possible use of William Painter's tr. in *The Palace of Pleasure*, 1566). PROBABLE SOURCE: Chaucer, *The Legend of Good Women* (lines 1680–1885).

Titus Andronicus 1593–94

Performed January 24, 1594 (Henslowe's *Diary*, where it is marked "ne," i.e. new). Entered on *S.R.* February 6, 1594; published 1594. Listed by Meres (*Palladis Tamia*, 1598) as by Shakespeare. Rival theories of authorship: (1) Shakespeare's thorough rewriting of an earlier play (c. 1589), probably by Peele; (2) wholly Shakespeare's. An allusion to a play on this subject in *A Knack to Know a Knave*, acted as "new" on June 10, 1592 (Henslowe, *Diary*), must, if we accept the dates 1593–94, be interpreted as a reference to the pre-Shakespearean play.

SOURCES: (1) Anon., *The History of Titus Andronicus* (known only from an eighteenth-century chapbook in the Folger Shakespeare Library). (2) Ovid, *Metamorphoses* (tr. Golding, 1567), Bk. VI. (3) Seneca, *Thyestes* (tr. Jasper Heywood, 1560). PROBABLE SOURCE: Plutarch, *Lives* (tr. North, 1579 ed.).

The Taming of the Shrew 1593–94

Entered on *S.R.* January 22, 1607; published in F1 (1623). A play called *The Taming of a Shrew* was entered on *S.R.* May 2, 1594, and published in the same year. Two general views of *A Shrew* have been held: (1) that it is a "bad" quarto text of a play that served as Shakespeare's source for *The Shrew*; (2) that *A Shrew* is a "bad" quarto version of Shakespeare's *The Shrew*. If the second view is accepted, a view that has steadily gained support in recent years, Shakespeare's play (*The Shrew*) would have to be dated not later than 1593. The performance of a play called "the tamynge of A shrowe" is recorded in Henslowe's *Diary* for June 11, 1594, at the Newington Butts theatre, where both Shakespeare's company (the Chamberlain's Men) and the Admiral's Men are believed to have been performing at this time. Significantly perhaps, Henslowe does not mark the play "ne" (i.e. new).

SOURCES: (1) *A Merry Jest of a Shrewd and Curst Wife Lapped in Morel's Skin for Her Good Behavior* (c. 1550). (2) Gascoigne, *Supposes* (1566). (3) *The Taming of a Shrew* (published 1594) [see above for a different view].

TITLE	PROPOSED DATE	EVIDENCE FOR DATING; SOURCES
The Taming of the Shrew (cont.)		(4) For the Sly framework: some version of a story that appears in P. Heuterus' *De Rebus Burgundicis* (1584; Bk. IV) that relates a very similar prank played by Philip the Good of Burgundy on a drunken country-man. Shakespeare may have got the story from a now-lost collection of tales by Richard Edwards published in 1570 (see Thomas Warton, *History of English Poetry* [1774–81], Section 52); a later fragment (c. 1620) with the title "The Waking Man's Dream" may be part of a reprint of Edwards' collection (see *Shakespeare's Library*, ed. W. C. Hazlitt [1875], IV, 406–14). A translation of Heuterus' version by Grimestone (from the French of S. Goulart) appeared in 1607.
The Two Gentlemen of Verona	1594	Published in F1 (1623). Noted by Meres (*Palladis Tamia*, 1598) as by Shakespeare. Generally admitted to be Shakespeare's earliest attempt at romantic comedy. Leech (New Arden ed.) suggests that it was composed in two stages, first stage 1592, second stage late 1593, and that it precedes *The Comedy of Errors*. The two stages, he believes, may explain some of the numerous inconsistencies in the play as we now have it. But a date earlier than 1594 remains problematical.
		SOURCES: (1) Montemayor, *Diana Enamorada* (possibly in Yonge's English tr., published 1598 but in MS sixteen years earlier). (2) Brooke, *Romeus and Juliet* (1562). (3) Lyly, *Midas* (c. 1589). PROBABLE SOURCES: (1) Elyot, *The Governor* (1531). (2) Edwards, *Damon and Pithias* (c. 1565).
Love's Labor's Lost	1594–95 (revised 1597 for court performance)	Published 1598. It seems likely that a "bad" quarto edition preceded the 1598 quarto, but no copy is extant. Meres (*Palladis Tamia*, 1598) mentions the play as Shakespeare's, coupled with what sounds like a companion play, "Loue labours wonne," of which, although we know it to have been published in quarto by 1603, no copy has survived (see T. W. Baldwin, *Shakspere's "Love's Labor's Won,"* 1957). There seems to be a reference in IV.iii.343–44 to Chapman's *Shadow of Night* (1594), which would place the play not earlier than that year. The Muscovite disguise in V.ii and Berowne's complaint in I.i.48 ("Not to see ladies") are thought to show the influence of the Gray's Inn Christmas revels of 1594–95 (see Appendix B, Number 14); and Berowne's remark in V.ii.460–62 may be taken as a reference to the ill-fated performance of *The Comedy of Errors* during those revels. Certainly the song in V.ii.889–924 cannot have been composed before 1597 since it draws from Gerard's *Herbal* published in that year. This song and other revisions were probably written for the court performance (not later than Christmas of 1597) referred to on the title-page of the 1598 quarto.
		SOURCE: None definite; some suggested analogues with French history of the sixteenth century; probable influence of *commedia dell'arte* in plot and character types and of the Gray's Inn Christmas revels of 1594–95; song in V.ii.889–924 based on Gerard's *Herbal* (1597).
Additions to *Sir Thomas More*	1594–95	Suggested dates for the play as a whole range from 1590 to 1605, but the most widely accepted dating for the original play is 1590–93, for the revisions 1594–95. Shakespeare's proposed part in the revisions is limited to a single scene (Addition II in Hand D) and a shorter passage (Addition III in Hand C). For a full discussion, see the critical introduction to Additions II and III in this edition.
		SOURCES (for the play as a whole): (1) Hall, *The Union . . . of Lancaster and York* (1548). (2) "Lives" of More. PROBABLE SOURCE: Foxe, *Acts and Monuments* (1570 ed.).
King John	1594–96	Published in F1 (1623). Listed by Meres (*Palladis Tamia*, 1598) as by Shakespeare. The dating problem for *King John* is exceptionally murky. Two widely different views are held about the relationship of Shakespeare's play to the anonymous two-part play called *The Troublesome Reign of John, King of England*, published in 1591: (1) *T.R.* is the principal source of *King John* (the orthodox and still most generally accepted opinion); (2) *T.R.* is a memorial imitation of Shakespeare's play (i.e. a "bad" quarto). The proponents of (2), who are few in number, would thus date *King John* not later

TITLE	PROPOSED DATE	EVIDENCE FOR DATING; SOURCES
King John (cont.)		than 1590. If they should ever prove their case, the chronology of Shakespeare's early plays would have to be reconsidered. SOURCES: (1) Anon., *The Troublesome Reign of John, King of England*, 2 pts. (published 1591) [see above for another view]. (2) Holinshed, *Chronicles* (2nd ed., 1587). PROBABLE SOURCE: Hall, *The Union of . . . Lancaster and York* (1548). POSSIBLE SOURCE: Foxe, *Acts and Monuments* (1570 ed.).
Richard II	1595	Entered on *S.R.* August 29, 1597; published 1597. Listed by Meres (*Palladis Tamia*, 1598) as by Shakespeare. Shakespeare is probably indebted to Daniel's *Civil Wars* (1595). It is possible that a performance of this play took place at the house of Sir Edward Hoby, December 9, 1595 (see Appendix B, Number 15). If the "K. Richard" of Hoby's letter is indeed Shakespeare's *Richard II*, this piece of evidence, coupled with the probable influence of Daniel, would give us the first definite year date for the composition of one of the plays. SOURCES: (1) *The Union of . . . Lancaster and York* (1548). (2) Holinshed, *Chronicles* (2nd ed., 1587). (3) Anon., *1 Richard II* (or *Thomas of Woodstock*) (c. 1592). PROBABLE SOURCE: Daniel, *Civil Wars* (1595). POSSIBLE SOURCES: (1) Baldwin, ed., *A Mirror for Magistrates* (1559). (2) Froissart, *Chronicles* (tr. Lord Berners, c. 1523–25).
Romeo and Juliet	1595–96	"Bad" quarto published 1597; "good" quarto published 1599. Listed by Meres (*Palladis Tamia*, 1598) as by Shakespeare. Several astrological references in the play and an allusion to the great earthquake of 1584 as having occurred eleven years earlier seem to point to 1595 or 1596. Baldwin (*Five-Act Structure*) suggests a date of 1591, between *The Two Gentlemen of Verona* and *Lucrece*, partly on the evidence of another quake in 1580. SOURCE: Brooke, *The Tragical History of Romeus and Juliet* (1562).
A Midsummer Night's Dream	1595–96	Entered on *S.R.* October 8, 1600; published 1600. Listed by Meres (*Palladis Tamia*, 1598) as by Shakespeare. The play suggests special composition for a wedding, and seven different weddings have been suggested, ranging in date from 1590 to 1600 (despite the fact that Meres's listing rules out any date after September 7, 1598, for the play except in a revised form). An allusion to bad summer weather (II.i.81–117) has been connected with conditions in 1594, 1595, and 1596, the most recent opinion favoring 1596. The only wedding late enough in that year is the double wedding of the daughters of the Earl of Worcester, November 8, 1596. SOURCE: No source known for the main plot; for the Pyramus and Thisbe story, Ovid, *Metamorphoses* (tr. Golding, 1567), Bk. IV. PROBABLE SOURCES: (1) Chaucer, "The Knight's Tale." (2) Plutarch, *Lives* (tr. North, 1579 ed.). (3) *Huon of Bordeaux* (tr. Lord Berners, c. 1533–42). (4) Scot, *Discovery of Witchcraft* (1584). POSSIBLE SOURCES: (1) Apuleius, *The Golden Ass* (tr. Adlington, 1566). (2) Robinson, ed., *A Handful of Pleasant Delights* (1584; for Pyramus and Thisbe).
The Merchant of Venice	1596–97	Entered on *S.R.* July 22, 1598; published 1600. Listed by Meres (*Palladis Tamia*, 1598) as by Shakespeare. Among various supposed allusions in the play, only one seems unambiguous evidence for dating. I.i.27–29 refers to a ship ("wealthy *Andrew*") and there is little doubt that Shakespeare is here glancing at a Spanish vessel called the *St. Andrew*, which was captured in the Cadiz expedition of 1596. News of the capture reached England by July 30, 1596. Late 1596, or early 1597, seems, therefore, a likely date of composition. SOURCE: Marlowe, *The Jew of Malta* (c. 1589; for some details only). PROBABLE SOURCES: (1) Giovanni Fiorentino, *Il Pecorone* (1558), first story of fourth day (no contemporary tr. known). (2) Masuccio, *Il Novellino* (1476), fourteenth story (no contemporary tr. known). (3) *Gesta Romanorum* (tr. Richard Robinson, 1577, 1595), story 66. POSSIBLE SOURCES: (1) Munday, *Zelauto* (1580). (2) Anon., *The Jew* (c. 1569–79; not extant).

1 Henry IV

PROPOSED DATE: 1596–97

Entered on *S.R.* February 25, 1598; published 1598. Meres (*Palladis Tamia*, 1598) refers to "Henry the 4." as by Shakespeare.

SOURCES: (1) Holinshed, *Chronicles* (2nd ed., 1587). (2) Anon., *The Famous Victories of Henry V* (c. 1586). (3) Anon., *1 Richard II* (or *Thomas of Woodstock*) (c. 1592). PROBABLE SOURCES: (1) Stow, *Chronicles of England* (1580). (2) Daniel, *Civil Wars* (1595). POSSIBLE SOURCE: Baldwin, ed. *A Mirror for Magistrates* (1559).

The Merry Wives of Windsor

PROPOSED DATE: 1597 (revised c. 1600–1)

Entered on *S.R.* January 18, 1602; "bad" quarto published 1602. Received text published in F1 (1623). Until relatively recently *Merry Wives* was regularly dated 1601–2, but Hotson's suggestion that the play was originally written specially for the Garter Feast held at Westminster April 23, 1597, is being more and more strongly supported (see New Arden ed.). On this theory, the play was revised for the public theatre about 1600–1, and it is the revised version that lies behind the "bad" quarto, while the F1 text represents in most essentials (except for the name Broome for Brooke) the earlier "court" performance. On this view, Shakespeare wrote *Merry Wives* shortly after he began work on *2 Henry IV*. Meres (*Palladis Tamia*) does not list *Merry Wives* among Shakespeare's plays as of September 7, 1598, but a special court production might not have been known to him.

SOURCES: None definite. PROBABLE SOURCES: (1) Ovid, *Metamorphoses* (tr. Golding, 1567), Bk. III. (2) J. Rathgeb's *Journal* (1602; an account of the Mompelgard visit, details of which could have been known earlier to Shakespeare). POSSIBLE SOURCES: (1) Tarlton, *News Out of Purgatory* (1590). (2) Rich, *His Farewell to Military Profession* (1581). (3) Lyly, *Endimion* (1588).

2 Henry IV

PROPOSED DATE: 1598

Entered on *S.R.* August 23, 1600; published 1600. Some traces of the name Oldcastle (the original name of Falstaff, changed, it is supposed, because of offense to the Cobham family) remain in the speech-prefixes in the early part of *2 Henry IV*; this indicates that Shakespeare must have started composition of *2 Henry IV* before Part 1 (containing the alteration to Falstaff) was entered on *S.R.* (February 25, 1598). That Part 2 was not much more than begun at this time is suggested by the omission of "First Part" on the title-page of the 1598 quarto. Meres's reference to "Henry the 4." (*Palladis Tamia*; see above under *1 Henry IV*) is ambiguous so far as Part 2 is concerned.

SOURCES: (1) Holinshed, *Chronicles* (2nd ed., 1587). (2) Anon., *The Famous Victories of Henry V* (c. 1586). PROBABLE SOURCES: (1) Hall, *The Union of . . . Lancaster and York* (1548). (2) Daniel, *Civil Wars* (1595). POSSIBLE SOURCES: (1) Elyot, *The Governor* (1531). (2) Stow, *Chronicles of England* (1580).

Much Ado about Nothing

PROPOSED DATE: 1598–99

Marked "to be staied" on *S.R.* August 4, 1600; registered for publication on *S.R.* August 23, 1600; published 1600. Not included by Meres (*Palladis Tamia*) as of September 7, 1598. This omission by Meres may be significant, but it need not be so, since he fails to include *The Taming of the Shrew* (1593–94).

PROBABLE SOURCES: (1) Ariosto, *Orlando Furioso* (tr. Harington, 1591), Bk. V. (2) Spenser, *The Faerie Queene*, Bk. II, Canto iv (1590). (3) Bandello, *Novelle*, Novella 22 (1554; no contemporary English tr. known; French tr. in Belleforest's *Histoires Tragiques*, vol. III, 1568, story 18). POSSIBLE SOURCE: Munday (?), *Fedele and Fortunio* (c. 1584).

Henry V

PROPOSED DATE: 1599

Published in F1 (1623). Marked "to be staied" on *S.R.* August 4, 1600. A "bad" quarto text (1600) had been published by Millington and Busby before August 14, when its transfer to Thomas Pavier was entered on *S.R.* Not included by Meres (*Palladis Tamia*) as of September 7, 1598. Imitation of certain scenes in *Henry V*, and verbal echoes from it, in *1 Sir John Oldcastle* give a definite *terminus ad quem* for Shakespeare's play, since the authors (Munday, Drayton, Wilson, and Hathaway) of *1 Oldcastle* were paid for the finished play on October 16, 1599, by Henslowe (*Diary*, fol. 65).

TITLE	PROPOSED DATE	EVIDENCE FOR DATING; SOURCES	
Henry V (cont.)		An allusion, usually taken as referring to Essex's Irish campaign, in the Chorus to Act V has been used to date the play between March 27 and September 28, 1599. This view has recently been challenged by W. D. Smith, who argues that the allusion is rather to Lord Mountjoy, Elizabeth's successful commander in Ireland between early 1600 and Elizabeth's death in 1603, and that the Choruses were added, by another hand, to Shakespeare's play during those years (hence their non-appearance in the "bad" quarto of 1600). The matter remains open.	
		SOURCES: (1) Holinshed, *Chronicles* (2nd ed., 1587). (2) Tacitus, *Annals*, Bks. I, II (tr. Grenewey, 1598). (3) Anon., *The Famous Victories of Henry V* (c. 1586). POSSIBLE SOURCES: (1) Anon., *The Battle of Agincourt* (c. 1530). (2) Daniel, *Civil Wars* (1595).	
Julius Caesar	1599	Published in F1 (1623). A performance, probably at the Globe, was witnessed by a German traveller, Thomas Platter, on September 21, 1599 (see Appendix B, Number 16). Not included by Meres (*Palladis Tamia*) as of September 7, 1598. Jonson appears to paraphrase III.ii.104–5 in *Every Man Out of His Humor* (1599).	
		SOURCE: Plutarch, *Lives* (tr. North, 1579; the lives of Caesar, Brutus, Antony, and Cicero). POSSIBLE SOURCES: (1) Tacitus, *Annals* (tr. Grenewey, 1598). (2) Appian, *Civil Wars* (tr. W. B., 1578). (3) Pescetti, *Il Cesare* (1594). (4) Anon., *Caesar and Pompey, or Caesar's Revenge* (c. 1595).	
As You Like It	1599	Published in F1 (1623). Marked "to be staied" on *S.R.* August 4, 1600. Not included by Meres (*Palladis Tamia*) as of September 7, 1598. Setting of the song "It was a lover and his lass" (V.iii.16–33), probably original to this play, was published in Thomas Morley's *First Book of Airs* (1600).	
		SOURCE: Lodge, *Rosalynde* (1590). PROBABLE SOURCE: Anon., *Sir Clyomon and Sir Clamydes* (c. 1570).	
Hamlet	1600–1	Entered on *S.R.* July 26, 1602; "bad" quarto published 1603; "good" quarto published 1604. A play on the Hamlet story existed at least as early as 1589, probably by Thomas Kyd (see Nashe's preface to Greene's *Menaphon*, 1589 [Appendix B, Number 17]). Topical references in the play to the players' "inhibition," which has arisen out of the "late innovation" (II.ii.332–33), and to the "aery of children, little eyases" (II.ii.339), have been used in dating. Two interpretations have been advanced for the "inhibition–innovation" reference: (1) that it refers to the abortive Essex rebellion of February 8, 1601; (2) that it refers to the Privy Council decree of June 22, 1600, which limited the number of playhouses in London to two and performances to twice weekly. The "little eyases" passage, since it occurs only in the F1 text and clearly comments on the so-called War of the Theatres (after the middle of 1601), may be a later addition. The two incidental allusions to Julius Caesar link closely with *Julius Caesar* (1599) and suggest that the material was still fresh in Shakespeare's mind when he turned to *Hamlet*. Gabriel Harvey's well-known reference to Shakespeare's *Hamlet* (see Appendix B, Number 18), which is usually dated before the execution of Essex (February 25, 1601), is perhaps more safely dated as not later than July 21, 1603.	
		SOURCES: (1) It is generally agreed that the principal source was the earlier Hamlet play (now lost) referred to above. (2) Bright, *A Treatise of Melancholy* (1586). (3) Lavater, *Of Ghosts and Spirits Walking by Night* (tr. R.H., 1572). (4) Scot, *Discovery of Witchcraft* (1584). (5) Nashe, *Pierce Penniless* (1592). (6) Montaigne, *Essays* (tr. Florio, 1603; used in MS). POSSIBLE SOURCE: Belleforest, *Histoires Tragiques* (vol. V, story 3, 1570; in the original, which was the source for the *Ur-Hamlet* play, or in the anonymous tr. *The History of Hamblet*, in an edition antedating the earliest now known [1608]).	
The Phoenix and Turtle	c. 1601	Published in Robert Chester's *Love's Martyr* (1601). It seems to have been written specifically for this volume.	53

Twelfth Night	1601–2	Published in F1 (1623). A performance at the Middle Temple, possibly the first, described by John Manningham in his *Diary* (see Appendix B, Number 19), took place February 2, 1602. The play is probably not earlier than 1600, since the snatches of songs in II.iii seem to derive from Robert Jones's *First Book of Songs and Airs*, published in that year. There is a possible allusion to Sir Toby Belch in Jonson's *Poetaster* (III.iv.345), acted in 1601. Not included by Meres (*Palladis Tamia*) as of September 7, 1598.

SOURCE: Rich, *His Farewell to Military Profession* (1581). PROBABLE SOURCE: *Gl'Ingannati* (1531; no contemporary tr. known). POSSIBLE SOURCE: Forde, *The Famous History of Parismus* (1598).

Troilus and Cressida	1601–2	Entered on *S.R.* February 7, 1603; published 1609. F1 text (1623) substantially different. The reference in the Prologue to the "prologue arm'd" is generally taken as pointing to Jonson's *Poetaster* (1601), in which an "armed Prologue" appears. The character of Ajax is by some thought to be Shakespeare's parting blow at Jonson in the War of the Theatres in answer to Jonson's attack on Shakespeare's company in *Poetaster*. What appears to be a reference to Gilbert's *De Magnete* (1600) in III.ii.179 and IV.ii.104–5 may be taken to support a date after that year.

SOURCES: (1) Caxton, *The Ancient History of the Destruction of Troy* (tr. of Le Fèvre; 1596 ed.). (2) Homer, *Iliads* (tr. Chapman, 1598; only Bks. I–II, VII–XI and *Achilles' Shield*). (3) Lydgate, *The Ancient History and Only True Chronicle of the Wars [of Troy]* (tr. of Guido delle Colonne; 1555 ed.). PROBABLE SOURCES: (1) Chaucer, *Troilus and Criseyde*. (2) Ovid, *Metamorphoses* (tr. Golding, 1567), Bks. XII, XIII. POSSIBLE SOURCES: (1) Chettle and Dekker, *Troilus and Cressida* (1599; extant only in a fragmentary MS "plot"). (2) Greene, *Planetomachia* (1585).

All's Well That Ends Well	1602–3	Published in F1 (1623). Some critics believe, on the basis of different styles, that Shakespeare first wrote this play, or parts of it, as early as 1594–95, and that the F1 text represents his reworking around 1602–3. The fact that the "bed trick" here used is found also in Shakespeare's source suggests that the play is at least earlier than *Measure for Measure*, where the "bed trick" is Shakespeare's addition to the plot he borrows.

SOURCE: Painter, *The Palace of Pleasure* (1566–67), Novel 38 (tr. of Boccaccio).

Measure for Measure	1604	Published in F1 (1623). Performed at court December 26, 1604. The Duke referred to in connection with the King of Hungary's peace (I.ii.1–5) has recently been identified with the Duke of Holstein, Queen Anne's brother, who was in England in 1604 to raise men in the Protestant cause against Rudolph II of Hungary.

SOURCE: Whetstone, *Promos and Cassandra* (1578; a play based on Giraldi Cinthio's *Hecatommithi* [1565], Decade 8, Novella 5, and Claude Rouillet's *Philanira* [1556]). PROBABLE SOURCES: (1) Cinthio, *Epitia* (1583; no contemporary tr. known). (2) Cinthio, *Hecatommithi* (1565; no contemporary tr. known, though Whetstone included a prose version in his *Heptameron of Civil Discourses* [1582], which Shakespeare may have known).

Othello	1604	Published 1622; F1 text (1623) substantially different. Performed at court November 1, 1604. Some possibility of an earlier date is suggested by what appear to be verbal borrowings from *Othello* in the "bad" quarto of *Hamlet* (1603).

SOURCES: (1) Giraldi Cinthio, *Hecatommithi* (1565), Decade 3, Novella 7 (no contemporary English tr. known; Shakespeare does not appear to have used the French tr. by Chappuys [1584]). (2) Pliny, *The History of the World* (tr. Holland, 1601). (3) Contareni, *The Commonwealth and Government of Venice* (tr. Lewkenor, 1599).

King Lear	1605	Entered on *S.R.* November 26, 1607; published 1608 in a text in many ways resembling a "bad" quarto. Received text published in F1 (1623). Performed at court December 26, 1606. The popularity of Shakespeare's play probably

King Lear (cont.)

led to the publication (entered on *S.R.* May 14, 1594, and again May 8, 1605) of the much earlier anonymous *Chronicle History of King Leir* (c. 1590) in 1605. Since Shakespeare's play uses material from Harsnett's *Declaration of Egregious Popish Impostures*, it cannot be earlier than 1603; and the imitation of *Lear* (I.iv) by Sharpham in *The Fleer*, entered on *S.R.* May 13, 1606, affords a terminal date.

SOURCES: (1) Anon., *The Chronicle History of King Leir* (c. 1590). (2) Holinshed, *Chronicles* (2nd ed., 1587). (3) Sidney, *Arcadia* (1590). (4) Spenser, *The Faerie Queene*, Bk. II, Canto x (1590). (5) *Mirror for Magistrates* (ed. Higgins, 1574, 1587). (6) Harsnett, *Declaration of Egregious Popish Impostures* (1603). (7) Montaigne, *Essays* (tr. Florio, 1603). POSSIBLE SOURCE: Marston, *The Malcontent* (1604).

Macbeth — 1606

Published in F1 (1623). Contains probable allusions to the equivocation issue at the trial of the Gunpowder Plot conspirators (January-March 1606). There is some evidence that the play was first performed before James I on August 7, 1606, in honor of the visit of King Christian of Denmark. Simon Forman has left a description of a performance seen by him April 20, 1611 (see Appendix B, Number 20).

SOURCES: (1) Holinshed, *Chronicles* (2nd ed., 1587). (2) Seneca, *Hercules Furens* and *Agamemnon* (the second in Studley's tr., 1565). PROBABLE SOURCE: Buchanan, *Rerum Scoticarum Historia* (1582).

Antony and Cleopatra — 1606–7

Entered on *S.R.* May 20, 1608; published in F1 (1623). Some influence of Shakespeare's play has been found in Daniel's revision of his *Cleopatra*, published in 1607.

SOURCES: (1) Plutarch, *Lives* (tr. North, 1579; the life of Antony). (2) Appian, *Civil Wars* (tr. W. B., 1578). PROBABLE SOURCES: (1) Plutarch, *Lives* (tr. North, 1603; the life of Octavius Caesar). (2) Daniel, *The Tragedy of Cleopatra* (1599 ed.).

Coriolanus — 1607–8

Published in F1 (1623). Apart from stylistic evidence, there is little to suggest a more exact date. The reference to "the coal of fire upon the ice" (I.i.173) has been taken as alluding to the great frost of 1607–8 (see Dekker (?), *The Great Frost*, 1608), when the Thames was frozen over and pans of coals were burned on it. An allusion to Hugh Middleton's project for bringing water into London (begun in February 1609 but discussed earlier) has been detected in III.i.95–97.

SOURCES: (1) Plutarch, *Lives* (tr. North, 1579; life of Coriolanus). (2) Averell, *A Marvellous Combat of Contrarieties* (1588; this and the two following for Menenius' fable of the belly). (3) Sidney, *An Apology for Poetry* (1595). (4) Camden, *Remains . . . Concerning Britain* (1605). PROBABLE SOURCE: Livy, *Roman History* (tr. Holland, 1600).

Timon of Athens — 1607–8

Published in F1 (1623). The play was probably left unfinished by Shakespeare and never acted. Stylistic evidence places it somewhere between 1605 and 1608; most critics favor 1607–8.

SOURCE: Plutarch, *Lives* (tr. North, 1579; life of Alcibiades). POSSIBLE SOURCES: (1) Lucian, *Timon, or the Misanthrope* (no contemporary English tr. known; Latin tr. by Erasmus, 1506; Italian by Lonigo, 1536; French by Bretin, 1583). (2) Lyly, *Campaspe* (c. 1584). (3) Anon., *Timon* (c. 1602; possible relationship to Shakespeare's play much debated).

Pericles — 1607–8

Entered on *S.R.* May 20, 1608; published, in a "bad" quarto text, 1609. The play was not included among Shakespeare's collected works until the second issue of F3 (1664). A performance was seen at court by the Venetian and French ambassadors between May 1606 and November 1608. George Wilkins' little novel, *The Painful Adventures of Pericles Prince of Tyre*, based in part on this play, was published in 1608. The problem of authorship is discussed in the introduction to the play.

SOURCES: (1) Gower, *Confessio Amantis* (1554 ed.). (2) Twine, *The Pattern of Painful Adventures* (n.d. [c. 1594] and 1607). POSSIBLE SOURCE: Sidney, *Arcadia* (1590).

TITLE	PROPOSED DATE	EVIDENCE FOR DATING; SOURCES
Cymbeline	1609–10	Published in F1 (1623). Simon Forman saw a performance probably between April 20 and 30, 1611 (see Appendix B, Number 20). Metrical and stylistic evidence links *Cymbeline* with *The Winter's Tale* and *The Tempest*.
		SOURCES: (1) Holinshed, *Chronicles* (2nd ed., 1587). (2) *Mirror for Magistrates* (ed. Blenerhasset, 1578, and Higgins, 1587). (3) Anon., *Frederyke of Jennen* (1560 ed.; based on Boccaccio's *Decameron*). (4) Anon., *The Rare Triumphs of Love and Fortune* (1582). PROBABLE SOURCE: Boccaccio, *Decameron*, Day 2, Tale 9 (no contemporary English tr. known; two in French, the one by Maçon [1545] frequently reprinted). POSSIBLE SOURCE: Anon., *Sir Clyomon and Clamydes* (c. 1570).
The Winter's Tale	1610–11	Published in F1 (1623). Simon Forman saw a performance on May 15, 1611 (see Appendix B, Number 20), and a court performance took place November 5, 1611. In IV.iv.783–91 the reference to a source probably used for *Cymbeline* (Boccaccio's *Decameron*, Day 2, Tale 9) would seem to indicate that *The Winter's Tale* is the later play.
		SOURCES: (1) Greene, *Pandosto, the Triumph of Time* (1588). (2) Sabie, *The Fisherman's Tale* (1594) and *Flora's Fortune* (1595). PROBABLE SOURCE: Greene, *The Second Part of Cony-Catching* (1591; for Autolycus' first trick on the Clown). POSSIBLE SOURCE: Forde, *The Famous History of Parismus* (1598).
The Tempest	1611	Published in F1 (1623). Performed at court November 1, 1611. The play makes use of sources not available before September 1610.
		SOURCES: None known for the main plot, but Shakespeare used: (1) Strachey, *True Repertory of the Wrack and Redemption of Sir Thomas Gates* (dated July 15, 1610, but not published until 1625 in *Purchas His Pilgrims*). (2) Jourdain, *A Discovery of the Bermudas* (1610). (3) [Virginia Council], *True Declaration of the Estate of the Colony in Virginia* (1610). (4) Montaigne, *Essays* (tr. Florio, 1603). (5) Ovid, *Metamorphoses*, Bk. VII (both in the original and in Golding's tr., 1567).
Henry VIII	1612–13	Published in F1 (1623). The Globe Theatre burned down during a performance of the play, probably the first, on June 29, 1613. An account of the play and the fire is contained in a letter (July 2, 1613) from Sir Henry Wotton to Sir Edmund Bacon (see Appendix B, Number 21A). The question of Shakespeare's collaboration with John Fletcher in *Henry VIII* is discussed in the introduction to the play.
		SOURCES: (1) Holinshed, *Chronicles* (2nd ed., 1587). (2) Foxe, *Acts and Monuments* (1570 ed.). PROBABLE SOURCE: Samuel Rowley, *When You See Me, You Know Me* (1604).
Cardenio (a lost play)	1612–13	A play called "Cardenno" or "Cardenna" was twice acted at court 1612–13 by the King's Men. It was attributed to Fletcher and Shakespeare in Humphrey Moseley's *S.R.* entry September 9, 1653. The play itself has been lost, but it is likely that Lewis Theobald's *Double Falsehood, or The Distress'd Lovers* (1728) represents a drastic reworking of the original *Cardenio*.
		SOURCE: Cervantes, *Don Quixote* (tr. Shelton, 1612), the story of Cardenio and Lucinda.
The Two Noble Kinsmen	1613	Entered on *S.R.* April 8, 1634; published 1634. Both the entry and the title-page describe the play as by Fletcher and Shakespeare; the question of their collaboration is discussed in the introduction to the play. A date not earlier than 1613 is indicated by the borrowing of the morris-dance in III.v from Beaumont's *Inner Temple and Gray's Inn Mask*, produced February 20 of that year.
		SOURCES: (1) Chaucer, "The Knight's Tale." (2) Beaumont, *Inner Temple and Gray's Inn Mask* (1613).

The opening pages of the Shakespeare First Folio (1623) are reproduced below, by kind permission of the Harvard College Library, from the copy in the Harry Elkins Widener Collection. The pages are here reduced by slightly more than one fourth; the dimensions of the original are approximately 13 by 8⅜ inches.

To the Reader.

This Figure, that thou here feeſt put,
    It was for gentle Shakeſpeare cut;
Wherein the Grauer had a ſtrife
    with Nature, to out-doo the life :
O, could he but haue drawne his wit
    As well in braſſe, as he hath hit
His face ; the Print would then ſurpaſſe
    All, that was euer writ in braſſe.
But, ſince he cannot, Reader, looke
    Not on his Picture, but his Booke.

B. I.

Mr. WILLIAM
SHAKESPEARES

COMEDIES,
HISTORIES, &
TRAGEDIES.

Published according to the True Originall Copies.

Martin Droeshout sculpsit London.

LONDON
Printed by Isaac Iaggard, and Ed. Blount. 1623.

TO THE MOST NOBLE
AND
INCOMPARABLE PAIRE
OF BRETHREN.

WILLIAM
Earle of Pembroke, &c. Lord Chamberlaine to the
Kings most Excellent Maiesty.

AND

PHILIP
Earle of Montgomery, &c. Gentleman of his Maiesties
Bed-Chamber. Both Knights of the most Noble Order
of the Garter, and our singular good
LORDS.

Right Honourable,

Hilst we studie to be thankful in our particular, for
the many fauors we haue receiued from your L.L.
we are falne vpon the ill fortune, to mingle
two the most diuerse things that can bee, feare,
and rashnesse; rashnesse in the enterprize, and
feare of the successe. For, when we valew the places your H.H.
sustaine, we cannot but know their dignity greater, then to descend to
the reading of these trifles: and, vvhile we name them trifles, we haue
depriu'd our selues of the defence of our Dedication. But since your
L.L. haue beene pleas'd to thinke these trifles some-thing, heereto-
fore; and haue prosequuted both them, and their Authour liuing,
vvith so much fauour: we hope, that (they out-liuing him, and he not
hauing the fate, common with some, to be exequutor to his owne writings) you will vse the like indulgence toward them, you haue done

A 2   vnto

vnto their parent. There is a great difference, vvhether any Booke choose his Patrones, or finde them : This hath done both. For, so much were your L.L. likings of the seuerall parts, vvhen they were acted, as before they vvere published, the Volume ask'd to be yours. We haue but collected them, and done an office to the dead, to procure his Orphanes, Guardians ; vvithout ambition either of selfe-profit, or fame : onely to keepe the memory of so worthy a Friend, & Fellow aliue, as was our SHAKESPEARE, by humble offer of his playes, to your most noble patronage. Wherein, as we haue iustly obserued, no man to come neere your L.L. but vvith a kind of religious addresse ; it hath bin the height of our care, vvho are the Presenters, to make the present worthy of your H.H. by the perfection. But, there we must also craue our abilities to be considerd, my Lords. We cannot go beyond our owne powers. Country hands reach foorth milke, creame, fruites, or what they haue : and many Nations (we haue heard) that had not gummes & incense, obtained their requests with a leauened Cake. It vvas no fault to approch their Gods, by what meanes they could : And the most, though meanest, of things are made more precious, when they are dedicated to Temples. In that name therefore, we most humbly consecrate to your H.H. these remaines of your seruant Shakespeare ; that what delight is in them, may be euer your L.L. the reputation his, & the faults ours, if any be committed, by a payre so carefull to shew their gratitude both to the liuing, and the dead, as is

Your Lordshippes most bounden,

IOHN HEMINGE.
HENRY CONDELL.

To the great Variety of Readers.

Rom the moſt able,to him that can but ſpell: There you are number'd.We had rather you were weighd. Eſpecially, when the fate of all Bookes depends vp-on your capacities : and not of your heads alone, but of your purſes. Well ! It is now publique, & you wil ſtand for your priuiledges wee know : to read, and cenſure. Do ſo,but buy it firſt. That doth beſt commend a Booke, the Stationer ſaies. Then,how odde ſoeuer your braines be, or your wiſedomes, make your licence the ſame,and ſpare not. Iudge your ſixe-pen'orth, your ſhillings worth, your fiue ſhil-lings worth at a time, or higher, ſo you riſe to the iuſt rates, and wel-come. But, what euer you do, Buy. Cenſure will not driue a Trade, or make the Iacke go. And though you be a Magiſtrate of wit, and ſit on the Stage at *Black-Friers*, or the *Cock-pit*, to arraigne Playes dailie, know, theſe Playes haue had their triall alreadie, and ſtood out all Ap-peales ; and do now come forth quitted rather by a Decree of Court, then any purchas'd Letters of commendation.

It had bene a thing, we confeſſe, worthie to haue bene wiſhed,that the Author himſelfe had liu'd to haue ſet forth, and ouerſeen his owne writings ; But ſince it hath bin ordain'd otherwiſe,and he by death de-parted from that right,we pray you do not envie his Friends,the office of their care, and paine, to haue collected & publiſh'd them ; and ſo to haue publiſh'd them, as where (before) you were abus'd with diuerſe ſtolne, and ſurreptitious copies, maimed,and deformed by the frauds and ſtealthes of iniurious impoſtors, that expos'd them : euen thoſe, are now offer'd to your view cur'd, and perfect of their limbes ; and all the reſt, abſolute in their numbers, as he conceiued thē.Who,as he was a happie imitator of Nature,was a moſt gentle expreſſer of it.His mind and hand went together: And what he thought, he vttered with that eaſineſſe, that wee haue ſcarſe receiued from him a blot in his papers. But it is not our prouince,who onely gather his works, and giue them you, to praiſe him. It is yours that reade him. And there we hope,to your diuers capacities, you will finde enough, both to draw, and hold you : for his wit can no more lie hid, then it could be loſt. Reade him, therefore ; and againe, and againe : And if then you doe not like him, ſurely you are in ſome manifeſt danger, not to vnderſtand him. And ſo we leaue you to other of his Friends, whom if you need,can bee your guides : if you neede them not, you can leade your ſelues,and others. And ſuch Readers we wiſh him.

A 3
Iohn Heminge.
Henrie Condell.

To the memory of my beloued,
The AVTHOR
Mr. William Shakespeare:
And
what he hath left vs.

*T*O *draw no enuy (*Shakespeare*) on thy name,*
  Am I thus ample to thy Booke, and Fame :
While I confesse thy writings to be such,
  As neither Man, *nor* Muse, *can praise too much.*
'*Tis true, and all mens suffrage. But these wayes*
  Were not the paths I meant vnto thy praise :
For seeliest Ignorance on these may light,
  Which, when it sounds at best, but eccho's right ;
Or blinde Affection, which doth ne're aduance
  The truth, but gropes, and vrgeth all by chance ;
Or crafty Malice, might pretend this praise,
  And thinke to ruine, where it seem'd to raise.
These are, as some infamous Baud, or whore,
  Should praise a Matron. What could hurt her more ?
But thou art proofe against them, and indeed
  Aboue th'ill fortune of them, or the need.
I, therefore will begin. Soule of the Age !
  The applause ! delight ! the wonder of our Stage !
My Shakespeare, *rise ; I will not lodge thee by*
  Chaucer, *or* Spenser, *or bid* Beaumont *lye*
A little further, to make thee a roome :
  Thou art a Moniment, without a tombe,
And art aliue still, while thy Booke doth liue,
  And we haue wits to read, and praise to giue.
That I not mixe thee so, my braine excuses ;
  I meane with great, but disproportion'd Muses :
For, if I thought my iudgement were of yeeres,
  I should commit thee surely with thy peeres,
And tell, how farre thou didst ß our Lily *out-shine,*
  Or sporting Kid, *or* Marlowes *mighty line.*
And though thou hadst small Latine, *and lesse* Greeke,
  From thence to honour thee, I would not seeke
For names ; but call forth thund'ring Æschilus,
  Euripides, *and* Sophocles *to vs,*
Paccuuius, Accius, *him of* Cordoua *dead,*
  To life againe, to heare thy Buskin *tread,*
And shake a Stage : Or, when thy Sockes *were on,*
  Loaue thee alone, for the comparison

Of all, that insolent Greece, *or haughtie* Rome
  sent forth, or since did from their ashes come.
Triumph, my Britaine, *thou hast one to showe,*
  To whom all Scenes of Europe *homage owe.*
He was not of an age, but for all time!
  And all the Muses still were in their prime,
When like Apollo *he came forth to warme*
  Our eares, or like a Mercury *to charme!*
Nature her selfe was proud of his designes,
  And ioy'd to weare the dressing of his lines!
Which were so richly spun, and wouen so fit,
  As, since, she will vouchsafe no other Wit.
The merry Greeke, *tart* Aristophanes,
  Neat Terence, *witty* Plautus, *now not please;*
But antiquated, and deserted lye
  As they were not of Natures family.
Yet must I not giue Nature all: Thy Art,
  My gentle Shakespeare, *must enioy a part.*
For though the Poets matter, Nature be,
  His Art doth giue the fashion. And, that he,
Who casts to write a liuing line, must sweat,
  (such as thine are) and strike the second heat
Vpon the Muses anuile : turne the same,
  (And himselfe with it) that he thinkes to frame;
Or for the lawrell, he may gaine a scorne,
  For a good Poet's made, as well as borne.
And such wert thou. Looke how the fathers face
  Liues in his issue, euen so, the race
Of Shakespeares *minde, and manners brightly shines*
  In his well torned, and true-filed lines :
In each of which, he seemes to shake a Lance,
  As brandish't at the eyes of Ignorance.
Sweet Swan of Auon! *what a sight it were*
  To see thee in our waters yet appeare,
And make those flights vpon the bankes of Thames,
  That so did take Eliza, *and our* Iames !
But stay, I see thee in the Hemisphere
  Aduanc'd, and made a Constellation there !
Shine forth, thou Starre of Poets, *and with rage,*
  Or influence, chide, or cheere the drooping Stage;
Which, since thy flight frō hence, hath mourn'd like night,
  And despaires day, but for thy Volumes light.

BEN: IONSON.

Vpon the Lines and Life of the Famous
Scenicke Poet, Maſter WILLIAM
SHAKESPEARE.

Hoſe hands, which you ſo clapt, go now, and wring
You *Britaines* braue; for done are *Shakeſpeares* dayes:
His dayes are done, that made the dainty Playes,
Which made the Globe of heau'n and earth to ring.
Dry'de is that veine, dry'd is the *Theſpian* Spring,
Turn'd all to teares, and *Phœbus* clouds his rayes:
That corp's, that coffin now beſticke thoſe bayes,
Which crown'd him *Poet* firſt, then *Poets* King.
If *Tragedies* might any *Prologue* haue,
All thoſe he made, would ſcarſe make one to this:
Where *Fame*, now that he gone is to the graue
(Deaths publique tyring-houſe) the *Nuncius* is.

     For though his line of life went ſoone about,
     The life yet of his lines ſhall neuer out.

          HVGH HOLLAND.

A CATALOGVE

of the seuerall Comedies, Histories, and Tragedies contained in this Volume.

TO THE MEMORIE

of the deceased Authour Maister
W. SHAKESPEARE.

SHake-speare, *at length thy pious fellowes giue*
The world thy Workes : thy Workes, by which, out-liue
Thy Tombe, thy name must · when that stone is rent,
And Time dissolues thy Stratford *Moniment,*
Here we aliue shall view thee still. This Booke,
When Brasse and Marble fade, shall make thee looke
Fresh to all Ages: when Posteritie
Shall loath what's new, thinke all is prodegie
That is not Shake-speares *; eu'ry Line, each Verse*
Here shall reuiue, redeeme thee from thy Herse.
Nor Fire, nor cankring Age, as Naso *said,*
Of his, thy wit-fraught Booke shall once inuade.
Nor shall I e're beleeue, or thinke thee dead
(Though mist) vntill our bankrout Stage be sped
(Impossible) with some new straine t'out-do
Passions of Iuliet, *and her* Romeo *;*
Or till J heare a Scene more nobly take,
Then when thy half-Sword parlying Romans *spake.*
Till these, till any of thy Volumes rest
Shall with more fire, more feeling be exprest,
Be sure, our Shake-speare, *thou canst neuer dye,*
But crown'd with Lawrell, liue eternally.

L. Digges.

To the memorie of M. *W. Shake-speare.*

WEE *wondred* (Shake-speare) *that thou went'st so soone*
From the Worlds-Stage, to the Graues-Tyring-roome.
Wee thought thee dead, but this thy printed worth,
Tels thy Spectators, that thou went'st but-forth
To enter with applause. An Actors Art,
Can dye, and liue, to acte a second part.
That's but an Exit of Mortalitie ;
This, a Re-entrance to a Plaudite.

I. M.

The Workes of William Shakespeare,

containing all his Comedies, Histories, and Tragedies: Truely set forth, according to their first *ORIGINALL*.

The Names of the Principall Actors
in all these Playes.

William Shakespeare.

Richard Burbadge.

John Hemmings.

Augustine Phillips.

William Kempt.

Thomas Poope.

George Bryan.

Henry Condell.

William Slye.

Richard Cowly.

John Lowine.

Samuell Crosse.

Alexander Cooke.

Samuel Gilburne.

Robert Armin.

William Ostler.

Nathan Field.

John Underwood.

Nicholas Tooley.

William Ecclestone.

Joseph Taylor.

Robert Benfield.

Robert Goughe.

Richard Robinson.

Iohn Shancke.

Iohn Rice.

THE TEMPEST.

Actus primus, Scena prima.

A tempestuous noise of Thunder and Lightning heard: Enter a Ship-master, and a Botefwaine.

Master.

BOte-fwaine.

Botef. Heere Master : What cheere ?

Maft. Good : Speake to th'Mariners : fall too't, yarely, or we run our felues a ground, beftirre, beftirre. *Exit.*

Enter Mariners.

Botef. Heigh my hearts, cheerely, cheerely my harts : yare, yare : Take in the toppe-fale : Tend to th'Masters whistle : Blow till thou burst thy winde, if roome enough.

Enter Alonso, Sebastian, Anthonio, Ferdinando, Gonzalo, and others.

Alon. Good Botefwaine haue care : where's the Master ? Play the men.

Botef. I pray now keepe below.

Anth. Where is the Master, Boson ?

Botef. Do you not heare him ? you marre our labour, Keepe your Cabines : you do affift the storme.

Gonz. Nay, good be patient.

Botef. When the Sea is : hence, what cares these roarers for the name of King ? to Cabine; filence : trouble vs not.

Gon. Good, yet remember whom thou haft aboord.

Botef. None that I more loue then my felfe. You are a Counfellor, if you can command these Elements to filence, and worke the peace of the present, wee will not hand a rope more, vfe your authoritie : If you cannot, giue thankes you haue liu'd fo long, and make your felfe readie in your Cabine for the mifchance of the houre, if it fo hap. Cheerely good hearts : out of our way I fay. *Exit.*

Gon. I haue great comfort from this fellow : methinks he hath no drowning marke vpon him, his complexion is perfect Gallowes : ftand faft good Fate to his hanging, make the rope of his destiny our cable, for our owne doth little aduantage : If he be not borne to bee hang'd, our cafe is miferable. *Exit.*

Enter Botefwaine.

Botef. Downe with the top-Maft : yare, lower, lower, bring her to Try with Maine-courfe. A plague————
A cry within. *Enter Sebastian, Anthonio & Gonzalo.*
vpon this howling : they are lowder then the weather, or our office : yet againe ? What do you heere ? Shal we giue ore and drowne, haue you a minde to finke ?

Sebaf. A poxe o'your throat, you bawling, blafphemous incharitable Dog.

Botef. Worke you then.

Anth. Hang cur, hang, you whorefon infolent Noyfemaker, we are leffe afraid to be drownde, then thou art.

Gonz. I'le warrant him for drowning, though the Ship were no ftronger then a Nutt-fhell, and as leaky as an vnftanched wench.

Botef. Lay her a hold, a hold, fet her two courfes off to Sea againe, lay her off.

Enter Mariners wet.

Mari. All loft, to prayers, to prayers, all loft.

Botef. What muft our mouths be cold ?

Gonz. The King, and Prince, at prayers, let's affift them, for our cafe is as theirs.

Sebaf. I'am out of patience.

An. We are meerly cheated of our liues by drunkards, This wide-chopt-rafcall, would thou mightft lye drowning the wafhing of ten Tides.

Gonz. Hee'l be hang'd yet,
Though euery drop of water fweare againft it,
And gape at widft to glut him. *A confufed noyfe within.*
Mercy on vs.
We fplit, we fplit, Farewell my wife, and children,
Farewell brother : we fplit, we fplit, we fplit.

Anth. Let's all finke with' King

Seb. Let's take leaue of him. *Exit.*

Gonz. Now would I giue a thousand furlongs of Sea, for an Acre of barren ground : Long heath, Browne firrs, any thing; the wills aboue be done, but I would faine dye a dry death. *Exit.*

Scena Secunda.

Enter Profpero and Miranda.

Mira. If by your Art (my deereft father) you haue
Put the wild waters in this Rore; alay them :
The skye it feemes would powre down ftinking pitch,
But that the Sea, mounting to th' welkins cheeke,
Dafhes the fire out. Oh ! I haue fuffered
With thofe that I faw fuffer : A braue veffell

A (Who

(Who had no doubt some noble creature in her)
Dash'd all to peeces : O the cry did knocke
Against my very heart : poore soules, they perish'd.
Had I byn any God of power, I would
Haue suncke the Sea within the Earth, or ere
It should the good Ship so haue swallow'd, and
The fraughting Soules within her.

Pros. Be collected,
No more amazement : Tell your pitteous heart
there's no harme done.

Mira. O woe, the day.

Pros. No harme?
I haue done nothing, but in care of thee
(Of thee my deere one ; thee my daughter) who
Art ignorant of what thou art . naught knowing
Of whence I am : nor that I am more better
Then *Prospero*, Master of a full poore cell,
And thy no greater Father.

Mira. More to know
Did neuer medle with my thoughts.

Pros. 'Tis time
I should informe thee farther : Lend thy hand
And plucke my Magick garment from me : So,
Lye there my Art : wipe thou thine eyes, haue comfort,
The direfull spectacle of the wracke which touch'd
The very vertue of compassion in thee :
I haue with such prouision in mine Art
So safely ordered, that there is no soule
No not so much perdition as an hayre
Betid to any creature in the vessell
Which thou heardst cry, which thou saw'st sinke : Sit
For thou must now know farther.   [downe,

Mira. You haue often
Begun to tell me what I am, but stopt
And left me to a bootelesse Inquisition,
Concluding, stay : not yet.

Pros. The howr's now come
The very minute byds thee ope thine eare,
Obey, and be attentiue. Canst thou remember
A time before we came vnto this Cell ?
I doe not thinke thou canst, for then thou was't not
Out three yeeres old.

Mira. Certainely Sir, I can.

Pros. By what ? by any other house, or person ?
Of any thing the Image, tell me, that
Hath kept with thy remembrance.

Mira. 'Tis farre off :
And rather like a dreame, then an assurance
That my remembrance warrants : Had I not
Fowre, or fiue women once, that tended me ?

Pros. Thou hadst ; and more *Miranda* : But how is it
That this liues in thy minde ? What seest thou els
In the dark-backward and Abisme of Time ?
Yf thou remembrest ought ere thou cam'st here,
How thou cam'st here thou maist.

Mira. But that I doe not.

Pros. Twelue yere since (*Miranda*) twelue yere since,
Thy father was the Duke of *Millaine* and
A Prince of power :

Mira. Sir, are not you my Father ?

Pros. Thy Mother was a peece of vertue, and
She said thou wast my daughter ; and thy father
Was Duke of *Millaine*, and his onely heire,
And Princesse ; no worse Issued.

Mira. O the heauens,
What fowle play had we, that we came from thence ?

Or blessed was't we did ?

Pros. Both, both my Girle.
By fowle-play (as thou saist) were we heau'd thence,
But blessedly holpe hither.

Mira. O my heart bleedes
To thinke oth' teene that I haue turn'd you to,
Which is from my remembrance, please you, farther ;

Pros. My brother and thy vncle, call'd *Anthonio* :
I pray thee marke me, that a brother should
Be so perfidious : he, whom next thy selfe
Of all the world I lou'd, and to him put
The mannage of my state, as at that time
Through all the signories it was the first,
And *Prospero*, the prime Duke, being so reputed
In dignity ; and for the liberall Artes,
Without a paralell ; those being all my studie,
The Gouernment I cast vpon my brother,
And to my State grew stranger, being transported
And rapt in secret studies, thy false vncle
(Do'st thou attend me ?)

Mira. Sir, most heedefully.

Pros. Being once perfected how to graunt suites,
how to deny them : who t'aduance, and who
To trash for ouer-topping ; new created
The creatures that were mine, I say, or chang'd 'em,
Or els new form'd 'em ; hauing both the key,
Of Officer, and office, set all hearts i'th state
To what tune pleas'd his eare, that now he was
The Iuy which had hid my princely Trunck,
And suckt my verdure out on't : Thou attend'st not ?

Mira. O good Sir, I doe.

Pros. I pray thee marke me :
I thus neglecting worldly ends, all dedicated
To closenes, and the bettering of my mind
with that, which but by being so retir'd
Ore-priz'd all popular rate : in my false brother
Awak'd an euill nature, and my trust
Like a good parent, did beget of him
A falsehood in it's contrarie, as great
As my trust was, which had indeede no limit,
A confidence sans bound. He being thus Lorded,
Not onely with what my reuenew yeelded,
But what my power might els exact. Like one
Who hauing into truth, by telling of it,
Made such a synner of his memorie
To credite his owne lie, he did beleeue
He was indeed the Duke, out o'th' Substitution
And executing th'outward face of Roialtie
With all prerogatiue : hence his Ambition growing ;
Do'st thou heare ?

Mira. Your tale, Sir, would cure deafenesse.

Pros. To haue no Schreene between this part he plaid,
And him he plaid it for, he needes will be
Absolute *Millaine*, Me (poore man) my Librarie
Was Dukedome large enough : of temporall roalties
He thinks me now incapable. Confederates
(so drie he was for Sway) with King of *Naples*
To giue him Annuall tribute, doe him homage
Subiect his Coronet, to his Crowne and bend
The Dukedom yet vnbow'd (alas poore *Millaine*)
To most ignoble stooping.

Mira. Oh the heauens :

Pros. Marke his condition, and th'euent, then tell me
If this might be a brother.

Mira. I should sinne
To thinke but Noblie of my Grand-mother,

Good

THE PLAYS

Comedies

Histories

Tragedies

Romances

Sir Thomas More
The Additions Ascribed to Shakespeare

The Comedy of Errors

ALTHOUGH *The Comedy of Errors* is the only play by Shakespeare which includes the word *comedy* in its title, critics have persistently wanted to dismiss it as a farce, unworthy of serious consideration, however great its success as a theatrical frolic. Coleridge claimed that the play was a virtual paradigm of the lesser genre: "in exactest consonance with the philosophical principles and character of farce, as distinguished from comedy and from entertainments." It would be hard to deny that *The Comedy of Errors* has some of the characteristics of farce. As Coleridge observed, the device of the identical Antipholuses which Shakespeare took from the *Menaechmi* of Plautus strains the verisimilitude usually thought appropriate to comedy. Shakespeare's insistence upon compounding this basic absurdity by inventing identical servants to wait upon the single pair of twins provided in his Latin source pushes the story still further in the direction of that cloud-cuckoo-land of farce where, by special agreement between dramatist and audience, even the wildest and most coincidental plot structures become acceptable.

Twelfth Night, a play no one has ever wished to categorize as farce, also turns in part upon the confusions generated by twins identical in appearance. Viola and Sebastian, however, are both strangers in Illyria. They are mistaken for one another, pardonably, by new acquaintances; not, as in *The Comedy of Errors*, by those who know them well. Moreover, Viola recognizes at once what has happened: "Prove true, imagination, O, prove true, / That I, dear brother, be now ta'en for you!" (III.iv.375-76). Antipholus of Syracuse, by contrast, is journeying through the world in search of his lost twin. The

extraordinary things that begin to happen to him as soon as he sets foot in Ephesus constitute a virtual proclamation that his seven-year quest is over, his missing brother found. Yet for almost five acts the Syracusan Antipholus fails to reach this glaringly obvious conclusion, preferring to invoke sorcery or hallucination to explain his situation. He is not meant to seem obtuse. His reactions are simply governed here, although not in other respects, by the rules of farce rather than comedy. Similarly, Shakespeare asks his audience to accept without question the fact that the Sicilian Antipholus and Dromio each manage to disembark at Ephesus in Asia Minor wearing clothes indistinguishable from those that the native Antipholus and Dromio happen to have put on that morning. In *Twelfth Night*, Viola goes out of her way to explain that her boy's disguise is a deliberate copy in its "fashion, color, ornament" of the garb habitually worn by her lost brother. No rationalization of this kind is even attempted in *The Comedy of Errors*. Again, the latitude of farce must be invoked, even as it must when considering that hail of blows and beatings which falls upon the perplexed and innocent Dromios without, as it seems, causing them any real physical or psychological harm.

Yet despite its emphasis on plot and situational absurdity, despite the merry violence in many of the scenes, it is not really possible to contain *The Comedy of Errors* within the bounds of farce as defined by the *Oxford English Dictionary*: "a dramatic work (usually short) which has as its sole object to excite laughter." A comparison here with Shakespeare's principal source is illuminating. Although William Warner's translation of Plautus' *Menaechmi* did not appear until 1595, Shakespeare had almost certainly read the play in Latin before that date. Probably the "comedy of errors (like to Plautus his Menaechmus)" referred to as part of the disordered Christmas revels at Gray's Inn on December 28, 1594,[1] was Shakespeare's. It may well have been written, and given its initial performance, two or three years before. By Shakespearean standards, *The Comedy of Errors* is a short play, indeed the shortest in the canon, but the *Menaechmi* is very considerably shorter still. Plautus' play is also far less complex, concentrating almost entirely upon plot mistakings. Its characters are simple and rigidly type-cast. Peniculus, a parasite, is virtually summed up by his anxiety over his next free meal; Erotium, a courtesan, by the cupidity associated with her trade; while Menaechmus' wife, who is not even honored with a name of her own, is insufferably shrewish because, according to the conventions of Plautine drama, wives always are. At the end, it seems quite natural that her exasperated husband should propose to auction her off to anyone foolish enough to bid for so tiresome a commodity. Unlike Shakespeare's Adriana, she has no feelings to be considered.

Even Plautus' two brothers Menaechmus are differentiated almost entirely in terms of the situation into which each is flung. For the stranger Menaechmus Epidamnum proves to be a kind of land of the heart's desire, a place where courtesans press their favors on him gratis, banquets spread themselves for free, and total strangers press valuable gifts into his hands and decline payment. Puzzled but delighted, he welcomes this unexpected largesse of fortune. Meanwhile his twin brother is undergoing precisely the opposite experience in a familiar world of business and domestic cares which seems all at once to have run mad. Unlike Shakespeare, who was to concentrate attention on the problems of the Syracusan Antipholus, Plautus spends more time on the uncomfortable experience of the native twin than he does on the golden dream briefly enjoyed by the traveller. The Roman play is tightly constructed, lively and inventive, full of the atmosphere of a bustling harbor town. It would be difficult, however, to claim that it has any object or concern other than to turn the normal world upside down and to evoke laughter of a simple and unreflective kind.

Shakespeare retained the conventional city street of Roman comedy with its separate and stylized houses. Probably, when the play was performed at Gray's Inn, there were free-standing structures of painted canvas to represent the Phoenix, where the native Antipholus and his family live, the Porpentine for the courtesan, and the priory or abbey which becomes so important in the fifth act. This setting, with its invisible but strongly contrasted off-stage localities—the mart with its world of business and, in the opposite direction, the more open and ambiguous sea-port—made it easy for Shakespeare to preserve the classical unity of place, while building up the image of a credible and populous town. He changed its name, however, from Epidamnum to Ephesus. Ephesus, as a number of commentators have pointed out, had specific associations in St. Paul's *Epistle to the Ephesians* with witchcraft and sorcery, as well as with St. Paul's discussion of Christian marriage. These are both important themes in *The Comedy of Errors.*

Shakespeare may well have felt in the early 1590's that it would be a useful discipline to submit himself to the three unities, even if (as it turned out) he saw no subsequent need to employ them until he wrote *The Tempest* at the end of his career. He may also have turned to Plautus, as other Elizabethan dramatists had done before him, in order to learn something about the construction of a finely engineered dramatic plot after the more rambling organization typical of his own Henry VI plays or, possibly, of *The Two Gentlemen of Verona.*[2] If so, he did not hesitate to create for himself technical problems far exceeding anything posed by his source. By supplying twin servants, borrowed from another play by Plautus, the *Amphitruo,* to the twin masters of the *Menaechmi* and so doubling the opportunities for planned confusion he made *The Comedy of Errors* structurally as much a tour de force as one of the great Bach fugues. Even more important, he added three characters—Egeon, Luciana, and the Abbess—who have little or nothing to do with laughter.

Egeon derives not from classical comedy but from the story of Apollonius of Tyre as retold by the fourteenth-century poet John Gower in his *Confessio Amantis* (a story to which Shakespeare was to return years later for the plot of *Pericles*). The two appearances of old Egeon, at the beginning and end of *The Comedy of Errors,* not only define its time-span from morning until the sunset hour appointed for his execution: they greatly deepen the basic Plautine material in ways that often seem to anticipate *Pericles* and its successors. Parents in Roman comedy, like wives, were usually nothing but a nuisance, repressing and causing trouble for the young. Egeon cannot be fitted into such a scheme. It is true that his long opening account of the shipwreck which was the source of all his woes is faintly absurd. A family of six scattered by Fortune in a fashion at once so implausible and so ingeniously patterned announces itself fairly clearly as material for a comedy resolution. Yet it is wrong for actors to make Egeon's explanation to the Duke overtly comic. The anguish of the old man is real, even if the verse he speaks suggests delicately to a theatre audience that his loss will not prove irremediable. Later, in Act V, he addresses the son he believes to be guilty of forgetfulness and ingratitude in lines so bitter that they seem to prefigure the reproaches of Antonio in *Twelfth Night,* or even those of King Lear. Most important of all, Egeon allowed Shakespeare to open the play under the shadow of death and to keep this threat alive in the background, like a sword that has been drawn and not sheathed, until it flashes into prominence again in Act V only to dissolve before the discoveries and accords of the final scene. Death is never a serious possibility in the

[1] See Appendix B, Number 14, below.

[2] See the discussion of the date of *The Two Gentlemen of Verona* on pages 143–44.

Menaechmi, or in most of Roman comedy. Shakespeare, even at the beginning of his dramatic career, seems to have been wedded to the idea that happy endings must, to carry conviction, be won from a serious confrontation with mortality, violence, and time.

Behind the *Menaechmi*, as behind all the plays of Plautus, lay a Greek original now lost. Mistaken identity and the recovery or reunion of lost children seem to have been almost obsessive preoccupations of the New Comedy written by Menander and his contemporaries towards the end of the 4th century B.C. A response, probably, to the political and economic chaos of a Hellenistic world that was filled with displaced persons, where children were often "lost" by parents too poor or too distracted to cope with them at the time of their birth, and where free citizens could become slaves overnight, the theme has an emotional resonance in the surviving Menandrian fragments which vanished in the later, Roman adaptations. For Plautus, living in a very different and more stable world, dealing with the Greek material at second hand, these plots became little more than an approved comic formula. *The Comedy of Errors* is remarkable on a number of counts, but not least because of the way it revitalizes and gives new meaning to a seemingly outworn dramatic convention. This meaning is not really Menandrian. Between Menander's *Epitrepontes* or *Periceiromene* and Shakespeare's play there stretches not only an immense gulf of space and time but also the fact of Christianity with its stress upon the inner life. Menander's characters were psychologically more complex than their Roman descendants but it is still true that identity for them is principally a matter of establishing parentage and social class. Their quest is accomplished when they achieve the equivalent of a birth certificate. Antipholus of Syracuse, by contrast, has voluntarily left a father and a defined and satisfactory social role in order to find a missing mother and twin brother without whom he feels psychologically incomplete.

> I to the world am like a drop of water,
> That in the ocean seeks another drop,
> Who, falling there to find his fellow forth
> (Unseen, inquisitive), confounds himself.
> So I, to find a mother and a brother,
> In quest of them (unhappy) ah, lose myself.
>
> (I.ii.35–40)

Discontented and uneasy, Antipholus of Syracuse declares in the first scene in which he appears that he will, as a temporary distraction, "lose myself" in the streets of Ephesus. This is exactly what happens to him, but it happens in ways that neither he nor the writers of classical comedy could possibly have anticipated.

Unlike Plautus, Shakespeare seems to have been less interested in the problems of the native twin angered by the perversity of a familiar world than he was in the more extreme situation of the traveller, especially vulnerable because far from home, who finds himself losing his own sense of self in an alien city of reputed sorcery and spells. Antipholus of Syracuse, claimed as husband by a woman he has never seen before and does not like, saluted familiarly by men whose names he does not know and by a courtesan who assumes old acquaintance, badgered about inexplicable rings and chains and gold, finds it increasingly difficult to remain sure of a personal identity which everyone, even his own servant Dromio, seems determined not to recognize. Where the equivalent character in the *Menaechmi* had thought Epidamnum bewildering but delightful, Antipholus of Syracuse comes to regard Ephesus as a nightmare country where "none but witches do inhabit" (III.ii.156). Before long his self-confidence has been so badly shaken that he is asking Luciana to give him a new identity through the transforming power of romantic love (III.ii.33–52).

Like Egeon, Luciana is a character for whom there is no analogue in Plautus. The voice of reason and tolerance in the play, sane in the midst of madness, she counters the possessiveness and jealous frenzy of her sister Adriana with counsels of generosity and patience. Her own ideal of marriage is strikingly like that of the reformed Katherina at the end of *The Taming of the Shrew*: a relationship of mutual trust in which the woman is frankly subservient to her husband, as St. Paul believed she should be, but finds her own liberty and independence within this circumscription. It does not seem to be an ideal which Luciana has had much opportunity to see in practice. Faced with a nagging and suspicious sister and a brother-in-law who is careless of his wife's feelings and quick to anger, not to mention the dubious bond between the Ephesian Dromio and his spherical Nell, Luciana has remained single rather than court "troubles of the marriage-bed" (II.i.27). At the end of the play, however, it seems to be assumed that she will marry the Syracusan Antipholus: the man who appealed to her in Act III to help him forge a new identity through union with her own.

Before this can happen, violence and disorder in Ephesus rise to a pitch that is both funny and frightening. Outsiders like Angelo the goldsmith, Balthasar the merchant, Dr. Pinch the schoolmaster, the courtesan, and finally the Duke himself are all drawn into what at first had seemed only a family affair. In the last movement of the play, images of restraint, humiliation, and death proliferate. Antipholus of Syracuse, threatened with bondage and believing that he has seen the devil in the person of the courtesan, takes sanctuary in the abbey. His brother of Ephesus, having tried to savage his own wife, is bound and cast into a dark vault. Adriana, determined to remove from the abbey the man she believes to be her husband, is betrayed by the Abbess into a demonstration of her own shrewishness and publicly shamed. Pinch is tortured by his enraged prisoner. Old Egeon, led in bonds to the place of execution, is apparently spurned by the son he has brought up, and the angry explanations of Antipholus of Ephesus are so crossed and contradicted by the testimony of other characters that the Duke can only conclude that everyone is bewitched: "I think you all have drunk of Circe's cup" (V.i.271). Words are incapable of dealing with this tangle: indeed, they make it worse. Only the stage presence of the Syracusan Antipholus, as he emerges from the abbey to confront his twin for the first time in the play, can make sense of the tangle.

After the tension and accumulated mistakings of nearly five acts, this discovery generates an enormous sense of relief. The theatre audience, of course, unlike the characters in the play, has possessed the key to the situation all along: the knowledge that there are really two Dromios and two Antipholuses in Ephesus. The one surprise is Aemilia. When the Abbess recognizes Egeon as her long-lost husband and the two Antipholuses as her sons, Shakespeare deals a shrewd blow at the seeming omniscience of the spectators. Plautus had not restored this missing bit of the puzzle. There have been no hints in Shakespeare's play that Egeon's wife was alive and living in Ephesus. The discovery that she has been there all the time, that the virtuous and reverend lady who governs the abbey and has such decided views about a wife's duty to her husband is really the mother of the twins, is comical in the fullest sense of the word. As with Egeon's initial narrative of shipwreck and loss, there is something consciously absurd about this reunion which happens not only beyond hope but beyond any expectation explicitly generated by the play. Almost always, the theatre audience laughs when Aemilia identifies Egeon, but the laughter is not the laughter of farce.

At its ending *The Comedy of Errors* admits its own artificiality, its participation in that special realm of fairy-tale where the lost are always found, while reminding the theatre audience that it has not been in complete control of the situation after all. This last scene is consciously contrived but also moving in a way that seems to anticipate the marvellous discoveries of *Cymbeline* and *The Winter's Tale*. Certainly the emotions liberated look forward to the last plays. In the final moments of the comedy, the Syracusan Dromio makes another mistake. He addresses to the Ephesian Antipholus the question he ought to ask his own Syracusan master: "shall I fetch your stuff from shipboard?" "Dromio, what stuff of mine hast thou embark'd?" the puzzled Antipholus returns. But, for the first time in the play, no altercation, no ferocious exchange of words and blows results. Instead, Antipholus of Syracuse points out gently,

> He speaks to me. I am your master, Dromio.
> Come go with us, we'll look to that anon.
> Embrace thy brother there, rejoice with him.

The basic situation of the play, the source of all the misunderstanding, remains but it has been robbed of its sting. There is no pain in this final confusion of identities and no violence, only delight: "After so long grief, such nativity!"

Anne Barton

A Renaissance performance of Terence. From Terence: *Comoediae* (Lyon, 1493). The woodcut above, from the earliest printed book containing illustrations depicting dramatic performance, is from Terence's *Phormio, or The Scheming Parasite* (I.ii). It shows the kind of staging that Shakespeare uses in *The Comedy of Errors*. At the rear of the stage, clearly marked, may be seen the "houses" of the principal characters: Demipho (left), Chremes (centre), and Dorio (right). These "houses" remain unchanged throughout the play, and the characters enter from them and exit into them, but all the action takes place on the stage in front of the "houses." For comparison with *The Comedy of Errors*, see the note at the beginning of I.i, below. (*By permission of the Harvard College Library*)

The Comedy of Errors

[Dramatis Personae

SOLINUS, *Duke of Ephesus*
EGEON, *a merchant of Syracuse*
ANTIPHOLUS OF EPHESUS ⎫ *twin brothers, and sons*
ANTIPHOLUS OF SYRACUSE ⎭ *to Egeon and Aemilia*
DROMIO OF EPHESUS ⎫ *twin brothers, and bondmen*
DROMIO OF SYRACUSE ⎭ *to the two Antipholuses*
BALTHAZAR, *a merchant*
ANGELO, *a goldsmith*
FIRST MERCHANT OF EPHESUS, *friend to Antipholus of Syracuse*
SECOND MERCHANT OF EPHESUS, *to whom Angelo is a debtor*

DOCTOR PINCH, *a conjuring schoolmaster*

AEMILIA, *wife to Egeon, an abbess at Ephesus*
ADRIANA, *wife to Antipholus of Ephesus*
LUCIANA, *her sister*
LUCE, *servant to Adriana (also known as NELL)*
COURTEZAN

JAILER, HEADSMAN, MESSENGER, OFFICERS, *and other*
ATTENDANTS

SCENE: *Ephesus*]

ACT I, SCENE I

Enter the DUKE OF EPHESUS *with* [EGEON] *the merchant of Syracusa,* JAILER [*with* OFFICERS], *and other Attendants.*

Ege.   Proceed, Solinus, to procure my fall,
And by the doom of death end woes and all.
Duke.   Merchant of Syracusa, plead no more.
I am not partial to infringe our laws;
The enmity and discord which of late   5
Sprung from the rancorous outrage of your Duke
To merchants, our well-dealing countrymen,
Who, wanting guilders to redeem their lives,
Have seal'd his rigorous statutes with their bloods,
Excludes all pity from our threat'ning looks: 10

For since the mortal and intestine jars
'Twixt thy seditious countrymen and us,
It hath in solemn synods been decreed,
Both by the Syracusians and ourselves,
To admit no traffic to our adverse towns: 15
Nay more, if any born at Ephesus be seen
At any Syracusian marts and fairs;
Again, if any Syracusian born
Come to the bay of Ephesus, he dies,
His goods confiscate to the Duke's dispose,   20
Unless a thousand marks be levied
To quit the penalty and to ransom him.
Thy substance, valued at the highest rate,
Cannot amount unto a hundred marks,
Therefore by law thou art condemn'd to die.   25
Ege.   Yet this my comfort, when your words are
     done,
My woes end likewise with the evening sun.
Duke.   Well, Syracusian; say in brief the cause
Why thou departedst from thy native home,
And for what cause thou cam'st to Ephesus.   30
Ege.   A heavier task could not have been impos'd
Than I to speak my griefs unspeakable:
Yet that the world may witness that my end

Words and passages enclosed in square brackets in the text above are either emendations of the copy-text or additions to it. The Textual Notes immediately following the play cite the earliest authority for every such change or insertion and supply the reading of the copy-text wherever it is emended in this edition.

I.i. Location: The mart of Ephesus. Following classical precedent, the action of this play takes place either (a) outside three "houses," perhaps merely doors (in the centre the house of Antipholus of Ephesus, marked as the Phoenix; to either side, the house of the Courtezan, marked as the Porpentine, and the priory, marked perhaps with a cross) or (b) on the open stage generally, which then serves as a more or less unlocalized playing place, here called "The mart," i.e. the marketplace or exchange.
2. **doom:** judgment, sentence.   4. **partial:** improperly inclined.
6. **outrage:** violent conduct.
7. **well-dealing:** doing business honestly and peaceably.
8. **wanting:** lacking.   **guilders:** Dutch coins, but here used in the general sense of "money."
9. **seal'd . . . bloods:** ratified his extremely harsh laws by payment of their lives.

11. **intestine:** violent, deadly.   (The usual meaning, "internal," i.e. "civil," does not fit the context here.)   **jars:** strife, quarrels.
15. **admit . . . to:** permit no trade between.   **adverse:** hostile.
17. **marts.** Synonymous here with *fairs.*
20. **confiscate:** confiscated.   **dispose:** disposal.
21. **marks.** A mark was two-thirds of a pound (an amount, not a coin).   22. **quit:** pay.
23. **Thy substance:** the sum total of your wealth.

The Comedy
of Errors
I.i

Was wrought by nature, not by vile offense,
I'll utter what my sorrow gives me leave.   35
In Syracusa was I born, and wed
Unto a woman, happy but for me,
And by me, had not our hap been bad:
With her I liv'd in joy; our wealth increas'd
By prosperous voyages I often made   40
To Epidamium, till my factor's death,
And [the] great care of goods at randon left,
Drew me from kind embracements of my spouse;
From whom my absence was not six months old
Before herself (almost at fainting under   45
The pleasing punishment that women bear)
Had made provision for her following me,
And soon, and safe, arrived where I was.
There had she not been long but she became
A joyful mother of two goodly sons: 50
And, which was strange, the one so like the other ·
As could not be distinguish'd but by names.
That very hour, and in the self-same inn,
A mean woman was delivered
Of such a burthen male, twins both alike.   55
Those, for their parents were exceeding poor,
I bought, and brought up to attend my sons.
My wife, not meanly proud of two such boys,
Made daily motions for our home return:
Unwilling I agreed. Alas! too soon   60
We came aboard.
A league from Epidamium had we sail'd
Before the always-wind-obeying deep
Gave any tragic instance of our harm:
But longer did we not retain much hope;   65
For what obscured light the heavens did grant
Did but convey unto our fearful minds
A doubtful warrant of immediate death,
Which though myself would gladly have embrac'd,
Yet the incessant weepings of my wife,   70
Weeping before for what she saw must come,
And piteous plainings of the pretty babes,
That mourn'd for fashion, ignorant what to fear,
Forc'd me to seek delays for them and me.
And this it was (for other means was none):   75
The sailors sought for safety by our boat,
And left the ship, then sinking-ripe, to us.
My wife, more careful for the latter-born,
Had fast'ned him unto a small spare mast,
Such as sea-faring men provide for storms;   80
To him one of the other twins was bound,
Whilst I had been like heedful of the other.
The children thus dispos'd, my wife and I,
Fixing our eyes on whom our care was fix'd,

Fast'ned ourselves at either end the mast,   85
And floating straight, obedient to the stream,
Was carried towards Corinth, as we thought.
At length the sun, gazing upon the earth,
Dispers'd those vapors that offended us,
And by the benefit of his wished light   90
The seas wax'd calm, and we discovered
Two ships from far, making amain to us,
Of Corinth that, of Epidaurus this.
But ere they came—O, let me say no more!
Gather the sequel by that went before.   95
Duke. Nay, forward, old man, do not break off so,
For we may pity, though not pardon thee.
Ege. O, had the gods done so, I had not now
Worthily term'd them merciless to us!   99
For ere the ships could meet by twice five leagues,
We were encount'red by a mighty rock,
Which being violently borne [upon],
Our helpful ship was splitted in the midst;
So that, in this unjust divorce of us,
Fortune had left to both of us alike   105
What to delight in, what to sorrow for.
Her part, poor soul! seeming as burdened
With lesser weight, but not with lesser woe,
Was carried with more speed before the wind,
And in our sight they three were taken up   110
By fishermen of Corinth, as we thought.
At length, another ship had seiz'd on us,
And knowing whom it was their hap to save,
Gave healthful welcome to their shipwrack'd guests,
And would have reft the fishers of their prey,   115
Had not their [bark] been very slow of sail;
And therefore homeward did they bend their course.
Thus have you heard me sever'd from my bliss,
That by misfortunes was my life prolong'd,
To tell sad stories of my own mishaps.   120
Duke. And for the sake of them thou sorrowest
      for,
Do me the favor to dilate at full
What have befall'n of them and [thee] till now.
Ege. My youngest boy, and yet my eldest care,
At eighteen years became inquisitive   125
After his brother; and importun'd me
That his attendant—so his case was like,
Reft of his brother, but retain'd his name—
Might bear him company in the quest of him:
Whom whilst I labored of a love to see,   130

34. **nature:** natural affection, i.e. a father's love.   38. **hap:** fortune.
41. **Epidamium:** Plautus' Epidamnum, modern Durrës (Italian Durazzo) in Albania. Shakespeare may have supposed, however, that it was in Greece; see note on line 93.   **factor's:** agent's.
42. **at randon:** at random, i.e. neglected, unattended.
43. **kind:** affectionate.   52. **As:** that they.   54. **mean:** low-born.
58. **not meanly:** in no small degree.   59. **motions:** proposals.
64. **instance:** indication, sign.   67. **fearful:** full of fear.
68. **doubtful:** frightening, dreadful.   72. **plainings:** wailings.
73. **for fashion:** in imitation.
74. **delays:** ways of deferring (the execution of the death warrant, line 68).   77. **sinking-ripe:** ready to sink.
78. **careful:** full of care, anxious.   **latter-born:** second-born.
84. **whom:** him on whom.

86. **straight:** at once.
89. **vapors that offended:** clouds that injured or assailed.
92. **making amain:** proceeding at full speed.
93. **Epidaurus:** possibly Dubrovnik on the Adriatic coast, north of Epidamnum; but if Shakespeare supposed the latter to be in Greece, he may mean here the Greek Epidaurus, not far from Corinth.
95. **that:** what.   96. **forward:** go on.   99. **Worthily:** justly.
103. **Our . . . midst:** i.e. the mast to which they were fastened was broken in half.   106. **What:** something.   107. **as:** as if.
114. **healthful:** saving.   115. **reft:** robbed.
122. **dilate at full:** relate in detail, i.e. amplify.
123. **have befall'n:** has become.
124. **youngest boy.** Lines 78 ff. have led the reader to suppose that Egeon's charge was the elder son.
127. **so . . . like:** whose situation was similar.
128. **Reft . . . name.** Although commentators have found difficulty with this line (in view of line 52), the meaning seems clear enough, i.e. Egeon, presuming his elder son lost (or dead), has conferred his name on his younger son, who is now his "eldest care" (line 124).
130. **labored . . . love:** i.e. was racked by a desire.

I hazarded the loss of whom I lov'd.
Five summers have I spent in farthest Greece,
Roaming clean through the bounds of Asia,
And coasting homeward, came to Ephesus;
Hopeless to find, yet loath to leave unsought   135
Or that, or any place that harbors men.
But here must end the story of my life,
And happy were I in my timely death,
Could all my travels warrant me they live.
  Duke. Hapless Egeon, whom the fates have
      mark'd   140
To bear the extremity of dire mishap!
Now trust me, were it not against our laws,
Against my crown, my oath, my dignity,
Which princes, would they, may not disannul,
My soul should sue as advocate for thee: 145
But though thou art adjudged to the death,
And passed sentence may not be recall'd
But to our honor's great disparagement,
Yet will I favor thee in what I can;
Therefore, merchant, I'll limit thee this day   150
To seek thy [health] by beneficial help.
Try all the friends thou hast in Ephesus;
Beg thou, or borrow, to make up the sum,
And live: if no, then thou art doom'd to die.
Jailer, take him to thy custody.   155
  Jail. I will, my lord.
  Ege. Hopeless and helpless doth Egeon wend,
But to procrastinate his liveless end.   *Exeunt.*

[SCENE II]

Enter Antipholus Erotes [*of Syracuse, First*] Merchant [*of* Ephesus], *and* Dromio [*of* Syracuse].

  [*1. E.*] *Mer.* Therefore give out you are of Epida-
      mium,
Lest that your goods too soon be confiscate:
This very day a Syracusian merchant
Is apprehended for [arrival] here;
And not being able to buy out his life,   5
According to the statute of the town,
Dies ere the weary sun set in the west.
There is your money that I had to keep.
  S. Ant. Go bear it to the Centaur, where we host,
And stay there, Dromio, till I come to thee.   10

---

133. **clean:** completely.   **bounds:** territories.
136. **Or:** either.   **harbors:** lodges.
138. **timely:** opportune or seasonable (in that he would now die
happy if he believed that his sons lived).
139. **travels:** (1) journeyings; (2) travails, hardships.   **warrant:**
assure.
144. **would they:** even if they wanted to.   **disannul:** annul, cancel.
150. **limit:** allot as a limit. (The Duke's statement sets up the time
scheme of the play.)
158. **procrastinate:** postpone.   **liveless:** lifeless.

I.ii. Location: The mart.
o.s.d. **Erotes.** Explained as deriving in some way (as by compositorial
misreading) from Latin *erraticus* or *errans* (genitive *errantis*), "wandering" (designating the twin who is travelling in search of his brother).
The F1 spelling *Errotis* at II.ii o.s.d. (see the Textual Notes) supports
this conjecture. See also the note to II.i o.s.d.   5. **buy out:** ransom.
9. **Centaur.** Named from the figure on the sign over the door. Not
only inns but shops had such signs; and below, I.ii.75, where we learn
that the house in which Antipholus of Ephesus lives and carries on
his business is called the Phoenix.   **host:** lodge.

Within this hour it will be dinner-time;
Till that, I'll view the manners of the town,
Peruse the traders, gaze upon the buildings,
And then return and sleep within mine inn,
For with long travel I am stiff and weary.   15
Get thee away.
  S. Dro. Many a man would take you at your word,
And go indeed, having so good a mean.   *Exit Dromio.*
  S. Ant. A trusty villain, sir, that very oft,
When I am dull with care and melancholy,   20
Lightens my humor with his merry jests.
What, will you walk with me about the town,
And then go to my inn and dine with me?
  [*1.*] *E. Mer.* I am invited, sir, to certain merchants,
Of whom I hope to make much benefit;   25
I crave your pardon. Soon at five a' clock,
Please you, I'll meet with you upon the mart,
And afterward consort you till bed-time:
My present business calls me from you now.
  S. Ant. Farewell till then. I will go lose myself,
And wander up and down to view the city.   31
  [*1.*] *E. Mer.* Sir, I commend you to your own
      content.   *Exit.*
  S. Ant. He that commends me to mine own
      content,
Commends me to the thing I cannot get:
I to the world am like a drop of water,   35
That in the ocean seeks another drop,
Who, falling there to find his fellow forth
(Unseen, inquisitive), confounds himself.
So I, to find a mother and a brother,
In quest of them (unhappy), ah, lose myself.   40

Enter Dromio of Ephesus.

Here comes the almanac of my true date.
What now? How chance thou art return'd so soon?
  E. Dro. Return'd so soon! rather approach'd too
      late:
The capon burns, the pig falls from the spit;
The clock hath strucken twelve upon the bell: 45
My mistress made it one upon my cheek:
She is so hot, because the meat is cold:
The meat is cold, because you come not home:
You come not home, because you have no stomach:
You have no stomach, having broke your fast: 50
But we that know what 'tis to fast and pray,
Are penitent for your default to-day.
  S. Ant. Stop in your wind, sir; tell me this, I pray:
Where have you left the money that I gave you?

---

11. **dinner-time:** i.e. about twelve o'clock; cf. line 45.
13. **Peruse:** inspect.
18. **mean:** means, i.e. the money entrusted to him.
19. **villain:** fellow (used here good-naturedly), but with some suggestion of "villein" or "bondman."   21. **humor:** mood.
25. **benefit:** profit.   26. **Soon:** in early evening.
28. **consort:** keep company with.   30. **lose myself:** roam at will.
35. **to:** in relation to.   37. **forth:** out.
38. **Unseen, inquisitive:** unknown and eagerly inquiring.   **confounds
himself:** destroys itself, i.e. loses its identity. (The play is much concerned with apparent loss of identity.)   40. **unhappy:** unlucky.
41. **almanac . . . date:** i.e. indicator of my age (since he and Dromio
were both born on the same day and in the same hour).
42. **How chance:** how does it come about that.
46. **made it one:** struck one o'clock.   49. **stomach:** appetite.
52. **penitent:** i.e. doing penance.   **default:** fault, sin.
53. **wind:** idle talk.

E. Dro. O—sixpence that I had a' We'n'sday last
To pay the saddler for my mistress' crupper?   56
The saddler had it, sir, I kept it not.

S. Ant. I am not in a sportive humor now:
Tell me, and dally not, where is the money?
We being strangers here, how dar'st thou trust   60
So great a charge from thine own custody?

E. Dro. I pray you jest, sir, as you sit at dinner.
I from my mistress come to you in post:
If I return, I shall be post indeed,
For she will [score] your fault upon my pate: 65
Methinks your maw, like mine, should be your [clock],
And strike you home without a messenger.

S. Ant. Come, Dromio, come, these jests are out
of season,
Reserve them till a merrier hour than this:
Where is the gold I gave in charge to thee?   70

E. Dro. To me, sir? Why, you gave no gold to me.

S. Ant. Come on, sir knave, have done your
foolishness,
And tell me how thou hast dispos'd thy charge.

E. Dro. My charge was but to fetch you from
the mart
Home to your house, the Phoenix, sir, to dinner;   75
My mistress and her sister stays for you.

S. Ant. Now, as I am a Christian, answer me,
In what safe place you have bestow'd my money;
Or I shall break that merry sconce of yours
That stands on tricks when I am undispos'd: 80
Where is the thousand marks thou hadst of me?

E. Dro. I have some marks of yours upon my pate;
Some of my mistress' marks upon my shoulders;
But not a thousand marks between you both.
If I should pay your worship those again,   85
Perchance you will not bear them patiently.

S. Ant. Thy mistress' marks? What mistress,
slave, hast thou?

E. Dro. Your worship's wife, my mistress at the
Phoenix;
She that doth fast till you come home to dinner;
And prays that you will hie you home to dinner.   90

S. Ant. What, wilt thou flout me thus unto my
face,
Being forbid? There, take you that, sir knave.

[*Strikes Dromio.*]

E. Dro. What mean you, sir? For God sake hold
your hands!
Nay, and you will not, sir, I'll take my heels.

Exit Dromio [*of*] *Ephesus.*

S. Ant. Upon my life, by some device or other   95
The villain is o'erraught of all my money.
They say this town is full of cozenage:
As nimble jugglers that deceive the eye,
Dark-working sorcerers that change the mind,

Soul-killing witches that deform the body,   100
Disguised cheaters, prating mountebanks,
And many such-like liberties of sin:
If it prove so, I will be gone the sooner.
I'll to the Centaur to go seek this slave;
I greatly fear my money is not safe.   *Exit.*   105

ACT II, [SCENE I]

Enter ADRIANA, *wife to Antipholus Sereptus* [*of Ephesus*],
with LUCIANA, *her sister.*

Adr. Neither my husband nor the slave return'd,
That in such haste I sent to seek his master?
Sure, Luciana, it is two a' clock.

Luc. Perhaps some merchant hath invited him,
And from the mart he's somewhere gone to dinner.   5
Good sister, let us dine, and never fret;
A man is master of his liberty:
Time is their master, and when they see time,
They'll go or come; if so, be patient, sister.   9

Adr. Why should their liberty than ours be more?

Luc. Because their business still lies out a' door.

Adr. Look when I serve him so, he takes it [ill].

Luc. O, know he is the bridle of your will.

Adr. There's none but asses will be bridled so.

Luc. Why, headstrong liberty is lash'd with woe:
There's nothing situate under heaven's eye   16
But hath his bound in earth, in sea, in sky.
The beasts, the fishes, and the winged fowls
Are their males' subjects and at their controls:
Man, more divine, the master of all these,   20
Lord of the wide world and wild wat'ry seas,
Indu'd with intellectual sense and souls,
Of more pre-eminence than fish and fowls,
Are masters to their females, and their lords:
Then let your will attend on their accords.   25

Adr. This servitude makes you to keep unwed.

Luc. Not this, but troubles of the marriage-bed.

Adr. But, were you wedded, you would bear
some sway.

Luc. Ere I learn love, I'll practice to obey.   29

Adr. How if your husband start some other where?

Luc. Till he come home again, I would forbear.

Adr. Patience unmov'd! no marvel though she
pause—
They can be meek that have no other cause:
A wretched soul, bruis'd with adversity,
We bid be quiet when we hear it cry;   35
But were we burd'ned with like weight of pain,

101. **prating mountebanks:** i.e. itinerant quack doctors crying up their
remedies.
102. **liberties of sin:** wicked transgressors (Kittredge).

II.i. **Location:** Before the house of Antipholus of Ephesus.
o.s.d. **Sereptus.** A verbal echo of Plautus, who in the prologue to the
Menaechmi describes the lost twin as *puer surreptus,* "the boy who
was snatched away."
11. **still:** constantly.   **out a' door:** i.e. away from home.
12. **serve:** treat.   15. **lash'd:** (1) scourged; (2) bound.
17. **his:** its.   22. **intellectual sense:** reason.
25. **accords:** assents, i.e. wishes.
30. **start...where:** go off in some other direction, i.e. after some
other woman.   32. **pause:** i.e. before marrying.
33. **other cause:** cause to be otherwise.

56. **crupper:** leather strap, attached to the back of a saddle and passed
under the horse's tail, to prevent the saddle from slipping forwards.
61. **from:** out of.   63. **post:** haste.
64. **post:** i.e. the doorpost on which tavern reckonings were marked.
65. **score:** mark, cut.   73. **dispos'd:** deposited.   79. **sconce:** head.
80. **stands:** insists.   **undispos'd:** i.e. not in a merry mood.
81. **thousand marks.** Ironically, this is the exact amount needed to
ransom his father.   93. **God:** God's.   94. **and:** if.
96. **o'erraught:** overreached, i.e. cheated.   97. **cozenage:** cheating.

As much, or more, we should ourselves complain:
So thou, that hast no unkind mate to grieve thee,
With urging helpless patience would relieve me;
But if thou live to see like right bereft,   40
This fool-begg'd patience in thee will be left.

Luc. Well, I will marry one day, but to try.
Here comes your man, now is your husband nigh.

Enter DROMIO [OF] EPHESUS.

Adr. Say, is your tardy master now at hand?
E. Dro. Nay, he's at [two] hands with me, and
that my two ears can witness.   46
Adr. Say, didst thou speak with him? Know'st
    thou his mind?
E. Dro. Ay, ay, he told his mind upon mine ear.
Beshrew his hand, I scarce could understand it.
Luc. Spake he so doubtfully, thou couldst not
feel his meaning?   51
E. Dro. Nay, he strook so plainly, I could too
well feel his blows; and withal so doubtfully, that
I could scarce understand them.
Adr. But say, I prithee, is he coming home?   55
It seems he hath great care to please his wife.
E. Dro. Why, mistress, sure my master is horn-
    mad.
Adr. Horn-mad, thou villain!
E. Dro.   I mean not cuckold-mad—
But sure he is stark mad:
When I desir'd him to come home to dinner,   60
He ask'd me for a [thousand] marks in gold:
"'Tis dinner-time," quoth I: "My gold!" quoth he.
"Your meat doth burn," quoth I: "My gold!"
    quoth he.
"Will you come?" quoth I: "My gold!" quoth he;
"Where is the thousand marks I gave thee, vil-
    lain?"   65
"The pig," quoth I, "is burn'd": "My gold!" quoth he.
"My mistress, sir," quoth I: "Hang up thy mistress!
I know not thy mistress, out on thy mistress!"
Luc. Quoth who?
E. Dro. Quoth my master.   70
"I know," quoth he, "no house, no wife, no mis-
    tress."
So that my arrant, due unto my tongue,
I thank him, I bare home upon my shoulders:
For, in conclusion, he did beat me there.
Adr. Go back again, thou slave, and fetch him
    home.   75
E. Dro. Go back again, and be new beaten home?
For God's sake send some other messenger.

Adr. Back, slave, or I will break thy pate across.
E. Dro. And he will bless that cross with other
    beating:
Between you I shall have a holy head.   80
Adr. Hence, prating peasant! fetch thy master
    home.
E. Dro. Am I so round with you, as you with me,
That like a football you do spurn me thus?
You spurn me hence, and he will spurn me hither: 84
If I last in this service, you must case me in leather.
                                                [*Exit.*]
Luc. Fie, how impatience low'reth in your face!
Adr. His company must do his minions grace,
Whilst I at home starve for a merry look:
Hath homely age th' alluring beauty took
From my poor cheek? Then he hath wasted it.   90
Are my discourses dull? Barren my wit?
If voluble and sharp discourse be marr'd,
Unkindness blunts it more than marble hard.
Do their gay vestments his affections bait?
That's not my fault, he's master of my state.   95
What ruins are in me that can be found,
By him not ruin'd? Then is he the ground
Of my defeatures. My decayed fair
A sunny look of his would soon repair.
But, too unruly deer, he breaks the pale,   100
And feeds from home; poor I am but his stale.
Luc. Self-harming jealousy—fie, beat it hence!
Adr. Unfeeling fools can with such wrongs dis-
    pense:
I know his eye doth homage otherwhere,
Or else what lets it but he would be here?   105
Sister, you know he promis'd me a chain;
Would that alone a' love he would detain,
So he would keep fair quarter with his bed!
I see the jewel best enamelled
Will lose his beauty; yet the gold bides still   110
That others touch and, often touching, will
Where gold; and no man that hath a name
By falsehood and corruption doth it shame.
Since that my beauty cannot please his eye,
I'll weep what's left away, and weeping die.   115
Luc. How many fond fools serve mad jealousy?
                                                Exeunt.

---

39. **helpless:** unavailing.
40. **see . . . bereft:** see yourself similarly deprived of your rights.
41. **fool-begg'd:** foolishly urged.   **left:** abandoned.
45-46. **he's . . . witness:** i.e. he boxed my ears.
48. **told.** With pun on *tolled.*
49. **Beshrew:** mischief take.   **understand.** With play on "stand under."   50. **doubtfully:** ambiguously.   52. **strook:** struck.
53. **doubtfully:** unsettledly (looking forward to the implied "madness" of lines 57 ff.).
57. **horn-mad:** acting like an infuriated horned animal (but Adriana is quick to suspect a reference to the horns cuckolds were supposed to have).
67. **Hang . . . mistress:** let your mistress go hang herself.
72. **my arrant:** my errand, what I have to deliver.   **due . . . tongue:** which I should have carried back by means of my tongue.

78. **across.** Dromio's reply quibbles on *a cross.*
79. **bless:** make happy (?) or sign with another cross (?); perhaps with a quibble on *bless* = wound, drub (from French *blesser*).
80. **holy:** (1) marked with a cross; (2) full of holes.
82. **round:** plainspoken (with quibble on "spherical").
87. **do . . . grace:** show favor to his paramours.
89. **homely age:** ugly old age.
90. **wasted:** (1) laid waste; (2) squandered.
91. **discourses:** conversations.
92. **voluble:** fluent, animated.   **sharp:** witty.
94. **affections:** passions.   **bait:** entice.
95. **state:** outward estate, i.e. clothes.   97. **ground:** cause.
98. **defeatures:** disfigurements.   **decayed fair:** perished beauty.
100. **pale:** enclosure.
101. **from:** away from.   **stale:** literally, stalking-horse; here, dupe, laughingstock.   103. **dispense:** put up.   105. **lets:** prevents.
107. **Would . . . detain:** would that he would withhold only that manifestation of love (?).
108. **So:** provided.   **keep . . . with:** be true to.
109-13. **I . . . shame.** A difficult, possibly corrupt, passage. Herford explains: "The best enamelled jewel tarnishes; but the gold setting keeps its lustre however it may be worn by the touch; similarly, a man of assured reputation can commit domestic infidelity without blasting it."   116. **fond:** doting.

87

[SCENE II]

Enter ANTIPHOLUS EROTES [OF SYRACUSE].

S. Ant. The gold I gave to Dromio is laid up
Safe at the Centaur, and the heedful slave
Is wand'red forth, in care to seek me out.
By computation and mine host's report,
I could not speak with Dromio since at first   5
I sent him from the mart! See, here he comes.

Enter DROMIO [OF] SYRACUSA.

How now, sir, is your merry humor alter'd?
As you love strokes, so jest with me again.
You know no Centaur? You receiv'd no gold?
Your mistress sent to have me home to dinner?   10
My house was at the Phoenix? Wast thou mad,
That thus so madly thou didst answer me?

S. Dro. What answer, sir? when spake I such a
     word?

S. Ant. Even now, even here, not half an hour
since.   14

S. Dro. I did not see you since you sent me hence
Home to the Centaur with the gold you gave me.

S. Ant. Villain, thou didst deny the gold's receipt,
And toldst me of a mistress, and a dinner,
For which I hope thou feltst I was displeas'd.

S. Dro. I am glad to see you in this merry vein. 20
What means this jest? I pray you, master, tell me.

S. Ant. Yea, dost thou jeer and flout me in the
     teeth?
Think'st thou I jest? Hold, take thou that, and
     that.   *Beats Dromio.*

S. Dro. Hold, sir, for God's sake! Now your
     jest is earnest,
Upon what bargain do you give it me?   25

S. Ant. Because that I familiarly sometimes
Do use you for my fool, and chat with you,
Your sauciness will jest upon my love,
And make a common of my serious hours.
When the sun shines, let foolish gnats make sport, 30
But creep in crannies, when he hides his beams:
If you will jest with me, know my aspect,
And fashion your demeanor to my looks,
Or I will beat this method in your sconce.   34

S. Dro. Sconce call you it? So you would leave
battering, I had rather have it a head. And you use
these blows long, I must get a sconce for my head, and
insconce it too, or else I shall seek my wit in my
shoulders. But I pray, sir, why am I beaten?

S. Ant. Dost thou not know?   40

S. Dro. Nothing, sir, but that I am beaten.

S. Ant. Shall I tell you why?

S. Dro. Ay, sir, and wherefore; for they say, every
why hath a wherefore.

S. Ant. Why first—for flouting me, and then
     wherefore—   45
For urging it the second time to me.

S. Dro. Was there ever any man thus beaten out
     of season,
When in the why and the wherefore is neither rhyme
     nor reason?
Well, sir, I thank you.

S. Ant. Thank me, sir, for what?   50

S. Dro. Marry, sir, for this something that you
gave me for nothing.

S. Ant. I'll make you amends next, to give you
nothing for something. But say, sir, is it dinner-time?

S. Dro. No, sir, I think the meat wants that I
have.   56

S. Ant. In good time, sir: what's that?

S. Dro. Basting.

S. Ant. Well, sir, then 'twill be dry.

S. Dro. If it be, sir, I pray you eat none of it.   60

S. Ant. Your reason?

S. Dro. Lest it make you choleric, and purchase
me another dry basting.

S. Ant. Well, sir, learn to jest in good time—
there's a time for all things.   65

S. Dro. I durst have denied that before you were
so choleric.

S. Ant. By what rule, sir?

S. Dro. Marry, sir, by a rule as plain as the plain
bald pate of Father Time himself.   70

S. Ant. Let's hear it.

S. Dro. There's no time for a man to recover his
hair that grows bald by nature.

S. Ant. May he not do it by fine and recovery?

S. Dro. Yes, to pay a fine for a periwig, and recover the lost hair of another man.   76

S. Ant. Why is Time such a niggard of hair, being
(as it is) so plentiful an excrement?

S. Dro. Because it is a blessing that he bestows on
beasts, and what he hath scanted [men] in hair he hath
given them in wit.   81

S. Ant. Why, but there's many a man hath more
hair than wit.

S. Dro. Not a man of those but he hath the wit to
lose his hair.   85

S. Ant. Why, thou didst conclude hairy men plain
dealers without wit.

S. Dro. The plainer dealer, the sooner lost; yet he
loseth it in a kind of jollity.

S. Ant. For what reason?   90

II.ii. Location: The mart.
4. **computation:** reckoning (of time).
22. **in the teeth:** to my face.
24. **earnest:** (1) serious; (2) money paid down to secure a bargain.
28. **jest . . . love:** trifle with my indulgence.
29. **common:** public playground.
32. **aspect:** (1) expression; (2) influence, favorable or unfavorable, of
the planets.
34. **sconce:** head; but Dromio plays on the meanings "fort" (line 35,
with accompanying quibble on *battering* as "beating" and "using a
battering ram") and "protective covering" (line 37).
38. **insconce:** fortify, protect.
38-39. **seek . . . shoulders:** i.e. because his head will be beaten into
his shoulders.

51. **Marry:** indeed (a weakened oath, "by the Virgin Mary").
55. **wants that:** lacks what.   57. **In good time:** indeed.
62. **choleric:** irascible. Overdone meat was believed to cause an excess
of the bodily fluid called choler, which produced irascibility.
63. **dry basting:** severe beating.
74. **fine and recovery:** a legal process by which an entailed estate
could be converted into a fee-simple.   78. **excrement:** outgrowth.
80. **scanted:** been niggardly of, stinted.
84-85. **hath . . . hair:** i.e. can manage to contract syphilis (which
causes loss of hair).
86-87. **plain dealers:** men who deal honestly and plainly.
88. **dealer:** i.e. dealer with women.

S. Dro. For two—and sound ones too.

S. Ant. Nay, not sound, I pray you.

S. Dro. Sure ones then.

S. Ant. Nay, not sure, in a thing falsing.

S. Dro. Certain ones then. 95

S. Ant. Name them.

S. Dro. The one, to save the money that he spends in [tiring]; the other, that at dinner they should not drop in his porridge. 99

S. Ant. You would all this time have prov'd there is no time for all things.

S. Dro. Marry, and did, sir: namely, [e'en] no time to recover hair lost by nature.

S. Ant. But your reason was not substantial, why there is no time to recover. 105

S. Dro. Thus I mend it: Time himself is bald, and therefore, to the world's end, will have bald followers.

S. Ant. I knew 'twould be a bald conclusion. But soft, who wafts us yonder? 109

Enter ADRIANA *and* LUCIANA.

Adr. Ay, ay, Antipholus, look strange and frown,
Some other mistress hath thy sweet aspects:
I am not Adriana, nor thy wife.
The time was once, when thou unurg'd wouldst vow
That never words were music to thine ear,
That never object pleasing in thine eye, 115
That never touch well welcome to thy hand,
That never meat sweet-savor'd in thy taste,
Unless I spake, or look'd, or touch'd, or carv'd to thee.
How comes it now, my husband, O, how comes it,
That thou art then estranged from thyself? 120
Thyself I call it, being strange to me,
That, undividable incorporate,
Am better than thy dear self's better part.
Ah, do not tear away thyself from me;
For know, my love, as easy mayst thou fall 125
A drop of water in the breaking gulf,
And take unmingled thence that drop again,
Without addition or diminishing,
As take from me thyself and not me too.
How dearly would it touch thee to the quick, 130
Shouldst thou but hear I were licentious,
And that this body, consecrate to thee,
By ruffian lust should be contaminate?
Wouldst thou not spit at me, and spurn at me,
And hurl the name of husband in my face, 135
And tear the stain'd skin [off] my harlot brow,
And from my false hand cut the wedding-ring,
And break it with a deep-divorcing vow?
I know thou canst, and therefore see thou do it.
I am possess'd with an adulterate blot; 140
My blood is mingled with the crime of lust:

For if we two be one, and thou play false,
I do digest the poison of thy flesh,
Being strumpeted by thy contagion.
Keep then fair league and truce with thy true bed, 145
I live dis-stain'd, thou undishonored.

S. Ant. Plead you to me, fair dame? I know you not:
In Ephesus I am but two hours old,
As strange unto your town as to your talk,
Who, every word by all my wit being scann'd, 150
Wants wit in all one word to understand.

Luc. Fie, brother, how the world is chang'd with you:
When were you wont to use my sister thus?
She sent for you by Dromio home to dinner.

S. Ant. By Dromio? 155

S. Dro. By me?

Adr. By thee, and this thou didst return from him,
That he did buffet thee, and in his blows
Denied my house for his, me for his wife.

S. Ant. Did you converse, sir, with this gentlewoman? 160
What is the course and drift of your compact?

S. Dro. I, sir? I never saw her till this time.

S. Ant. Villain, thou liest, for even her very words
Didst thou deliver to me on the mart.

S. Dro. I never spake with her in all my life. 165

S. Ant. How can she thus then call us by our names,
Unless it be by inspiration?

Adr. How ill agrees it with your gravity
To counterfeit thus grossly with your slave,
Abetting him to thwart me in my mood! 170
Be it my wrong you are from me exempt,
But wrong not that wrong with a more contempt.
Come, I will fasten on this sleeve of thine:
Thou art an elm, my husband, I a vine,
Whose weakness, married to thy [stronger] state, 175
Makes me with thy strength to communicate:
If aught possess thee from me, it is dross,
Usurping ivy, brier, or idle moss,
Who, all for want of pruning, with intrusion
Infect thy sap, and live on thy confusion. 180

S. Ant. To me she speaks, she moves me for her theme:
What, was I married to her in my dream?
Or sleep I now and think I hear all this?
What error drives our eyes and ears amiss?
Until I know this sure uncertainty, 185
I'll entertain the [offer'd] fallacy.

Luc. Dromio, go bid the servants spread for dinner.

S. Dro. O for my beads! I cross me for a sinner.

---

91. **sound:** valid (but Antipholus' objection quibbles on the sense "healthy"). 94. **falsing:** deceptive. 98. **tiring:** dressing the hair.
99. **porridge:** soup. 108. **bald:** lame, stupid.
109. **soft:** hold. **wafts:** beckons. 110. **strange:** distant.
122. **undividable:** indivisibly.
123. **better part:** spiritually or physically the best qualities of a man; cf. III.ii.61. 125. **fall:** let fall.
129. **As...too:** i.e. we are so indivisibly one that we cannot be separated without inevitable loss to each other.
130. **dearly:** deeply, keenly. 141. **crime:** sin.

144. **strumpeted:** made a strumpet. 146. **dis-stain'd:** unstained.
151. **all:** i.e. all that you have been saying. 153. **use:** treat.
161. **compact:** plot. 169. **grossly:** obviously. 170. **mood:** anger.
171. **exempt:** separated. 172. **more:** greater.
177. **aught...me:** anything (evil) hold a part in you which separates you from me. **dross:** impure matter mixed with a pure substance.
178. **idle:** barren, useless. 180. **confusion:** ruin.
181. **moves:** pleads with. **for her theme:** as the subject of what she is saying.
185. **know...uncertainty:** know this to be undeniable illusion.
186. **entertain:** accept. **fallacy:** delusive notion.
188. **beads:** rosary. **cross...sinner:** i.e. he makes the sign of the cross to protect himself as a mere sinning mortal.

This is the fairy land. O spite of spites!
We talk with goblins, owls, and sprites;   190
If we obey them not, this will ensue:
They'll suck our breath, or pinch us black and blue.
  Luc. Why prat'st thou to thyself, and answer'st
    not?
Dromio, thou [drumble,] thou snail, thou slug, thou
    sot!
  S. Dro. I am transformed, master, am [not I]? 195
  S. Ant. I think thou art in mind, and so am I.
  S. Dro. Nay, master, both in mind and in my
    shape.
  S. Ant. Thou hast thine own form.
  S. Dro.   No, I am an ape.
  Luc. If thou art chang'd to aught, 'tis to an ass.
  S. Dro. 'Tis true she rides me and I long for grass.
'Tis so, I am an ass, else it could never be   201
But I should know her as well as she knows me.
  Adr. Come, come, no longer will I be a fool,
To put the finger in the eye and weep,
Whilst man and master laughs my woes to scorn. 205
Come, sir, to dinner. Dromio, keep the gate.
Husband, I'll dine above with you to-day,
And shrive you of a thousand idle pranks.
Sirrah, if any ask you for your master,
Say he dines forth, and let no creature enter.   210
Come, sister. Dromio, play the porter well.
  S. Ant. Am I in earth, in heaven, or in hell?
Sleeping or waking, mad or well-advis'd?
Known unto these, and to myself disguis'd?
I'll say as they say, and persever so,   215
And in this mist at all adventures go.
  S. Dro. Master, shall I be porter at the gate?
  Adr. Ay, and let none enter, lest I break your
    pate.
  Luc. Come, come, Antipholus, we dine too late.
                                            [*Exeunt.*]

ACT III, Scene I

Enter Antipholus of Ephesus, *his man* Dromio [of
Ephesus], Angelo *the goldsmith, and* Balthazar
the merchant.

  E. Ant. Good Signior Angelo, you must excuse
    us all,
My wife is shrewish when I keep not hours:
Say that I linger'd with you at your shop
To see the making of her carcanet,
And that to-morrow you will bring it home.   5
But here's a villain that would face me down

192. **breath:** i.e. breath of life (probably connected with the folk
belief that the breath of man was his soul).
194. **drumble:** sluggish person, drone. **sot:** fool.
198. **ape:** counterfeit (aping myself).
204. **put . . . weep:** i.e. play the child.
207. **above.** The living quarters would be on the floor above the business quarters.
208. **shrive you of:** hear you confess and forgive you for.
209. **Sirrah:** term of address to inferiors.
210. **forth:** away from home. 213. **well-advis'd:** sane.
216. **at all adventures:** whatever happens.

III.i. **Location:** Before the house of Antipholus of Ephesus.
4. **carcanet:** jewelled necklace.
6. **face me down:** maintain to my face that.

He met me on the mart, and that I beat him,
And charg'd him with a thousand marks in gold,
And that I did deny my wife and house.   9
Thou drunkard, thou, what didst thou mean by this?
  E. Dro. Say what you will, sir, but I know what
    I know:
That you beat me at the mart, I have your hand
    to show;
If the skin were parchment, and the blows you gave
    were ink,
Your own handwriting would tell you what I think.
  E. Ant. I think thou art an ass.
  E. Dro.   Marry, so it doth appear
By the wrongs I suffer, and the blows I bear.   16
I should kick, being kick'd, and being at that pass,
You would keep from my heels, and beware of an ass.
  E. Ant. Y' are sad, Signior Balthazar, pray God
    our cheer
May answer my good will and your good welcome
    here.   20
  Balth. I hold your dainties cheap, sir, and your
    welcome dear.
  E. Ant. O, Signior Balthazar, either at flesh or
    fish,
A table full of welcome makes scarce one dainty
    dish.
  Balth. Good meat, sir, is common; that every
    churl affords.
  E. Ant. And welcome more common, for that's
    nothing but words.   25
  Balth. Small cheer and great welcome makes a
    merry feast.
  E. Ant. Ay, to a niggardly host and more spar-
    ing guest:
But though my cates be mean, take them in good
    part;
Better cheer may you have, but not with better
    heart.
But soft, my door is lock'd; go bid them let us in. 30
  E. Dro. Maud, Bridget, Marian, Cic'ly, Gillian,
    Ginn!
  S. Dro. [*Within.*] Mome, malt-horse, capon, cox-
    comb, idiot, patch!
Either get thee from the door, or sit down at the
    hatch;
Dost thou conjure for wenches, that thou call'st for
    such store,
When one is one too many? Go get thee from the
    door.   35
  E. Dro. What patch is made our porter? My
    master stays in the street.
  S. Dro. [*Within.*] Let him walk from whence he
    came, lest he catch cold on 's feet.
  E. Ant. Who talks within there? Ho, open the
    door!

8. **with:** i.e. with the possession of. 9. **deny:** disclaim.
17. **at that pass:** in that predicament.
19. **sad:** serious. **cheer:** fare. 20. **answer:** match.
27. **sparing:** frugal. 28. **cates:** provisions. **mean:** modest, plain.
32. **Mome:** blockhead. **malt-horse:** brewer's horse, i.e. heavy or
stupid creature. **patch:** fool.
33. **hatch:** bottom half of a divided door.
34. **conjure for:** summon up by magic. 37. **on 's:** in his.

S. Dro. [*Within.*] Right, sir, I'll tell you when,
and you'll tell me wherefore.

E. Ant. Wherefore? For my dinner: I have not
din'd to-day.   40

S. Dro. [*Within.*] Nor to-day here you must not,
come again when you may.

E. Ant. What art thou that keep'st me out from
the house I owe?

S. Dro. [*Within.*] The porter for this time, sir,
and my name is Dromio.

E. Dro. O villain, thou hast stol'n both mine
office and my name: 44
The one ne'er got me credit, the other mickle blame.
If thou hadst been Dromio to-day in my place,
Thou wouldst have chang'd thy face for a name, or
thy name for an ass.

Enter LUCE [*within*].

Luce. [*Within.*] What a coil is there, Dromio?
Who are those at the gate?

E. Dro. Let my master in, Luce.

Luce. [*Within.*] Faith, no, he comes too late,
And so tell your master.

E. Dro.   O Lord, I must laugh!   50
Have at you with a proverb—Shall I set in my staff?

Luce. [*Within.*] Have at you with another, that's—
When? can you tell?

S. Dro. [*Within.*] If thy name be called Luce—
Luce, thou hast answer'd him well.

E. Ant. Do you hear, you minion? You'll let us in,
I hope?   54

Luce. [*Within.*] I thought to have ask'd you.

S. Dro. [*Within.*]   And you said no.

E. Dro. So come help: well strook! there was
blow for blow.

E. Ant. Thou baggage, let me in.

Luce. [*Within.*]   Can you tell for whose sake?

E. Dro. Master, knock the door hard.

Luce. [*Within.*]   Let him knock till it ache.

E. Ant. You'll cry for this, minion, if I beat the
door down.

Luce. [*Within.*] What needs all that, and a pair
of stocks in the town?   60

Enter ADRIANA [*within*].

Adr. [*Within.*] Who is that at the door that keeps
all this noise?

S. Dro. [*Within.*] By my troth, your town is
troubled with unruly boys.

E. Ant. Are you there, wife? You might have
come before.

Adr. [*Within.*] Your wife, sir knave? Go get
you from the door.

E. Dro. If you went in pain, master, this knave
would go sore.   65

Ang. Here is neither cheer, sir, nor welcome: we
would fain have either.

Balth. In debating which was best, we shall part
with neither.

E. Dro. They stand at the door, master, bid them
welcome hither.

E. Ant. There is something in the wind, that we
cannot get in.

E. Dro. You would say so, master, if your garments were thin.   70
Your cake here is warm within: you stand here in
the cold.
It would make a man mad as a buck to be so bought
and sold.

E. Ant. Go fetch me something: I'll break ope
the gate.

S. Dro. [*Within.*] Break any breaking here, and
I'll break your knave's pate.

E. Dro. A man may break a word with [you],
sir, and words are but wind: 75
Ay, and break it in your face, so he break it not
behind.

S. Dro. [*Within.*] It seems thou want'st breaking,
out upon thee, hind!

E. Dro. Here's too much "out upon thee!"; I
pray thee let me in.

S. Dro. [*Within.*] Ay, when fowls have no feathers, and fish have no fin.   79

E. Ant. Well, I'll break in: go borrow me a crow.

E. Dro. A crow without feather? Master, mean
you so?
For a fish without a fin, there's a fowl without a
feather:
If a crow help us in, sirrah, we'll pluck a crow together.

E. Ant. Go, get thee gone, fetch me an iron crow.

Balth. Have patience, sir, O, let it not be so! 85
Herein you war against your reputation,
And draw within the compass of suspect
Th' unviolated honor of your wife.
Once this—your long experience of [her] wisdom,
Her sober virtue, years, and modesty,   90
Plead on [her] part some cause to you unknown;
And doubt not, sir, but she will well excuse

---

42. **owe:** own.   44. **office:** function.   45. **mickle:** much.
47. **chang'd . . . a name.** A puzzling passage. Dover Wilson suggests emending *a name* to *an aim*, i.e. a mark or target (for the blows Dromio has received); Foakes accepts his emendation and in addition reads *office* for *face* (a change supported by lines 44–45). **an ass:** i.e. the name of ass.
47 s.d. **Enter Luce within.** It seems probable that the entry of Luce here and of Adriana at line 60, although they speak from "within" and out of sight of Antipholus of Ephesus and his companions, was managed in such a way as to make them partly visible to the audience, and that they withdraw following line 64, as Dover Wilson has suggested.   48. **coil:** fuss.
51. **Have at you:** here I come at you.   **set . . . staff:** take up my residence here (with a bawdy innuendo).
52. **When . . . tell:** i.e. never (a conventional phrase of derision or defiance).
54. **minion:** hussy.   **hope.** No rhyming line follows. The loss of a line, supposed by Malone and others, would account for the obscurity of the next two lines. Alternatively, some editors follow Theobald in emending *hope* to *trow* (i.e. suppose), thus producing a rhyming triplet.
60. **What . . . town:** why do we put up with all this when the town provides means of punishment.

61. **keeps:** continues to make.
65. **If . . . sore:** if you were in pain, then this knave she mentions would be in pain; i.e. she means you.
67. **debating:** discussing.   **part:** depart.
72. **mad . . . buck.** Cf. *horn-mad*, II.i.57.   **bought and sold:** imposed upon.   75. **break a word:** exchange words.   77. **hind:** slave.
80. **crow:** crowbar (with following quibble by Dromio).
83. **pluck . . . together:** pick a bone, settle accounts.
87. **suspect:** suspicion.   89. **Once this:** in short.
90. **virtue:** merit.   92. **well excuse:** explain satisfactorily.

*The Comedy
of Errors
III.i*

Why at this time the doors are made against you.
Be rul'd by me, depart in patience,
And let us to the Tiger all to dinner,   95
And about evening come yourself alone
To know the reason of this strange restraint.
If by strong hand you offer to break in
Now in the stirring passage of the day,
A vulgar comment will be made of it;   100
And that supposed by the common rout
Against your yet ungalled estimation,
That may with foul intrusion enter in,
And dwell upon your grave when you are dead;
For slander lives upon succession,   105
For ever hous'd where it gets possession.
   E. Ant. You have prevail'd. I will depart in quiet,
And in despite of mirth mean to be merry.
I know a wench of excellent discourse,
Pretty and witty; wild, and yet, too, gentle;   110
There will we dine. This woman that I mean,
My wife (but, I protest, without desert)
Hath oftentimes upbraided me withal:
To her will we to dinner. [*To Angelo.*] Get you home
And fetch the chain; by this I know 'tis made.   115
Bring it, I pray you, to the Porpentine,
For there's the house. That chain will I bestow
(Be it for nothing but to spite my wife)
Upon mine hostess there. Good sir, make haste.
Since mine own doors refuse to entertain me,   120
I'll knock elsewhere, to see if they'll disdain me.
   Ang. I'll meet you at that place some hour hence.
   E. Ant. Do so. This jest shall cost me some
      expense.   *Exeunt.*

[SCENE II]

Enter [LUCIANA] *with* ANTIPHOLUS OF SYRACUSA.

[*Luc.*] And may it be that you have quite forgot
A husband's office? Shall, Antipholus,
Even in the spring of love, thy love-springs rot?
Shall love, in [building], grow so [ruinous]?
If you did wed my sister for her wealth,   5
Then for her wealth's sake use her with more kindness:
Or if you like elsewhere, do it by stealth,
Muffle your false love with some show of blindness:
Let not my sister read it in your eye;
Be not thy tongue thy own shame's orator: 10
Look sweet, speak fair, become disloyalty;
Apparel vice like virtue's harbinger;
Bear a fair presence, though your heart be tainted;
Teach sin the carriage of a holy saint;

Be secret-false: what need she be acquainted?   15
What simple thief brags of his own [attaint]?
'Tis double wrong, to truant with your bed,
And let her read it in thy looks at board:
Shame hath a bastard fame, well managed;
Ill deeds is doubled with an evil word.   20
Alas, poor women, make us [but] believe
(Being compact of credit) that you love us;
Though others have the arm, show us the sleeve:
We in your motion turn, and you may move us.
Then, gentle brother, get you in again;   25
Comfort my sister, cheer her, call her [wife]:
'Tis holy sport to be a little vain,
When the sweet breath of flattery conquers strife.
   S. Ant. Sweet mistress—what your name is else,
      I know not,
Nor by what wonder you do hit of mine—   30
Less in your knowledge and your grace you show not
Than our earth's wonder, more than earth divine.
Teach me, dear creature, how to think and speak:
Lay open to my earthy gross conceit,
Smoth'red in errors, feeble, shallow, weak,   35
The folded meaning of your words' deceit.
Against my soul's pure truth why labor you,
To make it wander in an unknown field?
Are you a god? Would you create me new?
Transform me then, and to your pow'r I'll yield.   40
But if that I am I, then well I know
Your weeping sister is no wife of mine,
Nor to her bed no homage do I owe:
Far more, far more, to you do I decline.
O, train me not, sweet mermaid, with thy note,   45
To drown me in thy [sister's] flood of tears.
Sing, siren, for thyself, and I will dote;
Spread o'er the silver waves thy golden hairs,
And as a [bed] I'll take [them], and there lie,
And in that glorious supposition think   50
He gains by death that hath such means to die:
Let Love, being light, be drowned if she sink!
   Luc. What, are you mad, that you do reason so?
   S. Ant. Not mad, but mated—how, I do not know.
   Luc. It is a fault that springeth from your eye.   55
   S. Ant. For gazing on your beams, fair sun, being
      by.
   Luc. Gaze when you should, and that will clear
      your sight.

93. **made:** fastened.   99. **stirring passage:** busy traffic.
100. **vulgar:** public.   101. **supposed:** conjectured.
102. **ungalled estimation:** unblemished reputation.
105. **For . . . succession:** i.e. one slander begets another, so that its
successors (heirs) never end.
108. **in . . . mirth:** though I do not feel like being merry.
112. **desert:** my deserving it.   116. **Porpentine:** porcupine.

III.ii. Location: Scene continues.
1. **may:** can.   3. **love-springs:** tender shoots of love.
8. **Muffle . . . blindness:** cover up the love you faithlessly feel for
another with an outward appearance that will keep it from being seen.
11. **fair:** courteously.   **become disloyalty:** carry infidelity gracefully.   12. **harbinger:** messenger.   14. **carriage:** demeanor.

15. **what:** why.
16. **What simple thief:** i.e. what thief is so simple (stupid) that he.
attaint: dishonor; or possibly, conviction of crime.
17. **truant with:** be unfaithful to.   18. **board:** table.
19. **bastard fame:** sham reputation.
22. **Being . . . credit:** i.e. as you easily may, for we are entirely
composed of credulity.
24. **motion:** i.e. orbit (referring to the motion of the spheres).
27. **vain:** false.   30. **wonder:** miracle.   **hit of:** hit on, guess.
32. **earth's wonder.** Perhaps an allusion to Queen Elizabeth, before
whom the play may have been performed.
34. **conceit:** understanding.
36. **folded:** hidden.   **deceit:** i.e. ambiguous, apparently misleading,
meaning.   44. **decline:** incline.
45. **train:** entice.   **mermaid:** i.e. siren.   **note:** music.
51. **death, die.** These words were frequently used with reference to
sexual intercourse.
52. **light:** (1) wanton; (2) buoyant. Antipholus suggests that Love
cannot possibly sink and thus cannot be drowned.
53. **reason:** argue.
54. **mated:** (1) amazed; (2) matched with a wife.   56. **by:** near.

S. Ant. As good to wink, sweet love, as look on
night.

Luc. Why call you me love? Call my sister so.

S. Ant. Thy sister's sister.

Luc.   That's my sister.

S. Ant.   No;
It is thyself, mine own self's better part: 61
Mine eye's clear eye, my dear heart's dearer heart,
My food, my fortune, and my sweet hope's aim,
My sole earth's heaven, and my heaven's claim.

Luc. All this my sister is, or else should be.   65

S. Ant. Call thyself sister, sweet, for I am thee:
Thee will I love and with thee lead my life;
Thou hast no husband yet, nor I no wife.
Give me thy hand.

Luc.   O soft, sir, hold you still;
I'll fetch my sister to get her good will. *Exit.* 70

Enter DROMIO [OF] SYRACUSA.

S. Ant. Why, how now, Dromio, where run'st
thou so fast?

S. Dro. Do you know me, sir? Am I Dromio?
Am I your man? Am I myself?   74

S. Ant. Thou art Dromio, thou art my man, thou
art thyself.

S. Dro. I am an ass, I am a woman's man, and
besides myself.

S. Ant. What woman's man, and how besides
thyself?   80

S. Dro. Marry, sir, besides myself, I am due to a
woman: one that claims me, one that haunts me, one
that will have me.

S. Ant. What claim lays she to thee?   84

S. Dro. Marry, sir, such claim as you would lay to
your horse, and she would have me as a beast; not that,
I being a beast, she would have me, but that she, being
a very beastly creature, lays claim to me.

S. Ant. What is she?   89

S. Dro. A very reverent body: ay, such a one as a
man may not speak of without he say "Sir-reverence."
I have but lean luck in the match, and yet is she a
wondrous fat marriage.

S. Ant. How dost thou mean a fat marriage?   94

S. Dro. Marry, sir, she's the kitchen wench and
all grease, and I know not what use to put her to but
to make a lamp of her and run from her by her own
light. I warrant, her rags and the tallow in them will
burn a Poland winter: if she lives till doomsday, she'll
burn a week longer than the whole world.   100

S. Ant. What complexion is she of?

S. Dro. Swart, like my shoe, but her face nothing
like so clean kept: for why? she sweats, a man may
go over shoes in the grime of it.

S. Ant. That's a fault that water will mend.   105

S. Dro. No, sir, 'tis in grain, Noah's flood could
not do it.

S. Ant. What's her name?

S. Dro. Nell, sir; but her name [and] three quarters, that's an ell and three quarters, will not measure
her from hip to hip.   111

S. Ant. Then she bears some breadth?

S. Dro. No longer from head to foot than from
hip to hip: she is spherical, like a globe; I could find
out countries in her.   115

S. Ant. In what part of her body stands Ireland?

S. Dro. Marry, sir, in her buttocks, I found it out
by the bogs.

S. Ant. Where Scotland?   119

S. Dro. I found it by the barrenness, hard in the
palm of the hand.

S. Ant. Where France?

S. Dro. In her forehead, arm'd and reverted,
making war against her heir.

S. Ant. Where England?   125

S. Dro. I look'd for the chalky cliffs, but I could
find no whiteness in them. But I guess, it stood in her
chin, by the salt rheum that ran between France
and it.

S. Ant. Where Spain?   130

S. Dro. Faith, I saw it not; but I felt it hot in
her breath.

S. Ant. Where America, the Indies?

S. Dro. O, sir, upon her nose, all o'er embellish'd
with rubies, carbuncles, sapphires, declining their rich
aspect to the hot breath of Spain, who sent whole
armadoes of carrects to be ballast at her nose.   137

S. Ant. Where stood Belgia, the Netherlands?

S. Dro. O, sir, I did not look so low. To conclude, this drudge or diviner laid claim to me,   140
call'd me Dromio, swore I was assur'd to her, told me
what privy marks I had about me, as the mark of my
shoulder, the mole in my neck, the great wart on my
left arm, that I, amaz'd, ran from her as a witch.
And I think, if my breast had not been made of faith,
       and my heart of steel,   145
She had transform'd me to a curtal dog, and made me
       turn i' th' wheel.

S. Ant. Go hie thee presently, post to the road,
And if the wind blow any way from shore,
I will not harbor in this town to-night.
If any bark put forth, come to the mart,   150

---

58. **wink:** close the eyes.
64. **My . . . claim:** my sole heaven on earth and my claim on heaven
hereafter.   78. **besides myself:** (1) out of my mind; (2) also myself.
90. **reverent:** reverend, worthy (used primarily for the sake of the
following quibble in *Sir-reverence*).
91. **without:** unless. **Sir-reverence:** save your reverence (a conventional phrase of apology before an offensive expression).
92. **lean:** poor.
99. **doomsday:** i.e. when the world was supposedly to be consumed
by fire. 102. **Swart:** swarthy, dark.

106. **in grain:** fast dyed, indelible.
109. **Nell.** Elsewhere she is called Luce.
110. **an ell:** a measure of 45 inches (with play on *a Nell*).
120. **barrenness.** Referring to the calluses on the palm of a kitchen
drudge, or to the hand's dryness (a moist hand was thought to denote
fruitfulness). Dover Wilson detects a pun on *barren ness* (i.e. promontory).
123–24. **arm'd . . . heir.** An allusion to the armed resistance of the
Catholic Holy League to Protestant Henry of Navarre, designated
heir to the French throne by Henry III in 1589.
123. **arm'd and reverted:** (1) in arms and revolted; (2) covered with
an eruption and receding (alluding to loss of hair from venereal
disease). 124. **heir.** With pun on *hair.* 127. **them:** i.e. her teeth.
128. **rheum:** mucus from the nose. 135. **declining:** bending.
137. **armadoes:** armadas, fleets. **carrects:** carracks, galleons. **ballast:** ballasted, loaded. 140. **diviner:** sorceress.
141. **assur'd:** betrothed. 142. **of:** on.
146. **curtal dog:** dog with a docked tail. **turn . . . wheel:** turn the
spit by running in a wheel.
147. **presently:** at once. **road:** roadstead, harbor.

**The Comedy
of Errors
III.ii**

Where I will walk till thou return to me.
If every one knows us, and we know none,
'Tis time, I think, to trudge, pack, and be gone.
    S. Dro. As from a bear a man would run for
      life,   154
So fly I from her that would be my wife.   *Exit.*
    S. Ant. There's none but witches do inhabit here,
And therefore 'tis high time that I were hence.
She that doth call me husband, even my soul
Doth for a wife abhor. But her fair sister,
Possess'd with such a gentle sovereign grace,   160
Of such enchanting presence and discourse,
Hath almost made me traitor to myself;
But lest myself be guilty to self-wrong,
I'll stop mine ears against the mermaid's song.

Enter ANGELO *with the chain.*

    Ang. Master Antipholus—
    S. Ant.   Ay, that's my name.
    Ang. I know it well, sir. Lo here's the chain.   166
I thought to have ta'en you at the Porpentine;
The chain unfinish'd made me stay thus long.
    S. Ant. What is your will that I shall do with this?
    Ang. What please yourself, sir; I have made it
      for you.   170
    S. Ant. Made it for me, sir! I bespoke it not.
    Ang. Not once, nor twice, but twenty times you
      have.
Go home with it, and please your wife withal,
And soon at supper-time I'll visit you,
And then receive my money for the chain.   175
    S. Ant. I pray you, sir, receive the money now,
For fear you ne'er see chain nor money more.
    Ang. You are a merry man, sir, fare you well.
                                Exit.
    S. Ant. What I should think of this, I cannot tell:
But this I think, there's no man is so vain   180
That would refuse so fair an offer'd chain.
I see a man here needs not live by shifts,
When in the streets he meets such golden gifts.
I'll to the mart and there for Dromio stay:
If any ship put out, then straight away.   *Exit.*   185

ACT IV, SCENE I

Enter a [SECOND] MERCHANT [*of* EPHESUS, ANGELO
the] *goldsmith, and an* OFFICER.

    [*2. E.*] *Mer.* You know since Pentecost the sum is
      due,
And since I have not much importun'd you,
Nor now I had not, but that I am bound
To Persia, and want guilders for my voyage:
Therefore make present satisfaction,   5
Or I'll attach you by this officer.

    Ang. Even just the sum that I do owe to you
Is growing to me by Antipholus,
And in the instant that I met with you
He had of me a chain. At five a' clock   10
I shall receive the money for the same:
Pleaseth you walk with me down to his house,
I will discharge my bond, and thank you too.

Enter ANTIPHOLUS [OF] EPHESUS, DROMIO [OF EPH-
ESUS] *from the Courtezan's.*

    Off. That labor may you save; see where he comes.
    E. Ant. While I go to the goldsmith's house, go
      thou   15
And buy a rope's end; that will I bestow
Among my wife and [her] confederates,
For locking me out of my doors by day.
But soft, I see the goldsmith. Get thee gone,
Buy thou a rope, and bring it home to me.   20
    E. Dro. I buy a thousand pound a year! I buy a
      rope!   *Exit Dromio.*
    E. Ant. A man is well holp up that trusts to you:
I promised your presence and the chain,
But neither chain nor goldsmith came to me:
Belike you thought our love would last too long   25
If it were chain'd together, and therefore came not.
    Ang. Saving your merry humor, here's the note
How much your chain weighs to the utmost charect,
The fineness of the gold, and chargeful fashion,
Which doth amount to three odd ducats more   30
Than I stand debted to this gentleman.
I pray you see him presently discharg'd,
For he is bound to sea, and stays but for it.
    E. Ant. I am not furnish'd with the present money:
Besides, I have some business in the town.   35
Good signior, take the stranger to my house,
And with you take the chain, and bid my wife
Disburse the sum on the receipt thereof.
Perchance I will be there as soon as you.
    Ang. Then you will bring the chain to her your-
      self?   40
    E. Ant. No, bear it with you, lest I come not
      time enough.
    Ang. Well, sir, I will. Have you the chain about
      you?
    E. Ant. And if I have not, sir, I hope you have:
Or else you may return without your money.
    Ang. Nay, come, I pray you, sir, give me the
      chain: 45
Both wind and tide stays for this gentleman,
And I, to blame, have held him here too long.
    E. Ant. Good Lord! you use this dalliance to
      excuse
Your breach of promise to the Porpentine:

---

153. **trudge, pack, be gone.** These words are synonymous.
160. **Possess'd with:** possessing.   163. **to:** of.
171. **bespoke:** requested.   180. **vain:** foolish.
182. **shifts:** stratagems, tricks.

IV.i. Location: The mart.
1. **Pentecost:** Whitsuntide.   5. **present:** immediate.
6. **attach:** arrest.

8. **growing...by:** due...from.
16. **bestow:** employ.
21. **I...year.** An obscure remark. Dromio may mean that in buying
the rope he will be purchasing an annuity that will yield him a thousand poundings (i.e. beatings) a year.   22. **holp:** helped.
25. **Belike:** probably.   28. **utmost charect:** last carat.
29. **chargeful fashion:** expensive design or workmanship.
30. **ducats:** gold (or sometimes silver) coins of varying value, widely
used in European countries.   41. **time enough:** in time.
48. **dalliance:** trifling, idle delay.

I should have chid you for not bringing it,   50
But like a shrew you first begin to brawl.
   [2. E.] Mer. The hour steals on, I pray you, sir,
     dispatch.
   Ang. You hear how he importunes me—the chain!
   E. Ant. Why, give it to my wife, and fetch your
     money.
   Ang. Come, come, you know I gave it you even
     now.   55
Either send the chain, or send me by some token.
   E. Ant. Fie, now you run this humor out of breath.
Come, where's the chain? I pray you let me see it.
   [2. E.] Mer. My business cannot brook this dalli-
     ance.
Good sir, say whe'r you'll answer me or no: 60
If not, I'll leave him to the officer.
   E. Ant. I answer you? What should I answer you?
   Ang. The money that you owe me for the chain.
   E. Ant. I owe you none, till I receive the chain.
   Ang. You know I gave it you half an hour since.
   E. Ant. You gave me none, you wrong me much
     to say so.   66
   Ang. You wrong me more, sir, in denying it.
Consider how it stands upon my credit.
   [2. E.] Mer. Well, officer, arrest him at my suit.
   Off. I do, and charge you in the Duke's name to
     obey me.   70
   Ang. This touches me in reputation.
Either consent to pay this sum for me
Or I attach you by this officer.
   E. Ant. Consent to pay thee that I never had!
Arrest me, foolish fellow, if thou dar'st.   75
   Ang. Here is thy fee, arrest him, officer.
I would not spare my brother in this case,
If he should scorn me so apparently.
   Off. I do arrest you, sir: you hear the suit.
   E. Ant. I do obey thee, till I give thee bail.   80
But, sirrah, you shall buy this sport as dear
As all the metal in your shop will answer.
   Ang. Sir, sir, I shall have law in Ephesus,
To your notorious shame, I doubt it not.

   Enter DROMIO [OF] SYRACUSA *from the bay.*

   S. Dro. Master, there's a bark of Epidamium   85
That stays but till her owner comes aboard,
And then, sir, she bears away. Our fraughtage, sir,
I have convey'd aboard, and I have bought
The oil, the balsamum, and aqua-vitae.
The ship is in her trim, the merry wind   90
Blows fair from land: they stay for nought at all
But for their owner, master, and yourself.
   E. Ant. How now? a madman? Why, thou pee-
     vish sheep,
What ship of Epidamium stays for me?   94
   S. Dro. A ship you sent me to, to hire waftage.

   E. Ant. Thou drunken slave, I sent thee for a rope,
And told thee to what purpose and what end.
   S. Dro. You sent me for a rope's end as soon:
You sent me to the bay, sir, for a bark.   99
   E. Ant. I will debate this matter at more leisure,
And teach your ears to list me with more heed.
To Adriana, villain, hie thee straight:
Give her this key, and tell her, in the desk
That's cover'd o'er with Turkish tapestry
There is a purse of ducats; let her send it.   105
Tell her I am arrested in the street,
And that shall bail me. Hie thee, slave, be gone!
On, officer, to prison till it come.
            Exeunt [all but Dromio of Syracuse].
   S. Dro. To Adriana! That is where we din'd,
Where Dowsabel did claim me for her husband: 110
She is too big, I hope, for me to compass.
Thither I must, although against my will,
For servants must their masters' minds fulfill.   *Exit.*

[SCENE II]

Enter ADRIANA *and* LUCIANA.

   Adr. Ah, Luciana, did he tempt thee so?
Mightst thou perceive austerely in his eye
That he did plead in earnest? yea or no?
Look'd he or red or pale, or sad or merrily?
What observation mad'st thou in this case   5
[Of] his heart's meteors tilting in his face?
   Luc. First he denied you had in him no right.
   Adr. He meant he did me none: the more my spite.
   Luc. Then swore he that he was a stranger here.
   Adr. And true he swore, though yet forsworn he
     were.   10
   Luc. Then pleaded I for you.
   Adr.   And what said he?
   Luc. That love I begg'd for you, he begg'd of me.
   Adr. With what persuasion did he tempt thy love?
   Luc. With words that in an honest suit might move.
First he did praise my beauty, then my speech.   15
   Adr. Didst speak him fair?
   Luc.   Have patience, I beseech.
   Adr. I cannot, nor I will not, hold me still,
My tongue, though not my heart, shall have his will.
He is deformed, crooked, old, and sere,
Ill-fac'd, worse bodied, shapeless every where;   20
Vicious, ungentle, foolish, blunt, unkind,
Stigmatical in making, worse in mind.
   Luc. Who would be jealous then of such a one?
No evil lost is wail'd when it is gone.
   Adr. Ah, but I think him better than I say,   25

---

98. **for . . . end:** i.e. to be hanged.   101. **list:** listen to.
110. **Dowsabel:** a name derived from French *douce et belle*, i.e.
gentle and beautiful, here applied ironically to Nell (Luce).
111. **compass:** (1) achieve; (2) put my arm round.

IV.ii. Location: Before the house of Antipholus of Ephesus.
2. **austerely:** seriously.
6. **heart's meteors:** i.e. passions.   **tilting:** contending.
7. **no:** i.e. any.   8. **spite:** grief, vexation.
16. **him fair:** to him courteously.   18. **his:** its.
19. **sere:** withered.   20. **shapeless:** misshapen.
22. **Stigmatical in making:** physically deformed by nature.

56. **send me . . . token:** send with me some object belonging to you
to prove that the request comes from you.   59. **brook:** tolerate.
60. **whe'r:** whether.   **answer:** satisfy, pay.
68. **stands . . . credit:** concerns my reputation for probity in business
dealings.   78. **apparently:** openly.   87. **fraughtage:** cargo.
89. **balsamum:** balm.   **aqua-vitae:** spirits.
90. **in her trim:** rigged and ready to sail.
93. **peevish:** silly.   **sheep.** With a pun on *ship* (line 94), pronounced
similarly.   95. **waftage:** passage.

The Comedy
of Errors
*IV.*ii

And yet would herein others' eyes were worse:
Far from her nest the lapwing cries away;
My heart prays for him, though my tongue do curse.

Enter DROMIO [OF] SYRACUSA.

S. Dro. Here, go: the desk, the purse! [Sweat]
now, make haste! 29
Luc. How hast thou lost thy breath?
S. Dro. By running fast.
Adr. Where is thy master, Dromio? Is he well?
S. Dro. No, he's in Tartar limbo, worse than hell:
A devil in an everlasting garment hath him;
[One] whose hard heart is button'd up with steel;
A fiend, a fairy, pitiless and rough; 35
A wolf, nay worse, a fellow all in buff;
A back-friend, a shoulder-clapper, one that counter-
mands
The passages of alleys, creeks, and narrow lands;
A hound that runs counter, and yet draws dry-foot
well;
One that before the judgment carries poor souls to
hell. 40
Adr. Why, man, what is the matter?
S. Dro. I do not know the matter, he is 'rested on
the case.
Adr. What, is he arrested? Tell me at whose suit.
S. Dro. I know not at whose suit he is arrested
well;
But ['a's] in a suit of buff which 'rested him, that can
I tell. 45
Will you send him, mistress, redemption, the money
in his desk?
Adr. Go fetch it, sister. (*Exit Luciana.*) This I
wonder at,
[That] he unknown to me should be in debt.
Tell me, was he arrested on a band?
S. Dro. Not on a band but on a stronger thing:
A chain, a chain! Do you not [hear] it ring? 51
Adr. What, the chain?
S. Dro. No, no, the bell, 'tis time that I were gone:
It was two ere I left him, and now the clock strikes one.
Adr. The hours come back! that did I never
[hear]. 55
S. Dro. O yes, if any hour meet a sergeant, 'a
turns back for very fear.

Adr. As if Time were in debt! How fondly dost
thou reason!
S. Dro. Time is a very bankrout and owes more
than he's worth to season.
Nay, he's a thief too: have you not heard men say,
That Time comes stealing on by night and day? 60
If ['a] be in debt and theft, and a sergeant in the way,
Hath he not reason to turn back an hour in a day?

Enter LUCIANA.

Adr. Go, Dromio, there's the money, bear it
straight,
And bring thy master home immediately.
Come, sister, I am press'd down with conceit— 65
Conceit, my comfort and my injury. *Exeunt.*

[SCENE III]

Enter ANTIPHOLUS [OF] SYRACUSA.

[*S. Ant.*] There's not a man I meet but doth salute
me
As if I were their well-acquainted friend,
And every one doth call me by my name:
Some tender money to me, some invite me;
Some other give me thanks for kindnesses; 5
Some offer me commodities to buy.
Even now a tailor call'd me in his shop,
And show'd me silks that he had bought for me,
And therewithal took measure of my body.
Sure these are but imaginary wiles, 10
And Lapland sorcerers inhabit here.

Enter DROMIO [OF] SYRACUSA.

S. Dro. Master, here's the gold you sent me for.
What, have you got the picture of old Adam new
apparell'd?
S. Ant. What gold is this? What Adam dost thou
mean? 16
S. Dro. Not that Adam that kept the Paradise,
but that Adam that keeps the prison; he that goes in
the calve's-skin that was kill'd for the Prodigal; he
that came behind you, sir, like an evil angel, and bid
you forsake your liberty. 21
S. Ant. I understand thee not.
S. Dro. No? Why, 'tis a plain case: he that went
like a base-viol in a case of leather; the man, sir, that
when gentlemen are tir'd, gives them a sob and 'rests

---

26. **herein . . . worse:** i.e. that in seeing him other women would view
him even less favorably (so that he would not be attractive to them).
27. **lapwing:** pewit, which tries to divert attention from the nest to
protect its young.
32. **Tartar:** Tartarean, infernal. **limbo:** loosely, hell; also a cant
term for prison.
33. **everlasting garment:** i.e. the arresting officer's buff-leather jerkin,
with a play on "suit of durance" (see IV.iii.27).
35. **fairy:** malevolent spirit.
37. **back-friend:** false friend; but also alluding to an officer's clapping
a man on the back or shoulder to signify arrest. **countermands:**
prohibits. 38. **creeks:** narrow winding passages.
39. **counter:** (1) following a scent in the opposite direction to that
taken by the game; (2) debtors' prison. **draws dry-foot:** tracks
game by the scent of the foot.
40. **judgment:** legal judgment (with a quibble on "Judgment Day").
hell: another term for a debtors' prison. 41. **matter:** cause.
42. **on the case:** a type of legal action, but with a quibble on *case* =
container (in contrast to *matter* = contents), i.e. skin or suit of
clothes (recalling "back-friend" and "shoulder-clapper").
45. **'a's:** he's.
49. **band:** bond (but Dromio quibbles on the sense "neck-band");
cf. IV.iii.31. 56. **sergeant:** arresting officer.

57. **fondly:** foolishly.
58. **bankrout:** bankrupt. **to season:** at any given moment.
65. **conceit:** thought, imaginings.

IV.iii. Location: The mart.
10. **imaginary wiles:** tricks of the imagination.
11. **Lapland.** Notorious for witchcraft and sorcery.
13. **have . . . apparell'd:** have you found the arresting officer (likened,
because of his leather jerkin, to Adam clothed in beasts' skins) a new
suit (with obvious pun) and thus got rid of him.
19. **calve's-skin . . . Prodigal.** Allusion to the story of the Prodigal
Son, for whom a fatted calf was killed (see Luke 15:11–32).
20. **evil angel.** Perhaps an allusion (by contraries) to the good angel who delivered Peter from prison (Acts 12:6–11), or (directly) to the Evil Angel in Marlowe's *Doctor Faustus*. See also lines 40–41.
25. **sob:** a rest given to a horse to recover its wind (with following pun on 'rests).

them; he, sir, that takes pity on decay'd men and   26
gives them suits of durance; he that sets up his rest to
do more exploits with his mace than a morris-pike.

S. Ant.   What, thou mean'st an officer?   29

S. Dro.   Ay, sir, the sergeant of the band: he that
brings any man to answer it that breaks his band; one
that thinks a man always going to bed and says, "God
give you good rest!"   33

S. Ant.   Well, sir, there rest in your foolery. Is
there any ships puts forth to-night? May we be
gone?   36

S. Dro.   Why, sir, I brought you word an hour
since that the bark *Expedition* put forth to-night, and
then were you hind'red by the sergeant to tarry for the
hoy *Delay*. Here are the angels that you sent for
to deliver you.   41

S. Ant.   The fellow is distract, and so am I,
And here we wander in illusions:
Some blessed power deliver us from hence!

Enter a COURTEZAN.

Cour.   Well met, well met, Master Antipholus.   45
I see, sir, you have found the goldsmith now.
Is that the chain you promis'd me to-day?

S. Ant.   Sathan, avoid, I charge thee tempt me not.

S. Dro.   Master, is this Mistress Sathan?

S. Ant.   It is the devil.   50

S. Dro.   Nay, she is worse, she is the devil's dam,
and here she comes in the habit of a light wench;
and thereof comes that the wenches say, "God damn
me," that's as much to say, "God make me a light
wench." It is written, they appear to men like angels of
light, light is an effect of fire, and fire will burn: *ergo*,
light wenches will burn. Come not near her.   57

Cour.   Your man and you are marvellous merry,
sir.
Will you go with me? we'll mend our dinner here.

S. Dro.   Master, if [you] do, expect spoon-meat,
or bespeak a long spoon.   61

S. Ant.   Why, Dromio?

S. Dro.   Marry, he must have a long spoon that
must eat with the devil.

S. Ant.   Avoid then, fiend, what tell'st thou me of
supping?   65
Thou art, as you are all, a sorceress:
I conjure thee to leave me and be gone.

Cour.   Give me the ring of mine you had at dinner,
Or, for my diamond, the chain you promis'd,
And I'll be gone, sir, and not trouble you.   70

S. Dro.   Some devils ask but the parings of one's
nail,
A rush, a hair, a drop of blood, a pin,
A nut, a cherry-stone;
But she, more covetous, would have a chain.
Master, be wise, and if you give it her,   75
The devil will shake her chain, and fright us with it.

Cour.   I pray you, sir, my ring, or else the chain;
I hope you do not mean to cheat me so?

S. Ant.   Avaunt, thou witch! Come, Dromio, let
us go.

S. Dro.   "Fly pride," says the peacock: mistress,
that you know.   80

Exit [*with Antipholus of Syracuse*].

Cour.   Now out of doubt Antipholus is mad,
Else would he never so demean himself.
A ring he hath of mine worth forty ducats,
And for the same he promis'd me a chain:
Both one and other he denies me now.   85
The reason that I gather he is mad,
Besides this present instance of his rage,
Is a mad tale he told to-day at dinner,
Of his own doors being shut against his entrance.
Belike his wife, acquainted with his fits,   90
On purpose shut the doors against his way.
My way is now to hie home to his house,
And tell his wife that, being lunatic,
He rush'd into my house, and took perforce
My ring away. This course I fittest choose,   95
For forty ducats is too much to lose.   [*Exit.*]

[SCENE IV]

Enter ANTIPHOLUS [OF] EPHESUS *with* [*the* OFFICER].

E. Ant.   Fear me not, man, I will not break away;
I'll give thee, ere I leave thee, so much money,
To warrant thee, as I am 'rested for.
My wife is in a wayward mood to-day,
And will not lightly trust the messenger,   5
That I should be attach'd in Ephesus;
I tell you, 'twill sound harshly in her ears.

Enter DROMIO [OF] EPHESUS *with a rope's end*.

Here comes my man: I think he brings the money.
How now, sir? have you that I sent you for?

E. Dro.   Here's that, I warrant you, will pay them
all.   10

E. Ant.   But where's the money?

E. Dro.   Why, sir, I gave the money for the rope.

E. Ant.   Five hundred ducats, villain, for a rope?

E. Dro.   I'll serve you, sir, five hundred at the rate.

E. Ant.   To what end did I bid thee hie thee
home?   15

27. **durance:** (1) durable cloth; (2) imprisonment. **sets . . . rest:**
ventures all (continuing the pun on *'rest*, which occurs once more in
line 33).
28. **mace:** club carried by a constable. **morris-pike:** kind of pike
supposedly of Moorish origin.
40. **hoy:** small vessel. **angels:** gold coins worth about 10 shillings.
42. **distract:** distracted, mad.
48. **Sathan, avoid:** Satan, be off (Matthew 4:10; the Geneva Version
is here quoted exactly).
52. **habit:** (1) dress; (2) demeanor, manner. **light:** wanton.
55–56. **angels of light.** See 2 Corinthians 11:14: ". . . Satan himself is
transformed into an angel of light." 56. **ergo:** therefore.
57. **burn:** communicate venereal disease.
59. **Will you:** if you will. **mend:** supplement.
60. **spoon-meat:** food for infants, hence delicacies.

75. **and if:** if.
80. **Fly . . . peacock:** i.e. an accusation of dishonesty coming from a
dishonest person is as out of place as a warning against pride would
be from the peacock. 82. **demean:** conduct. 87. **rage:** insanity.
94. **perforce:** forcibly.

IV.iv. **Location:** Scene continues.
3. **warrant thee:** give you security. 5. **trust:** credit.
6. **attach'd:** arrested. 14. **at the rate:** for that amount.

The Comedy of Errors
IV.iv

E. Dro. To a rope's end, sir, and to that end am
　I return'd.

E. Ant. And to that end, sir, I will welcome you.
　　　　　　　　　　　　　　　　　　　[*Beats Dromio.*]

Off. Good sir, be patient.

E. Dro. Nay, 'tis for me to be patient: I am in
adversity.　　　　　　　　　　　　　　　　　　　20

Off. Good now, hold thy tongue.

E. Dro. Nay, rather persuade him to hold his
hands.

E. Ant. Thou whoreson, senseless villain!　　24

E. Dro. I would I were senseless, sir, that I might
not feel your blows.

E. Ant. Thou art sensible in nothing but blows,
and so is an ass.

E. Dro. I am an ass indeed; you may prove it by
my long ears. I have serv'd him from the hour of　30
my nativity to this instant, and have nothing at his
hands for my service but blows. When I am cold, he
heats me with beating; when I am warm, he cools me
with beating. I am wak'd with it when I sleep,　34
rais'd with it when I sit, driven out of doors with it
when I go from home, welcom'd home with it when I
return; nay, I bear it on my shoulders, as a beggar
wont her brat; and I think when he hath lam'd me,
I shall beg with it from door to door.

Enter ADRIANA, LUCIANA, COURTEZAN, *and a schoolmaster call'd* PINCH.

E. Ant. Come go along, my wife is coming yon-
　der.　　　　　　　　　　　　　　　　　　　40

E. Dro. Mistress, *respice finem*, respect your end,
or rather, the prophecy like the parrot, "beware the
rope's end."

E. Ant. Wilt thou still talk?　*Beats Dromio.*　44

Cour. How say you now? Is not your husband mad?

Adr. His incivility confirms no less.
Good Doctor Pinch, you are a conjurer,
Establish him in his true sense again,
And I will please you what you will demand.

Luc. Alas, how fiery, and how sharp, he looks!　50

Cour. Mark, how he trembles in his ecstasy!

Pinch. Give me your hand, and let me feel your
　pulse.

E. Ant. There is my hand, and let it feel your ear.
　　　　　　　　　　　　　　　　　　　[*Strikes Pinch.*]

Pinch. I charge thee, Sathan, hous'd within this
　man,
To yield possession to my holy prayers,　　　55
And to thy state of darkness hie thee straight:
I conjure thee by all the saints in heaven!

E. Ant. Peace, doting wizard, peace! I am not
　mad.

Adr. O that thou wert not, poor distressed soul!

E. Ant. You minion, you, are these your cus-
　tomers?　　　　　　　　　　　　　　　　　　60
Did this companion with the saffron face
Revel and feast it at my house to-day,
Whilst upon me the guilty doors were shut,
And I denied to enter in my house?

Adr. O husband, God doth know you din'd at
　home,　　　　　　　　　　　　　　　　　　65
Where would you had remain'd until this time,
Free from these slanders and this open shame.

E. Ant. Din'd at home? Thou villain, what say-
　est thou?

E. Dro. Sir, sooth to say, you did not dine at home.

E. Ant. Were not my doors lock'd up, and I shut
　out?　　　　　　　　　　　　　　　　　　70

E. Dro. Perdie, your doors were lock'd, and you
　shut out.

E. Ant. And did not she herself revile me there?

E. Dro. Sans fable, she herself revil'd you there.

E. Ant. Did not her kitchen maid rail, taunt, and
　scorn me?

E. Dro. Certes she did, the kitchen vestal scorn'd
　you.　　　　　　　　　　　　　　　　　　75

E. Ant. And did not I in rage depart from thence?

E. Dro. In verity you did, my bones bears witness,
That since have felt the vigor of his rage.

Adr. Is't good to soothe him in these contraries?

Pinch. It is no shame; the fellow finds his vein,
And yielding to him, humors well his frenzy.　81

E. Ant. Thou hast suborn'd the goldsmith to arrest
　me.

Adr. Alas, I sent you money to redeem you,
By Dromio here, who came in haste for it.

E. Dro. Money by me? Heart and good will you
　might,　　　　　　　　　　　　　　　　　85
But surely, master, not a rag of money.

E. Ant. Went'st not thou to her for a purse of
　ducats?

Adr. He came to me, and I deliver'd it.

Luc. And I am witness with her that she did.

E. Dro. God and the rope-maker bear me witness
That I was sent for nothing but a rope!　　　91

Pinch. Mistress, both man and master is pos-
　sess'd:
I know it by their pale and deadly looks.
They must be bound and laid in some dark room.

E. Ant. Say wherefore didst thou lock me forth
　'to-day?　　　　　　　　　　　　　　　　95
And why dost thou deny the bag of gold?

---

21. **Good now:** pray you.
27. **sensible in:** (1) sensitive to; (2) made sensible by.
30.t **ears.** With pun on *years*; i.e. Dromio is an ass for not having left
Anphiolus' service long ago.
38. **wont:** is accustomed to (bear).
39. **I . . . it:** i.e. all I will get is a beating (the usual reward of beggars).
41. **respice finem:** look to your end (with pun on *respice funem*, look
to the hangman's rope).
42. **prophesy . . . parrot.** There are references to parrots' being taught
to say "rope," i.e. apparently prophesying that the hearer was destined
for hanging.
47. **conjurer.** Being able to speak Latin, Pinch could conjure evil
spirits.　49. **please:** pay.　50. **sharp:** angry.
51. **ecstasy:** madness.

60. **minion:** hussy.　61. **companion:** fellow.　**saffron:** yellow.
64. **denied . . . in:** refused admittance to.　67. **slanders:** disgraces.
71. **Perdie:** assuredly (a weakened oath, like French *pardieu*, originally "by God").　73. **Sans:** without.
75. **Certes:** certainly.　**kitchen vestal.** Johnson explains that Luce's
task was, "like that of the vestal virgins, to keep the fire burning."
There is obvious irony in the bracketing of Luce with virgins.
79. **soothe:** humor.
82. **suborn'd . . . me:** induced the goldsmith to lie for you in order to
have me arrested.　86. **rag:** scrap.　93. **deadly:** deathly.
94. **bound . . . room.** The regular treatment for the insane in Shakespeare's day.　95. **forth:** out.

Adr. I did not, gentle husband, lock thee forth.
E. Dro. And, gentle master, I receiv'd no gold;
But I confess, sir, that we were lock'd out.
Adr. Dissembling villain, thou speak'st false in
    both.   100
E. Ant. Dissembling harlot, thou art false in all,
And art confederate with a damned pack
To make a loathsome abject scorn of me;
But with these nails I'll pluck out these false eyes
That would behold in me this shameful sport. 105

Enter three or four, and offer to bind him; he strives.

Adr. O, bind him, bind him, let him not come near
    me.
Pinch. More company! the fiend is strong within
    him.
Luc. Ay me, poor man, how pale and wan he looks!
E. Ant. What, will you murther me? Thou jailer,
    thou,
I am thy prisoner. Wilt thou suffer them   110
To make a rescue?
Off.   Masters, let him go:
He is my prisoner, and you shall not have him.
Pinch. Go bind this man, for he is frantic too.
            [*They offer to bind Dromio of Ephesus.*]
Adr. What wilt thou do, thou peevish officer?
Hast thou delight to see a wretched man   115
Do outrage and displeasure to himself?
Off. He is my prisoner; if I let him go,
The debt he owes will be requir'd of me.
Adr. I will discharge thee ere I go from thee:
Bear me forthwith unto his creditor,   120
And knowing how the debt grows, I will pay it.
Good Master Doctor, see him safe convey'd
Home to my house. O most unhappy day!
E. Ant. O most unhappy strumpet!
E. Dro. Master, I am here ent'red in bond for you.
E. Ant. Out on thee, villain, wherefore dost thou
    mad me?   126
E. Dro. Will you be bound for nothing? Be mad,
    good master,
Cry "The devil!"
Luc. God help, poor souls, how idlely do they talk!
Adr. Go bear him hence. Sister, go you with me.
            *Exeunt. Manent Officer, Adriana,
                Luciana, Courtezan.*
Say now, whose suit is he arrested at?   131
Off. One Angelo, a goldsmith. Do you know
    him?
Adr. I know the man; what is the sum he owes?
Off. Two hundred ducats.
Adr.   Say, how grows it due?   134
Off. Due for a chain your husband had of him.
Adr. He did bespeak a chain for me, but had it not.
Cour. When as your husband all in rage to-day
Came to my house, and took away my ring—

The ring I saw upon his finger now—
Straight after did I meet him with a chain.   140
Adr. It may be so, but I did never see it.
Come, jailer, bring me where the goldsmith is,
I long to know the truth hereof at large.

Enter ANTIPHOLUS [OF] SYRACUSA, *with his rapier
    drawn, and* DROMIO [OF] SYRACUSA.

Luc. God for thy mercy! they are loose again.
Adr. And come with naked swords: let's call
    more help   145
To have them bound again.
Off.   Away, they'll kill us.
    *Exeunt omnes [but Antipholus of Syracuse and Dro-
    mio of Syracuse] as fast as may be, frighted.*
S. Ant. I see these witches are afraid of swords.
S. Dro. She that would be your wife now ran
    from you.
S. Ant. Come to the Centaur, fetch our stuff
    from thence;
I long that we were safe and sound aboard.   150
S. Dro. Faith, stay here this night, they will surely
do us no harm. You saw they speak us fair, give us
gold: methinks they are such a gentle nation that,
but for the mountain of mad flesh that claims marriage
of me, I could find in my heart to stay here still, and
turn witch.   156
S. Ant. I will not stay to-night for all the town:
Therefore away, to get our stuff aboard.   *Exeunt.*

ACT V, SCENE I

Enter the [SECOND] MERCHANT *and* [ANGELO] *the
    goldsmith.*

Ang. I am sorry, sir, that I have hind'red you,
But I protest he had the chain of me,
Though most dishonestly he doth deny it.
    [*2. E.*] *Mer.* How is the man esteem'd here in the
        city?
Ang. Of very reverent reputation, sir,   5
Of credit infinite, highly belov'd,
Second to none that lives here in the city:
His word might bear my wealth at any time.
    [*2. E.*] *Mer.* Speak softly, yonder, as I think, he
        walks.

Enter ANTIPHOLUS [OF SYRACUSE] *and* DROMIO [OF
    SYRACUSE] *again.*

Ang. 'Tis so; and that self chain about his neck,
Which he forswore most monstrously to have.   11
Good sir, draw near to me, I'll speak to him.
Signior Antipholus, I wonder much
That you would put me to this shame and trouble,
And, not without some scandal to yourself,   15
With circumstance and oaths so to deny
This chain which now you wear so openly.

102. **pack:** gang of conspirators.
111. **make a rescue:** forcibly remove a person from legal custody.
113 s.d. **offer:** make an attempt.
114. **peevish:** foolish.   116. **displeasure:** offense.
119. **discharge:** pay.
121. **knowing . . . grows:** as soon as I know how the debt arose.
126. **mad:** madden.   129. **idlely:** idly, irrationally.

143. **at large:** in full.   149. **stuff:** baggage.

V.i. Location: Before a priory.
8. **His . . . time:** his word would be sufficient security for as much as
I am worth.   10. **self:** same.   11. **forswore:** denied on oath.
16. **circumstance:** details, particulars.

*The Comedy
of Errors
V.i*

Beside the charge, the shame, imprisonment,
You have done wrong to this my honest friend,
Who, but for staying on our controversy,   20
Had hoisted sail and put to sea to-day.
This chain you had of me, can you deny it?
　　S. Ant.   I think I had, I never did deny it.
　　[*2. E.*] *Mer.*   Yes, that you did, sir, and forswore
　　　it too.
　　S. Ant.   Who heard me to deny it or forswear it?
　　[*2. E.*] *Mer.*   These ears of mine thou know'st did
　　　hear thee;   26
Fie on thee, wretch, 'tis pity that thou liv'st
To walk where any honest men resort.
　　S. Ant.   Thou art a villain to impeach me thus:
I'll prove mine honor and mine honesty   30
Against thee presently, if thou dar'st stand.
　　[*2. E.*] *Mer.*   I dare, and do defy thee for a villain.
　　　　　　　　　　　　　　　　　They draw.

Enter ADRIANA, LUCIANA, COURTEZAN, *and others.*

　　Adr.   Hold, hurt him not for God sake! he is mad.
Some get within him, take his sword away:
Bind Dromio too, and bear them to my house.   35
　　S. Dro.   Run, master, run, for God's sake take
　　　a house!
This is some priory, in, or we are spoil'd.
　　　　　　Exeunt [*Antipholus of Syracuse and
　　　　　　Dromio of Syracuse*] *to the priory.*

Enter LADY ABBESS.

　　Abb.   Be quiet, people. Wherefore throng you
　　　hither?
　　Adr.   To fetch my poor distracted husband hence.
Let us come in, that we may bind him fast,   40
And bear him home for his recovery.
　　Ang.   I knew he was not in his perfect wits.
　　[*2. E.*] *Mer.*   I am sorry now that I did draw on him.
　　Abb.   How long hath this possession held the man?
　　Adr.   This week he hath been heavy, sour, sad,
And much different from the man he was;   46
But till this afternoon his passion
Ne'er brake into extremity of rage.
　　Abb.   Hath he not lost much wealth by wrack of
　　　sea?
Buried some dear friend? Hath not else his eye   50
Stray'd his affection in unlawful love—
A sin prevailing much in youthful men,
Who give their eyes the liberty of gazing?
Which of these sorrows is he subject to?
　　Adr.   To none of these, except it be the last,   55
Namely, some love that drew him oft from home.
　　Abb.   You should for that have reprehended him.
　　Adr.   Why, so I did.
　　Abb.   Ay, but not rough enough.
　　Adr.   As roughly as my modesty would let me.
　　Abb.   Haply, in private.
　　Adr.   And in assemblies too.   60

　　Abb.   Ay, but not enough.
　　Adr.   It was the copy of our conference:
In bed he slept not for my urging it;
At board he fed not for my urging it;
Alone, it was the subject of my theme;   65
In company I often glanced it;
Still did I tell him it was vild and bad.
　　Abb.   And thereof came it that the man was mad.
The venom clamors of a jealous woman
Poisons more deadly than a mad dog's tooth.   70
It seems his sleeps were hind'red by thy railing,
And thereof comes it that his head is light.
Thou say'st his meat was sauc'd with thy upbraid-
　　ings:
Unquiet meals make ill digestions,
Thereof the raging fire of fever bred,   75
And what's a fever but a fit of madness?
Thou say'st his sports were hind'red by thy brawls:
Sweet recreation barr'd, what doth ensue
But moody and dull melancholy,
Kinsman to grim and comfortless despair,   80
And at her heels a huge infectious troop
Of pale distemperatures and foes to life?
In food, in sport, and life-preserving rest
To be disturb'd, would mad or man or beast:
The consequence is then, thy jealous fits   85
Hath scar'd thy husband from the use of wits.
　　Luc.   She never reprehended him but mildly,
When he demean'd himself rough, rude, and wildly.
Why bear you these rebukes, and answer not?
　　Adr.   She did betray me to my own reproof.   90
Good people, enter and lay hold on him.
　　Abb.   No, not a creature enters in my house.
　　Adr.   Then let your servants bring my husband
　　　forth.
　　Abb.   Neither. He took this place for sanctuary,
And it shall privilege him from your hands   95
Till I have brought him to his wits again,
Or lose my labor in assaying it.
　　Adr.   I will attend my husband, be his nurse,
Diet his sickness, for it is my office,
And will have no attorney but myself,   100
And therefore let me have him home with me.
　　Abb.   Be patient, for I will not let him stir
Till I have us'd the approved means I have,
With wholesome syrups, drugs, and holy prayers,
To make of him a formal man again: 105
It is a branch and parcel of mine oath,
A charitable duty of my order,
Therefore depart, and leave him here with me.
　　Adr.   I will not hence, and leave my husband here;
And ill it doth beseem your holiness   110
To separate the husband and the wife.
　　Abb.   Be quiet and depart, thou shalt not have him.
　　　　　　　　　　　　　　　　　[*Exit.*]
　　Luc.   Complain unto the Duke of this indignity.

---

18. charge: expense.   **20. staying on:** delaying as a result of.
29. impeach: accuse.   **31. presently:** immediately.
34. within him: under his guard.   **36. take:** take refuge in.
37. spoil'd: done for.   **47. passion:** disorder.   **48. rage:** madness.
49. wrack of: shipwreck at.   **51. Stray'd:** led astray.

62. copy . . . conference: theme of all our talk.
66. glanced: hinted at.   **67. Still:** continually.   **vild:** vile.
69. venom: venomous.   **82. distemperatures:** physical disorders.
84. mad or: madden either.   **99. office:** duty (as a wife).
100. attorney: agent.   **103. approved:** proved, tested.
105. formal: normal, sane.   **106. parcel:** part.

Adr. Come go: I will fall prostrate at his feet,
And never rise until my tears and prayers   115
Have won his Grace to come in person hither,
And take perforce my husband from the Abbess.
   [*2. E.*] *Mer.* By this I think the dial points at five.
Anon I'm sure the Duke himself in person
Comes this way to the melancholy vale,   120
The place of [death] and sorry execution,
Behind the ditches of the abbey here.
   Ang. Upon what cause?
   [*2. E.*] *Mer.* To see a reverent Syracusian mer-
      chant,
Who put unluckily into this bay   125
Against the laws and statutes of this town,
Beheaded publicly for his offense.
   Ang. See where they come, we will behold his
      death.
   Luc. Kneel to the Duke before he pass the abbey.

Enter the DUKE OF EPHESUS [*attended*] *and* [EGEON]
the merchant of Syracuse, bare-head, with the HEADS-
MAN *and other* OFFICERS.

   Duke. Yet once again proclaim it publicly,   130
If any friend will pay the sum for him,
He shall not die, so much we tender him.
   Adr. Justice, most sacred Duke, against the
      Abbess!
   Duke. She is a virtuous and a reverend lady,
It cannot be that she hath done thee wrong.   135
   Adr. May it please your Grace, Antipholus my
      husband,
Who I made lord of me and all I had,
At your important letters—this ill day
A most outrageous fit of madness took him,
That desp'rately he hurried through the street—   140
With him his bondman, all as mad as he—
Doing displeasure to the citizens
By rushing in their houses, bearing thence
Rings, jewels, any thing his rage did like.
Once did I get him bound, and sent him home,   145
Whilst to take order for the wrongs I went,
That here and there his fury had committed.
Anon, I wot not by what strong escape,
He broke from those that had the guard of him,
And with his mad attendant and himself,   150
Each one with ireful passion, with drawn swords,
Met us again, and madly bent on us
Chas'd us away; till raising of more aid,
We came again to bind them. Then they fled
Into this abbey, whither we pursu'd them,   155
And here the Abbess shuts the gates on us,
And will not suffer us to fetch him out,
Nor send him forth, that we may bear him hence.
Therefore, most gracious Duke, with thy command
Let him be brought forth, and borne hence for help.
   Duke. Long since thy husband serv'd me in my
      wars,   161

And I to thee engag'd a prince's word,
When thou didst make him master of thy bed,
To do him all the grace and good I could.
Go some of you, knock at the abbey-gate,   165
And bid the Lady Abbess come to me:
I will determine this before I stir.

Enter a MESSENGER.

   [*Mess.*] O mistress, mistress, shift and save your-
      self!
My master and his man are both broke loose,
Beaten the maids a-row, and bound the doctor,   170
Whose beard they have sing'd off with brands of fire,
And ever as it blaz'd, they threw on him
Great pails of puddled mire to quench the hair;
My master preaches patience to him, and the while
His man with scissors nicks him like a fool;   175
And sure (unless you send some present help)
Between them they will kill the conjurer.
   Adr. Peace, fool, thy master and his man are here,
And that is false thou dost report to us.
   Mess. Mistress, upon my life, I tell you true; 180
I have not breath'd almost since I did see it.
He cries for you, and vows, if he can take you,
To scorch your face, and to disfigure you.
                                        Cry within.
Hark, hark, I hear him, mistress; fly, be gone!
   Duke. Come stand by me, fear nothing. Guard
      with halberds!   185
   Adr. Ay me, it is my husband! Witness you,
That he is borne about invisible:
Even now we hous'd him in the abbey here,
And now he's there, past thought of human reason.

Enter ANTIPHOLUS [OF EPHESUS] *and* DROMIO OF
EPHESUS.

   E. Ant. Justice, most gracious Duke, O, grant me
      justice,—   190
Even for the service that long since I did thee,
When I bestrid thee in the wars, and took
Deep scars to save thy life; even for the blood
That then I lost for thee, now grant me justice.
   Ege. Unless the fear of death doth make me dote,
I see my son Antipholus and Dromio.   196
   E. Ant. Justice, sweet prince, against that woman
      there!
She whom thou gav'st to me to be my wife;
That hath abused and dishonored me,
Even in the strength and height of injury: 200
Beyond imagination is the wrong
That she this day hath shameless thrown on me.
   Duke. Discover how, and thou shalt find me just.
   E. Ant. This day, great Duke, she shut the doors
      upon me,
While she with harlots feasted in my house.   205

---

121. **sorry:** sad.   132. **tender:** have a concern for.
138. **important:** importunate, pressing.   **letters.** Possibly Adriana
had been a ward of the Duke.   140. **desp'rately:** recklessly.
142. **displeasure:** offense.   146. **take order:** make reparation.
148. **wot:** know.   160. **help:** cure.

162. **engag'd:** pledged.   164. **grace:** favor.
170. **a-row:** one after another.   173. **puddled:** foul.
175. **nicks . . . fool:** cuts his hair in a fantastic fashion, like a court
jester's.   185. **halberds:** long-handled spears with blades.
188. **hous'd him in:** drove him into.
192. **bestrid:** stood over (to defend when fallen).
199. **abused:** maltreated.   203. **Discover:** reveal.
205. **harlots:** lewd fellows.

The Comedy of Errors V.i

Duke. A grievous fault! Say, woman, didst thou so?

Adr. No, my good lord. Myself, he, and my sister
To-day did dine together: so befall my soul
As this is false he burthens me withal!

Luc. Ne'er may I look on day, nor sleep on night,
But she tells to your Highness simple truth! 211

Ang. O perjur'd woman! They are both forsworn:
In this the madman justly chargeth them.

E. Ant. My liege, I am advised what I say,
Neither disturbed with the effect of wine, 215
Nor heady-rash, provok'd with raging ire,
Albeit my wrongs might make one wiser mad.
This woman lock'd me out this day from dinner;
That goldsmith there, were he not pack'd with her,
Could witness it, for he was with me then, 220
Who parted with me to go fetch a chain,
Promising to bring it to the Porpentine,
Where Balthazar and I did dine together.
Our dinner done, and he not coming thither,
I went to seek him. In the street I met him, 225
And in his company that gentleman.
There did this perjur'd goldsmith swear me down
That I this day of him receiv'd the chain,
Which, God he knows, I saw not; for the which
He did arrest me with an officer. 230
I did obey, and sent my peasant home
For certain ducats; he with none return'd.
Then fairly I bespoke the officer
To go in person with me to my house.
By th' way we met 235
My wife, her sister, and a rabble more
Of vild confederates. Along with them
They brought one Pinch, a hungry lean-fac'd villain,
A mere anatomy, a mountebank,
A threadbare juggler and a fortune-teller, 240
A needy, hollow-ey'd, sharp-looking wretch,
A living dead man. This pernicious slave,
Forsooth, took on him as a conjurer,
And gazing in mine eyes, feeling my pulse,
And with no face, as 'twere, outfacing me, 245
Cries out, I was possess'd. Then all together
They fell upon me, bound me, bore me thence,
And in a dark and dankish vault at home
There left me and my man, both bound together,
Till gnawing with my teeth my bonds in sunder, 250
I gain'd my freedom; and immediately
Ran hither to your Grace, whom I beseech
To give me ample satisfaction
For these deep shames and great indignities.

Ang. My lord, in truth, thus far I witness with him: 255
That he din'd not at home, but was lock'd out.

Duke. But had he such a chain of thee, or no?

Ang. He had, my lord, and when he ran in here,
These people saw the chain about his neck.

[2. E.] Mer. Besides, I will be sworn these ears of mine 260
Heard you confess you had the chain of him,
After you first forswore it on the mart,
And thereupon I drew my sword on you;
And then you fled into this abbey here,
From whence I think you are come by miracle. 265

E. Ant. I never came within these abbey walls,
Nor ever didst thou draw thy sword on me;
I never saw the chain, so help me heaven;
And this is false you burthen me withal.

Duke. Why, what an intricate impeach is this!
I think you all have drunk of Circe's cup. 271
If here you hous'd him, here he would have been;
If he were mad, he would not plead so coldly.
You say he din'd at home; the goldsmith here
Denies that saying. Sirrah, what say you? 275

E. Dro. Sir, he din'd with her there, at the Porpentine.

Cour. He did, and from my finger snatch'd that ring.

E. Ant. 'Tis true, my liege, this ring I had of her.

Duke. Saw'st thou him enter at the abbey here?

Cour. As sure, my liege, as I do see your Grace.

Duke. Why, this is strange. Go call the Abbess hither. 281
I think you are all mated, or stark mad.

Exit one to the Abbess.

Ege. Most mighty Duke, vouchsafe me speak a word:
Haply I see a friend will save my life,
And pay the sum that may deliver me. 285

Duke. Speak freely, Syracusian, what thou wilt.

Ege. Is not your name, sir, call'd Antipholus?
And is not that your bondman, Dromio?

E. Dro. Within this hour I was his bondman, sir,
But he, I thank him, gnaw'd in two my cords: 290
Now am I Dromio, and his man, unbound.

Ege. I am sure you both of you remember me.

E. Dro. Ourselves we do remember, sir, by you;
For lately we were bound as you are now.
You are not Pinch's patient, are you, sir? 295

Ege. Why look you strange on me? You know me well.

E. Ant. I never saw you in my life till now.

Ege. O! grief hath chang'd me since you saw me last,
And careful hours with time's deformed hand
Have written strange defeatures in my face: 300
But tell me yet, dost thou not know my voice?

E. Ant. Neither.

Ege. Dromio, nor thou?

E. Dro.   No, trust me, sir, nor I.

Ege. I am sure thou dost! 304

208-9. so . . . As: I swear by my hope of salvation that.
209. burthens: burdens, charges.   withal: with.
214. liege: sovereign.   am advised: know very well.
219. pack'd: in league.   221. parted with: departed from.
231. peasant: servant.   233. fairly: civilly.   bespoke: requested.
239. mere anatomy: absolute skeleton.   mountebank: quack, charlatan.   240. juggler: sorcerer.
243. took . . . as: pretended to be.

270. impeach: accusation.
271. Circe's cup: i.e. the drink by means of which the sorceress Circe transformed men into beasts.   273. coldly: coolly, rationally.
282. mated: confounded, stupefied.
299. careful: full of care.   deformed: deforming.
300. defeatures: disfigurements.

E. Dro. Ay, sir, but I am sure I do not—and whatsoever a man denies, you are now bound to believe him.

Ege. Not know my voice! O time's extremity,
Hast thou so crack'd and splitted my poor tongue
In seven short years, that here my only son   310
Knows not my feeble key of untun'd cares?
Though now this grained face of mine be hid
In sap-consuming winter's drizzled snow,
And all the conduits of my blood froze up,
Yet hath my night of life some memory,   315
My wasting lamps some fading glimmer left,
My dull deaf ears a little use to hear:
All these old witnesses—I cannot err—
Tell me thou art my son Antipholus.

E. Ant. I never saw my father in my life.   320

Ege. But seven years since, in Syracusa, boy,
Thou know'st we parted, but perhaps, my son,
Thou sham'st to acknowledge me in misery.

E. Ant. The Duke, and all that know me in the city,
Can witness with me that it is not so.   325
I ne'er saw Syracusa in my life.

Duke. I tell thee, Syracusian, twenty years
Have I been patron to Antipholus,
During which time he ne'er saw Syracusa:
I see thy age and dangers make thee dote.   330

Enter the Abbess *with* Antipholus [of] Syracusa *and* Dromio [of] Syracusa.

Abb. Most mighty Duke, behold a man much
wrong'd.   *All gather to see them.*

Adr. I see two husbands, or mine eyes deceive me.

Duke. One of these men is genius to the other:
And so of these, which is the natural man,
And which the spirit? Who deciphers them?   335

S. Dro. I, sir, am Dromio, command him away.

E. Dro. I, sir, am Dromio, pray let me stay.

S. Ant. Egeon art thou not? or else his ghost?

S. Dro. O my old master, who hath bound him
here?

Abb. Whoever bound him, I will loose his bonds,
And gain a husband by his liberty.   341
Speak, old Egeon, if thou be'st the man
That hadst a wife once call'd Aemilia,
That bore thee at a burthen two fair sons.
O, if thou be'st the same Egeon, speak,   345
And speak unto the same Aemilia!

Ege. If I dream not, thou art Aemilia.
If thou art she, tell me, where is that son
That floated with thee on the fatal raft?

Abb. By men of Epidamium he and I,   350
And the twin Dromio, all were taken up;
But by and by rude fishermen of Corinth
By force took Dromio and my son from them,
And me they left with those of Epidamium.
What then became of them I cannot tell;   355
I to this fortune that you see me in.

Duke. Why, here begins his morning story right:

These two Antipholus', these two so like,
And these two Dromios, one in semblance—
Besides her urging of her wrack at sea—   360
These are the parents to these children,
Which accidentally are met together.
Antipholus, thou cam'st from Corinth first?

S. Ant. No, sir, not I, I came from Syracuse.

Duke. Stay, stand apart, I know not which is which.

E. Ant. I came from Corinth, my most gracious
lord—   366

E. Dro. And I with him.

E. Ant. Brought to this town by that most famous
warrior,
Duke Menaphon, your most renowned uncle.   369

Adr. Which of you two did dine with me to-day?

S. Ant. I, gentle mistress.

Adr.   And are not you my husband?

E. Ant. No, I say nay to that.

S. Ant. And so do I, yet did she call me so;
And this fair gentlewoman, her sister here,
Did call me brother. [*To Luciana.*] What I told you
then   375
I hope I shall have leisure to make good,
If this be not a dream I see and hear.

Ang. That is the chain, sir, which you had of me.

S. Ant. I think it be, sir, I deny it not.

E. Ant. And you, sir, for this chain arrested me.

Ang. I think I did, sir, I deny it not.   381

Adr. I sent you money, sir, to be your bail,
By Dromio, but I think he brought it not.

E. Dro. No, none by me.

S. Ant. This purse of ducats I receiv'd from you,
And Dromio my man did bring them me.   386
I see we still did meet each other's man,
And I was ta'en for him, and he for me,
And thereupon these errors are arose.   389

E. Ant. These ducats pawn I for my father here.

Duke. It shall not need, thy father hath his life.

Cour. Sir, I must have that diamond from you.

E. Ant. There take it, and much thanks for my
good cheer.

Abb. Renowned Duke, vouchsafe to take the pains
To go with us into the abbey here,   395
And hear at large discoursed all our fortunes;
And all that are assembled in this place
That by this sympathized one day's error
Have suffer'd wrong, go keep us company,
And we shall make full satisfaction.   400
Thirty-three years have I but gone in travail
Of you, my sons, and till this present hour
My heavy burthen [ne'er] delivered.
The Duke, my husband, and my children both,
And you the calendars of their nativity,   405
Go to a gossips' feast, and go with me—
After so long grief, such nativity!

Duke. With all my heart, I'll gossip at this feast.

*Exeunt omnes. Manent the two
Dromios and two brothers.*

---

308. **extremity:** extreme rigor.
311. **my . . . cares:** i.e. my voice enfeebled and made discordant by care.   312. **grained:** furrowed.   316. **lamps:** eyes.
333. **genius:** attendant spirit.   335. **deciphers:** distinguishes.
344. **burthen:** burden, birth.

387. **still:** continually.   398. **sympathized:** shared in (by all).
405. **calendars . . . nativity:** i.e. the Dromios; see note to I.ii.41.
406. **gossips' feast:** a feast of the godparents, a baptismal feast.   **go.** Some editors emend to *joy.*   407. **grief:** suffering.
408. **gossip:** make merry.

The Comedy
of Errors
V.i

S. Dro. Master, shall I fetch your stuff from
shipboard?

E. Ant. Dromio, what stuff of mine hast thou
embark'd?   410

S. Dro. Your goods that lay at host, sir, in the
Centaur.

S. Ant. He speaks to me. I am your master,
Dromio.
Come go with us, we'll look to that anon.
Embrace thy brother there, rejoice with him.

Exit [with Antipholus of Ephesus].

S. Dro. There is a fat friend at your master's
house,   415

411. **lay at host:** were put up.

That kitchen'd me for you to-day at dinner:
She now shall be my sister, not my wife.

E. Dro. Methinks you are my glass, and not my
brother:
I see by you I am a sweet-fac'd youth.
Will you walk in to see their gossiping?   420

S. Dro. Not I, sir, you are my elder.

E. Dro. That's a question; how shall we try it?

S. Dro. We'll draw cuts for the senior, till then,
lead thou first.

E. Dro. Nay then thus: 424
We came into the world like brother and brother;
And now let's go hand in hand, not one before another.

Exeunt.

416. **kitchen'd:** entertained in the kitchen.
418. **glass:** mirror.   423. **cuts:** lots.

NOTE ON THE TEXT

The only authority for the text of *The Comedy of Errors* is the First Folio (1623); all later texts are derived from that source. The manuscript behind the F1 text seems to have been some form of Shakespeare's autograph, probably his "foul papers." There is also perhaps some slight evidence of a book-keeper's hand in a few stage directions, notably that at IV.iv.146 (see Textual Notes). That the manuscript could ever have served as a prompt-book, however, seems highly unlikely, because there is a good deal of confusing variety, ambiguity, and inconsistency in the form of the speech-prefixes, and Luce is once referred to as Nel, Luciana as Juliana. The text as a whole is clean and presents few real difficulties.

For further information, see: W. W. Greg, *The Shakespeare First Folio* (Oxford, 1955); R. A. Foakes, ed., New Arden *The Comedy of Errors* (London, 1962).

TEXTUAL NOTES

Dramatis personae: *subs. as first given in Douai MS and Rowe*
Act-scene division: *F1 marks acts and first scene of each act, except Act II (act only); other scene divisions from Rowe and later editors (see first note to each scene); present act-scene arrangement as a whole first established by Capell*

I.i

Location: *ed.*
o.s.d. with Officers] *Capell*
1 **s.p. Ege.]** *Rowe (subs.);* Marchant. *F1 (*Mer. *or* Merch. *throughout scene)*
27 **sun]** *F2;* Sonne *F1*
38 **me]** mee too *F2*
42 **the . . . left]** *Theobald;* he . . . left *F1;* he great store of goods at randone leaving *F2*
54 **mean]** poor meane *F2*
55 **burthen male, twins]** burthen, Maletwins *F2*
59 **device]** *F2;* deuise *F1*
60 **agreed.]** *F4 (subs.);* agreed, *F1*
63 **always-wind-obeying]** *first hyphen, Theobald*
77 **sinking-ripe]** *hyphen, F2*
102 **upon]** *Pope (after F2* up upon); vp *F1*
116 **bark]** *F2;* backe *F1*
123 **thee]** *F2;* they *F1*
144 **princes, . . . they,]** *Theobald;* Princes . . . they *F1*
151 **health]** *Wilson;* helpe *F1*

I.ii

I.ii] *Pope*
Location: *Cambridge*
o.s.d. Antipholus] *Malone;* Antipholis *F1*
o.s.d. First] *Dyce;* a *F1*
1 **s.p. 1. E. Mer.]** *Dyce;* Mer. *F1*
4 **arrival]** *F2;* a riuall *F1 (F1 makes possible, but unlikely, sense)*

9 **s.p. S. Ant.]** *Kittredge (after Rowe, Capell; this s.p. is used throughout the present text for Antipholus of Syracuse);* Ant. *F1 (throughout this scene; in later scenes* Ant., An., Antip., Anti., S. Anti., S. Ant.); *adjustment to S. Ant. not generally recorded hereafter*
17 **s.p. S. Dro.]** *Kittredge (after Rowe, Capell);* Dro. *F1 (the s.p.* Dro. *occurs occasionally hereafter for S. Dro. in F1; adjustment to S. Dro. not generally further recorded)*
24, 32 **s.pp. 1. E. Mer.]** *Dyce;* E. Mar. *F1*
32 **s.d. Exit]** *Rowe;* Exeunt. *F1*
40 **(unhappy), ah,]** *ed.;* (vnhappie a) *F1;* (unhappie) *F2*
65 **score]** *Rowe;* scoure *F1*
66 **clock]** *Pope;* cooke *F1*
92 **s.d. Strikes Dromio.]** *Douai MS (subs.), Collier*
94 **s.d. Exit]** *F2;* Exeunt *F1*
95 **device]** *F2;* deuise *F1*
96 **o'erraught]** *Hanmer;* ore-wrought *F1*
99 **Dark-working]** *hyphen, F2*

II.i

II.i] *Rowe;* Actus Secundus, *F1*
Location: *Dyce (after Pope)*
o.s.d. Antipholus] *Malone;* Antipholis *F1*
11 **a' door]** *ed. (after F4* adoor); adore *F1*
12 **ill]** *F2;* thus *F1*
22 **Indu'd]** *Rowe;* Indued *F1*
23 **pre-eminence]** *Capell;* preheminence *F1*
45 **two]** *F2;* too *F1*
47–8 **Say . . . mind?]** *as verse, Steevens; as prose, F1*
61 **thousand]** *F2;* hundred *F1*
71–4 **I . . . there.]** *as verse, Pope; as prose, F1*
76 **s.p. E. Dro.]** *Rowe;* Dro. *F1 (the s.p.* Dro. *occurs occasionally hereafter for E. Dro. in F1; adjustment to E. Dro. not generally*

further recorded)
78 **across]** *F2;* a-crosse *F1 (perhaps to emphasize the pun in the next two lines)*
85 **s.d. Exit.]** *F2*
91 **wit?]** *F4;* wit, *F1*
107 **alone a' love]** *ed. (after Cunningham conj.);* alone, a loue *F1;* alone, alone *F2*
110–2 **yet . . . gold;]** *Alexander;* yet . . . touch, and . . . will, / Where gold *F1*
115 **what's left away,]** *Pope;* (what's left away) *F1*
116 **s.d. Exeunt.]** *F2;* Exit. *F1*

II.ii

II.ii] *Capell*
Location: *Wilson*
o.s.d. Antipholus] *Malone;* Antipholis *F1*
o.s.d. Erotes] *F2;* Errotis *F1*
3–4 **out. . . . report,]** *Rowe (after F4* report,); out . . . report. *F1*
6 **s.d. Dromio of Syracusa]** *ed. (after Rowe);* Dromio Siracusia *F1;* Dromio Siracusan *F2 (read as* Syracusa *hereafter)*
12 **didst]** *F2;* did didst *F1*
14 **s.p. S. Ant.]** *Capell (subs.);* E. Ant. *F1 (i.e. Antipholus Erotes)*
45–6 **Why . . . me.]** *as verse, Capell; as prose, F1*
47–9 **Was . . . you.]** *as verse, Rowe; as prose, F1*
80 **men]** *Theobald;* them *F1*
98 **tiring]** *Pope;* trying *F1*
102 **e'en]** *Capell conj.; in F1 (a Shakespearean spelling of* e'en)
136 **off]** *Hanmer;* of *F1*
146 **dis-stain'd]** *Theobald;* distain'd *F1*
156 **me?]** *Rowe;* me. *F1*
171 **wrong]** *Dyce;* wrong, *F1*
175 **stronger]** *F3;* stranger *F1*
186 **offer'd]** *Capell;* free'd *F1*

194 **drumble**] *ed.;* Dromio *F1*
195 **not I**] *Theobald;* I not *F1*
219 s.d. **Exeunt.**] *Rowe*

III.i

Location: *Pope (subs.)*
o.s.d. **Balthazar**] *F2;* Balthaser *F1*
24 **common;**] *Theobald;* common *F1*
25 s.p. **E. Ant.**] *Rowe (this s.p. is used throughout the present text for Antipholus of Ephesus);* Anti. *F1 (and later in F1 Ant., Anti., E. Ant.); adjustment to E. Ant. not generally recorded hereafter*
31 **Cic'ly**] *ed.;* Cisley *F1*
32, 37, etc. s.dd. **Within.**] *Rowe*
35 **many? Go**] *F4;* many, goe *F1*
41 **not,**] *F3;* not *F1*
47, 60 s.dd. **within**] *Rowe (subs.)*
54] *Malone suggests that a following rhyming line (probably ending in* rope*) is missing*
56 **So, . . . strook!**] *Dyce (subs.);* So come helpe, well strooke *F1*
60 s.d. **within**] *Rowe (subs.)*
75 **you**] *F2;* your *F1*
89 **this—**] *Theobald (subs., after Rowe);* this *F1*
89, 91 **her**] *Douai MS, Rowe;* your *F1*
110 **yet, too,**] *Rowe (subs.);* yet too *F1*
114 s.d. **To Angelo.**] *Cambridge*

III.ii

III.ii] *Pope*
Location: *ed. (after Wilson)*
o.s.d. **Luciana**] *F2;* Iuliana *F1*
1 s.p. **Luc.**] *Rowe;* Iulia. *F1*
4 **building**] *Theobald;* buildings *F1*
4 **ruinous**] *Theobald conj.;* ruinate *F1*
16 **attaint**] *Douai MS, Rowe;* attaine *F1*
21 **but**] *Theobald;* not *F1*
26 **wife**] *F2;* wise *F1*
46 **sister's**] *F2;* sister *F1*
49 **bed**] *F2;* bud *F1*
49 **them**] *Edwards;* thee *F1*
71–80 **Why . . . thyself?**] *as prose, Rowe; as verse, F1*
109 **and**] *Theobald;* is *F1*
126 **chalky**] *F2;* chalkle *F1*
145–6 **And . . . wheel.**] *as verse, Knight; as prose, F1*
146 **curtal**] *F2;* Curtull *F1*
157 **high**] *F4;* hie *F1*

IV.i

Location: *Wilson*
o.s.d. **Second**] *Dyce*
1, 52, etc. s.pp. **2. E. Mer.**] *Dyce;* Mar. *F1*
17 **her**] *Douai MS, Rowe;* their *F1*
84 s.d. **Syracusa**] *ed.;* Sira. *F1 (this form and Sir., Sirac. have been regularly expanded as* Syracusa *in the present text)*
108 s.d. **all . . . Syracuse**] *Kittredge (after Capell)*

IV.ii

IV.ii] *Capell*
Location: *Wilson (subs., after Pope)*
6 **Of**] *F2;* Oh, *F1*
28 s.d. **Dromio of Syracusa**] *ed.;* S. Dromio *F1*
29 **Sweat**] *Wilson;* sweet *F1*
34 **One**] *F2;* On *F1*
37 **back-friend**] *hyphen, F4*
38 **alleys**] *Capell;* allies *F1*
42, 45 **'rested**] *Theobald;* rested *F1*
44–6 **I . . . desk?**] *as verse, Capell; as prose, F1*
45 **'a's**] *Clark, Glover conj.;* is *F1*
46 **mistress,**] *Theobald;* Mistris *F1*
47 s.d. **Exit Luciana.**] *placed as in Cambridge; after l. 47, F1*
47 **at,**] *Rowe;* at. *F1*
48 **That**] *F2;* Thus *F1*
51 **hear**] *F3;* here *F1*
55 **hear**] *F2;* here *F1*
58 **bankrout**] *F2;* bankerout *F1*
61 **'a**] *Staunton;* I *F1*
66 s.d. **Exeunt.**] *Rowe;* Exit. *F1*

IV.iii

IV.iii] *Capell*
Location: *Wilson*
1 s.p. **S. Ant.**] *Rowe (after F2 An.S.)*
25 **'rests**] *Theobald;* rests *F1*
34 **Well . . . foolery.**] *as prose, Capell; as verse, F1*
40 **hoy**] *Pope;* Hoy *F1 (in italics)*
60 **you do,**] *F2;* do *F1*
71–6 **Some . . . it.**] *as verse, Capell (subs.); as prose, F1*
80 s.d. **with . . . Syracuse**] *Capell (subs.)*
96 s.d. **Exit.**] *F2*

IV.iv

IV.iv] *Capell*
Location: *ed. (after Wilson)*
o.s.d. **the Officer**] *Capell;* a lailor *F1*
3 **'rested**] *Theobald;* rested *F1*
6 **Ephesus;**] *Capell (subs.);* Ephesus, *F1*
17 s.d. **Beats Dromio.**] *Douai MS, Pope*
53 s.d. **Strikes Pinch.**] *Douai MS (subs.), Dyce*
56 **straight:**] *Capell (subs.);* straight, *F1*
75 **Certes**] *Rowe;* Certis *F1*
79 **contraries**] *F2;* crontraries *F1*
107 **him.**] *F2;* him *F1*
109 **me? . . . thou,**] *Rowe;* me, . . . thou? *F1*
110–1 **I . . . rescue!**] *as verse, Pope; as prose, F1*

113 s.d. **They . . . Ephesus.**] *Cambridge*
128 **Cry "The devil!"**] *Theobald (subs.);* cry the diuell. *F1*
129 **help,**] *Theobald;* help *F1*
130 s.d. **Manent**] *Rowe;* Manet *F1; F1 s.d. after l. 131; placed as in Theobald*
146 **again.**] *againe. / Runne all out. F1 (apparently anticipating the s.d. at the end of the line)*
146 s.d. **but . . . Syracuse**] *Cambridge*

V.i

Location: *ed. (after Pope)*
o.s.d. **Second**] *Dyce*
4, 9, etc. s.pp. **2. E. Mer.**] *Dyce;* Mar. *F1*
37 s.d. **Antipholus . . . Syracuse**] *Capell (subs.)*
38 **quiet,**] *Theobald;* quiet *F1*
45 **sour,**] *F2;* sower *F1*
77 **brawls**] *F2;* bralles *F1*
112 s.d. **Exit.**] *Hanmer (after Theobald)*
121 **death**] *F3;* depth *F1*
129 s.d. **attended**] *Capell*
138 **letters—**] *Theobald (subs.);* Letters *F1*
168 s.p. **Mess.**] *F2*
189 s.d. **Dromio**] *Rowe;* E. Dromio *F1*
195 s.p. **Ege.**] *Rowe (subs.);* Mar. Fat. *F1*
235 **By**] *F4;* By' *F1*
241 **needy . . . wretch**] needy-hollow-ey'd-sharpe-looking-wretch *F1*
245 **no face**] *Pope;* no-face *F1*
246 **all together**] *Rowe;* altogether *F1*
283, 287, etc. s.pp. **Ege.**] *Rowe (subs.);* Fa., Fath., *or* Father. *F1 (throughout rest of scene)*
305 **Ay, sir,**] *I sir, F1 (possibly we should read* I, sir?*)*
318 **witnesses . . . err—**] *Rowe (subs.);* witnesses, I cannot erre. *F1*
321 **Syracusa, boy,**] *Capell;* Siracusa boy *F1*
357–62 **Why . . . together.**] *placed as in Capell; these lines follow l. 346 in F1 (if we suppose a line or two lost, dealing with the "wrack," in Aemilia's speech, ll. 340–6, then the F1 order, with the Duke's speech as an aside, would make good sense)*
363 **Antipholus**] *Capell;* Duke. Antipholus *F1 (see preceding note)*
363 **first?**] *Capell;* first. *F1*
375 s.d. **To Luciana.**] *Cambridge (after Capell)*
397–9 **place . . . wrong,**] *Rowe (subs.);* place: . . . wrong. *F1*
403 **ne'er**] *Dyce;* are *F1*
406 **gossips'**] *Halliwell;* Gossips *F1*
408 s.d. **Manent**] *Rowe;* Manet *F1*
414 s.d. **with . . . Ephesus**] *Theobald (subs.)*
423 **senior**] *Rowe;* Signior *F1*
426 s.d. **Exeunt.**] Exeunt. / FINIS. *F1*

The Taming of the Shrew

 N THE YEAR 1594 there was published
an anonymous play entitled *The
Taming of a Shrew*, now generally
believed to be either a pirated and
inaccurate version of Shakespeare's
comedy or else a "bad" quarto of a
different play, now lost, which also
served Shakespeare as a source for his own *The Taming
of the Shrew*. In general outline, *A Shrew* is very close
to Shakespeare's play, although there are very few
verbal parallels and the entire comedy is markedly
inferior to the one published as Shakespeare's in the
First Folio of 1623. Shakespeare's fantasy about
courtship and marriage in Padua is clearly an early
comedy, part of the group which also includes *The
Two Gentlemen of Verona* and *The Comedy of Errors*.
None of these plays is easy to date, but *The Taming
of the Shrew* must have been written between 1590
and 1594. Like *The Comedy of Errors*, it displays a
complete assurance of technique within limits admittedly narrower, closer to farce, than those of the
comedies Shakespeare was to write later in the decade.
Inventive, witty, and vital, it has come honestly by its
enduring popularity in the theatre. Indeed, no other
play by Shakespeare depends so heavily upon theatrical
realization as opposed to mere reading. Attitudes
and turns of phrase that seem archaic, or even brutal,
on the printed page, have a way of becoming entirely
acceptable as soon as Katherina and Petruchio are
actually speaking. On the stage, unless the actor
deliberately coarsens his part, Petruchio comes over
far less as an aggressive male out to bully a refractory
wife into total submission than he does as a man who
genuinely prizes Katherina and, by exploiting an age-
old and basic antagonism between the sexes,
manoeuvres her into an understanding of his nature
and also her own.

Shrewish wives in English drama can trace their
descent from Mrs. Noah in the mystery plays, that
indomitable scold who would not leave her "gossips"
and get into the ark at her husband's bidding even
though the whole world was drowning in the Flood.
Intractable, violent, and sharp-tongued wives, some of
them fond of cuckolding their husbands as well as
merely ordering them about, represented a familiar
comic type in Tudor interludes and farces. Roman
comedy had also dealt with the termagant wife.
Elizabethan dramatists who adapted plays by Plautus
and Terence found it easy to graft the classical
shrew onto her native counterpart. Meanwhile,
outside the theatre, there was no decline in that
venerable and even more extensive tradition of shrew
literature which Chaucer had contributed to, as well
as the more humble compilers of jest-books or of
ballads like "A Merry Jest of a Shrewd and Curst
Wife Lapped in Morel's Skin for Her Good
Behavior" (c. 1550). Verbal similarities indicate that
Shakespeare knew this particular ballad; certainly
he knew others like it, in which the approved remedy
for a domineering wife was physical violence, the more
ingenious and excruciating the better. By comparison
with the husband who binds his erring spouse, beats
her, bleeds her into a state of debility, or (in the case
of the ballad mentioned above) incarcerates her
inside the salted skin of the dead horse Morel,
Petruchio—although no Romeo—is almost a model of
intelligence and humanity. His aim, moreover, is not
the crude one of the traditional wife-tamer, out to
pulverize the woman's will as well as, in most cases,
her body. What Petruchio wants, and ends up with,
is a Katherina of unbroken spirit and gaiety who has
suffered only minor physical discomfort and who has
learned the value of self-control and of caring about
someone other than herself.

Northrop Frye once remarked that the Katherina of Act I is not really dissimilar from the Katherina of Act V: at the beginning of the comedy she is persecuting her sister Bianca, and at the end she is engaged in precisely the same activity—except that now she has learned how to do it with social approval on her side. The remark is far from representing the whole truth about Katherina's progress in the course of the comedy, but it does usefully point to the way Petruchio's "method" has harmonized and ordered the elements of a personality without doing violence to its essential selfhood. Shakespeare's sympathy with and almost uncanny understanding of women characters is one of the distinguishing features of his comedy, as opposed to that of most of his contemporaries. His heroines not only tend to overshadow their male counterparts, as Rosalind overshadows Orlando, Julia Proteus, or Viola Orsino: they adumbrate and urge throughout the play values which, with their help, will triumph in the new, more enlightened society of the end. Nevertheless, there is no hint anywhere in his work that he would have dissented from the official position of the Elizabethan church as derived from the counsel of St. Paul in his letter to the Ephesians: "Let women be subject to their husbands, as to the Lord; for the husband is the head of the woman, as Christ is the head of the church." The attitude adopted by the reformed Katherina in the last scene of the comedy is strikingly like that of Luciana rebuking her nagging and possessive sister Adriana in *The Comedy of Errors*: both women see the subservience of a wife to her husband as an in-built law of nature, not to be transgressed, and both have the force of the entire comedy behind them in their belief.

Although it lacks the essential seriousness and the poetry of *As You Like It*, *Twelfth Night*, or even *Love's Labor's Lost*, *The Taming of the Shrew* is nonetheless psychologically discerning. Petruchio comes to Padua initially because he is looking for a rich wife. At the first sight of Katherina, however, this cold, unemotional project becomes something far more complex: Kate is not only a problem to be solved, but a prize, in ways that have nothing to do with the size of her dowry. She is, in fact, a far more honest and interesting person than her apparently docile and much-admired sister Bianca, although Petruchio is the only person in Padua, at least until Act V, to see that this is true. As for Katherina herself, the stage convention which allows the actress playing the part to show plainly in her face that she falls in love with Petruchio the moment she sets eyes on him has much to recommend it. Heartily sick of a single life, not to mention all the adulation showered on Bianca, she is really more than ready to give herself to a man but, imprisoned within a set of aggressive attitudes which have become habitual, has not the faintest idea how to do so. Petruchio's strategy is perceptively designed to make her abandon a shrew's role originally adopted as a defense, not intrinsic in her nature, and to permit her to escape into freedom and love within the bonds of marriage.

The two techniques he employs are complementary. First of all, he "kills her in her own humor" (IV.i.180), "is more shrew than she" (IV.i.85–86), beating the servants, hurling dinner plates, insulting tradesmen, scolding and complaining, throwing tantrums and changing his mind with the wind. Not only does he present her in all this with a masculine version of her own unreasonable and arbitrary behavior, he forces her to experience it objectively and to realize just how impossible it is for another person to tolerate. At the same time, he goes on assuring her, despite everything she can do and say to prove the contrary, that she herself is gentle, rational, and loving: exactly the hidden qualities in her that he needs to foster and encourage. Petruchio wins in the end not because of superior force but because he succeeds in showing Katherina both the unloveliness of the false personality she has adopted and the emotional truth of the self she has submerged. The method used is not exactly Freud's, but the integrated and quietly confident Kate who wins Petruchio's wager for him at the end of the comedy is a woman who has discovered and come to terms with her own genuine nature.

There are undeniable elements of farce in the Katherina/Petruchio plot, as well as a robust glee in that age-old motif of the battle between the sexes which Shakespeare does, at moments in the play, exploit for its own, eminently theatrical, sake. Nevertheless, all the exuberance and in-fighting ultimately serves an end poles apart from the mere vindictive savagery of "The Curst Wife Lapped in Morel's Skin." It is true that by comparison with Beatrice in *Much Ado about Nothing* (1598) Katherina is a character sketched in bold, rapid strokes, with none of Beatrice's sophistication, verbal brilliance, or emotional depth. She is nonetheless an important first study for Benedick's exasperating sparring partner, another woman who shelters behind a false aggressiveness and has to be tricked into accepting a man's love. The achievement of *The Taming of the Shrew* lies more on the surface, depends more upon stage incident and rough-and-tumble than was to be the case in the comedies of the later 1590's, yet both structurally and thematically it is a remarkably consistent and skillful play. Certainly Shakespeare seems to have taken pains not only to link those ideas about role-playing and transformation which are so important in the taming plot with the parallel story of Bianca and her three suitors, but also to extend them beyond the inset play into the strangely truncated adventure of Christopher Sly.

The Bianca plot is derived from a play by George Gascoigne, *Supposes* (1566), in itself an adaptation of Ariosto's comedy *I Suppositi* (1509). Both plays declare their Plautine ancestry. They are concerned almost entirely with plot "mistaking," false "supposes" about the identity of characters and the nature of situations. Polynesta, Gascoigne's equivalent to Bianca, is a shadowy figure and, like most of her prototypes in Roman comedy, rarely appears on stage. She is really the excuse for the intrigue, more than a character in her own right. When the comedy begins, she is pregnant by her lover Erostrato, who has changed identities with his servant Dulipo in order to gain access to Polynesta. The false Erostrato, posing as a suitor to Polynesta, defeats an elderly but rich rival by means of the same ruse that Tranio employs to help Lucentio in Shakespeare's play. As in Shakespeare, the real father then puts in an unexpected appearance and is horrified to discover his own identity usurped by a perfect stranger and his son's by the servant he has raised in his house. False suppositions proliferate but all ends happily at last with Polynesta married to her seducer Erostrato and Dulipo, suddenly revealed as the long-lost son of the Gremio figure, transformed from a servant into a man of rank and fortune.

In taking over Gascoigne's plot, Shakespeare obviously intended the various "supposes" inherent in it as a complement to those in the Katherina/Petruchio story. He rejected the idea that Tranio might be other than he seemed—the favorite New Comedy motif of the child lost in infancy and reared as a servant never appealed much to Elizabethans—but made up for the loss of this particular mistake of identity by providing Bianca with a third suitor, Hortensio, and having him woo her in the disguise of a music master. Elizabethan preferences must also have been partly responsible for the fact that Bianca, unlike Polynesta, is still a virgin and a much more active and developed character than her prototype. Less predictable was Shakespeare's decision to present her as a mirror image of her elder sister Katherina. Bianca's sweet submissiveness is no more integral to her character than Kate's bad temper is to hers. Already in the scene where she is wooed by the disguised Lucentio and Hortensio she displays a deviousness and cunning which suggest that the dutiful daughter and long-suffering, patient younger sister are roles that she knows how to play, rather than indications of her true character. Once married to Lucentio, she ceases abruptly to be "sweet Bianca." At the wedding feast itself she reveals an unexpected streak of bawdry, willfulness, and arrogance. Lucentio, as it turns out, and not Petruchio, has married the shrewish sister. As for Hortensio, his headstrong widow is clearly going to drive him to experiment with Petruchio's wife-taming methods before the first week of marriage is out.

In the marriage feast which concludes *The Taming of the Shrew* all the plot material of the comedy proper is woven together in a fashion that is thematically as well as structurally masterful. Spare and elegant, almost dance-like in form, the play transforms the Roman model from which, basically, it derives into a thing of grace and sophistication. Patently designed to be watched, not read, full of game-playing and visual humor, it is perhaps the most unequivocally light-hearted of all Shakespeare's comedies, the one whose qualities lie most obviously on the surface. If it is short on poetry and deep emotion, without the power to disturb of *Twelfth Night* or *Measure For Measure*, it makes up for these deficiencies by sheer theatrical brilliance—as the theatre itself has always

known. This pervading sense of symmetry and control is one of the things which make the abrupt disappearance of Christopher Sly and of the frame so elaborately set up in the Induction such a puzzle.

The idea of the play set within a frame seems to have been especially popular in the late 1580's and early 1590's. It was one way of exploring the new self-sufficiency of a stage world which had only recently become entirely secular and needed to redefine its relationship with an audience coming to the theatre now less for instruction than delight. *The Taming of a Shrew* is one of a number of plays surviving from this period which presented that audience with an image of itself in the form of one or more on-stage spectators who watch, and thereby help to distance, an illusion. In this text, Christopher Sly remains visible on stage almost to the end of the inset play, and takes a lively interest in the performance put on for his benefit. He inquires knowledgeably after the next appearance of the fool, refuses to have people sent to prison, and when it becomes necessary for the purposes of the lord's game with him that he fall asleep, he has to be plied with drink before he will remove his attention from the play. There is a certain charm about the conclusion of *A Shrew*, when Sly wakes from what he regards as the best dream he has ever had and resolves to go home and apply the lesson in shrew-taming to his own recalcitrant wife. In the theatre, directors often insert these additional Sly episodes into Shakespeare's play on the grounds that it is both illogical and unsatisfying to have him vanish without explanation after Act I and to miss out the moment when he regains his own humble identity. They may well be right.

The idea for Sly's transformation may have been suggested originally by a story (1570), now lost, by the early Elizabethan dramatist and Master of the Children of the Chapel, Richard Edwards. Shakespeare need not, however, have been dependent upon a specific source: the motif of the beggar who wakes to find himself inexplicably surrounded with wealth and comfort beyond his wildest imaginings was popular both in Europe and in the East. It is one of the tales told in *The Arabian Nights*, where the adventure-loving caliph Haroun Al Raschid engineers the trick, and it is reported that Philip the Good of Burgundy actually played a similar prank. Inherent in all versions is the return of the beggar to his original state and his conviction that all the wonders he has seen and enjoyed were only an exceptionally vivid dream. It is possible, of course, that in Shakespeare's play, as in *A Shrew*, the Sly framework continued to the end, and that the portion now missing was simply omitted from the Folio text as the result of some unexplained accident. Against this view is the fact that Shakespeare's Sly, unlike his namesake in *A Shrew*, is presented as bored with the comedy he watches from the beginning and already nodding off after the first scene. It has sometimes been suggested that Shakespeare decided to truncate the part so savagely because he discovered that he could not trust the actor who played it not to dominate the entire comedy. Hamlet is particularly scathing about clowns who persistently speak "more than is set down for them," even though "in the mean time some necessary question of the play be then to be consider'd." He calls them "villainous" (III.ii.38–45). Was the original Sly an actor of this kind, whose antics distracted attention from the inset play to such an extent that Shakespeare had to banish him from the stage as soon as possible? Alternatively, it has been argued that Sly was never intended to do more than lead the theatre audience into the play-world of Padua and, having done that, had fulfilled his function and might disappear, like the Fool in *King Lear*. Critics who are of this persuasion insist that in Shakespeare's richer and more resonant comedy it could only be disturbing to remain aware of Sly throughout, and a positive anticlimax to have to return from the wedding feast and the triumph of Petruchio and Kate to the bare heath at the end, and Sly's rueful awakening. On the whole, experimentation in the theatre with the extra dialogue from *A Shrew* (recorded in the Textual Notes below) suggests that this is not psychologically true, that Sly can lead us away from Shakespeare's Padua quite as subtly and effectively as Feste leads us from Illyria or Puck from the palace of Duke Theseus. The question of why, in the Folio text, he does not, seems likely to remain a source of controversy.

What does seem clear is that the Sly scenes, mysterious though their abbreviation is, lock into place in Shakespeare's play as part of an overall concern with transformation and questions of identity. Baptista discovers at the wedding feast that he does not recognize Kate, his own daughter, "for she is chang'd, as she had never been" (V.ii.115). Bianca too is "chang'd," although not for the better. These particular transformations have a psychological truth behind them of a kind alien to the situation comedy of Gascoigne or Plautus. Yet Shakespeare allows them to grow out of a series of more literal mistakings in the form of those multiple disguises associated with the Bianca plot and, on the outermost circle of the action, the confusion of the tinker who wakes to find he is a lord. It seems right that this ancient wish-dream of poverty translated to riches should introduce a play concerned throughout with role-playing, with the discrepancy between what people seem and what they really are. Interestingly enough, although the actors who entertain Sly in *A Shrew* are presented as bunglers, men who talk about performing a "Tragicall" or a "comodotie" and request the lord to provide them with a little vinegar to make their devil roar, their equivalents in the Folio text are men of dignity and skill. Precursors of the city-tragedians in *Hamlet*, they are honorably received by the lord, who commands that they should "want nothing that my house affords" (Induction i.104). It is difficult to say just why the players should be debased in *A Shrew*, but it is obviously fitting in Shakespeare's text that they should be what they are: magicians whose art is not confined to the stage but an integral part of life itself.

Anne Barton

The Taming of a Shrew by "J. R." (c. 1635). The program for "taming a shrew" advocated by the Father (left) in this woodcut from a broadside ballad differs sharply from the tactics employed by Petruchio: understanding and mutual forbearance as opposed to male chauvinism. (*The Folger Shakespeare Library*)

The Taming of the Shrew

[INDUCTION,] SCENE I

Enter beggar, CHRISTOPHERO SLY, *and* HOSTESS.

Sly. I'll pheeze you, in faith.

Host. A pair of stocks, you rogue!

Sly. Y' are a baggage, the Slys are no rogues. Look in the chronicles; we came in with Richard Conqueror. Therefore *paucas pallabris*, let the world slide. Sessa! 6

Host. You will not pay for the glasses you have burst?

Sly. No, not a denier. Go by, Saint Jeronimy! go to thy cold bed, and warm thee. 10

Host. I know my remedy; I must go fetch the [thirdborough]. [*Exit.*]

Sly. Third, or fourth, or fift borough, I'll answer

Words and passages enclosed in square brackets in the text above are either emendations of the copy-text or additions to it. The Textual Notes immediately following the play cite the earliest authority for every such change or insertion and supply the reading of the copy-text wherever it is emended in this edition.

Ind. i. Location: Before an alehouse on a heath.
1. **I'll pheeze you.** A vague threat, equivalent to modern "I'll fix you" or "I'll do for you."
2. **A pair of stocks:** i.e. I'll have you in the stocks.
4. **Richard.** Sly's blunder for *William.*
5. **paucas pallabris:** few words (Spanish *pocas palabras*).
6. **Sessa.** Of uncertain meaning; perhaps equivalent to "let it go" (from Spanish *cesar,* "cease"). 8. **burst:** broken.
9. **denier:** copper coin worth very little. **Go...Jeronimy.** Sly's variation of a stock tag signifying impatient dismissal; it stemmed from a line in Kyd's *Spanish Tragedy,* "Hieronimo, beware; go by, go by," but Sly confuses Hieronimo in the play with St. Jerome (Latin Hieronymus).
9-10. **Go...thee.** Cf. *Lear,* III.iv.48; probably proverbial.
12. **thirdborough:** constable. The first syllable evolved from the Old English word for "peace." 13. **fift:** fifth.
14. **boy:** here, a term of contempt, applicable to either sex.

him by law. I'll not budge an inch, boy; let him come, and kindly. *Falls asleep.* 15

Wind horns. Enter a LORD *from hunting, with his* TRAIN.

Lord. Huntsman, I charge thee, tender well my hounds
(Brach Merriman, the poor cur, is emboss'd),
And couple Clowder with the deep-mouth'd brach.
Saw'st thou not, boy, how Silver made it good
At the hedge-corner, in the coldest fault? 20
I would not lose the dog for twenty pound.

[1.] Hun. Why, Belman is as good as he, my lord;
He cried upon it at the merest loss,
And twice to-day pick'd out the dullest scent.
Trust me, I take him for the better dog. 25

Lord. Thou art a fool; if Echo were as fleet,
I would esteem him worth a dozen such.
But sup them well, and look unto them all,
To-morrow I intend to hunt again.

[1.] Hun. I will, my lord. 30

Lord. What's here? One dead, or drunk? See, doth he breathe?

2. Hun. He breathes, my lord. Were he not warm'd with ale,
This were a bed but cold to sleep so soundly.

Lord. O monstrous beast, how like a swine he lies!

15. **kindly:** i.e. welcome. s.d. **Wind:** blow. 16. **tender:** care for.
17. **Brach:** bitch hound. In view of the repetition of the word in the next line, most editors emend, commonly either to *Broach* (= bleed) or to *Breathe* (= allow to rest). **emboss'd:** foaming at the mouth.
20. **in...fault:** when the scent was coldest.
23. **cried upon it:** bayed, i.e. was the first to recover the scent. **at...loss:** when the scent had been completely lost.

Grim death, how foul and loathsome is thine image!
Sirs, I will practice on this drunken man.   36
What think you, if he were convey'd to bed,
Wrapp'd in sweet clothes, rings put upon his fingers,
A most delicious banquet by his bed,
And brave attendants near him when he wakes,   40
Would not the beggar then forget himself?
  1. Hun. Believe me, lord, I think he cannot
    choose.
  2. Hun. It would seem strange unto him when he
    wak'd.
  Lord. Even as a flatt'ring dream or worthless
    fancy.
Then take him up, and manage well the jest.   45
Carry him gently to my fairest chamber,
And hang it round with all my wanton pictures.
Balm his foul head in warm distilled waters,
And burn sweet wood to make the lodging sweet.
Procure me music ready when he wakes,   50
To make a dulcet and a heavenly sound;
And if he chance to speak, be ready straight,
And with a low submissive reverence
Say, "What is it your honor will command?"
Let one attend him with a silver basin   55
Full of rose-water and bestrew'd with flowers,
Another bear the ewer, the third a diaper,
And say, "Will't please your lordship cool your
    hands?"
Some one be ready with a costly suit,
And ask him what apparel he will wear;   60
Another tell him of his hounds and horse,
And that his lady mourns at his disease.
Persuade him that he hath been lunatic,
And when he says he is, say that he dreams,
For he is nothing but a mighty lord.   65
This do, and do it kindly, gentle sirs;
It will be pastime passing excellent,
If it be husbanded with modesty.
  1. Hun. My lord, I warrant you we will play our
    part
As he shall think by our true diligence   70
He is no less than what we say he is.
  Lord. Take him up gently and to bed with him,
And each one to his office when he wakes.
                    [*Some bear out Sly.*]   *Sound trumpets.*
Sirrah, go see what trumpet 'tis that sounds.
                              [*Exit Servingman.*]
Belike some noble gentleman that means   75
(Travelling some journey) to repose him here.

            Enter SERVINGMAN.

How now? who is it?
  Serv.   An't please your honor, players
That offer service to your lordship.

            Enter PLAYERS.

  Lord. Bid them come near. Now, fellows, you are
    welcome.
  Players. We thank your honor.   80
  Lord. Do you intend to stay with me to-night?
  2. Play. So please your lordship to accept our duty.
  Lord. With all my heart. This fellow I remember
Since once he play'd a farmer's eldest son.
'Twas where you woo'd the gentlewoman so well.   85
I have forgot your name; but sure that part
Was aptly fitted and naturally perform'd.
  [*1. Play.*] I think 'twas Soto that your honor
    means.
  Lord. 'Tis very true; thou didst it excellent.
Well, you are come to me in happy time,   90
The rather for I have some sport in hand,
Wherein your cunning can assist me much.
There is a lord will hear you play to-night;
But I am doubtful of your modesties,
Lest, over-eyeing of his odd behavior   95
(For yet his honor never heard a play),
You break into some merry passion,
And so offend him; for I tell you, sirs,
If you should smile, he grows impatient.
  [*1.*] *Play.* Fear not, my lord, we can contain our-
    selves,   100
Were he the veriest antic in the world.
  Lord. Go, sirrah, take them to the buttery,
And give them friendly welcome every one.
Let them want nothing that my house affords.
                        Exit one with the Players.
Sirrah, go you to Barthol'mew my page,   105
And see him dress'd in all suits like a lady;
That done, conduct him to the drunkard's chamber,
And call him madam, do him obeisance.
Tell him from me, as he will win my love,
He bear himself with honorable action,   110
Such as he hath observ'd in noble ladies
Unto their lords, by them accomplished;
Such duty to the drunkard let him do,
With soft low tongue and lowly courtesy,
And say, "What is't your honor will command,   115
Wherein your lady, and your humble wife,
May show her duty and make known her love?"
And then with kind embracements, tempting kisses,
And with declining head into his bosom,
Bid him shed tears, as being overjoyed   120
To see her noble lord restor'd to health,
Who for this seven years hath esteemed him
No better than a poor and loathsome beggar.

35. **image:** likeness (with reference to the ancient view that sleep was the image of death).   36. **practice:** play a joke.
38. **sweet:** perfumed.   39. **banquet:** light repast.
40. **brave:** finely dressed.   44. **worthless fancy:** empty fantasy.
48. **Balm:** anoint.   52. **straight:** immediately.
57. **diaper:** towel.   64. **is:** i.e. is indeed mad.
66. **kindly:** naturally, i.e. convincingly.   67. **passing:** surpassingly.
68. **husbanded with modesty:** managed with restraint.
73. **office:** duty.   74. **Sirrah:** ordinary form of address to inferiors.
75. **Belike:** probably.   77. **An't:** if it.

82. **duty:** expression of respect.   87. **naturally:** realistically.
88. **Soto.** A character of this name, with a role like that described by the Lord, appears in Fletcher's *Women Pleased*, but since that play was first acted around 1620, the reference here must either be a late addition or point to a much earlier play on which Fletcher's play was based.   90. **in happy time:** opportunely.
91. **The rather for:** the more so because.   92. **cunning:** skill.
93. **will:** who will (a frequent construction).
94. **modesties:** self-control.   95. **over-eyeing of:** observing.
97. **merry passion:** fit of laughter.
101. **antic:** grotesque creature, eccentric.   102. **buttery:** store room for liquor (kept in butts) and other provisions.   104. **want:** lack.   106. **in all suits:** in every detail.
110. **honorable:** becoming, decorous.
112. **accomplished:** performed.   122. **him:** himself.

111

And if the boy have not a woman's gift
To rain a shower of commanded tears,   125
An onion will do well for such a shift,
Which in a napkin (being close convey'd)
Shall in despite enforce a watery eye.
See this dispatch'd with all the haste thou canst;
Anon I'll give thee more instructions.   130

                                        Exit a Servingman.
I know the boy will well usurp the grace,
Voice, gait, and action of a gentlewoman.
I long to hear him call the drunkard husband,
And how my men will stay themselves from laughter
When they do homage to this simple peasant.   135
I'll in to counsel them; haply my presence
May well abate the over-merry spleen,
Which otherwise would grow into extremes.

                                        [*Exeunt.*]

[SCENE II]

Enter aloft the drunkard [SLY] *with* ATTENDANTS,
some with apparel, basin and ewer, and other appurte-
nances, and LORD.

Sly. For God's sake, a pot of small ale.
1. Serv. Will't please your [lordship] drink a cup
    of sack?
2. Serv. Will't please your honor taste of these
    conserves?
3. Serv. What raiment will your honor wear
    to-day?
Sly. I am Christophero Sly, call not me honor   5
nor lordship. I ne'er drank sack in my life; and
if you give me any conserves, give me conserves of
beef. Ne'er ask me what raiment I'll wear, for
I have no more doublets than backs, no more stockings than legs, nor no more shoes than feet—   10
nay, sometime more feet than shoes, or such shoes
as my toes look through the overleather.
Lord. Heaven cease this idle humor in your honor!
O that a mighty man of such descent,
Of such possessions, and so high esteem,   15
Should be infused with so foul a spirit!
Sly. What, would you make me mad? Am not
I Christopher Sly, old Sly's son of Burton-heath,
by birth a pedlar, by education a card-maker, by
transmutation a bear-herd, and now by present   20
profession a tinker? Ask Marian Hacket, the fat
ale-wife of Wincot, if she know me not. If she say

I am not fourteen pence on the score for sheer ale,
score me up for the lying'st knave in Christendom.
What! I am not bestraught. Here's—   25
3. Serv. O, this it is that makes your lady mourn!
2. Serv. O, this is it that makes your servants
    droop!
Lord. Hence comes it that your kindred shuns
    your house,
As beaten hence by your strange lunacy.
O noble lord, bethink thee of thy birth,   30
Call home thy ancient thoughts from banishment,
And banish hence these abject lowly dreams.
Look how thy servants do attend on thee,
Each in his office ready at thy beck.   34
Wilt thou have music? Hark, Apollo plays,   *Music.*
And twenty caged nightingales do sing.
Or wilt thou sleep? We'll have thee to a couch,
Softer and sweeter than the lustful bed
On purpose trimm'd up for Semiramis.
Say thou wilt walk; we will bestrow the ground.   40
Or wilt thou ride? Thy horses shall be trapp'd,
Their harness studded all with gold and pearl.
Dost thou love hawking? Thou hast hawks will soar
Above the morning lark. Or wilt thou hunt?
Thy hounds shall make the welkin answer them   45
And fetch shrill echoes from the hollow earth.
1. Serv. Say thou wilt course, thy greyhounds
    are as swift
As breathed stags; ay, fleeter than the roe.
2. Serv. Dost thou love pictures? We will fetch
    thee straight
Adonis painted by a running brook,   50
And Cytherea all in sedges hid,
Which seem to move and wanton with her breath,
Even as the waving sedges play with wind.
Lord. We'll show thee Io as she was a maid,
And how she was beguiled and surpris'd,   55
As lively painted as the deed was done.
3. Serv. Or Daphne roaming through a thorny
    wood,
Scratching her legs that one shall swear she bleeds,
And at that sight shall sad Apollo weep,
So workmanly the blood and tears are drawn.   60
Lord. Thou art a lord, and nothing but a lord.
Thou hast a lady far more beautiful
Than any woman in this waning age.
1. Serv. And till the tears that she hath shed for
    thee

---

126. **shift:** purpose.   127. **napkin:** handkerchief.
128. **in despite:** i.e. in spite of his inability to weep.
130. **Anon:** very shortly.   131. **usurp:** assume.
136. **haply:** perhaps.
137. **spleen:** impulse, mood. Fits of laughter (as of anger) were
supposed to originate in the spleen.

Ind. ii. Location: A bedchamber in the Lord's house.
o.s.d. **aloft:** i.e. in the gallery over the back of the stage.
1. **small:** weak.   2. **sack:** Spanish white wine.
3. **conserves:** sweetmeats of fruit.
7–8. **conserves of beef:** salt beef.   9. **doublets:** jackets.
12. **overleather:** upper leather.   13. **idle humor:** absurd fancy.
18. **Burton-heath:** perhaps Barton-on-the-Heath, a Warwickshire
village about sixteen miles from Stratford.
19. **card-maker:** maker of cards for combing wool.
20. **bear-herd:** keeper of a tame bear.
22. **Wincot:** a small village about four miles from Stratford; the
parish records indicate that Hackets were living there in the 1590's.

23. **on the score:** in debt (originally recorded by scoring or notching
a stick).   **sheer ale:** i.e. ale alone.
24. **score:** reckon.   **lying'st ... Christendom.** Cf. *2 Henry VI*,
II.i.126.   25. **bestraught:** distracted, mad.
31. **ancient thoughts:** former reason.   35. **Apollo:** god of music.
39. **Semiramis:** legendary queen of Assyria notorious for her volup-
tuousness.   40. **bestrow:** bestrew (with coverings).
41. **trapp'd:** adorned.   45. **welkin:** sky.   47. **course:** hunt hares.
48. **breathed:** in full breath, in good wind.   **roe:** a kind of small,
fleet deer.
50. **Adonis:** the young hunter beloved of Venus and slain by a wild
boar. The story is the subject of Shakespeare's *Venus and Adonis*.
51. **Cytherea:** Venus (so named from her traditional association with
the island Cythera).   52. **wanton:** play amorously.
54. **Io:** a Greek maiden loved by Jupiter, who turned her into a cow
in an unsuccessful attempt to conceal her from Juno.
56. **lively:** realistically.
57. **Daphne:** a nymph changed by Diana into a laurel tree to preserve
her from rape by Apollo.   63. **waning:** degenerate.

Like envious floods o'errun her lovely face,   65
She was the fairest creature in the world,
And yet she is inferior to none.

Sly.   Am I a lord, and have I such a lady?
Or do I dream? Or have I dream'd till now?
I do not sleep: I see, I hear, I speak;   70
I smell sweet savors, and I feel soft things.
Upon my life, I am a lord indeed,
And not a tinker, nor Christopher Sly.
Well, bring our lady hither to our sight,
And once again a pot o' th' smallest ale.   75

2. Serv.   Will't please your mightiness to wash
your hands?
O how we joy to see your wit restor'd!
O that once more you knew but what you are!
These fifteen years you have been in a dream,
Or when you wak'd, so wak'd as if you slept.   80

Sly.   These fifteen years! by my fay, a goodly nap,
But did I never speak of all that time?

1. Serv.   O yes, my lord, but very idle words,
For though you lay here in this goodly chamber,
Yet would you say ye were beaten out of door,   85
And rail upon the hostess of the house,
And say you would present her at the leet,
Because she brought stone jugs and no seal'd quarts.
Sometimes you would call out for Cicely Hacket.

Sly.   Ay, the woman's maid of the house.   90

3. Serv.   Why, sir, you know no house nor no such
maid,
Nor no such men as you have reckon'd up,
As Stephen Sly, and old John Naps of Greece,
And Peter Turph, and Henry Pimpernell,
And twenty more such names and men as these,   95
Which never were, nor no man ever saw.

Sly.   Now Lord be thanked for my good amends!
All.   Amen.

Enter [the Page *as a] lady, with* Attendants.

Sly.   I thank thee, thou shalt not lose by it.
Page.   How fares my noble lord?   100
Sly.   Marry, I fare well, for here is cheer enough.
Where is my wife?
Page.   Here, noble lord, what is thy will with her?
Sly.   Are you my wife and will not call me husband?
My men should call me "lord"; I am your goodman.
Page.   My husband and my lord, my lord and husband,   106
I am your wife in all obedience.
Sly.   I know it well. What must I call her?
Lord.   Madam.
Sly.   Al'ce madam, or Joan madam?   110

Lord.   Madam, and nothing else, so lords call
ladies.
Sly.   Madam wife, they say that I have dream'd,
And slept above some fifteen year or more.
Page.   Ay, and the time seems thirty unto me,
Being all this time abandon'd from your bed.   115
Sly.   'Tis much. Servants, leave me and her alone.
Madam, undress you, and come now to bed.
Page.   Thrice-noble lord, let me entreat of you
To pardon me yet for a night or two;
Or if not so, until the sun be set.   120
For your physicians have expressly charg'd,
In peril to incur your former malady,
That I should yet absent me from your bed.
I hope this reason stands for my excuse.   124
Sly.   Ay, it stands so that I may hardly tarry so
long. But I would be loath to fall into my dreams
again. I will therefore tarry in despite of the flesh
and the blood.

Enter a Messenger.

Mess.   Your honor's players, hearing your amendment,
Are come to play a pleasant comedy,   130
For so your doctors hold it very meet,
Seeing too much sadness hath congeal'd your blood,
And melancholy is the nurse of frenzy.
Therefore they thought it good you hear a play,
And frame your mind to mirth and merriment,   135
Which bars a thousand harms and lengthens life.
Sly.   Marry, I will, let them play it. Is not a
comonty a Christmas gambold, or a tumbling-trick?
Page.   No, my good lord, it is more pleasing stuff.
Sly.   What, household stuff?   140
Page.   It is a kind of history.
Sly.   Well, we'll see't. Come, madam wife, sit by
my side, and let the world slip, we shall ne'er be
younger.   *[They all sit.]* Flourish.

[ACT I, Scene I]

Enter Lucentio *and his man* Tranio.

Luc.   Tranio, since for the great desire I had
To see fair Padua, nursery of arts,
I am arriv'd for fruitful Lombardy,
The pleasant garden of great Italy,
And by my father's love and leave am arm'd   5
With his good will and thy good company,
My trusty servant, well approv'd in all,

---

65. **envious:** spiteful.   67. **yet:** still, even now.   81. **fay:** faith.
82. **of:** during.   86. **house:** tavern.
87. **present:** bring a charge against.   **leet:** manorial court (where complaints about short measure would be heard).
88. **seal'd:** officially stamped as a guarantee of full measure.
93. **Stephen Sly.** There was a Stratford citizen of this name.   **Greece.** Probably an error for *Greet*, the name of a village twenty miles from Stratford.
97. **amends:** Sly's error for *amendment*, i.e. recovery (as in line 129).
101. **Marry:** why, indeed (originally the name of the Virgin Mary used as an oath).   **cheer:** hospitable entertainment.
105. **goodman:** husband (a word in use among the lower classes).

115. **abandon'd:** banished.
122. **In...incur:** on peril of incurring.   130. **pleasant:** merry.
132. **sadness...blood.** That melancholy thickens the blood was a long-established medical belief.   133. **frenzy:** madness.
138. **gambold.** Perhaps Sly's blunder for *gambol* (as *comonty* is for *comedy*), but it is an old form of the word.
140. **household stuff.** The ordinary meaning is "house furnishings," but Sly may mean "domestic goings-on."   141. **history:** story.
144 s.d. **Flourish:** trumpet fanfare.

I.i. Location: Padua. A street before Baptista's house.
2. **nursery of arts.** Padua's university, founded in the thirteenth century, was famous throughout Europe.
3. **am arriv'd for:** have come here on my way to.   **fruitful:** fertile.
7. **approv'd:** tried, proved dependable.

Here let us breathe, and haply institute
A course of learning and ingenious studies.
Pisa, renowned for grave citizens,   10
Gave me my being and my father first,
A merchant of great traffic through the world,
Vincentio, come of the Bentivolii;
Vincentio's son, brought up in Florence,
It shall become to serve all hopes conceiv'd,   15
To deck his fortune with his virtuous deeds.
And therefore, Tranio, for the time I study,
Virtue and that part of philosophy
Will I apply that treats of happiness
By virtue specially to be achiev'd.   20
Tell me thy mind, for I have Pisa left
And am to Padua come, as he that leaves
A shallow plash to plunge him in the deep,
And with society seeks to quench his thirst.
    Tra. *Mi perdonato*, gentle master mine;   25
I am, in all affected as yourself,
Glad that you thus continue your resolve
To suck the sweets of sweet philosophy.
Only, good master, while we do admire
This virtue and this moral discipline,   30
Let's be no Stoics nor no stocks, I pray,
Or so devote to Aristotle's checks
As Ovid be an outcast quite abjur'd.
Balk logic with acquaintance that you have,
And practice rhetoric in your common talk,   35
Music and poesy use to quicken you,
The mathematics, and the metaphysics,
Fall to them as you find your stomach serves you:
No profit grows where is no pleasure ta'en.
In brief, sir, study what you most affect.   40
    Luc. Gramercies, Tranio, well dost thou advise.
If, Biondello, thou wert come ashore,
We could at once put us in readiness,
And take a lodging fit to entertain
Such friends as time in Padua shall beget.   45
But stay a while, what company is this?
    Tra. Master, some show to welcome us to town.

Enter Baptista *with his two daughters*, Katherina
and Bianca, Gremio, *a pantaloon*, Hortensio,
[*suitor*] *to* Bianca. Lucentio, Tranio *stand by*.

    Bap. Gentlemen, importune me no farther,
For how I firmly am resolv'd you know:
That is, not to bestow my youngest daughter   50

Before I have a husband for the elder.
If either of you both love Katherina,
Because I know you well, and love you well,
Leave shall you have to court her at your pleasure.
    Gre. To cart her rather; she's too rough for me.
There, there, Hortensio, will you any wife?   56
    Kath. [*To Baptista.*] I pray you, sir, is it your will
To make a stale of me amongst these mates?
    Hor. Mates, maid, how mean you that? No mates
        for you,
Unless you were of gentler, milder mould.   60
    Kath. I' faith, sir, you shall never need to fear.
Iwis it is not half way to her heart;
But if it were, doubt not her care should be
To comb your noddle with a three-legg'd stool,
And paint your face, and use you like a fool.   65
    Hor. From all such devils, good Lord deliver us!
    Gre. And me too, good Lord!
    Tra. Husht, master, here's some good pastime
        toward;
That wench is stark mad or wonderful froward.
    Luc. But in the other's silence do I see   70
Maid's mild behavior and sobriety.
Peace, Tranio!
    Tra. Well said, master, mum, and gaze your fill.
    Bap. Gentlemen, that I may soon make good
What I have said, Bianca, get you in,   75
And let it not displease thee, good Bianca,
For I will love thee ne'er the less, my girl.
    Kath. A pretty peat! it is best
Put finger in the eye, and she knew why.
    Bian. Sister, content you in my discontent.   80
Sir, to your pleasure humbly I subscribe;
My books and instruments shall be my company,
On them to look and practice by myself.
    Luc. Hark, Tranio, thou mayst hear Minerva
        speak.
    Hor. Signior Baptista, will you be so strange?   85
Sorry am I that our good will effects
Bianca's grief.
    Gre.   Why will you mew her up,
Signior Baptista, for this fiend of hell,
And make her bear the penance of her tongue?
    Bap. Gentlemen, content ye; I am resolv'd.   90
Go in, Bianca.   [*Exit Bianca.*]
And for I know she taketh most delight
In music, instruments, and poetry,
Schoolmasters will I keep within my house,
Fit to instruct her youth. If you, Hortensio,   95
Or, Signior Gremio, you, know any such,
Prefer them hither; for to cunning men

---

8. **breathe:** pause for breath, i.e. remain for a time. **institute:** embark upon. 9. **ingenious:** intellectual. 11. **first:** before me. 12. **traffic:** business. 15. **become:** befit. **serve:** fulfill. **conceiv'd:** i.e. entertained for him by his friends. 19. **apply:** study. 23. **plash:** pool. 24. **society:** satiety. 25. **Mi perdonato:** pardon me. 26. **affected:** disposed. 31. **stocks:** blocks of wood, i.e. beings destitute of feelings. The pun on *stoics/stocks* was commonplace. 32. **devote:** devoted. **checks:** restraints. 33. **As:** that. **Ovid:** the Latin love-poet; the antithesis is between an ascetic regimen of serious study (Aristotle) and lighter entertainment (Ovid). 34. **Balk logic:** chop logic, bandy arguments. 36. **quicken:** stimulate, enliven. 38. **Fall to:** partake of. **stomach:** appetite, inclination. 40. **affect:** find pleasing. 41. **Gramercies:** many thanks. 42. **come ashore.** Like a number of other inland cities, Padua is endowed by Shakespeare with a harbor. 47 s.d. **pantaloon:** foolish old man (a stock character in Italian comedy).

55. **cart.** Disorderly women were sometimes punished by being driven through the streets in a cart. 58. **stale:** laughingstock (but she has also in mind the sense "harlot," suggested by Gremio's jest about carting). **mates:** rude fellows. 59. **mates:** husbands. 62. **Iwis:** indeed. **it:** i.e. marriage. 65. **paint:** i.e. redden with scratches. 68. **Husht:** keep silent. **toward:** in view. 69. **froward:** perverse, refractory. 78. **peat:** pet, spoiled darling. 79. **Put . . . eye:** i.e. weep. **and:** if. 84. **Minerva:** goddess of wisdom. 85. **so strange:** i.e. so unnatural a father. 87. **mew:** shut (term for caging a falcon). 88. **for:** for the benefit of (?) or in place of (?). 89. **her . . . her:** i.e. Bianca . . . Katherina's. 97. **Prefer:** recommend. **cunning:** skillful, able.

I will be very kind, and liberal
To mine own children in good bringing-up,
And so farewell. Katherina, you may stay,   100
For I have more to commune with Bianca.   *Exit.*

Kath. Why, and I trust I may go too, may I not?
What, shall I be appointed hours, as though (belike)
I knew not what to take and what to leave? Ha! *Exit.*

Gre. You may go to the devil's dam; your gifts
are so good, here's none will hold you. Their   106
love is not so great, Hortensio, but we may blow our
nails together, and fast it fairly out. Our cake's
dough on both sides. Farewell; yet for the love
I bear my sweet Bianca, if I can by any means light
on a fit man to teach her that wherein she delights,
I will wish him to her father.   112

Hor. So will I, Signior Gremio. But a word, I
pray. Though the nature of our quarrel yet never
brook'd parle, know now upon advice, it toucheth
us both, that we may yet again have access to our
fair mistress, and be happy rivals in Bianca's love,
to labor and effect one thing specially.   118

Gre. What's that, I pray?

Hor. Marry, sir, to get a husband for her sister.

Gre. A husband! a devil.   121

Hor. I say, a husband.

Gre. I say, a devil. Think'st thou, Hortensio,
though her father be very rich, any man is so very
a fool to be married to hell?   125

Hor. Tush, Gremio; though it pass your patience
and mine to endure her loud alarums, why, man,
there be good fellows in the world, and a man could
light on them, would take her with all faults, and
money enough.   130

Gre. I cannot tell; but I had as lief take her
dowry with this condition: to be whipt at the high
cross every morning.

Hor. Faith, as you say, there's small choice
in rotten apples. But come, since this bar in   135
law makes us friends, it shall be so far forth friendly
maintain'd till by helping Baptista's eldest daughter
to a husband we set his youngest free for a husband,
and then have to't afresh. Sweet Bianca, happy man
be his dole! He that runs fastest gets the ring. How
say you, Signior Gremio?   141

Gre. I am agreed, and would I had given him the
best horse in Padua to begin his wooing that would
thoroughly woo her, wed her, and bed her, and rid
the house of her! Come on.   145

*Exeunt ambo [Gremio and Hortensio]. Manent
Tranio and Lucentio.*

101. **commune:** talk over.   105. **dam:** mother. **gifts:** endowments.
106–7. **Their love:** our love of them (i.e. women).
107–8. **blow our nails:** i.e. twiddle our thumbs, wait patiently.
108. **fast . . . out:** pass the time in abstinence.
108–9. **Our cake's dough.** Proverbial expression for failure.
109. **on both sides:** for both of us.   112. **wish:** commend.
115. **brook'd parle:** tolerated discussion. **advice:** reflection.
toucheth: behooves, concerns.   124. **very:** completely.
126. **pass:** exceeds.   128. **and:** if.
132–33. **high cross:** cross set on a pedestal in a marketplace.
135–36. **bar in law:** obstacle strong enough to halt a lawsuit.
139–40. **happy . . . dole:** may his (the successful suitor's) lot be that
of a happy man (proverbial).
140. **ring:** prize (alluding to the sport of running or riding at the ring,
which was carried off by a lance); with play on "wedding ring."
145 s.d. **ambo:** both.

Tra. I pray, sir, tell me, is it possible
That love should of a sudden take such hold?

Luc. O Tranio, till I found it to be true,
I never thought it possible or likely.
But see, while idly I stood looking on,   150
I found the effect of love in idleness,
And now in plainness do confess to thee,
That art to me as secret and as dear
As Anna to the Queen of Carthage was:
Tranio, I burn, I pine, I perish, Tranio,   155
If I achieve not this young modest girl.
Counsel me, Tranio, for I know thou canst;
Assist me, Tranio, for I know thou wilt.

Tra. Master, it is no time to chide you now,
Affection is not rated from the heart.   160
If love have touch'd you, nought remains but so,
"*Redime te captum quam queas minimo.*"

Luc. Gramercies, lad. Go forward, this contents;
The rest will comfort, for thy counsel's sound.

Tra. Master, you look'd so longly on the maid,
Perhaps you mark'd not what's the pith of all.   166

Luc. O yes, I saw sweet beauty in her face,
Such as the daughter of Agenor had,
That made great Jove to humble him to her hand,
When with his knees he kiss'd the Cretan strond.

Tra. Saw you no more? Mark'd you not how her
sister   171
Began to scold, and raise up such a storm
That mortal ears might hardly endure the din?

Luc. Tranio, I saw her coral lips to move,
And with her breath she did perfume the air.   175
Sacred and sweet was all I saw in her.

Tra. Nay, then 'tis time to stir him from his trance.
I pray, awake, sir; if you love the maid,
Bend thoughts and wits to achieve her. Thus it stands:
Her elder sister is so curst and shrewd   180
That till the father rid his hands of her,
Master, your love must live a maid at home,
And therefore has he closely mew'd her up,
Because she will not be annoy'd with suitors.

Luc. Ah, Tranio, what a cruel father's he!   185
But art thou not advis'd, he took some care
To get her cunning schoolmasters to instruct her?

Tra. Ay, marry, am I, sir; and now 'tis plotted.

Luc. I have it, Tranio.

Tra.   Master, for my hand,
Both our inventions meet and jump in one.   190

Luc. Tell me thine first.

Tra.   You will be schoolmaster,
And undertake the teaching of the maid:
That's your device.

154. **Anna:** the sister and confidante of Dido.
160. **rated:** driven away by scolding.
162. **Redime . . . minimo:** "Ransom yourself from captivity as
cheaply as you can" (Terence, *Eunuchus,* I.i.29; quoted here in the
version in Lily's Latin grammar).   163. **contents:** is satisfying.
165. **look'd . . . on:** i.e. spent so much of your time looking at.
168. **daughter of Agenor:** Europa, loved by Jupiter; he assumed the
form of a bull to carry her off.   170. **strond:** strand, shore.
180. **curst and shrewd.** The adjectives are synonyms, both meaning
here "ill-natured, shrewish."
183. **closely . . . up:** placed her in close confinement (cf. line 87).
184. **Because:** so that.   186. **advis'd:** aware.   189. **for:** by.
190. **inventions:** schemes.   **jump:** agree.

*The Taming
of the Shrew
I.i*

Luc.   It is; may it be done?

Tra. Not possible; for who shall bear your part,
And be in Padua here Vincentio's son,   195
Keep house and ply his book, welcome his friends,
Visit his countrymen, and banquet them?

Luc. *Basta,* content thee; for I have it full.
We have not yet been seen in any house,
Nor can we be distinguish'd by our faces   200
For man or master. Then it follows thus:
Thou shalt be master, Tranio, in my stead;
Keep house and port and servants, as I should.
I will some other be, some Florentine,
Some Neapolitan, or meaner man of Pisa.   205
'Tis hatch'd, and shall be so. Tranio, at once
Uncase thee; take my color'd hat and cloak.
When Biondello comes, he waits on thee,
But I will charm him first to keep his tongue.

Tra. So had you need.   210
In brief, sir, sith it your pleasure is,
And I am tied to be obedient—
For so your father charg'd me at our parting;
"Be serviceable to my son," quoth he,
Although I think 'twas in another sense—   215
I am content to be Lucentio,
Because so well I love Lucentio.

Luc. Tranio, be so, because Lucentio loves,
And let me be a slave, t' achieve that maid   219
Whose sudden sight hath thrall'd my wounded eye.

Enter BIONDELLO.

Here comes the rogue. Sirrah, where have you been?

Bion. Where have I been? Nay, how now, where
are you? Master, has my fellow Tranio stol'n your
clothes? or you stol'n his? or both? Pray what's
the news?   225

Luc. Sirrah, come hither, 'tis no time to jest,
And therefore frame your manners to the time.
Your fellow Tranio here, to save my life,
Puts my apparel and my count'nance on,
And I for my escape have put on his;   230
For in a quarrel since I came ashore
I kill'd a man, and fear I was descried.
Wait you on him, I charge you, as becomes,
While I make way from hence to save my life.
You understand me?

Bion.   Ay, sir!—[*aside*] ne'er a whit.   235

Luc. And not a jot of Tranio in your mouth,
Tranio is chang'd into Lucentio.

Bion. The better for him, would I were so too!

Tra. So could I, faith, boy, to have the next wish
after,
That Lucentio indeed had Baptista's youngest
daughter.   240
But, sirrah, not for my sake, but your master's, I
advise
You use your manners discreetly in all kind of companies.

198. **Basta:** enough. **full:** i.e. fully planned.
203. **port:** state, style of living. 205. **meaner:** of lower class.
207. **Uncase:** undress. 211. **sith:** since.
214. **serviceable:** diligent in service.
229. **count'nance:** outward appearance.

116

When I am alone, why then I am Tranio;
But in all places else [your] master Lucentio.

Luc. Tranio, let's go.   245
One thing more rests, that thyself execute—
To make one among these wooers. If thou ask me
why,
Sufficeth my reasons are both good and weighty.
                              Exeunt.

The Presenters above speaks.

1. Serv. My lord, you nod, you do not mind the
play.

Sly. Yes, by Saint Anne, do I. A good matter,
surely; comes there any more of it?   251

Page. My lord, 'tis but begun.

Sly. 'Tis a very excellent piece of work, madam
lady; would 'twere done!   *They sit and mark.*

[SCENE II]

Enter PETRUCHIO *and his man* GRUMIO.

Pet. Verona, for a while I take my leave
To see my friends in Padua, but of all
My best beloved and approved friend,
Hortensio; and I trow this is his house.
Here, sirrah Grumio, knock, I say.   5

Gru. Knock, sir? whom should I knock? Is there
any man has rebus'd your worship?

Pet. Villain, I say, knock me here soundly.

Gru. Knock you here, sir? Why, sir, what am I,
sir, that I should knock you here, sir?   10

Pet. Villain, I say, knock me at this gate,
And rap me well, or I'll knock your knave's pate.

Gru. My master is grown quarrelsome. I should
knock you first,
And then I know after who comes by the worst.

Pet. Will it not be?   15
Faith, sirrah, and you'll not knock, I'll ring it.
I'll try how you can *sol, fa,* and sing it.
                              He wrings him by the ears.

Gru. Help, [masters], help, my master is mad.

Pet. Now knock when I bid you, sirrah villain!

Enter HORTENSIO.

Hor. How now, what's the matter? My old   20
friend Grumio! and my good friend Petruchio!
How do you all at Verona?

Pet. Signior Hortensio, come you to part the fray?
Con tutto [il] core, ben trovato, may I say.   24

Hor. *Alla nostra casa ben venuto, molto honorato
signor mio Petrucio.*

248 s.d. **Presenters:** those who, by means of a prologue or an induction, introduce or present a play to the spectators.
249. **mind:** pay attention to.   254 s.d. **mark:** observe.

I.ii. Location: Padua. Before Hortensio's house.
4. **trow:** believe.   7. **rebus'd:** blunder for *abused.*
8, 11, 12. **me:** i.e. for me (but Grumio misunderstands, or pretends
to).   16. **ring.** With play on *wring.*
19. **villain:** base-born creature.
22. **How . . . all:** i.e. how are all your family.
24. **Con . . . trovato:** with all my heart, well met.
25–26. **Alla . . . Petrucio:** welcome to our house, my most honored
Signor Petruchio. (Note the spelling of the name; in Italian *ch* is
pronounced *k,* and *c* before *i* like English *ch.*)

Rise, Grumio, rise, we will compound this quarrel.

Gru. Nay, 'tis no matter, sir, what he 'leges in
Latin. If this be not a lawful cause for me to leave
his service, look you, sir. He bid me knock 30
him and rap him soundly, sir. Well, was it fit for a
servant to use his master so, being perhaps (for
aught I see) two and thirty, a peep out?
Whom would to God I had well knock'd at first,
Then had not Grumio come by the worst. 35

Pet. A senseless villain! Good Hortensio,
I bade the rascal knock upon your gate,
And could not get him for my heart to do it.

Gru. Knock at the gate? O heavens! Spake
you not these words plain, "Sirrah, knock me 40
here; rap me here; knock me well, and knock me
soundly"? And come you now with "knocking at
the gate"?

Pet. Sirrah, be gone, or talk not, I advise you.

Hor. Petruchio, patience, I am Grumio's pledge.
Why, this' a heavy chance 'twixt him and you, 46
Your ancient, trusty, pleasant servant Grumio.
And tell me now, sweet friend, what happy gale
Blows you to Padua here from old Verona?

Pet. Such wind as scatters young men through the
          world 50
To seek their fortunes farther than at home,
Where small experience grows. But in a few,
Signior Hortensio, thus it stands with me:
Antonio, my father, is deceas'd,
And I have thrust myself into this maze, 55
Happily to wive and thrive as best I may.
Crowns in my purse I have, and goods at home,
And so am come abroad to see the world.

Hor. Petruchio, shall I then come roundly to thee,
And wish thee to a shrewd ill-favor'd wife? 60
Thou'dst thank me but a little for my counsel;
And yet I'll promise thee she shall be rich,
And very rich. But th' art too much my friend,
And I'll not wish thee to her.

Pet. Signior Hortensio, 'twixt such friends as we
Few words suffice; and therefore, if thou know 66
One rich enough to be Petruchio's wife
(As wealth is burthen of my wooing dance),
Be she as foul as was Florentius' love,
As old as Sibyl, and as curst and shrowd 70
As Socrates' Xantippe, or a worse,
She moves me not, or not removes at least

Affection's edge in me. [Whe'er] she is as rough
As are the swelling Adriatic seas,
I come to wive it wealthily in Padua; 75
If wealthily, then happily in Padua.

Gru. Nay, look you, sir, he tells you flatly what
his mind is. Why, give him gold enough, and marry
him to a puppet or an aglet-baby, or an old trot with
ne'er a tooth in her head, though she have as many 80
diseases as two and fifty horses. Why, nothing comes
amiss, so money comes withal.

Hor. Petruchio, since we are stepp'd thus far in,
I will continue that I broach'd in jest.
I can, Petruchio, help thee to a wife 85
With wealth enough, and young and beauteous,
Brought up as best becomes a gentlewoman.
Her only fault, and that is faults enough,
Is that she is intolerable curst
And shrowd and froward, so beyond all measure, 90
That were my state far worser than it is,
I would not wed her for a mine of gold.

Pet. Hortensio, peace! thou know'st not gold's
          effect.
Tell me her father's name, and 'tis enough;
For I will board her, though she chide as loud 95
As thunder when the clouds in autumn crack.

Hor. Her father is Baptista Minola,
An affable and courteous gentleman.
Her name is Katherina Minola,
Renown'd in Padua for her scolding tongue. 100

Pet. I know her father, though I know not her,
And he knew my deceased father well.
I will not sleep, Hortensio, till I see her,
And therefore let me be thus bold with you
To give you over at this first encounter, 105
Unless you will accompany me thither.

Gru. I pray you, sir, let him go while the humor
lasts. A' my word, and she knew him as well as I do,
she would think scolding would do little good upon
him. She may perhaps call him half a score 110
knaves or so. Why, that's nothing; and he begin
once, he'll rail in his rope-tricks. I'll tell you what,
sir, and she stand him but a little, he will throw a
figure in her face, and so disfigure her with it, that she
shall have no more eyes to see withal than a cat.
You know him not, sir. 116

Hor. Tarry, Petruchio, I must go with thee,
For in Baptista's keep my treasure is.
He hath the jewel of my life in hold,
His youngest daughter, beautiful Bianca, 120
And her withholds from me [and] other more,

---

27. compound: settle.   28. 'leges: alleges.
33. two . . . out: slang for "drunk" (deriving from the card game
trentuno, or one and thirty; *peep* = pip, a spot on a playing card, and
a peep out = off by one).   45. pledge: surety.
46. this': this is.   heavy chance: sad happening.
47. ancient: of long standing.
52. in a few: in brief.   59. come roundly: speak plainly.
68. burthen: burden, ground bass or undersong.
69. foul: ugly.   Florentius' love. A reference to a story best known
from Chaucer's *Canterbury Tales*, where it is assigned to the Wife of
Bath. Sir Florent promises to marry an old hag if she will tell him the
answer to a riddle on which his life depends. After their marriage
she becomes young and beautiful. The story is told also by Chaucer's
contemporary John Gower in his *Confessio Amantis*, a book that
Shakespeare used as a source in another early play, *The Comedy of
Errors*.
70. Sibyl: prophetess of Cumae to whom Apollo gave as many years
of life as she could hold grains of sand in her hand.   shrowd: shrewd,
i.e. shrewish.   71. Xantippe. Proverbial for shrewishness.
72. moves: disturbs, troubles.

72-73. or . . . me: nor dulls in the least the keenness of my inclination
(to marry her for her wealth).   78. mind: intention.
79. aglet-baby: small metal figure serving as the tag on a lacing-cord.
trot: common prostitute.   82. withal: with it.   84. that: what.
91. state: estate, means.
95. board: accost, make advances to (literally, come alongside a
ship in order to attack).   chide: rail, brawl.   *Scold* (see line 100) is
synonymous.   105. give you over: leave you.
107. humor: mood, whim.
112. rope-tricks: blunder for *rhetorics* (an interpretation supported
by *figure* in line 114) (?) or tricks that deserve hanging (?).
113. stand: withstand.   115. withal: with.
118. keep: keeping, custody; perhaps also with the sense of "fortified
place" (cf. *dungeon keep*) or "strongroom." *Hold* in line 119 is
parallel.

The Taming
of the Shrew
I.ii

Suitors to her and rivals in my love;
Supposing it a thing impossible,
For those defects I have before rehears'd,
That ever Katherina will be woo'd.   125
Therefore this order hath Baptista ta'en,
That none shall have access unto Bianca
Till Katherine the curst have got a husband.
    Gru. Katherine the curst!
A title for a maid of all titles the worst.   130
    Hor. Now shall my friend Petruchio do me grace,
And offer me disguis'd in sober robes
To old Baptista as a schoolmaster
Well seen in music, to instruct Bianca,
That so I may by this device at least   135
Have leave and leisure to make love to her,
And unsuspected court her by herself.

Enter GREMIO, *and* LUCENTIO *disguised [as a school-*
master].

    Gru. Here's no knavery! See, to beguile the old
folks, how the young folks lay their heads together!
Master, master, look about you! Who goes there? ha!
    Hor. Peace, Grumio, it is the rival of my love.
Petruchio, stand by a while.   142
    Gru. A proper stripling, and an amorous!
                              [*They stand aside.*]
    Gre. O, very well, I have perus'd the note.
Hark you, sir, I'll have them very fairly bound— 145
All books of love, see that at any hand—
And see you read no other lectures to her.
You understand me. Over and beside
Signior Baptista's liberality,
I'll mend it with a largess. Take your paper too,
And let me have them very well perfum'd;   151
For she is sweeter than perfume itself
To whom they go to. What will you read to her?
    Luc. What e'er I read to her, I'll plead for you
As for my patron, stand you so assur'd,   155
As firmly as yourself were still in place,
Yea, and perhaps with more successful words
Than you—unless you were a scholar, sir.
    Gre. O this learning, what a thing it is!
    Gru. O this woodcock, what an ass it is!   160
    Pet. Peace, sirrah!
    Hor. Grumio, mum! [*Coming forward.*] God save
        you, Signior Gremio.
    Gre. And you are well met, Signior Hortensio.
Trow you whither I am going? To Baptista Minola.
I promis'd to inquire carefully   165
About a schoolmaster for the fair Bianca,
And by good fortune I have lighted well

On this young man; for learning and behavior
Fit for her turn, well read in poetry
And other books, good ones, I warrant ye.   170
    Hor. 'Tis well; and I have met a gentleman
Hath promis'd me to help [me] to another,
A fine musician to instruct our mistress;
So shall I no whit be behind in duty
To fair Bianca, so beloved of me.   175
    Gre. Beloved of me, and that my deeds shall prove.
    Gru. And that his bags shall prove.
    Hor. Gremio, 'tis now no time to vent our love;
Listen to me, and if you speak me fair,
I'll tell you news indifferent good for either.   180
Here is a gentleman whom by chance I met,
Upon agreement from us to his liking,
Will undertake to woo curst Katherine,
Yea, and to marry her, if her dowry please.
    Gre. So said, so done, is well.   185
Hortensio, have you told him all her faults?
    Pet. I know she is an irksome brawling scold.
If that be all, masters, I hear no harm.
    Gre. No, say'st me so, friend? What country-
        man?
    Pet. Born in Verona, old [Antonio's] son.   190
My father dead, my fortune lives for me,
And I do hope good days and long to see.
    Gre. O sir, such a life, with such a wife, were
        strange;
But if you have a stomach, to't a' God's name;
You shall have me assisting you in all.   195
But will you woo this wild-cat?
    Pet.   Will I live?
    Gru. Will he woo her? ay—or I'll hang her.
    Pet. Why came I hither but to that intent?
Think you a little din can daunt mine ears?
Have I not in my time heard lions roar?   200
Have I not heard the sea, puff'd up with winds,
Rage like an angry boar chafed with sweat?
Have I not heard great ordnance in the field,
And heaven's artillery thunder in the skies?
Have I not in a pitched battle heard   205
Loud 'larums, neighing steeds, and trumpets' clang?
And do you tell me of a woman's tongue,
That gives not half so great a blow to hear
As will a chestnut in a farmer's fire?
Tush, tush, fear boys with bugs.
    Gru.   For he fears none.
    Gre. Hortensio, hark.   211
This gentleman is happily arriv'd,
My mind presumes, for his own good and [ours].
    Hor. I promis'd we would be contributors,
And bear his charge of wooing, whatsoe'er.   215
    Gre. And so we will, provided that he win her.
    Gru. I would I were as sure of a good dinner.

---

131. **grace:** a favor.   134. **seen:** versed.
141. **love:** i.e. love-suit.
143. **proper stripling:** handsome young man (ironically alluding to
Gremio).
144. **note.** Evidently a memorandum from the supposed schoolmaster about books for Bianca.
145. **I'll have them:** I desire them to be, i.e. see that they are.   **fairly:**
handsomely.   146. **at any hand:** in any case.
147. **read . . . lectures:** teach . . . subjects.
150. **mend:** augment.   **largess:** liberal gift.   **paper:** i.e. the "note"
of line 144.   151. **them:** i.e. the books.
156. **as:** i.e. as if.   **in place:** present.
160. **woodcock.** A bird easily caught, hence proverbial for stupidity.
164. **Trow:** know.

177. **bags:** i.e. money bags.   178. **vent:** express.
179. **fair:** courteously, civilly.   180. **indifferent:** equally.
182. **Upon . . . liking:** who, if we will meet the terms he wants (see
lines 214–15).
194. **a':** of, i.e. in.   202. **chafed:** irritated.
203. **ordnance:** cannon.   206. **'larums:** alarums, calls to arms.
208. **blow:** blasting noise.
210. **fear . . . bugs:** frighten children with bogeymen.
212. **happily:** propitiously.   215. **charge:** expense.

Enter TRANIO *brave*, [*as Lucentio*,] *and* BIONDELLO.

Tra. Gentlemen, God save you. If I may be bold,
Tell me, I beseech you, which is the readiest way
To the house of Signior Baptista Minola?   220
Bion. He that has the two fair daughters? is't he
   you mean?
Tra. Even he, Biondello.
Gre. Hark you, sir, you mean not her to—
Tra. Perhaps him and her, sir; what have you
   to do?   224
Pet. Not her that chides, sir, at any hand, I pray.
Tra. I love no chiders, sir. Biondello, let's away.
Luc. [*Aside.*] Well begun, Tranio.
Hor.   Sir, a word ere you go.
Are you a suitor to the maid you talk of, yea or no?
Tra. And if I be, sir, is it any offense?
Gre. No; if without more words you will get you
   hence.   230
Tra. Why, sir, I pray, are not the streets as free
For me as for you?
Gre.   But so is not she.
Tra. For what reason, I beseech you?
Gre.   For this reason, if you'll know,
That she's the choice love of Signior Gremio.   234
Hor. That she's the chosen of Signior Hortensio.
Tra. Softly, my masters! If you be gentlemen,
Do me this right: hear me with patience.
Baptista is a noble gentleman,
To whom my father is not all unknown,
And were his daughter fairer than she is,   240
She may more suitors have, and me for one.
Fair Leda's daughter had a thousand wooers,
Then well one more may fair Bianca have;
And so she shall. Lucentio shall make one,
Though Paris came in hope to speed alone.   245
Gre. What, this gentleman will out-talk us all.
Luc. Sir, give him head, I know he'll prove a jade.
Pet. Hortensio, to what end are all these words?
Hor. Sir, let me be so bold as ask you,
Did you yet ever see Baptista's daughter?   250
Tra. No, sir, but hear I do that he hath two:
The one as famous for a scolding tongue,
As is the other for beauteous modesty.
Pet. Sir, sir, the first's for me, let her go by.
Gre. Yea, leave that labor to great Hercules,   255
And let it be more than Alcides' twelve.
Pet. Sir, understand you this of me, in sooth:
The youngest daughter, whom you hearken for,
Her father keeps from all access of suitors,
And will not promise her to any man,   260
Until the elder sister first be wed.
The younger then is free, and not before.
Tra. If it be so, sir, that you are the man
Must stead us all, and me amongst the rest;

And if you break the ice, and do this [feat],   265
Achieve the elder, set the younger free
For our access—whose hap shall be to have her
Will not so graceless be to be ingrate.
Hor. Sir, you say well, and well you do conceive,
And since you do profess to be a suitor,   270
You must, as we do, gratify this gentleman,
To whom we all rest generally beholding.
Tra. Sir, I shall not be slack; in sign whereof,
Please ye we may contrive this afternoon,
And quaff carouses to our mistress' health,   275
And do as adversaries do in law,
Strive mightily, but eat and drink as friends.
Gru., Bion. O excellent motion! Fellows, let's be
   gone.
Hor. The motion's good indeed, and be it so,
Petruchio, I shall be your *ben venuto.*   *Exeunt.*   280

[ACT II, SCENE I]

Enter KATHERINA *and* BIANCA.

Bian. Good sister, wrong me not, nor wrong
   yourself,
To make a bondmaid and a slave of me—
That I disdain; but for these other [gawds],
Unbind my hands, I'll pull them off myself,
Yea, all my raiment, to my petticoat,   5
Or what you will command me will I do,
So well I know my duty to my elders.
Kath. Of all thy suitors here I charge [thee] tell
Whom thou lov'st best; see thou dissemble not.
Bian. Believe me, sister, of all the men alive   10
I never yet beheld that special face
Which I could fancy more than any other.
Kath. Minion, thou liest. Is't not Hortensio?
Bian. If you affect him, sister, here I swear
I'll plead for you myself, but you shall have him.   15
Kath. O then belike you fancy riches more:
You will have Gremio to keep you fair.
Bian. Is it for him you do envy me so?
Nay then you jest, and now I well perceive
You have but jested with me all this while.   20
I prithee, sister Kate, untie my hands.
Kath. If that be jest, then all the rest was so.
                                   Strikes her.

Enter BAPTISTA.

Bap. Why, how now, dame, whence grows this
   insolence?
Bianca, stand aside. Poor girl, she weeps.
Go ply thy needle, meddle not with her.   25
For shame, thou hilding of a devilish spirit,

---

217. **s.d. brave:** finely dressed.   224. **what . . . do:** what is it to you.
236. **Softly:** gently.   237. **right:** justice.
242. **Fair Leda's daughter:** Helen of Troy.
245. **Paris:** Trojan prince who won Helen from her husband, King Menelaus of Sparta.   **came:** were to come.   **speed:** succeed.
247. **jade:** ill-conditioned horse (not likely to finish the course).
256. **Alcides' twelve:** i.e. the twelve labors of Hercules (the descendant of Alcaeus).   257. **sooth:** truth.
258. **hearken:** lie in wait.   264. **stead:** help.

267. **whose hap:** he whose good fortune.
269. **conceive:** understand.   271. **gratify:** reward.
272. **generally:** as a whole.   **beholding:** beholden, indebted.
274. **contrive:** spend, pass (time).   275. **carouses:** toasts.
276. **adversaries:** i.e. lawyers on opposite sides of a case.
280. **ben venuto:** welcome, i.e. host.

II.i. **Location:** Padua. Baptista's house.
3. **gawds:** ornaments.   12. **fancy:** love.   13. **Minion:** hussy.
14. **affect:** love.   17. **fair:** finely dressed.   18. **envy:** hate.
26. **hilding:** good-for-nothing jade.

The Taming of the Shrew II.i

*The Taming
of the Shrew*
II.i

Why dost thou wrong her that did ne'er wrong thee?
When did she cross thee with a bitter word?
    Kath. Her silence flouts me, and I'll be reveng'd.
                                Flies after Bianca.
    Bap. What, in my sight? Bianca, get thee in. 30
                                  Exit [*Bianca*].
    Kath. What, will you not suffer me? Nay, now I
    see
She is your treasure, she must have a husband;
I must dance barefoot on her wedding-day,
And for your love to her lead apes in hell.
Talk not to me, I will go sit and weep, 35
Till I can find occasion of revenge.   [*Exit.*]
    Bap. Was ever gentleman thus griev'd as I?
But who comes here?

Enter GREMIO, LUCENTIO *in the habit of a mean man,*
PETRUCHIO *with* [HORTENSIO *as a musician, and*]
TRANIO [*as Lucentio*] *with his boy* [BIONDELLO]
bearing a lute and books.

    Gre. Good morrow, neighbor Baptista. 39
    Bap. Good morrow, neighbor Gremio. God save
you, gentlemen!
    Pet. And you, good sir! Pray have you not a
    daughter
Call'd Katherina, fair and virtuous?
    Bap. I have a daughter, sir, call'd Katherina.
    Gre. You are too blunt, go to it orderly. 45
    Pet. You wrong me, Signior Gremio, give me leave.
I am a gentleman of Verona, sir,
That hearing of her beauty and her wit,
Her affability and bashful modesty,
Her wondrous qualities and mild behavior, 50
Am bold to show myself a forward guest
Within your house, to make mine eye the witness
Of that report which I so oft have heard.
And for an entrance to my entertainment,
I do present you with a man of mine, 55
                        [Presenting Hortensio.]
Cunning in music and the mathematics,
To instruct her fully in those sciences,
Whereof I know she is not ignorant.
Accept of him, or else you do me wrong.
His name is Litio, born in Mantua. 60
    Bap. Y' are welcome, sir, and he, for your good
    sake.
But for my daughter Katherine, this I know,
She is not for your turn, the more my grief.
    Pet. I see you do not mean to part with her,
Or else you like not of my company. 65
    Bap. Mistake me not, I speak but as I find.
Whence are you, sir? What may I call your name?
    Pet. Petruchio is my name, Antonio's son,
A man well known throughout all Italy.
    Bap. I know him well; you are welcome for his
    sake. 70

    Gre. Saving your tale, Petruchio, I pray
Let us that are poor petitioners speak too.
[Backare]! you are marvellous forward.
    Pet. O, pardon me, Signior Gremio, I would fain
    be doing.
    Gre. I doubt it not, sir; but you will curse your
    wooing. 75
[Neighbor], this is a gift very grateful, I am sure of
it. To express the like kindness, myself, that have
been more kindly beholding to you than any, freely
give unto [you] this young scholar [*presenting Lucentio*], that hath been long studying at Rheims, as 80
cunning in Greek, Latin, and other languages, as
the other in music and mathematics. His name is
Cambio; pray accept his service.
    Bap. A thousand thanks, Signior Gremio. Wel-
come, good Cambio. [*To Tranio.*] But, gentle 85
sir, methinks you walk like a stranger. May I be so
bold to know the cause of your coming?
    Tra. Pardon me, sir, the boldness is mine own,
That being a stranger in this city here,
Do make myself a suitor to your daughter, 90
Unto Bianca, fair and virtuous.
Nor is your firm resolve unknown to me,
In the preferment of the eldest sister.
This liberty is all that I request,
That upon knowledge of my parentage, 95
I may have welcome 'mongst the rest that woo,
And free access and favor as the rest;
And toward the education of your daughters,
I here bestow a simple instrument,
And this small packet of Greek and Latin books. 100
If you accept them, then their worth is great.
    Bap. Lucentio is your name, of whence, I pray?
    Tra. Of Pisa, sir, son to Vincentio.
    Bap. A mighty man of Pisa; by report
I know him well. You are very welcome, sir. 105
Take you the lute, and you the set of books.
You shall go see your pupils presently.
Holla, within!

                Enter a SERVANT.

          Sirrah, lead these gentlemen
To my daughters, and tell them both,
These are their tutors. Bid them use them well. 110
         [*Exit Servant with Lucentio and Hortensio,
         Biondello following.*]
We will go walk a little in the orchard,
And then to dinner. You are passing welcome,
And so I pray you all to think yourselves.
    Pet. Signior Baptista, my business asketh haste,
And every day I cannot come to woo. 115
You knew my father well, and in him me,
Left soly heir to all his lands and goods,
Which I have bettered rather than decreas'd.

33–34. **dance . . . hell.** Both proverbial fates assigned to old maids.
38 s.d. **mean:** of low rank (i.e. Lucentio is in his disguise as the schoolmaster Cambio).
45. **orderly:** properly, i.e. more ceremoniously.
50. **qualities:** natural gifts.
54. **for an entrance:** as an entrance fee.   **entertainment:** reception.
66. **as I find:** i.e. as the facts stand.
70. **I . . . well:** i.e. his name is well known to me.

71. **Saving:** with all respect for.
73. **Backare:** stand back (pseudo-Latin).
74. **would . . . doing:** am eager to get on with the business (*doing* is also slang for "having sexual intercourse").
86. **stranger:** foreigner.   97. **favor:** leave, permission.
102. **Lucentio . . . name.** As Baptista presumably learns from the inscriptions in the books.   104. **report:** reputation.
107. **presently:** immediately.   111. **orchard:** garden.
112. **passing:** exceedingly.   117. **soly:** solely.

Then tell me, if I get your daughter's love,
What dowry shall I have with her to wife?   120
  Bap. After my death, the one half of my lands,
And in possession twenty thousand crowns.
  Pet. And for that dowry, I'll assure her of
Her widowhood, be it that she survive me,
In all my lands and leases whatsoever.   125
Let specialties be therefore drawn between us,
That covenants may be kept on either hand.
  Bap. Ay, when the special thing is well obtain'd,
That is, her love; for that is all in all.
  Pet. Why, that is nothing; for I tell you, father,
I am as peremptory as she proud-minded;   131
And where two raging fires meet together,
They do consume the thing that feeds their fury.
Though little fire grows great with little wind,
Yet extreme gusts will blow out fire and all;   135
So I to her, and so she yields to me,
For I am rough, and woo not like a babe.
  Bap. Well mayst thou woo, and happy be thy
    speed!
But be thou arm'd for some unhappy words.
  Pet. Ay, to the proof, as mountains are for winds,
That [shake] not, though they blow perpetually.   141

Enter HORTENSIO [*as Litio*] *with his head broke.*

  Bap. How now, my friend, why dost thou look
    so pale?
  Hor. For fear, I promise you, if I look pale.
  Bap. What, will my daughter prove a good musi-
    cian?
  Hor. I think she'll sooner prove a soldier,   145
Iron may hold with her, but never lutes.
  Bap. Why then thou canst not break her to the lute?
  Hor. Why no, for she hath broke the lute to me.
I did but tell her she mistook her frets,
And bow'd her hand to teach her fingering;   150
When, with a most impatient devilish spirit,
"Frets, call you these?" quoth she, "I'll fume with
    them."
And with that word she strook me on the head,
And through the instrument my pate made way,
And there I stood amazed for a while,   155
As on a pillory, looking through the lute,
While she did call me rascal fiddler
And twangling Jack, with twenty such vild terms,
As had she studied to misuse me so.
  Pet. Now by the world, it is a lusty wench!   160
I love her ten times more than e'er I did.
O, how I long to have some chat with her!
  Bap. Well, go with me and be not so discomfited.
Proceed in practice with my younger daughter;

---

122. **possession**: i.e. immediate possession.
124. **widowhood**: widow's share of the estate.
126. **specialties**: express contracts.
133. **They . . . fury**: i.e. they cancel each other out (pride meets pride). 138. **speed**: fortune. 139. **unhappy**: hateful.
140. **to the proof**: in proved (tested) armor.
141 s.d. **with . . . broke**: with a bleeding cut on his head.
146. **hold with her**: stand her usage. 147. **break**: train.
149. **frets**: bars for fingering on a lute. 150. **bow'd**: bent.
152. **fume**. With obvious play on *fret* in the sense "be vexed."
155. **amazed**: in confusion.
158. **twangling Jack**: twanging knave. **vild**: vile.
159. **As**: as if. 160. **lusty**: lively, vigorous.

She's apt to learn, and thankful for good turns.   165
Signior Petruchio, will you go with us,
Or shall I send my daughter Kate to you?
  Pet. I pray you do. I'll attend her here,
    Exit [*Baptista with Gremio, Tranio, and Hortensio*].
    Manet Petruchio.
And woo her with some spirit when she comes.
Say that she rail, why then I'll tell her plain   170
She sings as sweetly as a nightingale;
Say that she frown, I'll say she looks as clear
As morning roses newly wash'd with dew;
Say she be mute, and will not speak a word,
Then I'll commend her volubility,   175
And say she uttereth piercing eloquence;
If she do bid me pack, I'll give her thanks,
As though she bid me stay by her a week;
If she deny to wed, I'll crave the day
When I shall ask the banes, and when be married.   180
But here she comes, and now, Petruchio, speak.

Enter KATHERINA.

Good morrow, Kate, for that's your name, I hear.
  Kath. Well have you heard, but something hard
    of hearing:
They call me Katherine that do talk of me.   184
  Pet. You lie, in faith, for you are call'd plain Kate,
And bonny Kate, and sometimes Kate the curst;
But Kate, the prettiest Kate in Christendom,
Kate of Kate-Hall, my super-dainty Kate,
For dainties are all Kates, and therefore, Kate,
Take this of me, Kate of my consolation—   190
Hearing thy mildness prais'd in every town,
Thy virtues spoke of, and thy beauty sounded,
Yet not so deeply as to thee belongs,
Myself am mov'd to woo thee for my wife.
  Kath. Mov'd! in good time! Let him that mov'd
    you hither   195
Remove you hence. I knew you at the first
You were a moveable.
  Pet.   Why, what's a moveable?
  Kath. A join'd-stool.
  Pet.   Thou hast hit it; come sit on me.
  Kath. Asses are made to bear, and so are you.
  Pet. Women are made to bear, and so are you.
  Kath. No such jade as you, if me you mean.   201
  Pet. Alas, good Kate, I will not burthen thee,
For knowing thee to be but young and light.

---

165. **apt**: willing, quick. 168. **attend**: await.
172. **clear**: cheerful, serene. 177. **pack**: be gone.
179. **deny**: refuse. **crave the day**: inquire the date.
180. **ask the banes**: have the banns read.
183. **something**: somewhat.
188. **Kate-Hall**. Kate is so well spoken of that her residence takes its name from her rather than from her family or her father.
189. **Kates**. A play on *cates*, "delicacies." Many editors read *cates*.
192. **sounded**: proclaimed (but *deeply* in the next line indicates a quibble on the sense "plumbed").
195. **in good time**: indeed, forsooth.
197. **moveable**. With pun on "piece of furniture."
198. **join'd-stool**: a stool with legs fitted into it, a good piece of joinery.
199. **bear**: carry (with following puns on "bear children" and "support a man during sexual intercourse").
201. **jade**: a horse that soon tires. 202. **burthen**: burden.
203. **For knowing**: because I know. **light**: (1) delicate, slight; (2) wanton; (3) lacking a burden in the musical sense of "having no ground bass."

The Taming of the Shrew II.i

Kath. Too light for such a swain as you to catch,
And yet as heavy as my weight should be. 205
Pet. Should be! should—buzz!
Kath.   Well ta'en, and like a buzzard.
Pet. O slow-wing'd turtle, shall a buzzard take thee?
Kath. Ay, for a turtle, as he takes a buzzard.
Pet. Come, come, you wasp, i' faith you are too angry.
Kath. If I be waspish, best beware my sting. 210
Pet. My remedy is then to pluck it out.
Kath. Ay, if the fool could find it where it lies.
Pet. Who knows not where a wasp does wear his sting?
In his tail.
Kath. In his tongue. 215
Pet. Whose tongue?
Kath. Yours, if you talk of tales, and so farewell.
Pet. What, with my tongue in your tail? Nay, come again,
Good Kate; I am a gentleman—
Kath.   That I'll try. *She strikes him.*
Pet. I swear I'll cuff you, if you strike again. 220
Kath. So may you lose your arms.
If you strike me, you are no gentleman,
And if no gentleman, why then no arms.
Pet. A herald, Kate? O, put me in thy books!
Kath. What is your crest? a coxcomb? 225
Pet. A combless cock, so Kate will be my hen.
Kath. No cock of mine, you crow too like a craven.
Pet. Nay, come, Kate, come; you must not look so sour.
Kath. It is my fashion when I see a crab.
Pet. Why, here's no crab, and therefore look not sour. 230
Kath. There is, there is.
Pet. Then show it me.
Kath. Had I a glass, I would.
Pet. What, you mean my face?
Kath. Well aim'd of such a young one. 235
Pet. Now, by Saint George, I am too young for you.
Kath. Yet you are wither'd.
Pet. 'Tis with cares.
Kath. I care not.
Pet. Nay, hear you, Kate. In sooth you scape not so. 240
Kath. I chafe you if I tarry. Let me go.

204. **light:** quick, elusive. **swain:** young rustic, country bumpkin.
206. **buzz.** Punning on *be/bee*, with the rude implication that her remark makes no more sense than a buzzing sound. **buzzard:** fool (figuratively). In line 207 the word denotes an inferior kind of hawk, in line 208 a buzzing insect (which prompts Petruchio's *wasp* in line 209). 207. **turtle:** turtledove.
217. **talk of tales:** talk idly (with obvious pun).
223. **arms:** coat of arms.
224. **herald:** authority on heraldry. **books:** (1) heraldic registers; (2) good books, i.e. favor.
225. **crest:** (1) heraldic device; (2) comb, as on a cock's head. **coxcomb.** The badge of the court fool.
226. **combless:** gentle, with crest cut down.
227. **craven:** a cock that will not fight. 229. **crab:** crab apple.
235. **aim'd of:** guessed for. 236. **young:** i.e. strong.
240. **scape:** escape.
241. **chafe:** (1) irritate; (2) inflame, excite.

122

Pet. No, not a whit, I find you passing gentle:
'Twas told me you were rough and coy and sullen,
And now I find report a very liar; 244
For thou art pleasant, gamesome, passing courteous,
But slow in speech, yet sweet as spring-time flowers.
Thou canst not frown, thou canst not look askaunce,
Nor bite the lip, as angry wenches will,
Nor hast thou pleasure to be cross in talk;
But thou with mildness entertain'st thy wooers, 250
With gentle conference, soft, and affable.
Why does the world report that Kate doth limp?
O sland'rous world! Kate like the hazel-twig
Is straight and slender, and as brown in hue
As hazel-nuts, and sweeter than the kernels. 255
O, let me see thee walk. Thou dost not halt.
Kath. Go, fool, and whom thou keep'st command.
Pet. Did ever Dian so become a grove
As Kate this chamber with her princely gait?
O, be thou Dian, and let her be Kate, 260
And then let Kate be chaste, and Dian sportful!
Kath. Where did you study all this goodly speech?
Pet. It is extempore, from my mother-wit.
Kath. A witty mother! witless else her son.
Pet. Am I not wise? 265
Kath. Yes, keep you warm.
Pet. Marry, so I mean, sweet Katherine, in thy bed;
And therefore setting all this chat aside,
Thus in plain terms: your father hath consented
That you shall be my wife; your dowry 'greed on;
And will you, nill you, I will marry you. 271
Now, Kate, I am a husband for your turn,
For by this light whereby I see thy beauty,
Thy beauty that doth make me like thee well,
Thou must be married to no man but me; 275
For I am he am born to tame you, Kate,
And bring you from a wild Kate to a Kate
Conformable as other household Kates.

Enter BAPTISTA, GREMIO, TRANIO [*as Lucentio*].

Here comes your father. Never make denial;
I must and will have Katherine to my wife. 280
Bap. Now, Signior Petruchio, how speed you with my daughter?
Pet. How but well, sir? how but well?
It were impossible I should speed amiss.
Bap. Why, how now, daughter Katherine, in your dumps? 284
Kath. Call you me daughter? Now I promise you
You have show'd a tender fatherly regard,
To wish me wed to one half lunatic,
A madcap ruffian and a swearing Jack,

243. **coy:** disdainful.
246. **But:** not other than. 247. **askaunce:** scornfully.
251. **conference:** conversation. 256. **halt:** limp.
257. **whom . . . command:** i.e. command your servants, not me.
258. **Dian:** Diana, goddess of the hunt and of chastity.
261. **sportful:** amorous.
266. **keep you warm.** Alluding to the proverbial "wit enough to keep oneself warm" (cf. "sense enough to come in out of the rain"), which she implies is as much wit as he possesses.
271. **nill you:** will you not. 272. **for your turn:** to suit you.
277. **wild Kate.** Perhaps with a pun on *wildcat*.
281. **speed:** succeed, fare. 284. **in your dumps:** downcast.
285. **promise:** assure.

That thinks with oaths to face the matter out.

Pet. Father, 'tis thus: yourself and all the world,
That talk'd of her, have talk'd amiss of her.   291
If she be curst, it is for policy,
For she's not froward, but modest as the dove;
She is not hot, but temperate as the morn;
For patience she will prove a second Grissel,   295
And Roman Lucrece for her chastity;
And to conclude, we have 'greed so well together
That upon Sunday is the wedding-day.

Kath. I'll see thee hang'd on Sunday first.

Gre. Hark, Petruchio, she says she'll see thee
hang'd first.   300

Tra. Is this your speeding? Nay then good night
our part!

Pet. Be patient, gentlemen, I choose her for myself.
If she and I be pleas'd, what's that to you?
'Tis bargain'd 'twixt us twain, being alone,
That she shall still be curst in company.   305
I tell you 'tis incredible to believe
How much she loves me. O, the kindest Kate,
She hung about my neck, and kiss on kiss
She vied so fast, protesting oath on oath,
That in a twink she won me to her love.   310
O, you are novices! 'tis a world to see
How tame, when men and women are alone,
A meacock wretch can make the curstest shrew.
Give me thy hand, Kate, I will unto Venice
To buy apparel 'gainst the wedding-day.   315
Provide the feast, father, and bid the guests,
I will be sure my Katherine shall be fine.

Bap. I know not what to say, but give me your
hands.
God send you joy, Petruchio, 'tis a match.

Gre., Tra. Amen, say we. We will be witnesses.

Pet. Father, and wife, and gentlemen, adieu.   321
I will to Venice, Sunday comes apace.
We will have rings and things, and fine array;
And kiss me, Kate, we will be married a' Sunday.

Exeunt Petruchio and Katherine [severally].

Gre. Was ever match clapp'd up so suddenly?   325

Bap. Faith, gentlemen, now I play a merchant's
part,
And venture madly on a desperate mart.

Tra. 'Twas a commodity lay fretting by you;
'Twill bring you gain, or perish on the seas.

Bap. The gain I seek is, quiet [in] the match.   330

Gre. No doubt but he hath got a quiet catch.
But now, Baptista, to your younger daughter;
Now is the day we long have looked for.
I am your neighbor, and was suitor first.

Tra. And I am one that love Bianca more   335
Than words can witness, or your thoughts can guess.

Gre. Youngling, thou canst not love so dear as I.

Tra. Greybeard, thy love doth freeze.

Gre.   But thine doth fry.
Skipper, stand back, 'tis age that nourisheth.

Tra. But youth in ladies' eyes that flourisheth.

Bap. Content you, gentlemen, I will compound
this strife.   341
'Tis deeds must win the prize, and he of both
That can assure my daughter greatest dower
Shall have my Bianca's love.
Say, Signior Gremio, what can you assure her?   345

Gre. First, as you know, my house within the city
Is richly furnished with plate and gold,
Basins and ewers to lave her dainty hands;
My hangings all of Tyrian tapestry;
In ivory coffers I have stuff'd my crowns;   350
In cypress chests my arras counterpoints,
Costly apparel, tents, and canopies,
Fine linen, Turkey cushions boss'd with pearl,
Valens of Venice gold in needle-work;
Pewter and brass, and all things that belongs   355
To house or house-keeping. Then at my farm
I have a hundred milch-kine to the pail,
Six score fat oxen standing in my stalls,
And all things answerable to this portion.
Myself am strook in years, I must confess,   360
And if I die to-morrow, this is hers,
If whilst I live she will be only mine.

Tra. That "only" came in well. Sir, list to me:
I am my father's heir and only son.
If I may have your daughter to my wife,   365
I'll leave her houses three or four as good,
Within rich Pisa walls, as any one
Old Signior Gremio has in Padua,
Besides two thousand ducats by the year
Of fruitful land, all which shall be her jointer.   370
What, have I pinch'd you, Signior Gremio?

Gre. Two thousand ducats by the year of land!
[Aside.] My land amounts not to so much in all.—
That she shall have, besides an argosy
That now is lying in Marsellis road.   375
What, have I chok'd you with an argosy?

Tra. Gremio, 'tis known my father hath no less
Than three great argosies, besides two galliasses
And twelve tight galleys. These I will assure her,
And twice as much, what e'er thou off'rest next.   380

Gre. Nay, I have off'red all, I have no more,
And she can have no more than all I have;
If you like me, she shall have me and mine.

289. **face:** brazen.   292. **policy:** crafty purpose.
295. **Grissel:** patient Griselda, a model of wifely submission. Her
story is told by the Clerk in Chaucer's *Canterbury Tales.*
296. **Lucrece:** Lucretia, who committed suicide after her rape by
Sextus Tarquinius. Shakespeare told the story in *The Rape of Lucrece.*
309. **vied:** i.e. kept matching in an effort to go me one better.
311. **a world:** worth a world, matter for wonder.
313. **meacock:** timid.   315. **'gainst:** in preparation for.
317. **fine:** handsomely dressed.   325. **clapp'd up:** settled.
327. **mart:** bargain.
328. **fretting:** decaying in disuse (with a play on "irritable").

337. **dear.** With a play on "expensively."
339. **Skipper:** flighty fellow.
341. **Content you:** be calm. **compound:** settle.
342-43. **he . . . That:** whichever of you two.
343. **assure:** convey (property).   349. **Tyrian:** purple or dark red.
351. **arras counterpoints:** tapestry counterpanes.
352. **tents:** bed hangings.   353. **boss'd:** embossed, studded.
354. **Valens:** valances, fringes or short draperies edging bed canopies.
357. **milch-kine . . . pail:** dairy cattle.
359. **all . . . portion:** i.e. everything else on the same scale.
360. **strook:** struck, i.e. advanced.
369. **ducats:** Venetian gold coins.
370. **jointer:** jointure, marriage settlement.
371. **pinch'd:** discomfited.   374. **argosy:** large merchant vessel.
375. **Marsellis road:** harbor of Marseilles.
376. **chok'd:** silenced.   378. **galliasses:** large galleys.
379. **tight:** watertight, sound.

Tra. Why then the maid is mine from all the
world,
By your firm promise; Gremio is outvied.   385
Bap.   I must confess your offer is the best,
And let your father make her the assurance,
She is your own, else you must pardon me;
If you should die before him, where's her dower?
Tra.   That's but a cavil; he is old, I young.   390
Gre.   And may not young men die as well as old?
Bap.   Well, gentlemen,
I am thus resolv'd: on Sunday next you know
My daughter Katherine is to be married.
Now on the Sunday following shall Bianca   395
Be bride to you, if you make this assurance;
If not, to Signior Gremio.
And so I take my leave, and thank you both.   *Exit.*
Gre.   Adieu, good neighbor. Now I fear thee not.
Sirrah, young gamester, your father were a fool   400
To give thee all, and in his waning age
Set foot under thy table. Tut, a toy!
An old Italian fox is not so kind, my boy.   *Exit.*
Tra.   A vengeance on your crafty withered hide!
Yet I have fac'd it with a card of ten.   405
'Tis in my head to do my master good.
I see no reason but suppos'd Lucentio
Must get a father, call'd suppos'd Vincentio;
And that's a wonder. Fathers commonly
Do get their children; but in this case of wooing,   410
A child shall get a sire, if I fail not of my cunning.
                                                  Exit.

ACT III, [SCENE I]

Enter LUCENTIO [*as Cambio*], HORTENSIO [*as Litio*],
and BIANCA.

Luc.   Fiddler, forbear, you grow too forward, sir.
Have you so soon forgot the entertainment
Her sister Katherine welcom'd you withal?
Hor.   But, wrangling pedant, this is
The patroness of heavenly harmony.   5
Then give me leave to have prerogative,
And when in music we have spent an hour,
Your lecture shall have leisure for as much.
Luc.   Preposterous ass, that never read so far
To know the cause why music was ordain'd!   10
Was it not to refresh the mind of man
After his studies or his usual pain?
Then give me leave to read philosophy,
And while I pause, serve in your harmony.
Hor.   Sirrah, I will not bear these braves of
thine.   15
Bian.   Why, gentlemen, you do me double wrong

To strive for that which resteth in my choice.
I am no breeching scholar in the schools,
I'll not be tied to hours, nor 'pointed times,
But learn my lessons as I please myself.   20
And to cut off all strife, here sit we down:
Take you your instrument, play you the whiles,
His lecture will be done ere you have tun'd.
Hor.   You'll leave his lecture when I am in tune?
Luc.   That will be never, tune your instrument.
Bian.   Where left we last?   26
Luc.   Here, madam:
      "*Hic ibat Simois; hic est [Sigeia] tellus;
      Hic steterat Priami regia celsa senis.*"
Bian.   Conster them.   30
Luc.   "*Hic ibat,*" as I told you before, "*Simois,*"
I am Lucentio, "*hic est,*" son unto Vincentio of Pisa,
"*[Sigeia] tellus,*" disguis'd thus to get your love,
"*Hic steterat,*" and that Lucentio that comes a-wooing,
"*Priami,*" is my man Tranio, "*regia,*" bearing 35
my port, "*celsa senis,*" that we might beguile the old
pantaloon.
Hor.   Madam, my instrument's in tune.
Bian.   Let's hear. O fie, the treble jars.
Luc.   Spit in the hole, man, and tune again.   40
Bian.   Now let me see if I can conster it:
"*Hic ibat Simois,*" I know you not, "*hic est [Sigeia]
tellus,*" I trust you not, "*Hic steterat Priami,*" take
heed he hear us not, "*regia,*" presume not, "*celsa
senis,*" despair not.   45
Hor.   Madam, 'tis now in tune.
Luc.   All but the base.
Hor.   The base is right, 'tis the base knave that jars.
[*Aside.*] How fiery and forward our pedant is!
Now, for my life, the knave doth court my love:
Pedascule, I'll watch you better yet.   50
[*Bian.*]   In time I may believe, yet I mistrust.
[*Luc.*]   Mistrust it not, for sure Aeacides
Was Ajax, call'd so from his grandfather.
[*Bian.*]   I must believe my master, else, I promise
you,
I should be arguing still upon that doubt.   55
But let it rest. Now, Litio, to you:
Good master, take it not unkindly, pray,
That I have been thus pleasant with you both.
Hor.   [*To Lucentio.*] You may go walk, and give
me leave a while;
My lessons make no music in three parts.   60
Luc.   Are you so formal, sir? Well, I must wait,

385. **outvied:** outdone.   387. **let your father:** if your father will.
400. **gamester.** Perhaps alluding to the fact that Tranio's offer rests
on a gamble, not a certainty.
402. **Set . . . table:** i.e. become your dependent.   **a toy:** nonsense.
405. **fac'd . . . ten:** bluffed with only a ten-spot.   410. **get:** beget.
411. See the Textual Notes for an episode in the Sly framework
preserved in *The Taming of a Shrew.*

III.i. Location: Padua. Baptista's house.
6. **prerogative:** precedence.   8. **lecture:** lesson.
9. **Preposterous:** reversing the natural order of things.
10. **ordain'd:** instituted.   12. **pain:** labor, toil.
15. **braves:** offensive remarks.

18. **breeching scholar:** schoolboy liable to be flogged.
22. **the whiles:** for the present.
24. **I . . . tune:** i.e. my instrument is in tune; but Lucentio pretends
to take *I* literally and *in tune* in the sense "in harmony" (with Bianca).
28–29. **Hic . . . senis:** "Here flowed the Simois; here is the Sigeian
land; here stood the lofty palace of old Priam" (Ovid, *Heroides,*
I.33–34).   30. **Conster:** construe.   36. **port:** demeanor.
37. **pantaloon:** foolish old man (Gremio).   39. **jars:** is out of tune.
40. **Spit . . . hole.** Perhaps to tighten the peg so that the string would
stay in tune longer, but the phrase may mean simply "get ready for a
fresh try."
50. **Pedascule:** pedant (a Latin coinage, with vocative ending).
52–53. **Aeacides . . . grandfather.** To mislead Hortensio, Lucentio
pretends to be concerned with the next line of his Latin passage.
Actually, he seems now to be referring to Ovid's *Metamorphoses,*
xiii.27–28. *Aeacides* = descendant of Aeacus.
58. **pleasant:** merry.   59. **give me leave:** allow me opportunity.
60. **in three parts:** for three voices.   61. **formal:** precise.

[*Aside*.] And watch withal, for but I be deceiv'd,
Our fine musician groweth amorous.
    Hor. Madam, before you touch the instrument,
To learn the order of my fingering,   65
I must begin with rudiments of art,
To teach you gamouth in a briefer sort,
More pleasant, pithy, and effectual,
Than hath been taught by any of my trade;
And there it is in writing, fairly drawn.   70
    Bian. Why, I am past my gamouth long ago.
    Hor. Yet read the gamouth of Hortensio.
    Bian. [*Reads*.]
        "*Gamouth* I am, the ground of all accord:
        A re, to plead Hortensio's passion;
        B mi, Bianca, take him for thy lord,   75
        C fa ut, that loves with all affection.
        D sol re, one cliff, two notes have I,
        E la mi, show pity, or I die."
Call you this gamouth? Tut, I like it not.
Old fashions please me best; I am not so nice   80
To [change] true rules for [odd] inventions.

Enter a MESSENGER.

    [*Mess*.] Mistress, your father prays you leave your
        books,
And help to dress your sister's chamber up.
You know to-morrow is the wedding-day.
    Bian. Farewell, sweet masters both, I must be
        gone.   [*Exeunt Bianca and Messenger*.] 85
    Luc. Faith, mistress, then I have no cause to
        stay.   [*Exit*.]
    Hor. But I have cause to pry into this pedant.
Methinks he looks as though he were in love;
Yet if thy thoughts, Bianca, be so humble
To cast thy wand'ring eyes on every stale,   90
Seize thee that list. If once I find thee ranging,
Hortensio will be quit with thee by changing.   *Exit*.

[SCENE II]

Enter BAPTISTA, GREMIO, TRANIO [*as Lucentio*],
    KATHERINE, BIANCA, [LUCENTIO *as Cambio*,] *and*
    others, attendants.

    Bap. [*To Tranio*.] Signior Lucentio, this is the
        'pointed day,
That Katherine and Petruchio should be married,
And yet we hear not of our son-in-law.
What will be said? What mockery will it be,
To want the bridegroom when the priest attends   5
To speak the ceremonial rites of marriage?
What says Lucentio to this shame of ours?
    Kath. No shame but mine. I must forsooth be
        forc'd
To give my hand oppos'd against my heart

Unto a mad-brain rudesby full of spleen,   10
Who woo'd in haste, and means to wed at leisure.
I told you, I, he was a frantic fool,
Hiding his bitter jests in blunt behavior;
And to be noted for a merry man,
He'll woo a thousand, 'point the day of marriage,   15
Make friends, invite, and proclaim the banes,
Yet never means to wed where he hath woo'd.
Now must the world point at poor Katherine,
And say, "Lo, there is mad Petruchio's wife,
If it would please him come and marry her!"   20
    Tra. Patience, good Katherine, and Baptista too.
Upon my life, Petruchio means but well,
Whatever fortune stays him from his word.
Though he be blunt, I know him passing wise;
Though he be merry, yet withal he's honest.   25
    Kath. Would Katherine had never seen him
        though!
            Exit weeping [*followed by Bianca and others*].
    Bap. Go, girl, I cannot blame thee now to weep,
For such an injury would vex a very saint,
Much more a shrew of [thy] impatient humor.

Enter BIONDELLO.

    Bion. Master, master, news, [old news,] and such
news as you never heard of!   31
    Bap. Is it new and old too? how may that be?
    Bion. Why, is it not news to [hear] of Petruchio's
coming?
    Bap. Is he come?   35
    Bion. Why, no, sir.
    Bap. What then?
    Bion. He is coming.
    Bap. When will he be here?
    Bion. When he stands where I am, and sees you
there.   41
    Tra. But say, what to thine old news?
    Bion. Why, Petruchio is coming in a new hat and
an old jerkin; a pair of old breeches thrice turn'd;
a pair of boots that have been candle-cases, one   45
buckled, another lac'd; an old rusty sword ta'en
out of the town armory, with a broken hilt, and
chapeless; with two broken points; his horse hipp'd,
with an old mothy saddle and stirrups of no kindred; besides, possess'd with the glanders and   50
like to mose in the chine, troubled with the lampass,
infected with the fashions, full of windgalls, sped
with spavins, ray'd with the yellows, past cure

---

62. **but:** unless.   67. **gamouth:** gamut, the diatonic scale.
73. **ground:** basis, foundation.   **accord:** harmony.
76. **ut:** the lowest note, now called *do*.   77. **cliff:** clef, key.
80. **nice:** capricious, or perhaps a late use of its earlier common
meaning "simple, foolish."   90. **stale:** decoy, bait.
91. **Seize . . . list:** let him take you that will.   **ranging:** inconstant.
92. **be quit:** be quits, get even.   **changing:** i.e. loving another.

III.ii. Location: Padua. Before Baptista's house.

---

10. **rudesby:** rude, boisterous fellow.   **spleen:** sudden impulse.
12. **frantic:** mad.   13. **blunt:** rude.
14. **be noted for:** gain a reputation as.   16. **banes:** banns.
23. **fortune:** chance.   25. **honest:** honorable.   30. **old:** rare.
44. **jerkin:** jacket.
45. **candle-cases:** receptacles for candle ends (because no longer fit to
wear).
48. **chapeless:** without a chape, the metal tip of the sheath.   **points:**
tagged laces for attaching hose to doublet.   **hipp'd:** lame in the hip.
(Most of the diseases here named are discussed in Gervase Markham's
How to Choose, Ride, Train, and Diet . . . Horses, 1593.)
50. **glanders:** swellings underneath the horse's jaw.
51. **mose . . . chine:** suffer from a dark discharge from the nostrils (a
characteristic of glanders).   **lampass:** a thick, spongy skin over a
horse's upper teeth, making eating almost impossible.
52. **fashions:** farcins, small tumors on the horse's body.   **windgalls:**
soft tumors generally found on the fetlock joint.   **sped:** far gone.
53. **spavins:** a disease of the hock.   **ray'd:** defiled.   **yellows:**
jaundice.

of the fives, stark spoil'd with the staggers, be- 55
gnawn with the bots, [sway'd] in the back, and
shoulder-shotten, near-legg'd before, and with a
half- [cheek'd] bit and a head-stall of sheep's leather,
which being restrain'd to keep him from stumbling,
hath been often burst, and now repair'd with knots;
one girth six times piec'd, and a woman's crupper 60
of velure, which hath two letters for her name fairly
set down in studs, and here and there piec'd with
packthread.

Bap. Who comes with him? 64

Bion. O, sir, his lackey, for all the world caparison'd like the horse; with a linen stock on one leg,
and a kersey boot-hose on the other, gart'red with
a red and blue list; an old hat, and the humor of
forty fancies prick'd in't for a feather: a monster, 69
a very monster in apparel, and not like a Christian
footboy or a gentleman's lackey.

Tra. 'Tis some odd humor pricks him to this
fashion;
Yet oftentimes he goes but mean apparell'd.

Bap. I am glad he's come, howsoe'er he comes.

Bion. Why, sir, he comes not. 75

Bap. Didst thou not say he comes?

Bion. Who? that Petruchio came?

Bap. Ay, that Petruchio came.

Bion. No, sir, I say his horse comes, with him on
his back. 80

Bap. Why, that's all one.

Bion. Nay, by Saint Jamy,
　　I hold you a penny,
　　A horse and a man
　　Is more than one, 85
　　And yet not many.

Enter PETRUCHIO *and* GRUMIO.

Pet. Come, where be these gallants? Who's at
home?

Bap. You are welcome, sir.

Pet. 　　　　　　And yet I come not well.

Bap. And yet you halt not.

Tra. 　　　　　　Not so well apparell'd
As I wish you were. 90

Pet. Were it better I should rush in thus:
　　　　　　　　[*Pretends great excitement.*]
But where is Kate? Where is my lovely bride?
How does my father?—Gentles, methinks you frown,

And wherefore gaze this goodly company,
As if they saw some wondrous monument, 95
Some comet or unusual prodigy?

Bap. Why, sir, you know this is your wedding-day.
First were we sad, fearing you would not come,
Now sadder, that you come so unprovided.
Fie, doff this habit, shame to your estate, 100
An eye-sore to our solemn festival!

Tra. And tell us what occasion of import
Hath all so long detain'd you from your wife,
And sent you hither so unlike yourself?

Pet. Tedious it were to tell, and harsh to hear—
Sufficeth I am come to keep my word, 106
Though in some part enforced to digress,
Which at more leisure I will so excuse
As you shall well be satisfied with all.
But where is Kate? I stay too long from her. 110
The morning wears, 'tis time we were at church.

Tra. See not your bride in these unreverent robes,
Go to my chamber, put on clothes of mine.

Pet. Not I, believe me, thus I'll visit her.

Bap. But thus, I trust, you will not marry her. 115

Pet. Good sooth, even thus; therefore ha' done
　　with words;
To me she's married, not unto my clothes.
Could I repair what she will wear in me,
As I can change these poor accoutrements,
'Twere well for Kate, and better for myself. 120
But what a fool am I to chat with you,
When I should bid good morrow to my bride,
And seal the title with a lovely kiss!

　　　　　　　　Exit [*with Grumio*].

Tra. He hath some meaning in his mad attire.
We will persuade him, be it possible, 125
To put on better ere he go to church.

Bap. I'll after him, and see the event of this.

　　　　　　　Exit [*with Gremio and Attendants*].

Tra. But, sir, love concerneth us to add
Her father's liking, which to bring to pass,
As before imparted to your worship, 130
I am to get a man—what e'er he be,
It skills not much, we'll fit him to our turn—
And he shall be Vincentio of Pisa,
And make assurance here in Padua
Of greater sums than I have promised. 135
So shall you quietly enjoy your hope,
And marry sweet Bianca with consent.

Luc. Were it not that my fellow schoolmaster
Doth watch Bianca's steps so narrowly,

---

54. **fives:** swellings at the base of the ear. **staggers:** a disease
causing a staggering gait.
55. **bots:** intestinal worms. **sway'd:** with a wrenched and depressed
backbone.
56. **shoulder-shotten:** with a dislocated shoulder. **near-legg'd
before:** with knock-kneed forelegs.
57. **half-cheek'd:** i.e. loose. **head-stall:** part of the bridle over the
head. **sheep's leather:** i.e. leather of inferior quality. Pigskin was
commonly used in fine saddlery. 58. **restrain'd:** drawn tight.
59. **burst:** broken.
60. **piec'd:** mended. **crupper:** strap fastened to the saddle and
passing under the horse's tail. 61. **velure:** velvet.
66. **stock:** stocking.
67. **kersey boot-hose:** coarse woollen stocking for wearing under
boots. 68. **list:** strip of cloth.
68–69. **humor . . . fancies:** i.e. some ornament of highly whimsical
design. 69. **prick'd:** pinned. **for:** in place of.
72. **humor:** whim, caprice. **pricks:** spurs, incites.
83. **hold:** wager. 87. **gallants:** gentlemen.
93. **Gentles:** gentlemen.

99. **unprovided:** poorly equipped.
100. **habit:** costume. **estate:** position, station.
101. **solemn:** ceremonious. 105. **harsh:** rough.
107. **digress:** deviate (from a promise).
112. **unreverent:** disrespectful.
116. **Good sooth:** indeed. **ha':** have.
118. **repair . . . me:** change for the better what she will take on in
having me for a husband. 123. **lovely:** loving.
127. **event:** outcome.
128–29. **But . . . liking.** Generally considered a crux, but the meaning
may be "But, sir, love [i.e. the love-suits for Bianca's hand; cf. *love*
in I.ii.141] makes us concerned to achieve her father's approval."
Many editors emend *But, sir, love* to *But, sir, to love* or *But to her love*,
to make easier sense and also regularize the metre.
130. **As.** Frequently emended to *As I*, again for metrical reasons.
132. **skills:** matters. 139. **narrowly:** closely.

'Twere good methinks to steal our marriage,   140
Which once perform'd, let all the world say no,
I'll keep mine own, despite of all the world.
    Tra. That by degrees we mean to look into,
And watch our vantage in this business.
We'll overreach the greybeard, Gremio,   145
The narrow-prying father, Minola,
The quaint musician, amorous Litio,
All for my master's sake, Lucentio.

                Enter GREMIO.

Signior Gremio, came you from the church?
    Gre. As willingly as e'er I came from school. 150
    Tra. And is the bride and bridegroom coming
        home?
    Gre. A bridegroom, say you? 'tis a groom indeed,
A grumbling groom, and that the girl shall find.
    Tra. Curster than she? why, 'tis impossible.
    Gre. Why, he's a devil, a devil, a very fiend. 155
    Tra. Why, she's a devil, a devil, the devil's dam.
    Gre. Tut, she's a lamb, a dove, a fool to him!
I'll tell you, Sir Lucentio: when the priest
Should ask if Katherine should be his wife,
"Ay, by gogs-wouns," quoth he, and swore so loud,
That all amaz'd the priest let fall the book,   161
And as he stoop'd again to take it up,
This mad-brain'd bridegroom took him such a cuff
That down fell priest and book, and book and priest.
"Now take them up," quoth he, "if any list." 165
    Tra. What said the wench when he rose again?
    Gre. Trembled and shook; for why, he stamp'd
        and swore
As if the vicar meant to cozen him.
But after many ceremonies done,
He calls for wine. "A health!" quoth he, as if 170
He had been aboard, carousing to his mates
After a storm, quaff'd off the muscadel,
And threw the sops all in the sexton's face,
Having no other reason
But that his beard grew thin and hungerly, 175
And seem'd to ask him sops as he was drinking.
This done, he took the bride about the neck,
And kiss'd her lips with such a clamorous smack
That at the parting all the church did echo.
And I seeing this, came thence for very shame, 180
And after me I know the rout is coming.
Such a mad marriage never was before.
Hark, hark, I hear the minstrels play.   *Music plays.*

Enter PETRUCHIO, KATE, BIANCA, HORTENSIO [*as Litio*],
    BAPTISTA, [GRUMIO, *and* TRAIN].

    Pet. Gentlemen and friends, I thank you for your
        pains.

I know you think to dine with me to-day,   185
And have prepar'd great store of wedding cheer,
But so it is, my haste doth call me hence,
And therefore here I mean to take my leave.
    Bap. Is't possible you will away to-night?
    Pet. I must away to-day, before night come. 190
Make it no wonder; if you knew my business,
You would entreat me rather go than stay.
And, honest company, I thank you all
That have beheld me give away myself
To this most patient, sweet, and virtuous wife. 195
Dine with my father, drink a health to me,
For I must hence, and farewell to you all.
    Tra. Let us entreat you stay till after dinner.
    Pet. It may not be.
    Gre.   Let me entreat you.
    Pet. It cannot be.
    Kath.   Let me entreat you. 200
    Pet. I am content.
    Kath.   Are you content to stay?
    Pet. I am content you shall entreat me stay,
But yet not stay, entreat me how you can.
    Kath. Now if you love me stay.
    Pet.   Grumio, my horse.
    Gru. Ay, sir, they be ready; the oats have eaten
the horses.   206
    Kath. Nay then,
Do what thou canst, I will not go to-day,
No, nor to-morrow—not till I please myself.
The door is open, sir, there lies your way;   210
You may be jogging whiles your boots are green.
For me, I'll not be gone till I please myself.
'Tis like you'll prove a jolly surly groom,
That take it on you at the first so roundly.   214
    Pet. O Kate, content thee, prithee be not angry.
    Kath. I will be angry; what hast thou to do?
Father, be quiet, he shall stay my leisure.
    Gre. Ay, marry, sir, now it begins to work.
    Kath. Gentlemen, forward to the bridal dinner.
I see a woman may be made a fool,   220
If she had not a spirit to resist.
    Pet. They shall go forward, Kate, at thy command.
Obey the bride, you that attend on her.
Go to the feast, revel and domineer,
Carouse full measure to her maidenhead,   225
Be mad and merry, or go hang yourselves;
But for my bonny Kate, she must with me.
Nay, look not big, nor stamp, nor stare, nor fret,
I will be master of what is mine own.
She is my goods, my chattels, she is my house, 230
My household stuff, my field, my barn,
My horse, my ox, my ass, my any thing;
And here she stands, touch her whoever dare,

---

140. **steal our marriage:** marry secretly.
144. **vantage:** advantage, opportunity.
147. **quaint:** skilled, clever.
152. **a groom indeed:** (1) a fine kind of bridegroom (ironic); (2) a
servingman actually.
157. **fool:** i.e. poor weak creature.   **to:** compared with.
160. **gogs-wouns:** God's (Christ's) wounds.
161. **amaz'd:** bewildered.   163. **took:** struck.   165. **list:** choose.
167. **for why:** because.
168. **cozen:** cheat (by making the ceremony invalid through some
irregularity).   171. **aboard:** aboard ship.   173. **sops:** dregs.
175. **hungerly:** sparsely.   181. **rout:** crowd (of guests).

191. **Make:** consider.   193. **honest:** worthy.   204. **horse.** Plural.
205–6. **oats . . . horses:** i.e. the horses are stuffed full of oats.
211. **be . . . green:** i.e. get an early start (proverbial); *green* = fresh,
new.   213. **jolly:** overbearing.
214. **roundly:** outspokenly, unceremoniously.
216. **what . . . do:** it's no concern of yours.   217. **stay:** await.
224. **domineer:** carouse.
228. **big:** threatening (said to the wedding guests, not to Katherine,
whose conduct it really describes).
232. **ox . . . thing.** Alluding to the Tenth Commandment.

I'll bring mine action on the proudest he
That stops my way in Padua. Grumio,   235
Draw forth thy weapon, we are beset with thieves;
Rescue thy mistress if thou be a man.
Fear not, sweet wench, they shall not touch thee,
    Kate!
I'll buckler thee against a million.

Exeunt Petruchio, Katherina, [and Grumio].

Bap. Nay, let them go, a couple of quiet ones. 240
Gre. Went they not quickly, I should die with
    laughing.
Tra. Of all mad matches never was the like.
Luc. Mistress, what's your opinion of your sister?
Bian. That being mad herself, she's madly mated.
Gre. I warrant him, Petruchio is Kated.   245
Bap. Neighbors and friends, though bride and
    bridegroom wants
For to supply the places at the table,
You know there wants no junkets at the feast.
Lucentio, you shall supply the bridegroom's place,
And let Bianca take her sister's room.   250
Tra. Shall sweet Bianca practice how to bride it?
Bap. She shall, Lucentio. Come, gentlemen, let's
    go.   *Exeunt.*

[ACT IV, Scene I]

Enter Grumio.

Gru. Fie, fie on all tir'd jades, on all mad masters, and all foul ways! Was ever man so beaten?
Was ever man so ray'd? Was ever man so weary?
I am sent before to make a fire, and they are coming after to warm them. Now were not I a   5
little pot and soon hot, my very lips might freeze
to my teeth, my tongue to the roof of my mouth,
my heart in my belly, ere I should come by a fire
to thaw me. But I with blowing the fire shall
warm myself; for considering the weather, 10
a taller man than I will take cold. Holla, ho,
Curtis!

Enter Curtis.

Curt. Who is that calls so coldly?
Gru. A piece of ice. If thou doubt it, thou mayst
slide from my shoulder to my heel with no greater
a run but my head and my neck. A fire, good 16
Curtis.
Curt. Is my master and his wife coming, Grumio?
Gru. O ay, Curtis, ay, and therefore fire, fire;
cast on no water.   20
Curt. Is she so hot a shrew as she's reported?
Gru. She was, good Curtis, before this frost;

but thou know'st winter tames man, woman, and
beast; for it hath tam'd my old master and my new
mistress and myself, fellow Curtis.   25
[*Curt.*] Away, you three-inch fool! I am no beast.
Gru. Am I but three inches? Why, thy horn
is a foot, and so long am I at the least. But wilt thou
make a fire, or shall I complain on thee to our mistress, whose hand (she being now at hand) thou 30
shalt soon feel, to thy cold comfort, for being slow
in thy hot office?
Curt. I prithee, good Grumio, tell me, how goes
the world?   34
Gru. A cold world, Curtis, in every office but
thine, and therefore fire. Do thy duty and have thy
duty, for my master and mistress are almost frozen
to death.
Curt. There's fire ready, and therefore, good
Grumio, the news.   40
Gru. Why, "Jack, boy! ho, boy!" and as much
news as wilt thou.
Curt. Come, you are so full of cony-catching!
Gru. Why, therefore fire, for I have caught
extreme cold. Where's the cook? Is supper 45
ready, the house trimm'd, rushes strew'd, cobwebs swept, the servingmen in their new fustian,
[their] white stockings, and every officer his wed-
ding garment on? Be the Jacks fair within, the
Gills fair without, the carpets laid, and every thing
in order?   51
Curt. All ready; and therefore I pray thee,
news.
Gru. First, know my horse is tir'd, my master
and mistress fall'n out.   55
Curt. How?
Gru. Out of their saddles into the dirt, and
thereby hangs a tale.
Curt. Let's ha't, good Grumio.
Gru. Lend thine ear.   60
Curt. Here.
Gru. There.   [*Strikes him.*]
Curt. This 'tis to feel a tale, not to hear a tale.
Gru. And therefore 'tis call'd a sensible tale;
and this cuff was but to knock at your ear, and 65
beseech list'ning. Now I begin: *Inprimis*, we came
down a foul hill, my master riding behind my mis-
tress—
Curt. Both of one horse?
Gru. What's that to thee?   70
Curt. Why, a horse.

---

234. **bring...on:** (1) attack; (2) bring legal action against.
239. **buckler:** shield.   246. **wants:** are lacking.   247. **For to:** to.
248. **junkets:** sweetmeats.

IV.i. Location: Petruchio's country house.
3. **ray'd:** dirtied.
6. **little...hot:** proverbial for a small person with a quick temper.
9. **blowing the fire:** i.e. keeping myself in a rage.
11. **taller.** With play on the sense " better."
19–20. **fire...water.** An allusion to the round or catch "Scotland's
burning," in which the words "Fire, fire!" are followed by "Cast on
water."

26. **I...beast:** i.e. don't call me your fellow, since you have just
admitted that you are a beast.
27. **horn:** cuckold's horn. (The passage is full of indelicate jesting.)
32. **hot office:** task of providing heat.   37. **duty:** due, reward.
41. **Jack...boy:** the first words of another catch.
43. **cony-catching:** trickery, evasion (perhaps with punning reference
to Grumio's fondness for catches).
46. **rushes.** Used as floor covering.
47. **fustian:** coarse cloth of cotton and flax.
48. **officer:** household servant.
49. **Jacks:** (1) servingmen; (2) drinking vessels.
50. **Gills:** (1) maidservants; (2) small drinking vessels (*gills*).   **carpets:** here, probably table coverings.
58. **thereby...tale:** there is a story connected with that.
64. **sensible:** (1) reasonable; (2) capable of being felt.
66. **Inprimis:** in the first place.   67. **foul:** muddy.   69. **of:** on.

Gru. Tell thou the tale. But hadst thou not cross'd me, thou shouldst have heard how her horse fell, and she under her horse; thou shouldst have heard in how miry a place, how she was be- 75 moil'd, how he left her with the horse upon her, how he beat me because her horse stumbled, how she waded through the dirt to pluck him off me; how he swore, how she pray'd that never pray'd before; how I cried, how the horses ran away, 80 how her bridle was burst; how I lost my crupper, with many things of worthy memory, which now shall die in oblivion, and thou return unexperienc'd to thy grave. 84

Curt. By this reck'ning he is more shrew than she.

Gru. Ay, and that thou and the proudest of you all shall find when he comes home. But what talk I of this? Call forth Nathaniel, Joseph, Nicholas, Philip, Walter, Sugarsop, and the rest; let their 90 heads be slickly comb'd, their blue coats brush'd, and their garters of an indifferent knit; let them curtsy with their left legs, and not presume to touch a hair of my master's horse-tail till they kiss their hands. Are they all ready? 95

Curt. They are.

Gru. Call them forth.

Curt. Do you hear, ho? You must meet my master to countenance my mistress.

Gru. Why, she hath a face of her own. 100

Curt. Who knows not that?

Gru. Thou, it seems, that calls for company to countenance her.

Curt. I call them forth to credit her. 104

Enter four or five SERVINGMEN.

Gru. Why, she comes to borrow nothing of them.

Nath. Welcome home, Grumio!

Phil. How now, Grumio?

Jos. What, Grumio!

Nich. Fellow Grumio!

Nath. How now, old lad? 110

Gru. Welcome, you; how now, you; what, you; fellow, you—and thus much for greeting. Now, my spruce companions, is all ready, and all things neat?

Nath. All things is ready. How near is our master? 116

Gru. E'en at hand, alighted by this; and therefore be not—Cock's passion, silence! I hear my master.

Enter PETRUCHIO *and* KATE.

Pet. Where be these knaves? What, no man at door 120
To hold my stirrup, nor to take my horse?
Where is Nathaniel, Gregory, Philip?

All Serv. Here, here, sir, here, sir.

Pet. Here, sir! here, sir! here, sir! here, sir!
You loggerheaded and unpolish'd grooms! 125
What? no attendance? no regard? no duty?
Where is the foolish knave I sent before?

Gru. Here, sir, as foolish as I was before.

Pet. You peasant swain, you whoreson malt-horse drudge!
Did I not bid thee meet me in the park, 130
And bring along these rascal knaves with thee?

Gru. Nathaniel's coat, sir, was not fully made,
And Gabr'el's pumps were all unpink'd i' th' heel;
There was no link to color Peter's hat, 134
And Walter's dagger was not come from sheathing;
There were none fine but Adam, Rafe, and Gregory;
The rest were ragged, old, and beggarly,
Yet, as they are, here are they come to meet you.

Pet. Go, rascals, go, and fetch my supper in.

Exeunt Servants.

[*Sings.*] "Where is the life that late I led? 140
Where are those"—
Sit down, Kate, and welcome. Soud, soud, soud, soud!

Enter SERVANTS *with supper.*

Why, when, I say? Nay, good sweet Kate, be merry.
Off with my boots, you rogues! You villains, when?
[*Sings.*] "It was the friar of orders grey, 145
As he forth walked on his way"—
Out, you rogue, you pluck my foot awry.
Take that, and mend the plucking [off] the other.

[*Strikes him.*]

Be merry, Kate. Some water here; what ho!

Enter one with water.

Where's my spaniel Troilus? Sirrah, get you hence,
And bid my cousin Ferdinand come hither; 151
One, Kate, that you must kiss, and be acquainted with.
Where are my slippers? Shall I have some water?
Come, Kate, and wash, and welcome heartily.
You whoreson villain, will you let it fall? 155

[*Strikes him.*]

Kath. Patience, I pray you, 'twas a fault unwilling.

Pet. A whoreson, beetle-headed, flap-ear'd knave!
Come, Kate, sit down, I know you have a stomach.
Will you give thanks, sweet Kate, or else shall I?
What's this? Mutton?

1. Serv.   Ay.

Pet.   Who brought it?

Peter.   I. 160

Pet. 'Tis burnt, and so is all the meat.

---

73. **cross'd:** interrupted.   75–76. **bemoil'd:** covered with mud.
88. **what:** why.
91. **blue coats.** The regular dress for menservants.
92. **indifferent knit:** i.e. ordinary pattern or texture.
99. **countenance:** pay your respects to (with obvious pun following).
104. **credit:** honor (again with following pun).
118. **Cock's passion:** by God's (Christ's) suffering.

125. **loggerheaded:** blockheaded.
129. **peasant swain:** rascally lout.   **malt-horse drudge:** slow, heavy horse, used to grind malt by working a treadmill.
133. **unpink'd:** without eyelets.
134. **link:** torch (the smoke of which could be used to blacken old hats).   135. **sheathing:** having a sheath made.
136. **fine:** well dressed.
140–41. **Where . . . those:** fragment of a song no longer extant; lines 145–46 are from another.
142. **Soud:** an expression of impatience (?). Some editors emend to *Food.*
157. **beetle-headed:** blockheaded (*beetle* = a heavy tool for ramming and pounding).   158. **stomach:** (1) appetite; (2) temper.

The Taming
of the Shrew
IV.i

What dogs are these? Where is the rascal cook?
How durst you, villains, bring it from the dresser
And serve it thus to me that love it not?
There, take it to you, trenchers, cups, and all.   165
    [*He throws down the table and meat and all,
        and beats them.*]
You heedless joltheads and unmanner'd slaves!
What, do you grumble? I'll be with you straight.
        [*Exeunt Servants.*]
    Kath. I pray you, husband, be not so disquiet.
The meat was well, if you were so contented.
    Pet. I tell thee, Kate, 'twas burnt and dried away,
And I expressly am forbid to touch it;   171
For it engenders choler, planteth anger,
And better 'twere that both of us did fast,
Since of ourselves, ourselves are choleric,
Than feed it with such overroasted flesh.   175
Be patient, to-morrow't shall be mended,
And for this night we'll fast for company.
Come, I will bring thee to thy bridal chamber.
                            Exeunt.

    Enter Servants *severally.*

    Nath. Peter, didst ever see the like?
    Peter. He kills her in her own humor.   180

    Enter Curtis, *a servant.*

    Gru. Where is he?
    Curt. In her chamber, making a sermon of con-
tinency to her,
And rails, and swears, and rates, that she, poor soul,
Knows not which way to stand, to look, to speak,   185
And sits as one new risen from a dream.
Away, away, for he is coming hither.   [*Exeunt.*]

    Enter Petruchio.

    Pet. Thus have I politicly begun my reign,
And 'tis my hope to end successfully.
My falcon now is sharp and passing empty,   190
And till she stoop, she must not be full-gorg'd,
For then she never looks upon her lure.
Another way I have to man my haggard,
To make her come, and know her keeper's call,
That is, to watch her, as we watch these kites   195
That bate and beat and will not be obedient.
She eat no meat to-day, nor none shall eat;
Last night she slept not, nor to-night she shall not;
As with the meat, some undeserved fault
I'll find about the making of the bed,   200
And here I'll fling the pillow, there the bolster,
This way the coverlet, another way the sheets.
Ay, and amid this hurly I intend

That all is done in reverend care of her,
And in conclusion, she shall watch all night,   205
And if she chance to nod I'll rail and brawl,
And with the clamor keep her still awake.
This is a way to kill a wife with kindness,
And thus I'll curb her mad and headstrong humor.
He that knows better how to tame a shrew,   210
Now let him speak; 'tis charity to shew.   *Exit.*

[Scene II]

Enter Tranio [*as Lucentio*] *and* Hortensio [*as Litio*].

    Tra. Is't possible, friend Litio, that Mistress Bianca
Doth fancy any other but Lucentio?
I tell you, sir, she bears me fair in hand.
    [*Hor.*] Sir, to satisfy you in what I have said,
Stand by and mark the manner of his teaching.   5
                        [*They stand aside.*]

    Enter Bianca [*and* Lucentio *as Cambio*].

    [*Luc.*] Now, mistress, profit you in what you read?
    Bian. What, master, read you? First resolve me
        that.
    [*Luc.*] I read that I profess, the Art to Love.
    Bian. And may you prove, sir, master of your art!
    Luc. While you, sweet dear, prove mistress of
        my heart!   [*They retire.*]   10
    Hor. Quick proceeders, marry! Now tell me,
        I pray,
You that durst swear that your mistress Bianca
Lov'd [none] in the world so well as Lucentio.
    Tra. O despiteful love, unconstant womankind!
I tell thee, Litio, this is wonderful.   15
    Hor. Mistake no more, I am not Litio,
Nor a musician, as I seem to be,
But one that scorn to live in this disguise
For such a one as leaves a gentleman,
And makes a god of such a cullion.   20
Know, sir, that I am call'd Hortensio.
    Tra. Signior Hortensio, I have often heard
Of your entire affection to Bianca,
And since mine eyes are witness of her lightness,
I will with you, if you be so contented,   25
Forswear Bianca and her love for ever.
    Hor. See how they kiss and court! Signior
        Lucentio,
Here is my hand, and here I firmly vow
Never to woo her more, but do forswear her
As one unworthy all the former favors   30
That I have fondly flatter'd [her] withal.
    Tra. And here I take the like unfeigned oath,
Never to marry with her though she would entreat.

163. **dresser:** sideboard.   165. **trenchers:** wooden dishes or plates.
166. **joltheads:** blockheads.
167. **with you straight:** after you straightway (to punish you).
172. **choler:** the humor, or bodily fluid, that was thought to make one
short-tempered.   174. **of ourselves:** by our nature.
180. **kills . . . humor:** i.e. masters her ill temper with a worse temper.
190. **sharp:** hungry.
191. **stoop:** fly to the lure (a baited device used to recall a falcon),
i.e. submit to authority.
193. **man:** tame.   **haggard:** wild female hawk.
195. **watch her:** keep her from sleeping.   **kites:** falcons.
196. **bate and beat:** flap and flutter the wings impatiently.
197. **She eat:** she ate.   203. **intend:** pretend.

207. **still:** always.   211. **shew:** show, i.e. reveal his method.

IV.ii. Location: Padua. Before Baptista's house.
3. **bears . . . hand:** treats me encouragingly (with suggestion of deceit).
6. **profit you:** do you make progress.   **read:** study.
7. **resolve:** answer.
8. **that:** what.   **Art to Love:** Ovid's *Ars Amandi.*
11. **proceeders.** Playing on the academic term "to proceed Master of
Arts," suggested by Bianca's "master of your art."
15. **wonderful:** a cause for wonder.   20. **cullion:** base fellow.
23. **entire:** unfeigned, sincere.   24. **lightness:** wantonness.
31. **fondly:** foolishly.

Fie on her, see how beastly she doth court him!

Hor.   Would all the world but he had quite for-
          sworn!   35
For me, that I may surely keep mine oath,
I will be married to a wealthy widow,
Ere three days pass, which hath as long lov'd me
As I have lov'd this proud disdainful haggard.
And so farewell, Signior Lucentio.   40
Kindness in women, not their beauteous looks,
Shall win my love, and so I take my leave,
In resolution as I swore before.   [*Exit.*]

Tra.   Mistress Bianca, bless you with such grace
As 'longeth to a lover's blessed case!   45
Nay, I have ta'en you napping, gentle love,
And have forsworn you with Hortensio.

Bian.   Tranio, you jest, but have you both for-
          sworn me?

Tra.   Mistress, we have.

Luc.   Then we are rid of Litio.

Tra.   I' faith, he'll have a lusty widow now,   50
That shall be woo'd and wedded in a day.

Bian.   God give him joy!

Tra.   Ay, and he'll tame her.

Bian.   He says so, Tranio?

Tra.   Faith, he is gone unto the taming-school.

Bian.   The taming-school! what, is there such a
          place?   55

Tra.   Ay, mistress, and Petruchio is the master,
That teacheth tricks eleven and twenty long,
To tame a shrew and charm her chattering tongue.

Enter BIONDELLO.

Bion.   O master, master, I have watch'd so long
That I am dog-weary, but at last I spied   60
An ancient angel coming down the hill,
Will serve the turn.

Tra.   What is he, Biondello?

Bion.   Master, a mercantant, or a pedant,
I know not what, but formal in apparel,
In gait and countenance surely like a father.   65

Luc.   And what of him, Tranio?

Tra.   If he be credulous, and trust my tale,
I'll make him glad to seem Vincentio,
And give assurance to Baptista Minola,
As if he were the right Vincentio.   70
Take [in] your love, and then let me alone.

          [*Exeunt Lucentio and Bianca.*]

Enter a PEDANT.

Ped.   God save you, sir!

Tra.   And you, sir! you are welcome.
Travel you far on, or are you at the farthest?

Ped.   Sir, at the farthest for a week or two,
But then up farther, and as far as Rome,   75
And so to Tripoli, if God lend me life.

Tra.   What countryman, I pray?

Ped.   Of Mantua.

Tra.   Of Mantua, sir? marry, God forbid!
And come to Padua, careless of your life?

Ped.   My life, sir? How, I pray? for that goes hard.

Tra.   'Tis death for any one in Mantua   81
To come to Padua. Know you not the cause?
Your ships are stay'd at Venice, and the Duke,
For private quarrel 'twixt your Duke and him,
Hath publish'd and proclaim'd it openly.   85
'Tis marvel, but that you are but newly come,
You might have heard it else proclaim'd about.

Ped.   Alas, sir, it is worse for me than so,
For I have bills for money by exchange
From Florence, and must here deliver them.   90

Tra.   Well, sir, to do you courtesy,
This will I do, and this I will advise you.
First, tell me, have you ever been at Pisa?

Ped.   Ay, sir, in Pisa have I often been,
Pisa renowned for grave citizens.   95

Tra.   Among them know you one Vincentio?

Ped.   I know him not, but I have heard of him;
A merchant of incomparable wealth.

Tra.   He is my father, sir, and sooth to say,
In count'nance somewhat doth resemble you.   100

Bion.   [*Aside.*]   As much as an apple doth an
oyster, and all one.

Tra.   To save your life in this extremity,
This favor will I do you for his sake;
And think it not the worst of all your fortunes   105
That you are like to Sir Vincentio.
His name and credit shall you undertake,
And in my house you shall be friendly lodg'd.
Look that you take upon you as you should;
You understand me, sir? So shall you stay   110
Till you have done your business in the city.
If this be court'sy, sir, accept of it.

Ped.   O sir, I do, and will repute you ever
The patron of my life and liberty.

Tra.   Then go with me to make the matter good.
This by the way I let you understand: 116
My father is here look'd for every day,
To pass assurance of a dow'r in marriage
'Twixt me and one Baptista's daughter here.
In all these circumstances I'll instruct you;   120
Go with me to clothe you as becomes you.   *Exeunt.*

SCENE [III]

Enter KATHERINA *and* GRUMIO.

Gru.   No, no, forsooth I dare not for my life.

---

34. **beastly:** i.e. lewdly.
35. **Would ... forsworn:** i.e. would that Bianca should be left an old
maid, since he does not believe that she will really marry Cambio-
Lucentio, whom he thinks to be a penniless musician (Bond).
45. **'longeth:** belongs.   50. **lusty:** spirited, vigorous.
54. **he ... taming-school.** How does Tranio know this, since
Hortensio has only just made his decision and has not mentioned his
intention to visit Petruchio? Imperfectly adjusted revision has been
suggested. See Textual Notes, line 53, for a curiously close textual
parallel here with *The Taming of a Shrew*.
57. **tricks ... long:** i.e. tricks that meet the need of the case; an
allusion to the card game trentuno (cf. I.ii.33).
61. **ancient angel:** i.e. a fellow of the good old stamp. The angel was
a gold coin bearing the figure of the archangel Michael.
62. **serve the turn:** answer our purpose.
63. **marcantant:** merchant (Italian *mercantante*).

80. **goes hard:** is serious.   102. **all one:** no matter.
107. **credit:** reputation.   **undertake:** assume.
109. **take upon you:** i.e. act your part.   113. **repute:** consider.
118. **pass:** convey.   120. **circumstances:** details.

IV.iii. Location: Petruchio's house.

The Taming
of the Shrew
IV.iii

Kath. The more my wrong, the more his spite
　　appears.
What, did he marry me to famish me?
Beggars that come unto my father's door
Upon entreaty have a present alms,　　　　5
If not, elsewhere they meet with charity;
But I, who never knew how to entreat,
Nor never needed that I should entreat,
Am starv'd for meat, giddy for lack of sleep,
With oaths kept waking, and with brawling fed;　10
And that which spites me more than all these wants,
He does it under name of perfect love;
As who should say, if I should sleep or eat,
'Twere deadly sickness, or else present death.
I prithee go, and get me some repast;　　　15
I care not what, so it be wholesome food.
　Gru. What say you to a neat's foot?
　Kath. 'Tis passing good, I prithee let me have it.
　Gru. I fear it is too choleric a meat.
How say you to a fat tripe finely broil'd?　　20
　Kath. I like it well, good Grumio, fetch it me.
　Gru. I cannot tell, I fear 'tis choleric.
What say you to a piece of beef and mustard?
　Kath. A dish that I do love to feed upon.
　Gru. Ay, but the mustard is too hot a little.　25
　Kath. Why then the beef, and let the mustard rest.
　Gru. Nay then I will not, you shall have the
　　mustard,
Or else you get no beef of Grumio.
　Kath. Then both or one, or any thing thou wilt.
　Gru. Why then the mustard without the beef.　30
　Kath. Go get thee gone, thou false deluding
　　slave,　　　　　　　　　　　*Beats him.*
That feed'st me with the very name of meat.
Sorrow on thee and all the pack of you
That triumph thus upon my misery!
Go get thee gone, I say.　　　　　　35

Enter Petruchio *and* Hortensio *with meat.*

　Pet. How fares my Kate? What, sweeting, all
　　amort?
　Hor. Mistress, what cheer?
　Kath.　　　　　　　Faith, as cold as can be.
　Pet. Pluck up thy spirits, look cheerfully upon me.
Here, love, thou seest how diligent I am
To dress thy meat myself, and bring it thee.　40
I am sure, sweet Kate, this kindness merits thanks.
What, not a word? Nay then, thou lov'st it not;
And all my pains is sorted to no proof.
Here, take away this dish.
　Kath.　　　　　　　I pray you let it stand.
　Pet. The poorest service is repaid with thanks,
And so shall mine before you touch the meat.　46
　Kath. I thank you, sir.
　Hor. Signior Petruchio, fie, you are to blame.
Come, Mistress Kate, I'll bear you company.

　Pet. [*Aside.*] Eat it up all, Hortensio, if thou
　　lovest me.—　　　　　　　50
Much good do it unto thy gentle heart!
Kate, eat apace. And now, my honey love,
Will we return unto thy father's house,
And revel it as bravely as the best,
With silken coats and caps, and golden rings,　55
With ruffs and cuffs, and fardingales, and things,
With scarfs and fans, and double change of brav'ry,
With amber bracelets, beads, and all this knav'ry.
What, hast thou din'd? The tailor stays thy leisure,
To deck thy body with his ruffling treasure.　60

Enter Tailor.

Come, tailor, let us see these ornaments;
Lay forth the gown.

Enter Haberdasher.

　　　　　　What news with you, sir?
　[*Hab.*] Here is the cap your worship did bespeak.
　Pet. Why, this was moulded on a porringer—
A velvet dish. Fie, fie, 'tis lewd and filthy.　65
Why, 'tis a cockle or a walnut-shell,
A knack, a toy, a trick, a baby's cap.
Away with it! come let me have a bigger.
　Kath. I'll have no bigger, this doth fit the time,
And gentlewomen wear such caps as these.　70
　Pet. When you are gentle, you shall have one too,
And not till then.
　Hor.　　　　[*Aside.*] That will not be in haste.
　Kath. Why, sir, I trust I may have leave to speak,
And speak I will. I am no child, no babe;
Your betters have endur'd me say my mind,　75
And if you cannot, best you stop your ears.
My tongue will tell the anger of my heart,
Or else my heart concealing it will break,
And rather than it shall, I will be free,
Even to the uttermost, as I please, in words.　80
　Pet. Why, thou say'st true, it is [a] paltry cap,
A custard-coffin, a bauble, a silken pie.
I love thee well in that thou lik'st it not.
　Kath. Love me, or love me not, I like the cap,
And it I will have, or I will have none.　85
　　　　　　　　　[*Exit Haberdasher.*]
　Pet. Thy gown? why, ay. Come, tailor, let us see't.
O mercy, God, what masquing stuff is here?
What's this? a sleeve? 'tis like [a] demi-cannon.
What, up and down carv'd like an apple-tart?
Here's snip and nip and cut and slish and slash,　90
Like to a censer in a barber's shop.
Why, what a' devil's name, tailor, call'st thou this?
　Hor. [*Aside.*] I see she's like to have neither cap
　　nor gown.

54. **bravely:** finely arrayed.
56. **fardingales:** farthingales, hooped petticoats.
57. **brav'ry:** finery.　58. **this knav'ry:** i.e. such tricks.
60. **ruffling:** gaily ruffled.　64. **porringer:** porridge bowl.
65. **lewd:** worthless.　66. **cockle:** cockleshell.
67. **knack:** knickknack.　**trick:** trifle.
69. **fit the time:** agree with the present fashion.
82. **custard-coffin:** crust over a custard (perhaps with pun on *costard*, slang for "head").
87. **masquing stuff:** i.e. material fit only for a masque.
88. **demi-cannon:** large cannon.　89. **up and down:** exactly.
91. **censer:** perfuming pan with a perforated lid.　92. **a':** in.

2. **more:** greater.　**my wrong:** the wrong done to me.
5. **present:** immediate.　11. **spites:** vexes.
13. **As . . . say:** as if to say.　17. **neat's:** ox's.
19. **choleric:** productive of temper. Cf. IV.i.172.　32. **very:** mere.
36. **all amort:** dispirited, dejected.
43. **sorted . . . proof:** i.e. fruitless.　44. **stand:** remain.

Tai. You bid me make it orderly and well,
According to the fashion and the time.   95
  Pet. Marry, and did; but if you be rememb'red,
I did not bid you mar it to the time.
Go hop me over every kennel home,
For you shall hop without my custom, sir.
I'll none of it; hence, make your best of it.   100
  Kath. I never saw a better fashion'd gown,
More quaint, more pleasing, nor more commendable.
Belike you mean to make a puppet of me.
  Pet. Why, true, he means to make a puppet of thee.
  Tai. She says your worship means to make a
puppet of her.   106
  Pet. O monstrous arrogance! Thou liest, thou
        thread, thou thimble,
Thou yard, three-quarters, half-yard, quarter, nail!
Thou flea, thou nit, thou winter-cricket thou!
Brav'd in mine own house with a skein of thread?
Away, thou rag, thou quantity, thou remnant,   111
Or I shall so bemete thee with thy yard
As thou shalt think on prating whilst thou liv'st!
I tell thee, I, that thou hast marr'd her gown.
  Tai. Your worship is deceiv'd, the gown is made
Just as my master had direction.   116
Grumio gave order how it should be done.
  Gru. I gave him no order, I gave him the stuff.
  Tai. But how did you desire it should be made?
  Gru. Marry, sir, with needle and thread.   120
  Tai. But did you not request to have it cut?
  Gru. Thou hast fac'd many things.
  Tai. I have.   123
  Gru. Face not me; thou hast brav'd many men,
brave not me; I will neither be fac'd nor brav'd. I
say unto thee, I bid thy master cut out the gown,
but I did not bid him cut it to pieces. *Ergo*, thou
liest.
  Tai. Why, here is the note of the fashion to
testify.   130
  Pet. Read it.
  Gru. The note lies in 's throat if he say I said
so.
  Tai. [*Reads.*] "Inprimis, a loose-bodied gown"—
  Gru. Master, if ever I said loose-bodied gown,
sew me in the skirts of it, and beat me to death with
a bottom of brown thread. I said a gown.   137
  Pet. Proceed.
  Tai. [*Reads.*] "With a small compass'd cape"—
  Gru. I confess the cape.   140
  Tai. [*Reads.*] "With a trunk sleeve"—
  Gru. I confess two sleeves.
  Tai. [*Reads.*] "The sleeves curiously cut."
  Pet. Ay, there's the villainy.   144

  Gru. Error i' th' bill, sir, error i' th' bill! I commanded the sleeves should be cut out, and sew'd up
again, and that I'll prove upon thee, though thy little
finger be arm'd in a thimble.
  Tai. This is true that I say; and I had thee in
place where, thou shouldst know it.   150
  Gru. I am for thee straight. Take thou the bill,
give me thy mete-yard, and spare not me.
  Hor. God-a-mercy, Grumio, then he shall have
no odds.   154
  Pet. Well, sir, in brief, the gown is not for me.
  Gru. You are i' th' right, sir, 'tis for my mistress.
  Pet. Go take it up unto thy master's use.
  Gru. Villain, not for thy life! Take up my mis-
tress' gown for thy master's use!
  Pet. Why, sir, what's your conceit in that?   160
  Gru. O, sir, the conceit is deeper than you think
        for:
Take up my mistress' gown to his master's use!
O fie, fie, fie!
  Pet. [*Aside.*] Hortensio, say thou wilt see the
        tailor paid.—
Go take it hence, be gone, and say no more.   165
  Hor. Tailor, I'll pay thee for thy gown to-morrow,
Take no unkindness of his hasty words.
Away, I say, commend me to thy master.

                                                Exit Tailor.

  Pet. Well, come, my Kate, we will unto your
        father's
Even in these honest mean habiliments;   170
Our purses shall be proud, our garments poor,
For 'tis the mind that makes the body rich;
And as the sun breaks through the darkest clouds,
So honor peereth in the meanest habit.
What, is the jay more precious than the lark,   175
Because his feathers are more beautiful?
Or is the adder better than the eel,
Because his painted skin contents the eye?
O no, good Kate; neither art thou the worse
For this poor furniture and mean array.   180
If thou accountedst it shame, lay it on me,
And therefore frolic, we will hence forthwith,
To feast and sport us at thy father's house.
Go call my men, and let us straight to him,
And bring our horses unto Long-lane end;   185
There will we mount, and thither walk on foot.
Let's see, I think 'tis now some seven a' clock,
And well we may come there by dinner-time.
  Kath. I dare assure you, sir, 'tis almost two,
And 'twill be supper-time ere you come there.   190
  Pet. It shall be seven ere I go to horse.
Look what I speak, or do, or think to do,
You are still crossing it. Sirs, let 't alone,
I will not go to-day, and ere I do,

---

94. **orderly:** properly.   96. **be rememb'red:** recollect.
98. **kennel:** gutter.   102. **quaint:** beautiful, elegant.
108. **nail:** measure of 2¼ inches.   109. **nit:** egg of a louse.
110. **Brav'd:** defied.   111. **quantity:** fragment.
112. **bemete:** measure, i.e. beat.   113. **yard:** yardstick.
113. **think on:** remember.   **whilst:** as long as.   122. **fac'd:** trimmed.
124. **Face:** bully.   **brav'd:** dressed splendidly.   125. **brave:** defy.
127. **Ergo:** therefore.
134. **loose-bodied gown:** loosely fitted gown (a style of dress worn by
prostitutes, among others).
137. **bottom:** ball (properly, the core on which the thread was wound).
139. **compass'd:** circular.   141. **trunk sleeve:** large, wide sleeve.
143. **curiously:** elaborately.

150. **place where:** the right place.
151. **bill.** With quibble on its sense as a kind of weapon—a blade
fixed onto a long staff.   152. **mete-yard:** measuring-stick.
157. **unto...use:** i.e. for whatever purpose the tailor's master can
find for it (but Gremio pretends to misunderstand).
160. **conceit:** idea, meaning.
174. **peereth:** appears.   **habit:** attire.
180. **furniture:** furnishing, i.e. costume.
188. **dinner-time:** i.e. around noon.   192. **Look what:** whatever.
193. **crossing:** contradicting.

It shall be what a' clock I say it is.   195
   Hor. [*Aside.*] Why, so this gallant will command
     the sun.   [*Exeunt.*]

[SCENE IV]

Enter TRANIO [*as Lucentio*]*, and the* PEDANT *dress'd like
Vincentio,* [*booted and bare-headed*]*.*

   Tra. [Sir], this is the house, please it you that I
   call?
   Ped. Ay, what else? And but I be deceived,
Signior Baptista may remember me
Near twenty years ago in Genoa,
Where we were lodgers at the Pegasus.   5
   Tra. 'Tis well, and hold your own in any case
With such austerity as 'longeth to a father.

Enter BIONDELLO.

   Ped. I warrant you. But, sir, here comes your boy;
'Twere good he were school'd.
   Tra. Fear you not him. Sirrah Biondello,   10
Now do your duty throughly, I advise you.
Imagine 'twere the right Vincentio.
   Bion. Tut, fear not me.
   Tra. But hast thou done thy errand to Baptista?
   Bion. I told him that your father was at Venice,
And that you look'd for him this day in Padua.   16
   Tra. Th' art a tall fellow; hold thee that to drink.
Here comes Baptista; set your countenance, sir.

Enter BAPTISTA *and* LUCENTIO [*as Cambio*]*.*

Signior Baptista, you are happily met.
[*To the Pedant.*] Sir, this is the gentleman I told you
     of.   20
I pray you stand good father to me now,
Give me Bianca for my patrimony.
   Ped. Soft, son!
Sir, by your leave, having come to Padua
To gather in some debts, my son Lucentio   25
Made me acquainted with a weighty cause
Of love between your daughter and himself;
And for the good report I hear of you,
And for the love he beareth to your daughter,
And she to him, to stay him not too long,   30
I am content, in a good father's care,
To have him match'd; and if you please to like
No worse than I, upon some agreement
Me shall you find ready and willing
With one consent to have her so bestowed;   35
For curious I cannot be with you,
Signior Baptista, of whom I hear so well.
   Bap. Sir, pardon me in what I have to say—

Your plainness and your shortness please me well.
Right true it is, your son Lucentio here   40
Doth love my daughter, and she loveth him,
Or both dissemble deeply their affections;
And therefore if you say no more than this,
That like a father you will deal with him,
And pass my daughter a sufficient dower,   45
The match is made, and all is done:
Your son shall have my daughter with consent.
   Tra. I thank you, sir. Where then do you know
   best
We be affied and such assurance ta'en
As shall with either part's agreement stand?   50
   Bap. Not in my house, Lucentio, for you know
Pitchers have ears, and I have many servants;
Besides, old Gremio is heark'ning still,
And happily we might be interrupted.
   Tra. Then at my lodging, and it like you.   55
There doth my father lie; and there this night
We'll pass the business privately and well.
Send for your daughter by your servant here;
My boy shall fetch the scrivener presently.
The worst is this, that at so slender warning,   60
You are like to have a thin and slender pittance.
   Bap. It likes me well. Cambio, hie you home,
And bid Bianca make her ready straight;
And if you will, tell what hath happened:
Lucentio's father is arriv'd in Padua,   65
And how she's like to be Lucentio's wife.
               [*Exit Lucentio.*]
   Bion. I pray the gods she may with all my heart!
   Tra. Dally not with the gods, but get thee gone.
                 Exit [*Biondello*]*.*

Enter PETER, [*a servant, who whispers to Tranio*]*.*

Signior Baptista, shall I lead the way?
Welcome! one mess is like to be your cheer.   70
Come, sir, we will better it in Pisa.
   Bap. I follow you.   *Exeunt.*

Enter LUCENTIO [*as Cambio*] *and* BIONDELLO.

   Bion. Cambio!
   Luc. What say'st thou, Biondello?
   Bion. You saw my master wink and laugh upon
you?   76
   Luc. Biondello, what of that?
   Bion. Faith, nothing; but h'as left me here behind
to expound the meaning or moral of his signs and
tokens.   80
   Luc. I pray thee moralize them.
   Bion. Then thus: Baptista is safe, talking with the
deceiving father of a deceitful son.
   Luc. And what of him?
   Bion. His daughter is to be brought by you to
the supper.   86

---

196. See the Textual Notes for an episode of the Sly framework
preserved in *The Taming of a Shrew.*

IV.iv. Location: Padua. Before Baptista's house.
2. **but:** unless.
5. **the Pegasus:** i.e. an inn so named, marked by a sign displaying the
winged horse of classical myth.
10. **Fear you not:** have no fears about. 11. **throughly:** thoroughly.
17. **tall:** clever. **hold . . . drink:** i.e. Tranio tips him.
18. **set your countenance:** look grave. 23. **Soft:** not so fast.
36. **curious:** particular about every detail.

49. **affied:** betrothed. 53. **heark'ning still:** always listening.
54. **happily:** haply, perchance. 55. **and it like:** if it please.
56. **lie:** lodge. 57. **pass:** transact.
59. **scrivener:** notary. **presently:** immediately.
61. **pittance:** scanty meal. 66. **like:** likely.
70. **mess:** dish. **cheer:** welcome, entertainment.
78. **h'as:** he has. 81. **moralize:** interpret.
82. **safe:** i.e. safely taken care of.

Luc. And then?

Bion. The old priest of Saint Luke's church is at your command at all hours.

Luc. And what of all this?　　　　　　90

Bion. I cannot tell, [except] they are busied about a counterfeit assurance. Take you assurance of her, *cum privilegio ad imprimendum solum;* to th' church take the priest, clerk, and some sufficient honest witnesses.　　　　　　95
If this be not that you look for, I have no more to say,
But bid Bianca farewell for ever and a day.

Luc. Hear'st thou, Biondello?

Bion. I cannot tarry. I knew a wench married in an afternoon as she went to the garden for　100 parsley to stuff a rabbit, and so may you, sir. And so adieu, sir; my master hath appointed me to go to Saint Luke's to bid the priest be ready to come against you come with your appendix.　　　*Exit.*

Luc. I may and will, if she be so contented.　105
She will be pleas'd, then wherefore should I doubt?
Hap what hap may, I'll roundly go about her;
It shall go hard if Cambio go without her.　　*Exit.*

[SCENE V]

Enter PETRUCHIO, KATE, HORTENSIO, [*and* SERVANTS].

Pet. Come on a' God's name, once more toward
　　our father's.
Good Lord, how bright and goodly shines the moon!

Kath. The moon! the sun—it is not moonlight now.

Pet. I say it is the moon that shines so bright.

Kath. I know it is the sun that shines so bright.

Pet. Now by my mother's son, and that's my-
　　self,　　　　　　6
It shall be moon, or star, or what I list,
Or ere I journey to your father's house.—
Go on, and fetch our horses back again.—
Evermore cross'd and cross'd, nothing but cross'd!　10

Hor. Say as he says, or we shall never go.

Kath. Forward, I pray, since we have come so far,
And be it moon, or sun, or what you please;
And if you please to call it a rush-candle,
Henceforth I vow it shall be so for me.　　　15

Pet. I say it is the moon.

Kath. 　　　　　I know it is the moon.

Pet. Nay then you lie; it is the blessed sun.

Kath. Then God be blest, it [is] the blessed sun,
But sun it is not, when you say it is not;
And the moon changes even as your mind.　　20
What you will have it nam'd, even that it is,
And so it shall be so for Katherine.

Hor. Petruchio, go thy ways, the field is won.

Pet. Well, forward, forward, thus the bowl should
　　run,
And not unluckily against the bias.　　　　25
But soft, company is coming here.

Enter VINCENTIO.

[*To Vincentio.*]　Good morrow, gentle mistress, where
　　away?
Tell me, sweet Kate, and tell me truly too,
Hast thou beheld a fresher gentlewoman?
Such war of white and red within her cheeks!　30
What stars do spangle heaven with such beauty,
As those two eyes become that heavenly face?
Fair lovely maid, once more good day to thee.
Sweet Kate, embrace her for her beauty's sake.

Hor. 'A will make the man mad, to make [a]
woman of him.　　　　　　36

Kath. Young budding virgin, fair, and fresh, and
　　sweet,
Whither away, or [where] is thy abode?
Happy the parents of so fair a child!
Happier the man whom favorable stars　　　40
Allots thee for his lovely bedfellow!

Pet. Why, how now, Kate, I hope thou art not mad.
This is a man, old, wrinkled, faded, withered,
And not a maiden, as thou say'st he is.

Kath. Pardon, old father, my mistaking eyes,　45
That have been so bedazzled with the sun,
That every thing I look on seemeth green;
Now I perceive thou art a reverent father.
Pardon, I pray thee, for my mad mistaking.

Pet. Do, good old grandsire, and withal make
　　known　　　　　　50
Which way thou travellest—if along with us,
We shall be joyful of thy company.

Vin. Fair sir, and you my merry mistress,
That with your strange encounter much amaz'd me,
My name is call'd Vincentio, my dwelling Pisa,　55
And bound I am to Padua, there to visit
A son of mine, which long I have not seen.

Pet. What is his name?

Vin. 　　　　　Lucentio, gentle sir.

Pet. Happily met, the happier for thy son.
And now by law, as well as reverent age,　　60
I may entitle thee my loving father.
The sister to my wife, this gentlewoman,
Thy son by this hath married. Wonder not,
Nor be not grieved; she is of good esteem,
Her dowry wealthy, and of worthy birth;　　65
Beside, so qualified as may beseem
The spouse of any noble gentleman.
Let me embrace with old Vincentio,
And wander we to see thy honest son,
Who will of thy arrival be full joyous.　　　70

Vin. But is this true, or is it else your pleasure,

---

91. **except:** unless.　92. **Take you assurance:** make yourself sure.
93. **cum . . . solum:** with exclusive rights to print.
103. **against:** by the time that.　104. **appendix:** addition, i.e. bride.
107. **about her:** i.e. about marrying her.

IV.v. Location: A road leading to Padua.
8. **Or ere:** before.
14. **rush-candle:** inferior candle made by dipping a rush into grease.
20. **moon . . . mind.** Under Kate's apparent acquiescence lies an ironic thrust, since the moon was thought to govern the moods of a lunatic.

24. **bowl:** ball in the game of bowls.
25. **bias:** an off-centre weight in the bowl which governs its course unless it is diverted by some obstacle; hence *against the bias* means "off its proper course."　47. **green:** young and fresh.
48. **reverent:** reverend.
54. **encounter:** manner of address, behavior.
63. **this:** this time.　64. **esteem:** reputation.
66. **so qualified:** of such qualities.

Like pleasant travellers, to break a jest
Upon the company you overtake?
   Hor. I do assure thee, father, so it is.
   Pet. Come go along and see the truth hereof,   75
For our first merriment hath made thee jealous.
                              Exeunt [all but Hortensio].
   Hor. Well, Petruchio, this has put me in heart.
Have to my widow! and if she [be] froward,
Then hast thou taught Hortensio to be untoward. *Exit.*

[ACT V, Scene I]

Enter Biondello, Lucentio, *and* Bianca; Gremio *is
out before.*

   Bion. Softly and swiftly, sir, for the priest is ready.
   Luc. I fly, Biondello; but they may chance to need
thee at home, therefore leave us.
   Bion. Nay, faith, I'll see the church a' your back,
and then come back to my [master's] as soon   5
as I can.   [*Exeunt Lucentio, Bianca, and Biondello.*]
   Gre. I marvel Cambio comes not all this while.

Enter Petruchio, Kate, Vincentio, Grumio, *with*
Attendants.

   Pet. Sir, here's the door, this is Lucentio's house.
My father's bears more toward the market-place;
Thither must I, and here I leave you, sir.   10
   Vin. You shall not choose but drink before you
go.
I think I shall command your welcome here;
And by all likelihood some cheer is toward.   *Knock.*
   Gre. They're busy within, you were best knock
louder.   15

Pedant looks out of the window.

   Ped. What's he that knocks as he would beat
down the gate?
   Vin. Is Signior Lucentio within, sir?
   Ped. He's within, sir, but not to be spoken
withal.   20
   Vin. What if a man bring him a hundred pound
or two, to make merry withal?
   Ped. Keep your hundred pounds to yourself, he
shall need none so long as I live.   24
   Pet. Nay, I told you your son was well belov'd
in Padua.   Do you hear, sir?—to leave frivolous
circumstances, I pray you tell Signior Lucentio that
his father is come from Pisa, and is here at the door
to speak with him.   29
   Ped. Thou liest, his father is come from Padua
and here looking out at the window.
   Vin. Art thou his father?
   Ped. Ay, sir, so his mother says, if I may believe
her.   34

   Pet. [*To Vincentio.*]   Why, how now, gentleman?
Why, this is flat knavery, to take upon you another
man's name.
   Ped. Lay hands on the villain. I believe 'a means
to cozen somebody in this city under my countenance.   40

Enter Biondello.

   Bion. I have seen them in the church together,
God send 'em good shipping! But who is here?
Mine old master Vincentio! Now we are undone
and brought to nothing.
   Vin. [*Seeing Biondello.*]   Come hither, crack-
hemp.   46
   Bion. I hope I may choose, sir.
   Vin. Come hither, you rogue. What, have you
forgot me?
   Bion. Forgot you? no, sir. I could not forget
you, for I never saw you before in all my life.   51
   Vin. What, you notorious villain, didst thou
never see thy [master's] father, Vincentio?
   Bion. What, my old worshipful old master?
Yes, marry, sir—see where he looks out of the
window.   56
   Vin. Is't so indeed?   *He beats Biondello.*
   Bion. Help, help, help! here's a madman will
murder me.   [*Exit.*]
   Ped. Help, son! help, Signior Baptista!   60
                                 [*Exit above.*]
   Pet. Prithee, Kate, let's stand aside and see the
end of this controversy.   [*They retire.*]

Enter Pedant [*below*] *with* Servants, Baptista,
Tranio [*as Lucentio*].

   Tra. Sir, what are you that offer to beat my
servant?   64
   Vin. What am I, sir? Nay, what are you, sir?
O immortal gods! O fine villain! A silken doublet,
a velvet hose, a scarlet cloak, and a copatain hat!
O, I am undone, I am undone! While I play the good
husband at home, my son and my servant spend all
at the university.   70
   Tra. How now, what's the matter?
   Bap. What, is the man lunatic?
   Tra. Sir, you seem a sober ancient gentleman by
your habit; but your words show you a madman.
Why, sir, what 'cerns it you if I wear pearl and   75
gold? I thank my good father, I am able to maintain it.
   Vin. Thy father! O villain, he is a sailmaker in
Bergamo.
   Bap. You mistake, sir, you mistake, sir. Pray
what do you think is his name?   80
   Vin. His name! as if I knew not his name! I
have brought him up ever since he was three years
old, and his name is Tranio.

---

76. **jealous:** suspicious.
78. **froward:** refractory.   79. **untoward:** unmannerly.

V.i. Location: Padua. Before Lucentio's house.
o.s.d. **out before:** on the forestage.
4. **I'll . . . back:** I'll see the church over you, i.e. I'll see you into the
church.   9. **bears:** lies (nautical term).
13. **cheer is toward:** entertainment is in preparation.
27. **circumstances:** matters.

36. **flat:** downright.   39–40. **under my countenance:** in my person.
42. **good shipping:** fair sailing.   43. **undone:** ruined.
45–46. **crack-hemp:** gallows bird.
47. **I hope . . . choose:** i.e. I am not subject to your orders.
63. **offer:** presume.   66. **fine:** consummate.
67. **copatain:** high-crowned.
68–69. **good husband:** careful manager.   75. **'cerns:** concerns.
76. **maintain:** afford.

Ped. Away, away, mad ass, his name is Lucentio,
and he is mine only son, and heir to the lands of me,
Signior Vincentio.   86

Vin. Lucentio! O, he hath murd'red his master!
Lay hold on him, I charge you, in the Duke's name.
O, my son, my son! Tell me, thou villain, where is
my son Lucentio?   90

Tra. Call forth an officer.

         [Exit Servant, who returns with an Officer.]
Carry this mad knave to the jail. Father Baptista,
I charge you see that he be forthcoming.

Vin. Carry me to the jail?

Gre. Stay, officer, he shall not go to prison.   95

Bap. Talk not, Signior Gremio; I say he shall go
to prison.

Gre. Take heed, Signior Baptista, lest you be
cony-catch'd in this business. I dare swear this is the
right Vincentio.   100

Ped. Swear if thou dar'st.

Gre. Nay, I dare not swear it.

Tra. Then thou wert best say that I am not
Lucentio.   104

Gre. Yes, I know thee to be Signior Lucentio.

Bap. Away with the dotard, to the jail with
him!

    Enter BIONDELLO, LUCENTIO, *and* BIANCA.

Vin. Thus strangers may be hal'd and abus'd. O
monstrous villain!   109

Bion. O, we are spoil'd and—yonder he is. Deny
him, forswear him, or else we are all undone.

    Exeunt Biondello, Tranio, and Pedant
      as fast as may be.

Luc. Pardon, sweet father.   *Kneel.*

Vin.   Lives my sweet son?

Bian. Pardon, dear father.

Bap.   How hast thou offended?
Where is Lucentio?

Luc.   Here's Lucentio,
Right son to the right Vincentio,   115
That have by marriage made thy daughter mine,
While counterfeit supposes blear'd thine eyne.

Gre. Here's packing, with a witness, to deceive us
all!

Vin. Where is that damned villain Tranio,   120
That fac'd and braved me in this matter so?

Bap. Why, tell me, is not this my Cambio?

Bian. Cambio is chang'd into Lucentio.

Luc. Love wrought these miracles. Bianca's love
Made me exchange my state with Tranio,   125
While he did bear my countenance in the town,
And happily I have arrived at the last
Unto the wished haven of my bliss.
What Tranio did, myself enforc'd him to;
Then pardon him, sweet father, for my sake.   130

---

93. **forthcoming:** ready to appear (in court) when required.
99. **cony-catch'd:** duped.
117. **supposes:** suppositions, conjectures; an allusion to Gascoigne's
play *Supposes* (itself based on Ariosto's *I Suppositi*), from which
Shakespeare took the Lucentio-Bianca plot. **blear'd thine eyne:**
hoodwinked you (*eyne* is an archaic plural of *eye*).
118. **packing:** conspiracy, plotting. **witness:** vengeance.
121. **fac'd and braved.** Cf. IV.iii.124-25.
125. **state:** rank and degree.

Vin. I'll slit the villain's nose, that would have
sent me to the jail.

Bap. But do you hear, sir? Have you married my
daughter without asking my good will?

Vin. Fear not, Baptista, we will content you, go
to; but I will in to be reveng'd for this villainy.   136
         Exit.

Bap. And I, to sound the depth of this knavery.
         Exit.

Luc. Look not pale, Bianca, thy father will not
frown.   *Exeunt [Lucentio and Bianca].*

Gre. My cake is dough, but I'll in among the
rest,   140
Out of hope of all but my share of the feast.   *[Exit.]*

Kath. Husband, let's follow, to see the end of
this ado.

Pet. First kiss me, Kate, and we will.

Kath. What, in the midst of the street?

Pet. What, art thou asham'd of me?   145

Kath. No, sir, God forbid, but asham'd to kiss.

Pet. Why then let's home again. Come, sirrah,
let's away.

Kath. Nay, I will give thee a kiss; now pray thee,
love, stay.

Pet. Is not this well? Come, my sweet Kate: 149
Better once than never, for never too late.   *Exeunt.*

         [SCENE II]

Enter BAPTISTA, VINCENTIO, GREMIO, *the* PEDANT,
  LUCENTIO, *and* BIANCA; [PETRUCHIO, KATHERINA,
  HORTENSIO,] TRANIO, BIONDELLO, GRUMIO, *and*
  WIDOW: *the servingmen with Tranio bringing in a
  banquet.*

Luc. At last, though long, our jarring notes agree,
And time it is, when raging war is [done],
To smile at scapes and perils overblown.
My fair Bianca, bid my father welcome,
While I with self-same kindness welcome thine.   5
Brother Petruchio, sister Katherina,
And thou, Hortensio, with thy loving widow,
Feast with the best, and welcome to my house.
My banket is to close our stomachs up
After our great good cheer. Pray you sit down,   10
For now we sit to chat as well as eat.

Pet. Nothing but sit and sit, and eat and eat!

Bap. Padua affords this kindness, son Petruchio.

Pet. Padua affords nothing but what is kind.

Hor. For both our sakes, I would that word were
true.   15

Pet. Now, for my life, Hortensio fears his widow.

Wid. Then never trust me if I be afeard.

Pet. You are very sensible, and yet you miss my
sense:
I mean Hortensio is afeard of you.

---

140. **My ... dough.** Proverbial expression for failure. Cf. I.i.108-9.
141. **Out ... but:** with hope of nothing except.

V.ii. Location: Padua. Lucentio's house.
3. **scapes:** escapes. **overblown:** blown over.
9. **banket:** banquet, i.e. light repast of sweets, fruit, and wine.
16. **fears.** The widow takes this word in its causative sense,
"frightens."

Wid. He that is giddy thinks the world turns
round.   20
Pet. Roundly replied.
Kath.   Mistress, how mean you that?
Wid. Thus I conceive by him.
Pet. Conceives by me! how likes Hortensio that?
Hor. My widow says, thus she conceives her tale.
Pet. Very well mended. Kiss him for that, good
widow.   25
Kath. "He that is giddy thinks the world turns
round":
I pray you tell me what you meant by that.
Wid. Your husband, being troubled with a shrew,
Measures my husband's sorrow by his woe:
And now you know my meaning.   30
Kath. A very mean meaning.
Wid.   Right, I mean you.
Kath. And I am mean indeed, respecting you.
Pet. To her, Kate!
Hor. To her, widow!
Pet. A hundred marks, my Kate does put her
down.   35
Hor. That's my office.
Pet. Spoke like an officer. Ha' to thee, lad!
                                                    Drinks to Hortensio.
Bap. How likes Gremio these quick-witted folks?
Gre. Believe me, sir, they butt together well.   39
Bian. Head, and butt! an hasty-witted body
Would say your head and butt were head and horn.
Vin. Ay, mistress bride, hath that awakened you?
Bian. Ay, but not frighted me, therefore I'll sleep
again.
Pet. Nay, that you shall not, since you have begun;
Have at you for a [bitter] jest or two!   45
Bian. Am I your bird? I mean to shift my bush,
And then pursue me as you draw your bow.
You are welcome all.
                                    Exit Bianca [with Katherina and Widow].
Pet. She hath prevented me. Here, Signior Tranio,
This bird you aim'd at, though you hit her not;   50
Therefore a health to all that shot and miss'd.
Tra. O, sir, Lucentio slipp'd me like his greyhound,
Which runs himself, and catches for his master.
Pet. A good swift simile, but something currish.
Tra. 'Tis well, sir, that you hunted for yourself;
'Tis thought your deer does hold you at a bay.   56
Bap. O, O, Petruchio, Tranio hits you now.
Luc. I thank thee for that gird, good Tranio.
Hor. Confess, confess, hath he not hit you here?
Pet. 'A has a little gall'd me, I confess;   60
And as the jest did glance away from me,
'Tis ten to one it maim'd you [two] outright.

21. **Roundly:** frankly, plainly.
22. **Thus . . . him:** that's what I take him for.
29. **Measures:** judges.   31. **very mean:** very contemptible.
32. **I . . . you:** i.e. I am moderate (in temper) compared with you.
35. **marks.** A mark was the sum of 13s. 4d.   37. **Ha':** i.e. here's.
45. **Have at you:** I shall come at you.   **bitter:** shrewd, sharp.
46. **your bird:** i.e. the bird you are aiming your darts at.   **shift my
bush:** fly to another tree (so that he will have to follow her if he
intends to keep her as his target).   49. **prevented:** forestalled.
52. **slipp'd:** unleashed.
54. **swift:** (1) ready-witted; (2) having reference to swiftness.
56. **hold you at a bay:** turn to make a stand against you (hunting
term).   58. **gird:** taunt; sharp, biting jest.   60. **gall'd:** wounded.

Bap. Now in good sadness, son Petruchio,
I think thou hast the veriest shrew of all.
Pet. Well, I say no; and therefore [for] assurance
Let's each one send unto his wife,   66
And he whose wife is most obedient,
To come at first when he doth send for her,
Shall win the wager which we will propose.
Hor. Content. What's the wager?
Luc.   Twenty crowns.
Pet. Twenty crowns!   71
I'll venture so much of my hawk or hound,
But twenty times so much upon my wife.
Luc. A hundred then.
Hor.   Content.
Pet.   A match! 'tis done.
Hor. Who shall begin?
Luc.   That will I.   75
Go, Biondello, bid your mistress come to me.
Bion. I go.   *Exit.*
Bap. Son, I'll be your half, Bianca comes.
Luc. I'll have no halves; I'll bear it all myself.

                                    Enter Biondello.

How now, what news?
Bion.   Sir, my mistress sends you word
That she is busy, and she cannot come.   81
Pet. How? she is busy, and she cannot come!
Is that an answer?
Gre.   Ay, and a kind one too.
Pray God, sir, your wife send you not a worse.
Pet. I hope better.   85
Hor. Sirrah Biondello, go and entreat my wife
To come to me forthwith.   *Exit Biondello.*
Pet.   O ho, entreat her!
Nay then she must needs come.
Hor.   I am afraid, sir,
Do what you can, yours will not be entreated.

                                    Enter Biondello.

Now, where's my wife?   90
Bion. She says you have some goodly jest in hand.
She will not come; she bids you come to her.
Pet. Worse and worse; she will not come! O vild,
Intolerable, not to be endur'd!
Sirrah Grumio, go to your mistress,   95
Say I command her come to me.   *Exit [Grumio].*
Hor. I know her answer.
Pet.   What?
Hor.   She will not.
Pet. The fouler fortune mine, and there an end.

                                    Enter Katherina.

Bap. Now, by my holidam, here comes Katherina!
Kath. What is your will, sir, that you send for
me?   100
Pet. Where is your sister, and Hortensio's wife?

63. **good sadness:** all seriousness.   65. **assurance:** proof.
74. **A match:** agreed.
78. **I'll . . . half:** I'll share the wager with you.   85. **hope:** expect.
93. **vild:** vile.
99. **holidam:** properly *halidom*, i.e. holiness; but, as the spelling
shows, the word had come to be taken as referring to the Virgin
Mary.

Kath. They sit conferring by the parlor fire.

Pet. Go fetch them hither. If they deny to come,
Swinge me them soundly forth unto their husbands.
Away, I say, and bring them hither straight.   105

[*Exit Katherina.*]

Luc. Here is a wonder, if you talk of a wonder.

Hor. And so it is; I wonder what it bodes.

Pet. Marry, peace it bodes, and love, and quiet life,
An aweful rule, and right supremacy;
And to be short, what not, that's sweet and happy.

Bap. Now fair befall thee, good Petruchio!   111
The wager thou hast won, and I will add
Unto their losses twenty thousand crowns,
Another dowry to another daughter,
For she is chang'd, as she had never been.   115

Pet. Nay, I will win my wager better yet,
And show more sign of her obedience,
Her new-built virtue and obedience.

Enter KATE, BIANCA, *and* WIDOW.

See where she comes, and brings your froward wives
As prisoners to her womanly persuasion.   120
Katherine, that cap of yours becomes you not;
Off with that bable, throw it under-foot.

[*Katherina throws down her cap.*]

Wid. Lord, let me never have a cause to sigh,
Till I be brought to such a silly pass!

Bian. Fie, what a foolish duty call you this?   125

Luc. I would your duty were as foolish too.
The wisdom of your duty, fair Bianca,
Hath cost me [a] hundred crowns since supper-time.

Bian. The more fool you for laying on my duty.

Pet. Katherine, I charge thee tell these head-
strong women   130
What duty they do owe their lords and husbands.

Wid. Come, come, you're mocking; we will have
no telling.

Pet. Come on, I say, and first begin with her.

Wid. She shall not.

Pet. I say she shall, and first begin with her.   135

Kath. Fie, fie, unknit that threat'ning unkind
brow,
And dart not scornful glances from those eyes,
To wound thy lord, thy king, thy governor.
It blots thy beauty, as frosts do bite the meads,
Confounds thy fame, as whirlwinds shake fair buds,
And in no sense is meet or amiable.   141
A woman mov'd is like a fountain troubled,
Muddy, ill-seeming, thick, bereft of beauty,
And while it is so, none so dry or thirsty
Will deign to sip, or touch one drop of it.   145
Thy husband is thy lord, thy life, thy keeper,

Thy head, thy sovereign; one that cares for thee,
And for thy maintenance; commits his body
To painful labor, both by sea and land;
To watch the night in storms, the day in cold,   150
Whilst thou li'st warm at home, secure and safe;
And craves no other tribute at thy hands
But love, fair looks, and true obedience—
Too little payment for so great a debt.
Such duty as the subject owes the prince,   155
Even such a woman oweth to her husband;
And when she is froward, peevish, sullen, sour,
And not obedient to his honest will,
What is she but a foul contending rebel,
And graceless traitor to her loving lord?   160
I am asham'd that women are so simple
To offer war where they should kneel for peace,
Or seek for rule, supremacy, and sway,
When they are bound to serve, love, and obey.
Why are our bodies soft, and weak, and smooth, 165
Unapt to toil and trouble in the world,
But that our soft conditions, and our hearts,
Should well agree with our external parts?
Come, come, you froward and unable worms!
My mind hath been as big as one of yours,   170
My heart as great, my reason haply more,
To bandy word for word and frown for frown;
But now I see our lances are but straws,
Our strength as weak, our weakness past compare,
That seeming to be most which we indeed least are.
Then vail your stomachs, for it is no boot,   176
And place your hands below your husband's foot;
In token of which duty, if he please,
My hand is ready, may it do him ease.

Pet. Why, there's a wench! Come on, and kiss
me, Kate.   180

Luc. Well, go thy ways, old lad, for thou shalt ha't.

Vin. 'Tis a good hearing when children are toward.

Luc. But a harsh hearing when women are froward.

Pet. Come, Kate, we'll to bed.
We three are married, but you two are sped.   185

[*To Lucentio.*] 'Twas I won the wager, though you hit
the white,
And being a winner, God give you good night!

Exit Petruchio [*with Katherina*].

Hor. Now go thy ways, thou hast tam'd a curst
shrow.

Luc. 'Tis a wonder, by your leave, she will be
tam'd so.   [*Exeunt.*]

---

157. **peevish:** obstinate, willful.   161. **simple:** foolish.
166. **Unapt:** unfit.   167. **conditions:** qualities.
169. **unable worms:** i.e. poor weak creatures.
170. **big:** haughty, arrogant.
176. **Then . . . boot:** Then lower your pride, for there is no help for it.
179. **do him ease:** give him pleasure.
182. **toward:** tractable, obedient.   185. **sped:** done for.
186. **white:** centre of the target; playing on Bianca's name, which in
Italian means "white."   188. **shrow:** shrew.
189. See the Textual Notes for the final episodes of the Sly framework
preserved in *The Taming of a Shrew*.

---

103. **deny:** refuse.   104. **Swinge:** whip.   **me.** The ethical dative.
109. **aweful rule:** order commanding respect.
111. **fair:** good fortune.   122. **bable:** bauble.
125. **duty:** obedience.   129. **laying:** betting.
140. **Confounds:** ruins.   **fame:** reputation.   142. **mov'd:** angry.

The basic authority for *The Taming of the Shrew* is the First Folio (1623); all later texts are derived essentially from that source. A quarto edition based on F1 (referred to as Q in the Textual Notes) was printed in 1631.

There has been much speculation about the relation between *The Shrew* and a play entitled *A Pleasant Conceited Historie, called The taming of a Shrew*, which was published in 1594 (referred to as (Q) in the Textual Notes). The once-popular theory that *A Shrew* is the direct source of Shakespeare's play is no longer accepted. Today scholars generally hold either (a) that *A Shrew* is a "bad" quarto derived by some form of memorial imitation from *The Shrew*, or (b) that both plays are derived from a common original, the 1594 text of *A Shrew* being indeed a "bad" quarto, but a "bad" quarto of Shakespeare's source. The first alternative seems to be gaining increasing support in the most recent assessments of the problem. Textually, *A Shrew* is of little value to an editor of Shakespeare's *Shrew*, since, whether or not we accept it as a "bad" quarto of *The Shrew*, there is only some occasional verbal correspondence between the two texts. It does, however, preserve, in mangled form, a conclusion of the Sly framework and four short Sly inter-scenes, all of which are lacking in the F1 text. The conclusion and two of the inter-scenes were inserted in the text of *The Shrew* by Pope; in the present edition the five passages are included in the Textual Notes (see II.i.411, IV.iii.196, V.ii.189). Other passages from (Q) are quoted at Induction, ii.129–44, IV.ii.50–6, V.ii.136–79. Two later editions of *A Shrew* appeared in 1596 and 1607.

The F1 text gives evidence of having been printed from Shakespeare's "foul papers" (perhaps from "foul papers" which had undergone some form of revision). Since there is also evidence of a book-keeper's hand at several places in the F1 text (for example, in the use of actors' names for character names, though "Sincklo" at Induction i.88 would appear to be authorial), it is further supposed that these "foul papers" had been annotated by a book-keeper in preparation for the production of an official prompt-book. Omissions in the stage directions and the palpable confusion in speech-prefixes at III.i.48–54 and IV.ii.4–8 make it most unlikely that the manuscript from which the F1 text was printed could itself have served as a prompt-book.

For further information, see: Peter Alexander, "*The Taming of a Shrew*," *TLS*, 16 September 1926, p. 614, and "The Original Ending of *The Taming of the Shrew*," *SQ*, XX (1969), 111–16; J. D. Wilson, ed., New Cambridge *The Taming of the Shrew* (Cambridge, 1928) [the preceding studies view *A Shrew* as a "bad" quarto of *The Shrew*]; R. A. Houk, "The Evolution of *The Taming of the Shrew*," *PMLA*, LVII (1942), 1009–38; G. I. Duthie, "*The Taming of a Shrew* and *The Taming of the Shrew*," *RES*, XIX (1943), 337–56 [the last two studies support the view that *A Shrew* and *The Shrew* are derived from a common source]; W. W. Greg, *The Shakespeare First Folio* (Oxford, 1955); J. W. Shroeder, "*The Taming of a Shrew* and *The Taming of the Shrew*: A Case Reopened," *JEGP*, LVII (1958), 424–43 [reopens the argument that *A Shrew* in its present form was one of the sources of *The Shrew*]; Richard Hosley, "Sources and Analogues of *The Taming of the Shrew*," *Huntington Library Quarterly*, XXVII (1964), 289–308 [points out new sources and defends the spelling *Litio* against the *Licio* of F2; in his Pelican edition, accepts the "bad" quarto relationship of *A Shrew* to *The Shrew*].

TEXTUAL NOTES

Dramatis personae: *subs. as first given by Rowe*
Act-scene division: *none in (Q); F1 gives headings for I.i (at the beginning of the Induction), Act III (at III.i of the present text), IV.i (at IV.iii), and Act V (at V.ii); other act-scene divisions from Rowe and later editors (see first note to each scene); present act-scene arrangement as a whole first established by Steevens*

Induction, i

Induction, i] *Pope;* Actus primus. Scoena Prima. *F1*
Location: *Theobald*
o.s.d. Enter ... Hostess.] *Kittredge (subs.);* Enter Begger and Hostes, Christophero Sly. *F1;* Enter a Tapster, beating out of his doores Slie Droonken. *(Q)*
1 s.p. Sly.] *Rowe;* Begger. *F1 (or Beg. throughout)*
9 Saint] *Dyce;* S. *F1*
12 thirdborough] *Theobald;* Head- / borough *F1*
12 s.d. Exit.] *Rowe;* (Q) *has* Exit Tapster.
17 (Brach ... cur, is emboss'd),] *White;* Brach ... Curre is imbost, *F1*
22, 30 s.pp. 1. Hun.] *Capell;* Hunts. *F1*
32–3 He ... soundly.] *as verse, Rowe; as prose, F1*
73 s.d. Some ... Sly.] *Theobald;* (Q) *has* Exeunt two with Slie.
74 s.d. Exit Servingman.] *Theobald*
78 s.d. Enter Players.] Enter two of the players with packs at their backs, and a boy. *(Q)*
88 s.p. 1. Play.] *Capell;* Sincklo. *F1 (the name of the actor who played this role)*
100 s.p. 1. Play.] *Capell;* Plai. *F1*

135 peasant.] *Johnson;* peasant, *F1*
138 s.d. Exeunt.] *Capell*

Induction, ii

Induction, ii] *Capell*
Location: *Theobald*
o.s.d. Enter ... Lord.] Enter two with a table and a banquet on it, and two other, with Slie asleepe in a chaire, richlie apparelled, & the musick plaieng. *(Q)*
2, 3, 76 Will't] *F3;* Wilt *F1*
2 lordship] *Q;* Lord *F1*
18 Sly's] *Q* (Slies); Sies *F1*
23 fourteen pence] *Rowe;* xiiii.d. *F1*
25 What!] *Hanmer (subs.);* What *F1*
26 s.p. 3. Serv.] *Capell;* 3. Man. *F1 (throughout scene)*
27 s.p. 2. Serv.] *Capell;* 2 Man. *F1 (throughout scene)*
47 s.p. 1. Serv.] *Capell;* 1 Man. *F1 (throughout scene)*
73 Christopher] Christophero *F2*
98 s.d. the Page as a] *Capell; s.d. in (Q) reads:* Enter the boy in Womans attire.
100 s.p. Page.] *Capell;* Lady. *F1 (or La. throughout scene)*
110 Al'ce] *Capell;* Alce *F1*
129–44] *(Q) gives the following equivalent of these lines:* Lord. May it please you, your honors plaiers be come / To offer your honour a plaie. / Slie. A plaie Sim, O braue, be they my plaiers? / Lord. I my Lord. / Slie. Is there not a foole in the plaie? / Lord. Yes my lord. / Slie. When wil they plaie Sim? / Lord. Euen when it please your honor, they be readie. / Boy. My lord Ile go bid them begin their plaie. / Slie. Doo, but looke that you come againe. / Boy. I warrant you my lord, I

wil not leaue you thus. / Exit boy. / Slie. Come Sim, where be the plaiers? Sim stand by / Me and weele flout the plaiers out of their cotes. / Lord. Ile cal them my lord. Hoe where are you there? / Sound Trumpets.
137 will, ... Is] *Capell;* will let them play, it is *F1*
138 comonty] *(Q), in Induction, i, calls a comedy a* comoditie
144 s.d. They all sit.] *Malone (subs.)*
144 s.d. Flourish.] *part of o.s.d. for I.i, F1;* Sound Trumpets. *(Q)*

I.i

I.i] *Pope*
Location: *Wilson (subs., after Theobald)*
o.s.d. Tranio] *F2;* Triano *F1*
13 Vincentio] *Hanmer;* Vincentio's *F1*
14 brought] *F2;* brough *F1*
25 Mi perdonato] *Capell (reading* perdonate); Me Pardonato *F1*
26 am,] *ed.;* am *F1*
33 Ovid] *F3;* Ouid; *F1*
47 Katherina] *F2;* Katerina *F1 (occasionally throughout; the form reflects Shakespeare's pronunciation)*
47 s.d. suitor] *F2* (shuiter); sister *F1*
57 s.p. Kath.] *Rowe;* Kate. *F1 (throughout)*
57 s.d. To Baptista.] *Capell*
71 Maid's] *Rowe;* Maids *F1*
78–9 A ... why.] *as verse, Capell; as prose, F1*
90 resolv'd] *Q;* resould *F1*
91 s.d. Exit Bianca.] *Theobald*
98 kind, and liberal] *Theobald, Hanmer;* kind and liberall, *F1*
108 cake's] *F3;* cakes *F1*
145 s.d. Manent] *Pope;* Manet *F1*
162 captum] *F2;* captam *F1*

163 **contents;]** *Theobald;* contents, *F1*
164 **counsel's]** *F2;* counsels *F1*
207 **color'd]** *F2;* Conlord *F1*
207 **cloak.]** *Pope;* cloake, *F1*
227 **time.]** *F2;* time *F1*
235 **Ay, sir!—[aside]]** *Munro (after Rowe, Dyce);* I sir, *F1 (F1 is ambiguous; most recent editors read I, sir!)*
239–44 **So...Lucentio.]** *as verse, Capell; as prose, F1*
244 **your]** *F2;* you *F1*
249 **s.p. 1. Serv.]** *Capell;* 1. Man. *F1*

I.ii

I.ii] *Capell*
Location: *Pope*
18 **masters]** *Theobald;* mistris *F1*
24 **Con . . . trovato]** *Theobald (after Rowe);* Contutti le core bene trobatto *F1*
25 **ben]** *F2;* bene *F1*
25 **molto]** *Theobald;* multo *F1*
25 **honorato]** *F2;* honorata *F1*
28 **'leges]** *Capell;* leges *F1*
34–5 **Whom . . . worst.]** *as verse, Rowe; as prose, F1*
46 **this' a]** *W. S. Walker conj.;* this a *F1*
50 **young men]** *F3;* yongmen *F1*
52 **grows. But . . . few,]** *Hanmer (subs.);* growes but . . . few. *F1*
70 **Sibyl]** *Theobald;* Sibell *F1*
71 **Xantippe]** *Theobald;* Zentippe *F1*
73 **Whe'er]** *ed.;* Were *F1*
74 **seas,]** *Rowe;* seas. *F1*
79 **aglet-baby]** *hyphen, Theobald*
112 **rope-tricks]** *hyphen, Theobald*
121 **me and other]** *Capell;* me. Other *F1*
137 s.d. **disguised]** *F2;* disgused *F1*
137 s.d. **as a schoolmaster]** *Wilson (subs.)*
138–9 **old folks]** *F2;* olde- / folkes *F1*
143 s.d. **They stand aside.]** *Kittredge (after Capell)*
162 s.d. **Coming forward.]** *Collier*
164 **Minola.]** *Rowe (subs.);* Minola, *F1*
172 **me]** *Rowe;* one *F1*
190 **Antonio's]** *Rowe;* Butonios *F1*
206 **trumpets']** *Capell;* trumpets *F1*
209 **chestnut]** *Singer;* Chesse-nut *F1*
213 **ours]** *Thirlby conj.;* yours *F1*
227 s.d. **Aside.]** *Capell*
264 **stead]** *Capell;* steed *F1*
265 **feat]** *Rowe;* seeke *F1*
279 **motion's]** *Rowe;* motions *F1*
280 **ben]** *F2;* Been *F1*

II.i

II.i] *Pope*
Location: *Pope*
3 **gawds]** *Theobald;* goods *F1*
8 **thee]** *F2*
30 s.d. **Bianca]** *Rowe*
36 s.d. **Exit.]** *Rowe*
38 s.d. **Hortensio . . . and]** *Rowe*
42–3 **And . . . virtuous?]** *as verse, Capell; as prose, F1*
55 s.d. **Presenting Hortensio.]** *Rowe*
60 **Litio]** Licio *F2*
71–3 **Saving . . . forward.]** *as verse, Steevens (after Capell); as prose, F1*
73 **Backare!]** *Craig;* Bacare *F1 (in italics)*
74 **O . . . doing.]** *as verse, Hanmer; as prose, F1*
75–6 **wooing. Neighbor,]** *Theobald;* wooing neighbors: *F1*
76–87 **Neighbor . . . coming?]** *as prose, Pope; as verse, F1*
77 **it.]** *Rowe (subs.);* it, *F1*
77 **kindness,]** *Cambridge;* kindnesse *F1*
79 **you]** *Capell*
79 s.d. **presenting Lucentio]** *Rowe*
85 s.d. **To Tranio.]** *Rowe*
90 **a suitor]** *Q;* as utor *F1*
104 **Pisa; by report]** *Rowe;* Pisa by report, *F1*
110 s.d. **Exit . . . following.]** *Capell*
131 **proud-minded]** *hyphen, Rowe*
141 **shake]** *F2;* shakes *F1*

153 **strook]** *Capell;* stroke *F1*
157 **rascal fiddler]** *Capell;* Rascall, Fidler, *F1*
168 s.d. **Baptista . . . Hortensio]** *Theobald (s.d. placed as in Rowe; after l. 167, F1)*
186 **bonny]** *F4;* bony *F1*
213–4 **Who . . . tail.]** *as verse, Rowe; as prose, F1*
247 **askaunce]** *ed. (after Capell);* a sconce *F1*
263 **mother-wit]** *hyphen, Capell*
278 s.d. **Tranio]** *Q;* Trayno *F1 (s.d. after l. 275, F1; placed as in Pcpe)*
301 **good night]** *F3;* godnight *F1*
324 s.d. **severally]** *Theobald*
330 **in]** *Rowe;* me *F1*
354 **Valens]** *ed.;* Vallens *F1*
357 **pail]** *F2;* pale *F1*
373 s.d. **Aside.]** *Warburton conj.*
375 **Marsellis]** *F2;* Marcellus *F1*
379 **tight]** *Rowe;* tite *F1*
411] *After this line Pope inserts the first five speeches of the following Sly framework from (Q); Capell, after III.ii: Then Slie speakes. / Slie. Sim, when will the foole come againe? / Lord. Heele come againe my Lord anon. / Slie. Gis some more drinke here, souns wheres / The Tapster, here Sim eate some of these things. / Lord. So I doo my Lord. / Slie. Here Sim, I drinke to thee. / Lord. My Lord heere comes the plaiers againe, / Slie. O braue, heers two fine gentlewomen.*

III.i

III.i] *Rowe;* Actus Tertia. *F1*
Location: *Theobald*
19 **'pointed]** *Hanmer;* pointed *F1*
28 **hic]** *Q;* hie *F1 (?)*
28, 33, 42 **Sigeia]** *F2 (subs.);* sigeria *F1*
43 **steterat]** *Q;* staterat *F1*
48–50 **How . . . yet.]** *continued to Hortensio, Rowe; assigned to Luc., F1*
48 s.d. **Aside.]** *Capell*
51 s.p. **Bian.]** *Theobald conj.; line given as part of preceding speech, F1*
52 s.p. **Luc.]** *Theobald conj.;* Bian. *F1*
54 s.p. **Bian.]** *Theobald conj.;* Hort. *F1*
59 s.d. **To Lucentio.]** *Capell*
62 s.d. **Aside.]** *Cambridge*
73 s.d. **Reads.]** *Capell*
74 **A re]** *Q;* Are *F1*
75 **B mi]** *Pope;* Beeme *F1*
76 **C fa ut]** *Q;* Cfavt *F1*
81 **change]** *F2;* charge *F1*
81 **odd]** *Theobald;* old *F1*
82 s.p. **Mess.]** *Neilson;* Nicke. *F1 (perhaps Nicholas Tooley, who may have played the role)*
85 s.d. **Exeunt . . . Messenger.]** *Neilson*
86 s.d. **Exit.]** *Rowe*
90–1 **stale, . . . list.]** *Capell (subs.);* stale: . . . List, *F1*

III.ii

III.ii] *Pope*
Location: *Malone (after Capell)*
o.s.d. **Lucentio]** *Rowe*
1 s.d. **To Tranio.]** *Capell*
1 **'pointed]** *Pope;* pointed *F1*
13 **behavior;]** *F4;* behauiour, *F1*
14 **man,]** *Rowe;* man; *F1*
15 **'point]** *Pope;* point *F1*
26 s.d. **followed . . . others]** *Capell (subs.)*
29 **thy]** *F2*
30 **old news]** *Capell*
33 **hear]** *Q;* heard *F1*
48 **hipp'd,]** *Hanmer;* hip'd *F1*
55 **sway'd]** *Hanmer;* Waid *F1*
56 **near-legg'd]** *hyphen, Rowe*
57 **half-cheek'd]** *Singer;* halfe-chekt *F1*
82–6 **Nay . . . many.]** *as verse, Collier (after Rowe); as prose, F1*
86 s.d. **Enter . . . Grumio.]** Enter Ferando baselie attired, and a red cap on his head. *(Q)*
87–90 **Come . . . were.]** *as verse, Capell; as prose, F1*
91 s.d. **Pretends great excitement.]** *ed.*
123 s.d. **with Grumio]** *Dyce (subs.)*

127 s.d. **with . . . Attendants]** *Cambridge (subs.)*
146 **narrow-prying]** *hyphen, Pope*
153 **grumbling]** *F2;* grumlling *F1*
167–83 **Trembled . . . play.]** *as verse, Steevens (after F2); as prose, F1*
183 s.d. **Grumio, and Train]** *Capell*
199 s.p. **Gre.]** *F2;* Gra. *F1*
209 **to-morrow—]** *Sisson;* to morrow, *F1*
239 s.d. **Petruchio, Katherina]** *Rowe (subs.);* P. Ka. *F1*
239 s.d. **and Grumio]** *Capell (subs.)*

IV.i

IV.i] *Pope*
Location: *Pope*
3 **ray'd]** *Johnson;* raide *F1;* raied *Q*
26 s.p. **Curt.]** *F2;* Gru. *F1*
41 **"Jack . . . boy!"]** *quotes, Warburton*
48 **their]** *F3;* the *F1*
62 s.d. **Strikes him.]** *Rowe*
117 s.p. **Gru.]** *F3;* Gre. *F1*
129 **peasant]** *Rowe;* pezant, *F1*
139 s.d. **Exeunt Servants.]** *Theobald;* Ex. Ser. *F1*
140 s.d. **Sings.]** *Theobald*
140–1 **"Where . . . those"]** *quotes, Theobald*
142 s.d. **Enter . . . supper.]** They couer the bord and fetch in the meate. *(Q)*
145 s.d. **Sings.]** *Rowe*
148 **off]** *Rowe;* of *F1*
148 s.d. **Strikes him.]** *Rowe;* He beates them all. *(Q)*
155 s.d. **Strikes him.]** *Capell*
165 s.d. **He . . . them.]** *(Q)*
167 s.d. **Exeunt Servants.]** *Dyce*
178 s.d. **Enter Servants severally.]** Manent seruingmen and eate vp all the meate. *(Q)*
180 s.d. **Enter . . . servant.]** *placed as in Capell; after l. 181, F1*
184–7 **And . . . hither.]** *as verse, Pope; as prose, F1*
187 s.d. **Exeunt.]** *Pope*

IV.ii

IV.ii] *Steevens*
Location: *Pope, Theobald*
1 **Litio]** *Pelican;* Lisio *F1 (throughout scene)*
4 s.p. **Hor.]** *F2;* Luc. *F1*
5 s.d. **They stand aside.]** *Theobald (subs.)*
6, 8 s.pp. **Luc.]** *F2;* Hor. *F1*
7 **What . . . First]** *Theobald;* What Master reade you first, *F1*
8 **read . . . profess,]** *Rowe (read F4);* reade, . . . professe *F1*
10 **prove]** *F2;* ptoue *F1*
10 s.d. **They retire.]** *Theobald (subs.)*
13 **none]** *Rowe;* me *F1*
31 **her]** *F3;* them *F1*
35 **forsworn!]** *Capell;* forsworn *F1*
36 **oath,]** *Rowe;* oath. *F1*
43 s.d. **Exit.]** *Rowe*
45 **'longeth]** *Hanmer;* longeth *F1*
50–6] *With these lines cf. the curiously close equivalent in (Q): [Valeria.] . . . But tell me my Lord, is Ferando married then? / Aurel. He is: and Polidor shortly shall be wed, / And he meanes to tame his wife ere long. / Vale. He saies so. / Aurel. Faith he's gon vnto the taming schoole. / Val. The taming schoole: why is there such a place? / Aurel. I: and Ferando is the Maister of the schoole.*
53 **Tranio?]** *ed.;* Tranio. *F1*
63 **mercantant]** *ed.;* Marcantant *F1; called marchant in (Q)*
65 **countenance]** *F2;* eountenance *F1*
71 **Take]** *F2;* Par. Take *F1*
71 **in]** *Theobald;* me *F1*
71 s.d. **Exeunt . . . Bianca.]** *Rowe*
101 s.d. **Aside.]** *Rowe*

IV.iii

IV.iii] *Steevens;* Actus Quartus. Scena Prima. *F1 ((Q) offers more frequent verbal links with this scene than usual)*
Location: *Capell (subs.)*
o.s.d. **Enter]** *Q;* Entor *F1*
19 **choleric]** phlegmaticke *F2*
50 s.d. **Aside.]** *Theobald*

62 s.d. **Enter Haberdasher.**] *placed as in Dyce; after l.* 61, *F1*

63 s.p. **Hab.**] *Rowe;* Fel. *F1*

72 s.d. **Aside.**] *Hanmer*

81 **a**] *Q*

82 **custard-coffin**] *hyphen, Warburton*

85 s.d. **Exit Haberdasher.**] *Cambridge*

86 **gown?**] *Rowe;* gowne, *F1*

88 **a**] *Q*

91 **censer**] *Rowe;* Censor *F1*

93 s.d. **Aside.**] *Theobald*

108 **yard,**] *F2;* yard *F1*

109 **winter-cricket**] *hyphen, Capell*

133, 141, etc. s.dd. **Reads.**] *Capell*

150 **where,**] *Q;* where *F1*

164 s.d. **Aside.**] *Rowe*

175 **What,**] *Theobald (after Pope);* What *F1*

181 **me.**] *F4;* me, *F1*

196 s.d. **Aside.**] *Globe*

196] *Pope here inserts part of the following Sly framework from* (Q); *Capell, after V.i:* Slie *sleepes.* / *Lord. Whose within there? come hither sirs my Lords* / *A sleepe againe: go take him easily vp,* / *And put him in his one apparell againe,* / *And lay him in the place where we did find him,* / *Iust vnderneath the alehouse side below,* / *But see you wake him not in any case.* / *Boy. It shall be don my Lord come helpe to beare him* / *hence, Exit.*

IV.iv

IV.iv] *Steevens*
Location: *Capell*

o.s.d. **booted and bare-headed**] *from F1 s.d. at l.* 18 *below:* Enter Baptista and Lucentio: Pedant booted and bare headed.

1 **Sir**] *Theobald;* Sirs *F1*

4 **Genoa,**] *Theobald;* Genoa. *F1*

5 **Where . . . Pegasus.**] *continued to Pedant, Theobald; part of Tranio's following speech, F1*

7 **'longeth**] *Hanmer;* longeth *F1*

19 **Signior**] *Capell;* Tra. Signior *F1 (repeated s.p.)*

20 s.d. **To the Pedant.**] *Capell*

64 **And, . . . will,**] *Rowe;* And . . . will *F1*

64 **happened:**] *Capell (subs.);* hapned, *F1*

66 s.d. **Exit Lucentio.**] *Nicholson conj. (in Cambridge)*

68 s.d. **Exit Biondello.**] *Cambridge;* Exit. *F1 (after l.* 67)

68 s.d. **a servant . . . Tranio**] *ed. (after Bond)*

78 **h'as**] *Hanmer;* has *F1*

91 **except**] *F2;* expect *F1*

93 **imprimendum solum**] *F2;* Impremendum solem *F1*

IV.v

IV.v] *Steevens*
Location: *Hanmer (subs.)*

o.s.d. **Hortensio**] *Q;* Hortentio *F1 (occasionally)*

o.s.d. **and Servants**] *Cambridge*

17 **then**] theu *F1*

18 **is**] *Q;* in *F1*

27 s.d. **To Vincentio.**] *Rowe*

35 **a**] *F2;* the *F1*

38 **where**] *F2;* whether *F1*

41 **Allots**] *Q;* A lots *F1*

76 s.d. **all but Hortensio**] *Cambridge*

78 **be**] *F2*

V.i

V.i] *Warburton*
Location: *Pope*

o.s.d. **Bianca**] *Q;* Bianea *F1*

5 **master's**] *Capell;* mistris *F1*

6 s.d. **Exeunt . . . Biondello.**] *Rowe;* Exit. *F1 (after l.* 4)

30 **liest,**] *F2;* liest *F1*

35 s.d. **To Vincentio.**] *Capell*

44 **brought**] *Q;* brough *F1*

45 s.d. **Seeing Biondello.**] *Rowe*

53 **master's**] *F2;* Mistris *F1*

55 **marry**] *F2;* marie *F1*

59 s.d. **Exit.**] *Capell*

60 s.d. **Exit above.**] *Capell*

62 s.d. **They retire.**] *Theobald*

62 s.d. **below**] *Capell*

74 **madman**] *Rowe;* mad man *F1*

75 **'cerns**] *Collier;* cernes *F1*

83 **Tranio**] *F2;* Tronio *F1*

91 s.d. **Exit . . . Officer.**] *ed.*

107 s.d. **Bianca**] *Q;* Biancu *F1*

110 **and—**] *Capell;* and *F1*

111 s.d. **Exeunt**] *Theobald;* Exit *F1*

139 s.d. **Lucentio and Bianca**] *Capell*

140 **dough, but**] *Q;* doug, h but *F1*

141 s.d. **Exit.**] *Rowe*

146 **No**] *Q;* Mo *F1*

V.ii

V.ii] *Steevens;* Actus Quintus. *F1*
Location: *Pope*

o.s.d. **Petruchio, Katherina, Hortensio**] *Rowe (subs.)*

2 **done**] *Rowe;* come *F1*

37 **thee,**] *F2 (comma, Theobald);* the *F1*

40 **butt!**] *Rowe (subs.);* but *F1*

45 **bitter**] *Theobald conj.;* better *F1*

48 s.d. **with . . . Widow**] *Rowe (subs.)*

62 **two**] *Rowe;* too *F1*

62 **outright**] *F3;* out right *F1*

65 **for**] *F2;* sir *F1*

82–8 **How . . . come.**] *as verse, Rowe; as prose, F1*

89 s.d. **Enter Biondello.**] *placed as in Capell; after can, l.* 89, *F1*

96 s.d. **Grumio**] *Rowe*

105 s.d. **Exit Katherina.**] *Rowe (subs.)*

122 s.d. **Katherina . . . cap.**] *Rowe (subs.)*

128 **a**] *Capell;* fiue *F1*

130–1 **Katherine . . . husband.**] *as verse, Rowe; as prose, F1*

132 **you're**] *F3;* your *F1*

136–79 *Cf.* (Q): *Kate. Then you that liue thus by your pompered wills,* / *Now list to me and marke what I shall say,* / *Theternall power that with his only breath,* / *Shall cause this end and this beginning frame,* / *Not in time, nor before time, but with time, confusd,* / *For all the course of yeares, of ages, moneths,* / *Of seasons temperate, of dayes and houres,* / *Are tund and stopt, by measure of his hand,* / *The first world was, a forme, without a forme,* / *A heape confusd a mixture all deformd,* / *A gulfe of gulfes, a body bodilies,* / *Where all the elements were orderles,* / *Before the great commander of the world,* / *The King of Kings the glorious God of heauen,* / *Who in six daies did frame his heauenly worke,* / *And made all things to stand in perfit course.* / *Then to his image he did make a man.* / *Olde*

Adam and from his side a sleepe, / *A rib was taken, of which the Lord did make,* / *The woe of man so termed by Adam then,* / *Woman for that, by her came sinne to vs,* / *And for her sin was Adam doomd to die,* / *As Sara to her husband, so should we,* / *Obey them, loue them, keepe, and nourish them,* / *If they by any meanes doo want our helpes,* / *Laying our handes vnder theire feete to tread,* / *If that by that we, might procure there ease,* / *And for a president Ile first begin,* / *And lay my hand vnder my husbands feete* / *She laies her hand vnder her husbands feete.*

136 **threat'ning**] *Q;* thretaning *F1*

186 s.d. **To Lucentio.**] *Malone*

187 s.d. **with Katherina**] *Rowe (subs.)*

189 s.d. **Exeunt.**] *Rowe;* FINIS. *F1*

189] *Pope here inserts the conclusion of the Sly framework from* (Q), *omitting the Tapster's opening speech:* Then enter two bearing of *Slie* in his / Owne apparrell againe, and leaues him / Where they found him, and then goes out. / Then enter the *Tapster.* / *Tapster. Now that the darkesome night is ouerpast,* / *And dawning day apeares in cristall sky,* / *Now must I hast abroad: but soft whose this?* / *What Slie oh wondrous hath he laine here allnight,* / *Ile wake him, I thinke he's starued by this,* / *But that his belly was so stuft with ale,* / *What how Slie, Awake for shame.* / *Slie. Sim gis some more wine: whats all the* / *Plaiers gon: am not I a Lord?* / *Tapster. A Lord with a murrin: come art thou* / *dronken still?* / *Slie. Whose this? Tapster, oh Lord sirra, I haue had* / *The brauest dreame to night, that euer thou* / *Hardest in all thy life.* / *Tapster. I marry but you had best get you home,* / *For your wife will course you for dreming here to night,* / *Slie Will she?* I know now how to tame a shrew, / *I dreamt vpon it all this night till now,* / *And thou hast wakt me out of the best dreame* / *That euer I had in my life, but Ile to my* / *Wife presently and tame her too* / *And if she anger me.* / *Tapster. Nay tarry Slie for Ile go home with thee,* / *And heare the rest that thou hast dreamt to night.* / *Exeunt Omnes.*

Two other Sly inter-scene passages occur in A Shrew:
(1) *after Scene xiv (not in* The Shrew): Slie. Sim *must they be married now?* / *Lord. I my Lord.* / Enter Ferando and Kate and Sander. / *Slie. Looke Sim the foole is come againe now.*
(2) *after the* (Q) *equivalent of V.i.87–95:* Phylotus *and* Valeria *runnes away.* / *Then Slie speakes.* / *Slie. I say wele haue no sending to prison.* / *Lord. My Lord this is but the play, theyre but in iest.* / *Slie. I tell thee Sim wele haue no sending,* / *To prison thats flat: why Sim am not I Don Christo Vary?* / *Therefore I say they shall not go to prison.* / *Lord. No more they shall not my Lord,* / *They be run away.* / *Slie. I say they run away Sim? thats well,* / *Then gis some more drinke, and let them play againe.* / *Lord. Here my Lord.* / *Slie drinkes and then falls a sleepe.*

The Two Gentlemen of Verona

THE TWO GENTLEMEN OF VERONA has
the unenviable distinction of being
the least loved and least regarded of
Shakespeare's comedies. Even *The
Comedy of Errors* and *The Taming
of the Shrew* have always enjoyed a
robust theatrical life. This fact has
enabled them to surmount, even to mock, the disparagements of critics more concerned to praise
Shakespeare's mature comedies at the expense of his
early work than to distinguish the special qualities
and merits of those early plays. As it happens, *The
Two Gentlemen of Verona* does, when sympathetically
acted and directed, possess a delicate, lyrical charm.
Launce and Julia are splendid acting parts and, on the
stage, the dog Crab is invariably seductive. There is
some fine verse and some excellent comic invention.
Nevertheless, that new critical assessment which has
rehabilitated *Love's Labor's Lost* and discovered that
The Comedy of Errors is more than knockabout farce
continues to hesitate over *The Two Gentlemen of
Verona*. Although there have been successful professional productions since William Poel demonstrated
in 1898 and 1910 that the play could hold an audience,
it is still infrequently performed. It continues to
engage academic attention less for itself than as a
limping forerunner of Shakespeare's developed romantic style in comedy.

There are some valid reasons for this comparative
neglect. The only text of *The Two Gentlemen of
Verona*, that of the First Folio, is a maze of contradictions and inconsistencies. Shakespeare seems to have
been unable to make up his mind whether the main
action of the play takes place in Verona, Milan, or
Padua. Silvia's father wavers disconcertingly between
being a Duke and an Emperor; Launce and his dog

were fairly obviously an afterthought, imperfectly
welded into a plot which originally employed only
one comic servant; and Sir Eglamour appears to be
two quite different people. The quality of the verse
is extremely uneven. Most puzzling of all, the play's
resolution is achieved through a movement of plot so
brusque, so destructive of the relationships of the
characters as they have been developed, that generations of commentators have tried to absolve Shakespeare from responsibility for Valentine's overgenerous
gift of his lady Silvia to his friend Proteus, the man
who had been doing his best to rape her only a moment
before.

There is no real case for assuming either that
Shakespeare had a collaborator at whose doorstep
the awkward moments of the comedy may conveniently be laid, or that the First Folio text seriously
misrepresents the lost original. Clifford Leech's
theory that the play was composed in two phases,
part of it written perhaps in 1592 and the rest added
hastily for performance late in 1593, has more to
recommend it but is still highly conjectural. Like
most of Shakespeare's early work, *The Two Gentlemen
of Verona* cannot be dated with any precision. The
first mention of it is in Meres's list of 1598. Because
of its romance elements, features which seem to
anticipate *As You Like It* and *Twelfth Night*, it is
generally placed after *The Comedy of Errors* and *The
Taming of the Shrew* in the chronology. But recent
commentators point to the fact that forests, journeys,
and heroines disguised as boys had figured in earlier
English comedy. There is no reason why experimentation with classical and Italian models should
necessarily have preceded Shakespeare's exploration,
in *The Two Gentlemen of Verona*, of the more native
tradition. The play is really neither more nor less

143

innovative than the two which have been claimed as its forerunners.

Dramatically, *The Two Gentlemen of Verona* seems in fact more tentative than either *The Comedy of Errors* or *The Taming of the Shrew*. Stanley Wells has pointed to the almost exclusive reliance of this comedy upon soliloquy, duologue, and the aside as comment. Thirteen of its twenty scenes are realized entirely in terms of these three relatively uncomplicated dramatic techniques. Where Shakespeare does attempt a more complex orchestration of voices, the result tends to be awkward and ill-sustained. Characters are left to stand about, forgotten, in uncomfortable silence as the dialogue shifts back by preference to those tête-à-tête conversations which the dramatist knew how to handle. Wells remarks that although a similar technique can be observed in some Tudor interludes, neither *The Comedy of Errors* nor *The Taming of the Shrew* is limited in this way. Both these latter comedies are assured and confident in their construction of scenes involving the interplay of three or more characters. So, for that matter, are the three Henry VI plays and *Richard III*. The contrasted failure of *The Two Gentlemen of Verona* to make a success out of anything more extended than the duet seems to suggest that it was the work of a man still more at home with narrative or lyrical verse than with drama: a man who might well have turned subsequently to the discipline of Roman comedy in order to acquire certain formal theatrical skills which he was conscious that he lacked. It is entirely possible that *The Two Gentlemen of Verona* was Shakespeare's first professional play.

Its ultimate source was the story of Felix and Felismena as told in the *Diana* of the Portuguese writer Jorge de Montemayor. The *Diana* would have been available to Shakespeare in a French translation, but he may have depended not upon it for the shadowy prototypes of Proteus, Julia, and Silvia but upon a lost play, "The history of felix & philiomena," which was performed at court by the Queen's Men in 1585. In Montemayor, the equivalent to Silvia had been conveniently killed off at the end, allowing the Proteus and Julia characters to return to their original pairing. By adding Valentine to the story, Shakespeare created the possibility of a symmetrical happy ending. At the same time, his introduction of the complementary theme of friendship betrayed greatly complicated Montemayor's original account of falsehood in love. Interestingly, Cervantes did much the same thing to the Felix and Felismena plot when he wove it into Part I of *Don Quixote*. He made Cardenio, Valentine's counterpart, an integral part of the imbroglio involving the treacherous friend Don Fernando, Cardenio's lady Luscinda, and Don Fernando's first love Dorothea. As Cervantes tells it, the story is one of unquestioned absolutes, of extreme but unexamined romantic implausibilities. As such, it raises no problems. For Shakespeare, on the other hand, working in a different medium and essentially more realistic in his attitude towards these characters, the love and friendship motifs proved less easy to reconcile.

The idea that blind love must necessarily win a victory over rational friendship (as it does, painfully, in Chaucer's "Knight's Tale") ran side by side in the Middle Ages with the contrasted idea that the wise man, however tempted, will always value friendship over love. One of these two distinct literary traditions was rooted in the code of *l'amour courtois*; the other arose from a more moralistic but equally powerful set of demands. That concentration upon the nature and accords of love characteristic of Shakespearean comedy should not be allowed to obscure the fact that most Elizabethans would have seconded the opinion of Francis Bacon in his *Essays* that friendship is a serious matter and passion a far more dangerous and ephemeral kind of commitment. Although it might seem less promising as a dramatic subject than love, friendship was in fact celebrated in a number of Elizabethan plays. Probably, Shakespeare knew Richard Edwards' *Damon and Pithias* (1565), described as "the excellent Comedy of Two the most Faithfullest Friends" and much admired by contemporaries. In Lyly's *Endimion* (1588) and Peele's *The Old Wive's Tale* (1590) he would have found a character racked by the choice between friendship and love who, because he correctly prefers friendship, is awarded love as well. There must have been other sixteenth-century plays, now lost, which derived from and extended the considerable body of non-dramatic friendship literature.

In *Endimion*, *The Old Wive's Tale* and, by implication, in *Damon and Pithias*, friendship and love were conceived of as warring absolutes. The Knight Eumenides in *Endimion* has only one magical wish and a difficult decision to make as to whether he should expend it on a beloved mistress or a friend. Peele's wandering knight is brought to the extreme point of raising his sword to cleave his lady in two rather than dishonor his promise to share everything obtained on his journey with his friend, before he is mercifully absolved. In *The Two Gentlemen of Verona*, by contrast, love and friendship are not rival values. Only the disordered vision of a Proteus insists that they cancel each other out.

> Methinks my zeal to Valentine is cold,
> And that I love him not as I was wont:
> O, but I love his lady too too much,
> And that's the reason I love him so little.
>
> (II.iv.203–6)

His challenging remark to Silvia, "In love / Who respects friend?", provokes a crushing reply: "All men but Proteus" (V.iv.53–54). Even the steadfast Valentine is mocked and chided when his passion temporarily deprives him of his sense of proportion and, in the braggardism of his praise of Silvia, of consideration for the feelings of a friend. His suggestion, in II.iv, that Proteus' lady Julia might just serve to carry Silvia's train is arrogant and unlovely. In order to reach the harmony of love and friendship that is proper, the "One feast, one house, one mutual happiness" of the play's conclusion, attitudes like these need to be castigated and amended.

Neither love nor friendship is allowed to establish itself in the comedy as an ideal. The servants Launce and Speed provide an ironic commentary throughout, grounding the fantasies of their masters in reality. Speed irreverently denies that Silvia's divine beauty has any objective existence, that it is any more than the result of a partial way of seeing. He pokes fun at Valentine's love melancholy, and at the consequent dulling of his perceptions. In II.i he has to explain the meaning of Silvia's letter-trick to a Valentine so absurdly far gone in a dream of love that he fails to recognize its palpable and inviting presence. On a lower, less exacting but also more honest level, the friendship between Launce and Speed echoes the bond which unites their masters. Like Proteus, Launce considers marriage, but his wooing of the milkmaid possessed of more hair than wit, more faults than hairs, and more wealth than faults, is the most loveless and practical of bargains. Launce's real devotion, his gestures of genuine self-sacrifice, are reserved for Crab, his dog.

In the comedies of John Lyly, servants and minor characters had sometimes been allowed to mimic the behavior of their betters. Shakespeare may well have learned from Lyly's technique of parallel and juxtaposition. The drama of Lyly, however, was essentially rigid and conservative. Although the sighings and posturings of a Sir Tophas at the bottom of the scale might momentarily render love ridiculous, this parody in no way qualified the celebration of Endimion's ideal love for Cynthia at the top. Plays like *Endimion* arranged their characters in a strict hierarchy. Themes of love or friendship could be refracted among the various levels without the dramatist ever suggesting, as Shakespeare had already begun to do in *The Two Gentlemen of Verona*, that the commentary provided by pages or fools might modify admiration of the more dignified central characters. Lyly would never have had the effrontery to hint that a comic servingman who volunteers to be whipped himself so that his dog will not have to pay for its social misdemeanors displays a generosity which puts a Proteus or a Valentine, for all their hyperbolic oaths, to shame.

If *The Two Gentlemen of Verona* was indeed Shakespeare's first comedy, his tendency to hand over most of the initiative and just judgment to the women in his cast of characters was already marked. Proteus is treacherous and Valentine, at least in the first half of the play, self-pitying and selfish. The Duke is mercenary and unfeeling: ready to push his daughter into marriage with a fool simply on the grounds of wealth. Even Sir Eglamour, the romantic knight faithful unto death, abruptly turns coward and abandons Silvia to her fate when they meet the outlaws in the forest. By contrast, Silvia herself remains unshakeably loyal to the lover she has chosen, whatever obstacles fortune, her father, or the scheming Proteus can invent. She is even tender of the rights and feelings of a Julia she has never met, but only heard of by report. As for Julia, the fact that she anticipates Rosalind and Viola by assuming a boy's disguise to follow her lover is really less important than the character Shakespeare

has given her: intrepid and sane, witty but sensitive, capable of committing follies but also of mocking them herself. She and Launce are the only two people in the play prepared with open eyes to suffer and be humiliated for love. The parallel between them is indicated subtly in IV.iv when Launce's rhetorical question hurled at the unrepentant Crab, "How many masters would do this for his servant?", is echoed soon after by Julia's cry as she prepares to deliver Proteus' ring to Silvia, as instructed: "How many women would do such a message?"

It is primarily because of the attitudes embodied in Julia, Silvia and Launce that Shakespeare's blunder in the final scene, when without warning he gives ideal friendship precedence over love, is so disastrous. Proteus' sudden repentance and Valentine's unquestioning forgiveness are entirely acceptable. The lightning reformation of evildoers was common in Elizabethan drama. It is even possible to read into Valentine's free pardon a new maturity, a fine tempering of spirit learned during his enforced exile in the forest. The gift of Silvia to his friend, on the other hand, is an intolerable clumsiness for which Shakespeare must take the blame. A gesture that would have been perfectly appropriate in Lyly or Peele, establishing a correct priority of values as a prelude to the happy ending, it has the effect here of negating the whole previous development of the comedy. Up to this point, *The Two Gentlemen of Verona* has placed small faith in love and friendship as abstract ideals. Only the false logic of Proteus, the braggardism and self-pity of Valentine, have coined generalizations of this kind. Certainly the play has not dignified friendship at the expense of love. If anything, it has suggested that as young men grow up and find themselves as individuals, love must and should come to dominate friendship in their lives, without cancelling out the earlier bond. And Silvia herself has never been portrayed as a chattel, a mere passive prize to be awarded to her would-be rapist without regard for her own feelings and inclinations.

As it happens, Proteus is given no opportunity to take up Valentine's excessive offer: "All that was mine in Silvia I give thee." Julia, as soon as the words are spoken, sinks fainting to the ground. The discovery of the true identity of Proteus' page drastically alters the situation. Proteus himself accepts Speed's doctrine of the relativity, the subjective nature of love: "What is in Silvia's face, but I may spy / More fresh in Julia's with a constant eye?" Valentine wins Silvia as the free gift of a Duke finally able to see what everyone else has known all along—that the preferred suitor Thurio, for all his wealth, is both a coward and a fool. Even the outlaws are forgiven and restored to favor in an ending which, after its one misstep, manages to achieve not only symmetry but joy.

The Two Gentlemen of Verona is not, by Shakespearean standards, a great comedy. More patchy and unsure than any of his other plays in the genre, it suggests a Shakespeare who at this stage in his career had not yet developed the full courage of his artistic convictions. Valentine's gift of Silvia to Proteus looks very like a nervous recourse to tradition, to the practice of older dramatists. Significantly, it occurs at the point which, in any comedy, is most difficult to handle with assurance: the resolution. The play's faults of tone and structure, its various inconsistencies and contradictions, should not however be allowed to obscure its very real merits. Although some of the verse is wooden, mechanically padded out to fill the line, the man who could give Proteus his description of Orpheus' lute,

> Whose golden touch could soften steel and stones,
> Make tigers tame, and huge leviathans
> Forsake unsounded deeps to dance on sands,
>
> (III.ii.78–80)

was already a dramatic poet worth the marking. Even more remarkable in its way is the supple, idiosyncratic prose spoken by Launce. In the prose comedy of Lyly, all the characters had employed the same distanced and deliberately artificial idiom. The prose of Launce, like that of Falstaff and Benedick later, seems to have been created by the character himself, to represent his particular and natural style of expression.

In innumerable ways, *The Two Gentlemen of Verona* looks forward to Shakespeare's later comedies. The character of Julia and her masculine disguise, the central position of the women in the play, the serious use of the clowns as commentators, and of music, themes of travel, and the transformation of people through love, the greenwood as the place where pretenses are dropped and characters appear for what they really are, the carefully calculated mixture of prose and verse: all of these motifs and devices were to be extended and developed in succeeding plays. Most important of all, when it is true to itself the comedy insists upon both the importance and the relativity of love. It fights shy of system and abstraction in favor of a meticulous, sensitive exploration of individual situations and reactions. The central issue, how to relate friendship and love, was one that Shakespeare returned to in the Sonnets, in *The Merchant of Venice*, *Much Ado about Nothing* and, near the end of his writing life, in *The Winter's Tale*. Arguably, these later treatments are all of them more assured and consistently successful. Yet *The Two Gentlemen of Verona* has a freshness and lyrical charm all its own, an uncertain glory that is no more to be despised than that of the April day described by Proteus, wavering between brilliance and cloud.

Anne Barton

A table-book for the year 1581. Harvard College Library. This is a fine example (shown actual size) of the kind of sixteenth-century pocket tables or table-book to which Hamlet refers when he says: "My tables—meet it is I set it down / That one may smile, and smile, and be a villain!" (*Hamlet*, I.v.107–8), and to which Julia metaphorically likens Lucetta in *The Two Gentlemen of Verona* (II.vii.2–4). It was called "tables" because it was made up of a number of thick, heavily waxed (hence erasable) cardboard leaves (each a table). The example above has an almanac for the year 1581 at the beginning and is handsomely bound in a typical Elizabethan stamped leather binding. Notice the brass clasps which hold it closed. (*By permission of the Harvard College Library*)

The Two Gentlemen of Verona

THE NAMES OF ALL THE ACTORS

DUKE [OF MILAN], *father to Silvia*
VALENTINE ⎱ *the two Gentlemen*
PROTEUS ⎰
ANTONIO, *father to Proteus*
THURIO, *a foolish rival to Valentine*
EGLAMOUR, *agent for Silvia in her escape*
HOST, *where Julia lodges*
OUTLAWS, *with Valentine*

SPEED, [*page*] *to Valentine*
LAUNCE, *a clownish servant to Proteus*
PANTHINO, *servant to Antonio*

JULIA, *beloved of Proteus*
SILVIA, *beloved of Valentine*
LUCETTA, *waiting-woman to Julia*

[ATTENDANTS; MUSICIANS]

[SCENE: *Verona; Milan; and a forest somewhere between Milan and Mantua*]

ACT I, SCENE I

[*Enter*] VALENTINE, PROTEUS.

Val. Cease to persuade, my loving Proteus:
Home-keeping youth have ever homely wits.
Were't not affection chains thy tender days
To the sweet glances of thy honor'd love,
I rather would entreat thy company, 5
To see the wonders of the world abroad,
Than (living dully sluggardiz'd at home)
Wear out thy youth with shapeless idleness.
But since thou lov'st, love still, and thrive therein,
Even as I would, when I to love begin. 10
Pro. Wilt thou be gone? Sweet Valentine, adieu,
Think on thy Proteus, when thou, happ'ly, seest
Some rare noteworthy object in thy travel.
Wish me partaker in thy happiness
When thou dost meet good hap; and in thy danger 15
(If ever danger do environ thee)
Commend thy grievance to my holy prayers,
For I will be thy beadsman, Valentine.
Val. And on a love-book pray for my success?
Pro. Upon some book I love I'll pray for thee. 20
Val. That's on some shallow story of deep love,

How young Leander cross'd the Hellespont.
Pro. That's a deep story of a deeper love,
For he was more than over shoes in love.
Val. 'Tis true; for you are over boots in love, 25
And yet you never swom the Hellespont.
Pro. Over the boots? nay, give me not the boots.
Val. No, I will not; for it boots thee not.
Pro. What?
Val. To be in love—where scorn is bought with groans;
Coy looks with heart-sore sighs; one fading moment's mirth 30
With twenty watchful, weary, tedious nights:
If happ'ly won, perhaps a hapless gain;
If lost, why then a grievous labor won;
However—but a folly bought with wit,
Or else a wit by folly vanquished. 35
Pro. So, by your circumstance, you call me fool.
Val. So, by your circumstance, I fear you'll prove.
Pro. 'Tis love you cavil at, I am not Love.
Val. Love is your master, for he masters you;
And he that is so yoked by a fool, 40
Methinks should not be chronicled for wise.
Pro. Yet writers say: as in the sweetest bud
The eating canker dwells, so eating love
Inhabits in the finest wits of all.
Val. And writers say: as the most forward bud
Is eaten by the canker ere it blow, 46

Words and passages enclosed in square brackets in the text above are either emendations of the copy-text or additions to it. The Textual Notes immediately following the play cite the earliest authority for every such change or insertion and supply the reading of the copy-text wherever it is emended in this edition.

I.i. Location: Verona. A street.
2. **homely:** simple.
3. **affection:** passion (stronger than the modern meaning). **tender:** youthful. 8. **shapeless:** lacking form, aimless.
9. **love still:** go on loving. 12. **happ'ly:** haply, perchance.
13. **object:** sight. 15. **hap:** fortune.
17. **Commend thy grievance:** commit your trouble.
18. **beadsman:** one who prays in another's behalf.
19. **love-book:** love-manual or love story (instead of a prayer book).

22. **Leander:** youth who nightly swam the Hellespont to visit Hero. One night he drowned in his attempt, whereupon Hero threw herself into the Hellespont and drowned also. 26. **swom:** swum.
27. **give . . . boots:** i.e. do not make fun of me. 28. **boots:** profits.
31. **watchful:** wakeful. 32. **hapless:** unfortunate.
34. **However:** whichever, either way.
36. **circumstance:** detailed proof (so also at line 84).
37. **circumstance:** condition, situation. 43. **canker:** cankerworm.
44. **Inhabits:** dwells. 46. **blow:** open.

Even so by love the young and tender wit
Is turn'd to folly, blasting in the bud,
Losing his verdure, even in the prime,
And all the fair effects of future hopes. 50
But wherefore waste I time to counsel thee
That art a votary to fond desire?
Once more adieu. My father at the road
Expects my coming, there to see me shipp'd.
  Pro. And thither will I bring thee, Valentine. 55
  Val. Sweet Proteus, no; now let us take our leave.
To Milan let me hear from thee by letters
Of thy success in love, and what news else
Betideth here in absence of thy friend;
And I likewise will visit thee with mine. 60
  Pro. All happiness bechance to thee in Milan.
  Val. As much to you at home; and so farewell.
  Exit.

  Pro. He after honor hunts, I after love:
He leaves his friends, to dignify them more;
I [leave] myself, my friends, and all, for love. 65
Thou, Julia, thou hast metamorphis'd me,
Made me neglect my studies, lose my time,
War with good counsel, set the world at nought;
Made wit with musing weak, heart sick with thought.

[Enter] Speed.

  Speed. Sir Proteus! 'save you! Saw you my
    master? 70
  Pro. But now he parted hence to embark for Milan.
  Speed. Twenty to one then he is shipp'd already,
And I have play'd the sheep in losing him.
  Pro. Indeed a sheep doth very often stray,
And if the shepherd be awhile away. 75
  Speed. You conclude that my master is a shepherd
then, and I [a] sheep?
  Pro. I do.
  Speed. Why then my horns are his horns, whether
I wake or sleep. 80
  Pro. A silly answer, and fitting well a sheep.
  Speed. This proves me still a sheep.
  Pro. True; and thy master a shepherd. 83
  Speed. Nay, that I can deny by a circumstance.
  Pro. It shall go hard but I'll prove it by another.
  Speed. The shepherd seeks the sheep, and not the
sheep the shepherd; but I seek my master, and my
master seeks not me: therefore I am no sheep. 88
  Pro. The sheep for fodder follow the shepherd,
the shepherd for food follows not the sheep; thou for
wages followest thy master, thy master for wages
follows not thee: therefore thou art a sheep. 92
  Speed. Such another proof will make me cry "baa."
  Pro. But dost thou hear? gav'st thou my letter
to Julia? 95
  Speed. Ay, sir; I (a lost mutton) gave your letter to
her (a lac'd mutton), and she (a lac'd mutton) gave
me (a lost mutton) nothing for my labor.
  Pro. Here's too small a pasture for such store of
muttons. 100
  Speed. If the ground be overcharg'd, you were best
stick her.
  Pro. Nay, in that you are astray; 'twere best
pound you. 104
  Speed. Nay, sir, less than a pound shall serve me
for carrying your letter.
  Pro. You mistake; I mean the pound—a pinfold.
  Speed. From a pound to a pin? fold it over and over,
'Tis threefold too little for carrying a letter to your
    lover.
  Pro. But what said she? 110
[Speed nods, and Proteus looks at him questioningly.]
  Speed. Ay.
  Pro. Nod-ay—why, that's "noddy."
  Speed. You mistook, sir: I say, she did nod; and
you ask me if she did nod, and I say, "Ay."
  Pro. And that set together is "noddy." 115
  Speed. Now you have taken the pains to set it
together, take it for your pains.
  Pro. No, no, you shall have it for bearing the
letter. 119
  Speed. Well, I perceive I must be fain to bear
with you.
  Pro. Why, sir, how do you bear with me?
  Speed. Marry, sir, the letter, very orderly,
having nothing but the word "noddy" for my pains.
  Pro. Beshrew me, but you have a quick wit. 125
  Speed. And yet it cannot overtake your slow purse.
  Pro. Come, come, open the matter in brief:
what said she?
  Speed. Open your purse, that the money and the
matter may be both at once deliver'd. 130
  Pro. Well, sir, here is for your pains. What said
she?
  Speed. Truly, sir, I think you'll hardly win her.
  Pro. Why? couldst thou perceive so much from
her? 135

---

48. **blasting:** withering.
49. **his verdure:** its fresh vigor. **prime:** early spring.
50. **effects:** fulfillments. **future hopes:** promise of future development. 52. **fond:** foolish, doting. 53. **road:** roadstead, harbor.
54. **Expects:** awaits. **shipp'd:** aboard. Shakespeare seems to have supposed that Verona was a seaport. 55. **bring:** accompany.
58. **success:** fortune (good or bad).
60. **visit:** bestow the same benefit on.
64. **friends.** Often used in reference to relatives. **dignify them more:** i.e. by improving himself. 65. **leave:** neglect.
66. **metamorphis'd:** variant form of *metamorphosed*.
67. **lose:** waste.
69. **thought:** melancholy (supposed typical of lovers).
70. **'save you:** God save you. 71. **parted:** departed.
72, 73. **shipp'd, sheep.** The pun would be obvious to the Elizabethans, who gave *ship* and *sheep* almost the same pronunciation.
75. **And if:** if.
79. **my . . . horns:** he owns my horns, i.e. he is a cuckold (referring to the notion that the husbands of unfaithful wives sprouted horns).
85. **It . . . I'll:** I'll fare ill indeed if I can't.

93. **cry "baa":** i.e. admit I am a sheep (with quibble on "say 'bah'").
94. **dost thou hear:** i.e. listen to me.
97. **lac'd mutton:** prostitute. 101. **overcharg'd:** overburdened.
102. **stick:** stab (with sexual innuendo).
103. **astray:** (1) straying (like a lost sheep); (2) deviating from propriety. 104. **pound you:** (1) put you in the pound; (2) beat you.
107. **pinfold:** enclosure for stray cattle.
108. **pin.** Proverbially worthless. **fold:** multiply.
112. **noddy:** (1) a simpleton; (2) the knave in various card games.
120. **fain:** willing.
120–21. **bear with:** (1) put up with; (2) act as bearer for.
123. **Marry:** indeed (originally the name of the Virgin Mary used as an oath). **orderly:** properly, duly.
125. **Beshrew me:** mischief take me (a weakened curse).
127. **open:** disclose. 133. **hardly win:** have a hard time winning.
134–35. **perceive . . . her:** deduce that from her behavior. Speed's reply quibbles on *perceive* in the now obsolete sense "receive." (Cf. the similar possibilities for wordplay in modern *gather* or *take in*.)

Speed. Sir, I could perceive nothing at all from her; no, not so much as a ducat for delivering your letter: and being so hard to me that brought your mind, I fear she'll prove as hard to you in telling your mind. Give her no token but stones, for she's as hard as steel. 141

Pro. What said she? nothing?

Speed. No, not so much as "Take this for thy pains." To testify your bounty, I thank you, you have [testern'd] me; in requital whereof, henceforth carry your letters yourself: and so, sir, I'll commend you to my master. 147

Pro. Go, go, be gone, to save your ship from wrack,
Which cannot perish having thee aboard,
Being destin'd to a drier death on shore. [*Exit Speed.*]
I must go send some better messenger: 151
I fear my Julia would not deign my lines,
Receiving them from such a worthless post.   *Exit.*

SCENE II

Enter JULIA *and* LUCETTA.

Jul. But say, Lucetta, now we are alone,
Wouldst thou then counsel me to fall in love?

Luc. Ay, madam, so you stumble not unheedfully.

Jul. Of all the fair resort of gentlemen
That every day with parle encounter me, 5
In thy opinion which is worthiest love?

Luc. Please you repeat their names, I'll show my mind
According to my shallow simple skill.

Jul. What think'st thou of the fair Sir Eglamour?

Luc. As of a knight well-spoken, neat, and fine;
But were I you, he never should be mine. 11

Jul. What think'st thou of the rich Mercatio?

Luc. Well of his wealth; but of himself, so, so.

Jul. What think'st thou of the gentle Proteus?

Luc. Lord, Lord! to see what folly reigns in us! 15

Jul. How now? what means this passion at his name?

Luc. Pardon, dear madam, 'tis a passing shame
That I (unworthy body as I am)
Should censure thus on lovely gentlemen.

Jul. Why not on Proteus, as of all the rest? 20

Luc. Then thus: of many good I think him best.

Jul. Your reason?

Luc. I have no other but a woman's reason:
I think him so, because I think him so.

Jul. And wouldst thou have me cast my love on him? 25

Luc. Ay—if you thought your love not cast away.

Jul. Why, he, of all the rest, hath never mov'd me.

Luc. Yet he, of all the rest, I think best loves ye.

Jul. His little speaking shows his love but small.

Luc. Fire that's closest kept burns most of all.

Jul. They do not love that do not show their love.

Luc. O, they love least that let men know their love. 32

Jul. I would I knew his mind.

Luc. Peruse this paper, madam.

Jul. "To Julia"—say, from whom? 35

Luc. That the contents will show.

Jul. Say, say; who gave it thee?

Luc. Sir Valentine's page; and sent, I think, from Proteus.
He would have given it you, but I, being in the way,
Did in your name receive it; pardon the fault, I pray.

Jul. Now, by my modesty, a goodly broker! 41
Dare you presume to harbor wanton lines?
To whisper and conspire against my youth?
Now trust me, 'tis an office of great worth,
And you an officer fit for the place. 45
There! take the paper; see it be return'd,
Or else return no more into my sight.

Luc. To plead for love deserves more fee than hate.

Jul. Will ye be gone?

Luc.   That you may ruminate.   *Exit.*

Jul. And yet I would I had o'erlook'd the letter; 50
It were a shame to call her back again,
And pray her to a fault for which I chid her.
What 'fool is she, that knows I am a maid,
And would not force the letter to my view!
Since maids, in modesty, say "no" to that 55
Which they would have the profferer construe "ay."
Fie, fie, how wayward is this foolish love,
That (like a testy babe) will scratch the nurse
And presently, all humbled, kiss the rod!
How churlishly I chid Lucetta hence, 60
When willingly I would have had her here!
How angerly I taught my brow to frown,
When inward joy enforc'd my heart to smile!
My penance is, to call Lucetta back
And ask remission for my folly past. 65
What ho! Lucetta!

[*Enter* LUCETTA.]

Luc.   What would your ladyship?

Jul. Is't near dinner-time?

---

137. **ducat:** here, a silver coin worth about 3*s.* 6*d.*
139. **mind:** intentions.   **in telling:** when you tell her.
140. **stones:** jewels.
145. **testern'd me:** given me a testern (sixpence).
146. **commend you:** deliver your greetings.
148. **wrack:** shipwreck.
150. **Being:** i.e. since you are. Lines 148–50 allude to the proverb "He that is born to be hanged shall never be drowned."
151. **some better messenger.** This (and the episode as a whole) seems to ignore the fact that Proteus has a servant of his own, Launce. It has been suggested that the character of Launce was an afterthought in Shakespeare's composition of the play.
152. **deign:** accept graciously.
153. **post:** (1) messenger; (2) blockhead.

I.ii. Location: Verona. The garden of Julia's house.
4. **resort:** company.   5. **parle:** talk.
12. **Mercatio.** The name suggests a merchant (from Italian *mercato,* "market").   16. **passion:** passionate outburst.
17. **passing:** surpassing.   19. **censure:** pass judgment.

27. **mov'd:** proposed marriage to.
34. **this paper:** i.e. the letter which in I.i Speed has assured Proteus he delivered personally to Julia. Another instance of confused plotting, unless lines 39–40 are interpreted to mean that Lucetta deceived Speed by pretending to be Julia, an interpretation which the word *broker* in line 41 makes unlikely.   39. **in the way:** at hand.
41. **broker:** go-between.   48. **more fee:** better recompense.
50. **o'erlook'd:** looked over, read.
52. **to a fault:** to commit a fault.   53. **'fool:** a fool.
58. **testy:** fretful.   59. **presently:** immediately.
62. **angerly:** angrily.

Luc.   I would it were,
That you might kill your stomach on your meat,
And not upon your maid.
    Jul.   What is't that you
Took up so gingerly?
    Luc.   Nothing.
    Jul.   Why didst thou stoop then?
    Luc.   To take a paper up that I let fall.   71
    Jul.   And is that paper nothing?
    Luc.   Nothing concerning me.
    Jul.   Then let it lie for those that it concerns.
    Luc.   Madam, it will not lie where it concerns
Unless it have a false interpreter.   75
    Jul.   Some love of yours hath writ to you in rhyme.
    Luc.   That I might sing it, madam, to a tune:
Give me a note, your ladyship can set.
    Jul.   As little by such toys as may be possible:
Best sing it to the tune of "Light o' love."   80
    Luc.   It is too heavy for so light a tune.
    Jul.   Heavy? belike it hath some burden then?
    Luc.   Ay; and melodious were it, would you sing
it.
    Jul.   And why not you?
    Luc.   I cannot reach so high.
    Jul.   Let's see your song. [*Takes the letter.*] How
        now, minion?   85
    Luc.   Keep tune there still, so you will sing it out.
And yet methinks I do not like this tune.
    Jul.   You do not?
    Luc.   No, madam, 'tis too sharp.
    Jul.   You, minion, are too saucy.
    Luc.   Nay, now you are too flat,   90
And mar the concord with too harsh a descant:
There wanteth but a mean to fill your song.
    Jul.   The mean is drown'd with [your] unruly bass.
    Luc.   Indeed I bid the base for Proteus.   94
    Jul.   This babble shall not henceforth trouble me.
Here is a coil with protestation!   [*Tears the letter.*]
Go, get you gone; and let the papers lie:
You would be fing'ring them, to anger me.
    Luc.   She makes it strange, but she would be best
        pleas'd
To be so ang'red with another letter.   [*Exit.*]   100
    Jul.   Nay, would I were so ang'red with the same.
O hateful hands, to tear such loving words!
Injurious wasps, to feed on such sweet honey,

And kill the bees that yield it with your stings!
I'll kiss each several paper for amends.   105
Look, here is writ "kind Julia." Unkind Julia,
As in revenge of thy ingratitude,
I throw thy name against the bruising stones,
Trampling contemptuously on thy disdain.
And here is writ "love-wounded Proteus."   110
Poor wounded name: my bosom as a bed
Shall lodge thee till thy wound be throughly heal'd;
And thus I search it with a sovereign kiss.
But twice, or thrice, was "Proteus" written down:
Be calm, good wind, blow not a word away   115
Till I have found each letter in the letter,
Except mine own name; that, some whirlwind bear
Unto a ragged, fearful, hanging rock,
And throw it thence into the raging sea.
Lo, here in one line is his name twice writ,   120
"Poor forlorn Proteus, passionate Proteus:
To the sweet Julia"—that I'll tear away—
And yet I will not, sith so prettily
He couples it to his complaining names.
Thus will I fold them one upon another;   125
Now kiss, embrace, contend, do what you will.

[*Enter* LUCETTA.]

    Luc.   Madam,
Dinner is ready, and your father stays.
    Jul.   Well, let us go.
    Luc.   What, shall these papers lie like tell-tales
        here?   130
    Jul.   If you respect them, best to take them up.
    Luc.   Nay, I was taken up for laying them down;
Yet here they shall not lie, for catching cold.
    Jul.   I see you have a month's mind to them.
    Luc.   Ay, madam, you may say what sights you see;
I see things too, although you judge I wink.   136
    Jul.   Come, come, will't please you go?   *Exeunt.*

SCENE III

Enter ANTONIO *and* PANTHINO.

    Ant.   Tell me, Panthino, what sad talk was that
Wherewith my brother held you in the cloister?
    Pan.   'Twas of his nephew Proteus, your son.
    Ant.   Why, what of him?
    Pan.   He wond'red that your lordship
Would suffer him to spend his youth at home,   5
While other men, of slender reputation,
Put forth their sons to seek preferment out:

68. **kill:** satisfy.   **stomach:** (1) appetite; (2) anger.
68, 69. **meat, maid.** A quibble, *meat* being pronounced as *mate*.
74. **concerns:** is of importance.
78. **note:** (1) musical note; (2) letter.   **set:** (1) set to music; (2)
write. Julia takes it in the sense of "set store."   79. **toys:** trifles.
80. **"Light o' Love":** a popular tune, mentioned also in *Much Ado*,
III.iv.44.   81. **heavy:** serious.
82. **burden:** (1) bass accompaniment; (2) load.
84. **reach so high:** (1) sing such high notes; (2) aspire to one of such
high rank.   85. **minion:** hussy.   86. **tune:** (1) pitch; (2) temper.
88. **sharp.** With quibble on the sense "pinching."
90. **flat.** With quibble on the sense "blunt."
91. **descant:** improvised harmony added to a melody.
92. **mean:** (1) tenor (i.e. Proteus); (2) opportunity.
93. **unruly bass.** With quibble on the sense "base misconduct."
94. **bid . . . for:** support the cause of (a figure from the game of prisoner's base), with obvious pun.
96. **coil with protestation:** fuss about protestations of love.
99. **makes it strange:** pretends to be indifferent.
101. **so . . . same:** i.e. I wish I still had the first letter to be so angered
by.   103. **wasps:** i.e. fingers.

105. **several paper:** separate fragment.
106. **Unkind:** unnatural, cruel.   107. **As:** as if.
112. **throughly:** thoroughly.
113. **search:** probe, cleanse.   **sovereign:** curative.
123. **sith:** since.   **prettily:** ingeniously.
124. **complaining:** lamenting.
128. **your father.** After one other reference to her father (I.iii.4–8),
Shakespeare seems to treat Julia as a wealthy orphan (see II.vii.86–87).
stays: waits.   131. **respect:** prize.   132. **taken up:** rebuked.
133. **for:** for fear of.   134. **month's mind:** strong desire.
136. **wink:** close my eyes.

I.iii. Location: Verona. Antonio's house.
1. **sad:** serious.
6. **slender reputation:** i.e. lower social station than yourself.
7. **Put forth:** send away from home.   **out:** abroad.

Some to the wars, to try their fortune there;
Some to discover islands far away;
Some to the studious universities.   10
For any or for all these exercises
He said that Proteus, your son, was meet;
And did request me to importune you
To let him spend his time no more at home,
Which would be great impeachment to his age,   15
In having known no travel in his youth.
  Ant. Nor need'st thou much importune me to that
Whereon this month I have been hammering.
I have consider'd well his loss of time,
And how he cannot be a perfect man,   20
Not being tried and tutor'd in the world:
Experience is by industry achiev'd,
And perfected by the swift course of time.
Then tell me, whither were I best to send him?
  Pan. I think your lordship is not ignorant   25
How his companion, youthful Valentine,
Attends the Emperor in his royal court.
  Ant. I know it well.
  Pan. 'Twere good, I think, your lordship sent him
      thither:
There shall he practice tilts and tournaments,   30
Hear sweet discourse, converse with noblemen,
And be in eye of every exercise
Worthy his youth and nobleness of birth.
  Ant. I like thy counsel; well hast thou advis'd;
And that thou mayst perceive how well I like it,   35
The execution of it shall make known:
Even with the speediest expedition
I will dispatch him to the Emperor's court.
  Pan. To-morrow, may it please you, Don Al-
      phonso
With other gentlemen of good esteem   40
Are journeying to salute the Emperor,
And to commend their service to his will.
  Ant. Good company; with them shall Proteus go—

[*Enter*] PROTEUS.

And in good time! now will we break with him.
  Pro. Sweet love, sweet lines, sweet life!   45
Here is her hand, the agent of her heart;
Here is her oath for love, her honor's pawn:
O that our fathers would applaud our loves,
To seal our happiness with their consents!
O heavenly Julia!   50
  Ant. How now? what letter are you reading there?
  Pro. May't please your lordship, 'tis a word or two
Of commendations sent from Valentine,
Deliver'd by a friend that came from him.   54
  Ant. Lend me the letter; let me see what news.
  Pro. There is no news, my lord, but that he writes

How happily he lives, how well-belov'd
And daily graced by the Emperor;
Wishing me with him, partner of his fortune.
  Ant. And how stand you affected to his wish?   60
  Pro. As one relying on your lordship's will,
And not depending on his friendly wish.
  Ant. My will is something sorted with his wish:
Muse not that I thus suddenly proceed;
For what I will, I will, and there an end.   65
I am resolv'd that thou shalt spend some time
With Valentinus in the Emperor's court;
What maintenance he from his friends receives,
Like exhibition thou shalt have from me.
To-morrow be in readiness to go—   70
Excuse it not, for I am peremptory.
  Pro. My lord I cannot be so soon provided:
Please you deliberate a day or two.
  Ant. Look what thou want'st shall be sent after
      thee.
No more of stay: to-morrow thou must go.   75
Come on, Panthino; you shall be employ'd
To hasten on his expedition.
              [*Exeunt Antonio and Panthino.*]
  Pro. Thus have I shunn'd the fire for fear of
      burning,
And drench'd me in the sea, where I am drown'd.
I fear'd to show my father Julia's letter,   80
Lest he should take exceptions to my love,
And with the vantage of mine own excuse
Hath he excepted most against my love.
O, how this spring of love resembleth
The uncertain glory of an April day,   85
Which now shows all the beauty of the sun,
And by and by a cloud takes all away.

[*Enter* PANTHINO.]

  Pan. Sir Proteus, your [father] calls for you:
He is in haste; therefore I pray you go.
  Pro. Why, this it is: my heart accords thereto, 90
And yet a thousand times it answers "no."   *Exeunt.*

ACT II, SCENE I

Enter VALENTINE, SPEED.

  Speed. Sir, your glove.
  Val.   Not mine: my gloves are on.
  Speed. Why then this may be yours—for this is
      but one.
  Val. Ha? let me see; ay, give it me, it's mine:
Sweet ornament that decks a thing divine—
Ah, Silvia, Silvia!   5
  Speed. [*Shouting.*] Madam Silvia! Madam Silvia!

---

15. **impeachment:** reproach. **to his age:** when he is old.
18. **hammering:** deliberating. 21. **tried:** tested, proved.
27. **Emperor.** Another inconsistency; Valentine has gone to Milan,
and in the next scene appears in the ducal court there. See the note on
II.iv.76, 77, 79. 30. **practice:** perform.
31. **discourse:** conversation, talk. **converse:** associate.
32. **be . . . of:** have an opportunity to see. 42. **commend:** commit.
44. **in good time:** at the right moment (often used of people arriving
opportunely). **break with:** disclose our purpose to.
47. **pawn:** pledge. 49. **seal:** ratify.
53. **commendations:** greetings.

---

58. **graced:** shown favor. 60. **affected:** disposed.
63. **something sorted:** rather in agreement.
64. **Muse:** wonder, grumble. 68. **friends:** relatives.
69. **exhibition:** allowance of money.
71. **Excuse it not:** offer no excuses. **peremptory:** resolved.
72. **provided:** equipped. 74. **Look what:** whatever.
83. **excepted most against:** set most strong impediments in the way of.

II.i. Location: Milan. The Duke's palace.
1, 2. **on, one.** A common pun, encouraged by the fact that the words
were similar in sound and often spelled alike (*on*).

The Two
Gentlemen
of Verona
II.i

Val. How now, sirrah?

Speed. She is not within hearing, sir.

Val. Why, sir, who bade you call her?

Speed. Your worship, sir, or else I mistook. 10

Val. Well—you'll still be too forward.

Speed. And yet I was last chidden for being too slow.

Val. Go to, sir; tell me, do you know Madam Silvia? 15

Speed. She that your worship loves?

Val. Why, how know you that I am in love?

Speed. Marry, by these special marks: first, you have learn'd, like Sir Proteus, to wreathe your arms, like a malecontent; to relish a love-song, like a 20 robin-redbreast; to walk alone, like one that had the pestilence; to sigh, like a schoolboy that had lost his A B C; to weep, like a young wench that had buried her grandam; to fast, like one that takes diet; to watch, like one that fears robbing; to speak puling, like a 25 beggar at Hallowmas. You were wont, when you laugh'd, to crow like a cock; when you walk'd, to walk like one of the lions; when you fasted, it was presently after dinner; when you look'd sadly, it was for want of money: and now you are metamorphis'd 30 with a mistress, that when I look on you, I can hardly think you my master.

Val. Are all these things perceiv'd in me?

Speed. They are all perceiv'd without ye.

Val. Without me? they cannot. 35

Speed. Without you? nay, that's certain; for without you were so simple, none else would: but you are so without these follies, that these follies are within you, and shine through you like the water in an urinal, that not an eye that sees you but is a physician to comment on your malady. 41

Val. But tell me: dost thou know my lady Silvia?

Speed. She that you gaze on so as she sits at supper?

Val. Hast thou observ'd that? Even she I mean.

Speed. Why, sir, I know her not. 45

Val. Dost thou know her by my gazing on her, and yet know'st her not?

Speed. Is she not hard-favor'd, sir?

Val. Not so fair, boy, as well-favor'd.

Speed. Sir, I know that well enough. 50

Val. What dost thou know?

Speed. That she is not so fair as (of you) well favor'd.

Val. I mean that her beauty is exquisite, but her favor infinite. 55

Speed. That's because the one is painted, and the other out of all count.

Val. How painted? and how out of count?

Speed. Marry, sir, so painted to make her fair, that no man counts of her beauty. 60

Val. How esteem'st thou me? I account of her beauty.

Speed. You never saw her since she was deform'd.

Val. How long hath she been deform'd?

Speed. Ever since you lov'd her. 65

Val. I have lov'd her ever since I saw her, and still I see her beautiful.

Speed. If you love her, you cannot see her.

Val. Why? 69

Speed. Because Love is blind. O that you had mine eyes, or your own eyes had the lights they were wont to have when you chid at Sir Proteus for going ungarter'd!

Val. What should I see then? 74

Speed. Your own present folly, and her passing deformity: for he, being in love, could not see to garter his hose; and you, being in love, cannot see to put on your hose.

Val. Belike, boy, then you are in love—for last morning you could not see to wipe my shoes. 80

Speed. True, sir; I was in love with my bed. I thank you, you swing'd me for my love, which makes me the bolder to chide you for yours.

Val. In conclusion, I stand affected to her. 84

Speed. I would you were set, so your affection would cease.

Val. Last night she enjoin'd me to write some lines to one she loves.

Speed. And have you?

Val. I have. 90

Speed. Are they not lamely writ?

Val. No, boy, but as well as I can do them.

[*Enter*] SILVIA.

Peace, here she comes.

Speed. [*Aside.*] O excellent motion! O exceeding puppet! Now will he interpret to her. 95

Val. Madam and mistress, a thousand good morrows.

Speed. [*Aside.*] O, give ye good ev'n! here's a million of manners. 99

Sil. Sir Valentine and servant, to you two thousand.

Speed. [*Aside.*] He should give her interest, and she gives it him.

Val. As you enjoin'd me, I have writ your letter

---

7. **sirrah:** usual form of address to an inferior.
14. **Go to:** an expression of remonstrance.
19. **wreathe:** fold. Folded arms conventionally betokened melancholy, particularly love melancholy.
20. **malecontent:** variant form of *malcontent.*   23. **A B C:** primer.
24. **watch:** lie awake.   25. **puling:** whiningly.
26. **Hallowmas:** All Saints' Day (November 1), when beggars asked for special alms.
28. **lions.** Possibly those kept in the Tower of London.
29. **presently:** immediately.   31. **with:** by.   **that:** so that.
34. **without ye:** outside you, i.e. by your external appearance.
36–37. **without:** unless.   37. **would:** i.e. would perceive them.
39–40. **urinal:** glass vessel for examining urine.
48. **hard-favor'd:** ugly.
49. **Not . . . well-favor'd.** Valentine explains his meaning in lines 54–55.   52. **of:** by.   55. **favor:** charm, graciousness of nature.

57. **out . . . count:** incalculable.
60. **counts of:** makes account of, esteems.
63. **deform'd:** i.e. altered by the lover's eye, which does not view the loved one realistically.   71. **lights:** sight.
73. **going ungarter'd.** Carelessness in dress was thought to be a sign of lovesickness.   75. **passing:** exceedingly great.
82. **swing'd:** beat (past of *swinge*).   85. **set:** seated.
94. **motion:** puppet show.
95. **interpret:** supply explanatory comment on the action (as a puppeteer did).   98. **give:** i.e. God give.
100. **servant:** one devoted to the service of a lady (who was not pledged by accepting it).
102–3. **He . . . him:** i.e. he ought to outdo her (in compliments), but she outdoes him.

Unto the secret, nameless friend of yours;   105
Which I was much unwilling to proceed in,
But for my duty to your ladyship.
     Sil. I thank you, gentle servant—'tis very clerkly
done.
     Val. Now trust me, madam, it came hardly off;
For being ignorant to whom it goes,   110
I writ at random, very doubtfully.
     Sil. Perchance you think too much of so much
pains?
     Val. No, madam; so it stead you, I will write
(Please you command) a thousand times as much;
And yet—   115
     Sil. A pretty period! Well—I guess the sequel;
And yet I will not name it—and yet I care not—
And yet take this again—and yet I thank you—
Meaning henceforth to trouble you no more.
     Speed. [*Aside.*] And yet you will; and yet another
"yet."   120
     Val. What means your ladyship? Do you not
like it?
     Sil. Yes, yes; the lines are very quaintly writ,
But (since unwillingly) take them again.
Nay, take them.
     Val. Madam, they are for you.   125
     Sil. Ay, ay; you writ them, sir, at my request,
But I will none of them; they are for you.
I would have had them writ more movingly.
     Val. Please you, I'll write your ladyship an-
other.   129
     Sil. And when it's writ, for my sake read it over,
And if it please you, so; if not, why, so.
     Val. If it please me, madam, what then?
     Sil. Why, if it please you, take it for your labor;
And so good morrow, servant.   *Exit Silvia.*
     Speed. O jest unseen, inscrutable; invisible,   135
As a nose on a man's face, or a weathercock on a
steeple!
My master sues to her; and she hath taught her suitor,
He being her pupil, to become her tutor.
O excellent device, was there ever heard a better,
That my master being scribe, to himself should write
the letter?   140
     Val. How now, sir? What are you reasoning with
yourself?
     Speed. Nay, I was rhyming; 'tis you that have
the reason.
     Val. To do what?   145
     Speed. To be a spokesman from Madam Silvia.
     Val. To whom?
     Speed. To yourself; why, she woos you by a figure.
     Val. What figure?
     Speed. By a letter, I should say.   150
     Val. Why, she hath not writ to me?
     Speed. What need she, when she hath made you

write to yourself? Why, do you not perceive the
jest?
     Val. No, believe me.   155
     Speed. No believing you indeed, sir: but did you
perceive her earnest?
     Val. She gave me none, except an angry word.
     Speed. Why, she hath given you a letter.
     Val. That's the letter I writ to her friend.   160
     Speed. And that letter hath she deliver'd, and there
an end.
     Val. I would it were no worse.
     Speed. I'll warrant you, 'tis as well: 164
"For often have you writ to her; and she in modesty,
Or else for want of idle time, could not again reply;
Or fearing else some messenger, that might her mind
discover,
Herself hath taught her love himself to write unto her
lover."
All this I speak in print, for in print I found it. Why
muse you, sir? 'tis dinner-time.   170
     Val. I have din'd.
     Speed. Ay, but hearken, sir; though the chameleon
Love can feed on the air, I am one that am nourish'd
by my victuals, and would fain have meat. O, be not
like your mistress—be mov'd, be mov'd. *Exeunt.*   175

SCENE II

Enter PROTEUS, JULIA.

     Pro. Have patience, gentle Julia.
     Jul. I must, where is no remedy.
     Pro. When possibly I can, I will return.
     Jul. If you turn not, you will return the sooner.
Keep this remembrance for thy Julia's sake.   5
                                        [*Giving a ring.*]
     Pro. Why then we'll make exchange: here, take
you this.
     Jul. And seal the bargain with a holy kiss.
     Pro. Here is my hand for my true constancy;
And when that hour o'erslips me in the day
Wherein I sigh not, Julia, for thy sake,   10
The next ensuing hour some foul mischance
Torment me for my love's forgetfulness!
My father stays my coming; answer not;
The tide is now—nay, not thy tide of tears,
That tide will stay me longer than I should.   15
Julia, farewell!   [*Exit Julia.*]
          What, gone without a word?
Ay, so true love should do: it cannot speak,
For truth hath better deeds than words to grace it.

[*Enter*] PANTHINO.

     Pan. Sir Proteus, you are stay'd for.

---

157. **earnest:** serious (but Valentine picks it up in the sense of
"pledge").   167. **her mind discover:** reveal her private intent.
169. **speak in print:** speak precisely.
171. **din'd:** i.e. feasted on Silvia's beauty.
172. **chameleon.** Popularly supposed to subsist on air.
174. **fain:** gladly.

II.ii. Location: Verona. Julia's house.
2. **is:** there is.   4. **turn:** prove unfaithful.   13. **stays:** waits for.
18. **hath ... it:** is adorned better by actions than by words.

---

107. **duty:** respect, submission.
108. **clerkly:** in a scholarly manner.   109. **hardly:** with difficulty.
111. **doubtfully:** uncertainty.   113. **stead:** benefit.
116. **A pretty period:** i.e. a fine point to stop your sentence, since
"And yet" implies that you regret your labor for me.   **Well:** very
well.   118. **again:** back.   122. **quaintly:** skillfully.
141. **reasoning:** discussing.   148. **figure:** device.

The Two
Gentlemen
of Verona
II.ii

Pro.   Go; I come, I come.   19
Alas, this parting strikes poor lovers dumb.   *Exeunt.*

Scene III

Enter Launce [*leading a dog*].

Launce. Nay, 'twill be this hour ere I have done weeping; all the kind of the Launces have this very fault. I have receiv'd my proportion, like the prodigious son, and am going with Sir Proteus to the Imperial's court. I think Crab my dog be the   5
sourest-natur'd dog that lives: my mother weeping, my father wailing, my sister crying, our maid howling, our cat wringing her hands, and all our house in a great perplexity, yet did not this cruel-hearted cur shed one tear. He is a stone, a very pibble stone, and has no   10
more pity in him than a dog. A Jew would have wept to have seen our parting; why, my grandam, having no eyes, look you, wept herself blind at my parting. Nay, I'll show you the manner of it. This shoe is my father; no, this left shoe is my father; no, no, this   15
left shoe is my mother; nay, that cannot be so neither; yes, it is so, it is so—it hath the worser sole. This shoe, with the hole in it, is my mother, and this my father—a vengeance on't! there 'tis. Now, sir, this staff is my sister, for, look you, she is as white as a lily and as   20
small as a wand. This hat is Nan, our maid. I am the dog—no, the dog is himself, and I am the dog—O! the dog is me, and I am myself; ay, so, so. Now come I to my father: "Father, your blessing." Now should not the shoe speak a word for weeping; now should I   25
kiss my father; well, he weeps on. Now come I to my mother. O that she could speak now like a [wood] woman! Well, I kiss her; why, there 'tis; here's my mother's breath up and down. Now come I to my sister; mark the moan she makes. Now the dog all   30
this while sheds not a tear, nor speaks a word; but see how I lay the dust with my tears.

[*Enter*] Panthino.

Pan. Launce, away, away! aboard! Thy master is shipp'd, and thou art to post after with oars. What's the matter? why weep'st thou, man? Away, ass, you'll lose the tide, if you tarry any longer.   36

Launce. It is no matter if the tied were lost; for it is the unkindest tied that ever any man tied.

Pan. What's the unkindest tide?   39

Launce. Why, he that's tied here, Crab, my dog.

Pan. Tut, man, I mean thou'lt lose the flood, and in losing the flood, lose thy voyage, and in losing thy voyage, lose thy master, and in losing thy master, lose thy service, and in losing thy service—Why dost thou stop my mouth?   45

Launce. For fear thou shouldst lose thy tongue.

Pan. Where should I lose my tongue?

Launce. In thy tale.

Pan. In thy tail!   49

Launce. Lose the tide, and the voyage, and the master, and the service, and the tied! Why, man, if the river were dry, I am able to fill it with my tears; if the wind were down, I could drive the boat with my sighs.   54

Pan. Come; come away, man—I was sent to call thee.

Launce. Sir—call me what thou dar'st.

Pan. Wilt thou go?

Launce. Well, I will go.   *Exeunt.*

Scene IV

Enter Valentine, Silvia, Thurio, Speed.

Sil. Servant!

Val. Mistress?

Speed. Master, Sir Thurio frowns on you.

Val. Ay, boy, it's for love.

Speed. Not of you.   5

Val. Of my mistress then.

Speed. 'Twere good you knock'd him.   [*Exit.*]

Sil. Servant, you are sad.

Val. Indeed, madam, I seem so.

Thu. Seem you that you are not?   10

Val. Happ'ly I do.

Thu. So do counterfeits.

Val. So do you.

Thu. What seem I that I am not?

Val. Wise.   15

Thu. What instance of the contrary?

Val. Your folly.

Thu. And how quote you my folly?

Val. I quote it in your jerkin.

Thu. My jerkin is a doublet.   29

Val. Well then I'll double your folly.

Thu. How?

Sil. What, angry, Sir Thurio? do you change color?

Val. Give him leave, madam, he is a kind of chameleon.   26

Thu. That hath more mind to feed on your blood than live in your air.

Val. You have said, sir.

Thu. Ay, sir, and done too—for this time.   30

Val. I know it well, sir; you always end ere you begin.

Sil. A fine volley of words, gentlemen, and quickly shot off.

Val. 'Tis indeed, madam, we thank the giver.   35

II.iii. Location: Verona. A street.
2. **kind:** kindred, family.
3–4. **proportion, prodigious:** blunders for *portion* and *prodigal*.
5. **Imperial's:** blunder for *Emperor's*. (See note on I.iii.27.)
10. **pibble:** pebble.
27. **wood:** distraught (with punning reference to a wooden shoe?).
29. **up and down:** exactly.   34. **post:** hasten.

II.iv. Location: Milan. The Duke's palace.
16. **instance:** proof.   18. **quote:** observe, "read" (Schmidt).
19. **jerkin:** short coat worn over, or instead of, the doublet. Valentine takes advantage of the fact that *quote* (often spelled *cote*) and *coat* were homophones.
28. **in your air:** i.e. on the air you breathe. Thurio alludes to the belief that the chameleon lives on air (see note on II.i.172), but he also draws on the commonplace that words are air to imply that he will challenge Valentine to a duel rather than swallow more of his insults.
30. **done:** The expected contrast with Valentine's sarcastic "said," but Thurio uses it in the sense "finished," though his "for this time" implies that next time he will act.
32. **begin:** i.e. get to the point of acting.

Sil. Who is that, servant?

Val. Yourself, sweet lady, for you gave the fire.
Sir Thurio borrows his wit from your ladyship's looks,
and spends what he borrows kindly in your com-
pany.   40

Thu. Sir, if you spend word for word with me, I
shall make your wit bankrupt.

Val. I know it well, sir; you have an exchequer of
words and, I think, no other treasure to give your
followers; for it appears by their bare liveries that
they live by your bare words.   46

Sil. No more, gentlemen, no more; here comes
my father.

[*Enter*] DUKE.

Duke. Now, daughter Silvia, you are hard beset.
Sir Valentine, your father is in good health: 50
What say you to a letter from your friends
Of much good news?

Val.   My lord, I will be thankful
To any happy messenger from thence.

Duke. Know ye Don Antonio, your countryman?

Val. Ay, my good lord, I know the gentleman   55
To be of worth and worthy estimation,
And not without desert so well reputed.

Duke. Hath he not a son?

Val. Ay, my good lord, a son that well deserves
The honor and regard of such a father.   60

Duke. You know him well?

Val. I knew him as myself: for from our infancy
We have convers'd and spent our hours together,
And though myself have been an idle truant,
Omitting the sweet benefit of time   65
To clothe mine age with angel-like perfection,
Yet hath Sir Proteus (for that's his name)
Made use and fair advantage of his days;
His years but young, but his experience old;
His head unmellowed, but his judgment ripe;   70
And in a word (for far behind his worth
Comes all the praises that I now bestow),
He is complete in feature and in mind
With all good grace to grace a gentleman.

Duke. Beshrew me, sir, but if he make this good,
He is as worthy for an empress' love   76
As meet to be an emperor's counsellor.
Well, sir—this gentleman is come to me
With commendation from great potentates,
And here he means to spend his time a while.   80
I think 'tis no unwelcome news to you.

Val. Should I have wish'd a thing, it had been he.

Duke. Welcome him then according to his worth—
Silvia, I speak to you, and you, Sir Thurio;

For Valentine, I need not cite him to it.   85
I will send him hither to you presently.   [*Exit.*]

Val. This is the gentleman I told your ladyship
Had come along with me, but that his mistress
Did hold his eyes lock'd in her crystal looks.

Sil. Belike that now she hath enfranchis'd them 90
Upon some other pawn for fealty.

Val. Nay sure, I think she holds them prisoners
    still.

Sil. Nay then he should be blind, and being blind,
How could he see his way to seek out you?   94

Val. Why, lady, Love hath twenty pair of eyes.

Thu. They say that Love hath not an eye at all.

Val. To see such lovers, Thurio, as yourself:
Upon a homely object Love can wink.

Sil. Have done, have done; here comes the gen-
    tleman.   [*Exit Thurio.*]

[*Enter*] PROTEUS.

Val. Welcome, dear Proteus! Mistress, I be-
    seech you   100
Confirm his welcome with some special favor.

Sil. His worth is warrant for his welcome hither,
If this be he you oft have wish'd to hear from.

Val. Mistress, it is: sweet lady, entertain him
To be my fellow-servant to your ladyship.   105

Sil. Too low a mistress for so high a servant.

Pro. Not so, sweet lady, but too mean a servant
To have a look of such a worthy mistress.

Val. Leave off discourse of disability.
Sweet lady, entertain him for your servant.   110

Pro. My duty will I boast of, nothing else.

Sil. And duty never yet did want his meed.
Servant, you are welcome to a worthless mistress.

Pro. I'll die on him that says so but yourself. 114

Sil. That you are welcome?

Pro.   That you are worthless.

[*Enter* THURIO.]

Thu. Madam, my lord your father would speak
    with you.

Sil. I wait upon his pleasure. Come, Sir Thurio,
Go with me. Once more, new servant, welcome;
I'll leave you to confer of home affairs;
When you have done, we look to hear from you. 120

Pro. We'll both attend upon your ladyship.
                              [*Exeunt Silvia and Thurio.*]

Val. Now tell me: how do all from whence you
    came?

Pro. Your friends are well and have them much
    commended.

Val. And how do yours?

Pro.   I left them all in health.

Val. How does your lady, and how thrives your
    love?   125

---

37. **fire:** spark (which set off the "volley").
39. **kindly:** naturally, properly.
45. **bare:** threadbare.   **liveries:** distinctive garments worn by a
gentleman's retainers.
49. **hard beset:** strongly besieged (by young men).
53. **happy messenger:** bearer of good news.
63. **convers'd:** been companions.   65. **Omitting:** neglecting.
70. **unmellowed:** i.e. without grey hairs.
73. **complete:** perfect.   **feature:** general personal appearance.
76, 77, 79. **empress' love, emperor's counsellor, great potentates.** The
language of these lines seems more suited to the Emperor of I.iii.27 ff.
than to a Duke of Milan. With line 76 cf. V.iv.141.

85. **cite:** urge.   86. **presently:** at once.   88. **Had:** would have.
90. **Belike that:** perhaps.   **enfranchis'd:** released from confinement.
91. **Upon...fealty:** i.e. for some other lover's vow of faithful
service.   104. **entertain:** engage.
109. **disability:** unworthiness.
112. **want his meed:** lack his reward.
114. **die on:** die fighting against.
123. **them much commended:** sent their kind regards.

The Two Gentlemen of Verona
II.iv

Pro. My tales of love were wont to weary you;
I know you joy not in a love-discourse.
  Val. Ay, Proteus, but that life is alter'd now:
I have done penance for contemning Love,
Whose high imperious thoughts have punish'd me
With bitter fasts, with penitential groans,   131
With nightly tears, and daily heart-sore sighs,
For in revenge of my contempt of love,
Love hath chas'd sleep from my enthralled eyes,
And made them watchers of mine own heart's sorrow.
O gentle Proteus, Love's a mighty lord,   136
And hath so humbled me as I confess
There is no woe to his correction,
Nor to his service no such joy on earth:
Now no discourse, except it be of love;   140
Now can I break my fast, dine, sup, and sleep,
Upon the very naked name of love.
  Pro. Enough; I read your fortune in your eye.
Was this the idol that you worship so?
  Val. Even she; and is she not a heavenly saint?
  Pro. No; but she is an earthly paragon.   146
  Val. Call her divine.
  Pro.   I will not flatter her.
  Val. O, flatter me; for love delights in praises.
  Pro. When I was sick, you gave me bitter pills,
And I must minister the like to you.   150
  Val. Then speak the truth by her; if not divine,
Yet let her be a principality,
Sovereign to all the creatures on the earth.
  Pro. Except my mistress.
  Val.   Sweet, except not any,
Except thou wilt except against my love.   155
  Pro. Have I not reason to prefer mine own?
  Val. And I will help thee to prefer her too:
She shall be dignified with this high honor—
To bear my lady's train, lest the base earth
Should from her vesture chance to steal a kiss,   160
And of so great a favor growing proud,
Disdain to root the summer-swelling flow'r,
And make rough winter everlastingly.
  Pro. Why, Valentine, what braggadism is this?
  Val. Pardon me, Proteus, all I can is nothing   165
To her, whose worth [makes] other worthies nothing:
She is alone.
  Pro.   Then let her alone.
  Val. Not for the world. Why, man, she is mine
own,
And I as rich in having such a jewel
As twenty seas, if all their sand were pearl,   170
The water nectar, and the rocks pure gold.
Forgive me, that I do not dream on thee,
Because thou seest me dote upon my love.
My foolish rival, that her father likes

(Only for his possessions are so huge),   175
Is gone with her along, and I must after,
For love, thou know'st, is full of jealousy.
  Pro. But she loves you?
  Val. Ay, and we are betroth'd: nay more, our
marriage hour,
With all the cunning manner of our flight,   180
Determin'd of—how I must climb her window,
The ladder made of cords, and all the means
Plotted and 'greed on for my happiness.
Good Proteus, go with me to my chamber,
In these affairs to aid me with thy counsel.   185
  Pro. Go on before; I shall inquire you forth.
I must unto the road, to disembark
Some necessaries that I needs must use,
And then I'll presently attend you.
  Val. Will you make haste?   190
  Pro. I will.   *Exit* [*Valentine*].
Even as one heat another heat expels,
Or as one nail by strength drives out another,
So the remembrance of my former love
Is by a newer object quite forgotten.   195
[Is it] mine [eye], or Valentinus' praise,
Her true perfection, or my false transgression,
That makes me reasonless, to reason thus?
She is fair; and so is Julia that I love
(That I did love, for now my love is thaw'd,   200
Which like a waxen image 'gainst a fire
Bears no impression of the thing it was).
Methinks my zeal to Valentine is cold,
And that I love him not as I was wont:
O, but I love his lady too too much,   205
And that's the reason I love him so little.
How shall I dote on her with more advice,
That thus without advice begin to love her?
'Tis but her picture I have yet beheld,
And that hath dazzled my reason's light;   210
But when I look on her perfections,
There is no reason but I shall be blind.
If I can check my erring love, I will;
If not, to compass her I'll use my skill.   *Exit*.

SCENE V

Enter SPEED *and* LAUNCE, [*meeting*].

Speed. Launce, by mine honesty, welcome to
[Milan].
  Launce. Forswear not thyself, sweet youth, for I
am not welcome. I reckon this always, that a man is
never undone till he be hang'd, nor never welcome   5
to a place till some certain shot be paid and the
hostess say "Welcome."
  Speed. Come on, you madcap, I'll to the alehouse

137. **as:** that.
138. **to his correction:** comparable to (the woe of) his punishment.
152. **principality:** a celestial being, belonging to one of the nine orders of angels.
155. **Except . . . love:** i.e. to place any as her equal is a detraction to her. 157. **prefer:** advance.
164. **braggadism:** braggartism, excessive praise.
165. **can:** i.e. can say of her.
166. **To her:** i.e. in comparison with her real worth.
167. **alone:** unique.
172. **do . . . thee:** seem careless of your welcome or your feelings.

175. **for:** because. 186. **forth:** out. 187. **road:** harbor.
189. **presently:** immediately.
192. **Even . . . expels.** It was thought that the application of external heat would ease the pain of a burn. 207. **advice:** deliberation.
209. **picture:** outer show. 212. **no reason but:** no doubt that.
214. **compass:** obtain.

II.v. Location. Milan. A street.
5. **undone:** ruined. 6. **shot:** fee, tavern reckoning.

with you presently; where, for one shot of five pence,
thou shalt have five thousand welcomes. But,   10
sirrah, how did thy master part with Madam Julia?

Launce. Marry, after they clos'd in earnest, they
parted very fairly in jest.

Speed. But shall she marry him?

Launce. No.   15

Speed. How then? shall he marry her?

Launce. No, neither.

Speed. What, are they broken?

Launce. No, they are both as whole as a fish.   19

Speed. Why then, how stands the matter with
them?

Launce. Marry, thus: when it stands well with
him, it stands well with her.

Speed. What an ass art thou! I understand thee
not.   25

Launce. What a block art thou, that thou canst
not! My staff understands me.

Speed. What thou say'st?

Launce. Ay, and what I do too. Look thee, I'll
but lean, and my staff understands me.   30

Speed. It stands under thee indeed.

Launce. Why, stand-under and under-stand is
all one.

Speed. But tell me true, will't be a match?   34

Launce. Ask my dog. If he say ay, it will; if he
say no, it will; if he shake his tail and say nothing,
it will.

Speed. The conclusion is then, that it will.

Launce. Thou shalt never get such a secret from
me but by a parable.   40

Speed. 'Tis well that I get it so. But, Launce, how
say'st thou that my master is become a notable lover?

Launce. I never knew him otherwise.

Speed. Than how?

Launce. A notable lubber—as thou reportest him
to be.   46

Speed. Why, thou whoreson ass, thou mistak'st
me.

Launce. Why, fool, I meant not thee, I meant thy
master.   50

Speed. I tell thee, my master is become a hot lover.

Launce. Why, I tell thee, I care not, though he
burn himself in love. If thou wilt, go with me to the
alehouse; if not, thou art an Hebrew, a Jew, and not
worth the name of a Christian.   55

Speed. Why?

Launce. Because thou hast not so much charity in
thee as to go to the ale with a Christian. Wilt thou go?

Speed. At thy service.   *Exeunt.*

SCENE VI

Enter PROTEUS *solus.*

Pro. To leave my Julia—shall I be forsworn?
To love fair Silvia—shall I be forsworn?
To wrong my friend, I shall be much forsworn.
And ev'n that pow'r which gave me first my oath
Provokes me to this threefold perjury.   5
Love bade me swear, and Love bids me forswear.
O sweet-suggesting Love, if thou hast sinn'd,
Teach me, thy tempted subject, to excuse it!
At first I did adore a twinkling star,
But now I worship a celestial sun.   10
Unheedful vows may heedfully be broken,
And he wants wit that wants resolved will
To learn his wit t' exchange the bad for better.
Fie, fie, unreverend tongue, to call her bad,
Whose sovereignty so oft thou hast preferr'd   15
With twenty thousand soul-confirming oaths.
I cannot leave to love, and yet I do;
But there I leave to love where I should love.
Julia I lose, and Valentine I lose:
If I keep them, I needs must lose myself;   20
If I lose them, thus find I by their loss—
For Valentine, myself; for Julia, Silvia.
I to myself am dearer than a friend,
For love is still most precious in itself,
And Silvia (witness heaven, that made her fair)   25
Shows Julia but a swarthy Ethiope.
I will forget that Julia is alive,
Rememb'ring that my love to her is dead;
And Valentine I'll hold an enemy,
Aiming at Silvia as a sweeter friend.   30
I cannot now prove constant to myself,
Without some treachery us'd to Valentine.
This night he meaneth with a corded ladder
To climb celestial Silvia's chamber-window,
Myself in counsel his competitor.   35
Now presently I'll give her father notice
Of their disguising and pretended flight,
Who, all enrag'd, will banish Valentine;
For Thurio, he intends, shall wed his daughter;
But, Valentine being gone, I'll quickly cross   40
By some sly trick blunt Thurio's dull proceeding.
Love, lend me wings to make my purpose swift,
As thou hast lent me wit to plot this drift.   *Exit.*

SCENE VII

Enter JULIA *and* LUCETTA.

Jul. Counsel, Lucetta; gentle girl, assist me;

---

12. **clos'd:** (1) came to terms; (2) embraced.
18. **are they broken:** have they fallen out (but Launce in his reply
quibbles on *broken* in the sense "in pieces").
19. **whole . . . fish.** A proverbial comparison.
22. **stands well.** One of Launce's numerous bawdy equivoques.
40. **by a parable:** i.e. indirectly, obscurely.
41–42. **how say'st thou:** what have you to say to this.
45. **lubber:** clumsy, stupid fellow.
47. **whoreson:** a term of abuse (literally bastard).
47–48. **thou mistak'st me:** you mistake my meaning (but Launce
replies to the sense "you misjudge me").   55. **worth:** worthy of.
58. **go . . . Christian.** Alluding to a "church-ale," a festival at which
ale was sold to raise funds for the church.

II.vi. Location: Milan. The Duke's palace.
5. **Provokes:** urges, incites.   7. **sweet-suggesting:** sweetly seductive.
11. **Unheedful . . . heedfully:** ill-considered . . . upon consideration.
12. **wants:** lacks.   13. **learn:** teach.   14. **unreverend:** irreverent.
15. **preferr'd:** recommend, urged.
16. **soul-confirming:** sworn on my soul.   17. **leave:** cease.
23–24. **I . . . itself.** Proteus, in saying that self-love is superior to love
for his friend, speaks like a villain and against the orthodox code of
friendship, just as lines 25–26 show him a traitor to the code of love.
24. **still:** always.   35. **counsel:** consultation.   **competitor:** ally.
37. **pretended:** intended.   40. **cross:** thwart.   41. **blunt:** stupid.

II.vii. Location: Verona. Julia's house.

The Two
Gentlemen
of Verona
II.vii

And ev'n in kind love I do conjure thee,
Who art the table wherein all my thoughts
Are visibly character'd and engrav'd,
To lesson me and tell me some good mean   5
How with my honor I may undertake
A journey to my loving Proteus.

Luc.   Alas, the way is wearisome and long.

Jul.   A true-devoted pilgrim is not weary
To measure kingdoms with his feeble steps;   10
Much less shall she that hath Love's wings to fly,
And when the flight is made to one so dear,
Of such divine perfection, as Sir Proteus.

Luc.   Better forbear till Proteus make return.

Jul.   O, know'st thou not his looks are my soul's
food?   15
Pity the dearth that I have pined in,
By longing for that food so long a time.
Didst thou but know the inly touch of love,
Thou wouldst as soon go kindle fire with snow
As seek to quench the fire of love with words.   20

Luc.   I do not seek to quench your love's hot fire,
But qualify the fire's extreme rage,
Lest it should burn above the bounds of reason.

Jul.   The more thou dam'st it up, the more it
burns:
The current that with gentle murmur glides,   25
Thou know'st, being stopp'd, impatiently doth rage;
But when his fair course is not hindered,
He makes sweet music with th' enamell'd stones,
Giving a gentle kiss to every sedge
He overtaketh in his pilgrimage;   30
And so by many winding nooks he strays
With willing sport to the wild ocean.
Then let me go, and hinder not my course:
I'll be as patient as a gentle stream,
And make a pastime of each weary step,   35
Till the last step have brought me to my love,
And there I'll rest, as after much turmoil
A blessed soul doth in Elysium.

Luc.   But in what habit will you go along?

Jul.   Not like a woman, for I would prevent   40
The loose encounters of lascivious men:
Gentle Lucetta, fit me with such weeds
As may beseem some well-reputed page.

Luc.   Why then your ladyship must cut your hair.

Jul.   No, girl, I'll knit it up in silken strings,   45
With twenty odd-conceited true-love knots:
To be fantastic may become a youth
Of greater time than I shall show to be.

Luc.   What fashion, madam, shall I make your
breeches?

Jul.   That fits as well as "Tell me, good my lord,
What compass will you wear your farthingale?"   51
Why, ev'n what fashion thou best likes, Lucetta.

Luc.   You must needs have them with a codpiece,
madam.

Jul.   Out, out, Lucetta, that will be ill-favor'd.

Luc.   A round hose, madam, now's not worth a
pin,   55
Unless you have a codpiece to stick pins on.

Jul.   Lucetta, as thou lov'st me, let me have
What thou think'st meet, and is most mannerly.
But tell me, wench, how will the world repute me
For undertaking so unstaid a journey?   60
I fear me it will make me scandaliz'd.

Luc.   If you think so, then stay at home and go not.

Jul.   Nay, that I will not.

Luc.   Then never dream on infamy, but go.
If Proteus like your journey when you come,   65
No matter who's displeas'd when you are gone:
I fear me he will scarce be pleas'd withal.

Jul.   That is the least, Lucetta, of my fear:
A thousand oaths, an ocean of his tears,
And instances of infinite of love,   70
Warrant me welcome to my Proteus.

Luc.   All these are servants to deceitful men.

Jul.   Base men, that use them to so base effect!
But truer stars did govern Proteus' birth:
His words are bonds, his oaths are oracles,   75
His love sincere, his thoughts immaculate,
His tears pure messengers sent from his heart,
His heart as far from fraud as heaven from earth.

Luc.   Pray heav'n he prove so when you come
to him!

Jul.   Now, as thou lov'st me, do him not that
wrong,   80
To bear a hard opinion of his truth:
Only deserve my love by loving him,
And presently go with me to my chamber,
To take a note of what I stand in need of,
To furnish me upon my longing journey.   85
All that is mine I leave at thy dispose,
My goods, my lands, my reputation;
Only, in lieu thereof, dispatch me hence.
Come; answer not; but to it presently,
I am impatient of my tarriance.   *Exeunt.*   90

ACT III, Scene I

Enter Duke, Thurio, Proteus.

Duke.   Sir Thurio, give us leave, I pray, a while,
We have some secrets to confer about. [*Exit Thurio.*]
Now tell me, Proteus, what's your will with me?

Pro.   My gracious lord, that which I would discover
The law of friendship bids me to conceal,   5
But when I call to mind your gracious favors

---

3. **table:** tablet, notebook.   4. **character'd:** written.
10. **measure:** traverse.   18. **inly:** inward.   22. **qualify:** moderate..
28. **enamell'd:** having naturally a hard shiny surface.
32. **wild ocean:** open sea.   40. **prevent:** forestall.
41. **encounters:** accostings.   42. **weeds:** clothes.
46. **odd-conceited:** strangely devised.
47. **fantastic:** capricious.   **become:** befit.
48. **greater time:** more years.
51. **compass:** circumference.   **farthingale:** hooped petticoat.

53. **codpiece:** a bag-like appendage at the front of breeches.
54. **ill-favor'd:** uncomely.   55. **round hose:** short padded breeches.
56. **stick pins on.** A common method of ornamenting the codpiece.
60. **unstaid:** unconventional.
61. **scandaliz'd:** disgraced (by becoming a source of scandal).
67. **withal:** with it.   70. **infinite:** an infinity.
85. **longing:** prompted by longing.
86. **at thy dispose:** in your charge.   90. **tarriance:** delay.

III.i. Location: Milan. The Duke's palace.
1. **give us leave:** polite form of dismissal.   4. **discover:** reveal.

Done to me (undeserving as I am),
My duty pricks me on to utter that
Which else no worldly good should draw from me.
Know, worthy prince, Sir Valentine, my friend,   10
This night intends to steal away your daughter;
Myself am one made privy to the plot.
I know you have determin'd to bestow her
On Thurio, whom your gentle daughter hates,
And should she thus be stol'n away from you,   15
It would be much vexation to your age.
Thus, for my duty's sake, I rather chose
To cross my friend in his intended drift,
Than, by concealing it, heap on your head
A pack of sorrows which would press you down,   20
Being unprevented, to your timeless grave.
   Duke. Proteus, I thank thee for thine honest care,
Which to requite, command me while I live.
This love of theirs myself have often seen,
Haply when they have judg'd me fast asleep,   25
And oftentimes have purpos'd to forbid
Sir Valentine her company and my court;
But fearing lest my jealous aim might err,
And so, unworthily, disgrace the man
(A rashness that I ever yet have shunn'd),   30
I gave him gentle looks, thereby to find
That which thyself hast now disclos'd to me.
And that thou mayst perceive my fear of this,
Knowing that tender youth is soon suggested,
I nightly lodge her in an upper tow'r,   35
The key whereof myself have ever kept;
And thence she cannot be convey'd away.
   Pro. Know, noble lord, they have devis'd a mean
How he her chamber-window will ascend,
And with a corded ladder fetch her down;   40
For which the youthful lover now is gone,
And this way comes he with it presently,
Where (if it please you) you may intercept him.
But, good my lord, do it so cunningly
That my discovery be not aimed at: 45
For love of you, not hate unto my friend,
Hath made me publisher of this pretense.
   Duke. Upon mine honor, he shall never know
That I had any light from thee of this.
   Pro. Adieu, my lord, Sir Valentine is coming.   50
                                                        [*Exit.*]

                [*Enter*] VALENTINE.

   Duke. Sir Valentine, whither away so fast?
   Val. Please it your Grace, there is a messenger
That stays to bear my letters to my friends,
And I am going to deliver them.
   Duke. Be they of much import?   55
   Val. The tenure of them doth but signify
My health and happy being at your court.
   Duke. Nay then no matter; stay with me a while;
I am to break with thee of some affairs

That touch me near, wherein thou must be secret.   60
'Tis not unknown to thee that I have sought
To match my friend Sir Thurio to my daughter.
   Val. I know it well, my lord, and sure the match
Were rich and honorable; besides, the gentleman
Is full of virtue, bounty, worth, and qualities   65
Beseeming such a wife as your fair daughter.
Cannot your Grace win her to fancy him?
   Duke. No, trust me, she is peevish, sullen, froward,
Proud, disobedient, stubborn, lacking duty,
Neither regarding that she is my child,   70
Nor fearing me as if I were her father;
And may I say to thee, this pride of hers
(Upon advice) hath drawn my love from her,
And where I thought the remnant of mine age
Should have been cherish'd by her child-like duty,   75
I now am full resolv'd to take a wife,
And turn her out to who will take her in:
Then let her beauty be her wedding-dow'r,
For me and my possessions she esteems not.
   Val. What would your Grace have me to do in
this?   80
   Duke. There is a lady in [Milano] here
Whom I affect; but she is nice and coy,
And nought esteems my aged eloquence.
Now therefore would I have thee to my tutor
(For long agone I have forgot to court;   85
Besides, the fashion of the time is chang'd)
How and which way I may bestow myself
To be regarded in her sun-bright eye.
   Val. Win her with gifts, if she respect not words:
Dumb jewels often in their silent kind   90
More than quick words do move a woman's mind.
   Duke. But she did scorn a present that I sent her.
   Val. A woman sometime scorns what best contents her.
Send her another; never give her o'er,
For scorn at first makes after-love the more.   95
If she do frown, 'tis not in hate of you,
But rather to beget more love in you.
If she do chide, 'tis not to have you gone,
For why, the fools are mad, if left alone.
Take no repulse, what ever she doth say;   100
For "get you gone," she doth not mean "away!"
Flatter and praise, commend, extol their graces;
Though ne'er so black, say they have angels' faces.
That man that hath a tongue, I say is no man,
If with his tongue he cannot win a woman.   105
   Duke. But she I mean is promis'd by her friends
Unto a youthful gentleman of worth,
And kept severely from resort of men,
That no man hath access by day to her.
   Val. Why then I would resort to her by night.
   Duke. Ay, but the doors be lock'd, and keys kept
safe,   111

18. **drift:** scheme.
21. **Being unprevented:** if they are not forestalled. **timeless:** untimely, premature.   28. **jealous aim:** suspicious conjecture.
34. **suggested:** tempted.   42. **presently:** even now.
45. **discovery:** disclosure.   **aimed at:** guessed.
47. **pretense:** intention.   56. **tenure:** tenor.
59. **break . . . of:** disclose to you.

65. **virtue:** good accomplishments.   **qualities:** attainments.
67. **fancy:** love.   68. **peevish:** willful.   **froward:** perverse.
73. **advice:** deliberation.   74. **where:** whereas.
82. **affect:** am fond of.   **nice:** difficult to please.   **coy:** offish, shy.
85. **agone:** ago (already rare in Shakespeare's day).   **forgot:** forgotten how.   87. **bestow:** conduct.   89. **respect:** heed.
90. **kind:** nature.   91. **quick:** lively.   99. **For why:** because.
101. **For:** i.e. for when she says.   103. **black:** dark-complexioned.
109, 112. **That:** so that.

The Two
Gentlemen
of Verona
III.i

That no man hath recourse to her by night.
Val. What lets but one may enter at her window?
Duke. Her chamber is aloft, far from the ground,
And built so shelving that one cannot climb it   115
Without apparent hazard of his life.
Val. Why then a ladder, quaintly made of cords,
To cast up, with a pair of anchoring hooks,
Would serve to scale another Hero's tow'r,
So bold Leander would adventure it.   120
Duke. Now as thou art a gentleman of blood,
Advise me where I may have such a ladder.
Val. When would you use it? pray, sir, tell me that.
Duke. This very night; for Love is like a child,
That longs for every thing that he can come by.   125
Val. By seven a' clock I'll get you such a ladder.
Duke. But hark thee: I will go to her alone.
How shall I best convey the ladder thither?
Val. It will be light, my lord, that you may bear it
Under a cloak that is of any length.   130
Duke. A cloak as long as thine will serve the turn?
Val. Ay, my good lord.
Duke.   Then let me see thy cloak—
I'll get me one of such another length.
Val. Why, any cloak will serve the turn, my lord.
Duke. How shall I fashion me to wear a cloak?   135
I pray thee let me feel thy cloak upon me.
What letter is this same? What's here? "To Silvia"?
And here an engine fit for my proceeding!
I'll be so bold to break the seal for once.   [*Reads.*]
"My thoughts do harbor with my Silvia nightly,   140
And slaves they are to me that send them flying:
O, could their master come and go as lightly,
Himself would lodge where, senseless, they are lying!
My herald thoughts in thy pure bosom rest them,
While I, their king, that thither them importune,   145
Do curse the grace that with such grace hath blest
         them,
Because myself do want my servants' fortune.
I curse myself, for they are sent by me,
   That they should harbor where their lord should be."
What's here?   150
"Silvia, this night I will enfranchise thee."
'Tis so; and here's the ladder for the purpose.
Why, Phaëton (for thou art Merops' son),
Wilt thou aspire to guide the heavenly car,
And with thy daring folly burn the world?   155
Wilt thou reach stars, because they shine on thee?
Go, base intruder, overweening slave,
Bestow thy fawning smiles on equal mates,

And think my patience (more than thy desert)
Is privilege for thy departure hence.   160
Thank me for this more than for all the favors
Which (all too much) I have bestowed on thee.
But if thou linger in my territories
Longer than swiftest expedition
Will give thee time to leave our royal court,   165
By heaven, my wrath shall far exceed the love
I ever bore my daughter, or thyself.
Be gone, I will not hear thy vain excuse,
But as thou lov'st thy life, make speed from hence.
                                                    [*Exit.*]
Val. And why not death, rather than living tor-
         ment?   170
To die is to be banish'd from myself,
And Silvia is myself: banish'd from her
Is self from self, a deadly banishment.
What light is light, if Silvia be not seen?
What joy is joy, if Silvia be not by?   175
Unless it be to think that she is by,
And feed upon the shadow of perfection.
Except I be by Silvia in the night,
There is no music in the nightingale;
Unless I look on Silvia in the day,   180
There is no day for me to look upon.
She is my essence, and I leave to be,
If I be not by her fair influence
Foster'd, illumin'd, cherish'd, kept alive.
I fly not death, to fly his deadly doom: 185
Tarry I here, I but attend on death,
But fly I hence, I fly away from life.

[*Enter* Proteus *and*] Launce.

Pro. Run, boy, run, run, and seek him out.
Launce. Soho, soho!
Pro. What seest thou?   190
Launce. Him we go to find. There's not a hair
on 's head but 'tis a Valentine.
Pro. Valentine?
Val. No.
Pro. Who then? his spirit?   195
Val. Neither.
Pro. What then?
Val. Nothing.
Launce. Can nothing speak? Master, shall I strike?
Pro. Who wouldst thou strike?   200
Launce. Nothing.
Pro. Villain, forbear.
Launce. Why, sir, I'll strike nothing. I pray
you—
Pro. Sirrah, I say forbear. Friend Valentine, a
         word.   205
Val. My ears are stopp'd and cannot hear good
         news,
So much of bad already hath possess'd them.

113. **lets:** hinders.   115. **shelving:** projecting.
116. **apparent:** obvious.   117. **quaintly:** skillfully.
119–20. **Hero's . . . Leander.** See note to I.i.22.
121. **blood:** good parentage.   131. **turn:** purpose.
133. **such another:** i.e. the same.
138. **engine:** contrivance (i.e. the rope ladder).
140. **harbor:** lodge.   142. **lightly:** quickly.
143. **senseless:** insensible.   **lying:** dwelling.
145. **importune:** urge, order.
146. **grace . . . grace:** good fortune . . . favor.   147. **want:** lack.
148. **for:** since.   151. **enfranchise thee:** set you free.
153. **Phaëton:** Phaëthon, the son of Helios, the sun-god, who made a
disastrous attempt to drive his father's chariot. A large portion of
the earth was scorched before Zeus intervened and slew Phaëthon.
Merops' son. Phaëthon's mother Clymene was the wife of Merops.
156. **reach:** reach for.   157. **overweening:** presumptuous.
158. **equal mates:** women of your own rank.

160. **Is privilege for:** licenses.   164. **expedition:** speed.
173. **deadly:** deathlike.   177. **shadow:** image, illusion.
182. **leave:** cease.
183. **fair influence:** beneficial effect (astrological figure).
185. **I . . . doom:** I do not elude death by fleeing from the Duke's
sentence of death.   186. **attend on:** wait.
189. **Soho:** a cry used in hunting the hare (note Launce's pun on *hair*
in line 191).
192. **Valentine.** With quibble on the sense "love token."

Pro. Then in dumb silence will I bury mine,
For they are harsh, untuneable, and bad.
  Val. Is Silvia dead?   210
  Pro. No, Valentine.
  Val. No Valentine indeed, for sacred Silvia.
Hath she forsworn me?
  Pro. No, Valentine.
  Val. No Valentine, if Silvia have forsworn me.
What is your news?   216
  Launce. Sir, there is a proclamation that you are
vanish'd.
  Pro. That thou art banish'd—O, that's the news!—
From hence, from Silvia, and from me thy friend.
  Val. O, I have fed upon this woe already,   221
And now excess of it will make me surfeit.
Doth Silvia know that I am banished?
  Pro. Ay, ay; and she hath offered to the doom
(Which unrevers'd stands in effectual force)   225
A sea of melting pearl, which some call tears;
Those at her father's churlish feet she tender'd,
With them, upon her knees, her humble self,
Wringing her hands, whose whiteness so became them
As if but now they waxed pale for woe: 230
But neither bended knees, pure hands held up,
Sad sighs, deep groans, nor silver-shedding tears
Could penetrate her uncompassionate sire;
But Valentine, if he be ta'en, must die.
Besides, her intercession chaf'd him so,   235
When she for thy repeal was suppliant,
That to close prison he commanded her,
With many bitter threats of biding there.
  Val. No more; unless the next word that thou
      speak'st
Have some malignant power upon my life;   240
If so—I pray thee breathe it in mine ear,
As ending anthem of my endless dolor.
  Pro. Cease to lament for that thou canst not help,
And study help for that which thou lament'st.
Time is the nurse and breeder of all good.   245
Here if thou stay, thou canst not see thy love;
Besides, thy staying will abridge thy life.
Hope is a lover's staff; walk hence with that
And manage it against despairing thoughts.
Thy letters may be here, though thou art hence,   250
Which, being writ to me, shall be deliver'd
Even in the milk-white bosom of thy love.
The time now serves not to expostulate:
Come, I'll convey thee through the city-gate;
And ere I part with thee, confer at large   255
Of all that may concern thy love-affairs.
As thou lov'st Silvia (though not for thyself)
Regard thy danger, and along with me.
  Val. I pray thee, Launce, and if thou seest my boy,
Bid him make haste and meet me at the North-gate.
  Pro. Go, sirrah, find him out. Come, Valentine.

  Val. O my dear Silvia! Hapless Valentine!   262
      [*Exeunt Valentine and Proteus.*]
  Launce. I am but a fool, look you, and yet I have
the wit to think my master is a kind of a knave; but
that's all one, if he be but one knave. He lives   265
not now that knows me to be in love, yet I am in
love, but a team of horse shall not pluck that from me;
nor who 'tis I love; and yet 'tis a woman; but what
woman, I will not tell myself; and yet 'tis a milkmaid;
yet 'tis not a maid, for she hath had gossips;   270
yet 'tis a maid, for she is her master's maid, and
serves for wages. She hath more qualities than a water-
spaniel, which is much in a bare Christian. [*Pulling out
a paper.*] Here is the cate-log of her condition.
"*Inprimis*, She can fetch and carry." Why, a   275
horse can do no more; nay, a horse cannot fetch, but
only carry, therefore is she better than a jade. "*Item*,
She can milk." Look you, a sweet virtue in a maid
with clean hands.

[*Enter*] SPEED.

  Speed. How now, Signior Launce? what news with
your mastership?   281
  Launce. With my [master's ship]? why, it is at
sea.
  Speed. Well, your old vice still: mistake the word.
What news then in your paper?   285
  Launce. The blackest news that ever thou heardst.
  Speed. Why, man? how black?
  Launce. Why, as black as ink.
  Speed. Let me read them.   289
  Launce. Fie on thee, jolthead, thou canst not
read.
  Speed. Thou liest; I can.
  Launce. I will try thee. Tell me this: who begot
thee?
  Speed. Marry, the son of my grandfather.   295
  Launce. O illiterate loiterer! it was the son of
thy grandmother. This proves that thou canst not
read.
  Speed. Come, fool, come; try me in thy paper.
  Launce. There—and Saint Nicholas be thy speed!
  Speed. [*Reads.*] "*Inprimis*, She can milk."   301
  Launce. Ay, that she can.
  Speed. "*Item*, She brews good ale."
  Launce. And thereof comes the proverb: "Blessing
of your heart, you brew good ale."   305
  Speed. "*Item*, She can sew."
  Launce. That's as much as to say, "Can she so?"
  Speed. "*Item*, She can knit."

208. mine: i.e. my news.
225. Which . . . force: which, if not reversed, will certainly be carried
out.   236. repeal: recall from banishment.
237. close: tightly shut.   238. biding: i.e. making her remain.
242. ending anthem: requiem.   243. that: what.
244. study help: devise a remedy.   249. manage: wield.
253. expostulate: discuss.   255. confer at large: discuss at length.
257. though . . . thyself: even if not for your own sake.

265. that's . . . knave: no matter, if his knavery be but slight.
270. gossips: godparents (to a child of hers).
272–73. water-spaniel. The spaniel was proverbial for fawning submissiveness.
273. bare: mere (perhaps with quibble on the sense "naked," in contrast to a spaniel's thick coat).
274. cate-log: catalogue (Launce's pronunciation).   condition: qualities.
275. Inprimis: *Imprimis*, in the first place (signalling the beginning of
a list, as *Item* distinguishes each later section).
277. jade: (1) ill-conditioned horse; (2) loose woman.
290. jolthead: blockhead.   296. loiterer: idler, truant.
300. Saint Nicholas: patron saint of scholars.   speed: protection,
help (with a play on Speed's name).

Launce. What need a man care for a stock with a wench, when she can knit him a stock?   310

Speed. "Item, She can wash and scour."

Launce. A special virtue; for then she need not be wash'd and scour'd.

Speed. "Item, She can spin."

Launce. Then may I set the world on wheels, when she can spin for her living.   316

Speed. "Item, She hath many nameless virtues."

Launce. That's as much as to say "bastard virtues," that indeed know not their fathers, and therefore have no names.   320

Speed. Here follow her vices.

Launce. Close at the heels of her virtues.

Speed. "Item, She is not to be [kiss'd] fasting, in respect of her breath."

Launce. Well, that fault may be mended with a breakfast. Read on.   326

Speed. "Item, She hath a sweet mouth."

Launce. That makes amends for her sour breath.

Speed. "Item, She doth talk in her sleep."

Launce. It's no matter for that, so she sleep not in her talk.   331

Speed. "Item, She is slow in words."

Launce. O villain, that set this down among her vices! To be slow in words is a woman's only virtue. I pray thee out with't, and place it for her chief virtue.   336

Speed. "Item, She is proud."

Launce. Out with that too; it was Eve's legacy, and cannot be ta'en from her.

Speed. "Item, She hath no teeth."   340

Launce. I care not for that neither, because I love crusts.

Speed. "Item, She is curst."

Launce. Well, the best is, she hath no teeth to bite.

Speed. "Item, She will often praise her liquor."   345

Launce. If her liquor be good, she shall; if she will not, I will; for good things should be prais'd.

Speed. "Item, She is too liberal."

Launce. Of her tongue she cannot, for that's writ down she is slow of; of her purse she shall not, for   350 that I'll keep shut. Now, of another thing she may, and that cannot I help. Well, proceed.

Speed. "Item, She hath more hair than wit, and more faults than hairs, and more wealth than faults."

Launce. Stop there; I'll have her. She was   355 mine and not mine twice or thrice in that last article. Rehearse that once more.

Speed. "Item, She hath more hair than wit"—

Launce. More hair than wit? It may be; I'll prove it: the cover of the salt hides the salt, and therefore it is more than the salt; the hair that covers the wit   361 is more than the wit, for the greater hides the less. What's next?

Speed. "And more faults than hairs"—

Launce. That's monstrous. O that that were out!   366

Speed. "And more wealth than faults."

Launce. Why, that word makes the faults gracious. Well, I'll have her; and if it be a match, as nothing is impossible—   370

Speed. What then?

Launce. Why, then will I tell thee—that thy master stays for thee at the North-gate.

Speed. For me?

Launce. For thee? ay, who art thou? He hath stay'd for a better man than thee.   376

Speed. And must I go to him?

Launce. Thou must run to him, for thou hast stay'd so long that going will scarce serve the turn.

Speed. Why didst not tell me sooner? Pox of your love-letters!   [*Exit.*]   381

Launce. Now will he be swing'd for reading my letter—an unmannerly slave, that will thrust himself into secrets. I'll after, to rejoice in the boy's correction.

Exit.

Scene II

Enter Duke, Thurio.

Duke. Sir Thurio, fear not but that she will love you
Now Valentine is banish'd from her sight.

Thu. Since his exile she hath despis'd me most,
Forsworn my company, and rail'd at me,
That I am desperate of obtaining her.   5

Duke. This weak impress of love is as a figure
Trenched in ice, which with an hour's heat
Dissolves to water, and doth lose his form.
A little time will melt her frozen thoughts,
And worthless Valentine shall be forgot.   10

[*Enter*] Proteus.

How now, Sir Proteus? is your countryman,
According to our proclamation, gone?

Pro. Gone, my good lord.

Duke. My daughter takes his going grievously.

Pro. A little time, my lord, will kill that grief.   15

Duke. So I believe; but Thurio thinks not so.
Proteus, the good conceit I hold of thee
(For thou hast shown some sign of good desert)
Makes me the better to confer with thee.

Pro. Longer than I prove loyal to your Grace   20
Let me not live to look upon your Grace.

Duke. Thou know'st how willingly I would effect
The match between Sir Thurio and my daughter?

Pro. I do, my lord.

Duke. And also, I think, thou art not ignorant   25
How she opposes her against my will?

309. **stock:** dowry.
310. **stock:** stocking.   315. **set . . . wheels:** take life easy.
317. **nameless:** inexpressible.   323–24. **in respect:** on account.
327. **sweet mouth:** sweet tooth (with an implication of wantonness).
330. **sleep.** With play on *slip,* pronounced similarly.
337. **proud.** With secondary meaning "lascivious."
343. **curst:** shrewish.   345. **praise:** appraise, i.e. sip or taste.
348. **liberal:** bold, wanton.

368. **gracious:** acceptable.
379. **going:** walking.   382. **swing'd:** thrashed (past of *swinge*).

III.ii. Location: Milan. The Duke's palace.
5. **That:** so that.   **am desperate:** despair.
6. **impress:** impression.   7. **Trenched:** cut.
14. **grievously:** bitterly, sorrowfully.   17. **conceit:** opinion.
19. **the better:** the more readily.   26. **opposes her against:** resists.

Pro.　She did, my lord, when Valentine was here.

Duke.　Ay, and perversely she persevers so.
What might we do to make the girl forget
The love of Valentine, and love Sir Thurio?　30

Pro.　The best way is to slander Valentine
With falsehood, cowardice, and poor descent,
Three things that women highly hold in hate.

Duke.　Ay, but she'll think that it is spoke in hate.

Pro.　Ay, if his enemy deliver it;　35
Therefore it must with circumstance be spoken
By one whom she esteemeth as his friend.

Duke.　Then you must undertake to slander him.

Pro.　And that, my lord, I shall be loath to do:
'Tis an ill office for a gentleman,　40
Especially against his very friend.

Duke.　Where your good word cannot advantage
him,
Your slander never can endamage him;
Therefore the office is indifferent,
Being entreated to it by your friend.　45

Pro.　You have prevail'd, my lord; if I can do it
By aught that I can speak in his dispraise,
She shall not long continue love to him.
But say this weed her love from Valentine,
It follows not that she will love Sir Thurio.　50

Thu.　Therefore, as you unwind her love from him,
Lest it should ravel and be good to none,
You must provide to bottom it on me;
Which must be done by praising me as much
As you in worth dispraise Sir Valentine.　55

Duke.　And, Proteus, we dare trust you in this kind,
Because we know (on Valentine's report)
You are already Love's firm votary,
And cannot soon revolt and change your mind.
Upon this warrant shall you have access　60
Where you with Silvia may confer at large—
For she is lumpish, heavy, melancholy,
And (for your friend's sake) will be glad of you—
Where you may temper her by your persuasion
To hate young Valentine and love my friend.　65

Pro.　As much as I can do, I will effect.
But you, Sir Thurio, are not sharp enough:
You must lay lime to tangle her desires
By wailful sonnets, whose composed rhymes
Should be full-fraught with serviceable vows.　70

Duke.　Ay, much is the force of heaven-bred poesy.

Pro.　Say that upon the altar of her beauty
You sacrifice your tears, your sighs, your heart;
Write till your ink be dry, and with your tears
Moist it again, and frame some feeling line　75
That may discover such integrity:
For Orpheus' lute was strung with poets' sinews,
Whose golden touch could soften steel and stones,

Make tigers tame, and huge leviathans
Forsake unsounded deeps to dance on sands.　80
After your dire-lamenting elegies,
Visit by night your lady's chamber-window
With some sweet consort; to their instruments
Tune a deploring dump—the night's dead silence　84
Will well become such sweet-complaining grievance.
This, or else nothing, will inherit her.

Duke.　This discipline shows thou hast been in love.

Thu.　And thy advice this night I'll put in practice:
Therefore, sweet Proteus, my direction-giver,
Let us into the city presently　90
To sort some gentlemen well skill'd in music.
I have a sonnet that will serve the turn
To give the onset to thy good advice.

Duke.　About it, gentlemen!

Pro.　We'll wait upon your Grace till after supper,
And afterward determine our proceedings.　96

Duke.　Even now about it! I will pardon you.

　　　　　　　　　　　　　　　　　Exeunt.

ACT IV, Scene I

Enter Valentine, Speed, *and certain* Outlaws.

1. Out.　Fellows, stand fast; I see a passenger.

2. Out.　If there be ten, shrink not, but down
　　　with 'em.

3. Out.　Stand, sir, and throw us that you have
　　　about ye.
If not, we'll make you sit, and rifle you.

Speed.　Sir, we are undone; these are the villains
That all the travellers do fear so much.　6

Val.　My friends—

1. Out.　That's not so, sir; we are your enemies.

2. Out.　Peace! we'll hear him.

3. Out.　Ay, by my beard, will we, for he is a
　　　proper man.　10

Val.　Then know that I have little wealth to lose.
A man I am cross'd with adversity;
My riches are these poor habiliments,
Of which if you should here disfurnish me,
You take the sum and substance that I have.　15

2. Out.　Whither travel you?

Val.　To Verona.

1. Out.　Whence came you?

Val.　From Milan.

3. Out.　Have you long sojourn'd there?　20

Val.　Some sixteen months, and longer might have
stay'd,
If crooked fortune had not thwarted me.

1. Out.　What, were you banish'd thence?

Val.　I was.

2. Out.　For what offense?　25

---

35. **deliver:** utter, speak.
36. **circumstance:** convincing detail.　41. **very:** special.
42. **advantage:** profit.
44. **indifferent:** neutral, neither good nor bad.　49. **weed:** remove.
53. **provide:** take care.　**bottom:** wind (as on a core).
62. **lumpish:** spiritless.　64. **Where:** whereas.　**temper:** mould.
68. **lime:** birdlime, a sticky substance smeared on twigs to entangle small birds.
70. **serviceable vows:** vows expressing readiness to serve.
75. **feeling:** impassioned.
76. **discover such integrity:** reveal such single-hearted devotion.
77. **sinews:** nerves.

79. **leviathans:** whales.　83. **consort:** band of musicians.
84. **deploring:** doleful.　**dump:** mournful tune.
85. **grievance:** sorrow.　86. **inherit:** gain, obtain.
87. **discipline:** instruction.　91. **sort:** choose.
93. **onset:** beginning.　95. **wait upon:** attend.
97. **pardon:** excuse from attendance.

IV.i. Location: A forest between Milan and Mantua.
1. **passenger:** traveller on foot, wayfarer.
3. **Stand:** halt (but *sit* in line 4 plays against the sense "stand up").
10. **proper:** good-looking, well made.　14. **disfurnish:** deprive.
22. **crooked:** malignant.

Val. For that which now torments me to rehearse:
I kill'd a man, whose death I much repent,
But yet I slew him manfully in fight,
Without false vantage, or base treachery.

1. Out. Why, ne'er repent it, if it were done so.
But were you banish'd for so small a fault?   31

Val. I was, and held me glad of such a doom.

2. Out. Have you the tongues?

Val. My youthful travel therein made me happy,
Or else I often had been miserable.   35

3. Out. By the bare scalp of Robin Hood's fat
        friar,
This fellow were a king for our wild faction!

1. Out. We'll have him. Sirs, a word.

Speed.   Master, be one of them;
It's an honorable kind of thievery.

Val.   Peace, villain.

2. Out. Tell us this: have you any thing to take to?

Val. Nothing but my fortune.   41

3. Out. Know then, that some of us are gentle-
        men,
Such as the fury of ungovern'd youth
Thrust from the company of aweful men.
Myself was from Verona banished   45
For practicing to steal away a lady,
[An] heir, and [near] allied unto the Duke.

2. Out. And I from Mantua, for a gentleman,
Who, in my mood, I stabb'd unto the heart.

1. Out. And I for such like petty crimes as these.
But to the purpose—for we cite our faults   51
That they may hold excus'd our lawless lives;
And partly, seeing you are beautified
With goodly shape, and by your own report
A linguist, and a man of such perfection   55
As we do in our quality much want—

2. Out. Indeed because you are a banish'd man,
Therefore, above the rest, we parley to you:
Are you content to be our general?
To make a virtue of necessity   60
And live as we do in this wilderness?

3. Out. What say'st thou? wilt thou be of our con-
        sort?
Say "ay" and be the captain of us all:
We'll do thee homage and be rul'd by thee,
Love thee as our commander and our king.   65

1. Out. But if thou scorn our courtesy, thou diest.

2. Out. Thou shalt not live to brag what we have
        offer'd.

Val. I take your offer, and will live with you,
Provided that you do no outrages

On silly women or poor passengers.   70

3. Out. No, we detest such vile base practices.
Come, go with us, we'll bring thee to our crews,
And show thee all the treasure we have got;
Which, with ourselves, all rest at thy dispose.

                                    Exeunt.

SCENE II

Enter PROTEUS.

Pro. Already have I been false to Valentine,
And now I must be as unjust to Thurio:
Under the color of commending him,
I have access my own love to prefer—
But Silvia is too fair, too true, too holy,   5
To be corrupted with my worthless gifts.
When I protest true loyalty to her,
She twits me with my falsehood to my friend;
When to her beauty I commend my vows,
She bids me think how I have been forsworn   10
In breaking faith with Julia whom I lov'd;
And notwithstanding all her sudden quips,
The least whereof would quell a lover's hope,
Yet, spaniel-like, the more she spurns my love,
The more it grows, and fawneth on her still.   15

[Enter] THURIO, MUSICIAN[s].

But here comes Thurio. Now must we to her window,
And give some evening music to her ear.

Thu. How now, Sir Proteus, are you crept before
        us?

Pro. Ay, gentle Thurio, for you know that love
Will creep in service where it cannot go.   20

Thu. Ay, but I hope, sir, that you love not here.

Pro. Sir, but I do; or else I would be hence.

Thu. Who? Silvia?

Pro.   Ay, Silvia—for your sake.

Thu. I thank you for your own. Now, gentlemen,
Let's tune, and to it lustily a while.   25

[Enter at one side] HOST, JULIA *[in boy's clothes, as
Sebastian]*.

Host. Now, my young guest, methinks you're
allycholly; I pray you, why is it?

Jul. Marry, mine host, because I cannot be
merry.   29

Host. Come, we'll have you merry: I'll bring you
where you shall hear music and see the gentleman
that you ask'd for.

Jul. But shall I hear him speak?

Host. Ay, that you shall.

Jul. That will be music.   *[Music plays.]*   35

Host. Hark, hark!

Jul. Is he among these?

Host. Ay; but peace, let's hear 'em.

---

27. **I . . . man.** Valentine's lie is presumably meant to impress the
outlaws.
32. **held . . . doom:** was pleased with such a sentence (i.e. to get off
so easily).
33. **the tongues:** knowledge of foreign languages.
34. **travel.** Perhaps correctly *travail*, i.e. laborious study; so F1 reads,
but ambiguously, since Elizabethan spelling did not distinguish the
two words. **happy:** skillful.
36. **friar:** i.e. Friar Tuck.   37. **faction:** company.
40. **any . . . take to:** any means of livelihood.
44. **aweful:** commanding respect (?) or law-abiding (?).
46. **practicing:** plotting.   49. **mood:** anger.
56. **quality:** profession.
58. **Therefore . . . rest:** for that reason chiefly.
60. **make . . . of:** embrace as if by choice.   62. **consort:** company.

70. **silly:** defenseless.   72. **crews:** bands.

IV.ii. Location: Milan. Outside the Duke's palace, under Silvia's
window.
2. **unjust:** false.   3. **color:** pretense.
9. **commend:** recommend, direct.   12. **quips:** sharp jests, sarcasms.
20. **go:** walk.   27. **allycholly:** blunder for *melancholy*.
32. **ask'd for:** inquired about.

Song

Who is Silvia? what is she,
That all our swains commend her?   40
Holy, fair, and wise is she;
The heaven such grace did lend her,
     That she might admired be.

Is she kind as she is fair?
For beauty lives with kindness.   45
Love doth to her eyes repair,
To help him of his blindness;
     And, being help'd, inhabits there.

Then to Silvia let us sing,
That Silvia is excelling;   50
She excels each mortal thing
Upon the dull earth dwelling.
     To her let us garlands bring.

Host. How now? are you sadder than you were
before? How do you, man? The music likes you
not.   56

Jul. You mistake; the musician likes me not.

Host. Why, my pretty youth?

Jul. He plays false, father.

Host. How, out of tune on the strings?   60

Jul. Not so; but yet so false that he grieves my
very heart-strings.

Host. You have a quick ear.

Jul. Ay, I would I were deaf; it makes me have
a slow heart.   65

Host. I perceive you delight not in music.

Jul. Not a whit, when it jars so.

Host. Hark, what fine change is in the music.

Jul. Ay; that change is the spite.

Host. You would have them always play but
one thing?   71

Jul. I would always have one play but one thing.
But, host, doth this Sir Proteus that we talk on
Often resort unto this gentlewoman?

Host. I tell you what Launce, his man, told me:
he lov'd her out of all nick.   76

Jul. Where is Launce?

Host. Gone to seek his dog, which to-morrow,
by his master's command, he must carry for a present
to his lady.   80

Jul. Peace, stand aside, the company parts.

Pro. Sir Thurio, fear not you, I will so plead,
That you shall say my cunning drift excels.

Thu. Where meet we?

Pro.   At Saint Gregory's well.

Thu.   Farewell.

[*Exeunt Thurio and Musicians.*]

[*Enter*] Silvia [*above at her window*].

Pro. Madam, good ev'n to your ladyship.   85

Sil. I thank you for your music, gentlemen.
Who is that that spake?

Pro. One, lady, if you knew his pure heart's truth,
You would quickly learn to know him by his voice.

Sil. Sir Proteus, as I take it.   90

Pro. Sir Proteus, gentle lady, and your servant.

Sil. What's your will?

Pro.   That I may compass yours.

Sil. You have your wish: my will is even this,
That presently you hie you home to bed.
Thou subtile, perjur'd, false, disloyal man,   95
Think'st thou I am so shallow, so conceitless,
To be seduced by thy flattery,
That hast deceiv'd so many with thy vows?
Return, return, and make thy love amends.
For me (by this pale queen of night I swear),   100
I am so far from granting thy request,
That I despise thee for thy wrongful suit,
And by and by intend to chide myself
Even for this time I spend in talking to thee.   104

Pro. I grant, sweet love, that I did love a lady;
But she is dead.

Jul.   [*Aside.*] 'Twere false, if I should speak it;
For I am sure she is not buried.

Sil. Say that she be; yet Valentine thy friend
Survives; to whom (thyself art witness)
I am betroth'd; and art thou not asham'd   110
To wrong him with thy importunacy?

Pro. I likewise hear that Valentine is dead.

Sil. And so suppose am I; for in [his] grave
Assure thyself my love is buried.

Pro. Sweet lady, let me rake it from the earth.   115

Sil. Go to thy lady's grave and call hers thence,
Or at the least, in hers sepulchre thine.

Jul. [*Aside.*] He heard not that.

Pro. Madam, if your heart be so obdurate,
Vouchsafe me yet your picture for my love,   120
The picture that is hanging in your chamber;
To that I'll speak, to that I'll sigh and weep;
For since the substance of your perfect self
Is else devoted, I am but a shadow;
And to your shadow will I make true love.   125

Jul. [*Aside.*] If 'twere a substance, you would
     sure deceive it,
And make it but a shadow, as I am.

Sil. I am very loath to be your idol, sir;
But since your falsehood shall become you well
To worship shadows and adore false shapes,   130
Send to me in the morning, and I'll send it;
And so, good rest.

Pro.   As wretches have o'ernight
That wait for execution in the morn.

[*Exeunt Proteus and Silvia.*]

Jul. Host, will you go?

Host. By my halidom, I was fast asleep.   135

Jul. Pray you, where lies Sir Proteus?

Host. Marry, at my house. Trust me, I think
'tis almost day.

---

43. **admired:** wondered at.
45. **For . . . kindness:** i.e. beauty without kindness dies unenjoyed,
and undelighting (Johnson). 55. **likes:** pleases.
65. **slow:** heavy. 67. **jars:** is discordant.
68. **fine change:** delicate modulation.
76. **out . . . nick:** beyond all reckoning. 83. **drift:** scheme.

92. **compass:** obtain. 95. **subtile:** crafty.
96. **conceitless:** witless.
111. **thy importunacy:** your importunity, i.e. the improper urging of
your own suit. 124. **else:** elsewhere. **shadow:** mere nothing.
125. **shadow:** i.e. picture. 126. **deceive:** be false to.
129. **become:** befit. 135. **halidom:** sanctity, salvation.
136. **lies:** lodges.

Jul. Not so; but it hath been the longest night
That e'er I watch'd, and the most heaviest.   140
                                        [*Exeunt.*]

SCENE III

Enter EGLAMOUR.

Egl. This is the hour that Madam Silvia
Entreated me to call and know her mind.
There's some great matter she'ld employ me in.
Madam, madam!

[*Enter*] SILVIA [*above at her window*].

Sil.   Who calls?
Egl.   Your servant and your friend;
One that attends your ladyship's command.   5
Sil. Sir Eglamour, a thousand times good morrow.
Egl. As many, worthy lady, to yourself.
According to your ladyship's impose,
I am thus early come to know what service
It is your pleasure to command me in.   10
Sil. O Eglamour, thou art a gentleman—
Think not I flatter, for I swear I do not—
Valiant, wise, remorseful, well accomplish'd,
Thou art not ignorant what dear good will
I bear unto the banish'd Valentine,   15
Nor how my father would enforce me marry
Vain Thurio, whom my very soul [abhors].
Thyself hast lov'd, and I have heard thee say
No grief did ever come so near thy heart
As when thy lady and thy true-love died,   20
Upon whose grave thou vow'dst pure chastity.
Sir Eglamour, I would to Valentine,
To Mantua, where I hear he makes abode;
And for the ways are dangerous to pass,
I do desire thy worthy company,   25
Upon whose faith and honor I repose.
Urge not my father's anger, Eglamour,
But think upon my grief, a lady's grief,
And on the justice of my flying hence,
To keep me from a most unholy match,   30
Which heaven and fortune still rewards with plagues.
I do desire thee, even from a heart
As full of sorrows as the sea of sands,
To bear me company, and go with me;
If not, to hide what I have said to thee,   35
That I may venture to depart alone.
Egl. Madam, I pity much your grievances,
Which since I know they virtuously are plac'd,
I give consent to go along with you,
Reaking as little what betideth me,   40

As much I wish all good befortune you.
When will you go?
Sil.   This evening coming.
Egl. Where shall I meet you?
Sil.   At Friar Patrick's cell,
Where I intend holy confession.   44
Egl. I will not fail your ladyship. Good morrow,
Gentle lady.
Sil.   Good morrow, kind Sir Eglamour.
                                        Exeunt.

SCENE IV

Enter LAUNCE [*with his dog*].

Launce. When a man's servant shall play the cur
with him, look you, it goes hard: one that I brought
up of a puppy; one that I sav'd from drowning, when
three or four of his blind brothers and sisters went to it.
I have taught him, even as one would say precisely,   5
"Thus I would teach a dog." I was sent to deliver him
as a present to Mistress Silvia from my master; and I
came no sooner into the dining-chamber but he steps
me to her trencher and steals her capon's leg. O, 'tis
a foul thing when a cur cannot keep himself in all   10
companies! I would have (as one should say) one
that takes upon him to be a dog indeed, to be, as it
were, a dog at all things. If I had not had more wit
than he, to take a fault upon me that he did, I think
verily he had been hang'd for't; sure as I live he had   15
suffer'd for't. You shall judge: he thrusts me himself
into the company of three or four gentleman-like dogs,
under the Duke's table. He had not been there
(bless the mark!) a pissing-while, but all the chamber
smelt him. "Out with the dog," says one. "What   20
cur is that?" says another. "Whip him out," says
the third. "Hang him up," says the Duke. I, having
been acquainted with the smell before, knew it was
Crab, and goes me to the fellow that whips the dogs:
"Friend," quoth I, "you mean to whip the dog?"   25
"Ay, marry, do I," quoth he. "You do him the more
wrong," quoth I, "'twas I did the thing you wot of."
He makes me no more ado, but whips me out of the
chamber. How many masters would do this for his
servant? Nay, I'll be sworn, I have sat in the stocks   30
for puddings he hath stol'n, otherwise he had been
executed; I have stood on the pillory for geese he
hath kill'd, otherwise he had suffer'd for't. Thou
think'st not of this now. Nay, I remember the
trick you serv'd me, when I took my leave of   35
Madam Silvia. Did not I bid thee still mark me, and
do as I do? When didst thou see me heave up my

---

140. **watch'd:** stayed awake. **heaviest:** grievous.

IV.iii. Location: The same, early the next morning.
o.s.d. **Eglamour.** Presumably not the Eglamour referred to in I.ii.9–11.
8. **impose:** command.   13. **remorseful:** compassionate.
14. **dear:** affectionate.
23. **Mantua.** Shakespeare here chose Mantua because he recalled that
Romeus fled in exile to that city in Brooke's *Romeus and Juliet*; the
detail reappears in *Romeo and Juliet*, a play for which Brooke's poem
is the principal source. This is only one of a substantial number of
echoes in *Two Gentlemen* from Brooke; another is the rendezvous at
Friar Patrick's (Friar Lawrence's in Brooke and *Romeo and Juliet*)
cell (lines 43–44 below).   24. **for:** because.   31. **still:** always.
37. **grievances:** trouble, distress.   40. **Reaking:** recking, caring.

41. **befortune:** befall.

IV.iv. The same, some hours later.
3. **of:** from.   4. **went to it:** met their death.
5. **even . . . precisely:** i.e. as one might say in the most perfect method
(of dog-training).   9. **trencher:** wooden plate.
10. **keep:** behave properly.
11–12. **one that:** i.e. such a dog as.
13. **a dog at:** adept at (but the joke obviously resides in the fact that
the words have their literal meaning also; so too for *pissing-while* in
line 19, slang for "a short time").
19. **bless the mark:** a phrase of apology for indecorous language.
27. **wot:** know.   31. **puddings:** stomachs or intestines of animals.

leg and make water against a gentlewoman's farthingale? Didst thou ever see me do such a trick?

[*Enter*] Proteus, Julia [*disguised as Sebastian*].

Pro. Sebastian is thy name? I like thee well,   40
And will employ thee in some service presently.

Jul. In what you please; I'll do what I can.

Pro. I hope thou wilt. [*To Launce.*] How now,
    you whoreson peasant,
Where have you been these two days loitering?

Launce. Marry, sir, I carried Mistress Silvia the
dog you bade me.   46

Pro. And what says she to my little jewel?

Launce. Marry, she says your dog was a cur,
and tells you currish thanks is good enough for such
a present.   50

Pro. But she receiv'd my dog?

Launce. No indeed did she not; here have I
brought him back again.

Pro. What, didst thou offer her this from me?

Launce. Ay, sir, the other squirrel was stol'n   55
from me by the hangman's boys in the market-place;
and then I offer'd her mine own, who is a dog as big
as ten of yours, and therefore the gift the greater.

Pro. Go, get thee hence, and find my dog again,
Or ne'er return again into my sight.   60
Away, I say! stayest thou to vex me here?

[*Exit Launce.*]

A slave, that still an end turns me to shame!
Sebastian, I have entertained thee,
Partly that I have need of such a youth
That can with some discretion do my business—   65
For 'tis no trusting to yond foolish lout—
But chiefly for thy face and thy behavior,
Which (if my augury deceive me not)
Witness good bringing up, fortune, and truth:
Therefore know [thou], for this I entertain thee.   70
Go presently, and take this ring with thee,
Deliver it to Madam Silvia—
She lov'd me well deliver'd it to me.

Jul. It seems you lov'd not her, [to] leave her
    token:
She is dead, belike?

Pro.   Not so; I think she lives.   75

Jul. Alas!

Pro. Why dost thou cry "alas"?

Jul.   I cannot choose
But pity her.

Pro.   Wherefore shouldst thou pity her?

Jul. Because methinks that she lov'd you as well
As you do love your lady Silvia: 80
She dreams on him that has forgot her love;
You dote on her that cares not for your love.
'Tis pity love should be so contrary;
And thinking on it makes me cry "alas!"

Pro. Well, give her that ring and therewithal   85
This letter; that's her chamber. Tell my lady

I claim the promise for her heavenly picture.
Your message done, hie home unto my chamber,
Where thou shalt find me sad and solitary.   [*Exit.*]

Jul. How many women would do such a message?
Alas, poor Proteus, thou hast entertain'd   91
A fox to be the shepherd of thy lambs.
Alas, poor fool, why do I pity him
That with his very heart despiseth me?
Because he loves her, he despiseth me;   95
Because I love him, I must pity him.
This ring I gave him when he parted from me,
To bind him to remember my good will;
And now am I (unhappy messenger)
To plead for that which I would not obtain,   100
To carry that which I would have refus'd,
To praise his faith which I would have disprais'd.
I am my master's true confirmed love;
But cannot be true servant to my master,
Unless I prove false traitor to myself.   105
Yet will I woo for him, but yet so coldly
As, heaven it knows, I would not have him speed.

[*Enter*] Silvia [*attended*].

Gentlewoman, good day; I pray you be my mean
To bring me where to speak with Madam Silvia.

Sil. What would you with her, if that I be she?

Jul. If you be she, I do entreat your patience   111
To hear me speak the message I am sent on.

Sil. From whom?

Jul. From my master, Sir Proteus, madam.

Sil. O, he sends you for a picture?   115

Jul. Ay, madam.

Sil. Ursula, bring my picture there.
Go give your master this. Tell him from me,
One Julia, that his changing thoughts forget,
Would better fit his chamber than this shadow.   120

Jul. Madam, please you peruse this letter—
Pardon me, madam, I have unadvis'd
Deliver'd you a paper that I should not:
This is the letter to your ladyship.

Sil. I pray thee let me look on that again.   125

Jul. It may not be; good madam, pardon me.

Sil. There, hold!
I will not look upon your master's lines;
I know they are stuff'd with protestations,
And full of new-found oaths, which he will break   130
As easily as I do tear his paper.

Jul. Madam, he sends your ladyship this ring.

Sil. The more shame for him that he sends it me;
For I have heard him say a thousand times
His Julia gave it him at his departure: 135
Though his false finger have profan'd the ring,
Mine shall not do his Julia so much wrong.

Jul. She thanks you.

Sil. What say'st thou?

Jul. I thank you, madam, that you tender her.   140
Poor gentlewoman, my master wrongs her much.

Sil. Dost thou know her?

41. **presently:** at once.
43. **whoreson peasant.** Coarsely playful rather than genuinely abusive.
55. **squirrel:** i.e. little dog.   56. **hangman's:** fit for the hangman.
62. **still an end:** continually.   63. **entertained:** taken into service.
73. **deliver'd:** who delivered.   74. **leave:** part with.
85. **therewithal:** at the same time.

93. **poor fool.** Referring to herself.   107. **speed:** succeed.
109. **where to speak:** where I may speak.
122. **unadvis'd:** inadvertently.
140. **tender:** regard sympathetically.

167

Jul. Almost as well as I do know myself.
To think upon her woes I do protest
That I have wept a hundred several times.   145
    Sil. Belike she thinks that Proteus hath forsook
her?
    Jul. I think she doth; and that's her cause of sor-
row.
    Sil. Is she not passing fair?
    Jul. She hath been fairer, madam, than she is:
When she did think my master lov'd her well,   150
She, in my judgment, was as fair as you;
But since she did neglect her looking-glass,
And threw her sun-expelling mask away,
The air hath starv'd the roses in her cheeks,
And pinch'd the lily-tincture of her face,   155
That now she is become as black as I.
    Sil. How tall was she?
    Jul. About my stature; for at Pentecost,
When all our pageants of delight were play'd,
Our youth got me to play the woman's part,   160
And I was trimm'd in Madam Julia's gown,
Which served me as fit, by all men's judgments,
As if the garment had been made for me;
Therefore I know she is about my height.
And at that time I made her weep agood,   165
For I did play a lamentable part,
Madam, 'twas Ariadne passioning
For Theseus' perjury and unjust flight;
Which I so lively acted with my tears
That my poor mistress, moved therewithal,   170
Wept bitterly; and would I might be dead
If I in thought felt not her very sorrow.
    Sil. She is beholding to thee, gentle youth.
Alas, poor lady, desolate and left!
I weep myself to think upon thy words.   175
Here, youth, there is my purse; I give thee this
For thy sweet mistress' sake, because thou lov'st her.
Farewell.
    Jul. And she shall thank you for't, if e'er you
know her.   [*Exit Silvia with Attendants.*]
A virtuous gentlewoman, mild and beautiful!   180
I hope my master's suit will be but cold,
Since she respects my mistress' love so much.
Alas, how love can trifle with itself!
Here is her picture: let me see; I think
If I had such a tire, this face of mine   185
Were full as lovely as is this of hers;
And yet the painter flatter'd her a little,
Unless I flatter with myself too much.
Her hair is auburn, mine is perfect yellow:
If that be all the difference in his love,   190
I'll get me such a color'd periwig.
Her eyes are grey as glass, and so are mine;

Ay, but her forehead's low, and mine's as high.
What should it be that he respects in her,
But I can make respective in myself,   195
If this fond Love were not a blinded god?
Come, shadow, come, and take this shadow up,
For 'tis thy rival. O thou senseless form,
Thou shalt be worshipp'd, kiss'd, lov'd, and ador'd;
And were there sense in his idolatry,   200
My substance should be statue in thy stead.
I'll use thee kindly for thy mistress' sake
That us'd me so; or else, by Jove I vow,
I should have scratch'd out your unseeing eyes,
To make my master out of love with thee.   *Exit.* 205

ACT V, Scene I

Enter Eglamour.

Egl. The sun begins to gild the western sky,
And now it is about the very hour
That Silvia at Friar Patrick's cell should meet me.
She will not fail, for lovers break not hours,
Unless it be to come before their time,   5
So much they spur their expedition.
See where she comes.

[*Enter*] Silvia.

                    Lady, a happy evening!
    Sil. Amen, amen! Go on, good Eglamour,
Out at the postern by the abbey wall;
I fear I am attended by some spies.   10
    Egl. Fear not: the forest is not three leagues off;
If we recover that, we are sure enough.   *Exeunt.*

Scene II

Enter Thurio, Proteus, Julia [*disguised as Sebastian*].

    Thu. Sir Proteus, what says Silvia to my suit?
    Pro. O, sir, I find her milder than she was,
And yet she takes exceptions at your person.
    Thu. What? that my leg is too long?
    Pro. No, that it is too little.   5
    Thu. I'll wear a boot, to make it somewhat
rounder.
    [*Jul. Aside.*] But love will not be spurr'd to what
it loathes.
    Thu. What says she to my face?
    Pro. She says it is a fair one.
    Thu. Nay then the wanton lies; my face is black.

---

154. **starv'd:** nipped.   156. **black:** dark-complexioned.
158. **Pentecost:** Whitsuntide (seven weeks after Easter).
159. **pageants of delight:** delightful entertainments.
161. **trimm'd:** decked out.   165. **agood:** in earnest.
166. **lamentable:** tragic.
167–68. **Ariadne . . . flight.** King Minos' daughter Ariadne, having
enabled Theseus to slay the Minotaur, fled with him from Crete, but
Theseus abandoned her on the island of Naxos, where she hanged
herself.   167. **passioning:** sorrowing.   168. **unjust:** faithless.
173. **beholding:** beholden, indebted.   181. **cold:** vain.
185. **tire:** headdress.

193. **as high:** i.e. as high as hers is low. High foreheads were greatly
admired.   194. **respects:** cares for.
195. **respective:** worthy of being cared for.
197. **shadow . . . shadow.** Cf. lines 124–25. **take . . . up:** (1) hold;
(2) oppose, challenge.   198. **senseless:** insensible.
200. **sense:** reason.   201. **statue:** i.e. idol.

V.i. Location: Milan. An abbey.
9. **postern:** small back or side door.
12. **recover:** reach.   **sure:** safe.

V.ii. Location: Milan. The Duke's palace.
3. **takes exceptions at:** objects to.
7. **spurr'd:** incited (with obvious quibble on Thurio's reference to
being booted).   9. **fair:** pale.

Pro. But pearls are fair; and the old saying is,   11
Black men are pearls in beauteous ladies' eyes.

  [*Jul. Aside.*] 'Tis true, such pearls as put out
ladies' eyes,
For I had rather wink than look on them.

Thu. How likes she my discourse?   15

Pro. Ill, when you talk of war.

Thu. But well, when I discourse of love and peace.

Jul. [*Aside.*] But better indeed, when you hold
[your] peace.

Thu. What says she to my valor?

Pro. O, sir, she makes no doubt of that.   20

Jul. [*Aside.*] She needs not, when she knows it
cowardice.

Thu. What says she to my birth?

Pro. That you are well deriv'd.

Jul. [*Aside.*] True: from a gentleman to a fool.

Thu. Considers she my possessions?   25

Pro. O ay; and pities them.

Thu. Wherefore?

Jul. [*Aside.*] That such an ass should owe them.

Pro. That they are out by lease.

Jul. Here comes the Duke.   30

[*Enter*] DUKE.

Duke. How now, Sir Proteus? how now, Thurio?
Which of you saw Eglamour of late?

Thu. Not I.

Pro.   Nor I.

Duke.   Saw you my daughter?

Pro.   Neither.

Duke. Why then
She's fled unto that peasant Valentine;   35
And Eglamour is in her company.
'Tis true; for Friar Laurence met them both,
As he in penance wander'd through the forest;
Him he knew well, and guess'd that it was she,
But being mask'd, he was not sure of it;   40
Besides, she did intend confession
At Patrick's cell this even, and there she was not.
These likelihoods confirm her flight from hence:
Therefore I pray you stand not to discourse,
But mount you presently and meet with me   45
Upon the rising of the mountain foot
That leads toward Mantua, whither they are fled.
Dispatch, sweet gentlemen, and follow me.   [*Exit.*]

Thu. Why, this it is to be a peevish girl,
That flies her fortune when it follows her.   50
I'll after, more to be reveng'd on Eglamour
Than for the love of reckless Silvia.   [*Exit.*]

Pro. And I will follow, more for Silvia's love
Than hate of Eglamour that goes with her.   [*Exit.*]

Jul. And I will follow, more to cross that love   55
Than hate for Silvia, that is gone for love.   *Exit.*

SCENE III

[*Enter*] SILVIA, OUTLAWS.

1. Out. Come, come,
Be patient; we must bring you to our captain.

Sil. A thousand more mischances than this one
Have learn'd me how to brook this patiently.

2. Out. Come, bring her away.   5

1. Out. Where is the gentleman that was with
her?

3. Out. Being nimble-footed, he hath outrun us,
But Moyses and Valerius follow him.
Go thou with her to the west end of the wood;   9
There is our captain. We'll follow him that's fled—
The thicket is beset, he cannot scape.

1. Out. Come, I must bring you to our captain's
cave.
Fear not; he bears an honorable mind,
And will not use a woman lawlessly.   14

Sil. O Valentine, this I endure for thee!   *Exeunt.*

SCENE IV

Enter VALENTINE.

Val. How use doth breed a habit in a man!
This shadowy desert, unfrequented woods,
I better brook than flourishing peopled towns:
Here can I sit alone, unseen of any,
And to the nightingale's complaining notes   5
Tune my distresses and record my woes.
O thou that dost inhabit in my breast,
Leave not the mansion so long tenantless,
Lest growing ruinous, the building fall
And leave no memory of what it was!   10
Repair me with thy presence, Silvia;
Thou gentle nymph, cherish thy forlorn swain.
                     [*Shouts within.*]
What hallowing and what stir is this to-day?
These are my mates, that make their wills their law,
Have some unhappy passenger in chase.   15
They love me well; yet I have much to do
To keep them from uncivil outrages.
Withdraw thee, Valentine: who's this comes here?
                     [*Steps aside.*]

[*Enter*] PROTEUS, SILVIA, JULIA [*disguised as Sebastian*].

Pro. Madam, this service I have done for you
(Though you respect not aught your servant doth)
To hazard life, and rescue you from him   21
That would have forc'd your honor and your love.
Vouchsafe me, for my meed, but one fair look:
A smaller boon than this I cannot beg,
And less than this, I am sure you cannot give.   25

---

12. **pearls:** i.e. things of great price.
13. **pearls:** cataracts.
20. **makes . . . of:** is in no uncertainty about (another double-edged
reply, like line 9).   **23. deriv'd:** descended.   **28. owe:** own.
37. **Friar Laurence.** Possibly a slip for Friar Patrick; see the note on
IV.iii.23.   **43. likelihoods:** indications.
49. **peevish:** silly, childish.
50. **fortune:** good fortune.
52. **reckless:** heedless, uncaring.   **55. cross:** frustrate.

V.iii. Location: The forest.
3. **more:** greater.   **4. learn'd:** taught.   **brook:** endure.
6. **gentleman:** i.e. Eglamour. His flight seems scarcely in character.
8. **Moyses:** variant of *Moses.*

V.iv. Location: The forest.
1. **use:** practice.   **2. desert:** deserted region.   **6. record:** sing.
7. **inhabit:** lodge.   **13. hallowing:** shouting.
15. **Have:** who have.   **unhappy passenger:** unfortunate traveller.
20. **respect:** heed.   **23. meed:** reward.   **fair:** kind.

The Two
Gentlemen
of Verona
V.iv

Val. [*Aside.*] How like a dream is this! I see,
 and hear:
Love, lend me patience to forbear a while.
 Sil. O miserable, unhappy that I am!
 Pro. Unhappy were you, madam, ere I came;
But by my coming I have made you happy. 30
 Sil. By thy approach thou mak'st me most un-
 happy.
 Jul. [*Aside.*] And me, when he approacheth to
 your presence.
 Sil. Had I been seized by a hungry lion,
I would have been a breakfast to the beast
Rather than have false Proteus rescue me. 35
O heaven be judge how I love Valentine,
Whose life's as tender to me as my soul!
And full as much (for more there cannot be)
I do detest false perjur'd Proteus.
Therefore be gone, solicit me no more. 40
 Pro. What dangerous action, stood it next to death,
Would I not undergo for one calm look?
O, 'tis the curse in love, and still approv'd,
When women cannot love where they're belov'd!
 Sil. When Proteus cannot love where he's be-
 lov'd! 45
Read over Julia's heart (thy first best love),
For whose dear sake thou didst then rend thy faith
Into a thousand oaths; and all those oaths
Descended into perjury, to love me.
Thou hast no faith left now, unless thou'dst two, 50
And that's far worse than none: better have none
Than plural faith, which is too much by one.
Thou counterfeit to thy true friend!
 Pro.   In love
Who respects friend?
 Sil.   All men but Proteus.
 Pro. Nay, if the gentle spirit of moving words 55
Can no way change you to a milder form,
I'll woo you like a soldier, at arm's end,
And love you 'gainst the nature of love—force ye.
 Sil. O heaven!
 Pro.   I'll force thee yield to my desire.
 Val. [*Coming forward.*] Ruffian! let go that rude
 uncivil touch, 60
Thou friend of an ill fashion!
 Pro.   Valentine!
 Val. Thou common friend, that's without faith
 or love,
For such is a friend now! treacherous man,
Thou hast beguil'd my hopes! Nought but mine eye
Could have persuaded me; now I dare not say 65
I have one friend alive; thou wouldst disprove me.
Who should be trusted, when one's right hand
Is perjured to the bosom? Proteus,
I am sorry I must never trust thee more,
But count the world a stranger for thy sake. 70

The private wound is deepest: O time most accurst!
'Mongst all foes that a friend should be the worst!
 Pro. My shame and guilt confounds me.
Forgive me, Valentine; if hearty sorrow
Be a sufficient ransom for offense, 75
I tender't here: I do as truly suffer
As e'er I did commit.
 Val.   Then I am paid;
And once again I do receive thee honest.
Who by repentance is not satisfied
Is nor of heaven nor earth, for these are pleas'd; 80
By penitence th' Eternal's wrath's appeas'd:
And that my love may appear plain and free,
All that was mine in Silvia I give thee.
 Jul. O me unhappy!   [*Swoons.*]
 Pro. Look to the boy. 85
 Val. Why, boy! why, wag! how now? what's the
matter? Look up; speak.
 Jul. O good sir, my master charg'd me to de-
liver a ring to Madam Silvia, which (out of my neglect)
was never done. 90
 Pro. Where is that ring, boy?
 Jul.   Here 'tis; this is it. [*Shows a ring.*]
 Pro. How? let me see.
Why, this is the ring I gave to Julia.
 Jul. O, cry you mercy, sir, I have mistook;
This is the ring you sent to Silvia. 95
        [*Shows another ring.*]
 Pro. But how cam'st thou by this ring? At my
 depart
I gave this unto Julia.
 Jul. And Julia herself did give it me,
And Julia herself hath brought it hither.
 Pro. How? Julia? 100
 Jul. Behold her that gave aim to all thy oaths,
And entertain'd 'em deeply in her heart.
How oft hast thou with perjury cleft the root?
O Proteus, let this habit make thee blush!
Be thou asham'd that I have took upon me 105
Such an immodest raiment—if shame live
In a disguise of love!
It is the lesser blot, modesty finds,
Women to change their shapes than men their minds.
 Pro. Than men their minds? 'tis true. O heaven,
 were man 110
But constant, he were perfect; that one error
Fills him with faults; makes him run through all
 th' sins:
Inconstancy falls off ere it begins.
What is in Silvia's face, but I may spy
More fresh in Julia's with a constant eye? 115
 Val. Come, come, a hand from either.
Let me be blest to make this happy close;
'Twere pity two such friends should be long foes.

31. **approach:** i.e. advances. 37. **tender:** dear.
42. **undergo:** undertake. **calm:** i.e. gentle.
43. **still approv'd:** ever attested by experience.
54. **respects:** considers.
57. **arm's end:** sword's point (with bawdy innuendo).
61. **fashion:** kind (perhaps with reference to the kind of friendship now fashionable; see lines 62–63).
62–63. **common . . . now:** i.e. ordinary, commonplace friend, which, as friendship is valued to-day, means one without faith or love.

73. **confounds:** destroys. 77. **commit:** transgress, sin.
78. **receive:** acknowledge, believe.
94. **cry you mercy:** I beg your pardon.
101. **gave aim to:** was the object of.
103. **root:** i.e. the bottom of the heart. 104. **habit:** garb.
106–7: **if . . . love:** if a disguise assumed for love's sake can produce shame.
113. **Inconstancy . . . begins:** an inconstant man begins to be faithless even before he has declared his love.
115. **constant:** steadfast, faithful. 117. **close:** union.

Pro. Bear witness, heaven, I have my wish for
ever.
Jul. And I mine. 120

[*Enter*] DUKE, THURIO, OUTLAWS.

Outlaws. A prize, a prize, a prize!
Val. Forbear, forbear, I say; it is my lord the
Duke.
Your Grace is welcome to a man disgrac'd,
Banished Valentine.
Duke.   Sir Valentine!
Thu. Yonder is Silvia; and Silvia's mine. 125
Val. Thurio, give back, or else embrace thy
death;
Come not within the measure of my wrath.
Do not name Silvia thine; if once again,
[Milan] shall not hold thee. Here she stands,
Take but possession of her with a touch: 130
I dare thee but to breathe upon my love.
Thu. Sir Valentine, I care not for her, I;
I hold him but a fool that will endanger
His body for a girl that loves him not.
I claim her not, and therefore she is thine. 135
Duke. The more degenerate and base art thou
To make such means for her as thou hast done,
And leave her on such slight conditions.
Now, by the honor of my ancestry,
I do applaud thy spirit, Valentine, 140
And think thee worthy of an empress' love.
Know then, I here forget all former griefs,
Cancel all grudge, repeal thee home again,
Plead a new state in thy unrivall'd merit,

To which I thus subscribe: Sir Valentine, 145
Thou art a gentleman and well deriv'd,
Take thou thy Silvia, for thou hast deserv'd her.
Val. I thank your Grace; the gift hath made me
happy.
I now beseech you (for your daughter's sake)
To grant one boon that I shall ask of you. 150
Duke. I grant it (for thine own) what e'er it be.
Val. These banish'd men, that I have kept withal,
Are men endu'd with worthy qualities.
Forgive them what they have committed here,
And let them be recall'd from their exile; 155
They are reformed, civil, full of good,
And fit for great employment, worthy lord.
Duke. Thou hast prevail'd, I pardon them and
thee;
Dispose of them as thou know'st their deserts.
Come, let us go, we will include all jars 160
With triumphs, mirth, and rare solemnity.
Val. And as we walk along, I dare be bold
With our discourse to make your Grace to smile.
What think you of this page, my lord?
Duke. I think the boy hath grace in him; he
blushes. 165
Val. I warrant you, my lord—more grace than
boy.
Duke. What mean you by that saying?
Val. Please you, I'll tell you as we pass along,
That you will wonder what hath fortuned.
Come, Proteus, 'tis your penance but to hear 170
The story of your loves discovered;
That done, our day of marriage shall be yours,
One feast, one house, one mutual happiness. *Exeunt.*

---

121. **A prize:** booty.   126. **give back:** stand back.
127. **measure:** reach (i.e. of his sword).
137. **make such means:** use such efforts.
138. **on . . . conditions:** so easily.   142. **griefs:** grievances.
143. **repeal:** recall from exile.
144. **Plead . . . state:** argue (that there is) a new condition of things
(Leech).

152. **kept withal:** lived with.
156–57. **They . . . employment.** An attempt to include everyone in the
happy ending, but a little awkward in view of Valentine's comment in
lines 14–17.   160. **include all jars:** conclude all discords.
161. **solemnity:** festivity.
169. **That:** so that.   **wonder:** marvel at.   **fortuned:** happened.

NOTE ON THE TEXT

The sole authority for *The Two Gentlemen of Verona* is the
First Folio (1623); all later texts are derived from that source.
On the whole, F1 offers a sound enough text, but there is
real confusion in the use of the place names Verona, Milan,
and Padua (see Textual Notes, II.v.2, III.i.81, V.iv.129).

As in the case of *The Tempest*, the manuscript underlying
the F1 text is believed to have been a transcript specially
prepared for the printers by Ralph Crane (for whose scribal
characteristics see the "Note on the Text" to *The Tempest*).
The transcript differed from the copy for *The Tempest*,
however, in one important respect: it employed (in common
with the copy for *The Merry Wives of Windsor* and that for
The Winter's Tale, two other probable Crane transcripts)
the so-called "massed entry" technique. Under this system,
the names of all the characters who are to take part in a
scene are grouped together, usually in order of appearance,
in a single inclusive entry direction at the opening of the
scene, and no points of entry are indicated in the text for
those characters in the group who actually enter later.

Exits within the scene are also generally ignored. Other
examples of the "massed entry" technique occur outside of
Shakespeare, but no entirely satisfactory explanation of its
employment has been advanced. The theory of "assembled
texts," principally developed by Dover Wilson, which holds
that it arose from the use of copy-text made up by assembling
players' parts, is now discredited. The prevailing current
view sees the practice as a misguided attempt by the scribe
(or, in some cases, the author) to imitate the formal aspects
of neo-classical scene division. By this convention, a new
scene was indicated upon the entrance of each major character or group of characters by means of a list which included, though without the direction "Enter," first the newly
entered character or characters (and, not infrequently,
those who were to enter later in the scene), then those
characters remaining on stage from the scene just ended;
and neither points of later entry within the scene nor exits
were marked. Since *The Two Gentlemen*, like *The Merry
Wives* and *The Winter's Tale*, is regularly divided in F1 into

acts and scenes on the usual Elizabethan principle (a new scene being indicated by a cleared stage), the "massed entry" technique produces only confusion.

There is nothing in the F1 text to suggest that the copy behind Crane's transcript was a prompt-book. Indeed, the kind of tangle represented by the Verona-Milan-Padua difficulties would probably have been cleared up in any copy associated with the stage.

For further information, see: J. D. Wilson, ed., New Cambridge *The Two Gentlemen of Verona* (Cambridge, 1921); W. W. Greg, *The Shakespeare First Folio* (Oxford, 1955); Clifford Leech, ed., New Arden *The Two Gentlemen of Verona* (London, 1969).

TEXTUAL NOTES

Dramatis personae: *as given in F1, following the play, with a few additions by Pope and later editors*
Proteus] *Steevens;* Protheus *F1 (throughout)*
Antonio] *Capell;* Anthonio *F1*
page] *Capell;* a clownish servant, *F1*
a clownish servant] *transferred, following Leech, from F1 description of Speed; the like F1*
Panthino] *Capell;* Panthion *F1*
Act-scene division: *from F1*

I.i

Location: *Wilson (after Theobald)*
o.s.d. **Enter . . . Proteus.]** *Rowe;* Valentine: Protheus, and Speed. *F1 (an example of the "massed entries" used throughout the F1 text; Speed does not actually enter until l. 69)*
2 **Home-keeping youth]** *F2;* Home-keeping-youth *F1*
13 **travel]** *F4;* trauaile *F1*
24 **over shoes]** *Rowe;* ouer-shooes *F1*
25 **over boots]** *Rowe;* ouer-bootes *F1*
57 **Milan]** *Rowe (subs.);* Millaine *F1 (generally throughout)*
65 **leave]** *Pope;* loue *F1*
65 **all,]** *Dyce;* all *F1*
69 s.d. **Enter Speed.]** *Rowe*
77 **a]** *F2*
93 **"baa."]** *Capell;* baâ. *F1 (F1 form suggests doubling of the "a" sound)*
109 **lover.]** *F2;* louer *F1*
110 s.d. **Speed . . . questioningly.]** *Sisson (subs.; after Theobald, Nicholson conj.)*
111 **Ay]** *Nicholson conj.;* I *F1*
112 **Nod-ay]** *Cambridge (subs.);* Nod-I *F1*
113–4 **You . . . "Ay."]** *as prose, Capell; as verse, F1*
123–4 **Marry . . . pains.]** *as prose, Capell; as verse, F1*
136–41 **Sir . . . steel.]** *as prose, Capell; as verse, F1*
142 **she? Nothing?]** *Cambridge;* she, nothing? *F1*
143–5 **No . . . me;]** *as prose, Capell; as verse, F1*
145 **testern'd]** *F2;* cestern'd *F1*
150 s.d. **Exit Speed.]** *Dyce*

I.ii

Location: *Capell*
5 **parle]** *Rowe;* par'le *F1*
56 **"ay"]** *Rowe (subs.);* I *F1*
66 s.d. **Enter Lucetta.]** *Rowe*
78 **set.]** *F2;* set *F1 (possibly the lack of pointing in F1 indicates an interrupted speech)*
80 **"Light o' love."]** *Theobald;* Light O, Loue. *F1*
85 s.d. **Takes the letter.]** *Kittredge (after Capell, Collier)*
93 **your]** *F2;* you *F1*
96 s.d. **Tears the letter.]** *Pope*
100 s.d. **Exit.]** *F2*
108 **bruising stones]** *F2;* bruzing-stones *F1*
126 s.d. **Enter Lucetta.]** *Pope*
137 **will't]** *Rowe;* wilt *F1*

I.iii

Location: *Theobald*
o.s.d. **Enter . . . Panthino.]** *Rowe (subs.);* Enter Antonio and Panthino. Protheus. *F1*
24 **whither]** *F2;* whether *F1*

43 s.d. **Enter Proteus.]** *F2*
50 **O]** *F2; Pro.* Oh *F1 (repeated s.p.)*
70 **readiness]** *F2;* readinesse, *F1*
77 s.d. **Exeunt . . . Panthino.]** *Rowe*
87 s.d. **Enter Panthino.]** *Rowe*
88 **father]** *F2;* Fathers *F1*
91 s.d. **Exeunt.]** Exeunt. Finis. *F1*

II.i

Location: *Pope, Theobald*
o.s.d. **Enter . . . Speed.]** *Rowe;* Enter Valentine, Speed, Siluia. *F1*
6 s.d. **Shouting.]** *Kittredge*
52–3 **well favor'd]** *F2;* well-fauourd *F1*
54–5 **I . . . infinite.]** *as prose, Capell; as verse, F1*
66–7 **I . . . beautiful.]** *as prose, Capell; as verse, F1*
79–80 **Belike . . . shoes.]** *as prose, Rowe; as verse, F1*
87–8 **Last . . . loves.]** *as prose, Pope; as verse, F1*
92 s.d. **Enter Silvia.]** *Rowe (after l. 93); placed as in Kittredge*
94, 98, 102 s.dd. **Aside.]** *Capell*
98 **ye good ev'n]** *Rowe (subs.);* ye-good-ev'n *F1*
109 **hardly off]** *F2;* hardly-off *F1*
113 **stead]** *Capell;* steed *F1*
119 s.d. **Aside.]** *Rowe*
139 **device]** *F4;* deuise *F1*
148 **woos]** *Rowe;* woes *F1 (generally)*
152–4 **What . . . jest?]** *as prose, Capell; as verse, F1*
156–7 **No . . . earnest?]** *as prose, Pope; as verse, F1*
165–8 **"For . . . lover."]** *quotes, Theobald*

II.ii

Location: *Pope, Theobald*
o.s.d. **Enter . . . Julia.]** *Rowe;* Enter Protheus, Iulia, Panthion. *F1*
5 s.d. **Giving a ring.]** *Rowe*
16 s.d. **Exit Julia.]** *Rowe*
18 s.d. **Enter Panthino.]** *Capell (after Rowe); note that the form is Panthion in F1 o.s.d.*

II.iii

Location: *Theobald*
o.s.d. **Enter . . . dog.]** *Pope (subs., after Rowe);* Enter Launce, Panthion. *F1*
27–8 **wood woman]** *Theobald;* would-woman *F1*
32 s.d. **Enter Panthino.]** *Capell (after Rowe); note that the form is Panthion in F1 o.s.d.*
33 **aboard]** *F4;* a Boord *F1*
37–8 **tied . . . unkindest tied]** *Theobald;* tide . . . vnkindest Tide *F1*
38 **tied.]** *Pope;* tide. *F1*
40 **tied]** *Pope;* tide *F1*
49 **tail!]** *Dyce;* Taile. *F1*
51 **tied]** *Singer;* tide *F1*

II.iv

Location: *Pope, Theobald*
o.s.d. **Enter . . . Speed.]** *Rowe;* Enter Valentine, Siluia, Thurio, Speed, Duke, Protheus. *F1*
7 s.d. **Exit.]** *Cambridge*
37–40 **Yourself . . . company.]** *as prose, Pope; as verse, F1*
43–8 **I . . . father.]** *as prose, Pope; as verse, F1*
48 s.d. **Enter Duke.]** *Rowe*

86 s.d. **Exit.]** *Rowe*
97 **yourself:]** *F4;* your selfe, *F1*
99 s.d. **Exit Thurio.]** *Collier*
99 s.d. **Enter Proteus.]** *Rowe*
108 **worthy]** *F2;* worthy a *F1*
115 s.d. **Enter Thurio.]** *Collier*
121 s.d. **Exeunt . . . Thurio.]** *Rowe*
166 **makes]** *F2;* make *F1*
191 s.d. **Exit Valentine.]** *Rowe;* Exit. *F1 (after l. 190)*
196 **Is . . . praise,]** *Malone (after F2* Is it mine then, *or Valentineans* praise?); It is mine, or Valentines praise? *F1*
205 **too too]** *Rowe;* too-too *F1*
210 **dazzled]** *Rowe;* dazel'd *F1;* dazel'd so *F2*
214 s.d. **Exit.]** *F2;* Exeunt. *F1*

II.v

Location: *Theobald*
o.s.d. **meeting]** *Capell*
2 **Milan]** *Pope;* Padua *F1*
8 **Come on]** *F4;* Come-on *F1*
42 **that]** *F2;* that that *F1*
53 **wilt,]** *Knight;* wilt *F1*

II.vi

Location: *Capell (subs.)*
1–2 **Julia—. . . Silvia—]** *Wilson;* Iulia; . . . Siluia; *F1*
35 **counsel]** *Theobald;* counsaile *F1*

II.vii

Location: *Pope, Theobald*
67 **withal]** *F2;* with all *F1*
70 **of infinite]** as infinite *F2*

III.i

Location: *Theobald*
o.s.d. **Enter . . . Proteus.]** *Rowe;* Enter Duke, Thurio, Protheus, Valentine, Launce, Speed. *F1*
2 s.d. **Exit Thurio.]** *Rowe*
50 s.d. **Exit.]** *Rowe*
50 s.d. **Enter Valentine.]** *Rowe;* Enter. *F2*
81 **Milano]** *Collier MS (after Pope);* Verona *F1*
83 **nought]** *F2;* naught *F1*
139 s.d. **Reads.]** *Rowe*
144 **rest them]** *F4;* rest-them *F1*
169 s.d. **Exit.]** *F2*
173 **self,]** *F2;* selfe. *F1*
187 s.d. **Enter . . . Launce.]** *F2*
189 **Soho, soho!]** *Theobald (subs.);* So-hough, Soa hough— *F1*
212 **Silvia.]** *F4 (subs.);* Siluia, *F1*
223 **banished]** *Rowe;* banish'd *F1*
246 **Here]** *F3;* Here, *F1*
262 s.d. **Exeunt . . . Proteus.]** *Theobald;* Exeunt. *F2*
273–4 s.d. **Pulling . . . paper.]** *Rowe*
278 **milk.]** *Rowe (subs.);* milke, *F1*
279 s.d. **Enter Speed.]** *F2*
282 **master's ship]** *Theobald;* Mastership *F1*
301 s.d. **Reads.]** *Capell*
318 **"bastard virtues"]** *Rowe;* Bastard-vertues *F1 (in italics)*
321 **follow]** *F1 (c);* followes *F1 (u) (the uncorrected form should perhaps be retained)*
323 **kiss'd]** *Rowe* (kist)
333–6 **O . . . virtue.]** *as prose, Pope; as verse, F1*
338–9 **Out . . . her.]** *as prose, Pope; as verse, F1*
353 **hair]** *F1 (c);* haires *F1 (u)*

356 **that last]** *F1 (c); that F1 (u)*
359 **be;]** *Theobald;* be *F1*
372 **then]** *F4;* then, *F1*
381 s.d. **Exit.]** *Capell*
384 s.d. **Exit.]** *Capell;* Exeunt. *F1*

III.ii

Location: *Capell (subs.)*
o.s.d. **Enter . . . Thurio.]** *Rowe;* Enter Duke, Thurio, Protheus. *F1*
10 s.d. **Enter Proteus.]** *Rowe*
14 **grievously.]** *Capell;* grieuously? *F1 (c);* heauily? *F1 (u)*
85 **sweet-complaining]** *hyphen, Capell*
93 **advice]** *F2;* aduise *F1*

IV.i

Location: *Neilson-Hill*
7 **friends—]** *Pope;* friends. *F1*
34 **travel]** *F3;* trauaile *F1*
35 **been]** *F2;* beene often *F1*
47 **An . . . near]** *Theobald;* And heire and Neece. *F1*
61 **this]** the *F2*

IV.ii

Location: *Theobald (subs.)*
o.s.d. **Enter Proteus.]** *Rowe;* Enter Protheus, Thurio, Iulia, Host, Musitian, Siluia. *F1*
15 s.d. **Enter . . . Musicians.]** *Rowe; note that F1 o.s.d. has* Musitian
25 s.d. **Enter . . . Sebastian.]** *ed. (after Rowe, Capell)*
35 s.d. **Music plays.]** *Capell*
38 **hear 'em]** *F3;* heare'm *F1*
61–2 **Not . . . heart-strings.]** *as prose, Pope; as verse, F1*
71 **thing?]** *Pope;* thing. *F1*
84 s.d. **Exeunt . . . Musicians.]** *Rowe*
84 s.d. **Enter . . . window.]** *Theobald (after Rowe)*
107, 118, 126 s.dd. **Aside.]** *Pope*
113 **his]** *F2;* her *F1*
133 s.d. **Exeunt . . . Silvia.]** *Rowe;* Exeunt. *F2*
137–8 **Marry . . . day.]** *as prose, Pope; as verse, F1*
140 s.d. **Exeunt.]** *F2*

IV.iii

Location: *ed. (after Capell)*
o.s.d. **Enter Eglamore.]** *Rowe;* Enter Eglamore, Siluia. *F1*
4 s.d. **Enter . . . window.]** *Theobald*
11–2 **gentleman— . . . not—]** *Pope (subs.);* Gentleman: / Thinke . . . flatter (for . . . not) *F1*
17 **abhors]** *Hanmer;* abhor'd *F1*
37–8 **grievances, Which]** *to ease the sense between ll. 37 and 38, Collier MS reads:* grievances, / And the most true affections that you bear: / Which
40 **Reaking]** *ed.;* Wreaking *F1*

IV.iv

Location: *ed. (after Wilson)*
o.s.d. **Enter . . . dog.]** *Pope (after Rowe);* Enter Launce, Protheus, Iulia, Siluia. *F1*
17 **gentleman-like dogs]** *Rowe;* gentleman-like-dogs *F1*
39 s.d. **Enter . . . Sebastian.]** *ed. (after Rowe)*
43 s.d. **To Launce.]** *Johnson*
47 **jewel]** *Pope;* Iewell *F1 (F4 italicizes; Wilson suggests that the F1 capital indicates that* Jewel *is the dog's name; evidently the compositor of F4 thought so)*
52–3 **No . . . again.]** *as prose, Pope; as verse, F1*
55–8 **Ay . . . greater.]** *as prose, Pope; as verse, F1*
61 s.d. **Exit Launce.]** *Rowe (after F2 Exit., both following l. 62); placed as in Capell*
70 **thou]** *F2;* thee *F1*
74 **to]** *F2;* not *F1*
89 s.d. **Exit.]** *F2*
107 s.d. **Enter Silvia attended.]** *Malone (after Rowe)*
149–50 **is: . . . well,]** *Rowe (subs.);* is, . . . well; *F1*
165 **agood]** *F2;* a good *F1*
179 s.d. **Exit . . . Attendants.]** *Dyce;* Exit. *F2 (after l. 178)*
205 s.d. **Exit.]** *F2;* Exeunt. *F1*

V.i

Location: *Pope, Capell*
o.s.d. **Enter Eglamour.]** *Rowe;* Enter Eglamoure, Siluia. *F1*

7 s.d. **Enter Silvia.]** *Rowe*

V.ii

Location: *Theobald (subs.)*
o.s.d. **Enter . . . Sebastian.]** *ed. (after Rowe);* Enter Thurio, Protheus, Iulia, Duke. *F1*
7 s.p., s.d. **Jul. Aside.]** *Boswell conj.;* Pro. *F1*
13 s.p., s.d. **Jul. Aside.]** *Rowe;* Thu. *F1*
18, 21, 24, 28 s.dd. **Aside.]** *Capell*
18 **your]** *F3;* you *F1*
30 s.d. **Enter Duke.]** *Rowe*
32 **saw]** say saw Sir *F2;* saw Sir *F4*
44 **stand]** *F2;* stand, *F1*
48 s.d. **Exit.]** *Rowe*
52 s.d. **Exit.]** *Capell*
54 s.d. **Exit.]** *Capell*
56 s.d. **Exit.]** *Capell;* Exeunt. *F1*

V.iii

Location: *Pope*
o.s.d. **Enter]** *Rowe*

V.iv

Location: *Pope*
o.s.d. **Enter Valentine.]** *Rowe;* Enter Valentine, Protheus, Siluia, Iulia, Duke, Thurio, Out-lawes. *F1*
12 s.d. **Shouts within.]** *Collier (subs.)*
18 s.d. **Steps aside.]** *Johnson*
18 s.d. **Enter . . . Sebastian.]** *ed. (after Rowe)*
26 s.d. **Aside.]** *Theobald*
32 s.d. **Aside.]** *Rowe*
49 **love]** deceive *F2*
49 **me.]** *F4 (subs.);* me, *F1*
57 **woo]** move *F2*
57 **arm's]** *Capell;* armes *F1*
60 s.d. **Coming forward.]** *Collier MS*
63 **Treacherous]** Thou treacherous *F2*
67 **trusted]** trusted now *F2*
84 s.d. **Swoons.]** *Pope*
91 s.d. **Shows a ring.]** *ed. (after Johnson)*
95 s.d. **Shows another ring.]** *Johnson*
113 **falls off]** *F2;* falls-off *F1*
120 s.d. **Enter . . . Outlaws.]** *Rowe*
121 s.p. **Outlaws]** *Dyce;* Out-l. *F1*
129 **Milan]** *Theobald;* Verona *F1*
144 **unrivall'd]** arrival'd *F2*
173 s.d. **Exeunt.]** Exeunt. *[list of actors]* FINIS. *F1*

Love's Labor's Lost

OVE'S LABOR'S LOST is perhaps the most relentlessly Elizabethan of all Shakespeare's plays. Filled with word games, elaborate conceits, parodies of spoken and written styles and obscure topical allusions, it continually requires—and baffles—scholarly explanation. Nothing can ever make most of the puns and witticisms of *Love's Labor's Lost* seem contemporary again. They are rooted too firmly in a specific society and moment of historical time. Hazlitt and Dr. Johnson thought the comedy wholly insignificant, a piece of linguistic self-indulgence which Shakespeare happily outgrew, and this view was shared until comparatively recently by the majority of critics. As with *Troilus and Cressida*, the rediscovery of the play seems to have originated in the postwar theatre. Despite the inaccessibility of much of the dialogue, *Love's Labor's Lost* has repeatedly demonstrated that it can communicate its quality and concerns to a modern audience which, although it may not be able to explain just why "a costard broken in a shin" (III.i.70) should be funny, responds to the freshness and brilliance of the comedy just the same. A major critical revaluation has accompanied this theatrical success. In particular, that old concern with the play as a supposed mine of concealed information about the activities and character of various prominent Elizabethans has fallen out of favor. There is, after all, not a shred of proof that Shakespeare was really satirizing Gabriel Harvey in the person of the pedant Holofernes, or that the famous crux at IV.iii.251 can be resolved through reference to a free-thinking "school of night" associated with Raleigh. Contemporary references of this kind, if and where they exist, are ultimately less important than the nature of *Love's Labor's Lost* as a complex and quite autonomous work of art.

Although the textual history of *Love's Labor's Lost* is unclear, scholars no longer regard it as a very early play. Theories that it was originally commissioned for performance outdoors in the grounds of some great country house are in many ways attractive, but remain hypothetical. Certainly it was played at court before the Queen during the Christmas revels of 1597 or 1598 and at Southampton's house to celebrate his release from prison in 1604. The Second Quarto also mentions public performances at the Globe and at Blackfriars. That the comedy was revised by Shakespeare at some point seems plain, but no agreement has ever been reached as to the date and extent of these alterations. The First Quarto of 1598 describes itself as "Newly corrected and augmented" and there are some obvious tracks in the snow registered at IV.iii.292–314 and again at V.ii.817–22 (see the Textual Notes). On the whole, a date around 1595 seems right for the main body of the play, although Shakespeare may have been tinkering with the text as late as 1597. A connection between Rosaline and the Dark Lady of the sonnets has long been recognized but, considering the notorious impossibility of arriving at a date for the sonnets, is scarcely helpful in placing the composition of *Love's Labor's Lost*. More promising are the stylistic affinities with *Romeo and Juliet*, *Richard II*, and *A Midsummer Night's Dream*. Different though they are in form and subject matter, the four plays nonetheless seem to constitute a natural group. All of them are lyrical and ornate, various and highly patterned in their verse forms. Quintessentially Elizabethan, they share a kind of linguistic exuberance and also a delight in exploring and extending their particular dramatic genres.

Between *A Midsummer Night's Dream* and *Love's Labor's Lost*, as might be expected, the connection is especially close. Both comedies belong to that small group of Shakespeare's plays for which there appears to be no narrative or dramatic source. Shakespeare could have read in the *Académie Française* of P. de la Primaudaye, translated into English in 1586, about the ideal of a league of study. Berowne, Dumaine, Longaville, Boyet, and Marcade are Anglicized versions of names belonging to actual French noblemen of the late sixteenth century. In 1578, Marguerite de Valois made a state visit with a retinue of ladies to her estranged husband Henry of Navarre, in the course of which they discussed the disposition of Aquitaine. One of Marguerite's ladies-in-waiting had a daughter, Hélène de Tournon, who seems, like Katherine's sister, to have died of love. Behind Holofernes lies a character type familiar in the *commedia dell'arte*, while Don Armado can trace his lineage back to the braggart warrior of Greek New Comedy. These few hints and suggestions do not provide much in the way of a narrative framework, and indeed the plot of *Love's Labor's Lost* is even more slender than that of *A Midsummer Night's Dream*. Action, in any sense that Aristotle would have understood, is confined to two arrivals: that of the Princess and her ladies in Act II, which destroys the Academe, and that of the messenger at the end, which destroys something even larger. Between these two very different invasions of the royal park the comedy unfolds entirely through the juxtaposition of attitudes and styles of wit, and through little, contrived shows: the masque of the Muscovites, or that Pageant of the Nine Worthies which stands in the equivalent position to the Pyramus and Thisby interlude in *A Midsummer Night's Dream*. In this play too a certain self-consciousness about comedy as a form becomes particularly striking in the fifth act.

As the title informs us from the start, love's labor will be lost, not won. In defiance of an immemorial comic convention, this play ends in partings, with the severance of people in love and not with marriage. Moreover, it draws attention to its own unorthodoxy.

Our wooing doth not end like an old play:
Jack hath not Gill. These ladies' courtesy
Might well have made our sport a comedy.

(V.ii.874–76)

Berowne's rueful comment stresses the violation of an accepted dramatic formula: "Jack shall have Jill; / Nought shall go ill; / The man shall have his mare again, and all shall be well" (*A Midsummer Night's Dream*, III.ii.461–63). Although there is hope at the end that these marriages may merely be postponed, a year, as Berowne recognizes, is "too long for a play" (V.ii.878). The gradual revelation of why this should be so, why the women must reject

their suitors and demand a resolution outside the limits of comedy, is the main business of *Love's Labor's Lost*: in fact, its plot.

The scheme of the Academe, through which Navarre and his friends hope to defeat Time and live forever in the memories of men, is both misguided and untenable. It is not, however, either ludicrous or contemptible. Navarre's image of "cormorant devouring Time" (I.i.4) is near-allied to that "devouring Time" of the sonnets which blunts the lion's paws and burns the long-lived phoenix in her blood. In the sonnets Shakespeare proposes two weapons against Time: children and, more persuasively, poetry. Navarre's Academe, significantly, has nothing to do either with the begetting of children or with the perpetuation of an actual love experience in verse. Navarre's attempt to prolong life by turning his back on it, forswearing women, liberty, festivity, and rest is not only paradoxical: it represents a sterile "treason 'gainst the kingly state of youth" (IV.iii.289). Three years of youth, as Berowne knows from the start, are too precious to sacrifice in the interests of a dubious memory on earth which will not even fall due until the king and his three friends are dead. Meanwhile, there is the sobering example of that dedicated scholar Holofernes: an embodiment of the pointless learning of those pedants who may be able to name all the stars in the firmament yet "have no more profit of their shining nights / Than those that walk and wot not what they are" (I.i.90–91).

The Academe, of course, is never in any real danger of succeeding. Almost before the ink is dry on the King's new edict forbidding any converse with women, the law is violated by Costard the clown. His trespass is immediately compounded by that of Don Armado, the haughty Spaniard who informs on Costard and then proceeds to court Jaquenetta himself. In the effort to escape punishment for his offense, Costard goes through a remarkable series of linguistic gyrations. If the proclamation specified a year's imprisonment for being taken with a wench, Costard will claim she was not a wench at all, but a damsel. Told that *damsel* too is covered by the law, he tries *virgin* and *maid* in rapid succession only to discover in the end that facts are facts and cannot be altered by verbal description. Navarre consigns him to prison and a diet of bran and water. Costard's defeat here constitutes a warning to the King and his courtiers, but they are not yet ready to heed it. Only with the entrance of the Princess of France and her ladies in Act II does the dangerous falsity of the language customarily employed by Navarre and his friends come under direct attack.

The Princess and her retinue come from a world outside the confines of Navarre that is colder and more realistic than the playground of the park. They too are witty, and they like to play with words. Unlike the men, however, they play their verbal games without ever losing sight of facts and situations. When Navarre bids the Princess "welcome to the court of Navarre," she reminds him sharply that "'welcome' I have not yet. The roof of this court is too high to be yours, and welcome to the wide fields too base to be mine" (II.i.91–94). Although she is cheerfully willing to accept a lodging in the open air because of the King's vow, she refuses to allow him to confuse her tent with the court. Throughout the comedy the women are ruthless in their dismemberment of the airy rhetoric, the unexamined conceits and images offered by the men. The King, rashly declaring that he and the other "Muscovites" have "measur'd many miles" (V.ii.184) to have the pleasure of dancing with the Princess and her ladies, is disconcerted to be asked the precise number of inches in these miles he claims to have "measured." Berowne requests "one sweet word" with the Princess and is given "honey," "milk," and "sugar" and told to consider himself overpaid. He speaks metaphorically of his heart and its sufferings, according to the immemorial language of love, and finds that Rosaline insists upon answering him in the manner of someone about to administer the Elizabethan equivalent of a cardiogram.

This feminine literal-mindedness may be exasperating, but it is not merely perverse. The Princess and her ladies do not trust the oaths and protestations of their suitors, do not credit the sincerity of their love. In a sense, they are right to be sceptical. High-spirited and inventive though it is, the wit of Berowne, Navarre, Dumaine, and Longaville is fatally self-indulgent. It exists at too great a remove from reality, and it can be not only imperceptive but cruel. The masque of the Muscovites, the first of the two plays within the play, demonstrates that although Navarre and his friends may be in love, they are not really in love with Rosaline, Katherine, Maria, and the Princess of France as individuals. These suitors judge by courtly outsides alone, in marked contrast to the women, who seize upon manners and traits of character in talking about the men they love and distrust in equal measure. When the women mask themselves and exchange favors, their lovers are completely and ignominiously taken in. Berowne woos the Princess instead of Rosaline; Dumaine mistakes Maria for Katherine; Longaville falls into the opposite error, and the King offers the realm of Navarre to Berowne's proper lady. By the end of the masque it has become apparent that the Academe, far from being the chief obstacle to love, was only a temporary and negligible block. Far more serious and disturbing are the habitual attitudes of the men and the verbal style which expresses and defines those attitudes.

With the failure of the masque of the Muscovites, a state of impasse seems to have been reached in the comedy. It is hard to see what the King and his friends can say to convince the women of their sincerity. Certainly their attempts at eloquence only work against them, and they have already proved the frailty of vows: "If love make me forsworn, how shall I swear to love?" (IV.ii.105). At this point of stalemate, Costard enters to announce that the Pageant of the Nine Worthies is at hand. On the politic ground that it will be as well to have one show worse than that of the King and his companions, Navarre agrees to see it. The decision is crucial.

Although the actors who participate in the pageant are an unpromising lot ("The pedant, the braggart, the hedge-priest, the fool, and the boy"), their intentions are of the very best, and they are also more sensitive and vulnerable to mockery than Bottom and the rude mechanicals of *A Midsummer Night's Dream*. In this audience, however, only the women are civil, refusing to take any part in the mounting storm of hilarity by which the actors are assailed. Indeed the Princess does all she can to counteract it, encouraging the performers and thanking them courteously for their pains. Her attitude is poles apart from that of the King and his courtiers, who begin by deriding the entertainment itself and end, inexcusably, by savaging individual actors not for their performances but for being the real-life people they are. Nathaniel the curate retires in dismay while Holofernes, in the role of Judas Maccabaeus, stumbles away through the gathering darkness with the reproach, "This is not generous, not gentle, not humble" (V.ii.629). Don Armado is treated worst of all but, significantly, he is concerned less for his own humiliation than for that of Hector, the hero he represents: "The sweet war-man is dead and rotten, sweet chucks, beat not the bones of the buried. When he breathed, he was a man" (V.ii.660–62). Navarre and his friends are not only forsworn; they are betraying precisely that ideal of immortality through fame which led them to found the Academe in the first place. It is Armado, eccentric though he is, who alone defends the dignity and worth of the dead, an issue about which the King once cared passionately, but which he appears to have forgotten now.

The Pageant of the Nine Worthies, naturally evocative of death and time, seems to concentrate and draw to itself all those images of mortality which have begun to make themselves felt in the last movement of the play. Although *Love's Labor's Lost* opens under the shadow of death, the great motivation for the Academe, it subsequently banishes not merely the threat but the very idea. Even the stag killed by the Princess becomes, in the alliterative verses of Holofernes, an unreal animal and its fate just about as credible as the executions ordered by the Queen at the garden party in *Alice in Wonderland*. Not until Act V do intimations of mortality begin to rise, slowly but disturbingly, through the fabric of the play, in the form of Katherine's sudden remembrance of her dead sister, Berowne's talk of plague symptoms, or his strident comparison of Holofernes to "a death's face in a ring" (V.ii.612). By way of this gradual massing of images, the triumph of Death in the person of Marcade is prepared for artistically without losing, in the theatre, any of its emotional shock:

I am sorry, madam, for the news I bring
Is heavy in my tongue. The King your father—
(V.ii.718–19)

The Princess, however, has intuitions independent of words: "Dead, for my life!" The messenger does not need to complete the sentence he began. Within a matter of seconds, the comedy is checked in full career.

Vows began the play of *Love's Labor's Lost* and vows of another kind end it. The artificial enclosure of the royal park violated now by death and time, the King and his friends accept the need to seek out a harsher and less protected world. They also accept penance for their faults. Navarre is dismissed by the Princess to "some forlorn and naked hermitage" where he is to try for twelve months "if frosts and fasts, hard lodging and thin weeds / Nip not the gaudy blossoms of your love." At the end of this period he may address her again on the basis of "these deserts": tangible proofs of constancy and endurance, not mere words and promises. Dumaine and Longaville accept similar conditions from Katherine and Maria. Berowne, the most brilliant and also the most deeply tainted of the men, receives a penance even more severe. He is sent by Rosaline to test his wit against the reality of sickness and disease, to "jest a twelve-month in a hospital." Intellectually, Berowne is entirely aware that "to move wild laughter in the throat of death" is impossible, something that cannot be. Emotionally, this is an experience which the man who led the assault upon the Nine Worthies needs to undergo. As Rosaline points out:

> A jest's prosperity lies in the ear
> Of him that hears it, never in the tongue
> Of him that makes it; then, if sickly ears,
> Deaf'd with the clamors of their own dear groans,
> Will hear your idle scorns, continue then,
> And I will have you and that fault withal;
> But if they will not, throw away that spirit,
> And I shall find you empty of that fault.
>
> (V.ii.861–68)

Language cannot exist in a vacuum. Even on what may seem to be its most trivial and humorous levels, it is an instrument of communication between people which demands that the speaker should consider the nature and feelings of the hearer. In love, above all, this is true—but it is also true in more ordinary relationships. Gently but firmly, the men are sent away to learn something that the women have known all along: how to accommodate speech to facts and to emotional realities, as opposed to using it as a means of evasion, idle amusement, or unthinking cruelty.

It may seem surprising that a play as verbally brilliant as *Love's Labor's Lost* should end by acknowledging the defeat of the word, but then the entire comedy is built upon paradox. The illogical scheme of the Academe at the beginning, the attempt to perpetuate life by denying it, is nicely balanced by the fact that it is the messenger at the end who breaks the impasse between the ladies of France and the suitors they cannot be persuaded to take seriously. Marcade, in his mourning clothes, makes it possible for the men's proposals of marriage to be entertained and for the redemptive trials and penances to be imposed. Only by accepting the reality of death as it exists in that world of plague and star-crossed love beyond the confines of the park can the men be freed from their self-imposed bondage. It is only by being, for a little while, lost that love's labor can eventually, and fully, be won.

As though conscious of the fact that in this resolution the arts of language have been subjected to an unfriendly scrutiny, Shakespeare allows them a restitution in the final song. Gathered together for the last time, before they disperse in their separate directions, all the characters of the comedy stand silently, for once, to hear the dialogue which the two learned men have composed in praise of the owl and the cuckoo. In doing so they seem to adumbrate that new social order, fragile and transitory but harmonious and at peace with itself, which the year of trial and penances may bring.

> When daisies pied, and violets blue,
>   And lady-smocks all silver-white,
> And cuckoo-buds of yellow hue
>   Do paint the meadows with delight,
> The cuckoo then on every tree
> Mocks married men, for thus sings he,
>   "Cuckoo;
> Cuckoo, cuckoo"—O word of fear,
> Unpleasing to a married ear!

In a sense, this song recapitulates the entire development of the comedy. It begins with the enamelled, deliberately fanciful meadows of spring, moves on to a summer of frank sensuality, "When turtles tread, and rooks and daws, / And maidens bleach their summer smocks." It ends, like the action itself, in winter-time: the season of chill and deprivation.

> When icicles hang by the wall,
>   And Dick the shepherd blows his nail,
> And Tom bears logs into the hall,
>   And milk comes frozen home in pail;
> When blood is nipp'd, and ways be foul,
> Then nightly sings the staring owl,
>   "Tu-whit, to-who"—
> A merry note,
> While greasy Joan doth keel the pot.

Yet despite this movement from spring towards winter, each season in the lyric contains a sense of its opposite. In the halcyon months of spring and summer the cuckoo's voice keeps human beings in touch with the realities of their condition in a world of time and mutability: with the threat of love grown old and bitter, with the metamorphosis of faith into infidelity and distrust. Conversely, winter is enlivened by the merry note of the owl, a voice of unexpected and compensating cheer in a dark season. The song presents a wholeness of outlook in which fact and fancy, youth and age, life and death are held in equilibrium. The unifying effect of the music must not be underestimated, but still this harmony is essentially verbal. The problem of how to create a truly meaningful language of love may still be unresolved for the people of the play: the year of penance remains to be lived through and its outcome cannot be predicted with confidence. Nevertheless, this final lyric stands as an encouraging indication of what language can do when handled rightly, of how finely—when it is honest and also disciplined by art—it can express the truth of the human condition. The balance held in the song is one which the women of France have possessed throughout, which Navarre and his friends have yet to acquire, and it holds the door open for a vindication of the arts of language after all.

Anne Barton

1 *Cardamine.*
Cockowe flowers.

5 *Cardamine lactea.*
Milke white Ladie smocks.

✱ *The description.*

1 THe first of the Cuckowe flowers, hath leaues at his springing vp somewhat rounde, and those that spring afterward grow iagged like the leaues of Greeke Valerian: among which riseth vp a stalke a foote long, set with the like leaues, but smaller and more iagged, resembling the leaues of Rocket. The flowers grow at the top in small bundels, white of colour, hollowe in the middle, resembling the white sweete Iohn: after which do come small chaffie huskes, or seede vessels, wherein the seede is conteined. The roote is small and threddie.

5 Milke white Ladie smockes hath stalkes rising immediately from the roote, deuiding themselues into sundrie small twiggie and hard braunches, set with leaues like those of Serpillum. The flowers growe at the top, made of fower leaues of a yellowish colour. The roote is tough and wooddy, with some fibres annexed thereto.

✱ *The place.*

These kinds of Cuckowe flowers, grow not so much in waters as they do in moist medowes, and in such places as be verie often ouerflowen not onely with raine water, but also with riuers and ponds.

✱ *The time.*

These flower for the most part in Aprill and Maie, when the Cuckowe doth begin to sing her pleasant notes without stammering.

In composing the song that ends *Love's Labor's Lost*, Shakespeare is thought to have had in mind the passages above from John Gerard's *Herbal*, published late in 1597. Despite Gerard, he seems to treat lady-smocks and cuckoo-flowers as distinct kinds, though in assigning to the cuckoo-flower "buds of yellow hue" he borrows a detail from Gerard's description of the "Milke white Ladie smockes." (*By permission of the Harvard College Library*)

Love's Labor's Lost

[Dramatis Personae

Ferdinand, *King of Navarre*
Berowne ⎫
Longaville ⎬ *lords attending on the King*
Dumaine ⎭
Boyet ⎫
Marcade ⎬ *lords attending on the Princess of France*

Don Adriano de Armado, *a fantastical Spaniard*
Sir Nathaniel, *a curate*
Holofernes, *a schoolmaster*
Dull, *a constable*

Costard, *a clown*
Moth, *page to Armado*
Forester

The Princess of France
Rosaline ⎫
Maria ⎬ *ladies attending on the Princess*
Katherine ⎭
Jaquenetta, *a country wench*

Lords, Attendants, *etc.*

Scene: *Navarre*]

[ACT I, Scene I]

Enter Ferdinand, *King of Navarre*, Berowne, Longaville, *and* Dumaine.

King. Let fame, that all hunt after in their lives,
Live regist'red upon our brazen tombs,
And then grace us in the disgrace of death;
When spite of cormorant devouring Time,
Th' endeavor of this present breath may buy   5
That honor which shall bate his scythe's keen edge,
And make us heirs of all eternity.
Therefore, brave conquerors—for so you are,
That war against your own affections
And the huge army of the world's desires—   10
Our late edict shall strongly stand in force:
Navarre shall be the wonder of the world;
Our court shall be a little academe,
Still and contemplative in living art.
You three, Berowne, Dumaine, and Longaville,   15
Have sworn for three years' term to live with me,
My fellow scholars, and to keep those statutes
That are recorded in this schedule here.
Your oaths are pass'd, and now subscribe your names,
That his own hand may strike his honor down   20
That violates the smallest branch herein.
If you are arm'd to do, as sworn to do,
Subscribe to your deep oaths, and keep it too.
Long. I am resolved, 'tis but a three years' fast:
The mind shall banquet, though the body pine;   25
Fat paunches have lean pates; and dainty bits
Make rich the ribs, but bankrout quite the wits.
Dum. My loving lord, Dumaine is mortified:
The grosser manner of these world's delights
He throws upon the gross world's baser slaves;   30
To love, to wealth, to pomp, I pine and die,
With all these living in philosophy.
Ber. I can but say their protestation over:
So much, dear liege, I have already sworn,
That is, to live and study here three years.   35
But there are other strict observances:
As not to see a woman in that term,
Which I hope well is not enrolled there;
And one day in a week to touch no food,
And but one meal on every day beside,   40
The which I hope is not enrolled there;
And then to sleep but three hours in the night,
And not be seen to wink of all the day—

*Words and passages enclosed in square brackets in the text above are
either emendations of the copy-text or additions to it. The Textual Notes
immediately following the play cite the earliest authority for every such
change or insertion and supply the reading of the copy-text wherever it is
emended in this edition.*

I.i. Location: Navarre. The King's park. (The action of the play
throughout takes place in the park.)
2. **brazen:** brass, i.e. enduring.
3. **grace:** honor.   **disgrace:** disfigurement, decay.
4. **spite of:** in spite of.   **cormorant:** ravenous.
5. **breath:** breathing-space, i.e. brief earthly life.   6. **bate:** dull.
9. **affections:** passions.   13. **academe:** academy.
14. **living art:** the art of living (i.e. the Stoic *ars vivendi*), or vital
learning (David).

18. **schedule:** document.   19. **pass'd:** pledged.
22. **arm'd:** prepared (for the combat; cf. the martial imagery of
lines 8–10).   27. **bankrout:** bankrupt (a variant form).
28. **mortified:** dead to worldly pleasures.
32. **With...living:** i.e. finding a substitute for love, wealth, and
pomp (?) or living with these companions (?).   34. **liege:** sovereign.
43. **wink of:** close the eyes during.

Love's
Labor's Lost
I.i

When I was wont to think no harm all night,
And make a dark night too of half the day— 45
Which I hope well is not enrolled there.
O, these are barren tasks, too hard to keep,
Not to see ladies, study, fast, not sleep.

King. Your oath is pass'd to pass away from
    these.

Ber. Let me say no, my liege, and if you please:
I only swore to study with your Grace, 51
And stay here in your court for three years' space.

Long. You swore to that, Berowne, and to the rest.

Ber. By yea and nay, sir, then I swore in jest.
What is the end of study, let me know. 55

King. Why, that to know which else we should
    not know.

Ber. Things hid and barr'd (you mean) from com-
    mon sense.

King. Ay, that is study's godlike recompense.

Ber. Com' on then, I will swear to study so,
To know the thing I am forbid to know: 60
As thus—to study where I well may dine,
When I to [feast] expressly am forbid;
Or study where to meet some mistress fine,
When mistresses from common sense are hid;
Or having sworn too hard-a-keeping oath, 65
Study to break it and not break my troth.
If study's gain be thus, and this be so,
Study knows that which yet it doth not know.
Swear me to this, and I will ne'er say no.

King. These be the stops that hinder study quite,
And train our intellects to vain delight. 71

Ber. Why? all delights are vain, but that most vain
Which, with pain purchas'd, doth inherit pain:
As, painfully to pore upon a book
To seek the light of truth, while truth the while 75
Doth falsely blind the eyesight of his look.
Light, seeking light, doth light of light beguile;
So ere you find where light in darkness lies,
Your light grows dark by losing of your eyes.
Study me how to please the eye indeed 80
By fixing it upon a fairer eye,
Who dazzling so, that eye shall be his heed,
And give him light that it was blinded by.
Study is like the heaven's glorious sun,
That will not be deep search'd with saucy looks; 85
Small have continual plodders ever won,
Save base authority from others' books.

These earthly godfathers of heaven's lights,
That give a name to every fixed star,
Have no more profit of their shining nights 90
Than those that walk and wot not what they are.
Too much to know is to know nought but fame;
And every godfather can give a name.

King. How well he's read, to reason against read-
    ing!

Dum. Proceeded well, to stop all good proceed-
    ing! 95

Long. He weeds the corn and still lets grow the
    weeding.

Ber. The spring is near when green geese are
    a-breeding.

Dum. How follows that?

Ber.   Fit in his place and time.

Dum. In reason nothing.

Ber.   Something then in rhyme.

King. Berowne is like an envious sneaping frost
That bites the first-born infants of the spring. 101

Ber. Well, say I am, why should proud summer
    boast
Before the birds have any cause to sing?
Why should I joy in any abortive birth?
At Christmas I no more desire a rose 105
Than wish a snow in May's new-fangled shows;
But like of each thing that in season grows.
So you, to study now it is too late,
Climb o'er the house to unlock the little gate.

King. Well, sit you out; go home, Berowne; adieu.

Ber. No, my good lord, I have sworn to stay with
    you; 111
And though I have for barbarism spoke more
Than for that angel knowledge you can say,
Yet, confident, I'll keep what I have sworn,
And bide the penance of each three years' day. 115
Give me the paper, let me read the same,
And to the strictest decrees I'll write my name.

King. How well this yielding rescues thee from
    shame!

Ber. [*Reads.*] "*Item*, That no woman shall come
within a mile of my court"—Hath this been proclaim'd? 121

Long. Four days ago.

Ber. Let's see the penalty. [*Reads.*] "—on pain of
losing her tongue." Who devis'd this penalty?

Long. Marry, that did I. 125

---

44. **think no harm:** i.e. sleep soundly.   47. **barren:** dull, fruitless.
50. **and if:** if.
54. **By . . . nay:** (1) most earnestly (a common meaning, derived from
Matthew 5:33–37); (2) equivocally, ambiguously.
57. **common sense:** ordinary perception.
59. **Com' on.** This, the quarto spelling, stresses the pun on *common
sense* (line 57).
70. **stops:** obstacles.   71. **train:** allure, entice.
73. **pain:** (1) labor; (2) suffering.   **purchas'd:** obtained.   **inherit:**
possess.   76. **falsely:** treacherously.   **his look:** its power to see.
77. **Light . . . beguile:** the eye, seeking enlightenment, deprives itself
of the power to see, i.e. excessive study frustrates the search for truth
by making the student blind.
80. **Study me:** i.e. study rather (as far as I am concerned).
81. **a fairer eye:** i.e. a sweetheart.
82. **Who dazzling so:** i.e. the man (who has fixed his eye "upon a
fairer eye") being thus dazzled.   **heed:** guard, protection.
83. **it:** i.e. his eye.   86. **Small:** little.
87. **base:** commonplace (because secondhand).

88. **earthly godfathers:** i.e. astronomers, who give names to stars as
godparents give names to children at baptism.   91. **wot:** know.
92. **fame:** hearsay, secondhand information.
95. **Proceeded:** advanced in a course of study (an academic term).
96. **He . . . weeding:** he pulls up the young wheat and leaves the weeds.
97. **green geese:** young geese, ready for sale about Whitsuntide; here,
simpletons, young fools.
99. **rhyme.** Berowne caps Dumaine's statement with a quibbling reference to the proverbial "neither rhyme nor reason."
100. **envious:** malicious.   **sneaping:** nipping.
101. **infants:** buds.   102. **proud:** splendid.
107. **like of:** am pleased with.
109. **Climb . . . gate:** i.e. act without any sense of fitness, behave
incongruously.
110. **sit you out:** don't take part (a term from cardplaying).
112. **barbarism:** ignorance, lack of culture.
115. **bide . . . day:** endure the hardship of each day of the three years.
119. **Item:** word preceding each part of a list or enumeration.
125. **Marry:** indeed (a weakened oath, "by the Virgin Mary").

Ber. Sweet lord, and why?

Long. To fright them hence with that dread penalty.

[*Ber.*] A dangerous law against gentility. [*Reads.*] "*Item*, If any man be seen to talk with a woman 129 within the term of three years, he shall endure such public shame as the rest of the court can possible devise."
This article, my liege, yourself must break,
For well you know here comes in embassy   134
The French king's daughter with yourself to speak—
A maid of grace and complete majesty—
About surrender up of Aquitaine
To her decrepit, sick, and bedred father;
Therefore this article is made in vain,
Or vainly comes th' admired Princess hither.   140

King. What say you, lords? Why, this was quite forgot.

Ber. So study evermore is overshot:
While it doth study to have what it would,
It doth forget to do the thing it should;
And when it hath the thing it hunteth most,   145
'Tis won as towns with fire—so won, so lost.

King. We must of force dispense with this decree,
She must lie here on mere necessity.

Ber. Necessity will make us all forsworn   149
Three thousand times within this three years' space;
For every man with his affects is born,
Not by might mast'red, but by special grace.
If I break faith, this word shall speak for me:
I am forsworn "on mere necessity."   154
So to the laws at large I write my name, [*Subscribes.*]
And he that breaks them in the least degree
Stands in attainder of eternal shame.
Suggestions are to other as to me;
But I believe, although I seem so loath,
I am the last that will last keep his oath.   160
But is there no quick recreation granted?

King. Ay, that there is. Our court you know is haunted
With a refined traveller of Spain,
A man in all the world's new fashion planted,
That hath a mint of phrases in his brain;   165
One who the music of his own vain tongue
Doth ravish like enchanting harmony;
A man of complements, whom right and wrong
Have chose as umpeer of their mutiny.
This child of fancy, that Armado hight,   170
For interim to our studies shall relate,

In high-borne words, the worth of many a knight
From tawny Spain, lost in the world's debate.
How you delight, my lords, I know not, I,
But I protest I love to hear him lie,   175
And I will use him for my minstrelsy.

Ber. Armado is a most illustrious wight,
A man of fire-new words, fashion's own knight.

Long. Costard the swain and he shall be our sport,
And so to study three years is but short.   180

Enter a Constable [DULL] *with a letter, with* COSTARD.

Dull. Which is the Duke's own person?

Ber. This, fellow. What wouldst?

Dull. I myself reprehend his own person, for I am his Grace's farborough; but I would see his own person in flesh and blood.

Ber. This is he.

Dull. Signior Arme—Arme—commends you.   187
There's villainy abroad; this letter will tell you more.

Cost. Sir, the contempts thereof are as touching me.

King. A letter from the magnificent Armado.   191

Ber. How low soever the matter, I hope in God for high words.

Long. A high hope for a low heaven. God grant us patience!   195

Ber. To hear, or forbear hearing?

Long. To hear meekly, sir, and to laugh moderately; or to forbear both.

Ber. Well, sir, be it as the style shall give us cause to climb in the merriness.   200

Cost. The matter is to me, sir, as concerning Jaquenetta: the manner of it is, I was taken with the manner.

Ber. In what manner?   204

Cost. In manner and form following, sir, all those three: I was seen with her in the manor-house, sitting with her upon the form, and taken following her into the park, which, put together, is in manner and form following. Now, sir, for the manner—it is the manner of a man to speak to a woman; for the form—in some form.   211

Ber. For the following, sir?

Cost. As it shall follow in my correction, and God defend the right!

King. Will you hear this letter with attention?

Ber. As we would hear an oracle.   216

Cost. Such is the simplicity of man to hearken after the flesh.

---

128. **gentility:** courtesy.   131. **possible:** possibly.
134. **in embassy:** as an ambassador.   136. **complete:** perfect.
138. **bedred:** bedridden.   142. **overshot:** wide of the mark, in error.
146. **with fire:** i.e. by destroying them with fire.
147. **of force:** necessarily.
148. **lie:** lodge, stay.   **mere:** absolute, utter.
151. **affects:** affections, passions.   152. **special grace:** divine aid.
153. **word:** motto, watchword.
155. **at large:** as a whole, in general.
157. **in attainder of:** condemned and disgraced to.
158. **Suggestions:** temptations.   161. **quick:** lively.
162–63. **haunted With:** frequented by.   166. **who:** whom.
168. **complements:** accomplishments.
169. **umpeer:** umpire.   **mutiny:** discord.
170. **child of fancy:** fantastic creature.   **hight:** is called.
171. **interim:** intermission, refreshing interval.

172. **high-borne:** lofty.
173. **tawny:** i.e. sunburned.   **debate:** warfare.
174. **How you delight:** what delights you.   177. **wight:** person.
178. **fire-new:** newly coined.
179. **Costard.** His name means a kind of large apple; also, humorously, the head.   **swain:** rustic youth.   181. **Duke's:** i.e. King's.
183. **reprehend:** blunder for *represent*.
184. **farborough:** apparently Dull's version of *thirdborough*, a petty constable.   190. **contempts:** blunder for *contents*.
191. **magnificent Armado:** grandiose or pompous Armado (the Spanish Armada was so called).
199. **style.** With play (in *climb*, line 200) on *stile*. Cf. IV.i.96–97.
202–3. **with the manner:** in the very act.   207. **form:** bench.
213. **correction:** punishment.

Love's
Labor's Lost
I.i

King. [*Reads.*] "Great deputy, the welkin's vicegerent, and sole dominator of Navarre, my soul's earth's god, and body's fost'ring patron"— 221

Cost. Not a word of Costard yet.

King. [*Reads.*] "So it is"—

Cost. It may be so; but if he say it is so, he is, in telling true—but so. 225

King. Peace!

Cost. —be to me, and every man that dares not fight!

King. No words!

Cost. —of other men's secrets, I beseech you. 230

King. [*Reads.*] "So it is, besieged with sable-colored melancholy, I did commend the black oppressing humor to the most wholesome physic of thy health-giving air; and as I am a gentleman, betook myself to walk: the time When? about the sixt 235 hour, when beasts most graze, birds best peck, and men sit down to that nourishment which is called supper: so much for the time When. Now for the ground Which? which, I mean, I walk'd upon: it is ycliped thy park. Then for the place Where? 240 where, I mean, I did encounter that obscene and most prepost'rous event that draweth from my snow-white pen the ebon-colored ink which here thou viewest, beholdest, surveyest, or seest. But to the place Where? It standeth north-north-east and by east 245 from the west corner of thy curious-knotted garden. There did I see that low-spirited swain, that base minnow of thy mirth"—

Cost. Me?

King. [*Reads.*] "that unlettered small-knowing soul"— 251

Cost. Me?

King. [*Reads.*] "that shallow vassal"—

Cost. Still me?

King. [*Reads.*] "which, as I remember, hight Costard"— 256

Cost. O! me.

King. [*Reads.*] "sorted and consorted, contrary to thy established proclaimed edict and continent canon; which with—O, with—but with this I passion to say wherewith"— 261

Cost. With a wench.

King. [*Reads.*] "with a child of our grandmother Eve, a female; or for thy more sweet understanding, a woman. Him I (as my ever-esteemed duty 265 pricks me on) have sent to thee, to receive the meed of punishment, by thy sweet Grace's officer, Anthony Dull, a man of good repute, carriage, bearing, and estimation."

Dull. Me, an't shall please you: I am Anthony Dull. 271

King. [*Reads.*] "For Jaquenetta (so is the weaker vessel called), which I apprehended with the aforesaid swain, I keep her as a vessel of thy law's fury, and shall, at the least of thy sweet notice, bring 275 her to trial. Thine, in all complements of devoted and heart-burning heat of duty,
　　　　　　Don Adriano de Armado."

Ber. This is not so well as I look'd for, but the best that ever I heard. 280

King. Ay, the best for the worst. But, sirrah, what say you to this?

Cost. Sir, I confess the wench.

King. Did you hear the proclamation?

Cost. I do confess much of the hearing it, but little of the marking of it. 286

King. It was proclaim'd a year's imprisonment to be taken with a wench.

Cost. I was taken with none, sir, I was taken with a damsel. 290

King. Well, it was proclaim'd damsel.

Cost. This was no damsel neither, sir, she was a virgin.

[*King.*] It is so varied too, for it was proclaim'd virgin. 295

Cost. If it were, I deny her virginity; I was taken with a maid.

King. This maid will not serve your turn, sir.

Cost. This maid will serve my turn, sir. 299

King. Sir, I will pronounce your sentence: you shall fast a week with bran and water.

Cost. I had rather pray a month with mutton and porridge.

King. And Don Armado shall be your keeper. My Lord Berowne, see him delivered o'er, 305 And go we, lords, to put in practice that Which each to other hath so strongly sworn.
　　　　　[*Exeunt King, Longaville, and Dumaine.*]

Ber. I'll lay my head to any good man's hat, These oaths and laws will prove an idle scorn. Sirrah, come on. 310

Cost. I suffer for the truth, sir; for true it is, I was taken with Jaquenetta, and Jaquenetta is a true girl, and therefore welcome the sour cup of prosperity! Affliction may one day smile again, and till then, sit thee down, sorrow! *Exeunt.* 315

[SCENE II]

Enter ARMADO *and* MOTH, *his page.*

Arm. Boy, what sign is it when a man of great spirit grows melancholy?

219–20. **welkin's vicegerent:** heaven's deputy.
225. **but so:** i.e. not saying much.　233. **physic:** medicine.
235. **sixt:** sixth.　240. **ycliped:** called.　241. **obscene:** disgusting.
242. **prepost'rous:** out of place, highly indecorous.
242–43. **snow-white pen:** i.e. white quill.
246. **curious-knotted:** intricately designed. Patterned garden beds were called knots.　247. **low-spirited:** base.
248. **minnow:** i.e. contemptible little creature.
250. **unlettered:** illiterate.　253. **vassal:** base slave.
258. **sorted:** associated.
259–60. **continent canon:** law enforcing restraint.
260. **passion:** grieve.　266. **meed:** reward.

272–73. **weaker vessel:** i.e. woman.
281. **best for:** best example of.　**sirrah:** form of address to inferiors.
294. **is so varied:** provides for that variation.
298. **This . . . turn:** this quibbling won't get you out of your difficulty (but Costard picks up the words in a ribald sense).
302–3. **mutton and porridge:** mutton soup (but *mutton* was also slang for "prostitute").　308. **lay:** wager.　312. **true:** honest.
315. **sit thee down:** i.e. settle down with me.

I.ii. o.s.d. **Moth.** Pronounced *mot* or *mote* by the Elizabethans and possibly intended by Shakespeare to represent the word now written *mote*, which he seems regularly to have spelled *moth*.

Moth. A great sign, sir, that he will look sad.

Arm. Why, sadness is one and the self-same thing, dear imp. 5

Moth. No, no, O Lord, sir, no.

Arm. How canst thou part sadness and melancholy, my tender juvenal?

Moth. By a familiar demonstration of the working, my tough signior. 10

Arm. Why tough signior? Why tough signior?

Moth. Why tender juvenal? Why tender juvenal?

Arm. I spoke it tender juvenal as a congruent epitheton appertaining to thy young days, which we may nominate tender. 15

Moth. And I tough signior as an appertinent title to your old time, which we may name tough.

Arm. Pretty and apt.

Moth. How mean you, sir? I pretty, and my saying apt? or I apt, and my saying pretty? 20

Arm. Thou pretty, because little.

Moth. Little pretty, because little. Wherefore apt?

Arm. And therefore apt, because quick.

Moth. Speak you this in my praise, master?

Arm. In thy condign praise. 25

Moth. I will praise an eel with the same praise.

Arm. What? that an eel is ingenious?

Moth. That an eel is quick.

Arm. I do say thou art quick in answers; thou heat'st my blood. 30

Moth. I am answer'd, sir.

Arm. I love not to be cross'd.

Moth. [*Aside.*] He speaks the mere contrary, crosses love not him.

Arm. I have promised to study three years with the Duke. 36

Moth. You may do it in an hour, sir.

Arm. Impossible.

Moth. How many is one thrice told?

Arm. I am ill at reck'ning, it fitteth the spirit of a tapster. 41

Moth. You are a gentleman and a gamester, sir.

Arm. I confess both, they are both the varnish of a complete man.

Moth. Then I am sure you know how much the gross sum of deuce-ace amounts to. 46

Arm. It doth amount to one more than two.

Moth. Which the base vulgar do call three.

Arm. True. 49

Moth. Why, sir, is this such a piece of study? Now here is three studied ere ye'll thrice wink; and how easy it is to put "years" to the word "three," and study three years in two words, the dancing horse will tell you.

Arm. A most fine figure! 55

Moth. [*Aside.*] To prove you a cipher.

Arm. I will hereupon confess I am in love; and as it is base for a soldier to love, so am I in love with a base wench. If drawing my sword against the humor of affection would deliver me from the 60 reprobate thought of it, I would take Desire prisoner, and ransom him to any French courtier for a new-devis'd cur'sy. I think scorn to sigh; methinks I should outswear Cupid. Comfort me, boy: what great men have been in love? 65

Moth. Hercules, master.

Arm. Most sweet Hercules! More authority, dear boy, name more; and, sweet my child, let them be men of good repute and carriage. 69

Moth. Sampson, master; he was a man of good carriage, great carriage, for he carried the town gates on his back like a porter; and he was in love.

Arm. O well-knit Sampson, strong-jointed Sampson! I do excel thee in my rapier as much as thou didst me in carrying gates. I am in love too. Who was Sampson's love, my dear Moth? 76

Moth. A woman, master.

Arm. Of what complexion?

Moth. Of all the four, or the three, or the two, or one of the four. 80

Arm. Tell me precisely of what complexion.

Moth. Of the sea-water green, sir.

Arm. Is that one of the four complexions?

Moth. As I have read, sir, and the best of them too. 85

Arm. Green indeed is the color of lovers; but to have a love of that color, methinks Sampson had small reason for it. He surely affected her for her wit.

Moth. It was so, sir, for she had a green wit. 89

Arm. My love is most immaculate white and red.

Moth. Most maculate thoughts, master, are mask'd under such colors.

Arm. Define, define, well-educated infant.

Moth. My father's wit and my mother's tongue assist me! 96

Arm. Sweet invocation of a child, most pretty and pathetical!

Moth. If she be made of white and red,
Her faults will ne'er be known, 100
For blush in cheeks by faults are bred,
And fears by pale white shown:
Then if she fear, or be to blame,
By this you shall not know,

---

5. **imp:** child (literally, sprig, shoot). 7. **part:** distinguish between. 8. **juvenal:** youth. 9. **familiar:** plain. 9–10. **working:** operation. 13–14. **congruent epitheton:** suitable epithet. 15. **nominate:** call. 16. **appertinent:** appropriate. 25. **condign:** worthily deserved. 29–30. **thou . . . blood:** you anger me. 34. **crosses:** i.e. coins (many of which were stamped with crosses). 39. **told:** counted, reckoned. 42. **gamester:** gambler. 43. **varnish:** finish, gloss. 46. **deuce-ace:** a two and a one, the second lowest throw at dice. 48. **vulgar:** common people. 53. **dancing horse.** Referring to a celebrated performing horse named Morocco, who had been trained to count by tapping with his hoof.

55. **figure:** example of verbal ingenuity (but the sense "numeral" probably inspires Moth's following aside). 56. **cipher:** nonentity. 58–59. **base . . . base:** morally reprehensible . . . low-born. 60. **humor of affection:** inclination to love. 63. **a new-devis'd cur'sy:** a new way of bowing, i.e. any new fashion. **think scorn:** disdain. 64. **outswear:** conquer by swearing. 69. **carriage:** behavior (with following quibble). 70. **Sampson:** Samson. For the exploit mentioned by Moth see Judges 16:3. 78. **complexion:** (1) color of skin; (2) temperament, disposition (supposed to be determined by the proportions of the four bodily fluids or "humors"—blood, phlegm, choler, and melancholy). 88. **affected:** loved. **wit:** intelligence. 89. **green:** immature. 92. **maculate:** stained, impure. 94. **Define:** explain your meaning. 98. **pathetical:** moving, touching.

Love's
Labor's Lost
I.ii

For still her cheeks possess the same   105
Which native she doth owe.

A dangerous rhyme, master, against the reason of white and red.

Arm. Is there not a ballet, boy, of the King and the Beggar?   110

Moth. The world was very guilty of such a ballet some three ages since, but I think now 'tis not to be found; or if it were, it would neither serve for the writing nor the tune.   114

Arm. I will have that subject newly writ o'er, that I may example my digression by some mighty president. Boy, I do love that country girl that I took in the park with the rational hind Costard. She deserves well.   119

Moth. [*Aside.*] To be whipt; and yet a better love than my master.

Arm. Sing, boy, my spirit grows heavy in love.

Moth. And that's great marvel, loving a light wench.

Arm. I say, sing.   125

Moth. Forbear till this company be past.

Enter Clown [COSTARD], *Constable* [DULL], *and Wench* [JAQUENETTA].

Dull. Sir, the Duke's pleasure is that you keep Costard safe, and you must suffer him to take no delight nor no penance, but 'a must fast three days a week. For this damsel, I must keep her at the   130 park; she is allow'd for the dey-woman. Fare you well.

Arm. I do betray myself with blushing. Maid.

Jaq. Man.

Arm. I will visit thee at the lodge.   135

Jaq. That's hereby.

Arm. I know where it is situate.

Jaq. Lord, how wise you are!

Arm. I will tell thee wonders.

Jaq. With that face?   140

Arm. I love thee.

Jaq. So I heard you say.

Arm. And so farewell.

Jaq. Fair weather after you!

[*Dull.*] Come, Jaquenetta, away.   145

Exeunt [*Dull and Jaquenetta*].

Arm. Villain, thou shalt fast for thy offenses ere thou be pardoned.

Cost. Well, sir, I hope when I do it I shall do it on a full stomach.

Arm. Thou shalt be heavily punished.   150

Cost. I am more bound to you than your fellows, for they are but lightly rewarded.

Arm. Take away this villain, shut him up.

Moth. Come, you transgressing slave, away.

Cost. Let me not be pent up, sir; I will fast, being loose.   156

Moth. No, sir, that were fast and loose; thou shalt to prison.

Cost. Well, if ever I do see the merry days of desolation that I have seen, some shall see.   160

Moth. What shall some see?

Cost. Nay, nothing, Master Moth, but what they look upon. It is not for prisoners to be too silent in their words, and therefore I will say nothing. I thank God I have as little patience as another man, and therefore I can be quiet.   *Exit* [*with Moth*].   166

Arm. I do affect the very ground (which is base) where her shoe (which is baser) guided by her foot (which is basest) doth tread. I shall be forsworn   (which is a great argument of falsehood) if I   170 love. And how can that be true love, which is falsely attempted? Love is a familiar; Love is a devil; there is no evil angel but Love. Yet was Sampson so tempted, and he had an excellent strength; yet was Salomon so seduced, and he had a very good wit. Cupid's   175 butt-shaft is too hard for Hercules' club, and therefore too much odds for a Spaniard's rapier. The first and second cause will not serve my turn; the passado he respects not, the duello he regards not: his disgrace is to be called boy, but his glory is to subdue men. Adieu, valor, rust, rapier, be still,   181 drum, for your manager is in love; yea, he loveth. Assist me, some extemporal god of rhyme, for I am sure I shall turn sonnet. Devise, wit, write, pen, for I am for whole volumes in folio.   *Exit.*   185

[ACT II, SCENE I]

Enter the PRINCESS OF FRANCE *with three attending Ladies* [ROSALINE, MARIA, KATHERINE] *and three* LORDS, [*one named* BOYET].

Boyet. Now, madam, summon up your dearest spirits;

---

106. **native:** naturally. **owe:** own. 109. **ballet:** ballad.
109–10. **King . . . Beggar:** i.e. King Cophetua and the beggar maid with whom he fell in love, the subjects of a popular ballad. Cf. IV.i.64–66. 113. **serve:** be acceptable.
116. **example:** give an example of. **digression:** lapse from propriety. 117. **president:** precedent.
118. **rational:** capable of thought. **hind:** rustic (perhaps with quibble on the sense "male deer"). 121. **love:** lover.
123. **light:** wanton.
129. **penance:** a blunder for *pleasance* (?) or perhaps Dull, like Costard elsewhere, is simply using a word that means the opposite of what he supposes. **'a:** he.
131. **allow'd . . . dey-woman:** approved to serve as dairy-woman.
136. **That's hereby.** It is clear from the rest of Jaquenetta's replies that some derisive sense is intended here, but the precise meaning is obscure.
140. **With that face:** a slang expression equivalent to "You don't say so."
146. **Villain:** (1) servant, peasant; (2) rascal.

148–49. **on . . . stomach.** With quibble on the secondary sense "with good courage." 151. **fellows:** servants. 152. **lightly:** slightly.
157. **fast and loose:** a cheating trick.
160. **desolation:** for *dissipation* (?) or *consolation* (?). But see note to line 129. 167. **affect:** love. 170. **argument:** proof.
172. **familiar:** attendant evil spirit, demon.
174. **Salomon:** Solomon.
176. **butt-shaft:** an arrow, without barb, for shooting at targets; often assigned to Cupid, perhaps because he was represented as a child.
177–78. **first . . . cause:** i.e. certain situations recognized in the code of honor as justifying a duel. Armado means that he is helpless against Cupid because Cupid will not be governed by the code.
178. **passado:** fencing thrust. 179. **duello:** duelling code.
182. **manager:** expert wielder. 183. **extemporal:** impromptu.
184. **turn sonnet:** i.e. become a sonneteer.
185. **folio:** i.e. the largest size of book.

II.i.1. **dearest spirits:** best wits.

Consider who the King your father sends,
To whom he sends, and what's his embassy:
Yourself, held precious in the world's esteem,
To parley with the sole inheritor   5
Of all perfections that a man may owe,
Matchless Navarre; the plea of no less weight
Than Aquitaine, a dowry for a queen.
Be now as prodigal of all dear grace
As Nature was in making graces dear,   10
When she did starve the general world beside
And prodigally gave them all to you.
   Prin. Good Lord Boyet, my beauty, though but
    mean,
Needs not the painted flourish of your praise:
Beauty is bought by judgment of the eye,   15
Not utt'red by base sale of chapmen's tongues.
I am less proud to hear you tell my worth
Than you much willing to be counted wise
In spending your wit in the praise of mine.
But now to task the tasker: good Boyet,   20
You are not ignorant all-telling fame
Doth noise abroad Navarre hath made a vow,
Till painful study shall outwear three years,
No woman may approach his silent court;
Therefore to 's seemeth it a needful course, 25
Before we enter his forbidden gates,
To know his pleasure; and in that behalf,
Bold of your worthiness, we single you
As our best-moving fair solicitor.
Tell him, the daughter of the King of France, 30
On serious business craving quick dispatch,
[Importunes] personal conference with his Grace.
Haste, signify so much, while we attend,
Like humble[-visag'd] suitors, his high will.
   Boyet. Proud of employment, willingly I go. 35
                        Exit Boyet.
   Prin. All pride is willing pride, and yours is so.
Who are the votaries, my loving lords,
That are vow-fellows with this virtuous Duke?
   [1.] Lord. [Lord] Longaville is one.
   Prin.   Know you the man?
   [Mar.] I know him, madam; at a marriage-feast,
Between Lord Perigort and the beauteous heir   41
Of Jaques Falconbridge, solemnized
In Normandy, saw I this Longaville,
A man of sovereign [parts, peerless] esteem'd,
Well fitted in arts, glorious in arms;   45
Nothing becomes him ill that he would well.
The only soil of his fair virtue's gloss,
If virtue's gloss will stain with any soil,
Is a sharp wit match'd with too blunt a will, 49

Whose edge hath power to cut, whose will still wills
It should none spare that come within his power.
   Prin. Some merry mocking lord belike, is't so?
   [Mar.] They say so most that most his humors
    know.
   Prin. Such short-liv'd wits do wither as they grow.
Who are the rest?   55
   [Kath.] The young Dumaine, a well-accomplish'd
    youth,
Of all that virtue love for virtue loved;
Most power to do most harm, least knowing ill;
For he hath wit to make an ill shape good,
And shape to win grace though he had no wit.   60
I saw him at the Duke Alanson's once,
And much too little of that good I saw
Is my report to his great worthiness.
   [Ros.] Another of these students at that time
Was there with him, if I have heard a truth.   65
Berowne they call him, but a merrier man,
Within the limit of becoming mirth,
I never spent an hour's talk withal.
His eye begets occasion for his wit,
For every object that the one doth catch   70
The other turns to a mirth-moving jest,
Which his fair tongue, conceit's expositor,
Delivers in such apt and gracious words
That aged ears play truant at his tales,
And younger hearings are quite ravished,   75
So sweet and voluble is his discourse.
   Prin. God bless my ladies! are they all in love,
That every one her own hath garnished
With such bedecking ornaments of praise?   79
   [1.] Lord. Here comes Boyet.

               Enter BOYET.

   Prin.   Now, what admittance, lord?
   Boyet. Navarre had notice of your fair approach,
And he and his competitors in oath
Were all address'd to meet you, gentle lady,
Before I came. Marry, thus much I have learnt:
He rather means to lodge you in the field,   85
Like one that comes here to besiege his court,
Than seek a dispensation for his oath,
To let you enter his [unpeopled] house.

   Enter [FERDINAND, *King of*] *Navarre,* LONGAVILLE,
    DUMAINE, *and* BEROWNE, [*and* ATTENDANTS].

Here comes Navarre.   [*The ladies-in-waiting mask.*]
   King. Fair Princess, welcome to the court of
    Navarre.   90

---

5. **inheritor:** possessor.   6. **owe:** own.
7. **plea:** that which is claimed.   10. **dear:** costly (because scarce).
11. **starve:** stint, deprive. **general:** whole. **beside:** apart (from
you). 14. **flourish:** embellishment.
16. **utt'red:** offered for sale. **chapmen's:** merchants'.
17. **proud:** pleased. **tell:** (1) describe; (2) reckon up.
20. **task the tasker:** i.e. set a task for you, who have been setting one
for me. 21. **fame:** rumor. 23. **painful:** laborious.
25. **to 's:** to us. 28. **Bold:** confident.
29. **best-moving:** most eloquent. **fair:** just.
37. **the votaries:** those who have taken vows.
45. **arts:** intellectual accomplishments. 46. **would:** wishes to do.
49. **too . . . will:** i.e. a disposition unwilling to spare others' feelings.

50. **still:** ever.
57. **Of . . . loved:** loved for his virtue by all who love virtue.
58. **Most . . . ill:** i.e. because of his innocence, possessed of the
greatest power to do the greatest harm.
59–60. **he . . . wit:** his intelligence is such that it would make up for
an ugly body, and his physical endowment is such that it would make
up for lack of brains. 61. **Duke Alanson's:** Duke of Alençon's.
62. **little:** short. 63. **report:** testimony.
66. **Berowne.** Here perhaps with a play on *brown* = sombre (David).
67. **becoming:** decorous. 68. **withal:** with.
72. **conceit's expositor:** fancy's interpreter.
74. **play truant at:** i.e. stop attending to serious matters in order to
listen to. 76. **voluble:** quick-witted. 80. **admittance:** reception.
82. **competitors:** associates. 83. **address'd:** made ready, prepared.
88. **unpeopled:** i.e. lacking the proper retinue of servants.

Love's
Labor's Lost
II.i

Prin. "Fair" I give you back again, and "welcome"
I have not yet. The roof of this court is too high to
be yours, and welcome to the wide fields too base to
be mine.

King. You shall be welcome, madam, to my
court.   95

Prin. I will be welcome then—conduct me thither.

King. Hear me, dear lady: I have sworn an oath.

Prin. Our Lady help my lord! he'll be forsworn.

King. Not for the world, fair madam, by my will.

Prin. Why, will shall break it, will, and nothing
else.   100

King. Your ladyship is ignorant what it is.

Prin. Were my lord so, his ignorance were wise,
Where now his knowledge must prove ignorance.
I hear your Grace hath sworn out house-keeping:
'Tis deadly sin to keep that oath, my lord,   105
And sin to break it.
But pardon me, I am too sudden bold;
To teach a teacher ill beseemeth me.
Vouchsafe to read the purpose of my coming,
And suddenly resolve me in my suit.   110

[*Giving a paper.*]

King. Madam, I will, if suddenly I may.

Prin. You will the sooner, that I were away,
For you'll prove perjur'd if you make me stay.

Ber. Did not I dance with you in Brabant once?

Kath. Did not I dance with you in Brabant
once?   115

Ber. I know you did.

Kath.   How needless was it then
To ask the question?

Ber.   You must not be so quick.

Kath. 'Tis long of you that spur me with such
questions.

Ber. Your wit's too hot, it speeds too fast, 'twill
tire.

Kath. Not till it leave the rider in the mire.   120

Ber. What time a' day?

Kath. The hour that fools should ask.

Ber. Now fair befall your mask!

Kath. Fair fall the face it covers!

Ber. And send you many lovers!   125

Kath. Amen, so you be none.

Ber. Nay then will I be gone.

King. Madam, your father here doth intimate
The payment of a hundred thousand crowns,
Being but the one half of an entire sum   130
Disbursed by my father in his wars.
But say that he, or we, as neither have,
Receiv'd that sum, yet there remains unpaid
A hundred thousand more, in surety of the which
One part of Aquitaine is bound to us,   135
Although not valued to the money's worth.
If then the King your father will restore
But that one half which is unsatisfied,

We will give up our right in Aquitaine,
And hold fair friendship with his Majesty.   140
But that, it seems, he little purposeth:
For here he doth demand to have repaid
A hundred thousand crowns, and not demands,
[On] payment of a hundred thousand crowns,
To have his title live in Aquitaine;   145
Which we much rather had depart withal,
And have the money by our father lent,
Than Aquitaine, so gelded as it is.
Dear Princess, were not his requests so far   149
From reason's yielding, your fair self should make
A yielding 'gainst some reason in my breast,
And go well satisfied to France again.

Prin. You do the King my father too much wrong,
And wrong the reputation of your name,
In so unseeming to confess receipt   155
Of that which hath so faithfully been paid.

King. I do protest I never heard of it;
And, if you prove it, I'll repay it back,
Or yield up Aquitaine.

Prin.   We arrest your word.
Boyet, you can produce acquittances   160
For such a sum from special officers
Of Charles his father.

King.   Satisfy me so.

Boyet. So please your Grace, the packet is not come
Where that and other specialties are bound:
To-morrow you shall have a sight of them.   165

King. It shall suffice me; at which interview
All liberal reason I will yield unto.
Mean time receive such welcome at my hand
As honor (without breach of honor) may
Make tender of to thy true worthiness.   170
You may not come, fair Princess, within my gates,
But here without you shall be so receiv'd
As you shall deem yourself lodg'd in my heart,
Though so denied fair harbor in my house.   174
Your own good thoughts excuse me, and farewell.
To-morrow shall we visit you again.

Prin. Sweet health and fair desires consort your
Grace!

King. Thy own wish wish I thee in every place.

Exit [*with Longaville, Dumaine,*
and Attendants].

Ber. Lady, I will commend you to [mine own]
heart.   180

Ros. Pray you, do my commendations—I would
be glad to see it.

Ber. I would you heard it groan.

Ros. Is the fool sick?

Ber. Sick at the heart.   185

Ros. Alack, let it blood.

Ber. Would that do it good?

Ros. My physic says ay.

---

92. **roof . . . court:** i.e. the sky.   99. **by my will:** willingly.
104. **sworn out house-keeping:** renounced hospitality.
107. **sudden:** rashly.
110. **suddenly:** immediately.   **resolve:** answer.
117. **quick:** sharp.   118. **long:** because.
123. **fair befall:** good fortune to.
128. **intimate:** suggest, discuss.   136. **valued:** equal in value.

146. **depart withal:** part with.   148. **gelded:** i.e. reduced in value.
155. **unseeming to:** seeming to be unwilling to.
159. **arrest:** take as security.
164. **specialties:** special terms or documents.
167. **liberal:** gentlemanlike, generous.   173. **As:** that.
177. **consort:** attend.   184. **the fool:** the poor thing.
186. **let it blood:** bleed it. Bloodletting was a common medical treatment.   188. **physic:** medical knowledge.

Ber. Will you prick't with your eye?

Ros. No point, with my knife. 190

Ber. Now God save thy life!

Ros. And yours from long living!

Ber. I cannot stay thanksgiving. *Exit.*

Enter DUMAINE.

Dum. Sir, I pray you a word. What lady is that
 same? 194

Boyet. The heir of Alanson, [Katherine] her name.

Dum. A gallant lady. Monsieur, fare you well.
               Exit.

[*Enter* LONGAVILLE.]

Long. I beseech you a word. What is she in the
 white?

Boyet. A woman sometimes, and you saw her in
 the light.

Long. Perchance light in the light. I desire her
 name.

Boyet. She hath but one for herself, to desire that
 were a shame. 200

Long. Pray you, sir, whose daughter?

Boyet. Her mother's, I have heard.

Long. God's blessing on your beard!

Boyet. Good sir, be not offended,
She is an heir of Falconbridge. 205

Long. Nay, my choler is ended.
She is a most sweet lady.

Boyet. Not unlike, sir, that may be.
        Exit Longaville.

Enter BEROWNE.

Ber. What's her name in the cap?

Boyet. [Rosaline,] by good hap. 210

Ber. Is she wedded or no?

Boyet. To her will, sir, or so.

Ber. O, you are welcome, sir, adieu.

Boyet. Farewell to me, sir, and welcome to you.
         Exit Berowne.

Mar. That last is Berowne, the merry madcap lord.
Not a word with him but a jest.

Boyet.   And every jest but a word. 216

Prin. It was well done of you to take him at his
 word.

Boyet. I was as willing to grapple as he was to
 board.

Kath. Two hot sheeps, marry.

Boyet.   And wherefore not ships?
No sheep, sweet lamb, unless we feed on your lips.

[*Kath.*] You sheep, and I pasture: shall that finish
 the jest? 221

Boyet. So you grant pasture for me.
     [*Offering to kiss her.*]

[*Kath.*]   Not so, gentle beast.
My lips are no common, though several they be.

Boyet. Belonging to whom?

[*Kath.*]   To my fortunes and me.

Prin. Good wits will be jangling, but, gentles,
 agree: 225
This civil war of wits were much better used
On Navarre and his book-men, for here 'tis abused.

Boyet. If my observation (which very seldom lies),
By the heart's still rhetoric, disclosed with eyes,
Deceive me not now, Navarre is infected. 230

Prin. With what?

Boyet. With that which we lovers entitle "affected."

Prin. Your reason?

Boyet. Why, all his behaviors did make their
 retire
To the court of his eye, peeping thorough desire: 235
His heart like an agot with your print impressed,
Proud with his form, in his eye pride expressed;
His tongue, all impatient to speak and not see,
Did stumble with haste in his eyesight to be;
All senses to that sense did make their repair, 240
To feel only looking on fairest of fair:
Methought all his senses were lock'd in his eye,
As jewels in crystal for some prince to buy,
Who tend'ring their own worth from where they
 were glass'd,
Did point you to buy them, along as you pass'd; 245
His face's own margent did cote such amazes
That all eyes saw his eyes enchanted with gazes.
I'll give you Aquitaine and all that is his,
And you give him for my sake but one loving kiss.

Prin. Come to our pavilion—Boyet is dispos'd.

Boyet. But to speak that in words which his eye
 hath disclos'd. 251
I only have made a mouth of his eye,
By adding a tongue which I know will not lie.

[*Mar.*] Thou art an old love-monger and speakest
 skillfully.

[*Kath.*] He is Cupid's grandfather, and learns news
 of him. 255

[*Ros.*] Then was Venus like her mother, for her
 father is but grim.

---

190. **No point:** (1) it is dull; (2) by no means.
193. **stay thanksgiving:** take time to thank you properly.
198. **and:** if. 199. **light . . . light:** wanton if clearly seen.
203. **God's . . . beard.** Jesting reference to a man's beard was thought
to be insulting. 208. **unlike:** unlikely.
212. **or so:** or something of the kind.
214. **welcome to you:** you are welcome to go (?).
217. **take . . . word:** give him word for word.
218. **grapple . . . board:** come to grips with him . . . attack (terms
from naval warfare).
219. **sheeps, ships.** Elizabethan puns on these near-homonyms are
numberless.

222. **So:** provided.
223. **common:** common land. **though:** inasmuch as (?). **several:**
(1) private enclosed land; (2) more than one; (3) parted.
225. **jangling:** disputing.
227. **book-men:** scholars. **abused:** misapplied.
229. **still rhetoric:** silent eloquence. 232. **affected:** being in love.
234. **retire:** withdrawal. 235. **thorough:** through.
236. **agot:** agate (often carved with small figures and set into rings).
impressed: engraved.
237. **his form:** the form imprinted on it, i.e. the image of the Princess.
238. **to . . . see:** at being able only to speak, not to see.
239. **in . . . be:** to participate in the sense of sight.
240. **repair:** resort. 241. **looking:** through looking.
244. **Who:** which. **tend'ring:** offering, showing forth. **glass'd:**
enclosed in glass. 245. **point:** direct.
246. **margent.** Margins of books often bore commentary upon the
adjoining text; hence the word is here applied to the King's looks of
amazement, which comment on what his eye beholds. **cote:** variant
form of *quote* (indicating the Elizabethan pronunciation), i.e. indicate.
250. **dispos'd:** inclined (to be merry). 254. **skillfully:** as an expert.
256. **her . . . grim:** i.e. Boyet is no "beauty."

Love's
Labor's Lost
II.i

Boyet. Do you hear, my mad wenches?
[Mar.]   No.
Boyet.   What then, do you see?
[Mar.] Ay, our way to be gone.
Boyet.   You are too hard for me.

Exeunt omnes.

[ACT III, SCENE I]

Enter Braggart [ARMADO] *and his Boy* [MOTH].

Arm. Warble, child, make passionate my sense
of hearing.
Moth. [*Sings the song*] "Concolinel."
Arm. Sweet air! Go, tenderness of years, take
this key, give enlargement to the swain, bring   5
him festinately hither. I must employ him in a letter
to my love.
Moth. Master, will you win your love with a
French brawl?
Arm. How meanest thou? Brawling in French?
Moth. No, my complete master, but to jig off   11
a tune at the tongue's end, canary to it with your
feet, humor it with turning up your eyelids, sigh
a note and sing a note, sometime through the throat,
[as] if you swallow'd love with singing love,   15
sometime through [the] nose, as if you snuff'd up
love by smelling love; with your hat penthouse-like
o'er the shop of your eyes; with your arms cross'd
on your thin[-bellied] doublet like a rabbit on a spit; or
your hands in your pocket like a man after the   20
old painting; and keep not too long in one tune, but
a snip and away: these are complements, these are
humors, these betray nice wenches that would be
betray'd without these; and make them men of note—
do you note?—men that most are affected to these.   25
Arm. How hast thou purchased this experience?
Moth. By my [penny] of observation.
Arm. But O—but O—
Moth. "The hobby-horse is forgot."
Arm. Call'st thou my love "hobby-horse"?   30
Moth. No, master, the hobby-horse is but a colt,
[*aside*] and your love perhaps a hackney.—But have you
forgot your love?

257. **mad wenches:** high-spirited girls.

III.i.1. **passionate:** impassioned, feeling.
3. **Concolinel.** Unexplained; probably the title of a song.
5. **enlargement:** freedom.   6. **festinately:** in haste.
9. **brawl:** one of the oldest of figure dances (from French *branle*).
11. **jig:** sing in the tune of a jig.
12. **canary:** dance in a very lively manner (from the name of a dance).   14. **sometime:** from time to time, at times.
17. **penthouse-like:** like a projecting roof.
18. **arms cross'd.** Folded arms betokened love melancholy.
19. **thin-bellied doublet:** (1) doublet with an unpadded belly or lower front; (2) doublet over a thin belly (suggestive of one wasted by love-longing).
22. **a snip and away:** a snatch and then on to another.   **complements:** gentlemanly actions.   23. **nice:** coy.
25. **affected:** inclined.
28-29. **But . . . forgot.** The line, a lament for the passing of the good old days, occurs again in *Hamlet* (III.ii.135) and elsewhere, and was probably the refrain of a song. The hobby-horse, a dancer costumed to suggest a horse, was a favorite figure in May-games and other traditional festivities which were falling into disuse, partly because of Puritan disapproval.
30. **hobby-horse:** slang for a wanton or a prostitute.
31. **colt:** (1) a young male horse; (2) a lascivious person.
32. **hackney:** (1) riding horse; (2) prostitute (slang).

Arm. Almost I had.
Moth. Negligent student, learn her by heart.   35
Arm. By heart and in heart, boy.
Moth. And out of heart, master; all those three I
will prove.
Arm. What wilt thou prove?   39
Moth. A man, if I live; and this, "by, in, and with-
out," upon the instant: by heart you love her, because
your heart cannot come by her; in heart you love her,
because your heart is in love with her; and out of
heart you love her, being out of heart that you cannot
enjoy her.   45
Arm. I am all these three.
Moth. And three times as much more—[*aside*]
and yet nothing at all.
Arm. Fetch hither the swain, he must carry me
a letter.   50
Moth. A message well sympathiz'd—a horse to
be embassador for an ass.
Arm. Ha, ha? what sayest thou?
Moth. Marry, sir, you must send the ass upon
the horse, for he is very slow-gaited. But I go.   55
Arm. The way is but short, away!
Moth. As swift as lead, sir.
Arm. The meaning, pretty ingenious?
Is not lead a metal heavy, dull, and slow?
Moth. *Minime*, honest master, or rather, master,
    no.   60
Arm. I say lead is slow.
Moth.   You are too swift, sir, to say so.
Is that lead slow which is fir'd from a gun?
Arm. Sweet smoke of rhetoric!
He reputes me a cannon, and the bullet, that's he;
I shoot thee at the swain.
Moth.   Thump then, and I flee. [*Exit.*]
Arm. A most acute juvenal, volable and free of
    grace!   66
By thy favor, sweet welkin, I must sigh in thy face:
Most rude melancholy, valor gives thee place.
My herald is return'd.

Enter Page [MOTH] *and Clown* [COSTARD].

Moth. A wonder, master! Here's a costard
    broken in a shin.   70
Arm. Some enigma, some riddle—come, thy
    l'envoy—begin.
Cost. No egma, no riddle, no l'envoy, no salve in
the mail, sir. O sir, plantan, a plain plantan; no
l'envoy, no l'envoy, no salve, sir, but a plantan!
Arm. By virtue thou enforcest laughter—thy   75

51. **sympathiz'd:** matched.   52. **embassador:** ambassador.
60. **Minime:** by no means.
65. **Thump:** i.e. make a noise like a gun going off.
66. **volable:** voluble, i.e. quick-witted.
67. **favor:** good will, leave (with a play, perhaps, on the sense "face")
68. **gives thee place:** yields its place to you.
70. **a costard . . . shin:** a head with a cut on its shin.
71. **l'envoy:** i.e. explanation; properly, a postscript to a literary composition, which sends the piece on its way to its intended readers and interprets or comments on its import (cf. lines 81-82).
72. **salve.** Possibly Costard here says *salvé* (a salute) when he means *salve* (a healing ointment); hence Armado in lines 78-79 points out that he has taken "salve for l'envoy," i.e. salutation for farewell.
73. **mail:** pouch, bag (of a seller of cures).   **plantan:** plantain, a healing herb. Costard wants the common home remedy, not strange remedies with foreign names.

silly thought, my spleen; the heaving of my lungs
provokes me to ridiculous smiling—O, pardon me,
my stars! Doth the inconsiderate take salve for
l'envoy, and the word "l'envoy" for a salve?

Moth. Do the wise think them other? is not l'envoy
a salve? 80

Arm. No, page, it is an epilogue or discourse, to
make plain
Some obscure precedence that hath tofore been sain.
I will example it:
The fox, the ape, and the humble-bee
Were still at odds, being but three. 85
There's the moral. Now the l'envoy.

Moth. I will add the l'envoy. Say the moral
again.

Arm. The fox, the ape, and the humble-bee
Were still at odds, being but three. 90

Moth. Until the goose came out of door,
And stayed the odds by adding four.
Now will I begin your moral, and do you follow
with my l'envoy:
The fox, the ape, and the humble-bee 95
Were still at odds, being but three.

Arm. Until the goose came out of door,
Staying the odds by adding four.

Moth. A good l'envoy, ending in the goose; would
you desire more? 100

Cost. The boy hath sold him a bargain, a goose,
that's flat.
Sir, your pennyworth is good, and your goose be fat.
To sell a bargain well is as cunning as fast and loose:
Let me see: a fat l'envoy—ay, that's a fat goose.

Arm. Come hither, come hither. How did this
argument begin? 105

Moth. By saying that a costard was broken in a
shin.
Then call'd you for the l'envoy.

Cost. True, and I for a plantan; thus came your
argument in;
Then the boy's fat l'envoy, the goose that you
bought,
And he ended the market. 110

Arm. But tell me, how was there a costard broken
in a shin?

Moth. I will tell you sensibly.

Cost. Thou hast no feeling of it, Moth. I will
speak that l'envoy: 115
I, Costard, running out that was safely within,
Fell over the threshold, and broke my shin.

Arm. We will talk no more of this matter.

Cost. Till there be more matter in the shin.

Arm. Sirrah Costard, I will enfranchise thee. 120

Cost. O, marry me to one Frances! I smell some
l'envoy, some goose, in this.

Arm. By my sweet soul, I mean setting thee at
liberty, enfreedoming thy person: thou wert immured,
restrained, captivated, bound. 125

Cost. True, true, and now you will be my purgation and let me loose.

Arm. I give thee thy liberty, set thee from durance, and in lieu thereof, impose on thee nothing
but this: bear this significant [*giving a letter*] to 130
the country maid Jaquenetta. There is remuneration, for the best ward of mine honor is rewarding
my dependants. Moth, follow.

Moth. Like the sequel, I. Signior Costard, adieu.
Exit [*Armado, followed by Moth*].

Cost. My sweet ounce of man's flesh, my incony
Jew! 135
Now will I look to his remuneration. Remuneration! O, that's the Latin word for three farthings:
three farthings—remuneration. "What's the price
of this inkle?"—"One penny."—"No, I'll give you
a remuneration": why, it carries it. Remuner- 140
ation: why, it is a fairer name than French crown!
I will never buy and sell out of this word.

Enter BEROWNE.

Ber. O, my good knave Costard, exceedingly well
met!

Cost. Pray you, sir, how much carnation ribbon
may a man buy for a remuneration? 146

Ber. O, what is a remuneration?

Cost. Marry, sir, halfpenny farthing.

Ber. O, why then three-farthing worth of silk.

Cost. I thank your worship, God be wi' you! 150

Ber. O, stay, slave; I must employ thee.
As thou wilt win my favor, good my knave,
Do one thing for me that I shall entreat.

Cost. When would you have it done, sir?

Ber. O, this afternoon. 155

Cost. Well, I will do it, sir; fare you well.

Ber. O, thou knowest not what it is.

Cost. I shall know, sir, when I have done it.

Ber. Why, villain, thou must know first. 159

Cost. I will come to your worship to-morrow
morning.

Ber. It must be done this afternoon. Hark, slave,
it is but this:
The Princess comes to hunt here in the park,
And in her train there is a gentle lady: 165
When tongues speak sweetly, then they name her
name,
And Rosaline they call her. Ask for her,
And to her white hand see thou do commend

---

76. **spleen.** Supposedly the organ in which laughter originated.
78. **inconsiderate:** unthinking one, dull-witted person.
82. **precedence:** preceding matter. (The second half of Armado's line
is redundant.) **sain:** said.
83. **example:** give an example of. (The example is thought by commentators to contain some topical reference, no longer clear.)
85. **still:** always. **at odds:** (1) quarrelling; (2) an odd number.
92. **stayed the odds:** (1) checked the quarrelling; (2) prevented an
odd number. **four:** i.e. a fourth.
101. **sold . . . goose:** made a fool of him.
102. **your . . . and:** you got your money's worth if.
103. **fast and loose:** cheating. 105. **argument:** topic, discussion.
113. **sensibly:** feelingly, with emotion. 119. **matter:** pus.

122. **goose:** slang for "whore."
126–27. **be my purgation:** clear me of wrongdoing (with obvious
second sense extending to *bound* and *let me loose*).
130. **significant:** token, sign. 132. **ward:** guard.
135. **incony:** fine, rare. **Jew.** Used playfully.
139. **inkle:** a kind of linen tape.
140. **it carries it:** it wins the day.
141. **French crown:** (1) a coin; (2) bald head (caused by syphilis,
often called "the French disease").
142. **out . . . word:** using any other word but this.
145. **carnation:** flesh-colored.

Love's
Labor's Lost
III.i

This seal'd-up counsel. There's thy guerdon; go. 169
  Cost. Gardon, O sweet gardon! better than re-
muneration, aleven-pence-farthing better; most sweet
gardon! I will do it, sir, in print. Gardon! Re-
muneration!   *Exit.*
  Ber. O, and I, forsooth, in love! I, that have been
love's whip,
A very beadle to a humorous sigh,   175
A critic, nay, a night-watch constable,
A domineering pedant o'er the boy,
Than whom no mortal so magnificent!
This wimpled, whining, purblind, wayward boy,
This senior[-junior], giant-dwarf, Dan Cupid,   180
Regent of love-rhymes, lord of folded arms,
Th' anointed sovereign of sighs and groans,
Liege of all loiterers and malecontents,
Dread prince of plackets, king of codpieces,
Sole imperator and great general   185
Of trotting paritors (O my little heart!),
And I to be a corporal of his field,
And wear his colors like a tumbler's hoop!
What! I love, I sue, I seek a wife—
A woman, that is like a German [clock],   190
Still a-repairing, ever out of frame,
And never going aright, being a watch,
But being watch'd that it may still go right!
Nay, to be perjur'd, which is worst of all;
And among three to love the worst of all,   195
A whitely wanton with a velvet brow,
With two pitch-balls stuck in her face for eyes;
Ay, and, by heaven, one that will do the deed
Though Argus were her eunuch and her guard.
And I to sigh for her, to watch for her,   200
To pray for her, go to! It is a plague
That Cupid will impose for my neglect
Of his almighty dreadful little might.
Well, I will love, write, sigh, pray, sue, groan:
Some men must love my lady, and some Joan.   205
                                                        [*Exit.*]

169. **counsel:** private communication.   **guerdon:** reward.
171. **aleven:** eleven.   172. **in print:** i.e. most exactly.
175. **beadle:** parish officer who whipped petty offenders.   **humorous:**
moody.   177. **pedant:** schoolmaster.
178. **magnificent:** proud, boastful.
179. **wimpled:** blindfolded.   **purblind:** totally blind.
180. **senior-junior.** Perhaps with play on *Signor Junior*, i.e. Mr.
Youngboy.   **Dan:** sir (from Latin *dominus*, "master").
181. **folded arms.** See note on III.i.18.
184. **plackets:** slits in petticoats, i.e. women (in bawdy sense).   **codpieces:** baggy appendages at the front of breeches, i.e. men (in bawdy
sense).
186. **paritors:** apparitors, officers who summoned offenders to an
ecclesiastical court.   187. **a corporal . . . field:** his field officer.
188. **tumbler's hoop.** Usually decorated with varicolored ribbons.
191. **Still:** ever.   **frame:** order.
193. **But . . . right:** i.e. unless an eye is kept on her to see that she
behaves herself.   196. **whitely:** pale, sallow.
198. **do the deed:** engage in sexual intercourse.
199. **Argus:** a monster with a hundred eyes, never all closed simultaneously.   200. **watch:** stay awake all night.
205. **my lady:** milady, i.e. a woman of gentle birth.   **Joan:** stock
name for a peasant wench.

[ACT IV, SCENE I]

Enter the PRINCESS, *a* FORESTER, *her Ladies* [ROSALINE,
MARIA, KATHERINE], *and her* LORDS, [*among them*
BOYET].

  Prin. Was that the King that spurr'd his horse so
    hard
Against the steep-up rising of the hill?
  For. I know not, but I think it was not he.
  Prin. Whoe'er 'a was, 'a show'd a mounting mind.
Well, lords, to-day we shall have our dispatch;   5
[On] Saturday we will return to France.
Then, forester, my friend, where is the bush
That we must stand and play the murtherer in?
  For. Hereby, upon the edge of yonder coppice,
A stand where you may make the fairest shoot.   10
  Prin. I thank my beauty, I am fair that shoot,
And thereupon thou speak'st the fairest shoot.
  For. Pardon me, madam, for I meant not so.
  Prin. What, what? First praise me, and again
    say no?
O short-liv'd pride! Not fair? alack for woe!   15
  For. Yes, madam, fair.
  Prin.   Nay, never paint me now;
Where fair is not, praise cannot mend the brow.
Here (good my glass), take this for telling true:
                              [*Giving him money.*]
Fair payment for foul words is more than due.
  For. Nothing but fair is that which you inherit.   20
  Prin. See, see, my beauty will be sav'd by merit.
O heresy in fair, fit for these days!
A giving hand, though foul, shall have fair praise.
But come, the bow: now mercy goes to kill,
And shooting well is then accounted ill.   25
Thus will I save my credit in the shoot:
Not wounding, pity would not let me do't;
If wounding, then it was to show my skill,
That more for praise than purpose meant to kill.
And out of question so it is sometimes: 30
Glory grows guilty of detested crimes,
When for fame's sake, for praise, an outward part,
We bend to that the working of the heart;
As I for praise alone now seek to spill
The poor deer's blood, that my heart means no ill.   35
  Boyet. Do not curst wives hold that self-sover-
    eignty
Only for praise' sake, when they strive to be
Lords o'er their lords?
  Prin. Only for praise—and praise we may afford
To any lady that subdues a lord.   40

                    Enter Clown [COSTARD].

IV.i.9. **coppice:** thicket.
10. **stand:** hunter's station.   **fairest:** most favorable.
16. **paint:** flatter.   17. **fair:** beauty.
18. **good my glass:** my good mirror (because he shows the Princess
her face at its true value).   20. **inherit:** own.
21. **by merit:** (1) by its own deserts; (2) by my giving of gratuities.
22. **heresy.** Because the Protestant Church teaches salvation by faith,
not by "merit," i.e. good works.   **in fair:** with regard to beauty.
25. **then:** i.e. when it is a merciful person who is doing the shooting.
30. **out of question:** undoubtedly.
31. **Glory:** i.e. the desire for too much glory.   **detested:** detestable.
36. **curst:** shrewish.

Boyet. Here comes a member of the common-
     wealth.

Cost. God dig-you-den all! Pray you, which is
the head lady?

Prin. Thou shalt know her, fellow, by the rest
that have no heads.   45

Cost. Which is the greatest lady, the highest?

Prin. The thickest and the tallest.

Cost. The thickest and the tallest! it is so, truth is
     truth.
And your waist, mistress, were as slender as my wit,
One a' these maids' girdles for your waist should be
     fit.   50
Are not you the chief woman? You are the thick-
     est here.

Prin. What's your will, sir? what's your will?

Cost. I have a letter from Monsieur Berowne to
     one Lady Rosaline.

Prin. O, thy letter, thy letter! He's a good
     friend of mine.
Stand aside, good bearer. Boyet, you can carve,   55
Break up this capon.

Boyet.   I am bound to serve.
This letter is mistook; it importeth none here.
It is writ to Jaquenetta.

Prin.   We will read it, I swear.
Break the neck of the wax, and every one give ear.

Boyet reads. "By heaven, that thou art fair,   60
is most infallible; true, that thou art beauteous; truth
itself, that thou art lovely. More fairer than fair,
beautiful than beauteous, truer than truth itself, have
commiseration on thy heroical vassal! The magnanimous and most illustrate King Cophetua set eye   65
upon the pernicious and indubitate beggar Zenelophon;
and he it was that might rightly say, *Veni, vidi,
vici;* which to annothanize in the vulgar—O base and
obscure vulgar!—*videlicet,* He came, [saw], and
overcame: he came, one; [saw], two; [overcame],   70
three. Who came? the king. Why did he come?
to see. Why did he see? to overcome. To whom
came he? to the beggar. What saw he? the beggar.
Who overcame he? the beggar. The conclusion is
victory; on whose side? the [king's]. The cap-   75
tive is enrich'd; on whose side? the beggar's. The
catastrophe is a nuptial; on whose side? the king's;
no, on both in one, or one in both. I am the king, for
so stands the comparison; thou the beggar, for so witnesseth thy lowliness. Shall I command thy love?   80
I may. Shall I enforce thy love? I could. Shall I
entreat thy love? I will. What shalt thou exchange
for rags? robes; for tittles? titles; for thyself? me.

Thus expecting thy reply, I profane my lips on thy
foot, my eyes on thy picture, and my heart on   85
thy every part. Thine, in the dearest design of industry,
                    Don Adriano de Armado.
Thus dost thou hear the Nemean lion roar
'Gainst thee, thou lamb, that standest as his prey;
Submissive fall his princely feet before,   90
And he from forage will incline to play.
But if thou strive, poor soul, what art thou then?
Food for his rage, repasture for his den."

Prin. What plume of feathers is he that indited
     this letter?
What vane? What weathercock? Did you ever hear
     better?   95

Boyet. I am much deceived but I remember the
     style.

Prin. Else your memory is bad, going o'er it ere-
     while.

Boyet. This Armado is a Spaniard that keeps here
     in court,
A phantasime, a Monarcho, and one that makes sport
To the Prince and his book-mates.

Prin.   Thou fellow, a word.
Who gave thee this letter?

Cost.   I told you: my lord.   101

Prin. To whom shouldst thou give it?

Cost.   From my lord to my lady.

Prin. From which lord to which lady?

Cost. From my Lord Berowne, a good master of
     mine,
To a lady of France that he call'd Rosaline.   105

Prin. Thou hast mistaken his letter. Come,
     lords, away.
[*To Rosaline.*] Here, sweet, put up this—'twill be
     thine another day.   [*Exeunt Princess and Train.*]

Boyet. Who is the shooter? Who is the shooter?

Ros.   Shall I teach you to know?

Boyet. Ay, my continent of beauty.

Ros.   Why, she that bears the bow.
Finely put off!   110

Boyet. My lady goes to kill horns, but if thou
     marry,
Hang me by the neck if horns that year miscarry.
Finely put on!

Ros. Well then I am the shooter.

Boyet.   And who is your deer?

---

41. **commonwealth:** common people.
42. **dig-you-den:** give you good evening.
56. **Break up:** cut up (a technical term in carving), i.e. open.   **capon:**
i.e. love letter (a play on French *poulet* in the same sense).
57. **mistook:** mis-taken, delivered to the wrong person (so also
mistaken in line 106).   **importeth:** concerns.
59. **Break . . . wax:** i.e. break the seal (with continuation of the
image in *capon*).   65. **illustrate:** illustrious.
65–66. **King . . . Zenelophon.** See note on I.ii.109–10.
66. **indubitate:** undoubted.
68. **annothanize:** anatomize, i.e. explain, interpret (?) or annotate,
gloss (?).   **vulgar:** vernacular.   69. **videlicet:** namely.
77. **catastrophe:** denouement, outcome.
82. **exchange:** obtain in exchange.   83. **tittles:** jots, points.

84. **expecting:** awaiting.   86. **industry:** zealous gallantry.
88. **Nemean lion:** the lion of Nemea, in Greece, slain by Hercules as
the first of his twelve labors.   91. **forage:** raging, ravening.
92. **strive:** resist.   93. **repasture:** food.
94. **What . . . feathers:** i.e. what kind of fine bird.
95. **vane:** weathervane (with play on *vain*).
96. **but I:** if I do not.   97. **erewhile:** i.e. so recently.
98. **keeps:** lives.
99. **phantasime:** one full of fantastic notions.   **Monarcho:** i.e. man
with a highly inflated sense of self-importance (from the nickname of a
hanger-on at court who had declared that he was monarch of the
world).   100. **To:** for.
107. **'twill . . . day:** i.e. your turn will come.
108. **shooter.** Many editors emend to *suitor* (then pronounced
shooter), but Boyet already knows (from lines 53, 104–5) that the
suitor is Berowne. As we know, the Princess is the shooter, and
Rosaline in line 114 only says *she* is the shooter to "take a shot" at
Boyet.   109. **continent:** container of all, sum of.
110. **put off:** answered, evaded.
112. **if . . . miscarry:** if there is a shortage of horns, i.e. if you don't
make your husband a cuckold.

Ros. If we choose by the horns, yourself come
not near.   115
Finely put on indeed!

Mar. You still wrangle with her, Boyet, and she
strikes at the brow.

Boyet. But she herself is hit lower. Have I hit
her now?

Ros. Shall I come upon thee with an old saying,
that was a man when King Pippen of France was a
little boy, as touching the hit it?   121

Boyet. So I may answer thee with one as old, that
was a woman when Queen Guinover of Britain was
a little wench, as touching the hit it.   124

Ros. [*Sings.*] Thou canst not hit it, hit it, hit it,
      Thou canst not hit it, my good man.

Boyet. [*Sings.*] And I cannot, cannot, cannot,
      And I cannot, another can.

                    Exeunt [*Rosaline and Katherine*].

Cost. By my troth, most pleasant. How both
did fit it!

Mar. A mark marvellous well shot, for they both
did hit [it].   130

Boyet. A mark! O, mark but that mark! a mark,
says my lady!
Let the mark have a prick in't, to mete at, if it may be.

Mar. Wide a' the bow-hand! I' faith, your hand
is out.

Cost. Indeed 'a must shoot nearer, or he'll ne'er
hit the clout.

Boyet. And if my hand be out, then belike your
hand is in.   135

Cost. Then will she get the upshoot by cleaving
the [pin].

Mar. Come, come, you talk greasily, your lips
grow foul.

Cost. She's too hard for you at pricks, sir, challenge her to bowl.

Boyet. I fear too much rubbing. Good night, my
good owl.   [*Exeunt Boyet and Maria.*] 139

Cost. By my soul, a swain, a most simple clown!
Lord, Lord, how the ladies and I have put him down!
O' my troth, most sweet jests, most incony vulgar
wit!   142
When it comes so smoothly off, so obscenely as it
were, so fit.

Armado [a' th' one] side—O, a most dainty man!
To see him walk before a lady and to bear her fan!
To see him kiss his hand! and how most sweetly 'a
will swear!   146
And his page a' t' other side, that handful of wit!
Ah, heavens, it is [a] most pathetical nit!

                         [*Shout*] *within.*
Sola, sola!   *Exit.*

[SCENE II]

Enter DULL, HOLOFERNES *the Pedant, and* NATHANIEL
[*from watching the hunt*].

Nath. Very reverent sport truly, and done in the
testimony of a good conscience.

Hol. The deer was (as you know) *sanguis*, in
blood, ripe as the pomewater, who now hangeth like
a jewel in the ear of *caelo*, the sky, the welkin, the   5
heaven, and anon falleth like a crab on the face of
terra, the soil, the land, the earth.

Nath. Truly, Master Holofernes, the epithites are
sweetly varied, like a scholar at the least; but, sir,
I assure ye it was a buck of the first head.   10

Hol. Sir Nathaniel, *haud credo.*

Dull. 'Twas not a haud credo, 'twas a pricket.

Hol. Most barbarous intimation! yet a kind of
insinuation, as it were *in via*, in way, of explication;
facere, as it were, replication, or rather *ostentare*, 15
to show, as it were, his inclination, after his un-
dressed, unpolished, uneducated, unpruned, untrained,
or rather unlettered, or ratherest unconfirmed fashion,
to insert again my *haud credo* for a deer.

Dull. I said the deer was not a haud credo, 'twas
a pricket.   21

Hol. Twice sod simplicity, *bis coctus!*
O thou monster Ignorance, how deformed dost thou
      look!

Nath. Sir, he hath never fed of the dainties that
      are bred in a book;   24
He hath not eat paper, as it were; he hath not drunk
ink; his intellect is not replenished; he is only an
animal, only sensible in the duller parts;
And such barren plants are set before us, that we
      thankful should be—

---

117. **still:** always. **strikes . . . brow:** (1) takes good aim; (2) taunts
you with being a cuckold.
118. **lower:** i.e. in the heart. **hit her:** read her situation accurately.
119. **come upon:** riposte against.
120. **a man:** i.e. already far from new. **Pippen:** Pepin (died 768),
father of Charlemagne.
121. **the hit it:** a popular catch, or round, to be sung dancing (with
obvious bawdy implication).
123. **Guinover.** Guinevere, legend has it, lived even earlier than Pepin;
in addition, Boyet has appropriately chosen the name of a woman
famous for being unfaithful to her husband.
132. **prick:** centre of the target, bull's-eye (with a bawdy quibble).
mete at: measure by, take aim at.
133. **Wide . . . bow-hand:** too far to the left. **out:** at fault, inaccurate.
134. **clout:** mark of cloth in the centre of the target.
136. **upshoot:** best shot. **pin:** i.e. the pin which held the clout.
137. **greasily:** grossly.
139. **rubbing:** in the game of bowls, encountering an obstacle.
142. **incony:** rare, fine.
143. **obscenely.** Whatever word Costard intends, this one describes
the preceding dialogue more accurately than he knows.

144. **dainty:** refined, elegant.
146. **swear.** A line to furnish the expected rhyme is presumably lost.
148. **pathetical nit:** touching little fellow. 149. **Sola:** a hunting cry.

IV.ii.1–2. **in the testimony:** with the warrant.
3–4. **in blood:** in excellent physical condition.
4. **pomewater:** a kind of apple.
4–6. **now . . . anon:** at one moment . . . at the next.
6. **crab:** crab apple. 8. **epithites:** epithets.
10. **buck . . . head:** a deer of the fifth year, with its first fully developed
antlers.
11. **Sir:** courtesy title for a priest. **haud credo:** I cannot believe it.
Dull misunderstands this as an assertion that the animal was a doe of
some kind. (A. L. Rowse, in the London *Times Literary Supplement*,
July 18, 1952, suggests that Dull hears *haud credo* as "awd (old)
gray doe.") 12. **pricket:** a deer of the second year.
13. **intimation:** intrusion.
15. **facere . . . replication:** to make . . . explanation.
18. **unconfirmed:** unconsolidated, i.e. his *fashion* is without the coherence proper to learning.
22. **Twice sod:** twice-seethed, i.e. twice-boiled (repeated in *bis coctus*),
probably referring to Dull's repeating his mistake. **simplicity:**
ignorance, rusticity.

Which we [of] taste and feeling are—for those parts
    that do fructify in us more than he.
For as it would ill become me to be vain, [indiscreet],
    or a fool,   30
So were there a patch set on learning, to see him in
    a school:
But *omne bene*, say I, being of an old father's mind:
Many can brook the weather that love not the wind.
    Dull. You two are book-men: can you tell me by
        your wit
What was a month old at Cain's birth, that's not
    five weeks old as yet?   35
    Hol. [Dictynna], goodman Dull, [Dictynna], good-
man Dull.
    Dull. What is [Dictynna]?
    Nath. A title to Phoebe, to Luna, to the moon.
    Hol. The moon was a month old when Adam was
    no more,
And raught not to five weeks when he came to five-
    score.   40
Th' allusion holds in the exchange.
    Dull. 'Tis true indeed, the collusion holds in the
exchange.
    Hol. God comfort thy capacity! I say, th' allu-
sion holds in the exchange.   45
    Dull. And I say, the pollution holds in the ex-
change, for the moon is never but a month old; and
I say beside that, 'twas a pricket that the Princess
kill'd.   49
    Hol. Sir Nathaniel, will you hear an extemporal
epitaph on the death of the deer? And to humor the
[ignorant, call I] the deer the Princess kill'd a pricket.
    Nath. *Perge*, good Master Holofernes, *perge*, so it
shall please you to abrogate squirility.
    Hol. I will something affect the letter, for it argues
facility.   55
The preyful Princess pierc'd and prick'd a pretty
    pleasing pricket;
Some say a sore, but not a sore, till now made sore
    with shooting.
The dogs did yell: put *l* to sore, then sorel jumps from
    thicket,
Or pricket sore, or else sorel; the people fall a-hooting.
If sore be sore, then L to sore makes fifty sores o' sorel:

Of one sore I an hundred make by adding but one
    more L.   61
    Nath. A rare talent!
    Dull. [*Aside.*] If a talent be a claw, look how he
claws him with a talent.   64
    [*Hol.*] This is a gift that I have, simple; simple,
a foolish extravagant spirit, full of forms, figures,
shapes, objects, ideas, apprehensions, motions, revolutions. These are begot in the ventricle of memory,
nourish'd in the womb of [pia mater], and delivered
upon the mellowing of occasion. But the gift is   70
good in those [in] whom it is acute, and I am thankful
for it.
    [*Nath.*] Sir, I praise the Lord for you, and so may
my parishioners, for their sons are well tutor'd by
you, and their daughters profit very greatly   75
under you. You are a good member of the commonwealth.
    [*Hol.*] *Mehercle*, if their sons be [ingenious], they
shall want no instruction; if their daughters be capable,
I will put it to them: but *vir* [*sapit*] *qui pauca loquitur.*
A soul feminine saluteth us.   81

    Enter JAQUENETTA *and the Clown* [COSTARD].

    Jaq. God give you good morrow, Master Person.
    [*Hol.*] Master Person, *quasi* [pers-one]. And if
one should be pierc'd, which is the one?
    Cost. Marry, Master Schoolmaster, he that is
likel'est to a hogshead.   86
    [*Hol.*] Of piercing a hogshead! a good lustre of
conceit in a turf of earth; fire enough for a flint,
pearl enough for a swine: 'tis pretty; it is well.
    Jaq. Good Master Person, be so good as read me
this letter. It was given me by Costard, and sent me
from Don Armado. I beseech you read it.   92
    [*Hol.*] *Facile, precor gelida quando* [*pecus omne*]
sub umbra ruminat, and so forth. Ah, good old
Mantuan! I may speak of thee as the traveller doth
of Venice: 96
    [*Venechia, Venechia*],
    Che non te [*vede*], *che non te* [*prechia*].
Old Mantuan, old Mantuan! who understandeth
thee not, loves thee not. *Ut, re, sol, la, mi, fa.* Under
pardon, sir, what are the contents? or rather, as
Horace says in his—What, my soul, verses?   102

---

29. **Which we:** we who.   **do fructify:** are fruitful.
31. **So . . . learning:** it would be putting a fool to learn (?) or it would
be setting a blemish on learning (?).
32. **omne bene:** all's well.   **an old father's mind:** the opinion of some
wise man of the past.
33. **brook:** endure. The proverb means that one must put up with
many things one does not like.
36. **Dictynna:** the moon (a rather rare classical name for her, appropriate in the mouth of the pedantic Holofernes).   **goodman:**
yeoman, or more generally any person below the rank of gentleman.
40. **raught:** reached.
41. **Th' allusion . . . exchange:** i.e. the riddle is not affected by the
substitution of Adam's name for Cain's.
42. **collusion:** Like *pollution* (line 46), another of Dull's "mistakings,"
but Shakespeare seems here to be commenting on the kind of in-game
that is being inflicted on Dull by Holofernes and Nathaniel.
50. **extemporal:** extempore.   53. **Perge:** proceed.
54. **abrogate squirility:** abstain from scurrility (with apparent reference to *pricket* = prick it).
55. **something:** somewhat.   **affect the letter:** use alliteration.
56. **preyful:** desirous of prey.   57. **sore:** a deer of the fourth year.
58. **sorel:** a deer of the third year.   59. **Or:** either.
60, 61. **L.** With reference to the Roman numeral for fifty.

63. **talent:** i.e. talon.   64. **claws:** scratches, i.e. flatters.
67. **motions:** impulses.
68. **ventricle of memory:** one of three divisions of the brain, supposed
to be the seat of memory.
69. **pia mater:** membrane surrounding the brain.
76. **under you:** under your instruction (with an equivoque carried on
in lines 79–80).   78. **Mehercle:** by Hercules.   79. **want:** lack.
80. **vir . . . loquitur:** that man is wise who speaks little.
82. **Person:** i.e. Parson.
83. **quasi:** as if, that is.   **pers-one:** i.e. pierce-one (*pierce* being
pronounced *perse*).
86. **likel'est:** likeliest, i.e. likest.   **hogshead.** "Piercing a hogshead"
was slang for getting drunk.
87–88. **lustre of conceit:** spark of imagination.
93–94. **Facile . . . ruminat.** The beginning of the first eclogue of
Mantuan, an Italian writer of pastorals who died in 1516. *Facile* is an
error for *Fauste*, and the line may be translated: "Faustus, while all
the cattle chew their cud in the cool shade." If the error is not a
misprint, Shakespeare is jibing at the pedant's Latin.
97–98. **Venechia . . . prechia:** Venice, Venice, he who has not seen
you cannot value you (a version of an Italian proverb).
100. **Ut . . . fa.** He sings the scale, in incorrect order. (*Ut* was the old
name for modern *do.*)

[*Nath.*]   Ay, sir, and very learned.

[*Hol.*]   Let me hear a staff, a stanze, a verse;
lege, domine.

[*Nath.*]   [*Reads.*]
"If love make me forsworn, how shall I swear to
    love?   105
Ah, never faith could hold, if not to beauty vowed!
Though to myself forsworn, to thee I'll faithful prove;
Those thoughts to me were oaks, to thee like osiers
    bowed.
Study his bias leaves, and makes his book thine eyes,
Where all those pleasures live that art would com-
    prehend.   110
If knowledge be the mark, to know thee shall suf-
    fice;
Well learned is that tongue that well can thee com-
    mend,
All ignorant that soul that sees thee without wonder;
Which is to me some praise that I thy parts admire.
Thy eye Jove's lightning bears, thy voice his dreadful
    thunder,   115
Which, not to anger bent, is music and sweet fire.
Celestial as thou art, O, pardon love this wrong,
That sings heaven's praise with such an earthly
    tongue."

Hol.   You find not the apostraphas, and so miss
the accent. Let me supervise the [canzonet]. [*He* 120
takes the letter.] Here are only numbers ratified, but for
the elegancy, facility, and golden cadence of poesy,
caret. Ovidius Naso was the man. And why indeed
"Naso," but for smelling out the odoriferous flowers
of fancy, the jerks of invention? *Imitari* is 125
nothing: so doth the hound his master, the ape his
keeper, the tired horse his rider. But, damosella virgin,
was this directed to you?

Jaq.   Ay, sir, from one Monsieur Berowne, one of
the strange queen's lords.   130

[*Hol.*]   I will overglance the superscript: "To
the snow-white hand of the most beauteous Lady
Rosaline." I will look again on the intellect of the
letter, for the nomination of the party [writing] to
the person written unto: "Your ladyship's in   135
all desired employment, Berowne." Sir [Nathaniel],
this Berowne is one of the votaries with the King, and
here he hath framed a letter to a sequent of the
stranger queen's, which accidentally, or by the way

of progression, hath miscarried. Trip and go,   140
my sweet, deliver this paper into the royal hand of
the King; it may concern much. Stay not thy compliment; I forgive thy duty. Adieu.

Jaq.   Good Costard, go with me. Sir, God save
your life!   145

Cost.   Have with thee, my girl.

                   Exit [*with Jaquenetta*].

[*Nath.*]   Sir, you have done this in the fear of God,
very religiously; and as a certain father saith—

Hol.   Sir, tell not me of the father, I do fear colorable colors. But to return to the verses: did they please
you, Sir Nathaniel?   151

Nath.   Marvellous well for the pen.

Hol.   I do dine to-day at the father's of a certain
pupil of mine, where, if (before repast) it shall please
you to gratify the table with a grace, I will, on   155
my privilege I have with the parents of the foresaid
child or pupil, undertake your *bien venuto*; where I
will prove those verses to be very unlearned, neither
savoring of poetry, wit, nor invention. I beseech your
society.   160

Nath.   And thank you too; for society, saith the
text, is the happiness of life.

Hol.   And certes the text most infallibly concludes it. [*To Dull.*] Sir, I do invite you too, you
shall not say me nay: *pauca verba*. Away, the   165
gentles are at their game, and we will to our recreation.

                         Exeunt.

[SCENE III]

Enter BEROWNE *with a paper in his hand, alone.*

Ber.   The King he is hunting the deer: I am coursing myself. They have pitch'd a toil: I am toiling in a
pitch—pitch that defiles—defile! a foul word. Well,
"set thee down, sorrow!" for so they say the fool
said, and so say I, and I the fool: well prov'd,   5
wit! By the Lord, this love is as mad as Ajax. It kills
sheep; it kills me, I a sheep: well prov'd again a' my
side! I will not love; if I do, hang me; i' faith, I will
not. O but her eye—by this light, but for her eye,
I would not love her; yes, for her two eyes.   10
Well, I do nothing in the world but lie, and lie in
my throat. By heaven, I do love, and it hath taught

---

104. staff, stanze. Both words mean "stanza."   **lege, domine:** read, master.
105–18. This sonnet was printed with some verbal changes in *The Passionate Pilgrim* (1599); so were the poems at IV.iii.58–71, 99–118 (the three being there numbered V, III, and XVI respectively).
108. to me were: i.e. which seemed to me as strong as.   **osiers:** willows.
109. Study . . . leaves: i.e. the student abandons his inclination (to learning).
119. find . . . apostraphas: disregard the marks indicating contractions. It has been suggested that Holofernes is reproving Nathaniel for reading *sings* when the metre of the last line requires *singès*, and that his technical term is therefore a blunder; but his complaint may be more general.   **120. supervise:** look over.
121. numbers ratified: verses metrically correct.
123. caret: it is lacking.   **124. Naso.** From Latin *nasus*, "nose."
125. jerks of invention: strokes of imagination.   **Imitari:** to imitate.
130. strange: foreign.   **131. superscript:** address, salutation.
133. intellect: meaning, i.e. contents.   **138. sequent:** follower.
139–40. by . . . progression: in going from hand to hand.

140. Trip and go: a common phrase, from a favorite song to accompany dancing.
142–43. Stay . . . compliment: do not take time for a polite leave taking.   **143. forgive thy duty:** waive the requirement of a curtsy.
146. Have with thee: I'll go with you.   **147. father:** church father.
149–50. colorable colors: plausible excuses.
152. for the pen: so far as the penmanship is concerned (cf. V.ii.40); or, perhaps, considering the writer (an example of the "learned" man's condescension to the courtier).   **155. gratify:** grace.
157. bien venuto: welcome (Italian *ben venuto*).
163. certes: certainly.   **165. pauca verba:** few words.
166. gentles: gentlefolk.

IV.iii.**1–2. coursing:** pursuing.   **2. pitch'd a toil:** set a snare.
2–3. toiling . . . pitch: a quibbling reference to Rosaline's eyes, which he has called two pitch-balls (III.i.197).
4. set thee down. See note on I.i.315.
6. mad as Ajax. Ajax, maddened by the refusal of the Greek leaders to give him the slain Achilles' armor, attacked a flock of sheep, thinking they were the Greek army.
11–12. in my throat: i.e. profoundly.

me to rhyme and to be mallicholy; and here is part
of my rhyme, and here my mallicholy. Well, she
hath one a' my sonnets already: the clown 15
bore it, the fool sent it, and the lady hath it: sweet
clown, sweeter fool, sweetest lady! By the world,
I would not care a pin, if the other three were in.
Here comes one with a paper, God give him 19
grace to groan! *He stands aside, [climbing into a tree].*

The KING *ent'reth [with a paper].*

King. Ay me!
Ber. [*Aside.*] Shot, by heaven! Proceed, sweet
Cupid, thou hast thump'd him with thy bird-bolt
under the left pap. In faith, secrets!
King. [*Reads.*]
"So sweet a kiss the golden sun gives not 25
To those fresh morning drops upon the rose,
As thy eye-beams, when their fresh rays have smote
The night of dew that on my cheeks down flows;
Nor shines the silver moon one half so bright
Through the transparent bosom of the deep, 30
As doth thy face through tears of mine give light.
Thou shin'st in every tear that I do weep,
No drop but as a coach doth carry thee;
So ridest thou triumphing in my woe.
Do but behold the tears that swell in me, 35
And they thy glory through my grief will show.
But do not love thyself, then thou [wilt] keep
My tears for glasses, and still make me weep.
O queen of queens, how far dost thou excel
No thought can think, nor tongue of mortal tell." 40
How shall she know my griefs? I'll drop the paper.
Sweet leaves, shade folly. Who is he comes here?

Enter LONGAVILLE *[with a paper]. The King steps aside.*

What, Longaville, and reading! Listen, ear.
Ber. [*Aside.*] Now in thy likeness, one more fool
appear!
Long. Ay me, I am forsworn! 45
Ber. [*Aside.*] Why, he comes in like a perjure,
wearing papers.
[*King.*] [*Aside.*] In love, I hope—sweet fellow-
ship in shame.
Ber. [*Aside.*] One drunkard loves another of the
name.
Long. Am I the first that have been perjur'd so?
Ber. [*Aside.*] I could put thee in comfort: not by
two that I know. 50
Thou makest the triumphery, the corner-cap of
society,
The shape of love's Tyburn that hangs up simplicity.
Long. I fear these stubborn lines lack power to
move.

O sweet Maria, empress of my love,
These numbers will I tear, and write in prose! 55
Ber. [*Aside.*] O, rhymes are guards on wanton
Cupid's hose:
Disfigure not his shop.
Long.   This same shall go. *He reads the sonnet.*
"Did not the heavenly rhetoric of thine eye,
'Gainst whom the world cannot hold argument,
Persuade my heart to this false perjury? 60
Vows for thee broke deserve not punishment.
A woman I forswore, but I will prove,
Thou being a goddess, I forswore not thee.
My vow was earthly, thou a heavenly love;
Thy grace being gain'd cures all disgrace in me. 65
Vows are but breath, and breath a vapor is;
Then thou, fair sun, which on my earth dost shine,
Exhal'st this vapor-vow; in thee it is.
If broken then, it is no fault of mine:
If by me broke, what fool is not so wise 70
To lose an oath to win a paradise?"
Ber. [*Aside.*] This is the liver-vein, which makes
flesh a deity,
A green goose a goddess; pure, pure [idolatry].
God amend us, God amend! we are much out a'
th' way. 74

Enter DUMAINE *[with a paper].*

Long. By whom shall I send this?—Company?
Stay.   [*Steps aside.*]
Ber. [*Aside.*] "All hid, all hid," an old infant play.
Like a demigod here sit I in the sky,
And wretched fools' secrets heedfully o'er-eye.
More sacks to the mill! O heavens, I have my wish!
Dumaine transformed! four woodcocks in a dish! 80
Dum. O most divine Kate!
Ber. [*Aside.*] O most profane coxcomb!
Dum. By heaven, the wonder in a mortal eye!
Ber. [*Aside.*] By earth, she is not, corporal,
there you lie.
Dum. Her amber hairs for foul hath amber coted.
Ber. [*Aside.*] An amber-color'd raven was well
noted. 86
Dum. As upright as the cedar.
Ber. [*Aside.*]   Stoop, I say,
Her shoulder is with child.
Dum.   As fair as day.
Ber. [*Aside.*] Ay, as some days, but then no sun
must shine.

13. **mallicholy:** melancholy.   18. **in:** i.e. in the same predicament.
23. **bird-bolt:** blunt arrow for killing birds. See note on I.ii.176.
24. **under . . . pap:** i.e. in the heart.
28. **night of dew:** night's allowance of tears.
38. **glasses:** mirrors.
46. **perjure:** perjurer.   **wearing papers.** Perjurers were sometimes
punished by being exposed to public view wearing paper placards
which set forth their offenses.
51. **triumphery:** triumvirate (an apparently unique variant of
triumviry).   **corner-cap:** three-cornered cap.
52. **Tyburn:** the site of public executions in London. There are many
references to its triangular gallows.

56. **guards:** trimmings.   **hose:** breeches.
57. **shop:** codpiece (slang).   58–71. See the note on IV.ii.105–18.
59. **whom:** which.   65. **grace:** favor.   68. **Exhal'st:** drawest up.
71. **To:** as to.
72. **liver-vein:** the style and manner of men in love (the liver being the
supposed seat of the affections).
73. **green goose:** young goose, i.e. gawky young girl.
74. **much . . . way:** gone far astray.
76. **All hid.** Alluding to the game of hide and seek.
79. **More . . . mill:** i.e. there's more to come (proverbial).
80. **woodcocks.** Proverbially silly birds.
84. **she . . . corporal:** i.e. field officer in Cupid's army (cf. III.i.187).
85. **coted:** quoted, i.e. set down as, caused to be regarded as. Her
amber-colored hair has made amber seem ugly by comparison.
86. **raven.** A quibble on *foul/fowl.*   **well noted:** accurately observed
(ironic).
87. **Stoop:** stooped (perhaps also suggesting that Dumaine should
come down to earth).
88. **is with child:** i.e. is humped.

Dum. O that I had my wish!
Long. [*Aside.*]   And I had mine! 90
King. [*Aside.*] And mine too, good Lord!
Ber. [*Aside.*] Amen, so I had mine. Is not that a
good word?
Dum. I would forget her, but a fever she
Reigns in my blood, and will rememb'red be.
Ber. [*Aside.*] A fever in your blood! why then
incision   95
Would let her out in saucers. Sweet misprision!
Dum. Once more I'll read the ode that I have writ.
Ber. [*Aside.*] Once more I'll mark how love can
vary wit.
Dum. (*Reads his sonnet.*)
    "On a day—alack the day!—
    Love, whose month is ever May,   100
    Spied a blossom passing fair
    Playing in the wanton air:
    Through the velvet leaves the wind,
    All unseen, can passage find;
    That the lover, sick to death,   105
    [Wish'd] himself the heavens' breath.
    Air, quoth he, thy cheeks may blow;
    Air, would I might triumph so!
    But, alack, my hand is sworn
    Ne'er to pluck thee from thy [thorn];   110
    Vow, alack, for youth unmeet,
    Youth so apt to pluck a sweet.
    Do not call it sin in me,
    That I am forsworn for thee;
    Thou for whom Jove would swear   115
    Juno but an Ethiop were,
    And deny himself for Jove,
    Turning mortal for thy love."
This will I send and something else more plain
That shall express my true love's fasting pain. 120
O would the King, Berowne, and Longaville
Were lovers too! Ill, to example ill,
Would from my forehead wipe a perjur'd note:
For none offend where all alike do dote.
Long. [*Advancing.*] Dumaine, thy love is far from
charity,   125
That in love's grief desir'st society:
You may look pale, but I should blush, I know,
To be o'erheard and taken napping so.
King. [*Advancing.*] Come, sir, you blush; as his
your case is such;
You chide at him, offending twice as much.   130
You do not love Maria? Longaville
Did never sonnet for her sake compile,
Nor never lay his wreathed arms athwart
His loving bosom to keep down his heart.
I have been closely shrouded in this bush   135
And mark'd you both, and for you both did blush.

I heard your guilty rhymes, observ'd your fashion,
Saw sighs reek from you, noted well your passion.
"Ay me!" says one, "O Jove!" the other cries;   139
One, her hairs were gold, crystal the other's eyes.
[*To Longaville.*] You would for paradise break faith
and troth,
[*To Dumaine.*] And Jove for your love would in-
fringe an oath.
What will Berowne say when that he shall hear
Faith infringed, which such zeal did swear?
How will he scorn! how will he spend his wit!   145
How will he triumph, leap, and laugh at it!
For all the wealth that ever I did see,
I would not have him know so much by me.
Ber. Now step I forth to whip hypocrisy.
            [*Descending and advancing.*]
Ah, good my liege, I pray thee pardon me!   150
Good heart, what grace hast thou thus to reprove
These worms for loving, that art most in love?
Your eyes do make no [coaches;] in your tears
There is no certain princess that appears;
You'll not be perjur'd, 'tis a hateful thing;   155
Tush, none but minstrels like of sonneting!
But are you not asham'd? Nay, are you not,
All three of you, to be thus much o'ershot?
You found his mote, the King your mote did see;
But I a beam do find in each of three.   160
O, what a scene of fool'ry have I seen,
Of sighs, of groans, of sorrow, and of teen!
O me, with what strict patience have I sat,
To see a king transformed to a gnat!
To see great Hercules whipping a gig,   165
And profound Salomon to tune a jig,
And Nestor play at push-pin with the boys,
And critic Timon laugh at idle toys!
Where lies thy grief, O, tell me, good Dumaine?
And, gentle Longaville, where lies thy pain?   170
And where my liege's? All about the breast!
A caudle ho!
King.   Too bitter is thy jest.
Are we betrayed thus to thy over-view?
Ber. Not you by me, but I betrayed to you:
I that am honest, I that hold it sin   175
To break the vow I am engaged in.
I am betrayed by keeping company
With men like [you], men of inconstancy.
When shall you see me write a thing in rhyme,
Or groan for Joan, or spend a minute's time   180
In pruning me? When shall you hear that I

---

92. **a good word:** i.e. kind.   95. **incision:** bloodletting.
96. **saucers:** bowls used to receive the blood.   **misprision:** mistake.
99–118. See note on IV.ii.105–18.   102. **wanton:** frolicsome.
104. **can:** gan, i.e. began to, did.   105. **That:** so that.
116. **Ethiop:** blackamoor.   120. **fasting:** caused by abstinence.
122. **example:** furnish a precedent for.
123. **perjur'd note.** See note on IV.iii.46.
125. **charity:** Christian love.
133. **wreathed arms.** See note on III.i.18.

138. **reek:** smoke.   145. **spend:** employ.   148. **by:** about.
153–54. **Your . . . appears.** Alluding to the King's sonnet (IV.iii.32–33).
158. **o'ershot:** wide of the mark, in error.
159. **You:** i.e. Longaville.   **his:** i.e. Dumaine's.
159,160. **mote, beam.** See Matthew 7:3–5: "And why seest thou the
mote that is in thy brother's eye, but perceivest not the beam that is
in thine own eye?" (Geneva).   162. **teen:** grief.
164. **gnat:** i.e. an insignificant little creature (perhaps quibbling on
"moth," which was pronounced *mote* [line 159]).   165. **gig:** top.
166. **Salomon:** Solomon, proverbial for wisdom.   **tune:** play.
167. **Nestor:** oldest and wisest of the Greeks in the Trojan war.
push-pin: a child's game with pins.
168. **critic:** cynic, censorious.   **Timon.** Noted for his misanthropy.
laugh . . . toys: take pleasure in foolish trifles.
172. **caudle:** a warm, thin gruel given to the sick.
176. **engaged in:** sworn to.   181. **pruning:** preening, dressing up.

Will praise a hand, a foot, a face, an eye,
A gait, a state, a brow, a breast, a waist,
A leg, a limb—
   King.   Soft, whither away so fast?
A true man, or a thief, that gallops so?   185
   Ber.   I post from love; good lover, let me go.

      Enter JAQUENETTA *and Clown* [COSTARD].

   Jaq.   God bless the King!
   King.   What present hast thou there?
   Cost.   Some certain treason.
   King.   What makes treason here?
   Cost.   Nay, it makes nothing, sir.
   King.   If it mar nothing neither,
The treason and you go in peace away together.   190
   Jaq.   I beseech your Grace let this letter be read:
Our person misdoubts it; 'twas treason, he said.
   King.   Berowne, read it over.
               He [*Berowne*] *reads the letter.*
               Where hadst thou it?
   Jaq.   Of Costard.
   King.   Where hadst thou it?
   Cost.   Of Dun Adramadio, Dun Adramadio.   195
              [*Berowne tears the letter.*]
   King.   How now, what is in you? Why dost thou
    tear it?
   Ber.   A toy, my liege, a toy; your Grace needs not
    fear it.
   Long.   It did move him to passion, and therefore
    let's hear it.
   Dum.   [*Gathering up the pieces.*] It is Berowne's
    writing, and here is his name.
   Ber.   [*To Costard.*] Ah, you whoreson loggerhead,
    you were born to do me shame.   200
Guilty, my lord, guilty! I confess, I confess.
   King.   What?
   Ber.   That you three fools lack'd me fool to make
    up the mess.
He, he, and you—and you, my liege!—and I,
Are pick-purses in love, and we deserve to die.   205
O, dismiss this audience, and I shall tell you more.
   Dum.   Now the number is even.
   Ber.   True, true, we are four.
Will these turtles be gone?
   King.   Hence, sirs, away!
   Cost.   Walk aside the true folk, and let the traitors
    stay.   [*Exeunt Costard and Jaquenetta.*]   209
   Ber.   Sweet lords, sweet lovers, O, let us embrace!
As true we are as flesh and blood can be.
The sea will ebb and flow, heaven show his face;
Young blood doth not obey an old decree.
We cannot cross the cause why we were born;
Therefore of all hands must we be forsworn.   215
   King.   What, did these rent lines show some love
    of thine?

   Ber.   Did they, quoth you? Who sees the heavenly
    Rosaline,
That (like a rude and savage man of Inde),
At the first op'ning of the gorgeous east,
Bows not his vassal head, and strooken blind,   220
Kisses the base ground with obedient breast?
What peremptory eagle-sighted eye
Dares look upon the heaven of her brow,
That is not blinded by her majesty?
   King.   What zeal, what fury, hath inspir'd thee
    now?   225
My love (her mistress) is a gracious moon,
She (an attending star) scarce seen a light.
   Ber.   My eyes are then no eyes, nor I Berowne.
O, but for my love, day would turn to night!
Of all complexions the cull'd sovereignty   230
Do meet as at a fair in her fair cheek,
Where several worthies make one dignity,
Where nothing wants that want itself doth seek.
Lend me the flourish of all gentle tongues—
Fie, painted rhetoric! O, she needs it not.   235
To things of sale a seller's praise belongs:
She passes praise, then praise too short doth blot.
A wither'd hermit, fivescore winters worn,
Might shake off fifty, looking in her eye:
Beauty doth varnish age, as if new born,   240
And gives the crutch the cradle's infancy.
O, 'tis the sun that maketh all things shine!
   King.   By heaven, thy love is black as ebony.
   Ber.   Is ebony like her? O [wood] divine!
A wife of such wood were felicity.   245
O, who can give an oath? Where is a book?
That I may swear beauty doth beauty lack,
If that she learn not of her eye to look:
No face is fair that is not full so black.
   King.   O paradox! Black is the badge of hell,   250
The hue of dungeons, and the school of night;
And beauty's crest becomes the heavens well.
   Ber.   Devils soonest tempt, resembling spirits of
    light.
O, if in black my lady's brows be deck'd,
It mourns that painting [and] usurping hair   255
Should ravish doters with a false aspect:
And therefore is she born to make black fair.

183. **state:** attitude, pose.   185. **true:** honest.   186. **post:** hasten.
187. **present:** i.e. writing.   188. **makes treason:** has treason to do.
192. **person:** parson. Actually, at IV.ii.140–42 it is Holofernes, not
Nathaniel, who comments on the letter, and treason is not mentioned,
but there is confusion in the text at that point (see the Textual Notes).
misdoubts: suspects.   203. **mess:** group of four at table.
205. **pick-purses:** i.e. cheaters.   208. **turtles:** turtledoves, lovers.
214. **cross . . . born:** i.e. hold out against love.
215. **of all hands:** in any case.

218. **rude:** ignorant.   **Inde:** India.   220. **strooken:** struck.
222. **peremptory:** determined.   **eagle-sighted.** The eagle was thought
to be able to gaze directly at the sun.
227. **scarce . . . light:** a light hardly to be seen.
230. **cull'd sovereignty:** those selected as supreme.
232. **worthies:** excellencies, i.e. beauties.   **dignity:** i.e. surpassing
beauty.
233. **wants . . . want:** is lacking . . . desire.
234. **flourish:** eloquence, embellishment.   **gentle:** noble.
235. **painted:** artificial.   236. **of sale:** for sale.
237. **She . . . blot:** i.e. she exceeds anything that can be said in her
praise; hence any praise of her will inevitably fall short, and be a
blemish instead of an ornament.   246. **book:** Bible.
248. **of her eye:** i.e. from Rosaline's black eyes.   **to look:** i.e. how
beauty should look.   249. **full so:** just as.
250. **badge of hell.** Devils were regularly represented as black.
251. **school of night.** Many emendations have been proposed for
school, but the phrase may allude to a group of writers whose chief
patron was Sir Walter Raleigh, a group that was called "Sir Walter
Rauley's Schoole of Atheisme."
252. **And beauty's crest:** but the badge of beauty (the sun?).
253. **Devils . . . light.** Cf. 2 Corinthians 11:14: "Satan himself is
transformed into an angel of light."   255. **usurping:** i.e. false.

Her favor turns the fashion of the days,
For native blood is counted painting now;
And therefore red, that would avoid dispraise, 260
Paints itself black, to imitate her brow.

 Dum. To look like her are chimney-sweepers black.

 Long. And since her time are colliers counted bright.

 King. And Ethiops of their sweet complexion crack.

 Dum. Dark needs no candles now, for dark is light. 265

 Ber. Your mistresses dare never come in rain,
For fear their colors should be wash'd away.

 King. 'Twere good yours did; for, sir, to tell you plain,
I'll find a fairer face not wash'd to-day. 269

 Ber. I'll prove her fair, or talk till doomsday here.

 King. No devil will fright thee then so much as she.

 Dum. I never knew man hold vile stuff so dear.

 Long. Look, here's thy love [*showing his boot*], my foot and her face see.

 Ber. O, if the streets were paved with thine eyes,
Her feet were much too dainty for such tread! 275

 Dum. O vile! then as she goes what upward lies
The street should see as she walk'd overhead.

 King. But what of this, are we not all in love?

 Ber. O, nothing so sure, and thereby all forsworn.

 King. Then leave this chat, and, good Berowne, now prove 280
Our loving lawful, and our faith not torn.

 Dum. Ay marry, there—some flattery for this evil.

 Long. O, some authority how to proceed;
Some tricks, some quillets, how to cheat the devil.

 Dum. Some salve for perjury.

 Ber.   O, 'tis more than need.
Have at you then, affection's men-at-arms. 286
Consider what you first did swear unto:
To fast, to study, and to see no woman—
Flat treason 'gainst the kingly state of youth.
Say, can you fast? Your stomachs are too young, 290
And abstinence engenders maladies.
⟨And where that you have vow'd to study, lords,
In that each of you have forsworn his book,
Can you still dream and pore and thereon look?
For when would you, my lord, or you, or you, 295
Have found the ground of study's excellence
Without the beauty of a woman's face?
From women's eyes this doctrine I derive:
They are the ground, the books, the academes, 299
From whence doth spring the true Promethean fire.

Why, universal plodding poisons up
The nimble spirits in the arteries,
As motion and long-during action tires
The sinowy vigor of the traveller.
Now for not looking on a woman's face, 305
You have in that forsworn the use of eyes,
And study too, the causer of your vow.
For where is any author in the world
Teaches such beauty as a woman's eye?
Learning is but an adjunct to ourself, 310
And where we are, our learning likewise is.
Then when ourselves we see in ladies' eyes,
With ourselves,
Do we not likewise see our learning there?⟩
O, we have made a vow to study, lords, 315
And in that vow we have forsworn our books.
For when would you, my liege, or you, or you,
In leaden contemplation have found out
Such fiery numbers as the prompting eyes
Of beauty's tutors have enrich'd you with? 320
Other slow arts entirely keep the brain;
And therefore, finding barren practicers,
Scarce show a harvest of their heavy toil;
But love, first learned in a lady's eyes,
Lives not alone immured in the brain, 325
But with the motion of all elements,
Courses as swift as thought in every power,
And gives to every power a double power,
Above their functions and their offices.
It adds a precious seeing to the eye: 330
A lover's eyes will gaze an eagle blind.
A lover's ear will hear the lowest sound,
When the suspicious head of theft is stopp'd.
Love's feeling is more soft and sensible
Than are the tender horns of cockled snails. 335
Love's tongue proves dainty Bacchus gross in taste.
For valor, is not Love a Hercules,
Still climbing trees in the Hesperides?
Subtile as Sphinx, as sweet and musical
As bright Apollo's lute, strung with his hair. 340
And when Love speaks, the voice of all the gods
Make heaven drowsy with the harmony.
Never durst poet touch a pen to write
Until his ink were temp'red with Love's sighs:
O then his lines would ravish savage ears 345
And plant in tyrants mild humility.
From women's eyes this doctrine I derive:

301. **up:** completely.
302. **spirits ... arteries.** The "spirits" that were thought to give life to man—natural (seated in the liver), vital (the heart), and animal (the brain)—supposedly coursed through the arteries.
303. **long-during:** long-continued. 304. **sinowy:** sinewy, muscular.
318. **leaden:** dull.
319. **fiery numbers:** i.e. the sonnets and other poems or verses.
321. **arts:** branches of knowledge. **keep:** remain in, dwell.
329. **Above ... offices:** over and above their usual functions (*functions* and *offices* are synonyms).
331. **gaze ... blind.** See the note on line 222.
333. **the suspicious ... stopp'd:** i.e. even the ears of a thief, apprehensive of danger, are deaf. 334. **sensible:** sensitive.
335. **cockled:** having a shell. With the line cf. *Venus and Adonis*, lines 1033–34.
338. **Hesperides:** i.e. the garden (as misunderstood by the Elizabethans) in which the golden apples grew, watched by the daughters of Hesperus. The last of Hercules' twelve labors was to gain possession of the fruit. 341. **voice:** i.e. responsive songs.

258. **favor:** face.
259. **native blood:** natural color. **counted:** accounted, taken to be.
264. **crack:** boast. 271. **then:** i.e. at doomsday.
284. **quillets:** verbal niceties, quibbles.
286. **Have at you:** here goes. **affection's:** love's.
289. **state:** majesty, power.
292–314. These lines are a first-draft version of part of lines 315–62.
293. **book:** true book, i.e. woman's face.
296. **ground:** basis, foundation.
300. **Promethean fire:** i.e. divine fire; from the legend that Prometheus stole fire from heaven and gave it to man.

They sparkle still the right Promethean fire;
They are the books, the arts, the academes,
That show, contain, and nourish all the world,   350
Else none at all in aught proves excellent.
Then fools you were these women to forswear,
Or keeping what is sworn, you will prove fools.
For wisdom's sake, a word that all men love,
Or for love's sake, a word that loves all men,   355
Or for men's sake, the [authors] of these women,
Or women's sake, by whom we men are men,
[Let] us once lose our oaths to find ourselves,
Or else we lose ourselves to keep our oaths.
It is religion to be thus forsworn: 360
For charity itself fulfills the law,
And who can sever love from charity?

    King. Saint Cupid, then! and, soldiers, to the field!
    Ber. Advance your standards, and upon them,
      lords;
Pell-mell, down with them! but be first advis'd,   365
In conflict that you get the sun of them.
    Long. Now to plain-dealing, lay these glozes by:
Shall we resolve to woo these girls of France?
    King. And win them too; therefore let us devise
Some entertainment for them in their tents.   370
    Ber. First, from the park let us conduct them
      thither;
Then homeward every man attach the hand
Of his fair mistress. In the afternoon
We will with some strange pastime solace them,
Such as the shortness of the time can shape,   375
For revels, dances, masks, and merry hours
Forerun fair Love, strewing her way with flowers.
    King. Away, away, no time shall be omitted
That will be time, and may by us be fitted.
    Ber. [*Allons! allons!*] Sow'd cockle reap'd no corn,
And justice always whirls in equal measure: 381
Light wenches may prove plagues to men forsworn;
If so, our copper buys no better treasure.   [*Exeunt.*]

[ACT V, Scene I]

Enter the Pedant [Holofernes], *the Curate* [Sir Na-
thaniel], *and* Dull.

    Hol. Satis quid sufficit.
    Nath. I praise God for you, sir. Your reasons at
dinner have been sharp and sententious: pleasant
without scurrility, witty without affection, audacious
without impudency, learned without opinion, and   5
strange without heresy. I did converse this *quondam*
day with a companion of the King's, who is intituled,
nominated, or called, Don Adriano de Armado.
    Hol. Novi [*hominem*] tanquam te. His humor is
lofty, his discourse peremptory, his tongue filed,   10
his eye ambitious, his gait majestical, and his general
behavior vain, ridiculous, and thrasonical. He is too
picked, too spruce, too affected, too odd as it were,
too peregrinate, as I may call it.
    Nath. A most singular and choice epithet.   15
          Draw out his table-book.
    Hol. He draweth out the thread of his verbosity
finer than the staple of his argument. I abhor such
fanatical phantasimes, such insociable and point-
devise companions, such rackers of ortography, as to
speak "dout," fine, when he should say "doubt";   20
"det," when he should pronounce "debt"—*d, e, b, t,*
not *d, e, t:* he clepeth a calf, "cauf"; half, "hauf";
neighbor *vocatur* "nebor"; neigh abbreviated "ne."
This is abhominable—which he would call "abbom-
inable"; it insinuateth me of [*insanie*]: *ne intelligis,*   25
domine? to make frantic, lunatic.
    Nath. Laus Deo, [*bone*] intelligo.
    Hol. [*Bone? bone* for *bene,*] Priscian a little
scratch'd, 'twill serve.

Enter Braggart [Armado], *Boy* [Moth, *and* Costard].

    Nath. Videsne quis venit?   30
    Hol. Video, et gaudeo.
    Arm. [*To Moth.*] Chirrah!
    Hol. [*Quare*] chirrah, not sirrah?
    Arm. Men of peace, well encount'red.
    Hol. Most military sir, salutation.   35
    Moth. [*Aside to Costard.*] They have been at a
great feast of languages, and stol'n the scraps.
    Cost. O, they have liv'd long on the alms-basket of
words. I marvel thy master hath not eaten thee for
a word, for thou art not so long by the head as   40

---

355. **loves.** Variously glossed, for example as "is a friend to," "is lovable to," "sets a value upon," "inspires with love."
361. **For . . . law.** Cf. Romans 13:8: "he that loveth another hath fulfilled the law."
366. **get . . . them:** i.e. get the sun in their eyes; hence, get the advantage of them.   367. **glozes:** pretenses, sophistries.
372. **attach:** seize.
380. **Allons:** come.   **cockle:** i.e. weeds.   **corn:** grain.
381. **measure:** proportion.   382. **Light:** frivolous.
383. **copper:** base coin.

V.i.1. **Satis quid sufficit:** properly, *satis (est) quod sufficit,* enough is as good as a feast. Some editors correct Holofernes' faulty Latin; others suppose a satiric intent on Shakespeare's part (see note on IV.ii.93–94).   2. **reasons:** discourses.
3. **sharp:** acute, subtle.   **sententious:** pithy.
4. **affection:** affectation.   **audacious:** spirited, bold (in a good sense).

5. **opinion:** self-conceit, arrogance.
6. **strange:** new, fresh.   **this quondam:** the other.
7. **intituled:** entitled.
9. **Novi . . . te:** I know the man as well as I know you.   **humor:** mental disposition.
10. **peremptory:** overbearing.   **filed:** polished.
11. **majestical:** stately.   12. **thrasonical:** boastful.
13. **picked:** fastidious.   14. **peregrinate:** foreign.
15. **singular:** unmatched.   s.d. **table-book:** notebook.
17. **staple:** fibre.   **argument:** subject matter.
18. **fanatical:** extravagant.   **phantasimes:** fantastic fellows.   **insociable:** not companionable.
18–19. **point-devise:** extremely precise.
19. **rackers of ortography:** tormentors of orthography. Holofernes represents the group of Renaissance educators who sought to bring the spelling and pronunciation of English words as close as possible to their Latin originals.   20. **fine:** mincingly.   22. **clepeth:** calls.
23. **vocatur:** is called.
25. **it . . . insanie:** (1) it suggests insanity to me; (2) it introduces frenzy into me (i.e. it drives me frantic).
25–26. **ne intelligis, domine:** do you understand, master.
27. **Laus . . . intelligo:** God be praised, I understand well.
28–29. **Priscian . . . scratch'd:** i.e. your Latin is a little faulty. Priscian's grammars (written about the beginning of the sixth century) were considered standard.
30. **Videsne quis venit:** do you see who comes.
31. **Video, et gaudeo:** I see and rejoice.   33. **Quare:** why.
38. **alms-basket:** baskets in which scraps were collected for the poor, i.e. public charity.

Love's
Labor's
Lost
V.i

honorificabilitudinitatibus: thou art easier swallow'd than a flap-dragon.

Moth. Peace, the peal begins.

Arm. [*To Holofernes.*] Monsieur, are you not lett'red?   45

Moth. Yes, yes, he teaches boys the horn-book. What is *a, b,* spell'd backward, with the horn on his head?

Hol. *Ba, pueritia,* with a horn added.   49

Moth. *Ba,* most silly sheep, with a horn. You hear his learning.

Hol. *Quis, quis,* thou consonant?

Moth. The last of the five vowels, if "you" repeat them; or the fift, if I.

Hol. I will repeat them—*a, e, I*—   55

Moth. The sheep: the other two concludes it—*o, U.*

Arm. Now by the salt [wave] of the Mediterraneum, a sweet touch, a quick venue of wit—snip, snap, quick and home. It rejoiceth my intellect. True wit!   61

Moth. Offer'd by a child to an old man: which is wit-old.

Hol. What is the figure? What is the figure?

Moth. Horns.   65

Hol. Thou disputes like an infant; go whip thy gig.

Moth. Lend me your horn to make one, and I will whip about your infamy, [*manu*] *cita*—a gig of a cuckold's horn.   70

Cost. And I had but one penny in the world, thou shouldst have it to buy gingerbread. Hold, there is the very remuneration I had of thy master, thou halfpenny purse of wit, thou pigeon-egg of discretion. O, and the heavens were so pleas'd that   75
thou wert but my bastard, what a joyful father wouldest thou make me! Go to, thou hast it *ad dunghill,* at the fingers' ends, as they say.

Hol. O, I smell false Latin, "dunghill" for *unguem.*   80

Arm. Arts-man, preambulate, we will be singuled from the barbarous. Do you not educate youth at the charge-house on the top of the mountain?

Hol. Or *mons,* the hill.   84

Arm. At your sweet pleasure, for the mountain.

Hol. I do, *sans question.*

Arm. Sir, it is the King's most sweet pleasure and affection to congratulate the Princess at her pavilion in the posteriors of this day, which the rude multitude call the afternoon.   90

Hol. The posterior of the day, most generous sir, is liable, congruent, and measurable for the afternoon. The word is well cull'd, chose, sweet, and apt, I do assure you, sir, I do assure.   94

Arm. Sir, the King is a noble gentleman, and my familiar, I do assure ye, very good friend; for what is inward between us, let it pass. I do beseech thee remember thy courtesy; I beseech thee apparel thy head; and among other [importunate] and most serious designs, and of great import indeed 100
too—but let that pass; for I must tell thee it will please his Grace (by the world) sometime to lean upon my poor shoulder, and with his royal finger, thus, dally with my excrement, with my mustachio; but, sweet heart, let that pass. By the world, I 105
recount no fable: some certain special honors it pleaseth his greatness to impart to Armado, a soldier, a man of travel, that hath seen the world; but let that pass. The very all of all is—but, sweet heart, I do implore secrety—that the King would have me present 110
the Princess (sweet chuck) with some delightful ostentation, or show, or pageant, or antic, or firework. Now, understanding that the curate and your sweet self are good at such eruptions and sudden breaking out of mirth (as it were), I have acquainted you withal, to the end to crave your assistance.   116

Hol. Sir, you shall present before her the Nine Worthies. Sir [Nathaniel], as concerning some entertainment of time, some show in the posterior of this day, to be [rend'red] by our [assistance,] the 120
King's command, and this most gallant, illustrate, and learned gentleman, before the Princess, I say none so fit as to present the Nine Worthies.

Nath. Where will you find men worthy enough to present them?   125

Hol. Joshua, yourself; myself; and this gallant gentleman, Judas Machabeus; this swain (because of

---

41. **honorificabilitudinitatibus:** dative (or ablative) plural of a medieval Latin word meaning "the state of being loaded with honors"; "often mentioned as the longest word known" (Johnson).
42. **flap-dragon:** a flaming raisin floating on wine or ale, to be snapped up with the mouth.   43. **peal:** peal of bells, i.e. babble of tongues.
45. **lett'red:** i.e. an educated man.
46. **horn-book:** printed sheet of paper, protected by a thin sheet of transparent horn, from which children learned their letters.
49. **pueritia:** childishness, child.
52. **Quis:** who.   **consonant:** i.e. nonentity, since a consonant requires a vowel to turn it into a pronounceable syllable.
53. **last.** Many editors emend to *third,* but they miss the jest. Moth is answering the question "Who is a sheep?" and (as David points out) "To Moth, Holofernes remains 'you' (and thus the sheep) no matter who repeats the vowels."   54. **fift:** fifth.
56. **concludes it:** (1) proves my contention; (2) completes the list of vowels.   57. **o, U:** oh, you.   59. **touch:** stroke.   **venue:** thrust.
60. **home:** to the point aimed at.
63. **wit-old.** With a quibble on *wittol,* a contented cuckold.
64. **figure:** figure of speech.   66. **disputes:** reasonest.
67. **gig:** top.   69. **manu cita:** with ready hand.
74. **halfpenny purse:** tiny purse just large enough for a small coin.
79–80. [ad] unguem: to a nicety, perfectly (literally, to the nail).
81. **Arts-man:** scholar.   **preambulate:** walk ahead (with me).
singuled: separated, singled out.   83. **charge-house:** school.

86. **sans:** without.   88. **congratulate:** give pleasure to.
91. **generous:** well-born.
92. **liable, congruent, and measurable.** All synonyms, meaning "suitable, fit."
93. **chose:** (well) chosen. Many editors read *choice,* following F2.
96. **familiar:** intimate friend.   97. **inward:** confidential, private.
98. **remember thy courtesy:** i.e. remember that you have removed your hat (see line 35).   101. **let that pass:** never mind about that.
104. **excrement:** outgrowth (of hair; used also of fingernails).
109. **all of all:** sum of all.   110. **secrety:** secrecy.
111. **chuck:** chick (a term of endearment).
112. **ostentation:** spectacular show.   **antic:** pageant or other entertainment with the characters in grotesque or fantastic costumes.
117–118. **Nine Worthies:** a group of nine famous conquerors often mentioned in literature or represented in pageants and plays. The usual list comprised three pagans, Hector of Troy, Alexander the Great, and Julius Caesar; three Jews, Joshua, David, and Judas Maccabeus; and three Christians, King Arthur, Charlemagne, and Godfrey of Bouillon. The list varied, but Hercules and Pompey make their first recorded appearance in it in Holofernes' next speech.
123. **present:** represent.
126–27. **Joshua . . . Machabeus.** Possibly an unrevised draft, since Holofernes assigns himself no role, and Nathaniel and Armado eventually play Alexander and Hector respectively.

his great limb or joint) shall pass Pompey the Great;
the page, Hercules.   129

Arm. Pardon, sir, error: he is not quantity
enough for that Worthy's thumb, he is not so big
as the end of his club.

Hol. Shall I have audience? He shall present
Hercules in minority; his enter and exit shall be   134
strangling a snake; and I will have an apology for
that purpose.

Moth. An excellent device! so if any of the
audience hiss, you may cry, "Well done, Hercules,
now thou crushest the snake!" That is the way to
make an offense gracious, though few have the grace
to do it.   141

Arm. For the rest of the Worthies?

Hol. I will play three myself.

Moth. Thrice-worthy gentleman!

Arm. Shall I tell you a thing?   145

Hol. We attend.

Arm. We will have, if this fadge not, an antic.
I beseech you follow.

Hol. *Via,* goodman Dull! thou hast spoken no
word all this while.   150

Dull. Nor understood none neither, sir.

Hol. [*Allons!*] we will employ thee.

Dull. I'll make one in a dance, or so; or I will
play
On the tabor to the Worthies, and let them dance
        the hay.   154

Hol. Most dull, honest Dull! to our sport; away!
                                            Exeunt.

[SCENE II]

Enter the Ladies: [*the* PRINCESS, MARIA, KATHERINE,
and ROSALINE].

Prin. Sweet hearts, we shall be rich ere we depart,
If fairings come thus plentifully in.
A lady wall'd about with diamonds!
Look you what I have from the loving King.   4

Ros. Madam, came nothing else along with that?

Prin. Nothing but this? Yes, as much love in
        rhyme
As would be cramm'd up in a sheet of paper,
Writ a' both sides the leaf, margent and all,
That he was fain to seal on Cupid's name.

Ros. That was the way to make his godhead
        wax,   10
For he hath been five thousand year a boy.

Kath. Ay, and a shrowd unhappy gallows too.

Ros. You'll ne'er be friends with him, 'a kill'd
        your sister.

Kath. He made her melancholy, sad, and heavy,
And so she died. Had she been light, like you,   15
Of such a merry, nimble, stirring spirit,
She might 'a' been [a] grandam ere she died.
And so may you; for a light heart lives long.

Ros. What's your dark meaning, mouse, of this
        light word?

Kath. A light condition in a beauty dark.   20

Ros. We need more light to find your meaning out.

Kath. You'll mar the light by taking it in snuff;
Therefore I'll darkly end the argument.

Ros. Look what you do, you do it still i' th'
        dark.   24

Kath. So do not you, for you are a light wench.

Ros. Indeed I weigh not you, and therefore light.

Kath. You weigh me not? O, that's you care not
        for me.

Ros. Great reason: for past care is still past
        cure.

Prin. Well bandied both, a set of wit well played.
But, Rosaline, you have a favor too?   30
Who sent it? and what is it?

Ros.   I would you knew.
And if my face were but as fair as yours,
My favor were as great: be witness this.
Nay, I have verses too, I thank Berowne;
The numbers true, and, were the numb'ring too,   35
I were the fairest goddess on the ground.
I am compar'd to twenty thousand fairs.
O, he hath drawn my picture in his letter!

Prin. Any thing like?

Ros. Much in the letters, nothing in the praise.   40

Prin. Beauteous as ink—a good conclusion.

Kath. Fair as a text B in a copy-book.

Ros. Ware pencils [ho]! let me not die your
        debtor,
My red dominical, my golden letter:
O that your face were not so full of O's!   45

Prin. A pox of that jest! and I beshrow all shrows.

---

128. **pass:** perform.   133. **have audience:** be heard.
134. **Hercules in minority.** Hercules' first exploit was to strangle two
serpents sent by the envious Juno to destroy him in his cradle.
enter: entrance.   147. **fadge:** turn out well.
149. **Via:** on! (a cry of encouragement).
153. **make one:** be one of the party.
154. **tabor:** a small drum.   **hay:** a country dance, something like
a reel.

V.ii.2. **fairings:** presents.
3. **A lady...diamonds.** A description of the King's gift; similar
gems are listed in extant inventories.
9. **That...name:** so that he was obliged to add Cupid's name (as
witness to his vows) on an attached slip of paper. Seals were often
thus attached to legal documents.
10. **wax:** grow (with play on the wax of the seal).
11. **five thousand year.** The supposed age of the world.

12. **shrowd:** shrewd, i.e. evilly disposed (or perhaps here used
adverbially, in the sense "grievously").   **unhappy:** bringing bad
luck.   **gallows:** knave fit to be hanged.   15. **light:** cheerful.
17. **'a':** have.
19. **dark:** obscure, hidden.   **light:** trivial, unimportant.
20. **light condition:** wanton nature.
22. **taking...snuff:** taking offense, with pun on snuffing a candle
(*light*).   24. **Look what:** whatever.
26. **I...you:** I do not weigh as much as you. (Katherine takes it in a
different sense, which she explains.)
28. **for...cure:** i.e. Katherine is beyond hope of cure.
30. **favor:** love token.
35. **numbers:** metre.   **numb'ring:** estimate.
37. **fairs:** beautiful women.
40. **letters:** penmanship.   **praise:** i.e. content.
41. **Beauteous as ink.** A jibe at Rosaline's dark complexion.
42. **text B.** The text hand was one of the more formal of the Elizabethan styles of writing. *B* is meant, perhaps, to suggest *black*.
43. **Ware pencils:** i.e. beware this sketching of portraits with the finely
pointed brushes used for make-up.   **let...debtor:** i.e. I owe you
one for that.
44. **red dominical:** the red letter used to mark Sundays on calendars.
The medieval Latin name for Sunday was *dies dominica.*   **golden
letter.** Also used to mark Sundays. Here used quibblingly with reference to Katherine's fair complexion.
45. **O's:** marks left by smallpox (hence the Princess' next remark).
46. **beshrow all shrows:** beshrew (i.e. mischief take) all shrews.

Love's
Labor's Lost
V.ii

But, Katherine, what was sent to you from fair
    Dumaine?
    Kath. Madam, this glove.
    Prin.   Did he not send you twain?
    Kath. Yes, madam, and moreover
Some thousand verses of a faithful lover.   50
A huge translation of hypocrisy,
Vildly compiled, profound simplicity.
    Mar. This, and these [pearls], to me sent Longa-
    ville.
The letter is too long by half a mile.
    Prin. I think no less. Dost thou not wish in heart
The chain were longer and the letter short?   56
    Mar. Ay, or I would these hands might never
    part.
    Prin. We are wise girls to mock our lovers so.
    Ros. They are worse fools to purchase mocking so.
That same Berowne I'll torture ere I go.   60
O that I knew he were but in by th' week!
How I would make him fawn, and beg, and seek,
And wait the season, and observe the times,
And spend his prodigal wits in bootless rhymes,
And shape his service wholly to my device,   65
And make him proud to make me proud that jests!
So pair-taunt-like would I o'ersway his state
That he should be my fool and I his fate.
    Prin. None are so surely caught, when they are
    catch'd,
As wit turn'd fool; folly, in wisdom hatch'd,   70
Hath wisdom's warrant and the help of school,
And wit's own grace to grace a learned fool.
    Ros. The blood of youth burns not with such
    excess
As gravity's revolt to [wantonness].
    Mar. Folly in fools bears not so strong a note   75
As fool'ry in the wise, when wit doth dote,
Since all the power thereof it doth apply
To prove, by wit, worth in simplicity.

Enter BOYET.

    Prin. Here comes Boyet, and mirth is in his face.
    Boyet. O, I am [stabb'd] with laughter! Where's
    her Grace?   80
    Prin. Thy news, Boyet?
    Boyet.   Prepare, madam, prepare!
Arm, wenches, arm! encounters mounted are
Against your peace. Love doth approach disguis'd,
Armed in arguments—you'll be surpris'd.
Muster your wits, stand in your own defense,   85
Or hide your heads like cowards, and fly hence.
    Prin. Saint Denis to Saint Cupid! What are they
That charge their breath against us? Say, scout, say.

    Boyet. Under the cool shade of a sycamore
I thought to close mine eyes some half an hour;   90
When lo, to interrupt my purpos'd rest,
Toward that shade I might behold address'd
The King and his companions. Warily
I stole into a neighbor thicket by,
And overheard what you shall overhear: 95
That by and by disguis'd [they] will be here.
Their herald is a pretty knavish page,
That well by heart hath conn'd his embassage.
Action and accent did they teach him there:
"Thus must thou speak," and "thus thy body bear";
And ever and anon they made a doubt   101
Presence majestical would put him out;
"For," quoth the King, "an angel shalt thou see;
Yet fear not thou, but speak audaciously."
The boy replied, "An angel is not evil;   105
I should have fear'd her had she been a devil."
With that all laugh'd, and clapp'd him on the shoulder,
Making the bold wag by their praises bolder.
One rubb'd his elbow thus, and fleer'd, and swore
A better speech was never spoke before.   110
Another, with his finger and his thumb,
Cried, "*Via!* we will do't, come what will come."
The third he caper'd, and cried, "All goes well."
The fourth turn'd on the toe, and down he fell.
With that they all did tumble on the ground,   115
With such a zealous laughter, so profound,
That in this spleen ridiculous appears,
To check their folly, passion's solemn tears.
    Prin. But what, but what, come they to visit us?
    Boyet. They do, they do; and are apparell'd thus,
Like Muscovites or Russians, as I guess.   121
Their purpose is to parley, to court, and dance,
And every one his love-feat will advance
Unto his several mistress, which they'll know
By favors several which they did bestow.   125
    Prin. And will they so? The gallants shall be
    task'd:
For, ladies, we will every one be mask'd,
And not a man of them shall have the grace,
Despite of suit, to see a lady's face.
Hold, Rosaline, this favor thou shalt wear,   130
And then the King will court thee for his dear.
Hold, take thou this, my sweet, and give me thine,
So shall Berowne take me for Rosaline.
And change you favors too, so shall your loves
Woo contrary, deceiv'd by these removes.   135
    Ros. Come on then, wear the favors most in sight.
    Kath. But in this changing, what is your intent?

51. **translation:** metaphor (a rhetorical term).
52. **Vildly:** vilely. **simplicity:** foolishness (cf. line 78).
57. **Ay . . . part.** Meaning not clear; perhaps "Yes, may I never give
one of my hands to a husband who can't be more generous."
61. **in . . . week:** caught for good. 64. **bootless:** unavailing.
66. **make him . . . jests:** make him dress himself splendidly to please
me when I am only acting in jest.
67. **pair-taunt-like:** i.e. holding the winning hand (from the name of a
winning combination of cards in the game of post and pair).
75. **note:** stigma. 82. **encounters:** assailants. **mounted:** raised.
84. **surpris'd:** overcome. 87. **Saint Denis:** patron saint of France.
88. **charge:** level (as a weapon).

92. **might:** could. **address'd:** directed.
95. **overhear:** hear over again. 96. **by and by:** soon.
98. **conn'd:** learned. **embassage:** message.
101. **made a doubt:** expressed fear.
102. **put him out:** make him forget his lines. 107. **clapp'd:** patted.
109. **rubb'd his elbow.** An indication of satisfaction. **fleer'd:**
grinned. 111. **with . . . thumb:** i.e. snapping his fingers.
117. **spleen ridiculous:** ridiculous fit of laughter.
118. **solemn:** melancholy.
121. **Like Muscovites.** Russian costumes were not uncommon in
court masquerades. 123. **love-feat:** act of courtship.
126. **task'd:** put to the test. 129. **suit:** pleading.
132–33. **Hold . . . Rosaline.** Possibly Shakespeare's revised version of
lines 130–31. 135. **removes:** exchanges.
136. **most in sight:** conspicuously.

Prin. The effect of my intent is to cross theirs:
They do it but in mockery merriment,
And mock for mock is only my intent.   140
Their several counsels they unbosom shall
To loves mistook, and so be mock'd withal
Upon the next occasion that we meet,
With visages display'd, to talk and greet.   144
     Ros. But shall we dance, if they desire us to't?
     Prin. No, to the death we will not move a foot,
Nor to their penn'd speech render we no grace,
But while 'tis spoke each turn away [her] face.
     Boyet. Why, that contempt will kill the speaker's
          heart,
And quite divorce his memory from his part.   150
     Prin. Therefore I do it, and I make no doubt
The rest will [ne'er] come in, if he be out.
There's no such sport as sport by sport o'erthrown,
To make theirs ours and ours none but our own;
So shall we stay, mocking intended game,   155
And they, well mock'd, depart away with shame.
                         Sound trumpet [within].
     Boyet. The trumpet sounds, be mask'd; the mask-
          ers come.   [*The Ladies mask.*]

Enter BLACKMOORS *with music, the Boy* [MOTH] *with
a speech,* [*the* KING] *and the rest of the* LORDS *disguised* [*as Russians*].

     Moth. "All hail, the richest beauties on the
          earth!"—
     [*Boyet*]. Beauties no richer than rich taffata.
     Moth. "A holy parcel of the fairest dames   160
                    The Ladies turn their backs to him.
That ever turn'd their—backs—to mortal views!"
     Ber. Their "eyes," villain, their "eyes."
     Moth. "That [ever] turn'd their eyes to mortal
          views!
Out"—
     Boyet. True, out indeed.   165
     Moth. "Out of your favors, heavenly spirits, vouch-
          safe
Not to behold"—
     Ber. "Once to behold," rogue.
     Moth. "Once to behold with your sun-beamed
          eyes,
—with your sun-beamed eyes"—   170
     Boyet. They will not answer to that epithet;
You were best call it "daughter-beamed eyes."
     Moth. They do not mark me, and that brings me
          out.
     Ber. Is this your perfectness?   Be gone, you
          rogue!   [*Exit Moth.*]

139. **mockery:** mocking.
141. **counsels:** private purposes, inmost thoughts.
146. **to the death:** as long as we live.
147. **penn'd speech:** speech written out with care.
152. **out:** put out of his part, i.e. confused.
155. **stay:** remain as visitors.
157 s.d. **Blackmoors:** black Africans.
159. **taffata:** i.e. masks of taffeta.   160. **parcel:** company.
172. **daughter-beamed.** Because they are women (quibbling on *sun*
and *son*).
173. **mark:** pay attention to.   **brings me out:** puts me off, makes me
forget my lines.
174. **your perfectness:** i.e. the perfect mastery of your lines that you
led us to expect.

     Ros. What would these strangers? Know their
          minds, Boyet.   175
If they do speak our language, 'tis our will
That some plain man recount their purposes.
Know what they would.
     Boyet.   What would you with the Princess?
     Ber. Nothing but peace, and gentle visitation.
     Ros. What would they, say they?   180
     Boyet. Nothing but peace, and gentle visitation.
     Ros. Why, that they have, and bid them so be
          gone.
     Boyet. She says, you have it, and you may be
          gone.
     King. Say to her we have measur'd many miles,
To tread a measure with her on this grass.   185
     Boyet. They say that they have measur'd many
          a mile
To tread a measure with you on this grass.
     Ros. It is not so. Ask them how many inches
Is in one mile: if they have measured many,
The measure then of one is eas'ly told.   190
     Boyet. If to come hither you have measur'd miles,
And many miles, the Princess bids you tell
How many inches doth fill up one mile.
     Ber. Tell her, we measure them by weary steps.
     Boyet. She hears herself.
     Ros.   How many weary steps   195
Of many weary miles you have o'ergone
Are numb'red in the travel of one mile?
     Ber. We number nothing that we spend for you;
Our duty is so rich, so infinite,
That we may do it still without accompt.   200
Vouchsafe to show the sunshine of your face,
That we (like savages) may worship it.
     Ros. My face is but a moon, and clouded too.
     King. Blessed are clouds, to do as such clouds do!
Vouchsafe, bright moon, and these thy stars, to
          shine   205
(Those clouds removed) upon our watery eyne.
     Ros. O vain petitioner! beg a greater matter,
Thou now requests but moonshine in the water.
     King. Then in our measure do but vouchsafe
          one change.
Thou bid'st me beg; this begging is not strange.   210
     Ros. Play, music, then! Nay, you must do it soon.
                              [*Music plays.*]
Not yet; no dance: thus change I like the moon.
     King. Will you not dance? How come you thus
          estranged?
     Ros. You took the moon at full, but now she's
          changed.   214
     King. Yet still she is the moon, and I the man.
The music plays, vouchsafe some motion to it.

177. **plain:** plainspoken.
179. **visitation:** visit.   184. **measur'd:** paced.
185. **tread a measure:** dance a stately dance.
200. **accompt:** reckoning.
203. **but a moon:** i.e. not a sun (the king symbol, proper to the real
Princess).   **clouded:** i.e. obscured by the mask.   206. **eyne:** eyes.
208. **moonshine . . . water:** i.e. nothing (proverbial).
209. **change:** (1) change of the moon; (2) round or figure in dancing.
210. **not strange:** not foreign (though done by a supposed foreigner).
215. **man:** i.e. man in the moon.
216. **motion.** Rosaline takes this in the sense "response."

[*Ros.*] Our ears vouchsafe it.

King.   But your legs should do it.

Ros. Since you are strangers, and come here by chance,
We'll not be nice; take hands. We will not dance.

King. Why take we hands then?

Ros.   Only to part friends. 220
Curtsy, sweet hearts—and so the measure ends.

King. More measure of this measure; be not nice.

Ros. We can afford no more at such a price.

King. Price you yourselves; what buys your company?

Ros. Your absence only.

King.   That can never be. 225

Ros. Then cannot we be bought; and so, adieu—
Twice to your visor, and half once to you.

King. If you deny to dance, let's hold more chat.

Ros. In private then.

King.   I am best pleas'd with that.
                    [*They converse apart.*]

Ber. White-handed mistress, one sweet word with thee. 230

Prin. Honey, and milk, and sugar: there is three.

Ber. Nay then two treys, and if you grow so nice,
Metheglin, wort, and malmsey; well run, dice!
There's half a dozen sweets.

Prin.   Seventh sweet, adieu.
Since you can cog, I'll play no more with you. 235

Ber. One word in secret.

Prin.   Let it not be sweet.

Ber. Thou grievest my gall.

Prin.   Gall! bitter.

Ber.   Therefore meet.
                    [*They converse apart.*]

Dum. Will you vouchsafe with me to change a word?

Mar. Name it.

Dum.   Fair lady—

Mar.   Say you so? Fair lord—
Take that for your fair lady.

Dum.   Please it you, 240
As much in private, and I'll bid adieu.
                    [*They converse apart.*]

[*Kath.*] What, was your vizard made without a tongue?

Long. I know the reason, lady, why you ask.

[*Kath.*] O for your reason! quickly, sir, I long!

Long. You have a double tongue within your mask, 245
And would afford my speechless vizard half.

[*Kath.*] "Veal," quoth the Dutchman. Is not veal a calf?

Long. A calf, fair lady!

[*Kath.*]   No, a fair lord calf.

Long. Let's part the word.

[*Kath.*]   No, I'll not be your half.
Take all and wean it, it may prove an ox. 250

Long. Look how you butt yourself in these sharp mocks!
Will you give horns, chaste lady? Do not so.

[*Kath.*] Then die a calf, before your horns do grow.

Long. One word in private with you ere I die.

[*Kath.*] Bleat softly then, the butcher hears you cry.   [*They converse apart.*] 255

Boyet. The tongues of mocking wenches are as keen
As is the razor's edge invisible,
Cutting a smaller hair than may be seen;
Above the sense of sense, so sensible
Seemeth their conference, their conceits have wings
Fleeter than arrows, bullets, wind, thought, swifter things. 261

Ros. Not one word more, my maids, break off, break off.

Ber. By heaven, all dry-beaten with pure scoff!

King. Farewell, mad wenches, you have simple wits. *Exeunt* [*King, Lords, and Blackmoors*].

Prin. Twenty adieus, my frozen Muscovits. 265
Are these the breed of wits so wondered at?

Boyet. Tapers they are, with your sweet breaths puff'd out.

Ros. Well-liking wits they have—gross gross, fat fat.

Prin. O poverty in wit, kingly-poor flout! 269
Will they not (think you) hang themselves to-night?
Or ever but in vizards show their faces?
This pert Berowne was out of count'nance quite.

Ros. They were all in lamentable cases!
The King was weeping-ripe for a good word. 274

Prin. Berowne did swear himself out of all suit.

Mar. Dumaine was at my service, and his sword:
"No point," quoth I; my servant straight was mute.

Kath. Lord Longaville said I came o'er his heart,
And trow you what he call'd me?

Prin.   Qualm, perhaps.

---

218. **strangers:** foreigners.   219. **nice:** coy.
222. **More measure:** a larger amount.
227. **visor:** mask. The line has not been satisfactorily explained.
228. **deny:** refuse.   232. **treys:** threes.
233. **Metheglin:** a Welsh drink brewed from honey.   **wort:** sweet unfermented beer.   **malmsey:** a strong sweet wine.
235. **cog:** cheat.
237. **Thou . . . gall:** you are causing me pain by chafing a sore place (but the Princess picks up *gall* in the sense of "bile"—cf. "bitter as gall").   **meet:** fitting.
242. **vizard:** mask.   **tongue.** W. J. Lawrence, in the *Times Literary Supplement,* June 7, 1923, explained that Elizabethan masks were kept in place by a tongue, or interior projection, held in the mouth.
245. **double.** With play on the sense "ambiguous, deceptive."
247. **Veal.** The Dutchman's pronunciation of "well," or the German *viel* (much). In addition to calling Longaville a calf, Katherine may

be punning on *veil,* i.e. the mask, and, in the combination of *long* (line 244) and *veal,* on Longaville's name.
249. **part the word:** divide the word *calf* between us.   **your half:** (1) half of something of which you are the other half; (2) your better half, i.e. wife.   250. **wean:** i.e. raise.
251. **butt:** injure (with play on the horns of the ox).
252. **give horns:** (1) attack with horns (developing the idea in *butt*); (2) make your husband a cuckold.
259. **Above . . . sense:** beyond the power of sense to perceive.   **sensible:** sensitive, quick-witted.   260. **conference:** conversation.
263. **dry-beaten:** beaten soundly without bloodshed.
268. **Well-liking:** plump.
269. **kingly-poor flout.** The Princess jibes at Rosaline's pun on *liking/like king* and caps it by reversing the syllables of *li-king* into *king-ly.*   272. **pert:** lively, brisk.
273. **cases:** (1) states; (2) costumes.
274. **weeping-ripe for:** ready to weep for lack of.
275. **out . . . suit:** past all propriety (with another play, perhaps, on costume).   277. **No point.** See note on II.i.190.
279. **trow you:** would you believe.   **Qualm:** i.e. heartburn. (Pronounced somewhat like *come,* and hence suggesting the Princess' "go" in the next line.)

Kath. Yes, in good faith.
Prin.   Go, sickness as thou art!
Ros. Well, better wits have worn plain statute-
         caps.   281
But will you hear? the King is my love sworn.
Prin. And quick Berowne hath plighted faith to me.
Kath. And Longaville was for my service born.
Mar. Dumaine is mine, as sure as bark on tree.
Boyet. Madam, and pretty mistresses, give ear:
Immediately they will again be here   287
In their own shapes; for it can never be
They will digest this harsh indignity.
Prin. Will they return?
Boyet.   They will, they will, God knows,
And leap for joy, though they are lame with blows:
Therefore change favors, and when they repair, 292
Blow like sweet roses in this summer air.
Prin. How blow? how blow? speak to be under-
         stood.
Boyet. Fair ladies mask'd are roses in their bud;
Dismask'd, their damask sweet commixture shown,
Are angels [vailing] clouds, or roses blown.   297
Prin. Avaunt, perplexity! What shall we do,
If they return in their own shapes to woo?
Ros. Good madam, if by me you'll be advis'd, 300
Let's mock them still, as well known as disguis'd.
Let us complain to them what fools were here,
Disguis'd like Muscovites, in shapeless gear;
And wonder what they were, and to what end
Their shallow shows and prologue vildly penn'd, 305
And their rough carriage so ridiculous,
Should be presented at our tent to us.
Boyet. Ladies, withdraw; the gallants are at hand.
Prin. Whip to our tents, as roes [run] o'er land.
                         Exeunt [*Princess and Ladies*].

Enter the KING *and the rest* [*of the* LORDS *in their
proper habits*].

King. Fair sir, God save you! Where's the
         Princess?   310
Boyet. Gone to her tent. Please it your Majesty
Command me any service to her thither?
King. That she vouchsafe me audience for one
         word.
Boyet. I will, and so will she, I know, my lord.
                                         Exit.
Ber. This fellow pecks up wit as pigeons pease,
And utters it again when God doth please.   316
He is wit's pedlar, and retails his wares
At wakes and wassails, meetings, markets, fairs:

And we that sell by gross, the Lord doth know,
Have not the grace to grace it with such show. 320
This gallant pins the wenches on his sleeve;
Had he been Adam, he had tempted Eve.
'A can carve too, and lisp; why, this is he
That kiss'd his hand away in courtesy;
This is the ape of form, monsieur the nice,   325
That when he plays at tables chides the dice
In honorable terms; nay, he can sing
A mean most meanly, and in hushering
Mend him who can. The ladies call him sweet;
The stairs as he treads on them kiss his feet. 330
This is the flow'r that smiles on every one,
To show his teeth as white as whalë's bone;
And consciences that will not die in debt
Pay him the due of honey-tongued Boyet.
King. A blister on his sweet tongue, with my
         heart,   335
That put Armado's page out of his part!

Enter the [PRINCESS, *ushered by* BOYET, *and her*]
LADIES.

Ber. See where it comes! Behavior, what wert
         thou
Till this madman show'd thee? And what art thou
         now?   338
King. All hail, sweet madam, and fair time of day!
Prin. "Fair" in "all hail" is foul, as I conceive.
King. Conster my speeches better, if you may.
Prin. Then wish me better, I will give you leave.
King. We came to visit you, and purpose now
To lead you to our court; vouchsafe it then.
Prin. This field shall hold me, and so hold your
         vow: 345
Nor God, nor I, delights in perjur'd men.
King. Rebuke me not for that which you provoke:
The virtue of your eye must break my oath.
Prin. You nickname virtue; vice you should have
         spoke,
For virtue's office never breaks men's troth.   350
Now by my maiden honor, yet as pure
As the unsallied lily, I protest,
A world of torments though I should endure,
I would not yield to be your house's guest:
So much I hate a breaking cause to be   355
Of heavenly oaths, vow'd with integrity.
King. O, you have liv'd in desolation here,
Unseen, unvisited, much to our shame.
Prin. Not so, my lord, it is not so, I swear;
We have had pastimes here and pleasant game,   360

---

281. **plain statute-caps:** perhaps the woollen caps required by law to
be worn by the London apprentices.
288. **shapes:** (1) forms; (2) clothes (cf. line 303).
289. **digest:** put up with, stomach.   292. **repair:** return.
293. **Blow:** bloom.
296. **damask:** red and white.   **commixture:** complexion.
297. **vailing:** letting fall, shedding.   **blown:** fully opened (cf. *full-
blown*).   298. **Avaunt, perplexity:** away, riddler.
301. **as . . . disguis'd:** as much in their real persons as when they were
disguised.   303. **shapeless gear:** ill-cut clothes.
309. **Whip:** dart, fly.   **land:** laund, open space in a wooded area.
315. **pease:** peas.
316. **utters:** puts forth, sells.   **when . . . please:** i.e. when the moment is propitious.   318. **wakes:** festivals.   **wassails:** revels.

319. **by gross:** wholesale.
321. **pins . . . sleeve:** gains the favor of all the girls (?) or has all the
girls hanging on his arm (?).   322. **had:** would have.
323. **carve:** i.e. woo with the most delicate courtesy.   **lisp:** talk
affectedly.   325. **form:** strict manners.   **nice:** punctilious.
326. **tables:** backgammon.   327. **honorable:** polite.
328. **mean:** tenor.   **meanly:** indifferently.   **hushering:** ushering,
introducing (the function of a gentleman usher).
329. **Mend:** better, improve on.   332. **whalë's:** i.e. walrus'.
337. **Behavior:** i.e. politeness, fine manners.
338. **madman:** droll fellow.   341. **Conster:** construe.
348. **virtue:** power (but the Princess picks up the word in the sense
"goodness").   349. **nickname:** misname, miscall.
350. **office:** operation.   352. **unsallied:** unsullied.

Love's
Labor's Lost
V.ii

A mess of Russians left us but of late.
   King. How, madam? Russians?
   Prin.   Ay, in truth, my lord;
Trim gallants, full of courtship and of state.
   Ros. Madam, speak true. It is not so, my lord.
My lady (to the manner of the days)   365
In courtesy gives undeserving praise.
We four indeed confronted were with four
In Russian habit; here they stay'd an hour,
And talk'd apace; and in that hour, my lord,
They did not bless us with one happy word.   370
I dare not call them fools; but this I think,
When they are thirsty, fools would fain have drink.
   Ber. This jest is dry to me. Gentle sweet,
Your wits makes wise things foolish. When we greet,
With eyes best seeing, heaven's fiery eye,   375
By light we lose light; your capacity
Is of that nature that to your huge store
Wise things seem foolish, and rich things but poor.
   Ros. This proves you wise and rich, for in my
     eye—
   Ber. I am a fool, and full of poverty.   380
   Ros. But that you take what doth to you belong,
It were a fault to snatch words from my tongue.
   Ber. O, I am yours, and all that I possess!
   Ros. All the fool mine?
   Ber.   I cannot give you less.   384
   Ros. Which of the vizards was it that you wore?
   Ber. Where? when? what vizard? why demand you
    this?
   Ros. There then, that vizard, that superfluous
    case,
That hid the worse, and show'd the better face.
   King. [*Aside.*] We were descried, they'll mock
    us now downright.   389
   Dum. [*Aside.*] Let us confess and turn it to a jest.
   Prin. Amaz'd, my lord? Why looks your High-
    ness sad?
   Ros. Help, hold his brows, he'll sound! Why
    look you pale?
Sea-sick, I think, coming from Muscovy.
   Ber. Thus pour the stars down plagues for perjury.
Can any face of brass hold longer out?   395
Here stand I, lady, dart thy skill at me,
Bruise me with scorn, confound me with a flout,
Thrust thy sharp wit quite through my ignorance,
Cut me to pieces with thy keen conceit;
And I will wish thee never more to dance,   400
Nor never more in Russian habit wait.
O, never will I trust to speeches penn'd,
Nor to the motion of a schoolboy's tongue,
Nor never come in vizard to my friend,
Nor woo in rhyme, like a blind harper's song!   405
Taffata phrases, silken terms precise,

Three-pil'd hyperboles, spruce affection,
Figures pedantical—these summer flies
Have blown me full of maggot ostentation.
I do forswear them, and I here protest,   410
By this white glove (how white the hand, God
    knows!),
Henceforth my wooing mind shall be express'd
In russet yeas and honest kersey noes.
And to begin, wench, so God help me law!
My love to thee is sound, sans crack or flaw.   415
   Ros. Sans "sans," I pray you.
   Ber.   Yet I have a trick
Of the old rage. Bear with me, I am sick;
I'll leave it by degrees. Soft, let us see—
Write "Lord have mercy on us" on those three:
They are infected, in their hearts it lies;   420
They have the plague, and caught it of your eyes.
These lords are visited; you are not free,
For the Lord's tokens on you do I see.
   Prin. No, they are free that gave these tokens
    to us.
   Ber. Our states are forfeit, seek not to undo us.
   Ros. It is not so, for how can this be true,   426
That you stand forfeit, being those that sue?
   Ber. Peace, for I will not have to do with you.
   Ros. Nor shall not, if I do as I intend.
   Ber. Speak for yourselves, my wit is at an end.
   King. Teach us, sweet madam, for our rude trans-
    gression   431
Some fair excuse.
   Prin.   The fairest is confession.
Were not you here but even now, disguis'd?
   King. Madam, I was.
   Prin.   And were you well advis'd?
   King. I was, fair madam.
   Prin.   When you then were here,
What did you whisper in your lady's ear?   436
   King. That more than all the world I did respect
    her.
   Prin. When she shall challenge this, you will
    reject her.
   King. Upon mine honor, no.
   Prin.   Peace, peace, forbear:
Your oath once broke, you force not to forswear.   440
   King. Despise me when I break this oath of mine.
   Prin. I will, and therefore keep it. Rosaline,
What did the Russian whisper in your ear?

---

361. **mess:** group of four.   365. **to...days:** in the current fashion.
370. **happy:** felicitous.
373. **dry:** dull, stupid (with pun on "thirsty").
374. **greet:** i.e. look at.   386. **demand:** question.
389. **downright:** out and out.   391. **Amaz'd:** confounded.
392. **sound:** swoon.   395. **face of brass:** i.e. guilty self-assurance.
397. **confound:** destroy.   400. **wish:** invite.
401. **wait:** attend upon.   404. **friend:** sweetheart.
405. **like...song.** Harping was proverbially the resource of the
blind.   406. **Taffata:** taffeta.

407. **Three-pil'd:** deep-piled, like velvet of the best quality.   **affection:** affectation.
409. **blown...ostentation:** i.e. deposited on me their eggs, which
have hatched into the maggots of vanity.
413. **russet:** rough homespun.   **kersey:** coarse woollen cloth.
414. **law:** la (an interjection).
416. **Sans "sans":** i.e. no affected foreign words.   **Yet:** still.
trick: touch.   417. **rage:** fever, infection.
419. **Lord...us.** The sign put on the door of a plague-stricken house.
422. **visited:** attacked by plague (the term officially used).   **free:**
(1) free of plague; (2) untouched by love, fancy-free.
423. **Lord's tokens:** (1) plague spots; (2) love tokens given by the
lords.   424. **free:** liberal (?) or free of obligation (?).
425. **states:** estates.   **undo us:** undo our forfeiture, i.e. reject our
yielding of ourselves.
427. **sue:** (1) bring the suit (it is the defendant who may have to
forfeit his lands, not the plaintiff); (2) plead.
434. **well advis'd:** in your right mind.   437. **respect:** value, prize.
438. **challenge:** lay claim to.   440. **force not:** i.e. find it easy.

Ros. Madam, he swore that he did hold me dear
As precious eyesight, and did value me   445
Above this world; adding thereto, moreover,
That he would wed me, or else die my lover.

Prin. God give thee joy of him! The noble lord
Most honorably doth uphold his word.

King. What mean you, madam? By my life, my
truth,   450
I never swore this lady such an oath.

Ros. By heaven, you did; and to confirm it plain,
You gave me this: but take it, sir, again.

King. My faith and this the Princess I did give;
I knew her by this jewel on her sleeve.   455

Prin. Pardon me, sir, this jewel did she wear,
And Lord Berowne (I thank him) is my dear.
What? will you have me, or your pearl again?

Ber. Neither of either; I remit both twain.
I see the trick an't; here was a consent,   460
Knowing aforehand of our merriment,
To dash it like a Christmas comedy.
Some carry-tale, some please-man, some slight zany,
Some mumble-news, some trencher-knight, some
    Dick,
That smiles his cheek in years and knows the
    trick   465
To make my lady laugh when she's dispos'd,
Told our intents before; which once disclos'd,
The ladies did change favors; and then we,
Following the signs, woo'd but the sign of she.
Now, to our perjury to add more terror,   470
We are again forsworn, in will and error.
Much upon this 'tis; [*to Boyet*] and might not you
Forestall our sport, to make us thus untrue?
Do not you know my lady's foot by th' squier,
And laugh upon the apple of her eye?   475
And stand between her back, sir, and the fire,
Holding a trencher, jesting merrily?
You put our page out. Go, you are allow'd;
Die when you will, a smock shall be your shroud.
You leer upon me, do you? There's an eye   480
Wounds like a leaden sword.

Boyet.   Full merrily
Hath this brave [manage], this career, been run.

Ber. Lo, he is tilting straight! Peace, I have done.

Enter Clown [COSTARD].

Welcome, pure wit, thou part'st a fair fray.

Cost. O Lord, sir, they would know   485
Whether the three Worthies shall come in or no.

Ber. What, are there but three?

Cost.   No, sir, but it is vara fine,
For every one pursents three.

Ber.   And three times thrice is nine.

Cost. Not so, sir, under correction, sir, I hope it
    is not so.
You cannot beg us, sir, I can assure you, sir, we know
    what we know.   490
I hope, sir, three times thrice, sir—

Ber. Is not nine.

Cost. Under correction, sir, we know whereuntil
it doth amount.   494

Ber. By Jove, I always took three threes for nine.

Cost. O Lord, sir, it were pity you should get
your living by reck'ning, sir.

Ber. How much is it?

Cost. O Lord, sir, the parties themselves, the
actors, sir, will show whereuntil it doth amount.   500
For mine own part, I am, as [they] say, but to parfect one man in one poor man, Pompion the Great,
sir.

Ber. Art thou one of the Worthies?   504

Cost. It pleas'd them to think me worthy of
Pompey the Great; for mine own part, I know
not the degree of the Worthy, but I am to stand
for him.

Ber. Go bid them prepare.

Cost. We will turn it finely off, sir; we will take
    some care.   *Exit.*   510

King. Berowne, they will shame us; let them not
    approach.

Ber. We are shame-proof, my lord; and 'tis some
    policy
To have one show worse than the King's and his
    company.

King. I say they shall not come.   514

Prin. Nay, my good lord, let me o'errule you now.
That sport best pleases that doth [least] know how:
Where zeal strives to content, and the contents
Dies in the zeal of that which it presents.
Their form confounded makes most form in mirth,
When great things laboring perish in their birth.   520

Ber. A right description of our sport, my lord.

Enter Braggart [ARMADO].

Arm. Anointed, I implore so much expense of thy
royal sweet breath as will utter a brace of words.

[*Converses apart with the King, and delivers
    him a paper.*]

Prin. Doth this man serve God?

---

459. **either:** the two.   **remit:** give up, surrender.
460. **an't:** on it, i.e. of it.   **consent:** agreement, i.e. conspiracy.
462. **dash:** destroy, frustrate.
463. **carry-tale:** talebearer.   **please-man:** sycophant.   **zany:** clown.
464. **mumble-news:** prattler, gossip.   **trencher-knight:** i.e. parasite
(a trencher is a wooden platter or dish).   **Dick:** silly person.
465. **smiles . . . years:** laughs his face into wrinkles.
469. **she:** i.e. each one's supposed mistress.
472. **Much . . . 'tis:** i.e. this must be substantially what happened.
474. **squier:** square, rule. Berowne means that Boyet knows well
what will please the Princess.
475. **apple:** pupil. Boyet is in a position to have private jokes with the
Princess.   477. **Holding a trencher:** i.e. dancing attendance.
478. **allow'd:** privileged to jest (as a fool was).
479. **smock:** woman's undergarment (either a charge of effeminacy or
equivalent to saying that women will be the death of him).
481. **leaden sword:** i.e. a stage sword, unable to wound.
482. **brave:** fine.   **manage:** piece of horsemanship.   **career:** running, course.
483. **tilting straight:** back immediately to his verbal sparring.

487. **vara:** very.
488. **pursents:** presents; i.e. represents.   489. **under:** subject to.
490. **beg us:** prove us fools.   494. **whereuntil:** whereunto, i.e. to
how much.
496. **it . . . get:** it would be too bad if you had to earn.
501-2. **parfect:** i.e. perform or present.
502. **Pompion:** pumpkin (error for *Pompey*).   512. **policy:** wise strategy.
517-18. **the contents . . . presents:** i.e. the substance of the play is
murdered by the actors in their excessive eagerness to please (which
makes them undertake too ambitious a project for their talents).
521. **right:** exact.   **our sport:** i.e. the Muscovite masque.

Ber. Why ask you?   525

Prin. 'A speaks not like a man of God his making.

Arm. That is all one, my fair, sweet, honey monarch; for I protest, the schoolmaster is exceeding fantastical, too too vain, too too vain: but we will put it (as they say) to *fortuna de la*   530 [*guerra*]. I wish you the peace of mind, most royal couplement.   *Exit.*

King. Here is like to be a good presence of Worthies: he presents Hector of Troy; the swain, Pompey the Great; the parish curate, Alexander;   535 Armado's page, Hercules; the pedant, Judas Machabeus;

And if these four Worthies in their first show thrive, These four will change habits, and present the other five.

Ber. There is five in the first show.   540

King. You are deceived, 'tis not so.

Ber. The pedant, the braggart, the hedge-priest, the fool, and the boy:

Abate throw at novum, and the whole world again Cannot pick out five such, take each one in his vein.

King. The ship is under sail, and here she comes amain.   546

Enter [Costard *for*] *Pompey.*

Cost. "I Pompey am"—

Ber.   You lie, you are not he.

Cost. "I Pompey am"—

Boyet.   With libbard's head on knee.

Ber. Well said, old mocker. I must needs be friends with thee.

Cost. "I Pompey am, Pompey surnam'd the Big"—   550

Dum. "The Great."

Cost. It is "Great," sir.

"Pompey surnam'd the Great, That oft in field with targe and shield did make my foe to sweat,

And travelling along this coast, I here am come by chance,

And lay my arms before the legs of this sweet lass of France."   555

If your ladyship would say, "Thanks, Pompey," I had done.

[*Prin.*] Great thanks, great Pompey.

Cost. 'Tis not so much worth; but I hope I was perfect. I made a little fault in "Great."

Ber. My hat to a halfpenny, Pompey proves the best Worthy.   561

Enter Curate [Sir Nathaniel] *for Alexander.*

Nath. "When in the world I liv'd, I was the world's commander;

By east, west, north, and south, I spread my conquering might.

My scutcheon plain declares that I am Alisander"—

Boyet. Your nose says, no, you are not; for it stands too right.   565

Ber. Your nose smells "no" in [this], most tender-smelling knight.

Prin. The conqueror is dismay'd. Proceed, good Alexander.

Nath. "When in the world I liv'd, I was the world's commander"—

Boyet. Most true, 'tis right; you were so, Alisander.

Ber. Pompey the Great—   570

Cost. Your servant, and Costard.

Ber. Take away the conqueror, take away Alisander.

Cost. [*To Nathaniel.*] O sir, you have overthrown Alisander the conqueror! You will be scrap'd   575 out of the painted cloth for this. Your lion, that holds his poll-axe sitting on a close-stool, will be given to Ajax; he will be the ninth Worthy. A conqueror, and afeard to speak! Run away for shame, Alisander. [*Nathaniel retires.*] There an't shall please you,   580 a foolish mild man, an honest man, look you, and soon dash'd. He is a marvellous good neighbor, faith, and a very good bowler; but for Alisander—alas, you see how 'tis—a little o'erparted. But there are Worthies a-coming will speak their mind in some other sort.   586

Prin. Stand aside, good Pompey.

Enter Pedant [Holofernes] *for Judas, and the Boy* [Moth] *for Hercules.*

Hol. "Great Hercules is presented by this imp, Whose club kill'd Cerberus, that three-headed *canus*; And when he was a babe, a child, a shrimp,   590 Thus did he strangle serpents in his *manus*.

Quoniam he seemeth in minority,

Ergo I come with this apology."

[*Aside.*] Keep some state in thy exit, and vanish.

[*Moth retires.*]

"Judas I am"—   595

Dum. A Judas!

Hol. Not Iscariot, sir.

"Judas I am, ycliped Machabeus."

---

526. **God his:** God's.
530–31. **fortuna . . . guerra:** the fortune of war.
532. **couplement:** couple.   533. **presence:** assembly, company.
542. **hedge-priest:** illiterate priest of low status.
544. **Abate . . . novum:** except for a lucky throw of the dice in the game of novum (from Latin *novem*, "nine"), played by five players and having nine and five as its principal throws. The quibble here is on the presentation of nine characters by five players.
545. **vein:** individual character.
548. **libbard's:** leopard's. An allusion to Pompey's coat of arms, which would properly be on his shield; perhaps Costard is holding the shield awkwardly low.
553. **targe:** light shield.   559. **perfect:** word-perfect.

565. **right:** straight (an allusion to a reputed physical characteristic of Alexander, a wry neck).
566. **Your . . . this.** Alexander was reputed to possess skin and breath of a "marvellous good savour" (North's Plutarch).   **tender-smelling:** endowed with a sensitive sense of smell.
575–76. **You . . . this.** An allusion to the frequent representation of the Nine Worthies on canvases or tapestries.
576–77. **lion . . . close-stool.** Alexander's arms showed a lion seated in a chair and holding a battle-axe.   **close-stool:** privy.
578. **Ajax.** With a pun on *a jakes,* i.e. a privy. Ajax, a Greek warrior, coveted the armor of the slain Achilles.
584. **o'erparted:** given too difficult a part.
588. **imp:** child (as at I.i.5).
589. **Cerberus:** the three-headed dog at the entrance to Hades, whose capture was one of Hercules' tasks.   **canus:** dog (properly *canis*).
591. **manus:** hands.   592. **Quoniam:** since.
593. **Ergo:** therefore.   594. **state:** dignity.
598. **ycliped:** called (as at I.i.240).

Dum. Judas Machabeus clipt is plain Judas.

Ber. A kissing traitor. How art thou prov'd Judas?

Hol. "Judas I am"— 601

Dum. The more shame for you, Judas.

Hol. What mean you, sir?

Boyet. To make Judas hang himself.

Hol. Begin, sir, you are my elder. 605

Ber. Well follow'd: Judas was hang'd on an elder.

Hol. I will not be put out of countenance.

Ber. Because thou hast no face.

Hol. What is this?

Boyet. A cittern-head. 610

Dum. The head of a bodkin.

Ber. A death's face in a ring.

Long. The face of an old Roman coin, scarce seen.

Boyet. The pommel of Caesar's falchion.

Dum. The carv'd-bone face on a flask. 615

Ber. Saint George's half-cheek in a brooch.

Dum. Ay, and in a brooch of lead.

Ber. Ay, and worn in the cap of a tooth-drawer.
And now forward, for we have put thee in countenance. 620

Hol. You have put me out of countenance.

Ber. False, we have given thee faces.

Hol. But you have out-fac'd them all.

Ber. And thou wert a lion, we would do so.

Boyet. Therefore as he is, an ass, let him go. 625
And so adieu, sweet Jude! Nay, why dost thou stay?

Dum. For the latter end of his name.

Ber. For the ass to the Jude; give it him. Jud-as,
away!

Hol. This is not generous, not gentle, not humble.

Boyet. A light for Monsieur Judas! It grows
dark, he may stumble. [*Holofernes retires.*]

Prin. Alas, poor Machabeus, how hath he been
baited! 631

Enter Braggart [ARMADO *for Hector*].

Ber. Hide thy head, Achilles, here comes Hector
in arms.

Dum. Though my mocks come home by me, I
will now be merry. 635

King. Hector was but a Troyan in respect of this.

Boyet. But is this Hector?

King. I think Hector was not so clean-timber'd.

Long. His leg is too big for Hector's.

Dum. More calf, certain. 640

Boyet. No, he is best indu'd in the small.

Ber. This cannot be Hector.

Dum. He's a god or a painter, for he makes faces.

Arm. "The armipotent Mars, of lances the almighty,
Gave Hector a gift"— 645

Dum. A [gilt] nutmeg.

Ber. A lemon.

Long. Stuck with cloves.

Dum. No, cloven.

Arm. Peace!— 650
"The armipotent Mars, of lances the almighty,
Gave Hector a gift, the heir of Ilion;
A man so breathed, that certain he would fight, yea,
From morn till night, out of his pavilion.
I am that flower"—

Dum. That mint.

Long. That columbine. 655

Arm. Sweet Lord Longaville, rein thy tongue.

Long. I must rather give it the rein, for it runs
against Hector.

Dum. Ay, and Hector's a greyhound. 659

Arm. The sweet war-man is dead and rotten,
sweet chucks, beat not the bones of the buried.
When he breathed, he was a man. But I will forward with my device. [*To the Princess.*] Sweet
royalty, bestow on me the sense of hearing. 664

Berowne steps forth [*to whisper to Costard and
then returns to his place*].

Prin. Speak, brave Hector, we are much delighted.

Arm. I do adore thy sweet Grace's slipper.

Boyet. Loves her by the foot.

Dum. He may not by the yard. 669

Arm. "This Hector far surmounted Hannibal.
The party is gone"—

Cost. Fellow Hector, she is gone; she is two
months on her way.

Arm. What meanest thou? 674

Cost. Faith, unless you play the honest Troyan,
the poor wench is cast away. She's quick, the child
brags in her belly already. 'Tis yours.

Arm. Dost thou infamonize me among potentates? Thou shalt die. 679

Cost. Then shall Hector be whipt for Jaquenetta that is quick by him, and hang'd for Pompey
that is dead by him.

Dum. Most rare Pompey!

Boyet. Renowned Pompey! 684

Ber. Greater than great, great, great, great
Pompey! Pompey the Huge!

Dum. Hector trembles.

---

599. **clipt:** abbreviated.
600. **A kissing traitor.** An allusion to the kiss by which Judas Iscariot betrayed Jesus, but perhaps also a quibble on *clipt* in the sense "embraced."
605. **Begin...elder:** i.e. hang yourself first, since you have pre-cedence as my senior.   606. **Judas...elder.** An old tradition.
609. **What is this.** Holofernes points to his face, provoking the quips which follow. All the replies allude to faces carved as ornaments on various objects.   610. **cittern:** cithern, guitar.
611. **bodkin:** a long pin or pin-shaped ornament for the hair, or a small dagger.   612. **death's face:** death's head.
613. **scarce seen:** worn almost indistinguishable.
614. **falchion:** curved sword.   615. **flask:** powder flask.
616. **half-cheek:** profile.
618. **tooth-drawer.** Evidently a brooch or badge in the tooth-drawer's cap was a distinguishing mark of his dress.
623. **out-fac'd them all:** put all the faces out of countenance (through mockery).   629. **gentle:** courteous.   **humble:** kind.
632. **Achilles:** the best warrior on the Greek side, as Hector was on the Trojan side.   634. **by me:** to me, i.e. to injure me.
636. **Troyan:** (1) Trojan; (2) cant term for boon companion, dis-solute fellow.   **respect of:** comparison with.
638. **clean-timber'd:** well built.

640. **calf:** (1) part of the leg; (2) stupid fellow, dolt.
641. **indu'd:** endowed, supplied.   **small:** the part of the leg below the calf.   644. **armipotent:** powerful in arms.
646. **gilt:** glazed with the yolk of an egg (an old cookery term).
652. **Ilion:** Troy.   653. **so breathed:** in such good condition.
654. **pavilion:** the tent which would be used by a combatant when not engaged in fighting.   669. **yard:** penis.   676. **quick:** pregnant.
678. **infamonize:** defame.
682. **that is dead:** i.e. whose hopes of winning Jaquenetta have been killed.

Ber. Pompey is mov'd. More Ates, more Ates!
stir them [on], stir them on!

Dum. Hector will challenge him.   690

Ber. Ay, if 'a have no more man's blood in his
belly than will sup a flea.

Arm. By the north pole, I do challenge thee.

Cost. I will not fight with a pole like a   694
Northren man; I'll slash, I'll do it by the sword.
I bepray you let me borrow my arms again.

Dum. Room for the incens'd Worthies!

Cost. I'll do it in my shirt.

Dum. Most resolute Pompey!   699

Moth. Master, let me take you a button-hole
lower. Do you not see Pompey is uncasing for the
combat? What mean you? You will lose your
reputation.

Arm. Gentlemen and soldiers, pardon me, I will
not combat in my shirt.   705

Dum. You may not deny it; Pompey hath made
the challenge.

Arm. Sweet bloods, I both may and will.

Ber. What reason have you for't?   709

Arm. The naked truth of it is, I have no shirt;
I go woolward for penance.

Boyet. True, and it was enjoin'd him in Rome
for want of linen; since when, I'll be sworn he wore
none but a dishclout of Jaquenetta's, and that 'a wears
next his heart for a favor.   715

Enter a Messenger, Monsieur MARCADE.

Marc. God save you, madam!

Prin.   Welcome, Marcade,
But that thou interruptest our merriment.

Marc. I am sorry, madam, for the news I bring
Is heavy in my tongue. The King your father—

Prin. Dead, for my life!

Marc.   Even so: my tale is told.   720

Ber. Worthies, away! the scene begins to cloud.

Arm. For mine own part, I breathe free breath.
I have seen the day of wrong through the little
hole of discretion, and I will right myself like a
soldier.   *Exeunt Worthies.*   725

King. How fares your Majesty?

Prin. Boyet, prepare, I will away to-night.

King. Madam, not so, I do beseech you stay.

Prin. Prepare, I say. I thank you, gracious lords,
For all your fair endeavors, and entreat,   730
Out of a new-sad soul, that you vouchsafe
In your rich wisdom to excuse, or hide,
The liberal opposition of our spirits,
If overboldly we have borne ourselves
In the converse of breath—your gentleness   735

Was guilty of it. Farewell, worthy lord!
A heavy heart bears not a humble tongue.
Excuse me so, coming too short of thanks
For my great suit so easily obtain'd.   739

King. The extreme parts of time extremely forms
All causes to the purpose of his speed,
And often, at his very loose, decides
That which long process could not arbitrate.
And though the mourning brow of progeny
Forbid the smiling courtesy of love   745
The holy suit which fain it would convince,
Yet since love's argument was first on foot,
Let not the cloud of sorrow justle it
From what it purpos'd; since to wail friends lost
Is not by much so wholesome-profitable   750
As to rejoice at friends but newly found.

Prin. I understand you not, my griefs are double.

Ber. Honest plain words best pierce the ear of
grief,
And by these badges understand the King.
For your fair sakes have we neglected time,   755
Play'd foul play with our oaths. Your beauty, ladies,
Hath much deformed us, fashioning our humors
Even to the opposed end of our intents;
And what in us hath seem'd ridiculous—
As love is full of unbefitting strains,   760
All wanton as a child, skipping and vain,
Form'd by the eye and therefore like the eye,
Full of straying shapes, of habits, and of forms,
Varying in subjects as the eye doth roll
To every varied object in his glance;   765
Which parti-coated presence of loose love
Put on by us, if, in your heavenly eyes,
Have misbecom'd our oaths and gravities,
Those heavenly eyes, that look into these faults,
Suggested us to make. Therefore, ladies,   770
Our love being yours, the error that love makes
Is likewise yours. We to ourselves prove false,
By being once false for ever to be true
To those that make us both—fair ladies, you;
And even that falsehood, in itself a sin,   775
Thus purifies itself and turns to grace.

Prin. We have receiv'd your letters full of love;
Your favors, embassadors of love;
And in our maiden council rated them
At courtship, pleasant jest, and courtesy,   780
As bombast and as lining to the time;
But more devout than this [in] our respects

688. **Ates.** Ate was the goddess of discord and strife.
695. **Northren man:** countryman from the north, boor.
700-701. **take . . . lower:** help you take off your doublet (with quibble on the sense "humiliate you"). 701. **uncasing:** undressing.
708. **bloods:** men of fire and spirit.
711. **go woolward:** wear no linen between the woollen outer clothing and the skin.
713. **want of linen.** Boyet suggests that the reason is not penance but a shortage of shirts.
723-25. **I . . . soldier:** i.e. I now perceive my wrongdoing and will make honorable amends. (See lines 883-84.)   732. **hide:** overlook.
733. **liberal opposition:** unrestrained antagonism.
735. **converse of breath:** conversation.   **gentleness:** courtesy.

737. **humble:** courteous.
739. **suit.** The King has apparently granted this.
740-41. **The extreme . . . speed:** i.e. the pressure of final moments demands quick decisions.   741. **his:** its, i.e. time's.
742. **loose:** moment of release (technical term for the discharge of an arrow).   746 **convince:** give proof of.   748. **justle:** jostle.
752. **double:** excessive (?).
754. **badges:** i.e. the plain words he is about to speak.
758. **Even . . . intents:** into the very opposite of what we intended.
760. **strains:** impulses.
763. **straying.** Perhaps an error for *strange*, arising from an authorial spelling *straing* (as in *Sir Thomas More*, Addition II, line 8).
766. **parti-coated:** dressed like a fool, in motley.   **loose:** unrestrained.   768. **misbecom'd:** been unbecoming to.
770. **Suggested:** tempted.   **make:** i.e. make them.   Word order and syntax in lines 766-70 are strained.
780. **At:** i.e. as merely.
781. **bombast:** wool used for padding or stuffing.
782. **devout:** serious.   **respects:** regard, consideration.

Have we not been, and therefore met your loves
In their own fashion, like a merriment.
　Dum.　Our letters, madam, show'd much more than
　　jest.　　　　　　　　　　　　　　　　　785
　Long.　So did our looks.
　Ros.　　　　　　　We did not cote them so.
　King.　Now at the latest minute of the hour,
Grant us your loves.
　Prin.　　　　　　A time methinks too short
To make a world-without-end bargain in.
No, no, my lord, your Grace is perjur'd much,　790
Full of dear guiltiness, and therefore this:
If for my love (as there is no such cause)
You will do aught, this shall you do for me:
Your oath I will not trust, but go with speed
To some forlorn and naked hermitage,　　　795
Remote from all the pleasures of the world;
There stay until the twelve celestial signs
Have brought about the annual reckoning.
If this austere insociable life
Change not your offer made in heat of blood;　800
If frosts and fasts, hard lodging and thin weeds
Nip not the gaudy blossoms of your love
But that it bear this trial, and last love;
Then at the expiration of the year,　　　　804
Come challenge me, challenge me by these deserts,
And by this virgin palm now kissing thine,
I will be thine; and till that [instant] shut
My woeful self up in a mourning house,
Raining the tears of lamentation
For the remembrance of my father's death.　810
If this thou do deny, let our hands part,
Neither intitled in the other's heart.
　King.　If this, or more than this, I would deny,
To flatter up these powers of mine with rest,
The sudden hand of death close up mine eye!　815
Hence [hermit] then—my heart is in thy breast.
　⟨*Ber.*　And what to me, my love? and what to me?
　Ros.　You must be purged too, your sins are rack'd,
You are attaint with faults and perjury:
Therefore if you my favor mean to get,　　820
A twelvemonth shall you spend, and never rest,
But seek the weary beds of people sick.⟩
　Dum.　But what to me, my love? but what to me?
A wife?
　Kath.　　　A beard, fair health, and honesty;
With threefold love I wish you all these three.　825
　Dum.　O, shall I say, I thank you, gentle wife?
　Kath.　Not so, my lord, a twelvemonth and a day
I'll mark no words that smooth-fac'd wooers say.
Come when the King doth to my lady come;
Then if I have much love, I'll give you some.　830
　Dum.　I'll serve thee true and faithfully till then.
　Kath.　Yet swear not, lest ye be forsworn again.
　Long.　What says Maria?

　Mar.　　　　　　　　At the twelvemonth's end
I'll change my black gown for a faithful friend.　834
　Long.　I'll stay with patience, but the time is long.
　Mar.　The liker you; few taller are so young.
　Ber.　Studies my lady? Mistress, look on me,
Behold the window of my heart, mine eye,
What humble suit attends thy answer there.
Impose some service on me for thy love.　　840
　Ros.　Oft have I heard of you, my Lord Berowne,
Before I saw you; and the world's large tongue
Proclaims you for a man replete with mocks,
Full of comparisons and wounding flouts,
Which you on all estates will execute　　　845
That lie within the mercy of your wit.
To weed this wormwood from your fructful brain,
And therewithal to win me, if you please,
Without the which I am not to be won,
You shall this twelvemonth term from day to day　850
Visit the speechless sick, and still converse
With groaning wretches; and your task shall be,
With all the fierce endeavor of your wit,
To enforce the pained impotent to smile.　　854
　Ber.　To move wild laughter in the throat of death?
It cannot be, it is impossible:
Mirth cannot move a soul in agony.
　Ros.　Why, that's the way to choke a gibing spirit,
Whose influence is begot of that loose grace
Which shallow laughing hearers give to fools.　860
A jest's prosperity lies in the ear
Of him that hears it, never in the tongue
Of him that makes it; then if sickly ears,
Deaf'd with the clamors of their own dear groans,
Will hear your idle scorns, continue then,　　865
And I will have you and that fault withal;
But if they will not, throw away that spirit,
And I shall find you empty of that fault,
Right joyful of your reformation.
　Ber.　A twelvemonth? Well, befall what will be-
　　fall,　　　　　　　　　　　　　　　　870
I'll jest a twelvemonth in an hospital.
　Prin.　[*To the King.*] Ay, sweet my lord, and so
　　I take my leave.
　King.　No, madam, we will bring you on your
　　way.
　Ber.　Our wooing doth not end like an old play:
Jack hath not Gill. These ladies' courtesy　　875
Might well have made our sport a comedy.
　King.　Come, sir, it wants a twelvemonth an' a
　　day,
And then 'twill end.
　Ber.　　　　　　That's too long for a play.

　　　　　Enter Braggart [ARMADO].

　Arm.　Sweet Majesty, vouchsafe me—
　Prin.　Was not that Hector?　　　　　　880

---

786. cote: quote, i.e. interpret.
789. world-without-end. Cf. Sonnet 57.5.　791. dear: grievous.
797-98. until . . . reckoning: i.e. one year. The "signs" are the signs
of the zodiac.　801. weeds: clothing.　802. gaudy: gay and showy.
803. last: continue as.　805. challenge: claim.
812. intitled: having a legal claim.
814. flatter up: pamper, coddle.　rest: easy living.
817-22. These lines are a first-draft version of lines 837-54.
818. rack'd: extended.

834. friend: sweetheart, lover.　835. stay: wait.
842. the world's large tongue: i.e. universal report.
844. comparisons: satirical similes.　845. estates: classes of people.
847. fructful: fruitful.　851. still converse: constantly associate.
853. fierce: ardent.
854. pained impotent: those made helpless by pain.
859. influence. Used in the astrological sense.
864. dear: intense, grievous.　866. withal: along with you.
873. bring: escort.

Love's
Labor's Lost
V.ii

Dum. The worthy knight of Troy.

Arm. I will kiss thy royal finger, and take leave. I am a votary; I have vow'd to Jaquenetta to hold the plough for her sweet love three year. But, most esteemed greatness, will you hear the dialogue 885 that the two learned men have compiled in praise of the owl and the cuckoo? It should have followed in the end of our show.

King. Call them forth quickly, we will do so.

Arm. Holla! approach. 890

Enter all.

This side is Hiems, Winter; this Ver, the Spring; the one maintained by the owl, th' other by the cuckoo. Ver, begin.

THE SONG

[*Spring.*] When daisies pied, and violets blue,
    And lady-smocks all silver-white, 895
And cuckoo-buds of yellow hue
    Do paint the meadows with delight,
The cuckoo then on every tree
Mocks married men; for thus sings he,
        "Cuckoo; 900
Cuckoo, cuckoo"—O word of fear,
Unpleasing to a married ear!

When shepherds pipe on oaten straws,
    And merry larks are ploughmen's clocks;

When turtles tread, and rooks and daws, 905
    And maidens bleach their summer smocks,
The cuckoo then on every tree
Mocks married men; for thus sings he,
        "Cuckoo;
Cuckoo, cuckoo"—O word of fear, 910
Unpleasing to a married ear!

Winter. When icicles hang by the wall,
    And Dick the shepherd blows his nail,
And Tom bears logs into the hall,
    And milk comes frozen home in pail; 915
When blood is nipp'd, and ways be [foul],
Then nightly sings the staring owl,
        "Tu-whit, to-who!"—
A merry note,
While greasy Joan doth keel the pot. 920

When all aloud the wind doth blow,
    And coughing drowns the parson's saw,
And birds sit brooding in the snow,
    And Marian's nose looks red and raw;
When roasted crabs hiss in the bowl, 925
Then nightly sings the staring owl,
        "Tu-whit, to-who!"—
A merry note,
While greasy Joan doth keel the pot.

[*Arm.*] The words of Mercury are harsh after the songs of Apollo. [You that way; we this way.] 931
        [*Exeunt omnes.*]

883–84. **hold the plough:** i.e. become a farmer.
885. **dialogue:** debate, statement of contrasting points of view.
892. **maintained:** represented.   894. **pied:** particolored.
895, 896. **lady-smocks, cuckoo-buds.** J. W. Lever, in *Review of English Studies*, n.s. III (1952), 117–20, has shown that Shakespeare took these flower-names from John Gerard's *Herbal* (1597). Modern commentators have identified them variously.
901. **word of fear:** i.e. because the cuckoo's call suggests the word *cuckold.*

905. **turtles:** turtle-doves.   **tread:** mate.
913. **blows his nail.** This phrase, meaning literally "blows on his finger-nails (for warmth)," had also the sense "waits patiently while he has nothing to do" (cf. *cools his heels*). Both meanings are probably present here.
920. **keel:** cool by stirring (to keep the pot from boiling over).
922. **saw:** moral platitude (in his sermon).
925. **roasted crabs:** roasted crab apples (which were added to a bowl or pot of warmed ale).

NOTE ON THE TEXT

Love's Labor's Lost was published in quarto (Q1) in 1598; the text of the First Folio (1623) is essentially a reprint of Q1, such corrections as it affords, even in speech-prefixes, being within the scope of any intelligent printing-house editor. A second quarto (Q2), printed in 1631, is based on the F1 text. There is, therefore, no question that Q1, as the only substantive text, must be the basis of any modern edition.

There is considerable internal evidence that Q1 was set, probably throughout, from some form of Shakespeare's "foul papers," and the text it presents is unfortunately far from satisfactory. It abounds in obvious misprints and textual cruxes, and there is a good deal of inconsistency in the use of speech-prefixes and considerable confusion in the assignment of speeches to Rosaline, Katherine, and Maria and to Holofernes and Sir Nathaniel (see Textual Notes, *passim,* especially II.i, IV.ii, V.ii).

One other complication must be noticed. It seems likely that Q1 was actually preceded by a "bad" quarto edition of which no copy is now extant. The statement "Newly corrected and augmented" on the Q1 title-page is suggestively similar to the claim "Newly corrected, augmented, and amended" on the title-page of the "good" quarto (1599) of *Romeo and Juliet*—there intended to repudiate the text of the earlier "bad" quarto of that play—and both quartos were printed for the same publisher, Cuthbert Burby. To what extent, if any, the postulated "bad" quarto may have affected the text of Q1 (as, for example, the "bad" quartos of both *Romeo and Juliet* and *Hamlet* can be shown to have influenced the texts of the "good" quartos of those plays) will have to remain a matter of conjecture, but that it may have done so and hence contributed in some degree to the difficulties of the Q1 text must be considered a possibility.

The complications and confusions in Q1 have led to various theories of revision, and revision there certainly was, but of exactly what kind and at what time made is not clear. At least two passages (see the text at IV.iii.292 and V.ii.817) preserve what are generally agreed to be Shakespeare's first drafts of later lines (corruption from the hypothetical "bad" quarto seems a less likely explanation), and it is probable that the characters Holofernes and Sir Nathaniel and the whole Worthies business were not part of Shakespeare's original play. On the whole it seems likely that some years elapsed between Shakespeare's first draft (perhaps 1594) and the play as we now have it (probably 1597); certainly the song "When daisies pied and violets blue" (V.ii.894–929) cannot have been written before 1597, for J. W. Lever has recently shown that Shakespeare here depends heavily on a passage in Gerard's *Herbal* first published in that year.

Although, as already noticed, F1 is basically nothing but a slightly corrected reprint of Q1, it contains one line—the last in the play—not found in Q1. The line may possibly be Shakespeare's, but it is more probably an unauthorized addition made with a view to clearing the stage expeditiously. The more significant F1 variants are recorded in the Textual Notes.

The spelling of the name of Armado's page raises a difficulty. Shakespeare regularly used the single spelling *moth* (and apparently the single pronunciation *mot* or *mote*; see H. Kökeritz, *Shakespeare's Pronunciation* [New Haven, 1953], p. 320) for the senses now differentiated by the spellings *moth* and *mote*. It seems highly likely that in naming the diminutive page (and also one of the fairies in *A Midsummer Night's Dream*) he intended the sense of *mote*, i.e. an atom or tiny particle; if so, consistency would require modernization of the spelling in this text (cf. the treatment of the same spelling in IV.iii.159). Since, however, there is a possibility that Shakespeare was thinking primarily of the insect (likewise a diminutive creature), it has seemed best not to depart from the traditional spelling.

For further information, see: J. D. Wilson, ed., New Cambridge *Love's Labour's Lost* (Cambridge, 1923); Richard David, ed., New Arden *Love's Labour's Lost* (London, 1951); W. W. Greg, *The Shakespeare First Folio* (Oxford, 1955).

TEXTUAL NOTES

Title: **Love's Labor's Lost]** *F3*; A Pleasant Conceited Comedie Called Loues labors lost. As it was presented before her Highnes this last Christmas. Newly corrected and augmented By W. Shakespere. *Q1 (title-page)*; Loues Labour's lost. *F1*
Dramatis personae: *subs. as first given by Rowe*
Act-scene division: *none in Q1; F1 marks acts only (Act V being mistakenly headed Actus Quartus.); scene divisions from F2 (I.i) and from Rowe and later editors (see first note to each scene); present act-scene arrangement as a whole first established by Steevens*

I.i

I.i] *F2; Actus primus. F1*
Location: *Cambridge (after Capell); so throughout the play*
1 s.p. **King.]** *Rowe*; Ferdinand. *Q1, F1 (or Ferd., Fer., throughout scene)*
5 **buy]** *F2*; buy: *Q1, F1*
13 **academe]** *Q2*; Achademe *Q1, F1 (throughout)*
16 **me,]** *F2*; me: *Q1, F1*
18 **schedule]** *Rowe*; sedule *Q1*; scedule *F1*
31 **pomp]** *F1*; pome *F1*
50 **please:]** *F4 (subs.)*; please, *Q1, F1*
55 **know.]** *Alexander (after Capell)*; know? *Q1, F1*
57 **barr'd]** *F4 (bar'd)*; bard *Q1, F1*
57 **common]** *F1*; cammon *Q1*
59 **Com' on]** Come on *F1*
62 **feast]** *Theobald*; fast *Q1, F1*
65 **hard-a-keeping]** *hyphens, Hanmer*
72 **but]** and *F1*
80 **indeed]** *F1*; in deede *Q1 (throughout, except IV.i.134)*
87 **authority]** *F1*; aucthoritie *Q1*
104 **abortive]** *F1*; abhortiue *Q1*
109 **Climb . . . gate.]** That were to clymbe ore the house to vnlocke the gate. *F1*
114 **sworn]** swore *F2*
119, 123, 128 s.dd. **Reads.]** *Pope (subs.)*
128 s.p. **Ber.]** *Theobald*; speech continued to Longaville, *Q1, F1*
128 **gentility]** *F1*; gentletie *Q1*
131 **can possible]** shall possibly *F1*
138 **bedred]** bed-rid *F1 (with Q1 form cf. Hamlet, I.ii.29, and Lucrece, l. 975)*
153 **speak]** break *F1*
155 s.d. **Subscribes.]** *Capell*
166 **One]** *F1*; On *Q1*
169 **umpeer]** umpire *F1*
172 **high-borne]** *hyphen, F1 (eds. usually adopt F3 high-born, but cf. high words in l. 193)*
178 **fire-new]** *Pope*; fier new *Q1*; fire, new *F1*
180 s.d. **Enter . . . Costard.]** *arranged as in Capell (Dull substituted for Constable by*

Rowe); Enter a Constable with Costard with a letter. *Q1, F1*
181 s.p. **Dull.]** *Rowe*; Constab. *Q1, F1 (or Const., throughout scene)*
184 **farborough]** Tharborough *F1 (the F1 form is closer to the standard form third-borough, but the Q1 reading is well within Dull's capacity for verbal blundering)*
190 s.p. **Cost.]** *Rowe*; Clowne. *Q1, F1 (throughout scene, except ll. 222, 224)*
190 **contempts]** *F1*; Contempls *Q1*
211 **form—]** *Capell*; forme *Q1, F1*
219 etc. s.dd. **Reads.]** *Rowe*
219–20 **welkin's vicegerent]** *F1*; welkis Vizgerent *Q1*
222 **Costard]** *F1*; Costart *Q1*
231 **besieged]** *F1*; besedged *Q1*
234 **health-giving]** *F1*; health-geuing *Q1*
242 **prepost'rous]** *F1 (preposterous)*; propostrous *Q1*
242 **snow-white]** *F1*; snowhite *Q1*
246 **curious-knotted]** *hyphen, Theobald*
250 **small-knowing]** *hyphen, F2*
277 **heart-burning]** *hyphen, F1*
281 **worst]** *F1*; wost *Q1*
294 s.p. **King.]** *from F1 Fer.*; Ber. *Q1*
307 s.d. **Exeunt . . . Dumaine.]** *Capell*; Exeunt. *F2*
313 **prosperity]** *F1*; prosperie *Q1*
314 **Affliction]** *F1*; affliccio *Q1*
314–5 **till . . . thee]** vntill then sit *F1*

I.ii

I.ii] *Capell*
3 s.p. **Moth.]** *Rowe*; Boy. *Q1, F1 (throughout scene)*
4 **Why,]** *Pope (subs.)*; Why? *Q1, F1*
14 **epitheton]** *F2*; apethaton *Q1*; apathaton *F1*
33, 56, 120 s.dd. **Aside.]** *Hanmer*
51 **ye'll]** *Cambridge*; yele *Q1*; you'll *F1*
101 **blush in]** *ed.*; blush-in *Q1, F1*; blushing *F2*
117 **president]** *F1*; presedent *Q1*
127 s.p. **Dull.]** *Rowe*; Constab. *Q1*; Const. *F1*
128 **suffer him to]** let him *F1*
131 **dey-woman]** *Wilson*; Day womand *Q1*; Day-woman *F1*
134 s.p. **Jaq.]** *Rowe*; Maide. *Q1, F1 (throughout scene)*
140 **that face?]** that face. *Q1*; what face? *F1*
145 s.p. **Dull.]** *Theobald*; Clo. *Q1, F1*
145 s.d. **Dull and Jaquenetta]** *Theobald*
148 s.p. **Cost.]** *Rowe*; Clo. *Q1, F1 (throughout scene)*
166 s.d. **with Moth]** *Pope (subs.)*
179 **duello]** *F1*; Duella *Q1*

II.i

II.i] *Rowe*; Actus Secunda. *F1*
o.s.d. **one named Boyet]** *Kittredge*

2 **Consider]** *F1*; Cosider *Q1*
13 s.p. **Prin.]** *F2*; Queene. *Q1, F1*
21–34] *F1 assigns these lines to Prin.*
21 **all-telling]** *hyphen, F1*
29 **best-moving]** *hyphen, Warburton*
32 **Importunes]** *F1*; Importuous *Q1*
34 **humble-visag'd]** *F1 (hyphen, Pope)*; humble visage *Q1*
37–8 **Who . . . Duke?]** *as verse, Rowe; as prose, Q1, F1*
39 s.p. **1. Lord.]** *Capell*; Lor. *Q1, F1*
39 **Lord]** *Capell*
40 s.p. **Mar.]** *Rowe*; 1. Lady. *Q1, F1*
40–2 **madam; . . . solemnized]** *Capell*; Maddame . . . solemnized. *Q1, F1*
44 **parts, peerless]** *Alexander*; peerelsse he is *Q1*; parts he is *F1*
53 s.p. **Mar.]** *Rowe*; Lad. *Q1*; Lad. 1. *F1*
54 **short-liv'd]** *F1 (hyphen, Rowe)*; short liued *Q1*
56 s.p. **Kath.]** *Rowe*; 2. Lad. *Q1, F1*
61 **Alanson's]** *Rowe (subs.)*; Alansoes *Q1, F1*
64 s.p. **Ros.]** *F1 (Rossa.)*; 3. Lad. *Q1*
80 s.p. **1. Lord.]** *Capell*; Lord. *Q1*; Ma. *F1*
88 **unpeopled]** *F1*; vnpeeled *Q1*
88 s.d. **and Attendants]** *Rowe*
89 **Here]** *F1*; Bo. Heere *Q1 (repeated s.p.)*
89 s.d. **The . . . mask.]** *ed. (after Capell)*
90 s.p. **King.]** Nauar. *Q1, F1 (or Nau. through l. 111)*
100 **it, will]** *Capell (subs.)*; it will, *Q1, F1*
110 s.d. **Giving a paper.]** *Collier MS (after Capell)*
115–27] *Katherine's speeches in these lines assigned to Rosaline, F1*
116 **needless]** *F1*; needles *Q1*
128 s.p. **King.]** *F1*; Ferd. *Q1 (through l. 167)*
140 **friendship]** *F1*; faiendship *Q1*
142 **demand]** *F1*; pemaund *Q1*
144 **On]** *Theobald*; One *Q1, F1*
167 **I will]** would I *F1*
173–4 **heart, . . . house.]** *F1*; hart. . . . house, *Q1*
178 s.p. **King.]** Na. *F1*
178 s.d. **with . . . Attendants]** *Capell (subs.)*
179 **mine own]** *Q2*; my none *Q1*; my owne *F1*
184 **fool]** soule *F1*
190 **No point]** No poynt *Q1, F1 (both in italics)*
195 **Katherine]** *Capell conj. (Catharine)*; Rosalin *Q1, F1*
196 **lady. Monsieur]** *Rowe (subs.)*; Lady Mounsir *Q1*; Lady, Mounsier *F1*
196 s.d. **Enter Longaville.]** *Wilson (subs.)*
210 **Rosaline]** *Brae conj. (in Cambridge)*; Katherin *Q1*; Katherine *F1*
219 s.p. **Kath.]** La. Ma. *F1*
219 **sheeps, marry.]** *Rowe (marry F4)*; Sheepes marie. *Q1*; Sheepes marie: *F1 (continuing the rest of l. 219 to La. Ma.)*
221, 222, 224 s.pp. **Kath.]** *Wilson*; La. or Lad. *Q1, F1*

222 s.d. **Offering . . . her.**] *Capell*
228–9 **lies), . . . eyes,**] *Theobald;* lyes / . . . eyes. *Q1;* lies / . . . eyes) *F1*
242 **lock'd**] *F3;* lokt *Q1;* lockt *F1*
245 **you to**] out to *F1*
254 s.p. **Mar.**] *Capell;* Lad. *Q1;* Lad. Ro. *F1*
255 s.p. **Kath.**] *Capell;* Lad. 2. *Q1;* La. Ma. *F1*
256 s.p. **Ros.**] *Rowe;* Lad. 3. *Q1;* Lad. 2. *F1*
257 s.p. **Mar.**] *Rowe;* Lad. *Q1;* La. 1. *F1*
258 s.p. **Mar.**] *Neilson;* Lad. *Q1;* Lad. 2. *F1*

III.i

III.i] *Rowe;* Actus Tertius. *F1*
1 s.p. **Arm.**] *Rowe;* Bra. *Q1, F1 (through l. 66)*
3 s.p. **Moth.**] *Rowe;* Boy. *Q1, F1 (throughout scene)*
3 s.d. **Sings . . . "Concolinel."**] *Wilson;* Concolinel. *Q1, F1 (F1 adds* Song. *centred above l. 1)*
13 **eyelids**] eie *F1*
15 **as**] *Theobald*
16 **through the**] *F2;* through: *Q1, F1*
19 **thin-bellied**] *ed.;* thinbellies *Q1;* thinbellie *F1*
25 **note?—**] *Neilson;* note *Q1, F1*
27 **penny**] *Hanmer;* penne *Q1, F1*
32 s.d. **aside**] *Nicholson conj. (in Cambridge)*
35 **Negligent**] *F1;* Necligent *Q1*
40 **and this,**] *Theobald;* (and this) *Q1, F1*
47 s.d. **aside**] *Nicholson conj. (in Cambridge)*
58–9 **The . . . slow?**] *as verse, Pope; as prose, Q1, F1*
58 **The**] Thy *F1*
65 s.d. **Exit.**] *Rowe*
66 **voluble**] voluble *F1*
71 **l'envoy—**] *Johnson;* Lenuoy *Q1, F1*
73 **the mail**] *Malone (after Johnson;* the *F2);* thee male *Q1, F1*
73 **plain**] *F1;* pline *Q1*
83–92 **I . . . four.**] *om. F1*
121 **Frances**] *Capell;* Francis *Q1, F1*
130 s.d. **giving a letter**] *Dyce (after Capell)*
134 s.d. **Armado . . . Moth**] *Kittredge*
138 **remuneration**] *F1;* remuration *Q1*
139 **One penny.**] *Cambridge;* i.d. *Q1, F1*
140–1 **it. Remuneration**] *Theobald;* it remuneration *Q1, F1*
171 **aleven-pence-farthing**] *ed.;* a leuenpence-farthing *Q1, F1*
176 **critic**] *F1;* Crietick *Q1*
180 **senior-junior**] *Hanmer (after Theobald);* signior Iunios *Q1, F1*
180 **giant-dwarf**] *hyphen, Theobald*
185 **imperator**] *Rowe;* Emperator *Q1, F1*
190 **German**] *F1 (subs.);* Iermane *Q1*
190 **clock**] *F2;* Cloake *Q1, F1*
196 **whitely**] *F3;* whitly *F1*
204 **sue**] *F2;* shue *Q1, F1*
205 s.d. **Exit.**] *Rowe*

IV.i

IV.i] *Rowe;* Actus Quartus. *F1*
o.s.d. **among them Boyet**] *ed. (after Capell)*
1 s.p. **Prin.**] Quee. *Q1, F1 (subs., throughout scene)*
2 **steep-up rising**] *Hart;* steepe vp rising *Q1;* steepe vprising *F1*
3 s.p. **For.**] Boy. *F1*
6 **On**] *F1;* Ore *Q1 (possibly correct = or in the early sense of "before")*
14 **and**] and then *F1*
18 s.d. **Giving him money.**] *Johnson*
32 **praise**] *Pope;* praise *Q1, F1*
42 s.p. **Cost.**] *Rowe;* Clo. *Q1, F1 (subs., throughout scene)*
69 **saw**] *F2;* See *Q1, F1*
70 **saw**] *Rowe;* see *Q1, F1*
70 **overcame**] *F3;* couercame *Q1, F1*
75 **king's**] *F3;* king *Q1, F1*
82 **What**] *F4;* What, *Q1, F1*
87 **Adriano**] *Q2;* Adriana *Q1, F1*
87 **Armado**] *F2;* Armatho *Q1, F1*
95 **vane**] *Rowe;* vaine *Q1;* veine *F1*
101 **you:**] *Theobald (subs.);* you, *Q1, F1*
107 s.d. **To Rosaline.**] *Capell*

107 s.d. **Exeunt . . . Train.**] *Theobald (subs.);* Exeunt. *F1*
125, 127 s.dd. **Sings.**] *Wilson*
128 s.d. **Exeunt . . . Katherine.**] *Capell;* Exit. *Q1, F1 (placed as in F1; after l. 126, Q1)*
130 **it**] *F4*
136 **pin**] *F2;* is in *Q1, F1*
139 s.d. **Exeunt . . . Maria.**] *Theobald (subs.)*
142 **O'**] *Rowe;* O *Q1, F1*
144 **Armado**] *Q1;* Armatho *F1*
144 **a' th' one**] *Rowe (subs.);* ath toothen *Q1;* ath to the *F1*
148 **a**] *F2*
148 s.d. **Shout**] *F2;* Shoot *Q1, F1 (s.d. placed as in Capell; after* Exeunt. *Q1, F1)*
149 **Sola, sola**] *Capell;* Sowla, sowla *Q1, F1*
149 s.d. **Exit.**] *Theobald;* Exeunt. *Q1, F1*

IV.ii

IV.ii] *Pope*
o.s.d. **from . . . hunt**] *ed. (after Alexander)*
3 s.p. **Hol.**] *Rowe;* Ped. *Q1, F1*
8 **epithites**] *F2;* epythithes *Q1, F1*
14–5 **explication; facere,**] *Theobald;* explication *facere: Q1, F1*
22–3 **Twice . . . look!**] *as verse, Dyce; as prose, Q1, F1*
28–9 **And . . . he.**] *as verse, Hanmer; as prose, Q1, F1*
29 **of**] *Tyrwhitt conj.*
30 **indiscreet**] *F1;* indistreell *Q1*
36, 37 **Dictynna**] *Rowe;* Dictisima . . . dictisima . . . dictima *Q1, F1*
40 **five weeks**] *Rowe;* fiue-weeks *Q1, F1*
46 **pollution**] *Rowe;* polusion *Q1, F1*
52 **ignorant, call I**] *Cambridge;* ignorault cald *Q1;* ignorant call'd *F1*
52 **deer**] *Rowe;* Deare: *Q1;* Deare, *F1*
54 **squirility**] *Rowe;* scurilitie *Q1, F1*
56 **preyful**] *Collier;* prayfull *Q1, F1*
58 **l**] *Capell;* ell *Q1, F1*
59 **pricket sore**] *Theobald;* Pricket-sore *Q1, F1*
59 **a-hooting**] *hyphen, Dyce*
60 **L**] *Pope;* el *Q1;* ell *F1*
60 **o' sorel**] *Wilson (after Warburton);* o sorell *Q1, F1*
61 **L**] *F1;* l *Q1*
63 s.d. **Aside.**] *Dyce (after Collier MS)*
65, 78, 83, 87, 104 s.pp. **Hol.**] *Rowe;* Nath. *Q1, F1*
69 **pia mater**] *Rowe;* prima- / ter *Q1;* primater *F1*
71 **in**] *F1*
73, 103 s.pp. **Nath.**] *Rowe;* Holo. *or* Hol. *Q1, F1*
78 **ingenious**] *Capell;* ingenous *Q1;* ingennous *F1*
80 **sapit**] *Q2;* sapis *Q1, F1*
83 **pers-one**] *Capell;* Person *Q1, F1;* Persone *F2*
85 s.p. **Cost.**] *Rowe;* Clo. *Q1, F1*
86 **likel'est**] *ed.;* liklest *Q1;* likest *F1*
92 **Armado**] *Collier;* Armatho *Q1, F1*
93 s.p. **Hol.**] *Thirlby conj.;* Nath. *Q1, F1*
93 **pecus omne**] *Theobald;* pecas omnia *Q1, F1*
97 **Venechia, Venechia**] *Sisson;* vemchie, vencha *Q1, F1*
98 **Che . . . che**] *Sisson;* que . . . que *Q1, F1*
98 **vede**] *Malone;* vnde *Q1, F1*
98 **prechia**] *Sisson;* perreche *Q1, F1*
100 **loves thee not.**] *om. F1*
104 **stanze**] *F1;* stauze *Q1*
105 s.p. **Nath.**] *Rowe; Q1, F1 make ll. 105–18 a continuation of the preceding speech, which they assign to* Nath. *(see note on ll. 65 etc., above)*
105 s.d. **Reads.**] *Capell*
105–18 **"If . . . tongue."**] *see a slightly variant version in* The Passionate Pilgrim, v
118 **That sings**] *F1;* That singes *Q1;* To sing *Passionate Pilgrim*
119 s.p. **Hol.**] *Rowe;* Pedan. *Q1;* Ped. *F1*
120 **canzonet**] *Theobald;* cangenet *F1 (correcting Q1* cangenct; *possibly intended as one of Holofernes' mispronunciations, like* apostraphas *in l. 119)*

120–1 s.d. **He . . . letter.**] *Wilson*
121–8 **Here . . . you?**] *continued to* Holofernes, *Theobald; given to* Nath. *Q1, F1*
125 **invention? Imitari**] *Theobald;* inuention imitarie *Q1, F1;* invention imitary *F2*
131 s.p. **Hol.**] *Theobald;* Nath. *Q1, F1*
134 **writing**] *Rowe;* written *Q1, F1*
136–43 **Sir . . . Adieu.**] *continued to* Holofernes, *Theobald (see note, l. 131); assigned to* Ped. *Q1 (Per. F1)*
136 **Nathaniel**] *Capell;* Holofernes *Q1, F1 (Theobald om. Sir Holofernes)*
144 s.p. **Jaq.**] *Theobald;* Mayd. *Q1, F1*
146 s.d. **with Jaquenetta**] *Rowe (subs.)*
147 s.p. **Nath.**] *Rowe;* Holo. *Q1;* Hol. *F1*
149, 153, 163 s.pp. **Hol.**] Ped. *or* Peda. *Q1, F1*
154 **before**] being *F1*
164 s.d. **To Dull.**] *Theobald*

IV.iii

IV.iii] *Steevens*
20 s.d. **climbing . . . tree**] *Wilson (after Collier MS)*
20, 42, 74 s.dd. **with a paper**] *Capell*
22, 44, etc. s.dd. **Aside.**] *Johnson*
24 s.d. **Reads.**] *Theobald*
37 **wilt**] *F1;* will *Q1*
47 s.p. **King.**] *Rowe;* Long. *Q1, F1*
51 **corner-cap**] *hyphen, Rowe*
58–71 **"Did . . . paradise?"**] *see a slightly variant version in* The Passionate Pilgrim, III
68 **vapor-vow;**] *F4;* vapour-vow *Q1;* vapor vow, *Passionate Pilgrim;* vapour-vow, *F1*
71 **lose**] *F4;* loose *Q1, F1*
72 **liver-vein**] *hyphen, Rowe*
73 **idolatry**] *F1;* ydotarie *Q1*
75 s.d. **Steps aside.**] *Johnson*
85 **hairs**] *F1;* heires *Q1*
86 **amber-color'd**] *hyphen, Rowe*
97 **ode**] *F1;* Odo *Q1*
99–118 **"On . . . love."**] *see a slightly variant version in* The Passionate Pilgrim, XVI
106 **Wish'd**] *Passionate Pilgrim, F2;* Wish *Q1, F1*
106 **heavens'**] *ed.;* heauens *Q1, Passionate Pilgrim, F1*
110 **thorn**] *England's Helicon, Rowe;* throne *Q1, Passionate Pilgrim, F1*
120 **true love's**] *Rowe;* trueloues *Q1;* trueloues *F1*
125, 129 s.dd. **Advancing.**] *Rowe (subs.)*
128 **o'erheard**] *F1;* ore-hard *Q1*
140 **One,**] *Malone;* One *Q1;* On *F1*
141 s.d. **To Longaville.**] *Johnson*
142 s.d. **To Dumaine.**] *Johnson*
149 s.d. **Descending and advancing.**] *Wilson (after Johnson)*
153 **coaches; . . . tears**] *Hanmer;* couches . . . teares. *Q1, F1*
159 **mote . . . mote**] *Rowe;* Moth . . . Moth *Q1, F1*
178 **men . . . men**] *S. Walker conj.;* men like men *Q1;* men, like men *F1*
180 **Joan**] *Q1 (c)* (Ione), *F1* (Ioane); Loue *Q1 (u)*
181 **me? When**] *F3;* mee when *Q1;* mee, when *F1*
195 s.d. **Berowne . . . letter.**] *Capell (subs.)*
199 s.d. **Gathering . . . pieces.**] *Capell (subs.)*
200 s.d. **To Costard.**] *Theobald*
209 s.d. **Exeunt . . . Jaquenetta.**] *Theobald*
222 **peremptory**] *F1;* peromptorie *Q1*
238 **hermit**] *F1;* Hermigtt *Q1*
244 **wood**] *Rowe;* word *Q1, F1*
255 **and**] *F4*
262 **black**] *F1;* blake *Q1*
264 **crack**] *Q2;* crake *Q1, F1*
273 s.d. **showing his boot**] *Wilson (subs., after Capell)*
292–314] *These lines (included in both Q1 and F1) clearly represent Shakespeare's first draft of parts of the speech which follows in ll. 315–62*
293 **book,**] *Hanmer;* Booke. *Q1, F1*
320 **beauty's**] *Rowe;* beautis *Q1;* beauties *F1*
336 **dainty Bacchus**] *F2;* daintie, Bachus *Q1, F1*

339 **Subtile]** *F1* (Subtill); Subtit *Q1*
356 **authors]** *Johnson;* authour *Q1, F1*
358 **Let]** *F2;* Lets *Q1;* Let's *F1* (*om.* us)
364 **standards]** *F1;* standars *Q1*
380 **Allons! allons!]** *Theobald;* Alone alone *Q1;* Alone, alone *F1*
380 **Sow'd]** *Capell;* sowed *Q1, F1*
383 s.d. **Exeunt.]** *F1*

V.i

V.i] *Rowe;* Actus Quartus. *F1*
1 s.p. **Hol.]** *Rowe;* Pedant. *Q1, F1* (or Ped., Peda., *throughout scene*)
2 s.p. **Nath.]** *Rowe;* Curat. *Q1, F1* (*throughout scene*)
8 **Armado]** *Rowe;* Armatho *Q1, F1*
9 **hominem]** *F3;* hominum *Q1, F1*
15 **epithet]** *F3;* Epithat *Q1, F1*
18–9 **point-devise]** *hyphen, Pope*
19 **ortography]** *ed.:* ortagriphie *Q1, F1*
25 **insanie]** *Theobald;* infamie *Q1, F1*
27 **bone]** *Theobald;* bene *Q1, F1* (bene *is correct Latin, but Holofernes' comment requires an error on Sir Nathaniel's part*)
28 **Bone . . . Priscian]** *Theobald;* Bome boon for boon prescian, *Q1, F1*
29 s.d. **and Costard]** *Rowe*
31 **gaudeo]** *Q2;* gaudio *Q1, F1*
32 s.p. **Arm.]** *Rowe;* Brag. *Q1, F1* (*throughout scene*)
32 s.d. **To Moth.]** *Capell*
33 **Quare]** *F2;* Quari *Q1, F1*
36 s.p. **Moth.]** *Rowe;* Boy. *Q1, F1*
36 s.d. **Aside to Costard.]** *Johnson*
38 s.p. **Cost.]** *Rowe;* Clow. *Q1, F1* (*throughout scene*)
43 s.p. **Moth.]** *Rowe;* Page. *Q1, F1* (*throughout scene*)
44 s.d. **To Holofernes.]** *Capell*
58 **wave]** *F1;* wane *Q1*
59 **venue]** *F2;* vene we *Q1, F1*
69 **manu cita]** *anon. conj.* (*in Cambridge*); vnū cita *Q1;* vnum cita *F1*
76 **wert]** *F1;* wart *Q1*
77 **dunghill]** *F4* (*subs.*); dungil *Q1, F1*
79 **dunghill]** *Rowe* (*subs.*); dunghel *Q1, F1*
81 **preambulate]** *Cambridge;* preambulat *Q1, F1* (*in italics*)
99 **importunate]** *F1;* importunt *Q1*
104 **mustachio]** *F1;* mustachie *Q1*
110 **secrety]** secretie *Q1;* secrecie *F1*
118 **Nathaniel]** *Capell;* Holofernes *Q1, F1*
120 **rend'red]** *F1;* rended *Q1*
120 **assistance,]** *Theobald conj.;* assistants *Q1, F1;* assistants at *F2*
126 **myself;]** *Sisson;* my selfe, *Q1, F1*
147 **antic]** *Theobald;* Antique *Q1, F1*
152 **Allons]** *Rowe;* Alone *Q1, F1*
153–4 **I'll . . . hay.]** *as verse, Dyce; as prose, Q1, F1*
155 **Most dull]** *Theobald;* Most *Dull Q1, F1*

V.ii

V.ii] *Steevens*
3–4 **A . . . King.]** *as verse, Pope; as prose, Q1, F1*
13 **ne'er]** *F1;* neare *Q1*
15–7 **And . . . died.]** *as verse, F2; as prose, Q1, F1*
17 **'a']** *Kittredge;* a *Q1, F1*
17 **been a]** *F1;* bin *Q1*
22 **You'll]** *F1;* Yole *Q1*
43 **pencils]** *Q2* (pensils); pensalls *Q1, F1*
43 **ho!]** *Hanmer;* How? *Q1, F1*
53, 57 s.pp. **Mar.]** *F1;* Marg. *Q1*
53 **pearls]** *F1;* Pearle *Q1*
65 **device]** *so Q1, F1, breaking the couplet rhyme; F2 reads the line as* And shape his service all to my behests; *Knight suggested* hests *for* deuice
67 **pair-taunt-like]** *Percy Simpson* (*in TLS*); perttaunt like *Q1, F1*
70 **fool; . . . hatch'd,]** *F2;* Foole, . . . hatcht: *Q1, F1*
74 **gravity's]** *Warburton;* grauities *Q1, F1*
74 **wantonness]** *F2;* wantons be *Q1, F1*
80 **stabb'd]** *F1;* stable *Q1*
82–3 **are . . . disguis'd,]** *Theobald* (*subs.*); are,

/ Against your Peace Loue doth approch, disguysd: *Q1* (*Q1 pointing makes some sense but is very awkward; F1 adds comma after* Peace)
89 **sycamore]** *F1;* Siccamone *Q1*
91 **purpos'd]** *F1;* purposed *Q1*
93 **companions. Warily]** *F1* (companions:); companions warely, *Q1*
96 **they]** *F1;* thy *Q1*
118 **folly, passion's]** *Theobald;* follie pashions *Q1;* folly passions *F1*
118 **solemn]** *F1;* solembe *Q1*
120 **apparell'd]** *F1;* appariled *Q1*
122 **parley]** *Rowe;* parlee *Q1, F1*
132–3 **Hold . . . Rosaline.]** *possibly a revised form of ll. 130–1*
134 **too]** *F1;* two *Q1*
135 **deceiv'd]** *F1;* deceyued *Q1*
139 **mockery]** mocking *Q1*
148 **her]** *F2;* his *Q1, F1*
149 **speaker's]** keepers *F1*
152 **ne'er]** *F2;* ere *Q1, F1*
156 s.d. **trumpet within]** *Capell* (Trumpets); Trom. *Q1; om. F1*
157 s.d. **The Ladies mask.]** *Johnson*
157 s.d. **the King]** *Rowe*
157 s.d. **as Russians]** *Capell* (*subs., after Rowe*)
158 s.p. **Moth.]** *Rowe;* Page. *Q1, F1* (*subs., throughout scene*)
159 s.p. **Boyet.]** *Theobald;* Berow. *Q1, F1*
161 **their—backs—]** *Capell;* their backes *Q1, F1*
163 **ever]** *F1;* euen *Q1*
169 **sun-beamed]** *hyphen, Rowe*
170 **sun-beamed]** *hyphen, F4*
171 **epithet]** *F4* (*subs.*); Epythat *Q1;* Epythite *F1*
172 **daughter-beamed]** *hyphen, F2*
174 s.d. **Exit Moth.]** *Capell*
175 **strangers]** *F1;* stranges *Q1*
178 **Princess]** *F4;* Princes *Q1, F1*
197 **travel]** *F1;* trauaile *Q1*
211 s.d. **Music plays.]** *Capell* (*subs.*)
212 **yet;]** *Capell;* yet *Q1, F1*
216 **The . . . it.]** *continued to the King, Theobald; assigned to Rosa. Q1, F1* (. . . it, *Q1;* . . . it: *F1*)
217 s.p. **Ros.]** *Theobald*
219 **nice; take hands.]** *Theobald* (*subs.*); nice, take handes, *Q1, F1*
222 **measure;]** *F3;* measue *Q1;* measure, *F1*
229, 237, 241, 255 s.dd. **They converse apart.]** *Capell*
230 **White-handed]** *hyphen, F4*
242, 244, 247, 248, 249, 253, 255 s.pp. **Kath.]** *Rowe;* Maria, Mari., *or* Mar. *Q1, F1*
258–9 **seen; . . . sense, so sensible]** *Theobald;* seene, . . . sense so sensible, *Q1,* (sensible:) *F1*
263 **dry-beaten]** *hyphen, Hanmer*
264 s.d. **Exeunt . . . Blackmoors.]** *Theobald* (*subs.*); Exe. *Q1;* Exeunt. *F1*
269 **kingly-poor]** *hyphen, Capell*
274 **weeping-ripe]** *hyphen, Rowe*
297 **vailing]** *F1;* varling *Q1*
309 **run]** *F4;* runs *Q1, F1*
309 s.d. **Princess and Ladies]** *Capell* (*subs.*)
309 s.d. **of . . . habits]** *Rowe* (*subs.*)
311–2 **Gone . . . thither?]** *as verse, Capell* (*F1 as irregular verse, om.* thither); *as prose, Q1*
316 **God]** Ioue *Q1*
328 **hushering]** Vshering *F1*
334 **due]** dutie *F1*
336 **Armado's]** *F2;* Armathoes *Q1, F1*
336 s.d. **Princess . . . her]** *Capell* (*subs.*)
338 **madman]** *F1;* mad man *Q1*
338 **show'd]** *F1;* shewed *Q1*
341 **Conster]** *ed.;* Consture *Q1;* Construe *F1*
352 **unsallied]** *cf. the form* sallied *in Hamlet* (*Q2, Q1*), I.ii.129; unsullied *F2*
356 **vow'd]** *F1;* vowed *Q1*
368 **stay'd]** *F4;* stayed *Q1, F1*
374 **foolish]** *Rowe* (*subs.*); foolish *Q1, F1*
375 **eye,]** *F3;* eie: *Q1, F1*
388 **show'd]** *F1;* shewed *Q1*
389, 390 s.dd. **Aside.]** *Capell*
407 **Three-pil'd]** *hyphen, F1*
407 **hyperboles]** *F1;* Hiberboles *Q1*

415 **sans]** *F1* (*in italics*); sance *Q1* (*in italics*)
416 **Sans]** *Tyrwhitt conj.;* Sans, *Q1, F1* (*in italics*)
439–40 **Peace . . . forswear.]** *as verse, F1; as prose, Q1*
463 **carry-tale]** *hyphen, F1*
463 **zany]** *F1;* saine *Q1*
464 **mumble-news]** *hyphen, F1*
464 **trencher-knight]** *hyphen, F1*
465 **smiles]** *F1;* smyles, *Q1*
472 s.d. **to Boyet]** *Rowe* (*after l. 472*); *placed as in Theobald*
478 **allow'd]** *F3;* aloude *Q1;* alowd *F1*
481 **merrily]** *F1;* merely *Q1*
482 **manage]** *Theobald;* nuage *Q1;* manager *F1*
485 s.p. **Cost.]** *Rowe;* Clow. *Q1, F1* (or Clowne., Clo., *throughout scene*)
490 **You . . . know.]** *as verse, Capell; as prose, Q1, F1*
501 **they]** *F1;* thy *Q1*
502–3 **Great,]** *Rowe;* great *Q1, F1*
512 **shame-proof]** *hyphen, F1*
516 **least]** *F1;* best *Q1*
523 s.d. **Converses . . . paper.]** *Capell*
530–1 **de la guerra]** *Theobald;* delaguar *Q1, F1*
532 **couplement]** *Capell* (*after Warburton*); cupplement *Q1, F1*
538–9 **And . . . five.]** *as verse, Rowe; as prose, Q1, F1*
545 **pick]** pricke *F1*
546 s.d. **Costard for]** *Rowe*
557 s.p. **Prin.]** *F2;* Lady. *Q1;* La. *F1*
566 **this]** *F1;* his *Q1*
566 **tender-smelling]** *hyphen, Capell*
568 **liv'd]** *Rowe;* liued *Q1, F1*
574 s.d. **To Nathaniel.]** *Capell*
579 **afeard]** *Capell;* a feard *Q1;* affraid *F1*
580 s.d. **Nathaniel retires.]** *Capell*
582 **faith]** insooth *F1*
586 **sort.]** *Rowe;* sort. Exit Curat. *Q1, F1;* Exit Clo. *F2*
588 s.p. **Hol.]** *Rowe;* Peda. *Q1, F1* (*throughout scene*)
589 **three-headed]** *hyphen, F1*
594 s.d. **Aside.]** *Neilson*
594 s.d. **Moth retires.]** *Capell;* Exit Boy. *Q1, F1* (*l. 594 in italics as part of Holofernes' role in Q1*)
600 **prov'd]** *F1;* proud *Q1*
606 **elder]** *F1;* Felder *Q1*
610 **cittern-head]** *hyphen, Knight*
614 **falchion]** *F1;* Fauchion *Q1*
616 **half-cheek]** *hyphen, Theobald*
623 **out-fac'd]** *F1;* outfaste *Q1*
628 **Jud-as]** *F1;* Iudas *Q1*
630 s.d. **Holofernes retires.]** *Capell*
631 s.d. **Enter]** *F1;* Eeter *Q1*
631 s.d. **Armado for Hector]** *Capell*
638 **clean-timber'd]** *hyphen, Warburton*
646 **gilt]** *F1;* gift *Q1*
654 **I . . . flower—]** *Capell* (*after Theobald, who included the line as part of Armado's role as Hector*); I . . . Flower. *Q1, F1* (*not distinguished by italics as part of Armado's role*)
662 **When . . . man.]** *om. F1*
663 s.d. **To the Princess.]** *Steevens* (*after Capell*)
664 s.d. **to . . . place]** *Capell* (*subs.*)
667 **I . . . slipper.]** *as F1; in italics as part of Armado's role, Q1*
671 **The . . . gone—]** *as part of Armado's speech, Pope; centred as s.d.* (*in italics*), *Q1, F1*
688–9 **mov'd. More . . . on,]** *Rowe* (*subs.*); mooued more Ates more Atees stir them or *Q1;* moued, more Atees more Atees stirre them, or *F1*
709 **for't]** *F1;* fort *Q1*
710 **have]** *F1;* hane *Q1*
716–7 **Welcome . . . merriment.]** *as verse, Capell; as prose, Q1, F1*
717 **interruptest]** *F1;* interrnpptest *Q1*
730 **endeavors, and entreat,]** *Rowe;* endeuors and entreat: *Q1;* endeuors and entreats: *F1*
731 **new-sad soul]** *Theobald;* new sad-soule *Q1, F1*

215

750 **wholesome-profitable**] *S. Walker conj.;* holdsome profitable *Q1;* wholsome profitable *F1*

759 **seem'd**] *F1;* seemed *Q1*

766 **parti-coated**] *hyphen, F1*

768 **misbecom'd**] *F1;* misbecombd *Q1*

768 **gravities,**] *Capell;* grauities. *Q1, F1*

774 **both—**] *Theobald (subs.);* both *Q1;* both, *F1*

778 **embassadors**] the Ambassadors *F1*

782 **this in**] *Hanmer;* this *Q1;* these are *F1*

785 **show'd**] *F1;* shewed *Q1*

807 **instant**] *F1;* instance *Q1*

812 **intitled**] *F1;* intiled *Q1*

816 **hermit**] *Pollard conj.* (in New Cambridge); herrite *Q1;* euer *F1*

817–22] *These lines (included in both Q1 and F1) clearly represent Shakespeare's first draft of ll. 837–54*

824 **A wife?**] *continued to Dumaine, Dyce; part of Katherine's next line, Q1, F1*

828 **smooth-fac'd**] *F3;* smothfast *Q1;* smoothfac'd *F1*

845 **estates**] *F1;* estetes *Q1*

847 **fructful**] fruitfull *F1*

872 s.d. **To the King.**] *Rowe*

879 s.p. **Arm.**] *Rowe;* Brag. *Q1, F1 (throughout scene)*

894 s.p. **Spring.**] *Theobald*

895–6 **And . . . hue**] *Theobald's arrangement; lines reversed, Q1, F1*

895 **silver-white**] *hyphen, Capell*

912 **icicles**] *F1* (Isicles); Isacles *Q1*

914 **Tom**] *F1;* Thom *Q1*

916 **foul**] *F1;* full *Q1*

930 s.p. **Arm.**] *F1* (Brag.)

930–1 **The . . . Apollo.**] *these lines set in larger roman type in Q1 without s.p.*

931 **You . . . way.**] *F1*

931 s.d. **Exeunt omnes.**] *F1* (Exeunt omnes. / FINIS.); FINIS. *Q1*

A sufferer from love melancholy. From Samuel Rowlands, *The Melancholy Knight* (1615). This representation of the fashionable and prescribed posture for the suffering lover matches almost perfectly Moth's advice to the infatuated Don Armado on how to win the love of Jaquenetta: he must sing "with your hat penthouse-like o'er the shop of your eyes; with your arms cross'd on your thin-bellied doublet like a rabbit on a spit" (*Love's Labor's Lost*, III.i.17–19). Similarly, in *The Two Gentlemen of Verona* (II.i.18–20), Speed knows by "special marks" that Valentine is in love, first of all, as he tells his master, because "you have learn'd . . . to wreathe your arms, like a malecontent." (*Curators of the Bodleian Library*)

A Midsummer Night's Dream

HEN Samuel Pepys saw *A Midsummer Night's Dream* in 1662, he reacted much as Hippolyta does to "the most lamentable comedy and most cruel death of Pyramus and Thisby" as performed by Bottom and his friends. "This is the silliest stuff that ever I heard," she says (V.i.210). Pepys's judgment, confided to his diary, that this was "the most insipid ridiculous play that ever I saw in my life" was extreme. Nevertheless, condescension to the comedy as a matter of gossamer and moonshine, a charming trifle to be eked out theatrically by as much music and spectacle as possible, dominated both the criticism and the stage representations of this play from the Restoration until the second half of the twentieth century. Only comparatively recently has it become possible to see that *A Midsummer Night's Dream* is a complex and exacting work of art. An extraordinary synthesis of material which, in itself, is challengingly diverse, the play embodies in its apparent effortlessness and poise Shakespeare's entire confidence at this time in his own comic form.

Although there is no identifiable narrative or dramatic source for the plot, a good deal of general reading seems to underlie the comedy. The influence of Ovid's *Metamorphoses* is evident both in the unifying theme of transformation and in the introduction of the Pyramus and Thisby story, which Ovid had related, and which Shakespeare must have known in the original Latin as well as in Golding's popular if rather ponderous translation of 1567. Hippolyta and her husband Theseus, that humane and practical hero, figure in Chaucer's "Knight's Tale" and also in North's translation of Plutarch's *Lives of the Noble Grecians and Romans* (1579), both of them works that

Shakespeare certainly knew. Bottom's transformation may have been inspired by the misfortune which overcomes Lucius in *The Golden Ass* of Apuleius, a Latin romance of the second century A.D. which existed in an early Elizabethan translation. Oberon had appeared in the old romance *Huon of Bordeaux*, and Bottom's fumbling attempt to characterize the marvellous dream he has had (IV.i.211–14) seems to depend upon a passage from St. Paul's *Epistle to the Corinthians* as it was rendered in the Bishops' Bible. The influence of St. Augustine and of some of the Renaissance Neo-Platonists has also been detected by certain recent commentators concerned to argue that in this comedy Shakespeare, for once, was handling ideas more usually associated with Spenser or with Jonson's masques at court. If, as is often supposed, *A Midsummer Night's Dream* was commissioned for a wedding celebration at Whitehall or in some great house, the presence of such literary and iconographical elements, most of them serving to define an ideal of Christian marriage, would obviously be appropriate. Unfortunately, neither a specific occasion nor the degree of Shakespeare's possible indebtedness to writers like Ficino and Pico della Mirandola has ever been satisfactorily established.

It would be a mistake, however, to regard the interwoven strands which make up the tapestry of the comedy as being predominantly literary and intellectual. By way of the title itself, and also through Theseus's suggestion that the lovers he finds sleeping in the forest might have come there early to "observe / The rite of May" (IV.i.132–33), the action of the play is associated with two traditional and distinct country festivals. Although Shakespeare cannily refuses to make any clear statement about the night or even the month of the year in which the lovers lose themselves in the forest (he was to be similarly evasive in *Twelfth Night*, despite the apparent clue provided, again, by the title), he was obviously concerned to evoke the audience's memories of holiday license and merriment, that atmosphere of madness and of magic, herb-lore and supernatural manifestations, which Elizabethans connected both with May-day and with the summer solstice. The comedy's concern with marriage and fertility is scarcely unique in Shakespeare, but the particular stress upon man's dependence on the natural world and its seasonal rhythms is at least as likely to have been dictated by the dramatist's awareness of the customs of May-day and Midsummer Eve as by any hypothetical noble wedding.

Athens, at the beginning of the play, is partly classical and partly Chaucer's somewhat quaint medieval dukedom. When the lovers return to it at the end, it seems to have transformed itself almost entirely into an Elizabethan great house. Here, despite references to Centaurs and "my kinsman Hercules" (V.i.47), Duke Theseus rules over his little kingdom more in the manner of Leicester at Kenilworth than as an antique hero. Like Athens, the wood nearby where most of the action takes place is both mythological and intensely English, alien and familiar. It is a compelling invention precisely because its true nature remains mysterious. Are its moonlit glades beneficent and beautiful, or merely frightening, the place of error and unreason? Certainly this sylvan world is complex. The fairies who attend upon Titania are, as Bottom makes clear, both spirits and common English insects and flowers. Even the moon which presides over the whole imbroglio contrives to be a simple source of light, a goddess, the subject of learned allusions to the triple Hecate, participant in an allegorical tableau in praise of Queen Elizabeth, a stage prop, and (in the rustic imagination at least) the place that an old man with a thorn-bush and a dog calls home.

Oberon and Titania, the sovereign spirits of the wood, are exotic personages who might well inhabit a court masque, or start out from the greenery of some nobleman's park to welcome Queen Elizabeth on one of her royal progresses. Shakespeare sees them as dangerous powers whose dissensions and quarrels can disorder the seasons and throw the natural world into chaos. They bless the human marriages at the end, but it should not be forgotten that they have also the power to destroy. Puck, on the other hand, is the far more homely product of rural superstition, the Robin Goodfellow of Shakespeare's Warwickshire childhood. An intruder into the more elegant fairy world, he does not belong properly to the forest at all, but to sixteenth-century village life as it was lived in dairies, orchards, and smoky cottage interiors. His victims in the play, Hermia and Lysander, Helena and Demetrius, would probably have reminded many of the members of Shakespeare's audience of equivalent characters in the court comedies of John Lyly. They are only slightly individualized, not because Shakespeare was incapable at this stage of fuller charac-

terization, but because he obviously wished to distance the lovers, subordinating them to the total pattern of the play. Ironically, although they themselves regard each other as strikingly different, objects of passionate love or hate, all four look and behave, from the point of view of the outsider—whether Puck or the theatre audience—remarkably alike. They present a deliberately generalized picture of love's unreason, a state governed less by individual disposition than by the madness appropriate to a particular time of life as well as of the year.

Bottom and his friends, the last and in a way the most surprising of the various groups of characters assembled in the wood, are plain Elizabethan workmen. The play which they present for the delectation of Theseus and his court is also, in essence, Elizabethan. Although most of the plays, both popular and courtly, written between 1560 and the new departure signalized by Marlowe's *Tamburlaine* in 1587 have been lost, enough of them survive to indicate that in the Pyramus and Thisby interlude Shakespeare was remembering, and mocking, actual plays which had formed part of the repertory of the children's companies and of the travelling groups of adult players when he was a boy. Some of Bottom's most grotesque speeches as Pyramus are surprisingly close to lines intended to be spoken in all seriousness in *Appius and Virginia* (1564) or in Preston's *Cambises* (1561). The mechanicals themselves are deeply confused about the nature of theatrical illusion. Probably only Bottom has ever seen a professional play. Their decision to add an explanatory Prologue, and to personify Moonshine and Wall, is unfortunate but the text they have chosen to perform is in any case hilarious, even without these blundering embellishments. Shakespeare the London professional backed by an acting company gradually outstripping its rivals and soon to build a dazzling new theatre on the Bankside and acquire a royal patent, could afford to burlesque the bad plays and outmoded acting styles of the recent past.

A Midsummer Night's Dream was first printed in a quarto edition in 1600. The comedy was first mentioned by Meres in 1598, but 1595–96 is usually accepted as the date of composition. It has certain stylistic affinities with *Richard II* and *Romeo and Juliet*, plays which must have been written at about the same time. More importantly, it seems to consolidate and conclude Shakespeare's first period of experiment with comic form. The synthesizing impulse characteristic of *A Midsummer Night's Dream* not only knits together a number of different historical times and places, literary traditions, character types, and modes of thought. It manifests itself in the play's unusual variety of metres and verse forms, as well as in the tendency, remarked on by several critics, for characters to stress the richness of their encompassing dramatic world by listing its components. Egeus is not content simply to state that Lysander has exchanged love-tokens with Hermia. He names them all: "bracelets of thy hair, rings, gawds, conceits, / Knacks, trifles, nosegays, sweetmeats" (I.i.33–34). Almost all the characters are given to list-making. Oberon painstakingly itemizes every kind of wild beast that might conceivably wake Titania; Hermia and Lysander count all the obstacles that have ever threatened true love, while the fairies almost bury Bottom alive under a deluge of honey and butterflies, glow-worms, apricots and figs.

Shakespeare's friend Ben Jonson was, in many of his plays, a compulsive maker of dramatic inventories of a superficially similar kind. *Volpone*, *The Alchemist* and *Bartholomew Fair* are filled with tallies, a sea of objects which continually threaten to engulf the characters. Nothing, however, could be more different in effect from the list-making of *A Midsummer Night's Dream.* Jonson's world of things is stifling and corrupt, inanimate, man-made and man-soiled, the dusty contents of some Gothic lumber-room of the imagination: "his copper rings, / His saffron jewel, with the toad-stone in't, / Or his embroidered suit, with the cope-stitch, / Made of a hearse-cloth, or his old tilt-feather" (*Volpone*, II.v.11–14). Almost invariably, Jonson's enumerations evoke an incoherent urban world, so overcrowded that it has become impossible for human beings to walk about naturally among the detritus of a civilization out of control. By contrast, the lists in Shakespeare's comedy create the sense of a country world that is inexhaustibly rich and various, occasionally grotesque, but basically fresh, creative, and young. Moreover, where Jonson's lists are deliberately disjunctive, images of chaos, Shakespeare's relate and interact without sacrificing the individuality of the separate components. In the remarkably generous and inclusive order of *A Midsummer Night's Dream*, where Bottom can converse amiably with the fairy queen without losing a jot of his own identity, there seems to be nothing which the shaping spirit of imagination cannot use and, in some way, make relevant to the whole.

Not surprisingly, a preoccupation with the idea of imagination, and with some of its products—dreams, the illusions of love, poetry and plays—is central to this comedy. Theseus may speak somewhat slightingly of "the lunatic, the lover, and the poet," beings "of imagination all compact" whose fantasies are literally incredible: "more strange than true" (V.i.2 ff). The play as a whole takes a far more complicated view of the matter. Theseus himself, for Shakespeare as for Chaucer and Sophocles, is preeminently the hero of a daylight world of practicalities, of the active as opposed to the contemplative life. His relationship with Hippolyta in the comedy presents an image of passion steadied by the relative maturity of the people involved. There are ages of love as well as of human life and Theseus and Hippolyta represent summer as opposed to the giddy spring fancies of the couples lost in the wood. Theseus is a wise ruler and a good man, but Shakespeare makes it plain that there are other, important areas of human experience with which he is incompetent to deal. When Theseus leads the bridal couples to bed at the end of Act V with the mocking reminder that " 'tis almost fairy time" (V.i.364), he intends the remark as a last jibe at Hermia and Lysander, Helena and Demetrius: people who, in his estimation, have been led all too easily by darkness and their own fear to suppose a bush a bear (V.i.22). The joke, however, is on Theseus. It is indeed almost fairy time. In fact, Puck, Oberon, and Titania have been waiting for this moment in order to take over the palace. For a few nocturnal hours the wood infiltrates the urban world. Even so, years before, a Titania in whom Theseus apparently does not believe led him "through the glimmering night / From Perigenia, whom he ravished," and made him "with fair Aegles break his faith, / With Ariadne, and Antiopa" (II.i.77–80). The life of the self-appointed critic of imagination and the irrational is permeated by exactly those qualities he is concerned to minimize or reject. Gently, the comedy suggests that while it is certainly possible to mistake a bush for a bear, one may also err as Theseus does by confounding a genuine bear with a bush. The second mistake is, on the whole, the more dangerous.

The last act of *A Midsummer Night's Dream* is concerned principally, and even somewhat self-consciously, with the relationship between art and life, dreams and the waking world. In terms of plot, this fifth act is superfluous. Almost all the business of the comedy has been concluded at the end of Act IV: the error of Titania's vision put right and she herself reconciled with Oberon, Hermia paired off happily with Lysander and Helena with Demetrius. Theseus has not only overruled the objections of old Egeus, but insisted upon associating these marriages with his own: "Away with us to Athens. Three and three, / We'll hold a feast in great solemnity" (IV.i.184–85). This couplet has the authentic ring of a comedy conclusion. Only one expectation generated by the action remains unfulfilled: the presentation of the Pyramus and Thisby play before the Duke and his bride. Out of this single remaining bit of material, Shakespeare constructs a fifth act which seems, in effect, to take place beyond the normal, plot-defined boundaries of comedy.

The new social order which has emerged from the ordeal of the wood makes its first public appearance at the performance of the mechanicals' play. It is sensitive and hopeful. Theseus, characteristically, is condescending about the actor's art: "The best in this kind are but shadows; and the worst are no worse, if imagination amend them" (V.i.211–12). Richard Burbage would scarcely have thanked him. Such a view of the theatre overstresses the audience's lordly willingness-to-be-fooled at the expense of the power of illusion. Certainly a quite extraordinary effort of imagination would be required to extract Aristotelian pity and fear from the tragedy of Pyramus and Thisby as enacted by Bottom and Flute. The courtly audience, like the theatre audience, laughs at the ineptitudes and absurdities of the play within the play. Unlike Berowne and his friends in the equivalent scene of *Love's Labor's Lost*, however, the on-stage spectators in *A Midsummer Night's Dream* remain courteous. Most of the remarks made by Theseus, Hippolyta, and the four lovers are not heard by the preoccupied actors. Those that do penetrate, suggestions as to the proper disposition of Moonshine's lantern, dog, and bush, cries of "Well roar'd, Lion" and "Well run, Thisby," are entirely in the spirit of the performance. It was Bottom, after all, back in the rehearsal stage, who fondly imagined a success for Lion so great that the audience would intervene to request an encore: "Let him roar again." Gratifyingly, this wish-dream just about comes true. As the play proceeds, tolerance ripens into geniality, into an unforced accord between actors and spectators based upon considerations far more complex than anything articulated by Theseus. Although the artistic merit of the Pyramus and Thisby play is virtually non-existent, the performance itself is a resounding success. No feelings have been hurt, and everyone has had a thoroughly good time. Even Theseus finds that "this palpable-gross play hath well beguil'd / The heavy gait of night" (V.i.367–68).

For the theatre audience, granted a perspective wider than the one enjoyed by Theseus and the members of his court, the Pyramus and Thisby story of love thwarted by parents and the enmity of the stars consolidates and in a sense defines the happy ending of *A Midsummer Night's Dream*. It reminds us of the initial dilemma of Hermia and Lysander, and also of how their story might well have ended: with blood and deprivation. The heavy rhetoric of the interlude fairly bristles with fate and disaster, introducing into Act V a massing of images of death. The entire action of the play within the play is tragic in intention, although not in execution. Without meaning to do so, Bottom and his associates transform tragedy into farce before our eyes, converting that litany of true love crossed which was rehearsed in the very first scene by Hermia and Lysander to laughter. In doing so, they recapitulate the development of *A Midsummer Night's Dream* as a whole, reenacting its movement from potential calamity to an ending in which quick bright things come not to confusion, as once seemed inevitable, but to joy. An intelligent director can and should ensure that the on-stage audience demonstrates some awareness of the ground-bass of mortality sounding underneath the hilarity generated by Bottom's performance, that a line like Lysander's "he is dead, he is nothing" (V.i.308–9) is not lost in the merriment. Only the theatre audience, however, can capture the full resonance of the Pyramus and Thisby play.

When Theseus dismisses the actors after the Bergomask, and the members of the stage audience depart to their chambers, *A Midsummer Night's Dream* seems once again to have arrived at its ending. For the second time Theseus is given a couplet which sounds like the last lines of a play (V.i.369–70). When something like this happened at the end of Act IV it was Bottom, starting up out of his sleep, who set the comedy going again. This time it is the entrance of the fairies, but again the prolongation has nothing to do with plot. The appearance of Puck, Oberon, Titania and their train in the heart of Athens lends a symmetry to the action which would otherwise have been lacking and also gives the lie to Theseus's scepticism. Most

important of all, however, is the way Puck's speech picks up and transforms precisely those ideas of death and destruction distanced through laughter in the Pyramus and Thisby play.

> Now the hungry lion roars,
> And the wolf behowls the moon;
> Whilst the heavy ploughman snores,
> All with weary task foredone.
> Now the wasted brands do glow,
> Whilst the screech-owl, screeching loud,
> Puts the wretch that lies in woe
> In remembrance of a shroud.
> Now it is the time of night
> That the graves, all gaping wide,
> Every one lets forth his sprite,
> In the church-way paths to glide.

All the images here are of sickness, toil, and death. Even the wasted brands, in context, suggest the inevitable running down of human life as it approaches the grave.

Once again, Shakespeare has adjusted the balance between art and life, reality and illusion. Puck's hungry lion is something genuinely savage, not at all the "very gentle beast, and of a good conscience" (V.i.227–28) impersonated by Snug. Even so, his talk of graves and shrouds, drudgery and exhaustion, brings the sense of mortality kept at bay in the Pyramus and Thisby interlude closer, preparing us for the true end of the comedy after so many feints and false conclusions. Puck's speech begins a modulation which will terminate, some fifty lines later, in direct address to the audience and in a player's request for applause. Actors and spectators alike will be turned out of Athens to face the workaday world. Yet Shakespeare refuses to concede that Theseus was right. In the first place, Puck's account of the terrors of the night is not final. It serves to introduce Oberon and Titania, the most fantastic characters in the play, and in their hands Puck's night fears turn into benediction and blessing. About the facts of mortality themselves the fairy king and queen can do nothing, even as Titania could do nothing to prevent the death, years before, of the votaress of her order. All they can do is to strengthen the fidelity and trust of the three pairs of lovers, to bless these marriages, and to stress the positive side of the night as a time for love and procreation as well as for death and fear. Certainly the emphasis on the fair, unblemished children to be born is not accidental, something to be explained purely in terms of the possible occasion of the play's first performance. These children summoned up by Oberon extend the comedy into the future, counteracting the artificial finality which always threatens to diminish happy endings. A beginning is made implicit in the final moments of the play, a further and wider circle.

Unlike characters in fairy-tale, Theseus and Hippolyta, Demetrius and Helena, Lysander and Hermia cannot live happily ever after. Only the qualified immortality to be obtained through offspring is available to them. It was an idea of survival in time which the Shakespeare of the sonnets came to distrust. Nevertheless, in the general atmosphere of celebration and blessing at the end of *A Midsummer Night's Dream*, it seems for the moment enough. It is only after this final coming together in Theseus' palace of the two poles of the comedy, a world of fantasy and one of fact, of immortality and of death, that Puck turns to speak to the theatre audience. Like Theseus, he describes the actors as "shadows" and sums up the play now concluded as a "weak and idle theme, / No more yielding than a dream." When John Lyly ended his court comedies with superficially similar words of deprecation and apology, he seems to have meant them literally. Shakespeare is far more devious. Images of sleep and dreams, shadows and illusions, have been used so constantly in the course of the comedy, examined and invested with such body and significance that they cannot be regarded now as simple terms of denigration and dismissal. As with that mock-apology for the author's "rough and all-unable pen" which concludes *Henry V*, Shakespeare seems to have felt able to trust his audience to take the point: to recognize the simplification, and to understand that the play has created its own reality, a reality touching our own at every point which

More witnesseth than fancy's images,
And grows to something of great constancy;
But howsoever, strange and admirable. (V.i.25–27)

Anne Barton

A Midsummer Night's Dream

[ACT I, SCENE I]

Enter THESEUS, HIPPOLYTA, [PHILOSTRATE,] *with others.*

The. Now, fair Hippolyta, our nuptial hour
Draws on apace. Four happy days bring in
Another moon; but O, methinks, how slow
This old moon [wanes]! She lingers my desires,
Like to a step-dame, or a dowager,   5
Long withering out a young man's revenue.
    Hip. Four days will quickly steep themselves in
        night;
Four nights will quickly dream away the time;
And then the moon, like to a silver bow
[New] bent in heaven, shall behold the night   10
Of our solemnities.
    The.   Go, Philostrate,
Stir up the Athenian youth to merriments,
Awake the pert and nimble spirit of mirth,
Turn melancholy forth to funerals:

The pale companion is not for our pomp.   15
                              [*Exit Philostrate.*]
Hippolyta, I woo'd thee with my sword,
And won thy love doing thee injuries;
But I will wed thee in another key,
With pomp, with triumph, and with revelling.

Enter EGEUS *and his daughter* HERMIA *and* LYSANDER *and* DEMETRIUS.

    Ege. Happy be Theseus, our renowned Duke!   20
    The. Thanks, good Egeus. What's the news with
        thee?
    Ege. Full of vexation come I, with complaint
Against my child, my daughter Hermia.
Stand forth, Demetrius. My noble lord,
This man hath my consent to marry her.   25
Stand forth, Lysander. And, my gracious Duke,
This man hath bewitch'd the bosom of my child.
Thou, thou, Lysander, thou hast given her rhymes,
And interchang'd love-tokens with my child;
Thou hast by moonlight at her window sung   30
With faining voice verses of faining love,
And stol'n the impression of her fantasy

I.i. Location: Athens. The palace of Theseus.
4. **lingers:** delays the fulfillment of.
5. **step-dame:** stepmother. **dowager:** widow with property rights charged upon an estate during her lifetime.
6. **withering out:** diminishing.   11. **solemnities:** i.e. marriage rites.
13. **pert:** lively, brisk.

15. **companion:** fellow (contemptuous).   **pomp:** ceremonial splendor.
16–17. **I . . . injuries.** Theseus had made war against the Amazons and taken their queen captive.   19. **triumph:** public spectacle.
31. **faining . . . faining:** (1) loving . . . longing; (2) feigning . . . feigned.
32. **stol'n . . . fantasy:** stealthily stamped your image on her imagination, i.e. made her fall in love with you.

With bracelets of thy hair, rings, gawds, conceits,
Knacks, trifles, nosegays, sweetmeats—messengers
Of strong prevailment in unhardened youth.   35
With cunning hast thou filch'd my daughter's heart,
Turn'd her obedience (which is due to me)
To stubborn harshness. And, my gracious Duke,
Be it so she will not here before your Grace
Consent to marry with Demetrius,   40
I beg the ancient privilege of Athens:
As she is mine, I may dispose of her;
Which shall be either to this gentleman,
Or to her death, according to our law
Immediately provided in that case.   45
The. What say you, Hermia? Be advis'd, fair maid.
To you your father should be as a god;
One that compos'd your beauties; yea, and one
To whom you are but as a form in wax,
By him imprinted, and within his power,   50
To leave the figure, or disfigure it.
Demetrius is a worthy gentleman.
Her. So is Lysander.
The.   In himself he is;
But in this kind, wanting your father's voice,
The other must be held the worthier.   55
Her. I would my father look'd but with my eyes.
The. Rather your eyes must with his judgment
          look.
Her. I do entreat your Grace to pardon me.
I know not by what power I am made bold,
Nor how it may concern my modesty,   60
In such a presence here to plead my thoughts;
But I beseech your Grace that I may know
The worst that may befall me in this case,
If I refuse to wed Demetrius.
The. Either to die the death, or to abjure   65
For ever the society of men.
Therefore, fair Hermia, question your desires,
Know of your youth, examine well your blood,
Whether (if you yield not to your father's choice)
You can endure the livery of a nun,   70
For aye to be in shady cloister mew'd,
To live a barren sister all your life,
Chaunting faint hymns to the cold fruitless moon.
Thrice blessed they that master so their blood
To undergo such maiden pilgrimage;   75
But earthlier happy is the rose distill'd,

Than that which withering on the virgin thorn
Grows, lives, and dies in single blessedness.
Her. So will I grow, so live, so die, my lord,
Ere I will yield my virgin patent up   80
Unto his lordship, whose unwished yoke
My soul consents not to give sovereignty.
The. Take time to pause, and by the next new
          moon—
The sealing-day betwixt my love and me
For everlasting bond of fellowship—   85
Upon that day either prepare to die
For disobedience to your father's will,
Or else to wed Demetrius, as he would,
Or on Diana's altar to protest
For aye austerity and single life.   90
Dem. Relent, sweet Hermia, and, Lysander, yield
Thy crazed title to my certain right.
Lys. You have her father's love, Demetrius,
Let me have Hermia's; do you marry him.
Ege. Scornful Lysander, true, he hath my love;   95
And what is mine, my love shall render him.
And she is mine, and all my right of her
I do estate unto Demetrius.
Lys. I am, my lord, as well deriv'd as he,
As well possess'd; my love is more than his;   100
My fortunes every way as fairly rank'd
(If not with vantage) as Demetrius';
And (which is more than all these boasts can be)
I am belov'd of beauteous Hermia.
Why should not I then prosecute my right?   105
Demetrius, I'll avouch it to his head,
Made love to Nedar's daughter, Helena,
And won her soul; and she, sweet lady, dotes,
Devoutly dotes, dotes in idolatry,
Upon this spotted and inconstant man.   110
The. I must confess that I have heard so much,
And with Demetrius thought to have spoke thereof;
But, being over-full of self-affairs,
My mind did lose it. But, Demetrius, come,
And come, Egeus, you shall go with me;   115
I have some private schooling for you both.
For you, fair Hermia, look you arm yourself
To fit your fancies to your father's will;
Or else the law of Athens yields you up
(Which by no means we may extenuate)   120
To death, or to a vow of single life.
Come, my Hippolyta; what cheer, my love?
Demetrius and Egeus, go along;
I must employ you in some business
Against our nuptial, and confer with you   125
Of something nearly that concerns yourselves.

33. **bracelets . . . hair.** Hair bracelets were a common love token. **gawds:** toys, trinkets.   **conceits:** ingenious trifles.
34. **Knacks:** knickknacks.
38. **harshness:** discordance, i.e. disobedience.   39. **Be it so:** if.
45. **Immediately:** expressly.   46. **Be advis'd:** consider well.
49. **a form:** i.e. the impression of a seal.
51. **leave:** i.e. leave unchanged.   **disfigure:** obliterate.
54. **in this kind:** in this respect, i.e. as your wooer.   **wanting:** lacking.   **voice:** authorization, consent.
60. **how . . . concern:** whether it befit.
65. **die the death:** be put to death by judicial sentence.
68. **Know . . . youth:** inquire of your youthful feelings.   **blood:** passions.
70. **livery:** dress, distinctive garb.   71. **mew'd:** shut up, confined.
73. **moon:** i.e. Diana, the virgin goddess, whose votary Hermia would become.
75. **maiden pilgrimage:** i.e. journey through life as a virgin. Lines 74–75 are a saving compliment to the Virgin Queen, Elizabeth, though lines 76–78 rather diminish its effect.
76. **distill'd:** made into perfume. With the image in this passage cf. Sonnet 5.

77. **thorn:** brier rose bush.
78. **single blessedness:** "divine blessing accorded to a life of celibacy" (*O.E.D.*).
80. **virgin patent:** privilege of virginity.   89. **protest:** vow.
92. **crazed:** cracked, flawed.   **title:** claim to possession.
98. **estate unto:** settle or bestow upon.
99. **well deriv'd:** well born.
100. **possess'd:** endowed with wealth.   101. **fairly:** handsomely.
102. **with vantage:** better.   106. **head:** face.
110. **spotted and inconstant:** stained with inconstancy.
113. **self-affairs:** my own affairs.   116. **schooling:** admonition.
117. **For:** as for.   **look you arm:** see that you prepare.
118. **fancies:** affections.   120. **extenuate:** mitigate.
123. **go along:** come with us.   125. **Against:** in preparation for.
126. **nearly that:** that closely.

A Midsummer
Night's Dream
I.i

Ege. With duty and desire we follow you.
                    Exeunt. [Manent Lysander and Hermia.]
Lys. How now, my love? why is your cheek so
pale?
How chance the roses there do fade so fast?
Her. Belike for want of rain; which I could well
Beteem them from the tempest of my eyes.   131
Lys. Ay me! for aught that I could ever read,
Could ever hear by tale or history,
The course of true love never did run smooth;
But either it was different in blood—   135
Her. O cross! too high to be enthrall'd to [low].
Lys. Or else misgraffed in respect of years—
Her. O spite! too old to be engag'd to young.
Lys. Or else it stood upon the choice of friends—
Her. O hell, to choose love by another's eyes!   140
Lys. Or if there were a sympathy in choice,
War, death, or sickness did lay siege to it,
Making it momentany as a sound,
Swift as a shadow, short as any dream,
Brief as the lightning in the collied night,   145
That, in a spleen, unfolds both heaven and earth;
And ere a man hath power to say "Behold!"
The jaws of darkness do devour it up:
So quick bright things come to confusion.
Her. If then true lovers have been ever cross'd,
It stands as an edict in destiny.   151
Then let us teach our trial patience,
Because it is a customary cross,
As due to love as thoughts and dreams and sighs,
Wishes and tears, poor fancy's followers.   155
Lys. A good persuasion; therefore hear me, Her-
mia:
I have a widow aunt, a dowager,
Of great revenue, and she hath no child.
From Athens is her house remote seven leagues;
And she respects me as her only son.   160
There, gentle Hermia, may I marry thee;
And to that place the sharp Athenian law
Cannot pursue us. If thou lovest me, then
Steal forth thy father's house to-morrow night;
And in the wood, a league without the town   165
(Where I did meet thee once with Helena
To do observance to a morn of May),
There will I stay for thee.
Her.   My good Lysander,
I swear to thee, by Cupid's strongest bow,

By his best arrow with the golden head,   170
By the simplicity of Venus' doves,
By that which knitteth souls and prospers loves,
And by that fire which burn'd the Carthage queen
When the false Troyan under sail was seen,
By all the vows that ever men have broke   175
(In number more than ever women spoke),
In that same place thou hast appointed me
To-morrow truly will I meet with thee.
Lys. Keep promise, love. Look, here comes Helena.

Enter HELENA.

Her. God speed fair Helena! whither away?   180
Hel. Call you me fair? That fair again unsay.
Demetrius loves your fair, O happy fair!
Your eyes are lodestars, and your tongue's sweet air
More tuneable than lark to shepherd's ear
When wheat is green, when hawthorn buds appear.
Sickness is catching; O, were favor so,   186
[Yours would] I catch, fair Hermia, ere I go;
My ear should catch your voice, my eye your eye,
My tongue should catch your tongue's sweet melody.
Were the world mine, Demetrius being bated,   190
The rest I'll give to be to you translated.
O, teach me how you look, and with what art
You sway the motion of Demetrius' heart.
Her. I frown upon him; yet he loves me still.
Hel. O that your frowns would teach my smiles
such skill!   195
Her. I give him curses; yet he gives me love.
Hel. O that my prayers could such affection move!
Her. The more I hate, the more he follows me.
Hel. The more I love, the more he hateth me.
Her. His folly, Helena, is no fault of mine.   200
Hel. None but your beauty; would that fault
were mine!
Her. Take comfort; he no more shall see my face;
Lysander and myself will fly this place.
Before the time I did Lysander see,
Seem'd Athens as a paradise to me;   205
O then, what graces in my love do dwell,
That he hath turn'd a heaven unto a hell!
Lys. Helen, to you our minds we will unfold:
To-morrow night, when Phoebe doth behold
Her silver visage in the wat'ry glass,   210
Decking with liquid pearl the bladed grass
(A time that lovers' flights doth still conceal),
Through Athens gates have we devis'd to steal.

127. **duty and desire:** eagerness to serve.   s.d. **Manent:** remain.
130. **Belike:** very likely.   131. **Beteem:** afford.
135. **blood:** birth, hereditary station.
136. **cross:** vexation, thwarting.
137. **misgraffed:** ill grafted, i.e. badly matched.
139. **friends:** i.e. relatives.   143. **momentany:** momentary.
145. **collied:** dark (literally, blackened with coal).
146. **in a spleen:** i.e. as if in a sudden fit of passion (?) or in a flash (?). The spleen was thought to be the seat of sudden impulsive feelings and actions.   **unfolds:** reveals.
149. **quick:** quickly, suddenly (perhaps with additional sense of "living" or "lively," modifying *things*).   **confusion:** ruin.
150. **ever:** always.
152. **teach...patience:** i.e. discipline ourselves to meet this trial patiently.
154. **As...love:** as much love's due.   **thoughts:** melancholy moods.   155. **fancy's:** love's.
156. **persuasion:** opinion, doctrine.   160. **respects:** regards.
167. **do...May:** perform the ceremonies of May-day.
168. **stay:** wait.

170. **arrow...head.** According to Ovid's *Metamorphoses*, Cupid's sharp, gold-tipped arrow produced love, his blunt, lead-tipped arrow aversion.   171. **simplicity:** harmlessness, innocence.
173. **Carthage queen:** Dido, who immolated herself on a funeral pyre after the Trojan hero Aeneas, her lover, secretly sailed away from Carthage.
182. **fair...fair:** beauty...fair one (with special reference to her blonde coloring).   **happy:** lucky.
183. **lodestars:** guiding stars.   **air:** melody, music.
184. **tuneable:** tuneful.
186. **favor:** attributes, features (with play on "being favored").
190. **bated:** excepted.   191. **translated:** transformed.
192. **art:** skill (i.e. in magic).   193. **motion:** impulse, desire.
197. **affection:** passion.   **move:** arouse.
209. **Phoebe:** Diana, the moon.   210. **glass:** mirror.
212. **still:** always.
213. **Athens.** Adjectival; cf. "Verona streets," *Romeo and Juliet,* III.i.89.   **devis'd:** decided.

Her. And in the wood, where often you and I
Upon faint primrose beds were wont to lie,   215
Emptying our bosoms of their counsel [sweet],
There my Lysander and myself shall meet;
And thence from Athens turn away our eyes,
To seek new friends and [stranger companies].
Farewell, sweet playfellow, pray thou for us;   220
And good luck grant thee thy Demetrius!
Keep word, Lysander; we must starve our sight
From lovers' food till morrow deep midnight.
    Lys. I will, my Hermia.   *Exit Hermia.*
                    Helena, adieu:
As you on him, Demetrius dote on you!   225
                    Exit Lysander.
    Hel. How happy some o'er other some can be!
Through Athens I am thought as fair as she.
But what of that? Demetrius thinks not so;
He will not know what all but he do know;
And as he errs, doting on Hermia's eyes,   230
So I, admiring of his qualities.
Things base and vile, holding no quantity,
Love can transpose to form and dignity.
Love looks not with the eyes but with the mind;
And therefore is wing'd Cupid painted blind.   235
Nor hath Love's mind of any judgment taste;
Wings, and no eyes, figure unheedy haste;
And therefore is Love said to be a child,
Because in choice he is so oft beguil'd.
As waggish boys in game themselves forswear,   240
So the boy Love is perjur'd every where;
For ere Demetrius look'd on Hermia's eyne,
He hail'd down oaths that he was only mine;
And when this hail some heat from Hermia felt,
So he dissolv'd, and show'rs of oaths did melt.   245
I will go tell him of fair Hermia's flight;
Then to the wood will he to-morrow night
Pursue her; and for this intelligence
If I have thanks, it is a dear expense.
But herein mean I to enrich my pain,   250
To have his sight thither and back again.   *Exit.*

[SCENE II]

Enter QUINCE *the carpenter and* SNUG *the joiner and*
BOTTOM *the weaver and* FLUTE *the bellows-mender
and* SNOUT *the tinker and* STARVELING *the tailor.*

    Quin. Is all our company here?

    Bot. You were best to call them generally, man
by man, according to the scrip.
    Quin. Here is the scroll of every man's name,
which is thought fit, through all Athens, to play in   5
our enterlude before the Duke and the Duchess, on
his wedding-day at night.
    Bot. First, good Peter Quince, say what the play
treats on; then read the names of the actors; and so
grow to a point.   10
    Quin. Marry, our play is *The most lamentable
comedy and most cruel death of Pyramus and Thisby.*
    Bot. A very good piece of work, I assure you, and
a merry. Now, good Peter Quince, call forth your
actors by the scroll. Masters, spread yourselves.   15
    Quin. Answer as I call you. Nick Bottom the
weaver.
    Bot. Ready. Name what part I am for, and pro-
ceed.
    Quin. You, Nick Bottom, are set down for Pyra-
mus.   21
    Bot. What is Pyramus? a lover, or a tyrant?
    Quin. A lover, that kills himself most gallant
for love.   24
    Bot. That will ask some tears in the true perform-
ing of it. If I do it, let the audience look to their eyes.
I will move storms; I will condole in some measure. To the rest—yet my chief humor is for a tyrant. I could play Ercles rarely, or a part to tear a
cat in, to make all split.   30
            "The raging rocks
                And shivering shocks
            Shall break the locks
                Of prison gates;
            And Phibbus' car   35
            Shall shine from far,
            And make and mar
                The foolish Fates."
This was lofty! Now name the rest of the players.
This is Ercles' vein, a tyrant's vein; a lover is more
condoling.   41
    Quin. Francis Flute the bellows-mender.
    Flu. Here, Peter Quince.
    Quin. Flute, you must take Thisby on you.
    Flu. What is Thisby? a wand'ring knight?   45
    Quin. It is the lady that Pyramus must love.

---

215. **faint:** pale (?) or faintly scented (?).
216. **counsel:** inmost thought.
219. **stranger companies:** the company of strangers.
222–23. **starve . . . food:** i.e. refrain from seeing each other.
231. **admiring of:** wondering at.
232. **holding no quantity:** lacking proportion, unshapely.
233. **transpose:** change, transform. **dignity:** worth.
236. **taste:** any trace. 237. **figure:** symbolize.
240. **game:** fun, sport.
242. **eyne:** eyes (archaic even in Elizabethan English; used for the
sake of rhyme). 248. **intelligence:** information.
249. **dear expense:** painful purchase, costly gain.
251. **his sight:** the sight of him.

I.ii. Location: Athens. Quince's house.
o.s.d. The names of the craftsmen are derived in one way or another
from their work. Quince's name is probably a form of *quoins* or
quines, wedge-shaped pieces of wood used in carpentry. Snug's name
suggests the expert joining of pieces of wood by a maker of fine
furniture. Bottom is named for the *bottom* or core on which thread is
wound. Flute would repair fluted church organs as well as domestic
bellows. Snout's name suggests the spout of a kettle, an article very
familiar to tinkers. Starveling takes his name from the proverbial
leanness of tailors ("Nine tailors make a man").
2. **You were best:** it would be best for you. **generally.** The first of
Bottom's characteristic verbal blunders. Here he obviously means
"individually"—just the opposite of what he says.
3. **scrip:** script, written list. 6. **enterlude:** interlude, brief play.
10. **grow . . . point:** come systematically to a conclusion.
11. **Marry:** why, indeed (originally the name of the Virgin Mary
used as an oath). **lamentable:** mournful.
26. **look . . . eyes:** take care not to injure their eyes with weeping.
27. **condole:** speak pathetically, arouse pity.
28. **humor:** temperamental bent.
29. **Ercles:** Hercules. The tradition for ranting in this part grew
from Seneca's *Hercules Furens.* 29–30. **tear a cat:** i.e. rant.
30. **make all split:** cause great commotion.
35. **Phibbus' car:** the chariot of Phoebus, the sun-god.
41. **condoling:** pathetic.
45. **What:** what sort of man. **wand'ring knight:** knight-errant.

A Midsummer
Night's Dream
I.ii

Flu. Nay, faith; let not me play a woman; I have a beard coming.

Quin. That's all one; you shall play it in a mask, and you may speak as small as you will.   50

Bot. And I may hide my face, let me play Thisby too. I'll speak in a monstrous little voice, "Thisne! Thisne! Ah, Pyramus, my lover dear! thy Thisby dear, and lady dear!"

Quin. No, no, you must play Pyramus; and, Flute, you Thisby.   56

Bot. Well, proceed.

Quin. Robin Starveling the tailor.

Star. Here, Peter Quince.

Quin. Robin Starveling, you must play Thisby's mother. Tom Snout the tinker.   61

Snout. Here, Peter Quince.

Quin. You, Pyramus' father; myself, Thisby's father; Snug the joiner, you the lion's part. And I hope here is a play fitted.   65

Snug. Have you the lion's part written? Pray you, if it be, give it me, for I am slow of study.

Quin. You may do it extempore, for it is nothing but roaring.   69

Bot. Let me play the lion too. I will roar, that I will do any man's heart good to hear me. I will roar, that I will make the Duke say, "Let him roar again; let him roar again."

Quin. And you should do it too terribly, you would fright the Duchess and the ladies, that 75 they would shrike; and that were enough to hang us all.

All. That would hang us, every mother's son.

Bot. I grant you, friends, if you should fright the ladies out of their wits, they would have no more 80 discretion but to hang us; but I will aggravate my voice so that I will roar you as gently as any sucking dove; I will roar you and 'twere any nightingale.   84

Quin. You can play no part but Pyramus; for Pyramus is a sweet-fac'd man; a proper man as one shall see in a summer's day; a most lovely gentleman-like man: therefore you must needs play Pyramus.

Bot. Well; I will undertake it. What beard were I best to play it in?   91

Quin. Why, what you will.

Bot. I will discharge it in either your straw-color beard, your orange-tawny beard, your purple-in-grain beard, or your French-crown-color 95 beard, your perfit yellow.

Quin. Some of your French crowns have no hair at all; and then you will play barefac'd. But, mas-

ters, here are your parts, and I am to entreat you, request you, and desire you, to con them by to- 100 morrow night; and meet me in the palace wood, a mile without the town, by moonlight; there will we rehearse; for if we meet in the city, we shall be dogg'd with company, and our devices known. In the mean time I will draw a bill of properties, such 105 as our play wants. I pray you fail me not.

Bot. We will meet, and there we may rehearse most obscenely and courageously. Take pains, be perfit; adieu.

Quin. At the Duke's oak we meet.   110

Bot. Enough; hold, or cut bow-strings.   *Exeunt.*

[ACT II, SCENE I]

Enter a FAIRY *at one door and* ROBIN GOODFELLOW [PUCK] *at another.*

Puck. How now, spirit, whither wander you?

Fairy.   Over hill, over dale,
            Thorough bush, thorough brier,
            Over park, over pale,
            Thorough flood, thorough fire,   5
            I do wander every where,
            Swifter than the moon's sphere;
            And I serve the Fairy Queen,
            To dew her orbs upon the green.
            The cowslips tall her pensioners be,   10
            In their gold coats spots you see:
            Those be rubies, fairy favors,
            In those freckles live their savors.
I must go seek some dewdrops here,
And hang a pearl in every cowslip's ear.   15
Farewell, thou lob of spirits; I'll be gone.
Our Queen and all her elves come here anon.

Puck. The King doth keep his revels here to-night;
Take heed the Queen come not within his sight;
For Oberon is passing fell and wrath,   20
Because that she as her attendant hath
A lovely boy stolen from an Indian king;
She never had so sweet a changeling.
And jealous Oberon would have the child
Knight of his train, to trace the forests wild;   25
But she, perforce, withholds the loved boy,
Crowns him with flowers, and makes him all her joy.
And now they never meet in grove or green,

47–48. **I . . . coming.** On the Elizabethan stage, female parts were played by boys.   49. **That's all one:** that makes no difference.
50. **small:** high-pitched.   51. **And:** if.   65. **fitted:** cast.
70. **that:** so that.   74. **terribly:** terrifyingly.   76. **shrike:** shriek.
81. **aggravate.** He means just the opposite.   83. **and:** as if.
86. **proper:** handsome.   90. **Well:** very well.
93. **discharge:** perform.   **your.** The indefinite use, meaning vaguely "that you know of"; a colloquialism.
94–95. **purple-in-grain:** dyed a fast purple or deep red.
95. **French-crown-color:** yellowish color of a gold coin.
96. **perfit:** perfect.
97–98. **Some . . . all.** Alluding to loss of hair from the "French disease," syphilis.

99. **am to:** must.   100. **con:** learn by heart.   105. **bill:** list.
108. **obscenely.** Bottom may connect this word with *seen* and mean "without being observed," or with *scene* and mean "dramatically."
109. **perfit:** i.e. letter-perfect in your parts.
111. **hold . . . bow-strings:** an expression of uncertain meaning, from archery; perhaps equivalent to "hold to our agreement or the project is done for."

II.i. Location: A wood near Athens.
3. **Thorough:** through.   4. **pale:** enclosure.
7. **sphere.** In the Ptolemaic system of astronomy, the moon and the other heavenly bodies were thought to revolve about the earth fixed in transparent spheres.   9. **orbs:** circles, i.e. fairy rings.
10. **pensioners.** Members of the royal bodyguard were called gentlemen pensioners.   12. **favors:** love tokens.   13. **savors:** perfumes.
16. **lob:** country bumpkin.   17. **anon:** at once.
20. **passing . . . wrath:** exceedingly fierce and angry.
23. **changeling:** child exchanged for another by fairies.
25. **trace:** traverse.   26. **perforce:** forcibly.

By fountain clear, or spangled starlight sheen,
But they do square, that all their elves for fear 30
Creep into acorn-cups, and hide them there.
   Fairy. Either I mistake your shape and making
     quite,
Or else you are that shrewd and knavish sprite
Call'd Robin Goodfellow. Are not you he
That frights the maidens of the villagery, 35
Skim milk, and sometimes labor in the quern,
And bootless make the breathless huswife churn,
And sometime make the drink to bear no barm,
Mislead night-wanderers, laughing at their harm?
Those that Hobgoblin call you, and sweet Puck, 40
You do their work, and they shall have good luck.
Are not you he?
   Puck.   Thou speakest aright;
I am that merry wanderer of the night.
I jest to Oberon and make him smile
When I a fat and bean-fed horse beguile, 45
Neighing in likeness of a filly foal;
And sometime lurk I in a gossip's bowl,
In very likeness of a roasted crab,
And when she drinks, against her lips I bob,
And on her withered dewlop pour the ale. 50
The wisest aunt, telling the saddest tale,
Sometime for three-foot stool mistaketh me;
Then slip I from her bum, down topples she,
And "tailor" cries, and falls into a cough;
And then the whole quire hold their hips and loff, 55
And waxen in their mirth, and neeze, and swear
A merrier hour was never wasted there.
But room, fairy! here comes Oberon.
   Fairy. And here my mistress. Would that he were
     gone!

Enter the King of Fairies [OBERON] *at one door with his*
TRAIN, *and the Queen* [TITANIA] *at another with hers.*

   Obe. Ill met by moonlight, proud Titania. 60
   Tita. What, jealous Oberon? [Fairies,] skip
     hence—
I have forsworn his bed and company.
   Obe. Tarry, rash wanton! Am not I thy lord?
   Tita. Then I must be thy lady; but I know
When thou hast stolen away from fairy land, 65
And in the shape of Corin sat all day,
Playing on pipes of corn, and versing love,
To amorous Phillida. Why art thou here

Come from the farthest steep of India?
But that, forsooth, the bouncing Amazon, 70
Your buskin'd mistress, and your warrior love,
To Theseus must be wedded, and you come
To give their bed joy and prosperity.
   Obe. How canst thou thus for shame, Titania,
Glance at my credit with Hippolyta, 75
Knowing I know thy love to Theseus?
Didst not thou lead him through the glimmering night
From Perigenia, whom he ravished?
And make him with fair [Aegles] break his faith,
With Ariadne, and Antiopa? 80
   Tita. These are the forgeries of jealousy;
And never, since the middle summer's spring,
Met we on hill, in dale, forest, or mead,
By paved fountain or by rushy brook,
Or in the beached margent of the sea, 85
To dance our ringlets to the whistling wind,
But with thy brawls thou hast disturb'd our sport.
Therefore the winds, piping to us in vain,
As in revenge, have suck'd up from the sea
Contagious fogs; which, falling in the land, 90
Hath every pelting river made so proud
That they have overborne their continents.
The ox hath therefore stretch'd his yoke in vain,
The ploughman lost his sweat, and the green corn
Hath rotted ere his youth attain'd a beard. 95
The fold stands empty in the drowned field,
And crows are fatted with the murrion flock;
The nine men's morris is fill'd up with mud,
And the quaint mazes in the wanton green,
For lack of tread, are undistinguishable. 100
The human mortals want their winter here;
No night is now with hymn or carol blest.
Therefore the moon (the governess of floods),

29. **fountain:** spring.   30. **square:** quarrel.   **that:** so that.
32. **making:** form.   33. **shrewd:** mischievous.
35. **villagery:** village folk, peasantry.
36. **quern:** handmill for grinding grain.
37. **bootless:** unavailingly.   **huswife:** housewife, woman who manages a household.
38. **sometime:** at times.   **bear no barm:** fail to ferment (?) or go flat (?). *Barm* yeast.   47. **gossip's:** garrulous old woman's.
48. **crab:** crab apple.   50. **dewlop:** dewlap, loose skin on the neck.
51. **aunt:** old woman, gossip.   **saddest:** soberest.
54. **tailor.** Probably referring to the fact that she finds herself sitting cross-legged on the floor as tailors did to sew.   **cough.** Probably with a suggestion of breaking wind.
55. **quire:** choir, i.e. company.   **loff:** laugh.
56. **waxen:** increase (with archaic plural ending in *-en*).   **neeze:** sneeze.   57. **wasted:** spent.
63. **rash wanton:** impetuous and willful creature.
66, 68. **Corin, Phillida.** Conventional names in pastoral poetry.
67. **corn:** oat stalks.   **versing love:** making love verses.

69. **steep:** mountain range.
71. **buskin'd:** wearing buskins or half-boots.
75. **Glance . . . Hippolyta:** cast aspersion on my good name by accusing me with Hippolyta.
78. **Perigenia:** Perigouna, daughter of the brigand Sinis, whom the youthful Theseus slew on his first journey to Athens. Shakespeare took this and the following names of Theseus' mistresses from the "Life of Theseus" in North's translation of Plutarch (which, however, reads *Perigouna*).
79. **Aegles:** Aegle, a nymph for whose love Theseus, in some accounts, deserted Ariadne.
80. **Ariadne:** daughter of Minos, king of Crete. Having slain the Minotaur with her aid, Theseus fled Crete with her, but abandoned her on the voyage back to Athens.   **Antiopa:** another name for the Amazon queen captured by Theseus; here obviously taken to be distinct from Hippolyta.
82. **middle summer's spring:** beginning of midsummer.
84. **paved fountain:** spring with pebbled bottom.   **rushy:** edged with rushes.   85. **in:** on.   **margent:** margin, edge.
86. **ringlets:** circular dances.
87. **brawls:** noisy quarrels (with probably play on *brawl* as the name of a dance [French *branle*] described as "base" by contemporary writers).   90. **Contagious:** noxious.   91. **pelting:** paltry.
92. **overborne their continents:** overflowed their banks.
94. **corn:** grain.   95. **his:** its.
97. **murrion:** dead of the murrain, a disease of cattle and sheep.
98. **nine men's morris:** i.e. the turf marked with squares on which the rustic game of this name was played.
99. **quaint mazes:** complicated pattern of paths to be traced rapidly by a line of boys as a sport.   **wanton:** luxuriant.
101. **want their winter here.** A controversial passage. Perhaps it means "lack under these circumstances their proper winter season" (with an allusion in *hymn or carol* in line 102 to Christmas observances). Most editors, following Theobald, emend *here* to *cheer.*
103. **Therefore.** As in lines 88 and 93, this means "in consequence of the breach between us."

Pale in her anger, washes all the air,
That rheumatic diseases do abound.   105
And thorough this distemperature, we see
The seasons alter: hoary-headed frosts
Fall in the fresh lap of the crimson rose,
And on old Hiems' [thin] and icy crown
An odorous chaplet of sweet summer buds   110
Is, as in mockery, set; the spring, the summer,
The childing autumn, angry winter, change
Their wonted liveries; and the mazed world,
By their increase, now knows not which is which.
And this same progeny of evils comes   115
From our debate, from our dissension;
We are their parents and original.
    Obe. Do you amend it then; it lies in you.
Why should Titania cross her Oberon?
I do but beg a little changeling boy,   120
To be my henchman.
    Tita.   Set your heart at rest;
The fairy land buys not the child of me.
His mother was a vot'ress of my order,
And in the spiced Indian air, by night,
Full often hath she gossip'd by my side,   125
And sat with me on Neptune's yellow sands,
Marking th' embarked traders on the flood;'
When we have laugh'd to see the sails conceive
And grow big-bellied with the wanton wind;
Which she, with pretty and with swimming gait,   130
Following (her womb then rich with my young squire)
Would imitate, and sail upon the land
To fetch me trifles, and return again,
As from a voyage, rich with merchandise.
But she, being mortal, of that boy did die,   135
And for her sake do I rear up her boy;
And for her sake I will not part with him.
    Obe. How long within this wood intend you stay?
    Tita. Perchance till after Theseus' wedding-day.
If you will patiently dance in our round,   140
And see our moonlight revels, go with us;
If not, shun me, and I will spare your haunts.
    Obe. Give me that boy, and I will go with thee.
    Tita. Not for thy fairy kingdom. Fairies, away!
We shall chide downright, if I longer stay.   145
                    Exeunt [Titania and her Train].
    Obe. Well; go thy way. Thou shalt not from this
        grove
Till I torment thee for this injury.
My gentle Puck, come hither. Thou rememb'rest
Since once I sat upon a promontory, ·
And heard a mermaid on a dolphin's back   150

Uttering such dulcet and harmonious breath
That the rude sea grew civil at her song,
And certain stars shot madly from their spheres,
To hear the sea-maid's music?
    Puck.   I remember.
    Obe. That very time I saw (but thou couldst not),
Flying between the cold moon and the earth,   156
Cupid all arm'd. A certain aim he took
At a fair vestal throned by [the] west,
And loos'd his love-shaft smartly from his bow,
As it should pierce a hundred thousand hearts;   160
But I might see young Cupid's fiery shaft
Quench'd in the chaste beams of the wat'ry moon,
And the imperial vot'ress passed on,
In maiden meditation, fancy-free.
Yet mark'd I where the bolt of Cupid fell.   165
It fell upon a little western flower,
Before milk-white, now purple with love's wound,
And maidens call it love-in-idleness.
Fetch me that flow'r; the herb I showed thee once.
The juice of it on sleeping eyelids laid   170
Will make or man or woman madly dote
Upon the next live creature that it sees.
Fetch me this herb, and be thou here again
Ere the leviathan can swim a league.
    Puck. I'll put a girdle round about the earth   175
In forty minutes.   *[Exit.]*
    Obe.   Having once this juice,
I'll watch Titania when she is asleep,
And drop the liquor of it in her eyes;
The next thing then she waking looks upon
(Be it on lion, bear, or wolf, or bull,   180
On meddling monkey, or on busy ape),
She shall pursue it with the soul of love.
And ere I take this charm from off her sight
(As I can take it with another herb),
I'll make her render up her page to me.   185
But who comes here? I am invisible,
And I will overhear their conference.

    Enter DEMETRIUS, HELENA *following him.*

    Dem. I love thee not; therefore pursue me not.
Where is Lysander and fair Hermia?
The one I'll [slay]; the other [slayeth] me.   190
Thou toldst me they were stol'n unto this wood;
And here am I, and wode within this wood,
Because I cannot meet my Hermia.
Hence, get thee gone, and follow me no more.

105. **That:** so that.   **rheumatic diseases:** colds, catarrh, and other such disorders characterized by a flow of watery "rheum."
106. **distemperature:** disturbance in the natural order, i.e. bad weather (perhaps with play on the sense "ill humor," harking back to the moon's "anger" in line 104).   109. **Hiems:** the god of winter.
112. **childing:** fruitful (literally, pregnant).
113. **wonted liveries:** customary apparel.   **mazed:** bewildered, confused.   114. **their increase:** what they produce.
116. **debate:** disagreement, quarrelling.
117. **original:** origin.   119. **cross:** thwart.
121. **henchman:** page of honor.   **Set . . . rest:** i.e. give up that notion.
127. **traders:** trading vessels.   **flood:** flood tide.
129. **wanton:** amorous.   140. **round:** circular dance.
142. **spare:** stay away from.   145. **chide:** quarrel.
146. **from:** go from.   147. **injury:** affront.   149. **Since:** when.

151. **breath:** voice, music.
152. **rude:** rough, boisterous.   **civil:** well-behaved, gentle.
157. **all:** fully, completely.
158. **vestal:** i.e. vestal virgin. The passage is a compliment to Queen Elizabeth, and may allude to some actual entertainment in her honor, such as the water pageant with which the Earl of Hertford amused her when she visited him at Elvetham in 1591.   160. **As:** as if.
162. **moon:** i.e. Diana, the virgin goddess, whose votaress the "fair vestal" is.   164. **fancy-free:** free of love-thoughts.
168. **love-in-idleness:** a name for the pansy.
171. **or . . . or:** either . . . or.
174. **leviathan:** gigantic sea-beast (see Job 41), usually identified with the whale.
176. **forty.** Used frequently as an indefinite number.
177. **watch . . . asleep:** i.e. watch for a time when I can catch her sleeping.
186. **I am invisible.** Spoken for the benefit of the audience, to explain how he can eavesdrop unseen.   192. **wode:** mad (pronounced *wood*).

Hel.   You draw me, you hard-hearted adamant;
But yet you draw not iron, for my heart   196
Is true as steel. Leave you your power to draw,
And I shall have no power to follow you.
Dem.   Do I entice you? Do I speak you fair?
Or rather do I not in plainest truth   200
Tell you I do not [nor] I cannot love you?
Hel.   And even for that do I love you the more:
I am your spaniel; and, Demetrius,
The more you beat me, I will fawn on you.
Use me but as your spaniel; spurn me, strike me,   205
Neglect me, lose me; only give me leave,
Unworthy as I am, to follow you.
What worser place can I beg in your love
(And yet a place of high respect with me)
Than to be used as you use your dog?   210
Dem.   Tempt not too much the hatred of my spirit,
For I am sick when I do look on thee.
Hel.   And I am sick when I look not on you.
Dem.   You do impeach your modesty too much,
To leave the city and commit yourself   215
Into the hands of one that loves you not;
To trust the opportunity of night,
And the ill counsel of a desert place,
With the rich worth of your virginity.
Hel.   Your virtue is my privilege. For that   220
It is not night when I do see your face,
Therefore I think I am not in the night,
Nor doth this wood lack worlds of company,
For you in my respect are all the world.
Then how can it be said I am alone,   225
When all the world is here to look on me?
Dem.   I'll run from thee, and hide me in the brakes,
And leave thee to the mercy of wild beasts.
Hel.   The wildest hath not such a heart as you.
Run when you will; the story shall be chang'd: 230
Apollo flies, and Daphne holds the chase;
The dove pursues the griffin; the mild hind
Makes speed to catch the tiger—bootless speed,
When cowardice pursues and valor flies.
Dem.   I will not stay thy questions. Let me go;
Or if thou follow me, do not believe   236
But I shall do thee mischief in the wood.
Hel.   Ay, in the temple, in the town, the field,
You do me mischief. Fie, Demetrius!
Your wrongs do set a scandal on my sex.   240
We cannot fight for love, as men may do.
We should be woo'd, and were not made to woo.
[*Exit Demetrius.*]

I'll follow thee and make a heaven of hell,
To die upon the hand I love so well.   [*Exit.*]
Obe.   Fare thee well, nymph. Ere he do leave this
grove,   245
Thou shalt fly him, and he shall seek thy love.

Enter PUCK.

Hast thou the flower there? Welcome, wanderer.
Puck.   Ay, there it is.
Obe.   I pray thee give it me.
I know a bank where the wild thyme blows,
Where oxlips and the nodding violet grows,   250
Quite over-canopied with luscious woodbine,
With sweet musk-roses and with eglantine;
There sleeps Titania sometime of the night,
Lull'd in these flowers with dances and delight;
And there the snake throws her enamell'd skin,   255
Weed wide enough to wrap a fairy in;
And with the juice of this I'll streak her eyes,
And make her full of hateful fantasies.
Take thou some of it, and seek through this grove:
A sweet Athenian lady is in love   260
With a disdainful youth; anoint his eyes,
But do it when the next thing he espies
May be the lady. Thou shalt know the man
By the Athenian garments he hath on.
Effect it with some care, that he may prove   265
More fond on her than she upon her love;
And look thou meet me ere the first cock crow.
Puck.   Fear not, my lord! your servant shall do so.
[*Exeunt.*]

[SCENE II]

Enter TITANIA, *Queen of Fairies, with her* TRAIN.

Tita.   Come, now a roundel and a fairy song;
Then, for the third part of a minute, hence,
Some to kill cankers in the musk-rose buds,
Some war with rere-mice for their leathren wings   4
To make my small elves coats, and some keep back
The clamorous owl, that nightly hoots and wonders
At our quaint spirits. Sing me now asleep;
Then to your offices, and let me rest.

FAIRIES *sing.*

[*1. Fairy.*]   You spotted snakes with double tongue,
Thorny hedgehogs, be not seen,   10
Newts and blind-worms, do no wrong,
Come not near our fairy queen.

---

195. **adamant:** (1) lodestone, magnet; (2) the hardest substance.
196. **you . . . iron:** i.e. what you draw (my heart) is not iron, but steel of the finest temper.   197. **Leave:** give up.
199. **fair:** courteously.   206. **Neglect:** ignore.
211. **Tempt:** try, put to the test.
214. **impeach:** discredit, call into question.
218. **desert:** deserted, unpeopled.
220. **Your . . . privilege:** your excellence in my eyes is my warrant for doing so.   **For that:** because.
224. **in my respect:** as far as I am concerned.   227. **brakes:** thickets.
231. **Apollo . . . chase.** According to the myth, Daphne, pursued by Apollo, was saved from rape by being transformed into a laurel tree.
232. **griffin:** fabulous monster with the body of a lion and the head of an eagle.   **hind:** female of the red deer.
235. **stay thy questions:** delay to listen to your talk.
240. **Your . . . sex.** Because he forces her to be the wooer instead of the wooed.

244. **upon:** by.   249. **blows:** blooms.
250. **oxlips:** flowering plant resembling the cowslip.
251. **woodbine:** honeysuckle.
252. **musk-roses:** variety of large, fragrant rose.   **eglantine:** sweet-brier, another variety of rose.
253. **sometime of:** at some time during.   255. **throws:** sheds.
256. **Weed:** garment.   257. **streak:** anoint.
266. **fond on:** infatuated with.

II.ii. Location: The wood.
1. **roundel:** dance in a circle.   3 **cankers:** cankerworms.
4. **rere-mice:** bats.   **leathren:** leathern.
7. **quaint:** pretty, dainty.   8. **offices:** duties.   9. **double:** forked.
11. **Newts:** water lizards. Newts, blind-worms, and spiders (line 20) were all thought to be poisonous.

A Midsummer
Night's Dream
II.ii

[*Cho.*] Philomele, with melody,
  Sing in our sweet lullaby,
 Lulla, lulla, lullaby, lulla, lulla, lullaby.   15
   Never harm,
   Nor spell, nor charm,
  Come our lovely lady nigh.
  So good night, with lullaby.

1. Fairy. Weaving spiders, come not here;   20
 Hence, you long-legg'd spinners, hence!
 Beetles black, approach not near;
 Worm nor snail, do no offense.

[*Cho.*] Philomele, with melody, etc.

2. Fairy. Hence, away! now all is well.   25
 One aloof stand sentinel.
    [*Exeunt Fairies. Titania sleeps.*]

Enter OBERON [*and squeezes the flower on Titania's
eyelids*].

Obe. What thou seest when thou dost wake,
 Do it for thy true-love take;
 Love and languish for his sake.
 Be it ounce, or cat, or bear,   30
 Pard, or boar with bristled hair,
 In thy eye that shall appear
 When thou wak'st, it is thy dear:
 Wake when some vile thing is near.   [*Exit.*]

Enter LYSANDER *and* HERMIA.

Lys. Fair love, you faint with wand'ring in the
  wood;   35
And to speak troth I have forgot our way.
We'll rest us, Hermia, if you think it good,
And tarry for the comfort of the day.
 Her. Be't so, Lysander. Find you out a bed;
For I upon this bank will rest my head.   40
 Lys. One turf shall serve as pillow for us both,
One heart, one bed, two bosoms, and one troth.
 Her. Nay, [good] Lysander; for my sake, my dear,
Lie further off yet; do not lie so near.
 Lys. O, take the sense, sweet, of my innocence!
Love takes the meaning in love's conference: 46
I mean, that my heart unto yours [is] knit,
So that but one heart we can make of it;
Two bosoms interchained with an oath,
So then two bosoms and a single troth.   50
Then by your side no bed-room me deny;
For lying so, Hermia, I do not lie.
 Her. Lysander riddles very prettily.
Now much beshrew my manners and my pride,
If Hermia meant to say Lysander lied.   55
But, gentle friend, for love and courtesy,
Lie further off, in humane modesty;

Such separation as may well be said
Becomes a virtuous bachelor and a maid,
So far be distant; and good night, sweet friend.   60
Thy love ne'er alter till thy sweet life end!
 Lys. Amen, amen, to that fair prayer, say I,
And then end life when I end loyalty!
Here is my bed; sleep give thee all his rest!
 Her. With half that wish the wisher's eyes be
  press'd!   [*They sleep.*]   65

Enter PUCK.

Puck. Through the forest have I gone,
 But Athenian found I none,
 On whose eyes I might approve
 This flower's force in stirring love.
 Night and silence—Who is here?   70
 Weeds of Athens he doth wear:
 This is he, my master said,
 Despised the Athenian maid;
 And here the maiden, sleeping sound,
 On the dank and dirty ground.   75
 Pretty soul, she durst not lie
 Near this lack-love, this kill-courtesy.
 Churl, upon thy eyes I throw
 All the power this charm doth owe.
 When thou wak'st, let love forbid   80
 Sleep his seat on thy eyelid.
 So awake when I am gone,
 For I must now to Oberon.   *Exit.*

Enter DEMETRIUS *and* HELENA, *running.*

Hel. Stay—though thou kill me, sweet Demetrius.
 Dem. I charge thee hence, and do not haunt me
  thus.   85
 Hel. O, wilt thou darkling leave me? do not so.
 Dem. Stay, on thy peril; I alone will go.   [*Exit.*]
 Hel. O, I am out of breath in this fond chase!
The more my prayer, the lesser is my grace.
Happy is Hermia, wheresoe'er she lies,   90
For she hath blessed and attractive eyes.
How came her eyes so bright? Not with salt tears;
If so, my eyes are oft'ner wash'd than hers.
No, no; I am as ugly as a bear;
For beasts that meet me run away for fear.   95
Therefore no marvel though Demetrius
Do, as a monster, fly my presence thus.
What wicked and dissembling glass of mine
Made me compare with Hermia's sphery eyne!
But who is here? Lysander! on the ground?   100
Dead, or asleep? I see no blood, no wound.
Lysander, if you live, good sir, awake.
 Lys. [*Awaking.*] And run through fire I will for
  thy sweet sake.

---

13. **Philomele:** the nightingale. Philomela, daughter of King Pandion of Athens, was transformed into a nightingale, according to Ovid, after her rape by her brother-in-law Tereus.   21. **spinners:** spiders or (Cairncross) daddy-longlegs.   30. **ounce:** lynx.   **cat:** wildcat.   31. **Pard:** leopard.   36. **troth:** truth.   42. **troth:** pledged faith.   45. **take . . . innocence:** interpret my meaning as entirely innocent.   46. **Love . . . conference:** i.e. a lover should be able to understand what is meant when he and his beloved talk together.   52. **I . . . lie:** i.e. I am not false.   53. **prettily:** ingeniously, skillfully.   54. **beshrew:** mischief take.   57. **humane:** courteous, decorous.

65. **With . . . press'd:** i.e. may half of all sleep's rest (which "all" you have wished for me) be yours.   68. **approve:** test.   73. **Despised:** who despised.   79. **owe:** possess.   85. **haunt:** follow persistently.   86. **darkling:** in the dark.   87. **Stay . . . peril:** i.e. it will be dangerous for you if you don't remain here.   88. **fond:** doting, foolishly loving.   89. **my grace:** the favor I am granted.   90. **lies:** dwells.   91. **attractive:** magnetic.   97. **as a monster:** i.e. as he would fly from a monster.   99. **Made me compare:** induced me to compare my eyes.   **sphery eyne:** eyes as bright as stars in their spheres.

Transparent Helena, nature shows art,
That through thy bosom makes me see thy heart.   105
Where is Demetrius? O, how fit a word
Is that vile name to perish on my sword!

Hel. Do not say so, Lysander, say not so.
What though he love your Hermia? Lord, what
        though?
Yet Hermia still loves you; then be content.   110

Lys. Content with Hermia? No; I do repent
The tedious minutes I with her have spent.
Not Hermia, but Helena I love.
Who will not change a raven for a dove?
The will of man is by his reason sway'd;   115
And reason says you are the worthier maid.
Things growing are not ripe until their season,
So I, being young, till now ripe not to reason;
And touching now the point of human skill,
Reason becomes the marshal to my will,   120
And leads me to your eyes, where I o'erlook
Love's stories written in Love's richest book.

Hel. Wherefore was I to this keen mockery born?
When at your hands did I deserve this scorn?
Is't not enough, is't not enough, young man,   125
That I did never, no, nor never can,
Deserve a sweet look from Demetrius' eye,
But you must flout my insufficiency?
Good troth, you do me wrong (good sooth, you do)
In such disdainful manner me to woo.   130
But fare you well; perforce I must confess
I thought you lord of more true gentleness.
O that a lady, of one man refus'd,
Should of another therefore be abus'd!   *Exit*.

Lys. She sees not Hermia. Hermia, sleep thou
        there,   135
And never mayst thou come Lysander near!
For as a surfeit of the sweetest things
The deepest loathing to the stomach brings,
Or as the heresies that men do leave
Are hated most of those they did deceive,   140
So thou, my surfeit and my heresy,
Of all be hated, but the most of me!
And, all my powers, address your love and might
To honor Helen and to be her knight.   *Exit*.

Her. [*Starting up*.] Help me, Lysander, help me!
        do thy best   145
To pluck this crawling serpent from my breast!
Ay me, for pity! what a dream was here!
Lysander, look how I do quake with fear.
Methought a serpent eat my heart away,
And you sate smiling at his cruel prey.   150
Lysander! what, remov'd? Lysander! lord!
What, out of hearing gone? No sound, no word?
Alack, where are you? Speak, and if you hear;

Speak, of all loves! I swoon almost with fear.
No? then I well perceive you are not nigh: 155
Either death, or you, I'll find immediately.   *Exit*.

[ACT III, SCENE I]

Enter the Clowns [QUINCE, SNUG, BOTTOM, FLUTE,
SNOUT, *and* STARVELING].

Bot. Are we all met?

Quin. Pat, pat; and here's a marvail's convenient place for our rehearsal. This green plot shall
be our stage, this hawthorn brake our tiring-house,
and we will do it in action as we will do it before
the Duke.   6

Bot. Peter Quince!

Quin. What sayest thou, bully Bottom?

Bot. There are things in this comedy of Pyramus
and Thisby that will never please. First, Pyramus   10
must draw a sword to kill himself; which the ladies
cannot abide. How answer you that?

Snout. By'r lakin, a parlous fear.

Star. I believe we must leave the killing out, when
all is done.   15

Bot. Not a whit! I have a device to make all well.
Write me a prologue, and let the prologue seem to
say we will do no harm with our swords, and that
Pyramus is not kill'd indeed; and for the more better assurance, tell them that I Pyramus am not   20
Pyramus, but Bottom the weaver. This will put
them out of fear.

Quin. Well; we will have such a prologue, and it
shall be written in eight and six.

Bot. No; make it two more; let it be written in
eight and eight.   26

Snout. Will not the ladies be afeard of the lion?

Star. I fear it, I promise you.

Bot. Masters, you ought to consider with your-
[selves], to bring in (God shield us!) a lion   30
among ladies, is a most dreadful thing; for there is
not a more fearful wild-fowl than your lion living;
and we ought to look to't.

Snout. Therefore another prologue must tell he is
not a lion.   35

Bot. Nay; you must name his name, and half his
face must be seen through the lion's neck, and he
himself must speak through, saying thus, or to the
same defect: "Ladies," or "Fair ladies, I would wish

---

104. **Transparent:** (1) bright, radiant; (2) capable of being seen
through.   109. **What though:** what does it matter if.
115. **will:** desire.
119. **point:** summit.   **skill:** discernment, judgment.
121. **o'erlook:** survey, read.   123. **keen:** bitter.
127. **Deserve:** earn.
129. **Good troth, good sooth.** Both phrases mean "in very truth."
132. **gentleness:** courtesy.
133. **of:** by (so also in lines 134, 140, 142).   134. **abus'd:** ill used.
149. **eat:** ate (common preterite form, pronounced *et*).
150. **sate:** sat.   **prey:** preying.   153. **and if:** if.

154. **of all loves:** for the sake of all true love.

III.i. Location: Scene continues. (Although F1 marks an act break
here, III.i is obviously a continuation of II.ii, since Titania remains
asleep on stage, to wake at line 129.)
2. **marvail's:** marvellous.   4. **tiring-house:** dressing room.
8. **bully:** a friendly term meaning "fine fellow."
13. **By'r lakin:** by our ladykin, i.e. the Virgin Mary.   **parlous:**
perilous.   14–15. **when . . . done:** after all.
24. **eight and six:** the common ballad measure of alternating eight-
and six-syllable lines.
30–31. **lion among ladies.** It has been suggested that Shakespeare
here alludes to an episode at a court entertainment in Scotland in
1594, when a tame lion which was to have drawn a chariot was
replaced by a black African so as not to frighten the spectators.
32. **fearful:** (1) dreadful (as referring to a lion); (2) full of fear (as
referring to a bird).   **your.** See note on I.ii.93.
39. **defect:** blunder for *effect*.

A Midsummer Night's Dream III.i

you," or "I would request you," or "I would 40
entreat you, not to fear, not to tremble: my life
for yours. If you think I come hither as a lion, it
were pity of my life. No! I am no such thing; I am
a man as other men are"; and there indeed let him
name his name, and tell them plainly he is Snug the
joiner. 46

Quin. Well; it shall be so. But there is two hard
things: that is, to bring the moonlight into a chamber; for you know, Pyramus and Thisby meet by
moonlight. 50

Snout. Doth the moon shine that night we play
our play?

Bot. A calendar, a calendar! Look in the almanac.
Find out moonshine, find out moonshine.

Quin. Yes; it doth shine that night. 55

[*Bot.*] Why then may you leave a casement of the
great chamber window (where we play) open; and the
moon may shine in at the casement.

Quin. Ay; or else one must come in with a bush
of thorns and a lantern, and say he comes to dis- 60
figure, or to present, the person of Moonshine. Then,
there is another thing: we must have a wall in the
great chamber; for Pyramus and Thisby (says the
story) did talk through the chink of a wall.

Snout. You can never bring in a wall. What say
you, Bottom? 66

Bot. Some man or other must present Wall; and
let him have some plaster, or some loam, or some
rough-cast about him, to signify wall; or let him hold
his fingers thus, and through that cranny shall Pyramus
and Thisby whisper. 71

Quin. If that may be, then all is well. Come, sit
down, every mother's son, and rehearse your parts.
Pyramus, you begin. When you have spoken your
speech, enter into that brake; and so every one according to his cue. 76

Enter ROBIN [PUCK, *behind*].

Puck. What hempen home-spuns have we swag-
g'ring here,
So near the cradle of the Fairy Queen?
What, a play toward? I'll be an auditor,
An actor too perhaps, if I see cause. 80

Quin. Speak, Pyramus. Thisby, stand forth.

Bot. "Thisby, the flowers of odious savors
sweet"—

Quin. [Odorous], odorous.

Bot. —"odors savors sweet;
So hath thy breath, my dearest Thisby dear. 85
But hark; a voice! Stay thou but here a while,
And by and by I will to thee appear." *Exit.*

[*Puck.*] A stranger Pyramus than e'er played here.
[Exit.]

Flu. Must I speak now? 89

Quin. Ay, marry, must you; for you must understand he goes but to see a noise that he heard, and is
to come again.

Flu. "Most radiant Pyramus, most lily-white of
hue,
Of color like the red rose on triumphant brier,
Most brisky juvenal, and eke most lovely Jew, 95
As true as truest horse, that yet would never tire,
I'll meet thee, Pyramus, at Ninny's tomb."

Quin. "Ninus' tomb," man. Why, you must not
speak that yet. That you answer to Pyramus. You
speak all your part at once, cues and all. Pyramus,
enter. Your cue is past; it is "never tire." 101

Flu. O—"As true as truest horse, that yet would
never tire."

[*Enter* PUCK, *and* BOTTOM *with an ass's head*.]

Bot. "If I were fair, Thisby, I were only thine."

Quin. O monstrous! O strange! We are haunted.
Pray, masters, fly, masters! Help! 105

[*Exeunt Quince, Snug, Flute, Snout, and Starveling.*]

Puck. I'll follow you, I'll lead you about a round,
Through bog, through bush, through brake, through
brier:
Sometime a horse I'll be, sometime a hound,
A hog, a headless bear, sometime a fire,
And neigh, and bark, and grunt, and roar, and burn,
Like horse, hound, hog, bear, fire, at every turn. 111
Exit.

Bot. Why do they run away? This is a knavery of
them to make me afeard.

Enter SNOUT.

Snout. O Bottom, thou art chang'd! What do I
see on thee? 115

Bot. What do you see? You see an ass-head of
your own, do you? [*Exit Snout.*]

Enter QUINCE.

Quin. Bless thee, Bottom, bless thee! Thou art
translated. *Exit.*

Bot. I see their knavery. This is to make an ass of
me, to fright me, if they could; but I will not stir 121
from this place, do what they can. I will walk up and
down here, and I will sing, that they shall hear I am
not afraid. [*Sings.*]
      The woosel cock so black of hue, 125
          With orange-tawny bill,
      The throstle with his note so true,
          The wren with little quill—

41–42. **my . . . yours:** I pledge my life in defense of yours.
43. **were . . . life:** would endanger my life.
59–60. **bush of thorns.** English peasants saw "the man in the moon"
as bearing a bundle of sticks on his back.
60–61. **disfigure:** blunder for *prefigure.* 61. **present:** represent.
69. **rough-cast:** plaster mixed with pebbles for coating the outside of
buildings.
77. **hempen home-spuns:** uncouth rustics (literally, persons wearing
home-spun cloth made of hemp). **swagg'ring:** blustering about.
79. **toward:** about to take place.
82. **odious:** blunder for *odorous.* Dogberry makes the reverse error
in *Much Ado,* III.v.16: "Comparisons are odorous."

95. **brisky juvenal:** lively youth. **eke:** also. **Jew.** Probably suggested by the first syllable of *juvenal* and used to provide a rhyme.
98. **Ninus:** mythical founder of Nineveh; his wife, Semiramis,
reputedly erected Babylon, the scene of the story of Pyramus and
Thisbe. 103. **fair:** handsome. **were:** would be.
106. **about a round:** roundabout. 109. **fire:** will-o'-the-wisp.
116–17. **an ass-head . . . own:** i.e. something dreamed up inside your
own asinine head. 119. **translated:** transformed.
125. **woosel cock:** male ousel or blackbird.
127. **throstle:** song thrush.
128. **quill:** piping voice (literally, pipe made of a hollow stalk).

Tita. [*Awaking.*] What angel wakes me from my
flow'ry bed?
Bot. [*Sings.*]
      The finch, the sparrow, and the lark,   130
        The plain-song cuckoo grey,
      Whose note full many a man doth mark,
        And dares not answer nay—
for indeed, who would set his wit to so foolish a bird?
Who would give a bird the lie, though he cry "cuckoo"
never so?   136
Tita. I pray thee, gentle mortal, sing again.
Mine ear is much enamored of thy note;
So is mine eye enthralled to thy shape;
And thy fair virtue's force (perforce) doth move me
On the first view to say, to swear, I love thee.   141
Bot. Methinks, mistress, you should have little
reason for that. And yet, to say the truth, reason
and love keep little company together now-a-days.
The more the pity that some honest neighbors   145
will not make them friends. Nay, I can gleek upon
occasion.
Tita. Thou art as wise as thou art beautiful.
Bot. Not so, neither; but if I had wit enough to
get out of this wood, I have enough to serve mine
owe turn.   151
Tita. Out of this wood do not desire to go;
Thou shalt remain here, whether thou wilt or no.
I am a spirit of no common rate;
The summer still doth tend upon my state;   155
And I do love thee; therefore go with me.
I'll give thee fairies to attend on thee;
And they shall fetch thee jewels from the deep,
And sing while thou on pressed flowers dost sleep.
And I will purge thy mortal grossness so,   160
That thou shalt like an aery spirit go.
Peaseblossom! Cobweb! Moth! and Mustardseed!

Enter four Fairies [Peaseblossom, Cobweb, Moth,
  and Mustardseed].

[*Peas.*] Ready.
[*Cob.*]   And I.
[*Moth.*]   And I.
[*Mus.*]   And I.
[*All.*]   Where shall we go?
Tita. Be kind and courteous to this gentleman,
Hop in his walks and gambol in his eyes;   165
Feed him with apricocks and dewberries,
With purple grapes, green figs, and mulberries;
The honey-bags steal from the humble-bees,
And for night-tapers crop their waxen thighs,
And light them at the fiery glow-worm's eyes,   170
To have my love to bed and to arise;

And pluck the wings from painted butterflies,
To fan the moonbeams from his sleeping eyes.
Nod to him, elves, and do him courtesies.
   [*Peas.*] Hail, mortal!   175
   [*Cob.*] Hail!
   [*Moth.*] Hail!
   [*Mus.*] Hail!
Bot. I cry your worships mercy, heartily. I be-
seech your worship's name.   180
Cob. Cobweb.
Bot. I shall desire you of more acquaintance, good
Master Cobweb. If I cut my finger, I shall make
bold with you. Your name, honest gentleman?
Peas. Peaseblossom.   185
Bot. I pray you commend me to Mistress Squash,
your mother, and to Master Peascod, your father.
Good Master Peaseblossom, I shall desire you of more
acquaintance too. Your name, I beseech you, sir?
Mus. Mustardseed.   190
Bot. Good Master Mustardseed, I know your
patience well. That same cowardly, giant-like ox-
beef hath devour'd many a gentleman of your house.
I promise you your kindred hath made my eyes water
ere now. I desire you [of] more acquaintance, good
Master Mustardseed.   196
Tita. Come wait upon him; lead him to my bower.
The moon methinks looks with a wat'ry eye;
And when she weeps, weeps every little flower,
Lamenting some enforced chastity.   200
Tie up my lover's tongue, bring him silently. *Exeunt.*

[Scene II]

Enter King of Fairies [Oberon].

Obe. I wonder if Titania be awak'd;
Then what it was that next came in her eye,
Which she must dote on in extremity.

[*Enter* Puck.]

Here comes my messenger. How now, mad spirit?
What night-rule now about this haunted grove?   5
Puck. My mistress with a monster is in love.
Near to her close and consecrated bower,
While she was in her dull and sleeping hour,
A crew of patches, rude mechanicals,
That work for bread upon Athenian stalls,   10
Were met together to rehearse a play
Intended for great Theseus' nuptial day.
The shallowest thick-skin of that barren sort,

---

131. **plain-song:** melody without variations.
132–33. **Whose . . . nay.** The similarity between *cuckoo* and *cuckold*
gave rise to a common jest.   135. **give . . . lie:** call a bird a liar.
136. **never so:** i.e. ever so much, continually.
140. **thy . . . force:** the power of your beauty.
146. **gleek:** gibe, jest.   151. **owe:** own.
154. **rate:** value, worth.
155. **still:** ever, always.   **doth . . . state:** attends upon me as one of
my retinue.   160. **grossness:** corporeal nature.
162. **Moth.** Pronounced *mote* or *mot* by the Elizabethans, and probably intended by Shakespeare to represent here the word now written
mote, which he seems regularly to have spelled *moth*.
166. **apricocks:** apricots.   171. **have:** i.e. attend (with lights).

179. **cry . . . mercy:** beg pardon of your honors.
182. **of more acquaintance:** to be better acquainted with me.
183–84. **If . . . you.** Cobwebs were applied to cuts to inhibit bleeding.
186. **commend me:** give my regards.   **Squash:** unripe pea pod.
187 **Peascod:** mature pea pod.
192. **patience:** calmness in suffering.
199. **she weeps:** i.e. causes dew.   200. **enforced:** violated.

III.ii. Location: The wood.
2. **next:** nearest, i.e. first.   3. **in extremity:** to the utmost degree.
5. **night-rule:** night activity, night sport.   **haunted:** much frequented.
7. **close:** secret.   8. **dull:** drowsy.
9. **patches:** clowns, fools.   **rude mechanicals:** ignorant working-
men.   10. **stalls:** street or market booths where wares were sold.
13. **thick-skin:** blockhead.   **barren sort:** stupid crew.

A Midsummer Night's Dream
III.ii

Who Pyramus presented, in their sport,
Forsook his scene, and ent'red in a brake;   15
When I did him at this advantage take,
An ass's nole I fixed on his head.
Anon his Thisby must be answered,
And forth my mimic comes. When they him spy,
As wild geese that the creeping fowler eye,   20
Or russet-pated choughs, many in sort
(Rising and cawing at the gun's report),
Sever themselves and madly sweep the sky,
So, at his sight, away his fellows fly;
And at our stamp, here o'er and o'er one falls;   25
He murther cries, and help from Athens calls.
Their sense thus weak, lost with their fears thus
          strong,
Made senseless things begin to do them wrong,
For briers and thorns at their apparel snatch;
Some sleeves, some hats, from yielders all things
          catch.   30
I led them on in this distracted fear,
And left sweet Pyramus translated there;
When in that moment (so it came to pass)
Titania wak'd, and straightway lov'd an ass.
    Obe. This falls out better than I could devise.   35
But hast thou yet latch'd the Athenian's eyes
With the love-juice, as I did bid thee do?
    Puck. I took him sleeping (that is finish'd too)
And the Athenian woman by his side;
That when he wak'd, of force she must be ey'd.   40

          Enter DEMETRIUS *and* HERMIA.

    Obe. Stand close; this is the same Athenian.
    Puck. This is the woman; but not this the man.
    Dem. O, why rebuke you him that loves you so?
Lay breath so bitter on your bitter foe.
    Her. Now I but chide; but I should use thee
          worse,   45
For thou (I fear) hast given me cause to curse.
If thou hast slain Lysander in his sleep,
Being o'er shoes in blood, plunge in the deep,
And kill me too.
The sun was not so true unto the day   50
As he to me. Would he have stolen away
From sleeping Hermia? I'll believe as soon
This whole earth may be bor'd, and that the moon
May through the centre creep, and so displease
Her brother's noontide with th' Antipodes.   55
It cannot be but thou hast murd'red him;
So should a murtherer look—so dead, so grim.
    Dem. So should the murthered look, and so should I,
Pierc'd through the heart with your stern cruelty.

Yet you, the murtherer, look as bright, as clear,   60
As yonder Venus in her glimmering sphere.
    Her. What's this to my Lysander? Where is he?
Ah, good Demetrius, wilt thou give him me?
    Dem. I had rather give his carcass to my hounds.
    Her. Out, dog, out, cur! thou driv'st me past the
          bounds   65
Of maiden's patience. Hast thou slain him then?
Henceforth be never numb'red among men!
O, once tell true; tell true, even for my sake!
Durst thou have look'd upon him being awake?
And hast thou kill'd him sleeping? O brave touch!
Could not a worm, an adder, do so much?   71
An adder did it! for with doubler tongue
Than thine, thou serpent, never adder stung.
    Dem. You spend your passion on a mispris'd mood.
I am not guilty of Lysander's blood;   75
Nor is he dead, for aught that I can tell.
    Her. I pray thee, tell me then that he is well.
    Dem. And if I could, what should I get therefore?
    Her. A privilege never to see me more.
And from thy hated presence part I [so]:   80
See me no more, whether he be dead or no.   *Exit.*
    Dem. There is no following her in this fierce vein.
Here therefore for a while I will remain.
So sorrow's heaviness doth heavier grow
For debt that bankrout [sleep] doth sorrow owe;   85
Which now in some slight measure it will pay,
If for his tender here I make some stay.
                    Lie down [*and sleep*].
    Obe. What hast thou done? Thou hast mistaken
          quite,
And laid the love-juice on some true-love's sight.
Of thy misprision must perforce ensue   90
Some true love turn'd, and not a false turn'd true.
    Puck. Then fate o'errules, that one man holding
          troth,
A million fail, confounding oath on oath.
    Obe. About the wood go swifter than the wind,
And Helena of Athens look thou find.   95
All fancy-sick she is and pale of cheer
With sighs of love, that costs the fresh blood dear.
By some illusion see thou bring her here.
I'll charm his eyes against she do appear.
    Puck. I go, I go, look how I go,   100
Swifter than arrow from the Tartar's bow.   [*Exit.*]
    Obe.   Flower of this purple dye,
          Hit with Cupid's archery,
          Sink in apple of his eye.
          When his love he doth espy,   105
          Let her shine as gloriously

15. scene: playing place.   17. nole: noddle, head.
19. mimic: actor.
21. russet-pated choughs: grey-headed jackdaws.   in sort: in company, together.
25. at our stamp. Puck's use of *our* instead of *my* has puzzled editors, as has the notion that a fairy's stamp would be frightening. (This is the first occurrence of the word in that sense recorded in the *O.E.D.*). Many editors adopt Theobald's conjecture *at a stump*.
26. calls: calls for.   36. latch'd: anointed.
40. of force: perforce, necessarily.
53. whole: solid.   be bor'd: have a hole bored through it.
55. her brother's: i.e. the sun's.   with th' Antipodes: among the people on the other side of the earth.
57. dead: deadly (?) or deathly pale (?).

60. clear: shining.
62. What's this to: what has all this to do with.
70. brave touch: noble exploit.   71. worm: snake, serpent.
74. passion: passionate outburst.   on . . . mood: in mistaken anger.
84. heavier. With play on the sense "drowsier."
85. bankrout: bankrupt.
87. for his tender: until sleep offers itself (in payment of the deficit).
90. misprision: mistake.   92. troth: faith.
93. confounding . . . oath: invalidating one oath with another.
96. fancy-sick: lovesick.   cheer: face.
97. costs . . . dear. Each sigh was thought to draw a drop of blood from the heart.
99. against . . . appear: in preparation for her coming.
101. arrow . . . bow. Proverbial for swiftness.

As the Venus of the sky.
When thou wak'st, if she be by,
Beg of her for remedy.

Enter PUCK.

Puck. Captain of our fairy band,   110
Helena is here at hand,
And the youth, mistook by me,
Pleading for a lover's fee.
Shall we their fond pageant see?
Lord, what fools these mortals be!   115
Obe. Stand aside. The noise they make
Will cause Demetrius to awake.
Puck. Then will two at once woo one;
That must needs be sport alone.
And those things do best please me   120
That befall prepost'rously.

Enter LYSANDER *and* HELENA.

Lys. Why should you think that I should woo in
 scorn?
Scorn and derision never come in tears.
Look when I vow, I weep; and vows so born,
In their nativity all truth appears.   125
How can these things in me seem scorn to you,
Bearing the badge of faith to prove them true?
Hel. You do advance your cunning more and more;
When truth kills truth, O devilish-holy fray!
These vows are Hermia's. Will you give her o'er?   130
Weigh oath with oath, and you will nothing weigh.
Your vows to her and me, put in two scales,
Will even weigh; and both as light as tales.
Lys. I had no judgment when to her I swore.
Hel. Nor none, in my mind, now you give her
 o'er.   135
Lys. Demetrius loves her; and he loves not you.
Dem. [*Awaking.*] O Helen, goddess, nymph, per-
 fect, divine!
To what, my love, shall I compare thine eyne?
Crystal is muddy. O, how ripe in show
Thy lips, those kissing cherries, tempting grow!   140
That pure congealed white, high Taurus' snow,
Fann'd with the eastern wind, turns to a crow
When thou hold'st up thy hand. O, let me kiss
This princess of pure white, this seal of bliss!
Hel. O spite! O hell! I see you all are bent   145
To set against me for your merriment.
If you were civil and knew courtesy,
You would not do me thus much injury.
Can you not hate me, as I know you do,
But you must join in souls to mock me too?   150
If you were men, as men you are in show,
You would not use a gentle lady so;

To vow, and swear, and superpraise my parts,
When I am sure you hate me with your hearts.
You both are rivals, and love Hermia;   155
And now both rivals, to mock Helena.
A trim exploit, a manly enterprise,
To conjure tears up in a poor maid's eyes
With your derision! None of noble sort
Would so offend a virgin, and extort   160
A poor soul's patience, all to make you sport.
Lys. You are unkind, Demetrius; be not so;
For you love Hermia; this you know I know.
And here, with all good will, with all my heart,
In Hermia's love I yield you up my part;   165
And yours of Helena to me bequeath,
Whom I do love, and will do till my death.
Hel. Never did mockers waste more idle breath.
Dem. Lysander, keep thy Hermia; I will none.
If e'er I lov'd her, all that love is gone.   170
My heart to her but as guest-wise sojourn'd,
And now to Helen is it home return'd,
There to remain.
Lys.   Helen, it is not so.
Dem. Disparage not the faith thou dost not know,
Lest, to thy peril, thou aby it dear.   175
Look where thy love comes; yonder is thy dear.

Enter HERMIA.

Her. Dark night, that from the eye his function
 takes,
The ear more quick of apprehension makes;
Wherein it doth impair the seeing sense,
It pays the hearing double recompense.   180
Thou art not by mine eye, Lysander, found;
Mine ear, I thank it, brought me to thy sound.
But why unkindly didst thou leave me so?
Lys. Why should he stay, whom love doth press
 to go?
Her. What love could press Lysander from my
 side?   185
Lys. Lysander's love, that would not let him bide—
Fair Helena! who more engilds the night
Than all yon fiery oes and eyes of light.
Why seek'st thou me? Could not this make thee know,
The hate I bare thee made me leave thee so?   190
Her. You speak not as you think. It cannot be.
Hel. Lo! she is one of this confederacy.
Now I perceive, they have conjoin'd all three
To fashion this false sport, in spite of me.
Injurious Hermia, most ungrateful maid!   195
Have you conspir'd, have you with these contriv'd
To bait me with this foul derision?
Is all the counsel that we two have shar'd,
The sisters' vows, the hours that we have spent,
When we have chid the hasty-footed time   200
For parting us—O, is all forgot?
All school-days friendship, childhood innocence?

113. **fee:** right, privilege. 114. **fond pageant:** foolish show.
119. **alone:** unparalleled.
121. **prepost'rously:** out of the natural order.
124–25. **vows . . . appears:** i.e. when vows are so born, the nature of
their birth makes their sincerity manifest.
127. **badge:** identifying mark (like the family crest or other device
worn on livery to identify a gentleman's retainers).
128. **advance:** hold high, i.e. display. 133. **tales:** lies.
141. **Taurus:** a mountain range in Asiatic Turkey.
142. **turns . . . crow:** i.e. seems black in comparison.
144. **seal:** pledge. 151. **show:** appearance.

153. **superpraise:** overpraise. **parts:** qualities.
157. **trim:** fine. 160. **extort:** wring, torture.
169. **none:** i.e. of her. 175. **aby:** pay for, atone for.
177. **his:** its. 188. **oes:** circles, i.e. stars.
194. **in . . . me:** to vex me. 195. **Injurious:** insulting.
196. **contriv'd:** plotted. 197. **bait:** torment.
198. **counsel:** private thoughts, confidences.

A Midsummer Night's Dream III.ii

We, Hermia, like two artificial gods,
Have with our needles created both one flower,
Both on one sampler, sitting on one cushion,   205
Both warbling of one song, both in one key,
As if our hands, our sides, voices, and minds
Had been incorporate. So we grew together,
Like to a double cherry, seeming parted,
But yet an union in partition,   210
Two lovely berries moulded on one stem;
So with two seeming bodies, but one heart,
Two of the first, [like] coats in heraldry,
Due but to one, and crowned with one crest.
And will you rent our ancient love asunder,   215
To join with men in scorning your poor friend?
It is not friendly, 'tis not maidenly.
Our sex, as well as I, may chide you for it,
Though I alone do feel the injury.
    Her. I am amazed at your [passionate] words. 220
I scorn you not; it seems that you scorn me.
    Hel. Have you not set Lysander, as in scorn,
To follow me and praise my eyes and face?
And made your other love, Demetrius
(Who even but now did spurn me with his foot), 225
To call me goddess, nymph, divine and rare,
Precious, celestial? Wherefore speaks he this
To her he hates? And wherefore doth Lysander
Deny your love (so rich within his soul)
And tender me (forsooth) affection,   230
But by your setting on, by your consent?
What though I be not so in grace as you,
So hung upon with love, so fortunate
(But miserable most, to love unlov'd)?
This you should pity rather than despise.   235
    Her. I understand not what you mean by this.
    Hel. Ay, do! persever, counterfeit sad looks,
Make mouths upon me when I turn my back,
Wink each at other, hold the sweet jest up;
This sport, well carried, shall be chronicled.   240
If you have any pity, grace, or manners,
You would not make me such an argument.
But fare ye well; 'tis partly my own fault,
Which death, or absence, soon shall remedy.
    Lys. Stay, gentle Helena; hear my excuse,   245
My love, my life, my soul, fair Helena!
    Hel. O excellent!
    Her.   Sweet, do not scorn her so.
    Dem. If she cannot entreat, I can compel.
    Lys. Thou canst compel no more than she entreat.
Thy threats have no more strength than her weak
    [prays].   250
Helen, I love thee, by my life I do!

203. **artificial:** skilled in art, able to create.
208. **incorporate:** united in one body.   209. **seeming:** apparently.
211. **lovely:** loving.
213–14. **Two . . . crest:** "we had *two of the first,* i.e. bodies, like double coats in heraldry that belong to a man and wife as *one person,* but which, like our *single heart,* have but *one crest*" (Douce).
215. **rent:** rend.   220. **amazed:** utterly bewildered.
225. **even but now:** just now.   229. **your love:** his love of you.
232. **grace:** favor.   237. **sad:** serious, grave.
238. **mouths:** a common corruption of *mows,* "grimaces."   **upon:** at.
239. **hold . . . up:** carry . . . on.   240. **carried:** managed.
242. **argument:** subject matter (for jesting).
248. **If . . . compel:** i.e. if Hermia cannot influence you by pleas, I can do so by force.   250. **prays:** prayings, prayers.

I swear by that which I will lose for thee,
To prove him false that says I love thee not.
    Dem. I say I love thee more than he can do.   254
    Lys. If thou say so, withdraw, and prove it too.
    Dem. Quick, come!
    Her.   Lysander, whereto tends all this?
    Lys. Away, you Ethiop!
    Dem.   No, no; he'll
Seem to break loose—take on as you would follow,
But yet come not. You are a tame man, go!
    Lys. Hang off, thou cat, thou bur! Vile thing,
let loose;   260
Or I will shake thee from me like a serpent!
    Her. Why are you grown so rude? What change
is this,
Sweet love?
    Lys.   Thy love? Out, tawny Tartar, out!
Out, loathed med'cine! O hated potion, hence!
    Her. Do you not jest?
    Hel.   Yes, sooth; and so do you.   265
    Lys. Demetrius, I will keep my word with thee.
    Dem. I would I had your bond, for I perceive
A weak bond holds you. I'll not trust your word.
    Lys. What? should I hurt her, strike her, kill her
dead?
Although I hate her, I'll not harm her so.   270
    Her. What? can you do me greater harm than hate?
Hate me, wherefore? O me, what news, my love!
Am not I Hermia? Are not you Lysander?
I am as fair now as I was erewhile.
Since night you lov'd me; yet since night you left
me: 275
Why then, you left me (O, the gods forbid!)
In earnest, shall I say?
    Lys.   Ay, by my life;
And never did desire to see thee more.
Therefore be out of hope, of question, of doubt;
Be certain! nothing truer; 'tis no jest   280
That I do hate thee, and love Helena.
    Her. O me, you juggler, you canker-blossom,
You thief of love! What, have you come by night
And stol'n my love's heart from him?
    Hel.   Fine, i' faith!
Have you no modesty, no maiden shame,   285
No touch of bashfulness? What, will you tear
Impatient answers from my gentle tongue?
Fie, fie, you counterfeit, you puppet, you!
    Her. "Puppet"? Why so? Ay, that way goes
the game.
Now I perceive that she hath made compare   290
Between our statures: she hath urg'd her height,
And with her personage, her tall personage,
Her height, forsooth, she hath prevail'd with him.
And are you grown so high in his esteem,

257. **Ethiop:** blackamoor. Hermia is a brunette.
260. **Hang off:** let go.
268. **weak bond:** i.e. Hermia's arms. Demetrius implies that Lysander is not trying very hard to break away from her.
272. **what news:** what is the matter.
275. **Since night:** i.e. last night.
282. **canker-blossom:** worm that destroys the bud.
288. **puppet:** i.e. a mere doll rather than a woman (cf. the preceding *counterfeit*), but Hermia takes it as a reference to her small stature.
292. **personage:** figure.

Because I am so dwarfish and so low?　295
How low am I, thou painted maypole? Speak!
How low am I? I am not yet so low
But that my nails can reach unto thine eyes.
　Hel. I pray you, though you mock me, [gentlemen],
Let her not hurt me. I was never curst;　300
I have no gift at all in shrewishness;
I am a right maid for my cowardice.
Let her not strike me. You perhaps may think,
Because she is something lower than myself,
That I can match her.
　Her.　　　　　　"Lower"? hark again.　305
　Hel. Good Hermia, do not be so bitter with me.
I evermore did love you, Hermia,
Did ever keep your counsels, never wrong'd you;
Save that, in love unto Demetrius,
I told him of your stealth unto this wood.　310
He followed you; for love I followed him.
But he hath chid me hence, and threat'ned me
To strike me, spurn me, nay, to kill me too.
And now, so you will let me quiet go,
To Athens will I bear my folly back,　315
And follow you no further. Let me go.
You see how simple and how fond I am.
　Her. Why, get you gone. Who is't that hinders
　　you?
　Hel. A foolish heart, that I leave here behind.
　Her. What, with Lysander?
　Hel.　　　　　　　With Demetrius.　320
　Lys. Be not afraid; she shall not harm thee, Helena.
　Dem. No, sir; she shall not, though you take her
　　part.
　Hel. O, when she is angry, she is keen and shrewd!
She was a vixen when she went to school;
And though she be but little, she is fierce.　325
　Her. "Little" again? Nothing but "low" and
　　"little"?
Why will you suffer her to flout me thus?
Let me come to her.
　Lys.　　　　　Get you gone, you dwarf;
You minimus, of hind'ring knot-grass made;
You bead, you acorn.
　Dem.　　　　　You are too officious　330
In her behalf that scorns your services.
Let her alone; speak not of Helena,
Take not her part. For if thou dost intend
Never so little show of love to her,
Thou shalt aby it.
　Lys.　　　　Now she holds me not;　335
Now follow, if thou dar'st, to try whose right,
Of thine or mine, is most in Helena.
　Dem. Follow? Nay; I'll go with thee, cheek by
　　jowl.　　　[*Exeunt Lysander and Demetrius.*]

　Her. You, mistress, all this coil is long of you.
Nay, go not back.
　Hel.　　　　　I will not trust you, I,　340
Nor longer stay in your curst company.
Your hands than mine are quicker for a fray;
My legs are longer though, to run away.　[*Exit.*]
　Her. I am amaz'd, and know not what to say. *Exit.*
　Obe. This is thy negligence. Still thou mistak'st,
Or else commit'st thy knaveries willfully.　346
　Puck. Believe me, king of shadows, I mistook.
Did not you tell me I should know the man
By the Athenian garments he had on?
And so far blameless proves my enterprise,　350
That I have 'nointed an Athenian's eyes;
And so far am I glad it so did sort,
As this their jangling I esteem a sport.
　Obe. Thou seest these lovers seek a place to fight;
Hie therefore, Robin, overcast the night;　355
The starry welkin cover thou anon
With drooping fog as black as Acheron,
And lead these testy rivals so astray
As one come not within another's way.
Like to Lysander sometime frame thy tongue;　360
Then stir Demetrius up with bitter wrong;
And sometime rail thou like Demetrius;
And from each other look thou lead them thus,
Till o'er their brows death-counterfeiting sleep
With leaden legs and batty wings doth creep.　365
Then crush this herb into Lysander's eye;
Whose liquor hath this virtuous property,
To take from thence all error with his might,
And make his eyeballs roll with wonted sight.
When they next wake, all this derision　370
Shall seem a dream and fruitless vision,
And back to Athens shall the lovers wend
With league whose date till death shall never end.
Whiles I in this affair do thee employ,
I'll to my queen and beg her Indian boy;　375
And then I will her charmed eye release
From monster's view, and all things shall be peace.
　Puck. My fairy lord, this must be done with haste,
For Night's swift dragons cut the clouds full fast,
And yonder shines Aurora's harbinger;　380
At whose approach, ghosts, wand'ring here and there,
Troop home to churchyards. Damned spirits all,
That in crossways and floods have burial,
Already to their wormy beds are gone.
For fear lest day should look their shames upon,　385

---

295. **low:** short.　300. **curst:** shrewish, sharp-tongued.
302. **right:** real, true.　**for:** with respect to.
304. **something:** somewhat.　305. **match:** be a match for.
310. **stealth:** stealing away.
323. **shrewd:** sharp-tongued (synonymous with *curst* in line 300).
324. **vixen:** shrew (literally, she-fox).
329. **minimus:** diminutive creature.　**knot-grass:** a weed that was thought to stunt the growth of animals or children.
333. **intend:** offer; or, possibly, pretend.　335. **aby:** pay for.
338. **cheek by jowl:** side by side.

339. **coil:** uproar.　**long of:** because of.　345. **Still:** continually.
350. **so far:** to this extent.　352. **sort:** turn out.
353. **As:** that.　**jangling:** disputing, wrangling.
355. **Hie:** hasten.　356. **welkin:** sky.
357. **Acheron:** a river of Hades; here, Hades itself.
361. **wrong:** insults.　365. **batty:** batlike.
366. **this herb:** i.e. the herb that Oberon has mentioned (II.i.184) as the antidote to love-in-idleness.　367. **virtuous:** powerful.
368. **with his might:** by its efficacy.
370. **derision:** laughable mockery.
371. **fruitless:** having no effect, inconsequential.
373. **date:** duration.
379. **dragons:** i.e. those that were supposed to draw the chariot of the goddess of night.　**full:** very.
380. **Aurora's harbinger:** the precursor of dawn, i.e. the morning star.
382-83. **Damned . . . burial.** Suicides were commonly buried at crossroads; to these Puck adds those who have drowned themselves and whose bodies have not been recovered.

A Midsummer
Night's Dream
III.ii

They willfully themselves exile from light,
And must for aye consort with black-brow'd Night.
  Obe. But we are spirits of another sort.
I with the Morning's love have oft made sport,
And like a forester, the groves may tread   390
Even till the eastern gate, all fiery red,
Opening on Neptune with fair blessed beams,
Turns into yellow gold his salt green streams.
But notwithstanding, haste, make no delay;
We may effect this business yet ere day.   [*Exit.*]
  Puck. Up and down, up and down,   396
    I will lead them up and down;
    I am fear'd in field and town.
    Goblin, lead them up and down.
Here comes one.   400

Enter LYSANDER.

  Lys. Where art thou, proud Demetrius? Speak
    thou now.
  Puck. Here, villain, drawn and ready. Where
    art thou?
  Lys. I will be with thee straight.
  Puck.   Follow me then
To plainer ground.
        [*Exit Lysander, as following the voice.*]

Enter DEMETRIUS.

  Dem.   Lysander, speak again!
Thou runaway, thou coward, art thou fled?   405
Speak! In some bush? Where dost thou hide thy head?
  Puck. Thou coward, art thou bragging to the stars,
Telling the bushes that thou look'st for wars,
And wilt not come? Come, recreant, come, thou child,
I'll whip thee with a rod. He is defil'd   410
That draws a sword on thee.
  Dem.   Yea, art thou there?
  Puck. Follow my voice; we'll try no manhood
    here.   *Exeunt.*

[*Enter* LYSANDER.]

  Lys. He goes before me, and still dares me on.
When I come where he calls, then he is gone.
The villain is much lighter-heel'd than I;   415
I followed fast, but faster he did fly,
That fallen am I in dark uneven way,
And here will rest me. [*Lie down.*] Come, thou gentle
    day!
For if but once thou show me thy grey light,   419
I'll find Demetrius and revenge this spite.   [*Sleeps.*]

[*Enter*] ROBIN [PUCK] *and* DEMETRIUS.

  Puck. Ho, ho, ho! Coward, why com'st thou not?
  Dem. Abide me, if thou dar'st; for well I wot
Thou run'st before me, shifting every place,

And dar'st not stand, nor look me in the face.
Where art thou now?
  Puck.   Come hither; I am here.   425
  Dem. Nay then thou mock'st me. Thou shalt buy
    this dear,
If ever I thy face by daylight see.
Now, go thy way. Faintness constraineth me
To measure out my length on this cold bed.
By day's approach look to be visited.   430
               [*Lies down and sleeps.*]

Enter HELENA.

  Hel. O weary night, O long and tedious night,
Abate thy hours! Shine, comforts, from the east,
That I may back to Athens by daylight,
From these that my poor company detest.
And sleep, that sometimes shuts up sorrow's eye,   435
Steal me a while from mine own company.   *Sleep.*
  Puck. Yet but three? Come one more;
    Two of both kinds makes up four.

[*Enter* HERMIA.]

    Here she comes, curst and sad.
    Cupid is a knavish lad,   440
    Thus to make poor females mad.
  Her. Never so weary, never so in woe,
Bedabbled with the dew and torn with briers,
I can no further crawl, no further go;
My legs can keep no pace with my desires.   445
Here will I rest me till the break of day.
Heavens shield Lysander, if they mean a fray!
              [*Lies down and sleeps.*]
  Puck.   On the ground,
    Sleep sound;
    I'll apply,   450
    [To] your eye,
  Gentle lover, remedy.
     [*Squeezing the juice on Lysander's eyes.*]
    When thou wak'st,
    Thou tak'st
    True delight   455
    In the sight
  Of thy former lady's eye;
  And the country proverb known,
  That every man should take his own,
  In your waking shall be shown.   460
    Jack shall have Jill;
    Nought shall go ill:
The man shall have his mare again, and all shall be
    well.   [*Exit.*]

[ACT IV, SCENE I]

Enter Queen of Fairies [TITANIA] *and Clown* [BOTTOM],
and Fairies [PEASEBLOSSOM, COBWEB, MOTH, MUS-
TARDSEED, *and others, attending*]; *and the King*
[OBERON] *behind them* [*unseen*].

  Tita. Come sit thee down upon this flow'ry bed,

---

389. **the Morning's love:** Cephalus, a mighty hunter, and lover of
Aurora; or perhaps Aurora herself. If the first, Oberon means that
he has often hunted in early morning with Cephalus; if the second,
he means that he has often enjoyed the pleasures of the dawn, instead
of being driven off by it.
390. **like:** in the guise of.   **forester:** keeper of a royal forest or
hunting preserve.   402. **drawn:** with drawn sword.
403. **straight:** straightway.   404. **plainer:** more level.
409. **recreant:** coward.   412. **try:** test.   417. **uneven:** rough.
422. **Abide me:** face me in fight.   **wot:** know.

429. **measure . . . length:** i.e. stretch out.   432. **Abate:** shorten.
439. **curst:** ill-tempered.   444. **go:** walk.

While I thy amiable cheeks do coy,
And stick musk-roses in thy sleek smooth head,
And kiss thy fair large ears, my gentle joy.

Bot. Where's Peaseblossom?   5

Peas. Ready.

Bot. Scratch my head, Peaseblossom. Where's
Mounsieur Cobweb?

Cob. Ready.   9

Bot. Mounsieur Cobweb, good mounsieur, get you
your weapons in your hand, and kill me a red-hipp'd
humble-bee on the top of a thistle; and, good mounsieur,
bring me the honey-bag. Do not fret yourself too much
in the action, mounsieur; and, good mounsieur, have a
care the honey-bag break not, I would be loath   15
to have you overflowen with a honey-bag, signior.
Where's Mounsieur Mustardseed?

Mus. Ready.

Bot. Give me your neaf, Mounsieur Mustardseed.
Pray you, leave your curtsy, good mounsieur.   20

Mus. What's your will?

Bot. Nothing, good mounsieur, but to help
Cavalery Cobweb to scratch. I must to the barber's,
mounsieur; for methinks I am marvail's hairy   24
about the face; and I am such a tender ass, if my hair
do but tickle me, I must scratch.

Tita. What, wilt thou hear some music, my sweet
love?

Bot. I have a reasonable good ear in music. Let's
have the tongs and the bones.   29

                    [*Music. Tongs. Rural music.*]

Tita. Or say, sweet love, what thou desirest to eat.

Bot. Truly, a peck of provender; I could munch
your good dry oats. Methinks I have a great desire
to a bottle of hay. Good hay, sweet hay, hath no
fellow.

Tita. I have a venturous fairy that shall seek   35
The squirrel's hoard, and fetch thee new nuts.

Bot. I had rather have a handful or two of dried
peas. But, I pray you, let none of your people stir
me; I have an exposition of sleep come upon me.   39

Tita. Sleep thou, and I will wind thee in my arms.
Fairies, be gone, and be [all ways] away.

                                    [*Exeunt Fairies.*]

So doth the woodbine the sweet honeysuckle
Gently entwist; the female ivy so
Enrings the barky fingers of the elm.   44
O, how I love thee! how I dote on thee! [*They sleep.*]

Enter Robin Goodfellow [Puck].

Obe. [*Advancing.*] Welcome, good Robin. Seest
       thou this sweet sight?
Her dotage now I do begin to pity.
For meeting her of late behind the wood,
Seeking sweet favors for this hateful fool,
I did upbraid her, and fall out with her.   50
For she his hairy temples then had rounded
With coronet of fresh and fragrant flowers;
And that same dew which sometime on the buds
Was wont to swell like round and orient pearls,
Stood now within the pretty flouriets' eyes,   55
Like tears that did their own disgrace bewail.
When I had at my pleasure taunted her,
And she in mild terms begg'd my patience,
I then did ask of her her changeling child;
Which straight she gave me, and her fairy sent   60
To bear him to my bower in fairy land.
And now I have the boy, I will undo
This hateful imperfection of her eyes.
And, gentle Puck, take this transformèd scalp
From off the head of this Athenian swain,   65
That he, awaking when the other do,
May all to Athens back again repair,
And think no more of this night's accidents
But as the fierce vexation of a dream.
But first I will release the Fairy Queen.   70

                                    [*Touching her eyes.*]
       Be as thou wast wont to be;
       See as thou wast wont to see.
       Dian's bud [o'er] Cupid's flower
       Hath such force and blessèd power.
Now, my Titania, wake you, my sweet queen.   75

Tita. My Oberon, what visions have I seen!
Methought I was enamor'd of an ass.

Obe. There lies your love.

Tita.   How came these things to pass?
O, how mine eyes do loathe his visage now!

Obe. Silence a while. Robin, take off this head.
Titania, music call, and strike more dead   81
Than common sleep of all these [five] the sense.

Tita. Music, ho, music, such as charmeth sleep!

                                    [*Music, still.*]

Puck. Now, when thou wak'st, with thine own
       fool's eyes peep.

Obe. Sound, music! [*Louder music.*] Come, my
       queen, take hands with me,   85
And rock the ground whereon these sleepers be.
Now thou and I are new in amity,
And will to-morrow midnight solemnly
Dance in Duke Theseus' house triumphantly,
And bless it to all fair prosperity.   90

IV.i. Location: Scene continues. (Again F1 marks an act break
where the action is clearly continuous, the lovers remaining asleep
on the stage. The F1 act division is preceded by the notation "They
sleepe all the Act."; this may mean that they sleep during some kind
of inter-act music, as well as into the next scene, but it need be nothing
more than an inexact reference to the fact that they sleep during the
first 138 lines of the next scene.)
2. amiable: lovely.   **coy:** caress.
16. overflowen with: submerged by.   **19. neaf:** fist.
20. leave your curtsy: i.e. put on your hat.
23. Cavalery: cavalier (form of address for a fashionable gentleman).
Cobweb. Peaseblossom has been asked to do the scratching. This may
be Shakespeare's slip or Bottom's.
29. tongs, bones: rustic musical instruments; the tongs were struck
with a key (as a triangle), and the bones were rattled between the
fingers (as clappers).   **33. bottle:** bundle.   **34. fellow:** equal.
39. exposition: blunder for *disposition*, i.e. desire, inclination.
41. all ways away: off in all directions.
42. woodbine. Obviously not the honeysuckle here (as at II.i.251).
Various vines were known by this name.

49. favors: i.e. flowers as love gifts.   **51. rounded:** encircled.
53. sometime: formerly.
54. orient pearls: i.e. the most beautiful of pearls.
55. flouriets': flowerets'.   **64. scalp:** skull.
66. other: others.   **68. accidents:** events, incidents.
69. fierce: excessive, wild.
73. Dian's bud: i.e. the herb of II.i.184, III.ii.366, perhaps the flower
of the *agnus castus* or chaste tree, thought to preserve chastity.
82. these five: i.e. the four lovers and Bottom.
83 s.d. Music, still: i.e. soft music.   **88. solemnly:** ceremoniously.
89. triumphantly: festively.

A Midsummer
Night's Dream
IV.i

There shall the pairs of faithful lovers be
Wedded, with Theseus, all in jollity.
  Puck.　Fairy King, attend and mark;
I do hear the morning lark.
  Obe.　Then, my queen, in silence sad,　　　95
Trip we after night's shade.
We the globe can compass soon,
Swifter than the wand'ring moon.
  Tita.　Come, my lord, and in our flight,
Tell me how it came this night　　　100
That I sleeping here was found,
With these mortals on the ground.
　　　　　　　　Exeunt. Wind horn [within].

Enter THESEUS, [HIPPOLYTA, EGEUS,] *and all his* TRAIN.

  The.　Go, one of you, find out the forester,
For now our observation is perform'd,
And since we have the vaward of the day,　　　105
My love shall hear the music of my hounds.
Uncouple in the western valley, let them go.
Dispatch, I say, and find the forester.
　　　　　　　　[*Exit an Attendant.*]
We will, fair queen, up to the mountain's top,
And mark the musical confusion　　　110
Of hounds and echo in conjunction.
  Hip.　I was with Hercules and Cadmus once,
When in a wood of Crete they bay'd the bear
With hounds of Sparta. Never did I hear
Such gallant chiding; for besides the groves,　　　115
The skies, the fountains, every region near
Seem all one mutual cry. I never heard
So musical a discord, such sweet thunder.
  The.　My hounds are bred out of the Spartan kind;
So flew'd, so sanded; and their heads are hung　　　120
With ears that sweep away the morning dew;
Crook-knee'd, and dewlapp'd like Thessalian bulls;
Slow in pursuit; but match'd in mouth like bells,
Each under each. A cry more tuneable
Was never hollow'd to, nor cheer'd with horn,　　　125
In Crete, in Sparta, nor in Thessaly.
Judge when you hear. But soft! What nymphs are
　　　these?
  Ege.　My lord, this' my daughter here asleep,
And this Lysander, this Demetrius is,
This Helena, old Nedar's Helena.　　　130
I wonder of their being here together.
  The.　No doubt they rose up early to observe
The rite of May; and hearing our intent,
Came here in grace of our solemnity.
But speak, Egeus, is not this the day　　　135
That Hermia should give answer of her choice?
  Ege.　It is, my lord.

  The.　Go, bid the huntsmen wake them with their
　　　horns.
　　　　[*Exit an Attendant.*] *Shout within. Wind horns.*
　　　　　They all start up.
Good morrow, friends. Saint Valentine is past;
Begin these wood-birds but to couple now?　　　140
  Lys.　Pardon, my lord.　　　　[*They kneel.*]
  The.　　　　　　　　　I pray you all, stand up.
I know you two are rival enemies.
How comes this gentle concord in the world,
That hatred is so far from jealousy
To sleep by hate and fear no enmity?　　　145
  Lys.　My lord, I shall reply amazedly,
Half sleep, half waking; but, as yet, I swear,
I cannot truly say how I came here.
But, as I think—for truly would I speak,
And now I do bethink me, so it is—　　　150
I came with Hermia hither. Our intent
Was to be gone from Athens, where we might,
Without the peril of the Athenian law—
  Ege.　Enough, enough, my lord; you have enough.
I beg the law, the law, upon his head.　　　155
They would have stol'n away, they would, Deme-
　　　trius,
Thereby to have defeated you and me:
You of your wife, and me of my consent,
Of my consent that she should be your wife.
  Dem.　My lord, fair Helen told me of their stealth,
Of this their purpose hither to this wood,　　　161
And I in fury hither followed them,
Fair Helena in fancy following me.
But, my good lord, I wot not by what power
(But by some power it is), my love to Hermia　　　165
(Melted as the snow) seems to me now
As the remembrance of an idle gaud,
Which in my childhood I did dote upon;
And all the faith, the virtue of my heart,
The object and the pleasure of mine eye,　　　170
Is only Helena. To her, my lord,
Was I betrothed ere I [saw] Hermia;
But like a sickness did I loathe this food;
But, as in health, come to my natural taste,
Now I do wish it, love it, long for it,　　　175
And will for evermore be true to it.
  The.　Fair lovers, you are fortunately met;
Of this discourse we more will hear anon.
Egeus, I will overbear your will;
For in the temple, by and by, with us　　　180
These couples shall eternally be knit.
And, for the morning now is something worn,
Our purpos'd hunting shall be set aside.
Away with us to Athens. Three and three,
We'll hold a feast in great solemnity.　　　185
Come, Hippolyta.
　　　　[*Exeunt Theseus, Hippolyta, Egeus, and Train.*]

95. **sad:** sober.　102 s.d. **Wind:** blow.
104. **observation:** observance, May-day rites (cf. I.i.167).
105. **vaward:** early part.　107. **Uncouple:** unleash them.
108. **Dispatch:** make haste.　113. **bay'd:** brought to bay.
114. **hounds of Sparta.** Famous for hunting ability.
115. **chiding:** baying.　117. **Seem.** Usually emended to *Seem'd.*
120. **flew'd:** having large chaps.　**sanded:** of a sandy color.
122. **dewlapp'd:** having a pendulous flap of skin at the throat.
123–24. **match'd . . . each:** with voices of varying but harmonious
pitch, like a peal of bells.
124. **cry:** pack of hounds.　**tuneable:** melodious.
127. **soft:** stop.　128. **this':** this is.
134. **in . . . solemnity:** to honor our observance of the same rites.

139. **Saint Valentine.** It was supposed that birds chose their mates on
St. Valentine's Day.
144. **jealousy:** suspicion, apprehension of evil.
145. **To . . . hate:** as to sleep side by side with a foe.
146. **amazedly:** perplexedly.
152. **where we might:** wherever we could.
153. **Without the peril:** beyond the dangerous reach.
157. **defeated:** defrauded.　163. **fancy:** love.
167. **idle gaud:** worthless trinket.　182. **for:** since.

Dem. These things seem small and undistinguish-
    able,
Like far-off mountains turned into clouds.
  Her. Methinks I see these things with parted eye,
When every thing seems double.
  Hel.   So methinks;   190
And I have found Demetrius like a jewel,
Mine own, and not mine own.
  Dem.   Are you sure
That we are awake? It seems to me
That yet we sleep, we dream. Do not you think
The Duke was here, and bid us follow him?   195
  Her. Yea, and my father.
  Hel.   And Hippolyta.
  Lys. And he did bid us follow to the temple.
  Dem. Why then, we are awake. Let's follow him,
And by the way let's recount our dreams.
                                  [*Exeunt Lovers.*]
  Bot. [*Awaking.*] When my cue comes, call   200
me, and I will answer. My next is, "Most fair Pyramus." Heigh-ho! Peter Quince! Flute the bellows-
mender! Snout the tinker! Starveling! God's my life,
stol'n hence, and left me asleep! I have had a most
rare vision. I have had a dream, past the wit of   205
man to say what dream it was. Man is but an ass,
if he go about [t'] expound this dream. Methought
I was—there is no man can tell what. Methought I
was, and methought I had—but man is but [a patch'd]
fool, if he will offer to say what methought I   210
had. The eye of man hath not heard, the ear of man
hath not seen, man's hand is not able to taste, his
tongue to conceive, nor his heart to report, what
my dream was. I will get Peter Quince to write a
ballet of this dream. It shall be call'd "Bot-   215
tom's Dream," because it hath no bottom; and I will
sing it in the latter end of a play, before the Duke.
Peradventure, to make it the more gracious, I shall
sing it at her death.   [*Exit.*]

[Scene II]

Enter Quince, *Thisby* [Flute], *and the rabble* [Snout,
Starveling].

  Quin. Have you sent to Bottom's house? Is he
come home yet?
  [*Star.*] He cannot be heard of. Out of doubt he is
transported.
  Flu. If he come not, then the play is marr'd. It
goes not forward, doth it?   6

Quin. It is not possible. You have not a man in
all Athens able to discharge Pyramus but he.
  Flu. No, he hath simply the best wit of any
handicraft man in Athens.   10
  Quin. Yea, and the best person too; and he is a
very paramour for a sweet voice.
  Flu. You must say "paragon." A paramour is
(God bless us!) a thing of naught.   14

Enter Snug *the joiner.*

  Snug. Masters, the Duke is coming from the temple,
and there is two or three lords and ladies more married. If our sport had gone forward, we had all been
made men.
  Flu. O sweet bully Bottom! Thus hath he lost
sixpence a day during his life; he could not   20
have scap'd sixpence a day. And the Duke had not
given him sixpence a day for playing Pyramus, I'll be
hang'd. He would have deserv'd it. Sixpence a day in
Pyramus, or nothing.   24

Enter Bottom.

  Bot. Where are these lads? Where are these
hearts?
  Quin. Bottom! O most courageous day! O most
happy hour!
  Bot. Masters, I am to discourse wonders; but
ask me not what; for if I tell you, I am [no] true   30
Athenian. I will tell you every thing, right as it
fell out.
  Quin. Let us hear, sweet Bottom.
  Bot. Not a word of me. All that I will tell you
is, that the Duke hath din'd. Get your apparel   35
together, good strings to your beards, new ribands
to your pumps; meet presently at the palace; every
man look o'er his part; for the short and the long
is, our play is preferr'd. In any case, let Thisby
have clean linen; and let not him that plays the   40
lion pare his nails, for they shall hang out for the
lion's claws. And, most dear actors, eat no onions
nor garlic, for we are to utter sweet breath; and I do
not doubt but to hear them say, it is a sweet comedy.
No more words. Away, go, away! [*Exeunt.*]   45

[ACT V, Scene I]

Enter Theseus, Hippolyta, *and* Philostrate, [Lords,
and Attendants].

  Hip. 'Tis strange, my Theseus, that these lovers
    speak of.
  The. More strange than true. I never may believe

---

189. parted: out of focus.
191–92. like . . . mine own: like some precious thing found by
accident, and hence not certainly belonging to me, though in my
possession. 202. Heigh-ho: A yawn. 203. God's: God save.
207. go about: attempt. 209. patch'd: wearing motley.
210. offer: venture.
211–14. The eye . . . was. A parody of 1 Corinthians 2:9: "The eye
hath not seen, and the ear hath not heard, neither have entered into
the heart of man . . ." (Bishops'). 215. ballet: ballad.
216. hath no bottom: i.e. is all tangled up because it lacks a core
(*bottom*). 218. gracious: attractive, elegant.
219. her: i.e. Thisbe's.

IV.ii. Location: Athens. Quince's house.
4. transported: carried away by the fairies.

---

8. discharge: successfully perform the role of.
14. a thing of naught: something wicked.
20. sixpence a day: i.e. as a royal pension.
20–21. he . . . scap'd: his reward would certainly not have been less
than. 21. And: if. 26. hearts: good fellows.
29. am . . . wonders: have wonders to recount.
31. right: exactly, just. 34. of: from.
36. strings: To attach their false beards (?). ribands: ribbons.
37. presently: immediately.
39. preferr'd: recommended, put forward.

V.i. Location: Athens. The palace of Theseus.
1. that: what. 2. may: can.

*A Midsummer
Night's Dream
V.i*

These antic fables, nor these fairy toys.
Lovers and madmen have such seething brains,
Such shaping fantasies, that apprehend   5
More than cool reason ever comprehends.
The lunatic, the lover, and the poet
Are of imagination all compact.
One sees more devils than vast hell can hold;
That is the madman. The lover, all as frantic,   10
Sees Helen's beauty in a brow of Egypt.
The poet's eye, in a fine frenzy rolling,
Doth glance from heaven to earth, from earth to
    heaven;
And as imagination bodies forth
The forms of things unknown, the poet's pen   15
Turns them to shapes, and gives to aery nothing
A local habitation and a name.
Such tricks hath strong imagination,
That if it would but apprehend some joy,
It comprehends some bringer of that joy;   20
Or in the night, imagining some fear,
How easy is a bush suppos'd a bear!
    Hip. But all the story of the night told over,
And all their minds transfigur'd so together,
More witnesseth than fancy's images,   25
And grows to something of great constancy;
But howsoever, strange and admirable.

Enter lovers, LYSANDER, DEMETRIUS, HERMIA, *and*
    HELENA.

    The. Here come the lovers, full of joy and mirth.
Joy, gentle friends, joy and fresh days of love
Accompany your hearts!
    Lys.   More than to us   30
Wait in your royal walks, your board, your bed!
    The. Come now; what masques, what dances
        shall we have,
To wear away this long age of three hours
Between [our] after-supper and bed-time?
Where is our usual manager of mirth?   35
What revels are in hand? Is there no play
To ease the anguish of a torturing hour?
Call Philostrate.
    Phil.   Here, mighty Theseus.
    The. Say, what abridgment have you for this
        evening?
What masque? what music? How shall we be-
        guile   40
The lazy time, if not with some delight?
    Phil. There is a brief how many sports are ripe.

Make choice of which your Highness will see first.
                                    [*Giving a paper.*]
    The. [*Reads.*] "The battle with the Centaurs, to
        be sung
By an Athenian eunuch to the harp."   45
We'll none of that: that have I told my love,
In glory of my kinsman Hercules.
"The riot of the tipsy Bacchanals,
Tearing the Thracian singer in their rage."
That is an old device; and it was play'd   50
When I from Thebes came last a conqueror.
"The thrice three Muses mourning for the death
Of Learning, late deceas'd in beggary."
That is some satire, keen and critical,
Not sorting with a nuptial ceremony.   55
"A tedious brief scene of young Pyramus
And his love Thisby; very tragical mirth."
Merry and tragical? Tedious and brief?
That is hot ice and wondrous strange snow.
How shall we find the concord of this discord?   60
    Phil. A play there is, my lord, some ten words
        long,
Which is as brief as I have known a play;
But by ten words, my lord, it is too long,
Which makes it tedious; for in all the play
There is not one word apt, one player fitted.   65
And tragical, my noble lord, it is;
For Pyramus therein doth kill himself;
Which when I saw rehears'd, I must confess,
Made mine eyes water; but more merry tears
The passion of loud laughter never shed.   70
    The. What are they that do play it?
    Phil. Hard-handed men that work in Athens here,
Which never labor'd in their minds till now;
And now have toiled their unbreathed memories
With this same play, against your nuptial.   75
    The. And we will hear it.
    Phil.   No, my noble lord,
It is not for you. I have heard it over,
And it is nothing, nothing in the world;
Unless you can find sport in their intents,
Extremely stretch'd, and conn'd with cruel pain,   80
To do you service.
    The.   I will hear that play;
For never any thing can be amiss,
When simpleness and duty tender it.
Go bring them in; and take your places, ladies.
                                    [*Exit Philostrate.*]

---

3. **antic:** grotesque. **fairy toys:** trifling tales about fairy doings.
5. **shaping fantasies:** fertile imaginations. **apprehend:** perceive, imagine. 6. **comprehends:** takes in, includes.
8. **compact:** formed, composed.
11. **Helen:** Helen of Troy, a paragon of beauty. **brow of Egypt:** gipsy's face. 19. **would but:** merely wishes to.
20. **comprehends . . . joy:** has no trouble including or creating in his fantasy some source of the joy.
21. **some fear:** something to be feared.
25. **More witnesseth:** gives evidence of more. **fancy's images:** ideas created by imagination.
26. **grows to:** arrives at. **constancy:** consistency, hence certainty.
27. **howsoever:** in any event. **admirable:** to be wondered at.
34. **after-supper:** light repast following supper (?).
39. **abridgment:** pastime (to abridge or shorten the time).
42. **brief:** list, abstract. **ripe:** ready for presentation.

44. **battle . . . Centaurs:** battle between the Centaurs and the Lapithae at the wedding feast of Theseus' friend Pirithous, when the Centaurs attempted to carry off the bride, Hippodamia.
47. **glory . . . kinsman.** One version of the tradition placed Hercules at the battle against the Centaurs. He and Theseus, according to Plutarch's life of the latter, were kinsmen.
48–49. **The riot . . . rage.** Orpheus, the Thracian musician, was torn to pieces by Bacchantes at the height of their orgiastic frenzy.
50. **device:** i.e. something devised for dramatic representation.
52–53. **The thrice . . . beggary.** Perhaps a topical allusion, though laments on the low estate of learning were commonplace.
54. **critical:** censorious.   55. **sorting with:** befitting.
59. **strange.** Perhaps an error, replacing some word which with *snow* would produce a "discord" similar to *hot ice.*
65. **fitted:** well cast.   74. **toiled:** taxed.   **unbreathed:** unexercised.
75. **against:** in preparation for.
80. **Extremely stretch'd:** strained to the uttermost.   **conn'd:** learned by heart.   83. **simpleness:** sincerity.

Hip. I love not to see wretchedness o'ercharged,
And duty in his service perishing.   86
The. Why, gentle sweet, you shall see no such
thing.
Hip. He says they can do nothing in this kind.
The. The kinder we, to give them thanks for
nothing.
Our sport shall be to take what they mistake;   90
And what poor duty cannot do, noble respect
Takes it in might, not merit.
Where I have come, great clerks have purposed
To greet me with premeditated welcomes;
Where I have seen them shiver and look pale,   95
Make periods in the midst of sentences,
Throttle their practic'd accent in their fears,
And in conclusion dumbly have broke off,
Not paying me a welcome. Trust me, sweet,
Out of this silence yet I pick'd a welcome;   100
And in the modesty of fearful duty
I read as much as from the rattling tongue
Of saucy and audacious eloquence.
Love, therefore, and tongue-tied simplicity
In least speak most, to my capacity.   105

[*Enter* PHILOSTRATE.]

Phil. So please your Grace, the Prologue is address'd.
The. Let him approach.   [*Flourish trumpet.*]

Enter [QUINCE *for*] *the Prologue.*

Pro. If we offend, it is with our good will.
That you should think, we come not to offend,
But with good will. To show our simple skill,   110
That is the true beginning of our end.
Consider then, we come but in despite.
We do not come, as minding to content you,
Our true intent is. All for your delight
We are not here. That you should here repent you,
The actors are at hand; and, by their show,   116
You shall know all, that you are like to know.
The. This fellow doth not stand upon points.
Lys. He hath rid his prologue like a rough colt;
he knows not the stop. A good moral, my lord: it is
not enough to speak, but to speak true.   121
Hip. Indeed he hath play'd on this prologue like

a child on a recorder—a sound, but not in government.
The. His speech was like a tangled chain;   125
nothing impair'd, but all disorder'd. Who is next?

Enter [*with a Trumpet before them*] PYRAMUS *and*
THISBY *and* WALL *and* MOONSHINE *and* LION.

Pro. Gentles, perchance you wonder at this show;
But wonder on till truth make all things plain.
This man is Pyramus, if you would know;
This beauteous lady Thisby is certain.   130
This man, with lime and rough-cast, doth present
Wall, that vile Wall, which did these lovers sunder;
And through Wall's chink, poor souls, they are con-
tent
To whisper. At the which let no man wonder.
This man, with lantern, dog, and bush of thorn,   135
Presenteth Moonshine; for if you will know,
By moonshine did these lovers think no scorn
To meet at Ninus' tomb, there, there to woo.
This grisly beast, which Lion hight by name,
The trusty Thisby, coming first by night,   140
Did scare away, or rather did affright;
And as she fled, her mantle she did fall,
Which Lion vile with bloody mouth did stain.
Anon comes Pyramus, sweet youth and tall,
And finds his trusty Thisby's mantle slain;   145
Whereat, with blade, with bloody blameful blade,
He bravely broach'd his boiling bloody breast;
And Thisby, tarrying in mulberry shade,
His dagger drew, and died. For all the rest,
Let Lion, Moonshine, Wall, and lovers twain   150
At large discourse, while here they do remain.
                Exit [*with Pyramus,*] *Thisby, Lion,*
                        and Moonshine.
The. I wonder if the lion be to speak.
Dem. No wonder, my lord; one lion may, when
many asses do.
Wall. In this same enterlude it doth befall   155
That I, one [Snout] by name, present a wall;
And such a wall, as I would have you think,
That had in it a crannied hole or chink,
Through which the lovers, Pyramus and Thisby,
Did whisper often, very secretly.   160
This loam, this rough-cast, and this stone doth show
That I am that same wall; the truth is so;
And this the cranny is, right and sinister,
Through which the fearful lovers are to whisper.   164
The. Would you desire lime and hair to speak
better?
Dem. It is the wittiest partition that ever I heard
discourse, my lord.

85. **wretchedness o'ercharged:** feebleness overburdened.
86. **his service:** its attempt to perform due service.
88. **in this kind:** of this sort.
91. **noble respect:** generous consideration.
92. **Takes . . . merit:** judges it in relation to the abilities of the performers, not the merit of the performance.   93. **clerks:** scholars.
101. **fearful:** timorous, frightened.
105. **least:** i.e. saying least.   **to my capacity:** in my opinion. In
the kindly speech of Theseus, a tribute was very likely intended to the
graciousness of Queen Elizabeth. Attempts have been made to
identify the passage with some particular occasion.
106. **Prologue:** speaker of the prologue.   **address'd:** ready.
107 s.d. **Flourish:** sound a fanfare.
108–17. **If . . . know.** The humor of the passage is in the blunders of
its punctuation.   112. **despite:** ill will, defiance of your wishes.
113. **minding:** intending.
118. **stand upon points:** (1) bother about trifles; (2) heed his punctuation.   119. **rough:** unbroken.
120. **stop:** (1) reining in a horse to a quick halt; (2) period.
121. **true:** (1) the truth; (2) correctly.

123. **recorder:** wind instrument resembling a flute or flageolet.
123–24. **government:** control, management.
126. **nothing impair'd:** i.e. still unbroken (*nothing* is here, as often,
adverbial, meaning "in no respect, not at all").
137. **think no scorn:** regard it as no disgrace.   139. **hight:** is called.
142. **fall:** let fall.   144. **tall:** brave.   147. **broach'd:** stabbed.
151. **At large:** at length.
154. **No wonder:** it will be no wonder if he does.
163. **right and sinister:** running right and left, i.e. horizontal.
167. **wittiest:** cleverest.

[Enter PYRAMUS.]

The. Pyramus draws near the wall. Silence!

Pyr. O grim-look'd night! O night with hue so
    black!   170
O night, which ever art when day is not!
O night, O night! alack, alack, alack,
I fear my Thisby's promise is forgot!
And thou, O wall, O sweet, O lovely wall,   174
That stand'st between her father's ground and mine!
Thou wall, O wall, O sweet and lovely wall,
Show me thy chink, to blink through with mine eyne!
    [Wall holds up his fingers.]
Thanks, courteous wall; Jove shield thee well for this!
But what see I? No Thisby do I see.
O wicked wall, through whom I see no bliss!   180
Curs'd be thy stones for thus deceiving me!

The. The wall methinks, being sensible, should
curse again.

Pyr. No, in truth, sir, he should not. "Deceiving
me" is Thisby's cue. She is to enter now, and   185
I am to spy her through the wall. You shall see it
will fall pat as I told you. Yonder she comes.

Enter THISBY.

This. O wall, full often hast thou heard my moans,
For parting my fair Pyramus and me!
My cherry lips have often kiss'd thy stones,   190
Thy stones with lime and hair knit [up in thee].

Pyr. I see a voice! Now will I to the chink,
To spy and I can hear my Thisby's face.
Thisby!

This.   My love thou art, my love I think.   194

Pyr. Think what thou wilt, I am thy lover's grace;
And, like Limander, am I trusty still.

This. And I, like Helen, till the Fates me kill.

Pyr. Not Shafalus to Procrus was so true.

This. As Shafalus to Procrus, I to you.   199

Pyr. O, kiss me through the hole of this vild wall!

This. I kiss the wall's hole, not your lips at all.

Pyr. Wilt thou at Ninny's tomb meet me straight-
    way?

This. 'Tide life, 'tide death, I come without delay.
    [Exeunt Pyramus and Thisby.]

Wall. Thus have I, Wall, my part discharged so;
And being done, thus Wall away doth go. *[Exit.]* 205

The. Now is the moon used between the two
neighbors.

Dem. No remedy, my lord, when walls are so
willful to hear without warning.

Hip. This is the silliest stuff that ever I heard.   210

The. The best in this kind are but shadows; and
the worst are no worse, if imagination amend them.

Hip. It must be your imagination then, and not
theirs.   214

The. If we imagine no worse of them than they
of themselves, they may pass for excellent men.
Here come two noble beasts in, a man and a
lion.   218

Enter LION *and* MOONSHINE.

Lion. You, ladies, you, whose gentle hearts do fear
The smallest monstrous mouse that creeps on floor,
May now, perchance, both quake and tremble here,
When lion rough in wildest rage doth roar.   222
Then know that I as Snug the joiner am
A lion fell, nor else no lion's dam,
For, if I should, as lion, come in strife   225
Into this place, 'twere pity on my life.

The. A very gentle beast, and of a good conscience.

Dem. The very best at a beast, my lord, that e'er
I saw.   230

Lys. This lion is a very fox for his valor.

The. True; and a goose for his discretion.

Dem. Not so, my lord; for his valor cannot carry
his discretion, and the fox carries the goose.   234

The. His discretion, I am sure, cannot carry his
valor; for the goose carries not the fox. It is well;
leave it to his discretion, and let us listen to the
Moon.

Moon. This lanthorn doth the horned moon
    present—

Dem. He should have worn the horns on his
head.   241

The. He is no crescent, and his horns are invisible
within the circumference.

Moon. This lanthorn doth the horned moon
    present;
Myself the man i' th' moon do seem to be.   245

The. This is the greatest error of all the rest.
The man should be put into the lanthorn. How is
it else the man i' th' moon?

Dem. He dares not come there for the candle; for,
you see, it is already in snuff.   250

Hip. I am a-weary of this moon. Would he would
change!

The. It appears, by his small light of discretion,
that he is in the wane; but yet in courtesy, in all
reason, we must stay the time.   255

---

170. **grim-look'd:** grim-looking.   182. **sensible:** capable of feeling.
183. **again:** in return.   187. **fall pat:** happen exactly.
193. **and:** if.
194. **My...think.** The Q1 punctuation is here retained, although it
"doth not stand upon points."   195. **lover's grace:** i.e. lover.
196, 197. **Limander, Helen:** blunders for *Leander* and *Hero.*
198. **Shafalus, Procrus:** blunders for *Cephalus* and *Procris.*
200. **vild:** vile.   203. **'Tide:** betide, come.
206. **Now...used:** i.e. Moonshine, Wall being down, will now come
into play. Most editors follow Pope in emending *moon used* to *mural*
[i.e. wall] *down* (which is close to the F1 reading, *morall downe*).
208–9. **so...hear:** so willing to hear (?) or so perverse as to hear
(?)—in either case, with humorous allusion to the proverb "Walls
have ears" (certainly true of Snout!).   209. **without warning:** surrep-
titiously (?) or without warning the parents (?).

211. **in this kind:** of this profession, i.e. actors.   **shadows:** likenesses,
representations.
223–24. **I...dam:** i.e. only as Snug the joiner am I a lion, or even a
lioness.
224. **lion fell:** cruel lion (but with additional sense "lionskin"—an
unintentionally humorous reference to Snug's costume).
227. **gentle:** polite.
231. **very...valor:** i.e. more crafty (diplomatic) than courageous.
232. **goose...discretion:** i.e. more foolish than crafty.
239. **lanthorn:** a variant of *lantern,* influenced by the fact that lanterns usually had sides of transparent horn rather than glass; hence
there is wordplay in the reference to the "horned" (i.e. crescent) moon,
as well as in the jest about the cuckold's horns in the next speech.
249. **for the candle:** on account of the candle.
250. **in snuff:** (1) offended; (2) in need of snuffing.
255. **stay:** wait for.

Lys.　Proceed, Moon.

Moon.　All that I have to say is to tell you that the lanthorn is the moon, I the man i' th' moon, this thorn-bush my thorn-bush, and this dog my dog.　259

Dem.　Why, all these should be in the lanthorn; for all these are in the moon. But silence! here comes Thisby.

Enter THISBY.

This.　This is old Ninny's tomb. Where is my love?

Lion.　O!　　　　[*The Lion roars. Thisby runs off.*]

Dem.　Well roar'd, Lion.　265

The.　Well run, Thisby.

Hip.　Well shone, Moon. Truly, the moon shines with a good grace. [*The Lion shakes Thisby's mantle.*]

The.　Well mous'd, Lion.

Enter PYRAMUS.

Dem.　And then came Pyramus. [*Exit Lion.*]　270

Lys.　And so the lion vanish'd.

Pyr.　Sweet Moon, I thank thee for thy sunny beams;

I thank thee, Moon, for shining now so bright;

For by thy gracious, golden, glittering [gleams],

I trust to take of truest Thisby sight.　275

But stay! O spite!

But mark, poor knight,

What dreadful dole is here!

Eyes, do you see?

How can it be?　280

O dainty duck! O dear!

Thy mantle good,

What, stain'd with blood?

Approach, ye Furies fell!

O Fates, come, come,　285

Cut thread and thrum,

Quail, crush, conclude, and quell!

The.　This passion, and the death of a dear friend, would go near to make a man look sad.

Hip.　Beshrew my heart, but I pity the man.　290

Pyr.　O, wherefore, Nature, didst thou lions frame?

Since lion vild hath here deflow'r'd my dear;

Which is—no, no—which was the fairest dame

That liv'd, that lov'd, that lik'd, that look'd with cheer.

Come, tears, confound,　295

Out, sword, and wound

The pap of Pyramus;

Ay, that left pap,

Where heart doth hop.　[*Stabs himself.*]

Thus die I, thus, thus, thus.　300

Now am I dead,

Now am I fled;

My soul is in the sky.

Tongue, lose thy light,　304

Moon, take thy flight, [*Exit Moonshine.*]

Now die, die, die, die, die.　[*Dies.*]

Dem.　No die, but an ace, for him; for he is but one.

Lys.　Less than an ace, man; for he is dead, he is nothing.

The.　With the help of a surgeon he might yet recover, and yet prove an ass.　311

Hip.　How chance Moonshine is gone before Thisby comes back and finds her lover?

[*Enter* THISBY.]

The.　She will find him by starlight. Here she comes, and her passion ends the play.　315

Hip.　Methinks she should not use a long one for such a Pyramus. I hope she will be brief.

Dem.　A mote will turn the balance, which Pyramus, which Thisby, is the better: he for a man, God warr'nt us; she for a woman, God bless us.　320

Lys.　She hath spied him already with those sweet eyes.

Dem.　And thus she means, *videlicet*—

This.　Asleep, my love?

What, dead, my dove?　325

O Pyramus, arise!

Speak, speak! Quite dumb?

Dead, dead? A tomb

Must cover thy sweet eyes.

These lily lips,　330

This cherry nose,

These yellow cowslip cheeks,

Are gone, are gone!

Lovers, make moan;

His eyes were green as leeks.　335

O Sisters Three,

Come, come to me,

With hands as pale as milk;

Lay them in gore,

Since you have shore　340

With shears his thread of silk.

Tongue, not a word!

Come, trusty sword,

Come, blade, my breast imbrue!

[*Stabs herself.*]

And farewell, friends;　345

Thus Thisby ends;

Adieu, adieu, adieu.　[*Dies.*]

The.　Moonshine and Lion are left to bury the dead.

Dem.　Ay, and Wall too.　350

[*Bot.*] [*Starting up.*] No, I assure you, the wall is down that parted their fathers. Will it please you to

269. **mous'd:** shaken, torn (like a mouse in the jaws of a cat).
276. **spite:** malicious stroke of fortune.
278. **dole:** grievous sight.
286. **thread and thrum:** warp and the loose ends of the warp; here, the complete thread (of life).
287. **Quail:** overpower. **conclude:** bring to an end. **quell:** kill.
288. **passion:** violent expression of sorrow.
289. **go . . . make:** almost succeed in making.
294. **cheer.** Almost certainly the meaning here is "countenance."
295. **confound:** destroy (me).

304–5. **Tongue . . . flight.** Pyramus reverses the order of *Tongue* and *Moon*, with the result that Moonshine receives his walking orders. "Tongue, take your flight" would mean "be made dumb (by death)."
307. **No . . . ace:** not a whole die but a single face—the one-spot.
one: (1) a single person; (2) in a class by himself.
311. **ass.** With pun on *ace*. 315. **passion:** passionate speech.
318–19. **which . . . which:** whether . . . or.
320. **warr'nt:** defend. "God warrant us" and "God bless us" were both used conventionally to ward off an evil omen, and hence here imply Demetrius' opinion of the performances.
323. **means:** laments. **videlicet:** as follows.
336. **Sisters Three:** the Fates. 340. **shore:** shorn.
344. **imbrue:** stain with blood.

A Midsummer Night's Dream
V.i

see the epilogue, or to hear a Bergomask dance between
two of our company?　　　　　　　　　　　　　　　354

　　The.　No epilogue, I pray you; for your play needs
no excuse. Never excuse; for when the players are
all dead, there need none to be blam'd. Marry, if
he that writ it had play'd Pyramus, and hang'd him-
self in Thisby's garter, it would have been a fine
tragedy; and so it is, truly, and very notably　360
discharg'd. But come, your Bergomask; let your
epilogue alone.　　　　　　　　　　　　　[*A dance.*]
The iron tongue of midnight hath told twelve.
Lovers, to bed, 'tis almost fairy time.
I fear we shall outsleep the coming morn　　　365
As much as we this night have overwatch'd.
This palpable-gross play hath well beguil'd
The heavy gait of night. Sweet friends, to bed.
A fortnight hold we this solemnity,
In nightly revels and new jollity.　　*Exeunt.*　370

Enter PUCK.

　　Puck.　Now the hungry [lion] roars,
　　　　And the wolf [behowls] the moon;
　　　　Whilst the heavy ploughman snores,
　　　　All with weary task foredone.
　　　　Now the wasted brands do glow,　　　375
　　　　Whilst the screech-owl, screeching loud,
　　　　Puts the wretch that lies in woe
　　　　In remembrance of a shroud.
　　　　Now it is the time of night
　　　　That the graves, all gaping wide,　　　380
　　　　Every one lets forth his sprite,
　　　　In the church-way paths to glide.
　　　　And we fairies, that do run
　　　　By the triple Hecat's team
　　　　From the presence of the sun,　　　385
　　　　Following darkness like a dream,
　　　　Now are frolic. Not a mouse
　　　　Shall disturb this hallowed house.
　　　　I am sent with broom before,
　　　　To sweep the dust behind the door.　　390

Enter King and Queen of Fairies [OBERON *and* TITANIA]
with all their TRAIN.

　　Obe.　Through the house give glimmering light
　　　　By the dead and drowsy fire,
　　　　Every elf and fairy sprite
　　　　Hop as light as bird from brier,

And this ditty, after me,　　　　　　　　　　　395
Sing, and dance it trippingly.

　　Tita.　First, rehearse your song by rote,
　　　　To each word a warbling note.
　　　　Hand in hand, with fairy grace,
　　　　Will we sing, and bless this place.　　　400
　　　　　　　　　　　　　[*Song and dance.*]

　　Obe.　Now, until the break of day,
　　　　Through this house each fairy stray.
　　　　To the best bride-bed will we,
　　　　Which by us shall blessed be;
　　　　And the issue, there create,　　　405
　　　　Ever shall be fortunate.
　　　　So shall all the couples three
　　　　Ever true in loving be;
　　　　And the blots of Nature's hand
　　　　Shall not in their issue stand;　　　410
　　　　Never mole, hare-lip, nor scar,
　　　　Nor mark prodigious, such as are
　　　　Despised in nativity,
　　　　Shall upon their children be.
　　　　With this field-dew consecrate,　　　415
　　　　Every fairy take his gait,
　　　　And each several chamber bless,
　　　　Through this palace, with sweet peace,
　　　　And the owner of it blest
　　　　Ever shall in safety rest.　　　420
　　　　Trip away; make no stay;
　　　　Meet me all by break of day.
　　　　　Exeunt [*Oberon, Titania, and Train*].

　　Puck.　If we shadows have offended,
　　　　Think but this, and all is mended,
　　　　That you have but slumb'red here　　　425
　　　　While these visions did appear.
　　　　And this weak and idle theme,
　　　　No more yielding but a dream,
　　　　Gentles, do not reprehend.
　　　　If you pardon, we will mend.　　　430
　　　　And, as I am an honest Puck,
　　　　If we have unearned luck
　　　　Now to scape the serpent's tongue,
　　　　We will make amends ere long;
　　　　Else the Puck a liar call.　　　435
　　　　So, good night unto you all.
　　　　Give me your hands, if we be friends,
　　　　And Robin shall restore amends.　　[*Exit.*]

---

353. **see, hear.** Order reversed by Bottom. **Bergomask dance:** a
rustic dance taking its name from Bergamo in Italy.
356. **no excuse:** no extenuation of faults. 363. **told:** struck.
366. **overwatch'd:** stayed up too late.
367. **palpable-gross:** obviously dull.
368. **heavy:** torpid, dull. 374. **foredone:** exhausted.
375. **wasted . . . glow:** logs have burned down into glowing embers.
381. **his sprite:** its ghost.
384. **triple Hecat's team.** Hecate ruled in three capacities: as Luna
(or Cynthia) in heaven, as Diana on earth, and as Proserpina in hell.
Here she is the queen of night, drawn by her team of dragons (cf.
III.ii.379). 387. **frolic:** merry.
390. **behind:** i.e. from behind. Robin Goodfellow was a household
spirit, and was thus sent to clean the house in preparation for the
coming of his king and queen.

405. **create:** created. 412. **prodigious:** abnormal.
416. **take his gait:** go his way. 417. **several:** separate.
425. **That . . . here:** i.e. that it is but a "midsummer night's dream."
428. **No . . . but:** yielding nothing more than.
430. **mend:** do better the next time.
433. **serpent's tongue:** hissing. 437. **Give . . . hands:** applaud.
438. **restore amends:** make amends in the future.

A Midsummer Night's Dream was first published in quarto (Q1) in 1600 by Thomas Fisher; this edition is here used as copy-text. A second quarto (Q2), set from a copy of Q1, was printed by James Roberts in 1619 with the fraudulent date 1600; it is essentially a reprint of Q1, with a few added stage directions and an occasional correction of obvious errors. The text of the First Folio (1623) was based on a copy of Q2 which had either itself served as a prompt-book or, more probably, been corrected against an official prompt-book.

Q1 displays the kinds of stage directions and inconsistencies in speech-prefixes and character names which are generally associated with Shakespeare's "foul papers," though the text is unusually clean and may have been printed from some sort of "fair copy" of the "foul papers." It has been suggested that Q1 also shows evidence of a book-keeper's hand in a few stage directions, but nothing in these directions makes it impossible to accept them as authorial notations.

The theatrical provenience of certain aspects of the copy-text for F1 is unquestionable (see, for example, the Textual Notes, III.ii.416, 463, IV.i.101, IV.ii o.s.d., V.i.126, 264; the omission of the double reference to God in V.i.319–20 probably points in the same direction). The two most substantial changes are both found in V.i: the substitution of Egeus for Philostrate, except in 76–81, throughout the scene, and the alternating distribution of Theseus' speech at ll. 44–60 between Lysander and Theseus. The more significant F1 variants are recorded in the Textual Notes. In the present text the excessively heavy use of phrasal commas in the Q1 copy-text has been considerably lightened.

For further information, see: J. D. Wilson, ed., New Cambridge, *A Midsummer Night's Dream* (Cambridge, 1924); W. W. Greg, *The Shakespeare First Folio* (Oxford, 1955); R. K. Turner, "Printing Methods and Textual Problems in *A Midsummer Night's Dream* Q1," *SB*, XV (1962), 34–8.

TEXTUAL NOTES

Title: A . . . Dream] *F1*; A Midsommer nights dreame. As it hath been sundry times publickely acted, by the Right honourable, the Lord Chamberlaine his seruants. Written by William Shakespeare. *Q1 (title-page)*
Dramatis personae: *subs. as first given by Rowe*
Act-scene division: *none in Q1–2; F1 marks acts only; scene divisions from Rowe and later editors (see first note to each scene); present act-scene arrangement as a whole first established by Capell*

I.i

I.i] *Rowe;* Actus primus. *F1*
Location: *Theobald*
o.s.d. Philostrate] *Theobald*
4 wanes] *Q2, F1;* waues *Q1*
10 New] *Rowe;* Now *Q1–2, F1*
15 s.d. Exit Philostrate.] *Theobald*
19 s.d. Lysander and Demetrius] *F1;* Lysander and Helena, and Demetrius *Q1–2 (Helena does not enter until l. 179)*
24 Stand forth, Demetrius.] *Rowe; in italics as s.d., Q1–2, F1*
26 Stand forth, Lysander.] *Rowe; in italics as s.d., Q1–2, F1*
29 love-tokens] *hyphen, F1*
84 sealing-day] *hyphen, Capell*
113 over-full] *hyphen, F1*
113 self-affairs] *hyphen, Q2, F1*
127 s.d. Manent . . . Hermia.] *F1 (Manet)*
132 Ay me!] *Dyce;* Eigh me: *Q1;* Eigh me: *Q2; om. F1;* Hermia *F2*
136 low] *Theobald;* loue *Q1–2, F1*
139 friends] merit *F1*
143 momentany] momentarie *F1*
159 remote] remou'd *F1*
187 Yours would] *Hanmer;* Your words *Q1–2, F1*
200 no fault] none *Q2, F1*
216 sweet] *Theobald;* sweld *Q1–2, F1 (a barely possible reading)*
219 stranger companies] *Theobald;* strange companions *Q1–2, F1*
224 s.d. Exit Hermia.] *placed as in Dyce; after l. 223, Q1–2, F1*
226 other some] *Hanmer;* othersome *Q1–2, F1*
237 figure] *Rowe;* figure, *Q1–2, F1*
247 wood] *Q2, F1;* wodde *Q1*

I.ii

I.ii] *Capell*
Location: *Capell*

10 grow] grow on *F1*
11 Marry] *Q2, F1;* Mary *Q1*
11–2 The . . . Thisby.] *distinguished as a title, Capell*
23 gallant] gallantly *F1*
28 rest—yet] *Theobald (subs.);* rest yet, *Q1–2, F1*
30–1 split. "The] *Theobald (subs.);* split the *Q1–2, F1*
31–8 "The . . . Fates."] *as verse, Johnson; as prose, Q1–2, F1*
42 bellows-mender] *hyphen, F1*
86 sweet-fac'd] *hyphen, F1*
92 Why,] *Q2, F1;* Why? *Q1*
93 straw-color] *hyphen, F1*
94 orange-tawny] *hyphen, F4*
94–5 purple-in-grain] *hyphens, Rowe*
95 French-crown-color] *first hyphen, F1; second hyphen, Rowe*
104 devices] *F3;* deuises *Q1–2, F1*

II.i

II.i] *Rowe;* Actus Secundus. *F1*
Location: *Theobald*
o.s.d. Puck] *Rowe*
1 s.p. Puck.] *Rowe;* Robin. *Q1–2, F1 (until l. 154)*
2–9 Over . . . green.] *arranged as in Pope; as four verse lines, Q1–2, F1*
22 stolen] *Q2;* stollen, *Q1;* stolne *F1*
52 three-foot] *hyphen, F1*
61 s.p. Tita.] *Capell;* Qu. *Q1–2, F1 (through-out scene)*
61 Fairies] *Theobald;* Fairy *Q1–2, F1*
69 steep] *Q2, F1;* steppe *Q1*
79 Aegles] *Chambers (after North's Plutarch);* Eagles *Q1–2, F1*
91 pelting] petty *F1*
107 hoary-headed] *hyphen, Rowe;* hoared headed *Q2, F1*
109 thin] *Tyrwhitt conj.;* chinne *Q1–2, F1*
115 evils comes] *F2;* euils, / Comes *Q1–2, F1*
145 s.d. Titania . . . Train] *Theobald*
158 the] *F1*
164 fancy-free] *hyphen, F2*
168 love-in-idleness] *hyphens, Capell*
176 s.d. Exit.] *F2*
183 from off] off from *Q2, F1*
183 off] *Q2, F1 (see preceding note);* of *Q1*
190 slay . . . slayeth] *Thirlby conj.;* stay . . . stayeth *Q1–2, F1 (cf. Romeo and Juliet, IV.i.72)*
194 thee] *Q2, F1;* the *Q1*
201 nor] *F1;* not *Q1–2*
210 use] doe *F1*
242 s.d. Exit Demetrius.] *Capell*
244 s.d. Exit.] *Q2, F1*

246 s.d. Enter Puck.] *placed as in Capell; after l. 247, Q1–2, F1*

II.ii

II.ii] *Capell*
Location: *Pelican (after Capell)*
1 s.p. Tita.] *Capell;* Quee. *Q1–2, F1*
4 leathren] *Wilson;* lethten *Q1;* leathern *Q2, F1*
9 s.p. 1. Fairy.] *Capell*
13, 24 s.pp. Cho.] *Capell*
14 our] your *F1*
20 s.p. 1. Fairy.] 2. Fairy. *F1*
25 s.p. 2. Fairy.] 1. Fairy. *F1*
26 s.d. Exeunt Fairies.] *Rowe*
26 s.d. Titania sleeps.] *F1 (Shee sleepes.)*
26 s.d. and . . . eyelids] *Capell*
27 dost] *Q2, F1;* doest *Q1*
28 true-love] *hyphen, Harness*
34 s.d. Exit.] *Rowe*
38 comfort] *Q2, F1;* comfor *Q1*
39 Be't] *Pope;* Bet it *Q1;* Be it *Q2, F1*
43 good] *Q2, F1;* god *Q1*
47 is] *Q2, F1;* it *Q1*
48 we can] can you *F1*
49 interchained] interchanged *F1*
65 s.d. They sleep.] *F1*
87 s.d. Exit.] *F1 (Exit Demetrius.)*
103 s.d. Awaking.] *Rowe*
119 human] *F4;* humane *Q1–2, F1*
145 s.d. Starting up.] *Capell*
152 hearing] *Theobald;* hearing, *Q1–2, F1*

III.i

III.i] *Rowe;* Actus Tertius. *F1*
Location: *ed. (after Wilson)*
2 marvail's] *Kittredge;* maruailes *Q1;* maruailous *Q2, F1*
13 By'r lakin] *Pope (subs.);* Berlakin *Q1;* Berlaken *Q2, F1*
16 device] *Q2, F1;* deuise *Q1*
29 yourselves] *F1;* your selfe *Q1–2*
32 wild-fowl] *hyphen, Pope*
51 s.p. Snout.] *Cambridge;* Sn. *Q1–2, F1;* Snug. *F2*
56 s.p. Bot.] *Q2, F1;* Cet. *Q1*
76 s.d. behind] *Theobald; F1 gives an earlier duplicate s.d.* Enter Pucke. *after l. 54*
82, 84, 89, 93, 102, 103 s.pp. Bot., Flu.] *Q1–2, F1 give as s.pp. the character names in the play-within-the-play:* Pyra., This.
83 Odorous, odorous] *Collier conj.;* Odours, odorous *Q1–2;* Odours, odours *F1*
88 s.p. Puck.] *F1;* Quin. *Q1–2*
88 s.d. Exit.] *Capell*
90, 98, 104 s.pp. Quin.] Pet. *Q2, F1*

102 s.d. **Enter . . . head.**] *Capell (after Rowe);* Enter Piramus with the Asse head. *F1 (after l. 111)*

105 s.d. **Exeunt . . . Starveling.**] *Dyce;* The Clownes all Exit. *F1*

117 s.d. **Exit Snout.**] *Dyce*

124, 129 s.dd. **Sings.**] *Pope*

126 **orange-tawny**] *hyphen, F1*

129 s.d. **Awaking.**] *Rowe (subs.)*

139–41] *Ordered as 141, 139, 140, Q2, F1*

162 s.d. **Peaseblossom . . . Mustardseed**] *Dyce; F1 om. l. 162 and has as s.d.:* Enter Pease-blossom, Cobweb, Moth, Mustardseede, and foure Fairies.

163 **Peas. Ready . . . go?**] *Dyce (after Capell); Fairies.* [Fai. *Q2, F1*] Readie: and I, and I, and I. Where shall we goe? *Q1–2, F1*

175 s.p. **Peas.**] *Dyce;* 1. Fai. *Q1–2, F1*

176 s.p. **Cob.**] *Dyce (after Capell 2. Fairy); continued to* 1. Fai., *Q1–2, F1*

177 s.p. **Moth.**] *Dyce;* 2. Fai. *Q1–2, F1*

178 s.p. **Mus.**] *Dyce;* 3. Fai. *Q1–2, F1*

195 **of**] *Collier*

201 s.d. **Exeunt.**] *Rowe;* Exit. *Q1–2, F1*

III.ii

III.ii] *Capell*

Location: *Pelican (after Capell)*

o.s.d. **Enter . . . Oberon.**] Enter King of Fairies, and Robin goodfellow. *Q1–2;* Enter King of Pharies, solus. *F1*

3 s.d. **Enter Puck.**] *F1 (see preceding note)*

6–7 **love. . . . bower,**] *Rowe;* loue, . . . bower. *Q1;* loue, . . . bower, *Q2, F1*

14 **sport**] *Rowe;* sport, *Q1–2, F1*

15–6 **brake; . . . take,**] *Pope;* brake, . . . take: *Q1;* brake, . . . take, *Q2, F1*

19 **mimic**] *F1;* Minnick *Q1;* Minnock *Q2*

37, 89 **love-juice**] *hyphen, Theobald*

38 s.p. **Puck.**] *Rob. Q1–2, F1 (until l. 110)*

52 **From**] *Q1, F1;* Frow *Q2*

80 **so**] *Pope*

84 **grow**] *Pope;* grow. *Q1–2;* grow: *F1*

85 **sleep**] *Rowe;* slippe *Q1;* slip *Q2, F1*

87 s.d. **and sleep**] *ed. (after Collier)*

89 **true-love's**] *hyphen, Capell*

96 **fancy-sick**] *hyphen, F2*

101 s.d. **Exit.**] *Q2, F1*

104 **eye.**] *Rowe (subs.);* eye, *Q1–2, F1*

109 **her**] *Q2, F1;* her, *Q1*

129 **devilish-holy**] *hyphen, Capell*

137 s.d. **Awaking.**] *Rowe;* Awa. *F1 (after l. 136)*

137 **perfect**] *Q2, F1;* perfect *Q1*

159 **derision! None**] *F1 (subs.);* derision None, *Q1;* derision, none *Q2*

164 **here**] *Q2, F1;* heare *Q1*

175 **aby**] abide *F1 (again at l. 335)*

199 **sisters'**] *Steevens;* sisters *Q1–2, F1*

213 **first, like**] *Theobald (Folkes conj.);* first life *Q1–2, F1*

220 **passionate**] *F1*

227 **Precious,**] *Q2, F1;* Pretious *Q1*

237 **Ay, do!**] *Rowe (subs.);* I doe. *Q1;* I, do, *Q2, F1*

252 **thee,**] *Q2, F1;* thee; *Q1*

257 **no; he'll**] no, hee'l *Q2;* no, Sir, *F1*

260 **off**] *Q2, F1;* of *Q1*

279 **Therefore**] *Q2, F1;* Thefore *Q1*

282 **canker-blossom**] *hyphen, F3*

299 **gentlemen**] *Q2, F1;* gentleman *Q1*

338 s.d. **Exeunt . . . Demetrius.**] *F1* (Exit); Exit. *Q2*

343 s.d. **Exit.**] *Capell*

344 **Her. I . . . say.**] *om. F1 (following l. 343 F1 reads:* Enter Oberon and Pucke.)

344 s.d. **Exit.**] *Capell;* Exeunt. *Q1–2*

346 **willfully**] willingly *F1*

364 **death-counterfeiting**] *Q2, F1;* death-counterfaiting. *F1*

383 **all,**] *Q2, F1;* all; *Q1*

385 **lest**] *F4;* least *Q1–2, F1 (a possible reading, meaning* smallest amount of*)*

387 **black-brow'd**] *Q2, F1 (hyphen, F3);* black browed *Q1*

394 **notwithstanding**] *Q2, F1;* notwistanding *Q1*

---

395 s.d. **Exit.**] *Rowe*

402 s.p. **Puck.**] *Rob. Q1–2, F1 (throughout rest of scene)*

404 s.d. **Exit . . . voice.**] *Cambridge (after Capell)*

406 **Speak! . . . bush?**] *Capell;* Speake in some bush. *Q1–2, F1* (bush:)

406 **dost**] *Q2, F1;* doest *Q1*

412 s.d. **Enter Lysander.**] *Theobald (subs.)*

416] *Opposite this line F1 reads:* shifting places. *(presumably a prompter's note)*

418 s.d. **Lie down.**] *F1 (after l. 418); placed as in Capell*

420 s.d. **Sleeps.**] *Capell*

420 s.d. **Enter**] *F1*

426 **shalt**] *Q2, F1;* shat *Q1*

430 s.d. **Lies . . . sleeps.**] *Malone (after Rowe and Capell)*

432 **Shine, comforts,**] *Theobald;* shine comforts, *Q1;* shine comforts *Q2, F1*

438 s.d. **Enter Hermia.**] *Q2, F1 (after l. 440); placed as in Neilson*

447 s.d. **Lies . . . sleeps.**] *Dyce (after Rowe and Capell)*

451 **To**] *Rowe*

452 s.d. **Squeezing . . . eyes.**] *Rowe*

463 s.d. **Exit.**] *Rowe (following l. 463 F1 reads:* They sleepe all the Act.)

IV.i

IV.i] *Rowe;* Actus Quartus. *F1*

Location: *ed.*

o.s.d. **Peaseblossom . . . attending**] *Dyce (after Rowe)*

o.s.d. **unseen**] *Capell*

24 **marvail's**] *Kittredge;* Maruailes *Q1;* maruailous *Q2;* maruellous *F1*

29 s.d. **Music. . . . music.**] *F1 (no period after* Music)

41 **all ways**] *Theobald;* alwaies *Q1–2, F1*

41 s.d. **Exeunt Fairies.**] *Capell*

42 **woodbine . . . honeysuckle**] *Rowe;* woodbine, . . . Honisuckle, *Q1–2, F1*

45 s.d. **They sleep.**] *Capell*

45 s.d. **Enter . . . Puck.**] Enter Robin goodfellow and Oberon. *F1*

46 s.d. **Advancing.**] *Collier*

70 s.d. **Touching her eyes.**] *Capell*

71 **Be**] Be thou *F1*

73 **bud . . . flower**] *Thirlby conj.;* budde, or Cupids flower, *Q1–2, F1*

82 **sleep . . . five**] *Theobald;* sleepe: of all these, fine *Q1,* (sleepe;) *Q2, F1*

83 **ho**] *Q2, F1;* howe *Q1*

83 s.d. **Music, still.**] *F1*

84, 93 s.pp. **Puck.**] *Rowe;* Rob. *Q1–2, F1*

85 s.d. **Louder music.**] *ed. (after Wilson)*

96 **night's**] the nights *Q2, F1*

101] *After this line F1 adds s.d.:* Sleepers Lye still. *(i.e. remain lying down)*

102 s.d. **horn**] hornes *Q1*

102 s.d. **within**] *Capell*

102 s.d. **Hippolyta, Egeus,**] *F1 (in reverse order)*

107 **Uncouple**] *Q2, F1;* Vncouple, *Q1*

108 s.d. **Exit an Attendant.**] *Dyce*

113 **bay'd**] *Rowe;* bayed *Q1–2, F1*

122 **Crook-knee'd**] *hyphen, F2*

128 **this'**] *ed.;* this *Q1;* this is *Q2, F1*

133 **rite**] *Pope;* right *Q1–2, F1*

138 s.d. **Exit an Attendant.**] *Dyce*

138 s.d. **Shout . . . up.**] *arranged as in Kittredge;* Shoute within: they all start vp. Winde hornes. *Q1–2;* Hornes and they wake. Shout within, they all start vp. *F1*

141 s.d. **They kneel.**] *Capell (subs.)*

149–50 **for . . . is—**] *Capell;* (for . . . speake) / And . . . is; *Q1–2, F1*

152 **might,**] *Dyce;* might *Q1;* might be *Q2, F1*

153 **law—**] *Dyce;* lawe, *Q1;* Law. *Q2, F1*

172 **saw**] *Steevens (after Rowe);* see *Q1–2, F1*

186 s.d. **Exeunt . . . Train.**] *Capell;* Exit. *Q2;* Exit Duke and Lords. *F1*

192–3 **Are . . . awake?**] *om. F1*

198–9 **Why . . . dreams.**] *as verse, Rowe; as prose, Q1–2, F1*

199 **let's**] let vs *Q2, F1*

199 s.d. **Exeunt Lovers.**] *F1* (Exit); Exit. *Q2*

---

200 s.p., s.d. **Bot. Awaking.**] *from F1:* Bottome wakes. / *Clo.;* Clo. *Q1–2*

205 **have**] *om. F1*

207 **t' expound**] *ed.;* expound *Q1;* to expound *Q2, F1*

209 **a patch'd**] *F1;* patcht a *Q1–2*

219 s.d. **Exit.**] *Q2, F1*

IV.ii

IV.ii] *Capell*

Location: *Capell*

o.s.d. **and the rabble**] *om. F1*

o.s.d. **Snout, Starveling**] *F1* (Snout and Starueling)

3 s.p. **Star.**] *F1;* Flut. *Q1–2*

5 s.p. **Flu.**] *Rowe;* Thys. *Q1–2, F1 (throughout scene)*

6 **forward,**] *Q2, F1;* forward. *Q1*

14 **naught**] *F2;* nought *Q1–2, F1*

30 **no**] *F1;* not *Q1–2*

45 **go,**] *Theobald;* go *Q1–2, F1*

45 s.d. **Exeunt.**] *F1*

V.i

V.i] *Rowe;* Actus Quintus. *F1*

Location: *Theobald*

o.s.d. **Philostrate**] Egeus *F1 (see l. 38)*

o.s.d. **Lords**] *F1* (and his Lords)

o.s.d. **and Attendants**] *Capell*

3 **antic**] *Q2, F1;* antique *Q1*

4 **madmen**] *Rowe;* mad men *Q1–2, F1*

5–8, 12–7] *As Wilson suggests, the mislining in Q1 (followed in Q2, F1) probably shows that Shakespeare at some stage added these lines on the poet to the original speech; on similar evidence other insertions can also be traced in the first 84 lines of the scene*

10 **madman**] *F3* (mad-man); mad man *Q1–2, F1*

30–1 **More . . . bed!**] *as verse, F2; as prose, Q1–2, F1*

34 **our**] *F1;* Or *Q1;* or *Q2*

34 **after-supper**] *hyphen, F4*

38 **Philostrate**] Egeus *F1 (all Philostrate's lines, except 76–81, are given to Egeus in F1)*

43 s.d. **Giving a paper.**] *Theobald*

44–5, 48–9, 52–3, 56–7] *These lines are assigned to* Lis. *(i.e. Lysander) in F1*

44 s.d. **Reads.**] *Theobald*

50 **device**] *Q2, F1;* deuise *Q1*

58–60 **Merry . . . discord?**] *as regular verse, Pope (om. l. 59); as irregular verse, Q1; as mixed irregular verse and prose, Q2; as prose, F1*

84 s.d. **Exit Philostrate.**] *Pope*

105 s.d. **Enter Philostrate.**] *Capell*

107 s.d. **Flourish trumpet.**] *ed.;* Flor. Trum. *F1*

107 s.d. **Quince for**] *Rowe (F1 places* Quince. *opposite* Enter the Prologue.)

122 **this**] his *F1*

126 s.d. **with . . . them**] *from F1* Tawyer with a Trumpet before them. *(Tawyer was a servant in Shakespeare's company who died in 1625)*

141 **scare**] *F3;* scarre *Q1–2, F1*

145 **trusty**] *om. F1;* gentle *F2*

151 s.d. **with Pyramus**] *Cambridge (subs.); Q1–2 s.d. after l. 154 (here placed as in F1); F1 s.d.:* Exit all but Wall.

156 **Snout**] *Q2, F1;* Flute *Q1*

168 s.d. **Enter Pyramus.**] *F1 (after l. 169); placed as in Neilson*

170 **grim-look'd**] *hyphen, Theobald*

177 s.d. **Wall . . . fingers.**] *Capell*

184–7 **No . . . comes.**] *as prose, Pope; as verse, Q1–2, F1*

187 s.d. **Enter Thisby.**] *after fall l. 187, F1*

191 **hair**] *Q2, F1;* hayire *Q1*

191 **up in thee**] *F1;* now againe *Q1–2*

203 s.d. **Exeunt . . . Thisby.**] *Dyce*

205 s.d. **Exit.**] *Dyce;* Exit Clow. *F1 (i.e. the* Clowns: Pyramus, Thisby, and Wall)

206 s.p. **The.**] *Rowe;* Duk. (or Duke.) *Q1–2, F1 (throughout rest of scene)*

206 **moon used**] morall downe *F1 (both readings are corrupt; some eds. read* mural down [*Pope*]*, others* wall down [*Collier MS*])

210 s.p. **Hip.**] *Rowe;* Dutch. *Q1–2, F1 (throughout rest of scene)*
217 **beasts in,**] *Rowe;* beasts, in *Q1–2, F1*
223 **as**] one *F1*
263, 328 **tomb**] *Q2 (subs.), F1;* tumbe *Q1*
264 s.d. **The . . . off.**] *F1*
268 s.d. **The . . . mantle.**] *Capell*
269 s.d. **Enter Pyramus.**] *placed as in Alexander; after l. 271, Q1–2, F1*
270 s.d. **Exit Lion.**] *ed. (after Wilson)*
274 **gleams**] *Knight conj.;* beames *Q1–2, F1*
275 **take**] taste *F1*
299 s.d. **Stabs himself.**] *Dyce (after Collier MS)*

305 s.d. **Exit Moonshine.**] *Capell*
306 s.d. **Dies.**] *Capell*
311 **yet**] *om. F1*
312–3 **before**] *Rowe;* before? *Q1–2, F1*
313 s.d. **Enter Thisby.**] *F1*
318 **mote**] *Heath conj.;* moth *Q1–2, F1*
319–20 **he . . . us.**] *om. F1*
320 **warr'nt**] *Wilson;* warnd *Q1–2*
335 **leeks.**] *Q2, F1;* leekes, *Q1*
344 s.d. **Stabs herself.**] *Dyce*
347 s.d. **Dies.**] *Warburton*
351 s.p. **Bot.**] *F1;* Lyon. *Q1–2*
351 s.d. **Starting up.**] *Capell*
357 **Marry**] *Q2, F1;* Mary *Q1*

362 s.d. **A dance.**] *Rowe*
367 **palpable-gross**] *hyphen, Capell*
371 **lion**] *Rowe;* Lyons *Q1–2, F1*
372 **behowls**] *Theobald;* beholds *Q1–2, F1*
384 **Hecat's**] *Johnson;* Hecates *Q1–2, F1*
400 s.d. **Song and dance.**] *Capell*
401–22] *Called* The Song. *and not assigned to* Oberon, *F1*
419–20 **And . . . rest.**] *arranged as in Staunton; lines reversed in Q1–2, F1*
422 s.d. **Oberon . . . Train**] *Capell*
423 s.p. **Puck.**] *Rowe;* Robin. *Q1–2, F1*
438 s.d. **Exit.**] *Capell;* FINIS. *Q1–2, F1*

The Merchant of Venice

THE MERCHANT OF VENICE combines two folk-tales of great age. The story of the savage creditor who tries but fails to obtain a pound of human flesh as payment of a debt came originally from the East. It was widespread in Europe by the early Middle Ages. Shakespeare's immediate source for Shylock's bond was probably the first story of the fourth day in Ser Giovanni's prose collection *Il Pecorone*, written at the end of the fourteenth century and printed in Milan in 1558. There is no record of any English translation that Shakespeare could have known. He may have read the story in Italian, or he may have depended upon a lost work in English which derived from *Il Pecorone*. An anonymous play called *The Jew*, now lost, was described by Stephen Gosson in 1579 as exhibiting "the greedinesse of worldly choosers, and bloody minds of usurers." Perhaps Shakespeare knew it. The second folk-tale, that of the lover who gains his lady because he chooses the right casket among three in a riddle game, was also traditional long before it came to be exploited by Boccaccio and Gower in the fourteenth century. Probably Shakespeare drew upon the version available in the medieval *Gesta Romanorum* (translated into English in 1577) when he devised the love trial at Belmont.

Jews had been officially banished from England for three centuries, since the reign of Edward I. In the popular imagination they figured almost as mythical beasts: strange, evil beings who had once crucified Christ and might be expected to persevere in anti-Christian activities. Although a few Jews continued to inhabit Shakespeare's London, they were forced to make a secret of their race and religion. In 1594, two or three years before the probable date of composition of *The Merchant of Venice*, they achieved an unwelcome notoriety when Roderigo Lopez, a Portuguese Jew who had been Queen Elizabeth's physician, was tried and executed for his part in a supposed poisoning plot aimed against her. Marlowe's tragedy *The Jew of Malta*, originally performed about 1589, was revived at this time in an obvious attempt to capitalize on the public interest aroused by the Lopez case. The original stimulus for *The Merchant of Venice* may have come from Shakespeare's memory of the trial. More important, probably, was the influence of Marlowe's play.

Barabas, the hero-villain of *The Jew of Malta*, is a figure of fantastic evil. Half Machiavel, half Vice, a brilliant caricature more than a credible human being, he rockets from one outrage to the next within a society of Christians who are fundamentally as corrupt as he but considerably less clever. Despite their pious professions, "desire of gold" motivates all of them. Even the holy friars squabble among themselves over the possession of Barabas' enormous wealth. This wealth is the product of trade, not usury, and Barabas' attitude towards it is that of an artist and sensualist more than a miser. Although he is directly responsible for seven murders in the course of the action, not to mention poisoning an entire convent of nuns, it is surprisingly difficult for an audience to dissociate itself from this witty and inventive villain, or to feel much sympathy for his victims. Even the death of his daughter Abigail, murdered by Barabas because (like Shakespeare's Jessica) she loves a Christian and has been converted to his faith, is made to seem wryly funny the moment after it occurs. The unquestioned centre of his play, Barabas has no real rivals in Malta either in the form of other characters or of attitudes contrasted to his own. He can be condemned only in the light of values which exist outside the play he dominates.

By contrast with Barabas, Shylock is a closely observed human being, not a bogeyman to frighten children in the nursery. In the theatre, the part has always attracted actors, and it has been played in a variety of ways. Shylock has sometimes been presented as the devil incarnate, sometimes as a comic villain gabbling absurdly about ducats and daughters. He has also been sentimentalized as a wronged and suffering father nobler by far than the people who triumph over him. Roughly the same range of interpretation can be found in criticism on the play. Shakespeare's text suggests a truth more complex than any of these extremes. A sober, cautious man, as sparing of speech as he is of the ducats he has amassed by lending money at interest, Shylock has nursed a not unjustified hatred of the Christians in Venice over long years. Even the magnanimous Antonio freely confesses that he is accustomed to revile Shylock, to spit at him and kick him, when they meet on the Rialto. Treated as something inhuman, a "dog" or "cur," Shylock not unnaturally responds, when the opportunity presents itself, with tooth and claw. Behind the "merry bond" he offers Antonio there lurks an inchoate impulse towards revenge which events, unexpectedly, transform into a real possibility.

The antipathy between Shylock and the citizens of Venice is not simply racial, nor is it a matter only of the conflict between a merchant and a usurer. Shylock is an alien in a society whose religion, pleasures, aims, and attitudes are radically different from his own. Restrained and frugal by nature, he holds the expansive way of life characteristic of the Christians in contempt: their masques and music, the wealth lavished on feasts, the upkeep of great households, jewels and fine attire. Even his economical, unadorned style of speech, a style distrustful of metaphor or figurative language, sets him off from Antonio, Portia, Bassanio and their friends as much as does his plain Jewish gaberdine in a city where the merchants were accustomed to dress like princes. Although he shares their vocabulary, at least up to a point, Shylock tends to narrow its meaning. When he decides that he may accept Antonio's bond because "Antonio is a good man," Bassanio is indignant: "Have you heard any imputation to the contrary?" (I.iii.12–14). The question elicits from Shylock one of his rare laughs. For him, the word *good* has only one meaning: financial sufficiency. The moral implications which for Bassanio are primary do not count in Shylock's estimation of a man's worth. Later on in the play, it will become apparent that the word *mercy* has no meaning for him at all.

By comparison with Shylock, the Christians may at first sight appear wasteful and superficial. Bassanio makes no attempt to conceal the fact that he has squandered all his money on good living and now needs to repair his fortunes by way of a rich marriage. Although it matters that Portia is both beautiful and good, Bassanio takes himself to Belmont primarily because she is enormously wealthy, and he does not scruple to ask for yet another loan from his indulgent friend Antonio in order that he may shine there with rich gifts, liveried servants in attendance, and splendid clothes. Lorenzo loves Shylock's daughter Jessica, but also the jewels and ducats she has promised to steal from her father on the night of their elopement. Gratiano is an unabashedly worldly chatterbox and the conversation of those shadowy figures Salerio and Solanio hovers continually around the subject of wealth. Antonio's existence, apart from his irrational love of Bassanio, seems wholly bounded by his activities as a merchant. When it seems that he has lost both his friend to Portia and all his ships to Fortune he accepts the idea of death with the passivity of a man for whom life holds nothing else of interest.

Yet it would be wrong to see Shylock as the hero of *The Merchant of Venice* even in the special sense in which Barabas, for all his wickedness, is the hero of Marlowe's play. The Christians in Venice are far from perfect, but they are not hypocrites like their coreligionists of Malta and, despite their surface materialism and occasional failure to be kind, they do embody values which make Shylock's outlook seem limited and impoverished. Although usury was a relatively common financial practice in Elizabethan England, the medieval conviction that it was wrong to take interest remained emotionally powerful. For Shakespeare's audience, Antonio's policy of lending large sums of money gratis was something rapidly fading into the past, but they could respond nonetheless to the comedy's celebration of an attitude towards wealth still honored in principle if less and less frequently in practice. Shylock accumulates money for its own sake. In his hands it remains passive, inert and cold. The Christians, by contrast, transform barren metal into other and more interesting things: silks and spices, ships that venture across the world, and, at Belmont, into a way of life that is generous and vital. On each side, the ethic involved affects areas of life other than the financial.

Shylock's relations with other people are negative and suspicious—where they are not positively destructive. Both his servant Launcelot and his daughter Jessica describe his house as hell (II.ii.22–30, II.iii.2) and both flee from it to a more spacious existence. Characteristically, Shylock cannot see the human losses he has sustained apart from their economic consequences. The abrupt departure of Launcelot means, primarily, a welcome diminution in his household expenses and an equally welcome increase in those of the hated Bassanio. Speaking of Jessica's elopement, he constantly confuses the material with the personal loss, ducats with daughters, in a fashion more grotesque than pathetic. The happiest ending he can imagine for her story would be to see her "hears'd at my foot, and the ducats in her coffin" (III.i.89–90).

Among the Christians, ideas of wealth exist in a similarly close association with personal relations, but the effect is very different. Bassanio has been a spendthrift but this fault, Shakespeare suggests, is ultimately less crippling than Shylock's avarice. It is precisely because he does not fear the ominous inscription on the third casket—"Who chooseth me must give and hazard all he hath" (II.vii.16)—that Bassanio is able to win Portia. His original in *Il Pecorone* had won the lady by underhand means: one of her maids revealed to him the secret of the drugged wine which on two earlier attempts had caused him to fail the wooing test. Bassanio, by contrast, faces the riddle-game honestly. His choice of the leaden casket demonstrates that he does in fact love Portia for herself and not simply for her golden exterior. Failure to choose rightly would have condemned him to perpetual celibacy as well as to the loss of Portia and all his hopes. The risk, however, was shared. Behind Bassanio stands Antonio, the merchant who habitually entrusts his wealth to the hazard of sea-storms, rocks, and treacherous sands and who has now literally risked all he has, including his own life, to help his friend.

Most of Shakespeare's comedies involve, at some point, a journey to a place where life is heightened, of an extraordinary quality. Belmont is a locality of this kind. Portia's house lies in an indeterminate place reached across the sea, among trees and lawns and under an open sky. With its music and its riddle-game out of the past, its possession of the kind of limitless, inexplicable wealth proper to fairy-tale, it forms an obvious contrast with the crowded, urban world of Venice where money is a commodity to be counted and painfully earned. There is a sense, however, in which Belmont is really the better self of Venice: a world of clarity, order, and materialism transfigured, presided over by a lady in whom the virtues characteristic of the Christians in the comedy manifest themselves in their most complete and realized form. As generous as Antonio and as reflective, equally capable of self-sacrificing love, she has perceptions and energies, an emotional wholeness and range of response, which he lacks. It is only Portia, in her disguise as the young lawyer, who can rescue Venice from its dilemma. She does so by demonstrating the inadequacy of Shylock's attitudes to protect even the man who believes in them. Shylock will have nothing to do with the essentially Christian quality of generosity, as defined and urged by Portia in her speech on mercy. He insists upon the letter of the law, upon the kind of literal and narrow, essentially impersonal, interpretation of words characteristic of him throughout, and finds that Portia—when forced to do so—can easily turn this game against him. Her claim that Shylock's undeniable legal right to a pound of Antonio's living flesh does not entitle him to spill even a single drop of Antonio's blood, like her warning about the peril involved in the weighing, comes from a folk tradition. In Shakespeare's hands, however, it is no longer a device to be admired in itself. Portia's triumph is really an indication of the insufficiency and mechanical nature of Shylock's own values, of how unworthy they were of the trust he placed in them.

When Shylock stumbles from the court near the end of Act IV, stripped of almost everything, including his religion, it may seem as though *The*

Merchant of Venice had reached its logical, if somewhat disquieting end. In terms of plot, the comedy is over. Of the two folk-tales upon which it was based, one has already come to its conclusion in Act III, with Bassanio's success in the riddle-game. Comedies usually end with marriages, but all three of the unions with which the play is concerned have been accomplished by that point: Portia and Bassanio, Nerissa and Gratiano, Jessica and Lorenzo. Act IV is concerned to conduct the other story, that of the savage creditor and the pound of flesh, to its preordained ending. Shylock himself does not reappear after the court scene, nor does Shakespeare make any attempt to smooth over the raggedness and pain of his final exit, to make it look more like a preliminary to any genuine accommodation of Shylock within the Venetian social order. Like the last act of *A Midsummer Night's Dream*, the fifth act of *The Merchant of Venice* takes place outside the normal limits of a comedy plot. The material for it is not articulated until Act IV, and it is material of an essentially thematic rather than a narrative kind.

The Merchant of Venice is a play about contrasted attitudes towards wealth and the life-styles dictated by each, but it is also a comedy which returns to that question of love and friendship and the rivalry between them which Shakespeare had first explored in *The Two Gentlemen of Verona*. There seems little point in trying to extract from the play any explicit statement that Antonio's love for Bassanio is homosexual in origin. What is clear is that Antonio's unexplained melancholy in the opening scene is somehow connected with Bassanio's recently expressed intention to seek a wife, although Antonio himself never says so directly, and although he himself is far too magnanimous to refuse to help Bassanio in his enterprise. Nevertheless, his letter sent to Belmont in Act III is emotional in ways that seem to reflect a response to the loss of Bassanio to Portia quite as much as his anxiety over what will become of him at the hands of Shylock. There is almost a sense that Antonio welcomes death as an incontrovertible proof that he has done something for Bassanio that Portia can never hope to rival, has elevated his love above hers. But he does not know Portia.

Bassanio does not tell Portia about Antonio until he has to: when Salerio arrives at Belmont with the news of their friend's deadly peril. Her response is immediate and predictable. Freely she offers Bassanio enough money to pay Antonio's debt twenty times over and dispatches him to Venice at once, postponing their wedding night: "For never shall you lie by Portia's side / With an unquiet soul" (III.ii.305–6). To Lorenzo, after Bassanio's departure, she explains her attitude towards Antonio:

> in companions
> That do converse and waste the time together,
> Whose souls do bear an egall yoke of love,
> There must be needs a like proportion
> Of lineaments, of manners, and of spirit;
> Which makes me think that this Antonio,
> Being the bosom lover of my lord,

Must needs be like my lord. If it be so,
How little is the cost I have bestowed
In purchasing the semblance of my soul,
From out the state of hellish cruelty.

(III.iv.11–21)

This generosity, this willingness to accommodate Antonio within the newly formed husband and wife relationship, is not merely abstract. Disguised as a man of law and accompanied by Nerissa, she sets off secretly for Venice in order to make absolutely sure that Bassanio will not lose a friend as a consequence of gaining a wife.

Antonio owes his life to Portia. Bassanio could not have saved him. Yet both Bassanio and his friend say things in the course of the trial which Portia has every right to find alarming. Antonio's hidden jealousy of the "honorable wife" emerges when he bids Bassanio return to Belmont with the story of his sacrifice and death "and when the tale is told, bid her be judge / Whether Bassanio had not once a love" (IV.i.276–77). Bassanio, in his remorse, makes it clear that he values Antonio's life not only above his own, but also above that of his wife—a priority for which, as the pretended Balthazar remarks dryly, "your wife would give you little thanks" (IV.i.288). It is because she realizes that the situation must be clarified that she resorts to the ring trick: a test which forces Bassanio to weigh his obligations to his wife against those to his friend and to recognize the latent antagonism between them.

Bassanio, to do him credit, struggles hard to keep his promise to Portia and her ring. Significantly, it is Antonio who finally persuades him otherwise: "let him have the ring. / Let his deservings and my love withal / Be valued 'gainst your wive's commandement" (IV.i.449–51). Obedient to old loyalties, Bassanio yields. He is wrong to do so and, back in Belmont, Portia plagues him for it. The contretemps over the rings is funny—indeed, in the case of Gratiano and Nerissa it is little more than an excuse for some bawdy jokes—but Portia uses it for a serious purpose. In the end, Bassanio is forgiven. It was to Portia all the time, a Portia unknown to him in her man's disguise, that he gave away the ring of love. Looked at rightly, there was no betrayal at all. Yet Portia does not reveal the truth until she has brought Antonio to the point of confessing his responsibility for the quarrel, and of swearing, "My soul upon the forfeit, that your lord / Will never more break faith advisedly" (V.i.252–53). Only then does she relent, returning the ring to Bassanio through the hands of Antonio, who discovers that he has become the surety for Bassanio's faith, in a relationship which, although it does not cancel out friendship, relegates it nonetheless to a subordinate place. There is room for friendship within the house of love, but love holds the upper and controlling hand.

The hand, however, is Portia's and it is characteristically generous and full of gifts. At the same time that she gently but firmly excludes Antonio from priority of place in Bassanio's affections, she com-

pensates him with the news that three of the ships he had given up for lost are miraculously, and richly, arrived in port. When Antonio thanks Portia he does so as if, in some mysterious way, she were the agent of his good fortune: "Sweet lady, you have given me life and living" (V.i.286). Whether this mercantile prosperity can fully compensate Antonio for the loss of Bassanio, for the fact that he must make his exit singly behind the three couples who, at the end of the scene, move off joyously to bed, the comedy does not attempt to judge. The solitude of Antonio at the end of Act V is without the tragic overtones of Shylock's last appearance but it suggests a link between the two arch-enemies after all: both are voices somehow missing in the final chord.

There are false notes in this chord, as well as some omissions. Even at Belmont, life is not perfect.

> If to do were as easy as to know what were good to do, chapels had been churches, and poor men's cottages princes' palaces. It is a good divine that follows his own instructions; I can easier teach twenty what were good to be done, than to be one of the twenty to follow mine own teaching. The brain may devise laws for the blood, but a hot temper leaps o'er a cold decree. (I.ii.12–19)

Portia's rueful assessment of human frailty is a just one. Generosity is the great principle by which the Christians try to live and yet, at Belmont, no one remembers or pities Shylock, not even Portia. During the trial itself, she seemed to forget her own eloquent celebration of mercy as soon as it came to sentencing her victim, and she does not spare him a thought now. Gratiano, the most thoughtless of the Christians, would increase Shylock's punishment if he could. His own relationship with Nerissa is a coarsened and trivialized version of the one that binds Portia and Bassanio. Lorenzo and Jessica let money slip through their hands like water, and then depend upon other people to take them in and put the situation right. Their love-duet in the night at the beginning of Act V is beautiful, but the myths they invoke are all, disturbingly, stories of infidelity and misunderstanding: Dido and Aeneas, Troilus and Cressida, Pyramus and Thisby, Medea and Jason. There is hope embodied in the new society which forms at Belmont at the end of *The Merchant of Venice*, but there is also a consciousness that while the music of the spheres, the flawless, immutable harmony of a world better than this, exists and may even be sensed on clear nights as an influence, it remains fundamentally inaudible:

> Such harmony is in immortal souls,
> But whilst this muddy vesture of decay
> Doth grossly close it in, we cannot hear it.

(V.i.63–65)

Under circumstances like these, the best one can do is to accept and rejoice in the music of earth, transitory and imperfect though it is.

Anne Barton

The Merchant of Venice

[Dramatis Personae

The Duke *of* Venice
The Prince *of* Morocco
The Prince *of* Arragon } *suitors to Portia*
Antonio, *a merchant of Venice*
Bassanio, *his friend, suitor to Portia*
Solanio
Gratiano } *friends to Antonio and Bassanio*
Salerio
Lorenzo, *in love with Jessica*
Shylock, *a rich Jew*
Tubal, *a Jew, his friend*

Launcelot Gobbo, *a clown, servant to Shylock*
Old Gobbo, *father to Launcelot*
Leonardo, *servant to Bassanio*
Balthazar
Stephano } *servants to Portia*

Portia, *a rich heiress, of Belmont*
Nerissa, *her waiting-gentlewoman*
Jessica, *daughter to Shylock*

Magnificoes *of Venice,* Officers *of the Court of Justice,*
Jailer, Servants *to Portia, and other* Attendants

Scene: *Partly at Venice and partly at Belmont, the seat of Portia*]

[ACT I, Scene I]

Enter Antonio, Salerio, *and* Solanio.

Ant. In sooth, I know not why I am so sad;
It wearies me, you say it wearies you;
But how I caught it, found it, or came by it,
What stuff 'tis made of, whereof it is born,
I am to learn;   5
And such a want-wit sadness makes of me,
That I have much ado to know myself.
Sal. Your mind is tossing on the ocean,
There where your argosies with portly sail
Like signiors and rich burghers on the flood,   10
Or as it were the pageants of the sea,
Do overpeer the petty traffickers
That cur'sy to them, do them reverence,
As they fly by them with their woven wings.
Sol. Believe me, sir, had I such venture forth,   15
The better part of my affections would
Be with my hopes abroad. I should be still

Plucking the grass to know where sits the wind,
Piring in maps for ports and piers and roads;
And every object that might make me fear   20
Misfortune to my ventures, out of doubt
Would make me sad.
Sal.   My wind cooling my broth
Would blow me to an ague when I thought
What harm a wind too great might do at sea.
I should not see the sandy hour-glass run   25
But I should think of shallows and of flats,
And see my wealthy *Andrew* [dock'd] in sand,
Vailing her high top lower than her ribs
To kiss her burial. Should I go to church
And see the holy edifice of stone,   30
And not bethink me straight of dangerous rocks,
Which touching but my gentle vessel's side
Would scatter all her spices on the stream,
Enrobe the roaring waters with my silks,
And in a word, but even now worth this,   35
And now worth nothing? Shall I have the thought
To think on this, and shall I lack the thought
That such a thing bechanc'd would make me sad?
But tell not me; I know Antonio
Is sad to think upon his merchandise.   40

*Words and passages enclosed in square brackets in the text above are
either emendations of the copy-text or additions to it. The Textual Notes
immediately following the play cite the earliest authority for every such
change or insertion and supply the reading of the copy-text wherever it is
emended in this edition.*

I.i. Location: Venice. A street.
1. **sooth:** truth. **sad:** melancholy.
5. **I . . . learn:** I have still to find out, i.e. I don't know.
9. **argosies:** large merchant ships. **portly:** stately.
10. **signiors:** gentlemen of substance.
11. **pageants:** high mobile stages used for the miracle plays and other
entertainments, something like modern floats.
12. **overpeer:** tower over, look down upon.
13. **cur'sy:** curtsy, i.e. bob up and down on the waves. **do them
reverence:** make obeisance to them.
15. **venture:** speculative commercial enterprise.
16. **affections:** thoughts and feelings. 17. **still:** constantly.

19. **Piring:** peering, prying. **roads:** roadsteads, anchorages.
21. **out of doubt:** undoubtedly. 26. **flats:** shoals.
27. **wealthy:** richly laden. **Andrew.** This was the name of one of
two very large Spanish galleons captured by the English in the Cadiz
expedition of 1596; news of the exploit created great excitement in
England, and it is doubtless alluded to here.
28. **Vailing:** lowering. **high top:** topmast.
29. **kiss her burial:** do homage to her place of burial.
31. **bethink me straight:** be put in mind straightway.
32. **gentle:** noble. 35. **but even now:** i.e. just a moment ago.
38. **bechanc'd:** should it happen.

Ant.   Believe me, no. I thank my fortune for it,
My ventures are not in one bottom trusted,
Nor to one place; nor is my whole estate
Upon the fortune of this present year:
Therefore my merchandise makes me not sad.   45
Sol.   Why then you are in love.
Ant.   Fie, fie!
Sol.   Not in love neither? Then let us say you are
    sad
Because you are not merry; and 'twere as easy
For you to laugh and leap, and say you are merry
Because you are not sad. Now by two-headed Janus,
Nature hath fram'd strange fellows in her time: 51
Some that will evermore peep through their eyes,
And laugh like parrots at a bagpiper;
And other of such vinegar aspect
That they'll not show their teeth in way of smile   55
Though Nestor swear the jest be laughable.

Enter Bassanio, Lorenzo, *and* Gratiano.

Here comes Bassanio, your most noble kinsman,
Gratiano, and Lorenzo. Fare ye well,
We leave you now with better company.
Sal.   I would have stay'd till I had made you
    merry,   60
If worthier friends had not prevented me.
Ant.   Your worth is very dear in my regard.
I take it your own business calls on you,
And you embrace th' occasion to depart.
Sal.   Good morrow, my good lords.   65
Bass.   Good signiors both, when shall we laugh?
    say, when?
You grow exceeding strange. Must it be so?
Sal.   We'll make our leisures to attend on yours.
                    Exeunt Salerio and Solanio.
Lor.   My Lord Bassanio, since you have found
    Antonio,
We two will leave you, but at dinner-time   70
I pray you have in mind where we must meet.
Bass.   I will not fail you.
Gra.   You look not well, Signior Antonio,
You have too much respect upon the world.
They lose it that do buy it with much care.   75
Believe me you are marvellously chang'd.
Ant.   I hold the world but as the world, Gratiano,
A stage, where every man must play a part,
And mine a sad one.
Gra.   Let me play the fool,
With mirth and laughter let old wrinkles come,   80
And let my liver rather heat with wine

Than my heart cool with mortifying groans.
Why should a man, whose blood is warm within,
Sit like his grandsire cut in alablaster?
Sleep when he wakes? and creep into the jaundies   85
By being peevish? I tell thee what, Antonio—
I love thee, and 'tis my love that speaks—
There are a sort of men whose visages
Do cream and mantle like a standing pond,
And do a willful stillness entertain,   90
With purpose to be dress'd in an opinion
Of wisdom, gravity, profound conceit,
As who should say, "I am Sir Oracle,
And when I ope my lips let no dog bark!"
O my Antonio, I do know of these   95
That therefore only are reputed wise
For saying nothing; when I am very sure
If they should speak, would almost damn those ears
Which hearing them would call their brothers fools.
I'll tell thee more of this another time;   100
But fish not with this melancholy bait
For this fool gudgeon, this opinion.
Come, good Lorenzo. Fare ye well a while,
I'll end my exhortation after dinner.
Lor.   Well, we will leave you then till dinner-time.
I must be one of these same dumb wise men,   106
For Gratiano never lets me speak.
Gra.   Well, keep me company but two years moe,
Thou shalt not know the sound of thine own tongue.
Ant.   Fare you well! I'll grow a talker for this gear.
Gra.   Thanks, i' faith, for silence is only commend-
    able   111
In a neat's tongue dried and a maid not vendible.
                    Exeunt [Gratiano and Lorenzo].
Ant.   It is that—any thing now!
Bass.   Gratiano speaks an infinite deal of nothing,
more than any man in all Venice. His reasons are as
two grains of wheat hid in two bushels of chaff;   116
you shall seek all day ere you find them, and when
you have them, they are not worth the search.
Ant.   Well, tell me now what lady is the same
To whom you swore a secret pilgrimage,   120
That you to-day promis'd to tell me of?
Bass.   'Tis not unknown to you, Antonio,
How much I have disabled mine estate,

---

82. **mortifying:** killing.   Groans and sighs were thought to draw blood from the heart.
84. **alablaster:** alabaster.   Stone effigies were common on tombs in churches.
85. **jaundies:** jaundice (thought to be caused by an excess of one of the humors, choler or yellow bile, as melancholy was by an excess of black bile).
89. **cream and mantle:** i.e. acquire a set expression (literally, grow a scum).   **standing:** stagnant.
90. **willful stillness:** self-imposed and persistent silence.   **entertain:** maintain.   91. **opinion:** reputation.   92. **conceit:** thought.
95. **of these:** some men.   96. **therefore:** therefor, for that reason.
98–99. **would . . . fools:** would speak such nonsense that those who heard them would immediately call them fools and so risk damnation. The allusion is to Matthew 5:22: "And whosoever saith unto his brother, . . . Fool, shall be worthy to be punished with hell fire" (Geneva).   101. **melancholy bait:** bait of melancholy.
102. **gudgeon:** a small fish easily caught.
104. **exhortation:** sermon.   108. **keep:** if you keep.   **moe:** more.
110. **for this gear:** as a consequence of all this talk of yours.
112. **neat's:** ox's.   **vendible:** salable, i.e. marriageable.
113. **It . . . now:** i.e. it is as you say—or indeed whatever you care to make it.   115. **reasons:** reasonable statements, sensible ideas.

---

42. **bottom:** ship.   44. **fortune:** chance.
50. **Janus:** Roman god represented with two faces looking in opposite directions.
52. **peep . . . eyes:** i.e. look out through eyes half closed by laughter. Cf. line 80.
53. **like parrots:** i.e. raucously.   **bagpiper.** Bagpipe music was regarded as melancholy.
56. **Nestor:** the oldest and gravest of the Greek heroes at Troy.
61. **prevented:** forestalled.
64. **embrace th' occasion:** take advantage of the opportunity.
66. **when . . . laugh:** i.e. when shall we next have a merry time together.
67. **strange:** like strangers, i.e. reserved, distant.
74. **respect . . . world:** concern for business affairs.
80. **old:** typical of old age (?) or plentiful (as in IV.ii.15) (?).
81. **liver.** Regarded as the seat of the emotions.

By something showing a more swelling port
Than my faint means would grant continuance.   125
Nor do I now make moan to be abridg'd
From such a noble rate, but my chief care
Is to come fairly off from the great debts
Wherein my time something too prodigal
Hath left me gag'd. To you, Antonio,   130
I owe the most in money and in love,
And from your love I have a warranty
To unburthen all my plots and purposes
How to get clear of all the debts I owe.
    Ant. I pray you, good Bassanio, let me know it,
And if it stand, as you yourself still do,   136
Within the eye of honor, be assur'd
My purse, my person, my extremest means,
Lie all unlock'd to your occasions.
    Bass. In my school-days, when I had lost one shaft,
I shot his fellow of the self-same flight   141
The self-same way with more advised watch
To find the other forth, and by adventuring both
I oft found both. I urge this childhood proof,
Because what follows is pure innocence.   145
I owe you much, and like a willful youth,
That which I owe is lost, but if you please
To shoot another arrow that self way
Which you did shoot the first, I do not doubt,
As I will watch the aim, or to find both   150
Or bring your latter hazard back again,
And thankfully rest debtor for the first.
    Ant. You know me well, and herein spend but time
To wind about my love with circumstance,
And out of doubt you do me now more wrong   155
In making question of my uttermost
Than if you had made waste of all I have.
Then do but say to me what I should do
That in your knowledge may by me be done,
And I am prest unto it; therefore speak.   160
    Bass. In Belmont is a lady richly left,
And she is fair, and fairer than that word,
Of wondrous virtues. Sometimes from her eyes
I did receive fair speechless messages.
Her name is Portia, nothing undervalu'd   165
To Cato's daughter, Brutus' Portia.
Nor is the wide world ignorant of her worth,
For the four winds blow in from every coast
Renowned suitors, and her sunny locks
Hang on her temples like a golden fleece,   170

Which makes her seat of Belmont Colchis' strond,
And many Jasons come in quest of her.
O my Antonio, had I but the means
To hold a rival place with one of them,
I have a mind presages me such thrift   175
That I should questionless be fortunate!
    Ant. Thou know'st that all my fortunes are at sea,
Neither have I money nor commodity
To raise a present sum; therefore go forth,
Try what my credit can in Venice do.   180
That shall be rack'd, even to the uttermost,
To furnish thee to Belmont, to fair Portia.
Go presently inquire, and so will I,
Where money is, and I no question make
To have it of my trust, or for my sake. *Exeunt.*   185

[SCENE II]

Enter PORTIA *with her waiting-woman,* NERISSA.

    Por. By my troth, Nerissa, my little body is
a-weary of this great world.
    Ner. You would be, sweet madam, if your mis-
eries were in the same abundance as your good fortunes are; and yet for aught I see, they are as   5
sick that surfeit with too much as they that starve
with nothing. It is no mean happiness therefore
to be seated in the mean: superfluity comes sooner by
white hairs, but competency lives longer.
    Por. Good sentences, and well pronounc'd.   10
    Ner. They would be better if well follow'd.
    Por. If to do were as easy as to know what were
good to do, chapels had been churches, and poor
men's cottages princes' palaces. It is a good divine
that follows his own instructions; I can easier   15
teach twenty what were good to be done, than to
be one of the twenty to follow mine own teaching.
The brain may devise laws for the blood, but a hot
temper leaps o'er a cold decree—such a hare is madness the youth, to skip o'er the meshes of good   20
counsel the cripple. But this reasoning is not in
the fashion to choose me a husband. O me, the
word choose! I may neither choose who I would, nor
refuse who I dislike; so is the will of a living daughter
curb'd by the will of a dead father. Is it not hard, 25
Nerissa, that I cannot choose one, nor refuse none?
    Ner. Your father was ever virtuous, and holy

---

124. **something:** somewhat (modifies *more*). Another example of this
common adverbial use occurs in line 129.   **swelling port:** splendid
style of living.   126. **to be abridg'd:** at being reduced.
127. **rate:** manner of living.
128. **fairly:** fitly, honorably; or perhaps completely (cf. line 134).
129. **time:** youth.   130. **gag'd:** pledged.
133. **unburthen:** variant form of *unburden.*   136. **still:** always.
137. **eye:** sight, view.   139. **occasions:** needs.
141. **his:** its.   **flight:** range.   142. **advised:** careful, deliberate.
143. **forth:** out.
144. **urge:** put forward, bring up.   **proof:** experience.
145. **innocence:** childish folly (?) or childlike sincerity (?).
146. **like . . . youth:** i.e. because I have behaved recklessly, as youth
does.   148. **self:** same.   150. **or:** either.
151. **latter hazard:** second risk.   153. **spend but:** only waste.
154. **circumstance:** elaborate reasoning.
156. **making question of:** questioning whether I will do.
160. **prest unto:** ready for.
162. **fairer . . . word:** what is better still.   163. **Sometimes:** formerly.
165. **nothing undervalu'd:** in no way inferior.

171. **Colchis:** the country, at the eastern end of the Black Sea,
where Jason won the Golden Fleece.   **strond:** strand, shore.
175. **thrift:** thriving, success.   176. **questionless:** undoubtedly.
178. **commodity:** merchandise.   181 **rack'd:** stretched.
183. **presently:** immediately.
184-85. **no . . . To:** have no doubt that I shall.
185. **of . . . sake:** on my credit as a businessman, or as a friendly
loan.

I.ii. Location: Belmont. Portia's house.
8. **in the mean:** between the extremes of too little and too much.
comes sooner by: sooner gets.   9. **competency:** moderate means.
10. **sentences:** maxims.   14. **divine:** clergyman.
15. **follows . . . instructions:** practices what he preaches.
18. **for the blood:** to control passion.
18-19. **hot temper:** impetuous temperament.
20. **meshes:** nets, snares.
20-21. **good . . . cripple:** wisdom the old man incapable of action.
21-22. **this . . . me:** this line of reasoning is not of a kind to help me
in choosing.   24-25. **will . . . will:** desire . . . testament.

men at their death have good inspirations; therefore the lott'ry that he hath devis'd in these three
chests of gold, silver, and lead, whereof who 30
chooses his meaning chooses you, will no doubt
never be chosen by any rightly but one who you shall
rightly love. But what warmth is there in your
affection towards any of these princely suitors that
are already come? 35

Por. I pray thee over-name them, and as thou
namest them, I will describe them; and according to
my description level at my affection.

Ner. First, there is the Neapolitan prince. 39

Por. Ay, that's a colt indeed, for he doth nothing
but talk of his horse, and he makes it a great appropriation to his own good parts that he can shoe
him himself. I am much afeard my lady his mother
play'd false with a smith.

Ner. Then is there the County Palentine. 45

Por. He doth nothing but frown, as who should
say, "And you will not have me, choose." He hears
merry tales and smiles not. I fear he will prove the
weeping philosopher when he grows old, being so
full of unmannerly sadness in his youth. I had 50
rather be married to a death's-head with a bone in
his mouth than to either of these. God defend me from
these two!

Ner. How say you by the French lord, Monsieur
Le [Bon]? 55

Por. God made him, and therefore let him pass
for a man. In truth, I know it is a sin to be a mocker,
but he! why, he hath a horse better than the Neapolitan's, a better bad habit of frowning than the Count
Palentine; he is every man in no man. If a throstle 60
sing, he falls straight a-cap'ring. He will fence with
his own shadow. If I should marry him, I should
marry twenty husbands. If he would despise me,
I would forgive him, for if he love me to madness,
I shall never requite him. 65

Ner. What say you then to Falconbridge, the
young baron of England?

Por. You know I say nothing to him, for he
understands not me, nor I him. He hath neither Latin,
French, nor Italian, and you will come into the 70
court and swear that I have a poor pennyworth in
the English. He is a proper man's picture, but alas,
who can converse with a dumb show? How oddly he
is suited! I think he bought his doublet in Italy, his
round hose in France, his bonnet in Germany, and his
behavior every where. 76

Ner. What think you of the Scottish lord, his
neighbor?

Por. That he hath a neighborly charity in him, for
he borrow'd a box of the ear of the Englishman, 80
and swore he would pay him again when he was able.
I think the Frenchman became his surety and seal'd
under for another.

Ner. How like you the young German, the Duke
of Saxony's nephew? 85

Por. Very vildly in the morning, when he is sober,
and most vildly in the afternoon, when he is drunk.
When he is best, he is a little worse than a man, and
when he is worst, he is little better than a beast. And
the worst fall that ever fell, I hope I shall make shift
to go without him. 91

Ner. If he should offer to choose, and choose the
right casket, you should refuse to perform your
father's will, if you should refuse to accept him. 94

Por. Therefore for fear of the worst, I pray thee
set a deep glass of Rhenish wine on the contrary
casket, for if the devil be within, and that temptation without, I know he will choose it. I will do any
thing, Nerissa, ere I will be married to a spunge. 99

Ner. You need not fear, lady, the having any of
these lords. They have acquainted me with their
determinations, which is indeed to return to their
home, and to trouble you with no more suit, unless
you may be won by some other sort than your father's
imposition depending on the caskets. 105

Por. If I live to be as old as Sibylla, I will die as
chaste as Diana, unless I be obtain'd by the manner
of my father's will. I am glad this parcel of wooers
are so reasonable, for there is not one among them
but I dote on his very absence, and I pray God grant
them a fair departure. 111

Ner. Do you not remember, lady, in your father's
time, a Venetian, a scholar and a soldier, that came
hither in company of the Marquis of Montferrat?

Por. Yes, yes, it was Bassanio—as I think, so was
he call'd. 116

Ner. True, madam; he, of all the men that ever
my foolish eyes look'd upon, was the best deserving
a fair lady.

Por. I remember him well, and I remember him
worthy of thy praise. 121

Enter a SERVINGMAN.

How now, what news?

Serv. The four strangers seek for you, madam,
to take their leave; and there is a forerunner come
from a fift, the Prince of Morocco, who brings word
the Prince his master will be here to-night. 126

30. **whereof:** among which chests.
31. **chooses his meaning:** i.e. guesses your father's intention correctly.
36. **over-name them:** name them over. With lines 36 ff. compare *The Two Gentlemen of Verona,* I.ii.7 ff. 38. **level:** guess.
40. **colt:** i.e. young, inexperienced creature. The Neapolitans in Shakespeare's day were famous for horsemanship.
41-42. **appropriation:** addition. 42. **good parts:** accomplishments.
45. **County Palentine:** Count Palatine.
47. **And:** if. **choose:** i.e. do what you please.
49. **weeping philosopher:** Heraclitus.
51-52. **death's-head . . . mouth.** Probably referring to the skull and cross-bones frequently cut on tombstones. 54. **by:** concerning.
60. **throstle:** thrush. 72. **is . . . picture:** is handsome in appearance.
74. **suited:** apparelled. **doublet:** coat, upper garment.
75. **round hose:** short breeches. **bonnet:** soft, cap-like hat. The satire in this passage on the international character of an English gallant's costume was a commonplace at this time.

82-83. **became . . . another:** guaranteed the Scot's payment and pledged himself to pay the Englishman with another blow (an allusion to French promises to back the Scots in their quarrels with the English). 86. **vildly:** vilely. 89. **And:** if.
90. **fall . . . fell:** befall . . . befell. **make shift:** contrive.
96. **contrary:** wrong. 99. **spunge:** sponge.
104. **sort:** manner, way.
105. **imposition:** conditions (if they fail to choose the right casket); see II.i.38-42.
106. **Sibylla:** the Cumaean Sibyl. Apollo promised her that her years would equal the number of grains of sand she held in her hand.
123. **four.** Nerissa has named six. **strangers:** foreigners.
125. **fift:** fifth.

257

The Merchant
of Venice
I.ii

Por. If I could bid the fift welcome with so good heart as I can bid the other four farewell, I should be glad of his approach. If he have the condition of a saint, and the complexion of a devil, I had rather he should shrive me than wive me. 131
Come, Nerissa. Sirrah, go before.
Whiles we shut the gate upon one wooer, another
    knocks at the door. *Exeunt.*

[SCENE III]

Enter BASSANIO *with* SHYLOCK *the Jew.*

Shy. Three thousand ducats, well.
Bass. Ay, sir, for three months.
Shy. For three months, well.
Bass. For the which, as I told you, Antonio shall be bound. 5
Shy. Antonio shall become bound, well.
Bass. May you stead me? Will you pleasure me? Shall I know your answer?
Shy. Three thousand ducats for three months, and Antonio bound. 10
Bass. Your answer to that.
Shy. Antonio is a good man.
Bass. Have you heard any imputation to the contrary? 14
Shy. Ho, no, no, no, no! my meaning in saying he is a good man is to have you understand me that he is sufficient. Yet his means are in supposition: he hath an argosy bound to Tripolis, another to the Indies; I understand moreover upon the Rialto, he hath a third at Mexico, a fourth for England, 20 and other ventures he hath, squand'red abroad. But ships are but boards, sailors but men; there be land-rats and water-rats, water-thieves and land-thieves, I mean pirates, and then there is the peril of waters, winds, and rocks. The man is notwith- 25 standing sufficient. Three thousand ducats: I think I may take his bond.
Bass. Be assur'd you may.
Shy. I will be assur'd I may; and that I may be assur'd, I will bethink me. May I speak with Antonio? 31
Bass. If it please you to dine with us.
Shy. Yes, to smell pork, to eat of the habitation which your prophet the Nazarite conjur'd the devil

into. I will buy with you, sell with you, talk 35 with you, walk with you, and so following; but I will not eat with you, drink with you, nor pray with you. What news on the Rialto? Who is he comes here?

Enter ANTONIO.

Bass. This is Signior Antonio. 40
Shy. [*Aside.*] How like a fawning publican he
    looks!
I hate him for he is a Christian;
But more, for that in low simplicity
He lends out money gratis, and brings down
The rate of usance here with us in Venice. 45
If I can catch him once upon the hip,
I will feed fat the ancient grudge I bear him.
He hates our sacred nation, and he rails
Even there where merchants most do congregate
On me, my bargains, and my well-won thrift, 50
Which he calls interest. Cursed be my tribe
If I forgive him!
Bass.   Shylock, do you hear?
Shy. I am debating of my present store,
And by the near guess of my memory,
I cannot instantly raise up the gross 55
Of full three thousand ducats. What of that?
Tubal, a wealthy Hebrew of my tribe,
Will furnish me. But soft, how many months
Do you desire? [*To Antonio.*] Rest you fair, good
    signior,
Your worship was the last man in our mouths. 60
Ant. Shylock, albeit I neither lend nor borrow
By taking nor by giving of excess,
Yet to supply the ripe wants of my friend,
I'll break a custom. [*To Bassanio.*] Is he yet possess'd
How much ye would?
Shy.   Ay, ay, three thousand ducats.
Ant. And for three months. 66
Shy. I had forgot—three months—[*to Bassanio*]
    you told me so.
Well then, your bond; and let me see—but hear you,
Methoughts you said you neither lend nor borrow
Upon advantage.
Ant.   I do never use it. 70
Shy. When Jacob graz'd his uncle Laban's sheep—
This Jacob from our holy Abram was
(As his wise mother wrought in his behalf)

---

129. **condition**: disposition.
130. **complexion . . . devil.** Devils were always represented as black in Shakespeare's day.
131. **shrive me**: hear my confession and grant me absolution.
132. **Sirrah**: form of address used to inferiors.

I.iii. Location: Venice. A public place.
1. **ducats**: in this play, gold coins (there were also silver ducats); their value has been variously estimated, usually at something between a quarter and a half of an English pound apiece.
7. **stead**: assist, supply.
17. **in supposition**: i.e. not certainly in existence.
19. **Rialto**: commercial and business exchange of Venice.
21. **squand'red**: unwisely scattered.
29. **assur'd**: sure, satisfied (but Shylock takes it up in the sense "guaranteed by adequate security").
33–38. **Yes . . . you.** Perhaps these lines are spoken aside while Shylock "bethinks him" (see line 30).
34. **Nazarite**: Nazarene. *Nazarite* is the form used in both the Geneva and Bishops' versions (in Matthew 2:23). The allusion here is to Jesus' casting devils into a herd of swine (see Mark 5:1–13).
41. **fawning publican.** A controversial passage. Presumably Shylock regards Antonio as one who, like a publican (a tax collector for the Romans), deprives him of his rightful profits, but who now (like the publican in Luke 18:10–14 who prayed for mercy) assumes an ingratiating demeanor because he is asking a favor.
42. **for**: because.
43. **low simplicity.** Both words have good and bad meanings: *low* = (1) humble, (2) base; *simplicity* = (1) honest plainness (the opposite of duplicity), (2) folly. Shylock may be speaking straightforwardly or ironically. 45. **usance**: usury.
46. **upon the hip**: at a disadvantage (a wrestling term).
50. **thrift**: thriving, profit (so also at line 90).
55. **gross**: total amount. 62. **excess**: interest.
63. **ripe**: immediate. 64. **possess'd**: informed.
69. **Methoughts**: it seemed to me (a variant of *methought*).
70. **advantage**: interest. **use it**: make it my practice.
71. **Jacob.** See Genesis 27, 30:25–43.

The third possessor; ay, he was the third—
Ant. And what of him? did he take interest? 75
Shy. No, not take interest, not as you would say
Directly int'rest. Mark what Jacob did:
When Laban and himself were compremis'd
That all the eanlings which were streak'd and pied
Should fall as Jacob's hire, the ewes being rank 80
In end of autumn turned to the rams,
And when the work of generation was
Between these woolly breeders in the act,
The skillful shepherd pill'd me certain wands,
And in the doing of the deed of kind, 85
He stuck them up before the fulsome ewes,
Who then conceiving did in eaning time
Fall parti-color'd lambs, and those were Jacob's.
This was a way to thrive, and he was blest;
And thrift is blessing, if men steal it not. 90
Ant. This was a venture, sir, that Jacob serv'd for,
A thing not in his power to bring to pass,
But sway'd and fashion'd by the hand of heaven.
Was this inserted to make interest good?
Or is your gold and silver ewes and rams? 95
Shy. I cannot tell, I make it breed as fast.
But note me, signior.
Ant.   Mark you this, Bassanio,
The devil can cite Scripture for his purpose.
An evil soul producing holy witness
Is like a villain with a smiling cheek, 100
A goodly apple rotten at the heart.
O, what a goodly outside falsehood hath!
Shy. Three thousand ducats—'tis a good round
        sum.
Three months from twelve; then let me see, the
        rate—
Ant. Well, Shylock, shall we be beholding to you?
Shy. Signior Antonio, many a time and oft 106
In the Rialto you have rated me
About my moneys and my usances.
Still have I borne it with a patient shrug
(For suff'rance is the badge of all our tribe). 110
You call me misbeliever, cut-throat dog,
And spet upon my Jewish gaberdine,
And all for use of that which is mine own.
Well then, it now appears you need my help.
Go to then, you come to me, and you say, 115
"Shylock, we would have moneys," you say so—
You, that did void your rheum upon my beard,
And foot me as you spurn a stranger cur

Over your threshold; moneys is your suit.
What should I say to you? Should I not say, 120
"Hath a dog money? Is it possible
A cur can lend three thousand ducats?" Or
Shall I bend low and in a bondman's key,
With bated breath and whisp'ring humbleness,
Say this: 125
"Fair sir, you spet on me on Wednesday last,
You spurn'd me such a day, another time
You call'd me dog; and for these courtesies
I'll lend you thus much moneys"?
Ant. I am as like to call thee so again, 130
To spet on thee again, to spurn thee too.
If thou wilt lend this money, lend it not
As to thy friends, for when did friendship take
A breed for barren metal of his friend?
But lend it rather to thine enemy, 135
Who if he break, thou mayst with better face
Exact the penalty.
Shy.   Why, look you how you storm!
I would be friends with you, and have your love,
Forget the shames that you have stain'd me with,
Supply your present wants, and take no doit 140
Of usance for my moneys, and you'll not hear me.
This is kind I offer.
Bass. This were kindness.
Shy.   This kindness will I show.
Go with me to a notary, seal me there
Your single bond; and in a merry sport 145
If you repay me not on such a day,
In such a place, such sum or sums as are
Express'd in the condition, let the forfeit
Be nominated for an equal pound
Of your fair flesh, to be cut off and taken 150
In what part of your body pleaseth me.
Ant. Content, in faith, I'll seal to such a bond,
And say there is much kindness in the Jew.
Bass. You shall not seal to such a bond for me,
I'll rather dwell in my necessity. 155
Ant. Why, fear not, man, I will not forfeit it.
Within these two months, that's a month before
This bond expires, I do expect return
Of thrice three times the value of this bond.
Shy. O father Abram, what these Christians are,
Whose own hard dealings teaches them suspect 161
The thoughts of others! Pray you tell me this:
If he should break his day, what should I gain
By the exaction of the forfeiture?
A pound of man's flesh taken from a man 165
Is not so estimable, profitable neither,
As flesh of muttons, beefs, or goats. I say,
To buy his favor, I extend this friendship.
If he will take it, so, if not, adieu;

---

78. **compremis'd:** agreed (a variant form of *compromised*).
79. **eanlings:** new-born lambs.   **pied:** variegated in color (cf. *parti-color'd* in line 88).   80. **hire:** wages.   **rank:** in heat.
84. **pill'd:** peeled.   **me.** The so-called ethical dative; a colloquialism.
85. **kind:** nature.   87. **eaning:** lambing.
88. **Fall:** let fall, give birth to.
91. **venture . . . for:** commercial enterprise with an unpredictable outcome on which Jacob risked his time as a servant.
94. **inserted:** put into the Bible (?) or injected into the discussion (?). **make interest good:** justify taking interest.
97–102. **Mark . . . hath.** Perhaps another aside.
105. **beholding:** beholden, indebted.   107. **rated:** reviled.
110. **badge:** distinctive mark.
112. **spet:** spit. (The same form could be the past tense; see line 126.) **gaberdine:** a loose upper garment of coarse material.
113. **use.** With play on "usury."
115. **Go to:** term of remonstrance.   117. **rheum:** spittle.
118. **spurn:** kick.

134. **A breed:** offspring, increase (cf. line 96). The figure continues in *barren*. One of the oldest arguments against taking interest was that it is against nature for money to breed money.
136. **break:** go bankrupt.   140. **doit:** coin of trifling value.
143. **were kindness:** would be kindness (if the offer were seriously meant).
145. **single bond:** bond signed only by the debtor, without sureties.
149. **nominated for:** stipulated as.   **equal:** exact.
155. **dwell:** remain.
163. **break his day:** fail to pay on the due date.
164. **forfeiture:** forfeit, amount stipulated as penalty.

The Merchant
of Venice
I.iii

And for my love I pray you wrong me not.   170
   Ant.   Yes, Shylock, I will seal unto this bond.
   Shy.   Then meet me forthwith at the notary's;
Give him direction for this merry bond,
And I will go and purse the ducats straight,
See to my house, left in the fearful guard   175
Of an unthrifty knave, and presently
I'll be with you.   *Exit.*
   Ant.   Hie thee, gentle Jew.
The Hebrew will turn Christian, he grows kind.
   Bass.   I like not fair terms and a villain's mind.
   Ant.   Come on, in this there can be no dismay,   180
My ships come home a month before the day.
                               Exeunt.

[ACT II, Scene I]

*[Flourish cornets.] Enter [the Prince of] Morocco,
a tawny Moor, all in white, and three or four Followers accordingly, with Portia, Nerissa, and their
Train.*

   Mor.   Mislike me not for my complexion,
The shadowed livery of the burnish'd sun,
To whom I am a neighbor and near bred.
Bring me the fairest creature northward born,
Where Phoebus' fire scarce thaws the icicles,   5
And let us make incision for your love,
To prove whose blood is reddest, his or mine.
I tell thee, lady, this aspect of mine
Hath fear'd the valiant; by my love, I swear
The best-regarded virgins of our clime   10
Have lov'd it too. I would not change this hue,
Except to steal your thoughts, my gentle queen.
   Por.   In terms of choice I am not soly led
By nice direction of a maiden's eyes;
Besides, the lott'ry of my destiny   15
Bars me the right of voluntary choosing.
But if my father had not scanted me,
And hedg'd me by his wit to yield myself
His wife who wins me by that means I told you,
Yourself, renowned Prince, then stood as fair   20
As any comer I have look'd on yet
For my affection.
   Mor.   Even for that I thank you;
Therefore I pray you lead me to the caskets
To try my fortune. By this scimitar
That slew the Sophy and a Persian prince   25

That won three fields of Sultan Solyman,
I would o'erstare the sternest eyes that look,
Outbrave the heart most daring on the earth,
Pluck the young sucking cubs from the she-bear,
Yea, mock the lion when 'a roars for prey,   30
To win [thee], lady. But alas the while!
If Hercules and Lichas play at dice
Which is the better man, the greater throw
May turn by fortune from the weaker hand:
So is Alcides beaten by his [page],   35
And so may I, blind fortune leading me,
Miss that which one unworthier may attain,
And die with grieving.
   Por.   You must take your chance,
And either not attempt to choose at all,
Or swear before you choose, if you choose wrong   40
Never to speak to lady afterward
In way of marriage; therefore be advis'd.
   Mor.   Nor will not. Come bring me unto my
   chance.
   Por.   First, forward to the temple; after dinner
Your hazard shall be made.
   Mor.   Good fortune then!   45
To make me blest or cursed'st among men.
                        [Cornets.] Exeunt.

[Scene II]

Enter the Clown [Launcelot Gobbo] alone.

   Laun.   Certainly my conscience will serve me to
run from this Jew my master. The fiend is at mine
elbow and tempts me, saying to me, "[Gobbo],
Launcelot [Gobbo], good Launcelot," or "good
[Gobbo]," or "good Launcelot [Gobbo], use your   5
legs, take the start, run away." My conscience
says, "No; take heed, honest Launcelot, take heed,
honest [Gobbo]," or as aforesaid, "honest Launcelot
[Gobbo], do not run, scorn running with thy heels."
Well, the most courageous fiend bids me pack.   10
"*Fia!*" says the fiend; "away!" says the fiend;
"for the heavens, rouse up a brave mind," says the
fiend, "and run." Well, my conscience, hanging
about the neck of my heart, says very wisely to me,
"My honest friend Launcelot, being an honest   15
man's son"—or rather an honest woman's son, for
indeed my father did something smack, something
grow to, he had a kind of taste—well, my conscience says, "Launcelot, bouge not." "Bouge," says

---

170. **wrong me not:** do not impute evil motives to me.
175. **fearful:** arousing anxiety, i.e. untrustworthy.
177. **Hie thee:** hasten.

II.i. Location: Belmont. Portia's house.
o.s.d. **Flourish:** sound a fanfare.   **cornets:** horns (not the modern
brass instrument).   **accordingly:** in accord, i.e. dark-skinned and
dressed in white like Morocco.
2. **shadowed . . . sun:** dark distinctive dress worn by the sun's retainers, i.e. black skin.   3. **near bred:** closely related.
5. **Phoebus:** the sun-god.
7. **whose . . . reddest:** i.e. who is most courageous.
8. **aspect:** visage.   9. **fear'd:** frightened.
12. **steal your thoughts:** gain possession of your thoughts (so that they
would become more favorable to me).
13. **terms:** respect.   **soly:** solely.   14. **nice:** fastidious.
15. **lott'ry . . . destiny:** game of chance on which my fate depends.
17. **scanted:** restricted.   18. **wit:** wisdom.
25. **Sophy:** Shah of Persia.

26. **fields:** battles.   **Solyman:** Suleiman II, the Magnificent (1496?–
1566).   27. **o'erstare:** outstare.   30. **'a:** he.
32. **Lichas:** the servant of Hercules (Alcides).
32–33. **play . . . Which:** throw dice to decide which.
42. **be advis'd:** take careful thought.
43. **will not:** i.e. will not violate the condition.
44. **to the temple:** i.e. to take the oath.
46. **blest or cursed'st:** most blessed or most cursed (the superlative
ending affects both adjectives).

II.ii. Location: Venice. A street.
1. **serve:** allow, encourage.
9. **with thy heels:** indignantly (with obvious pun).
10. **pack:** begone.   11. **Fia:** away (properly *via*).
12. **for the heavens:** in heaven's name (with special effect in the
devil's mouth).
17–18. **smack . . . taste:** i.e. his father is given to lechery.
19. **bouge:** budge.

the fiend. "Bouge not," says my conscience. 20
"Conscience," say I, "you counsel well." "Fiend,"
say I, "you counsel well." To be rul'd by my
conscience, I should stay with the Jew my master,
who (God bless the mark) is a kind of devil; and to
run away from the Jew, I should be rul'd by the 25
fiend, who, saving your reverence, is the devil himself. Certainly the Jew is the very devil incarnation, and in my conscience, my conscience is but a
kind of hard conscience, to offer to counsel me to
stay with the Jew. The fiend gives the more 30
friendly counsel: I will run, fiend; my heels are at
your commandement, I will run.

Enter OLD GOBBO *with a basket.*

Gob. Master young man, you, I pray you, which
is the way to Master Jew's? 34

Laun. [*Aside.*] O heavens, this is my true-begot-
ten father, who being more than sand-blind, high
gravel-blind, knows me not. I will try confusions
with him.

Gob. Master young gentleman, I pray you, which
is the way to Master Jew's? 40

Laun. Turn up on your right hand at the next
turning, but at the next turning of all, on your left;
marry, at the very next turning, turn of no hand, but
turn down indirectly to the Jew's house. 44

Gob. Be God's sonties, 'twill be a hard way to
hit. Can you tell me whether one Launcelot, that
dwells with him, dwell with him or no?

Laun. Talk you of young Master Launcelot?
[*Aside.*] Mark me now, now will I raise the waters.
—Talk you of young Master Launcelot? 50

Gob. No master, sir, but a poor man's son. His
father, though I say 't, is an honest exceeding poor
man and, God be thank'd, well to live.

Laun. Well, let his father be what 'a will, we talk
of young Master Launcelot. 55

Gob. Your worship's friend and Launcelot, sir.

Laun. But I pray you, *ergo*, old man, *ergo*, I beseech you, talk you of young Master Launcelot.

Gob. Of Launcelot, an't please your mastership.

Laun. Ergo, Master Launcelot. Talk not of 60
Master Launcelot, father, for the young gentleman,
according to Fates and Destinies, and such odd
sayings, the Sisters Three, and such branches of
learning, is indeed decceas'd, or as you would say in
plain terms, gone to heaven. 65

Gob. Marry, God forbid, the boy was the very
staff of my age, my very prop.

Laun. [*Aside.*] Do I look like a cudgel or a hovel-
post, a staff, or a prop?—Do you know me, father?

Gob. Alack the day, I know you not, young gentleman, but I pray you tell me, is my boy, God rest
his soul, alive or dead? 72

Laun. Do you not know me, father?

Gob. Alack, sir, I am sand-blind, I know you not.

Laun. Nay, indeed if you had your eyes 75
you might fail of the knowing me; it is a wise father
that knows his own child. Well, old man, I will
tell you news of your son. Give me your blessing;
truth will come to light; murder cannot be hid long;
a man's son may, but in the end truth will out. 80

Gob. Pray you, sir, stand up. I am sure you are
not Launcelot, my boy.

Laun. Pray you let's have no more fooling about
it, but give me your blessing. I am Launcelot, your
boy that was, your son that is, your child that shall
be. 86

Gob. I cannot think you are my son.

Laun. I know not what I shall think of that; but
I am Launcelot, the Jew's man, and I am sure Margery
your wife is my mother. 90

Gob. Her name is Margery indeed. I'll be sworn,
if thou be Launcelot, thou art mine own flesh and
blood. Lord worshipp'd might he be, what a beard
hast thou got! Thou hast got more hair on thy chin
than Dobbin my fill-horse has on his tail. 95

Laun. It should seem then that Dobbin's tail grows
backward. I am sure he had more hair of his tail than
I have of my face when I [last] saw him.

Gob. Lord, how art thou chang'd! How dost
thou and thy master agree? I have brought him a
present. How 'gree you now? 101

Laun. Well, well; but for mine own part, as I
have set up my rest to run away, so I will not rest
till I have run some ground. My master's a very
Jew. Give him a present! give him a halter. 105
I am famish'd in his service; you may tell every
finger I have with my ribs. Father, I am glad you
are come; give me your present to one Master
Bassanio, who indeed gives rare new liveries. If
I serve not him, I will run as far as God has any 110
ground. O rare fortune, here comes the man. To
him, father, for I am a Jew if I serve the Jew any
longer.

Enter BASSANIO *with a follower or two,* [*one of them*
LEONARDO].

---

24. **God . . . mark.** This expression, originally used to avert ill omen, was also employed, like *saving your reverence* (line 26), as a conventional apology before an offensive expression.
27-28. **incarnation:** blunder for *incarnate.*   28. **in:** by.
36. **sand-blind:** partly blind.   **high:** i.e. fully (an intensive).
37. **gravel-blind.** Launcelot's coinage for the degree of poor vision between sand-blind and stone-blind.   **try confusions.** Launcelot's adaptation of *try conclusions* = make experiments.
43. **marry:** indeed (originally the name of the Virgin Mary used as an oath).   45. **Be:** by.   **sonties:** little saints (?).
49. **raise the waters:** stir things up (?) or induce tears (?).
53. **well to live:** with a good livelihood (a contradiction of his preceding remark; perhaps Gobbo supposes that the phrase means "in good health").
56. **Your . . . Launcelot.** Another disclaimer of the title "Master" for Launcelot.   57. **ergo:** therefore.   59. **an:** if.
61. **father:** common form of address to an old person; hence it does not reveal to Gobbo that Launcelot is his son.
63. **Sisters Three:** the Fates.

68-69. **hovel-post:** post supporting a shed.
76-77. **it . . . child.** Launcelot reverses the usual form of the proverb, "It is a wise child that knows his own father."
85-86. **child . . . be.** Alluding to second childhood.
93. **what a beard.** Gobbo mistakes Launcelot's long hair for a beard; perhaps Launcelot has bowed his head deeply.
95. **fill-horse:** shaft horse.
96-97. **grows backward:** (1) gets shorter instead of longer; (2) grows at the wrong end (referring to Gobbo's error).
103. **set . . . rest:** boldly resolved (from a term meaning "stake everything" in the card game primero).
105. **halter:** hangman's noose.   106. **tell:** count.
108. **give me:** give (see note on I.iii.84).
109. **liveries:** distinctive garb worn by a gentleman's servants.

The Merchant
of Venice
II.ii

Bass. You may do so, but let it be so hasted that supper be ready at the farthest by five of the 115 clock. See these letters deliver'd, put the liveries to making, and desire Gratiano to come anon to my lodging. [*Exit one of his men.*]

Laun. To him, father.

Gob. God bless your worship! 120

Bass. Gramercy, wouldst thou aught with me?

Gob. Here's my son, sir, a poor boy—

Laun. Not a poor boy, sir, but the rich Jew's man, that would, sir, as my father shall specify—

Gob. He hath a great infection, sir, as one would say, to serve— 126

Laun. Indeed the short and the long is, I serve the Jew, and have a desire, as my father shall specify—

Gob. His master and he (saving your worship's reverence) are scarce cater-cousins— 131

Laun. To be brief, the very truth is that the Jew, having done me wrong, doth cause me, as my father, being I hope an old man, shall frutify unto you—

Gob. I have here a dish of doves that I would bestow upon your worship, and my suit is— 136

Laun. In very brief, the suit is impertinent to myself, as your worship shall know by this honest old man, and though I say it, though old man, yet poor man, my father. 140

Bass. One speak for both. What would you?

Laun. Serve you, sir.

Gob. That is the very defect of the matter, sir.

Bass. I know thee well, thou hast obtain'd thy suit.

Shylock thy master spoke with me this day, 145
And hath preferr'd thee, if it be preferment
To leave a rich Jew's service, to become
The follower of so poor a gentleman.

Laun. The old proverb is very well parted between my master Shylock and you, sir: you have the grace of God, sir, and he hath enough. 151

Bass. Thou speak'st it well. Go, father, with thy son.
Take leave of thy old master, and inquire
My lodging out.—Give him a livery
More guarded than his fellows'; see it done. 155

Laun. Father, in. I cannot get a service, no, I have ne'er a tongue in my head, well! [*Looking on his palm.*] If any man in Italy have a fairer table, which doth offer to swear upon a book, I shall have good fortune. Go to, here's a simple line of 160

121. **Gramercy:** many thanks.
125. **infection:** blunder for *affection*, i.e. desire.
131. **cater-cousins:** good friends.
134. **frutify:** blunder for *certify* (?) or *notify* (?).
137. **impertinent.** He means the opposite.
143. **defect:** blunder for *effect*, i.e. gist.
144. **suit:** (1) request; (2) livery.
146. **preferr'd thee:** put you forward, recommended you.   **preferment:** being put forward, i.e. a promotion.
149. **proverb:** i.e. "He that hath the grace of God hath enough."
parted: divided.
155. **guarded:** ornamented (with braid or the like). It has been suggested that Bassanio takes Launcelot into service as his fool, who would wear a motley coat "guarded" with yellow.
158. **table:** part of the palm of the hand.
159. **swear . . . book:** i.e. tell the truth (about the future); with play on placing the palm upon a Bible for oath-taking.
160. **simple:** plain, unremarkable (ironic).

life! Here's a small trifle of wives! Alas, fifteen wives is nothing! Aleven widows and nine maids is a simple coming-in for one man. And then to scape drowning thrice, and to be in peril of my life with the edge of a feather-bed, here are simple scapes. 165 Well, if Fortune be a woman, she's a good wench for this gear. Father, come, I'll take my leave of the Jew in the twinkling. *Exit Clown [with Old Gobbo].*

Bass. I pray thee, good Leonardo, think on this: These things being bought and orderly bestowed, 170 Return in haste, for I do feast to-night My best esteem'd acquaintance. Hie thee, go.

Leon. My best endeavors shall be done herein.

Enter GRATIANO.

Gra. Where's your master?

Leon.   Yonder, sir, he walks. *Exit Leonardo.*

Gra. Signior Bassanio! 175

Bass. Gratiano!

Gra. I have suit to you.

Bass.   You have obtain'd it.

Gra. You must not deny me; I must go with you to Belmont.

Bass. Why then you must. But hear thee, Gratiano: 180
Thou art too wild, too rude, and bold of voice—
Parts that become thee happily enough,
And in such eyes as ours appear not faults,
But where thou art not known, why, there they show
Something too liberal. Pray thee take pain 185
To allay with some cold drops of modesty
Thy skipping spirit, lest through thy wild behavior
I be misconst'red in the place I go to,
And lose my hopes.

Gra.   Signior Bassanio, hear me:
If I do not put on a sober habit, 190
Talk with respect, and swear but now and then,
Wear prayer-books in my pocket, look demurely,
Nay more, while grace is saying hood mine eyes
Thus with my hat, and sigh and say amen,
Use all the observance of civility, 195
Like one well studied in a sad ostent
To please his grandam, never trust me more.

Bass. Well, we shall see your bearing.

Gra. Nay, but I bar to-night, you shall not gauge me
By what we do to-night.

Bass.   No, that were pity. 200
I would entreat you rather to put on
Your boldest suit of mirth, for we have friends
That purpose merriment. But fare you well,
I have some business.

Gra. And I must to Lorenzo and the rest, 205
But we will visit you at supper-time. *Exeunt.*

162. **Aleven:** eleven (a variant spelling that occurs a number of times in Shakespeare's texts).
163. **simple coming-in:** modest income (with a ribald innuendo).
165. **edge . . . feather-bed:** i.e. some sexual escapade.
167. **gear:** business.   182. **Parts:** qualities.
185. **liberal:** unrestrained.   188. **misconst'red:** misconstrued.
190. **habit:** behavior, demeanor (with play on "suit"; cf. line 201).
193-94. **hood . . . hat.** Hats were worn during meals but removed during grace.   196. **sad ostent:** sober appearance.
197. **more:** again..

[SCENE III]

Enter JESSICA *and the Clown* [LAUNCELOT].

Jes. I am sorry thou wilt leave my father so.
Our house is hell, and thou, a merry devil,
Didst rob it of some taste of tediousness.
But fare thee well, there is a ducat for thee,
And, Launcelot, soon at supper shalt thou see   5
Lorenzo, who is thy new master's guest.
Give him this letter, do it secretly,
And so farewell. I would not have my father
See me in talk with thee.
 Laun. Adieu, tears exhibit my tongue. Most   10
beautiful pagan, most sweet Jew! if a Christian do
not play the knave and get thee, I am much deceiv'd.
But adieu, these foolish drops do something drown
my manly spirit. Adieu!   14
 Jes. Farewell, good Launcelot. [*Exit Launcelot.*]
Alack, what heinous sin is it in me
To be ashamed to be my father's child!
But though I am a daughter to his blood,
I am not to his manners. O Lorenzo,
If thou keep promise, I shall end this strife,   20
Become a Christian and thy loving wife. *Exit.*

[SCENE IV]

Enter GRATIANO, LORENZO, SALERIO, *and* SOLANIO.

Lor. Nay, we will slink away in supper-time,
Disguise us at my lodging, and return
All in an hour.
 Gra. We have not made good preparation.   4
 Sal. We have not spoke us yet of torch-bearers.
 Sol. 'Tis vile, unless it may be quaintly ordered,
And better in my mind not undertook.
 Lor. 'Tis now but four of clock, we have two hours
To furnish us.

Enter LAUNCELOT [*with a letter*].

    Friend Launcelot, what's the news?
 Laun. And it shall please you to break up this, it
shall seem to signify.   11
 Lor. I know the hand; in faith, 'tis a fair hand,
And whiter than the paper it writ on
Is the fair hand that writ.
 Gra.   Love-news, in faith.
 Laun. By your leave, sir.   15
 Lor. Whither goest thou?
 Laun. Marry, sir, to bid my old master the Jew
to sup to-night with my new master the Christian.
 Lor. Hold here, take this. Tell gentle Jessica
I will not fail her, speak it privately. *Exit Clown.*   20
Go, gentlemen,
Will you prepare you for this masque to-night?

I am provided of a torch-bearer.
 Sal. Ay, marry, I'll be gone about it straight.
 Sol. And so will I.
 Lor.   Meet me and Gratiano   25
At Gratiano's lodging some hour hence.
 Sal. 'Tis good we do so.   *Exit* [*with Solanio*].
 Gra. Was not that letter from fair Jessica?
 Lor. I must needs tell thee all. She hath directed
How I shall take her from her father's house,   30
What gold and jewels she is furnish'd with,
What page's suit she hath in readiness.
If e'er the Jew her father come to heaven,
It will be for his gentle daughter's sake,
And never dare misfortune cross her foot,   35
Unless she do it under this excuse,
That she is issue to a faithless Jew.
Come go with me, peruse this as thou goest.
Fair Jessica shall be my torch-bearer.   *Exeunt.*

[SCENE V]

Enter [SHYLOCK *the*] *Jew and his man that was, the
Clown* [LAUNCELOT].

Shy. Well, thou shalt see, thy eyes shall be thy
  judge,
The difference of old Shylock and Bassanio.—
What, Jessica!—Thou shalt not gurmandize,
As thou hast done with me—What, Jessica!—
And sleep and snore, and rend apparel out—   5
Why, Jessica, I say!
 Laun.   Why, Jessica!
 Shy. Who bids thee call? I do not bid thee call.
 Laun. Your worship was wont to tell me I could
do nothing without bidding.

Enter JESSICA.

 Jes. Call you? what is your will?   10
 Shy. I am bid forth to supper, Jessica.
There are my keys. But wherefore should I go?
I am not bid for love, they flatter me,
But yet I'll go in hate, to feed upon
The prodigal Christian. Jessica, my girl,   15
Look to my house. I am right loath to go;
There is some ill a-brewing towards my rest,
For I did dream of money-bags to-night.
 Laun. I beseech you, sir, go. My young master
doth expect your reproach.   20
 Shy. So do I his.
 Laun. And they have conspir'd together. I will
not say you shall see a masque, but if you do, then
it was not for nothing that my nose fell a-bleeding

II.iii. Location: Venice. Shylock's house.
5. **soon at supper:** at supper this evening.
10. **exhibit:** blunder for *inhibit.* 19. **manners:** character.

II.iv. Location: Venice. A street.
5. **spoke . . . of:** yet bespoken.
6. **quaintly ordered:** skillfully managed. 10. **break up:** open.
19. **Hold here.** Synonymous with *take this.*

24. **straight:** straightway, at once.
34. **gentle.** With pun on *Gentile.* 35. **foot:** i.e. path, way.
37. **faithless:** unbelieving.

II.v. Location: Venice. Before Shylock's house.
o.s.d. **man that was:** former servant.
3. **gurmandize:** gormandize.
5. **rend apparel out;** ruin your clothes by rough use.
18. **dream of money-bags.** It was considered unlucky to dream of
money. **to-night:** last night.
20. **reproach:** blunder for *approach,* i.e. coming.
24. **nose fell a-bleeding.** A sign of bad luck.

The Merchant
of Venice
II.v

on Black Monday last at six a' clock i' th' morn- 25
ing, falling out that year on Ash We'n'sday was four
year in th' afternoon.

Shy. What, are there masques? Hear you me,
    Jessica:
Lock up my doors, and when you hear the drum
And the vile squealing of the wry-neck'd fife, 30
Clamber not you up to the casements then,
Nor thrust your head into the public street
To gaze on Christian fools with varnish'd faces;
But stop my house's ears, I mean my casements;
Let not the sound of shallow fopp'ry enter 35
My sober house. By Jacob's staff I swear
I have no mind of feasting forth to-night;
But I will go. Go you before me, sirrah,
Say I will come.

Laun. I will go before, sir. Mistress, look out at
window for all this— 41
        There will come a Christian by,
        Will be worth a Jewess' eye. [*Exit.*]

Shy. What says that fool of Hagar's offspring, ha?

Jes. His words were "Farewell, mistress!"—noth-
    ing else. 45

Shy. The patch is kind enough, but a huge feeder,
Snail-slow in profit, and he sleeps by day
More than the wild-cat. Drones hive not with me,
Therefore I part with him, and part with him
To one that I would have him help to waste 50
His borrowed purse. Well, Jessica, go in,
Perhaps I will return immediately.
Do as I bid you, shut doors after you;
Fast bind, fast find—
A proverb never stale in thrifty mind. *Exit.* 55

Jes. Farewell, and if my fortune be not cross'd,
I have a father, you a daughter, lost. *Exit.*

[SCENE VI]

Enter [*two of*] *the masquers,* GRATIANO *and* SALERIO.

Gra. This is the penthouse under which Lorenzo
Desir'd us to make stand.

Sal.   His hour is almost past.

Gra. And it is marvel he out-dwells his hour,
For lovers ever run before the clock.

Sal. O, ten times faster Venus' pigeons fly 5
To seal love's bonds new made, than they are wont
To keep obliged faith unforfeited!

Gra. That ever holds. Who riseth from a feast
With that keen appetite that he sits down?
Where is the horse that doth untread again 10
His tedious measures with the unbated fire
That he did pace them first? All things that are,
Are with more spirit chased than enjoy'd.
How like a younger or a prodigal
The scarfed bark puts from her native bay, 15
Hugg'd and embraced by the strumpet wind!
How like the prodigal doth she return,
With over-weather'd ribs and ragged sails,
Lean, rent, and beggar'd by the strumpet wind!

Enter LORENZO.

Sal. Here comes Lorenzo, more of this hereafter.

Lor. Sweet friends, your patience for my long
    abode; 21
Not I but my affairs have made you wait.
When you shall please to play the thieves for wives,
I'll watch as long for you then. Approach,
Here dwells my father Jew. Ho! who's within? 25

[*Enter*] JESSICA *above* [*in boy's clothes*].

Jes. Who are you? tell me for more certainty,
Albeit I'll swear that I do know your tongue.

Lor. Lorenzo, and thy love.

Jes. Lorenzo, certain, and my love indeed,
For who love I so much? And now who knows 30
But you, Lorenzo, whether I am yours?

Lor. Heaven and thy thoughts are witness that
    thou art.

Jes. Here, catch this casket, it is worth the pains.
I am glad 'tis night, you do not look on me,
For I am much asham'd of my exchange. 35
But love is blind, and lovers cannot see
The pretty follies that themselves commit,
For if they could, Cupid himself would blush
To see me thus transformed to a boy. 39

Lor. Descend, for you must be my torch-bearer.

Jes. What, must I hold a candle to my shames?
They in themselves, good sooth, are too too light.
Why, 'tis an office of discovery, love,
And I should be obscur'd.

Lor.   So are you, sweet,
Even in the lovely garnish of a boy. 45
But come at once,
For the close night doth play the runaway,
And we are stay'd for at Bassanio's feast.

Jes. I will make fast the doors, and gild myself
With some moe ducats, and be with you straight.
                        [*Exit above.*]

Gra. Now by my hood, a gentle, and no Jew. 51

---

25. **Black Monday:** Easter Monday (so called because of a particular Easter Monday, in 1360, when bitterly cold weather caused many deaths). Launcelot's nonsense in this passage derides Shylock's superstition about his dream.
30. **wry-neck'd fife:** fife-player (or fife played) with head twisted to one side. Like *drum* in line 29, *fife* can refer either to the instrument or to the player. 33. **varnish'd faces:** i.e. masks.
35. **fopp'ry:** foolishness.
36. **Jacob's staff.** See Genesis 32:10 and Hebrews 11:21.
41. **for all this:** i.e. despite all that Shylock has said.
44. **Hagar's offspring.** Hagar was a Gentile, and Ishmael, her son by Abraham, became an outcast. 46. **patch:** fool.
47. **profit:** improvement, proficiency.

II.vi. Location: Scene continues.
1. **penthouse:** projecting roof offering shelter from the weather.
5. **Venus' pigeons:** the doves which drew Venus' chariot.
7. **obliged:** pledged.

10. **untread:** retrace.
14. **younger:** i.e. younger son. Cf. the parable of the prodigal son in Luke 15.
15. **scarfed:** decked with streamers (suggesting the extravagant dress of the prodigal).
16. **Hugg'd . . . wind.** Continuing the parallel between the ship and the prodigal; cf. *ribs* (line 18) and *beggar'd* (line 19).
21. **abode:** delay. 25. **father:** father-in-law. 35. **exchange:** i.e. change into boy's clothes.
42. **light:** wanton (with play on "clear").
43. **'tis . . . discovery:** i.e. the whole function of torch-bearing is to bring things to view. 45. **garnish:** dress. 47. **close:** secret.
51. **gentle.** With pun on *Gentile* (as at II.iv.34).

Lor.   Beshrow me but I love her heartily,
For she is wise, if I can judge of her,
And fair she is, if that mine eyes be true,
And true she is, as she hath prov'd herself;   55
And therefore, like herself, wise, fair, and true,
Shall she be placed in my constant soul.

                    Enter JESSICA.

What, art thou come? On, [gentlemen], away!
Our masquing mates by this time for us stay.
                    Exit [with Jessica and Salerio].

                    Enter ANTONIO.

Ant.   Who's there?   60
Gra.   Signior Antonio!
Ant.   Fie, fie, Gratiano, where are all the rest?
'Tis nine a' clock—our friends all stay for you.
No masque to-night, the wind is come about,
Bassanio presently will go aboard.   65
I have sent twenty out to seek for you.
Gra.   I am glad on't. I desire no more delight
Than to be under sail, and gone to-night.   *Exeunt.*

                    [SCENE VII]

[*Flourish cornets.*] *Enter* PORTIA *with* [*the* PRINCE OF]
MOROCCO *and both their* TRAINS.

Por.   Go, draw aside the curtains and discover
The several caskets to this noble prince.
Now make your choice.
Mor.   This first, of gold, who this inscription bears,
"Who chooseth me shall gain what many men de-
    sire";   5
The second, silver, which this promise carries,
"Who chooseth me shall get as much as he deserves";
This third, dull lead, with warning all as blunt,
"Who chooseth me must give and hazard all he hath."
How shall I know if I do choose the right?   10
Por.   The one of them contains my picture, Prince:
If you choose that, then I am yours withal.
Mor.   Some god direct my judgment! Let me see,
I will survey th' inscriptions back again.
What says this leaden casket?   15
"Who chooseth me must give and hazard all he hath."
Must give—for what? for·lead, hazard for lead?
This casket threatens. Men that hazard all
Do it in hope of fair advantages;
A golden mind stoops not to shows of dross.   20
I'll then nor give nor hazard aught for lead.
What says the silver with her virgin hue?
"Who chooseth me shall get as much as he deserves."
As much as he deserves! pause there, Morocco,
And weigh thy value with an even hand.   25
If thou beest rated by thy estimation,
Thou dost deserve enough, and yet enough

May not extend so far as to the lady;
And yet to be afeard of my deserving
Were but a weak disabling of myself.   30
As much as I deserve! why, that's the lady.
I do in birth deserve her, and in fortunes,
In graces, and in qualities of breeding;
But more than these, in love I do deserve.
What if I stray'd no farther, but chose here?   35
Let's see once more this saying grav'd in gold:
"Who chooseth me shall gain what many men desire."
Why, that's the lady, all the world desires her.
From the four corners of the earth they come
To kiss this shrine, this mortal breathing saint.   40
The Hyrcanian deserts and the vasty wilds
Of wide Arabia are as throughfares now
For princes to come view fair Portia.
The watery kingdom, whose ambitious head
Spets in the face of heaven, is no bar   45
To stop the foreign spirits, but they come
As o'er a brook to see fair Portia.
One of these three contains her heavenly picture.
Is't like that lead contains her? 'Twere damnation
To think so base a thought; it were too gross   50
To rib her cerecloth in the obscure grave.
Or shall I think in silver she's immur'd,
Being ten times undervalued to tried gold?
O sinful thought! never so rich a gem
Was set in worse than gold. They have in England   56
A coin that bears the figure of an angel
Stamp'd in gold, but that's insculp'd upon;
But here an angel in a golden bed
Lies all within. Deliver me the key.
Here do I choose, and thrive I as I may!   60
Por.   There take it, Prince, and if my form lie there,
Then I am yours.   [*He unlocks the golden casket.*]
Mor.   O hell! what have we here?
A carrion Death, within whose empty eye
There is a written scroll! I'll read the writing.
[*Reads.*] "All that glisters is not gold,   65
            Often have you heard that told;
            Many a man his life hath sold
            But my outside to behold.
            Gilded [tombs] do worms infold.
            Had you been as wise as bold,   70
            Young in limbs, in judgment old,
            Your answer had not been inscroll'd.
            Fare you well, your suit is cold."
        Cold indeed, and labor lost:
        Then farewell heat, and welcome frost!   75
Portia, adieu. I have too griev'd a heart
To take a tedious leave; thus losers part.
                    Exit [with his Train].

52. **Beshrow:** beshrew, evil befall (a weakened curse).
65. **presently:** at once.

II.vii. Location: Belmont. Portia's house.
1. **discover:** reveal.   8. **all as:** equally.   12. **withal:** therewith.
25. **even:** impartial.   26. **estimation:** valuation.

30. **disabling:** undervaluing.   40. **shrine:** image.
41. **Hyrcanian:** pertaining to a desolate area southeast of the Caspian
Sea.   **deserts:** unpopulated areas, wastes.
42. **throughfares:** thoroughfares.
51. **rib:** enclose.   **cerecloth:** shroud.
53. **Being . . . gold:** which is worth only one tenth as much as.
56. **angel:** a gold coin which bore the figure of the archangel Michael
treading on the dragon.
57. **insculp'd upon:** engraved on the surface.
63. **Death:** death's-head.
72. **inscroll'd:** set down here; i.e. you would have made a different
choice and received a different answer.

265

Por. A gentle riddance. Draw the curtains, go.
Let all of his complexion choose me so.   *Exeunt.*

[SCENE VIII]

Enter SALERIO *and* SOLANIO.

Sal. Why, man, I saw Bassanio under sail,
With him is Gratiano gone along;
And in their ship I am sure Lorenzo is not.
Sol. The villain Jew with outcries rais'd the Duke,
Who went with him to search Bassanio's ship.   5
Sal. He came too late, the ship was under sail,
But there the Duke was given to understand
That in a gondilo were seen together
Lorenzo and his amorous Jessica.
Besides, Antonio certified the Duke   10
They were not with Bassanio in his ship.
Sol. I never heard a passion so confus'd,
So strange, outrageous, and so variable
As the dog Jew did utter in the streets.
"My daughter! O my ducats! O my daughter!   15
Fled with a Christian! O my Christian ducats!
Justice! the law! my ducats, and my daughter!
A sealed bag, two sealed bags of ducats,
Of double ducats, stol'n from me by my daughter!
And jewels, two stones, two rich and precious stones,
Stol'n by my daughter! Justice! find the girl,   21
She hath the stones upon her, and the ducats."
Sal. Why, all the boys in Venice follow him,
Crying, his stones, his daughter, and his ducats.
Sol. Let good Antonio look he keep his day,   25
Or he shall pay for this.
Sal.   Marry, well rememb'red.
I reason'd with a Frenchman yesterday,
Who told me, in the Narrow Seas that part
The French and English, there miscarried
A vessel of our country richly fraught.   30
I thought upon Antonio when he told me,
And wish'd in silence that it were not his.
Sol. You were best to tell Antonio what you hear,
Yet do not suddenly, for it may grieve him.
Sal. A kinder gentleman treads not the earth.   35
I saw Bassanio and Antonio part:
Bassanio told him he would make some speed
Of his return; he answered, "Do not so,
[Slubber] not business for my sake, Bassanio,
But stay the very riping of the time;   40
And for the Jew's bond which he hath of me,
Let it not enter in your mind of love.
Be merry, and employ your chiefest thoughts
To courtship, and such fair ostents of love
As shall conveniently become you there."   45
And even there, his eye being big with tears,
Turning his face, he put his hand behind him,

And with affection wondrous sensible
He wrung Bassanio's hand, and so they parted.
Sol. I think he only loves the world for him.   50
I pray thee let us go and find him out
And quicken his embraced heaviness
With some delight or other.
Sal.   Do we so.   *Exeunt.*

[SCENE IX]

Enter NERISSA *and a* SERVITOR.

Ner. Quick, quick, I pray thee, draw the curtain
        straight;
The Prince of Arragon hath ta'en his oath,
And comes to his election presently.

[*Flourish cornets.*]   *Enter* [*the* PRINCE OF] ARRAGON,
his TRAIN, *and* PORTIA.

Por. Behold, there stand the caskets, noble Prince·
If you choose that wherein I am contain'd,   5
Straight shall our nuptial rites be solemniz'd;
But if you fail, without more speech, my lord,
You must be gone from hence immediately.
Ar. I am enjoin'd by oath to observe three things:
First, never to unfold to any one   10
Which casket 'twas I chose; next, if I fail
Of the right casket, never in my life
To woo a maid in way of marriage;
Lastly,
If I do fail in fortune of my choice,   15
Immediately to leave you, and be gone.
Por. To these injunctions every one doth swear
That comes to hazard for my worthless self.
Ar. And so have I address'd me. Fortune now
To my heart's hope! Gold, silver, and base lead.   20
"Who chooseth me must give and hazard all he hath."
You shall look fairer ere I give or hazard.
What says the golden chest? Ha, let me see:
"Who chooseth me shall gain what many men desire."
What many men desire! That many may be meant   25
By the fool multitude that choose by show,
Not learning more than the fond eye doth teach,
Which pries not to th' interior, but like the martlet
Builds in the weather on the outward wall,
Even in the force and road of casualty.   30
I will not choose what many men desire,
Because I will not jump with common spirits,
And rank me with the barbarous multitudes.
Why then to thee, thou silver treasure house,
Tell me once more what title thou dost bear: 35
"Who chooseth me shall get as much as he deserves."
And well said too; for who shall go about

8. **gondilo:** gondola.   9. **amorous:** loving.
12. **passion:** passionate outburst.   27. **reason'd:** talked.
28. **Narrow Seas:** English Channel.   29. **miscarried:** perished.
34. **suddenly:** without preparation.
39. **Slubber:** hurry over, do in a slovenly manner.   41. **for:** as for.
42. **enter . . . love:** i.e. intrude into your thoughts of love.
44. **ostents:** shows.   45. **conveniently:** properly.

48. **sensible:** evident, intense.   50. **for him:** on his account.
52. **quicken . . . heaviness:** enliven the sorrow he clings to.

II.ix. Location: Belmont. Portia's house.
1. **straight:** immediately.   3. **election:** choice.   **presently:** at once.
19. **address'd me:** prepared myself.   26. **By:** for.
27. **fond:** foolish.   28. **martlet:** martin.
29. **in the weather:** exposed to the elements.
30. **force:** power.   **casualty:** mischance.   32. **jump:** agree.

To cozen fortune, and be honorable
Without the stamp of merit? Let none presume
To wear an undeserved dignity.   40
O that estates, degrees, and offices
Were not deriv'd corruptly, and that clear honor
Were purchas'd by the merit of the wearer!
How many then should cover that stand bare?
How many be commanded that command?   45
How much low peasantry would then be gleaned
From the true seed of honor? and how much honor
Pick'd from the chaff and ruin of the times
To be new varnish'd? Well, but to my choice:
"Who chooseth me shall get as much as he deserves."
I will assume desert. Give me a key for this,   51
And instantly unlock my fortunes here.

[_He unlocks the silver casket._]

Por. Too long a pause for that which you find
    there.
_Ar._ What's here? the portrait of a blinking idiot,
Presenting me a schedule! I will read it.   55
How much unlike art thou to Portia!
How much unlike my hopes and my deservings!
"Who chooseth me shall have as much as he de-
    serves"!
Did I deserve no more than a fool's head?
Is that my prize? Are my deserts no better?   60
Por. To offend and judge are distinct offices,
And of opposed natures.
_Ar._   What is here?
[_Reads._] "The fire seven times tried this:
        Seven times tried that judgment is,
        That did never choose amiss.
        Some there be that shadows kiss,   65
        Such have but a shadow's bliss.
        There be fools alive, iwis,
        Silver'd o'er, and so was this.
        Take what wife you will to bed,   70
        I will ever be your head.
        So be gone, you are sped."
Still more fool I shall appear
By the time I linger here.
With one fool's head I came to woo,   75
But I go away with two.
Sweet, adieu. I'll keep my oath,
Patiently to bear my wroth.

[_Exit with his Train._]

Por. Thus hath the candle sing'd the moth.
O, these deliberate fools, when they do choose,   80
They have the wisdom by their wit to lose.

Ner. The ancient saying is no heresy,
Hanging and wiving goes by destiny.
Por. Come draw the curtain, Nerissa.

Enter MESSENGER.

Mess. Where is my lady?
Por.   Here; what would my lord?   85
Mess. Madam, there is alighted at your gate
A young Venetian, one that comes before
To signify th' approaching of his lord,
From whom he bringeth sensible regreets:
To wit (besides commends and courteous breath),   90
Gifts of rich value. Yet I have not seen
So likely an embassador of love.
A day in April never came so sweet,
To show how costly summer was at hand,
As this fore-spurrer comes before his lord.   95
Por. No more, I pray thee. I am half afeard
Thou wilt say anon he is some kin to thee,
Thou spend'st such high-day wit in praising him.
Come, come, Nerissa, for I long to see
Quick Cupid's post that comes so mannerly.   100
Ner. Bassanio, Lord Love, if thy will it be!

Exeunt.

[ACT III, SCENE I]

[_Enter_] SOLANIO _and_ SALERIO.

Sol. Now what news on the Rialto?
Sal. Why, yet it lives there uncheck'd that Antonio hath a ship of rich lading wrack'd on the Narrow Seas; the Goodwins I think they call the place,
a very dangerous flat, and fatal, where the carcasses   5
of many a tall ship lie buried, as they say, if my
gossip Report be an honest woman of her word.
Sol. I would she were as lying a gossip in that
as ever knapp'd ginger or made her neighbors believe
she wept for the death of a third husband. But   10
it is true, without any slips of prolixity, or crossing the
plain highway of talk, that the good Antonio, the
honest Antonio—O that I had a title good enough to
keep his name company!—
Sal. Come, the full stop.   15
Sol. Ha, what sayest thou? Why, the end is,
he hath lost a ship.
Sal. I would it might prove the end of his losses.
Sol. Let me say amen betimes, lest the devil
cross my prayer, for here he comes in the likeness of
a Jew.   21

---

38. **cozen:** cheat. 39. **stamp:** official seal (as on a document).
41. **estates:** status. **degrees:** ranks.
42. **deriv'd:** inherited, gained. **clear:** illustrious.
44. **cover . . . bare:** wear their hats, who must now bare their heads
(in the presence of their social superiors).
45. **be . . . command:** become servants instead of masters.
46. **gleaned:** separated. 47. **seed of honor:** nobility.
48. **ruin:** refuse. 51. **assume:** claim (in a bad sense).
55. **schedule:** paper with writing.
61–62. **To . . . natures:** i.e. the offender should not judge his own
case. 68. **iwis:** certainly.
71. **I . . . head:** i.e. you will always be a fool.
72. **sped:** taken care of (in a bad sense).
73–74. **Still . . . here:** i.e. the longer I stay here, the greater fool I
will appear to be. 78. **wroth:** unhappy lot (a variant of _ruth_).
80. **deliberate:** calculating.

89. **sensible regreets:** tangible greetings. 90. **breath:** speech.
91. **Yet:** up till now.
92. **likely:** promising. **embassador:** ambassador.
94. **costly:** rich, lavish.
98. **high-day:** holiday, i.e. appropriate for some special occasion.
100. **post:** messenger.

III.i. Location: Venice. A street.
2. **uncheck'd:** unhindered, i.e. not denied.
4. **Goodwins:** Goodwin Sands, off the mouth of the Thames.
6–7. **my gossip Report:** i.e. Dame Rumor. _Gossip_, literally "godparent," was used of a female crony or confidante and thus developed
its present sense. 9. **knapp'd:** chewed.
11. **slips of prolixity:** lapses into prolixity; or perhaps (as Kittredge
suggests), wordy lies (_slip_ can mean "false coin").
11–12. **crossing . . . talk:** departing from plain speech.

Enter SHYLOCK.

How now, Shylock, what news among the merchants?

Shy. You knew, none so well, none so well as you, of my daughter's flight. 25

Sal. That's certain. I for my part knew the tailor that made the wings she flew withal.

Sol. And Shylock for his own part knew the bird was flidge, and then it is the complexion of them all to leave the dam. 30

Shy. She is damn'd for it.

Sal. That's certain, if the devil may be her judge.

Shy. My own flesh and blood to rebel!

Sol. Out upon it, old carrion, rebels it at these years? 36

Shy. I say, my daughter is my flesh and my blood.

Sal. There is more difference between thy flesh and hers than between jet and ivory, more between your bloods than there is between red wine and 41 Rhenish. But tell us, do you hear whether Antonio have had any loss at sea or no?

Shy. There I have another bad match. A bankrout, a prodigal, who dare scarce show his head on 45 the Rialto; a beggar, that was us'd to come so smug upon the mart: let him look to his bond. He was wont to call me usurer, let him look to his bond. He was wont to lend money for a Christian cur'sy, let him look to his bond. 50

Sal. Why, I am sure if he forfeit thou wilt not take his flesh. What's that good for?

Shy. To bait fish withal—if it will feed nothing else, it will feed my revenge. He hath disgrac'd me, and hind'red me half a million, laugh'd at my 55 losses, mock'd at my gains, scorn'd my nation, thwarted my bargains, cool'd my friends, heated mine enemies; and what's his reason? I am a Jew. Hath not a Jew eyes? Hath not a Jew hands, organs, dimensions, senses, affections, passions; fed with 60 the same food, hurt with the same weapons, subject to the same diseases, heal'd by the same means, warm'd and cool'd by the same winter and summer, as a Christian is? If you prick us, do we not bleed? If you tickle us, do we not laugh? If you 65 poison us, do we not die? And if you wrong us, shall we not revenge? If we are like you in the rest, we will resemble you in that. If a Jew wrong a Christian, what is his humility? Revenge. If a Christian wrong a Jew, what should his sufferance be by Chris- 70 tian example? Why, revenge. The villainy you teach me, I will execute, and it shall go hard but I will better the instruction.

Enter a [SERVING]MAN *from Antonio.*

[*Serv.*] Gentlemen, my master Antonio is at his house, and desires to speak with you both. 75

Sal. We have been up and down to seek him.

Enter TUBAL.

Sol. Here comes another of the tribe; a third cannot be match'd, unless the devil himself turn Jew.
Exeunt Gentlemen [*Solanio and Salerio,
with Servingman*].

Shy. How now, Tubal, what news from Genoa? Hast thou found my daughter? 80

Tub. I often came where I did hear of her, but cannot find her.

Shy. Why, there, there, there, there! A diamond gone, cost me two thousand ducats in Frankford! The curse never fell upon our nation till 85 now, I never felt it till now. Two thousand ducats in that, and other precious, precious jewels. I would my daughter were dead at my foot, and the jewels in her ear! Would she were hears'd at my foot, and the ducats in her coffin! No news 90 of them? Why, so—and I know not what's spent in the search. Why, thou loss upon loss! the thief gone with so much, and so much to find the thief, and no satisfaction, no revenge, nor no ill luck stirring but what lights a' my shoulders, no sighs but a' my breathing, no tears but a' my shedding. 96

Tub. Yes, other men have ill luck too. Antonio, as I heard in Genoa—

Shy. What, what, what? ill luck, ill luck?

Tub. Hath an argosy cast away, coming from Tripolis. 101

Shy. I thank God, I thank God. Is it true, is it true?

Tub. I spoke with some of the sailors that escap'd the wrack. 105

Shy. I thank thee, good Tubal, good news, good news! Ha, ha! [Heard] in Genoa?

Tub. Your daughter spent in Genoa, as I heard, one night fourscore ducats. 109

Shy. Thou stick'st a dagger in me. I shall never see my gold again. Fourscore ducats at a sitting, fourscore ducats!

Tub. There came divers of Antonio's creditors in my company to Venice that swear he cannot choose but break. 115

Shy. I am very glad of it. I'll plague him, I'll torture him. I am glad of it.

Tub. One of them show'd me a ring that he had of your daughter for a monkey. 119

Shy. Out upon her! Thou torturest me, Tubal. It was my turkis, I had it of Leah when I was a bachelor. I would not have given it for a wilderness of monkeys.

Tub. But Antonio is certainly undone. 124

Shy. Nay, that's true, that's very true. Go, Tubal,

---

27. **wings.** With play on *wing* = an ornamental flap above the upper end of the sleeve. **withal:** with.
29. **flidge:** fledged, ready to fly. **complexion:** natural tendency.
35-36. **rebels . . . years.** Solanio pretends to misunderstand: "Do you have sensual desires at your age?"
42. **Rhenish:** i.e. white wine. 44. **match:** bargain.
44-45. **bankrout:** bankrupt. 46. **smug:** neat, spruce.
49. **for . . . cur'sy:** out of Christian courtesy.
60. **dimensions:** bodily proportions.
69-70. **his . . . his:** the Christian's . . . the Jew's.
69. **humility:** patient endurance.

78. **match'd:** found to match them.
84-85. **Frankford:** Frankfort, famous for its fairs.
89. **hears'd:** coffined. 95. **a':** of, on.
114-15. **choose but break:** avoid going bankrupt.
121. **turkis:** turquoise.

fee me an officer; bespeak him a fortnight before.
I will have the heart of him if he forfeit, for were
he out of Venice I can make what merchandise I
will.   Go, Tubal, and meet me at our synagogue;
go, good Tubal, at our synagogue, Tubal.   130

Exeunt.

[SCENE II]

Enter BASSANIO, PORTIA, GRATIANO, [NERISSA,] *and all
their* TRAINS.

Por.   I pray you tarry, pause a day or two
Before you hazard, for in choosing wrong
I lose your company; therefore forbear a while.
There's something tells me (but it is not love)
I would not lose you, and you know yourself,   5
Hate counsels not in such a quality.
But lest you should not understand me well—
And yet a maiden hath no tongue but thought—
I would detain you here some month or two
Before you venture for me.   I could teach you   10
How to choose right, but then I am forsworn.
So will I never be, so may you miss me,
But if you do, you'll make me wish a sin,
That I had been forsworn.   Beshrow your eyes,
They have o'erlook'd me and divided me: 15
One half of me is yours, the other half yours—
Mine own, I would say; but if mine, then yours,
And so all yours.   O, these naughty times
Puts bars between the owners and their rights!
And so though yours, not yours.   Prove it so,   20
Let fortune go to hell for it, not I.
I speak too long, but 'tis to peize the time,
To eche it, and to draw it out in length,
To stay you from election.
Bass.   Let me choose,
For as I am, I live upon the rack.   25
Por.   Upon the rack, Bassanio! then confess
What treason there is mingled with your love.
Bass.   None but that ugly treason of mistrust,
Which makes me fear th' enjoying of my love;
There may as well be amity and life   30
'Tween snow and fire, as treason and my love.
Por.   Ay, but I fear you speak upon the rack,
Where men enforced do speak any thing.
Bass.   Promise me life, and I'll confess the truth.
Por.   Well then, confess and live.
Bass.   Confess and love
Had been the very sum of my confession.   36
O happy torment, when my torturer
Doth teach me answers for deliverance!
But let me to my fortune and the caskets.
Por.   Away then!   I am lock'd in one of them;
If you do love me, you will find me out.   41

126. **fee . . . officer:** i.e. engage a sheriff's officer for me.
128. **make what merchandise:** drive what bargain.

III.ii. Location: Belmont. Portia's house.
2. **in choosing:** if you choose.   6. **quality:** manner.
15. **o'erlook'd:** bewitched.   18. **naughty:** wicked.
20. **Prove it so:** should it prove so.   22. **peize:** weigh down, retard.
23. **eche:** eke, augment.
26–27. **confess What treason.** The rack was used to extort confessions
of treason.   28. **mistrust:** doubt, uncertainty.
29. **fear:** feel apprehensive about.

Nerissa and the rest, stand all aloof.
Let music sound while he doth make his choice;
Then if he lose he makes a swan-like end,
Fading in music.   That the comparison   45
May stand more proper, my eye shall be the stream
And wat'ry death-bed for him.   He may win,
And what is music then?   Then music is
Even as the flourish when true subjects bow
To a new-crowned monarch; such it is   50
As are those dulcet sounds in break of day
That creep into the dreaming bridegroom's ear,
And summon him to marriage.   Now he goes,
With no less presence, but with much more love,
Than young Alcides, when he did redeem   55
The virgin tribute paid by howling Troy
To the sea-monster.   I stand for sacrifice;
The rest aloof are the Dardanian wives,
With bleared visages, come forth to view
The issue of th' exploit.   Go, Hercules,   60
Live thou, I live; with much, much more dismay
I view the fight than thou that mak'st the fray.

[*Here music.*]

*A song, the whilst Bassanio comments on the
caskets to himself.*

    Tell me where is fancy bred,
    Or in the heart or in the head?
    How begot, how nourished?   65
      [*All.*] Reply, reply.
    It is engend'red in the [eyes],
    With gazing fed, and fancy dies
    In the cradle where it lies.
    Let us all ring fancy's knell.   70
    I'll begin it.   Ding, dong, bell.
      All.   Ding, dong, bell.

Bass.   So may the outward shows be least them-
selves—
The world is still deceiv'd with ornament.
In law, what plea so tainted and corrupt   75
But, being season'd with a gracious voice,
Obscures the show of evil?   In religion,
What damned error but some sober brow
Will bless it, and approve it with a text,
Hiding the grossness with fair ornament?   80
There is no [vice] so simple but assumes
Some mark of virtue on his outward parts.
How many cowards, whose hearts are all as false
As stairs of sand, wear yet upon their chins
The beards of Hercules and frowning Mars,   85
Who inward search'd, have livers white as milk,

44. **swan-like end.** The swan was thought to sing before dying.
49. **flourish:** fanfare of trumpets.
54. **presence:** nobility of appearance.
54–57. **much . . . monster.** Hercules' motive in rescuing the Trojan
princess Hesione from a sea-monster to which she was to be sacrificed
was not love for her but a desire to possess the horses which Laomedon,
her father, had promised him as a reward.   56. **howling:** lamenting.
58. **Dardanian:** Trojan.   59. **bleared:** weeping.
61. **Live thou:** if you live.   63. **fancy:** love.
67. **engend'red . . . eyes.** The eyes were considered the entry-port of
love.
69. **In the cradle:** (1) in the eyes where it was born; (2) in infancy.
73. **be least themselves:** i.e. falsify the inner reality.
74. **still:** ever, continually.   79. **approve:** prove, confirm.
81. **simple:** unmixed.   83. **all:** just.

The Merchant
of Venice
III.ii

And these assume but valor's excrement
To render them redoubted! Look on beauty,
And you shall see 'tis purchas'd by the weight,
Which therein works a miracle in nature,   90
Making them lightest that wear most of it.
So are those crisped snaky golden locks,
Which [make] such wanton gambols with the wind
Upon supposed fairness, often known
To be the dowry of a second head,   95
The skull that bred them in the sepulchre.
Thus ornament is but the guiled shore
To a most dangerous sea; the beauteous scarf
Veiling an Indian beauty; in a word,
The seeming truth which cunning times put on   100
To entrap the wisest. Therefore then, thou gaudy gold,
Hard food for Midas, I will none of thee;
Nor none of thee, thou pale and common drudge
'Tween man and man; but thou, thou meagre lead,
Which rather threaten'st than dost promise aught,
Thy paleness moves me more than eloquence,   106
And here choose I. Joy be the consequence!
    Por. [*Aside.*] How all the other passions fleet
          to air,
As doubtful thoughts, and rash-embrac'd despair,
And shudd'ring fear, and green-eyed jealousy!   110
O love, be moderate, allay thy ecstasy,
In measure rain thy joy, scant this excess!
I feel too much thy blessing; make it less,
For fear I surfeit.
    Bass.   What find I here?
          [*Opening the leaden casket.*]
Fair Portia's counterfeit! What demigod   115
Hath come so near creation? Move these eyes?
Or whether, riding on the balls of mine,
Seem they in motion? Here are sever'd lips,
Parted with sugar breath; so sweet a bar
Should sunder such sweet friends. Here in her hairs
The painter plays the spider, and hath woven   121
A golden mesh t' entrap the hearts of men
Faster than gnats in cobwebs. But her eyes—
How could he see to do them? Having made one,
Methinks it should have power to steal both his   125
And leave itself unfurnish'd. Yet look how far
The substance of my praise doth wrong this shadow

In underprizing it, so far this shadow
Doth limp behind the substance. Here's the scroll,
The continent and summary of my fortune.   130
[*Reads.*] "You that choose not by the view,
          Chance as fair, and choose as true:
          Since this fortune falls to you,
          Be content, and seek no new.
          If you be well pleas'd with this,   135
          And hold your fortune for your bliss,
          Turn you where your lady is,
          And claim her with a loving kiss."
A gentle scroll. Fair lady, by your leave,
I come by note, to give and to receive.   140
Like one of two contending in a prize,
That thinks he hath done well in people's eyes,
Hearing applause and universal shout,
Giddy in spirit, still gazing in a doubt
Whether those peals of praise be his or no,   145
So, thrice-fair lady, stand I, even so,
As doubtful whether what I see be true,
Until confirm'd, sign'd, ratified by you.
    Por. You see me, Lord Bassanio, where I stand,
Such as I am. Though for myself alone   150
I would not be ambitious in my wish
To wish myself much better, yet for you,
I would be trebled twenty times myself,
A thousand times more fair, ten thousand times more
          rich,
That only to stand high in your account,   155
I might in virtues, beauties, livings, friends,
Exceed account. But the full sum of me
Is sum of something; which, to term in gross,
Is an unlesson'd girl, unschool'd, unpractic'd,
Happy in this, she is not yet so old   160
But she may learn; happier than this,
She is not bred so dull but she can learn;
Happiest of all, is that her gentle spirit
Commits itself to yours to be directed,
As from her lord, her governor, her king.   165
Myself, and what is mine, to you and yours
Is now converted. But now I was the lord
Of this fair mansion, master of my servants,
Queen o'er myself; and even now, but now,
This house, these servants, and this same myself   170
Are yours—my lord's!—I give them with this ring,
Which when you part from, lose, or give away,
Let it presage the ruin of your love,
And be my vantage to exclaim on you.   174
    Bass. Madam, you have bereft me of all words,
Only my blood speaks to you in my veins,
And there is such confusion in my powers,

87. **excrement:** outgrowth (such as beards [see line 85] or fingernails), i.e. external attributes.
88. **render them redoubted:** make themselves feared.
91. **lightest:** most wanton (with obvious wordplay).
92. **crisped:** curled. **snaky:** long and waving (but with a suggestion of the snake's deceptive nature).
94. **supposed fairness:** i.e. a supposedly beautiful woman.
95. **dowry:** possession. **a second:** another. With lines 95–96 cf. Sonnet 68.5–8 (where *second* has its more usual meaning).
97. **guiled:** guileful, treacherous.
99. **Indian:** i.e. dark-complexioned. Elizabethans had a particular dislike for dusky skins.
102. **Midas:** Phrygian king who turned whatever he touched to gold.
103. **common drudge:** public slave (when coined).
106. **Thy paleness.** Stress *Thy*, to give the required contrast with *pale* as applied to silver in line 103. Many editors emend *paleness* to *plainness*, following Theobald.
109. **As:** such as. **doubtful:** fearful.
112. **In . . . joy:** pour out your joy moderately. **scant:** diminish.
115. **counterfeit:** portrait. 117. **Or whether:** or.
118. **sever'd:** separated. 123. **Faster:** more firmly.
126. **unfurnish'd:** i.e. without its mate. **look how far:** however far, as far as.
127. **substance:** i.e. verbal expression. **shadow:** portrait.

128. **underprizing it:** i.e. understating its beauty.
129. **the substance:** i.e. Portia herself. 130. **continent:** container.
132. **Chance as fair:** hazard as fortunately.
140. **note:** authorization in writing (i.e. the scroll). **give . . . receive:** i.e. proffer a kiss and receive one in return. 141. **prize:** competition.
145. **his:** for him. 155. **account:** estimation.
156. **livings:** possessions. 157. **account:** calculation.
158. **Is . . . something:** i.e. adds up to something (how little, her following lines describe). Many editors adopt the Folio reading *nothing* in place of *something*. **term in gross:** state in full.
160. **Happy:** fortunate. 165. **from:** by.
167. **But now:** just now. 173. **ruin:** decay.
174. **vantage:** opportunity. **exclaim on:** accuse, reproach.
177. **powers:** faculties.

As after some oration fairly spoke
By a beloved prince, there doth appear
Among the buzzing pleased multitude,   180
Where every something, being blent together,
Turns to a wild of nothing, save of joy
Express'd and not express'd. But when this ring
Parts from this finger, then parts life from hence;
O then be bold to say Bassanio's dead!   185
    Ner. My lord and lady, it is now our time,
That have stood by and seen our wishes prosper,
To cry good joy. Good joy, my lord and lady!
    Gra. My Lord Bassanio and my gentle lady,
I wish you all the joy that you can wish;   190
For I am sure you can wish none from me;
And when your honors mean to solemnize
The bargain of your faith, I do beseech you
Even at that time I may be married too.   194
    Bass. With all my heart, so thou canst get a wife.
    Gra. I thank your lordship, you have got me one.
My eyes, my lord, can look as swift as yours:
You saw the mistress, I beheld the maid;
You lov'd, I lov'd; for intermission
No more pertains to me, my lord, than you;   200
Your fortune stood upon the caskets there,
And so did mine too as the matter falls;
For wooing here until I sweat again,
And swearing till my very [roof] was dry
With oaths of love, at last, if promise last,   205
I got a promise of this fair one here
To have her love—provided that your fortune
Achiev'd her mistress.
    Por.   Is this true, Nerissa?
    Ner. Madam, it is, so you stand pleas'd withal.
    Bass. And do you, Gratiano, mean good faith?
    Gra. Yes, faith, my lord.   211
    Bass. Our feast shall be much honored in your
        marriage.
    Gra. We'll play with them the first boy for a
thousand ducats.
    Ner. What, and stake down?   215
    Gra. No, we shall ne'er win at that sport, and
stake down.
But who comes here? Lorenzo and his infidel?
What, and my old Venetian friend Salerio?

Enter Lorenzo, Jessica, *and* Salerio, *a messenger
    from Venice.*

    Bass. Lorenzo and Salerio, welcome hither,   220
If that the youth of my new int'rest here
Have power to bid you welcome. By your leave,
I bid my very friends and countrymen,
Sweet Portia, welcome.
    Por.   So do I, my lord,

They are entirely welcome.   225
    Lor. I thank your honor. For my part, my lord,
My purpose was not to have seen you here,
But meeting with Salerio by the way,
He did entreat me, past all saying nay,
To come with him along.
    Sal.   I did, my lord,   230
And I have reason for it. Signior Antonio
Commends him to you.   [*Gives Bassanio a letter.*]
    Bass.   Ere I ope his letter,
I pray you tell me how my good friend doth.
    Sal. Not sick, my lord, unless it be in mind,
Nor well, unless in mind. His letter there   235
Will show you his estate.   [*Bassanio*] *open the letter.*
    Gra. Nerissa, cheer yond stranger, bid her wel-
        come.
Your hand, Salerio. What's the news from Venice?
How doth that royal merchant, good Antonio?
I know he will be glad of our success;   240
We are the Jasons, we have won the fleece.
    Sal. I would you had won the fleece that he hath
lost.
    Por. There are some shrowd contents in yond
        same paper
That steals the color from Bassanio's cheek—
Some dear friend dead, else nothing in the world   245
Could turn so much the constitution
Of any constant man. What, worse and worse!
With leave, Bassanio, I am half yourself,
And I must freely have the half of any thing
That this same paper brings you.
    Bass.   O sweet Portia,   250
Here are a few of the unpleasant'st words
That ever blotted paper! Gentle lady,
When I did first impart my love to you,
I freely told you all the wealth I had
Ran in my veins: I was a gentleman;   255
And then I told you true. And yet, dear lady,
Rating myself at nothing, you shall see
How much I was a braggart: when I told you
My state was nothing, I should then have told you
That I was worse than nothing; for indeed   260
I have engag'd myself to a dear friend,
Engag'd my friend to his mere enemy,
To feed my means. Here is a letter, lady,
The paper as the body of my friend,
And every word in it a gaping wound   265
Issuing life-blood. But is it true, Salerio?
Hath all his ventures fail'd? What, not one hit?
From Tripolis, from Mexico, and England,
From Lisbon, Barbary, and India,
And not one vessel scape the dreadful touch   270
Of merchant-marring rocks?

---

181. blent: blended, confused.
185. be . . . say: say with confidence.
191. you . . . me: i.e. you feel no need to be wished more joy by me
(than you have already wished for yourselves).   195. so: provided.
199. intermission: delay (in falling in love).
203. sweat again: sweated repeatedly.
204. roof: i.e. roof of the mouth.   213. play: make a wager.
215. stake down: money to cover the bet paid down in advance (but
Gratiano makes a bawdy pun on the term).
221-22. If . . . power: i.e. if my place in this household, still so new,
gives me the right.   223. very: true.

225. entirely: heartily.   232. Commends him: sends his greetings.
236. estate: condition, situation.
239. royal merchant: i.e. prince of merchants (?). Cf. IV.i.29, where
the phrase seems to mean "the richest of merchants."
241. Jasons . . . fleece. Cf. I.i.169-72.
243. shrowd: shrewd, grievous.   246. constitution: state of mind.
247. constant: steadfast.   259. state: estate, property.
262. mere: absolute.
264. The paper . . . friend: i.e. the letter, like my friend's body, torn
open.   267. hit: successful venture.
271. merchant-marring: destructive to merchant ships.

**The Merchant
of Venice
III.ii**

Sal.   Not one, my lord.
Besides, it should appear, that if he had
The present money to discharge the Jew,
He would not take it. Never did I know
A creature that did bear the shape of man   275
So keen and greedy to confound a man.
He plies the Duke at morning and at night,
And doth impeach the freedom of the state,
If they deny him justice. Twenty merchants,
The Duke himself, and the magnificoes   280
Of greatest port, have all persuaded with him,
But none can drive him from the envious plea
Of forfeiture, of justice, and his bond.
  Jes.   When I was with him I have heard him swear
To Tubal and to Chus, his countrymen,   285
That he would rather have Antonio's flesh
Than twenty times the value of the sum
That he did owe him; and I know, my lord,
If law, authority, and power deny not,
It will go hard with poor Antonio.   290
  Por.   Is it your dear friend that is thus in trouble?
  Bass.   The dearest friend to me, the kindest man,
The best-condition'd and unwearied spirit
In doing courtesies, and one in whom
The ancient Roman honor more appears   295
Than any that draws breath in Italy.
  Por.   What sum owes he the Jew?
  Bass.   For me, three thousand ducats.
  Por.   What, no more?
Pay him six thousand, and deface the bond;
Double six thousand, and then treble that,   300
Before a friend of this description
Shall lose a hair through Bassanio's fault.
First go with me to church and call me wife,
And then away to Venice to your friend;
For never shall you lie by Portia's side   305
With an unquiet soul. You shall have gold
To pay the petty debt twenty times over.
When it is paid, bring your true friend along.
My maid Nerissa and myself mean time
Will live as maids and widows. Come away!   310
For you shall hence upon your wedding-day.
Bid your friends welcome, show a merry cheer—
Since you are dear bought, I will love you dear.
But let me hear the letter of your friend.   314
  [*Bass. (Reads.*)]   "Sweet Bassanio, my ships have
all miscarried, my creditors grow cruel, my estate
is very low, my bond to the Jew is forfeit; and since
in paying it, it is impossible I should live, all debts
are clear'd between you and I, if I might but   319
see you at my death. Notwithstanding, use your
pleasure; if your love do not persuade you to come,
let not my letter."
  Por.   O love! dispatch all business and be gone.

273. **present:** ready.   **discharge:** settle his obligation to.
274. **He:** i.e. the Jew.   276. **keen:** savage.   **confound:** destroy.
278. **impeach . . . state:** i.e. accuse the state of failing to support the
liberties of its citizens.   280. **magnificoes:** grandees.
281. **port:** state, dignity.   **persuaded:** pleaded.
282. **envious:** malicious.
293. **best-condition'd:** best-natured.   **unwearied:** i.e. most unwearied.   299. **deface:** destroy.   312. **cheer:** countenance.
313. **dear bought:** obtained at a high price.
320–21. **use your pleasure:** follow your own inclination.

Bass.   Since I have your good leave to go away,
I will make haste; but till I come again,   325
No bed shall e'er be guilty of my stay,
Nor rest be interposer 'twixt us twain.   *Exeunt.*

[SCENE III]

Enter [SHYLOCK] *the Jew and* [SOLANIO] *and* ANTONIO
and the JAILER.

  Shy.   Jailer, look to him, tell not me of mercy.
This is the fool that lent out money gratis.
Jailer, look to him.
  Ant.   Hear me yet, good Shylock.
  Shy.   I'll have my bond, speak not against my bond,
I have sworn an oath that I will have my bond.   5
Thou call'dst me dog before thou hadst a cause,
But since I am a dog, beware my fangs.
The Duke shall grant me justice. I do wonder,
Thou naughty jailer, that thou art so fond
To come abroad with him at his request.   10
  Ant.   I pray thee hear me speak.
  Shy.   I'll have my bond; I will not hear thee speak.
I'll have my bond, and therefore speak no more.
I'll not be made a soft and dull-ey'd fool
To shake the head, relent, and sigh, and yield   15
To Christian intercessors. Follow not,
I'll have no speaking, I will have my bond.   *Exit Jew.*
  Sol.   It is the most impenetrable cur
That ever kept with men.
  Ant.   Let him alone,
I'll follow him no more with bootless prayers.   20
He seeks my life; his reason well I know:
I oft deliver'd from his forfeitures
Many that have at times made moan to me;
Therefore he hates me.
  [*Sol.*]   I am sure the Duke
Will never grant this forfeiture to hold.   25
  Ant.   The Duke cannot deny the course of law;
For the commodity that strangers have
With us in Venice, if it be denied,
Will much impeach the justice of the state,
Since that the trade and profit of the city   30
Consisteth of all nations. Therefore go.
These griefs and losses have so bated me
That I shall hardly spare a pound of flesh
To-morrow to my bloody creditor.
Well, jailer, on. Pray God Bassanio come   35
To see me pay his debt, and then I care not!   *Exeunt.*

[SCENE IV]

Enter PORTIA, NERISSA, LORENZO, JESSICA, *and* [BAL-
THAZAR,] *a man of Portia's.*

  Lor.   Madam, although I speak it in your presence,

III.iii. Location: Venice. A street.
9. **naughty:** good-for-nothing.   14. **dull-ey'd:** i.e. easily put upon.
19. **kept:** dwelt.   20. **bootless:** unavailing.   26. **deny:** refuse.
27. **commodity:** commercial privileges.   **strangers:** aliens.
29. **impeach . . . state.** Cf. III.ii.278.   32. **bated:** reduced.

III.iv. Location: Belmont. Portia's house.

You have a noble and a true conceit
Of godlike amity, which appears most strongly
In bearing thus the absence of your lord.
But if you knew to whom you show this honor,   5
How true a gentleman you send relief,
How dear a lover of my lord your husband,
I know you would be prouder of the work
Than customary bounty can enforce you.
    Por. I never did repent for doing good,   10
Nor shall not now: for in companions
That do converse and waste the time together,
Whose souls do bear an egall yoke of love,
There must be needs a like proportion
Of lineaments, of manners, and of spirit;   15
Which makes me think that this Antonio,
Being the bosom lover of my lord,
Must needs be like my lord. If it be so,
How little is the cost I have bestowed
In purchasing the semblance of my soul,   20
From out the state of hellish cruelty.
This comes too near the praising of myself,
Therefore no more of it. [Hear] other things:
Lorenzo, I commit into your hands
The husbandry and manage of my house   25
Until my lord's return. For mine own part,
I have toward heaven breath'd a secret vow
To live in prayer and contemplation,
Only attended by Nerissa here,
Until her husband and my lord's return.   30
There is a monast'ry two miles off,
And there we will abide. I do desire you
Not to deny this imposition,
The which my love and some necessity
Now lays upon you.
    Lor.   Madam, with all my heart,   35
I shall obey you in all fair commands.
    Por. My people do already know my mind,
And will acknowledge you and Jessica
In place of Lord Bassanio and myself.
So fare you well till we shall meet again.   40
    Lor. Fair thoughts and happy hours attend on you!
    Jes. I wish your ladyship all heart's content.
    Por. I thank you for your wish, and am well pleas'd
To wish it back on you. Fare you well, Jessica.
        Exeunt [*Jessica and Lorenzo*].
Now, Balthazar,   45
As I have ever found thee honest-true,
So let me find thee still. Take this same letter,
And use thou all th' endeavor of a man
In speed to [Padua]. See thou render this
Into my [cousin's] hands, Doctor Bellario,   50
And look what notes and garments he doth give thee,
Bring them, I pray thee, with imagin'd speed

Unto the [traject], to the common ferry
Which trades to Venice. Waste no time in words,
But get thee gone. I shall be there before thee.   55
    Balth. Madam, I go with all convenient speed.
        [*Exit.*]
    Por. Come on, Nerissa, I have work in hand
That you yet know not of. We'll see our husbands
Before they think of us.
    Ner.   Shall they see us?
    Por. They shall, Nerissa; but in such a habit   60
That they shall think we are accomplished
With that we lack. I'll hold thee any wager,
When we are both accoutered like young men,
I'll prove the prettier fellow of the two,
And wear my dagger with the braver grace,   65
And speak between the change of man and boy
With a reed voice, and turn two mincing steps
Into a manly stride; and speak of frays
Like a fine bragging youth, and tell quaint lies,
How honorable ladies sought my love,   70
Which I denying, they fell sick and died.
I could not do withal. Then I'll repent,
And wish, for all that, that I had not kill'd them;
And twenty of these puny lies I'll tell,
That men shall swear I have discontinued school   75
Above a twelvemonth. I have within my mind
A thousand raw tricks of these bragging Jacks,
Which I will practice.
    Ner.   Why, shall we turn to men?
    Por. Fie, what a question's that,
If thou wert near a lewd interpreter!   80
But come, I'll tell thee all my whole device
When I am in my coach, which stays for us
At the park-gate; and therefore haste away,
For we must measure twenty miles to-day.   *Exeunt.*

[SCENE V]

Enter Clown [LAUNCELOT] *and* JESSICA.

    Laun. Yes, truly, for look you, the sins of the
father are to be laid upon the children; therefore, I
promise you, I fear you. I was always plain with
you, and so now I speak my agitation of the matter;
therefore be a' good cheer, for truly I think you   5
are damn'd. There is but one hope in it that can do
you any good, and that is but a kind of bastard hope
neither.
    Jes. And what hope is that, I pray thee?   9

---

2. **conceit**: conception, understanding.
9. **bounty**: benevolence.   **enforce**: urge upon.   12. **waste**: spend.
13. **egall**: equal.
14. **needs**: of necessity.   **proportion**: agreement, correspondence.
20. **semblance**: likeness, double.   **my soul**: i.e. Bassanio.
25. **husbandry and manage**: care and management (the two nouns are near synonyms).   33. **deny this imposition**: refuse this charge.
49. **Padua**. A famed centre for the study of civil law.
50. **cousin's**: kinsman's.   51. **look what**: whatever.
52. **imagin'd speed**: speed as quick as thought.

53. **traject**. Explained as from Italian *traghetto*, "ferry."   **common**:
public.   54. **trades**: plies back and forth.
56. **convenient**: due, appropriate.   60. **a habit**: apparel.
61. **accomplished**: equipped.
69. **quaint**: skillfully contrived, elaborate.
72. **do withal**: help it.   74. **puny**: petty, childish.
75–76. **I . . . twelvemonth**: I have been out of school at least a year (ironic).   77. **Jacks**: ill-mannered fellows.

III.v. Location: Belmont. Portia's garden.
1–2. **sins . . . children**. Referring to the Second Commandment in the Second Prayer Book (1552); "and visit the sin of the father upon the children." 3. **fear**: fear for.
4. **agitation**: blunder for *cogitation* (?).
8. **neither**. Emphasizing the negative implication of what precedes (= that isn't much of a hope either).

Laun. Marry, you may partly hope that your father got you not, that you are not the Jew's daughter.

Jes. That were a kind of bastard hope indeed; so the sins of my mother should be visited upon me.

Laun. Truly then I fear you are damn'd both 15
by father and mother; thus when I shun Scylla, your father, I fall into Charybdis, your mother. Well, you are gone both ways.

Jes. I shall be sav'd by my husband, he hath made me a Christian! 20

Laun. Truly, the more to blame he; we were Christians enow before, e'en as many as could well live one by another. This making of Christians will raise the price of hogs. If we grow all to be pork-eaters, we shall not shortly have a rasher on the coals for money. 26

Enter LORENZO.

Jes. I'll tell my husband, Launcelot, what you say. Here he [comes].

Lor. I shall grow jealous of you shortly, Launcelot, if you thus get my wife into corners! 30

Jes. Nay, you need not fear us, Lorenzo, Launcelot and I are out. He tells me flatly there's no mercy for me in heaven because I am a Jew's daughter; and he says you are no good member of the commonwealth, for in converting Jews to Christians, you raise the price of pork. 36

Lor. I shall answer that better to the commonwealth than you can the getting up of the Negro's belly; the Moor is with child by you, Launcelot.

Laun. It is much that the Moor should be 40
more than reason; but if she be less than an honest woman, she is indeed more than I took her for.

Lor. How every fool can play upon the word! I think the best grace of wit will shortly turn into silence, and discourse grow commendable in 45
none only but parrots. Go in, sirrah, bid them prepare for dinner.

Laun. That is done, sir, they have all stomachs!

Lor. Goodly Lord, what a wit-snapper are you! then bid them prepare dinner. 50

Laun. That is done too, sir, only "cover" is the word.

Lor. Will you cover then, sir?

Laun. Not so, sir, neither, I know my duty. 54

Lor. Yet more quarrelling with occasion! wilt thou show the whole wealth of thy wit in an instant? I pray thee understand a plain man in his plain meaning: go to thy fellows, bid them cover the table, serve in the meat, and we will come in to dinner. 60

Laun. For the table, sir, it shall be serv'd in; for the meat, sir, it shall be cover'd; for your coming in to dinner, sir, why, let it be as humors and conceits shall govern. *Exit Clown.* 64

Lor. O dear discretion, how his words are suited! The fool hath planted in his memory An army of good words, and I do know A many fools, that stand in better place, Garnish'd like him, that for a tricksy word Defy the matter. How cheer'st thou, Jessica? 70
And now, good sweet, say thy opinion, How dost thou like the Lord Bassanio's wife?

Jes. Past all expressing. It is very meet The Lord Bassanio live an upright life, For having such a blessing in his lady, 75
He finds the joys of heaven here on earth, And if on earth he do not [merit] it, In reason he should never come to heaven! Why, if two gods should play some heavenly match, And on the wager lay two earthly women, 80
And Portia one, there must be something else Pawn'd with the other, for the poor rude world Hath not her fellow.

Lor.   Even such a husband Hast thou of me as she is for [a] wife.

Jes. Nay, but ask my opinion too of that. 85

Lor. I will anon, first let us go to dinner.

Jes. Nay, let me praise you while I have a stomach.

Lor. No, pray thee, let it serve for table-talk; Then howsome'er thou speak'st, 'mong other things I shall disgest it.

Jes.   Well, I'll set you forth. *Exeunt.* 90

[ACT IV, SCENE I]

Enter the DUKE, *the* MAGNIFICOES, ANTONIO, BASSANIO, [SALERIO,] *and* GRATIANO [*with others*].

Duke. What, is Antonio here?

Ant. Ready, so please your Grace.

Duke. I am sorry for thee. Thou art come to answer

---

11. **got:** begot.
16–17. **Scylla . . . Charybdis.** Scylla was a sea-monster and Charybdis a whirlpool in the strait between Italy and Sicily. The difficulty of avoiding one without falling prey to the other is still proverbial.
18. **gone:** done for, lost.
19–20. **I . . . Christian.** Cf. 1 Corinthians 7:14: "the unbelieving wife is sanctified by the husband."
22. **enow:** enough. Shakespeare uses this form only as a modifier of plural nouns; see another example in IV.i.29.
23. **live . . . another:** (1) dwell side by side; (2) make a living off one another.   25. **rasher:** slice of bacon.
26. **for money:** at any price.   29. **jealous:** jealous.
32. **out:** at odds.
41. **more than reason:** larger than is reasonable. Note the wordplay on *much, more, Moor.*   41–42. **honest:** chaste.
44. **best grace:** highest excellence.   48. **stomachs:** appetites.
51. **cover:** lay the table.
54. **I . . . duty.** Launcelot now takes *cover* in the sense "put on your hat." Cf. II.ix.44.

55. **quarrelling with occasion:** taking issue at every opportunity.
59. **meat:** food.
61. **table.** Here used in the sense "food," as is shown by *serv'd in.*
62. **cover'd:** i.e. served in covered dishes.
63–64. **as . . . govern:** as your whims and notions shall determine.
65. **discretion:** discrimination.   **suited:** adapted to suit the occasion.
68. **A many:** many.   **better place:** higher rank.
69. **Garnish'd:** furnished (with words).   **tricksy:** ingenious, clever.
70. **Defy:** disdain, set at nought.   **matter:** substance, meaning.
How cheer'st thou: what cheer.   82. **Pawn'd:** staked.
87. **stomach:** (1) appetite; (2) inclination.
89. **howsome'er:** howsoever.
90. **disgest:** digest.   **set you forth:** (1) serve you up; (2) praise you highly.

IV.i. Location: Venice. A court of justice.
3. **answer:** satisfy.

A stony adversary, an inhuman wretch,
Uncapable of pity, void and empty   5
From any dram of mercy.
   Ant.   I have heard
Your Grace hath ta'en great pains to qualify
His rigorous course; but since he stands obdurate,
And that no lawful means can carry me
Out of his envy's reach, I do oppose   10
My patience to his fury, and am arm'd
To suffer, with a quietness of spirit,
The very tyranny and rage of his.
   Duke. Go one, and call the Jew into the court.
   Sal. He is ready at the door; he comes, my lord.

           Enter SHYLOCK.

   Duke. Make room, and let him stand before our
      face.   16
Shylock, the world thinks, and I think so too,
That thou but leadest this fashion of thy malice
To the last hour of act, and then 'tis thought
Thou'lt show thy mercy and remorse more strange
Than is thy strange apparent cruelty;   21
And where thou now exacts the penalty,
Which is a pound of this poor merchant's flesh,
Thou wilt not only loose the forfeiture,
But touch'd with humane gentleness and love,   25
Forgive a moi'ty of the principal,
Glancing an eye of pity on his losses,
That have of late so huddled on his back,
Enow to press a royal merchant down,
And pluck commiseration of [his state]   30
From brassy bosoms and rough hearts of flints,
From stubborn Turks, and Tartars never train'd
To offices of tender courtesy.
We all expect a gentle answer, Jew!
   Shy. I have possess'd your Grace of what I pur-
      pose,   35
And by our holy Sabaoth have I sworn
To have the due and forfeit of my bond.
If you deny it, let the danger light
Upon your charter and your city's freedom!
You'll ask me why I rather choose to have   40
A weight of carrion flesh than to receive
Three thousand ducats. I'll not answer that;
But say it is my humor, is it answer'd?
What if my house be troubled with a rat,
And I be pleas'd to give ten thousand ducats   45
To have it ban'd? What, are you answer'd yet?
Some men there are love not a gaping pig;
Some that are mad if they behold a cat;

And others, when the bagpipe sings i' th' nose,
Cannot contain their urine: for affection,   50
[Mistress] of passion, sways it to the mood
Of what it likes or loathes. Now for your answer:
As there is no firm reason to be rend'red
Why he cannot abide a gaping pig;
Why he, a harmless necessary cat;   55
Why he, a woollen bagpipe, but of force
Must yield to such inevitable shame
As to offend, himself being offended;
So can I give no reason, nor I will not,
More than a lodg'd hate and a certain loathing   60
I bear Antonio, that I follow thus
A losing suit against him. Are you answered?
   Bass. This is no answer, thou unfeeling man,
To excuse the current of thy cruelty.
   Shy. I am not bound to please thee with my
      answers.   65
   Bass. Do all men kill the things they do not love?
   Shy. Hates any man the thing he would not kill?
   Bass. Every offense is not a hate at first.
   Shy. What, wouldst thou have a serpent sting
      thee twice?
   Ant. I pray you think you question with the Jew:
You may as well go stand upon the beach   71
And bid the main flood bate his usual height;
You may as well use question with the wolf
Why he hath made the ewe bleak for the lamb;
You may as well forbid the mountain pines   75
To wag their high tops, and to make no noise
When they are fretten with the gusts of heaven;
You may as well do any thing most hard
As seek to soften that—than which what's harder?—
His Jewish heart! Therefore I do beseech you   80
Make no moe offers, use no farther means,
But with all brief and plain conveniency
Let me have judgment and the Jew his will.
   Bass. For thy three thousand ducats here is six.
   Shy. If every ducat in six thousand ducats   85
Were in six parts, and every part a ducat,
I would not draw them, I would have my bond.
   Duke. How shalt thou hope for mercy, rend'ring
      none?
   Shy. What judgment shall I dread, doing no wrong?
You have among you many a purchas'd slave,   90
Which like your asses, and your dogs and mules,
You use in abject and in slavish parts,
Because you bought them. Shall I say to you,
"Let them be free! Marry them to your heirs!
Why sweat they under burthens? Let their beds   95
Be made as soft as yours, and let their palates
Be season'd with such viands"? You will answer,
"The slaves are ours." So do I answer you:
The pound of flesh which I demand of him
Is dearly bought as mine, and I will have it.   100

---

6. **dram:** i.e. smallest amount.   7. **qualify:** moderate.
10. **envy's:** malice's.   13. **tyranny:** violence, cruelty.
16. **our.** The "royal" plural.
18. **leadest:** carriest, maintainest.   **fashion:** pretense.
19. **act:** performance.
20. **remorse:** pity.   **strange:** extraordinary.
24. **loose:** release, i.e. waive; or, since *loose* and *lose* are doublets in
Elizabethan spelling, Shakespeare may have intended *lose* = forget.
forfeiture: forfeit.   26. **moi'ty:** portion.   28. **huddled:** crowded.
32. **stubborn:** unyielding.   33. **offices:** acts.
35. **possess'd:** informed.
36. **Sabaoth:** for *Sabbath* (here = Saturday). *Sabaoth* (a Hebrew
word) properly means "armies" or "hosts" but was frequently confused with *Sabbath*.   38. **danger:** harm.   43. **humor:** whim.
46. **ban'd:** poisoned.
47. **gaping pig:** roasted pig with its mouth open.

50. **affection:** instinctual feelings.
54–56. **he . . . he . . . he:** one . . . another . . . still another.
60. **lodg'd:** deep-seated.   62. **losing:** unprofitable.
64. **current:** tenor, drift.
70. **think:** bear in mind.   **question:** argue.
72. **main flood:** high tide.   **bate:** diminish.   74. **bleak:** bleat.
77. **fretten:** fretted.   82. **conveniency:** fitness.   87. **draw:** take.
92. **parts:** tasks.   95. **burthens:** burdens.   97. **season'd:** gratified.

The Merchant of Venice
IV.i

If you deny me, fie upon your law!
There is no force in the decrees of Venice.
I stand for judgment. Answer—shall I have it?
 Duke. Upon my power I may dismiss this court,
Unless Bellario, a learned doctor,   105
Whom I have sent for to determine this,
Come here to-day.
 Sal.   My lord, here stays without
A messenger with letters from the doctor,
New come from Padua.
 Duke. Bring us the letters; call the messenger.   110
 Bass. Good cheer, Antonio! what, man, courage
yet!
The Jew shall have my flesh, blood, bones, and all,
Ere thou shalt lose for me one drop of blood.
 Ant. I am a tainted wether of the flock,
Meetest for death; the weakest kind of fruit   115
Drops earliest to the ground, and so let me.
You cannot better be employ'd, Bassanio,
Than to live still and write mine epitaph.

 Enter NERISSA [*dressed like a lawyer's clerk*].

 Duke. Came you from Padua, from Bellario?
 Ner. From both, my lord. Bellario greets your
Grace.   [*Presenting a letter*.]
 Bass. Why dost thou whet thy knife so ear-
nestly?   121
 Shy. To cut the forfeiture from that bankrout
there.
 Gra. Not on thy sole, but on thy soul, harsh Jew,
Thou mak'st thy knife keen; but no metal can,   124
No, not the hangman's axe, bear half the keenness
Of thy sharp envy. Can no prayers pierce thee?
 Shy. No, none that thou hast wit enough to make.
 Gra. O, be thou damn'd, inexecrable dog!
And for thy life let justice be accus'd.
Thou almost mak'st me waver in my faith   130
To hold opinion with Pythagoras,
That souls of animals infuse themselves
Into the trunks of men. Thy currish spirit
Govern'd a wolf, who hang'd for human slaughter,
Even from the gallows did his fell soul fleet,   135
And whilst thou layest in thy unhallowed dam,
Infus'd itself in thee; for thy desires
Are wolvish, bloody, starv'd, and ravenous.
 Shy. Till thou canst rail the seal from off my bond,
Thou but offend'st thy lungs to speak so loud.   140
Repair thy wit, good youth, or it will fall
To cureless ruin. I stand here for law.
 Duke. This letter from Bellario doth commend
A young and learned doctor to our court.
Where is he?
 Ner.   He attendeth here hard by   145
To know your answer, whether you'll admit him.

 Duke. With all my heart. Some three or four of
you
Go give him courteous conduct to this place.
Mean time the court shall hear Bellario's letter.   149
[*Reads*.] "Your Grace shall understand that at
the receipt of your letter I am very sick, but in
the instant that your messenger came, in loving
visitation was with me a young doctor of Rome.
His name is Balthazar. I acquainted him with the
cause in controversy between the Jew and   155
Antonio the merchant. We turn'd o'er many books
together. He is furnish'd with my opinion, which
better'd with his own learning, the greatness
whereof I cannot enough commend, comes with
him, at my importunity, to fill up your Grace's   160
request in my stead. I beseech you let his lack of
years be no impediment to let him lack a reverend
estimation, for I never knew so young a body with
so old a head. I leave him to your gracious acceptance, whose trial shall better publish his commendation."   166

 Enter PORTIA *for Balthazar*.

You hear the learn'd Bellario, what he writes,
And here I take it is the doctor come.
Give me your hand. Come you from old Bellario?
 Por. I did, my lord.
 Duke.   You are welcome, take your place.
Are you acquainted with the difference   171
That holds this present question in the court?
 Por. I am informed throughly of the cause.
Which is the merchant here? and which the Jew?   174
 Duke. Antonio and old Shylock, both stand forth.
 Por. Is your name Shylock?
 Shy.   Shylock is my name.
 Por. Of a strange nature is the suit you follow,
Yet in such rule that the Venetian law
Cannot impugn you as you do proceed.—
You stand within his danger, do you not?   180
 Ant. Ay, so he says.
 Por.   Do you confess the bond?
 Ant. I do.
 Por.   Then must the Jew be merciful.
 Shy. On what compulsion must I? tell me that.
 Por. The quality of mercy is not strain'd,
It droppeth as the gentle rain from heaven   185
Upon the place beneath. It is twice blest:
It blesseth him that gives and him that takes.
'Tis mightiest in the mightiest, it becomes
The throned monarch better than his crown.
His sceptre shows the force of temporal power,   190
The attribute to awe and majesty,
Wherein doth sit the dread and fear of kings;
But mercy is above this sceptred sway,
It is enthroned in the hearts of kings,

---

104. **Upon**: by, in accordance with.
107. **stays without**: waits outside.
108. **letters**: a letter (Latin *litterae*).
114. **tainted**: infected with disease, sickly.   **wether**: sheep (properly, a castrated ram).
118. **live still**: go on living.   125. **hangman's**: executioner's.
128. **inexecrable**: that cannot be execrated enough.
129. **for thy life**: because you are permitted to live.
135. **fell**: cruel.   140. **offend'st**: injurest.
142. **cureless**: incurable.

148. **conduct**: escort.   162. **to . . . lack**: which will deprive him of.
165. **trial**: testing.   **publish**: make known.
171. **difference**: dispute.
173. **throughly**: thoroughly.   **cause**: case.   178. **rule**: order.
180. **within his danger**: at his mercy.
184. **strain'd**: constrained, compelled.
186. **is twice blest**: i.e. bestows a double blessing.
191. **attribute to**: visible symbol of.

It is an attribute to God himself;   195
And earthly power doth then show likest God's
When mercy seasons justice. Therefore, Jew,
Though justice be thy plea, consider this,
That in the course of justice, none of us
Should see salvation. We do pray for mercy,   200
And that same prayer doth teach us all to render
The deeds of mercy. I have spoke thus much
To mitigate the justice of thy plea,
Which if thou follow, this strict court of Venice   204
Must needs give sentence 'gainst the merchant there.
  Shy. My deeds upon my head! I crave the law,
The penalty and forfeit of my bond.
  Por. Is he not able to discharge the money?
  Bass. Yes, here I tender it for him in the court,
Yea, twice the sum. If that will not suffice,   210
I will be bound to pay it ten times o'er,
On forfeit of my hands, my head, my heart.
If this will not suffice, it must appear
That malice bears down truth. [*To the Duke.*] And I
  beseech you
Wrest once the law to your authority: 215
To do a great right, do a little wrong,
And curb this cruel devil of his will.
  Por. It must not be, there is no power in Venice
Can alter a decree established.
'Twill be recorded for a precedent,   220
And many an error by the same example
Will rush into the state. It cannot be.
  Shy. A Daniel come to judgment! yea, a Daniel!
O wise young judge, how I do honor thee!
  Por. I pray you let me look upon the bond.   225
  Shy. Here 'tis, most reverend doctor, here it is.
  Por. Shylock, there's thrice thy money off'red thee.
  Shy. An oath, an oath, I have an oath in heaven!
Shall I lay perjury upon my soul?
[No], not for Venice.
  Por.   Why, this bond is forfeit,   230
And lawfully by this the Jew may claim
A pound of flesh, to be by him cut off
Nearest the merchant's heart. Be merciful,
Take thrice thy money, bid me tear the bond.
  Shy. When it is paid according to the tenure.   235
It doth appear you are a worthy judge;
You know the law, your exposition
Hath been most sound. I charge you by the law,
Whereof you are a well-deserving pillar,
Proceed to judgment. By my soul I swear   240
There is no power in the tongue of man
To alter me: I stay here on my bond.

---

195. **attribute to:** quality or characteristic of.
197. **seasons:** tempers.
201. **that same prayer:** i.e. the Lord's Prayer.
203. **mitigate . . . plea:** i.e. soften your plea for strict justice.
206. **My . . . head:** i.e. I ask no mercy for my deeds (a rejection of Portia's "we do pray for mercy"; cf. lines 88–89).
214. **bears down truth:** overthrows righteousness.
215. **Wrest:** strain, forcibly subject.
223. **Daniel.** In the Apocryphal story of Susannah and the Elders, the youthful Daniel acts as judge when the Elders accuse Susannah. By the time Gratiano picks up the term (lines 333, 340 below), the parallel has become closer, for Daniel turned the tables on the accusers just as Portia has done.   235. **tenure:** tenor.
242. **stay . . . on:** make a stand on, i.e. insist upon the fulfillment of.

  Ant. Most heartily I do beseech the court
To give the judgment.
  Por.   Why then thus it is:
You must prepare your bosom for his knife—   245
  Shy. O noble judge, O excellent young man!
  Por. For the intent and purpose of the law
Hath full relation to the penalty,
Which here appeareth due upon the bond.
  Shy. 'Tis very true. O wise and upright judge!
How much more elder art thou than thy looks!   251
  Por. Therefore lay bare your bosom.
  Shy.   Ay, his breast,
So says the bond, doth it not, noble judge?
"Nearest his heart," those are the very words.
  Por. It is so. Are there balance here to weigh
The flesh?
  Shy.   I have them ready.   256
  Por. Have by some surgeon, Shylock, on your
  charge,
To stop his wounds, lest he do bleed to death.
  Shy. Is it so nominated in the bond?
  Por. It is not so express'd, but what of that?   260
'Twere good you do so much for charity.
  Shy. I cannot find it, 'tis not in the bond.
  Por. You, merchant, have you any thing to say?
  Ant. But little; I am arm'd and well prepar'd.
Give me your hand, Bassanio, fare you well.   265
Grieve not that I am fall'n to this for you;
For herein Fortune shows herself more kind
Than is her custom. It is still her use
To let the wretched man outlive his wealth,
To view with hollow eye and wrinkled brow   270
An age of poverty; from which ling'ring penance
Of such misery doth she cut me off.
Commend me to your honorable wife,
Tell her the process of Antonio's end,
Say how I lov'd you, speak me fair in death;   275
And when the tale is told, bid her be judge
Whether Bassanio had not once a love.
Repent but you that you shall lose your friend,
And he repents not that he pays your debt;
For if the Jew do cut but deep enough,   280
I'll pay it instantly with all my heart.
  Bass. Antonio, I am married to a wife
Which is as dear to me as life itself,
But life itself, my wife, and all the world,
Are not with me esteem'd above thy life.   285
I would lose all, ay, sacrifice them all
Here to this devil, to deliver you.
  Por. Your wife would give you little thanks for
  that
If she were by to hear you make the offer.
  Gra. I have a wife who I protest I love;   290
I would she were in heaven, so she could
Entreat some power to change this currish Jew.
  Ner. 'Tis well you offer it behind her back,
The wish would make else an unquiet house.

---

248. **Hath . . . to:** i.e. fully authorizes.
255. **balance:** scales (construed as plural).
257. **on your charge:** at your expense.
268. **still:** regularly. **use:** habit, custom.   274. **process:** story.
277. **love:** i.e. friend.   278. **Repent but you:** grieve only.

Shy. [*Aside.*] These be the Christian husbands.
I have a daughter— 295
Would any of the stock of Barrabas
Had been her husband rather than a Christian!
—We trifle time. I pray thee pursue sentence.
   Por. A pound of that same merchant's flesh is
   thine,
The court awards it, and the law doth give it. 300
   Shy. Most rightful judge!
   Por. And you must cut this flesh from off his
   breast,
The law allows it, and the court awards it.
   Shy. Most learned judge, a sentence! Come pre-
   pare!
   Por. Tarry a little, there is something else. 305
This bond doth give thee here no jot of blood;
The words expressly are "a pound of flesh."
Take then thy bond, take thou thy pound of flesh,
But in the cutting it, if thou dost shed
One drop of Christian blood, thy lands and goods 310
Are by the laws of Venice confiscate
Unto the state of Venice.
   Gra. O upright judge! Mark, Jew. O learned
   judge!
   Shy. Is that the law?
   Por.   Thyself shalt see the act;
For as thou urgest justice, be assur'd 315
Thou shalt have justice more than thou desir'st.
   Gra. O learned judge! Mark, Jew, a learned judge!
   Shy. I take this offer then; pay the bond thrice
And let the Christian go.
   Bass.   Here is the money.
   Por. Soft, 320
The Jew shall have all justice. Soft, no haste.
He shall have nothing but the penalty.
   Gra. O Jew! an upright judge, a learned judge!
   Por. Therefore prepare thee to cut off the flesh.
Shed thou no blood, nor cut thou less nor more 325
But just a pound of flesh. If thou tak'st more
Or less than a just pound, be it but so much
As makes it light or heavy in the substance
Or the division of the twentith part
Of one poor scruple, nay, if the scale do turn 330
But in the estimation of a hair,
Thou diest, and all thy goods are confiscate.
   Gra. A second Daniel! a Daniel, Jew!
Now, infidel, I have you on the hip. 334
   Por. Why doth the Jew pause? Take thy forfeiture.
   Shy. Give me my principal, and let me go.
   Bass. I have it ready for thee, here it is.
   Por. He hath refus'd it in the open court;
He shall have merely justice and his bond.

   Gra. A Daniel, still say I, a second Daniel! 340
I thank thee, Jew, for teaching me that word.
   Shy. Shall I not have barely my principal?
   Por. Thou shalt have nothing but the forfeiture,
To be so taken at thy peril, Jew.
   Shy. Why then the devil give him good of it!
I'll stay no longer question.
   Por.   Tarry, Jew, 346
The law hath yet another hold on you.
It is enacted in the laws of Venice,
If it be proved against an alien,
That by direct or indirect attempts 350
He seek the life of any citizen,
The party 'gainst the which he doth contrive
Shall seize one half his goods; the other half
Comes to the privy coffer of the state,
And the offender's life lies in the mercy 355
Of the Duke only, 'gainst all other voice:
In which predicament I say thou stand'st;
For it appears, by manifest proceeding,
That indirectly, and directly too,
Thou hast contrived against the very life 360
Of the defendant; and thou hast incurr'd
The danger formerly by me rehears'd.
Down therefore, and beg mercy of the Duke.
   Gra. Beg that thou mayst have leave to hang thy-
   self,
And yet thy wealth being forfeit to the state, 365
Thou hast not left the value of a cord;
Therefore thou must be hang'd at the state's charge.
   Duke. That thou shalt see the difference of our
   spirit,
I pardon thee thy life before thou ask it.
For half thy wealth, it is Antonio's; 370
The other half comes to the general state,
Which humbleness may drive unto a fine.
   Por. Ay, for the state, not for Antonio.
   Shy. Nay, take my life and all, pardon not that:
You take my house when you do take the prop 375
That doth sustain my house; you take my life
When you do take the means whereby I live.
   Por. What mercy can you render him, Antonio?
   Gra. A halter gratis—nothing else, for God sake.
   Ant. So please my lord the Duke and all the court
To quit the fine for one half of his goods, 381
I am content; so he will let me have
The other half in use, to render it
Upon his death unto the gentleman
That lately stole his daughter. 385
Two things provided more, that for this favor
He presently become a Christian;
The other, that he do record a gift,

296. **Barrabas:** a criminal (whose name is properly spelled *Barabbas*)
whom the Jews asked Pontius Pilate to release in preference to Jesus
(see Mark 15:6–15); also the villainous chief character (*Barabas*) of
Marlowe's *Jew of Malta*. Here and in Marlowe the name is pronounced with main stress on the first syllable.
298. **trifle:** waste on trifles.   **pursue:** proceed with.
320. **Soft:** not so fast.   321. **all:** only.   327. **just:** exact.
328. **substance:** gross weight.
329. **division:** fraction.   **twentith:** twentieth.
330. **scruple:** twenty grains, a very small amount.
331. **in . . . hair:** by a hair's breadth (?) or by the weight of a hair (?).
334. **on the hip.** See I.iii.46.

346. **stay . . . question:** await no further determination of the case.
352. **contrive:** plot.   353. **seize:** take possession of.
369. **pardon:** remit (a penalty).   372. **drive:** reduce.
373. **Ay . . . Antonio:** i.e. yes, with respect to the state's portion, but
not Antonio's.
376–77. **you . . . live.** Cf. Ecclesiasticus 34:23: "He that taketh away
his neighbor's living, slayeth him" (Geneva; verse 22 in King James).
380–85. **So . . . daughter.** Antonio's stipulations here are not clear.
The principal ambiguities lie in *quit* (line 381) and in *use* (line 383);
quit may mean either "remit" or "(have him) pay," and *in use* may
mean either "in trust" or "to be used as a source of income." Commentators generally favor the first interpretation in each case.
387. **presently:** immediately.

Here in the court, of all he dies possess'd
Unto his son Lorenzo and his daughter.   390
  Duke.   He shall do this, or else I do recant
The pardon that I late pronounced here.
  Por.   Art thou contented, Jew? what dost thou say?
  Shy.   I am content.
  Por.   Clerk, draw a deed of gift.
  Shy.   I pray you give me leave to go from hence,
I am not well. Send the deed after me,   396
And I will sign it.
  Duke.   Get thee gone, but do it.
  [*Gra.*]   In christ'ning shalt thou have two god-
    fathers:
Had I been judge, thou shouldst have had ten more,
To bring thee to the gallows, not to the font.   400
                                    Exit [*Shylock*].
  Duke.   Sir, I entreat you home with me to dinner.
  Por.   I humbly do desire your Grace of pardon,
I must away this night toward Padua,
And it is meet I presently set forth.
  Duke.   I am sorry that your leisure serves you not.
Antonio, gratify this gentleman,   406
For in my mind you are much bound to him.
                          Exeunt Duke and his Train.
  Bass.   Most worthy gentleman, I and my friend
Have by your wisdom been this day acquitted
Of grievous penalties, in lieu whereof   410
Three thousand ducats, due unto the Jew,
We freely cope your courteous pains withal.
  Ant.   And stand indebted, over and above,
In love and service to you evermore.
  Por.   He is well paid that is well satisfied,   415
And I, delivering you, am satisfied,
And therein do account myself well paid.
My mind was never yet more mercenary.
I pray you know me when we meet again;
I wish you well, and so I take my leave.   420
  Bass.   Dear sir, of force I must attempt you further.
Take some remembrance of us as a tribute,
Not as fee. Grant me two things, I pray you,
Not to deny me, and to pardon me.   424
  Por.   You press me far, and therefore I will yield.
[*To Antonio.*]   Give me your gloves, I'll wear them for
    your sake,
[*To Bassanio.*]   And for your love I'll take this ring
    from you.
Do not draw back your hand, I'll take no more,
And you in love shall not deny me this!
  Bass.   This ring, good sir, alas, it is a trifle!   430
I will not shame myself to give you this.
  Por.   I will have nothing else but only this,
And now methinks I have a mind to it.
  Bass.   There's more depends on this than on the
    value.
The dearest ring in Venice will I give you,   435
And find it out by proclamation;
Only for this, I pray you pardon me.

  Por.   I see, sir, you are liberal in offers.
You taught me first to beg, and now methinks
You teach me how a beggar should be answer'd.   440
  Bass.   Good sir, this ring was given me by my wife,
And when she put it on, she made me vow
That I should neither sell, nor give, nor lose it.
  Por.   That 'scuse serves many men to save their
    gifts,
And if your wife be not a mad woman,   445
And know how well I have deserv'd this ring,
She would not hold out enemy for ever
For giving it to me. Well, peace be with you!
                          Exeunt [*Portia and Nerissa*].
  Ant.   My Lord Bassanio, let him have the ring.
Let his deservings and my love withal   450
Be valued 'gainst your wive's commandement.
  Bass.   Go, Gratiano, run and overtake him;
Give him the ring, and bring him, if thou canst,
Unto Antonio's house. Away, make haste.
                                    Exit Gratiano.
Come, you and I will thither presently,   455
And in the morning early will we both
Fly toward Belmont. Come, Antonio.   *Exeunt.*

[SCENE II]

Enter [PORTIA *and*] NERISSA [*disguised as before*].

  Por.   Inquire the Jew's house out, give him this
    deed,
And let him sign it. We'll away to-night,
And be a day before our husbands home.
This deed will be well welcome to Lorenzo.

Enter GRATIANO.

  Gra.   Fair sir, you are well o'erta'en.   5
My Lord Bassanio upon more advice
Hath sent you here this ring, and doth entreat
Your company at dinner.
  Por.   That cannot be.
His ring I do accept most thankfully,
And so I pray you tell him; furthermore,   10
I pray you show my youth old Shylock's house.
  Gra.   That will I do.
  Ner.   Sir, I would speak with you.
[*Aside to Portia.*]   I'll see if I can get my husband's
    ring,
Which I did make him swear to keep for ever.
  Por. [*Aside to Nerissa.*]   Thou mayst, I warrant.
    We shall have old swearing   15
That they did give the rings away to men;
But we'll outface them, and outswear them too.—
Away, make haste. Thou know'st where I will tarry.
  Ner.   Come, good sir, will you show me to this
    house?   [*Exeunt.*]

*The Merchant
of Venice
IV.ii*

399. **ten more**: i.e. a jury of twelve.   406. **gratify**: reward.
407. **mind**: opinion.   410. **lieu**: return.
412. **cope**: match, requite.   421. **attempt**: urge.
436. **proclamation**: advertisement (by a herald).

448. **For giving**: because you gave.
451. **wive's**: wife's.   **commandement.** Quadrisyllabic, as frequently
in Shakespeare.

IV.ii. Location: Venice. A street.
6. **more advice**: further consideration.
15. **old**: plentiful (a colloquialism).

[ACT V, SCENE I]

Enter LORENZO *and* JESSICA.

Lor. The moon shines bright. In such a night as
　　　this,
When the sweet wind did gently kiss the trees,
And they did make no noise, in such a night
Troilus methinks mounted the Troyan walls,
And sigh'd his soul toward the Grecian tents,　　5
Where Cressid lay that night.
Jes.　　　　　　　　　　　In such a night
Did Thisby fearfully o'ertrip the dew,
And saw the lion's shadow ere himself,
And ran dismayed away.
Lor.　　　　　　　In such a night
Stood Dido with a willow in her hand　　　　10
Upon the wild sea-banks, and waft her love
To come again to Carthage.
Jes.　　　　　　　　　　In such a night
Medea gathered the enchanted herbs
That did renew old Aeson.
Lor.　　　　　　　　In such a night
Did Jessica steal from the wealthy Jew,　　　15
And with an unthrift love did run from Venice,
As far as Belmont.
Jes.　　　　　　In such a night
Did young Lorenzo swear he lov'd her well,
Stealing her soul with many vows of faith,
And ne'er a true one.
Lor.　　　　　　In such a night　　　20
Did pretty Jessica (like a little shrow)
Slander her love, and he forgave it her.
Jes. I would out-night you, did nobody come;
But hark, I hear the footing of a man.

Enter a MESSENGER.

Lor. Who comes so fast in silence of the night?　25
Mess. A friend.
Lor. A friend! what friend? your name, I pray you,
　　　friend?
Mess. Stephano is my name, and I bring word
My mistress will before the break of day
Be here at Belmont. She doth stray about　　30
By holy crosses, where she kneels and prays
For happy wedlock hours.
Lor.　　　　　　　　Who comes with her?
Mess. None but a holy hermit and her maid.
I pray you, is my master yet return'd?
Lor. He is not, nor we have not heard from him.
But go we in, I pray thee, Jessica,　　　　36
And ceremoniously let us prepare
Some welcome for the mistress of the house.

Enter Clown [LAUNCELOT].

Laun. Sola, sola! wo ha, ho! sola, sola!
Lor. Who calls?　　　　　　　　　　　　40
Laun. Sola! did you see Master Lorenzo? Master
Lorenzo, sola, sola!
Lor. Leave hollowing, man—here.
Laun. Sola! where, where?
Lor. Here!　　　　　　　　　　　　　　45
Laun. Tell him there's a post come from my mas-
ter, with his horn full of good news. My master will
be here ere morning.　　　　　　　　[*Exit.*]
Lor. Sweet soul, let's in, and there expect their
　　　coming.
And yet no matter; why should we go in?　　50
My friend [Stephano], signify, I pray you,
Within the house, your mistress is at hand,
And bring your music forth into the air.

　　　　　　　　　　　　[*Exit Messenger.*]

How sweet the moonlight sleeps upon this bank!
Here will we sit, and let the sounds of music　55
Creep in our ears. Soft stillness and the night
Become the touches of sweet harmony.
Sit, Jessica. Look how the floor of heaven
Is thick inlaid with patens of bright gold.
There's not the smallest orb which thou behold'st　60
But in his motion like an angel sings,
Still quiring to the young-ey'd cherubins;
Such harmony is in immortal souls,
But whilst this muddy vesture of decay
Doth grossly close it in, we cannot hear it.　　65

[*Enter* MUSICIANS.]

Come ho, and wake Diana with a hymn,
With sweetest touches pierce your mistress' ear,
And draw her home with music.　　*Play Music.*
Jes. I am never merry when I hear sweet music.
Lor. The reason is, your spirits are attentive;　70
For do but note a wild and wanton herd
Or race of youthful and unhandled colts,
Fetching mad bounds, bellowing and neighing loud,
Which is the hot condition of their blood,
If they but hear perchance a trumpet sound,　　75
Or any air of music touch their ears,
You shall perceive them make a mutual stand,
Their savage eyes turn'd to a modest gaze,
By the sweet power of music; therefore the poet
Did feign that Orpheus drew trees, stones, and floods;
Since nought so stockish, hard, and full of rage,　81
But music for the time doth change his nature.
The man that hath no music in himself,

V.i. Location: Belmont. The avenue before Portia's house.
4. **Troilus:** Trojan prince and lover of Cressida, who proved faithless
to him after she had been sent from Troy to the Greek camp.
7. **Thisby:** Thisbe, beloved of Pyramus; their story is the subject of
the play performed by Bottom and his fellows in *A Midsummer
Night's Dream* (V.i).
10. **Dido:** queen of Carthage who loved Aeneas and was deserted by
him. **willow.** The emblem of slighted love.　11. **waft:** beckoned.
13. **Medea:** an enchantress who helped Jason win the Golden Fleece.
14. **Aeson:** Jason's father, whose youth was restored by Medea's
magic arts.　16. **unthrift:** prodigal.　21. **shrow:** shrew.
24. **footing:** footsteps.
31. **crosses:** wayside crosses (common both in England and in Italy).

39. **Sola.** Perhaps the imitation of a post horn (see lines 46–48).
49. **expect:** await.　51. **signify:** give notice.
57. **Become:** befit.　**touches:** notes (literally, the fingering of a
musical instrument).　59. **patens:** metal plates or disks.
62. **quiring:** singing in harmony.　**young-ey'd:** i.e. eternally keen-
sighted.　64. **muddy . . . decay:** i.e. mortal flesh.
65. **it . . . it:** man's immortal soul . . . the music of the spheres.
66. **Diana:** here, the moon-goddess.
68 s.d. **Music:** musicians (so also in line 98).
70. **spirits are attentive:** faculties are concentrated.
71. **wanton:** untrained (cf. *unhandled,* line 72).　72. **race:** herd.
77. **mutual:** common.
79. **the poet:** perhaps Ovid, who tells the story of the Thracian
musician Orpheus in his *Metamorphoses.*
81. **stockish:** resembling a block of wood, i.e. unfeeling.

Nor is not moved with concord of sweet sounds,
Is fit for treasons, stratagems, and spoils;   85
The motions of his spirit are dull as night,
And his affections dark as [Erebus]:
Let no such man be trusted. Mark the music.

Enter PORTIA *and* NERISSA.

Por. That light we see is burning in my hall.
How far that little candle throws his beams!
So shines a good deed in a naughty world.   90
Ner. When the moon shone, we did not see the
    candle.
Por. So doth the greater glory dim the less:
A substitute shines brightly as a king
Until a king be by, and then his state   95
Empties itself, as doth an inland brook
Into the main of waters. Music, hark!
Ner. It is your music, madam, of the house.
Por. Nothing is good, I see, without respect;
Methinks it sounds much sweeter than by day. 100
Ner. Silence bestows that virtue on it, madam.
Por. The crow doth sing as sweetly as the lark
When neither is attended; and I think
The nightingale, if she should sing by day
When every goose is cackling, would be thought 105
No better a musician than the wren.
How many things by season season'd are
To their right praise and true perfection!
Peace ho! the Moon sleeps with Endymion,
And would not be awak'd.   [*Music ceases.*]
Lor.   That is the voice,   110
Or I am much deceiv'd, of Portia.
Por. He knows me as the blind man knows the
    cuckoo,
By the bad voice!
Lor.   Dear lady, welcome home!
Por. We have been praying for our husbands'
    welfare,
Which speed we hope the better for our words. 115
Are they return'd?
Lor.   Madam, they are not yet;
But there is come a messenger before,
To signify their coming.
Por.   Go in, Nerissa.
Give order to my servants that they take
No note at all of our being absent hence—   120
Nor you, Lorenzo—Jessica, nor you.

[*A tucket sounds.*]

Lor. Your husband is at hand, I hear his trumpet.
We are no tell-tales, madam, fear you not.
Por. This night methinks is but the daylight sick,
It looks a little paler. 'Tis a day,   125
Such as the day is when the sun is hid.

Enter BASSANIO, ANTONIO, GRATIANO, *and their* FOL-
    LOWERS.

Bass. We should hold day with the Antipodes,
If you would walk in absence of the sun.
Por. Let me give light, but let me not be light,
For a light wife doth make a heavy husband,   130
And never be Bassanio so for me—
But God sort all! You are welcome home, my lord.
Bass. I thank you, madam. Give welcome to my
    friend;
This is the man, this is Antonio,
To whom I am so infinitely bound.   135
Por. You should in all sense be much bound to him,
For as I hear he was much bound for you.
Ant. No more than I am well acquitted of.
Por. Sir, you are very welcome to our house.
It must appear in other ways than words,   140
Therefore I scant this breathing courtesy.
Gra. [*To Nerissa.*] By yonder moon I swear you do
    me wrong;
In faith, I gave it to the judge's clerk.
Would he were gelt that had it, for my part,
Since you do take it, love, so much at heart.   145
Por. A quarrel ho already! what's the matter?
Gra. About a hoop of gold, a paltry ring
That she did give me, whose posy was
For all the world like cutler's poetry
Upon a knife, "Love me, and leave me not."   150
Ner. What talk you of the posy or the value?
You swore to me, when I did give [it] you,
That you would wear it till your hour of death,
And that it should lie with you in your grave.
Though not for me, yet for your vehement oaths, 155
You should have been respective and have kept it.
Gave it a judge's clerk! no, God's my judge,
The clerk will ne'er wear hair on 's face that had it.
Gra. He will, and if he live to be a man.
Ner. Ay, if a woman live to be a man.   160
Gra. Now, by this hand, I gave it to a youth,
A kind of boy, a little scrubbed boy,
No higher than thyself, the judge's clerk,
A prating boy, that begg'd it as a fee.
I could not for my heart deny it him.   165
Por. You were to blame, I must be plain with you,
To part so slightly with your wive's first gift,
A thing stuck on with oaths upon your finger,
And so riveted with faith unto your flesh.
I gave my love a ring, and made him swear   170
Never to part with it, and here he stands.
I dare be sworn for him he would not leave it,
Nor pluck it from his finger, for the wealth
That the world masters. Now, in faith, Gratiano,
You give your wife too unkind a cause of grief; 175
And 'twere to me I should be mad at it.

---

85. **stratagems:** deceptive tricks.   **spoils:** acts of plunder.
87. **Erebus:** the hell of classical mythology.   91. **naughty:** wicked.
97. **main of waters:** ocean.
99. **respect:** reference to other circumstances.
103. **When . . . attended:** i.e. when each sings alone.
107. **by . . . are:** are matured by favorable occasion.
109. **Endymion:** a shepherd loved by the moon-goddess, who caused
him to be cast into a perpetual sleep in a cave on Mount Latmos.
115. **Which speed:** who thrive.
121 s.d. **tucket:** distinctive series of notes on a trumpet.

127-28. **We . . . sun:** i.e. if you always walked at night (when it is
day on the other side of the world), we would have day then too.
129. **be light:** be wanton.   130. **heavy:** sorrowful.
132. **sort:** dispose.   136. **sense:** reason.
141. **scant:** make brief.   **breathing courtesy:** utterance of welcome.
144. **gelt:** gelded.
148. **posy:** motto, sometimes in verse (*posy = poesy*), inscribed inside
a ring.   150. **leave:** part with.   156. **respective:** careful.
162. **scrubbed:** scrubby, stunted.   174. **masters:** possesses.

The Merchant of Venice
V.i

Bass. [*Aside.*] Why, I were best to cut my left
    hand off,
And swear I lost the ring defending it.
    Gra. My Lord Bassanio gave his ring away
Unto the judge that begg'd it, and indeed   180
Deserv'd it too; and then the boy, his clerk,
That took some pains in writing, he begg'd mine,
And neither man nor master would take aught
But the two rings.
    Por.   What ring gave you, my lord?
Not that, I hope, which you receiv'd of me.   185
    Bass. If I could add a lie unto a fault,
I would deny it; but you see my finger
Hath not the ring upon it, it is gone.
    Por. Even so void is your false heart of truth.
By heaven, I will ne'er come in your bed   190
Until I see the ring!
    Ner.   Nor I in yours
Till I again see mine!
    Bass.   Sweet Portia,
If you did know to whom I gave the ring,
If you did know for whom I gave the ring,
And would conceive for what I gave the ring,   195
And how unwillingly I left the ring,
When nought would be accepted but the ring,
You would abate the strength of your displeasure.
    Por. If you had known the virtue of the ring,
Or half her worthiness that gave the ring,   200
Or your own honor to contain the ring,
You would not then have parted with the ring.
What man is there so much unreasonable,
If you had pleas'd to have defended it
With any terms of zeal, wanted the modesty   205
To urge the thing held as a ceremony?
Nerissa teaches me what to believe—
I'll die for't but some woman had the ring!
    Bass. No, by my honor, madam, by my soul,
No woman had it, but a civil doctor,   210
Which did refuse three thousand ducats of me,
And begg'd the ring, the which I did deny him,
And suffer'd him to go displeas'd away—
Even he that had held up the very life
Of my dear friend. What should I say, sweet lady?
I was enforc'd to send it after him,   216
I was beset with shame and courtesy,
My honor would not let ingratitude
So much besmear it. Pardon me, good lady,
For by these blessed candles of the night,   220
Had you been there, I think you would have begg'd
The ring of me to give the worthy doctor.
    Por. Let not that doctor e'er come near my house.
Since he hath got the jewel that I loved,
And that which you did swear to keep for me,   225
I will become as liberal as you,
I'll not deny him any thing I have,
No, not my body nor my husband's bed.
Know him I shall, I am well sure of it.

Lie not a night from home. Watch me like Argus;
If you do not, if I be left alone,   231
Now by mine honor, which is yet mine own,
I'll have that doctor for [my] bedfellow.
    Ner. And I his clerk; therefore be well advis'd
How you do leave me to mine own protection.   235
    Gra. Well, do you so; let not me take him then,
For if I do, I'll mar the young clerk's pen.
    Ant. I am th' unhappy subject of these quarrels.
    Por. Sir, grieve not you, you are welcome not-
    withstanding.
    Bass. Portia, forgive me this enforced wrong,   240
And in the hearing of these many friends
I swear to thee, even by thine own fair eyes,
Wherein I see myself—
    Por.   Mark you but that!
In both my eyes he doubly sees himself,
In each eye, one. Swear by your double self,   245
And there's an oath of credit.
    Bass.   Nay, but hear me.
Pardon this fault, and by my soul I swear
I never more will break an oath with thee.
    Ant. I once did lend my body for his wealth,
Which but for him that had your husband's ring   250
Had quite miscarried. I dare be bound again,
My soul upon the forfeit, that your lord
Will never more break faith advisedly.
    Por. Then you shall be his surety. Give him this,
And bid him keep it better than the other.   255
    Ant. Here, Lord Bassanio, swear to keep this ring.
    Bass. By heaven, it is the same I gave the doctor!
    Por. I had it of him. Pardon me, Bassanio,
For by this ring, the doctor lay with me.
    Ner. And pardon me, my gentle Gratiano,   260
For that same scrubbed boy, the doctor's clerk,
In lieu of this last night did lie with me.
    Gra. Why, this is like the mending of highways
In summer, where the ways are fair enough.
What, are we cuckolds ere we have deserv'd it?   265
    Por. Speak not so grossly, you are all amaz'd.
Here is a letter, read it at your leisure.
It comes from Padua, from Bellario.
There you shall find that Portia was the doctor,
Nerissa there her clerk. Lorenzo here   270
Shall witness I set forth as soon as you,
And even but now return'd; I have not yet
Enter'd my house. Antonio, you are welcome,
And I have better news in store for you
Than you expect. Unseal this letter soon;   275
There you shall find three of your argosies
Are richly come to harbor suddenly.
You shall not know by what strange accident
I chanced on this letter.
    Ant.   I am dumb.   279
    Bass. Were you the doctor, and I knew you not?

---

199. **virtue:** power, efficacy.   201. **contain:** retain.
205. **wanted the modesty:** who would have been so lacking in moderation as.
206. **urge:** insist on being given.   **ceremony:** sacred pledge.
210. **civil doctor:** doctor of civil law.
226. **liberal:** (1) generous; (2) sexually free.

230. **from:** away from.   **Argus:** a hundred-eyed monster.
237. **pen.** With ribald second sense.
245. **double.** With play on the double reflection and the sense
"deceitful."   246. **of credit:** to be believed.
249. **wealth:** welfare.   253. **advisedly:** deliberately.
262. **In lieu of:** in return for.
263–64. **this . . . enough:** this development makes what was fairly
bad before even worse.   266. **amaz'd:** bewildered.

Gra. Were you the clerk that is to make me
cuckold?

Ner. Ay, but the clerk that never means to do it,
Unless he live until he be a man.

Bass. Sweet doctor, you shall be my bedfellow—
When I am absent, then lie with my wife.   285

Ant. Sweet lady, you have given me life and living,
For here I read for certain that my ships
Are safely come to road.

Por.   How now, Lorenzo?
My clerk hath some good comforts too for you.

Ner. Ay, and I'll give them him without a fee.   290
There do I give to you and Jessica,
From the rich Jew, a special deed of gift,
After his death, of all he dies possess'd of.

286. **living**: possessions.   288. **road**: harbor.

Lor. Fair ladies, you drop manna in the way
Of starved people.

Por.   It is almost morning,   295
And yet I am sure you are not satisfied
Of these events at full. Let us go in,
And charge us there upon inter'gatories,
And we will answer all things faithfully.

Gra. Let it be so. The first inter'gatory   300
That my Nerissa shall be sworn on is,
Whether till the next night she had rather stay,
Or go to bed now, being two hours to day.
But were the day come, I should wish it dark
Till I were couching with the doctor's clerk.   305
Well, while I live I'll fear no other thing
So sore, as keeping safe Nerissa's ring.   *Exeunt.*

298. **charge . . . inter'gatories**: question us under oath.
306. **fear**: be concerned about.

NOTE ON THE TEXT

The Merchant of Venice was first published in quarto (Q1) in 1600 by Thomas Heyes; this edition is here used as copy-text. A second quarto (Q2), set from a copy of Q1, was printed in 1619 by J. Roberts with the fraudulent date 1600.[1] The text of the First Folio (1623) was based on a slightly corrected and edited copy of Q1. A third quarto (Q3), printed from a copy of Q1, appeared in 1637.

There has been disagreement about the exact nature of the manuscript underlying Q1. It seems most reasonable to believe that it was set either from Shakespeare's "foul papers" or from a "fair copy" of these, perhaps one made by Shakespeare himself. "Fair copy" rather than the usual "foul papers" is suggested because the text of Q1 is remarkably clean and, with the exception of the Salarino-Salerio tangle (see below), presents few difficulties. That tangle points clearly to the use of some kind of authorial copy; so do the occasional use of variant speech-prefixes for Shylock and Launcelot and the permissive nature of several stage directions (see, for example, II.i o.s.d. and II.ii.113 s.d.). Some scholars detect slight traces of playhouse annotation, but the evidence is ambiguous, and the Salerio-Salarino confusion makes it highly unlikely that the manuscript behind Q1 could ever have served as an actual prompt-book.

The problem concerning the names Salarino and Salerio has engaged the attention of a long line of editors. Until Dover Wilson's edition (1926), either Salerio was absorbed into Salarino or the names were taken as representing two different characters. The form *Salarino* (once *Salerino*, at

II.vi o.s.d.) never occurs in the text proper but only in stage directions and speech-prefixes (*Sal.*, *Salar.*, *Salari.*, and once [III.i.79] *Saleri.*), and not even in these after III.i. At III.ii.219 s.d. a character with the name Salerio enters as a messenger from Antonio, whose friend he is, and this name occurs five times in the remaining lines of the scene. Wilson suggested that at this stage in the composition of the play Shakespeare made up his mind to alter the name Salarino to Salerio, neglecting, not uncharacteristically, to make the necessary adjustments in the earlier stage directions and speech-prefixes. The present text, like that of all other recent editions, adopts Wilson's solution.

Q2 and F1 both show a certain amount of editing: Q2 tidies the text and adds a few new unauthorized readings and some stage directions; F1 introduces several sound effects which suggest the theatre, and gets rid of a couple of oaths. Neither text, however, shows evidence of a serious attempt at correction against an independent manuscript, though it is possible that F1 was printed from a copy of Q1 which had had some direct connection with the theatre. The more significant variants in Q2 and F1 are recorded in the Textual Notes.

For further information, see: J. D. Wilson, ed., New Cambridge *The Merchant of Venice* (Cambridge, 1926); J. R. Brown, "The Compositors of *Hamlet* Q2 and *The Merchant of Venice*," *SB*, VII (1955), 17–40, and ed., New Arden *The Merchant of Venice* (London, 1955); W. W. Greg, *The Shakespeare First Folio* (Oxford, 1955); D. F. McKenzie, "Compositor B's Role in *The Merchant of Venice*," *SB*, XII (1958), 75–90; Christopher Spencer, "Shakespeare's *Merchant of Venice* in Sixty-three Editions," *SB*, XXV (1972), 89–106.

[1] It should be noted that the collations of Q1 and Q2 which appear in the Cambridge *Shakespeare* (Vol. II, 1863 and 1891) and in the Furness *Variorum* (1888) reverse the correct order of the two quartos.

TEXTUAL NOTES

Title: The . . . Venice] *F1*; The most excellent Historie of the Merchant of Venice. With the extreame crueltie of Shylocke the Iewe towards the sayd Merchant, in cutting a iust pound of his flesh: and the obtayning of Portia by the choyse of three chests. As it hath beene diuers times acted by the Lord Chamberlaine his Seruants. Written by William

Shakespeare. *Q1 (title-page)*; The comicall History of the Merchant of Venice. *Q1 (title on sig. A2ʳ)*
Dramatis personae: *subs. as first given in Q3*
Act-scene division: *none in Q1–2; F1 marks acts only; scene divisions from Rowe and later editors (see first note to each scene); present act-scene arrangement as a whole first established by Capell*

I.i
I.i] *Rowe*; Actus Primus. *F1*
Location: *Theobald*
o.s.d. Antonio] *Capell*; Anthonio *Q1–2, F1 (throughout in s.dd. and text)*
o.s.d. Salerio] *Wilson*; Salaryno *Q1–2*; Salarino *F1*
o.s.d. Solanio] *Capell*; Salanio *Q1–2, F1*
8 s.p. Sal.] *Wilson (and F1 for Salarino);*

Salarino. (or Salar., Sala., Sal. *throughout scene*) *Q1–2, F1*
13 them,... reverence,] *F3 (after F1)*; them ... reuerence *Q1*; them, ... reuerence *Q2, P1*
15 s.p. Sol.] *Capell*; Salanio. *Q1–2*; Salar. *F1*
27 dock'd] *Rowe*; docks *Q1–2, F1*
47 neither?] *Q2*; neither: *Q1, F1*
56 s.d. Lorenzo] *Rowe*; Lorenso *Q1–2, F1 (sporadically throughout, but usually Lorenzo)*
93 Sir] sir an *F1*
98 damn] *F4*; dam *Q1–2, F1*
112 vendible] *F1*; vendable *Q1–2*
112 s.d. Gratiano and Lorenzo] *Theobald*
113 that—] *ed. (after Collier)*; that *Q1–2, F1*
114 nothing,] *Q2, F1*; nothing *Q1*
146 youth,] *Q2, F1*; youth *Q1*

I.ii

I.ii] *Rowe*
Location: *Rowe, Capell*
7 mean] smal *F1*
21 reasoning] reason *F1*
32 you] *om. Q2*
45, 60 Palentine] Palatine *Q2*
55 Bon] *Capell*; Boune *Q1–2, F1*
60 throstle] *Pope*; Trassell *Q1–2, F1*
61 a-cap'ring] hyphen, *Dyce*
77 Scottish] other *F1*
110 pray God grant] wish *F1*

I.iii

I.iii] *Rowe*
Location: *Rowe, Theobald*
19 Indies;] *F3 (subs.)*; Indies, *Q1–2, F1*
19 Rialto] *F2*; Ryalta *Q1–2, F1*
21 hath,] *Theobald*; hath *Q1–2, F1*
29, 33, 41 s.pp. Shy.] *Q2*; Iew. *Q1, F1*
41 s.d. Aside.] *Rowe*
50 well-won] *Q2*; well-wone *Q1*; well-worne *F1*
59 s.d. To Antonio.] *Rowe*
59 fair,] *Rowe*; faire *Q1–2, F1*
64 s.d. To Bassanio.] *Staunton*
64–5 Is ... would?] are you resolu'd, / How much he would haue? *Q2*; is he yet possest / How much he would? *F1*
67 s.d. To Bassanio.] *Brown*
79 eanlings] *Capell*; eanelings *Q1–2, F1*
84 pill'd] *Knight*; pyld *Q1–2*; pil'd *F1*
104 see, the rate—] *Lloyd conj. (in Cambridge)*; see the rate. *Q1–2, F1*
127 day, another time] *F1* (day;); day another time, *Q1–2*
129 moneys''?] *Theobald*; moneyes. *Q1–2, F1*

II.i

II.i] *Rowe*; Actus Secundus. *F1*
Location: *Rowe, Capell*
o.s.d. Flourish cornets.] *F1 (at end of s.d.)*; placed as in *Malone*
o.s.d. the Prince of Morocco] *Capell*; Morochus *Q1–2, F1*
9 valiant; by ... swear] *Steevens (subs.)*; valiant, (by ... sweare) *Q1, Q2 (valiant), F1*
10 best-regarded] hyphen, *Malone*
31 thee] *Rowe*; the *Q1–2, F1*
31 alas the while!] *Pope*; alas, the while *Q1–2, F1*
35 page] *Theobald*; rage *Q1–2, F1*
46 s.d. Cornets.] *F1 (after l. 45)*; placed as in *Dyce*

II.ii

II.ii] *Rowe*
Location: *Rowe, Capell*
1 s.p. Laun.] *Rowe*; Clowne. *Q1–2, F1*
3, 4, 5, 8, 9 Gobbo] *Q2*; Iobbe *Q1, F1*; Job *F3*
4 Launcelot] *Rowe*; Launcelet or Lancelet *Q1–2, F1 (throughout)*
12 heavens,] *Collier*; heauens *Q1–2, F1*
22 well] ill *Q2*
27 incarnation] incarnal *Q2*
32 confusions] conclusions *Q2*
33 young man] *Q2*; young-man *Q1, F1*
35, 49 s.dd. Aside.] *Johnson*

36 sand-blind] hyphen, *F1*
37 gravel-blind] hyphen, *Rowe*
68 s.d. Aside] *Collier*
74 sand-blind] hyphen, *Rowe*
75 indeed] *F1*; in deede *Q1–2*
79 murder] *F1*; muder *Q1*; Murther *Q2*
80 in the end] at the length *Q2*
91, 109 indeed] *Q2, F1*; in deede *Q1*
95 fill-horse] *Pope*; philhorse *Q1, F1*; pilhorse *Q2*
95 has] *Q2, F1*; hase *Q1*
98 last] lost *Q1, F1*
113 s.d. one ... Leonardo] *ed. (after Theobald)*
118 s.d. Exit ... men.] *Q2*
157 head, well!] head. Well, *Q2*
157–8 s.d. Looking ... palm.] *Johnson*
162 Aleven] *Brown*; a leuen *Q1, F1*; eleuen *Q2*
163 coming-in] hyphen, *Theobald*
168 twinkling] twinkling of an eye *Q2*
168 s.d. with Old Gobbo] *Rowe (subs.)*
174 s.d. Exit Leonardo.] placed as in *Theobald*; after l. 173, *Q1–2, F1*
180 must.] *Q2*; must *Q1*; must: *F1*
183 faults,] *Q2*; faults *Q1*; faults, *F1*
184 known,] *F1*; knowne; *Q1*; knowne. *Q2*

II.iii

II.iii] *Capell*
Location: *Theobald*
10 s.p. Laun.] *Q2*; Clowne. *Q1, F1*
10–1 tongue. Most ... Jew!] *Johnson (subs.)*; tongue, most ... Iewe, *Q1–2, F1*
13 something] somewhat *F1*
15 s.d. Exit Launcelot.] *Capell*; Exit. *Q2, F1 (after l. 14)*

II.iv

II.iv] *Capell*
Location: *Theobald*
o.s.d. Salerio] *Wilson*; Salaryno *Q1*; Salarino *Q2*; Slarino *F1*
o.s.d. Solanio] *Capell*; Salanio *Q1–2, F1*
5 s.p. Sal.] *Wilson (and F1 for Salarino; throughout scene)*; Salari. *Q1 (or Sal. throughout scene)*; Salar. *Q2 (throughout scene)*
9 s.d. with a letter] *F1*; s.d. placed as in *Q2*; after l. 9, *Q1*
14 Love-news,] *Q2 (subs.; hyphen, F2)*; Loue, newes *Q1*; Loue newes *F1*
19 here,] *F1*; heere *Q1–2*
20 privately.] *Q2*; priuatly, *Q1*; priuately: *F1*
20 s.d. Exit Clown.] placed as in *White*; after l. 23, *Q1–2, F1*
27 s.d. with Solanio] *Wilson (subs., after Capell)*
39 s.d. Exeunt.] *Rowe*; Exit. *Q1–2, F1*

II.v

II.v] *Capell*
Location: *Capell (after Theobald)*
o.s.d. was,] *ed.*; was *Q1, F1*; *Q2 s.d. reads:* Enter the Iew and Lancelet.
1 s.p. Shy.] *Q2*; Iewe. *Q1, F1*
22 together.] *Johnson*; together, *Q1–2, F1*
28 What are there] *Q2*; What are there *Q1*; What are their *F1*
43 Jewess'] *Pope*; Iewes *Q1*
43 s.d. Exit.] *Rowe*
47 Snail-slow] hyphen, *Q2, F1*

II.vi

II.vi] *Capell*
Location: *ed. (after Halliwell)*
o.s.d. two of] *ed.*
o.s.d. Salerio] *Wilson*; Salarino *Q1–2*; Salino *F1 (and s.p. at l. 20)*
2 Desir'd] *Q2*; desired *Q1, F1*
18 over-weather'd] *Q3*; ouer-wetherd *Q1–2*; ouer-wither'd *F1*
25 Ho] *Q2*; Howe *Q1*; Hoa *F1*
25 s.d. Enter] *Capell*
25 s.d. in boy's clothes] *Rowe*
50 s.d. Exit above.] *Theobald*
58 gentlemen] *Q2, F1*; gentleman *Q1*
59 s.d. with ... Salerio] *Wilson (after Capell)*

66 I ... you.] *om. Q2 (which continues ll. 67–8 to Antonio)*

II.vii

II.vii] *Capell*
Location: *Rowe, Capell*
o.s.d. Flourish cornets.] *Malone (after Capell; but F1, probably in error, places Flo. Cornets. after Scene viii o.s.d.)*
o.s.d. the Prince of] *Capell*
17 give—] *Capell*; giue, *Q1, Q2, (c), F1*; giue *Q2 (u)*
18 threatens.] *Rowe*; threatens *Q1–2, F1*
62 s.d. He ... casket.] *Rowe (subs.)*
65 s.d. Reads.] *Dyce*
69 tombs] *Johnson conj.*; timber *Q1–2, F1*
74 Cold] *Capell*; Mor. Cold *Q1–2, F1 (repeated s.p.)*
77 s.d. with his Train] *Dyce*

II.viii

II.viii] *Capell*
Location: *Rowe, Capell*
o.s.d. Salerio] *Wilson*; Salarino *Q1–2, F1*
o.s.d. Solanio] *Capell*; Salanio *Q2*
1 s.p. Sal.] *Wilson (and Q1, F1 for Salarino)*; Salar. *Q2*; so throughout scene
39 Slubber] *Q2, F1*; slumber *Q1*

II.ix

II.ix] *Capell*
Location: *Rowe, Capell*
o.s.d. Servitor] *Q2*; Seruiture *Q1, F1*
3 s.d. Flourish cornets.] *F1 (at end of s.d.)*; placed as in *Malone (after Capell)*
3 s.d. the Prince of] *Capell*
3 s.d. Arragon] *Q2, F1*; Arrogon *Q1*
6 rites] *Pope*; rights *Q1–2, F1*
19 me.] *Q3* (me;); me, *Q1–2, F1*
48 chaff] *Q2, F1*; chaft *Q1*
49 varnish'd] *F1*; varnist *Q1*; vernish'd *Q2*
52 s.d. He ... casket.] *Rowe (subs.; after l. 53)*; placed as in *Collier*
55 schedule] *F4*; shedule *Q1*; sedule *Q2*; scedule *F1*
63 s.d. Reads.] *Q2* (hee reads.)
64 judgment] *Q2*; iudement *Q1, F1*
73 Still] *Capell*; Arrag. Still *Q1–2, F1 (repeated s.p.)*
78 wroth] *Q3*; wroath *Q1–2, F1*
78 s.d. Exit ... Train.] *Capell (subs., after Rowe)*
98 high-day] hyphen, *F1*
101 Bassanio, Lord Love,] *Rowe*; Bassanio Lord, loue *Q1–2, F1*

III.i

III.i] *Rowe*; Actus Tertius. *F1*
Location: *Rowe, Theobald*
o.s.d. Enter] *Q2, F1*
o.s.d. Solanio] Salanio *Q2*
o.s.d. Salerio] *Wilson*; Salarino *Q1–2, F1*
2 s.p. Sal.] *Wilson (and F1 for Salarino)*; Salari. *Q1*; Salar. *Q2*; so throughout scene, except Saleri. at l. 79, *Q1*
7 gossip] gossips *Q2, F1*
7 Report] *Q3*; report *Q1–2, F1*
14 company!—] *Capell (after F1 company!)*; company. *Q1–2*
21 s.d. Enter Shylock.] placed as in *Q2*; after l. 23, *Q1, F1*
29 fldge] fledg'd *Q2, F1*
69 humility? Revenge.] *Rowe*; humillity, reuenge? *Q1–2, F1*
71 example? Why, revenge.] *F2*; example, why reuenge? *Q1–2, F1*
73 s.d. Servingman] *Brown*; man *Q1–2, F1*
74 s.p. Serv.] *Rowe*
78 s.d. Solanio ... Servingman] *Wilson (after Capell)*; *Q1 repeats* Enter Tuball. *after this exit*
91 them? Why, so—] *Capell (subs.)*; them, why so? *Q1, F1*; them, why so: *Q2*
91 what's] how much is *F1*
98 Genoa—] *Rowe*; Genowa? *Q1, F1*; Genoway. *Q2*

107 Heard] *Kellner conj.*; heere *Q1–2*; here *F1*
107 Genoa?] *Rowe*; Genowa. *Q1, F1*; Genoway. *Q2*
109 one] in one *Q2*
121 turkis] *ed.*; Turkies *Q1–2, F1*

III.ii

III.ii] *Rowe*
Location: *Rowe, Capell*
o.s.d. Nerissa] *Capell*
56 paid] *Q2*; payed *Q1*; paied *F1*
61 live;] *Rowe*; liue *Q1–2, F1*
62 s.d. Here music.] *F1*
66 s.p. All.] *W. J. Lawrence conj. (in Brown)*; *Q1–2, F1* place Replie, replie. *to the right opposite l. 65*
67 eyes] *F1*; eye *Q1–2*
68 dies] *F4*; dies: *Q1–2*; dies, *F1*
69 lies.] *F1* (lies:); lies *Q1*; lyes, *Q2*
71 I'll begin it.] *in roman, as if not part of the song* (which is in italics), *Q1–2, F1*; *Johnson first included it in the song*
81 vice] *F2*; voyce *Q1–2, F1*
84 stairs] *F4*; stayers *Q1–2, F1*
93 make] *Pope*; maketh *Q1–2*; makes *F1*
108 s.d. Aside.] *from Granville's version (1701)*
109 rash-embrac'd] *hyphen, Theobald*
110 shudd'ring] *F1*; shyddring *Q1–2*
114 s.d. Opening . . . casket.] *Rowe*
117 whether] *F1*; whither *Q1–2*
122 t' entrap] *Q2, F1* (t'intrap); tyntrap *Q1*
131 s.d. Reads.] *Dyce*
142 eyes,] *Capell*; eyes: *Q1, F1*; eyes; *Q2*
158 something] nothing *F1*
161 than] *Johnson*; then *Q1–2, F1*; then in *F2*
171 yours—my lord's!—] *Wilson*; yours, my Lords, *Q1*; yours, my Lord, *Q2, F1*
199 lov'd; for intermission] *Theobald*; lou'd for intermission, *Q1–2, F1*
201 caskets] Casket *Q2*
203 sweat] *F3*; swet *Q1–2, F1*
204 roof] *Q2*; rough *Q1, F1*
232 s.d. Gives . . . letter.] *Theobald*
236 s.d. Bassanio] *Rowe*
258 braggart:] *Pope*; Braggart, *Q1–2, F1*
266 life-blood] *hyphen, Rowe*
267 hit?] *Theobald*; hit, *Q1–2, F1*
293 best-condition'd] *hyphen, 1734 ed., Capell*
315 s.p., s.d. Bass. (Reads.)] *Rowe*
327 Nor] No *Q2*

III.iii

III.iii] *Rowe*
Location: *Rowe, Theobald*
o.s.d. Solanio] *F1*; Salerio *Q1*; Salarino *Q2*
1 s.p. Shy.] *Rowe*; Iew. *Q1–2, F1 (throughout scene)*
14 dull-ey'd] *hyphen, Q2*
24 s.p. Sol.] *F1*; Sal. *Q1–2*

III.iv

III.iv] *Rowe*
Location: *Rowe, Capell*
o.s.d. Balthazar] *Theobald*
20 soul] *Q2*; soule; *Q1, F1*
21 cruelty] misery *Q2*
23 Hear] *Thirlby conj.*; heere *Q1–2, F1*
44 s.d. Jessica and Lorenzo] *Rowe*
45 Balthazar] *F2*; Balthaser *Q1–2, F1*
46 honest-true] *hyphen, Theobald*
49 Padua] *Theobald*; Mantua *Q1–2, F1*
50 cousin's] *Q2, F1*; cosin *Q1*
53 traject] *Rowe*; Tranect *Q1–2, F1*
56 s.d. Exit.] *Q2*

63 accoutered] apparreld *Q2*
80 near] *F3*; nere *Q1–2, F1*

III.v

III.v] *Capell*
Location: *Capell (subs.)*
1 s.p. Laun.] *Rowe*; Clowne. *Q1–2, F1 (throughout scene)*
13 indeed] *Q2, F1*; in deede *Q1*
22 e'en] *Q2, F1*; in *Q1* (*a Shakespearean form for e'en*)
28 comes.] *Q2, F1*; come? *Q1*
29 jealious] iealous *Q1*
49 wit-snapper] *hyphen, Q2, F1*
70 cheer'st] *F1*; cherst *Q1*; far'st *Q2*
74 life,] *Q2*; life *F1*
77 merit it] *Pope*; meane it, it *Q1, F1*; meane it, then *Q2*
78 In] Is *F1*
84 a] *F1*
89 howsome'er] *F4*; how so mere *Q1*; howsoere *Q2*; how som ere *F1*
90 s.d. Exeunt.] *F1*; Exit. *Q1–2*

IV.i

IV.i] *Rowe*; Actus Quartus. *F1*
Location: *Rowe, Capell*
o.s.d. Salerio] *Cambridge*
o.s.d. with others] *Capell (subs.)*
4 inhuman] *Rowe*; inhumaine, *Q1*; inhumane, *Q2, F1*
22 exacts] exact'st *F1*
24 loose] lose *F4*
30 his state] *Q2, F1*; this states *Q1*
31 flints] flint *Q2*
35 s.p. Shy.] *Rowe*; Iewe. *Q1–2 (until l. 183, except ll. 65, 67, 69 in Q2), F1 (until l. 206)*
36 Sabaoth] Sabbath *Q2, F1*
50 urine: for affection,] *Thirlby conj.*; vrine for affection. *Q1–2, F1*
51 Mistress] *Thirlby and Waldron conj.*; Maisters *Q1–2, F1*
56 bagpipe,] *Alexander*; bagpipe *Q1, F1*; Bagpipe; *Q2*
58 offend,] *Q2*; offend *Q1, F1*
69 What,] *F3*; What *Q1–2, F1*
74 bleak] bleate *Q1*
75 You may] Or even *F1*
75 mountain] *F1*; mountaine of *Q1–2*
79 that—] *Rowe (subs.)*; that *Q1*; that, *Q2, F1*
79 what's harder?] *F1* (what harder?); what's harder: *Q1–2*
100 bought as mine,] *ed.*; bought, as mine *Q1*; bought, tis mine *Q2, F1*
118 s.d. dressed . . . clerk] *Rowe*
120 both, my lord. Bellario] *Pope*; both? my L. Bellario *Q1*; both, my L. Bellario *Q2*; both. / My Lord Bellario *F1*
120 s.d. Presenting a letter.] *Capell*
123 sole] *F1* (soale); soule *Q1–2*
134 human] *Rowe*; humaine *Q1*; humane *Q2, F1*
136 whilst] *Q2, F1*; whilest *Q1*
136 dam,] *Q2, F1*; dam; *Q1*
142 cureless] endlesse *F1*
150 s.d. Reads.] *Collier MS* (Duke reades)
154, 166 s.d. Balthazar] *Boswell*; Balthazer *Q1–2*; Balthasar *F1* (*but Balthazar in l. 166 s.d.*)
167 You] *Wilson*; Duke. You *Q1–2, F1* (*repeated s.p.*)
214 s.d. To the Duke.] *ed.*
230 No] *Q2, F1*; Not *Q1*
239 well-deserving] *hyphen, F1*
250 s.p. Shy.] *Q2*; Iew. *Q1, F1 (until l. 314), Q2 (ll. 294, 301, 304)*
258 do] should *F1*

259 Is it so] It is not *F1*
263 You] Come *F1*
281 instantly] presently *Q2*
295 s.d. Aside.] *Rowe*
318 s.p. Shy.] *Rowe*; Iew. *Q1–2, F1*
324 off] *Q2, F1*; of *Q1*
326 tak'st] cutst *Q2*
329 twentith] twentieth *F1*
346 question] heere in question *Q2*
398 s.p. Gra.] *Q2, F1*; Shy. *Q1*
400 s.d. Shylock] *Rowe*
407 s.d. Exeunt] *Capell*; Exit *Q1–2, F1*
426 s.d. To Antonio.] *Cambridge (after Capell)*
427 s.d. To Bassanio.] *Cambridge (after Capell)*
448 s.d. Portia and Nerissa] *Theobald (subs.)*

IV.ii

IV.ii] *Capell*
Location: *Capell (subs.)*
o.s.d. Portia and] *F1*
o.s.d. disguised as before] *Kittredge*
13 s.d. Aside to Portia.] *Capell, Pope*
15 s.d. Aside to Nerissa.] *Capell (subs.)*
19 s.d. Exeunt.] *F1*

V.i

V.i] *Rowe*; Actus Quintus. *F1*
Location: *Rowe, Capell*
6 Cressid] *Theobald*; Cressed *Q1, F1*; Cressada *Q2*
18 lov'd] *F1*; loued *Q1–2*
39 s.p. Laun.] *Rowe*; Clowne. *Q1–2, F1 (throughout scene)*
41–2 Master . . . sola,] *Cambridge*; M. Lorenzo, & M. Lorenzo sola, *Q1, F1*; M. Lorenzo, M. Lorenzo, sola, *Q2*; M. Lorenzo, and M. Lorenzo, sola, *F2*; M. Lorenzo, and Mrs. Lorenza, sola, *F3*
48 s.d. Exit.] *Capell*
49 Sweet soul] *arranged as in Rowe, who, however, reads* Sweet Love, *following F2; last words of Launcelot's speech, Q1–2, F1*
51 Stephano] *Q2*; Stephen *Q1, F1*
53 s.d. Exit Messenger.] *Johnson*
56 ears. Soft stillness] *F2 (subs.)*; eares soft stilnes, *Q1–2, F1*
59 inlaid] *Rowe*; inlayed *Q1–2, F1*
62 young-ey'd] *hyphen, Q3*
65 in] in it *Q2, F1*
65 s.d. Enter Musicians.] *Malone (after Capell)*
81 stockish, hard,] *F1*; stockish hard *Q1–2*
87 Erebus] *F2*; Terebus *Q1–2*; Erobus *F1*
106 wren] *Q2, F1*; Renne *Q1*
109 ho!] *Malone (subs.)*; how *Q1–2, F1*
110 s.d. Music ceases.] *F1*
114 husbands' welfare] husband health *Q2*
121 s.d. A tucket sounds.] *F1*
142 s.d. To Nerissa.] *Rowe*
152 it] *Q2, F1*
157 no . . . judge,] but wel I know *F1*
177 s.d. Aside.] *Theobald*
214 had held up] did vphold *Q2*
223 house.] *Johnson*; house *Q1*; house, *Q2, F1*
230 Argus] *F2*; Argos *Q1–2, F1*
233 my] *Q2, F1*; mine *Q1*
244 himself,] *Neilson*; himselfe: *Q1–2, F1*
245 one. Swear] *Rowe (subs.)*; one, sweare *Q1–2, F1*
288 road] *Pope*; Rode *Q1–2, F1*; Rodes *F2*; Rhodes *F3*
298 inter'gatories] *F1*; intergotories *Q1–2*
300 inter'gatory] *F1*; intergotory *Q2*
303 bed now,] *Q2*; bed now *Q1*; bed, now *F1*
305 Till] That *Q2*
307 s.d. Exeunt.] Exeunt. / FINIS. *Q1–2, F1*

The Merry Wives of Windsor

No TWO COMEDIES by Shakespeare are alike, yet there is a sense in which *The Merry Wives of Windsor* is more of a play apart than any of its companions. It is true that Elizabethan England is often clearly visible beneath the disguise of Venice, Athens, the corrupt Vienna of Duke Vincentio, Messina, or even the geographically indistinct shores of Illyria. *The Merry Wives of Windsor*, however, is unique among the comedies in that it is set explicitly in an English town well known to members of Shakespeare's audience. Moreover, it set out to remind this audience of local topography and detail. Not only Windsor Castle and its great park, but Datchet Mead, the road to Frogmore, the Garter Inn, even the great oak, the sawpit nearby, and the castle ditch where Page conceals himself with Shallow and Slender were names and places possessed of an independent, contemporary existence outside Shakespeare's play. On the whole, the most successful productions of *The Merry Wives of Windsor* are those which recognize and are concerned to build up a stage picture of ordinary, middle-class life in a small country town, among innkeepers and doctors, country magistrates, parsons, citizens and their wives and children: people who exist on the periphery of a royal residence without themselves belonging to the court.

The comedy may reflect a specific occasion as well as a particular place. The Folio, although not the quarto, text refers to the necessity of putting the town in order in preparation for a visit from the Queen (V.v.43–46) and to forthcoming ceremonies at Windsor Castle connected with the Knights of the Garter (V.v.56–73). Leslie Hotson has argued that these passages indicate a first performance before Elizabeth at Westminster during the Garter Feast of April 23, 1597, one month before the newly elected knights were formally installed at Windsor. Among the noblemen named that April was the second Lord Hunsdon, Elizabeth's Lord Chamberlain and official patron of Shakespeare's company. There is a well-known theatrical tradition, first recorded by John Dennis in 1702, to the effect that Shakespeare wrote *The Merry Wives of Windsor* at royal command, because the Queen had asked for a play about Falstaff in love, and that he completed it within fourteen days. Hotson speculates that Hunsdon commissioned and paid for the first performance of the comedy as a way of thanking his sovereign for the favor she had shown him. If this is so, Shakespeare would have had to put the piece together at great speed in order to get it ready and rehearsed in the few weeks between Hunsdon's realization of the honor in store for him and the Garter Feast of April 23.

Hotson's theory is in many ways attractive, and it has the merit of explaining the presence of two passages in the Folio text which otherwise seem puzzling. One might also argue that a comedy concerned, as this one is, with the punishment of a knight whose principles and behavior contravene all the ideals of his rank would be appropriate, almost as a kind of antimasque, at a Garter feast. Nor is Falstaff the only character in the play who inverts the values celebrated by the Order of the Garter and makes himself ridiculous in the process. The Garter motto, "*Honi soit qui mal y pense*" (evil be to him who thinks evil), applies neatly to the jealous Ford, a man who persists in seeing evil where none exists and, in the effort to prove that his own wife is unfaithful, covers himself with shame.

Acceptance of the hypothesis that *The Merry Wives of Windsor* was originally conceived as a court entertainment on the occasion of a Garter feast, and subsequently transferred to the public stage, does not necessarily involve agreement with Hotson that the first performance occurred on April 23, 1597. A number of scholars, perplexed by the problem of the play's relation to *1* and *2 Henry IV* and to *Henry V*, have preferred a date closer to the quarto edition of 1602. Falstaff appears, of course, in both the Henry IV plays and his death is reported in *Henry V*. Bardolph is present in all three of the histories as well as in *The Merry Wives of Windsor*, and so is Mistress Quickly. Pistol swaggers through both *2 Henry IV* and *Henry V*, while Justice Shallow and Nym have another existence in *2 Henry IV* and *Henry V* respectively. Hotson's date for *The Merry Wives of Windsor* would place it between the first and second parts of *Henry IV* and well before *Henry V*. Is it reasonable to suppose that Shakespeare interrupted his work on *2 Henry IV* in order to exhibit Falstaff in a wholly different dramatic context, and that Pistol, Justice Shallow, and Nym made their first appearance in the comedy and were then displayed more extensively in the later histories? For some commentators, the idea is palpably absurd; for others, it represents an entirely plausible account of what happened.

Those who regard *The Merry Wives of Windsor* as a play of 1597 and those who see it as a work composed after *Henry V* do manage to agree on one point: Falstaff's adventures in Windsor do not lock into the historical sequence at any moment that is even vaguely definable. Anne Page's suitor Fenton is disapproved of by her father on the grounds that he is "of too high a region," impoverished, and once "kept company with the wild Prince and Poins" (III.ii.72–73). The reference is tantalizing but not very helpful. Fenton himself is never mentioned in the histories and, in *The Merry Wives of Windsor* itself, the past tense implied in the verb *kept* resolutely refuses to explain itself. Not only is there no talk of rebellion and civil war in the comedy, no mention of Prince Hal apart from this one, let alone of Henry V and preparations for the invasion of France, but the throne is occupied (at least in the Folio text) by a queen. Falstaff worries at one point (IV.v.94 ff.) that he will become a laughingstock at court should the news of his discomfitures extend so far, but we are never enlightened as to his position there or the reasons behind his present sojourn at the Garter Inn. Even odder is the fact that Mistress Quickly—and just what she is doing acting as servant to a French physician in Windsor is anybody's guess—and Falstaff do not appear to know each other or to share any common memories of the Boar's Head at Eastcheap in *1 Henry IV*.

Most readers have found that Mistress Quickly, Shallow, Bardolph, Pistol, and Nym are not quite the same people as their namesakes in the histories, although they share certain characteristics and speech habits. In the case of Falstaff, the sense of disappointment has been marked. The Windsor version of Sir John seems so tame and unresourceful compared with his far greater self of Eastcheap, Shrewsbury, Gaultree, and even Gloucestershire that critics have often wanted to explain the falling-off in terms of Shakespeare's artistic dismay at having to resurrect a character he had finished with, and officially buried in *Henry V*, simply in order to comply with a not very perceptive royal command. Arguments of this kind tend to isolate character from plot and to stress the former at the expense of the latter in a way that Elizabethans (and indeed most audiences before 1850) would not have understood. In Sophocles' tragedy *Ajax*, Odysseus is a hero by virtue of exactly those qualities of rationalism and flexibility which, in Sophocles' *Philoctetes*, make him despicable. The basic outline of the character is the same in both plays, but the plots happen to be very different and Sophocles (with the later approval of Aristotle) obviously thought of character not as an end in itself but as the servant and expressive agent of plot. Aeschylus and even Euripides operated in a similar fashion, and so did medieval dramatists. Shakespeare may never have come any closer to Aristotle's *Poetics* than the version at several removes in Sidney's *Apology for Poetry* (1595), but for him too character, although developed to an extent that would have been unthinkable even in Euripides, was still largely dependent upon plot and dramatic genre. Falstaff is probably another and a lesser creature in *The Merry Wives of Windsor* than that cunning destroyer of illusions familiar in the Henry IV plays not because his creator had tired of him but because in this play he inhabits and is subject to a world of comedy, as opposed to representing a comic viewpoint in the alien but vulnerable world of historical event.

No one has ever been able to find a specific source for the plot of *The Merry Wives of Windsor*, although the tradition to which it belongs has never been in doubt. It is a *fabliau*, a merry tale dealing with sexual misadventure, and as such it has analogues in most of the literatures of the world. Probably Shakespeare derived part of the plot for *The Merchant of Venice* from the prose collection *Il Pecorone* by Ser Giovanni. He could also have found there, in the second story told on the first day, a version of the Falstaff/Ford situation that is closer than most. In the Italian story, a young law student called Bucciuolo asks his professor for advice in conducting a love affair. The lady he selects turns out to be the professor's wife, although the student (and, for a time, the professor himself) is ignorant of this fact. When the professor realizes at last that he has been teaching the student how to seduce his own wife, he raids the house, but the lady conceals her lover under a heap of wet washing. The next day, the unsuspecting student tells the professor of his narrow escape, and also of the night of illicit love which followed. The professor learns that his wife has made a second assignation with the young man for that evening, collects a band of neighbors and relations, and makes an ignominious and fruitless assault upon the pile of washing. The lover, on this occasion, had already been smuggled out of the house by the guilty wife. Publicly humiliated, a cuckold without being able to prove it, the professor goes mad. Only then does the student discover what he has done. He flees from Bologna.

This story may well have helped to shape *The Merry Wives of Windsor*. Yet the basic situation in Shakespeare's play is really very different. The Italian professor was genuinely cuckolded, but Shakespeare's Ford is merely fool enough to think he is. Bucciuolo succeeded in committing adultery but Falstaff is tricked by a pair of wives who may be merry but are also fiercely chaste. It is the would-be lover in Shakespeare who is cleverly deceived, not the husband. There are, of course, *fabliaux* in which wives intrigue against and not for their suitors, and in some of them the baffled lecher is subjected to three separate humiliations, as Falstaff is. Moreover, Lyly's *Endimion* (1588), a comedy Shakespeare almost certainly knew, had already staged the scene of a nobleman pinched and tormented by fairies—real ones, in Lyly—as a punishment for lust. Ultimately, however, *The Merry Wives of Windsor* is a strikingly independent creation: a play which extends and, in a sense, violates the calculatedly limited form of the merry tale. Although it is perhaps the lightest of Shakespeare's comedies, a play which contains no threat of death, in which nothing much is at risk and no one, not even Falstaff, is left out of the feast at the end, it presents a vivid and detailed picture of small-town society which, if it does not exactly invite the term *realism*, nonetheless cannot be dismissed as farce.

The Falstaff of the Henry IV plays is a carnival king fighting to maintain his equilibrium in a hostile world of political intrigue. When events force him out of his tavern-citadel, he discovers that as a master of illusions himself he can survive, at least for a time, in a cold climate by recognizing and turning to his own advantage the illusions—of honor, justice, military glory, or swashbuckling youth—which other people mistake for realities. The citizens of Windsor are not without some misconceptions of their own, notably about the tractability of Anne Page or, in the case of Ford, about his wife's light-mindedness, but essentially they are clear-eyed and entirely aware of the need to band together against Falstaff, the intruder from another social and moral sphere. They see in him, rightly, a threat to the established order of a community which, although far from perfect, has nonetheless a wholeness and sanity lacking in the diseased and fragmented world of *1* and *2 Henry IV*. This society is an active force in *The Merry Wives of Windsor*. Falstaff, after launching his complacent and imperceptive assault upon the virtue of Mistress Page and Mistress Ford, is passive: an unwitting victim who merely deludes himself into thinking that he is initiating events.

The comic pattern here is unusual. Although Falstaff is without the mental agility he displays in the histories, he remains a larger-than-life, mythic figure. He is the spirit of festive inconsequence: self-indulgent, amoral, anarchic, a reveller who is out to disrupt the everyday social order. This order

refuses, however, to capitulate or be changed by him in the slightest. It simply closes ranks and reaffirms its original values against an outsider who, like Malvolio in *Twelfth Night*, is made ridiculous, although his sins are of a wholly different kind. The end of the play does not accord with Shakespeare's usual comic practice. Anne Page may have managed to marry the man she loves, and Ford has learned to trust his wife, but there is no sense that a new or transformed society leaves Herne's oak. All that has happened is that a pre-existing society whose values Falstaff tried and failed to subvert has triumphed, without losing its vitality or gaiety of heart.

This solidarity is the more remarkable in that it unites characters of a somewhat prickly individuality, some of whom do not even find it easy to make themselves verbally understood. Evans, the Welsh parson, is a man who "makes fritters of English" (V.v.143). Dr. Caius, the French physician, one of his rivals for the hand of Anne Page, is even less comprehensible most of the time, a foreigner engaged in a desperate grapple with the English tongue. Slender is not only bashful almost to the point of nonexistence but has a vocabulary as slight as everything else about him, while Nym has latched onto the word *humor* as though it were a diamond discovered among the pebbles on a beach and uses it to cope with all contingencies, with the result that it rapidly ceases to have any meaning whatever. Mistress Quickly is scandalized by what seem to her to be the bawdy syllables uttered by a small boy rehearsing his Latin declension, but herself habitually blunders into unconscious obscenities about which Freud might have had a good deal to say. Bardolph confuses *sentences* with *senses*, and his associate Pistol is so lost in a private linguistic fantasy, made up of scraps and borrowings from old plays, as to be virtually impossible to engage in normal conversation. Among all these characters occupied, in their several ways, in hacking and misconstruing the English language, Falstaff stands out as a man who can make words do exactly what he wants them to do. The Fords, the Pages, and the jovial Host of the Garter are verbally competent as Evans or Mistress Quickly are not, but it is only Falstaff who fully understands the resources of language and can speak in a fashion that is genuinely creative. In this play, however, as opposed to the histories, his skill gains him nothing. Almost as much as Pistol, he is a man playing with words in a vacuum, wholly out of touch with a society whose values are no less powerful because they are never clearly articulated by the people who uphold them.

It is difficult to believe that the hard-headed Falstaff of the history plays could possibly have mistaken the amateur dramatics of the Herne the Hunter scene for reality. The *fabliau* Falstaff temporarily resident in Windsor is still witty in himself, but he is also "the cause that wit is in other men" in a different and more ignominious sense. Although the actors in the play within the play have had their squabbles and differences, they unite without question at the end to dramatize the triumph of the community. Falstaff is not merely frightened: the horns he imagined he would plant on the brows of his cuckolds Ford and Page are made, quite literally, to adorn his own forehead. In punishing their victim, the citizens of Windsor not only bury past animosities and mistrusts. They also exchange their previous verbal clumsiness, their cacophony of prose styles, for a lyrical, assured, and uniform verse inconceivable as the invention of the individual characters who speak it. Amateur theatricals have a way of being unfortunate in Shakespeare, as witness the Pageant of the Nine Worthies in *Love's Labor's Lost,* or the efforts of Bottom and his friends in *A Midsummer Night's Dream.* The potentiality for chaos and mismanagement in the show of Herne the Hunter is at least as great as it was in those earlier comedies, considering the actors who participate, but the result is very different.

Fairies, black, grey, green, and white,
You moonshine revellers, and shades of night,
You orphan heirs of fixed destiny,
Attend your office and your quality.   (V.v.37–40)

This is certainly not the idiom of the Mistress Quickly we know, nor do Pistol and Evans seem to suffer, in the play scene, from their customary idiosyncrasies of expression. *The Merry Wives of Windsor* is in some ways the most realistic of Shakespeare's comedies, but we are patently not meant to puzzle over the question of just which Windsor citizen wrote the dialogue for the Herne the Hunter play, let alone what speech therapist elicited performances of such unexpected skill from Evans, Pistol, and Quickly. The verse here stands as the embodiment of a social and moral order allowed, in its moment of triumph, an expression that is appropriately impersonal and communal.

In the English histories, moral judgments are difficult and equivocal. This is one reason why Falstaff can be, at least in part, successful. In the particular comic world of Windsor, on the other hand, they are fixed and unalterable poles and Falstaff, trying to run against them, is broken. Yet there is a remarkable air of geniality and good humor about the end of the play. After all, there have been two intruders from another social sphere in the little world of Windsor. Falstaff may be baffled, but Fenton wins. Exactly the play-within-the-play that undoes the fat knight provides the young courtier with the opportunity to steal away Anne Page. Unlike Falstaff, Fenton has not misprized or trampled upon the life of Windsor. Although he sought Anne Page in marriage initially because of her father's wealth, he has come to love her for herself, and he has tried to obtain her by honorable means. Failing this, he concludes a bargain with Anne herself and then asks for and obtains the forgiveness of the society he has breached. There is some comfort here for Falstaff in discovering that the Herne the Hunter play has deceived not only himself but, unexpectedly, its own masters. When Verdi came to the end of his last opera, *Falstaff,* based on Shakespeare's play, he united all the characters in a great fugal chorus. The words of the chorus are those of Boito, Verdi's librettist, not Shakespeare, but their frank and unforced admission that every man is in some sense a fool and vulnerable to the laughter of others is entirely in the spirit of the last scene of *The Merry Wives of Windsor.* And so, even more profoundly, is the enormous vitality and expansiveness of the music Verdi found at this point: music which flowers out of and celebrates the values of this comic society.

Anne Barton

The Merry Wives of Windsor

ACT I, SCENE I

Enter JUSTICE SHALLOW, SLENDER, SIR HUGH EVANS.

Shal. Sir Hugh, persuade me not; I will make a Star Chamber matter of it. If he were twenty Sir John Falstaffs, he shall not abuse Robert Shallow, esquire.

Slen. In the county of Gloucester, Justice of Peace and Coram. 6

Shal. Ay, cousin Slender, and *Custa-lorum.*

Slen. Ay, and *Rato-lorum* too; and a gentleman born, Master Parson, who writes himself *Armigero*, in any bill, warrant, quittance, or obligation, *Armigero*. 11

Shal. Ay, that I do, and have done any time these three hundred years.

Slen. All his successors (gone before him) hath done't; and all his ancestors (that come after him) may. They may give the dozen white luces in their coat. 15

Shal. It is an old coat.

Evans. The dozen white louses do become an old coat well; it agrees well, passant. It is a familiar beast to man, and signifies love. 21

Shal. The luce is the fresh fish, the salt fish is an old coat.

Slen. I may quarter, coz.

Shal. You may, by marrying. 25

Evans. It is marring indeed, if he quarter it.

Shal. Not a whit.

Evans. Yes, py'r lady. If he has a quarter of your coat, there is but three skirts for yourself, in my simple conjectures. But that is all one. If 30 Sir John Falstaff have committed disparagements unto you, I am of the church, and will be glad to

---

Words and passages enclosed in square brackets in the text above are either emendations of the copy-text or additions to it. The Textual Notes immediately following the play cite the earliest authority for every such change or insertion and supply the reading of the copy-text wherever it is emended in this edition.

I.i. Location: Windsor. Before Page's house.
o.s.d. **Sir:** courtesy title for a priest.
1. **persuade:** plead with.
2. **Star Chamber.** The court of Star Chamber, composed mainly of the King's Council, was the highest civil court in England.
6. **Coram:** i.e. quorum, a justice who sat on the bench at county sessions.
7. **Custa-lorum:** i.e. *custos rotulorum*, keeper of the rolls. The principal justice in the county had custody of the records.
8. **Rato-lorum:** i.e. *rotulorum*.
10. **Armigero:** esquire; literally, one entitled to bear (heraldic) arms. **bill:** bill of exchange. **quittance:** discharge from debt.
10–11. **obligation:** contract.

16. **give:** display as an armorial bearing. **luces:** pikes (fish).
17. **coat:** coat of arms. Evans misunderstands both *coat* (as a garment) and *luces* (as *louses*).
20. **passant.** Perhaps Evans means *passing*, i.e. exceedingly; if so, he unintentionally enriches his picture of the old coat and the lice by using the heraldic term for "walking." **familiar:** (1) domestic; (2) overintimate.
22–23. **The luce . . . coat.** Shallow's meaning has not been satisfactorily explained.
24. **quarter:** add to one's coat of arms the arms of another family by placing them in one of the four sections of the escutcheon. **coz:** cousin. 28. **py'r lady:** by Our Lady.
29. **skirts:** the full lower part of some doublets.
30. **simple:** humble (with a play on "foolish").

do my benevolence to make atonements and com-promises between you.

Shal. The Council shall hear it, it is a riot. 35

Evans. It is not meet the Council hear a riot; there is no fear of Got in a riot. The Council, look you, shall desire to hear the fear of Got, and not to hear a riot. Take your vizaments in that.

Shal. Ha! o' my life, if I were young again, the sword should end it. 41

Evans. It is petter that friends is the sword, and end it; and there is also another device in my prain, which peradventure prings goot discretions with it: there is Anne Page, which is daughter to Master [George] Page, which is pretty virginity. 46

Slen. Mistress Anne Page? She has brown hair, and speaks small like a woman.

Evans. It is that fery person for all the orld, as just as you will desire, and seven hundred pounds 50 of moneys, and gold, and silver, is her grandsire upon his death's-bed (Got deliver to a joyful resurrec-tions!) give, when she is able to overtake seven-teen years old. It were a goot motion if we leave our pribbles and prabbles, and desire a mar- 55 riage between Master Abraham and Mistress Anne Page.

Slen. Did her grandsire leave her seven hundred pound?

Evans. Ay, and her father is make her a petter penny. 61

Slen. I know the young gentlewoman, she has good gifts.

Evans. Seven hundred pounds, and possibilities, is goot gifts. 65

Shal. Well, let us see honest Master Page. Is Falstaff there?

Evans. Shall I tell you a lie? I do despise a liar as I do despise one that is false, or as I despise one that is not true. The knight Sir John is there, and 70 I beseech you be rul'd by your well-willers. I will peat the door for Master Page. [*Knocks.*] What ho! Got pless your house here!

Page. [*Within.*] Who's there? 74

[*Enter*] PAGE.

Evans. Here is Got's plessing, and your friend, and Justice Shallow, and here young Master Slender, that peradventures shall tell you another tale, if mat-ters grow to your likings.

Page. I am glad to see your worships well. I thank you for my venison, Master Shallow. 80

Shal. Master Page, I am glad to see you. Much good do it your good heart! I wish'd your veni-son better, it was ill kill'd. How doth good Mis-tress Page?—and I thank you always with my heart, la! with my heart. 85

Page. Sir, I thank you.

Shal. Sir, I thank you; by yea and no, I do.

Page. I am glad to see you, good Master Slender.

Slen. How does your fallow greyhound, sir? I heard say he was outrun on Cotsall. 90

Page. It could not be judg'd, sir.

Slen. You'll not confess, you'll not confess.

Shal. That he will not. 'Tis your fault, 'tis your fault; 'tis a good dog.

Page. A cur, sir. 95

Shal. Sir! he's a good dog, and a fair dog—can there be more said? He is good, and fair. Is Sir John Falstaff here?

Page. Sir, he is within; and I would I could do a good office between you. 100

Evans. It is spoke as a Christians ought to speak.

Shal. He hath wrong'd me, Master Page.

Page. Sir, he doth in some sort confess it.

Shal. If it be confess'd, it is not redress'd. Is not that so, Master Page? He hath wrong'd me, indeed he hath, at a word he hath. Believe me, Robert Shallow, esquire, saith he is wrong'd. 107

Page. Here comes Sir John.

[*Enter* SIR JOHN] FALSTAFF, BARDOLPH, NYM, PISTOL.

Fal. Now, Master Shallow, you'll complain of me to the King? 110

Shal. Knight, you have beaten my men, kill'd my deer, and broke open my lodge.

Fal. But not kiss'd your keeper's daughter?

Shal. Tut, a pin! this shall be answer'd. 114

Fal. I will answer it straight: I have done all this. That is now answer'd.

Shal. The Council shall know this.

Fal. 'Twere better for you if it were known in counsel. You'll be laugh'd at.

Evans. *Pauca verba*; Sir John, good worts. 120

Fal. Good worts? good cabbage. Slender, I broke your head; what matter have you against me?

Slen. Marry, sir, I have matter in my head against you, and against your cony-catching ras-

33-34. **compremises:** compromises (a variant form), settlements by arbitration.
35. **The Council . . . riot.** The Privy Council sitting as Star Chamber heard such cases. But Evans supposes that Shallow is talking about an ecclesiastical council or synod.
39. **vizaments:** Evans' version of *advisements* = considerations.
42. **that . . . sword:** i.e. that the quarrel be settled by the intervention of friends.
47. **Mistress.** Used of unmarried as well as married women.
48. **small:** in a high-pitched voice.
49. **orld.** Evans frequently (though not consistently) omits initial *w*; see *ork* (line 145), *oman* (line 227), *ord* and its variant *ort* (line 254).
50. **just:** precisely. 54. **motion:** move, plan.
55. **pribbles and prabbles:** bribbles and brabbles, i.e. petty disputings.
60. **is:** i.e. will. 63. **gifts:** qualities of mind and body.
64. **possibilities:** expectations (of additional inheritance).
66. **honest:** worthy. 71. **well-willers:** well-wishers.
78. **grow:** develop.

83. **ill:** i.e. illegally (see lines 111-12 below).
87. **by . . . no:** most certainly (a common usage, based on Matthew 5:37). 89. **fallow:** of a fawn color.
90. **Cotsall:** Cotswold. The Cotswolds are a range of hills in Glouces-tershire.
93. **fault:** misfortune (with quibble on the sense "loss of scent").
100. **office:** service. 103. **sort:** manner.
106. **at a word:** in short.
114. **pin:** trifle. **answer'd:** accounted for.
115. **answer it straight:** (1) account for it strictly; (2) reply to it straightway. 118-19. **in counsel:** secretly, privately.
120. **Pauca verba:** few words.
121. **worts:** vegetables (a pun on Evans' pronunciation of *words*). **cabbage:** i.e. cabbage head, fool.
122. **broke:** cut open. **matter:** grievance, complaint.
123. **Marry:** indeed (originally the name of the Virgin Mary used as an oath). **matter:** issue from the wound.
124. **cony-catching:** cheating.

cals, Bardolph, Nym, and Pistol. [They carried me to the tavern and made me drunk, and afterward pick'd my pocket.]   127

Bard. You Banbury cheese!

Slen. Ay, it is no matter.

Pist. How now, Mephostophilus?

Slen. Ay, it is no matter.

Nym. Slice, I say! *Pauca, pauca.* Slice, that's my humor.   133

Slen. Where's Simple, my man? can you tell, cousin?

Evans. Peace, I pray you. Now let us understand. There is three umpires in this matter, as I understand: that is, Master Page (*fidelicet*   138 Master Page) and there is myself (*fidelicet* myself) and the three party is (lastly and finally) mine host of the Garter.

Page. We three to hear it and end it between them.   143

Evans. Fery goot. I will make a prief of it in my note-book, and we will afterwards ork upon the cause with as great discreetly as we can.

Fal. Pistol!

Pist. He hears with ears.   148

Evans. The tevil and his tam! what phrase is this? "He hears with ear"? Why, it is affectations.

Fal. Pistol, did you pick Master Slender's purse?   152

Slen. Ay, by these gloves, did he, or I would I might never come in mine own great chamber again else, of seven groats in mill-sixpences, and two Edward shovel-boards, that cost me two shilling and two pence a-piece of Yead Miller—by these gloves.

Fal. Is this true, Pistol?

Evans. No, it is false, if it is a pick-purse.   160

Pist. Ha, thou mountain-foreigner! Sir John, and master mine,

I combat challenge of this latten bilbo.

Word of denial in thy *labras* here!

Word of denial! Froth and scum, thou liest!

Slen. By these gloves, then 'twas he.   165

Nym. Be avis'd, sir, and pass good humors.

I will say "marry trap" with you, if you run the nuthook's humor on me—that is the very note of it.   169

Slen. By this hat, then he in the red face had it; for though I cannot remember what I did when you made me drunk, yet I am not altogether an ass.

Fal. What say you, Scarlet and John?

Bard. Why, sir, for my part, I say the gentleman had drunk himself out of his five sentences.   175

Evans. It is his five senses. Fie, what the ignorance is!

Bard. And being fap, sir, was (as they say) cashier'd; and so conclusions pass'd the careers.   179

Slen. Ay, you spake in Latin then too: but 'tis no matter; I'll ne'er be drunk whilst I live again, but in honest, civil, godly company, for this trick. If I be drunk, I'll be drunk with those that have the fear of God, and not with drunken knaves.   184

Evans. So Got udge me, that is a virtuous mind.

Fal. You hear all these matters denied, gentlemen; you hear it.

[*Enter*] ANNE PAGE [*with wine*], MISTRESS FORD, MISTRESS PAGE.

Page. Nay, daughter, carry the wine in, we'll drink within.   [*Exit Anne Page.*]

Slen. O heaven! this is Mistress Anne Page.   190

Page. How now, Mistress Ford?

Fal. Mistress Ford, by my troth, you are very well met. By your leave, good mistress. [*Kisses her.*]

Page. Wife, bid these gentlemen welcome. Come, we have a hot venison pasty to dinner. Come, gentlemen, I hope we shall drink down all unkindness.   197

[*Exeunt all except Shallow, Slender, and Evans.*]

Slen. I had rather than forty shillings I had my Book of Songs and Sonnets here.

[*Enter*] SIMPLE.

How now, Simple, where have you been? I must wait on myself, must I? You have not the Book of Riddles about you, have you?   202

Sim. Book of Riddles? Why, did you not lend it to Alice Shortcake upon All-hallowmas last, a fortnight afore Michaelmas?   205

Shal. Come, coz, come, coz, we stay for you. A word with you, coz; marry, this, coz: there is as

125. **carried:** took, accompanied.
128. **Banbury cheese.** Proverbially thin; a hit at Slender which indicates that his physique matches his name.
130. **Mephostophilus:** Mephistopheles, the devil in Marlowe's *Dr. Faustus.*
132. **Slice.** Another hit at Slender's thinness (?) or Nym's threat to slice the "Banbury cheese" with his sword (?) or (as suggested by the following *Pauca*) an order to Slender to cut short his remarks (?).
133. **humor:** whim, mood.   138. **fidelicet:** *videlicet,* namely.
141. **Garter:** the name of an inn in Windsor.
154. **great chamber:** hall.
155. **groats:** coins worth fourpence.   **mill-sixpences:** newly introduced machine-made coins with fluted edges.
156. **Edward shovel-boards:** old broad shillings of Edward VI, worn smooth by long use and therefore convenient for the game of shovel-board.   157. **Yead:** Ed.
160. **false.** Evans takes *true* in the sense "honest."
161. **mountain-foreigner:** i.e. Welshman.
162. **latten bilbo:** sword made of a soft alloy resembling brass (a hit at Slender's cowardice and perhaps another glance at his thinness). *Bilbo* comes from the name of the Spanish city Bilbao, where fine swords were manufactured.
163. **Word ... labras:** i.e. I call you a liar to your face (*labras* = lips).
166. **avis'd:** advised, i.e. prudent.   **pass good humors:** do nothing disagreeable.

167. **marry trap:** probably an exclamation from a children's game, meaning "now you're caught."
167–68. **run ... me:** act like the constable, i.e. accuse me of stealing.
168. **very note:** exact information.
173. **Scarlet and John.** Will Scarlet and Little John were two of Robin Hood's companions. "Scarlet" alludes to the color of Bardolph's face.
178. **fap:** drunk.
179. **cashier'd:** deprived (of his senses).   **conclusions ... careers:** inferences galloped off at full speed, i.e. he drew the wrong conclusions.
185. **udge:** Evans' version of *judge.*   192. **troth:** faith.
195. **to:** for.
199. **Book ... Sonnets.** Probably an allusion to the book better known as Tottel's *Miscellany* (1557), a collection of poems by Wyatt, Surrey, and others.
201–2. **Book of Riddles.** Another popular but scarcely up-to-the-minute book; although not extant in any edition older than 1629, it first appeared at least as early as 1575.
204–5. **All-hallowmas ... Michaelmas.** Simple errs: Michaelmas is September 29; All-hallowmas, or All Saints' Day, November 1.
206. **stay:** wait.

'twere a tender, a kind of tender, made afar off by Sir Hugh here. Do you understand me?

Slen. Ay, sir, you shall find me reasonable. If it be so, I shall do that that is reason. 211

Shal. Nay, but understand me.

Slen. So I do, sir.

Evans. Give ear to his motions: Master Slender, I will description the matter to you, if you be capacity of it. 216

Slen. Nay, I will do as my cousin Shallow says. I pray you pardon me; he's a Justice of Peace in his country, simple though I stand here.

Evans. But that is not the question: the question is concerning your marriage. 221

Shal. Ay, there's the point, sir.

Evans. Marry, is it; the very point of it—to Mistress Anne Page. 224

Slen. Why, if it be so, I will marry her upon any reasonable demands.

Evans. But can you affection the oman? Let us command to know that of your mouth, or of your 228 lips; for divers philosophers hold that the lips is parcel of the mouth. Therefore precisely, can you carry your good will to the maid?

Shal. Cousin Abraham Slender, can you love her?

Slen. I hope, sir, I will do as it shall become one that would do reason. 234

Evans. Nay, Got's lords and his ladies, you must speak possitable, if you can carry her your desires towards her.

Shal. That you must. Will you, upon good dowry, marry her?

Slen. I will do a greater thing than that, upon your request, cousin, in any reason. 241

Shal. Nay, conceive me, conceive me, sweet coz; what I do is to pleasure you, coz. Can you love the maid?

Slen. I will marry her, sir, at your request; but if there be no great love in the beginning, yet heaven may decrease it upon better acquaintance, 247 when we are married and have more occasion to know one another. I hope, upon familiarity will grow more content. But if you say, "Marry her," I will marry her; that I am freely dissolv'd, and dissolutely. 252

Evans. It is a fery discretion answer, save the fall is in the ord "dissolutely." The ort is (according to our meaning) "resolutely." His meaning is good. 256

Shal. Ay—I think my cousin meant well.

Slen. Ay, or else I would I might be hang'd, la!

Shal. Here comes fair Mistress Anne. 259

[Enter ANNE PAGE.*]*

Would I were young for your sake, Mistress Anne!

Anne. The dinner is on the table. My father desires your worships' company. 262

Shal. I will wait on him, fair Mistress Anne.

Evans. 'Od's plessed will! I will not be absence at the grace. *[Exeunt Shallow and Evans.]* 265

Anne. Will't please your worship to come in, sir?

Slen. No, I thank you, forsooth, heartily; I am very well.

Anne. The dinner attends you, sir.

Slen. I am not a-hungry, I thank you, forsooth. Go, sirrah, for all you are my man, go wait 271 upon my cousin Shallow. *[Exit Simple.]* A Justice of Peace sometime may be beholding to his friend for a man. I keep but three men and a boy yet, till my mother be dead. But what though? yet I live like a poor gentleman born. 276

Anne. I may not go in without your worship; they will not sit till you come.

Slen. I' faith, I'll eat nothing. I thank you as much as though I did. 280

Anne. I pray you, sir, walk in.

Slen. I had rather walk here, I thank you. I bruis'd my shin th' other day with playing at sword and dagger with a master of fence (three veneys for a dish of stew'd prunes) and by my troth, I cannot abide the smell of hot meat since. Why do your dogs bark so? be there bears i' th' town? 287

Anne. I think there are, sir, I heard them talk'd of.

Slen. I love the sport well, but I shall as soon quarrel at it as any man in England. You are 291 afraid if you see the bear loose, are you not?

Anne. Ay indeed, sir.

Slen. That's meat and drink to me, now. I have seen Sackerson loose twenty times, and have taken him by the chain; but (I warrant you) the women 296 have so cried and shriek'd at it, that it pass'd. But women, indeed, cannot abide 'em, they are very ill-favor'd rough things.

[Enter PAGE.*]*

Page. Come, gentle Master Slender, come; we stay for you. 301

Slen. I'll eat nothing, I thank you, sir.

Page. By cock and pie, you shall not choose, sir! come, come.

Slen. Nay, pray you lead the way. 305

Page. Come on, sir.

Slen. Mistress Anne, yourself shall go first.

Anne. Not I, sir, pray you keep on.

---

208. afar off: indirectly.
219. simple . . . here: i.e. humble though I (his kinsman) be (but with unintentional suggestion of *simple* = simple-minded).
230. parcel: part.   **236. possitable:** Evans' version of *positively*.
242. conceive: understand.   **243. pleasure:** please.
247. decrease: blunder for *increase*.
250. content. Many editors adopt Theobald's emendation *contempt* as more in line with Slender's mode of expression in the surrounding prose. In either case there is an echo of the proverb "Familiarity breeds contempt."   **251. dissolv'd:** blunder for *resolved.*
252. dissolutely: blunder for *resolutely.*
254. fall: Evans' version of *fault.*

264. 'Od's: God's.   **269. attends:** awaits.
271. sirrah: customary form of address to an inferior.
273. beholding: beholden, indebted.
275. what though: what does it matter.
284. fence: fencing.   **veneys:** bouts.
285. stew'd prunes. A favorite dish in brothels, hence slang for *prostitutes.*   **290. sport:** i.e. bear-baiting.
295. Sackerson: a famous bear at Paris Garden near the Globe and other theatres on the Bankside.   **297. pass'd:** defied description.
299. ill-favor'd: ugly.
303. By . . . pie: a mild oath of disputed origin.   **shall not choose:** must.

Slen. Truly I will not go first; truly la! I will not do you that wrong.   310

Anne. I pray you, sir.

Slen. I'll rather be unmannerly than troublesome. You do yourself wrong indeed la!   *Exeunt.*

SCENE II

Enter EVANS *and* SIMPLE [*from dinner*].

Evans. Go your ways, and ask of Doctor Caius' house which is the way; and there dwells one Mistress Quickly, which is in the manner of his nurse—or his dry nurse—or his cook—or his laundry—his washer and his wringer.   5

Sim. Well, sir.

Evans. Nay, it is petter yet. Give her this letter; for it is a oman that altogether's acquaintance with Mistress Anne Page; and the letter is to desire and require her to solicit your master's desires   10 to Mistress Anne Page. I pray you be gone. I will make an end of my dinner; there's pippins and cheese to come.   *Exeunt.*

SCENE III

Enter FALSTAFF, HOST, BARDOLPH, NYM, PISTOL, [ROBIN, *Falstaff's*] *page.*

Fal. Mine host of the Garter!

Host. What says my bully-rook? Speak scholarly and wisely.

Fal. Truly, mine host, I must turn away some of my followers.   5

Host. Discard, bully Hercules, cashier; let them wag; trot, trot.

Fal. I sit at ten pounds a week.

Host. Thou'rt an emperor—Caesar, Keiser, and Pheazar. I will entertain Bardolph; he shall draw, he shall tap. Said I well, bully Hector?   11

Fal. Do so, good mine host.

Host. I have spoke; let him follow. [*To Bardolph.*] Let me see thee froth and [lime]. I am at a word; follow.   [*Exit.*] 15

Fal. Bardolph, follow him. A tapster is a good trade. An old cloak makes a new jerkin; a wither'd servingman a fresh tapster. Go, adieu.

Bard. It is a life that I have desir'd. I will thrive.

I.ii. Location: Scene continues.
1. **ask of:** inquire concerning.
4. **dry nurse.** Evans means someone who looks after an adult, as opposed to a wet nurse who cares for an infant.
8. **altogether's acquaintance:** is very well acquainted.
12. **pippins:** kind of apple.

I.iii. Location: Windsor. The Garter Inn.
2. **bully-rook:** fine fellow.   **scholarly:** as befits a scholar.
6. **cashier:** dismiss.   7. **wag:** go their way.
8. **I sit at:** my expenses come to.   9. **Keiser:** kaiser, emperor.
10. **Pheazar:** vizier (?) or perhaps simply a word invented by the host to rhyme with the others.   **entertain:** hire.   **draw:** draw liquor.
11. **tap:** serve as tapster.
14. **froth and lime.** Serving beer with a heavy froth allowed short measure; adding lime to cheap wine masked its sour taste.   **I . . . word:** i.e. I am a man of action and few words.
17. **jerkin:** close-fitting jacket.

Pist. O base Hungarian wight! wilt thou the spigot wield?   [*Exit Bardolph.*] 21

Nym. He was gotten in drink. Is not the humor conceited?

Fal. I am glad I am so acquit of this tinderbox; his thefts were too open; his filching was like an unskillful singer, he kept not time.   26

Nym. The good humor is to steal at a minute's rest.

Pist. "Convey," the wise it call. "Steal"? foh! a *fico* for the phrase!   30

Fal. Well, sirs, I am almost out at heels.

Pist. Why then let kibes ensue.

Fal. There is no remedy; I must cony-catch, I must shift.

Pist. Young ravens must have food.   35

Fal. Which of you know Ford of this town?

Pist. I ken the wight; he is of substance good.

Fal. My honest lads, I will tell you what I am about.

Pist. Two yards, and more.   40

Fal. No quips now, Pistol! Indeed I am in the waist two yards about; but I am now about no waste; I am about thrift. Briefly—I do mean to   43 make love to Ford's wife. I spy entertainment in her. She discourses, she carves, she gives the leer of invitation. I can construe the action of her familiar style, and the hardest voice of her behavior (to be English'd rightly) is, "I am Sir John Falstaff's."

Pist. He hath studied her [well], and translated her will, out of honesty into English.   50

Nym. The anchor is deep. Will that humor pass?

Fal. Now, the report goes she has all the rule of her husband's purse. He hath a legend of angels.

Pist. As many devils entertain; and "To her, boy," say I.   55

Nym. The humor rises; it is good. Humor me the angels.

---

20. **Hungarian:** i.e. beggarly (from the phonetic similarity of *Hungary* and *hungry*).   **wight:** person, man.
22. **gotten in drink:** conceived when his parents were drunk (an origin attributed to cowards).   23. **conceited:** ingenious.
24. **acquit:** rid.   **tinderbox.** Another allusion to Bardolph's red face.
27-28. **minute's rest.** Some editors emend to *minim's rest* or *minim-rest,* the shortest rest in music, but the F1 reading is supported by Q1-2.   29. **Convey:** steal.
30. **fico:** fig (Italian), an obscene gesture to show contempt, made by thrusting the thumb between two fingers.
31. **out at heels:** i.e. out of money, but Pistol quibbles on the literal meaning.   32. **kibes:** chilblains.
33. **cony-catch:** trick fools out of their money (literally, snare rabbits).
34. **shift:** devise a stratagem.
35. **Young . . . food.** Proverbial and Biblical, with reference to the raven's habits as a voracious scavenger.
37. **ken:** know.   **of substance good:** well-to-do.
43. **thrift:** profit.   44. **entertainment:** willingness to receive me.
45. **carves:** shows courtesy (?) or speaks affectedly (?).   **leer:** amorous side-glance.
46-47. **construe . . . style:** i.e. interpret the informality of her behavior (with an elaborate grammatical pun that extends to *voice* and *English'd* in the following lines).
47. **hardest voice:** (1) severest expression; (2) most difficult construction.   48. **English'd:** (1) put into words; (2) translated into English.
50. **honesty:** chastity.
51. **The anchor is deep.** A crux. The phrase may mean "the scheme is firmly set" or that Falstaff is getting out of his depth (as he soon does).   **Will . . . pass:** i.e. will my figure of speech pass muster.
53. **legend:** legion (a variant spelling).   **angels:** gold coins, worth about 10 shillings, stamped with the figure of the archangel Michael.
54. **entertain:** take into service.

Fal. I have writ me here a letter to her; and here another to Page's wife, who even now gave me good eyes too, examin'd my parts with most judicious iliads; sometimes the beam of her view gilded my foot, sometimes my portly belly. 62

Pist. Then did the sun on dunghill shine.

Nym. I thank thee for that humor.

Fal. O, she did so course o'er my exteriors with such a greedy intention, that the appetite of her eye did seem to scorch me up like a burning-glass! 66 Here's another letter to her. She bears the purse too; she is a region in Guiana, all gold and bounty. I will be cheaters to them both, and they shall be 70 exchequers to me. They shall be my East and West Indies, and I will trade to them both. Go, bear thou this letter to Mistress Page; and thou this to Mistress Ford. We will thrive, lads, we will thrive. 74

Pist. Shall I Sir Pandarus of Troy become, And by my side wear steel? Then Lucifer take all!

Nym. I will run no base humor. Here, take the humor-letter; I will keep the havior of reputation.

Fal. [*To Robin.*] Hold, sirrah, bear you these letters tightly;
Sail like my pinnace to these golden shores. 80
Rogues, hence, avaunt, vanish like hailstones; go!
Trudge! Plod away i' th' hoof! Seek shelter, pack!
Falstaff will learn the [humor] of the age,
French thrift, you rogues—myself and skirted page.
[*Exeunt Falstaff and Robin.*]

Pist. Let vultures gripe thy guts! for gourd and fullam holds, 85
And high and low beguiles the rich and poor.
Tester I'll have in pouch when thou shalt lack,
Base Phrygian Turk!

Nym. I have operations [in my head] which be humors of revenge. 90

Pist. Wilt thou revenge?

Nym. By welkin and her star!

Pist. With wit or steel?

Nym. With both the humors, I.
I will discuss the humor of this love to [Page]. 95

Pist. And I to [Ford] shall eke unfold
How Falstaff (varlet vile)

His dove will prove, his gold will hold,
And his soft couch defile.

Nym. My humor shall not cool. I will incense [Page] to deal with poison; I will possess him 101 with yallowness, for the revolt of mine is dangerous—that is my true humor.

Pist. Thou art the Mars of malecontents. I second thee; troop on. *Exeunt.* 105

SCENE IV

Enter MISTRESS QUICKLY, SIMPLE.

Quick. What, John Rugby!

[*Enter*] JOHN RUGBY.

I pray thee go to the casement, and see if you can see my master, Master Doctor Caius, coming. If he do, i' faith, and find any body in the house, here will be an old abusing of God's patience and the King's English. 6

Rug. I'll go watch.

Quick. Go, and we'll have a posset for't soon at night, in faith, at the latter end of a sea-coal fire. [*Exit Rugby.*] An honest, willing, kind fellow 10 as ever servant shall come in house withal; and I warrant you, no tell-tale nor no breed-bate. His worst fault is, that he is given to prayer; he is something peevish that way; but nobody but has his fault—but let that pass. Peter Simple, you say your name is? 16

Sim. Ay, for fault of a better.

Quick. And Master Slender's your master?

Sim. Ay, forsooth.

Quick. Does he not wear a great round beard, like a glover's paring-knife? 21

Sim. No, forsooth; he hath but a little [whey]-face, with a little yellow beard, a Cain-color'd beard.

Quick. A softly-sprighted man, is he not?

Sim. Ay, forsooth; but he is as tall a man of his hands as any is between this and his head. He hath fought with a warrener. 27

Quick. How say you? O, I should remember him. Does he not hold up his head (as it were) and strut in his gait? 30

Sim. Yes indeed does he.

Quick. Well, heaven send Anne Page no worse fortune! Tell Master Parson Evans I will do what

---

61. **iliads:** oeillades, amorous glances.
66. **intention:** intentness of regard.
67. **burning-glass:** a glass which focuses the rays of the sun and produces intense heat.
69. **Guiana.** A possible compliment to Sir Walter Raleigh, who in 1596, on his return from his voyage to South America, published an account entitled *The Discovery of the Large, Rich, and Beautiful Empire of Guiana.*
70. **cheaters:** escheators, officers appointed to oversee lands forfeited to the king, called *escheats*; with play on the ordinary meaning.
71. **exchequers:** treasuries; the escheator was an official of the Exchequer.
75. **Sir Pandarus:** the uncle of Cressida, who brought her and Troilus together as lovers; from his name is derived the word *pander.*
76. **And . . . steel:** i.e. and I a soldier.
78. **keep . . . reputation:** behave in a reputable fashion.
79. **tightly:** skillfully. 82. **pack:** be off.
84. **French thrift:** an economy measure, practiced in France, of having one page rather than a retinue of servingmen. **skirted:** wearing a skirted doublet, a style popular in France.
85. **gripe:** grip, seize. **gourd:** hollow dice. **fullam:** loaded dice.
86. **high and low:** the roll of the dice (?) or false dice (?). Cf. *The Winter's Tale,* V.i.207. 87. **Tester:** sixpence. **pouch:** purse.
88. **Phrygian Turk:** a term of abuse.
89. **operations:** plans, schemes. 92. **welkin:** heaven, sky.
95. **discuss:** disclose. 96. **eke:** also.

98. **prove:** try, test. 100. **incense:** incite.
101. **deal with:** use. **possess him:** cause him to be possessed.
102. **yallowness:** yellowness (a variant spelling), i.e. jealousy. **revolt of mine:** casting off of my allegiance (?).
104. **the Mars:** i.e. the most warlike.

I.iv. Location: Dr. Caius' house.
5. **old:** great, plentiful.
8. **posset:** hot milk curdled with ale or wine.
9. **sea-coal:** mineral coal as opposed to charcoal.
11. **withal:** with. 12. **breed-bate:** mischief maker.
13–14. **something peevish:** somewhat silly.
22. **whey-face:** pallid face.
23. **Cain-color'd beard.** Cain was traditionally represented with a yellow or reddish beard. 24. **softly-sprighted:** mild-spirited.
25–26. **as . . . hands:** as valiant a man.
26. **between . . . head.** Not satisfactorily explained; probably a disparaging witticism. 27. **warrener:** gamekeeper, especially of rabbits.

I can for your master. Anne is a good girl, and
I wish— 35

[*Enter* RUGBY.]

Rug. Out alas! here comes my master.
Quick. We shall all be shent. Run in here, good
young man; go into this closet. He will not stay
long. [*Shuts Simple in the closet.*] What, John Rugby!
John! what, John, I say! Go, John, go inquire for 40
my master; I doubt he be not well, that he comes
not home.
[*Singing.*] And down, down, adown-a, etc.

[*Enter*] DOCTOR CAIUS.

Caius. Vat is you sing? I do not like des toys.
Pray you go and vetch me in my closet [*une boîte* 45
en] *verd*, a box, a green-a box. Do intend vat I speak?
A green-a box.
Quick. Ay, forsooth, I'll fetch it you. [*Aside.*]
I am glad he went not in himself; if he had found the
young man, he would have been horn-mad. 50
Caius. Fe, fe, fe, fe! *ma foi, il fait fort* [*chaud. O,
je m'en*] *vois à la cour—la grande affaire.*
Quick. Is it this, sir?
Caius. *Oui, mette le au mon pocket; dépêche,* quickly.
Vere is dat knave Rugby? 55
Quick. What, John Rugby! John!
Rug. Here, sir!
Caius. You are John Rugby, and you are Jack
Rugby. Come, take-a your rapier, and come after
my heel to the court. 60
Rug. 'Tis ready, sir, here in the porch.
Caius. By my trot, I tarry too long. 'Od's me!
Qu'ai-je oublié? Dere is some simples in my closet,
dat I vill not for the varld I shall leave behind.
Quick. Ay me, he'll find the young man there,
and be mad! 66
Caius. O *diable, diable!* vat is in my closet?
Villainy! laroon! [*Pulling Simple out.*] Rugby, my
rapier!
Quick. Good master, be content. 70
Caius. Wherefore shall I be content-a?
Quick. The young man is an honest man.
Caius. What shall de honest man do in my closet?
Dere is no honest man dat shall come in my closet.
Quick. I beseech you be not so phlegmatic. Hear
the truth of it: he came of an errand to me from
Parson Hugh. 77
Caius. Vell?
Sim. Ay, forsooth; to desire her to—
Quick. Peace, I pray you. 80

Caius. Peace-a your tongue.—Speak-a your tale.
Sim. To desire this honest gentlewoman, your
maid, to speak a good word to Mistress Anne Page
for my master in the way of marriage.
Quick. This is all indeed la! but I'll ne'er put
my finger in the fire, and need not. 86
Caius. Sir Hugh send-a you? Rugby, [*baillez*] me
some paper. Tarry you a little-a while. [*Writes.*]
Quick. [*Aside to Simple.*] I am glad he is so quiet.
If he had been throughly mov'd, you should 90
have heard him so loud and so melancholy. But
notwithstanding, man, I'll do [you] your master
what good I can; and the very yea and the no is,
the French doctor, my master (I may call him my
master, look you, for I keep his house; and I 95
wash, wring, brew, bake, scour, dress meat and
drink, make the beds, and do all myself)—
Sim. [*Aside to Quickly.*] 'Tis a great charge to
come under one body's hand. 99
Quick. [*Aside to Simple.*] Are you avis'd o' that?
You shall find it a great charge; and to be up early
and down late; but notwithstanding (to tell you
in your ear, I would have no words of it) my master himself is in love with Mistress Anne Page; 104
but notwithstanding that, I know Anne's mind—
that's neither here nor there.
Caius. You jack'nape, give-a this letter to Sir
Hugh. By gar, it is a shallenge. I will cut his troat in
de park; and I will teach a scurvy jack-a-nape 109
priest to meddle or make—You may be gone; it is
not good you tarry here. By gar, I will cut all his
two stones; by gar, he shall not have a stone to throw
at his dog. [*Exit Simple.*]
Quick. Alas! he speaks but for his friend. 114
Caius. It is no matter-a ver dat. Do not you
tell-a me dat I shall have Anne Page for myself?
By gar, I vill kill de Jack priest; and I have appointed mine host of de Jarteer to measure our
weapon. By gar, I will myself have Anne Page. 119
Quick. Sir, the maid loves you, and all shall be
well. We must give folks leave to prate; what the
good-jer!
Caius. Rugby, come to the court with me. By
gar, if I have not Anne Page, I shall turn your head
out of my door. Follow my heels, Rugby. 125

[*Exeunt Caius and Rugby.*]

Quick. You shall have Anne—fool's-head of your
own. No, I know Anne's mind for that. Never
a woman in Windsor knows more of Anne's mind
than I do, nor can do more than I do with her, I
thank heaven. 130

---

37. shent: scolded. **41. doubt:** fear. **44. toys:** trifles.
45-46. une . . . verd: a green box.
46. intend: hear, understand (from French *entendre*).
50. horn-mad: as mad as an enraged bull.
51-52. ma . . . affaire: my word, it is very hot; I am going to the court,
the great affair.
54. Oui . . . dépêche: yes, put it in my pocket; be quick about it.
59. your rapier: i.e. your master's rapier. **62. trot:** troth.
63. Qu'ai-je oublié: what have I forgotten. **simples:** medicinal
herbs. **67. diable:** devil. **68. laroon:** robber (French *larron*).
70. content: calm.
75. phlegmatic. A blunder, probably for *choleric*, which in the old
"humors" physiology designated the temperament diametrically opposed to the phlegmatic.

86. and need not: if I don't have to. **87. baillez:** fetch.
90. throughly mov'd: thoroughly angered.
91. melancholy: irascible (?) or a blunder like *phlegmatic* in line 75 (?).
93. the very . . . no: i.e. what is certain (see note to I.i.87).
96. dress meat: prepare food. **98. charge:** burden.
100. Are . . . that: i.e. you may well say so.
107. jack'nape: coxcomb, fop. **110. make:** have to do, interfere.
111-12. cut . . . stones: castrate him.
117. Jack: contemptuous epithet, meaning "knavish."
118. Jarteer: Garter (French *jarretière*).
118-19. measure our weapon: i.e. act as a second.
122. good-jer: expletive of uncertain origin.
126. Anne. A quibble on *Anne / an.* Mistress Quickly means that the
only result of his wooing of Anne will be his being made a fool of.

Fenton. [*Within.*] Who's within there, ho?

Quick. Who's there, I trow? Come near the house, I pray you.

[*Enter*] FENTON.

Fent. How now, good woman, how dost thou?

Quick. The better that it pleases your good worship to ask.　136

Fent. What news? How does pretty Mistress Anne?

Quick. In truth, sir, and she is pretty, and honest, and gentle, and one that is your friend; I can tell you that by the way, I praise heaven for it.　141

Fent. Shall I do any good, think'st thou? shall I not lose my suit?

Quick. Troth, sir, all is in His hands above. But notwithstanding, Master Fenton, I'll be sworn　145 on a book she loves you. Have not your worship a wart above your eye?

Fent. Yes, marry, have I, what of that?

Quick. Well, thereby hangs a tale. Good faith, it is such another Nan; but (I detest) an honest　150 maid as ever broke bread. We had an hour's talk of that wart. I shall never laugh but in that maid's company! But, indeed, she is given too much to allicholy and musing; but for you—well—go to.　154

Fent. Well; I shall see her to-day. Hold, there's money for thee. Let me have thy voice in my behalf. If thou seest her before me, commend me.

Quick. Will I? I' faith, that we will; and I will tell your worship more of the wart the next time we have confidence, and of other wooers.　160

Fent. Well, farewell, I am in great haste now.

Quick. Farewell to your worship. [*Exit Fenton.*] Truly, an honest gentleman; but Anne loves him not; for I know Anne's mind as well as another does. Out upon't! what have I forgot?　*Exit.*　165

ACT II, SCENE I

Enter MISTRESS PAGE [*reading of a letter*].

Mrs. Page. What, have [I] scap'd love-letters in the holiday-time of my beauty, and am I now a subject for them? Let me see.　[*Reads.*]

"Ask me no reason why I love you, for though Love use Reason for his precisian, he admits him　5 not for his counsellor. You are not young, no more am I; go to then, there's sympathy. You are merry, so am I; ha, ha! then there's more sympathy. You love sack, and so do I; would you desire better

sympathy? Let it suffice thee, Mistress Page　10 —at the least if the love of soldier can suffice —that I love thee. I will not say, pity me—'tis not a soldier-like phrase—but I say, love me. By me,

　　　Thine own true knight,
　　　By day or night,　　　　　　15
　　　Or any kind of light,
　　　With all his might
　　　For thee to fight,
　　　　　John Falstaff."

What a Herod of Jewry is this! O wicked, wicked world! One that is well-nigh worn to pieces　21 with age to show himself a young gallant! What an unweigh'd behavior hath this Flemish drunkard pick'd (with the devil's name!) out of my conversation, that he dares in this manner assay me?　25 Why, he hath not been thrice in my company! What should I say to him? I was then frugal of my mirth. Heaven forgive me! Why, I'll exhibit a bill in the parliament for the putting down of men. How shall I be reveng'd on him? for　30 reveng'd I will be! as sure as his guts are made of puddings.

[*Enter*] MISTRESS FORD.

Mrs. Ford. Mistress Page, trust me, I was going to your house.　34

Mrs. Page. And trust me, I was coming to you. You look very ill.

Mrs. Ford. Nay, I'll ne'er believe that; I have to show to the contrary.

Mrs. Page. Faith, but you do, in my mind.　39

Mrs. Ford. Well—I do then; yet I say I could show you to the contrary. O Mistress Page, give me some counsel!

Mrs. Page. What's the matter, woman?

Mrs. Ford. O woman—if it were not for one trifling respect, I could come to such honor!　45

Mrs. Page. Hang the trifle, woman, take the honor. What is it? Dispense with trifles. What is it?

Mrs. Ford. If I would but go to hell for an eternal moment or so, I could be knighted.　50

Mrs. Page. What? thou liest! Sir Alice Ford! These knights will hack, and so thou shouldst not alter the article of thy gentry.

Mrs. Ford. We burn daylight. Here, read, read; perceive how I might be knighted. I shall think　55

---

132. **trow:** wonder.　　**Come near:** enter.　　139. **honest:** chaste.
140. **gentle:** well-mannered.
150. **it . . . Nan:** i.e. what a lively Anne she is.　　**detest:** blunder for *protest.*
154. **allicholy:** blunder for *melancholy.*　　**go to:** enough (a term of rebuke).　　160. **confidence:** blunder for *conference.*

II.i. Location: Windsor. Before Page's house.
2. **holiday-time:** playtime, i.e. youthful days.
4–6. **though . . . counsellor:** i.e. though Love listens to the puritanical sermons of Reason, he doesn't follow Reason's advice; in other words, the lover knows the rational objections to his course but yields to his irrational impulses nevertheless.
7. **sympathy:** agreement, congeniality.　　9. **sack:** Spanish wine.

20. **Herod of Jewry:** i.e. a ranting villain (like Herod in the mystery plays).
23. **unweigh'd:** ill-considered.　　**Flemish drunkard:** i.e. one who drinks enough to rival the Flemish (proverbially heavy drinkers).
24. **with . . . name:** may the name of devil go with him (?).
24–25. **conversation:** behavior, conduct.
25. **assay:** make advances to.
27. **What . . . say:** what could I have said.　　28. **exhibit:** submit.
29. **putting down:** suppression.
32. **puddings:** sausages, stuffed intestines.
36. **very ill:** i.e. not very well.
37–38. **have to show:** have evidence.
39. **in my mind:** to my way of thinking.
52. **hack.** Of uncertain meaning; possibly "attack with swords," with sexual innuendo, matching Mrs. Ford's quibble in *knighted* = (1) given the title of knight, (2) provided with a knight as lover.
53. **article . . . gentry:** character of your station.
54. **burn daylight:** waste time.

the worse of fat men, as long as I have an eye to make difference of men's liking: and yet he would not swear; [prais'd] women's modesty; and gave such orderly and well-behav'd reproof to all uncomeliness, that I would have sworn his disposition 60 would have gone to the truth of his words; but they do no more adhere and keep place together than the hundred Psalms to the tune of "Green-sleeves." What tempest, I trow, threw this whale (with so many tuns of oil in his belly) ashore at Windsor? 65 How shall I be reveng'd on him? I think the best way were to entertain him with hope, till the wicked fire of lust have melted him in his own grease. Did you ever hear the like? 69

Mrs. Page. Letter for letter; but that the name of Page and Ford differs! To thy great comfort in this mystery of ill opinions, here's the twin-brother of thy letter; but let thine inherit first, for I protest mine never shall. I warrant he hath a thou- 74 sand of these letters, writ with blank space for different names (sure, more!); and these are of the second edition. He will print them, out of doubt; for he cares not what he puts into the press, when he would put us two. I had rather be a giantess, and lie 79 under Mount Pelion. Well—I will find you twenty lascivious turtles ere one chaste man.

Mrs. Ford. Why, this is the very same: the very hand; the very words. What doth he think of us?

Mrs. Page. Nay, I know not; it makes me almost ready to wrangle with mine own honesty. 85 I'll entertain myself like one that I am not acquainted withal; for sure unless he know some strain in me that I know not myself, he would never have boarded me in this fury.

Mrs. Ford. "Boarding," call you it? I'll be sure to keep him above deck. 91

Mrs. Page. So will I; if he come under my hatches, I'll never to sea again. Let's be reveng'd on him: let's appoint him a meeting, give him a show of comfort in his suit, and lead him on with a fine-baited 95 delay, till he hath pawn'd his horses to mine host of the Garter.

Mrs. Ford. Nay, I will consent to act any villainy against him, that may not sully the chariness of our honesty. O that my husband saw this letter! it would give eternal food to his jealousy. 101

Mrs. Page. Why, look where he comes; and my good man too. He's as far from jealousy as I am from

giving him cause, and that (I hope) is an unmeasurable distance. 105

Mrs. Ford. You are the happier woman.

Mrs. Page. Let's consult together against this greasy knight. Come hither. [*They retire.*]

[*Enter*] FORD [*with*] PISTOL; PAGE [*with*] NYM.

Ford. Well, I hope it be not so.

Pist. Hope is a curtal dog in some affairs. 110 Sir John affects thy wife.

Ford. Why, sir, my wife is not young.

Pist. He woos both high and low, both rich and poor,
Both young and old, one with another, Ford.
He loves the gallimaufry, Ford. Perpend. 115

Ford. Love my wife?

Pist. With liver burning hot. Prevent; or go thou Like Sir Actaeon he, with Ringwood at thy heels— O, odious is the name!

Ford. What name, sir? 120

Pist. The horn, I say. Farewell.
Take heed, have open eye, for thieves do foot by night.
Take heed, ere summer comes or cuckoo-birds do sing.
Away, Sir Corporal Nym!
Believe it, Page, he speaks sense. [*Exit.*] 125

Ford. [*Aside.*] I will be patient; I will find out this.

Nym. [*To Page.*] And this is true; I like not the humor of lying. He hath wrong'd me in some humors. I should have borne the humor'd letter to her; but I have a sword, and it shall bite upon my neces- 131 sity. He loves your wife: there's the short and the long. My name is Corporal Nym; I speak, and I avouch; 'tis true; my name is Nym, and Falstaff loves your wife. Adieu. I love not the humor of bread and cheese [and there's the humor of it]. Adieu. [*Exit.*] 137

Page. "The humor of it," quoth 'a! Here's a fellow frights English out of his wits.

Ford. I will seek out Falstaff. 140

Page. I never heard such a drawling, affecting rogue.

Ford. If I do find it—well.

Page. I will not believe such a Cataian, though the priest o' th' town commended him for a true man. 146

Ford. 'Twas a good sensible fellow—well.

[*Mrs. Page and Mrs. Ford come forward.*]

57. **make difference of:** discriminate among. **liking:** physiques.
61. **gone . . . of:** supported, confirmed.
63. **hundred Psalms.** Many editors read *Hundredth Psalm* (*hundred* is a common variant of *hundredth*). **Green-sleeves:** a popular love song, still current. 67. **entertain . . . hope:** lead him on.
72. **mystery . . . opinions:** i.e. mysterious situation in which you have acquired such a questionable reputation. 77. **out of:** without.
78. **into the press.** With second meaning "under his weight."
80. **Pelion:** mountain in Thessaly which (according to one version of the Greek myth) the giants tried to pile upon its neighbor Mount Ossa.
81. **turtles:** turtledoves, proverbially faithful to their mates.
86. **entertain:** treat. 87. **withal:** with.
88. **boarded:** made advances to (a naval term, meaning to come alongside or aboard a ship, usually in order to attack).
95. **fine-baited:** subtly alluring.
98. **Nay.** Not a refusal but an expression of willingness to go farther.
99. **chariness:** scrupulous integrity.

110. **curtal:** with tail docked. 111. **affects:** loves.
115. **gallimaufry:** hodgepodge, miscellaneous assortment (term from cookery). **Perpend:** consider.
117. **liver.** The supposed seat of the passions.
118. **Actaeon:** Greek hunter who accidentally saw Diana as she was bathing, and was punished by being turned into a stag. He was killed by his own dogs. Pistol warns Ford that he is in danger of acquiring the horns of a cuckold. **Ringwood:** common name for a dog.
119. **the name:** i.e. the name of cuckold. 122. **foot:** walk.
123. **cuckoo-birds.** The cuckoo's call supposedly foretold cuckoldry.
131–32. **upon my necessity:** when I need to use it.
136. **bread and cheese:** i.e. the daily fare Falstaff has allowed him, with, Wilson suggests, some reference to the name of the cuckoo-bread flower. 139. **his:** its. 141. **affecting:** affected.
143. **If . . . well:** if I find it to be true, I'll take proper measures.
144. **Cataian:** scoundrel (literally, a person from Cathay, i.e. China).

Page. How now, Meg?

Mrs. Page. Whither go you, George, hark you?

Mrs. Ford. How now, sweet Frank, why art thou melancholy? 151

Ford. I melancholy? I am not melancholy. Get you home; go.

Mrs. Ford. Faith, thou hast some crotchets in thy head now. Will you go, Mistress Page? 155

Mrs. Page. Have with you. You'll come to dinner, George? [*Aside to Mrs. Ford.*] Look who comes yonder. She shall be our messenger to this paltry knight. 159

Mrs. Ford. [*Aside to Mrs. Page.*] Trust me, I thought on her. She'll fit it.

[*Enter* Mistress] Quickly.

Mrs. Page. You are come to see my daughter Anne?

Quick. Ay, forsooth; and I pray, how does good Mistress Anne? 165

Mrs. Page. Go in with us and see. We have an hour's talk with you.

[*Exeunt Mrs. Page, Mrs. Ford, and Mrs. Quickly.*]

Page. How now, Master Ford?

Ford. You heard what this knave told me, did you not? 170

Page. Yes, and you heard what the other told me?

Ford. Do you think there is truth in them?

Page. Hang 'em, slaves! I do not think the knight would offer it; but these that accuse him in his intent towards our wives are a yoke of his discarded men —very rogues, now they be out of service. 176

Ford. Were they his men?

Page. Marry, were they.

Ford. I like it never the better for that. Does he lie at the Garter? 180

Page. Ay, marry, does he. If he should intend this voyage toward my wife, I would turn her loose to him; and what he gets more of her than sharp words, let it lie on my head. 184

Ford. I do not misdoubt my wife; but I would be loath to turn them together. A man may be too confident. I would have nothing lie on my head. I cannot be thus satisfied.

[*Enter*] Host.

Page. Look where my ranting host of the Garter comes. There is either liquor in his pate, or money in his purse, when he looks so merrily. How now, mine host? 192

Host. How now, bully-rook? thou'rt a gentleman. Cavaleiro Justice, I say!

[*Enter*] Shallow.

Shal. I follow, mine host, I follow. Good even

and twenty, good Master Page! Master Page, will you go with us? we have sport in hand. 197

Host. Tell him, Cavaleiro Justice; tell him, bully-rook.

Shal. Sir, there is a fray to be fought between Sir Hugh the Welsh priest and Caius the French doctor. 202

Ford. Good mine host o' th' Garter, a word with you.

Host. What say'st thou, my bully-rook? 205

[*Ford and the Host talks.*]

Shal. [*To Page.*] Will you go with us to behold it? My merry host hath had the measuring of their weapons, and, I think, hath appointed them contrary places; for, believe me, I hear the parson is no jester. Hark, I will tell you what our sport shall be. [*They converse apart.*] 211

Host. Hast thou no suit against my knight, my guest-cavalier?

[*Ford.*] None, I protest; but I'll give you a pottle of burnt sack to give me recourse to him and tell him my name is [Brook]—only for a jest. 216

Host. My hand, bully; thou shalt have egress and regress—said I well?—and thy name shall be [Brook]. It is a merry knight. Will you go, An-heires? 220

Shal. Have with you, mine host.

Page. I have heard the Frenchman hath good skill in his rapier.

Shal. Tut, sir; I could have told you more. In these times you stand on distance: your passes, stoccadoes, and I know not what. 'Tis the heart, Master Page, 'tis here, 'tis here. I have seen 227 the time, with my long sword I would have made you four tall fellows skip like rats.

Host. Here, boys, here, here! shall we wag?

Page. Have with you. I had rather hear them scold than fight. [*Exeunt Host, Shallow, and Page.*] 232

Ford. Though Page be a secure fool, and stands so firmly on his wive's frailty, yet I cannot put off my opinion so easily. She was in his company at Page's house; and what they made there, I know not. Well, I will look further into't, and I 237 have a disguise to sound Falstaff. If I find her honest, I lose not my labor; if she be otherwise, 'tis labor well bestow'd. *Exit.*

154. **crotchets:** whims.
156. **Have with you:** I'll go with you (a conventional expression; see lines 221 and 231 and III.ii.92). 174. **offer:** venture.
175. **yoke:** pair. 180. **lie:** lodge. 181. **intend:** propose making.
184. **lie . . . head:** be my own responsibility. In line 187 Ford turns the words into an allusion to the cuckold's horns.
185. **misdoubt:** mistrust.
194. **Cavaleiro:** a gentleman expert in arms, a gallant.
195–96. **Good . . . twenty:** i.e. many returns of the day.

208–9. **contrary places:** different meeting-places.
214. **pottle:** two-quart tankard.
215. **burnt:** warmed. **recourse:** access.
216. **Brook.** That this form of Ford's alias, preserved in the quartos, was Shakespeare's original choice is shown by the wordplay at II.ii.150–51. Its alteration to *Broom*, to which F1 testifies, was presumably made to meet the wishes of the same Lord Cobham who is thought to have forced the replacement of *Oldcastle* by *Falstaff* in the Henry IV plays; in the latter case he would have been objecting to the use of an ancestor's name, in the former to the use of his own surname.
220. **An-heires.** A crux. The most widely adopted emendation is Theobald's *Mynheers*, Dutch for "sirs."
225. **stand:** rely. **distance:** prescribed space maintained between combatants. **passes:** lunges. **stoccadoes:** thrusts.
229. **tall:** valiant. 230. **wag:** be on our way.
232. **scold:** quarrel noisily. 233. **secure:** overconfident.
233–34. **stands . . . frailty:** trusts his susceptible wife so firmly.
234. **wive's:** wife's. **put off:** dismiss from my mind.
235. **She:** i.e. Mrs. Ford. 236. **made:** did.
238. **sound:** plumb, measure the depth of.

SCENE II

Enter FALSTAFF, PISTOL.

[*Pist.* I will retort the sum in equipage.]

Fal. I will not lend thee a penny.

Pist. Why then the world's mine oyster,
Which I with sword will open.

Fal. Not a penny. I have been content, sir, you
should lay my countenance to pawn. I have 6
grated upon my good friends for three reprieves for
you and your coach-fellow Nym; or else you had
look'd through the grate, like a geminy of baboons.
I am damn'd in hell for swearing to gentlemen my
friends, you were good soldiers and tall fellows; 11
and when Mistress Bridget lost the handle of her
fan, I took't upon mine honor thou hadst it not.

Pist. Didst not thou share? Hadst thou not
fifteen pence? 14

Fal. Reason, you rogue, reason; think'st thou
I'll endanger my soul gratis? At a word, hang no
more about me, I am no gibbet for you. Go—a
short knife and a throng!—to your manor of Pickt-
hatch! Go. You'll not bear a letter for me, you
rogue? You stand upon your honor! Why, 20
thou unconfinable baseness, it is as much as I can
do to keep the terms of my honor precise. I, I, I
myself sometimes, leaving the fear of [God] on the
left hand, and hiding mine honor in my necessity,
am fain to shuffle, to hedge, and to lurch; and 25
yet you, rogue, will ensconce your rags, your cat-a-
mountain looks, your red-lattice phrases, and your
bold-beating oaths, under the shelter of your honor!
You will not do it? You! 29

Pist. I do relent. What would thou more of man?

[*Enter*] ROBIN.

Rob. Sir, here's a woman would speak with you.

Fal. Let her approach.

[*Enter* MISTRESS] QUICKLY.

Quick. Give your worship good morrow.

Fal. Good morrow, goodwife.

Quick. Not so, and't please your worship. 35

Fal. Good maid then.

Quick. I'll be sworn,
As my mother was the first hour I was born.

Fal. I do believe the swearer. What with me? 39

Quick. Shall I vouchsafe your worship a word or
two?

Fal. Two thousand, fair woman, and I'll vouchsafe thee the hearing. 43

Quick. There is one Mistress Ford, sir—I pray
come a little nearer this ways. I myself dwell with
Master Doctor Caius—

Fal. Well, on. Mistress Ford, you say—

Quick. Your worship says very true. I pray
your worship come a little nearer this ways. 49

Fal. I warrant thee, nobody hears—mine own
people, mine own people.

Quick. Are they so? [God] bless them and make
them his servants!

Fal. Well; Mistress Ford, what of her? 54

Quick. Why, sir, she's a good creature. Lord,
Lord, your worship's a wanton! Well—heaven forgive you, and all of us, I pray—

Fal. Mistress Ford; come, Mistress Ford—

Quick. Marry, this is the short and the long
of it: you have brought her into such a canaries as 60
'tis wonderful. The best courtier of them all (when
the court lay at Windsor) could never have brought
her to such a canary; yet there has been knights,
and lords, and gentlemen, with their coaches; I
warrant you, coach after coach, letter after 65
letter, gift after gift; smelling so sweetly, all musk,
and so rushling, I warrant you, in silk and gold,
and in such alligant terms, and in such wine and
sugar of the best, and the fairest, that would have
won any woman's heart; and I warrant you, 70
they could never get an eye-wink of her. I had
myself twenty angels given me this morning, but
I defy all angels (in any such sort, as they say) but
in the way of honesty; and I warrant you, they
could never get her so much as sip on a cup with 75
the proudest of them all, and yet there has been earls,
nay (which is more) pensioners, but I warrant you
all is one with her.

Fal. But what says she to me? Be brief, my good
she-Mercury. 80

Quick. Marry, she hath receiv'd your letter—for
the which she thanks you a thousand times—and
she gives you to notify that her husband will be
absence from his house between ten and eleven.

Fal. Ten and eleven? 85

Quick. Ay, forsooth; and then you may come
and see the picture, she says, that you wot of. Master
Ford her husband will be from home. Alas, the
sweet woman leads an ill life with him. He's a very

II.ii. Location: Windsor. The Garter Inn.
1. **retort**: i.e. repay. **in equipage.** Meaning uncertain; conjectures
include "in military supplies," "in stolen goods," "in regular install-
ments."
6. **lay . . . pawn**: i.e. incur debts on the strength of my patronage.
7. **grated upon**: made a nuisance of myself with.
8. **coach-fellow**: close associate (literally, a horse teamed with another
in drawing a coach).
9. **grate**: i.e. grated window in a debtor's prison. **like . . . geminy**:
i.e. like a pair of baboons in a cage.
13. **took't . . . honor**: swore by my honor.
18. **short . . . throng**: i.e. with a small knife suitable for cutting purses
in a crowd.
18-19. **Pickt-hatch**: an area of London noted for its brothels. The
houses sometimes had the lower halves (hatches) of their divided doors
guarded with spikes (piked). 21. **unconfinable**: i.e. infinite.
22. **terms**: state. **precise.** Possibly punning on the meaning "puritanical."
25. **shuffle**: practice trickery. **hedge**: dodge. **lurch**: pilfer.
26-27. **cat-a-mountain**: catamount, wildcat.
27. **red-lattice phrases**: tavern talk (from the red-latticed windows
that distinguished an alehouse).
28. **bold-beating.** This word, which occurs only here, has been explained as a telescoping of *bold-faced* and *browbeating*.
35. **Not so**: i.e. I am not a wife.

40. **vouchsafe**: grant the favor of (misused by Quickly).
60. **canaries.** Not certainly explained; perhaps "state of excitement,"
from the lively dance called the canary. 62. **lay**: was in residence.
66. **musk**: i.e. heavy perfume (based on a highly odoriferous substance secreted by the male musk-deer).
67. **rushling**: Quickly's version of *rustling*.
68. **alligant.** She may intend either *elegant* or *eloquent*.
72. **twenty angels**: i.e. as a bribe to gain access to Mistress Ford.
77. **pensioners**: gentlemen of the royal bodyguard.
80. **she-Mercury**: female messenger. The winged Mercury was the
messenger of the gods. 87. **wot**: know.

jealousy man. She leads a very frampold life with him, good heart.   91

Fal. Ten and eleven. Woman, commend me to her, I will not fail her.

Quick. Why, you say well. But I have another messenger to your worship. Mistress Page hath 95 her hearty commendations to you too; and let me tell you in your ear, she's as fartuous a civil modest wife, and one (I tell you) that will not miss you morning nor evening prayer, as any is in Windsor, whoe'er be the other; and she bade me tell your 100 worship that her husband is seldom from home, but she hopes there will come a time. I never knew a woman so dote upon a man; surely I think you have charms, la; yes, in truth.

Fal. Not I, I assure thee. Setting the attraction of my good parts aside, I have no other charms. 106

Quick. Blessing on your heart for't!

Fal. But I pray thee tell me this: has Ford's wife and Page's wife acquainted each other how they love me?   110

Quick. That were a jest indeed! They have not so little grace, I hope. That were a trick indeed! But Mistress Page would desire you to send her your little page, of all loves. Her husband has a marvellous infection to the little page; and 115 truly Master Page is an honest man. Never a wife in Windsor leads a better life than she does: do what she will, say what she will, take all, pay all, go to bed when she list, rise when she list, all is as she will; and truly she deserves it, for if there be a 120 kind woman in Windsor, she is one. You must send her your page, no remedy.

Fal. Why, I will.

Quick. Nay, but do so then, and look you, he may come and go between you both; and in 125 any case have a nay-word, that you may know one another's mind, and the boy never need to understand any thing; for 'tis not good that children should know any wickedness. Old folks, you know, have discretion, as they say, and know the world. 130

Fal. Fare thee well, commend me to them both. There's my purse, I am yet thy debtor. Boy, go along with this woman. [*Exeunt Mrs. Quickly and Robin.*] This news distracts me!

Pist. [*Aside.*] This punk is one of Cupid's carriers. Clap on more sails, pursue; up with your fights; 136 Give fire! She is my prize, or ocean whelm them all!
                                                        [*Exit.*]

Fal. Say'st thou so, old Jack? go thy ways. I'll make more of thy old body than I have done. Will they yet look after thee? Wilt thou, after 140 the expense of so much money, be now a gainer?

Good body, I thank thee. Let them say 'tis grossly done, so it be fairly done, no matter.

[*Enter*] BARDOLPH.

Bard. Sir John, there's one Master [Brook] below would fain speak with you, and be acquainted 145 with you; and hath sent your worship a morning's draught of sack.

Fal. [Brook] is his name?

Bard. Ay, sir.

Fal. Call him in. [*Exit Bardolph.*] Such [Brooks] are welcome to me, that o'erflows such liquor. 151 Ah, ha! Mistress Ford and Mistress Page, have I encompass'd you? Go to, *via!*

[*Enter* BARDOLPH *with*] FORD [*disguised like Brook*].

Ford. [God save] you, sir!   154

Fal. And you, sir! Would you speak with me?

Ford. I make bold, to press with so little preparation upon you.

Fal. You're welcome. What's your will? Give us leave, drawer.   [*Exit Bardolph.*] 159

Ford. Sir, I am a gentleman that have spent much. My name is [Brook].

Fal. Good Master [Brook], I desire more acquaintance of you.

Ford. Good Sir John, I sue for yours—not to charge you, for I must let you understand I think 165 myself in better plight for a lender than you are; the which hath something embold'ned me to this unseason'd intrusion; for they say, if money go before, all ways do lie open.

Fal. Money is a good soldier, sir, and will on. 170

Ford. Troth, and I have a bag of money here troubles me. If you will help to bear it, Sir John, take all, or half, for easing me of the carriage.

Fal. Sir, I know not how I may deserve to be your porter.   175

Ford. I will tell you, sir, if you will give me the hearing.

Fal. Speak, good Master [Brook], I shall be glad to be your servant.   179

Ford. Sir, I hear you are a scholar (I will be brief with you), and you have been a man long known to me, though I had never so good means as desire to make myself acquainted with you. I shall discover a thing to you, wherein I must very much lay open mine own imperfection; but, good Sir John, as you have one eye upon my follies, as you hear them unfolded, 186 turn another into the register of your own, that I may pass with a reproof the easier, sith you yourself know how easy it is to be such an offender.

Fal. Very well, sir, proceed.   190

Ford. There is a gentlewoman in this town, her husband's name is Ford.

Fal. Well, sir.

90. **frampold:** disagreeable.
97. **fartuous:** Quickly's laughable version of *virtuous.* **modest:** proper.   103–4. **have charms:** employ magic spells.
106. **parts:** qualities.   114. **of all loves:** for love's sake.
115. **infection:** blunder for *affection.*   119. **list:** pleases.
126. **nay-word:** password. The first recorded use of the word, which occurs again at V.ii.5; cf. *an ayword* (= byword), *Twelfth Night,* II.iii.135.   134. **distracts:** confounds (with joy).
135. **punk:** whore.   **carriers:** messengers.
136. **Clap:** put.   **fights:** canvas screens raised during naval action to conceal and protect the sailors.   137. **prize:** booty.

142. **grossly:** clumsily.   143. **fairly:** fortunately.
153. **encompass'd you:** got round you, taken you in.   **via:** go on.
156–57. **preparation:** prearrangement, advance notice.
158–59. **Give us leave.** A polite dismissal.   159. **drawer:** tapster.
165. **charge you:** put you to any expense.
168. **unseason'd:** unseasonable.   183. **discover:** reveal.
187. **register:** record.   188. **sith:** since.

Ford. I have long lov'd her, and I protest to you, bestow'd much on her; follow'd her with a doting observance; engross'd opportunities to meet her; 196 fee'd every slight occasion that could but niggardly give me sight of her; not only bought many presents to give her, but have given largely to many to know what she would have given; briefly, I have pursu'd her as love hath pursu'd me, which hath been on the 201 wing of all occasions. But whatsoever I have merited, either in my mind or in my means, meed I am sure I have receiv'd none, unless experience be a jewel— that I have purchas'd at an infinite rate, and that hath taught me to say this: 206 "Love like a shadow flies when substance love pursues, Pursuing that that flies, and flying what pursues."

Fal. Have you receiv'd no promise of satisfaction at her hands? 210

Ford. Never.

Fal. Have you importun'd her to such a purpose?

Ford. Never.

Fal. Of what quality was your love then? 214

Ford. Like a fair house built on another man's ground, so that I have lost my edifice by mistaking the place where I erected it.

Fal. To what purpose have you unfolded this to me?

Ford. When I have told you that, I have told you all. Some say that, though she appear 221 honest to me, yet in other places she enlargeth her mirth so far that there is shrewd construction made of her. Now, Sir John, here is the heart of my purpose: you are a gentleman of excellent breeding, admirable discourse, of great admittance, authen- 226 tic in your place and person, generally allow'd for your many war-like, court-like, and learned preparations.

Fal. O sir! 230

Ford. Believe it, for you know it. There is money, spend it, spend it; spend more; spend all I have; only give me so much of your time in exchange of it, as to lay an amiable siege to the honesty of this Ford's wife. Use your art of wooing; win her to consent to you; if any man may, you may as soon as any. 237

Fal. Would it apply well to the vehemency of your affection, that I should win what you would enjoy? Methinks you prescribe to yourself very preposterously. 241

Ford. O, understand my drift. She dwells so securely on the excellency of her honor, that the folly of my soul dares not present itself; she is too bright to be look'd against. Now, could I come to her with any detection in my hand, my desires 246

had instance and argument to commend themselves. I could drive her then from the ward of her purity, her reputation, her marriage vow, and a thousand other her defenses, which now are too too strong- 250 ly embattled against me. What say you to't, Sir John?

Fal. Master [Brook], I will first make bold with your money; next, give me your hand; and last, as I am a gentleman, you shall, [and] you will, enjoy Ford's wife. 255

Ford. O good sir!

Fal. I say you shall.

Ford. Want no money, Sir John, you shall want none.

Fal. Want no Mistress Ford, Master [Brook], you shall want none. I shall be with her (I may 261 tell you) by her own appointment; even as you came in to me, her assistant or go-between parted from me. I say I shall be with her between ten and eleven; for at that time the jealous rascally knave her husband will be forth. Come you to me at night, you shall know how I speed. 267

Ford. I am blest in your acquaintance. Do you know Ford, sir?

Fal. Hang him, poor cuckoldly knave, I know him not. Yet I wrong him to call him poor. They 271 say the jealous wittolly knave hath masses of money, for the which his wife seems to me well-favor'd. I will use her as the key of the cuckoldly rogue's coffer, and there's my harvest-home. 275

Ford. I would you knew Ford, sir, that you might avoid him if you saw him.

Fal. Hang him, mechanical salt-butter rogue! I will stare him out of his wits; I will awe him with my cudgel; it shall hang like a meteor o'er the cuckold's horns. Master [Brook], thou shalt know I 281 will predominate over the peasant, and thou shalt lie with his wife. Come to me soon at night. Ford's a knave, and I will aggravate his style; thou, Master [Brook], shalt know him for knave, and cuckold. Come to me soon at night. [*Exit.*] 286

Ford. What a damn'd Epicurean rascal is this! My heart is ready to crack with impatience. Who says this is improvident jealousy? My wife hath sent to him, the hour is fix'd, the match is made. Would any man have thought this? See the hell of 291 having a false woman! My bed shall be abus'd, my coffers ransack'd, my reputation gnawn at, and I shall not only receive this villainous wrong, but stand under the adoption of abominable terms, and

196. **engross'd:** monopolized.   197. **fee'd:** made use of, bought.
199. **largely:** generously.
200. **what . . . given:** i.e. what gifts she would like to receive.
203. **meed:** reward.
207-8. **Love . . . pursues.** The idea is proverbial.
222. **enlargeth:** gives scope to, extends.   223. **shrewd:** malicious.
226. **of great admittance:** i.e. having ready entry into good society.
226-27. **authentic:** recognized.   227. **allow'd:** acknowledged.
228-29. **preparations:** accomplishments.   234. **amiable:** amorous.
243. **securely:** confidently.
245. **look'd against:** looked at directly (i.e. she is like the sun).

247. **instance:** evidence, proof.
248. **ward:** posture of defense in fencing.
251. **embattled:** arrayed.   254. **and:** if.   258. **Want:** lack.
265. **jealous:** jealous (a variant form).
266. **forth:** away from home.   272. **wittolly:** cuckoldly.
273. **for the which:** for which reason.   **well-favor'd:** beautiful.
275. **harvest-home:** time for reaping a profit.
278. **mechanical:** base (literally, referring to a manual worker).
salt-butter: another contemptuous epithet, perhaps meaning "having coarse tastes" or "malodorous."
282. **predominate:** have the ascendancy (like a planet at the time of its greatest influence).
284. **aggravate his style:** expand his title (by adding the word *cuckold* to it).   287. **Epicurean:** sensual.
289. **improvident jealousy:** rash suspicion.
295. **stand under.** With a play on his bearing of a cuckold's horns.

by him that does me this wrong. Terms! names! 296
Amaimon sounds well; Lucifer, well; Barbason,
well; yet they are devils' additions, the names of
fiends; but Cuckold! Wittol!—Cuckold! the devil
himself hath not such a name. Page is an ass, a secure
ass; he will trust his wife, he will not be jealous. 301
I will rather trust a Fleming with my butter, Parson
Hugh the Welshman with my cheese, an Irishman
with my aqua-vitae bottle, or a thief to walk my
ambling gelding, than my wife with herself. Then
she plots, then she ruminates, then she devises; 306
and what they think in their hearts they may effect,
they will break their hearts but they will effect.
[God] be prais'd for my jealousy! Eleven o' clock
the hour. I will prevent this, detect my wife, be
reveng'd on Falstaff, and laugh at Page. I 311
will about it; better three hours too soon than a
minute too late. Fie, fie, fie! cuckold, cuckold,
cuckold!   *Exit.*

Scene III

Enter Caius, Rugby.

Caius. Jack Rugby!
Rug. Sir?
Caius. Vat is the clock, Jack?
Rug. 'Tis past the hour, sir, that Sir Hugh
promis'd to meet.   5
Caius. By gar, he has save his soul, dat he is no
come; he has pray his Pible well, dat he is no come.
By gar, Jack Rugby, he is dead already, if he be
come.   9
Rug. He is wise, sir; he knew your worship would
kill him if he came.
Caius. By gar, de herring is no dead so as I vill
kill him. Take your rapier, Jack, I vill tell you how
I vill kill him.
Rug. Alas, sir, I cannot fence.   15
Caius. Villainy, take your rapier.
Rug. Forbear; here's company.

[*Enter*] Page, Shallow, Slender, Host.

Host. [God] bless thee, bully-doctor!
Shal. [God] save you, Master Doctor Caius!
Page. Now, good Master Doctor!   20
Slen. Give you good morrow, sir.
Caius. Vat be all you, one, two, tree, four, come
for?
Host. To see thee fight, to see thee foin, to see
thee traverse, to see thee here, to see thee there, 25
to see thee pass thy puncto, thy stock, thy reverse, thy

distance, thy montant. Is he dead, my Ethiopian?
Is he dead, my Francisco? Ha, bully? What says my
Aesculapius? my Galien? my heart of elder? Ha?
is he dead, bully-stale? is he dead?   30
Caius. By gar, he is de coward Jack priest of de
vorld; he is not show his face.
Host. Thou art a Castalion-King-Urinal! Hector
of Greece, my boy!   34
Caius. I pray you bear witness that me have
stay six or seven, two, tree hours for him, and he is
no come.
Shal. He is the wiser man, Master Doctor:
he is a curer of souls, and you a curer of bodies. 39
If you should fight, you go against the hair of your
professions. Is it not true, Master Page?
Page. Master Shallow, you have yourself been a
great fighter, though now a man of peace.
Shal. Bodykins, Master Page, though I now be
old and of the peace, if I see a sword out, my finger 45
itches to make one. Though we are justices and
doctors and churchmen, Master Page, we have some
salt of our youth in us, we are the sons of women,
Master Page.
Page. 'Tis true, Master Shallow.   50
Shal. It will be found so, Master Page. Master
Doctor Caius, I am come to fetch you home. I am
sworn of the peace. You have show'd yourself a
wise physician, and Sir Hugh hath shown himself
a wise and patient churchman. You must go with
me, Master Doctor.   56
Host. Pardon, guest-justice. A [word], Mounseur
Mock-water.
Caius. Mock-vater? vat is dat?
Host. Mock-water, in our English tongue, is
valor, bully.   61
Caius. By gar, then I have as much mock-vater
as de Englishman. Scurvy Jack-dog priest! By gar,
me vill cut his ears.
Host. He will clapper-claw thee tightly, bully. 65
Caius. Clapper-de-claw? vat is dat?
Host. That is, he will make thee amends.
Caius. By gar, me do look he shall clapper-de-claw
me, for, by gar, me vill have it.
Host. And I will provoke him to't, or let him
wag.   71

297. **Amaimon, Lucifer, Barbason:** names of devils.
298. **additions:** titles.   300. **secure:** overconfident.
303. **cheese.** The Welshman's love of cheese was proverbial.
304. **aqua-vitae:** brandy, spirits.   **walk:** i.e. exercise.
310. **prevent:** forestall.

II.iii. Location: A field near Windsor.
12–13. **de herring . . . him:** i.e. I will kill him deader than a herring.
("As dead as a herring" was proverbial.)   24. **foin:** thrust.
25. **traverse:** shift position from side to side.
26. **puncto:** thrust with the point of the sword.   **stock:** stoccado,
thrust.   **reverse:** backhand stroke.

27. **distance:** keeping the prescribed space between fencers.   **montant:** upward blow.   **Ethiopian.** Alluding to Caius' dark complexion (?).   28. **Francisco:** Frenchman.
29. **Aesculapius:** Greek god of medicine.   **Galien:** Galen, famous
Greek physician and medical authority.   **heart of elder:** i.e. coward,
since the elder has soft pith at its centre.
30. **bully-stale:** i.e. fine Master Doctor, *stale* being used for "physician" (from the sense "urine").
33. **Castalion-King-Urinal.** Like *stale* in *bully-stale, urinal* (= a vessel
for the inspection of urine) is used for "physician." *Castalion* seems
to be the Host's version of *Castilian* = Spanish = cowardly.
40. **go . . . of:** behave contrary to (from brushing an animal's hair the
wrong way).
44. **Bodykins:** by God's little body (a weakened oath).
46. **make one:** join in.   48. **salt:** wantonness.
58. **Mock-water.** A crux. Obviously connected with *stale* (line 30)
and Urinal (line 33), with a play on *make-water*, implying cowardice
(like *Castalion,* line 33). The Host's equation with valor (line 61) is of
course ironic.
63. **Jack-dog:** mongrel (hence Caius' threat to "cut his ears").
65. **clapper-claw:** thrash.   **tightly:** soundly.
70. **provoke:** incite, urge.

Caius. Me tank you for dat.

Host. And moreover, bully—but first, Master Guest, and Master Page, and eke Cavaleiro Slender, go you through the town to Frogmore.   75
[*Aside to them.*]

Page. Sir Hugh is there, is he?

Host. He is there. See what humor he is in; and I will bring the doctor about by the fields. Will it do well?

Shal. We will do it.   80

All [*Page, Shal., Slen.*]. Adieu, good Master Doctor.
[*Exeunt all but the Host, Caius, and Rugby.*]

Caius. By gar, me vill kill de priest, for he speak for a jack-an-ape to Anne Page.

Host. Let him die; [but first] sheathe thy impatience, throw cold water on thy choler. Go about the fields with me through Frogmore, I will bring   86 thee where Mistress Anne Page is, at a farm-house a-feasting; and thou shalt woo her. Cried game? Said I well?

Caius. By gar, me dank you vor dat. By gar, I love you; and I shall procure-a you de good   91 guest: de earl, de knight, de lords, de gentlemen, my patients.

Host. For the which I will be thy adversary toward Anne Page. Said I well?   95

Caius. By gar, 'tis good; vell said.

Host. Let us wag then.

Caius. Come at my heels, Jack Rugby.   *Exeunt.*

ACT III, Scene I

Enter Evans, Simple.

Evans. I pray you now, good Master Slender's servingman, and friend Simple by your name, which way have you look'd for Master Caius, that calls himself Doctor of Physic?   4

Sim. Marry, sir, the pittie-ward, the park-ward—every way; Old Windsor way, and every way but the town way.

Evans. I most fehemently desire you you will also look that way.

Sim. I will, sir.   [*Exit.*]   10

Evans. [Jeshu] pless my soul! how full of chollors I am and trempling of mind! I shall be glad if he have deceiv'd me. How melancholies I am! I will knog his urinals about his knave's costard when I have good opportunities for the ork. Pless my soul!   [*Sings.*]   16

"To shallow rivers, to whose falls
    Melodious birds sings madrigals;
    There will we make our peds of roses,

And a thousand fragrant posies.   20
    To shallow—"
Mercy on me! I have a great dispositions to cry.
[*Sings.*]
"Melodious birds sing madrigals—
    When as I sat in Pabylon—
    And a thousand vagram posies.   25
    To shallow, etc."

[*Enter* Simple.]

Sim. Yonder he is coming, this way, Sir Hugh.

Evans. He's welcome.   [*Sings.*]
"To shallow rivers, to whose falls—"
Heaven prosper the right! What weapons is he?   30

Sim. No weapons, sir. There comes my master, Master Shallow, and another gentleman—from Frogmore, over the stile, this way.

Evans. Pray you give me my gown, or else keep it in your arms.   [*Reads in a book.*]   35

[*Enter*] Page, Shallow, Slender.

Shal. How now, Master Parson? Good morrow, good Sir Hugh. Keep a gamester from the dice, and a good student from his book, and it is wonderful.

Slen. [*Aside.*] Ah, sweet Anne Page!   40

Page. [God] save you, good Sir Hugh!

Evans. [God] pless you from his mercy sake, all of you!

Shal. What? the sword and the word? Do you study them both, Master Parson?   45

Page. And youthful still, in your doublet and hose, this raw rheumatic day?

Evans. There is reasons and causes for it.

Page. We are come to you to do a good office, Master Parson.   50

Evans. Fery well; what is it?

Page. Yonder is a most reverend gentleman, who, belike having receiv'd wrong by some person, is at most odds with his own gravity and patience that ever you saw.   55

Shal. I have liv'd fourscore years and upward; I never heard a man of his place, gravity, and learning, so wide of his own respect.

Evans. What is he?   59

Page. I think you know him: Master Doctor Caius, the renown'd French physician.

Evans. Got's will, and his passion of my heart! I had as lief you would tell me of a mess of porridge.

Page. Why?   64

Evans. He has no more knowledge in Hibocrates and Galen—and he is a knave besides, a cowardly knave as you would desires to be acquainted withal.

---

75. **Frogmore:** a small village near Windsor.
88. **Cried game:** i.e. have I promised good sport?

III.i. Location: A field near Frogmore.
5. **pittie-ward:** towards the Petty or Little Park.
5–6. **park-ward:** towards Windsor Great Park.
11. **chollors:** choler, anger.
14. **knog:** knock.   **costard:** apple, i.e. head.
15. **ork:** work.
17–20. **To . . . posies.** From Marlowe's poem "Come live with me and be my love."

24. **When . . . Pabylon.** The first line of a metrical version of Psalm 137.
25. **vagram:** Evans' version of *vagrant*, with which he confuses *fragrant*.   38. **student:** student (a variant form).
44. **the word:** the Bible. Line 42 seems to echo Psalm 6:4: "Return, O Lord: deliver my soul: save me for thy mercies' sake" (Geneva).
46. **doublet and hose:** close-fitting jacket and breeches. In cold weather a cloak would ordinarily be worn over them.
54. **odds:** strife.   **gravity:** dignity.
58. **wide of:** at variance with.   **respect:** reputation.
65. **Hibocrates:** Hippocrates, famous Greek physician and writer on medicine.

Page. I warrant you, he's the man should fight with him.

Slen. [*Aside.*] O sweet Anne Page! 70

[*Enter*] HOST, CAIUS, RUGBY.

Shal. It appears so by his weapons. Keep them asunder; here comes Doctor Caius.

[*Evans and Caius offer to fight.*]

Page. Nay, good Master Parson, keep in your weapon.

Shal. So do you, good Master Doctor. 75

Host. Disarm them, and let them question. Let them keep their limbs whole and hack our English.

Caius. I pray you let-a me speak a word with your ear. Vherefore vill you not meet-a me? 80

Evans. [*Aside to Caius.*] Pray you use your patience in good time.

Caius. By gar, you are de coward, de Jack dog, John ape. 84

Evans. [*Aside to Caius.*] Pray you let us not be laughing-stocks to other men's humors. I desire you in friendship, and I will one way or other make you amends. [*Aloud.*] I will knog your [urinals] about your knave's cogscomb [for missing your meetings and appointments]. 90

Caius. Diable! Jack Rugby—mine host de Jarteer—have I not stay for him to kill him? Have I not, at de place I did appoint? 93

Evans. As I am a Christians-soul, now look you; this is the place appointed. I'll be judgment by mine host of the Garter.

Host. Peace, I say, Gallia and Gaul, French and Welsh, soul-curer and body-curer!

Caius. Ay, dat is very good, excellant. 99

Host. Peace, I say! hear mine host of the Garter. Am I politic? Am I subtle? Am I a Machivel? Shall I lose my doctor? No, he gives me the potions and the motions. Shall I lose my parson? my priest? my Sir Hugh? No, he gives me the proverbs and the no-verbs. [Give me thy hand, 105 terrestial; so.] Give me thy hand, celestial; so. Boys of art, I have deceiv'd you both; I have directed you to wrong places. Your hearts are mighty, your skins are whole, and let burnt sack be the issue. Come, lay their swords to pawn. Follow me, [lads] of peace; follow, follow, follow. [*Exit.*] 111

Shal. [Afore God], a mad host. Follow, gentlemen, follow.

Slen. [*Aside.*] O sweet Anne Page!

[*Exeunt Shallow, Slender, and Page.*]

Caius. Ha, do I perceive dat? Have you make-a de sot of us, ha, ha? 116

Evans. This is well! he has made us his vlouting-stog. I desire you that we may be friends; and let us knog our prains together to be revenge on this same scall, scurvy, cogging companion, the host of the Garter. 121

Caius. By gar, with all my heart. He promise to bring me where is Anne Page; by gar, he deceive me too.

Evans. Well, I will smite his noddles. Pray you follow. [*Exeunt.*] 126

SCENE II

[*Enter*] MISTRESS PAGE, ROBIN.

Mrs. Page. Nay, keep your way, little gallant; you were wont to be a follower, but now you are a leader. Whether had you rather lead mine eyes, or eye your master's heels?

Rob. I had rather, forsooth, go before you like a man than follow him like a dwarf. 6

Mrs. Page. O, you are a flattering boy, now I see you'll be a courtier.

[*Enter*] FORD.

Ford. Well met, Mistress Page. Whither go you? 10

Mrs. Page. Truly, sir, to see your wife. Is she at home?

Ford. Ay, and as idle as she may hang together, for want of company. I think if your husbands were dead, you two would marry. 15

Mrs. Page. Be sure of that—two other husbands.

Ford. Where had you this pretty weathercock?

Mrs. Page. I cannot tell what the dickens his name is my husband had him of. What do you call your knight's name, sirrah? 21

Rob. Sir John Falstaff.

Ford. Sir John Falstaff!

Mrs. Page. He, he—I can never hit on 's name. There is such a league between my goodman and he! Is your wife at home indeed? 26

Ford. Indeed she is.

Mrs. Page. By your leave, sir. I am sick till I see her. [*Exeunt Mrs. Page and Robin.*] 29

Ford. Has Page any brains? Hath he any eyes? Hath he any thinking? Sure they sleep, he hath no use of them. Why, this boy will carry a letter twenty mile, as easy as a cannon will shoot point-blank twelve score. He pieces out his wive's inclination; he gives her folly motion and advantage; 35

---

68. **he:** i.e. Evans.   **should:** who is to.
72 s.d. **offer:** make as if.   76. **question:** discuss.
81–82. **use . . . time:** i.e. the occasion calls for patience.
92. **stay:** waited.
95. **judgment by:** i.e. governed by the judgment of.
97. **Gallia and Gaul:** Wales and France.
101. **politic:** crafty.   **Machivel:** Machiavel, i.e. intriguer.
103. **motions:** purges.
105. **proverbs . . . no-verbs:** i.e. what I should and should not do (with perhaps some sarcastic comment on Evans' vocabulary).
106. **terrestial:** terrestrial (a variant form, by analogy with *celestial*).
107. **art:** learning.   109. **issue:** outcome.   116. **sot:** fool.

117–18. **vlouting-stog:** flouting-stock, i.e. laughingstock.
120. **scall:** scald, scurvy.   **cogging:** dissembling.

III.ii. Location: Windsor. A street.
3. **Whether.** Signalling a choice of alternatives.
13. **may hang together:** can be and still survive.
18. **weathercock.** Referring probably to Robin's feathered hat; weathercocks often had a pennon attached.
25. **league:** friendship.   **goodman:** i.e. husband.
34. **twelve score:** i.e. 240 yards.   **pieces out:** augments.
34–35. **inclination:** natural disposition.
35. **folly:** wantonness.   **motion:** prompting.   **advantage:** opportunity.

and now she's going to my wife, and Falstaff's boy with her. A man may hear this show'r sing in the wind. And Falstaff's boy with her! Good plots, they are laid, and our revolted wives share damnation together. Well, I will take him, then torture 40 my wife, pluck the borrow'd veil of modesty from the so-seeming Mistress Page, divulge Page himself for a secure and willful Actaeon; and to these violent proceedings all my neighbors shall cry aim. [*Clock heard.*] The clock gives me my cue, and my 45 assurance bids me search—there I shall find Falstaff. I shall be rather prais'd for this than mock'd; for it is as positive as the earth is firm that Falstaff is there. I will go.

[*Enter*] PAGE, SHALLOW, SLENDER, HOST, EVANS, CAIUS, [RUGBY].

Shal., *Page, etc.*   Well met, Master Ford.   50
Ford.   Trust me, a good knot. I have good cheer at home, and I pray you all go with me.
Shal.   I must excuse myself, Master Ford.
Slen.   And so must I, sir. We have appointed to dine with Mistress Anne, and I would not break with her for more money than I'll speak of.   56
Shal.   We have linger'd about a match between Anne Page and my cousin Slender, and this day we shall have our answer.   59
Slen.   I hope I have your good will, father Page.
Page.   You have, Master Slender, I stand wholly for you; but my wife, Master Doctor, is for you altogether.
Caius.   Ay, be-gar, and de maid is love-a me. My nursh-a Quickly tell me so mush.   65
Host.   What say you to young Master Fenton? He capers, he dances, he has eyes of youth; he writes verses, he speaks holiday, he smells April and May—he will carry't, he will carry't—'tis in his buttons—he will carry't.   70
Page.   Not by my consent, I promise you. The gentleman is of no having. He kept company with the wild Prince and Poins; he is of too high a region, he knows too much. No, he shall not knit a knot in his fortunes with the finger of my substance. 75 If he take her, let him take her simply. The wealth I have waits on my consent, and my consent goes not that way.
Ford.   I beseech you heartily, some of you go home with me to dinner. Besides your cheer, you 80 shall have sport; I will show you a monster. Master

Doctor, you shall go, so shall you, Master Page, and you, Sir Hugh.
Shal.   Well, fare you well. We shall have the freer wooing at Master Page's.   85
                    [*Exeunt Shallow and Slender.*]
Caius.   Go home, John Rugby, I come anon.
                    [*Exit Rugby.*]
Host.   Farewell, my hearts. I will to my honest knight Falstaff, and drink canary with him.   [*Exit.*]
Ford.   [*Aside.*] I think I shall drink in pipe-wine first with him; I'll make him dance.—Will you go, gentles?   91
All.   Have with you to see this monster.   *Exeunt.*

SCENE III

Enter MISTRESS FORD, MISTRESS PAGE.

Mrs. Ford.   What, John! What, Robert!
Mrs. Page.   Quickly, quickly! Is the buck-basket—
Mrs. Ford.   I warrant. What, Robin, I say!

[*Enter*] SERVANTS [*with a great buck-basket*].

Mrs. Page.   Come, come, come.   5
Mrs. Ford.   Here, set it down.
Mrs. Page.   Give your men the charge, we must be brief.
Mrs. Ford.   Marry, as I told you before, John and Robert, be ready here hard by in the brew- 10 house, and when I suddenly call you, come forth, and (without any pause or staggering) take this basket on your shoulders. That done, trudge with it in all haste, and carry it among the whitsters in Datchet-mead, and there empty it in the muddy ditch close by the Thames side.   16
Mrs. Page.   You will do it?
Mrs. Ford.   I ha' told them over and over, they lack no direction. Be gone, and come when you are call'd.   [*Exeunt Servants.*]   20
Mrs. Page.   Here comes little Robin.

[*Enter*] ROBIN.

Mrs. Ford.   How now, my eyas-musket, what news with you?
Rob.   My master, Sir John, is come in at your back door, Mistress Ford, and requests your company.   26
Mrs. Page.   You little Jack-a-Lent, have you been true to us?
Rob.   Ay, I'll be sworn. My master knows not of your being here, and hath threat'ned to put 30

37-38. **hear . . . wind:** tell that a rain shower is coming by the rising wind, i.e. tell by these tokens that trouble is imminent.
42. **divulge:** reveal.   43. **Actaeon.** See note to II.i.118.
44. **cry aim:** applaud.   46. **assurance:** foreknowledge.
51. **knot:** company.   **cheer:** fare.
68. **speaks holiday:** talks merrily.   69. **carry't:** win the day.
69-70. **in his buttons.** A crux; perhaps = in his very nature (as a fresh young *button*, i.e. bud).
72. **having:** wealth, property.
73. **Prince and Poins.** An allusion to *1* and *2 Henry IV*, where Falstaff is a companion of Prince Hal and Poins.
73-74. **he . . . much:** i.e. he comes from too rarefied a social level and is too sophisticated and worldly.   74-75. **knit . . . in:** mend.
76. **simply:** by herself (without dowry).
81. **show . . . monster.** Alluding to the sort of abnormal births exhibited at fairs.

86. **anon:** immediately.
88. **canary:** a sweet wine from the Canary Islands.
89. **pipe-wine:** wine in the cask (with pun on *pipe* in the musical sense, suggested by a second meaning of *canary*, i.e. a lively dance).

III.iii. Location: Windsor. Ford's house.
2-3. **buck-basket:** basket for dirty clothes.   7. **charge:** order.
10. **hard:** near.   14. **whitsters:** bleachers of linen.
15. **Datchet-mead:** a meadow along the Thames near Windsor Park.
22. **eyas-musket:** young sparrow hawk.
27. **Jack-a-Lent:** a figure set up to be used as a target; here, puppet.
30-31. **put . . . liberty:** i.e. discharge me.

me into everlasting liberty if I tell you of it; for he swears he'll turn me away.

Mrs. Page. Thou'rt a good boy. This secrecy of thine shall be a tailor to thee, and shall make thee a new doublet and hose. I'll go hide me.   35

Mrs. Ford. Do so. Go tell thy master I am alone. [*Exit Robin.*] Mistress Page, remember you your cue.

Mrs. Page. I warrant thee, if I do not act it, hiss me.   [*Exit.*]   39

Mrs. Ford. Go to then. We'll use this unwholesome humidity, this gross wat'ry pumpion. We'll teach him to know turtles from jays.

[*Enter*] FALSTAFF.

Fal. "Have I caught thee, my heavenly jewel?" Why, now let me die, for I have liv'd long   44 enough. This is the period of my ambition. O this blessed hour!

Mrs. Ford. O sweet Sir John!

Fal. Mistress Ford, I cannot cog, I cannot prate, Mistress Ford. Now shall I sin in my wish: I would thy husband were dead. I'll speak it before the best lord, I would make thee my lady.   51

Mrs. Ford. I your lady, Sir John? Alas, I should be a pitiful lady!

Fal. Let the court of France show me such another. I see how thine eye would emulate the diamond. Thou hast the right arch'd beauty of the brow   56 that becomes the ship-tire, the tire-valiant, or any tire of Venetian admittance.

Mrs. Ford. A plain kerchief, Sir John. My brows become nothing else, nor that well neither.   60

Fal. [By the Lord,] thou art a tyrant to say so. Thou wouldst make an absolute courtier, and the firm fixture of thy foot would give an excellent motion to thy gait in a semicircled farthingale. I see what thou wert, if Fortune thy foe were not, Nature thy friend. Come, thou canst not hide it.

Mrs. Ford. Believe me, there's no such thing in me.

Fal. What made me love thee? Let that persuade thee there's something extraordinary in thee.   69 Come, I cannot cog and say thou art this and that, like a many of these lisping hawthorn buds, that come like women in men's apparel, and smell like Bucklersbury in simple time—I cannot; but I love thee, none but thee; and thou deserv'st it.   74

41. **humidity.** Cf. the description of Falstaff in *1 Henry IV*, II.iv.450, as "that swoll'n parcel of dropsies." **pumpion:** pumpkin.
42. **turtles:** turtledoves, i.e. constant wives. **jays:** i.e. loose women.
43. **Have . . . jewel.** From Sidney's *Astrophel and Stella* (1591).
45. **period:** goal. 48. **cog:** flatter.
57. **ship-tire:** woman's head-dress (*tire*) in the form of a ship. **tire-valiant:** another style of head-dress.
58. **of Venetian admittance:** which is the vogue in Venice (a leader in fashion). 62. **absolute:** finished, perfect. 63. **fixture:** setting.
64. **semicircled farthingale:** petticoat with half-hoops to hold out the skirt behind and at the sides.
64–65. **what thou wert:** what you would be, i.e. what a figure you would cut at court.
65. **if . . . not:** i.e. if Fortune had not made you a lowly citizen's wife. *Fortune thy foe* contains an allusion to a very popular ballad tune, "Fortune My Foe." **Nature thy friend:** i.e. Nature having been so bountiful in her gifts to you.
71. **hawthorn buds:** i.e. young dandies (see the note on III.ii.69–70).
72. **Bucklersbury:** a street in London off Cheapside, inhabited by herbalists.
73. **simple time:** i.e. midsummer, when the annual supply of fresh herbs or simples would be scenting the air as they dried.

Mrs. Ford. Do not betray me, sir. I fear you love Mistress Page.

Fal. Thou mightst as well say I love to walk by the Counter-gate, which is as hateful to me as the reek of a lime-kill.   79

Mrs. Ford. Well, heaven knows how I love you, and you shall one day find it.

Fal. Keep in that mind, I'll deserve it.

Mrs. Ford. Nay, I must tell you, so you do; or else I could not be in that mind.   84

[*Enter* ROBIN.]

Rob. Mistress Ford, Mistress Ford! here's Mistress Page at the door, sweating, and blowing, and looking wildly, and would needs speak with you presently.

Fal. She shall not see me, I will ensconce me behind the arras.   90

Mrs. Ford. Pray you do so, she's a very tattling woman.   [*Falstaff stands behind the arras.*]

[*Enter* MISTRESS PAGE.]

What's the matter? How now?

Mrs. Page. O Mistress Ford, what have you done? You're sham'd, y' are overthrown, y' are undone for ever!   96

Mrs. Ford. What's the matter, good Mistress Page?

Mrs. Page. O well-a-day, Mistress Ford, having an honest man to your husband, to give him such cause of suspicion!   101

Mrs. Ford. What cause of suspicion?

Mrs. Page. What cause of suspicion? Out upon you! How am I mistook in you!

Mrs. Ford. Why, alas, what's the matter?   105

Mrs. Page. Your husband's coming hither, woman, with all the officers in Windsor, to search for a gentleman that he says is here now in the house, by your consent, to take an ill advantage of his absence. You are undone.

Mrs. Ford. 'Tis not so, I hope.

Mrs. Page. Pray heaven it be not so, that you have such a man here; but 'tis most certain your husband's coming, with half Windsor at his heels, to search for such a one. I come before to tell you.   115 If you know yourself clear, why, I am glad of it; but if you have a friend here, convey, convey him out. Be not amaz'd, call all your senses to you, defend your reputation, or bid farewell to your good life for ever.   120

Mrs. Ford. What shall I do? There is a gentleman, my dear friend; and I fear not mine own shame so much as his peril. I had rather than a thousand pound he were out of the house.   124

Mrs. Page. For shame, never stand "you had rather" and "you had rather." Your husband's here

75. **betray:** deceive.
78. **Counter-gate:** gate of the debtors' prison in London.
79. **lime-kill:** lime-kiln. 88. **presently:** at once.
89. **ensconce:** hide, conceal. 90. **arras:** tapestry wall-hanging.
95. **undone:** ruined. 100. **to:** for. 116. **clear:** innocent.
118. **amaz'd:** bewildered. 125. **stand:** lose time over.

at hand, bethink you of some conveyance. In the house you cannot hide him. O, how have you deceiv'd me! Look, here is a basket; if he be of any 129 reasonable stature, he may creep in here, and throw foul linen upon him, as if it were going to bucking; or—it is whiting-time—send him by your two men to Datchet-mead.

Mrs. Ford. He's too big to go in there. What shall I do? 135

Fal. [*Starting from his concealment.*] Let me see't, let me see't, O, let me see't! I'll in, I'll in. Follow your friend's counsel. I'll in.

Mrs. Page. What, Sir John Falstaff? [*Aside.*] Are these your letters, knight? 140

Fal. [*To Mrs. Page.*] I love thee. Help me away. —Let me creep in here. I'll never—

[*Goes into the basket; they put clothes over him.*]

Mrs. Page. Help to cover your master, boy. Call your men, Mistress Ford. You dissembling knight!

Mrs. Ford. What, John! Robert! John! 145

[*Exit Robin.*]

[*Enter* Servants.]

Go take up these clothes here quickly. Where's the cowl-staff? Look how you drumble! Carry them to the laundress in Datchet-mead; quickly, come.

[*Enter*] Ford, Page, Caius, Evans.

Ford. Pray you come near. If I suspect without cause, why then make sport at me, then let 150 me be your jest, I deserve it. How now? Whither bear you this?

Serv. To the laundress, forsooth.

Mrs. Ford. Why, what have you to do whither they bear it? You were best meddle with buck-washing. 156

Ford. Buck! I would I could wash myself of the buck! Buck, buck, buck! ay, buck! I warrant you, buck, and of the season too, it shall appear. [*Exeunt Servants with the basket.*] Gentlemen, 160 I have dream'd to-night; I'll tell you my dream. Here, here, here be my keys. Ascend my chambers, search, seek, find out. I'll warrant we'll unkennel the fox. Let me stop this way first. [*Locking the door.*] So, now uncape. 165

Page. Good Master Ford, be contented. You wrong yourself too much.

Ford. True, Master Page. Up, gentlemen, you shall see sport anon. Follow me, gentlemen. [*Exit.*]

Evans. This is fery fantastical humors and jealousies. 171

Caius. By gar, 'tis no the fashion of France; it is not jealous in France.

Page. Nay, follow him, gentlemen, see the issue of his search. [*Exeunt Page, Caius, and Evans.*] 175

Mrs. Page. Is there not a double excellency in this?

Mrs. Ford. I know not which pleases me better, that my husband is deceiv'd, or Sir John.

Mrs. Page. What a taking was he in when your husband ask'd who was in the basket! 181

Mrs. Ford. I am half afraid he will have need of washing, so throwing him into the water will do him a benefit.

Mrs. Page. Hang him, dishonest rascal! I would all of the same strain were in the same distress. 186

Mrs. Ford. I think my husband hath some special suspicion of Falstaff's being here, for I never saw him so gross in his jealousy till now.

Mrs. Page. I will lay a plot to try that, and we will yet have more tricks with Falstaff. His dissolute disease will scarce obey this medicine. 192

Mrs. Ford. Shall we send that foolish carrion, Mistress Quickly, to him, and excuse his throwing into the water, and give him another hope, to betray him to another punishment? 196

Mrs. Page. We will do it. Let him be sent for to-morrow, eight a' clock, to have amends.

[*Enter* Ford, Page, Caius, *and* Evans.]

Ford. I cannot find him. May be the knave bragg'd of that he could not compass. 200

Mrs. Page. [*Aside to Mrs. Ford.*] Heard you that?

Mrs. Ford. You use me well, Master Ford, do you?

Ford. Ay, I do so.

Mrs. Ford. Heaven make you better than your thoughts! 205

Ford. Amen!

Mrs. Page. You do yourself mighty wrong, Master Ford.

Ford. Ay, ay; I must bear it.

Evans. If there be any pody in the house, and in the chambers, and in the coffers, and in the 211 presses, heaven forgive my sins at the day of judgment!

Caius. Be-gar, nor I too; there is no-bodies.

Page. Fie, fie, Master Ford, are you not asham'd? What spirit, what devil suggests this imagina- 215 tion? I would not ha' your distemper in this kind for the wealth of Windsor Castle.

Ford. 'Tis my fault, Master Page. I suffer for it.

Evans. You suffer for a pad conscience. Your wife is as honest a omans as I will desires among five thousand, and five hundred too. 221

Caius. By gar, I see 'tis an honest woman.

Ford. Well, I promis'd you a dinner. Come, come, walk in the park. I pray you pardon me; 224 I will hereafter make known to you why I have done this. Come, wife, come, Mistress Page, I pray you pardon me; pray heartly pardon me.

---

127. **bethink:** devise.   **conveyance:** expedient, stratagem.
131. **bucking:** washing.   132. **whiting-time:** bleaching time.
147. **cowl-staff:** pole for carrying a basket (*cowl*) between two persons. **drumble:** move sluggishly.
155–56. **buck-washing:** washing clothes (but Ford picks it up in the sense of "getting rid of a cuckold's horns").   159. **of the:** in.
161. **to-night:** last night.   163. **unkennel:** uncover.
165. **uncape.** Meaning uncertain; possibly "unleash," i.e. start the chase.   166. **be contented:** calm yourself.

180. **taking:** state of agitation.   186. **strain:** character.
189. **gross:** open, obvious.
192. **obey this medicine:** i.e. yield to this single dose.
193. **carrion:** bawd, i.e. go-between, messenger (?) or piece of old flesh (?).   194. **excuse:** make excuses for.
212. **presses:** clothes-presses.   215. **suggests:** stirs up.
216. **distemper:** disorder (here, of mind).   **in this kind:** of this sort.
224. **walk . . . park:** i.e. take a stroll until dinner is ready.
227. **heartly:** heartily.

Page. Let's go in, gentlemen, but (trust me) we'll mock him. I do invite you to-morrow morning 229 to my house to breakfast; after, we'll a-birding together. I have a fine hawk for the bush. Shall it be so?

Ford. Any thing.

Evans. If there is one, I shall make two in the company. 235

Caius. If there be one or two, I shall make-a the turd.

Ford. Pray you go, Master Page.

           [Exit with Page.]

Evans. I pray you now remembrance to-morrow on the lousy knave, mine host. 240

Caius. Dat is good, by gar; with all my heart!

Evans. A lousy knave, to have his gibes and his mockeries!   *Exeunt.*

Scene IV

Enter Fenton, Anne Page.

Fent. I see I cannot get thy father's love,
Therefore no more turn me to him, sweet Nan.

Anne. Alas, how then?

Fent.   Why, thou must be thyself.
He doth object I am too great of birth,
And that my state being gall'd with my expense, 5
I seek to heal it only by his wealth.
Besides these, other bars he lays before me,
My riots past, my wild societies,
And tells me 'tis a thing impossible
I should love thee but as a property. 10

Anne. May be he tells you true.

[Fent.] No, heaven so speed me in my time to
           come!
Albeit I will confess thy father's wealth
Was the first motive that I woo'd thee, Anne;
Yet wooing thee, I found thee of more value 15
Than stamps in gold, or sums in sealed bags;
And 'tis the very riches of thyself
That now I aim at.

Anne.   Gentle Master Fenton,
Yet seek my father's love, still seek it, sir.
If opportunity and humblest suit 20
Cannot attain it, why then hark you hither!

           [They converse apart.]

[Enter] Shallow, Slender, [Mistress] Quickly.

Shal. Break their talk, Mistress Quickly, my kinsman shall speak for himself.

Slen. I'll make a shaft or a bolt on't. 'Slid, 'tis but venturing. 25

Shal. Be not dismay'd.

Slen. No, she shall not dismay me. I care not for that, but that I am afeard.

Quick. Hark ye, Master Slender would speak a word with you. 30

Anne. I come to him. *[Aside.]* This is my father's choice.
O, what a world of vild ill-favor'd faults
Looks handsome in three hundred pounds a year!

Quick. And how does good Master Fenton? Pray you a word with you. 35

Shal. She's coming; to her, coz. O boy, thou hadst a father!

Slen. I had a father, Mistress Anne, my uncle can tell you good jests of him. Pray you, uncle, tell Mistress Anne the jest how my father stole two geese out of a pen, good uncle. 41

Shal. Mistress Anne, my cousin loves you.

Slen. Ay, that I do—as well as I love any woman in Gloucestershire.

Shal. He will maintain you like a gentlewoman.

Slen. Ay, that I will, come cut and long-tail, under the degree of a squire. 47

Shal. He will make you a hundred and fifty pounds jointure.

Anne. Good Master Shallow, let him woo for himself. 51

Shal. Marry, I thank you for it; I thank you for that good comfort. She calls you, coz. I'll leave you.

Anne. Now, Master Slender—

Slen. Now, good Mistress Anne— 55

Anne. What is your will?

Slen. My will? 'Od's heartlings, that's a pretty jest indeed! I ne'er made my will yet, I thank heaven. I am not such a sickly creature, I give heaven praise.

Anne. I mean, Master Slender, what would you with me? 61

Slen. Truly, for mine own part, I would little or nothing with you. Your father and my uncle hath made motions. If it be my luck, so; if not, happy man be his dole! They can tell you how things go better than I can. You may ask your father, here he comes.

[Enter] Page, Mistress Page.

Page. Now, Master Slender. Love him, daughter Anne. 67
Why, how now? What does Master Fenton here?
You wrong me, sir, thus still to haunt my house.
I told you, sir, my daughter is dispos'd of.

Fent. Nay, Master Page, be not impatient. 71

---

228. **go in:** i.e. accept his invitation (?).
230. **a-birding:** hawking with a sparrow hawk at small birds which were thus driven out of the bushes and shot.
III.iv. Location: Windsor. Before Page's house.
1. **love:** i.e. good will, consent.   2. **turn:** direct.
3. **be thyself:** i.e. decide for yourself.
5. **my . . . expense:** my estate being wounded by my extravagance.
8. **societies:** companionships.
10. **property:** (mere) possession (with play perhaps on a stage property and a means to an end).   12. **speed:** be favorable to.
16. **stamps:** coins.
20. **opportunity:** taking advantage of opportune times for your suit.
22. **Break:** interrupt.

24. **I'll . . . on't:** i.e. I may do a good job or a bad, but I'll make a stab at it (proverbial). A shaft was a slender, sharp arrow; a bolt, a thick, blunt arrow.   **'Slid:** by God's eyelid (a weakened oath).
32. **vild:** vile (a variant form).   **ill-favor'd:** ugly.
36–37. **thou . . . father:** i.e. be as resolute as your father must have been in approaching a woman.
46. **come . . . long-tail:** i.e. whatever happens (proverbial). Literally, *cut and long-tail* = animals with docked and undocked tails, i.e. all animals.   48. **make:** give.
57. **'Od's heartlings:** by God's little heart (a weakened oath).
64. **motions:** proposals.   **so:** well and good.
64–65. **happy . . . dole:** good luck to him (who gets you) (proverbial).

Mrs. Page. Good Master Fenton, come not to my
  child.
Page. She is no match for you.
Fent. Sir, will you hear me?
Page.   No, good Master Fenton.
Come, Master Shallow; come, son Slender, in.   75
Knowing my mind, you wrong me, Master Fenton.
                   [*Exeunt Page, Shallow, and Slender.*]
Quick. Speak to Mistress Page.
Fent. Good Mistress Page, for that I love your
  daughter
In such a righteous fashion as I do,
Perforce, against all checks, rebukes, and manners,
I must advance the colors of my love,   81
And not retire. Let me have your good will.
Anne. Good mother, do not marry me to yond fool.
Mrs. Page. I mean it not, I seek you a better
  husband.
Quick. That's my master, Master Doctor.   85
Anne. Alas, I had rather be set quick i' th' earth,
And bowl'd to death with turnips!
Mrs. Page. Come, trouble not yourself. Good
  Master Fenton,
I will not be your friend nor enemy.
My daughter will I question how she loves you, 90
And as I find her, so am I affected.
Till then farewell, sir; she must needs go in,
Her father will be angry.
Fent. Farewell, gentle mistress; farewell, Nan. 94
                          [*Exeunt Mrs. Page and Anne.*]
Quick. This is my doing now. "Nay," said I,
"will you cast away your child on a fool, and a
physician? Look on Master Fenton." This is my
doing.   98
Fent. I thank thee; and I pray thee, once to-night
Give my sweet Nan this ring. There's for thy pains.
Quick. Now heaven send thee good fortune!
[*Exit Fenton.*] A kind heart he hath. A woman 102
would run through fire and water for such a kind
heart. But yet I would my master had Mistress
Anne; or I would Master Slender had her; or, in
sooth, I would Master Fenton had her. I will do what
I can for them all three, for so I have promis'd, 107
and I'll be as good as my word, but speciously for
Master Fenton. Well, I must of another errand to
Sir John Falstaff from my two mistresses. What a
beast am I to slack it!   *Exit.* 111

SCENE V

Enter FALSTAFF.

Fal. Bardolph, I say!

[*Enter*] BARDOLPH.

Bard. Here, sir.

---

80. checks: reproofs.   81. colors: banners.
86. set: firmly planted; here probably = buried up to the neck.
quick: alive.   87. bowl'd: pelted.   91. affected: inclined.
99. once: sometime.   108. speciously: blunder for *specially*.
111. slack: be remiss in.

III.v. Location: Windsor. The Garter Inn.

Fal. Go fetch me a quart of sack, put a toast
in't. [*Exit Bardolph.*] Have I liv'd to be carried in a
basket like a barrow of butcher's offal? and to 5
be thrown in the Thames? Well, [and] I be serv'd such
another trick, I'll have my brains ta'en out and
butter'd, and give them to a dog for a new-year's
gift. The rogues slighted me into the river with as
little remorse as they would have drown'd a 10
blind bitch's puppies, fifteen i' th' litter; and you
may know by my size that I have a kind of alacrity
in sinking; [and] the bottom were as deep as hell, I
should down. I had been drown'd, but that the
shore was shelvy and shallow—a death that I 15
abhor; for the water swells a man; and what a thing
should I have been when I had been swell'd! I should
have been a mountain of mummy.

[*Enter* BARDOLPH *with sack.*]

Bard. Here's Mistress Quickly, sir, to speak with
you.   20
Fal. Come, let me pour in some sack to the
Thames water; for my belly's as cold as if I had
swallow'd snowballs for pills to cool the reins.
Call her in.
Bard. Come in, woman!   25

[*Enter* MISTRESS] QUICKLY.

Quick. By your leave; I cry you mercy! Give your
worship good morrow.
Fal. Take away these chalices. Go, brew me a
pottle of sack finely.
Bard. With eggs, sir?   30
Fal. Simple of itself; I'll no pullet-sperm in my
brewage. [*Exit Bardolph.*] How now?
Quick. Marry, sir, I come to your worship from
Mistress Ford.   34
Fal. Mistress Ford? I have had ford enough. I
was thrown into the ford; I have my belly full of
ford.
Quick. Alas the day! good heart, that was not her
fault. She does so take on with her men; they mistook their erection.   40
Fal. So did I mine, to build upon a foolish woman's
promise.
Quick. Well, she laments, sir, for it, that it would
yearn your heart to see it. Her husband goes this
morning a-birding; she desires you once more 45
to come to her, between eight and nine. I must carry
her word quickly. She'll make you amends, I warrant
you.
Fal. Well, I will visit her, tell her so. And bid
her think what a man is: let her consider his frailty,
and then judge of my merit.   51
Quick. I will tell her.
Fal. Do so. Between nine and ten, say'st thou?

---

3. toast: piece of toast.   9. slighted: tossed carelessly.
10. remorse: compassion.   15. shelvy: made of sandbanks.
18. mummy: dead flesh.   23. reins: kidneys.
26. cry you mercy: beg your pardon.
29. pottle: half a gallon.   finely: so as to taste well.
39. take . . . men: scold her servants.
40. erection. Quickly means *direction*, i.e. instructions; Falstaff
quibbles on the word.   44. yearn: vex, grieve.
50. his frailty: i.e. the weakness of the flesh.

Quick. Eight and nine, sir.

Fal. Well, be gone; I will not miss her.   55

Quick. Peace be with you, sir.   [*Exit.*]

Fal. I marvel I hear not of Master [Brook]; he sent me word to stay within. I like his money well. O, here he comes.

[*Enter*] Ford [*disguised*].

Ford. Bless you, sir!   60

Fal. Now, Master [Brook], you come to know what hath pass'd between me and Ford's wife?

Ford. That indeed, Sir John, is my business.

Fal. Master [Brook], I will not lie to you. I was at her house the hour she appointed me.   65

Ford. And sped you, sir?

Fal. Very ill-favoredly, Master [Brook].

Ford. How so, sir? Did she change her determination?   69

Fal. No, Master [Brook], but the peaking cornuto her husband, Master [Brook], dwelling in a continual 'larum of jealousy, comes me in the instant of our encounter, after we had embrac'd, kiss'd, protested, and, as it were, spoke the prologue of 74 our comedy; and at his heels a rabble of his companions, thither provok'd and instigated by his distemper, and, forsooth, to search his house for his wive's love.

Ford. What? While you were there?

Fal. While I was there.   80

Ford. And did he search for you, and could not find you?

Fal. You shall hear. As good luck would have it, comes in one Mistress Page; gives intelligence 84 of Ford's approach; and in her invention, and Ford's wive's distraction, they convey'd me into a buck-basket.

Ford. A buck-basket?   88

Fal. [By the Lord], a buck-basket! Ramm'd me in with foul shirts and smocks, socks, foul stockings, greasy napkins, that, Master [Brook], there was the rankest compound of villainous smell that ever offended nostril.

Ford. And how long lay you there?   94

Fal. Nay, you shall hear, Master [Brook], what I have suffer'd to bring this woman to evil for your good. Being thus cramm'd in the basket, a couple of Ford's knaves, his hinds, were call'd forth by their mistress to carry me in the name of foul clothes 99 to Datchet-lane. They took me on their shoulders; met the jealous knave their master in the door, who ask'd them once or twice what they had in their basket. I quak'd for fear, lest the lunatic knave would have search'd it; but fate (ordaining he 104 should be a cuckold) held his hand. Well, on went he for a search, and away went I for foul clothes. But mark the sequel, Master [Brook]. I suffer'd the pangs of three several deaths: first, an intolerable fright, to be detected with a jealous rotten 109

bell-wether; next, to be compass'd like a good bilbo in the circumference of a peck, hilt to point, heel to head; and then to be stopp'd in like a strong distillation with stinking clothes that fretted 113 in their own grease. Think of that—a man of my kidney. Think of that—that am as subject to heat as butter; a man of continual dissolution and thaw. It was a miracle to scape suffocation. And in the height of this bath (when I was more than 118 half stew'd in grease, like a Dutch dish) to be thrown into the Thames, and cool'd, glowing-hot, in that surge, like a horse-shoe; think of that—hissing-hot—think of that, Master [Brook].

Ford. In good sadness, sir, I am sorry that for my sake you have suffer'd all this. My suit then is desperate; you'll undertake her no more?   125

Fal. Master [Brook], I will be thrown into Etna, as I have been into Thames, ere I will leave her thus. Her husband is this morning gone a-birding. I have receiv'd from her another ambassy of 129 meeting. 'Twixt eight and nine is the hour, Master [Brook].

Ford. 'Tis past eight already, sir.

Fal. Is it? I will then address me to my appointment. Come to me at your convenient leisure, 134 and you shall know how I speed; and the conclusion shall be crown'd with your enjoying her. Adieu. You shall have her, Master [Brook]. Master [Brook], you shall cuckold Ford.   [*Exit.*] 138

Ford. Hum! ha? Is this a vision? Is this a dream? Do I sleep? Master Ford, awake! awake, Master Ford! There's a hole made in your best coat, Master Ford. This 'tis to be married! This 'tis to have linen and buck-baskets! Well, I will proclaim myself what I am. I will now take the lecher; 144 he is at my house. He cannot scape me; 'tis impossible he should; he cannot creep into a halfpenny purse, nor into a pepper-box. But lest the devil that guides him should aid him, I will search impossible places. Though what I am I cannot avoid, yet to be 149 what I would not shall not make me tame. If I have horns to make one mad, let the proverb go with me: I'll be horn-mad.   *Exit.*

ACT IV, SCENE I

Enter Mistress Page, [Mistress] Quickly, William.

Mrs. Page. Is he at Master Ford's already, think'st thou?

110. **bell-wether.** Alluding both to Ford's clamor and to his leading a flock of followers.
111. **peck:** container holding a quarter of a bushel.   **hilt to point.** The test of a well-tempered sword (*bilbo*) was that it could be so bent.
112. **stopp'd:** shut.   113. **fretted:** decayed.
115. **kidney:** constitution.   116. **dissolution:** liquefaction.
123. **good sadness:** all seriousness.
125. **undertake:** have to do with.
129. **ambassy:** embassy, message.
133. **address me to:** prepare myself for.
146. **halfpenny purse:** a tiny novelty purse.
152. **horn-mad:** as mad as an angry bull, with punning allusion to the cuckold's horns.

67. **ill-favoredly:** badly.
70. **peaking:** sneaking (perhaps with a quibble on *peak* = point of a horn).   **cornuto:** cuckold (literally, horned creature).
98. **hinds:** servants.   108. **several:** separate.   109. **with:** by.

IV.i. Location: Windsor. A street.

Quick. Sure he is by this—or will be presently. But truly he is very courageous mad about his throwing into the water. Mistress Ford desires you to come suddenly.   6

Mrs. Page. I'll be with her by and by; I'll but bring my young man here to school.

[*Enter*] EVANS.

Look where his master comes; 'tis a playing-day, I see. How now, Sir Hugh, no school to-day?   10

Evans. No; Master Slender is let the boys leave to play.

Quick. Blessing of his heart!

Mrs. Page. Sir Hugh, my husband says my son profits nothing in the world at his book. I   15 pray you ask him some questions in his accidence.

Evans. Come hither, William; hold up your head; come.

Mrs. Page. Come on, sirrah; hold up your head. Answer your master, be not afraid.   20

Evans. William, how many numbers is in nouns?

Will. Two.

Quick. Truly, I thought there had been one number more, because they say, "'Od's nouns."

Evans. Peace your tattlings! What is "fair," William?   26

Will. Pulcher.

Quick. Poulcats? There are fairer things than poulcats sure.

Evans. You are a very simplicity oman; I pray you peace. What is *lapis*, William?   31

Will. A stone.

Evans. And what is "a stone," William?

Will. A pebble.

Evans. No; it is *lapis*. I pray you remember in your prain.   36

Will. Lapis.

Evans. That is a good William. What is he, William, that does lend articles?   39

Will. Articles are borrow'd of the pronoun, and be thus declin'd, *Singulariter, nominativo, hic, haec, hoc.*

Evans. *Nominativo, hig, hag, hog;* pray you mark; *genitivo, hujus.* Well, what is your accusative case?

Will. *Accusativo, hinc.*   45

Evans. I pray you have your remembrance, child. *Accusativo,* [*hung*], *hang, hog.*

Quick. "Hang-hog" is Latin for bacon, I warrant you.   49

Evans. Leave your prabbles, oman. What is the focative case, William?

Will. O—*vocativo,* O.

Evans. Remember, William, focative is *caret.*

Quick. And that's a good root.

Evans. Oman, forbear.   55

Mrs. Page. Peace!

Evans. What is your genitive case plural, William?

Will. Genitive case?

Evans. Ay.   60

Will. [*Genitivo,*] *horum, harum, horum.*

Quick. Vengeance of Jinny's case! Fie on her! never name her, child, if she be a whore.

Evans. For shame, oman.   64

Quick. You do ill to teach the child such words. He teaches him to "hic" and to "hac," which they'll do fast enough of themselves, and to call "horum," —fie upon you!   68

Evans. Oman, art thou [*lunatics*]? Hast thou no understandings for thy cases and the numbers of the genders? Thou art as foolish Christian creatures as I would desires.

Mrs. Page. Prithee hold thy peace.

Evans. Show me now, William, some declensions of your pronouns.   75

Will. Forsooth, I have forgot.

Evans. It is *qui,* [*quae*], *quod:* if you forget your *qui*'s, your [*quae*'s], and your *quod*'s, you must be preeches. Go your ways and play, go.

Mrs. Page. He is a better scholar than I thought he was.   81

Evans. He is a good sprag memory. Farewell, Mistress Page.

Mrs. Page. Adieu, good Sir Hugh. [*Exit Evans.*] Get you home, boy. Come, we stay too long.   85

Exeunt.

SCENE II

Enter FALSTAFF, MISTRESS FORD,

Fal. Mistress Ford, your sorrow hath eaten up my sufferance. I see you are obsequious in your love, and I profess requital to a hair's breadth, not only, Mistress Ford, in the simple office of love, but in all the accoustrement, complement, and   5 ceremony of it. But are you sure of your husband now?

Mrs. Ford. He's a-birding, sweet Sir John.

Mrs. Page. [*Within.*] What ho, gossip Ford! What ho!   10

Mrs. Ford. Step into th' chamber, Sir John.

[*Exit Falstaff.*]

[*Enter*] MISTRESS PAGE.

Mrs. Page. How now, sweet heart, who's at home besides yourself?

Mrs. Ford. Why, none but mine own people.

Mrs. Page. Indeed?   15

---

4. **courageous.** Perhaps she means *outrageous.*
6. **suddenly:** at once.   9. **playing-day:** holiday.
11. **leave:** permission.   16. **accidence:** Latin grammar.
24. **'Od's nouns:** by God's wounds (a weakened oath); with play on odd numbers (i.e. three).
28. **Poulcats:** polecats, fitches (slang for "prostitutes").
30. **very:** complete.   **simplicity:** fool.
41. **Singulariter:** in the singular number.   **nominativo:** in the nominative case. The Latin names of other cases are in lines 43, 45, 52.
53. **caret:** is wanting, does not occur. Quickly takes it for *carrot.*

66. **hic . . . hac:** hiccup . . . hack, cough (from too much to drink).
79. **preeches:** i.e. breeched, whipped.
82. **sprag:** sprack, i.e. lively, alert.

IV.ii. Windsor: Ford's house.
2. **sufferance:** suffering.   **obsequious:** devoted.
5. **accoustrement:** accoutrement.   9. **gossip:** friend.

Mrs. Ford. No, certainly. [*Aside to her.*] Speak louder.

Mrs. Page. Truly, I am so glad you have nobody here.

Mrs. Ford. Why?   20

Mrs. Page. Why, woman, your husband is in his old lines again. He so takes on yonder with my husband; so rails against all married mankind; so curses all Eve's daughters, of what complexion soever; and so buffets himself on the forehead, 25 crying, "Peer out, peer out!", that any madness I ever yet beheld seem'd but tameness, civility, and patience to this his distemper he is in now. I am glad the fat knight is not here.

Mrs. Ford. Why, does he talk of him?   30

Mrs. Page. Of none but him, and swears he was carried out, the last time he search'd for him, in a basket; protests to my husband he is now here, and hath drawn him and the rest of their company from their sport, to make another experiment of his 35 suspicion. But I am glad the knight is not here. Now he shall see his own foolery.

Mrs. Ford. How near is he, Mistress Page?

Mrs. Page. Hard by, at street end; he will be here anon.   40

Mrs. Ford. I am undone! the knight is here.

Mrs. Page. Why then you are utterly sham'd, and he's but a dead man. What a woman are you? Away with him, away with him! Better shame than murther.   45

Mrs. Ford. Which way should he go? How should I bestow him? Shall I put him into the basket again?

[*Enter* Falstaff.]

Fal. No, I'll come no more i' th' basket. May I not go out ere he come?   50

Mrs. Page. Alas! three of Master Ford's brothers watch the door with pistols, that none shall issue out; otherwise you might slip away ere he came. But what make you here?   54

Fal. What shall I do? I'll creep up into the chimney.

Mrs. Ford. There they always use to discharge their birding-pieces. Creep into the kill-hole.

Fal. Where is it?   59

Mrs. Ford. He will seek there, on my word. Neither press, coffer, chest, trunk, well, vault, but he hath an abstract for the remembrance of such places, and goes to them by his note. There is no hiding you in the house.

Fal. I'll go out then.   65

[*Mrs. Page.*] If you go out in your own semblance, you die, Sir John—unless you go out disguis'd.

Mrs. Ford. How might we disguise him?   68

Mrs. Page. Alas the day, I know not! There is no woman's gown big enough for him; otherwise he might put on a hat, a muffler, and a kerchief, and so escape.

Fal. Good hearts, devise something; any extremity rather than a mischief.   74

Mrs. Ford. My maid's aunt, the fat woman of Brainford, has a gown above.

Mrs. Page. On my word, it will serve him; she's as big as he is. And there's her thrumm'd hat and her muffler too. Run up, Sir John.   79

Mrs. Ford. Go, go, sweet Sir John. Mistress Page and I will look some linen for your head.

Mrs. Page. Quick, quick! we'll come dress you straight. Put on the gown the while. [*Exit Falstaff.*]

Mrs. Ford. I would my husband would meet him in this shape. He cannot abide the old woman 85 of Brainford. He swears she's a witch, forbade her my house, and hath threat'ned to beat her.

Mrs. Page. Heaven guide him to thy husband's cudgel; and the devil guide his cudgel afterwards!

Mrs. Ford. But is my husband coming?   90

Mrs. Page. Ay, in good sadness, is he, and talks of the basket too, howsoever he hath had intelligence.

Mrs. Ford. We'll try that; for I'll appoint my men to carry the basket again, to meet him at the door with it, as they did last time.   96

Mrs. Page. Nay, but he'll be here presently. Let's go dress him like the witch of Brainford.

Mrs. Ford. I'll first direct my men what they shall do with the basket. Go up, I'll bring linen for him straight.   [*Exit.*] 101

Mrs. Page. Hang him, dishonest varlet! we cannot misuse [him] enough.

We'll leave a proof, by that which we will do,
Wives may be merry, and yet honest too: 105
We do not act that often jest and laugh;
'Tis old, but true: still swine eats all the draff. [*Exit.*]

[*Enter* Mistress Ford *with two*] Servants.

Mrs. Ford. Go, sirs, take the basket again on your shoulders. Your master is hard at door. If he bid you set it down, obey him. Quickly, dispatch.
          [*Exit.*]

1. Serv. Come, come, take it up.   111

2. Serv. Pray heaven it be not full of knight again.

1. Serv. I hope not, I had lief as bear so much lead.

[*Enter*] Ford, Page, Caius, Evans, Shallow.

Ford. Ay, but if it prove true, Master Page, have you any way then to unfool me again? Set down the basket, villain! Somebody call my wife. Youth in a basket! O you panderly rascals, there's a 117 knot, a [ging], a pack, a conspiracy against me.

---

22. **lines:** fits of temper, jealous rages.   24. **complexion:** type.
26. **Peer out.** An order to his horns to become visible.
43. **What a:** what kind of.   45. **murther:** murder.
54. **make you:** are you doing.   57. **use:** are accustomed.
58. **kill-hole:** kiln-hole, oven.   62. **abstract:** list.

73–74. **extremity:** extreme measure.
76. **Brainford:** Brentford, a village near Windsor. There is an allusion (see lines 86, 98) to the notorious "witch of Brentford," who kept a tavern there. **above:** upstairs.
78. **thrumm'd:** made of coarse yarn.
85. **shape:** disguise.   97. **presently:** at once.
107. **still:** quiet.   **draff:** swill.   110. **dispatch:** make haste.
113. **lief as:** as lief (possibly a misprint).
115. **unfool me:** make me a sound man.
118. **knot:** company.   **ging:** gang.   **pack:** confederacy.

Now shall the devil be sham'd. What, wife, I say! Come, come forth! Behold what honest clothes you send forth to bleaching! 121

Page. Why, this passes, Master Ford. You are not to go loose any longer, you must be pinion'd.

Evans. Why, this is lunatics! this is mad as a mad dog! 125

Shal. Indeed, Master Ford, this is not well indeed.

Ford. So say I too, sir.

[*Enter* MISTRESS FORD.]

Come hither, Mistress Ford, Mistress Ford, the honest woman, the modest wife, the virtuous 130 creature, that hath the jealous fool to her husband! I suspect without cause, mistress, do I?

Mrs. Ford. Heaven be my witness you do, [and] if you suspect me in any dishonesty. 134

Ford. Well said, brazen-face! hold it out. Come forth, sirrah! [*Pulling clothes out of the basket.*]

Page. This passes!

Mrs. Ford. Are you not asham'd? Let the clothes alone.

Ford. I shall find you anon. 140

Evans. 'Tis unreasonable! Will you take up your wive's clothes? Come away.

Ford. Empty the basket, I say!

Mrs. Ford. Why, man, why? 144

Ford. Master Page, as I am a man, there was one convey'd out of my house yesterday in this basket. Why may not he be there again? In my house I am sure he is. My intelligence is true, my jealousy is reasonable. Pluck me out all the linen. 149

Mrs. Ford. If you find a man there, he shall die a flea's death.

Page. Here's no man.

Shal. By my fidelity, this is not well, Master Ford; this wrongs you. 154

Evans. Master Ford, you must pray, and not follow the imaginations of your own heart. This is jealousies.

Ford. Well, he's not here I seek for.

Page. No, nor no where else but in your brain. 159

Ford. Help to search my house this one time. If I find not what I seek, show no color for my extremity; let me for ever be your table-sport. Let them say of me, "As jealous as Ford, that search'd a hollow walnut for his wive's leman." Satisfy me once more, once more search with me. 165

Mrs. Ford. What ho, Mistress Page! come you and the old woman down; my husband will come into the chamber.

Ford. Old woman? What old woman's that?

Mrs. Ford. Why, it is my maid's aunt of Brainford. 171

Ford. A witch, a quean, an old cozening quean! Have I not forbid her my house? She comes of errands, does she? We are simple men, we do not know what's brought to pass under the profession of fortune-telling. She works by charms, by 176 spells, by th' figure, and such daub'ry as this is, beyond our element; we know nothing. Come down, you witch, you hag you, come down, I say!

Mrs. Ford. Nay, good, sweet husband! Good gentlemen, let him [not] strike the old woman. 181

[*Enter* FALSTAFF *disguised like an old woman, and* MISTRESS PAGE *with him.*]

Mrs. Page. Come, Mother Prat, come give me your hand.

Ford. I'll prat her. Out of my door, you witch, you rag, you baggage, you poulcat, you runnion! out, out! I'll conjure you, I'll fortune-tell you! 186
[*Ford beats him, and he runs away.*]

Mrs. Page. Are you not asham'd? I think you have kill'd the poor woman.

Mrs. Ford. Nay, he will do it.—'Tis a goodly credit for you. 190

Ford. Hang her, witch!

Evans. By yea and no, I think the oman is a witch indeed. I like not when a oman has a great peard. I spy a great peard under his muffler. 194

Ford. Will you follow, gentlemen? I beseech you follow; see but the issue of my jealousy. If I cry out thus upon no trail, never trust me when I open again.

Page. Let's obey his humor a little further. Come, gentlemen. 200
[*Exeunt Ford, Page, Shallow, Caius, and Evans.*]

Mrs. Page. Trust me, he beat him most pitifully.

Mrs. Ford. Nay, by th' mass, that he did not; he beat him most unpitifully, methought.

Mrs. Page. I'll have the cudgel hallow'd and hung o'er the altar; it hath done meritorious service. 205

Mrs. Ford. What think you? May we, with the warrant of womanhood and the witness of a good conscience, pursue him with any further revenge?

Mrs. Page. The spirit of wantonness is sure scar'd out of him. If the devil have him not in feesimple, with fine and recovery, he will never, I 211 think, in the way of waste, attempt us again.

Mrs. Ford. Shall we tell our husbands how we have serv'd him? 214

Mrs. Page. Yes, by all means; if it be but to scrape the figures out of your husband's brains. If

---

119. **Now . . . sham'd:** i.e. now the truth will come out (alluding to the proverb "Tell the truth and shame the devil").
122. **passes:** goes beyond all bounds.
135. **hold it out:** keep up the pretense.
140. **find:** unmask, reveal. **anon:** now.
148. **intelligence:** information.
154. **wrongs you:** does you dishonor.
155. **you must pray:** i.e. for grace to conquer your jealousy.
156. **follow . . . heart.** Cf. Jeremiah 13:10, "They [the Jews] follow the wicked imaginations of their own heart" (Bishops').
161–62. **show . . . extremity:** make no attempt to extenuate my extravagant behavior.
162. **table-sport:** laughingstock of the group. 164. **leman:** lover.

172. **quean:** hussy. **cozening:** cheating.
177. **by th' figure:** by drawing up astrological charts (?) or, possibly, by making wax figures of her victims to induce sickness or death by sticking pins into them. **daub'ry:** imposture.
184. **prat:** beat (?) or practice tricks on (?).
185. **runnion:** ronyon, scabby woman.
196–97. **cry out:** give tongue (like a hound); *open* later in the sentence has the same meaning. 197. **trail:** scent.
210–11. **fee-simple:** i.e. absolute possession.
211. **fine and recovery:** procedures by which an entailed estate was converted into a fee-simple. 212. **waste:** spoliation.
216. **scrape:** erase. **figures:** figments of the imagination.

[2098-2132]

[2133-2181]

*The
Merry Wives
of Windsor
IV.iv*

they can find in their hearts the poor unvirtuous fat knight shall be any further afflicted, we two will still be the ministers. 219

Mrs. Ford. I'll warrant they'll have him publicly sham'd, and methinks there would be no period to the jest, should he not be publicly sham'd.

Mrs. Page. Come, to the forge with it, then shape it. I would not have things cool. *Exeunt.* 224

Scene III

Enter Host *and* Bardolph.

Bard. Sir, the [Germans desire] to have three of your horses. The Duke himself will be to-morrow at court, and they are going to meet him.

Host. What duke should that be comes so secretly? I hear not of him in the court. Let me speak with the gentlemen; they speak English? 6

Bard. Ay, sir; I'll call [them] to you.

Host. They shall have my horses, but I'll make them pay; I'll sauce them. They have had my [house] a week at command. I have turn'd away my other guests; they must come off. I'll sauce them, come. *Exeunt.*

Scene IV

Enter Page, Ford, Mistress Page, Mistress Ford, *and* Evans.

Evans. 'Tis one of the best discretions of a oman as ever I did look upon.

Page. And did he send you both these letters at an instant?

Mrs. Page. Within a quarter of an hour. 5

Ford. Pardon me, wife, henceforth do what thou wilt.
I rather will suspect the sun with [cold]
Than thee with wantonness. Now doth thy honor stand,
In him that was of late an heretic,
As firm as faith.

219. **ministers:** agents. 221. **period:** fitting conclusion.
223. **to . . . it:** i.e. let us strike while the iron is hot.

IV.iii. **Location:** Windsor. The Garter Inn.
2. **The Duke.** This scene and IV.v.63–92 may allude to Frederick, Duke of Württemberg, who had been elected to the Order of the Garter in 1597, at the same time as Lord Hunsdon (see the introduction to the play), but *in absentia*. From 1592, when as Count Mompelgard he visited England, he exerted every possible influence at court to have himself elected a Garter knight, in the process apparently making himself a theme for laughter. Elizabeth finally yielded, for political reasons, in 1597, but not in time for Frederick to attend the investiture and installation, nor did he in fact receive his Garter insignia until after Elizabeth's death. Evidence for this identification is found in the otherwise inexplicable quarto reading *three sorts of cosen gar-mombles*, replaced in the Folio text by *three Cozen-Iermans* (see Textual Notes, IV.v.77), *cousin* being a form of address between ruling princes. Other alleged topical allusions have been found in the horse-stealing itself, which is not connected with the Duke.
9. **sauce them:** make it hot for them, i.e. make them pay dearly.
10. **at command:** i.e. to be ready for their use whenever they should arrive. 11. **come off:** pay up.

IV.iv. **Location:** Windsor. Ford's house.
1–2. **best . . . oman:** i.e. most discreet women.
3–4. **at an instant:** at the same time.

Page. 'Tis well, 'tis well, no more. 10
Be not as extreme in submission as in offense;
But let our plot go forward. Let our wives
Yet once again (to make us public sport)
Appoint a meeting with this old fat fellow,
Where we may take him, and disgrace him for it. 15

Ford. There is no better way than that they spoke of.

Page. How? to send him word they'll meet him in the park at midnight? Fie, fie, he'll never come. 19

Evans. You say he has been thrown in the rivers, and has been grievously peaten as an old oman. Methinks there should be terrors in him that he should not come; methinks his flesh is punish'd, he shall have no desires.

Page. So think I too. 25

Mrs. Ford. Devise but how you'll use him when he comes,
And let us two devise to bring him thither.

Mrs. Page. There is an old tale goes, that Herne the Hunter
(Sometime a keeper here in Windsor forest)
Doth all the winter-time, at still midnight, 30
Walk round about an oak, with great ragg'd horns,
And there he blasts the tree, and takes the cattle,
And [makes] milch-kine yield blood, and shakes a chain
In a most hideous and dreadful manner. 34
You have heard of such a spirit, and well you know
The superstitious idle-headed eld
Receiv'd and did deliver to our age
This tale of Herne the Hunter for a truth.

Page. Why, yet there want not many that do fear
In deep of night to walk by this Herne's oak. 40
But what of this?

Mrs. Ford. Marry, this is our device:
That Falstaff at that oak shall meet with us,
[Disguis'd like [Herne], with huge horns on his head].

Page. Well, let it not be doubted but he'll come,
And in this shape when you have brought him thither,
What shall be done with him? What is your plot? 46

Mrs. Page. That likewise have we thought upon, and thus:
Nan Page (my daughter) and my little son,
And three or four more of their growth, we'll dress
Like urchins, ouphes, and fairies, green and white,
With rounds of waxen tapers on their heads, 51
And rattles in their hands. Upon a sudden,
As Falstaff, she, and I are newly met,
Let them from forth a sawpit rush at once
With some diffused song. Upon their sight, 55
We two in great amazedness will fly;
Then let them all encircle him about,
And fairy-like to pinch the unclean knight;
And ask him why, that hour of fairy revel,

31. **ragg'd:** jagged, pronged.
32. **blasts the tree:** causes the tree to be blighted. **takes:** bewitches.
36. **idle-headed:** silly, crazy. **eld:** people of an earlier generation.
39. **want:** lack. 45. **shape:** disguise.
50. **urchins:** goblins. **ouphes:** elves.
54. **sawpit:** a pit over which wood is sawed.
55. **diffused:** confused, wild.

In their so sacred paths he dares to tread   60
In shape profane.
    [*Mrs.*] *Ford.*   And till he tell the truth,
Let the supposed fairies pinch him sound,
And burn him with their tapers.
    Mrs. Page.   The truth being known,
We'll all present ourselves; dis-horn the spirit,
And mock him home to Windsor.
    Ford.   The children must   65
Be practic'd well to this, or they'll nev'r do't.
    Evans. I will teach the children their behaviors;
and I will be like a jack-an-apes also, to burn the
knight with my taber.
    Ford. That will be excellent. I'll go buy them
vizards.   70
    Mrs. Page. My Nan shall be the queen of all the
fairies,
Finely attired in a robe of white.
    Page. That silk will I go buy. [*Aside.*] And in
that time
Shall Master Slender steal my Nan away,   74
And marry her at Eton.—Go, send to Falstaff straight.
    Ford. Nay, I'll to him again in name of [Brook];
He'll tell me all his purpose. Sure he'll come.
    Mrs. Page. Fear not you that. Go get us properties
And tricking for our fairies.   79
    Evans. Let us about it. It is admirable pleasures
and fery honest knaveries.
        [*Exeunt Page, Ford, and Evans.*]
    Mrs. Page. Go, Mistress Ford,
Send Quickly to Sir John, to know his mind.
        [*Exit Mrs. Ford.*]
I'll to the doctor, he hath my good will,
And none but he, to marry with Nan Page.   85
That Slender (though well landed) is an idiot;
And he my husband best of all affects.
The doctor is well money'd, and his friends
Potent at court. He, none but he, shall have her,   89
Though twenty thousand worthier come to crave her.
        [*Exit.*]

Scene V

Enter Host, Simple.

    Host. What wouldst thou have, boor? What,
thick-skin? Speak, breathe, discuss; brief, short,
quick, snap.
    Sim. Marry, sir, I come to speak with Sir John
Falstaff from Master Slender.   5
    Host. There's his chamber, his house, his castle,
his standing-bed and truckle-bed; 'tis painted about
with the story of the Prodigal, fresh and new. Go,

knock and call; he'll speak like an Anthropophaginian
unto thee. Knock, I say.   10
    Sim. There's an old woman, a fat woman, gone
up into his chamber. I'll be so bold as stay, sir,
till she come down. I come to speak with her
indeed.   14
    Host. Ha? a fat woman? The knight may be
robb'd. I'll call. Bully-knight! bully Sir John! speak
from thy lungs military. Art thou there? It is thine
host, thine Ephesian, calls.
    Fal. [*Above.*] How now, mine host?   19
    Host. Here's a Bohemian-Tartar tarries the com-
ing down of thy fat woman. Let her descend, bully,
let her descend; my chambers are honorable. Fie,
privacy? fie!

[Enter] Falstaff.

    Fal. There was, mine host, an old fat woman
even now with me, but she's gone.   25
    Sim. Pray you, sir, was't not the wise woman of
Brainford?
    Fal. Ay, marry, was it, mussel-shell, what would
you with her?   29
    Sim. My master, sir, my Master Slender, sent
to her, seeing her go thorough the streets, to know,
sir, whether one Nym, sir, that beguil'd him of a chain,
had the chain or no.
    Fal. I spake with the old woman about it.
    Sim. And what says she, I pray, sir?   35
    Fal. Marry, she says that the very same man
that beguil'd Master Slender of his chain cozen'd him
of it.
    Sim. I would I could have spoken with the woman
herself. I had other things to have spoken with her too
from him.   41
    Fal. What are they? let us know.
    Host. Ay; come; quick.
    [*Sim.*] I may not conceal them, sir.
    Host. Conceal them, or thou diest.   45
    Sim. Why, sir, they were nothing but about
Mistress Anne Page, to know if it were my master's
fortune to have her or no.
    Fal. 'Tis, 'tis his fortune.
    Sim. What, sir?   50
    Fal. To have her, or no. Go; say the woman told
me so.
    Sim. May I be bold to say so, sir?
    Fal. Ay, sir; like who more bold?   54
    Sim. I thank your worship. I shall make my
master glad with these tidings.   [*Exit.*]
    Host. Thou [art] clerkly, thou art clerkly, Sir
John. Was there a wise woman with thee?   58
    Fal. Ay, that there was, mine host, one that hath
taught me more wit than ever I learn'd before in my
life; and I paid nothing for it neither, but was paid for
my learning.

---

62. **sound:** soundly.
68. **like a jack-an-apes:** disguised as a monkey (but he later appears as a satyr).   70. **vizards:** masks.
75. **Eton:** a town across the Thames from Windsor.
78. **properties:** i.e. stage properties.   79. **tricking:** adornments.
87. **he:** i.e. him.   **affects:** likes.

IV.v **Location:** Windsor. The Garter Inn.
3. **snap:** sudden.
7. **truckle-bed:** trundle bed, low bed that slides under a bed of normal height (**standing-bed**).
8. **story . . . Prodigal.** See Luke 15:11–32. This parable is also asso-
ciated with Falstaff in *2 Henry IV*, II.i.144–45.

9. **Anthropophaginian:** cannibal.   18. **Ephesian:** boon companion.
20. **Bohemian-Tartar:** i.e. wild man.
28. **mussel-shell:** i.e. gaping creature (resembling an open bivalve).
31. **thorough:** through.   32. **beguil'd:** cheated, robbed.
44. **conceal:** blunder for *reveal.*
54. **like . . . bold:** like the boldest.   57. **clerkly:** scholarly, wise.
61. **was paid:** was rewarded (with a beating).

[Enter] BARDOLPH.

Bard. Out alas, sir, cozenage! mere cozenage.

Host. Where be my horses? Speak well of them,
varletto.　　　　　65

Bard. Run away with the cozeners; for so soon
as I came beyond Eton, they threw me off from
behind one of them, in a slough of mire; and set spurs
and away, like three German devils, three Doctor
Faustuses.　　　　　70

Host. They are gone but to meet the Duke, villain,
do not say they be fled. Germans are honest men.

[Enter] EVANS.

Evans. Where is mine host?

Host. What is the matter, sir?　　　　　74

Evans. Have a care of your entertainments.
There is a friend of mine come to town, tells me
there is three cozen-germans that has cozen'd all
the hosts of Readins, of Maidenhead, of Colebrook,
of horses and money. I tell you for good will, look
you. You are wise and full of gibes and vlout-　80
ing-stocks, and 'tis not convenient you should be
cozen'd. Fare you well.　　　　　*[Exit.]*

[Enter] CAIUS.

Caius. Vere is mine host de Jarteer?

Host. Here, Master Doctor, in perplexity and
doubtful dilemma.　　　　　85

Caius. I cannot tell vat is dat; but it is tell-a me
dat you make grand preparation for a duke de Jamany.
By my trot, dere is no duke that the court is know to
come. I tell you for good will; adieu.　　　*[Exit.]*

Host. Hue and cry, villain, go! Assist me, knight,
I am undone! Fly, run, hue and cry, villain! I am　91
undone!　　　　　*[Exeunt Host and Bardolph.]*

Fal. I would all the world might be cozen'd,
for I have been cozen'd and beaten too. If it should
come to the ear of the court, how I have been transform'd, and how my transformation hath been　96
wash'd and cudgell'd, they would melt me out of
my fat drop by drop, and liquor fishermen's boots
with me. I warrant they would whip me with their
fine wits till I were as crestfall'n as a dried pear.
I never prosper'd since I forswore myself at　101
primero. Well, if my wind were but long enough
[to say my prayers], I would repent.

[Enter MISTRESS] QUICKLY.

Now? whence come you?

Quick. From the two parties, forsooth.　　　105

Fal. The devil take one party and his dam the
other! and so they shall be both bestow'd. I have
suffer'd more for their sakes—more than the villainous
inconstancy of man's disposition is able to bear.

Quick. And have not they suffer'd? Yes, I warrant; speciously one of them. Mistress Ford,　111
good heart, is beaten black and blue, that you cannot
see a white spot about her.

Fal. What tellest thou me of black and blue?
I was beaten myself into all the colors of the rainbow; and I was like to be apprehended for the　116
witch of Brainford. But that my admirable dexterity of
wit, my counterfeiting the action of an old woman,
deliver'd me, the knave constable had set me i' th'
stocks, i' th' common stocks, for a witch.　　120

Quick. Sir—let me speak with you in your chamber. You shall hear how things go, and, I warrant,
to your content. Here is a letter will say somewhat. Good hearts, what ado here is to bring you
together! Sure, one of you does not serve heaven well,
that you are so cross'd.　　　126

Fal. Come up into my chamber.　　　*Exeunt.*

SCENE VI

Enter FENTON, HOST.

Host. Master Fenton, talk not to me, my mind is
heavy; I will give over all.

Fent. Yet hear me speak. Assist me in my purpose,
And (as I am a gentleman) I'll give thee
A hundred pound in gold more than your loss.　　5

Host. I will hear you, Master Fenton, and I will
(at the least) keep your counsel.

Fent. From time to time I have acquainted you
With the dear love I bear to fair Anne Page,
Who mutually hath answer'd my affection　　10
(So far forth as herself might be her chooser)
Even to my wish. I have a letter from her
Of such contents as you will wonder at;
The mirth whereof so larded with my matter,
That neither, singly, can be manifested　　15
Without the show of both. Fat Falstaff
Hath a great scene; the image of the jest
I'll show you here at large. Hark, good mine host:
To-night at Herne's oak, just 'twixt twelve and one,
Must my sweet Nan present the Fairy Queen;　　20
The purpose why, is here; in which disguise,
While other jests are something rank on foot,
Her father hath commanded her to slip
Away with Slender, and with him at Eton
Immediately to marry. She hath consented.　　25
Now, sir,
Her mother (even strong against that match

---

63. **mere:** sheer, absolute.　**65. varletto:** knave.
69–70. **Doctor Faustuses.** Referring to the scholar-magician Faustus
in Marlowe's play.
75. **your entertainments:** those you receive as guests.
77. **cozen-germans.** A pun on "cousin-germans," i.e. close relatives,
and "cozening Germans."
78. **Readins:** Reading. Like Maidenhead and Colnbrook (*Colebrook*),
it was near Windsor.
80–81. **vlouting-stocks.** See note on III.i.117–18; but here Evans
probably means *flouts*, i.e. jibes.　**81. convenient:** fitting.
85. **doubtful:** apprehensive.　**87. Jamany:** Germany.
88. **trot:** troth.
90. **Hue and cry:** the cry raised during pursuit of a felon.
98. **liquor:** oil.　**101. forswore myself:** cheated.
102. **primero:** a popular card game.

111. **speciously:** blunder for *specially*.　126. **cross'd:** thwarted.

IV.vi. **Location:** Scene continues.
2. **give over:** abandon.
7. **keep your counsel:** not divulge what you tell me.
10. **mutually:** in return.
14. **larded:** intermingled.　**my matter:** the part that concerns me.
17. **image:** idea.　18. **at large:** in detail.　20. **present:** represent.
22. **something . . . foot:** being carried out in some number.
27. **even:** equally.

And firm for Doctor Caius) hath appointed
That he shall likewise shuffle her away,
While other sports are tasking of their minds,   30
And at the dean'ry, where a priest attends,
Straight marry her. To this her mother's plot
She (seemingly obedient) likewise hath
Made promise to the doctor. Now, thus it rests:
Her father means she shall be all in white;   35
And in that habit, when Slender sees his time
To take her by the hand and bid her go,
She shall go with him. Her mother hath intended
(The better to [denote] her to the doctor,
For they must all be mask'd and vizarded)   40
That quaint in green she shall be loose enrob'd,
With ribands pendant, flaring 'bout her head;
And when the doctor spies his vantage ripe,
To pinch her by the hand, and on that token,
The maid hath given consent to go with him.   45
  Host. Which means she to deceive, father or
    mother?
  Fent. Both, my good host, to go along with me.
And here it rests, that you'll procure the vicar
To stay for me at church, 'twixt twelve and one,
And in the lawful name of marrying,   50
To give our hearts united ceremony.
  Host. Well, husband your device; I'll to the vicar.
Bring you the maid, you shall not lack a priest.
  Fent. So shall I evermore be bound to thee;
Besides, I'll make a present recompense. *Exeunt.* 55

ACT V, SCENE I

Enter FALSTAFF, [MISTRESS] QUICKLY.

  Fal. Prithee no more prattling. Go, I'll hold.
This is the third time; I hope good luck lies in odd
numbers. Away, go. They say there is divinity in odd
numbers, either in nativity, chance, or death. Away!
  Quick. I'll provide you a chain, and I'll do what
I can to get you a pair of horns.   6
  Fal. Away, I say, time wears, hold up your head
and mince.   [*Exit Mrs. Quickly.*]

[*Enter*] FORD [*disguised*].

How now, Master [Brook]? Master [Brook], the
matter will be known to-night, or never. Be you in   10
the park about midnight, at Herne's oak, and you shall
see wonders.
  Ford. Went you not to her yesterday, sir, as you
told me you had appointed?   14
  Fal. I went to her, Master [Brook], as you see,
like a poor old man, but I came from her, Master
[Brook], like a poor old woman. That same knave
Ford, her husband, hath the finest mad devil of jealousy

in him, Master [Brook], that ever govern'd frenzy.
I will tell you—he beat me grievously, in the shape   20
of a woman; for in the shape of man, Master [Brook],
I fear not Goliah with a weaver's beam, because
I know also life is a shuttle. I am in haste, go along
with me, I'll tell you all, Master [Brook]. Since I
pluck'd geese, play'd truant, and whipt top,   25
I knew not what 'twas to be beaten till lately. Follow
me, I'll tell you strange things of this knave Ford, on
whom to-night I will be reveng'd, and I will deliver his
wife into your hand. Follow. Strange things in hand,
Master [Brook]! Follow.   *Exeunt.* 30

SCENE II

Enter PAGE, SHALLOW, SLENDER.

  Page. Come, come; we'll couch i' th' castle-ditch
till we see the light of our fairies. Remember, son
Slender, my [daughter].
  Slen. Ay, forsooth, I have spoke with her, and we
have a nay-word how to know one another. I come   5
to her in white, and cry "mum"; she cries "budget";
and by that we know one another.
  Shal. That's good too; but what needs either your
"mum" or her "budget"? The white will decipher her
well enough. It hath strook ten a' clock.   10
  Page. The night is dark, light and spirits will
become it well. Heaven prosper our sport! No man
means evil but the devil, and we shall know him by
his horns. Let's away; follow me.   *Exeunt.*

SCENE III

Enter MISTRESS PAGE, MISTRESS FORD, CAIUS.

  Mrs. Page. Master Doctor, my daughter is in
green. When you see your time, take her by the hand,
away with her to the deanery, and dispatch it quickly.
Go before into the park; we two must go together.
  Caius. I know vat I have to do. Adieu.   5
  Mrs. Page. Fare you well, sir. [*Exit Caius.*] My
husband will not rejoice so much at the abuse of
Falstaff as he will chafe at the doctor's marrying my
daughter. But 'tis no matter; better a little chiding
than a great deal of heart-break.   10
  Mrs. Ford. Where is Nan now, and her troop of
fairies, and the Welsh devil [Hugh]?
  Mrs. Page. They are all couch'd in a pit hard by
Herne's oak, with obscur'd lights; which, at the very

---

30. **tasking of:** fully occupying.   41. **quaint:** prettily.
42. **ribands:** ribbons.   **flaring:** streaming in the wind.
51. **united ceremony:** union of the marriage rite.
52. **husband:** manage carefully.   55. **present:** immediate.

V.i. Location: Scene continues.
1. **hold:** keep (the appointment).
3. **divinity:** i.e. mysterious quality or power.   8. **mince:** trip it.
13. **yesterday:** Actually, Falstaff's last encounter was earlier the same
day.   18. **finest:** most consummate.

22. **Goliah . . . beam.** An allusion to 1 Samuel 17:7, "the shaft of his
[the giant Goliath's] spear was like a weaver's beam" (Geneva). A
weaver's beam is a large wooden cylinder on a loom.
23. **life . . . shuttle.** An allusion to Job 7:6, "My days are swifter than
a weaver's shuttle."
25. **pluck'd . . . top:** i.e. indulged in boyhood pranks.

V.ii. Location: Outskirts of Windsor Park.
1. **couch:** lie hidden.
6. **mum . . . budget.** Mumbudget was a children's game in which
silence was required.   9. **decipher:** make known.
10. **strook:** struck.

V.iii. Location: Scene continues.
3. **dispatch:** conclude.   14. **obscur'd:** darkened.

instant of Falstaff's and our meeting, they will at once display to the night. 16

Mrs. Ford. That cannot choose but amaze him.

Mrs. Page. If he be not amaz'd, he will be mock'd; if he be amaz'd, he will every way be mock'd.

Mrs. Ford. We'll betray him finely. 20

Mrs. Page. Against such lewdsters, and their lechery,
Those that betray them do no treachery.

Mrs. Ford. The hour draws on. To the oak, to the oak! *Exeunt.*

SCENE IV

Enter EVANS [*like a satyr*] *and* [*others as*] *fairies.*

Evans. Trib, trib, fairies; come, and remember your parts. Be pold, I pray you. Follow me into the pit, and when I give the watch-ords, do as I pid you. Come, come, trib, trib. *Exeunt.*

SCENE V

Enter FALSTAFF [*with a buck's head upon him*].

Fal. The Windsor bell hath strook twelve; the minute draws on. Now the hot-bloodied gods assist me! Remember, Jove, thou wast a bull for thy Europa, love set on thy horns. O powerful love, that in some respects makes a beast a man; in some other, a man 5 a beast. You were also, Jupiter, a swan for the love of Leda. O omnipotent love, how near the god drew to the complexion of a goose! A fault done first in the form of a beast (O Jove, a beastly fault!) and then another fault in the semblance of a fowl—think 10 on't, Jove, a foul fault! When gods have hot backs, what shall poor men do? For me, I am here a Windsor stag, and the fattest, I think, i' th' forest. Send me a cool rut-time, Jove, or who can blame me to piss my tallow? Who comes here? My doe? 15

[*Enter*] MISTRESS PAGE, MISTRESS FORD.

Mrs. Ford. Sir John? art thou there, my deer? my male deer?

Fal. My doe with the black scut? Let the sky rain potatoes; let it thunder to the tune of "Green-sleeves,"

hail kissing-comfits, and snow eringoes; let there 20 come a tempest of provocation, I will shelter me here.
[*Embracing her.*]

Mrs. Ford. Mistress Page is come with me, sweet heart.

Fal. Divide me like a brib'd-buck, each a haunch. I will keep my sides to myself, my shoulders for 25 the fellow of this walk—and my horns I bequeath your husbands. Am I a woodman, ha? Speak I like Herne the hunter? Why, now is Cupid a child of conscience, he makes restitution. As I am a true spirit, welcome!
[*There is a noise of horns.*]

Mrs. Page. Alas, what noise? 30

Mrs. Ford. Heaven forgive our sins!

Fal. What should this be?

Mrs. Ford, Mrs. Page. Away, away!
[*The two women run away.*]

Fal. I think the devil will not have me damn'd, lest the oil that's in me should set hell on fire; he would never else cross me thus. 36

Enter EVANS [*like a satyr*], ANNE PAGE [*and* BOYS *dressed like fairies*], PISTOL [*as Hobgoblin,* MISTRESS] QUICKLY [*like the Queen of Fairies; they sing a song about him and afterward speak*].

Quick. Fairies, black, grey, green, and white,
You moonshine revellers, and shades of night,
You orphan heirs of fixed destiny,
Attend your office and your quality. 40
Crier Hobgoblin, make the fairy Oyes.

Pist. Elves, list your names; silence, you aery toys!
Cricket, to Windsor chimneys shalt thou leap;
Where fires thou find'st unrak'd and hearths unswept,
There pinch the maids as blue as bilberry; 45
Our radiant Queen hates sluts and sluttery.

Fal. They are fairies, he that speaks to them shall die.
I'll wink and couch; no man their works must eye.
[*Lies down upon his face.*]

Evans. Where's Bede? Go you, and where you find a maid
That ere she sleep has thrice her prayers said, 50
Raise up the organs of her fantasy,
Sleep she as sound as careless infancy;
But those as sleep and think not on their sins,

---

17. **amaze:** bewilder, strike panic in.
18. **mock'd:** (1) deceived; (2) ridiculed.   21. **lewdsters:** lechers.

V.iv. Location: Windsor Park.
3. **watch-ords:** watchwords.

V.v. Location: Scene continues.
2. **hot-bloodied:** hot-blooded.
3. **Jove . . . Europa.** Jupiter transformed himself into a white bull to carry off the Phoenician princess Europa.
4. **set on:** instigated, i.e. impelled you to assume.
6–7. **a swan . . . Leda.** Leda, whose husband was king of Sparta, was ravished by Jupiter in the form of a swan; their children were Helen of Troy and Pollux.
8. **complexion:** temperament.   **A fault:** a sin (with special reference to sex).   11. **hot:** lustful.
14. **rut-time:** period of sexual excitement in deer.
15. **tallow:** fat of an animal. Stags grew thin in rutting time.
18. **scut:** tail (of a deer); slang for the female pudenda.
19. **potatoes:** sweet potatoes (which were thought to stimulate sexuality).   **Green-sleeves.** See note to II.i.63.

20. **kissing-comfits:** perfumed candies, used by women to sweeten their breath.   **eringoes:** candied roots of sea-holly (another supposed aphrodisiac).   21. **provocation:** sexual incitement.
24. **brib'd-buck:** stolen deer, which poachers would hurriedly cut up after shooting; hence, a cut-up deer.
25–26. **my shoulders . . . walk:** my shoulders for the keeper of this forest (with punning sense that he will fight with the keeper if necessary).
27. **woodman:** i.e. one who knows how to take care of himself in a forest.
28. **Cupid . . . conscience:** i.e. Cupid is at last behaving honorably to Falstaff.
39. **orphan . . . destiny.** Variously explained. Fairies were supposedly of spontaneous birth and thus would be orphans by "fixed destiny."
40. **Attend:** heed.   **office:** duty.   **quality:** business.
41. **Oyes:** hear ye (the call of the official crier).
42. **toys:** things of no substance.
44. **unrak'd:** not raked together and banked with fuel to keep them alive during the night.
45. **bilberry:** blueberry.   48. **wink:** shut my eyes.
51. **Raise . . . fantasy:** i.e. elevate her dream-producing faculties so that she will be free of nightmares.   52. **careless:** free from care.

*The
Merry Wives
of Windsor
V.v*

Pinch them, arms, legs, backs, shoulders, sides, and
shins.
Quick.   About, about;   55
Search Windsor Castle, elves, within and out.
Strew good luck, ouphes, on every sacred room,
That it may stand till the perpetual doom
In state as wholesome as in state 'tis fit,
Worthy the owner, and the owner it.   60
The several chairs of order look you scour
With juice of balm and every precious flow'r;
Each fair installment, coat, and sev'ral crest,
With loyal blazon, evermore be blest!
And nightly, meadow-fairies, look you sing,   65
Like to the Garter's compass, in a ring.
Th' expressure that it bears, green let it be,
More fertile-fresh than all the field to see;
And *"Honi soit qui mal y pense"* write
In em'rald tuffs, flow'rs purple, blue, and white,   70
Like sapphire, pearl, and rich embroidery,
Buckled below fair knighthood's bending knee:
Fairies use flow'rs for their charactery.
Away, disperse! but till 'tis one a' clock,
Our dance of custom, round about the oak   75
Of Herne the hunter, let us not forget.
Evans.   Pray you lock hand in hand; yourselves
in order set;
And twenty glow-worms shall our lanthorns be,
To guide our measure round about the tree.
But stay, I smell a man of middle-earth.   80
Fal.   Heavens defend me from that Welsh fairy,
lest he transform me to a piece of cheese!
Pist.   Vild worm, thou wast o'erlook'd even in thy
birth.
Quick.   With trial-fire touch me his finger-end.
If he be chaste, the flame will back descend   85
And turn him to no pain; but if he start,
It is the flesh of a corrupted heart.
Pist.   A trial, come.
Evans.   Come, will this wood take fire?
[*They put the tapers to his fingers, and he starts.*]
Fal.   O, O, O!
Quick.   Corrupt, corrupt, and tainted in desire!   90
About him, fairies, sing a scornful rhyme,
And as you trip, still pinch him to your time.

THE SONG

Fie on sinful fantasy!
Fie on lust and luxury!

Lust is but a bloody fire,   95
Kindled with unchaste desire,
Fed in heart, whose flames aspire,
As thoughts do blow them, higher and higher.
Pinch him, fairies, mutually!
Pinch him for his villainy!   100
Pinch him, and burn him, and turn him about,
Till candles, and starlight, and moonshine be out.

[*Here they pinch him and sing about him. And the
Doctor*] CAIUS [*comes one way, and steals away a boy
in green; and*] SLENDER [*another way; he takes a boy
in white; and*] FENTON [*steals Mistress Anne Page.
And a noise of hunting is made within; and all the
fairies run away. Falstaff pulls off his buck's head,
and rises up.*]

[*Enter*] PAGE, FORD, [MISTRESS PAGE, *and* MISTRESS
FORD].

Page.   Nay, do not fly, I think we have watch'd
you now.
Will none but Herne the hunter serve your turn?
Mrs. Page.   I pray you come, hold up the jest no
higher.   105
Now, good Sir John, how like you Windsor wives?
See you these, husband? Do not these fair yokes
Become the forest better than the town?
Ford.   Now, sir, who's a cuckold now? Master
[Brook], Falstaff's a knave, a cuckoldly knave;   110
here are his horns, Master [Brook]; and, Master
[Brook], he hath enjoy'd nothing of Ford's but his
buck-basket, his cudgel, and twenty pounds of money,
which must be paid to Master [Brook]. His horses are
arrested for it, Master [Brook].   115
Mrs. Ford.   Sir John, we have had ill luck; we
could never meet. I will never take you for my love
again, but I will always count you my deer.   118
Fal.   I do begin to perceive that I am made an ass.
Ford.   Ay, and an ox too; both the proofs are extant.
Fal.   And these are not fairies? I was three or four
times in the thought they were not fairies, and yet the
guiltiness of my mind, the sudden surprise of my
powers, drove the grossness of the foppery into a
receiv'd belief, in despite of the teeth of all rhyme   125
and reason, that they were fairies. See now how wit
may be made a Jack-a-Lent, when 'tis upon ill employment!
Evans.   Sir John Falstaff, serve Got, and leave your
desires, and fairies will not pinse you.   130
Ford.   Well said, fairy Hugh.
Evans.   And leave you your jealousies too, I pray you.
Ford.   I will never mistrust my wife again, till thou
art able to woo her in good English.

---

61. **several . . . order:** i.e. the individual stalls assigned in St. George's
Chapel, Windsor, to the members of the Order of the Garter.
63. **installment:** stall.   **coat:** coat of arms.
64. **blazon:** armorial bearings.
66. **Like . . . compass:** i.e. like the round garter which was worn below
the left knee by members of the Order.
67. **expressure:** imprint (literally, expression).
69. **Honi . . . pense:** Evil to him who evil thinks (motto of the Order
of the Garter); *pense* is here disyllabic.
70. **tuffs:** tufts, bunches.   73. **charactery:** writing.
78. **lanthorns:** lanterns.   79. **measure:** stately dance.
80. **a man of middle-earth:** i.e. a mortal. "Spirits are supposed to
inhabit the ethereal regions, and fairies to dwell underground; men
therefore are in a middle station" (Johnson).
82. **cheese.** See note to II.ii.303.
83. **o'erlook'd:** bewitched by the "evil eye."
86. **turn him to:** cause him.   92. **still:** continually.
94. **luxury:** lechery.

95. **bloody fire:** fire in the blood.
99. **mutually:** jointly, all together.
103. **watch'd you:** caught you in the act.
105. **hold . . . higher:** continue the joke no longer.
107. **fair yokes:** i.e. the horns.
115. **arrested:** seized by warrant as security.
120. **ox:** i.e. fool, with punning reference to the horns (line 107).
extant: present.   123. **surprise:** confounding.
124. **powers:** faculties.   **grossness:** flagrant character, obviousness.
foppery: dupery, deceit.   125. **despite . . . teeth:** defiance.
127. **Jack-a-Lent:** butt (see note on III.iii.27).

Fal. Have I laid my brain in the sun and dried it, that it wants matter to prevent so gross o'er- 136 reaching as this? Am I ridden with a Welsh goat too? Shall I have a coxcomb of frieze? 'Tis time I were chok'd with a piece of toasted cheese.

Evans. Seese is not good to give putter; your belly is all putter. 141

Fal. "Seese" and "putter"! Have I liv'd to stand at the taunt of one that makes fritters of English? This is enough to be the decay of lust and late-walking through the realm. 145

Mrs. Page. Why, Sir John, do you think, though we would have thrust virtue out of our hearts by the head and shoulders, and have given ourselves without scruple to hell, that ever the devil could have made you our delight? 150

Ford. What, a hodge-pudding? A bag of flax?

Mrs. Page. A puff'd man?

Page. Old, cold, wither'd, and of intolerable entrails?

Ford. And one that is as slanderous as Sathan? 155

Page. And as poor as Job?

Ford. And as wicked as his wife?

Evans. And given to fornications, and to taverns, and sack, and wine, and metheglins, and to drinkings and swearings and starings, pribbles and prabbles? 160

Fal. Well, I am your theme. You have the start of me, I am dejected. I am not able to answer the Welsh flannel; ignorance itself is a plummet o'er me. Use me as you will.

Ford. Marry, sir, we'll bring you to Windsor, to one Master [Brook] that you have cozen'd of 166 money, to whom you should have been a pander. Over and above that you have suffer'd, I think to repay that money will be a biting affliction.

Page. Yet be cheerful, knight. Thou shalt eat a posset to-night at my house, where I will desire 171 thee to laugh at my wife, that now laughs at thee. Tell her Master Slender hath married her daughter.

Mrs. Page. [*Aside.*] Doctors doubt that. If Anne Page be my daughter, she is, by this, Doctor Caius' wife. 176

[*Enter* SLENDER.]

Slen. Whoa ho, ho! father Page!

Page. Son? how now? how now, son? have you dispatch'd?

138. **coxcomb:** fool's cap.   **frieze:** a coarse woollen cloth made in Wales.   139. **piece . . . cheese.** See note on II.ii.303.
144. **late-walking:** keeping late hours.
151. **hodge-pudding:** large pork sausage.
153–54. **intolerable entrails:** i.e. a monstrous belly.
155. **Sathan:** Satan.
157. **wicked . . . wife.** Job's wife counselled him to curse God and die (Job 2.9).
159. **metheglins:** Welsh drink of fermented honey, resembling mead.
160. **starings:** swaggerings.
161. **your theme:** the object of your mirth.   **start:** advantage.
162. **dejected:** abased, humbled.
163. **flannel.** Of Welsh origin.   **ignorance itself:** i.e. Evans.   **plummet:** plummet line, for fathoming, probably with play (suggested by *flannel* and by *frieze*, line 138) on *plumbet*, a woollen fabric.
167. **should have been:** were to have been.
168. **that:** what.   170. **eat:** consume.
171. **posset.** See note on I.iv.8.
174. **Doctors doubt that.** Proverbial expression of disbelief. *Doctors =* learned men.   175. **this:** this time.

Slen. Dispatch'd? I'll make the best in Gloucestershire know on't. Would I were hang'd la, else! 181

Page. Of what, son?

Slen. I came yonder at Eton to marry Mistress Anne Page, and she's a great lubberly boy. If it had not been i' th' church, I would have swing'd him, 185 or he should have swing'd me. If I did not think it had been Anne Page, would I might never stir!—and 'tis a postmaster's boy. 188

Page. Upon my life then, you took the wrong.

Slen. When need you tell me that? I think so, when I took a boy for a girl. If I had been married to him (for all he was in woman's apparel) I would not have had him. 193

Page. Why, this is your own folly. Did not I tell you how you should know my daughter by her garments?

Slen. I went to her in [white] and cried "mum," and she cried "budget," as Anne and I had appointed, and yet it was not Anne, but a postmaster's boy. 199

Mrs. Page. Good George, be not angry. I knew of your purpose; turn'd my daughter into [green]; and indeed she is now with the Doctor at the dean'ry, and there married.

[*Enter* CAIUS.]

Caius. Vere is Mistress Page? By gar, I am cozen'd. I ha' married oon garsoon, a boy; oon 205 pesant, by gar. A boy! It is not Anne Page. By gar, I am cozen'd.

Mrs. Page. Why? did you take her in [green]?

Caius. Ay, be-gar, and 'tis a boy. Be-gar, I'll raise all Windsor. [*Exit.*] 210

Ford. This is strange. Who hath got the right Anne?

Page. My heart misgives me. Here comes Master Fenton.

[*Enter* FENTON *and* ANNE PAGE.]

How now, Master Fenton? 215

Anne. Pardon, good father! good my mother, pardon!

Page. Now, mistress, how chance you went not with Master Slender?

Mrs. Page. Why went you not with Master Doctor, maid?

Fent. You do amaze her. Hear the truth of it. 220
You would have married her most shamefully,
Where there was no proportion held in love.
The truth is, she and I (long since contracted)
Are now so sure that nothing can dissolve us.
Th' offense is holy that she hath committed, 225
And this deceit loses the name of craft,
Of disobedience, or unduteous title,
Since therein she doth evitate and shun

181. **else:** if I don't.   184. **lubberly:** loutish.
185. **swing'd:** beaten (past tense of *swinge*).
188. **postmaster:** master of the post-horses.
205. **oon garsoon:** *un garçon*, a boy.
205–6. **oon pesant:** *un paysan*, a peasant.   220. **amaze:** confuse.
222. **proportion:** balance, equality.   223. **contracted:** betrothed.
224. **sure:** i.e. firmly bound.
227. **unduteous title:** designation of undutifulness.
228. **evitate:** avoid.

A thousand irreligious cursed hours
Which forced marriage would have brought upon her.
　Ford.　Stand not amaz'd; here is no remedy.　231
In love, the heavens themselves do guide the state;
Money buys lands, and wives are sold by fate.
　Fal.　I am glad, though you have ta'en a special
stand to strike at me, that your arrow hath glanc'd.
　Page.　Well, what remedy? Fenton, heaven give
thee joy!　236
What cannot be eschew'd must be embrac'd.

235. **stand:** concealed position for shooting at game.

　Fal.　When night-dogs run, all sorts of deer are
chas'd.
　Mrs. Page.　Well, I will muse no further. Master
Fenton,
Heaven give you many, many merry days!　240
Good husband, let us every one go home,
And laugh this sport o'er by a country fire—
Sir John and all.
　Ford.　　　　Let it be so. Sir John,
To Master [Brook] you yet shall hold your word,
For he to-night shall lie with Mistress Ford. *Exeunt.*

239. **muse:** complain.

NOTE ON THE TEXT

The Merry Wives of Windsor was printed in a drastically shortened, memorially reconstructed form in 1602 (Q1). This "bad" quarto was reprinted in 1619 (Q2). The full text of the play, essentially the same as that from which Q1 was reported, appeared for the first time in the First Folio (1623). A third quarto (Q3), based on F1, was published in 1630.

Although the F1 text is the principal authority for any modern edition, Q1, debased as it undoubtedly is, furnishes several short passages perhaps accidentally omitted from F1, as well as many stage directions, suggests corrections for a number of faulty readings, and restores some oaths and the name Brook (Broom in F1) as the original form of Ford's alias. Pope and Theobald first began the practice of inserting tempting bits and pieces from Q1 into the F1 text. A few such passages have been admitted into the present text; others are recorded in the Textual Notes.

The F1 text is believed to have been printed from a transcript specially prepared for the publishers by Ralph Crane (see the "Note on the Text" to *The Tempest*). Evidence of Crane's hand may be seen in the frequent parentheses, in such hyphenated forms as *drawling-affecting, carry-her, idle-headed-Eld*, etc. (not completely recorded in the Textual Notes), and perhaps most conspicuously in the consistent use of "massed entries" (on which see the "Note on the Text" to *The Two Gentlemen of Verona*). Scholars seem generally to agree that Crane based his transcript on some kind of prompt-book, but the evidence for this view is slender.

In the F1 text thirty-seven short prose passages are wrongly printed as verse. Since the play is basically in prose, they raise no difficult problems, and with a few exceptions they are not recorded in the Textual Notes. F3 (particularly in III.iii) and Pope are responsible for adjusting these passages to prose.

Except as noted above, Q1–2 are in general cited only in connection with readings of F1. The absence of Q1–2 from the sigla cited in a textual note indicates that the reading of the lemma occurs in a passage which in Q1–2 is either omitted or so differently worded that it offers no recognizable equivalent. Some longer passages from Q1–2 which differ markedly from the F1 text are included in the Textual Notes for comparison (see I.i.1–108, III.ii.8 s.d., III.iii.1–21, IV.iv.42, V.v.49–54, 84–102, 104, 169, 236–45).

For further information, see: W. W. Greg, ed., *The Merry Wives of Windsor, 1602* (Oxford, 1910) [first full statement of the memorial reconstruction theory], and *The Shakespeare First Folio* (Oxford, 1955); J. D. Wilson, ed., New Cambridge *The Merry Wives of Windsor* (Cambridge, 1921); William Bracy, *"The Merry Wives of Windsor": The History and Transmission of Shakespeare's Text* (Columbia, Mo., 1952) [argues unsuccessfully against the memorial reconstruction theory]; William Green, *Shakespeare's "Merry Wives of Windsor"* (Princeton, 1962); J. M. Nosworthy, *Shakespeare's Occasional Plays* (London, 1965); H. J. Oliver, ed., New Arden *The Merry Wives of Windsor* (London, 1971).

TEXTUAL NOTES

Title: The . . . Windsor] A Most pleasaunt and excellent conceited Comedie, of Syr Iohn Falstaffe, and the merrie Wiues of Windsor. Entermixed with sundrie variable and pleasing humors, of Syr Hugh the Welch Knight, Iustice Shallow, and his swaggering Cousin M. Slender. With the swaggering vaine of Auncient Pistoll, and Corporall Nym. By William Shakespeare. As it hath bene diuers times Acted by the right Honorable my Lord Chamberlaines seruants. Both before her Maiestie, and else-where. *Q1 (title-page)*
Dramatis personae: *subs. as first given in Folger MS (ca. 1650) and Rowe*
Act-scene division: *from F1*

I.i

Location: *Theobald*
o.s.d. Enter . . . Evans.] *Rowe;* Enter Iustice

Shallow, Slender, Sir Hugh Euans, Master Page, Falstoffe, Bardolph, Nym, Pistoll, Anne Page, Mistresse Ford, Mistresse Page, Simple. *F1 (an example of the "massed entries" used throughout the F1 text; all but the first three characters actually enter at later points in the scene);* Enter Iustice Shallow, Syr Hugh, Maister Page, and Slender. *Q1–2*
1–108] *Except for ll. 1–2, these opening lines appear in a different form in Q1–2:* Shal. Nere talke to me, Ile make a star-chamber matter of it. / The Councell shall know it. *[cf. l. 117]* / Pag. Nay good maister Shallow be perswaded by mee. / Slen. Nay surely my vncle shall not put it vp so. / Sir Hu. Wil you not heare reasons M. Slenders *[Slender Q2]*? / You should heare reasons. / Shal. Tho he be a knight, he shall not thinke to carrie it so away. / M.

Page I will not be wronged. For you / Syr, I loue you, and for my cousen / He comes to looke vpon your daughter. / Pa. And heres my hand, and if my daughter / Like him so well as I, wee'l quickly haue it *[haue't Q2]* a match: / In the meane time let me intreat you to soiourne / Here a while. And on my life Ile vndertake / To make you friends. / Sir Hu. I pray you M. Shallowes *[Shallow Q2]* let it be so. / The matter is pud *[put Q2]* to arbitraments. / The first man is M. Page, videlicet M. Page. / The second is my selfe, videlicet my selfe. / And *[om. Q2]* the third and last man, is mine host of the gartyr. *[the last three lines are a version of ll. 138–41]* / Enter Syr Iohn Falstaffe, Pistoll, Bardolfe, and Nim. / Here is sir Iohn himselfe now, look you.

3 Falstaffs] *F2;* Falstoffs *F1*
28 py'r lady] *Capell;* per-lady *F1*

39 **vizaments]** *Capell;* viza-ments *F1*
46 **George]** *Theobald;* Thomas *F1*
72 s.d. **Knocks.]** *Rowe*
73 **Got pless]** *F2* (Got blesse); Got-plesse *F1* (these hyphenated forms, characteristic of Crane, are not generally noted)
74 s.d. **Within.]** *Dyce*
74 s.d. **Enter Page.]** *Collier*
75 **Got's]** *F2;* go't's *F1*
108 s.d. **Enter . . . Pistol.]** *Q1–2* (subs.)
119 **counsel]** *Q1–2;* councell *F1*
125–7 **They . . . pocket.]** *Q1–2* (first inserted, Malone)
141 **Garter]** *Q2;* Gater *F1;* gartyr *Q1*
161 **mountain-foreigner]** *hyphen, Hanmer*
162 **latten]** *Q2;* (laten) *Latine F1*
168–9 **that . . . note]** And there's the humor *Q1–2*
179 **careers]** *Capell* (subs.); Car-eires *F1*
180 **Latin]** *F2;* Latten *F1*
187 s.d. **Enter . . . Page.]** *Capell;* Enter Mistresse Foord, Mistresse Page, and her daughter Anne. *Q1–2*
189 s.d. **Exit Anne Page.]** *Theobald*
193 s.d. **Kisses her.]** *Q1–2* (Syr Iohn kisses her.)
197 s.d. **Exeunt . . . Evans.]** *Rowe* (subs.); Exit all, but Slender and mistresse Anne. *Q1–2*
199 s.d. **Enter Simple.]** *Rowe*
208 **afar off]** *F2;* a farre-off *F1*
227 **oman]** *Rowe* ('oman); 'o-man *F1*
236 **carry her]** *Pope;* carry-her *F1*
253 **discretion answer]** *F2;* descetion-answere *F1*
259 s.d. **Enter Anne Page.]** *Rowe*
262 **worships']** *Capell;* worships *F1*
265 s.d. **Exeunt . . . Evans.]** *Rowe*
272 s.d. **Exit Simple.]** *Theobald*
285 **prunes)]** *followng this, Wilson inserts from Q1–2:* and I with my ward / Defending my head, he hot my shin.
299 s.d. **Enter Page.]** *Q1–2*

I.ii

Location: *ed.* (after Wilson)
o.s.d. **from dinner]** *Q1–2*
8 **altogether's]** *Tyrwhitt conj.;* altogeathers *F1*

I.iii

Location: *Pope*
13 s.d. **To Bardolph.]** *Cambridge*
14 **lime]** *Q1–2* (lyme); liue *F1*
15 s.d. **Exit.]** *Q1–2*
19 s.d. **Exit.]** *Q1–2* (Exit Bardolph.)
20 **Hungarian]** gongarian *F1*
21 s.d. **Exit Bardolph.]** *Q1–2* (after l. 19); placed as in *Dyce*
23 **conceited?]** *following this, Theobald inserts from Q1–2:* His minde is not heroick. And theres the humor of it.
49 **well]** *Q1–2;* will *F1*
53 **He]** She *Q1–2*
53 **a legend]** legians *Q1;* Legions *Q2; most eds. read* a legion *(Rowe), but* legend *misused for* legion *occurs outside of Shakespeare*
54 **entertain]** attend her. *Q1–2*
61 **iliads]** *ed.;* illiads *F1*
78 **reputation.]** reputation. And theres the humor of it. *Q1–2*
79 s.d. **To Robin.]** *Theobald*
83 **humor]** *Q1–2;* honor *F1*
84 **page]** *Q1–2* (Page)? Page *F1* (in italics)
84 s.d. **Exeunt . . . Robin.]** *Q1–2* (. . . the Boy.)
89–90 **I . . . revenge.]** *as prose, Pope; as verse, F1, Q1–2*
89 **in my head]** *Q1–2* (first inserted, Pope)
95 **Page]** *Q1–2;* Ford *F1*
96 **Ford]** *Q1–2;* Page *F1*
101 **Rann]** Ford *F1*
102–3 **yallowness . . . humor.]** Iallowes, / And theres the humor of it. *Q1–2*

I.iv

Location: *Pope*
o.s.d. **Enter . . . Simple.]** *Q1–2;* Enter Mistris Quickly, Simple, Iohn Rugby, Doctor, Caius, Fenton. *F1*
1 s.d. **Enter John Rugby.]** *Wilson*
10 s.d. **Exit Rugby.]** *Rowe*
22 **whey-face]** *Capell;* wee-face *F1* (Q1–2 refer here to a whay coloured beard)
23 **Cain-color'd]** *hyphen, F2;* kane colored *Q1–2*
35 s.d. **Enter Rugby.]** *Rowe*
38, 63, 67 **closet]** Counting-house *Q1–2*
39 s.d. **Shuts . . . closet.]** *Rowe;* He steps into the Counting-house. *Q1–2*
43 s.d. **Singing.]** *Theobald*
43 s.d. **Enter Doctor Caius.]** *Rowe*
44 **des toys]** *F3;* des-toyes *F1*
45–6 **une boite en]** *Hart;* vnboyteene *F1*
51–2 **chaud . . . vois]** *ed.* (after *Rowe*); chando, Ie man voi *F1*
52 **affaire]** *Rowe;* affaires *F1*
54 **quickly]** *Pope;* quickly *F1* (in italics)
58 **and]** *Q1–2;* aad *F1*
68 **laroon]** *Wilson;* La-roone *F1*
68 s.d. **Pulling Simple out.]** *Theobald*
78 **Vell?]** *Neilson;* Vell. *F1*
87 **baillez]** *Theobald;* ballow *F1*
88 s.d. **Writes.]** *Q1–2* (The Doctor writes.)
89, 100 s.dd. **Aside to Simple.]** *Cambridge*
92 **you]** *Cambridge;* yoe *F1*
98 s.d. **Aside to Quickly.]** *Cambridge*
105 **that,]** *Rowe;* that *F1*
113 s.d. **Exit Simple.]** *Rowe*
125 s.d. **Exeunt . . . Rugby.]** *Rowe;* Exit Doctor. *Q1–2*
126 **Anne—fool's-head]** *Daniel conj.* (subs.); An-fooles head *F1;* Anne-fools head *F3*
131 s.d. **Within.]** *Rowe*
132 **trow]** *Rowe;* troa *F1*
133 s.d. **Enter Fenton.]** *Rowe*
154 **to.]** *Capell;* too——— *F1*
157 **me.]** *Knight;* me.——— *F1*
162 s.d. **Exit Fenton.]** *Rowe* (after l. 161); placed as in *Dyce*
163 **him]** *F2;* hiim *F1*

II.i

Location: *Pope*
o.s.d. **Enter . . . letter.]** *Q1–2;* Enter Mistris Page, Mistris Ford, Master Page, Master Ford, Pistoll, Nim, Quickly, Host, Shallow. *F1*
1 **I]** *Q3*
3 s.d. **Reads.]** *Capell*
20–8 **What . . . me!]** *as prose, Pope* (after *F3*), *Q1–2; as irregular verse, F1*
32 s.d. **Enter Mistress Ford.]** *Rowe*
51 **What?]** *Johnson;* What *F1*
58 **prais'd]** *Theobald;* praise *F1*
64 **trow]** *Rowe;* troa *F1*
65 **ashore]** *Capell* (subs.); a'shoare *F1*
95 **fine-baited]** *hyphen, Capell*
108 s.d. **They retire.]** *Theobald*
108 s.d. **Enter . . . Nym.]** *Rowe* (after *Q1–2:* Enter Ford, Page, Pistoll and Nym.)
113–5 **He . . . Perpend.]** *as verse, Pope, Q1–2; as prose, F1*
114 **Ford.]** *Rowe* (subs.); (Ford) *F1*
115 **gallimaufry, Ford. Perpend.]** *ed.* (after *Sisson*); Gally-mawfry (Ford) perpend. *F1*
125 s.d. **Exit.]** *Q1–2* (Exit Pistoll:)
126 s.d. **Aside.]** *Capell*
128 s.d. **To Page.]** *Hanmer*
136 **and . . . it.]** *Q1–2* (first inserted, Capell)
137 s.d. **Exit.]** *Q1–2* (Exit Nym.)
141 **drawling, affecting]** *F2;* drawling-affecting *F1*
147 s.d. **Mrs. . . . forward.]** *Theobald*
155 **head now. Will]** *Johnson;* head, Now: will *F1*
157 s.d. **Aside . . . Ford.]** *Capell*
160 s.d. **Aside . . . Page.]** *Capell*
161 s.d. **Enter Mistress Quickly.]** *Rowe; Q1–2 enter* Mrs. Quickly *around l. 149*
167 s.d. **Exeunt . . . Quickly.]** *Q1–2* (Exit)
188 s.d. **Enter Host.]** *Dyce; Q1–2 enter* Host and Shallow *here* (after confident. l. 187)
189 **ranting]** ramping *Q1–2*
193–4 **gentleman. Cavaleiro]** *Hanmer* (subs.); Gentleman. Caueleiro *F1; Q1–2 read*

ll. 193–4 as: God blesse you my bully rookes, God blesse / Cauelera Iustice I say.
194 s.d. **Enter Shallow.]** *Dyce*
205 s.d. **Ford . . . talks.]** *Q1–2* (Q1–2 reverse order of speeches in ll. 203–5)
206 s.d. **To Page.]** *Johnson*
211 s.d. **They converse apart.]** *Capell*
213 **guest-cavalier]** My guest, my cauellira *Q1–2*
214 s.p. **Ford.]** *Q1–2;* Shal. *F1*
216 **Brook]** *Q2* (misprinted Rrooke in *Q1*); Broome *F1*
219 **Brook]** *Q1–2;* Broome *F1*
220 **An-heires]** *an unsolved crux; Theobald's conj.* Mynheers *is the most popular emendation*
232 s.d. **Exeunt . . . Page.]** *Rowe;* Exit Host and Shallow. *Q1–2*
240 s.d. **Exit.]** *Rowe;* Exeunt. *F1;* Exit omnes. *Q1–2*

II.ii

Location: *Pope*
o.s.d. **Enter . . . Pistol.]** *Q1–2* (subs.); Enter Falstaffe, Pistoll, Robin, Quickly, Bardolffe, Ford. *F1*
1 **Pist. I . . . equipage.]** *Q1–2* (after l. 2); first inserted, *Theobald* (after l. 4); placed as in *Wilson*
3–4 **Why . . . open.]** *as verse, Steevens; as prose, F1*
13–4 **Didst . . . pence?]** *as verse, Capell; as prose, F1*
22 **honor]** *Q1–2;* hononor *F1*
22 **I, I, I]** I, I *Q1–2*
23 **God]** *Q1–2;* heauen *F1*
25 **shuffle,]** *Q1–2;* shuffle: *F1*
26 **you,]** *Pope;* you *F1*
30 s.d. **Enter Robin.]** *Rowe*
32 s.d. **Enter Mistress Quickly.]** *Q1–2*
52 **God bless]** *Q1–2;* heauen-blesse *F1*
66 **gift; . . . sweetly,]** *Capell;* gift, . . . sweetly; *F1*
90 **jealousy man]** *Theobald;* iealousie-man *F1*
112 **hope.]** *Rowe* (subs.); hope, *F1*
114 **page,]** *F4;* Page *F1*
133–4 s.d. **Exeunt . . . Robin.]** *Rowe;* Exit Mistresse Quickly.
135 s.d. **Aside.]** *Wilson*
137 s.d. **Exit.]** *Rowe*
138 **so, old Jack?]** *F4* (subs.); so (old Iacke) *F1*
143 s.d. **Enter Bardolph.]** *Q1–2*
148 **Brook]** *Q1–2;* Broome *F1* (throughout scene)
150 s.d. **Exit Bardolph.]** *Theobald*
150 **Brooks]** *Q1–2;* Broomes *F1*
153 s.d. **Enter . . . Brook.]** *Theobald* (subs.); Enter Foord disguised like Brooke. *Q1–2*
154 **God save]** *Q1–2;* 'Blesse *F1*
159 s.d. **Exit Bardolph.]** *Theobald*
204 **jewel—]** *Theobald* (subs.); Iewell, *F1*
207–8 **"Love . . . pursues."]** *marked with gnomic quotes, F1*
233 **exchange]** *Q3;* enchange *F1*
246–7 **hand, . . . themselves.]** *Rowe* (subs., after *F4*); hand; . . . themselues, *F1*
254 **and]** *Q1;* if *F1, Q2*
257 **I]** M. Brooke, I *Q1–2*
286 s.d. **Exit.]** *Q1–2* (Exit Falstaffe)
295 **abominable]** *F4;* abhominable *F1*
299 **Wittol!—Cuckold!]** *Cambridge;* Wittoll, Cuckold? *F1*
309 **God]** *Q1–2;* Heauen *F1*
314 s.d. **Exit.]** *Q1–2* (Exit Ford); Exti. *F1*

II.iii

Location: *Dyce*
o.s.d. **Enter . . . Rugby.]** *Q1–2* (Enter the Doctor and his man.); Enter Caius, Rugby, Page, Shallow, Slender, Host. *F1*
17 s.d. **Enter . . . Host.]** *Q1–2* (Enter Shallow, Page, my [om. Q2] Host, and Slender.)
18 **God bless]** *Q1–2;* 'Blesse *F1*
19 **God save]** *Q1–2* (in speech by Page); 'Saue *F1*
28 **Francisco]** francoyes *Q1–2* (possibly correct = "Frenchman")

38–9 **Doctor: he**] *F4;* Docto)rhe *F1*
57 **word**] *Q1–2*
75 s.d. **Aside to them.**] *Capell*
81 s.p. **Page, Shal., Slen.**] *Malone (the line is spoken by Shallow in Q1–2)*
81 s.d. **Exeunt . . . Rugby.**] *ed. (after Q1–2: Exit all but the Host and Doctor.)*
84 **but first**] *Q1–2*
88 **Cried game?**] *Sisson;* Cride-game, *F1;* cried game: *Q1–2*
92 **guest**] gesse *Q1;* guests *Q2*
93 **patients**] patinces *Q1*

III.i

Location: *Malone (after Pope)*
o.s.d. **Enter . . . Simple.**] *Q1–2 (Enter Syr Hugh and Simple.); Enter Euans, Simple, Page, Shallow, Slender, Host, Caius, Rugby. F1*
10 s.d. **Exit.**] *Cambridge*
11 **Jeshu pless**] *Q1–2;* 'Plesse *F1*
16, 22, 28 s.dd. **Sings.**] *Dyce (after Pope)*
24 **When . . . Babylon—**] There dwelt a man in Babylon, *Q1–2*
26 s.d. **Enter Simple.**] *Cambridge*
35 s.d. **Reads in a book.**] *Dyce (after Collier MS)*
35 s.d. **Enter . . . Slender.**] *Q1–2*
40 s.d. **Aside.**] *Cambridge*
41 **God save**] *Q1–2;* 'Saue *F1*
42 **God pless**] *Q1–2;* 'Plesse *F1*
42 **mercy sake**] *Capell (subs.);* mercy-sake *F1;* mercies sake *Q1–2*
70 s.d. **Aside.**] *Cambridge*
70 s.d. **Enter . . . Rugby.**] *Q1–2 (Enter Doctor and the Host, they offer to fight.)*
72 s.d. **Evans . . . fight.**] *from Q1–2 (see preceding note)*
77–8 **Let . . . English.**] *given to Shallow in Q1–2, perhaps correctly*
81 s.d. **Aside to Caius.**] *Cambridge*
85 s.d. **Aside to Caius.**] *Staunton*
88 s.d. **Aloud.**] *Staunton*
88 **urinals**] *Q1–2;* Vrinal *F1*
89 **cogscomb**] cockcomes *Q1;* coxcomb *Q2*
89–90 **for . . . appointments**] *Q1–2 (first inserted, Pope)*
105–6 **Give . . . so.**] *Q1–2* (Giue . . . hand terestial, / So); *first inserted, Theobald, who punctuates subs. as here*
106 **hand, celestial; so.**] *Theobald (subs., after Rowe);* hand (Cellestiall) so: *F1;* hand celestiall: / So *Q1–2*
110 **lads**] *Q1–2;* Lad *F1*
111 s.d. **Exit.**] *Q1–2 (Exit Host.)*
112 **Afore God**] *Q1–2;* Trust me *F1*
114 s.d. **Aside.**] *Cambridge*
114 s.d. **Exeunt . . . Page.**] *Rowe (who, however, includes the Host; Neilson first om. the Host)*
120 **scall, . . . companion,**] *Capell (subs.);* scall scuruy-cogging-companion *F1*
126 s.d. **Exeunt.**] *Pope;* Exit omnes *Q1–2*

III.ii

Location: *Theobald (after Pope)*
o.s.d. **Enter . . . Robin.**] *Rowe;* Mist. Page, Robin, Ford, Page, Shallow, Slender, Host, Euans, Caius. *F1*
8 s.d. **Enter Ford.**] *Q1–2 (Enter M. Foord.); Q1–2 begin the scene with Ford's entry and offer the following lines in place of ll. 1–59: Enter M. Foord. / For. The time drawes on he shuld come to my house, / Well wife, you had best worke closely, / Or I am like to goe beyond your cunning: / I now wil seek my guesse that comes [guests that come Q2] to dinner, / And in good time see where they all are come. / Enter Shallow, Page, and sir Hugh. / By my faith a knot well met: your welcome all. [cf. l. 51] / Pa. I thanke you good M. Ford. / For. Welcome good M. Page, / I would your daughter were here. / Pa. I thank you sir, she is very well at home.*
29 s.d. **Exeunt . . . Robin.**] *Rowe*

33 **mile, as easy**] *F4;* mile as easie, *F1*
44–5 s.d. **Clock heard.**] *Capell*
49 s.d. **Enter . . . Rugby.**] *Capell (after Q1–2, which like F1 fail to enter Rugby here)*
70 **buttons**] betmes *Q1–2*
73 **Poins**] *F3* (Poinz); Pointz *F1; Q1–2 om. the whole reference to the Prince and Poins*
84 **fare you well**] God be with you *Q1–2*
85 s.d. **Exeunt . . . Slender.**] *Q1–2 (Exit)*
86 s.d. **Exit Rugby.**] *Capell*
88 s.d. **Exit.**] *Q1–2 (Exit host.)*
89 s.d. **Aside.**] *Johnson*

III.iii

Location: *Pope*
o.s.d. **Enter . . . Page.**] *Capell;* Enter M. Ford, M. Page, Seruants, Robin, Falstaffe, Ford, Page, Caius, Euans. *F1;* Enter Mistrise Ford, with two of her men, and a great buck basket. *Q1–2*
4 s.d. **Enter . . . buck-basket.**] *Capell (after Q1–2; see preceding note)*
15 **Datchet-mead**] *Rowe;* Dotchet Mead *F1*
20 s.d. **Exeunt Servants.**] *Folger MS, Johnson;* Exit seruant. *F1*
21 s.d. **Enter Robin.**] *Rowe*
37 s.d. **Exit Robin.**] *Rowe*
39 s.d. **Exit.**] *Rowe*
42 s.d. **Enter Falstaff.**] *Q1–2 (Enter Sir Iohn.)*
43–4 **"Have . . . jewel?"**] *Q1–2 om. thee as in Sidney's original line*
48–9 **prate, . . . Now**] *F4 (subs.);* prate (Mist. Ford) now *F1*
50 **dead.**] *Theobald (subs.);* dead, *F1*
56 **beauty**] bent *Q1–2*
61 **By the Lord**] *Q1–2*
61 **tyrant**] traitor *Q1–2*
65 **foe were not,**] *F2;* foe, were not *F1*
69 **thee**] *Q1–2;* thee. *F1*
84 s.d. **Enter Robin.**] *Capell;* Within. *F2*
92 s.d. **Falstaff . . . arras.**] *Q1–2*
92 s.d. **Enter Mistress Page.**] *Q1–2 (before Falstaff hides himself); placed as in F2*
111 **'Tis . . . hope.**] Speak louder. But I hope tis not true Mistris Page. *Q1–2*
125 **For shame**] Gode [Gods *Q2*] body woman *Q1–2*
136 s.d. **Starting . . . concealment.**] *Capell*
139 s.d. **Aside.**] *Q1–2*
141 s.d. **To Mrs. Page.**] *Malone conj.*
141 **thee.**] thee, and none but thee: *Q1–2*
142 s.d. **Goes . . . him.**] *from Q1–2 s.d.:* Sir Iohn goes into the basket, they put cloathes ouer him, the two men carries it away: Foord meetes it, and all the rest, Page, Doctor, Priest, Slender, Shallow.
145 s.d. **Exit Robin.**] *Malone*
145 s.d. **Enter Servants.**] *Capell*
148 s.d. **Enter . . . Evans.**] *Folger MS, Rowe (see l. 142 above for Q1–2)*
151 **now?**] now who goes heare? *Q1–2*
160 s.d. **Exeunt . . . basket.**] *Rowe (see l. 142 above for Q1–2)*
164 s.d. **Locking the door.**] *Capell*
169 s.d. **Exit.**] *Capell*
170 **This**] By Ieshu these *Q1–2*
175 s.d. **Exeunt . . . Evans.**] *Capell;* Exit omnes. *Q1–2*
193 **foolish**] *F2;* foolishion *F1*
198 s.d. **Enter . . . Evans.**] *Rowe;* Enter all. *Q1–2*
201 s.d. **Aside . . . Ford.**] *Capell*
202 **You . . . you?**] I, I, peace. *Q1–2 (as a separate speech for Mrs. Ford; Theobald inserts these words at the beginning of the F1 speech)*
210 **If**] By Ieshu if *Q1–2*
220 **omans**] *Capell* ('omans); o'mans *F1 (so generally)*
227 **me.**] *following this speech Q1–2 read:* Sir Hu. By so kad vdgme, M. Fordes [Foord *Q2*] is / Not in his right wittes:
230 **after,**] *Theobald;* after *F1*
237 **turd.**] tird: / *Sir. Hu.* In your teeth for shame. *Q1–2*
238 s.d. **Exit with Page.**] *Wilson*
241 **with all**] *F2;* withall *F1*

III.iv

Q1–2 reverse the order of Scenes iv and v
Location: *Pope (subs.)*
o.s.d. **Enter . . . Page.**] *Rowe;* Enter Fenton, Anne, Page, Shallow, Slender, Quickly, Page, Mist. Page. *F1;* Enter M. Fenton, Page [Anne Page *Q2*], and mistresse Quickly. *Q1–2*
1–21] *These lines are replaced in Q1–2 by the following essentially different lines:* Fen: Tell me sweet *Nan,* how doest thou yet resolue, / Shall foolish *Slender* haue thee to his wife? / Or one as wise as he, the learned Doctor? / Such such as they enioy thy maiden hart? / Thou knowst that I haue alwaies loued thee deare, / And thou hast oft times swore the like to me. / An: Good M. *Fenton,* you may assure your selfe / My hart is setled vpon none but you, / Tis as my father and my mother please: / Get their consent, you quickly shall haue mine. / Fen: Thy father thinks I loue thee for his wealth, / Tho I must needs confesse at first that drew me, / But since thy vertues wiped that trash away, / I loue thee *Nan,* and so deare is it set, / That whilst I liue, I nere shall thee forget. / Quic: Godes pitie here comes her father. *[In Q1–2 the rough equivalent of ll. 22–66 follows the exit of Mrs. Page (with Page, who has remained on stage) about l. 94.]*
12 s.p. **Fent.**] *Q3*
21 s.d. **They converse apart.**] *Capell*
21 s.d. **Enter . . . Quickly.**] *Rowe*
31 s.d. **Aside.**] *Capell*
58 **heaven**] God *Q1–2*
66 s.d. **Enter . . . Page.**] *Rowe;* Enter M. Page his wife, M. Shallow, and Slender. *Q1–2*
74 **Fenton**] *Q3;* Fenter *F1*
76 s.d. **Exeunt . . . Slender.**] *Rowe;* in Q1–2 instead of exiting they whisper.
88 **yourself.**] *Warburton (subs.);* your selfe *F1*
94 s.d. **Exeunt . . . Anne.**] *Rowe*
102 s.d. **Exit Fenton.**] *Q1–2 (after the equivalent of l. 100); placed as in Dyce*
111 s.d. **Exit.**] *Rowe;* Exeunt *F1*
121 **surge**] *Pope;* serge *F1*

III.v

Location: *Pope*
o.s.d. **Enter Falstaff.**] *Q1* (Enter Sir Iohn Falstaffe); Enter Falstaffe, Bardolfe, Quickly, Ford. *F1;* Enter Sir Iohn Falstaffe and Bardolfe. *Q1–2*
1 s.d. **Enter Bardolph.**] *Wilson*
4 s.d. **Exit Bardolph.**] *Theobald*
6, 13 **and**] *Q1;* if *F1,* Q2
9 **slighted**] slided *Q1–2*
18 **mummy.**] money. Now is the Sacke brewed? *Q1–2*
18 s.d. **Enter . . . sack.**] *Dyce (after Theobald)*
25 s.d. **Enter Mistress Quickly.**] *Q1–2*
31 **pullet-sperm**] *F2;* Pullet-Spersme *F1;* pullets sperme *Q1–2*
32 s.d. **Exit Bardolph.**] *Capell*
56 s.d. **Exit.**] *Q1–2 (Exit mistresse Quickly.)*
57 **Brook**] *Q1–2;* Broome *F1 (throughout scene)*
59 s.d. **Enter Ford disguised.**] *Dyce (after F2);* Enter Brooke. *Q1–2*
60 **Bless**] God saue *Q1–2*
70 **cornuto**] *F2;* Curnuto *F1*
83 **good luck**] God *Q1–2*
89 **By the Lord**] *Q1–2;* Yes: *F1*
108 **several**] egregious *Q1–2*
138 s.d. **Exit.**] *Q1–2 (Exit Falstaffe.)*
152 s.d. **Exit.**] *Rowe;* Exeunt. *F1;* Exit omnes. *Q1–2*

IV.i

Scene om. Q1–2
Location: *Capell*
o.s.d. **Enter . . . William.**] Enter Mistris Page, Quickly, William, Euans. *F1*
8 s.d. **Enter Evans.**] *Rowe (after l. 10); placed as in Neilson*
9 **playing-day**] hyphen, *F4*

28–9 Poulcats . . . poulcats] *F2;* Powlcats . . . Powlcats *F1*
43 hujus] *F2;* huius *F1*
47 hung] *Pope;* hing *F1*
48 Latin] *F3;* latten *F1*
52 O—] *Capell;* O, *F1*
61 Genitivo] *Folger MS, Singer;* Genitiue *F1*
62 Jinny's] *Kittredge;* Ginyes *F1*
69 lunatics] *Folger MS, Capell;* Lunaties *F1*
77 quae] *Folger MS, Pope;* que *F1*
78 quae's] *Pope;* Ques *F1*
84–5 s.d. Exit Evans.] *Steevens (subs.)*

IV.ii

Location: *Pope*
o.s.d. Enter . . . Ford.] Enter Falstaffe, Mist. Ford, Mist. Page, Seruants, Ford, Page, Caius, Euans, Shallow. *F1;* Enter misteris Ford and her two men. *Q1–2 (followed by the equivalent of ll. 108–10, before the entry of Falstaff)*
9 s.d. Within.] *Rowe*
11 into th' chamber] behind the arras *Q1–2*
11 s.d. Exit Falstaff.] *Rowe;* He steps behind the arras. *Q1–2*
11 s.d. Enter Mistress Page.] *Q1–2 (after l. 10); placed as in Rowe*
16 s.d. Aside to her.] *Dyce (after Theobald)*
22 lines] vaine *Q1–2 (Theobald's lunes is frequently adopted by eds.)*
48 s.d. Enter Falstaff.] *Rowe*
66 s.p. Mrs. Page.] *Malone;* Mist. Ford. *F1*
73 Good hearts] For Gods sake *Q1–2*
75–6 aunt . . . Brainford] Aunt Gillian of Brainford *Q1–2*
83 s.d. Exit Falstaff.] *F2 (Exit.)*
99 direct] *Q3;* direct direct *F1*
101 s.d. Exit.] *Capell*
103 him] *F2*
107 draff] *Capell;* draugh *F1*
107 s.d. Exit.] *Capell*
107 s.d. Enter . . . Servants.] *Capell (subs.); for Q1–2 see note on o.s.d.*
110 s.d. Exit.] *Capell*
113 lief as] as leife *F2*
113 s.d. Enter . . . Shallow.] *Rowe;* Enter M. Ford, Page, Priest [Hugh *Q2*], Shallow, the two men carries the basket, and Ford meets it. *Q1–2*
116–7 Youth . . . basket!] You youth in a basket, come out here, *Q1–2*
118 ging] *F2;* gin *F1*
119 What,] *Hanmer (after Theobald);* What *F1*
126 this] *Q3;* thi *F1*
128 s.d. Enter Mistress Ford.] *Theobald (after l. 125); placed as in Dyce*
133 Heaven . . . do,] I Gods my record do you. *Q1–2*
133 and if] *Q1;* if *F1, Q2*
136 s.d. Pulling . . . basket.] *Rowe; in Q1–2 Ford says:* Pull out the cloathes, search.
139 clothes] *F2;* cloths *F1*
141 'Tis unreasonable] Ieshu plesse me *Q1–2*
142 Come] *Rowe;* Come, *F1*
145] *Preceding this speech of Ford's, Q1–2 read:* Sir Hu. By [By om. *Q2*] so kad vdge me, tis verie necessarie / He were put in pethlem.
145 a man] an honest man *Q1–2*
170 maid's aunt] maidens [maids *Q2*] Ant, Gillian *Q1–2*
172 s.p. Ford] *om. Q1*
181 not] *Q3*
181 s.d. Enter . . . him.] *Q1–2*
184 prat her] *Steevens;* Prat-her *F1*
186 s.d. Ford . . . away.] *Q1–2 (part of s.d. at l. 181); placed as in Neilson*
192 By . . . no] By Ieshu *Q1–2*
199 his] her *Q1–2*
200 s.d. Exeunt . . . Evans.] *Dyce;* Exit omnes. *Q1–2*
201 Trust me] By my Troth *Q1–2*
210 him.] *F4 (subs.);* him, *F1*

IV.iii

Location: *Pope*

1 Germans desire] *Capell;* Germane desires *F1;* three Gentlemen *Q1–2*
7 them] *Q1–2;* him *F1*
9 house] *Q1–2;* houses *F1*

IV.iv

Location: *Pope*
7 cold] *Rowe;* gold *F1*
28 Herne] Horne *Q1–2 (throughout; possibly, as in the Brook-Broom substitution, the original name)*
33 makes] *F2;* make *F1*
41 device] *F3;* deuise *F1*
42] *At this point Q1–2 explain why the meeting must take place in the park:* Now for that Falstaffe hath bene so deceiued, / As that he dares not venture to the house, / Weele send him word to meet vs in the field,
43 Disguis'd . . . head.] *Q1–2 (Disguised like Horne, with huge horns on his head,); first inserted by Theobald, who also includes the preceding line (Weele . . . field,); Malone as here*
45 shape] *F2;* shape, *F1*
61 s.p. Mrs. Ford.] *Rowe;* Ford. *F1*
62 him] *F2;* him, *F1*
71 My . . . fairies] my daughter *Anne,* / Shall like a litle Fayrie be disguised *Q1–2 (Page speaking)*
73 s.d. Aside.] *Pope*
81 s.d. Exeunt . . . Evans.] *Rowe*
83 Quickly] *Theobald;* quickly *F1 (not in italics as a proper name)*
83 s.d. Exit Mrs. Ford.] *Rowe*
90 s.d. Exit.] *F2;* Exit omnes. *Q1–2*

IV.v

Location: *Pope*
o.s.d. Enter Host and Simple.] *Q1–2;* Enter Host, Simple, Falstaffe, Bardolfe, Euans, Caius, Quickly. *F1*
2 thick-skin] *hyphen, Q1–2*
19 s.d. Above.] *Theobald (from Q2 he speakes aboue.)*
23 s.d. Enter Falstaff.] *Q1–2 (Enter Sir Iohn.; after l. 25); placed as in Theobald*
44 s.p. Sim.] *Folger MS, Rowe;* Fal. *F1*
54 Ay, sir; like] *F1 (I Sir: like);* I tike *Q1–2*
56 s.d. Exit.] *Q2*
57 Thou art] *Q1–2;* Thou are *F1*
58 John. Was] *Rowe (subs.);* Iohn) was *F1*
59 Ay . . . was] *F1 (I . . . was);* Marry was there *Q1–2*
62 s.d. Enter Bardolph.] *Q1–2*
70 Faustuses] *F2;* Faustasses *F1*
72 s.d. Enter Evans.] *Q1–2; in Q1–2 the order of entry for Evans and Caius (see l. 82) is reversed*
77 three cozen-germans] three Cozen-Iermans *F1;* three sorts of cosen garmombles *Q1–2*
82 s.d. Exit.] *Q1–2*
82 s.d. Enter Caius.] *Q1–2 (Enter Doctor.)*
87 duke de Jamany] Germaine Duke *Q1–2*
89 s.d. Exit.] *Q1–2*
90, 91 Hue] *Rowe;* Huy *F1*
92 s.d. Exeunt . . . Bardolph.] *Capell;* Exit. *Q1–2*
103 to . . . prayers] *Q1–2; first inserted, Pope*
103 s.d. Enter Mistress Quickly.] *Q1–2 (after l. 104); placed as in Theobald*
117 Brainford.] *Theobald (subs.);* Brainford, *F1*

IV.vi

Location: *ed. (after Wilson)*
16–7 Fat . . . scene.] Wherein fat Falstaffe had a mightie scare, *Q1–2*
39 denote] *Capell;* deuote *F1*
41 green] red *Q1–2*

V.i

Scene om. *Q1–2*
Location: *ed. (after Wilson)*
o.s.d. Enter . . . Quickly.] *Rowe;* Enter Falstaffe, Quickly, and Ford. *F1*
8 s.d. Exit Mrs. Quickly.] *Rowe (after l. 7); placed as in Capell*

8 s.d. Enter Ford disguised.] *Dyce (after Rowe)*

V.ii

Scene om. *Q1–2*
Location: *Wilson*
3 my daughter] *F2;* my *F1*

V.iii

Scene om. *Q1–2*
Location: *ed. (after Pelican)*
6 s.d. Exit Caius.] *Rowe (after l. 6); placed as in Capell*
12 Hugh] *Capell;* Herne *F1*

V.iv

Scene om. *Q1–2*
Location: *Capell (after Pope)*
o.s.d. like a satyr] *Q1–2 (see V.v.36 s.d. below)*
o.s.d. others as] *Capell (subs.)*

V.v

In Q1–2 the dialogue for this scene contains only occasional echoes of the F1 text and omits all reference to the Garter Feast and the Queen
Location: *ed. (after Wilson)*
o.s.d. Enter . . . him.] *Q1–2 (sir Iohn);* Enter Falstaffe, Mistris Page, Mistris Ford, Euans, Anne Page, Fairies, Page, Ford, Quickly, Slender, Fenton, Caius, Pistoll. *F1*
1 strook] *Capell;* stroke *F1*
15 s.d. Enter . . . Ford.] *Q1–2*
20 hail kissing-comfits] *Rowe;* haile-kissing Comfits *F1*
21 s.d. Embracing her.] *Capell*
29 s.d. There . . . horns.] *Q1–2 (There is a noise of hornes, the two women run away.)*
33 s.d. The . . . away.] *Q1–2 (see preceding note)*
34–6 I . . . thus.] as prose, *Pope;* as verse, *F1*
36 s.d. Enter . . . speak.] *Q1–2 (with addition of Anne Page [ed. (after Alexander)] and Pistol as Hobgoblin [Dyce];* Enter Fairies. *F1*
48 s.d. Lies . . . face.] *Rowe*
49–54 Evans. Where's . . . shins.] *Q1–2 assign Evans two speeches of direction to the "Fairies," one perhaps substituting for Pistol's speech (ll. 42–6); Pistol has no part in the Q1–2 scene:* Sir Hu. Come hither *Peane,* go to the countrie houses, / And when you finde a slut that lies a sleepe, / And all her dishes foule, and roome vnswept, / With your long nailes pinch her till she crie, / And sweare to mend her sluttish huswiferie. / *Fai.* I warrant you I will performe your will. / *Hu.* Where is [Wher's *Q2*] Pead? go you & see where Brokers sleep, / And Foxe-eyed Seriants with their mase, / Goe laie the Proctors in the street, / And pinch the lowsie Seriants face: / Spare none of these when they are [th' are *Q2*] a bed, / But such whose nose lookes plew and red.
62 balm, . . . flow'r;] *Rowe (subs.);* Balme; . . . flowre, *F1*
65 nightly, meadow-fairies] *Capell;* Nightly-meadow-Fairies *F1*
66–7 ring. . . . bears,] *Rowe (subs.);* ring, . . . beares: *F1*
68 More] *F2;* Mote *F1*
70 em'rald tuffs] *Kittredge (tufts; hyphen dropped, Capell);* Emrold-tuffes *F1*
71 sapphire, pearl] *Theobald;* Saphire-pearle *F1*
80 middle-earth] *hyphen, Dyce*
81 Heavens defend] God Blesse *Q1–2*
81–2 Heavens . . . cheese!] as prose, *Pope;* as verse, *F1*
84–102] *Cf. the Q1–2 version of these lines:* Quic. Looke euery one about this round. / And if that any here be found, / For his presumption in this place, / Spare neither legge, arme, head, nor face. / Sir Hu. See

I haue spied one by good luck, / His bodie man, his head a buck. / *Fal.* God send me good fortune now, and I care not. / *Quic.* Go strait, and do as I commaund, / And take a Taper in your hand, / And set it to his fingers endes, / And if you see it him offends, / And that he starteth at the flame, / Then is he mortall, know his name: / If with an F. it doth begin, / Why then be shure he is [hee's *Q2*] full of sin. / About it then, and know the truth, / Of this same metamorphised [metamorphosed *Q2*] youth. / *Sir Hu.* Giue me the Tapers, I will try / And if that he loue venery. / *They put the Tapers [Torches Q2] to his fingers, and he starts. / Sir Hu.* It is [Tis *Q2*] right indeed, he is full of lecheries and iniquitie. / *Quic.* A little distant from him stand, / And euery one take hand in hand, / And compasse him within a ring, / First pinch him well, and after sing.

88 s.d. **They . . . starts.**] *Q1–2* (Torches *Q2*)

92] *Following this line Theobald inserts from Q1–2: Sir Hu.* It is [Tis *Q2*] right indeed, he is full of lecheries and iniquitie.

102 s.d. **Here . . . up.**] *Q1–2 (with green . . . white [Theobald] substituted for Q1–2's red . . . greene; Q1–2 also describe Anne Page as being in white)*

102 s.d. **Enter . . . Ford.**] *Capell (after Rowe);* And enters M. Page M. Ford, and their wiues, M. Shallow, and Sir Hugh. *Q1–2*

104 **Will . . . turn?**] *Q1–2 give Falstaff a speech which reads like an answer to this query: Fal.* Horne the hunter quoth you: am I a ghost? / Sblood the Fairies hath made a ghost of me: / What [What, *Q2*] hunting at this time at night? / Ile lay my life the mad Prince of *Wales* / Is stealing his fathers Deare. How now who haue / we here, what is all *Windsor* stirring? Are you there?

110 **Brook**] *Q1–2;* Broome *F1 (throughout scene)*

169] *Following this line Theobald inserts from Q1–2: Mi. For.* Nay husband let that go to make amends, / Forgiue that sum, and so weele let be friends. / *For.* Well here is my hand, all's forgiuen at last.; *and Keightley adds also the following speech from Q1–2: Fal.* It hath cost me well, / I haue bene well pinched and washed.

174 s.d. **Aside.**] *Theobald*

176 s.d. **Enter Slender.**] *Q1–2; in Q1–2 the order of entry for Slender and Caius (see l. 203) is reversed*

182 **what,**] *F2;* what *F1*

197 **white**] *Rowe;* greene *F1;* red *Q1–2*

199] *Following this line Theobald inserts from Q1–2: Sir. Hu.* Ieshu M. *Slender,* cannot you see but marrie boyes? / *Pa.* O I am vext at hart, what shal I do?

201 **green**] *Rowe;* white *F1*

203 s.d. **Enter Caius.**] *Q1–2* (Enter the Doctor.)

208 **green**] *Pope;* white *F1*

209 **be-gar . . . Be-gar**] *hyphens, ed.*

210 s.d. **Exit.**] *Capell*

214 s.d. **Enter . . . Page.**] *Q1–2*

232 **state;**] *Rowe;* state, *F1*

236–8 **Well . . . chas'd.**] *as verse, Rowe (after F4); as prose, F1*

236–45] *Cf. the concluding lines in Q1–2: Mi. For.* Come mistris *Page,* Ile be bold with you, / Tis pitie to part loue that is so true. / *Mis. Pa.* Altho that I haue missed in my intent, / Yet I am glad my husbands match was crossed, / Here M. *Fenton,* take her, and God giue thee ioy. / *Sir. Hu:* Come M. *Page,* you must needs agree. / *Fo.* I yfaith [Ifaith *Q2*] sir come, you see your wife is wel [wel *om. Q2*] pleased: / *Pa.* I cannot tel, and yet my hart's well eased, / And yet it doth me good the Doctor missed. / Come hither *Fenton,* and come hither daughter, / Go too you might haue stai'd for my good will, / But since your choise is made of one you loue, / Here take her *Fenton,* & both happie proue. / *Sir. Hu.* I wil also [also *om. Q2*] dance & eat plums at your weddings. / *Ford.* All parties pleased, now let vs in to feast, / And laugh at *Slender,* and the Doctors ieast. / He hath got the maiden, each of you a boy / To waite vpon you, so God giue you ioy, / And sir *Iohn Falstaffe* now shal you keep your word, / For *Brooke* this night shall lye with mistris *Ford. (Pope first inserted Sir Hugh's* I wil . . . weddings. *after l. 237)*

243 **so. Sir John,**] *Theobald (subs.);* so (Sir Iohn:) *F1*

245 s.d. **Exeunt.**] Exeunt / FINIS. *F1;* Exit omnes. / FINIS. *Q1–2*

Horns, the cuckold's curse. From *Roxburghe Ballads,* ed. W. Chappell, I (1869), 151. Elizabethans seemed never to tire of comic or serious allusions to the horns of the cuckold, the badge figuratively worn by the husband of an unfaithful wife, and in *The Merry Wives of Windsor,* the theme of which is Falstaff's abortive attempt to cuckold Master Ford and Master Page, the horn image occurs frequently. In the woodcut above, horns are everywhere: the cornuted (horned) husband appears at the upstairs lattice window; the huntsman's rousing peal (which, like the cuckoo's call elsewhere, becomes a symbolic warning to cuckolds) issues from a horn; the house sign is a pair of antlers; and the devil tempting the wife is horned. As Master Page says of Falstaff, who has been instructed to wear a pair of antlers at the pretended assignation in Windsor Park: "No man means evil but the devil, and we shall know him by his horns" (V.ii.12–14).

Much Ado about Nothing

When Berlioz, in 1861, turned *Much Ado about Nothing* into an opera, he retitled it *Béatrice et Bénédict*. He omitted Don John entirely and replaced Dogberry and Verges with a comic musician named Somarone. Claudio, Hero, and Don Pedro he kept, but purely as the agents who trick Beatrice and Benedick into matrimony. In the opera, the course of Hero's and Claudio's love is quite smooth and, also, patently subordinate to the bickerings and dissension of the rival pair. Berlioz' emphasis on Beatrice and Benedick at the expense of what is, strictly speaking, the main plot of Shakespeare's comedy is familiar: a reflection of the way actors, audiences, and readers have tended to react for several hundred years. Even King Charles I, in his personal copy of Shakespeare's Second Folio, altered the play's title as Berlioz did, proclaiming his own interest in the witty lovers rather than their romantic opposites. Shakespeare himself cannot have been unaware of the disproportionate amount of interest generated by the subplot. More important, however, is the fact that he obviously meant each plot to interconnect with and gain interest from the other. Taken by itself, without the vital undercurrent of the Beatrice and Benedick story, the relationship between Hero and Claudio seems flat and thin. On the other hand, Beatrice and Benedick cannot really sustain the play by themselves. Musically splendid though it is, Berlioz' opera is nonetheless a demonstration of the extent to which their odd and intensely individual agreement is impoverished as soon as you separate it from that skein of villainy, deceit, and misunderstanding which Don Pedro's bastard brother weaves about the more conventional lovers in Shakespeare's comedy. A Beatrice who has

no need to ask Benedick to "Kill Claudio" (IV.i.289), forcing him to choose abruptly between his old world of male friendships and the new world of love, cannot fully reveal either her own nature or the depth of her lover's commitment.

In its basic outline, the Hero and Claudio plot is of great age, tracing its ancestry back to the romance literature of ancient Greece. It seems, however, to have acquired an especial popularity during the Renaissance. In constructing his own version of this archetypal story of the lady falsely accused of unchastity, cast off by her lover, and after many vicissitudes restored to him again, Shakespeare probably had at least four non-dramatic variants of the tale somewhere in mind. Ariosto's account, in Canto V of *Orlando Furioso*, of how the Scottish princess Genevra was mistaken for her maid Dalinda, seen keeping a tryst with another man, and so abandoned by her own love Ariodante, would have been available to him in Sir John Harington's translation of 1591. He must also have known Spenser's sombre version, the story of Phedon, Claribell, and the false Philemon in Book II of *The Faerie Queene* (1590), as well as that of Timbreo and Fenicia in Bandello's twenty-second novella (1554), translated into French and adapted generally by Belleforest in his *Histoires Tragiques* of 1574. George Whetstone drew upon both Bandello and Ariosto in his related tale of Rinaldo and Giletta, included in his collection *The Rock of Regard* (1576). There were also several plays, in French, Latin, and Italian, based upon this plot. In 1585, an anonymous Elizabethan dramatist (possibly Anthony Munday) produced a version of the most famous of these, Pasqualigo's *Il Fedele* (1579), under the title *Fedele and Fortunio*. Shakespeare almost certainly knew this play.

Although the essential shape of the story remains the same through all these different tellings, it was in fact subject to variation and also to marked changes in interpretation. Usually, although by no means always, the villain of the piece is the lover's friend: a man treacherously in love with the lady himself who slanders her in order to break off the match. The injured heroine is commonly a fiancée, less usually a wife. In at least one version, that of Spenser, she does actually die. More often, her death is merely symbolic: the prelude to a joyous reunion with her lover, disabused at last of his belief that she was untrue. In a significant number of cases, the lover is blamed quite specifically for the ease with which he gave credence to the false report, and for yielding himself to jealousy without sifting the matter thoroughly. Most versions deal, to some extent, with a conflict between love and friendship in which the more fiery and irrational force of love overthrows not only a former bond of trust but the integrity of a personality.

In *Much Ado about Nothing* Shakespeare transferred the rivalry between love and friendship to a position slightly outside the main imbroglio. Don John, the source of a misunderstanding that comes close to being fatal, has no interest whatever in Hero herself. A man incapable of any genuine human relationship, he is not even Claudio's friend, let alone his rival in love. Don John is a malcontent pure and simple, a man who might say with the cold duke in Thurber's story *The Thirteen Clocks*: "We all have faults, and mine is doing wickedness." Certainly, Shakespeare makes no attempt to provide him with even the kind of fairy-tale motivation that Oliver has for practicing against the life of his younger brother in *As You Like It*. The fact that Don John was born a bastard becomes an all-sufficient explanation of why it is that he is treacherous, scheming, savage, and morose. A thing of darkness, out of step with his society, he hates the children of light simply because they generate radiance in a world he prefers to see dark. This is why he plans to wreck the intended marriage of Claudio and Hero. He has nothing to gain personally from such a tactic, except the pleasure of annoying his brother, grieving Claudio, turning laughter to tears, and reducing everyone around him to the state of misery and gloom in which he languishes himself. A plot mechanism more than a complex character in his own right, Don John appears in the play as a kind of anti-comic force, the official enemy of all happy endings.

Much Ado about Nothing represents a variant on the more usual Shakespearean comic pattern of a journey from an urban to a rural, an ordinary to a heightened world, and back again. All the action of the play takes place in Messina, but it is a town temporarily lifted out of its normal habits and atmosphere by the fact that it happens to be filled with glamorous strangers resting there for a time after a triumphant military campaign, and by the sense of gaiety and elation attendant upon a newly concluded peace. Don Pedro, the prince, comes from Aragon. Benedick hails from Padua, while Claudio is a Florentine. The three are old friends, however, as well as comrades in arms. Moreover, they are quite at home in Messina. Don Pedro has stayed with Leonato before. Claudio has an uncle in the town, and he had his eye on Hero before he went off to war. Beatrice and Benedick appear to have been insulting one another joyously for years.

In the Messina of the comedy, masked faces, revels, and dances are the order of the day. Apart from Dogberry and his associates, this is a courtly world enjoying a period of carnival. Some of the deceits, like the one that brings Beatrice and Benedick together, are harmless and even beneficent. Others are not. The general atmosphere, however, is conducive to eavesdropping, mistaken identity, game-playing, and conversations reported wrongly, even as it is to music, feasting, and marriage. Claudio's wooing of Hero seems almost like an expected and conventional response to the times: an acknowledgment that, when wars are over, it is advisable to begin replenishing a population diminished by bullets and swords. Certainly, Claudio's courtship of Hero is of the most formal and socially proper kind. He takes her wealth and position as Leonato's only child into careful account, seeks the advice and approbation of his prince before embarking on the match, and behaves in every way like a sober, prudent man contracting a dynastic alliance in which the charms of the lady matter, of course, but scarcely inspire in him the recklessness of a Romeo. A man does not allow his prince, however respected, to propose marriage for him in disguise unless he sees that marriage in social more than in personal terms. This, however, is what Claudio does. Only when Don Pedro has secured the consent of both the lady and her father does the prospective bridegroom speak to Hero himself. With the war happily ended, Claudio feels that the time is right for matrimony and for begetting an heir. His practicality in this respect is not exactly held against him, but it does explain the ease with which he believes Don John's slanders, and the unconsidered violence with which he shames Hero and casts her off. Essentially, Claudio is a man who thinks he has been duped in a bargain, not a Troilus whose whole world shatters around him because he has to recognize that the goddess of his idolatry is false.

Hero too is docile and passive. She welcomes the alliance with Claudio, but there is no suggestion that she has been pining with love for the young Florentine while he has been away at the war. When it is falsely reported that Don Pedro is interested in her himself, she seems entirely willing to accept the prince as a suitor, despite the discrepancy in their ages. Like Claudio, presumably, she thinks it is high time she got married. Beatrice tells her that she has a right to her own judgment in such matters (II.i.52–6) but Hero's will conforms entirely to her father's. Elizabethans must have detected a certain irony in the name Shakespeare bestowed upon this singularly dutiful daughter. In Greek mythology, Hero was the lady beloved of Leander, who broke her religious vows in order to enjoy a clandestine love affair with him. When, through the enmity of the gods, Leander was drowned while swimming the Hellespont one night to a secret meeting with her, Hero killed herself. Shakespeare knew Marlowe's great narrative poem on the subject and, in *As You Like It*, quoted a line from it: "Who ever lov'd that lov'd not at first sight?" It would be hard to imagine an attitude further away from the caution and circumspection of Claudio's Hero.

The affairs of these two lovers, often conducted through third parties, are inveterately public. The rupture between them, when it comes, is public too. Claudio denounces Hero in church, on their wedding day, before a crowd of people, and with the backing of the prince. Even Leonato, Hero's own father, is convinced. In the bitterest speech of the comedy, he begs his own child at least to have the decency to die, and tries to prevent anyone from reviving her. The friar has some difficulty in persuading him that this condemnation may be too hasty. Apart from the friar, only Beatrice and Benedick suspect, from the first, that Hero is really innocent and the prince and Claudio misled. Beatrice, in particular, reacts violently against Claudio's public denunciation of her cousin: "What, bear her in hand until they come to take hands, and then with public accusation, uncover'd slander, unmitigated rancor—O God, that I were a man! I would eat his heart in the market-place" (IV.i.303–7). Her indignation is, in a sense, just but it also serves to indicate the distance between her own intensely personal attachment to Benedick and the more formal, outward bond which unites Claudio and Hero. Claudio's atonement when the truth is known, even his reunion with Hero, are wholly consistent with the nature of this plot: his penitence before Hero's tomb in V.iii is again public, a ritual demonstration of sorrow, and he gets his lady back only because he agrees to ally himself, sight unseen, with another daughter of Leonato's house.

Much Ado about Nothing is usually dated 1598. There is no specific source for the Beatrice and Benedick underplot, but it is important to remember that several years earlier, in *The Taming of the Shrew*, Shakespeare had already experimented with the idea of an unconventional couple who arrive at love and understanding by way of insult and aggression. Like Katherina and Petruchio before them, Beatrice and Benedick use protestations of enmity and distaste to conceal a powerful, underlying attraction. There is a suggestion in the text that these "two bears" were once, at some indeterminate past time, in love with each other (II.i.280–82). Shakespeare does not say why the relationship broke down but, in the comedy itself, each one is obsessed with and continually talking about the other in a manner which makes it clear from the start that their animosity is a cloak for feelings of a very different kind. This is why they can be tricked with such ease. All that the conspirators have to do is to suggest to each that the other has yielded first, has taken the first step towards an admission and acknowledgment of love, and all

defenses crumble. Both Beatrice and Benedick, for all their surface gaiety, their scorn of the married state, are essentially lonely people. They are older than Claudio and Hero, and in danger of finding themselves imprisoned for life within a set of attitudes and social responses which, though witty and amusing, are nonetheless inhibiting and sterile. Neither can break these self-imposed fetters without help from outside. When this help arrives, they turn joyously to one another with a freedom and a depth of engagement lacking in the relationship of Hero and Claudio.

In several important respects, Beatrice and Benedick are prototypes of the witty lovers in Restoration comedy: source characters for that impressive line of skirmishing gallants and ladies which extends from Etherege and the early comedies of Dryden to Congreve's Mirabell and Millamant in *The Way of the World*. Like their Restoration descendants, they converse by preference in prose: a prose sharply distinguished from the blank-verse rhapsodies of the younger pair of lovers. Their wit is imaginative and easy, but it is also analytic: a yoking together of judgment and fancy which, again, looks forward to the period of Charles II. Essentially, Beatrice and Benedick are—like Mirabell and Millamant, or Etherege's Dorimant and Harriet—romantics who need to keep this weakness dark. For all its surface aggression, its deflationary quality, their wit is really defensive: a way of protecting a self that they know to be vulnerable. Beatrice savages Benedick in public, and mocks him behind his back, because she cannot help thinking about him and needs to camouflage this interest. Benedick defends the bachelor state, inveighs against women and even against the courtly art of music, affecting a spirit of bluff, masculine camaraderie on all social occasions, in order to fend off alternative ways of thinking and feeling. Like Restoration lovers, Beatrice and Benedick use wit to distance emotions which they recognize as potentially dangerous. They cling to the society of their own sex because there they feel safe, but they cannot resist launching provocative shafts of ridicule or inquiry into the enemy's terrain.

Although Beatrice has no evidence to advance against the damning account of how Don Pedro, Don John and Claudio actually saw Hero talk with a ruffian at her chamber window after midnight, she never for an instant believes that her cousin is guilty. Her logic here is that of the instincts and the heart, but it happens to be entirely right. Benedick, understandably, is slower to commit himself to the defense of Hero, although from the first he is puzzled by the charge against her. He makes an important decision, however, when he does not leave the church with Claudio, Don Pedro, and the bastard, as might be expected. He chooses, instead, to remain behind with Hero, Leonato, the friar, and Beatrice. In doing so, he breaks with that little all-male society of soldiers which has hitherto claimed his allegiance. He behaves in this seemingly uncharacteristic fashion although he and Beatrice have not yet, in fact, reached an understanding, simply because he is beginning to see the

329

world through different eyes. Leonato, in the last scene of all, will claim: "The sight whereof I think you had from me, / From Claudio, and the Prince" (V.iv.25–26). This is true, however, only in the sense that had it not been for the conspiracy, Benedick would never have been able to liberate and admit responses buried deep inside himself.

At the end of the play, Claudio and Don Pedro are still inflicting upon Benedick their somewhat heavy-handed badinage about "the savage bull" and "the married man." For them, the capitulation of the confirmed bachelor is primarily a matter for laughter and self-congratulation, even as it was in the first scene of Act V when, with Hero newly "dead," they indulged their "gossip-like humor" (V.i.186) on the same subject, in order to raise their spirits, and found Benedick icily still and unresponsive. There is no evil in Claudio and the prince, but there is something schoolboyish and immature. The flight of Don John from Messina, together with Borachio's confession of the plot against Hero, relieves Benedick of the necessity of turning his sword against his former friend, but it is important that he should have accepted Beatrice's passionate and impulsive commission. We in the audience never really believe that Benedick will "kill Claudio." Law and justice in Messina are, to put it mildly, inefficient, but it is nonetheless evident, even in the scene where the challenge is formally delivered, that Hero's innocence will shortly be vindicated without any help from Benedick. What his engagement in her cause demonstrates is the new priority in his life of love, and the extent to which this love supersedes and cancels out older ties. As for Beatrice, the woman who pretended, early in the comedy, that she could not imagine why anyone should think her life incomplete without a man, a mere "clod of wayward marl" (II.i.62–63), she finds herself in Act IV wishing no fewer than three times "that I were a man." Her appeal to Benedick to do what, as a woman, she cannot herself manage, and her gratitude to him, represent, on her part, as radical a transformation of attitude as does his challenge to Claudio.

Virtually all of Shakespeare's comedies involve some kind of confrontation with death before the characters are allowed to win through to the happiness of the final scene. *Much Ado about Nothing* enacts this movement through darkness to light in a particularly striking way. The penultimate scene takes place before the monument of Leonato, the supposed burial place of Hero. The characters involved all wear mourning and they carry tapers to lighten the gloom of the place. The scene occurs at night, but once the dirge for Hero has been sung, the sun rises at once.

> Good morrow, masters, put your torches out.
> The wolves have preyed, and look, the gentle day,
> Before the wheels of Phoebus, round about
> Dapples the drowsy east with spots of grey.
>
> (V.iii.24–27)

As an indication of the turning point of the comedy, the moment when it begins to move irreversibly towards joy, Don Pedro's description of the new dawn could scarcely be clearer in its effect. Yet there is a sense in which the threat of death and disaster in this play has never possessed the kind of seriousness or urgency which it has, for instance, in *The Merchant of Venice* or *Measure for Measure*. This is partly because the wickedness of Don John is so fantastic and oddly remote, and partly because it is no sooner committed than revealed. It is only a matter of time before someone more intelligent than Dogberry and his ancient and most quiet watch hears Borachio's confession and understands the truth.

A town which appears to manage quite nicely despite the fact that its police force spends its time on duty sleeping, and would require another police force to prevent its halberds from being stolen by frisky citizens, is scarcely a town where evil flourishes. The ineptitudes of Dogberry and his partner Verges are not merely funny in themselves: they reassure the theatre audience that comedy remains in control of the action, even when the potential for tragedy seems greatest. Dogberry's linguistic muddles are also important in the light of the play's treatment of language and the multiple meanings of words. When Beatrice, early in Act V, makes the word *foul* jump through an astonishing series of hoops as part of her teasing refusal to give Benedick a kiss, her lover complains: "Thou hast frighted the word out of his right sense, so forcible is thy wit" (V.ii.55–56). Benedick's comment is both rueful and admiring. Both he and Beatrice are adept at verbal game-playing, although her skill, arguably, is even greater than his. Certainly the wit of both is a conscious exploration of the resources and also the illogicalities of language. Dogberry too is a character who customarily frights words out of their proper meaning. In the course of the comedy, he contrives to strike terror into the words *redemption, excommunication, suspect, opinioned, tedious,* and *blunt*, to list only a few of his victims. He does so, of course, not because he is witty but because he is ignorant. A man with an exaggerated idea of his own merits and importance—"I am a wise fellow, and which is more, an officer, and which is more, a householder, and which is more, as pretty a piece of flesh as any is in Messina" (IV.ii.80–82)—he relies upon language to overawe and impress the people with whom he deals. To some extent, his verbal habits seem to have rubbed off on his associates: Verges gets himself into some terrible linguistic tangles, and even the watch, although content in general with the simplest kind of speech, run headlong into the word *deformed* as though it were a kind of brier-patch. Only Dogberry, however, consistently misemploys the grandest words he can think of as a way of magnifying himself.

Frequently, Dogberry lunges at a glittering and distant term and misses. The result is a glorious collection of non-words, bastard compounds which hover bewilderingly on the edge of sense: *decerns, suffigance, dissembly,* or *vigitant*. Verbal mistaking of this kind is associated, on the whole, only with the most dim-witted of Shakespeare's clowns. There is, nevertheless, something almost touching about Dogberry's unrequited passion for words in a play in which other characters possess a mastery of language that is positively dazzling. The suggestion that he is a man who "hath had losses" (IV.ii.84) is made only once, and not elaborated on by Shakespeare, but it is enough to explain the compulsion behind his speech style. Dogberry is a man who has, at some time in the past, suffered heavy financial and social setbacks. He has struggled onto his feet again, owns his own house, and has two gowns "and every thing handsome about him" (IV.ii.85–86), but the doubt and the insecurity remain and cannot be banished. This is why he deals so constantly in self-magnification, bullies

Verges, and becomes positively obsessed with the fact that he has publicly been described as an ass. Words are his one defense against the possibility that he may be slighted or misprized by the world. He uses them to keep the reality of his self and his situation at bay. The activity is familiar. Beatrice and Benedick happen to be masters of a linguistic game whose first principles Dogberry has never been able to grasp, but for them too words have been a way of keeping people at a distance, of protecting and isolating a vulnerable inner self. Shakespeare never allows the paragons of wit to share a scene with the man who declares that "Comparisons are odorous" (III.v.16), but he makes it clear that, for all the surface dissimilarity, there is an affinity between them.

Anne Barton

MATRIMONIO.

Matrimony. From Cesare Ripa, *Iconologia* (1603). "In time the savage bull doth bear the yoke," quips Don Pedro, quoting inaccurately a line from Kyd's *Spanish Tragedy*, in answer to Benedick's vigorous flouting of the suggestion that he, too, will some day "look pale with love" and become a "married man" (*Much Ado*, I.i.245–68)—as, of course, he eventually does. Not only does the emblem above show the yoke, it includes also another common symbol of marriage—the clog, a heavy piece of wood attached to the leg or neck to prevent escape. Bertram makes the allusion clear when, as his wife Helena enters, he jibes: "Here comes my clog" (*All's Well*, II.v.53). (*By permission of the Harvard College Library*)

Much Ado about Nothing

[ACT I, Scene I]

Enter Leonato, *governor of Messina,* Hero *his daughter, and* Beatrice *his niece, with a* Messenger.

Leon. I learn in this letter that Don [Pedro] of Arragon comes this night to Messina.

Mess. He is very near by this, he was not three leagues off when I left him.

Leon. How many gentlemen have you lost in this action? 6

Mess. But few of any sort, and none of name.

Leon. A victory is twice itself when the achiever brings home full numbers. I find here that Don [Pedro] hath bestow'd much honor on a young Florentine call'd Claudio. 11

Mess. Much deserv'd on his part, and equally rememb'red by Don Pedro. He hath borne himself beyond the promise of his age, doing in the figure of a lamb the feats of a lion. He hath indeed better bett'red expectation than you must expect of me to tell you how. 17

Leon. He hath an uncle here in Messina will be very much glad of it.

Mess. I have already deliver'd him letters, and there appears much joy in him, even so much that joy could not show itself modest enough without a badge of bitterness.

Leon. Did he break out into tears?

Mess. In great measure. 25

Leon. A kind overflow of kindness. There are no faces truer than those that are so wash'd. How much better is it to weep at joy than to joy at weeping!

Beat. I pray you, is Signior Mountanto return'd from the wars or no? 31

Mess. I know none of that name, lady. There was none such in the army of any sort.

Leon. What is he that you ask for, niece?

Hero. My cousin means Signior Benedick of Padua. 36

Mess. O, he's return'd, and as pleasant as ever he was.

Beat. He set up his bills here in Messina, and challeng'd Cupid at the flight, and my uncle's 40 fool, reading the challenge, subscrib'd for Cupid, and challeng'd him at the burbolt. I pray you, how

---

22. **modest:** moderate.
23. **badge of bitterness:** sign of sorrow. Leonato's next question translates these words into literal terms. 26. **kind:** natural.
30. **Mountanto.** From Italian *montanto*, a fencing term meaning an upward blow or thrust. 37. **pleasant:** jocular.
39. **bills:** public notices.
40. **at the flight:** to an archery contest. Perhaps she means that Benedick proclaimed himself immune to love.
41. **fool:** jester. It has been suggested that perhaps Beatrice means herself, and is referring obliquely to an earlier romantic encounter with Benedick. See lines 61–64 and II.i.278–82. **subscrib'd for:** made an undertaking on behalf of.
42. **burbolt:** bird-bolt, a blunt-headed arrow for shooting birds at short distance. The bird-bolt was allowed to fools and children as being less dangerous than the barbed long-distance arrow, and was frequently assigned to Cupid, perhaps because he was represented as a child.

Words and passages enclosed in square brackets in the text above are either emendations of the copy-text or additions to it. The Textual Notes immediately following the play cite the earliest authority for every such change or insertion and supply the reading of the copy-text wherever it is emended in this edition.

I.i. Location: Messina. Before Leonato's house.
6. **action:** battle.
7. **sort:** rank (so also in line 33). **name:** reputation, prominence.
14. **figure:** appearance. 16. **bett'red:** surpassed.
18. **will:** who will (a frequent construction).

many hath he kill'd and eaten in these wars? But how many hath he kill'd? for indeed I promis'd to eat all of his killing. 45

Leon. Faith, niece, you tax Signior Benedick too much, but he'll be meet with you, I doubt it not.

Mess. He hath done good service, lady, in these wars. 49

Beat. You had musty victual, and he hath holp to eat it. He is a very valiant trencherman, he hath an excellent stomach.

Mess. And a good soldier too, lady.

Beat. And a good soldier to a lady, but what is he to a lord? 55

Mess. A lord to a lord, a man to a man, stuff'd with all honorable virtues.

Beat. It is so indeed, he is no less than a stuff'd man. But for the stuffing—well, we are all mortal. 60

Leon. You must not, sir, mistake my niece. There is a kind of merry war betwixt Signior Benedick and her; they never meet but there's a skirmish of wit between them. 64

Beat. Alas, he gets nothing by that. In our last conflict four of his five wits went halting off, and now is the whole man govern'd with one; so that if he have wit enough to keep himself warm, let him bear it for a difference between himself and his horse, for it is all the wealth that he hath left 70 to be known a reasonable creature. Who is his companion now? he hath every month a new sworn brother.

Mess. Is't possible? 74

Beat. Very easily possible. He wears his faith but as the fashion of his hat: it ever changes with the next block.

Mess. I see, lady, the gentleman is not in your books. 79

Beat. No, and he were, I would burn my study. But I pray you, who is his companion? Is there no young squarer now that will make a voyage with him to the devil?

Mess. He is most in the company of the right noble Claudio. 85

Beat. O Lord, he will hang upon him like a disease; he is sooner caught than the pestilence, and the taker runs presently mad. God help the noble Claudio! If he have caught the Benedick, it will cost him a thousand pound ere 'a be cur'd. 90

Mess. I will hold friends with you, lady.

Beat. Do, good friend.

Leon. You will never run mad, niece.

Beat. No, not till a hot January.

Mess. Don Pedro is approach'd. 95

Enter Don Pedro, Claudio, Benedick, Balthasar, *and* [Don] John *the Bastard.*

D. Pedro. Good Signior Leonato, are you come to meet your trouble? The fashion of the world is to avoid cost, and you encounter it.

Leon. Never came trouble to my house in the likeness of your Grace, for trouble being gone, 100 comfort should remain; but when you depart from me, sorrow abides and happiness takes his leave.

D. Pedro. You embrace your charge too willingly. I think this is your daughter. 104

Leon. Her mother hath many times told me so.

Bene. Were you in doubt, sir, that you ask'd her?

Leon. Signior Benedick, no, for then were you a child. 108

D. Pedro. You have it full, Benedick. We may guess by this what you are, being a man. Truly the lady fathers herself. Be happy, lady, for you are like an honorable father. 112

Bene. If Signior Leonato be her father, she would not have his head on her shoulders for all Messina, as like him as she is. 115

Beat. I wonder that you will still be talking, Signior Benedick, nobody marks you.

Bene. What, my dear Lady Disdain! are you yet living? 119

Beat. Is it possible disdain should die while she hath such meet food to feed it as Signior Benedick? Courtesy itself must convert to disdain, if you come in her presence.

Bene. Then is courtesy a turncoat. But it is certain I am lov'd of all ladies, only you excepted; 125 and I would I could find in my heart that I had not a hard heart, for truly I love none.

Beat. A dear happiness to women, they would else have been troubled with a pernicious suitor. I thank God and my cold blood, I am of your 130 humor for that: I had rather hear my dog bark at a crow than a man swear he loves me.

Bene. God keep your ladyship still in that mind! so some gentleman or other shall scape a predestinate scratch'd face. 135

Beat. Scratching could not make it worse, and 'twere such a face as yours were.

44–45. **promis'd . . . killing:** i.e. predicted that he wouldn't kill anyone.   46. **tax:** take to task, censure.   47. **meet:** even, quits.
50. **musty:** stale.   **holp:** helped.   51. **trencherman:** good eater.
52. **stomach:** appetite.   54. **to:** in comparison with.
58–59. **stuff'd man:** i.e. a dummy, not a real man.
59–60. **for . . . mortal:** as for his character—well, we all have our faults.
66. **five wits.** Usually listed as memory, fantasy, judgment, imagination, and common wit.   **halting:** limping.
68. **wit . . . warm.** Proverbial for minimal intelligence.
69. **difference:** a variation in a coat of arms to distinguish a junior member or branch of a family from the chief line.
71. **known:** recognized as.
72–73. **sworn brother:** friend with whom he has exchanged vows of lifelong fidelity.   75. **faith:** loyalty.
77. **block:** wooden mould for shaping hats; hence, fashion.
79. **books:** i.e. good books, favor.   80. **and:** if.
82. **squarer:** quarreller.   88. **presently:** immediately.   90. **'a:** he.

91. **hold friends:** keep on friendly terms (so as not to incur your wrath).   93. **run mad:** i.e. "catch the Benedick."
98. **cost:** expense.   **encounter:** go to meet.
103. **embrace your charge:** welcome your burden.
109. **have it full:** are well answered, have got back as good as you gave.
111. **fathers herself:** shows who her father is (by her resemblance to him).   114. **his head:** i.e. with its marks of age.
116. **still:** always.   122. **convert:** change.
128. **dear happiness:** great stroke of good fortune.
131. **humor for that:** inclination in that respect.
134. **scape:** escape.
134–35. **predestinate:** foreordained, inevitable (for anyone who marries Beatrice).
137. **were:** i.e. is (the verb has been attracted into the subjunctive by the preceding *'twere*).

Bene. Well, you are a rare parrot-teacher.

Beat. A bird of my tongue is better than a beast of yours.   140

Bene. I would my horse had the speed of your tongue, and so good a continuer. But keep your way a' God's name, I have done.

Beat. You always end with a jade's trick, I know you of old.   145

D. Pedro. That is the sum of all: Leonato—Signior Claudio and Signior Benedick—my dear friend Leonato hath invited you all. I tell him we shall stay here at the least a month, and he heartily prays some occasion may detain us longer. I   150 dare swear he is no hypocrite, but prays from his heart.

Leon. If you swear, my lord, you shall not be forsworn. [*To Don John.*] Let me bid you welcome, my lord, being reconcil'd to the Prince your brother: I owe you all duty.   156

D. John. I thank you. I am not of many words, but I thank you.

Leon. Please it your Grace lead on?   159

D. Pedro. Your hand, Leonato, we will go together.   *Exeunt. Manent Benedick and Claudio.*

Claud. Benedick, didst thou note the daughter of Signior Leonato?

Bene. I noted her not, but I look'd on her.

Claud. Is she not a modest young lady?   165

Bene. Do you question me, as an honest man should do, for my simple true judgment? or would you have me speak after my custom, as being a profess'd tyrant to their sex?   169

Claud. No, I pray thee speak in sober judgment.

Bene. Why, i' faith, methinks she's too low for a high praise, too brown for a fair praise, and too little for a great praise; only this commendation I can afford her, that were she other than she is, she were unhandsome, and being no other but as she is, I do not like her.   176

Claud. Thou thinkest I am in sport. I pray thee tell me truly how thou lik'st her.

Bene. Would you buy her, that you inquire after her?   180

Claud. Can the world buy such a jewel?

Bene. Yea, and a case to put it into. But speak you this with a sad brow? or do you play the flouting Jack, to tell us Cupid is a good hare-finder and Vulcan a rare carpenter? Come, in what key shall a man take you to go in the song?   186

Claud. In mine eye, she is the sweetest lady that ever I look'd on.

Bene. I can see yet without spectacles, and I see no such matter. There's her cousin, and she   190 were not possess'd with a fury, exceeds her as much in beauty as the first of May doth the last of December. But I hope you have no intent to turn husband, have you?   194

Claud. I would scarce trust myself, though I had sworn the contrary, if Hero would be my wife.

Bene. Is't come to this? In faith, hath not the world one man but he will wear his cap with suspicion? Shall I never see a bachelor of threescore again? Go to, i' faith, and thou wilt needs thrust   200 thy neck into a yoke, wear the print of it, and sigh away Sundays. Look, Don Pedro is return'd to seek you.

Enter DON PEDRO.

D. Pedro. What secret hath held you here, that you follow'd not to Leonato's?   205

Bene. I would your Grace would constrain me to tell.

D. Pedro. I charge thee on thy allegiance.

Bene. You hear, Count Claudio, I can be secret as a dumb man; I would have you think so; but   210 on my allegiance, mark you this, on my allegiance, he is in love. With who? Now that is your Grace's part. Mark how short his answer is: with Hero, Leonato's short daughter.

Claud. If this were so, so were it utt'red.   215

Bene. Like the old tale, my lord: "It is not so, nor 'twas not so, but indeed, God forbid it should be so."

Claud. If my passion change not shortly, God forbid it should be otherwise.   220

D. Pedro. Amen, if you love her, for the lady is very well worthy.

Claud. You speak this to fetch me in, my lord.

D. Pedro. By my troth, I speak my thought.

Claud. And in faith, my lord, I spoke mine.   225

Bene. And by my two faiths and troths, my lord, I spoke mine.

Claud. That I love her, I feel.

D. Pedro. That she is worthy, I know.

Bene. That I neither feel how she should be lov'd, nor know how she should be worthy, is the   231 opinion that fire cannot melt out of me; I will die in it at the stake.

D. Pedro. Thou wast ever an obstinate heretic in the despite of beauty.   235

---

138. **rare:** excellent.   **parrot-teacher:** i.e. one who says the same thing over and over.
139–40. **A bird . . . yours:** i.e. a bird taught to speak like me would be better than an animal taught to speak like you, for he would say nothing.   142. **so . . . continuer:** (were) so tireless.
144. **jade's trick.** A jade is an ill-conditioned horse, likely to drop out of a race before the end, as Benedick here lamely drops out of the contest of wits.
146. **That . . . all.** Don Pedro and Leonato have been conversing aside.
155. **being:** since you are.
164. **noted her not:** didn't observe her in particular.
169. **tyrant:** one pitiless and cruel.   171. **low:** short.
183. **sad:** serious.   183–84. **flouting Jack:** mocking fellow.
184–85. **to . . . carpenter:** i.e. by saying something as obviously wide of the truth as that Cupid has sharp eyes, or calling Vulcan a carpenter. (Cupid was blind, Vulcan the blacksmith of the gods.)
186. **go . . . song:** sing in harmony with you.

198–99. **wear . . . suspicion.** An allusion to the popular jest that a cuckold (husband of an unfaithful wife) grew horns.
202. **Sundays:** i.e. the day a husband would be expected to spend with his wife.
213. **part:** speaking part (namely, to ask "With who?").
215. **If . . . utt'red:** i.e. if it were true and I had told him so in confidence, he would have violated my confidence in just this manner.
216. **old tale.** Apparently some form of the Bluebeard story. In an eighteenth-century version cited by Furness, a lady who has discovered the bodies of the victims describes her experience, under the fiction that she is recalling a dream, and at intervals the murderer, who is among the listeners, interjects the words here quoted.
223. **fetch me in:** trick me, take me in.
235. **despite:** despising, contempt.

Claud. And never could maintain his part but in the force of his will.

Bene. That a woman conceiv'd me, I thank her; that she brought me up, I likewise give her most humble thanks; but that I will have a rechate 240 winded in my forehead, or hang my bugle in an invisible baldrick, all women shall pardon me. Because I will not do them the wrong to mistrust any, I will do myself the right to trust none; and the fine is (for the which I may go the finer), I will live a bachelor. 246

D. Pedro. I shall see thee, ere I die, look pale with love.

Bene. With anger, with sickness, or with hunger, my lord, not with love. Prove that ever I lose more blood with love than I will get again with drink- 251 ing, pick out mine eyes with a ballad-maker's pen, and hang me up at the door of a brothel-house for the sign of blind Cupid.

D. Pedro. Well, if ever thou dost fall from this faith, thou wilt prove a notable argument. 256

Bene. If I do, hang me in a bottle like a cat, and shoot at me, and he that hits me, let him be clapp'd on the shoulder, and call'd Adam.

D. Pedro. Well, as time shall try: 260
"In time the savage bull doth bear the yoke."

Bene. The savage bull may, but if ever the sensible Benedick bear it, pluck off the bull's horns, and set them in my forehead, and let me be vildly painted, and in such great letters as they write "Here is good horse to hire," let them signify 266 under my sign, "Here you may see Benedick the married man."

Claud. If this should ever happen, thou wouldst be horn-mad. 270

D. Pedro. Nay, if Cupid have not spent all his quiver in Venice, thou wilt quake for this shortly.

Bene. I look for an earthquake too then.

D. Pedro. Well, you will temporize with the

hours. In the mean time, good Signior Benedick, 275 repair to Leonato's, commend me to him, and tell him I will not fail him at supper, for indeed he hath made great preparation.

Bene. I have almost matter enough in me for such an embassage, and so I commit you— 280

Claud. To the tuition of God. From my house— if I had it—

D. Pedro. The sixt of July. Your loving friend, Benedick. 284

Bene. Nay, mock not, mock not. The body of your discourse is sometime guarded with fragments, and the guards are but slightly basted on neither. Ere you flout old ends any further, examine your conscience, and so I leave you. *Exit.*

Claud. My liege, your Highness now may do me good. 290

D. Pedro. My love is thine to teach; teach it but how,
And thou shalt see how apt it is to learn
Any hard lesson that may do thee good.

Claud. Hath Leonato any son, my lord?

D. Pedro. No child but Hero, she's his only heir.
Dost thou affect her, Claudio?

Claud.   O my lord, 296
When you went onward on this ended action,
I look'd upon her with a soldier's eye,
That lik'd, but had a rougher task in hand
Than to drive liking to the name of love. 300
But now I am return'd, and that war-thoughts
Have left their places vacant, in their rooms
Come thronging soft and delicate desires,
All prompting me how fair young Hero is,
Saying I lik'd her ere I went to wars. 305

D. Pedro. Thou wilt be like a lover presently,
And tire the hearer with a book of words.
If thou dost love fair Hero, cherish it,
And I will break with her, and with her father,
And thou shalt have her. Was't not to this end 310
That thou began'st to twist so fine a story?

Claud. How sweetly you do minister to love,
That know love's grief by his complexion!
But lest my liking might too sudden seem,
I would have salv'd it with a longer treatise. 315

236–37. **in . . . will:** i.e. by willful obstinacy (not by rational argument). Willful adherence to heterodox opinion was the essential element of heresy.
240–41. **that . . . forehead:** i.e. that I should wear a cuckold's horns. A rechate (or recheat) is a series of notes sounded (*winded*) on the horn for calling the hounds together.
241–42. **hang . . . baldrick:** i.e. carry my horn not in the usual place on the usual strap (*baldrick*) but where no strap is seen (because none is present)—on my forehead.
242. **shall pardon me:** must excuse me from.   245. **fine:** end.
250. **Prove:** if you can show.
250–52. **I . . . drinking.** It was a common belief that sighing (characteristic of lovers) consumed the blood, but that wine generated fresh blood.   252. **a ballad-maker's pen.** An instrument of satire.
254. **sign.** Inns, shops, etc. were identified by painted signs.
256. **notable argument:** outstanding example in discussions of the topic.
257. **bottle:** wicker case. Sometimes a cat was suspended in such a container as a target for archers.
259. **Adam.** Probably an allusion to Adam Bell, an archer celebrated in ballads for his skill.   260. **try:** test, show.
261. **In . . . yoke.** Inaccurately quoted from Kyd's *The Spanish Tragedy*, II.i.3.
262–63. **sensible:** rational.   264. **vildly:** vilely, wretchedly.
270. **horn-mad:** mad as a horned beast, stark mad (with the common allusion to cuckold's horns).
271–72. **spent . . . quiver:** used up all his arrows (with play following on *quiver* = tremble).
272. **Venice.** Noted at the time for its licentiousness.
273. **I . . . too:** i.e. it will take an earthquake as well.
274. **temporize:** come to terms, compromise.

276. **commend me:** present my compliments.
279. **matter:** substance, i.e. intelligence.
280. **and . . . you.** A conventional form of words which Claudio and Don Pedro jeer at by extending it into a stock complimentary closing for a letter.
281. **tuition:** protection.   283. **sixt:** sixth.
286. **guarded with fragments:** trimmed with odds and ends (a metaphor from dressmaking, looking back to *body* in the sense "bodice," and continued in *basted on*; but suggesting also that Don Pedro can guard his serious concerns from exposure by talking inanities when it suits him).
287. **the guards . . . neither:** the trimmings are very insecurely stitched on too (i.e. they have little connection with what is being said).
288. **flout:** mock, jeer at.   **old ends:** (1) old tags (= the *fragments* of line 286); (2) conventional closings (of letters).
288–89. **examine your conscience:** i.e. consider whether you have ever been guilty of the same thing.   296. **affect:** love.
297. **ended action:** campaign now ended.   301. **now I:** now that I.
306. **presently:** any moment now.
307. **book of words:** whole book of lover's set speeches.
309. **break with:** broach the subject to.
311. **twist:** spin.   313. **his complexion:** its outward appearance.
315. **salv'd:** smoothed, i.e. put a better face on.   **treatise:** discourse.

Much Ado
about Nothing
I.i

D. *Pedro.* What need the bridge much broader
    than the flood?
The fairest grant is the necessity.
Look what will serve is fit: 'tis once, thou lovest,
And I will fit thee with the remedy.
I know we shall have revelling to-night;   320
I will assume thy part in some disguise,
And tell fair Hero I am Claudio,
And in her bosom I'll unclasp my heart,
And take her hearing prisoner with the force
And strong encounter of my amorous tale;   325
Then after to her father will I break,
And the conclusion is, she shall be thine.
In practice let us put it presently.   *Exeunt.*

[SCENE II]

Enter LEONATO *and an old man* [ANTONIO], *brother
to Leonato,* [*meeting*].

Leon. How now, brother, where is my cousin,
your son? Hath he provided this music?
Ant. He is very busy about it. But, brother, I
can tell you strange news that you yet dreamt not
of.   5
Leon. Are they good?
Ant. As the [event] stamps them, but they have
a good cover; they show well outward. The Prince
and Count Claudio, walking in a thick-pleach'd
alley in mine orchard, were thus much over-   10
heard by a man of mine. The Prince discover'd to
Claudio that he lov'd my niece your daughter, and
meant to acknowledge it this night in a dance; and
if he found her accordant, he meant to take the
present time by the top, and instantly break with
you of it.   16
Leon. Hath the fellow any wit that told you this?
Ant. A good sharp fellow. I will send for him,
and question him yourself.   19
Leon. No, no, we will hold it as a dream till it
appear itself; but I will acquaint my daughter withal,
that she may be the better prepar'd for an answer,
if peradventure this be true. Go you and tell her
of it. [*Several persons cross the stage.*] Cousins, you
know what you have to do. O, I cry you mercy,   25
friend, go you with me, and I will use your skill.
Good cousin, have a care this busy time.   *Exeunt.*

[SCENE III]

Enter [DON] JOHN *the Bastard and* CONRADE, *his companion.*

Con. What the good-year, my lord, why are
you thus out of measure sad?
D. John. There is no measure in the occasion
that breeds, therefore the sadness is without limit.
Con. You should hear reason.   5
D. John. And when I have heard it, what blessing
brings it?
Con. If not a present remedy, at least a patient
sufferance.   9
D. John. I wonder that thou (being, as thou
say'st thou art, born under Saturn) goest about to
apply a moral medicine to a mortifying mischief.
I cannot hide what I am: I must be sad when I
have cause, and smile at no man's jests; eat   14
when I have stomach, and wait for no man's leisure;
sleep when I am drowsy, and tend on no man's business; laugh when I am merry, and claw no man in
his humor.   18
Con. Yea, but you must not make the full show
of this till you may do it without controlment.
You have of late stood out against your brother,
and he hath ta'en you newly into his grace, where
it is impossible you should take true root but by
the fair weather that you make yourself. It is needful that you frame the season for your own harvest.   26
D. John. I had rather be a canker in a hedge
than a rose in his grace, and it better fits my blood
to be disdain'd of all than to fashion a carriage to
rob love from any. In this (though I cannot be   30
said to be a flattering honest man) it must not be
denied but I am a plain-dealing villain. I am trusted
with a muzzle, and enfranchis'd with a clog, therefore
I have decreed not to sing in my cage. If I had my
mouth, I would bite; if I had my liberty, I would   35
do my liking. In the mean time let me be that I am,
and seek not to alter me.
Con. Can you make no use of your discontent?
D. John. I make all use of it, for I use it only.
Who comes here?   40

Enter BORACHIO.

317. **The fairest . . . necessity:** the best gift is the one that fills the need of the occasion.
318. **Look what:** whatever.   **'tis once:** i.e. the simple fact is.
323. **in . . . unclasp:** to her private hearing I'll disclose the contents (*unclasp* = open the book) of.

I.ii. Location: Leonato's house.
1. **cousin.** Used of aunt, uncle, niece, or nephew, as well as of cousin in the modern sense.   7. **event:** outcome.
7–8. **stamps . . . cover.** Antonio uses the figure of news printed and bound in a book.
9–10. **thick-pleach'd alley:** walk bordered with bushes or small trees and overarched with their densely entwined boughs.
10. **orchard:** garden.   11. **discover'd:** revealed.
14. **accordant:** consenting.   15. **top:** forelock.
17. **wit:** intelligence.
21. **appear itself:** make itself evident (as a face).   **withal:** with it.
25. **cry you mercy:** beg your pardon.

I.iii. Location: Leonato's house.
1. **What the good-year.** An unexplained expletive.
2. **out of measure:** immoderately.   4. **breeds:** causes it.
5. **hear:** listen to.   8. **present:** immediate.
9. **sufferance:** endurance.
11. **born under Saturn:** born when the planet Saturn was predominant, hence supposedly morose (cf. *saturnine*).
11–12. **goest . . . mischief:** dost endeavor to cure a deadly ill by means of moralizing platitudes.
16. **tend on:** attend to.   17. **claw:** flatter, humor.
18. **humor:** whims.   20. **controlment:** restraint.
21. **stood out:** rebelled.   22. **grace:** favor.   25. **frame:** create.
27. **canker:** wild rose (considered a weed).
28. **blood:** mood, temper.
29. **fashion a carriage:** counterfeit a behavior.
32–33. **trusted . . . muzzle:** trusted as a muzzled dog is trusted, i.e. not trusted at all.
33. **enfranchis'd:** given my freedom.   **clog:** a heavy block of wood attached to an animal to restrict its movement.
34. **decreed:** made up my mind.
40 s.d. **Borachio.** Spanish *borracho* means "drunkard."

What news, Borachio?

Bora. I came yonder from a great supper. The Prince your brother is royally entertain'd by Leonato, and I can give you intelligence of an intended marriage.   45

D. John. Will it serve for any model to build mischief on? What is he for a fool that betroths himself to unquietness?

Bora. Marry, it is your brother's right hand.

D. John. Who, the most exquisite Claudio?   50

Bora. Even he.

D. John. A proper squire! And who, and who? which way looks he?·

Bora. Marry, one Hero, the daughter and heir of Leonato.   55

D. John. A very forward March-chick! How came you to this?

Bora. Being entertain'd for a perfumer, as I was smoking a musty room, comes me the Prince and Claudio, hand in hand in sad conference. I whipt 60 me behind the arras, and there heard it agreed upon that the Prince should woo Hero for himself, and having obtain'd her, give her to Count Claudio.   64

D. John. Come, come, let us thither, this may prove food to my displeasure. That young start-up hath all the glory of my overthrow. If I can cross him any way, I bless myself every way. You are both sure, and will assist me?

Con. To the death, my lord.   70

D. John. Let us to the great supper, their cheer is the greater that I am subdu'd. Would the cook were a' my mind! Shall we go prove what's to be done?

Bora. We'll wait upon your lordship.   *Exeunt.* 75

[ACT II, SCENE I]

Enter LEONATO, [ANTONIO] *his brother,* HERO *his daughter, and* BEATRICE *his niece,* [MARGARET, URSULA,] *and a* KINSMAN.

Leon. Was not Count John here at supper?

Ant. I saw him not.

Beat. How tartly that gentleman looks! I never can see him but I am heart-burn'd an hour after.

Hero. He is of a very melancholy disposition.   5

Beat. He were an excellent man that were made

just in the midway between him and Benedick: the one is too like an image and says nothing, and the other too like my lady's eldest son, evermore tattling.   10

Leon. Then half Signior Benedick's tongue in Count John's mouth, and half Count John's melancholy in Signior Benedick's face—

Beat. With a good leg and a good foot, uncle, and money enough in his purse, such a man would 15 win any woman in the world, if 'a could get her good will.

Leon. By my troth, niece, thou wilt never get thee a husband, if thou be so shrewd of thy tongue.

Ant. In faith, she's too curst.   20

Beat. Too curst is more than curst. I shall lessen God's sending that way, for it is said, "God sends a curst cow short horns"—but to a cow too curst he sends none.   24

Leon. So, by being too curst, God will send you no horns.

Beat. Just, if he send me no husband, for the which blessing I am at him upon my knees every morning and evening. Lord, I could not endure 29 a husband with a beard on his face, I had rather lie in the woollen!

Leon. You may light on a husband that hath no beard.

Beat. What should I do with him? dress him in my apparel and make him my waiting-gentle- 35 woman? He that hath a beard is more than a youth, and he that hath no beard is less than a man; and he that is more than a youth is not for me, and he that is less than a man, I am not for him; therefore I will even take sixpence in earnest of the berrord, and lead his apes into hell.   41

Leon. Well then, go you into hell.

Beat. No, but to the gate, and there will the devil meet me like an old cuckold with horns on his head, and say, "Get you to heaven, Beatrice, 45 get you to heaven, here's no place for you maids." So deliver I up my apes, and away to Saint Peter. For the heavens, he shows me where the bachelors sit, and there live we as merry as the day is long.   49

Ant. [*To Hero.*] Well, niece, I trust you will be rul'd by your father.

Beat. Yes, faith, it is my cousin's duty to make cur'sy and say, "Father, as it please you." But yet for all that, cousin, let him be a handsome fellow, or else make another cur'sy and say, "Father, as it please me."   56

Leon. Well, niece, I hope to see you one day fitted with a husband.

---

47. **What . . . fool:** what kind of fool is he.
49. **Marry:** indeed (originally the name of the Virgin Mary used as an oath).
52. **proper squire:** handsome young fellow (spoken sneeringly).
56. **forward:** precocious.   **March-chick:** chick which has hatched prematurely.   58. **entertain'd for:** hired as.
59. **smoking:** refreshing the air of (by burning some aromatic substance).   60. **sad:** serious.   61. **arras:** tapestry wall-hanging.
66. **displeasure:** anger, hatred.   **start-up:** upstart.
67. **cross:** thwart (with following quibble on the sense "make the sign of the cross").   69. **sure:** loyal, to be counted on.
73. **prove:** try, discover.   75. **wait upon:** attend.

II.i. Location: Leonato's house.
3. **tartly.** Modern idiom would require the adjectival form.
4. **am heart-burn'd:** suffer from heartburn (caused by Don John's sour looks).

---

9. **my . . . son:** i.e. a spoiled child.   19. **shrewd:** sharp, satirical.
20. **curst:** ill-tempered; here, sharp-tongued; in line 23, vicious, savage.
27. **Just:** precisely, just so.   **if . . . husband.** She implies that God, in sending her a husband, would also send horns—i.e. that her husband would certainly be a cuckold.
30–31. **in the woollen:** between woollen blankets, without sheets.
40. **in earnest:** as advance payment.   **berrord:** bear-ward, one who keeps and trains bears (and sometimes apes).
41. **lead . . . hell.** The proverbial fate of old maids.
48. **For the heavens:** so far as heaven is concerned.   **bachelors:** unmarried persons of either sex.   53. **cur'sy:** curtsy.

Beat. Not till God make men of some other
mettle than earth. Would it not grieve a woman 60
to be overmaster'd with a piece of valiant dust? to
make an account of her life to a clod of wayward
marl? No, uncle, I'll none. Adam's sons are my
brethren, and truly I hold it a sin to match in my
kinred. 65

Leon. Daughter, remember what I told you. If
the Prince do solicit you in that kind, you know
your answer.

Beat. The fault will be in the music, cousin, if
you be not woo'd in good time. If the Prince be 70
too important, tell him there is measure in every
thing, and so dance out the answer. For hear me,
Hero: wooing, wedding, and repenting, is as a
Scotch jig, a measure, and a cinquepace; the first
suit is hot and hasty, like a Scotch jig, and full 75
as fantastical; the wedding, mannerly-modest, as
a measure, full of state and ancientry; and then
comes repentance, and with his bad legs falls into
the cinquepace faster and faster, till he sink into
his grave. 80

Leon. Cousin, you apprehend passing shrewdly.

Beat. I have a good eye, uncle, I can see a church
by daylight.

Leon. The revellers are ent'ring, brother, make
good room. [*They put on their masks.*] 85

Enter Prince [DON] PEDRO, CLAUDIO, *and* BENEDICK,
and [DON] JOHN, [*and* BORACHIO *as maskers, with a
Drum*].

D. Pedro. Lady, will you walk about with your
friend?

Hero. So you walk softly, and look sweetly, and
say nothing, I am yours for the walk, and especially
when I walk away. 90

D. Pedro. With me in your company?

Hero. I may say so when I please.

D. Pedro. And when please you to say so?

Hero. When I like your favor, for God defend
the lute should be like the case! 95

D. Pedro. My visor is Philemon's roof, within
the house is Jove.

Hero. Why then your visor should be thatch'd.

D. Pedro. Speak low if you speak love.
[*They move aside.*]

[*Bora.*] Well, I would you did like me. 100

---

60. **mettle:** substance.   63. **marl:** clay.
64–65. **match . . . kinred:** i.e. marry within the forbidden degrees of
relationship; *kinred* = kindred.
70. **in good time:** with propriety (with obvious pun).
71. **important:** importunate, pressing.   **measure:** (1) moderation;
(2) slow, stately dance.
74. **cinquepace:** lively dance (trisyllabic).   75. **full:** fully, quite.
76. **mannerly-modest:** becomingly moderate in tempo.
77. **state and ancientry:** traditional stateliness.
81. **apprehend passing shrewdly:** perceive with unusual sharpness.
85 s.d. **Drum:** drummer.
87. **friend.** Often used in the sense "lover," and perhaps so here.
88. **softly:** gently.   94. **favor:** face.
94–95. **God . . . case:** i.e. God forbid that your face should not be
handsomer than your mask.
96. **visor:** mask.   **Philemon's roof.** Philemon and his wife Baucis
entertained Jove in their peasant cottage, unaware of his identity
(Ovid, *Metamorphoses*, viii).
98. **thatch'd:** (1) roofed with thatch (as peasant cottages generally
were); (2) bearded.

Marg. So would not I for your own sake, for I
have many ill qualities.

[*Bora.*] Which is one?

Marg. I say my prayers aloud. 104

[*Bora.*] I love you the better; the hearers may
cry amen.

Marg. God match me with a good dancer!

[*Bora.*] Amen.

Marg. And God keep him out of my sight when
the dance is done! Answer, clerk. 110

[*Bora.*] No more words; the clerk is answer'd.
[*They move aside.*]

Urs. I know you well enough, you are Signior
Antonio.

Ant. At a word, I am not. 114

Urs. I know you by the waggling of your head.

Ant. To tell you true, I counterfeit him.

Urs. You could never do him so ill-well, unless
you were the very man. Here's his dry hand up and
down. You are he, you are he.

Ant. At a word, I am not. 120

Urs. Come, come, do you think I do not know
you by your excellent wit? Can virtue hide itself?
Go to, mum, you are he. Graces will appear, and
there's an end. [*They move aside.*]

Beat. Will you not tell me who told you so? 125

Bene. No, you shall pardon me.

Beat. Nor will you not tell me who you are?

Bene. Not now.

Beat. That I was disdainful, and that I had my
good wit out of the "Hundred Merry Tales"—well,
this was Signior Benedick that said so. 131

Bene. What's he?

Beat. I am sure you know him well enough.

Bene. Not I, believe me.

Beat. Did he never make you laugh? 135

Bene. I pray you, what is he?

Beat. Why, he is the Prince's jester, a very dull
fool; only his gift is in devising impossible slanders.
None but libertines delight in him, and the commendation is not in his wit, but in his villainy, 140
for he both pleases men and angers them, and then
they laugh at him and beat him. I am sure he is in the
fleet; I would he had boarded me.

Bene. When I know the gentleman, I'll tell him
what you say. 145

Beat. Do, do, he'll but break a comparison or
two on me, which peradventure, not mark'd, or not
laugh'd at, strikes him into melancholy, and then

---

102. **ill:** bad.
110. **Answer, clerk:** i.e. say amen (= so be it) again. It was the duty
of the parish clerk to say the responses at church services.
114. **At:** in.
117. **do . . . ill-well:** imitate his imperfections so perfectly.
118. **dry hand.** A sign of age.   118–19. **up and down:** exactly.
122. **virtue:** excellence (of any kind).   123. **mum:** silence.
124. **an end:** no more to be said.
130. **Hundred Merry Tales:** a popular collection of jests and tales,
first published in 1526.   137. **dull:** stupid.
138. **only his gift:** i.e. his only talent.   **impossible:** incredible.
139. **libertines:** i.e. those who reject the customary restraints upon
thought and behavior.   140. **villainy:** satiric rudeness.
143. **fleet:** i.e. company drifting about the room.   **boarded:** come
alongside (a ship) to attempt an attack on it; here, tried his wit on.
146. **break a comparison:** crack a joke.

there's a partridge wing sav'd, for the fool will eat
no supper that night. [*Music for the dance begins.*] We
must follow the leaders. 151

Bene. In every good thing.

Beat. Nay, if they lead to any ill, I will leave
them at the next turning.

> *Dance.* [*Then*] *exeunt* [*all but Don John,*
> *Borachio, and Claudio*].

D. John. Sure my brother is amorous on Hero,
and hath withdrawn her father to break with him 156
about it. The ladies follow her, and but one visor
remains.

Bora. And that is Claudio. I know him by his
bearing. 160

D. John. Are not you Signior Benedick?

Claud. You know me well, I am he.

D. John. Signior, you are very near my brother
in his love. He is enamor'd on Hero, I pray you
dissuade him from her, she is no equal for his birth.
You may do the part of an honest man in it. 166

Claud. How know you he loves her?

D. John. I heard him swear his affection.

Bora. So did I too, and he swore he would marry
her to-night. 170

D. John. Come let us to the banquet.

> *Exeunt. Manet Claudio.*

Claud. Thus answer I in name of Benedick,
But hear these ill news with the ears of Claudio.
'Tis certain so, the Prince woos for himself.
Friendship is constant in all other things 175
Save in the office and affairs of love;
Therefore all hearts in love use their own tongues.
Let every eye negotiate for itself,
And trust no agent; for beauty is a witch
Against whose charms faith melteth into blood. 180
This is an accident of hourly proof,
Which I mistrusted not. Farewell therefore Hero!

> *Enter* BENEDICK.

Bene. Count Claudio?

Claud. Yea, the same.

Bene. Come, will you go with me? 185

Claud. Whither?

Bene. Even to the next willow, about your own
business, County. What fashion will you wear
the garland of? about your neck, like an usurer's
chain? or under your arm, like a lieutenant's scarf?
You must wear it one way, for the Prince hath got
your Hero. 192

Claud. I wish him joy of her.

Bene. Why, that's spoken like an honest drovier;
so they sell bullocks. But did you think the Prince

would have serv'd you thus? 196

Claud. I pray you leave me.

Bene. Ho, now you strike like the blind man.
'Twas the boy that stole your meat, and you'll beat
the post. 200

Claud. If it will not be, I'll leave you.   *Exit.*

Bene. Alas, poor hurt fowl, now will he creep
into sedges. But that my Lady Beatrice should
know me, and, not know me! The Prince's fool!
hah, it may be I go under that title because I am
merry. Yea, but so I am apt to do myself wrong. 206
I am not so reputed. It is the base (though bitter)
disposition of Beatrice that puts the world into her
person, and so gives me out. Well, I'll be reveng'd
as I may. 210

> *Enter the Prince* [DON PEDRO].

D. Pedro. Now, signior, where's the Count? Did
you see him?

Bene. Troth, my lord, I have play'd the part of
Lady Fame. I found him here as melancholy as a
lodge in a warren. I told him, and I think I told
him true, that your Grace had got the good will of 216
this young lady, and I off'red him my company to
a willow-tree, either to make him a garland, as being
forsaken, or to bind him up a rod, as being worthy
to be whipt.

D. Pedro. To be whipt? What's his fault?

Bene. The flat transgression of a schoolboy, 222
who being overjoy'd with finding a bird's nest,
shows it his companion, and he steals it.

D. Pedro. Wilt thou make a trust a transgression?
The transgression is in the stealer. 226

Bene. Yet it had not been amiss the rod had
been made, and the garland too, for the garland
he might have worn himself, and the rod he might
have bestow'd on you, who (as I take it) have stol'n
his bird's nest. 231

D. Pedro. I will but teach them to sing, and restore them to the owner.

Bene. If their singing answer your saying, by my
faith you say honestly. 235

D. Pedro. The Lady Beatrice hath a quarrel to
you. The gentleman that danc'd with her told her
she is much wrong'd by you. 238

Bene. O, she misus'd me past the endurance of

---

151. **leaders:** i.e. of the dance.
163–64. **very . . . love:** a very close friend of my brother's
171. **banquet:** light repast of sweets, fruit, and wine.
176. **office:** business.   177. **all:** let all.
180. **Against whose charms:** in the face of whose spells. **blood:** passion.
181. **accident . . . proof:** occurrence of a sort that takes place every hour.   182. **mistrusted:** suspected.
187. **next:** nearest. **willow.** The emblem of unrequited love.
188. **County:** count.   189. **garland:** i.e. of willow.
191. **one way:** one way or another.
194. **drovier:** drover, cattle dealer.

198. **blind man.** The particular story has not been identified. In the Spanish romance *Lazarillo de Tormes*, the hero steals a sausage from his master, a blind beggar, and is so severely punished by him that, in revenge, he causes the blind man to jump against a stone pillar.
200. **post:** pillar (but with a quibble on the sense "messenger").
202–3. **creep into sedges:** i.e. find himself a hiding-place, as an injured bird seeks refuge in the rushes along a river bank.
207. **base (though bitter):** low, yet capable of stinging its victim (?). The locution is not very natural, and Johnson emended it to *base, the bitter.*
208–9. **puts . . . person:** i.e. assumes that everyone is of her opinion.
209. **gives me out:** represents me.   213. **Troth:** in truth.
214. **Lady Fame:** Dame Rumor.
215. **lodge . . . warren:** burrow in a rabbit warren. Rabbits were proverbially melancholy.
222. **flat:** simple, silly.
225. **a trust:** i.e. the placing of one's trust in a person.
230. **bestow'd:** i.e. used   232. **them:** i.e. the nestlings.
234. **answer:** correspond to.   236. **to:** with.
239. **misus'd:** abused.

a block; an oak but with one green leaf on it would have answer'd her. My very visor began to assume life, and scold with her. She told me, not thinking I had been myself, that I was the Prince's jester, that I was duller than a great thaw, huddling jest upon jest with such impossible conveyance upon me that I stood like a man at a mark, with a 246 whole army shooting at me. She speaks poniards, and every word stabs. If her breath were as terrible as her terminations, there were no living near her, she would infect to the north star. I would not marry her, though she were endow'd with all 251 that Adam had left him before he transgress'd. She would have made Hercules have turn'd spit, yea, and have cleft his club to make the fire too. Come, talk not of her; you shall find her the infernal Ate in good apparel. I would to God some scholar 256 would conjure her, for certainly, while she is here, a man may live as quiet in hell as in a sanctuary, and people sin upon purpose, because they would go thither; so indeed all disquiet, horror, and perturbation follows her. 261

Enter CLAUDIO *and* BEATRICE, [LEONATO *and* HERO].

D. Pedro. Look here she comes.

Bene. Will your Grace command me any service to the world's end? I will go on the slightest arrand now to the Antipodes that you can devise to send me on; I will fetch you a toothpicker now from 266 the furthest inch of Asia, bring you the length of Prester John's foot, fetch you a hair off the great Cham's beard, do you any embassage to the Pigmies, rather than hold three words' conference with this harpy. You have no employment for me? 271

D. Pedro. None, but to desire your good company.

Bene. O God, sir, here's a dish I love not, I cannot endure my Lady Tongue. *Exit.* 275

D. Pedro. Come, lady, come, you have lost the heart of Signior Benedick.

Beat. Indeed, my lord, he lent it me awhile, and I gave him use for it, a double heart for his single one. Marry, once before he won it of me with false dice, therefore your Grace may well say I have lost it. 282

D. Pedro. You have put him down, lady, you have put him down.

Beat. So I would not he should do me, my lord, lest I should prove the mother of fools. I have 286 brought Count Claudio, whom you sent me to seek.

D. Pedro. Why, how now, Count, wherefore are you sad?

Claud. Not sad, my lord. 290

D. Pedro. How then? sick?

Claud. Neither, my lord.

Beat. The Count is neither sad, nor sick, nor merry, nor well; but civil count, civil as an orange, and something of that jealous complexion. 295

D. Pedro. I' faith, lady, I think your blazon to be true, though I'll be sworn, if he be so, his conceit is false. Here, Claudio, I have woo'd in thy name, and fair Hero is won. I have broke with her father, and his good will obtain'd. Name the day of marriage, and God give thee joy! 301

Leon. Count, take of me my daughter, and with her my fortunes. His Grace hath made the match, and all grace say amen to it.

Beat. Speak, Count, 'tis your cue. 305

Claud. Silence is the perfectest herald of joy; I were but little happy, if I could say how much! Lady, as you are mine, I am yours. I give away myself for you, and dote upon the exchange. 309

Beat. Speak, cousin, or (if you cannot) stop his mouth with a kiss, and let not him speak neither.

D. Pedro. In faith, lady, you have a merry heart.

Beat. Yea, my lord, I thank it—poor fool, it keeps on the windy side of care. My cousin tells him in his ear that he is in her heart. 316

Claud. And so she doth, cousin.

Beat. Good Lord, for alliance! Thus goes every one to the world but I, and I am sunburnt. I may sit in a corner and cry "Heigh-ho for a husband!" 320

D. Pedro. Lady Beatrice, I will get you one.

Beat. I would rather have one of your father's getting. Hath your Grace ne'er a brother like you? Your father got excellent husbands, if a maid could come by them. 325

D. Pedro. Will you have me, lady?

Beat. No, my lord, unless I might have another for working-days. Your Grace is too costly to wear every day. But I beseech your Grace pardon me, I was born to speak all mirth and no matter. 330

D. Pedro. Your silence most offends me, and to be merry best becomes you, for out a' question, you were born in a merry hour.

Beat. No, sure, my lord, my mother cried, but

240. **but ... it:** i.e. with the slightest vestige of life in it.
244. **a great thaw.** When impassable roads would prevent the usual activities and pastimes. **huddling:** piling up.
245. **impossible conveyance:** incredible adeptness.
246. **at a mark:** set up as a target. 249. **terminations:** terms, words.
250. **north star.** Supposedly the remotest star.
252. **left:** bestowed upon.
253. **Hercules ... spit.** Omphale forced the captive Hercules to put on women's clothes and spin among her maids. Turning the spit was work of a far more menial order.
256. **Ate:** goddess of mischief and discord. **scholar:** i.e. one familiar with the Latin formulas for exorcising evil spirits.
264. **arrand:** errand.
268. **Prester John:** a legendary Far Eastern ruler who was both emperor and Christian priest (*Prester* is a shortened form of *Presbyter*, i.e. priest).
269. **Cham:** Khan of Tartary, ruler of the Mongols. **Pigmies.** Supposed to inhabit the mountains of India.
271. **harpy:** i.e. creature of prey; literally a mythical monster with the face and trunk of a woman and the wings and claws of a bird. In heraldry the harpy was assigned to one who had committed manslaughter (= Beatrice's crime!). 279. **use:** usury, interest.
280. **false:** loaded.

284. **put him down:** got the better of him (with following quibble by Beatrice).
294. **civil:** (1) grave, serious; (2) Seville (a homophone); oranges of Seville are bitter.
295. **something:** somewhat, to some degree. **jealous complexion:** i.e. yellow, the color associated with jealousy.
296. **blazon:** description. 297. **so:** i.e. jealous. **conceit:** idea.
304. **all grace:** i.e. the grace of God. 306. **heralt:** herald.
315. **windy:** windward, i.e. safe.
318-19. **goes ... world:** i.e. everyone gets married.
319. **sunburnt:** i.e. unattractive.
320. **Heigh-ho ... husband:** the title of a ballad.
323. **getting:** begetting. 330. **matter:** substance, sense.

then there was a star danc'd, and under that was I born.
Cousins, God give you joy!   336

Leon. Niece, will you look to those things I told
you of?

Beat. I cry you mercy, uncle. By your Grace's
pardon.   *Exit Beatrice.* 340

D. Pedro. By my troth, a pleasant-spirited lady.

Leon. There's little of the melancholy element
in her, my lord. She is never sad but when she sleeps,
and not ever sad then; for I have heard my daughter
say, she hath often dreamt of unhappiness, and wak'd
herself with laughing.   346

D. Pedro. She cannot endure to hear tell of a
husband.

Leon. O, by no means, she mocks all her wooers
out of suit.   350

D. Pedro. She were an excellent wife for Benedick.

Leon. O Lord, my lord, if they were but a week
married, they would talk themselves mad.

D. Pedro. County Claudio, when mean you to go
to church?   356

Claud. To-morrow, my lord. Time goes on
crutches till love have all his rites.

Leon. Not till Monday, my dear son, which is
hence a just sevennight, and a time too brief too, to
have all things answer my mind.   361

D. Pedro. Come, you shake the head at so long
a breathing, but I warrant thee, Claudio, the time
shall not go dully by us. I will in the interim undertake one of Hercules' labors, which is, to 365
bring Signior Benedick and the Lady Beatrice into
a mountain of affection th' one with th' other. I
would fain have it a match, and I doubt not but to
fashion it, if you three will but minister such assistance as I shall give you direction.   370

Leon. My lord, I am for you, though it cost me
ten nights' watchings.

Claud. And I, my lord.

D. Pedro. And you too, gentle Hero?

Hero. I will do any modest office, my lord, to help
my cousin to a good husband.   376

D. Pedro. And Benedick is not the unhopefullest
husband that I know. Thus far can I praise him: he is
of a noble strain, of approv'd valor, and confirm'd
honesty. I will teach you how to humor your 380
cousin, that she shall fall in love with Benedick, and I,
with your two helps, will so practice on Benedick
that, in despite of his quick wit and his queasy stomach, he shall fall in love with Beatrice. If we can do
this, Cupid is no longer an archer; his glory shall 385
be ours, for we are the only love-gods. Go in with
me, and I will tell you my drift.   *Exeunt.*

---

344. **ever:** always.
345. **unhappiness:** "some amusing roguery or other" (Kittredge).
350. **suit:** courtship.   355–56. **go to church:** marry.
360. **a just sevennight:** exactly a week.
361. **answer my mind:** correspond with my wishes.
363. **breathing:** interval, delay.   369. **minister:** furnish, supply.
372. **watchings:** lying awake.   379. **approv'd:** tested.
382. **practice on:** scheme against.
383. **in despite of:** notwithstanding.
383–84. **his queasy stomach:** i.e. his squeamishness about partaking of
love.   387. **drift:** intent.

[SCENE II]

Enter [DON] JOHN *and* BORACHIO.

D. John. It is so, the Count Claudio shall marry
the daughter of Leonato.

Bora. Yea, my lord, but I can cross it.

D. John. Any bar, any cross, any impediment
will be med'cinable to me. I am sick in displeas- 5
ure to him, and whatsoever comes athwart his affection ranges evenly with mine. How canst thou cross
this marriage?

Bora. Not honestly, my lord, but so covertly that
no dishonesty shall appear in me.   10

D. John. Show me briefly how.

Bora. I think I told your lordship a year since,
how much I am in the favor of Margaret, the waiting-
gentlewoman to Hero.

D. John. I remember.   15

Bora. I can, at any unseasonable instant of the
night, appoint her to look out at her lady's chamber-
window.

D. John. What life is in that, to be the death of
this marriage?   20

Bora. The poison of that lies in you to temper.
Go you to the Prince your brother; spare not to tell
him that he hath wrong'd his honor in marrying the
renown'd Claudio—whose estimation do you mightily
hold up—to a contaminated stale, such a one as
Hero.   26

D. John. What proof shall I make of that?

Bora. Proof enough to misuse the Prince, to vex
Claudio, to undo Hero, and kill Leonato. Look you
for any other issue?   30

D. John. Only to despite them, I will endeavor
any thing.

Bora. Go then, find me a meet hour to draw
Don Pedro and the Count Claudio alone, tell them
that you know that Hero loves me, intend a 35
kind of zeal both to the Prince and Claudio—as
in love of your brother's honor, who hath made
this match, and his friend's reputation, who is thus
like to be cozen'd with the semblance of a maid—
that you have discover'd thus. They will scarcely 40
believe this without trial. Offer them instances,
which shall bear no less likelihood than to see me
at her chamber-window, hear me call Margaret
Hero, hear Margaret term me Claudio; and bring
them to see this the very night before the in- 45
tended wedding—for in the mean time I will so fashion
the matter that Hero shall be absent—and there shall
appear such seeming truth of Hero's disloyalty, that

II.ii. Location: Leonato's house.
1. **shall:** is going to.   3. **cross:** thwart.
5. **med'cinable:** medicinal, healing.
5–6. **displeasure to:** anger against.
6–7. **comes . . . affection:** goes contrary to his desires.
7. **ranges evenly:** runs parallel.   11. **briefly:** quickly.
21. **lies in:** depends upon.   **temper:** mix.
24. **estimation:** worth.
25. **contaminated stale:** common prostitute.
28. **misuse:** deceive.   **vex:** torment.   35. **intend:** pretend.
39. **cozen'd:** deceived.   **semblance:** outward appearance.
41. **instances:** proofs.
44. **term me Claudio.** Apparently a slip. Many editors emend to
Borachio (following Theobald).

jealousy shall be call'd assurance, and all the preparation overthrown.   50

D. John. Grow this to what adverse issue it can,
I will put it in practice. Be cunning in the working
this, and thy fee is a thousand ducats.

Bora. Be you constant in the accusation, and my
cunning shall not shame me.   55

D. John. I will presently go learn their day of
marriage.   *Exeunt.*

[SCENE III]

Enter BENEDICK *alone.*

Bene. Boy!

[*Enter* BOY.]

Boy. Signior?

Bene. In my chamber-window lies a book, bring
it hither to me in the orchard.

Boy. I am here already, sir.   *Exit.* 5

Bene. I know that, but I would have thee hence,
and here again. I do much wonder that one man,
seeing how much another man is a fool when he
dedicates his behaviors to love, will, after he hath
laugh'd at such shallow follies in others, become 10
the argument of his own scorn by falling in love—
and such a man is Claudio. I have known when
there was no music with him but the drum and the
fife, and now had he rather hear the tabor and the
pipe; I have known when he would have walk'd 15
ten mile afoot to see a good armor, and now will
he lie ten nights awake carving the fashion of a
new doublet; he was wont to speak plain and to the
purpose (like an honest man and a soldier), and now
is he turn'd ortography—his words are a very 20
fantastical banquet, just so many strange dishes.
May I be so converted and see with these eyes?
I cannot tell; I think not. I will not be sworn but
love may transform me to an oyster, but I'll take
my oath on it, till he have made [an] oyster of 25
me, he shall never make me such a fool. One woman
is fair, yet I am well; another is wise, yet I am
well; another virtuous, yet I am well; but till all
graces be in one woman, one woman shall not come
in my grace. Rich she shall be, that's certain; 30
wise, or I'll none; virtuous, or I'll never cheapen
her; fair, or I'll never look on her; mild, or come
not near me; noble, or not I for an angel; of good

discourse, an excellent musician, and her hair shall
be of what color it please God. Hah! the Prince 35
and Monsieur Love. I will hide me in the arbor.

[*Withdraws.*]

Enter Prince [DON PEDRO], LEONATO, CLAUDIO. *Music*
[*within*].

D. Pedro. Come, shall we hear this music?

Claud. Yea, my good lord. How still the evening
is,
As hush'd on purpose to grace harmony!

D. Pedro. See you where Benedick hath hid himself?   40

Claud. O, very well, my lord. The music ended,
We'll fit the [hid]-fox with a pennyworth.

Enter BALTHASAR *with Music.*

D. Pedro. Come, Balthasar, we'll hear that song
again.

Balth. O good my lord, tax not so bad a voice
To slander music any more than once.   45

D. Pedro. It is the witness still of excellency
To put a strange face on his own perfection.
I pray thee sing, and let me woo no more.

Balth. Because you talk of wooing, I will sing,
Since many a wooer doth commence his suit   50
To her he thinks not worthy, yet he woos,
Yet will he swear he loves.

D. Pedro.   Nay, pray thee come,
Or if thou wilt hold longer argument,
Do it in notes.

Balth.   Note this before my notes:
There's not a note of mine that's worth the noting.

D. Pedro. Why, these are very crotchets that he
speaks—   56
Note notes, forsooth, and nothing.   [*Air.*]

Bene. Now, divine air! now is his soul ravish'd!
Is it not strange that sheep's guts should hale souls
out of men's bodies? Well, a horn for my money
when all's done.   61

THE SONG

[*Balth.*] Sigh no more, ladies, sigh no more,
     Men were deceivers ever,
One foot in sea, and one on shore,
     To one thing constant never.   65
Then sigh not so, but let them go,
     And be you blithe and bonny,
Converting all your sounds of woe
     Into hey nonny nonny.

---

49. **jealousy:** suspicion.   **assurance:** certainty.
49–50. **preparation:** i.e. for the wedding.
53. **ducats:** continental gold coins, variously valued (but Borachio's reward is clearly to be a large one).   56. **presently:** at once.

II.iii. Location: Leonato's garden.
4. **orchard:** garden.
5. **I . . . already:** i.e. I'll be back before you know I've gone.
11. **argument:** subject.
14. **tabor:** small drum. The tabor and pipe were used for social merriment, in contrast to the martial drum and fife.
16. **armor:** suit of armor.   17. **carving:** planning.
18. **doublet:** close-fitting jacket.
20. **turn'd ortography:** i.e. become a faddist in language.
31. **I'll none:** I'll have none of her.   **cheapen:** bargain for.
33. **for an angel:** (1) though she be an angel; (2) for ten shillings

(involving a play on *noble* as the name of another coin, worth two thirds as much as an angel).
34–35. **hair . . . God:** i.e. if she satisfies all these requirements, I won't stipulate what color her hair must be.
39. **grace harmony:** do honor to music.
42. **hid-fox.** An allusion to a children's game; cf. *Hamlet,* IV.ii.30–31: "Hide fox, and all after."   **pennyworth:** a good bargain, i.e. more than he bargained for.
44. **tax:** task.   47. **To . . . on:** i.e. not to admit.
48. **woo:** entreat.   54. **notes:** i.e. musical notes.
56. **crotchets:** (1) whims; (2) quarter notes in music.
57. **nothing.** With homophonic pun on *noting.*
59. **sheep's guts:** violin or lute strings.   **hale:** draw, drag.
60. **horn:** i.e. hunting horn (but an audience always alive to the cuckold jest would have found the remark comically incongruous in Benedick's mouth).

Sing no more ditties, sing no moe, 70
   Of dumps so dull and heavy;
The fraud of men was ever so,
   Since summer first was leavy.
Then sigh not so, etc.

D. Pedro. By my troth, a good song. 75

Balth. And an ill singer, my lord.

D. Pedro. Ha, no, no, faith, thou sing'st well enough for a shift.

Bene. And he had been a dog that should have howl'd thus, they would have hang'd him, and 80 I pray God his bad voice bode no mischief. I had as live have heard the night-raven, come what plague could have come after it.

D. Pedro. Yea, marry, dost thou hear, Balthasar? I pray thee get us some excellent music; for 85 to-morrow night we would have it at the Lady Hero's chamber-window.

Balth. The best I can, my lord.   *Exit Balthasar.*

D. Pedro. Do so, farewell. Come hither, Leonato. What was it you told me of to-day, that your niece Beatrice was in love with Signior Benedick? 91

Claud. [*Aside.*] O ay, stalk on, stalk on, the fowl sits.—I did never think that lady would have lov'd any man. 94

Leon. No, nor I neither, but most wonderful that she should so dote on Signior Benedick, whom she hath in all outward behaviors seem'd ever to abhor.

Bene. Is't possible? Sits the wind in that corner?

Leon. By my troth, my lord, I cannot tell what to think of it but that she loves him with an enrag'd affection; it is past the infinite of thought. 101

D. Pedro. May be she doth but counterfeit.

Claud. Faith, like enough.

Leon. O God! counterfeit? There was never counterfeit of passion came so near the life of passion as she discovers it. 106

D. Pedro. Why, what effects of passion shows she?

Claud. [*Aside.*] Bait the hook well, this fish will bite.

Leon. What effects, my lord? She will sit you— you heard my daughter tell you how. 111

Claud. She did indeed.

D. Pedro. How, how, I pray you? You amaze me, I would have thought her spirit had been invincible against all assaults of affection. 115

Leon. I would have sworn it had, my lord, especially against Benedick.

Bene. I should think this a gull, but that the white-bearded fellow speaks it. Knavery cannot sure hide himself in such reverence. 120

Claud. [*Aside.*] He hath ta'en th' infection. Hold it up.

---

70. **moe:** more (in number).   71. **dumps:** mournful tunes.
73. **leavy:** leafy.   78. **for a shift:** to make do.
82. **live:** lief.   **night-raven:** a bird, variously identified, whose cry presaged disaster.
92–93. **stalk . . . sits:** walk stealthily, the bird has settled (in a bush).
98. **Sits . . . corner:** is that how the wind blows.
100. **enrag'd:** mad with passion.
101. **infinite:** infinity, boundlessness.   106. **discovers:** reveals.
107. **effects:** manifestations.   110. **sit you:** sit (a colloquialism).
118. **gull:** trick.   121–22. **Hold it up:** keep it up.

D. Pedro. Hath she made her affection known to Benedick?

Leon. No, and swears she never will. That's her torment. 126

Claud. 'Tis true indeed, so your daughter says. "Shall I," says she, "that have so oft encount'red him with scorn, write to him that I love him?" 129

Leon. This says she now when she is beginning to write to him, for she'll be up twenty times a night, and there will she sit in her smock till she have writ a sheet of paper. My daughter tells us all.

Claud. Now you talk of a sheet of paper, I remember a pretty jest your daughter told [us of]. 135

Leon. O, when she had writ it, and was reading it over, she found "Benedick" and "Beatrice" between the sheet?

Claud. That. 139

Leon. O, she tore the letter into a thousand halfpence; rail'd at herself, that she should be so immodest to write to one that she knew would flout her. "I measure him," says she, "by my own spirit, for I should flout him, if he writ to me, yea, though I love him, I should." 145

Claud. Then down upon her knees she falls, weeps, sobs, beats her heart, tears her hair, prays, curses: "O sweet Benedick! God give me patience!" 149

Leon. She doth indeed, my daughter says so; and the ecstasy hath so much overborne her that my daughter is sometime afeard she will do a desperate outrage to herself. It is very true.

D. Pedro. It were good that Benedick knew of it by some other, if she will not discover it. 155

Claud. To what end? he would make but a sport of it, and torment the poor lady worse.

D. Pedro. And he should, it were an alms to hang him. She's an excellent sweet lady, and (out of all suspicion) she is virtuous. 160

Claud. And she is exceeding wise.

D. Pedro. In every thing but in loving Benedick.

Leon. O my lord, wisdom and blood combating in so tender a body, we have ten proofs to 164 one that blood hath the victory. I am sorry for her, as I have just cause, being her uncle and her guardian.

D. Pedro. I would she had bestow'd this dotage on me, I would have daff'd all other respects, and made her half myself. I pray you tell Benedick of it, and hear what 'a will say. 171

Leon. Were it good, think you?

Claud. Hero thinks surely she will die, for she says she will die if he love her not, and she will die ere she make her love known, and she will die if he woo her, rather than she will bate one breath of her accustom'd crossness. 177

---

132. **smock:** undergarment.
140–41. **halfpence:** i.e. very small bits.   151. **ecstasy:** madness.
153. **outrage:** act of violence.   158. **alms:** good deed.
159. **out of:** beyond.   163. **blood:** natural feeling.
168. **dotage:** doting.
169. **daff'd:** doffed, put aside.   **respects:** considerations.
170. **half myself:** i.e. my wife.   176. **bate:** abate.
177. **crossness:** perversity.

D. Pedro. She doth well. If she should make tender of her love, 'tis very possible he'll scorn it, for the man (as you know all) hath a contemptible spirit.   181

Claud. He is a very proper man.

D. Pedro. He hath indeed a good outward happiness.

Claud. Before God, and in my mind, very wise.

D. Pedro. He doth indeed show some sparks that are like wit.   187

Claud. And I take him to be valiant.

D. Pedro. As Hector, I assure you, and in the managing of quarrels you may say he is wise, for either he avoids them with great discretion, or undertakes them with a most Christian-like fear.   192

Leon. If he do fear God, 'a must necessarily keep peace; if he break the peace, he ought to enter into a quarrel with fear and trembling.   195

D. Pedro. And so will he do, for the man doth fear God, howsoever it seems not in him by some large jests he will make. Well, I am sorry for your niece. Shall we go seek Benedick, and tell him of her love?   200

Claud. Never tell him, my lord. Let her wear it out with good counsel.

Leon. Nay, that's impossible, she may wear her heart out first.

D. Pedro. Well, we will hear further of it by your daughter, let it cool the while. I love   206 Benedick well, and I could wish he would modestly examine himself, to see how much he is unworthy so good a lady.

Leon. My lord, will you walk? Dinner is ready.

Claud. [*Aside.*] If he do not dote on her upon this, I will never trust my expectation.   212

D. Pedro. [*Aside.*] Let there be the same net spread for her, and that must your daughter and her gentlewomen carry. The sport will be, when   215 they hold one an opinion of another's dotage, and no such matter; that's the scene that I would see, which will be merely a dumb show. Let us send her to call him in to dinner.

[*Exeunt Don Pedro, Claudio, and Leonato.*]

Bene. [*Coming forward.*] This can be no trick: the conference was sadly borne; they have   221 the truth of this from Hero; they seem to pity the lady. It seems her affections have their full bent. Love me? why, it must be requited. I hear how I am censur'd; they say I will bear myself proudly, if I perceive the love come from her; they say too that she will rather die than give any sign of   227 affection. I did never think to marry. I must not

seem proud; happy are they that hear their detractions, and can put them to mending. They say the lady is fair; 'tis a truth, I can bear them witness; and virtuous; 'tis so, I cannot reprove it; and   232 wise, but for loving me; by my troth, it is no addition to her wit, nor no great argument of her folly, for I will be horribly in love with her. I may chance have some odd quirks and remnants of wit broken on me, because I have rail'd so long against marriage; but doth not the appetite alter? A man loves   238 the meat in his youth that he cannot endure in his age. Shall quips and sentences and these paper bullets of the brain awe a man from the career of his humor? No, the world must be peopled. When I said I would die a bachelor, I did not think   243 I should live till I were married. Here comes Beatrice. By this day, she's a fair lady. I do spy some marks of love in her.

Enter BEATRICE.

Beat. Against my will I am sent to bid you come in to dinner.   248

Bene. Fair Beatrice, I thank you for your pains.

Beat. I took no more pains for those thanks than you take pains to thank me. If it had been painful, I would not have come.   252

Bene. You take pleasure then in the message?

Beat. Yea, just so much as you may take upon a knive's point, and choke a daw withal. You have no stomach, signior, fare you well.   *Exit.* 256

Bene. Ha! "Against my will I am sent to bid you come in to dinner"—there's a double meaning in that. "I took no more pains for those thanks than you took pains to thank me"—that's as much as to say, "Any pains that I take for you is as easy as thanks." If I do not take pity of her, I am   262 a villain; if I do not love her, I am a Jew. I will go get her picture.   *Exit.*

[ACT III, SCENE I]

Enter HERO *and two gentlewomen,* MARGARET *and* URSLEY.

Hero. Good Margaret, run thee to the parlor,
There shalt thou find my cousin Beatrice
Proposing with the Prince and Claudio.
Whisper her ear, and tell her I and Ursley
Walk in the orchard, and our whole discourse   5
Is all of her. Say that thou overheardst us,
And bid her steal into the pleached bower,
Where honeysuckles, ripened by the sun,
Forbid the sun to enter, like favorites

---

179. **tender:** offer.   180. **contemptible:** contemptuous.
182. **proper:** handsome.
183–84. **hath . . . happiness:** is fortunate in his appearance.
189. **Hector.** The greatest of the Trojan warriors.
198. **large:** broad, indelicate.
202. **good counsel:** i.e. giving herself good advice.   210. **walk:** go.
215. **carry:** undertake.
216–17. **no such matter:** nothing of the kind exists.
218. **merely . . . show:** entirely pantomime (because with no occasion for satiric exchange they will have nothing to say).
221. **sadly borne:** seriously conducted.
223. **have . . . bent:** are at full stretch.

229–30. **their detractions:** unfavorable criticisms of themselves.
230. **put . . . mending:** i.e. apply themselves to correcting their faults.
232. **reprove:** disprove, deny.   236. **quirks:** jests.
240. **sentences:** maxims.
240–41. **paper . . . brain:** verbal ammunition.
241–42. **career . . . humor:** course of his inclination.
255. **daw:** jackdaw.   256. **stomach:** appetite.

III.i. Location: Leonato's garden.
o.s.d. **Ursley:** variant form of *Ursula*.   3. **Proposing:** talking.

Made proud by princes, that advance their pride   10
Against that power that bred it. There will she
    hide her,
To listen our propose. This is thy office;
Bear thee well in it, and leave us alone.

Marg. I'll make her come, I warrant you, presently.   [*Exit.*]

Hero. Now, Ursula, when Beatrice doth come,   15
As we do trace this alley up and down,
Our talk must only be of Benedick.
When I do name him, let it be thy part
To praise him more than ever man did merit.
My talk to thee must be how Benedick   20
Is sick in love with Beatrice. Of this matter
Is little Cupid's crafty arrow made,
That only wounds by hearsay.

Enter BEATRICE [*behind*].

Now begin,
For look where Beatrice like a lapwing runs
Close by the ground, to hear our conference.   25

Urs. The pleasant'st angling is to see the fish
Cut with her golden oars the silver stream,
And greedily devour the treacherous bait;
So angle we for Beatrice, who even now
Is couched in the woodbine coverture.   30
Fear you not my part of the dialogue.

Hero. Then go we near her, that her ear lose
    nothing
Of the false sweet bait that we lay for it.

[*They advance to the bower.*]

No, truly, Ursula, she is too disdainful,
I know her spirits are as coy and wild   35
As haggards of the rock.

Urs.   But are you sure
That Benedick loves Beatrice so entirely?

Hero. So says the Prince and my new-trothed lord.

Urs. And did they bid you tell her of it, madam?

Hero. They did entreat me to acquaint her of it,
But I persuaded them, if they lov'd Benedick,   41
To wish him wrastle with affection,
And never to let Beatrice know of it.

Urs. Why did you so? Doth not the gentleman
Deserve as full as fortunate a bed   45
As ever Beatrice shall couch upon?

Hero. O god of love! I know he doth deserve
As much as may be yielded to a man;
But nature never fram'd a woman's heart
Of prouder stuff than that of Beatrice.   50
Disdain and scorn ride sparkling in her eyes,
Misprising what they look on, and her wit
Values itself so highly that to her
All matter else seems weak. She cannot love,
Nor take no shape nor project of affection,   55

She is so self-endeared.

Urs.   Sure I think so,
And therefore certainly it were not good
She knew his love, lest she'll make sport at it.

Hero. Why, you speak truth. I never yet saw man,
How wise, how noble, young, how rarely featur'd,
But she would spell him backward. If fair-fac'd,   61
She would swear the gentleman should be her sister;
If black, why, Nature, drawing of an antic,
Made a foul blot; if tall, a lance ill-headed;
If low, an agot very vildly cut;   65
If speaking, why, a vane blown with all winds;
If silent, why, a block moved with none.
So turns she every man the wrong side out,
And never gives to truth and virtue that
Which simpleness and merit purchaseth.   70

Urs. Sure, sure, such carping is not commendable.

Hero. No, not to be so odd, and from all fashions,
As Beatrice is, cannot be commendable.
But who dare tell her so? If I should speak,
She would mock me into air; O, she would laugh me
Out of myself, press me to death with wit.   76
Therefore let Benedick, like cover'd fire,
Consume away in sighs, waste inwardly.
It were a better death than die with mocks,
Which is as bad as die with tickling.   80

Urs. Yet tell her of it, hear what she will say.

Hero. No, rather I will go to Benedick,
And counsel him to fight against his passion,
And truly I'll devise some honest slanders
To stain my cousin with. One doth not know   85
How much an ill word may empoison liking.

Urs. O, do not do your cousin such a wrong.
She cannot be so much without true judgment—
Having so swift and excellent a wit
As she is priz'd to have—as to refuse   90
So rare a gentleman as Signior Benedick.

Hero. He is the only man of Italy,
Always excepted my dear Claudio.

Urs. I pray you be not angry with me, madam,
Speaking my fancy: Signior Benedick,   95
For shape, for bearing, argument, and valor,
Goes foremost in report through Italy.

Hero. Indeed he hath an excellent good name.

Urs. His excellence did earn it, ere he had it.
When are you married, madam?   100

Hero. Why, every day to-morrow. Come go in,
I'll show thee some attires, and have thy counsel
Which is the best to furnish me to-morrow.

---

12. **listen our propose:** listen to our conversation.
23. **only . . . hearsay:** wounds by hearsay only.
30. **woodbine coverture:** honeysuckle bower.   35. **coy:** shy.
36. **haggards . . . rock:** mature female hawks snared in their mountain
habitats, hence very difficult to tame.
42. **wish him wrastle:** advise him to wrestle.
45. **as full as:** fully as.   52. **Misprising:** undervaluing, despising.
54. **All matter else:** i.e. what anyone else has to say.
55. **take . . . affection:** formulate any mental image or idea of what
love is.

56. **self-endeared:** full of self-love.
60. **How:** however.   **rarely featur'd:** excellent in face and form.
61. **spell him backward:** i.e. say the reverse of him, turn his merits into
faults.   63. **black:** dark.   **antic:** grotesque figure.
65. **agot:** agate; here, a small figure incised in agate for a seal or a
ring.   70. **simpleness:** sincerity.   **purchaseth:** deserve.
72. **from all fashions:** contrary to all accepted behavior.
76. **press . . . death.** Accused felons who refused to plead either guilty
or not guilty were pressed to death by heavy weights.
78. **Consume . . . sighs.** An allusion to the belief that each sigh cost
the heart one drop of blood.   84. **honest:** harmless.
90. **priz'd:** esteemed.   92. **only:** i.e. very best.
96. **argument:** skills in conversation.
97. **report:** reputation (so also *name*, line 98).
101. **every day to-morrow:** i.e. to-morrow I shall be able to say that I
am married every day.

Urs. [*Aside.*] She's limed, I warrant you. We
have caught her, madam.

Hero. [*Aside.*] If it prove so, then loving goes
by haps: 105
Some Cupid kills with arrows, some with traps.

[*Exeunt Hero and Ursula.*]

Beat. [*Coming forward.*] What fire is in mine ears?
Can this be true?
Stand I condemn'd for pride and scorn so much?
Contempt, farewell, and maiden pride, adieu!
No glory lives behind the back of such.   110
And, Benedick, love on, I will requite thee,
Taming my wild heart to thy loving hand.
If thou dost love, my kindness shall incite thee
To bind our loves up in a holy band;
For others say thou dost deserve, and I   115
Believe it better than reportingly.   *Exit.*

[SCENE II]

Enter Prince [DON PEDRO], CLAUDIO, BENEDICK, *and*
LEONATO.

D. Pedro. I do but stay till your marriage be
consummate, and then go I toward Arragon.

Claud. I'll bring you thither, my lord, if you'll
vouchsafe me.   4

D. Pedro. Nay, that would be as great a soil
in the new gloss of your marriage as to show a child
his new coat and forbid him to wear it. I will only
be bold with Benedick for his company, for from
the crown of his head to the sole of his foot, he is all
mirth. He hath twice or thrice cut Cupid's   10
bow-string, and the little hangman dare not shoot
at him. He hath a heart as sound as a bell, and his
tongue is the clapper, for what his heart thinks, his
tongue speaks.

Bene. Gallants, I am not as I have been.   15

Leon. So say I, methinks you are sadder.

Claud. I hope he be in love.

D. Pedro. Hang him, truant, there's no true
drop of blood in him to be truly touch'd with love.
If he be sad, he wants money.   20

Bene. I have the toothache.

D. Pedro. Draw it.

Bene. Hang it!

Claud. You must hang it first, and draw it afterwards.   25

D. Pedro. What? sigh for the toothache?

Leon. Where is but a humor or a worm.

Bene. Well, every one [can] master a grief but
he that has it.

Claud. Yet say I, he is in love.   30

D. Pedro. There is no appearance of fancy in
him, unless it be a fancy that he hath to strange
disguises—as to be a Dutchman to-day, a Frenchman to-morrow, or in the shape of two countries
at once, as a German from the waist downward,
all slops, and a Spaniard from the hip upward,   36
no doublet. Unless he have a fancy to this foolery,
as it appears he hath, he is no fool for fancy, as you
would have it appear he is.   39

Claud. If he be not in love with some woman,
there is no believing old signs. 'A brushes his hat
a' mornings; what should that bode?

D. Pedro. Hath any man seen him at the barber's?

Claud. No, but the barber's man hath been   45
seen with him, and the old ornament of his cheek hath
already stuff'd tennis-balls.

Leon. Indeed he looks younger than he did, by
the loss of a beard.

D. Pedro. Nay, 'a rubs himself with civet. Can
you smell him out by that?   51

Claud. That's as much as to say, the sweet youth's
in love.

[*D. Pedro.*] The greatest note of it is his melancholy.   55

Claud. And when was he wont to wash his face?

D. Pedro. Yea, or to paint himself? for the which
I hear what they say of him.

Claud. Nay, but his jesting spirit, which is now
crept into a lute-string, and now govern'd by stops.

D. Pedro. Indeed that tells a heavy tale for him.
Conclude, conclude, he is in love.   62

Claud. Nay, but I know who loves him.

D. Pedro. That would I know too. I warrant
one that knows him not.   65

Claud. Yes, and his ill conditions, and in despite
of all, dies for him.

D. Pedro. She shall be buried with her face upwards.   69

---

104. **limed:** caught, like a bird entangled in birdlime.
105. **haps:** chance.
107. **What . . . ears.** Alluding to the folk belief that being talked about
in one's absence causes one's ears to burn.
110. **No . . . such:** nothing good is said about such a person when his
back is turned.
112. **Taming . . . hand.** Beatrice has been termed a "haggard" and
now acknowledges the justness of the epithet by her use of another
image from falconry.   114. **band:** bond.
116. **better than reportingly:** on better evidence than mere rumor.

III.ii. **Location:** Leonato's house.
3. **bring:** escort.   4. **vouchsafe:** allow.
8. **be bold with:** take the liberty of asking.
11. **hangman:** i.e. rogue (with play on Cupid as torturer, a role played
also by the public hangman).   16. **sadder:** more serious.
18-19. **there's . . . him:** he hasn't enough natural feeling.
20. **wants:** lacks.
21. **toothache.** Lovers were commonly supposed to suffer from toothaches, but Benedick may only be inventing an excuse for his changed
appearance.   23. **Hang it:** confound it.

24-25. **hang . . . afterwards.** Alluding to the execution of traitors, who
were hanged, cut down while still alive, drawn (disembowelled), and
quartered.
27. **humor . . . worm.** Toothaches were supposedly caused by abnormal
secretions or by actual worms in the teeth.
31. **fancy:** love (with following quibble).   36. **slops:** loose breeches.
37. **no doublet:** i.e. with his doublet completely covered by a cloak.
46. **old . . . cheek:** i.e. his beard.
50. **civet:** perfume derived from the civet cat.
51. **smell him out:** discover his true nature (with obvious play on the
literal sense).
52. **sweet.** With quibble on the sense "perfumed."
54. **greatest note:** most conspicuous mark.
56, 57. **wash, paint:** i.e. with cosmetics.
59-60. **now crept.** Some editors emend to *new-crept* (following Boas)
in view of the second *now* in the sentence.
60. **lute-string.** The lute commonly provided the accompaniment for
love songs.   **govern'd by stops:** regulated by frets (on the finger-
board of the lute), i.e. subjected to restraints.
66. **Yes:** i.e. she does know him.   **ill conditions:** bad characteristics.
68-69. **She . . . upwards.** Sexual double-entendre, taking off from a
quibble on Claudio's *dies* in the sense "experiences sexual climax."

Bene. Yet is this no charm for the toothache. Old signior, walk aside with me, I have studied eight or nine wise words to speak to you, which these hobby-horses must not hear.

[*Exeunt Benedick and Leonato*.]

D. Pedro. For my life, to break with him about Beatrice. 75

Claud. 'Tis even so. Hero and Margaret have by this play'd their parts with Beatrice, and then the two bears will not bite one another when they meet. 79

Enter [DON] JOHN *the Bastard*.

D. John. My lord and brother, God save you!

D. Pedro. Good den, brother.

D. John. If your leisure serv'd, I would speak with you.

D. Pedro. In private? 84

D. John. If it please you, yet Count Claudio may hear, for what I would speak of concerns him.

D. Pedro. What's the matter?

D. John. [*To Claudio*.] Means your lordship to be married to-morrow?

D. Pedro. You know he does. 90

D. John. I know not that, when he knows what I know.

Claud. If there be any impediment, I pray you discover it. 94

D. John. You may think I love you not; let that appear hereafter, and aim better at me by that I now will manifest. For my brother, I think he holds you well, and in dearness of heart hath holp to effect your ensuing marriage—surely suit ill spent and labor ill bestow'd. 100

D. Pedro. Why, what's the matter?

D. John. I came hither to tell you, and circumstances short'ned (for she has been too long a-talking of), the lady is disloyal.

Claud. Who, Hero? 105

D. John. Even she—Leonato's Hero, your Hero, every man's Hero.

Claud. Disloyal?

D. John. The word is too good to paint out her wickedness. I could say she were worse; think 110 you of a worse title, and I will fit her to it. Wonder not till further warrant. Go but with me to-night, you shall see her chamber-window ent'red, even the night before her wedding-day. If you love her then, to-morrow wed her; but it would better fit your honor to change your mind. 116

Claud. May this be so?

D. Pedro. I will not think it.

D. John. If you dare not trust that you see, confess not that you know. If you will follow me, 120

I will show you enough, and when you have seen more, and heard more, proceed accordingly.

Claud. If I see any thing to-night why I should not marry her, to-morrow in the congregation, where I should wed, there will I shame her. 125

D. Pedro. And as I woo'd for thee to obtain her, I will join with thee to disgrace her.

D. John. I will disparage her no farther till you are my witnesses. Bear it coldly but till midnight, and let the issue show itself. 130

D. Pedro. O day untowardly turn'd!

Claud. O mischief strangely thwarting!

D. John. O plague right well prevented! So will you say when you have seen the sequel. [*Exeunt*.]

[SCENE III]

Enter DOGBERRY *and his compartner* [VERGES] *with the* WATCH.

Dog. Are you good men and true?

Verg. Yea, or else it were pity but they should suffer salvation, body and soul.

Dog. Nay, that were a punishment too good for them, if they should have any allegiance in them, being chosen for the Prince's watch. 6

Verg. Well, give them their charge, neighbor Dogberry.

Dog. First, who think you the most desartless man to be constable? 10

1. Watch. Hugh Oatcake, sir, or George Seacole, for they can write and read.

Dog. Come hither, neighbor Seacole. God hath blest you with a good name. To be a well-favor'd man is the gift of fortune, but to write and read comes by nature. 16

2. Watch. Both which, Master Constable—

Dog. You have: I knew it would be your answer. Well, for your favor, sir, why, give God thanks, and make no boast of it, and for your writing 20 and reading, let that appear when there is no need of such vanity. You are thought here to be the most senseless and fit man for the constable of the watch; therefore bear you the lanthorn. This is your charge: you shall comprehend all vagrom men; you are to bid any man stand, in the Prince's name. 26

2. Watch. How if 'a will not stand?

Dog. Why then take no note of him, but let him go, and presently call the rest of the watch together, and thank God you are rid of a knave. 30

Verg. If he will not stand when he is bidden, he is none of the Prince's subjects.

---

129. **coldly**: calmly.   131. **untowardly turn'd**: perversely altered.

---

73. **hobby-horses**: i.e. buffoons (from the name of a performer in the morris-dance whose costume and antics suggested a horse).
74. **For**: upon.   81. **Good den**: good evening.
94. **discover**: reveal.   96. **aim better at**: judge better of.
98. **well**: in high esteem.   **dearness**: affection.
102–3. **circumstances short'ned**: without unnecessary details.
103–4. **has . . . of**: i.e. is not worth even the short time we have spent in mentioning her.   109. **paint out**: depict.
112. **warrant**: proof (is shown).   119. **that**: what.

III.iii. Location: A street.
1. **true**: loyal.
3. **salvation**: blunder for *damnation*. Dogberry's and Verges' words frequently mean precisely the opposite of what the speaker intends; witness *allegiance* (line 5), *desartless* (line 9), *senseless* (line 23).
14. **well-favor'd**: good-looking.   19. **favor**: appearance.
24. **lanthorn**: variant form of *lantern* (by popular etymology from the fact that lanterns often had sides made of transparent sheets of horn).
25. **comprehend**: i.e. apprehend.   **vagrom**: i.e. vagrant.
26. **stand**: stop.

Dog. True, and they are to meddle with none but the Prince's subjects. You shall also make no noise in the streets; for, for the watch to babble 35 and to talk, is most tolerable, and not to be endur'd.

[2.] Watch. We will rather sleep than talk, we know what belongs to a watch.

Dog. Why, you speak like an ancient and most quiet watchman, for I cannot see how sleeping 40 should offend; only have a care that your bills be not stol'n. Well, you are to call at all the alehouses, and bid those that are drunk get them to bed.

[2.] Watch. How if they will not?

Dog. Why then let them alone till they are sober. If they make you not then the better 46 answer, you may say they are not the men you took them for.

[2.] Watch. Well, sir.

Dog. If you meet a thief, you may suspect him, by virtue of your office, to be no true man; and 51 for such kind of men, the less you meddle or make with them, why, the more is for your honesty.

[2.] Watch. If we know him to be a thief, shall we not lay hands on him? 55

Dog. Truly by your office you may, but I think they that touch pitch will be defil'd. The most peaceable way for you, if you do take a thief, is to let him show himself what he is, and steal out of your company. 60

Verg. You have been always call'd a merciful man, partner.

Dog. Truly, I would not hang a dog by my will, much more a man who hath any honesty in him.

Verg. If you hear a child cry in the night, you must call to the nurse and bid her still it. 66

[2.] Watch. How if the nurse be asleep and will not hear us?

Dog. Why then depart in peace, and let the child wake her with crying, for the ewe that will not hear her lamb when it baes will never answer a calf when he bleats. 72

Verg. 'Tis very true.

Dog. This is the end of the charge: you, constable, are to present the Prince's own person. If you meet the Prince in the night, you may stay him. 76

Verg. Nay, by'r lady, that I think 'a cannot.

Dog. Five shillings to one on't, with any man that knows the [statues], he may stay him; marry, not without the Prince be willing, for indeed the watch ought to offend no man, and it is an offense to stay a man against his will. 82

Verg. By'r lady, I think it be so.

Dog. Ha, ah ha! Well, masters, good night. And there be any matter of weight chances, call up me. Keep your fellows' counsels and your own, and good night. Come, neighbor. 87

[2.] Watch. Well, masters, we hear our charge. Let us go sit here upon the church-bench till two, and then all to bed. 90

Dog. One word more, honest neighbors. I pray you watch about Signior Leonato's door, for the wedding being there to-morrow, there is a great coil to-night. Adieu! Be vigitant, I beseech you.

Exeunt [Dogberry and Verges].

Enter BORACHIO *and* CONRADE.

Bora. What, Conrade! 95

[2.] Watch. [Aside.] Peace, stir not.

Bora. Conrade, I say!

Con. Here, man, I am at thy elbow.

Bora. Mass, and my elbow itch'd; I thought there would a scab follow. 100

Con. I will owe thee an answer for that, and now forward with thy tale.

Bora. Stand thee close then under this penthouse, for it drizzles rain, and I will, like a true drunkard, utter all to thee. 105

[2.] Watch. [Aside.] Some treason, masters, yet stand close.

Bora. Therefore know I have earn'd of Don John a thousand ducats.

Con. Is it possible that any villainy should be so dear? 111

Bora. Thou shouldst rather ask if it were possible any villainy should be so rich; for when rich villains have need of poor ones, poor ones may make what price they will. 115

Con. I wonder at it.

Bora. That shows thou art unconfirm'd. Thou knowest that the fashion of a doublet, or a hat, or a cloak, is nothing to a man.

Con. Yes, it is apparel. 120

Bora. I mean the fashion.

Con. Yes, the fashion is the fashion.

Bora. Tush, I may as well say the fool's the fool. But seest thou not what a deformed thief this fashion is?

[2.] Watch. [Aside.] I know that Deformed; 'a has been a vile thief this seven year; 'a goes up and down like a gentleman. I remember his name. 127

Bora. Didst thou not hear somebody?

Con. No, 'twas the vane on the house.

Bora. Seest thou not, I say, what a deformed thief this fashion is, how giddily 'a turns about all the hot-bloods between fourteen and five-and- 132 thirty, sometimes fashioning them like Pharaoh's soldiers in the reechy painting, sometime like god Bel's priests in the old church-window, sometime

33. **meddle:** have to do.   36. **tolerable:** for *intolerable.*
38. **belongs to:** are the duties of.
41. **bills:** hooked blades fastened on long poles.
46–47. **make . . . answer:** . . . don't then agree to go home.
51. **true:** honest.   53. **is:** it is.
57. **they . . . defil'd.** A commonplace, derived from the Apocryphal book Ecclesiasticus (13:1).   64. **more:** for *less.*   66. **still:** quiet.
75. **present:** represent.   79. **statues:** i.e. statutes.
80. **without:** unless.

94. **coil:** fuss, to-do.   **vigitant:** i.e. vigilant.
99. **Mass:** by the Mass.   100. **scab:** scurvy fellow.
103. **penthouse:** a kind of porch structure, projecting from the main building.
104–5. **like . . . all.** Referring to the Latin tag "In vino veritas."
107. **stand close:** keep concealed.   111. **dear:** costly.
113. **villainy:** i.e. one wanting villainy to be committed.
117. **unconfirm'd:** inexperienced.
119. **is . . . man:** i.e. does not make the man.
124. **deformed thief:** ill-formed thief (because fashion assumes such fantastic shapes [lines 133–38] and robs men of their money by changing so often).   134. **reechy:** smoky, dirty.
135. **Bel's priests.** An allusion to the Apocryphal story of Bel (Baal) and the Dragon.

like the shaven Hercules in the smirch'd worm-eaten tapestry, where his codpiece seems as massy as his club?   138

Con. All this I see, and I see that the fashion wears out more apparel than the man. But art not thou thyself giddy with the fashion too, that thou hast shifted out of thy tale into telling me of the fashion?   143

Bora. Not so neither, but know that I have to-night woo'd Margaret, the Lady Hero's gentle-woman, by the name of Hero. She leans me out at her mistress' chamber-window, bids me a thousand 147 times good night—I tell this tale vildly, I should first tell thee how the Prince, Claudio, and my master, planted and plac'd and possess'd by my master Don John, saw afar off in the orchard this amiable encounter.   152

Con. And thought they Margaret was Hero?

Bora. Two of them did, the Prince and Claudio, but the devil my master knew she was Margaret; and partly by his oaths, which first possess'd them, partly by the dark night, which did deceive them, but 157 chiefly by my villainy, which did confirm any slander that Don John had made, away went Claudio enrag'd; swore he would meet her as he was appointed next morning at the temple, and there, before the whole congregation, shame her with what he saw o'er- 162 night, and send her home again without a husband.

[2.] Watch. We charge you, in the Prince's name, stand!

[1.] Watch. Call up the right Master Constable. We have here recover'd the most dangerous piece 167 of lechery that ever was known in the commonwealth.

[2.] Watch. And one Deformed is one of them; I know him, 'a wears a lock.

Con. Masters, masters—   171

2. Watch. You'll be made bring Deformed forth, I warrant you.

Con. Masters—

[2. Watch.] Never speak, we charge you; let us obey you to go with us.   176

Bora. We are like to prove a goodly commodity, being taken up of these men's bills.

Con. A commodity in question, I warrant you. Come, we'll obey you.   *Exeunt.*

[SCENE IV]

Enter HERO *and* MARGARET *and* URSULA.

Hero. Good Ursula, wake my cousin Beatrice, and desire her to rise.

Urs. I will, lady.

Hero. And bid her come hither.

Urs. Well.   [*Exit.*] 5

Marg. Troth, I think your other rebato were better.

Hero. No, pray thee, good Meg, I'll wear this.

Marg. By my troth 's not so good, and I warrant your cousin will say so.   10

Hero. My cousin's a fool, and thou art another. I'll wear none but this.

Marg. I like the new tire within excellently, if the hair were a thought browner; and your gown's a most rare fashion, i' faith. I saw the Duchess of Milan's gown that they praise so.   16

Hero. O, that exceeds, they say.

Marg. By my troth 's but a night-gown [in] respect of yours: cloth a' gold and cuts, and lac'd with silver, set with pearls, down sleeves, side 20 sleeves, and skirts, round underborne with a bluish tinsel; but for a fine, quaint, graceful, and excellent fashion, yours is worth ten on't.

Hero. God give me joy to wear it, for my heart is exceeding heavy.   25

Marg. 'Twill be heavier soon by the weight of a man.

Hero. Fie upon thee, art not asham'd?

Marg. Of what, lady? of speaking honorably? Is not marriage honorable in a beggar? Is not 30 your lord honorable without marriage? I think you would have me say, "saving your reverence, a husband." And bad thinking do not wrest true speaking, I'll offend nobody. Is there any harm in "the heavier for a husband"? None, I think, 35 and it be the right husband and the right wife; otherwise 'tis light, and not heavy. Ask my Lady Beatrice else, here she comes.

Enter BEATRICE.

Hero. Good morrow, coz.

Beat. Good morrow, sweet Hero.   40

Hero. Why, how now? Do you speak in the sick tune?

Beat. I am out of all other tune, methinks.

Marg. Clap 's into "Light a' love"; that goes without a burden. Do you sing it, and I'll dance it.   46

---

136. **shaven Hercules.** This allusion has not been identified; probably the reference is to the Omphale episode (see note to II.i.253).
137. **codpiece:** the bag-like flap at the front of men's breeches.
139–40. **fashion . . . man.** i.e. clothes are more often discarded because the fashion has changed than because they are worn-out.
142. **shifted.** With a quibble on the meaning "changed (clothing)."
150. **possess'd:** informed. 151. **amiable:** loving.
166. **right Master.** By mistaken analogy with such honorifics as "right honorable" and "right worshipful."
167. **recover'd:** for *discovered.* 168. **lechery:** for *treachery* (?).
170. **lock:** i.e. a love-lock of hair. 176. **obey.** He means *command.*
177. **commodity:** goods. 178. **taken up:** (1) taken on credit; (2) arrested. **bills:** (1) bonds; (2) pikes.
179. **in question:** (1) questionable; (2) about to be tried at law.

III.iv. Location: Hero's apartment in Leonato's house.
5. **Well:** very well. 6. **rebato:** stiff collar supporting a ruff.
9. **'s:** it is. 13. **tire:** headdress. **within:** in the inner room.
17. **exceeds:** is beyond comparison.
18. **night-gown:** dressing gown.
18–19. **in respect of:** compared with.
19. **cuts:** slashed openings, showing the fabric underneath. **lac'd:** trimmed. 20. **down sleeves:** long tight sleeves.
20–21. **side sleeves:** wide ornamental sleeves hanging open from the shoulder.
21. **round underborne:** lined around the bottom of the skirt.
22. **quaint:** elegant. 30. **in:** i.e. even in.
32. **saving your reverence:** a phrase of apology before an improper expression.
33. **And bad:** if bawdy. **wrest:** twist, misinterpret.
37. **light.** Punning on the meaning "wanton."
38. **else:** i.e. if this isn't true.
42. **sick tune:** i.e. voice of a sick person.
44. **Clap 's:** let's shift. **Light a' love:** a popular song.
45. **burden:** bass undersong (but with punning reference to "weight of a man").

Beat. Ye light a' love with your heels! then if your husband have stables enough, you'll see he shall lack no barns.

Marg. O illegitimate construction! I scorn that with my heels.   51

Beat. 'Tis almost five a' clock, cousin, 'tis time you were ready. By my troth, I am exceeding ill. Heigh-ho!

Marg. For a hawk, a horse, or a husband?   55

Beat. For the letter that begins them all, H.

Marg. Well, and you be not turn'd Turk, there's no more sailing by the star.

Beat. What means the fool, trow?

Marg. Nothing I, but God send every one their heart's desire!   61

Hero. These gloves the Count sent me, they are an excellent perfume.

Beat. I am stuff'd, cousin, I cannot smell.

Marg. A maid, and stuff'd! There's goodly catching of cold.   66

Beat. O, God help me, God help me, how long have you profess'd apprehension?

Marg. Ever since you left it. Doth not my wit become me rarely?   70

Beat. It is not seen enough, you should wear it in your cap. By my troth, I am sick.

Marg. Get you some of this distill'd *carduus benedictus*, and lay it to your heart; it is the only thing for a qualm.   75

Hero. There thou prick'st her with a thistle.

Beat. Benedictus! why *benedictus?* You have some moral in this *benedictus.*

Marg. Moral? no, by my troth I have no moral meaning, I meant plain holy-thistle. You   80
may think perchance that I think you are in love. Nay, by'r lady, I am not such a fool to think what I list, nor I list not to think what I can, nor indeed I cannot think, if I would think my heart out of thinking, that you are in love, or that you will be   85
in love, or that you can be in love. Yet Benedick was such another, and now is he become a man. He swore he would never marry, and yet now in despite of his heart he eats his meat without grudging; and how you may be converted I know   90
not, but methinks you look with your eyes as other women do.

Beat. What pace is this that thy tongue keeps?

Marg. Not a false gallop.   94

Enter URSULA.

Urs. Madam, withdraw, the Prince, the Count, Signior Benedick, Don John, and all the gallants of the town are come to fetch you to church.

Hero. Help to dress me, good coz, good Meg, good Ursula.   [*Exeunt.*]

[SCENE V]

Enter LEONATO *and the Constable* [DOGBERRY] *and the Headborough* [VERGES].

Leon. What would you with me, honest neighbor?

Dog. Marry, sir, I would have some confidence with you that decerns you nearly.

Leon. Brief, I pray you, for you see it is a busy time with me.   5

Dog. Marry, this it is, sir.

Verg. Yes, in truth it is, sir.

Leon. What is it, my good friends?

Dog. Goodman Verges, sir, speaks a little [off] the matter; an old man, sir, and his wits are not so blunt as, God help, I would desire they were, but in faith, honest as the skin between his brows.   12

Verg. Yes, I thank God I am as honest as any man living, that is an old man, and no honester than I.

Dog. Comparisons are odorous—*palabras,* neighbor Verges.   17

Leon. Neighbors, you are tedious.

Dog. It pleases your worship to say so, but we are the poor Duke's officers; but truly, for mine own part, if I were as tedious as a king, I could find in my heart to bestow it all of your worship.   22

Leon. All thy tediousness on me, ah?

Dog. Yea, and 'twere a thousand pound more than 'tis, for I hear as good exclamation on your worship as of any man in the city, and though I be but a poor man, I am glad to hear it.   27

Verg. And so am I.

Leon. I would fain know what you have to say.

Verg. Marry, sir, our watch to-night, excepting your worship's presence, ha' ta'en a couple of as arrant knaves as any in Messina.

Dog. A good old man, sir, he will be talking; as they say, "When the age is in, the wit is out."   34
God help us, it is a world to see! Well said, i' faith,

---

47. **Ye . . . heels:** i.e you are light-heeled (slang for "unchaste").
49. **barns.** With pun on *bairns,* "children."
51. **with my heels:** contemptuously.
56. **H.** With pun on *ache,* which was pronounced *aitch* in Shakespeare's day.
57. **turn'd Turk:** i.e. abandoned your faith (which was that you would never fall in love).
58. **no . . . star:** no more navigating by the north star, i.e. no more trusting to anything.   59. **trow:** I wonder.
64. **I am stuff'd:** i.e. I have a cold (with bawdy pun by Margaret following).
68. **profess'd apprehension:** made wit your profession.
71–72. **wear . . . cap:** i.e. as a fool does his coxcomb.
73–74. **carduus benedictus:** blessed (or holy) thistle, a medicinal herb.
78. **moral:** hidden meaning.   83. **list:** please.
87. **a man:** i.e. like other men.
89–90. **eats . . . grudging:** i.e. has an appetite like any other man.
94. **a false gallop:** (1) a canter; (2) running on untruthfully.

III.v. **Location:** Leonato's house.
o.s.d. **Headborough:** petty constable.
2. **confidence:** for *conference.*
3. **decerns:** for *concerns.*   **nearly:** intimately.
9. **Goodman:** regular title for one just below the rank of gentleman.
12. **honest . . . brows.** A proverbial comparison.
16. **odorous:** for *odious.*   **palabras:** a shortening of Spanish *pocas palabras,* "few words."   20. **poor Duke's.** He intends *Duke's poor.*
22. **of:** on.   24. **and:** even if.
25. **exclamation:** for *acclamation* (?). Dogberry's word is an unfortunate choice, since it normally meant "accusation" or "reproach."
30. **to-night:** last night.   **excepting:** for *respecting.* Dogberry here intends a polite phrase meaning "If I may speak of such things without offending your worship," but he says something far different.
34. **When . . . out:** an adaptation of the proverb "When ale is in, wit is out."
35. **it . . . see:** a proverbial phrase equivalent to "It is wonderful to behold"; but Dogberry seems to mean "What a world we live in."

neighbor Verges. Well, God's a good man; and
two men ride of a horse, one must ride behind.
An honest soul, i' faith, sir, by my troth he is, as
ever broke bread; but God is to be worshipp'd; all
men are not alike, alas, good neighbor!   40
Leon. Indeed, neighbor, he comes too short of
you.
Dog. Gifts that God gives.
Leon. I must leave you.   44
Dog. One word, sir. Our watch, sir, have indeed
comprehended two aspicious persons, and we would
have them this morning examin'd before your worship.   48
Leon. Take their examination yourself, and bring
it me. I am now in great haste, as it may appear
unto you.   51
Dog. It shall be suffigance.
Leon. Drink some wine ere you go; fare you well.

[*Enter a* MESSENGER.]

Mess. My lord, they stay for you to give your
daughter to her husband.   55
Leon. I'll wait upon them, I am ready.
                    [*Exeunt Leonato and Messenger.*]
Dog. Go, good partner, go, get you to Francis
Seacole, bid him bring his pen and inkhorn to the
jail. We are now to examination these men.
Verg. And we must do it wisely.   60
Dog. We will spare for no wit, I warrant you.
Here's that shall drive some of them to a non-come;
only get the learned writer to set down our excom-
munication, and meet me at the jail.   [*Exeunt.*]

[ACT IV, SCENE I]

Enter Prince [DON PEDRO, DON JOHN *the*] *Bastard,*
LEONATO, FRIAR [FRANCIS], CLAUDIO, BENEDICK,
HERO, *and* BEATRICE [*with* ATTENDANTS].

Leon. Come, Friar Francis, be brief—only to the
plain form of marriage, and you shall recount their
particular duties afterwards.
Friar. You come hither, my lord, to marry this
lady.   5
Claud. No.
Leon. To be married to her. Friar, you come to
marry her.
Friar. Lady, you come hither to be married to
this count.   10
Hero. I do.
Friar. If either of you know any inward impedi-

ment why you should not be conjoin'd, I charge you
on your souls to utter it.
Claud. Know you any, Hero?   15
Hero. None, my lord.
Friar. Know you any, Count?
Leon. I dare make his answer, none.
Claud. O, what men dare do! What men may
do! What men daily do, not knowing what they do!
Bene. How now! interjections? Why then, some
be of laughing, as, ah, ha, he!   22
Claud. Stand thee by, friar. Father, by your leave,
Will you with free and unconstrained soul
Give me this maid, your daughter?   25
Leon. As freely, son, as God did give her me.
Claud. And what have I to give you back whose
          worth
May counterpoise this rich and precious gift?
D. Pedro. Nothing, unless you render her again.
Claud. Sweet Prince, you learn me noble thank-
          fulness.   30
There, Leonato, take her back again.
Give not this rotten orange to your friend,
She's but the sign and semblance of her honor.
Behold how like a maid she blushes here!
O, what authority and show of truth   35
Can cunning sin cover itself withal!
Comes not that blood as modest evidence
To witness simple virtue? Would you not swear,
All you that see her, that she were a maid,
By these exterior shows? But she is none: 40
She knows the heat of a luxurious bed;
Her blush is guiltiness, not modesty.
Leon. What do you mean, my lord?
Claud.   Not to be married,
Not to knit my soul to an approved wanton.
Leon. Dear my lord, if you, in your own proof,
Have vanquish'd the resistance of her youth,   46
And made defeat of her virginity—
Claud. I know what you would say. If I have
          known her,
You will say, she did embrace me as a husband,
And so extenuate the 'forehand sin.   50
No, Leonato,
I never tempted her with word too large,
But as a brother to his sister, show'd
Bashful sincerity and comely love.
Hero. And seem'd I ever otherwise to you?   55
Claud. Out on thee seeming! I will write against
          it:
You seem to me as Dian in her orb,
As chaste as is the bud ere it be blown;

---

36. **God's . . . man:** God is good (proverbial).
37. **of a horse:** on one horse.
39. **God . . . worshipp'd:** i.e. we must praise God for whatever he sees
fit to bestow (?).
46. **comprehended:** for *apprehended.* **aspicious:** for *suspicious.*
52. **suffigance:** for *sufficient.* 56. **wait upon:** attend.
62. **non-come:** shortened form of *non compos mentis,* "not of sound
mind," but Dogberry seems to intend *nonplus.*
63–64. **excommunication:** for *examination,* or (perhaps) *communication.*

IV.i. Location: A church.
12. **inward:** secret, private.

21–22. **some . . . he.** Grammars classified the interjections according to the emotions they expressed; Benedick's sample is quoted from
Lily's Latin grammar.
28. **counterpoise:** balance, be equivalent to. 30. **learn:** teach.
35. **authority:** authenticity.
37. **modest evidence:** evidence of modesty. 41. **luxurious:** lustful.
44. **approved:** proved. 45. **proof:** i.e. test or trial of her.
50. **extenuate:** lessen, excuse. **'forehand sin:** i.e. premarital sex
relations. 52. **large:** broad, immodest.
56. **thee seeming:** i.e. you in your mere appearance (of good).
57. **Dian:** Diana, emblematic of virginity. **orb:** sphere. Diana, in
one of her aspects, was the moon-goddess.
58. **be blown:** open.

But you are more intemperate in your blood
Than Venus, or those pamp'red animals   60
That rage in savage sensuality.
    Hero. Is my lord well, that he doth speak so wide?
    Leon. Sweet Prince, why speak not you?
    D. Pedro.   What should I speak?
I stand dishonor'd, that have gone about
To link my dear friend to a common stale.   65
    Leon. Are these things spoken, or do I but dream?
    D. John. Sir, they are spoken, and these things
    are true.
    Bene. This looks not like a nuptial.
    Hero.   "True"! O God!
    Claud. Leonato, stand I here?
Is this the Prince? is this the Prince's brother?   70
Is this face Hero's? are our eyes our own?
    Leon. All this is so, but what of this, my lord?
    Claud. Let me but move one question to your
    daughter,
And by that fatherly and kindly power
That you have in her, bid her answer truly.   75
    Leon. I charge thee do so, as thou art my child.
    Hero. O God defend me, how am I beset!
What kind of catechizing call you this?
    Claud. To make you answer truly to your name.
    Hero. Is it not Hero? Who can blot that name
With any just reproach?
    Claud.   Marry, that can Hero,   81
Hero itself can blot out Hero's virtue.
What man was he talk'd with you yesternight
Out at your window betwixt twelve and one?
Now if you are a maid, answer to this.   85
    Hero. I talk'd with no man at that hour, my lord.
    D. Pedro. Why then are you no maiden. Leonato,
I am sorry you must hear. Upon mine honor,
Myself, my brother, and this grieved count
Did see her, hear her, at that hour last night   90
Talk with a ruffian at her chamber-window,
Who hath indeed, most like a liberal villain,
Confess'd the vile encounters they have had
A thousand times in secret.
    D. John. Fie, fie, they are not to be named, my
    lord,   95
Not to be spoke of;
There is not chastity enough in language
Without offense to utter them. Thus, pretty lady,
I am sorry for thy much misgovernment.
    Claud. O Hero! what a Hero hadst thou been,   100
If half thy outward graces had been placed
About thy thoughts and counsels of thy heart!
But fare thee well, most foul, most fair! Farewell,
Thou pure impiety and impious purity!
For thee I'll lock up all the gates of love,   105

And on my eyelids shall conjecture hang,
To turn all beauty into thoughts of harm,
And never shall it more be gracious.
    Leon. Hath no man's dagger here a point for me?
                        [Hero swoons.]
    Beat. Why, how now, cousin, wherefore sink you
    down?   110
    D. John. Come, let us go. These things, come
    thus to light,
Smother her spirits up.
      [Exeunt Don Pedro, Don John, and Claudio.]
    Bene. How doth the lady?
    Beat.   Dead, I think. Help, uncle!
Hero, why, Hero! Uncle! Signior Benedick! Friar!
    Leon. O Fate! take not away thy heavy hand,   115
Death is the fairest cover for her shame
That may be wish'd for.
    Beat.   How now, cousin Hero?
    Friar. Have comfort, lady.
    Leon. Dost thou look up?
    Friar.   Yea, wherefore should she not?
    Leon. Wherefore? why, doth not every earthly
    thing   120
Cry shame upon her? could she here deny
The story that is printed in her blood?
Do not live, Hero, do not ope thine eyes;
For did I think thou wouldst not quickly die,   124
Thought I thy spirits were stronger than thy shames,
Myself would, on the rearward of reproaches,
Strike at thy life. Griev'd I, I had but one?
Chid I for that at frugal nature's frame?
O, one too much by thee! Why had I one?
Why ever wast thou lovely in my eyes?   130
Why had I not with charitable hand
Took up a beggar's issue at my gates,
Who smirched thus and mir'd with infamy,
I might have said, "No part of it is mine;
This shame derives itself from unknown loins"?   135
But mine, and mine I lov'd, and mine I prais'd,
And mine that I was proud on, mine so much
That I myself was to myself not mine,
Valuing of her—why, she, O she is fall'n
Into a pit of ink, that the wide sea   140
Hath drops too few to wash her clean again,
And salt too little which may season give
To her foul tainted flesh!
    Bene.   Sir, sir, be patient.
For my part I am so attir'd in wonder,
I know not what to say.   145
    Beat. O, on my soul, my cousin is belied!
    Bene. Lady, were you her bedfellow last night?
    Beat. No, truly, not, although until last night,
I have this twelvemonth been her bedfellow.
    Leon. Confirm'd, confirm'd! O, that is stronger
    made   150

62. **wide:** wide of the mark, far from the truth.
64. **gone about:** endeavored.   65. **stale:** whore.
73. **move:** propose.   74. **kindly:** natural.
79. **answer . . . name:** tell truthfully by what name you should be called (?) or acknowledge that the name you have been called ("common stale") belongs to you (?).
82. **Hero itself:** the name Hero (now the name of an unchaste woman).
89. **grieved:** aggrieved, wronged.   92. **liberal:** gross, licentious.
99. **much misgovernment:** great misconduct.
102. **thoughts and counsels:** i.e. secret thoughts (hendiadys).
105. **For thee:** because of my experience with you.

106. **conjecture:** suspicion.   108. **be gracious:** seem beautiful.
112. **spirits:** vital forces.   122. **blood:** blushes.
125. **shames:** feelings of shame.
126. **on . . . reproaches:** after reproaching you.
128. **frame:** design (with respect to the number of my offspring).
138. **I . . . mine:** i.e. that I was nothing to myself.
139. **Valuing of her:** since I valued her so exclusively.
142. **season give:** act as a preservative, i.e. as a restorative.
144. **attir'd:** wrapped.

Which was before barr'd up with ribs of iron!
Would the two princes lie, and Claudio lie,
Who lov'd her so, that speaking of her foulness,
Wash'd it with tears? Hence from her, let her die.
    Friar. Hear me a little,   155
For I have only been silent so long,
And given way unto this course of fortune,
By noting of the lady. I have mark'd
A thousand blushing apparitions   159
To start into her face, a thousand innocent shames
In angel whiteness beat away those blushes,
And in her eye there hath appear'd a fire
To burn the errors that these princes hold
Against her maiden truth. Call me a fool,
Trust not my reading, nor my observations,   165
Which with experimental seal doth warrant
The tenure of my book; trust not my age,
My reverence, calling, nor divinity,
If this sweet lady lie not guiltless here
Under some biting error.
    Leon.   Friar, it cannot be.   170
Thou seest that all the grace that she hath left
Is that she will not add to her damnation
A sin of perjury; she not denies it.
Why seek'st thou then to cover with excuse
That which appears in proper nakedness?   175
    Friar. Lady, what man is he you are accus'd of?
    Hero. They know that do accuse me, I know
            none.
If I know more of any man alive
Than that which maiden modesty doth warrant,
Let all my sins lack mercy! O my father,   180
Prove you that any man with me convers'd
At hours unmeet, or that I yesternight
Maintain'd the change of words with any creature,
Refuse me, hate me, torture me to death!
    Friar. There is some strange misprision in the
            princes.   185
    Bene. Two of them have the very bent of honor,
And if their wisdoms be misled in this,
The practice of it lives in John the Bastard,
Whose spirits toil in frame of villainies.   189
    Leon. I know not. If they speak but truth of her,
These hands shall tear her; if they wrong her honor,
The proudest of them shall well hear of it.
Time hath not yet so dried this blood of mine,
Nor age so eat up my invention,
Nor fortune made such havoc of my means,   195
Nor my bad life reft me so much of friends,
But they shall find, awak'd in such a kind,
Both strength of limb, and policy of mind,

Ability in means, and choice of friends,
To quit me of them throughly.
    Friar.   Pause awhile,   200
And let my counsel sway you in this case.
Your daughter here the [princes] left for dead,
Let her awhile be secretly kept in,
And publish it that she is dead indeed.
Maintain a mourning ostentation,   205
And on your family's old monument
Hang mournful epitaphs, and do all rites
That appertain unto a burial.
    Leon. What shall become of this? what will this do?
    Friar. Marry, this well carried shall on her behalf
Change slander to remorse; that is some good.   211
But not for that dream I on this strange course,
But on this travail look for greater birth:
She dying, as it must be so maintain'd,
Upon the instant that she was accus'd,   215
Shall be lamented, pitied, and excus'd
Of every hearer; for it so falls out
That what we have we prize not to the worth
Whiles we enjoy it, but being lack'd and lost,
Why then we rack the value; then we find   220
The virtue that possession would not show us
Whiles it was ours. So will it fare with Claudio:
When he shall hear she died upon his words,
Th' idea of her life shall sweetly creep
Into his study of imagination,   225
And every lovely organ of her life
Shall come apparell'd in more precious habit,
More moving, delicate, and full of life,
Into the eye and prospect of his soul,   229
Than when she liv'd indeed. Then shall he mourn,
If ever love had interest in his liver,
And wish he had not so accused her;
No, though he thought his accusation true.
Let this be so, and doubt not but success
Will fashion the event in better shape   235
Than I can lay it down in likelihood.
But if all aim but this be levell'd false,
The supposition of the lady's death
Will quench the wonder of her infamy.
And if it sort not well, you may conceal her,   240
As best befits her wounded reputation,
In some reclusive and religious life,
Out of all eyes, tongues, minds, and injuries.
    Bene. Signior Leonato, let the friar advise you,
And though you know my inwardness and love   245

156–58. **I . . . lady.** I have kept silence so long, allowing these events
to take their free course, only because I have been occupied in
observing the lady (?). The passage has difficulties and may be
textually corrupt (see the Textual Notes).
166–67. **experimental . . . book:** the seal of experience guarantees as
genuine the conclusions I have drawn from my reading (of her face).
Tenure = tenor, import.   175. **proper:** its own.
182. **unmeet:** improper.   183. **change:** exchange.
184. **Refuse:** renounce, cast off.   185. **misprision:** misapprehension.
186. **the very bent of:** a perfect inclination toward.
188. **practice:** plotting.   189. **frame:** contriving.
194. **eat:** eaten.   **invention:** power of devising (retaliation); cf.
policy of mind, line 198.   197. **kind:** manner, degree.
198. **policy of mind:** shrewdness in contriving.

200. **quit . . . throughly:** settle my account with them thoroughly.
205. **mourning ostentation:** show of mourning.
209. **become of:** result from.   210. **carried:** managed.
213. **travail:** labor (in the double sense of "effort" and "pain of
childbirth").   220. **rack:** stretch.   223. **upon:** as a result of.
225. **study of imagination:** imaginative study, i.e. musing, reverie.
226. **organ . . . life:** aspect of her as she was when she lived.
229. **prospect:** view.
231. **interest in:** any claim upon (a legal term).   **liver.** The supposed
seat of the passion of love.
234. **success:** the happy working out (of my plan).
235. **event:** outcome.
236. **lay . . . likelihood:** suggest its probable consequences.
237. **if . . . false:** if we miss our aim in every other respect.
240. **sort:** turn out.
242. **reclusive:** retired, secluded (as a religious recluse).
243. **injuries:** insults.
245. **inwardness and love:** close friendship (hendiadys).

Is very much unto the Prince and Claudio,
Yet, by mine honor, I will deal in this
As secretly and justly as your soul
Should with your body.

Leon. 　　　　　　Being that I flow in grief,
The smallest twine may lead me. 　　　　250

Friar. 'Tis well consented; presently away,
For to strange sores strangely they strain the cure.
Come, lady, die to live; this wedding-day
Perhaps is but prolong'd, have patience and endure.
　　　　　　Exit [with all but Benedick and Beatrice].

Bene. Lady Beatrice, have you wept all this while?

Beat. Yea, and I will weep a while longer. 　256

Bene. I will not desire that.

Beat. You have no reason, I do it freely.

Bene. Surely I do believe your fair cousin is
wrong'd. 　　　　　　　　　　　　　260

Beat. Ah, how much might the man deserve of me
that would right her!

Bene. Is there any way to show such friendship?

Beat. A very even way, but no such friend.

Bene. May a man do it? 　　　　　　265

Beat. It is a man's office, but not yours.

Bene. I do love nothing in the world so well as
you—is not that strange? 　　　　　　268

Beat. As strange as the thing I know not. It
were as possible for me to say I lov'd nothing so
well as you, but believe me not; and yet I lie not:
I confess nothing, nor I deny nothing. I am sorry
for my cousin.

Bene. By my sword, Beatrice, thou lovest me.

Beat. Do not swear and eat it. 　　　275

Bene. I will swear by it that you love me, and I
will make him eat it that says I love not you.

Beat. Will you not eat your word?

Bene. With no sauce that can be devis'd to it. I
protest I love thee. 　　　　　　　　280

Beat. Why then God forgive me!

Bene. What offense, sweet Beatrice?

Beat. You have stay'd me in a happy hour, I was
about to protest I lov'd you.

Bene. And do it with all thy heart. 　　285

Beat. I love you with so much of my heart that
none is left to protest.

Bene. Come, bid me do any thing for thee.

Beat. Kill Claudio.

Bene. Ha, not for the wide world. 　　290

Beat. You kill me to deny it. Farewell.

Bene. Tarry, sweet Beatrice.

Beat. I am gone, though I am here; there is no love
in you. Nay, I pray you let me go.

Bene. Beatrice— 　　　　　　　　295

Beat. In faith, I will go.

Bene. We'll be friends first.

---

249. **Being that:** since. 　**flow in:** am dissolved in (?) or am afloat
on (?).
252. **For . . . cure:** strange diseases require strange and desperate
cures. 　254. **prolong'd:** postponed. 　264. **even:** level, easy.
269. **As strange:** as much a stranger (playing on Benedick's use of
strange). 　275. **eat it:** go back on your oath.
280. **protest:** declare (but Beatrice pretends to take it in the sense of
"object," as she uses it herself in line 287).
283. **in . . . hour:** at just the right moment, opportunely.
291. **deny:** refuse. 　293. **am gone:** have left you (in spirit).

Beat. You dare easier be friends with me than fight
with mine enemy.

Bene. Is Claudio thine enemy?　　　　300

Beat. Is 'a not approv'd in the height a villain,
that hath slander'd, scorn'd, dishonor'd my kinswoman? O that I were a man! What, bear her in
hand until they come to take hands, and then 　304
with public accusation, uncover'd slander, unmitigated
rancor—O God, that I were a man! I would eat his
heart in the market-place.

Bene. Hear me, Beatrice—

Beat. Talk with a man out at a window! a proper
saying! 　　　　　　　　　　　　310

Bene. Nay, but, Beatrice—

Beat. Sweet Hero, she is wrong'd, she is sland'red,
she is undone.

Bene. Beat—

Beat. Princes and counties! Surely a princely
testimony, a goodly count, Count Comfect, a 　316
sweet gallant surely! O that I were a man for his sake!
or that I had any friend would be a man for my sake!
But manhood is melted into cur'sies, valor into compliment, and men are only turn'd into tongue, and 　320
trim ones too. He is now as valiant as Hercules that
only tells a lie, and swears it. I cannot be a man with
wishing, therefore I will die a woman with grieving.

Bene. Tarry, good Beatrice. By this hand, I love
thee. 　　　　　　　　　　　　　325

Beat. Use it for my love some other way than
swearing by it.

Bene. Think you in your soul the Count Claudio
hath wrong'd Hero?

Beat. Yea, as sure as I have a thought or a soul. 　330

Bene. Enough, I am engag'd, I will challenge
him. I will kiss your hand, and so I leave you. By
this hand, Claudio shall render me a dear account.
As you hear of me, so think of me. Go comfort
your cousin. I must say she is dead; and so farewell. 　　　　　　　　　　*[Exeunt.]* 　336

[SCENE II]

Enter the Constables [DOGBERRY *and* VERGES] *and the
Town Clerk* [*or* SEXTON] *in gowns,* [*and the* WATCH
with CONRADE *and*] BORACHIO.

Dog. Is our whole dissembly appear'd?

Verg. O, a stool and a cushion for the sexton.

Sex. Which be the malefactors?

Dog. Marry, that am I and my partner.

Verg. Nay, that's certain, we have the exhibition
to examine. 　　　　　　　　　　6

---

301. **approv'd:** proved. 　**height:** highest degree.
303–4. **bear . . . hand:** deceive her with false hopes.
305. **uncover'd:** unconcealed, open. 　315. **counties:** counts.
316. **count:** (1) the title; (2) legal indictment; (3) story. 　**Comfect:**
comfit, sweetmeat. 　317. **for his sake:** i.e. to deal with him.
321. **trim:** fine. 　331. **engag'd:** bound by a pledge.
333. **render . . . account:** make a very costly settlement with me.

IV.ii. Location: A prison.
o.s.d. **gowns:** robes of office. 　1. **dissembly:** for *assembly.*
5. **exhibition:** possibly for *commission,* but *exhibition* could mean "an
allowance of money"; in either case Verges blunders.

Sex. But which are the offenders that are to be examin'd? Let them come before Master Constable.

Dog. Yea, marry, let them come before me. What is your name, friend? 　　10

Bora. Borachio.

Dog. Pray write down Borachio. Yours, sirrah?

Con. I am a gentleman, sir, and my name is Conrade.

Dog. Write down Master Gentleman Conrade. Masters, do you serve God? 　　16

Both [*Con., Bora.*]. Yea, sir, we hope.

Dog. Write down, that they hope they serve God; and write God first, for God defend but God should go before such villains! Masters, it is prov'd 20 already that you are little better than false knaves, and it will go near to be thought so shortly. How answer you for yourselves?

Con. Marry, sir, we say we are none. 　　24

Dog. A marvellous witty fellow, I assure you, but I will go about with him. Come you hither, sirrah; a word in your ear, sir. I say to you, it is thought you are false knaves.

Bora. Sir, I say to you, we are none. 　　29

Dog. Well, stand aside. 'Fore God, they are both in a tale. Have you writ down, that they are none?

Sex. Master Constable, you go not the way to examine; you must call forth the watch that are their accusers. 　　35

Dog. Yea, marry, that's the eftest way; let the watch come forth. Masters, I charge you in the Prince's name accuse these men.

1. Watch. This man said, sir, that Don John, the Prince's brother, was a villain. 　　40

Dog. Write down Prince John a villain. Why, this is flat perjury, to call a prince's brother villain.

Bora. Master Constable—

Dog. Pray thee, fellow, peace. I do not like thy look, I promise thee. 　　45

Sex. What heard you him say else?

2. Watch. Marry, that he had receiv'd a thousand ducats of Don John for accusing the Lady Hero wrongfully.

Dog. Flat burglary as ever was committed. 　　50

Verg. Yea, by mass, that it is.

Sex. What else, fellow?

1. Watch. And that Count Claudio did mean, upon his words, to disgrace Hero before the whole assembly, and not marry her. 　　55

Dog. O villain! thou wilt be condemn'd into everlasting redemption for this.

Sex. What else?

[*1. and 2.*] *Watch.* This is all. 　　59

Sex. And this is more, masters, than you can deny. Prince John is this morning secretly stol'n away. Hero was in this manner accus'd, in this very manner

refus'd, and upon the grief of this suddenly died. Master Constable, let these men be bound, and brought to Leonato's. I will go before and show him their examination. [*Exit.*] 66

[*Dog.*] Come let them be opinion'd.

Verg. Let them be in the hands—

[*Con.*] [Off,] coxcomb!

Dog. God's my life, where's the sexton? Let 70 him write down the Prince's officer coxcomb. Come, bind them. Thou naughty varlet!

[*Con.*] Away, you are an ass, you are an ass.

Dog. Dost thou not suspect my place? Dost thou not suspect my years? O that he were here to 75 write me down as ass! But, masters, remember that I am an ass; though it be not written down, yet forget not that I am an ass. No, thou villain, thou art full of piety, as shall be prov'd upon thee by good witness. I am a wise fellow, and which is more, an officer, 80 and which is more, a householder, and which is more, as pretty a piece of flesh as any is in Messina, and one that knows the law, go to, and a rich fellow enough, go to, and a fellow that hath had losses, and one that hath two gowns, and every thing hand- 85 some about him. Bring him away. O that I had been writ down an ass! *Exeunt.*

[ACT V, SCENE I]

Enter LEONATO *and his brother* [ANTONIO].

Ant. If you go on thus, you will kill yourself,
And 'tis not wisdom thus to second grief
Against yourself.

Leon. 　　　　　　I pray thee cease thy counsel,
Which falls into mine ears as profitless
As water in a sieve. Give not me counsel, 　　5
Nor let no comforter delight mine ear
But such a one whose wrongs do suit with mine.
Bring me a father that so lov'd his child,
Whose joy of her is overwhelm'd like mine,
And bid him speak of patience; 　　10
Measure his woe the length and breadth of mine,
And let it answer every strain for strain,
As thus for thus, and such a grief for such,
In every lineament, branch, shape, and form;
If such a one will smile and stroke his beard, 　　15
And, sorrow wag, cry "hem!" when he should groan,
Patch grief with proverbs, make misfortune drunk
With candle-wasters, bring him yet to me,
And I of him will gather patience.
But there is no such man, for, brother, men 　　20

---

12. **sirrah**: form of address to inferiors. 　19. **defend**: forbid.
25. **witty**: clever, cunning. 　26. **go about with**: outmaneuver.
31. **in a tale**: agreed on the same lie.
36. **eftest**. It is clear that he means something like "easiest" or "quickest," but not what word he may be mangling.
54. **upon his words**: on the basis of his accusation.
57. **redemption**. He means the opposite.

63. **refus'd**: renounced. 　67. **opinion'd**: for *pinioned.*
70. **God's**: God save. 　72. **naughty**: wicked.
74. **suspect**: for *respect.* 　79. **piety**: for *impiety.*
82. **as . . . flesh**: as fine a fellow.

V.i. Location: Near Leonato's house.
2. **second**: aid. 　6. **delight**: try to please. 　7. **suit with**: match.
11. **Measure his woe**: let his woe equal in its dimensions.
12. **strain**: strong feeling.
16. **And, sorrow wag**: and, letting sorrow go hang. Many editors emend to *Bid sorrow wag* (after Capell), i.e. bid sorrow be off.
17. **drunk**: i.e. insensible.
18. **candle-wasters**: those who sit up late over books; here, those who write moral treatises, and by extension, their good advice itself.

Can counsel and speak comfort to that grief
Which they themselves not feel, but tasting it,
Their counsel turns to passion, which before
Would give preceptial med'cine to rage,
Fetter strong madness in a silken thread,   25
Charm ache with air, and agony with words.
No, no, 'tis all men's office to speak patience
To those that wring under the load of sorrow,
But no man's virtue nor sufficiency
To be so moral when he shall endure   30
The like himself. Therefore give me no counsel,
My griefs cry louder than advertisement.
   Ant. Therein do men from children nothing differ.
   Leon. I pray thee peace. I will be flesh and blood,
For there was never yet philosopher   35
That could endure the toothache patiently,
However they have writ the style of gods,
And made a push at chance and sufferance.
   Ant. Yet bend not all the harm upon yourself;
Make those that do offend you suffer too.   40
   Leon. There thou speak'st reason; nay, I will do so.
My soul doth tell me Hero is belied,
And that shall Claudio know; so shall the Prince,
And all of them that thus dishonor her.   44

Enter Prince [Don Pedro] *and* Claudio.

   Ant. Here comes the Prince and Claudio hastily.
   D. Pedro. Good den, good den.
   Claud.   Good day to both of you.
   Leon. Hear you, my lords—
   D. Pedro.   We have some haste, Leonato.
   Leon. Some haste, my lord! Well, fare you well,
      my lord.
Are you so hasty now? well, all is one.
   D. Pedro. Nay, do not quarrel with us, good old
      man.   50
   Ant. If he could right himself with quarrelling,
Some of us would lie low.
   Claud.   Who wrongs him?
   Leon. Marry, thou dost wrong me, thou dis-
      sembler, thou—
Nay, never lay thy hand upon thy sword,
I fear thee not.
   Claud.   Marry, beshrew my hand,   55
If it should give your age such cause of fear.
In faith, my hand meant nothing to my sword.
   Leon. Tush, tush, man, never fleer and jest at me;
I speak not like a dotard nor a fool,
As under privilege of age to brag   60
What I have done being young, or what would do
Were I not old. Know, Claudio, to thy head,
Thou hast so wrong'd mine innocent child and me
That I am forc'd to lay my reverence by,

And with grey hairs and bruise of many days,   65
Do challenge thee to trial of a man.
I say thou hast belied mine innocent child!
Thy slander hath gone through and through her heart,
And she lies buried with her ancestors—
O, in a tomb where never scandal slept,   70
Save this of hers, fram'd by thy villainy!
   Claud. My villainy?
   Leon.   Thine, Claudio, thine, I say.
   D. Pedro. You say not right, old man.
   Leon.   My lord, my lord,
I'll prove it on his body, if he dare,
Despite his nice fence and his active practice,   75
His May of youth and bloom of lustihood.
   Claud. Away, I will not have to do with you.
   Leon. Canst thou so daff me? Thou hast kill'd
      my child.
If thou kill'st me, boy, thou shalt kill a man.
   Ant. He shall kill two of us, and men indeed; 80
But that's no matter, let him kill one first.
Win me and wear me, let him answer me.
Come follow me, boy; come, sir boy, come follow me.
Sir boy, I'll whip you from your foining fence,
Nay, as I am a gentleman, I will.   85
   Leon. Brother—
   Ant. Content yourself. God knows I lov'd my
      niece,
And she is dead, slander'd to death by villains,
That dare as well answer a man indeed
As I dare take a serpent by the tongue.   90
Boys, apes, braggarts, Jacks, milksops!
   Leon.   Brother Anthony—
   Ant. Hold you content. What, man! I know
      them, yea,
And what they weigh, even to the utmost scruple—
Scambling, outfacing, fashion-monging boys,
That lie and cog and flout, deprave and slander,   95
Go anticly, and show outward hideousness,
And speak [off] half a dozen dang'rous words,
How they might hurt their enemies—if they durst—
And this is all.
   Leon. But, brother Anthony—
   Ant.   Come, 'tis no matter;
Do not you meddle, let me deal in this.   101
   D. Pedro. Gentlemen both, we will not wake your
      patience.
My heart is sorry for your daughter's death;
But on my honor she was charg'd with nothing

24. **preceptial:** comprised of precepts.   26. **air:** breath, i.e. words.
28. **wring:** writhe.   29. **sufficiency:** ability.
30. **moral:** full of moral sentiments.   32. **advertisement:** counsel.
37. **style of gods:** language worthy of gods (who are above human suffering).
38. **a push at:** an onslaught against (?), or an expression of contempt toward (*push* being a common form of *pish*) (?), (an expression of contempt).   **sufferance:** suffering.
49. **all is one:** it does not matter.
52. **Some of us.** He means Don Pedro and Claudio.
55. **beshrew:** curse.   57. **to:** i.e. in grasping.   58. **fleer:** jeer.
62. **head:** face.

66. **trial . . . man:** i.e. text (or combat) worthy of a man.
75. **nice fence:** dextrous fencing (probably with a sneer in *nice* at the new Italian fashion of duelling with rapier and dagger in place of the older native half-sword and dagger; cf. line 84).
76. **lustihood:** bodily vigor.   78. **daff:** doff, i.e. thrust aside.
80. **men indeed:** true men (cf. line 89).
82. **Win . . . wear me:** i.e. if he wants to have me, he'll have to overcome me first (a proverbial phrase used as a summons to action). **answer me:** meet me in response to my challenge.
84. **foining:** thrusting.
87. **Content yourself:** i.e. don't try to stop me.
94. **Scambling:** contentious.   **outfacing:** insolent.   **fashion-monging:** following the fashions, foppish.
95. **cog:** cheat.   **deprave:** vilify.
96. **Go anticly:** go about fantastically dressed.   **outward hideousness:** a threatening appearance.   97. **dang'rous:** arrogant, threatening.
102. **wake your patience:** i.e. test your patience further, add to your troubles.

But what was true, and very full of proof.   105

Leon. My lord, my lord—

D. Pedro. I will not hear you.

Leon. No? Come, brother, away! I will be heard.

Ant. And shall, or some of us will smart for it.

Exeunt ambo [Leonato and Antonio].

Enter BENEDICK.

D. Pedro. See, see, here comes the man we went
to seek.   110

Claud. Now, signior, what news?

Bene. Good day, my lord.

D. Pedro. Welcome, signior, you are almost come
to part almost a fray.   114

Claud. We had lik'd to have had our two noses
snapp'd off with two old men without teeth.

D. Pedro. Leonato and his brother. What think'st
thou? Had we fought, I doubt we should have been
too young for them.

Bene. In a false quarrel there is no true valor.
I came to seek you both.   121

Claud. We have been up and down to seek thee,
for we are high-proof melancholy, and would fain
have it beaten away. Wilt thou use thy wit?

Bene. It is in my scabbard, shall I draw it?   125

D. Pedro. Dost thou wear thy wit by thy side?

Claud. Never any did so, though very many have
been beside their wit. I will bid thee draw, as we do
the minstrels, draw to pleasure us.

D. Pedro. As I am an honest man, he looks pale.
Art thou sick, or angry?   131

Claud. What, courage, man! What though care
kill'd a cat, thou hast mettle enough in thee to kill
care.

Bene. Sir, I shall meet your wit in the career, and
you charge it against me. I pray you choose another
subject.   137

Claud. Nay then give him another staff, this last
was broke cross.

D. Pedro. By this light, he changes more and
more. I think he be angry indeed.

Claud. If he be, he knows how to turn his girdle.

Bene. Shall I speak a word in your ear?

Claud. God bless me from a challenge!   144

Bene. [*Aside to Claudio.*] You are a villain. I jest
not; I will make it good how you dare, with what you
dare, and when you dare. Do me right; or I will protest your cowardice. You have kill'd a sweet lady,
and her death shall fall heavy on you. Let me hear
from you.   150

Claud. Well, I will meet you, so I may have good
cheer.

D. Pedro. What, a feast, a feast?

Claud. I' faith, I thank him, he hath bid me to a
calve's-head and a capon, the which if I do not carve
most curiously, say my knife's naught. Shall I not
find a woodcock too?   157

Bene. Sir, your wit ambles well, it goes easily.

D. Pedro. I'll tell thee how Beatrice prais'd thy
wit the other day. I said thou hadst a fine wit.   160
"True," said she, "a fine little one." "No," said I,
"a great wit." "Right," says she, "a great gross
one." "Nay," said I, "a good wit." "Just," said
she, "it hurts nobody." "Nay," said I, "the gentleman is wise." "Certain," said she, "a wise   165
gentleman." "Nay," said I, "he hath the tongues."
"That I believe," said she, "for he swore a thing to
me on Monday night, which he forswore on Tuesday
morning. There's a double tongue, there's two
tongues." Thus did she an hour together trans-   170
shape thy particular virtues, yet at last she concluded with a sigh, thou wast the proper'st man in
Italy.

Claud. For the which she wept heartily and said
she car'd not.   175

D. Pedro. Yea, that she did, but yet for all that,
and if she did not hate him deadly, she would love
him dearly. The old man's daughter told us all.

Claud. All, all, and, moreover, God saw him
when he was hid in the garden.   180

D. Pedro. But when shall we set the savage bull's
horns on the sensible Benedick's head?

Claud. Yea, and text underneath, "Here dwells
Benedick the married man"?   184

Bene. Fare you well, boy, you know my mind. I
will leave you now to your gossip-like humor. You
break jests as braggards do their blades, which, God
be thank'd, hurt not. My lord, for your many
courtesies I thank you. I must discontinue your company. Your brother the bastard is fled from   190
Messina. You have among you kill'd a sweet and
innocent lady. For my Lord Lack-beard there, he
and I shall meet, and till then peace be with him.

[Exit.]

D. Pedro. He is in earnest.   194

Claud. In most profound earnest, and I'll warrant you, for the love of Beatrice.

D. Pedro. And hath challeng'd thee?

Claud. Most sincerely.   198

---

109 s.d. **ambo:** both.   118. **doubt:** fear.
123. **high-proof:** at a high level of.
128. **beside their wit:** out of their minds.
129. **minstrels.** Who are bidden to draw their bows across the strings
of their instruments.
135. **in the career:** at full speed (an expression from jousting).
136. **charge:** direct, level.   138. **staff:** lance.
139. **broke cross:** broken crosswise, athwart his opponent's shield.
Claudio means that Benedick has performed wretchedly in this first
exchange.
142. **he knows . . . girdle.** Proverbial, but of uncertain meaning;
generally explained as meaning "it's up to him to get himself into a
better frame of mind; I shall make no effort to placate him" (*girdle* =
belt).   147. **Do me right:** give me satisfaction.
147–8. **protest:** proclaim.

151–52. **so . . . cheer:** so long as I may have good cheer.
155, 157. **calve's-head, capon, woodcock.** Types of stupidity.
156. **curiously:** daintily.   **naught:** worthless.
158. **your . . . easily:** your wit moves smoothly like an ambling horse
(i.e. it shows no mettle or fire like a horse at the gallop).
162. **gross:** coarse.   164. **hurts nobody:** i.e. has no bite.
165–66. **a wise gentleman.** One of the established uses of this phrase
was in an ironic sense.
166. **hath the tongues:** is a master of languages.
170–71. **trans-shape:** distort.   172. **proper'st:** handsomest.
177. **and if:** if.   **deadly:** mortally.
179–80. **God . . . garden.** This reference to the action of III.i contains
also an echo of Genesis 3:8.
181–84. **But . . . man.** Benedick is put on notice that his lordly
assertion at I.i.262–68 has not been forgotten.
187. **braggards:** braggarts, i.e. those better at boasting of their
prowess than of demonstrating it.

D. Pedro. What a pretty thing man is when he goes in his doublet and hose and leaves off his wit!

Enter Constables [DOGBERRY *and* VERGES, *and the* WATCH *with*] CONRADE *and* BORACHIO.

Claud. He is then a giant to an ape, but then is an ape a doctor to such a man.   202

D. Pedro. But soft you, let me be. Pluck up, my heart, and be sad. Did he not say my brother was fled?   205

Dog. Come you, sir. If justice cannot tame you, she shall ne'er weigh more reasons in her balance. Nay, and you be a cursing hypocrite once, you must be look'd to.   209

D. Pedro. How now? two of my brother's men bound? Borachio one!

Claud. Hearken after their offense, my lord.

D. Pedro. Officers, what offense have these men done?   214

Dog. Marry, sir, they have committed false report; moreover they have spoken untruths; secondarily, they are slanders; sixt and lastly, they have belied a lady; thirdly, they have verified unjust things; and to conclude, they are lying knaves.

D. Pedro. First, I ask thee what they have   220 done; thirdly, I ask thee what's their offense; sixt and lastly, why they are committed; and to conclude, what you lay to their charge.

Claud. Rightly reason'd, and in his own division, and by my troth there's one meaning well suited.   225

D. Pedro. Who have you offended, masters, that you are thus bound to your answer? This learned constable is too cunning to be understood. What's your offense?   229

Bora. Sweet Prince, let me go no farther to mine answer: do you hear me, and let this count kill me. I have deceiv'd even your very eyes. What your wisdoms could not discover, these shallow fools have brought to light, who in the night overheard me confessing to this man how Don John your   235 brother incens'd me to slander the Lady Hero, how you were brought into the orchard, and saw me court Margaret in Hero's garments, how you disgrac'd her when you should marry her. My villainy   240 they have upon record, which I had rather seal with my death than repeat over to my shame. The lady is dead upon mine and my master's false accusation; and briefly, I desire nothing but the reward of a villain.

D. Pedro. Runs not this speech like iron through your blood?   245

Claud. I have drunk poison whiles he utter'd it.

D. Pedro. But did my brother set thee on to this?

Bora. Yea, and paid me richly for the practice of it.

D. Pedro. He is compos'd and fram'd of treachery, And fled he is upon this villainy.   250

Claud. Sweet Hero, now thy image doth appear In the rare semblance that I lov'd it first.

Dog. Come, bring away the plaintiffs. By this time our sexton hath reform'd Signior Leonato of the matter; and, masters, do not forget to specify,   255 when time and place shall serve, that I am an ass.

Verg. Here, here comes Master Signior Leonato, and the sexton too.

Enter LEONATO, *his brother* [ANTONIO], *and the* SEXTON.

Leon. Which is the villain? Let me see his eyes, That when I note another man like him   260 I may avoid him. Which of these is he?

Bora. If you would know your wronger, look on me.

Leon. Art thou the slave that with thy breath hast kill'd
Mine innocent child?

Bora.   Yea, even I alone.

Leon. No, not so, villain, thou beliest thyself.   265
Here stand a pair of honorable men,
A third is fled, that had a hand in it.
I thank you, princes, for my daughter's death;
Record it with your high and worthy deeds.
'Twas bravely done, if you bethink you of it.   270

Claud. I know not how to pray your patience,
Yet I must speak. Choose your revenge yourself,
Impose me to what penance your invention
Can lay upon my sin; yet sinn'd I not,
But in mistaking.

D. Pedro.   By my soul, nor I,   275
And yet, to satisfy this good old man,
I would bend under any heavy weight
That he'll enjoin me to.

Leon. I cannot bid you bid my daughter live—
That were impossible—but I pray you both,   280
Possess the people in Messina here
How innocent she died, and if your love
Can labor aught in sad invention,
Hang her an epitaph upon her tomb,
And sing it to her bones, sing it to-night.   285
To-morrow morning come you to my house,
And since you could not be my son-in-law,
Be yet my nephew. My brother hath a daughter,
Almost the copy of my child that's dead,
And she alone is heir to both of us.   290
Give her the right you should have giv'n her cousin,
And so dies my revenge.

Claud.   O noble sir!
Your overkindness doth wring tears from me.
I do embrace your offer, and dispose
For henceforth of poor Claudio.   295

---

200. **goes . . . wit:** i.e. forgets to put on his good sense along with his clothes.
201. **a giant to:** i.e. much larger than (*to* = in comparison with).
202. **doctor:** scholar, learned man.   203. **soft you:** wait a minute.
203–4. **Pluck . . . heart:** collect yourself, my mind.
204. **sad:** serious.
207. **reasons:** i.e. legal cases (Dogberry seems to have confused *reasons* and *causes*). Perhaps *reasons* quibbles on *raisins*, which it closely resembled in pronunciation.   **balance:** scale.
212. **Hearken after:** inquire into.   217. **slanders:** i.e. slanderers.
218. **verified:** affirmed as true (but perhaps a blunder for *testified*).
225. **well suited:** i.e. in several garbs.
227. **bound . . . answer:** bound over for trial (perhaps with puns on *bound* in the senses "pinioned" and "on the way").
236. **incens'd:** incited.   242. **upon:** as a result of.

248. **practice:** execution.   253. **plaintiffs:** blunder for *defendants*.
254. **reform'd:** for *informed*.   255. **specify:** for *testify* (?).
266. **honorable:** of distinguished rank.   273. **Impose:** subject.
281. **Possess:** inform.
290. **heir to both.** Antonio's son (mentioned in I.ii.1–2) has apparently been forgotten.   291. **should:** were to.

Leon. To-morrow then I will expect your coming,
To-night I take my leave. This naughty man
Shall face to face be brought to Margaret,
Who I believe was pack'd in all this wrong,   299
Hir'd to it by your brother.

Bora.   No, by my soul she was not,
Nor knew not what she did when she spoke to me,
But always hath been just and virtuous
In any thing that I do know by her.   303

Dog. Moreover, sir, which indeed is not under
white and black, this plaintiff here, the offender,
did call me ass. I beseech you let it be remem-
b'red in his punishment. And also, the watch heard
them talk of one Deformed. They say he wears a key
in his ear and a lock hanging by it, and borrows   309
money in God's name, the which he hath us'd so
long and never paid that now men grow hard-hearted
and will lend nothing for God's sake. Pray you
examine him upon that point.   313

Leon. I thank thee for thy care and honest pains.

Dog. Your worship speaks like a most thankful
and reverent youth, and I praise God for you.

Leon. There's for thy pains.

Dog. God save the foundation!

Leon. Go, I discharge thee of thy prisoner, and I
thank thee.   320

Dog. I leave an arrant knave with your worship,
which I beseech your worship to correct yourself, for
the example of others. God keep your worship! I
wish your worship well. God restore you to health!
I humbly give you leave to depart, and if a merry   325
meeting may be wish'd, God prohibit it! Come,
neighbor.   [*Exeunt Dogberry and Verges.*]

Leon. Until to-morrow morning, lords, farewell.

Ant. Farewell, my lords, we look for you to-
morrow.

D. Pedro. We will not fail.

Claud.   To-night I'll mourn with Hero.

Leon. [*To the Watch.*] Bring you these fellows on.
—We'll talk with Margaret,   331
How her acquaintance grew with this lewd fellow.

                              Exeunt [*severally*].

[SCENE II]

Enter BENEDICK *and* MARGARET, [*meeting*].

Bene. Pray thee, sweet Mistress Margaret, deserve well at my hands by helping me to the speech
of Beatrice.

Marg. Will you then write me a sonnet in praise
of my beauty?   5

Bene. In so high a style, Margaret, that no man
living shall come over it, for in most comely truth
thou deservest it.

Marg. To have no man come over me? Why,
shall I always keep below stairs?   10

Bene. Thy wit is as quick as the greyhound's
mouth, it catches.

Marg. And yours as blunt as the fencer's foils,
which hit, but hurt not.   14

Bene. A most manly wit, Margaret, it will not
hurt a woman. And so I pray thee call Beatrice;
I give thee the bucklers.

Marg. Give us the swords, we have bucklers of
our own.   19

Bene. If you use them, Margaret, you must put
in the pikes with a vice, and they are dangerous
weapons for maids.

Marg. Well, I will call Beatrice to you, who I
think hath legs.   *Exit Margaret.*

Bene. And therefore will come.   25
[*Sings.*] "The god of love,
                    That sits above,
          And knows me, and knows me,
               How pitiful I deserve"—   29
I mean in singing; but in loving, Leander the good
swimmer, Troilus the first employer of pandars,
and a whole bookful of these quondam carpet-
mongers, whose names yet run smoothly in the
even road of a blank verse, why, they were never
so truly turn'd over and over as my poor self in   35
love. Marry, I cannot show it in rhyme; I have tried.
I can find out no rhyme to "lady" but "baby," an
innocent rhyme; for "scorn," "horn," a hard rhyme;
for "school," "fool," a babbling rhyme: very ominous
endings. No, I was not born under a rhyming planet,
nor I cannot woo in festival terms.   41

Enter BEATRICE.

Sweet Beatrice, wouldst thou come when I call'd
thee?

Beat. Yea, signior, and depart when you bid me.

Bene. O, stay but till then!   45

Beat. "Then" is spoken; fare you well now.
And yet ere I go, let me go with that I came, which

---

297. naughty: wicked.   **299. pack'd:** involved as a conspirator.
303. by: concerning.   **304–5. under . . . black:** in writing.
308–9. key . . . it. Dogberry's transmutation of the *lock* of III.iii.170.
310. in God's name: i.e. like a professional beggar (who commonly
used this phrase).   **us'd:** made a practice.
316. reverent. Perhaps another blunder, but *reverent* was commonly
used in the sense "reverend" (see V.iv.123).
318. God . . . foundation: a phrase used by those who received alms
from a charitable foundation.
321–22. I . . . yourself. Dogberry here makes use of locutions which,
contrary to his intention, permit the interpretation that he is calling
Leonato a knave and urging him to reform.
326. prohibit. One last example of Dogberry saying precisely the
opposite of what he means.   **332. lewd:** low, worthless.

V.ii. Location: Leonato's orchard.

7. come over: (1) exceed: (2) get across (pointing to a quibble on
style / stile in line 6). Margaret then plays on a third sense, with
characteristic ribaldry.   **in . . . comely truth:** (1) in good truth; (2)
by virtue of your beauty.
10. keep: dwell, stay.   **below stairs:** i.e. in the servants' quarters.
17. give . . . bucklers: i.e. give up (*buckler* = a kind of shield).
21. pikes: spikes in the centre of a shield.   **vice:** screw.
26–29. The first lines of a contemporary song.
29. How . . . deserve: how much I deserve pity (but Benedick twists
the meaning to "how pitifully small my deserts are").
30. Leander. Who swam the Hellespont nightly to see his love Hero.
31. Troilus. Whose union with Cressida was arranged by her uncle
Pandarus.   **32. quondam:** of former days.
32–33. carpet-mongers. Knights who avoided military service were
contemptuously called carpet knights. Benedick's use of the term for
storied lovers of old implies that they were contemptible performers
compared with himself.
38. innocent: childish.   **hard:** (1) harsh, unpleasant (because associated with the idea of the cuckold's horn); (2) solid.
41. festival terms: elevated language suitable for a special occasion.
47. that I came: what I came for.

is, with knowing what hath pass'd between you
and Claudio.

Bene. Only foul words—and thereupon I will
kiss thee.   51

Beat. Foul words is but foul wind, and foul wind
is but foul breath, and foul breath is noisome; therefore
I will depart unkiss'd.   54

Bene. Thou hast frighted the word out of his
right sense, so forcible is thy wit. But I must tell
thee plainly, Claudio undergoes my challenge, and
either I must shortly hear from him, or I will subscribe him a coward. And I pray thee now tell me,
for which of my bad parts didst thou first fall in love
with me?   61

Beat. For them all together, which maintain'd
so politic a state of evil that they will not admit any
good part to intermingle with them. But for which
of my good parts did you first suffer love for me?   65

Bene. Suffer love! a good epithite! I do suffer
love indeed, for I love thee against my will.

Beat. In spite of your heart, I think. Alas, poor
heart, if you spite it for my sake, I will spite it for
yours, for I will never love that which my friend
hates.   71

Bene. Thou and I are too wise to woo peaceably.

Beat. It appears not in this confession; there's
not one wise man among twenty that will praise
himself.   75

Bene. An old, an old instance, Beatrice, that
liv'd in the time of good neighbors. If a man do
not erect in this age his own tomb ere he dies, he
shall live no longer in monument than the bell rings
and the widow weeps.   80

Beat. And how long is that, think you?

Bene. Question: why, an hour in clamor and
a quarter in rheum; therefore is it most expedient   83
for the wise, if Don Worm (his conscience) find no
impediment to the contrary, to be the trumpet of
his own virtues, as I am to myself. So much for
praising myself, who I myself will bear witness is
praiseworthy. And now tell me, how doth your
cousin?   89

Beat. Very ill.

Bene. And how do you?

Beat. Very ill too.

Bene. Serve God, love me, and mend. There
will I leave you too, for here comes one in haste.   94

Enter URSULA.

Urs. Madam, you must come to your uncle,
yonder's old coil at home. It is prov'd my Lady
Hero hath been falsely accus'd, the Prince and
Claudio mightily abus'd, and Don John is the   98
author of all, who is fled and gone. Will you come
presently?

Beat. Will you go hear this news, signior?

Bene. I will live in thy heart, die in thy lap, and
be buried in thy eyes; and moreover I will go with
thee to thy uncle's.   *Exeunt.* 104

[SCENE III]

Enter CLAUDIO, *Prince* [DON PEDRO], *and three or four
with tapers.*

Claud. Is this the monument of Leonato?

[*A*] *Lord.* It is, my lord.

[*Claud.   Reading out of a scroll.*]

EPITAPH

"Done to death by slanderous tongues
      Was the Hero that here lies.
Death, in guerdon of her wrongs,   5
      Gives her fame which never dies.
So the life that died with shame
Lives in death with glorious fame."

Hang thou there upon the tomb,
                        [*Hangs up the scroll.*]
Praising her when I am [dumb].   10
Now, music, sound, and sing your solemn hymn.

SONG

Pardon, goddess of the night,
Those that slew thy virgin knight,
For the which, with songs of woe,
Round about her tomb they go.   15
      Midnight, assist our moan,
      Help us to sigh and groan,
            Heavily, heavily.
      Graves, yawn and yield your dead,
      Till death be uttered,   20
            Heavily, heavily.

[*Claud.*] Now, unto thy bones good night!
      Yearly will I do this rite.

D. Pedro. Good morrow, masters, put your
      torches out.
The wolves have preyed, and look, the gentle day,   25
Before the wheels of Phoebus, round about
Dapples the drowsy east with spots of grey.
Thanks to you all, and leave us. Fare you well.

---

53. **noisome:** ill-smelling.
55–56. **his right sense:** (1) its senses, its right mind; (2) its correct
meaning.   57. **undergoes:** is subject to.
58–59. **subscribe:** formally proclaim.
63. **politic:** shrewdly managed.
65. **suffer:** (1) experience: (2) suffer from.
66. **epithite:** epithet, i.e. expression.
73. **It . . . confession:** your wisdom is not shown by this declaration
that you are wise.
76. **instance:** proverb, maxim (i.e. that a wise man does not praise
himself).
77. **time . . . neighbors:** good old days when neighbors were willing to
speak well of one another.
82. **Question:** that is the question.   **clamor:** sound (of the bell).
83. **rheum:** tears (of the widow).
84. **Don . . . conscience.** It was a commonplace to describe the conscience as a gnawing worm.   85. **trumpet:** trumpeter.

96. **old coil:** great confusion, much ado.   98. **abus'd:** deceived.
100. **presently:** immediately.
102. **die.** Used with the common sexual implication.

V.iii. Location: A churchyard.
5. **guerdon:** recompense.   12. **goddess . . . night.** See note to IV.i.57.
18. **Heavily:** mournfully.
19. **yield your dead:** i.e. so that they too may "assist our moan."
20. **uttered:** fully expressed, i.e. adequately lamented.
25. **have preyed:** i.e. have finished their night's preying.
26. **Before . . . Phoebus:** i.e. preceding the chariot of the sun.

Claud. Good morrow, masters—each his several way.

D. Pedro. Come let us hence, and put on other weeds,   30
And then to Leonato's we will go.

Claud. And Hymen now with luckier issue speed 's
Than this for whom we rend'red up this woe.

                        Exeunt.

[SCENE IV]

Enter LEONATO, BENEDICK, [BEATRICE,] MARGARET, URSULA, *old man* [ANTONIO], FRIAR [FRANCIS], HERO.

Friar. Did I not tell you she was innocent?

Leon. So are the Prince and Claudio, who accus'd her
Upon the error that you heard debated.
But Margaret was in some fault for this,
Although against her will, as it appears   5
In the true course of all the question.

Ant. Well, I am glad that all things sorts so well.

Bene. And so am I, being else by faith enforc'd
To call young Claudio to a reckoning for it.   9

Leon. Well, daughter, and you gentlewomen all,
Withdraw into a chamber by yourselves,
And when I send for you, come hither masked.
The Prince and Claudio promis'd by this hour
To visit me. You know your office, brother:
You must be father to your brother's daughter,   15
And give her to young Claudio.   *Exeunt Ladies.*

Ant. Which I will do with confirm'd countenance.

Bene. Friar, I must entreat your pains, I think.

Friar. To do what, signior?

Bene. To bind me, or undo me—one of them.   20
Signior Leonato, truth it is, good signior,
Your niece regards me with an eye of favor.

Leon. That eye my daughter lent her, 'tis most true.

Bene. And I do with an eye of love requite her.

Leon. The sight whereof I think you had from me,   25
From Claudio, and the Prince. But what's your will?

Bene. Your answer, sir, is enigmatical,
But for my will, my will is your good will
May stand with ours, this day to be conjoin'd
In the state of honorable marriage,   30
In which, good friar, I shall desire your help.

Leon. My heart is with your liking.

Friar.   And my help.
Here comes the Prince and Claudio.

Enter Prince [DON PEDRO] *and* CLAUDIO *and two or three other.*

D. Pedro. Good morrow to this fair assembly.

Leon. Good morrow, Prince; good morrow, Claudio;
                                         35
We here attend you. Are you yet determined
To-day to marry with my brother's daughter?

Claud. I'll hold my mind were she an Ethiope.

Leon. Call her forth, brother, here's the friar ready.   [*Exit Antonio.*]

D. Pedro. Good morrow, Benedick. Why, what's the matter,   40
That you have such a February face,
So full of frost, of storm, and cloudiness?

Claud. I think he thinks upon the savage bull.
Tush, fear not, man, we'll tip thy horns with gold,
And all Europa shall rejoice at thee,   45
As once Europa did at lusty Jove,
When he would play the noble beast in love.

Bene. Bull Jove, sir, had an amiable low,
And some such strange bull leapt your father's cow,
And got a calf in that same noble feat   50
Much like to you, for you have just his bleat.

Enter Brother [ANTONIO], HERO, BEATRICE, MARGARET, URSULA, [*the ladies masked*].

Claud. For this I owe you: here comes other reck'nings.
Which is the lady I must seize upon?

[*Ant.*] This same is she, and I do give you her.

Claud. Why then she's mine. Sweet, let me see your face.   55

Leon. No, that you shall not till you take her hand,
Before this friar, and swear to marry her.

Claud. Give me your hand before this holy friar—
I am your husband if you like of me.   59

Hero. [*Unmasking.*] And when I liv'd, I was your other wife,
And when you lov'd, you were my other husband.

Claud. Another Hero!

Hero.   Nothing certainer:
One Hero died defil'd, but I do live,
And surely as I live, I am a maid.   64

D. Pedro. The former Hero! Hero that is dead!

Leon. She died, my lord, but whiles her slander liv'd.

Friar. All this amazement can I qualify,
When after that the holy rites are ended,
I'll tell you largely of fair Hero's death.
Mean time let wonder seem familiar,   70
And to the chapel let us presently.

Bene. Soft and fair, friar. Which is Beatrice?

Beat. [*Unmasking.*] I answer to that name. What is your will?

---

30. **weeds:** clothes.
32. **Hymen:** the god of marriage.   **with . . . speed 's:** favor us with better fortune.

V.iv. Location: Leonato's house.
3. **Upon:** because of.   **debated:** publicly discussed.
5. **against her will:** unintentionally.
6. **question:** judicial examination.   7. **sorts:** turn out.
8. **faith:** i.e. his pledge to Beatrice.   14. **office:** function, role.
17. **confirm'd:** steadfast, i.e. serious.   **countenance:** demeanor.
20. **undo:** (1) ruin; (2) unbind.

36. **yet:** still.
43. **savage bull.** Another reference to Benedick's complacent statement at I.i.262–68.   45. **Europa:** Europe.
46. **Europa:** a Phoenician princess whom Jove, in the form of a white bull, carried off from her native land.
48. **amiable low:** winning voice.
52. **owe you:** i.e. will repay you later.
52–53. **other reck'nings:** other accounts (that I must settle first).
59. **like of:** like, are willing to take.
63. **defil'd:** disgraced, slandered.   67. **qualify:** moderate.
69. **largely:** fully, in detail.
70. **let . . . familiar:** accept these amazing events as natural.

Bene.   Do not you love me?

Beat.   Why, no, no more than reason.

Bene.   Why then your uncle and the Prince and
    Claudio   75
Have been deceived. They swore you did.

Beat.   Do not you love me?

Bene.   Troth, no, no more than reason.

Beat.   Why then my cousin, Margaret, and Ursula
Are much deceiv'd, for they did swear you did.

Bene.   They swore that you were almost sick
    for me.   80

Beat.   They swore that you were well-nigh dead
    for me.

Bene.   'Tis no such matter. Then you do not
    love me?

Beat.   No, truly, but in friendly recompense.

Leon.   Come, cousin, I am sure you love the gentle-
    man.

Claud.   And I'll be sworn upon't that he loves her,
For here's a paper written in his hand,   86
A halting sonnet of his own pure brain,
Fashion'd to Beatrice.

Hero.   And here's another
Writ in my cousin's hand, stol'n from her pocket,
Containing her affection unto Benedick.   90

Bene.   A miracle! here's our own hands against
our hearts. Come, I will have thee, but by this light,
I take thee for pity.

Beat.   I would not deny you, but by this good
day, I yield upon great persuasion, and partly   95
to save your life, for I was told you were in a consumption.

[*Bene.*]   Peace, I will stop your mouth.

                                        [*Kissing her.*]

D. Pedro.   How dost thou, Benedick the married
    man?   99

Bene.   I'll tell thee what, Prince: a college of

91–92. **our . . . hearts:** i.e. our own written testimony to prove our
hearts guilty as charged.   99. **How . . . man.** Cf. I.i.267–68.
100. **college:** company, assemblage.

wit-crackers cannot flout me out of my humor.
Dost thou think I care for a satire or an epigram?
No, if a man will be beaten with brains, 'a shall
wear nothing handsome about him. In brief,   104
since I do purpose to marry, I will think nothing to
any purpose that the world can say against it, and
therefore never flout at me for what I have said
against it; for man is a giddy thing, and this is my
conclusion. For thy part, Claudio, I did think 109
to have beaten thee, but in that thou art like to be
my kinsman, live unbruis'd, and love my cousin.

Claud.   I had well hop'd thou wouldst have denied
Beatrice, that I might have cudgell'd thee out   113
of thy single life, to make thee a double-dealer,
which out of question thou wilt be, if my cousin
do not look exceeding narrowly to thee.

Bene.   Come, come, we are friends. Let's have a
dance ere we are married, that we may lighten our
own hearts and our wives' heels.

Leon.   We'll have dancing afterward.   120

Bene.   First, of my word; therefore play, music.
Prince, thou art sad, get thee a wife, get thee a wife.
There is no staff more reverent than one tipp'd with
horn.

Enter MESSENGER.

Mess.   My lord, your brother John is ta'en in flight,
And brought with armed men back to Messina.   126

Bene.   Think not on him till to-morrow. I'll
devise thee brave punishments for him. Strike up,
pipers.   *Dance.* [*Exeunt.*]

101. **wit-crackers:** jokesters (cf. *crack a joke*).
103–4. **if . . . him:** if a man is going to allow himself to be beaten up
by wit, he will never dare wear good clothes; i.e. if a man allows
ridicule to dictate his actions, he will deprive himself of many desirable
things.   108. **giddy:** fickle, changeable.
108–9. **my conclusion:** the position I have finally come to.
114. **double-dealer:** (1) married man (cf. *single man*); (2) unfaithful
husband.   115. **out of question:** without doubt.
116. **narrowly:** closely.   121. **of:** on.
123. **reverent:** reverend, honorable.
124. **horn.** The cuckold joke once more.
128. **brave:** capital, fine.

NOTE ON THE TEXT

Much Ado about Nothing was first published in quarto in
1600 by Andrew Wise and William Aspley; this edition (Q)
is here used as copy-text. The First Folio text (1623) was
printed from a copy of Q into which had been introduced
some stage directions from a manuscript prompt-book (see,
for example, Textual Notes, II.i.85, II.iii.36). The textual
changes found in F1 are of the kind probably attributable to
compositorial tinkering or error and cannot be accorded any
authority, though something like stage censorship may lie
behind the F1 omissions at III.ii.34–37 and IV.ii.17–20. Only
the more significant F1 variants are recorded in the Textual
Notes.

The considerable confusions in Q (particularly in the
speech-prefixes for Antonio and for Dogberry, Verges, and
the Watch) and the many indefinite and vaguely descriptive
stage directions point clearly to Shakespeare's "foul papers"

as the copy-text. As further evidence of "foul papers," it
may be noticed that the opening stage direction of I.i
introduces a character called "Innogen" as Leonato's wife
(referred to again at the beginning of II.i as "his wife")
who has no speaking part in the play; presumably Shakespeare, following his source in Bandello's *Novelle*, at one time
intended to include Hero's mother in his version of the story.
It has been suggested that the "foul papers" had received
a few additions to the stage directions by a book-keeper,
perhaps as a preliminary to having a "fair copy" transcribed
for the official prompt-book (see the opening stage directions of I.ii and II.i), but the evidence for a second hand is
very slight.

Dover Wilson's elaborate revision theory, advanced in
1923 to explain some of the obvious difficulties and confusions in Q, has never been generally accepted, and recent

bibliographical work, showing that Q was set from cast-off copy by a single compositor, has gone far to discredit it entirely.

For further information, see: J. D. Wilson, ed., New Cambridge *Much Ado about Nothing* (Cambridge, 1923); W. W. Greg, *The Shakespeare First Folio* (Oxford, 1955); W. C. Ferguson, "The Compositors of *Henry IV, Part 2, Much*

Ado about Nothing, The Shoemakers' Holiday, and *The First Part of the Contention*," *SB*, XIII (1960), 19–29; J. H. Smith, "The Composition of the Quarto of *Much Ado about Nothing*," *SB*, XVI (1963), 9–26; Charlton Hinman, ed., *Much Ado about Nothing* (1600) [facsimile of Q] (Oxford, 1971).

TEXTUAL NOTES

Title: **Much . . . Nothing**] Much adoe about Nothing. As it hath been sundrie times publikely acted by the right honourable, the Lord Chamberlaine his seruants. Written by William Shakespeare. *Q1 (title-page)*
Dramatis personae: *subs. as first given in Rowe*

Act-scene division: *none in Q; F1, except for I.i, marks only acts; other scene divisions from Rowe and later editors (see first note to each scene); present act-scene arrangement as a whole first established by Capell*

I.i

I.i] *F1*
Location: *Pope*
o.s.d. **Messina**] Messina, Innogen his wife *Q, F1 (Innogen has no lines in the play and appears only once again, in II.i o.s.d. as his wife; first om. by Theobald)*
1, 10 **Pedro**] *Rowe*; Peter *Q, F1*
50 **victual**] *F1*; vittaile *Q*
51 **eat**] ease *F1*
65 **that.**] *F1*; that, *Q*
71 **creature**] *F1*; creature, *Q*
89 **Benedick**] *F2*; Benedict *Q, F1*
92 **Do,**] *Theobald*; Do *Q, F1*
96 **are you**] you are *F1*
138 **parrot-teacher**] *hyphen, F2*
146–7 **Leonato— . . . Benedick—**] *Theobald*; Leonato, . . . Benedicke, *Q*; Leonato, . . . Benedicke, *F1*
154 s.d. **To Don John.**] *Hanmer*
172 **high**] *F3*; hie *Q, F1*
203 s.d. **Enter Don Pedro.**] *Hanmer*; Enter don Pedro, Iohn the bastard. *Q, F1*
210–2 **so . . . allegiance,**] *Nicholson conj. (in Cambridge)*; so (but . . . allegiance) *Q, F1*
227 **spoke**] speake *F1*
281 **house—**] *Capell (subs.)*; house *Q*; house, *F1*
301 **war-thoughts**] *F1*; warre-thoughts, *Q*
302 **vacant,**] *Capell*; vacant, *Q*
309–10 **and . . . her.**] *om. F1*

I.ii

I.ii] *Capell*
Location: *Capell (subs.)*
o.s.d. **Antonio**] *Rowe*
o.s.d. **meeting**] *Cambridge*
3 s.p. **Ant.**] *Rowe*; Old *Q, F1 (throughout scene)*
7 **event**] *F2*; euents *Q, F1*
9 **thick-pleach'd**] *hyphen, Theobald*
24 s.d. **Several . . . stage.**] *Theobald (subs.)*
26 **skill**] *F1*; shill *Q*

I.iii

I.iii] *Capell*
Location: *Theobald (subs.)*
o.s.d. **Don**] *Rowe*; sir *Q, F1*
1 **good-year**] *hyphen, Malone*
8 **at least**] yet *F1*
33 **muzzle**] *F4 (muzzel)*; mussell *Q, F1*
39 **make**] will make *F1*
40 s.d. **Enter Borachio.**] *placed as in Dyce; after l. 41, Q, F1*
49 **Marry**] *F2*; Mary *Q, F1 (generally)*
49 **brother's**] *F1*; bothers *Q*
54 **one**] on *F1*
69 **me?**] *F1*; me. *Q*

II.i

II.i] *Rowe*; Actus Secundus. *F1*
Location: *Pope*

o.s.d. **his brother**] *Rowe (subs.)*; his brother, his wife *Q, F1*
o.s.d. **Margaret, Ursula,**] *Rowe*
2 s.p. **Ant.**] *Rowe*; brother *Q, F1 (until l. 114)*
50 s.d. **To Hero.**] *Rowe*
60 **mettle**] *Wilson*; mettal *Q, F1*
66 **you.**] *Rowe (subs.)*; you, *Q, F1*
76 **mannerly-modest**] *hyphen, Theobald*
77 **ancientry**] *Johnson*; aunchentry *Q, F1*
85 s.d. **They . . . masks.**] *Capell (subs.)*
85 s.d. **Prince Don Pedro**] *Rowe (subs.)*; prince, Pedro *Q, F1*
85 s.d. **Don John, and Borachio**] *Wilson*; Balthasar, or dumb Iohn. *Q, F1*
85 s.d. **as . . . Drum**] *after F1*: Maskers with a drum.
88 **So**] *F1*; So, *Q*
91 **company?**] *Rowe*; company. *Q, F1*
99 s.d. **They move aside.**] *ed. (after Hanmer)*
100, 103, 105 s.pp. **Bora.**] *Wilson*; Bene. *Q, F1*
108, 111 s.pp. **Bora.**] *Wilson*; Balth. *Q, F1*
111, 124 s.dd. **They move aside.**] *ed. (after Capell)*
113 **Antonio**] *Pope*; Anthonio *Q, F1*
117 **ill-well**] *hyphen, Theobald*
150 s.d. **Music . . . begins.**] *Capell (subs.); F1 gives Musicke for the dance. after l. 153*
154 s.d. **Then . . . Claudio.**] *Steevens (subs.)*; exeunt *Q, F1*
183 **Claudio?**] *Rowe*; Claudio. *Q, F1*
198 **blind man**] *Rowe*; blindman *Q, F1*
210 s.d. **Enter . . . Pedro.**] *from F1*: Enter the Prince.; Enter the Prince, Hero, Leonato. Iohn and Borachio, and Conrade. *Q*
223, 231 **bird's**] *Rowe*; birds *Q, F1*
244 **that**] and that *F1*
261 s.d. **Leonato and Hero**] *F1 (subs.)*
300 **obtain'd.**] *Theobald (subs.)*; obtained, *Q, F1*
314 **it—**] *Wilson*; it, *Q, F1*
320 **"Heigh-ho . . . husband!"**] *quotes, Staunton*
326 s.p. **D. Pedro.**] *Rowe (subs.)*; Prince *Q, F1 (throughout rest of scene)*
374 **too,**] *Rowe*; too *Q*; to *F1*
387 s.d. **Exeunt.**] *F2*; exit. *Q, F1*

II.ii

II.ii] *Capell*
Location: *Cambridge (after Theobald)*
o.s.d. **Don**] *Rowe*
37 **in**] in a *F1*
38–9 **match, . . . maid—**] *Capell (after Rowe)*; match) . . . maid. *Q, F1*
44 **Margaret**] *F1*; Marg. *Q*
57 s.d. **Exeunt.**] *Rowe*; exit *Q, F1*

II.iii

II.iii] *Capell*
Location: *Theobald*
1 s.d. **Enter Boy.**] *Collier*
25 **an**] *F1*; and *Q*
36 s.d. **Withdraws.**] *Theobald*
36 s.d. **Claudio**] Claudio and Iacke Wilson *F1 (i.e. the actor who played Balthasar; F1 omits Q's entry for Balthasar at l. 42)*
36 s.d. **within**] *Neilson*
42 **hid-fox**] *Warburton*; kid-foxe *Q, F1 (a reading defended by some eds.)*
42 s.d. **Balthasar**] *Neilson*; Balthasar *Q (for F1 see second note on l. 36 s.d.)*
43 **Balthasar**] *F1*; Balthaser *Q*
57 s.d. **Air.**] *Capell*
62 s.p. **Balth.**] *Capell*

92 s.d. **Aside.**] *Johnson*
108, 121, 211, 213 s.dd. **Aside.**] *Theobald*
135 **us of**] *F1*; of vs *Q*
190 **say**] see *F1*
199 **seek**] see *F1*
208 **unworthy**] vnworthy to haue *F1*
219 s.d. **Exeunt . . . Leonato.**] *Capell (after F1 Exeunt.)*
220 s.d. **Coming forward.**] *Theobald (subs.)*

III.i

III.i] *Rowe*; Actus Tertius. *F1*
Location: *Theobald*
o.s.d. **Ursley**] Vrsula *F1*
12 **propose**] purpose *F1*
14 s.d. **Exit.**] *F2*
23 s.d. **behind**] *Steevens; s.d. placed as in Cambridge; after l. 25, Q; after l. 23, F1*
33 s.d. **They . . . bower.**] *Steevens*
38 **new-trothed**] *hyphen, Theobald*
58 **she'll**] she *F1*
60 **featur'd**] *F1*; featured *Q*
61 **fair-fac'd**] *F1 (hyphen, F4)*; faire faced *Q*
63 **antic**] *F1 (anticke)*; antique *Q*
96 **bearing**] *F4*; bearing *Q, F1*
104, 105 s.dd. **Aside.**] *Capell*
104 **limed**] tane *F1*
106 s.d. **Exeunt . . . Ursula.**] *Capell (after Rowe)*; Exit. *F1*
107 s.d. **Coming forward.**] *Theobald (subs.)*
111 **on**] *Q (c), F1*; one *Q (u)*

III.ii

III.ii] *Pope*
Location: *Theobald*
1 s.p. **D. Pedro.**] *Rowe (subs.)*; Prince *Q, (or Prin.) F1 (throughout scene)*
28 **can**] *Pope*; cannot *Q, F1*
34–7 **or . . . doublet.**] *om. F1*
39 **it**] it to *F1*
54 s.p. **D. Pedro.**] *F1 (Prin.)*; Bene. *Q*
73 s.d. **Exeunt . . . Leonato.**] *Theobald*
79 s.d. **Don**] *Rowe*
80 s.p. **D. John.**] *Rowe (subs.)*; Bastard *Q, F1 (or Bast. throughout scene)*
88 s.d. **To Claudio.**] *Rowe*
97–8 **brother, I . . . heart**] *Rowe*; brother (I . . . heart) *Q, F1*
114 **her then,**] *Hanmer*; her, then *Q, F1*
124 **her,**] *Alexander (after Capell)*; her *Q, F1*
129 **midnight**] night *F1*
134 s.d. **Exeunt.**] *F2*

III.iii

III.iii] *Capell*
Location: *Pope*
37, 44, 49, 54, 67, 88 s.pp. **2. Watch.**] *Rowe*; Watch *Q, F1*
79 **statues**] *F1*; statutes *Q*
86 **fellows'**] *Hanmer*; fellowes *Q, F1*
94 s.d. **Dogberry and Verges**] *Pope*
96, 106 s.pp. **2. Watch.**] *Capell*; Watch *Q, F1*
96 s.d. **Aside.**] *Rowe*
108 **Don**] *F1*; Dun *Q*
125 s.p. **2. Watch.**] *Wilson*; Watch *Q, F1*
125 s.d. **Aside.**] *Capell*
127 **gentleman**] *F2*; gentle man *Q, F1*
164, 169 s.pp. **2. Watch.**] *Wilson*; Watch 1 *Q, F1*
166 s.p. **1. Watch.**] *Wilson*; Watch 2 *Q, F1*
175 s.d. **2. Watch.**] *ed. (after Theobald 1. Watch.); speech continued to Conrade, Q, F1*
175 **you;**] *Wilson (subs.)*; you, *Q, F1*

III.iv

III.iv] Capell
Location: *Theobald*
5 s.d. **Exit.**] *Hanmer*
18 **in**] *F1*; it *Q*
32-3 **"saving . . . husband."**] *quotes, Cambridge*
48 **see**] looke *F1*
54 **Heigh-ho!**] *Dyce*; hey ho. *Q, F1*
80 **holy-thistle**] *hyphen, Rowe*
99 s.d. **Exeunt.**] *Rowe*

III.v

III.v] *Capell*
Location: *Theobald*
2 s.p. **Dog.**] *Rowe*; Const. Dog. *Q, F1 (or Con. Do., Const. Do., Constable until l. 57)*
7 s.p. **Verg.**] *Rowe*; Headb. *Q, F1 (or Head. until l. 60)*
9 **off**] *Capell conj.*; of *Q, F1*
24 **and 'twere**] *F1*; and't twere *Q*
24 **pound**] times *F1*
33 **talking;**] *Capell*; talking *Q, F1*
39 **worshipp'd;**] *Rowe*; worshipt, *Q, F1*
53 s.d. **Enter a Messenger.**] *Rowe*
56 s.d. **Exeunt . . . Messenger.**] *Capell (after Rowe)*; exit *Q, F1 (following l. 52)*
59 **examination**] examine *F1*
62 **non-come**] *hyphen, Rowe*
64 s.d. **Exeunt.**] *F1*

IV.i

IV.i] *Rowe*; Actus Quartus. *F1*
Location: *Pope*
o.s.d. **with Attendants**] *Staunton (subs.)*
4 s.p. **Friar.**] *Rowe*; Fran. *Q, F1*
20 **not . . . do!**] *om. F1*
29 s.p. **D. Pedro.**] *Rowe (subs.)*; Prince *Q (here misprinted* Princn*), F1 (throughout scene)*
53 **show'd**] *Rowe*; shewed *Q, F1*
56 **seeming!**] *Collier (after Knight)*; seeming, *Q, F1*
56 **it:**] *Theobald*; it, *Q, F1*
68 **"True"!**] *F3 (quotes, Wilson)*; True, *Q, F1*
77 **me,**] *F2*; me *Q, F1*
109 s.d. **Hero swoons.**] *Hanmer*
112 s.d. **Exeunt . . . Claudio.**] *Rowe*
120 **why,**] *Theobald*; why *Q, F1*
127 **Griev'd**] *F1*; Grieued *Q*
133 **smirched**] smeered *F1*
133 **mir'd**] *F1*; mired *Q*
136 **lov'd**] *F1*; loued *Q*
137-9 **on, . . . her,**] *Rowe (subs.*; on, *F2)*; on . . . mine: . . . her, *Q, F1*
144 **attir'd**] *Pope*; attired *Q, F1*
144-6 **Sir . . . say.**] *as verse, Pope; as prose, Q, F1*
148 **truly, not,**] *Sisson*; truly, not *Q*; truly: not *F1*
153 **lov'd**] *F1*; loued *Q*
155-8 **Hear . . . mark'd**] *as verse, Pope (after Rowe); as prose, Q, F1 (in Q these lines fall at the bottom of sig. G1, where, in order to squeeze them in, G1ᵛ, as part of the inner forme, being already printed off (the result of printing from cast-off copy), the compositor had to set them as prose, even so extending the usual number of lines per page by two; he may, indeed, have been forced to omit some of the MS text, thus leaving the passage difficult to explain satisfactorily)*
158 **lady,**] *Rowe (subs.)*; lady, *Q, F1*
158 **mark'd**] *F2*, markt, *Q*; markt. *F1*
161 **beat**] beare *F1*
180 **mercy!**] *F1 (mercy.)*; mercie, *Q*
190 **not.**] *F1 (not:)*; not, *Q*
202 **princes . . . dead,**] *Theobald*; princesse

(left for dead,) *Q*; Princesse (left for dead) *F1*
228 **moving,**] *F2*; moouing *Q, F1*
254 s.d. **with . . . Beatrice**] *Rowe (subs.)*
271 **not; . . . not:**] *F4 (subs.)*; not, . . . not, *Q, F1*
275 **swear**] sweare by it *F1*
306 **rancor**] *Rowe*; rancour? *Q, F1*
314 **Beat—**] *Theobald*; Beat? *Q, F1*
319 **compliment**] *Rowe*; complement *Q, F1*
336 s.d. **Exeunt.**] *F2*

IV.ii

IV.ii] *Capell*
Location: *Theobald*
o.s.d. **or Sexton**] *Capell (subs.)*
o.s.d. **and the Watch . . . and**] *Capell (after Rowe); s.d. in Q, F1 reads:* Enter the Constables, Borachio, and the Towne clearke in gownes.
1 s.p. **Dog.**] *Capell*; Keeper *Q, F1 (an error for Kemp, the actor who played Dogberry; see l. 9 below)*
2 s.p. **Verg.**] *Capell*; Cowley *Q, F1 (or Couley throughout scene; Cowley was the actor who played Verges)*
4 s.p. **Dog.**] *Capell*; Andrew *Q, F1 (another error for Kemp, perhaps from his role as a Merry Andrew or Fool)*
9 s.p. **Dog.**] *Capell*; Kemp *Q, F1 (or Ke., Kem. throughout rest of scene)*
17-20 **Con., Bora. Yea . . . villains!**] *om. F1*
17 s.p. **Con., Bora.**] *Capell*
51 **by**] by th' *F1*
59 s.p. **1. and 2. Watch.**] *ed.*; Watch *Q, F1*
66 s.d. **Exit.**] *Theobald*
67 s.p. **Dog.**] *Rowe*; Constable *Q, F1*
68-9 **in the hands— / Con. Off, coxcomb!**] *Warburton (reading in hand.)*; in the hands of Coxcombe. *Q, F1*
72 **them.**] *F3 (subs.)*; them, *Q*; them *F1*
73 s.p. **Con.**] *Rowe*; Couley *Q, F1*
87 s.d. **Exeunt.**] *Rowe*; exit. *Q, F1*

V.i

V.i] *Rowe*; Actus Quintus. *F1*
Location: *ed. (after Pope)*
1 s.p. **Ant.**] *Rowe*; Brother *Q, F1 (throughout scene)*
6 **comforter**] comfort *F1*; comfort els *F2*
6 **ear**] *Dyce*; eare, *Q, F1*
16 **And, sorrow**] *Johnson*; And sorrow, *Q, F1*
46 s.p. **D. Pedro.**] *Rowe (subs.)*; Prince *Q, F1 (throughout scene)*
47 **lords—**] *Capell*; Lords? *Q, F1*
87 **lov'd**] *F1*; loued *Q*
96 **anticly**] *F3 (antickly)*; antiquely *Q, F1*
97 **off**] *Theobald*; of *Q, F1*
98 **enemies— . . . durst—**] *ed.*; enemies, . . . durst, *Q*; enemies, . . . durst. *F1*
108 **No?**] *F1*; No *Q, F1*
109 s.d. **ambo**] *F1*; amb. *Q (s.d. placed as in Rowe; after l. 108, Q, F1)*
109 s.d. **Enter Benedick.**] *after l. 107, F1*
115 **lik'd**] *Q, F1 (likt)*; like *F2*
117 **brother.**] *F4 (subs.)*; brother *Q*; brother, *F1*
123 **high-proof**] *hyphen, Theobald*
126 **Dost**] *F4*; Doest *Q, F1*
132 **What,**] *F1*; What *Q*
136 **me.**] *F4 (me:)*; me, *Q, F1*
145 s.d. **Aside to Claudio.**] *Cambridge*
169 **there's**] *F1*; theirs *Q*
182 **on**] *F1*; one *Q*
193 s.d. **Exit.**] *Rowe*
200 s.d. **Dogberry . . . with**] *Hanmer*
203 **up,**] *Steevens*; vp *Q, F1*
206 s.p. **Dog.**] *Rowe*; Const. *Q, F1 (throughout scene)*
257 s.p. **Verg.**] *Rowe*; Con. 2 *Q, F1*
263 **thou**] thou thou *F1*

293 **overkindness**] *F1*; ouer kindnesse *Q*
300 **Hir'd**] *Pope*; Hyred *Q*; Hired *F1*
316 **reverent**] reuerend *F1*
327 s.d. **Enter . . . Verges.**] *Cambridge (placed as in Rowe)*; Exeunt. *F1 (after l. 328)*
331 s.d. **To the Watch.**] *Cambridge*
331-2 **Bring . . . fellow.**] *as verse, Pope; as prose, Q, F1*
332 s.d. **severally**] *Theobald*

V.ii

V.ii] *Capell*
Location: *Brooke*
o.s.d. **meeting**] *Capell*
9 **me? Why,**] *Rowe*; me, why *Q, F1*
23 s.d. **Margaret**] *F3*; Margarite *Q, F1*
26 s.d. **Sings.**] *Pope*
26-9 **The . . . deserve—**] *as verse, Capell; as prose, Q, F1*
41 **nor**] for *F1*
41 s.d. **Enter Beatrice.**] *placed as in F1; after l. 43, Q*
86 **myself.**] *Rowe (subs.)*; my selfe *Q, F1*
88 **praiseworthy**] *F4*; praise worthie *Q, F1*
104 **uncle's**] *Malone*; vncles *Q, F1*
104 s.d. **Exeunt.**] *F1*; exit. *Q*

V.iii

V.iii] *Capell*
Location: *Kittredge*
2 s.p. **A Lord.**] *Cambridge*; Lord *Q, F1*
3 s.p. s.d. **Claud. Reading . . . scroll.**] *Capell*
9-10 **Hang . . . dumb.**] *distinguished as not part of the Epitaph, Capell*
9 s.d. **Hangs . . . scroll.**] *Kittredge (after Capell)*
10 **dumb**] *F1 (dombe)*; dead *Q*
11 **Now**] *Capell*; Claudio Now *Q, F1 (repeated s.p.)*
17 **groan,**] *Capell (after Theobald)*; grone. *Q, F1*
21 **Heavily, heavily.**] Heauenly, heauenly. *F1*
22 s.p. **Claud.**] *Rowe*; Lo. *Q, F1*
23 **rite**] *Pope*; right *Q, F1*
24, 30 s.pp. **D. Pedro.**] *Rowe (subs.)*; Prince *Q, F1*
32 **speed 's**] *Thirlby conj.*; speeds *Q, F1*

V.iv

V.iv] *Capell*
Location: *Pope*
o.s.d. **Beatrice**] *Capell*
o.s.d. **Antonio**] *Rowe*
5 **will, . . . appears**] *Capell (will, Theobald)*; will . . . appeares, *Q, F1*
7 s.p. **Ant.**] *Rowe*; Old *Q, F1 (throughout scene)*
7 **sorts**] sort *F1*
33 **Here . . . Claudio.**] *om. F1*
34 s.p. **D. Pedro.**] *Rowe (subs.)*; Prince *Q, F1 (throughout scene)*
39 s.d. **Exit Antonio.**] *Theobald*
40 **Benedick**] *F1*; Bened. *Q*
50 **And**] *A F1*
51 s.d. **the ladies masked**] *Kittredge (subs., after Theobald)*
54 s.p. **Ant.**] *Theobald*; Leo. *Q, F1*
60 s.d. **Unmasking.**] *Rowe*
61 **lov'd**] *F1*; loued *Q*
73 s.d. **Unmasking.**] *Capell*
78 **cousin,**] *Rowe*; cosin *Q, F1*
88 **Fashion'd**] *Rowe*; Fashioned *Q, F1*
98 s.p. **Bene.**] *Thirlby conj.*; Leon. *Q, F1*
98 s.d. **Kissing her.**] *Theobald*
121 **play,**] *Pope*; plaie *Q, F1*
121 **music.**] *F1*; musicke, *Q*
123 **reverent**] reuerend *F1*
129 s.d. **Exeunt.**] *Rowe*; FINIS. *Q, F1*

As You Like It

THOMAS LODGE'S ROMANCE *Rosalynde or Euphues' Golden Legacy* (1590), Shakespeare's source for *As You Like It*, is one of the minor classics of Elizabethan prose. Lodge himself was a borrower. A fourteenth-century poem, *The Tale of Gamelyn*, underlies his own story, although it was Lodge who expanded and altered what had originally been an exclusively masculine tale about outlaws and revengeful brothers into a pastoral concerned chiefly with love. There is no equivalent to Shakespeare's Jaques, or to Touchstone, Audrey, or William, in *Rosalynde*, but all the other main characters are there at least in outline, some of them under the same names. The plot of *As You Like It* is also derived almost entirely from Lodge, although Shakespeare made it more obviously a family affair. His Duke Frederick and Duke Senior are brothers, which they are not in Lodge, and his Celia and Rosalind, as a result, are first cousins. Shakespeare also mitigated the violence of his source. In *Rosalynde*, three men are actually killed during the wrestling match; Aliena has to be rescued, at some cost in terms of bloodshed and death, from outlaws who intend to deliver her as an unwitting incestuous gift to her own lecherous father; and at the end this father is slain in battle. There are no deaths in *As You Like It*, no hint of incest, and the only blood spilled (Orlando's and that of Charles the wrestler and his two anonymous opponents) has a distanced, fairy-tale quality. There are no outlaws either, only banished courtiers sufficiently tender-hearted to worry about preying upon the deer in the forest, let alone upon other human beings; and the usurping duke, Celia's father, never reaches the fatal battlefield because an old religious man meets and peaceably converts him on the way.

In *Love's Labor's Lost* and *A Midsummer Night's Dream* earlier, Shakespeare had experimented with the reduction of plot entanglement, actual story line, to a minimum. *As You Like It* too is a play which stresses "Words above action, matter above words," as Ben Jonson once urged, although the effect produced is not at all like that of Jonsonian comedy. There is a flurry of events at the beginning—Oliver's various attempts to rid himself of his virtuous younger brother, the banishment of Rosalind and then of Oliver himself—but these are transparently devices for getting all the major characters away from the familiar world and into the forest of Arden, rather than incidents exploited for their own sake. Near the end, another little explosion of events precipitates four marriages and releases all the exiles from their pastoral life. In between, Shakespeare seems to go out of his way to avoid generating suspense. Celia and Oliver, Audrey and Touchstone have agreed to marry almost before we realize what is happening. Rosalind has only to abandon her disguise as Ganymede—and there is no reason on the level of plot why she should not do this as soon as she is safe in Arden—for Orlando to declare himself and Phebe to recognize that she must be content with her faithful Silvius after all.

As You Like It replaces a developing intrigue, of the kind exemplified by *Much Ado about Nothing* or *Twelfth Night*, with a structure of cunningly juxtaposed characters and attitudes which Shakespeare has elaborated until it becomes a substitute for plot. As the days go by in Arden, two or more characters meet, converse and part, to be succeeded on the stage by another group of people concerned to explore a different, but related, point of view. Without being in the least undramatic, as Jonson's early comedies often were, *As You Like It* is singulariy still at the centre in a way that focuses attention upon ideas and thematic material. Unlike the Elizabethan Jonson, Shakespeare refuses to legislate or even to take sides in the various rivalries the comedy sets up: between court and country, nature and fortune, youth and age, realism and romanticism, inherent nobility and the virtue that is acquired, the active and the contemplative life, laughter and melancholy. These polarities, the subject of ceaseless debate and meditation, tend to be identified with particular characters, but the comedy as a whole is far more interested in doing justice to the complexity of the argument than in prescribing correct choices.

No society, if it is honest with itself, can pretend that these antinomies do not exist. Equally, no society can have any true cohesion or self-respect if it does not try to accommodate them all, fairly, within its total structure. Rosalind is extraordinarily important in *As You Like It*, as central and dominating a figure in her fashion as Hamlet is in his own, very different play, because in her these warring opposites are reconciled and live at peace without for an instant losing their force or individuality. Like Jaques, Rosalind knows that human beings die and that worms eat them. Like old Corin, she is aware that even the most passionate love diminishes with time, and like Touchstone, that lovers are objectively ridiculous and their airiest flights grounded in the senses. She knows these things immediately and emotionally, not merely in the abstract, and yet they do not sour her gaiety or trivialize the essential seriousness of her commitment to Orlando. Speculative and thoughtful, she is nonetheless able to give a positive shape to her own existence and to that of several other people as well. Detached but involved, she laughs at herself as much as she does at Phebe, Silvius, or Jaques, yet manages to be gentle and generous to them and perceptive in her own affairs. Life is at best imperfect, even in Arden, but Rosalind suggests that there are ways of living it well and to some purpose, despite the pessimism of Jaques. This is why she matters so much in the play, and why the resolution of the plot, such as it is, is placed almost entirely in her hands.

As You Like It was one of four plays which the Lord Chamberlain's Men formally requested to be stayed from publication in 1600. Presumably, the confidence implied by the title was justified: the play was popular with Elizabethan audiences and the actors wanted to retain their profitable monopoly of the text. *As You Like It* is absent from Meres's list of 1598, so that 1599 seems likely as the date of its composition. By then, Shakespeare had already written at least seven comedies, most of them built upon the idea of two localities, one heightened and more remarkable than the other. Like Belmont, Navarre, the wood in *The Two Gentlemen of Verona* or *A Midsummer Night's Dream*, Arden is a place set apart from the ordinary world. It is emphatically not a paradise. Winter, cold winds and rain, the penalty incurred by the Old Testament Adam, come to it. Some of its native inhabitants are churlish and stupid. Yet the forest is essentially a good place, not because it possesses limitless wealth or supernatural power, but simply because in Arden fortune does not oppress and stifle nature. People are free here, as they are not in the nervous court of Duke Frederick, to realize their own potentialities. Worldly assets and success cease to matter. In the forest, judgments are made only in terms of what people really are. Some characters, like Orlando and Rosalind, gain from the opportunity. Others do not.

The idea that sophisticated people, suddenly made part of a rustic life of which previously they had the most distant and imperfect knowledge, may discover truths obscured or undisclosed in the court is a very old one. Pastoral is a complex and enduring form, not because it is escapist, but because it is basically tough: it is a way of testing both the self and the assumptions of ordinary, urban society. *As You Like It* is a pastoral in this sense. It begins with a disordered society, a corrupt court in which violence and broken ribs are considered entertaining and men like Le Beau have to hide their own intuitive sense of justice under a foppish mask; where Oliver, simply because he is an elder son, can treat his servants and younger brother like animals. It moves from this nightmare world into Arden, an exile which is really a liberation, where ideas and relationships can be honestly examined. Long after such a masculine impersonation is necessary, Rosalind clings to the part of Ganymede because of the freedom it allows her. In her boy's disguise, she escapes (for a time) the limitations of being a woman, Duke Senior's daughter, the conscious object of Orlando's love. She learns a great deal about herself, about Orlando, and about love itself which she could not have done within the normal conventions of society. This knowledge is, in a sense, the gift of the forest but it can only come to full fruition in the world outside. Sooner or later, Rosalind must stop playacting, must reveal herself to Orlando in her own person, and recognize the fact that Hymen, the god of marriage, presides not over the fields and woods but over the town (V,iv.141–46).

There is some truth in Jaques' accusation that Duke Senior and his companions in exile are as much usurpers in a world whose natural balance they have disturbed as Duke Frederick himself. Arden is not a place where people who are not really farmers or goat-herds can live permanently, however useful it may be as a temporary refuge. At the end, most of the characters return joyously to an urban world which, thanks to what they have learned during their banishment, they will transform. The pattern here is one that is standard in pastoral literature, and one of the sources of its enduring fascination. Shakespeare must have known Spenser's particularly haunting version of it in Book VI of *The Faerie Queene*. He returned to it himself in *Cymbeline*, *The Winter's Tale*, and *The Tempest*. *As You Like It*, however, stands out among the other plays of Shakespeare which might be described, at least in part, as pastorals by its essential optimism and by its insistence upon the tolerance and inclusiveness of the new society epitomized in the final dance.

It is true that there are some ungainly participants in this concluding ritual. The elephantine caperings of Audrey are no more "seemly" than they ever were. More important, the relativism, the sceptical attitude of Touchstone remains unchanged. Like all Shakespeare's fools, Touchstone is a corruptor of words. Language itself is one of his main preoccupations, and he likes to bewilder simple souls like Corin by demonstrating the superiority of words over facts. It is entirely characteristic of Touchstone that he does not care on which side of a question he argues. In fact, he reverses himself twice in the course of the court-versus-country dispute with Corin. What matters to him is a denial of the single, objective nature of reality: the reality believed in by men like Corin who earn what they eat, get what they wear, owe no man hate, envy no man's happiness, and never question either the values implied by these attitudes or the words used to express them. Corin is finally silenced by Touchstone's "courtly" wit. He is not, however, exactly defeated. He and the fool simply represent antithetical ways of looking at the world. Neither perspective is advanced as a model. Corin's simplicity is obviously limited, but then so is the willful complication of Touchstone's verbal kingdom.

Shakespeare's fools are usually solitaries, men who can comment on society in the way they do partly because they themselves are set apart, free of domestic entanglement or even of a personal past. Touchstone is unusual in that he does not merely talk about getting married: he actually does it, pressing in among the other "country copulatives" at the end to accept the social bond of matrimony. The bride of this man for whom words are all-important is a girl unable to comprehend or make effective use of even the simplest verbal constructs. In the first scene in which she appears, Audrey manages to misunderstand the words *poetical*, *features*, *honest*, and *foul* in rapid succession. Her mistakings are comic, but her relationship to Touchstone gives them a special significance. Audrey cannot find meanings for words; Touchstone can find too many. Both, however, are "sure together, / As the winter to foul weather" (V.iv.135–36) because when it comes to the point of choice, of action, they fall back upon appetite, non-verbal sense experience of the kind that man shares with the brute creation. Both characters make us laugh, Audrey unwittingly, Touchstone because it is his profession, but there is in both cases a fundamental misadjustment between language and fact. Certainly Touchstone does not represent a point of view to be trusted in this play, as Feste or Lear's fool do in theirs. Although the scepticism of Touchstone does distinguish gold from dross in a whole series of different encounters—with Le Beau, with Jaques, with Corin, Rosalind, and Orlando—the agent is in no sense to be confused either in nature or quality with what it is there to verify or expose. The touchstone identifies the gold: it is not in itself a precious substance. The man totally without illusions is ultimately as much a fool as his

romantic opposite, Silvius. Even the most skillful use of words, the most intelligent awareness of the multiple nature of reality, if it is without commitment or generosity, leads in the end to a rigid and reductive kind of behavior, imprisoning man within the skin of the animal.

There are two important absentees from the final dance, as well as two erratic performers. Orlando's faithful servant Adam is simply too old to help initiate the new social order. Silently, he has vanished from the play. As for Jaques, although he is present in the final scene, he is adamant in his refusal to join the dance. It is one of the few absolutely just and perceptive decisions he announces in the course of the comedy. A man unbalanced in his pessimism, delighting in his own melancholy and unsociability, Jaques has hitherto dealt in judgments that were somehow incomplete or askew. Oliver confounded men with beasts but Jaques, in his reported soliloquy on the herd-abandoned deer, makes the opposite mistake of interpreting animal behavior as though it were human. Throughout Act II he clings perversely to prose and discordant sounds while all around him the play is lifting into verse and song. As the comedy progresses, he continues to fare badly. Only Jaques fails to recognize that, in their encounter in the forest, Touchstone has cleverly parodied his own style:

> And then he drew a dial from his poke,
> And looking on it, with lack-lustre eye,
> Says very wisely, "It is ten a' clock.
> Thus we may see," quoth he, "how the world wags.
> 'Tis but an hour ago since it was nine,
> And after one hour more 'twill be elevèn,
> And so from hour to hour, we ripe and ripe,
> And then from hour to hour, we rot and rot;
> And thereby hangs a tale." (II.vii.20–28)

These melancholy certainties which Jaques so admires are platitudes of the most obvious kind. Even without the Duke's barbed reminder that Jaques' own libertine past scarcely qualifies him to scourge vice in others, it would be hard to see what value a satirist could have who relied upon moralizings so dusty.

Jaques' famous account of the seven ages of man, for all its verbal poise and inventiveness, is also a set piece which, for Elizabethans, must have verged on the banal. Moreover, it is generalized and demonstrably untrue. Orlando, as Touchstone is quick to point out, may be absurd when he hangs love sonnets on trees. There is still far more value in his relationship with Rosalind than Jaques accounts for in his dismissal of man as lover. Again, Jaques reduces old age to "second childishness and mere oblivion, / Sans teeth, sans eyes, sans taste, sans every thing" (II.vii.165–66). The words are no sooner spoken than Orlando enters bearing old Adam: a man enfeebled by his years, dependent now upon a younger life, but also the living image of all that Jaques has left out of his type picture: loyal, honest, and discriminating. His age has its own kind of value, "frosty but kindly," and the tenderness of Orlando, as well as the respect paid Adam by Duke Senior, ridicules Jaques' despair. With Orlando and Rosalind, Jaques makes even less headway. Orlando flatly declines the satirist's invitation to join him in a verbal assault upon the world "and all our misery": "I will chide no breather in the world but myself, against whom I know most faults" (III.ii.278–81). Rosalind, even more crushingly, points out that Jaques' ideal of silent unresponsiveness is one realized by the average fence-post (IV.i.8–9).

Throughout *As You Like It* Jaques has functioned less as the representative of a valid point of view than as a measure of the essential sanity and balance of those characters who stand closer than he to the centre of the play. He too is a kind of touchstone, testing the strength of that optimism and faith in the future characteristic of Rosalind, Orlando, Celia, and Duke Senior with his continual reminders of mortality and decay. None of them attempt to deny the facts of death and time, but all reject the hopelessness of Jaques: the notion that life is without purpose or meaning because it finishes in the grave. The new society forged in Arden is not flawless. Nevertheless, the final dance is a triumph, an image of harmony, and its movements, disciplined and artful though they are, are flexible enough to accommodate the awkwardness of the goat-girl and the fool. Jaques is respectful of what has been achieved, yet he insists at the end that there is a world elsewhere, beyond the scope of comedy. This is why he casts in his lot with the penitent Duke Frederick, a man who is still asking questions, as opposed to celebrating a resolution. Jaques' response here is, for once, justifiable. He is right to remind us that the comic dance, for all its generosity, its vigor and grace, cannot hope to contain all aspects of human experience.

"The truest poetry is the most feigning." This is what Touchstone tells an uncomprehending Audrey (III.iii.19–20). On her, as might be expected, the paradox is lost. What the fool is playfully gesturing towards is the orthodox Aristotelianism of Sidney's *Apology for Poetry* (1580). The most quintessential, and most truthful, poetry is that which is most clearly imaginary, which mirrors an ideal world of absolutes rather than an untidy world of fact. This, of course, is the argument by which Aristotle originally tried to vindicate poets and painters against Plato's dismissal of them as liars: mere copyists at secondhand of a world of sense which is itself nothing but an inferior imitation. Characteristically, Touchstone no sooner summons up Sidney's position than he proceeds to undercut and confuse it. Lovers are given to addressing their ladies in verse. What is the objective value of the promises they make in this form? By the time Touchstone has finished ringing the changes on that ambiguous word *feigning*, a wiser head than Audrey's might well be perplexed. Poetry is left in an uncertain position, partly redeemed from Plato's

charge—picked up by Elizabethan Puritans—that it was an art of lies, partly called into question.

Touchstone's juggling with the counters of truth and falsehood, in their relation to reality and the imagination, is immensely relevant to *As You Like It* as a whole. This is a comedy which emphasizes its own dependence upon artifice and convention, upon openly literary modes. It goes far beyond Lodge in this respect. At a number of points, the psychology is unequivocally that of fairy-tale. Oliver, like any wicked witch, hates his brother Orlando simply because he is good and people like him. Duke Frederick banishes Rosalind for much the same nonreason. Both wicked brothers are converted in a flash, while Oliver and Celia give themselves to each other so suddenly that even Rosalind and Orlando are startled. With the exception of Rosalind, most of the characters resolve themselves when looked at closely into familiar Elizabethan types: the melancholy traveller, the fool, the scornful shepherdess and adoring swain, the romantic lover, the rustic, the good brother and the bad. Shakespeare changed the name of Lodge's Rosader to Orlando probably because he wished to remind his audience of Ariosto's hero in *Orlando Furioso* (English translation 1591): a man who runs mad in the woods for love of his lady Angelica. He reduced the character Lodge had called Adam Spencer to Adam, pure and simple, thus increasing the suggestion of primal old age: fundamental and original humanity. The informing mode of the play is pastoral, with all that the word implies of distance and fabrication. Lions and palm trees do not ordinarily exist in chilly northern forests, but then Arden cannot be located on any map. It is a place associated with the English Robin Hood ballads, but also with classical legends of the Golden World, while the folk ritual of killing the stag and enveloping the successful hunter in its skin (IV.ii) awakens echoes as old as some of the cave paintings at Lascaux.

Yet it would be a mistake to think of *As You Like It* only as a fairy-tale, a fantasy of love and game-playing in the open air. The comedy is essentially serious, concerned to examine the nature of people, emotions, and ideas. It capitalizes, as the title announces from the start, upon the familiarity and resonance possessed by certain character types and situations and moves through them to an analysis of experience which Philip Sidney would almost certainly have found insufficiently didactic: overgenerous in its attitudes and in its admission of the relativity of judgment. In *As You Like It*, however, the most feigning poetry is indeed the truest in a sense different from the one outlined in Sidney's *Apology*: out of artifice, out of convention frankly admitted as such, Shakespeare has gradually elicited a complex and subtle vision of reality.

Anne Barton

As You Like It

[DRAMATIS PERSONAE

DUKE SENIOR, *living in banishment*
DUKE FREDERICK, *his brother, and usurper of his
dominions*
AMIENS }
JAQUES } *lords attending on the banished Duke*
LE BEAU, *a courtier attending upon Duke Frederick*
CHARLES, *wrestler to Duke Frederick*
OLIVER }
JAQUES } *sons of Sir Rowland de Boys*
ORLANDO }
ADAM }
DENNIS } *servants to Oliver*

TOUCHSTONE, *a clown*
SIR OLIVER MARTEXT, *a vicar*
CORIN }
SILVIUS } *shepherds*
WILLIAM, *a country fellow, in love with Audrey*
A person representing HYMEN

ROSALIND, *daughter to the banished Duke*
CELIA, *daughter to Duke Frederick*
PHEBE, *a shepherdess*
AUDREY, *a country wench*

LORDS, PAGES, FORESTERS, *and* ATTENDANTS

SCENE: *Oliver's house; Duke Frederick's court; and the forest of Arden*]

ACT I, SCENE I

Enter ORLANDO and ADAM.

Orl. As I remember, Adam, it was upon this
fashion bequeath'd me by will but poor a thousand
crowns, and, as thou say'st, charg'd my brother,
on his blessing, to breed me well; and there begins
my sadness. My brother Jaques he keeps at 5
school, and report speaks goldenly of his profit.
For my part, he keeps me rustically at home, or (to
speak more properly) stays me here at home unkept; for call you that keeping for a gentleman of
my birth, that differs not from the stalling of an 10
ox? His horses are bred better, for besides that
they are fair with their feeding, they are taught
their manage, and to that end riders dearly hir'd;
but I (his brother) gain nothing under him but growth,
for the which his animals on his dunghills are 15
as much bound to him as I. Besides this nothing

that he so plentifully gives me, the something that
nature gave me his countenance seems to take from
me. He lets me feed with his hinds, bars me the
place of a brother, and as much as in him lies, 20
mines my gentility with my education. This is it,
Adam, that grieves me, and the spirit of my father,
which I think is within me, begins to mutiny against
this servitude. I will no longer endure it, though
yet I know no wise remedy how to avoid it. 25

Enter OLIVER.

Adam. Yonder comes my master, your brother.
Orl. Go apart, Adam, and thou shalt hear how
he will shake me up.
Oli. Now, sir, what make you here? 29
Orl. Nothing. I am not taught to make any thing.
Oli. What mar you then, sir?
Orl. Marry, sir, I am helping you to mar that
which God made, a poor unworthy brother of yours,
with idleness. 34
Oli. Marry, sir, be better employ'd, and be naught
a while.
Orl. Shall I keep your hogs and eat husks with

I.i. Location. The garden of Oliver's house.
2, 3. **bequeath'd, charg'd.** The understood subject is *he*, i.e. Orlando's
father. 2. **poor a:** a poor.
4. **on his blessing:** i.e. on pain of losing his blessing. **breed me:**
bring me up. 5–6. **keeps at school:** maintains at the university.
6. **goldenly:** in glowing terms. **profit:** progress.
7. **rustically:** like a peasant; cut off from civilized society.
8. **stays:** detains. 8–9. **unkept:** without proper maintenance.
12. **fair:** in fine physical condition.
13. **manage:** manege, paces and movements of a trained horse.
dearly: at great expense. 16. **bound:** indebted.

18. **countenance:** behavior, or (ironically) favor, patronage.
19. **hinds:** farm laborers. **bars me:** excludes me from.
21. **mines:** undermines. **with my education:** by the way I am
brought up. 28. **shake me up:** berate me (cf. *blow me up*).
29. **make you:** are you doing (but Orlando quibbles on the more
usual sense of *make*).
31. **mar.** Commonly used in antithesis to *make*, as in *Othello*, I.v.4:
"It makes us, or it mars us."
32. **Marry:** why, indeed (originally the name of the Virgin Mary
used as an oath).
35. **be naught:** a mild curse, equivalent to "Go to the devil."

them? What prodigal portion have I spent, that I should come to such penury?

Oli. Know you where you are, sir? 40

Orl. O, sir, very well; here in your orchard.

Oli. Know you before whom, sir?

Orl. Ay, better than him I am before knows me. I know you are my eldest brother, and in the gentle condition of blood you should so know me. 45 The courtesy of nations allows you my better, in that you are the first born, but the same tradition takes not away my blood, were there twenty brothers betwixt us. I have as much of my father in me as you, albeit I confess your coming before me is nearer to his reverence. 51

Oli. What, boy! [*Strikes him.*]

Orl. Come, come, elder brother, you are too young in this. [*Collaring him.*]

Oli. Wilt thou lay hands on me, villain? 55

Orl. I am no villain; I am the youngest son of Sir Rowland de Boys. He was my father, and he is thrice a villain that says such a father begot villains. Wert thou not my brother, I would not take this hand from thy throat till this other had pull'd out thy tongue for saying so. Thou hast rail'd on thyself. 62

Adam. Sweet masters, be patient, for your father's remembrance, be at accord.

Oli. Let me go, I say. 65

Orl. I will not till I please. You shall hear me. My father charg'd you in his will to give me good education. You have train'd me like a peasant, obscuring and hiding from me all gentleman-like qualities. The spirit of my father grows strong 70 in me, and I will no longer endure it; therefore allow me such exercises as may become a gentleman, or give me the poor allottery my father left me 73 by testament, with that I will go buy my fortunes.

Oli. And what wilt thou do? beg, when that is spent? Well, sir, get you in. I will not long be troubled with you; you shall have some part of your will. I pray you leave me.

Orl. I will no further offend you than becomes me for my good. 80

Oli. Get you with him, you old dog.

Adam. Is "old dog" my reward? Most true, I have lost my teeth in your service. God be with my old master, he would not have spoke such a word. 84

Exeunt Orlando, Adam.

Oli. Is it even so? Begin you to grow upon me?

I will physic your rankness, and yet give no thousand crowns neither. Holla, Dennis!

Enter DENNIS.

Den. Calls your worship?

Oli. Was not Charles, the Duke's wrastler, here to speak with me? 90

Den. So please you, he is here at the door, and importunes access to you.

Oli. Call him in. [*Exit Dennis.*] 'Twill be a good way; and to-morrow the wrastling is.

Enter CHARLES.

Cha. Good morrow to your worship. 95

Oli. Good Monsieur Charles, what's the new news at the new court?

Cha. There's no news at the court, sir, but the old news: that is, the old Duke is banish'd by his younger brother the new Duke, and three or 100 four loving lords have put themselves into voluntary exile with him, whose lands and revenues enrich the new Duke; therefore he gives them good leave to wander.

Oli. Can you tell if Rosalind, the Duke's daughter, be banish'd with her father? 106

Cha. O no; for the Duke's daughter, her cousin, so loves her, being ever from their cradles bred together, that [she] would have follow'd her exile, or have died to stay behind her. She is at the court, 110 and no less belov'd of her uncle than his own daughter, and never two ladies lov'd as they do.

Oli. Where will the old Duke live?

Cha. They say he is already in the forest of Arden, and a many merry men with him; and there 115 they live like the old Robin Hood of England. They say many young gentlemen flock to him every day, and fleet the time carelessly, as they did in the golden world.

Oli. What, you wrastle to-morrow before the new Duke? 121

Cha. Marry, do I, sir; and I came to acquaint you with a matter. I am given, sir, secretly to understand that your younger brother, Orlando, 124 hath a disposition to come in disguis'd against me to try a fall. To-morrow, sir, I wrastle for my credit, and he that escapes me without some broken limb shall acquit him well. Your brother is but young and tender, and for your love I would 129 be loath to foil him, as I must for my own honor if he come in; therefore out of my love to you, I came hither to acquaint you withal, that either

---

37–39. **Shall . . . penury.** An allusion to the parable of the prodigal son (Luke 15:11–32), who, having wasted his portion of his father's possessions, was forced to become a swineherd and envied the hogs their husks.
40. **where:** i.e. in whose presence (but Orlando again quibbles).
41. **orchard:** garden.
44–45. **gentle . . . blood:** feeling proper to gentle birth.
46. **courtesy of nations:** generally accepted convention; here, the custom of primogeniture. **allows:** acknowledges.
50–51. **your . . . reverence:** i.e. your being my senior gives you a better claim to the respect which was due him.
54. **young in this:** i.e. inexperienced in fighting.
56. **villain:** person of low birth (not the sense Oliver intended).
63. **be patient:** control yourselves. 70. **qualities:** accomplishments.
72. **exercises:** occupations, training. 73. **allottery:** portion.
78. **your will:** what you want.
85. **grow upon me:** i.e. get so big that you crowd me.

86. **physic your rankness:** administer a dose that will cure your overgrowth. 89. **wrastler:** wrestler. 95. **morrow:** morning.
104. **leave:** permission. 110. **to stay:** at being forced to stay.
114. **forest of Arden.** The setting of much of the action of Lodge's *Rosalynde*, where it signifies the forest of Ardennes in present-day Belgium, Luxembourg, and France; but Shakespeare (and his audience) would doubtless have in mind as well the forest of Arden in Warwickshire. 118. **fleet:** pass. **carelessly:** free from care.
118–19. **the golden world:** the Golden Age, i.e. the primal age of innocence and ease. 126. **fall:** bout.
127. **credit:** professional reputation. 128. **shall:** must.
130. **foil:** defeat. 132. **withal:** therewith.

you might stay him from his intendment, or brook such disgrace well as he shall run into, in that it is a thing of his own search, and altogether against my will.   134

Oli. Charles, I thank thee for thy love to me, which thou shalt find I will most kindly requite. I had myself notice of my brother's purpose herein, and have by underhand means labor'd to dissuade him from it; but he is resolute. I'll tell thee, Charles, it is the stubbornest young fellow of France, full of ambition, an envious emulator of every man's good parts, a secret and villainous contriver against me his natural brother; therefore use thy discretion—I had as lief thou didst break his neck as his finger. And thou wert best look to't; for if thou dost him any slight disgrace, or if he do not mightily grace himself on thee, he will practice against thee by poison, entrap thee by some treacherous device, and never leave thee till he hath ta'en thy life by some indirect means or other; for I assure thee (and almost with tears I speak it) there is not one so young and so villainous this day living. I speak but brotherly of him, but should I anatomize him to thee as he is, I must blush and weep, and thou must look pale and wonder.   139–159

Cha. I am heartily glad I came hither to you. If he come to-morrow, I'll give him his payment. If ever he go alone again, I'll never wrastle for prize more. And so God keep your worship!   *Exit.*   160

[*Oli.*] Farewell, good Charles. Now will I stir this gamester. I hope I shall see an end of him; for my soul (yet I know not why) hates nothing more than he. Yet he's gentle, never school'd and yet learned, full of noble device, of all sorts enchantingly belov'd, and indeed so much in the heart of the world, and especially of my own people, who best know him, that I am altogether mispris'd. But it shall not be so long, this wrastler shall clear all. Nothing remains but that I kindle the boy thither, which now I'll go about.   *Exit.*   164

SCENE II

Enter ROSALIND *and* CELIA.

Cel. I pray thee, Rosalind, sweet my coz, be merry.

Ros. Dear Celia—I show more mirth than I am mistress of, and would you yet [I] were merrier? Unless you could teach me to forget a banish'd father, you must not learn me how to remember any extraordinary pleasure.   5

Cel. Herein I see thou lov'st me not with the full weight that I love thee. If my uncle, thy banish'd father, had banish'd thy uncle, the Duke my father, so thou hadst been still with me, I could have taught my love to take thy father for mine; so wouldst thou, if the truth of thy love to me were so righteously temper'd as mine is to thee.   10–14

Ros. Well, I will forget the condition of my estate, to rejoice in yours.

Cel. You know my father hath no child but I, nor none is like to have; and truly when he dies, thou shalt be his heir; for what he hath taken away from thy father perforce, I will render thee again in affection. By mine honor, I will, and when I break that oath, let me turn monster. Therefore, my sweet Rose, my dear Rose, be merry.   19

Ros. From henceforth I will, coz, and devise sports. Let me see—what think you of falling in love?

Cel. Marry, I prithee do, to make sport withal. But love no man in good earnest, nor no further in sport neither, than with safety of a pure blush thou mayst in honor come off again.   27

Ros. What shall be our sport then?

Cel. Let us sit and mock the good huswife Fortune from her wheel, that her gifts may henceforth be bestow'd equally.   31

Ros. I would we could do so; for her benefits are mightily misplac'd, and the bountiful blind woman doth most mistake in her gifts to women.   36

Cel. 'Tis true, for those that she makes fair she scarce makes honest, and those that she makes honest she makes very ill-favoredly.

Ros. Nay, now thou goest from Fortune's office to Nature's. Fortune reigns in gifts of the world, not in the lineaments of Nature.   42

Enter Clown [TOUCHSTONE].

Cel. No; when Nature hath made a fair creature, may she not by Fortune fall into the fire? Though Nature hath given us wit to flout at Fortune, hath not Fortune sent in this fool to cut off the argument?   45

Ros. Indeed there is Fortune too hard for Nature,

133. **brook:** endure.
135. **search:** seeking.   140. **underhand:** indirect.
143. **emulator:** rival.   144. **parts:** qualities.
145. **contriver:** schemer.   **natural:** own.   146. **lief:** willingly.
147. **thou . . . look:** you had better give serious attention.
149. **grace . . . thee:** gain honor at your expense.
150. **practice:** plot, act treacherously.
155. **brotherly:** i.e. with brotherly reticence about his vices.
156. **anatomize:** dissect, lay open.
161. **go alone:** walk without help.
164. **stir:** stir up (to compete in the wrestling).   **gamester:** sportive fellow.   166. **gentle:** of gentlemanly character.
167. **device:** devising, purposes.   **of all sorts:** by people of every rank.   168. **enchantingly:** as if by enchantment.
171. **mispris'd:** despised.   172. **clear:** settle.   **kindle:** incite.
173. **thither:** i.e. to court, for the wrestling.

I.ii. Location: Lawn before the Duke's palace.
1. **sweet my coz:** my dear cousin.

3–4. **am mistress of:** have at my command, i.e. actually feel.
6. **learn:** instruct.   11. **so:** provided that.
14. **righteously temper'd:** rightly compounded.
15. **estate:** state, circumstances.   20. **perforce:** by force.
25. **sports:** amusements.   28. **safety:** safeguard.   **pure:** innocent.
29. **come off:** escape.
31. **huswife:** housewife, manager of household affairs. The conventional image of Fortune with her wheel is playfully altered (by the adjective *good*) to a domestic picture of an industrious matron at her spinning wheel. Cf. *the false huswife Fortune* in *Antony and Cleopatra*, IV.xv.44, where *huswife* = hussy.
38. **honest:** chaste.   39. **ill-favoredly:** ugly.   40. **office:** function.
41. **gifts . . . world:** i.e. wealth, power, and the like, as contrasted with beauty and intelligence, the gifts of Nature. This distinction was an Elizabethan commonplace.
42 s.d. **Touchstone.** The audience does not learn the Clown's name until II.iv.19.   45. **flout:** mock, jeer.
47. **argument:** discussion, witty exchange.

when Fortune makes Nature's natural the cutter-off
of Nature's wit.   50

Cel. Peradventure this is not Fortune's work
neither, but Nature's, who perceiveth our natural
wits too dull to reason of such goddesses, [and] hath
sent this natural for our whetstone; for always the
dullness of the fool is the whetstone of the wits.   55
How now, wit, whither wander you?

Touch. Mistress, you must come away to your
father.

Cel. Were you made the messenger?

Touch. No, by mine honor, but I was bid to
come for you.   61

Ros. Where learn'd you that oath, fool?

Touch. Of a certain knight, that swore by his
honor they were good pancakes, and swore by his
honor the mustard was naught. Now I'll stand to it,
the pancakes were naught, and the mustard was good,
and yet was not the knight forsworn.   67

Cel. How prove you that, in the great heap of
your knowledge?

Ros. Ay, marry, now unmuzzle your wisdom.

Touch. Stand you both forth now. Stroke your
chins, and swear by your beards that I am a   72
knave.

Cel. By our beards (if we had them) thou art.

Touch. By my knavery (if I had it) then I were.
But if you swear by that that is not, you are not   76
forsworn. No more was this knight, swearing by
his honor, for he never had any; or if he had, he
had sworn it away before ever he saw those pancakes
or that mustard.   80

Cel. Prithee, who is't that thou mean'st?

Touch. One that old Frederick, your father, loves.

[*Cel.*] My father's love is enough to honor him
enough. Speak no more of him, you'll be whipt for
taxation one of these days.   85

Touch. The more pity that fools may not speak
wisely what wise men do foolishly.

Cel. By my troth, thou sayest true; for since the
little wit that fools have was silenc'd, the little   89
foolery that wise men have makes a great show.
Here comes Monsieur [Le] Beau.

Enter Le Beau.

Ros. With his mouth full of news.

Cel. Which he will put on us, as pigeons feed
their young.

Ros. Then shall we be news-cramm'd.   95

Cel. All the better; we shall be the more marketable. *Bon jour*, Monsieur Le Beau. What's the
news?

Le Beau. Fair princess, you have lost much good
sport.   100

Cel. Sport! of what color?

Le Beau. What color, madam? How shall I answer you?

Ros. As wit and fortune will.

Touch. Or as the Destinies decrees.   105

Cel. Well said—that was laid on with a trowel.

Touch. Nay, if I keep not my rank—

Ros. Thou losest thy old smell.

Le Beau. You amaze me, ladies. I would have
told you of good wrastling, which you have lost
the sight of.   111

Ros. Yet tell us the manner of the wrastling.

Le Beau. I will tell you the beginning; and if it
please your ladyships, you may see the end, for   114
the best is yet to do, and here where you are, they
are coming to perform it.

Cel. Well, the beginning, that is dead and buried.

Le Beau. There comes an old man and his three
sons—

Cel. I could match this beginning with an old tale.

Le Beau. Three proper young men, of excellent
growth and presence.   122

Ros. With bills on their necks, "Be it known unto
all men by these presents."

Le Beau. The eldest of the three wrastled with
Charles, the Duke's wrastler, which Charles in a
moment threw him, and broke three of his ribs,   127
that there is little hope of life in him. So he serv'd
the second, and so the third. Yonder they lie, the
poor old man, their father, making such pitiful dole
over them that all the beholders take his part with
weeping.   132

Ros. Alas!

Touch. But what is the sport, monsieur, that the
ladies have lost?   135

Le Beau. Why, this that I speak of.

Touch. Thus men may grow wiser every day.
It is the first time that ever I heard breaking of ribs
was sport for ladies.

Cel. Or I, I promise thee.   140

Ros. But is there any else longs to see this broken
music in his sides? Is there yet another dotes upon
rib-breaking? Shall we see this wrastling, cousin?

Le Beau. You must if you stay here, for here is
the place appointed for the wrastling, and they are
ready to perform it.   146

Cel. Yonder sure they are coming. Let us now
stay and see it.

Flourish. Enter Duke [Frederick], Lords, Orlando,
Charles, *and* Attendants.

---

49. **natural:** idiot, simpleton.
56. **wit . . . you.** Celia turns to her purpose an expression ordinarily
addressed to one who was talking too much or not to the point,
or giving other such evidence that his wits were deserting him. For
another example see IV.i.166, "Wit, whither wilt?" (i.e. whither wilt
thou go?).   65. **naught:** bad.   67. **forsworn:** perjured.
85. **taxation:** censure, slander.   88. **troth:** faith.
93. **put:** force.
96–97. **more marketable.** As a fowl fattened by forced feeding
would be.

101. **color:** sort.
106. **with a trowel.** Deliberately ambiguous: (1) with telling force;
(2) unsubtly. Touchstone blandly ignores the second possibility.
107. **rank:** i.e. status as a witty jester. Rosalind puns on the sense
"bad-smelling."   109. **amaze:** bewilder.   115. **to do:** to be done.
120. **I . . . tale:** i.e. that isn't a very original beginning. The motif
of the father with three sons is common in folktales.
121. **proper:** handsome.   123. **bills:** placards.
124. **these presents:** this present document (with obvious pun on
presence).   128. **that:** so that.   130. **dole:** lamentation.
141–42. **broken music:** i.e. noisy breaking of ribs. Rosalind twists to
her own purposes a term used of music arranged for instruments of
more than one kind.
148 s.d. **Flourish:** trumpet fanfare (announcing an important personage).

Duke F. Come on. Since the youth will not be entreated, his own peril on his forwardness. 150

Ros. Is yonder the man?

Le Beau. Even he, madam.

Cel. Alas, he is too young! yet he looks successfully.

Duke F. How now, daughter and cousin? are you crept hither to see the wrestling? 156

Ros. Ay, my liege, so please you give us leave.

Duke F. You will take little delight in it, I can tell you, there is such odds in the man. In pity of the challenger's youth I would fain dissuade 160 him, but he will not be entreated. Speak to him, ladies, see if you can move him.

Cel. Call him hither, good Monsieur Le Beau.

Duke F. Do so; I'll not be by.

Le Beau. Monsieur the challenger, the princess calls for you. 166

Orl. I attend them with all respect and duty.

Ros. Young man, have you challeng'd Charles the wrestler?

Orl. No, fair princess; he is the general challenger. I come but in, as others do, to try with him the strength of my youth. 172

Cel. Young gentleman, your spirits are too bold for your years. You have seen cruel proof of this man's strength. If you saw yourself with your eyes, or knew yourself with your judgment, the 176 fear of your adventure would counsel you to a more equal enterprise. We pray you for your own sake to embrace your own safety, and give over this attempt.

Ros. Do, young sir, your reputation shall 180 not therefore be mispris'd. We will make it our suit to the Duke that the wrestling might not go forward.

Orl. I beseech you, punish me not with your hard thoughts, wherein I confess me much guilty to deny so fair and excellent ladies any thing. But let your fair eyes and gentle wishes go with me to my 186 trial; wherein if I be foil'd, there is but one sham'd that was never gracious; if kill'd, but one dead that is willing to be so. I shall do my friends no wrong, for I have none to lament me; the world no injury, for in it I have nothing. Only in the world I fill up a place, which may be better supplied when I have made it empty. 193

Ros. The little strength that I have, I would it were with you.

Cel. And mine, to eke out hers.

Ros. Fare you well; pray heaven I be deceiv'd in you! 198

Cel. Your heart's desires be with you!

Cha. Come, where is this young gallant that is so desirous to lie with his mother earth? 201

Orl. Ready, sir, but his will hath in it a more modest working.

Duke F. You shall try but one fall.

Cha. No, I warrant your Grace, you shall not entreat him to a second, that have so mightily persuaded him from a first. 207

Orl. You mean to mock me after; you should not have mock'd me before. But come your ways.

Ros. Now Hercules be thy speed, young man!

Cel. I would I were invisible, to catch the strong fellow by the leg.   *Wrastle.* 212

Ros. O excellent young man!

Cel. If I had a thunderbolt in mine eye, I can tell who should down.   [*Charles is thrown.*] *Shout.*

Duke F. No more, no more. 216

Orl. Yes, I beseech your Grace, I am not yet well breath'd.

Duke F. How dost thou, Charles?

Le Beau. He cannot speak, my lord. 220

Duke F. Bear him away. What is thy name, young man?

Orl. Orlando, my liege, the youngest son of Sir Rowland de Boys.

Duke F. I would thou hadst been son to some man else:

The world esteem'd thy father honorable, 225
But I did find him still mine enemy.
Thou shouldst have better pleas'd me with this deed
Hadst thou descended from another house.
But fare thee well, thou art a gallant youth.
I would thou hadst told me of another father. 230

Exit Duke [*with Train and Le Beau*].

Cel. Were I my father, coz, would I do this?

Orl. I am more proud to be Sir Rowland's son,
His youngest son, and would not change that calling
To be adopted heir to Frederick.

Ros. My father lov'd Sir Rowland as his soul, 235
And all the world was of my father's mind.
Had I before known this young man his son,
I should have given him tears unto entreaties,
Ere he should thus have ventur'd.

Cel.   Gentle cousin,
Let us go thank him, and encourage him. 240
My father's rough and envious disposition
Sticks me at heart. Sir, you have well deserv'd.
If you do keep your promises in love
But justly as you have exceeded all promise,
Your mistress shall be happy.

Ros.   Gentleman, 245
[*Giving him a chain from her neck.*]

150. **entreated:** persuaded (to desist).   **his own ... forwardness:** i.e. let him assume the risk for his own rashness.
151. **yonder.** A demonstrative pronoun, not an adverb.
153–54. **successfully:** like a winner.   157. **liege:** sovereign.
159. **odds:** disparity, i.e. superiority.   **the man:** i.e. Charles.
160. **fain:** gladly.
175–76. **If ... judgment:** i.e. if you used your powers of observation and your judgment on yourself.
177. **fear:** danger.   **your adventure:** your venture, the risk you are taking.   178. **equal:** commensurate with your powers.
181. **therefore:** on that account.   **mispris'd:** despised.
183–84. **punish ... thoughts:** don't think ill of me if I refuse to withdraw.   184. **wherein:** with reference to which.
188. **gracious:** in favor, esteemed.   196. **eke out:** supplement.
197–98. **deceiv'd in you:** i.e. mistaken about your chances.

203. **modest working:** decorous operation (Orlando is playing on the sexual implications of line 201).
209. **come your ways:** come along and begin.
210. **be thy speed:** aid you, give you success.
218. **well breath'd:** i.e. warmed up.   226. **still:** ever, always.
231. **do this:** behave thus.   233. **calling:** name.
238. **unto:** in addition to.   241. **envious:** malicious.
242. **Sticks:** stabs.
244. **But justly as:** to the same degree in which.   **promise:** expectation (of success in the wrestling match).

As You Like It
I.ii

Wear this for me: one out of suits with Fortune,
That could give more, but that her hand lacks means.
Shall we go, coz?

Cel.   Ay. Fare you well, fair gentleman.

Orl. Can I not say, I thank you? My better
          parts
Are all thrown down, and that which here stands up
Is but a quintain, a mere liveless block.   251

Ros. He calls us back. My pride fell with my
          fortunes,
I'll ask him what he would. Did you call, sir?
Sir, you have wrastled well, and overthrown
More than your enemies.

Cel.   Will you go, coz?   255

Ros. Have with you.—Fare you well.

                         Exit [*with Celia*].

Orl. What passion hangs these weights upon my
          tongue?
I cannot speak to her, yet she urg'd conference.

Enter Le Beau.

O poor Orlando! thou art overthrown,
Or Charles, or something weaker, masters thee.   260

Le Beau. Good sir, I do in friendship counsel you
To leave this place. Albeit you have deserv'd
High commendation, true applause, and love,
Yet such is now the Duke's condition
That he misconsters all that you have done.   265
The Duke is humorous—what he is indeed
More suits you to conceive than I to speak of.

Orl. I thank you, sir; and pray you tell me this:
Which of the two was daughter of the Duke,
That here was at the wrastling?   270

Le Beau. Neither his daughter, if we judge by
          manners,
But yet indeed the [smaller] is his daughter.
The other is daughter to the banish'd Duke,
And here detain'd by her usurping uncle
To keep his daughter company, whose loves   275
Are dearer than the natural bond of sisters.
But I can tell you that of late this Duke
Hath ta'en displeasure 'gainst his gentle niece,
Grounded upon no other argument
But that the people praise her for her virtues,   280
And pity her for her good father's sake;
And on my life his malice 'gainst the lady
Will suddenly break forth. Sir, fare you well.
Hereafter, in a better world than this,
I shall desire more love and knowledge of you.   285

Orl. I rest much bounden to you; fare you well.

                    [*Exit Le Beau.*]

246. one . . . Fortune: one whose petitions to Fortune are rejected (?)
or one who no longer wears the livery of Fortune, i.e. one cast out of
Fortune's favor (?).   247. could: would wish to.
251. quintain: wooden figure used as a target in tilting.   liveless:
lifeless.
256. Have with you: let us go together.
257. passion: violent emotion.
258. urg'd conference: invited conversation.
260. Or: either.   264. condition: state of mind.
265. misconsters: misconstrues.
266. humorous: temperamental, given to shifting moods or notions.
279. argument: reason, grounds.
284. in . . . world: i.e. when circumstances are more favorable.
286. bounden: indebted.

Thus must I from the smoke into the smother,
From tyrant Duke unto a tyrant brother.
But heavenly Rosalind!   *Exit.*

SCENE III

Enter Celia *and* Rosalind.

Cel. Why, cousin, why, Rosalind! Cupid have
mercy, not a word?

Ros. Not one to throw at a dog.

Cel. No, thy words are too precious to be cast
away upon curs, throw some of them at me. Come
lame me with reasons.   6

Ros. Then there were two cousins laid up, when
the one should be lam'd with reasons, and the other
mad without any.

Cel. But is all this for your father?   10

Ros. No, some of it is for my child's father. O
how full of briers is this working-day world!

Cel. They are but burs, cousin, thrown upon
thee in holiday foolery; if we walk not in the trodden paths, our very petticoats will catch them.   15

Ros. I could shake them off my coat; these
burs are in my heart.

Cel. Hem them away.

Ros. I would try, if I could cry "hem" and have
him.   20

Cel. Come, come, wrastle with thy affections.

Ros. O, they take the part of a better wrastler
than myself!

Cel. O, a good wish upon you! you will try in
time, in despite of a fall. But turning these   25
jests out of service, let us talk in good earnest. Is
it possible, on such a sudden, you should fall into so
strong a liking with old Sir Rowland's youngest son?

Ros. The Duke my father lov'd his father
dearly.   30

Cel. Doth it therefore ensue that you should
love his son dearly? By this kind of chase, I should
hate him, for my father hated his father dearly;
yet I hate not Orlando.

Ros. No, faith, hate him not, for my sake.   35

Cel. Why should I not? Doth he not deserve
well?

Enter Duke [Frederick] *with* Lords.

Ros. Let me love him for that, and do you love

287. from . . . smother: i.e. out of the frying pan into the fire.

I.iii. Location: The Duke's palace.
6. reasons: explanations (of your silence).
11. my child's father: i.e. Orlando. In her love melancholy Rosalind
is dreaming of the future.
14. holiday foolery. In retort to *working-day world*, line 12 (Wilson).
18. Hem them away: i.e. cough them away, like any other choking
obstruction in the throat or chest.
19–20. cry . . . him: win him merely by clearing my throat (with a
play on *hem* and *him*).
22. take . . . of: (1) side with; (2) require the agency of.
25. in despite of: notwithstanding the danger of.
25–26. turning . . . service: dismissing this levity.
31. therefore ensue: follow as a consequence.
32. By . . . chase: by pursuing this course of argument.
33. dearly: intensely.
36–37. deserve well: i.e. well deserve to be hated (but Rosalind
pretends to misunderstand).

him because I do. Look, here comes the Duke.

Cel. With his eyes full of anger.   40

Duke F. Mistress, dispatch you with your safest haste,
And get you from our court.

Ros.   Me, uncle?

Duke F.   You, cousin.
Within these ten days if that thou beest found
So near our public court as twenty miles,
Thou diest for it.

Ros.   I do beseech your Grace   45
Let me the knowledge of my fault bear with me:
If with myself I hold intelligence,
Or have acquaintance with mine own desires;
If that I do not dream, or be not frantic
(As I do trust I am not), then, dear uncle,   50
Never so much as in a thought unborn
Did I offend your Highness.

Duke F.   Thus do all traitors:
If their purgation did consist in words,
They are as innocent as grace itself.
Let it suffice thee that I trust thee not.   55

Ros. Yet your mistrust cannot make me a traitor.
Tell me whereon the [likelihood] depends.

Duke F. Thou art thy father's daughter, there's enough.

Ros. So was I when your Highness took his duke-dom,
So was I when your Highness banish'd him.   60
Treason is not inherited, my lord,
Or if we did derive it from our friends,
What's that to me? my father was no traitor.
Then, good my liege, mistake me not so much
To think my poverty is treacherous.   65

Cel. Dear sovereign, hear me speak.

Duke F. Ay, Celia, we stay'd her for your sake,
Else had she with her father rang'd along.

Cel. I did not then entreat to have her stay,
It was your pleasure and your own remorse.   70
I was too young that time to value her,
But now I know her. If she be a traitor,
Why, so am I. We still have slept together,
Rose at an instant, learn'd, play'd, eat together,
And wheresoe'er we went, like Juno's swans,   75
Still we went coupled and inseparable.

Duke F. She is too subtile for thee, and her smooth-ness,
Her very silence, and her patience

Speak to the people, and they pity her.
Thou art a fool; she robs thee of thy name,   80
And thou wilt show more bright and seem more vir-tuous
When she is gone. Then open not thy lips:
Firm and irrevocable is my doom
Which I have pass'd upon her; she is banish'd.

Cel. Pronounce that sentence then on me, my liege,
I cannot live out of her company.   86

Duke F. You are a fool. You, niece, provide your-self;
If you outstay the time, upon mine honor,
And in the greatness of my word, you die.

                    Exit Duke [*with Lords*].

Cel. O my poor Rosalind, whither wilt thou go?
Wilt thou change fathers? I will give thee mine.   91
I charge thee be not thou more griev'd than I am.

Ros. I have more cause.

Cel.   Thou hast not, cousin,
Prithee be cheerful. Know'st thou not the Duke
Hath banish'd me, his daughter?

Ros.   That he hath not.   95

Cel. No, hath not? Rosalind lacks then the love
Which teacheth thee that thou and I am one.
Shall we be sund'red? shall we part, sweet girl?
No, let my father seek another heir.
Therefore devise with me how we may fly,   100
Whither to go, and what to bear with us,
And do not seek to take your change upon you,
To bear your griefs yourself, and leave me out;
For by this heaven, now at our sorrows pale,
Say what thou canst, I'll go along with thee.   105

Ros. Why, whither shall we go?

Cel. To seek my uncle in the forest of Arden.

Ros. Alas, what danger will it be to us,
Maids as we are, to travel forth so far!
Beauty provoketh thieves sooner than gold.   110

Cel. I'll put myself in poor and mean attire,
And with a kind of umber smirch my face;
The like do you. So shall we pass along
And never stir assailants.

Ros.   Were it not better,
Because that I am more than common tall,   115
That I did suit me all points like a man?
A gallant curtle-axe upon my thigh,
A boar-spear in my hand, and—in my heart
Lie there what hidden woman's fear there will—
We'll have a swashing and a martial outside,   120
As many other mannish cowards have
That do outface it with their semblances.

Cel. What shall I call thee when thou art a man?

---

41. **your safest haste:** i.e. utmost speed, since in speed lies your safety.
42. **cousin.** Used of aunts, uncles, nieces, and nephews, as well as cousins in the modern sense.
47. **hold intelligence:** am in communication.
49. **If that:** if.   **frantic:** raving mad.   53. **purgation:** exoneration.
54. **grace:** virtue.   57. **likelihood:** supposition that it is likely.
62. **friends:** relatives.
64. **good my liege:** my good lord duke (*liege* = sovereign).
65. **To:** as to.   67. **stay'd her:** kept her here.
68. **rang'd:** roamed.
70. **remorse:** pity, compassion (prompted by conscience).
71. **that time:** at that time. The line suggests that some considerable time has passed since Duke Senior was banished. This is not the impression conveyed by I.i, but cf. II.i.2.   73. **still:** always.
74. **at an instant:** at the same moment.
75. **Juno's swans.** Swans were associated with Venus, not Juno.
77. **subtile:** subtle, cunning.

---

80. **name:** i.e. due praise.
81. **show:** appear.   **virtuous:** filled with admirable qualities.
83. **doom:** judgment, sentence.
87. **provide yourself:** make your preparations.
89. **in ... word:** upon my word as duke.   91. **change:** exchange.
102. **change:** i.e. of fortune.   110. **provoketh:** arouses.
111. **mean:** lowly.   112. **umber:** brown pigment.
116. **suit:** dress.   **all points:** in every respect.
117. **curtle-axe:** short sword.
120. **swashing:** blustering, swashbuckling.
121. **mannish:** pretending manly courage.
122. **outface it:** boldly carry off a situation.   **semblances:** (mere) appearances.

As You Like It
I.iii

Ros. I'll have no worse a name than Jove's own
  page,
And therefore look you call me Ganymed. 125
But what will you [be] call'd?
  Cel. Something that hath a reference to my state:
No longer Celia, but Aliena.
  Ros. But, cousin, what if we assay'd to steal
The clownish fool out of your father's court? 130
Would he not be a comfort to our travel?
  Cel. He'll go along o'er the wide world with me;
Leave me alone to woo him. Let's away,
And get our jewels and our wealth together,
Devise the fittest time and safest way 135
To hide us from pursuit that will be made
After my flight. Now go [we in] content
To liberty, and not to banishment. *Exeunt.*

ACT II, SCENE I

Enter DUKE SENIOR, AMIENS, *and two or three* LORDS,
  like foresters.

  Duke S. Now, my co-mates and brothers in exile,
Hath not old custom made this life more sweet
Than that of painted pomp? Are not these woods
More free from peril than the envious court?
Here feel we not the penalty of Adam, 5
The seasons' difference, as the icy fang
And churlish chiding of the winter's wind,
Which when it bites and blows upon my body
Even till I shrink with cold, I smile and say,
"This is no flattery: these are counsellors 10
That feelingly persuade me what I am."
Sweet are the uses of adversity,
Which like the toad, ugly and venomous,
Wears yet a precious jewel in his head;
And this our life, exempt from public haunt, 15
Finds tongues in trees, books in the running brooks,
Sermons in stones, and good in every thing.
  Ami. I would not change it. Happy is your Grace,
That can translate the stubbornness of fortune
Into so quiet and so sweet a style. 20
  Duke S. Come, shall we go and kill us venison?
And yet it irks me the poor dappled fools,
Being native burghers of this desert city,
Should in their own confines with forked heads

Have their round haunches gor'd.
  1. Lord.   Indeed, my lord,
The melancholy Jaques grieves at that, 26
And in that kind swears you do more usurp
Than doth your brother that hath banish'd you.
To-day my Lord of Amiens and myself
Did steal behind him as he lay along 30
Under an oak, whose antique root peeps out
Upon the brook that brawls along this wood,
To the which place a poor sequest'red stag,
That from the hunter's aim had ta'en a hurt,
Did come to languish; and indeed, my lord, 35
The wretched animal heav'd forth such groans
That their discharge did stretch his leathern coat
Almost to bursting, and the big round tears
Cours'd one another down his innocent nose
In piteous chase; and thus the hairy fool, 40
Much marked of the melancholy Jaques,
Stood on th' extremest verge of the swift brook,
Augmenting it with tears.
  Duke S.   But what said Jaques?
Did he not moralize this spectacle?
  1. Lord. O yes, into a thousand similes. 45
First, for his weeping into the needless stream:
"Poor deer," quoth he, "thou mak'st a testament
As worldlings do, giving thy sum of more
To that which had too [much]." Then being there
  alone,
Left and abandoned of his velvet [friends]: 50
"'Tis right," quoth he, "thus misery doth part
The flux of company." Anon a careless herd,
Full of the pasture, jumps along by him
And never stays to greet him. "Ay," quoth Jaques,
"Sweep on, you fat and greasy citizens, 55
'Tis just the fashion. Wherefore do you look
Upon that poor and broken bankrupt there?"
Thus most invectively he pierceth through
The body of [the] country, city, court,
Yea, and of this our life, swearing that we 60
Are mere usurpers, tyrants, and what's worse,
To fright the animals and to kill them up
In their assign'd and native dwelling-place.
  Duke S. And did you leave him in this contempla-
  tion?
  2. Lord. We did, my lord, weeping and com-
  menting 65
Upon the sobbing deer.

---

125. **Ganymed:** Ganymede, the boy whom Jupiter made cupbearer
to the gods. 128. **Aliena:** the estranged one (Latin).
129. **assay'd:** attempted. 133. **woo:** coax, persuade.
137. **content:** contentment.

II.i. Location: The forest of Arden.
o.s.d. **like:** in the guise of. 2. **old:** long-continued.
3. **painted:** artificial, specious. 4. **envious:** malicious, spiteful.
5. **feel we not:** i.e. we do not suffer seriously from. Many editors
emend *not* to *but* (after Theobald).
5–6. **penalty . . . difference.** In Eden it was perpetual spring.
6. **as:** such as. 7. **churlish:** rough, rude.
11. **feelingly:** through my senses. 12. **uses:** benefits.
13–14. **toad . . . head.** A widespread belief. The jewel was supposed
to have great curative power against disease. 14. **his:** its.
15. **exempt:** cut off. **public haunt:** the society of men.
19. **translate:** transform.
22. **irks:** distresses. **fools:** innocents (expressive of affectionate
pity). 23. **desert:** uninhabited by men, "unpeopled" (III.ii.126).
24. **confines:** territories. **forked heads:** two-pronged hunting arrows.

26. **Jaques.** Pronounced as a dissyllable throughout.
30. **along:** stretched out. 31. **antique:** ancient.
32. **brawls:** noisily courses.
33. **sequest'red:** separated from the herd.
39. **Cours'd:** pursued (a hunting metaphor, picked up by *chase*,
line 40). 41. **marked of:** observed by.
42. **extremest verge:** very edge of the bank.
44. **moralize:** interpret morally or symbolically.
46. **needless:** having no need (of additional water).
48. **worldlings:** mortals; worldly men. **sum of more:** additional
amount.
50. **of:** by. **velvet:** i.e. in flourishing condition. There is perhaps
an allusion to the so-called "velvet" on the antlers of deer during
the stage of rapid growth, as well as to the rich clothing of "worldlings." 51. **'Tis right:** just so. **part:** depart from.
52. **flux:** continuous stream. **Anon:** just then; presently. **careless:** carefree. 56. **just:** exactly. 57. **broken:** ruined.
58. **invectively:** in abusive language.
61. **mere:** out-and-out. **what's worse:** whatever may be worse.
62. **up:** off (intensive).

Duke S.   Show me the place.
I love to cope him in these sullen fits,
For then he's full of matter.
   1. Lord. I'll bring you to him straight.   *Exeunt.*

SCENE II

Enter DUKE [FREDERICK] *with* LORDS.

   Duke F. Can it be possible that no man saw them?
It cannot be. Some villains of my court
Are of consent and sufferance in this.
   1. Lord. I cannot hear of any that did see her.
The ladies, her attendants of her chamber,   5
Saw her a-bed, and in the morning early
They found the bed untreasur'd of their mistress.
   2. Lord. My lord, the roynish clown, at whom
     so oft
Your Grace was wont to laugh, is also missing.
Hisperia, the princess' gentlewoman,   10
Confesses that she secretly o'erheard
Your daughter and her cousin much commend
The parts and graces of the wrastler
That did but lately foil the sinowy Charles,
And she believes, where ever they are gone,   15
That youth is surely in their company.
   Duke F. Send to his brother; fetch that gallant
     hither.
If he be absent, bring his brother to me;
I'll make him find him. Do this suddenly;
And let not search and inquisition quail   20
To bring again these foolish runaways.   *Exeunt.*

SCENE III

Enter ORLANDO *and* ADAM, [*meeting*].

   Orl. Who's there?
   Adam. What, my young master? O my gentle
     master,
O my sweet master, O you memory
Of old Sir Rowland! Why, what make you here?
Why are you virtuous? Why do people love you?   5
And wherefore are you gentle, strong, and valiant?
Why would you be so fond to overcome
The bonny priser of the humorous Duke?
Your praise is come too swiftly home before you.
Know you not, master, to [some] kind of men   10
Their graces serve them but as enemies?
No more do yours. Your virtues, gentle master,
Are sanctified and holy traitors to you.

---

67. **cope:** deal with, converse with.   **sullen:** melancholy.
68. **matter:** substance, good sense.   69. **straight:** straightway.

II.ii. Location: The Duke's palace.
3. **Are . . . in:** i.e. have connived at.   8. **roynish:** scurvy, paltry.
13. **parts and graces:** talents and accomplishments.
14. **sinowy:** sinewy.   19. **suddenly:** quickly.
20. **inquisition:** inquiry.   **quail:** slacken.   21. **again:** back.

II.iii. Location: Before Oliver's house.
3. **memory:** reminder.   4. **make you:** are you doing.
5. **virtuous:** full of good qualities.   7. **fond:** foolish.   **to:** as to.
8. **bonny priser:** strapping prize-fighter.   **humorous:** capricious.
11. **graces:** virtues.   12. **more:** i.e. better.

O, what a world is this, when what is comely
Envenoms him that bears it!   15
   [*Orl.*] Why, what's the matter?
   Adam.   O unhappy youth,
Come not within these doors! Within this roof
The enemy of all your graces lives.
Your brother—no, no brother, yet the son
(Yet not the son, I will not call him son)   20
Of him I was about to call his father—
Hath heard your praises, and this night he means
To burn the lodging where you use to lie,
And you within it. If he fail of that,
He will have other means to cut you off;   25
I overheard him, and his practices.
This is no place, this house is but a butchery;
Abhor it, fear it, do not enter it.
   [*Orl.*] Why, whither, Adam, wouldst thou have
     me go?
   Adam. No matter whither, so you come not
     here.   30
   Orl. What, wouldst thou have me go and beg my
     food?
Or with a base and boist'rous sword enforce
A thievish living on the common road?
This I must do, or know not what to do;
Yet this I will not do, do how I can.   35
I rather will subject me to the malice
Of a diverted blood and bloody brother.
   Adam. But do not so. I have five hundred crowns,
The thrifty hire I sav'd under your father,
Which I did store to be my foster-nurse,   40
When service should in my old limbs lie lame,
And unregarded age in corners thrown.
Take that, and He that doth the ravens feed,
Yea, providently caters for the sparrow,
Be comfort to my age! Here is the gold,   45
All this I give you, let me be your servant.
Though I look old, yet I am strong and lusty;
For in my youth I never did apply
Hot and rebellious liquors in my blood,
Nor did not with unbashful forehead woo   50
The means of weakness and debility;
Therefore my age is as a lusty winter,
Frosty, but kindly. Let me go with you,
I'll do the service of a younger man
In all your business and necessities.   55
   Orl. O good old man, how well in thee appears
The constant service of the antique world,
When service sweat for duty, not for meed!
Thou art not for the fashion of these times,
Where none will sweat but for promotion,   60
And having that do choke their service up
Even with the having. It is not so with thee.

---

23. **use:** are accustomed.   26. **practices:** treacherous plots.
27. **place:** dwelling place.   **butchery:** slaughterhouse.
32. **boist'rous:** violent.   35. **do . . . can:** whatever happens to me.
37. **diverted blood:** disaffected kinship.
39. **thrifty . . . sav'd:** money I thriftily saved from my wages.
41. **When . . . lame:** when my duties as a servant would be performed
haltingly because of my aged limbs.   42. **thrown:** be thrown.
43–44. **He . . . sparrow.** Alluding to such Biblical passages as Job
38:41, Luke 12:6, 24.   47. **lusty:** vigorous.
49. **rebellious:** injurious to health.
53. **kindly:** (1) natural; (2) pleasant.   57. **constant:** faithful.
58. **sweat:** sweated.   **meed:** reward.

As You Like It
II.iii

But, poor old man, thou prun'st a rotten tree,
That cannot so much as a blossom yield
In lieu of all thy pains and husbandry.   65
But come thy ways, we'll go along together,
And ere we have thy youthful wages spent,
We'll light upon some settled low content.
    Adam.   Master, go on, and I will follow thee
To the last gasp, with truth and loyalty.   70
From [seventeen] years till now almost fourscore
Here lived I, but now live here no more.
At seventeen years many their fortunes seek,
But at fourscore it is too late a week;
Yet fortune cannot recompense me better   75
Than to die well, and not my master's debtor.
                                                Exeunt.

SCENE IV

Enter ROSALIND *for Ganymed,* CELIA *for Aliena, and Clown, alias* TOUCHSTONE.

    Ros.   O Jupiter, how [weary] are my spirits!
    Touch.   I care not for my spirits, if my legs were not weary.
    Ros.   I could find in my heart to disgrace my man's apparel and to cry like a woman; but I   5
must comfort the weaker vessel, as doublet and hose
ought to show itself courageous to petticoat; therefore courage, good Aliena.
    Cel.   I pray you bear with me, I cannot go no
further.   10
    Touch.   For my part, I had rather bear with you
than bear you. Yet I should bear no cross if I did
bear you, for I think you have no money in your
purse.
    Ros.   Well, this is the forest of Arden.   15
    Touch.   Ay, now am I in Arden, the more fool I.
When I was at home, I was in a better place, but
travellers must be content.

Enter CORIN *and* SILVIUS.

    Ros.   Ay, be so, good Touchstone. Look you,
who comes here, a young man and an old in solemn
talk.   21
    Cor.   That is the way to make her scorn you still.
    Sil.   O Corin, that thou knew'st how I do love her!
    Cor.   I partly guess; for I have lov'd ere now.
    Sil.   No, Corin, being old, thou canst not guess,
Though in thy youth thou wast as true a lover   26
As ever sigh'd upon a midnight pillow.
But if thy love were ever like to mine—
As sure I think did never man love so—
How many actions most ridiculous   30
Hast thou been drawn to by thy fantasy?
    Cor.   Into a thousand that I have forgotten.
    Sil.   O, thou didst then never love so heartily!

65. **lieu of:** return for.
68. **low content:** lowly contented state.   74. **a week:** i.e. a time.

II.iv. Location: The forest of Arden.
6. **weaker vessel:** i.e. woman (see 1 Peter 3:7).   **doublet and hose:**
jacket and breeches.   9. **cannot go no.** Elizabethan double negative.
12. **cross:** (1) burden; (2) the device stamped on a penny.
20. **solemn:** serious.   31. **fantasy:** fanciful love-thoughts.

If thou rememb'rest not the slightest folly
That ever love did make thee run into,   35
Thou hast not lov'd;
Or if thou hast not sat as I do now,
Wearing thy hearer in thy mistress' praise,
Thou hast not lov'd;
Or if thou hast not broke from company   40
Abruptly, as my passion now makes me,
Thou hast not lov'd.
O Phebe, Phebe, Phebe!   *Exit.*
    Ros.   Alas, poor shepherd, searching of [thy
wound],
I have by hard adventure found mine own.   45
    Touch.   And I mine. I remember when I was
in love, I broke my sword upon a stone, and bid him
take that for coming a-night to Jane Smile; and I
remember the kissing of her batler and the cow's
dugs that her pretty chopp'd hands had milk'd;   50
and I remember the wooing of a peascod instead of
her, from whom I took two cods, and giving her
them again, said with weeping tears, "Wear these
for my sake." We that are true lovers run into
strange capers; but as all is mortal in nature,   55
so is all nature in love mortal in folly.
    Ros.   Thou speak'st wiser than thou art ware of.
    Touch.   Nay, I shall ne'er be ware of mine own
wit till I break my shins against it.
    Ros.   Jove, Jove! this shepherd's passion   60
            Is much upon my fashion.
    Touch.   And mine, but it grows something stale
with me.
    Cel.   I pray you, one of you question yond man,
If he for gold will give us any food;   65
I faint almost to death.
    Touch.   Holla! you clown!
    Ros.   Peace, fool, he's not thy kinsman.
    Cor.   Who calls?
    Touch.   Your betters, sir.
    Cor.   Else are they very wretched.
    Ros.   Peace, I say. Good even to [you], friend.
    Cor.   And to you, gentle sir, and to you all.   70
    Ros.   I prithee, shepherd, if that love or gold
Can in this desert place buy entertainment,
Bring us where we may rest ourselves and feed.
Here's a young maid with travel much oppressed,
And faints for succor.
    Cor.   Fair sir, I pity her,   75
And wish, for her sake more than for mine own,
My fortunes were more able to relieve her;
But I am shepherd to another man,

38. **Wearing:** wearying.   44. **searching of:** probing.
45. **hard adventure:** ill chance.   48. **a-night:** at night.
49. **batler:** a club for beating clothes while washing them.
50. **chopp'd:** chapped.
51. **peascod:** pea pod; but here apparently the whole plant. Country
swains thought that peascods presented to and worn by their mistresses brought good luck in their wooing. There is, Wilson suggests,
a bawdy undertone in the lines as a whole, turning on *peascod* and
codpiece.   52. **whom, her.** Both words refer to the pea plant.
55. **mortal:** subject to death.   56. **mortal:** i.e. humanly faulty.
57. **ware:** aware. Touchstone then quibbles on the sense "wary."
61. **upon:** after.   62. **something:** somewhat.
66. **clown:** country fellow. Rosalind quibbles on the sense "jester."
68. **wretched:** low in rank and means.
72. **entertainment:** accommodation.
75. **faints for succor:** is faint for lack of aid (i.e. food)

And do not shear the fleeces that I graze.
My master is of churlish disposition,   80
And little reaks to find the way to heaven
By doing deeds of hospitality.
Besides, his cote, his flocks, and bounds of feed
Are now on sale, and at our sheep-cote now
By reason of his absence there is nothing   85
That you will feed on; but what is, come see,
And in my voice most welcome shall you be.
    Ros. What is he that shall buy his flock and pasture?
    Cor. That young swain that you saw here but
    erewhile,
That little cares for buying any thing.   90
    Ros. I pray thee, if it stand with honesty,
Buy thou the cottage, pasture, and the flock,
And thou shalt have to pay for it of us.
    Cel. And we will mend thy wages. I like this
    place,
And willingly could waste my time in it.   95
    Cor. Assuredly the thing is to be sold.
Go with me; if you like upon report
The soil, the profit, and this kind of life,
I will your very faithful feeder be,   99
And buy it with your gold right suddenly. *Exeunt.*

SCENE V

Enter AMIENS, JAQUES, *and others.*

SONG

[*Ami.*] Under the greenwood tree
          Who loves to lie with me,
          And turn his merry note
          Unto the sweet bird's throat,
     Come hither, come hither, come hither!   5
          Here shall he see
               No enemy
          But winter and rough weather.

    Jaq. More, more, I prithee more.
    Ami. It will make you melancholy, Monsieur
Jaques.   11
    Jaq. I thank it. More, I prithee more. I can
suck melancholy out of a song, as a weasel sucks eggs.
More, I prithee more.
    Ami. My voice is ragged, I know I cannot   15
please you.
    Jaq. I do not desire you to please me, I do desire
you to sing. Come, more, another stanzo. Call you
'em stanzos?

    Ami. What you will, Monsieur Jaques.   20
    Jaq. Nay, I care not for their names, they owe
me nothing. Will you sing?
    Ami. More at your request than to please myself.   24
    Jaq. Well then, if ever I thank any man, I'll
thank you; but that they call compliment is like th'
encounter of two dog-apes; and when a man thanks
me heartily, methinks I have given him a penny, and
he renders me the beggarly thanks. Come, sing;
and you that will not, hold your tongues.   30
    Ami. Well, I'll end the song. Sirs, cover the
while; the Duke will drink under this tree. He hath
been all this day to look you.
    Jaq. And I have been all this day to avoid him.
He is too disputable for my company. I think   35
of as many matters as he, but I give heaven thanks,
and make no boast of them. Come, warble, come.

SONG   *All together here.*

          Who doth ambition shun,
          And loves to live i' th' sun,
          Seeking the food he eats,   40
          And pleas'd with what he gets,
     Come hither, come hither, come hither!
          Here shall he see
               [No enemy
          But winter and rough weather].   45

    Jaq. I'll give you a verse to this note, that I made
yesterday in despite of my invention.
    Ami. And I'll sing it.
    [*Jaq.*] Thus it goes:

          If it do come to pass   50
          That any man turn ass,
          Leaving his wealth and ease
          A stubborn will to please,
          Ducdame, ducdame, ducdame!
          Here shall he see   55
               Gross fools as he,
          And if he will come to me.

    Ami. What's that "ducdame"?

21-22. **they . . . nothing.** Debtors signed their names in the lender's record book.   26. **compliment:** formal courtesy.
27. **dog-apes:** baboons.
29. **beggarly:** i.e. excessive, like those of an effusively grateful beggar.
31. **cover:** set the table.   31-32. **the while:** meanwhile.
33. **look:** look for.   35. **disputable:** fond of argument.
39. **i' th' sun:** i.e. live a free open-air life.   46. **note:** tune.
47. **in . . . invention:** notwithstanding my lack of imagination.
50-57. **If . . . me.** Jaques' stanza serves as a realistic, if cynical, antidote to the outright romanticism of Amiens' song. Such undercutting of the romantic attitude is an important function of Jaques' role throughout.
54. **Ducdame.** Trisyllabic. Not satisfactorily explained, despite numerous ingenious suggestions, e.g. that it is related to Latin *duc ad me,* "lead (him) to me"; to Welsh *dewch da mi,* "come to me"; or to Gipsy *dukrā mē,* a fortuneteller's cry to attract customers. The last of these is temptingly appropriate for an invitation to a gipsy existence in the forest and would clarify the reference in line 61 to "all the first-born of Egypt," i.e. all highborn persons who have adopted a gipsy life; but there is no evidence that an audience could have recognized any such derivation. *Ducdame* may well be a meaningless invented word; when Jaques tells Amiens that it serves "to call fools into a circle" (lines 59-60), probably part of his meaning is that only fools will draw round to ask what it means.
57. **And if:** if only.

---

79. **do . . . graze:** i.e. am not the owner who profits from the shearing of the sheep I graze.   80. **churlish:** miserly.
81. •**reaks:** recks, cares.
83. **cote:** cottage.   **bounds of feed:** areas in which he has grazing rights.
87. **in my voice:** as far as my word carries weight.
88. **What:** who.   89. **erewhile:** a short time ago.
91. **stand:** be consonant.   93. **to pay:** i.e. the money to pay.
94. **mend:** increase.   95. **waste:** spend.   99. **feeder:** servant.
100. **suddenly:** speedily.

II.v. Location: The forest.
3. **turn:** adapt, i.e. attune.   15. **ragged:** raspy.
18. **stanzo:** stanza.

Jaq. 'Tis a Greek invocation, to call fools into a circle. I'll go sleep, if I can; if I cannot, I'll rail against all the first-born of Egypt.   61

Ami. And I'll go seek the Duke, his banket is prepar'd.   *Exeunt.*

SCENE VI

Enter ORLANDO *and* ADAM.

Adam. Dear master, I can go no further. O, I die for food! Here lie I down, and measure out my grave. Farewell, kind master.

Orl. Why, how now, Adam? no greater heart in thee? Live a little, comfort a little, cheer thy-   5
self a little. If this uncouth forest yield any thing savage, I will either be food for it, or bring it for food to thee. Thy conceit is nearer death than thy powers. For my sake be comfortable, hold death a while at the arm's end. I will here be with   10
thee presently, and if I bring thee not something to eat, I will give thee leave to die; but if thou diest before I come, thou art a mocker of my labor. Well said, thou look'st cheerly, and I'll be with thee quickly. Yet thou liest in the bleak air. Come,   15
I will bear thee to some shelter, and thou shalt not die for lack of a dinner if there live any thing in this desert. Cheerly, good Adam!   *Exeunt.*

SCENE VII

[*A table set out.*] *Enter* DUKE SENIOR, [AMIENS,] *and* LORD[s], *like outlaws.*

Duke S. I think he be transform'd into a beast, For I can no where find him like a man.

1. Lord. My lord, he is but even now gone hence; Here was he merry, hearing of a song.

Duke S. If he, compact of jars, grow musical,   5
We shall have shortly discord in the spheres.
Go seek him, tell him I would speak with him.

Enter JAQUES.

1. Lord. He saves my labor by his own approach.

Duke S. Why, how now, monsieur, what a life is this,

That your poor friends must woo your company?   10
What, you look merrily!

Jaq. A fool, a fool! I met a fool i' th' forest,
A motley fool. A miserable world!
As I do live by food, I met a fool,
Who laid him down, and bask'd him in the sun,   15
And rail'd on Lady Fortune in good terms,
In good set terms, and yet a motley fool.
"Good morrow, fool," quoth I. "No, sir," quoth he,
"Call me not fool till heaven hath sent me fortune."
And then he drew a dial from his poke,   20
And looking on it, with lack-lustre eye,
Says very wisely, "It is ten a' clock.
Thus we may see," quoth he, "how the world wags.
'Tis but an hour ago since it was nine,
And after one hour more 'twill be eleven,   25
And so from hour to hour, we ripe and ripe,
And then from hour to hour, we rot and rot;
And thereby hangs a tale." When I did hear
The motley fool thus moral on the time,
My lungs began to crow like chanticleer,   30
That fools should be so deep contemplative;
And I did laugh sans intermission
An hour by his dial. O noble fool!
A worthy fool! Motley's the only wear.

Duke S. What fool is this?   35

Jaq. O worthy fool! One that hath been a courtier,
And says, if ladies be but young and fair,
They have the gift to know it; and in his brain,
Which is as dry as the remainder biscuit
After a voyage, he hath strange places cramm'd   40
With observation, the which he vents
In mangled forms. O that I were a fool!
I am ambitious for a motley coat.

Duke S. Thou shalt have one.

Jaq.   It is my only suit—
Provided that you weed your better judgments   45
Of all opinion that grows rank in them
That I am wise. I must have liberty
Withal, as large a charter as the wind,
To blow on whom I please, for so fools have;
And they that are most galled with my folly,   50
They most must laugh. And why, sir, must they so?
The why is plain as way to parish church:
He that a fool doth very wisely hit
Doth very foolishly, although he smart,
[Not to] seem senseless of the bob; if not,   55
The wise man's folly is anatomiz'd
Even by the squand'ring glances of the fool.

---

59. **Greek.** This word could be used of any unintelligible utterance, or, more specifically, of sharpers' cant.
61. **first-born of Egypt.** See note to line 54. *First-born* would suggest in particular the elder of the two dukes. The phrase itself is a Biblical echo, from the account of the death of all the first-born of Egypt in Exodus 11–12.
62. **banket:** banquet, i.e. light repast of fruit, sweetmeats, and wine.

II.vi. Location: The forest.
5. **comfort:** take heart. (So also *be comfortable* in line 9.)
6. **uncouth:** strange, wild. 8. **conceit:** imagination.
11. **presently:** immediately. 13–14. **Well said:** well done.
14. **cheerly:** cheerful.

II.vii. Location: The forest.
2. **like:** in the form of.
5. **compact of jars:** composed entirely of discords.
6. **discord . . . spheres.** It was thought that a ravishingly beautiful harmony was produced by the movement of the crystal spheres in which, according to the Ptolemaic system, the planets and stars revolved round the earth. It was inaudible to human ears.

13. **motley:** wearing motley, the parti-colored costume of professional jesters. 17. **set:** forthright, outspoken.
19. **Call . . . fortune.** An allusion to the proverb "Fortune favors fools." 20. **dial:** portable sundial. **poke:** pocket, pouch.
23. **wags:** goes on its way. 29. **moral:** moralize.
30. **crow:** i.e. with laughter. **chanticleer:** a cock.
31. **deep:** profoundly. 32. **sans:** without. 34. **wear:** costume.
39. **dry.** Dryness of the brain was supposedly connected with good memory. **remainder biscuit:** stale hardtack. 41. **vents:** utters.
44. **suit:** (1) petition; (2) clothing (cf. line 34). 46. **rank:** wild.
48. **Withal:** also. **charter:** privilege, license.
50. **galled:** rubbed on a sensitive spot.
53. **He . . . hit:** he that is wittily attacked by a fool.
54. **Doth:** acts, behaves.
55. **senseless of:** insensible to. **bob:** jibe, taunt.
56. **anatomiz'd:** dissected, laid bare.
57. **squand'ring glances:** random hits.

Invest me in my motley; give me leave
To speak my mind, and I will through and through
Cleanse the foul body of th' infected world,   60
If they will patiently receive my medicine.
  Duke S.   Fie on thee! I can tell what thou wouldst
do.
  Jaq.   What, for a counter, would I do but good?
  Duke S.   Most mischievous foul sin, in chiding sin:
For thou thyself hast been a libertine,   65
As sensual as the brutish sting itself,
And all th' embossed sores, and headed evils,
That thou with license of free foot hast caught,
Wouldst thou disgorge into the general world.
  Jaq.   Why, who cries out on pride   70
That can therein tax any private party?
Doth it not flow as hugely as the sea,
Till that the weary very means do ebb?
What woman in the city do I name,
When that I say the city-woman bears   75
The cost of princes on unworthy shoulders?
Who can come in and say that I mean her,
When such a one as she, such is her neighbor?
Or what is he of basest function,
That says his bravery is not on my cost,   80
Thinking that I mean him, but therein suits
His folly to the mettle of my speech?
There then! how then? what then?   Let me see
    wherein
My tongue hath wrong'd him; if it do him right,
Then he hath wrong'd himself. If he be free,   85
Why then my taxing like a wild goose flies,
Unclaim'd of any man. But who [comes] here?

  Enter ORLANDO [*with his sword drawn*].

  Orl.   Forbear, and eat no more.
  Jaq.   Why, I have eat none yet.
  Orl.   Nor shalt not, till necessity be serv'd.
  Jaq.   Of what kind should this cock come of?   90
  Duke S.   Art thou thus bolden'd, man, by thy dis-
tress?
Or else a rude despiser of good manners,
That in civility thou seem'st so empty?
  Orl.   You touch'd my vein at first.   The thorny
    point
Of bare distress hath ta'en from me the show   95
Of smooth civility; yet am I inland bred,

And know some nurture.   But forbear, I say,
He dies that touches any of this fruit
Till I and my affairs are answered.
  Jaq.   And you will not be answer'd with reason,
I must die.   101
  Duke S.   What would you have?   Your gentleness
    shall force,
More than your force move us to gentleness.
  Orl.   I almost die for food, and let me have it.
  Duke S.   Sit down and feed, and welcome to our
    table.   105
  Orl.   Speak you so gently?   Pardon me, I pray you.
I thought that all things had been savage here,
And therefore put I on the countenance
Of stern command'ment.   But what e'er you are
That in this desert inaccessible,   110
Under the shade of melancholy boughs,
Lose and neglect the creeping hours of time;
If ever you have look'd on better days,
If ever been where bells have knoll'd to church,
If ever sate at any good man's feast,   115
If ever from your eyelids wip'd a tear,
And know what 'tis to pity, and be pitied,
Let gentleness my strong enforcement be,
In the which hope I blush, and hide my sword.
  Duke S.   True is it that we have seen better days,
And have with holy bell been knoll'd to church,   121
And sat at good men's feasts, and wip'd our eyes
Of drops that sacred pity hath engend'red;
And therefore sit you down in gentleness,
And take upon command what help we have   125
That to your wanting may be minist'red.
  Orl.   Then but forbear your food a little while,
Whiles, like a doe, I go to find my fawn,
And give it food.   There is an old poor man,
Who after me hath many a weary step   130
Limp'd in pure love; till he be first suffic'd,
Oppress'd with two weak evils, age and hunger,
I will not touch a bit.
  Duke S.   Go find him out,
And we will nothing waste till you return.
  Orl.   I thank ye, and be blest for your good com-
fort!   [*Exit.*] 135
  Duke S.   Thou seest we are not all alone unhappy:
This wide and universal theatre
Presents more woeful pageants than the scene
Wherein we play in.
  Jaq.   All the world's a stage,
And all the men and women merely players;   140
They have their exits and their entrances,
And one man in his time plays many parts,
His acts being seven ages.   At first the infant,

63. **counter:** a disk or coin of no value, used in computation. Jaques humorously adapts a betting formula: "I'll wager a counter you can't tell me . . ."   66. **sting:** lust.
67. **embossed:** swollen.   **headed evils:** sores that have come to a head.
68. **license . . . foot:** i.e. the privilege of living like a libertine (uncontrolled).   69. **general:** whole.
70. **pride:** ostentation and extravagance.
71. **tax:** take to task, censure.   **private party:** particular individual.
73. **the weary very means:** i.e. the source itself, becoming exhausted (?). Various emendations have been proposed, e.g. *wearer's* for *weary*.
75. **city-woman:** citizen's wife.
79. **basest function:** lowest office or rank.
80. **bravery:** splendid dress.   **on my cost:** at my expense.
81. **suits:** (1) dresses; (2) makes conformable.
82. **mettle:** substance, tenor.   84. **right:** justice.
85. **free:** innocent.
94. **vein:** condition, state of mind.   **at first:** i.e. in the first explanation you suggested.
96. **smooth:** mild.   **inland bred:** i.e. reared in a centre of civilized behavior, not on the wild or rustic outskirts.

97. **nurture:** education, good training.   99. **answered:** satisfied.
100. **And:** if.   **reason.** With a pun on *raisin* (then closer in pronunciation to *reason* than now). The fruits on the table may well have included grapes.
102. **force:** press home, urge.   104. **for food:** i.e. for lack of food.
109. **command'ment:** command, authority.   114. **knoll'd:** rung.
115. **sate:** sat.
118. **enforcement:** compulsion.   125. **upon command:** at your will.
126. **wanting:** need.   132. **weak:** enfeebling.
134. **waste:** consume.
137. **This . . . theatre.** Thought to be a reference to the Globe theatre, built in 1599, and its motto, *Totus mundus agit histrionem* (The whole world plays the actor).

Mewling and puking in the nurse's arms.
Then the whining schoolboy, with his satchel 145
And shining morning face, creeping like snail
Unwillingly to school. And then the lover,
Sighing like furnace, with a woeful ballad
Made to his mistress' eyebrow. Then a soldier,
Full of strange oaths, and bearded like the pard, 150
Jealous in honor, sudden, and quick in quarrel,
Seeking the bubble reputation
Even in the cannon's mouth. And then the justice,
In fair round belly with good capon lin'd,
With eyes severe and beard of formal cut, 155
Full of wise saws and modern instances;
And so he plays his part. The sixt age shifts
Into the lean and slipper'd pantaloon,
With spectacles on nose, and pouch on side,
His youthful hose, well sav'd, a world too wide 160
For his shrunk shank, and his big manly voice,
Turning again toward childish treble, pipes
And whistles in his sound. Last scene of all,
That ends this strange eventful history,
Is second childishness, and mere oblivion, 165
Sans teeth, sans eyes, sans taste, sans every thing.

Enter ORLANDO *with* ADAM.

Duke S. Welcome. Set down your venerable bur-
 then,
And let him feed.
 Orl. I thank you most for him.
 Adam. So had you need,
I scarce can speak to thank you for myself. 170
 Duke S. Welcome, fall to. I will not trouble you
As yet to question you about your fortunes.
Give us some music, and, good cousin, sing.

SONG

[*Ami.*] Blow, blow, thou winter wind,
 Thou art not so unkind 175
 As man's ingratitude;
 Thy tooth is not so keen,
 Because thou art not seen,
 Although thy breath be rude.
Heigh-ho, sing heigh-ho! unto the green holly, 180
Most friendship is feigning, most loving mere folly.
 [Then] heigh-ho, the holly!
 This life is most jolly.

 Freeze, freeze, thou bitter sky,
 That dost not bite so nigh 185
 As benefits forgot;
 Though thou the waters warp,

Thy sting is not so sharp
 As friend rememb'red not.
Heigh-ho, sing, etc. 190

 Duke S. If that you were the good Sir Rowland's
 son,
As you have whisper'd faithfully you were,
And as mine eye doth his effigies witness
Most truly limn'd and living in your face,
Be truly welcome hither. I am the Duke 195
That lov'd your father. The residue of your fortune,
Go to my cave and tell me. Good old man,
Thou art right welcome as thy [master] is.
Support him by the arm. Give me your hand,
And let me all your fortunes understand. *Exeunt.* 200

ACT III, SCENE I

Enter DUKE [FREDERICK], LORDS, *and* OLIVER.

 Duke F. Not see him since? Sir, sir, that cannot
 be.
But were I not the better part made mercy,
I should not seek an absent argument
Of my revenge, thou present. But look to it:
Find out thy brother, wheresoe'er he is; 5
Seek him with candle; bring him dead or living
Within this twelvemonth, or turn thou no more
To seek a living in our territory.
Thy lands and all things that thou dost call thine
Worth seizure do we seize into our hands, 10
Till thou canst quit thee by thy brother's mouth
Of what we think against thee.
 Oli. O that your Highness knew my heart in this!
I never lov'd my brother in my life.
 Duke F. More villain thou. Well, push him out
 of doors, 15
And let my officers of such a nature
Make an extent upon his house and lands.
Do this expediently, and turn him going. *Exeunt.*

SCENE II

Enter ORLANDO [*with a paper*].

 Orl. Hang there, my verse, in witness of my love,
And thou, thrice-crowned queen of night, survey
With thy chaste eye, from thy pale sphere above,

144. **Mewling:** crying. **puking:** vomiting.
148. **Sighing like furnace:** i.e. emitting sighs as a furnace emits smoke.
150. **bearded . . . pard:** with long mustaches like the feelers of the leopard or panther.
151. **Jealous in honor:** jealously protective of his honor. **sudden:** rash.
154. **with . . . lin'd.** Perhaps with satiric reference to the bribing of judges with capons.
156. **saws:** maxims. **modern instances:** trite illustrations.
157. **sixt:** sixth.
158. **pantaloon:** foolish old man (from the name of a stock character in Italian comedy). 163. **his:** its. 164. **history:** chronicle play.
165. **mere:** utter. 167. **burthen:** burden.
180. **holly.** An emblem of mirth.
187. **warp:** freeze (?) or contort by freezing (?).

192. **faithfully:** with assurances of good faith.
193. **effigies:** likeness, image. 194. **limn'd:** portrayed.

III.i. Location: The Duke's palace.
2. **better:** i.e. greater. **made:** made of. 3. **argument:** subject.
6. **with candle.** An allusion to the parable in Luke 15:8 which describes how a woman who has lost a coin lights a candle and diligently searches the house until she has found it.
7. **turn:** return. 11. **quit:** acquit. **mouth:** testimony.
15. **More villain thou.** The irony of this charge nicely points up the parallel between Oliver and Duke Frederick.
16. **of . . . nature:** whose duty it is to see to such matters.
17. **extent:** seizure by writ.
18. **expediently:** quickly. **turn him going:** get him on his way.

III.ii. Location: The forest.
2. **thrice-crowned queen:** i.e. the divinity who ruled on earth as Diana, in the heavens as Cynthia the moon-goddess, and in the underworld as Hecate or Proserpina.

Thy huntress' name that my full life doth sway.
O Rosalind, these trees shall be my books,　5
And in their barks my thoughts I'll character,
That every eye which in this forest looks
Shall see thy virtue witness'd every where.
Run, run, Orlando, carve on every tree
The fair, the chaste, and unexpressive she.　*Exit.*　10

Enter CORIN *and Clown* [TOUCHSTONE].

Cor.　And how like you this shepherd's life, Master
Touchstone?

Touch.　Truly, shepherd, in respect of itself, it is
a good life; but in respect that it is a shepherd's life,
it is naught. In respect that it is solitary, I like　15
it very well; but in respect that it is private, it is a
very vild life. Now in respect it is in the fields, it
pleaseth me well; but in respect it is not in the court,
it is tedious. As it is a spare life (look you) it fits my
humor well; but as there is no more plenty in it,　20
it goes much against my stomach. Hast any philosophy
in thee, shepherd?

Cor.　No more but that I know the more one
sickens the worse at ease he is; and that he that　24
wants money, means, and content is without three
good friends; that the property of rain is to wet and
fire to burn; that good pasture makes fat sheep; and
that a great cause of the night is lack of the sun; that
he that hath learn'd no wit by nature, nor art, may
complain of good breeding, or comes of a very dull
kindred.　31

Touch.　Such a one is a natural philosopher.
Wast ever in court, shepherd?

Cor.　No, truly.

Touch.　Then thou art damn'd.　35

Cor.　Nay, I hope.

Touch.　Truly, thou art damn'd, like an ill-roasted
egg, all on one side.

Cor.　For not being at court? Your reason.　39

Touch.　Why, if thou never wast at court, thou
never saw'st good manners; if thou never saw'st
good manners, then thy manners must be wicked,
and wickedness is sin, and sin is damnation. Thou
art in a parlous state, shepherd.　44

Cor.　Not a whit, Touchstone. Those that are
good manners at the court are as ridiculous in the
country as the behavior of the country is most
mockable at the court. You told me you salute
not at the court but you kiss your hands; that　49
courtesy would be uncleanly if courtiers were shepherds.

Touch.　Instance, briefly; come, instance.

Cor.　Why, we are still handling our ewes, and
their fells you know are greasy.　54

Touch.　Why, do not your courtier's hands sweat?
And is not the grease of a mutton as wholesome as
the sweat of a man? Shallow, shallow. A better
instance, I say; come.

Cor.　Besides, our hands are hard.　59

Touch.　Your lips will feel them the sooner.
Shallow again. A more sounder instance, come.

Cor.　And they are often tarr'd over with the
surgery of our sheep; and would you have us kiss
tar? The courtier's hands are perfum'd with civet.　64

Touch.　Most shallow man! thou worm's-meat,
in respect of a good piece of flesh indeed! Learn
of the wise, and perpend: civet is of a baser birth
than tar, the very uncleanly flux of a cat. Mend
the instance, shepherd.　69

Cor.　You have too courtly a wit for me, I'll rest.

Touch.　Wilt thou rest damn'd? God help thee,
shallow man! God make incision in thee, thou art raw.

Cor.　Sir, I am a true laborer: I earn that I eat,
get that I wear, owe no man hate, envy no man's　74
happiness, glad of other men's good, content with my
harm, and the greatest of my pride is to see my ewes
graze and my lambs suck.

Touch.　That is another simple sin in you, to bring
the ewes and the rams together, and to offer to get　79
your living by the copulation of cattle; to be bawd to a
bell-wether, and to betray a she-lamb of a twelvemonth to a crooked-pated old cuckoldly ram, out of
all reasonable match. If thou beest not damn'd　83
for this, the devil himself will have no shepherds;
I cannot see else how thou shouldst scape.

Cor.　Here comes young Master Ganymed, my
new mistress's brother.

Enter ROSALIND [*with a paper, reading*].

Ros.　"From the east to western Inde,
　　No jewel is like Rosalind.
　　Her worth, being mounted on the wind,　90
　　Through all the world bears Rosalind.
　　All the pictures fairest lin'd

4. **Thy huntress'**. It was a commonplace to represent Diana's maiden votaries as her companions in the hunt, of which she was patron.
6. **character**: inscribe. Orlando is making literal Duke Senior's metaphor of "tongues in trees" (II.i.16); cf. also line 127 below.
8. **virtue**: excellence. 10. **unexpressive**: inexpressible.
13. **in . . . itself**: considered in and for itself.
14. **in respect that**: with regard to the fact that, in so far as.
15. **naught**: bad. 16. **private**: lonely.
17. **vild**: vile, wretched. 20. **humor**: fancy.
21. **stomach**: inclination (with play on the sense "appetite").
29. **wit**: knowledge. **art**: study. 30. **complain**: lament the lack.
32. **natural**: born (with play on the sense "fool").
37–38. **damn'd . . . side**: ruined, like an egg roasted in the ashes that when opened proves to be done on one side but still raw on the other.
41. **manners**: (1) deportment; (2) morals. 44. **parlous**: perilous.
49. **but you kiss**: without kissing.

52. **Instance**: proof. **briefly**: quickly.
53. **still**: always. 54. **fells**: skins.
61. **more sounder**. Double comparatives were common in Elizabethan usage.
62. **tarr'd over**. Tar was applied to the sores and cuts of sheep.
64. **civet**: perfume derived from the civet cat.
66. **in respect of**: in comparison with. 67. **perpend**: consider.
68. **flux**: secretion. **Mend**: improve.
70. **rest**: stop, argue no further. Touchstone then quibbles on the sense "remain, continue."
72. **make incision**: i.e. to let out his folly, as a surgeon let out "bad" blood. **raw**: untutored, simple; with a play on the sense "sore" (hence requiring surgery). 73. **that**: what.
75–76. **content . . . harm**: patient in my own misfortune.
78. **simple**: (1) foolish; (2) unadulterated, out-and-out.
79. **offer**: undertake.
82. **cuckoldly**: i.e. horned, as cuckolds supposedly were (?) or like one who cuckolds, i.e. lecherous (?). **out of**: beyond the limits of, contrary to. 83. **match**: (1) correspondence, likeness; (2) mating.
84. **the devil . . . shepherds**: it will be because the devil refuses to have shepherds in hell. 85. **scape**: escape. 88. **Inde**: Indies.
92. **fairest**. There is play on two senses of *fair*, "beautiful" and "blonde." Lines 92–93 say that all other beautiful women are ugly, all other blondes dark-complexioned, in comparison with (*to*) Rosalind. Blonde beauty was the Elizabethan ideal. See Rosalind's disparagement of Phebe's looks in III.v.46–47. **lin'd**: drawn.

As You Like It
III.ii

Are but black to Rosalind.
Let no face be kept in mind
But the fair of Rosalind." 95

Touch. I'll rhyme you so eight years together, dinners and suppers and sleeping-hours excepted. It is the right butter-women's rank to market.

Ros. Out, fool!

Touch. For a taste: 100

If a hart do lack a hind,
Let him seek out Rosalind.
If the cat will after kind,
So be sure will Rosalind.
Wint'red garments must be lin'd, 105
So must slender Rosalind.
They that reap must sheaf and bind,
Then to cart with Rosalind.
Sweetest nut hath sourest rind,
Such a nut is Rosalind. 110
He that sweetest rose will find,
Must find love's prick and Rosalind.

This is the very false gallop of verses; why do you infect yourself with them? 114

Ros. Peace, you dull fool, I found them on a tree.

Touch. Truly, the tree yields bad fruit.

Ros. I'll graff it with you, and then I shall graff 118 it with a medlar. Then it will be the earliest fruit i' th' country; for you'll be rotten ere you be half ripe, and that's the right virtue of the medlar.

Touch. You have said; but whether wisely or no, let the forest judge.

Enter CELIA *with a writing.*

Ros. Peace,
Here comes my sister reading, stand aside.

Cel. [*Reads.*]
"Why should this [a] desert be? 125
For it is unpeopled? No!
Tongues I'll hang on every tree,
That shall civil sayings show:
Some, how brief the life of man
Runs his erring pilgrimage, 130
That the stretching of a span
Buckles in his sum of age;
Some, of violated vows
'Twixt the souls of friend and friend;
But upon the fairest boughs, 135

Or at every sentence end,
Will I 'Rosalinda' write,
Teaching all that read to know
The quintessence of every sprite
Heaven would in little show. 140
Therefore heaven Nature charg'd
That one body should be fill'd
With all graces wide-enlarg'd.
Nature presently distill'd
Helen's cheek, but not [her] heart, 145
Cleopatra's majesty,
Atalanta's better part,
Sad Lucretia's modesty.
Thus Rosalind of many parts
By heavenly synod was devis'd, 150
Of many faces, eyes, and hearts,
To have the touches dearest priz'd.
Heaven would that she these gifts should have,
And I to live and die her slave." 154

Ros. O most gentle Jupiter, what tedious homily of love have you wearied your parishioners withal, and never cried, "Have patience, good people!"

Cel. How now? back, friends! Shepherd, go off a little. Go with him, sirrah. 159

Touch. Come, shepherd, let us make an honorable retreat, though not with bag and baggage, yet with scrip and scrippage.   *Exit* [*with Corin*].

Cel. Didst thou hear these verses?

Ros. O yes, I heard them all, and more too, for some of them had in them more feet than the verses would bear. 166

Cel. That's no matter; the feet might bear the verses.

Ros. Ay, but the feet were lame, and could not bear themselves without the verse, and therefore stood lamely in the verse. 171

Cel. But didst thou hear without wondering how thy name should be hang'd and carv'd upon these trees?

Ros. I was seven of the nine days out of the wonder before you came; for look here what I found on a palm tree. I was never so berhym'd since Pythagoras' 176 time, that I was an Irish rat, which I can hardly remember.

96. **together:** without intermission.
98. **the right . . . market:** i.e. precisely like dairy-women riding along one behind another at the same pace on their way to market.
100. **taste:** sample.
101. **hart . . . hind:** (1) male deer . . . female deer; (2) man . . . woman. (The verses are a series of double entendres.)
103. **will after kind:** will behave in accordance with its nature (proverbial).   105. **Wint'red:** readied for winter use.
108. **to cart.** The harvest was transported on farm-carts, but Touchstone is alluding here to the practice of exposing disreputable women to public derision by driving them about the town in carts.
113. **very false gallop:** true canter (suggesting effortlessly regular movement, hence a mechanical and monotonous effect).
117. **graff:** graft. What follows is a triple pun: "with *yew*, and afterward with a *medlar*"; "with *you*, and *in that case* with a *meddler*." The medlar is an apple-like fruit that is not ready to eat until it is on the verge of decay.
120. **right virtue:** characteristic quality.   126. **For:** because.
130. **his erring:** its wandering.
131. **span:** distance from the tip of the thumb to the tip of the little finger of a spread hand.   132. **Buckles in:** encompasses.

139. **quintessence:** ultimate essence; highest perfection. **sprite:** spirit.
140. **in little:** in small space; probably with reference to man as microcosm or miniature universe.
143. **wide-enlarg'd:** extended to the fullest (?) or hitherto dispersed at large, i.e. gathered from everywhere (?).   144. **presently:** at once.
145. **Helen's cheek:** Helen of Troy's beauty.   **her heart:** i.e. her falseness in love.
147. **Atalanta's better part:** i.e. her fleetness of foot (see lines 276–77 below), as contrasted with her greed. Hippomenes defeated her in a race, and thus won her as his bride, by dropping in her way three golden apples which she paused thrice to pick up.
148. **modesty:** scrupulous chastity. The story of Lucretia's rape and suicide is told by Shakespeare in *The Rape of Lucrece*.
152. **touches:** features, traits.   153. **would:** desired.
155. **Jupiter.** Many editors read *pulpiter* (first suggested by Spedding).
156. **withal:** with.   159. **sirrah:** form of address to inferiors.
161. **not . . . baggage:** i.e. not with as much equipment as a retreating army would carry.
162. **scrip and scrippage:** a pouch and its contents.
166. **bear:** permit (with following pun on the sense "carry").
170. **without:** (1) without the help of; (2) outside.
173. **should be:** came to be.
176–77. **Pythagoras' time.** An allusion to the Pythagorean doctrine of transmigration of souls.
177. **that:** when.   **Irish rat.** Alluding to an old belief that Irish enchanters could rhyme rats and other animals to death.

Cel. Trow you who hath done this?

Ros. Is it a man?   180

Cel. And a chain, that you once wore, about his neck. Change you color?

Ros. I prithee who?

Cel. O Lord, Lord, it is a hard matter for friends to meet; but mountains may be remov'd with earthquakes, and so encounter.   186

Ros. Nay, but who is it?

Cel. Is it possible?

Ros. Nay, I prithee now, with most petitionary vehemence, tell me who it is.   190

Cel. O wonderful, wonderful, and most wonderful wonderful! and yet again wonderful, and after that, out of all hooping!

Ros. Good my complexion, dost thou think, though I am caparison'd like a man, I have a doublet and hose in my disposition? One inch of delay more is a South-sea of discovery. I prithee tell me who is   197 it quickly, and speak apace. I would thou couldst stammer, that thou mightst pour this conceal'd man out of thy mouth, as wine comes out of a narrow-mouth'd bottle, either too much at once, or none at all. I prithee take the cork out of thy mouth that I may drink thy tidings.   203

Cel. So you may put a man in your belly.

Ros. Is he of God's making? What manner of man? Is his head worth a hat? or his chin worth a beard?   207

Cel. Nay, he hath but a little beard.

Ros. Why, God will send more, if the man will be thankful. Let me stay the growth of his beard, if thou delay me not the knowledge of his chin.   211

Cel. It is young Orlando, that tripp'd up the wrastler's heels, and your heart, both in an instant.

Ros. Nay, but the devil take mocking. Speak sad brow and true maid.   215

Cel. I' faith, coz, 'tis he.

Ros. Orlando?

Cel. Orlando.

Ros. Alas the day, what shall I do with my doublet and hose? What did he when thou saw'st him?   220 What said he? How look'd he? Wherein went he? What makes he here? Did he ask for me? Where remains he? How parted he with thee? And when shalt thou see him again? Answer me in one word.

Cel. You must borrow me Gargantua's mouth first; 'tis a word too great for any mouth of this   226

age's size. To say ay and no to these particulars is more than to answer in a catechism.

Ros. But doth he know that I am in this forest and in man's apparel? Looks he as freshly as he did the day he wrastled?   231

Cel. It is as easy to count atomies as to resolve the propositions of a lover. But take a taste of my finding him, and relish it with good observance. I found him under a tree, like a dropp'd acorn.   235

Ros. It may well be call'd Jove's tree, when it drops [such] fruit.

Cel. Give me audience, good madam.

Ros. Proceed.

Cel. There lay he, stretch'd along, like a wounded knight.   241

Ros. Though it be pity to see such a sight, it well becomes the ground.

Cel. Cry "holla" to [thy] tongue, I prithee; it curvets unseasonably. He was furnish'd like a hunter.

Ros. O ominous! he comes to kill my heart.   246

Cel. I would sing my song without a burthen; thou bring'st me out of tune.

Ros. Do you not know I am a woman? when I think, I must speak. Sweet, say on.   250

Enter ORLANDO *and* JAQUES.

Cel. You bring me out. Soft, comes he not here?

Ros. 'Tis he. Slink by, and note him.

Jaq. I thank you for your company, but, good faith, I had as lief have been myself alone.

Orl. And so had I; but yet for fashion sake I thank you too for your society.   256

Jaq. God buy you, let's meet as little as we can.

Orl. I do desire we may be better strangers.

Jaq. I pray you mar no more trees with writing love-songs in their barks.   260

Orl. I pray you mar no moe of my verses with reading them ill-favoredly.

Jaq. Rosalind is your love's name?

Orl. Yes, just.

Jaq. I do not like her name.   265

Orl. There was no thought of pleasing you when she was christen'd.

Jaq. What stature is she of?

Orl. Just as high as my heart.   269

Jaq. You are full of pretty answers; have you not been acquainted with goldsmiths' wives, and conn'd them out of rings?

---

179. **Trow you:** have you any idea.
181. **And a chain:** i.e. yes, it is a man, and one with a chain.
185. **remov'd with:** moved by.
189–190. **petitionary vehemence:** urgent entreaty.
193. **out of:** beyond.   **hooping:** whooping, i.e. power to utter.
194. **Good my complexion:** have mercy on my temperament, i.e. on my woman's impatient curiosity.
195. **caparison'd:** decked out (ordinarily used of a horse's ornamental trappings).
196–97. **is . . . discovery:** will seem as long as the time needed to explore the South Seas.
205. **of God's making:** i.e. not of the tailor's making (the usual antithesis).   210. **stay:** await.
214–15. **sad . . . maid:** seriously and truly.
221. **Wherein went he:** how was he dressed.
222. **makes he:** is he doing.
225. **Gargantua's mouth.** Rabelais' giant swallowed five pilgrims in a salad.

228. **catechism:** catechizing.
230. **freshly:** fresh, youthfully vigorous.
232. **atomies:** atoms, minute specks.   233. **propositions:** questions.
234. **relish it:** enhance its flavor.   **good observance:** close attention.
236. **Jove's tree:** i.e. the oak, the king of trees, as the eagle, also connected with Jove, is the king of birds.
238. **audience:** hearing, attention.   240. **along:** full length.
244. **holla:** stop.
244–45. **curvets unseasonably:** frisks about at the wrong time.
245. **furnish'd:** dressed, equipped.
246. **heart.** With pun on *hart* (and so spelled in F1).
247. **burthen:** burden, ground-bass, repeated undersong.
248. **bring'st:** puttest.   251. **bring me out:** put me off, confuse me.
257. **God buy you:** God be with you; goodbye.   261. **moe:** more.
262. **ill-favoredly:** in an unattractive way, badly.
264. **just:** just so, exactly.
271–72. **conn'd . . . rings:** i.e. memorized the mottoes or "posies" (i.e. poesies) engraved on rings.

As You Like It
III.ii

Orl. Not so; but I answer you right painted cloth, from whence you have studied your questions.   275

Jaq. You have a nimble wit; I think 'twas made of Atalanta's heels. Will you sit down with me? and we two will rail against our mistress the world, and all our misery.

Orl. I will chide no breather in the world but myself, against whom I know most faults.   281

Jaq. The worst fault you have is to be in love.

Orl. 'Tis a fault I will not change for your best virtue. I am weary of you.

Jaq. By my troth, I was seeking for a fool when I found you.   286

Orl. He is drown'd in the brook; look but in, and you shall see him.

Jaq. There I shall see mine own figure.

Orl. Which I take to be either a fool or a cipher.

Jaq. I'll tarry no longer with you. Farewell, good Signior Love.   292

Orl. I am glad of your departure. Adieu, good Monsieur Melancholy.   [*Exit Jaques.*]

Ros. [*Aside to Celia.*] I will speak to him like a saucy lackey, and under that habit play the knave with him.—Do you hear, forester?   297

Orl. Very well. What would you?

Ros. I pray you, what is't a' clock?

Orl. You should ask me what time o' day; there's no clock in the forest.   301

Ros. Then there is no true lover in the forest, else sighing every minute and groaning every hour would detect the lazy foot of Time as well as a clock.   305

Orl. And why not the swift foot of Time? Had not that been as proper?

Ros. By no means, sir. Time travels in divers paces with divers persons. I'll tell you who Time ambles withal, who Time trots withal, who Time gallops withal, and who he stands still withal.   311

Orl. I prithee, who doth he trot withal?

Ros. Marry, he trots hard with a young maid between the contract of her marriage and the day it is solemniz'd. If the interim be but a se'nnight, Time's pace is so hard that it seems the length of seven year.   317

Orl. Who ambles Time withal?

Ros. With a priest that lacks Latin, and a rich man that hath not the gout; for the one sleeps easily because he cannot study, and the other lives merrily because he feels no pain; the one lacking the   322 burthen of lean and wasteful learning, the other knowing no burthen of heavy tedious penury. These Time ambles withal.   325

Orl. Who doth he gallop withal?

Ros. With a thief to the gallows; for though he go as softly as foot can fall, he thinks himself too soon there.

Orl. Who stays it still withal?   330

Ros. With lawyers in the vacation; for they sleep between term and term, and then they perceive not how Time moves.

Orl. Where dwell you, pretty youth?   334

Ros. With this shepherdess, my sister; here in the skirts of the forest, like fringe upon a petticoat.

Orl. Are you native of this place?

Ros. As the cony that you see dwell where she is kindled.   340

Orl. Your accent is something finer than you could purchase in so remov'd a dwelling.

Ros. I have been told so of many; but indeed an old religious uncle of mine taught me to speak, who was in his youth an inland man, one that knew courtship too well, for there he fell in love. I have heard him read many lectures against it, and I   347 thank God I am not a woman, to be touch'd with so many giddy offenses as he hath generally tax'd their whole sex withal.   350

Orl. Can you remember any of the principal evils that he laid to the charge of women?

Ros. There were none principal, they were all like one another as halfpence are, every one fault seeming monstrous till his fellow-fault came to match it.   356

Orl. I prithee recount some of them.

Ros. No; I will not cast away my physic but on those that are sick. There is a man haunts the forest, that abuses our young plants with carving "Rosalind" on their barks; hangs odes upon hawthorns, and elegies on brambles; all, forsooth,   362 [deifying] the name of Rosalind. If I could meet that fancy-monger, I would give him some good counsel, for he seems to have the quotidian of love upon him.   366

Orl. I am he that is so love-shak'd, I pray you tell me your remedy.

Ros. There is none of my uncle's marks upon you. He taught me how to know a man in love; in which cage of rushes I am sure you [are] not prisoner.   371

Orl. What were his marks?

Ros. A lean cheek, which you have not; a blue eye and sunken, which you have not; an unquestionable spirit, which you have not; a beard neglected, which you have not (but I pardon you for that,   376 for simply your having in beard is a younger broth-

---

273. **right:** true, genuine.
273–74. **painted cloth.** The cheapest type of wall-hanging, customarily decorated with scenes and mottoes, and thus another source of clichés.   280. **breather:** living person.
290. **cipher:** zero (punning on a second sense of *figure*), nonentity.
296. **habit:** guise.   299. **a' clock:** by (of) the clock.
304. **detect:** reveal.   310. **withal:** with.
313. **hard:** with an uneasy pace (the discomfort of the pace making the ride seem long).   315. **se'nnight:** week.
323. **wasteful:** consuming.

328. **go as softly:** walk as slowly.
332. **term:** session.   339. **cony:** rabbit.   340. **kindled:** born.
342. **purchase:** acquire.   **remov'd:** remote.
344. **religious:** belonging to a religious order.
346. **courtship:** (1) the ways of court life; (2) wooing.
348. **touch'd:** tainted.   349. **generally:** universally.
358. **physic:** knowledge of medicine.
364. **fancy-monger:** dealer in love.
365. **quotidian:** an ague with daily attacks of chills and fever.
371. **cage of rushes:** i.e. insubstantial prison, easy to escape from.
373. **blue:** i.e. with dark circles caused by weeping and lack of sleep.
374–75. **unquestionable:** disinclined to converse.
377. **simply:** frankly.   **your having in:** what you own in the way of.

er's revenue); then your hose should be ungarter'd, your bonnet unbanded, your sleeve unbutton'd, your shoe untied, and every thing about you demonstrating a careless desolation. But you are 381 no such man; you are rather point-device in your accoutrements, as loving yourself, than seeming the lover of any other.

Orl. Fair youth, I would I could make thee believe I love. 386

Ros. Me believe it? You may as soon make her that you love believe it, which I warrant she is apter to do than to confess she does. That is one of the points in the which women still give the lie to their consciences. But in good sooth, are 391 you he that hangs the verses on the trees, wherein Rosalind is so admir'd?

Orl. I swear to thee, youth, by the white hand of Rosalind, I am that he, that unfortunate he. 395

Ros. But are you so much in love as your rhymes speak?

Orl. Neither rhyme nor reason can express how much. 399

Ros. Love is merely a madness, and I tell you, deserves as well a dark house and a whip as madmen do; and the reason why they are not so punish'd and cur'd is, that the lunacy is so ordinary that the whippers are in love too. Yet I profess curing it by counsel. 405

Orl. Did you ever cure any so?

Ros. Yes, one, and in this manner. He was to imagine me his love, his mistress; and I set him every day to woo me. At which time would I, being but a moonish youth, grieve, be effeminate, 410 changeable, longing and liking, proud, fantastical, apish, shallow, inconstant, full of tears, full of smiles; for every passion something, and for no passion truly any thing, as boys and women are for the most part cattle of this color; would now like 415 him, now loathe him; then entertain him, then forswear him; now weep for him, then spit at him; that I drave my suitor from his mad humor of love to a living humor of madness, which was, to forswear 419 the full stream of the world, and to live in a nook merely monastic. And thus I cur'd him, and this way will I take upon me to wash your liver as clean as a sound sheep's heart, that there shall not be one spot of love in't.

Orl. I would not be cur'd, youth. 425

Ros. I would cure you, if you would but call me Rosalind, and come every day to my cote and woo me.

Orl. Now, by the faith of my love, I will. Tell me where it is. 429

Ros. Go with me to it, and I'll show it you; and by the way, you shall tell me where in the forest you live. Will you go?

Orl. With all my heart, good youth.

Ros. Nay, you must call me Rosalind. Come, sister, will you go?   *Exeunt.* 435

SCENE III

Enter Clown [TOUCHSTONE], AUDREY; *and* JAQUES [*behind*].

Touch. Come apace, good Audrey; I will fetch up your goats, Audrey. And how, Audrey? am I the man yet? Doth my simple feature content you?

Aud. Your features, Lord warrant us! what features? 6

Touch. I am here with thee and thy goats as the most capricious poet, honest Ovid, was among the Goths.

Jaq. [*Aside.*] O knowledge ill-inhabited, worse than Jove in a thatch'd house! 11

Touch. When a man's verses cannot be understood, nor a man's good wit seconded with the forward child, understanding, it strikes a man more dead than a great reckoning in a little room. Truly, I would the gods had made thee poetical. 16

Aud. I do not know what "poetical" is. Is it honest in deed and word? Is it a true thing?

Touch. No, truly; for the truest poetry is the most feigning, and lovers are given to poetry; 20 and what they swear in poetry may be said as lovers they do feign.

Aud. Do you wish then that the gods had made me poetical?

Touch. I do, truly; for thou swear'st to me 25 thou art honest. Now if thou wert a poet, I might have some hope thou didst feign.

Aud. Would you not have me honest? 28

Touch. No, truly, unless thou wert hard-favor'd; for honesty coupled to beauty is to have honey a sauce to sugar.

---

379. **bonnet unbanded:** hat without a band around the crown, a fashion described by Stubbes in *The Anatomy of Abuses* as "unseemly (I will not say how assy)."
381. **careless:** i.e. heedless of appearance.
382. **point-device:** very correct.
383. **accoutrements:** accoutrements.
389. **apter:** readier.   390. **still:** regularly.
391. **consciences:** inmost thoughts, "hearts."   **sooth:** truth.
400. **merely a:** an utter.
401. **dark . . . whip.** The common treatment for the insane.
404. **profess:** claim to have skill in.
410. **moonish:** given to changing moods.   **be effeminate:** act like a woman.   411. **fantastical:** fanciful, capricious.
412. **apish:** affected.   416. **entertain:** welcome, admit.
418. **drave:** drove.   **humor:** whim.
419. **living humor:** actual state.
421. **merely monastic:** exactly like a hermit.
422. **liver.** The supposed seat of the passions.
423. **sound sheep's heart.** Perhaps suggesting that Orlando, by being freed of love, will be reduced to one of the stupidest of animals.

425. **would not:** do not wish to be. Rosalind then picks up *would* in the ordinary sense.

III.iii. Location: The forest.
3. **feature:** form and appearance.   5. **warrant:** protect.
5–6. **what features?** To Audrey the noun is simply unintelligible.
8. **capricious:** ingenious, full of witty conceits; with play on Latin *caper*, "he-goat," which further suggests the sense "goatish, lascivious."   9. **Goths.** Pronounced *goats.*
10. **ill-inhabited:** meanly lodged.
11. **Jove . . . house.** Jupiter and Mercury, disguised, stayed as guests in the lowly cottage of Baucis and Philemon.
13–14. **forward:** precocious.
15. **great . . . room:** exorbitant bill for food in a small, mean tavern. Some find here an allusion to Christopher Marlowe's death at the hands of Ingram Frizer in 1593 in a quarrel over a tavern bill.
18. **honest:** honorable, true.   20. **feigning:** based on imagination.
26. **honest:** chaste.   29. **hard-favor'd:** ugly.

Jaq. [*Aside.*] A material fool!

Aud. Well, I am not fair, and therefore I pray the gods make me honest. 34

Touch. Truly, and to cast away honesty upon a foul slut were to put good meat into an unclean dish.

Aud. I am not a slut, though I thank the gods I am foul. 39

Touch. Well, prais'd be the gods for thy foulness! sluttishness may come hereafter. But be it as it may be, I will marry thee; and to that end I have been with Sir Oliver Martext, the vicar of the next village, who hath promis'd to meet me in this place of the forest and to couple us. 45

Jaq. [*Aside.*] I would fain see this meeting.

Aud. Well, the gods give us joy!

Touch. Amen. A man may, if he were of a fearful heart, stagger in this attempt; for here we have no temple but the wood, no assembly but horn- 50 beasts. But what though? Courage! As horns are odious, they are necessary. It is said, "Many a man knows no end of his goods." Right! many a man has good horns, and knows no end of them. Well, that is the dowry of his wife, 'tis none of 55 his own getting. Horns? even so. Poor men alone? No, no, the noblest deer hath them as huge as the rascal. Is the single man therefore bless'd? No, as a wall'd town is more worthier than a village, so is the forehead of a married man more honor- 60 able than the bare brow of a bachelor; and by how much defense is better than no skill, by so much is a horn more precious than to want.

Enter Sir Oliver Martext.

Here comes Sir Oliver. Sir Oliver Martext, you are well met. Will you dispatch us here under 65 this tree, or shall we go with you to your chapel?

Sir Oli. Is there none here to give the woman?

Touch. I will not take her on gift of any man.

Sir Oli. Truly, she must be given, or the marriage is not lawful. 70

Jaq. [*Discovering himself.*] Proceed, proceed. I'll give her.

Touch. Good even, good Master What-ye-call't; how do you, sir? You are very well met. God 74 'ild you for your last company. I am very glad to see you. Even a toy in hand here, sir. Nay, pray be cover'd.

Jaq. Will you be married, motley?

Touch. As the ox hath his bow, sir, the horse his 80 curb, and the falcon her bells, so man hath his desires; and as pigeons bill, so wedlock would be nibbling.

Jaq. And will you (being a man of your breeding) be married under a bush like a beggar? Get you to church, and have a good priest that can tell 85 you what marriage is. This fellow will but join you together as they join wainscot; then one of you will prove a shrunk panel, and like green timber warp, warp. 89

Touch. [*Aside.*] I am not in the mind but I were better to be married of him than of another, for he is not like to marry me well; and not being well married, it will be a good excuse for me hereafter to leave my wife. 94

Jaq. Go thou with me, and let me counsel thee.

[*Touch.*] Come, sweet Audrey,
We must be married, or we must live in bawdry.
Farewell, good Master Oliver: not

>   "O sweet Oliver,
>   O brave Oliver,   100
>   Leave me not behind thee;"

but

>   "Wind away,
>   Be gone, I say,
>   I will not to wedding with thee."   105
>   [*Exeunt Jaques, Touchstone, and Audrey.*]

Sir Oli. 'Tis no matter; ne'er a fantastical knave of them all shall flout me out of my calling.   *Exit.*

Scene IV

Enter Rosalind *and* Celia.

Ros. Never talk to me, I will weep.

Cel. Do, I prithee, but yet have the grace to consider that tears do not become a man.

Ros. But have I not cause to weep?

Cel. As good cause as one would desire, therefore weep. 6

Ros. His very hair is of the dissembling color.

Cel. Something browner than Judas's. Marry, his kisses are Judas's own children.

Ros. I' faith, his hair is of a good color. 10

Cel. An excellent color. Your chestnut was ever the only color.

Ros. And his kissing is as full of sanctity as the touch of holy bread. 14

---

32. **material:** full of "matter" or good sense.   36. **foul:** ugly.
43. **Sir:** courtesy title for a priest.   49. **stagger:** hesitate, waver.
50–51. **horn-beasts.** With allusion to the horns of the cuckolded husband.   51. **what though:** what of that.   **As:** though.
52. **necessary:** inevitable.
53. **knows . . . goods:** thinks his wealth inexhaustible.
54. **knows . . . them:** isn't aware of their points coming into view on his forehead.   55. **dowry:** i.e. what his wife brings him.
56. **getting.** With play on "begetting," with reference to his wife's children.   58. **rascal:** young, lean deer, hence inferior.
62. **defense:** skill in self-defense.   63. **want:** i.e. lack one.
65. **dispatch:** i.e. marry.   71 s.d. **Discovering:** revealing.
75. **'ild:** yield, i.e. reward.   **your last company.** Referring to their earlier meeting (II.vii.12 ff.).
76. **Even . . . hand:** first a trifling matter is being undertaken.
77. **be cover'd:** put on your hat. Touchstone speaks as if to a social inferior who has respectfully bared his head.

79. **bow:** yoke.
85–86. **tell . . . is:** instruct you in the responsibilities of marriage (as the ignorant Sir Oliver cannot).
90–91. **not . . . better:** not sure but that it would be better for me.
97. **married:** i.e. properly in church.   **in bawdry:** i.e. in sin.
99–101. **O . . . thee.** From a ballad of the 1580's, now lost; but lines 103–5 may be Touchstone's improvisation.   103. **Wind:** wander, go.
106. **fantastical:** full of ridiculous notions.

III.iv. Location: The forest.
7. **of . . . color:** i.e. red—like Judas Iscariot's, according to tradition.
8. **Something:** somewhat.
9. **Judas's own children:** i.e. traitorous, like the kiss with which Judas betrayed Jesus.   11. **Your.** The indefinite use; a colloquialism.
14. **holy bread:** ordinary leavened bread which was blessed after the Eucharist and given to non-communicants.

Cel. He hath bought a pair of cast lips of Diana.
A nun of winter's sisterhood kisses not more religiously, the very ice of chastity is in them.

Ros. But why did he swear he would come this
morning, and comes not?

Cel. Nay certainly there is no truth in him.   20

Ros. Do you think so?

Cel. Yes, I think he is not a pick-purse nor a
horse-stealer, but for his verity in love, I do think
him as concave as a cover'd goblet or a worm-eaten
nut.   25

Ros. Not true in love?

Cel. Yes, when he is in—but I think he is not
in.

Ros. You have heard him swear downright he was.

Cel. "Was" is not "is." Besides, the oath of [a]
lover is no stronger than the word of a tapster;
they are both the confirmer of false reckonings.   32
He attends here in the forest on the Duke your
father.

Ros. I met the Duke yesterday, and had much
question with him. He ask'd me of what parentage
I was. I told him of as good as he, so he laugh'd   37
and let me go. But what talk we of fathers, when
there is such a man as Orlando?

Cel. O, that's a brave man! he writes brave
verses, speaks brave words, swears brave oaths, and
breaks them bravely, quite traverse, athwart   42
the heart of his lover, as a puisne tilter, that spurs
his horse but on one side, breaks his staff like a
noble goose. But all's brave that youth mounts and
folly guides. Who comes here?   46

Enter CORIN.

Cor. Mistress and master, you have oft inquired
After the shepherd that complain'd of love,
Who you saw sitting by me on the turf,
Praising the proud disdainful shepherdess   50
That was his mistress.

Cel.   Well; and what of him?

Cor. If you will see a pageant truly play'd
Between the pale complexion of true love
And the red glow of scorn and proud disdain,
Go hence a little, and I shall conduct you,   55
If you will mark it.

Ros.   O, come, let us remove,
The sight of lovers feedeth those in love.
Bring us to this sight, and you shall say
I'll prove a busy actor in their play.   *Exeunt.*

---

15. **cast:** cast-off; i.e. one whom he kissed might think that his lips
had once belonged to Diana, the goddess of chastity.
16. **of winter's sisterhood:** i.e. devoted to cold and barren chastity.
23. **verity:** truthfulness.
24. **concave:** hollow.   **cover'd goblet.** A goblet would have its cover
on only when not in use, hence empty.   36. **question:** conversation.
38. **what:** why.
40. **brave:** excellent, splendid (but used with irony and some suggestion of the related word *bravado* [= boasting without intention of
action]).   42. **traverse:** awry.
43. **puisne:** inexperienced (literally, younger).   44. **staff:** spear.
45. **noble goose:** young, foolish courtier.
52. **pageant:** drama, scene.
53. **pale.** Every sigh was thought to draw a drop of blood from the
heart.   56. **will mark:** desire to witness.

SCENE V

Enter SILVIUS *and* PHEBE.

Sil. Sweet Phebe, do not scorn me, do not,
          Phebe;
Say that you love me not, but say not so
In bitterness. The common executioner,
Whose heart th' accustom'd sight of death makes hard,
Falls not the axe upon the humbled neck   5
But first begs pardon. Will you sterner be
Than he that dies and lives by bloody drops?

Enter, [*behind,*] ROSALIND, CELIA, *and* CORIN.

Phe. I would not be thy executioner;
I fly thee for I would not injure thee.
Thou tell'st me there is murder in mine eye: 10
'Tis pretty, sure, and very probable,
That eyes, that are the frail'st and softest things,
Who shut their coward gates on atomies,
Should be called tyrants, butchers, murtherers!
Now I do frown on thee with all my heart,   15
And if mine eyes can wound, now let them kill thee.
Now counterfeit to swound; why, now fall down,
Or if thou canst not, O, for shame, for shame,
Lie not, to say mine eyes are murtherers!
Now show the wound mine eye hath made in thee;   20
Scratch thee but with a pin, and there remains
Some scar of it; lean upon a rush,
The cicatrice and capable impressure
Thy palm some moment keeps; but now mine eyes,
Which I have darted at thee, hurt thee not,   25
Nor I am sure there is no force in eyes
That can do hurt.

Sil.   O dear Phebe,
If ever (as that ever may be near)
You meet in some fresh cheek the power of fancy,
Then shall you know the wounds invisible   30
That love's keen arrows make.

Phe.   But till that time
Come not thou near me; and when that time comes,
Afflict me with thy mocks, pity me not,
As till that time I shall not pity thee.

Ros. [*Advancing.*] And why, I pray you? Who
          might be your mother,   35
That you insult, exult, and all at once,
Over the wretched? What though you have no
          beauty—
As, by my faith, I see no more in you
Than without candle may go dark to bed—
Must you be therefore proud and pitiless?   40
Why, what means this? why do you look on me?
I see no more in you than in the ordinary
Of nature's sale-work. 'Od's my little life,
I think she means to tangle my eyes too!

III.v. Location: The forest.
5. **Falls:** lets fall.   6. **But first begs:** without first asking.
7. **dies and lives:** spends his whole life and thus earns his whole living.
9. **for:** because.   11. **pretty:** clever (ironic).   **sure:** surely.
17. **counterfeit to swound:** pretend to swoon.
23. **cicatrice:** i.e. mark.   **capable impressure:** perceptible impression.   29. **fresh:** young and beautiful.   **fancy:** love.
33. **mocks:** ridicule.   36. **all at once:** i.e. in the same breath.
38–39. **no . . . bed:** i.e. not enough beauty to lighten the dark.
43. **sale-work:** run-of-the-mill products.   **'Od's:** God save.
44. **tangle:** ensnare.

As You Like It
III.v

No, faith, proud mistress, hope not after it.   45
'Tis not your inky brows, your black silk hair,
Your bugle eyeballs, nor your cheek of cream
That can entame my spirits to your worship.
You foolish shepherd, wherefore do you follow her,
Like foggy south, puffing with wind and rain?   50
You are a thousand times a properer man
Than she a woman. 'Tis such fools as you
That makes the world full of ill-favor'd children.
'Tis not her glass, but you that flatters her,
And out of you she sees herself more proper   55
Than any of her lineaments can show her.
But, mistress, know yourself, down on your knees,
And thank heaven, fasting, for a good man's love;
For I must tell you friendly in your ear,
Sell when you can, you are not for all markets.   60
Cry the man mercy, love him, take his offer;
Foul is most foul, being foul to be a scoffer.
So take her to thee, shepherd. Fare you well.

Phe. Sweet youth, I pray you chide a year together,
I had rather hear you chide than this man woo.   65

Ros. He's fall'n in love with your foulness—and
she'll fall in love with my anger. If it be so, as
fast as she answers thee with frowning looks, I'll
sauce her with bitter words.—Why look you so
upon me?   70

Phe. For no ill will I bear you.

Ros. I pray you do not fall in love with me,
For I am falser than vows made in wine.
Besides, I like you not. If you will know my house,
'Tis at the tuft of olives here hard by.   75
Will you go, sister? Shepherd, ply her hard.
Come, sister. Shepherdess, look on him better,
And be not proud; though all the world could see,
None could be so abus'd in sight as he.
Come, to our flock.   *Exit [with Celia and Corin].*   80

Phe. Dead shepherd, now I find thy saw of might,
"Who ever lov'd that lov'd not at first sight?"

Sil. Sweet Phebe—

Phe.   Hah! what say'st thou, Silvius?

Sil. Sweet Phebe, pity me.

Phe. Why, I am sorry for thee, gentle Silvius.   85

Sil. Where ever sorrow is, relief would be.
If you do sorrow at my grief in love,
By giving love, your sorrow and my grief
Were both extermin'd.

Phe. Thou hast my love; is not that neighborly?   90

Sil. I would have you.

Phe.   Why, that were covetousness.
Silvius, the time was that I hated thee;
And yet it is not that I bear thee love,
But since that thou canst talk of love so well,
Thy company, which erst was irksome to me,   95
I will endure; and I'll employ thee too.
But do not look for further recompense
Than thine own gladness that thou art employ'd.

Sil. So holy and so perfect is my love,
And I in such a poverty of grace,   100
That I shall think it a most plenteous crop
To glean the broken ears after the man
That the main harvest reaps. Loose now and then
A scatt'red smile, and that I'll live upon.

Phe. Know'st thou the youth that spoke to me
yerwhile?   105

Sil. Not very well, but I have met him oft,
And he hath bought the cottage and the bounds
That the old carlot once was master of.

Phe. Think not I love him, though I ask for him;
'Tis but a peevish boy—yet he talks well—   110
But what care I for words? Yet words do well
When he that speaks them pleases those that hear.
It is a pretty youth—not very pretty—
But sure he's proud—and yet his pride becomes him.
He'll make a proper man. The best thing in him   115
Is his complexion; and faster than his tongue
Did make offense, his eye did heal it up.
He is not very tall—yet for his years he's tall;
His leg is but so so—and yet 'tis well;
There was a pretty redness in his lip,   120
A little riper and more lusty red
Than that mix'd in his cheek; 'twas just the difference
Betwixt the constant red and mingled damask.
There be some women, Silvius, had they mark'd him
In parcels as I did, would have gone near   125
To fall in love with him; but for my part
I love him not, nor hate him not; and yet
Have more cause to hate him than to love him,
For what had he to do to chide at me?
He said mine eyes were black and my hair black,
And, now I am rememb'red, scorn'd at me.   131
I marvel why I answer'd not again.
But that's all one; omittance is no quittance.
I'll write to him a very taunting letter,
And thou shalt bear it; wilt thou, Silvius?   135

---

47. **bugle eyeballs:** eyes like shiny black beads.   **cream:** yellow.
48. **entame:** subdue.   **your worship:** worship of you.
50. **south:** south wind (which in England brings fog and rain).   **wind and rain:** i.e. sighs and tears.   51. **properer:** handsomer.
54. **glass:** mirror.   55. **out of you:** i.e. with you as her mirror.
59. **friendly:** as a friend.   61. **Cry...mercy:** beg the man's pardon.
62. **Foul...scoffer:** i.e. an ugly woman is seen at her worst when, ugly though she is, she scoffs at proffered love.
64. **together:** without intermission.   69. **sauce:** rebuke sharply.
78. **could see:** should be able to look (on you).
79. **abus'd in sight:** deceived by his eyes.
81. **Dead shepherd:** i.e. Marlowe (died 1593); line 82 is quoted from his *Hero and Leander* (I.176), published in 1598.   **find...might:** perceive the force of your saying.
86. **Where...be:** i.e. wherever sorrow is felt, a desire to give relief should follow.   89. **Were both extermin'd:** would both be banished.
90. **is...neighborly:** i.e. doesn't that follow from the fact that I am

your neighbor (and hence, with reference to Christ's second commandment, am bound as a good Christian to love you).
91. **covetousness.** Referring to the Mosaic tenth commandment, "Thou shalt not covet...anything that is thy neighbor's." Phebe thus makes it appear that she is following the Biblical injunctions, while Silvius is breaking them.
93. **yet...that:** the time has not yet come when.
95. **erst:** once, before.   100. **poverty of grace:** dearth of favor.
103–104. **Loose...scatt'red:** let fly...random (a figure from archery).   105. **yerwhile:** erewhile, just now.
107. **bounds:** pasturage.   108. **carlot:** peasant.
123. **constant:** uniform.   **mingled damask:** mixture of red and white.
125. **In parcels:** part by part, in detail.
125–26. **gone...fall:** come close to falling.
129. **what...do:** what business had he.
131. **am rememb'red:** recall.
133. **omittance...quittance:** failure to assert a claim does not imply renunciation of the claim (legal proverb); i.e. I am still entitled to reply.

Sil. Phebe, with all my heart.
Phe. 　　　　　　　　　　　　I'll write it straight;
The matter's in my head and in my heart.
I will be bitter with him and passing short.
Go with me, Silvius.　　　　　　　　　　*Exeunt.*

ACT IV, SCENE I

Enter ROSALIND *and* CELIA *and* JAQUES.

Jaq. I prithee, pretty youth, let me [be] better
acquainted with thee.
Ros. They say you are a melancholy fellow.
Jaq. I am so; I do love it better than laughing. 4
Ros. Those that are in extremity of either are
abominable fellows, and betray themselves to every
modern censure worse than drunkards.
Jaq. Why, 'tis good to be sad and say nothing.
Ros. Why then 'tis good to be a post. 9
Jaq. I have neither the scholar's melancholy,
which is emulation; nor the musician's, which is
fantastical; nor the courtier's, which is proud; nor
the soldier's, which is ambitious; nor the lawyer's,
which is politic; nor the lady's, which is nice; nor
the lover's, which is all these: but it is a melan- 15
choly of mine own, compounded of many simples,
extracted from many objects, and indeed the sundry contemplation of my travels, in which [my]
often rumination wraps me in a most humorous
sadness. 20
Ros. A traveller! By my faith, you have great
reason to be sad. I fear you have sold your own
lands to see other men's; then to have seen much,
and to have nothing, is to have rich eyes and poor
hands. 25
Jaq. Yes, I have gain'd my experience.

Enter ORLANDO.

Ros. And your experience makes you sad. I had
rather have a fool to make me merry than experience
to make me sad—and to travel for it too!
Orl. Good day and happiness, dear Rosalind! 30
Jaq. Nay then God buy you, and you talk in
blank verse.
Ros. Farewell, Monsieur Traveller: look you
lisp and wear strange suits; disable all the benefits of
your own country; be out of love with your 35
nativity, and almost chide God for making you
that countenance you are; or I will scarce think

you have swam in a gundello. [*Exit Jaques.*] Why,
how now, Orlando, where have you been all this
while? You a lover! And you serve me such another
trick, never come in my sight more. 41
Orl. My fair Rosalind, I come within an hour of
my promise.
Ros. Break an hour's promise in love! He that
will divide a minute into a thousand parts, and 45
break but a part of the thousand part of a minute
in the affairs of love, it may be said of him that
Cupid hath clapp'd him o' th' shoulder, but I'll
warrant him heart-whole.
Orl. Pardon me, dear Rosalind. 50
Ros. Nay, and you be so tardy, come no more in
my sight. I had as lief be woo'd of a snail.
Orl. Of a snail?
Ros. Ay, of a snail; for though he comes slowly,
he carries his house on his head; a better join- 55
ture I think than you make a woman. Besides,
he brings his destiny with him.
Orl. What's that?
Ros. Why, horns! which such as you are fain to
be beholding to your wives for. But he comes 60
arm'd in his fortune, and prevents the slander of
his wife.
Orl. Virtue is no horn-maker; and my Rosalind
is virtuous.
Ros. And I am your Rosalind. 65
Cel. It pleases him to call you so; but he hath a
Rosalind of a better leer than you.
Ros. Come, woo me, woo me; for now I am in a
holiday humor, and like enough to consent. What
would you say to me now, and I were your very very
Rosalind? 71
Orl. I would kiss before I spoke.
Ros. Nay, you were better speak first, and when
you were gravell'd for lack of matter, you might
take occasion to kiss. Very good orators when 75
they are out, they will spit, and for lovers lacking
(God warn us!) matter, the cleanliest shift is to kiss.
Orl. How if the kiss be denied?
Ros. Then she puts you to entreaty, and there
begins new matter. 80
Orl. Who could be out, being before his belov'd
mistress?
Ros. Marry, that should you if I were your mistress, or I should think my honesty ranker than
my wit. 85
Orl. What, of my suit?
Ros. Not out of your apparel, and yet out of your
suit. Am not I your Rosalind?

138. **passing short:** exceedingly curt.

IV.i. Location: The forest.
5. **are . . . of:** go to extremes in.
7. **modern censure:** ordinary judgment.
8. **sad:** sober-minded. Rosalind then quibbles on the sense "heavy."
11. **emulation:** envy.　12. **fantastical:** highly fanciful.
14. **politic:** shrewd, calculated.　**nice:** delicate, fastidious.
16. **simples:** ingredients.　17. **objects:** sights, observations.
17–18. **sundry contemplation of:** contemplation of various details during (?) or various ways of thinking about (?).
18–19. **in . . . rumination:** in which (melancholy) my frequent medita-tion.　19. **humorous:** moody.
29. **travel.** With pun on *travail*, "labor."
31. **God buy you:** goodbye.　**and:** if.
34. **lisp:** speak affectedly.　**disable:** disparage.
36. **nativity:** birth, i.e. nationality.

38. **swam . . . gundello:** ridden in a gondola, i.e. seen Venice (a very popular resort of foreign travellers).　46. **thousand:** thousandth.
48. **clapp'd . . . shoulder:** i.e. struck him in the back (with his arrow). Cf. *clapp'd i' th' clout* (hit the bull's-eye), *2 Henry IV*, III.ii.46.
49. **heart-whole:** not wounded in the heart.
55–56. **jointure:** marriage settlement.
59. **horns:** i.e. cuckold's horns.　**fain:** obliged.
60. **beholding:** beholden, indebted.
61. **arm'd . . . fortune:** already equipped for his future.　**prevents:** forestalls.　**slander:** ill repute.　67. **of . . . leer:** better-looking.
74. **gravell'd:** stuck, at a loss.　76. **out:** i.e. out of "matter."
77. **warn:** warrant, protect.　**cleanliest shift:** cleverest device (with a play in *cleanliest* on kissing versus spitting).
84. **honesty:** chastity.　**ranker:** more corrupt.

As You Like It
IV.i

Orl. I take some joy to say you are, because I would be talking of her.   90

Ros. Well, in her person, I say I will not have you.

Orl. Then in mine own person, I die.

Ros. No, faith, die by attorney. The poor world is almost six thousand years old, and in all this time there was not any man died in his own   96 person, *videlicet*, in a love-cause. Troilus had his brains dash'd out with a Grecian club, yet he did what he could to die before, and he is one of the patterns of love. Leander, he would have liv'd   100 many a fair year though Hero had turn'd nun, if it had not been for a hot midsummer night; for, good youth, he went but forth to wash him in the Hellespont, and being taken with the cramp was drown'd; and the foolish chroniclers of that age found it was—   105 Hero of Sestos. But these are all lies: men have died from time to time, and worms have eaten them, but not for love.

Orl. I would not have my right Rosalind of this mind, for I protest her frown might kill me.   110

Ros. By this hand, it will not kill a fly. But come, now I will be your Rosalind in a more coming-on disposition; and ask me what you will, I will grant it.

Orl. Then love me, Rosalind.   115

Ros. Yes, faith, will I, Fridays and Saturdays and all.

Orl. And wilt thou have me?

Ros. Ay, and twenty such.

Orl. What sayest thou?   120

Ros. Are you not good?

Orl. I hope so.

Ros. Why then, can one desire too much of a good thing? Come, sister, you shall be the priest, and marry us. Give me your hand, Orlando. What do you say, sister?   126

Orl. Pray thee marry us.

Cel. I cannot say the words.

Ros. You must begin, "Will you, Orlando"—

Cel. Go to! Will you, Orlando, have to wife this Rosalind?   131

Orl. I will.

Ros. Ay, but when?

Orl. Why, now, as fast as she can marry us.

Ros. Then you must say, "I take thee, Rosalind, for wife."   136

Orl. I take thee, Rosalind, for wife.

Ros. I might ask you for your commission, but I do take thee, Orlando, for my husband. There's

a girl goes before the priest, and certainly a woman's thought runs before her actions.   141

Orl. So do all thoughts, they are wing'd.

Ros. Now tell me how long you would have her after you have possess'd her.

Orl. For ever and a day.   145

Ros. Say "a day," without the "ever." No, no, Orlando, men are April when they woo, December when they wed; maids are May when they are maids, but the sky changes when they are wives. I will be more jealous of thee than a Barbary cock-   150 pigeon over his hen, more clamorous than a parrot against rain, more new-fangled than an ape, more giddy in my desires than a monkey. I will weep for nothing, like Diana in the fountain, and I will do that when you are dispos'd to be merry. I will laugh   155 like a hyen, and that when thou art inclin'd to sleep.

Orl. But will my Rosalind do so?

Ros. By my life, she will do as I do.

Orl. O, but she is wise.   159

Ros. Or else she could not have the wit to do this; the wiser, the waywarder. Make the doors upon a woman's wit, and it will out at the casement; shut that, and 'twill out at the key-hole; stop that, 'twill fly with the smoke out at the chimney.

Orl. A man that had a wife with such a wit, he might say, "Wit, whither wilt?"   166

Ros. Nay, you might keep that check for it, till you met your wive's wit going to your neighbor's bed.

Orl. And what wit could wit have to excuse that?

Ros. Marry, to say she came to seek you there. You shall never take her without her answer,   172 unless you take her without her tongue. O, that woman that cannot make her fault her husband's occasion, let her never nurse her child herself, for she will breed it like a fool!   176

Orl. For these two hours, Rosalind, I will leave thee.

Ros. Alas, dear love, I cannot lack thee two hours!

Orl. I must attend the Duke at dinner. By two a' clock I will be with thee again.

Ros. Ay, go your ways, go your ways; I knew what you would prove; my friends told me as   183 much, and I thought no less. That flattering tongue of yours won me. 'Tis but one cast away, and so come death! Two a' clock is your hour?

Orl. Ay, sweet Rosalind.   187

Ros. By my troth, and in good earnest, and so God mend me, and by all pretty oaths that are not

---

94. **attorney:** proxy.
94–95. **The poor . . . old.** This was the view of some Biblical commentators.
97. **videlicet:** namely.   **Troilus:** the lover of Cressida, who proved faithless to him.
98. **brains . . . club.** Troilus died of a wound inflicted by Achilles' spear. Rosalind makes his end, and Leander's, as unromantic as possible.
98–99. **did . . . before:** i.e. vainly did his utmost to die earlier of frustrated love.   100. **patterns:** models.
105. **found:** gave the verdict (the customary term for the handing down of a verdict by a coroner's jury).   109. **right:** real.
138. **for your commission:** i.e. by what authority you presume to take her (since no one has given her away).

140. **goes before:** anticipates.
150–51. **Barbary cock-pigeon:** a kind of pigeon originally from the Barbary coast of Africa; but the term *Barbary* was also more widely applied to Eastern non-Christians, particularly Moslems, and is suggestive here of the vigilance of Eastern husbands in secluding their wives from other men.
152. **against:** before.   **new-fangled:** delighted by novelty.
153. **giddy:** variable.
154. **Diana . . . fountain.** There may be some specific reference here; but the figure of Diana was probably common in garden fountains.
156. **hyen:** hyena.   161. **Make:** make fast, bar.
166. **Wit, whither wilt.** See note to I.ii.56.   168. **wive's:** wife's.
174–75. **her husband's occasion:** a chance to put her husband in the wrong.   179. **lack:** do without.
189. **pretty:** pleasant-sounding, inoffensive.

dangerous, if you break one jot of your promise, or come one minute behind your hour, I will think you the most pathetical break-promise, and the most hollow lover, and the most unworthy of her 193 you call Rosalind, that may be chosen out of the gross band of the unfaithful; therefore beware my censure, and keep your promise.

Orl. With no less religion than if thou wert indeed my Rosalind; so adieu. 198

Ros. Well, Time is the old justice that examines all such offenders, and let Time try. Adieu.

Exit [Orlando].

Cel. You have simply misus'd our sex in your love-prate. We must have your doublet and hose 202 pluck'd over your head, and show the world what the bird hath done to her own nest.

Ros. O coz, coz, coz, my pretty little coz, that thou didst know how many fathom deep I am 206 in love! But it cannot be sounded; my affection hath an unknown bottom, like the bay of Portugal.

Cel. Or rather, bottomless—that as fast as you pour affection in, [it] runs out.

Ros. No, that same wicked bastard of Venus that was begot of thought, conceiv'd of spleen, and 212 born of madness, that blind rascally boy that abuses every one's eyes because his own are out, let him be judge how deep I am in love. I'll tell thee, Aliena, I cannot be out of the sight of Orlando. I'll go find a shadow, and sigh till he come. 217

Cel. And I'll sleep. *Exeunt.*

Scene II

Enter Jaques *and* Lords [*as*] foresters.

Jaq. Which is he that kill'd the deer?

[1.] *Lord.* Sir, it was I.

Jaq. Let's present him to the Duke like a Roman conqueror, and it would do well to set the deer's horns upon his head, for a branch of victory. Have you no song, forester, for this purpose? 6

[2.] *Lord.* Yes, sir.

Jaq. Sing it. 'Tis no matter how it be in tune, so it make noise enough. *Music.*

Song

[2. *Lord.*] What shall he have that kill'd the deer?
His leather skin and horns to wear. 11
Then sing him home.
The rest shall bear this burthen.

Take thou no scorn to wear the horn,
It was a crest ere thou wast born;
Thy father's father wore it, 15
And thy father bore it.
The horn, the horn, the lusty horn
Is not a thing to laugh to scorn. *Exeunt.*

Scene III

Enter Rosalind *and* Celia.

Ros. How say you now? Is it not past two a' clock? And here much Orlando!

Cel. I warrant you, with pure love and troubled brain, he hath ta'en his bow and arrows and is gone forth—to sleep. Look who comes here. 5

Enter Silvius.

Sil. My errand is to you, fair youth,
My gentle Phebe did bid me give you this.

[*Gives a letter.*]

I know not the contents, but as I guess
By the stern brow and waspish action
Which she did use as she was writing of it, 10
It bears an angry tenure. Pardon me,
I am but as a guiltless messenger.

Ros. Patience herself would startle at this letter,
And play the swaggerer: bear this, bear all!
She says I am not fair, that I lack manners; 15
She calls me proud, and that she could not love me
Were man as rare as phoenix. 'Od's my will,
Her love is not the hare that I do hunt;
Why writes she so to me? Well, shepherd, well,
This is a letter of your own device. 20

Sil. No, I protest, I know not the contents,
Phebe did write it.

Ros.　　　　　Come, come, you are a fool,
And turn'd into the extremity of love.
I saw her hand, she has a leathern hand,
A freestone-colored hand. I verily did think 25
That her old gloves were on, but 'twas her hands;
She has a huswive's hand—but that's no matter.
I say she never did invent this letter,
This is a man's invention and his hand.

Sil. Sure it is hers. 30

Ros. Why, 'tis a boisterous and a cruel style,
A style for challengers. Why, she defies me,
Like Turk to Christian. Women's gentle brain
Could not drop forth such giant-rude invention,
Such Ethiop words, blacker in their effect 35
Than in their countenance. Will you hear the letter?

Sil. So please you, for I never heard it yet;
Yet heard too much of Phebe's cruelty.

Ros. She Phebes me. Mark how the tyrant writes.

---

192. **pathetical:** pitiable, miserable. 195. **gross:** entire.
197. **religion:** faithfulness. 200. **try:** determine.
201. **simply:** stupidly (?) or utterly (?). **misus'd:** abused, slandered.
202–4. **We . . . nest:** i.e. we must expose you as a member of the sex that you have defamed. There is an allusion to the proverb "It is a foul bird that fouls its own nest." 211. **bastard of Venus:** Cupid.
212. **thought:** melancholy. **spleen:** caprice, waywardness.
213. **abuses:** deludes. 214. **his . . . out:** he himself is blind.
217. **shadow:** shady place.

IV.ii. Location: The forest. This short scene is introduced to indicate the passing of the specified two hours between Scenes i and iii.
8. **how . . . tune:** whether you sing it on key (?) or whether the tune be good or bad (?).
12 s.d. **bear this burthen:** i.e. sing the words "Then sing him home"

as a ground-bass or undersong throughout (?). On the stage direction see the Textual Notes. 13. **Take . . . scorn:** do not disdain.
14. **crest:** (1) heraldic device; (2) something growing on the head.

IV.iii. Location: The forest.
11. **tenure:** tenor. 17. **phoenix.** Supposedly unique.
23. **turn'd:** brought. 25. **freestone-colored:** brownish-yellow.
35. **Ethiop:** black. 36. **countenance:** physical appearance.
39. **Phebes me:** behaves like Phebe towards me, i.e. addresses me in cruel words.

(*Read.*) "Art thou god to shepherd turn'd,   40
    That a maiden's heart hath burn'd?"
Can a woman rail thus?
    Sil.   Call you this railing?
    Ros.   (*Read.*)
    "Why, thy godhead laid apart,
        Warr'st thou with a woman's heart?"   45
Did you ever hear such railing?
    "Whiles the eye of man did woo me,
        That could do no vengeance to me."
Meaning me a beast.
    "If the scorn of your bright eyne   50
        Have power to raise such love in mine,
    Alack, in me what strange effect
        Would they work in mild aspect?
    Whiles you chid me, I did love;
        How then might your prayers move?   55
    He that brings this love to thee
        Little knows this love in me;
    And by him seal up thy mind,
        Whether that thy youth and kind
    Will the faithful offer take   60
        Of me, and all that I can make,
    Or else by him my love deny,
        And then I'll study how to die."
    Sil.   Call you this chiding?
    Cel.   Alas, poor shepherd!   65
    Ros.   Do you pity him? No, he deserves no pity.
Wilt thou love such a woman? What, to make thee
an instrument, and play false strains upon thee? not
to be endur'd! Well, go your way to her (for I see
love hath made thee a tame snake) and say this to her:
that if she love me, I charge her to love thee; if she   71
will not, I will never have her unless thou entreat for
her. If you be a true lover, hence, and not a word;
for here comes more company.   *Exit Silvius*

Enter OLIVER.

    Oli.   Good morrow, fair ones. Pray you (if you
know)   75
Where in the purlieus of this forest stands
A sheep-cote fenc'd about with olive-trees?
    Cel.   West of this place, down in the neighbor
bottom,
The rank of osiers by the murmuring stream
Left on your right hand brings you to the place.   80
But at this hour the house doth keep itself,
There's none within.
    Oli.   If that an eye may profit by a tongue,
Then should I know you by description—
Such garments and such years. "The boy is fair,   85
Of female favor, and bestows himself
Like a ripe sister; the woman low,

And browner than her brother." Are not you
The owner of the house I did inquire for?
    Cel.   It is no boast, being ask'd, to say we are.   90
    Oli.   Orlando doth commend him to you both,
And to that youth he calls his Rosalind
He sends this bloody napkin. Are you he?
    Ros.   I am. What must we understand by this?
    Oli.   Some of my shame, if you will know of me
What man I am, and how, and why, and where   96
This handkercher was stain'd.
    Cel.   I pray you tell it.
    Oli.   When last the young Orlando parted from you
He left a promise to return again
Within an hour, and pacing through the forest,   100
Chewing the food of sweet and bitter fancy,
Lo what befell! He threw his eye aside,
And mark what object did present itself
Under an old oak, whose boughs were moss'd with
    age
And high top bald with dry antiquity: 105
A wretched ragged man, o'ergrown with hair,
Lay sleeping on his back; about his neck
A green and gilded snake had wreath'd itself,
Who with her head nimble in threats approach'd
The opening of his mouth; but suddenly   110
Seeing Orlando, it unlink'd itself,
And with indented glides did slip away
Into a bush, under which bush's shade
A lioness, with udders all drawn dry,
Lay couching, head on ground, with cat-like watch
When that the sleeping man should stir; for 'tis   116
The royal disposition of that beast
To prey on nothing that doth seem as dead.
This seen, Orlando did approach the man,
And found it was his brother, his elder brother.   120
    Cel.   O, I have heard him speak of that same brother,
And he did render him the most unnatural
That liv'd amongst men.
    Oli.   And well he might so do,
For well I know he was unnatural.
    Ros.   But to Orlando: did he leave him there,   125
Food to the suck'd and hungry lioness?
    Oli.   Twice did he turn his back, and purpos'd so;
But kindness, nobler ever than revenge,
And nature, stronger than his just occasion,
Made him give battle to the lioness,   130
Who quickly fell before him, in which hurtling
From miserable slumber I awaked.
    Cel.   Are you his brother?
    Ros.   Was't you he rescu'd?
    Cel.   Was't you that did so oft contrive to kill him?
    Oli.   'Twas I; but 'tis not I. I do not shame   135
To tell you what I was, since my conversion
So sweetly tastes, being the thing I am.

---

44. **laid apart**: put aside (for human shape).   48. **vengeance**: harm.
50. **eyne**: eyes (archaic even in Elizabethan English; used here for
the sake of rhyme).   53. **aspect**: looks.
58. **seal . . . mind**: i.e. send your decision in a letter.
59. **youth and kind**: youthful nature.
68. **instrument**: (1) tool; (2) musical instrument.
76. **purlieus**: cleared land bordering a forest.
78. **neighbor bottom**: neighboring dell.
79. **rank of osiers**: row of willows.
86. **female favor**: feminine features.   **bestows**: conducts.
87. **ripe**: mature, i.e. elder.   **low**: short.

93. **napkin**: handkerchief.   103. **what object**: what a sight.
111. **unlink'd**: uncoiled.   112. **indented**: undulating.
114. **udders . . . dry**. Hence hungry.
122. **render him**: depict him as.   **unnatural**: devoid of natural
feeling. Cf. **nature** (= natural affection) in line 129.
125. **to**: with regard to.
128. **kindness**: feeling proper to his (human) kind.
129. **just occasion**: chance to get even.   131. **hurtling**: commotion.
134. **contrive**: plan, devise ways.

Ros. But for the bloody napkin?

Oli.   By and by.
When from the first to last betwixt us two
Tears our recountments had most kindly bath'd,   140
As how I came into that desert place—
[In] brief, he led me to the gentle Duke,
Who gave me fresh array and entertainment,
Committing me unto my brother's love,
Who led me instantly unto his cave,   145
There stripp'd himself, and here upon his arm
The lioness had torn some flesh away,
Which all this while had bled; and now he fainted,
And cried in fainting upon Rosalind.
Brief, I recover'd him, bound up his wound,   150
And after some small space, being strong at heart,
He sent me hither, stranger as I am,
To tell this story, that you might excuse
His broken promise, and to give this napkin,
Dy'd in [his] blood, unto the shepherd youth   155
That he in sport doth call his Rosalind.

[*Rosalind faints.*]

Cel. Why, how now, Ganymed, sweet Ganymed?

Oli. Many will swoon when they do look on blood.

Cel. There is more in it. Cousin Ganymed!

Oli. Look, he recovers.   160

Ros. I would I were at home.

Cel.   We'll lead you thither.
I pray you, will you take him by the arm?

Oli. Be of good cheer, youth. You a man?
You lack a man's heart.

Ros. I do so, I confess it. Ah, sirrah, a body
would think this was well counterfeited! I pray   166
you tell your brother how well I counterfeited.
Heigh-ho!

Oli. This was not counterfeit, there is too great
testimony in your complexion that it was a passion
of earnest.   171

Ros. Counterfeit, I assure you.

Oli. Well then, take a good heart and counterfeit
to be a man.

Ros. So I do; but i' faith, I should have been a
woman by right.   176

Cel. Come, you look paler and paler. Pray you
draw homewards. Good sir, go with us.

Oli. That will I, for I must bear answer back
How you excuse my brother, Rosalind.   180

Ros. I shall devise something; but I pray you
commend my counterfeiting to him. Will you go?

Exeunt.

ACT V, SCENE I

Enter Clown [TOUCHSTONE] *and* AUDREY.

Touch. We shall find a time, Audrey, patience,
gentle Audrey.

Aud. Faith, the priest was good enough, for all
the old gentleman's saying.   4

Touch. A most wicked Sir Oliver, Audrey, a most
vile Martext. But, Audrey, there is a youth here
in the forest lays claim to you.

Aud. Ay, I know who 'tis; he hath no interest
in me in the world. Here comes the man you mean.

Enter WILLIAM.

Touch. It is meat and drink to me to see a clown.
By my troth, we that have good wits have much to
answer for; we shall be flouting; we cannot hold.   12

Will. Good ev'n, Audrey.

Aud. God ye good ev'n, William.

Will. And good ev'n to you, sir.   15

Touch. Good ev'n, gentle friend. Cover thy head,
cover thy head; nay, prithee be cover'd. How old
are you, friend?

Will. Five and twenty, sir.

Touch. A ripe age. Is thy name William?   20

Will. William, sir.

Touch. A fair name. Wast born i' the forest
here?

Will. Ay, sir, I thank God.   24

Touch. "Thank God"—a good answer. Art rich?

Will. Faith, sir, so, so.

Touch. "So, so" is good, very good, very excellent
good; and yet it is not, it is but so, so. Art thou wise?

Will. Ay, sir, I have a pretty wit.   29

Touch. Why, thou say'st well. I do now remember a saying, "The fool doth think he is wise,
but the wise man knows himself to be a fool." The
heathen philosopher, when he had a desire to eat a
grape, would open his lips when he put it into   34
his mouth, meaning thereby that grapes were made
to eat and lips to open. You do love this maid?

Will. I do, [sir].

Touch. Give me your hand. Art thou learned?

Will. No, sir.   39

Touch. Then learn this of me: to have, is to have.
For it is a figure in rhetoric that drink, being pour'd out
of a cup into a glass, by filling the one doth empty the
other. For all your writers do consent that *ipse* is he:
now, you are not *ipse*, for I am he.

Will. Which he, sir?   45

Touch. He, sir, that must marry this woman.
Therefore, you clown, abandon—which is in the
vulgar leave—the society—which in the boorish is
company—of this female—which in the common   49
is woman; which together is, abandon the society of
this female, or, clown, thou perishest; or to thy better

---

138. **for**: i.e. what about.
140. **recountments**: stories told to each other.
150. **Brief**: in brief. **recover'd**: revived.
159. **Cousin**. In her excitement Celia forgets that Rosalind is supposed to be her brother.
165. **I do so.** She lacks a man's heart in two senses not suspected
by Oliver. 170–71. **passion of earnest**: genuine seizure.

V.i. Location: The forest.
8–9 **interest in**: claim to.   10. **clown**: country yokel.
12. **shall**: must. **flouting**: making sport. **hold**: hold back, refrain.   14. **God ye**: God give you.
16. **Cover thy head**: William has respectfully removed his hat.
27. **good, very good.** Touchstone is punning on another meaning of
so, so: "just so; very good."
33–35. **heathen . . . mouth.** Capell suggests that this notion occurs to
Touchstone because William is standing with his mouth open,
gaping at him in bewilderment. The inference is that Audrey is no
grape for William's swallowing.
43. **your writers**: authorities (the indefinite *your*, as in III.iv.12).
ipse: he himself.

understanding, diest; or (to wit) I kill thee, make thee away, translate thy life into death, thy liberty into bondage. I will deal in poison with thee, or in basti-nado, or in steel; I will bandy with thee in faction; I 55 will o'errun thee with [policy]; I will kill thee a hundred and fifty ways: therefore tremble and depart.

Aud. Do, good William.

Will. God rest you merry, sir.　　　　　　*Exit.*

Enter CORIN.

Cor. Our master and mistress seeks you. Come away, away!　　　　　　61

Touch. Trip, Audrey, trip, Audrey! I attend, I attend.　　　　　　*Exeunt.*

SCENE II

Enter ORLANDO *and* OLIVER.

Orl. Is't possible that on so little acquaintance you should like her? that but seeing, you should love her? and loving, woo? and wooing, she should grant? and will you persever to enjoy her?　　4

Oli. Neither call the giddiness of it in question, the poverty of her, the small acquaintance, my sudden wooing, nor [her] sudden consenting; but say with me, I love Aliena; say with her that she loves me; consent with both that we may enjoy each other. It shall be to your good; for my father's house and all the 10 revenue that was old Sir Rowland's will I estate upon you, and here live and die a shepherd.

Enter ROSALIND.

Orl. You have my consent. Let your wedding be to-morrow; thither will I invite the Duke and 14 all 's contented followers. Go you and prepare Aliena; for look you, here comes my Rosalind.

Ros. God save you, brother.

Oli. And you, fair sister.　　　　　　[*Exit.*]

Ros. O my dear Orlando, how it grieves me to see thee wear thy heart in a scarf!　　20

Orl. It is my arm.

Ros. I thought thy heart had been wounded with the claws of a lion.

Orl. Wounded it is, but with the eyes of a lady.

Ros. Did your brother tell you how I counter-feited to sound when he show'd me your handker-cher?　　27

Orl. Ay, and greater wonders than that.

Ros. O, I know where you are. Nay, 'tis true. There was never any thing so sudden but the fight of two rams, and Caesar's thrasonical brag of "I came, saw, and [overcame]." For your brother and my sister no sooner met but they look'd; no sooner look'd but they lov'd; no sooner lov'd but they sigh'd; no sooner sigh'd but they ask'd one another the 35 reason; no sooner knew the reason but they sought the remedy: and in these degrees have they made a pair of stairs to marriage, which they will climb inconti-nent, or else be incontinent before marriage. They 39 are in the very wrath of love, and they will together. Clubs cannot part them.

Orl. They shall be married to-morrow; and I will bid the Duke to the nuptial. But O, how bitter a thing it is to look into happiness through another 44 man's eyes! By so much the more shall I to-morrow be at the height of heart-heaviness, by how much I shall think my brother happy in having what he wishes for.

Ros. Why then to-morrow I cannot serve your turn for Rosalind?

Orl. I can live no longer by thinking.　　50

Ros. I will weary you then no longer with idle talking. Know of me then (for now I speak to some purpose) that I know you are a gentleman of good conceit. I speak not this that you should bear a 54 good opinion of my knowledge, insomuch I say I know you are; neither do I labor for a greater esteem than may in some little measure draw a belief from you, to do yourself good, and not to grace me. Believe then, if you please, that I can do strange things. I have, 59 since I was three year old, convers'd with a magician, most profound in his art, and yet not damnable. If you do love Rosalind so near the heart as your gesture cries it out, when your brother marries Aliena, shall you marry her. I know into what straits of fortune 64 she is driven, and it is not impossible to me, if it appear not inconvenient to you, to set her before your eyes to-morrow, human as she is, and without any danger.

Orl. Speak'st thou in sober meanings?　　69

Ros. By my life I do, which I tender dearly, though I say I am a magician. Therefore put you in your best array, bid your friends; for if you will

52. **to wit:** namely.　53. **translate:** change.
54-55. **bastinado:** beating with a stick.
55. **bandy:** vie, contend.　**faction:** factious spirit.
56. **o'errun:** overwhelm.　**policy:** craftiness.
59. **God . . . merry.** A common form of greeting or leavetaking.

V.ii. Location: The forest.
4. **persever:** persevere.　5. **giddiness:** dizzying speed.
6. **sudden:** swift.　11. **estate:** bestow as an estate.
15. **all 's:** all his.　**contented:** ready, willing.
17. **brother:** (prospective) brother-in-law.
18. **sister.** Oliver is presumably entering into the supposed Ganymed's pretense of being Rosalind.
20. **heart . . . scarf.** Rosalind pretends to assume that any bandage (*scarf*) worn by Orlando must cover the part that he has long pro-claimed wounded—his heart—and further that he has been wearing it on his sleeve.　26. **sound:** swoon.

29. **where you are:** what you mean.
31. **thrasonical:** vaunting. Thraso is a braggart soldier in Terence's *Eunuchus.*
37. **degrees.** With a pun on the meaning "steps."　**pair:** flight.
38-39. **incontinent:** immediately (with following pun on the sense "unchaste").　40. **wrath:** rage, passionate ardor.
41. **Clubs.** Regularly used for breaking up street fights.
43. **bid:** invite.　52-53. **to some purpose:** with serious intent.
54. **conceit:** understanding.　.55. **insomuch:** inasmuch as.
58. **grace:** do honor to.　60. **convers'd:** associated.
61. **not damnable:** i.e. not a practicer of black magic, which involved trafficking with evil spirits and invited damnation.
62. **gesture:** bearing.　63. **cries it out:** plainly reveals.
66. **inconvenient:** unfitting.
67-68. **human . . . danger:** i.e. in her own person, not a spirit in her shape who might endanger Orlando's soul (cf. the apparition of Helen in Marlowe's *Doctor Faustus*).　69. **sober:** serious.
70. **tender dearly:** value highly.
71. **though . . . magician:** i.e. though I endanger my life by saying openly that I practice magic (some forms of which were punishable by death).

be married to-morrow, you shall; and to Rosalind, if you will.   74

Enter SILVIUS *and* PHEBE.

Look, here comes a lover of mine and a lover of hers.

Phe. Youth, you have done me much ungentleness,
To show the letter that I writ to you.

Ros. I care not if I have. It is my study
To seem despiteful and ungentle to you.   80
You are there followed by a faithful shepherd—
Look upon him, love him; he worships you.

Phe. Good shepherd, tell this youth what 'tis to
love.

Sil. It is to be all made of sighs and tears,
And so am I for Phebe.   85

Phe. And I for Ganymed.

Orl. And I for Rosalind.

Ros. And I for no woman.

Sil. It is to be all made of faith and service,
And so am I for Phebe.   90

Phe. And I for Ganymed.

Orl. And I for Rosalind.

Ros. And I for no woman.

Sil. It is to be all made of fantasy,
All made of passion, and all made of wishes,   95
All adoration, duty, and observance,
All humbleness, all patience, and impatience,
All purity, all trial, all observance;
And so am I for Phebe.

Phe. And so am I for Ganymed.   100

Orl. And so am I for Rosalind.

Ros. And so am I for no woman.

Phe. If this be so, why blame you me to love you?

Sil. If this be so, why blame you me to love you?

Orl. If this be so, why blame you me to love you?

Ros. Why do you speak too, "Why blame you
me to love you?"   107

Orl. To her that is not here, nor doth not hear.

Ros. Pray you no more of this, 'tis like the howling of Irish wolves against the moon. [*To Silvius.*] I
will help you if I can. [*To Phebe.*] I would love   111
you if I could.—To-morrow meet me all together.
[*To Phebe.*] I will marry you, if ever I marry woman,
and I'll be married to-morrow. [*To Orlando.*] I will
satisfy you, if ever I satisfied man, and you shall be
married to-morrow. [*To Silvius.*] I will content   116
you, if what pleases you contents you, and you
shall be married to-morrow. [*To Orlando.*] As you
love Rosalind, meet. [*To Silvius.*] As you love Phebe,
meet. And as I love no woman, I'll meet. So fare
you well; I have left you commands.   121

Sil. I'll not fail, if I live.

Phe. Nor I.

Orl. Nor I.   *Exeunt.*

SCENE III

Enter Clown [TOUCHSTONE] *and* AUDREY.

Touch. To-morrow is the joyful day, Audrey, to-
morrow will we be married.

Aud. I do desire it with all my heart; and I hope
it is no dishonest desire to desire to be a woman
of the world. Here come two of the banish'd Duke's
pages.   6

Enter two PAGES.

1. Page. Well met, honest gentleman.

Touch. By my troth, well met. Come, sit, sit,
and a song.

2. Page. We are for you, sit i' th' middle.   10

1. Page. Shall we clap into't roundly, without
hawking or spitting or saying we are hoarse, which
are the only prologues to a bad voice?

2. Page. I' faith, i' faith, and both in a tune, like
two gipsies on a horse.   15

SONG

It was a lover and his lass,
   With a hey, and a ho, and a hey nonino,
That o'er the green corn-field did pass,
   In spring time, the only pretty [ring]
      time,
When birds do sing, hey ding a ding, ding,   20
Sweet lovers love the spring.

Between the acres of the rye,
   With a hey, and a ho, and a hey nonino,
These pretty country folks would lie,
   In spring time, etc.   25

This carol they began that hour,
   With a hey, and a ho, and a hey nonino,
How that a life was but a flower,
   In spring time, etc.

And therefore take the present time,   30
   With a hey, and a ho, and a hey nonino,
For love is crowned with the prime,
   In spring time, etc.

Touch. Truly, young gentlemen, though there
was no great matter in the ditty, yet the note was
very untuneable.   36

1. Page. You are deceiv'd, sir, we kept time, we
lost not our time.

Touch. By my troth, yes; I count it but time lost
to hear such a foolish song. God buy you, and God
mend your voices! Come, Audrey.   *Exeunt.* 41

---

77. **ungentleness:** discourtesy.
79. **study:** diligent endeavor.   80. **despiteful:** cruel.
96. **observance:** devoted service.
98. **trial:** being tested, proving one's constancy.   **observance.** Some editors, taking this repetition as an error, emend to *obedience.*
106–7. **Why . . . to.** Emended by some editors to *Who . . . to,* to accord with Orlando's reply.

V.iii. Location: The forest.
4. **dishonest:** immodest.   4–5. **woman . . . world:** married woman.
10. **We . . . you:** i.e. that suits us.
11. **clap into't roundly:** strike into it briskly.
13. **only:** i.e. only proper, i.e. customary.
14. **in a tune:** (1) in unison; (2) keeping in time. Both here and in the next line *a* = one.   18. **corn-field:** wheatfield.
19. **ring time:** season for weddings.
22. **Between . . . rye:** i.e. on the unploughed strips separating the planted fields.   30. **take:** seize for enjoyment.
32. **prime:** springtime.   35. **ditty:** words.   **note:** music.
36. **untuneable:** untuneful.
39. **yes:** i.e. yes, you did lose (waste) your time.

As You Like It
V.iv

SCENE IV

Enter DUKE SENIOR, AMIENS, JAQUES, ORLANDO, OLIVER, CELIA.

Duke S. Dost thou believe, Orlando, that the boy
Can do all this that he hath promised?

Orl. I sometimes do believe, and sometimes do not,
As those that fear they hope, and know they fear.

Enter ROSALIND, SILVIUS, *and* PHEBE.

Ros. Patience once more, whiles our compact is
    urg'd: 5
You say, if I bring in your Rosalind,
You will bestow her on Orlando here?

Duke S. That would I, had I kingdoms to give
    with her.

Ros. And you say you will have her, when I
    bring her.   9

Orl. That would I, were I of all kingdoms king.

Ros. You say you'll marry me, if I be willing?

Phe. That will I, should I die the hour after.

Ros. But if you do refuse to marry me,
You'll give yourself to this most faithful shepherd?

Phe. So is the bargain.   15

Ros. You say that you'll have Phebe, if she will?

Sil. Though to have her and death were both one
    thing.

Ros. I have promis'd to make all this matter even:
Keep you your word, O Duke, to give your daughter;
You, yours, Orlando, to receive his daughter;   20
Keep you your word, Phebe, that you'll marry me,
Or else, refusing me, to wed this shepherd;
Keep your word, Silvius, that you'll marry her
If she refuse me; and from hence I go
To make these doubts all even.   25

Exeunt Rosalind and Celia.

Duke S. I do remember in this shepherd boy
Some lively touches of my daughter's favor.

Orl. My lord, the first time that I ever saw him
Methought he was a brother to your daughter.
But, my good lord, this boy is forest-born,   30
And hath been tutor'd in the rudiments
Of many desperate studies by his uncle,
Whom he reports to be a great magician,
Obscured in the circle of this forest.   34

Enter Clown [TOUCHSTONE] *and* AUDREY.

Jaq. There is sure another flood toward, and
these couples are coming to the ark. Here comes a
pair of very strange beasts, which in all tongues are
call'd fools.

Touch. Salutation and greeting to you all!   39

Jaq. Good my lord, bid him welcome. This is
the motley-minded gentleman that I have so often

met in the forest. He hath been a courtier, he swears.

Touch. If any man doubt that, let him put me to my
purgation. I have trod a measure, I have flatt'red a   44
lady, I have been politic with my friend, smooth with
mine enemy, I have undone three tailors, I have had
four quarrels, and like to have fought one.

Jaq. And how was that ta'en up?

Touch. Faith, we met, and found the quarrel was
upon the seventh cause.   50

Jaq. How seventh cause? Good my lord, like
this fellow.

Duke S. I like him very well.

Touch. God 'ild you, sir, I desire you of the like.
I press in here, sir, amongst the rest of the country   55
copulatives, to swear and to forswear, according as
marriage binds and blood breaks. A poor virgin, sir, an
ill-favor'd thing, sir, but mine own; a poor humor of
mine, sir, to take that that no man else will. Rich   59
honesty dwells like a miser, sir, in a poor house, as
your pearl in your foul oyster.

Duke S. By my faith, he is very swift and sententious.

Touch. According to the fool's bolt, sir, and such
dulcet diseases.   65

Jaq. But for the seventh cause—how did you find
the quarrel on the seventh cause?

Touch. Upon a lie seven times remov'd (bear your
body more seeming, Audrey), as thus, sir. I did dislike the cut of a certain courtier's beard. He sent   70
me word, if I said his beard was not cut well, he was in
the mind it was: this is call'd the Retort Courteous.
If I sent him word again, it was not well cut, he
would send me word he cut it to please himself: this
is call'd the Quip Modest. If again, it was not well
cut, he disabled my judgment: this is call'd the   76
Reply Churlish. If again, it was not well cut, he
would answer I spake not true: this is call'd the
Reproof Valiant. If again, it was not well cut, he
would say I lie: this is call'd the Countercheck   80
Quarrelsome; and so to Lie Circumstantial and the Lie
Direct.

Jaq. And how oft did you say his beard was not
well cut?   84

Touch. I durst go no further than the Lie Circumstantial, nor he durst not give me the Lie Direct;
and so we measur'd swords and parted.

Jaq. Can you nominate in order now the degrees
of the lie?   89

V.iv. Location: The forest.
4. **fear they hope:** fear they are merely hoping (without prospect of fulfillment).   5. **urg'd:** put forward.   8. **had I:** even if I had.
18. **even:** smooth, unobstructed by difficulty.
26. **do remember:** am reminded (of).
27. **lively:** lifelike.   **touches:** aspects, details.   **favor:** appearance.   32. **desperate:** dangerous.
34. **Obscured:** hidden; with a possible allusion in *Obscured in the circle* to the magic circle within which a magician was supposed safe during his dealing with spirits.   35. **toward:** on the way.

43–44. **put . . . purgation:** challenge me to clear myself (of the charge of lying).   44. **measure:** a slow, stately dance.
46. **undone:** bankrupted (by running up huge bills and failing to pay).
47. **like . . . fought:** almost had to fight.   48. **ta'en up:** settled.
54. **desire . . . like:** wish you the same.
56. **copulatives:** people about to marry.   57. **blood:** passion.
58. **humor:** whim.   60. **honesty:** chastity.
62–63. **swift and sententious:** ready-witted and pithy.
64. **fool's bolt.** Alluding to the proverb "A fool's bolt [arrow] is soon shot."
65. **dulcet diseases:** pleasing discomfort. A jester's shafts of wit are entertaining but can strike painfully home.
69. **more seeming:** in a more seemly fashion.
69–70. **dislike:** find fault with.   75. **Modest:** moderate.
76. **disabled:** belittled, declared incompetent.
80. **Countercheck:** counter-rebuff, contradiction.
81. **Circumstantial:** indirect.
87. **measur'd swords:** i.e. prepared for duelling.
88. **nominate:** name over.

Touch. O sir, we quarrel in print, by the book—
as you have books for good manners. I will name you
the degrees. The first, the Retort Courteous; the
second, the Quip Modest; the third, the Reply
Churlish; the fourth, the Reproof Valiant; the   94
fift, the Countercheck Quarrelsome; the sixt, the
Lie with Circumstance; the seventh, the Lie Direct.
All these you may avoid but the Lie Direct; and you
may avoid that too, with an If. I knew when seven
justices could not take up a quarrel, but when the   99
parties were met themselves, one of them thought but
of an If, as, "If you said so, then I said so"; and they
shook hands and swore brothers. Your If is the only
peacemaker; much virtue in If.

Jaq. Is not this a rare fellow, my lord? He's as
good at any thing, and yet a fool.   105

Duke S. He uses his folly like a stalking-horse,
and under the presentation of that he shoots his wit.

Enter HYMEN, ROSALIND, *and* CELIA. *Still music.*

Hym.   Then is there mirth in heaven,
When earthly things made even
Atone together.   110
Good Duke, receive thy daughter,
Hymen from heaven brought her,
Yea, brought her hither,
That thou mightst join [her] hand with his
Whose heart within his bosom is.   115

Ros. [*To Duke Senior.*] To you I give myself, for I
am yours.

[*To Orlando.*] To you I give myself, for I am yours.

Duke S. If there be truth in sight, you are my
daughter.

Orl. If there be truth in sight, you are my Rosalind.

Phe.   If sight and shape be true,   120
Why then my love adieu!

Ros. I'll have no father, if you be not he;
I'll have no husband, if you be not he;
Nor ne'er wed woman, if you be not she.

Hym.   Peace ho! I bar confusion,   125
'Tis I must make conclusion
Of these most strange events.
Here's eight that must take hands
To join in Hymen's bands,
If truth holds true contents.   130

[*To Orlando and Rosalind.*]
You and you no cross shall part;

[*To Oliver and Celia.*]
You and you are heart in heart;

[*To Phebe.*]
You to his love must accord,

Or have a woman to your lord;
[*To Touchstone and Audrey.*]
You and you are sure together,   135
As the winter to foul weather.—
Whiles a wedlock-hymn we sing,
Feed yourselves with questioning;
That reason wonder may diminish
How thus we met, and these things finish.

SONG

Wedding is great Juno's crown,   141
O blessed bond of board and bed!
'Tis Hymen peoples every town,
High wedlock then be honored.
Honor, high honor, and renown   145
To Hymen, god of every town!

Duke S. O my dear niece, welcome thou art to me,
Even daughter, welcome, in no less degree.

Phe. I will not eat my word, now thou art mine,
Thy faith my fancy to thee doth combine.   150

Enter Second Brother [JAQUES DE BOYS].

Jaq. de B. Let me have audience for a word or two.
I am the second son of old Sir Rowland,
That bring these tidings to this fair assembly.
Duke Frederick, hearing how that every day
Men of great worth resorted to this forest,   155
Address'd a mighty power, which were on foot
In his own conduct, purposely to take
His brother here, and put him to the sword;
And to the skirts of this wild wood he came;
Where, meeting with an old religious man,   160
After some question with him, was converted
Both from his enterprise and from the world,
His crown bequeathing to his banish'd brother,
And all their lands restor'd to [them] again
That were with him exil'd. This to be true,   165
I do engage my life.

Duke S.   Welcome, young man;
Thou offer'st fairly to thy brothers' wedding:
To one his lands withheld, and to the other
A land itself at large, a potent dukedom.
First, in this forest let us do those ends   170
That here were well begun and well begot;
And after, every of this happy number,
That have endur'd shrewd days and nights with us,
Shall share the good of our returned fortune,
According to the measure of their states.   175

---

90. **by the book:** according to established rules. There were, in fact, such books, hardly less fantastic than Touchstone's "lie seven times remov'd." One which may be glanced at here is Vincent Saviolo's *Practice of the Rapier and Dagger* (1594–5), the second part of which treats of "Honor and Honorable Quarrels," with a section headed "Of the manner and diversity of Lies." 99. **take up:** settle.
102. **swore brothers:** i.e. became sworn brothers, pledged to the mutual loyalty proper to actual brothers.
106. **stalking-horse:** any deceptive cover used by a game-stalker to get within shooting distance of his quarry.
107. **under . . . that:** i.e. using his assumed folly as a protective disguise. 107 s.d. **Hymen:** god of marriage. **Still:** soft.
108. **mirth:** joy. 110. **Atone:** are at one, accord.
130. **If . . . contents:** i.e. if truth is true. 131. **cross:** disagreement.
133. **accord:** assent.

134. **to:** for.
135. **sure together:** securely joined. 138. **Feed:** satisfy.
139. **reason:** rational explanation.
141. **Juno's.** Juno was the goddess of marriage.
144. **High:** solemn.
148. **Even . . . degree:** i.e. you are no whit less welcome to me than a daughter. 150. **combine:** unite.
156. **Address'd:** made ready, levied. **power:** army.
157. **In . . . conduct:** under his personal command.
161. **question:** conversation. 166. **engage:** pledge.
167. **Thou offer'st fairly:** you bring handsome gifts.
169. **A land . . . large:** a whole country in itself. The restoration of the dukedom to Rosalind's father means that her husband will be the next duke.
170. **do those ends:** bring to a conclusion those purposes.
171. **begot:** conceived. 172. **every:** every one.
173. **shrewd:** sorely difficult. 175. **states:** rank.

As You Like It
V.iv

Mean time, forget this new-fall'n dignity,
And fall into our rustic revelry.
Play, music, and you brides and bridegrooms all,
With measure heap'd in joy, to th' measures fall.
　　Jaq. Sir, by your patience.—If I heard you rightly,
The Duke hath put on a religious life,　　　181
And thrown into neglect the pompous court?
　　Jaq. de B. He hath.
　　Jaq. To him will I. Out of these convertites
There is much matter to be heard and learn'd.　　185
　　[*To Duke Senior.*] You to your former honor I be-
　　　　queath,
Your patience and your virtue well deserves it;
　　[*To Orlando.*] You to a love, that your true faith doth
　　　　merit;
　　[*To Oliver.*] You to your land, and love, and great
　　　　allies;　　　189
　　[*To Silvius.*] You to a long and well-deserved bed;
　　[*To Touchstone.*] And you to wrangling, for thy loving
　　　　voyage
Is but for two months victuall'd.—So to your pleas-
　　　　ures,
I am for other than for dancing measures.
　　Duke S. Stay, Jaques, stay.　　　194
　　Jaq. To see no pastime I. What you would have
I'll stay to know at your abandon'd cave. *Exit.*
　　Duke S. Proceed, proceed. We'll begin these rites,
As we do trust they'll end, in true delights.
　　　　　　[*A dance.*] *Exeunt* [*all but Rosalind*].

176. **new-fall'n:** newly acquired.　178. **music:** musicians.
180. **patience:** indulgence, permission.
182. **pompous:** ceremonious.　184. **convertites:** converts.

[EPILOGUE]

　　Ros. It is not the fashion to see the lady the epilogue; but it is no more unhandsome than to see the lord the prologue. If it be true that good wine needs no bush, 'tis true that a good play needs no epilogue. Yet to good wine they do use good 5 bushes; and good plays prove the better by the help of good epilogues. What a case am I in then, that am neither a good epilogue, nor cannot insinuate with you in the behalf of a good play! I am not furnish'd like a beggar, therefore to beg will not 10 become me. My way is to conjure you, and I'll begin with the women. I charge you, O women, for the love you bear to men, to like as much of this play as please you; and I charge you, O men, for the love you bear to women (as I perceive 15 by your simp'ring, none of you hates them), that between you and the women the play may please. If I were a woman I would kiss as many of you as had beards that pleas'd me, complexions that lik'd me, and breaths that I defied not; and I am 20 sure, as many as have good beards, or good faces, or sweet breaths, will for my kind offer, when I make curtsy, bid me farewell.　　　　　　　　　　*Exit.*

Epi. 2. **unhandsome:** unfitting.
3–4. **good . . . bush.** Proverbial. The ivy bush was formerly the vintner's sign.　7. **case:** predicament.
8. **insinuate:** ingratiate myself.　10. **furnish'd:** dressed, equipped.
11. **conjure:** earnestly charge.
18. **If . . . woman.** Women's parts were played by boys.
19. **lik'd:** pleased.　20. **defied:** disliked.
23. **bid me farewell:** i.e. by applauding.

NOTE ON THE TEXT

The First Folio (1623) is the only authority for *As You Like It*; all later texts are derived from that source. The F1 text seems to be based on a careful transcript prepared from some form of Shakespeare's manuscript (perhaps "fair copy"), and it probably shows traces of the prompter's hand in a few stage directions (see those at I.ii.212, 215; II.v.37; IV.ii.12; V.iv.107). On the whole, the text appears sound and presents no serious textual problems.

For further information, see W. W. Greg, *The Shakespeare First Folio* (Oxford, 1955).

TEXTUAL NOTES

Dramatis personae: *subs. as first given by Rowe; an earlier list, which describes Duke Senior as* Ferdinand Old duke of Burgundy, *appears in the Douai MS*
Act-scene division: *from F1*

I.i

Location: *Rowe, Pope*
52 **What,**] *Theobald;* What *F1*
52 s.d. **Strikes him.**] *White*
54 s.d. **Collaring him.**] *Johnson*
93 s.d. **Exit Dennis.**] *Johnson*
109 **she**] *F3;* hee *F1*
151, 167 **device**] *F3;* deuise *F1*
156 **anatomize**] *F3;* anathomize *F1*
163 s.p. **Oli.**] *F2*

I.ii

Location: *Capell (after Rowe)*
4 **I**] *Rowe*
31 **huswife**] *Capell;* houswife *F1*
53 **and**] *Malone*

57 s.p. **Touch.**] *Malone;* Clow. *F1 (through-out)*
81 **mean'st**] *Rowe;* means't *F1*
83 s.p. **Cel.**] *Theobald;* Ros. *F1*
84 s.d. **Exeunt**] *Rowe (subs.);* Ex. *F1*
87 **wise men**] *F3;* Wisemen *F1*
91 **Le**] *F2;* the *F1*
91 **Beau**] *Steevens;* Beu *F1 (throughout, except in s.d. following l. 91)*
97 **Bon jour**] *Rowe (subs.);* Boon-iour *F1*
149 s.p. **Duke F.**] *Malone;* Duke. *F1 (through-out)*
149–56 **Come . . . wrastling.**] *as prose, Pope; as verse, F1*
208 **You . . . after;**] *Cambridge, following Theobald, suggests reading* And you . . . after, *(i.e.* If you . . . after,*) on the supposition that the compositor took* And *to be part of the speech-prefix* Orland.; *though not necessary, the emendation makes for easier sense*
215 s.d. **Charles is thrown.**] *Rowe*

230 s.d. **with . . . Beau**] *Capell (subs.)*
242 **deserv'd.**] *Pope (subs.);* deseru'd, *F1*
243 **love**] *Singer;* loue; *F1;* love, *F2*
244 **all**] all in *F2*
245 s.d. **Giving . . . neck.**] *Theobald*
251 **quintain**] *Theobald;* quintine *F1*
256 s.d. **with Celia**] *Rowe (subs.)*
272 **smaller**] *Malone;* taller *F1*
286 s.d. **Exit Le Beau.**] *Capell*
289 **Rosalind**] *Rowe;* Rosaline *F1 (through II.v; Compositor D's spelling)*

I.iii

Location: *Theobald (subs.)*
1–2 **Why . . . word?**] *as prose, Rowe; as verse, F1*
12 **working-day**] *hyphen, Rowe*
42 **uncle?**] *Capell;* Vncle. *F1*
52 **traitors:**] *Theobald (subs.);* Traitors, *F1*
57 **likelihood**] *F2;* likelihoods *F1*
78 **her**] *F2;* per *F1*
82 **lips:**] *Pope;* lips *F1;* lips, *F2*

83 **doom**] *Rowe;* doombe *F1*
89 **s.d. with Lords**] *Malone (subs.);* &c. *F1*
126 **be**] *F2;* by *F1*
131 **travel**] *F3;* trauaile *F1*
133 **woo**] *F2* (wooe); woe *F1* (*sporadically throughout*)
137 **we in**] *F2;* in we *F1*

II.i

Location: *Theobald (after Rowe)*
6 **fang**] *Johnson;* phange *F1*
18 **I . . . it.**] *Upton suggested giving these words to Duke Senior and has been followed by many eds.*
18 **it. Happy**] *Rowe (subs.);* it, happy *F1*
31 **antique**] *Pope;* anticke *F1*
45 **similes**] *Steevens;* similies *F1*
49 **much**] *F2;* must *F1*
50 **friends**] *Rowe;* friend *F1*
59 **the**] *F2*

II.ii

Location: *Rowe (subs.)*

II.iii

Location: *Capell (after Rowe)*
o.s.d. meeting] *Capell*
10 **some**] *F2;* seeme *F1*
16 **s.p. Orl.**] *F2; continued to Adam, F1*
29 **s.p. Orl.**] *F2;* Ad. *F1*
35 **can.**] *F3* (can:); can, *F1*
39 **sav'd**] *Rowe;* saued *F1*
46 **servant.**] *Theobald (subs.);* seruant, *F1*
71 **seventeen**] *Rowe;* seauentie *F1*

II.iv

Location: *Theobald (after Rowe)*
1 **weary**] *Theobald;* merry *F1*
19 **so,**] *Rowe;* so *F1*
33 **heartily!**] *Dyce (after F4);* hartily, *F1*
38 **Wearing**] Wearying *F2 (adopted by some eds.)*
44 **shepherd!**] *F2;* Shepheard *F1*
44 **thy**] *Rowe;* they *F1;* their *F2*
44 **wound**] *F2;* would *F1*
48 **a-night**] *hyphen, Collier*
69 **you**] *F2;* your *F1*
74 **travel**] *F3;* trauaile *F1*
81 **reaks**] *ed.;* wreakes *F1*
83 **Besides,**] *Rowe;* Besides *F1*

II.v

Location: *Capell (after Rowe)*
1 **s.p. Ami.**] *Capell*
12–4, 17–9, 34–7, 46–7] *as prose, Pope; as irregular verse, F1*
26 **compliment**] *Pope;* complement *F1*
44–5 **No . . . weather.**] *from ll. 7–8 above; &c. F1*
49 **s.p. Jaq.**] *F2;* Amy. *F1*

II.vi

Location: *Capell (after Rowe)*
1–18] *as prose, Pope; as irregular verse, F1*
14, 18 **cheerly**] *F4;* cheerely *F1*

II.vii

Location: *Capell (after Rowe)*
o.s.d. A . . . out.] *Rowe*
o.s.d. Amiens] *Capell*
o.s.d. Lords] *Rowe;* Lord *F1*
38 **brain**] *F2;* braiue *F1*
48 **Withal**] *F2,* Wiithall *F1*
55 **Not to**] *Theobald*
56 **wise man's**] *Rowe;* Wise-mans *F1*
56 **anatomiz'd**] *F3;* anathomiz'd *F1*
64 **sin**] *F2;* fin *F1*
75 **city-woman**] *hyphen, Pope*
83 **then! . . . what then?**] *Wilson (after Theobald);* then, how then, what then, *F1*
87 **any man. But**] *F1* any. man But *F1* (*Furness claims that some copies of F1 have been corrected, but Hinman records no corrected state*)
87 **comes**] *F2;* come *F1*
87 **s.d. with . . . drawn**] *Douai MS, Theobald*
100–1 **and . . . die.**] *as prose, Capell; as verse, F1*
135 **s.d. Exit.**] *Rowe*

167–8 **Welcome . . . feed.**] *as verse, Pope; as prose, F1*
174 **s.p. Ami.**] *Johnson*
182 **Then**] *Rowe;* The *F1*
198 **master**] *F2;* masters *F1*

III.i

Location: *Rowe (subs.)*

III.ii

Location: *Rowe*
o.s.d. with a paper] *Capell*
27 **good**] *F2;* pood *F1*
32–3 **Such . . . shepherd?**] *as prose, Pope; as verse, F1*
87 **s.d. with . . . reading**] *Capell*
89 **Rosalind**] *Kittredge points out that F1 here, and through l. 112, spells the name as* Rosalinde *to emphasize the pronunciation*
92 **lin'd**] *Pope;* Linde *F1*
97 **sleeping-hours**] *hyphen, Dyce*
125 **s.d. Reads.**] *Dyce*
125 **a desert be?**] *Rowe;* Desert bee, *F1*
128 **show**] *F4;* shoe *F1*
135 **boughs**] *Rowe;* bowes *F1*
143 **wide-enlarg'd.**] *Rowe (subs.; hyphen, Dyce);* wide enlarg'd, *F1*
145 **her**] *Douai MS, Rowe;* his *F1*
148 **Lucretia's**] *F4;* Lucrecia's *F1*
158 **now?**] *Theobald;* now! now *F1;* now! now! *F2*
158 **back,**] *Dyce;* backe *F1*
162 **s.d. with Corin**] *Rowe (subs.)*
196 **hose**] a hose *F2*
227 **size.**] *F3 (subs.);* size, *F1*
237 **such**] *Capell;* forth *F1;* forth such *F2*
244 **thy**] *Rowe;* the *F1*
246 **heart**] *Rowe;* Hart *F1*
294 **s.d. Exit Jaques.**] *Douai MS, Rowe*
295 **s.d. Aside to Celia.**] *Capell*
347 **lectures**] *F3;* Lectors *F1;* Lecturs *F2*
363 **deifying**] *F2;* defying *F1*
371 **are**] *F2;* art *F1*
382 **point-device**] *hyphen, Theobald*

III.iii

Location: *Capell (after Rowe)*
o.s.d. behind] *Collier*
2 **Audrey?**] *Capell;* Audrey *F1*
7 **goats**] *Munro;* Goats, *F1*
10, 32, 46 **s.dd. Aside.**] *Johnson*
14–5 **God 'ild**] *Theobald (after F2 godild);* goddild *F1*
56–7 **Horns? . . . alone?**] *Theobald (subs., after Rowe);* hornes, euen so poore men alone? *F1*
67 **s.p. Sir Oli.**] *Rowe;* Ol. *F1 (throughout)*
71 **s.d. Discovering himself.**] *Johnson*
90 **s.d. Aside.**] *Capell*
90 **mind**] *Capell;* minde, *F1*
96 **s.p. Touch.**] *F2* (Clo.); Ol. *F1*
99–105 **O . . . thee.**] *subs. as verse, Warburton conj.; as prose, F1*
105 **s.d. Exeunt . . . Audrey.**] *Capell*
107 **s.d. Exit.**] *Capell;* Exeunt. *F1*

III.iv

Location: *Capell (after Rowe)*
5–14 **As . . . bread.**] *as prose, Pope; as irregular verse, F1*
30 **a**] *F2*

III.v

Location: *Rowe (implied)*
1 **Phebe;**] *Rowe;* Phebe *F1;* Phebe, *F3*
7 **s.d. behind**] *Collier (after Capell)*
9 **thee**] *ed.;* thee, *F1*
10 **eye:**] *F4 (subs.);* eye, *F1*
11 **pretty,**] *Theobald;* pretty *F1*
17 **why,**] *Theobald;* why *F1*
20 **thee;**] *thee, F1*
22 **lean**] Leane but *F2*
35 **s.d. Advancing.**] *Capell*
37 **have**] *F2;* hau *F1*
37 **beauty—**] *Pope (subs.);* Beauty *F1*
66–70 **He's . . . me?**] *as prose, Pope; as irregular verse, F1*
80 **s.d. with . . . Corin**] *Hanmer (subs.)*
88 **love,**] *F4;* loue *F1*

108 **carlot**] *Steevens;* Carlot *F1 (in italics, as a proper name)*
128 **Have**] I haue *F2*
134 **taunting**] *F4;* tanting *F1*

IV.i

Location: *Rowe*
1 **be**] *F2*
6 **abominable**] *F3;* abhominable *F1*
18 **my**] *F2;* by *F1*
19 **rumination**] *Rowe (the comma is very faint in F4);* rumination, *F1*
29 **travel**] *F3;* trauaile *F1*
38 **s.d. Exit Jaques.**] *Dyce;* Exit. *F2 (after l. 32)*
49 **heart-whole**] *F4;* heart hole *F1*
55 **jointure**] *F2;* ioyncture *F1*
69 **holiday**] *Capell;* holy-day *F1*
97 **love-cause**] *hyphen, Theobald*
105 **chroniclers**] *F2;* Chronoclers *F1*
105 **was—**] *Theobald (subs.);* was *F1*
106 **Sestos**] *Capell;* Cestos *F1*
138 **I . . . commission,**] *as prose, Pope; as verse, F1*
200 **s.d. Orlando**] *Rowe*
210 **it**] *F2;* in *F1*

IV.ii

Location: *Capell (after Rowe)*
o.s.d. as] *Malone*
2 **s.p. 1. Lord.**] *Malone (after Capell);* Lord. *F1*
7 **s.p. 2. Lord.**] *Malone (after Capell);* Lord. *F1*
10 **s.p. 2. Lord.**] *C. J. Hill (in Riverside Six Plays)*
12 **s.d. The . . . burthen.**] *as s.d., Theobald; as concluding part of l. 12, F1*

IV.iii

Location: *Capell (after Rowe)*
1–5 **How . . . here.**] *as prose, Pope; as verse, F1*
5 **forth—to**] *Capell;* forth / To *F1*
5 **s.d. Enter Silvius.**] *placed as in Pope; after* brain, *l. 4, F1*
7 **did**] *om. F2*
7 **s.d. Gives a letter.**] *Johnson (subs.)*
34 **giant-rude**] *hyphen, Capell*
44 **apart**] *F2;* a part *F1*
73 **lover,**] *F4;* louer *F1*
78 **bottom,**] *Rowe;* bottom *F1*
87 **the**] But the *F2*
105 **top**] *F2;* top, *F1*
142 **In**] *F2;* I *F1*
155 **his**] *F2;* this *F1*
156 **s.d. Rosalind faints.**] *Pope*
165 **I . . . it.**] *as prose, Pope; as verse, F1*
170 **a**] *om. F2*

V.i

Location: *Rowe*
10 **clown.**] *F4 (subs.);* Clowne, *F1*
22 **Wast**] *Pope;* Was't *F1*
32 **wise man**] *F4;* wiseman *F1*
37 **sir**] *F2;* sit *F1*
56 **policy**] *F2;* police *F1*
58 **Do,**] *F4;* Do *F1*
59 **merry,**] *F4;* merry *F1*

V.ii

Location: *Capell (after Rowe)*
7 **her**] *Douai MS, Rowe*
13–6 **You . . . Rosalind.**] *as prose, Pope; as verse, F1*
18 **s.d. Exit.**] *Capell*
32 **overcame**] *F2;* ouercome *F1*
46 **heart-heaviness**] *hyphen, Rowe*
56 **are**] *F2;* arc *F1*
67 **human**] *Rowe;* humane *F1*
110 **s.d. To Silvius.**] *Douai MS, Capell*
111 **s.d. To Phebe.**] *Douai MS, Johnson*
112 **all together**] *F4;* altogether *F1*
113 **s.d. To Phebe.**] *Pope*
114 **s.d. To Orlando.**] *Pope*
116 **s.d. To Silvius.**] *Pope*
118 **s.d. To Orlando.**] *Johnson*
119 **s.d. To Silvius.**] *Douai MS, Johnson*

V.iii

Location: *Capell (after Rowe)*
16 It was] Twas *Morley* (*in* First Booke of Ayres, *1600*)
17 hey, and] haye with *Morley, Adv. MS 5.2.14, fol. 18* (*in* National Library, Edinburgh)
18 corn-field] corne fields *Morley*
19 In] *Knight (after Adv. MS), Morley;* In the *F1*
19 ring] *Steevens conj. and Morley, Adv. MS;* rang *F1*
20 a ding, ding] ading ading *Morley, Adv. MS*
23, 27, 31 hey, and] hay, with *Morley*
24 folks] fooles *Morley, Adv. MS*
24 would] did *Adv. MS*
30–3 And . . . etc.] *Johnson's arrangement* (*as in Morley and Adv. MS*); *in F1 these lines follow l. 21*

30 And . . . time] Then prettie louers take the time *Morley, Adv. MS*
36 untuneable.] *F2;* vntunable *F1*

V.iv

Location: *Capell (after Rowe)*
25 s.d. Exeunt] *Hanmer;* Exit *F1*
34 s.d. Enter . . . Audrey.] *placed as in Rowe; after l. 33, F1*
81 to] *F2* (to the); ro *F1*
114 her] *F3;* his *F1*
116 s.d. To Duke Senior.] *Douai MS, Rowe*
117 s.d. To Orlando.] *Douai MS, Rowe*
121 adieu!] *Theobald;* adieu *F1;* adiev. *F2*
130 s.d. To . . . Rosalind.] *Johnson*
131 s.d. To . . . Celia.] *Johnson*
132 s.d. To Phebe.] *Johnson*
134 s.d. To . . . Audrey.] *Johnson*
148 daughter,] *F4;* daughter *F1*
150 s.d. Jaques de Boys] *Rowe*

151, 183 s.pp. Jaq. de B.] *Rowe;* 2. Bro. *F1*
164 them] *Douai MS, Rowe;* him *F1*
171 were] *F2;* vvete *F1*
186 s.d. To Duke Senior.] *Rowe*
186 bequeath,] *Rowe;* bequeath *F1;* bequeath; *F2*
188 s.d. To Orlando.] *Rowe*
189 s.d. To Oliver.] *Rowe*
190 s.d. To Silvius.] *Rowe*
191 s.d. To Touchstone.] *Rowe*
197 rites] *Rowe;* rights *F1*
198 trust they'll end,] *Pope;* trust, they'l end *F1*
198 s.d. A dance.] *Capell*
198 s.d. Exeunt.] *Craig;* Exit *F1*
198 s.d. all but Rosalind.] *ed.*

Epilogue

Epilogue] *so titled by Theobald*
23 s.d. Exit.] Exit. / FINIS. *F1*

CANTVS.   VI.   THO. MORLEY.

T was a louer and his lasse, With a haye, with a hoe and a haye nonie no and a haye nonie nonie no , That o're the green corne fields did passe in spring time, ij, ij. the only pretiring time whē birds do sing, hay ding ading ading ij.   ij.   sweete louers loue the springe in spring time,   ij.   The onely pretiring time whē birds do sing, Haye ding ading ading, ij.   ij.   sweete louers loue the spring.

"It was a lover and his lass." From the unique copy of Thomas Morley's *First Book of Airs, or Little Short Songs* (1600) in the Folger Shakespeare Library. This setting by Thomas Morley (1557–1603) of "It was a lover and his lass" (*As You Like It*, V.iii.16–33) is one of the very few contemporary settings for a Shakespearean lyric that have survived. The melody is scored in the upper staff, the lute accompaniment in the lower staff. A setting without words for a song called "O mistress mine" in Morley's *First Book of Consort Lessons* (1599) may be for Shakespeare's lyric in *Twelfth Night* (II.iii. 39–52). There are also contemporary settings for "Where the bee sucks" and "Full fadom five" in *The Tempest*; these are by Robert Johnson, one of the Musicians of the Lute to James I, and may have been specially written for the court performance of *The Tempest* in 1613 in honor of the marriage of the Lady Elizabeth, James I's daughter, to the Elector Palatine.

Twelfth Night

TWELFTH NIGHT, OR WHAT YOU WILL is the only play for which Shakespeare provided an alternative title. As with *Much Ado about Nothing*, *As You Like It*, and *All's Well That Ends Well*, his other late Elizabethan comedies, the title as a whole is more serious than its offhand and casual manner would suggest. The word *will* possessed for Elizabethans its modern sense of "wish" or "inclination," and this is its primary significance here: an airy invitation to reader or audience to rechristen the comedy according to individual taste and reaction. (King Charles I was one of those who responded: he insisted upon describing it, in his personal copy of the Second Folio, as *Malvolio*.) Elizabethans, however, also used the noun *will* for irrational desire, passion (often physical) uncontrolled by judgment. Shakespeare puns elaborately on the word in several of his sonnets to the Dark Lady. In this sense, the comedy is indeed about what people—Olivia, Orsino, Antonio, Malvolio, and even Viola—"will," the frightening suddenness with which "the pales and forts of reason," as Hamlet termed them, may be swept away by a kind of emotional thunderstorm.

The first mention of *Twelfth Night* comes from the diary of the lawyer John Manningham. "At our feast," he noted, "we had a play called 'Twelve Night, or What You Will,' much like the Comedy of Errors, or Menechmi in Plautus, but most like and near to that in Italian called *Inganni*." The feast in question here was Candlemas, February 2, 1602, and the place was the Middle Temple. Probably this was not the first performance of the comedy. On stylistic grounds, and also from the evidence provided by certain topical allusions contained within it, a date of 1600 or 1601 seems more likely. Leslie Hotson, in his book *The First Night of "Twelfth Night,"* has attempted to place the first performance more precisely. He believes that Shakespeare wrote the play at royal command in honor of the state visit of Don Virginio Orsino, Duke of Bracciano, and that it was first presented on Twelfth Night (January 6) in 1601. As it happened, news of Orsino's projected visit did not reach England until December 26, 1600. Hotson's theory implies that Shakespeare wrote the comedy, and that the Lord Chamberlain's Men somehow managed to learn their parts and rehearse for a performance at court, within a space of ten or eleven days. This seems hard to believe. Hotson also argues that this original audience was meant to recognize Olivia as Queen Elizabeth, Orsino as the visiting Italian Duke, and Malvolio as the pompous Comptroller of the Royal Household, Sir William Knollys. The comedy as a whole set out to compliment the visitor from Italy, flatter the aging queen, and bait an unpopular court official. Again, the theory seems forced and implausible. It is difficult to believe that either Elizabeth or her foreign guest would have welcomed the association with Olivia and Orsino, given the folly of both characters and the extent to which they are humiliated in the course of the action. As for Malvolio, to identify him with a real individual and suggest that this is the key to the character is to limit his function and impact and sadly to inhibit that complexity of response which an audience normally feels towards him in the theatre.

Even if the comedy received its first performance on Twelfth Night, Shakespeare is most unlikely to have given it this name purely for so accidental and ephemeral a reason. Within the play itself there are no specific references to the Feast of the Epiphany, the twelfth and culminating day of the Christmas season. The action, from Viola's arrival on the sea-coast of Illyria to the discoveries of the final scene, seems to occupy about three months. This is the length of time that Antonio claims to have known the youth Sebastian and that Cesario, by "his" own testimony, has served the Duke. Shakespeare could easily have made it clear, had he wished, that Sir Toby's disorderly revel in the third scene of Act II was a Twelfth Night celebration, but he did not. Probably, he deliberately avoided any such pinpointing of the time of year because he wished to draw the attention of his audience to the Twelfth Night theme in ways that were more pervasive and subtle.

Epiphany was originally a major Christian feast, even more important than Christmas. It commemorated not only the coming of the Magi with gifts to Bethlehem, but two later events in the life of Christ: his baptism, and the miracle at Cana. Human nature being what it is, it was perhaps inevitable that a celebration which initially was wholly pious should, with time, alter its complexion, attracting to itself in the process a good deal of the license and even the specific customs of the pagan Saturnalia. Before long, the Church found itself struggling to suppress what had gradually become a kind of annual orgy within sacred precincts: the celebration of a world turned ritually upside down. The effort was, in part, successful. By the end of the fifteenth century the riotous Feast of Fools, now associated with Epiphany, had at least been driven out of the church itself and forced to adopt less overtly blasphemous forms. In secular society, however, especially in the Inns of Court and the universities and in princely gatherings, it continued to flourish during Shakespeare's lifetime. If he christened a comedy *Twelfth Night*, it seems reasonable to assume that he intended that title to summon up images of Epiphany as it was kept in his own time: a period of holiday abandon in which the normal rules and order of life were suspended or else deliberately inverted, in which serious issues and events mingled perplexingly with revelry and apparent madness. This, in effect, is the atmosphere in Illyria: a country where everyone (except, perhaps, Feste) is very much in earnest, but also a little insane.

Manningham was not wholly imperceptive in pointing out the resemblance between *Twelfth Night* and *Inganni*. In 1537 there was published an Italian comedy of disguise and mistaken identity called *Gl'Ingannati*. It reappeared throughout the century in a number of different adaptations and languages (sometimes called *Inganni*) and left its mark on at least one work of English fiction known to Shakespeare: Barnabe Rich's prose tale "Apolonius and Silla" in his collection entitled *Rich His Farewell to Military Profession* (1581). *Gl'Ingannati* involves a brother and sister parted by accident and eventually reunited; its heroine disguises herself as a boy and finds that she has to pay court to an embarrassingly susceptible lady in the name of the master she herself loves. These are things that happen in *Twelfth Night* too, and yet neither *Gl'Ingannati* nor any of the works that derive from it can really be regarded as a source for Shakespeare's play. *Gl'Ingannati* and all its tribe are heavily indebted to Plautine comedy: they are slick, fast-moving, unemotional, and certainly unpoetic, concerned primarily with plot and intrigue. In general shape, let alone in tone and spirit, they are worlds away from *Twelfth Night*. There is no more reason to suppose that Shakespeare was thinking of *Gl'Ingannati* or any of its descendants when he conceived his own play than that *The Comedy of Errors* or *The Two Gentlemen of Verona* earlier borrowed from this source in creating the dilemma of the two Antipholuses or Julia's reluctant embassy to Silvia in her boy's disguise. This is plot material of the most ownerless and ancient kind: the very stuff of Comedy since Menander.

The words "Twelfth Night" not only suggest a carnival world; they warn an audience that it is not to ask too many awkward questions about the miraculous resemblance of boy and girl twins who, on the stage, will almost invariably look less than identical. Nor are we to question love at first sight, a duke who accepts as his wife a servant he thought, only five minutes before, was a boy, or the feasibility of persuading a man that he can make his fortune forever by way of yellow stockings and crossed garters. In a world that is ritually upside down, almost anything can happen. There is a sense in which Sir Toby Belch is the master of these disorderly revels, a man literally intoxicated throughout most of the play, for whom Time in its logical, workaday aspect has simply ceased to exist: "To be up after midnight and to go to bed then, is early; so that to go to bed after midnight is to go to bed betimes" (II.iii.7–9). As a kind of carnival, or temporary, king, Sir Toby rules his sector of Olivia's household according to the rules of holiday inconsequence. His chief enemy, of course, is Malvolio. Olivia's steward is not only dedicated to work, sobriety, and regular hours: he insists that all the world should follow his example, that there should be no cakes and ale, no tang of ginger on the tongue, and no relaxation of discipline in man's progress from cradle to grave. He has no use for folly, whether it is that of Feste the professional, or Fabian's low taste for the sport of bear-baiting, or the nightly songs and carousals of Sir Toby and his companion Aguecheek.

Toby himself is a parasite sponging off a young and wealthy niece. He uses this position to deceive and profit from the ridiculous ambitions of a hanger-on of his own, Sir Andrew Aguecheek. In the final scene he will turn viciously on this supposed friend: "Will you help?—an ass-head and a coxcomb and a knave, a thin-fac'd knave, a gull!" (V.i.206–7). There is nothing lovely, or even honest, about Sir Toby's riotous little court. Yet a theatre audience will always, at least up to the point of Malvolio's incarceration in the dark house in Act IV, support Sir Toby, Sir Andrew, Maria, Feste, and Fabian in their plot against the steward. In the study it is possible to be more soft-hearted. To watch *Twelfth Night* on the stage, however, is to participate and delight in a heightened world temporarily free from Time and normal responsibility. At a party where everyone is joyously drunk, Malvolio is the guest who insists on remaining cold sober, who reads long lectures on temperance to everyone else, and threatens to summon the police. As such, he is our enemy as well as Sir Toby's, not only because he tries to suppress music and revelry which we find entertaining, but because we recognize that, in his view, we ought not to be indulging ourselves by going to the theatre at all. This is why his downfall, in its early stages, is so delicious. Yellow-stockinged and cross-gartered, trying to learn how to smile, Malvolio has become the unconscious victim of precisely that irrational spirit of holiday which he so despises. He has harbored a private folly all along—his conceit, born of self-love and isolation, that Olivia adores him—and when his enemies employ it against him, his behavior becomes at least as mad as theirs.

Madness in Illyria is by no means confined to Sir Toby, his entourage, and the deceived Malvolio. The very first scene of the comedy introduces Orsino, a nobleman committed to a course of wild extravagancy, in the Elizabethan sense of that word. He is bound up within a fiction, a dream of romantic passion, in which the voyage itself is really more important than its specific goal. *Twelfth Night* is not Jonsonian comedy. Whatever some critics may say, the lovelorn Orsino is not a figure of fun. Indeed, the verse he speaks at the beginning of the play is seductively beautiful: intense, metaphoric, and imaginative. Only by the slightest touches—the way his hunting image, for instance, threatens to overbalance into an Actaeon/cuckold joke which the speaker certainly does not intend—does Shakespeare hint at something that Feste, later, will make explicit: the fact that Orsino's love-melancholy is essentially sterile and self-induced, a state of mind dependent upon that very absence and lack of response from Olivia which it affects to lament.

On the whole, Olivia will suffer greater humiliation than Orsino in the course of the comedy, although her lack of self-knowledge is no more acute than his. She is described from the beginning in words that evoke a complex response:

> The element itself, till seven years' heat,
> Shall not behold her face at ample view;
> But like a cloistress she will veiled walk,
> And water once a day her chamber round
> With eye-offending brine; all this to season
> A brother's dead love, which she would keep fresh
> And lasting in her sad remembrance.   (I.i.25–31)

The underlying image here is homely, even a little grotesque. Like a housewife who carefully turns a piece of pickled meat once a day in its brine bath, Olivia intends through salt tears to preserve the memory of her dead brother beyond the normal span of grief. There is something forced and abnormal about such mourning, but there is also—as Orsino's reaction makes clear—something noble. Like the King of Navarre and his courtiers in *Love's Labor's Lost*, Olivia is engaged in a war against Time and

human forgetfulness. In her case, the struggle takes the form not of a league of study but of resistance to that natural psychological process by which, gradually, we cease to grieve for the dead. The attempt fails, even as the Academe fails. Olivia finds that she "cannot cross the cause why we were born" (*Love's Labor's Lost*, IV.iii.214). At the first sight of Cesario she abandons her veil and, in rapid succession after that, her tears, her rites of memory, her pride, and even her modesty. It is right and proper, in accord with all the laws of comedy, that this should happen, that Sebastian ultimately should fill up the place of the dead brother in Olivia's heart. Seven years is a long time, and youth is very short. The world, as Benedick observed, "must be peopled" (*Much Ado about Nothing*, II.iii.242). Yet Olivia's ignominious collapse, while necessary, is also sad. Man has his glimpses of the ideal, whether of love or of fidelity to the dead. Not even in Illyria, however, can such ideals be sustained.

In the comedies that he wrote before *Twelfth Night*, Shakespeare had created a number of fantasy worlds, places that never were on sea or land, where life has some of the qualities of a dream. He invented Portia's house over the sea at Belmont, with its riddle-game, its music, and its limitless wealth; the forests of *As You Like It*, *The Two Gentlemen of Verona*, and *A Midsummer Night's Dream*; the withdrawn, artificially enclosed park of *Love's Labor's Lost*. Even in *The Comedy of Errors*, *The Taming of the Shrew*, *The Merry Wives of Windsor*, and *Much Ado about Nothing*, there are shadowy traces of this pattern of movement from an ordinary world to a second, somehow magical, environment in which characters are transformed, but which they must leave at the end of the comedy to take up the burden of the everyday. The people who set out from Arden, Navarre, Oberon's wood, Windsor Great Park, or the nightmare house of Petruchio are not quite the same as those who, briefly, have sojourned there. Their experiences in this second, heightened world have altered them, usually for the better. It is clear, however, that their future lies in a harsher, more realistic society, subject to imperfection, death, human limitation, and Time, which we accept as an image of our own.

In the final romances, Shakespeare abandoned this comic pattern. *The Tempest* is the only play which even approximates to it, and it does so in a very peculiar sense indeed. The characters of the last plays are continually travelling, but the places from which they set out, to which they journey, and to which they return are all equally marvellous. There is no distinction in this particular sense between Tharsus, Tyre, and Mytilene in *Pericles*, between Sicily and Bohemia in *The Winter's Tale*, between Cymbeline's court and the forest to which Imogen flees. It is, in fact, the second world entirely that we meet in the last plays: the world of the mythical and the strange. People may be transformed within it, but their transformation no longer depends upon their experience of an extraordinary place where the demands of life as they know it are, for a time, suspended and which they must leave at the end.

In ways that go beyond the implications of its title, *Twelfth Night* is a kind of Janus-faced play, mediating between the early comedies and the last romances. Viola's disguise as Cesario recalls the masculine impersonations of Julia and Rosalind. Yet in her strange passivity, her insistence upon enduring events rather than creating them, she is like Perdita and Miranda, Marina and Imogen. The theme of mistaken identity, that confusion between twins which finally gives Sebastian to Olivia, Viola to Orsino, Shakespeare had exploited years before in *The Comedy of Errors*. Its emotional quality in *Twelfth Night*, however, prefigures the highly charged reunions of *Pericles* and *The Winter's Tale*. With respect to the idea of two comic worlds, one of them heightened, the other an analogue to our own reality, *Twelfth Night* also seems to strike a balance between the practice of early and of late Shakespearean comedy. Viola and Sebastian are shipwrecked into Illyria, even as (metaphorically at least) Hermia, Helena, Demetrius, and Lysander were shipwrecked into the forest by the harsh laws of society, or Bassanio fled the poverty of his condition in Venice in search of the Golden Fleece at Belmont. But the *Twelfth Night* characters remain in Illyria; they do not return. Nor do we gain any sense of what Messaline, the place from which they say they have come, is like. Any contrasts between the heightened and the ordinary must be found within Illyria itself.

Both Viola and Sebastian, the two intruders from the sea, accept Illyria more or less as they find it. They may be momentarily baffled by the topsy-turvy world of the revels: both yield themselves to the current without even trying, as Malvolio tries, to alter its course. Sebastian cheerfully marries a woman he doesn't know, and who may well be mad, simply because she is lovely and lays passionate claim to him. Viola, once committed to her role as Orsino's page, conscientiously does whatever she is told, however painful, without trying to impose her own will upon events. She is careful to keep at arm's length from the love-crazed Olivia, but essentially she plays a waiting game, believing that Time "must untangle this, not I" (II.ii.40). When circumstances provide her with virtual proof that her twin brother is not only alive but the source of considerable confusion and misunderstanding in Illyria, she not only makes no attempt to explain, let alone find him: she sits almost unnaturally still, leaving the wretched Antonio to flounder in an agony of mind, and her own love Orsino to entertain the most murderous suspicions and intents. Hopelessly entangled herself in the rough-and-tumble world of the underplot, deceived by the false challenge of Sir Toby, terrified by the bare prospect of combat with Sir Andrew, her efforts are all to evade action rather than, like Rosalind, to initiate it. Even her boy's disguise operates not as a liberation but merely as a way of going underground in a difficult situation, of waiting to see what Time will bring. This attitude, as it turns out, is the best she could have adopted. By surrendering herself unquestioningly to the madness of Illyria, by remaining aware but passive, she contrives to win Olivia for her brother, redeem Antonio's life,

and marry Orsino herself. Time does untangle the knot without her help: she was right to believe, against all chance and probability, that tempests might be kind, and salt waves fresh in love (III.iv.384).

Time, however, is a twofold entity in *Twelfth Night*. Even Viola, for all her faith in Time as a redemptive and beneficent force, can see that it has another face. When she tells Orsino about that supposed sister who never told her love, but sat "like Patience on a monument, / Smiling at grief" (II.iv.114–15), until it was too late, or agrees with him sadly that women are indeed like summer roses which "die, even when they to perfection grow" (II.iv.41), her words are filled with a bitter consciousness that for her too the months are passing and slowly diminishing her beauty and her youth, hidden in a boy's disguise. The chief spokesman in the play for this second, realistic kind of Time is not, however, Viola but Feste. Feste is not only a wise fool, a man in complete intellectual and emotional control of himself, who has chosen the part of professional jester: he operates throughout the comedy as a truth-teller who reminds the other characters that holiday, by its very nature, is not eternal. It is Feste who points out to the revellers that the future is uncertain, laughter momentary, and youth "a stuff will not endure" (II.iii.52). He tells Olivia something she does not want to hear, that "beauty's a flower" (I.v.52), and suggests ominously beneath his seeming lightness that "pleasure will be paid, one time or another" (II.iv.70–71). An isolated figure, with no discernible loyalties, involvements, or private life, he seems to be as much (or as little) at home in Orsino's house as in Olivia's. In both he remains watchful, observant, and essentially detached.

Elizabethans would naturally have expected Feste to be heavily involved in the plot against Malvolio, not only because he had a personal grudge against the steward, but because such behavior was appropriate to a fool. Real-life fools, if they had sufficient wit, were much given to the perpetration of practical jokes, as witness some of the stories told in *A Nest of Ninnies* (1605), that scarifying anthology compiled by Robert Armin, the actor who originally played Feste. Shakespeare, however, keeps Feste apart from the gulling of Malvolio until the Sir Topas scene, just before the end. This, of course, is the scene in which it is first intimated that the spirit of carnival may be about to break. Even Sir Toby can scent the morning air. He begins to worry that they have gone too far by imprisoning Malvolio in the dark house, and wishes that they "were well rid of this knavery" (IV.ii.67–68). In Act V images of death and violence proliferate. Antonio appears bound, anguished, and facing the prospect of execution. His presence summons up the memory of war and destruction, that sea-fight in which Orsino's young nephew had been maimed for life. Maddened by jealousy, Orsino himself threatens to kill Cesario. Sir Toby and Sir Andrew, having narrowly escaped serious injury at the hands of Sebastian, arrive on the scene covered with blood and calling for a surgeon. The party, as it seems, is over. Suddenly sober and disillusioned, Sir Andrew wishes pathetically that he were at home. Two broken revellers, even their friendship destroyed, they vanish from the stage, not to reappear. Maria does not appear either, to give us any indication of how she feels about her marriage-bargain with Sir Toby. As for Malvolio, he intrudes briefly upon the scene of joy at the end, without understanding any of it, and departs as a figure of violence, threatening revenge upon this society in which he is an alien.

At the end of *Twelfth Night*, the two kinds of Time which have coexisted throughout the comedy suddenly diverge. They are used to distinguish a world of fiction from one of fact. For Viola and Orsino, Olivia and Sebastian, there will be no awakening from the dream, no need to leave a heightened realm. The clock by which they live is that of fairy-tale: beneficent, unhurried, and admittedly unreal. Shakespeare goes out of his way to stress the formal, distanced quality of their story at its conclusion. This is why Sebastian and Viola, twins parted for only three months, put one another through a question-and-answer test of the most artificial kind, why Viola (unlike Rosalind) does not return to her girl's clothes. Orsino simply accepts a woman he has never, in fact, seen. Olivia accepts as husband a stranger she has mistaken for someone else. These resolutions and accords are powerful and emotionally charged, but they are also deliberately playlike and literary, not to be confused with the way of the world as we know it to be. Olivia and Sebastian, Viola and Orsino confront us at the end less as representatives of a new society than as people who, by the special dispensation of Comedy, have been allowed to escape from death and time.

There is a disturbingly large number of important absentees in the ending of *Twelfth Night*, more than in any other Shakespearean comedy. Sir Andrew, Sir Toby, Maria, and Malvolio do not participate in this happy ending. Antonio is present, but seems to have no part to play. Feste is absent too during the revelations and explanations, but he seems (characteristically) to understand and accept what has happened when he reappears to end the comedy. We in the theatre audience have also to face expulsion from Illyria, along with Sir Andrew and Sir Toby, Maria and the steward. Our revels, too, have ended. It is the task of Feste in his final song to tell us this, and to build a bridge from that remote, enchanted place where the two romantic couples remain forever in the very different world outside the theatre which is our own. Like Jaques' summary of the seven ages of life from cradle to grave, Feste's account of man's inexorable progress from a child's holiday realm of irresponsibility and joy into age, vice, disillusionment, and death draws upon an old, didactic tradition. Its basic pessimism is informed and sweetened, however, not only by the music to which it is set, but by the tolerance and acceptance of Feste himself. Precisely because of his anonymity and aloofness in the play now ended, he can be trusted to speak for all mankind, and not simply for himself. There is nothing that can be done about those harsh facts of existence to which Feste points, any more than about the wind and the rain. They must simply be endured. Like childhood happiness, all comedies come to an end. The great and consoling difference lies in the fact that one can, after all, as Feste points out, return to the theatre: and there, "we'll strive to please you every day."

Anne Barton

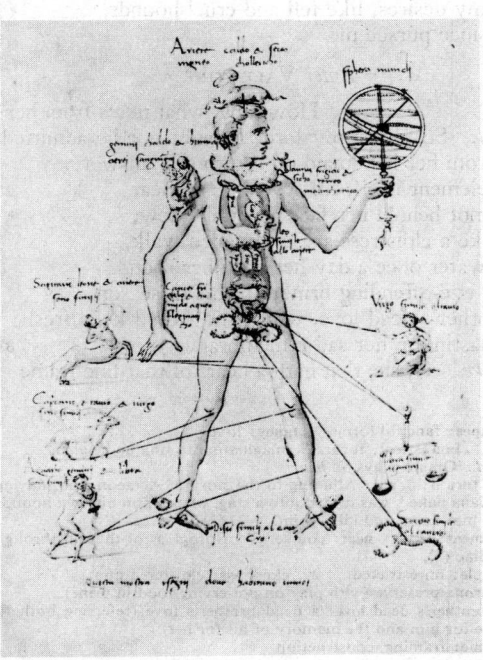

Man and the zodiac. From *Grilandus Inventum Libri IV*, MS Harvard College Library, 1506–8. Sir Toby, in answer to Sir Andrew's proposal for "some revels," says, "What shall we do else? were we not born under Taurus?" Sir Andrew asks: "Taurus? That's sides and heart." And Sir Toby rejoins: "No, sir, it is legs and thighs. Let me see thee caper" (*Twelfth Night*, I.iii.137–41). Shakespeare's reference is to the commonly held belief (by no means dead today) that individual parts of man's body were under the particular influence of one or another of the twelve signs of the zodiac. In the drawing here reproduced, which details the scheme, the relation of man (microcosm) to the universe (macrocosm) is emphasized by the "sphaera mundi" that the youth holds in his left hand.

Both Sir Toby and Sir Andrew are wrong according to the standard manuals (Taurus governing neck and throat, and Leo, sides and heart), but a minority view agreed with Sir Toby. Obviously Shakespeare is out for fun, not "science," and Sir Toby's choice of Taurus, instead of Sagittarius or Aquarius, probably is intended to carry a bawdy allusion as applied to legs and thighs. Nor does Shakespeare miss the opportunity for a play on "caper" and "Capricorn," the goat, which, as the picture indicates, governs the knees. (*By permission of the Harvard College Library*)

Twelfth Night, or What You Will

[Dramatis Personae

Orsino, *Duke of Illyria*
Sebastian, *brother to Viola*
Antonio, *a sea captain, friend to Sebastian*
Sea Captain, *friend to Viola*
Valentine ⎱
Curio ⎰ *gentlemen attending on the Duke*
Sir Toby Belch, *uncle to Olivia*
Sir Andrew Aguecheek
Malvolio, *steward to Olivia*

Fabian ⎱
Feste, *a clown* ⎰ *servants to Olivia*

Olivia, *a rich countess*
Viola, *sister to Sebastian*
Maria, *Olivia's gentlewoman*

Lords, Priests, Sailors, Officers, Musicians, Gentlewoman, Servant, *and other* Attendants

Scene: *A city in Illyria, and the sea-coast near it*]

ACT I, Scene I

Enter Orsino, *Duke of Illyria,* Curio, *and other* Lords;
  [Musicians *attending*].

Duke. If music be the food of love, play on,
Give me excess of it; that surfeiting,
The appetite may sicken, and so die.
That strain again, it had a dying fall;
O, it came o'er my ear like the sweet sound   5
That breathes upon a bank of violets,
Stealing and giving odor. Enough, no more,
'Tis not so sweet now as it was before.
O spirit of love, how quick and fresh art thou,
That notwithstanding thy capacity   10
Receiveth as the sea, nought enters there,
Of what validity and pitch soe'er,
But falls into abatement and low price

Even in a minute. So full of shapes is fancy
That it alone is high fantastical.   15
  Cur. Will you go hunt, my lord?
  Duke.   What, Curio?
  Cur.   The hart.
  Duke. Why, so I do, the noblest that I have.
O, when mine eyes did see Olivia first,
Methought she purg'd the air of pestilence!
That instant was I turn'd into a hart,   20
And my desires, like fell and cruel hounds,
E'er since pursue me.

Enter Valentine.

                        How now, what news from her?
  Val. So please my lord, I might not be admitted,
But from her handmaid do return this answer:
The element itself, till seven years' heat,   25
Shall not behold her face at ample view;
But like a cloistress she will veiled walk,
And water once a day her chamber round
With eye-offending brine; all this to season
A brother's dead love, which she would keep fresh
And lasting in her sad remembrance.   31
  Duke. O, she that hath a heart of that fine frame

---

*Words and passages enclosed in square brackets in the text above are
either emendations of the copy-text or additions to it. The Textual Notes
immediately following the play cite the earliest authority for every such
change or insertion and supply the reading of the copy-text wherever it is
emended in this edition.*

I.i. Location: The Duke's palace.
o.s.d. **Illyria**: a country extending along the east coast of the Adriatic,
in large part approximating modern Jugoslavia.
1. **music . . . love.** Cf. *Antony and Cleopatra*, II.v. 1–2, "music, moody
food / Of us that trade in love." The whole speech is concerned,
using a figure of nausea (surfeiting), with the insatiable, but paradoxically quickly sated, quality of love as Orsino here sees it—a kind
of glutton that devours dainties only to vomit them up. In a real
sense, the play is about a rectification of this view of love.
3. **appetite**: i.e. love's appetite for music.
4. **fall**: cadence.
9. **quick**: lively, vigorous. **fresh**: keen.
10. **capacity**: power to take in.
12. **validity**: value. **pitch**: high worth (a term from falconry,
designating the highest point of a hawk's flight; or perhaps *validity
and pitch* is better taken as a hendiadys, meaning "high valuation."
13. **abatement**: depreciation. **price**: esteem.

14. **shapes**: fanciful forms. **fancy**: love.
15. **it . . . fantastical**: it carries imagination to unique heights.
16. **hart.** Orsino plays on *heart.*
20–22. **turn'd . . . me.** Alluding to the story of Actaeon who, having
seen Diana naked, was turned into a stag, whereupon his own hounds
hunted him down and killed him. 21. **fell**: fierce.
25. **element**: sky. **heat**: course (?) or progress of the sun through
the zodiac (?).
26. **ample**: unrestricted. 27. **cloistress**: cloistered nun.
29. **season**: preserve (with play on preserving food in brine).
30. **A brother's dead love**: a dead brother's love (referring both to
her love for him and the memory of his for her).
32. **frame**: framing, construction.

To pay this debt of love but to a brother,
How will she love when the rich golden shaft
Hath kill'd the flock of all affections else   35
That live in her; when liver, brain, and heart,
These sovereign thrones, are all supplied and fill'd
Her sweet perfections with one self king!
Away before me to sweet beds of flow'rs,
Love-thoughts lie rich when canopied with bow'rs.   40
                                        Exeunt.

SCENE II

Enter VIOLA, *a* CAPTAIN, *and* SAILORS.

Vio. What country, friends, is this?
Cap. This is Illyria, lady.
Vio. And what should I do in Illyria?
My brother he is in Elysium.   4
Perchance he is not drown'd—what think you, sailors?
Cap. It is perchance that you yourself were saved.
Vio. O my poor brother! and so perchance may
    he be.
Cap. True, madam, and to comfort you with
    chance,
Assure yourself, after our ship did split,   9
When you, and those poor number saved with you,
Hung on our driving boat, I saw your brother,
Most provident in peril, bind himself
(Courage and hope both teaching him the practice)
To a strong mast that liv'd upon the sea;
Where like [Arion] on the dolphin's back,   15
I saw him hold acquaintance with the waves
So long as I could see.
Vio.   For saying so, there's gold.
Mine own escape unfoldeth to my hope,
Whereto thy speech serves for authority,   20
The like of him. Know'st thou this country?
Cap. Ay, madam, well, for I was bred and born
Not three hours' travel from this very place.
Vio. Who governs here?
Cap. A noble duke, in nature as in name.   25
Vio. What is his name?
Cap. Orsino.
Vio. Orsino! I have heard my father name him.
He was a bachelor then.

Cap. And so is now, or was so very late;   30
For but a month ago I went from hence,
And then 'twas fresh in murmur (as you know
What great ones do, the less will prattle of)
That he did seek the love of fair Olivia.
Vio. What's she?   35
Cap. A virtuous maid, the daughter of a count
That died some twelvemonth since, then leaving her
In the protection of his son, her brother,
Who shortly also died; for whose dear love,
They say, she hath abjur'd the [company]   40
And [sight] of men.
Vio.   O that I serv'd that lady,
And might not be delivered to the world
Till I had made mine own occasion mellow
What my estate is!
Cap.   That were hard to compass,
Because she will admit no kind of suit,   45
No, not the Duke's.
Vio. There is a fair behavior in thee, captain,
And though that nature with a beauteous wall
Doth oft close in pollution, yet of thee
I will believe thou hast a mind that suits   50
With this thy fair and outward character.
I prithee (and I'll pay thee bounteously)
Conceal me what I am, and be my aid
For such disguise as haply shall become
The form of my intent. I'll serve this duke;   55
Thou shalt present me as an eunuch to him,
It may be worth thy pains; for I can sing
And speak to him in many sorts of music
That will allow me very worth his service.
What else may hap, to time I will commit,   60
Only shape thou thy silence to my wit.
Cap. Be you his eunuch, and your mute I'll be;
When my tongue blabs, then let mine eyes not see.
Vio. I thank thee. Lead me on.   *Exeunt.*

SCENE III

Enter SIR TOBY [BELCH] *and* MARIA.

Sir To. What a plague means my niece to take the
death of her brother thus? I am sure care's an enemy
to life.
Mar. By my troth, Sir Toby, you must come in
earlier a' nights. Your cousin, my lady, takes great
exceptions to your ill hours.   6

---

34. **golden shaft:** Cupid's gold-tipped arrow, which caused love. He had also a lead-tipped arrow, which produced loathing.
35. **affections else:** other emotions (than love) (?) or other loves (?).
36. **liver . . . heart.** The supposed seats of the passions (and especially love), thought or judgment, and the feelings or sentiments respectively.
37. **supplied.** Synonymous with *fill'd.*
37–38. **and . . . perfections:** and her sweet perfections filled.
38. **one self king:** one and the same lord, the person whom she loves wholly.

I.ii. Location: The sea-coast.
4. **Elysium:** i.e. heaven. The classical name is used to play on *Illyria.*
5–6. **Perchance . . . perchance:** perhaps . . . by mere chance.
8. **chance:** i.e. a favorable possibility.   11. **driving:** drifting.
12. **Most provident:** showing great foresight.
14. **liv'd:** i.e. remained afloat.
15. **Arion . . . back.** Arion, a Greek poet and musician, on a voyage from Sicily to Greece charmed dolphins with his singing and playing on the lyre. When he leaped overboard to escape murder by the sailors, he was saved by a dolphin on whose back he rode to shore.
19. **unfoldeth:** discloses.
21. **like of him:** i.e. chance that he escaped likewise.

32. **murmur:** rumor.
42–44. **might . . . is:** that my position in life (*estate*) might not be revealed to the world until the moment is ripe for me.
44. **compass:** achieve.   46. **not:** not even.
47. **behavior:** appearance and conduct, the "outward character" of line 51.   54. **become:** be suitable to.
55. **form . . . intent:** nature of my purpose (with *form* in the sense of "shape" looking back to *disguise,* line 54).
56. **as an eunuch:** i.e. as a *castrato* or male soprano singer; thus her high voice will not be incongruous with her male disguise. Actually, Viola becomes his page.
59. **allow . . . service:** cause me to be acknowledged as worthy to serve him.   61. **shape:** fashion.   **wit:** plan, device.
62. **mute:** i.e. silent servant (suggested by *eunuch,* both being servants in the Turkish court).

I.iii. Location: Olivia's house.
5. **a':** of.   **cousin:** kinswoman.

Twelfth Night
I.iii

Sir To. Why, let her except before excepted.

Mar. Ay, but you must confine yourself within the modest limits of order. 9

Sir To. Confine? I'll confine myself no finer than I am. These clothes are good enough to drink in, and so be these boots too; and they be not, let them hang themselves in their own straps. 13

Mar. That quaffing and drinking will undo you. I heard my lady talk of it yesterday; and of a foolish knight that you brought in one night here to be her wooer.

Sir To. Who, Sir Andrew Aguecheek?

Mar. Ay, he.

Sir To. He's as tall a man as any's in Illyria. 20

Mar. What's that to th' purpose?

Sir To. Why, he has three thousand ducats a year.

Mar. Ay, but he'll have but a year in all these ducats. He's a very fool and a prodigal. 24

Sir To. Fie, that you'll say so! He plays o' th' viol-de-gamboys, and speaks three or four languages word for word without book, and hath all the good gifts of nature. 28

Mar. He hath indeed, almost natural; for besides that he's a fool, he's a great quarreller; and but that he hath the gift of a coward to allay the gust he hath in quarrelling, 'tis thought among the prudent he would quickly have the gift of a grave.

Sir To. By this hand, they are scoundrels and substractors that say so of him. Who are they? 35

Mar. They that add moreov'r, he's drunk nightly in your company.

Sir To. With drinking healths to my niece. I'll drink to her as long as there is a passage in my throat, and drink in Illyria. He's a coward and a coystrill that will not drink to my niece till his brains turn 41 o' th' toe like a parish-top. What, wench! *Castiliano vulgo!* for here comes Sir Andrew Agueface.

Enter Sir Andrew [Aguecheek].

Sir And. Sir Toby Belch! How now, Sir Toby Belch? 45

Sir To. Sweet Sir Andrew!

Sir And. Bless you, fair shrew.

Mar. And you too, sir.

Sir To. Accost, Sir Andrew, accost.

Sir And. What's that? 50

Sir To. My niece's chambermaid.

[*Sir And.*] Good Mistress Accost, I desire better acquaintance.

Mar. My name is Mary, sir.

Sir And. Good Mistress Mary Accost— 55

Sir To. You mistake, knight. "Accost" is front her, board her, woo her, assail her.

Sir And. By my troth, I would not undertake her in this company. Is that the meaning of "accost"?

Mar. Fare you well, gentlemen. 60

Sir To. And thou let part so, Sir Andrew, would thou mightst never draw sword again.

Sir And. And you part so, mistress, I would I might never draw sword again. Fair lady, do you think you have fools in hand? 65

Mar. Sir, I have not you by th' hand.

Sir And. Marry, but you shall have—and here's my hand.

Mar. Now, sir, thought is free. I pray you 69 bring your hand to th' butt'ry-bar, and let it drink.

Sir And. Wherefore, sweetheart? What's your metaphor?

Mar. It's dry, sir.

Sir And. Why, I think so. I am not such an ass but I can keep my hand dry. But what's your jest? 75

Mar. A dry jest, sir.

Sir And. Are you full of them?

Mar. Ay, sir, I have them at my fingers' ends. Marry, now I let go your hand, I am barren. 79

Exit Maria.

Sir To. O knight, thou lack'st a cup of canary. When did I see thee so put down?

Sir And. Never in your life I think, unless you see canary put me down. Methinks sometimes I have no more wit than a Christian or an ordinary man has; but I am a great eater of beef, and I believe that does harm to my wit. 86

Sir To. No question.

---

7. **except before excepted.** A quibble on the legal phrase *exceptis excipiendis* = with the exceptions aforesaid. Sir Toby apparently means that Olivia's objections are an old story and that she is welcome to go on making them.
9. **modest:** moderate. **order:** orderly conduct.
10. **confine.** Quibbling on the sense "dress." 12. **and:** if.
14. **undo you:** be the ruin of you.
18. **Aguecheek.** Suggestive of a thin, pale face, like that of a man with ague. 20. **tall:** valiant, stalwart.
23–24. **he'll . . . ducats:** i.e. he'll run though his estate in a year (at the rate he's going). 24. **very:** true, utter.
26. **viol-de-gamboys:** *viola da gamba* ("leg-viol"), the bass of the viol family. 27. **without book:** by memory.
29. **almost natural:** almost like a "natural" or halfwit.
31. **gust:** relish, gusto. 34–35. **substractors:** i.e. detractors.
40. **coystrill:** knave.
42. **parish-top.** Parishes kept large tops for the amusement and exercise of their people in winter; they were made to spin by means of whips.
42–43. **Castiliano vulgo.** Meaning uncertain; perhaps Maria is urged to act with the proverbial gravity and decorum of the Castilians to impress Sir Andrew.
43. **Agueface.** Perhaps a slip on Shakespeare's part which was later received into the text as an intentional jest.

49. **Accost:** address (her). Sir Toby's gloss (lines 56–57) includes the several suggestive connotations of the word.
51. **chambermaid:** lady in waiting. In a household like Olivia's such a term does not imply low social position. Maria is clearly a gentlewoman.
57. **board:** approach closely (as in boarding a ship in naval warfare). **assail:** i.e. attack with offers of love. Both *board* and *assail* illustrate the common practice of applying the language of war to amorous activity.
58. **undertake:** have to do (a word frequently used in a bawdy sense).
61. **And . . . so:** i.e. if you let her go thus.
65. **have . . . hand:** are dealing with fools.
67. **Marry:** indeed (a weakened oath," by the Virgin Mary"). **you shall have.** An unfortunate choice of words.
69. **thought is free:** i.e. I may think what I like (proverbial); an unreassuring answer to his question in lines 64–65.
70. **butt'ry-bar:** entrance to the buttery, the room where butts of ale and wine were stored and from which drinks were dispensed.
73. **dry:** (1) thirsty; (2) lacking in moisture (a dry hand was associated with age and impotence).
74–75. **I . . . dry.** Alluding to a proverb to the effect that even a fool knows enough to come in out of the rain.
76. **dry jest:** (1) ironic joke; (2) barren old laughingstock.
78. **at . . . ends:** (1) in readiness; (2) held by my hand.
79. **barren:** i.e. destitute of dry jests.
80. **canary:** a sweet wine from the Canary Islands.
81. **put down:** confounded, overcome.
83. **put me down:** make me drunk.
85–86. **I . . . wit.** This reflects a current belief.

Sir And. And I thought that, I'd forswear it. I'll ride home to-morrow, Sir Toby.

Sir To. *Pourquoi*, my dear knight? 90

Sir And. What is "*pourquoi*"? Do, or not do? I would I had bestow'd that time in the tongues that I have in fencing, dancing, and bear-baiting. O had I but follow'd the arts! 94

Sir To. Then hadst thou had an excellent head of hair.

Sir And. Why, would that have mended my hair?

Sir To. Past question, for thou seest it will not [curl by] nature. 99

Sir And. But it becomes [me] well enough, does't not?

Sir To. Excellent, it hangs like flax on a distaff; and I hope to see a huswife take thee between her legs, and spin it off. 104

Sir And. Faith, I'll home to-morrow, Sir Toby. Your niece will not be seen, or if she be, it's four to one she'll none of me. The Count himself here hard by woos her. 108

Sir To. She'll none o' th' Count. She'll not match above her degree, neither in estate, years, nor wit; I have heard her swear't. Tut, there's life in't, man.

Sir And. I'll stay a month longer. I am a fellow o' th' strangest mind i' th' world; I delight in masques and revels sometimes altogether. 114

Sir To. Art thou good at these kickshawses, knight?

Sir And. As any man in Illyria, whatsoever he be, under the degree of my betters, and yet I will not compare with an old man. 119

Sir To. What is thy excellence in a galliard, knight?

Sir And. Faith, I can cut a caper.

Sir To. And I can cut the mutton to't.

Sir And. And I think I have the back-trick simply as strong as any man in Illyria. 124

Sir To. Wherefore are these things hid? Wherefore have these gifts a curtain before 'em? Are they like to take dust, like Mistress Mall's picture? Why dost thou not go to church in a galliard, and come home in a coranto? My very walk should be a jig. 129

I would not so much as make water but in a sink-a-pace. What dost thou mean? Is it a world to hide virtues in? I did think by the excellent constitution of thy leg, it was form'd under the star of a galliard. 133

Sir And. Ay, 'tis strong; and it does indifferent well in a [dun-]color'd stock. Shall we [set] about some revels?

Sir To. What shall we do else? were we not born under Taurus?

Sir And. Taurus? That['s] sides and heart. 139

Sir To. No, sir, it is legs and thighs. Let me see thee caper. Ha, higher! Ha, ha, excellent! *Exeunt.*

SCENE IV

Enter VALENTINE, *and* VIOLA *in man's attire.*

Val. If the Duke continue these favors towards you, Cesario, you are like to be much advanc'd; he hath known you but three days, and already you are no stranger. 4

Vio. You either fear his humor or my negligence, that you call in question the continuance of his love. Is he inconstant, sir, in his favors?

Val. No, believe me.

Enter DUKE, CURIO, *and* ATTENDANTS.

Vio. I thank you. Here comes the Count.

Duke. Who saw Cesario, ho? 10

Vio. On your attendance, my lord, here.

Duke. Stand you awhile aloof. Cesario,
Thou know'st no less but all. I have unclasp'd
To thee the book even of my secret soul.
Therefore, good youth, address thy gait unto her, 15
Be not denied access, stand at her doors,
And tell them, there thy fixed foot shall grow
Till thou have audience.

Vio. 　　　　　　Sure, my noble lord,
If she be so abandon'd to her sorrow
As it is spoke, she never will admit me. 20

Duke. Be clamorous, and leap all civil bounds,
Rather than make unprofited return.

Vio. Say I do speak with her, my lord, what then?

Duke. O then, unfold the passion of my love,

88. **forswear:** swear off. 90. **Pourquoi:** why.
92. **bestow'd:** employed. **tongues:** languages.
94. **follow'd the arts:** applied myself to learning.
97. **mended:** improved.
98–99. **it . . . nature.** Sir Toby's jest takes advantage of the phonetic similarity of *tongues* and *tongs* (= curling-tongs) and of a second meaning of *arts*, "artificial methods."
102. **distaff:** three-foot cleft staff used in spinning wool or flax.
103–4. **huswife . . . off.** With second meaning involving *huswife* (housewife) in the sense "hussy, whore" and a reference to loss of hair from venereal disease.
107. **hard by:** near by.
110. **above her degree:** with her superior. **estate:** social position.
115. **kickshawses:** elegant trifles (the singular *kickshaws* is an anglicization of French *quelque chose*).
118. **under . . . betters:** except for those that excel me.
119. **old man:** experienced man, expert (?).
120. **galliard:** a lively dance in triple time.
121. **cut a caper:** execute a leap. Sir Toby's reply quibbles on *caper* as a condiment often served with mutton.
123. **back-trick:** steps taken backwards in the galliard.
127. **like:** likely. **take:** gather. **Mistress Mall's picture.** A topical allusion has been suspected, but the reference is probably general (*Mall* = Moll). Pictures were often protected from fading by curtains; see I.v.233.
129. **coranto:** a quick running dance. **should:** would.

130–31. **sink-a-pace:** cinquepace (French *cinque-pas*), a dance resembling the galliard.
132. **virtues:** talents, accomplishments. There is probably an allusion here to Jesus' parable of the talents (Matthew 25:14–30).
133. **star . . . galliard:** i.e. a star favorable to dancing. Cf. Beatrice's "There was a star danc'd, and under that was I born" (*Much Ado*, II.i.335). 134. **indifferent:** moderately. 135. **stock:** stocking.
138. **Taurus:** the zodiacal sign that according to a few authorities controls "legs and thighs" (line 140), but neck and throat according to the majority. See the illustration on p. 407 for the signs commonly associated with the legs.
139. **sides and heart.** Sir Andrew errs as usual; the sign for this region is Leo.

I.iv. Location: The Duke's palace.
5. **his humor . . . negligence:** change of mood on his part or neglect of duty on mine.
11. **On your attendance:** waiting to attend upon you.
12. **you.** Addressed to all except Viola-Cesario.
15. **address thy gait:** go.
18. **audience:** a hearing (of the Duke's love-suit).
21. **civil bounds:** i.e. bounds of good manners.
22. **unprofited:** profitless.

Twelfth Night
I.iv

Surprise her with discourse of my dear faith;   25
It shall become thee well to act my woes:
She will attend it better in thy youth
Than in a nuntio's of more grave aspect.

 Vio. I think not so, my lord.

 Duke.   Dear lad, believe it;
For they shall yet belie thy happy years,   30
That say thou art a man. Diana's lip
Is not more smooth and rubious; thy small pipe
Is as the maiden's organ, shrill and sound,
And all is semblative a woman's part.
I know thy constellation is right apt   35
For this affair. Some four or five attend him—
All, if you will; for I myself am best
When least in company. Prosper well in this,
And thou shalt live as freely as thy lord,
To call his fortunes thine.

 Vio.   I'll do my best   40
To woo your lady. [*Aside.*] Yet a barful strife!
Whoe'er I woo, myself would be his wife.   *Exeunt.*

SCENE V

Enter MARIA *and* CLOWN [FESTE].

 Mar. Nay, either tell me where thou hast been, or
I will not open my lips so wide as a bristle may enter,
in way of thy excuse. My lady will hang thee for
thy absence.

 Clo. Let her hang me! He that is well hang'd in
this world needs to fear no colors.   6

 Mar. Make that good.

 Clo. He shall see none to fear.

 Mar. A good lenten answer. I can tell thee where
that saying was born, of "I fear no colors."   10

 Clo. Where, good Mistress Mary?

 Mar. In the wars, and that may you be bold to say
in your foolery.

 Clo. Well, God give them wisdom that have it; and
those that are fools, let them use their talents.   15

 Mar. Yet you will be hang'd for being so long
absent, or to be turn'd away—is not that as good as a
hanging to you?

 Clo. Many a good hanging prevents a bad marriage; and for turning away, let summer bear it out.

 Mar. You are resolute then?   21

25. **Surprise:** overpower. **dear:** loving, heartfelt.
27. **attend:** heed, give ear to. 28. **nuntio's:** messenger's.
30. **yet:** as yet. 32. **rubious:** ruby-red. **pipe:** throat.
33. **shrill and sound:** high and clear (uncracked).
34. **semblative:** resembling. **part:** role (cf. *act*, line 26).
35. **constellation:** i.e. nature (as determined by position of the stars
at one's birth). 39. **freely:** generously.
41. **barful strife:** i.e. an endeavor to which there is (for me) a serious
impediment.

I.v. Location: Olivia's house.
o.s.d. **Feste.** This name is known only from II.iv.11.
6. **fear no colors.** Proverbial for "fear nothing" (*colors* = worldly
deceptions). Feste puns on *collars* = hangman's nooses.
9. **lenten:** meagre (in wit).
12. **In the wars.** Maria quibbles on *colors* in the sense "military
standards."
15. **talents:** (1) natural abilities; (2) talons (with a pun on *fools /
fowls*). 17. **turn'd away.** With a play on *turned off* = hanged.
20. **for:** as for. **let...out:** let the fact that summer is coming
make it endurable.

 Clo. Not so, neither, but I am resolv'd on two
points—

 Mar. That if one break, the other will hold; or if
both break, your gaskins fall.   25

 Clo. Apt, in good faith, very apt. Well, go thy
way, if Sir Toby would leave drinking, thou wert as
witty a piece of Eve's flesh as any in Illyria.   28

 Mar. Peace, you rogue, no more o' that. Here
comes my lady. Make your excuse wisely, you were
best.   [*Exit.*]

Enter LADY OLIVIA *with* MALVOLIO [*and* ATTENDANTS].

 Clo. Wit, and't be thy will, put me into good fooling! Those wits that think they have thee do   33
very oft prove fools; and I that am sure I lack thee,
may pass for a wise man. For what says Quinapalus?
"Better a witty fool than a foolish wit."—God bless
thee, lady!

 Oli. Take the fool away.

 Clo. Do you not hear, fellows? Take away the
lady.   40

 Oli. Go to, y' are a dry fool; I'll no more of you.
Besides, you grow dishonest.

 Clo. Two faults, madonna, that drink and good
counsel will amend; for give the dry fool drink, then is
the fool not dry; bid the dishonest man mend himself:
if he mend, he is no longer dishonest; if he cannot, let
the botcher mend him. Any thing that's mended is but
patch'd; virtue that transgresses is but patch'd with   48
sin, and sin that amends is but patch'd with virtue.
If that this simple syllogism will serve, so; if it will not,
what remedy? As there is no true cuckold but calamity, so beauty's a flower. The lady bade take away the
fool, therefore I say again, take her away.   53

 Oli. Sir, I bade them take away you.

 Clo. Misprision in the highest degree! Lady,
"*Cucullus non facit monachum*": that's as much to say
as I wear not motley in my brain. Good madonna,
give me leave to prove you a fool.

 Oli. Can you do it?

 Clo. Dexteriously, good madonna.   60

 Oli. Make your proof.

 Clo. I must catechize you for it, madonna. Good
my mouse of virtue, answer me.

23. **points.** Maria's rejoinder quibbles on the sense "laces supporting
the breeches or hose." 25. **gaskins:** breeches.
26–27. **go thy way:** run along.
27–28. **thou...Illyria:** i.e. you'd make him a good match.
32. **and't:** if it. 32–33. **good fooling:** good form for jesting.
33. **thee:** i.e. wit. 35. **Quinapalus.** Feste's invention.
41. **Go to:** a conventional phrase of reproof. **dry:** dull, stale.
42. **dishonest:** wanton, wicked.
43. **madonna:** my lady (Italian *mia donna*). 45. **mend:** reform.
46–47. **let...him:** let him be mended by someone who can do the job
(*botcher* = one who mends shoes or clothes, a cobbler or a tailor).
48–49. **virtue...virtue.** Feste warns that he, like all men, will be
imperfect after he reforms, as he was before. *Patch'd* plays on Feste's
motley, the conventional parti-colored dress for jesters.
50. **so:** well and good.
51. **what remedy:** i.e. there's nothing more I can say or do.
51–52. **As...flower.** A difficult passage. Dover Wilson explains:
"Olivia has wedded calamity by taking her vow, and has proved
herself a fool, since women are proverbially unfaithful to their weeds
and beauty fades like the flower."
55. **Misprision:** mistaking one thing for another.
56. **Cucullus...monachum:** the cowl does not make the monk.
60. **Dexteriously:** dexterously (a true variant, not Feste's coinage).
62–63. **Good...virtue:** my good virtuous mouse. The transposition
in *Good my* is common in forms of address (e.g. *good my lord*).

Oli. Well, sir, for want of other idleness, I'll bide your proof.   65

Clo. Good madonna, why mourn'st thou?

Oli. Good fool, for my brother's death.

Clo. I think his soul is in hell, madonna.

Oli. I know his soul is in heaven, fool.   69

Clo. The more fool, madonna, to mourn for your brother's soul, being in heaven. Take away the fool, gentlemen.

Oli. What think you of this fool, Malvolio? doth he not mend?   74

Mal. Yes, and shall do till the pangs of death shake him. Infirmity, that decays the wise, doth ever make the better fool.

Clo. God send you, sir, a speedy infirmity, for the better increasing your folly! Sir Toby will be sworn that I am no fox, but he will not pass his word for twopence that you are no fool.   81

Oli. How say you to that, Malvolio?

Mal. I marvel your ladyship takes delight in such a barren rascal. I saw him put down the other day with an ordinary fool that has no more brain than a stone. Look you now, he's out of his guard already. Unless you laugh and minister occasion to him, he is   87 gagg'd. I protest I take these wise men that crow so at these set kind of fools no better than the fools' zanies.

Oli. O, you are sick of self-love, Malvolio, and taste with a distemper'd appetite. To be generous, guiltless, and of free disposition, is to take those things for bird-bolts that you deem cannon-bullets.   93 There is no slander in an allow'd fool, though he do nothing but rail; nor no railing in a known discreet man, though he do nothing but reprove.

Clo. Now Mercury indue thee with leasing, for thou speak'st well of fools!

Enter MARIA.

Mar. Madam, there is at the gate a young gentleman much desires to speak with you.   100

Oli. From the Count Orsino, is it?

Mar. I know not, madam. 'Tis a fair young man, and well attended.

Oli. Who of my people hold him in delay?

Mar. Sir Toby, madam, your kinsman.   105

Oli. Fetch him off, I pray you, he speaks nothing but madman; fie on him! [*Exit Maria.*] Go you, Malvolio; if it be a suit from the Count, I am sick, or

not at home—what you will, to dismiss it. (*Exit Malvolio.*) Now you see, sir, how your fooling grows old, and people dislike it.   111

Clo. Thou hast spoke for us, madonna, as if thy eldest son should be a fool; whose skull Jove cram with brains! for—here he comes—

Enter SIR TOBY.

one of thy kin has a most weak *pia mater*.   115

Oli. By mine honor, half drunk. What is he at the gate, cousin?

Sir To. A gentleman.

Oli. A gentleman? What gentleman?

Sir To. 'Tis a gentleman here—a plague o' these pickle-herring! How now, sot?   121

Clo. Good Sir Toby!

Oli. Cousin, cousin, how have you come so early by this lethargy?

Sir To. Lechery! I defy lechery. There's one at the gate.   126

Oli. Ay, marry, what is he?

Sir To. Let him be the devil and he will, I care not; give me faith say I. Well, it's all one.   *Exit.*

Oli. What's a drunken man like, fool?   130

Clo. Like a drown'd man, a fool, and a madman. One draught above heat makes him a fool, the second mads him, and a third drowns him.

Oli. Go thou and seek the crowner, and let him sit o' my coz; for he's in the third degree of drink, he's drown'd. Go look after him.   136

Clo. He is but mad yet, madonna, and the fool shall look to the madman.   [*Exit.*]

Enter MALVOLIO.

Mal. Madam, yond young fellow swears he will speak with you. I told him you were sick; he takes on him to understand so much, and therefore comes to speak with you. I told him you were asleep;   142 he seems to have a foreknowledge of that too, and therefore comes to speak with you. What is to be said to him, lady? he's fortified against any denial.   145

Oli. Tell him he shall not speak with me.

Mal. H'as been told so; and he says he'll stand at your door like a sheriff's post, and be the supporter to a bench, but he'll speak with you.

Oli. What kind o' man is he?   150

Mal. Why, of mankind.

Oli. What manner of man?

Mal. Of very ill manner: he'll speak with you, will you or no.

Oli. Of what personage and years is he?   155

---

64. **other idleness:** any other way of wasting time.
71. **being:** when it is.
74. **mend:** equivalent to "become a better fool"; Olivia uses it in the sense "become a more amusing fool," Malvolio in the sense "become more and more foolish."
80. **fox:** crafty fellow.   **pass:** pledge.   84. **with:** by.
86. **out . . . guard:** without a witty riposte (a figure from fencing).
87. **minister occasion:** give opportunity, provide openings.
88. **protest:** declare, avow.
89. **set kind:** artificial sort.   **fools' zanies:** fools' fools. A zany (a character in the *commedia dell'arte*) was a clown's attendant who aped his master on stage.
90. **of:** with.   **self-love.** The key to Malvolio's character.
91. **distemper'd:** unhealthy.   92. **free:** open.
93. **bird-bolts:** blunt-headed arrows for shooting birds. The passage has reference to the proverb "A fool's bolt is soon shot."
94. **allow'd:** given license to speak his mind.
95. **known discreet:** of recognized judgment.
97. **Mercury:** god of guile and trickery.   **leasing:** lying.
107. **madman:** i.e. mad talk.

111. **old:** i.e. stale (cf. line 41).
115. **pia mater:** brain (properly, the membrane enveloping the brain).
116. **What:** what sort of man.
120-21. **a plague . . . pickle-herring.** Sir Toby thus excuses a belch.
121. **sot:** fool.   124. **lethargy:** stupor.
129. **give me faith.** As protection in confrontation with the devil. **it's all one:** no matter.
132. **above heat:** i.e. above the point of feeling a pleasant warmth.
134. **crowner:** coroner.
134-35. **sit . . . coz:** i.e. hold an inquest on my kinsman.
141. **therefore:** for that very reason.   147. **H'as:** he has.
148. **sheriff's post:** a decorative post set up outside the sheriff's office.
151. **of mankind:** of the human race, i.e. just an ordinary man.
155. **personage:** physical appearance.

Twelfth Night
I.v

Mal. Not yet old enough for a man, nor young enough for a boy; as a squash is before 'tis a peascod, or a codling when 'tis almost an apple. 'Tis with him in standing water, between boy and man. He is very well-favor'd, and he speaks very shrewishly. One would think his mother's milk were scarce out of him.　　162

Oli. Let him approach. Call in my gentlewoman.

Mal. Gentlewoman, my lady calls.　　　*Exit.*

Enter MARIA.

Oli. Give me my veil; come throw it o'er my face.　　165
We'll once more hear Orsino's embassy.

Enter [VIOLA].

Vio. The honorable lady of the house, which is she?

Oli. Speak to me, I shall answer for her. Your will?　　169

Vio. Most radiant, exquisite, and unmatchable beauty—I pray you tell me if this be the lady of the house, for I never saw her. I would be loath to cast away my speech; for besides that it is excellently well penn'd, I have taken great pains to con it. Good beauties, let me sustain no scorn; I am very comptible, even to the least sinister usage.　　176

Oli. Whence came you, sir?

Vio. I can say little more than I have studied, and that question's out of my part. Good gentle one, give me modest assurance if you be the lady of the house, that I may proceed in my speech.　　181

Oli. Are you a comedian?

Vio. No, my profound heart; and yet (by the very fangs of malice I swear) I am not that I play. Are you the lady of the house?　　185

Oli. If I do not usurp myself, I am.

Vio. Most certain, if you are she, you do usurp yourself; for what is yours to bestow is not yours to reserve. But this is from my commission. I will on with my speech in your praise, and then show you the heart of my message.　　191

Oli. Come to what is important in't. I forgive you the praise.

Vio. Alas, I took great pains to study it, and 'tis poetical.　　195

Oli. It is the more like to be feign'd, I pray you keep it in. I heard you were saucy at my gates, and allow'd your approach rather to wonder at you than to hear you. If you be not mad, be gone. If you have

reason, be brief. 'Tis not that time of moon with me to make one in so skipping a dialogue.　　201

Mar. Will you hoist sail, sir? Here lies your way.

Vio. No, good swabber, I am to hull here a little longer. Some mollification for your giant, sweet lady. Tell me your mind—I am a messenger.　　205

Oli. Sure you have some hideous matter to deliver, when the courtesy of it is so fearful. Speak your office.

Vio. It alone concerns your ear. I bring no overture of war, no taxation of homage; I hold the　209 olive in my hand; my words are as full of peace as matter.

Oli. Yet you began rudely. What are you? What would you?　　213

Vio. The rudeness that hath appear'd in me have I learn'd from my entertainment. What I am, and what I would, are as secret as maidenhead: to your ears, divinity; to any other's, profanation.　　217

Oli. Give us the place alone, we will hear this divinity. [*Exeunt Maria and Attendants.*] Now, sir, what is your text?　　220

Vio. Most sweet lady—

Oli. A comfortable doctrine, and much may be said of it. Where lies your text?

Vio. In Orsino's bosom.　　224

Oli. In his bosom? In what chapter of his bosom?

Vio. To answer by the method, in the first of his heart.

Oli. O, I have read it; it is heresy. Have you no more to say?

Vio. Good madam, let me see your face.　　230

Oli. Have you any commission from your lord to negotiate with my face? You are now out of your text; but we will draw the curtain, and show you the picture. Look you, sir, such a one I was this present. [*Unveiling.*] Is't not well done?　　235

Vio. Excellently done, if God did all.

Oli. 'Tis in grain, sir, 'twill endure wind and weather.

Vio. 'Tis beauty truly blent, whose red and white Nature's own sweet and cunning hand laid on.　　240

157. **squash:** unripe pea pod.　157–58. **peascod:** pea pod.
158. **codling:** unripe apple.
159. **in standing water:** i.e. at the turn of the tide.
160. **well-favor'd:** handsome.　**shrewishly:** ill-temperedly, sharply.
172–73. **cast away:** waste (by delivering it to the wrong person).
174. **con:** memorize.　175. **comptible:** sensitive, susceptible.
176. **least sinister usage:** slightest uncivil treatment.
179. **out . . . part:** not in my lines.　180. **modest:** befitting.
182. **comedian:** actor (continuing the theatrical metaphor of line 179).
183. **my profound heart:** my very wise lady (?).
186. **do . . . myself:** am not an impostor.
187–88. **usurp yourself:** possess yourself wrongfully (by refusing to give yourself to a husband).
189. **from my commission:** i.e. beyond my instructions.
192. **forgive you:** excuse you from.　197. **keep it in:** do not utter it.
199. **not mad:** i.e. not utterly mad (?). Some editors emend to *but mad* (Staunton conjecture).

200. **reason:** your wits.　**time of moon.** Certain phases of the moon were supposed to have a bad influence, particularly on lunacy.
201. **make one:** take part.　**skipping:** flighty.
203. **swabber.** Continuing Maria's nautical metaphor. A swabber was a petty officer charged with keeping the decks clean.　**hull:** drift with sails furled.
204. **mollification:** appeasement.　**your giant.** Referring ironically to Maria, who is apparently diminutive (see II.v.13, III.ii.66), and alluding to giants as guardians of ladies in romantic tales.
205. **Tell . . . mind.** Assigned by many editors (following Warburton) to Olivia.
207. **when . . . fearful:** i.e. when what should be the courteous manner of its introduction is so threatening (?).　**office:** business.
209. **taxation of homage:** demand for tribute.
211. **matter:** significant meaning.
215. **entertainment:** manner of reception.
216. **maidenhead:** virginity.
220. **what . . . text.** Picking up *divinity* (line 217), Olivia suggests that Viola-Cesario is going to proceed like a preacher in setting forth the text of a sermon. She continues this figure, with Viola's cooperation, through line 228.　222. **comfortable:** full of comfort.
226. **by the method:** according to the accepted form in beginning a sermon.　232. **out of:** wandering from.
234. **such . . . present.** Olivia begins as if displaying a portrait of herself painted at an earlier time, then ends with "at the present time" (*this present*).
236. **if . . . all:** if it is all natural (unaided by cosmetics).
237. **'Tis in grain:** it is fast-dyed, i.e. it won't wash off.
239. **blent:** blended.　240. **cunning:** skilled.

Lady, you are the cruell'st she alive
If you will lead these graces to the grave,
And leave the world no copy.

Oli. O, sir, I will not be so hard-hearted; I will
give out divers schedules of my beauty. It shall 245
be inventoried, and every particle and utensil labell'd to
my will: as, *item*, two lips, indifferent red; *item*, two
grey eyes, with lids to them; *item*, one neck, one chin,
and so forth. Were you sent hither to praise me?

Vio. I see you what you are, you are too proud;
But if you were the devil, you are fair. 251
My lord and master loves you. O, such love
Could be but recompens'd, though you were crown'd
The nonpareil of beauty.

Oli.   How does he love me?

Vio. With adorations, fertile tears, 255
With groans that thunder love, with sighs of fire.

Oli. Your lord does know my mind, I cannot love
　　him,
Yet I suppose him virtuous, know him noble,
Of great estate, of fresh and stainless youth;
In voices well divulg'd, free, learn'd, and valiant, 260
And in dimension, and the shape of nature,
A gracious person. But yet I cannot love him.
He might have took his answer long ago.

Vio. If I did love you in my master's flame,
With such a suff'ring, such a deadly life, 265
In your denial I would find no sense,
I would not understand it.

Oli.   Why, what would you?

Vio. Make me a willow cabin at your gate,
And call upon my soul within the house;
Write loyal cantons of contemned love, 270
And sing them loud even in the dead of night;
Hallow your name to the reverberate hills,
And make the babbling gossip of the air
Cry out "Olivia!" O, you should not rest
Between the elements of air and earth 275
But you should pity me!

Oli.   You might do much.
What is your parentage?

Vio. Above my fortunes, yet my state is well:
I am a gentleman.

Oli.   Get you to your lord.
I cannot love him; let him send no more— 280
Unless (perchance) you come to me again
To tell me how he takes it. Fare you well.
I thank you for your pains. Spend this for me.

Vio. I am no fee'd post, lady; keep your purse;
My master, not myself, lacks recompense. 285
Love make his heart of flint that you shall love,
And let your fervor like my master's be
Plac'd in contempt! Farewell, fair cruelty.   *Exit.*

Oli. "What is your parentage?"
"Above my fortunes, yet my state is well: 290
I am a gentleman." I'll be sworn thou art;
Thy tongue, thy face, thy limbs, actions, and spirit
Do give thee fivefold blazon. Not too fast! soft, soft!
Unless the master were the man. How now?
Even so quickly may one catch the plague? 295
Methinks I feel this youth's perfections
With an invisible and subtle stealth
To creep in at mine eyes. Well, let it be.
What ho, Malvolio!

Enter MALVOLIO.

Mal.   Here, madam, at your service.

Oli. Run after that same peevish messenger, 300
The [County's] man. He left this ring behind him,
Would I or not. Tell him I'll none of it.
Desire him not to flatter with his lord,
Nor hold him up with hopes: I am not for him.
If that the youth will come this way to-morrow, 305
I'll give him reasons for't. Hie thee, Malvolio.

Mal. Madam, I will.   *Exit.*

Oli. I do I know not what, and fear to find
Mine eye too great a flatterer for my mind.
Fate, show thy force: ourselves we do not owe; 310
What is decreed must be; and be this so.   [*Exit.*]

ACT II, SCENE I

Enter ANTONIO *and* SEBASTIAN.

Ant. Will you stay no longer? nor will you not
that I go with you?

Seb. By your patience, no. My stars shine darkly
over me. The malignancy of my fate might perhaps
distemper yours; therefore I shall crave of you 5
your leave, that I may bear my evils alone. It were a
bad recompense for your love, to lay any of them
on you.

241–43. **Lady . . . copy.** Reminiscent of the argument in Shakespeare's
first seventeen sonnets.   241. **she:** woman.
243. **copy:** i.e. a child inheriting your beauty. Olivia plays on the
sense "transcript, record."
245 **schedules:** itemized lists, inventories.
246. **particle and utensil:** particular and item.   **labell'd:** attached.
247. **item:** a term (= also) usually preceding each item after the first
(signalled by *imprimis* = in the first place) in a list, but sometimes,
as here, preceding the first as well.   **indifferent:** moderately.
249. **praise.** With a quibble on "appraise."
251. **if:** even if.   **the devil.** The supreme example of pride.
253. **Could . . . though:** could be no more than evenly repaid even
though.   254. **nonpareil:** one that has no equal.
255. **fertile:** abundant, ever-flowing.   259. **stainless:** unstained.
260. **In . . . divulg'd:** well reputed by general opinion (*voices*).
261. **dimension . . . nature:** form and physique.
262. **gracious person:** pleasing figure of a man.
264. **flame:** passion.   265. **deadly:** death-like.
268. **willow cabin:** hut of willow boughs. Willow was the symbol of
unrequited love.   269. **my soul:** i.e. Olivia.
270. **cantons:** cantos, songs.   **contemned:** despised, scornfully rejected.   272. **Hallow:** halloo, shout.   **reverberate:** resounding.
273. **babbling . . . air:** echo.
275. **Between . . . earth:** i.e. anywhere on the face of the earth.
276. **But:** but that.   278. **state:** condition.

284. **fee'd post:** messenger who should be tipped.
286. **Love . . . love:** may love give a heart of flint to the man you fall
in love with.   288. **cruelty:** cruel person.
293. **give . . . blazon:** i.e. proclaim you a gentleman five times over
as surely as if they were coats of arms. A blazon is a heraldic description of armorial bearings.   **soft:** stay.
298. **creep . . . eyes.** It was a conventional idea that love entered
through the eyes.
300. **peevish:** pettish, childish.   301. **County's:** Count's, i.e. Duke's.
303. **flatter with:** encourage.   306. **Hie:** hasten.
308–9. **fear . . . mind:** am afraid I shall find that my eyes (i.e. senses)
have seduced my mind.   310. **owe:** own, control.

II.i. Location: The sea-coast.
3. **patience:** sufferance.
4. **malignancy:** virulent condition, (1) in its medical sense = deadly
contagion, (2) in its astrological sense = evil stellar influence.
5. **distemper:** infect.

Ant. Let me yet know of you whither you are bound. 10

Seb. No, sooth, sir; my determinate voyage is mere extravagancy. But I perceive in you so excellent a touch of modesty, that you will not extort from me what I am willing to keep in; therefore it charges me in manners the rather to express myself. You 15 must know of me then, Antonio, my name is Sebastian, which I call'd Rodorigo; my father was that Sebastian of Messaline, whom I know you have heard of. He left behind him myself and a sister, both born in an hour. If the heavens had been pleas'd, would we had so 20 ended! But you, sir, alter'd that, for some hour before you took me from the breach of the sea was my sister drown'd.

Ant. Alas the day! 24

Seb. A lady, sir, though it was said she much resembled me, was yet of many accounted beautiful; but though I could not with such estimable wonder overfar believe that, yet thus far I will boldly publish her: she bore a mind that envy could not but call fair. She is drown'd already, sir, with salt water, 30 though I seem to drown her remembrance again with more.

Ant. Pardon me, sir, your bad entertainment.

Seb. O good Antonio, forgive me your trouble.

Ant. If you will not murther me for my love, let me be your servant. 36

Seb. If you will not undo what you have done, that is, kill him whom you have recover'd, desire it not. Fare ye well at once; my bosom is full of kindness, and I am yet so near the manners of my 40 mother, that upon the least occasion more mine eyes will tell tales of me. I am bound to the Count Orsino's court. Farewell. *Exit.*

Ant. The gentleness of all the gods go with thee! I have many enemies in Orsino's court, 45 Else would I very shortly see thee there. But come what may, I do adore thee so That danger shall seem sport, and I will go. *Exit.*

Scene II

Enter Viola *and* Malvolio *at several doors.*

Mal. Were you not ev'n now with the Countess Olivia?

Vio. Even now, sir; on a moderate pace I have since arriv'd but hither. 4

Mal. She returns this ring to you, sir. You might have sav'd me my pains, to have taken it away yourself. She adds moreover, that you should put your lord into a desperate assurance she will none of him. And one thing more, that you be never so hardy to come again in his affairs, unless it be to report your lord's taking of this. Receive it so. 11

Vio. She took the ring of me, I'll none of it.

Mal. Come, sir, you peevishly threw it to her; and her will is, it should be so return'd. If it be worth stooping for, there it lies, in your eye; if not, be it his that finds it. *Exit.* 16

Vio. I left no ring with her. What means this lady? Fortune forbid my outside have not charm'd her! She made good view of me; indeed so much That methought her eyes had lost her tongue, 20 For she did speak in starts distractedly. She loves me sure, the cunning of her passion Invites me in this churlish messenger. None of my lord's ring? Why, he sent her none. I am the man! If it be so, as 'tis, 25 Poor lady, she were better love a dream. Disguise, I see thou art a wickedness Wherein the pregnant enemy does much. How easy is it for the proper-false In women's waxen hearts to set their forms! 30 Alas, [our] frailty is the cause, not we, For such as we are made [of,] such we be. How will this fadge? My master loves her dearly, And I (poor monster) fond as much on him; And she (mistaken) seems to dote on me. 35 What will become of this? As I am man, My state is desperate for my master's love; As I am woman (now alas the day!), What thriftless sighs shall poor Olivia breathe! O time, thou must untangle this, not I, 40 It is too hard a knot for me t' untie. [*Exit.*]

Scene III

Enter Sir Toby *and* Sir Andrew.

Sir To. Approach, Sir Andrew. Not to be a-bed

---

11. **sooth:** truly (shortened form of *in sooth*). **determinate:** intended. 12. **mere extravagancy:** utter vagabondage.
13. **touch:** feeling.
14. **willing . . . in:** desirous of keeping secret. **it charges me:** it is incumbent on me.
15. **in manners:** by the requirements of good manners, in courtesy.
18. **Messaline.** Not identified.
19. **in an hour:** within the same hour.
22. **breach . . . sea:** breaking waves, surf.
27. **such estimable wonder:** estimation reflecting so much admiration.
28. **publish:** proclaim. 29. **envy:** i.e. even malice.
33. **your bad entertainment:** the humble hospitality I have offered you. 35. **murther me:** i.e. be the cause of my death.
38. **recover'd:** rescued.
39–40. **kindness:** natural feeling, i.e. a brother's grief.
40–41. **yet . . . mother:** i.e. still so newly a man. Such apologies by men for womanish tears are numerous in Shakespeare.

II.ii. Location: A street.
o.s.d. **several:** separate.

3. **on:** at.   6. **to have taken:** by taking.
8. **desperate assurance:** certainty without hope of change.
9. **hardy:** bold.
11. **taking of this:** i.e. reception of Olivia's message of rejection.
14. **so return'd:** i.e. thrown back at you.
15. **in your eye:** in plain view.
18. **forbid . . . not.** Modern idiom would omit *not*.
19. **made . . . me:** examined me closely.
20. **lost:** i.e. made her lose.
21. **in starts:** by fits and starts. **distractedly:** disjointedly.
23. **in:** by means of, through.
28. **the pregnant enemy:** the devil, always ready (to take advantage of our evil for his own evil ends).
29. **proper-false:** i.e. men who are handsome but false.
30. **waxen:** i.e. impressionable. The image is from sealing. **set their forms:** stamp their images. 31. **frailty:** human weakness.
32. **such . . . of:** i.e. frail flesh. 33. **fadge:** work out, come off.
34. **monster:** i.e. being both a man and woman. **fond:** dote.
39. **thriftless:** unprofitable.

II.iii. Location: Olivia's house.

after midnight is to be up betimes, and "*deliculo surgere,*" thou know'st—

Sir And. Nay, by my troth, I know not; but I know, to be up late is to be up late.   5

Sir To. A false conclusion. I hate it as an unfill'd can. To be up after midnight and to go to bed then, is early; so that to go to bed after midnight is to go to bed betimes. Does not our lives consist of the four elements?   10

Sir And. Faith, so they say, but I think it rather consists of eating and drinking.

Sir To. Th' art a scholar; let us therefore eat and drink. Marian, I say, a stoup of wine!

Enter Clown.

Sir And. Here comes the fool, i' faith.   15

Clo. How now, my hearts? Did you never see the picture of "we three"?

Sir To. Welcome, ass. Now let's have a catch.

Sir And. By my troth, the fool has an excellent breast. I had rather than forty shillings I had such   20 a leg, and so sweet a breath to sing, as the fool has. In sooth, thou wast in very gracious fooling last night, when thou spok'st of Pigrogromitus, of the Vapians passing the equinoctial of Queubus. 'Twas very good, i' faith. I sent thee sixpence for thy leman; hadst it?   25

Clo. I did impeticos thy gratillity; for Malvolio's nose is no whipstock. My lady has a white hand, and the Mermidons are no bottle-ale houses.

Sir And. Excellent! Why, this is the best fooling, when all is done. Now a song.   30

Sir To. Come on, there is sixpence for you. Let's have a song.

Sir And. There's a testril of me too. If one knight give a—

Clo. Would you have a love-song, or a song of good life?   36

Sir To. A love-song, a love-song.

Sir And. Ay, ay. I care not for good life.

Clown sings.

O mistress mine, where are you roaming?
O, stay and hear, your true-love's coming,   40

That can sing both high and low.
Trip no further, pretty sweeting;
Journeys end in lovers meeting,
    Every wise man's son doth know.

Sir And. Excellent good, i' faith.   45
Sir To. Good, good.

Clown [*sings*].

What is love? 'Tis not hereafter;
Present mirth hath present laughter;
    What's to come is still unsure.
In delay there lies no plenty,   50
Then come kiss me sweet and twenty;
    Youth's a stuff will not endure.

Sir And. A mellifluous voice, as I am true knight.
Sir To. A contagious breath.
Sir And. Very sweet and contagious, i' faith.   55
Sir To. To hear by the nose, it is dulcet in contagion. But shall we make the welkin dance indeed? Shall we rouse the night-owl in a catch that will draw three souls out of one weaver? Shall we do that?   59
Sir And. And you love me, let's do't. I am dog at a catch.
Clo. By'r lady, sir, and some dogs will catch well.
Sir And. Most certain. Let our catch be "Thou knave."   64
Clo. "Hold thy peace, thou knave," knight? I shall be constrain'd in't to call thee knave, knight.
Sir And. 'Tis not the first time I have constrain'd one to call me knave. Begin, fool. It begins, "Hold thy peace."
Clo. I shall never begin if I hold my peace.   70
Sir And. Good, i' faith. Come, begin.

Catch sung.

Enter Maria.

Mar. What a caterwauling do you keep here! If my lady have not call'd up her steward Malvolio and bid him turn you out of doors, never trust me.   74
Sir To. My lady's a Catian, we are politicians, Malvolio's a Peg-a-Ramsey, and [*sings*] "Three merry men be we." Am not I consanguineous? Am I not of

---

2. **betimes:** in good season.
2–3. **deliculo surgere.** From a well-known Latin maxim, *Diluculo surgere saluberrimum est,* "to get up at dawn is very healthful."
4. **by my troth:** on my word.   7. **can:** tankard.
10. **four elements:** earth, water, air, and fire, supposed the constituents of all created things.
13. **Th' art a scholar:** i.e. I'll accept your authority on that point.
14. **stoup:** large drinking-cup.
17. **picture of "we three":** i.e. a picture of two fools or ass-heads inscribed "we three," the viewer being the third.
18. **catch:** round.   20. **breast:** i.e. breath, voice.
21. **leg:** graceful bow or obeisance (?) or fine leg for dancing (?). Relevance uncertain.   22. **gracious:** delightful.
23–24. **Pigrogromitus . . . Queubus.** Feste's mock scholarship.
24. **equinoctial:** equator.   25. **leman:** sweetheart.
26. **impeticos:** impetticoat, i.e. pocket (?) or, possibly, spend on a woman (?).   **gratillity:** little tip (invented diminutive of *gratuity*).
27. **whipstock:** whip handle, i.e. whip. The apparent meaning is that Malvolio's nose is stuck into everything but is no real deterrent. **has . . . hand:** is gently bred (?) or has ladylike tastes (?).
28. **Mermidons.** Presumably a tavern, with a sign displaying Myrmidons (Achilles' troop).   **bottle-ale houses:** i.e. low-class taverns.
33. **testril:** sixpence (invented diminutive of *tester*; Sir Andrew seems to be aping Feste, with absurd effect).
35–36. **of good life:** conducive to virtue, edifying.

42. **sweeting:** sweet one.   43. **in lovers meeting:** when lovers meet.
49. **still:** ever, always.
51. **sweet and twenty:** sweet and twenty more times sweet. *Twenty* is used as an intensive.
54. **contagious breath:** (1) catchy song; (2) bad breath.
56–57. **To . . . contagion:** if we could both hear and smell with our noses, we could call it sweetly stinking.
57. **welkin:** heavens, i.e. heavenly bodies.
58–59. **draw three souls.** It was a conventional notion that music could draw the soul from the body. These three singers will have three times that effect.   **weaver.** Weavers were supposedly given to singing psalms.
60. **dog:** i.e. very good, expert.   62. **By'r lady:** by Our Lady.
63–64. **"Thou knave."** The words of the catch are: "Hold thy peace, thou knave; and I prithee hold thy peace." Each singer in turn thus calls another a knave.
67–68. **constrain'd . . . knave:** compelled someone to challenge me to a duel (but as usual Sir Andrew's form of words is unfortunate).
72. **keep:** keep up.
75. **Catian:** Cathayan (i.e., Chinese); slang for one whose word cannot be trusted (?).   **politicians:** schemers, intriguers.
76. **Peg-a-Ramsey.** A term of contempt, alluding to a character in a coarse ballad.
76–77. **"Three . . . we."** A fragment of an old song.

417

Twelfth Night
II.iii

her blood? Tilly-vally! Lady! [*Sings.*] "There dwelt
a man in Babylon, lady, lady."   79

Clo. Beshrew me, the knight's in admirable fooling.

Sir And. Ay, he does well enough if he be dispos'd, and so do I too. He does it with a better grace,
but I do it more natural.

Sir To. [*Sings.*] "O the twelf day of December"—

Mar. For the love o' God, peace!   85

Enter MALVOLIO.

Mal. My masters, are you mad? Or what are you?
Have you no wit, manners, nor honesty, but to gabble
like tinkers at this time of night? Do ye make an
alehouse of my lady's house, that ye squeak out your
coziers' catches without any mitigation or remorse   90
of voice? Is there no respect of place, persons, nor
time in you?

Sir To. We did keep time, sir, in our catches.
Sneck up!   94

Mal. Sir Toby, I must be round with you. My
lady bade me tell you, that though she harbors you as
her kinsman, she's nothing allied to your disorders.
If you can separate yourself and your misdemeanors,
you are welcome to the house; if not, and it would
please you to take leave of her, she is very willing to
bid you farewell!   101

Sir To. [*Sings.*] "Farewell, dear heart, since I
must needs be gone."

Mar. Nay, good Sir Toby.

Clo. [*Sings.*] "His eyes do show his days are
almost done."

Mal. Is't even so?   105

Sir To. [*Sings.*] "But I will never die."

Clo. Sir Toby, there you lie.

Mal. This is much credit to you.

Sir To. [*Sings.*] "Shall I bid him go?"

Clo. [*Sings.*] "What and if you do?"   110

Sir To. [*Sings.*] "Shall I bid him go, and spare
not?"

Clo. [*Sings.*] "O no, no, no, no, you dare not."

Sir To. [*To Clown.*] Out o' tune, sir! ye lie.
[*To Malvolio.*] Art any more than a steward? Dost
thou think because thou art virtuous there shall be no
more cakes and ale?   116

Clo. Yes, by Saint Anne, and ginger shall be hot i'
th' mouth too.

Sir To. Th' art i' th' right. Go, sir, rub your chain
with crumbs. A stope of wine, Maria!   120

Mal. Mistress Mary, if you priz'd my lady's
favor at any thing more than contempt, you would
not give means for this uncivil rule. She shall know of
it, by this hand.   *Exit.*

Mar. Go shake your ears.   125

Sir And. 'Twere as good a deed as to drink when
a man's a-hungry, to challenge him the field, and then
to break promise with him, and make a fool of him.

Sir To. Do't, knight. I'll write thee a challenge,
or I'll deliver thy indignation to him by word of mouth.

Mar. Sweet Sir Toby, be patient for to-night.
Since the youth of the Count's was to-day with   132
my lady, she is much out of quiet. For Monsieur
Malvolio, let me alone with him. If I do not gull him
into an ayword, and make him a common recreation,
do not think I have wit enough to lie straight in my
bed. I know I can do it.   137

Sir To. Possess us, possess us, tell us something
of him.

Mar. Marry, sir, sometimes he is a kind of puritan.

Sir And. O, if I thought that, I'd beat him like a
dog!

Sir To. What, for being a puritan? Thy exquisite
reason, dear knight?   144

Sir And. I have no exquisite reason for't, but I
have reason good enough.

Mar. The dev'l a puritan that he is, or any thing
constantly but a time-pleaser, an affection'd ass, that
cons state without book, and utters it by great   149
swarths; the best persuaded of himself, so cramm'd
(as he thinks) with excellencies, that it is his grounds
of faith that all that look on him love him; and on that
vice in him will my revenge find notable cause to work.

Sir To. What wilt thou do?   154

Mar. I will drop in his way some obscure epistles
of love, wherein by the color of his beard, the shape
of his leg, the manner of his gait, the expressure of his

---

78. **Tilly-vally! Lady!:** fiddle-faddle, lady indeed! Perhaps Sir Toby
is annoyed by Maria's "my lady" instead of "your cousin" as elsewhere.
78–79. **There . . . lady.** The first line of the *Ballad of Constant Susanna*,
with the song's "burden" (*lady, lady*) added.
80. **Beshrew me:** a mild oath (originally = curse me).
81–82. **dispos'd:** inclined to mirth.
83. **natural:** (1) naturally; (2) like a fool.
84. **"O . . . December."** The opening line of another ballad (*twelf* =
twelfth).   87. **honesty:** decorum, decency.
90. **coziers':** cobblers'.   **mitigation or remorse:** i.e. softening.
91. **respect:** regard.   94. **Sneck up:** go hang.
95. **round:** plain-spoken.
96. **harbors you:** allows you residence.
97. **nothing allied:** no kin at all.
102. **Farewell . . . gone.** From the ballad *Corydon's Farewell to
Phillis.* The subsequent lines sung by Sir Toby and Feste are slightly
adapted to the occasion.
107. **Sir . . . lie.** It seems likely that Feste sings this line too.
110. **and if:** if.
113. **Out o' tune:** i.e. false (quibbling on *false* as in "a false note,"
but with intended meaning "lying"); like the following *ye lie*, a
reference to Feste's "you dare not [bid him go]."
116. **cakes and ale.** Proverbial for revelry.

117. **ginger.** A common addition to ale.
119–20. **rub . . . crumbs:** i.e. polish your steward's chain (a reminder
of his position as a servant).   120. **stope:** stoup.
123. **give means:** i.e. provide drinks.   **rule:** course of conduct.
125. **Go . . . ears.** Implying that Malvolio is an ass.
127. **field:** i.e. duelling-ground.
134. **let . . . him:** leave him to me.   **gull:** befool.
135. **an ayword:** a byword or proverb (*ay* = ever). The F1 form is
here retained, since Shakespeare seems to have been the first to use
the phrase and its etymology is doubtful. Editors (following Rowe)
usually read *a nayword*, a form that occurs twice in *The Merry Wives
of Windsor*, where, however, the sense required seems to be "password."   **common recreation:** general laughingstock.
138. **Possess:** tell, inform.
140. **puritan:** i.e. one who professes to be extremely precise in morals;
frequently (as Malvolio has just shown himself to be), one who is
complacent about his own moral superiority and highly censorious
of the lapses or fancied lapses of others. Apparently Sir Andrew in
lines 140–42 takes Maria to be charging him with being a member of
the Puritan party in the Anglican Church, and Maria in line 147
rejects the idea.   143. **exquisite:** ingenious.
148. **constantly:** consistently, steadily.   **time-pleaser:** self-seeking flatterer.   **affection'd:** full of affectation.
149. **cons . . . book:** commits to memory the speech and behavior of
the great.   **utters:** (1) repeats; (2) discharges.
150. **swarths:** swaths, i.e. masses.   **the best . . . himself:** having the
highest opinion of himself.   151–52. **grounds of faith:** firm belief.
157. **expressure:** expressive quality.

418

eye, forehead, and complexion, he shall find himself most feelingly personated. I can write very like my lady your niece; on a forgotten matter we can hardly make distinction of our hands.　161

Sir To. Excellent, I smell a device.

Sir And. I have't in my nose too.

Sir To. He shall think by the letters that thou wilt drop that they come from my niece, and that she's in love with him.　166

Mar. My purpose is indeed a horse of that color.

Sir And. And your horse now would make him an ass.

Mar. Ass, I doubt not.　170

Sir And. O, 'twill be admirable!

Mar. Sport royal, I warrant you. I know my physic will work with him. I will plant you two, and let the fool make a third, where he shall find the letter; observe his construction of it. For this night, to bed, and dream on the event. Farewell.　*Exit.*　176

Sir To. Good night, Penthesilea.

Sir And. Before me, she's a good wench.

Sir To. She's a beagle true-bred, and one that adores me. What o' that?　180

Sir And. I was ador'd once too.

Sir To. Let's to bed, knight. Thou hadst need send for more money.

Sir And. If I cannot recover your niece, I am a foul way out.　185

Sir To. Send for money, knight; if thou hast her not i' th' end, call me cut.

Sir And. If I do not, never trust me, take it how you will.　189

Sir To. Come, come, I'll go burn some sack, 'tis too late to go to bed now. Come, knight, come, knight.　*Exeunt.*

Scene IV

Enter Duke, Viola, Curio, *and others.*

Duke. Give me some music. Now good morrow, friends.
Now, good Cesario, but that piece of song,
That old and antique song we heard last night;

159. **feelingly personated**: exactly represented.
161. **hands**: handwriting.
170. **Ass.** A quibble on *as / ass* (= Sir Andrew).
173. **physic**: medicine.
174. **fool . . . third.** Actually it is not Feste but Fabian who makes the third (see II.v). Maria's words imply that Feste is no longer present. He last speaks at lines 117–18; perhaps Malvolio waves him out as he leaves at line 124.
175. **construction**: interpretation.　176. **event**: outcome.
177. **Penthesilea**: queen of the Amazons (an ironical allusion to Maria's size).
178. **Before me**: i.e. on my soul (formed on the pattern of such oaths as *before God* and *before heaven*).　197. **beagle**: small hunting-dog.
181. **I . . . too.** A line that suddenly, as elsewhere in Shakespeare, reveals the human being in a hitherto ridiculous figure of fun.
184. **recover**: win (with a suggestion of making good on his expenditure, as in *recover a debt*).
185. **foul way out**: wretchedly out of pocket.
187. **cut**: a horse with a docked tail.
190. **burn some sack**: prepare some warm sack (Spanish wine) and sugar.

II.iv. Location: The Duke's palace.
2. **but**: just (let us have).　3. **antique**: quaint.

Methought it did relieve my passion much,
More than light airs and recollected terms　5
Of these most brisk and giddy-paced times.
Come, but one verse.

Cur. He is not here, so please your lordship, that should sing it.

Duke. Who was it?　10

Cur. Feste the jester, my lord, a fool that the Lady Olivia's father took much delight in. He is about the house.

Duke. Seek him out, and play the tune the while.
　　　　　　　　　　[Exit Curio.]　Music plays.
Come hither, boy. If ever thou shalt love,　15
In the sweet pangs of it remember me;
For such as I am, all true lovers are,
Unstaid and skittish in all motions else,
Save in the constant image of the creature
That is belov'd. How dost thou like this tune?　20

Vio. It gives a very echo to the seat
Where Love is thron'd.

Duke. 　　　　　　Thou dost speak masterly.
My life upon't, young though thou art, thine eye
Hath stay'd upon some favor that it loves.
Hath it not, boy?

Vio. 　　　　　A little, by your favor.　25

Duke. What kind of woman is't?

Vio. 　　　　　　　　Of your complexion.

Duke. She is not worth thee then. What years, i' faith?

Vio. About your years, my lord.

Duke. Too old, by heaven. Let still the woman take
An elder than herself, so wears she to him;　30
So sways she level in her husband's heart.
For, boy, however we do praise ourselves,
Our fancies are more giddy and unfirm,
More longing, wavering, sooner lost and worn,
Than women's are.

Vio. 　　　　　I think it well, my lord.　35

Duke. Then let thy love be younger than thyself,
Or thy affection cannot hold the bent;
For women are as roses, whose fair flow'r
Being once display'd, doth fall that very hour.

Vio. And so they are; alas, that they are so!　40
To die, even when they to perfection grow!

Enter Curio *and* Clown.

5. **light**: trivial (?) or quick in tempo (?). **recollected.** Meaning uncertain; variously explained as "refined," "studied," "farfetched," and so on.
18. **Unstaid and skittish**: giddy and fickle. **motions else**: other thoughts and feelings.
21–22. **gives . . . thron'd**: i.e. it expresses what the heart feels.
22. **masterly**: like one who has had experience (of love).
24. **stay'd upon**: attended (?) or lingered upon (?). **favor**: face.
25. **by your favor**: if you please (a polite phrase), but with obvious quibbles on "near your face" and "thanks to you."
26. **complexion**: appearance, good looks.
29. **still**: ever, always.
30. **wears**: adapts herself (like a garment adjusting itself to the wearer).
31. **sways**: (1) holds sway; (2) swings. **level**: in perfect balance.
33. **fancies**: loves. **unfirm**: fickle.
34. **worn**: spent.　35. **think it well**: think so too.
37. **hold the bent**: maintain its fullness and intensity (as a bow is kept bent to its full extent under high tension).
39. **display'd**: fully opened.　41. **even when**: just when.

Twelfth Night
II.iv

Duke. O fellow, come, the song we had last night.
Mark it, Cesario, it is old and plain.
The spinsters and the knitters in the sun,   44
And the free maids that weave their thread with bones,
Do use to chaunt it. It is silly sooth,
And dallies with the innocence of love,
Like the old age.
Clo. Are you ready, sir?
Duke. Ay, prithee sing.   *Music.*

THE SONG

[*Clo.*] Come away, come away, death,   51
        And in sad cypress let me be laid.
    [Fly] away, [fly] away, breath,
        I am slain by a fair cruel maid.
    My shroud of white, stuck all with yew,   55
        O, prepare it!,
    My part of death, no one so true
        Did share it.

    Not a flower, not a flower sweet
        On my black coffin let there be strown.   60
    Not a friend, not a friend greet
        My poor corpse, where my bones
            shall be thrown.
    A thousand thousand sighs to save,
        Lay me, O, where
    Sad true lover never find my grave,   65
        To weep there.

Duke. There's for thy pains.
Clo. No pains, sir, I take pleasure in singing, sir.
Duke. I'll pay thy pleasure then.   69
Clo. Truly, sir, and pleasure will be paid, one time
or another.
Duke. Give me now leave to leave thee.
Clo. Now the melancholy god protect thee, and
the tailor make thy doublet of changeable taffata,   74
for thy mind is a very opal. I would have men of such
constancy put to sea, that their business might be
every thing and their intent every where, for that's it
that always makes a good voyage of nothing. Farewell.
                                                    Exit.
Duke. Let all the rest give place.
                              [*Curio and Attendants retire.*]

Once more, Cesario,
Get thee to yond same sovereign cruelty.   80
Tell her, my love, more noble than the world,
Prizes not quantity of dirty lands;
The parts that fortune hath bestow'd upon her,
Tell her, I hold as giddily as fortune;
But 'tis that miracle and queen of gems   85
That nature pranks her in attracts my soul.
Vio. But if she cannot love you, sir?
Duke. [I] cannot be so answer'd.
Vio.   Sooth, but you must.
Say that some lady, as perhaps there is,
Hath for your love as great a pang of heart   90
As you have for Olivia. You cannot love her;
You tell her so. Must she not then be answer'd?
Duke. There is no woman's sides
Can bide the beating of so strong a passion
As love doth give my heart; no woman's heart   95
So big, to hold so much; they lack retention.
Alas, their love may be call'd appetite,
No motion of the liver, but the palate,
That suffer surfeit, cloyment, and revolt,
But mine is all as hungry as the sea,   100
And can digest as much. Make no compare
Between that love a woman can bear me
And that I owe Olivia.
Vio.   Ay, but I know—
Duke. What dost thou know?   104
Vio. Too well what love women to men may owe;
In faith, they are as true of heart as we.
My father had a daughter lov'd a man
As it might be perhaps, were I a woman,
I should your lordship.
Duke.   And what's her history?   109
Vio. A blank, my lord; she never told her love,
But let concealment like a worm i' th' bud
Feed on her damask cheek; she pin'd in thought,
And with a green and yellow melancholy
She sate like Patience on a monument,
Smiling at grief. Was not this love indeed?   115
We men may say more, swear more, but indeed
Our shows are more than will; for still we prove
Much in our vows, but little in our love.
Duke. But died thy sister of her love, my boy?
Vio. I am all the daughters of my father's house,

---

42. **fellow:** here, a familiar term of address to one of lower station
(without derogatory implication).
44. **spinsters:** spinning-women.
45. **free:** carefree.   **weave . . . bones:** make bone or thread lace
with bone bobbins.
46. **Do use:** are accustomed.   **silly sooth:** simple truth.
47. **dallies:** plays lovingly.
48. **Like . . . age:** as in the good old days.
51. **Come away:** come hither.
52. **cypress:** i.e. a coffin of cypress wood, or a bier covered with
cypress trees, like yews (line 55), were often planted
in graveyards and were emblematic of death.
57–58. **My . . . it:** i.e. I had to enact alone my role of dying, unsupported by one of equal constancy.
70–71. **pleasure . . . another:** i.e. indulgence exacts payment sooner
or later.   72. **leave to leave:** permission to take leave of.
73. **the melancholy god:** i.e. the god to whom you pay your devotion.
Feste clearly implies that Orsino's melancholy is a self-indulgence.
74. **doublet:** close-fitting jacket.   **changeable taffata:** taffata (thin
silk) woven of threads of different colors, so that its color shifts
with movement.
75–78. **I . . . nothing.** Intended ironically; men of such changeable
mind arrive at no destination and bring nothing home.
79. **give place:** withdraw.

80. **sovereign cruelty:** supremely cruel person, "cruell'st she alive"
(I.v.241).   83. **parts:** worldly goods.
84. **hold . . . fortune:** esteem as lightly as fortune does (which could
sweep them away in a moment).
85. **miracle . . . gems:** i.e. her beauty.
86. **nature.** As contrasted with fortune.   **pranks:** adorns.
90. **for your love:** for love of you.
92. **be answer'd:** accept your answer.
93–103. **There . . . Olivia.** True to his changeable nature, the Duke
now contradicts the opinion he voiced in lines 32–35.
94. **bide:** endure.   96. **retention:** power of retaining.
98. **No . . . liver:** no impulse of the liver, i.e. not the passion of true
love.   **the palate:** i.e. a motion of the palate, a sensual appetite.
99. **suffer:** experience.   **cloyment:** satiety.   **revolt:** revulsion of
appetite. Cf. lines 98–101 with Orsino's opening speech in I.i; there
is considerable irony in what he here attributes to women's love and
what to his own.   103. **owe:** bear.
112. **damask:** pink and white, like a damask rose.
113. **green and yellow:** pale and sallow.
114. **sate:** sat.   **like . . . monument:** like a sculptured figure of
Patience on a tomb.
117. **more than will:** greater than our desire.   **still:** ever, always.

And all the brothers too—and yet I know not.   121
Sir, shall I to this lady?
   Duke.   Ay, that's the theme,
To her in haste; give her this jewel; say
My love can give no place, bide no denay.   *Exeunt.*

SCENE V

Enter SIR TOBY, SIR ANDREW, *and* FABIAN.

Sir To.   Come thy ways, Signior Fabian.

Fab.   Nay, I'll come. If I lose a scruple of this sport, let me be boil'd to death with melancholy.

Sir To.   Wouldst thou not be glad to have the niggardly rascally sheep-biter come by some notable shame?   6

Fab.   I would exult, man. You know he brought me out o' favor with my lady about a bear-baiting here.

Sir To.   To anger him we'll have the bear again, and we will fool him black and blue, shall we not, Sir Andrew?   11

Sir And.   And we do not, it is pity of our lives.

Enter MARIA.

Sir To.   Here comes the little villain. How now, my metal of India?   14

Mar.   Get ye all three into the box-tree; Malvolio's coming down this walk. He has been yonder i' the sun practicing behavior to his own shadow this half hour. Observe him, for the love of mockery; for   18 I know this letter will make a contemplative idiot of him. Close, in the name of jesting! [*The men hide themselves.*] Lie thou there [*throws down a letter*]; for here comes the trout that must be caught with tickling.
                                        Exit.

Enter MALVOLIO.

Mal.   'Tis but fortune, all is fortune. Maria once told me she did affect me, and I have heard herself   24 come thus near, that should she fancy, it should be one of my complexion. Besides, she uses me with a more exalted respect than any one else that follows her. What should I think on't?

Sir To.   Here's an overweening rogue!

Fab.   O, peace! Contemplation makes a rare   30

turkey-cock of him. How he jets under his advanc'd plumes!

Sir And.   'Slight, I could so beat the rogue!

Sir To.   Peace, I say!

Mal.   To be Count Malvolio!   35

Sir To.   Ah, rogue!

Sir And.   Pistol him, pistol him!

Sir To.   Peace, peace!

Mal.   There is example for't: the Lady of the Strachy married the yeoman of the wardrobe.   40

Sir And.   Fie on him, Jezebel!

Fab.   O, peace! now he's deeply in. Look how imagination blows him.

Mal.   Having been three months married to her, sitting in my state—   45

Sir To.   O, for a stone-bow, to hit him in the eye!

Mal.   Calling my officers about me, in my branch'd velvet gown; having come from a day-bed, where I have left Olivia sleeping—

Sir To.   Fire and brimstone!   50

Fab.   O, peace, peace!

Mal.   And then to have the humor of state; and after a demure travel of regard—telling them I know my place as I would they should do theirs—to ask for my kinsman Toby—   55

Sir To.   Bolts and shackles!

Fab.   O, peace, peace, peace! Now, now.

Mal.   Seven of my people, with an obedient start, make out for him. I frown the while, and perchance wind up my watch, or play with my—some rich jewel. Toby approaches; curtsies there to me—   61

Sir To.   Shall this fellow live?

Fab.   Though our silence be drawn from us with cars, yet peace.

Mal.   I extend my hand to him thus, quenching my familiar smile with an austere regard of control—   66

Sir To.   And does not Toby take you a blow o' the lips then?

Mal.   Saying, "Cousin Toby, my fortunes, having

124. **give . . . denay:** yield no ground and endure no denial.
II.v. Location: Olivia's garden.
1. **Come thy ways:** come along.
2. **Nay.** Implying that Sir Toby need not urge. **scruple:** tiniest bit.
3. **boil'd . . . melancholy.** With a pun on *boil / bile* (pronounced alike). Black bile was the cause of melancholy.
5. **sheep-biter:** i.e. malicious sneak.
8. **bear-baiting.** A type of entertainment that Malvolio would naturally disapprove of (with some reason).
10. **fool:** mock. **black and blue:** i.e. thoroughly (used figuratively with *fool* instead of the usual *beat*).
12. **it . . . lives:** "life won't be worth living" (Kittredge).
14. **metal of India:** i.e. gold; here = girl worth her weight in gold.
17. **behavior:** courtly manners.
19–20. **make . . . him:** make him sit and daydream like an idiot staring into space. 20. **Close:** keep hidden.
22. **tickling:** (1) stroking under the gills (trout were actually taken by this means); (2) flattery.
24. **she:** i.e. Olivia. **did affect:** was fond of.
25. **fancy:** fall in love. 27. **follows her:** is in her service.
29. **overweening:** arrogant, presumptuous.
30. **Contemplation.** Looking back to lines 19–20.

31. **jets:** struts. **advanc'd:** raised. 33. **'Slight:** by God's light.
39. **example:** precedent. 39–40. **Lady . . . Strachy.** Not certainly identified.
40. **yeoman . . . wardrobe:** servant in charge of clothing and linen in a nobleman's household.
41. **Jezebel:** the cruel and arrogant wife of Ahab, king of Israel (the application of the word to Malvolio is typical of Sir Andrew).
43. **blows him:** puffs him up. 45. **state:** chair of state (as Count).
46. **stone-bow:** crossbow that shot stones instead of arrows.
47. **officers:** household staff. **branch'd:** figured with a pattern of leaves or flowers. 48. **day-bed:** couch.
52. **have . . . state:** i.e. adopt the manner of the great.
53. **after . . . regard:** having gravely allowed my eyes to travel from one to another. **telling:** indicating to.
58. **start:** in obedient haste.
59. **make out:** sally forth.
60. **my— . . . jewel.** Malvolio is on the verge of saying "my chain" (his insignia of office as steward) but catches himself in time.
63–64. **with cars.** The general meaning is clearly "by main force." *Cars* is sometimes explained as meaning "carts" (with citation of III.ii.59–60, "oxen and wain-ropes cannot hale them together"), but Shakespeare elsewhere uses *car* only in the sense *chariot*, usually with reference to the sun-god's chariot; Johnson therefore proposed emending to *carts*. Possibly a reference to some form of torture is intended; the line would then mean "it is torture to remain silent" and would present a witty reversal of the usual purpose of torture, which is to draw speech from the silent. The emendation most often adopted, however, is Hanmer's *by th' ears*, which implies reluctance or resistance on the part of what is drawn.
66. **familiar:** friendly. **austere . . . control:** look of stern authority.
67. **take:** give.

Twelfth Night
II.v

421

Twelfth Night
II. v

cast me on your niece, give me this prerogative of
speech"—   71

Sir To. What, what?

Mal. "You must amend your drunkenness."

Sir To. Out, scab!

Fab. Nay, patience, or we break the sinews of
our plot!   76

Mal. "Besides, you waste the treasure of your
time with a foolish knight"—

Sir And. That's me, I warrant you.

Mal. "One Sir Andrew"—   80

Sir And. I knew 'twas I, for many do call me fool.

Mal. What employment have we here?

[*Taking up the letter.*]

Fab. Now is the woodcock near the gin.

Sir To. O, peace, and the spirit of humors intimate
reading aloud to him!   85

Mal. By my life, this is my lady's hand. These be
her very c's, her u's, and her t's, and thus makes she
her great P's. It is, in contempt of question, her hand.

Sir And. Her c's, her u's, and her t's: why that?

Mal. [*Reads.*] "To the unknown belov'd, this, and
my good wishes":—her very phrases! By your   91
leave, wax. Soft! And the impressure her Lucrece,
with which she uses to seal. 'Tis my lady. To
whom should this be?

Fab. This wins him, liver and all.   95

Mal. [*Reads.*]

  "Jove knows I love,
      But who?
    Lips, do not move;
    No man must know."   99

"No man must know." What follows? The numbers
alter'd! "No man must know." If this should be thee,
Malvolio?

Sir To. Marry, hang thee, brock!

Mal. [*Reads.*]

  "I may command where I adore,
    But silence, like a Lucrece knife,   105
  With bloodless stroke my heart doth gore;
    M. O. A. I. doth sway my life."

Fab. A fustian riddle!

Sir To. Excellent wench, say I.   109

Mal. "M. O. A. I. doth sway my life." Nay, but
first let me see, let me see, let me see.

Fab. What dish a' poison has she dress'd him!

Sir To. And with what wing the [staniel] checks
at it!   114

Mal. "I may command where I adore." Why, she
may command me: I serve her, she is my lady. Why,
this is evident to any formal capacity, there is no
obstruction in this. And the end—what should that
alphabetical position portend? If I could make that
resemble something in me! Softly! M. O. A. I.—

Sir To. O ay, make up that. He is now at a cold
scent.   122

Fab. Sowter will cry upon't for all this, though it
be as rank as a fox.

Mal. M—Malvolio; M—why, that begins my
name.   126

Fab. Did not I say he would work it out? The cur
is excellent at faults.

Mal. M—but then there is no consonancy in the
sequel that suffers under probation: A should follow,
but O does.   131

Fab. And O shall end, I hope.

Sir To. Ay, or I'll cudgel him, and make him
cry O!

Mal. And then I comes behind.   135

Fab. Ay, and you had any eye behind you, you
might see more detraction at your heels than fortunes
before you.

Mal. M. O. A. I. This simulation is not as the
former; and yet, to crush this a little, it would bow to
me, for every one of these letters are in my name.
Soft, here follows prose.   142

[*Reads.*] "If this fall into thy hand, revolve. In my
stars I am above thee, but be not afraid of greatness.
Some are [born] great, some [achieve] greatness, and
some have greatness thrust upon 'em. Thy Fates open
their hands, let thy blood and spirit embrace them, and
to inure thyself to what thou art like to be, cast   148
thy humble slough and appear fresh. Be opposite with
a kinsman, surly with servants; let thy tongue tang
arguments of state; put thyself into the trick of
singularity. She thus advises thee that sighs for thee.
Remember who commended thy yellow stock-   153

74. **scab:** scurvy fellow. 82. **employment:** business.
83. **woodcock.** A proverbially stupid bird, easily caught. **gin:** trap,
snare (short form of *engine* = contrivance). 84. **humors:** caprice.
87. **c's . . . t's.** Malvolio has unwittingly spelled out *cut*, slang for
the female pudenda. The "joke" is compounded by *great P's*, line 88.
88. **great:** capital. **in . . . question:** beyond dispute.
91–92. **By your leave:** with your permission (addressed to the seal
as he breaks it).
92. **Soft:** not so fast, wait a moment. **impressure:** device impressed on the wax. **Lucrece:** i.e. a figure of the virtuous Roman
matron Lucretia, who stabbed herself after her rape by Tarquin—an
emblem of chastity. 93. **uses:** is accustomed.
95. **wins:** conquers. **liver:** i.e. his love.
100–101. **The numbers alter'd:** the metre changed.
103. **brock:** badger, i.e. stinker.
108. **fustian:** worthless, nonsensical.
112. **What:** what a. **dress'd:** prepared.
113. **wing:** flight, i.e. speed. **staniel:** inferior hawk. **checks:** is
diverted from its proper quarry by an inferior prey, i.e. is led astray.

117. **formal capacity:** normal understanding.
118. **obstruction:** obstacle, difficulty.
119. **alphabetical position:** arrangement of letters.
121. **O, ay.** Sir Toby seems to echo two of the letters that Malvolio
has just read (*ay* is spelled *I*, as usual, in F1). **make up that:** piece
that together, work that out.
121–22. **cold scent:** faint, hence difficult, trail.
123. **Sowter:** a hound's name; literally, cobbler, i.e. bungler. **cry
upon't:** give tongue as if he had found the scent.
123–24. **though . . . fox:** though the deception is as easy to smell out
as a stinking (*rank*) fox.
128. **excellent at faults:** not put off the trail by breaks in the scent
(with ironic implication that he is very likely to pick up a false scent).
129. **consonancy:** agreement, correspondence.
130. **sequel:** i.e. following letter(s). **suffers:** endures, stands up.
probation: testing, examination. 132. **O:** i.e. a hangman's noose.
137. **detraction:** defamation.
139. **simulation:** representation, disguised meaning.
140. **crush:** force. **bow to:** (1) yield its meaning to; (2) point to,
indicate. 143. **revolve:** consider.
144. **stars:** fortunes, i.e. rank and wealth.
146–47. **open their hands:** i.e. are ready to give.
147. **let . . . them:** i.e. welcome their gifts with the whole force of
your being. *Blood and spirit* = either "body and soul" or "passion
and mettle." 148. **inure:** accustom.
148–49. **cast . . . slough:** cast off your lowly demeanor. The figure is
of a snake sloughing off its old skin. 149. **opposite:** quarrelsome.
150. **tang:** sound loud with.
151. **arguments of state:** political topics, matters of statecraft.
trick: custom, habit.
151–52. **put . . . singularity:** cultivate individuality, adopt eccentric
habits.

ings, and wish'd to see thee ever cross-garter'd: I say, remember. Go to, thou art made if thou desir'st to be so; if not, let me see thee a steward still, the fellow of servants, and not worthy to touch Fortune's fingers. Farewell. She that would alter services with thee,

> The Fortunate-Unhappy."   159

Daylight and champian discovers not more. This is open. I will be proud, I will read politic authors, I will baffle Sir Toby, I will wash off gross   162 acquaintance, I will be point-devise the very man. I do not now fool myself, to let imagination jade me; for every reason excites to this, that my lady loves me. She did commend my yellow stockings of late, she did praise my leg being cross-garter'd, and in this   167 she manifests herself to my love, and with a kind of injunction drives me to these habits of her liking. I thank my stars, I am happy. I will be strange, stout, in yellow stockings, and cross-garter'd, even   171 with the swiftness of putting on. Jove and my stars be prais'd! Here is yet a postscript.
[*Reads.*] "Thou canst not choose but know who I am. If thou entertain'st my love, let it appear in thy smiling; thy smiles become thee well. Therefore in my presence still smile, dear my sweet, I prithee." Jove, I thank thee. I will smile, I will do every   178 thing that thou wilt have me.   *Exit.*

Fab. I will not give my part of this sport for a pension of thousands to be paid from the Sophy.

Sir To. I could marry this wench for this device—

Sir And. So could I too.

Sir To. And ask no other dowry with her but such another jest.   185

Enter MARIA.

Sir And. Nor I neither.

Fab. Here comes my noble gull-catcher.

Sir To. Wilt thou set thy foot o' my neck?

Sir And. Or o' mine either?

Sir To. Shall I play my freedom at tray-trip, and become thy bond-slave?   191

Sir And. I' faith, or I either?

Sir To. Why, thou hast put him in such a dream, that when the image of it leaves him he must run mad.

Mar. Nay, but say true, does it work upon him?

Sir To. Like aqua-vitae with a midwife.   196

Mar. If you will then see the fruits of the sport, mark his first approach before my lady. He will come to her in yellow stockings, and 'tis a color she abhors, and cross-garter'd, a fashion she detests; and he will smile upon her, which will now be so unsuitable   201 to her disposition, being addicted to a melancholy as she is, that it cannot but turn him into a notable contempt. If you will see it, follow me.

Sir To. To the gates of Tartar, thou most excellent devil of wit!   206

Sir And. I'll make one too.   *Exeunt.*

ACT III, SCENE I

Enter VIOLA, *and* CLOWN [*with a tabor*].

Vio. 'Save thee, friend, and thy music! Dost thou live by thy tabor?

Clo. No, sir, I live by the church.

Vio. Art thou a churchman?   4

Clo. No such matter, sir. I do live by the church; for I do live at my house, and my house doth stand by the church.

Vio. So thou mayst say the [king] lies by a beggar, if a beggar dwells near him; or the church stands by thy tabor, if thy tabor stand by the church.   10

Clo. You have said, sir. To see this age! A sentence is but a chev'ril glove to a good wit. How quickly the wrong side may be turn'd outward!

Vio. Nay, that's certain. They that dally nicely with words may quickly make them wanton.   15

Clo. I would therefore my sister had had no name, sir.

Vio. Why, man?   18

Clo. Why, sir, her name's a word, and to dally with that word might make my sister wanton. But indeed, words are very rascals since bonds disgrac'd them.

Vio. Thy reason, man?

Clo. Troth, sir, I can yield you none without words, and words are grown so false, I am loath to prove reason with them.   25

Vio. I warrant thou art a merry fellow, and car'st for nothing.

154. **cross-garter'd:** wearing the garters crossed at the back so that in front they pass both above and below the knee.
156. **still:** always (so also in line 177).
158. **alter services:** exchange duties, i.e. make you master and myself your servant.
160. **champian:** champaign, open country.   **discovers:** reveals.
161. **open:** evident, obvious.   **proud:** lofty.   **politic authors:** writers on political science.
162. **baffle:** treat with disdain.   **wash off:** rid myself of.   **gross:** low.   163. **point-devise:** correctly in every detail, precisely.
164. **I . . . me:** I am not foolishly allowing imagination to trick me.
165. **every . . . this:** every piece of evidence urges this conclusion.
170. **happy:** blessed by fortune.   **strange:** distant, reserved.   **stout:** haughty.
172, 178. **Jove.** Here and elsewhere (III.iv.74–75, 82, and particularly IV.ii.11), possibly a replacement for an original *God*, to comply with the anti-profanity statute of 1606.
175. **entertain'st:** acceptest.   181. **Sophy:** the Shah of Persia.
187. **gull-catcher:** tricker of credulous fools.
188. **set . . . neck:** i.e. as a symbol of conquest.
190. **play:** gamble.   **tray-trip:** a game of dice in which the best throw was three (*tray = trey*).
196. **aqua-vitae:** brandy or other spirits.

205. **Tartar:** Tartarus, hell.   207. **make one:** go along.

III.i. Location: Olivia's garden.
o.s.d. **tabor:** small drum.
1. **'Save:** God save.   **music.** Feste probably has also a pipe (played with the help of one hand while the tabor was beaten with the other).
3. **live by:** earn a living by. Feste quibbles on "dwell near."
4. **churchman:** man in holy orders.
8. **So . . . beggar:** in the same fashion you could say what would be taken to mean "the king lies with a beggar." (Similarly, *stands by*, line 9, could be taken to mean "is supported by.")
11–12. **A sentence:** any utterance.
12. **chev'ril:** kidskin (soft and pliable).
14. **dally nicely:** play sophistically.
15. **make them wanton:** allow them to get out of hand.
19. **dally:** toy amorously.
20. **wanton:** unchaste. Dover Wilson suggests a pun on *want one*, i.e. lack a (good) name.
21. **bonds disgrac'd them.** Quibbling on *bonds* as (1) sworn statements (in place of a man's plain word or promise); (2) fetters (betokening criminality).
25. **reason:** "the reasonableness of any proposition" (Kittredge).
26–27. **car'st for nothing:** dost not worry about anything. Feste then proceeds to play on other meanings of *care*.

Twelfth Night
III.i

Clo. Not so, sir, I do care for something; but in my conscience, sir, I do not care for you. If that be to care for nothing, sir, I would it would make you invisible.

Vio. Art not thou the Lady Olivia's fool?   31

Clo. No, indeed, sir, the Lady Olivia has no folly. She will keep no fool, sir, till she be married, and fools are as like husbands as pilchers are to herrings, the husband's the bigger. I am indeed not her fool, but her corrupter of words.   36

Vio. I saw thee late at the Count Orsino's.

Clo. Foolery, sir, does walk about the orb like the sun, it shines every where. I would be sorry, sir, but the fool should be as oft with your master as with my mistress. I think I saw your wisdom there.   41

Vio. Nay, and thou pass upon me, I'll no more with thee. Hold, there's expenses for thee.

Clo. Now Jove, in his next commodity of hair, send thee a beard!   45

Vio. By my troth, I'll tell thee, I am almost sick for one—[*aside*] though I would not have it grow on my chin. Is thy lady within?

Clo. Would not a pair of these have bred, sir?

Vio. Yes, being kept together, and put to use.   50

Clo. I would play Lord Pandarus of Phrygia, sir, to bring a Cressida to this Troilus.

Vio. I understand you, sir. 'Tis well begg'd.

Clo. The matter, I hope, is not great, sir—begging but a beggar: Cressida was a beggar. My lady is within, sir. I will conster to them whence you come; who you are, and what you would, are out of my welkin—I might say "element," but the word is overworn.   *Exit.*   59

Vio. This fellow is wise enough to play the fool,
And to do that well craves a kind of wit.
He must observe their mood on whom he jests,
The quality of persons, and the time;

And like the haggard, check at every feather
That comes before his eye. This is a practice   65
As full of labor as a wise man's art;
For folly that he wisely shows is fit,
But wise [men], folly-fall'n, quite taint their wit.

Enter Sir Toby *and* Andrew.

Sir To. 'Save you, gentleman.

Vio. And you, sir.   70

Sir And. *Dieu vous garde, monsieur.*

Vio. *Et vous aussi; votre serviteur.*

Sir And. I hope, sir, you are, and I am yours.

Sir To. Will you encounter the house? My niece is desirous you should enter, if your trade be to her.

Vio. I am bound to your niece, sir; I mean she is the list of my voyage.   77

Sir To. Taste your legs, sir, put them to motion.

Vio. My legs do better understand me, sir, than I understand what you mean by bidding me taste my legs.

Sir To. I mean, to go, sir, to enter.   81

Vio. I will answer you with gait and entrance—but we are prevented.

Enter Olivia *and* Gentlewoman.

Most excellent accomplish'd lady, the heavens rain odors on you!   85

Sir And. That youth's a rare courtier—"rain odors," well.

Vio. My matter hath no voice, lady, but to your own most pregnant and vouchsafed ear.

Sir And. "Odors," "pregnant," and "vouchsafed"; I'll get 'em all three all ready.   91

Oli. Let the garden door be shut, and leave me to my hearing. [*Exeunt all but Olivia and Viola.*] Give me your hand, sir.

Vio. My duty, madam, and most humble service.

Oli. What is your name?   96

Vio. Cesario is your servant's name, fair princess.

Oli. My servant, sir? 'Twas never merry world Since lowly feigning was call'd compliment. Y' are servant to the Count Orsino, youth.   100

Vio. And he is yours, and his must needs be yours: Your servant's servant is your servant, madam.

Oli. For him, I think not on him. For his thoughts, Would they were blanks, rather than fill'd with me.

28–29. **in my conscience:** to let you into a secret.
30. **I . . . invisible.** Viola ought to be invisible, by Feste's process of thought, since if he cares for something and does not care for Viola, then Viola is nothing.
34. **pilchers:** pilchards, small fish resembling herring.
37. **late:** recently.
38. **orb:** earth, as the centre about which the sun courses (*walks*) in the Ptolemaic system.   39. **but:** unless.
41. **your wisdom.** An ironic form of address on the model of *your honor* or *your worship*.
42. **pass upon me:** fence with me (using sharp words as your weapon).
43. **Hold:** take this.   **expenses:** something for you to spend.
44–45. **Jove . . . beard.** Feste follows the usual practice of one who received alms by invoking God's blessing on the giver.
44. **commodity:** consignment, lot.
47. **one:** a beard, i.e. a man (Orsino).
48. **my chin.** The stress belongs on *my*.
49. **pair of these:** i.e. two coins.   **bred:** multiplied.
50. **put to use:** loaned at interest.
51. **Pandarus:** Cressida's uncle, and the go-between in her love affair with Troilus.
54. **The matter:** i.e. the amount begged.
55. **Cressida . . . beggar.** Alluding to the tradition stemming from Henryson's *Testament of Cresseid* that Cressida became a leper and a beggar.   56. **conster:** construe, explain.
58. **welkin, element.** *Element* in the sense "sky" is synonymous with *welkin*, but it can have other senses as well, as of course it has in the phrase *out of my element* (= here "outside the range of my information"). Feste gives a final example of how words can be made "wanton."
60. **play the fool.** Feste, like Touchstone in *As You Like It*, is a shrewd, sharp person who makes his living by playing the fool; he is not, like the Fool in *King Lear*, a "natural" or halfwit.
61. **wit:** intelligence.   62. **their mood:** the mood of those.
63. **quality:** character.

64. **haggard:** a hawk taken in maturity and hence difficult to train. **check.** See the note on II.v.113.
65. **practice:** exercise of skill.   66. **art:** skill.
67. **wisely shows:** assumes judiciously.   **fit:** proper.
68. **folly-fall'n:** lapsed into folly.   **taint:** discredit.
71. **Dieu . . . monsieur:** God keep you, sir.
72. **Et . . . serviteur:** And you too; your servant.
74. **encounter.** Pedantry for "enter."
75. **trade:** business. The word suggests to Viola a trading voyage.
76. **I . . . to:** i.e. my destination is.
77. **list:** limit, utmost point.   78. **Taste:** i.e. make trial of, test.
79. **understand me:** stand under me, hold me up.
82. **gait and entrance:** going and entering (answering to *go* and *enter* in line 81); with a play on "gate and entrance."
83. **prevented:** anticipated.   88. **hath no voice:** cannot be spoken.
89. **pregnant and vouchsafed:** receptive and graciously bestowed.
91. **all ready:** i.e. all ready for use in future conversation.
93. **hearing:** audience, interview.
98. **'Twas . . . world:** life has never been as pleasant (proverbial).
99. **lowly feigning:** pretending humility, i.e. calling oneself "your servant."   **was call'd:** was first called, began to be called.
103. **For:** as for.

Vio. Madam, I come to whet your gentle thoughts
On his behalf.
  Oli.   O, by your leave, I pray you: 106
I bade you never speak again of him;
But would you undertake another suit,
I had rather hear you to solicit that
Than music from the spheres.
  Vio.   Dear lady—   110
  Oli. Give me leave, beseech you. I did send,
After the last enchantment you did here,
A ring in chase of you; so did I abuse
Myself, my servant, and I fear me you.
Under your hard construction must I sit,   115
To force that on you in a shameful cunning
Which you knew none of yours. What might you
    think?
Have you not set mine honor at the stake,
And baited it with all th' unmuzzled thoughts
That tyrannous heart can think? To one of your
    receiving   120
Enough is shown; a cypress, not a bosom,
Hides my heart. So let me hear you speak.
  Vio. I pity you.
  Oli.   That's a degree to love.
  Vio. No, not a grize; for 'tis a vulgar proof
That very oft we pity enemies.   125
  Oli. Why then methinks 'tis time to smile again.
O world, how apt the poor are to be proud!
If one should be a prey, how much the better
To fall before the lion than the wolf!   *Clock strikes.*
The clock upbraids me with the waste of time.   130
Be not afraid, good youth, I will not have you,
And yet when wit and youth is come to harvest,
Your wife is like to reap a proper man.
There lies your way, due west.
  Vio.   Then westward-ho!
Grace and good disposition attend your ladyship!   135
You'll nothing, madam, to my lord by me?
  Oli. Stay!
I prithee tell me what thou think'st of me.
  Vio. That you do think you are not what you are.
  Oli. If I think so, I think the same of you.   140

Vio. Then think you right: I am not what I am.
  Oli. I would you were as I would have you be.
  Vio. Would it be better, madam, than I am?
I wish it might, for now I am your fool.
  Oli. [*Aside.*] O, what a deal of scorn looks beau-
    tiful   145
In the contempt and anger of his lip!
A murd'rous guilt shows not itself more soon
Than love that would seem hid: love's night is noon.—
Cesario, by the roses of the spring,
By maidhood, honor, truth, and every thing,   150
I love thee so, that maugre all thy pride,
Nor wit nor reason can my passion hide.
Do not extort thy reasons from this clause,
For that I woo, thou therefore hast no cause;
But rather reason thus with reason fetter: 155
Love sought is good, but given unsought is better.
  Vio. By innocence I swear, and by my youth,
I have one heart, one bosom, and one truth,
And that no woman has, nor never none
Shall mistress be of it, save I alone.   160
And so adieu, good madam, never more
Will I my master's tears to you deplore.
  Oli. Yet come again; for thou perhaps mayst move
That heart which now abhors, to like his love.

                                   Exeunt.

SCENE II

Enter Sir Toby, Sir Andrew, *and* Fabian.

Sir And. No, faith, I'll not stay a jot longer.
Sir To. Thy reason, dear venom, give thy reason.
Fab. You must needs yield your reason, Sir
Andrew.
Sir And. Marry, I saw your niece do more 5
favors to the Count's servingman than ever she
bestow'd upon me. I saw't i' th' orchard.
Sir To. Did she see [thee] the while, old boy?
tell me that.
Sir And. As plain as I see you now.   10
Fab. This was a great argument of love in her
toward you.
Sir And. 'Slight! will you make an ass o' me?
Fab. I will prove it legitimate, sir, upon the oaths
of judgment and reason.   15
Sir To. And they have been grand-jurymen since
before Noah was a sailor.
Fab. She did show favor to the youth in your sight

---

106. **by your leave:** a polite phrase of interruption: "please say no more" (so also *Give me leave*, line 111).
110. **music . . . spheres.** A reference to the notion that the revolution of the spheres in which the heavenly bodies were fixed produced ravishing music, inaudible to human ears.
112. **enchantment you did:** charm you worked, spell you cast.
113. **abuse:** dishonor.   115. **construction:** interpretation.
116. **To force:** for forcing.
118. **at the stake.** The figure in 118–19 is from bear-baiting; Olivia's honor is set upon by Cesario's thoughts as the bear is set upon by dogs to tear and worry it.
120. **tyrannous:** cruel.   **receiving:** power to apprehend.
121. **cypress:** a nearly transparent black fabric.
123. **degree:** step; *grize* in line 124 is a synonym.
124. **'tis . . . proof:** i.e. everybody knows from experience.
126. **then:** i.e. if you are my enemy.   **smile:** i.e. abandon love and its pangs.   127. **apt:** ready.   128. **should be:** were to be.
129. **lion . . . wolf:** i.e. Orsino . . . Cesario.
131. **have you:** have you for a husband.   133. **proper:** worthy.
134. **due west:** i.e. where the sun disappears from sight; a clear dismissal.   **westward-ho:** the cry of watermen on the Thames when they were about to put off westward.
135. **good disposition:** a tranquil mind.
139. **That . . . what you are:** i.e. that you are mistaken in supposing you are in love with a man, not a woman.
140. **If . . . you.** Presumably she interprets his remark as meaning that she is mad but doesn't know it.

144. **now . . . fool:** i.e. you have put me into a foolish position (in a sense that she cannot guess).   145. **deal:** large amount.
148. **love's . . . noon:** love's attempted secrecy is like broad daylight to everybody else.   151. **maugre:** in spite of.   153. **Nor:** neither.
153–54. **Do . . . cause:** do not wrest reasons for not loving me from this proposition: that because I woo, you have no cause to accept my love.
155. **rather . . . fetter:** instead bind together these two reasons (to accept my love).
156. **Love . . . better.** Olivia will receive a love that she sued for, which is good; Cesario will receive a love for which he did not have to sue, which is better.   162. **deplore:** lament, describe.

III.ii. Location: Olivia's house.
2. **venom:** venomous one.   7. **orchard:** garden.
11. **argument:** evidence.   14. **oaths:** i.e. sworn testimony.
16. **grand-jurymen:** i.e. experts in evaluating evidence.

Twelfth Night
III.ii

only to exasperate you, to awake your dormouse 19
valor, to put fire in your heart, and brimstone in your
liver. You should then have accosted her, and with
some excellent jests, fire-new from the mint, you
should have bang'd the youth into dumbness. This was
look'd for at your hand, and this was balk'd. 24
The double gilt of this opportunity you let time wash
off, and you are now sail'd into the north of my lady's
opinion, where you will hang like an icicle on a
Dutchman's beard, unless you do redeem it by some
laudable attempt either of valor or policy. 29

Sir And. And't be any way, it must be with
valor, for policy I hate. I had as lief be a Brownist as
a politician.

Sir To. Why then build me thy fortunes upon the
basis of valor. Challenge me the Count's youth 34
to fight with him, hurt him in eleven places—my
niece shall take note of it, and assure thyself, there is
no love-broker in the world can more prevail in man's
commendation with woman than report of valor.

Fab. There is no way but this, Sir Andrew. 39

Sir And. Will either of you bear me a challenge to
him?

Sir To. Go, write it in a martial hand, be curst and
brief. It is no matter how witty, so it be eloquent and
full of invention. Taunt him with the license of 44
ink. If thou thou'st him some thrice, it shall not be
amiss; and as many lies as will lie in thy sheet of paper,
although the sheet were big enough for the bed of
Ware in England, set 'em down. Go about it. Let
there be gall enough in thy ink, though thou write with
a goose-pen, no matter. About it. 50

Sir And. Where shall I find you?

Sir To. We'll call thee at the cubiculo. Go.

Exit Sir Andrew.

Fab. This is a dear manikin to you, Sir Toby.

Sir To. I have been dear to him, lad, some two
thousand strong, or so. 55

19. **dormouse:** i.e. sleepy.   22. **fire-new:** brand-new.
24. **balk'd:** neglected, let slip.
25. **double gilt:** double plating with gold; perhaps referring to Sir
Andrew's double opportunity to prove his love and valor.
26. **north:** i.e. cold regions (of disfavor).
27–28. **icicle . . . beard.** Perhaps an allusion to William Barentz, a
Dutchman who travelled to the Arctic in 1596–97 and wrote an
account of his experiences which was entered in the Stationers'
Register in June 1598 (earliest extant edition, 1609).
29. **policy:** cunning, strategy.
31. **Brownist:** a follower of Robert Browne, founder of the Con-
gregationalist sect.   32. **politician:** contriver, schemer.
33. **build me:** build (a colloquialism); cf. *Challenge me,* line 34.
37. **love-broker:** go-between in love matters.
38. **report:** reputation.   42. **curst:** bad-tempered, insulting.
43. **so:** provided that, so long as.
44. **invention:** imagination. (Sir Toby is being intentionally contradictory in lines 43–44.)
44–45. **with . . . ink:** i.e. with the freedom that writing affords (arising
in this case from its comparative safety).
45. **If . . . him.** *Thou* instead of *you* was the form of address used to
friends and to social inferiors, hence an insult to a comparative
stranger.
47–48. **bed of Ware.** This bed (which may be seen in the Victoria
and Albert Museum, London) is eleven feet square.
49. **gall:** (1) an ingredient of ink; (2) acrimony.
50. **goose-pen:** quill pen made from a goose feather (with an implication that the letter will be couched in foolish terms).
52. **call thee:** call for you.   **cubiculo:** little chamber.
53. **dear . . . you:** puppet dear to you (referring to Sir Toby's manipulation of him).   54. **dear:** expensive.

Fab. We shall have a rare letter from him; but
you'll not deliver't?

Sir To. Never trust me then; and by all means stir
on the youth to an answer. I think oxen and wain- 59
ropes cannot hale them together. For Andrew, if he
were open'd and you find so much blood in his liver as
will clog the foot of a flea, I'll eat the rest of th'
anatomy.

Fab. And his opposite, the youth, bears in his
visage no great presage of cruelty. 65

Enter MARIA.

Sir To. Look where the youngest wren of [nine]
comes.

Mar. If you desire the spleen, and will laugh yourselves into stitches, follow me. Yond gull 69
Malvolio is turn'd heathen, a very renegado; for there
is no Christian that means to be sav'd by believing
rightly can ever believe such impossible passages of
grossness. He's in yellow stockings.

Sir To. And cross-garter'd? 74

Mar. Most villainously; like a pedant that keeps a
school i' th' church. I have dogg'd him like his
murtherer. He does obey every point of the letter that
I dropp'd to betray him. He does smile his face 78
into more lines than is in the new map, with the
augmentation of the Indies; you have not seen such a
thing as 'tis. I can hardly forbear hurling things at him.
I know my lady will strike him. If she do, he'll smile,
and take't for a great favor.

Sir To. Come bring us, bring us where he is. 84

Exeunt omnes.

SCENE III

Enter SEBASTIAN *and* ANTONIO.

Seb. I would not by my will have troubled you,
But since you make your pleasure of your pains,
I will no further chide you.

Ant. I could not stay behind you. My desire
(More sharp than filed steel) did spur me forth, 5
And not all love to see you (though so much
As might have drawn one to a longer voyage)

58. **then:** i.e. if I don't.   59–60. **wain-ropes:** wagon ropes.
60. **hale:** drag.
61. **blood . . . liver.** Cowards were thought to have white (bloodless)
livers.
63. **anatomy:** a medical term meaning either "body" or "skeleton."
In view of Sir Andrew's thinness, Sir Toby may intend the latter.
64. **opposite:** adversary.
66. **youngest . . . nine:** i.e. the very smallest of wrens.
68. **the spleen:** extreme mirth. The spleen was regarded as the source
of immoderate or uncontrollable laughter.   69. **gull:** dupe.
70. **renegado:** renegade, i.e. renouncer of his religion.
72–73. **such . . . grossness:** such obviously impossible expressions (as
the letter contains).
75. **pedant:** schoolmaster (the point of the reference to his holding a
school in the church is unexplained).   78. **betray:** expose, ensnare.
79–80. **lines . . . Indies.** Probably referring to a map prepared by
Edward Wright, Richard Hakluyt, and John Davis, and printed in
1600. It was the first English map based on Mercator's projection, and
therefore showed North America (*the Indies*) as proportionately
larger than in earlier maps. It is crisscrossed by numerous rhumb
lines.

III.iii. Location: A street.
6. **all:** entirely, only.

426

But jealousy what might befall your travel,
Being skilless in these parts; which to a stranger,
Unguided and unfriended, often prove   10
Rough and unhospitable. My willing love,
The rather by these arguments of fear,
Set forth in your pursuit.
    Seb.   My kind Antonio,
I can no other answer make but thanks,
And thanks; and ever oft good turns   15
Are shuffled off with such uncurrent pay;
But were my worth as is my conscience firm,
You should find better dealing. What's to do?
Shall we go see the reliques of this town?
    Ant. To-morrow, sir; best first go see your
        lodging.   20
    Seb. I am not weary, and 'tis long to night;
I pray you let us satisfy our eyes
With the memorials and the things of fame
That do renown this city.
    Ant.   Would you'ld pardon me.
I do not without danger walk these streets.   25
Once in a sea-fight 'gainst the Count his galleys
I did some service, of such note indeed,
That were I ta'en here, it would scarce be answer'd.
    Seb. Belike you slew great number of his people?
    Ant. Th' offense is not of such a bloody nature,
Albeit the quality of the time and quarrel   31
Might well have given us bloody argument.
It might have since been answer'd in repaying
What we took from them, which for traffic's sake
Most of our city did. Only myself stood out,   35
For which if I be lapsed in this place
I shall pay dear.
    Seb.   Do not then walk too open.
    Ant. It doth not fit me. Hold, sir, here's my purse.
In the south suburbs at the Elephant
Is best to lodge. I will bespeak our diet,   40
Whiles you beguile the time, and feed your knowledge
With viewing of the town. There shall you have me.
    Seb. Why I your purse?
    Ant. Haply your eye shall light upon some toy
You have desire to purchase; and your store   45
I think is not for idle markets, sir.
    Seb. I'll be your purse-bearer, and leave you
For an hour.

    Ant.   To th' Elephant.
    Seb.   I do remember. *Exeunt.*

SCENE IV

Enter OLIVIA *and* MARIA.

    Oli. [*Aside.*] I have sent after him; he says he'll
        come.
How shall I feast him? What bestow of him?
For youth is bought more oft than begg'd or borrow'd.
I speak too loud.—
Where's Malvolio? He is sad and civil,   5
And suits well for a servant with my fortunes.
Where is Malvolio?
    Mar. He's coming, madam, but in very strange
manner. He is sure possess'd, madam.
    Oli. Why, what's the matter? does he rave?   10
    Mar. No, madam, he does nothing but smile.
Your ladyship were best to have some guard about you,
if he come, for sure the man is tainted in 's wits.
    Oli. Go call him hither.

Enter MALVOLIO.

                        I am as mad as he,
If sad and merry madness equal be.   15
How now, Malvolio?
    Mal. Sweet lady, ho, ho.
    Oli. Smil'st thou? I sent for thee upon a sad
occasion.   19
    Mal. Sad, lady? I could be sad. This does make
some obstruction in the blood, this cross-gartering, but
what of that? If it please the eye of one, it is with me
as the very true sonnet is, "Please one, and please all."
    [*Oli.*] Why, how dost thou, man? What is the
matter with thee?   25
    Mal. Not black in my mind, though yellow in my
legs. It did come to his hands, and commands shall be
executed. I think we do know the sweet Roman hand.
    Oli. Wilt thou go to bed, Malvolio?
    Mal. To bed? Ay, sweet heart, and I'll come to
thee.   31
    Oli. God comfort thee! Why dost thou smile so,
and kiss thy hand so oft?
    Mar. How do you, Malvolio?
    Mal. At your request! Yes, nightingales answer
daws.   36

---

8. **jealousy:** suspicion, anxiety.   9. **skilless in:** unfamiliar with.
15. **And . . . turns.** A much-emended line. Sense can be made of it
by taking *ever oft* as "it has always been true that frequently," but
the awkwardness of this and the metrical deficiency of the line
strongly suggest corruption. Most editors adopt Theobald's *And
thanks, and ever thanks; and oft good turns.*
16. **shuffled off:** shrugged off.   **uncurrent pay:** payment in worthless
money, i.e. mere thanks. An uncurrent coin is one not accepted as
legal tender.
17. **worth:** wealth.   **conscience:** awareness (of my indebtedness).
19. **reliques:** relics of the past, ancient monuments (see line 23).
24. **renown:** make famous.   26. **Count his:** Count's.
28. **it . . . answer'd:** it would be difficult for me to make a defense.
29. **Belike:** probably.   31. **quality:** i.e. circumstances.
32. **bloody argument:** occasion for bloodshed.
34. **for traffic's sake:** in order to resume trading.
36. **lapsed:** caught napping, taken by surprise (literally, slipped).
38. **fit:** behoove.   39. **Elephant:** the name of an inn.
40. **bespeak our diet:** order our food.
42. **have me:** know where to find me.
44. **Haply:** perchance.   **toy:** trifle.   45. **store:** supply of money.
46. **idle markets:** luxuries.

III.iv. Location: Olivia's garden.
1. **he . . . come.** In view of lines 57–58, this apparently means "if he
says he'll come."
5. **sad:** sober, serious (so also in line 18).   **civil:** seemly, decorous.
6. **suits:** accords.   9. **possess'd:** i.e. possessed of an evil spirit.
10. **rave:** talk incoherently.   13. **tainted:** infected, disordered.
23. **sonnet:** poem.   **Please . . . all:** i.e. if I please you, I please
everyone I care to please (the first line and refrain of a popular ballad
published in 1592).
26–27. **Not . . . legs.** Meaning not entirely clear. *To wear yellow hose*
meant "to be jealous," and Malvolio may mean "Though I wear
yellow on my legs, my thoughts are not black, i.e. I don't wear
yellow because I am jealous." His main intent, of course, is to call
attention to the stockings.
28. **Roman hand.** The Italian script, resembling our own, which was
beginning to replace the English or secretary hand.
35–36. **At . . . daws:** i.e. am I to notice a question from you? O,
certainly, a nightingale should answer a crow. (Malvolio is being
"surly with servants," as instructed.)

Twelfth Night
III.iv

Mar. Why appear you with this ridiculous boldness before my lady?

Mal. "Be not afraid of greatness": 'twas well writ.

Oli. What mean'st thou by that, Malvolio? 40

Mal. "Some are born great"—

Oli. Ha?

Mal. "Some achieve greatness"—

Oli. What say'st thou?

Mal. "And some have greatness thrust upon them."

Oli. Heaven restore thee! 46

Mal. "Remember who commended thy yellow stockings"—

Oli. Thy yellow stockings?

Mal. "And wish'd to see thee cross-garter'd." 50

Oli. Cross-garter'd?

Mal. "Go to, thou art made, if thou desir'st to be so"—

Oli. Am I made?

Mal. "If not, let me see thee a servant still." 55

Oli. Why, this is very midsummer madness.

Enter SERVANT.

Serv. Madam, the young gentleman of the Count Orsino's is return'd. I could hardly entreat him back. He attends your ladyship's pleasure. 59

Oli. I'll come to him. [*Exit Servant.*] Good Maria, let this fellow be look'd to. Where's my cousin Toby? Let some of my people have a special care of him. I would not have him miscarry for the half of my dowry.

Exit [*with Maria*].

Mal. O ho, do you come near me now? No worse man than Sir Toby to look to me! This concurs 65 directly with the letter: she sends him on purpose, that I may appear stubborn to him; for she incites me to that in the letter. "Cast thy humble slough," says she; "be opposite with a kinsman, surly with servants; 69 let thy tongue [tang] with arguments of state; put thyself into the trick of singularity"; and consequently sets down the manner how: as a sad face, a reverend carriage, a slow tongue, in the habit of some sir of note, and so forth. I have lim'd her, but it is Jove's 74 doing, and Jove make me thankful! And when she went away now, "Let this fellow be look'd to"; "fellow"! not "Malvolio," nor after my degree, but "fellow." Why, every thing adheres together, that no dram of a scruple, no scruple of a scruple, no ob- 79 stacle, no incredulous or unsafe circumstance—What can be said? Nothing that can be can come between me

and the full prospect of my hopes. Well, Jove, not I, is the doer of this, and he is to be thank'd.

Enter TOBY, FABIAN, *and* MARIA.

Sir To. Which way is he, in the name of sanctity? If all the devils of hell be drawn in little, and Legion himself possess'd him, yet I'll speak to him. 86

Fab. Here he is, here he is. How is't with you, sir?

[*Sir To.*] How is't with you, man?

Mal. Go off, I discard you. Let me enjoy my private. Go off. 90

Mar. Lo, how hollow the fiend speaks within him! Did not I tell you? Sir Toby, my lady prays you to have a care of him.

Mal. Ah ha, does she so?

Sir To. Go to, go to; peace, peace, we must deal gently with him. Let me alone. How do you, 96 Malvolio? How is't with you? What, man, defy the devil! Consider, he's an enemy to mankind.

Mal. Do you know what you say?

Mar. La you, and you speak ill of the devil, how he takes it at heart! Pray God he be not bewitch'd! 101

Fab. Carry his water to th' wise woman.

Mar. Marry, and it shall be done to-morrow morning if I live. My lady would not lose him for more than I'll say. 105

Mal. How now, mistress?

Mar. O Lord!

Sir To. Prithee hold thy peace, this is not the way. Do you not see you move him? Let me alone with him.

Fab. No way but gentleness, gently, gently. The fiend is rough, and will not be roughly us'd. 111

Sir To. Why, how now, my bawcock? How dost thou, chuck?

Mal. Sir!

Sir To. Ay, biddy, come with me. What, man, 'tis not for gravity to play at cherry-pit with Sathan. Hang him, foul collier! 117

Mar. Get him to say his prayers, good Sir Toby, get him to pray.

Mal. My prayers, minx! 120

Mar. No, I warrant you, he will not hear of godliness.

---

56. **midsummer madness.** Proverbial; the midsummer moon was traditionally associated with insanity.　59. **attends:** awaits.
61. **fellow:** man (used of a servant or social inferior, without contemptuous sense).　63. **miscarry:** come to harm.
64. **come near:** begin to understand.
67. **stubborn:** rude, harsh.　**incites:** encourages.
71. **consequently:** thereafter.　72. **reverend:** dignified.
73. **slow tongue:** deliberate manner of speaking.　**habit...note:** attire of a kind suitable for a distinguished gentleman.
74. **lim'd:** caught as with birdlime (a sticky substance spread on bushes to ensnare small birds).
77. **fellow.** Malvolio takes the word to mean "companion."　**after my degree:** according to my place, i.e. "steward."
78. **adheres together:** hangs together.
79. **dram:** small quantity (one-eighth of a fluid ounce).　**scruple:** (1) doubt; (2) smallest quantity (one-third of a dram).
80. **incredulous:** incredible.　**unsafe:** uncertain.

82. **prospect:** range, scope.
84. **in...sanctity:** in the name of all that is holy.
85. **drawn in little:** contracted into small compass (so that they could all find room in Malvolio's bosom).　**Legion.** Alluding to Mark 5:8–9: "For he [Jesus] said unto him, Come out of the man, thou unclean spirit. And he asked him, What is thy name? And he answered, saying, My name is Legion: for we are many" (Geneva).
89. **discard:** cast off, want nothing to do with.
89–90. **private:** privacy.　91. **hollow:** deep, resounding (adverbial).
93. **have...of:** be attentive to, take care of.
96. **Let me alone:** leave him to me.　97. **defy:** renounce.
100. **La you:** an exclamation.　**and:** if, when.
101. **bewitch'd.** Demoniac possession was sometimes attributed to witchcraft.　102. **water:** urine (for analysis).
109. **move him:** make him angry.
111. **rough:** violent.　**us'd:** treated.
112. **bawcock:** fine fellow (from French *beau coq*).
113. **chuck:** chick (a term of endearment).
115. **biddy:** child's name for a chicken.
116. **gravity:** a grave man.　**cherry-pit:** a child's game in which cherry stones are thrown into a hole. Sir Toby provokingly talks to Malvolio as if he were a child and at the same time warns him that his soul is in danger.
117. **foul collier:** filthy coal-miner. Devils were always represented as coal-black, and they worked in hell-pit.
120. **minx:** impudent woman.

Mal. Go hang yourselves all! You are idle shallow things, I am not of your element. You shall know more hereafter.   *Exit.* 125

Sir To. Is't possible?

Fab. If this were play'd upon a stage now, I could condemn it as an improbable fiction.

Sir To. His very genius hath taken the infection of the device, man.   130

Mar. Nay, pursue him now, lest the device take air, and taint.

Fab. Why, we shall make him mad indeed.

Mar. The house will be the quieter.   134

Sir To. Come, we'll have him in a dark room and bound. My niece is already in the belief that he's mad. We may carry it thus, for our pleasure and his 137 penance, till our very pastime, tir'd out of breath, prompt us to have mercy on him; at which time we will bring the device to the bar and crown thee for a finder of madmen. But see, but see.   141

Enter Sir Andrew.

Fab. More matter for a May morning.

Sir And. Here's the challenge, read it. I warrant there's vinegar and pepper in't.

Fab. Is't so saucy?   145

Sir And. Ay, is't! I warrant him. Do but read.

Sir To. Give me. [*Reads.*] "Youth, whatsoever thou art, thou art but a scurvy fellow."

Fab. Good, and valiant.   149

Sir To. [*Reads.*] "Wonder not, nor admire not in thy mind, why I do call thee so, for I will show thee no reason for't."

Fab. A good note, that keeps you from the blow of the law.   154

Sir To. [*Reads.*] "Thou com'st to the Lady Olivia, and in my sight she uses thee kindly. But thou liest in thy throat, that is not the matter I challenge thee for."

Fab. Very brief, and to exceeding good sense—less.

Sir To. [*Reads.*] "I will waylay thee going home, where if it be thy chance to kill me"—   160

Fab. Good.

Sir To. [*Reads.*] "Thou kill'st me like a rogue and a villain."

Fab. Still you keep o' th' windy side of the law; good.   165

Sir To. [*Reads.*] "Fare thee well, and God have mercy upon one of our souls! He may have mercy

upon mine, but my hope is better, and so look to thyself. Thy friend as thou usest him, and thy sworn enemy,   Andrew Aguecheek." 170 If this letter move him not, his legs cannot. I'll give't him.

Mar. You may have very fit occasion for't; he is now in some commerce with my lady, and will by and by depart.   175

Sir To. Go, Sir Andrew, scout me for him at the corner of the orchard like a bum-baily. So soon as ever thou seest him, draw, and as thou draw'st, swear horrible; for it comes to pass oft that a terrible oath, with a swaggering accent sharply twang'd off, gives manhood more approbation than ever proof itself would have earn'd him. Away!   182

Sir And. Nay, let me alone for swearing. *Exit.*

Sir To. Now will not I deliver his letter; for the behavior of the young gentleman gives him out to 185 be of good capacity and breeding; his employment between his lord and my niece confirms no less. Therefore this letter, being so excellently ignorant, will breed no terror in the youth; he will find it comes from a clodpole. But, sir, I will deliver his 190 challenge by word of mouth, set upon Aguecheek a notable report of valor, and drive the gentleman (as I know his youth will aptly receive it) into a most hideous opinion of his rage, skill, fury, and impetuosity. This will so fright them both that they will kill one another by the look, like cockatrices. 196

Enter Olivia *and* Viola.

Fab. Here he comes with your niece. Give way till he take leave, and presently after him.

Sir To. I will meditate the while upon some horrid message for a challenge.   200

[*Exeunt Sir Toby, Fabian, and Maria.*]

Oli. I have said too much unto a heart of stone,
And laid mine honor too unchary on't.
There's something in me that reproves my fault;
But such a headstrong potent fault it is
That it but mocks reproof.   205

Vio. With the same havior that your passion bears
Goes on my master's griefs.

Oli. Here, wear this jewel for me, 'tis my picture.

123. **idle:** foolish.
124. **I . . . element:** i.e. I do not belong to your earthy level.   **know more:** hear about this.
129. **genius:** governing principle of his being (literally, attendant spirit).
131–32. **take . . . taint:** (1) be exposed to (noxious) air and corrupt; (2) become known and be spoiled.
135–36. **dark . . . bound.** A common treatment at this time for the insane.   137. **carry it:** keep it going.
140. **bar:** i.e. bar of judgment.
142. **matter . . . morning:** material for a May-day comedy.
145. **saucy:** (1) highly spiced; (2) insolent.
146. **I warrant him:** I guarantee he (Cesario) will be taken care of.
150. **admire:** marvel.
153–54. **A . . . law:** i.e. a carefully worded challenge, that safeguards you from a charge of slander.
156–57. **in thy throat:** in the most heinous degree.
164. **windy side:** windward, i.e. safe (because, as before, the abuse is too feeble to be defamatory; but perhaps also because *like a rogue and a villain* can be taken to modify *me*, not *thou*).

169. **Thy . . . him:** your friend insofar as you behave in a friendly fashion toward him.
171. **move him:** stir him up (with following quibble).
173. **fit:** convenient.   174. **commerce:** dealing, business.
174–75. **will . . . depart:** is on the verge of departing.
176. **scout me:** keep watch.
177. **bum-baily:** petty sheriff's officer who arrested for debt.
180–81. **gives . . . approbation:** gives valor a higher reputation. i.e. gives a man a higher reputation for valor.
181. **proof:** actual trial, performance.
183. **let . . . swearing:** have no fears about my ability to swear.
185. **gives him out:** declares him.   186. **capacity:** ability.
189. **find:** detect, see.
190. **clodpole:** knucklehead (variant form of *clodpoll*).
193. **youth:** i.e. inexperience.   **aptly receive it:** readily credit the report.
196. **cockatrices:** basilisks, fabulous serpents that were supposedly able to kill by their glance alone.
197–98. **Give them way:** stay out of their way.
198. **presently:** immediately.
202. **laid:** hazarded.   **unchary:** carelessly.
204. **potent:** powerful.   206. **havior:** behavior.
208. **jewel.** Used of any product of the jeweller's art; here a brooch or locket with Olivia's picture set in it.

Twelfth Night
III.iv

Refuse it not, it hath no tongue to vex you;
And I beseech you come again to-morrow.   210
What shall you ask of me that I'll deny,
That honor, sav'd, may upon asking give?

    Vio. Nothing but this—your true love for my
master.

    Oli. How with mine honor may I give him that
Which I have given to you?

    Vio.   I will acquit you.   215

    Oli. Well, come again to-morrow. Fare thee well.
A fiend like thee might bear my soul to hell. [*Exit.*]

Enter Toby *and* Fabian.

    Sir To. Gentleman, God save thee!

    Vio. And you, sir.

    Sir To. That defense thou hast, betake thee to't.
Of what nature the wrongs are thou hast done   221
him, I know not; but thy intercepter, full of despite,
bloody as the hunter, attends thee at the orchard-end.
Dismount thy tuck, be yare in thy preparation, for thy
assailant is quick, skillful, and deadly.   225

    Vio. You mistake, sir, I am sure; no man hath any
quarrel to me. My remembrance is very free and clear
from any image of offense done to any man.

    Sir To. You'll find it otherwise, I assure you;
therefore, if you hold your life at any price, betake you
to your guard; for your opposite hath in him   231
what youth, strength, skill, and wrath can furnish man
withal.

    Vio. I pray you, sir, what is he?   234

    Sir To. He is knight, dubb'd with unhatch'd rapier,
and on carpet consideration, but he is a devil in private
brawl. Souls and bodies hath he divorc'd three, and his
incensement at this moment is so implacable, that
satisfaction can be none but by pangs of death and   239
sepulchre. Hob, nob, is his word; give't or take't.

    Vio. I will return again into the house, and desire
some conduct of the lady. I am no fighter. I have
heard of some kind of men that put quarrels purposely
on others, to taste their valor. Belike this is a man of
that quirk.   245

    Sir To. Sir, no; his indignation derives itself out of
a very [competent] injury; therefore get you on, and
give him his desire. Back you shall not to the house,
unless you undertake that with me which with as much
safety you might answer him; therefore on, or   250

strip your sword stark naked; for meddle you must,
that's certain, or forswear to wear iron about you.

    Vio. This is as uncivil as strange. I beseech you
do me this courteous office, as to know of the knight
what my offense to him is. It is something of my
negligence, nothing of my purpose.   256

    Sir To. I will do so. Signior Fabian, stay you by
this gentleman till my return.   *Exit Toby.*

    Vio. Pray you, sir, do you know of this matter?

    Fab. I know the knight is incens'd against you,
even to a mortal arbitrement, but nothing of the
circumstance more.   262

    Vio. I beseech you, what manner of man is he?

    Fab. Nothing of that wonderful promise, to read
him by his form, as you are like to find him in the   265
proof of his valor. He is indeed, sir, the most skillful,
bloody, and fatal opposite that you could possibly have
found in any part of Illyria. Will you walk towards
him? I will make your peace with him if I can.   269

    Vio. I shall be much bound to you for't. I am one
that had rather go with sir priest than sir knight.
I care not who knows so much of my mettle.

                            Exeunt.

Enter Toby *and* Andrew.

    Sir To. Why, man, he's a very devil, I have not
seen such a firago. I had a pass with him, rapier,
scabbard, and all; and he gives me the stuck in with
such a mortal motion that it is inevitable; and   276
on the answer, he pays you as surely as your feet
hits the ground they step on. They say he has been
fencer to the Sophy.

    Sir And. Pox on't, I'll not meddle with him.   280

    Sir To. Ay, but he will not now be pacified.
Fabian can scarce hold him yonder.

    Sir And. Plague on't, and I thought he had been
valiant, and so cunning in fence, I'd have seen him
damn'd ere I'd have challeng'd him. Let him let the
matter slip, and I'll give him my horse, grey   286
Capilet.

    Sir To. I'll make the motion. Stand here, make a
good show on't; this shall end without the perdition
of souls. [*Aside.*] Marry, I'll ride your horse as   290
well as I ride you.

Enter Fabian *and* Viola.

212. **sav'd:** i.e. without injury to itself, safely.
215. **acquit:** waive all claim to.
217. **like thee:** in your likeness.   **might:** i.e. could without resistance
from me.
220. **That defense:** whatever skill in fencing.
222. **intercepter:** ambusher.   **despite:** contempt and hatred.
223. **bloody . . . hunter:** i.e. as intent on bloodshed as the hunting dog
tracking down its prey.
224. **Dismount thy tuck:** draw your rapier.   **yare:** ready, brisk.
227. **quarrel to:** reason to quarrel with.   **remembrance:** memory.
230. **price:** value.   231. **opposite:** adversary.
233. **withal:** with.
235. **unhatch'd:** unhacked, undented (i.e. never used in battle).
236. **on carpet consideration.** A carpet knighthood was one not given
on the battlefield for services performed there, hence often one given
for political reasons; *consideration* suggests a bought knighthood.
240. **Hob, nob:** have it, have it not; i.e. "give't or take't."   **word:**
motto.   242. **conduct:** protective escort.
244. **taste:** make trial of.
247. **competent:** sufficient.   249. **that:** i.e. a duel.

251. **strip . . . naked:** draw your sword now (and fight with me).
meddle: have to do, be involved. Cf. line 280, where *not meddle
with* = have nothing to do with.
252. **forswear . . . you:** renounce your right to wear a sword.
254. **know of:** ascertain from.   255. **of:** arising from.
256. **purpose:** intention.
261. **to . . . arbitrement:** to a point requiring settlement by a duel to
the death.   264–65. **read . . . form:** judge him by his appearance.
271. **sir priest.** Priests were often addressed by the courtesy title *sir.*
272. **mettle:** temperament.
274. **firago:** virago. Schmidt suggests that Sir Toby uses this word,
applicable only to a woman (its original meaning is "acting like a
man"), as a linguistic joke on Sir Andrew, who has not studied
languages (I.iii.92–93); if so, there is a joke on Sir Toby also.   **pass:**
bout.
275. **gives me:** gives.   **stuck in:** stoccado (or stoccato), thrust.
277. **answer:** return hit.   **pays:** repays.
283. **and . . . been:** if I had supposed he was.
287. **Capilet:** a name meaning "little horse." It is typical of Sir
Andrew's imagination that he should name a little horse "little horse."
288. **motion:** offer.   288–89. **make . . . show:** put a good face.
289–90. **perdition of souls:** loss of lives.

[*To Fabian.*] I have his horse to take up the quarrel.
I have persuaded him the youth's a devil.

Fab. He is as horribly conceited of him; and pants
and looks pale, as if a bear were at his heels. 295

Sir To. [*To Viola.*] There's no remedy, sir, he will
fight with you for 's oath sake. Marry, he hath better
bethought him of his quarrel, and he finds that 298
now scarce to be worth talking of; therefore draw,
for the supportance of his vow. He protests he will
not hurt you. 301

Vio. [*Aside.*] Pray God defend me! A little thing
would make me tell them how much I lack of a man.

Fab. Give ground if you see him furious. 304

Sir To. Come, Sir Andrew, there's no remedy, the
gentleman will for his honor's sake have one bout with
you. He cannot by the duello avoid it; but he has
promis'd me, as he is a gentleman and a soldier, he will
not hurt you. Come on, to't.

Sir And. Pray God he keep his oath! 310

> *Enter* ANTONIO.

Vio. I do assure you, 'tis against my will.
　　　　　　　　　　　　　　　[*They draw.*]

Ant. Put up your sword. If this young gentleman
Have done offense, I take the fault on me;
If you offend him, I for him defy you.

Sir To. You, sir? Why, what are you? 315

Ant. One, sir, that for his love dares yet do more
Than you have heard him brag to you he will.

Sir To. Nay, if you be an undertaker, I am for you.
　　　　　　　　　　　　　　　[*They draw.*]

> *Enter* OFFICERS.

Fab. O good Sir Toby, hold! here come the officers.

Sir To. [*To Antonio.*] I'll be with you anon. 320
　　　　　　　[*Steps aside to avoid the Officers.*]

Vio. Pray, sir, put your sword up, if you please.

Sir And. Marry, will I, sir; and for that I promis'd you, I'll be as good as my word. He will bear you
easily, and reins well.

1. Off. This is the man, do thy office. 325

2. Off. Antonio, I arrest thee at the suit of Count
Orsino.

Ant. You do mistake me, sir.

1. Off. No, sir, no jot. I know your favor well,
Though now you have no sea-cap on your head. 330
Take him away, he knows I know him well.

Ant. I must obey. [*To Viola.*] This comes with
　　seeking you;
But there's no remedy, I shall answer it.
What will you do, now my necessity 334
Makes me to ask you for my purse? It grieves me
Much more for what I cannot do for you

Than what befalls myself. You stand amaz'd,
But be of comfort.

2. Off. Come, sir, away. 339

Ant. I must entreat of you some of that money.

Vio. What money, sir?
For the fair kindness you have show'd me here,
And part being prompted by your present trouble,
Out of my lean and low ability
I'll lend you something. My having is not much; 345
I'll make division of my present with you.
Hold, there's half my coffer.

Ant. 　　　　　　　Will you deny me now?
Is't possible that my deserts to you
Can lack persuasion? Do not tempt my misery,
Lest that it make me so unsound a man 350
As to upbraid you with those kindnesses
That I have done for you.

Vio. 　　　　　I know of none,
Nor know I you by voice or any feature.
I hate ingratitude more in a man
Than lying, vainness, babbling, drunkenness, 355
Or any taint of vice whose strong corruption
Inhabits our frail blood.

Ant. 　　　　　O heavens themselves!

2. Off. Come, sir, I pray you go.

Ant. Let me speak a little. This youth that you
　　see here
I snatch'd one half out of the jaws of death, 360
Reliev'd him with such sanctity of love,
And to his image, which methought did promise
Most venerable worth, did I devotion.

1. Off. What's that to us? The time goes by;
　　away!

Ant. But O, how vild an idol proves this god! 365
Thou hast, Sebastian, done good feature shame.
In nature there's no blemish but the mind;
None can be call'd deform'd but the unkind.
Virtue is beauty, but the beauteous evil
Are empty trunks o'erflourish'd by the devil. 370

1. Off. The man grows mad, away with him!
　　Come, come, sir.

Ant. Lead me on. 　　　　*Exit* [*with Officers*].

Vio. Methinks his words do from such passion fly
That he believes himself; so do not I.
Prove true, imagination, O, prove true, 375
That I, dear brother, be now ta'en for you!

---

292. **take up:** settle.
294. **He . . . him:** i.e. the youth has as dreadful a conception of Sir
Andrew. 297. **for 's:** for his.
298. **bethought . . . quarrel:** considered the grounds for his challenge.
300. **supportance:** upholding. **protests:** solemnly promises.
307. **duello:** the code of duelling.
318. **undertaker:** i.e. one who takes up a challenge for another.
320. **be . . . anon:** be back right away.
322–23. **that . . . you:** i.e. the horse Capilet (about which of course
Viola knows nothing). 324. **easily:** smoothly.
325. **office:** duty, function. 329. **favor:** face.
333. **answer it:** i.e. make what defense I can.

337. **amaz'd:** bewildered. 343. **part:** in part.
344. **ability:** means. 345. **My having:** what I possess.
346. **present:** ready money.
347. **coffer:** store of wealth (literally, strong-box).
349. **lack persuasion:** fail to persuade you. **tempt:** try too far.
350. **unsound:** unhealthy (used figuratively).
355. **vainness:** vanity. **babbling:** foolish, loose talk.
356. **any . . . vice:** the taint of any fault.
360. **one . . . death:** out of the jaws of death which had half-swallowed
him. 361. **such.** Used here with intensive force.
362. **his image:** what he appeared to be (with play on *image* in the
sense "religious statue").
363. **venerable worth:** worthiness of veneration. 365. **vild:** vile.
366. **Thou . . . shame.** Alluding to the belief that physical beauty is a
reflection of spiritual beauty. **feature:** physical form.
368. **unkind:** unnatural. The unnatural quality with which he is
charging the supposed Sebastian is of course ingratitude.
370. **trunks o'erflourish'd:** (1) chests covered over with elaborate
carvings; (2) bodies made externally beautiful.
374. **so . . . I:** I do not believe myself, i.e. I don't quite dare to
believe what all this suggests to me (that my brother is alive).

Twelfth Night
III.iv

Sir To. Come hither, knight; come hither, Fabian; we'll whisper o'er a couplet or two of most sage saws.

Vio. He nam'd Sebastian. I my brother know
Yet living in my glass; even such and so　　380
In favor was my brother, and he went
Still in this fashion, color, ornament,
For him I imitate. O, if it prove,
Tempests are kind and salt waves fresh in love.　384
　　　　　　　　　　　　　　　　[*Exit.*]

Sir To. A very dishonest paltry boy, and more a coward than a hare. His dishonesty appears in leaving his friend here in necessity, and denying him; and for his cowardship, ask Fabian.

Fab. A coward, a most devout coward, religious in it.　　390

Sir And. 'Slid, I'll after him again, and beat him.

Sir To. Do, cuff him soundly, but never draw thy sword.

Sir And. And I do not—　　　　　[*Exit.*]

Fab. Come, let's see the event.　　395

Sir To. I dare lay any money 'twill be nothing yet.
　　　　　　　　　　　　　　　　Exeunt.

ACT IV, Scene I

Enter Sebastian *and* Clown.

Clo. Will you make me believe that I am not sent for you?

Seb. Go to, go to, thou art a foolish fellow,
Let me be clear of thee.　　　　　4

Clo. Well held out, i' faith! No, I do not know you, nor I am not sent to you by my lady, to bid you come speak with her, nor your name is not Master Cesario, nor this is not my nose neither: nothing that is so is so.

Seb. I prithee vent thy folly somewhere else,　10
Thou know'st not me.

Clo. Vent my folly! He has heard that word of some great man, and now applies it to a fool. Vent my folly! I am afraid this great lubber the world will prove a cockney. I prithee now ungird thy strangeness, and tell me what I shall vent to my lady. Shall I vent to her that thou art coming?　　17

Seb. I prithee, foolish Greek, depart from me.
There's money for thee. If you tarry longer,
I shall give worse payment.　　　　20

Clo. By my troth, thou hast an open hand. These

wise men that give fools money get themselves a good report—after fourteen years' purchase.

Enter Andrew, Toby, *and* Fabian.

Sir And. Now, sir, have I met you again? There's for you.　　　　　　[*Strikes Sebastian.*]　25

Seb. Why, there's for thee, and there, and there.
[*Strikes Sir Andrew.*] Are all the people mad?
　　　　　　　　　　　　　[*Draws his dagger.*]

Sir To. Hold, sir, or I'll throw your dagger o'er the house.　　　　[*Seizes Sebastian's arm.*]　29

Clo. This will I tell my lady straight; I would not be in some of your coats for twopence.　[*Exit.*]

Sir To. Come on, sir, hold!

Sir And. Nay, let him alone. I'll go another way to work with him; I'll have an action of battery against him, if there be any law in Illyria. Though I strook him first, yet it's no matter for that.　　36

Seb. Let go thy hand.

Sir To. Come, sir, I will not let you go. Come, my young soldier, put up your iron; you are well flesh'd.
Come on.　　　　　　　　　40

Seb. I will be free from thee. [*Breaks away and draws his sword.*] What wouldst thou now?
If thou dar'st tempt me further, draw thy sword.

Sir To. What, what? Nay then I must have an ounce or two of this malapert blood from you.　44
　　　　　　　　　　　　　　　　[*Draws.*]

Enter Olivia.

Oli. Hold, Toby, on thy life I charge thee hold!

Sir To. Madam—

Oli. Will it be ever thus? Ungracious wretch,
Fit for the mountains and the barbarous caves,
Where manners ne'er were preach'd! Out of my sight!
Be not offended, dear Cesario.　　　50
Rudesby, be gone!
　　[*Exeunt Sir Toby, Sir Andrew, and Fabian.*]
　　　　　　　　　　　　I prithee, gentle friend,
Let thy fair wisdom, not thy passion, sway
In this uncivil and unjust extent
Against thy peace. Go with me to my house,
And hear thou there how many fruitless pranks　55
This ruffian hath botch'd up, that thou thereby
Mayst smile at this. Thou shalt not choose but go;

378. **saws:** sayings, maxims.
379–80. **I . . . glass:** I know that the appearance of my brother is still alive every time I look in a mirror (i.e. I am the living image of my brother).　381–82. **went Still in:** always wore.
383. **prove:** prove true.　385. **dishonest:** dishonorable.
385–86. **more a coward:** more cowardly.
391. **'Slid:** by God's eyelid.　394. **And:** if.
395. **event:** outcome.
396. **yet:** now as before (?) or nevertheless (?) or after all (?).

IV.i. Location: Before Olivia's house.
4. **clear:** rid.　5. **held out:** persisted in.
10. **vent thy folly:** utter your foolish talk. *Vent* was in common use, and it is hard to understand why Feste chooses to think it affected.
14. **lubber:** clumsy stupid fellow, lout.
15. **cockney:** overnice, effeminate fellow.
15–16. **ungird thy strangeness:** put off your pretense of being a stranger.　18. **Greek:** i.e. jester.

23. **report:** reputation.　**after . . . purchase:** i.e. provided they give generously enough. "Fourteen years' purchase" would be a high price for a piece of land, since the ordinary purchase price was based on twelve years' rental.
28. **Hold:** stop.　30. **straight:** straightway, at once.
31. **be . . . coats:** i.e. be in the shoes of some of you.
33–34. **go . . . him:** get at him in another way.
34. **action of battery:** a lawsuit for assault and battery.
35. **strook:** struck (a common variant).
37. **Let . . . hand:** let go of me.
38–39. **Come, my . . . flesh'd.** Addressed ironically, some commentators believe, to Sir Andrew (who would then have "flesh'd" or used for the first time in battle his "unhatch'd rapier" [III.iv.235]). But it is far from evident that Sir Andrew has drawn his "iron," and certainly it is Sebastian whom Sir Toby is intent on restraining from line 28 on. If these words are addressed to him, as seems far more likely, *you are well flesh'd* = you have had a sufficient taste of combat.
44. **malapert:** impudent, saucy.　47. **Ungracious:** graceless.
51. **Rudesby:** unmannerly fellow.　52. **fair:** clear, equitable.
53. **uncivil:** barbarous (cf. lines 48–49). **unjust:** unlawful. **extent:** show of violence.　55. **fruitless:** idle.
56. **botch'd up:** patched together, clumsily contrived.

Do not deny. Beshrew his soul for me,
He started one poor heart of mine, in thee.   59
  Seb. What relish is in this? How runs the stream?
Or I am mad, or else this is a dream.
Let fancy still my sense in Lethe steep;
If it be thus to dream, still let me sleep!
  Oli. Nay, come, I prithee. Would thou'dst be
    rul'd by me!   64
  Seb. Madam, I will.
  Oli.   O, say so, and so be! *Exeunt.*

Scene II

Enter Maria *and* Clown.

  Mar. Nay, I prithee put on this gown and this
beard, make him believe thou art Sir Topas the curate,
do it quickly. I'll call Sir Toby the whilst. [*Exit.*]
  Clo. Well, I'll put it on, and I will dissemble myself in't, and I would I were the first that ever dis-   5
sembled in such a gown. I am not tall enough to become
the function well, nor lean enough to be thought a good
student; but to be said an honest man and a good
house-keeper goes as fairly as to say a careful man and
a great scholar. The competitors enter.   10

Enter Toby [*and* Maria].

  Sir To. Jove bless thee, Master Parson.
  Clo. *Bonos dies*, Sir Toby: for as the old hermit of
Prague, that never saw pen and ink, very wittily said
to a niece of King Gorboduc, "That that is is";   14
so I, being Master Parson, am Master Parson; for
what is "that" but "that," and "is" but "is"?
  Sir To. To him, Sir Topas.
  Clo. What ho, I say! Peace in this prison!
  Sir To. The knave counterfeits well; a good knave.
  Mal. (*Within.*) Who calls there?   20
  Clo. Sir Topas the curate, who comes to visit
Malvolio the lunatic.

  Mal. Sir Topas, Sir Topas, good Sir Topas, go to
my lady.
  Clo. Out, hyperbolical fiend! how vexest thou this
man! Talkest thou nothing but of ladies?   26
  Sir To. Well said, Master Parson.
  Mal. Sir Topas, never was man thus wrong'd.
Good Sir Topas, do not think I am mad; they have laid
me here in hideous darkness.   30
  Clo. Fie, thou dishonest Sathan! I call thee by the
most modest terms, for I am one of those gentle ones
that will use the devil himself with courtesy. Say'st
thou that house is dark?
  Mal. As hell, Sir Topas.   35
  Clo. Why, it hath bay windows transparent as
barricadoes, and the [clerestories] toward the south
north are as lustrous as ebony; and yet complainest
thou of obstruction?   39
  Mal. I am not mad, Sir Topas, I say to you this
house is dark.
  Clo. Madman, thou errest. I say there is no darkness but ignorance, in which thou art more puzzled than
the Egyptians in their fog.   44
  Mal. I say this house is as dark as ignorance,
though ignorance were as dark as hell; and I say there
was never man thus abus'd. I am no more mad   47
than you are; make the trial of it in any constant
question.
  Clo. What is the opinion of Pythagoras concerning
wild-fowl?   51
  Mal. That the soul of our grandam might happily
inhabit a bird.
  Clo. What think'st thou of his opinion?
  Mal. I think nobly of the soul, and no way ap-
prove his opinion.   56
  Clo. Fare thee well. Remain thou still in darkness.
Thou shalt hold th' opinion of Pythagoras ere I will
allow of thy wits, and fear to kill a woodcock lest thou
dispossess the soul of thy grandam. Fare thee well.
  Mal. Sir Topas, Sir Topas!   61
  Sir To. My most exquisite Sir Topas!
  Clo. Nay, I am for all waters.
  Mar. Thou mightst have done this without thy
beard and gown, he sees thee not.   65
  Sir To. To him in thine own voice, and bring me
word how thou find'st him. I would we were well rid
of this knavery. If he may be conveniently deliver'd,
I would he were, for I am now so far in offense with

---

58. Beshrew. Here much closer to its original sense "curse" than in II.iii.80.
59. He . . . thee: "He that offends thee, attacks one of my hearts, or as the ancients expressed it, half my heart" (Johnson). There may also be a glancing play on *hart*, suggested by *started.*
60. relish: taste, i.e. quality, nature. **61. Or:** either.
62. fancy: imagination. **Lethe:** the river of forgetfulness in the underworld.

IV.ii. Location: Olivia's house.
2. Sir Topas. Shakespeare may have borrowed the name from Chaucer's "Rime of Sir Thopas" in *The Canterbury Tales.* On *Sir* see the note to III.iv.271. **3. the whilst:** in the meantime.
4. dissemble: disguise.
5–6. dissembled: created a false impression, concealed his true nature.
6. tall. The sense here is probably "large, well-fleshed," in contrast to *lean*, line 7. Feste seems to be glancing jestingly at two traditional notions, that clerics are given to the pleasures of the table and that scholars lead ascetic lives.
6–7. become . . . well: grace the priestly office.
8. studient: scholar (a variant form of *student*, not Feste's invention). Most scholars were churchmen. **said:** known as.
8–9. good house-keeper: good manager of his household.
9. goes as fairly: sounds as well. **careful:** highly regardful of his duties. **10. competitors:** partners, confederates.
12. Bonos dies: for *bonus dies*, good day.
12–13. hermit of Prague. Now that Feste is a priest, the authority he invents is a man of religion. **13. wittily:** cleverly.
14. Gorboduc: a legendary king of England.

25. hyperbolical: vehement (a rhetorical term, meaning "exaggerated in style"). **fiend:** i.e. the devil by whom Malvolio is possessed.
32. modest: moderate. **34. house:** i.e. room.
37. barricadoes: barricades. **clerestories:** windows in the upper wall. **39. obstruction:** shutting out of light.
43. puzzled: greatly perplexed.
44. Egyptians . . . fog. An allusion to Exodus 10:22, "And Moses stretched forth his hand toward heaven; and there was a black darkness in all the land of Egypt three days" (Geneva).
48–49. constant question: topic for rational discourse.
50–51. Pythagoras . . . wild-fowl. Referring to the Pythagorean doctrine of transmigration of souls.
52. happily: haply, perchance.
59. allow . . . wits: grant that you are sane. **woodcock.** Proverbial for its stupidity.
62. exquisite: consummately accomplished.
63. for all waters: i.e. ready for anything (a phrase of unknown origin). **68. deliver'd:** set free.
69. far in offense: deeply in disgrace.

my niece that I cannot pursue with any safety this
sport [t'] the upshot. Come by and by to my chamber.

Exit [with Maria].

Clo. [*Sings.*]

"Hey, Robin, jolly Robin,   72
    Tell me how thy lady does."

Mal. Fool!

Clo. "My lady is unkind, perdie."   75

Mal. Fool!

Clo. "Alas, why is she so?"

Mal. Fool, I say!

Clo. "She loves another"—Who calls, ha?   79

Mal. Good fool, as ever thou wilt deserve well at
my hand, help me to a candle, and pen, ink, and paper.
As I am a gentleman, I will live to be thankful to
thee for't.

Clo. Master Malvolio?

Mal. Ay, good fool.   85

Clo. Alas, sir, how fell you besides your five wits?

Mal. Fool, there was never man so notoriously
abus'd; I am as well in my wits, fool, as thou art.

Clo. But as well! Then you are mad indeed, if you
be no better in your wits than a fool.   90

Mal. They have here propertied me, keep me in
darkness, send ministers to me, asses, and do all they
can to face me out of my wits.

Clo. Advise you what you say; the minister is here.
—Malvolio, Malvolio, thy wits the heavens restore!
Endeavor thyself to sleep, and leave thy vain bibble
babble.   97

Mal. Sir Topas!

Clo. Maintain no words with him, good fellow.—
Who, I, sir? Not I, sir. God buy you, good Sir
Topas.—Marry, amen.—I will, sir, I will.

Mal. Fool, fool, fool, I say!   102

Clo. Alas, sir, be patient. What say you, sir?
I am shent for speaking to you.

Mal. Good fool, help me to some light and some
paper. I tell thee I am as well in my wits as any man
in Illyria.

Clo. Well-a-day that you were, sir!   108

Mal. By this hand, I am. Good fool, some ink,
paper, and light; and convey what I will set down to
my lady. It shall advantage thee more than ever the
bearing of letter did.

Clo. I will help you to't. But tell me true, are you
not mad indeed, or do you but counterfeit?

Mal. Believe me I am not, I tell thee true.   115

Clo. Nay, I'll ne'er believe a madman till I see his
brains. I will fetch you light and paper and ink.

Mal. Fool, I'll requite it in the highest degree.
I prithee be gone.

Clo. [*Sings.*]

I am gone, sir,   120
And anon, sir,
    I'll be with you again;
In a trice,
Like to the old Vice,
    Your need to sustain;   125

Who with dagger of lath,
In his rage and his wrath,
    Cries, ah, ha! to the devil;
Like a mad lad,
Pare thy nails, dad.   130
    Adieu, goodman devil.   *Exit.*

SCENE III

Enter SEBASTIAN.

[*Seb.*] This is the air, that is the glorious sun,
This pearl she gave me, I do feel't and see't,
And though 'tis wonder that enwraps me thus,
Yet 'tis not madness. Where's Antonio then?
I could not find him at the Elephant,   5
Yet there he was, and there I found this credit,
That he did range the town to seek me out.
His counsel now might do me golden service,
For though my soul disputes well with my sense,
That this may be some error, but no madness,   10
Yet doth this accident and flood of fortune
So far exceed all instance, all discourse,
That I am ready to distrust mine eyes,
And wrangle with my reason that persuades me
To any other trust but that I am mad,   15
Or else the lady's mad; yet if 'twere so,
She could not sway her house, command her followers,
Take and give back affairs, and their dispatch,
With such a smooth, discreet, and stable bearing
As I perceive she does. There's something in't   20
That is deceivable. But here the lady comes.

71. **upshot:** conclusion (the decisive shot in an archery contest).
72–73. **Hey . . . does.** These lines, with 75, 77, 79, are from an old
song, a version of which is attributed to Sir Thomas Wyatt.
75. **perdie:** indeed (a weakened oath, like French *pardieu,* literally
"by God").
86. **besides:** out of. **five wits.** Usually listed as common wit
(common sense) fantasy, memory, judgment, and imagination.
87–88. **notoriously abus'd:** egregiously misused.
91. **propertied me:** i.e. stowed me away like a piece of furniture
(perhaps with play on stage properties).
93. **face . . . wits:** brazenly deny that I am sane.
94. **Advise you:** consider well.
95–97. **Malvolio . . . babble.** Feste here impersonates Sir Topas again,
and in his next speech takes both parts in a dialogue between Sir Topas
and himself. 96. **Endeavor thyself:** strive.
100. **God buy you:** God be with you, goodby.
104. **shent:** rebuked. 108. **Well-a-day:** alas.
111. **advantage:** benefit.

123. **trice:** moment.
124. **Vice:** the comic character in the morality plays and interludes,
in which he often beat the Devil with his "dagger of lath" and
threatened to trim his long nails with it. Feste here compares himself
to the Vice (whose role was an ancestor of the Clown's role), and his
impudent remarks to the devil by whom Malvolio is supposedly
possessed are by implication addressed to Malvolio himself.
131. **goodman devil.** A final insult to Malvolio, who is addressed by
the title proper for those below the rank of gentleman.

IV.iii. Location: Olivia's garden.
6. **was:** had been. **found this credit:** learned that they believed as
follows. 7. **range:** go about.
9. **my soul . . . sense:** i.e. my reason and my senses both maintain
(*disputes with* = "argues together with").
11. **accident . . . fortune:** chance occurrence and (i.e. which is a)
brimming over of good fortune.
12. **instance:** example, precedent. **discourse:** reasoning, logic.
15. **trust:** belief, conviction.
17. **sway:** rule, manage. **followers:** servants.
18. **Take . . . dispatch:** i.e. take business in hand and give instructions
for its prompt execution. *Take* governs *affairs; give back* governs
dispatch. 19. **discreet:** judicious. 21. **deceivable:** deceptive.

Enter OLIVIA *and* PRIEST.

Oli. Blame not this haste of mine. If you mean
well,
Now go with me, and with this holy man,
Into the chantry by; there, before him,
And underneath that consecrated roof,   25
Plight me the full assurance of your faith,
That my most jealous and too doubtful soul
May live at peace. He shall conceal it
Whiles you are willing it shall come to note,
What time we will our celebration keep   30
According to my birth. What do you say?
Seb. I'll follow this good man, and go with you,
And having sworn truth, ever will be true.
Oli. Then lead the way, good father, and heavens
so shine   34
That they may fairly note this act of mine!   *Exeunt.*

ACT V, SCENE I

Enter CLOWN *and* FABIAN.

Fab. Now as thou lov'st me, let me see his letter.
Clo. Good Master Fabian, grant me another re-
quest.
Fab. Any thing.
Clo. Do not desire to see this letter.   5
Fab. This is to give a dog and in recompense
desire my dog again.

Enter DUKE, VIOLA, CURIO, *and* LORDS.

Duke. Belong you to the Lady Olivia, friends?
Clo. Ay, sir, we are some of her trappings.
Duke. I know thee well; how dost thou, my good
fellow?   11
Clo. Truly, sir, the better for my foes and the
worse for my friends.
Duke. Just the contrary: the better for thy friends.
Clo. No, sir, the worse.   15
Duke. How can that be?
Clo. Marry, sir, they praise me, and make an ass
of me. Now my foes tell me plainly I am an ass; so
that by my foes, sir, I profit in the knowledge of   19
myself, and by my friends I am abus'd; so that, conclusions to be as kisses, if your four negatives make

your two affirmatives, why then the worse for my
friends and the better for my foes.
Duke. Why, this is excellent.   24
Clo. By my troth, sir, no; though it please you to
be one of my friends.
Duke. Thou shalt not be the worse for me, there's
gold.
Clo. But that it would be double-dealing, sir, I
would you could make it another.   30
Duke. O, you give me ill counsel.
Clo. Put your grace in your pocket, sir, for this
once, and let your flesh and blood obey it.
Duke. Well, I will be so much a sinner to be a
double-dealer. There's another.   35
Clo. *Primo, secundo, tertio,* is a good play, and
the old saying is, the third pays for all. The triplex, sir, is a good tripping measure, or the bells of
Saint Bennet, sir, may put you in mind—one, two,
three.   40
Duke. You can fool no more money out of me at
this throw. If you will let your lady know I am here to
speak with her, and bring her along with you, it may
awake my bounty further.   44
Clo. Marry, sir, lullaby to your bounty till I come
again. I go, sir, but I would not have you to think that
my desire of having is the sin of covetousness; but as
you say, sir, let your bounty take a nap, I will awake
it anon.   *Exit.*

Enter ANTONIO *and* OFFICERS.

Vio. Here comes the man, sir, that did rescue me.
Duke. That face of his I do remember well,   51
Yet when I saw it last, it was besmear'd
As black as Vulcan in the smoke of war.
A baubling vessel was he captain of,
For shallow draught and bulk unprizable,   55
With which such scathful grapple did he make
With the most noble bottom of our fleet,
That very envy, and the tongue of loss,
Cried fame and honor on him. What's the matter?
1. Off. Orsino, this is that Antonio   60
That took the *Phoenix* and her fraught from Candy,
And this is he that did the *Tiger* board,
When your young nephew Titus lost his leg.

24. chantry: a small private chapel where mass was sung daily for the
souls of the dead.   **by:** near by.
26. Plight: pledge. The ceremony in question here is the betrothal,
regarded as a binding contract; the marriage will be solemnized later
(lines 30–31).
27. jealous: mistrustful (variant form of *jealous*).   **doubtful:**
apprehensive.
29. Whiles: until.   **come to note:** become publicly known.
30. What: at which.   **31. birth:** rank, social position.
V.i. Location: Before Olivia's house.
6–7. This . . . again. Manningham in his *Diary* (in which the Middle
Temple performance of *Twelfth Night* is recorded; see the introduction)
relates a similar incident involving Queen Elizabeth and a Dr. Bullein,
her kinsman, the owner of the dog. But whether Shakespeare knew of
the incident is uncertain.   **20. abus'd:** deceived.
20–23. so . . . foes. This jest has never been satisfactorily paraphrased.
Dover Wilson's explication may be given as one of many: "a kiss is
made by four lips (contraries or negatives) brought together by two
ardent mouths (affirmatives); if conclusions are like this, says Feste,
then the conclusion that I am not an ass is only half the value of the
conclusion that I am one."

29. But: except for the fact.   **double-dealing:** (1) duplicity; (2) giving two coins.
32. Put . . . pocket: (1) pocket up (set aside) your virtue; (2) let your
Grace dip into your purse (with further sense in *grace* of "favor" or
"generosity").
33. flesh and blood: frail human nature.   **it:** i.e. the "ill counsel."
36. Primo, secundo, tertio. Perhaps with reference to a game of dice,
perhaps to a child's game.
37. the third . . . all. Proverbial; cf. "The third time's the charm."
37–38. triplex: triple time in music.
39. Saint Bennet: Saint Benedict; possibly alluding to the London
parish church of St. Bennet Hithe on Paul's Wharf, just across the
Thames from the Globe.
41. fool: (1) befool, cheat; (2) obtain by your jester's wit.
42. throw: (1) time; (2) throw of the dice.
53. Vulcan: the smith of the gods, blackened by the smoky fire in his
smithy.   **54. baubling:** trifling, toylike.
55. For . . . unprizable: valueless because of its shallow draught and
small size. For another *bauble / shallow / bulk* cluster see *Troilus and
Cressida,* I.iii.34–37.   **56. scathful:** damaging.
57. bottom: ship.
58. envy: enmity, i.e. (we) his enemies.   **loss:** i.e. the losers.
61. fraught: freight, cargo.   **from Candy:** returning from Candia
(Crete).

435

Twelfth Night
V.i

Here in the streets, desperate of shame and state,
In private brabble did we apprehend him.   65
    Vio. He did me kindness, sir, drew on my side,
But in conclusion put strange speech upon me.
I know not what 'twas but distraction.
    Duke. Notable pirate, thou salt-water thief!
What foolish boldness brought thee to their mercies
Whom thou in terms so bloody and so dear   71
Hast made thine enemies?
    Ant.   Orsino, noble sir,
Be pleas'd that I shake off these names you give me.
Antonio never yet was thief or pirate,
Though I confess, on base and ground enough,   75
Orsino's enemy. A witchcraft drew me hither:
That most ingrateful boy there by your side
From the rude sea's enrag'd and foamy mouth
Did I redeem; a wrack past hope he was.
His life I gave him, and did thereto add   80
My love, without retention or restraint,
All his in dedication. For his sake
Did I expose myself (pure for his love)
Into the danger of this adverse town,
Drew to defend him when he was beset;   85
Where being apprehended, his false cunning
(Not meaning to partake with me in danger)
Taught him to face me out of his acquaintance,
And grew a twenty years removed thing
While one would wink; denied me mine own purse,
Which I had recommended to his use   91
Not half an hour before.
    Vio.   How can this be?
    Duke. When came he to this town?
    Ant. To-day, my lord; and for three months before,
No int'rim, not a minute's vacancy,   95
Both day and night did we keep company.

Enter OLIVIA *and* ATTENDANTS.

    Duke. Here comes the Countess, now heaven walks
        on earth.
But for thee, fellow—fellow, thy words are madness.
Three months this youth hath tended upon me,
But more of that anon. Take him aside.   100
    Oli. What would my lord, but that he may not
        have,
Wherein Olivia may seem serviceable?
Cesario, you do not keep promise with me.

    Vio. Madam—
    Duke. Gracious Olivia—   105
    Oli. What do you say, Cesario? Good my lord—
    Vio. My lord would speak, my duty hushes me.
    Oli. If it be aught to the old tune, my lord,
It is as fat and fulsome to mine ear
As howling after music.
    Duke.   Still so cruel?   110
    Oli. Still so constant, lord.
    Duke. What, to perverseness? You uncivil lady,
To whose ingrate and unauspicious altars
My soul the faithfull'st off'rings have breath'd out
That e'er devotion tender'd! What shall I do?   115
    Oli. Even what it please my lord, that shall become
        him.
    Duke. Why should I not (had I the heart to do it),
Like to th' Egyptian thief at point of death,
Kill what I love? (a savage jealousy
That sometime savors nobly), but hear me this: 120
Since you to non-regardance cast my faith,
And that I partly know the instrument
That screws me from my true place in your favor,
Live you the marble-breasted tyrant still.
But this your minion, whom I know you love,   125
And whom, by heaven I swear, I tender dearly,
Him will I tear out of that cruel eye,
Where he sits crowned in his master's spite.
Come, boy, with me, my thoughts are ripe in mischief.
I'll sacrifice the lamb that I do love,   130
To spite a raven's heart within a dove.
    Vio. And I most jocund, apt, and willingly,
To do you rest, a thousand deaths would die.
    Oli. Where goes Cesario?
    Vio.   After him I love
More than I love these eyes, more than my life,   135
More by all mores than e'er I shall love wife.
If I do feign, you witnesses above
Punish my life for tainting of my love!
    Oli. Ay me, detested! how am I beguil'd!
    Vio. Who does beguile you? who does do you
        wrong?   140
    Oli. Hast thou forgot thyself? Is it so long?
Call forth the holy father.
    Duke.   Come, away!
    Oli. Whither, my lord? Cesario, husband, stay.
    Duke. Husband?
    Oli.   Ay, husband. Can he that deny?
    Duke. Her husband, sirrah?

---

64. **desperate . . . state:** i.e. with reckless disregard of disgrace and danger. *Shame* refers perhaps to his involvement in a street brawl, *state* to his dangerous position as a public enemy.
65. **brabble:** brawl.
66. **drew . . . side:** drew his sword in my defense.
67. **put . . . me:** spoke very strangely to me.
68. **but distraction:** unless it was insanity.
69. **Notable:** notorious.
71. **in terms:** in a manner.   **dear:** grievous.
73. **Be pleas'd:** permit.
75. **base and ground.** The nouns are synonyms.
79. **wrack:** wreck.   81. **retention:** reservation.
83. **pure:** solely.   84. **Into:** to.   **adverse:** hostile.
87. **Not . . . partake:** having no intention of sharing.
88. **face . . . acquaintance:** deny brazenly that he knew me.
89–90. **grew . . . wink:** in the twinkling of an eye became as distant as if we had not seen each other for twenty years.
91. **recommended:** commended, committed.
95. **vacancy:** gap, interval.
101. **but . . . have:** i.e. except what I cannot give him (i.e. her love).
102. **seem serviceable:** show her duty.

109. **fat and fulsome:** gross and distasteful.
112. **uncivil:** inhumane.
113. **ingrate:** ungrateful.   **unauspicious:** unpropitious.
115. **tender'd:** offered.
118. **Egyptian thief.** Referring to an episode in Heliodorus' *Ethiopica*, in which Thyamis, an Egyptian robber captain who has taken Chariclea captive and fallen in love with her, finds himself in danger of death at his enemies' hands and attempts to kill Chariclea first.
120. **savors nobly:** has a noble quality about it.
121. **non-regardance:** disregard, neglect.   **faith:** constancy.
122. **that.** Repeating the sense of *Since*, line 121.
123. **screws:** forces.   124. **marble-breasted:** stony-hearted.
125. **minion:** darling.   126. **tender:** regard.
128. **in . . . spite:** in defiance of his master.   132. **apt:** ready.
133. **do you rest:** give you peace.   136. **mores:** (such) comparisons.
138. **tainting . . . love:** bringing my love into discredit.
139. **detested:** renounced, rejected.
145. **sirrah:** form of address to an inferior.

Vio.   No, my lord, not I.

Oli. Alas, it is the baseness of thy fear   146
That makes thee strangle thy propriety.
Fear not, Cesario, take thy fortunes up,
Be that thou know'st thou art, and then thou art
As great as that thou fear'st.

Enter PRIEST.

                O, welcome, father!
Father, I charge thee by thy reverence   151
Here to unfold, though lately we intended
To keep in darkness what occasion now
Reveals before 'tis ripe, what thou dost know
Hath newly pass'd between this youth and me.   155

Priest. A contract of eternal bond of love,
Confirm'd by mutual joinder of your hands,
Attested by the holy close of lips,
Strength'ned by interchangement of your rings,
And all the ceremony of this compact   160
Seal'd in my function, by my testimony;
Since when, my watch hath told me, toward my grave
I have travell'd but two hours.

Duke. O thou dissembling cub! what wilt thou be
When time hath sow'd a grizzle on thy case?   165
Or will not else thy craft so quickly grow,
That thine own trip shall be thine overthrow?
Farewell, and take her, but direct thy feet
Where thou and I (henceforth) may never meet.   169

Vio. My lord, I do protest—

Oli.   O, do not swear!
Hold little faith, though thou hast too much fear.

Enter SIR ANDREW.

Sir And. For the love of God, a surgeon! Send
one presently to Sir Toby.

Oli. What's the matter?   174

Sir And. H'as broke my head across, and has given
Sir Toby a bloody coxcomb too. For the love of God,
your help! I had rather than forty pound I were at
home.

Oli. Who has done this, Sir Andrew?   179

Sir And. The Count's gentleman, one Cesario.
We took him for a coward, but he's the very devil
incardinate.

Duke. My gentleman, Cesario?

Sir And. 'Od's lifelings, here he is! You broke
my head for nothing, and that that I did, I was set on
to do't by Sir Toby.   186

Vio. Why do you speak to me? I never hurt you.

You drew your sword upon me without cause,
But I bespake you fair, and hurt you not.   189

Enter TOBY *and* CLOWN.

Sir And. If a bloody coxcomb be a hurt, you have
hurt me. I think you set nothing by a bloody coxcomb.
Here comes Sir Toby halting—you shall hear more.
But if he had not been in drink, he would have tickled
you othergates than he did.   194

Duke. How now, gentleman? how is't with you?

Sir To. That's all one. H'as hurt me, and there's
th' end on't. Sot, didst see Dick surgeon, sot?

Clo. O, he's drunk, Sir Toby, an hour agone; his
eyes were set at eight i' th' morning.   199

Sir To. Then he's a rogue, and a passy-measures
[pavin]. I hate a drunken rogue.

Oli. Away with him! Who hath made this havoc
with them?

Sir And. I'll help you, Sir Toby, because we'll be
dress'd together.   205

Sir To. Will you help?—an ass-head and a coxcomb and a knave, a thin-fac'd knave, a gull!

Oli. Get him to bed, and let his hurt be look'd to.
[*Exeunt Clown, Fabian, Sir Toby, and Sir Andrew.*]

Enter SEBASTIAN.

Seb. I am sorry, madam, I have hurt your kinsman,
But had it been the brother of my blood,   210
I must have done no less with wit and safety.
You throw a strange regard upon me, and by that
I do perceive it hath offended you.
Pardon me, sweet one, even for the vows
We made each other but so late ago.   215

Duke. One face, one voice, one habit, and two
                persons,
A natural perspective, that is and is not!

Seb. Antonio, O my dear Antonio!
How have the hours rack'd and tortur'd me,
Since I have lost thee!   220

Ant. Sebastian are you?

Seb.   Fear'st thou that, Antonio?

Ant. How have you made division of yourself?
An apple, cleft in two, is not more twin
Than these two creatures. Which is Sebastian?

Oli. Most wonderful!   225

Seb. Do I stand there? I never had a brother;

147. **strangle thy propriety:** i.e. disown your identity as my husband.
148. **take . . . up:** receive your fortune.
150. **that thou fear'st:** i.e. Orsino. 153. **occasion:** necessity.
155. **newly:** recently. 157. **joinder:** joining. 158. **close:** union.
161. **Seal'd:** ratified, attested. **in my function:** i.e. by my authority as priest.
165. **a grizzle:** grey hair. **case:** skin (of a fox); Orsino is thus calling Viola-Cesario a fox-cub.
167. **trip:** attempt to trip up (or trap) another.
170. **protest:** avow, swear. 171. **Hold little:** keep a little.
173. **presently:** immediately.
175. **H'as . . . across:** he has given me a cut on the head.
176. **coxcomb:** head (with a suggestion of the cap traditionally worn by the professional fool in its applicability to Sir Toby and Sir Andrew).
182. **incardinate.** Apparently Sir Andrew's slip for *incarnate.*
184. **'Od's lifelings:** by God's little lives.

189. **bespake you fair:** spoke courteously to you.
191. **set nothing by:** regard as nothing. 192. **halting:** limping.
193. **But if:** if only. **in drink:** drunk. **tickled:** chastised.
194. **othergates:** otherwise. 196. **That's all one:** no matter.
196–97. **there's . . . on't:** that's that. 197. **Sot:** fool.
199. **set:** extinguished (as in *the sun sets*), i.e. closed.
200–201. **passy-measures pavin.** Naylor explains *passy-measures* (from Italian *passamezzo*) as a dance tune with "strains" consisting of eight bars each (hence suggested to Sir Toby by Feste's "set at eight"). The pavin or pavan(e) was a slow and stately dance. Sir Toby obviously expects no speedy aid from Dick surgeon.
204–5. **be dress'd:** have our wounds cared for.
206–7. **coxcomb:** fool. 207. **gull:** dupe.
211. **with . . . safety:** i.e. with due regard for my own safety.
212. **throw . . . me:** look at me as if I were a stranger.
216. **habit:** dress.
217. **natural perspective:** i.e. an optical illusion produced by nature, not by a perspective glass (an optical device that makes the viewer see an object differently). **that . . . not:** i.e. that must be an illusion and yet is not.

Twelfth Night
V.i

Nor can there be that deity in my nature
Of here and every where. I had a sister,
Whom the blind waves and surges have devour'd.
Of charity, what kin are you to me?   230
What countryman? What name? What parentage?
     Vio. Of Messaline; Sebastian was my father,
Such a Sebastian was my brother too;
So went he suited to his watery tomb.
If spirits can assume both form and suit,   235
You come to fright us.
     Seb.   A spirit I am indeed,
But am in that dimension grossly clad
Which from the womb I did participate.
Were you a woman, as the rest goes even,
I should my tears let fall upon your cheek,   240
And say, "Thrice welcome, drowned Viola!"
     Vio. My father had a mole upon his brow.
     Seb. And so had mine.
     Vio. And died that day when Viola from her birth
Had numb'red thirteen years.   245
     Seb. O, that record is lively in my soul!
He finished indeed his mortal act
That day that made my sister thirteen years.
     Vio. If nothing lets to make us happy both
But this my masculine usurp'd attire,   250
Do not embrace me till each circumstance
Of place, time, fortune, do cohere and jump
That I am Viola—which to confirm,
I'll bring you to a captain in this town,
Where lie my maiden weeds; by whose gentle help
I was preserv'd to serve this noble count.   256
All the occurrence of my fortune since
Hath been between this lady and this lord.
     Seb. [*To Olivia.*] So comes it, lady, you have been
                        mistook;
But Nature to her bias drew in that.   260
You would have been contracted to a maid,
Nor are you therein, by my life, deceiv'd,
You are betroth'd both to a maid and man.
     Duke. Be not amaz'd, right noble is his blood.
If this be so, as yet the glass seems true,   265
I shall have share in this most happy wrack.
[*To Viola.*] Boy, thou hast said to me a thousand times
Thou never shouldst love woman like to me.
     Vio. And all those sayings will I over swear,
And all those swearings keep as true in soul   270
As doth that orbed continent the fire

That severs day from night.
     Duke.   Give me thy hand,
And let me see thee in thy woman's weeds.
     Vio. The captain that did bring me first on shore
Hath my maid's garments. He upon some action 275
Is now in durance, at Malvolio's suit,
A gentleman, and follower of my lady's.
     Oli. He shall enlarge him; fetch Malvolio hither.
And yet, alas, now I remember me,
They say, poor gentleman, he's much distract.   280

Enter CLOWN *with a letter, and* FABIAN.

A most extracting frenzy of mine own
From my remembrance clearly banish'd his.
How does he, sirrah?
     Clo. Truly, madam, he holds Belzebub at the
stave's end as well as a man in his case may do. H'as
here writ a letter to you; I should have given't 286
you to-day morning. But as a madman's epistles are no
gospels, so it skills not much when they are deliver'd.
     Oli. Open't and read it.
     Clo. Look then to be well edified when the fool
delivers the madman. [*Reads madly.*] "By the Lord,
madam"—   292
     Oli. How now, art thou mad?
     Clo. No, madam, I do but read madness. And your
ladyship will have it as it ought to be, you must allow
vox.   296
     Oli. Prithee read i' thy right wits.
     Clo. So I do, madonna; but to read his right wits is
to read thus; therefore perpend, my princess, and give
ear.   300
     Oli. [*To Fabian.*] Read it you, sirrah.
     Fab. (*Reads.*) "By the Lord, madam, you wrong
me, and the world shall know it. Though you have put
me into darkness, and given your drunken cousin rule
over me, yet have I the benefit of my senses as well as
your ladyship. I have your own letter that induc'd me
to the semblance I put on; with the which I doubt 307
not but to do myself much right, or you much shame.
Think of me as you please. I leave my duty a little
unthought of, and speak out of my injury.
                        The madly-us'd Malvolio."
     Oli. Did he write this?   312
     Clo. Ay, madam.
     Duke. This savors not much of distraction.
     Oli. See him deliver'd, Fabian, bring him hither.
                        [*Exit Fabian.*]
My lord, so please you, these things further thought on,

227. **deity:** divine attribute.   228. **here . . . where:** omnipresence.
229. **blind:** ruthless.   230. **Of charity:** (tell me) out of kindness.
234. **suited:** dressed.
237. **in . . . clad:** clothed in that corporeal frame.
238. **participate:** share existence with.
239. **as . . . even:** i.e. as (is likely since) all the rest accords. A common type of ellipsis; for another example see line 265.
246. **lively:** vivid.   249. **lets:** hinders.
252. **cohere:** agree.   **jump:** coincide, agree.
255. **Where:** at whose house.   **weeds:** clothes.
260. **Nature . . . that:** i.e. your nature was true to its own bent when you fell in love with one who is the perfect likeness of me.
261. **contracted:** betrothed.
263. **maid:** virgin (here applied to a man).
264. **amaz'd:** astounded, dazed (a much stronger word than in modern usage).
265. **glass:** i.e. the "natural perspective" of line 217.
269. **over:** again.
271. **As . . . fire:** i.e. as the sun's sphere keeps the fire. *Continent* = container.

275. **action:** legal charge.   276. **durance:** prison.
278. **enlarge:** release.   279. **remember me:** recall.
280. **distract:** distracted, out of his wits.
281. **extracting frenzy:** i.e. madness that took other things out of my mind.   282. **his:** i.e. remembrance of his frenzy.
284–85. **holds . . . end:** keeps the devil (who possesses him) at a distance. "To hold the devil at stave's end" was proverbial.
287–88. **a madman's . . . gospels:** i.e. a madman's letters are not to be taken as gospel truth (with play on the reading of appointed passages from the epistles and the gospels in a church service).
288. **it . . . much:** it doesn't matter much.
291. **delivers:** presents, speaks the words of.
294. **And:** if.   296. **vox:** voice, i.e. dramatic reading.
299. **perpend:** consider.   307. **the which:** i.e. the letter (as proof).
309. **my duty:** the duty I owe you as your servant.
315. **deliver'd:** released.

To think me as well a sister as a wife, 317
One day shall crown th' alliance on't, so please you,
Here at my house and at my proper cost.
 Duke. Madam, I am most apt t' embrace your offer.
[*To Viola.*] Your master quits you; and for your
   service done him, 321
So much against the mettle of your sex,
So far beneath your soft and tender breeding,
And since you call'd me master for so long,
Here is my hand—you shall from this time be 325
Your master's mistress.
 Oli.   A sister! you are she.

    Enter [FABIAN *with*] MALVOLIO.

 Duke. Is this the madman?
 Oli.   Ay, my lord, this same.
How now, Malvolio?
 Mal.   Madam, you have done me wrong,
Notorious wrong.
 Oli.   Have I, Malvolio? No. 329
 Mal. Lady, you have. Pray you peruse that letter.
You must not now deny it is your hand;
Write from it if you can, in hand or phrase,
Or say 'tis not your seal, not your invention.
You can say none of this. Well, grant it then,
And tell me, in the modesty of honor, 335
Why you have given me such clear lights of favor,
Bade me come smiling and cross-garter'd to you,
To put on yellow stockings, and to frown
Upon Sir Toby and the lighter people;
And acting this in an obedient hope, 340
Why have you suffer'd me to be imprison'd,
Kept in a dark house, visited by the priest,
And made the most notorious geck and gull
That e'er invention play'd on? Tell me why!
 Oli. Alas, Malvolio, this is not my writing, 345
Though I confess much like the character;
But out of question 'tis Maria's hand.
And now I do bethink me, it was she
First told me thou wast mad. Then cam'st in smiling,
And in such forms which here were presuppos'd 350
Upon thee in the letter. Prithee be content.
This practice hath most shrewdly pass'd upon thee;
But when we know the grounds and authors of it,
Thou shalt be both the plaintiff and the judge
Of thine own cause.
 Fab.   Good madam, hear me speak,
And let no quarrel nor no brawl to come 356
Taint the condition of this present hour,
Which I have wond'red at. In hope it shall not,

Most freely I confess, myself and Toby
Set this device against Malvolio here, 360
Upon some stubborn and uncourteous parts
We had conceiv'd against him. Maria writ
The letter at Sir Toby's great importance,
In recompense whereof he hath married her.
How with a sportful malice it was follow'd 365
May rather pluck on laughter than revenge,
If that the injuries be justly weigh'd
That have on both sides pass'd.
 Oli. Alas, poor fool, how have they baffled thee!
 Clo. Why, "some are born great, some achieve
greatness, and some have greatness thrown upon
them." I was one, sir, in this enterlude—one Sir Topas,
sir, but that's all one. "By the Lord, fool, I am 373
not mad." But do you remember? "Madam, why
laugh you at such a barren rascal? And you smile not,
he's gagg'd." And thus the whirligig of time brings in
his revenges.
 Mal. I'll be reveng'd on the whole pack of you.
           [*Exit.*]
 Oli. He hath been most notoriously abus'd. 379
 Duke. Pursue him, and entreat him to a peace;
He hath not told us of the captain yet.
When that is known, and golden time convents,
A solemn combination shall be made
Of our dear souls. Mean time, sweet sister,
We will not part from hence. Cesario, come— 385
For so you shall be while you are a man;
But when in other habits you are seen,
Orsino's mistress, and his fancy's queen.
       Exeunt [*all but Clown*].

     Clown sings.

When that I was and a little tine boy,
 With hey ho, the wind and the rain, 390
A foolish thing was but a toy,
 For the rain it raineth every day.

But when I came to man's estate,
 With hey ho, etc.
'Gainst knaves and thieves men shut
  their gate, 395
 For the rain, etc.

But when I came, alas, to wive,
 With hey ho, etc.
By swaggering could I never thrive,
 For the rain, etc. 400

---

317. **think ... wife:** regard me as favorably as a sister-in-law as you would have as a wife.
318. **crown ... on't:** i.e. see the performance of the two weddings that will create that relationship. 319. **proper cost:** own expense.
320. **apt:** ready. 321. **quits:** frees, withdraws all claim to.
322. **mettle:** disposition.
332. **from it:** differently. **hand or phrase:** handwriting or phraseology. 333. **invention:** composition.
335. **in ... honor:** with the sense of propriety of an honorable person. 336. **clear lights:** i.e. sure signs.
339. **lighter:** lesser. 343. **geck:** fool.
344. **invention:** devising. 347. **out of:** beyond.
349. **cam'st:** cam'st thou.
350. **which:** as. **presuppos'd:** suggested beforehand.
352. **shrewdly:** grievously. **pass'd upon:** imposed upon.
358. **wond'red:** marvelled.

361. **Upon:** (which) in consequence of. **stubborn:** rude, haughty. **parts:** acts. 362. **conceiv'd:** devised.
363. **importance:** importunity.
365. **sportful:** jesting. **follow'd:** carried through.
366. **pluck on:** draw on, induce.
369. **baffled thee:** put you down.
372. **enterlude:** interlude, i.e. comedy.
376. **whirligig of time:** i.e. time's circling course. A whirligig is a spinning top or toy.
379. **He ... abus'd.** Olivia thus repeats Malvolio's own judgment at IV.ii.87–88. 381. **captain.** See lines 253–56, 274–77.
382. **convents:** suits. 383. **combination:** marriage.
389. **tine:** tiny. Cf. with lines 389 ff. the song in *King Lear*, III.ii.74–77, in which the variant spelling *tine* again appears.
391. **A ... toy:** i.e. my mischief was not taken seriously.
395. **'Gainst ... gate:** i.e. my mischief caused men to shut their doors against me as a knave and a thief.
399. **swaggering:** bullying, blustering.

Twelfth Night
V.i

But when I came unto my beds,
    With hey ho, etc.
With toss-pots still had drunken heads,
    For the rain, etc.

A great while ago the world begun,   405
    [With] hey ho, etc.
But that's all one, our play is done,
    And we'll strive to please you every day.
                        [*Exit.*]

401. **unto my beds**: to old age (?)   403. **toss-pots**: drunkards.

NOTE ON THE TEXT

The First Folio (1623) is our only authority for *Twelfth Night*; all later texts are derived from that source. The copy-text for F1 seems to have been either a prompt-book or a transcript of a prompt-book, although the evidence of theatre provenience is comparatively slight. There is no reason to suppose that the prompt-book was in Shakespeare's autograph.

The F1 text is unusually clean and presents few significant problems to the editor. The play is carefully divided into acts and scenes, though the cleared stage at III.iv.272 suggests the possibility that a new scene should have been marked at that point. The present text, however, adheres to the F1 division. The mildness of the profanity in such a role as Sir Toby's is probably the result of a book-keeper's attempt to meet the provisions of the anti-profanity act of 1606.

For further information, see W. W. Greg, *The Shakespeare First Folio* (Oxford, 1955).

TEXTUAL NOTES

Title: **Twelfth**] Twelfe *F1*
Dramatis personae: *subs. as first given in Douai MS and Rowe*
Act-scene division: *from F1*

I.i

Location: *Rowe (subs.)*
o.s.d. **Musicians attending**] *Malone (after Rowe)*
10-1 **capacity . . . sea,**] *Rowe*; capacitie, . . . Sea. *F1*
22 s.d. **Enter Valentine.**] *placed as in Dyce; after l. 22, F1*
38 **self**] selfe same *F2*

I.ii

Location: *Capell*
15 **Arion**] *Pope*; Orion *F1*
23 **travel**] *F3*; trauaile *F1*
40-1 **company And sight**] *Hanmer*; sight / And company *F1*

I.iii

Location: *Rowe*
7 **except**] *Hanmer*; except, *F1*
17 **wooer.**] *F2*; woer *F1*
43 s.d. **Aguecheek**] *Malone*
52 s.p. **Sir And.**] *F2 (An.)*; Ma. *F1*
52 **Accost**] *Rowe*; accost *F1*
55 **Mary Accost**] *Rowe*; Mary, accost *F1*
57 **woo**] *F2 (wooe)*; woe *F1 (frequently)*
90, 91 **Pourquoi**] *Rowe (subs.)*; Pur-quoy and purquoy *F1*
99 **curl by**] *Theobald*; coole my *F1*
100 **me**] *F2*; we *F1*
100 **does't**] *Rowe*; dost *F1*
107 **Count**] *F2*; Connt *F1*
115 **kickshawses**] *F3*; kicke-chawses *F1*
129 **coranto**] *Rowe*; Carranto *F1*
131 **dost**] *F3*; dooest *F1*
135 **dun-color'd**] *Collier MS*; dam'd colour'd *F1*
135 **set**] *Rowe*; sit *F1*
139 **That's**] *F3*; That *F1*

I.iv

Location: *Rowe (subs.)*

I.v

Location: *Rowe*
9 **lenten**] *Douai MS, Rowe*; lenton *F1*
17 **away—**] *Dyce*; away: *F1*
31 s.d. **Exit.**] *Pope*

31 s.d. **and Attendants**] *Staunton (after Capell)*
88 **wise men**] *F3*; Wisemen *F1*
92 **guiltless**] *F3*; guiltlesse *F1*
107 s.d. **Exit Maria.**] *Capell*
114 **for— . . . comes—**] *Cambridge*; for . . . comes. *F1*
120 **here—**] *Steevens*; heere. *F1*
131 **madman**] *Rowe*; madde man *F1*
138 s.d. **Exit.**] *Rowe*
147 **H'as**] *Staunton*; Ha's *F1*
166 s.d. **Viola.**] *F2*; Violenta *F1*
166 **beauty—**] *Rowe*; beau- / tie. *F1*
184 **fangs**] *Rowe*; phangs *F1*
210 **olive**] *Rowe*; Olyffe *F1*
219 s.d. **Exeunt . . . Attendants.**] *Capell*
234-5 s.d. **Unveiling.**] *Rowe*
245 **schedules**] *Rowe*; scedules *F1*
257 **him,**] *F3*; him *F1*
301 **County's**] *Capell*; Countes *F1*
311 s.d. **Exit.**] *Rowe*; Finis, Actus primus. *F1*

II.i

Location: *Capell*

II.ii

Location: *Capell*
3 **sir,**] *Rowe*; sir, *F1*
20 **That**] That sure *F2*
25 **man! If**] *Rowe (subs.)*; man, if *F1*
29 **proper-false**] *hyphen, Malone*
31 **our**] *F2*; O *F1*
32 **made of,**] *Thirlby conj.*; made, if *F1*
41 s.d. **Exit.**] *Rowe*

II.iii

Location: *Rowe*
1 **a-bed**] *hyphen, Rowe*
3 **know'st**] *Theobald*; know'st. *F1*
17 **"we three"**] *quotes, Cambridge*
22 **In sooth**] *Theobald*; Insooth *F1*
25, 31 **sixpence**] *Theobald (subs.)*; sixe pence *F1*
25 **leman**] *Theobald*; Lemon *F1*
34 **give a—**] *F2*; giue a *F1*
40 **true-love's**] *Rowe (hyphen, Capell)*; true loues *F1*
46 s.d. **sings**] *Cambridge*
65 **knight?**] *Capell*; knight. *F1*
76 s.d. **sings**] *Wilson*
78 **Tilly-vally!**] *Capell*; tilly vally. *F1*
78 **Lady!**] *F2*; Ladie, *F1*
78, 84 s.d. **Sings.**] *Rowe*
84 **O'**] *W. S. Walker conj.*; O *F1*
102, 104, 106 s.dd. **Sings.**] *Hanmer*

102, 104, 106] *Quotes, Theobald*
109, 110, 111, 112 s.dd. **Sings.**] *Rowe*
113 s.d. **To Clown.**] *Collier conj.*
114 s.d. **To Malvolio.**] *Collier conj.*
143 **What,**] *Rowe*; What *F1*
151 **grounds**] ground *F2*
179 **true-bred**] *hyphen, Theobald*

II.iv

Location: *Rowe (subs.)*
3 **antique**] *Pope*; Anticke *F1*
14 s.d. **Exit Curio.**] *Pope*
22 **masterly.**] *Rowe*; masterly, *F1*
50 **Ay, prithee**] *Warburton (subs.)*; I prethee *F1*
51 s.p. **Clo.**] *Capell*
53 **Fly away, fly**] *Rowe*; Fye away, fie *F1*
60 **strown**] *Rowe*; strewne *F1*
79 s.d. **Curio . . . retire.**] *Cambridge*
82-3 **lands; . . . her,**] *Pope (her, F2)*; lands, . . . her: *F1*
88 **I**] *Hanmer*; It *F1*
96 **much;**] *Rowe*; much, *F1*

II.v

Location: *Pope*
14 **metal**] *Malone*; Mettle *F1*; Nettle *F2*
20 **Close,**] *Rowe*; Close *F1*
20-1 **jesting! Lie**] *Theobald*; ieasting, lye *F1*
20-1 s.d. **The . . . themselves.**] *Capell*
21 s.d. **Throws . . . letter.**] *Theobald*
53 **travel**] *F4*; trauaile *F1*
60 **my—**] *Collier*; my *F1*
82 s.d. **Taking . . . letter.**] *Rowe*
87, 89 **c's . . . u's . . . t's**] *Wilson*; C's . . . V's . . . T's *F1 (the italic capital V is ambiguous and could stand for either U or V; F3 first gives a capital U)*
90, 96, 103, 143 s.dd. **Reads.**] *Capell*
96-9 **"Jove . . . know."**] *as verse, Capell (after Hanmer); as prose, F1*
98 **Lips,**] *Capell MS*; Lips *F1*
105 **knife,**] *F2*; knife: *F1*
113 **staniel**] *Hanmer*; stallion *F1*
119-20 **portend? . . . me!**] *Capell (after Rowe)*; portend, . . . me ? *F1*
121 **O ay**] *Rowe (subs.)*; O I *F1*
139 **M. O. A. I.**] *F2*; M, O, A, I. *F1*
143-59 **In . . . Fortunate-Unhappy."**] *as part of the letter, Capell (after F3, Hanmer); not distinguished by italics as part of the letter, F1*
145 **born**] *Douai MS, Rowe*; become *F1*
145 **achieve**] *F2*; atcheeues *F1*

148 **be,]** *Rowe;* be: *F1*
155 **remember.]** *Rowe (subs.);* remember, *F1*
159–60 **The . . . Daylight]** *Capell (after Hanmer);* tht [the *F2*] fortunate vnhappy daylight *F1*
161 **politic]** *F2;* pollticke *F1*
163 **point-devise]** hyphen, *Capell*
174 s.d. **Reads.]** *Collier*
177 **dear]** *F2;* deero *F1 (Daniel conj. dear, O)*
196 **aqua-vitae]** *F2;* Aqua vite *F1*
207 s.d. **Exeunt.]** Exeunt / Finis Actus secundus *F1*

III.i

Location: Pope
o.s.d. **with a tabor]** *Malone*
8 **king]** *F2;* King s *F1*
47 s.d. **aside]** *Cambridge*
66 **wise man's]** *Hanmer;* Wise-mans *F1*
68 **wise men, folly-fall'n]** *Capell (after Theobald conj.);* wisemens folly falne *F1*
71 **vous]** *Rowe;* vou *F1*
72 **aussi]** *Theobald (after Rowe);* ousie *F1*
72 **votre]** *Johnson;* vostre *F1*
82 **gait]** *Johnson (subs.);* gate *F1*
91 **all ready]** *Malone;* already *F1*
93 s.d. **Exeunt . . . Viola.]** *Rowe (subs.)*
99 **compliment]** *Pope;* complement *F1*
112 **here]** *Thirlby conj.;* heare *F1*
142 **were]** *Pope;* were, *F1*
145 s.d. **Aside.]** *Staunton (after Capell)*
145–6 **beautiful . . . lip!]** *Rowe (subs.);* beautifull? . . . lip, *F1*

III.ii

Location: Rowe
8 **thee]** *F3*
16 **grand-jurymen]** *Dyce;* grand Iurie men *F1*
57 **deliver't?]** *Dyce;* deliuer't. *F1*
66 **nine]** *Theobald;* mine *F1*
70 **renegado]** *Rowe;* Renegatho *F1*

III.iii

Location: Rowe
o.s.d. **Antonio]** *Hanmer;* Anthonio *F1 (throughout scene)*
8 **travel]** *F2;* rrauell *F1*
15–6 **And . . . pay;]** *om. F2–4*

III.iv

Location: Capell
1 s.d. **Aside.]** *Neilson*
8–9 **He's . . . madam.]** *as prose, Pope; as verse, F1*
15 **merry]** *F3;* metry *F1;* mercy *F2*
20–5 **Sad . . . thee?]** *as prose, Pope; as verse, F1*
20 **Sad, lady?]** *Theobald;* Sad Lady, *F1*
24 s.p. **Oli.]** *F2;* Mal. *F1*
24 **dost]** *F3 (do'st);* doest *F1*
55 **let]** *F2;* ler *F1*

60 s.d. **Exit Servant.]** *Capell*
63 s.d. **with Maria]** *Capell (subs.)*
70 **tang]** *F2;* langer *F1*
88 s.p. **Sir To.]** *anon. conj. (in Cambridge); line continued to Fabian, F1*
137 **thus,]** *Capell;* thus *F1*
147, 150, etc. s.dd. **Reads.]** *Rowe*
158 **sense—less]** *Dyce;* sence-lesse *F1*
171 **If]** *Hanmer; To.* If *F1 (repeated s.p.)*
173 **You]** *F2;* Yon *F1*
173 **fit]** *F2;* sit *F1*
200 s.d. **Exeunt . . . Maria.]** *Capell*
217 s.d. **Exit.]** *F2*
220 **thee]** *F2;* the *F1*
237 **brawl]** *F3;* brall *F1*
247 **competent]** *F4;* computent *F1*
281–2 **Ay . . . yonder.]** *as prose, Capell; as verse, F1*
290 s.d. **Aside.]** *Theobald*
292 s.d. **To Fabian.]** *Douai MS, Rowe*
296 s.d. **To Viola.]** *Douai MS, Capell*
302 s.d. **Aside.]** *Capell*
311 s.d. **They draw.]** *Rowe*
318 s.d. **They draw.]** *Cambridge*
320 s.d. **To Antonio.]** *Capell*
326 **Antonio]** *Rowe;* Anthonio *F1*
332 s.d. **To Viola.]** *Collier*
334–5 **do, . . . purse?]** *Dyce;* do: . . . purse. *F1*
355 **babbling,]** *Steevens;* babling *F1*
372 s.d. **with Officers]** *Theobald*
375 **prove true]** *F2;* proue ttue *F1*
384 s.d. **Exit.]** *F2*
394 s.d. **Exit.]** *Theobald*
396 s.d. **Exeunt.]** *Rowe;* Exit *F1*

IV.i

Location: Capell (subs.)
10–1 **I . . . me.]** *as verse, Capell; as prose, F1*
17–20 **I . . . payment.]** *as verse, Capell; as prose, F1*
22 **wise men]** *Rowe;* Wise- / men *F1*
25 s.d. **Strikes Sebastian.]** *Douai MS, Rowe*
27 s.d. **Strikes Sir Andrew.]** *Douai MS, Rowe*
27 s.d. **Draws his dagger.]** *ed. (after Collier)*
29 s.d. **Seizes Sebastian's arm.]** *ed. (after Rowe, following l. 32); placed as in Wilson*
31 s.d. **Exit.]** *Rowe*
35 **strook]** *F3;* stroke *F1*
41 s.d. **Breaks . . . sword.]** *ed. (after Capell, Collier MS)*
44 s.d. **Draws.]** *Steevens (after Rowe)*
51 s.d. **Exeunt . . . Fabian.]** *Capell (after Rowe)*

IV.ii

Location: Rowe
3 s.d. **Exit.]** *Theobald*
6 **in such]** *F2; F1 accidentally repeats* in *before* such

10 s.d. **and Maria]** *Theobald*
14 **Gorboduc]** *Pope;* Gorbodacke *F1*
20 s.p., s.d. **Mal. (Within.)]** *F1 gives separate s.d.* Maluolio within. *and then s.p.*
37 **clerestories]** *Blakeway conj. (in Boswell);* cleere stores *F1;* cleare stones *F2*
60 **soul]** house *F1*
71 **t' the]** *ed.;* the *F1*
71 s.d. **with Maria]** *Theobald*
71, 119 s.dd. **Sings.]** *Rowe*
119 **gone]** *F2;* goue *F1*
131 **goodman]** *Capell;* good man *F1*

IV.iii

Location: Capell
1 s.p. **Seb.]** *F2*
4 **Antonio]** *Hanmer;* Anthonio *F1*
35 s.d. **Exeunt.]** Exeunt. / Finis Actus Quartus. *F1*

V.i

Location: Capell
10 **dost]** *F3 (do'st);* doest *F1*
49 s.d. **Antonio]** *Rowe;* Anthonio *F1 (throughout scene)*
104 **Madam—]** *ed.;* Madam; *F1*
118 **thief . . . death,]** *Collier;* theefe, . . . death *F1*
123 **favor,]** *Capell;* fauour: *F1*
139 **me,]** *Rowe;* me *F1*
154 **ripe,]** *Cambridge (after Pope);* ripe: *F1*
182 **incardinate]** *F2;* incardinatc *F1*
194 **othergates]** *Capell;* other gates *F1*
196 **H'as]** *Rowe;* has *F1*
200–1 **passy-measures pavin]** *Malone;* passy measures panyn *F1*
206 **help?—]** *Malone;* helpe *F1*
208 s.d. **Exeunt . . . Andrew.]** *Dyce*
244 **died]** *F2 (di'd);* dide *F1*
250 **attire,]** *Capell;* attyre: *F1*
259 s.d. **To Olivia.]** *Rowe*
267 s.d. **To Viola.]** *Rowe*
271 **continent the fire]** *Rowe;* Continent, the fire, *F1*
285 **H'as]** *Rowe;* has *F1*
291 s.d. **Reads madly.]** *Alexander*
301 s.d. **To Fabian.]** *Rowe*
311 **madly-us'd]** hyphen, *Steevens*
315 s.d. **Exit Fabian.]** *Capell*
321 s.d. **To Viola.]** *Rowe*
324 **long,]** *Pope;* long: *F1*
326 **sister!]** *Dyce;* sister, *F1*
326 s.d. **Fabian with]** *Capell*
359 **confess, myself]** *Theobald;* confesse my selfe, *F1*
373 **Lord, fool]** *Rowe;* Lotd Foole *F1 (Lord F2)*
378 s.d. **Exit.]** *Rowe*
388 s.d. **all but Clown]** *Dyce (subs.)*
405 **begun]** *Rowe;* begon *F1*
406 **With]** *F2*
408 s.d. **Exit.]** *Rowe;* FINIS. *F1*

A three-part song. From Robert Jones, *The First Book of Songs and Airs* (1600). This is a three-part (tenor, alto, bass) setting of the first stanza of an old song called "Corydon's Farewell to Phyllis." Sir Toby and Feste alternately sing snatches of the first two stanzas in *Twelfth Night* (II.iii.102–12). Whether they used the present melody (published shortly before the play was first performed) cannot be determined. (*The Folger Shakespeare Library*)

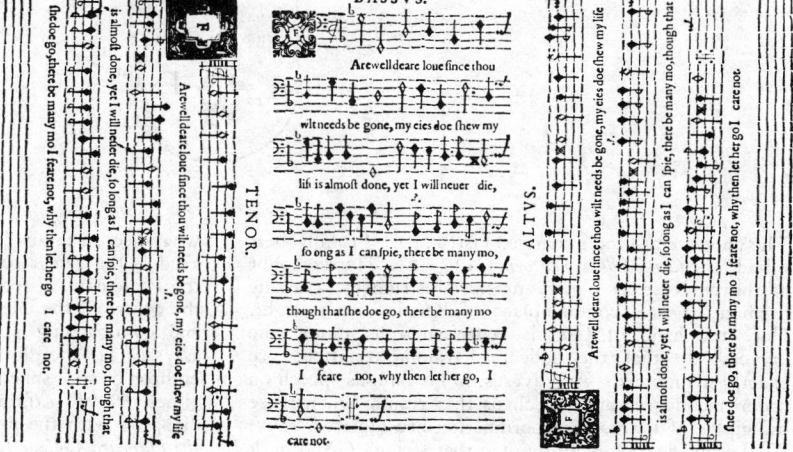

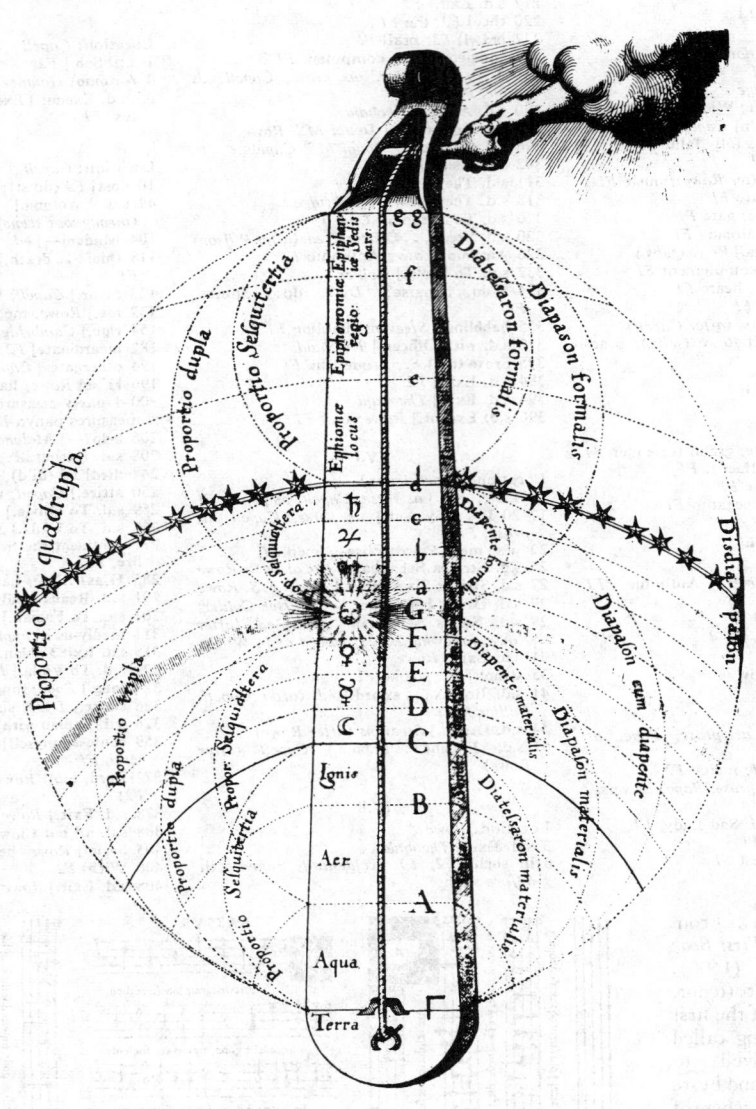

The universe as God's stringed instrument. From Robert Fludd, *Utriusque Cosmi Historia* (1617–19). The metaphor of the universe as a giant musical instrument, a divine harmony, was a commonplace of Renaissance thought. Here the hand of God is represented as tuning the universe so that the delicate harmonic relations are exactly maintained. As Ulysses, in his famous speech on order and degree and the chaos that results when these principles of harmonic subordination are violated, says: "Take but degree away, untune that string, / And hark what discord follows" (*Troilus and Cressida*, I.iii.109–10). Fludd's diagram also illustrates the principal outlines of the Ptolemaic system (see Plate 10), with the Earth as the centre of the universe. Note particularly the central and commanding position of the Sun, referred to by Ulysses as "the glorious planet Sol / In noble eminence enthron'd and spher'd / Amidst the other [planets]" (lines 89–91), through which it links the heavenly diapason with the material diapason. (*By permission of the Harvard College Library*)

442

Troilus and Cressida

MORE THAN ANY OTHER PLAY by Shake-speare, *Troilus and Cressida* is the discovery of the twentieth century. Its unconventional form, neither comedy, tragedy, history, nor satire, its intellectualism, savagery, and disillusion speak forcefully to contemporary audiences naturally sceptical about ideas of honor, nobility, and military glory. There is no record of any performance of this play before 1898. Since the Second World War it has scarcely left the stage, despite the large cast required for its performance and the considerable technical problems involved. Critics continue to disagree about the tone and meaning of *Troilus and Cressida*. The modern theatre has decided firmly, and surely rightly, that the play is a brilliant but scarifying vision of a world in pieces, all value and coherence gone. Despite its energy and wit, the picture of man which it presents is pessimistic almost to the point of nihilism.

On the evidence of the Stationers' Register, *Troilus and Cressida* was in existence by February 1603, although it may have been written a year or two earlier. The 1603 entry grants permission to James Roberts to print, "when he hath gotten sufficient aucthority for yt, The booke of Troilus and Cresseda, as yt is acted by my lord Chamberlens Men." Perhaps this authority (probably the permission of Shakespeare and his fellow shareholders at the Globe) was not forthcoming or perhaps the entry was a blocking entry; in any case the play did not appear in print until 1609, in a quarto edition published not by Roberts but by two partners named Richard Bonian and Henry Walley. Although they duly registered their manuscript (on January 28, 1609), they almost certainly had no legal title to it, a fact which they tried to brazen out

in a preface congratulating prospective readers on their good fortune in gaining access to a work which "by the grand possessors' wills" would never have escaped.

The 1609 quarto is mysterious in ways that go beyond the problem of how Bonian and Walley secured the forbidden text. When printing began, a title-page was provided which described *Troilus and Cressida* as a play "acted by the King's Majesty's servants at the Globe." This claim accords with the specific mention of professional performances in the 1603 Stationers' Register entry. During the course of printing, however, a decision was made to replace this title-page by another, in which the reference to actors and theatre was suppressed. Moreover, following this second title-page an address to the reader was inserted which hailed *Troilus and Cressida* as "a new play, never stal'd with the stage, never clapper-claw'd with the palms of the vulgar" and urged the reader not to "like this the less for not being sullied with the smoky breath of the multitude."[1]

No satisfactory explanation of this contradiction has yet been given, although a number of hypotheses have been advanced. Were Bonian and Walley simply correcting an initial error? If so, Roberts had made the same mistake in 1603. In any case, why should a hard-working man of the theatre like Shakespeare compose a full-length drama not intended for the stage which he also declined to release for publication? It has been suggested that the play was intended for the Globe, put into rehearsal, and then withdrawn before the first performance because it proved too difficult; alternatively, that it was written for a single private

---

[1] For the entire address, as well as the wording of both title-pages, see the Textual Notes.

performance either at Whitehall or for the lawyers at one of the Inns of Court and was considered unsuitable for the general public. Neither theory seems convincing in the light of Shakespeare's artistic practicality, his canny sense of what a given company of actors could manage, and also his ability to please the most diverse tastes with the same play.

Nevill Coghill has argued that *Troilus and Cressida* was originally acted at the Globe but that for a later, Inns of Court performance Shakespeare added a mocking, cynical prologue and epilogue designed to protect his work against possible sneers from a more sophisticated, critical audience accustomed to the metaphysical urbanities of Donne's *Songs and Sonnets*. According to Coghill, the publishers were appealing directly to this audience when they devised their preface and second title-page. They pretended that the addition of a prologue and epilogue made *Troilus and Cressida* a new play and one that was the particular property of the lawyers. As it happens there is textual evidence in the First Folio version to suggest that originally Pandarus made his final exit in V.iii and that his re-entry to speak the epilogue was an afterthought. The prologue, on the other hand, was printed for the first time in the Folio; it does not appear in the 1609 quarto at all. Elizabethan publishers were no paragons of truth-telling. All the same, it seems hard to believe that Bonian and Walley would have gone to the trouble and expense of cancelling their title-page after printing had begun in order to announce, purely on the basis of a prologue which they were not even offering their readers and a brief epilogue which they were, that this was a fashionable new play substantially different from the one seen at the Globe.

Although Coghill's argument is ultimately unsatisfactory, it is interesting as an example of the lengths to which some critics have gone in the attempt to demonstrate that *Troilus and Cressida*, looked at properly, is really a straightforward tragedy and not a "problem play" at all. Coghill contends that once stripped of its sardonic and "misleading" prologue and epilogue, *Troilus and Cressida* becomes the play seen at the Globe: a drama about good but doomed Trojans suffering at the hands of nasty but victorious Greeks. Like G. Wilson Knight, he believes in the Trojans as heroes, the keepers of important human values tragically destroyed by an adverse fate. It is difficult to see how a mere prologue and epilogue could distort the whole character of a play, especially a play as clear and unequivocal in its sympathies as Coghill believes this one to be. The truth is that the prologue, with its abrupt shifts of tone and style, its dizzying blend of celebration and mockery, the grandiloquent and the deliberately off-hand, is a microcosm of the play it serves to introduce: a finely judged preparation for the mixed and unclassifiable experience to come. Pandarus' epilogue, by contrast, is monolithic and brutal. But it too has a structural relevance. Calculatedly shocking though it is, a theatrically brilliant last twist of the knife, it can nonetheless stand as a logical conclusion requiring no external excuse: the final step in that inexorable

coarsening of action and characters evident throughout Act V. Dryden appraised the situation here more justly than Coghill and other modern critics of his persuasion. When, in 1679, Dryden set himself to convince an audience that *Troilus and Cressida* was an unmistakable tragedy, a dignified lament for Troy, he did more than merely jettison Shakespeare's prologue and epilogue. He rewrote the whole play.

The seventeenth-century editors of *Troilus and Cressida* are of small help in establishing its genre. Both the first and the corrected title-page of the 1609 quarto describe it as a "history." The preface, on the other hand, insists vigorously that it is "passing full of the palm comical; for it is a birth of . . . [that] brain that never undertook anything comical vainly." The First Folio editors, just to make the confusion complete, designed for it a place in the midst of the tragedy section, transferring it to a makeshift position between the Histories and the Tragedies only as the result of some undetermined emergency while the book was going through the press. *Troilus and Cressida* is by no means the only play of its period to be classified in a random and contradictory fashion. For Shakespeare and his contemporaries, the terms *comedy*, *history*, and *tragedy* were vaguer and less precise than they became for Dryden. All the same, one can see why this particular play invited difference of opinion. Certainly the fence-sitting position it occupies in the First Folio, although apparently the result of practical rather than esthetic uncertainties, proved to be prophetic.

To the three categories proposed by the original editors the twentieth century has added a fourth: satire. O. J. Campbell has made out a case for *Troilus and Cressida* as a play deriving from the temporary vogue for satire so marked in the last years of Elizabeth's reign. He accepts the idea of performance at one of the Inns of Court and proceeds to develop from this premise a series of parallels associating Shakespeare's play with the non-dramatic satires of writers like Marston, and with the early humor comedies of Ben Jonson. There are, undoubtedly, satiric elements in *Troilus and Cressida* (although the notion that Achilles is a malicious portrait of Elizabeth's truant favorite, the Earl of Essex, is firmly to be discounted). Yet the end of the play scarcely "leaves the audience suffused with cynical amusement" in the way Campbell suggests. Tragic pity and fear may manifest themselves only fitfully in *Troilus and Cressida*, but they are present all the same. The death of Hector is as horrifying as anything Shakespeare ever wrote, the final appearance of Cassandra has the spine-chilling quality of high tragedy, and even the young lovers of the title—flawed though they are—make undeniable emotional demands upon an audience. It is simply not possible to watch this play with unbroken intellectual detachment.

Campbell's idea that *Troilus and Cressida* belongs to the same breed as Jonson's *Every Man Out of His Humor* and *Cynthia's Revels*, that it is a work dedicated to the service of moral education, ridiculing Trojan sensuality and Greek individualism, has the merit of seeing that Shakespeare did not side with Priam and his sons. On the other hand, the comparison with Jonson only points up the absence in Shakespeare's play of any spokesman-character like Jonson's Asper, Crites, or Horace: conservative and well-balanced men of righteousness and moral sense who guide the just judgment of the theatre audience at the same time that they ridicule and correct the aberrant humors of the comedy. The fact that no one character or group of characters in *Troilus and Cressida* can be regarded as being either morally or structurally central is one of the problems of the play. Here, critics like L. C. Knights, A. P. Rossiter, Una Ellis-Fermor, and W. R. Elton would seem to be more accurate when they point to the stubborn relativism of the work, its presentation of a society in which fixed or objective values no longer operate. Elizabethan orthodoxies may be mouthed from time to time by the characters. Ulysses' speech on degree in I.iii has long been regarded as the cornerstone of the "Elizabethan world-picture," evidence of Shakespeare's fundamental conservatism. Looked at in context, however, this speech reveals itself as an adroit stringing together of pious platitudes: a piece of rhetoric which is applauded by all but to which no one, least of all Ulysses himself, pays the smallest practical attention. The abortive scheme to stir Achilles into action by making him jealous of Ajax is, in fact, a further violation of "degree, priority, and place." It derives from a disabused pragmatism of the kind advocated by Thomas Hobbes. As Elton has said, absolutes of good or evil are grotesquely out of place in this world. People and things, no matter how elevated they may sound, all come to the marketplace to be weighed and priced according to a fluctuating standard dependent upon laws of supply and demand, and the condition of the market at a given moment of time.

Neither tragedy nor satire, celebration nor parody, *Troilus and Cressida* is innovatory and experimental, yet assured. Its intellectualism does not diminish its emotional force. In the theatre it demands a dazzling variety of response from its audience, a combination of detachment and involvement, sympathy and criticism, more exacting than is usual with Shakespeare. In part the complexity which characterizes the play springs from its subject matter and from the ironies generated by the audience's detailed foreknowledge of the destiny reserved for each character. The myth of Troy was already vast and susceptible of widely divergent interpretation in the Athens of Euripides. Shakespeare received it further augmented by all the commentary and literary reworkings of the Middle Ages and early Renaissance. In writing his own play he almost certainly drew upon Chaucer's *Troilus and Criseyde* for the love story, although his own approach to the three principals was far less indulgent than Chaucer's. Probably he also knew Henryson's *Testament of Cresseid*, a fifteenth-century Scottish poem which deals movingly with the fortunes of Cressida after she has been abandoned by Diomed. For the Trojan war and its heroes he was in part dependent upon translations of Homer. The first installment of Chapman's had appeared in 1598, and there was also available Arthur Hall's translation of ten books. Virgil's *Aeneid* and the material scattered through Ovid's *Metamorphoses* which deals with Troy must also have been in his mind. But he drew upon medieval as well as classical sources, primarily upon Caxton's compendium translated from the French, the *Recuyell of the Histories of Troy*, with some consultation also of Lydgate's moralizing version of the war in his *Troy Book*. There is evidence of the existence of several earlier Elizabethan plays dealing with the story of Troilus and Cressida, but all have been lost, so that there is no way of telling what influence (if any) they exerted on Shakespeare when he came to construct his own account.

More speculative, but tantalizing, is the possible influence of Euripides. In play after play Euripides took up the matter of Troy. Elizabethans knew many of these plays, in translations and adapted versions. If Shakespeare himself ever encountered the *Orestes* he would have found there an attitude towards the myth strikingly like his own. For Euripides too, the Trojan war was an expense of spirit in a waste of shame. His Helen is a vain and light-minded flirt, manifestly not worth a fraction of the trouble she has caused, and the other "heroes" are similarly debased. Everywhere, Euripides measures the epic grandeur of the story against the unlovely reality of these events and people when seen up close. Like Shakespeare's, his play is brilliant and savage, without any clear-cut moral or structural centre. It is also mixed in form, a combination of tragedy, comedy, and satire so extreme that until recently it was as much an embarrassment to the classicists as *Troilus and Cressida* was to the Shakespeareans of the eighteenth and nineteenth centuries.

Among Shakespeare's own plays, *Hamlet* seems closely associated with *Troilus and Cressida*. Although these two plays, written about the same time, are radically different in tone and structure, they share a predilection for images of disease and physical corruption. They are also alike in exploring the hiatus between a character's words and actions, between the verbal formulation of intent and subsequent behavior. Oaths and vows are essentially an attempt to order and dictate the future by linguistic means. In *Troilus and Cressida* they exist only to be broken. Because Shakespeare does not let us forget for an instant how this story will end, the verbal contract entered into by Troilus, Pandarus, and Cressida in III.ii becomes positively hideous in its irony. Achilles, too, vows to Queen Hecuba and Polyxena that he will not go out to battle on the day which follows the single combat between Ajax and Hector. When Patroclus is killed, Achilles sweeps aside his oath. Even Thersites takes pains to remind us of the bitter end of Diomedes' pact with Cressida when he describes Diomedes as one who "will spend his mouth and promise like Brabbler the hound, but when he performs, astronomers foretell it: . . . the sun borrows of the moon when Diomed keeps his word" (V.i.90–94).

This derisory treatment of promises simply concentrates the general idea, even more widespread in this play than it is in *Hamlet*, of the irrelevance of

445

words to deeds. Ulysses may analyze the malaise which distempers all the Greek host in traditional and lofty terms; he tries to correct it through a sordid, Machiavellian stratagem which Nestor can describe in terms of two mastiffs snarling over a bone. Hector, in the Trojan council scene, demonstrates irrefutably that Helen "is not worth what she doth cost the keeping," then ignores his own reasoning and votes to continue the war. Cressida tells Troilus that she will be "a woeful Cressid 'mongst the merry Greeks," but begins to play the coquette the moment she sets foot in the Greek camp. There is a sense in which Troilus' contemptuous dismissal of Cressida's letter as "Words, words, mere words" near the end of the play (V.iii.108) applies to all the rhetoric and oratory in it.

The words of objective observers, as Ulysses tells Achilles in III.iii, are not only the source of a man's reputation: they are the only means by which he can be confirmed in his private estimation of himself. Ulysses seems to regard this state of affairs with complacency. The play as a whole is less approving. Indeed, most of those verbal descriptions through which value is established prove to be false visions, without substance in reality. When, in III.i, Pandarus is told that the palace musicians play for Lord Paris and for his companion, "the mortal Venus, the heart-blood of beauty, love's invisible soul," he replies: "Who? my cousin Cressida?" The right answer, of course, is Helen. Pandarus is an old fool, filled with misplaced family pride, and yet his mistake is not incomprehensible. The Helen of the play is no goddess, no Platonic essence of Beauty. She is not even Homer's troubled plaything of the gods, so lovely that the mere sight of her walking by momentarily justified the entire war for the elders at the Skaian gates. An idle, pretty girl in Shakespeare, she likes to amuse herself by counting the hairs on Troilus' chin and can express a languorous opinion that "this love will undo us all" without reflecting that, in all seriousness, it might. In Marlowe's *Dr. Faustus*, Helen had been celebrated as a deity who "launched a thousand ships, / And burnt the topless towers of Ilium." For Shakespeare—and he deliberately echoed Marlowe's line—she is the source not only of destruction but debasement, a woman valueless in herself who has "turn'd crown'd kings to merchants." Cressida, whatever Pandarus may think and Troilus falsely urge upon her, comes no closer to being an ideal: "love's invisible soul." The formula itself is a distorted invention, not a reflection of truth. Yet it is for empty words like these that Troy will burn.

A similar and comic discrepancy between reputation and fact creates the impasse of I.iii where Aeneas, bearing Hector's challenge to the Greeks, inquires elaborately how he may find "that god in office, guiding men . . . the high and mighty Agamemnon." As it happens, the man he has singled out as an informant is Agamemnon himself: an Agamemnon considerably less godlike and awe-inspiring in the flesh than in the hyperbolic language of Aeneas. Just so, the heroic stature of Achilles about which everyone

but Thersites talks seems to be a verbal chimera. Pompously invited, in IV.v, to feast his eyes on the splendors of Achilles' physique, Hector finds that the briefest perusal will do quite nicely. When Achilles at last takes the field and engages Hector, he has to accept the clemency of his foe. He does manage to kill Hector in their second encounter, but only through recourse to treachery, in an unfair fight. Achilles' instructions to his Myrmidons after the butchery ensure, however, that what was really a scene from the abattoir will be blazoned to the world in epic terms. This, as it seems, is how myths originate.

No Homeric reputation emerges from this play unscathed. Even Hector betrays the hopes invested in him at the beginning of the play. In the Trojan council he perversely turns his back on the truth he sees, merely because he is besotted with a cozening idea of honor and glory to be won. Worse still, his death is the result of his own greed. Hector's magnanimity, his generosity in battle to a wounded or retreating adversary, has been stressed throughout the play; indeed, this characteristic of his has been one of the few things which have rescued the war from Thersites' descriptions of it as the mere "clapper-clawing" of animals. Hector's chivalry is not proof, however, against the temptation provided by the Greek in splendid armor who crosses his path in V.vi. In order to possess this armor, he brutally kills a man who was only trying to run away. It is while Hector is gloating over his spoils, defenseless and unprepared, that Achilles catches his advantage.

In the love plot, Troilus may be more constant than Cressida: he is equally flawed. Although in the Trojan council he advances the proposition, "I take to-day a wife," it remains the illustration for an argument only. He never mentions marriage to Cressida and this silence, in a world where Chaucer's courtly-love convention does not obtain, seems strange. Fatally self-absorbed from the start, Troilus idealizes his own sensuality and, in the process, omits to notice what kind of person his beloved really is. For all their exaltation, Troilus' lines anticipating the bliss of union with Cressida in III.ii reduce love to a matter of appetite. "Love's thrice-repured nectar" may seem far removed from "the fragments, scraps, the bits and greasy relics / Of her o'er-eaten faith" which he will summon up in V.ii. The paradisal banquet has given place to the disgusting remnants, the unlovely litter of the morning after. But in both cases, before and after her treachery, Cressida is regarded by her lover principally as matter for ingestion, an object to be devoured by the senses. As the knowing presence of Pandarus continually reminds us.

The systematic undercutting and diminution of every other principal character leaves one, uncomfortably enough, to face Thersites as the one man who assesses the situation correctly. An allowed fool of the most savage kind, Thersites has only two functions in the play: to observe and to rail. He is there to remind us that love is lechery, that man is an animal, the body a sink of filth and diseases, and the human intellect a bad joke. A voice more than a person, he operates almost in the manner of a chemical agent: the addition of one dram of Thersites will turn any situation instantly into mud. If he believes that there may be some other country in which men are not wholly taken up with war and lechery, he gives no sign of it. The human condition, in his view, is faithfully mirrored in the events and personalities of the Trojan war.

No audience, at first, puts much faith in his scabrous evaluation of the loves and wars of Troy. The voice is too obviously distorted, the imagination too foul, and his own position too ignominious. In his early scenes Thersites is consistently the object of physical abuse, beaten and kicked. Yet as the play unfolds he gains both independence and a disconcerting strength. The very idea of an armed Hector seriously inquiring of Thersites on the field of battle "Art thou of blood and honor?" is absurd in a way that diminishes Hector, not Thersites. By the end, although one scarcely rejoices as he does over his discoveries, it is hard to challenge his sweeping indictment of both sides. The weakness of Cressida, the overwrought sensuality of Troilus, and the lip-smacking services of Pandarus have betrayed Love. Paris is a selfish voluptuary, Ajax a lout, and Menelaus so obviously a figure of fun that no one, not even the courteous Hector, can resist laughing at him to his face. The rationalism of Ulysses is hollow and ineffective. Only an accident, the death of Patroclus in battle, gets Achilles out of his tent and into his armor: not Ulysses' stratagem. Achilles' heroic stature is a fraud. Even Hector has looked truth in the eye and then dishonored both it and the knightly generosity of which he seemed the embodiment. Agamemnon is a nonentity and Helen, for all the poetry lavished on her, a trivial fool. Men may talk like gods. They end up behaving like those beasts to which Thersites so persistently compares them.

Argumentative and intensely verbal, almost self-consciously intellectual, *Troilus and Cressida* moves towards a position of profound scepticism. The play which contains, in Ulysses' speech on order, Shakespeare's most elaborate presentation of the medieval great chain of being, finishes by portraying a chaos which can no longer be remedied by traditional means. Accepted ideas of degree and rule, of personal honor, reputation, and love, do not, in this society, require reaffirmation so much as radical redefinition. Even the mode of speech favored by the characters is shown to be dangerously inappropriate and misjudged. In *The Language Poets Use*, Winifred Nowottny has argued that simile, a process of likening stable, defined objects to one another without ever suggesting that their identity merges in a new creation, is a figure particularly suited to the description of a familiar, ordered world. Metaphor, by contrast, is creative and exploratory: a way of mapping a fluid, uncertain reality for which there are, as yet, no categories or fixed terms. *Troilus and Cressida*, although concerned with disintegration and change, stands out among Shakespeare's plays by not employing metaphor as its dominant figure of speech. Simile, extended comparisons introduced by *like*, or *as*, or some other formal indication of parallel, seems to be the preferred idiom of both Greece and Troy. Characters often play at simile-making, as Troilus and Cressida do in their vows, or Thersites when he tries to decide to which of the many possible base or animal forms malicious wit may most effectively liken Menelaus. The speeches of Ulysses are a tissue of analogy and seemingly judicial parallel. In every case, despite the surface logic, nothing is really discovered about the focal term in the comparison. Essentially an instrument of analysis, simile as it is used in this play merely obscures identity and evades truth. When Achilles says that his mind is troubled, "like a fountain stirred," when Ajax declares that he hates proud men "as I do hate the engend'ring of toads," or Troilus pictures Cressida as a pearl embedded in India, to be reached by way of "this sailing Pandar," simile is being employed falsely to describe a world whose values are not stable, a world of chaos and relativity with which only metaphor can cope.

There are right and wrong ways of ordering the complexities of human experience at a given moment of time. In *Troilus and Cressida* the only order which ultimately passes muster and stands firm would seem to be the artistic order of the play itself. Although Shakespeare concedes much (too much, as far as earlier critics were concerned) to the formless and unorthodox in the structuring of his five acts, the logic of the play is nevertheless far more effective and impressive than anything Ulysses represents. Individual characters may be bewilderingly inconsistent; their dramatic treatment is not. Silently, through the juxtaposition and contrast of different characters and ideas, through the placing of scenes and the implicit comment they make upon one another, an order is affirmed which envelops and, in a sense, contradicts the nihilism of the action. The distortions of epic celebration, the inadequacy of simile as a way of anatomizing situations demanding a flexible, intuitive language, do not prevent Shakespeare from demonstrating that words, rightly used, can be the sensitive and precise registers of experience. Ultimately, Thersites' reductivist view of man is refuted by the simple fact that *Troilus and Cressida* exists. The disorder of the subject is not, as in so many twentieth-century works, reflected in its structure. This sense of mastery and control over difficult material is why, for all its pessimism and savagery, the experience of *Troilus and Cressida* is finally exhilarating. Despite the bleakness of the ending and the bitter prophecies of Pandarus, this great play dismisses its audience fundamentally reassured.

Anne Barton

The History of Troilus and Cressida

PRIAM, *King of Troy*
HECTOR
TROILUS
PARIS ⎬ *his sons*
DEIPHOBUS
HELENUS
MARGARELON, *a bastard son of Priam*
AENEAS ⎱ *Trojan commanders*
ANTENOR ⎰
CALCHAS, *a Trojan priest, taking part with the Greeks*
PANDARUS, *uncle to Cressida*
ALEXANDER, *servant to Cressida*
SERVANT *and* BOY *to Troilus*
SERVANT *to Paris*

AGAMEMNON, *the Greek general*
MENELAUS, *his brother*
NESTOR
ULYSSES
ACHILLES
AJAX ⎬ *Greek commanders*
DIOMEDES
PATROCLUS
THERSITES, *a deformed and scurrilous Greek*
SERVANT *to Diomedes*

HELEN, *wife to Menelaus*
ANDROMACHE, *wife to Hector*
CASSANDRA, *daughter to Priam, a prophetess*
CRESSIDA, *daughter to Calchas*

TROJAN *and* GREEK SOLDIERS, *and* ATTENDANTS

SCENE: *Troy, and the Greek camp before it*]

[THE PROLOGUE

In Troy, there lies the scene. From isles of Greece
The princes orgillous, their high blood chaf'd,
Have to the port of Athens sent their ships
Fraught with the ministers and instruments
Of cruel war. Sixty and nine, that wore   5
Their crownets regal, from th' Athenian bay
Put forth toward Phrygia, and their vow is made
To ransack Troy, within whose strong immures
The ravish'd Helen, Menelaus' queen,
With wanton Paris sleeps—and that's the quarrel. 10
To Tenedos they come,
And the deep-drawing [barks] do there disgorge
Their warlike fraughtage. Now on Dardan plains
The fresh and yet unbruised Greeks do pitch
Their brave pavilions. Priam's six-gated city,   15
Dardan and Timbria, Helias, Chetas, Troien,
And [Antenorides], with massy staples
And corresponsive and fulfilling bolts
[Sperr] up the sons of Troy.
Now expectation, tickling skittish spirits,   20
On one and other side, Troyan and Greek,
Sets all on hazard—and hither am I come,
A prologue arm'd, but not in confidence
Of author's pen or actor's voice, but suited
In like conditions as our argument,   25
To tell you, fair beholders, that our play

---

*Words and passages enclosed in square brackets in the text above are
either emendations of the copy-text or additions to it. The Textual Notes
immediately following the play cite the earliest authority for every such
change or insertion and supply the reading of the copy-text wherever it is
emended in this edition.*

Pro. 2. **orgillous:** proud (variant of *orgulous*). Note that the Prologue
contains no reference to the Troilus and Cressida story. **high blood:**
(1) noble lineage; (2) temperament readily fired by honorable exploits.
4. **Fraught:** freighted, loaded. Cf. *fraughtage* (= cargo) in line 13.
ministers: soldiers (who operate the "instruments" or weapons).
6. **crownets:** coronets.
7. **Phrygia:** in Elizabethan usage, the land of the Trojans.
8. **immures:** walls, defenses.
11. **Tenedos:** an island off the northwest coast of Asia Minor, close
to Troy; here described as the naval base of the Greek invasion.
12. **deep-drawing:** low in the water (because of their heavy cargo).

13. **Dardan:** Trojan (from the name of Dardanus, ancestor of the
Trojan kings).
15. **brave:** splendid. **pavilions:** large peaked tents.
16–17. **Dardan . . . Antenorides.** The names of the six gates of Troy.
17–18. **massy . . . bolts:** i.e. heavy, solid sockets into which correspondingly heavy and solid bolts fitted.
19. **Sperr up:** lock up (defensively) with bolts and bars.
23. **arm'd:** in armor. Lines 23–25 are usually taken as a stroke at
Ben Jonson, who in *Poetaster* (1601) introduces an "armed prologue,"
suggesting his own embattled position in the War of the Theatres
then at its height. If so, *confidence* signifies overconfidence or
arrogance, the attitude for which Jonson was most often attacked.
The characterization of Ajax is thought by some to be a further attack on Jonson.
24–25. **suited . . . argument:** i.e. dressed to match our (martial) subject
matter.

Leaps o'er the vaunt and firstlings of those broils,
Beginning in the middle; starting thence away
To what may be digested in a play.
Like or find fault, do as your pleasures are,   30
Now good or bad, 'tis but the chance of war.]

[ACT I, SCENE I]

Enter PANDARUS *and* TROILUS.

Tro.   Call here my varlet, I'll unarm again.
Why should I war without the walls of Troy,
That find such cruel battle here within?
Each Troyan that is master of his heart,
Let him to field, Troilus, alas, hath none.   5
Pan.   Will this gear ne'er be mended?
Tro.   The Greeks are strong, and skillful to their
          strength,
Fierce to their skill, and to their fierceness valiant,
But I am weaker than a woman's tear,
Tamer than sleep, fonder than ignorance,   10
Less valiant than the virgin in the night,
And skilless as unpractic'd infancy.
Pan.   Well, I have told you enough of this. For my
part, I'll not meddle nor make no farther. He that will
have a cake out of the wheat must tarry the grinding.
Tro.   Have I not tarried?   16
Pan.   Ay, the grinding; but you must tarry the bolt-
ing.
Tro.   Have I not tarried?
Pan.   Ay, the bolting; but you must tarry the leav-
ening.   21
Tro.   Still have I tarried.
Pan.   Ay, to the leavening, but here's yet in the
word "hereafter" the kneading, the making of the cake,
the heating the oven, and the baking; nay, you must
stay the cooling too, or ye may chance burn your lips.
Tro.   Patience herself, what goddess e'er she be,   27
Doth lesser blench at suff'rance than I do.
At Priam's royal table do I sit,
And when fair Cressid comes into my thoughts—
So, traitor, then she comes when she is thence.   31
Pan.   Well, she look'd yesternight fairer than ever
I saw her look, or any woman else.

Tro.   I was about to tell thee—when my heart,
As wedged with a sigh, would rive in twain,   35
Lest Hector or my father should perceive me,
I have (as when the sun doth light a-scorn)
Buried this sigh in wrinkle of a smile,
But sorrow that is couch'd in seeming gladness
Is like that mirth fate turns to sudden sadness.   40
Pan.   And her hair were not somewhat darker than
Helen's—well, go to!—there were no more compar-
ison between the women! But for my part, she is
my kinswoman; I would not, as they term it, praise
her, but I would somebody had heard her talk yester-
day as I did. I will not dispraise your sister Cas-
sandra's wit, but—   47
Tro.   O Pandarus! I tell thee, Pandarus—
When I do tell thee there my hopes lie drown'd,
Reply not in how many fadoms deep   50
They lie indrench'd. I tell thee I am mad
In Cressid's love; thou answer'st she is fair,
Pourest in the open ulcer of my heart
Her eyes, her hair, her cheek, her gait, her voice,
Handlest in thy discourse, O, that her hand,   55
In whose comparison all whites are ink
Writing their own reproach; to whose soft seizure
The cygnet's down is harsh, and spirit of sense
Hard as the palm of ploughman. This thou tell'st me,
As true thou tell'st me, when I say I love her,   60
But saying thus, in stead of oil and balm,
Thou lay'st in every gash that love hath given me
The knife that made it.
Pan.   I speak no more than truth.
Tro.   Thou dost not speak so much.   65
Pan.   Faith, I'll not meddle in it, let her be as she
is; if she be fair, 'tis the better for her; and she be not,
she has the mends in her own hands.
Tro.   Good Pandarus! How now, Pandarus?   69
Pan.   I have had my labor for my travail; ill thought
on of her, and ill thought [on] of you; gone between
and between, but small thanks for my labor.
Tro.   What, art thou angry, Pandarus? What, with
          me?   73
Pan.   Because she's kin to me, therefore she's not
so fair as Helen. And she were [not] kin to me, she
would be as fair a' Friday as Helen is on Sunday.

---

27. vaunt: beginnings (originally a prefix = "first part of," like *van-* in *vanguard*). **firstlings:** first fruits (synonymous with *vaunt*). **28. Beginning . . . middle:** i.e. after seven years' siege (see I.iii.12); probably alluding to the fact that epic poems traditionally (since the *Iliad*) leap "into the middle of things" (*in medias res*).

I.i. Location: Troy. Before Priam's palace. **1. varlet:** page or servant to a knight. **5. hath none.** Because he has given his heart to Cressida. **6. gear:** business. **7, 8. to:** in addition to, or in proportion to. **10. fonder:** more foolish. **14. not . . . nor . . . no.** Elizabethan multiple negative, implying simple negation. **meddle nor make.** A proverbial phrase (*make* = do, undertake). **15. cake:** a kind of bread, flattened and shaped, baked hard on both sides. **17–18. bolting:** sifting. **20–21. leavening:** fermenting (of the dough). **27. what . . . be:** however much a goddess she is. **28. lesser . . . suff'rance:** i.e. flinch more under suffering. *Lesser* apparently carries the sense "worse" or "with less fortitude." **31. So . . . thence:** i.e. I am a traitor to say "when she comes," for by saying so I admit that she is sometimes absent from my thoughts. Most editors emend (after Rowe) to *When she comes! When is she thence?*

35. As wedged: as if cleft (as by a wedge). **rive:** split. **37. a-scorn:** in mockery (?). The image seems to be of the sun gleaming momentarily through the clouds, deceptively promising fair weather. Most editors emend (after Rowe) to *a storm.* **39. is couch'd:** lies low or hidden. **41. And:** if. **hair . . . darker.** Blonde beauty was the Elizabethan ideal. **42. go to:** enough said. **42–43. no more comparison:** (they are) not to be compared (Cressida is so superior to Helen). **47. wit:** powers of intellect. **50. fadoms:** fathoms. **55. that her hand:** that hand of hers. **56. In whose comparison:** in comparison with which. **57. to:** in comparison with. **seizure:** clasp. **58. cygnet's:** young swan's. **spirit of sense:** i.e. spirit of the sense of touch or feeling. The spirits of the senses, in Elizabethan physiology, were subtle vapors, transmitted through the nerves (thought of as hollow tubes), and believed to be the intermediaries between man's body and soul. **65. speak so much:** tell the whole truth (with the implication that the whole truth about Cressida's beauty can never be told). **68. has . . . hands:** (1) must make the best of it (proverbial); (2) has the remedy (i.e. cosmetics) available. **70. travail:** pains, efforts. **70–71. thought on of:** thought of by. **76. as fair . . . Sunday:** i.e. as beautiful at her plainest as Helen in her Sunday best.

Troilus
and Cressida
I.i

But what [care] I? I care not and she were a blackamoor, 'tis all one to me.

Tro. Say I she is not fair?   79

Pan. I do not care whether you do or no. She's a
fool to stay behind her father, let her to the Greeks;
and so I'll tell her the next time I see her. For my part,
I'll meddle nor make no more i' th' matter.

Tro. Pandarus—

Pan. Not I.   85

Tro. Sweet Pandarus—

Pan. Pray you speak no more to me, I will leave
all as I found it, and there an end.

Exit. Sound alarum.

Tro. Peace, you ungracious clamors! peace, rude
sounds!
Fools on both sides, Helen must needs be fair,   90
When with your blood you daily paint her thus.
I cannot fight upon this argument;
It is too starv'd a subject for my sword.
But Pandarus—O gods! how do you plague me!
I cannot come to Cressid but by Pandar,   95
And he's as teachy to be woo'd to woo,
As she is stubborn-chaste against all suit.
Tell me, Apollo, for thy Daphne's love,
What Cressid is, what Pandar, and what we:
Her bed is India, there she lies, a pearl;   100
Between our Ilium and where she [resides],
Let it be call'd the wild and wand'ring flood,
Ourself the merchant, and this sailing Pandar
Our doubtful hope, our convoy, and our bark.

Alarum. Enter AENEAS.

Aene. How now, Prince Troilus, wherefore not
a-field?   105

Tro. Because not there. This woman's answer
sorts,
For womanish it is to be from thence.
What news, Aeneas, from the field to-day?

Aene. That Paris is returned home and hurt.   109

Tro. By whom, Aeneas?

Aene.   Troilus, by Menelaus.

Tro. Let Paris bleed, 'tis but a scar to scorn;
Paris is gor'd with Menelaus' horn.   *Alarum.*

Aene. Hark what good sport is out of town to-day.

Tro. Better at home, if "would I might" were
"may."
But to the sport abroad—are you bound thither?   115

Aene. In all swift haste.

Tro.   Come go we then together. *Exeunt.*

[SCENE II]

Enter CRESSID *and her man* [ALEXANDER].

Cres. Who were those went by?

Alex.   Queen Hecuba and Helen.

Cres. And whither go they?

Alex.   Up to the eastern tower,
Whose height commands as subject all the vale,
To see the battle. Hector, whose patience
Is as a virtue fix'd, to-day was mov'd: 5
He chid Andromache and strook his armorer,
And like as there were husbandry in war,
Before the sun rose he was harness'd light,
And to the field goes he; where every flower
Did as a prophet weep what it foresaw   10
In Hector's wrath.

Cres.   What was his cause of anger?

Alex. The noise goes, this: there is among the
Greeks
A lord of Troyan blood, nephew to Hector,
They call him Ajax.

Cres.   Good; and what of him?

Alex. They say he is a very man *per se* and stands
alone.   16

Cres. So do all men, unless th' are drunk, sick, or
have no legs.

Alex. This man, lady, hath robb'd many beasts of
their particular additions: he is as valiant as the   20
lion, churlish as the bear, slow as the elephant; a man
into whom nature hath so crowded humors that his
valor is crush'd into folly, his folly sauc'd with discretion. There is no man hath a virtue that he hath not
a glimpse of, nor any man an attaint but he carries   25
some stain of it. He is melancholy without cause, and
merry against the hair; he hath the joints of every
thing, but every thing so out of joint that he is a gouty
Briareus, many hands and no use, or purblind Argus,
all eyes and no sight.   30

Cres. But how should this man, that makes me
smile, make Hector angry?

---

81. **stay . . . father:** remain (here) after her father is gone. Cressida's
father Calchas, forewarned by the Delphic oracle that Troy would be
defeated, had defected to the Greeks.
88. s.d. **alarum:** trumpet call to arms.
92. **upon this argument:** in defense of this cause.
93. **starv'd:** thin, empty (of sustenance).
96. **teachy:** quick to take offense, touchy (variant of *tetchy*).
98. **for . . . love:** for the sake of your love of Daphne (a nymph
who was turned into a laurel or bay tree to escape Apollo's importunate love).   99. **we:** I.
101. **Ilium.** This name, usually in its Greek form *Ilion*, is used
throughout for Priam's palace, hence to be distinguished from Troy,
for which it is properly a poetic name.
104. **convoy:** protective escort, conductor.
105. **Troilus.** Dissyllabic throughout, except at V.ii.161 (see the
note there).
111. **a scar to scorn:** (1) a wound too slight to be taken seriously;
(2) a wound given in return for scorn.
112. **Menelaus' horn:** i.e. the cuckold's horn that Paris himself has
scornfully given Menelaus.

I.ii. Location: Troy. A street.
5. **Is . . . fix'd:** is (ordinarily) a constant quality.   **mov'd:** angry.
6. **strook:** struck (a common variant).
7. **husbandry:** careful management, thrift (with play on the sense
"tillage" developing in *harness'd* and *field* in lines 8–9).
8. **harness'd light:** dressed in armor swiftly.   12. **noise:** rumor.
13. **nephew.** Actually Ajax, according to the tradition followed in this
play, was Hector's first cousin; see the note on II.ii.73.
15. **man per se:** man in a class by himself (for excellence).
20. **particular additions:** special attributes or descriptive titles.
22. **humors:** temperamental bents.
23. **sauc'd:** flavored, spiced. The context, however, implies a more
even mixture of "folly" and "discretion," and Theobald's conjecture
forc'd (another culinary term, meaning "stuffed,") is attractive.
25. **glimpse:** flash, i.e. trace.   **attaint:** vice.
26. **stain:** tincture, slight admixture.
27. **against the hair:** contrary to his natural disposition (or to the
particular occasion); equivalent to *against the grain.*   **joints:** limbs.
28–29. **a gouty Briareus:** i.e. a man with a hundred hands (such as
the giant Briareus was reputed to have), all disabled by gout.
29. **purblind Argus:** i.e. a man with a hundred eyes (such as Argus
was reputed to have), all sightless.

Alex. They say he yesterday cop'd Hector in the battle and strook him down, the disdain and shame 34 whereof hath ever since kept Hector fasting and waking.

[*Enter* PANDARUS.]

Cres. Who comes here?

Alex. Madam, your uncle Pandarus.

Cres. Hector's a gallant man.

Alex. As may be in the world, lady. 40

Pan. What's that? what's that?

Cres. Good morrow, uncle Pandarus.

Pan. Good morrow, cousin Cressid. What do you talk of? Good morrow, Alexander. How do you, cousin? When were you at Ilium? 45

Cres. This morning, uncle.

Pan. What were you talking of when I came? Was Hector arm'd and gone ere ye came to Ilium? Helen was not up, was she?

Cres. Hector was gone, but Helen was not up. 50

Pan. E'en so; Hector was stirring early.

Cres. That were we talking of, and of his anger.

Pan. Was he angry?

Cres. So he says here. 54

Pan. True, he was so; I know the cause too. He'll lay about him to-day, I can tell them that, and there's Troilus will not come far behind him. Let them take heed of Troilus; I can tell them that too.

Cres. What, is he angry too?

Pan. Who, Troilus? Troilus is the better man of the two. 61

Cres. O Jupiter, there's no comparison.

Pan. What, not between Troilus and Hector? Do you know a man if you see him?

Cres. Ay, if I ever saw him before and knew him.

Pan. Well, I say Troilus is Troilus. 66

Cres. Then you say as I say, for I am sure he is not Hector.

Pan. No, nor Hector is not Troilus in some degrees. 70

Cres. 'Tis just to each of them; he is himself.

Pan. Himself? alas, poor Troilus, I would he were!

Cres. So he is.

Pan. Condition I had gone barefoot to India.

Cres. He is not Hector. 75

Pan. Himself? no! he's not himself. Would 'a were himself! Well, the gods are above, time must friend or end. Well, Troilus, well, I would my heart were in her body. No, Hector is not a better man than Troilus. 80

Cres. Excuse me.

Pan. He is elder.

Cres. Pardon me, pardon me.

33. **cop'd:** met and fought with.   34. **disdain:** ignominy.
43. **cousin:** kinswoman; here, niece.
65. **before and knew.** There is a bawdy quibble on *before* (= from the front) and *knew* (= had sexual intercourse with).
71. **he:** i.e. each one.
74. **Condition:** on that condition (i.e. to make Troilus himself again); continues Pandarus' preceding speech.   **had:** would have.
76. **'a:** he.
78. **friend or end:** bring him to a happy condition or kill him (proverbial).   **heart:** feelings.
81. **Excuse me:** i.e. I disagree; so *Pardon me* in line 83.

Pan. Th' other's not come to't. You shall tell me another tale when th' other's come to't. Hector shall not have his [wit] this year. 86

Cres. He shall not need it if he have his own.

Pan. Nor his qualities.

Cres. No matter.

Pan. Nor his beauty. 90

Cres. 'Twould not become him, his own's better.

Pan. You have no judgment, niece. Helen herself swore th' other day that Troilus, for a brown favor (for so 'tis, I must confess)—not brown neither—

Cres. No, but brown. 95

Pan. Faith, to say truth, brown and not brown.

Cres. To say the truth, true and not true.

Pan. She prais'd his complexion above Paris.

Cres. Why, Paris hath color enough.

Pan. So he has. 100

Cres. Then Troilus should have too much: if she prais'd him above, his complexion is higher than his. He having color enough, and the other higher, is too flaming a praise for a good complexion. I had as lieve Helen's golden tongue had commended Troilus for a copper nose. 106

Pan. I swear to you, I think Helen loves him better than Paris.

Cres. Then she's a merry Greek indeed.

Pan. Nay, I am sure she does. She came to him th' other day into the compass'd window—and you know he has not past three or four hairs on his chin— 112

Cres. Indeed a tapster's arithmetic may soon bring his particulars therein to a total.

Pan. Why, he is very young, and yet will he, within three pound, lift as much as his brother Hector.

Cres. Is he so young a man and so old a lifter? 117

Pan. But to prove to you that Helen loves him: she came and puts me her white hand to his cloven chin—

Cres. Juno have mercy! how came it cloven? 120

Pan. Why, you know 'tis dimpled. I think his smiling becomes him better than any man in all Phrygia.

Cres. O, he smiles valiantly.

Pan. Does he not? 125

Cres. O yes, and 'twere a cloud in autumn.

Pan. Why, go to then. But to prove to you that Helen loves Troilus—

Cres. Troilus will stand to the proof, if you'll prove it so. 130

86. **this year:** i.e. ever (indefinite use).
93. **for a brown favor:** considering that he has a dark complexion.
98. **above:** beyond that of.
102. **his . . . his:** i.e. Troilus' . . . Paris'.   **higher:** more highly colored, ruddier.   104. **as lieve:** just as soon.
106. **copper nose:** red nose resulting from intemperance.
109. **merry Greek:** person of loose life (slang); the phrase, ordinarily having nothing to do with Greeks, is peculiarly apposite here.
111. **compass'd window:** semicircular bay-window.
112. **past:** more than.
113. **tapster's arithmetic:** i.e. reckoning of the easiest sort. A tapster scored drinks one at a time on a board; the score never got very high before payment was demanded.
117. **old:** experienced.   **lifter:** (a) weight lifter; (b) thief; perhaps with the further sense "fornicator" (cf. *stand to the proof*, line 129, where *stand*, as frequently, has a bawdy implication).
119. **puts me:** puts (a colloquialism).   **cloven:** cleft.
126. **and:** as if (so also *an'* in lines 173, 175).   **cloud in autumn:** i.e. one that threatens a storm, unlike a summer cloud.

Pan. Troilus! why, he esteems her no more than I esteem an addle egg.

Cres. If you love an addle egg as well as you love an idle head, you would eat chickens i' th' shell.

Pan. I cannot choose but laugh to think how she tickled his chin. Indeed she has a marvell's white hand, I must needs confess.   137

Cres. Without the rack.

Pan. And she takes upon her to spy a white hair on his chin.   140

Cres. Alas, poor chin! many a wart is richer.

Pan. But there was such laughing! Queen Hecuba laugh'd that her eyes ran o'er.

Cres. With millstones.

Pan. And Cassandra laugh'd.   145

Cres. But there was a more temperate fire under the pot of her eyes. Did her eyes run o'er too?

Pan. And Hector laugh'd.

Cres. At what was all this laughing?

Pan. Marry, at the white hair that Helen spied on Troilus' chin.   151

Cres. And't had been a green hair, I should have laugh'd too.

Pan. They laugh'd not so much at the hair as at his pretty answer.   155

Cres. What was his answer?

Pan. Quoth she, "Here's but two and fifty hairs on your chin—and one of them is white."   159

Cres. This is her question.

Pan. That's true, make no question of that. "Two and fifty hairs," quoth he, "and one white. That white hair is my father, and all the rest are his sons." "Jupiter," quoth she, "which of these hairs is Paris my husband?" "The fork'd one," quoth he, "pluck't out, and give it him." But there was such laughing!   165 and Helen so blush'd, and Paris so chaf'd, and all the rest so laugh'd, that it pass'd.

Cres. So let it now, for it has been a great while going by.

Pan. Well, cousin, I told you a thing yesterday, think on't.   171

Cres. So I do.

Pan. I'll be sworn 'tis true; he will weep you an' 'twere a man born in April.   *Sound a retreat.*

Cres. And I'll spring up in his tears an' 'twere a nettle against May.   176

Pan. Hark, they are coming from the field. Shall

we stand up here and see them as they pass toward Ilion? Good niece, do, sweet niece Cressida.

Cres. At your pleasure.   180

Pan. Here, here, here's an excellent place, here we may see most bravely. I'll tell you them all by their names as they pass by, but mark Troilus above the rest.

Enter AENEAS [*and passes over the stage*].

Cres. Speak not so loud.   185

Pan. That's Aeneas; is not that a brave man? He's one of the flowers of Troy, I can tell you. But mark Troilus; you shall see anon.

Cres. Who's that?   189

Enter ANTENOR [*and passes over the stage*].

Pan. That's Antenor. He has a shrowd wit, I can tell you, and he's man good enough. He's one o' th' soundest judgments in Troy, whosoever, and a proper man of person. When comes Troilus? I'll show you Troilus anon. If he see me, you shall see him nod at me.   195

Cres. Will he give you the nod?

Pan. You shall see.

Cres. If he do, the rich shall have more.   198

Enter HECTOR [*and passes over the stage*].

Pan. That's Hector, that, that, look you, that; there's a fellow! Go thy way, Hector! There's a brave man, niece. O brave Hector! look how he looks! There's a countenance! Is't not a brave man?   202

Cres. O, a brave man!

Pan. Is 'a not? It does a man['s] heart good. Look you what hacks are on his helmet! Look you yonder, do you see? Look you there, there's no jesting; there's laying on, take't off who will, as they say. There be hacks!   208

Cres. Be those with swords?

Pan. Swords! any thing, he cares not; and the devil come to him, it's all one. By God's lid, it does one's heart good. Yonder comes Paris, yonder comes Paris.

Enter PARIS [*and passes over the stage*].

Look ye yonder, niece; is't not a gallant man too, is't not? Why, this is brave now. Who said he came   214 hurt home to-day? He's not hurt. Why, this will do Helen's heart good now, ha? Would I could see Troilus now! You shall see Troilus anon.

Cres. Who's that?   218

Enter HELENUS [*and passes over the stage*].

---

134. **idle:** empty, foolish (applied both to Pandarus' head and Troilus'), with play on *addle/idle*.   136. **marvell's:** marvellous.
138. **Without the rack:** i.e. without being put to the torture.
141. **is richer:** i.e. has more hairs in it.
144. **millstones.** Proverbially shed by those too hard-hearted to shed tears. Here the point seems to be that there was nothing to make anyone laugh hard enough to cry.
150. **Marry:** why (originally an oath, "by the Virgin Mary").
162. **his sons.** Priam's sons traditionally numbered fifty; presumably the "fork'd" hair of line 164 is counted as two.
164. **fork'd:** (1) bifurcated; (2) horned (implying the likelihood that Paris, like Menelaus, will be made a cuckold by Helen).
165. **give it him.** With a quibble on "present him with horns."
166. **so chaf'd:** became so angry.
167. **pass'd:** was beyond description.
174. s.d. **retreat:** trumpet signal for withdrawal of forces.
176. **nettle.** Cressida twists the proverbial "April showers bring May flowers," perhaps also with a pun on *tears/tares* in line 175.   **against:** in anticipation of.

182. **bravely:** admirably, capitally. Cf. Pandarus' application of the adjectival form to Aeneas, Hector, and Troilus below.
188. **anon:** presently, at once.
190. **shrowd:** sharp, biting (variant of *shrewd*).
192. **whosoever:** i.e. bar none.
193. **proper . . . person:** fine-looking man.
196. **give . . . nod:** i.e. call you fool (or noddy).
198. **rich . . . more:** i.e. one already rich (in folly) will be made richer.
205. **hacks:** dents, scars.
207. **laying . . . will:** i.e. a vigorous dealing of blows, whatever anyone may say to the contrary. The phrase *lay on* regularly attracts the phrase *take off*.   210. **and:** if.
211. **all one:** all the same to him.   **By God's lid:** by God's eyelid (a mild oath).

Pan. That's Helenus. I marvel where Troilus is. That's Helenus. I think he went not forth to-day. That's Helenus.   221

Cres. Can Helenus fight, uncle?

Pan. Helenus? no. Yes, he'll fight indifferent well. I marvel where Troilus is. Hark, do you not hear the people cry "Troilus"? Helenus is a priest.   225

Cres. What sneaking fellow comes yonder?

Enter TROILUS [*and passes over the stage*].

Pan. Where? Yonder? That's Deiphobus. 'Tis Troilus! There's a man, niece! Hem! Brave Troilus, the prince of chivalry!

Cres. Peace, for shame, peace!   230

Pan. Mark him, note him. O brave Troilus! Look well upon him, niece. Look you how his sword is bloodied, and his helm more hack'd than Hector's, and how he looks, and how he goes! O admirable   234 youth! he never saw three and twenty. Go thy way, Troilus, go thy way! Had I a sister were a grace, or a daughter a goddess, he should take his choice. O admirable man! Paris? Paris is dirt to him, and I warrant Helen, to change, would give an eye to boot.

[*Enter* COMMON SOLDIERS *and pass over the stage*.]

Cres. Here comes more.   240

Pan. Asses, fools, dolts! chaff and bran, chaff and bran! porridge after meat! I could live and die in the eyes of Troilus. Ne'er look, ne'er look, the eagles are gone; crows and daws, crows and daws! I had rather be such a man as Troilus than Agamemnon and all Greece.   246

Cres. There is amongst the Greeks Achilles, a better man than Troilus.

Pan. Achilles! a drayman, a porter, a very camel.

Cres. Well, well.

Pan. Well, well! Why, have you any discretion? have you any eyes? do you know what a man is? Is not birth, beauty, good shape, discourse, manhood,   253 learning, gentleness, virtue, youth, liberality, and such-like, the spice and salt that season a man?

Cres. Ay, a minc'd man, and then to be bak'd with no date in the pie, for then the man's date is out.

Pan. You are such a woman, a man knows not at what ward you lie.   259

Cres. Upon my back, to defend my belly, upon my wit, to defend my wiles, upon my secrecy, to defend mine honesty, my mask, to defend my beauty, and you, to defend all these; and at all these wards I lie, at a thousand watches.

Pan. Say one of your watches.   265

Cres. Nay, I'll watch you for that; and that's one of the chiefest of them too. If I cannot ward what I would not have hit, I can watch you for telling how I took the blow—unless it swell past hiding, and then it's past watching.   270

Pan. You are such another!

Enter [*Troilus'*] BOY.

Boy. Sir, my lord would instantly speak with you.

Pan. Where?

Boy. At your own house, there he unarms him.

Pan. Good boy, tell him I come. [*Exit Boy.*] I doubt he be hurt. Fare ye well, good niece.   276

Cres. Adieu, uncle.

Pan. I will be with you, niece, by and by.

Cres. To bring, uncle?

Pan. Ay, a token from Troilus.   280

Cres. By the same token, you are a bawd.

[*Exit Pandarus.*]

Words, vows, gifts, tears, and love's full sacrifice,
He offers in another's enterprise,
But more in Troilus thousandfold I see
Than in the glass of Pandar's praise may be;   285
Yet hold I off. Women are angels, wooing:
Things won are done, joy's soul lies in the doing.
That she belov'd knows nought that knows not this:
Men prize the thing ungain'd more than it is.
That she was never yet that ever knew   290
Love got so sweet as when desire did sue.
Therefore this maxim out of love I teach:
Achievement is command; ungain'd, beseech;

220. **he:** i.e. Troilus.   223. **indifferent:** moderately.
233. **helm:** helmet.   234. **goes:** walks.
236. **a grace:** one of the three Graces.
237. **take his choice:** have her if he chose.
239. **to change:** to be able to exchange (Paris for Troilus).   **to boot:** into the bargain.   242. **porridge:** soup.
242–43. **in the eyes of:** in the sight of, either looking at or being looked at by (Troilus).
249. **drayman:** one who drives a dray (brewer's cart).
253. **discourse:** wit in conversation.
256. **minc'd man.** Cressida means that if he is made up of so many different ingredients he resembles nothing so much as a meat pie; perhaps with a suggestion that the meat is tainted to require so much "spice and salt" to disguise the taste.
256–57. **bak'd . . . out.** Dates were one of the commonest ingredients of Elizabethan cookery, and the implication here is that a pie without dates is no proper pie. Cressida's showing that the pie contains no dates rests on the quibble in *date is out*: (1) date is wanting; (2) time is past, i.e. Troilus is out of date (and hence not a man for Cressida).
258. **such:** so unpredictable.
259. **ward:** posture of defense (a term from fencing). Note the revealing language of physical conflict with which Cressida (through line 270) describes her attitude toward men.

261–62. **secrecy . . . honesty.** Cressida here seems to imply that her reputation for chastity (*honesty*) depends upon her ability to keep her own counsel.
262. **mask.** Elizabethan ladies wore silk masks to protect their faces from sun and wind.
263–64. **at a thousand watches:** in a thousand ways guarding (watching) myself (from attack).
265. **watches:** i.e. night watches (with bawdy innuendo).
266–67. **Nay . . . too:** i.e. no, I will keep an eye on you in such a situation as one of the greatest threats to my security.
268. **watch . . . telling:** guard against your revealing.
270. **watching:** concealing (by guarding the secret).
271. **You . . . another:** equivalent to modern "you're a one."
276. **doubt:** fear.
279. **To bring.** Cressida's enigmatic rejoinder has been much discussed. *Be with* (line 278) could mean not only "visit" but also "be even with," and there was an expression *be with you to bring*, in which *to bring* meant something like "with a vengeance." Possibly therefore Cressida means "Is that a threat?" On the other hand, she may be saying simply, "To bring something?" (the sense to which Pandarus replies), with the hint that she expects him to return with something from Troilus.
281. **bawd:** procurer or pander (implying that the token is a bribe).
286. **wooing:** being wooed. The active participle with passive sense was common; cf. "the house is building," an example still current.
287. **doing:** process of achieving (with bawdy play on the sense "having sexual intercourse").
289. **Men . . . is:** i.e. men value the sexual object more in anticipation than in realization.
290–91. **That . . . sue:** the woman never lived who did not know that love granted (to a man) is less sweet (to him) than love desired.
292. **out of:** derived from.
293. **Achievement . . . beseech:** i.e. physical consummation once attained makes a man a tyrant; withheld, it makes him a suppliant.

*Troilus
and Cressida
I.ii*

Then though my heart's content firm love doth bear,
Nothing of that shall from mine eyes appear.   295

Exit [with Alexander].

[SCENE III]

[*Sennet.*] *Enter* AGAMEMNON, NESTOR, ULYSSES, DIO-
MEDES, MENELAUS, *with others.*

Agam.   Princes:
What grief hath set these jaundies o'er your cheeks?
The ample proposition that hope makes
In all designs begun on earth below
Fails in the promis'd largeness. Checks and disasters
Grow in the veins of actions highest rear'd,   6
As knots, by the conflux of meeting sap,
Infects the sound pine, and diverts his grain
Tortive and errant from his course of growth.
Nor, princes, is it matter new to us   10
That we come short of our suppose so far
That after seven years' siege yet Troy walls stand,
Sith [every] action that hath gone before,
Whereof we have record, trial did draw
Bias and thwart, not answering the aim   15
And that unbodied figure of the thought
That gave't surmised shape. Why then, you princes,
Do you with cheeks abash'd behold our works,
And call them shames which are indeed nought else
But the protractive trials of great Jove   20
To find persistive constancy in men?
The fineness of which metal is not found
In fortune's love; for then the bold and coward,
The wise and fool, the artist and unread,
The hard and soft, seem all affin'd and kin;   25
But in the wind and tempest of her frown,
Distinction, with a broad and powerful fan,
Puffing at all, winnows the light away,
And what hath mass or matter, by itself
Lies rich in virtue and unmingled.   30

Nest. With due observance of [thy] godlike seat,
Great Agamemnon, Nestor shall apply
Thy latest words. In the reproof of chance
Lies the true proof of men: the sea being smooth,
How many shallow bauble boats dare sail   35
Upon her [patient] breast, making their way
With those of nobler bulk!
But let the ruffian Boreas once enrage
The gentle Thetis, and anon behold
The strong-ribb'd bark through liquid mountains cut,
Bounding between the two moist elements,   41
Like Perseus' horse. Where's then the saucy boat
Whose weak untimber'd sides but even now
Corrivall'd greatness? Either to harbor fled,
Or made a toast for Neptune. Even so   45
Doth valor's show and valor's worth divide
In storms of fortune; for in her ray and brightness
The herd hath more annoyance by the breeze
Than by the tiger; but when the splitting wind
Makes flexible the knees of knotted oaks,   50
And flies fled under shade, why then the thing of
          courage,
As rous'd with rage, with rage doth sympathize,
And with an accent tun'd in self-same key
Retires to chiding fortune.
Ulyss.   Agamemnon,
Thou great commander, nerves and bone of Greece,
Heart of our numbers, soul and only sprite   56
In whom the tempers and the minds of all
Should be shut up, hear what Ulysses speaks.
Besides th' applause and approbation
The which, [*to Agamemnon*] most mighty for thy place
          and sway,   60
[*To Nestor.*] And thou most reverend for [thy]
          stretch'd-out life,
I give to both your speeches, which were such
As Agamemnon and the hand of Greece
Should hold up high in brass, and such again

294. **content . . . bear:** the form and body of my heart carries the firm impress of love.

I.iii. Location: The Greek camp. Before Agamemnon's tent.
o.s.d. **Sennet:** series of trumpet notes signalling the entrance or exit of a procession or important person.
2. **jaundies:** jaundice (considered at this time as a plural). Both Agamemnon and Nestor speak repetitive commonplaces concealed in high-sounding and opaque language.
3. **proposition:** offer.
6. **highest rear'd:** aimed at the highest goal (cf. *aim*, line 15).
7. **conflux:** flowing together. Used by Shakespeare only here; so also *Tortive* (line 9), *protractive* (line 20), *persistive* (line 21), and other Latinisms in Agamemnon's vocabulary.
8. **Infects:** infect (Elizabethan third person plural in -*s*, or singular by proximity to *sap*, line 7). **his:** its (Shakespeare's almost invariable form of the neuter possessive pronoun).
9. **Tortive and errant:** twisted and wandering. **course:** natural direction.   11. **suppose:** expectation, estimate.
13. **Sith:** since.   14. **trial:** attempted performance.
15. **Bias and thwart:** awry and crosswise (cf. *tortive and errant*, line 9).   18. **works:** actions, deeds.
20. **protractive trials:** long-drawn-out testings.
21. **persistive:** persisting, enduring.
22. **metal:** i.e. constancy (using a metaphor for the refining of gold).
23. **In fortune's love:** i.e. when fortune smiles (cf. *frown*, line 26).
24. **artist:** scholar.   25. **affin'd:** joined by affinity, closely related.
27. **Distinction:** discrimination. **fan:** basket-shaped device for winnowing grain.
28. **light:** things of no "mass or matter" (line 29), i.e. chaff.
30. **virtue:** quality. **unmingled.** Quadrisyllabic.

31. **observance of:** deference to.   **seat:** throne.
32. **apply:** illustrate with examples.
33. **reproof:** confutation, rebuffing.   34. **proof:** test, proving.
35. **shallow bauble boats:** flat-bottomed toy boats.
38. **Boreas:** the north wind.
39. **Thetis:** a sea-nymph, mother of Achilles, here representing the sea itself, probably by a long-standing confusion with Tethys, wife of Oceanus.   41. **two moist elements:** water and air.
42. **Perseus' horse.** Pegasus, the winged horse, which belonged to Bellerophon, was regularly associated with Perseus in Elizabethan references. **saucy:** presumptuous.
43. **untimber'd sides:** sides not supported with strong timbers (cf. *strong-ribb'd*, line 40).   44. **Corrivall'd:** vied with.
45. **toast:** a tasty morsel (alluding to pieces of toasted bread floated in a flagon of liquor). **Neptune:** god of the sea, here = the sea itself.
46. **Doth.** Singular verb preceding a plural subject. **valor's show:** the mere appearance of valor.
47. **In . . . fortune:** when fortune frowns.   48. **breeze:** gadfly.
51. **fled:** are fled. **shade:** shelter. **thing of courage:** courageous creature.
52. **As . . . sympathize:** being itself roused to rage reacts sympathetically with the rage of the elements.
54. **Retires:** returns, i.e. answers (?). Of the several emendations proposed, most editors adopt *retorts* (Dyce conjecture).
55. **nerves:** sinews.   56. **numbers:** armies. **sprite:** spirit.
57. **tempers:** temperaments, dispositions.
58. **shut up:** contained as in a single body.
61. **stretch'd-out life.** Nestor is described by Homer as "third-ag'd" (Chapman's translation, *Iliad*, I, 249).
62. **such:** i.e. of such quality and significance.
63. **and . . . Greece.** This phrase has caused much difficulty, but if *and* is taken in the sense "who is," the meaning is perfectly clear. With *hand* cf. *nerves and bone* in line 55.

454

As venerable Nestor, hatch'd in silver,   65
Should with a bond of air strong as the axle-tree
On which heaven rides, knit all the Greekish ears
To his experienc'd tongue, yet let it please both,
Thou great, and wise, to hear Ulysses speak.
  [*Agam.* Speak, prince of Ithaca, and be't of less
      expect   70
That matter needless, of importless burthen,
Divide thy lips, than we are confident,
When rank Thersites opes his mastic jaws,
We shall hear music, wit, and oracle.]   74
  [*Ulyss.*]   Troy, yet upon his bases, had been down,
And the great Hector's sword had lack'd a master,
But for these instances:
The specialty of rule hath been neglected,
And look how many Grecian tents do stand
Hollow upon this plain, so many hollow factions.   80
When that the general is not like the hive
To whom the foragers shall all repair,
What honey is expected? Degree being vizarded,
Th' unworthiest shows as fairly in the mask.
The heavens themselves, the planets, and this centre
Observe degree, priority, and place,   86
Insisture, course, proportion, season, form,
Office, and custom, in all line of order;
And therefore is the glorious planet Sol
In noble eminence enthron'd and spher'd   90
Amidst the other; whose med'cinable eye
Corrects the [ill aspects] of [planets evil],
And posts like the commandment of a king,
Sans check, to good and bad. But when the planets
In evil mixture to disorder wander,   95
What plagues and what portents, what mutiny!

What raging of the sea, shaking of earth!
Commotion in the winds! frights, changes, horrors
Divert and crack, rend and deracinate
The unity and married calm of states   100
Quite from their fixure! O, when degree is shak'd,
Which is the ladder of all high designs,
The enterprise is sick. How could communities,
Degrees in schools, and brotherhoods in cities,
Peaceful commerce from dividable shores,   105
The primogenity and due of birth,
Prerogative of age, crowns, sceptres, laurels,
But by degree stand in authentic place?
Take but degree away, untune that string,
And hark what discord follows. Each thing [meets]
In mere oppugnancy: the bounded waters   111
Should lift their bosoms higher than the shores,
And make a sop of all this solid globe;
Strength should be lord of imbecility,
And the rude son should strike his father dead;   115
Force should be right, or rather, right and wrong
(Between whose endless jar justice resides)
Should lose their names, and so should justice too!
Then every thing include itself in power,
Power into will, will into appetite,   120
And appetite, an universal wolf
(So doubly seconded with will and power),
Must make perforce an universal prey,
And last eat up himself. Great Agamemnon,
This chaos, when degree is suffocate,   125
Follows the choking,
And this neglection of degree it is
That by a pace goes backward with a purpose
It hath to climb. The general's disdain'd
By him one step below, he by the next,   130
That next by him beneath; so every step,
Exampled by the first pace that is sick
Of his superior, grows to an envious fever

65. **hatch'd in silver:** engraved in silver (referring to Nestor's white hair).
66. **bond of air:** i.e. his words, to which the listeners' ears are tied. **axle-tree:** axis.   67. **rides:** turns, revolves.
70–74. **be't . . . oracle.** A typically wordy, involved, and negative way for Agamemnon to say: when Ulysses speaks we can expect good sense and sound counsel as certainly as we can anticipate discord, railing, and lies when Thersites speaks.   70. **expect:** expectation.
71. **burthen:** tenor.
73. **rank:** corrupt, coarse, foul.   **mastic.** Probably connected with *mastix* (= a scourge), hence "abusive."
74. **oracle:** i.e. truth.   75. **bases:** foundations.
77. **But:** except, if it were not.   **instances:** reasons, facts.
78. **specialty of rule:** the prerogative of command which belongs to the ruler.   **neglected:** disregarded, not properly respected.
79–80. **look . . . factions:** i.e. there are precisely as many empty pretenses of individual authority as there are tents on this plain. *Look how many* = however many, just as many. The first *Hollow* in line 80 may be intrusive; if not, it must mean "empty at the moment."
81. **like the hive:** i.e. the centre to which all energy is directed and from which all order emanates. The bee-state analogy was a favorite with the Elizabethans; cf. *Henry V*, I.ii.187–204.
82. **foragers:** workers (drones), all those subordinate to the "general" or ruler.
83–84. **Degree . . . mask:** i.e. when persons of various degrees are masked, the lowest is undistinguishable from the highest.
85. **this centre:** i.e. the earth (the centre of the Ptolemaic universe).
87. **Insisture:** steady continuance.   **proportion:** relationship.
88. **Office:** proper function or service.   **custom:** established practice.   89. **Sol:** the sun (the king of planets).
90. **spher'd:** set in a sphere.
91. **other:** others.   **med'cinable:** healing, restorative.
92. **ill . . . evil:** threatening glances of malign planets (i.e. their individual way of looking upon the earth). Some editors prefer the Q reading *influence of evil planets*, where *influence* = the unceasing effect of the planets on man and all other sublunary things, supposedly through a material emanation from them (*O.E.D.*).
93. **posts:** speeds.   94. **Sans:** without.
95. **evil mixture:** threatening conjunction.
96. **portents:** (bad) omens.

99. **Divert:** turn awry.   **deracinate:** tear up by the roots.
101. **fixure:** fixed position, stability.   **degree:** the principle of proper subordination.
103. **The enterprise:** i.e. any undertaking.
104. **Degrees:** academic rank.   **brotherhoods:** trade guilds, corporations.   105. **dividable:** dividing (?) or divided, separated (?).
106. **primogenity . . . birth:** the rights of the eldest-born.
107. **laurels:** i.e. high distinctions.
108. **authentic place:** position of acknowledged authority.
109. **untune that string.** The Elizabethans thought of the universe as a great musical instrument tuned by the hand of God, of which order, or degree, was an attribute. See the illustration on p. 442.
111. **mere oppugnancy:** absolute opposition.
112. **Should:** would (as a result); so in lines 114, 115, 116, 118.
113. **sop:** a toast, or cake, floated in liquor.
114. **Strength . . . imbecility:** physical strength would always dominate physical weakness (as in the example in line 115). *Imbecility* (used only here by Shakespeare) did not yet refer to mental weakness.
115. **rude:** violent, brutal (with some underlying sense of "unmannerly").
117. **Between . . . resides:** i.e. justice, by securing the right, stands as a shield against the continual onslaughts of the wrong.
118. **names:** i.e. their identity.
119. **include itself in:** would become one with.
120. **will . . . appetite:** uncontrolled desire or lust, which finds expression in an all-devouring appetite.
123. **perforce:** of necessity.   **prey:** act of preying, devouring.
125. **suffocate:** suffocated, strangled.
126. **choking:** the act of suffocation.
128. **by a pace:** step by step (Johnson), as the next sentence describes.
131. **step.** Meaning now the person on the step, not the step itself.
132. **Exampled:** given a precedent.   **first pace:** i.e. the person next below the general.   **sick:** i.e. distempered by disdain.

*Troilus
and Cressida
I.iii*

Of pale and bloodless emulation,
And 'tis this fever that keeps Troy on foot,   135
Not her own sinews. To end a tale of length,
Troy in our weakness stands, not in her strength.

Nest. Most wisely hath Ulysses here discover'd
The fever whereof all our power is sick.

Agam. The nature of the sickness found, Ulysses,
What is the remedy?   141

Ulyss. The great Achilles, whom opinion crowns
The sinow and the forehand of our host,
Having his ear full of his airy fame,
Grows dainty of his worth, and in his tent   145
Lies mocking our designs. With him Patroclus
Upon a lazy bed the livelong day
Breaks scurril jests,
And with ridiculous and [awkward] action,
Which, slanderer, he imitation calls,   150
He pageants us. Sometime, great Agamemnon,
Thy topless deputation he puts on,
And like a strutting player, whose conceit
Lies in his hamstring, and doth think it rich
To hear the wooden dialogue and sound   155
'Twixt his stretch'd footing and the scaffolage,
Such to-be-pitied and o'er-wrested seeming
He acts thy greatness in; and when he speaks,
'Tis like a chime a-mending, with terms [unsquar'd],
Which from the tongue of roaring Typhon dropp'd
Would seem hyperboles. At this fusty stuff   161
The large Achilles, on his press'd bed lolling,
From his deep chest laughs out a loud applause,
Cries, "Excellent! 'tis Agamemnon right!
Now play me Nestor, hem, and stroke thy beard,   165
As he being dress'd to some oration."
That's done, as near as the extremest ends
Of parallels, as like as Vulcan and his wife;
Yet god Achilles still cries, "Excellent!
'Tis Nestor right. Now play him me, Patroclus,   170

Arming to answer in a night alarm."
And then forsooth the faint defects of age
Must be the scene of mirth; to cough and spit,
And with a palsy fumbling on his gorget,
Shake in and out the rivet; and at this sport   175
Sir Valor dies; cries, "O, enough, Patroclus,
Or give me ribs of steel! I shall split all
In pleasure of my spleen." And in this fashion,
All our abilities, gifts, natures, shapes,
Severals and generals of grace exact,   180
Achievements, plots, orders, preventions,
Excitements to the field, or speech for truce,
Success or loss, what is or is not, serves
As stuff for these two to make paradoxes.

Nest. And in the imitation of these twain—   185
Who, as Ulysses says, opinion crowns
With an imperial voice—many are infect.
Ajax is grown self-will'd, and bears his head
In such a rein, in full as proud a place
As broad Achilles; keeps his tent like him,   190
Makes factious feasts, rails on our state of war,
Bold as an oracle, and sets Thersites,
A slave whose gall coins slanders like a mint,
To match us in comparisons with dirt,
To weaken [or] discredit our exposure,   195
How rank soever rounded in with danger.

Ulyss. They tax our policy, and call it cowardice,
Count wisdom as no member of the war,
Forestall prescience, and esteem no act
But that of hand. The still and mental parts,   200
That do contrive how many hands shall strike
When fitness calls them on, and know by measure
Of their observant toil the enemies' weight—
Why, this hath not a finger's dignity.
They call this bed-work, mapp'ry, closet-war,   205
So that the ram that batters down the wall,

---

134. **pale . . . emulation.** Pallor was traditionally associated with envy personified, and also with the chills that alternated with fever (cf., e.g., *agues pale* in *Venus and Adonis*, line 739). *Emulation* = jealous rivalry.
135. **on foot:** standing.   136. **tale of length:** long tale.
138. **discover'd:** revealed.   139. **power:** army.
143. **sinow . . . forehand:** i.e. foremost in strength (*sinow* is a variant form of *sinew*).
144. **his airy fame:** i.e. talk of his prowess. Like line 66, an allusion to the commonplace that words are breath and breath is air.
145. **dainty . . . worth:** oversolicitous of his (self-supposed) value.
147. **Upon . . . bed:** lazily upon a bed.
151. **pageants:** mimics (as in a theatrical exhibition).
152. **topless deputation:** supreme office (as general).
153. **strutting player.** Cf. *Macbeth*, V.v.24–25.
153–54. **conceit . . . hamstring:** intelligence is located in his leg muscles (literally, the tendons at the back of the knee); with a play on *conceit* in the modern sense.
154. **rich:** something magnificent, admirable.
155–56. **wooden . . . scaffolage:** i.e. the echoing noise of his mighty strides on the boards of the stage (*scaffolage* is a variant of *scaffoldage*).
157. **to-be-pitied . . . seeming:** pitifully overstrained mimicry.
159. **chime a-mending:** the cacophony produced by chimes while being retuned or repaired.   **terms unsquar'd:** ill-fitting expressions. Literally, *unsquar'd* = untrimmed (as applied to building stones).
160. **from:** i.e. even from.   **Typhon:** a giant with a hundred heads (mouths).
161. **fusty:** mouldy, stale. Unfortunately, there are no grounds for relating the word to *fustian*, "bombastic," which would suit the context admirably.
162. **press'd:** weighed down (with "large Achilles").
164. **right:** exactly.   165. **hem:** clear your throat.
166. **As . . . to:** as if he were about to begin.
168. **wife:** Venus. Vulcan was misshapen and lame.

172. **forsooth:** in truth.   **faint:** feeble.
174. **palsy:** tremorous.   **gorget:** armor for protecting the throat.
175. **rivet:** metal bolt fastening the gorget.
176. **Sir Valor:** Achilles (ironic).
178. **spleen.** The supposed seat of fits of laughter.
180. **Severals . . . exact:** (our) individual and general qualities of unexceptionable excellence (?). The phrase *of grace exact* has been variously explained and emended.
181. **preventions:** precautions.
182. **Excitements:** urgings, exhortations.
184. **paradoxes:** ways of treating a subject to make the truth appear absurd or the absurd appear like the truth.
186–87. **crowns . . . voice:** adjudges supreme.
187. **infect:** infected, diseased.
189. **In . . . rein:** as haughtily (like a proud-spirited horse bridling).
190. **broad:** physically large.   **keeps:** stays in.
191. **state:** council.
192. **Bold . . . oracle:** as confident as if he were the source of truth.
193. **gall:** rancor.   **like a mint:** as fast as a mint coins money.
194. **in comparisons:** by analogies ("false" implied).
195. **our exposure:** i.e. as exposed as we are.
196. **How . . . danger:** however thickly (*rank*) we are hemmed in by danger.   197. **policy:** prudent conduct of affairs.
198. **member:** part, element.
199. **Forestall prescience:** obstruct attempts to exercise foresight.
199–200. **esteem . . . hand:** value no performance that is not merely physical.   200. **still:** quiet (as opposed to the violent).
202. **fitness:** suitable occasion.   **measure:** computation.
203. **observant toil:** laborious observation.   **weight:** strength.
204. **not . . . dignity:** no greater worth than a finger has in relation to the whole body.
205. **bed-work:** "planning out action and war, as a man might do on his pillow" (Theobald).   **mapp'ry:** mere drawing of charts and diagrams.   **closet-war:** war for the study; cf. *closet-drama.*
206. **ram:** i.e. battering-ram.

For the great swinge and rudeness of his poise,
They place before his hand that made the engine,
Or those that with the fineness of their souls
By reason guide his execution.   210
  Nest. Let this be granted, and Achilles' horse
Makes many Thetis' sons.   [*Tucket.*]
  Agam. What trumpet? Look, Menelaus.
  Men. From Troy.

[*Enter* AENEAS.]

  Agam. What would you 'fore our tent?   215
  Aene. Is this great Agamemnon's tent, I pray you?
  Agam. Even this.
  Aene. May one that is a herald and a prince
Do a fair message to his kingly eyes?   219
  Agam. With surety stronger than Achilles' arm,
'Fore all the Greekish heads, which with one voice
Call Agamemnon head and general.
  Aene. Fair leave and large security. How may
A stranger to those most imperial looks
Know them from eyes of other mortals?
  Agam.   How?   225
  Aene. Ay,
I ask, that I might waken reverence,
And bid the cheek be ready with a blush
Modest as morning when she coldly eyes
The youthful Phoebus.   230
Which is that god in office, guiding men?
Which is the high and mighty Agamemnon?
  Agam. This Troyan scorns us, or the men of Troy
Are ceremonious courtiers.
  Aene. Courtiers as free, as debonair, unarm'd, 235
As bending angels; that's their [fame] in peace.
But when they would seem soldiers, they have galls,
Good arms, strong joints, true swords, and, great
          Jove's accord,
Nothing so full of heart. But peace, Aeneas,
Peace, Troyan, lay thy finger on thy lips!   240
The worthiness of praise distains his worth,
If that the prais'd himself bring the praise forth;
But what the repining enemy commends,
That breath fame blows, that praise, sole pure, tran-
          scends.
  Agam. Sir, you of Troy, call you yourself Aeneas?
  Aene. Ay, Greek, that is my name.   246
  Agam. What's your affairs, I pray you?
  Aene. Sir, pardon, 'tis for Agamemnon's ears.
  Agam. He hears nought privately that comes from
Troy.

  Aene. Nor I from Troy come not to whisper with
        him.   250
I bring a trumpet to awake his ear,
To set his [sense] on [the] attentive bent,
And then to speak.
  Agam.   Speak frankly as the wind,
It is not Agamemnon's sleeping hour.
That thou shalt know, Troyan, he is awake,   255
He tells thee so himself.
  Aene.   Trumpet, blow [loud],
Send thy brass voice through all these lazy tents,
And every Greek of mettle, let him know,
What Troy means fairly shall be spoke aloud.

                              Sound trumpet.

We have, great Agamemnon, here in Troy   260
A prince call'd Hector—Priam is his father—
Who in [this] dull and long-continued truce
Is resty grown. He bade me take a trumpet,
And to this purpose speak: kings, princes, lords!
If there be one among the fair'st of Greece   265
That holds his honor higher than his ease,
And [seeks] his praise more than he fears his peril,
That knows his valor, and knows not his fear,
That loves his mistress more than in confession
With truant vows to her own lips he loves,   270
And dare avow her beauty and her worth
In other arms than hers—to him this challenge!
Hector, in view of Troyans and of Greeks,
Shall make it good, or do his best to do it:
He hath a lady, wiser, fairer, truer,   275
Than ever Greek did couple in his arms,
And will to-morrow with his trumpet call,
Midway between your tents and walls of Troy,
To rouse a Grecian that is true in love.
If any come, Hector shall honor him;   280
If none, he'll say in Troy when he retires,
The Grecian dames are sunburnt, and not worth
The splinter of a lance. Even so much.
  Agam. This shall be told our lovers, Lord Aeneas.
If none of them have soul in such a kind,   285
We left them all at home. But we are soldiers,
And may that soldier a mere recreant prove,
That means not, hath not, or is not in love!
If then one is, or hath, [or] means to be,
That one meets Hector; if none else, I am he.   290
  Nest. Tell him of Nestor, one that was a man
When Hector's grandsire suck'd. He is old now,
But if there be not in our Grecian [mould]
A noble man that hath no spark of fire

---

207. **swinge:** impetus.   **rudeness:** rough violence.   **his poise:** its weight.   208. **place before:** prefer above.
209. **fineness . . . souls:** subtlety of their "mental parts" (line 200).
210. **his execution:** its operation.
211–12. **Achilles' horse . . . sons:** i.e. Achilles' horse is worth as much as many Achilleses (sons of Thetis, Achilles' mother).
212 s.d. **Tucket:** distinctive series of notes on a trumpet.
219. **fair:** courteous.
220. **surety:** security.   221. **'Fore:** in the presence of.
224. **looks:** glances (of the eyes).
227. **waken reverence:** prepare to be reverent.
229. **morning:** i.e. Aurora, goddess of the dawn.
235. **debonair:** gentle, meek.   236. **fame:** reputation.
237. **galls:** spirits resenting injuries.
238. **great Jove's accord:** great Jove consenting.
239. **Nothing . . . heart:** nothing has greater courage than they.
241. **distains his worth:** taints its value.
243. **repining:** begrudging.   244. **sole:** completely, utterly.

251. **trumpet.** Used both of the instrument and the player.
252. **set . . . bent:** make him bend an attentive ear.
253. **frankly:** freely.   258. **mettle:** spirit, courage.
259. **fairly:** honorably.   263. **resty:** sluggish (from lack of action).
265. **fair'st:** most illustrious.   267. **praise:** honorable reputation.
269–70. **in . . . loves:** i.e. in avowal made with idle vows to the lips of her whom he loves.
272. **In . . . hers:** i.e. not in his mistress' arms but in armor.
276. **couple . . . arms:** embrace (with sexual implication).
280. **honor him:** i.e. engage him in combat.
282. **sunburnt.** A sunburned skin was not a mark of beauty to the Elizabethans.   283. **splinter:** breaking.
285. **soul . . . kind:** such a spirit.   287. **mere recreant:** utter traitor.
288. **means not, hath not:** doesn't intend to be, or has not been.
292. **suck'd:** was a baby at the breast.
293–94. **not . . . no.** Modern usage would require the omission of no.
293. **mould:** characteristic cast, native constitution. Cf. lines 349–50. Most editors prefer host, an easier but flatter reading.

To answer for his love, tell him from me   295
I'll hide my silver beard in a gold beaver,
And in my vambrace put my withered brawns,
And meeting him [will] tell him that my lady
Was fairer than his grandam, and as chaste
As may be in the world. His youth in flood,   300
I'll prove this troth with my three drops of blood.
   Aene. Now heavens forfend such scarcity of
      [youth]!
   Ulyss. Amen.
   [*Agam.*] Fair Lord Aeneas, let me touch your hand;
To our pavilion shall I lead you, sir.   305
Achilles shall have word of this intent,
So shall each lord of Greece, from tent to tent.
Yourself shall feast with us before you go,
And find the welcome of a noble foe.
                  [*Exeunt. Manent Ulysses and Nestor.*]
   Ulyss. Nestor!   310
   Nest. What says Ulysses?
   Ulyss. I have a young conception in my brain,
Be you my time to bring it to some shape.
   Nest. What is't?
   Ulyss. [*This 'tis:*]   315
Blunt wedges rive hard knots; the seeded pride
That hath to this maturity blown up
In rank Achilles must or now be cropp'd,
Or shedding, breed a nursery of like evil,
To overbulk us all.
   Nest.   Well, and how?   320
   Ulyss. This challenge that the gallant Hector
      sends,
However it is spread in general name,
Relates in purpose only to Achilles.
   Nest. True, the purpose is perspicuous as sub-
      stance,
Whose grossness little characters sum up;   325
And in the publication make no strain
But that Achilles, were his brain as barren
As banks of Libya (though, Apollo knows,
'Tis dry enough), will with great speed of judgment,
Ay, with celerity, find Hector's purpose   330
Pointing on him.
   Ulyss. And wake him to the answer, think you?
   Nest. Why, 'tis most meet; who may you else
      oppose
That can from Hector bring those honors off,

If not Achilles? Though't be a sportful combat,   335
Yet in the trial much opinion dwells;
For here the Troyans taste our dear'st repute
With their fin'st palate; and trust to me, Ulysses,
Our imputation shall be oddly pois'd
In this vild action, for the success,   340
Although particular, shall give a scantling
Of good or bad unto the general,
And in such indexes (although small pricks
To their subsequent volumes) there is seen
The baby figure of the giant mass   345
Of things to come at large. It is suppos'd
He that meets Hector issues from our choice,
And choice (being mutual act of all our souls)
Makes merit her election, and doth boil
(As 'twere from forth us all) a man distill'd   350
Out of our virtues, who miscarrying,
What heart receives from hence a conquering part
To steel a strong opinion to themselves?
[Which entertain'd, limbs are his instruments,
In no less working than are swords and bows   355
Directive by the limbs.]
   Ulyss.   Give pardon to my speech:
Therefore 'tis meet Achilles meet not Hector.
Let us like merchants first show foul wares,
And think perchance they'll sell; if not,
The lustre of the better shall exceed   360
By showing the worse first. Do not consent
That ever Hector and Achilles meet,
For both our honor and our shame in this
Are dogg'd with two strange followers.
   Nest. I see them not with my old eyes, what are
      they?   365
   Ulyss. What glory our Achilles shares from
      Hector,
Were he not proud, we all should share with him.
But he already is too insolent;
And it were better parch in Afric sun
Than in the pride and salt scorn of his eyes,   370
Should he scape Hector fair. If he were foil'd,

295. **answer for:** testify to.   296. **beaver:** face guard of a helmet.
297. **vambrace:** i.e. vantbrace, armor for the front part of the arm.
brawns: muscles; here, arms.
300. **His . . . flood:** he being at the height of youthful strength.
301. **troth:** truth.   302. **forfend:** forbid.
313. **Be . . . time:** act as a midwife (as for a woman whose "time" has
come).
316. **Blunt . . . knots:** proverbial (referring to "knots" in timber).
seeded: run to seed.
317. **blown up:** become overexpanded and ready to burst (like the
seed pod of a plant past full bloom).
318. **rank:** puffed-up, swollen.   **or:** either.   **cropp'd:** cut off.
319. **shedding:** scattering its seeds.   **nursery:** training ground.
320. **overbulk:** overwhelm.   **and how:** what then follows?
324-25. **perspicuous . . . up:** as clearly to be seen as great wealth,
the quantity of which may be expressed in a few small figures.
326. **in the publication:** when it is proclaimed publicly.   **make no
strain:** have no doubt.
328. **banks of Libya:** sandbanks of the Libyan desert.
329. **dry.** A dry brain was equated with dullness.
332. **wake him:** rouse himself.

336. **in . . . dwells:** in the combat (seen as a test of relative merit) the
question of reputation is importantly involved.
337-38. **taste . . . palate:** i.e. are putting to the test our best by means
of their best (*dear'st repute* = Achilles; *fin'st palate* = Hector).
339. **Our imputation:** the honor or discredit imputed to us.   **oddly
pois'd:** i.e. unjustly or wrongly weighed (because quite disproportionate to the cause).
340. **vild:** paltry (variant of *vile*).   **success:** outcome (good or bad).
341. **particular:** belonging to an individual.   **give a scantling:** i.e.
be taken as a sample (of what is to come).
342. **general:** the whole army.   343. **indexes:** tables of contents.
343-44. **small . . . volumes:** slight indicators of the content that
follows. *Subsequent* is accented on the second syllable.
345. **baby figure:** embryonic form.   346. **is:** will be.
349. **election:** basis of selection.
351. **miscarrying:** losing to his opponent.
352. **conquering part:** share of victory.
353. **steel . . . themselves:** i.e. attach firmly to themselves a conviction
of their prowess.
354-56. **limbs . . . limbs:** limbs become its instruments of (victorious)
action, no less responsive to it than swords and bows are subject to
direction by the limbs.
357. **Therefore 'tis meet:** for this very reason it is proper.
358. **foul:** poor in quality.
360. **lustre . . . exceed:** the comparative fineness of the superior
wares will be enhanced.
364. **strange followers:** i.e. unexpected or surprising corollaries.
369. **better parch:** better to scorch.   370. **salt:** bitter, corroding.
371. **scape Hector fair:** escape from Hector with victory.

Why then we do our main opinion crush
In taint of our best man. No, make a lott'ry,
And by device let blockish Ajax draw
The sort to fight with Hector; among ourselves   375
Give him allowance for the better man,
For that will physic the great Myrmidon,
Who broils in loud applause, and make him fall
His crest that prouder than blue Iris bends.
If the dull brainless Ajax come safe off,   380
We'll dress him up in voices; if he fail,
Yet go we under our opinion still
That we have better men. But hit or miss,
Our project's life this shape of sense assumes:
Ajax employ'd plucks down Achilles' plumes.   385
    Nest. Now, Ulysses, I begin to relish thy advice,
And I will give a taste thereof forthwith
To Agamemnon. Go we to him straight.
Two curs shall tame each other; pride alone
Must [tarre] the mastiffs on, as 'twere a bone.   390
                                    Exeunt.

[ACT II, Scene I]

Enter Ajax *and* Thersites.

    Ajax. Thersites!
    Ther. Agamemnon, how if he had biles—full, all
over, generally?
    Ajax. Thersites!   4
    Ther. And those biles did run—say so—did not
the general run then? Were not that a botchy core?
    Ajax. Dog!
    Ther. Then would come some matter from him; I
see none now.   9
    Ajax. Thou bitch-wolf's son, canst thou not hear?
Feel then.   [*Strikes him.*]
    Ther. The plague of Greece upon thee, thou
mongrel beef-witted lord!
    Ajax. Speak then, thou [whinid'st] leaven, speak; I

will beat thee into handsomeness.   15
    Ther. I shall sooner rail thee into wit and holiness,
but I think thy horse will sooner con an oration without book than thou learn [a] prayer without book.
Thou canst strike, canst thou? A red murrion a' thy
jade's tricks!   20
    Ajax. Toadstool! learn me the proclamation.
    Ther. Dost thou think I have no sense, thou
strikest me thus?
    Ajax. The proclamation!
    Ther. Thou art proclaim'd fool, I think.   25
    Ajax. Do not, porpentine, do not, my fingers itch.
    Ther. I would thou didst itch from head to foot;
and I had the scratching of thee, I would make thee the
loathsomest scab in Greece. When thou art forth in
the incursions, thou strikest as slow as another.   30
    Ajax. I say, the proclamation!
    Ther. Thou grumblest and railest every hour on
Achilles, and thou art as full of envy at his greatness as
Cerberus is at Proserpina's beauty, ay, that thou
bark'st at him.   35
    Ajax. Mistress Thersites!
    Ther. Thou shouldst strike him.
    Ajax. Cobloaf!
    [*Ther.*] He would pun thee into shivers with his
fist, as a sailor breaks a biscuit.   40
    [*Ajax.*] [*Beating him.*] You whoreson cur!
    [*Ther.*] Do! do! thou stool for a witch! ay, do! do!
thou sodden-witted lord! Thou hast no more brain than
I have in mine elbows, an asinico may tutor thee. You
scurvy valiant ass! thou art here but to thrash   45
Troyans, and thou art bought and sold among those of
any wit, like a barbarian slave. If thou use to beat me,
I will begin at thy heel, and tell what thou art by
inches, thou thing of no bowels, thou!
    Ajax. You dog!   50
    Ther. You scurvy lord!
    Ajax. [*Beating him.*] You cur!
    Ther. Mars his idiot! Do, rudeness, do, camel,
do, do.

[*Enter* Achilles *and* Patroclus.]

372–73. **our . . . taint**: destroy our general reputation by the dishonor.   374. **by device**: by a trick.   **blockish**: stupid, dull-witted.
375. **sort**: lot.   376. **Give . . . for**: acknowledge him as.
377. **physic**: act as a medicinal purge to.   **great Myrmidon**: Achilles.
The Myrmidons, a people of Thessaly, were special followers of
Achilles.
378. **broils**: bakes (as in the sunshine), with a strong suggestion of
being overcooked.
378–79. **fall His crest**: i.e. bow his pride. *Crest* = the tuft of feathers
on a bird's head; here, the plumes on Achilles' helmet (cf. *plumes* in
line 385).
379. **blue Iris**. The messenger of Juno, here used for the rainbow,
with which she was identified; perhaps "blue" as associated with the
sky; but cf. *Lucrece*, line 1587: "Blue circles streamed, like rainbows
in the sky."   **bends**: arches.   381. **voices**: words of praise.
383. **hit or miss**: win or lose, either way (earliest use of this phrase).
384. **life**: success.   **this . . . assumes**: takes on this semblance of
rational meaning.   388. **straight**: straightway.
390. **tarre . . . on**: set the dogs fighting against each other.

II.i. **Location**: The Greek camp.
2. **biles**: boils (a variant form).
6. **botchy**: ulcerous.   **core**: boil (properly, the hard mass of tissue
at the centre of a boil); perhaps with play on *corps* = body.
8. **matter**: (a) meaning; (b) pus.
12. **plague of Greece**. Perhaps referring to a plague visited by Apollo
on the Greeks (described in the *Iliad*, Bk. I).
13. **mongrel**. Ajax was part Greek and part Trojan.   **beef-witted**:
stupid as an ox.
14. **whinid'st**: mouldiest (variant of *vinewed'st*).   **leaven**: a batch
of fermenting dough, here associated with the Biblical "leaven of
maliciousness and wickedness," 1 Corinthians, 5:8 (Geneva).

15. **handsomeness**: (1) proper manners; (2) proper shape (alluding to
Thersites' physical deformity).
17–18. **con . . . book**: learn a speech by heart.
19. **murrion**: plague (variant of *murrain*).   **a'**: on.
20. **jade's tricks**. A jade was a bad-tempered horse and his "tricks"
were rearing and kicking.
21. **Toadstool**. Referring to Thersites as (1) poisonous, (2) deformed
in shape, (3) an upstart.   **learn me**: find out for me the tenor of
(see lines 90–91).   22. **sense**: feeling.   26. **porpentine**: porcupine.
28. **and**: if.
30. **incursions**: military encounters.   **another**: anyone else.
34. **Cerberus**: the three-headed dog that was porter-guardian of the
underworld.   **Proserpina**: queen of the underworld.   **that**: so
that.
36. **Mistress**. Implying cowardice (?) or a termagant's tongue (?).
38. **Cobloaf**: a little loaf made with a round head (Minsheu).
39. **pun . . . shivers**: pound you into fragments.
41. **whoreson**: term of general abuse (literally, son of a whore).
42. **stool . . . witch**: privy used by a witch, hence especially stinking;
probably suggested by the common Elizabethan pun on *Ajax/a jakes*
(= privy).   43. **sodden-witted**: boiled-brained, stupid.
44. **asinico**: blockhead; literally, little ass (Spanish).
45. **scurvy valiant**: scabby vainglorious.
46. **bought and sold**: treated like a piece of merchandise.
47. **use**: continue.   49. **bowels**: tender feeling, mercy.
53. **Mars his idiot**: Mars's fool, creature good only for brainless
violence.

Achil. Why, how now, Ajax, wherefore do ye
thus?   55
How now, Thersites, what's the matter, man?

Ther. You see him there? Do you?

Achil. Ay, what's the matter?

Ther. Nay, look upon him.

Achil. So I do. What's the matter?   60

Ther. Nay, but regard him well.

Achil. Well? why, so I do.

Ther. But yet you look not well upon him, for
whosomever you take him to be, he is Ajax.

Achil. I know that, fool.   65

Ther. Ay, but that fool knows not himself.

Ajax. Therefore I beat thee.

Ther. Lo, lo, lo, lo, what modicums of wit he
utters! his evasions have ears thus long. I have bobb'd
his brain more than he has beat my bones. [I] will   70
buy nine sparrows for a penny, and his *pia mater* is not
worth the ninth part of a sparrow. This lord, Achilles,
Ajax, who wears his wit in his belly and his guts in his
head, [I'll] tell you what I say of him.

Achil. What?   75

Ther. I say, this Ajax—

[*Ajax offers to strike him.*]

Achil. Nay, good Ajax.

Ther. Has not so much wit—

Achil. Nay, I must hold you.   79

Ther. As will stop the eye of Helen's needle, for
whom he comes to fight.

Achil. Peace, fool!

Ther. I would have peace and quietness, but the
fool will not—he there, that he! Look you there.

Ajax. O thou damn'd cur! I shall—   85

Achil. Will you set your wit to a fool's?

Ther. No, I warrant you, the fool's will shame it.

Patr. Good words, Thersites.

Achil. What's the quarrel?   89

Ajax. I bade the vile owl go learn me the tenor of
the proclamation, and he rails upon me.

Ther. I serve thee not.

Ajax. Well, go to, go to.

Ther. I serve here voluntary.   94

Achil. Your last service was suff'rance, 'twas not
voluntary; no man is beaten voluntary. Ajax was here
the voluntary, and you as under an impress.   97

Ther. E'en so; a great deal of your wit, too, lies in
your sinews, or else there be liars. Hector shall have
a great catch, and ['a] knock [out] either of your

brains; 'a were as good crack a fusty nut with no
kernel.   102

Achil. What, with me too, Thersites?

Ther. There's Ulysses and old Nestor, whose wit
was mouldy ere [your] grandsires had nails [on their
toes], yoke you like draught-oxen, and make you
plough up the wars.   107

Achil. What? what?

Ther. Yes, good sooth. To, Achilles! to, Ajax! to—

Ajax. I shall cut out your tongue.   110

Ther. 'Tis no matter, I shall speak as much as thou
afterwards.

Patr. No more words, Thersites, peace!

Ther. I will hold my peace when Achilles' [brach]
bids me, shall I?   115

Achil. There's for you, Patroclus.

Ther. I will see you hang'd like clatpoles ere I
come any more to your tents. I will keep where there
is wit stirring, and leave the faction of fools.   *Exit.*

Patr. A good riddance.   120

Achil. Marry, this, sir, is proclaim'd through all
our host:
That Hector, by the [fift] hour of the sun,
Will with a trumpet 'twixt our tents and Troy
To-morrow morning call some knight to arms
That hath a stomach, and such a one that dare   125
Maintain—I know not what, 'tis trash. Farewell.

Ajax. Farewell. Who shall answer him?

Achil. I know not, 'tis put to lott'ry. Otherwise,
He knew his man.

Ajax. O, meaning you? I will go learn more of
it.   [*Exeunt.*]   130

[SCENE II]

Enter PRIAM, HECTOR, TROILUS, PARIS, *and* HELENUS.

Pri. After so many hours, lives, speeches spent,
Thus once again says Nestor from the Greeks:
"Deliver Helen, and all damage else—
As honor, loss of time, travail, expense,
Wounds, friends, and what else dear that is consum'd
In hot digestion of this cormorant war—   6
Shall be strook off." Hector, what say you to't?

Hect. Though no man lesser fears the Greeks than I
As far as toucheth my particular,
Yet, dread Priam,   10
There is no lady of more softer bowels,
More spungy to suck in the sense of fear,
More ready to cry out, "Who knows what follows?"

64. **whosomever:** whosoever.
65. **I . . . fool.** Thersites quibbles on "I know that fool."
67. **Therefore . . . thee:** i.e. I beat you because I am not a fool (?) or
I stoop to beat you because I don't know my own superiority (?).
69. **his . . . long:** i.e. his attempts to get out of it are asinine.   **bobb'd:**
thumped.   70. **will:** can.
71. **pia mater:** i.e. brain (properly, the membrane that covers the
brain).   73–74. **wears . . . head:** probably proverbial.
86. **set . . . to:** match your wits with.
88. **Good words:** i.e. speak temperately (from Plautus, *bona verba*).
93. **go to:** interjection expressing disapproval or protest.
94, 96. **voluntary.** Adverbial.
95. **suff'rance:** the endurance of something imposed (with play on
the sense "suffering pain").
97. **impress:** (a) impressment, conscription; (b) imprint (of Ajax'
blows).   98. **E'en so:** true.
100. **and 'a:** if he.   100–101. **either . . . brains:** the brains of either
one of you (Achilles or Ajax).

101. **'a . . . good:** it would be as much worth his while to.
109. **To:** i.e. to it (as if urging on draught oxen).
111. **as much:** i.e. as much sense.
114. **brach:** bitch dog. Cf. *masculine whore* applied to Patroclus in
V.i.17.   117. **clatpoles:** blockheads, dolts (variant of *clotpolls*).
122. **fift:** fifth.   125. **a stomach:** courage (appetite for a fight).

II.ii. Location: Troy. Priam's palace.
4. **travail:** painful labor.
6. **cormorant:** gluttonous, devouring (from the large voracious sea-
bird of that name).   9. **my particular:** my personal concerns.
11. **more softer bowels:** tenderer feelings (the Elizabethan double
comparative was used for emphasis).
12. **spungy:** absorbent (variant of *spongy*).

Than Hector is. The wound of peace is [surety],
[Surety] secure, but modest doubt is call'd   15
The beacon of the wise, the tent that searches
To th' bottom of the worst. Let Helen go.
Since the first sword was drawn about this question,
Every tithe soul, 'mongst many thousand dismes,
Hath been as dear as Helen; I mean, of ours.   20
If we have lost so many tenths of ours,
To guard a thing not ours nor worth to us
(Had it our name) the value of one ten,
What merit's in that reason which denies
The yielding of her up?
    Tro.   Fie, fie, my brother!   25
Weigh you the worth and honor of a king
So great as our dread father's in a scale
Of common ounces? Will you with compters sum
The past-proportion of his infinite,
And buckle in a waist most fathomless   30
With spans and inches so diminutive
As fears and reasons? Fie, for godly shame!
    Hel.   No marvel though you bite so sharp [at] rea-
     sons,
You are so empty of them. Should not our father
Bear the great sway of his affairs with reason,   35
Because your speech hath none that tell him so?
    Tro.   You are for dreams and slumbers, brother
     priest,
You fur your gloves with reason. Here are your
     reasons:
You know an enemy intends you harm;
You know a sword employ'd is perilous,   40
And reason flies the object of all harm.
Who marvels then, when Helenus beholds
A Grecian and his sword, if he do set
The very wings of reason to his heels
And fly like chidden Mercury from Jove,   45
Or like a star disorb'd? Nay, if we talk of reason,
[Let's] shut our gates and sleep. Manhood and honor

Should have hare hearts, would they but fat their
    thoughts
With this cramm'd reason; reason and respect
Make livers pale and lustihood deject.   50
    Hect. Brother, she is not worth what she doth cost
The keeping.
    Tro.   What's aught but as 'tis valued?
    Hect. But value dwells not in particular will,
It holds his estimate and dignity
As well wherein 'tis precious of itself   55
As in the prizer. 'Tis mad idolatry
To make the service greater than the god,
And the will dotes that is attributive
To what infectiously itself affects,
Without some image of th' affected merit.   60
    Tro.   I take to-day a wife, and my election
Is led on in the conduct of my will,
My will enkindled by mine eyes and ears,
Two traded pilots 'twixt the dangerous [shores]
Of will and judgment: how may I avoid   65
(Although my will distaste what it elected)
The wife I chose? There can be no evasion
To blench from this and to stand firm by honor.
We turn not back the silks upon the merchant
When we have soil'd them, nor the remainder viands
We do not throw in unrespective sieve,   71
Because we now are full. It was thought meet
Paris should do some vengeance on the Greeks.
Your breath with full consent bellied his sails;
The seas and winds, old wranglers, took a truce,   75
And did him service; he touch'd the ports desir'd,

14. **wound . . . surety:** i.e. the danger of peace lies in a sense of security.
15. **secure:** careless, overconfident. **modest doubt:** a reasonable measure of wariness.
16. **beacon:** warning light (like a fire set on a hilltop). **tent:** probe (medical).
19. **tithe . . . dismes:** (literally) tenth . . . tenths, The meaning of lines 19–20 has been much debated. Deighton's explanation is most widely accepted: "The meaning seems to be not that every tenth soul *only*, but every soul *that has been taken as a tithe by war* is as dear as Helen, and of such tithes there have been many thousands."
23. **Had . . . name:** i.e. even if Helen were a Trojan. **one ten:** one "tithe," i.e. a single Trojan life.
28. **compters:** counters (variant form), tokens, false coins. **sum:** add up, total.
29. **past-proportion:** immeasurability.
31. **spans:** i.e. hand spans, the distance between the extended thumb and little finger (reckoned as nine inches).
33. **bite . . . at:** talk so cuttingly of. **reasons.** Perhaps with a quibble on *raisins* (pronounced similarly); snapping up burning raisins floating in a glass of wine was an Elizabethan pastime.
34. **Should . . . father:** should our father *not*.
36. **tell him so:** i.e. tell him how (to conduct his affairs with reason).
37. **dreams and slumbers.** Cf. *bed-work,* I.iii.205.
38. **fur . . . reason:** i.e. employ your kind of reason to secure a comfortable life for yourself. *Fur* means "line with fur." Troilus goes on to charge Helenus with rationalizing his counsel of prudence.
41. **object . . . harm:** sight of anything dangerous.
45. **Mercury:** Jove's messenger, who was pictured as wearing shoes with wings on the heels.
46. **star disorb'd:** star cast out of its proper orb or sphere, i.e. shooting star.

48. **Should:** would certainly. **hare:** timid.
49. **cramm'd.** A transferred modifier, rightly describing the thoughts, which are compared to fowl fattened for market by overfeeding. **respect:** cautious consideration (of consequences).
50. **livers pale.** A white (*bloodless*) liver was symbolic of cowardice. **lustihood:** bodily vigor. **deject:** dejected, abated.
51–52. **what . . . keeping:** her keep, her living expenses.
52. **What's . . . valued:** what gives worth to anything except the value at which someone esteems it.
53. **particular will:** the arbitrary preference of any single person.
54. **dignity:** worth. 55. **wherein . . . itself:** in its intrinsic value.
56. **the prizer:** i.e. the value placed on it by someone who prizes it.
57. **To . . . god:** i.e. to pay greater honor to a thing than in its essential nature it is worth.
58. **dotes:** is mad. **is attributive:** pays tribute.
59. **infectiously.** This may refer to the will (behaving as if diseased) or to the object of esteem (given supposed value by contagion from the will's valuation of it). **affects:** likes, admires.
60. **image:** appearance (within itself).
61. **I . . . wife.** Troilus sets up a hypothetical analogy. **election:** choice. **led . . . will:** guided by my desire.
64. **traded pilots:** intermediaries constantly going back and forth.
65. **judgment:** the rational faculty (as opposed to *will*). **avoid:** get rid of. 66. **distaste:** (come to) dislike.
67. **evasion:** contrived excuse, subterfuge.
68. **blench:** turn aside. **and:** and at the same time.
70. **remainder viands:** food left uneaten.
71. **unrespective sieve:** i.e. the refuse basket, into which only worthless (*unrespective* = unregarded) things are thrown (?). Perhaps *unrespective* in the sense "unregarding" is a transferred modifier, rightly describing those who throw away the food.
73. **vengeance.** Paris had gone to Greece to avenge the Greeks' refusal to return Priam's sister Hesione (the "old aunt" of line 77), taken captive by Hercules and given by him to Telamon, king of Salamis. Telamon was Ajax' father, and according to the medieval and Renaissance tradition followed in this play Hesione was his mother. His relationship to Hector becomes of dramatic interest in IV.v.
74. **breath:** i.e. approving speeches or votes (again the commonplace that words are air). **bellied:** filled out, distended.
75. **old wranglers:** long-time opponents or quarrellers.

*Troilus
and Cressida
II.ii*

And for an old aunt whom the Greeks held captive,
He brought a Grecian queen, whose youth and fresh-
     ness
Wrinkles Apollo's, and makes pale the morning.
Why keep we her? The Grecians keep our aunt. 80
Is she worth keeping? Why, she is a pearl,
Whose price hath launch'd above a thousand ships,
And turn'd crown'd kings to merchants.
If you'll avouch 'twas wisdom Paris went—
As you must needs, for you all cried "Go, go"— 85
If you'll confess [he] brought home worthy prize—
As you must needs, for you all clapp'd your hands,
And cried "Inestimable!"—why do you now
The issue of your proper wisdoms rate,
And do a deed that never Fortune did, 90
Beggar the estimation which you priz'd
Richer than sea and land? O theft most base,
That we have stol'n what we do fear to keep!
But thieves unworthy of a thing so stol'n,
That in their country did them that disgrace 95
We fear to warrant in our native place!
    Cassandra. [*Within.*] Cry, Troyans, cry!
    Pri.   What noise? what shrike is this?
    Tro. 'Tis our mad sister, I do know her voice.
    Cas. [*Within.*] Cry, Troyans!
    Hect. It is Cassandra. 100

Enter CASSANDRA *raving* [*with her hair about her ears*].

    Cas. Cry, Troyans, cry! lend me ten thousand eyes,
And I will fill them with prophetic tears.
    Hect. Peace, sister, peace!
    Cas. Virgins and boys, mid-age and wrinkled [eld],
Soft infancy, that nothing canst but cry, 105
Add to my clamors! Let us pay betimes
A moi'ty of that mass of moan to come.
Cry, Troyans, cry! practice your eyes with tears!
Troy must not be, nor goodly Ilion stand.
Our fire-brand brother Paris burns us all. 110
Cry, Troyans, cry! a Helen and a woe!
Cry, cry! Troy burns, or else let Helen go. *Exit.*
    Hect. Now, youthful Troilus, do not these high
     strains

Of divination in our sister work
Some touches of remorse? or is your blood 115
So madly hot that no discourse of reason,
Nor fear of bad success in a bad cause,
Can qualify the same?
    Tro.   Why, brother Hector,
We may not think the justness of each act
Such and no other than event doth form it, 120
Nor once deject the courage of our minds
Because Cassandra's mad. Her brain-sick raptures
Cannot distaste the goodness of a quarrel
Which hath our several honors all engag'd
To make it gracious. For my private part, 125
I am no more touch'd than all Priam's sons;
And Jove forbid there should be done amongst us
Such things as might offend the weakest spleen
To fight for and maintain.
    Par. Else might the world convince of levity 130
As well my undertakings as your counsels,
But I attest the gods, your full consent
Gave wings to my propension, and cut off
All fears attending on so dire a project.
For what, alas, can these my single arms? 135
What propugnation is in one man's valor
To stand the push and enmity of those
This quarrel would excite? Yet I protest,
Were I alone to pass the difficulties,
And had as ample power as I have will, 140
Paris should ne'er retract what he hath done,
Nor faint in the pursuit.
    Pri.   Paris, you speak
Like one besotted on your sweet delights.
You have the honey still, but these the gall;
So to be valiant, is no praise at all. 145
    Par. Sir, I propose not merely to myself
The pleasures such a beauty brings with it,
But I would have the soil of her fair rape
Wip'd off, in honorable keeping her.
What treason were it to the ransack'd queen, 150
Disgrace to your great worths, and shame to me,
Now to deliver her possession up
On terms of base compulsion! Can it be
That so degenerate a strain as this
Should once set footing in your generous bosoms? 155

---

79. **Wrinkles Apollo's:** makes Apollo's youth and freshness look aged by comparison. **morning:** i.e. rosy dawn.
82. **price:** value. **launch'd . . . ships.** There is no necessary connection with Marlowe's *Doctor Faustus* ("Was this the face that launch'd a thousand ships?"); there is a classical source in Lucian's *Dialogue of the Dead*, and Marlowe was not alone in drawing from it. But Shakespeare elsewhere quotes Marlowe and borrows from his work.
83. **turn'd . . . merchants.** An echo of Matthew 13:45: "Again, the kingdome of heaven is like unto a marchant man, seeking goodly pearls: which when he had found one precious pearl, went and sold all he had, and bought it" (Geneva). 84. **avouch:** affirm.
89. **issue . . . rate:** repudiate the outcome of your own good judgments.
90. **do . . . did:** i.e. be more inconstant than even Fortune herself.
91. **Beggar . . . which:** esteem as worthless what.
93. **That:** in that.
95–96. **That . . . place:** who gave the Greeks in their own country a disgrace that we are now afraid to ratify.
97. **Cry:** weep and lament. **shrike:** shriek (variant form).
104. **eld:** old age. 105. **canst:** can do. 106. **betimes:** in advance.
107. **moi'ty:** portion. **moan:** lamentation.
108. **practice . . . tears:** accustom your eyes to weeping.
110. **fire-brand brother Paris.** The reference is to Hecuba's dream, when she was pregnant with Paris, that she would be delivered of a fire-brand which would be the destruction of Troy.

115. **remorse:** compunction.
116. **discourse of reason:** faculty of reason, reason itself.
117. **success:** outcome. 118. **qualify:** moderate.
119–20. **We . . . it:** i.e. we must not judge the propriety of every action by its result (*event*). 121. **once deject:** ever abate.
122. **brain-sick raptures:** mad, ecstatic fits.
123. **distaste:** make unpalatable.
124. **our . . . engag'd:** the honor of each of us bound by oath.
125. **gracious:** righteous. 126. **touch'd:** affected. **all:** any of.
128. **spleen:** temper. 130. **convince:** convict.
132. **attest the gods:** call the gods to witness.
133. **propension:** inclination.
134. **attending on:** i.e. which might accompany.
135. **can . . . arms:** can my unaided arms do.
136. **propugnation.** defense. 137. **push and enmity:** hostile onset.
139. **pass:** experience, go through with.
141. **retract:** disavow, wish undone.
142. **faint:** weary, lose heart. 143. **besotted:** doting.
145. **So:** under such circumstances.
146. **propose . . . myself:** set before my mind, have in view.
148. **her fair rape:** the abduction of her fair self (?).
150. **ransack'd:** carried off as plunder.
152. **deliver . . . up:** return her, having once possessed her.
154. **strain:** impulse. 155. **once:** for a moment. **generous:** noble.

There's not the meanest spirit on our party
Without a heart to dare, or sword to draw,
When Helen is defended; nor none so noble
Whose life were ill bestow'd, or death unfam'd,
Where Helen is the subject. Then I say, 160
Well may we fight for her whom we know well
The world's large spaces cannot parallel.

Hect. Paris and Troilus, you have both said well,
And on the cause and question now in hand
Have gloz'd, but superficially, not much 165
Unlike young men, whom Aristotle thought
Unfit to hear moral philosophy.
The reasons you allege do more conduce
To the hot passion of distemp'red blood
Than to make up a free determination 170
'Twixt right and wrong; for pleasure and revenge
Have ears more deaf than adders to the voice
Of any true decision. Nature craves
All dues be rend'red to their owners: now,
What nearer debt in all humanity 175
Than wife is to the husband? If this law
Of nature be corrupted through affection,
And that great minds, of partial indulgence
To their benumbed wills, resist the same,
There is a law in each well-order'd nation 180
To curb those raging appetites that are
Most disobedient and refractory.
If Helen then be wife to Sparta's king,
As it is known she is, these moral laws
Of nature and of nations speak aloud 185
To have her back return'd. Thus to persist
In doing wrong extenuates not wrong,
But makes it much more heavy. Hector's opinion
Is this in way of truth; yet ne'er the less,
My spritely brethren, I propend to you 190
In resolution to keep Helen still,
For 'tis a cause that hath no mean dependance
Upon our joint and several dignities.

Tro. Why, there you touch'd the life of our design!
Were it not glory that we more affected 195
Than the performance of our heaving spleens,
I would not wish a drop of Troyan blood
Spent more in her defense. But, worthy Hector,

She is a theme of honor and renown,
A spur to valiant and magnanimous deeds, 200
Whose present courage may beat down our foes,
And fame in time to come canonize us,
For I presume brave Hector would not lose
So rich advantage of a promis'd glory
As smiles upon the forehead of this action 205
For the wide world's revenue.

Hect.   I am yours,
You valiant offspring of great Priamus.
I have a roisting challenge sent amongst
The dull and factious nobles of the Greeks
Will [strike] amazement to their drowsy spirits. 210
I was advertis'd their great general slept,
Whilst emulation in the army crept:
This I presume will wake him.   *Exeunt.*

[SCENE III]

Enter THERSITES *solus.*

[*Ther.*] How now, Thersites? What, lost in the
labyrinth of thy fury? Shall the elephant Ajax carry it
thus? He beats me, and I rail at him. O worthy
satisfaction! Would it were otherwise: that I could
beat him, whilst he rail'd at me. 'Sfoot, I'll learn to 5
conjure and raise devils, but I'll see some issue of my
spiteful execrations. Then there's Achilles, a rare
enginer! If Troy be not taken till these two undermine
it, the walls will stand till they fall of themselves.
O thou great thunder-darter of Olympus, forget 10
that thou art Jove, the king of gods, and, Mercury, lose
all the serpentine craft of thy caduceus, if ye take not
that little little less than little wit from them that they
have, which short-arm'd ignorance itself knows is so
abundant scarce, it will not in circumvention 15
deliver a fly from a spider, without drawing their
massy irons and cutting the web! After this, the
vengeance on the whole camp! or rather, the Neapolitan bone-ache! for that methinks is the curse depending on those that war for a placket. I have said my 20
prayers, and devil Envy say amen. What ho! my
Lord Achilles!

---

156. **party:** side.
158. **When . . . defended:** when it is a question of defending Helen.
159. **bestow'd:** employed.   165. **gloz'd:** commented.
166. **Aristotle:** The mention of Aristotle in ancient Troy is, of course, an anachronism. The reference is to a passage in the *Nicomachean Ethics* (I,3).   168–69. **conduce To:** tend towards.
169. **distemp'red blood:** diseased appetite.   170. **free:** unbiased.
172. **more . . . adders:** There was a tradition that the adder could make itself deaf by laying one ear on the ground and inserting its tail in the other. Cf. Psalm 58:4–5: "like the deaf adder that stoppeth his ear. Which heareth not the voice of the enchanter, though he be most expert in charming" (Geneva).
173. **Nature:** i.e. natural law, *jus naturae*; joined in line 180 with *jus gentium*, the law of nations or civil law.   **craves:** requires.
177. **affection:** passion (as opposed to reason).
178. **that.** Repeating the sense of *If* (line 176).   **of partial:** out of a biased (or self-interested) one.
179. **benumbed:** i.e. rendered insensitive to right by passion.
185. **aloud:** loudly.   187. **extenuates:** mitigates.
189. **in . . . truth:** considered in terms of abstract right.
190. **spritely:** spirited.
190–91. **propend . . . resolution:** incline to your resolve.
192–93. **cause . . . dignities:** i.e. cause upon which our combined and individual honors depend in no slight measure.   194. **life:** heart.
195. **glory:** honor, fame.   **affected:** aimed at.
196. **performance . . . spleens:** carrying out of our angry impulses.

199. **theme of:** subject encouraging.
201. **Whose present courage:** the bravery of which in the present time.
202. **canonize:** memorialize (us) as heroes (accented on the second syllable; so also *revenue*, line 206, and *advertis'd*, line 211).
205. **smiles . . . action.** The image seems to have been suggested by the idea of seizing time (favorable opportunity) by the forelock; cf. III.iii.146 ff.   208. **roisting:** boisterous.   210. **Will:** which will.
211. **advertis'd:** informed   212. **emulation:** factious envy.

II.iii. Location: The Greek camp. Before Achilles' tent.
2. **carry it:** bear off the honors, have the advantage.
5. **'Sfoot:** by God's foot (mild oath).
8. **enginer:** contriver, strategist (variant of *engineer*).
10. **thunder-darter.** With reference to one of Jove's titles, *Jupiter Tonans* (= thundering).
12. **serpentine . . . caduceus.** The caduceus was the wand bearing two intertwined serpents which was carried by Mercury, who was also associated with cunning and deception; hence *serpentine craft*.
14. **short-arm'd ignorance:** i.e. ignorance such that almost everything is beyond its grasp.
17. **massy irons:** massive swords (which they use in place of intelligence).
18–19. **Neapolitan bone-ache:** syphilis (believed to have originated in Naples).   19–20. **depending on:** hanging over.
20. **placket:** woman (literally, a slit or opening in a petticoat).

Troilus
and Cressida
II.iii

Patr. [*Within.*] Who's there? Thersites? Good Thersites, come in and rail. 24

Ther. If I could 'a' remem'red a gilt counterfeit, thou [wouldst] not have slipp'd out of my contemplation. But it is no matter, thyself upon thyself! The common curse of mankind, folly and ignorance, be thine in great revenue! Heaven bless thee from a tutor, and discipline come not near thee! Let thy blood 30 be thy direction till thy death; then if she that lays thee out says thou art a fair corse, I'll be sworn and sworn upon't she never shrouded any but lazars. Amen.

[*Enter* PATROCLUS.]

Where's Achilles? 34
Patr. What, art thou devout? Wast thou in prayer?
Ther. Ay, the heavens hear me!
Patr. Amen.

Enter ACHILLES.

Achil. Who's there?
Patr. Thersites, my lord. 39
Achil. Where? where? O, where? Art thou come? Why, my cheese, my digestion, why hast thou not serv'd thyself in to my table so many meals? Come, what's Agamemnon?
Ther. Thy commander, Achilles. Then tell me, Patroclus, what's Achilles? 45
Patr. Thy lord, Thersites. Then tell me, I pray thee, what's Thersites?
Ther. Thy knower, Patroclus. Then tell me, Patroclus, what art thou?
Patr. Thou must tell that knowest. 50
Achil. O, tell, tell.
Ther. I'll decline the whole question: Agamemnon commands Achilles, Achilles is my lord, I am Patroclus' knower, and Patroclus is a fool.
[*Patr.* You rascal! 55
Ther. Peace, fool, I have not done.
Achil. He is a privileg'd man. Proceed, Thersites.
Ther. Agamemnon is a fool, Achilles is a fool, Thersites is a fool, and, as aforesaid, Patroclus is a fool.] 60
Achil. Derive this; come.
Ther. Agamemnon is a fool to offer to command Achilles, Achilles is a fool to be commanded [of Agamemnon], Thersites is a fool to serve such a fool, and this Patroclus is a fool positive. 65

Patr. Why am I a fool?
Ther. Make that demand of the prover, it suffices me thou art. Look you, who comes here?

Enter AGAMEMNON, ULYSSES, NESTOR, DIOMED, AJAX, *and* CALCHAS.

Achil. Come, Patroclus, I'll speak with nobody. Come in with me, Thersites. [*Exit.*] 70
Ther. Here is such patchery, such juggling, and such knavery! All the argument is a whore and a cuckold, a good quarrel to draw emulous factions and bleed to death upon. [Now the dry suppeago on the subject, and war and lechery confound all!] [*Exit.*]
Agam. Where is Achilles? 76
Patr. Within his tent, but ill dispos'd, my lord.
Agam. Let it be known to him that we are here. He [shent] our messengers, and we lay by Our appertainings, visiting of him. 80
Let him be told so, lest perchance he think We dare not move the question of our place, Or know not what we are.
Patr. I shall say so to him. [*Exit.*]
Ulyss. We saw him at the opening of his tent, He is not sick. 85
Ajax. Yes, lion-sick, sick of proud heart. You may call it melancholy, if you will favor the man; but by my head, 'tis pride. But why, why? Let him show us a cause. [A word, my lord.] [*Takes Agamemnon aside.*]
Nest. What moves Ajax thus to bay at him? 90
Ulyss. Achilles hath inveigled his fool from him.
Nest. Who, Thersites?
Ulyss. He.
Nest. Then will Ajax lack matter, if he have lost his argument. 95
Ulyss. No, you see he is his argument that has his argument, Achilles.
Nest. All the better, their fraction is more our wish than their faction. But it was a strong composure a fool could disunite. 100
Ulyss. The amity that wisdom knits not, folly may easily untie.

[*Enter* PATROCLUS.]

Here comes Patroclus.
Nest. No Achilles with him. 104

---

25. **'a':** have.
25–27. **If . . . contemplation:** i.e. he has been "praying" for Ajax and Achilles, forgetting the worthless Patroclus (= *gilt counterfeit*, i.e. a coin made of base metal gilded over).
26. **slipp'd.** With a play on *slip* = a counterfeit coin.
27. **thyself upon thyself.** Thersites calls down upon Patroclus the worst plague he can imagine—Patroclus himself.
29. **great revenue:** generous incoming quantities. **bless:** i.e. preserve. 30. **blood:** lust, violent passion. 32. **corse:** corpse.
33. **lazars:** lepers. 41. **cheese.** Supposed an aid to digestion.
48. **Thy knower:** one who knows you for what you really are.
52. **decline . . . question:** state in order all the points of the subject; a technical grammatical term, like *Derive* (line 61) and *positive* (line 65).
57. **privileg'd man:** i.e. a man given license to rail, just as an "allow'd fool," like Feste in *Twelfth Night*, was permitted to speak his mind with relative impunity.
61. **Derive this:** show how this follows. 62. **offer:** undertake.
65. **fool positive:** absolute fool (without any reason outside himself for being so).

67. **Make that demand:** ask that question. **of the prover:** i.e. of yourself (the one who can prove it positively). Many editors prefer the simpler F1 reading *to the Creator*.
69. **Come.** Omitted in F1, probably rightly.
71. **patchery:** trickery, hypocrisy (?).
72–73. **whore . . . cuckold:** i.e. Helen and Menelaus.
73. **draw:** attract.
74. **suppeago:** serpigo, a disfiguring skin disease.
77. **ill dispos'd:** ill; with possible play on "unfavorably inclined."
78. **we.** The royal plural. 79. **shent:** abused, berated.
79–80. **lay . . . appertainings:** waive the honor properly due to us.
82. **move the question:** insist upon the rights.
86. **lion-sick.** The lion, as king of beasts, was traditionally proud.
87–88. **melancholy . . . pride:** "i.e. not a 'humour' but a deadly sin" (A. Walker).
94–95. **matter . . . argument:** i.e. he will lack subject matter if he has lost the theme of his railing.
96–97. **he . . . Achilles:** i.e. he has a new theme for railing—Achilles, the man who took his former theme, Thersites.
98–99. **fraction . . . faction:** division . . . alliance.
99. **strong composure:** firm alliance (spoken ironically).
101. **amity:** union.

Ulyss. The elephant hath joints, but none for cour-
tesy; his legs are legs for necessity, not for flexure.
  Patr. Achilles bids me say he is much sorry,
If any thing more than your sport and pleasure
Did move your greatness and this noble state
To call upon him. He hopes it is no other   110
But for your health and your disgestion sake,
An after-dinner's breath.
  Agam.   Hear you, Patroclus:
We are too well acquainted with these answers,
But his evasion, wing'd thus swift with scorn,
Cannot outfly our apprehensions.   115
Much attribute he hath, and much the reason
Why we ascribe it to him; yet all his virtues,
Not virtuously on his own part beheld,
Do in our eyes begin to lose their gloss,
Yea, like fair fruit in an unwholesome dish,   120
Are like to rot untasted. Go and tell him
We come to speak with him, and you shall not sin
If you do say we think him over-proud
And under-honest, in self-assumption greater
Than in the note of judgment; and worthier than him-
        self   125
Here tend the savage strangeness he puts on,
Disguise the holy strength of their command,
And underwrite in an observing kind
His humorous predominance; yea, watch
His [pettish lines], his ebbs, [his] flows, [as] if 130
The passage and whole [carriage of this action]
Rode on his tide. Go tell him this, and add,
That if he overhold his price so much,
We'll none of him; but let him, like an engine
Not portable, lie under this report: 135
"Bring action hither, this cannot go to war."
A stirring dwarf we do allowance give
Before a sleeping giant. Tell him so.
  Patr. I shall, and bring his answer presently.
                                         [*Exit.*]
  Agam. In second voice we'll not be satisfied,   140
We come to speak with him. Ulysses, [enter you].
                                 [*Exit Ulysses.*]

105–6. **elephant . . . flexure.** It was traditionally believed, despite
Aristotle, that the elephant had no knee-joints and had to sleep
standing up, leaning against a tree.   109. **state:** noble retinue.
110–11. **no other But:** for no other reason except.
111. **disgestion:** digestion (variant form).
112. **breath:** breathing, exercise.
115. **apprehensions:** understanding (of the truth); with sense also of
"capture, arrest." An example of the plural use of an abstract noun
when it relates to more than one person; modern usage requires the
singular. For another example see III.ii.174.
116. **attribute:** reputation, honor.
118. **on . . . beheld:** viewed by himself.
120. **unwholesome:** foul, dirty.
125. **note of judgment:** quality that is characteristic of judgment.
126. **tend:** wait upon.   **savage strangeness:** rude aloofness.
128–29. **underwrite . . . predominance:** i.e. subscribe to his capricious
assumption of superior authority by their deference.
130. **pettish lines:** ill-tempered behavior (line = course of action).
Many editors accept Hanmer's emendation *lunes* (= fits of madness,
influenced by the moon). The Q reading *course, and time* lends some
support to the F1 reading here adopted.
131. **passage . . . action:** whole success of this undertaking (the siege
of Troy). Note that *passage, carriage,* and *Rode* (line 132) are all part
of the image of transport by sea.
133. **overhold his price:** overestimate his value.
134–35. **engine Not portable:** war machine too heavy to transport.
135. **lie . . . report:** suffer the stigma of this pronouncement.
137. **allowance:** approbation.   139. **presently:** at once.
140. **second voice:** someone speaking for him.

  Ajax. What is he more than another?
  Agam. No more than what he thinks he is.
  Ajax. Is he so much? Do you not think he thinks
himself a better man than I am?   145
  Agam. No question.
  Ajax. Will you subscribe his thought, and say he is?
  Agam. No, noble Ajax, you are as strong, as
valiant, as wise, no less noble, much more gentle, and
altogether more tractable.   150
  Ajax. Why should a man be proud? how doth pride
grow? I know not what pride is.
  Agam. Your mind is the clearer, [Ajax,] and your
virtues the fairer. He that is proud eats up himself.
Pride is his own glass, his own trumpet, his own   155
chronicle, and whatever praises itself but in the deed,
devours the deed in the praise.

              Enter ULYSSES.

  Ajax. I do hate a proud man, as I do hate the en-
gend'ring of toads.   159
  Nest. [*Aside.*] And yet he loves himself. Is't not
strange?
  Ulyss. Achilles will not to the field to-morrow.
  Agam. What's his excuse?
  Ulyss.   He doth rely on none,
But carries on the stream of his dispose
Without observance or respect of any,   165
In will peculiar and in self-admission.
  Agam. Why will he not upon our fair request
Untent his person and share th' air with us?
  Ulyss. Things small as nothing, for request's sake
        only,
He makes important. Possess'd he is with greatness,
And speaks not to himself but with a pride   171
That quarrels at self-breath. Imagin'd worth
Holds in his blood such swoll'n and hot discourse
That 'twixt his mental and his active parts
Kingdom'd Achilles in commotion rages,   175
And batters down himself. What should I say?
He is so plaguy proud that the death-tokens of it
Cry "No recovery."
  Agam.   Let Ajax go to him.
Dear lord, go you and greet him in his tent.
'Tis said he holds you well, and will be led   180
At your request a little from himself.
  Ulyss. O Agamemnon, let it not be so!
We'll consecrate the steps that Ajax makes

143. **No . . . is.** This may be taken in two ways: (1) his worth lies only
in his self-estimation; (2) he is as worthy as he thinks he is (as a covert
rebuke to Ajax, who, of course, takes the statement in the first sense).
147. **subscribe:** endorse.
155. **glass:** mirror (self-reflecting).   **trumpet:** i.e. praiser.
156. **chronicle:** record.   **praises . . . deed:** praises itself in any way
except by silently doing the deed.   158. **engend'ring:** copulation.
164. **dispose:** inclination.
166. **In . . . self-admission:** in accordance with what he himself desires and approves.
169. **for . . . only:** merely because they are requested of him.
170. **Possess'd.** With reference to being possessed by the devil, in this
case pride (= greatness).
172. **quarrels at self-breath:** find fault even with what he says of
himself (as inadequate to his greatness).   173. **blood:** passions.
175. **Kingdom'd Achilles:** i.e. Achilles seen as a microcosm of a regal
state caught in civil war; cf. *Julius Caesar,* II.i.67–69.
177. **plaguy:** confoundedly, pestilently.   **death-tokens:** plague spots
(betokening death).
181. **from himself:** i.e. away from his characteristic arrogance.

*Troilus
and Cressida*
II.iii

When they go from Achilles. Shall the proud lord
That bastes his arrogance with his own seam,   185
And never suffers matter of the world
Enter his thoughts, save such as doth revolve
And ruminate himself, shall he be worshipp'd
Of that we hold an idol more than he?
No! this thrice worthy and right valiant lord   190
Shall not so [stale] his palm, nobly acquir'd,
Nor, by my will, assubjugate his merit,
As amply [titled] as Achilles' is,
By going to Achilles.
That were to enlard his fat-already pride,   195
And add more coals to Cancer when he burns
With entertaining great Hyperion.
This lord go to him! Jupiter forbid,
And say in thunder, "Achilles go to him."
  Nest. [*Aside to Diomedes.*] O, this is well. He rubs
    the vein of him.   200
  Dio. [*Aside to Nestor.*] And how his silence drinks
    up his applause!
  Ajax. If I go to him, with my armed fist
I'll [pash] him o'er the face.
  Agam. O no, you shall not go.
  Ajax. And he be proud with me, I'll pheese his
    pride.   205
Let me go to him.
  Ulyss. Not for the worth that hangs upon our
    quarrel.
  Ajax. A paltry, insolent fellow!
  Nest. [*Aside.*] How he describes himself!
  Ajax. Can he not be sociable?   210
  Ulyss. [*Aside.*] The raven chides blackness.
  Ajax. I'll [let] his [humors] blood.
  Agam. [*Aside.*] He will be the physician that
should be the patient.
  Ajax. And all men were of my mind—   215
  Ulyss. [*Aside.*] Wit would be out of fashion.
  Ajax. 'A should not bear it so, 'a should eat swords
first. Shall pride carry it?
  Nest. [*Aside.*] And 'twould, you'd carry half.   219
  [*Ulyss.*] [*Aside.*] 'A would have ten shares. I will
knead him, I'll make him supple. He's not yet through
warm.

  Nest. [*Aside.*] Force him with [praises]—pour in,
pour [in], his ambition is dry.   224
  Ulyss. [*To Agamemnon.*] My lord, you feed too
    much on this dislike.
  Nest. Our noble general, do not do so.
  Dio. You must prepare to fight without Achilles.
  Ulyss. Why, 'tis this naming of him does him harm.
Here is a man—but 'tis before his face,
I will be silent.
  Nest.   Wherefore should you so?   230
He is not emulous, as Achilles is.
  Ulyss. Know the whole world, he is as valiant—
  Ajax. A whoreson dog, that shall palter with us
    thus!
Would he were a Troyan!
  Nest. What a vice were it in Ajax now—   235
  Ulyss. If he were proud—
  Dio. Or covetous of praise—
  Ulyss. Ay, or surly borne—
  Dio. Or strange, or self-affected!
  Ulyss. Thank the heavens, lord, thou art of sweet
    composure.   240
Praise him that gat thee, she that gave thee suck;
Fam'd be thy tutor, and thy parts of nature
Thrice fam'd beyond, [beyond] all erudition;
But he that disciplin'd thine arms to fight,
Let Mars divide eternity in twain,   245
And give him half; and for thy vigor,
Bull-bearing Milo his addition yield
To sinowy Ajax. I will not praise thy wisdom,
Which like a [bourn], a pale, a shore, confines
[Thy] spacious and dilated parts. Here's Nestor,   250
Instructed by the antiquary times;
He must, he is, he cannot but be wise.
But pardon, father Nestor, were your days
As green as Ajax', and your brain so temper'd,
You should not have the eminence of him,   255
But be as Ajax.
  Ajax.   Shall I call you father?
  Nest. Ay, my good son.
  Dio.   Be rul'd by him, Lord Ajax.

185. **seam:** fat, lard.
187–88. **revolve And ruminate.** The verbs are synonymous, meaning "to turn over and over in the mind."
189. **Of:** by.   **idol more:** greater object of worship.
191. **stale his palm:** cheapen his honors.
192. **assubjugate:** debase.
193. **As . . . is:** having a name as great as Achilles'.
196–97. **add . . . Hyperion:** i.e. intensify the heat of what is already hot in its own nature. The sun (*Hyperion*) enters into Cancer (a sign of the zodiac associated with heat) on June 21, the beginning of summer.   200. **rubs . . . him:** tickles his desire for praise.
203. **pash:** smash.
205. **pheese:** do for, settle the business of (*O.E.D.*).
207. **hangs . . . quarrel:** is involved in our quarrel with the Trojans.
211. **raven chides blackness:** i.e. the pot calls the kettle black.
212. **let . . . blood:** purge his fantasies of greatness by bleeding them. *Let blood* is a medical term for bleeding a patient.
215, 219. **And:** if.
217. **bear it so:** get away with it in such a manner; cf. "carry it," line 218.
217–18. **eat swords first:** be stabbed before that should be permitted to happen.
220. **'A . . . shares:** i.e. he is too proud to share but could qualify for all (*ten shares* = the whole).
221–22. **through warm:** thoroughly warmed up.

223. **Force:** stuff.   224. **dry:** thirsty.
225. **this dislike:** i.e. Achilles' aloofness.
228. **this naming of him:** i.e. the continual reference to Achilles as though he were the Greeks' sole hope.   **does him harm:** has this bad effect.   231. **emulous:** covetous of praise, envious.
233. **palter:** trifle, play fast and loose.
238. **surly borne:** of arrogant bearing.
239. **strange:** unfriendly, distant.   **self-affected:** in love with himself.
240. **composure:** composition (in mind and body).
241. **gat:** got, i.e. begot.
242. **parts of nature:** natural endowments.
243. **beyond all erudition:** above all learning; i.e. Ajax's natural endowments are such that they far surpass anything that learning could add to them (with ironical double sense).
244. **But he:** but for him.
245. **eternity:** i.e. his eternal fame as a warrior.
247. **Bull-bearing . . . yield:** let Milo yield his title "bull-bearing." Milo, a famous athlete of Crotona, carried a four-year-old bull on his shoulders forty yards, killed it with one blow of his fist, and ate the bull, all in one day.
248. **sinowy:** sinewy, muscular.   **I will not:** I will forbear to (but again with ironic second sense).
249. **bourn:** boundary.   **pale:** fence.
250. **spacious . . . parts:** ample and extensive qualities.
251. **antiquary:** ancient (first recorded use as an adjective).
254. **green:** youthful.   **so temper'd:** i.e. at a correspondingly youthful stage of development.
255. **eminence of:** superiority over.

Ulyss. There is no tarrying here, the hart Achilles
Keeps thicket. Please it our great general
To call together all his state of war.						260
Fresh kings are come to Troy; to-morrow
We must with all our main of power stand fast;
And here's a lord—come knights from east to west,
And [cull] their flower, Ajax shall cope the best.

Agam. Go we to council. Let Achilles sleep:	265
Light boats sail swift, though greater hulks draw
deep.					*Exeunt.*

[ACT III, Scene I]

[*Music sounds within.*]	*Enter* PANDARUS [*and a*
SERVANT].

Pan. Friend, you! pray you a word. Do you not
follow the young Lord Paris?

Serv. Ay, sir, when he goes before me.

Pan. You depend upon him, I mean.

Serv. Sir, I do depend upon the Lord.		5

Pan. You depend upon a notable gentleman; I must
needs praise him.

Serv. The Lord be prais'd!

Pan. You know me, do you not?

Serv. Faith, sir, superficially.			10

Pan. Friend, know me better, I am the Lord
Pandarus.

Serv. I hope I shall know your honor better!

Pan. I do desire it.

Serv. You are in the state of grace.		15

Pan. Grace? Not so, friend, honor and lordship
are my titles. What music is this?

Serv. I do but partly know, sir, it is music in parts.

Pan. Know you the musicians?

Serv. Wholly, sir.					20

Pan. Who play they to?

Serv. To the hearers, sir.

Pan. At whose pleasure, friend?

Serv. At mine, sir, and theirs that love music.

Pan. Command, I mean, [friend].			25

Serv. Who shall I command, sir?

Pan. Friend, we understand not one another; I am
too courtly and thou too cunning. At whose request do
these men play?						29

Serv. That's to't indeed, sir. Marry, sir, at the request of Paris my lord, who is there in person; with

him, the mortal Venus, the heart-blood of beauty,
love's invisible soul.

Pan. Who? my cousin Cressida?			34

Serv. No, sir, Helen. Could not you find out that
by her attributes?

Pan. It should seem, fellow, thou hast not seen the
Lady Cressid. I come to speak with Paris from the
Prince Troilus. I will make a complimental assault
upon him, for my business seethes.			40

Serv. Sodden business! there's a stew'd phrase indeed!

Enter PARIS *and* HELEN [*attended*].

Pan. Fair be to you, my lord, and to all this fair
company! fair desires, in all fair measure, fairly guide
them! Especially to you, fair queen, fair thoughts be
your fair pillow!					46

Helen. Dear lord, you are full of fair words.

Pan. You speak your fair pleasure, sweet queen.
Fair prince, here is good broken music.		49

Par. You have broke it, cousin; and by my life
you shall make it whole again—you shall piece it out
with a piece of your performance. Nell, he is full of
harmony.

Pan. Truly, lady, no.

Helen. O sir—						55

Pan. Rude, in sooth, in good sooth, very rude.

Par. Well said, my lord, well, you say so in fits.

Pan. I have business to my lord, dear queen. My
lord, will you vouchsafe me a word?			59

Helen. Nay, this shall not hedge us out, we'll hear
you sing, certainly.

Pan. Well, sweet queen, you are pleasant with me.
But marry thus, my lord: my dear lord and most
esteem'd friend, your brother Troilus—		64

Helen. My Lord Pandarus, honey-sweet lord—

Pan. Go to, sweet queen, go to—commends himself most affectionately to you—

Helen. You shall not bob us out of our melody. If
you do, our melancholy upon your head!		69

Pan. Sweet queen, sweet queen, that's a sweet
queen—i' faith—

Helen. And to make a sweet lady sad is a sour
offense.

Pan. Nay, that shall not serve your turn, that shall
it not, in truth la! Nay, I care not for such words,	75
no, no. And, my lord, he desires you, that if the King

---

260. **state:** council.
262. **main of power:** principal strength. This line seems to ignore the truce and the single combat set for the next day.
263. **come knights:** let knights come.
264. **cull their flower:** choose out the best of them.	**cope the best:** encounter with the best on equal terms.
266. **hulks:** large unwieldy vessels.

III.i. Location: Troy. Priam's palace.
2. **follow:** i.e. serve.	3. **goes:** walks.
4. **You . . . him:** a conceited way of saying, "you are his servant."
5. **Lord:** (1) master; (2) God (with the same quibble in line 8).
13. **know . . . better.** With a quibble on "see you become a better man" (continued in the next exchange).
15. **state of grace:** spiritual state necessary to salvation. Pandarus takes it as referring to social rank and replies that he is not entitled to be addressed as "your Grace" (used to one of royal blood) but only as "your honor" and "your lordship."
18. **in parts:** having a different scoring for each voice or instrument.
30. **to't:** to the point (in contrast to "too courtly").

33. **love's invisible soul:** i.e. the quintessence of love made visible in her only.
36. **her attributes:** i.e. the qualities I have just ascribed to her.
39. **complimental assault:** ceremonial attack.
40. **seethes:** boils, i.e. is urgent. The Servant derides the word with his *Sodden* (= boiled) and *stew'd*, both implying connection with stews, i.e. brothels, and the sweating treatment for venereal disease.
43. **Fair:** i.e. fair fortune.
49. **broken music:** music, particularly of a courtly nature, employing several different varieties of instruments.
50. **broke:** interrupted.	**cousin:** familiar term of address among social equals, not necessarily implying actual kinship.
51. **piece it out:** mend it.	56. **Rude:** unpolished, amateurish.
57. **in fits:** by fits, when the humor takes you (?); perhaps with play on "in musical strains."
60. **hedge us out:** deprive us (by a subterfuge).
62. **pleasant:** merry, jocose.
66. **Go to:** an expression of remonstrance.	68. **bob:** cheat.
75. **care not for:** pay no heed to.

call for him at supper, you will make his excuse.

Helen.   My Lord Pandarus—

Pan.   What says my sweet queen, my very very
sweet queen?   80

Par.   What exploit's in hand?   Where sups he to-
night?

Helen.   Nay, but, my lord—

Pan.   What says my sweet queen?   My cousin will
fall out with you.   85

Helen.   You must not know where he sups.

Par.   I'll lay my life, with my disposer Cressida.

Pan.   No, no! no such matter, you are wide.   Come,
your disposer is sick.

Par.   Well, I'll make 's excuse.   90

Pan.   Ay, good my lord.   Why should you say
Cressida?   No, your [poor] disposer's sick.

Par.   I spy!

Pan.   You spy? what do you spy?—Come, give me
an instrument.—Now, sweet queen.   95

Helen.   Why, this is kindly done.

Pan.   My niece is horribly in love with a thing you
have, sweet queen.

Helen.   She shall have it, my lord, if it be not my
Lord Paris.   100

Pan.   He? no! she'll none of him.   They two are
twain.

Helen.   Falling in, after falling out, may make them
three.   104

Pan.   Come, come, I'll hear no more of this, I'll
sing you a song now.

Helen.   Ay, ay, prithee now.   By my troth, sweet
[lord], thou hast a fine forehead.

Pan.   Ay, you may, you may.   109

Helen.   Let thy song be love.   This love will undo
us all.   O Cupid, Cupid, Cupid!

Pan.   Love? ay, that it shall, i' faith.

Par.   Ay, good now, love, love, nothing but love.

[*Pan.*   In good troth, it begins so.]   [*Sings.*]

          "Love, love, nothing but love, still love,
                    still more!
          For O, love's bow   116
          Shoots buck and doe.
          The [shaft confounds]
                    Not that it wounds,
          But tickles still the sore.   120
          These lovers cry, O ho, they die!
          Yet that which seems the wound to kill,
          Doth turn O ho! to ha, ha, he!
          So dying love lives still.

O ho! a while, but ha, ha, ha!   125
O ho! groans out for ha, ha, ha!—hey ho!"

Helen.   In love, i' faith, to the very tip of the nose.

Par.   He eats nothing but doves, love, and that
breeds hot blood, and hot blood begets hot thoughts,
and hot thoughts beget hot deeds, and hot deeds is love.

Pan.   Is this the generation of love—hot blood, hot
thoughts, and hot deeds?   Why, they are vipers.   Is
love a generation of vipers?   Sweet lord, who's a-field
to-day?   134

Par.   Hector, Deiphobus, Helenus, Antenor, and
all the gallantry of Troy.   I would fain have arm'd to-
day, but my Nell would not have it so.   How chance
my brother Troilus went not?

Helen.   He hangs the lip at something.   You know
all, Lord Pandarus.   140

Pan.   Not I, honey-sweet queen.   I long to hear how
they sped to-day.   You'll remember your brother's
excuse?

Par.   To a hair.

Pan.   Farewell, sweet queen.   145

Helen.   Commend me to your niece.

Pan.   I will, sweet queen.   [*Exit.*]   *Sound a retreat.*

Par.   They're come from the field.   Let us to
          Priam's hall
To greet the warriors.   Sweet Helen, I must woo you
To help unarm our Hector.   His stubborn buckles,
With [these] your white enchanting fingers touch'd,
Shall more obey than to the edge of steel,   152
Or force of Greekish sinews.   You shall do more
Than all the island kings—disarm great Hector.

Helen.   'Twill make us proud to be his servant,
          Paris!   155
Yea, what he shall receive of us in duty
Gives us more palm in beauty than we have,
Yea, overshines ourself.

Par.   Sweet, above thought I love [thee]!   *Exeunt.*

[SCENE II]

Enter PANDARUS, *Troilus'* MAN, [*meeting*].

Pan.   How now, where's thy master?   At my
cousin Cressida's?

Man.   No, sir, [he] stays for you to conduct him
thither.

[*Enter* TROILUS.]

Pan.   O, here he comes!   How now, how now?   5

84–85. **My . . . you:** my cousin (i.e. Paris; cf. line 50) will be annoyed
with you if you don't stop interrupting.
87. **lay:** wager.   **my disposer Cressida.** Meaning uncertain; probably
a courtly turn of phrase meaning that he is always at her disposal or
command.   90. **make 's:** make his.
93. **I spy.** Alluding to the children's game of that name.
102. **twain:** i.e. at odds; cf. *falling out*, line 103.
103–4. **Falling . . . three:** i.e. sexual relations, after a lover's quarrel,
may result in a child, thus making two into three.
108. **fine forehead.** Considered a mark of manly beauty, though the
reference here probably carries some kind of bawdy implication.
109. **you may:** go on, keep it up.   113. **good now:** if you please.
118–20. **The shaft . . . sore:** i.e. Love's arrow does not kill what it
wounds but it continues to irritate the wound.   There is probably a
play on *sore* = a buck of the fourth year; cf. line 117.
121. **cry, O ho:** i.e. sigh.   **die.** Here and in *dying* (= by dying) in
line 124 the word has its sexual sense "experience orgasm."

128. **doves.** Doves or pigeons were believed to be especially amorous.
love: i.e. Helen.
129. **hot blood:** lustful feelings.   131. **generation:** progeny.
132. **they are vipers.** Probably with reference to Acts 28:3: "And
when Paul had gathered a number of sticks, and laid them on the fire,
there came a viper out of the heat, and leapt on his hand" (Geneva).
133. **generation of vipers.** Cf., among other New Testament passages,
Matthew 23:33: "O serpents, the generation of vipers, how should
ye escape the damnation of hell?" (Geneva).
136. **gallantry:** gallants.   139. **hangs the lip:** sulks.
142. **sped:** succeeded, prospered.
154. **island kings:** the Greek leaders.
157. **Gives . . . palm:** affords greater preeminence to us.

III.ii. Location: Troy. Calchas' garden.
3. **stays:** waits.

Tro. Sirrah, walk off. [*Exit Man.*]

Pan. Have you seen my cousin?

Tro. No, Pandarus, I stalk about her door,
Like to a strange soul upon the Stygian banks
Staying for waftage. O, be thou my Charon, 10
And give me swift transportance to these fields
Where I may wallow in the lily-beds
Propos'd for the deserver! O gentle Pandar,
From Cupid's shoulder pluck his painted wings,
And fly with me to Cressid! 15

Pan. Walk here i' th' orchard, I'll bring her
straight. [*Exit.*]

Tro. I am giddy; expectation whirls me round;
Th' imaginary relish is so sweet
That it enchants my sense; what will it be, 20
When that the wat'ry palates taste indeed
Love's thrice-repured nectar? Death, I fear me,
Sounding destruction, or some joy too fine,
Too subtile, potent, tun'd too sharp in sweetness
For the capacity of my ruder powers. 25
I fear it much, and I do fear besides
That I shall lose distinction in my joys,
As doth a battle, when they charge on heaps
The enemy flying. 29

[*Enter* PANDARUS.]

Pan. She's making her ready, she'll come straight.
You must be witty now: she does so blush, and fetches
her wind so short, as if she were fray'd with a spirit.
I'll fetch her. It is the prettiest villain, she fetches her
breath as short as a new-ta'en sparrow. [*Exit.*] 34

Tro. Even such a passion doth embrace my bosom:
My heart beats thicker than a feverous pulse,
And all my powers do their bestowing lose,
Like vassalage at [unawares] encount'ring
The eye of majesty. 39

Enter PANDAR *and* CRESSID.

Pan. Come, come, what need you blush? Shame's
a baby. Here she is now, swear the oaths now to her
that you have sworn to me. [*Cressida draws backward.*]
What, are you gone again? You must be watch'd ere

you be made tame, must you? Come your ways, come
your ways; and you draw backward, we'll put you 45
i' th' fills. Why do you not speak to her? Come, draw
this curtain, and let's see your picture. Alas the day,
how loath you are to offend daylight! And 'twere
dark you'd close sooner. So, so, rub on and kiss the
mistress. How now, a kiss in fee-farm? Build 50
there, carpenter, the air is sweet. Nay, you shall fight
your hearts out ere I part you—the falcon as the tercel,
for all the ducks i' th' river. Go to, go to.

Tro. You have bereft me of all words, lady. 54

Pan. Words pay no debts, give her deeds; but
she'll bereave you a' th' deeds too, if she call your
activity in question. What, billing again? Here's
"In witness whereof the parties interchangeably"—
Come in, come in, I'll go get a fire. [*Exit.*]

Cres. Will you walk in, my lord? 60

Tro. O Cressid, how often have I wish'd me thus!

Cres. Wish'd, my lord? The gods grant—O my
lord!

Tro. What should they grant? What makes this
pretty abruption? What too curious dreg espies my
sweet lady in the fountain of our love? 66

Cres. More dregs than water, if my [fears] have
eyes.

Tro. Fears make devils of cherubins, they never
see truly. 70

Cres. Blind fear that seeing reason leads finds
safer footing than blind reason stumbling without fear.
To fear the worst oft cures the worse.

Tro. O, let my lady apprehend no fear. In all
Cupid's pageant there is presented no monster. 75

Cres. Nor nothing monstrous neither?

Tro. Nothing but our undertakings, when we vow
to weep seas, live in fire, eat rocks, tame tigers; thinking it harder for our mistress to devise imposition
enough than for us to undergo any difficulty im- 80
pos'd. This [is] the monstruosity in love, lady, that
the will is infinite and the execution confin'd, that the
desire is boundless and the act a slave to limit.

Cres. They say all lovers swear more performance
than they are able, and yet reserve an ability that 85

---

6. **Sirrah:** form of address to an inferior. **walk off:** leave us.
8. **stalk:** walk restlessly.
9. **Stygian banks:** the shore of the lake called Styx, traditionally
listed as one of the four rivers of the underworld.
10. **Charon:** the ferryman of Hell, who for a fee gave transportation
(*waftage*) to the souls of the dead across Styx.
11. **fields:** the Elysian fields, the pagan heaven and a part of hell, to
which the souls of the good were transported after death. It was
thought of as a place of great sensuous delight; cf. "wallow in the
lily-beds," line 12. The lily image is both Virgilian and Biblical (Song
of Solomon). 13. **Propos'd for:** promised to.
16. **orchard:** garden.
21. **wat'ry palates:** senses (= tastes) watering with anticipation.
23. **Sounding destruction:** swooning disintegration.
24. **subtile:** rarefied (variant of *subtle*).
27. **distinction . . . joys:** the power of distinguishing between greater
and lesser pleasures. 29. **flying:** in flight.
31. **witty:** clever in small talk (to put Cressida at her ease).
32. **fray'd . . . spirit:** frightened by a ghost.
33. **villain.** Like *wretch*, used as a term of endearment.
36. **thicker:** faster.
37. **powers . . . lose:** faculties, mental and physical, lose their use.
38–39. **vassalage . . . majesty:** vassal(s) . . . king. Cf. *gallantry* in
III.1.136. 40. **what:** for what reason, why.
43. **watch'd.** To "watch" a hawk was to prevent it from sleeping in
order to tame it.

44. **Come your ways:** come along.
46. **fills:** shafts (as of a horse-drawn wagon).
47. **curtain:** i.e. the veil Cressida is wearing. Curtains were hung in
front of pictures. 49. **close:** (1) come to terms; (2) come together.
49–50. **rub . . . mistress.** A metaphor from bowling, describing the
action of the bowl as it rolls (*rubs*) on its way to touch (*kiss*) the Jack
or small ball (*mistress*).
50. **in fee-farm:** i.e. of unlimited duration. *Fee-farm* = a grant of
lands in fee, i.e. in perpetuity.
52. **falcon . . . tercel:** the female as well as the male hawk.
56–57. **bereave . . . question:** i.e. she'll wear you out physically. *In
question* = into the matter.
58. **"In . . . interchangeably":** the formula for concluding indentures
signed between two parties. The implied image of lips as seals is a
common one.
65. **abruption:** breaking off. **too curious dreg:** speck of dirt (i.e.
bad omen) overscrupulously imagined.
69. **make . . . cherubins:** i.e. can distort good into evil.
71. **seeing:** clear-eyed.
74–75. **In . . . monster:** i.e. nothing like a monster (i.e. a frightening
figure) takes part in Cupid's masque or procession. Spenser, however,
describes a "Masque of Cupid" (*Faerie Queene*, III.xii.3–26) in
which many "monsters" appear (Danger, Fear, Suspect, Fury,
Cruelty, etc.), and earlier examples of Cupid's court offer similar
"monsters." 77. **undertakings:** vows, promises.
81. **monstruosity:** monstrosity, i.e. something unnatural.
85. **able:** capable of.

they never perform; vowing more than the perfection
of ten, and discharging less than the tenth part of one.
They that have the voice of lions and the act of hares,
are they not monsters?   89

Tro. Are there such? Such are not we. Praise us
as we are tasted, allow us as we prove. Our head shall
go bare till merit [crown it]. No [perfection] in reversion shall have a praise in present; we will not name
desert before his birth, and being born, his addition
shall be humble. Few words to fair faith. Troilus   95
shall be such to Cressid as what envy can say worst
shall be a mock for his truth, and what truth can speak
truest not truer than Troilus.

Cres. Will you walk in, my lord?   99

[*Enter* PANDARUS.]

Pan. What, blushing still? Have you not done
talking yet?

Cres. Well, uncle, what folly I commit, I dedicate
to you.

Pan. I thank you for that; if my lord get a boy of
you, you'll give him me. Be true to my lord; if he
flinch, chide me for it.   106

Tro. You know now your hostages: your uncle's
word and my firm faith.

Pan. Nay, I'll give my word for her too. Our
kindred, though they be long ere they be woo'd,   110
they are constant being won. They are burs, I can tell
you, they'll stick where they are thrown.

Cres. Boldness comes to me now, and brings me
heart.
Prince Troilus, I have lov'd you night and day
For many weary months.   115

Tro. Why was my Cressid then so hard to win?

Cres. Hard to seem won; but I was won, my lord,
With the first glance that ever—pardon me,
If I confess much, you will play the tyrant.
I love you now, but till now not so much   120
But I might master it. In faith I lie,
My thoughts were like unbridled children grown
Too headstrong for their mother. See, we fools!
Why have I blabb'd? Who shall be true to us,
When we are so unsecret to ourselves?   125
But though I lov'd you well, I woo'd you not,
And yet, good faith, I wish'd myself a man,
Or that we women had men's privilege
Of speaking first. Sweet, bid me hold my tongue,
For in this rapture I shall surely speak   130
The thing I shall repent. See, see, your silence,
[Cunning] in dumbness, from my weakness draws
My very soul of counsel! Stop my mouth.

Tro. And shall, albeit sweet music issues thence.
                                                    [*Kisses her.*]

Pan. Pretty, i' faith.   135

Cres. My lord, I do beseech you pardon me,
'Twas not my purpose thus to beg a kiss.
I am asham'd. O heavens, what have I done!
For this time will I take my leave, my lord.

Tro. Your leave, sweet Cressid!   140

Pan. Leave! And you take leave till to-morrow
morning—

Cres. Pray you content you.

Tro. What offends you, lady?

Cres. Sir, mine own company.   145

Tro. You cannot shun yourself.

Cres. Let me go and try.
I have a kind of self resides with you;
But an unkind self, that itself will leave
To be another's fool. I would be gone.   150
Where is my wit? I know not what I speak.

Tro. Well know they what they speak that speak
so wisely.

Cres. Perchance, my lord, I show more craft than
love,
And fell so roundly to a large confession,
To angle for your thoughts, but you are wise,   155
Or else you love not; for to be wise and love
Exceeds man's might; that dwells with gods above.

Tro. O that I thought it could be in a woman—
As, if it can, I will presume in you—
To feed for [aye] her lamp and flames of love,   160
To keep her constancy in plight and youth,
Outliving beauties outward, with a mind
That doth renew swifter than blood decays!
Or that persuasion could but thus convince me
That my integrity and truth to you   165
Might be affronted with the match and weight
Of such a winnowed purity in love!
How were I then uplifted! but alas,
I am as true as truth's simplicity,
And simpler than the infancy of truth.   170

Cres. In that I'll war with you.

Tro.   O virtuous fight,
When right with right wars who shall be most right!
True swains in love shall in the world to come
Approve their truth by Troilus. When their rhymes,
Full of protest, of oath and big compare,   175

86–87. **perfection of ten:** performance of ten perfect lovers.
88. **voice . . . hares:** i.e. roar out their promises like the king of beasts
and perform like the timorous and cowardly hare. Lions and hares
are proverbially contrasted. 91. **allow us:** give us approbation.
92–93. **perfection in reversion:** promise of future perfection.
94. **addition:** title of honor.
97. **mock . . . truth:** ridiculing of his faithfulness.
106. **flinch:** prove untrue. 121. **But:** but that.
130. **rapture:** delirious state (earliest use in this sense).
133. **soul of counsel:** innermost feelings.

141. **And:** if. 143. **content you:** be still.
148–50. **I have . . . fool:** i.e. half of me is yours, but an unnatural
half, that will thus desert its other half to become your fool (or dupe).
154. **roundly:** outspoken, frankly.
155. **wise:** i.e. too wise to be taken in by such "craft."
156. **Or . . . not.** In view of the next line and a half, *Or else* creates
difficulty. It has been emended in various ways (e.g. *And then*
[Capell]) or given strained interpretations (e.g. "or in other words"
[Staunton]), but the confusion is probably Shakespeare's, who from
time to time corners himself syntactically in this way.
156–57. **to . . . above.** A saying popular in various wordings; the
ultimate source is Publilius Syrus (*Amare et sapere vix deo conceditur*,
"To love and be wise is scarcely granted to a god").
161. **in . . . youth:** in youthful condition (hendiadys), i.e. unchanged
by the passage of time.
162. **beauties outward:** external marks of beauty.
163. **blood decays:** the physical attributes decline.
166. **affronted:** faced, balanced. **match and weight:** equal amount.
168. **uplifted:** exalted in spirit.
169. **simplicity:** purity, state of being unmixed.
170. **infancy of truth:** i.e. truth at its most pure.
171. **war:** i.e. vie as an equal. 173. **True:** constant.
174. **Approve . . . Troilus:** use Troilus as a touchstone for proving
their faithfulness.
175. **protest:** protestations (of love). **big compare:** i.e. comparisons
of their love with things of great magnitude.

Wants similes, truth tir'd with iteration,
As true as steel, as plantage to the moon,
As sun to day, as turtle to her mate,
As iron to adamant, as earth to th' centre,
[Yet] after all comparisons of truth   180
(As truth's authentic author to be cited)
"As true as Troilus" shall crown up the verse,
And sanctify the numbers.
   Cres.   Prophet may you be!
If I be false, or swerve a hair from truth,
When time is old [and] hath forgot itself,   185
When water-drops have worn the stones of Troy,
And blind oblivion swallow'd cities up,
And mighty states characterless are grated
To dusty nothing, yet let memory,
From false to false among false maids in love,   190
Upbraid my falsehood! When th' have said as false
As air, as water, wind, or sandy earth,
As fox to lamb, or wolf to heifer's calf,
Pard to the hind, or step-dame to her son,
Yea, let them say, to stick the heart of falsehood,   195
"As false as Cressid."
   Pan.   Go to, a bargain made, seal it, seal it, I'll be
the witness. Here I hold your hand, here my cousin's.
If ever you prove false one to another, since I have
taken such pain to bring you together, let all piti-   200
ful goers-between be call'd to the world's end after my
name; call them all Pandars. Let all constant men be
Troiluses, all false women Cressids, and all brokers-
between Pandars! Say, amen.
   Tro.   Amen.   205
   Cres.   Amen.
   Pan.   Amen. Whereupon I will show you a chamber, which bed, because it shall not speak of your pretty
encounters, press it to death. Away!
                   Exeunt [*Troilus and Cressida*].
And Cupid grant all tongue-tied maidens here   210
Bed, chamber, Pandar to provide this gear!   *Exit.*

[SCENE III]

Enter ULYSSES, DIOMED, NESTOR, AGAMEMNON,
[AJAX, MENELAUS, *and*] CALCHAS. [*Flourish.*]

   Cal.   Now, princes, for the service I have done,

Th' advantage of the time prompts me aloud
To call for recompense. Appear it to [your] mind,
That through the sight I bear in things to [come],
I have abandon'd Troy, left my possession,   5
Incurr'd a traitor's name, expos'd myself
From certain and possess'd conveniences
To doubtful fortunes, sequest'ring from me all
That time, acquaintance, custom, and condition
Made tame and most familiar to my nature;   10
And here, to do you service, am become
As new into the world, strange, unacquainted.
I do beseech you, as in way of taste,
To give me now a little benefit
Out of those many regist'red in promise,   15
Which you say live to come in my behalf.
   Agam.   What wouldst thou of us, Troyan? Make
      demand.
   Cal.   You have a Troyan prisoner call'd Antenor,
Yesterday took; Troy holds him very dear.
Oft have you (often have you thanks therefore)   20
Desir'd my Cressid in right great exchange,
Whom Troy hath still denied, but this Antenor,
I know, is such a wrest in their affairs
That their negotiations all must slack,
Wanting his manage, and they will almost   25
Give us a prince of blood, a son of Priam,
In change of him. Let him be sent, great princes,
And he shall buy my daughter; and her presence
Shall quite strike off all service I have done,
In most accepted pain.
   Agam.   Let Diomedes bear him,   30
And bring us Cressid hither; Calchas shall have
What he requests of us. Good Diomed,
Furnish you fairly for this interchange;
Withal bring word if Hector will to-morrow
Be answered in his challenge: Ajax is ready.   35
   Dio.   This shall I undertake, and 'tis a burthen
Which I am proud to bear.   *Exit* [*with Calchas*].

[*Enter*] ACHILLES *and* PATROCLUS [*and*] *stand in* [*the
door of*] *their tent.*

   Ulyss.   Achilles stands i' th' entrance of his tent.
Please it our general pass strangely by him,
As if he were forgot, and, princes all,
Lay negligent and loose regard upon him.   40
I will come last; 'tis like he'll question me
Why such unplausive eyes are bent, why turn'd on
      him?

---

176. **Wants similes:** run out of comparisons.
177. **plantage:** vegetation (earliest use).
178. **turtle:** turtledove (emblematic of constancy).
179. **adamant:** loadstone, magnet. **as earth . . . centre:** as objects
on the surface of the earth to the centre of the earth. Cf. IV.ii.103–5.
The earth was believed to be a "great magnet" with a core of homo-
geneous matter (see William Gilbert, *De Magnete*, 1600, Bk. I, Chap.
17).   181. **authentic author:** authoritative source or prototype.
183. **numbers:** measures, verses.
188. **characterless:** i.e. without any written records left.
190. **false maids in love:** maids who are false in love.
191. **th':** they.   194. **Pard:** panther or leopard.
195. **stick:** pierce, stab.
202. **constant.** The immediate context demands *inconstant,* but
Shakespeare has allowed his knowledge of the story's outcome to
take precedence.
208. **chamber, which bed.** Most editors insert *with a bed* (Hanmer)
after *chamber;* but that Pandarus in the context should think of a
chamber as essentially a bed is not out of character.
208–9. **because . . . death.** Alluding to pressing to death with weights
as the penalty for persons arraigned for felony who refused to plead.
210. **maidens:** virgins (of either sex).   211. **gear:** equipment.

III.iii. Location: The Greek camp.
2. **Th' advantage . . . time:** this propitious moment.
4. **sight:** spiritual vision, second sight.
5. **my possession:** all I own.
7. **From:** in exchange for. **certain:** secure.
8. **sequest'ring:** separating.   10. **tame:** domestic.
12. **new:** new-born. **strange:** foreign. 13. **taste:** foretaste.
20. **therefore:** therefor, for it.
21. **in . . . exchange:** in exchange for someone of high rank.
23. **wrest:** tuning key (producing harmony or order).
25. **Wanting his manage:** lacking his directing hand.
27. **change of:** exchange for. 29. **strike off:** cancel out.
30. **most accepted pain:** i.e. labors that you have found highly
acceptable. 34. **Withal:** furthermore.
35. **Be answered in:** meet the answerer of. 36. **burthen:** burden.
39. **strangely:** as if he were a stranger.
41. **Lay . . . regard:** i.e. look at him negligently and carelessly.
43. **unplausive:** disapproving.

Troilus and Cressida
III.iii

If so, I have derision medicinable
To use between your strangeness and his pride,   45
Which his own will shall have desire to drink.
It may do good, pride hath no other glass
To show itself but pride; for supple knees
Feed arrogance and are the proud man's fees.
    Agam. We'll execute your purpose, and put on   50
A form of strangeness as we pass along.
So do each lord, and either greet him not,
Or else disdainfully, which shall shake him more
Than if not look'd on. I will lead the way.   54
    Achil. What comes the general to speak with me?
You know my mind, I'll fight no more 'gainst Troy.
    Agam. What says Achilles? Would he aught with
        us?
    Nest. Would you, my lord, aught with the general?
    Achil. No.
    Nest. Nothing, my lord.   60
    Agam. The better.
                    [*Exeunt Agamemnon and Nestor.*]
    Achil. Good day, good day.
    Men. How do you? how do you?   [*Exit.*]
    Achil. What, does the cuckold scorn me?
    Ajax. How now, Patroclus?   65
    Achil. Good morrow, Ajax.
    Ajax. Ha?
    Achil. Good morrow.
    Ajax. Ay, and good next day too.   *Exit.*
    Achil. What mean these fellows? Know they not
        Achilles?   70
    Patr. They pass by strangely. They were us'd to
        bend,
To send their smiles before them to Achilles,
To come as humbly as they us'd to creep
To holy altars.
    Achil.   What, am I poor of late?
'Tis certain, greatness, once fall'n out with fortune,   75
Must fall out with men too. What the declin'd is,
He shall as soon read in the eyes of others
As feel in his own fall; for men, like butterflies,
Show not their mealy wings but to the summer,
And not a man, for being simply man,   80
Hath any honor, but honor for those honors
That are without him, as place, riches, and favor—
Prizes of accident as oft as merit,
Which when they fall, as being slippery standers,
The love that lean'd on them as slippery too,   85
Doth one pluck down another, and together
Die in the fall. But 'tis not so with me,
Fortune and I are friends. I do enjoy
At ample point all that I did possess,

Save these men's looks, who do methinks find out   90
Some thing not worth in me such rich beholding
As they have often given. Here is Ulysses,
I'll interrupt his reading.
How now, Ulysses?
    Ulyss.   Now, great Thetis' son!
    Achil. What are you reading?
    Ulyss.   A strange fellow here
Writes me that man, how dearly ever parted,   96
How much in having, or without or in,
Cannot make boast to have that which he hath,
Nor feels not what he owes, but by reflection;
As when his virtues, aiming upon others,   100
Heat them, and they retort that heat again
To the first [giver].
    Achil.   This is not strange, Ulysses.
The beauty that is borne here in the face
The bearer knows not, but commends itself
To others' eyes; nor doth the eye itself,   105
That most pure spirit of sense, behold itself,
Not going from itself; but eye to eye opposed,
Salutes each other with each other's form;
For speculation turns not to itself,
Till it hath travell'd and is [mirror'd] there   110
Where it may see itself. This is not strange at all.
    Ulyss. I do not strain at the position—
It is familiar—but at the author's drift,
Who in his circumstance expressly proves
That no man is the lord of any thing,   115
Though in and of him there be much consisting,
Till he communicate his parts to others;
Nor doth he of himself know them for aught,
Till he behold them formed in th' applause
Where th' are extended; who like an arch reverb'rate
The voice again, or like a gate of steel,   121
Fronting the sun, receives and renders back
His figure and his heat. I was much rapt in this,
And apprehended here immediately
Th' unknown Ajax.   125
Heavens, what a man is there! A very horse,
That has he knows not what. Nature, what things
        there are
Most [abject] in regard, and dear in use!
What things again most dear in the esteem,   129
And poor in worth! Now shall we see to-morrow—
An act that very chance doth throw upon him—
Ajax renown'd! O heavens, what some men do,
While some men leave to do!

44–45. **I . . . pride:** i.e. I can reply that it is scorn (*derision*) of his arrogance that causes the aloofness, and this will have the effect of curing his arrogance.
47–48. **no . . . pride:** no mirror to view itself in except an answering pride (the *strangeness* of line 45).
49. **fees:** assumed perquisites.   50. **We'll.** The royal plural.
55. **What:** why.   69. **next day.** Quibbling on *morrow* = to-morrow.
71. **us'd:** accustomed.
73. **us'd.** Perhaps an error for *use* = are accustomed.
75. **fall'n out:** out of favor (with reference to Fortune's wheel).
79. **mealy:** powdery.   82. **without:** external to.
84. **slippery standers:** of uncertain footing.
85. **love that lean'd:** admiration that depended.
89. **At ample point:** i.e. at the top of Fortune's wheel.

91. **rich beholding:** noble observance.
96. **Writes me:** writes (a colloquialism).   **how . . . parted:** however richly endowed with virtues.   97. **having:** possessions.
99. **owes:** owns, possesses.   **by reflection:** i.e. by the value placed on his virtues by others.   101. **retort:** turn back, return.
106. **most . . . sense.** See note on I.i.58. Sight was considered the highest of the five senses.
107. **Not . . . itself:** unless it goes out from itself.   **eye to eye opposed:** i.e. one man's eye looking upon another man's eye.
109. **speculation:** sight.   112. **strain at:** find difficulty in.
113. **drift:** aim, tenor.
114. **circumstance:** argument.   115. **lord:** master, possessor.
119. **formed in:** given form or substance by.
120. **Where:** i.e. of those to whom (providing the implied antecedent of the following *who*).   123. **rapt:** caught up.
125. **unknown:** i.e. because his excellences are not yet seen by others.
128. **abject . . . use:** mean in estimation and valuable in practice.
133. **leave to do:** leave undone.

How some men creep in skittish Fortune's hall,
Whiles others play the idiots in her eyes!　　　135
How one man eats into another's pride,
While pride is fasting in his wantonness!
To see these Grecian lords!—why, even already
They clap the lubber Ajax on the shoulder,
As if his foot were on brave Hector's breast,　　140
And great Troy shriking.

Achil.　I do believe it, for they pass'd by me
As misers do by beggars, neither gave to me
Good word nor look. What, are my deeds forgot?

Ulyss.　Time hath, my lord, a wallet at his back,
Wherein he puts alms for oblivion,　　　146
A great-siz'd monster of ingratitudes.
Those scraps are good deeds past, which are devour'd
As fast as they are made, forgot as soon
As done. Perseverance, dear my lord,　　　150
Keeps honor bright; to have done is to hang
Quite out of fashion, like a rusty mail
In monumental mock'ry. Take the instant way,
For honor travels in a strait so narrow,
Where one but goes abreast. Keep then the path,　155
For emulation hath a thousand sons
That one by one pursue. If you give way,
Or [hedge] aside from the direct forthright,
Like to an ent'red tide, they all rush by
And leave you [hindmost];　　　160
[Or like a gallant horse fall'n in first rank,
Lie there for pavement to the abject [rear],
O'errun and trampled on.] Then what they do in
　　　present,
Though less than yours in [past], must o'ertop yours;
For Time is like a fashionable host　　　165
That slightly shakes his parting guest by th' hand,
And with his arms outstretch'd as he would fly,
Grasps in the comer. The welcome ever smiles,
And farewell goes out sighing. Let not virtue seek
Remuneration for the thing it was;　　　170
For beauty, wit,
High birth, vigor of bone, desert in service,
Love, friendship, charity, are subjects all
To envious and calumniating Time.
One touch of nature makes the whole world kin,　175

That all with one consent praise new-born gawds,
Though they are made and moulded of things past,
And [give] to dust, that is a little gilt,
More laud than gilt o'erdusted.
The present eye praises the present object.　　180
Then marvel not, thou great and complete man,
That all the Greeks begin to worship Ajax;
Since things in motion sooner catch the eye
[Than] what stirs not. The cry went once on thee,
And still it might, and yet it may again,　　185
If thou wouldst not entomb thyself alive
And case thy reputation in thy tent,
Whose glorious deeds but in these fields of late
Made emulous missions 'mongst the gods themselves,
And drave great Mars to faction.

Achil.　　　　　　　　Of this my privacy
I have strong reasons.

Ulyss.　　　　　But 'gainst your privacy　191
The reasons are more potent and heroical.
'Tis known, Achilles, that you are in love
With one of Priam's daughters.

Achil.　　　　　　Ha? known?

Ulyss.　Is that a wonder?　　　195
The providence that's in a watchful state
Knows almost every [grain of Pluto's gold],
Finds bottom in th' uncomprehensive depth,
Keeps place with thought and almost, like the gods,
Do thoughts unveil in their dumb cradles.　　200
There is a mystery (with whom relation
Durst never meddle) in the soul of state,
Which hath an operation more divine
Than breath or pen can give expressure to.
All the commerce that you have had with Troy　205
As perfectly is ours as yours, my lord,
And better would it fit Achilles much
To throw down Hector than Polyxena.
But it must grieve young Pyrrhus now at home,
When fame shall in our islands sound her trump,　210
And all the Greekish girls shall tripping sing,
"Great Hector's sister did Achilles win,
But our great Ajax bravely beat down him."
Farewell, my lord; I as your lover speak:
The fool slides o'er the ice that you should break.　215

　　　　　　　　　　　　　　　　　[*Exit.*]

---

134. **creep:** move so as to attract no notice.　**skittish:** fickle.
135. **play...eyes:** i.e. make fools of themselves to attract her attention.
137. **fasting...wantonness:** abstaining out of capriciousness (?) or arrogance (?).　141. **shriking:** shrieking (variant form).
145. **wallet...back.** Such a wallet appears in a number of earlier sources (e.g. Spenser's *Faerie Queene*, VI.viii.23–24), but is there symbolic of things man would be glad to forget, not his good deeds.
146. **alms for oblivion:** good deeds to be forgotten.
147. **monster:** i.e. Time.
150. **Perseverance.** Accented on the second syllable.　**dear my:** my dear (a common type of transposition).
152–53. **rusty...mock'ry:** a suit of armor grown rusty from disuse set up as a mocking trophy of past action.
153. **Take...way:** move forward continually.
155. **one...abreast:** i.e. men must walk in single file.　**Keep... path:** maintain your place on the path against competitors (*O.E.D.*, *v*., 33b).　158. **forthright:** straight path.
161–63. **Or...on.** These lines, which add little and disturb the metre, may represent a first thought later cancelled by Shakespeare.
162. **abject rear:** inferior rear ranks.
167. **as...fly.** The image suggests the fickleness of time; cf. the Latin tag *Tempus fugit* (= time flies).
172. **vigor of bone:** physical strength.
175. **One...kin:** i.e. there is one natural trait that all men share.

176. **gawds:** toys, trifles.　178. **a little gilt:** thinly gilded over.
179. **gilt o'erdusted:** true gold obscured with dust.
181. **complete:** perfect.　184. **cry:** applause.
187. **case:** enclose (as in a coffin, dead and buried).
189. **Made...themselves:** i.e. caused the very gods to take part in the battles in emulation.
190. **drave...faction:** drove...taking sides. Possibly a reference to the *Iliad*, Bk. V, where Mars interferes on the side of the Trojans.
192. **heroical:** becoming to a hero.
194. **one...daughters:** i.e. Polyxena.
196. **providence:** foresight. Cf. *prescience*, I.iii.199.
197. **Pluto:** god of the underworld; perhaps here confused, as elsewhere, even in antiquity, with Plutus, god of riches.
198. **uncomprehensive:** incomprehensible.
199–200. **Keeps...cradles:** keeps abreast of what is being thought and can even anticipate it before it is uttered.
201–2. **with...meddle:** i.e. of which no report can be given.
205. **commerce:** dealings.
209. **must:** will certainly.　**Pyrrhus:** Achilles' son, called also Neoptolemus.　214. **lover:** friend, well-wisher.
215. **The fool...break.** Meaning uncertain; perhaps, "The fool (Ajax) seems to be getting away with an apparently dangerous game, which you should take action to stop."

*Troilus
and Cressida
III.iii*

Patr. To this effect, Achilles, have I mov'd you.
A woman impudent and mannish grown
Is not more loath'd than an effeminate man
In time of action. I stand condemn'd for this;
They think my little stomach to the war,   220
And your great love to me, restrains you thus.
Sweet, rouse yourself, and the weak wanton Cupid
Shall from your neck unloose his amorous fold,
And like [a] dewdrop from the lion's mane,
Be shook to air.

Achil.   Shall Ajax fight with Hector?   225

Patr. Ay, and perhaps receive much honor by him.

Achil. I see my reputation is at stake,
My fame is shrowdly gor'd.

Patr.   O then beware!
Those wounds heal ill that men do give themselves.
Omission to do what is necessary   230
Seals a commission to a blank of danger,
And danger like an ague subtly taints
Even then when they sit idly in the sun.

Achil. Go call Thersites hither, sweet Patroclus.
I'll send the fool to Ajax and desire him   235
T' invite the Troyan lords after the combat
To see us here unarm'd. I have a woman's longing,
An appetite that I am sick withal,
To see great Hector in his weeds of peace,
To talk with him, and to behold his visage,   240
Even to my full of view.

Enter THERSITES.

            A labor sav'd!

Ther. A wonder!

Achil. What?

Ther. Ajax goes up and down the field, asking for
himself.   245

Achil. How so?

Ther. He must fight singly to-morrow with
Hector, and is so prophetically proud of an heroical
cudgelling that he raves in saying nothing.

Achil. How can that be?   250

Ther. Why, 'a stalks up and down like a peacock—
a stride and a stand; ruminates like an hostess that
hath no arithmetic but her brain to set down her
reckoning; bites his lip with a politic regard, as who
should say there were wit in this head and   255
'twould out—and so there is; but it lies as coldly in him
as fire in a flint, which will not show without knocking.
The man's undone for ever, for if Hector break not his
neck i' th' combat, he'll break't himself in vainglory.
He knows not me. I said, "Good morrow,   260
Ajax"; and he replies, "Thanks, Agamemnon." What
think you of this man that takes me for the general?
He's grown a very land-fish, languageless, a monster.

A plague of opinion! a man may wear it on both sides,
like a leather jerkin.   265

Achil. Thou must be my ambassador [to him],
Thersites.

Ther. Who, I? Why, he'll answer nobody; he professes not answering. Speaking is for beggars; he
wears his tongue in 's arms. I will put on his   270
presence, let Patroclus make demands to me; you shall
see the pageant of Ajax.

Achil. To him, Patroclus. Tell him I humbly
desire the valiant Ajax to invite the [most] valorous
Hector to come unarm'd to my tent, and to pro-   275
cure safe-conduct for his person of the magnanimous
and most illustrious six-or-seven-times-honor'd cap-
tain-general of the army, Agamemnon, [et cetera].
Do this.

Patr. Jove bless great Ajax!   280

Ther. Hum?

Patr. I come from the worthy Achilles—

Ther. Ha?

Patr. Who most humbly desires you to invite
Hector to his tent—   285

Ther. Hum?

Patr. And to procure safe-conduct from Agamemnon.

Ther. Agamemnon?

Patr. Ay, my lord.   290

Ther. Ha?

Patr. What say you to't?

Ther. God buy you, with all my heart.

Patr. Your answer, sir.   294

Ther. If to-morrow be a fair day, by aleven of the
clock it will go one way or other. Howsoever, he shall
pay for me ere he has me.

Patr. Your answer, sir.

Ther. Fare ye well, with all my heart.

Achil. Why, but he is not in this tune, is he?   300

Ther. No; but [he's] out of tune thus. What music
will be in him when Hector has knock'd out his brains,
I know not; but I am sure none, unless the fiddler
Apollo get his sinews to make catlings on.

Achil. Come, thou shalt bear a letter to him
straight.   305

Ther. Let me bear another to his horse, for that's
the more capable creature.

Achil. My mind is troubled, like a fountain stirr'd,
And I myself see not the bottom of it.   309

                        [*Exeunt Achilles and Patroclus.*]

Ther. Would the fountain of your mind were clear
again, that I might water an ass at it! I had rather be a
tick in a sheep than such a valiant ignorance. [*Exit.*]

---

218. **effeminate:** unmanly.   220. **stomach to:** appetite for.
223. **fold:** embrace.
228. **shrowdly gor'd:** sorely (variant form of *shrewdly*) wounded (as
by an animal's horn).
231. **Seals . . . danger:** i.e. licenses danger to do as it pleases. The
reference is to a warrant with blanks to be filled in at the recipient's
pleasure.   238. **withal:** with.   239. **weeds:** garments.
252. **hostess:** hostess of an inn.
254. **politic regard:** an appearance of being judicious.
257. **knocking:** striking.   258. **his:** i.e. Ajax'.
263. **land-fish:** a fish that lives on land, hence an unnatural creature
(*O.E.D.*); cf. *monster* later in the line.

264. **opinion:** reputation.
268–69. **professes:** makes a particular point of.
270. **in 's:** in his.   271. **presence:** demeanor, bearing.
293. **God buy you:** God be with you, i.e. goodby.
295. **aleven:** eleven (a characteristic Shakespearean spelling).
296. **Howsoever:** whichever way.
297. **pay . . . has me:** i.e. pay dearly before he has the better of me.
301. **out of tune:** completely disordered (unharmonious).
303–4. **fiddler Apollo.** Apollo was the god of music.
304. **make catlings on:** make lute strings (made of catgut) of.
307. **capable:** intelligent.
311. **might . . . ass.** Even an ass would refuse to drink the present
muddy water.   312. **valiant ignorance:** vainglorious fool.

[ACT IV, Scene I]

Enter at one door Aeneas [*with a torch*]; *at another,*
Paris, Deiphobus, Antenor, Diomed *the Grecian,*
[*and others*] *with torches.*

Par. See ho! who is that there?

Dei. It is the Lord Aeneas.

Aene. Is the Prince there in person?
Had I so good occasion to lie long
As [you], Prince Paris, nothing but heavenly business
Should rob my bed-mate of my company.   6

Dio. That's my mind too. Good morrow, Lord
Aeneas.

Par. A valiant Greek, Aeneas, take his hand,
Witness the process of your speech, wherein
You told how Diomed, a whole week by days,   10
Did haunt you in the field.

Aene.   Health to you, valiant sir,
During all question of the gentle truce;
But when I meet you arm'd, as black defiance
As heart can think or courage execute.

Dio. The one and other Diomed embraces.   15
Our bloods are now in calm, and, so long, health!
[But] when contention and occasion meet,
By Jove I'll play the hunter for thy life,
With all my force, pursuit, and policy.

Aene. And thou shalt hunt a lion that will fly   20
With his face backward. In humane gentleness,
Welcome to Troy! now, by Anchises' life,
Welcome indeed! By Venus' hand I swear,
No man alive can love in such a sort
The thing he means to kill, more excellently.   25

Dio. We sympathize. Jove, let Aeneas live,
If to my sword his fate be not the glory,
A thousand complete courses of the sun!
But in mine emulous honor let him die,
With every joint a wound, and that to-morrow!   30

Aene. We know each other well.

Dio. We do, and long to know each other worse.

Par. This is the most despiteful gentle greeting,
The noblest hateful love, that e'er I heard of.
What business, lord, so early?   35

Aene. I was sent for to the King, but why, I know
not.

Par. His purpose meets you; 'twas to bring this
Greek
To Calchas' house, and there to render him,
For the enfreed Antenor, the fair Cressid.
Let's have your company, or if you please,   40
Haste there before us. I constantly believe
(Or rather call my thought a certain knowledge)
My brother Troilus lodges there to-night.
Rouse him and give him note of our approach,

With the whole quality wherefore. I fear   45
We shall be much unwelcome.

Aene.   That I assure you.
Troilus had rather Troy were borne to Greece
Than Cressid borne from Troy.

Par.   There is no help.
The bitter disposition of the time
Will have it so. On, lord, we'll follow you.   50

Aene. Good morrow, all.   [*Exit.*]

Par. And tell me, noble Diomed—faith, tell me
true,
Even in soul of sound good-fellowship—
Who, in your thoughts, deserves fair Helen best,
Myself, or Menelaus?

Dio.   Both alike.   55
He merits well to have her that doth seek her,
Not making any scruple of her soil,
With such a hell of pain and world of charge;
And you as well to keep her that defend her,
Not palating the taste of her dishonor,   60
With such a costly loss of wealth and friends.
He like a puling cuckold would drink up
The lees and dregs of a flat tamed piece;
You like a lecher out of whorish loins
Are pleas'd to breed out your inheritors.   65
Both merits pois'd, each weighs nor less nor more,
But he as he, the heavier for a whore.

Par. You are too bitter to your country-woman.

Dio. She's bitter to her country. Hear me, Paris:
For every false drop in her bawdy veins,   70
A Grecian's life hath sunk; for every scruple
Of her contaminated carrion weight,
A Troyan hath been slain. Since she could speak,
She hath not given so many good words breath
As for her Greeks and Troyans suff'red death.   75

Par. Fair Diomed, you do as chapmen do,
Dispraise the thing that they desire to buy,
But we in silence hold this virtue well,
We'll not commend what we intend to sell.
Here lies our way.   *Exeunt.*   80

[Scene II]

Enter Troilus *and* Cressida.

Tro. Dear, trouble not yourself, the morn is cold.

IV.i. Location: Troy. A street.
9. **process:** course, tenor.
10. **a whole . . . days:** every day for a week.
12. **During . . . of:** in all our talk during.   19. **policy:** cunning.
20–21. **lion . . . backward:** i.e. if he retreats, Aeneas will retreat like
the lion, without turning his back in flight. His failure to reject the
idea that he might retreat under any circumstances is perhaps a
courteous gesture to Diomedes as a guest.
22, 23. **Anchises, Venus.** Aeneas' father and mother.
26. **We sympathize:** I am of the same mind.
37. **meets you:** is here before you.   41. **constantly:** firmly.

45. **quality wherefore:** occasion of it.
49. **disposition . . . time:** state of present affairs.
53. **in soul:** in the spirit.   57. **soil:** moral stain, dishonor.
58. **world of charge:** tremendous cost.
60. **palating the taste:** tasting the (foul) taste.
63. **flat tamed piece:** (1) opened cask of dead wine, (2) stale used-up
whore.   65. **inheritors:** descendants.
67. **he as he:** i.e. one as the other.
71. **scruple:** smallest unit of weight.
72. **carrion:** rotten, putrefied (as a dead body).
76. **chapmen:** buyers, hagglers.
77. **Dispraise . . . buy.** Cf. Proverbs 20:14: "It is naught, it is naught,
sayeth the buyer: but when he is gone apart, he boasteth" (Geneva).
78–79. **But . . . sell:** i.e. we think there is great virtue in silence and
will not commend (like cheap hawkers) what we intend to sell (at the
highest cost, our lives if necessary). Some editors emend *not* to *but*
(after Jackson's conjecture in Cambridge) for easier sense: we'll
commend only what we want to dispose of (not Helen). Cf. Sonnet
21.14, "I will not praise that purpose not to sell."

IV.ii. Location: Troy. The court of Calchas' house.

Cres. Then, sweet my lord, I'll call mine uncle
    down,
He shall unbolt the gates.
   Tro.   Trouble him not;
To bed, to bed. Sleep kill those pretty eyes,
And give as soft attachment to thy senses   5
As infants empty of all thought!
   Cres.   Good morrow then.
   Tro. I prithee now to bed.
   Cres.   Are you a-weary of me?
   Tro. O Cressida! but that the busy day,
Wak'd by the lark, hath rous'd the ribald crows,
And dreaming night will hide our joys no longer,   10
I would not from thee.
   Cres.   Night hath been too brief.
   Tro. Beshrew the witch! with venomous wights
    she stays
As tediously as hell, but flies the grasps of love
With wings more momentary-swift than thought.
You will catch cold and curse me.
   Cres.   Prithee tarry,   15
You men will never tarry.
O foolish Cressid! I might have still held off,
And then you would have tarried. Hark, there's one
    up.
   Pan. [*Within.*] What's all the doors open here?
   Tro. It is your uncle.   20

[*Enter* PANDARUS.]

   Cres. A pestilence on him! now will he be mocking.
I shall have such a life!
   Pan. How now, how now, how go maidenheads?
Here, you maid! where's my cousin Cressid?
   Cres. Go hang yourself, you naughty mocking
    uncle!   25
You bring me to do—and then you flout me too.
   Pan. To do what, to do what? let her say what.
What have I brought you to do?
   Cres. Come, come, beshrew your heart, you'll
    ne'er be good,
Nor suffer others.   30
   Pan. Ha, ha! Alas, poor wretch! a poor [*capocchia*]!
hast not slept to-night? Would he not, a naughty man,
let it sleep? A bugbear take him!
   Cres. Did not I tell you? Would he were knock'd i'
    th' head!   *One knocks.*
Who's that at door? Good uncle, go and see.   35
My lord, come you again into my chamber.
You smile and mock me, as if I meant naughtily.
   Tro. Ha, ha!
   Cres. Come, you are deceived, I think of no such
    thing.   *Knock.*
How earnestly they knock! Pray you come in.   40
I would not for half Troy have you seen here.
          Exeunt [*Troilus and Cressida*].

   Pan. Who's there? What's the matter? Will you
beat down the door? How now, what's the matter?

[*Enter* AENEAS.]

   Aene. Good morrow, lord, good morrow.
   Pan. Who's there? My Lord Aeneas! By my
    troth,   45
I knew you not. What news with you so early?
   Aene. Is not Prince Troilus here?
   Pan. Here? what should he do here?
   Aene. Come, he is here, my lord, do not deny him.
It doth import him much to speak with me.   50
   Pan. Is he here, say you? It's more than I know,
I'll be sworn. For my own part, I came in late. What
should he do here?
   Aene. Who!—nay then. Come, come, you'll do
him wrong ere you are ware. You'll be so true to   55
him, to be false to him. Do not you know of him, but
yet go fetch him hither, go.

[*Enter* TROILUS.]

   Tro. How now, what's the matter?
   Aene. My lord, I scarce have leisure to salute you,
My matter is so rash. There is at hand   60
Paris your brother, and Deiphobus,
The Grecian Diomed, and our Antenor
Deliver'd to [us]; and [for him] forthwith,
Ere the first sacrifice, within this hour,
We must give up to Diomedes' hand   65
The Lady Cressida.
   Tro.   Is it so concluded?
   Aene. By Priam and the general state of Troy.
They are at hand and ready to effect it.
   Tro. How my achievements mock me!
I will go meet them; and, my Lord Aeneas,   70
We met by chance, you did not find me here.
   Aene. Good, good, my lord, the secrets of neighbor
    Pandar
Have not more gift in taciturnity.
          Exeunt [*Troilus and Aeneas*].
   Pan. Is't possible? No sooner got but lost? The
devil take Antenor! the young prince will go mad.   75
A plague upon Antenor! I would they had broke 's
neck!

Enter CRESSID.

[*Cres.*] How now? what's the matter? who was here?
   Pan. Ah, ah!   79
   Cres. Why sigh you so profoundly? Where's my
lord? Gone? Tell me, sweet uncle, what's the matter?
   Pan. Would I were as deep under the earth as I am
above!
   Cres. O the gods! what's the matter?   84
   Pan. Pray thee get thee in. Would thou hadst
ne'er been born! I knew thou wouldest be his death.
O poor gentleman! A plague upon Antenor!

---

4. **kill:** put to rest (by closing).   5. **attachment:** imprisonment.
9. **ribald:** scurrilous, irreverent.
12. **Beshrew:** curses on.   **venomous wights:** people who dislike each
other.   24. **maid:** (1) waiting-woman; (2) maiden, virgin.
26. **do:** (1) act; (2) have sexual relations (slang).
30. **suffer others:** allow others (to be good).
31. **capocchia:** simpleton, innocent (Italian).
33. **bugbear:** hobgoblin.

50. **import:** concern.   54. **Who:** stop, hold (a form of *ho*).
56. **to:** as to.   **know of him:** i.e. admit that he is here.
60. **rash:** urgent.   67. **state:** council of state.
73. **Have . . . taciturnity:** are no more characterized by a proper
silence (than I will be).

Cres. Good uncle, I beseech you, on my knees [I
beseech you], what's the matter?   89
Pan. Thou must be gone, wench, thou must be
gone; thou art chang'd for Antenor. Thou must to thy
father, and be gone from Troilus. 'Twill be his death,
'twill be his bane, he cannot bear it.
Cres. O you immortal gods! I will not go.
Pan. Thou must.   95
Cres. I will not, uncle. I have forgot my father,
I know no touch of consanguinity;
No kin, no love, no blood, no soul so near me
As the sweet Troilus. O you gods divine,
Make Cressid's name the very crown of falsehood,   100
If ever she leave Troilus! Time, force, and death,
Do to this body what extremes you can;
But the strong base and building of my love
Is as the very centre of the earth,
Drawing all things to it. I'll go in and weep.   105
Pan. Do, do.
Cres. Tear my bright hair, and scratch my praised
          cheeks,
Crack my clear voice with sobs, and break my heart,
With sounding Troilus. I will not go from Troy.
                                          [*Exeunt.*]

[Scene III]

Enter Paris, Troilus, Aeneas, Deiphobus, Antenor,
Diomedes.

Par. It is great morning, and the hour prefix'd
For her delivery to this valiant Greek
Comes fast upon. Good my brother Troilus,
Tell you the lady what she is to do,
And haste her to the purpose.
Tro.   Walk into her house.
I'll bring her to the Grecian presently;   6
And to his hand when I deliver her,
Think it an altar, and thy brother Troilus
A priest there off'ring to it his own heart.   [*Exit.*]
Par. I know what 'tis to love,   10
And would, as I shall pity, I could help!
Please you walk in, my lords.   *Exeunt.*

[Scene IV]

Enter Pandarus *and* Cressida.

Pan. Be moderate, be moderate.
Cres. Why tell you me of moderation?
The grief is fine, full, perfect, that I taste,
And violenteth in a sense as strong
As that which causeth it. How can I moderate it?   5
If I could temporize with my affections,

Or brew it to a weak and colder palate,
The like allayment could I give my grief:
My love admits no qualifying dross,
No more my grief, in such a precious loss.   10

Enter Troilus.

Pan. Here, here, here he comes. [Ah], sweet
ducks!
Cres. O Troilus, Troilus!   [*Embracing him.*]
Pan. What a pair of spectacles is here! Let me
embrace too. "O heart," as the goodly saying is,   15
     "O heart, heavy heart,
         Why sigh'st thou without breaking?"
where he answers again,
     "Because thou canst not ease thy smart
         By friendship nor by speaking."   20
There was never a truer rhyme. Let us cast away
nothing, for we may live to have need of such a verse.
We see it, we see it. How now, lambs?
Tro. Cressid, I love thee in so strain'd a purity
That the blest gods, as angry with my fancy,   25
More bright in zeal than the devotion which
Cold lips blow to their deities, take thee from me.
Cres. Have the gods envy?
Pan. Ay, ay, ay, ay, 'tis too plain a case.
Cres. And is it true that I must go from Troy?   30
Tro. A hateful truth.
Cres.   What, and from Troilus too?
Tro. From Troy and Troilus.
Cres.   Is't possible?
Tro. And suddenly, where injury of chance
Puts back leave-taking, justles roughly by
All time of pause, rudely beguiles our lips   35
Of all rejoindure, forcibly prevents
Our lock'd embrasures, strangles our dear vows
Even in the birth of our own laboring breath.
We two, that with so many thousand sighs
Did buy each other, must poorly sell ourselves   40
With the rude brevity and discharge of one.
Injurious time now with a robber's haste
Crams his rich thiev'ry up, he knows not how.
As many farewells as be stars in heaven,
With distinct breath and consign'd kisses to them,   45
He fumbles up into a loose adieu;
And scants us with a single famish'd kiss,
Distasted with the salt of broken tears.
Aene. (*Within.*) My lord, is the lady ready?
Tro. Hark, you are call'd. Some say the Genius [so]
Cries ["come"] to him that instantly must die.   51
—Bid them have patience, she shall come anon.

7. **it:** i.e. the affections (viewed as a whole).   **palate:** taste.
10. **in . . . loss:** in the loss of so precious an object.
14. **pair of spectacles:** two (sad) sights (with play on "eye-glasses").
21. **rhyme.** No source is known for these verses.
23. **We see it:** i.e. we can see such a situation coming, alas.
24. **strain'd:** refined.   25. **fancy:** love.
26. **bright in zeal:** burning in ardor.   33. **suddenly:** immediately.
34. **Puts back leave-taking:** forestalls farewells.
36. **rejoindure:** (1) answering farewells; (2) being rejoined (in a kiss).
37. **embrasures:** embraces.
43. **he . . . how:** helter-skelter, without discrimination.
45. **With . . . them:** each separately uttered and ratified with an
accompanying kiss.   46. **loose:** casual.
48. **Distasted:** made bitter.
50. **Genius.** Each man was believed to have his own attendant spirit
who presided over his destiny from birth to death.

93. **bane:** death (properly, by poison).
97. **touch of consanguinity:** feeling of blood relationship.
104-5. **centre . . . it.** See the note on III.ii.179.
109. **sounding:** uttering.

IV.iii. Location: Troy. Before Calchas' house.
1. **great morning:** broad daylight.   6. **presently:** at once.

IV.iv. Location: Calchas' house.
3. **fine:** refined, pure.
4. **violenteth:** rages with violence.   **sense:** emotional feeling.
6. **affections:** emotions, passions.

*Troilus
and Cressida
IV.iv*

Pan. Where are my tears? Rain, to lay this wind,
or my heart will be blown up by [th' root].   [*Exit.*]
Cres.   I must then to the Grecians?
Tro.   No remedy.   55
Cres.   A woeful Cressid 'mongst the merry Greeks!
When shall we see again?
Tro.   Hear me, love. Be thou but true of heart—
Cres.   I true? How now? what wicked deem is this?
Tro.   Nay, we must use expostulation kindly,   60
For it is parting from us.
I speak not "be thou true" as fearing thee,
For I will throw my glove to Death himself
That there is no maculation in thy heart;
But "be thou true" say I to fashion in   65
My sequent protestation: be thou true,
And I will see thee.
Cres.   O, you shall be expos'd, my lord, to dangers
As infinite as imminent! but I'll be true.
Tro.   And I'll grow friend with danger. Wear this
          sleeve.   70
Cres.   And you this glove. When shall I see you?
Tro.   I will corrupt the Grecian sentinels,
To give thee nightly visitation.
But yet be true.
Cres.   O heavens, "be true" again?
Tro.   Hear why I speak it, love.   75
The Grecian youths are full of quality;
[Their loving well compos'd with gift of nature,
Flowing] and swelling o'er with arts and exercise.
How novelty may move, and parts with [person],
Alas, a kind of godly jealousy   80
(Which I beseech you call a virtuous sin)
Makes me afeard.
Cres.   O heavens, you love me not.
Tro.   Die I a villain then!
In this I do not call your faith in question
So mainly as my merit. I cannot sing,   85
Nor heel the high lavolt, nor sweeten talk,
Nor play at subtile games—fair virtues all,
To which the Grecians are most prompt and preg-
          nant—
But I can tell that in each grace of these

There lurks a still and dumb-discoursive devil   90
That tempts most cunningly, but be not tempted.
Cres.   Do you think I will?
Tro.   No,
But something may be done that we will not,
And sometimes we are devils to ourselves,   95
When we will tempt the frailty of our powers,
Presuming on their changeful potency.
Aene.   (*Within.*) Nay, good my lord!
Tro.   Come kiss, and let us part.
Par.   (*Within.*) Brother Troilus!
Tro.   Good brother, come you hither,
And bring Aeneas and the Grecian with you.   100
Cres.   My lord, will you be true?
Tro.   Who, I? Alas, it is my vice, my fault:
Whiles others fish with craft for great opinion,
I with great truth catch mere simplicity;
Whilst some with cunning gild their copper crowns,
With truth and plainness I do wear mine bare.   106
Fear not my truth: the moral of my wit
Is "plain and true"; there's all the reach of it.

[*Enter* AENEAS, PARIS, ANTENOR, DEIPHOBUS, *and*
DIOMEDES.]

Welcome, Sir Diomed! Here is the lady
Which for Antenor we deliver you.   110
At the port, lord, I'll give her to thy hand,
And by the way possess thee what she is.
Entreat her fair, and, by my soul, fair Greek,
If e'er thou stand at mercy of my sword,
Name Cressid, and thy life shall be as safe   115
As Priam is in Ilion.
Dio.   Fair Lady Cressid,
So please you, save the thanks this prince expects.
The lustre in your eye, heaven in your cheek,
Pleads your fair usage, and to Diomed
You shall be mistress, and command him wholly.   120
Tro.   Grecian, thou dost not use me courteously,
To shame the seal of my petition to thee
In praising her. I tell thee, lord of Greece,
She is as far high-soaring o'er thy praises
As thou unworthy to be call'd her servant.   125
I charge thee use her well, even for my charge;
For by the dreadful Pluto, if thou dost not,
Though the great bulk Achilles be thy guard,
I'll cut thy throat.
Dio.   O, be not mov'd, Prince Troilus.

---

53. **Rain . . . wind:** i.e. tears to allay this sighing.
54. **my . . . root.** It was believed that sighing shortened life by drawing blood from the heart. Pandarus ludicrously inflates his sighs into a gale that threatens to uproot his heart as if it were a tree.
56. **merry Greeks.** See the note on I.ii.109.
59. **deem:** surmise, thought.
61. **it:** i.e. the opportunity to "use expostulation."
62. **fearing thee:** doubting your faith.   63. **throw . . . to:** challenge.
64. **maculation:** stain of inconstancy.
65. **fashion in:** prepare the way for.
70, 71. **sleeve, glove.** Common love tokens, though a sleeve was commonly given by the woman. Both men's and women's sleeves were detachable.   72. **corrupt:** bribe.
73. **To:** in order to.   **nightly:** at night.
76. **quality:** admirable qualities.
77–78. **Their . . . exercise:** i.e. in their pursuit of love they have the advantage of fine natural endowments, increased to overflowing by acquired graces in which they are well practiced.
79. **novelty:** the new manner (of their wooing).   **parts with person:** accomplishments in addition to good looks.
80. **godly jealousy.** A Biblical echo; see 2 Corinthians 11:2: "For I am jealous over you, with godly jealousy" (Geneva).
86. **high lavolt.** The lavolta was a dance for two persons, requiring a good deal of bounding (hence "high").
88. **prompt and pregnant:** inclined and ready.

90. **dumb-discoursive:** communicating without speech.
96. **will tempt:** insist upon tempting.   **frailty:** susceptibility.
97. **Presuming . . . potency:** relying presumptuously on their strength, which is in fact very unstable.
103. **craft:** cunning.   **opinion:** reputation, approbation.
104. **I . . . simplicity:** "my use of bare truth wins for me the character of a plain, simple man" (Deighton).
107. **moral . . . wit:** the maxim that expresses my mind.
108. **all the reach:** the whole extent.   111. **port:** city gate.
112. **possess thee:** explain to you.
113. **Entreat:** treat.   **fair:** courteously, honorably.
117. **So please:** if it please.
122–23. **shame . . . her:** i.e. disdain to ratify my request by praising her (in those terms), i.e. fail to "entreat her fair" by addressing her at once as a professed lover (the *servant* of line 125). Many editors unnecessarily adopt Theobald's emendation of *seal* to *zeal*.
126. **use:** treat.   **even . . . charge:** i.e. on the basis of my demand alone.   128. **great bulk:** huge-framed.   129. **mov'd:** angry.

Let me be privileg'd by my place and message,　130
To be a speaker free. When I am hence,
I'll answer to my lust, and know you, lord,
I'll nothing do on charge. To her own worth
She shall be priz'd; but that you say, "Be't so,"
I speak it in my spirit and honor, "No."　135
　　Tro.　Come, to the port. I'll tell thee, Diomed,
This brave shall oft make thee to hide thy head.
Lady, give me your hand, and as we walk,
To our own selves bend we our needful talk.　139
　　　　　[*Exeunt Troilus, Cressida, and Diomedes.*
　　　　　　Sound trumpet.]
　　Par.　Hark, Hector's trumpet!
　　Aene.　　　　　　How have we spent this morning!
The Prince must think me tardy and remiss,
That swore to ride before him to the field.
　　Par.　'Tis Troilus' fault. Come, come, to field
　　　with him.
　　[[*Dei.*]　Let us make ready straight.
　　Aene.　Yea, with a bridegroom's fresh alacrity　145
Let us address to tend on Hector's heels.
The glory of our Troy doth this day lie
On his fair worth and single chivalry.]　　　*Exeunt.*

　　　　　　[SCENE V]

Enter AJAX *armed,* ACHILLES, PATROCLUS, AGAMEM-
NON, MENELAUS, ULYSSES, NESTOR, *etc.*

　　Agam.　Here art thou in appointment fresh and fair,
Anticipating time. With starting courage,
Give with thy trumpet a loud note to Troy,
Thou dreadful Ajax, that the appalled air
May pierce the head of the great combatant,　5
And hale him hither.
　　Ajax.　　　　　Thou, trumpet, there's my purse.
Now crack thy lungs, and split thy brazen pipe.
Blow, villain, till thy sphered bias cheek
Outswell the colic of puff'd Aquilon;
Come, stretch thy chest, and let thy eyes spout blood;
Thou blowest for Hector.　　　[*Trumpet sounds.*]　11
　　Ulyss.　No trumpet answers.
　　Achil.　　　　　　　'Tis but early days.

130. **place and message:** office and errand, i.e. status as an ambassador.
132. **answer . . . lust:** be answerable (on the battlefield) for what I
please to do (?). *Lust* = pleasure, desire.
133. **To:** in accordance with.　　137. **brave:** defiance.
140. **spent:** used up.　146. **address:** make ready.
148. **single chivalry:** knightly prowess as shown in single combat.

IV.v. Location: The Greek camp. Lists set out.
1. **appointment:** equipment (suitable to a knight).
2. **starting courage:** rousing spirit.
3. **trumpet:** (probably) trumpeter (as in line 6).
4. **dreadful:** inspiring dread.
6. **hale:** pull (alluding to the notion, already seen in I.iii.66-68, that
words or sounds tie the hearer's ear to the speaker or source of the
sound).
7. **brazen pipe:** i.e. the trumpeter's throat; "brazen" by transference
from the instrument.
8. **villain:** fellow (not derogatory).　**sphered bias cheek:** cheek
puffed out like a weighted bowl (used in the game of bowls).
9. **colic . . . Aquilon:** i.e. the tremendously distended cheeks of
puffing Aquilon (Greek name for Boreas, the north wind). The comparison is drawn from the representations of Boreas and other winds
in the corners of old maps, to which Ajax ludicrously adds the round-
ness of a belly distended by the wind of colic.
11. **for:** to summon.

[*Enter* DIOMED *and* CRESSID.]

　　Agam.　Is not yond Diomed, with Calchas'
　　　daughter?
　　Ulyss.　'Tis he, I ken the manner of his gait,
He rises on the toe. That spirit of his　15
In aspiration lifts him from the earth.
　　Agam.　Is this the Lady Cressid?
　　Dio.　　　　　　　Even she.
　　Agam.　Most dearly welcome to the Greeks, sweet
　　　lady.　　　　　　　　　　　　[*Kisses her.*]
　　Nest.　Our general doth salute you with a kiss.
　　Ulyss.　Yet is the kindness but particular,　20
'Twere better she were kiss'd in general.
　　Nest.　And very courtly counsel. I'll begin.
So much for Nestor.　　　　　　[*Kisses her.*]
　　Achil.　I'll take that winter from your lips, fair
　　　lady;
Achilles bids you welcome.　　　[*Kisses her.*]　25
　　Men.　I had good argument for kissing once.
　　Patr.　But that's no argument for kissing now,
For thus popp'd Paris in his hardiment,
And parted thus you and your argument. [*Kisses her.*]
　　Ulyss.　O deadly gall, and theme of all our scorns,
For which we lose our heads to gild his horns!　31
　　Patr.　The first was Menelaus' kiss, this, mine;
Patroclus kisses you.　　　　[*Kisses her again.*]
　　Men.　　　　　　O, this is trim!
　　Patr.　Paris and I kiss evermore for him.
　　Men.　I'll have my kiss, sir. Lady, by your leave.
　　Cres.　In kissing, do you render or receive?　36
　　Patr.　Both take and give.
　　Cres.　　　　　　I'll make my match to live,
The kiss you take is better than you give;
Therefore no kiss.　39
　　Men.　I'll give you boot, I'll give you three for one.
　　Cres.　You are an odd man, give even or give none.
　　Men.　An odd man, lady? Every man is odd.
　　Cres.　No, Paris is not, for you know 'tis true
That you are odd, and he is even with you.　44
　　Men.　You fillip me a' th' head.
　　Cres.　　　　　　No, I'll be sworn.
　　Ulyss.　It were no match, your nail against his horn.
May I, sweet lady, beg a kiss of you?
　　Cres.　You may.
　　Ulyss.　　　　　I do desire it.
　　Cres.　　　　　　　Why, beg then.
　　Ulyss.　Why then for Venus' sake, give me a kiss
When Helen is a maid again and his.　50
　　Cres.　I am your debtor, claim it when 'tis due.
　　Ulyss.　Never's my day, and then a kiss of you.

13. **yond:** yonder man.
20. **but particular:** limited only to one (playing on *general*).
24. **winter:** i.e. the cold lips of ancient Nestor.
26. **good argument:** good reason, i.e. Helen.
28. **thus . . . hardiment:** in this manner Paris popped in his bold stroke
(with bawdy equivoque).
30. **theme . . . scorns:** the subject that has brought scorn upon all
of us.　33. **this is trim:** a fine thing (ironic).
37. **I'll . . . live:** I'll wager my life that (?).
40. **boot:** something in addition.
41. **odd:** (1) singular, strange; (2) single (because he has lost his wife
Helen).
45. **fillip . . . head:** snap your fingernail against my head, i.e. twit
me for my cuckold's horns.　**No . . . sworn:** no, indeed, I don't
imply any such thing.　50. **his:** i.e. Menelaus'.

*Troilus
and Cressida
IV.v*

Dio. Lady, a word. I'll bring you to your father.
　　　　　　　　　　　　　　　[Exit with Cressida.]
Nest. A woman of quick sense.
Ulyss.　　　　　　　　　　　　Fie, fie upon her!
There's language in her eye, her cheek, her lip,　55
Nay, her foot speaks; her wanton spirits look out
At every joint and motive of her body.
O, these encounterers, so glib of tongue,
That give a coasting welcome ere it comes,
And wide unclasp the tables of their thoughts　60
To every ticklish reader! set them down
For sluttish spoils of opportunity,
And daughters of the game.　　　　　*Flourish.*
All.　The Troyans' trumpet.

Enter all of Troy: [HECTOR *armed*, PARIS, AENEAS,
HELENUS, TROILUS, *and* ATTENDANTS].

Agam.　　　　　　　　Yonder comes the troop.
Aene.　Hail, all the state of Greece! What shall
　　be done　　　　　　　　　　　　　　65
To him that victory commands? or do you purpose
A victor shall be known? Will you the knights
Shall to the edge of all extremity
Pursue each other, or shall they be divided
By any voice or order of the field?　　　70
Hector bade ask.
Agam.　　　　Which way would Hector have it?
Aene.　He cares not, he'll obey conditions.
Agam.　'Tis done like Hector.
[Achil.]　　　　　　But securely done,
A little proudly, and great deal misprising
The knight oppos'd.
Aene.　　　　　If not Achilles, sir,　　75
What is your name?
Achil.　　　　If not Achilles, nothing.
Aene.　Therefore Achilles, but what e'er, know
　　this:
In the extremity of great and little,
Valor and pride excel themselves in Hector,
The one almost as infinite as all,　　　80
The other blank as nothing. Weigh him well,
And that which looks like pride is courtesy.
This Ajax is half made of Hector's blood,
In love whereof, half Hector stays at home;
Half heart, half hand, half Hector comes to seek　85
This blended knight, half Troyan and half Greek.

Achil.　A maiden battle then? O, I perceive you.

[Enter DIOMEDES.]

Agam.　Here is Sir Diomed. Go, gentle knight,
Stand by our Ajax. As you and Lord Aeneas
Consent upon the order of their fight,　　　90
So be it, either to the uttermost,
Or else a breath. The combatants being kin
Half stints their strife before their strokes begin.
　　　　　　　　[Ajax and Hector enter the lists.]
[Ulyss.　They are oppos'd already.]
[Agam.]　What Troyan is that same that looks so
　　heavy?　　　　　　　　　　　　95
Ulyss.　The youngest son of Priam, a true knight,
Not yet mature, yet matchless, firm of word,
Speaking [in] deeds, and deedless in his tongue,
Not soon provok'd, nor being provok'd soon calm'd;
His heart and hand both open and both free,　100
For what he has he gives, what thinks he shows,
Yet gives he not till judgment guide his bounty,
Nor dignifies an impare thought with breath;
Manly as Hector, but more dangerous,
For Hector in his blaze of wrath subscribes　105
To tender objects, but he in heat of action
Is more vindicative than jealous love.
They call him Troilus, and on him erect
A second hope, as fairly built as Hector.
Thus says Aeneas, one that knows the youth　110
Even to his inches, and with private soul
Did in great Ilion thus translate him to me.
　　　　　　　　Alarum. [Hector and Ajax fight.]
Agam.　They are in action.
Nest.　Now, Ajax, hold thine own!
Tro.　　　　　　　Hector, thou sleep'st,
Awake thee!　　　　　　　　　　　115
Agam.　His blows are well dispos'd. There, Ajax!
　　　　　　　　　　　　Trumpets cease.
Dio.　You must no more.
Aene.　　　　Princes, enough, so please you.
Ajax.　I am not warm yet, let us fight again.
Dio.　As Hector pleases.
Hect.　　　　Why then will I no more.
Thou art, great lord, my father's sister's son,　120
A cousin-german to great Priam's seed;
The obligation of our blood forbids
A gory emulation 'twixt us twain.
Were thy commixtion Greek and Troyan so
That thou couldst say, "This hand is Grecian all,　125
And this is Troyan; the sinews of this leg
All Greek, and this all Troy; my mother's blood

---

54. **quick sense:** lively wit (but the words also mean "wanton sensuality," which accords with Ulysses' judgment).
57. **motive:** moving part (a sense found only in Shakespeare, according to *O.E.D.*).　59. **a coasting:** an (amorous) approach.
60. **wide . . . thoughts:** i.e. open wide the book of their minds (*tables* = tablets).　61. **ticklish:** prurient, lustful.
62. **sluttish . . . opportunity:** "corrupt wenches, of whose chastity every opportunity may make prey" (Johnson).
63. **the game:** sexual sport.　65. **state:** nobility.
65–66. **What . . . commands:** i.e. how shall the victor be honored. The phrasing is Biblical; cf. 1 Samuel 17:26: "What shall be done to the man that killeth this Philistim, and taketh away the shame from Israel?" (Geneva).　67. **Will you:** is it your will.
69. **divided:** separated (if the combat becomes dangerous).
73. **securely:** overconfidently.
74. **misprising:** undervaluing, i.e. scorning.
77. **what e'er:** whoever you may be.
78. **In . . . little:** i.e. at the two extremes on the scale of magnitude.
79. **excel:** outdo, surpass.
83. **Ajax . . . blood.** See the note on II.ii.73.

87. **maiden battle:** a fight not carried to a bloody outcome.
90. **order of:** rules governing.　92. **breath:** gentle exercise.
95. **heavy:** sad.
98. **Speaking . . . tongue:** i.e. he acts rather than talks about acting.
100. **free:** generous; so also in line 139.
103. **impare:** unconsidered (Lat. *imparatus*).
105–6. **subscribes . . . objects:** i.e. shows the "vice of mercy" (V.iii.37) to those (such as defeated opponents) who arouse his pity (*tender objects* = objects of tenderness).
107. **vindicative:** vindictive, vengeful.
111. **to his inches:** i.e. minutely, intimately.　**with private soul:** in personal confidence.　112. **translate:** interpret.
116. **dispos'd:** placed.　121. **cousin-german:** first cousin.
124. **so:** ordered in such a way.

Runs on the dexter cheek, and this sinister
Bounds in my father's": by Jove multipotent,
Thou shouldst not bear from me a Greekish member
Wherein my sword had not impressure made   131
[Of our rank feud]; but the just gods gainsay
That any [drop] thou borrow'dst from thy mother,
My sacred aunt, should by my mortal sword
Be drained! Let me embrace thee, Ajax.   135
By him that thunders, thou hast lusty arms!
Hector would have them fall upon him thus.
Cousin, all honor to thee!
  Ajax.   I thank thee, Hector.
Thou art too gentle and too free a man.
I came to kill thee, cousin, and bear hence   140
A great addition earned in thy death.
  Hect. Not Neoptolemus so mirable,
On whose bright crest Fame with her loud'st Oyes
Cries, "This is he," could promise to himself
A thought of added honor torn from Hector.   145
  Aene. There is expectance here from both the sides,
What further you will do.
  Hect.   We'll answer it:
The issue is embracement. Ajax, farewell.
  Ajax. If I might in entreaties find success,
As seld I have the chance, I would desire   150
My famous cousin to our Grecian tents.
  Dio. 'Tis Agamemnon's wish, and great Achilles
Doth long to see unarm'd the valiant Hector.
  Hect. Aeneas, call my brother Troilus to me,
And signify this loving interview   155
To the expecters of our Troyan part;
Desire them home. Give me thy hand, my cousin.
I will go eat with thee and see your knights.

[AGAMEMNON *and the rest come forward.*]

  Ajax. Great Agamemnon comes to meet us here.
  Hect. The worthiest of them tell me name by name;
But for Achilles, my own searching eyes   161
Shall find him by his large and portly size.
  Agam. Worthy all arms! as welcome as to one
That would be rid of such an enemy.
[But that's no welcome. Understand more clear,   165
What's past and what's to come is strew'd with husks
And formless ruin of oblivion;
But in this extant moment, faith and troth,
Strain'd purely from all hollow bias-drawing,
Bids thee, with most divine integrity,]   170
From heart of very heart, great Hector, welcome.
  Hect. I thank thee, most imperious Agamemnon.

  Agam. [*To Troilus.*] My well-fam'd lord of Troy,
  no less to you.
  Men. Let me confirm my princely brother's greet-
  ing:
You brace of warlike brothers, welcome hither.   175
  Hect. Who must we answer?
  Aene.   The noble Menelaus.
  Hect. O, you, my lord? By Mars his gauntlet,
  thanks!
Mock not [that I] affect th' untraded [oath],
Your quondam wife swears still by Venus' glove.
She's well, but bade me not commend her to you.   180
  Men. Name her not now, sir, she's a deadly theme.
  Hect. O, pardon, I offend.
  Nest. I have, thou gallant Troyan, seen thee oft,
Laboring for destiny, make cruel way
Through ranks of Greekish youth, and I have seen
  thee,   185
As hot as Perseus, spur thy Phrygian steed,
Despising many forfeits and subduements,
When thou hast hung [thy] advanced sword i' th' air,
Not letting it decline on the declined,
That I have said to some my standers-by   190
"Lo Jupiter is yonder, dealing life!"
And I have seen thee pause and take thy breath,
When that a ring of Greeks have [hemm'd] thee in,
Like an Olympian wrestling. This have I seen,
But this thy countenance, still lock'd in steel,   195
I never saw till now. I knew thy grandsire,
And once fought with him. He was a soldier good,
But, by great Mars, the captain of us all,
Never like thee. O, let an old man embrace thee,
And, worthy warrior, welcome to our tents.   200
  Aene. 'Tis the old Nestor.
  Hect. Let me embrace thee, good old chronicle,
That hast so long walk'd hand in hand with time.
Most reverend Nestor, I am glad to clasp thee.
  Nest. I would my arms could match thee in con-
  tention,   205
[As they contend with thee in courtesy].
  Hect. I would they could.
  Nest. Ha!
By this white beard, I'd fight with thee to-morrow.
Well, welcome, welcome!—I have seen the time.   210
  Ulyss. I wonder now how yonder city stands
When we have here her base and pillar by us.
  Hect. I know your favor, Lord Ulysses, well.
Ah, sir, there's many a Greek and Troyan dead
Since first I saw yourself and Diomed   215
In Ilion, on your Greekish embassy.
  Ulyss. Sir, I foretold you then what would ensue.
My prophecy is but half his journey yet,

---

128. **dexter:** right. **sinister:** left (here accented on the second
syllable). 129. **multipotent:** all-powerful.
132. **rank:** intemperate. **gainsay:** forbid.
136. **him that thunders:** Jove. 137. **thus:** i.e. in a friendly embrace.
141. **great addition:** title of honor.
142. **Neoptolemus so mirable:** i.e. Achilles so worthy of admiration.
As Johnson suggests, Shakespeare seems to have taken Neoptolemus
as Achilles' family name because his son was called Pyrrhus Neoptolemus. 143. **Oyes:** hear ye (from French *oyez*).
156. **expecters . . . part:** i.e. those of our Troyan side who are waiting
to learn the outcome. 162. **portly:** imposing.
163. **Worthy all arms:** worthy of all honor belonging to the profession
of a knight. **as to:** i.e. as you can be to.
169. **Strain'd . . . bias-drawing:** rendered free of all insincere deviations
from straightforward truth. *Bias-drawing* = the curved course of a
bowl weighted on one side. 170. **divine:** godlike.
172. **imperious:** imperial.

178. **untraded:** unfamiliar (i.e. not worn out by frequent usage).
179. **quondam:** former.
184. **Laboring for destiny:** i.e. like an agent of fate (in ending lives).
186. **Perseus.** See the note on I.iii.42.
187. **Despising . . . subduements:** disdaining to slay or subjugate
many (who had been overcome in combat). Cf. lines 105–6.
188. **advanced:** raised.
194. **Olympian:** i.e. one of the gods, dwellers on Mount Olympus.
wrestling: wrestling (variant form). 195. **still:** always hitherto.
202. **chronicle:** storehouse of history.
210. **I . . . time:** i.e. the time has been (when I would have fought with
you). 213. **favor:** countenance.

For yonder walls that pertly front your town,   219
Yon towers, whose wanton tops do buss the clouds,
Must kiss their own feet.
  Hect.   I must not believe you.
There they stand yet, and modestly I think
The fall of every Phrygian stone will cost
A drop of Grecian blood. The end crowns all,
And that old common arbitrator, Time,   225
Will one day end it.
  Ulyss.   So to him we leave it.
Most gentle and most valiant Hector, welcome!
After the general, I beseech you next
To feast with me and see me at my tent.
  Achil. I shall forestall thee, Lord Ulysses, thou!
Now, Hector, I have fed mine eyes on thee;   231
I have with exact view perus'd thee, Hector,
And quoted joint by joint.
  Hect.   Is this Achilles?
  Achil. I am Achilles.   234
  Hect. Stand fair, I pray thee, let me look on thee.
  Achil. Behold thy fill.
  Hect.   Nay, I have done already.
  Achil. Thou art too brief. I will the second time,
As I would buy thee, view thee limb by limb.
  Hect. O, like a book of sport thou'lt read me o'er;
But there's more in me than thou understand'st.   240
Why dost thou so oppress me with thine eye?
  Achil. Tell me, you heavens, in which part of his
     body
Shall I destroy him—whether there, or there, or
     there?—
That I may give the local wound a name,
And make distinct the very breach whereout   245
Hector's great spirit flew. Answer me, heavens!
  Hect. It would discredit the blest gods, proud man,
To answer such a question. Stand again.
Think'st thou to catch my life so pleasantly
As to prenominate in nice conjecture   250
Where thou wilt hit me dead?
  Achil.   I tell thee, yea.
  Hect. Wert thou an oracle to tell me so,
I'd not believe thee. Henceforth guard thee well,
For I'll not kill thee there, nor there, nor there,
But by the forge that [stithied] Mars his helm,   255
I'll kill thee every where, yea, o'er and o'er.
You wisest Grecians, pardon me this brag.
His insolence draws folly from my lips,
But I'll endeavor deeds to match these words,
Or may I never—
  Ajax.   Do not chafe thee, cousin,   260
And you, Achilles, let these threats alone,
Till accident or purpose bring you to't.
You may have every day enough of Hector,

If you have stomach. The general state, I fear,
Can scarce entreat you to be odd with him.   265
  Hect. I pray you let us see you in the field;
We have had pelting wars since you refus'd
The Grecians' cause.
  Achil.   Dost thou entreat me, Hector?
To-morrow do I meet thee, fell as death;
To-night all friends.
  Hect.   Thy hand upon that match.   270
  Agam. First, all you peers of Greece, go to my
     tent;
There in the full convive we. Afterwards,
As Hector's leisure and your bounties shall
Concur together, severally entreat him.
[Beat loud the taborins,] let the trumpets blow,   275
That this great soldier may his welcome know.
               Exeunt [all but Troilus and Ulysses].
  Tro. My Lord Ulysses, tell me, I beseech you,
In what place of the field doth Calchas keep?
  Ulyss. At Menelaus' tent, most princely Troilus.
There Diomed doth feast with him to-night,   280
Who neither looks upon the heaven nor earth,
But gives all gaze and bent of amorous view
On the fair Cressid.
  Tro. Shall I, sweet lord, be bound to you so much,
After we part from Agamemnon's tent,   285
To bring me thither?
  Ulyss.   You shall command me, sir.
But gentle tell me, of what honor was
This Cressida in Troy? Had she no lover there
That wails her absence?
  Tro. O, sir, to such as boasting show their scars
A mock is due. Will you walk on, my lord?   291
She was belov'd, [she lov'd]; she is, and doth:
But still sweet love is food for fortune's tooth.
               Exeunt.

[ACT V, SCENE I]

Enter ACHILLES *and* PATROCLUS.

  Achil. I'll heat his blood with Greekish wine to-
     night,
Which with my scimitar I'll cool to-morrow.
Patroclus, let us feast him to the height.
  Patr. Here comes Thersites.

Enter THERSITES.

  Achil.   How now, thou [core] of envy?
Thou crusty batch of nature, what's the news?   5

---

219. **pertly front:** boldly serve as a front to.   220. **buss:** kiss.
222. **modestly:** at a modest estimate, without exaggeration.
224. **The end crowns all.** A version of the Latin *Finis coronat opus,*
"the end crowns the work."   232. **perus'd:** thoroughly surveyed.
233. **quoted:** scrutinized.   235. **fair:** i.e. still.
239. **like . . . sport:** i.e. as material for a game, deciding by what rules
of combat he may be killed.
248. **Stand again:** i.e. let me view you again.
249. **pleasantly:** easily.
250. **prenominate:** name in advance of the fact.   **nice:** precise.
255. **stithied:** forged.

264. **stomach:** the inclination.   **general state:** the Greek leaders.
265. **be odd:** be at odds, i.e. meet in combat.
267. **pelting:** paltry, slight.   **refus'd:** renounced.
269. **fell:** ruthless, terrible.   272. **in . . . we:** we all feast together.
274. **severally entreat:** individually invite him (to visit you).
275. **taborins:** a kind of drums, struck with a single stick.
278. **keep:** dwell.   282. **bent:** inclination.   284. **bound:** indebted.
287. **gentle:** in courtesy.   **honor:** position, reputation.
290–91. **to . . . due:** those who boast of their wounds justly incur
derision. Troilus thus indirectly admits that he is the lover in question.
293. **fortune's:** i.e. ill fortune's.

V.i. **Location:** The Greek camp. Before Achilles' tent.
4. **core.** See the note on II.i.6.
5. **crusty batch of nature:** scabbed lump of nature's dough (a metaphor from baking bread; cf. *cobloaf,* II.i.38). Some editors, following
Theobald, emend *batch* to *botch* (= ulcer or sore).

Ther. Why, thou picture of what thou seemest, and idol of idiot-worshippers, here's a letter for thee.

Achil. From whence, fragment?

Ther. Why, thou full dish of fool, from Troy.

Patr. Who keeps the tent now?   10

Ther. The surgeon's box, or the patient's wound.

Patr. Well said, adversity! and what needs [these] tricks?

Ther. Prithee be silent, [boy], I profit not by thy talk. Thou art said to be Achilles' male varlot.   15

Patr. Male varlot, you rogue! What's that?

Ther. Why, his masculine whore. Now the rotten diseases of the south, the guts-griping, ruptures, [catarrhs,] loads a' gravel in the back, lethargies, cold palsies, raw eyes, dirt-rotten livers, whissing   20 lungs, bladders full of imposthume, sciaticas, lime-kills i' th' palm, incurable bone-ache, and the rivell'd fee-simple of the tetter, take and take again such preposterous discoveries!   24

Patr. Why, thou damnable box of envy, thou, what means thou to curse thus?

Ther. Do I curse thee?

Patr. Why, no, you ruinous butt, you whoreson indistinguishable cur, no.   29

Ther. No? why art thou then exasperate, thou idle immaterial skein of sleave-silk, thou green sarcenet flap for a sore eye, thou tossel of a prodigal's purse, thou? Ah, how the poor world is pest'red with such water-flies, diminutives of nature!

Patr. Out, gall!   35

Ther. Finch-egg!

Achil. My sweet Patroclus, I am thwarted quite From my great purpose in to-morrow's battle. Here is a letter from Queen Hecuba,

---

A token from her daughter, my fair love,   40
Both taxing me and gaging me to keep
An oath that I have sworn. I will not break it.
Fall Greeks, fail fame, honor or go or stay,
My major vow lies here; this I'll obey.
Come, come, Thersites, help to trim my tent;   45
This night in banqueting must all be spent.
Away, Patroclus!   [*Exeunt Achilles and Patroclus.*]

Ther. With too much blood and too little brain, these two may run mad, but, if with too much brain and too little blood they do, I'll be a curer of mad- 50 men. Here's Agamemnon, an honest fellow enough, and one that loves quails, but he has not so much brain as ear-wax; and the goodly transformation of Jupiter there, his [brother,] the bull, the primitive statue and oblique memorial of cuckolds, a thrifty shoeing-   55 horn in a chain, [hanging] at his [brother's] leg—to what form but that he is, should wit larded with malice, and malice fac'd with wit, turn him to? To an ass, were nothing, he is both ass and ox; to an ox, were nothing, [he is] both ox and ass. To be   60 a [dog], a moile, a cat, a fitchook, a toad, a lezard, an owl, a puttock, or a herring without a roe, I would not care; but to be Menelaus, I would conspire against destiny. Ask me [not] what I would be if I were not Thersites, for I care not to be the louse of a lazar, so I were not Menelaus. Hey-day! sprites and fires!   66

Enter AGAMEMNON, [HECTOR, TROILUS, AJAX,] ULYSSES, NESTOR, [MENELAUS,] *and* DIOMED, *with lights.*

Agam. We go wrong, we go wrong.

Ajax.   No, yonder 'tis,
There where we see the lights.

Hect.   I trouble you.

Ajax. No, not a whit.

[*Enter* ACHILLES.]

Ulyss.   Here comes himself to guide you.

Achil. Welcome, brave Hector, welcome, princes all.   70

Agam. So now, fair Prince of Troy, I bid good night.
Ajax commands the guard to tend on you.

6–7. **picture . . . idiot-worshippers**: i.e. you look like a man, but you are only an image of a man, and of a man who is an idiot.
8. **fragment**: crust (following the metaphor of line 5).
9. **full . . . fool**: container brimming over with foolishness (with a pun on *fool*/*full* and a play on *fool* as the name of a dessert made of custard, a trifle).
10. **Who . . . now.** Perhaps an indication that Ajax has been aping Achilles' arrogant behavior (cf. V.iv.14–15). Its principal purpose seems to be the opportunity it gives Thersites for his pun on *tent* (= surgical probe) in the next line.
12. **adversity**: i.e. one who talks at cross-purposes (referring to the quibble on *tent*).
15. **varlot**: attendant (variant form of *varlet*). Cf. *boy* in line 14.
18. **south.** The south wind was traditionally associated with disease, but the reference here is probably to Italy, specifically Naples (see the note on II.iii.18–19).
18–23. **guts-griping . . . tetter.** This "preposterous" catalogue of diseases arising from sexual license apparently draws on a passage in Greene's *Planetomachia*, 1585 (ed. Grosart, V, 103–4) listing "peculiar diseases" associated with the planet Venus.
19. **loads . . . back**: kidney stones.   **lethargies**: comatose states.
20. **whissing**: wheezing.   21. **imposthume**: abscesses.
21–22. **lime-kills . . . palm**: i.e. the burning sensation of psoriasis of the palm. *Lime-kills* is a variant spelling of *lime-kilns* (operated at exceedingly high heat).
22–23. **rivell'd . . . tetter**: shrivelled perpetual legacy of eczema, ringworm, etc.   23. **take**: afflict, plague (used of diseases).
23–24. **preposterous discoveries**: revelations of perversion (such as the relationship that Thersites alleges between Achilles and Patroclus).
26. **means thou**: meanest thou (colloquial elision).
28. **ruinous butt**: broken-down wine cask.
29. **indistinguishable**: shapeless, deformed.
30. **exasperate**: exasperated.
31. **immaterial . . . sleave-silk**: worthless (because unwoven) loose knot of raw, untwisted silk.   **sarcenet**: fine silk cloth of taffeta weave.   32. **tossel**: tassel.   33. **pest'red**: overrun.
35. **gall**: blister, or oak-gall (a round excrescence).
36. **Finch-egg.** Perhaps extending the idea of *diminutives of nature*; the finch was a very small bird and would lay a very small egg.

41. **taxing . . . gaging**: i.e. enjoining . . . binding.
48. **blood**: passion, irrational impulses.
50–51. **I'll . . . madmen.** The point is that the contingency just mentioned is an impossibility.   52. **quails**: prostitutes (slang).
53–54. **goodly . . . bull.** With ironic reference to Jupiter's taking the form of a bull in order to carry off Europa; Menelaus resembles the metamorphosed Jupiter only in being horned.
54. **primitive statue**: prototype, prime example.
55. **oblique.** Not satisfactorily explained; possibly referring to the slanting horns of the cuckold.
55–56. **thrifty . . . leg**: i.e. a serviceable tool ready to Agamemnon's hand. One kind of horn leads Shakespeare to another.
57. **larded**: interlarded.
58. **fac'd**: lined. Most editors adopt the F1 reading *forced* (= stuffed), perhaps correctly.
61. **moile**: mule (variant form).   **fitchook**: fitch, polecat (variant of *fitchew*).   **lezard**: lizard (variant form).
62. **puttock**: chicken-hawk, kite.   **herring . . . roe**: i.e. a herring of the least valuable sort.
63. **care**: mind (so *care . . . be* in line 65 = wouldn't mind being).
to be: if I had to be (or, perhaps, to escape being).
65. **lazar**: leper.
66. **sprites and fires.** Referring to those entering with torches (like will-o'-the-wisps); *sprites* = spirits.   72. **to**: that will.

Hect.   Thanks and good night to the Greeks' general.

Men.   Good night, my lord.

Hect.   Good night, sweet Lord Menelaus.

Ther.   Sweet draught! "Sweet," quoth 'a! Sweet sink, sweet sewer.   76

Achil.   Good night and welcome, both [at once], to those
That go or tarry.

Agam.   Good night.
                    Exeunt Agamemnon, Menelaus.

Achil.   Old Nestor tarries; and you too, Diomed,
Keep Hector company an hour or two.   81

Dio.   I cannot, lord, I have important business,
The tide whereof is now. Good night, great Hector.

Hect.   Give me your hand.

Ulyss.   [*Aside to Troilus.*]   Follow his torch, he
goes to Calchas' tent.   85
I'll keep you company.

Tro.   Sweet sir, you honor me.

Hect.   And so good night.
                [*Exit Diomedes, Ulysses and Troilus following.*]

Achil.   Come, come, enter my tent.
                Exeunt [*Achilles, Hector, Ajax, and Nestor*].

Ther.   That same Diomed's a false-hearted rogue, a most unjust knave. I will no more trust him when he leers than I will a serpent when he hisses. He will spend his mouth and promise, like Brabbler the   91 hound, but when he performs, astronomers foretell it: it is prodigious, there will come some change; the sun borrows of the moon when Diomed keeps his word. I will rather leave to see Hector than not to dog him. They say he keeps a Troyan drab, and uses the   96 traitor Calchas' tent. I'll after—nothing but lechery! all incontinent varlots!   [*Exit.*]

[Scene II]

Enter Diomed.

Dio.   What, are you up here, ho? Speak!

Cal.   [*Within.*] Who calls?

Dio.   Diomed. Calchas, I think. Where's your daughter?

Cal.   [*Within.*] She comes to you.

[*Enter* Troilus *and* Ulysses *at a distance; after them,* Thersites.]

Ulyss.   Stand where the torch may not discover us.

Enter Cressid.

Tro.   Cressid comes forth to him.

Dio.   How now, my charge?   6

Cres.   Now, my sweet guardian, hark, a word with you.   [*Whispers.*]

Tro.   Yea, so familiar?

Ulyss.   She will sing any man at first sight.

Ther.   And any man may sing her, if he can take her cliff; she's noted.   11

Dio.   Will you remember?

[*Cres.*]   Remember? yes.

Dio.   Nay, but do then,
And let your mind be coupled with your words.   15

Tro.   What shall she remember?

Ulyss.   List!

Cres.   Sweet honey Greek, tempt me no more to folly.

Ther.   Roguery!

Dio.   Nay then—   20

Cres.   I'll tell you what—

Dio.   Fo, fo, come, tell a pin. You are forsworn.

Cres.   In faith, I cannot. What would you have me do?

Ther.   A juggling trick—to be secretly open.

Dio.   What did you swear you would bestow on me?   25

Cres.   I prithee do not hold me to mine oath,
Bid me do any thing but that, sweet Greek.

Dio.   Good night.

Tro.   Hold, patience.

Ulyss.   How now, Troyan?   30

Cres.   Diomed—

Dio.   No, no, good night, I'll be your fool no more.

Tro.   Thy better must.

Cres.   Hark a word in your ear.

Tro.   O plague and madness!   35

Ulyss.   You are moved, Prince, let us depart, I pray,
Lest your displeasure should enlarge itself
To wrathful terms. This place is dangerous,
The time right deadly. I beseech you go.

Tro.   Behold, I pray you.

Ulyss.   Now, good my lord, go off;
You flow to great [distraction]. Come, my lord. 41

Tro.   I prithee stay.

Ulyss.   You have not patience, come.

Tro.   I pray you stay. By hell and all hell's torments,
I will not speak a word.

Dio.   And so good night.

Cres.   Nay, but you part in anger.

Tro.   Doth that grieve thee?   45
O withered truth!

Ulyss.   How now, my lord?

Tro.   By Jove
I will be patient.

Cres.   Guardian! Why, Greek!

---

75. **draught:** privy.   76. **sink:** cesspool.
77. **at once:** at the same time.   83. **tide:** right time.
89. **unjust:** false.   90. **leers:** looks seductively.
91-92. **Brabbler the hound.** *Brabbler* is here confused with *babbler,* i.e. one who like an ill-trained dog "spends his mouth," promising much and performing little.   93. **prodigious:** portentous, an omen.
93-94. **sun . . . moon:** i.e. natural order is reversed.
95. **leave to see:** give up seeing.   96. **drab:** whore.
98. **incontinent varlots:** sexually promiscuous rogues.

9. **sing . . . sight:** i.e. Cressida is "familiar," like an expert sight reader of music, with any man on first acquaintance.
11. **cliff:** (1) clef, key; (2) pudenda.   **noted:** notorious, with play on musical notation.   22. **tell a pin:** don't trifle.
24. **secretly open.** "Juggling" with two senses of *open,* "unsecret" and "yielding access."
38. **wrathful terms:** angry words, i.e. an open quarrel.
40. **Behold:** go on watching.
41. **flow:** are carried as on the swelling tide of your emotions. **great:** full, complete.

V.ii. Location: The Greek camp. Before Calchas' tent.

Dio. Fo, fo, [adieu,] you palter.
Cres. In faith, I do not. Come hither once again.
Ulyss. You shake, my lord, at something; will you
    go?   50
You will break out.
Tro.   She strokes his cheek.
Ulyss.   Come, come.
Tro. Nay, stay; by Jove I will not speak a word.
There is between my will and all offenses
A guard of patience. Stay a little while.   54
Ther. How the devil Luxury, with his fat rump
and potato finger, tickles [these] together! Fry,
lechery, fry!
Dio. [But] will you then?
Cres. In faith I will lo, never trust me else.
Dio. Give me some token for the surety of it.   60
Cres. I'll fetch you one.   *Exit.*
Ulyss. You have sworn patience.
Tro.   Fear me not, my lord.
I will not be myself, nor have cognition
Of what I feel; I am all patience.

              Enter CRESSID.

Ther. Now the pledge, now, now, now!   65
Cres. Here, Diomed, keep this sleeve.
Tro. O beauty, where is thy faith?
Ulyss.   My lord—
[*Tro.* I will be patient, outwardly I will.]
[*Cres.*] You look upon that sleeve, behold it well.
He lov'd me—O false wench!—Give't me again.   70
Dio. Whose was't?
Cres. It is no matter now I ha't again.
I will not meet with you to-morrow night.
I prithee, Diomed, visit me no more.
Ther. Now she sharpens. Well said, whetstone!   74
Dio. I shall have it.
Cres.   What, this?
Dio.   Ay, that.
Cres. O all you gods! O pretty, pretty pledge!
Thy master now lies thinking on his bed
Of thee and me, and sighs, and takes my glove,
And gives memorial dainty kisses to it,   80
As I kiss thee. Nay, do not snatch it from me.
He that takes that doth take my heart withal.
Dio. I had your heart before, this follows it.
Tro. I did swear patience.
[*Cres.*] You shall not have it, Diomed, faith, you
    shall not.   85
I'll give you something else.
Dio. I will have this. Whose was it?
Cres.   It is no matter.
Dio. Come, tell me whose it was.
Cres. 'Twas one's that lov'd me better than you
    will.
But now you have it, take it.
Dio.   Whose was it?   90

Cres. By all Diana's waiting-women yond,
And by herself, I will not tell you whose.
Dio. To-morrow will I wear it on my helm,
And grieve his spirit that dares not challenge it.
Tro. Wert thou the devil, and wor'st it on thy
    horn,   95
It should be challeng'd.
Cres. Well, well, 'tis done, 'tis past. And yet it is
    not;
I will not keep my word.
Dio.   Why then farewell,
Thou never shalt mock Diomed again.   99
Cres. You shall not go. One cannot speak a word
But it straight starts you.
Dio.   I do not like this fooling.
Ther. Nor I, by Pluto; but that that likes not you
pleases me best.
Dio. What, shall I come? The hour—
Cres. Ay, come—O Jove!—do come.—I shall be
    plagued.   105
Dio. Farewell till then.
Cres.   Good night. I prithee come.
                              [*Exit Diomedes.*]
Troilus, farewell! one eye yet looks on thee,
But with my heart the other eye doth see.
Ah, poor our sex! this fault in us I find,
The error of our eye directs our mind.   110
What error leads must err; O then conclude,
Minds sway'd by eyes are full of turpitude.   *Exit.*
Ther. A proof of strength she could not publish
    more,
Unless she said, "My mind is now turn'd whore."
Ulyss. All's done, my lord.
Tro.   It is.
Ulyss.   Why stay we then?
Tro. To make a recordation to my soul   116
Of every syllable that here was spoke.
But if I tell how these two did [co-act],
Shall I not lie in publishing a truth?
Sith yet there is a credence in my heart,   120
An esperance so obstinately strong,
That doth invert th' attest of eyes and ears,
As if those organs [had deceptious] functions,
Created only to calumniate.
Was Cressid here?
Ulyss.   I cannot conjure, Troyan.   125
Tro. She was not, sure.
Ulyss.   Most sure she was.
Tro. Why, my negation hath no taste of madness.

48. **palter:** equivocate.   53. **will:** desire (to speak and act).
55. **Luxury:** lechery (one of the Seven Deadly Sins).
56. **potato finger:** finger inciting to lust, potatoes being regarded as
an aphrodisiac.   59. **lo:** an exclamation equivalent to *indeed.*
60. **for the surety:** as an assurance.
63. **cognition:** rational apprehension.   72. **ha't:** have it.
80. **memorial:** commemorative.   **dainty:** delightful.

91. **Diana's waiting-women:** i.e. the stars (*Diana* = the moon).
101. **starts you:** impels you to abrupt action.   102. **likes:** pleases.
105. **I . . . plagued.** Equivalent to her "I shall have such a life!" at
IV.ii.22.
107–8. **one . . . see:** i.e. Cressida still has Troilus' image in her mind's
eye, but the eye of her heart (reacting to passion of the moment)
prefers Diomedes.   109. **poor our:** our poor.
113. **proof . . . more:** she could not offer a stronger proof (of her
"conclusion").
116–17. **make . . . Of:** fix firmly in my memory.
119. **lie . . . truth:** i.e. declare as true something that only seems (to
my senses) to be true.
120. **credence:** faith, belief.   121. **esperance:** hope.
122. **invert:** change to the contrary.   123. **deceptious:** deceiving.
125. **conjure:** call up spirits, i.e. raise a false Cressida.
127. **negation:** refusal to believe.

Ulyss. Nor mine, my lord; Cressid was here but
  now.

Tro. Let it not be believ'd for womanhood!
Think we had mothers, do not give advantage   130
To stubborn critics, apt without a theme
For depravation, to square the general sex
By Cressid's rule. Rather think this not Cressid.

Ulyss. What hath she done, Prince, that can [soil]
  our mothers?

Tro. Nothing at all, unless that this were she.   135

Ther. Will 'a swagger himself out on 's own eyes?

Tro. This she? no, this is Diomed's Cressida.
If beauty have a soul, this is not she;
If souls guide vows, if vows be sanctimonies,
If sanctimony be the gods' delight,   140
If there be rule in unity itself,
This was not she. O madness of discourse,
That cause sets up with and against itself!
Bi-fold authority, where reason can revolt
Without perdition, and loss assume all reason   145
Without revolt. This is, and is not, Cressid!
Within my soul there doth conduce a fight
Of this strange nature, that a thing inseparate
Divides more wider than the sky and earth,
And yet the spacious breadth of this division   150
Admits no orifex for a point as subtle
As Ariachne's broken woof to enter.
Instance, O instance, strong as Pluto's gates,
Cressid is mine, tied with the bonds of heaven;
Instance, O instance, strong as heaven itself,   155
The bonds of heaven are slipp'd, dissolv'd, and loos'd,
And with another knot, [five]-finger-tied,
The fractions of her faith, orts of her love,
The fragments, scraps, the bits and greasy relics
Of her o'er-eaten faith, are given to Diomed.   160

Ulyss. May worthy Troilus be half attached

With that which here his passion doth express?

Tro. Ay, Greek, and that shall be divulged well
In characters as red as Mars his heart
Inflam'd with Venus. Never did young man fancy
With so eternal and so fix'd a soul.   166
Hark, Greek: as much [as] I do Cressid love,
So much by weight hate I her Diomed.
That sleeve is mine that he'll bear on his helm.
Were it a casque compos'd by Vulcan's skill,   170
My sword should bite it. Not the dreadful spout
Which shipmen do the hurricano call,
Constring'd in mass by the almighty sun,
Shall dizzy with more clamor Neptune's ear,
In his descent, than shall my prompted sword   175
Falling on Diomed.

Ther. He'll tickle it for his concupy.

Tro. O Cressid! O false Cressid! false, false, false!
Let all untruths stand by thy stained name,
And they'll seem glorious.

Ulyss.   O, contain yourself;   180
Your passion draws ears hither.

Enter AENEAS.

Aene. I have been seeking you this hour, my lord.
Hector by this is arming him in Troy;
Ajax, your guard, stays to conduct you home.

Tro. Have with you, Prince. My courteous lord,
  adieu.   185
Farewell, revolted fair! and, Diomed,
Stand fast, and wear a castle on thy head!

Ulyss. I'll bring you to the gates.

Tro. Accept distracted thanks.   189

Exeunt Troilus, Aeneas, and Ulysses.

Ther. Would I could meet that rogue Diomed! I
would croak like a raven, I would bode, I would bode.
Patroclus will give me any thing for the intelligence of
this whore. The parrot will not do more for an almond
than he for a commodious drab. Lechery, lechery, still
wars and lechery, nothing else holds fashion. A burning devil take them!   *Exit.*   196

[SCENE III]

Enter HECTOR *and* ANDROMACHE.

And. When was my lord so much ungently
  temper'd

---

129. **for:** for the sake of.   130. **Think:** remember that.
131–32. **apt . . . depravation:** always ready, even when they have no
grounds for denigration.
132–33. **square . . . rule:** measure all women by the yardstick of
Cressida's behavior.
136. **Will . . . eyes:** will he bluster himself out of believing what he
has just seen with his own eyes. *On* = of.
139. **sanctimonies:** sacred things.
140. **sanctimony:** sanctity of life and character.
141. **If . . . unity:** i.e. if one is one and not dividable into two.
142. **discourse:** reason.
143. **That . . . up:** that sets up a contest (or debate).
144. **Bi-fold:** double, ambiguous (first recorded use).
144–46. **where . . . revolt:** i.e. where reason can revolt against itself
(i.e. deny the senses' evidence that this is Cressida) without loss
(*perdition*) of reason, and where loss of reason (inability to trust
the senses) can, without revolt against reason, arrogate to itself the
appearance of the highest (*all*) reason (belief that this is not Cressida).
147. **there . . . fight:** a battle is joined (the only recorded non-transitive
use of *conduce*).
148. **this:** i.e. the following.   **inseparate:** indivisible.
151. **orifex:** aperture (erroneous variant of *orifice*).   **subtle:** delicate,
fine.
152. **Ariachne's broken woof:** i.e. a fragment of a spider's web.
Ariachne appears to be Shakespeare's error for the name of Arachne,
who according to Ovid (*Metamorphoses*, VI, 1–145) was turned into
a spider by Pallas for daring to challenge her successfully in a weaving
contest.   155. **Instance:** proof, evidence.
157. **five-finger-tied:** i.e. tied by human hands (referring to the
physical contact Troilus has just witnessed between Diomedes and
Cressida) as opposed to the "bonds of heaven" of lines 154, 156.
158. **orts:** leavings, scraps.
160. **o'er-eaten:** that she has sickened of.
161–62. **May . . . With:** can it be that worthy Troilus half believes
(literally, is half possessed by). *Troilus* is trisyllabic here for the only

time in the play: the anomaly has led some editors to insert *but* before
half.   165. **fancy:** love.   168. **by weight:** precisely.
170. **casque:** helmet.   **Vulcan's skill.** Vulcan was armorer to the
gods.   171. **spout:** waterspout.
173. **Constring'd in mass:** compressed into a dense body.
175. **prompted:** sword driven by the will to destroy.
177. **He'll tickle it:** Troilus will tickle Diomedes' helmet (?) or
Diomedes will tickle (i.e. be tickled) (?). *Tickle* is of course used in
ironic understatement.   **Concupy.** Shakespeare's coinage, presumably meaning either "concupiscence" or "concubine" (= Cressida).
181. **passion:** lamentation.
185. **Have with you:** let us go together.   186. **revolted:** traitorous.
187. **castle:** i.e. a helmet giving more than ordinary protection.
191. **bode:** prophesy. The croaking of ravens was looked upon as a
portent of evil.
192. **the intelligence:** news.   194. **commodious:** accommodating.
195–96. **burning devil:** i.e. venereal disease.

V.iii. Location: Troy. Before Priam's palace.
1. **ungently temper'd:** unkindly disposed.

To stop his ears against admonishment?
Unarm, unarm, and do not fight to-day.

Hect. You train me to offend you, get you in.
By all the everlasting gods, I'll go! 5

And. My dreams will sure prove ominous to the
day.

Hect. No more, I say.

Enter CASSANDRA.

Cas. Where is my brother Hector?

And. Here, sister, arm'd, and bloody in intent.
Consort with me in loud and dear petition,
Pursue we him on knees; for I have dreamt 10
Of bloody turbulence, and this whole night
Hath nothing been but shapes and forms of slaughter.

Cas. O, 'tis true.

Hect. Ho! bid my trumpet sound!

[*Cas.*] No notes of sally, for the heavens, sweet
brother. 14

Hect. Be gone, I say, the gods have heard me swear.

Cas. The gods are deaf to hot and peevish vows;
They are polluted off'rings, more abhorr'd
Than spotted livers in the sacrifice.

And. O, be persuaded! do not count it holy
[To hurt by being just; it is as lawful, 20
For we would give much, to [use] violent thefts,
And rob in the behalf of charity.]

[*Cas.*] It is the purpose that makes strong the vow,
But vows to every purpose must not hold;
Unarm, sweet Hector.

Hect. Hold you still, I say; 25
Mine honor keeps the weather of my fate.
Life every man holds dear, but the dear man
Holds honor far more precious-dear than life.

Enter TROILUS.

How now, young man, meanest thou to fight to-day?

And. Cassandra, call my father to persuade. 30

Exit Cassandra.

Hect. No, faith, young Troilus, doff thy harness,
youth,
I am to-day i' th' vein of chivalry.
Let grow thy sinews till their knots be strong,
And tempt not yet the brushes of the war.
Unarm thee, go, and doubt thou not, brave boy, 35
I'll stand to-day for thee and me and Troy.

Tro. Brother, you have a vice of mercy in you,
Which better fits a lion than a man.

Hect. What vice is that? Good Troilus, chide me
for it.

Tro. When many times the captive Grecian falls,
Even in the fan and wind of your fair sword, 41
You bid them rise and live.

Hect. O, 'tis fair play.

Tro. Fool's play, by heaven, Hector.

Hect. How now? how now?

Tro. For th' love of all the gods,
Let's leave the hermit pity with our mother, 45
And when we have our armors buckled on,
The venom'd vengeance ride upon our swords,
Spur them to ruthful work, rein them from ruth.

Hect. Fie, savage, fie!

Tro. Hector, then 'tis wars.

Hect. Troilus, I would not have you fight to-day.

Tro. Who should withhold me? 51
Not fate, obedience, nor the hand of Mars
Beck'ning with fiery truncheon my retire,
Not Priamus and Hecuba on knees,
Their eyes o'ergalled with recourse of tears, 55
Nor you, my brother, with your true sword drawn,
Oppos'd to hinder me, should stop my way,
[But by my ruin].

Enter PRIAM *and* CASSANDRA.

Cas. Lay hold upon him, Priam, hold him fast,
He is thy crutch. Now if thou lose thy stay, 60
Thou on him leaning, and all Troy on thee,
Fall all together.

Pri. Come, Hector, come, go back.
Thy wife hath dreamt, thy mother hath had visions,
Cassandra doth foresee, and I myself
Am like a prophet suddenly enrapt 65
To tell thee that this day is ominous:
Therefore come back.

Hect. Aeneas is a-field,
And I do stand engag'd to many Greeks,
Even in the faith of valor, to appear
This morning to them.

Pri. Ay, but thou shalt not go.

Hect. I must not break my faith. 71
You know me dutiful, therefore, dear sir,
Let me not shame respect, but give me leave
To take that course by your consent and voice,
Which you do here forbid me, royal Priam. 75

Cas. O Priam, yield not to him.

And. Do not, dear father.

Hect. Andromache, I am offended with you,
Upon the love you bear me, get you in.

Exit Andromache.

Tro. This foolish, dreaming, superstitious girl
Makes all these bodements.

Cas. O, farewell, dear Hector.
Look how thou diest, look how thy eye turns pale. 81
Look how thy wounds do bleed at many vents,
Hark how Troy roars, how Hecuba cries out,
How poor Andromache shrills her dolors forth.
Behold, [distraction], frenzy, and amazement, 85
Like witless antics, one another meet,

---

4. **train:** draw, induce.   9. **dear:** loving.   16. **peevish:** foolish.
17. **abhorr'd:** abhorrent.
20. **hurt . . . just:** to commit injury by observing your vow.
21. **For . . . much:** because we would like to give generously.
23. **purpose:** i.e. the quality of the cause.
24. **vows . . . hold:** not all vows should be held inviolate.
26. **keeps the weather:** keeps to windward, i.e. takes precedence.
27. **dear man:** man who is held dear; noble man.
34. **brushes:** encounters.
37. **vice of mercy:** fault of being merciful.
38. **lion.** The lion, according to Pliny, spared any adversary that
made submission to it.   40. **captive:** conquered.

48. **ruthful . . . ruth:** woeful . . . mercy.
49. **then 'tis wars:** i.e. it is an attitude proper to war.
53. **truncheon:** marshal's baton or staff.   **retire:** withdrawal.
55. **recourse:** repeated coursing or flowing.   58. **ruin:** death.
62. **Fall all:** i.e. all will fall.   65. **enrapt:** inspired.
69. **faith of valor:** the honor proper to a man of courage.
73. **shame respect:** disgrace the respect (due to you).
80. **Makes . . . bodements:** is the cause of all these prophecies of
disaster.   84. **dolors:** griefs.   86. **antics:** fools.

Troilus
and Cressida
V.iii

And all cry, Hector! Hector's dead! O Hector!
 Tro. Away, away.
 Cas. Farewell; yet soft: Hector, I take my leave.
Thou dost thyself and all our Troy deceive. [*Exit.*]
 Hect. You are amaz'd, my liege, at her exclaim.
Go in and cheer the town. We'll forth and fight, 92
Do deeds worth praise, and tell you them at night.
 Pri. Farewell, the gods with safety stand about
  thee!
   [*Exeunt severally Priam and Hector.*] *Alarum.*
 Tro. They are at it, hark! Proud Diomed, believe,
I come to lose my arm, or win my sleeve. 96

Enter PANDAR.

 Pan. Do you hear, my lord? Do you hear?
 Tro. What now?
 Pan. Here's a letter come from yond poor girl.
 Tro. Let me read. 100
 Pan. A whoreson tisick, a whoreson rascally tisick
so troubles me, and the foolish fortune of this girl, and
what one thing, what another, that I shall leave you
one a' th's days; and I have a rheum in mine eyes too,
and such an ache in my bones, that unless a man were
curs'd, I cannot tell what to think on't. What says
she there? 107
 Tro. Words, words, mere words, no matter from
  the heart;
Th' effect doth operate another way.
           [*Tearing the letter.*]
Go, wind, to wind, there turn and change together.
My love with words and errors still she feeds, 111
But edifies another with her deeds. *Exeunt* [*severally*].

[SCENE IV]

[*Alarum.*] *Enter* THERSITES. *Excursions.*

 Ther. Now they are clapper-clawing one another;
I'll go look on. That dissembling abominable varlet,
Diomed, has got that same scurvy doting foolish
[young] knave's sleeve of Troy there in his helm.
I would fain see them meet, that that same young 5
Troyan ass, that loves the whore there, might send
that Greekish whoremasterly villain with the sleeve
back to the dissembling luxurious drab, of a sleeveless
arrant. A' th' t' other side, the policy of those crafty

swearing rascals, that stale old mouse-eaten dry 10
cheese, Nestor, and that same dog-fox, Ulysses, is not
prov'd worth a blackberry. They set me up, in policy,
that mongril cur, Ajax, against that dog of as bad a
kind, Achilles; and now is the cur Ajax prouder than
the cur Achilles, and will not arm to-day; where- 15
upon the Grecians began to proclaim barbarism, and
policy grows into an ill opinion.

[*Enter* DIOMED, *and* TROILUS *following*.]

Soft, here comes sleeve and t' other.
 Tro. Fly not, for shouldst thou take the river Styx,
I would swim after.
 Dio.   Thou dost miscall retire. 20
I do not fly, but advantageous care
Withdrew me from the odds of multitude.
Have at thee!
 Ther. Hold thy whore, Grecian!—now for thy
whore, Troyan!—now the sleeve, now the sleeve! 25
[*Exeunt Troilus and Diomedes fighting.*]

Enter HECTOR.

 Hect. What art [thou], Greek? Art thou for
  Hector's match?
Art thou of blood and honor?
 Ther. No, no, I am a rascal, a scurvy railing knave,
a very filthy rogue.
 Hect. I do believe thee, live.   [*Exit.*] 30
 Ther. God-a-mercy, that thou wilt believe me, but
a plague break thy neck—for frighting me! What's
become of the wenching rogues? I think they have
swallow'd one another. I would laugh at that miracle—
yet in a sort lechery eats itself. I'll seek them. 35
                Exit.

[SCENE V]

Enter DIOMED *and* SERVANT.

 Dio. Go, go, my servant, take thou Troilus' horse,
Present the fair steed to my lady Cressid.
Fellow, commend my service to her beauty;
Tell her I have chastis'd the amorous Troyan,
And am her knight by proof.
 Serv.   I go, my lord. [*Exit.*] 5

Enter AGAMEMNON.

 Agam. Renew, renew! The fierce Polydamas
Hath beat down Menon; bastard Margarelon
Hath Doreus prisoner,
And stands Colossus-wise, waving his beam,

---

89. **yet soft:** i.e. pause a moment.
91. **amaz'd:** stunned (speechless). **exclaim:** outcries.
101. **tisick:** a severe cough or asthma (variant of *phthisic*).
103. **leave you:** i.e. die.
104. **a' th's:** of these. **rheum:** mucous discharge.
105. **ache . . . bones.** Implying syphilis.
106. **curs'd:** under a witch's malediction.
109. **Th' effect . . . way:** i.e. her actions give the lie to what she says.
112. **edifies:** profits, supports.

V.iv. Location: Plains between Troy and the Greek camp.
o.s.d. **Excursions:** sallies. 1. **clapper-clawing:** thrashing, mauling.
2. **abominable.** Supposedly derived from *ab homine*, "not like a man," hence "unnatural."
4. **knave's . . . Troy:** i.e. knave of Troy's (Troilus') sleeve. **in:** on.
7. **whoremasterly:** fornicating. 8. **luxurious:** lecherous.
8–9. **sleeveless arrant:** futile errand (variant form of *errand*).
9. **policy:** stratagem.
9–10. **crafty swearing:** i.e. given to making crafty or deceptive statements (like the plan to smoke Achilles out of his tent by paying court to Ajax).

11. **dog-fox:** male fox (a symbol of craft). 12. **set me:** set.
13. **mongril:** mongrel. Used (as at II.i.13) with reference to Ajax' mixed parentage.
16. **began.** Most editors adopt Rowe's emendation *begin*. **proclaim barbarism:** declare a state of anarchy.
17. **policy:** polity, organized government. **grows . . . opinion:** begins to be looked upon with disfavor.
20. **miscall retire:** i.e. misinterpret my moving back (as retreat).
21. **advantageous care:** concern to find an advantageous position.
27. **blood:** noble descent.
31. **God-a-mercy:** an exclamation expressing thanks (literally, God have mercy, i.e. God reward you). 35. **in a sort:** in a kind of way.

V.v. Location: Scene continues.
9. **beam:** lance.

Upon the pashed corses of the kings   10
Epistrophus and Cedius; Polyxenes is slain,
Amphimachus and Thoas deadly hurt,
Patroclus ta'en or slain, and Palamedes
Sore hurt and bruised. The dreadful Sagittary
Appalls our numbers. Haste we, Diomed,   15
To reinforcement, or we perish all.

Enter NESTOR.

Nest. Go bear Patroclus' body to Achilles,
And bid the snail-pac'd Ajax arm for shame.
There is a thousand Hectors in the field:
Now here he fights on Galathe his horse,   20
And there lacks work; anon he's there afoot,
And there they fly or die, like scaling sculls
Before the belching whale; then is he yonder,
And there the strawy Greeks, ripe for his edge,
Fall down before him like a mower's swath.   25
Here, there, and every where, he leaves and takes,
Dexterity so obeying appetite
That what he will he does, and does so much
That proof is call'd impossibility.

Enter ULYSSES.

Ulyss. O, courage, courage, princes! Great
    Achilles   30
Is arming, weeping, cursing, vowing vengeance.
Patroclus' wounds have rous'd his drowsy blood,
Together with his mangled Myrmidons,
That noseless, handless, hack'd and chipp'd, come to
    him,
Crying on Hector. Ajax hath lost a friend,   35
And foams at mouth, and he is arm'd and at it,
Roaring for Troilus, who hath done to-day
Mad and fantastic execution,
Engaging and redeeming of himself
With such a careless force, and forceless care,   40
As if that [luck], in very spite of cunning,
Bade him win all.

Enter AJAX.

[*Ajax.*] Troilus, thou coward Troilus!   *Exit.*
Dio.   Ay, there, there.
Nest. So, so, we draw together.   *Exit.*

Enter ACHILLES.

Achil.   Where is this Hector?
Come, come, thou boy-queller, show thy face,   45
Know what it is to meet Achilles angry.

---

10. **pashed corses:** battered corpses.
14. **Sagittary:** "a marvellous beast" that had accompanied King Epistrophus to Troy (not the same Epistrophus of line 11); it was half man, half horse, and "shot right well with a bowe" (Caxton).
15. **Appalls our numbers:** dismays our soldiers.
22. **scaling sculls:** scattering shoals of fish.
26. **leaves and takes:** i.e. leaves the dead and attacks the living (?) or spares some and kills others as he chooses (?).
29. **proof . . . impossibility:** i.e. the accomplished fact is deemed an impossibility.
39. **Engaging:** pawning (forming with *redeeming* a commercial metaphor).
40. **careless force:** confident strength. **forceless care:** i.e. recklessness (?) or effortless skill (?).
44. **draw together:** begin to act as a team.
45. **boy-queller:** boy-killer (referring, with exaggeration, to his killing of Patroclus).

Hector, where's Hector? I will none but Hector.
                                        Exeunt.

[SCENE VI]

Enter AJAX.

[*Ajax.*] Troilus, thou coward Troilus, show thy
    head!

Enter DIOMED.

[*Dio.*] Troilus, I say, where's Troilus?
Ajax.   What wouldst thou?
Dio. I would correct him.
Ajax. Were I the general, thou shouldst have my
    office
Ere that correction. Troilus, I say, what, Troilus!   5

Enter TROILUS.

Tro. O traitor Diomed! turn thy false face, thou
    traitor,
And pay thy life thou owest me for my horse.
Dio. Ha, art thou there?
Ajax. I'll fight with him alone. Stand, Diomed.
Dio. He is my prize, I will not look upon.   10
Tro. Come both you cogging Greeks, have at you
    both!   [*Exeunt fighting.*]

[*Enter* HECTOR.]

Hect. Yea, Troilus? O, well fought, my youngest
    brother!

Enter ACHILLES.

[*Achil.*] Now do I see thee, ha! Have at thee,
    Hector!   [*They fight.*]
Hect. Pause if thou wilt.
Achil. I do disdain thy courtesy, proud Troyan.
Be happy that my arms are out of use;   16
My rest and negligence befriends thee now,
But thou anon shalt hear of me again;
Till when, go seek thy fortune.   *Exit.*
Hect.   Fare thee well.
I would have been much more a fresher man,   20
Had I expected thee. How now, my brother?

Enter TROILUS.

Tro. Ajax hath ta'en Aeneas! Shall it be?
No, by the flame of yonder glorious heaven,
He shall not carry him; I'll be ta'en too,
Or bring him off. Fate, hear me what I say!   25
I reak not though I end my life to-day.   *Exit.*

Enter one in armor.

Hect. Stand, stand, thou Greek, thou art a goodly
    mark.

V.vi. Location: Scene continues.
4–5. **thou . . . correction:** i.e. I would yield you my generalship sooner than the privilege of chastising him.   9. **Stand:** stand aside.
10. **look upon:** be an onlooker.
11. **cogging:** cheating (applicable only to Diomedes).   **have at you:** here I come at you (a stock expression of warning).
14. **if thou wilt:** if you wish. Hector is offering a favor, not asking one.
23. **flame:** i.e. the sun.   24. **carry:** defeat.
25. **bring him off:** rescue him.
26. **reak:** care (variant form of *reck*).   27. **mark:** target.

489

No? wilt thou not? I like thy armor well;
I'll frush it and unlock the rivets all,
But I'll be master of it. [*Exit one in armor.*] Wilt thou
   not, beast, abide?   30
Why then fly on, I'll hunt thee for thy hide.   *Exit.*

[SCENE VII]

Enter ACHILLES *with* MYRMIDONS.

[*Achil.*] Come here about me, you my Myrmidons,
Mark what I say. Attend me where I wheel;
Strike not a stroke, but keep yourselves in breath,
And when I have the bloody Hector found,
Empale him with your weapons round about,   5
In fellest manner execute your arms.
Follow me, sirs, and my proceedings eye,
It is decreed Hector the great must die.   *Exeunt.* 8

Enter THERSITES; MENELAUS [*and*] PARIS [*fighting*].

Ther. The cuckold and the cuckold-maker are at it.
Now, bull! now, dog! 'Loo, Paris, 'loo! Now my
double-henn'd Spartan! 'Loo, Paris, 'loo! The bull
has the game, ware horns ho!   12
              Exeunt Paris and Menelaus.

Enter Bastard [MARGARELON].

Mar. Turn, slave, and fight.
Ther. What art thou?
Mar. A bastard son of Priam's.   15
Ther. I am a bastard too, I love bastards. I am
bastard begot, bastard instructed, bastard in mind,
bastard in valor, in every thing illegitimate. One bear
will not bite another, and wherefore should one
bastard? Take heed, the quarrel's most ominous 20
to us. If the son of a whore fight for a whore, he
tempts judgment. Farewell, bastard.   [*Exit.*]
Mar. The devil take thee, coward!   *Exit.*

[SCENE VIII]

Enter HECTOR.

Hect. Most putrefied core, so fair without,
Thy goodly armor thus hath cost thy life.
Now is my day's work done, I'll take [good] breath.
Rest, sword, thou hast thy fill of blood and death.
  [*Puts off his helmet and hangs his shield behind him.*]

29. **frush:** batter.

V.vii. Location: Scene continues.
2. **wheel:** range around the battlefield. 5. **Empale:** fence.
6. **execute your arms:** employ your weapons.
10. **bull:** i.e. Menelaus (the horned one). Thersites talks in terms of
bull-baiting with dogs, the sort of entertainment Londoners were
familiar with at Paris Garden. '**Loo:** a cry to urge on the dogs
(i.e. Paris).
11. **double-henn'd Spartan:** i.e. Menelaus is henned by Helen and
"double-henn'd" because Helen has played false (= *double*). Many
editors prefer F1 *sparrow* to *Spartan*; the phrase then refers to Paris,
who is a lecher (the sparrow was proverbially a lascivious bird) with
two wives, Oenone (whom he deserted) and Helen.
21. **for a whore:** i.e. for Helen. 22. **tempts:** invites.

V.viii. Location: Scene continues.
1. **core:** i.e. the body inside the armor.

490

Enter ACHILLES *and* MYRMIDONS.

Achil. Look, Hector, how the sun begins to set, 5
How ugly night comes breathing at his heels;
Even with the vail and dark'ning of the sun,
To close the day up, Hector's life is done.
Hect. I am unarm'd, forgo this vantage, Greek.
Achil. Strike, fellows, strike, this is the man I
   seek.   [*Hector falls.*] 10
So, Ilion, fall thou next! Come, Troy, sink down!
Here lies thy heart, thy sinews, and thy bone.
On, Myrmidons, and cry you all amain,
"Achilles hath the mighty Hector slain!"   *Retreat.*
Hark, a retire upon our Grecian part. 15
[*Myr.*] The Troyans' trumpet sound the like, my
   lord.
Achil. The dragon wing of night o'erspreads the
   earth,
And stickler-like the armies separates.
My half-supp'd sword that frankly would have fed,
Pleas'd with this dainty bait, thus goes to bed. 20
               [*Sheathes his sword.*]
Come tie his body to my horse's tail,
Along the field I will the Troyan trail.   *Exeunt.*

[SCENE IX]

[*Sound retreat. Shout.*] *Enter* AGAMEMNON, AJAX,
  MENELAUS, NESTOR, DIOMED, *and the rest, marching.*

Agam. Hark, hark, what [shout] is this?
Nest. Peace, drums!
Soldiers. (*Within.*) Achilles! Achilles! Hector's
   slain! Achilles!
Dio. The bruit is, Hector's slain, and by Achilles.
Ajax. If it be so, yet bragless let it be, 5
Great Hector was as good a man as he.
Agam. March patiently along; let one be sent
To pray Achilles see us at our tent.
If in his death the gods have us befriended,
Great Troy is ours, and our sharp wars are ended. 10
                     Exeunt.

[SCENE X]

Enter AENEAS, PARIS, ANTENOR, DEIPHOBUS.

Aene. Stand ho! yet are we masters of the field.

Enter TROILUS.

Tro. Never go home, here starve we out the night—
Hector is slain.
All.   Hector! the gods forbid!
Tro. He's dead, and at the murtherer's horse's tail,

7. **vail:** descent.
14 s.d. **Retreat:** trumpet signal for the withdrawal of forces (= *retire*,
line 15). 18. **stickler-like:** like an umpire.
19. **frankly:** freely, generously.
20. **dainty bait:** light meal or snack.

V.ix. Location: Scene continues.
4. **bruit:** noise, rumor. 10. **sharp:** bitter.

V.x. Location: Scene continues.
2. **starve . . . night:** let us pass the night here in the killing cold (in
preference to breaking the news to Troy; see lines 15–21).

In beastly sort, dragg'd through the shameful field. 5
Frown on, you heavens, effect your rage with speed!
Sit, gods, upon your thrones, and smile at Troy!
I say, at once, let your brief plagues be mercy,
And linger not our sure destructions on!

Aene. My lord, you do discomfort all the host. 10
Tro. You understand me not that tell me so.
I do not speak of flight, of fear, of death,
But dare all imminence that gods and men
Address their dangers in. Hector is gone.
Who shall tell Priam so, or Hecuba? 15
Let him that will a scritch-owl aye be call'd
Go in to Troy and say [there,] "Hector's dead!"
There is a word will Priam turn to stone,
Make wells and Niobes of the maids and wives,
Cold statues of the youth, and in a word, 20
Scare Troy out of itself. [But march away.
Hector is dead;] there is no more to say.
Stay yet. You [vile] abominable tents,
Thus proudly [pight] upon our Phrygian plains,
Let Titan rise as early as he dare, 25
I'll through and through you! and, thou great-siz'd
     coward,
No space of earth shall sunder our two hates.
I'll haunt thee like a wicked conscience still,
That mouldeth goblins swift as frenzy's thoughts.
Strike a free march. To Troy with comfort go; 30
Hope of revenge shall hide our inward woe.

           Enter PANDARUS.

7. **smile:** mock. In view of lines 6, 8-9, many editors emend *smile at* to *smite at* (Warburton) or *smite all* (Hanmer).
13. **imminence:** threats of impending disaster.
14. **Address . . . in:** level their threats with.
16. **scritch-owl:** screech-owl.
19. **Niobes.** Niobe wept herself into a stone after her fourteen children were slaughtered by Apollo and Diana.   24. **pight:** pitched.
26. **coward:** i.e. Achilles, because he did not kill Hector in fair fight.
30. **comfort:** reassurance.

Pan. But hear you, hear you!
Tro. Hence, broker, lackey! [*Strikes him.*] Igno-
     miny, shame
Pursue thy life, and live aye with thy name! 34

          Exeunt all but Pandarus.

Pan. A goodly medicine for my aching bones!
O world, world, [world!] thus is the poor agent
despis'd! O [traders] and bawds, how earnestly are
you set a-work, and how ill requited! Why should our
endeavor be so lov'd and the performance so loath'd?
What verse for it? What instance for it? Let me see:
     Full merrily the humble-bee doth sing, 41
     Till he hath lost his honey and his sting;
     And being once subdu'd in armed tail,
     Sweet honey and sweet notes together fail.
Good traders in the flesh, set this in your painted
cloths: 46
As many as be here of Pandar's hall,
Your eyes, half out, weep out at Pandar's fall;
Or if you cannot weep, yet give some groans,
Though not for me, yet for [your] aching bones. 50
Brethren and sisters of the hold-[door] trade,
Some two months hence my will shall here be made.
It should be now, but that my fear is this,
Some galled goose of Winchester would hiss.
Till then I'll sweat and seek about for eases, 55
And at that time bequeath you my diseases. [*Exit.*]

33. **broker:** go-between, bawd.   **lackey:** servant, slave.
37. **traders:** i.e. "traders in the flesh," line 45.
40. **instance:** example, case in point.
43. **subdu'd . . . tail:** having his sting removed (with sexual implication).
45-46. **painted cloths:** cheap wall-hangings painted with scenes and mottoes.   47. **hall:** guild, fraternity.
48. **half out:** i.e. already half blind from venereal disease.
51. **hold-door trade:** prostitution.
54. **galled:** (1) offended; (2) having venereal sores.   **goose of Winchester:** prostitute (so called because the brothels in Southwark were under the jurisdiction of the Bishop of Winchester).
55. **sweat.** Sweating was one of the treatments for venereal disease.

NOTE ON THE TEXT

The textual situation in *Troilus and Cressida* presents unusual difficulties. Two good texts of ambiguously related authority exist: the quarto, of which there are two states, printed in 1609 by George Eld for Bonian and Walley (Q); and the First Folio text (1623). With respect to the provenience and relation of Q and F1 there has been general agreement on only two points: (1) Q was based on a transcript (perhaps literary) of Shakespeare's "foul papers"; (2) F1, except for I.i.1–I.ii.234, which was printed directly from an uncorrected copy of Q, was printed from a copy of Q which had been corrected by collation with Shakespeare's "foul papers." Thus both Q and F1 are derived ultimately from the same source. Such being the case, how are we to account for the roughly 500 verbal variants which distinguish the two texts? One possible answer is revision, but at what stage? Individual examples of what appears to be revision can be pointed out in both Q and F1. Some critics (Alexander, Williams, Greg) believe that the transcript from which Q was printed was a "fair copy" made by Shakespeare himself and that he revised stylistically in the process of copying; others (notably Hillebrand) argue for a double revision by Shakespeare, first in the transcript from which Q was set, then later, and more heavily, in the "foul papers" themselves. Finally, Miss Walker, one of the latest editors of the play, reverting to a view proposed by Chambers in 1930, denies the revision theory and Shakespeare's hand in the transcript for Q, and suggests that the verbal differences between Q and F1 are merely the result of printers' errors in both texts, the difficulty (chiefly affecting the scribal transcript behind Q) experienced in deciphering Shakespeare's hand, and, in F1, editorial or compositorial sophistication of a kind not uncommon in F1 texts. Unlike other recent editors, Miss Walker leans, where variants seem to be of equal merit, toward F1 as the more authoritative text.

Although Q is here accepted as the basic copy-text, with general preference given to Q variants, the present text, like all modern editions of the play, is eclectic, admitting some forty-four lines or part-lines unique to F1 and adopting F1 readings where they seem in the editor's judgment significantly better than those in Q. Such a compromise may not perhaps be defensible on purely theoretical grounds, but, given the uncertain relations and relative authority of Q and F1, it would be even less defensible to adhere stubbornly to Q for the sake of mere consistency.

Because of the ambiguous authority of Q and F1 the Textual Notes record all significant variants in the F1 text. The reader is thus in a position to study the evidence and form his own judgment. I.i.1–92 survives in F1 in two settings of type; they are referred to in the Textual Notes as "first setting" and "second setting."

For further information, see: Peter Alexander, "*Troilus and Cressida*, 1609," *The Library*, IX (1928), 267–86; E. K.

Chambers, *William Shakespeare* (Oxford, 1930), I, 438–49; Philip Williams, "Shakespeare's *Troilus and Cressida*: the Relationship of Quarto and Folio," *SB*, III (1950–51), 131–43; H. N. Hillebrand, ed., New Variorum *Troilus and Cressida* (Philadelphia, 1953); Alice Walker, *Textual Problems of the First Folio* (Cambridge, 1953), and ed., New Cambridge *Troilus and Cressida* (Cambridge, 1957); W. W. Greg, *The Shakespeare First Folio* (Oxford, 1955); E. A. J. Honigmann, *The Stability of Shakespeare's Text* (London, 1965); J. M. Nosworthy, *Shakespeare's Occasional Plays* (London, 1965).

TEXTUAL NOTES

Title: The . . . Cressida] The Historie of Troylus and Cresseida. As it was acted by the Kings Maiesties seruants at the Globe. Written by William Shakespeare. *Q (title-page, first state)*; The Famous Historie of Troylus and Cresseid. Excellently expressing the beginning of their loues, with the conceited wooing of Pandarus Prince of Licia. Written by William Shakespeare. *Q (title-page, second state)*; The Tragedie of Troylus and Cressida. *F1*
The second state of Q contains the following advertisement: A neuer writer, to an euer reader. Newes. Eternall reader, you haue heere a new play, neuer stal'd with the Stage, neuer clapper-clawd with the palmes of the vulger, and yet passing full of the palme comicall; for it is a birth of your braine, that neuer vnder-tooke any thing commicall, vainely: And were but the vaine names of commedies changde for the titles of Commodities, or of Playes for Pleas; you should see all those grand censors, that now stile them such vanities, flock to them for the maine grace of their grauities: especially this authors Commedies, that are so fram'd to the life, that they serue for the most common Commentaries, of all the actions of our liues, shewing such a dexteritie, and power of witte, that the most displeased with Playes, are pleasd with his Commedies. And all such dull and heauy-witted worldlings, as were neuer capable of the witte of a Commedie, comming by report of them to his representations, haue found that witte there, that they neuer found in them-selues, and haue parted better wittied then they came: feeling an edge of witte set vpon them, more then euer they dreamd they had braine to grinde it on. So much and such sauored salt of witte is in his Commedies, that they seeme (for their height of pleasure) to be borne in that sea that brought forth *Venus*. Amongst all there is none more witty then this: And had I time I would comment vpon it, though I know it needs not, (for so much as will make you thinke your testerne well bestowd) but for so much worth, as euen poore I know to be stuft in it. It deserues such a labour, as well as the best Commedy in *Terence* or *Plautus*. And beleeue this, that when hee is gone, and his Commedies out of sale, you will scramble for them, and set vp a new English Inquisition. Take this for a warning, and at the perrill of your pleasures losse, and Iudgements, refuse not, nor like this the lesse, for not being sullied, with the smoaky breath of the multitude; but thanke fortune for the scape it hath made amongst you. Since by the grand possessors wills I beleeue you should haue prayd for them rather then beene prayd. And so I leaue all such to bee prayd for (for the states of their wits healths) that will not praise it, *Vale.*

492

Dramatis personae: subs. as given in Capell, following Rowe
Act-scene division: *none in Q; only I.i marked in F1; other act-scene divisions by Rowe and later editors (see first note to each scene); present act-scene arrangement as a whole first established by Dyce*

Prologue

From F1; om. Q
8 immures] *F2;* emures *F1*
12 barks] *F2;* Barke *F1*
17 Antenorides] *Theobald;* Antenonidus *F1*
19 Sperr] *Theobald;* Stirre *F1*
31 good] *Kittredge;* good, *F1*

I.i

I.i] *F1*
Location: *Capell (after Theobald)*
3 within?] *F1;* within, *Q*
5 field,] *F1;* field *Q*
15 must] must needes *F1*
20–1 leauening] leau'ning *F1 (first setting);* leau'ing *F1 (second setting)*
24 "hereafter"] *Dyce;* here- / after, *Q, F1*
25 heating] heating of *F1 (second setting)*
26 ye] *ed.;* yea *Q (cf. I.ii.48 Q, F1);* you *F1*
26 burn] to burne *F1*
28 suff'rance] *Kittredge;* suffrance *Q;* sufferance *F1*
30 thoughts—] *Rowe;* thoughts, *Q, F1*
31 comes] comes, *F1*
32 Well,] *F1;* Well *Q*
34 thee—] *Capell;* thee *Q;* thee, *F1*
36 me,] *Rowe;* me: *Q, F1*
37 a-scorn] *F1;* a scorne *Q*
45 her] it *F1*
46 Cassandra's] *F1;* Cassandraes *Q*
48 Pandarus!] *F1;* Pandarus *Q*
51–2 mad . . . love;] *F1 (subs.);* madde: . . . loue? *Q*
53 heart] *Theobald;* heart: *Q;* heart, *F1*
55 discourse,] *Malone;* discourse: *Q;* discourse. *F1*
58 sense] *F1;* sence: *Q*
66 in it] in't *F1*
70 travail] *Collier;* trauell *Q, F1*
71 on] *F1*
75 not] *F1 (second setting)*
76 a'] on *F1*
77 care] *F1*
80 s.p. Pan.] Troy. *F1 (second setting)*
82 her. For] *F1 (subs.);* her for *Q*
90 Helen] *F1;* Helleu *Q*
94 me!] *Rowe;* me *Q;* me? *F1*
96 woo] *Theobald;* woe *Q, F1 (generally)*
97 stubborn-chaste] *Theobald;* stubborne, chast, *Q, F1*
98 Daphne's] *F1;* Daphues *Q*
101 resides] *F2;* reides *Q;* recides *F1*
105 a-field] *F2 (subs.);* a field *Q, F1*
115 abroad—] *Rowe;* abrode *Q;* abroad, *F1*

I.ii

I.ii] *Capell*
Location: *Capell (after Theobald)*
o.s.d. Alexander] *Theobald*

1 s.p. Alex.] *Malone;* Man. *Q, F1 (throughout scene)*
6 chid] chides *F1*
8 light] *F2;* lyte *Q, F1*
17 th' are] *ed.;* the are *Q;* they are *F1*
29 purblind] purblinded *F1*
34 strook] *F2;* stroke *Q, F1*
34 disdain] disdaind *F1*
36 s.d. Enter Pandarus.] *F1*
45 Ilium] *F1;* Illum *Q*
48 ye] *F2;* yea *Q, F1*
51 so;] *F1;* so, *Q*
69 nor] not *F1*
71 just . . . them;] *Johnson (subs.; F4 just);* iust, . . . them *Q*
72 Himself?] *F1;* Himselfe, *Q*
78 end.] *F1 (subs.);* end *Q*
84, 85 other's] *Rowe;* others *Q, F1*
84 come] *F1;* eome *Q*
86 wit] *Rowe;* will *Q, F1*
101 much:] *Rowe (subs.);* much, *Q, F1*
115 will he] *F1;* will hc *Q*
116 lift] *F1;* liste *Q*
121 Why . . . dimpled.] *as prose, Pope; as verse, Q, F1*
124 valiantly] *F1;* valianty *Q*
129 the] *F2;* thee *Q, F1*
139 hair] *F1;* heare *Q (sporadically; not hereafter recorded)*
146 a more] more *F1*
147 pot] *F1;* por *Q*
157 hairs] *F1;* heires *Q (sporadically; not hereafter recorded)*
164 pluck't] *F3;* pluckt *Q, F1*
168 for it] For is *F1*
172 do] does *F1*
179 Ilion] Illium *F1*
179 Cressida] *F1;* Cresseida *Q (throughout, except at III.ii.2 and IV.v.288)*
184, 189, 198, 212, 218, 226, 239 s.dd. and . . . stage] *Rowe (subs.)*
187 tell] *om. F1*
191 man] a man *F1*
192 judgments] iudgement *F1*
194 him] him him *F1*
198 have] haue, *F1*
199–200 that; there's] *Pope (subs.);* that, thers *Q;* that there's *F1*
200 fellow!] *Rowe;* fellow *Q;* fellow. *F1*
203 a brave] braue *F1*
204 man's] *F1;* man *Q*
206 there's] *Pope;* thers *Q;* om. *F1*
207 will] ill *F1*
210 thing,] *Rowe;* thing *Q, F1*
212 s.d. Enter Paris] *placed as in Capell; after l. 209, Q, F1*
217 see] *om. F1*
223 indifferent] *F2;* indifferent, *Q, F1*
223 well.] *Rowe (subs.);* well, *Q, F1*
231 note] not *F1*
233–4 and how he] *following these words the F1 text ceases to be essentially a reprint of Q (see "Note on the Text")*
235 never] ne're *F1*
237 choice] *F1;* choiee *Q*
239 an eye] money *F1*
239 s.d. Enter Common Soldiers] *F1*

240 comes] come *F1*
242 in the] i'th' *F1*
247 amongst] among *F1*
251 Why,] *F4*; why *Q, F1*
254–5 such-like] so forth *F1*
255 season] seasons *F1*
257 date is] dates *F1*
258 a woman] another woman *F1*
258 a man] one *F1*
263 lie, at] lye at, at *F1*
267 too] *F1*; two *Q*
270 it's] *F1*; its *Q*
271 s.d. Troilus'] *Capell*
274 there . . . him] om. *F1*
275 s.d. Exit Boy.] *Capell*
278 I will be] *Cambridge*; I wilbe *Q*; Ile be *F1*
279 uncle?] *Hudson*; vncle: *Q*; Vnkle. *F1*
281 s.d. Exit Pandarus.] *F1*
287, 290] *Marked with gnomic quotes, Q*
288 nought] *F1*; naught *Q*
289 prize] *F1*; price *Q*
294] *Marked with gnomic quotes and in italics, Q, F1*
294 Then] That *F1*
294 content] Contents *F1*
295 s.d. with Alexander] *ed.*

I.iii

I.iii] *Capell*
Location: *Capell (after Rowe)*
o.s.d. Sennet.] *F1*
2 these jaundies o'er] (o'er, *Kittredge* for *Q* ore); the Iaundies on *F1*
6 rear'd,] *Cambridge*; reard. *Q, F1*
8 Infects] Infect *F1*
13 every] *F1*; euer *Q*
19 call them shames] thinke them shame, *F1*
19 nought] *F1*; naught *Q*
27 broad] lowd *F1*
28 winnows] *F1*; winnowes *Q*
29 matter, by itself] *Hanmer*; matter by it selfe, *Q, F1*
31 thy] *F1*; the *Q*
31 godlike] godly *F1*
36 patient] *F1*; ancient *Q*
40 strong-ribb'd] hyphen, *Pope*
44 Corrivall'd] Co-riual'd *F1*
48 breeze] *ed. (after Dyce)*; Bryze *Q*; Brieze *F1*
55 nerves] nerue *F1 (in support of Q reading cf. V.viii.12)*
56 sprite] spirit *F1*
58 speaks.] *Rowe*; speakes, *Q, F1*
59 th'] the *F1*
60 s.d. to Agamemnon] *Rowe*
60–1 for . . . reverend] *F1*; (for . . . reuerend) *Q*
61 s.d. To Nestor.] *Rowe*
61 thy] *F1*; the *Q*
61 stretch'd-out] hyphen, *F1*
67 On] In *F1*
67 heaven . . . Greekish] the Heauens ride, knit all Greekes *F1*
70–4 Agam. Speak . . . oracle.] *F1*
70 expect] *Rowe (subs.)*; expect: *F1*
72 lips, than] *Pope*; lips; then *F1*
75 s.p. Ulyss.] *F1*
75 bases] basis *F1*
86 priority,] *F1*; prioritie *Q*
87 Insisture] *F1*; In sisture *Q*
92 ill . . . evil] *F1*; influence of euill Planets *Q*
94 check,] *F1*; check *Q*
102 of] to *F1*
106 primogenity] primogenitiue *F1*
110 meets] *F1*; melts *Q*
117 (Between . . . resides)] *in italics, Q*
117 resides] *F2*; recides *Q*
118 their] her *F1*
119 include] includes *F1*
127 it is] is it *F1*
128 with] in *F1*
137 stands] liues *F1*
143 sinow] sinew *F1*
144 airy] ayery *F1*
149 awkward] *F1*; sillie *Q*
156 scaffolage] *F1*; scoaffollage *Q*
157 to-be-pitied] hyphens, *F2*
157 o'er-wrested] *Pope*; ore-rested *Q, F1*
159 unsquar'd] *F1*; vnsquare *Q*

161 seem] seemes *F1*
164 right] iust *F1*
165 hem] hum *F1*
176 Valor] *F1*; valour *Q*
176–8 "O . . . spleen."] *quotes, Johnson (after Pope)*
179 natures,] *F1*; natures *Q*
188 self-will'd] *F1*; selfe-wild *Q*
190 keeps] and keepes *F1*
195 or] *anon. conj. (in Cambridge)*; our *Q*; and *F1*
199 Forestall] *F1*; Forstall *Q*
202 calls] call *F1*
203 enemies'] *Warburton*; enemies *Q, F1*
205 closet-war] hyphen *F1*
207 swinge] swing *F1*
209 fineness] *F1*; finesse *Q*
212 s.d. Tucket.] *F1*
214 s.d. Enter Aeneas.] *F1*
219 eyes] eares *F1*
223 security.] *F1*; security, *Q*
228 bid] on *F1*
231 god in office,] *Rowe*; god, in office *Q*; God in office *F1*
236 fame] *F1*; same *Q*
238 great] om. *F1*
238 accord,] *F1*; accord *Q*
242 that the] that he *F1*
244 praise, sole pure,] *Capell*; praise sole pure *Q, F1*
247 affairs] affayre *F1*
249 nought] *F1*; naught *Q*
250 with] om. *F1*
252 sense on the] *F1*; seat on that *Q*
256 loud] alowd *F1*
262 this] *F1*; his *Q*
262 long-continued] hyphen, *F1*
263 resty] rusty *F1*
265 among] among'st *F1*
267 And] That *F1*
267 seeks] *F1*; feeds *Q* (seeds ed. conj.)
269–70 confession . . . loves,] *Pope*; confession, (With . . . loues) *Q*
276 couple] compasse *F1*
289 or] *F1*; a *Q*
290 I am] Ile be *F1*
293 mould] *F1*; hoste *Q*
294 A . . . no] One . . . one *F1*
295 me] *Cambridge*; me. *Q*; me, *F1*
297 vambrace] Vantbrace *F1*
297 my withered brawns] this wither'd brawne *F1*
298 will] *F1*
301 prove] pawne *F1*
301 troth] truth *F1*
302 forfend] *Kittredge*; for-fend *Q*; forbid *F1*
302 nought] *F1*; men *Q*
304 s.p. Agam.] *F1*; *speech continued to Ulysses, Q*
305 sir] first *F1*
309 s.d. Exeunt . . . Nestor.] *F1* (Manet, Manent *F2*)
315 This 'tis:] *F1*
324 True] om. *F1*
324 as] euen as *F1*
327 Achilles, . . . barren] *F1*; Achilles weare his braine, as barren, *Q*
328–9 (though . . . enough)] *in italics (except Apollo), Q*
333 Why] Yes *F1*
334 those honors] his Honor *F1*
336 the] this *F1*
340 vild] wilde *F1*
352 receives . . . a] from hence receyues the *F1*
354–6 Which . . . limbs.] *F1*
354 are] *F2*; are in *F1*
356 speech:] *F1*; speech? *Q*
358 first . . . wares] shew our fowlest Wares *F1*
360–1 shall . . . first.] yet to shew, / Shall shew the better. *F1*
363–4 For . . . followers.] *as verse, F1; as prose, Q*
367 share] weare *F1*
369 it] we *F1*
372 do] did *F1*
374 device] *F1*; deuise *Q*
376 for the better] as the worthier *F1*

386 advice] *F1*; aduise *Q*
387 thereof] of it *F1*
390 tarre] *F1*; arre *Q*
390 a] their *F1*

II.i

II.i] *Rowe*
Location: *Rowe*
2 biles—full,] *Rowe*; biles, full, *Q*; Biles (ful) *F1*
5 run—say so—] *Rowe*; run (say so), *Q*; runne, say so; *F1*
6 then] om. *F1*
8 would] there would *F1*
11 s.d. Strikes him.] *F1*
13 beef-witted] hyphen, *F1*
14 thou] you *F1*
14 whinid'st] *F1*; vnsalted *Q*
17 con] *F1*; cunne *Q*
17–8 without book] om. *F1*
18 a] *F1*
19 murrion] Murren *F1*
19 a' thy] *Sisson*; ath thy *Q*; o'th thy *F1*
21 Toadstool] Toads stoole *F1*
23 strikest] strik'st *F1*
25 fool] a foole *F1*
26 porpentine] *F1*; Forpentin *Q*
27 foot;] *anon. conj. (in Cambridge)*; foote, *Q, F1*
28 of thee] *F1*; of the *Q*
29 loathsomest] lothsom'st *F1*
29–30 When . . . another.] om. *F1*
32 grumblest] *F1*; gromblest *Q*
38 Ajax. Cobloaf!] *F1*; Aiax Coblofe, *Q (in italics, as part of Thersites' preceding line)*
39, 41, 42 s.pp. Ther. . . . Ajax. . . . Ther.] *F1*; *ll. 39–42 (through do!) continued to Thersites, Q (see preceding note and l. 42 below)*
41 s.d. Beating him.] *Pope*
42 do! thou . . . ay,] *A. Walker*; do? / Aiax. Thou . . . witch: / Ther. I, *Q*; do. / Aia. Thou . . . Witch. / Ther. I, *F1*
43 sodden-witted] hyphen, *F1*
44 thee.] *F1*; thee, *Q*
44 You] Thou *F1*
45 thrash] thresh *F1*
52 s.d. Beating him.] *Rowe*
54 s.d. Enter . . . Patroclus.] *F1*
55 ye thus] you this *F1*
62 Well?] *Kittredge*; Well, *Q, F1*
62 so I do] so I do so *F1*
64 whosomever] *Kittredge*; who some euer *Q, F1*
65 that,] *Rowe*; that *Q, F1*
70 I] *F1*; It *Q*
74 I'll] *F1*; I *Q*
76 Ajax—] *F1*; Aiax. *Q*
76 s.d. Ajax . . . him.] *Rowe*
85 damn'd] *F1*; damned *Q*
87 the] for a *F1*
88 Thersites] *F1*; Thesites *Q*
90 the] thee *F1*
90 tenor] tenure *F1*
95 suff'rance] *Kittredge*; suffrance *Q*; sufferance *F1*
98 so;] *Knight (after Rowe)*; so, *Q, F1*
100 and . . . out] *Cambridge conj.*; and knocke at *Q*; if he knocke out *F1*
101 brains] *F1*; beains *Q*
101 'a] he *F1*
103 too, Thersites?] *F4*; to Thersites. *Q*; to Thersites? *F1*
105 your] *Theobald*; their *Q, F1*
105–6 on their toes] *F1*
106 draught-oxen] hyphen, *F1*
107 wars] warre *F1*
109 To . . . Ajax!] *Theobald*; to Achilles, to Aiax, *Q, F1*
113 peace] *F1*
114 brach] *Rowe*; brooch *Q, F1*
117 clatpoles] Clotpoles *F1*
122 fift] *F1*; first *Q*
126 Maintain—] *Hanmer*; Maintaine *Q, F1*
130 s.d. Exeunt.] *Pope*; Exit. *F1*

II.ii

II.ii] *Capell*
Location: *Rowe*
3 damage] *F1*; domage *Q*

493

4 travail] *F1*; trauell *Q*
7 strook] *Capell*; stroke *Q, F1*
9 toucheth] touches *F1*
14–5 surety, Surety] *F1*; surely / Surely *Q*
17 worst.] *F1*; worst *Q*
24 merit's] *F1*; merits *Q*
26 king] *Craig*; King: *Q*; King *F1* (*but followed by a parenthesis*)
27 father's] *anon. conj.* (*in Cambridge*); fathers *Q*; Father *F1*
28 compters] Counters *F1*
29 past-proportion] *hyphen, Johnson*
30 in] *F1*; in, *Q*
30 waist] *Johnson*; waste *Q, F1*
31 diminutive] *F1*; dyminutue *Q*
33 at] *F1*; of *Q*
34 them.] *Rowe*; them *Q*; them, *F1*
34 father] *F1*; father; *Q*
35 reason] reasons *F1*
36 tell] tells *F1*
38 reasons.] *Pope (subs.)*; reasons *Q, F1*
43 Grecian] *F1*; Gretian *Q*
45, 46] *Lines transposed, F1*
47 Let's] *F1*; Sets *Q*
48 hare] hard *F1*
50 Make] Makes *F1*
51–2 Brother . . . keeping.] *as verse, Theobald (after F1); as prose, Q*
52 keeping] holding *F1*
56 mad] made *F1*
58 attributive] inclineable *F1*
64 shores] *F1*; shore *Q*
67 chose] *F1*; choose *Q*
70 soil'd] spoyl'd *F1*
71 unrespective] *F1*; vnrespectiue *Q*
71 sieve] *Johnson*; siue *Q*; same *F1*
72 full.] *F1*; full, *Q*
74 with] of *Q*
75 truce,] *F1*; ttuce: *Q*
79 pale] stale *F1*
82 launch'd] *F1*; lansh't *Q*
86 he] *F1*; be *Q*
86 worthy] Noble *F1*
87 all clapp'd] *F1*; all, clapt *Q*
90 never fortune] Fortune neuer *F1*
94 stol'n,] *F1*; stolne: *Q*
97, 99 s.dd. Within.] *Theobald*
97 shrike] shreeke *F1*
100 Cassandra] *F1*; Crssandra *Q*
100 s.d. with . . . ears] *F1*; *s.d. after l. 96, Q, F1*; *placed as in Theobald*
104 eld] *Theobald conj.*; elders *Q*; old *F1*
105 canst] can *F1*
106 clamors] clamour *F1*
122 mad.] *Rowe (subs.)*; madde, *Q, F1*
178–9 minds, . . . indulgence . . . wills,] *Rowe*; mindes . . . indulgence, . . . wills *Q, F1*
180 well-order'd] well-ordred *F1*
182 refractory] *F2*; refracturie *Q, F1*
185 nations] Nation *F1*
210 strike] *F1*; shrike *Q*

II.iii

II.iii] *Capell*
Location: *Rowe, Theobald*
1 s.p. Ther.] *Hanmer*
4 satisfaction! Would] *Craig*; satisfaction, would *Q, F1*
8 enginer] *F1*; inginer *Q*
12 ye] thou *F1*
15 abundant] *F1*; abaundant *Q*
16 their] the *F1*
18 Neapolitan] *Johnson (in a note)*; Neopolitan *Q*; *om. F1*
19 depending] dependant *F1*
23 s.d. Within.] *anon. conj.* (*in Cambridge*)
25 'a'] *Kittredge*; a *Q*; haue *F1*
26 wouldst] *F1*; couldst *Q*
32 art] *F1*; art not *Q*
32 corse] *Capell*; course *Q*; coarse *F1*
33 s.d. Enter Patroclus.] *F1 (after l. 22); placed after anon. conj.* (*in Cambridge*)
35 prayer] a prayer *F1*
37 Patr. Amen.] *om. F1*
40 O, where?] *om. F1*
40 come?] *F1*; come *Q*
42 in to] *Capell*; into *Q, F1*
47 Thersites] thy selfe *F1*

50 must] maist *F1*
50 knowest] know'st *F1*
55–60 Patr. You . . . fool.] *F1*
61 this; come.] *Rowe*; this? come? *Q, F1*
63–4 of Agamemnon] *F1* (Agamemon)
65 this] *om. F1*
67 of the prover] to the Creator *F1*
68 s.d. Diomed] Diomedes *F1 (this variation frequent in F1 s.dd.; not hereafter recorded); s.d. after l. 66, F1*
68 s.d. Calchas] *Pope*; Calcas *Q*; Chalcas *F1*
69 Come] *om. F1*
70 s.d. Exit.] *F1*
72–3 whore . . . cuckold] Cuckold . . . Whore *F1*
73 emulous] emulations, *F1*
74–5 Now . . . all!] *F1*
75 s.d. Exit.] *Theobald*
79 shent] *Theobald*; sate *Q*; sent *F1*
80 appertainings] appertainments *F1*
80 him.] *F1* (him:); him *Q*
81 so, lest] of, so *F1*
83 say so] so say *F1*
83 s.d. Exit.] *Rowe*
86 lion-sick] *hyphen, F4*
87 you will] will *F1*
88 'tis] it is *F1*
88 a] the *F1*
89 A . . . lord.] *F1*
89 s.d. Takes Agamemnon aside.] *Capell (subs.)*
92 Who] *F1*; Who *Q*
96 argument] *F1*; argument, *Q*
97 argument,] *F3*; argument *Q, F1*
99 their] *F1*; theit *Q*
99 composure] counsell that *F1*
101 knits not,] knits, not *F1*
102 s.d. Enter Patroclus.] *F1*
104 him.] him? *F1*
105–6 The . . . flexure.] *as prose, Malone; as verse, Q*
106 legs are] legge are *F1*
106 flexure] flight *F1*
111 disgestion] digestion *F1*
112 after-dinner's] *hyphen and apostrophe, Rowe*
112 Hear] *F1*; Heere *Q*
114 wing'd] *F2*; winged *Q, F1*
118 on] of *F1*
120 Yea] Yea, and *F1*
120 unwholesome] unholdsome *F1*
122 come] came *F1*
124 self-assumption] *hyphen, F1*
126 tend] tends *F1*
126–7 on, Disguise] *F1*; on / Disguise, *Q*
130 pettish lines, . . . his flows, as] *F1*; course, and time, . . . and flowes, and *Q*
131 carriage . . . action] *F1*; streame of his commencement, *Q*
136 "Bring . . . war."] *quotes, Hanmer*
139 s.d. Exit.] *Rowe*
141 enter you] entertaine *Q*
141 s.d. Exit Ulysses.] *F1*
144 much?] *F3*; much: *Q*; much, *F1*
152 pride] it *F1*
153 Ajax] *F1*
156 whatever] *Rowe*; what euer *Q, F1*
158 do hate] hate *F1*
160 s.d. Aside.] *Capell*
160 And] *om. F1*
166 self-admission] *hyphen, F4*
168 th'] the *F1*
169 request's] *Pope*; requests *Q, F1*
172 self-breath] *hyphen, F1*
172 worth] wroth *F1*
176 down himself] gainst it selfe *F1*
177 death-tokens] *hyphen, F3*
180 led] *F1*; lead *Q*
187 doth] doe *F1*
191 Shall] Must *F1*
191 stale] *Rowe*; staule *Q, F1*
193 titled] *F1*; liked *Q*
193 is,] is: *F1*
194 Achilles.] *Rowe (subs.)*; Achilles, *Q, F1*
195 fat-already] *hyphen, Capell*; fat already, *F1*
200 s.d. Aside to Diomedes.] *Johnson (subs.)*
201 s.d. Aside to Nestor.] *Johnson (subs.)*

201 his] this *F1*
202–3 If . . . face.] *as verse, Rowe; as prose, Q, F1*
203 pash] *F1*; push *Q*
205 he] a *F1*
209, 211, 213, 216, 219, 220, 223 s.dd. Aside.] *Capell*
212 let his humors] *F1*; tell his humorous *Q*
215 of] a *F1*
219 'twould] *F1*; two'od *Q*
220 s.p. Ulyss.] *F1*; Aiax. *Q* (*Q gives 'A would . . . warm. to Ajax*)
220–1 I will . . . warm.] *assigned to Ajax, F1*
223 praises] *F1*; praiers *Q*
224 in] *F1*
225 s.d. To Agamemnon.] *Capell*
226 so.] *F1*; so? *Q*
227 You] *F1*; Yon *Q*
228 does] doth *F1*
229 man—] *Rowe*; man *Q*; man, *F1*
233–4 A . . . Troyan!] *as verse, Pope; as prose, Q, F1*
233 with us thus] thus with vs *F1*
239 self-affected] *hyphen, F3*
241 gat] got *F1*
242 Fam'd] Fame *F1*
242–3 nature . . . all] *F1*; nature, / Thrice fam'd beyond all thy *Q*
244 thine] thy *F1*
246 half; . . . vigor,] *Rowe*; halfe, . . . vigour: *Q*; halfe, . . . vigour, *F1*
249 bourn] *F1*; boord *Q*
250 Thy] *F1*; This *Q*
254 Ajax'] *Hanmer*; Aiax *Q, F1*
257 s.p. Nest.] Vlis. *F1*
258 here,] *F1*; here *Q*
259 great] *om. F1*
263 lord—] *Capell*; Lord *Q*; Lord, *F1*
264 cull] *F1*; call *Q*
266 sail] may saile *F1*
266 hulks] bulkes *F1*

III.i

III.i] *Rowe*
Location: *Capell (subs.)*
o.s.d. Music sounds within.] *F1 (after Exeunt. at end of II.iii); placed as in Rowe*
o.s.d. and a Servant] *F1*
1 you not] not you *F1*
3 s.p. Serv.] *F1*; Man. *Q* (*throughout scene*)
6 notable] noble *F1*
6 gentleman;] *F1 (subs.)*; gentleman *Q*
15 grace.] *Warburton*; grace? *Q, F1*
17 titles] title *F1*
25 friend] *F1*
28 thou] thou art *F1*
31 who is] who's *F1*
32 heart-blood] *hyphen, Rowe*
34 Who?] *F1*; Who *Q*
35 not you] you not *F1*
37 thou] that thou *F1*
38 Cressid.] *from F1* Cressida.; Cressid *Q*
39 complimental] *Johnson*; complementall *Q, F1*
40 seethes] *F1*; seeth's *Q*
41 there's] *F1*; theirs *Q*
42 s.d. Helen] Helena *F1*
42 s.d. attended] *Theobald*
44–5 company! . . . them!] *Theobald (subs.)*; company, . . . them, *Q*; company: . . . them, *F1*
52 Nell, he] *F1*; Nel. he *Q* (*Q may intend Nel. as s.p.*)
57 lord,] Lord: *F1*
58 lord, dear queen.] *F1 (subs.)*; Lord deere Queene? *Q*
63 lord:] *Theobald (subs.)*; Lord *Q*; Lord, *F1*
65, 141 honey-sweet] *hyphen, F4*
66–7 Go . . . you—] *as prose, Capell; as verse, Q, F1*
68–9 You . . . head!] *as prose, Hanmer; as verse, Q, F1*
71 queen—i' faith—] *Collier*; Queene I faith—*Q, F1*
77 supper, you] *F1*; super. You *Q*
79 queen, my] *F1*; Queenem, y *Q*
87 I'll . . . life,] *om. F1*
87 life,] *Theobald*; life *Q*

The Folger Shakespeare Library

By permission of the Harvard College Library

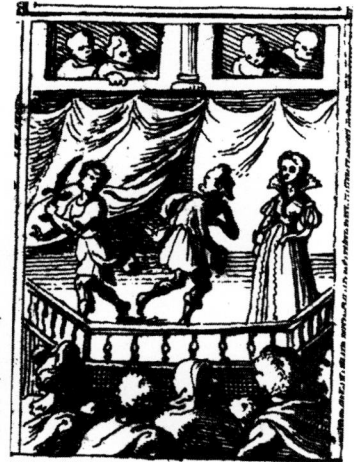

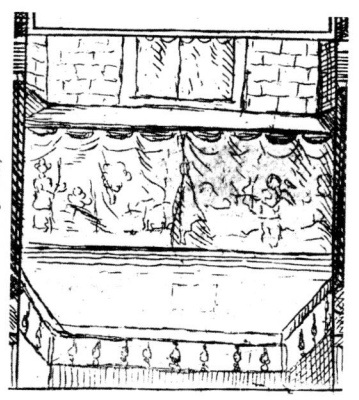

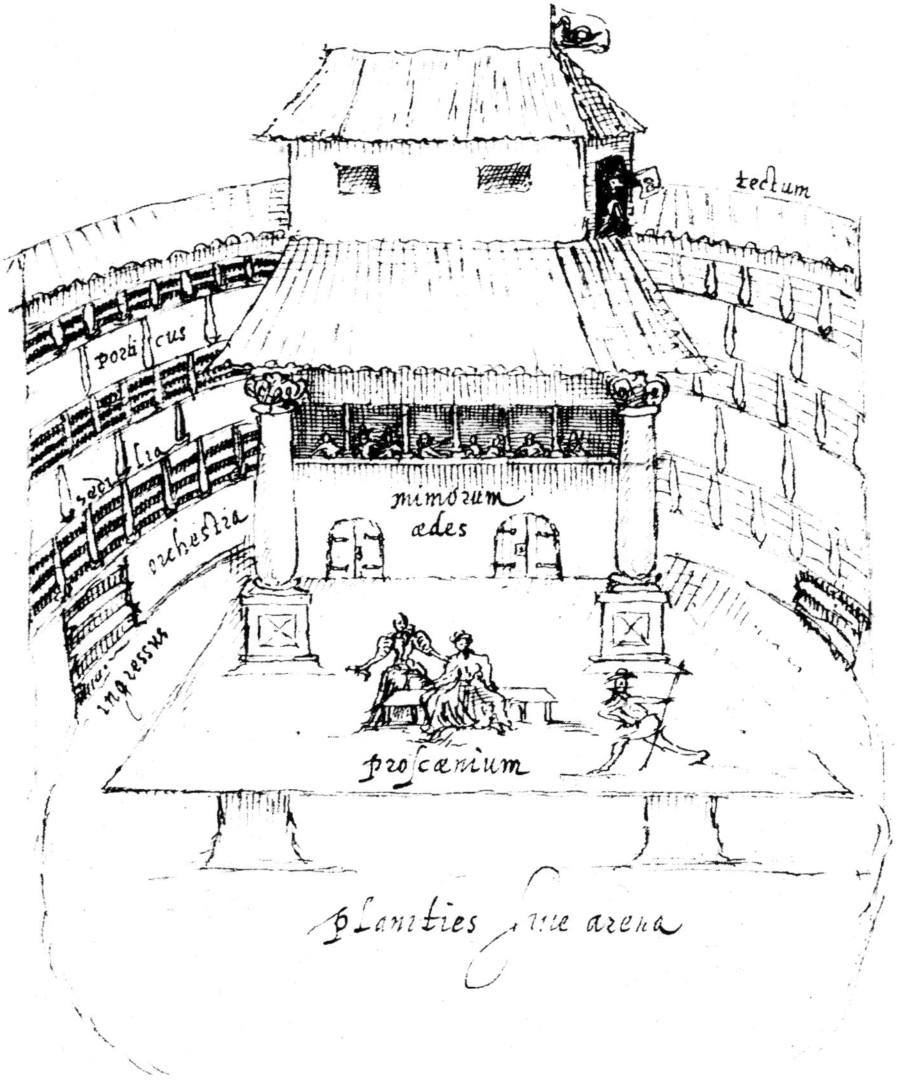

University Library, Utrecht

(Above) Johannes de Witt's sketch of the Swan Theatre (c. 1596; preserved in an early copy by his friend Arend van Buchell) is the only Elizabethan representation we possess of the interior of a public theatre. Its larger outlines confirm other kinds of contemporary evidence: the circular (or polygonal) structure, open to the sky, with three tiers of galleries, the uppermost roofed; the spectators' entrances ("*ingressus*"); the raised platform stage (wider than deep) projecting into the "yard" ("*planities siue arena*"), with two pillars supporting a roof (the "heavens") that covered the rear of the stage, and with standing-room on three sides for the "groundlings"; the tiring-house ("*mimorum aedes*"); and the "hut," from which a flag was flown during the times of performance and a trumpeter announced the beginning (on the third call) of a play. In certain details, however, the drawing is controversial, particularly in its depiction of the rear stage wall (the "scene").

The two stages shown to the left are from the title-pages of William Alabaster's *Roxana*, 1632 (upper), and Nathaniel Richards' *Messalina*, 1640. The *Roxana* stage is interesting for the curtains at the rear (perhaps concealing an inner playing area), the groundlings standing in the yard and other spectators seated above the stage (as in De Witt), and the railing surrounding the stage (as at the Globe). The *Messalina* stage also has curtains (in this case decorated with figures) and a stage railing, but adds what appears to be a curtained upper playing level and a trapdoor in the centre of the stage.

The pen-and-ink sketch shown above is the earliest known illustration (perhaps as early as 1594–95) of a scene from one of Shakespeare's plays. The artist (possibly, though probably not, Henry Peacham) has confused the action of the moment in *Titus Andronicus*, Act I: Tamora is apparently pleading with Titus to spare two of her sons, not one, and Aaron the Moor, with drawn sword in hand, is taking a more active part than his mute role in Act I allows him. Note particularly the mixture of more or less Roman costumes on the principal figures with the Elizabethan military garb on the two guards behind Titus, who also hold most un-Roman halberds. The illustration at the left (from G. Borgetto, *The Devil's Legend*, 1595) depicts two characters from the Italian *commedia dell'arte*: the Capitano (left) and the Zany. Both are associated with and may have influenced such Elizabethan comic figures as Falstaff and Parolles (who, like the Capitano, are descendants of the Roman comedy *miles gloriosus* or boasting soldier) and Costard or Launce (types of the rustic clown) and Touchstone or Feste (types of the professional fool).

The engraving opposite (c. 1662), later adapted to serve as frontispiece to Francis Kirkman's *The Wits, or Sport upon Sport* (1672), includes the earliest published depiction of Shakespearean characters, Sir John Falstaff and Mistress Quickly. Note also the stage lighting (by candelabra and footlights) and the upper curtained area, presumably a playing place, with spectators on either side.

PLATE 9

The Theatre of Compliment

Changling   Simpleton

French Dancing...

Sr I. Falstafe   Hostes   Clause

PLATE 10

On these two pages are shown contemporary portraits of eight well-known Elizabethan-Jacobean actors. Six of them were members of Shakespeare's company, the Lord Chamberlain's (later the King's) Men and are listed in the First Folio (1623) as among the "Principall Actors in all these Playes." William Kemp (above, left, with a taborer) and Robert Armin (above, right) were famous comedians, Kemp being associated with the roles of Costard, Bottom, Peter (in *Romeo and Juliet*), Dogberry, and possibly Falstaff; Armin with Feste and the Fool in *King Lear*. (Kemp's portrait is from his *Nine Days' Wonder*, 1600, an account of his celebrated hundred-mile morris-dance from London to Norwich in that year; Armin's is from the title-page of his play *The Two Maids of More-Clacke*, 1609). William Sly and John Lowin (below, centre and right) are more shadowy figures, though there is a tradition that Lowin created the role of Henry VIII, having "his instructions from Mr. Shakespeare himself." Nathan Field (below, left) joined the King's Men about 1615, having been a boy actor in the Queen's Revels.

Edward Alleyn (right centre) was the leading actor of the Admiral's Men. He was famous as Tamburlaine, Barabas (in Marlowe's *The Jew of Malta*), and Faustus, and his acting style is perhaps glanced at in the role of Lucianus in the play-within-the-play in *Hamlet*. He was closely associated with the theatrical business ventures of Philip Henslowe, his father-in-law, and was the founder of Dulwich College.

PLATE 11

(Above) Richard Burbage (c. 1567–1619), whose father James built The Theatre, the first London playhouse, in 1576, was the leading actor in the Chamberlain's-King's Men from the organization of the company in 1594 until shortly before his death. He created many of the greatest roles in Shakespeare's plays, including Richard III, Romeo, Hamlet, Othello, and Lear. Two well-known epitaphs survive; the shorter, "Exit Burbage." An extract from the longer runs: "Hee's gone & with him what a world are dead, / Which he reuiud, to be reuiued soe. / No more young Hamlett, ould Heironymoe. / Kind Leer, the greued Moore, and more beside, / That liued in him, haue now for euer dy'de."

The little sketch to the right depicts Richard Tarlton, a low comedian of the preceding generation, who died in 1588, but whose reputation continued to live well into the seventeenth century.

PLATE 12

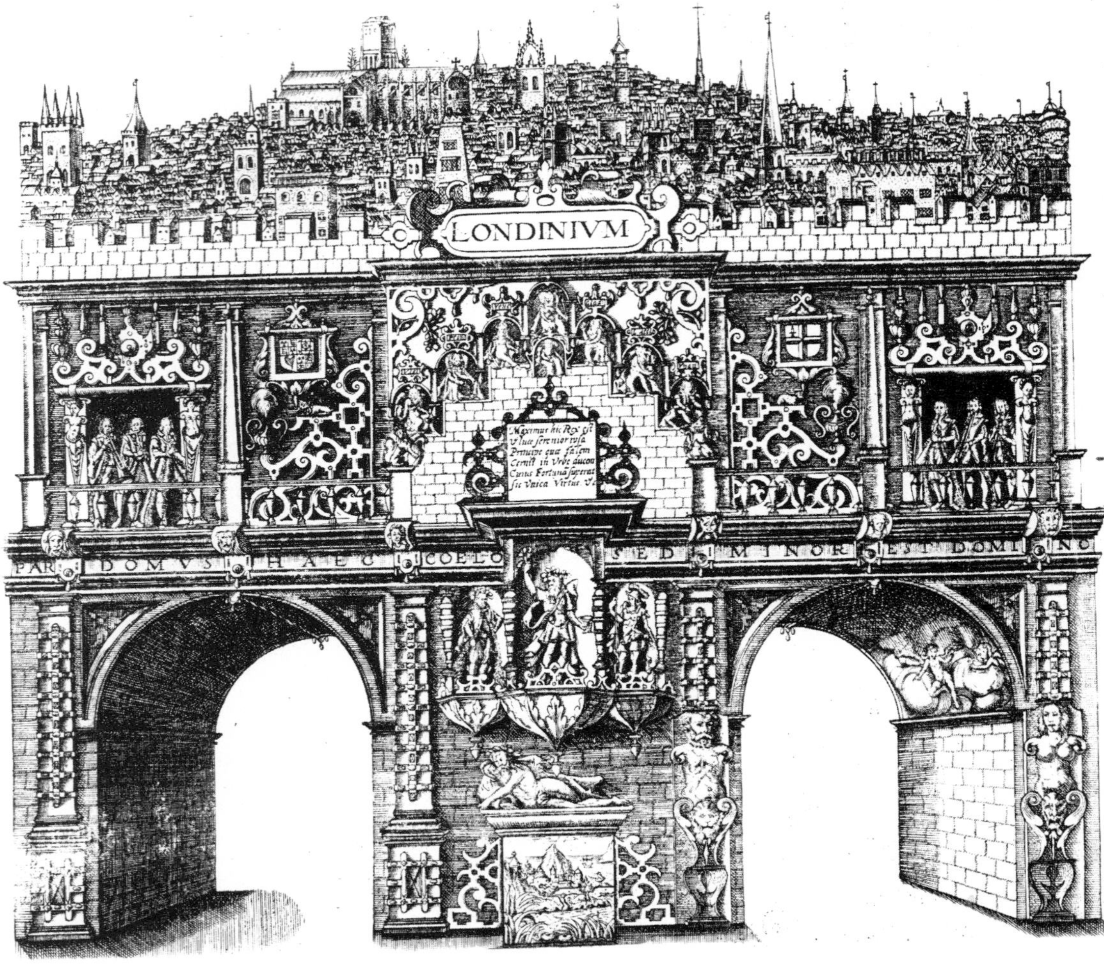

The Huntington Library, San Marino, California

Fishmongers' Company, London

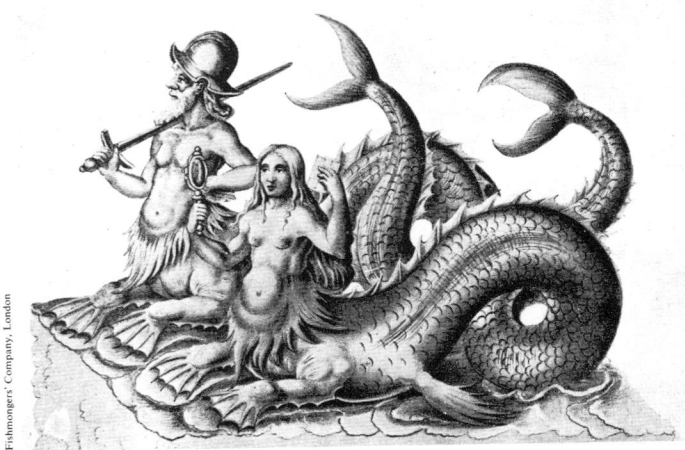

Two examples of London street pageantry are shown here: above, one of the seven triumphal arches erected to welcome King James I on his first state progress through the City, in 1604 (from Stephen Harrison, *Arches of Triumph*, 1604); at left, one of eight pageants (or floats) devised by the Fishmongers' Company for the Lord Mayor's show in 1616. The print opposite (from *Scarron's Comical Romance of a Company of Stage Players*, 1676) shows two scenes familiar in the provinces: the arrival of a group of strolling players at an inn and their later performance on a bare platform stage in the village square. Such a company in Shakespeare's England, however, would not have included an actress; this is a French troupe.

PLATE 14

These three drawings are by the well-known scenic artist and costume designer Inigo Jones (1573–1652), who during the first four decades of the seventeenth century produced sumptuous and very costly court masques and entertainments for James I and Charles I. Unlike plays in the public theatres, the court masques employed very sophisticated scenery, set behind a proscenium arch similar to that in use today. The setting above was designed for William Davenant's masque *Britannia Triumphans* (1638). It shows the use of moveable wings (three on each side), so arranged as to suggest perspective, and a painted backdrop picturing "London afar off." The two figures at the right were drawn for the same masque and represent a ballad singer and a man playing the "tongs and key" (who recalls Bottom's liking for "the tongs and the bones" in *A Midsummer Night's Dream*, IV.i.28–29).

PLATE 15

90 make 's] *Capell conj.;* makes *Q;* make *F1*
92 poor disposer's] *F1;* disposers *Q*
93 spy.] *F1;* spie? *Q*
95 instrument.] *Johnson;* instrument, *Q;* Instrument *F1*
97 horribly] horrible *F1*
102 twain] *F1;* tawine *Q*
107 prithee now.] *F1 (subs.);* prethee, now *Q*
108 lord] *F1;* lad *Q*
114 Pan. In . . . so.] *F1*
114 s.d. Sings.] *Capell (subs.)*
115 still love] *om. F1*
116 bow] *F4;* bow. *Q;* Bow, *F1*
118 shaft confounds] *F1;* shafts confound *Q*
128 doves,] *F3;* doues *Q*
133 a-field] *Warburton (after Rowe);* a field *Q, F1*
135 Deiphobus] Deiphoebus *F1*
135 Antenor] *Pope;* Anthenor *Q, F1 (frequently; not hereafter recorded)*
147 s.d. Exit.] *Rowe*
147 s.d. retreat.] *F1;* retreat? *Q*
148 They're] *F1;* Their *Q*
148 the] *om. F1*
151 these] *F1;* this *Q*
157 have,] *Pope;* haue. *Q;* haue: *F1*
159 s.p. Par.] *om. F1*
159 Sweet,] *Rowe;* Sweet *Q, F1*
159 thee] *F1;* her *Q*

III.ii

III.ii] *Capell*
Location: *ed.*
o.s.d. Troilus' Man] *F1;* Troylus, man *Q*
o.s.d. meeting] *Capell*
3 he] *F1*
4 s.d. Enter Troilus.] *F1*
6 s.d. Exit Man.] *Kittredge (after Capell)*
9 to] *om. F1*
11 these] those *F1*
13 Pandar] Pandarus *F1 (this variation frequent in F1 s.dd.; not hereafter recorded)*
17 s.d. Exit.] *F1 (Exit Pandarus.)*
22 thrice-repured] *hyphen, Collier;* thrice reputed *F1*
22 Death,] *F4;* Death *Q, F1*
22 me,] *White (after Rowe);* me *Q, F1*
24 subtile] *F1;* subtill *Q*
24 tun'd] and *F1*
29 s.d. Enter Pandarus.] *F1*
31 now:] *Wilson (after Pope);* now, *Q, F1*
32 fray'd] *Capell;* fraid *Q*
32 spirit] sprite *F1*
34 as short] so short *F1*
34 s.d. Exit.] *F1 (Exit Pand.)*
38 unawares] *F1;* vnwares *Q*
39 s.d. with] *Capell;* and *Q, F1*
39 s.d. Cressid] Cressida *F1 (this variation frequent in F1 s.dd.; not hereafter recorded)*
40 Come . . . blush?] *as prose, Pope; as verse, Q, F1*
42 s.d. Cressida draws backward.] *White*
47 day,] *F1;* day? *Q*
52 you—the] *A. Walker;* you. The *Q, F1*
52 tercel,] *F1;* tercell: *Q*
56 a' th'] 'oth' *Q*
58 "In . . . interchangeably"] *quotes, Hanmer*
58 interchangeably"—] *Rowe;* interchangeably. *Q, F1*
59 s.d. Exit.] *F2*
61 Cressid] *Kittredge;* Cressed *Q;* Cressida *F1*
62 grant—] *Pope;* graunt? *Q*
67 fears] *Pope;* teares *Q, F1*
72 safer] safe *F1*
74–5 O . . . monster.] *as prose, Pope; as verse, Q, F1*
76 Nor] Not *F1*
76 neither?] *F1;* neither *Q*
81 is] *F1*
92 crown it. No perfection] *F1* (it:); louer part no affection *Q*
99 s.d. Enter Pandarus.] *F1*
110 be woo'd] *Q* (woed); are wooed *F1*
114 lov'd] *F1;* loued *Q*
114–5 Prince . . . months.] *as verse, Rowe; as prose, Q, F1 (l. 113 also as prose, F1)*

118 glance . . . me—] *Rowe;* glance; that euer pardon me *Q,* (me,) *F1*
120 till now not] not till now *F1*
122 unbridled] *F3;* vnbrideled *Q, F1*
122 grown] *F2;* grone *Q;* grow *F1*
123 See, we fools!] *Theobald;* see wee fooles *Q, F1*
126 woo'd] *Rowe;* woed *Q, F1*
132 Cunning] *Pope;* Comming *Q, F1*
133 very . . . counsel!] soule of counsell from me. *Q*
133 counsel] *F1;* councell *Q*
134 s.d. Kisses her.] *Rowe (subs.)*
148 resides] *F2;* recids *Q;* recides *F1*
150–1 I . . . speak.] Where is my wit? / I would be gone: I speake I know not what. *F1*
152 that speak] that speakes *F1*
154 confession,] *F1;* confession. *Q*
157 might;] *Capell;* might *Q;* might, *F1*
160 aye] *F1;* age *Q*
160 love,] *F2;* loue. *Q, F1*
161 youth,] *F1;* youth. *Q*
167 purity] puriritie *Q*
174 truth] *Kittredge;* trueth *Q;* truths *F1*
174 Troilus.] *Rowe (subs.);* Troylus, *Q, F1*
176 Wants similes, truth] *F1;* Wants simele's truth *Q*
180 Yet] *F1*
180 truth] *ed.;* truth. *Q;* truth, *F1*
181 truth's] *Rowe;* truths *Q, F1*
185 and] *F1;* or *Q*
191 th' have] they'aue *F1*
192 wind, or] as Winde, as *F1*
193 or] as *F1*
198 witness.] *Rowe;* witnes *Q, F1*
200 pain] paines *F1*
201 goers-between] *hyphen, Rowe*
202, 204 Pandars] *Pope;* Panders *Q, F1*
203 brokers-between] *hyphen, Theobald*
209 s.d. Troilus and Cressida] *Capell; s.d. om. F1*
211 Pandar] *Pope;* Pander *Q;* and Pander *F1*
211 s.d. Exit.] Exeunt. *F1*

III.iii

III.iii] *Capell*
Location: *Rowe*
o.s.d. Ajax] *Theobald*
o.s.d. Menelaus, and] *F1*
o.s.d. Calchas] *Rowe;* Chalcas *Q, F1*
o.s.d. Flourish.] *F1*
1 done] done you *F1*
3 your] *F1*
4 come] *F4 (supported by Caxton);* loue *Q, F1*
17 demand.] *Rowe;* demand? *Q, F1*
31 Calchas] *Rowe;* Calcas *Q, F1 (generally; not hereafter recorded)*
35 answered] answer'd *F1*
37 s.d. with Calchas] *Capell (subs.)*
37 s.d. Enter] *F1*
37 s.d. stand] *om. F1*
37 s.d. the door of] *Neilson*
39 pass] to passe *F1*
42–3 me . . . him?] *F1* (me,); me. / . . . him, *Q*
43 unplausive] *F1;* vnpaulsiue *Q*
61 s.d. Exeunt . . . Nestor.] *Capell*
63 s.d. Exit.] *Capell*
66 Ajax.] *F4;* Aiax? *Q, F1*
67 Ha?] *Rowe;* Ha: *Q;* Ha. *F1*
69 s.d. Exit.] *Capell;* Exeunt. *Q, F1*
70 fellows?] *F1;* fellowes *Q*
81 but honor] but honour'd *F1*
88 friends.] *Theobald (subs.);* friends, *Q, F1*
88 enjoy] *F1;* enioy: *Q*
90 out] *F1;* out: *Q*
91 Some thing] Something *F1*
100 aiming] shining *F1*
102 giver] *F1;* giuers *Q*
105–6 To . . . itself,] *om. F1*
110 mirror'd] *Singer MS, Collier MS;* married *Q, F1*
110 there] *F1;* there? *Q*
112 at] it at *F1*
115 man] may *F1*
116 be] is *F1*
118 aught,] *F1* (ought,); aught: *Q*

119 th' applause] *F1* (th' applause,); the applause. *Q*
120 th' are] they are *F1*
121 steel] *Pope;* steele: *Q;* steele, *F1*
124 immediately] *F2;* immediately, *Q;* immediately: *F1*
125 Th'] The *F1*
127 what. Nature,] *F1;* what / Nature *Q*
127 are] *F2;* are. *Q, F1*
128 abject] *F1;* obiect *Q*
129 esteem,] *F1;* esteeme: *Q*
130–1 to-morrow— . . . him—] *Cambridge;* to morrow, . . . him *Q;* to morrow, . . . him? *F1*
137 fasting] feasting *F1*
140 on] *F1;* one *Q*
141 shriking] shrinking *F1*
146–7 oblivion, . . . ingratitudes.] *Hanmer (reading ingratitude);* obliuion: . . . ingratitudes, *Q;* obliuion: . . . ingratitudes: *F1*
152 mail] *Pope;* male *Q*
154 narrow,] *F1;* narrow: *Q*
155 one] *F1;* on *Q*
155 abreast.] *F3 (period, Pope, subs.);* a brest. *Q*
158 hedge aside] *F1;* turne a side *Q*
158 forthright] *F4 (subs.);* forth right *Q, F1*
160 hindmost] *F1;* him, most *Q*
161–3 Or . . . on.] *F1*
162 abject rear,] *Hanmer;* abiect, neere *F1*
164 past] *F1;* passe *Q*
169 farewell] farewels *F1*
169 Let] O let *F1*
178 give] *Thirlby conj.;* goe *Q, F1*
183 sooner] begin to *F1*
184 Than] *F1* (Then); That *Q*
184 stirs not] not stirs *F1*
184 once] out *F1*
194 known?] *F1;* knowne. *Q*
197 grain . . . gold] *F1;* thing *Q*
198 th'] *F1;* the *Q*
198 depth] deepes *F1*
210 our islands] her Iland *F1*
215 s.d. Exit.] *Pope*
219 this;] *F1;* this *Q*
224 a] *F1*
225 air] ayrie ayre *F1*
233 they] we *F1*
241 s.d. Enter Thersites.] *placed as in Globe; after sav'd! l. 241, Q; after l. 239, F1*
251 'a] he *F1*
255 this] his *F1*
259 break't] *F1;* breakt *Q*
259 vainglory] *F1 (subs.);* vaine glory *Q*
266 to him] *F1*
270 on his] on hii *F1*
271 demands] his demands *F1*
274 most] *F1*
276 magnanimous] magnanimious *F1*
277 six-or-seven-times-honor'd] *hyphens, Capell*
277 captain-general] *Hanmer;* Captaine Generall *Q;* Captaine, Generall *F1*
278 army,] *comma from F4;* armie. *Q;* Grecian Armie *F1*
278 et cetera.] *F1* (&c.)
287 safe-conduct] *hyphen, Capell*
295 aleven] *ed.;* a leuen *Q;* eleuen *F1*
295 of the] a *F1*
299 ye] you *F1*
301 he's] *F1*
301 of] a *F1*
306 bear] carry *F1*
309 s.d. Exeunt . . . Patroclus.] *Capell*
312 s.d. Exit.] *Capell*

IV.i

IV.i] *Rowe*
Location: *Rowe, Theobald*
o.s.d. with a torch] *F1*
o.s.d. Antenor] *Pope;* Autemor *Q;* Anthenor *F1*
o.s.d. and others] *Malone*
5 you] *F1;* your *Q*
6 bed-mate] *hyphen, F1*
8 Greek . . . hand,] *F1 (subs.);* Greeke Aeneas take his hand. *Q*

9 wherein] within; F1
10 a] in a F1
16 and, so long,] Rowe (subs.); and so long Q, F1
17 But] F1; Lul'd Q
17 meet] meetes F1
21 backward. . . . gentleness,] Theobald; back-ward, in humane gentlenesse: Q, F1
30 to-morrow!] Capell; to morrow— Q; to morrow. F1
33 despiteful] despightful'st F1
34-5 The . . . early?] as verse, F1; as prose, Q
37 'twas] it was F1
38 Calchas'] Pope; Calcho's Q; Calcha's F1
38 him,] F1; him: Q
41 believe] doe thinke F1
45 wherefore] whereof F1
46-8 That . . . Troy.] as verse, F1; as prose, Q
51 s.d. Exit.] F1 (Exit Aeneas)
53 soul] soule F1
54 deserves . . . best] merits . . . most F1
57 soil] soylure F1
61 friends.] F1 (friends:); friends, Q
66 nor less] no lesse F1
67 the] which F1
70 false] F1; falfe Q
77 they] you F1
79-80 We'll . . . way.] as verse, F1; as prose, Q

IV.ii

IV.ii] Pope
Location: ed. (after Capell)
7 now,] Theobald; now Q, F1
7 a-weary] Capell (subs.); a weary Q, F1
10 joys] eyes F1
13 tediously] hidiously F1
14 momentary-swift] hyphen, Pope; momentary, swift F1
17 off] F1; of Q
19 s.d. Within.] F1
19 What's] F1; Whats F1
20 s.d. Enter Pandarus.] F1
23-4 How . . . Cressid?] as prose, Pope; as verse, Q, F1
24 Here] Heare F1
27-8 To . . . do?] as prose, Pope; as verse, Q, F1
29-30 Come . . . others.] as verse, Capell; as prose, Q, F1
31 capocchia] Theobald; chipochia Q, F1
34 s.d. One knocks.] placed as in Capell; after l. 35, Q; after l. 33, F1
39 s.d. Knock.] placed as in Capell; after l. 40, Q, F1
41 s.d. Troilus and Cressida] Capell
43 s.d. Enter Aeneas] Rowe
45 there?] Pope; there Q, F1
45 Aeneas!] Collier; Aeneas: Q; Aeneas? F1
45-6 Who's . . . early?] as verse, Pope; as prose, Q, F1
48 Here?] F1; Here, Q
51 It's] Kittredge; its Q; 'tis F1
52 sworn. For] F1 (subs.); sworne / For Q
54 Who!—nay then.] Capell (after Rowe); Who, nay then! Q; Who, nay then: F1
55 you are] y'are F1
57 s.d. Enter Troilus.] F1
63 us . . . him] F1; him, and Q
66 so concluded] concluded so F1
72 neighbor Pandar] nature F1
73 s.d. Troilus and Aeneas] Capell
74 lost?] Hanmer; lost, Q; lost: F1
77 s.d. Enter Cressid.] Enter Cress. Q (Cress. serving as s.p.); Enter Pandarus and Cressid. F1 (after l. 73)
78 s.p. Cres.] F1
79 Ah, ah!] Ah, ha! F1
85 Pray thee] Prythee F1
86 wouldest] would'st F1
88-9 I beseech you] F1
101 force] orce F1
102 extremes] extremitie F1
105 I'll] I will F1
109 s.d. Exeunt.] F1

IV.iii

IV.iii] Capell

Location: ed. (after Theobald)
2 For] Of F1
9 own] om. F1
9 s.d. Exit.] Capell
12 lords.] F1; Lords? Q

IV.iv

IV.iv] Capell
Location: ed.
3 full, perfect] full perfect F1
4 violenteth] no lesse F1
6 affections] affection F1
9 dross] crosse F1
10 s.d. Enter Troilus.] after l. 9, F1
11 Ah] Johnson; a Q, F1
12 ducks] ducke F1
13 s.d. Embracing him.] Malone (after Capell)
16-7 "O . . . breaking."] as verse, Pope; as prose, Q, F1
17 sigh'st] sighest F1
19-20 "Because . . . speaking."] as verse, Pope; as prose, Q, F1
24 strain'd] strange F1
27 deities] F1; dieties Q
34 back . . . by] F1; back, leaue taking, iussles roughly by: Q
40-1 ourselves . . . one.] Pope; our selues: . . . one, Q; our selues, . . . our F1
42 time] time; F1
44 heaven,] F1; heauen. Q
48 Distasted] Distasting F1
50 Genius] F1 (genius); Genius Q (in italics)
50 so] F1
51 "come"] F1 (quotes, Hanmer); so Q
53 tears? Rain] F1 (raine,); teares raine Q
54 th' root] Alexander; my throate Q; the root F1
54 s.d. Exit.] Theobald
57 When . . . again?] assigned to Troilus, F1
58 me,] me my F1
58 heart—] Rowe; heart. Q, F1
64 there is] there's F1
70 Wear] F1; were Q
75 it, love.] F3 (subs.); it loue, Q; it; Loue: F1
77-8 Their . . . Flowing] F1 (Flawing F1; Flowing F2)
79 novelty] nouelties F1
79 person,] F1 (person.; comma, F3); por-tion, Q
82 afeard] Capell; a feard Q; affraid F1
87 subtile] F3; subtill Q, F1
101] Following this line F1 reads Exit.
102 Who, I?] F1 (comma, Capell); Who I, Q
106 wear] F1; were Q
108 "plain and true"] quotes, Johnson
108 s.d. Enter . . . Diomedes.] Malone (after Rowe); Enter the Greekes. F1 (after l. 108)
112 is.] F1; is Q
116 Ilion] F3; Illion? Q, F1
119 usage] visage F1
122-3 to thee In] towards, / I I F1
131 free.] F2 (free;); free? Q, F1
132 you] my F1
133 charge.] F1 (charge:); charge, Q
135 I] Ile F1
136 port.] F1; port Q
139 s.d. Exeunt . . . Diomedes.] Ritson conj.
139 s.d. Sound trumpet.] F1
140 Hark,] F1; Harke Q
142 to the] in the F1
143] Following this line F1 reads Exeunt.
144-8 Dei. Let . . . chivalry.] F1
144 s.p. Dei.] Ritson conj.; Dio. F1
148 s.d. Exeunt.] Exeu. Q (after l. 143); om. F1

IV.v

IV.v] Capell
Location: Capell (after Rowe)
o.s.d. Nestor] Theobald; Nester, Calcas Q; Nestor, Calcas F1
5-6 May . . . hither.] as verse, F1; as prose, Q
11 s.d. Trumpet sounds.] Hanmer
12 s.d. Enter . . . Cressid.] F4 (from F2 Enter Dio. Cres.)
13 yond] yong F1
15 toe] F1; too Q

18, 23, 25, 29 s.dd. Kisses her.] Collier MS (subs.)
20-3 Yet . . . Nestor.] as verse, Pope; as prose, Q, F1
29 And . . . argument.] om. F1
33 Patroclus] F1; Patrolus Q
33 s.d. Kisses her again.] Collier MS (subs.)
38-9 The . . . kiss.] as verse, Pope; as prose, Q, F1
43 not] F1; nor Q
48 then?] then? F1
49 kiss] Kittredge; kisse, Q; kisse: F1
50 his.] Capell; his— Q, F1
53 s.d. Exit with Cressida.] Dyce (after Pope)
55 language] a language F1
60 unclasp] F1; vnclapse Q
61 ticklish] tickling F1
63 s.d. Flourish.] after following entry direction in F1
64 Troyans'] Theobald; Troyans Q, F1
64 s.d. Hector . . . Attendants] F1 (armed Capell; Troilus Rowe); s.d. after l. 63, Q, F1; placed as in Alexander
65 the] you F1
69 they] om. F1
70-1 field? . . . ask.] Rowe; field, . . . aske? Q; field: . . . aske? F1
73 s.p. Achil.] A. Walker (after Theobald conj.); speech continued to Agamemnon, Q, F1
74 misprising] disprising F1
77-8 this: . . . little,] Pope (subs.); this, . . . little: Q, F1
81 nothing. Weigh] F1 (subs.); nothing, way Q
85 seek] F1; seeke: Q
87 then?] F1; then, Q
87 s.d. Enter Diomedes.] Pope
88 Sir] sir, F1
89 Aeneas] F1; Eneas Q
92 breath] breach F1
93 s.d. Ajax . . . lists.] Capell
94 Ulyss. They . . . already.] F1
95 s.p. Agam.] F1; Vlisses: Q (in italics; perhaps intended as a vocative, with l. 95 as the last line of Agamemnon's speech in the Q arrangement)
96 knight,] Knight; they call him Troylus; F1 (the F1 addition occurs again at l. 108 in both F1 and Q)
97 matchless,] F1; matchlesse Q
98 in] F1
103 impare] impaire F1
112 s.d. Hector . . . fight.] Rowe
116 dispos'd.] Rowe (subs.); dispo'd Q; dispos'd F1
121 cousin-german] hyphen, Pope
124 commixtion] commixion F1
124 so] Pope; so, Q, F1
132 Of . . . feud;] F1
133 drop] F1; day Q
142 Neoptolemus] F2; Neoptolymus Q, F1
143 Oyes] Dyce; (O yes) Q, F1
144 could] could'st F1
158 s.d. Agamemnon . . . forward.] Rowe; Enter Agamemnon and the rest. F1
161 my] mine F1
163 all] of F1
165-70 But . . . integrity,] F1
169 bias-drawing] hyphen, Theobald
173 s.d. To Troilus.] Rowe
177 lord?] Capell; Lord, Q, F1
178 that . . . oath] F1; thy affect, the vntraded earth) Q
179 quondam] F1; quandom Q
179 glove.] F3 (subs.); gloue, Q; Gloue F1
187 Despising many] And seene thee scorning F1
188 thy] F1; th' Q (probably intended as an elided form of thy)
190 to some] vnto F1
190 standers-by] hyphen, Rowe
193 hemm'd] F1; shrupd Q
199 O] om. F1
206 As . . . courtesy.] F1
220 Yon] Yond F1
235 pray thee] prythee F1
241 dost] Rowe; doost Q; doest F1

252 **an]** the *F1*
255 **stithied]** *F1*; stichied *Q*
263 **have]** *om. F1*
272 **we]** you *F1*
274 **him.]** *F1*; him *Q*
274–5 **him. Beat . . . taborins]** *F1*; him / To taste your bounties *Q*
276 **s.d. all . . . Ulysses]** *Malone (after Rowe)*
281 **upon . . . nor]** on heauen, nor on *F1*
284 **you]** thee *F1*
287 **But]** As *F1*
292 **belov'd, she lov'd;]** *F1*; beloued my Lord, *Q*

V.i

V.i] *Rowe*
Location: *Rowe (subs.)*
2 **scimitar]** *Rowe*; Cemitar *Q*, *F1*
4 **core]** *F1*; curre *Q*
6 **seemest]** seem'st *F1*
7 **idiot-worshippers]** *hyphen, F1*
12 **needs]** need *F1*
12 **these]** *F1*; this *Q*
14 **boy]** *F1*; box *Q*
15 **said]** thought *F1*
18 **the guts-griping,]** *Capell (comma, F4)*; the guts griping *Q*; guts-griping *F1*
19 **catarrhs,]** *F1*
19 **in the]** i'th' *F1*
20–3 **raw . . . tetter,]** and the like, *F1*
20 **dirt-rotten]** *Pope*; durtrotten *Q*
23 **preposterous]** prepostrous *F1*
26 **means]** mean'st *F1*
29 **no]** *om. F1*
30 **No?]** *F1*; No *Q*
31 **sleave-silk]** *Collier (hyphen, Dyce)*; sleiue silke *Q*; Sleyd silke *F1*
31 **sarcenet]** *F1*; sacenet *Q*
32 **tossel]** *F2*; toslell *Q*; tassell *F1*
32–3 **purse, thou? Ah]** *F3 (subs.)*; purse-thou ah *Q*; purse thou: Ah *F1*
36 **Finch-egg]** *hyphen, Theobald*
38 **in to-morrow's]** *F1 (to morrowes)*; into morrowes *Q*
47 **s.d. Exeunt . . . Patroclus.]** *Hanmer*; Exit. *F1*
51 **Here's]** *F1*; her's *Q*
54 **brother,]** *F1*; be *Q*
56 **hanging]** *F1*
56 **brother's]** *F1*; bare *Q*
58 **fac'd]** *ed.*; faced *Q*; forced *F1*
60 **he is]** *F1*; her's *Q*
61 **dog]** *F1*; day *Q*
61 **moile]** Mule *F1*
61 **fitchook]** *Kittredge*; Fichooke *Q*; Fitchew *F1*
64 **not]** *F1*
66 **Menelaus.]** *F1*; Menelaus— *Q*
66 **Hey-day]** Hoy-day *F1*
66 **sprites]** spirits *F1*
66 **s.d. Hector, Troilus, Ajax]** *Theobald*; Hector, Aiax *F1*
66 **s.d. Menelaus]** *Capell*
67–8 **We . . . you.]** *as verse, Capell*; *as prose*, *Q*, *F1*
67 **'tis]** *F1*; tis *Q*
68 **lights]** light *F1*
69 **s.d. Enter Achilles.]** *F1*
71 **now,]** *Capell*; now *Q*, *F1*
71 **good night]** *F1 (subs.)*; God night *Q*
73 **Greeks']** *Theobald*; Greekes *Q*, *F1*
76 **sewer]** *Rowe*; sure *Q*, *F1*
77–8 **Good . . . tarry.]** *as verse, Theobald*; *as prose*, *Q*, *F1*
77 **at once]** *F1*
79 **s.d. Exeunt Agamemnon, Menelaus.]** *om. F1*
80 **too, Diomed,]** *F1 (subs.)*; to Diomed. *Q*
85 **s.d. Aside to Troilus.]** *Capell (after Rowe)*
85–6 **Follow . . . company.]** *as verse, F1*; *as prose*, *Q*, *F1*
87 **s.d. Exit . . . following.]** *Capell*
87 **s.d. Achilles . . . Nestor]** *Capell (after Hanmer)*
88 **false-hearted]** *hyphen, F1*
93 **it]** that it *F1*
93 **sun]** *F1*; Sonne *Q*
98 **varlots]** Varlets *F1*

98 **s.d. Exit.]** *Hanmer*; Exeunt *F1*

V.ii

V.ii] *Rowe*
Location: *Capell (after Rowe)*
2, 4 **s.pp. Cal.]** *Rowe*; Chal. *Q*, *F1*
2, 4 **s.dd. Within.]** *Hanmer*
3 **Diomed. Calchas, I think.]** *Rowe (subs.*; Calchas *F4)*; Diomed, Chalcas I thinke *Q*; Diomed, Chalcas (I thinke) *F1*
3 **your]** you *F1*
4 **s.d. Enter . . . Ulysses]** *F1*
4 **s.d. at . . . Thersites]** *Capell*
5 **s.d. Enter Cressid]** *placed as in F1*; *after him. l. 6, Q*
7 **s.d. Whispers.]** *Rowe*
10–1 **sing . . . cliff]** finde . . . life *F1*
13 **s.p. Cres.]** *F2*; Cal. *Q*, *F1*
13 **Remember?]** *F1*; Remember *Q*
16 **shall]** should *F1*
18 **Greek,]** *F1*; Greeke *Q*
22 **come,]** *Theobald*; come *Q*; eome *F1*
22 **pin.]** *Johnson*; pin *Q*; pin, *F1*
22 **forsworn.]** a forsworne.— *F1*
24 **trick—]** *Collier*; tricke *Q*; tricke, *F1*
27 **do]** doe not *F1*
29 **Hold,]** *F1*; Hold *Q*
34 **a]** one *F1*
36 **pray]** pray you *F1*
40 **Now]** Nay *F1*
41 **distraction]** *F1*; distruction *Q*
42 **prithee]** pray thee *F1*
43 **all hell's]** hell *F1*
46 **How now, my]** Why, how now *F1*
48 **adieu,]** *F1* ⁓
50–1 **You . . . out.]** *as verse, F2*; *as prose*, *Q*, *F1*
56 **these]** *F1*
58 **But]** *F1*
62 **my]** sweete *F1*
64 **s.d. Cressid.]** *F1*; Cress. *Q*
68 **Tro. I . . . will.]** *F1*
69 **s.p. Cres.]** *F1*; Troy: *Q*
71 **was't]** *F1*; wast *Q*
72 **ha't]** haue't *F1*
78 **on]** in *F1*
81 **Nay . . . me.]** *continued to Cressida, Thirlby conj.*; *given to Diomedes*, *Q*, *F1 (a strained sense can be made out of the original; see Honigmann, pp. 81–2)*
82 **doth take]** rakes *F1*
85 **s.p. Cres.]** *F1*; *speech continued to Troilus, Q*
89 **one's]** *Johnson*; on's *Q*; one *F1*
91 **By]** *F1*; And by *Q*
98–101 **Why . . . you.]** *as verse, F1*; *as prose, Q*
102 **you]** me *F1*
106 **s.d. Exit Diomedes.]** *Capell*; Exit. *F1 (after then. l. 106)*
112 **Minds . . . turpitude.]** *F1*; *with gnomic quotes, Q*
113 **strength]** *F1*; strength, *Q*
114 **said]** say *F1*
118 **co-act]** *F4*; Court *Q*; coact *F1*
122 **th' attest]** that test *F1*
123 **had deceptious]** *F1*; were deceptions *Q*
126 **not,]** *Theobald*; not *Q*, *F1*
134 **soil]** *F1*; spoile *Q*
136 **'a]** he *F1*
139 **be sanctimonies]** are sanctimonie *F1*
142 **was]** is *F1*
143 **up]** vp, *F1*
143 **itself!]** *Capell (after Pope)*; it selfe *Q*; thy selfe *F1*
144 **Bi-fold]** By foule *F1*
152 **Ariachne's]** *F1*; Ariathna's *Q (u)*; Ariachna's *Q (c)*
157 **five-finger-tied]** *F1 (hyphens, Pope)*; finde finger tied *Q*
159 **relics]** *Dyce*; reliques *Q*, *F1*
160 **given]** bound *F1*
167 **as]** *F2*
167 **Cressid]** Cressida *F1*
169 **on]** in *F1*
173 **sun]** Fenne *F1*
181 **s.d. Aeneas]** *F1*; Eneas *Q*
189 **s.d. Aeneas]** *F1*; Eeneas *Q*

196 **s.d. Exit.]** *om. F1*

V.iii

V.iii] *Rowe*
Location: *Capell (after Theobald)*
4 **in]** gone *F1*
5 **all]** *om. F1*
7 **brother]** *F1*; brothet *Q*
8 **intent]** *F1*; intenr *Q*
14 **s.p. Cas.]** *F1*; Cres. *Q*
15 **Be gone]** *F4*; Begon *Q*, *F1*
20–2 **To . . . charity.]** *F1*
21 **lawful,]** *Tyrwhitt conj.*; lawfull: *F1*
21 **give . . . use]** *Tyrwhitt conj.*; count giue much to as *F1*
23 **s.p. Cas.]** *F1*; *speech continued to Andromache, Q*
27 **dear]** *F1*; deere *Q*, *F1*
28 **precious-dear]** *hyphen, F3*; precious, deere, *F1*
29 **meanest]** mean'st *F1*
31 **No, faith,]** *Theobald (after F4)*; No faith *Q*, *F1*
45 **mother]** Mothers *F1*
58 **But . . . ruin.]** *F1*
67 **a-field]** *F3*; a field *Q*, *F1*
82 **do]** doth *F1*
84 **dolors]** dolour *F1*
85 **distraction]** *F1*; destruction *Q*
86 **antics]** *F1*; antiques *Q*
89 **yet]** yes *F1*
90 **s.d. Exit.]** *F1*
93 **worth]** of *F1*
94 **s.d. Exeunt . . . Hector.]** *Malone (after Capell)*
104 **a' th's]** o'th's *F1*
109 **s.d. Tearing the letter.]** *Rowe*
110 **Go, wind,]** *Capell (after Theobald)*; Go winde *Q*, *F1*
112 **Following this line F1 adds:** Pand. Why, but heare you? / Troy. Hence brother lackie; ignomie and shame / Pursue thy life, and liue aye with thy name.; *these lines are found in a slightly different version in Q at V.x.32–4 (see the text) and are repeated (reading, as in Q, broker, for brother) in F1 at the same point*
112 **s.d. severally]** *Malone*

V.iv

V.iv] *Rowe*
Location: *Rowe (subs.)*
o.s.d. Alarum.] *F1 (A Larum.; preceding Exeunt. at V.iii.112); placed as in Rowe*
o.s.d. Excursions.] in excursion. *F1*
2 **abominable]** *F4*; abhominable *Q*, *F1*
4 **young]** *F1*
9 **arrant]** errant *F1*
9 **A' th' t' other]** *ed. (after Rowe)*; Ath'tother *Q*; O'th'tother *F1*
10 **stale]** stole *F1*
17 **s.d. Enter . . . following.]** *Capell (from F1 s.d. Enter Diomed and Troylus.)*
18 **t' other]** *Rowe*; tother *Q*; th'other *F1*
19–20 **Fly . . . after.]** *as verse, F1*; *as prose, Q*
24–5 **Hold . . . sleeve!]** *as prose, F1*; *as verse, Q*
25 **s.d. Exeunt . . . fighting.]** *Capell (after Rowe)*
26 **thou]** *F1*
30 **s.d. Exit.]** *Rowe*

V.v

V.v] *Capell*
Location: *ed. (after Rowe)*
o.s.d. Servant] Seruants *F1*
5 **s.p. Serv.]** *F1*; Man. *Q*
5 **s.d. Exit.]** *Hanmer*
5 **s.d. Enter Agamemnon.]** *placed as in F1*; *after proof. l. 5, Q*
6 **Polydamas]** Polidamus *F1*
9 **Colossus-wise]** *hyphen, F1*
10 **kings]** *Hanmer*; Kings: *Q*, *F1*
11 **Epistrophus]** *Steevens*; Epistropus *Q*, *F1*
11 **Cedius]** *Capell*; Cedus *Q*, *F1*
11 **Polyxenes]** *Dyce*; Polixines *Q*, *F1*
12 **Thoas]** *Pope*; Thous *Q*, *F1*
21 **afoot]** *F3*; a foote *Q*, *F1*

22 **scaling**] scaled *F1*
24 **strawy**] straying *F1*
25 **a**] the *F1*
34 **him,**] *Rowe;* him. *Q;* him; *F1*
35 **Hector.**] *F1;* Hector, *Q*
41 **luck**] *F1;* lust *Q*
43 s.p. **Ajax.**] *F1; Q treats* Enter Aiax. *as s.p.*
47 s.d. **Exeunt.**] *Capell;* Exit. *Q, F1*

V.vi

V.vi] *Capell*
Location: *ed. (after Rowe)*
1 s.p. **Ajax.**] *F1; Q treats* Enter Aiax. *as s.p.*
1 s.d. **Diomed**] *F1;* Diom.
2 s.p. **Dio.**] *F1; Q treats* Enter Diom. *as s.p.*
5 **what, Troilus!**] *Hanmer;* what Troylus. *Q;* what Troylus? *F1*
11 s.d. **Exeunt fighting.**] *Rowe;* Exit Troylus. *F1*
11 s.d. **Enter Hector.**] *F1*
12 **Troilus?**] *F1;* Troylus, *Q*
13 s.p. **Achil.**] *F1; Q treats* Enter Achil. *as s.p.*
13 **ha!**] *om. F1*
13 s.d. **They fight.**] *Rowe (subs.)*
24 **him;**] *F1 (subs.);* him *Q*
26 **reak**] *ed.;* wreake *Q, F1*
26 **I end**] thou end *F1*
30 s.d. **Exit . . . armor.**] *ed. (after A. Walker)*

V.vii

V.vii] *Capell*
Location: *ed. (after Rowe)*
1 s.p. **Achil.**] *F1*
6 **execute**] *F1;* execut *Q*
6 **arms**] arme *F1*
8 s.d. **Exeunt.**] *Pope;* Exit. *Q, F1*
8 s.d. **fighting**] *Capell*
9 **cuckold . . . cuckold-maker**] *F1 (subs.);* cuck-old . . . cuck-old-maker *Q*
10 **dog!**] *Rowe (subs.);* dogge *Q;* dogge, *F1*
10, 11 **'Loo, Paris, 'loo! . . . 'Loo, Paris, 'loo!**] *F4 (subs. but with semicolon after first 'loo);* lowe, *Paris* lowe, . . . lowe *Paris,* lowe *Q;* lowe, *Paris* lowe; . . . lowe, *Paris,* lowe; *F1*
11 **double-henn'd**] *hyphen, Pope*
11 **Spartan**] sparrow *F1*

12 s.d. **Exeunt**] *Hanmer;* Exit *Q, F1*
12 s.d. **Menelaus**] *F1;* Menelus *Q*
12 s.d. **Margarelon**] *Capell*
13, 15, 23 s.pp. **Mar.**] *Capell;* Bast. *Q, F1*
16–7 **am bastard**] am a Bastard *F1*
20 **quarrel's**] *F1;* quarrells *Q*
22 s.d. **Exit.**] *Capell*
23 s.d. **Exit.**] Exeunt. *F1*

V.viii

V.viii] *Dyce*
Location: *ed. (after Rowe)*
3 **good**] *F1;* my *Q*
4 s.d. **Puts . . . him.**] *Malone (after Capell)*
4 s.d. **Myrmidons**] his Myrmidons *F1*
5 **Look**] *F1;* Loke *Q*
6 **ugly**] *F1;* ougly *Q*
6 **heels**] *Rowe (subs.);* heeles *Q;* heeles, *F1*
7 **dark'ning**] darking *F1*
10 s.d. **Hector falls.**] *Capell*
11 **thou next! Come**] thou: now *F1*
13 **and**] *om. F1*
13 **amain**] a maine *F1*
15 **retire**] retreat *F1*
15 **part**] *F1;* prat *Q*
16 s.p. **Myr.**] *Rowe;* One: *Q;* Gree. *F1*
16 **Troyans' trumpet sound**] Troian Trumpets sounds *F1*
19 **half-supp'd**] *hyphen, Pope*
20 **bait,**] *comma, F3;* baite: *Q;* bed; *F1*
20 s.d. **Sheathes his sword.**] *Capell (subs.)*

V.ix

V.ix] *Dyce*
Location: *ed. (after Rowe)*
o.s.d. **Sound retreat. Shout.**] *F1*
o.s.d. **Diomed**] *F1;* Diom: *Q*
1 **shout**] *F1*
1 **this**] that *F1*
3 s.p. **Soldiers.**] *Neilson;* Sould: *Q;* Sold. *F1*
3 s.d. **Within.**] *om. F1*
3, 4 **Hector's**] *F1;* Hectors *Q*
3 **slain! Achilles!**] *Pope;* slaine Achilles. *Q;* slaine, Achilles. *F1*
6 **as . . . man**] a man as good *F1*

V.x

V.x] *Dyce*

Location: *ed. (after Rowe)*
o.s.d. **Deiphobus**] *F2;* Diephobus *Q;* Deiphoebus *F1*
1 **field.**] *ed.;* field, *Q, F1*
1 s.d. **Enter Troilus.**] *after l. 2, F1*
2 **Never . . . night—**] *F1 continues line to* Aeneas, *but assigns to Troilus* Hector is slaine. *in l. 3*
5 **beastly**] *F1;* bestly *Q*
8 **say,**] *Theobald;* say *Q, F1*
12 **fear,**] *F1;* feare *Q*
16 **scritch-owl**] *ed.;* scrich-ould *Q;* screech-oule *F1 (no hyphen)*
17 **in to**] *F1;* into *Q*
17 **there, "Hector's**] *F1 (subs.);* their Hectors *Q*
20 **Cold**] *Pope;* Could *Q;* Coole *F1*
21 **Scare**] *F3;* Scarre *Q, F1*
21–2 **But . . . dead;**] *F1*
23 **yet.**] *F1 (subs.);* yet *Q*
23 **vile**] *F1;* proud *Q*
23 **abominable**] *F4;* abhominable *Q, F1*
23 **tents,**] *F1;* tents: *Q*
24 **pight**] *F1;* pitcht *Q*
26 **great-siz'd**] *hyphen, Pope*
29 **frenzy's**] *Pope;* frienzes *Q;* frensies *F1*
30 **march. To Troy**] *ed.;* march, to Troy *Q;* march to Troy, *F1*
32 **hear you, hear**] *F1;* here you, here *Q*
33 s.d. **Strikes him.**] *Rowe*
33 **Ignominy,**] ignomy, and *F1*
34 s.d. **Exeunt . . . Pandarus.**] Exeunt. *F1*
35 **my**] mine *F1*
36 **world, world!**] *F1;* world— *Q*
37 **traders**] *Craig conj.;* traitors *Q, F1*
38 **a-work**] *F1* (aworke); a worke *Q*
39 **lov'd**] desir'd *F1*
39 **loath'd**] *F1;* loathed *Q*
41 **humble-bee**] *hyphen, Pope*
46 **cloths**] *Rowe;* cloathes *Q, F1*
47 **Pandar's**] *Rowe;* Pandars *Q;* Panders *F1 (not in italics as a proper name)*
50 **your**] *F1;* my *Q*
51 **hold-door**] *F1;* hold-ore *Q*
54 **galled**] *F1;* gauled *Q*
56 s.d. **Exit.**] *Rowe;* Exeunt. / FINIS. *F1;* FINIS. *Q*

Hector, Ajax, and Thersites. From the title-pages of Thomas Heywood's *The Iron Age, Parts 1 and 2* (1632). The combat of Hector and Ajax here pictured (left) is in marked contrast to their chivalric encounter in *Troilus and Cressida* (IV.v). Hector's boulder may be found in Homer (*Iliad*, Book VII), but Ajax' "farre greater stone" (Chapman's translation) has been replaced with a tree torn up by its roots (a detail perhaps original with Heywood, who had earlier used it in his *Troia Britannica*, 1609). In the second woodcut (only part of which is reproduced) notice Thersites' unabashedly Elizabethan costume, with rapier, boots, and spurs, typical of the mixed costuming tradition of the period. (*By permission of the Harvard College Library*)

All's Well That Ends Well

THE PLOT OF *All's Well That Ends Well* is a tissue of traditional folk motifs. The story of the abandoned wife who performs a seemingly impossible series of tasks in order to regain her husband is at least as old as the myth of Eros and Psyche. It has analogues in many of the literatures of the world. The hero or heroine who achieves great good fortune by knowing how to cure the sickness of the king when everyone else has failed, the bed-trick, the exchange of rings, and the association of virginity with magical power are all story elements with reverberations originating far back in the past. In shaping them into a dramatic plot, Shakespeare was strongly influenced by the story of Giletta of Narbona, told as the ninth story of the third day in Boccaccio's *Decameron*. It is possible that he read the Italian original, but his chief source was probably the English translation, in William Painter's collection *The Palace of Pleasure* (1566–67, 1575).

Giletta of Narbona is the daughter of a wealthy and celebrated physician. She falls in love with Beltramo, the only son of the noble count by whom her father is employed. The count dies and Beltramo goes to Paris as a ward of the French king, who is suffering from an apparently incurable disease. When Giletta's own father also dies, she follows Beltramo to Paris, heals the king with the help of a remedy she has inherited, and then claims Beltramo as her reward. Beltramo himself is horrified by the idea, and even the king is reluctant to agree to a marriage so unequal. He keeps his word to Giletta, however, and Beltramo is forced to yield. Immediately after the wedding, Beltramo flees to Italy and enters the service of the Florentines against the Sienese. Giletta, an unhappy virgin wife, remains for a time in Rossiglione, where she wins the love and respect of all her husband's subjects. Hearing, however, of Beltramo's bitter jest, that he would consent to live with his wife when she possessed herself of a ring from which he was never parted and came to him with their son in her arms, conditions impossible (as he thought) to fulfill, she disguises herself as a pilgrim and journeys to Florence. There, discovering that Beltramo is paying court to the daughter of an impoverished gentlewoman of the city, she persuades the two women to help her. The daughter exacts Beltramo's ring as the price of her surrender, and Giletta then, for some time, secretly supplies her place in Beltramo's bed. When she is sure she is pregnant, she puts an end to these nocturnal meetings, rewards the gentlewoman and her daughter, and sends them out of Florence. Beltramo returns to Rossiglione where, some time later, Giletta suddenly appears to confront him with the ring and twin sons so like their father that Beltramo cannot help but recognize them as his own. All the courtiers and ladies of Rossiglione plead that Giletta should be accepted, and Beltramo, "perceiving her constant mind and good wit, and the two fair young boys," gladly agrees: he sets up a great feast and "from that time forth he loved and honored her as his dear spouse and wife."

As told by Boccaccio and Painter, this story has a simple shape and a clarity which are satisfying and wholly unproblematic. Everyone, even the king, is agreed at the beginning that Giletta, though wealthy, is too low-born to be Countess of Rossiglione. In her first attempt, made as the physician's daughter, she fails to win anything more than the outward appearance of rank. Subsequently, while administering Beltramo's estates, and then in Florence, she demonstrates an innate aristocracy of wit and enterprise so compelling that it annihilates the class barrier. She

499

wins over Beltramo's household and subjects, then Beltramo himself, through sheer intellect and resourcefulness. No one in the story blames Beltramo for his initial repudiation. The king forced him into a demeaning marriage, and it rests entirely with Giletta to prove by her "diligence" that there might be something to recommend such a misalliance after all. It is true that the reader wants Giletta to succeed, but no blame attaches itself to Beltramo for being hard to persuade. Only through sheer intelligence, and by demonstrating that she can give her husband sons who inherit his face as well as his name, can Giletta make herself Beltramo's equal, his wife in fact and not in law only.

As usual, Shakespeare greatly compressed the time-span of Boccaccio's story, reducing it to a more manageably dramatic compass. He also made some significant changes in the situation and characters of the two protagonists. Helena, unlike Giletta, is poor as well as low-born, and she lacks the total self-sufficiency and some of the cunning of her prototype. Bertram, her reluctant husband, stands convicted of faults considerably more damning than Beltramo's aristocratic pride. He is callow and insensitive, a lecher, an oath-breaker, and a liar, who not only misprizes Helena but makes other serious mistakes of judgment as well. Shakespeare also added four major characters for whom there were no equivalents in his source; the old Countess of Rossillion, Lafew, Parolles, and the fool Lavatch. All four have one thing in common: they operate in their different ways, throughout the comedy, to raise Helena in our estimation and to degrade Bertram. The play that results has sacrificed the simplicity and clear emotional emphasis of the folk-tale from which it derives. Indeed it seems positively to stress the incompatibility between characters who are sophisticated and complex and a plot which is neither of these things. Like its successor *Measure for Measure*, *All's Well That Ends Well* often seems to be questioning its own story material and, particularly in the final scene, to look ironically at its own title and at the very nature of comedy.

It is virtually axiomatic in comedy since the time of Menander that when a young man or woman wishes to marry purely for love, overleaping disparities of birth, wealth, and position, the older generation represented by fathers, mothers, uncles, and guardians will strenuously oppose such an attempted infringement of the laws of established society. *All's Well That Ends Well*, with no help whatever from its source, insists upon inverting this pattern. Boccaccio's king, though grateful for his cure, did not relish bestowing Beltramo upon a rich physician's daughter. Shakespeare's King, by contrast, is warmly approving of the match, even though Helena, unlike Giletta, is not only a commoner but poor. The old lord Lafew, the most eminent of the King's courtiers, also adopts the attitude that nothing can be too good for her. Most surprising of all, the old Countess of Rossillion, Bertram's mother, greets the news that her only son has been married to her waiting-gentlewoman with unfeigned delight. In this

play it is the old who are generous and flexible in their social attitudes while the young—Bertram, Parolles, and (according to one view) the young lords whose constraint and inner fear at the prospect of being chosen by Helena are mocked by Lafew—tend to be class-conscious snobs.

All's Well That Ends Well is a play filled with nostalgia for the past, concerned to evoke the remembrance of better times. Rossillion, where the action begins and ends, is an almost Chekhovian backwater, elegiac and autumnal, a world preserved in amber. It derives its character chiefly from the old Countess, from the shrewd and "unhappy" fool favored by her late husband, and from memories of the dead: Bertram's father, or that wonder-working physician Gerard de Narbon whose skill, ultimately, was not proof against his own mortality. It is understandable, to some extent, that young Bertram should be impatient to leave this place, even as it is understandable that he should experience an initial psychological shock when told he must marry a girl he has known there all his life as a dependent, a kind of inferior sister. Yet neither Paris nor Florence, the two places to which he tries to escape, functions for him as that heightened, more extraordinary world familiar in so many of Shakespeare's comedies. In neither is he transformed.

In Paris as at Rossillion, the Golden Age lies in the past. The King is old and fretful, a man who has outlived his health, his friends, and his pleasure in living. The court which surrounds him is hard-headed and rational and Lafew summarizes its ordinary way of thinking when he complains, from the standpoint of an older generation, that

> They say miracles are past, and we have our philosophical persons, to make modern and familiar, things supernatural and causeless. Hence is it that we make trifles of terrors, ensconcing ourselves into seeming knowledge, when we should submit ourselves to an unknown fear. (II.iii.1–6)

Into this sceptical, hard-headed world comes Helena, offering something quite alien to it, in the form of a miraculous cure, and demanding a fairy-tale marriage as her reward. The cure, achieved by way of a secret transmitted to her from the past, is unexpectedly successful. The marriage is not. Bertram refuses to accommodate himself to the archetypal story pattern, to recognize any return of the Golden Age. A struggle develops between the demands of romance, or comic form, and the stubborn resistance set up by a realistic, everyday world in which merit is not always rewarded, or even recognized for what it is. In this world, unicorns do not exist to testify to the mystic power of virginity, and Prince Charming is likely to prefer the fashionably dressed elder sisters to beauty in rags. Love itself is not simply the servant of a fantastic plot, but a matter of complex adjustments within the personality.

From Paris, Bertram flees to Florence, a place to which his thoughts inclined him even before Helena's arrival. Like the other young lords, he is susceptible for all his rationalism to the glamour of war, and the

Florentines and the Sienese are, as the King puts it, "by th' ears" (I.ii.1). The phrase suggests a dogfight more than it does an epic combat out of the pages of chivalry, but the noble youth of France are still eager to go and fight on either side of this dispute, purely for the sake of personal honor. Honor is an important word in *All's Well That Ends Well* generally, but it is also one that takes some hard, Falstaffian knocks. The King of France will have nothing to do himself with the Italian imbroglio, for hard-headed political reasons, nor does he care if his courtiers join the Florentines or the Sienese. The First Lord tells the Duke of Florence at the beginning of Act III, after he has heard (but the theatre audience has not) "the fundamental reasons of this war," that "Holy seems the quarrel / Upon your Grace's part; black and fearful / On the opposer," and the words are recognizably a parody of what anyone involved in any war, for whatever reason, always says. Basically, Italy is a kind of gymnasium where the youth of France may exercise idle limbs and minds and indulge the only romanticism in which they still believe. The conflict itself ends in a peace treaty of an unspecified kind, after the usual quantity of bloodshed and embarrassing accidents: "There was excellent command—to charge in with our horse upon our own wings, and to rend our own soldiers!" (III.vi.48–50). Helena comes close to echoing Falstaff's words at Shrewsbury, although the emotion which prompts them is very different, when she laments that "honor but of danger wins a scar, / As oft it loses all" (III.ii.121–22). Moreover, as Lavatch points out (IV.v.94–101), even honor's scar may be ambiguous. The velvet patch on the face of the returning warrior may conceal wounds inflicted by syphilis rather than the sword.

Although Lafew, the King, and the old Countess fondly remember an age in which martial honor was something tangible and significant, it seems to have declined now into a matter of game-playing and mere words. Honor is not the only quality to be trivialized in this way. Shakespeare is concerned throughout to contrast a vanished world of the past in which words were subordinate to facts with a debased, present-day society in which language has become an empty and often a lying substitute for deeds. The King remembers and praises Bertram's father, his dead friend, as a man whose "tongue obey'd his hand" (I.ii.41). This proper subservience of speech to behavior tends now to be reversed or else, even more disturbingly, there is simply no connection at all between what people say and what they think and do. The King, Lafew, and the Countess constantly stress the rightful primacy of facts and intrinsic qualities over misleading verbal descriptions. All these members of an older generation know what the King later tries to tell Bertram, that

> Good alone
> Is good, without a name; vileness is so:
> The property by what it is should go,
> Not by the title.   (II.iii.128–31)

"The mere word's a slave," he goes on, trying to make

Bertram see that the fact that Helena is young, wise, and fair matters far more than the superficial social description of her as "a poor physician's daughter." He wastes his breath, however, on a young man whose best friend and greatest influence is called, entirely accurately, Parolles.

Parolles is an embodiment of that discrepancy between words and deed which plays so important a part in the play as a whole. The glorious, swashbuckling past upon which he lives, dines out at ordinaries, and attracts rich young patrons like Bertram is nothing but a verbal construct. He is really a parasite and a coward, sheltering behind a facade of language and fine clothes. He talks constantly of honor but has none, of guns and drums and wounds but in fact is timorous as a mouse. Parolles descends from a venerable line of braggart warriors, talkers and not doers, who originate with Aristophanes and then swagger their way through Menander, Plautus, and Terence into Elizabethan comedy. Shakespeare had already experimented with the *miles gloriosus* type in Don Armado, Ancient Pistol, and (with a difference) Falstaff. Parolles, however, is the most severely criticized of them all. He bears a heavy weight of moral blame for encouraging Bertram to corrupt "a well-derived nature" (III.ii.88), for upholding snobbery and vice. Lafew is entirely accurate when he declares that "there can be no kernel in this light nut; the soul of this man is his clothes" (II.v.43–44). Here, as elsewhere in the comedy, an extravagance of dress concealing emptiness or corruption within is used as a variant on the theme of fine words cloaking innate baseness. It is the way of the world that, for a time, the deception should pass, that Parolles should convince Bertram with words and clothes, while "virtue's steely bones / Looks bleak i' th' cold wind" (I.i.103–4). Lafew, Helena, Lavatch, and the Countess are never deceived by him, however, and ultimately he is subjected to a public exposure and humiliation that is crushing in a manner more usually associated with the "comical satires" of Ben Jonson than with Shakespeare. At the end, this "manifold linguist" is forced ignominiously into the position that Helena has maintained gracefully all along: "Simply the thing I am / Shall make me live" (IV.iii.333–34).

Helena herself is prized by the older generation not only because they recognize her intrinsic worth, but because she is a living example of the attitudes of the past. Certainly she makes her distrust of disembodied words plain from the start. In her imagination, the court to which Bertram has been despatched is a place of verbal conceits, "Of pretty, fond, adoptious christendoms" (I.i.174) which dress love up in fashionable disguises, losing the substance in the show. Left behind at Rossillion, she worries with some cause about what may happen to Bertram there and laments, characteristically, that "wishing well had not a body in't, / Which might be felt" (I.i.181–82). In Paris, she achieves the man she loves through an action, the healing of the King, and then discovers that her victory is hollow, a matter of words alone. She is only "the shadow of a wife . . . The name, and not the thing" (V.iii.307–8). Defeated and self-accusing, she attires herself as a pilgrim and makes her way towards Saint Jaques le Grand. Unlike Giletta, who intended quite specifically to find her husband and accomplish the task set, Helena seems to arrive in Florence more by accident than purpose. Once there, however, she proceeds to make the same use of Diana and her mother that Giletta had done, and with the same success. It is at this point that problems of a kind non-existent in Boccaccio's story rear themselves in Shakespeare's play.

Although some scholars have tried to identify *All's Well That Ends Well* with the mysterious *Love's Labor's Won*, a play mentioned by Meres in 1598 among the other early comedies of Shakespeare, its whole quality and verbal character really argue for a date around 1602–3, after *Hamlet* and *Troilus and Cressida* and just before *Measure for Measure*. The verse of *All's Well That Ends Well*—compressed, elliptical, abstract, often tortuous and obscure—is very different from the fluid, concrete, and playful language of the early comedies but, in some respects, like that of *Troilus and Cressida* and *Measure for Measure*. Even more important, the comedy ends by using the folk-motif of the bed-trick to force a clash between those opposing elements of fairy-tale and realism, of romance motivation and psychological probability, which have existed in so uneasy a harmony throughout. In the final scene of *All's Well That Ends Well*, romance wins a kind of pyrrhic victory, even as it does, again through the bed-trick, in a blatantly fictional last act of *Measure for Measure* a year later. Both victories are disturbing, because they raise in a particularly acute and deliberate fashion doubts as to the validity of comedy as an image of truth.

Bertram pays adulterous court to Diana with vows and false promises which she recognizes as such: "therefore your oaths / Are words and poor conditions, but unseal'd" (IV.ii.29–30). Back in France, he will deny that he ever made them. Helena, by contrast, takes words which Bertram originally intended only as a formula, a heightened way of declaring that he would never accept her as his wife, and interprets them literally. She forces language to become fact and confronts Bertram at the end not with words but with two talismanic things: the ring and the child she has conceived. Thematically, in terms of the debate between words and deeds which has been sustained throughout the play, this resolution is entirely right and proper. Psychologically, and in dramatic terms, it is difficult in ways that Shakespeare seems to have wanted to emphasize rather than to conceal.

In Boccaccio's story, Giletta is never believed to be dead. She reappears at Rossiglione after a long absence but not, as Helena seems to do, from the grave. Helena's supposed death is credited by other characters in the play on the best evidence: letters received from her at Saint Jaques le Grand describing her grief and illness and finally, confirmation of her decease from "the rector of the place" (IV.iii.58–59). Critics who do not like Helena often point out that she has apparently not only concocted a monstrous lie in these

letters but, apparently, has bribed the rector to forge a death certificate. Helena's "death," however, will not bear investigation in such literal terms, any more than will Hermione's in *The Winter's Tale*, and for much the same reasons. Helena dies so that Diana in the final scene can expound her riddle, "one that's dead is quick" (V.iii.303), and so that the transformation of Helena herself from a condition of nothingness—a "ghost," a "shadow," a wife in name alone—into a condition replete with life and joy may be as striking as possible. There is a powerful emotionalism in the last scene of this play. It derives, however, from an accord which, unlike the wholly consistent ending of *The Winter's Tale*, seems to ignore and leave unresolved the major issues of the play.

By introducing Helena's mock-death and resurrection, Shakespeare debased Bertram in a way for which there was no precedent in his source. In Boccaccio, the poor gentlewoman and her daughter remained in Florence after helping Giletta. Diana and her mother, on the other hand, appear in Rossillion to remind Bertram that he has sworn to marry Diana after his wife's death, and to claim fulfillment now of that promise. Bertram's behavior in these straits is very like that of Angelo when faced with Isabella and Mariana at the end of *Measure for Measure*: he turns and twists, lies and calumniates, providing an entirely realistic demonstration of just how far he can go in prevarication and meanness. The revelation of Helena, her fairy-tale task accomplished, clears him of a murder charge, but it does not elicit from him anything but the most perfunctory indication of acceptance and apology. Shakespeare might easily have made Bertram eloquent here, but he did not choose to. He was perhaps too conscious of the fact that the second winning of Bertram, although more arduous, nonetheless belongs to exactly the same world of fairy-tale and romance as the first. In terms of psychological truth, there is no more reason for Bertram to accept Helena because of the bed-trick than because of the miraculous healing of the King. This second clash between realism and fable, the old world and the new, is suggested but comes to no issue. Instead, the entire scene gradually fades away and becomes dim, retreating visibly into the realm of romance.

The character of the verse of *All's Well That Ends Well* alters markedly in the last fifty lines of the play. It becomes simple, direct, and archaic: the transparent language of riddle-games and fables. Most of it is further distanced by being cast in the form of rhyming couplets whose inevitability of sound and rhythm help to characterize the larger inevitability of the archetypal happy ending. Diana plays with the situation like a good fairy about to restore a princess who vanished long ago, teasing the baffled King, enjoying mystification for its own sake. By the time Helena appears with her two talismans, the ring and the unborn child, the comedy has loosed its moorings and floated off into a poignant, but attenuated, world of unbelief. Blithely, the King turns to Diana and enjoins her to select any husband she fancies from among the nobles of his court. One might think that the misfortunes of

Helena would make him wary of this particular matrimonial method, but no one moves to break the spell. Only in the odd conditional introduced into the King's final couplet, the unexpectedly tentative "seems" and "if," is a shadow of doubt allowed to return:

All yet seems well, and if it end so meet,
The bitter past, more welcome is the sweet.

The title of the comedy itself, referred to now by the King as it was previously, but more confidently, by Helena herself (IV.iv.33–36,V.i.25), was proverbial. Like the proverbs continually employed in a perverse and contradictory fashion by the bitter fool Lavatch—traditional bits of lore existing uneasily in a world grown too complex for such simplifications—it serves as a gentle reminder that fairy-tales, ultimately, are not true.

Anne Barton

The table of the heart. From Geffrey Whitney, *A Choice of Emblems* (1586). When Helena in *All's Well* (I.i.94–95) describes how she sits and draws Bertram's "arched brows, his hawking eye, his curls, / In our heart's table," she is referring metaphorically to the idea expressed in the emblem above, which shows a man inscribing the lineaments of his friend on a wax tablet held against the friend's heart. So too, Hamlet, when he exclaims, "My tables—meet it is I set it down / That one may smile, and smile, and be a villain!" (*Hamlet*, I.v.107–8), is literally applying Whitney's advice, in the verses accompanying the emblem, to record "His wordes and deedes, that beares the face of frende," though in Hamlet's case the "friend" is his bitter enemy Claudius. For a picture of a contemporary pocket "tables" or table-book, see p. 146.

All's Well That Ends Well

[DRAMATIS PERSONAE

KING OF FRANCE
DUKE OF FLORENCE
BERTRAM, *Count of Rossillion*
LAFEW, *an old lord*
PAROLLES, *a parasitical follower of Bertram*
Two French LORDS, *in the Florentine service*
RINALDO, *a steward* ⎱ *servants to the Countess of*
LAVATCH, *a clown* ⎰ *Rossillion*
PAGE
GENTLEMAN, *an astringer*

COUNTESS OF ROSSILLION, *mother to Bertram*
HELENA, *a gentlewoman protected by the Countess*
An old WIDOW *of Florence*
DIANA, *daughter to the Widow*
VIOLENTA ⎱ *neighbors and friends to the Widow*
MARIANA ⎰
LORDS, OFFICERS, SOLDIERS, *etc., French and Florentine*

SCENE: *Rossillion; Paris; Florence; Marseilles*]

ACT I, SCENE I

Enter young BERTRAM, *Count of Rossillion, his mother* [*the* COUNTESS OF ROSSILLION], *and* HELENA, LORD LAFEW, *all in black.*

Count. In delivering my son from me, I bury a second husband.

Ber. And I in going, madam, weep o'er my father's death anew; but I must attend his Majesty's command, to whom I am now in ward, evermore in subjection. 5

Laf. You shall find of the King a husband, madam; you, sir, a father. He that so generally is at all times good must of necessity hold his virtue to you, whose worthiness would stir it up where it wanted rather than lack it where there is such abundance. 10

Count. What hope is there of his Majesty's amendment?

Laf. He hath abandon'd his physicians, madam, under whose practices he hath persecuted time with hope, and finds no other advantage in the process but only the losing of hope by time. 16

Count. This young gentlewoman had a father—O, that "had," how sad a passage 'tis!—whose skill was almost as great as his honesty; had it stretch'd so far, would have made nature immortal, and death 20 should have play for lack of work. Would for the King's sake he were living! I think it would be the death of the King's disease.

Laf. How call'd you the man you speak of, madam? 25

Count. He was famous, sir, in his profession, and it was his great right to be so—Gerard de Narbon.

Laf. He was excellent indeed, madam. The King very lately spoke of him admiringly and mourningly. He was skillful enough to have liv'd still, if knowledge could be set up against mortality. 31

Ber. What is it, my good lord, the King languishes of?

Laf. A fistula, my lord.

Ber. I heard not of it before. 35

Words and passages enclosed in square brackets in the text above are either emendations of the copy-text or additions to it. The Textual Notes immediately following the play cite the earliest authority for every such change or insertion and supply the reading of the copy-text wherever it is emended in this edition.

I.i. Location: Rossillion. The Count's palace. (Shakespeare's *Rossillion* is an anglicized form of *Rousillon*, the name of a former province of southern France, just north of the eastern end of the Pyrenees.)
1. **In . . . husband:** The Countess means (in the courtly language that she and Lafew use in this scene and elsewhere) that her son's departure from home causes her as much sorrow as her husband's death; but it has often been pointed out that in her form of words and especially the several possible meanings of *deliver* (not only "send" but also "give birth to" and "liberate") can be found the germ of themes—birth and death, growing up and the relationship between the generations—that are to assume great importance in the play.   4. **attend:** heed, obey.
5. **to . . . ward:** whose ward I now am. On the old Count's death the King has become the guardian of his son (as a minor) and his estates.   **evermore in subjection:** i.e. whose subject I shall always be (but the words suggest also his impatience at being still under authority).   6. **of:** in.   7. **generally:** universally, i.e. to one and all.
8. **hold:** maintain, be consistent in extending.
9. **stir . . . wanted:** arouse goodness even in one who lacked it.

11–12. **amendment:** recovery.
13. **He . . . physicians.** A reversal of the usual "His physicians have abandoned him (i.e. given up hope of his recovery)."
14. **practices:** professional ministrations.
14–15. **persecuted . . . hope:** afflicted his days (with painful treatments) in hope of cure (?). Alternatively, *persecuted* (used nowhere else by Shakespeare) may mean simply "followed out, spent."
18. **passage:** expression, i.e. word (with additional suggestion of "passing away").   19. **honesty:** integrity, honor.
19–20. **stretch'd so far:** i.e. been as great as his "honesty" (which was absolute).   21. **should:** would certainly.
27. **his great right:** i.e. his right by reason of his greatness.
30. **still:** forever.   34. **fistula:** a kind of ulcer.

Laf. I would it were not notorious. Was this gentlewoman the daughter of Gerard de Narbon?

Count. His sole child, my lord, and bequeath'd to my overlooking. I have those hopes of her good that her education promises; her dispositions she 40 inherits, which makes fair gifts fairer; for where an unclean mind carries virtuous qualities, there commendations go with pity: they are virtues and traitors too. In her they are the better for their simpleness; she derives her honesty, and achieves her goodness. 45

Laf. Your commendations, madam, get from her tears.

Count. 'Tis the best brine a maiden can season her praise in. The remembrance of her father never approaches her heart but the tyranny of her sorrows 50 takes all livelihood from her cheek. No more of this, Helena; go to, no more, lest it be rather thought you affect a sorrow than to have—

Hel. I do affect a sorrow indeed, but I have it too.

Laf. Moderate lamentation is the right of the dead, excessive grief the enemy to the living. 56

Count. If the living be enemy to the grief, the excess makes it soon mortal.

Ber. Madam, I desire your holy wishes.

Laf. How understand we that? 60

Count. Be thou blest, Bertram, and succeed thy father
In manners as in shape! Thy blood and virtue

Contend for empire in thee, and thy goodness
Share with thy birthright! Love all, trust a few,
Do wrong to none. Be able for thine enemy 65
Rather in power than use, and keep thy friend
Under thy own life's key. Be check'd for silence,
But never tax'd for speech. What heaven more will,
That thee may furnish, and my prayers pluck down,
Fall on thy head!—Farewell, my lord. 70
'Tis an unseason'd courtier, good my lord,
Advise him.

Laf.   He cannot want the best
That shall attend his love.

Count.   Heaven bless him!
Farewell, Bertram.

Ber.   The best wishes that can
Be forged in your thoughts be servants to you! 75

[*Exit Countess.*]

[*To Helena.*]   Be comfortable to my mother, your mistress,
And make much of her.

Laf.   Farewell, pretty lady,
You must hold the credit of your father.

[*Exeunt Bertram and Lafew.*]

Hel. O, were that all! I think not on my father,
And these great tears grace his remembrance more
Than those I shed for him. What was he like? 81
I have forgot him. My imagination
Carries no favor in't but Bertram's.
I am undone, there is no living, none,
If Bertram be away. 'Twere all one 85
That I should love a bright particular star
And think to wed it, he is so above me.
In his bright radiance and collateral light
Must I be comforted, not in his sphere.
Th' ambition in my love thus plagues itself: 90
The hind that would be mated by the lion
Must die for love. 'Twas pretty, though a plague,
To see him every hour, to sit and draw
His arched brows, his hawking eye, his curls,
In our heart's table—heart too capable 95

---

36. I ... notorious: I wish it were not so settled a fact that everyone knows of it.   **39. overlooking:** supervision.
40. education: upbringing.
40–41. her dispositions she inherits: her inborn traits and tendencies. Modern idiom would require *the* for *her*.
41. which ... fairer: which (i.e. education) enhances fine natural qualities.
42. unclean mind: i.e. bad nature.   **virtuous qualities:** acquired excellences, benefits of good training.
43. go with pity: are mingled with regret.   **traitors.** Because "the advantages of education enable an ill mind to go further in wickedness than it would have done without them" (Warburton).
44. simpleness: being unmixed (with vice).
45. derives: inherits.   **achieves:** attains by her own efforts.
48. season: preserve (a culinary image).   **50. tyranny:** severity.
51. livelihood: (1) liveliness, animation; (2) means of living, i.e. blood.
52. Helena. Elsewhere in the dialogue the heroine's name is invariably *Helen* (F1 *Hellen*), though the longer form occurs several times in the stage directions.   **go to:** a stock expression of reproof or remonstrance.
53. affect ... have. The Countess does not mean that Helena will be suspected of hypocritically pretending a grief she has never felt (the first use of *affect* in this sense recorded in *O.E.D.* is from 1661), but that she will be suspected of making an outward show of grief in excess of what she now (after a lapse of time) feels. The situation strongly recalls *Hamlet*, I.ii.68 ff., where Gertrude urges Hamlet to put off his external show of mourning.   **have—.** The F1 dash, here retained, is a puzzle. The sense of the sentence is complete (although modern idiom would require *than have it* in place of *than to have*), as Helena's reply, picking up the contrast between *affect* and *have*, confirms. A similar dash at I.iii.153 has been interpreted as signalling a pause for a reply that is slow to come, and the same explanation might serve here.
54. I ... too. Like Hamlet, Helena acknowledges that she does make outward show of sorrow but asserts that the show is not in excess of what she feels. Not until lines 79 ff. do we learn that the sorrow is not for her father.
55. right: rightful due. Lafew's speech continues the parallel with *Hamlet* (I.ii.87 ff.).   **57. be ...:** i.e. resist excessive grief.
57–58. the excess ... mortal: it soon dies of its own excess.
60. How ... that. The reason for this remark is obscure; some commentators suggest that the line is misplaced in F1, others that Lafew considers Bertram's request an impolite interruption.
61–70. Be ... head. With these lines cf. Polonius' advice to Laertes (*Hamlet*, I.iii.57–81).
62. manners: behavior, moral conduct.   **blood and virtue:** inherited

and acquired good qualities (synonymous with *birthright* and *goodness* in the second half of the sentence).
63. Contend for empire: vie for rule.
64. Share: divide the rule.   **Love:** behave amiably to.
65. able for: competent to deal with.
66. in power: in capability, potentially.
66–67. keep ... key: safeguard your friend's life as you safeguard your own.   **67. check'd:** rebuked.
68. tax'd for speech: taken to task for excessive or injudicious talk.
69. furnish: supply advantageously.   **pluck:** draw.
71. unseason'd: unripe.
72–73. He ... love. Variously interpreted; perhaps "He shall not lack the best advice that my good will toward him can produce."
75. forged: shaped, devised.   **be ... you:** be at your command, i.e. be realized.   **76. comfortable:** serviceable.
77. make ... her: pay her great respect, devote yourself to her.
78. hold the credit: maintain the high reputation.   **79. on:** of.
80. grace his remembrance. Because they are taken by others to be a tribute to him (?).   **more.** Because more numerous (?).
81. shed. Past tense.
83. Carries no favor: contains no face (perhaps with play on "wears no love-token").   **85–86. 'Twere ... That:** it is just as if.
88. collateral: indirect; here, shining from a different sphere. The heavenly bodies, supposedly revolving in concentric spheres, were said to move collaterally.   **90. ambition:** loftiness of aim.
91. hind: female deer.   **94. hawking:** keen, piercing.
95. table: drawing-board. Cf. Sonnet 24.1–2: "My heart hath play'd the painter and hath stell'd / Thy beauty's form in table of my heart."   **capable:** receptive of impressions, susceptible.

Of every line and trick of his sweet favor.
But now he's gone, and my idolatrous fancy
Must sanctify his reliques. Who comes here?

Enter PAROLLES.

[*Aside.*] One that goes with him. I love him for his
      sake,
And yet I know him a notorious liar,   100
Think him a great way fool, soly a coward;
Yet these fix'd evils sit so fit in him,
That they take place when virtue's steely bones
Looks bleak i' th' cold wind. Withal, full oft we see
Cold wisdom waiting on superfluous folly.   105
      Par. 'Save you, fair queen!
      Hel. And you, monarch!
      Par. No.
      Hel. And no.
      Par. Are you meditating on virginity?   110
      Hel. Ay. You have some stain of soldier in you;
let me ask a question. Man is enemy to virginity; how
may we barricado it against him?
      Par. Keep him out.
      Hel. But he assails, and our virginity though
valiant, in the defense yet is weak. Unfold to us some
warlike resistance.   117
      Par. There is none. Man, setting down before you,
will undermine you and blow you up.
      Hel. Bless our poor virginity from underminers
and blowers-up! Is there no military policy how
virgins might blow up men?   122
      Par. Virginity being blown down, man will
quicklier be blown up. Marry, in blowing him down
again, with the breach yourselves made, you lose your
city. It is not politic in the commonwealth of   126
nature to preserve virginity. Loss of virginity is
rational increase, and there was never virgin [got] till
virginity was first lost. That you were made of is
metal to make virgins. Virginity, by being once lost,
may be ten times found; by being ever kept, it is   131
ever lost. 'Tis too cold a companion; away with't!

      Hel. I will stand for't a little, though therefore
I die a virgin.
      Par. There's little can be said in't, 'tis against the
rule of nature. To speak on the part of virginity is to
accuse your mothers, which is most infallible   137
disobedience. He that hangs himself is a virgin;
virginity murthers itself, and should be buried in high-
ways out of all sanctified limit, as a desperate offend-
ress against nature. Virginity breeds mites, much like
a cheese, consumes itself to the very paring, and   142
so dies with feeding his own stomach. Besides,
virginity is peevish, proud, idle, made of self-love,
which is the most inhibited sin in the canon. Keep it
not, you cannot choose but lose by't. Out with't!
Within [t' one] year it will make itself two,   147
which is a goodly increase, and the principal itself not
much the worse. Away with't!
      Hel. How might one do, sir, to lose it to her own
liking?   151
      Par. Let me see. Marry, ill, to like him that ne'er
it likes. 'Tis a commodity will lose the gloss with
lying: the longer kept, the less worth. Off with't
while 'tis vendible; answer the time of request.
Virginity, like an old courtier, wears her cap out of
fashion, richly suited, but unsuitable—just like   157
the brooch and the toothpick, which [wear] not now.
Your date is better in your pie and your porridge than
in your cheek; and your virginity, your old virginity,
is like one of our French wither'd pears, it looks ill,
it eats drily, marry, 'tis a wither'd pear; it was   162
formerly better, marry, yet 'tis a wither'd pear. Will
you any thing with it?
      Hel. Not my virginity yet: [. . . .]   165
There shall your master have a thousand loves,
A mother, and a mistress, and a friend,

---

96. **trick:** characteristic trait or expression.   97. **fancy:** love.
98. **sanctify his reliques:** worship whatever reminders of him remain.
s.d. **Parolles.** The name means "words" (French *paroles*), with an appropriateness that quickly becomes evident.
99. **love:** am well disposed toward.
101. **a great way:** largely a.   **soly:** solely, wholly.
102. **fix'd evils:** firmly established vices.   **sit . . . him:** fit him so becomingly (the first occurrence of the clothing imagery with which Parolles is associated).
103. **take place:** find acceptance (?) or take precedence (?).
104. **Looks.** Shakespeare frequently uses a verb in -*s* with a noun that is plural in form but may be taken as singular in sense.   **Withal:** therewith, i.e. in consequence of this.
105. **Cold . . . superfluous:** unprovided . . . enjoying superabundance; or (more specifically) naked . . . overdressed.
106. **'Save:** God save.   **queen.** An inflated form of address such as a courtier might use to his lady.
107. **monarch.** A match for *queen.*
108. **No:** i.e. I am no monarch.
109. **And no:** i.e. nor am I a queen.   111. **stain:** tinge, trace.
118. **setting down before:** laying siege to. The military figure, continued for some lines, gives good opportunity for bawdy quibbles.
121. **policy:** stratagem, craft.
124. **Marry:** to be sure (originally an oath, "by the Virgin Mary").
126. **politic:** expedient.
128. **rational increase:** (1) judicious increase; (2) increase of rational beings.   **got:** begotten.   129. **That:** that which.
130. **metal:** substance.
131. **may . . . found:** i.e. may be the means of creating ten more virgins.

133. **stand for't:** defend it.
136. **on the part:** in behalf.   137. **infallible:** certain.
138. **He . . . virgin:** i.e. a suicide and a virgin adopt the same course.
139. **murthers:** murders.
140. **sanctified limit:** boundaries of consecrated ground.
143. **his:** its (Shakespeare's all but invariable form).   **stomach.** With second sense "arrogance."
145. **inhibited:** prohibited.   **canon:** ecclesiastical law (?) or Scriptures (?).   **Keep:** hoard.
146. **Out with't:** put it out at interest.   147. **t' one:** the one, a single.
152–53. **ill . . . likes:** i.e. one would have to do ill, by liking a man who does not like virginity.
153. **will:** that will.   **gloss:** look of newness.
154. **lying:** being kept unsold.
155. **answer . . . request:** offer it while it is in demand.
157. **suited:** dressed (?) or (referring to *cap*) adorned (?).   **unsuitable:** not adapted to the time, unfashionable.
158. **brooch.** Long a fashionable ornament for hats.   **toothpick.** The use of toothpicks, a foreign invention, was for a time an affectation of travellers, who sometimes displayed their toothpicks in their hats.   **wear not:** are not worn.
159. **Your.** The indefinite use, as in "Your worm is your only emperor for diet" (*Hamlet*, IV.iii.21), but used here with continual suggestion of the personal sense. Helena's "Not *my* virginity yet" vigorously rejects that implication.   **date:** (1) the fruit (a very common ingredient in Elizabethan cookery); (2) age or sign of age.
161. **ill:** unappetizing.   162. **eats drily:** tastes dry.
163–64. **Will you:** will you do.
165. **Not . . . yet:** not with my virginity (?) or my virginity isn't a withered pear yet (?). Perhaps incomplete; there is an apparent gap in sense before the next line.
166. **There:** i.e. at court (as appears at line 177).
167. **mistress:** lady whom he serves.   **friend:** sweetheart, mistress. The terms of amorous address in Helena's catalogue in lines 167–73 are abundantly paralleled in the conventional love poetry of Shakespeare's day.

A phoenix, captain, and an enemy,
A guide, a goddess, and a sovereign,
A counsellor, a traitress, and a dear;   170
His humble ambition, proud humility;
His jarring concord, and his discord dulcet;
His faith, his sweet disaster; with a world
Of pretty, fond, adoptious christendoms
That blinking Cupid gossips. Now shall he—   175
I know not what he shall—God send him well!
The court's a learning place, and he is one—
  Par. What one, i' faith?
  Hel. That I wish well. 'Tis pity—
  Par. What's pity?   180
  Hel. That wishing well had not a body in't,
Which might be felt, that we, the poorer born,
Whose baser stars do shut us up in wishes,
Might with effects of them follow our friends,
And show what we alone must think, which never
Returns us thanks.   186

Enter PAGE.

  Page. Monsieur Parolles, my lord calls for you.
                                                    [*Exit.*]
  Par. Little Helen, farewell. If I can remember
thee, I will think of thee at court.
  Hel. Monsieur Parolles, you were born under a
charitable star.   191
  Par. Under Mars, I.
  Hel. I especially think, under Mars.
  Par. Why under Mars?
  Hel. The wars hath so kept you under that you
must needs be born under Mars.   196
  Par. When he was predominant.
  Hel. When he was retrograde, I think rather.
  Par. Why think you so?
  Hel. You go so much backward when you fight.
  Par. That's for advantage.   201
  Hel. So is running away, when fear proposes the
safety. But the composition that your valor and fear
makes in you is a virtue of a good wing, and I like the
wear well.

  Par. I am so full of businesses, I cannot answer thee
acutely. I will return perfect courtier, in the   207
which my instruction shall serve to naturalize thee, so
thou wilt be capable of a courtier's counsel, and understand what advice shall thrust upon thee, else thou diest
in thine unthankfulness, and thine ignorance makes
thee away. Farewell. When thou hast leisure,   212
say thy prayers; when thou hast none, remember thy
friends. Get thee a good husband, and use him as he
uses thee. So farewell.   [*Exit.*] 215
  Hel. Our remedies oft in ourselves do lie,
Which we ascribe to heaven. The fated sky
Gives us free scope, only doth backward pull
Our slow designs when we ourselves are dull.
What power is it which mounts my love so high,   220
That makes me see, and cannot feed mine eye?
The mightiest space in fortune nature brings
To join like likes, and kiss like native things.
Impossible be strange attempts to those
That weigh their pains in sense, and do suppose   225
What hath been cannot be. Who ever strove
To show her merit, that did miss her love?
The King's disease—my project may deceive me,
But my intents are fix'd, and will not leave me. *Exit.*

[SCENE II]

Flourish cornets. Enter the KING OF FRANCE *with letters*,
[LORDS,] *and divers* ATTENDANTS.

  King. The Florentines and Senoys are by th' ears,
Have fought with equal fortune, and continue
A braving war.
  1. Lord.   So 'tis reported, sir.
  King. Nay, 'tis most credible; we here receive it
A certainty, vouch'd from our cousin Austria,   5
With caution, that the Florentine will move us
For speedy aid; wherein our dearest friend

---

168. **phoenix:** i.e. nonpareil (the phoenix was unique). **captain:**
general (cf. "our great captain's captain [i.e. Desdemona]," *Othello*,
II.i.74). 172. **jarring:** discordant. **dulcet:** harmonious.
173. **sweet disaster:** dear misfortune.
174. **adoptious christendoms:** adopted nicknames or pet names
(*christendoms* = Christian names, hence familiar names generally).
175. **blinking:** i.e. blind. **gossips:** stands sponsor for, bestows
(*gossip* as a noun = godparent, who gives names at baptism).
176. **send him well:** grant him good fortune.
182. **might be felt:** could be perceived by the senses. **that:** so that.
183. **baser stars:** lower fortunes. **shut . . . wishes:** limit us to mere
wishing.
184. **with . . . them:** i.e. by means of our corporealized wishes.
185. **show . . . think:** make manifest what we can in fact only think.
186. **Returns us thanks:** wins us gratitude.
196. **under:** down, in an inferior position.
197. **predominant:** ascendant, in his position of greatest influence.
198. **retrograde:** moving backward (referring to a planet's apparent
movement in a direction opposite to that of the zodiac).
201. **advantage:** strategic gain.
203. **composition:** compound, mixture (with quibble on "truce,"
"terms for ending the fighting").
204. **virtue . . . wing:** characteristic excellence of a good wing, i.e.
rapid flight.
205. **wear:** practice, fashion. The choice of this word suggests that
wing (line 204) quibbles on the sense "decorative flap of material at
the shoulder"; some commentators suppose that Parolles is wearing
such wings.

207. **perfect:** complete.
208. **which:** i.e. courtly behavior. **naturalize:** familiarize. **so:**
provided that.
209. **capable:** receptive (with bawdy wordplay that takes in *understand*, *thrust*, and *diest* and makes plain what the subject of the
"instruction" will be).
211–12. **makes thee away:** puts an end to you.
212. **leisure:** opportunity.
213–14. **when . . . friends.** Precisely what Parolles means by this has
not been satisfactorily explained. 214. **use:** treat.
217. **fated:** instrumental to destiny. 219. **dull:** sluggish.
220. **mounts . . . high:** raises my desire to so lofty an object.
221. **makes me see:** enables me to perceive so distant an object (?).
cannot . . . eye: will not allow my eye to feed on it.
222. **The mightiest . . . fortune:** i.e. persons separated by the greatest
disparity of fortune. **brings:** causes.
223. **like likes:** as if they were alike in fortune. **native things:**
creatures of the same origin. 224. **strange:** extraordinary.
225. **That . . . sense:** who make a commonsense judgment of the
difficulties (i.e. the likelihood of success) of the "strange attempts"(?)
or who calculate the painful cost to themselves (?).
225–26. **do . . . be:** i.e. deem impossible what in fact resolute men
have done before (?). 227. **miss:** fail to achieve.

I.ii. Location: Paris. The King's palace.
o.s.d. **Flourish:** sound a fanfare. **cornets:** horns (not the modern
brass instruments).
1. **Senoys:** Sienese. **by th' ears:** at odds, quarrelling.
3. **braving:** marked by mutual defiance. 4. **we.** The royal plural.
5. **our cousin Austria:** my fellow sovereign the Duke of Austria.
6. **the Florentine:** the Florentines (?) or (like *Florence* in line 12) the
Duke of Florence (?). **move:** press, entreat.

Prejudicates the business, and would seem
To have us make denial.
  1. Lord. His love and wisdom,
Approv'd so to your Majesty, may plead   10
For amplest credence.
  King. He hath arm'd our answer,
And Florence is denied before he comes.
Yet for our gentlemen that mean to see
The Tuscan service, freely have they leave
To stand on either part.
  2. Lord. It well may serve   15
A nursery to our gentry, who are sick
For breathing and exploit.
  King. What's he comes here?

   Enter BERTRAM, LAFEW, *and* PAROLLES.

  1. Lord. It is the Count [Rossillion], my good lord,
Young Bertram.
  King. Youth, thou bear'st thy father's face;
Frank Nature, rather curious than in haste,   20
Hath well compos'd thee. Thy father's moral parts
Mayst thou inherit too! Welcome to Paris.
  Ber. My thanks and duty are your Majesty's.
  King. I would I had that corporal soundness now
As when thy father and myself in friendship   25
First tried our soldiership! He did look far
Into the service of the time, and was
Discipled of the bravest. He lasted long,
But on us both did haggish age steal on,
And wore us out of act. It much repairs me   30
To talk of your good father. In his youth
He had the wit which I can well observe
To-day in our young lords; but they may jest
Till their own scorn return to them unnoted
Ere they can hide their levity in honor.   35
So like a courtier, contempt nor bitterness
Were in his pride or sharpness; if they were,
His equal had awak'd them, and his honor,
Clock to itself, knew the true minute when
Exception bid him speak, and at this time   40
His tongue obey'd his hand. Who were below him
He us'd as creatures of another place,

And bow'd his eminent top to their low ranks,
Making them proud of his humility,
In their poor praise he humbled. Such a man   45
Might be a copy to these younger times;
Which followed well, would demonstrate them now
But goers backward.
  Ber. His good remembrance, sir,
Lies richer in your thoughts than on his tomb.
So in approof lives not his epitaph   50
As in your royal speech.
  King. Would I were with him! He would always
   say—
Methinks I hear him now; his plausive words
He scatter'd not in ears, but grafted them,
To grow there and to bear—"Let me not live"—   55
This his good melancholy oft began,
On the catastrophe and heel of pastime,
When it was out—"Let me not live," quoth he,
"After my flame lacks oil, to be the snuff
Of younger spirits, whose apprehensive senses   60
All but new things disdain; whose judgments are
Mere fathers of their garments; whose constancies
Expire before their fashions." This he wish'd.
I, after him, do after him wish too,
Since I nor wax nor honey can bring home,   65
I quickly were dissolved from my hive,
To give some laborers room.
  2. Lord. You're loved, sir;
They that least lend it you shall lack you first.
  King. I fill a place, I know't. How long is't, Count,
Since the physician at your father's died?   70
He was much fam'd.
  Ber. Some six months since, my lord.
  King. If he were living, I would try him yet.—
Lend me an arm.—The rest have worn me out
With several applications. Nature and sickness
Debate it at their leisure. Welcome, Count,   75
My son's no dearer.
  Ber. Thank your Majesty. *Exeunt. Flourish.*

---

10. Approv'd so: so fully proved.
11. arm'd our answer: made me determine on an adverse answer (i.e. hostile, hence armed); with further suggestion that the refusal will be proof against pleas.
13. for: as for, with respect to. **see:** i.e. take part in.
15. stand . . . part: fight on either side.
15–16. Serve A nursery: serve as a training school.
16. sick: pining. **17. breathing:** exercise.
20. Frank: bountiful. **curious:** working with careful skill.
21. parts: qualities. **25. As:** that I had.
26–27. look far Into: become deeply experienced in (?) or have profound insight into (?).
27–28. was Discipled of: was taught by (?) or had as followers (?).
29. on . . . on. A not uncommon type of redundancy. **haggish:** repulsive. **30. act:** action, activity. **repairs:** restores, refreshes.
34. return . . . unnoted: comes to be scornfully ignored (?).
35. hide . . . honor: submerge their levity in honorable action (?).
36. courtier: representative of true courtesy.
36–37. contempt . . . sharpness: there was no contempt in his pride, no wounding asperity in his keenness of wit.
38. equal: i.e. equal in rank.
39. Clock to itself: i.e. requiring no external cue. **true:** exact.
40. Exception: taking exception, disapproval.
41. obey'd his hand: said no more than his hand was willing to maintain. **Who:** those who.
42. us'd as: treated like. **of another place:** i.e. not of lower rank.

43. top: head.
45. In . . . humbled. A much-debated passage; perhaps "(which [i.e. humility]) he assumed in praise of (i.e. to do honor to) their poor selves." (The redundancy in "humbled his humility" would not be exceptional.)
46. copy: model, example to be followed (as in *copy-text*).
48. goers backward: regressive, inferior to him.
50. So . . . epitaph: i.e. the praise inscribed on his tomb is nowhere else so surely confirmed. **53. plausive:** praiseworthy.
54. scatter'd not: did not merely strew casually.
55. bear: bear fruit.
57. catastrophe: conclusion (synonymous with *heel*).
58. out: at an end (perhaps with play on "out at heel," but also leading into the candle figure that follows).
59. snuff: (1) burnt end of wick (which keeps the lower part of the wick from burning properly); (2) source of offense.
60. apprehensive: quick to seize upon ideas, hence capricious, inconstant.
62. Mere . . . garments: i.e. productive of nothing but new modes of dress.
63. Expire . . . fashions: shift even more quickly than fashions change.
64. after him . . . after him: surviving him . . . in agreement with his view. **65. nor . . . nor:** neither . . . nor.
66. dissolved: separated, departed.
67. laborers: i.e. workers, not drones.
68. lend it you: give you love. **lack:** miss, feel the want of.
74. with several applications: each with a different treatment.
75. Debate . . . leisure: fight it out in their own good time.

[SCENE III]

Enter COUNTESS, STEWARD [RINALDO], *and* CLOWN
[LAVATCH].

Count. I will now hear. What say you of this
gentlewoman?

Stew. Madam, the care I have had to even your
content, I wish might be found in the calendar of my
past endeavors, for then we wound our modesty, 5
and make foul the clearness of our deservings, when of
ourselves we publish them.

Count. What does this knave here? Get you gone,
sirrah. The complaints I have heard of you I do not all
believe. 'Tis my slowness that I do not, for I know 10
you lack not folly to commit them, and have ability
enough to make such knaveries yours.

Clo. 'Tis not unknown to you, madam, I am a poor
fellow.

Count. Well, sir. 15

Clo. No, madam, 'tis not so well that I am poor,
though many of the rich are damn'd, but if I may have
your ladyship's good will to go to the world, Isbel the
woman and [I] will do as we may.

Count. Wilt thou needs be a beggar? 20

Clo. I do beg your good will in this case.

Count. In what case?

Clo. In Isbel's case and mine own. Service is no
heritage, and I think I shall never have the blessing of
God till I have issue a' my body; for they say barnes
are blessings. 26

Count. Tell me thy reason why thou wilt marry.

Clo. My poor body, madam, requires it. I am
driven on by the flesh, and he must needs go that the
devil drives. 30

Count. Is this all your worship's reason?

Clo. Faith, madam, I have other holy reasons, such
as they are.

Count. May the world know them?

Clo. I have been, madam, a wicked creature, as you
and all flesh and blood are, and indeed I do marry that
I may repent. 37

Count. Thy marriage, sooner than thy wickedness.

Clo. I am out a' friends, madam, and I hope to have
friends for my wive's sake. 40

Count. Such friends are thine enemies, knave.

Clo. Y' are shallow, madam—in great friends, for
the knaves come to do that for me which I am a-weary
of. He that ears my land spares my team, and gives me
leave to inn the crop. If I be his cuckold, he's my 45
drudge. He that comforts my wife is the cherisher of
my flesh and blood; he that cherishes my flesh and
blood loves my flesh and blood; he that loves my flesh
and blood is my friend: *ergo*, he that kisses my wife is
my friend. If men could be contented to be what 50
they are, there were no fear in marriage, for young
Charbon the puritan and old Poysam the papist, howsome'er their hearts are sever'd in religion, their heads
are both one: they may jowl horns together like any
deer i' th' herd. 55

Count. Wilt thou ever be a foul-mouth'd and
calumnious knave?

Clo. A prophet I, madam, and I speak the truth
the next way:

>   For I the ballad will repeat, 60
>   Which men full true shall find:
>   Your marriage comes by destiny,
>   Your cuckoo sings by kind.

Count. Get you gone, sir, I'll talk with you more
anon. 65

Stew. May it please you, madam, that he bid Helen
come to you. Of her I am to speak.

Count. Sirrah, tell my gentlewoman I would speak
with her—Helen, I mean.

Clo. [*Sings.*]

>   "Was this fair face the cause," quoth she, 70
>   "Why the Grecians sacked Troy?
>   Fond done, done fond,
>   Was this King Priam's joy?"
>   With that she sighed as she stood,
>   With that she sighed as she stood, 75
>   And gave this sentence then:
>   "Among nine bad if one be good,

I.iii. Location: Rossillion. The Count's palace.

3–4. **even your content:** measure up to your wishes, serve you to your
complete satisfaction. 4. **calendar:** record.

6. **make . . . clearness:** sully the brightness.

9. **sirrah:** form of address used to inferiors. **all:** entirely. Dover
Wilson (following Maxwell's conjecture) reads *if I do not all believe,—*
a very attractive emendation. 18. **go . . . world:** marry.

19. **woman:** i.e. servingwoman. **do . . . may:** do the best we can
(doubtless with quibble on *do* in its frequent slang sense "have sexual
intercourse").

23. **case.** With another bawdy quibble; the Clown's talk is full of
equivoques.

23–24. **Service . . . heritage.** Proverbial, signifying that a servant's
lot brings him in very little to bequeath to his heirs.

24–25. **have . . . God:** have anything to show that God has blessed me.

25. **a':** of. **barnes:** bairns, children.

29–30. **he . . . drives.** Another proverb.

32. **other holy reasons.** "He reminds the Countess that his first
'reason' is to be found in the marriage service" (Dover Wilson); but
at the same time he perpetrates ribald puns in *holy* and *reasons*
(= *raisings*, a near homophone in Shakespeare's pronunciation).

37. **repent:** i.e. reform, make my sexual activity lawful. The
Countess' reply alludes to the proverb "Marry in haste and repent
at leisure." 40. **wive's:** wife's.

42. **Y' are . . . friends:** you have a superficial understanding of true
friendship (?). In Shakespeare's texts *in* is sometimes a variant
spelling of *e'en*, and many editors follow Hanmer in reading *e'en*
here, perhaps rightly. 44. **ears:** ploughs.

45. **inn:** harvest, get in.

49. **ergo:** therefore (signalling a logical conclusion).

50–51. **what they are:** i.e. cuckolds.

52. **Charbon, Poysam.** The names have been interpreted as derived
from *chair bonne* (good flesh) and *poisson* (fish), hence appropriate,
respectively, for the puritan, who rejected the ordinance of fasting,
and the papist, who followed it.

52–53. **howsome'er:** howsoever, however widely.

54. **both one:** identical (in bearing horns, the mark of the cuckold).
The statement about hearts and heads, as Hunter points out, comically
inverts the proverb "Hearts may agree though heads differ." **jowl:**
knock, bump. 56. **ever:** always.

59. **next:** nearest, most direct. Prophets spoke by immediate divine
inspiration.

62–63. **Your . . . kind.** A parallel to these lines has been pointed out
in a ballad of 1577, and perhaps they were a commonplace.

63. **by kind:** in accordance with its nature. The cuckoo's call was
conventionally regarded as announcing to married men that they
were cuckolds (see *Love's Labor's Lost*, V.ii.898–902), and this line
says in effect that cuckoldry is part of the course of nature.

69. **Helen.** This suggests to the Clown Helen of Troy, a good example
of what he has been talking about, and he extends his argument in
the song. No source is extant, but lines 80–81 indicate that the stanza
adapts some ballad known to the audience.

70. **she.** Perhaps Hecuba, wife of King Priam of Troy and mother
of Paris. 72. **Fond:** foolishly. 73. **this:** i.e. Paris, who stole Helen from her husband, King
Menelaus of Sparta, and thus caused the Trojan war.

76. **sentence:** judgment (?) or maxim (?).

Among nine bad if one be good,
There's yet one good in ten." 79
Count. What, one good in ten? You corrupt the
song, sirrah.
Clo. One good woman in ten, madam, which is a
purifying a' th' song. Would God would serve the
world so all the year! we'd find no fault with the 84
tithe-woman if I were the parson. One in ten, quoth
'a? And we might have a good woman born but [or]
every blazing star or at an earthquake, 'twould mend
the lottery well; a man may draw his heart out ere 'a
pluck one. 89
Count. You'll be gone, sir knave, and do as I command you.
Clo. That man should be at woman's command, and
yet no hurt done! Though honesty be no puritan, yet
it will do no hurt; it will wear the surplice of 94
humility over the black gown of a big heart. I am
going, forsooth. The business is for Helen to come
hither. *Exit.*
Count. Well, now.
Stew. I know, madam, you love your gentlewoman entirely. 100
Count. Faith, I do. Her father bequeath'd her to
me, and she herself, without other advantage, may lawfully make title to as much love as she finds. There is
more owing her than is paid, and more shall be paid her
than she'll demand. 105
Stew. Madam, I was very late more near her than I
think she wish'd me. Alone she was, and did communicate to herself her own words to her own ears;
she thought, I dare vow for her, they touch'd not any
stranger sense. Her matter was, she lov'd your 110
son. Fortune, she said, was no goddess, that had put
such difference betwixt their two estates; Love no god,
that would not extend his might only where qualities
were level; [Diana no] queen of virgins, that 114
would suffer her poor knight surpris'd without rescue
in the first assault or ransom afterward. This she
deliver'd in the most bitter touch of sorrow that e'er

I heard virgin exclaim in, which I held my duty
speedily to acquaint you withal, sithence in the 119
loss that may happen, it concerns you something
to know it.
Count. You have discharg'd this honestly, keep it
to yourself. Many likelihoods inform'd me of this
before, which hung so tott'ring in the balance that I
could neither believe nor misdoubt. Pray you 125
leave me. Stall this in your bosom, and I thank you for
your honest care. I will speak with you further anon.
Exit Steward.

Enter HELEN.

Even so it was with me when I was young.
If ever we are nature's, these are ours. This thorn
Doth to our rose of youth rightly belong; 130
Our blood to us, this to our blood is born.
It is the show and seal of nature's truth,
Where love's strong passion is impress'd in youth.
By our remembrances of days foregone,
Such were our faults, or then we thought them none.
Her eye is sick on't; I observe her now. 136
Hel. What is your pleasure, madam?
Count.　　　　　　　　　You know, Helen,
I am a mother to you.
Hel. Mine honorable mistress.
Count.　　　　　　　　　　　Nay, a mother,
Why not a mother? When I said "a mother," 140
Methought you saw a serpent. What's in "mother,"
That you start at it? I say I am your mother,
And put you in the catalogue of those
That were enwombed mine. 'Tis often seen
Adoption strives with nature, and choice breeds 145
A native slip to us from foreign seeds.
You ne'er oppress'd me with a mother's groan,
Yet I express to you a mother's care.
God's mercy, maiden! does it curd thy blood
To say I am thy mother? What's the matter, 150
That this distempered messenger of wet,
The many-color'd Iris, rounds thine eye?
—Why, that you are my daughter?
Hel.　　　　　　　　　　That I am not.
Count. I say I am your mother.
Hel.　　　　　　　　　Pardon, madam;

The Count Rossillion cannot be my brother: 155
I am from humble, he from honored name;
No note upon my parents, his all noble.
My master, my dear lord he is, and I
His servant live, and will his vassal die.
He must not be my brother.
   Count.   Nor I your mother? 160
   Hel. You are my mother, madam; would you
were—
So that my lord your son were not my brother—
Indeed my mother! Or were you both our mothers,
I care no more for than I do for heaven,
So I were not his sister. Can 't no other,   165
But, I your daughter, he must be my brother?
   Count. Yes, Helen, you might be my daughter-in-
     law.
God shield you mean it not! "daughter" and "mother"
So strive upon your pulse. What, pale again?
My fear hath catch'd your fondness! Now I see   170
The myst'ry of your [loneliness], and find
Your salt tears' head, now to all sense 'tis gross:
You love my son. Invention is asham'd,
Against the proclamation of thy passion,
To say thou dost not: therefore tell me true,   175
But tell me then 'tis so; for look, thy cheeks
Confess it, [t' one] to th' other, and thine eyes
See it so grossly shown in thy behaviors
That in their kind they speak it. Only sin
And hellish obstinacy tie thy tongue,   180
That truth should be suspected. Speak, is 't so?
If it be so, you have wound a goodly clew;
If it be not, forswear 't; howe'er, I charge thee,
As heaven shall work in me for thine avail,
To tell me truly.
   Hel.   Good madam, pardon me!   185
   Count. Do you love my son?
   Hel.   Your pardon, noble mistress!
   Count. Love you my son?
   Hel.   Do not you love him, madam?
   Count. Go not about; my love hath in 't a bond
Whereof the world takes note. Come, come, disclose

The state of your affection, for your passions   190
Have to the full appeach'd.
   Hel.   Then I confess
Here on my knee, before high heaven and you,
That before you, and next unto high heaven,
I love your son.
My friends were poor, but honest, so's my love.   195
Be not offended, for it hurts not him
That he is lov'd of me; I follow him not
By any token of presumptuous suit,
Nor would I have him till I do deserve him,
Yet never know how that desert should be.   200
I know I love in vain, strive against hope;
Yet in this captious and intenible sieve
I still pour in the waters of my love
And lack not to lose still. Thus Indian-like,
Religious in mine error, I adore   205
The sun, that looks upon his worshipper,
But knows of him no more. My dearest madam,
Let not your hate encounter with my love
For loving where you do; but if yourself,
Whose aged honor cites a virtuous youth,   210
Did ever in so true a flame of liking
Wish chastely, and love dearly, that your Dian
Was both herself and Love, O then give pity
To her whose state is such that cannot choose
But lend and give where she is sure to lose;   215
That seeks not to find that her search implies,
But riddle-like lives sweetly where she dies.
   Count. Had you not lately an intent—speak
     truly—
To go to Paris?
   Hel.   Madam, I had.
   Count.   Wherefore? tell true.
   Hel. I will tell truth, by grace itself I swear.   220
You know my father left me some prescriptions
Of rare and prov'd effects, such as his reading
And manifest experience had collected
For general sovereignty; and that he will'd me

157. **note:** mark of distinction.   **parents:** forebears.
162. **So:** provided.
163. **both our mothers:** the mother of us both.
164. **I . . . heaven.** Helena seems at first to use *care for* in the sense "mind" ("I wouldn't mind that") but shifts in mid-career with retroactive effect, so that at the end she has said, "I would value that as I value heaven."   165. **Can 't no other:** can it not be otherwise.
168. **shield:** defend, i.e. forbid. The *not* at the end of the sentence would ordinarily strengthen the negative sense already present; but perhaps the Countess is being deliberately ambiguous (as in line 170) in order to see what Helena can be brought to say before she knows that the Countess is not hostile.   169. **strive upon:** agitate.
170. **My . . . fondness.** This can mean "my apprehensiveness has caught out your foolishness" or "my concern has perceived your love."   171. **loneliness:** seclusion from people.
172. **head:** source.   **sense:** perception.   **gross:** obvious.
173. **Invention:** ability to find plausible answers.
174. **Against:** in the face of.   **thy.** Note the shift to the familiar form, continued to the end of the speech.
176. **then:** in that case (i.e. if you tell me true).
179. **in their kind:** in the way natural to them.
181. **suspected:** doubted, rendered suspect.
182. **wound . . . clew:** wound up a fine ball of thread (proverbial, with ironic sense; but the Countess may again be playing the ironic against the literal sense).
183. **forswear 't:** affirm that it is untrue.   **Howe'er:** whichever it is, in either case.   188. **Go not about:** don't evade.
189. **Whereof . . . note:** which society recognizes.

190. **affection:** feelings.   191. **appeach'd:** informed against you.
193. **before you:** more than (I love) you.   **next unto:** second only to.
195. **friends:** relatives, family.   **honest:** honorable.
197–98. **I . . . suit:** I do not pursue him with any manifestations of presumptuous love (?).
201. **hope:** expectation, what can reasonably be looked for.
202. **captious:** readily receptive (probably with added sense of "capacious").   **intenible:** unretentive.
203. **still pour:** go on pouring.
204. **lack . . . still:** (1) don't fail to go on losing it; (2) have no dearth of love to go on pouring away.   **Indian-like.** Probably referring to American Indians.
208. **encounter with:** stand against, oppose.
210. **aged honor:** honorable old age.   **cites:** testifies to.
211. **liking:** love.
212. **that:** so that.   **Dian:** Diana, goddess of chastity.
213. **Love:** i.e. Venus.   214. **such that:** such as.
216. **that . . . implies:** what causes her search (Schmidt), i.e. the object of her search.
217. **riddle-like:** paradoxically (referring to the following words) (?) or with her secret unguessed (?). The *flame of liking* of line 211, and the paradoxes of lines 212–13 and this line, suggest what Donne calls the "phoenix riddle" as Shakespeare treats it in "The Phoenix and Turtle." The passage is also reminiscent of Viola's description of a woman's concealed love in *Twelfth Night*, II.iv.110–15.
220. **grace:** God's grace.
223. **manifest experience:** experience of what is evident to the eye, i.e. clinical experience, in contrast to *reading* (line 222) (?). The usual gloss for *manifest* is, however, "widely known" or "notable."
224. **for general sovereignty:** for universal efficacy.   **will'd me:** desired me.

All's Well
That Ends Well
I.iii

In heedfull'st reservation to bestow them,   225
As notes whose faculties inclusive were
More than they were in note. Amongst the rest,
There is a remedy, approv'd, set down,
To cure the desperate languishings whereof
The King is render'd lost.
 Count.   This was your motive 230
For Paris, was it? speak.
 Hel. My lord your son made me to think of this;
Else Paris, and the medicine, and the King,
Had from the conversation of my thoughts
Happily been absent then.
 Count.   But think you, Helen, 235
If you should tender your supposed aid,
He would receive it? He and his physicians
Are of a mind; he, that they cannot help him,
They, that they cannot help. How shall they credit
A poor unlearned virgin, when the schools,   240
Embowell'd of their doctrine, have left off
The danger to itself?
 Hel.   There's something in't
More than my father's skill, which was the great'st
Of his profession, that his good receipt
Shall for my legacy be sanctified   245
By th' luckiest stars in heaven, and would your honor
But give me leave to try success, I'd venture
The well-lost life of mine on his Grace's cure
By such a day, an hour.
 Count.   Dost thou believe't?
 Hel. Ay, madam, knowingly.   250
 Count. Why, Helen, thou shalt have my leave and
  love,
Means and attendants, and my loving greetings
To those of mine in court. I'll stay at home
And pray God's blessing into thy attempt.
Be gone to-morrow, and be sure of this,   255
What I can help thee to thou shalt not miss. *Exeunt.*

ACT II, [SCENE I]

Enter the KING, *with divers young* LORDS *taking leave
for the Florentine war,* [BERTRAM] *Count Rossillion,
and* PAROLLES. *Flourish cornets.*

 King. Farewell, young lords, these warlike prin-
  ciples
Do not throw from you; and you, my lords, farewell.
Share the advice betwixt you; if both gain all,
The gift doth stretch itself as 'tis receiv'd,
And is enough for both.
 1. Lord.   'Tis our hope, sir,   5
After well-ent'red soldiers, to return
And find your Grace in health.
 King. No, no, it cannot be; and yet my heart
Will not confess he owes the malady
That doth my life besiege. Farewell, young lords, 10
Whether I live or die, be you the sons
Of worthy Frenchmen. Let higher Italy
(Those bated that inherit but the fall
Of the last monarchy) see that you come
Not to woo honor, but to wed it, when   15
The bravest questant shrinks. Find what you seek,
That fame may cry you loud. I say farewell.
 [2.] *Lord.* Health, at your bidding, serve your
  Majesty!
 King. Those girls of Italy, take heed of them.
They say our French lack language to deny   20
If they demand. Beware of being captives
Before you serve.
 Both [*Lords*]. Our hearts receive your warnings.
 King. Farewell.—Come hither to me.
    [*The King retires apart with some Lords.*]
 1. Lord. O my sweet lord, that you will stay be-
  hind us!
 Par. 'Tis not his fault, the spark.
 2. Lord.   O, 'tis brave wars! 25
 Par. Most admirable! I have seen those wars.
 Ber. I am commanded here, and kept a coil with,
"Too young" and "the next year" and "'tis too early."
 Par. And thy mind stand to't, boy, steal away
  bravely.
 Ber. I shall stay here the forehorse to a smock, 30
Creaking my shoes on the plain masonry,

1. **warlike principles:** military precepts. The King is taking leave of
two groups, those who go to aid the Florentines and those who go to
aid the Sienese (see I.ii.13–15).
3. **Share:** divide. **gain all:** wish to take advantage of the whole
of it. 4. **receiv'd:** accepted.
6. **After well-ent'red soldiers:** when we have become properly initiated
soldiers. 9. **owes:** possesses.
10. **besiege.** The King thinks of his illness as another form of warfare.
11. **be you:** show yourselves.
12. **worthy.** A transferred modifier, properly referring to *sons*.
higher Italy: the nobles of Italy (?) or mountainous Tuscany (?).
13. **Those . . . fall:** those excepted who have merely fallen heir to
places left empty by the collapse (?). The passage is variously interpreted and *the last monarchy* (line 14) variously identified.
15. **wed it:** i.e. achieve it, make it your own.
16. **questant:** seeker, i.e. mere wooer.
17. **cry you loud:** acclaim you loudly. 21. **demand:** ask.
21–22. **captives . . . serve.** Both words belong both to the language
of war and the language of love; here the first refers to love, the second
to war.
24. **sweet.** Used by the Elizabethans often as *dear* is used today;
but here probably an affectation.
25. **spark:** spirited young man. **brave:** splendid.
26. **seen:** had experience of.
27. **commanded here:** ordered to remain here. **kept . . . with:**
fussed over.
29. **And:** if. **stand to't:** is resolute. **bravely:** as would be fitting,
becomingly.
30. **forehorse . . . smock:** teamed up (like the leading horse of a
team) with a female. Perhaps the picture in his mind is of leading the
lady in a dance, hence the particular complaint in the next line.
31. **plain:** smooth.

225. **In . . . them:** to put them away and keep them with the utmost
care (for use in special cases). *Bestow* = stow away, treasure up. It
can also mean "give" and "employ" (senses that some give it here),
but Shakespeare regularly uses *reservation* in the sense "holding
back," "keeping to oneself." See II.i.108 below.
226–27. **As . . . note:** as prescriptions for remedies which had more
extensive curative properties than had yet been observed.
228. **approv'd:** proved, tested.
230. **render'd lost:** reported to be dying.
234. **conversation:** interchange, give-and-take.
235. **Happily:** haply, perhaps.
236. **your supposed aid:** the aid you envisage or propose.
238. **of a mind:** in agreement. **help:** cure.
241. **Embowell'd:** disembowelled, drained.
241–42. **left . . . itself:** abandoned the disease to its own course.
244. **receipt:** recipe, prescription.
245. **sanctified:** blessed. 246. **luckiest:** most benignant.
247. **try success:** test what the outcome will be.
248. **well-lost . . . mine:** i.e. my life which, if my venture fails, will be
lost in a good cause. 249. **such a:** a specified.
250. **knowingly:** with full awareness of what I am doing.
254. **into:** upon. 256. **miss:** lack.

II.i. Location: Paris. The King's palace.

Till honor be bought up, and no sword worn
But one to dance with! By heaven, I'll steal away.
1. Lord. There's honor in the theft.
Par.   Commit it, Count.
2. Lord. I am your accessary, and so farewell. 35
Ber. I grow to you, and our parting is a tortur'd
body.
1. Lord. Farewell, captain.
2. Lord. Sweet Monsieur Parolles!   39
Par. Noble heroes! my sword and yours are kin.
Good sparks and lustrous, a word, good metals: you
shall find in the regiment of the Spinii one Captain
Spurio, [with] his cicatrice, an emblem of war, here
on his sinister cheek; it was this very sword entrench'd
it. Say to him I live, and observe his reports for me.
[*1.*] *Lord.* We shall, noble captain.   46
Par. Mars dote on you for his novices!
                                    [*Exeunt Lords.*]
What will ye do?
Ber. Stay the King.   49
Par. Use a more spacious ceremony to the noble
lords; you have restrain'd yourself within the list of
too cold an adieu. Be more expressive to them, for
they wear themselves in the cap of the time, there do
muster true gait; eat, speak, and move under the
influence of the most receiv'd star, and though the 55
devil lead the measure, such are to be follow'd. After
them, and take a more dilated farewell.
Ber. And I will do so.
Par. Worthy fellows, and like to prove most
sinewy swordmen. *Exeunt* [*Bertram and Parolles*]. 60

Enter LAFEW. [*The* KING *comes forward.*]

Laf. [*Kneeling.*] Pardon, my lord, for me and for
my tidings.
King. I'll see thee to stand up.
Laf. Then here's a man stands that has brought his
pardon.
I would you had kneel'd, my lord, to ask me mercy,
And that at my bidding you could so stand up. 65

King. I would I had, so I had broke thy pate,
And ask'd thee mercy for't.
Laf.   Good faith, across!
But, my good lord, 'tis thus: will you be cur'd
Of your infirmity?
King.   No.
Laf.   O, will you eat
No grapes, my royal fox? Yes, but you will   70
My noble grapes, and if my royal fox
Could reach them. I have seen a medicine
That's able to breathe life into a stone,
Quicken a rock, and make you dance canary
With sprutely fire and motion, whose simple touch 75
Is powerful to araise King Pippen, nay,
To give great Charlemain a pen in 's hand
And write to her a love-line.
King.   What her is this?
Laf. Why, Doctor She! My lord, there's one
arriv'd,
If you will see her. Now by my faith and honor, 80
If seriously I may convey my thoughts
In this my light deliverance, I have spoke
With one, that in her sex, her years, profession,
Wisdom, and constancy, hath amaz'd me more
Than I dare blame my weakness. Will you see her—
For that is her demand—and know her business? 86
That done, laugh well at me.
King.   Now, good Lafew,
Bring in the admiration, that we with thee
May spend our wonder too, or take off thine
By wond'ring how thou took'st it.
Laf.   Nay, I'll fit you,
And not be all day neither.   [*Goes to the door.*] 91
King. Thus he his special nothing ever prologues.
Laf. Nay, come your ways.

Enter HELEN.

King.   This haste hath wings indeed.
Laf. Nay, come your ways;
This is his Majesty, say your mind to him.   95
A traitor you do look like, but such traitors
His Majesty seldom fears. I am Cressid's uncle,

32. **Till...up:** until others have monopolized all the available honor.   33. **one...with:** i.e. one worn for ornament, not use.
34. **theft.** A play on *steal*, continued in *Commit* and *accessary.*
36. **grow:** have become attached.
36–37. **a tortur'd body:** as painful as the rending of a body by torture. This speech comes oddly from Bertram and is perhaps misassigned.
41. **metals:** (1) swords(men); (2) mettlesome fellows. For the Elizabethans, *metal* and *mettle* were variants of the same word.
43. **Spurio.** The Italian word for "spurious."
44. **sinister:** left.   45. **observe his reports:** take note of his reply.
47. **novices:** young devotees.
49. **Stay the King:** attend (or support) the King. Some editors read *Stay;* (following F2), explained either as a telegraphic "Stay here; King's orders" or as "Stop talking; the King is approaching." Dover Wilson supposes that lines 50–60 are intended for the King's ear as he slowly comes forward with his attendants.
50. **ceremony:** courtesy.   51. **list:** boundary, limit.
52. **expressive:** outgoing.
53. **wear...time:** are conspicuous ornaments of the fashionable world.   54. **muster true gait:** exhibit the true (courtly) bearing.
55. **receiv'd:** accepted, fashionable.   56. **measure:** dance.
57. **dilated:** expansive (synonymous with *spacious*, line 50).
59. **like:** likely.   61. **Pardon:** i.e. indulgence.
62. **I'll...up:** i.e. let me see you rise. (The infinitive with *to* was common after verbs of perceiving.) Many editors emend *see* to *fee* (Theobald) or *sue* (Staunton conjecture).
63. **brought his pardon:** i.e. brought something that will win your indulgence.

66. **broke thy pate:** i.e. given you a blow on the head that brought blood.
67. **across.** "A word...used when any pass of wit miscarries" (Johnson). In tilting, a proper blow was delivered with the spear's point, not with the spear held athwart the adversary.
69–70. **will...fox:** i.e. do you pretend lack of interest in a cure because you suppose that a cure is beyond your reach (an allusion to Aesop's fable of the fox and the grapes).   71. **and if:** if.
72. **medicine.** This word can mean "physician" and perhaps does so here.
74. **Quicken:** give life to.   **canary:** a particularly energetic dance.
75. **simple:** mere (but perhaps with suggestion of its sense "medicinal herb".)
76. **Is...Pippen:** i.e. has the potency to bring back to life a man who has been dead for centuries. The Frankish king Pepin, father of Charlemagne, died in 768.
82. **light deliverance:** frivolous manner of reporting.
83. **profession:** what she professes to be able to do.
85. **blame my weakness:** lay to my enfeebled faculties (?) or to my susceptibility (?).   88. **admiration:** marvel.
89. **spend:** expend.   **take off:** take away, dispel (with following play on *take* in another sense, "receive into the mind, conceive").
90. **fit:** accommodate, furnish.
92. **special nothing:** remarkable trifle.
93. **come your ways:** come along.
97. **Cressid's uncle:** i.e. Pandarus, who brought Cressida and Troilus together.

All's Well
That Ends Well
II.i

That dare leave two together; fare you well.   *Exit.*
   King. Now, fair one, does your business follow us?
   Hel. Ay, my good lord.   100
Gerard de Narbon was my father,
In what he did profess, well found.
   King.   I knew him.
   Hel. The rather will I spare my praises towards
      him,
Knowing him is enough. On 's bed of death
Many receipts he gave me; chiefly one,   105
Which as the dearest issue of his practice,
And of his old experience th' only darling,
He bade me store up, as a triple eye,
Safer than mine own two, more dear. I have so,
And hearing your high Majesty is touch'd   110
With that malignant cause wherein the honor
Of my dear father's gift stands chief in power,
I come to tender it, and my appliance,
With all bound humbleness.
   King.   We thank you, maiden,
But may not be so credulous of cure,   115
When our most learned doctors leave us, and
The congregated college have concluded
That laboring art can never ransom nature
From her inaidible estate; I say we must not
So stain our judgment, or corrupt our hope,   120
To prostitute our past-cure malady
To empirics, or to dissever so
Our great self and our credit, to esteem
A senseless help when help past sense we deem.
   Hel. My duty then shall pay me for my pains.   125
I will no more enforce mine office on you,
Humbly entreating from your royal thoughts
A modest one, to bear me back again.
   King. I cannot give thee less, to be call'd grateful.
Thou thought'st to help me, and such thanks I give
As one near death to those that wish him live.   131
But what at full I know, thou know'st no part,
I knowing all my peril, thou no art.
   Hel. What I can do can do no hurt to try,
Since you set up your rest 'gainst remedy.   135

He that of greatest works is finisher
Oft does them by the weakest minister:
So holy writ in babes hath judgment shown,
When judges have been babes; great floods have flown
From simple sources; and great seas have dried   140
When miracles have by the great'st been denied.
Oft expectation fails, and most oft there
Where most it promises; and oft it hits
Where hope is coldest, and despair most [fits].
   King. I must not hear thee; fare thee well, kind
      maid,   145
Thy pains not us'd must by thyself be paid.
Proffers not took reap thanks for their reward.
   Hel. Inspired merit so by breath is barr'd.
It is not so with Him that all things knows
As 'tis with us that square our guess by shows;   150
But most it is presumption in us when
The help of heaven we count the act of men.
Dear sir, to my endeavors give consent,
Of heaven, not me, make an experiment.
I am not an imposture that proclaim   155
Myself against the level of mine aim,
But know I think, and think I know most sure,
My art is not past power, nor you past cure.
   King. Art thou so confident? Within what space
Hop'st thou my cure?
   Hel.   The greatest grace lending grace,
Ere twice the horses of the sun shall bring   161
Their fiery torcher his diurnal ring,
Ere twice in murk and occidental damp
Moist Hesperus hath quench'd her sleepy lamp,
Or four and twenty times the pilot's glass   165
Hath told the thievish minutes how they pass,
What is infirm from your sound parts shall fly,
Health shall live free, and sickness freely die.
   King. Upon thy certainty and confidence
What dar'st thou venter?
   Hel.   Tax of impudence,   170
A strumpet's boldness, a divulged shame,

99. **follow:** i.e. have as its object.
102. **well found:** found to be skilled.
106. **dearest issue:** (1) most precious product; (2) favorite child (equivalent to *only* [= chief, supreme] *darling* in line 107).
107. **old:** long.   108. **triple:** third.
109. **Safer:** with greater attention to its security.
110. **touch'd:** infected.
111. **cause:** disease.   **honor:** quality for which it is esteemed, particular efficacy.   112. **chief:** chiefly, particularly.
113. **my appliance:** my skill in administering it.
114. **bound:** dutiful.   116. **leave:** abandon hope for.
117. **congregated college:** assembled society of physicians.
118. **laboring art:** the efforts of human skill (here specifically medical science).   119. **inaidible estate:** incurable condition.
120. **stain:** pervert.   121. **prostitute:** basely submit.
122. **empirics:** quacks (accented on the first syllable).
123. **credit.** Usually explained as "reputation," but Schmidt's "belief, faith" seems superior in the context. The King's concern in this passage is his own integrity.
123-24. **esteem . . . deem:** trust to a highly unlikely remedy when I consider any remedy at all to be beyond reason.
125. **My duty:** i.e. my sense that I have performed my duty.
126. **enforce mine office:** press my professional services.
128. **A modest one:** a moderately favorable one (?) or one acknowledging that I have not impaired my modesty (?).   131. **live:** to live.
132. **no part:** in no degree, not at all.
135. **set . . . rest:** stake everything (a term from the game of primero), i.e. are resolved at all costs.

138-39. **holy . . . babes.** See Matthew 11:25: "thou hast hid these things from the wise and men of understanding, and hast opened them unto babes" (Geneva). Perhaps Shakespeare has in mind Daniel's triumphant defense of Susanna against the judgment of the Elders, to which he refers in *The Merchant of Venice,* IV.i.
139-40. **great . . . sources.** Perhaps alluding to Moses' smiting of the rock in Horeb (Exodus 17:1-7).
140-41. **great . . . denied.** Probably a reference to the parting of the Red Sea to permit the departure of the Israelites from Egypt (Exodus 15); *the great'st* then = Pharoah.
142. **fails:** is disappointed. Johnson points out that line 142 has no rhyming line; possibly there is a lacuna after line 141.
143. **hits:** proves true.
148. **Inspired:** bestowed by the breath of God.   **breath:** human breath, i.e. words.
150. **square:** regulate, shape.   **shows:** appearances.
152. **count:** account.   154. **experiment:** trial.
155. **imposture:** impostor.
155-56. **proclaim . . . aim:** i.e. announce an intention not in accordance with my actual one. *Level* = direction.
158. **My . . . power:** what I profess is not past my power to perform.
160. **The greatest . . . grace:** with God's help.
161. **horses . . . sun:** horses that draw the sun-god's chariot.
161-62. **bring . . . his diurnal ring:** bring . . . to the end of his daily circuit.
164. **Hesperus:** the evening star (actually Venus; hence, perhaps, the use of *her* rather than the expected *his*).   165. **glass:** hourglass.
166. **thievish.** Because in their passage they steal away life.
168. **freely:** of its own accord.
170. **venter:** venture, hazard.   **Tax of impudence:** accusation of shamelessness.   171. **divulged:** exposed, made public.

Traduc'd by odious ballads; my maiden's name
Sear'd otherwise; ne worse of worst—extended
With vildest torture, let my life be ended.

King. Methinks in thee some blessed spirit doth
    speak   175
His powerful sound within an organ weak;
And what impossibility would slay
In common sense, sense saves another way.
Thy life is dear, for all that life can rate
Worth name of life in thee hath estimate: 180
Youth, beauty, wisdom, courage, all
That happiness and prime can happy call.
Thou this to hazard needs must intimate
Skill infinite, or monstrous desperate.
Sweet practicer, thy physic I will try,   185
That ministers thine own death if I die.

Hel. If I break time, or flinch in property
Of what I spoke, unpitied let me die,
And well deserv'd. Not helping, death's my fee,
But if I help, what do you promise me?   190

King. Make thy demand.

Hel.   But will you make it even?

King. Ay, by my sceptre and my hopes of
[heaven].

Hel. Then shalt thou give me with thy kingly hand
What husband in thy power I will command.
Exempted be from me the arrogance   195
To choose from forth the royal blood of France,
My low and humble name to propagate
With any branch or image of thy state;
But such a one thy vassal, whom I know
Is free for me to ask, thee to bestow.   200

King. Here is my hand, the premises observ'd,
Thy will by my performance shall be serv'd.
So make the choice of thy own time, for I,
Thy resolv'd patient, on thee still rely.
More should I question thee, and more I must—   205
Though more to know could not be more to trust—
From whence thou cam'st, how tended on, but rest
Unquestion'd welcome and undoubted blest.—
Give me some help here ho!—If thou proceed
As high as word, my deed shall match thy deed.   210
        Flourish. Exeunt.

[SCENE II]

Enter COUNTESS *and* CLOWN.

Count. Come on, sir, I shall now put you to the
height of your breeding.

Clo. I will show myself highly fed and lowly
taught. I know my business is but to the court.   4

Count. To the court! Why, what place make you
special, when you put off that with such contempt?
But to the court!

Clo. Truly, madam, if God have lent a man any
manners, he may easily put it off at court. He that
cannot make a leg, put off 's cap, kiss his hand,   10
and say nothing, has neither leg, hands, lip, nor cap;
and indeed such a fellow, to say precisely, were not for
the court; but for me, I have an answer will serve all
men.   14

Count. Marry, that's a bountiful answer that fits all
questions.

Clo. It is like a barber's chair that fits all buttocks:
the pin-buttock, the quatch-buttock, the brawn-
buttock, or any buttock.   19

Count. Will your answer serve fit to all questions?

Clo. As fit as ten groats is for the hand of an attorney, as your French crown for your taffety punk, as
Tib's rush for Tom's forefinger, as a pancake for
Shrove Tuesday, a morris for May-day, as the nail to
his hole, the cuckold to his horn, as a scolding   25
quean to a wrangling knave, as the nun's lip to the
friar's mouth, nay, as the pudding to his skin.

Count. Have you, I say, an answer of such fitness
for all questions?

Clo. From below your duke to beneath your
constable, it will fit any question.   31

Count. It must be an answer of most monstrous
size that must fit all demands.

Clo. But a trifle neither, in good faith, if the learned
should speak truth of it. Here it is, and all that belongs
to't. Ask me if I am a courtier: it shall do you no harm
to learn.   37

Count. To be young again, if we could, I will be a
fool in question, hoping to be the wiser by your answer.

---

173. **Sear'd otherwise:** branded in other ways, i.e. with other shameful names. **ne . . . worst:** nor would this be worse than what is
worst (i.e. dishonor). **extended:** stretched out (as on the rack)
(?) or lingered out (?). 174. **vildest:** vilest.
177–78. **what . . . way:** what common sense would reject as impossible, reason declares feasible on other grounds.
179–80. **rate . . . life:** value as worthy of being called "life."
180. **hath estimate:** must be accounted present.
182. **happiness and prime:** good fortune and youth.
183. **Thou . . . hazard:** that you are willing to risk all this. **intimate:**
argue.
184. **monstrous desperate:** (that you are) horribly reckless.
185. **physic:** medicine.
187. **break time:** fail to perform within the specified time (of two
days). **flinch in property:** fall short in some particular.
189. **Not helping:** if I do not cure you.
191. **make it even:** fulfill it.
195. **Exempted:** far removed.
198. **image:** likeness, copy (?). Hunter suggests that *branch or image*
refers to family trees with portraits hanging from the various branches.
state: high place.
201. **premises observ'd:** conditions fulfilled.
204. **resolv'd:** with mind made up. **still:** ever.
207. **tended on:** attended.
208. **Unquestion'd:** (1) in advance of being asked these questions; (2)
unquestionably. 210. **word:** promise.

II.ii. Location: Rossillion. The Count's palace.
1–2. **put . . . height:** make a thorough trial. The Countess is referring
to the Clown's errand to the court.
2. **your breeding:** (the results of) your upbringing.
3–4. **highly . . . taught.** "Better fed than taught" was a proverbial
description of a child reared overindulgently. The Clown probably
implies that he will do well at court because his "breeding" has been
that of the pampered young courtiers.
5–6. **make you special:** do you rate as choice. 6. **put off:** dismiss.
9. **put it off:** pull it off, make a go of it.
10. **make a leg:** bend his knee, make obeisance. **put off:** take off.
13. **for:** as for.
17. **like . . . chair.** A common comparison for what suits all comers.
In the following line *pin* = pointed; *quatch* perhaps = broad and flat;
brawn = fleshy or fatty. 21. **ten groats:** forty pence.
22. **French crown:** (1) a coin; (2) bald head (resulting from syphilis,
commonly called "the French disease"). **taffety punk:** taffeta-clad
prostitute.
23. **Tib's rush:** i.e. a ring made by twisting a rush, for a love-token
or for use in a mock marriage. *Tib* is a stock name for a country
wench. **pancake.** Traditional fare for Shrove Tuesday, the day
before the beginning of Lent.
24. **morris:** morris-dance (a traditional feature of May-games).
25, 27. **his:** its. 26. **quean:** hussy. 27. **pudding:** sausage.
30–31. **below . . . constable.** Probably with bawdy innuendo.
34. **But . . . neither:** on the contrary it is a mere trifle.

I pray you, sir, are you a courtier?   40
Clo. O Lord, sir!—There's a simple putting off.
More, more, a hundred of them.
Count. Sir, I am a poor friend of yours that loves
you.
Clo. O Lord, sir!—Thick, thick, spare not me.   45
Count. I think, sir, you can eat none of this homely
meat.
Clo. O Lord, sir!—Nay, put me to't, I warrant
you.
Count. You were lately whipt, sir, as I think.   50
Clo. O Lord, sir!—Spare not me.
Count. Do you cry, "O Lord, sir!" at your whip-
ping, and "Spare not me"? Indeed your "O Lord, sir!"
is very sequent to your whipping; you would   54
answer very well to a whipping, if you were but
bound to't.
Clo. I ne'er had worse luck in my life in my "O
Lord, sir!" I see things may serve long, but not serve
ever.
Count. I play the noble huswife with the time,   60
To entertain it so merrily with a fool.
Clo. O Lord, sir!—Why, there't serves well again.
Count. [An] end, sir; to your business: give
Helen this,
And urge her to a present answer back.
Commend me to my kinsmen and my son.   65
This is not much.
Clo. Not much commendation to them.
Count. Not much employment for you.   You
understand me?
Clo. Most fruitfully, I am there before my legs.
Count. Haste you again.   *Exeunt.* 71

[SCENE III]

Enter COUNT [BERTRAM], LAFEW, *and* PAROLLES.

Laf. They say miracles are past, and we have our
philosophical persons, to make modern and familiar,
things supernatural and causeless. Hence is it that we
make trifles of terrors, ensconcing ourselves into seeming knowledge, when we should submit ourselves to an
unknown fear.   6

Par. Why, 'tis the rarest argument of wonder that
hath shot out in our latter times.
Ber. And so 'tis.
Laf. To be relinquish'd of the artists—   10
Par. So I say, both of Galen and Paracelsus.
Laf. Of all the learned and authentic fellows—
Par. Right, so I say.
Laf. That gave him out incurable—
Par. Why, there 'tis, so say I too.   15
Laf. Not to be help'd—
Par. Right, as 'twere a man assur'd of a—
Laf. Uncertain life, and sure death.
Par. Just, you say well; so would I have said. 19
Laf. I may truly say it is a novelty to the world.
Par. It is indeed; if you will have it in showing,
you shall read it in what-do-ye-call there.

         [*Pointing to a ballad in Lafew's hand.*]

Laf. [*Reading the title.*] "A showing of a heavenly
effect in an earthly actor."   24
Par. That's it I would have said, the very same.
Laf. Why, your dolphin is not lustier. 'Fore me,
I speak in respect—
Par. Nay, 'tis strange, 'tis very strange, that is the
brief and the tedious of it, and he's of a most facinerious
spirit that will not acknowledge it to be the—   30
Laf. Very hand of heaven.
Par. Ay, so I say.
Laf. In a most weak—
Par. And debile minister, great power, great   34
transcendence, which should indeed give us a further
use to be made than alone the recov'ry of the King,
as to be—
Laf. Generally thankful.

Enter KING, HELEN, *and* ATTENDANTS.

Par. I would have said it; you say well.   Here
comes the King.   40
Laf. *Lustick*, as the Dutchman says.   I'll like a
maid the better whilst I have a tooth in my head.
Why, he's able to lead her a coranto.

---

41. **O Lord, sir.** "A ridicule on that foolish expletive of speech then
in vogue at court" (Warburton). It evades an answer to a yes-or-no
question by appearing to deprecate either reply.   **putting off:**
evasion.   45. **Thick:** quick.   **spare not me:** i.e. keep them coming.
46–47. **homely meat:** plain food.
54. **is . . . to:** follows very logically from.   "O Lord, sir" during a
whipping would be a plea for mercy (quite the opposite of "Spare
not me").
55. **answer . . . to:** (1) have a very good answer to; (2) be a very
appropriate subject for.
56. **bound to't:** (1) required to answer; (2) tied to a post for a
whipping.
60. **I . . . time:** I am employing my time in a worthy manner indeed.
64. **present:** immediate.
65. **Commend me:** give my loving greetings.
70. **fruitfully.** The word *understand* routinely elicits a bawdy quibble
from the Clown.   71. **again:** back.

II.iii. Location: Paris. The King's palace.
2. **modern:** commonplace.
3. **causeless:** i.e. inexplicable in terms of natural law.
4. **terrors:** i.e. occurrences that should inspire awe.   **ensconcing . . .
into:** sheltering . . . in.
6. **unknown fear:** awe in the face of the unknown.

7. **rarest:** most extraordinary.   **argument:** theme, subject.
8. **latter:** recent, modern.
9. **And so 'tis.** This is Bertram's only speech until after the entrance
of the other lords at line 51. It has been conjectured that Shakespeare,
after beginning the scene, altered his intention to have Bertram present
from the start, and that Bertram should make his entrance with the
other lords.
10. **relinquish'd . . . artists:** given up by the learned (physicians).
11. **both . . . Paracelsus:** i.e. both those who follow the traditional
doctrine of Galen (Greek physician of the second century A.D. who
in Shakespeare's day was still the preeminent medical authority) and
those who favor the new methods of Paracelsus (Swiss-born alchemist
and physician [1493–1541] who had undertaken to reform the Galenic
system). Some editors would add these words to Lafew's next speech,
limiting Parolles again to mere assent.
12. **authentic fellows:** i.e. duly qualified members of the society of
physicians.   16. **help'd:** cured.   19. **Just:** exactly.
21. **in showing:** visible, i.e. set forth in print.
26. **lustier:** more vigorous and sportive.   Commentators suggest a
pun on *Dauphin* (regularly spelled *Dolphin* in Shakespeare's texts).
'Fore me: i.e. on my soul (a form of oath derived from such expressions as *'fore God* [line 45] and *'fore heaven*).
29. **brief . . . tedious:** short . . . long.   Parolles suddenly gets into his
stride with this speech and follows it up in his next, turning the tables
on Lafew. Some editors reassign the speeches, to Lafew's advantage.
facinerious: extremely wicked (variant of *facinorous*).
34. **debile minister:** feeble agent.   38. **Generally:** universally.
41. **Lustick:** lusty.   42. **tooth . . . head:** i.e. a taste (for girls).
43. **coranto:** a lively dance.

Par. *Mort du vinaigre!* is not this Helen?
Laf. 'Fore God, I think so.   45
King.   Go call before me all the lords in court.
Sit, my preserver, by thy patient's side,
And with this healthful hand, whose banish'd sense
Thou hast repeal'd, a second time receive
The confirmation of my promis'd gift,   50
Which but attends thy naming.

Enter three or four LORDS.

Fair maid, send forth thine eye. This youthful parcel
Of noble bachelors stand at my bestowing,
O'er whom both sovereign power and father's voice
I have to use. Thy frank election make;   55
Thou hast power to choose, and they none to forsake.
Hel.   To each of you one fair and virtuous mistress
Fall, when Love please! Marry, to each but one!
Laf.   I'd give bay Curtal and his furniture,
My mouth no more were broken than these boys',   60
And writ as little beard.
King.   Peruse them well.
Not one of those but had a noble father.
Hel.   Gentlemen,
Heaven hath through me restor'd the King to health.
All.   We understand it, and thank heaven for you.
Hel.   I am a simple maid, and therein wealthiest
That I protest I simply am a maid.   67
Please it your Majesty, I have done already.
The blushes in my cheeks thus whisper me,
"We blush that thou shouldst choose; but be refused,
Let the white death sit on thy cheek for ever,   71
We'll ne'er come there again."
King.   Make choice and see,
Who shuns thy love shuns all his love in me.
Hel.   Now, Dian, from thy altar do I fly,
And to imperial Love, that god most high,   75
Do my sighs stream. (*She addresses her to a Lord.*) Sir,
        will you hear my suit?
1. Lord.   And grant it.
Hel.   Thanks, sir; all the rest is mute.
Laf.   I had rather be in this choice than throw
ames-ace for my life.
Hel.   [*To a second Lord.*] The honor, sir, that flames
        in your fair eyes,
Before I speak, too threat'ningly replies.   81
Love make your fortunes twenty times above

Her that so wishes, and her humble love!
2. Lord.   No better, if you please.
Hel.   My wish receive,
Which great Love grant, and so I take my leave.   85
Laf.   Do all they deny her? And they were sons of
mine, I'd have them whipt, or I would send them to
th' Turk to make eunuchs of.
Hel.   [*To a third Lord.*] Be not afraid that I your
        hand should take,
I'll never do you wrong for your own sake.   90
Blessing upon your vows, and in your bed
Find fairer fortune, if you ever wed!
Laf.   These boys are boys of ice, they'll none have
[her]. Sure they are bastards to the English, the
French ne'er got 'em.   95
Hel.   [*To a fourth Lord.*] You are too young, too
        happy, and too good,
To make yourself a son out of my blood.
4. Lord.   Fair one, I think not so.
Laf.   There's one grape yet; I am sure thy father
drunk wine—but if thou be'st not an ass, I am a
youth of fourteen. I have known thee already.   101
Hel.   [*To Bertram.*] I dare not say I take you, but
        I give
Me and my service, ever whilst I live,
Into your guiding power.—This is the man.
King.   Why then, young Bertram, take her, she's
        thy wife.   105
Ber.   My wife, my liege? I shall beseech your
        Highness,
In such a business, give me leave to use
The help of mine own eyes.
King.   Know'st thou not, Bertram,
What she has done for me?
Ber.   Yes, my good lord,
But never hope to know why I should marry her.   110
King.   Thou know'st she has rais'd me from my
        sickly bed.
Ber.   But follows it, my lord, to bring me down
Must answer for your raising? I know her well;
She had her breeding at my father's charge—
A poor physician's daughter my wife! Disdain   115
Rather corrupt me ever!

---

44. Mort du vinaigre: a pseudo-French oath (= death of the vinegar) of obscure origin, presumably referring to the Crucifixion. Paroles' amazement shows that he has not yet learned the means of the King's cure.   **48. healthful:** healthy.   **sense:** power of feeling.
49. repeal'd: called back (carrying on the figure in *banish'd*).
51. attends: awaits.
53. stand . . . bestowing: are in my power to give. A guardian had authority to marry his ward to any woman of equal rank. Helen, of course, does not meet this condition.
55. frank election: free choice.   **56. forsake:** i.e. refuse.
58. to . . . one: only one to each (but with the private meaning "to all except one").
59. Curtal. The name means "having a docked tail."   **furniture:** trappings.
60. My . . . broken: if my teeth showed no more gaps (perhaps with the same reference to sensual appetite as in line 42) (?) or if I were no more broken to the bit (?) or if my voice were no more broken (?).
61. writ: (if I) claimed title to.   **67. protest:** avow.
69. whisper: whisper to.   **70. be:** if you are.
77. all . . . mute: i.e. I have no further words for you. There are two schools of thought about Helena's exchanges with the young lords. Some commentators take Lafew's comments at lines 86–88,

93–95 at face value and suppose that the lords, though they make politely acquiescent replies, show by their demeanor their disdain of Helen. The scene can certainly be played in this way, but the weight of the lines themselves seems to favor the view that Lafew, out of earshot, misinterprets the reason for Helena's speedy passing from one to another.
79. ames-ace: two aces (the lowest throw at dice). Lafew is making a jocular understatement: "I'd rather make a losing throw with my life at stake."
80–81. honor . . . threat'ningly. Susceptible of two interpretations: that the pride of rank which he displays threatens refusal, or that the honor his look pays Helena (i.e. his evident willingness to be chosen, or his obvious admiration) threatens embarrassment to one who has made another choice.
83. so wishes: pronounces this wish.
84. No . . . please: I wish for no one better than you if you will have me.   **receive:** accept.
86. Do . . . her: Helena's exchanges with the lords cannot be heard by the others.   **95. got:** begot.
99–100. There's . . . wine: "There is one yet into whom his father put good blood" (Johnson). "Good wine makes good blood" was proverbial.   **101. known:** come to know, i.e. seen through.
106. liege: sovereign.   **110. hope:** expect.
114. breeding: upbringing.   **charge:** expense.
115–16. Disdain . . . ever: let the consequences of my disdain rather spoil my fortunes forever.

All's Well
That Ends Well
II.iii

King. 'Tis only title thou disdain'st in her, the
    which
I can build up. Strange is it that our bloods,
Of color, weight, and heat, pour'd all together,
Would quite confound distinction, yet stands off 120
In differences so mighty. If she be
All that is virtuous—save what thou dislik'st,
A poor physician's daughter—thou dislik'st
Of virtue for the name. But do not so. 124
From lowest place [when] virtuous things proceed,
The place is dignified by th' doer's deed.
Where great additions swell 's, and virtue none,
It is a dropsied honor. Good alone
Is good, without a name; vileness is so:
The property by what [it] is should go, 130
Not by the title. She is young, wise, fair,
In these to nature she's immediate heir;
And these breed honor. That is honor's scorn,
Which challenges itself as honor's born,
And is not like the sire. Honors thrive, 135
When rather from our acts we them derive
Than our foregoers. The mere word's a slave
Debosh'd on every tomb, on every grave
A lying trophy, and as oft is dumb
Where dust and damn'd oblivion is the tomb 140
Of honor'd bones indeed. What should be said?
If thou canst like this creature as a maid,
I can create the rest. Virtue and she
Is her own dower; honor and wealth from me.
    Ber. I cannot love her, nor will strive to do't. 145
    King. Thou wrong'st thyself, if thou shouldst
        strive to choose.
    Hel. That you are well restor'd, my lord, I'm glad.
Let the rest go.
    King. My honor's at the stake, which to defeat,
I must produce my power. Here, take her hand, 150
Proud scornful boy, unworthy this good gift,
That dost in vile misprision shackle up
My love and her desert; that canst not dream,
We poising us in her defective scale,
Shall weigh thee to the beam; that wilt not know 155

It is in us to plant thine honor where
We please to have it grow. Check thy contempt;
Obey our will, which travails in thy good;
Believe not thy disdain, but presently
Do thine own fortunes that obedient right 160
Which both thy duty owes and our power claims,
Or I will throw thee from my care for ever
Into the staggers and the careless lapse
Of youth and ignorance; both my revenge and hate
Loosing upon thee, in the name of justice, 165
Without all terms of pity. Speak, thine answer.
    Ber. Pardon, my gracious lord; for I submit
My fancy to your eyes. When I consider
What great creation and what dole of honor
Flies where you bid it, I find that she, which late 170
Was in my nobler thoughts most base, is now
The praised of the King, who so ennobled,
Is as 'twere born so.
    King.   Take her by the hand,
And tell her she is thine; to whom I promise
A counterpoise—if not to thy estate 175
A balance more replete.
    Ber.   I take her hand.
    King. Good fortune and the favor of the King
Smile upon this contract, whose ceremony
Shall seem expedient on the now-born brief,
And be perform'd to-night. The solemn feast 180
Shall more attend upon the coming space,
Expecting absent friends. As thou lov'st her,
Thy love's to me religious; else, does err.
    Exeunt. Lafew and Parolles stay behind,
        commenting of this wedding.
    Laf. Do you hear, monsieur? A word with you.
    Par. Your pleasure, sir? 185
    Laf. Your lord and master did well to make his
recantation.
    Par. Recantation? My lord? My master?
    Laf. Ay; is it not a language I speak?
    Par. A most harsh one, and not to be understood
without bloody succeeding. My master? 191
    Laf. Are you companion to the Count Rossillion?
    Par. To any count, to all counts: to what is man.

117. **title:** i.e. lack of title. Cf. *name* (i.e. lack of name) in line 124.
119. **Of . . . heat.** Modifies *distinction* (line 120); *Of* = in respect of.
120. **stands off:** stand separated.   125. **proceed:** issue.
127. **additions:** honorific titles and other marks of distinction.
128. **dropsied:** i.e. unhealthily swollen.   **alone:** of itself, by its own essential nature.   129. **vileness is so:** vileness is vile of itself.
130. **property:** quality.   **go:** i.e. be accepted.
132. **In . . . heir:** she inherits these qualities directly from nature.
133. **honor's scorn:** i.e. an object of contempt in the eyes of the truly honorable.   134. **challenges:** makes claims for.
138. **Debosh'd:** debauched, debased.   139. **trophy:** memorial.
140. **damn'd:** damnable, hateful.
141. **honor'd bones indeed:** i.e. the remains of men who had truly possessed honor.
143. **Virtue and she:** she herself with her natural endowments of youth, wisdom, and beauty (line 130) and her honorable attainments.
145. **strive to do't:** attempt to do so.
146. **strive to choose:** endeavor to make your own choice, i.e. to follow your own wishes.
149. **at the stake:** under attack (a figure from bear-baiting).   **which:** i.e. which attack.
152. **misprision:** (1) scorn; (2) error, taking one thing for another. Sometimes spelled, and probably pronounced, *misprison*; hence the following *shackle up*.
154–55. **We . . . beam:** I, adding my weight to her overlight (*defective* = deficient) side of the balance, shall outweigh your side and send it up to the cross-beam. The figure of the balance recurs at lines 175–76.

156. **in us:** in my royal power.   158. **travails in:** labors for.
159. **Believe not:** do not credit, i.e. do not be governed by.   **presently:** at once.
160. **Do . . . right:** do your fortunes justice by yielding that obedience.
163. **staggers . . . lapse.** These words may mean "giddiness and heedless downward course" or "sick confusion and reckless ruin" (Dyce emended *careless* to *cureless* for "irreparable ruin"). *Of youth and ignorance* (line 164) supports the milder reading, but the rest of the sentence accords with the bleaker prediction.
166. **all . . . pity:** any concessions to mercy.   168. **fancy:** liking.
169. **great creation:** creating of greatness.   **dole:** dealing out.
170. **which late:** who a short time ago.   171. **base:** low in station.
175–76. **A counterpoise . . . replete:** an equal weight, if not a weight even heavier than your possessions come to.
179. **Shall . . . brief.** A much-debated line; perhaps "shall show itself speedily (*expedient* = expedition) in the wake of this just-completed contract."   180. **solemn:** ceremonial.
181. **more attend:** wait longer.   **space:** time.
182. **Expecting absent friends:** awaiting relatives who are not now here.
183. **to me:** in my interpretation.   **religious:** i.e. directed toward the proper object of worship.   **does err:** strays from the truth, is sinful or idolatrous.   s.d. **Lafew . . . wedding.** An unusual type of stage direction; possibly Shakespeare broke off work on the scene at this point and left a memorandum to guide himself when he resumed.
191. **succeeding:** sequel, consequences.

Laf. To what is count's man. Count's master is of another style.   195

Par. You are too old, sir; let it satisfy you, you are too old.

Laf. I must tell thee, sirrah, I write man; to which title age cannot bring thee.

Par. What I dare too well do, I dare not do.   200

Laf. I did think thee, for two ordinaries, to be a pretty wise fellow. Thou didst make tolerable vent of thy travel; it might pass: yet the scarfs and the   203 bannerets about thee did manifoldly dissuade me from believing thee a vessel of too great a burthen. I have now found thee. When I lose thee again, I care not; yet art thou good for nothing but taking up, and that thou'rt scarce worth.

Par. Hadst thou not the privilege of antiquity upon thee—   210

Laf. Do not plunge thyself too far in anger, lest thou hasten thy trial; which if—Lord have mercy on thee for a hen! So, my good window of lettice, fare thee well. Thy casement I need not open, for I look through thee. Give me thy hand.   215

Par. My lord, you give me most egregious indignity.

Laf. Ay, with all my heart, and thou art worthy of it.

Par. I have not, my lord, deserv'd it.   220

Laf. Yes, good faith, ev'ry dram of it, and I will not bate thee a scruple.

Par. Well, I shall be wiser.   223

Laf. Ev'n as soon as thou canst, for thou hast to pull at a smack a' th' contrary. If ever thou be'st bound in thy scarf and beaten, thou shall find what it is to be proud of thy bondage. I have a desire to hold my acquaintance with thee, or rather my knowledge, that I may say in the default, "He is a man I know."   228

Par. My lord, you do me most insupportable vexation.

Laf. I would it were hell-pains for thy sake, and my poor doing eternal; for doing I am past, as I will by thee, in what motion age will give me leave.   234

Exit.

Par. Well, thou hast a son shall take this disgrace off me, scurvy, old, filthy, scurvy lord! Well, I must be patient, there is no fettering of authority. I'll beat him, by my life, if I can meet him with any con-   238 venience, and he were double and double a lord. I'll have no more pity of his age than I would have of—I'll beat him, and if I could but meet him again.

Enter LAFEW.

Laf. Sirrah, your lord and master's married, there's news for you. You have a new mistress.   243

Par. I most unfeignedly beseech your lordship to make some reservation of your wrongs. He is my good lord; whom I serve above is my master.

Laf. Who? God?

Par. Ay, sir.   248

Laf. The devil it is that's thy master. Why dost thou garter up thy arms a' this fashion? Dost make hose of thy sleeves? Do other servants so? Thou wert best set thy lower part where thy nose stands. By mine honor, if I were but two hours younger, I'd beat   253 thee. Methink'st thou art a general offense, and every man should beat thee. I think thou wast created for men to breathe themselves upon thee.   256

Par. This is hard and undeserv'd measure, my lord.

Laf. Go to, sir, you were beaten in Italy for picking a kernel out of a pomegranate. You are a vagabond and no true traveller. You are more saucy with   260 lords and honorable personages than the commission of your birth and virtue gives you heraldry. You are not worth another word, else I'd call you knave. I leave you.

Exit.

Enter [BERTRAM] *Count Rossillion.*

Par. Good, very good, it is so then. Good, very good, let it be conceal'd awhile.   266

Ber. Undone, and forfeited to cares for ever!

194. **man:** servant.
196. **let . . . you:** i.e. don't force me to take action.
198. **write man:** style myself "man," claim manhood.
200. **What . . . not do:** i.e. what I have all too much courage for, your age inhibits me from doing.
201. **ordinaries:** meals.   202. **make . . . of:** talk passably about.
203, 204. **scarfs, bannerets.** Scarfs were often worn by soldiers, but Parolles, to judge by various references to his attire, evidently goes in for excessively showy adornment. His streamers suggest to Lafew pennants on a ship; hence his figure of a vessel in line 205. Cf. *The Merchant of Venice,* II.vi.14–15, where a "scarfed bark" conversely brings to mind a young gallant.
205. **burthen:** cargo (variant of *burden*).
206. **found thee:** found you out, seen through you (with following quibble).
207. **taking up.** The meaning may be "contradicting," "berating," or "taking into custody," and there is a final quibble on "picking up" (in contrast to *lose,* line 206).
209. **privilege of antiquity:** license permitted to old age.
212. **hasten thy trial:** be (tested and) found out sooner.
213. **hen:** coward (?). **lettice:** lattice. Lafew calls Parolles a lattice window because he has seen through him; perhaps also his scarfs and bannerets suggest latticework and advertise his character as red-lattice windows advertised taverns, of which they were a regular feature.
214. **Thy . . . open.** The casement was made of wood. Perhaps there is a play on *case* = body.
222. **bate:** abate, remit.   **scruple:** the smallest unit of weight, one-third of a dram.
223. **be wiser.** Parolles means something like "I'll avoid dotards in future," but Lafew replies to the simple sense "grow wiser."
225. **pull . . . contrary:** swallow a fair amount of the opposite quality.
227. **hold:** continue.
229. **in the default:** when you default (or fail). Lafew takes it for granted that that day will come. Cf. line 212, where he assumes that Parolles' *trial* (testing) will result in his being found wanting.

232. **I . . . sake.** Lafew adopts the verbal pattern of one who has been thanked for a kindness and who replies that he has done far less than the recipient deserves.
233. **my poor doing:** i.e. my very inadequate vexing of you. Lafew here picks up Parolles' *do* (line 230), then (in *for doing*) plays on the word in its slang sexual sense. **will:** i.e. will now pass.
234. **in . . . leave:** with whatever gait or speed my advanced age permits (alluding to Parolles' stress on his "antiquity").
235–36. **shall . . . me:** i.e. on whom I will retaliate.
238–39. **with any convenience:** on any suitable occasion.
239. **and:** even if.
245. **make . . . wrongs:** keep your affronts in some degree to yourself (Schmidt).   245–46. **my good lord:** i.e. my patron.
250. **garter . . . arms.** Presumably Parolles has tied a scarf around each arm.
254. **Methink'st.** The impersonal verb *methinks* (= it seems to me) is here treated as personal, drawn into the second person singular by attraction of the following *thou,* as if with the sense "thou seemest to me."   **general offense:** public nuisance.
256. **breathe . . . thee:** get their exercise by beating you.
257. **measure:** meting out of judgment, i.e. treatment.
258–59. **you . . . pomegranate.** The point seems to be that people find Parolles so worthy of beating that they beat him on the slightest pretext.   261. **commission:** warrant.
262. **gives you heraldry:** entitles you to be.

Par. What's the matter, sweet heart?

Ber. Although before the solemn priest I have sworn,
I will not bed her.   270

Par. What, what, sweet heart?

Ber. O my Parolles, they have married me!
I'll to the Tuscan wars, and never bed her.

Par. France is a dog-hole, and it no more merits
The tread of a man's foot. To th' wars!   275

Ber. There's letters from my mother; what th' import is,
I know not yet.

Par. Ay, that would be known. To th' wars, my boy, to th' wars!
He wears his honor in a box unseen,
That hugs his kicky-wicky here at home,   280
Spending his manly marrow in her arms,
Which should sustain the bound and high curvet
Of Mars's fiery steed. To other regions!
France is a stable, we that dwell in't jades,
Therefore to th' war!   285

Ber. It shall be so. I'll send her to my house,
Acquaint my mother with my hate to her,
And wherefore I am fled; write to the King
That which I durst not speak. His present gift
Shall furnish me to those Italian fields   290
Where noble fellows strike. Wars is no strife
To the dark house and the [detested] wife.

Par. Will this *capriccio* hold in thee, art sure?

Ber. Go with me to my chamber, and advise me.
I'll send her straight away. To-morrow,   295
I'll to the wars, she to her single sorrow.

Par. Why, these balls bound, there's noise in it.
'Tis hard!
A young man married is a man that's marr'd;
Therefore away, and leave her bravely; go.
The King has done you wrong; but hush, 'tis so.   300
Exeunt.

[SCENE IV]

Enter HELENA *and* CLOWN.

Hel. My mother greets me kindly. Is she well?

Clo. She is not well, but yet she has her health.
She's very merry, but yet she is not well; but thanks be

given, she's very well, and wants nothing i' th' world;
but yet she is not well.   5

Hel. If she be very well, what does she ail that she's not very well?

Clo. Truly, she's very well indeed, but for two things.

Hel. What two things?   10

Clo. One, that she's not in heaven, whither God send her quickly! the other, that she's in earth, from whence God send her quickly!

Enter PAROLLES.

Par. Bless you, my fortunate lady!

Hel. I hope, sir, I have your good will to have mine own good [fortunes].   16

Par. You had my prayers to lead them on, and to keep them on, have them still. O, my knave, how does my old lady?

Clo. So that you had her wrinkles and I her money, I would she did as you say.   21

Par. Why, I say nothing.

Clo. Marry, you are the wiser man; for many a man's tongue shakes out his master's undoing. To say nothing, to do nothing, to know nothing, and to have nothing, is to be a great part of your title, which is within a very little of nothing.   27

Par. Away, th' art a knave.

Clo. You should have said, sir, "Before a knave th' art a knave," that's "Before me th' art a knave." This had been truth, sir.   31

Par. Go to, thou art a witty fool, I have found thee.

Clo. Did you find me in yourself, sir, [*Parolles nods.*] or were you taught to find me? [*Parolles shakes his head.*]
The search, sir, was profitable, and much fool   35
may you find in you, even to the world's pleasure and the increase of laughter.

Par. A good knave, i' faith, and well fed.
Madam, my lord will go away to-night,
A very serious business calls on him.   40
The great prerogative and rite of love,
Which, as your due, time claims, he does acknowledge,
But puts it off to a compell'd restraint;
Whose want, and whose delay, is strew'd with sweets,
Which they distill now in the curbed time,   45
To make the coming hour o'erflow with joy,
And pleasure drown the brim.

Hel.   What's his will else?

Par. That you will take your instant leave a' th' King,
And make this haste as your own good proceeding,

---

276. **letters:** a letter (Latin *litterae*).
279. **in . . . unseen.** With sexual innuendo.
280. **kicky-wicky.** Apparently Shakespeare's invention.
281. **Spending:** expending, using up.   **his manly marrow:** the essence of his manliness.
282. **curvet:** a difficult leap in which all four legs are off the ground.
284. **jades:** inferior horses.
289. **His present gift:** the gift he has just made me.
290. **furnish me to:** equip me for.
292. **To:** compared with.   **dark house.** Perhaps this = dismal house, but probably the reference is to a madhouse (the mad were often kept in darkness) and Bertram means that living with Helena would drive him crazy. In *Twelfth Night* the room where Malvolio is confined is called a dark house (see IV.ii.34, 41; V.i.342).
293. **capriccio:** caprice (Italian).   295. **straight:** at once.
296. **single:** (1) solitary; (2) husbandless.
297. **these . . . it:** i.e. this shows spirit.   *Balls* = tennis balls.
298. **A young . . . marr'd.** Proverbial.   299. **bravely.** As at II.i.29.

II.iv. Location: Paris. The King's palace.
1. **kindly:** affectionately.
2. **well.** The Clown quibbles on the Elizabethan sense "in heaven."

4. **wants:** lacks.   6. **what:** in what, how.   24. **man's:** servant's.
26. **title:** worth.
29–30. **You . . . knave.** The Clown plays on the oath *before me* (= on my soul; see II.iii.26). He says, in effect, "You're another."
33. **in yourself.** Parolles unwarily takes this to mean "by your own efforts."   36. **pleasure:** merriment.
38. **well fed:** i.e. better fed than taught (see the note on II.ii.3).
42. **time:** the occasion.   43. **puts . . . to:** delays its because of.
44. **Whose want:** the lack of which (rite).   **sweets:** fragrant flowers. Parolles uses an elaborate figure based on the distillation of perfume.
45. **they:** i.e. the want and the delay.   **curbed time:** time of restraint; Hunter suggests that there is also a reference to the flask or *cucurbita* of the still.
47. **else:** besides.   49. **make:** represent.

Strength'ned with what apology you think   50
May make it probable need.

Hel.   What more commands he?

Par.   That having this obtain'd, you presently
Attend his further pleasure.

Hel.   In every thing I wait upon his will.   54

Par.   I shall report it so.   *Exit Parolles.*

Hel.   I pray you. Come, sirrah. *Exeunt.*

[SCENE V]

Enter LAFEW *and* BERTRAM.

Laf.   But I hope your lordship thinks not him a
soldier.

Ber.   Yes, my lord, and of very valiant approof.

Laf.   You have it from his own deliverance.

Ber.   And by other warranted testimony.   5

Laf.   Then my dial goes not true. I took this lark
for a bunting.

Ber.   I do assure you, my lord, he is very great in
knowledge, and accordingly valiant.   9

Laf.   I have then sinn'd against his experience, and
transgress'd against his valor, and my state that way is
dangerous, since I cannot yet find in my heart to repent.
Here he comes. I pray you make us friends, I will
pursue the amity.   14

Enter PAROLLES.

Par.   [*To Bertram.*] These things shall be done, sir.

Laf.   Pray you, sir, who's his tailor?

Par.   Sir!

Laf.   O, I know him well, I, sir, he, sir, 's a good
workman, a very good tailor.   19

Ber.   [*Aside to Parolles.*] Is she gone to the King?

Par.   She is.

Ber.   Will she away to-night?

Par.   As you'll have her.

Ber.   I have writ my letters, casketed my treasure,
Given order for our horses, and to-night,   25
When I should take possession of the bride,
[End] ere I do begin.

Laf.   A good traveller is something at the latter end
of a dinner, but [one] that lies three thirds, and uses a
known truth to pass a thousand nothings with, should

be once heard and thrice beaten. God save you, captain.

Ber.   Is there any unkindness between my lord and
you, monsieur?   33

Par.   I know not how I have deserv'd to run into
my lord's displeasure.

Laf.   You have made shift to run into't, boots and
spurs and all, like him that leapt into the custard; and
out of it you'll run again, rather than suffer question
for your residence.   39

Ber.   It may be you have mistaken him, my lord.

Laf.   And shall do so ever, though I took him at 's
prayers. Fare you well, my lord, and believe this of
me: there can be no kernel in this light nut; the soul of
this man is his clothes. Trust him not in matter of
heavy consequence; I have kept of them tame, and   45
know their natures. Farewell, monsieur, I have
spoken better of you than you have or will to deserve
at my hand, but we must do good against evil. [*Exit.*]

Par.   An idle lord, I swear.

Ber.   I think so.   50

Par.   Why, do you not know him?

Ber.   Yes, I do know him well, and common speech
Gives him a worthy pass. Here comes my clog.

Enter HELENA.

Hel.   I have, sir, as I was commanded from you,
Spoke with the King, and have procur'd his leave   55
For present parting; only he desires
Some private speech with you.

Ber.   I shall obey his will.
You must not marvel, Helen, at my course,
Which holds not color with the time, nor does
The ministration and required office   60
On my particular. Prepar'd I was not
For such a business; therefore am I found
So much unsettled. This drives me to entreat you
That presently you take your way for home,
And rather muse than ask why I entreat you,   65
For my respects are better than they seem,
And my appointments have in them a need
Greater than shows itself at the first view
To you that know them not. This to my mother.
[*Giving a letter.*]

---

36. **made shift:** contrived.
37. **like . . . custard.** "It was a Foolery practis'd at City-Entertainments, whilst the Jester or Zany was in Vogue, for him to leap into a large deep Custard" (Theobald).
38. **you'll run:** you wish to run.
38–39. **suffer . . . residence:** tolerate inquiry as to why you are in it.
40. **mistaken him:** misjudged him (or, perhaps, mistaken him for someone else). Lafew quibbles on "taken his actions amiss."
45. **heavy:** serious.   **kept . . . tame:** had some of them in my household (*tame* = domesticated).
47. **have . . . deserve:** have deserved or intend to deserve (?). Singer's conjecture *have or* [i.e. either] *wit or will to deserve* is tempting.
48. **do . . . evil:** return good for evil.
50. **I think so.** Singer's emendation *I think not so* would make the following remarks easier to account for.
52–53. **common . . . pass:** general report esteems him a worthy man.
53. **clog:** trammel; literally, a heavy block of wood attached to an animal to restrict its liberty of movement. Cf. *ball-and-chain* as slang for a wife.   56. **present parting:** immediate departure.
59. **holds . . . with:** does not match, is not in keeping with.   **time:** occasion.
59–61. **nor . . . particular:** i.e. nor does it permit the performance of the duty incumbent upon me as a private person (i.e. as a husband).
65. **muse:** wonder.   66. **respects:** considerations, i.e. reasons.
67. **appointments:** purposes, affairs.

---

50. **apology:** explanation.
51. **make . . . need:** make your alleged need for haste plausible.
52. **presently:** immediately.
53. **Attend . . . pleasure:** wait upon him to hear his further command.
54. **wait upon:** am ready to serve.

II.v. Location: Paris. The King's palace.
3. **valiant approof:** proved valor.   4. **deliverance:** report.
6. **dial:** clock.
6–7. **took . . . bunting.** "To take a bunting for a lark" was proverbial for mistakenly ascribing worth to what is worthless. The bunting resembles the lark but lacks the lark's beautiful song. Lafew reverses the proverb but with tongue in cheek.
9. **accordingly:** correspondingly.
10–12. **I . . . repent.** Lafew adopts the language of religious confession.
16. **who's his tailor.** Suggesting that Parolles is no more than the product of his tailor's skill.
18. **I . . . well.** Lafew pretends to take Parolles' reply for the name of the tailor.
28. **A good traveller:** a man who has travelled widely, i.e. a man with many tales to tell.

'Twill be two days ere I shall see you, so   70
I leave you to your wisdom.
　　Hel.　　　　　　　　　Sir, I can nothing say,
But that I am your most obedient servant.
　　Ber.　Come, come, no more of that.
　　Hel.　　　　　　　　　　And ever shall
With true observance seek to eke out that
Wherein toward me my homely stars have fail'd   75
To equal my great fortune.
　　Ber.　　　　　　　　Let that go.
My haste is very great. Farewell; hie home.
　　Hel.　Pray, sir, your pardon.
　　Ber.　　　　　　　　　Well, what would you say?
　　Hel.　I am not worthy of the wealth I owe,
Nor dare I say 'tis mine; and yet it is;   80
But like a timorous thief, most fain would steal
What law does vouch mine own.
　　Ber.　　　　　　　　　What would you have?
　　Hel.　Something, and scarce so much; nothing in-
　　deed.
I would not tell you what I would, my lord.
Faith, yes: 85
Strangers and foes do sunder, and not kiss.
　　Ber.　I pray you stay not, but in haste to horse.
　　Hel.　I shall not break your bidding, good my lord.
　　[*Ber.*] Where are my other men, monsieur?—
　　Farewell.   *Exit* [*Helena*].
Go thou toward home, where I will never come   90
Whilst I can shake my sword or hear the drum.
Away, and for our flight.
　　Par.　　　　　　　Bravely, *coraggio!* [*Exeunt.*]

ACT III, [SCENE I]

Flourish. Enter the DUKE OF FLORENCE, *the two French*
[LORDS], *with a troop of soldiers.*

　　Duke.　So that from point to point now have you
　　heard
The fundamental reasons of this war,
Whose great decision hath much blood let forth
And more thirsts after.
　　1. Lord.　　　　　　Holy seems the quarrel
Upon your Grace's part; black and fearful   5
On the opposer.
　　Duke.　Therefore we marvel much our cousin
　　France
Would in so just a business shut his bosom
Against our borrowing prayers.
　　[*2. Lord.*]　　　　　　　　Good my lord,
The reasons of our state I cannot yield   10
But like a common and an outward man

74. **observance**: devoted service.　**eke out**: piece out; add to.
75. **homely stars**: i.e. humble birth.　77. **hie**: hasten.
79. **owe**: possess.　81. **fain**: gladly.　87. **stay**: delay.
92. **Bravely**: splendidly done, bravo.　*Coraggio* (Italian "courage")
apparently has much the same sense here.

III.i. Location: Florence. The Duke's palace.
3. **decision**: war to decide the issue.　4. **Holy**: righteous.
6. **opposer**: opposer's.　8. **bosom**: heart.
9. **borrowing prayers**: entreaties for aid.
10. **yield**: produce, furnish.
11. **But . . . man**: except like a member of the general public on the
outside.

That the great figure of a council frames
By self-unable motion, therefore dare not
Say what I think of it, since I have found
Myself in my incertain grounds to fail   15
As often as I guess'd.
　　Duke.　　　　　　　Be it his pleasure.
　　[*1. Lord.*]　But I am sure the younger of our nature,
That surfeit on their ease, will day by day
Come here for physic.
　　Duke.　　　　　　Welcome shall they be;
And all the honors that can fly from us   20
Shall on them settle.—You know your places well;
When better fall, for your avails they fell.
To-morrow to th' field.   *Flourish.* [*Exeunt.*]

[SCENE II]

Enter COUNTESS *and* CLOWN.

　　Count.　It hath happen'd all as I would have had it,
save that he comes not along with her.
　　Clo.　By my troth, I take my young lord to be a
very melancholy man.
　　Count.　By what observance, I pray you?   5
　　Clo.　Why, he will look upon his boot and sing,
mend the ruff and sing, ask questions and sing, pick his
teeth and sing. I know a man that had this trick of
melancholy [sold] a goodly manor for a song.   9
　　Count.　Let me see what he writes, and when he
means to come.   [*Opening a letter.*]
　　Clo.　I have no mind to Isbel since I was at court.
Our old [ling] and our Isbels a' th' country are nothing
like your old ling and your Isbels a' th' court. The
brains of my Cupid's knock'd out, and I begin to   15
love, as an old man loves money, with no stomach.
　　Count.　What have we here?
　　Clo.　[E'en] that you have there.   *Exit.*
　　[*Count. Reads* a letter.] "I have sent you a daughter-
in-law; she hath recover'd the King, and undone   20
me. I have wedded her, not bedded her, and sworn to
make the 'not' eternal. You shall hear I am run away;
know it before the report come. If there be breadth
enough in the world, I will hold a long distance. My
duty to you.   25
　　　　　　Your unfortunate son,
　　　　　　　　　　　Bertram."

12. **figure**: shape, scheme.　**frames**: constructs.
13. **self-unable motion**: his own inadequate conjectures (*motion* =
motion of the mind, thought).
16. **guess'd**: made a guess (not "guessed right").　**Be . . . pleasure**:
i.e. let us simply say that it is his will.　17. **nature**: temperament.
18. **surfeit on**. Equivalent to "are fed up with, are sick of," but with
the metaphorical sense less faded. It was a commonplace that both
in the body politic and in individuals the self-indulgent life of peace-
time led to disorders that were cured by the bloodletting of war.
20. **that . . . us**: i.e. that are in my power to bestow.
22. **better fall**: better places fall vacant.　**fell**: will have fallen.

III.ii. Location: Rossillion. The Count's palace.
1. **all**: entirely.　3. **troth**: faith.　5. **observance**: observation.
7. **mend**: adjust.　**ruff**: ruffle, turned-over portion at the top of a
boot.
7–8. **pick his teeth**. A fashionable affectation; see the note on I.i.158.
13. **old ling**: salt cods (a bawdy pun: *salt* = lascivious; *cod* = male
sex organ).　14–15. **The brains . . . out**: my love is done for.
16. **stomach**: appetite.　20. **recover'd**: cured.
22. **not**. Probably punning on *knot*.

This is not well, rash and unbridled boy,
To fly the favors of so good a king,
To pluck his indignation on thy head   30
By the misprising of a maid too virtuous
For the contempt of empire.

Enter CLOWN.

Clo. O madam, yonder is heavy news within between two soldiers and my young lady!
Count. What is the matter?   35
Clo. Nay, there is some comfort in the news, some
comfort. Your son will not be kill'd so soon as I
thought he would.
Count. Why should he be kill'd?   39
Clo. So say I, madam, if he run away, as I hear he
does. The danger is in standing to't; that's the loss of
men, though it be the getting of children. Here they
come will tell you more; for my part, I only hear your
son was run away.   [*Exit.*]

Enter HELEN *and two Gentlemen,* [*the French* LORDS].

[*2. Lord.*] 'Save you, good madam.   45
Hel. Madam, my lord is gone, for ever gone.
[*1. Lord.*] Do not say so.
Count. Think upon patience. Pray you, gentlemen,
I have felt so many quirks of joy and grief
That the first face of neither on the start   50
Can woman me unto't. Where is my son, I pray you?
[*1. Lord.*] Madam, he's gone to serve the Duke of
Florence.
We met him thitherward, for thence we came;
And after some dispatch in hand at court,
Thither we bend again.   55
Hel. Look on his letter, madam, here's my pass-
port.
[*Reads.*] "When thou canst get the ring upon my
finger, which never shall come off, and show me a child
begotten of thy body that I am father to, then call me
husband; but in such a 'then' I write a 'never.'"   60
This is a dreadful sentence.
Count. Brought you this letter, gentlemen?
1. [*Lord*].   Ay, madam,
And for the contents' sake are sorry for our pains.
Count. I prithee, lady, have a better cheer;
If thou engrossest all the griefs are thine,   65
Thou robb'st me of a moi'ty. He was my son,
But I do wash his name out of my blood,
And thou art all my child. Towards Florence is he?
[*1. Lord.*] Ay, madam.
Count.   And to be a soldier?
[*1. Lord.*] Such is his noble purpose, and believe't,

The Duke will lay upon him all the honor   71
That good convenience claims.
Count.   Return you thither?
[*2. Lord.*] Ay, madam, with the swiftest wing of
speed.
Hel. [*Reads.*] "Till I have no wife, I have nothing
in France."   75
'Tis bitter.
Count. Find you that there?
Hel.   Ay, madam.
[*2. Lord.*] 'Tis but the boldness of his hand haply,
Which his heart was not consenting to.
Count. Nothing in France, until he have no wife!
There's nothing here that is too good for him   80
But only she, and she deserves a lord
That twenty such rude boys might tend upon,
And call her hourly mistress. Who was with him?
[*2. Lord.*] A servant only, and a gentleman
Which I have sometime known.
Count.   Parolles, was it not?
[*2. Lord.*] Ay, my good lady, he.   86
Count. A very tainted fellow, and full of wicked-
ness.
My son corrupts a well-derived nature
With his inducement.
[*2. Lord.*]   Indeed, good lady,
The fellow has a deal of that too much,   90
Which holds him much to have.
Count.   Y' are welcome, gentlemen.
I will entreat you, when you see my son,
To tell him that his sword can never win
The honor that he loses. More I'll entreat you
Written to bear along.
[*1. Lord.*]   We serve you, madam,   95
In that and all your worthiest affairs.
Count. Not so, but as we change our courtesies.
Will you draw near?   *Exit* [*with Lords*].
Hel. "Till I have no wife, I have nothing in France."
Nothing in France, until he has no wife!   100
Thou shalt have none, Rossillion, none in France;
Then hast thou all again. Poor lord, is't I
That chase thee from thy country, and expose
Those tender limbs of thine to the event
Of the none-sparing war? And is it I   105
That drive thee from the sportive court, where thou
Wast shot at with fair eyes, to be the mark
Of smoky muskets? O you leaden messengers,
That ride upon the violent speed of fire,
Fly with false aim, move the still-peering air   110

---

30. **pluck:** draw down.   31. **misprising:** scorning.
32. **empire:** i.e. an emperor.   33. **heavy:** sad.
41. **standing to't:** i.e. not running away (with a bawdy equivoque
which indicates that *be kill'd* in line 37 plays on the sexual sense of *die*).
42. **getting:** begetting.   48. **Think upon patience:** control yourself.
49. **quirks:** sudden strokes.
50. **face:** appearance.   **on the start:** with startling suddenness.
51. **woman me unto't:** make me respond like a (weak) woman, i.e.
with tears.   53. **thitherward:** on his way thither.
56. **passport:** voucher, written confirmation.
61. **sentence:** judicial sentence.
64. **have . . . cheer:** do not look so sad.
65. **If thou engrossest:** if you monopolize.   **are:** that are.
66. **moi'ty:** share, half.   68. **all my:** my only.

72. **convenience:** propriety, what is fitting.   77. **haply:** perhaps.
90–91. **has . . . have:** has altogether too much power of persuasion,
which proves very advantageous to him.
97. **but . . . courtesies:** i.e. except as I repay your courtesies with
mine (*change* = exchange).   98. **draw near:** come with me.
101. **Rossillion.** Helena appropriately designates her husband by the
title that sums up what he has in France.
104. **event:** all that occurs, i.e. accidents, hazards.
108. **leaden messengers:** i.e. bullets.
110. **still-peering.** A controversial reading. If correct, it could mean
"always looking on" or "looking on unmoved"; or *peering* may
represent a shortened form of *appearing* and the compound may
mean "motionless in appearance" or "always presenting itself (as a
mark)." But most apposite would be a reference to the air's invul-
nerability, and editors usually adopt the emendation *still-piecing* =
constantly closing itself up again (an anonymous conjecture first
recorded by Steevens). Many other emendations have been proposed.

That sings with piercing, do not touch my lord.
Whoever shoots at him, I set him there;
Whoever charges on his forward breast,
I am the caitiff that do hold him to't;
And though I kill him not, I am the cause   115
His death was so effected. Better 'twere
I met the ravin lion when he roar'd
With sharp constraint of hunger; better 'twere
That all the miseries which nature owes   119
Were mine at once. No, come thou home, Rossillion,
Whence honor but of danger wins a scar,
As oft it loses all. I will be gone.
My being here it is that holds thee hence.
Shall I stay here to do't? No, no, although
The air of paradise did fan the house,   125
And angels offic'd all. I will be gone,
That pitiful rumor may report my flight
To consolate thine ear. Come night, end day!
For with the dark, poor thief, I'll steal away.   *Exit.*

[SCENE III]

Flourish. Enter the DUKE OF FLORENCE, [BERTRAM,
Count of] *Rossillion, Drum and Trumpets, Soldiers,*
PAROLLES.

Duke. The general of our horse thou art, and we,
Great in our hope, lay our best love and credence
Upon thy promising fortune.
Ber.   Sir, it is
A charge too heavy for my strength, but yet
We'll strive to bear it for your worthy sake   5
To th' extreme edge of hazard.
Duke.   Then go thou forth,
And Fortune play upon thy prosperous helm
As thy auspicious mistress!
Ber.   This very day,
Great Mars, I put myself into thy file;
Make me but like my thoughts, and I shall prove   10
A lover of thy drum, hater of love.   *Exeunt omnes.*

[SCENE IV]

Enter COUNTESS *and* STEWARD.

Count. Alas! and would you take the letter of her?

Might you not know she would do as she has done
By sending me a letter? Read it again.
[*Stew. Reads*] *letter.*
"I am Saint Jaques' pilgrim, thither gone.
Ambitious love hath so in me offended   5
That barefoot plod I the cold ground upon
With sainted vow my faults to have amended.
Write, write, that from the bloody course of war
My dearest master, your dear son, may hie.
Bless him at home in peace, whilst I from far   10
His name with zealous fervor sanctify.
His taken labors bid him me forgive;
I, his despiteful Juno, sent him forth
From courtly friends, with camping foes to live,
Where death and danger dogs the heels of worth.   15
He is too good and fair for death and me,
Whom I myself embrace to set him free."
[*Count.*] Ah, what sharp stings are in her mildest
                                        words!
Rinaldo, you did never lack advice so much
As letting her pass so. Had I spoke with her,   20
I could have well diverted her intents,
Which thus she hath prevented.
Stew.   Pardon me, madam,
If I had given you this at overnight,
She might have been o'erta'en; and yet she writes,
Pursuit would be but vain.
Count.   What angel shall   25
Bless this unworthy husband? He cannot thrive,
Unless her prayers, whom heaven delights to hear
And loves to grant, reprieve him from the wrath
Of greatest justice. Write, write, Rinaldo,
To this unworthy husband of his wife.   30
Let every word weigh heavy of her worth,
That he does weigh too light. My greatest grief,
Though little he do feel it, set down sharply.
Dispatch the most convenient messenger.
When haply he shall hear that she is gone,   35
He will return, and hope I may that she,
Hearing so much, will speed her foot again,
Led hither by pure love. Which of them both

111. **sings.** Referring to the whistling sound made by the passage of the bullet, but with implication that the air, far from being injured, sings for joy.   **with piercing:** when it is pierced.
113. **forward:** (1) in the front ranks; (2) advancing; (3) facing the enemy.   114. **caitiff:** base wretch.   **hold:** force.
117. **ravin:** ravening.
119. **nature owes:** flesh is heir to (owes = owns).
121–22. **Whence . . . all:** i.e. from the war, where one can win at best no more than a scar, and often loses everything.
126. **offic'd all:** performed all the household duties.
127. **pitiful:** compassionate.
129. **thief, steal.** Cf. II.i.33–35.

III.iii. *Location:* Florence. Before the Duke's palace.
o.s.d. **Drum and Trumpets:** drummer and trumpeters.
2. **Great . . . hope:** expecting a highly favorable issue (an image of pregnancy).   **lay:** wager (but Bertram quibbles on the sense "place, load").   6. **edge of hazard:** limit of danger.
7. **helm:** helmet.   9. **file:** line of soldiers, i.e. ranks.

III.iv. *Location:* Rossillion. The Count's palace.

4–17. **I . . . free.** These lines make a sonnet in the Shakespearean form.
4. **Saint Jaques' pilgrim:** a pilgrim to the shrine of St. James, presumably (in view of the references in III.v.34, 95 to "Saint Jaques le Grand" and "great Saint Jaques") to the famous shrine at Compostela in northwestern Spain. It is never made clear why Helena's route should in III.v bring her to Florence. *Jaques,* as elsewhere in Shakespeare, is dissyllabic.
7. **sainted vow.** This may mean "vow to the saint (James)" or simply "sacred."   **my . . . amended:** to cause my sins to be pardoned (modifying not *vow* but *barefoot . . . vow*).
8. **course.** Perhaps with a play on *curse.*
10. **Bless him:** make him happy.   **in peace:** (1) removed from war; (2) unvexed by a "detested wife" (II.iii.292).
11. **sanctify:** invoke blessing upon.   12. **taken:** undertaken.
13. **despiteful:** cruel.   **Juno.** It was Juno's hostility that caused Hercules to undertake his labors (cf. line 12).
17. **Whom:** i.e. death.   **embrace:** (1) undergo; (2) welcome; (3) receive as a lover (in place of Bertram).
19. **lack . . . much:** show such poor judgment.
22. **prevented:** forestalled.   23. **at overnight:** yesterday evening.
27. **whom.** Apparently referring first to Helena (as the object of *hear*) and then to her prayers (as the object of *grant*).
29. **greatest justice:** i.e. the supreme Judge.
30. **unworthy . . . wife:** husband unworthy of his wife.
32. **weigh too light:** (1) consider inadequate; (2) judge too lightly.   **greatest:** extreme.   33. **sharply:** so as to make it keenly felt.
34. **convenient:** fit.   35. **When haply:** perhaps when.

Is dearest to me, I have no skill in sense
To make distinction. Provide this messenger. 40
My heart is heavy, and mine age is weak;
Grief would have tears, and sorrow bids me speak.

　　　　　　　　　　　　　　　　　Exeunt.

[SCENE V]

A tucket afar off. Enter *old* WIDOW *of Florence, her daughter* [DIANA], VIOLENTA, *and* MARIANA, *with other* CITIZENS.

　Wid. Nay, come, for if they do approach the city, we shall lose all the sight.
　Dia. They say the French count has done most honorable service. 4
　Wid. It is reported that he has taken their great'st commander, and that with his own hand he slew the Duke's brother. [*Tucket.*] We have lost our labor, they are gone a contrary way. Hark! you may know by their trumpets. 9
　Mar. Come, let's return again and suffice ourselves with the report of it. Well, Diana, take heed of this French earl. The honor of a maid is her name, and no legacy is so rich as honesty.
　Wid. I have told my neighbor how you have been solicited by a gentleman his companion. 15
　Mar. I know that knave, hang him! one Parolles, a filthy officer he is in those suggestions for the young earl. Beware of them, Diana; their promises, enticements, oaths, tokens, and all these engines of lust, 19 are not the things they go under. Many a maid hath been seduc'd by them, and the misery is, example, that so terrible shows in the wrack of maidenhood, cannot for all that dissuade succession, but that they are lim'd with the twigs that threatens them. I hope 24 I need not to advise you further, but I hope your own grace will keep you where you are, though there were no further danger known but the modesty which is so lost.
　Dia. You shall not need to fear me. 29

　　　Enter HELEN [*habited like a pilgrim*].

　Wid. I hope so. Look here comes a pilgrim. I

know she will lie at my house; thither they send one another. I'll question her. God save you, pilgrim, whither are bound?
　Hel. To Saint Jaques le Grand.
Where do the palmers lodge, I do beseech you? 35
　Wid. At the Saint Francis here beside the port.
　Hel. Is this the way?　　　　　*A march afar.*
　Wid. Ay, marry, is't. Hark you, they come this way.
If you will tarry, holy pilgrim,
But till the troops come by,
I will conduct you where you shall be lodg'd, 40
The rather for I think I know your hostess
As ample as myself.
　Hel.　　　　　Is it yourself?
　Wid. If you shall please so, pilgrim. 44
　Hel. I thank you, and will stay upon your leisure.
　Wid. You came I think from France?
　Hel.　　　　　　　　I did so.
　Wid. Here you shall see a countryman of yours
That has done worthy service.
　Hel.　　　　　His name, I pray you?
　Dia. The Count Rossillion. Know you such a one?
　Hel. But by the ear, that hears most nobly of him.
His face I know not.
　Dia.　　　　　Whatsome'er he is, 51
He's bravely taken here. He stole from France,
As 'tis reported, for the King had married him
Against his liking. Think you it is so?
　Hel. Ay, surely, mere the truth, I know his lady.
　Dia. There is a gentleman that serves the Count
Reports but coarsely of her.
　Hel.　　　　　What's his name? 57
　Dia. Monsieur Parolles.
　Hel.　　　　　O, I believe with him.
In argument of praise, or to the worth
Of the great Count himself, she is too mean 60
To have her name repeated. All her deserving
Is a reserved honesty, and that
I have not heard examin'd.
　Dia.　　　　　Alas, poor lady,
'Tis a hard bondage to become the wife
Of a detesting lord. 65
　Wid. I [warr'nt,] good creature, wheresoe'er she is,
Her heart weighs sadly. This young maid might do her
A shrewd turn, if she pleas'd.

---

39. **I . . . sense:** I am unable on the basis of what I feel.
41–42. **My . . . speak.** Contrast these lines with III.ii.49–51.
42. **bids me speak:** i.e. governs my words.

III.v. Location: Outside the walls of Florence.
o.s.d. **tucket:** series of trumpet notes.　**Violenta.** No lines are assigned to a character so named, and Helena's speech at the end of the scene makes it clear that the Widow has only two companions. Perhaps Shakespeare abandoned an original intention to add a character or, alternatively, to call the Widow's daughter by this name.　5. **their:** i.e. the Sienese'.
10. **return again:** go back, return home.
12. **her name:** her reputation (?) or the name of maid(en), i.e. virgin (?).　13. **honesty:** chastity.
17. **officer:** agent.　**suggestions:** solicitings.　**for:** on behalf of.
19. **oaths:** vows.　**tokens:** presents, bribes.　**engines of lust:** devisings to serve lust.
20. **go under:** masquerade as.　22. **wrack:** ruin.
23. **dissuade succession:** stop others from following the same course.
24. **lim'd . . . twigs:** i.e. caught in the trap. Birds were caught by means of birdlime, a sticky substance, smeared on the twigs of bushes.
26. **grace:** virtue.
26–28. **though . . . lost:** i.e. even if there were not the further danger of pregnancy.　29. **fear:** fear for.
30. **hope so.** Modern idiom would require *hope not.*

31. **lie:** lodge.　32. **question:** speak to.
33. **are bound:** are you bound (perhaps by analogy with the corresponding singular construction *art bound*, where *art* represents a telescoping of *art thou*).
35. **palmers:** pilgrims (strictly speaking, those returning from the Holy Land, who brought back palm leaves as tokens).
36. **Saint Francis:** i.e. an inn with a figure of the saint for its sign. **port:** city gate.　43. **ample:** amply, well.
44. **please so:** i.e. be good enough to let me be your hostess.
45. **stay . . . leisure:** await your convenience.
51. **Whatsome'er:** whatever sort of man.
52. **bravely taken:** excellently regarded.　53. **for:** because.
55. **mere the truth:** absolutely true.
57. **coarsely:** harshly, slightingly.　58. **believe:** agree.
59. **In . . . praise:** with respect to her own praiseworthiness.　**to:** in comparison with.　61. **repeated:** spoken.
61–62. **All . . . honesty:** her sole merit is a carefully guarded chastity.
63. **examin'd:** questioned.　67. **weighs sadly:** is heavy.
68. **shrewd:** hurtful.　**turn.** Frequently used with sexual implication.

Hel.   How do you mean?
May be the amorous Count solicits her
In the unlawful purpose.
 Wid.   He does indeed,   70
And brokes with all that can in such a suit
Corrupt the tender honor of a maid.
But she is arm'd for him, and keeps her guard
In honestest defense.

 Drum and Colors. Enter [BERTRAM] *Count Rossillion,*
  PAROLLES, *and the whole army.*

 Mar.   The gods forbid else!
 Wid. So, now they come.   75
That is Antonio, the Duke's eldest son,
That, Escalus.
 Hel.   Which is the Frenchman?
 Dia.   He,
That with the plume; 'tis a most gallant fellow.
I would he lov'd his wife. If he were honester
He were much goodlier. Is't not a handsome gentle-
 man?   80
 Hel. I like him well.
 Dia. 'Tis pity he is not honest. Yond's that same
  knave
That leads him to these places. Were I his lady,
I would poison that vile rascal.
 Hel.   Which is he?
 Dia. That jack-an-apes with scarfs. Why is he
 melancholy?   86
 Hel. Perchance he's hurt i' th' battle.
 Par. Lose our drum! Well.
 Mar. He's shrewdly vex'd at something. Look, he
has spied us.   90
 Wid. Marry, hang you!
 Mar. And your courtesy, for a ring-carrier!
  Exeunt [*Bertram, Parolles, and army*].
 Wid. The troop is past. Come, pilgrim, I will
  bring you
Where you shall host. Of enjoin'd penitents
There's four or five, to great Saint Jaques bound,   95
Already at my house.
 Hel.   I humbly thank you.
Please it this matron and this gentle maid
To eat with us to-night, the charge and thanking
Shall be for me, and to requite you further,
I will bestow some precepts of this virgin   100
Worthy the note.
 Both. We'll take your offer kindly. *Exeunt.*

[SCENE VI]

Enter [BERTRAM] *Count Rossillion and the* [*two*] *French*
[LORDS].

 [*2. Lord.*] Nay, good my lord, put him to't; let him
have his way.
 [*1. Lord.*] If your lordship find him not a hilding,
hold me no more in your respect.
 [*2. Lord.*] On my life, my lord, a bubble.   5
 Ber. Do you think I am so far deceiv'd in him?
 [*2. Lord.*] Believe it, my lord, in mine own direct
knowledge, without any malice, but to speak of him
as my kinsman, he's a most notable coward, an   9
infinite and endless liar, an hourly promise-breaker,
the owner of no one good quality worthy your
lordship's entertainment.   12
 [*1. Lord.*] It were fit you knew him, lest reposing
too far in his virtue, which he hath not, he might at
some great and trusty business in a main danger fail
you.   16
 Ber. I would I knew in what particular action to
try him.
 [*1. Lord.*] None better than to let him fetch off his
drum, which you hear him so confidently undertake
to do.   21
 [*2. Lord.*] I, with a troop of Florentines, will suddenly surprise him; such I will have, whom I am sure
he knows not from the enemy. We will bind and   24
hoodwink him so, that he shall suppose no other but
that he is carried into the leaguer of the adversaries,
when we bring him to our own tents. Be but your
lordship present at his examination, if he do not, for
the promise of his life, and in the highest compul-   29
sion of base fear, offer to betray you, and deliver all
the intelligence in his power against you, and that with
the divine forfeit of his soul upon oath, never trust my
judgment in any thing.   33
 [*1. Lord.*] O, for the love of laughter, let him fetch
his drum; he says he has a stratagem for't. When your
lordship sees the bottom of [his] success in't, and to
what metal this counterfeit lump of [ore] will be
melted, if you give him not John Drum's entertainment, your inclining cannot be remov'd. Here he
comes.   40

Enter PAROLLES.

 [*2. Lord.*] O, for the love of laughter, hinder not
the honor of his design. Let him fetch off his drum
in any hand.

---

71. **brokes:** does business (ordinarily used of a middleman, but here of the principal himself).
73. **guard:** ward, posture of defense (a technical term in weaponry).
74. **honestest defense:** utmost defense of virginity. s.d. **Colors:** flagbearer. **else:** that it should be otherwise.
79. **honester:** more honorable in his behavior.
82. **Yond:** that one, the one there (demonstrative pronoun).
85. **jack-an-apes:** monkey. 89. **shrewdly:** sorely.
92. **courtesy:** bow or salute. **ring-carrier:** go-between who brings presents or promises of marriage.
94. **host:** lodge. **enjoin'd penitents:** i.e. persons vowed to a pilgrimage as penance for their sins. 97. **Please it:** if it please.
98. **charge:** cost.
100. **precepts:** i.e. good advice. **of:** upon.
101. **Worthy the note:** worth listening to.
102. **take:** accept. **kindly:** gratefully.

III.vi. Location: Camp before Florence.
1. **to't:** to the test. 3. **hilding:** base wretch.
5. **a bubble:** i.e. empty and worthless despite his external glitter.
9. **as:** as if he were. **notable:** egregious.
12. **entertainment:** maintenance, patronage.
15. **trusty:** requiring trustworthiness.
23. **surprise him:** take him captive. 25. **hoodwink:** blindfold.
26. **leaguer:** camp.
30–31. **deliver . . . power:** report all the information at his command.
36. **bottom:** i.e. full extent.
37. **counterfeit.** A displaced modifier, rightly describing *ore*. **ore.** Perhaps "gold," by confusion with the heraldic term *or*.
38–39. **John Drum's entertainment:** being beaten away from the door, i.e. ignominious dismissal (found also with *Jack* or *Tom* in place of *John*). 39. **inclining:** liking, partiality.
43. **in any hand:** by all means.

Ber. How now, monsieur? This drum sticks sorely in your disposition. 45

[*1. Lord.*] A pox on't, let it go, 'tis but a drum.

Par. But a drum! Is't but a drum? A drum so lost! There was excellent command—to charge in with our horse upon our own wings, and to rend our own soldiers! 50

[*1. Lord.*] That was not to be blam'd in the command of the service; it was a disaster of war that Caesar himself could not have prevented, if he had been there to command. 54

Ber. Well, we cannot greatly condemn our success. Some dishonor we had in the loss of that drum, but it is not to be recover'd.

Par. It might have been recover'd.

Ber. It might, but it is not now. 59

Par. It is to be recover'd. But that the merit of service is seldom attributed to the true and exact performer, I would have that drum or another, or *hic jacet*. 63

Ber. Why, if you have a stomach, to't, monsieur: if you think your mystery in stratagem can bring this instrument of honor again into his native quarter, be magnanimious in the enterprise and go on; I will 67 grace the attempt for a worthy exploit. If you speed well in it, the Duke shall both speak of it, and extend to you what further becomes his greatness, even to the utmost syllable of your worthiness. 71

Par. By the hand of a soldier, I will undertake it.

Ber. But you must not now slumber in it.

Par. I'll about it this evening, and I will presently pen down my dilemmas, encourage myself in my certainty, put myself into my mortal preparation; and by midnight look to hear further from me. 77

Ber. May I be bold to acquaint his Grace you are gone about it?

Par. I know not what the success will be, my lord, but the attempt I vow.

Ber. I know th' art valiant, and to the possibility of thy soldiership will subscribe for thee. Farewell. 83

Par. I love not many words. *Exit.*

[*2. Lord.*] No more than a fish loves water. Is not this a strange fellow, my lord, that so confidently seems to undertake this business, which he knows is not to be done, damns himself to do, and dares better be damn'd than to do't? 89

[*1. Lord.*] You do not know him, my lord, as we do. Certain it is that he will steal himself into a man's favor, and for a week escape a great deal of discoveries, but when you find him out, you have him ever after.

Ber. Why, do you think he will make no deed at all of this that so seriously he does address himself unto? 96

[*2. Lord.*] None in the world, but return with an invention, and clap upon you two or three probable lies. But we have almost emboss'd him, you shall see his fall to-night; for indeed he is not for your lordship's respect. 101

[*1. Lord.*] We'll make you some sport with the fox ere we case him. He was first smok'd by the old Lord Lafew. When his disguise and he is parted, tell me what a sprat you shall find him, which you shall see this very night. 106

[*2. Lord.*] I must go look my twigs. He shall be caught.

Ber. Your brother he shall go along with me.

[*2. Lord.*] As't please your lordship. I'll leave you. [*Exit.*]

Ber. Now will I lead you to the house, and show you 110
The lass I spoke of.

[*1. Lord.*] But you say she's honest.

Ber. That's all the fault. I spoke with her but once, And found her wondrous cold, but I sent to her, By this same coxcomb that we have i' th' wind, Tokens and letters which she did re-send, 115
And this is all I have done. She's a fair creature; Will you go see her?

[*1. Lord.*] With all my heart, my lord. *Exeunt.*

[Scene VII]

Enter HELEN *and* WIDOW.

Hel. If you misdoubt me that I am not she,
I know not how I shall assure you further
But I shall lose the grounds I work upon.

Wid. Though my estate be fall'n, I was well born,
Nothing acquainted with these businesses, 5
And would not put my reputation now
In any staining act.

Hel.   Nor would I wish you.
First give me trust, the Count he is my husband,
And what to your sworn counsel I have spoken
Is so from word to word; and then you cannot, 10

44–45. **sticks . . . disposition:** is a sore point with you (cf. *a thorn in one's flesh*), keeps you in an irritated state of mind.
46. **A pox on't:** plague take it.   49. **wings:** flanks.
51–52. **That . . . service:** i.e. the orders for the action were not to blame for that.   52. **disaster:** mischance.
55–56. **we . . . success:** i.e. we came out pretty well (*success* = outcome).   60. **But that:** were it not that.
62–63. **hic jacet:** here lies (opening words of an epitaph), i.e. I would die in the attempt.   65. **mystery:** skill.
67. **magnanimious:** great-hearted, valiant (variant of *magnanimous*).
68. **grace:** do honor to.   **speed:** succeed.   70. **becomes:** befits.
74. **presently:** at once.
75. **dilemmas:** perplexities (as opposed to the *certainty* of line 76). It is uncertain whether Parolles is planning to work out his plan of attack or to prepare himself for possible death (so *mortal preparation* in line 76 may mean either readying his death-dealing weapons or taking the sacrament); the latter would give him the better opportunity for solemn posturing.   82. **possibility:** full capacity, utmost.
83. **subscribe:** vouch.   88. **damns:** condemns.

92. **escape . . . discoveries:** to a great extent escape being revealed for what he is.   94. **make no deed:** perform no part.
98. **probable:** plausible.
99. **emboss'd:** closed round, cornered (used of a hunted animal).
101. **respect:** regard.   103. **case:** skin.   **smok'd:** smelled out.
105. **sprat:** contemptible creature (literally, a kind of small fish).
107. **look my twigs:** collect my twigs for liming (see the note on III.v. 24), i.e. prepare the trap.
114. **have . . . wind:** are to the windward of, i.e. are stalking from an advantageous position which prevents his scenting us.
115. **re-send:** send back.

III.vii. Location: Florence. The Widow's house.
3. **But . . . upon:** i.e. without cutting the ground from under my feet (by publicly revealing my identity).
4. **my . . . fall'n:** my fortunes have declined.   8. **trust:** credence.
9. **counsel:** secrecy.   10. **so . . . to word:** true in every word.

All's Well
That Ends Well
III.vii

By the good aid that I of you shall borrow,
Err in bestowing it.
   Wid.   I should believe you,
For you have show'd me that which well approves
Y' are great in fortune.
   Hel.   Take this purse of gold,
And let me buy your friendly help thus far,   15
Which I will over-pay and pay again
When I have found it. The Count he woos your
    daughter,
Lays down his wanton siege before her beauty,
[Resolv'd] to carry her. Let her in fine consent,
As we'll direct her how 'tis best to bear it.   20
Now his important blood will nought deny
That she'll demand. A ring the County wears,
That downward hath succeeded in his house
From son to son, some four or five descents,
Since the first father wore it. This ring he holds   25
In most rich choice; yet in his idle fire,
To buy his will, it would not seem too dear,
Howe'er repented after.
   Wid.   Now I see
The bottom of your purpose.
   Hel.   You see it lawful then. It is no more   30
But that your daughter, ere she seems as won,
Desires this ring; appoints him an encounter;
In fine, delivers me to fill the time,
Herself most chastely absent. After,
To marry her, I'll add three thousand crowns   35
To what is pass'd already.
   Wid.   I have yielded.
Instruct my daughter how she shall persever,
That time and place with this deceit so lawful
May prove coherent. Every night he comes
With musics of all sorts, and songs compos'd   40
To her unworthiness. It nothing steads us
To chide him from our eaves, for he persists
As if his life lay on't.
   Hel.   Why then to-night
Let us assay our plot, which if it speed,
Is wicked meaning in a lawful deed,   45
And lawful meaning in a lawful act,
Where both not sin, and yet a sinful fact.
But let's about it.   *[Exeunt.]*

---

11. By: with respect to.   **13. approves:** proves.
15. thus far: to this point.
16. over-pay . . . again: pay again twice over, double.
17. found it: i.e. received from you the help I still require.
19. carry: conquer.   **in fine:** in the end.
20. bear it: manage the business.
21. important blood: importunate passion.
26. choice: estimation.   **his idle fire:** the mad folly of his passion.
27. his will: (the object of) his lust.
29. bottom: full extent.
35. To marry her: to provide her with a dowry.
37. persever: carry on the scheme (variant of *persevere*).
39. coherent: suitable, in accord.
40. musics: groups of musicians.
41. To her unworthiness: to her, who is not his social equal (?) or toward her undoing (?) or much to her disrepute (with the neighbors) (?).   **nothing steads us:** avails us not at all.
44. assay: try.
45, 46. meaning: intention (wicked on Bertram's part, lawful on Helena's).
47. both not sin: i.e. their mutual act is lawful intercourse between husband and wife.   **sinful fact:** sinful deed (with respect to Bertram's intention).

ACT IV, [SCENE I]

*Enter [Second] French [*Lord*] with five or six other* Soldiers *in ambush.*

   [2.] *Lord.* He can come no other way but by this hedge-corner. When you sally upon him, speak what terrible language you will. Though you understand it not yourselves, no matter; for we must not seem to understand him, unless some one among us, whom we must produce for an interpreter.   6
   1. Sold. Good captain, let me be th' interpreter.
   [2.] *Lord.* Art not acquainted with him? Knows he not thy voice?
   1. Sold. No, sir, I warrant you.   10
   [2.] *Lord.* But what linsey-woolsey hast thou to speak to us again?
   1. Sold. E'en such as you speak to me.
   [2.] *Lord.* He must think us some band of strangers i' th' adversary's entertainment. Now he hath a   15 smack of all neighboring languages; therefore we must every one be a man of his own fancy, not to know what we speak one to another; so we seem to know, is to know straight our purpose: choughs' language, gabble enough, and good enough. As for you,   20 interpreter, you must seem very politic. But couch ho, here he comes, to beguile two hours in a sleep, and then to return and swear the lies he forges.
                        [They stand aside.]

Enter Parolles.

   Par. Ten a' clock: within these three hours 'twill be time enough to go home. What shall I say I   25 have done? It must be a very plausive invention that carries it. They begin to smoke me, and disgraces have of late knock'd too often at my door. I find my tongue is too foolhardy, but my heart hath the fear of Mars before it, and of his creatures, not daring the reports of my tongue.   31
   [2.] *Lord.* [*Aside.*] This is the first truth that e'er thine own tongue was guilty of.
   Par. What the devil should move me to undertake the recovery of this drum, being not ignorant of the   35 impossibility, and knowing I had no such purpose? I must give myself some hurts, and say I got them in exploit. Yet slight ones will not carry it. They will say, "Came you off with so little?" And great ones I dare not give; wherefore what's the instance?   40 Tongue, I must put you into a butter-woman's mouth

---

IV.i. Location: Outside the Florentine camp.
11. linsey-woolsey: cloth made of linen and wool, hence a mixture or medley (of words).   **14. strangers:** foreigners.
15. entertainment: service.
16. smack: taste, smattering.
17. to know: knowing, understanding.
19. know: see effected, achieve.   **straight:** at once.   **choughs' language:** i.e. the chattering of jackdaws that have been taught to speak.
20. gabble . . . enough: enough gabble is all we need.
21. politic: cunning.   **couch:** conceal yourselves.
22. beguile: while away.   **a sleep:** a nap.
26. plausive: plausible.   **27. disgraces:** insults, humiliations.
30. his creatures: i.e. soldiers.
30–31. not . . . tongue: i.e. afraid to perform what my tongue utters.
40. what's the instance. This may mean either "what evidence can suffice?" or "what motive can I have had?" (repeating the question with which the speech begins).
41. butter-woman: dairy-woman (presumably garrulous).

and buy myself another of Bajazeth's mule, if you
prattle me into these perils.

[2.] *Lord.* [*Aside.*] Is it possible he should know
what he is, and be that he is?   45

Par. I would the cutting of my garments would
serve the turn, or the breaking of my Spanish sword.

[2.] *Lord.* [*Aside.*] We cannot afford you so.

Par. Or the baring of my beard, and to say it was in
stratagem.   50

[2.] *Lord.* [*Aside.*] 'Twould not do.

Par. Or to drown my clothes, and say I was
stripp'd.

[2.] *Lord.* [*Aside.*] Hardly serve.   54

Par. Though I swore I leapt from the window of
the citadel—

[2.] *Lord.* [*Aside.*] How deep?

Par. Thirty fadom.

[2.] *Lord.* [*Aside.*] Three great oaths would scarce
make that be believ'd.   60

Par. I would I had any drum of the enemy's.
I would swear I recover'd it.

[2.] *Lord.* [*Aside.*] You shall hear one anon.

Par. A drum now of the enemy's—

                 Alarum within.

[2.] *Lord.* *Throca movousus, cargo, cargo, cargo.*   65

All. *Cargo, cargo, cargo, villianda par corbo, cargo.*

Par. O, ransom, ransom! [*They seize him.*] Do not
hide mine eyes.   [*They blindfold him.*]

[1. *Sold. as*] *Interpreter. Boskos thromuldo boskos.*

Par. I know you are the Muskos' regiment,
And I shall lose my life for want of language.   70
If there be here German, or Dane, Low Dutch,
Italian, or French, let him speak to me,
I'll discover that which shall undo the Florentine.

Interp. *Boskos vauvado.* I understand thee, and can
speak thy tongue. *Kerelybonto,* sir, betake thee to thy
faith, for seventeen poniards are at thy bosom.   76

Par. O!

Interp. O, pray, pray, pray! *Manka revania dulche.*

[2.] *Lord.* *Oscorbidulchos volivorco.*

Interp. The general is content to spare thee yet,   80
And hoodwink'd as thou art, will lead thee on
To gather from thee. Haply thou mayst inform
Something to save thy life.

Par.   O, let me live,
And all the secrets of our camp I'll show,
Their force, their purposes; nay, I'll speak that   85
Which you will wonder at.

Interp.   But wilt thou faithfully?

Par. If I do not, damn me.

Interp.   *Acordo linta.*
Come on, thou [art] granted space.

         Exit [with Parolles guarded].
           A short alarum within.

[2.] *Lord.* Go tell the Count Rossillion, and my
brother,
We have caught the woodcock, and will keep him
muffled   90
Till we do hear from them.

[2.] *Sold.*   Captain, I will.

[2.] *Lord.* 'A will betray us all unto ourselves:
Inform on that.

[2.] *Sold.*   So I will, sir.

[2.] *Lord.* Till then I'll keep him dark and safely
lock'd.   *Exeunt.*

[SCENE II]

Enter BERTRAM *and the maid called* DIANA.

Ber. They told me that your name was Fontibell.

Dia. No, my good lord, Diana.

Ber.   Titled goddess,
And worth it, with addition! But, fair soul,
In your fine frame hath love no quality?
If the quick fire of youth light not your mind,   5
You are no maiden, but a monument.
When you are dead, you should be such a one
As you are now; for you are cold and stern,
And now you should be as your mother was
When your sweet self was got.   10

Dia. She then was honest.

Ber.   So should you be.

Dia.   No;
My mother did but duty, such, my lord,
As you owe to your wife.

Ber.   No more a' that.
I prithee do not strive against my vows.
I was compell'd to her, but I love thee   15
By love's own sweet constraint, and will for ever
Do thee all rights of service.

Dia.   Ay, so you serve us
Till we serve you; but when you have our roses,
You barely leave our thorns to prick ourselves,
And mock us with our bareness.

Ber.   How have I sworn!   20

Dia. 'Tis not the many oaths that makes the truth,
But the plain single vow that is vow'd true.
What is not holy, that we swear not by,
But take the High'st to witness. Then pray you tell me,

---

42. **Bajazeth's mule.** Bajazeth is a Turkish name, and the Turks used
mules extensively, but no one has explained satisfactorily why Parolles
should use this phrase, though what he signifies by it is clear enough.
Some editors emend *mule* to *mute* (Warburton conjecture), citing
Henry V, I.ii.231–32, "our grave, / Like Turkish mute, shall have a
tongueless mouth."   **45. that:** what.
48. **afford you so:** allow you that, let you off so easily.
49. **baring:** shaving off.
58. **fadom:** fathom (plural). A fathom is a measure of six feet.
64. s.d. **Alarum:** call to arms.   69. **Muskos':** Muscovites' (?).
73. **discover:** reveal.
75–76. **betake . . . faith:** i.e. say your prayers.
81. **hoodwink'd.** A play on "taken in" is just possible (earliest use
recorded in *O.E.D.,* 1610). **lead thee on:** take you to another place.
82. **gather:** obtain information.
86. **faithfully:** truthfully (with sharp irony provided by the second
sense "loyally").

88. **space:** a reprieve.
90. **woodcock.** A proverbially foolish bird, easily caught. **muffled:**
blindfolded.   93. **Inform on:** report.

IV.ii. Location: Florence. The Widow's house.
2. **Titled goddess:** bearing a goddess' name. That the goddess was
the patroness of virgins seems to escape Bertram's notice.
3. **worth:** worthy of. **addition:** (1) augmentation; (2) added titles
of honor.   4. **quality:** power, operation.   5. **quick:** lively, vital.
6. **monument:** effigy (stone, not flesh and blood).
14. **vows.** In view of lines 12–13, this probably refers to his vows to
live apart from Helena, not to his marriage vows.
18. **serve.** With sexual implication.   19. **barely:** bare, exposed.
22. **single:** (1) one (in contrast to *many*); (2) sincere.

All's Well
That Ends Well
IV.ii

If I should swear by Jove's great attributes   25
I lov'd you dearly, would you believe my oaths
When I did love you ill? This has no holding,
To swear by Him whom I protest to love
That I will work against Him; therefore your oaths
Are words and poor conditions, but unseal'd—   30
At least in my opinion.
Ber.   Change it, change it!
Be not so holy-cruel. Love is holy,
And my integrity ne'er knew the crafts
That you do charge men with. Stand no more off,
But give thyself unto my sick desires,   35
Who then recovers. Say thou art mine, and ever
My love, as it begins, shall so persever.
Dia. I see that men make rope's in such a scarre,
That we'll forsake ourselves. Give me that ring.
Ber. I'll lend it thee, my dear; but have no power
To give it from me.
Dia.   Will you not, my lord?   41
Ber. It is an honor 'longing to our house,
Bequeathed down from many ancestors,
Which were the greatest obloquy i' th' world
In me to lose.
Dia.   Mine honor's such a ring,   45
My chastity's the jewel of our house,
Bequeathed down from many ancestors,
Which were the greatest obloquy i' th' world
In me to lose. Thus your own proper wisdom
Brings in the champion Honor on my part,   50
Against your vain assault.
Ber.   Here, take my ring!
My house, mine honor, yea, my life, be thine,
And I'll be bid by thee.
Dia. When midnight comes, knock at my chamber-
    window;
I'll order take my mother shall not hear.   55
Now will I charge you in the band of truth,
When you have conquer'd my yet maiden bed,
Remain there but an hour, nor speak to me.
My reasons are most strong, and you shall know
    them
When back again this ring shall be deliver'd;   60
And on your finger in the night I'll put
Another ring, that what in time proceeds
May token to the future our past deeds.
Adieu till then, then fail not. You have won

A wife of me, though there my hope be done.   65
Ber. A heaven on earth I have won by wooing thee.
                                    [*Exit.*]
Dia. For which live long to thank both heaven and
    me!
You may so in the end.
My mother told me just how he would woo,
As if she sate in 's heart. She says all men   70
Have the like oaths. He had sworn to marry me
When his wife's dead; therefore I'll lie with him
When I am buried. Since Frenchmen are so braid,
Marry that will, I live and die a maid.
Only in this disguise I think 't no sin   75
To cozen him that would unjustly win.   *Exit.*

[SCENE III]

Enter the two French [LORDS] *and some two or three*
SOLDIERS.

[*1. Lord.*] You have not given him his mother's
letter?
[*2. Lord.*] I have deliv'red it an hour since. There
is something in 't that stings his nature; for on the
reading it he chang'd almost into another man.   5
[*1. Lord.*] He has much worthy blame laid upon
him for shaking off so good a wife and so sweet a lady.
[*2. Lord.*] Especially he hath incurr'd the everlasting displeasure of the King, who had even tun'd his
bounty to sing happiness to him. I will tell you a thing,
but you shall let it dwell darkly with you.   11
[*1. Lord.*] When you have spoken it, 'tis dead, and
I am the grave of it.
[*2. Lord.*] He hath perverted a young gentlewoman here in Florence, of a most chaste renown,
and this night he fleshes his will in the spoil of her   16
honor. He hath given her his monumental ring, and
thinks himself made in the unchaste composition.
[*1. Lord.*] Now God delay our rebellion! As we
are ourselves, what things are we!   20

25. **Jove's.** Perhaps (as elsewhere) a replacement for *God's* in con-
formity with a statute of 1606 which forbade profane use of God's
name.
27. **ill:** wickedly, in a way unsanctioned by religion. **holding:**
binding power (?) or consistency (?).
30. **words:** mere words. **poor ... unseal'd:** invalid contracts, without the seal that would give them binding force.
32. **so holy-cruel:** cruel by reason of your religious scruples.
36. **Who then recovers:** which then recover. For the form of the verb
see the note on I.i.104.
38. **I ... scarre.** A notable crux, here reprinted unchanged. See the
Textual Notes.
42. **honor ... house:** i.e. a symbol of family honor ('*longing* = belonging). 45. **honor:** chastity.
49–50. **your ... part:** i.e. Honor, called in by Bertram to defend his
refusal, instead becomes Diana's champion in defense of her refusal.
Proper = pertaining to oneself; *part* = side.
53. **be ... thee:** do whatever you ask.
55. **order:** measures. 56. **band:** bond, obligation.
62. **that ... proceeds:** which no matter what may happen in the
future (*what* = whatever).

65. **of:** in. **my ... done:** my hope of marriage is destroyed (with
second meaning, Dover Wilson suggests, of "my hope of aiding
Helena is accomplished"). 70. **sate:** sat.
71. **had:** would have (?). Some editors read *has* (following Grant
White), perhaps rightly, since in V.iii. Diana alleges that Bertram
made such a promise (lines 139–41) and Parolles confirms the charge
(lines 262–64). 73. **braid:** braided, plaited, i.e. deceitful.
74. **Marry:** let those marry. 75. **disguise:** pretense.
76. **cozen:** cheat. **unjustly:** dishonorably.

IV.iii. *Location:* The Florentine camp.
4. **stings his nature.** Rinaldo has known how to carry out the Countess'
instructions in III.iv.31–33. 6. **worthy:** well-deserved.
11. **darkly:** in secrecy. 14. **perverted:** corrupted.
15. **renown:** reputation.
16. **fleshes his will:** feeds his lust (a figure from hunting; to flesh a
dog (or a hawk) was to give him a piece of meat from the prey he
had hunted down). **spoil:** (1) quarry, "kill"; (2) laying waste,
destruction.
17. **monumental:** i.e. serving as a token or reminder of who and
what he is.
18. **made:** a made man. **composition:** compact, bargain.
19. **God ... rebellion.** Schmidt's gloss is "God make us slow to
sin," but *rebellion* here (as often elsewhere) probably refers specifically to urgent sexual appetite (as a rebel against the government of
reason), and *delay* may mean "allay, assuage." Dover Wilson,
conjecturing that the manuscript read *Godde lay*, emended *delay* to *lay*
(= exorcise, as in *lay a spirit*), a reading that involves a bawdy equivoque.

[*2. Lord.*]　Merely our own traitors. And as in the common course of all treasons, we still see them reveal themselves, till they attain to their abhorr'd ends; so he that in this action contrives against his own nobility in his proper stream o'erflows himself.　25

[*1. Lord.*]　Is it not meant damnable in us, to be trumpeters of our unlawful intents? We shall not then have his company to-night?

[*2. Lord.*]　Not till after midnight; for he is dieted to his hour.　30

[*1. Lord.*]　That approaches apace. I would gladly have him see his company anatomiz'd, that he might take a measure of his own judgments, wherein so curiously he had set this counterfeit.　34

[*2. Lord.*]　We will not meddle with him till he come; for his presence must be the whip of the other.

[*1. Lord.*]　In the mean time, what hear you of these wars?

[*2. Lord.*]　I hear there is an overture of peace.　39

[*1. Lord.*]　Nay, I assure you a peace concluded.

[*2. Lord.*]　What will Count Rossillion do then? Will he travel higher, or return again into France?

[*1. Lord.*]　I perceive by this demand, you are not altogether of his counsel.　44

[*2. Lord.*]　Let it be forbid, sir, so should I be a great deal of his act.

[*1. Lord.*]　Sir, his wife some two months since fled from his house. Her pretense is a pilgrimage to Saint Jaques le Grand; which holy undertaking with most austere sanctimony she accomplish'd; and there　50 residing, the tenderness of her nature became as a prey to her grief; in fine, made a groan of her last breath, and now she sings in heaven.

[*2. Lord.*]　How is this justified?　54

[*1. Lord.*]　The stronger part of it by her own letters, which makes her story true, even to the point of her death. Her death itself, which could not be her office to say is come, was faithfully confirm'd by the rector of the place.　59

[*2. Lord.*]　Hath the Count all this intelligence?

[*1. Lord.*]　Ay, and the particular confirmations, point from point, to the full arming of the verity.

[*2. Lord.*]　I am heartily sorry that he'll be glad of this.

[*1. Lord.*]　How mightily sometimes we make us comforts of our losses!　66

[*2. Lord.*]　And how mightily some other times we drown our gain in tears! The great dignity that his valor hath here acquir'd for him shall at home be encount'red with a shame as ample.　70

[*1. Lord.*]　The web of our life is of a mingled yarn, good and ill together: our virtues would be proud, if our faults whipt them not, and our crimes would despair, if they were not cherish'd by our virtues.

Enter a MESSENGER.

How now? where's your master?　75

[*Mess.*]　He met the Duke in the street, sir, of whom he hath taken a solemn leave. His lordship will next morning for France. The Duke hath offer'd him letters of commendations to the King.　79

[*2. Lord.*]　They shall be no more than needful there, if they were more than they can commend.

Enter [BERTRAM] *Count Rossillion.*

[*1. Lord.*]　They cannot be too sweet for the King's tartness. Here's his lordship now. How now, my lord, is't not after midnight?　84

Ber.　I have to-night dispatch'd sixteen businesses, a month's length a-piece, by an abstract of success: I have congied with the Duke, done my adieu with his nearest; buried a wife, mourn'd for her, writ to my lady mother I am returning, entertain'd my con-　89 voy, and between these main parcels of dispatch [effected] many nicer needs. The last was the greatest, but that I have not ended yet.

[*2. Lord.*]　If the business be of any difficulty, and this morning your departure hence, it requires haste of your lordship.　95

Ber.　I mean the business is not ended, as fearing to hear of it hereafter. But shall we have this dialogue between the fool and the soldier? Come, bring forth this counterfeit module, h'as deceiv'd me like a double-meaning prophesier.　100

[*2. Lord.*]　Bring him forth, h'as sate i' th' stocks all night, poor gallant knave.　[*Exeunt Soldiers.*]

Ber.　No matter, his heels have deserv'd it, in usurping his spurs so long. How does he carry himself?　104

[*2. Lord.*]　I have told your lordship already: the stocks carry him. But to answer you as you would be

---

21–25. Merely . . . himself: i.e. we are out-and-out betrayers of our own natures to evil. And we are traitors to ourselves in a second way: we reveal our self-treachery to others. Just as we see it happen that political traitors give themselves away, thus achieving their shameful deaths, so Bertram, who is plotting treason against his own nobleness of nature, by his own talk (*in his proper stream*) reveals his treason (and will reap dishonor). (Not all commentators accept this interpretation.)　**26. meant damnable**: damnably minded (?).
29–30. dieted . . . hour: restricted to his appointed time (and so unable to meet us earlier). This is better in context than "limited to a single hour."
32. company: companion.　**anatomiz'd**: dissected, laid open.
34. curiously: carefully, artfully.　**counterfeit**: fake gem.
35–36. him . . . he . . . his: i.e. Parolles . . . Bertram . . . Bertram's.
40. Nay: nay, more.
42. higher: farther (?). See the note on *higher Italy*, II.i.12.
43. demand: question.
44. of his counsel: in his confidence.
45–46. a great . . . act: in great part his accessory in the deed (with a quibble in *act* on *counsel / council*).
48. pretense: intention.　**50. sanctimony**: piety.
52. in fine: in the end (?) or to sum up (?).
54. justified: verified.　**58. office**: function.
59. rector: priest, or (less probably) governor.
62. arming: strengthening against attack, i.e. irrefutable proof.

68. dignity: honor.　**70. encount'red**: met, opposed.
71. web: fabric.　**73. whipt**: chastened.　**crimes**: sins.
74. cherish'd: looked after tenderly.
77. solemn: ceremonious, formal.　**will**: i.e. will set out.
78. offer'd: tendered.
81. if . . . commend: even if they commended him more highly than they possibly can.　**82. for**: i.e. to offset.
86. by . . . success: by a successful summary proceeding (Schmidt). Some editors connect the phrase with the next sentence and explain: "to give a summary of my successes" or "to give a summary of the successive items."　**87. congied with**: taken leave of.
89–90. entertain'd my convoy: engaged my travel aides (?) or hired means of conveyance (?).
90. between . . . dispatch: i.e. in the intervals of winding up these major pieces of business.　**91. nicer**: more delicate.
99. module: model (of soldiership).　**h'as**: he has.
99–100. double-meaning prophesier: i.e. ambiguous oracle.
102. gallant: showy, flamboyant.
103–4. usurping his spurs: wrongfully wearing spurs (symbolic of knightly valor).
104. carry: conduct (with following quibble).

All's Well
That Ends Well
IV.iii

understood, he weeps like a wench that had shed her milk. He hath confess'd himself to Morgan, whom he supposes to be a friar, from the time of his remem- 109 brance to this very instant disaster of his setting i' th' stocks; and what think you he hath confess'd?

Ber. Nothing of me, has 'a?

[*2. Lord.*] His confession is taken, and it shall be read to his face. If your lordship be in't, as I believe you are, you must have the patience to hear it. 115

Enter [SOLDIERS *and*] PAROLLES, *with* [*First Soldier as*] *his* INTERPRETER.

Ber. A plague upon him! Muffled! He can say nothing of me.

[*1. Lord.*] Hush, hush! Hoodman comes! *Porto-tartarossa.* 119

Interp. He calls for the tortures. What will you say without 'em?

Par. I will confess what I know without constraint. If ye pinch me like a pasty, I can say no more.

Interp. *Bosko chimurcho.*

[*1. Lord.*] *Boblibindo chicurmurco.* 125

Interp. You are a merciful general. Our general bids you answer to what I shall ask you out of a note.

Par. And truly, as I hope to live. 128

Interp. [*Reads.*] "First demand of him, how many horse the Duke is strong." What say you to that?

Par. Five or six thousand, but very weak and un-serviceable. The troops are all scatter'd, and the com-manders very poor rogues, upon my reputation and credit and as I hope to live. 134

Interp. Shall I set down your answer so?

Par. Do, I'll take the sacrament on't, how and which way you will.

Ber. All's one to him. What a past-saving slave is this! 139

[*1. Lord.*] Y' are deceiv'd, my lord, this is Mon-sieur Parolles, the gallant militarist—that was his own phrase—that had the whole theoric of war in the knot of his scarf, and the practice in the chape of his dagger.

[*2. Lord.*] I will never trust a man again for keep-ing his sword clean, nor believe he can have every thing in him by wearing his apparel neatly. 146

Interp. Well, that's set down.

Par. "Five or six thousand horse," I said—I will say true—"or thereabouts," set down, for I'll speak truth. 150

[*1. Lord.*] He's very near the truth in this.

Ber. But I con him no thanks for't, in the nature he delivers it.

Par. "Poor rogues," I pray you say.

Interp. Well, that's set down. 155

Par. I humbly thank you, sir. A truth's a truth, the rogues are marvellous poor.

Interp. [*Reads.*] "Demand of him, of what strength they are afoot." What say you to that? 159

Par. By my troth, sir, if I were to live this present hour, I will tell true. Let me see: Spurio, a hundred and fifty; Sebastian, so many; Corambus, so many; Jaques, so many; Guiltian, Cosmo, Lodowick, and Gratii, two hundred fifty each; mine own company, Chitopher, Vaumond, Bentii, two hundred fifty 165 each; so that the muster-file, rotten and sound, upon my life, amounts not to fifteen thousand pole, half of the which dare not shake the snow from off their cassocks, lest they shake themselves to pieces.

Ber. What shall be done to him? 170

[*1. Lord.*] Nothing, but let him have thanks. De-mand of him my condition, and what credit I have with the Duke.

Interp. Well, that's set down. 174
[*Reads.*] "You shall demand of him, whether one Captain Dumaine be i' th' camp, a Frenchman; what his reputation is with the Duke; what his valor, honesty, and expertness in wars; or whether he 178 thinks it were not possible with well-weighing sums of gold to corrupt him to a revolt." What say you to this? What do you know of it?

Par. I beseech you let me answer to the particular of the inter'gatories. Demand them singly.

Interp. Do you know this Captain Dumaine? 184

Par. I know him. 'A was a botcher's prentice in Paris, from whence he was whipt for getting the shrieve's fool with child, a dumb innocent, that could not say him nay. 188

Ber. Nay, by your leave, hold your hands—though I know his brains are forfeit to the next tile that falls.

Interp. Well, is this captain in the Duke of Florence's camp? 193

Par. Upon my knowledge, he is, and lousy.

[*1. Lord.*] Nay, look not so upon me; we shall hear of your [lordship] anon. 196

Interp. What is his reputation with the Duke?

Par. The Duke knows him for no other but a poor officer of mine, and writ to me this other day to turn him out a' th' band. I think I have his letter in my pocket. 201

Interp. Marry, we'll search.

107–8. **shed her milk:** i.e. accidentally spilled the milk she was taking to market.
109–10. **the time . . . remembrance:** as far back as he can remember.
110. **instant disaster:** present stroke of misfortune.
118. **Hoodman:** the blindfold player in blind man's buff (which is therefore also called hoodman blind).
123. **pinch . . . pasty.** Referring to pinching together the top and bottom crusts of a pasty (meat pie).
127. **note:** list, memorandum. 130. **horse:** horsemen.
136–37. **how . . . will:** i.e. according to any rite you prefer. This comes close to saying "I'll swear by whatever you hold sacred."
138. **All's . . . him:** it's all the same to him. 142. **theoric:** theory.
143. **chape:** metal tip of the scabbard. 145. **clean:** polished.
146. **neatly:** elegantly.
152. **con . . . thanks:** feel no gratitude to him. *Con* (used only in this idiom) means literally "know." **nature:** fashion, manner.

160–61. **live . . . hour.** The sense is "live *only* this present hour"; editors disagree as to whether emendation is necessary and, if it is, what form it should take.
162. **so many:** as many, the same number.
166. **muster-file:** total roll. **rotten and sound:** diseased and able-bodied.
167. **pole:** poll, heads. 169. **cassocks:** military cloaks.
172. **condition:** character.
179. **well-weighing:** (1) heavy; (2) persuasive.
180. **corrupt . . . revolt:** suborn him to commit treason.
182. **particular:** individual items.
185. **botcher's:** cobbler's or clothes-mender's.
187. **shrieve's fool:** mental defective in the official care of the sheriff. **innocent:** idiot.
190–91. **his . . . falls:** i.e. such a liar is subject to sudden death at any moment.
194. **lousy:** i.e. a contemptible fellow.

Par. In good sadness, I do not know. Either it is there, or it is upon a file with the Duke's other letters in my tent. 205

Interp. Here 'tis, here's a paper. Shall I read it to you?

Par. I do not know if it be it or no.

Ber. Our interpreter does it well.

[*1. Lord.*] Excellently. 210

Interp. [*Reads.*] "Dian, the Count's a fool, and full of gold"—

Par. That is not the Duke's letter, sir; that is an advertisement to a proper maid in Florence, 213 one Diana, to take heed of the allurement of one Count Rossillion, a foolish idle boy, but for all that very ruttish. I pray you, sir, put it up again.

Interp. Nay, I'll read it first, by your favor. 217

Par. My meaning in't, I protest, was very honest in the behalf of the maid; for I knew the young Count to be a dangerous and lascivious boy, who is a whale to virginity, and devours up all the fry it finds. 221

Ber. Damnable both-sides rogue!

Interp. [*Reads*] *letter.*

"When he swears oaths, bid him drop gold, and take it;
After he scores, he never pays the score.
Half won is match well made; match, and well make it;
He ne'er pays after-debts, take it before, 226
And say a soldier, Dian, told thee this:
Men are to mell with, boys are not to kiss;
For count of this, the Count's a fool, I know it,
Who pays before, but not when he does owe it. 230
  Thine, as he vow'd to thee in thine ear,
                                        Parolles."

Ber. He shall be whipt through the army with this rhyme in 's forehead. 234

[*2. Lord.*] This is your devoted friend, sir, the manifold linguist and the armipotent soldier.

Ber. I could endure any thing before but a cat, and now he's a cat to me.

Interp. I perceive, sir, by [the] general's looks, we shall be fain to hang you. 240

Par. My life, sir, in any case! Not that I am afraid to die, but that my offenses being many, I would repent out the remainder of nature. Let me live, sir, in a dungeon, i' th' stocks, or any where, so I may live. 245

Interp. We'll see what may be done, so you confess freely; therefore once more to this Captain

Dumaine. You have answer'd to his reputation with the Duke, and to his valor; what is his honesty? 249

Par. He will steal, sir, an egg out of a cloister. For rapes and ravishments he parallels Nessus. He professes not keeping of oaths; in breaking 'em he is stronger than Hercules. He will lie, sir, with such volubility, that you would think truth were a fool. 254 Drunkenness is his best virtue, for he will be swine-drunk, and in his sleep he does little harm, save to his bed-clothes about him; but they know his conditions, and lay him in straw. I have but little more to say, sir, of his honesty. He has every thing that an honest 259 man should not have; what an honest man should have, he has nothing.

[*1. Lord.*] I begin to love him for this.

Ber. For this description of thine honesty? A pox upon him for me, he's more and more a cat. 264

Interp. What say you to his expertness in war?

Par. Faith, sir, h'as led the drum before the English tragedians. To belie him I will not, and more of his soldiership I know not, except in that country 268 he had the honor to be the officer at a place there call'd Mile-end, to instruct for the doubling of files. I would do the man what honor I can, but of this I am not certain. 272

[*1. Lord.*] He hath out-villain'd villainy so far, that the rarity redeems him.

Ber. A pox on him, he's a cat still. 275

Interp. His qualities being at this poor price, I need not to ask you if gold will corrupt him to revolt.

Par. Sir, for a cardecue he will sell the fee-simple of his salvation, the inheritance of it, and cut th' entail from all remainders, and a perpetual succession for it perpetually. 281

Interp. What's his brother, the other Captain Dumaine?

[*2. Lord.*] Why does he ask him of me?

Interp. What's he? 285

Par. E'en a crow a' th' same nest; not altogether so great as the first in goodness, but greater a great deal in evil. He excels his brother for a coward, yet 288 his brother is reputed one of the best that is. In a

203. **In good sadness:** in all seriousness.
213. **advertisement:** admonition, warning.   **proper:** respectable.
214. **take heed:** be wary.
216. **ruttish:** lustful.   **up again:** back in the pocket.
217. **favor:** leave.   221. **fry:** young fish.
224. **scores:** incurs a debt, obtains goods on credit.   **score:** bill.
225. **Half . . . made:** a match well started (i.e. with all the conditions clearly set forth and agreed to in advance) is a match halfway to success. *Match* may mean a game, a bargain, or the coming together of a man and a woman.
226. **after-debts:** debts payable after the goods have been taken.
228. **mell:** meddle (in sexual sense).   229. **count of:** pay heed to.
230. **pays before:** i.e. can be made to pay in advance.   **when . . . it:** after he has incurred the debt.   234. **in:** i.e. attached to.
236. **manifold linguist:** speaker of many languages.   **armipotent:** mighty in action.   238. **cat:** i.e. object of aversion.
240. **fain:** obliged.
242–43. **would . . . nature:** want the rest of my natural life to repent in.

250. **an egg . . . cloister:** "anything, however trifling, from any place, however holy" (Johnson).
251. **Nessus:** the Centaur who attempted to rape Hercules' wife Dejanira and was killed by him.   The Centaurs, half man and half horse, figure in myth as ravishers of the women of the Lapithae.
252. **professes . . . of:** makes a regular practice of not keeping.
252–53. **in . . . Hercules.** The parallelism is not in the breaking of oaths but in the strength.
257. **they:** i.e. his attendants.   **conditions:** habits.
261. **nothing:** not at all.
266–67. **led . . . tragedians:** i.e. all his knowledge of the drum (symbolic of war) consists in his having beaten it at the head of a troupe of English actors (to announce their entry into a village or a playing place).
270. **Mile-end:** Mile-end Green, a large open area to the east of London, where the citizens received elementary military training.   **doubling of files.** The simplest of drill exercises.
274. **rarity:** peerlessness of his performance.
278. **cardecue:** French coin worth a quarter of a French crown (*quart d'écu*), about two shillings.
278–81. **sell . . . perpetually:** i.e. renounce forever salvation for himself, his heirs, and his heirs' heirs to the end of the line.   Fee-simple is the nearest thing in English property law to absolute and perpetual possession; an entail is a provision establishing that an estate is to pass successively to a series of predetermined heirs; remainders are certain residual property rights.
282. **What's:** what kind of man is.

retreat he outruns any lackey; marry, in coming on he
has the cramp.   291
  Interp. If your life be sav'd, will you undertake to
betray the Florentine?
  Par. Ay, and the captain of his horse, Count
Rossillion.   295
  Interp. I'll whisper with the general, and know his
pleasure.
  Par. [*Aside*.] I'll no more drumming, a plague of
all drums! Only to seem to deserve well, and to beguile
the supposition of that lascivious young boy the
Count, have I run into this danger. Yet who would
have suspected an ambush where I was taken?   302
  Interp. There is no remedy, sir, but you must die.
The general says, you that have so traitorously discover'd the secrets of your army, and made such
pestiferous reports of men very nobly held, can serve
the world for no honest use; therefore you must die.
Come, headsman, off with his head.   308
  Par. O Lord, sir, let me live, or let me see my
death!
  Interp. That shall you, and take your leave of all
your friends. [*Unblinding him*.] So, look about you.
Know you any here?   313
  Ber. Good morrow, noble captain.
  [*2. Lord*.] God bless you, Captain Parolles.
  [*1. Lord*.] God save you, noble captain.
  [*2. Lord*.] Captain, what greeting will you to my
Lord Lafew? I am for France.   318
  [*1. Lord*.] Good captain, will you give me a copy
of the sonnet you writ to Diana in behalf of the Count
Rossillion? And I were not a very coward, I'd compel
it of you, but fare you well.   322
                              Exeunt [*Bertram and Lords*].
  Interp. You are undone, captain, all but your
scarf; that has a knot on't yet.
  Par. Who cannot be crush'd with a plot?   325
  Interp. If you could find out a country where but
women were that had receiv'd so much shame, you
might begin an impudent nation. Fare ye well, sir, I
am for France too. We shall speak of you there. 329
                                        Exit [*with Soldiers*].
  Par. Yet am I thankful. If my heart were great,
'Twould burst at this. Captain I'll be no more,
But I will eat and drink, and sleep as soft
As captain shall. Simply the thing I am
Shall make me live. Who knows himself a braggart,
Let him fear this; for it will come to pass   335
That every braggart shall be found an ass.
Rust sword, cool blushes, and, Parolles, live
Safest in shame! Being fool'd, by fool'ry thrive!
There's place and means for every man alive.
I'll after them.   *Exit*. 340

290. **lackey:** running servant.   **coming on:** advancing.
292. **undertake:** engage yourself.
299–300. **beguile the supposition:** deceive the opinion, create a false
impression in the mind.
304–5. **discover'd:** revealed.
306. **pestiferous:** pernicious.   **very nobly held:** esteemed very noble.
317. **will you:** do you desire to send.   318. **for:** off to.
328. **impudent:** shameless.
334. **make me live:** gain me a livelihood.
338. **in shame:** by shameful means.   **fool'd:** made a fool of.

[SCENE IV]

Enter HELEN, WIDOW, *and* DIANA.

  Hel. That you may well perceive I have not
    wrong'd you,
One of the greatest in the Christian world
Shall be my surety; 'fore whose throne 'tis needful,
Ere I can perfect mine intents, to kneel.
Time was, I did him a desired office,   5
Dear almost as his life, which gratitude
Through flinty Tartar's bosom would peep forth,
And answer thanks. I duly am inform'd
His Grace is at Marsellis, to which place
We have convenient convoy. You must know   10
I am supposed dead. The army breaking,
My husband hies him home, where heaven aiding,
And by the leave of my good lord the King,
We'll be before our welcome.
  Wid.   Gentle madam,
You never had a servant to whose trust   15
Your business was more welcome.
  Hel.   Nor [you], mistress,
Ever a friend whose thoughts more truly labor
To recompense your love. Doubt not but heaven
Hath brought me up to be your daughter's dower,
As it hath fated her to be my motive   20
And helper to a husband. But O, strange men,
That can such sweet use make of what they hate,
When saucy trusting of the cozen'd thoughts
Defiles the pitchy night; so lust doth play
With what it loathes for that which is away—   25
But more of this hereafter. You, Diana,
Under my poor instructions yet must suffer
Something in my behalf.
  Dia.   Let death and honesty
Go with your impositions, I am yours
Upon your will to suffer.
  Hel.   Yet, I pray you: 30
But with the word the time will bring on summer,
When briers shall have leaves as well as thorns,
And be as sweet as sharp. We must away:
Our waggon is prepar'd, and time revives us.   34

IV.iv. Location: Florence. The Widow's house.
6. **which gratitude:** gratitude for which.
7. **Through . . . bosom:** even from the stony heart of a Tartar.
8. **answer:** respond with.
9. **Marsellis:** Marseilles.
10. **convenient:** suitable.   11. **breaking:** disbanding.
14. **before our welcome:** i.e. before we are expected.
19. **brought me up:** raised me up (Dover Wilson).
20. **motive:** means.
23. **saucy:** lascivious.   **cozen'd:** cheated, deluded (referring both
to the general delusiveness of lust and to Bertram's delusion about the
identity of his sexual partner).
24. **Defiles . . . night.** A reversal of the proverbial "He that touches
pitch will be defiled."
25. **for:** in the place of, taking it to be.
27. **yet:** still for a time (repeated in line 30).
28. **death and honesty:** an honest death, a death that leaves virtue
intact.
30. **Upon your will:** at your will, as you determine.
31. **with . . . summer:** i.e. with the promise that the time of further
suffering will lead on to a time of fulfillment (?). The line, especially
with the word, has been variously interpreted and much emended. It
should be noted that *word* is used in the sense "promise" at II.i.210.
32. **leaves:** petals.   33. **sweet:** fragrant.
34. **time revives us:** the interval of rest has restored us (?) or the
coming time will give us new life (?).

All's well that ends well! still the fine's the crown;
What e'er the course, the end is the renown. *Exeunt.*

[SCENE V]

Enter CLOWN, *old Lady* [COUNTESS], *and* LAFEW.

Laf. No, no, no, your son was misled with a snipt-taffata fellow there, whose villainous saffron would have made all the unbak'd and doughy youth of a nation in his color. Your daughter-in-law had been alive at this hour, and your son here at home, more 5
advanc'd by the King than by that red-tail'd humble-bee I speak of.

Count. I would I had not known him; it was the death of the most virtuous gentlewoman that ever nature had praise for creating. If she had partaken 10
of my flesh, and cost me the dearest groans of a mother, I could not have ow'd her a more rooted love.

Laf. 'Twas a good lady, 'twas a good lady. We may pick a thousand sallets ere we light on such another herb. 15

Clo. Indeed, sir, she was the sweet marjorom of the sallet, or rather the herb of grace.

Laf. They are not herbs, you knave, they are nose-herbs.

Clo. I am no great Nebuchadnezzar, sir, I have not much skill in [grass]. 21

Laf. Whether dost thou profess thyself—a knave or a fool?

Clo. A fool, sir, at a woman's service, and a knave at a man's. 25

Laf. Your distinction?

Clo. I would cozen the man of his wife and do his service.

Laf. So you were a knave at his service indeed.

Clo. And I would give his wife my bauble, sir, to do her service. 31

Laf. I will subscribe for thee, thou art both knave and fool.

Clo. At your service.

Laf. No, no, no. 35

Clo. Why, sir, if I cannot serve you, I can serve as great a prince as you are.

Laf. Who's that? a Frenchman?

Clo. Faith, sir, 'a has an English [name], but his fisnomy is more hotter in France than there. 40

Laf. What prince is that?

Clo. The black prince, sir, alias the prince of darkness, alias the devil.

Laf. Hold thee, there's my purse. I give thee not this to suggest thee from thy master thou talk'st of; serve him still. 46

Clo. I am a woodland fellow, sir, that always lov'd a great fire, and the master I speak of ever keeps a good fire. But sure he is the prince of the world; let his nobility remain in 's court. I am for the house 50
with the narrow gate, which I take to be too little for pomp to enter. Some that humble themselves may, but the many will be too chill and tender, and they'll be for the flow'ry way that leads to the broad gate and the great fire. 55

Laf. Go thy ways, I begin to be a-weary of thee, and I tell thee so before, because I would not fall out with thee. Go thy ways, let my horses be well look'd to, without any tricks. 59

Clo. If I put any tricks upon 'em, sir, they shall be jades' tricks, which are their own right by the law of nature. *Exit.*

Laf. A shrewd knave and an unhappy. 63

Count. So 'a is. My lord that's gone made himself much sport out of him. By his authority he remains here, which he thinks is a patent for his sauciness, and indeed he has no pace, but runs where he will.

Laf. I like him well, 'tis not amiss. And I was about to tell you, since I heard of the good lady's 69
death, and that my lord your son was upon his return home, I mov'd the King my master to speak in the behalf of my daughter, which in the minority of them both, his Majesty, out of a self-gracious remembrance, did first propose. His Highness hath promis'd me 74
to do it, and to stop up the displeasure he hath conceiv'd against your son, there is no fitter matter. How does your ladyship like it?

Count. With very much content, my lord, and I wish it happily effected. 79

Laf. His Highness comes post from Marsellis, of as able body as when he number'd thirty. 'A will be

---

35. All's . . . well. Proverbial. **the fine's the crown.** Also proverbial (*fine* = end); cf. *Troilus and Cressida*, IV.v.224, "the end crowns all," and the Latin *Finis coronat opus*, "the end crowns the work."
36. the renown: i.e. what determines the praise.

IV.v. Location: Rossillion. The Count's palace.
1. with: by.
1–2. snipt-taffata: wearing a garment of taffeta slashed to show a rich lining of contrasting color, i.e. showy.
2. saffron. Alluding to a fad for wearing ruffs and collars stiffened with saffron-colored starch. Saffron was also much used for coloring pastry; hence the figure from baking in line 3.
6. red-tail'd. Perhaps a further reference to Parolles' brilliant garments, but the bumble-bee is called "red-hipp'd" in *A Midsummer Night's Dream*, IV.i.111–12.
6–7. humble-bee: a wild bee with a particularly loud buzz.
11. dearest: most intense, sorest.
14. sallets: herbs or greens for salads. **16. marjorom:** marjoram.
17. herb of grace: rue (called herb of grace because its name was identified with *rue* = repentance).
18. herbs: i.e. salad herbs as distinguished from "nose-herbs," planted in gardens for their fragrance. Dover Wilson emends *not herbs* to *knot-herbs* = herbs for planting in garden knots (elaborately patterned beds).
21. grass. With a pun on *grace*, then pronounced similarly. For Nebuchadnezzar, the king of Babylon who "did eat grass as the oxen," see Daniel 4. **22. Whether:** which of the two.
28. service. Bawdy wordplay on *service* and *serve* was very common.
30. bauble: fool's rod of office (with a bawdy innuendo).
32. subscribe: vouch.

40. fisnomy: face (variant of *physiognomy*). **more hotter.** Perhaps alluding to the facial sores of syphilis (the "French disease").
42. black prince. "An English name" (line 39) because it was the nickname of Edward III's eldest son Edward, the father of Richard II.
45. suggest: lure.
49. prince . . . world. See John 12:31. The Biblical language continues in the references to heaven and hell in lines 50–55; cf. Matthew 7:13–14. **53. chill and tender:** sensitive to cold and comfort-loving.
56. Go thy ways: go along.
57. before: i.e. before I get thoroughly tired of you.
61. jades' tricks: (1) contemptible tricks; (2) tricks played on jades (ill-trained and ill-natured horses).
63. shrewd: biting, bitter. **unhappy:** morose, discontented.
66. patent: license.
67. has no pace: will not observe the reins (a figure from horse training). **68. 'tis not amiss:** there's no harm done.
73. a self-gracious remembrance: his own kindly thoughtfulness.
80. post: at utmost speed.

*All's Well
That Ends Well
IV.v*

here to-morrow, or I am deceiv'd by him that in such
intelligence hath seldom fail'd.   83

Count. It rejoices me, that I hope I shall see him
ere I die. I have letters that my son will be here
to-night. I shall beseech your lordship to remain with
me till they meet together.

Laf. Madam, I was thinking with what manners
I might safely be admitted.   89

Count. You need but plead your honorable privilege.

Laf. Lady, of that I have made a bold charter,
but I thank my God it holds yet.   93

Enter CLOWN.

Clo. O madam, yonder's my lord your son with a
patch of velvet on 's face. Whether there be a scar
under't or no, the velvet knows, but 'tis a goodly
patch of velvet. His left cheek is a cheek of two pile
and a half, but his right cheek is worn bare.   98

Laf. A scar nobly got, or a noble scar, is a good
liv'ry of honor; so belike is that.

Clo. But it is your carbinado'd face.

Laf. Let us go see your son I pray you. I long to
talk with the young noble soldier.   103

Clo. Faith, there's a dozen of 'em, with delicate
fine hats, and most courteous feathers, which bow the
head, and nod at every man.   *Exeunt.*

ACT V, [SCENE I]

Enter HELEN, WIDOW, *and* DIANA, *with two* ATTEND-
ANTS.

Hel. But this exceeding posting day and night
Must wear your spirits low; we cannot help it.
But since you have made the days and nights as one,
To wear your gentle limbs in my affairs,
Be bold you do so grow in my requital   5
As nothing can unroot you.

Enter a [GENTLEMAN, *an*] *astringer.*

In happy time!
This man may help me to his Majesty's ear,
If he would spend his power. God save you, sir.

Gent. And you.   9

Hel. Sir, I have seen you in the court of France.

Gent. I have been sometimes there.

Hel. I do presume, sir, that you are not fall'n
From the report that goes upon your goodness,
And therefore goaded with most sharp occasions,
Which lay nice manners by, I put you to   15
The use of your own virtues, for the which
I shall continue thankful.

Gent.   What's your will?

Hel. That it will please you
To give this poor petition to the King,
And aid me with that store of power you have   20
To come into his presence.

Gent. The King's not here.

Hel.   Not here, sir?

Gent.   Not indeed.
He hence remov'd last night, and with more haste
Than is his use.

Wid.   Lord, how we lose our pains!

Hel. All's well that ends well yet,   25
Though time seem so adverse and means unfit.
I do beseech you, whither is he gone?

Gent. Marry, as I take it, to Rossillion,
Whither I am going.

Hel.   I do beseech you, sir,
Since you are like to see the King before me,   30
Commend the paper to his gracious hand,
Which I presume shall render you no blame,
But rather make you thank your pains for it.
I will come after you with what good speed
Our means will make us means.

Gent.   This I'll do for you.   35

Hel. And you shall find yourself to be well thank'd,
What e'er falls more. We must to horse again.
Go, go, provide.   [*Exeunt.*]

[SCENE II]

Enter CLOWN *and* PAROLLES.

Par. Good Master Lavatch, give my Lord Lafew
this letter. I have ere now, sir, been better known to
you, when I have held familiarity with fresher clothes;
but I am now, sir, muddied in Fortune's mood, and
smell somewhat strong of her strong displeasure.   5

Clo. Truly, Fortune's displeasure is but sluttish
if it smell so strongly as thou speak'st of. I will hence-

---

82. **him:** a man, one. 83. **intelligence:** information.
84. **that . . . shall:** that I can hope to.
88–89. **thinking . . . admitted:** i.e. trying to think of a polite way to
obtain that favor.
90–91. **honorable privilege:** privilege due your honored self.
92. **of . . . charter:** i.e. I have stretched it to the limit.
95. **patch of velvet.** Used to cover a facial wound.
97–98. **two . . . half.** The thickest velvet was three-piled; the Clown
invents a quality between that and two-piled. 100. **belike:** probably.
101. **carbinado'd:** carbonadoed, slashed (used of meat scored for
broiling); here alluding to surgical treatment of syphilitic sores on the
face.

V.i. Location: Marseilles. A street.
1. **posting:** speedy travelling. 4. **wear:** weary.
5. **bold:** confident. **requital:** debt (literally, repayment).
6 s.d. **astringer:** falconer (strictly speaking, a trainer of goshawks, a
large, short-winged variety of hawk). It is not clear why his profession
should be stated, since it has no bearing on the action and is never
mentioned in the dialogue. Many editors therefore omit the designation, or emend it to *a stranger* (F3), i.e. a foreigner (or possibly an
authorial memorandum that this gentleman is not one who has
appeared earlier). **In happy time:** most opportune.
8. **spend:** expend, use.

---

13. **From . . . goodness:** from the goodness that current report
ascribes to you. 14. **sharp:** urgent. **occasions:** necessities.
15. **lay . . . by:** put aside scrupulous politeness. **put:** press.
24. **use:** custom. 31. **Commend:** commit.
32. **presume:** venture to say.
35. **Our . . . means:** our resources will secure us ways of achieving.

V.ii. Location: Rossillion. Before the Count's palace.
1. **Lavatch.** This is the only occurrence of the Clown's name in the
dialogue.
4. **mood:** i.e. bad mood (synonymous with *displeasure* in line 5).
Note the play in *muddied* / *mood*, which apparently suggests to the
Clown a further play on *moat*; this would explain his references below
to fish (since moats served as fish ponds) and to excrement (since
sewage was discharged into the moat).
6. **displeasure.** The Clown seems to use this word as interchangeable
with *mood* and hence with *moat*. Fortune is sluttish in not keeping her
moat cleaned out, and the Clown will therefore eat none of her fish.

forth eat no fish of Fortune's butt'ring. Prithee allow the wind.

Par. Nay, you need not to stop your nose, sir; I spake but by a metaphor.　11

Clo. Indeed, sir, if your metaphor stink, I will stop my nose, or against any man's metaphor. Prithee get thee further.

Par. Pray you, sir, deliver me this paper.　15

Clo. Foh, prithee stand away. A paper from Fortune's close-stool to give to a nobleman! Look here he comes himself.

Enter LAFEW.

Here is a purr of Fortune's, sir, or of Fortune's cat—but not a musk-cat—that has fall'n into the unclean fishpond of her displeasure, and as he says, is　21 muddied withal. Pray you, sir, use the carp as you may, for he looks like a poor, decay'd, ingenious, foolish, rascally knave. I do pity his distress in my [similes] of comfort, and leave him to your lordship.
　　　　　　　　　　　　　　　　[*Exit.*]

Par. My lord, I am a man whom Fortune hath cruelly scratch'd.　27

Laf. And what would you have me to do? 'Tis too late to pare her nails now. Wherein have you play'd the knave with Fortune that she should scratch you, who of herself is a good lady, and would not　31 have knaves thrive long under [her]? There's a cardecue for you. Let the justices make you and Fortune friends; I am for other business.

Par. I beseech your honor to hear me one single word.　36

Laf. You beg a single penny more. Come, you shall ha't; save your word.

Par. My name, my good lord, is Parolles.　39

Laf. You beg more than "word" then. Cox my passion! give me your hand. How does your drum?

Par. O my good lord, you were the first that found me!

Laf. Was I, in sooth? And I was the first that lost thee.　45

Par. It lies in you, my lord, to bring me in some grace, for you did bring me out.

Laf. Out upon thee, knave! Dost thou put upon me at once both the office of God and the devil? one

---

brings thee in grace, and the other brings thee out. [*Trumpets sound.*] The King's coming, I know　51 by his trumpets. Sirrah, inquire further after me. I had talk of you last night; though you are a fool and a knave, you shall eat. Go to, follow.

Par. I praise God for you.　　　[*Exeunt.*]　55

[SCENE III]

Flourish. Enter KING, *old Lady* [COUNTESS], LAFEW, *the two French* LORDS, *with* ATTENDANTS.

King. We lost a jewel of her, and our esteem
Was made much poorer by it; but your son,
As mad in folly, lack'd the sense to know
Her estimation home.

Count.　　　　　　'Tis past, my liege,
And I beseech your Majesty to make it　5
Natural rebellion, done i' th' blade of youth,
When oil and fire, too strong for reason's force,
O'erbears it, and burns on.

King.　　　　　　　　My honor'd lady,
I have forgiven and forgotten all,
Though my revenges were high bent upon him,　10
And watch'd the time to shoot.

Laf.　　　　　　　This I must say—
But first I beg my pardon—the young lord
Did to his Majesty, his mother, and his lady
Offense of mighty note; but to himself
The greatest wrong of all. He lost a wife　15
Whose beauty did astonish the survey
Of richest eyes, whose words all ears took captive,
Whose dear perfection hearts that scorn'd to serve
Humbly call'd mistress.

King.　　　　　　Praising what is lost
Makes the remembrance dear. Well, call him hither,
We are reconcil'd, and the first view shall kill　21
All repetition. Let him not ask our pardon,
The nature of his great offense is dead,
And deeper than oblivion we do bury
Th' incensing relics of it. Let him approach　25
A stranger, no offender; and inform him
So 'tis our will he should.

Gent.　　　　　　I shall, my liege. [*Exit.*]

King. What says he to your daughter? Have you
　　spoke?

Laf. All that he is hath reference to your Highness.

8–9. **allow the wind:** keep to the windward of me.
17. **close-stool:** predecessor of the water-closet.
19. **purr:** piece of dung (with quibble on "cat's purr"). The play on *purr* continues in *knave* (lines 24, 30, 32), since it was the name given to the jack in the card-game of post and pair.
20. **musk-cat:** musk-deer, the animal from which perfumers obtained musk.
22. **withal:** with it, in consequence. **carp:** (1) a fish (said by Hunter to have been bred in manured fishponds); (2) carper, chatterer.
23. **ingenious.** Out of place in the series, and not satisfactorily explained; possibly an error for *ingenerous,* "ignoble."
24–25. **pity . . . comfort:** show my compassion for his misery in my comforting similes, i.e. in saying that he is *like* a knave, not that he *is* a knave.
33. **cardecue.** See the note on IV.iii.278. **justices:** justices of the peace, who were empowered to relieve the worthy poor.
40. **more than "word":** i.e. "words" (a jest on Parolles' name).
40–41. **Cox my passion:** a weakened oath derived from an original "by God's (Christ's) suffering."
42, 44. **found, lost.** Cf. II.iii.205–6.　44. **sooth:** truth.
46–47. **in some grace:** into some favor. Lafew answers with a quibble.

---

52. **inquire . . . me:** come to see me later.

V.iii. Location: Rossillion. The Count's palace.
1. **of:** in. **our esteem:** my own worth.
3. **As . . . folly:** carrying folly to the point of madness.
4. **Her estimation home:** her worth to the full.
6. **rebellion.** Line 7 shows that the rebellion is of the passions against the reason, not of the youth against external authority. Cf. *God delay our rebellion,* IV.iii.19. **blade:** green shoot, i.e. immaturity, callowness. Theobald proposed reading *blaze,* Sisson *blood* (= passion).
10. **high bent:** bent to the utmost (a figure from archery).
11. **watch'd the time:** vigilantly waited for the right moment.
14. **of mighty note:** egregious.
16. **astonish the survey:** dazzle the sight.
17. **richest eyes:** eyes that had seen most.
22. **repetition:** reviewing of past wrongs.
25. **incensing . . . it:** reminders of it that would inflame my anger.
26. **A stranger:** i.e. one whose past is a closed book.
29. **hath reference to:** is submitted for decision to, is at the disposal of.

King. Then shall we have a match. I have letters
    sent me   30
That sets him high in fame.

          Enter COUNT BERTRAM.

Laf.   He looks well on't.
King. I am not a day of season,
For thou mayst see a sunshine and a hail
In me at once. But to the brightest beams
Distracted clouds give way, so stand thou forth, 35
The time is fair again.
    Ber.   My high-repented blames,
Dear sovereign, pardon to me.
    King.   All is whole,
Not one word more of the consumed time.
Let's take the instant by the forward top;
For we are old, and on our quick'st decrees 40
Th' inaudible and noiseless foot of time
Steals ere we can effect them. You remember
The daughter of this lord?
    Ber. Admiringly, my liege. At first
I stuck my choice upon her, ere my heart 45
Durst make too bold a herald of my tongue;
Where the impression of mine eye infixing,
Contempt his scornful perspective did lend me,
Which warp'd the line of every other favor,
Scorn'd a fair color, or express'd it stol'n, 50
Extended or contracted all proportions
To a most hideous object. Thence it came
That she whom all men prais'd, and whom myself,
Since I have lost, have lov'd, was in mine eye
The dust that did offend it.
    King.   Well excus'd. 55
That thou didst love her, strikes some scores away
From the great compt; but love that comes too late,
Like a remorseful pardon slowly carried,
To the great sender turns a sour offense, 59
Crying, "That's good that's gone." Our rash faults
Make trivial price of serious things we have,
Not knowing them until we know their grave,
Oft our displeasures, to ourselves unjust,
Destroy our friends, and after weep their dust;
Our own love waking cries to see what's done, 65
While shameful hate sleeps out the afternoon.

Be this sweet Helen's knell, and now forget her.
Send forth your amorous token for fair Maudlin.
The main consents are had, and here we'll stay
To see our widower's second marriage-day. 70
    [*Count.*] Which better than the first, O dear
    heaven, bless!
Or, ere they meet, in me, O nature, cesse!
    Laf. Come on, my son, in whom my house's name
Must be digested; give a favor from you
To sparkle in the spirits of my daughter, 75
That she may quickly come. [*Bertram gives a ring.*]
      By my old beard,
And ev'ry hair that's on't, Helen, that's dead,
Was a sweet creature; such a ring as this,
The last that e'er I took her leave at court,
I saw upon her finger.
    Ber.   Hers it was not. 80
    King. Now pray you let me see it; for mine eye,
While I was speaking, oft was fasten'd to't.
This ring was mine, and when I gave it Helen,
I bade her, if her fortunes ever stood
Necessitied to help, that by this token 85
I would relieve her. Had you that craft to reave her
Of what should stead her most?
    Ber.   My gracious sovereign,
Howe'er it pleases you to take it so,
The ring was never hers.
    Count.   Son, on my life,
I have seen her wear it, and she reckon'd it 90
At her live's rate.
    Laf.   I am sure I saw her wear it.
    Ber. You are deceiv'd, my lord, she never saw it.
In Florence was it from a casement thrown me,
Wrapp'd in a paper, which contain'd the name
Of her that threw it. Noble she was, and thought 95
I stood engag'd; but when I had subscrib'd
To mine own fortune, and inform'd her fully
I could not answer in that course of honor
As she had made the overture, she ceas'd
In heavy satisfaction, and would never 100
Receive the ring again.
    King.   Plutus himself,
That knows the tinct and multiplying med'cine,
Hath not in nature's mystery more science

---

32. **of season:** i.e. of any one season, of settled weather.
35. **Distracted . . . way:** i.e. clouds break and give way (*Distracted* [= broken] is proleptic).   **stand thou forth:** (1) come forth (from the place where you shelter from the storm); (2) come forward.
36. **time:** weather.   **high-repented:** bitterly repented.
37. **whole:** well.
39. **take . . . top:** take time by the forelock, grasp the opportunity while we can (proverbial).   Opportunity was represented as bald behind.   45. **stuck:** fixed.
47. **Where:** i.e. in my heart.   **the impression . . . eye:** the image (of Lafew's daughter) received by my eye. It was a commonplace that love entered the heart by way of the eye.
48. **perspective:** optical glass that distorts whatever is seen through it.
49. **favor:** face.
50. **Scorn'd:** made mock of.   **express'd it stol'n:** i.e. declared it painted.   52. **object:** sight.   53. **she:** i.e. Helena.
56. **scores:** debits.   57. **great compt:** total account.
58. **remorseful:** compassionate.   **slowly carried:** i.e. arriving too late.
59. **turns . . . offense.** Like milk turning sour or food going bad.
61. **Make . . . of:** place a trifling value on.
62. **know their grave:** i.e. lose them irrevocably.
64. **weep their dust:** weep over their ashes.
66. **sleeps . . . afternoon:** rests peacefully after its hateful work.

68. **Maudlin:** form of *Magdalen*.
72. **cesse:** cease (an archaic form, used for the sake of rhyme).
74. **digested:** absorbed.
79. **last:** last time.   **took her leave:** took leave of her.
85. **Necessitied to:** in need of.   86. **reave:** despoil.
87. **stead:** help.
90–91. **reckon'd . . . rate:** valued it as highly as her life (*live's* = *life's*).
96. **engag'd:** pledged (to her) (?). It has been suggested that the F1 spelling *ingag'd* may mean *not gaged* or may be an error for *ungag'd*, i.e. not pledged to anyone else.
96–97. **subscrib'd . . . fortune:** i.e. told her of my situation.
98–99. **I . . . overture:** i.e. I could not in honor accept the invitation that she had tendered in honor.
100. **heavy satisfaction:** sorrowful conviction that no other course was open.
101. **Plutus:** the god of riches, i.e. the being most knowledgeable about gold.
102. **tinct . . . med'cine:** i.e. the "grand elixir" or "philosopher's stone," sought by the alchemists as the means of turning base metals to gold (*tinct* = tincture). Cf. *Antony and Cleopatra*, I.v.36–37, "that great med'cine hath / With his tinct gilded thee."
103. **more science:** deeper knowledge.

Than I have in this ring. 'Twas mine, 'twas Helen's,
Whoever gave it you. Then if you know   105
That you are well acquainted with yourself,
Confess 'twas hers, and by what rough enforcement
You got it from her. She call'd the saints to surety
That she would never put it from her finger,
Unless she gave it to yourself in bed,   110
Where you have never come, or sent it us
Upon her great disaster.
    Ber.   She never saw it.
    King. Thou speak'st it falsely, as I love mine
        honor,
And mak'st [conjectural] fears to come into me,
Which I would fain shut out. If it should prove   115
That thou art so inhuman—'twill not prove so;
And yet I know not: thou didst hate her deadly,
And she is dead, which nothing but to close
Her eyes myself could win me to believe,
More than to see this ring. Take him away.   120
                    [*Guards seize Bertram.*]
My fore-past proofs, howe'er the matter fall,
Shall [tax] my fears of little vanity,
Having vainly fear'd too little. Away with him!
We'll sift this matter further.
    Ber.   If you shall prove
This ring was ever hers, you shall as easy   125
Prove that I husbanded her bed in Florence,
Where yet she never was.   [*Exit guarded.*]

    Enter a GENTLEMAN, [*the astringer*].

    King. I am wrapp'd in dismal thinkings.
    Gent.   Gracious sovereign,
Whether I have been to blame or no, I know not.
Here's a petition from a Florentine,   130
Who hath for four or five removes come short
To tender it herself. I undertook it,
Vanquish'd thereto by the fair grace and speech
Of the poor suppliant, who by this I know
Is here attending. Her business looks in her   135
With an importing visage, and she told me,
In a sweet verbal brief, it did concern
Your Highness with herself.
    [*King. Reads*] *a letter.* "Upon his many protesta-
tions to marry me when his wife was dead, I blush to
say it, he won me. Now is the Count Rossillion   141
a widower, his vows are forfeited to me, and my
honor's paid to him. He stole from Florence, taking
no leave, and I follow him to his country for justice.
Grant it me, O King, in you it best lies; otherwise a
seducer flourishes, and a poor maid is undone.   146
                    Diana Capilet."

    Laf. I will buy me a son-in-law in a fair, and toll
for this. I'll none of him.
    King. The heavens have thought well on thee,
        Lafew,   150
To bring forth this discov'ry. Seek these suitors.
Go speedily, and bring again the Count.
                    [*Exeunt some Attendants.*]
I am afeard the life of Helen, lady,
Was foully snatch'd.
    Count.   Now, justice on the doers!

    Enter BERTRAM [*guarded*].

    King. I wonder, sir, [sith] wives are monsters to
        you,   155
And that you fly them as you swear them lordship,
Yet you desire to marry. What woman's that?

    Enter WIDOW, DIANA.

    Dia. I am, my lord, a wretched Florentine,
Derived from the ancient Capilet.
My suit, as I do understand, you know,   160
And therefore know how far I may be pitied.
    Wid. I am her mother, sir, whose age and honor
Both suffer under this complaint we bring,
And both shall cease, without your remedy.
    King. Come hither, Count, do you know these
        women?   165
    Ber. My lord, I neither can nor will deny
But that I know them. Do they charge me further?
    Dia. Why do you look so strange upon your wife?
    Ber. She's none of mine, my lord.
    Dia.   If you shall marry,
You give away this hand, and that is mine;   170
You give away heaven's vows, and those are mine;
You give away myself, which is known mine;
For I by vow am so embodied yours,
That she which marries you must marry me,
Either both or none.   175
    Laf. Your reputation comes too short for my
daughter, you are no husband for her.
    Ber. My lord, this is a fond and desp'rate creature,
Whom sometime I have laugh'd with. Let your High-
        ness
Lay a more noble thought upon mine honor   180
Than for to think that I would sink it here.
    King. Sir, for my thoughts, you have them ill to
        friend
Till your deeds gain them; fairer prove your honor
Than in my thought it lies.
    Dia.   Good my lord,
Ask him upon his oath, if he does think   185

105–7. **if . . . hers.** The sense of this seems to be: "If you know anything at all, you know that it is her ring; confess it."
112. **Upon . . . disaster:** in the event of some dire misfortune.
114. **conjectural fears:** dreadful surmises.
121–23. **My . . . little:** however this matter turns out, the evidence I already have shows that my fears cannot be censured as foolish; the folly lies in my not having been apprehensive enough.
128. **dismal:** ill-boding.
131. **removes:** stopping places on a royal progress.   **come short:** failed to arrive in time.   133. **Vanquish'd:** won.
134. **by this:** by this time.   135. **looks:** shows itself.
136. **importing:** (1) full of import; (2) urgent.
137. **verbal brief:** summary statement.
142. **his . . . me:** I am entitled to performance of what he vowed.

148. **in a fair:** at a fair (implying that even in a place where mis-representation of merchandise is routine he can buy his daughter a better husband than Bertram).
148–49. **toll for:** i.e. pay a tax for the privilege of selling. Merchandise to be sold in a market had to be entered in the toll-book for a fee.
151. **these suitors.** The King has been told of only one suitor.
155. **sith:** since.
156. **that.** Replacing a second *sith*; a frequent Elizabethan usage. **swear them lordship:** i.e. speak your marriage vows.
164. **both:** i.e. age and honor.   170. **this hand:** i.e. Bertram's.
178. **fond and desp'rate:** foolish and reckless.   181. **sink:** debase.
182. **you . . . friend:** they are not at all friendly.
183. **gain them:** win their friendship.

He had not my virginity.

King. What say'st thou to her?

Ber.　　　　　　　She's impudent, my lord,
And was a common gamester to the camp.

Dia. He does me wrong, my lord; if I were so,
He might have bought me at a common price. 190
Do not believe him. O, behold this ring,
Whose high respect and rich validity
Did lack a parallel; yet for all that
He gave it to a commoner a' th' camp,
If I be one.

Count. He blushes, and 'tis hit. 195
Of six preceding ancestors, that gem,
Conferr'd by testament to th' sequent issue,
Hath it been owed and worn. This is his wife,
That ring's a thousand proofs.

King.　　　　　　Methought you said
You saw one here in court could witness it. 200

Dia. I did, my lord, but loath am to produce
So bad an instrument. His name's Parolles.

Laf. I saw the man to-day, if man he be.

King. Find him, and bring him hither.

　　　　　　　　　　　[*Exit an Attendant.*]

Ber.　　　　　　　　　What of him?
He's quoted for a most perfidious slave, 205
With all the spots a' th' world tax'd and debosh'd,
Whose nature sickens but to speak a truth.
Am I or that or this for what he'll utter,
That will speak any thing?

King.　　　　　She hath that ring of yours.

Ber. I think she has. Certain it is I lik'd her, 210
And boarded her i' th' wanton way of youth.
She knew her distance, and did angle for me,
Madding my eagerness with her restraint,
As all impediments in fancy's course
Are motives of more fancy, and in fine, 215
Her [inf'nite cunning,] with her modern grace,
Subdu'd me to her rate. She got the ring,
And I had that which any inferior might
At market-price have bought.

Dia.　　　　　　　　I must be patient.
You that have turn'd off a first so noble wife, 220
May justly diet me. I pray you yet
(Since you lack virtue, I will lose a husband)
Send for your ring, I will return it home,
And give me mine again.

Ber.　　　　　　　I have it not.

King. What ring was yours, I pray you?

Dia.　　　　　　　　Sir, much like

187. **impudent:** shameless.
192. **high respect:** high place in his regard.　**validity:** value.
195. **'tis hit:** that went home, she has hit the mark.　196. **Of:** by.
198. **owed:** possessed.
199–200. **Methought . . . it.** Diana has not said this.
205. **quoted for:** set down as.
206. **With . . . debosh'd:** i.e. accused of being corrupted with all the vices there are (*debosh'd* is a variant spelling of *debauched*).
207. **sickens . . . truth:** is made sick by telling a truth.
208. **or . . . or:** either . . . or.　**for:** in consequence of.
211. **boarded:** made advances to.
212. **knew her distance:** knew how to keep tantalizingly out of reach (?).　213. **Madding:** maddening, i.e. inflaming.
214. **fancy's:** love's.　215. **motives:** causes, sources.
216. **modern:** commonplace.
217. **Subdu'd . . . rate:** made me submit to her price.
219. **be patient:** keep my self-control.
221. **diet:** restrict, deprive (?).

The same upon your finger. 226

King. Know you this ring? This ring was his of
late.

Dia. And this was it I gave him, being a-bed.

King. The story then goes false, you threw it him
Out of a casement.

Dia.　　　　　　I have spoke the truth. 230

Enter PAROLLES.

Ber. My lord, I do confess the ring was hers.

King. You boggle shrewdly, every feather starts
you.
Is this the man you speak of?

Dia.　　　　　　　Ay, my lord.

King. Tell me, sirrah—but tell me true, I charge
you,
Not fearing the displeasure of your master, 235
Which on your just proceeding I'll keep off—
By him and by this woman here what know you?

Par. So please your Majesty, my master hath been
an honorable gentleman. Tricks he hath had in him,
which gentlemen have. 240

King. Come, come, to th' purpose. Did he love
this woman?

Par. Faith, sir, he did love her, but how?

King. How, I pray you?

Par. He did love her, sir, as a gentleman loves a
woman. 246

King. How is that?

Par. He lov'd her, sir, and lov'd her not.

King. As thou art a knave, and no knave. What
an equivocal companion is this! 250

Par. I am a poor man, and at your Majesty's command.

Laf. He's a good drum, my lord, but a naughty
orator.

Dia. Do you know he promis'd me marriage? 255

Par. Faith, I know more than I'll speak.

King. But wilt thou not speak all thou know'st?

Par. Yes, so please your Majesty. I did go between
them as I said, but more than that, he lov'd her, for
indeed he was mad for her, and talk'd of Sathan and of
Limbo and of Furies and I know not what. 261
Yet I was in that credit with them at that time that I
knew of their going to bed, and of other motions, as
promising her marriage, and things which would
derive me ill will to speak of; therefore I will not
speak what I know. 266

King. Thou hast spoken all already, unless thou
canst say they are married. But thou art too fine in thy
evidence, therefore stand aside.
This ring you say was yours?

Dia.　　　　　　　Ay, my good lord. 270

King. Where did you buy it? Or who gave it you?

Dia. It was not given me, nor I did not buy it.

King. Who lent it you?

Dia.　　　　　　It was not lent me neither.

232. **boggle:** shy, take fright.　**shrewdly:** violently, excessively.
starts you: makes you jump.　237. **By:** about.
250. **companion:** fellow.
253. **drum:** drummer.　**naughty:** execrable.
260. **Sathan:** Satan.　262. **that:** such.
263. **motions:** things urged.　268. **fine:** hairsplitting.

King. Where did you find it then?

Dia.   I found it not.

King. If it were yours by none of all these ways,
How could you give it him?

Dia.   I never gave it him.   276

Laf. This woman's an easy glove, my lord, she
goes off and on at pleasure.

King. This ring was mine, I gave it his first wife.

Dia. It might be yours or hers for aught I know.

King. Take her away, I do not like her now,   281
To prison with her; and away with him.
Unless thou tell'st me where thou hadst this ring,
Thou diest within this hour.

Dia.   I'll never tell you.

King. Take her away.

Dia.   I'll put in bail, my liege.   285

King. I think thee now some common customer.

Dia. By Jove, if ever I knew man, 'twas you.

King. Wherefore hast thou accus'd him all this
while?

Dia. Because he's guilty, and he is not guilty.
He knows I am no maid, and he'll swear to't;   290
I'll swear I am a maid, and he knows not.
Great King, I am no strumpet, by my life;
I am either maid, or else this old man's wife.
                         [*Pointing to Lafew.*]

King. She does abuse our ears. To prison with her!

Dia. Good mother, fetch my bail. [*Exit Widow.*]
      Stay, royal sir.   295
The jeweller that owes the ring is sent for,
And he shall surety me. But for this lord,
Who hath abus'd me, as he knows himself,
Though yet he never harm'd me, here I quit him.
He knows himself my bed he hath defil'd,   300
And at that time he got his wife with child.
Dead though she be, she feels her young one kick.
So there's my riddle: one that's dead is quick—
And now behold the meaning.

            Enter Widow *and* Helen.

King.   Is there no exorcist
Beguiles the truer office of mine eyes?   305
Is't real that I see?

Hel.   No, my good lord,
'Tis but the shadow of a wife you see,

---

286. **common customer:** prostitute.   287. **knew:** knew carnally.
299. **quit:** (1) acquit; (2) pay back.
303. **quick:** (1) alive; (2) pregnant.   304. **exorcist:** conjurer.

The name, and not the thing.

Ber.   Both, both. O, pardon!

Hel. O my good lord, when I was like this maid,
I found you wondrous kind. There is your ring,   310
And look you, here's your letter. This it says:
"When from my finger you can get this ring,
And [are] by me with child, etc." This is done.
Will you be mine now you are doubly won?

Ber. If she, my liege, can make me know this
      clearly,   315
I'll love her dearly, ever, ever dearly.

Hel. If it appear not plain and prove untrue,
Deadly divorce step between me and you!
O my dear mother, do I see you living?   319

Laf. Mine eyes smell onions, I shall weep anon.
[*To Parolles.*] Good Tom Drum, lend me a handkercher. So, I thank thee; wait on me home, I'll make
sport with thee. Let thy curtsies alone, they are
scurvy ones.   324

King. Let us from point to point this story know,
To make the even truth in pleasure flow.
[*To Diana.*] If thou beest yet a fresh uncropped
      flower,
Choose thou thy husband, and I'll pay thy dower,
For I can guess that by thy honest aid
Thou kept'st a wife herself, thyself a maid.   330
Of that and all the progress, more and less,
Resolvedly more leisure shall express.
All yet seems well, and if it end so meet,
The bitter past, more welcome is the sweet. *Flourish.*

            [EPILOGUE]

[*King. Advancing.*] The king's a beggar, now the
      play is done;
All is well ended, if this suit be won,
That you express content; which we will pay,
With strife to please you, day exceeding day.
Ours be your patience then, and yours our parts;   5
Your gentle hands lend us, and take our hearts.
                              Exeunt omnes.

---

309. **like:** i.e. taking the place of.
315. **make . . . clearly:** prove to me that this is true.
318. **Deadly divorce:** divorcing death.   322. **So:** very good.
326. **even:** plain.
331. **Of . . . less:** the course of that and everything, both greater and
smaller details.
332. **Resolvedly:** in a fashion that will resolve all questions.

Epi. 3. **express content:** i.e. applaud.   4. **strife:** striving, effort.

NOTE ON THE TEXT

The First Folio (1623) is the sole authority for *All's Well
That Ends Well*; all later texts are derived from that source.
Occasional permissive stage directions and frequent variations in speech-prefixes (particularly those designating the
Countess, the French Lords, and Bertram), not to mention
other confusions and a probable ghost character (Violenta in
III.v), indicate clearly enough that some stage of Shakespeare's "foul papers" underlies the F1 text, but whether
that text was set directly from the "foul papers" or from some
kind of transcript of them (which would explain the general
absence of characteristic Shakespearean spellings in F1;
but see the Textual Notes, II.v.29, III.ii.18, 126) is a debat-
able question, with some probability in favor of a direct use
of the "foul papers." The hand of a book-keeper has been

seen by some scholars in a few directions calling for stage noises and in the use of "G." and "E." (supposed to represent actors' initials) to distinguish, not consistently nor always accurately, the two French Lords. If this view is correct, it points to nothing more than a preliminary rough annotation of the "foul papers"; certainly, the manuscript from which F1 was printed could never have served as an official prompt-book.

For further information, see: J. D. Wilson, ed., New Cambridge *All's Well That Ends Well* (Cambridge, 1929) [Wilson's elaborate revision theory is no longer generally accepted]; W. W. Greg, *The Shakespeare First Folio* (Oxford, 1955); G. K. Hunter, ed., New Arden *All's Well That Ends Well* (London, 1959).

TEXTUAL NOTES

Title: All's . . . Well] *F3*; Alls Well, that Ends Well *F1*
Dramatis personae: *subs. as first given by Rowe*
Act-scene division: *F1 marks acts only, except for I.i; other scene divisions from Rowe and later editors (see first note to each scene); present act-scene arrangement as a whole first established by Capell*

I.i

Location: *Cambridge*
1 s.p. Count.] *Rowe*; Mother. *F1 (or Mo. throughout scene)*
3 s.p. Ber.] *Rowe*; Ros. *F1 (throughout scene)*
73–8 Heaven . . . father.] *as verse, ed.; as prose, F1*
75 forged] *ed. (after Malone)*; forg'd *F1 (the F1 line is extremely crowded, thoughts being reduced to thoghts)*
75 s.d. Exit Countess.] *Neilson-Hill*; Exit. *F2 (after Bertram. l. 74)*
76 s.d. To Helena.] *Nicholson conj. (in Cambridge; other eds., following Rowe, include ll. 74–5 as addressed to Helena)*
78 s.d. Exeunt . . . Lafew.] *Rowe*
79 all!] *Capell (after Rowe)*; all, *F1*
87 me.] *Rowe (subs.)*; me *F1*
93 hour,] *Pope*; houre *F1*
99 s.d. Aside.] *Cambridge*
113 barricado] *Rowe*; barracado *F1*
128 got] *F2*; goe *F1*
142 paring] *Rowe*; payring *F1*
147 t' one] *ed.*; ten *F1*
155 request.] *F4*; request, *F1*
158 wear] *Capell (after Rowe)*; were *F1*
165 yet : . . . .] *some words or lines seem to be missing here*
170 traitress] *F2*; Traitoresse *F1*
172 jarring . . . discord] *F4*; iarring, . . . discord, *F1*
177 one—] *Rowe*; one. *F1*
187 s.d. Exit.] *Theobald*
209 counsel] *F2*; councell *F1*
215 s.d. Exit.] *F2*
223 like likes] *F4*; like, likes *F1*

I.ii

I.ii] *Capell*
Location: *Capell (after Pope)*
o.s.d. Lords] *Capell*
3 s.p. 1. Lord.] *Rowe*; 1. Lo. G. *F1 (throughout scene; G. is perhaps an actor's initial)*
4–5 it A certainty,] *Capell*; it, / A certaintie *F1*
15, 67 s.pp. 2. Lord.] *Rowe*; 2. Lo. E. *and* L. 2. E. *F1 (E. is perhaps an actor's initial)*
18 Rossillion] *F2*; Rosignoll *F1*
52 him!] *F2 (subs.)*; him *F1*
76 s.d. Exeunt.] *Rowe*; Exit *F1*

I.iii

I.iii] *Capell*
Location: *Pope, Capell (subs.)*
10 believe.] *F4 (subs.)*; beleeue, *F1*
19 I will] *F2*; w will *F1*
42 madam—] *Alexander*; Madam *F1*
60–4 For . . . kind.] *as verse, Rowe (subs.); as prose, F1*
67 you.] *Theobald (subs.)*; you, *F1*
75] *The repetition of this line is indicated in F1 by bis following l. 74*

76–9 And . . . ten.] *as verse, Rowe; as prose, F1*
85 tithe-woman] *hyphen, Theobald*
86 or] *Capell*; ore *F1*
90 be gone] *F2*; begone *F1*
95 black gown] *F3*; blacke-Gowne *F1*
114 level; Diana no] *Theobald*; leuell, *F1*
128 Even] *Singer*; Old Cou. Euen *F1 (repeated s.p.)*
130 belong;] *Theobald*; belong *F1*
134 foregone] *Rowe*; forgon *F1*
137 s.p. Count.] *Rowe*; Ol. Cou. *F1 (or Old Cou. through l. 167)*
161 madam;] *Rowe*; Madam, *F1*
171 loneliness] *Theobald*; louelinesse *F1*
177 t' one] *Hunter*; 'ton tooth *F1*
183 forswear't; howe'er] *F3 (subs.)*; forsweare't how ere *F1*
189 disclose] *F3*; disclose: *F1*
202 intenible] *F2*; intemible *F1 (some recent eds., following Nicholson's conj. [in Cambridge], read inteemible, the F1 -tem- being a variant of teem [= to pour out]; neither intenible nor inteemible is recorded apart from this passage)*
202 sieve] *F3*; Siue. *F1*
204 lose] *F4*; loose *F1*
231 it? speak.] *Steevens*; it, speake? *F1*
248 well-lost] *hyphen, Pope*
249 an] and *F2*
255 Be gone] *F3*; Begon *F1*

II.i

II.i] *Rowe*; Actus Secundus. *F1*
Location: *Capell*
o.s.d. Count Rossillion] *ed.*; Count, Rosse *F1*; Count Rosse *F2*
3 you;] *Rowe (subs.)*; you, *F1*
3 gain all,] *Johnson*; gaine, all *F1*
5 s.p. 1. Lord.] *Rowe*; Lord. G. *F1*
12 Frenchmen] *Warburton*; French men *F1*
18 s.p. 2. Lord.] *Rowe*; L.G. *F1*
22 s.p. Both Lords.] *Capell (subs.)*; Bo. *F1*
23 s.d. The . . . Lords.] *ed. (after Capell)*
24 s.p. 1. Lord.] *Rowe*; 1. Lo. G. *F1 (until l. 46)*
25 fault,] *F3*; fault *F1*
25 s.p. 2. Lord.] *Rowe*; 2. Lo. E. *F1 (throughout scene)*
30 forehorse] *F3*; for-horse *F1*
40 kin.] *Rowe (subs.)*; kinne, *F1*
43 with . . . an] *Theobald*; his sicatrice, with an *F1*
46 s.p. 1. Lord.] *Rowe*; Lo. G. *F1*
47 s.d. Exeunt Lords.] *Theobald (after l. 49); placed as in Capell*
60 s.d. Bertram and Parolles] *Capell*
60 s.d. The . . . forward.] *Hunter (after Collier MS)*
61 s.d. Kneeling.] *Johnson*
70 will] *Knight*; will, *F1*
79 Doctor She] *White*; doctor she *F1*
81 convey] *Rowe*; conuay *F1*
91 s.d. Goes to the door.] *Sisson*
97 Cressid's] *Pope*; Cresseds *F1*
109 two, more dear.] *Steevens*; two: more deare *F1*
144 fits] *Theobald conj.*; shifts *F1*
155 imposture] *Capell*; Impostrue *F1*; Impostor *F3*
171 shame,] *Capell (Johnson conj.)*; shame *F1*

173 otherwise;] *Capell*; otherwise, *F1*
173 ne] no *F2*
173 worst—] *Alexander (after Wilson)*; worst *F1*
192 heaven] *Thirlby conj.*; helpe *F1*
210 s.d. Exeunt.] *F2*; Exit. *F1*

II.ii

II.ii] *Capell*
Location: *Pope, Capell*
1 s.p. Count.] *Rowe*; Lady. *F1 (or La. throughout scene)*
13 court;] *Rowe*; Court, *F1*
40 I] *Rowe*; La. I *F1 (repeated s.p.)*
60–1 I . . . fool.] *as verse, Knight; as prose, F1*
63 An] *Rowe*; And *F1*
63 sir;] *Rowe (after F3, which places a semicolon after end); sir *F1*
70 legs] *F2*; legegs *F1*

II.iii

II.iii] *Capell*
Location: *Pope, Capell (subs.)*
1 s.p. Laf.] Ol. Laf. *F1 (or Old Laf. until l. 184, except Ol. Lord., l. 99)*
2 familiar,] *Theobald*; familiar *F1*
9 s.p. Ber.] *Rowe*; Ros. *F1*
11 say,] *Rowe*; say *F1*
21 indeed] *Capell (subs.)*; indeede *F1*
22 what-do-ye-call] *hyphens, Glover conj.*
22 s.d. Pointing . . . hand.] *ed. (after Wilson)*
23 s.d. Reading the title.] *Alexander*
25 it] *Steevens*; it, *F1*
26 dolphin] *Theobald*; Dolphin *F1 (it is just possible that the reference is to the French Dauphin)*
26 'Fore] *Capell*; fore *F1*
41 Lustick] *F3*; Lustique *F1*
43 coranto] *Rowe (subs.)*; Carranto *F1*
44 Mort du vinaigre] *Rowe*; Mor du vinager *F1*
45 'Fore] *Pope*; Fore *F1*
57 mistress] *Rowe*; Mistris *F1*
60 boys'] *Capell*; boyes *F1*
63–4 Gentlemen . . . health.] *as verse, Capell (after Theobald); as prose, F1*
70 choose; . . . refused,] *Rann*; choose, . . . refused; *F1*
75 imperial Love] *Pope*; imperial loue *F1*; imperiall Ioue *F1*; impartiall Ioue *F3*
76 s.d. She . . . Lord.] *placed as in Wilson; after l. 62, F1*
78–9 I . . . life.] *as prose, Pope; as verse. F1*
80, 89, 96 s.dd. To a second Lord., etc.] *Capell*
84 better,] *Rowe*; better *F1*
94 her] *F2*; heere *F1*
96 s.p. Hel.] *F3*; La. *F1*
102 s.d. To Bertram.] *Rowe*
125 place when] *Thirlby conj.*; place, whence *F1*
128–9 alone . . . name;] *Capell (subs.)*; a lone, / Is good without a name? *F1*
130 it is] *F2*; is is *F1*
133, 134 honor's] *Rowe*; honours *F1*
137 word's] *F2*; words, *F1*
138 grave] *Knight (after Steevens)*; graue: *F1*
140–1 tomb . . . indeed.] *Theobald*; Tombe. . . . indeed, *F1*
168 eyes,] *Rowe*; eies, *F1*
175 counterpoise— . . . estate] *ed. (after Globe)*; counterpoize: . . . estate, *F1*

179 **now-born**] *Rowe;* now borne *F1*
201 **ordinaries,**] *F3 (subs.);* ordinaries: *F1*
213 **hen!**] *F3 (subs.);* hen, *F1*
249 **dost**] *Rowe;* dooest *F1*
267 **s.p. 1. Ber.**] *Rowe;* Ros. *F1 (throughout rest of scene)*
268 **sweet heart**] *F4;* sweet-heart *F1*
280 **kicksie-wicky**] *hyphen, Theobald;* kicksie wicksie *F2*
283 **regions!**] *Capell;* Regions, *F1*
292 **detested**] *Rowe;* detected *F1*
294 **advise**] *F3;* aduice *F1;* advize *F2*
300 **s.d. Exeunt.**] *Rowe;* Exit *F1*

II.iv

II.iv] *Capell*
Location: *Pope, Capell*
16 **fortunes**] *Heath conj.;* fortune *F1*
33 **s.d. Parolles nods.**] *Sisson*
34 **s.d. Parolles ... head.**] *Sisson*
35 **The**] *Rowe; Clo.* The *F1 (repeated s.p.)*
56 **you. Come**] *Theobald;* you come *F1*
56 **s.d. Exeunt.**] *Pope;* Exit *F1*

II.v

II.v] *Capell*
Location: *Pope, Capell*
15 **s.d. To Bertram.**] *Capell*
20 **s.d. Aside to Parolles.**] *Rowe*
27 **End**] *Collier MS;* And *F1*
28 **traveller**] *F3;* Trauailer *F1*
29 **one**] *Rowe;* on *F1*
31 **heard**] *F2;* hard *F1*
48 **s.d. Exit.**] *Rowe*
69 **s.d. Giving a letter.**] *Rowe*
89 **Ber. Where ... Farewell.**] *Theobald conj.;* Where are my other men? Monsieur, farewell. *F1 (continued to Helena)*
89 **s.d. Exit Helena.**] *Theobald conj., after F1* Exit *following a line assigned to Helena (see preceding note)*
90 **Go**] *Theobald conj.; Ber.* Go *F1*
92 **s.d. Exeunt.**] *Rowe*

III.i

III.i] *Rowe;* Actus Tertius. *F1*
Location: *Pope, Capell*
o.s.d. **French Lords**] *Rowe;* Frenchmen *F1*
9 **s.p. 2. Lord.**] *Rowe;* French E. *F1*
12 **council**] *F3;* Counsaile *F1*
13 **self-unable**] *hyphen, F4*
17 **s.p. 1. Lord.**] *Cambridge;* Fren. G. *F1*
23 **to th'**] *F2* (to the); to'th the *F1*
23 **s.d. Exeunt.**] *Rowe*

III.ii

III.ii] *Pope*
Location: *Pope, Capell*
9 **sold**] *F3;* hold *F1*
10 **s.p. Count.**] *Rowe;* Lad. *F1 (or La. throughout rest of scene, except Old. La., l. 64)*
11 **s.d. Opening a letter.**] *Capell*
13 **ling**] *F2;* Lings *F1*
18 **E'en**] *Theobald;* In *F1*
19 **s.p., s.d. Count. Reads**] *Rowe*
44 **s.d. Exit.**] *Rowe*
44 **s.d. the French Lords**] *Neilson (subs.)*
45, 73, 77, 84, 86, 89 **s.pp. 2. Lord.**] *Kittredge;* French E. *or* Fren. E. *F1*
47, 52, 69, 70, 95 **s.pp. 1. Lord.**] *Kittredge;* French G. *or* Fren. G. *F1*
48 **patience.**] *F3 (subs.);* patience, *F1*
57 **s.d. Reads.**] *Capell*
62 **s.p. 1. Lord.**] *Kittredge;* 1. G. *F1*
65 **engrossest**] *F4;* engrossest, *F1*
74 **s.d. Reads.**] *Rowe (subs.)*
74–5 **"Till ... France."**] *as prose, Capell; as verse, F1*
77–8 **'Tis ... to.**] *as verse, ed.; as prose, F1*
84–5 **A ... known.**] *as verse, Pope; as prose, F1*
88 **well-derived**] *hyphen, Pope*
89–96 **Indeed ... affairs.**] *as verse, Capell; as prose, F1*
90 **that**] *Rowe;* that, *F1*
98 **s.d. with Lords**] *Neilson (after Rowe)*
117 **ravin**] *Capell;* rauine *F1*
126 **angels**] *F2;* Angles *F1*

III.iii

III.iii] *Capell*
Location: *Capell (after Pope, Theobald)*

III.iv

III.iv] *Capell*
Location: *Pope, Capell*
1 **s.p. Count.**] *Rowe;* La. *F1 (throughout scene)*
4 **s.p., s.d. Stew. Reads**] *Collier (after Capell)*
7 **have**] *F2;* hane *F1*
10 **peace, whilst**] *F3;* peace. Whilst *F1*
18 **s.p. Count.**] *Capell*

III.v

III.v] *Capell*
Location: *Capell (after Pope)*
o.s.d. **Diana**] *Rowe*
1–15 **Nay ... companion.**] *as prose, Pope; as irregular verse, F1*
7 **s.d. Tucket.**] *Capell*
8 **way.**] ways *may be the reading of some copies of F1, but other copies clearly read* way:
21 **is,**] *Rowe;* is *F1*
29 **s.d. habited ... pilgrim**] *Capell (after Rowe)*
33 **are**] are you *F2*
34 **le**] *F3;* la *F1*
66 **warr'nt**] *ed. (after Globe);* write *F1*
76 **Antonio**] *F2;* Anthonio *F1*
82 **Yond's**] *Rowe;* yonds *F1*
92 **s.d. Exeunt ... army.**] *Rowe (subs.);* Exit. *F1*

III.vi

III.vi] *Capell*
Location: *Capell (subs.)*
o.s.d. **and ... Lords**] *Rowe;* and the Frenchmen, as at first *F1*
1, 5, 7, 41, 85 **s.pp. 2. Lord.**] *Capell;* Cap. E. *F1*
3, 13, 19, 46, 51, 90 **s.pp. 1. Lord.**] *Capell;* Cap. G. *F1*
6 **Do ... him?**] *as prose, Pope; as verse, F1*
22 **s.p. 2. Lord.**] *Cambridge;* C. E. *F1*
34 **s.p. 1. Lord.**] *Cambridge (Rowe in error);* Cap. G. *F1*
36 **his**] *Rowe;* this *F1*
37 **metal**] *F4;* mettle *F1*
37 **ore**] *Theobald* (oar); ours *F1*
39 **inclining**] *F2;* inlining *F1 (?)*
48 **command—**] *Rowe (subs.);* command, *F1*
82–3 **I ... Farewell.**] *as prose, Pope; as verse, F1*
97, 107 **s.pp. 2. Lord.**] *Rowe;* Cap. E. *F1*
102 **s.p. 1. Lord.**] *Rowe;* Cap. G. *F1*
109 **s.p. 2. Lord.**] *Rowe;* Cap. G. *F1*
109 **s.d. Exit.**] *Theobald*
111, 117 **s.pp. 1. Lord.**] *Rowe;* Cap. E. *F1*

III.vii

III.vii] *Capell*
Location: *Theobald*
19 **Resolv'd**] *Collier (Egerton MS);* Resolue *F1*
34 **After,**] *Hunter;* after *F1;* after this *F2*
41 **steads**] *F4;* steeds *F1*
48 **s.d. Exeunt.**] *Rowe*

IV.i

IV.i] *Rowe;* Actus Quartus. *F1*
Location: *Capell*
o.s.d. **Second French Lord**] *Cambridge;* one of the Frenchmen *F1*
1 **s.p. 2. Lord.**] *Cambridge;* 1. Lord E. *F1*
7 **captain**] *F3;* Captaiue *F1*
8, 11, etc. **s.pp. 2. Lord.**] *Cambridge;* Lor. E., Lo. E., *or* L. E. *F1*
19 **choughs'**] *Dyce;* Choughs *F1;* Chough's *F3*
23 **s.d. They stand aside.**] *Collier (subs.)*
32 **s.d. Aside.**] *Rowe*
42 **Bajazeth's**] *F2 (subs.);* Baiazeths *F1*
44, 48, etc. **s.dd. Aside.**] *Pope*
61, 64 **enemy's**] *Malone;* enemies *F1*
67 **s.d. They seize him.**] *Hunter (after Rowe)*
67 **s.d. They blindfold him.**] *Hunter (after Rowe)*

III.iii (col 3)

68 **s.p. 1. Sold. as Interpreter.**] *Kittredge (after Capell);* Inter. *F1*
69 **Muskos'**] *Capell;* Muskos *F1*
88 **art**] *F3;* are *F1*
88 **s.d. with Parolles guarded**] *Capell*
91, 94 **s.pp. 2. Sold.**] *Capell;* Sol. *F1*
95 **s.d. Exeunt.**] *Rowe;* Exit *F1*

IV.ii

IV.ii] *Pope*
Location: *Capell, Theobald*
6 **monument.**] *F2 (subs.);* monument *F1*
28, 29 **Him ... Him**] *Neilson;* him ... him *F1*
32 **holy-cruel**] *hyphen, Theobald*
38 **make ... scarre**] *so F1; no satisfactory explanation or emendation has been offered; Daniel's reading may rope 's in such a snare is perhaps the best*
42 **'longing**] *Rowe;* longing *F1*
57 **maiden bed**] *Theobald;* maiden-bed *F1*
66 **s.d. Exit.**] *F2*

IV.iii

IV.iii] *Pope*
Location: *Capell (after Theobald)*
o.s.d. **Lords**] *Rowe;* Captaines *F1*
1, 6, etc. (except ll. 82, 125) **s.pp. 1. Lord.**] *Rowe;* Cap. G. *F1*
2 **letter?**] *Rowe;* letter. *F1*
3, 8, etc. (except ll. 315, 317) **s.pp. 2. Lord.**] *Rowe;* Cap. E. *F1*
19 **rebellion!**] *Hanmer (after Rowe);* rebellion *F1*
24–5 **nobility, ... stream**] *Theobald;* nobility ... streame, *F1*
32 **anatomiz'd**] *Rowe;* anathomiz'd *F1*
76 **s.p. Mess.**] *Neilson;* Ser. *F1*
82 **s.p. 1. Lord.**] *Rowe;* Ber. *F1;* Cap. G. *F3*
91 **effected**] *F3;* affected *F1*
99 **h'as**] *Rowe;* ha s *F1*
101 **h'as**] *Rowe;* ha's *F1*
102 **s.d. Exeunt Soldiers.**] *Capell (after forth, l. 101);* placed by ed.
115 **s.d. Soldiers and**] *Capell (subs.)*
115 **s.d. First Soldier as**] *Capell (subs.)*
118 **Hush, hush!**] *assigned to 1. Lord, Walker conj.; continued to Bertram, F1*
125 **s.p. 1. Lord.**] *Rowe;* Cap. *F1*
129, 158, 175, 211 **s.dd. Reads.**] *Cambridge (after Capell)*
138 **All's ... him.**] *assigned to Bertram, Capell; continued to Parolles, F1*
196 **lordship**] *Pope;* Lord *F1*
223 **s.d. Reads the letter.**] *Rowe (subs.);* Let. *F1*
236 **armipotent**] *Capell;* army-potent *F1*
239 **the**] *F3;* your *F1*
266 **h'as**] *Rowe;* ha's *F1*
278 **cardecue**] *F2;* Cardecue *F1*
298 **s.d. Aside.**] *Rowe*
312 **s.d. Unblinding him.**] *Rowe*
315, 317 **s.pp. 2. Lord.**] *Rowe;* Lo. E. *F1*
322 **s.d. Bertram and Lords**] *Capell*
329 **s.d. with Soldiers**] *Cambridge*

IV.iv

IV.iv] *Capell*
Location: *Pope*
3 **'fore**] *F2 (subs.);* for *F1*
9 **Marsellis**] *F2;* Marcellae *F1*
16 **you**] *F4;* your *F1*
35 **fine's**] *Theobald;* fines *F1*

IV.v

IV.v] *Capell*
Location: *Pope, Capell*
8 **s.p. Count.**] *Rowe;* La. *F1 (or Lady. throughout scene)*
21 **grass**] *Rowe;* grace *F1*
39 **name**] *Rowe;* maine *F1*
45 **of**] *F3;* off *F1*
80 **Marsellis**] *F2;* Marcellus *F1*
84 **It**] *F3;* Ir *F1*
99–100 **A ... that.**] *as prose, Pope; as verse, F1*

102–3 **Let . . . soldier.**] *as prose, Pope; as verse, F1*

V.i

V.i] *Rowe;* Actus Quintus. *F1*
Location: *Capell*
6 s.d. **Enter . . . astringer.**] *ed. (from F3 s.d.* Enter a Gentleman a stranger.); Enter a gentle Astringer. *F1 (after line 6; placed as in Kittredge)*
38 s.d. **Exeunt.**] *F2*

V.ii

V.ii] *Pope*
Location: *Pope, Cambridge*
1 **Master**] *Neilson;* Mr *F1*
8 **allow**] *F2;* alow *F1*
19 **Here**] *Theobald;* Clo. Heere *F1 (repeated s.p.)*
20 **musk-cat**] *Theobald;* Muscat *F1*
25 **similes**] *Theobald;* smiles *F1*
25 s.d. **Exit.**] *Capell*
32 **her**] *F2*
40 **"word"**] *quotes, Cambridge*
44 **in sooth**] *Johnson;* insooth *F1*
48 **Dost**] *Rowe;* doest *F1*
51 s.d. **Trumpets sound.**] *Theobald (subs.)*
51 **coming,**] *Rowe;* comming *F1*
55 s.d. **Exeunt.**] *Rowe*

V.iii

V.iii] *Pope*
Location: *Capell (subs.)*
o.s.d. **Countess**] *Rowe*

4 s.p. **Count.**] *Rowe;* Old La. *F1 (throughout scene, except l. 195)*
25 **relics**] *F3;* reliques *F1*
27 s.d. **Exit.**] *Capell*
36 **high-repented**] *hyphen, Pope*
44 **liege.**] *Rowe;* Liege. *F1*
54 **lov'd,**] *F2;* lou'd; *F1*
58–9 **carried, . . . sender**] *Theobald;* carried . . . sender, *F1*
71 s.p. **Count.**] *Theobald; lines continued to the King, F1*
72 **meet, . . . nature,**] *Rowe;* meete in me, O Nature *F1*
76 s.d. **Bertram . . . ring.**] *Hanmer*
101 **Plutus**] *Rowe;* Platus *F1*
113 **falsely,**] *Rowe;* falsely: *F1*
114 **conjectural**] *F2;* connecturall *F1*
115 **out.**] *F4 (subs.);* out, *F1*
116–7 **inhuman— . . . not:**] *Rowe (subs.);* inhumane, . . . not, *F1*
120 s.d. **Guards seize Bertram.**] *Rowe*
122 **tax**] *F2;* taze *F1*
127 s.d. **Exit guarded.**] *Rowe*
127 s.d. **the astringer**] *ed. (see V.i.6 s.d.)*
139 s.p., s.d. **King. Reads**] *Rowe*
143 **honor's**] *Rowe;* honors *F1*
148 **toll**] *Rowe;* toule *F1*
151 **discov'ry.**] *Rowe;* discou'rie, *F1*
152 s.d. **Exeunt some Attendants.**] *Capell*
154 s.d. **guarded**] *Capell; s.d. placed as in Capell; after l. 152, F1*
155 **sith**] *Dyce;* sir *F1*
157 s.d. **Diana**] *Rowe;* Diana, and Parrolles *F1 (Parolles is later entered by F1 at l. 230)*

183 **them; fairer**] *Theobald conj.;* them fairer: *F1*
204 s.d. **Exit an Attendant.**] *Dyce*
204 s.p. **Ber.**] *Rowe;* Ros. *F1 (throughout rest of scene)*
207 **sickens . . . truth.**] *Hanmer (subs.);* sickens: . . . truth, *F1*
216 **inf'nite cunning**] *Hunter (after Walker conj.);* insuite comming *F1*
217 **rate.**] *F3 (subs.);* rate, *F1*
228 **a-bed**] *Rowe;* a bed *F1*
245 **gentleman**] *Rowe;* Gent. *F1*
249 **knave.**] *Rowe (subs.);* knaue, *F1*
259 **that,**] *F3;* that *F1*
276 **him.**] *Rowe;* him, *F1*
293 s.d. **Pointing to Lafew.**] *Rowe*
295 s.d. **Exit Widow.**] *Pope (after l. 295); placed as in Craig*
313 **are**] *Rowe;* is *F1*
321 s.d. **To Parolles.**] *Rowe*
321 **Good . . . handkercher.**] *as prose, Capell; as verse, F1*
327 s.d. **To Diana.**] *Rowe*
332 **Resolvedly**] *F4;* Resolduedly *F1*

Epilogue

Epilogue] *so titled by Rowe*
1 s.p., s.d. **King. Advancing.**] *Capell (after Pope)*
4 **strife**] *F2;* strift *F1 (a possible form, but not occurring elsewhere in Shakespeare)*
6 s.d. **Exeunt omnes.**] Exeunt omn. / FINIS. *F1*

Measure for Measure

MEASURE FOR MEASURE was performed at court on December 26, 1604, and probably was written earlier in that year. It is the last of Shakespeare's comedies. After it come *Othello*, *King Lear*, *Macbeth*, *Antony and Cleopatra*, *Coriolanus*, and *Timon of Athens*: an unbroken progression of tragedies halted only with the composition of *Pericles* in 1607–8. *Pericles* and its three successors among the romances are not tragedies, but neither are they plays which seem to fit into the category of comedy as we understand it in Shakespeare's earlier work. In tone and structure they constitute a race apart: a new and different species of play. *Measure for Measure* stands then as the end of a development, the last word spoken in a particular kind of dramatic investigation which seems to have begun in the early 1590's and which extended itself through some eleven comedies before reaching this terminus. The play itself has some of the qualities of a farewell: a sense of dissatisfaction with its own dramatic mode, concentrated in its notoriously troublesome final scene, and a predominant harshness of tone, a savagery even in its clowning. Frequently, it has been classed as a "dark" comedy, or as a "problem play." Certainly the shadow of the tragedies Shakespeare was to write after *Measure for Measure* seems to hang over it. Much of the action takes place in a prison, and the comedy as a whole is obsessed with the idea of death.

Measure for Measure is the only one of Shakespeare's twelve comedies which can be said to have aroused as much disagreement over interpretation as any of the great tragedies. The language of the play is particularly rich in religious imagery and reference and, of the major characters, one makes her first appearance as a novice in a convent, while another spends most of his time acting the part of a holy friar. Ideas of Christian mercy, atonement, chastity, and sin are constantly invoked. A passage from Christ's Sermon on the Mount in Matthew's gospel seems to underlie, not simply Shakespeare's shaping of the Angelo story, but the entire play: "Judge not, that ye be not judged. For with what judgment ye judge, ye shall be judged: and with what measure ye mete, it shall be measured unto you again" (Geneva). Not surprisingly, attempts have sometimes been made to see *Measure for Measure* as a Christian allegory. The Duke takes his role as the deputy of God on earth, a prince bearing the sword of heaven, with the utmost seriousness, but not even he goes as far as those commentators who have insisted upon identifying him quite literally with Christ. This theory, taken to its logical extreme, produces readings of the play in which Isabella comes to represent Man's Soul (or else the Church), with Lucio functioning as a rather shabby Satan. On the whole, doctrinaire Christian interpretations of this kind are unactable without drastic cutting and distortion of individual roles. More important, they have a way of reducing one of Shakespeare's most profound and disturbing plays to a collection of pious and undramatic platitudes.

The story of the corrupt governor who perverts justice in order to gratify his own lust, the central plot element in *Measure for Measure*, exists in a great many versions and in a variety of European languages. Shakespeare undoubtedly knew the story of Juriste, Epitia, and her brother Vico as told by Cinthio in his prose collection *Hecatommithi* (1565). Cinthio also completed a dramatic version of the story, a tragicomedy called *Epitia* after its heroine, published in Italy in 1583. Shakespeare may have seen it. The most important influence on *Measure for Measure*, however, was undoubtedly the English *Promos and Cassandra* (1578), a two-part play by George Whetstone. Whetstone himself drew upon Cinthio's *novella*, and possibly upon a sixteenth-century Latin play, *Philanira*. As in all other known versions before Shakespeare, Cassandra, the Isabella character, does in fact sleep with the unjust judge in order to save the life of her brother. (In some stories it is her husband who is in danger.) There is no real equivalent for Shakespeare's disguised Duke, although Whetstone's plot does contain a virtuous king who appears in Part II to redress Cassandra's wrongs. Most important of all, there is no hint of a Mariana. Reparation is made at the end by a marriage between Cassandra and Promos, the man who has treated her so badly.

Whetstone's play raises no problems of interpretation. It is a straightforward moral drama, perfectly summed up by the description provided on the title-page:

> The Right Excellent and famous Historye, of *Promos* and *Cassandra*: Devided into two Commicall Discourses, In the fyrste parte is showne, the unsufferable abuse, of a lewde Magistrate: The vertuous behaviours of a chaste Ladye: the uncontrowled leawdnes of a favoured Curtisan. And the undeserved estimation of a pernicious Parasyte. In the second parte is discoursed, the perfect magnanimitye of a noble Kinge, in checking Vice and favouring Vertue: Wherein is showne, the Ruyne and overthrowe, of dishonest practises: with the advauncement of upright dealing.

It is worth noting, in view of the claim still often made for Isabella as an unexamined absolute, a girl who could not possibly have behaved better in an agonizing situation, that Whetstone's Cassandra does sacrifice herself for her brother but is still described as a "chaste Ladye" and her behavior as "vertuous." To say categorically that Shakespeare's heroine ought to have emulated Cassandra (and, for that matter, all her predecessors in the same predicament) by yielding to Angelo, in the knowledge that the sin would be cancelled out by the circumstances of victimization and constraint, would obviously be to create yet another simplification of a decision which Shakespeare presents as complex. Yet the argument that Elizabethans (as opposed to our permissive twentieth-century society) must necessarily have endorsed Isabella's attitude in the prison scene with Claudio because they believed that fornication, on whatever grounds, involved the perdition of the soul, is simply not borne out by *Promos and Cassandra*. Nor, for that matter, is it a view sanctioned by *Measure for Measure*.

Shakespearean comedy is in general deeply distrustful of absolutes, of characters who attempt to guide their lives according to rigid (and usually unexamined) ideals of conduct. *Measure for Measure* is no exception. Angelo's absolute of icy self-control is suspect from the beginning; it is an idea, not a fact,

and it gives way entirely as soon as he faces a real temptation. There is an ironic correctness, however, in the fact that it is Isabella who brings him down. She is a kindred spirit, another virtuous absolutist. Like calls to like between them, and it is precisely this affinity which, as he senses himself, makes her so deadly to him: "O cunning enemy, that to catch a saint, / With saints dost bait thy hook" (II.ii.179–80). Beneath the sober and inflexible deportment of the lawgiver lurks a frustrated sensualist. Beneath the habit of the nun there is a narrow-minded but passionate girl afflicted with an irrational terror of sex which she has never admitted to herself. In collision over Claudio's fate, these two absolutists elicit from each other the unacknowledged and destructive aspects of their respective personalities. Angelo plunges into depravity, Isabella merely into hysteria and intolerance.

In the course of the play both undergo a painful process of education. By the end, Angelo stands humiliated and exposed before everyone: convicted of hypocrisy, avarice, lust, and a criminal perversion of justice. His only wish is for death. Isabella, the girl who could not bring herself even to name her brother's sin directly in her initial interview with Angelo, is brought to the point of urging another woman to behave like Juliet, and also consents to make, in public, a false declaration of her own loss of virginity. The Isabella who kneels beside Mariana in the final scene to beg for the life of Angelo is a different person from the chilly maiden who had to be coaxed by Lucio into pleading her brother's cause with any vigor, or from the terrified virgin who turned on Claudio like a Fury when he ventured to suggest that death might be worse than an enforced loss of chastity. Like Angelo, she has arrived at a new and juster knowledge of herself and also, by implication, of a world of compromise and imperfection which has, at least to some extent, to be accepted on its own terms.

Society in Vienna is demonstrably corrupt, but energetic. It looks, in fact, all too familiar: a recognizable image of almost any big city. When Angelo and his partner Escalus, as justices, try to set it right they become enmeshed in a web of detail. The wrong (if there was one) done to Elbow's wife cannot be disentangled from two stewed prunes—the others having been eaten—in a threepenny fruit-dish which was not china but was a good dish all the same. Justice as an abstract concept, which is how Angelo sees it, wants nothing to do with an inn-room called the Bunch of Grapes, with its low chair and its fire in winter, nor with Master Caper's four suits of peach-colored satin, as yet unpaid for, nor with young Master Rash and his commodity of brown paper and old ginger. Yet it is only by entering into this concrete world of individualized instances, of stubborn particularity, that anything like justice can be done. Angelo soon becomes exasperated when asked to make sense of the Froth/Elbow/Pompey imbroglio, and leaves the court, "hoping you'll find good cause to whip them all." It is not a very constructive

approach. His far more diffident colleague Escalus, left alone to make sense of the matter, is patient and intuitive. The sheer stupidity of Constable Elbow makes a conviction impossible (much as it did in the analogous case of Mistress Quickly, Falstaff, and the Lord Chief Justice in *2 Henry IV*), but Escalus does reach the bottom of the matter. He has to turn Pompey loose, for lack of evidence, with nothing more than a warning, but he knows how to deal with him on the next encounter, and he has uncovered at least one civic abuse, in the form of those house-holders who pay Elbow to do their job for them, which can be set right.

Vienna is certainly in need of more magistrates like Escalus. What it emphatically does not require are draconic, inhuman laws of the kind that Angelo, with the Duke's sanction, attempts to enforce. The view that the Duke is a character who exists on a plane different from that of everyone else in the play, a personification of Christian Providence and not really a human being, is not easy to sustain from the text. It becomes particularly implausible in the theatre. What an audience actually sees is a man who has delivered up his authority to another man— and a man he has reason to suspect—in order that this surrogate should bear the opprobrium of reactivating certain harsh statutes which the Duke himself has let slip. He is a false friar, not a real one, but this does not prevent him from playing upon the credulity of his victims and hearing confession. He also tends to play upon people's emotions, displaying a kind of scientific curiosity as to how they will behave under stress. He even devises special tests for them in which pressure can be applied to points he knows, or guesses, are weak. So, he torments Isabella by withholding from her the information that her brother is really alive. Most baffling of all, he carefully arranges a bed-trick, the substitution of Mariana for Isabella, which is not only a sin in the eyes of the Church; in terms of Elizabethan common law it represents a union considerably more dubious (even without taking into account the fraud involved) than the *de praesenti* contract which allows Claudio to claim perfectly correctly, in secular terms, that Juliet "is fast my wife" (I.ii.147).

If the Duke is an image of Providence, there would seem to be chaos in heaven. Certainly, error and miscalculation are rife in his plot. In the second scene of Act IV, he talks to the Provost in terms of complete confidence about Claudio's pardon: "As near the dawning, Provost, as it is, / You shall hear more ere morning" (94–95). While the Provost reads Angelo's message, the Duke indulges in some rather complacent rhyming couplets: "This is his pardon, purchas'd by such sin / For which the par-doner himself is in" (108–9). Angelo has not, how-ever, sent a pardon, only a reaffirmation of the original order for Claudio's execution. Providence, if that is what the Duke is, finds itself at this juncture seriously embarrassed. Clutching at straws, he decides that the long-term prisoner Barnardine must die in place of Claudio. The trouble with this is that Barnardine,

understandably enough, happens not to like the idea. He sees no reason why he should suddenly go to the block at a moment convenient for the Duke's pur-poses, and says so. Indeed, like Juliet in an earlier scene, he interrupts the Duke in mid-sentence, then turns on his heel and departs. It is the Provost who finds a solution to the dilemma by way of the con-veniently dead pirate Ragozine.

Like Angelo and Isabella, the Duke is a virtuous absolutist. He is in fact a kind of comic dramatist: a man trying to impose the order of art upon a reality which stubbornly resists such schematization. As such, he is continually being surprised by the un-predictability, not to mention rank insubordination, of his elected cast of characters. Angelo and Isabella, Barnardine, Juliet and Claudio get out of control; they do things that are not in their parts as conceived by the Duke and, as they do so, they force upon him a series of hasty rearrangements and patchings: re-writings of the script characterized by their makeshift quality. Reality in Vienna resists patterning. It can and should be cleaned up a bit, as Escalus tries to do, but essentially it remains its own vigorous, untidy self. Barnardine refuses to die at the moment re-quired by the scenario. Claudio is won over by the rhetorical persuasion of the Duke's speech, "Be absolute for death" (III.i.5–41) but soon after is fighting for life on any terms as though he had never spoken to the friar. Angelo promises one thing and then, unexpectedly, tries to write his own fourth act. Moreover, there is one character for whom there is no place in the design as the Duke sees it, but who nonetheless refuses to get off the stage. Lucio does nothing at all for the Duke's godlike detachment, his pretense of being above ordinary human emotions and responses. He clings like a burr, breathing into the ear of the supposed friar all the scandal that this some-what irresponsible disguise has made possible. In the final scene, where the Duke's role as a manipulator of action is most apparent, Lucio threatens continually to divert or interrupt the unfolding of the plot. He has to be shouted down before the scene can proceed as planned. With all his faults, he stands here as a man instinctively opposed to the artificial ordering of a dramatist duke. In his presence, the resolution im-posed upon the comedy in its last moments looks even odder and more perfunctory than it might otherwise have done.

The long and notoriously difficult last scene of *Measure for Measure* seems to offer a strong hint as to why this was the last comedy Shakespeare ever wrote. As a comic dramatist, remaking reality in the arbi-trary image of art, conducting events towards the happy ending required by this particular form, the Duke suggests an obvious parallel with Shakespeare himself. There is something forced and blatantly fictional about the Duke's ultimate disposition of people and events—and so there is about Shake-speare's. The Duke refuses to admit failure, but Shakespeare seems perversely to stress the hollowness, in a sense the falsehood, of the happy ending of this comedy. He suddenly imposes upon a play which

Measure
for Measure

hitherto has probed uncomfortably deep into the dark places of society and the human mind, which has been essentially realistic, an ending which is that of fairy-tale: conventional, suspect in its very tidiness, full of pyschological gaps and illogicalities.

There is, after all, nothing to prepare one for a marriage between the Duke and Isabella. There have been no love passages of even the shyest and most inarticulate kind between them. She has never expressed any dissatisfaction with her original choice of a religious life, nor has the Duke retracted his statement at the beginning of the play that he, personally, is impervious to love: "Believe not that the dribbling dart of love / Can pierce a complete bosom" (I.iii.2–3). When he abruptly asks her to "be mine" (characteristically choosing the worst possible moment to do so, when Isabella is wholly taken up with Claudio, restored to her beyond hope) and when he tells her, "I have a motion much imports your good," what seems to confront us is not an emotional reality, but simply an obeisance to the laws of comic form. It is in effect an outbreak of that pairing-off disease so prevalent in the fifth acts of Elizabethan comedy which here openly declares itself as such. The situation is not made more credible by the fact that, even as Angelo has uttered no word of love or acceptance to the faithful Mariana, so Isabella says nothing whatever in response to the Duke's proposal of marriage. Like the theatre audience, presumably, she is dumb with surprise.

Almost all of Shakespeare's comedies before *Measure for Measure* end with the formation of what Northrop Frye has called a "new society." This society is never flawless, but it is based upon tolerance and self-knowledge and it faces the future with optimism. In the dance at the end of *As You Like It* or *Much Ado about Nothing*, in the blessing of the marriage beds in *A Midsummer Night's Dream*, or the last of the entertainments in *Love's Labor's Lost*—that dialogue between the Owl and the Cuckoo where everyone, at last, has learned to listen courteously—we see the play projecting itself into the future, beyond the formal limits of its fifth act. There is continuity and promise, not simply arbitrary resolution. *Measure for Measure*, by contrast, does not really create anything that can be understood as a new society. Of the three marriages set up in its final moments, only the previous bond between Claudio and Juliet has any reality for us. The other two are ciphers. Most important of all, the play has admitted in its fifth act that it is only a play, a false geometry.

Measure for Measure departs from the norm of Shakespearean comedy in another important way. Most of its predecessors had been structured upon the idea of two contrasted localities of which one was heightened and more extraordinary than the other. The shape of the comedy was dictated by a journey from one realm into the other with, usually, a return to the normal world either implied or actually accomplished at the end. Almost all of *Measure for Measure*, however, takes place in Vienna: a city which is an image of the ordinary, the sordidly everyday. There is only one other place in the comedy. With its music and its gentle melancholy, its sense of isolation from an urban society which has passed it by, Mariana's moated grange seems to stand in the same relation to Vienna as Belmont to Venice, the wood to Duke Theseus' Athens, or Arden to the court of Duke Frederick. The great difference lies in the fact that the grange is not at all a place where people come and are transformed. It is a sealed-off enclosure, consciously thin in texture: literary and artificial. Mariana is taken away from it and transported to Vienna, a world to which she does not belong. A kind of fairy-tale princess, the mechanism of a happy ending unlikely in more realistic terms, she is made to take Isabella's place in Angelo's bed—an imaginary character substituting for a real one—and then to force a resolution which is contradictory and psychologically improbable, no matter how gratifying it may be in terms of the symmetry of plot.

Mariana is the only absolutist character in the play who escapes criticism. Her undeviating single-mindedness, the obsessive emotionalism which Tennyson explored so brilliantly in "Mariana" and "Mariana in the South" are, in Shakespeare, simply the servants of plot. Because of Mariana, there is a happy ending. It is an ending, however, which seems to create as many problems as it solves. Isabella, kneeling beside Mariana at the close, begs for Angelo's life on the grounds that

> My brother had but justice,
> In that he did the thing for which he died;
> For Angelo,
> His act did not o'ertake his bad intent,
> And must be buried but as an intent
> That perish'd by the way. (V.i.448–53)

It is hard to make sense of this argument. At best, it is special pleading of an illogical kind. That Angelo has not slept with Isabella, as he intended, is true. He has, however, slept with Mariana outside the bonds of holy matrimony, even as Claudio did with Juliet. How, then, can Isabella claim that her brother "had but justice" when he has died (as she thinks) for exactly the same sin, fornication on a pre-contract, committed by Angelo with Mariana?

There seems to be a desperate, and surely deliberate, confusion of values in *Measure for Measure*. Isabella perhaps speaks more truly than she knows when she says, in Act II, that the laws of heaven often seem oddly incompatible with those of society: "'Tis set down so in heaven, but not in earth" (II.iv.50). There is in this play an unresolved conflict between religious and secular law, between absolutes and anarchy, between a necessary but sterile order and a vigorous but suspect world of self-gratification and individualism. There is also a clash between fairy-tale and realism, the simplifications of plot and the horrifying complexities of character. In the midst of all this, Mariana seems like an exile from a land of fiction. Her moated grange is like Isabella's nunnery, or Angelo's impossible court of justice, in that it too deals with absolutes: with clear-cut black and white. It will not bear close examination of the kind urged elsewhere in the play. As for the Duke, an absolutist of an artistic as opposed to a moral, religious, or emotional kind, he appears to embody some of the problems of a Shakespeare now seemingly disillusioned with that art of comedy which, in the past, had served him so well.

Anne Barton

Pressing to death. From the title-page of the anonymous *The Life and Death of Griffin Flood Informer* (1623). This barbarous form of execution was resorted to for felons who refused to plead and was practiced as late as 1736. The so-called Press-yard in old Newgate Prison was the original scene of such tortures. With this woodcut before us, we can better understand the full force of Lucio's anguished protest when he is ordered by the Duke to marry a prostitute whom he has got with child: "Marrying a punk, my lord, is pressing to death, whipping, and hanging" (*Measure for Measure*, V.i.522–23). (*The Folger Shakespeare Library*)

Measure for Measure

THE NAMES OF ALL THE ACTORS

VINCENTIO, *the Duke*
ANGELO, *the Deputy*
ESCALUS, *an ancient lord*
CLAUDIO, *a young gentleman*
LUCIO, *a fantastic*
Two other like GENTLEMEN
PROVOST
THOMAS ⎫
PETER ⎬ *two friars*
[JUSTICE]
[VARRIUS]
ELBOW, *a simple constable*

FROTH, *a foolish gentleman*
[POMPEY,] *clown,* [*servant to Mistress Overdone*]
ABHORSON, *an executioner*
BARNARDINE, *a dissolute prisoner*
[SERVANT]

ISABELLA, *sister to Claudio*
MARIANA, *betrothed to Angelo*
JULIET, *beloved of Claudio*
FRANCISCA, *a nun*
MISTRESS OVERDONE, *a bawd*

[LORDS, OFFICERS, CITIZENS, BOY, *and* ATTENDANTS]

THE SCENE: *Vienna* [*and its environs*]

ACT I, SCENE I

Enter DUKE, ESCALUS, LORDS, [*and* ATTENDANTS].

Duke. Escalus.
Escal. My lord.
Duke. Of government the properties to unfold
Would seem in me t' affect speech and discourse,
Since I am put to know that your own science   5
Exceeds, in that, the lists of all advice
My strength can give you. Then no more remains
But that, to your sufficiency, as your worth is able,
And let them work. The nature of our people,
Our city's institutions, and the terms   10
For common justice, y' are as pregnant in
As art and practice hath enriched any
That we remember. There is our commission,

From which we would not have you warp. Call hither,
I say, bid come before us Angelo.   15
[*Exit an Attendant.*]
What figure of us think you he will bear?
For you must know, we have with special soul
Elected him our absence to supply,
Lent him our terror, dress'd him with our love,
And given his deputation all the organs   20
Of our own pow'r. What think you of it?
Escal. If any in Vienna be of worth
To undergo such ample grace and honor,
It is Lord Angelo.

Enter ANGELO.

Duke.   Look where he comes.
Ang. Always obedient to your Grace's will,   25
I come to know your pleasure.
Duke.   Angelo:
There is a kind of character in thy life,
That to th' observer doth thy history

Words and passages enclosed in square brackets in the text above are either emendations of the copy-text or additions to it. The Textual Notes immediately following the play cite the earliest authority for every such change or insertion and supply the reading of the copy-text wherever it is emended in this edition.

I.i. Location: Vienna. The Duke's palace.
3. **Of . . . unfold:** to expound the qualities required for governing well.
4. **seem . . . discourse:** i.e. make me appear to be fond of talking for its own sake.
5. **put to know:** forced to recognize. **science:** expert knowledge.
6. **lists:** boundaries. 7. **strength:** capability.
8–9. **But . . . work.** A crux that has inspired many emendations, none satisfactory. To provide a referent for *them*, commentators have explained *sufficiency . . . worth* as "authority . . . qualifications" (or "qualifications . . . authority"), but in fact both words probably mean "qualifications." There is now wide agreement that a lacuna exists after *sufficiency*, or, less probably, after *able*.
9–11. **The nature . . . justice:** i.e. our social, political, and judicial usages. *Terms* probably means "modes of procedure." The Duke shifts in this sentence to the "royal" plural.
11. **pregnant:** ready, i.e. well versed. 12. **art:** study, theory.

14. **warp:** deviate.
16. **What . . . bear:** i.e. how do you think he will represent me as my deputy. The figure is of the royal likeness stamped on wax or metal, to validate a seal or a coin.
17. **soul:** conviction (that the choice is right) (?).
18. **Elected . . . supply:** chosen him to fill my place in my absence.
19. **Lent . . . love:** i.e. bestowed on him the royal attributes that inspire terror and those that inspire love. Cf. the list of the "servants" of kings in *Henry VIII*, V.v.48: "peace, plenty, love, truth, terror."
20. **his deputation:** to him as my deputy. **organs:** instruments.
23. **undergo:** sustain, bear up.
27. **character:** writing, i.e. clear indication.
28–29. **to . . . unfold:** i.e. enables an observer to predict what your future behavior will be. This is Johnson's explanation, strongly supported by *2 Henry IV*, III.i.80–85.

Fully unfold. Thyself and thy belongings
Are not thine own so proper as to waste　　30
Thyself upon thy virtues, they on thee.
Heaven doth with us as we with torches do,
Not light them for themselves; for if our virtues
Did not go forth of us, 'twere all alike　　34
As if we had them not. Spirits are not finely touch'd
But to fine issues; nor Nature never lends
The smallest scruple of her excellence,
But like a thrifty goddess, she determines
Herself the glory of a creditor,
Both thanks and use. But I do bend my speech　　40
To one that can my part in him advertise.
Hold therefore, Angelo:
In our remove be thou at full ourself.
Mortality and mercy in Vienna
Live in thy tongue and heart. Old Escalus,　　45
Though first in question, is thy secondary.
Take thy commission.
　　Ang.　　　　　　　Now, good my lord,
Let there be some more test made of my mettle
Before so noble and so great a figure
Be stamp'd upon it.
　　Duke.　　　　　No more evasion.　　50
We have with a leaven'd and prepared choice
Proceeded to you; therefore take your honors.
Our haste from hence is of so quick condition
That it prefers itself, and leaves unquestion'd
Matters of needful value. We shall write to you,　　55
As time and our concernings shall importune,
How it goes with us, and do look to know
What doth befall you here. So fare you well.
To th' hopeful execution do I leave you
Of your commissions.
　　Ang.　　　　　　Yet give leave, my lord,　　60
That we may bring you something on the way.
　　Duke. My haste may not admit it,
Nor need you (on mine honor) have to do

With any scruple. Your scope is as mine own,
So to enforce or qualify the laws　　65
As to your soul seems good. Give me your hand,
I'll privily away. I love the people,
But do not like to stage me to their eyes;
Though it do well, I do not relish well
Their loud applause and aves vehement;　　70
Nor do I think the man of safe discretion
That does affect it. Once more fare you well.
　　Ang. The heavens give safety to your purposes!
　　Escal. Lead forth and bring you back in happiness!
　　Duke. I thank you. Fare you well.　　*Exit.*　　75
　　Escal. I shall desire you, sir, to give me leave
To have free speech with you; and it concerns me
To look into the bottom of my place.
A pow'r I have, but of what strength and nature
I am not yet instructed.　　80
　　Ang. 'Tis so with me. Let us withdraw together,
And we may soon our satisfaction have
Touching that point.
　　Escal.　　　　　I'll wait upon your honor.　　*Exeunt.*

Scene II

Enter Lucio *and two other* Gentlemen.

　　Lucio. If the Duke with the other dukes come not
to composition with the King of Hungary, why then
all the dukes fall upon the King.
　　1. Gent. Heaven grant us its peace, but not the
King of Hungary's!　　5
　　2. Gent. Amen.
　　Lucio. Thou conclud'st like the sanctimonious
pirate, that went to sea with the Ten Commandments,
but scrap'd one out of the table.
　　2. Gent. "Thou shalt not steal"?　　10
　　Lucio. Ay, that he raz'd.
　　1. Gent. Why, 'twas a commandement to command
the captain and all the rest from their functions; they

29. **belongings:** qualities, attributes (the *virtues* of line 31).
30. **proper:** exclusively.　**waste:** expend.
34. **all alike:** precisely the same.
35. **finely touch'd:** excellently endowed (with play on testing gold for
fineness by means of a touchstone).　36. **issues:** purposes, ends.
37. **scruple:** a very small unit of weight.
38. **determines:** allots (to).　39. **glory:** proud due.
40. **use:** interest.
41. **can . . . advertise:** can instruct that part of me now vested in him,
i.e. knows more about how to govern than I can tell him (cf. lines 5–7).
Advertise is accented on the second syllable.
42. **Hold:** i.e. maintain your worthiness (?) or take this (the document, as in lines 13, 47) (?).
43. **remove:** absence.　**at full.** Perhaps with play on *part* in line 41.
44. **Mortality and mercy:** i.e. authority to pronounce sentence of
death and freedom to temper justice with mercy. Cf. *terror . . . love*
in line 19.
45. **tongue** and **heart.** With reference to *Mortality* and *mercy* respectively.　46. **first in question:** i.e. first appointed.
48. **mettle.** In Elizabethan English *mettle* and *metal* were variants of
the same word, with primary meaning "substance." Here the sense
now spelled *metal* carries on the coining imagery of lines 16, 35–36.
51. **leaven'd:** i.e. pervaded by the gradual working of judgment (like
the action of yeast in dough).
53. **so quick condition:** so urgent a nature.
54. **prefers:** advances, gives priority to.　**unquestion'd:** undiscussed,
uninvestigated.
56. **our concernings:** matters of concern to us.　**importune:** urge,
require.　57. **look to know:** expect to be informed of.
59. **hopeful.** A transferred modifier, rightly describing the Duke's
expectations.
61. **bring . . . way:** escort you some distance on your way.

64. **scruple:** misgiving.　**scope:** freedom to act; here, breadth of
authority (a word that occurs five times in this play).
65. **enforce or qualify:** i.e. apply with greater or lesser severity.
67–72. **I . . . it:** Usually taken to allude to King James's dislike of
effusive English crowds. See II.iv.24–30.
68. **stage me:** make public show of myself.
69. **do well:** i.e. show their good will.
70. **aves:** acclamations (Latin *ave*, "hail," connected with acclaim of
Caesar).　71. **safe discretion:** sound judgment.
72. **does affect:** is fond of.　73. **give safety to:** protect, safeguard.
77. **free:** frank.
78. **look . . . place:** determine how far my duties and authority
extend.　82. **satisfaction:** dispelling of uncertainty.
83. **wait upon:** attend, accompany.

I.ii. Location: A street.
2. **composition:** agreement, treaty.
4. **its.** With the exception of one occurrence in *2 Henry VI* (III.ii.393),
this is Shakespeare's earliest recorded use of *its*, in a total of eleven.
Elsewhere, save for an occasional appearance of *it* (as in *King Lear*,
I.iv.216), he uses *his* as the possessive form of *it*.
7. **sanctimonious.** The earliest example of the modern ironic sense
listed in *O.E.D.*; the word's only other occurrence in Shakespeare—
sanctimonious ceremonies in *The Tempest*, IV.i.16—shows the original
straightforward meaning "marked by sanctity."
8. **Commandements.** A variant spelling, perhaps here (as often in
verse) quadrisyllabic.
9. **table:** tablet (referring to the tablets of stone on which the Ten
Commandments were traditionally represented).
11. **raz'd:** erased, "scrap'd out."
13. **functions:** professional duties.　Leisi sees an extended wordplay
on *steal/stale* (= urinate), *functions*, and *put forth*.

put forth to steal. There's not a soldier of us all, that in the thanksgiving before meat, do relish the petition well that prays for peace.   16

2. Gent.   I never heard any soldier dislike it.

Lucio.   I believe thee; for I think thou never wast where grace was said.

2. Gent.   No? a dozen times at least.   20

1. Gent.   What? in metre?

Lucio.   In any proportion, or in any language.

1. Gent.   I think, or in any religion.

Lucio.   Ay, why not? Grace is grace, despite of all controversy; as for example, thou thyself art a wicked villain, despite of all grace.   26

1. Gent.   Well; there went but a pair of shears between us.

Lucio.   I grant; as there may between the lists and the velvet. Thou art the list.   30

1. Gent.   And thou the velvet—thou art good velvet; thou'rt a three-pil'd piece, I warrant thee. I had as lief be a list of an English kersey as be pil'd, as thou art pil'd, for a French velvet. Do I speak feelingly now?   35

Lucio.   I think thou dost; and indeed with most painful feeling of thy speech. I will, out of thine own confession, learn to begin thy health; but, whilst I live, forget to drink after thee.

1. Gent.   I think I have done myself wrong, have I not?   41

2. Gent.   Yes, that thou hast; whether thou art tainted or free.

Enter Bawd [MISTRESS OVERDONE].

Lucio.   Behold, behold, where Madam Mitigation comes!   45

[*1. Gent.*]   I have purchas'd as many diseases under her roof as come to—

2. Gent.   To what, I pray?

Lucio.   Judge.

2. Gent.   To three thousand dolors a year.   50

1. Gent.   Ay, and more.

Lucio.   A French crown more.

1. Gent.   Thou art always figuring diseases in me; but thou art full of error, I am sound.   54

Lucio.   Nay, not (as one would say) healthy; but so sound as things that are hollow. Thy bones are hollow; impiety has made a feast of thee.

1. Gent.   How now, which of your hips has the most profound sciatica?   59

Mrs. Ov.   Well, well; there's one yonder arrested and carried to prison was worth five thousand of you all.

2. Gent.   Who's that, I pray thee?

Mrs. Ov.   Marry, sir, that's Claudio, Signior Claudio.   65

1. Gent.   Claudio to prison? 'tis not so.

Mrs. Ov.   Nay, but I know 'tis so. I saw him arrested; saw him carried away; and which is more, within these three days his head to be chopp'd off.

Lucio.   But after all this fooling, I would not have it so. Art thou sure of this?   71

Mrs. Ov.   I am too sure of it; and it is for getting Madam Julietta with child.

Lucio.   Believe me, this may be. He promis'd to meet me two hours since, and he was ever precise in promise-keeping.   76

2. Gent.   Besides, you know, it draws something near to the speech we had to such a purpose.

1. Gent.   But most of all agreeing with the proclamation.   80

Lucio.   Away! let's go learn the truth of it.

Exit [*with Gentlemen*].

Mrs. Ov.   Thus, what with the war, what with the sweat, what with the gallows, and what with poverty, I am custom-shrunk.

Enter Clown [POMPEY].

How now? what's the news with you?   85

Pom.   Yonder man is carried to prison.

Mrs. Ov.   Well; what has he done?

Pom.   A woman.

Mrs. Ov.   But what's his offense?

Pom.   Groping for trouts in a peculiar river.   90

Mrs. Ov.   What? is there a maid with child by him?

---

17. dislike: express dislike of.   **22. proportion:** form.
24–26. Grace . . . grace. Lucio shifts the sense of *grace* to "God's grace": grace remains grace despite all the debates about its nature—just as, to cite a parallel, in you villainy remains villainy despite the availability of grace.
27. Well. Often used to show that note has been taken of an insult; cf. line 60.
27–28. there . . . us: we are cut from the same cloth (proverbial).
29. lists: selvages, plain strips along the edge (from the basic sense "boundaries" seen in I.i.6).
32. three-pil'd: having a pile or nap of triple thickness.
33. lief: willingly.   **kersey:** plain woollen fabric (named for Kersey in Suffolk, where it was first made).   **pil'd.** Lucio plays on *piled*, "napped," and *pilled*, "bald." Loss of hair was an effect of the treatment for syphilis, which was called the "French disease"—hence *French velvet* in line 34.
34. speak feelingly: speak to the purpose, i.e. touch the quick; but Lucio quibbles on "speak painfully" (i.e. because his mouth is affected by the lesions of venereal disease).
38. begin thy health: begin drinking to your health.
39. forget . . . thee: remember not to drink out of your glass.
40. done myself wrong: i.e. laid myself open to that.
43. tainted: infected (in which case he has "done himself wrong" in a different sense).
44. Mitigation. So called because she allays sexual desire.
50. dolors: (1) pains; (2) dollars (continental coins).
52. French crown: (1) French gold coin; (2) bald head (in consequence of the "French disease").

53. figuring: (1) reckoning (with reference to the preceding lines); (2) imagining.
56. sound: resounding.   **Thy . . . hollow.** Another effect of syphilis.
58. How now. Probably addressed to Mrs. Overdone; "How now" is a casual greeting, and sciatica (another supposed effect of venereal disease) is elsewhere associated with bawds.
60. one yonder: a man back there (not limited to what is in view).
61. carried: conducted.
64. Marry: indeed (originally the name of the Virgin Mary used as an oath).
70. after . . . fooling: to return to seriousness.
77–78. draws . . . purpose: fits fairly closely with the conversation we had about that situation (i.e. the relation between Claudio and Juliet? or the increasing rigor of law enforcement?).
79–80. proclamation. Apparently the public announcement of the revived penalty for fornication.
83. sweat: sweating sickness, a form of the plague (which had been rampant in 1603 and until the middle of 1604).
84. custom-shrunk: short on customers.
86. Yonder man. This cannot be anyone but Claudio, since later we hear repeatedly that he is the first and still the only victim of the new dispensation. Mrs. Overdone's ignorance of his arrest (an event which she herself has announced shortly before), together with other obvious discrepancies, has been made the basis of various theories of revision.
87. done. Pompey quibbles on the slang sense "copulated" (a sense to which Mrs. Overdone's name is related).
90. peculiar: private (i.e. where fishing is against the law).

Pom. No; but there's a woman with maid by him. You have not heard of the proclamation, have you?

Mrs. Ov. What proclamation, man?

Pom. All houses in the suburbs of Vienna must be pluck'd down. 96

Mrs. Ov. And what shall become of those in the city?

Pom. They shall stand for seed. They had gone down too, but that a wise burgher put in for them.

Mrs. Ov. But shall all our houses of resort in the suburbs be pull'd down? 102

Pom. To the ground, mistress.

Mrs. Ov. Why, here's a change indeed in the commonwealth! What shall become of me? 105

Pom. Come; fear not you; good counsellors lack no clients. Though you change your place, you need not change your trade; I'll be your tapster still. Courage! there will be pity taken on you. You that have worn your eyes almost out in the service, you will be consider'd. 111

Mrs. Ov. What's to do here, Thomas tapster? Let's withdraw.

Pom. Here comes Signior Claudio, led by the Provost to prison; and there's Madam Juliet. *Exeunt.*

Enter PROVOST, CLAUDIO, JULIET, OFFICERS.

Claud. Fellow, why dost thou show me thus to
    th' world? 116
Bear me to prison, where I am committed.

Prov. I do it not in evil disposition,
But from Lord Angelo by special charge.

Claud. Thus can the demigod, Authority, 120
Make us pay down for our offense by weight
The words of heaven: on whom it will, it will;
On whom it will not, so; yet still 'tis just.

[*Enter*] LUCIO *and two* GENTLEMEN.

Lucio. Why, how now, Claudio? whence comes
    this restraint? 124

Claud. From too much liberty, my Lucio, liberty:
As surfeit is the father of much fast,
So every scope by the immoderate use
Turns to restraint. Our natures do pursue,

Like rats that ravin down their proper bane,
A thirsty evil, and when we drink we die. 130

Lucio. If I could speak so wisely under an arrest, I would send for certain of my creditors; and yet, to say the truth, I had as lief have the foppery of freedom as the mortality of imprisonment. What's thy offense, Claudio? 135

Claud. What but to speak of would offend again.

Lucio. What, is't murder?

Claud. No.

Lucio. Lechery?

Claud. Call it so. 140

Prov. Away, sir, you must go.

Claud. One word, good friend. Lucio, a word with
    you.

Lucio. A hundred! if they'll do you any good. Is lechery so look'd after?

Claud. Thus stands it with me: upon a true con-
    tract 145
I got possession of Julietta's bed.
You know the lady; she is fast my wife,
Save that we do the denunciation lack
Of outward order. This we came not to,
Only for propagation of a dow'r 150
Remaining in the coffer of her friends,
From whom we thought it meet to hide our love
Till time had made them for us. But it chances
The stealth of our most mutual entertainment
With character too gross is writ on Juliet. 155

Lucio. With child, perhaps?

Claud.   Unhappily, even so.
And the new deputy now for the Duke—
Whether it be the fault and glimpse of newness,
Or whether that the body public be
A horse whereon the governor doth ride, 160
Who, newly in the seat, that it may know
He can command, lets it straight feel the spur;
Whether the tyranny be in his place,
Or in his eminence that fills it up,
I stagger in—but this new governor 165

129. **ravin down:** devour greedily.   **proper bane:** particular poison.
130. **A thirsty . . . die.** Rat poison does not kill directly; it makes the rat thirsty, and taking water is fatal. So too much liberty stimulates lust, and the satisfying of lust incurs death.
132. **send . . . creditors:** i.e. take steps to bring about my own arrest.
133. **foppery:** folly.
134. **mortality:** being subject to death (?) or deadliness (?). Most editors from Rowe onward emend to *morality,* "moralizing talk," which provides an apt antithesis to *foppery* in the sense "idle talk." Shakespeare never uses the word *morality* elsewhere, but he does not use *mortality* in the precise sense required here either.
144. **look'd after:** kept watch upon.
145. **a true contract.** Claudio and Juliet have declared themselves husband and wife in the presence of witnesses. Under the common law such a declaration created a valid marriage (*sponsalia per verba de praesenti*), but the church required a religious ceremony before such a marriage could be consummated without incurring a penalty.
147. **fast:** firmly bound (perhaps with reference to making a contract of marriage by handfasting or joining hands).
148. **denunciation:** public announcement.
150. **propagation:** breeding, bringing to birth. Many editors adopt Malone's conjecture *prorogation,* i.e. delay; but figures of breeding and pregnancy are frequent in the play.   151. **friends:** relatives.
153. **made . . . us:** won them to our side.
155. **character:** writing, letters.   **gross:** large, obvious.
158. **Whether . . . newness:** i.e. whether it is the sudden brilliance (*glimpse*) of his new honor that is to blame.
162. **straight:** straightway.   163. **in his place:** inherent in his office.
164. **eminence:** distinction, superiority.
165. **stagger in:** am at a loss to decide.

92. **with maid.** Playing on *maid* = young fish (suggested by the trouts of line 90).
95. **houses:** i.e. houses of prostitution.   **suburbs.** The site of the London brothels (which were thus beyond the reach of city regulations).   96. **pluck'd:** pulled.
99. **stand for seed:** remain standing to assure the continuance of prostitution (like grain left uncut to provide seed for another season), with a bawdy equivoque.
100. **put . . . them:** intervened in their behalf (?) or made an offer for their purchase (?).
112. **What's to do here:** what to-do is this.   **Thomas tapster.** A stock name for a tapster; but Shakespeare may have changed his mind about Pompey's name.
120. **the demigod, Authority.** Reflecting the Elizabethan view of earthly rulers and magistrates as God's vicegerents.
121–22. **pay . . . heaven.** The oddness of *pay down . . . the words of heaven* has provoked various emendations. Johnson conjectured a lacuna between the two lines. If a period is placed after *weight,* lines 120–21 make a complete sentence; *pay down by weight* = pay the precise amount due.
122. **words of heaven.** Explained as a reference to Romans 9:15: "I will have mercy on him to whom I will show mercy" (Geneva).
123. **so:** similarly, i.e. it will not.   **still:** always, in every case.
124. **whence . . . restraint.** This is inconsistent with lines 60 ff., where Lucio learns of Claudio's arrest and its cause.
127. **scope:** freedom (see note on I.i.64).

Awakes me all the enrolled penalties
Which have, like unscour'd armor, hung by th' wall
So long that nineteen zodiacs have gone round
And none of them been worn; and for a name
Now puts the drowsy and neglected act   170
Freshly on me—'tis surely for a name.

Lucio.   I warrant it is; and thy head stands so tickle
on thy shoulders that a milkmaid, if she be in love, may
sigh it off. Send after the Duke, and appeal to him.

Claud.   I have done so, but he's not to be found.
I prithee, Lucio, do me this kind service: 176
This day my sister should the cloister enter,
And there receive her approbation.
Acquaint her with the danger of my state;
Implore her, in my voice, that she make friends   180
To the strict deputy; bid herself assay him.
I have great hope in that; for in her youth
There is a prone and speechless dialect,
Such as move men; beside, she hath prosperous art
When she will play with reason and discourse,   185
And well she can persuade.

Lucio.   I pray she may; as well for the encouragement of the like, which else would stand under grievous
imposition, as for the enjoying of thy life, who I would
be sorry should be thus foolishly lost at a game of tick-
tack. I'll to her.   191

Claud.   I thank you, good friend Lucio.

Lucio.   Within two hours.

Claud.   Come, officer, away! *Exeunt.*

Scene [III]

Enter Duke *and* Friar Thomas.

Duke.   No; holy father, throw away that thought;
Believe not that the dribbling dart of love
Can pierce a complete bosom. Why I desire thee
To give me secret harbor, hath a purpose

More grave and wrinkled than the aims and ends   5
Of burning youth.

Fri. T.   May your Grace speak of it?

Duke.   My holy sir, none better knows than you
How I have ever lov'd the life removed,
And held in idle price to haunt assemblies
Where youth, and cost, witless bravery keeps.   10
I have deliver'd to Lord Angelo
(A man of stricture and firm abstinence)
My absolute power and place here in Vienna,
And he supposes me travell'd to Poland
(For so I have strew'd it in the common ear,   15
And so it is receiv'd). Now, pious sir,
You will demand of me why I do this.

Fri. T.   Gladly, my lord.

Duke.   We have strict statutes and most biting laws
(The needful bits and curbs to headstrong weeds),   20
Which for this fourteen years we have let slip,
Even like an o'ergrown lion in a cave,
That goes not out to prey. Now, as fond fathers,
Having bound up the threat'ning twigs of birch,
Only to stick it in their children's sight   25
For terror, not to use, in time the rod
[Becomes] more mock'd than fear'd; so our decrees,
Dead to infliction, to themselves are dead,
And liberty plucks justice by the nose;
The baby beats the nurse, and quite athwart   30
Goes all decorum.

Fri. T.   It rested in your Grace
To unloose this tied-up justice when you pleas'd:
And it in you more dreadful would have seem'd
Than in Lord Angelo.

Duke.   I do fear—too dreadful;
Sith 'twas my fault to give the people scope,   35
'Twould be my tyranny to strike and gall them
For what I bid them do; for we bid this be done,
When evil deeds have their permissive pass,

---

166. **Awakes me:** awakes (a colloquialism). The figure is continued in *drowsy,* line 170.   167. **unscour'd:** unpolished, i.e. rusty.
168. **zodiacs . . . round:** i.e. years have passed.
169. **worn:** i.e. used (continuing the parallel between penalties and armor; cf. *puts . . . on,* lines 170–71).   **for a name:** for the sake of his reputation.   172. **tickle:** unstable, precariously attached.
173–74. **a milkmaid . . . off:** i.e. the merest breath of wind (a lovesick milkmaid's sigh) will blow it off (?). But the combination of *milkmaid* and *head* suggests a common play on *head* = maidenhead (as in IV.ii.5), and the passage may be an elliptical way of saying "a milkmaid, if her virginity were as unstable as your head, would lose it with her first sigh of love."   178. **approbation:** probation, novice's status.
180. **in my voice:** i.e. as persuasively as I would.
181. **assay him:** make trial of him (?) or assail him with words (?). Probably both senses are present: try how he will respond to your urging.
183. **prone:** eager, ready (?) or apt, expressive (?). Some commentators take the word to suggest the prostrate or bowed posture of supplication, but Shakespeare never uses *prone* in the sense of "recumbent."
184. **move.** Plural after a singular noun modified by two adjectives; for another example see III.i.126–27.
187–88. **encouragement . . . like:** giving comfort to offenders like yourself.   188. **which:** who (as often).
188–89. **stand . . . imposition:** be subject to very serious accusation.
190–91. **tick-tack:** a game resembling backgammon, scored by means of pegs set into holes; here, sexual intercourse.

I.iii. Location: A friary.
2. **dribbling:** falling too feebly to pierce its mark.
3. **complete:** fully defended (as if in complete armor, hence invulnerable).

5. **wrinkled:** i.e. befitting one of mature years.
8. **removed:** secluded, private.   9. **in idle price:** as of trifling value.
10. **cost:** lavish expenditure.   **bravery:** display. Many editors improve the metre by inserting *a* before *witless bravery.*   **keeps:** maintains. The verb in *–s* with a plural subject is common in Shakespeare.
12. **stricture:** strictness, keeping a tight rein (on oneself).
15. **strew'd:** scattered (an image from sowing seed).   **common:** general.   16. **receiv'd:** accepted, believed.
17. **demand:** ask (without the modern note of peremptoriness).
20. **weeds.** A type of lawlessness, because of their rank growth and resistance to control. Almost all editors, however, find the metaphor too mixed even for Shakespeare, and emend—most often to *steeds* (Theobald), which fits well with *bits and curbs,* but is unlikely to have been mistaken for *weeds* by a compositor. More attractive is *wills* (S. Walker), which with *curb* produces a figure found elsewhere in Shakespeare, e.g. in *The Merchant of Venice,* IV.i.215–17, where *law, curb* (verb), and *will* are found in conjunction. The discrepancy could have arisen from a confusion of *xiv* and *xix* in the manuscript.
21. **fourteen.** Cf. *nineteen zodiacs* in I.ii.168.   **let slip:** allowed to go lax, i.e. left unapplied.
22. **o'ergrown:** grown too fat, hence inactive.
23. **fond:** foolish, doting.
25. **it:** i.e. the switch made up of the twigs.
28. **Dead . . . dead:** since they are not enforced, are as if non-existent.
29. **liberty:** license.   **plucks . . . nose.** An action indicating the highest degree of contempt and defiance.
30. **athwart:** contrary, topsyturvey.
31. **decorum:** appropriateness of behavior.
32. **tied-up:** leashed (but also recalling the bound-up birch twigs).
33. **dreadful:** inspiring a proper terror of punishment (cf. *terror* in line 26 and, as a royal attribute, in I.i.19).   35. **Sith:** since.
36. **strike and gall.** Recalling respectively "twigs of birch" and "bits and curbs" (*gall* = chafe, cause physical irritation).
37. **we . . . done:** i.e. it is tantamount to ordering that a thing be done.

And not the punishment. Therefore indeed, my father,
I have on Angelo impos'd the office,　　　　　　　40
Who may, in th' ambush of my name, strike home,
And yet my nature never in the fight
To do in slander. And to behold his sway,
I will, as 'twere a brother of your order,
Visit both prince and people; therefore I prithee　45
Supply me with the habit, and instruct me
How I may formally in person bear
Like a true friar. Moe reasons for this action
At our more leisure shall I render you;
Only, this one: Lord Angelo is precise;　　　　　50
Stands at a guard with envy; scarce confesses
That his blood flows; or that his appetite
Is more to bread than stone: hence shall we see
If power change purpose: what our seemers be.

　　　　　　　　　　　　　　　　　Exeunt.

Scene [IV]

Enter Isabel *and* Francisca, *a nun.*

Isab.　And have you nuns no farther privileges?
Fran.　Are not these large enough?
Isab.　　　　　　　　Yes, truly; I speak not as desiring more,
But rather wishing a more strict restraint
Upon the sisterhood, the votarists of Saint Clare.　5
Lucio. (*Within.*) Ho! Peace be in this place!
Isab.　　　　　　　Who's that which calls?
Fran.　It is a man's voice. Gentle Isabella,
Turn you the key, and know his business of him;
You may, I may not; you are yet unsworn.　　　9
When you have vow'd, you must not speak with men
But in the presence of the prioress;
Then if you speak, you must not show your face,
Or if you show your face, you must not speak.
He calls again; I pray you answer him. [*Exit.*]　14
Isab.　Peace and prosperity! Who is't that calls?

[*Enter* Lucio.]

Lucio.　Hail, virgin, if you be, as those cheek-roses
Proclaim you are no less! Can you so stead me
As bring me to the sight of Isabella,
A novice of this place, and the fair sister
To her unhappy brother Claudio?　　　　　20

Isab.　Why "her unhappy brother"? let me ask,
The rather for I now must make you know
I am that Isabella, and his sister.
Lucio.　Gentle and fair, your brother kindly greets
　　you.
Not to be weary with you, he's in prison.　　　25
Isab.　Woe me! for what?
Lucio.　For that which, if myself might be his judge,
He should receive his punishment in thanks:
He hath got his friend with child.
Isab.　Sir, make me not your story.
Lucio.　　　　　　　　　　　'Tis true.　30
I would not—though 'tis my familiar sin
With maids to seem the lapwing, and to jest,
Tongue far from heart—play with all virgins so.
I hold you as a thing enskied, and sainted,
By your renouncement an immortal spirit,　　35
And to be talk'd with in sincerity,
As with a saint.
Isab.　You do blaspheme the good in mocking me.
Lucio.　Do not believe it. Fewness and truth, 'tis
　　thus:
Your brother and his lover have embrac'd.　　40
As those that feed grow full, as blossoming time
That from the seedness the bare fallow brings
To teeming foison, even so her plenteous womb
Expresseth his full tilth and husbandry.
Isab.　Some one with child by him? My cousin
　　Juliet?　　　　　　　　　　　　　45
Lucio.　Is she your cousin?
Isab.　Adoptedly, as school-maids change their
　　names
By vain though apt affection.
Lucio.　　　　　　　　She it is.
Isab.　O, let him marry her.
Lucio.　　　　　　　This is the point.
The Duke is very strangely gone from hence;　50
Bore many gentlemen (myself being one)
In hand, and hope of action; but we do learn
By those that know the very nerves of state,
His [givings]-out were of an infinite distance
From his true-meant design. Upon his place,　55
And with full line of his authority,
Governs Lord Angelo, a man whose blood
Is very snow-broth; one who never feels
The wanton stings and motions of the sense;

---

41. **in th' ambush:** under cover.　**home:** to the target.
42. **nature:** i.e. person (contrasted with *name*).
43. **do in slander:** put in disrepute.
45. **prince:** the one who has sovereign power, i.e. Angelo.
47. **formally:** in external appearance and demeanor.　**bear:** comport (myself).
48–49. **Moe . . . more:** more in number . . . greater in amount.
50. **precise:** punctiliously correct in manners and morals; in Shakespeare's day, often applied to Puritans.
51. **Stands . . . with:** maintains a wary defense against (a fencing term).　**envy:** malice.
52–53. **that . . . stone:** i.e. that he has any sensual desires.
54. **If . . . be:** i.e. whether possession of power will alter intention, and whether certain persons are what they seem to be.

I.iv. Location: A nunnery.
o.s.d. **Isabel.** Although commentators on the play always refer to its heroine as Isabella, that form of her name appears only five times in the dialogue (three times in this scene), *Isabel* five times as often, though only twice in the stage directions. There is a similar variation of *Juliet / Julietta.*　2. **large:** liberal.
5. **Saint Clare:** thirteenth-century foundress of an order of nuns (the Franciscan "poor Clares") having a rule of extreme austerity.
17. **stead:** help.

25. **weary:** wearisome.　29. **friend:** sweetheart.
30. **story:** i.e. theme for jesting or deception.
32. **lapwing:** This bird misled predators about the whereabouts of its young by fluttering about at some distance from the nest.
34. **enskied:** dwelling in heaven.
38. **You . . . me:** in mockingly calling me a saint you blaspheme against the true saints.
39. **Fewness and truth:** to speak briefly and truthfully.
42. **seedness:** state or time of being sown.
43. **foison:** abundance, i.e. harvest.　**plenteous:** fruitful.
44. **tilth:** tillage.　**husbandry:** (1) tillage; (2) husband's duties. Cf. Sonnet 3.5–6.　47. **change:** exchange.
48. **vain:** idle, i.e. producing no change in their relationship.　**apt:** i.e. natural to their age.
51–52. **Bore . . . action:** i.e. misled them about his intentions so that they kept expecting to see military action; a telescoping of *bore in hand* (= deluded) and *bore in hope* (= maintained in expectation).
53. **nerves:** sinews, i.e. inner workings.　**state:** policy.
56. **full line:** free range (as of a tether so long that it imposes no restraint).
58. **snow-broth:** melted snow.　59. **motions:** urgings.

But doth rebate and blunt his natural edge   60
With profits of the mind: study and fast.
He (to give fear to use and liberty,
Which have for long run by the hideous law,
As mice by lions) hath pick'd out an act,
Under whose heavy sense your brother's life   65
Falls into forfeit; he arrests him on it,
And follows close the rigor of the statute,
To make him an example. All hope is gone,
Unless you have the grace by your fair prayer
To soften Angelo. And that's my pith   70
Of business 'twixt you and your poor brother.
    Isab. Doth he so seek his life?
    Lucio.   H'as censur'd him
Already, and as I hear, the Provost hath
A warrant for 's execution.
    Isab. Alas, what poor ability's in me   75
To do him good!
    Lucio.   Assay the pow'r you have.
    Isab. My power? Alas, I doubt—
    Lucio.   Our doubts are traitors,
And makes us lose the good we oft might win,
By fearing to attempt. Go to Lord Angelo,
And let him learn to know, when maidens sue,   80
Men give like gods; but when they weep and kneel,
All their petitions are as freely theirs
As they themselves would owe them.
    Isab. I'll see what I can do.
    Lucio.   But speedily.
    Isab. I will about it straight;   85
No longer staying but to give the Mother
Notice of my affair. I humbly thank you.
Commend me to my brother. Soon at night
I'll send him certain word of my success.   89
    Lucio. I take my leave of you.
    Isab.   Good sir, adieu. *Exeunt* [*severally*].

ACT II, Scene I

Enter Angelo, Escalus, *and* Servants, Justice.

    Ang. We must not make a scarecrow of the law,
Setting it up to fear the birds of prey,
And let it keep one shape, till custom make it
Their perch and not their terror.
    Escal.   Ay, but yet
Let us be keen, and rather cut a little,   5
Than fall, and bruise to death. Alas, this gentleman,
Whom I would save, had a most noble father!
Let but your honor know
(Whom I believe to be most strait in virtue)

That in the working of your own affections,   10
Had time coher'd with place, or place with wishing,
Or that the resolute acting of [your] blood
Could have attain'd th' effect of your own purpose,
Whether you had not sometime in your life
Err'd in this point which now you censure him,   15
And pull'd the law upon you.
    Ang. 'Tis one thing to be tempted, Escalus,
Another thing to fall. I not deny
The jury, passing on the prisoner's life,
May in the sworn twelve have a thief or two   20
Guiltier than him they try. What's open made to
    justice,
That justice seizes. What knows the laws
That thieves do pass on thieves? 'Tis very pregnant,
The jewel that we find, we stoop and take't,
Because we see it; but what we do not see   25
We tread upon, and never think of it.
You may not so extenuate his offense
For I have had such faults; but rather tell me,
When I, that censure him, do so offend,
Let mine own judgment pattern out my death,   30
And nothing come in partial. Sir, he must die.

Enter Provost.

    Escal. Be it as your wisdom will.
    Ang.   Where is the Provost?
    Prov. Here, if it like your honor.
    Ang.   See that Claudio
Be executed by nine to-morrow morning.
Bring him his confessor, let him be prepar'd,   35
For that's the utmost of his pilgrimage.
                [*Exit Provost.*]
    Escal. Well; heaven forgive him! and forgive us all!
Some rise by sin, and some by virtue fall;
Some run from brakes of ice and answer none,
And some condemned for a fault alone.   40

Enter Elbow, Froth, *Clown* [Pompey], Officers.

    Elb. Come, bring them away. If these be good
people in a commonweal that do nothing but use their

---

60. **rebate.** Synonymous with *blunt.*   **edge:** keenness of desire.
62. **use and liberty:** license that has become customary.
64. **act:** law.   65. **heavy sense:** severe tenor.
70-71. **my . . . business:** the heart of my errand.
72. **H'as censur'd:** he has passed judgment.
82. **their petitions:** the things they sue for.   83. **owe:** own.
88. **Commend me:** give my loving greetings.   **Soon at night:** early
this evening.
89. **certain . . . success:** definite word of the outcome.

II.i. Location: A court of justice.
2. **fear:** frighten.   5. **keen:** sharp.
6. **fall.** Like bludgeons or heavy weights.   **bruise:** i.e. crush.
8. **know:** consider and decide.

10. **affections:** desires.
12. **that:** i.e. if (repeating the conditional sense of *Had time,* line 11).
blood: passions.   13. **effect:** effectuation, fulfillment.
14. **had not:** would not have.
15. **which:** for which.   **censure:** condemn.
20. **thief.** Often used in the more general sense "criminal."
21. **open:** manifest.
22. **What . . . laws:** how can the laws take cognizance.
23. **pregnant:** readily perceived, obvious.   28. **For:** because.
30. **judgment:** sentence (decreed for Claudio).   **pattern out:** be the
precedent for.   31. **come in partial:** be admitted in my favor.
33. **like:** please.   35. **prepar'd:** given spiritual preparation.
36. **utmost . . . pilgrimage:** limit of his life's journey.
39. **brakes of ice.** A famous crux. Attempts to relate the phrase to
punishment in hell (cf. III.i.121–22), taking *brakes* as "cages" or
"means of confinement," are unpersuasive, since it is clearly the
inequalities of temporal justice that Escalus is talking about. Many
editors adopt Rowe's *brakes of vice,* meaning "thickets (i.e. a multiplicity) of crimes," which provides the expected contrast with *a fault
alone,* "a single fault." Others follow Collier in reading "breaks of
ice." In its literal sense this image lacks the element of moral responsibility that the context requires; but ice is symbolic of virginity (cf.
the very ice of chastity in *As You Like It,* III.iv.18; *as chaste as ice* in
Hamlet, III.i.140), and the reference may be to breaches of virginity,
with *fault* in line 40 meaning "a mere crack," i.e. a slighter sexual
offense.   **answer none:** i.e. are not called to account.
41. **away:** along, this way.
42–43. **use . . . houses:** practice their improprieties in brothels.

abuses in common houses, I know no law. Bring them away.   44

Ang. How now, sir, what's your name? and what's the matter?

Elb. If it please your honor, I am the poor Duke's constable, and my name is Elbow. I do lean upon justice, sir, and do bring in here before your good honor two notorious benefactors.   50

Ang. Benefactors? Well; what benefactors are they? Are they not malefactors?

Elb. If it please your honor, I know not well what they are; but precise villains they are, that I am sure of, and void of all profanation in the world that good Christians ought to have.   56

Escal. This comes off well. Here's a wise officer.

Ang. Go to; what quality are they of? Elbow is your name? [*A pause.*] Why dost thou not speak, Elbow?   60

Pom. He cannot, sir; he's out at elbow.

Ang. What are you, sir?

Elb. He, sir! A tapster, sir; parcel-bawd; one that serves a bad woman; whose house, sir, was (as they say) pluck'd down in the suburbs; and now she professes a hot-house; which, I think, is a very ill house too.   67

Escal. How know you that?

Elb. My wife, sir, whom I detest before heaven and your honor—   70

Escal. How? thy wife?

Elb. Ay, sir; whom I thank heaven is an honest woman.

Escal. Dost thou detest her therefore?   74

Elb. I say, sir, I will detest myself also, as well as she, that this house, if it be not a bawd's house, it is pity of her life, for it is a naughty house.

Escal. How dost thou know that, constable? 78

Elb. Marry, sir, by my wife, who, if she had been a woman cardinally given, might have been accus'd in fornication, adultery, and all uncleanliness there.

Escal. By the woman's means?

Elb. Ay, sir, by Mistress Overdone's means; but

as she spit in his face, so she defied him.   84

Pom. Sir, if it please your honor, this is not so.

Elb. Prove it before these varlets here, thou honorable man, prove it.

Escal. Do you hear how he misplaces?   88

Pom. Sir, she came in great with child; and longing (saving your honors' reverence) for stew'd pruins. Sir, we had but two in the house, which at that very distant time stood, as it were, in a fruit-dish, a dish of some threepence—your honors have seen such dishes; they are not china dishes, but very good dishes. 94

Escal. Go to, go to; no matter for the dish, sir.

Pom. No indeed, sir, not of a pin; you are therein in the right. But to the point. As I say, this Mistress Elbow, being (as I say) with child, and being great-bellied, and longing (as I said) for pruins; and having but two in the dish (as I said), Master Froth here, this very man, having eaten the rest (as I said) and (as I say) paying for them very honestly; for, as you know, Master Froth, I could not give you three-pence again.

Froth. No indeed.   105

Pom. Very well; you being then (if you be rememb'red) cracking the stones of the foresaid pruins—

Froth. Ay, so I did indeed.

Pom. Why, very well; I telling you then (if you be rememb'red) that such a one and such a one were   110 past cure of the thing you wot of, unless they kept very good diet, as I told you—

Froth. All this is true.

Pom. Why, very well then—   114

Escal. Come; you are a tedious fool. To the purpose: what was done to Elbow's wife, that he hath cause to complain of? Come me to what was done to her.

Pom. Sir, your honor cannot come to that yet.

Escal. No, sir, nor I mean it not.   120

Pom. Sir, but you shall come to it, by your honor's leave. And I beseech you, look into Master Froth here, sir; a man of fourscore pound a year; whose father died at Hallowmas. Was't not at Hallowmas, Master Froth?   125

Froth. All-hallond eve.

Pom. Why, very well; I hope here be truths. He, sir, sitting (as I say) in a lower chair, sir— 'twas in the Bunch of Grapes, where indeed you have a delight to sit, have you not?   130

Froth. I have so, because it is an open room and good for winter.

46. **matter:** i.e. complaints.
47–48. **poor Duke's constable.** Elbow intends to depreciate himself, not the Duke.
48. **lean upon.** Probably a blunder for *uphold* or some such word that means the opposite of what he says; cf. *benefactors* for *malefactors* in line 50.
54. **precise.** This word has been used of Angelo in I.iii.50. It is not clear whether Elbow is blundering ("morally strict villain") or not ("neither more nor less than a villain"); certainly *profanation* is his blunder; but the whole sentence ironically recalls the Duke's comment on Angelo's icy, almost inhuman virtue.
57. **comes off well:** is well said.
58. **Go to:** a conventional phrase of rebuke, equivalent to "come, come" (spoken, of course, to Elbow). **quality:** occupation or station.
61. **out at elbow:** (1) impoverished (in his wits?); (2) rendered speechless (*out*) at the sound of his name.
62. **What:** of what quality (as in line 58).
63. **parcel-bawd:** a part-time bawd. The word *bawd* was used of men as well as women.
65–66. **she . . . hot-house:** i.e. her profession is the operation of a bath-house (but *professes* already had the meaning "falsely professes," and many brothels masqueraded as bath-houses).
69. **detest:** blunder for *attest* or *protest*, "avow."
77. **pity . . . life:** a very sad thing for her. Again Elbow says something other than what he intends. **naughty:** wicked.
80. **cardinally:** blunder for *carnally*.
82. **means.** Elbow takes this to mean "instrument, agent," i.e. the procurer Pompey.

88. **misplaces:** i.e. transposes *varlets* (= rascals) and *honorable men*.
90. **saving . . . reverence:** conventional phrase of apology preceding an expression that may give offense. **stew'd pruins.** Stewed prunes were a favorite dish in brothels; hence the term became a slang designation for prostitutes.
92. **distant:** blunder for *instant* (*instant time* = precise moment).
96. **pin.** Proverbial for worthlessness, but here with an equivoque, like *point* in the next line. Pompey's speeches are full of such ribaldry.
111. **the thing . . . of:** you-know-what; here, venereal disease.
112. **good diet:** strict regimen.
117. **Come me:** come (a colloquialism); but Pompey replies to the sense "let me come," with a bawdy quibble on *come*.
124. **Hallowmas:** All Saints' Day, November 1.
126. **All-hallond eve:** the day before Hallowmas.
128. **lower chair.** Not satisfactorily explained.
129. **Bunch of Grapes.** Rooms in taverns were often given names.
131. **open:** public (where a fire would be kept burning in winter).

Pom. Why, very well then; I hope here be truths.

Ang. This will last out a night in Russia
When nights are longest there. I'll take my leave, 135
And leave you to the hearing of the cause,
Hoping you'll find good cause to whip them all.

Escal. I think no less. Good morrow to your lordship. *Exit* [*Angelo*].
Now, sir, come on. What was done to Elbow's wife,
once more? 140

Pom. Once, sir? There was nothing done to her
once.

Elb. I beseech you, sir, ask him what this man did
to my wife.

Pom. I beseech your honor, ask me. 145

Escal. Well, sir, what did this gentleman to her?

Pom. I beseech you, sir, look in this gentleman's
face. Good Master Froth, look upon his honor; 'tis for
a good purpose. Doth your honor mark his face?

Escal. Ay, sir, very well. 150

Pom. Nay, I beseech you mark it well.

Escal. Well, I do so.

Pom. Doth your honor see any harm in his face?

Escal. Why, no. 154

Pom. I'll be suppos'd upon a book, his face is the
worst thing about him. Good then; if his face be the
worst thing about him, how could Master Froth do
the constable's wife any harm? I would know that of
your honor. 159

Escal. He's in the right, constable. What say you
to it?

Elb. First, and it like you, the house is a respected
house; next, this is a respected fellow; and his mistress
is a respected woman. 164

Pom. By this hand, sir, his wife is a more respected
person than any of us all.

Elb. Varlet, thou liest! thou liest, wicked varlet!
The time is yet to come that she was ever respected
with man, woman, or child. 169

Pom. Sir, she was respected with him before he
married with her.

Escal. Which is the wiser here: Justice or Iniquity?
Is this true? 173

Elb. O thou caitiff! O thou varlet! O thou wicked
Hannibal! I respected with her before I was married to
her? If ever I was respected with her, or she with me,
let not your worship think me the poor Duke's officer.
Prove this, thou wicked Hannibal, or I'll have mine
action of batt'ry on thee. 179

Escal. If he took you a box o' th' ear, you might
have your action of slander too.

Elb. Marry, I thank your good worship for it.
What is't your worship's pleasure I shall do with this
wicked caitiff? 184

Escal. Truly, officer, because he hath some offenses
in him that thou wouldst discover if thou couldst, let
him continue in his courses till thou know'st what
they are. 188

Elb. Marry, I thank your worship for it. Thou
seest, thou wicked varlet, now, what's come upon thee.
Thou art to continue now, thou varlet, thou art to
continue.

Escal. Where were you born, friend?

Froth. Here in Vienna, sir.

Escal. Are you of fourscore pounds a year? 195

Froth. Yes, and't please you, sir.

Escal. So. [*To Pompey.*] What trade are you of, sir?

Pom. A tapster, a poor widow's tapster.

Escal. Your mistress' name?

Pom. Mistress Overdone. 200

Escal. Hath she had any more than one husband?

Pom. Nine, sir; Overdone by the last.

Escal. Nine? Come hither to me, Master Froth.
Master Froth, I would not have you acquainted with
tapsters; they will draw you, Master Froth, and you
will hang them. Get you gone, and let me hear no
more of you. 207

Froth. I thank your worship. For mine own part,
I never come into any room in a tap-house, but I am
drawn in. 210

Escal. Well; no more of it, Master Froth. Farewell. [*Exit Froth.*] Come you hither to me, Master
Tapster. What's your name, Master Tapster?

Pom. Pompey.

Escal. What else? 215

Pom. Bum, sir.

Escal. Troth, and your bum is the greatest thing
about you, so that in the beastliest sense you are
Pompey the Great. Pompey, you are partly a bawd,
Pompey, howsoever you color it in being a tapster,
are you not? Come, tell me true, it shall be the better
for you. 222

Pom. Truly, sir, I am a poor fellow that would live.

Escal. How would you live, Pompey? by being a
bawd? What do you think of the trade, Pompey? is it
a lawful trade? 226

Pom. If the law would allow it, sir.

Escal. But the law will not allow it, Pompey; nor
it shall not be allow'd in Vienna.

Pom. Does your worship mean to geld and splay
all the youth of the city? 231

Escal. No, Pompey.

137. **whip them all:** i.e. find them all guilty. Whipping was a common
penalty for bawds and prostitutes.
138. **think no less:** expect that will be the outcome.
155. **suppos'd:** blunder for *depos'd,* i.e. sworn. **book:** Bible.
162. **and it like:** if it please. **respected:** blunder for *suspected* (and
so several times in lines 163–76). 165. **By this hand.** A common oath.
172. **Justice or Iniquity.** Elbow and Pompey are referred to in terms
of stock characters in the morality plays. 174. **caitiff:** wretch.
175. **Hannibal:** blunder for *cannibal,* i.e. savage; but the pairing of
the names of the celebrated generals Pompey and Hannibal would not
go unnoted.
179. **batt'ry:** blunder for *slander,* as Escalus points out obliquely.
180. **took:** struck.

186. **discover:** expose.
191. **continue.** Dover Wilson suggests that Elbow confuses this with
contain, i.e. be sexually continent. But perhaps he simply confuses
the word with its opposite, as elsewhere.
202. **Overdone . . . last.** With a bawdy quibble deriving from *do* =
copulate.
205. **draw:** deplete, drain dry; with a play on Froth's name and the
drawing of liquor, and a second quibble (signalled by *hang* in line 206)
on "disembowel" or, alternatively, "drag to execution" (*draw* was
used in both senses in judicial sentences).
206. **will hang them:** will be the cause of their being hanged (?) or
will have no recourse but to say "Hang them!" (?).
210. **drawn in:** (1) attracted to enter; (2) cheated.
217–18. **your . . . about you.** Probably with a reference to the fashion
of wearing thickly padded trunk-hose.
220. **color:** try to put a better appearance on.
223. **would live:** want to earn a living. 230. **splay:** spay.

Pom.   Truly, sir, in my poor opinion, they will to't then. If your worship will take order for the drabs and the knaves, you need not to fear the bawds.　　235

Escal.   There is pretty orders beginning, I can tell you: it is but heading and hanging.

Pom.   If you head and hang all that offend that way but for ten year together, you'll be glad to give out a commission for more heads. If this law hold in 240 Vienna ten year, I'll rent the fairest house in it after threepence a bay. If you live to see this come to pass, say Pompey told you so.　　243

Escal.   Thank you, good Pompey; and in requital of your prophecy, hark you: I advise you let me not find you before me again upon any complaint whatso-ever; no, not for dwelling where you do. If I do, Pompey, I shall beat you to your tent, and prove a 248 shrewd Caesar to you; in plain-dealing, Pompey, I shall have you whipt. So for this time, Pompey, fare you well.

Pom.   I thank your worship for your good counsel; [*aside*] but I shall follow it as the flesh and fortune shall better determine.

Whip me? No, no, let carman whip his jade,　　255
The valiant heart's not whipt out of his trade.　　*Exit.*

Escal.   Come hither to me, Master Elbow; come hither, Master Constable. How long have you been in this place of constable?

Elb.   Seven year and a half, sir.　　260

Escal.   I thought, by the readiness in the office, you had continu'd in it some time. You say seven years together?

Elb.   And a half, sir.　　264

Escal.   Alas, it hath been great pains to you. They do you wrong to put you so oft upon't. Are there not men in your ward sufficient to serve it?　　267

Elb.   Faith, sir, few of any wit in such matters. As they are chosen, they are glad to choose me for them. I do it for some piece of money, and go through with all.　　271

Escal.   Look you bring me in the names of some six or seven, the most sufficient of your parish.

Elb.   To your worship's house, sir?

Escal.   To my house. Fare you well. [*Exit El-bow.*] What's a' clock, think you?　　276

Just.   Eleven, sir.

Escal.   I pray you home to dinner with me.

Just.   I humbly thank you.

Escal.   It grieves me for the death of Claudio, But there's no remedy.　　281

---

234. **take order for:** see to. 237. **heading:** beheading.
240. **commission:** mandate. 241. **after:** at the rate of.
242. **bay:** portion of a house lying under one gable or between two party walls.
248–49. **beat . . . Caesar.** Alluding to Pompey's defeat by Caesar at Pharsalus in 48 B.C. *Shrewd* = harsh.
255. **carman:** carter. **jade:** worthless horse.
261. **readiness:** proficiency.
266. **put . . . upon't:** make you serve so many times. The constable was elected annually. **sufficient:** suitably qualified.
269–70. **choose . . . them:** i.e. engage me as their deputy (an ironic reminder of the Duke's deputizing of Angelo). 270. **piece:** coin.
277. **Eleven, sir.** The Justice's brief entry into the dialogue after nearly 300 lines of silence has been variously explained as an after-thought (see the rather awkward attachment of his name to the open-ing stage direction) and as evidence of revision.
278. **dinner.** The Elizabethan dinner was at midday.

Just.   Lord Angelo is severe.

Escal.　　　　　　　　　　　　　It is but needful.
Mercy is not itself, that oft looks so;
Pardon is still the nurse of second woe.
But yet, poor Claudio; there is no remedy.　　285
Come, sir.　　　　　　　　　　　　　*Exeunt.*

SCENE II

Enter PROVOST, SERVANT.

Serv.   He's hearing of a cause; he will come straight.
I'll tell him of you.

Prov.　　　　　Pray you do. [*Exit Servant.*] I'll know
His pleasure, may be he will relent. Alas,
He hath but as offended in a dream!
All sects, all ages smack of this vice, and he　　5
To die for't!

Enter ANGELO.

Ang.　　　　Now, what's the matter, Provost?

Prov.   Is it your will Claudio shall die to-morrow?

Ang.   Did not I tell thee yea? Hadst thou not order?
Why dost thou ask again?

Prov.　　　　　　　　　Lest I might be too rash.
Under your good correction, I have seen　　10
When, after execution, judgment hath
Repented o'er his doom.

Ang.　　　　　　　Go to; let that be mine.
Do you your office, or give up your place,
And you shall well be spar'd.

Prov.　　　　　　　　　　I crave your honor's pardon.
What shall be done, sir, with the groaning Juliet?　　15
She's very near her hour.

Ang.　　　　　　　　Dispose of her
To some more fitter place; and that with speed.

[*Enter* SERVANT.]

Serv.   Here is the sister of the man condemn'd
Desires access to you.

Ang.　　　　　　Hath he a sister?

Prov.   Ay, my good lord, a very virtuous maid, 20
And to be shortly of a sisterhood,
If not already.

Ang.　　Well; let her be admitted. [*Exit Servant.*]
See you the fornicatress be remov'd.
Let her have needful but not lavish means;
There shall be order for't.

Enter LUCIO *and* ISABELLA.

Prov.　　　　　　　　'Save your honor!　　25

Ang.   Stay a little while. [*To Isabella.*] Y' are wel-come; what's your will?

---

283. **Mercy . . . so:** i.e. to extend mercy too often is to prove un-merciful in the long run (since it encourages wrongdoers).

II.ii. Location: Angelo's house.
4. **He:** i.e. Claudio. **in a dream:** i.e. without conscious intent.
5. **sects:** classes. **vice:** sin.
10. **Under:** subject to. **seen:** known cases.
12. **doom:** sentence. **mine:** my responsibility.
16. **Dispose of her:** arrange for her to go. 25. **'Save:** God save.

Isab. I am a woeful suitor to your honor,
Please but your honor hear me.
Ang.   Well; what's your suit?
Isab. There is a vice that most I do abhor,
And most desire should meet the blow of justice;   30
For which I would not plead, but that I must;
For which I must not plead, but that I am
At war 'twixt will and will not.
Ang.   Well; the matter?
Isab. I have a brother is condemn'd to die;
I do beseech you let it be his fault,   35
And not my brother.
Prov.   [*Aside.*] Heaven give thee moving graces!
Ang.   Condemn the fault, and not the actor of it?
Why, every fault's condemn'd ere it be done.
Mine were the very cipher of a function,
To fine the faults whose fine stands in record,   40
And let go by the actor.
Isab.   O just but severe law!
I had a brother then. Heaven keep your honor!
Lucio. [*Aside to Isabella.*] Give't not o'er so. To
    him again, entreat him,
Kneel down before him, hang upon his gown;
You are too cold. If you should need a pin,   45
You could not with more tame a tongue desire it;
To him, I say!
Isab. Must he needs die?
Ang.   Maiden, no remedy.
Isab. Yes; I do think that you might pardon him,
And neither heaven nor man grieve at the mercy.   50
Ang. I will not do't.
Isab.   But can you if you would?
Ang. Look what I will not, that I cannot do.
Isab. But might you do't, and do the world no
    wrong,
If so your heart were touch'd with that remorse
As mine is to him?
Ang.   He's sentenc'd; 'tis too late.   55
Lucio. [*Aside to Isabella.*] You are too cold.
Isab. Too late? Why, no; I that do speak a word
May call it again. Well, believe this,
No ceremony that to great ones 'longs,
Not the king's crown, nor the deputed sword,   60
The marshal's truncheon, nor the judge's robe,
Become them with one half so good a grace
As mercy does.
If he had been as you, and you as he,
You would have slipp'd like him, but he, like you,   65
Would not have been so stern.
Ang.   Pray you be gone.
Isab. I would to heaven I had your potency,
And you were Isabel! Should it then be thus?
No; I would tell what 'twere to be a judge,

And what a prisoner.
Lucio.   [*Aside to Isabella.*] Ay, touch him;
    there's the vein.   70
Ang. Your brother is a forfeit of the law,
And you but waste your words.
Isab.   Alas, alas!
Why, all the souls that were were forfeit once,
And He that might the vantage best have took
Found out the remedy. How would you be   75
If He, which is the top of judgment, should
But judge you as you are? O, think on that,
And mercy then will breathe within your lips,
Like man new made.
Ang.   Be you content, fair maid,
It is the law, not I, condemn your brother.   80
Were he my kinsman, brother, or my son,
It should be thus with him: he must die to-morrow.
Isab. To-morrow? O, that's sudden! Spare him,
    spare him!
He's not prepar'd for death. Even for our kitchens
We kill the fowl of season. Shall we serve heaven
With less respect than we do minister   86
To our gross selves? Good, good my lord, bethink
    you:
Who is it that hath died for this offense?
There's many have committed it.
Lucio.   [*Aside to Isabella.*] Ay, well said.
Ang. The law hath not been dead, though it hath
    slept.   90
Those many had not dar'd to do that evil
If the first that did th' edict infringe
Had answer'd for his deed. Now 'tis awake,
Takes note of what is done, and like a prophet
Looks in a glass that shows what future evils,   95
Either now, or by remissness new conceiv'd,
And so in progress to be hatch'd and born,
Are now to have no successive degrees,
But here they live, to end.
Isab.   Yet show some pity.
Ang. I show it most of all when I show justice;
For then I pity those I do not know,   101
Which a dismiss'd offense would after gall,

---

35. let . . . fault: let his fault be condemned.
40. fine . . . fine: impose a penalty upon . . . penalty.
45. a pin: i.e. the merest trifle.   49. might: could.
52. Look what: whatsoever.   54. remorse: pity.
59. ceremony: symbolic appurtenance.   'longs: belongs.
60. deputed sword: i.e. sword of justice, symbolizing an authority
deputed by God.
61. marshal's truncheon: military commander's staff of office.
62. grace: appropriateness.
65–66. he . . . not: he would not, like you.
67. potency: power, authority to act.   69. tell: i.e. let people see.

70. there's the vein: that's the right style; but also with reference to
finding a vein in bloodletting, as *touch* suggests (cf. *As You Like It,*
II.vii.94, "you touch'd my vein at first").
74. vantage: advantage.   76. top of judgment: supreme judge.
78. breathe within: (1) come to life within; (2) breathe forth from
within.
79. Like . . . made. Explained by Malone as referring to man newly
created, but by most commentators as referring to man made new by
God's redeeming mercy; suggesting also the transformation of Angelo
into a different man.   Be you content: i.e. be satisfied that further
objection is vain.
81. kinsman. Often used of a relative more remote than a brother or
sister, who in turn was more remote than a parent or a child. The
nouns in this line are thus in ascending order.
83. sudden: (too) soon.
85. of season: i.e. of the proper degree of maturity.   serve. With
a quibble on serving food.   86. respect: thoughtful care.
87. gross: corporal.   bethink you: consider.
93. answer'd: paid.   94. prophet: fortune-teller.
95. glass: prospective glass or magic crystal.
96. Either . . . conceiv'd: i.e. both those that are already conceived
and those that will be conceived if lax enforcement of law (*remissness*)
continues.   98. have . . . degrees: propagate themselves no further.
99. here: i.e. in the potential offenders. Many editors emend to *ere*
(following Hanmer) or *where* (Malone).
102. dismiss'd: forgiven.   gall: injure.

And do him right that, answering one foul wrong,
Lives not to act another. Be satisfied;
Your brother dies to-morrow; be content. 105

Isab. So you must be the first that gives this sentence,
And he, that suffers. O, it is excellent
To have a giant's strength; but it is tyrannous
To use it like a giant.

Lucio. [*Aside to Isabella.*] That's well said.

Isab. Could great men thunder 110
As Jove himself does, Jove would never be quiet,
For every pelting, petty officer
Would use his heaven for thunder,
Nothing but thunder! Merciful heaven,
Thou rather with thy sharp and sulphurous bolt 115
Splits the unwedgeable and gnarled oak
Than the soft myrtle; but man, proud man,
Dress'd in a little brief authority,
Most ignorant of what he's most assur'd
(His glassy essence), like an angry ape 120
Plays such fantastic tricks before high heaven
As makes the angels weep; who, with our spleens,
Would all themselves laugh mortal.

Lucio. [*Aside to Isabella.*] O, to him, to him, wench!
he will relent. 124
He's coming; I perceive't.

Prov. [*Aside.*] Pray heaven she win him!

Isab. We cannot weigh our brother with ourself.
Great men may jest with saints; 'tis wit in them,
But in the less foul profanation.

Lucio. [*Aside to Isabella.*] Thou'rt i' th' right, girl,
more o' that.

Isab. That in the captain's but a choleric word,
Which in the soldier is flat blasphemy. 131

Lucio. [*Aside to Isabella.*] Art avis'd o' that? more
on't.

Ang. Why do you put these sayings upon me?

Isab. Because authority, though it err like others,
Hath yet a kind of medicine in itself, 135

That skins the vice o' th' top. Go to your bosom,
Knock there, and ask your heart what it doth know
That's like my brother's fault. If it confess
A natural guiltiness such as is his,
Let it not sound a thought upon your tongue 140
Against my brother's life.

Ang. [*Aside.*] She speaks, and 'tis
Such sense that my sense breeds with it.—Fare you well.

Isab. Gentle my lord, turn back.

Ang. I will bethink me. Come again to-morrow.

Isab. Hark how I'll bribe you. Good my lord,
turn back. 145

Ang. How? bribe me?

Isab. Ay, with such gifts that heaven shall share
with you.

Lucio. [*Aside to Isabella.*] You had marr'd all else.

Isab. Not with fond sicles of the tested gold,
Or stones, whose rate are either rich or poor 150
As fancy values them; but with true prayers,
That shall be up at heaven, and enter there
Ere sun-rise, prayers from preserved souls,
From fasting maids, whose minds are dedicate 154
To nothing temporal.

Ang. Well; come to me to-morrow.

Lucio. [*Aside to Isabella.*] Go to; 'tis well. Away!

Isab. Heaven keep your honor safe!

Ang. [*Aside.*] Amen!
For I am that way going to temptation,
Where prayers cross.

Isab. At what hour to-morrow
Shall I attend your lordship?

Ang. At any time 'fore noon. 160

Isab. 'Save your honor!

[*Exeunt Isabella, Lucio, and Provost.*]

Ang. From thee: even from thy virtue.
What's this? what's this? Is this her fault, or mine?
The tempter, or the tempted, who sins most, ha?
Not she; nor doth she tempt; but it is I
That, lying by the violet in the sun, 165
Do as the carrion does, not as the flow'r,
Corrupt with virtuous season. Can it be
That modesty may more betray our sense
Than woman's lightness? Having waste ground enough,
Shall we desire to raze the sanctuary 170

---

103. **right:** justice.
107. **that suffers:** (the first) that undergoes the penalty.
109. **like a giant:** i.e. without restraint. If (as Isabella's next speech suggests) there is an allusion here to the giants who warred against the gods, the phrase would mean "without the divine attribute of mercy."
110. **great men:** men in high place. 111. **be quiet:** have any quiet.
112. **pelting:** paltry. **officer:** official.
115. **bolt.** The damage done by lightning was formerly attributed to thunderbolts.
116. **Splits:** for *splitst.* A frequent type of simplification for euphony; cf. *exists*, III.i.20. 118. **brief:** short-lived.
119. **assur'd:** assured of.
120. **glassy essence:** i.e. man's essential being or rational soul, which, mirror-like (*glassy*), will show the man who contemplates it what he is. *Glassy* has probably the additional sense of "fragile, highly susceptible of damage." **like . . . ape.** The point is that men who undertake to act like gods make as ludicrous (or as sad) a spectacle as apes imitating what they have seen men do.
122. **with our spleens:** if they had spleens like us. The spleen was regarded as the seat of laughter as well as of irascibility.
123. **themselves laugh mortal:** laugh themselves into a resemblance of mortals, i.e. laugh as much at men as men laugh at apes (?).
125. **coming:** coming round, beginning to yield.
126. **cannot . . . ourself:** refuse to judge ourselves and other men by the same standard.
127. **may:** can with impunity. **jest with:** treat with levity.
130. **captain:** general. **choleric:** angry.
131. **blasphemy:** defamation.
132. **Art avis'd o':** are you informed of, have you discovered.
133. **put . . . upon:** apply . . . to.

136. **skins . . . top:** causes a new skin to grow over the sore.
136–41. **Go . . . life.** The same argument for mercy that Escalus put forward in II.i.8–16.
141–42. **'tis Such sense:** its import is such.
142. **my sense breeds:** my sensual desire multiplies.
143. **Gentle my lord:** my noble lord. 147. **that:** as.
148. **had . . . else:** would have spoiled everything otherwise (i.e. if you had used *bribe* in the normal sense).
149. **fond:** foolish, i.e. foolishly valued. **sicles:** shekels, i.e. coins. **tested:** i.e. purest (as confirmed by the touchstone).
150. **rate are.** The context establishes a collective sense for *rate*; hence the plural verb. 153. **preserved:** kept safe from the world.
159. **cross:** thwart, i.e. impede.
160. **'fore noon.** Note that this implies a change in the hour of Claudio's execution (see II.i.33–34), but the Provost is given no change of instruction.
167. **Corrupt:** putrefy. **virtuous season:** season or weather that has power (*virtue*) to make things grow (perhaps with play on *season* = preservative). 168. **sense:** sensual nature.
169. **lightness:** wantonness.

And pitch our evils there? O fie, fie, fie!
What dost thou? or what art thou, Angelo?
Dost thou desire her foully for those things
That make her good? O, let her brother live!
Thieves for their robbery have authority   175
When judges steal themselves. What, do I love her,
That I desire to hear her speak again?
And feast upon her eyes? What is't I dream on?
O cunning enemy, that to catch a saint,
With saints dost bait thy hook! Most dangerous   180
Is that temptation that doth goad us on
To sin in loving virtue. Never could the strumpet,
With all her double vigor, art and nature,
Once stir my temper; but this virtuous maid
Subdues me quite. Ever till now,   185
When men were fond, I smil'd and wond'red how.
                                        Exit.

SCENE III

Enter DUKE [*disguised as a friar*] *and* PROVOST,
[*meeting*].

  Duke. Hail to you, Provost! so I think you are.
  Prov. I am the Provost. What's your will, good
    friar?
  Duke. Bound by my charity and my blest order,
I come to visit the afflicted spirits
Here in the prison. Do me the common right   5
To let me see them, and to make me know
The nature of their crimes, that I may minister
To them accordingly.
  Prov. I would do more than that, if more were
    needful.

Enter JULIET.

Look, here comes one; a gentlewoman of mine,   10
Who, falling in the flaws of her own youth,
Hath blister'd her report. She is with child,
And he that got it, sentenc'd; a young man
More fit to do another such offense
Than die for this.   15
  Duke. When must he die?
  Prov.   As I do think, to-morrow.
[*To Juliet.*] I have provided for you. Stay a while,
And you shall be conducted.
  Duke. Repent you, fair one, of the sin you carry?
  Jul. I do; and bear the shame most patiently.   20
  Duke. I'll teach you how you shall arraign your
    conscience,

And try your penitence, if it be sound,
Or hollowly put on.
  Jul.   I'll gladly learn.
  Duke. Love you the man that wrong'd you?   24
  Jul. Yes, as I love the woman that wrong'd him.
  Duke. So then it seems your most offenseful act
Was mutually committed?
  Jul.   Mutually.
  Duke. Then was your sin of heavier kind than his.
  Jul. I do confess it, and repent it, father.
  Duke. 'Tis meet so, daughter, but lest you do
    repent   30
As that the sin hath brought you to this shame,
Which sorrow is always toward ourselves, not heaven,
Showing we would not spare heaven as we love it,
But as we stand in fear—
  Jul. I do repent me as it is an evil,   35
And take the shame with joy.
  Duke.   There rest.
Your partner, as I hear, must die to-morrow,
And I am going with instruction to him.
Grace go with you, *Benedicite!*   *Exit.*
  Jul. Must die to-morrow? O injurious love,   40
That respites me a life whose very comfort
Is still a dying horror!
  Prov.   'Tis pity of him.   *Exeunt.*

SCENE IV

Enter ANGELO.

  Ang. When I would pray and think, I think and
    pray
To several subjects. Heaven hath my empty words,
Whilst my invention, hearing not my tongue,
Anchors on Isabel; heaven in my mouth,
As if I did but only chew his name,   5
And in my heart the strong and swelling evil
Of my conception. The state, whereon I studied,
Is like a good thing, being often read,
Grown [sere] and tedious; yea, my gravity,
Wherein (let no man hear me) I take pride,   10
Could I, with boot, change for an idle plume,
Which the air beats for vain. O place, O form,
How often dost thou with thy case, thy habit,

171. **pitch our evils.** Variously explained as "cast our offensive waste matter" or "erect our privies." Those who prefer the second explanation cite *Henry VIII*, II.i.67, "Nor build our evils on the graves of great men," but no certain evidence for *evils* = privies has been found.
175–76. **Thieves . . . themselves.** Cf. II.i.18–23.
183. **art and nature:** i.e. her artifice as a prostitute added to her sexual appeal as a woman.
184. **stir my temper:** disturb my mental composure.
185. **Subdues:** overcomes.   186. **fond:** infatuated.

II.iii. Location: A prison.
3. **charity:** obligation to perform works of Christian charity.
5. **the common right:** i.e. the right of all persons in holy orders.
6. **make me know:** inform me.
11. **flaws:** sudden gusts (of passion).
12. **blister'd her report:** blighted her reputation.   13. **got:** begot.
21. **arraign:** accuse, bring to trial.

23. **hollowly:** not sincerely.   28. **heavier:** graver.
31. **As that:** because (so also *as* in lines 33–35).
33. **spare heaven:** i.e. relieve by your repentance the sorrow felt in heaven for sin.   36. **There rest:** continue in that frame of mind.
40. **love.** The result of love, her pregnancy, is presumably what saves her from execution. Many editors adopt Hanmer's emendation *law*.
42. **still:** ever.

II.iv. Location: Angelo's house.
2. **several:** separate.
3. **invention:** imagination.
4–5. **heaven . . . his name.** *His name* could of course mean "its name" (see the note on I.ii.4), but it seems more likely that *heaven* has here displaced an earlier *God*, in accordance with the statute of 1606 prohibiting the use of God's name in stage performances; so also in line 45, and perhaps elsewhere in the play where the context affords no clue.
6, 7. **swelling, conception.** Another pregnancy figure.
7. **The state:** statecraft, politics.
9. **sere:** arid.   **gravity:** dignified demeanor.
11. **boot:** advantage.
12. **for vain:** for vanity (with pun on *for vane*).   **place . . . form:** rank . . . dignity.

Wrench awe from fools, and tie the wiser souls
To thy false seeming! Blood, thou art blood.   15
Let's write "good angel" on the devil's horn,
'Tis not the devil's crest.

Enter SERVANT.

              How now? who's there?
Serv.   One Isabel, a sister, desires access to you.
Ang.   Teach her the way. [*Exit Servant.*]   O
heavens!
Why does my blood thus muster to my heart,   20
Making both it unable for itself,
And dispossessing all my other parts
Of necessary fitness?
So play the foolish throngs with one that swounds,
Come all to help him, and so stop the air   25
By which he should revive; and even so
The general subject to a well-wish'd king
Quit their own part, and in obsequious fondness
Crowd to his presence, where their untaught love
Must needs appear offense.

Enter ISABELLA.

             How now, fair maid?   30
Isab.   I am come to know your pleasure.
Ang.   That you might know it, would much better
    please me
Than to demand what 'tis. Your brother cannot live.
Isab.   Even so. Heaven keep your honor!
Ang.   Yet may he live a while; and it may be   35
As long as you or I. Yet he must die.
Isab.   Under your sentence?
Ang.   Yea.
Isab.   When, I beseech you? that in his reprieve,
Longer or shorter, he may be so fitted   40
That his soul sicken not.
Ang.   Ha? fie, these filthy vices! It were as good
To pardon him that hath from nature stol'n
A man already made, as to remit
Their saucy sweetness that do coin heaven's image 45
In stamps that are forbid. 'Tis all as easy
Falsely to take away a life true made
As to put metal in restrained means
To make a false one.   49
Isab.   'Tis set down so in heaven, but not in earth.

Ang.   Say you so? Then I shall pose you quickly.
Which had you rather, that the most just law
Now took your brother's life, [or,] to redeem him,
Give up your body to such sweet uncleanness
As she that he hath stain'd?
Isab.   Sir, believe this,   55
I had rather give my body than my soul.
Ang.   I talk not of your soul; our compell'd sins
Stand more for number than for accompt.
Isab.   How say you?
Ang.   Nay, I'll not warrant that; for I can speak
Against the thing I say. Answer to this: 60
I (now the voice of the recorded law)
Pronounce a sentence on your brother's life;
Might there not be a charity in sin
To save this brother's life?
Isab.   Please you to do't,
I'll take it as a peril to my soul,   65
It is no sin at all, but charity.
Ang.   Pleas'd you to do't at peril of your soul,
Were equal poise of sin and charity.
Isab.   That I do beg his life, if it be sin,
Heaven let me bear it! You granting of my suit, 70
If that be sin, I'll make it my morn-prayer
To have it added to the faults of mine,
And nothing of your answer.
Ang.   Nay, but hear me,
Your sense pursues not mine. Either you are ignorant,
Or seem so [craftily]; and that's not good.   75
Isab.   Let [me] be ignorant, and in nothing good,
But graciously to know I am no better.
Ang.   Thus wisdom wishes to appear most bright
When it doth tax itself; as these black masks
Proclaim an enshield beauty ten times louder   80
Than beauty could, displayed. But mark me:
To be received plain, I'll speak more gross:
Your brother is to die.
Isab.   So.
Ang.   And his offense is so, as it appears,   85
Accountant to the law upon that pain.
Isab.   True.
Ang.   Admit no other way to save his life
(As I subscribe not that, nor any other,
But in the loss of question), that you, his sister, 90
Finding yourself desir'd of such a person,
Whose credit with the judge, or own great place,
Could fetch your brother from the manacles

---

15. Blood . . . blood: i.e. under the external trappings lie the basic passions common to all men.
16. Let's write: i.e. say that we write.   **good angel.** With a play on Angelo's name.
17. 'Tis . . . crest: it is no true mark of his identity (as a heraldic crest is), i.e. it doesn't make an angel of him.
20. muster to: assemble in.   **21. it:** i.e. the heart.
24. swounds: faints.
26–30. and . . . offense. Apparently an allusion to a visit made by James I in March 1604 to the Royal Exchange in London, where a tremendous throng got out of control and nearly overwhelmed him.
27. subject: body of subjects.
28. Quit . . . part: leave their proper functions.   **obsequious fondness:** foolish eagerness to pay homage.   **29. untaught:** ignorant.
40. fitted: equipped, prepared.
43–44. him . . . made: i.e. a murderer.   **44. remit:** pardon.
45. saucy sweetness: lascivious pleasure.
45–46. coin . . . forbid: i.e. beget children unlawfully. The image is of counterfeiting coins (*stamps*).   **46. all as:** just as.
48. metal. With the same double sense of *metal / mettle* as at I.i.48.   **restrained:** forbidden.
50. 'Tis . . . earth: i.e. divine law forbids them equally, but in earthly law murder is more heinous.

51. pose: put a question to (shortened form of *appose*).
58. Stand . . . accompt: are recorded but are not charged against our account.
59–60. I'll . . . say: i.e. I don't necessarily subscribe to that view; I can assert any position in order to test you.
64. Please you: if you are willing. Isabella thinks he is talking about the possible guilt involved in pardoning Claudio.
68. Were: there would be.   **poise:** weight.
73. nothing. Perhaps adverbial, "in no way."   **your answer:** what you are answerable for.
74. Your . . . mine: i.e. you don't follow my meaning.
77. graciously: by God's grace.
79. tax itself: charge itself (with ignorance).   **these black masks.** The generic use: "the black masks that women wear."
80. enshield: enshielded, shielded from view.
82. received: understood.   **gross:** obviously, plainly.
86. Accountant: accountable.   **pain:** penalty.
90. in . . . question: to avoid lack of matter for argument, i.e. for the sake of discussion (?).   Singer's proposed change of *loss* to *loose* (= freedom) is tempting.

Of the all-[binding] law; and that there were
No earthly mean to save him, but that either   95
You must lay down the treasures of your body
To this supposed, or else to let him suffer—
What would you do?
    Isab.   As much for my poor brother as myself:
That is, were I under the terms of death,   100
Th' impression of keen whips I'ld wear as rubies,
And strip myself to death, as to a bed
That longing have been sick for, ere I'ld yield
My body up to shame.
    Ang.   Then must your brother die.
    Isab.   And 'twere the cheaper way: 105
Better it were a brother died at once,
Than that a sister, by redeeming him,
Should die for ever.
    Ang.   Were not you then as cruel as the sentence
That you have slander'd so?   110
    Isab.   Ignomy in ransom and free pardon
Are of two houses: lawful mercy
Is nothing kin to foul redemption.
    Ang.   You seem'd of late to make the law a tyrant,
And rather prov'd the sliding of your brother   115
A merriment than a vice.
    Isab.   O, pardon me, my lord, it oft falls out,
To have what we would have, we speak not what we
mean.
I something do excuse the thing I hate,
For his advantage that I dearly love.   120
    Ang.   We are all frail.
    Isab.   Else let my brother die,
If not a fedary, but only he,
Owe and succeed thy weakness.
    Ang.   Nay, women are frail too.
    Isab.   Ay, as the glasses where they view them-
selves,   125
Which are as easy broke as they make forms.
Women? Help heaven! men their creation mar
In profiting by them. Nay, call us ten times frail,
For we are soft as our complexions are,
And credulous to false prints.
    Ang.   I think it well;   130
And from this testimony of your own sex
(Since I suppose we are made to be no stronger

Than faults may shake our frames), let me be bold.
I do arrest your words. Be that you are,
That is a woman; if you be more, you're none;   135
If you be one (as you are well express'd
By all external warrants), show it now,
By putting on the destin'd livery.
    Isab.   I have no tongue but one; gentle my lord,
Let me entreat you speak the former language.   140
    Ang.   Plainly conceive, I love you.
    Isab.   My brother did love Juliet,
And you tell me that he shall die for't.
    Ang.   He shall not, Isabel, if you give me love.
    Isab.   I know your virtue hath a license in't,   145
Which seems a little fouler than it is,
To pluck on others.
    Ang.   Believe me, on mine honor,
My words express my purpose.
    Isab.   Ha? little honor to be much believ'd,
And most pernicious purpose! Seeming, seeming!   150
I will proclaim thee, Angelo, look for't!
Sign me a present pardon for my brother,
Or with an outstretch'd throat I'll tell the world aloud
What man thou art.
    Ang.   Who will believe thee, Isabel?
My unsoil'd name, th' austereness of my life,   155
My vouch against you, and my place i' th' state,
Will so your accusation overweigh,
That you shall stifle in your own report,
And smell of calumny. I have begun,
And now I give my sensual race the rein.   160
Fit thy consent to my sharp appetite,
Lay by all nicety and prolixious blushes
That banish what they sue for. Redeem thy brother
By yielding up thy body to my will,
Or else he must not only die the death,   165
But thy unkindness shall his death draw out
To ling'ring sufferance. Answer me to-morrow,
Or by the affection that now guides me most,
I'll prove a tyrant to him. As for you,
Say what you can: my false o'erweighs your true.   170
                                        Exit.

97. **him:** i.e. Claudio.   100. **the terms:** sentence.
103. **longing have.** If the text is correct, *have* = I have. Of the various emendations proposed, Sisson's *long I have* is perhaps the best.
105. **the cheaper way:** a better bargain.
106. **at once:** once (and then proceeded to eternal life).
108. **die for ever:** incur damnation.
110. **slander'd so:** i.e. accused of the same thing (cruelty).
111. **Ignomy:** ignominy (a frequent variant).
112. **two houses:** different families.
113. **nothing:** in no way. Cf. *something* (= somewhat) in line 119.
114. **of late:** not long ago.   115. **prov'd:** argued.
116. **A merriment:** something to be taken lightly.
121. **frail:** morally weak, unable to resist temptation.
122. **fedary:** confederate, i.e. one guilty of the same offense.
123. **Owe and succeed:** possess and hold by succession.   **thy weakness:** this frailty you speak of (but with an unintended second meaning).
126. **make forms:** (1) reflect images (as referring to mirrors); (2) produce children (as referring to women). The comparison of virginity to glass is a commonplace.
127. **men . . . mar.** Since it is women who create them.
129. **complexions:** constitutions, physical and mental.
130. **credulous:** readily receptive.   **false prints.** A recurrence of the figure of lines 45–49.   **think it well:** hold the same opinion.

133. **Than:** than that.
134. **arrest your words:** hold you to what you have said.   **that:** what.
135. **be more:** i.e. insist on keeping your chastity.   **none:** no women (in terms of what you have just said of them).
136. **express'd:** shown to be.   137. **warrants:** assurances.
138. **putting . . . livery:** i.e. accepting the role that women are born to.   139. **tongue:** language.
145. **license:** allowed freedom.
146. **seems . . . fouler:** looks . . . uglier.
147. **pluck on:** draw on, tempt.   148. **purpose:** true intent.
151. **proclaim thee:** denounce you publicly.
152. **present:** immediate.
153. **with . . . aloud.** This faintly ludicrous image of a cock crowing loudly shows the pitch of Isabella's excited indignation. The rhetorical fitness of the hexameter line has been pointed out.
154. **What:** what manner of.   156. **vouch:** sworn statement.
157. **overweigh:** outweigh.
158. **in . . . report:** in your own story (implying that it has polluted or poisoned the air) (?) or, with respect to your own reputation (?).
160. **race:** strain.   **the rein:** free rein.
162. **nicety:** fastidious reserve.   **prolixious:** prolix, i.e. excessive, tiresome. This word (ordinarily applied to language), taken with the next line, ironically recalls that Isabella will succeed by virtue of her youth's "prone and speechless dialect / Such as move men" (I.ii.183–84).
166. **unkindness:** unnaturalness (as a woman and as a sister).
167. **sufferance:** suffering (by torture).
168. **affection:** passion.

Isab.   To whom should I complain? Did I tell this,
Who would believe me? O perilous mouths,
That bear in them one and the self-same tongue,
Either of condemnation or approof,
Bidding the law make curtsy to their will,   175
Hooking both right and wrong to th' appetite,
To follow as it draws! I'll to my brother.
Though he hath fall'n by prompture of the blood,
Yet hath he in him such a mind of honor
That had he twenty heads to tender down   180
On twenty bloody blocks, he'ld yield them up,
Before his sister should her body stoop
To such abhorr'd pollution.
Then, Isabel, live chaste, and, brother, die;
More than our brother is our chastity.   185
I'll tell him yet of Angelo's request,
And fit his mind to death, for his soul's rest.   *Exit.*

ACT III, Scene I

Enter Duke [*disguised as a friar*], Claudio, *and*
Provost.

Duke.   So then you hope of pardon from Lord
   Angelo?
Claud.   The miserable have no other medicine
But only hope:
I have hope to live, and am prepar'd to die.
Duke.   Be absolute for death: either death or life 5
Shall thereby be the sweeter. Reason thus with life:
If I do lose thee, I do lose a thing
That none but fools would keep. A breath thou art,
Servile to all the skyey influences,
That dost this habitation where thou keep'st   10
Hourly afflict. Merely, thou art death's fool,
For him thou labor'st by thy flight to shun,
And yet run'st toward him still. Thou art not noble,
For all th' accommodations that thou bear'st
Are nurs'd by baseness. Thou'rt by no means valiant,
For thou dost fear the soft and tender fork   16
Of a poor worm. Thy best of rest is sleep,
And that thou oft provok'st, yet grossly fear'st

Thy death, which is no more. Thou art not thyself,
For thou exists on many a thousand grains   20
That issue out of dust. Happy thou art not,
For what thou hast not, still thou striv'st to get,
And what thou hast, forget'st. Thou art not certain,
For thy complexion shifts to strange effects,
After the moon. If thou art rich, thou'rt poor,   25
For like an ass, whose back with ingots bows,
Thou bear'st thy heavy riches but a journey,
And death unloads thee. Friend hast thou none,
For thine own bowels, which do call thee [sire],
The mere effusion of thy proper loins,   30
Do curse the gout, sapego, and the rheum
For ending thee no sooner. Thou hast nor youth nor
         age,
But as it were an after-dinner's sleep,
Dreaming on both, for all thy blessed youth
Becomes as aged, and doth beg the alms   35
Of palsied eld; and when thou art old and rich,
Thou hast neither heat, affection, limb, nor beauty,
To make thy riches pleasant. What's yet in this
That bears the name of life? Yet in this life
Lie hid moe thousand deaths; yet death we fear   40
That makes these odds all even.
Claud.   I humbly thank you.
To sue to live, I find I seek to die,
And seeking death, find life. Let it come on.
Isab.   [*Within.*] What ho! Peace here; grace and
   good company!
Prov.   Who's there? Come in, the wish deserves a
   welcome.   45
Duke.   Dear sir, ere long I'll visit you again.
Claud.   Most holy sir, I thank you.

Enter Isabella.

Isab.   My business is a word or two with Claudio.
Prov.   And very welcome. Look, signior, here's
   your sister.
Duke.   Provost, a word with you.   50
Prov.   As many as you please.
Duke.   Bring [me] to hear [them] speak, where I
may be conceal'd.   [*Exeunt Duke and Provost.*]
Claud.   Now, sister, what's the comfort?
Isab.   Why,
As all comforts are: most good, most good indeed. 55

171. **Did I:** if I were to.
174. **Either . . . approof:** i.e. now condemning, now sanctioning.
175. **make curtsy:** bow, make obeisance.
176. **Hooking.** Cf. *Anchor* in line 4.   177. **draws:** drags.
178. **prompture:** urging.   179. **mind of honor:** honorable mind.

III.i. Location: The prison.
5. **absolute for death:** certain that you must die.
9. **Servile to:** the slave of.   **skyey influences:** influence of the stars
(supposedly a physical emanation or flow, hence the name).
10. **dost.** The subject is *influences*. A singular verb with such a
subject is common enough; here it has been attracted into the second
person by the surrounding matter.   **habitation:** (1) the earth;
(2) the body.   **keep'st:** dwellest.
11. **Merely:** utterly.   **fool:** plaything.   13. **still:** continually.
14. **accommodations:** comforts, sophistications of civilized life.
Cf. *King Lear*, III.iv.106–8, "unaccommodated man is no more
but . . . a poor, bare, fork'd animal . . . ."   **bear'st.** The meaning
may be "possessest" or, more narrowly, "wearest," which would
make clothing the dominant idea in *accommodations* (as in the *Lear*
passage); but *bear'st* also suggests bearing a child (in two senses)
and leads to the next image.
15. **nurs'd by baseness:** fed by lowly means. Cf. *Antony and
Cleopatra*, V.ii.7–8, "which sleeps, and never palates more the dung,
/ The beggar's nurse and Caesar's."   17. **worm:** snake.
18. **grossly:** stupidly.

19. **not thyself:** not your own, not self-contained and independent.
20. **exists.** See the note on II.ii.116.   **grains:** seeds.
23. **certain:** stable, of fixed character.
24. **complexion:** physical and mental constitution.   **effects:** manifestations.
25. **After the moon:** (1) influenced by the moon; (2) resembling the
moon, constantly changing.
26. **ingots:** bars of precious metal.
29. **bowels:** i.e. offspring.   30. **mere:** very.   **proper:** own.
31. **sapego:** serpigo, a disfiguring skin disease.   **rheum:** catarrh,
running eyes, and other disorders associated with excess bodily fluid.
32. **nor youth:** neither youth.
33–34. **an after-dinner's . . . both.** "Our life . . . resembles our dreams
after dinner [i.e. the noonday meal], when the events of the morning
are mingled with the designs of the evening" (Johnson).
35. **as aged:** as if aged, i.e. no different from age (since young men
must beg for money from their elders, just as feeble old men must
look to younger men for physical assistance) (?). The passage may be
corrupt and has been variously emended.   36. **eld:** old age.
37. **heat:** vigor, vitality. It was thought that in old age the blood
became cold and thick.   **affection:** passion.   **limb:** i.e. proper use
of any bodily member.
41. **makes . . . even:** i.e. removes all these ills.   42. **To sue:** suing.

Measure
for Measure
III.i

Lord Angelo, having affairs to heaven,
Intends you for his swift ambassador,
Where you shall be an everlasting leiger;
Therefore your best appointment make with speed,
To-morrow you set on.
   Claud.   Is there no remedy?   60
   Isab. None, but such remedy as, to save a head,
To cleave a heart in twain.
   Claud.   But is there any?
   Isab. Yes, brother, you may live;
There is a devilish mercy in the judge,
If you'll implore it, that will free your life,   65
But fetter you till death.
   Claud.   Perpetual durance?
   Isab. Ay, just, perpetual durance, a restraint,
[Though] all the world's vastidity you had,
To a determin'd scope.
   Claud.   But in what nature?
   Isab. In such a one as, you consenting to't,   70
Would bark your honor from that trunk you bear,
And leave you naked.
   Claud.   Let me know the point.
   Isab. O, I do fear thee, Claudio, and I quake,
Lest thou a feverous life shouldst entertain,
And six or seven winters more respect   75
Than a perpetual honor. Dar'st thou die?
The sense of death is most in apprehension,
And the poor beetle that we tread upon
In corporal sufferance finds a pang as great   79
As when a giant dies.
   Claud.   Why give you me this shame?
Think you I can a resolution fetch
From flow'ry tenderness? If I must die,
I will encounter darkness as a bride,
And hug it in mine arms.
   Isab. There spake my brother; there my father's
       grave   85
Did utter forth a voice. Yes, thou must die:
Thou art too noble to conserve a life
In base appliances. This outward-sainted deputy,
Whose settled visage and deliberate word
Nips youth i' th' head, and follies doth [enew]   90
As falcon doth the fowl, is yet a devil;
His filth within being cast, he would appear

A pond as deep as hell.
   Claud.   The prenzie Angelo?
   Isab. O, 'tis the cunning livery of hell,
The damned'st body to invest and cover   95
In prenzie guards! Dost thou think, Claudio,
If I would yield him my virginity,
Thou mightst be freed!
   Claud.   O heavens, it cannot be.
   Isab. Yes, he would give't thee, from this rank
       offense,
So to offend him still. This night's the time   100
That I should do what I abhor to name,
Or else thou diest to-morrow.
   Claud.   Thou shalt not do't.
   Isab. O, were it but my life,
I'd throw it down for your deliverance
As frankly as a pin.
   Claud.   Thanks, dear Isabel.   105
   Isab. Be ready, Claudio, for your death to-morrow.
   Claud. Yes. Has he affections in him,
That thus can make him bite the law by th' nose,
When he would force it? Sure it is no sin,
Or of the deadly seven it is the least.   110
   Isab. Which is the least?
   Claud. If it were damnable, he being so wise,
Why would he for the momentary trick
Be perdurably fin'd? O Isabel!
   Isab. What says my brother?
   Claud.   Death is a fearful thing.
   Isab. And shamed life a hateful.   116
   Claud. Ay, but to die, and go we know not where;
To lie in cold obstruction, and to rot;
This sensible warm motion to become
A kneaded clod; and the delighted spirit   120
To bathe in fiery floods, or to reside
In thrilling region of thick-ribbed ice;
To be imprison'd in the viewless winds
And blown with restless violence round about
The pendant world; or to be worse than worst   125

---

56. **affairs to:** business with.   58. **leiger:** resident ambassador.
59. **appointment:** preparation.   60. **set on:** set forth.
66. **durance:** confinement.   67. **just:** exactly.
68. **vastidity:** vastness (apparently Shakespeare's coinage).
69. **a determin'd scope:** fixed limits, i.e. the ever-present consciousness of the means by which he had gained his life.
71. **bark:** strip off (as bark from a tree).   **trunk:** body (with play on "tree trunk").   73. **fear:** fear for.
74. **feverous life.** Cf. "life's fitful fever," *Macbeth*, III.ii.23. **entertain:** cherish, cling to.   75. **respect:** regard, value.
77. **apprehension:** i.e. the idea of it (literally, "taking hold").
78–80. **the poor . . . dies:** i.e. as for the physical pain of death, a giant feels proportionately no greater pain than a beetle feels.
81. **a resolution fetch:** achieve resoluteness of mind.
82. **flow'ry tenderness:** soothing flowers of rhetoric.
88. **In base appliances:** by applying ignoble remedies. **outward-sainted:** outwardly saintly.
89. **settled visage:** composed and unaltering expression.
90. **Nips . . . head.** The image is of a falcon striking its prey; it continues in *enew* = drive prey into the water (*in-eau*) or covert.
92. **cast.** Variously explained as "vomited," "calculated" (as in *casting accounts*), "examined for diagnosis" (as in *casting urine*), etc. But in view of *pond* in line 93, the likeliest meaning is "cleared out," as mud and refuse is cleared out of a ditch or pond and cast up on the bank (*O.E.D., v.*, 28, 29).

93. **pond.** The linking of a dirty pond and a hypocritical "settled visage" (line 89) occurs again in *The Merchant of Venice*, I.i.88–89, where men desirous of a reputation for "wisdom, gravity, profound conceit" are said to assume "visages" that "cream and mantle like a standing [stagnant] pool."
93, 96. **prenzie.** A word found nowhere else, and not satisfactorily explained. Among the many emendations, the two most favored by editors have been *princely* (F2) and *precise* (Tieck conjecture in Cambridge). Some proposed readings, e.g. *proxy* (Bulloch conjecture in Cambridge), fit one line but not the other, and some editors adopt different readings in the two lines.
94. **livery:** distribution of clothing to retainers.   95. **invest:** clothe.
96. **guards:** trimmings, external trappings. **Dost thou think:** i.e. can you believe.
99–100. **give't . . . still:** grant you freedom, in return for my foul offense, to go on offending in the same fashion.
104. **deliverance:** liberation from prison.
105. **As . . . pin:** as freely as I would throw away a pin.
108. **bite . . . nose:** flout the law. An ironic reversal of the "biting laws" of I.iii.19; cf. also I.iii.29.   109. **force:** enforce.
113. **trick:** trifle.   114. **perdurably fin'd:** punished eternally.
118. **obstruction:** darkness (as in *Twelfth Night*, IV.iii.39) (?). More often explained as stoppage of blood, i.e. cessation of all vital activity.
119. **sensible warm motion:** i.e. body endowed with feeling and heat and movement.
120. **kneaded:** reduced to a common mass (*O.E.D.*). **delighted:** having (capacity for) delight (?) or now experiencing delight (?).
122. **thrilling:** piercingly cold.   123. **viewless:** invisible.
124–25. **blown . . . world.** Cf. the punishment of sexual offenders in Dante's *Inferno*, Canto V.   124. **restless:** never-resting.
125. **pendant:** hanging in space.

Of those that lawless and incertain thought
Imagine howling—'tis too horrible!
The weariest and most loathed worldly life
That age, ache, [penury], and imprisonment
Can lay on nature is a paradise   130
To what we fear of death.
    Isab. Alas, alas!
    Claud.   Sweet sister, let me live.
What sin you do to save a brother's life,
Nature dispenses with the deed so far,
That it becomes a virtue.
    Isab.   O you beast!   135
O faithless coward! O dishonest wretch!
Wilt thou be made a man out of my vice?
Is't not a kind of incest, to take life
From thine own sister's shame? What should I think?
Heaven shield my mother play'd my father fair!   140
For such a warped slip of wilderness
Ne'er issu'd from his blood. Take my defiance!
Die, perish! Might but my bending down
Reprieve thee from thy fate, it should proceed.
I'll pray a thousand prayers for thy death,   145
No word to save thee.
    Claud. Nay, hear me, Isabel.
    Isab.   O fie, fie, fie!
Thy sin's not accidental, but a trade.
Mercy to thee would prove itself a bawd,   149
'Tis best that thou diest quickly.
    Claud.   O, hear me, Isabella!

[Enter Duke *disguised as a friar.]*

    Duke. Vouchsafe a word, young sister, but one
        word.
    Isab. What is your will?   152
    Duke. Might you dispense with your leisure, I
would by and by have some speech with you. The
satisfaction I would require is likewise your own
benefit.   156
    Isab. I have no superfluous leisure; my stay must
be stolen out of other affairs; but I will attend you a
while.   *[Walks apart.]*   159
    Duke. Son, I have overheard what hath pass'd
between you and your sister. Angelo had never the
purpose to corrupt her; only he hath made an assay of
her virtue to practice his judgment with the disposition
of natures. She (having the truth of honor in her) hath
made him that gracious denial which he is most   165
glad to receive. I am confessor to Angelo, and I know
this to be true; therefore prepare yourself to death.
Do not satisfy your resolution with hopes that are

fallible, to-morrow you must die; go to your knees,
and make ready.   170
    Claud. Let me ask my sister pardon. I am so out of
love with life that I will sue to be rid of it.
    Duke. Hold you there! Farewell. *[Exit Claudio.]*
Provost, a word with you.

[Enter Provost.*]*

    Prov. What's your will, father?   175
    Duke. That now you are come, you will be gone.
Leave me a while with the maid. My mind promises
with my habit, no loss shall touch her by my company.
    Prov. In good time.   *Exit.*   179
    Duke. *[Turning to Isabella.]* The hand that hath
made you fair hath made you good; the goodness that
is cheap in beauty makes beauty brief in goodness; but
grace, being the soul of your complexion, shall keep the
body of it ever fair. The assault that Angelo hath made
to you, fortune hath convey'd to my understand-   185
ing; and but that frailty hath examples for his falling,
I should wonder at Angelo. How will you do to content this substitute, and to save your brother?
    Isab. I am now going to resolve him. I had rather
my brother die by the law than my son should be   190
unlawfully born. But O, how much is the good Duke
deceiv'd in Angelo! If ever he return, and I can speak
to him, I will open my lips in vain, or discover his
government.   194
    Duke. That shall not be much amiss; yet, as the
matter now stands, he will avoid your accusation: he
made trial of you only. Therefore fasten your ear on
my advisings: to the love I have in doing good a remedy
presents itself. I do make myself believe that you may
most uprighteously do a poor wrong'd lady a   200
merited benefit; redeem your brother from the angry
law; do no stain to your own gracious person; and
much please the absent Duke, if peradventure he shall
ever return to have hearing of this business.   204
    Isab. Let me hear you speak farther. I have spirit
to do any thing that appears not foul in the truth of my
spirit.   207
    Duke. Virtue is bold, and goodness never fearful.
Have you not heard speak of Mariana, the sister of
Frederick, the great soldier who miscarried at sea?
    Isab. I have heard of the lady, and good words went
with her name.   212
    Duke. She should this Angelo have married; was

---

126. **lawless . . . thought:** unrestrained and dubious conjecture.
127. **Imagine.** On the plural form see the note on I.ii.84.
134. **dispenses with:** excuses.
137. **made a man:** i.e. given life (with a play on "conceived" or "born"). 140. **shield:** defend.
141. **warped:** deviating from what is natural, deformed, perverted.
slip of wilderness: shoot of a wild stock.
142. **defiance:** rejection, declaration of enmity.
143. **Might . . . down:** even if a mere bow from me could.
148. **accidental:** a chance happening. **trade:** established practice.
149. **prove . . . bawd:** procure further sexual indulgence for you.
153. **dispense with:** forgo. 158. **attend:** await.
162. **only he hath:** he has only. **assay:** test.
163. **disposition:** manner of thought and behavior.
164. **truth:** integrity. 165. **gracious:** virtuous.
167. **to death:** for death.

173. **Hold you there:** continue in that resolution.
178. **habit:** friar's gown.
179. **In good time.** A phrase of acquiescence, "very well."
181–82. **the goodness . . . in beauty:** the kindness that beauty is free with (?).
182. **makes . . . goodness:** makes virtue short-lived in beauty.
183. **complexion:** makeup, nature.
186. **but that:** except for the fact that. **hath examples:** furnishes precedents. **falling.** This word, taken with Angelo's name, has prompted the suggestion that an allusion to the fallen angels is intended. 188. **substitute:** deputy.
189. **resolve him:** give him a definite answer. 193. **discover:** expose.
194. **government:** conduct.
196–97. **avoid . . . only:** i.e. get round your accusation by saying that he was merely testing you. 206. **foul:** ugly. 208. **fearful:** timid.
210. **miscarried:** was lost.
213. **She . . . married.** The closest modern rendering would be "Her was this Angelo to have married." Nominative for accusative in emphatic initial position is not unusual.

*Measure
for Measure
III.i*

affianc'd to her [by] oath, and the nuptial appointed; between which time of the contract and limit of 215 the solemnity, her brother Frederick was wrack'd at sea, having in that perish'd vessel the dowry of his sister. But mark how heavily this befell to the poor gentlewoman: there she lost a noble and renown'd brother, in his love toward her ever most kind and 220 natural; with him, the portion and sinew of her fortune, her marriage-dowry; with both, her combinate-husband, this well-seeming Angelo. 223

Isab. Can this be so? Did Angelo so leave her?

Duke. Left her in her tears, and dried not one of them with his comfort; swallow'd his vows whole, pretending in her discoveries of dishonor; in few, bestow'd her on her own lamentation, which she yet wears for his sake; and he, a marble to her tears, is wash'd with them, but relents not. 230

Isab. What a merit were it in death to take this poor maid from the world! What corruption in this life, that it will let this man live! But how out of this can she avail? 234

Duke. It is a rupture that you may easily heal; and the cure of it not only saves your brother, but keeps you from dishonor in doing it.

Isab. Show me how, good father.

Duke. This forenam'd maid hath yet in her the continuance of her first affection; his unjust un- 240 kindness (that in all reason should have quench'd her love) hath (like an impediment in the current) made it more violent and unruly. Go you to Angelo, answer his requiring with a plausible obedience, agree with his demands to the point; only refer yourself to this 245 advantage: first, that your stay with him may not be long; that the time may have all shadow and silence in it; and the place answer to convenience. This being granted in course—and now follows all—we shall advise this wrong'd maid to stead up your appoint- 250 ment, go in your place. If the encounter acknowledge itself hereafter, it may compel him to her recompense;

and here, by this is your brother sav'd, your honor untainted, the poor Mariana advantag'd, and the corrupt deputy scal'd. The maid will I frame, and 255 make fit for his attempt. If you think well to carry this as you may, the doubleness of the benefit defends the deceit from reproof. What think you of it? 258

Isab. The image of it gives me content already, and I trust it will grow to a most prosperous perfection.

Duke. It lies much in your holding up. Haste you speedily to Angelo; if for this night he entreat you to his bed, give him promise of satisfaction. I will presently to Saint Luke's; there, at the moated grange, resides this dejected Mariana. At that place 265 call upon me, and dispatch with Angelo, that it may be quickly.

Isab. I thank you for this comfort. Fare you well, good father.   *Exit.* [*Manet Duke.*]

[SCENE II]

Enter ELBOW, *Clown* [POMPEY], OFFICERS.

Elb. Nay, if there be no remedy for it but that you will needs buy and sell men and women like beasts, we shall have all the world drink brown and white bastard.

Duke. O heavens, what stuff is here?

Pom. 'Twas never merry world since of two 5 usuries the merriest was put down, and the worser allow'd by order of law; a furr'd gown to keep him warm; and furr'd with fox and lambskins too, to signify that craft, being richer than innocency, stands for the facing. 10

Elb. Come your way, sir. Bless you, good father friar.

Duke. And you, good brother father. What offense hath this man made you, sir? 14

Elb. Marry, sir, he hath offended the law; and, sir, we take him to be a thief too, sir, for we have found upon him, sir, a strange picklock, which we have sent to the deputy.

Duke. Fie, sirrah, a bawd, a wicked bawd! The evil that thou causest to be done, 20 That is thy means to live. Do thou but think What 'tis to cram a maw or clothe a back From such a filthy vice; say to thyself,

---

214. **affianc'd . . . oath.** The contract between Angelo and Mariana, unlike that between Claudio and Juliet, appears to have been *sponsalia per verba de futuro*, a betrothal which could be cancelled by mutual consent or broken for cause by either party at any time before the marriage was solemnized. Mariana's alleged unchastity (line 227) would have been adequate cause if the allegation had been true. Sexual intercourse between a betrothed pair created a valid marriage at common law.   **the nuptial appointed:** the wedding day set.
215–16. **limit . . . solemnity:** day set for solemnizing the marriage.
221. **natural:** i.e. brotherly.   **sinew:** i.e. strength, mainstay.
222–23. **her combinate-husband:** the man bound by oath to be her husband.   226. **swallow'd:** retracted (cf. *eat one's words*).
227. **pretending . . . dishonor:** alleging she had been discovered to be unchaste.   **in few:** in short.
227–28. **bestow'd her on:** gave her over to (with ironic play on "gave her in marriage").
229. **wears:** makes her habit.   **a marble:** i.e. impervious.
234. **avail:** benefit.
235. **rupture:** breach (with play on the medical sense, as indicated by *heal* and *cure*).
240–41. **unjust unkindness:** unnatural degree of faithlessness.
244. **plausible obedience:** convincing pretense of obedience.
245. **to the point:** in every detail.   **refer yourself to:** commit yourself to, i.e. impose (?) or rely on (?).
246. **advantage:** favorable condition.   247. **shadow:** darkness.
247, 248. **time, place.** It has been suggested that these words are transposed.   249. **all:** i.e. the heart of the matter.
250. **stead up:** fulfill in your stead.
251. **encounter:** sexual encounter (as often; cf. line 83).
251–52. **acknowledge itself:** make itself known (by Mariana's pregnancy).

255. **scal'd:** weighed (and found wanting).   **frame:** shape, prepare.
259. **image:** i.e mental image, idea.
261. **holding up:** sustaining, ability to carry it through.
264. **moated:** surrounded by a ditch (not necessarily filled with water). **grange:** country house.
265. **dejected:** (1) low-spirited; (2) humbled.
266. **dispatch:** settle affairs.   269 s.d. **Manet:** remains.

III.ii. Location: Scene continues.
3. **bastard:** sweet Spanish wine (with obvious pun).
5. **'Twas . . . world:** things have never gone well (proverbial).
5–6. **two usuries:** i.e. lending money at interest and fornication, both of which produce increase.
7. **furr'd gown.** Associated with usurers.
8. **fox and lambskins.** Most editors read *on* for *and*, for closer agreement with *facing* (line 10).
9–10. **stands . . . facing:** sanctions the trimming (with a bawdy equivoque).
11–12. **father friar.** *Friar* = brother. The Duke answers Elbow's blunder in kind.
15. **the law:** i.e. not me but the law (a literal-minded reply).
16. **take.** With a quibble on "arrest." A precise equivalent would be *apprehend.*   17. **picklock:** skeleton key.   22. **maw:** stomach.

From their abominable and beastly touches
I drink, I eat, [array] myself, and live.   25
Canst thou believe thy living is a life,
So stinkingly depending? Go mend, go mend.

Pom. Indeed, it does stink in some sort, sir; but
yet, sir, I would prove—

Duke. Nay, if the devil have given thee proofs for
sin,   30
Thou wilt prove his. Take him to prison, officer.
Correction and instruction must both work
Ere this rude beast will profit.

Elb. He must before the deputy, sir, he has given
him warning. The deputy cannot abide a whore-   35
master. If he be a whoremonger, and comes before
him, he were as good go a mile on his errand.

Duke. That we were all, as some would seem to be,
From our faults, as faults from seeming, free!   39

Enter LUCIO.

Elb. His neck will come to your waist—a cord, sir.

Pom. I spy comfort, I cry bail. Here's a gentleman, and a friend of mine.

Lucio. How now, noble·Pompey? What, at the
wheels of Caesar? Art thou led in triumph? What,
is there none of Pygmalion's images newly made 45
woman to be had now, for putting the hand in the
pocket and extracting [it] clutch'd? What reply? Ha?
What say'st thou to this tune, matter, and method?
Is't not drown'd i' th' last rain? Ha? What say'st
thou, Trot? Is the world as it was, man? Which   50
is the way? Is it sad, and few words? or how?
The trick of it?

Duke. Still thus, and thus; still worse!

Lucio. How doth my dear morsel, thy mistress?
Procures she still? Ha?   55

Pom. Troth, sir, she hath eaten up all her beef, and
she is herself in the tub.

Lucio. Why, 'tis good; it is the right of it; it must
be so. Ever your fresh whore and your powder'd
bawd, an unshunn'd consequence; it must be so. Art

going to prison, Pompey?   61

Pom. Yes, faith, sir.

Lucio. Why, 'tis not amiss, Pompey. Farewell. Go
say I sent thee thither. For debt, Pompey? or how?

Elb. For being a bawd, for being a bawd.   65

Lucio. Well, then imprison him. If imprisonment
be the due of a bawd, why, 'tis his right. Bawd is he
doubtless, and of antiquity too; bawd-born. Farewell,
good Pompey. Commend me to the prison, Pompey.
You will turn good husband now, Pompey, you will
keep the house.   71

Pom. I hope, sir, your good worship will be my
bail.

Lucio. No indeed will I not, Pompey, it is not the
wear. I will pray, Pompey, to increase your   75
bondage. If you take it not patiently, why, your mettle
is the more. Adieu, trusty Pompey. Bless you, friar.

Duke. And you.

Lucio. Does Bridget paint still, Pompey? Ha?

Elb. Come your ways, sir, come.   80

Pom. You will not bail me then, sir?

Lucio. Then, Pompey, nor now. What news
abroad, friar? what news?

Elb. Come your ways, sir, come.

Lucio. Go to kennel, Pompey, go. [*Exeunt Elbow,
Pompey, and Officers.*] What news, friar, of the Duke?

Duke. I know none. Can you tell me of any?   87

Lucio. Some say he is with the Emperor of Russia;
other some, he is in Rome; but where is he, think you?

Duke. I know not where; but wheresoever, I wish
him well.   91

Lucio. It was a mad fantastical trick of him to steal
from the state, and usurp the beggary he was never
born to. Lord Angelo dukes it well in his absence; he
puts transgression to't.   95

Duke. He does well in't.

Lucio. A little more lenity to lechery would do no
harm in him. Something too crabbed that way, friar.

Duke. It is too general a vice, and severity must
cure it.   100

Lucio. Yes, in good sooth, the vice is of a great
kindred; it is well allied; but it is impossible to extirp
it quite, friar, till eating and drinking be put down.
They say this Angelo was not made by man and
woman after this downright way of creation. Is it true,
think you?   106

Duke. How should he be made then?

Lucio. Some report a sea-maid spawn'd him; some,
that he was begot between two stock-fishes. But it is
certain that when he makes water his urine is con-

24. **abominable.** Supposedly derived from *ab homine*, "alien to man, inhuman," a sense here reinforced by *beastly*.
29. **prove**: i.e. try to prove, argue.
30. **proofs for**: arguments in support of.   31. **prove**: turn out to be.
32. **Correction**: punishment.   **both work**: operate together, make their joint effect felt. Probably *work* in I.i.9 has the same meaning.
37. **he . . . errand**: i.e. things will go hard with him.
38–39. **That . . . free**: would that we were all free of faults, as some make themselves appear, and that faults were free of dissembling. Many editors adopt the F2 reading *Free from* in place of *From* (line 39); this improves the metre but does not alter the sense.
40. **come . . . waist**: come to the condition of your waist, i.e. be encircled by a cord.
43–44. **at . . . triumph.** Cf. II.i.248–49. The historical Pompey was never led in triumph by Caesar, though his sons were.
45–46. **Pygmalion's . . . woman.** Alluding to the legend of the sculptor Pygmalion's female statue that came to life; with a play on *become a woman* in the sense "lose one's virginity."
47. **clutch'd**: i.e. grasping a coin.
49. **drown'd . . . rain**: i.e. out of fashion (?).
50. **Trot**: old bawd (ordinarily applied to a woman).
50–51. **Which . . . way**: how does the world go. *The trick of it* (line 52) is another way of saying the same thing.   51. **sad**: melancholy.
56. **eaten . . . beef**: worn out all her prostitutes.
57. **tub**: (1) pickling-tub (for beef); (2) sweating-tub (for treating venereal disease).
59. **fresh . . . powder'd**: (1) young; (2) not preserved . . . (1) made-up; (2) pickled, corned.
60. **unshunn'd**: unshunnable (i.e. the young whore inevitably turns into the old bawd).

68. **antiquity**: long standing.
69. **Commend.** Playing on the senses "give my regards to" and "commit."   70. **husband**: master of a household.
71. **keep the house**: (1) manage the household; (2) stay indoors.
75. **wear**: fashion.   76. **mettle**: (1) spirit; (2) metal, i.e. shackles.
77. **trusty**: faithful.   80. **Come your ways**: come along.
82. **Then**: i.e. neither then.
93. **usurp the beggary.** It is not clear why Lucio should say this.
95. **puts transgression to't**: applies extreme measures to lawbreaking.
98. **crabbed**: harsh.   99. **general**: common.   101. **sooth**: truth.
101–2. **great kindred**: (1) large family; (2) good family (*well allied*, line 102, has the same meanings).   102. **extirp**: extirpate.
105. **this.** The generic use, as in II.iv.79.   **downright**: plain, ordinary (with a play on "horizontal").
107. **should he be**: is he said to have been.
108. **sea-maid**: mermaid.   109. **stock-fishes**: dried cod.

geal'd ice, that I know to be true; and he is a motion
generative, that's infallible.   112

Duke. You are pleasant, sir, and speak apace.

Lucio. Why, what a ruthless thing is this in him,
for the rebellion of a codpiece to take away the life of a
man! Would the Duke that is absent have done   116
this? Ere he would have hang'd a man for the getting a
hundred bastards, he would have paid for the nursing a
thousand. He had some feeling of the sport; he knew
the service, and that instructed him to mercy.   120

Duke. I never heard the absent Duke much detected for women, he was not inclin'd that way.

Lucio. O, sir, you are deceiv'd.

Duke. 'Tis not possible.

Lucio. Who? not the Duke? Yes, your beggar of
fifty; and his use was to put a ducat in her clack- 126
dish. The Duke had crotchets in him. He would be
drunk too, that let me inform you.

Duke. You do him wrong, surely.

Lucio. Sir, I was an inward of his. A shy fellow
was the Duke, and I believe I know the cause of his
withdrawing.   132

Duke. What, I prithee, might be the cause?

Lucio. No, pardon; 'tis a secret must be lock'd
within the teeth and the lips. But this I can let you
understand, the greater file of the subject held the Duke
to be wise.   137

Duke. Wise? Why, no question but he was.

Lucio. A very superficial, ignorant, unweighing
fellow.   140

Duke. Either this is envy in you, folly, or mistaking. The very stream of his life, and the business he
hath helm'd, must, upon a warranted need, give him a
better proclamation. Let him be but testimonied in his
own bringings-forth, and he shall appear to the envious
a scholar, a statesman, and a soldier. Therefore   146
you speak unskillfully; or, if your knowledge be more,
it is much dark'ned in your malice.

Lucio. Sir, I know him, and I love him.

Duke. Love talks with better knowledge, and
knowledge with [dearer] love.   151

Lucio. Come, sir, I know what I know.

Duke. I can hardly believe that, since you know
not what you speak. But if ever the Duke return (as

our prayers are he may), let me desire you to 155
make your answer before him. If it be honest you have
spoke, you have courage to maintain it. I am bound to
call upon you, and I pray you your name?

Lucio. Sir, my name is Lucio, well known to the
Duke.   160

Duke. He shall know you better, sir, if I may live
to report you.

Lucio. I fear you not.

Duke. O, you hope the Duke will return no more;
or you imagine me too unhurtful an opposite.   165
But indeed I can do you little harm; you'll forswear
this again.

Lucio. I'll be hang'd first; thou art deceiv'd in me,
friar. But no more of this. Canst thou tell if Claudio
die to-morrow, or no?   170

Duke. Why should he die, sir?

Lucio. Why? For filling a bottle with a tun-dish.
I would the Duke we talk of were return'd again.
This ungenitur'd agent will unpeople the province with
continency. Sparrows must not build in his   175
house-eaves, because they are lecherous. The Duke
yet would have dark deeds darkly answer'd, he would
never bring them to light. Would he were return'd!
Marry, this Claudio is condemn'd for untrussing.
Farewell, good friar, I prithee pray for me.   180
The Duke (I say to thee again) would eat mutton on
Fridays. He's now past it, yet (and I say to thee) he
would mouth with a beggar, though she smelt brown
bread and garlic. Say that I said so. Farewell. *Exit.*

Duke. No might nor greatness in mortality 185
Can censure scape; back-wounding calumny
The whitest virtue strikes. What king so strong
Can tie the gall up in the slanderous tongue?
But who comes here?

Enter ESCALUS, PROVOST, *and* [OFFICERS *with*] *Bawd*
[MISTRESS OVERDONE].

Escal. Go, away with her to prison.   190

Mrs. Ov. Good my lord, be good to me, your
honor is accounted a merciful man. Good my lord.

Escal. Double and treble admonition, and still forfeit in the same kind! This would make mercy swear
and play the tyrant.   195

Prov. A bawd of eleven years' continuance, may
it please your honor.

---

111. **motion:** puppet.
112. **generative:** male (?). Many editors adopt Theobald's *ungenera-tive* (= sexless); cf. *ungenitur'd* in line 174.   **infallible:** certain.
113. **pleasant:** jocose.   **apace:** rapidly, i.e. heedlessly.
115. **codpiece:** baggy appendage at the front of breeches; hence slang for "penis."   118. **nursing:** rearing.
121–22. **detected for:** accused of.
125. **your.** The indefinite use (but comically applicable, if Lucio but knew it, to the person he is addressing).   126. **use:** custom.
126–27. **clack-dish:** beggar's bowl with a wooden cover that could be "clacked" to attract the attention of passers-by.
127. **crotchets:** whims, odd notions.   129. **wrong:** injustice.
130. **inward:** intimate.   **shy:** warily reserved (*O.E.D.*). Used by Shakespeare only here and at V.i.54, where the context helps to define its sense.   132. **withdrawing:** departure, i.e. absence.
136. **greater . . . subject:** majority of his subjects.
139. **unweighing:** injudicious.   141. **envy:** malice.
142. **stream:** course.
143. **helm'd:** steered, directed.   **upon . . . need:** if a warrant were needed.
143–44. **give . . . proclamation:** proclaim him a better man (than you allow).
145. **bringings-forth:** achievements.   **to the envious:** even to the malicious.   147. **unskillfully:** in ignorance.

156–57. **If . . . spoke:** if what you have said is true.
157. **I am bound:** it is my duty.   165. **opposite:** opponent.
166. **forswear:** deny on oath.   172. **tun-dish:** funnel.
174. **ungenitur'd:** incapable of sex (see the note on line 112).   **agent:** deputy.   175. **Sparrows.** Proverbially lecherous.
177. **darkly:** secretly.
179. **untrussing:** untying the laces that fastened hose to doublet, i.e. undressing.
181. **I . . . again.** Here and in lines 182 (*and . . . thee*) and 184 (*Say . . . so*) Lucio brashly underlines his slanders to show his lack of concern about having them reported to the Duke.
181–82. **eat . . . Fridays:** eat forbidden meat, i.e. have recourse to prostitutes. *Mutton* is slang for "whore"; cf. *beef* in line 56.
183. **smelt:** smelt of.
183–84. **brown bread:** bread made of flour with most of the bran left in it, hence soon musty.   185. **mortality:** humankind.
186. **back-wounding:** backbiting.   187. **whitest:** purest.
188. **tie . . . up:** restrain the bitterness (or venom).
193–94. **forfeit . . . kind:** found guilty of the same offense.
194–95. **make . . . tyrant:** turn mercy itself to cruelty (with allusion to the raging and ranting of conventional tyrants, notably Herod, in early drama).

Mrs. Ov. My lord, this is one Lucio's information against me. Mistress Kate Keepdown was with child by him in the Duke's time; he promis'd her 200 marriage. His child is a year and a quarter old come Philip and Jacob. I have kept it myself; and see how he goes about to abuse me!

Escal. That fellow is a fellow of much license; let him be call'd before us. Away with her to prison! 205 Go to, no more words. [*Exeunt Officers with Mistress Overdone.*] Provost, my brother Angelo will not be alter'd, Claudio must die to-morrow. Let him be furnish'd with divines, and have all charitable preparation. If my brother wrought by my pity, it should not be so with him. 211

Prov. So please you, this friar hath been with him, and advis'd him for th' entertainment of death.

Escal. Good even, good father.

Duke. Bliss and goodness on you! 215

Escal. Of whence are you?

Duke. Not of this country, though my chance is now
To use it for my time. I am a brother
Of gracious order, late come from the [See],
In special business from his Holiness. 220

Escal. What news abroad i' th' world?

Duke. None, but that there is so great a fever on goodness, that the dissolution of it must cure it. Novelty is only in request, and, as it is, as dangerous to be ag'd in any kind of course, as it is virtuous to 225 be constant in any undertaking. There is scarce truth enough alive to make societies secure, but security enough to make fellowships accurs'd. Much upon this riddle runs the wisdom of the world. This news is old enough, yet it is every day's news. I pray you, sir, of what disposition was the Duke? 231

Escal. One that, above all other strifes, contended especially to know himself.

Duke. What pleasure was he given to? 234

Escal. Rather rejoicing to see another merry, than merry at any thing which profess'd to make him rejoice; a gentleman of all temperance. But leave we him to his

events, with a prayer they may prove prosperous, and let me desire to know how you find Claudio prepar'd. I am made to understand that you have lent him visitation. 241

Duke. He professes to have receiv'd no sinister measure from his judge, but most willingly humbles himself to the determination of justice; yet had he fram'd to himself (by the instruction of his 245 frailty) many deceiving promises of life, which I (by my good leisure) have discredited to him, and now is he resolv'd to die.

Escal. You have paid the heavens your function, and the prisoner the very debt of your calling. I 250 have labor'd for the poor gentleman to the extremest shore of my modesty, but my brother-justice have I found so severe, that he hath forc'd me to tell him he is indeed Justice. 254

Duke. If his own life answer the straitness of his proceeding, it shall become him well; wherein if he chance to fail, he hath sentenc'd himself.

Escal. I am going to visit the prisoner. Fare you well.

Duke. Peace be with you! 260

[*Exeunt Escalus and Provost.*]
  He who the sword of heaven will bear
  Should be as holy as severe;
  Pattern in himself to know,
  Grace to stand, and virtue go;
  More nor less to others paying 265
  Than by self-offenses weighing.
  Shame to him whose cruel striking
  Kills for faults of his own liking!
  Twice treble shame on Angelo,
  To weed my vice, and let his grow! 270
  O, what may man within him hide,
  Though angel on the outward side!
  How may likeness made in crimes,
  Making practice on the times,
  To draw with idle spiders' strings 275
  Most ponderous and substantial things!
  Craft against vice I must apply.

202. **Philip and Jacob:** the Feast of St. Philip and St. James, May 1. This was also May-day, celebrated with traditional festivities that were the occasion of much sexual license.   204. **license:** licentiousness.
207. **brother:** i.e. colleague in office, cf. *brother-justice*, line 252.
209. **charitable:** required by Christian charity.
210. **wrought . . . pity:** exercised his function as compassionately as I.
213. **entertainment:** acceptance.
218. **for my time:** to serve my particular occasion.
219. **late:** recently.   **the See:** the Holy See, Rome.
223. **the dissolution . . . cure it:** i.e. goodness can get rid of the disease only by dying.
224. **Novelty . . . request:** newfangledness alone is in demand.   **as . . . as:** as things stand, (it is) as.   225. **ag'd:** settled, constant.
226. **constant.** Many editors, following Staunton, emend to *inconstant*, so that *virtuous* (line 225) means "deemed virtuous by the new scale of values." But the F1 reading makes excellent sense: "constancy is now as dangerous as it is in actuality virtuous." **truth.** Perhaps meaning here "keeping one's plain word," in contrast to the following *security*, "giving security to bind an obligation." The sentence could then mean "There is hardly enough integrity left alive to make friendships possible, but enough security demanded to make commercial partnerships burdensome."
228-29. **upon this riddle:** after this paradoxical fashion.
231. **disposition:** inclination, temperament.
232. **strifes:** strivings, endeavors.
236. **which profess'd:** whose declared purpose was.
237. **temperance:** moderation.
237-38. **his events:** the outcome of his affairs.

240-41. **lent him visitation:** bestowed a visit upon him.
242-43. **sinister measure:** unjust treatment.
244. **determination:** decision.
245. **fram'd to himself:** formed in his mind.
245-46. **instruction . . . frailty:** prompting of natural human weakness.   246-47. **by . . . leisure:** as time gave me opportunity.
248. **resolv'd to die:** resolute for death.
249. **You . . . function.** Recalling the Duke's remarks in I.i.29 ff.
250. **the very . . . calling:** what you are obligated to give him.   252. **shore:** limit.   **modesty:** propriety.
255-56. **answer . . . proceeding:** matches the strictness of his official acts (cf. line 262).
261. **sword of heaven:** i.e. authority to execute justice (the "deputed sword" of II.ii.60).
263. **Pattern . . . know:** to find a precedent (for his judgment of others) in his judgment of his own behavior (?).
264. **Grace . . . go:** (to find in himself) grace to stand firm and virtue to go forward (?) or grace to stand firm if virtue fail (in others) (?).
265-66. **More . . . weighing:** allotting neither more nor less to others than is determined by weighing his own offenses. Cf. II.ii.126.
270. **my vice:** i.e. another's sin.
272. **angel.** Another play on Angelo's name.
273-76. **How . . . things.** Not satisfactorily explained. A major obstacle is the meaning of *likeness made in crimes*. Line 274 means "practicing deception on the world." The language of lines 275-76 is clear in itself, but not its grammatical or logical relation to what precedes. Lever's theory that two lines are missing after line 274 may well be correct.

With Angelo to-night shall lie
His old betrothed (but despised);
So disguise shall by th' disguised   280
Pay with falsehood false exacting,
And perform an old contracting.   *Exit.*

ACT IV, SCENE I

Enter MARIANA, *and* BOY *singing.*

SONG

Take, O, take those lips away,
  That so sweetly were forsworn,
And those eyes, the break of day,
  Lights that do mislead the morn;
But my kisses bring again, bring again,   5
  Seals of love, but seal'd in vain, seal'd
    in vain.

Enter DUKE [*disguised as a friar*].

Mari. Break off thy song, and haste thee quick
    away.
Here comes a man of comfort, whose advice
Hath often still'd my brawling discontent. [*Exit Boy.*]
I cry you mercy, sir, and well could wish   10
You had not found me here so musical.
Let me excuse me, and believe me so,
My mirth it much displeas'd, but pleas'd my woe.
  Duke. 'Tis good; though music oft hath such a
    charm
To make bad good, and good provoke to harm.   15
I pray you tell me, hath any body inquir'd for me here
to-day? Much upon this time have I promis'd here to
meet.
  Mari. You have not been inquir'd after. I have sat
here all day.   20

Enter ISABEL.

  Duke. I do constantly believe you. The time is
come even now. I shall crave your forbearance a little.
May be I will call upon you anon for some advantage
to yourself.
  Mari. I am always bound to you.   *Exit.* 25
  Duke. Very well met, and well come.
What is the news from this good deputy?
  Isab. He hath a garden circummur'd with brick,
Whose western side is with a vineyard back'd;
And to that vineyard is a planched gate,   30
That makes his opening with this bigger key.

This other doth command a little door,
Which from the vineyard to the garden leads;
There have I made my promise upon the heavy
Middle of the night to call upon him.   35
  Duke. But shall you on your knowledge find this
    way?
  Isab. I have ta'en a due and wary note upon't.
With whispering and most guilty diligence,
In action all of precept, he did show me
The way twice o'er.
  Duke.   Are there no other tokens   40
Between you 'greed concerning her observance?
  Isab. No; none but only a repair i' th' dark,
And that I have possess'd him my most stay
Can be but brief; for I have made him know
I have a servant comes with me along,   45
That stays upon me, whose persuasion is
I come about my brother.
  Duke.   'Tis well borne up.
I have not yet made known to Mariana
A word of this. What ho, within! come forth!

Enter MARIANA.

I pray you be acquainted with this maid,   50
She comes to do you good.
  Isab.   I do desire the like.
  Duke. Do you persuade yourself that I respect you?
  Mari. Good friar, I know you do, and have found
    it.
  Duke. Take then this your companion by the hand,
Who hath a story ready for your ear.   55
I shall attend your leisure, but make haste,
The vaporous night approaches.
  Mari. Will't please you walk aside?
        Exit [*with Isabella*].
  Duke. O place and greatness! millions of false eyes
Are stuck upon thee. Volumes of report   60
Run with these false, and most contrarious quest
Upon thy doings; thousand escapes of wit
Make thee the father of their idle dream,
And rack thee in their fancies.

Enter MARIANA *and* ISABELLA.

        Welcome, how agreed?   64

---

281. **falsehood:** deception, illusion.

IV.i. Location: The moated grange at St. Luke's.
2. **were forsworn:** swore falsely (to be true).
4. **mislead the morn:** i.e. make morning think that the sun has risen.
9. **brawling:** clamorous. 10. **cry you mercy:** beg your pardon.
12. **excuse me:** excuse myself (by saying).
13. **My . . . woe:** i.e. it was a song to ease my grief, not to make me merry. 14. **charm:** magic spell.
15. **make bad good:** make evil attractive. 17. **upon:** about.
21. **constantly:** assuredly.
22. **crave . . . little:** ask you to withdraw for a short time.
25. **bound to you:** in your debt.
26. **well come:** a common variant of *welcome*, and here paralleling *well met.* 28. **circummur'd:** walled about.
30. **planched:** made of planks.

37. **wary:** careful, attentive.
39. **In . . . precept:** i.e. with explanatory gestures.
41. **her observance:** the conditions she is to observe.
42. **repair:** coming.
43. **possess'd:** informed. **most:** longest possible.
46. **stays upon:** waits for. **persuasion:** belief. Cf. *persuade yourself,* line 52.
47. **borne up:** sustained, carried on. Cf. *holding up,* III.i.261.
52. **respect you:** have concern for your welfare.
53. **found it:** had proof of it. Editors have repaired the metrical deficiency of this line by inserting a word (*oft, so,* or *I*) before *have.*
57. **vaporous.** Night mists were considered noxious.
59–64. O . . . fancies. Most commentators agree that these lines, not appropriate to the context, were originally part of the Duke's soliloquy at III.i.185–88, perhaps preceding line 185.
60. **stuck:** fixed, fastened. **Volumes:** quantities. **report:** rumor.
61. **these false:** i.e. these false (= distorting) eyes. **contrarious.** A word (probably adverbial here) of many shades of meaning; the sense here may be that the rumormongers are hostile or perverse, that the rumors are false or inconsistent with one another or adverse, or all of these. **quest:** give tongue (like hunting dogs when they sight their quarry). 62. **escapes:** scapes, transgressions.
63. **idle dream:** foolish fantasy.
64. **rack:** stretch on the rack, i.e. distort, tear apart.

Isab. She'll take the enterprise upon her, father,
If you advise it.
Duke.   It is not my consent,
But my entreaty too.
Isab.   Little have you to say
When you depart from him, but soft and low,
"Remember now my brother."
Mari.   Fear me not.   69
Duke. Nor, gentle daughter, fear you not at all.
He is your husband on a pre-contract:
To bring you thus together 'tis no sin,
Sith that the justice of your title to him
Doth flourish the deceit. Come, let us go,
Our corn's to reap, for yet our tithe's to sow.   75
                                        Exeunt.

Scene II

Enter PROVOST *and Clown* [POMPEY].

Prov. Come hither, sirrah; can you cut off a man's
head?
Pom. If the man be a bachelor, sir, I can; but if he
be a married man, he's his wive's head, and I can never
cut off a woman's head.   5
Prov. Come, sir, leave me your snatches, and yield
me a direct answer. To-morrow morning are to die
Claudio and Barnardine. Here is in our prison a
common executioner, who in his office lacks a helper.
If you will take it on you to assist him, it shall   10
redeem you from your gyves; if not, you shall have
your full time of imprisonment, and your deliverance
with an unpitied whipping, for you have been a
notorious bawd.   14
Pom. Sir, I have been an unlawful bawd time out of
mind, but yet I will be content to be a lawful hangman.
I would be glad to receive some instruction from my
fellow partner.
Prov. What ho, Abhorson! Where's Abhorson
there?   20

Enter ABHORSON.

Abhor. Do you call, sir?
Prov. Sirrah, here's a fellow will help you to-
morrow in your execution. If you think it meet,
compound with him by the year, and let him abide here

with you; if not, use him for the present and dis-   25
miss him. He cannot plead his estimation with you;
he hath been a bawd.
Abhor. A bawd, sir? fie upon him, he will discredit
our mystery.   29
Prov. Go to, sir, you weigh equally; a feather will
turn the scale.   *Exit.*
Pom. Pray, sir, by your good favor—for surely,
sir, a good favor you have, but that you have a hanging
look—do you call, sir, your occupation a mystery?
Abhor. Ay, sir, a mystery.   35
Pom. Painting, sir, I have heard say, is a mystery;
and your whores, sir, being members of my occupation,
using painting, do prove my occupation a mystery;
but what mystery there should be in hanging, if I
should be hang'd, I cannot imagine.   40
Abhor. Sir, it is a mystery.
Pom. Proof.
Abhor. Every true man's apparel fits your thief.
If it be too little for your thief, your true man thinks it
big enough; if it be too big for your thief, your   45
thief thinks it little enough; so every true man's
apparel fits your thief.

Enter PROVOST.

Prov. Are you agreed?
Pom. Sir, I will serve him; for I do find your hangman is a more penitent trade than your bawd: he doth
oft'ner ask forgiveness.   51
Prov. You, sirrah, provide your block and your axe
to-morrow, four a' clock.
Abhor. Come on, bawd, I will instruct thee in my
trade; follow.   55
Pom. I do desire to learn, sir; and I hope, if you
have occasion to use me for your own turn, you shall
find me yare; for truly, sir, for your kindness, I owe
you a good turn.
Prov. Call hither Barnardine and Claudio.   60
                        Exeunt [*Abhorson and Pompey*].
Th' one has my pity; not a jot the other,
Being a murtherer, though he were my brother.

Enter CLAUDIO.

Look, here's the warrant, Claudio, for thy death.

66. **not:** not only.
67. **Little . . . say:** say little (*have you* is imperative).
69. **Fear me not:** i.e. have no fears about my management of it.
71. **husband . . . pre-contract:** i.e. affianced husband. Cf. Claudio's "true contract" (I.ii.145), which made him Juliet's actual husband.
73. **title to him:** right to possess him.
74. **flourish:** make fair, justify.
75. **Our . . . sow:** our grain is still to be reaped, for the seed that will produce our tithe dues isn't even sown yet, i.e. we have work to do before we can enjoy the fruits of our endeavor.

IV.ii. Location: The prison.
4. **wive's: wife's.** Cf. Ephesians 5:23: "For the husband is the wive's head" (Geneva).   5. **head:** i.e. maidenhead.
6. **leave me:** leave, cease (a colloquialism).   **snatches:** quibbles.
9. **common:** public.   **office:** duties.
11. **gyves:** shackles; here (apparently), imprisonment.
12. **deliverance:** release.   13. **unpitied:** pitiless, severe.
19. **Abhorson.** A telescoping of *abhor* and *whoreson*.
23. **execution.** In view of the context the sense may be "execution of official duties" rather than "judicial killing," but for an executioner the distinction is academic.
24. **compound:** come to an agreement.   **abide:** lodge.

25. **present:** immediate occasion.
26. **estimation:** worthiness, claim to consideration.
29. **mystery:** skilled craft.   32-33. **favor . . . favor:** leave . . . face.
33-34. **a hanging look:** (1) a melancholy expression; (2) the look of a hangman.
37. **your.** The indefinite use (as also in lines 43 ff.).
43-47. **Every . . . thief.** Abhorson begins his proof by showing that a thief is a "fitter" of clothes, hence a tailor, hence a member of a mystery. Presumably he would continue by arguing that thieves are "members of [his] occupation" (picking up Pompey's argument in line 37), and that his occupation is therefore a mystery. The argument from clothes is doubtless related to the fact that the clothes of an executed man were the due of the executioner.
43. **true man:** honest man (regularly used in antithesis to *thief*).
45. **big enough:** i.e. a big enough loss.
46. **thinks . . . enough:** i.e. doesn't think much of it.
51. **ask forgiveness.** The executioner always asked forgiveness of the condemned man.
57. **use . . . turn:** (1) make use of my professional expertise to serve your own purpose; (2) employ me for your own hanging (commonly called "turning off").   58. **yare:** nimble, adroit.
59. **a good turn.** Referring to the proverbial "one good turn deserves another," but with play on *turn* in its senses of "sexual satisfaction" and "hanging" (as in line 57).

'Tis now dead midnight, and by eight to-morrow   64
Thou must be made immortal. Where's Barnardine?
    Claud.   As fast lock'd up in sleep as guiltless labor
When it lies starkly in the traveller's bones.
He will not wake.
    Prov.   Who can do good on him?
Well, go, prepare yourself. [*Knocking within.*] But
        hark, what noise?
Heaven give your spirits comfort! [*Exit Claudio.*] By
        and by.—   70
I hope it is some pardon or reprieve
For the most gentle Claudio.

            Enter DUKE [*disguised as a friar*].
                        Welcome, father.
    Duke.   The best and wholesom'st spirits of the night
Envelop you, good Provost! Who call'd here of late?
    Prov.   None since the curfew rung.   75
    Duke.   Not Isabel?
    Prov.   No.
    Duke.   They will then ere't be long.
    Prov.   What comfort is for Claudio?
    Duke.   There's some in hope.
    Prov.   It is a bitter deputy.
    Duke.   Not so, not so; his life is parallel'd
Even with the stroke and line of his great justice.   80
He doth with holy abstinence subdue
That in himself which he spurs on his pow'r
To qualify in others. Were he meal'd with that
Which he corrects, then were he tyrannous,
But this being so, he's just. [*Knocking within.*] Now
        are they come.   [*Exit Provost.*]   85
This is a gentle Provost: seldom when
The steeled jailer is the friend of men.
                            [*Knocking within.*]
How now? what noise? That spirit's possess'd with
        haste
That wounds th' unsisting postern with these strokes.

            [*Enter* PROVOST.]

    Prov.   There he must stay until the officer   90
Arise to let him in; he is call'd up.
    Duke.   Have you no countermand for Claudio yet,
But he must die to-morrow?
    Prov.   None, sir, none.

---

64. **eight.** Cf. *four* in line 53. The discrepancy has been taken to indicate careless revision, but possibly it is for Barnardine, who is also to die in the morning (line 7–8), that the block and axe are to be ready at four.
67. **starkly:** stiffly. A transferred modifier, rightly describing the "traveller." **traveller's:** laborer's (*travel* and *travail* were still variant spellings of a single word). Cf. Ecclesiastes 5:12, "The sleep of him that travaileth is sweet" (Geneva; "a laboring man" in King James).   68. **do good on:** bestow a benefit on, aid.
70. **By and by:** coming; just a minute (called out to the one who knocks).
73. **best . . . spirits.** Contrasted with the harmful vapors alluded to in IV.i.57.   79–80. **is . . . with:** runs precisely parallel with.
80. **stroke.** Synonymous with *line* in the image evoked by *parallel'd.* But *stroke* also recalls the *cruel striking* of Angelo's justice as it has been described in III.ii.267, and perhaps *stroke and line* has the second meaning "headsman's stroke and hangman's rope."
83. **qualify:** abate.   **meal'd:** stained.
86. **gentle:** kindly.   **seldom when:** it rarely happens that.
87. **steeled:** hardened.
89. **unsisting:** shortened form of *unassisting* (?). Of several proposed emendations the best are *unshifting* (Capell) and *resisting* (Collier). **postern:** small door.

    Duke.   As near the dawning, Provost, as it is,
You shall hear more ere morning.
    Prov.   Happily   95
You something know, yet I believe there comes
No countermand; no such example have we.
Besides, upon the very siege of justice
Lord Angelo hath to the public ear   99
Profess'd the contrary.

            Enter a MESSENGER.
                    This is his [Lordship's] man.
[*Duke.*]   And here comes Claudio's pardon.
    Mess.   My lord hath sent you this note, and by me
this further charge: that you swerve not from the
smallest article of it, neither in time, matter, or   104
other circumstance. Good morrow; for as I take it,
it is almost day.
    Prov.   I shall obey him.   [*Exit Messenger.*]
    Duke. [*Aside.*] This is his pardon, purchas'd by
        such sin
For which the pardoner himself is in.
Hence hath offense his quick celerity,   110
When it is borne in high authority.
When vice makes mercy, mercy's so extended,
That for the fault's love is th' offender friended.
Now, sir, what news?   114
    Prov.   I told you: Lord Angelo (belike) thinking me
remiss in mine office, awakens me with this unwonted
putting-on, methinks strangely, for he hath not us'd it
before.
    Duke.   Pray you let's hear.   119
[*Prov. Reads*] *the letter.*
    "Whatsoever you may hear to the contrary, let
Claudio be executed by four of the clock, and in the
afternoon Barnardine. For my better satisfaction, let
me have Claudio's head sent me by five. Let this be
duly perform'd, with a thought that more de-   124
pends on it than we must yet deliver. Thus fail not to
do your office, as you will answer it at your peril."
What say you to this, sir?
    Duke.   What is that Barnardine who is to be ex-
ecuted in th' afternoon?   129
    Prov.   A Bohemian born; but here nurs'd up and
bred, one that is a prisoner nine years old.
    Duke.   How came it that the absent Duke had not
either deliver'd him to his liberty or executed him?
I have heard it was ever his manner to do so.   134
    Prov.   His friends still wrought reprieves for him;
and indeed his fact, till now in the government of
Lord Angelo, came not to an undoubtful proof.
    Duke.   It is now apparent?
    Prov.   Most manifest, and not denied by himself.
    Duke.   Hath he borne himself penitently in prison?
How seems he to be touch'd?   141

---

95. **Happily:** haply, perhaps.
97. **example:** precedent.   98. **siege:** seat.
110. **his quick celerity.** Explained as "its lively speed" in order to clear the phrase of the charge of tautology, but cf. *swift celerity* in V.i.394.   115. **belike:** I suppose.   117. **putting-on:** pressure.
122. **satisfaction:** assurance.   125. **deliver:** declare, make known.
130. **here:** i.e. in Vienna.
131. **is . . . old:** has been a prisoner for nine years.
135. **wrought:** managed to obtain.   136. **fact:** deed, i.e. crime.
141. **touch'd:** affected.

Prov. A man that apprehends death no more dreadfully but as a drunken sleep, careless, reakless, and fearless of what's past, present, or to come; insensible of mortality, and desperately mortal.   145

Duke. He wants advice.

Prov. He will hear none. He hath evermore had the liberty of the prison; give him leave to escape hence, he would not. Drunk many times a day, if not many days entirely drunk. We have very oft awak'd him, as if to carry him to execution, and show'd him a seeming warrant for it; it hath not mov'd him at all.   152

Duke. More of him anon. There is written in your brow, Provost, honesty and constancy; if I read it not truly, my ancient skill beguiles me; but in the boldness of my cunning, I will lay myself in hazard. Claudio, whom here you have warrant to execute, is no   157 greater forfeit to the law than Angelo who hath sentenc'd him. To make you understand this in a manifested effect, I crave but four days' respite; for the which you are to do me both a present and a dangerous courtesy.   162

Prov. Pray, sir, in what?

Duke. In the delaying death.

Prov. Alack, how may I do it, having the hour limited, and an express command, under penalty, to deliver his head in the view of Angelo? I may make my case as Claudio's, to cross this in the smallest.   168

Duke. By the vow of mine order I warrant you, if my instructions may be your guide. Let this Barnardine be this morning executed, and his head borne to Angelo.

Prov. Angelo hath seen them both, and will discover the favor.   173

Duke. O, death's a great disguiser, and you may add to it. Shave the head, and tie the beard, and say it was the desire of the penitent to be so bar'd before his death. You know the course is common. If any   177 thing fall to you upon this, more than thanks and good fortune, by the saint whom I profess, I will plead against it with my life.   180

Prov. Pardon me, good father, it is against my oath.

Duke. Were you sworn to the Duke, or to the deputy?

Prov. To him, and to his substitutes.

Duke. You will think you have made no offense, if the Duke avouch the justice of your dealing?   186

Prov. But what likelihood is in that?

Duke. Not a resemblance, but a certainty; yet since I see you fearful, that neither my coat, integrity, nor persuasion can with ease attempt you, I will go further than I meant, to pluck all fears out of you. Look you, sir, here is the hand and seal of the Duke; you know the character, I doubt not, and the signet is not strange to you.   194

Prov. I know them both.

Duke. The contents of this is the return of the Duke. You shall anon over-read it at your pleas-   197 ure; where you shall find, within these two days he will be here. This is a thing that Angelo knows not, for he this very day receives letters of strange tenor, perchance of the Duke's death, perchance entering into some monastery, but by chance nothing of what   202 is writ. Look, th' unfolding star calls up the shepherd. Put not yourself into amazement how these things should be; all difficulties are but easy when they are known. Call your executioner, and off with Barnardine's head. I will give him a present shrift, and   207 advise him for a better place. Yet you are amaz'd, but this shall absolutely resolve you. Come away, it is almost clear dawn.   *Exeunt.*

SCENE III

Enter Clown [POMPEY].

Pom. I am as well acquainted here as I was in our house of profession. One would think it were Mistress Overdone's own house, for here be many of her old customers. First, here's young Master Rash, he's in for a commodity of brown paper and old ginger,   5 ninescore and seventeen pounds, of which he made five marks ready money. Marry, then ginger was not much in request, for the old women were all dead. Then is there here one Master Caper, at the suit of Master Three-pile the mercer, for some four suits   10 of peach-color'd satin, which now peaches him a beggar. Then have we here young Dizzy, and young Master Deep-vow, and Master Copper-spur, and Master Starve-lackey the rapier and dagger man, and young Drop-heir that kill'd lusty Pudding,   15 and Master Forthlight the tilter, and brave Master Shoe-tie the great traveller, and wild Half-can that stabb'd Pots, and I think forty more, all great doers

142–43. **apprehends . . . as:** conceives of death as no more dreadful than.
143. **careless:** without anxiety. **reakless:** reckless, unconcerned.
145. **insensible of mortality:** with no feeling about what death means (?). **desperately mortal:** without hope of escaping execution (?) or in a desperate state of mortal sin (?).
146. **wants advice:** lacks (spiritual) counsel.
156. **lay . . . hazard:** risk my all.
159–60. **in . . . effect:** through concrete evidence, by a clear demonstration.
160. **four days' respite.** Cf. *two days* in line 198. It is difficult to account for *four*. 161. **present:** immediate. 166. **limited:** fixed.
168. **cross:** go contrary to.
169. **warrant you:** guarantee you against harm.
172–73. **discover the favor:** recognize the face.
175. **tie.** Not satisfactorily explained. Many editors emend to *trim* or *dye*. 178. **fall to:** befall. **upon:** in consequence of.
186. **avouch:** confirm, uphold. **justice:** justness.
188. **resemblance:** probability (?).

190. **attempt:** tempt. 193. **character:** handwriting.
203. **writ:** i.e. written here (?). **unfolding star:** morning star, whose appearance tells the shepherd that it is time to release his sheep from the fold. 204. **amazement:** perplexity.
209. **absolutely resolve you:** dispel your doubts completely.

IV.iii. Location: Scene continues.
1. **am . . . acquainted:** have as wide an acquaintance.
5. **a commodity . . . ginger.** A moneylender could circumvent the statute limiting interest on loans to ten percent by forcing a borrower to take a substantial part of the loan in some "commodity" at a valuation determined by the lender. Rash has had to agree to a valuation of 197 pounds on merchandise which on resale has brought little more than three pounds (a mark was two-thirds of a pound).
8. **old women.** Traditionally fond of ginger. The sentence has been taken as a reference to the heavy plague mortality in 1603.
9. **Caper:** i.e. frolic. The names of the prisoners are more or less suggestive of their particular bents.
10. **Three-pile.** See the note on I.ii.32.
11. **peaches him:** accuses him (of being).
16. **Forthlight.** Perhaps an error for *Forthright*, i.e. straight ahead (as a tilter, or jouster, might ride). **brave:** showily dressed.
17. **Shoe-tie . . . traveller.** Gaudy decorations on shoes were a foreign importation.

Measure
for Measure
IV.iii

in our trade, and are now "for the Lord's sake."

Enter ABHORSON.

Abhor. Sirrah, bring Barnardine hither.   20

Pom. Master Barnardine! You must rise and be hang'd, Master Barnardine!

Abhor. What ho, Barnardine!

Bar. (*Within.*) A pox o' your throats! Who makes that noise there? What are you?   25

Pom. Your friends, sir, the hangman. You must be so good, sir, to rise, and be put to death.

Bar. [*Within.*] Away, you rogue, away! I am sleepy.

Abhor. Tell him he must awake, and that quickly too.   31

Pom. Pray, Master Barnardine, awake till you are executed, and sleep afterwards.

Abhor. Go in to him, and fetch him out.

Pom. He is coming, sir, he is coming. I hear his straw rustle.   36

Enter BARNARDINE.

Abhor. Is the axe upon the block, sirrah?

Pom. Very ready, sir.

Bar. How now, Abhorson? What's the news with you?   40

Abhor. Truly, sir, I would desire you to clap into your prayers; for look you, the warrant's come.

Bar. You rogue, I have been drinking all night, I am not fitted for't.

Pom. O, the better, sir; for he that drinks all night, and is hang'd betimes in the morning, may sleep the sounder all the next day.   47

Enter DUKE [*disguised as a friar*].

Abhor. Look you, sir, here comes your ghostly father. Do we jest now, think you?

Duke. Sir, induc'd by my charity, and hearing how hastily you are to depart, I am come to advise you, comfort you, and pray with you.   52

Bar. Friar, not I; I have been drinking hard all night, and I will have more time to prepare me, or they shall beat out my brains with billets. I will not consent to die this day, that's certain.   56

Duke. O sir, you must; and therefore I beseech you Look forward on the journey you shall go.

Bar. I swear I will not die to-day for any man's persuasion.   60

Duke. But hear you—

Bar. Not a word. If you have any thing to say to me, come to my ward; for thence will not I to-day.   *Exit.*

Enter PROVOST.

Duke. Unfit to live, or die; O gravel heart! After him, fellows, bring him to the block.   65

[*Exeunt Abhorson and Pompey.*]

Prov. Now, sir, how do you find the prisoner?

Duke. A creature unprepar'd, unmeet for death; And to transport him in the mind he is Were damnable.

Prov.   Here in the prison, father, There died this morning of a cruel fever   70 One Ragozine, a most notorious pirate, A man of Claudio's years; his beard and head Just of his color. What if we do omit This reprobate till he were well inclin'd, And satisfy the deputy with the visage   75 Of Ragozine, more like to Claudio?

Duke. O, 'tis an accident that heaven provides! Dispatch it presently, the hour draws on Prefix'd by Angelo. See this be done, And sent according to command, whiles I   80 Persuade this rude wretch willingly to die.

Prov. This shall be done, good father, presently. But Barnardine must die this afternoon; And how shall we continue Claudio, To save me from the danger that might come   85 If he were known alive?

Duke.   Let this be done: Put them in secret holds, both Barnardine and Claudio. Ere twice the sun hath made his journal greeting To yond generation, you shall find Your safety manifested.   90

Prov. I am your free dependant.

Duke. Quick, dispatch, and send the head to Angelo.   *Exit* [*Provost*]. Now will I write letters to Angelo (The Provost, he shall bear them), whose contents Shall witness to him I am near at home;   95 And that by great injunctions I am bound To enter publicly. Him I'll desire To meet me at the consecrated fount, A league below the city; and from thence, By cold gradation and weal-balanc'd form,   100 We shall proceed with Angelo.

Enter PROVOST [*with Ragozine's head*].

Prov. Here is the head, I'll carry it myself.

Duke. Convenient is it. Make a swift return, For I would commune with you of such things That want no ear but yours.

Prov.   I'll make all speed. *Exit.*

19. "for . . . sake": the cry with which prisoners, who had to supply their own food and other necessities, besought the charity of those who passed by their barred windows.   27. to: as to.
41. clap into: speedily begin.   46. betimes: early.
48. ghostly: spiritual.   55. billets: blocks of wood, clubs.
63. ward: cell.   64. gravel: stony.

68. transport him: send him to the next world.
73. omit: pass over.   74. well inclin'd: in a proper state of mind.
77. accident: event.
78. Dispatch it presently: put it into execution at once.
79. Prefix'd: set in advance.   84. continue: keep.
87. holds: cells.   88. journal: daily.
89. yond generation: i.e. men outside the prison, on whom the sunlight falls (?). Some editors adopt Rowe's *yonder generation* (to mend the metre); others follow Hanmer in reading *th' under generation*, meaning either "people under the sun" or "people in the Antipodes" (so that lines 88 would mean either "before two days are past" or "before two nights are past").
91. free dependant: willing follower.
93. Angelo. Since in V.i the Duke enters the city with Varrius, it is conjectured that *Angelo* is an error for *Varrius*, picked up inadvertently from the end of line 92.
96. by great injunctions: for compelling reasons (?).
98. fount: spring.
100. cold gradation: coolly reasoned steps (?).   weal-balanc'd form: formalities required by considerations of state (?). Most editors follow Rowe in reading *well-balanced form*, "all due formalities."
101. with: in the affair of, against.   103. Convenient: fitting.
105. want: require.

Isab. (*Within.*) Peace, ho, be here!   106

Duke.   The tongue of Isabel. She's come to know
If yet her brother's pardon be come hither.
But I will keep her ignorant of her good,
To make her heavenly comforts of despair,   110
When it is least expected.

Enter ISABELLA.

Isab.   Ho, by your leave!
Duke.   Good morning to you, fair and gracious
daughter.
Isab.   The better, given me by so holy a man.
Hath yet the deputy sent my brother's pardon?
Duke.   He hath releas'd him, Isabel, from the world,
His head is off, and sent to Angelo.   116
Isab.   Nay, but it is not so.
Duke.   It is no other.
Show your wisdom, daughter, in your close patience.
Isab.   O, I will to him, and pluck out his eyes!
Duke.   You shall not be admitted to his sight.   120
Isab.   Unhappy Claudio! Wretched Isabel!
Injurious world! Most damned Angelo!
Duke.   This nor hurts him, nor profits you a jot.
Forbear it therefore, give your cause to heaven.
Mark what I say, which you shall find   125
By every syllable a faithful verity.
The Duke comes home to-morrow—nay, dry your
            eyes—
One of our covent, and his confessor,
Gives me this instance: already he hath carried
Notice to Escalus and Angelo,   130
Who do prepare to meet him at the gates,
There to give up their pow'r. If you can pace your
            wisdom
In that good path that I would wish it go,
And you shall have your bosom on this wretch,
Grace of the Duke, revenges to your heart,   135
And general honor.
Isab.   I am directed by you.
Duke.   This letter then to Friar Peter give;
'Tis that he sent me of the Duke's return.
Say, by this token, I desire his company
At Mariana's house to-night. Her cause and yours
I'll perfect him withal, and he shall bring you   141
Before the Duke; and to the head of Angelo
Accuse him home and home. For my poor self,
I am combined by a sacred vow,
And shall be absent. Wend you with this letter.   145
Command these fretting waters from your eyes
With a light heart; trust not my holy order

110. **of:** out of.   111. **it:** i.e. comfort.
118. **close patience:** silent fortitude.   121. **Unhappy:** unfortunate.
124. **give:** commit, entrust.
128. **covent:** convent, religious house.   **and:** i.e. who is.
129. **instance:** evidence.
132. **pace your wisdom:** teach your wisdom to go (a figure from riding).
133. **go.** Some such expression as *do so* must be understood after this word—a not uncommon type of ellipsis.
134. **have your bosom:** have your desire fulfilled.
137. **Peter.** Probably Shakespeare had in mind the friar of I.iii but had forgotten that he is there named Thomas.
141. **perfect him withal:** fully acquaint him with.
142. **head:** i.e. face.   143. **home and home:** to the utmost.
144. **combined:** bound (cf. *combinate-husband,* III.i.222–23).
146. **fretting:** corrosive.

If I pervert your course. Who's here?

Enter LUCIO.

Lucio.   Good even. Friar, where's the Provost?
Duke.   Not within, sir.   150
Lucio.   O pretty Isabella, I am pale at mine heart to see thine eyes so red; thou must be patient. I am fain to dine and sup with water and bran; I dare not for my head fill my belly; one fruitful meal would set me to't. But they say the Duke will be here to-morrow.   155 By my troth, Isabel, I lov'd thy brother. If the old fantastical Duke of dark corners had been at home, he had liv'd.   [*Exit Isabella.*]   158
Duke.   Sir, the Duke is marvellous little beholding to your reports, but the best is, he lives not in them.
Lucio.   Friar, thou knowest not the Duke so well as I do; he's a better woodman than thou tak'st him for.
Duke.   Well; you'll answer this one day. Fare ye well.   164
Lucio.   Nay, tarry, I'll go along with thee. I can tell thee pretty tales of the Duke.
Duke.   You have told me too many of him already, sir, if they be true; if not true, none were enough.
Lucio.   I was once before him for getting a wench with child.   170
Duke.   Did you such a thing?
Lucio.   Yes, marry, did I; but I was fain to forswear it. They would else have married me to the rotten medlar.
Duke.   Sir, your company is fairer than honest. Rest you well.   176
Lucio.   By my troth, I'll go with thee to the lane's end. If bawdy talk offend you, we'll have very little of it. Nay, friar, I am a kind of bur, I shall stick.
                            Exeunt.

SCENE IV

Enter ANGELO *and* ESCALUS.

Escal.   Every letter he hath writ hath disvouch'd other.
Ang.   In most uneven and distracted manner. His actions show much like to madness, pray heaven his wisdom be not tainted! And why meet him at the gates, and [redeliver] our authorities there?   6
Escal.   I guess not.
Ang.   And why should we proclaim it in an hour before his ent'ring, that if any crave redress of injustice, they should exhibit their petitions in the street?

148. **pervert:** direct wrongly.
149. **Good even.** A striking discrepancy.
151. **pale . . . heart.** Grief was thought to draw blood from the heart.
152. **fain:** obliged.   153. **bran:** coarse brown bread.
153–54. **for my head:** i.e. for fear of being beheaded.
157. **of dark corners.** Cf. Lucio's earlier allegations of the Duke's secret lechery.   159. **beholding:** beholden, indebted.
160. **he . . . them:** i.e. they do not describe him.
162. **woodman:** forester, i.e. hunter (of women).
163. **answer:** be held answerable.
174. **medlar:** an apple-like fruit that was not edible until it had begun to rot.   175. **fairer:** more amusing.

IV.iv. Location: Angelo's house.
1. **disvouch'd:** disavowed.   3. **uneven:** irregular.
5. **wisdom . . . tainted:** reason . . . impaired.
7. **guess not:** cannot guess.
8. **in an hour:** "leaving a clear hour" (Lever).

Escal. He shows his reason for that: to have a   11
dispatch of complaints, and to deliver us from devices
hereafter, which shall then have no power to stand
against us.   14

Ang. Well; I beseech you let it be proclaim'd
betimes i' th' morn. I'll call you at your house. Give
notice to such men of sort and suit as are to meet him.

Escal. I shall, sir. Fare you well.

Ang. Good night.   *Exit* [*Escalus*].
This deed unshapes me quite, makes me unpregnant
And dull to all proceedings. A deflow'red maid!   21
And by an eminent body that enforc'd
The law against it! But that her tender shame
Will not proclaim against her maiden loss,
How might she tongue me! Yet reason dares her no,
For my authority bears of a credent bulk,   26
That no particular scandal once can touch
But it confounds the breather. He should have liv'd,
Save that his riotous youth with dangerous sense
Might in the times to come have ta'en revenge,   30
By so receiving a dishonor'd life
With ransom of such shame. Would yet he had liv'd!
Alack, when once our grace we have forgot,
Nothing goes right—we would, and we would not.
                                                    Exit.

SCENE V

Enter DUKE [*in his own habit*] *and* FRIAR PETER.

Duke. These letters at fit time deliver me.
                                        [*Giving letters.*]
The Provost knows our purpose and our plot.
The matter being afoot, keep your instruction,
And hold you ever to our special drift,
Though sometimes you do blench from this to that,   5
As cause doth minister. Go call at Flavio's house,
And tell him where I stay. Give the like notice
To Valentius, Rowland, and to Crassus,
And bid them bring the trumpets to the gate.
But send me Flavius first.

Fri. P.   It shall be speeded well. [*Exit.*]

Enter VARRIUS.

Duke. I thank thee, Varrius, thou hast made good
      haste.   11
Come, we will walk. There's other of our friends

---

12. **dispatch:** speedy settlement.   **devices:** contrived charges.
17. **sort:** rank.   **suit:** following (?) or service at court (?).
20. **unpregnant:** unready, unapt.
22. **body:** person.   **enforc'd:** executed rigorously.
23. **But that:** were it not that.
24. **her maiden loss:** the loss of her virginity.
25. **tongue:** i.e. denounce.   **dares her no.** Not satisfactorily explained, but the sense is clear: reason forbids it.
26. **bears of a:** bears a (cf. *allow of, accept of,* etc.). Some editors read *bears a* for metrical reasons.   **credent bulk:** massive credibility, great power to win belief.
27. **no particular scandal:** no scandal whatever (*particular* = single, as in V.i.243).
28. **But . . . breather:** without destroying the one who uttered it. **should:** would.   29. **sense:** passion (?) or perceptiveness (?).
31. **By:** at, for.

IV.v. Location: Fields outside the town.
1. **deliver me:** deliver for me.   3. **keep:** keep to, follow.
4. **drift:** course, intention.   5. **blench:** turn aside.
6. **minister:** give occasion.   9. **trumpets:** trumpeters.

Will greet us here anon. My gentle Varrius!
                                                Exeunt.

SCENE VI

Enter ISABELLA *and* MARIANA.

Isab. To speak so indirectly I am loath.
I would say the truth, but to accuse him so,
That is your part. Yet I am advis'd to do it,
He says, to veil full purpose.

Mari.   Be rul'd by him.

Isab. Besides, he tells me that if peradventure   5
He speak against me on the adverse side,
I should not think it strange, for 'tis a physic
That's bitter to sweet end.

Enter [FRIAR] PETER.

Mari. I would Friar Peter—

Isab.   O, peace, the friar is come.

Fri. P. Come, I have found you out a stand most fit,
Where you may have such vantage on the Duke,   11
He shall not pass you. Twice have the trumpets
      sounded;
The generous and gravest citizens
Have hent the gates, and very near upon
The Duke is ent'ring; therefore hence away!   15
                                                Exeunt.

ACT V, SCENE I

[*Flourish.*] *Enter* DUKE, VARRIUS, LORDS, ANGELO,
ESCALUS, LUCIO, [PROVOST, OFFICERS,] CITIZENS
at several doors.

Duke. My very worthy cousin, fairly met!
Our old and faithful friend, we are glad to see you.

Ang., Escal. Happy return be to your royal Grace!

Duke. Many and hearty thankings to you both.
We have made inquiry of you, and we hear   5
Such goodness of your justice, that our soul
Cannot but yield you forth to public thanks,
Forerunning more requital.

Ang.   You make my bonds still greater.

Duke. O, your desert speaks loud, and I should
      wrong it
To lock it in the wards of covert bosom,   10
When it deserves with characters of brass
A forted residence 'gainst the tooth of time
And razure of oblivion. Give [me] your hand,
And let the subject see, to make them know
That outward courtesies would fain proclaim   15

IV.vi. Location: A street near the city gate.
3. **advis'd:** well-advised.   10. **stand:** place to stand.
11. **have . . . on:** be in so favorable a position for accosting.
13. **generous and gravest:** noblest and worthiest (the superlative ending of *gravest* governs both adjectives).
14. **hent:** taken places at.   **very near upon:** at just about this time.

V.i. Location: The city gate.
1. **cousin.** Form of address by a sovereign to one of his lords.
6. **goodness:** good reports.
7. **yield . . . thanks:** i.e. offer you public thanks.
8. **more requital:** greater reward.   **bonds:** obligations.
10. **wards:** cells.   **covert bosom:** private thoughts and feelings.
11. **characters:** letters, inscription.
12. **forted:** fortified.   **tooth of time.** Time devours all things.
13. **razure:** obliteration.   15. **fain:** gladly.

Favors that keep within. Come, Escalus,
You must walk by us on our other hand;
And good supporters are you.

Enter [FRIAR] PETER *and* ISABELLA.

Fri. P. Now is your time: speak loud, and kneel
  before him.
Isab. Justice, O royal Duke! Vail your regard 20
Upon a wrong'd—I would fain have said a maid!
O worthy Prince, dishonor not your eye
By throwing it on any other object,
Till you have heard me in my true complaint,
And given me justice, justice, justice, justice! 25
Duke. Relate your wrongs. In what? By whom?
  Be brief.
Here is Lord Angelo shall give you justice;
Reveal yourself to him.
Isab.   O worthy Duke,
You bid me seek redemption of the devil.
Hear me yourself; for that which I must speak 30
Must either punish me, not being believ'd,
Or wring redress from you. Hear me, O hear me, here.
Ang. My lord, her wits, I fear me, are not firm.
She hath been a suitor to me for her brother,
Cut off by course of justice—
Isab.   By course of justice! 35
Ang. And she will speak most bitterly and strange.
Isab. Most strange! but yet most truly will I speak:
That Angelo's forsworn, is it not strange?
That Angelo's a murtherer, is't not strange?
That Angelo is an adulterous thief, 40
An hypocrite, a virgin-violator,
Is it not strange? and strange?
Duke.   Nay, it is ten times strange.
Isab. It is not truer he is Angelo
Than this is all as true as it is strange;
Nay, it is ten times true, for truth is truth 45
To th' end of reck'ning.
Duke.   Away with her! Poor soul,
She speaks this in th' infirmity of sense.
Isab. O Prince, I conjure thee, as thou believ'st
There is another comfort than this world,
That thou neglect me not, with that opinion 50
That I am touch'd with madness. Make not impossible
That which but seems unlike; 'tis not impossible
But one the wicked'st caitiff on the ground,
May seem as shy, as grave, as just, as absolute
As Angelo. Even so may Angelo, 55
In all his dressings, caracts, titles, forms,
Be an arch-villain. Believe it, royal Prince,
If he be less, he's nothing, but he's more,
Had I more name for badness.
Duke.   By mine honesty,

If she be mad, as I believe no other, 60
Her madness hath the oddest frame of sense,
Such a dependancy of thing on thing,
As e'er I heard in madness.
Isab.   O gracious Duke,
Harp not on that; nor do not banish reason
For inequality, but let your reason serve 65
To make the truth appear, where it seems hid,
And hide the false seems true.
Duke.   Many that are not mad
Have sure more lack of reason. What would you
  say?
Isab. I am the sister of one Claudio,
Condemn'd upon the act of fornication 70
To lose his head, condemn'd by Angelo.
I (in probation of a sisterhood)
Was sent to by my brother; one Lucio
As then the messenger—
Lucio.   That's I, and't like your Grace.
I came to her from Claudio, and desir'd her 75
To try her gracious fortune with Lord Angelo,
For her poor brother's pardon.
Isab.   That's he indeed.
Duke. [*To Lucio.*] You were not bid to speak.
Lucio.   No, my good lord,
Nor wish'd to hold my peace.
Duke.   I wish you now then.
Pray you take note of it; and when you have 80
A business for yourself, pray heaven you then
Be perfect.
Lucio. I warrant your honor.
Duke. The warrant's for yourself; take heed to't.
Isab. This gentleman told somewhat of my tale—
Lucio. Right. 85
Duke. It may be right, but you are i' the wrong
To speak before your time. Proceed.
Isab.   I went
To this pernicious caitiff deputy—
Duke. That's somewhat madly spoken.
Isab.   Pardon it,
The phrase is to the matter. 90
Duke. Mended again. The matter; proceed.
Isab. In brief, to set the needless process by—
How I persuaded, how I pray'd, and kneel'd,
How he refell'd me, and how I replied

---

16. **keep:** dwell.
18. **supporters.** A heraldic term, designating the figures at either side
of the shield.   20. **Vail your regard:** bend your look.
28. **Reveal yourself:** i.e. disclose your suit.   44. **all as:** just as.
47. **sense:** intellect, reason.   48. **conjure:** adjure.   51. **Make:** deem.
52. **unlike:** unlikely.
53. **one the wicked'st:** the most wicked (an old idiom).   **caitiff:**
wretch.
54. **shy.** See the note on III.ii.130.   **absolute:** without defect.
56. **dressings . . . forms:** robes of office, insignia, titles, ceremonies.
58. **If . . . nothing:** i.e. he could be less a villain than he is, yet wicked.
59. **more:** i.e. worse (than *arch-villain*).

61. **frame of sense:** rational form.
62. **dependancy . . . thing:** logical order.   64. **that:** i.e. madness.
64–65. **do . . . inequality:** i.e. do not declare my reason gone because
of discrepancy (between her report of Angelo and the general report)
(?). This interpretation seems preferable to those that take *reason*
as referring to the Duke's reason and *inequality* as "injustice" or
"partiality" or "disparity" (between Isabella's status and Angelo's);
it permits Isabella a more respectful address to her sovereign and
furnishes an effective contrast rather than mere repetition in *reason /
your reason*: "Do not adjudge me lacking in reason, but rather employ
your own reason to find out the truth."
67. **hide:** remove from sight.   **seems:** that seems.
70. **upon:** in consequence of.   72. **probation:** novitiate.
79. **wish'd:** asked, bidden (cf. *desir'd* in line 75).   **wish you now:** bid
you now to do so.
81. **A business for yourself:** a matter in which you are involved.
82. **perfect:** fully prepared.   **warrant:** assure. The Duke quibbles
on the sense "warrant for arrest."
90. **to the matter:** to the point, germane.
91. **Mended:** i.e. speaking sanely.   **The matter:** get to the point
(since you say it is to the point).
92. **set . . . by:** omit unnecessary details of the story.
93. **persuaded:** pleaded.   94. **refell'd:** refuted.

579

(For this was of much length)—the vild conclusion 95
I now begin with grief and shame to utter.
He would not, but by gift of my chaste body
To his concupiscible intemperate lust,
Release my brother; and after much debatement,
My sisterly remorse confutes mine honor, 100
And I did yield to him; but the next morn betimes,
His purpose surfeiting, he sends a warrant
For my poor brother's head.

Duke.   This is most likely!

Isab.   O that it were as like as it is true!

Duke.   By heaven, fond wretch, thou know'st not
         what thou speak'st, 105
Or else thou art suborn'd against his honor
In hateful practice. First, his integrity
Stands without blemish; next, it imports no reason
That with such vehemency he should pursue
Faults proper to himself. If he had so offended, 110
He would have weigh'd thy brother by himself,
And not have cut him off. Some one hath set you on;
Confess the truth, and say by whose advice
Thou cam'st here to complain.

Isab.   And is this all?
Then, O you blessed ministers above, 115
Keep me in patience, and with ripened time
Unfold the evil which is here wrapp'd up
In countenance! Heaven shield your Grace from woe,
As I, thus wrong'd, hence unbelieved go!

Duke. I know you'ld fain be gone. An officer!
To prison with her! Shall we thus permit 121
A blasting and a scandalous breath to fall
On him so near us? This needs must be a practice.
Who knew of your intent and coming hither? 124

Isab.   One that I would were here, Friar Lodowick.

Duke.   A ghostly father, belike. Who knows that
         Lodowick?

Lucio.   My lord, I know him, 'tis a meddling friar.
I do not like the man; had he been lay, my lord,
For certain words he spake against your Grace
In your retirement, I had swing'd him soundly. 130

Duke.   Words against me? This' a good friar, be-
         like!
And to set on this wretched woman here
Against our substitute! Let this friar be found.

Lucio.   But yesternight, my lord, she and that friar,
I saw them at the prison. A saucy friar, 135
A very scurvy fellow.

Fri. P.   Blessed be your royal Grace!
I have stood by, my lord, and I have heard
Your royal ear abus'd. First, hath this woman
Most wrongfully accus'd your substitute, 140
Who is as free from touch or soil with her

As she from one ungot.

Duke.   We did believe no less.
Know you that Friar Lodowick that she speaks of?

Fri. P.   I know him for a man divine and holy,
Not scurvy, nor a temporary meddler, 145
As he's reported by this gentleman;
And on my trust, a man that never yet
Did (as he vouches) misreport your Grace.

Lucio.   My lord, most villainously, believe it.

Fri. P.   Well; he in time may come to clear himself;
But at this instant he is sick, my lord, 151
Of a strange fever. Upon his mere request,
Being come to knowledge that there was complaint
Intended 'gainst Lord Angelo, came I hither,
To speak as from his mouth, what he doth know 155
Is true and false; and what he with his oath
And all probation will make up full clear,
Whensoever he's convented. First, for this woman,
To justify this worthy nobleman,
So vulgarly and personally accus'd, 160
Her shall you hear disproved to her eyes,
Till she herself confess it.

Duke.   Good friar, let's hear it.
         [*Isabella is carried off guarded.*]
Do you not smile at this, Lord Angelo?
O heaven, the vanity of wretched fools!
Give us some seats. Come, cousin Angelo, 165
In this I'll be impartial. Be you judge
Of your own cause.

         Enter MARIANA [*veiled*].

                    Is this the witness, friar?
First, let her show [her] face, and after speak.

Mari.   Pardon, my lord, I will not show my face
Until my husband bid me. 170

Duke.   What, are you married?

Mari.   No, my lord.

Duke.   Are you a maid?

Mari.   No, my lord.

Duke.   A widow then? 175

Mari.   Neither, my lord.

Duke.   Why, you are nothing then: neither maid,
widow, nor wife?

Lucio.   My lord, she may be a punk; for many of
them are neither maid, widow, nor wife. 180

Duke.   Silence that fellow. I would he had some
         cause
To prattle for himself.

Lucio.   Well, my lord.

Mari.   My lord, I do confess I ne'er was married,
And I confess besides I am no maid. 185
I have known my husband, yet my husband
Knows not that ever he knew me.

---

95. **vild:** vile (a variant form).   100. **remorse:** pity.
105. **fond:** foolish.   107. **practice:** conspiracy.
108. **it . . . reason:** it is irrational.   109. **pursue:** persecute.
110. **proper to himself:** that he himself possessed.
111. **weigh'd . . . himself.** Cf. II.ii.126, III.ii.265–66.
115. **ministers:** angels.   117. **Unfold:** unwrap, disclose.
118. **In countenance:** in the Duke's authority (?) or by the Duke's
allowance (?).   122. **blasting:** blighting (like a destructive wind).
127. **meddling.** Perhaps (as often) with an implication of sexual
impropriety; cf. *saucy* (line 135), which can mean both "impudent"
and "lecherous."   130. **swing'd:** beaten (from *swinge*).
131. **This':** this is.   139. **abus'd:** deceived.
141. **touch or soil:** impure contact.

142. **ungot:** unbegotten.
145. **temporary meddler:** meddler in temporal affairs.
148. **as he vouches:** i.e. as Lucio affirms.
152. **Upon . . . request:** solely at his request.
153. **Being . . . knowledge:** since he had learned.
157. **probation:** proof.   158. **convented:** summoned.
160. **vulgarly:** publicly.   164. **vanity:** folly.
166. **be impartial:** not take part.   176. **Neither:** nor that either.
179. **punk:** prostitute.
181–82. **some . . . himself:** some necessity to speak in his own defense.
186. **known:** known carnally.

Lucio. He was drunk then, my lord, it can be no
better.

Duke. For the benefit of silence, would thou wert
so too!   191

Lucio. Well, my lord.

Duke. This is no witness for Lord Angelo.

Mari. Now I come to't, my lord.
She that accuses him of fornication,   195
In self-same manner doth accuse my husband,
And charges him, my lord, with such a time
When I'll depose I had him in mine arms
With all th' effect of love.

Ang. Charges she moe than me?

Mari.   Not that I know.

Duke. No? You say your husband.   201

Mari. Why, just, my lord, and that is Angelo,
Who thinks he knows that he ne'er knew my body,
But knows he thinks that he knows Isabel's.

Ang. This is a strange abuse. Let's see thy face.

Mari. My husband bids me, now I will unmask.

                                                    [*Unveiling.*]
This is that face, thou cruel Angelo,   207
Which once thou swor'st was worth the looking on;
This is the hand which, with a vow'd contract,
Was fast belock'd in thine; this is the body   210
That took away the match from Isabel,
And did supply thee at thy garden-house
In her imagin'd person.

Duke.   Know you this woman?

Lucio. Carnally, she says.

Duke.   Sirrah, no more!

Lucio. Enough, my lord.   215

Ang. My lord, I must confess I know this woman,
And five years since there was some speech of marriage
Betwixt myself and her; which was broke off,
Partly for that her promised proportions
Came short of composition, but in chief   220
For that her reputation was disvalued
In levity. Since which time of five years
I never spake with her, saw her, nor heard from her,
Upon my faith and honor.

Mari.   Noble Prince,
As there comes light from heaven, and words from
          breath,   225
As there is sense in truth, and truth in virtue,
I am affianc'd this man's wife as strongly
As words could make up vows; and, my good lord,
But Tuesday night last gone, in 's garden-house,
He knew me as a wife. As this is true,   230
Let me in safety raise me from my knees,
Or else for ever be confixed here,
A marble monument!

Ang.   I did but smile till now.

Now, good my lord, give me the scope of justice,
My patience here is touch'd. I do perceive   235
These poor informal women are no more
But instruments of some more mightier member
That sets them on. Let me have way, my lord,
To find this practice out.

Duke.   Ay, with my heart,
And punish them to your height of pleasure.   240
Thou foolish friar, and thou pernicious woman,
Compact with her that's gone, think'st thou thy oaths,
Though they would swear down each particular saint,
Were testimonies against his worth and credit
That's seal'd in approbation? You, Lord Escalus,   245
Sit with my cousin; lend him your kind pains
To find out this abuse, whence 'tis deriv'd.
There is another friar that set them on,
Let him be sent for.

Fri. P. Would he were here, my lord, for he indeed
Hath set the women on to this complaint.   251
Your Provost knows the place where he abides,
And he may fetch him.

Duke.   Go, do it instantly. [*Exit Provost.*]
And you, my noble and well-warranted cousin,
Whom it concerns to hear this matter forth,   255
Do with your injuries as seems you best,
In any chastisement. I for a while will leave you;
But stir not you till you have well determin'd
Upon these slanderers.

Escal.   My lord, we'll do it throughly.   259

                                                    Exit [*Duke*].
Signior Lucio, did not you say you knew that Friar
Lodowick to be a dishonest person?

Lucio. *Cucullus non facit monachum:* honest in
nothing but in his clothes, and one that hath spoke most
villainous speeches of the Duke.   264

Escal. We shall entreat you to abide here till he
come, and enforce them against him. We shall find this
friar a notable fellow.

Lucio. As any in Vienna, on my word.   268

Escal. Call that same Isabel here once again, I
would speak with her. [*Exit an Attendant.*] Pray you,
my lord, give me leave to question, you shall see how
I'll handle her.

Lucio. Not better than he, by her own report.

Escal. Say you?   274

Lucio. Marry, sir, I think if you handled her privately she would sooner confess; perchance publicly
she'll be asham'd.

Enter DUKE [*in his friar's habit*], PROVOST, [OFFICERS
with] ISABELLA.

Escal. I will go darkly to work with her.

---

197. with . . . time: with committing the offense at the very time.
198. depose: testify on oath.   199. effect: manifestations.
200. moe: more (persons).   202. just: just so, exactly.
210. fast belock'd. See note on I.ii.147.
211. match: appointed meeting (but also with reference to the
marriage thus consummated).
212. supply thee: (1) fill her place with you; (2) satisfy your wants.
219. for that: because.   proportions: portion, dowry.
220. composition: the agreed amount.   221. disvalued: debased.
222. levity: lightness, wantonness.
232. confixed: firmly fixed.   233. marble: immovable.

234. scope: full authority.   235. touch'd: wounded, i.e. tried beyond its limit.   236. informal: distracted.
242. Compact: leagued.   243. each particular: every single.
245. seal'd in approbation. "Angelo's faith has been tried, approved,
and sealed in testimony of that approbation, and . . . is no more to be
called in question" (Johnson).   255. forth: to the end, thoroughly.
256. with your injuries: with respect to the wrongs done you.
258. determin'd: reached a judgment.   259. throughly: thoroughly.
262. Cucullus . . . monachum: the hood does not make the monk
(proverbial). Lucio does not know how truly he speaks.
266. enforce them: put them strongly.   267. notable: notorious.
271. give. Probably with conditional sense: "if you will give."
278. darkly: secretly, cunningly.

Lucio. That's the way; for women are light at midnight. 280

Escal. Come on, mistress. Here's a gentlewoman denies all that you have said.

Lucio. My lord, here comes the rascal I spoke of, here with the Provost. 284

Escal. In very good time. Speak not you to him till we call upon you.

Lucio. Mum.

Escal. Come, sir, did you set these women on to slander Lord Angelo? They have confess'd you did.

Duke. 'Tis false. 290

Escal. How! know you where you are?

Duke. Respect to your great place! and let the devil Be sometime honor'd for his burning throne! Where is the Duke? 'tis he should hear me speak.

Escal. The Duke's in us; and we will hear you speak: 295
Look you speak justly.

Duke. Boldly, at least. But O, poor souls, Come you to seek the lamb here of the fox, Good night to your redress! Is the Duke gone? Then is your cause gone too. The Duke's unjust 300 Thus to retort your manifest appeal, And put your trial in the villain's mouth Which here you come to accuse.

Lucio. This is the rascal; this is he I spoke of.

Escal. Why, thou unreverend and unhallowed friar, Is't not enough thou hast suborn'd these women 306 To accuse this worthy man, but in foul mouth, And in the witness of his proper ear, To call him villain, and then to glance from him To th' Duke himself, to tax him with injustice? 310 Take him hence; to th' rack with him! We'll touze you Joint by joint, but we will know his purpose. What? "unjust"?

Duke. Be not so hot. The Duke Dare no more stretch this finger of mine than he Dare rack his own. His subject am I not, 315 Nor here provincial. My business in this state Made me a looker-on here in Vienna, Where I have seen corruption boil and bubble, Till it o'errun the stew; laws for all faults, But faults so countenanc'd, that the strong statutes Stand like the forfeits in a barber's shop, 321

As much in mock as mark.

Escal. Slander to th' state! Away with him to prison.

Ang. What can you vouch Against him, Signior Lucio? Is this the man That you did tell us of?

Lucio. 'Tis he, my lord. 325 Come hither, goodman bald-pate, do you know me?

Duke. I remember you, sir, by the sound of your voice; I met you at the prison, in the absence of the Duke.

Lucio. O, did you so? And do you remember what you said of the Duke? 331

Duke. Most notedly, sir.

Lucio. Do you so, sir? And was the Duke a flesh-monger, a fool, and a coward, as you then reported him to be? 335

Duke. You must, sir, change persons with me, ere you make that my report. You indeed spoke so of him, and much more, much worse.

Lucio. O thou damnable fellow! Did not I pluck thee by the nose for thy speeches? 340

Duke. I protest I love the Duke as I love myself.

Ang. Hark how the villain would close now, after his treasonable abuses! 343

Escal. Such a fellow is not to be talk'd withal. Away with him to prison! Where is the Provost? Away with him to prison! Lay bolts enough upon him. Let him speak no more. Away with those giglets too, and with the other confederate companion!

[*The Provost lays hands on the Duke.*]

Duke. Stay, sir, stay a while.

Ang. What, resists he? Help him, Lucio. 350

Lucio. Come, sir, come, sir, come, sir; foh, sir, why, you bald-pated, lying rascal, you must be hooded, must you? Show your knave's visage, with a pox to you! Show your sheep-biting face, and be hang'd an hour! Will't not off? [*Pulls off the friar's hood.*] 355

Duke. Thou art the first knave that e'er mad'st a duke.
First, Provost, let me bail these gentle three.
[*To Lucio.*] Sneak not away, sir, for the friar and you Must have a word anon.—Lay hold on him.

Lucio. This may prove worse than hanging. 360

Duke. [*To Escalus.*] What you have spoke I pardon. Sit you down,
We'll borrow place of him.—Sir, by your leave.

[*Takes Angelo's seat.*]

Hast thou or word, or wit, or impudence,
That yet can do thee office? If thou hast,
Rely upon it till my tale be heard, 365

279–80. **light at midnight**: i.e. wanton in the dark.
290. **'Tis false.** Equivocal: apparently a denial that he set the women on, but actually a denial that Angelo has been slandered, i.e. charged falsely.
292–93. **let . . . throne.** The Duke ironically extends the principle to its logical conclusion. 296. **justly**: truthfully.
298. **Come you**: if you come.
301. **retort**: throw back, refuse to accept. **manifest**: obviously just.
302–3. **the villain's mouth Which**: the mouth of the villain whom.
308. **in . . . ear**: in his own hearing. 309. **glance**: ricochet.
311. **touze**: tear, jerk. 313. **hot**: hasty.
316. **provincial**: subject to local religious authority.
319. **stew**: (1) pot; (2) brothel. 320. **countenanc'd**: tolerated.
321. **forfeits . . . shop.** Usually explained as extracted teeth (barber-surgeons also pulled teeth), which like disused laws have lost their power to bite. But the comparison is forced and gives a weak sense for line 322. More likely is the earlier explanation that barbers hung up in their shops, which were often thronged, a list of penalties for various kinds of misbehavior. Hart (*Notes and Queries*, July 1908, p. 64) cites from *Plain Percival*: "Speake a bloody word in a Barbers shop, you make a forfet" (quoted by Lever).

322. **As . . . mark**: i.e. as often broken as observed.
326. **goodman**: term of address, here ironic, to one below the rank of a gentleman. **bald-pate.** Lucio supposes that there is a tonsure under the Duke's hood. 341. **protest**: affirm.
342. **close**: come to terms. 347. **giglets**: wantons.
348. **confederate companion**: i.e. Friar Peter.
354. **Show . . . face.** Probably alluding to the fable of the wolf in sheep's clothing.
354–55. **hang'd an hour.** Presumably a jocular version of "hanged"; examples of "hanged awhile" have been cited. For another reference to the hanging of an animal, see *The Merchant of Venice*, IV.i.133–35, "Thy currish spirit / Govern'd a wolf, who hang'd for human slaughter, / Even from the gallows did his fell soul fleet. . . ."
357. **gentle three**: i.e. Isabella, Mariana, and Friar Peter.
362. **We'll.** The royal plural.

And hold no longer out.

Ang.   O my dread lord,
I should be guiltier than my guiltiness,
To think I can be undiscernible,
When I perceive your Grace, like pow'r divine,
Hath look'd upon my passes. Then, good Prince, 370
No longer session hold upon my shame,
But let my trial be mine own confession.
Immediate sentence then, and sequent death,
Is all the grace I beg.

Duke.   Come hither, Mariana.
Say: wast thou e'er contracted to this woman? 375

Ang. I was, my lord.

Duke. Go take her hence, and marry her instantly.
Do you the office, friar, which consummate,
Return him here again. Go with him, Provost.

            Exeunt [*Angelo, Mariana, Friar Peter, Provost*].

Escal. My lord, I am more amaz'd at his dishonor
Than at the strangeness of it.

Duke.   Come hither, Isabel, 381
Your friar is now your prince. As I was then
Advertising and holy to your business,
Not changing heart with habit, I am still
Attorneyed at your service.

Isab.   O, give me pardon, 385
That I, your vassal, have employ'd and pain'd
Your unknown sovereignty!

Duke.   You are pardon'd, Isabel;
And now, dear maid, be you as free to us.
Your brother's death I know sits at your heart;
And you may marvel why I obscur'd myself, 390
Laboring to save his life, and would not rather
Make rash remonstrance of my hidden pow'r
Than let him so be lost. O most kind maid,
It was the swift celerity of his death,
Which I did think with slower foot came on, 395
That brain'd my purpose. But peace be with him!
That life is better life, past fearing death,
Than that which lives to fear. Make it your comfort,
So happy is your brother.

Enter ANGELO, MARIANA, [FRIAR] PETER, *Provost*.

Isab.   I do, my lord. 399

Duke. For this new-married man approaching here,
Whose salt imagination yet hath wrong'd
Your well-defended honor, you must pardon
For Mariana's sake; but as he adjudg'd your brother—
Being criminal, in double violation
Of sacred chastity and of promise-breach, 405
Thereon dependant, for your brother's life—
The very mercy of the law cries out
Most audible, even from his proper tongue,

"An Angelo for Claudio, death for death!"
Haste still pays haste, and leisure answers leisure; 410
Like doth quit like, and *Measure* still *for Measure*.
Then, Angelo, thy fault's thus manifested;
Which though thou wouldst deny, denies thee vantage.
We do condemn thee to the very block 414
Where Claudio stoop'd to death, and with like haste.
Away with him!

Mari.   O my most gracious lord,
I hope you will not mock me with a husband!

Duke. It is your husband mock'd you with a husband.
Consenting to the safeguard of your honor,
I thought your marriage fit; else imputation, 420
For that he knew you, might reproach your life,
And choke your good to come. For his possessions,
Although by [confiscation] they are ours,
We do enstate and widow you with all,
To buy you a better husband.

Mari.   O my dear lord, 425
I crave no other, nor no better man.

Duke. Never crave him, we are definitive.

Mari. [*Kneeling.*] Gentle my liege—

Duke.   You do but lose your labor.
Away with him to death! [*To Lucio.*] Now, sir, to
    you.

Mari. O my good lord! Sweet Isabel, take my
    part! 430
Lend me your knees, and all my life to come
I'll lend you all my life to do you service.

Duke. Against all sense you do importune her.
Should she kneel down in mercy of this fact,
Her brother's ghost his paved bed would break, 435
And take her hence in horror.

Mari.   Isabel!
Sweet Isabel, do yet but kneel by me.
Hold up your hands, say nothing; I'll speak all.
They say best men are moulded out of faults,
And for the most, become much more the better 440
For being a little bad; so may my husband.
O Isabel! will you not lend a knee?

Duke. He dies for Claudio's death.

Isab. [*Kneeling.*]   Most bounteous sir:
Look, if it please you, on this man condemn'd
As if my brother liv'd. I partly think 445
A due sincerity governed his deeds,
Till he did look on me. Since it is so,
Let him not die. My brother had but justice,
In that he did the thing for which he died;

370. **passes:** transgressions.   383. **Advertising:** attentive.   **holy:** devoted.   384. **habit:** attire.   385. **Attorneyed at:** acting as agent in. 386. **pain'd:** given trouble to.   388. **free to:** i.e. quick to pardon. 392. **rash remonstrance:** quick manifestation. 394. **swift celerity.** See the note on IV.ii.110. 396. **brain'd:** dashed out the brains of, brought to a shattering end. 399. **So:** thus, in this way.   401. **salt:** lecherous. 403. **adjudg'd:** condemned. 405–6. **promise-breach . . . for:** breaking his promise, conditional on the former action, to save. Strict syntax would require *promise* in place of *promise-breach*. 407. **very mercy.** Angelo's crime is such that not only justice but mercy itself demands his death.   408. **proper:** own.

410. **Haste . . . haste:** haste is always repaid with haste. 411. **quit:** requite, retaliate with.   **Measure . . . Measure.** Cf. Matthew 7:2: "with what judgment ye judge, ye shall be judged, and with what measure ye mete, it shall be measured unto you again" (Geneva). 413. **though . . . deny:** even if you wished to deny it (which Angelo does not wish to do).   **vantage:** i.e. a lesser penalty than was imposed on Claudio. 417. **mock . . . husband:** i.e. tantalize me by offering, and then immediately withdrawing, the gift of a husband. 420. **imputation:** imputation of sin. 424. **enstate . . . you:** i.e. endow you by virtue of a widow's rights. 427. **we are definitive:** my decision is final. 428. **liege:** sovereign. 433. **all sense:** rationality and natural feeling. 434. **in . . . fact:** to beg mercy for this crime. 435. **his paved bed:** the stone paving above his grave.

Measure
for Measure
V.i

For Angelo,   450
His act did not o'ertake his bad intent,
And must be buried but as an intent
That perish'd by the way. Thoughts are no subjects,
Intents but merely thoughts.
    Mari.   Merely, my lord.   454
    Duke. Your suit's unprofitable; stand up, I say.
I have bethought me of another fault.
Provost, how came it Claudio was beheaded
At an unusual hour?
    Prov.   It was commanded so.
    Duke. Had you a special warrant for the deed?
    Prov. No, my good lord; it was by private mes-
      sage.   460
    Duke. For which I do discharge you of your office;
Give up your keys.
    Prov.   Pardon me, noble lord,
I thought it was a fault, but knew it not,
Yet did repent me, after more advice,
For testimony whereof, one in the prison,   465
That should by private order else have died,
I have reserv'd alive.
    Duke.   What's he?
    Prov.   His name is Barnardine.
    Duke. I would thou hadst done so by Claudio.
Go fetch him hither, let me look upon him.
                          [Exit Provost.]
    Escal. I am sorry, one so learned and so wise   470
As you, Lord Angelo, have still appear'd,
Should slip so grossly, both in the heat of blood
And lack of temper'd judgment afterward.
    Ang. I am sorry that such sorrow I procure,
And so deep sticks it in my penitent heart   475
That I crave death more willingly than mercy:
'Tis my deserving, and I do entreat it.

Enter BARNARDINE *and* PROVOST, CLAUDIO *[muffled]*,
JULIETTA.

    Duke. Which is that Barnardine?
    Prov.   This, my lord.
    Duke. There was a friar told me of this man.
Sirrah, thou art said to have a stubborn soul   480
That apprehends no further than this world,
And squar'st thy life according. Thou'rt condemn'd,
But for those earthly faults, I quit them all,
And pray thee take this mercy to provide
For better times to come. Friar, advise him,   485
I leave him to your hand. What muffled fellow's that?
    Prov. This is another prisoner that I sav'd,
Who should have died when Claudio lost his head,
As like almost to Claudio as himself.
                        [Unmuffles Claudio.]
    Duke. *[To Isabella.]* If he be like your brother, for
      his sake   490
Is he pardon'd, and for your lovely sake,
Give me your hand, and say you will be mine,
He is my brother too. But fitter time for that.

By this Lord Angelo perceives he's safe;
Methinks I see a quick'ning in his eye.   495
Well, Angelo, your evil quits you well.
Look that you love your wife; her worth worth yours.
I find an apt remission in myself;
And yet here's one in place I cannot pardon.
[To Lucio.] You, sirrah, that knew me for a fool, a
    coward,   500
One all of luxury, an ass, a madman,
Wherein have I so deserv'd of you,
That you extol me thus?
    Lucio. Faith, my lord, I spoke it but according to
the trick. If you will hang me for it, you may; but I
had rather it would please you I might be whipt.   506
    Duke. Whipt first, sir, and hang'd after.
Proclaim it, Provost, round about the city,
If any woman wrong'd by this lewd fellow
(As I have heard him swear himself there's one   510
Whom he begot with child), let her appear,
And he shall marry her. The nuptial finish'd,
Let him be whipt and hang'd.   513
    Lucio. I beseech your Highness do not marry me to
a whore. Your Highness said even now I made you a
duke; good my lord, do not recompense me in making
me a cuckold.
    Duke. Upon mine honor, thou shalt marry her.
Thy slanders I forgive, and therewithal
Remit thy other forfeits. Take him to prison,   520
And see our pleasure herein executed.
    Lucio. Marrying a punk, my lord, is pressing to
death, whipping, and hanging.
    Duke. Slandering a prince deserves it.
                  [Exeunt Officers with Lucio.]
She, Claudio, that you wrong'd, look you restore. 525
Joy to you, Mariana! Love her, Angelo!
I have confess'd her, and I know her virtue.
Thanks, good friend Escalus, for thy much goodness,
There's more behind that is more gratulate.
Thanks, Provost, for thy care and secrecy,   530
We shall employ thee in a worthier place.
Forgive him, Angelo, that brought you home
The head of Ragozine for Claudio's,
Th' offense pardons itself. Dear Isabel,
I have a motion much imports your good,   535
Whereto if you'll a willing ear incline,
What's mine is yours, and what is yours is mine.
So bring us to our palace, where we'll show
What's yet behind, that['s] meet you all should know.
                              [Exeunt.]

453. **no subjects:** i.e. not answerable to authority.
463. **knew it not:** was not certain of it.
464. **more advice:** further consideration.
471. **still:** always (heretofore).   473. **temper'd:** balanced.
481. **apprehends:** understands.   482. **squar'st:** shapest.
483. **quit:** remit.   492. **Give:** if you will give.

495. **quick'ning:** renewal of life.
496. **quits you well:** (1) is well rewarded; (2) is requited with good (in
contrast to "measure for measure").
497. **her . . . yours:** making your worth equal to hers (?).
498. **apt remission:** readiness to pardon.
499. **in place:** at hand, before me.   501. **luxury:** lechery.
505. **trick:** fashion.   519. **therewithal:** in addition.
522-23. **pressing to death.** One accused of felony who refused to
plead guilty or not guilty was secured on his back and weights were
piled on him in increasing number until he pleaded or died.
527. **confess'd her:** been her confessor.
529. **behind:** beyond, i.e. to come (so also in line 539).
532-34. **Forgive . . . itself.** This distinction between the offender and
the offense recalls II.ii.34-41.
535. **a motion:** something to propose.
538. **bring:** accompany.   **show:** make known.

The First Folio (1623) is the only authority for *Measure for Measure*; all later texts are derived from that source. It is believed that the F1 text was printed from a transcript, possibly, like the copy-texts for the first three plays in F1, by Ralph Crane (for whose scribal characteristics see the "Note on the Text" to *The Tempest*). The evidence for Crane's hand is not strong, but the fairly heavy use of parentheses, a number of hyphenated forms, and an occasional "Jonsonian elision" (see Textual Notes, III.i.4, IV.iii.149) point in his direction, as do the act-scene division and the presence of a list of dramatis personae. The source of the transcript is also uncertain. W. W. Greg favors copy based on Shakespeare's "foul papers," but it is likewise possible that the scribe used a prompt-book and omitted the usual prompt-notations associated with theatre copy. There are, at any rate, no confusions in the F1 text serious enough to rule out a prompt-copy source; and the absence of a substantial number of exit directions cannot be considered a serious stumbling block, since, on the whole, prompters were not overly concerned about getting characters off the stage.

Dover Wilson's ingenious theory of abridgment and later expansion (1922), evolved to explain the curious mixture of prose and verse passages in the play, is no longer generally accepted, but his suggestion that the role of Lucio (in II.ii and V.i) has at some stage in the composition been "fattened" is probably correct, and it might be further suggested that in I.iv Lucio has taken the role originally belonging to the Provost.

For further information, see: J. D. Wilson, ed., New Cambridge *Measure for Measure* (Cambridge, 1922); W. W. Greg, *The Shakespeare First Folio* (Oxford, 1955); J. W. Lever, ed., New Arden *Measure for Measure* (1965).

TEXTUAL NOTES

Dramatis personae: *subs. as given in F1, following the play, with a few additions by Rowe and later editors*
Act-scene division: *from F1, with the following exceptions: I.iii, iv (numbered I.iv, v in F1, which divides I.ii into two scenes, with the break after l. 115); III.ii (no scene division in F1); see first note to each scene; present act-scene arrangement as a whole first established by Dyce*

I.i

Location: *Theobald (after Pope)*
o.s.d. and Attendants] *Capell*
15 s.d. Exit an Attendant.] *Capell*
35 touch'd] *F2;* tonch'd *F1*
75 s.d. Exit.] *placed as in F2; after l. 74, F1*

I.ii

Location: *Rowe*
12 Why,] *Pope;* Why? *F1*
15 relish] *F3;* rallish *F1*
32 three-pil'd piece] *Rowe;* three pild-peece *F1*
46 s.p. 1. Gent.] *Theobold; continued to Lucio, F1*
46–7 I . . . to—] *as prose, Pope; as verse, F1*
60 s.p. Mrs. Ov.] Bawd. *F1 (subs. throughout)*
76 promise-keeping] *hyphen, F2*
81 s.d. with Gentlemen] *Capell (subs.)*
84 s.d. Enter Clown] *placed as in Dyce (after Capell); after l. 85, F1*
86 s.p. Pom.] *Dyce;* Clo. *F1 (subs. throughout)*
115] *Following this line F1 inserts* Scena Tertia. *before entry of Provost, etc.; no scene break observed in Padua First Folio prompt-book, Rowe*
115 s.d. Enter . . . Officers.] *Dyce (after Rowe; implied in Padua prompt-book);* Enter Prouost, Claudio, Iuliet, Officers, Lucio, & 2. Gent. *F1*
123 s.d. Enter . . . Gentlemen.] *Padua prompt-book, Dyce (after Davenant); F1 is ambiguous (see preceding note) about whether only the Second Gentleman or both Gentlemen re-enter here; Padua prompt-book gives only* Gent *(also ambiguous); F2 reads two* Gent.
125 liberty:] *Rowe (subs.);* Liberty *F1*
150 propagation] *F2;* propogation *F1*
185 reason] *Pope;* reason, *F1*

I.iii

I.iii] *Rowe;* Scena Quarta. *F1*
Location: *ed. (after Wilson)*
3 Why] *Rowe;* why, *F1*
10 cost,] cost, and *F2*

14 travell'd] *Rowe;* trauaild *F1*
27 Becomes] *Pope (after Davenant)*
54 s.d. Exeunt.] *F2;* Exit. *F1*

I.iv

I.iv] *Rowe;* Scena Quinta. *F1*
Location: *Rowe*
2, 7 s.pp. Fran.] *Capell;* Nun. *F1*
5 sisterhood] *F2;* Sisterstood *F1*
14 s.d. Exit.] *Rowe*
15 s.d. Enter Lucio.] *Rowe*
17 stead] *Rowe;* steed *F1*
54 givings-out] *Rowe (subs.);* giuing-out *F1*
55 true-meant] *hyphen, Pope*
61 fast.] *F2;* fast *F1*
63 run by] *Rowe;* run-by *F1*
72 so seek] *Rowe;* so, / Seeke *F1*
72 H'as] *Theobald;* Has *F1*
90 s.d. severally] *ed.*

II.i

Location: *Wilson*
12 your] *Rowe (after Davenant);* our *F1*
20 sworn twelve] *Rowe;* sworne-twelue *F1*
36 s.d. Exit Provost.] *Rowe*
38 Some . . . fall;] *in italics, F1*
59 s.d. A pause.] *ed. (suggested by line arrangement in F1)*
63 parcel-bawd] *hyphen, Theobald*
65 suburbs] *F2;* Suborbs *F1*
69 sir,] *F2;* Sir? *F1*
90 honors'] *Capell;* honors *F1*
94 china dishes] *Rowe (subs.);* China-dishes *F1*
98 great-bellied] *hyphen, Capell*
126 All-hallond eve] *Rowe (after F2);* Allhallond-Eue *F1*
138 s.d. Exit Angelo.] *Theobald;* Exit. *F1 (after l. 137)*
160 right, constable. What!] *ed.;* right (Constable) what *F1*
197 s.d. To Pompey.] *Rowe*
212 s.d. Exit Froth.] *Rowe*
253 s.d. aside] *Staunton*
275 s.d. Exit Elbow.] *Rowe*

II.ii

Location: *Johnson*
2 s.d. Exit Servant.] *Capell*
17 s.d. Enter Servant.] *Padua prompt-book, Capell*
22 s.d. Exit Servant.] *Theobald*
36 s.d. Aside.] *Collier*
37 it?] *Rowe;* it, *F1*
43, 56, etc. s.dd. Aside to Isabella.] *Collier (after Johnson)*
58 it] it backe *F2*
59 'longs] *Theobald;* longs *F1*

87 gross selves] *F4;* grosse-selues *F1*
102 gall,] *Craig;* gaule *F1*
125 s.d. Aside.] *Collier*
141, 157 s.dd. Aside.] *Johnson*
149 tested gold] *Rowe;* tested-gold *F1*
153 sun-rise] *hyphen, Theobald*
160 'fore noon] *Rowe;* 'fore-noone *F1*
161 s.d. Exeunt . . . Provost.] *Capell (after Rowe);* Exeunt. *F2*
163 most,] *Kittredge;* most? *F1*
183 art] *Pope;* Art, *F1*

II.iii

Location: *Rowe*
o.s.d. disguised . . . friar] *Rowe (subs.)*
o.s.d. meeting] *ed. (after Dyce)*
17 s.d. To Juliet.] *Theobald*
26 offenseful] *F2;* offence full *F1*
34 fear—] *Capell;* feare. *F1*

II.iv

Location: *Capell*
9 sere] *Heath conj. (after Hanmer);* feard *F1*
17 s.d. Enter Servant.] *placed as in Theobald; after l. 17, F1*
19 s.d. Exit Servant.] *Capell (after Johnson)*
30 s.d. Enter Isabella.] *placed as in Johnson; after l. 30, F1*
48 metal] *Theobald;* mettle *F1*
53 or] *Rowe (after Davenant);* and *F1*
75 craftily] *Rowe (after Davenant);* crafty *F1*
76 me] *F2*
94 all-binding law] *Johnson;* all-building-Law *F1*
122–3 he, Owe] *Theobald (subs.);* he / Owe, *F1*
158 report] *F2;* reporr *F1*
185] *Line marked with gnomic quotes, F1*

III.i

Location: *Rowe*
o.s.d. disguised . . . friar] *Collier (subs.)*
4 I have] *Capell;* I'haue *F1*
9 skyey influences] *F4;* skyie-influences *F1*
29 thee sire] *F4;* thee, fire *F1*
44 s.d. Within.] *Capell*
47 s.d. Enter Isabella.] *placed as in Dyce; after l. 43, F1*
52 me . . . them] *Steevens conj. (after Davenant);* them . . . me *F1; for ll. 52–3 F2 reads:* Bring them to speake, where I may be conceal'd, yet heare them.
53 s.d. Exeunt . . . Provost.] *Rowe;* Exeunt. *F2*
55 indeed.] *F4 (subs.);* indeede, *F1*
68 Though . . . had,] *Rowe;* Through . . . had *F1*

88 **outward-sainted]** *hyphen, Pope*
90 **enew]** *Keightley;* emmew *F1*
93, 96 **prenzie]** *Princely Pope; among other emendations suggested,* precise *(Tieck conj. in Cambridge) and* puny *(Drew conj. in SQ) are perhaps the best*
95 **damned'st]** *F2;* damnest *F1*
98 **freed!]** *Staunton;* freed? *F1*
99 **thee,]** *Capell;* thee; *F1*
99 **offense,]** *Hanmer;* offence *F1*
129 **penury]** *F2;* periury *F1*
150 s.d. **Enter ... friar.]** *Capell (subs.);* Duke steps in. *F2*
159 s.d. **Walks apart.]** *Capell*
173 s.d. **Exit Claudio.]** *Capell;* Exit. *F2 (after l. 172)*
174 s.d. **Enter Provost.]** *Capell (before l. 174); placed as in Dyce*
180 s.d. **Turning to Isabella.]** *Wilson*
191 **born]** *F3;* borne *F1*
198 **advisings: ... good]** *Pope;* aduisings, ... good; *F1*
214 **by]** *F2*
250 **stead]** *Rowe;* steed *F1*
264 **moated grange]** *F4;* moated-Grange *F1*
269 s.d. **Manet Duke.]** *ed.*

III.ii

III.ii] *Capell (after Pope); F1 (followed by the Padua prompt-book) correctly continues the scene without a new entry for the Duke*
Location: *ed. (after Wilson)*
24 **abominable]** *F3;* abhominable *F1*
25 **eat, array]** *Theobald (Bishop conj.);* eate away *F1*
28–9 **Indeed ... prove—]** *as prose, Pope; as verse, F1*
39 **seeming,]** *ed.;* seeming *F1*
40 **waist—]** *Dyce (waist Johnson);* wast, *F1*
47 **it]** *Rowe*
68 **bawd-born]** *F3 (hyphen, Steevens);* Baud borne *F1*
76 **bondage ... patiently,]** *Theobald (subs.);* bondage ... patiently: *F1*
85–6 s.d. **Exeunt ... Officers.]** *Rowe;* Exeunt. *F2*
145 **bringings-forth]** *hyphen, Dyce*
151 **dearer]** *Hanmer;* deare *F1*
183–4 **brown bread]** *Rowe;* browne-bread *F1*
189 s.d. **Officers with]** *Dyce (after Hanmer)*
206–7 s.d. **Exeunt ... Overdone.]** *Rowe (subs.)*
219 **See]** *Theobald;* Sea *F1*
224 **and, ... is,]** *Alexander;* and ... is *F1*
232–3 **One ... himself.]** *as prose, Capell; as verse, F1*
255–7 **If ... himself.]** *as prose, Pope; as verse, F1*
260 s.d. **Exeunt ... Provost.]** *Capell;* Exit. *F2*

IV.i

Location: *Cambridge (after Theobald)*
3 **eyes, ... day,]** *Rowe;* eyes: ... day *F1*
9 s.d. **Exit Boy.]** *Capell*
37 **upon't.]** *Rowe (subs.);* vpon't, *F1*
49 s.d. **Enter Mariana.]** *placed as in Rowe; after l. 48, F1*
58 **Will't]** *Steevens;* Wilt *F1*
58 s.d. **with Isabella]** *Rowe (subs.)*
64 s.d. **Enter ... Isabella.]** *placed as in Johnson; after l. 64, F1*
75 **tithe's]** *Pope;* Tithes *F1*

IV.ii

Location: *Rowe*
3–5 **If ... head.]** *as prose, Pope; as verse, F1*
44–7 **If ... thief.]** *continued to Abhorson, Capell; assigned to Clo., F1*
58 **yare,]** *Theobald;* y'are *F1*

---

60 s.d. **Exeunt ... Pompey.]** *Capell;* Exit. *F1 (after l. 59)*
69 s.d. **Knocking within.]** *Rowe (subs.)*
70 s.d. **Exit Claudio.]** *Capell*
70 **by.]** *F4 (subs.);* by, *F1*
72 s.d. **Enter ... friar.]** *placed as in Dyce; F1 s.d. (Enter Duke.) after l. 72*
85 s.d. **Knocking within.]** *Padua prompt-book (Knock), Rowe (subs.)*
85 s.d. **Exit Provost.]** *Theobald (subs.)*
87 s.d. **Knocking within.]** *Dyce (after Collier)*
89 s.d. **Enter Provost.]** *Theobald (subs.)*
95 **Happily]** *F3;* Happely *F1*
100 **This ... man.]** *continued to Provost, Tyrwhitt conj.; assigned to Duke., F1*
100 **Lordship's]** *Rowe;* Lords *F1*
101 s.p. **Duke.]** *Tyrwhitt conj.;* Pro. *F1*
102–6 **My ... day.]** *as prose, Pope; as verse, F1*
107 s.d. **Exit Messenger.]** *Rowe*
108 s.d. **Aside.]** *Johnson*
113 **fault's]** *Rowe;* faults *F1*
115–8 **I ... before.]** *as prose, Pope; as verse, F1*
117 **putting-on]** *hyphen, Dyce*
119 s.p., s.d. **Prov. Reads]** *Rowe*
130–1 **A ... old.]** *as prose, Pope; as verse, F1*
143 **reakless]** *ed.;* wreaklesse *F1*
169–73 **By ... favor.]** *as prose, Pope; as verse, F1*
170 **guide]** *F4 (subs.);* guide, *F1*
176 **bar'd]** *Malone (bared);* bar'de *F1*
198 **find, ... days]** *Theobald (after Rowe);* finde ... daies, *F1*
210 s.d. **Exeunt.]** *Pope;* Exit. *F1*

IV.iii

Location: *ed. (after Rowe)*
7 **Marry, then]** *Dyce;* marrie then, *F1*
17 **Shoe-tie]** *Capell (subs.);* Shootie *F1*
18 **Pots]** *as proper name, Rowe; not in italics, F1*
19 **"for ... sake."]** *quotes, Dyce*
26–7 **Your ... death.]** *as prose, Pope; as verse, F1*
28 s.d. **Within.]** *Theobald*
39–40 **How ... you?]** *as prose, Pope; as verse, F1*
43–4 **You ... for't.]** *as prose, Pope; as verse, F1*
65 s.d. **Exeunt ... Pompey.]** *Capell*
92 s.d. **Exit Provost.]** *Pope;* Exit. *F1 (after l. 91)*
101 s.d. **with Ragozine's head]** *Dyce (Padua prompt-book calls for a prop head)*
149 **Good ... Provost?]** *as prose, Hudson; as verse, F1*
149 **Good even]** *Rowe;* Good'euen *F1*
158 s.d. **Exit Isabella.]** *Theobald*
165–6 **Nay ... Duke.]** *as prose, Pope; as verse, F1*
172–4 **Yes ... medlar.]** *as prose, Pope; as verse, F1*

IV.iv

Location: *Capell*
3 **manner.]** *Rowe;* manner, *F1*
6 **redeliver]** *Capell;* re- / liuer *F1*
19 s.d. **Exit Escalus.]** *Capell;* Exit. *F1 (after l. 18)*
32 **liv'd]** *F2;* liued *F1*

IV.v

Location: *Pope*
o.s.d. **in ... habit]** *Rowe*
1 s.d. **Giving letters.]** *Johnson*
2 **plot.]** *F4 (subs.);* plot, *F1*
6 **Flavio's]** *ed.;* Flauia's *F1*
8 **Valentius]** *Pope;* Valencius *F1*

---

10 s.d. **Exit.]** *Theobald*

IV.vi

Location: *Capell*
4 **veil]** *Malone;* vaile *F1*

V.i

Location: *Capell*
o.s.d. **Flourish.]** *ed. (from Padua prompt-book)*
o.s.d. **Escalus]** *F2;* Esculus *F1*
o.s.d. **Provost, Officers]** *Capell (subs.)*
13 **me]** *F3;* we *F1*
41 **virgin-violator]** *hyphen, Theobald*
54 **absolute]** *F4;* absolute: *F1*
78 s.d. **To Lucio.]** *Rowe*
159 **nobleman]** *F2;* Noble man *F1*
162 s.d. **Isabella ... guarded.]** *Theobald (after l. 167); placed as in Capell*
167 s.d. **veiled]** *Rowe; s.d. placed as in Wilson; after l. 167, F1*
168 **her]** *F2;* your *F1*
181–2 **Silence ... himself.]** *as verse, Capell; as prose, F1*
206 s.d. **Unveiling.]** *Rowe*
215 **Enough]** *F2;* Enoug *F1*
219 **promised]** *Rowe;* promis'd *F1*
227 **affianc'd]** *Rowe;* affianced *F1*
253 s.d. **Exit Provost.]** *Capell*
259 **My ... throughly.]** *as verse, Wilson; as prose, F1*
259 s.d. **Exit Duke.]** *Capell;* Exit. *F1 (after slanderers. l. 259)*
270 s.d. **Exit an Attendant.]** *Dyce (after Capell)*
277 s.d. **in ... habit.]** *Pope (subs.)*
277 s.d. **Officers with]** *Capell (after Theobald)*
281–2 **Come ... said.]** *as prose, F3; as verse, F1*
283–2 **My ... Provost.]** *as prose, Pope; as verse, F1*
295 **speak:]** *F4;* speake, *F1*
298 **fox,]** *Dyce;* Fox; *F1;* Fox? *F2*
317 **looker-on]** *hyphen, Pope*
325–6 **'Tis ... me?]** *as verse, ed. (after Pope); as prose, F1*
348 s.d. **The ... Duke.]** *Johnson*
355 s.d. **Pulls ... hood.]** *Rowe*
358 s.d. **To Lucio.]** *Johnson*
361 s.d. **To Escalus.]** *Rowe*
362 s.d. **Takes Angelo's seat.]** *Neilson (after Capell)*
379 s.d. **Exeunt ... Provost.]** *Pope (after Rowe);* Exit. *F1*
384 **Not ... habit,]** *Rowe;* (Not ... habit) *F1*
399 s.d. **Mariana]** *Rowe;* Maria *F1*
411 **for]** *italics, Capell*
418 **husband.]** *Rowe;* husband, *F1*
423 **confiscation]** *F2;* confutation *F1*
428 s.d. **Kneeling.]** *Johnson*
429 s.d. **To Lucio.]** *Johnson*
443 s.d. **Kneeling.]** *Rowe*
449 **died]** *F2 (di'd);* dide *F1*
453–4 **subjects, Intents]** *Wilson;* subiects / Intents, *F1;* subjects; / Intents, *F4*
469 s.d. **Exit Provost.]** *Johnson*
472 **grossly]** *F2;* grosselie *F1*
477 s.d. **muffled]** *Dyce (after Capell)*
489 s.d. **Unmuffles Claudio.]** *Capell (subs.)*
490 s.d. **To Isabella.]** *Johnson*
491 **sake.]** *Rowe;* sake *F1*
497 **yours.]** *F2;* yours *F1*
500 s.d. **To Lucio.]** *Rowe*
501 **madman]** *Rowe;* mad man *F1*
522–3 **Marrying ... hanging.]** *as prose, Pope; as verse, F1*
524 s.d. **Exeunt ... Lucio.]** *Dyce*
539 **that's]** *F2;* that *F1*
539 s.d. **Exeunt.]** *Rowe;* FINIS. *F1 (after list of actors)*

Henry VI, Parts 1, 2, and 3

THE THREE HENRY VI PLAYS ascribed to Shakespeare in the Folio of 1623 have prompted much more scholarship than admiration. Indeed, the first, which had not appeared in print before, was esteemed so little that until fairly recent times it was virtually excluded from the canon. Warburton and other eighteenth-century editors, repelled by its coarse depiction of Joan of Arc and by its alleged inelegance of style, assumed that Shakespeare could not have written such a sorry thing; and despite Johnson's warning that "from mere inferiority nothing can be inferred," Edmond Malone's influential *Dissertation on the Three Parts of Henry VI* (1787) led most subsequent commentators either to assign the play to someone else or to regard Shakespeare's part in it as small and unimportant. Thus its authorship has been ascribed, on such evidence as style and use of sources, to a dizzying list of candidates: to Greene, to Greene assisted by Peele and Shakespeare, to Peele and Shakespeare working as a team, to a syndicate comprising Marlowe, Peele, Nashe, Shakespeare, and certain unknown writers. The names of Chapman, Drayton, Kyd, and Lodge have also crept into the discussion. The other two plays in the trilogy had been first printed almost thirty years before: Part 2 as *The First Part of the Contention betwixt the two famous Houses of Yorke and Lancaster* (1594) and Part 3 as *The true Tragedie of Richard Duke of Yorke . . . as it was sundrie times acted by the Right Honourable the Earle of Pembrooke his seruants* (1595). Each was reprinted in 1600, and in 1619 they appeared together as *The Whole Contention betweene the two Famous Houses, Lancaster and Yorke.* These quarto texts, however, vary so strikingly from the versions printed in the

Folio of 1623 that they were long thought to be old plays that Shakespeare had revised (as Malone had argued); only in recent years have they come to be generally regarded as reported texts or "bad" quartos of Shakespeare's works as they were first presented and, with minor alterations, exhumed by Heminge and Condell for publication in the Folio.

The evidence that bears upon and therefore complicates the authorship and date of Part 1 also involves Parts 2 and 3. Although in our present state of knowledge we cannot be certain of the circumstances under which these works were written and produced, any meaningful conjecture must rest upon the facts that follow:

(1) On March 3, 1592, Philip Henslowe, manager of the Rose theatre, recorded in his diary the presentation by Lord Strange's men of a "ne" (i.e. new) play, "Harey the vj." It was repeated fourteen times by June 19, shortly after which all the theatres were closed by an outbreak of the plague.

(2) In *Pierce Penniless*, which was entered in the Stationers' Register on August 8, 1592, and published soon thereafter, Nashe wrote that it would have "joyed brave Talbot, the terror of the French, to think that after he had lain two hundred years in his tomb he should triumph again on the stage, and have his bones new embalmed with the tears of ten thousand spectators at least (at several times) who in the tragedian that represents his person imagine they behold him fresh bleeding." The allusion would seem to fit *1 Henry VI*, in which Talbot plays a leading part.

(3) Shortly before his death on September 3, 1592, Greene, in *A Groatsworth of Wit*, warned certain of his fellow playwrights—presumably Marlowe,

587

Nashe, and Peele—about "an upstart crow, beautified with our feathers, that with his *tiger's heart wrapp'd in a player's hide* supposes he is as well able to bombast out a blank verse as the best of you; and being an absolute *Johannes fac totum*, is in his own conceit the only Shake-scene in a country." The allusion to Shakespeare is reinforced by the parody of a line in *3 Henry VI* (I.iv.137), which appears also in *The True Tragedy*: "O tiger's heart wrapt in a woman's hide."

Efforts to align these data and to ascertain their relevance to the three Henry VI plays in the Folio have led to a staggering mass of inference, interpretation, and conjecture. To rehearse all of this material, some of it extremely knotty, would be inappropriate here, but even a small sampling will indicate its scope. It has been suggested, for example, that Greene's misquotation from Part 3 makes it impossible to identify "Harey the vj" with *1 Henry VI*, since otherwise we must assume that the entire trilogy had been brought before the public between March 1592 (when the Henslowe play was "new") and the following June (when all theatrical production was halted by the plague); that Greene, ill and crotchety and jealous of a younger man's success, was only sneering at Shakespeare's pretensions as an actor; that Greene was charging Shakespeare with plagiarizing his and his associates' work, in which case *2* and *3 Henry VI* should be regarded as unauthorized adaptations of *The Contention* and *The True Tragedy*, and *1 Henry VI* either as a potboiler intended as a prologue to the plays that had been pilfered or (in Malone's words) as "the entire or nearly the entire production of some ancient dramatist"; that *1 Henry VI*, hastily thrown together to exploit the rival Pembroke troupe's success with *2* and *3 Henry VI*, was begun by Greene and Nashe and completed by Shakespeare (perhaps with Nashe's aid) for presentation by Strange's men in 1592; that Greene had blocked out the whole trilogy and written much of it when Nashe was called in to provide the first act of Part 1, Peele to supply certain things in Parts 2 and 3, and Shakespeare to touch up all three plays; that since Shakespeare was probably connected with Pembroke's troupe as early as 1592, "Harey the vj," which belonged to Strange's men, could not have been his work; that since *The Contention* and *The True Tragedy*—the latter certainly and the former probably belonging to Pembroke's men—contain many borrowings from Part 1, all three plays must have been in the Pembroke repertory, and therefore the Strange troupe's "Harey the vj" could not have been Part 1; that *The Contention* and *The True Tragedy*, formerly the property of Pembroke's men, were somehow acquired by Strange's men and revised by Shakespeare (who was a member of their troupe) as Parts 2 and 3 in 1592, when he also touched up an old Talbot play that Greene had written about 1589 and revised in 1591.

With some notable exceptions, modern scholars are agreed that *The Contention* and *The True Tragedy* are corrupt memorial reconstructions, not sources, of *2* and *3 Henry VI*. Thus Malone's once widely shared opinion that Shakespeare reworked a pair of older plays has now been generally abandoned for Peter Alexander's view that *2* and *3 Henry VI* are Shakespeare's own creation, and that the two quartos are reported texts which were pieced together from memory and perhaps from actors' parts in the possession of former members of the Pembroke troupe. In short, mutilation has replaced revision as a principle of explanation. But if Alexander (and Madeleine Doran working independently of him) have enabled us to redefine the problem, the problem still remains, and the precise connection between the six related works —"Harey the vj," the two quartos of 1594–95, and the three Henry VI plays ascribed to Shakespeare in the Folio of 1623—is still a matter of dispute. Perhaps, as certain scholars think, Shakespeare wrote *2* and *3 Henry VI* for Pembroke's men and then, encouraged by their success, prefaced them with a revision of "Harey the vj" that had somehow been secured from Strange's men. On the other hand, it is tempting to believe, with A. S. Cairncross, that *1 Henry VI* (which is unrelated to "Harey the vj") preceded Parts 2 and 3 in point of composition, that all three plays were written about 1590 for Pembroke's men or for their predecessors, and that they are mainly if not entirely Shakespeare's work. But unless new data come to light such educated guesses must take the place of knowledge.

Fortunately, the sources of these plays do not pose so many problems. The fact that different parts of *1 Henry VI* seem to draw on different works—for example, the Joan of Arc material in I.ii and V.iv from the second (1587) edition of Holinshed and certain details about the unruly servingmen in I.iii and III.i from Richard Fabyan's *Chronicle* (1559 ed.)—has been advanced as proof that several writers were involved; but it is easier to assume that here as elsewhere Shakespeare consulted various books and took from each what he most liked or needed. Thus in *1 Henry VI* Bullough finds traces of Holinshed and Geoffrey of Monmouth's *Historia Regum Britanniae*; in *2 Henry VI*, of Foxe's *Acts and Monuments*, Grafton's *Chronicle at Large* (for the spurious miracle of St. Albans in II.i), and Holinshed; and in *3 Henry VI*, of *A Mirror for Magistrates*. Despite these and other signs of Shakespeare's varied reading, the major source for all three plays is Edward Hall's *Union of the Two Noble and Illustre Families of Lancaster and York* (1548).

This famous book exemplifies the notion—as old as Augustine's *City of God*—that history, which seems to reel from one disaster to another, reveals a steady moral purpose because its course is set by God. To be sure, most fifteenth-century chroniclers had buttressed their political aspirations and attachments with deific sanctions. For example, Thomas Walsingham, the last of the line of historians produced by the great Benedictine monastery of St. Albans, was so incorrigibly hostile to Richard II and so sympathetic to Henry IV that he records the rise of the House of Lancaster as preordained by God; and John Hardyng, a shifty politician whose last patron was Richard, Duke of York, and whose clumsily versified chronicle represents almost the nadir of fifteenth-century historiography, views the savage Yorkists as instruments of providence. Compared to these, Polydore Vergil marks a real advance. This learned Italian, whose *Historia Anglica* was commissioned by Henry VII, divorced the interpretation of recent English history from partisan politics to advance the no less providential but more objective notion of divine justice as impartially punishing sin and rewarding virtue. But it was Edward Hall who most insistently depicted the triumphs of the house of Tudor and of the English Reformation as reciprocal signs of God's benign control. Like the Book of Genesis and the *Aeneid*, his *Union* tells the story of a people that, under divine guidance, fulfills its destiny. Hall's subject, like Shakespeare's in eight of the ten plays that he wrote on English history, is England in the fifteenth century, when two great ducal houses were competing for the throne. Dealing as it does with crime and retribution, with disorder and misrule, the *Union* is diffuse and episodic; but it generates real power, and its climax is impressive: the accession of the Lancastrian Earl of Richmond as Henry VII and his marriage to a daughter of the house of York are, as Hall presents them, blessings sent by God. From this union of the red rose with the white, peace descended "out of heaven into England" and the House of Tudor was secured upon the throne. Thus Hall had a double purpose: to expound the providential theme that "as by discord great things decay and fall to ruin, so the same by concord be revived and erected," and to celebrate the glories of the Tudors. Like many other writers of his age, Hall considered politics to be a branch of morals.

That Shakespeare, near the start of his career, should have been attracted to this patriotic theme is not at all surprising, and that it so clearly underlies the three parts of Henry VI and their sequel *Richard III* reinforces the conjecture that these four plays —the so-called first tetralogy—were conceived and written by one man. Shakespeare himself implies as much when, in the epilogue to *Henry V*, he speaks of the tumultuous events of Henry VI's reign "Which oft our stage hath shown"; and Johnson, who knew nothing about critical bibliography but had an ample fund of common sense, pointed to the fact that all three Henry VI plays are built upon a "series of transactions" that laces them together. Viewed as a cycle on the political disorders of fifteenth-century England, they have more merit than some of their detractors, including Coleridge and Hazlitt, have been willing to concede. For a young writer to undertake so big a subject as fifty years of English history required both skill and valor; and if the skill is sometimes lacking, the valor certifies his bold intention. Indeed, the bold intention, which imparts an almost epic sweep and power to plays so anecdotal and diffuse, may be said almost to justify the flaws. If Shakespeare, in the strength and plumage of his youth, had taken fewer chances he would not have done so much.

The audacity of youth is everywhere apparent: in the big, unwieldy canvas filled with an enormous cast of characters, in the convolutions of the plot, in the pageantry and violent action, in sheer theatricality. But it is most apparent in the style, which tends towards high and sometimes tedious declamation. Normally, all the characters speak alike, and their undifferentiated speech—a blank verse in which the unit is the single line stuffed with epithets and adorned with Latin tags and classical allusions—owes much to Seneca and Marlowe. It often gets beyond control, as in the imagistic chaos of the opening lines of *1 Henry VI* and in the bombast that Greene (of all people) saw fit to ridicule. More often, however, it is merely strident and inflated, and heavy in its metronomic beat:

> Is Talbot slain, the Frenchmen's only scourge,
> Your kingdom's terror and black Nemesis?
> O, were mine eyeballs into bullets turn'd,
> That I in rage might shoot them at your faces!
> O, that I could but call these dead to life,
> It were enough to fright the realm of France!
> Were but his picture left amongst you here,
> It would amaze the proudest of you all.
> Give me their bodies, that I may bear them hence
> And give them burial as beseems their worth.
>
> (IV.vii.77–86)

This kind of language, the basic idiom of these plays, continually approaches oratory. We hear it, for example, when Talbot baits the French before Bordeaux (Part 1, IV.ii), when York defends his title to the throne (Part 2, II.iii), even when Young Clifford soliloquizes on his fate (Part 3, II.vi). An even stiffer formalism appears in the monotonous stichomythy of King Edward's wooing (Part 3, III.ii), in the almost ritualistic comments on the carnage wrought at Towton (Part 3, II.v), and in the antiphonal couplets that Talbot and his son exchange before they die (Part 1, IV.v–vi). When, occasionally, Shakespeare goes beyond this sort of thing we are duly gratified. The prose of the Jack Cade scenes in Part 2, like all of Shakespeare's prose, reveals an ear so sharp that the language, in its supple, idiomatic precision, sounds not written but transcribed. Sometimes, too, the verse reminds us of Shakespeare's later work in its concentrated power, as when Young Clifford comes upon his slaughtered father:

> O, let the vile world end,
> And the premised flames of the last day
> Knit earth and heaven together!
> Now let the general trumpet blow his blast,
> Particularities and petty sounds
> To cease! Wast thou ordain'd, dear father,
> To lose thy youth in peace, and to achieve
> The silvery livery of advised age,
> And in thy reverence, and thy chair-days, thus
> To die in ruffian battle? (Part 2, V.ii.40–49)

These plays, so long derided or condemned, reveal an arc of structure. The action of Part 1, which carries through Parts 2 and 3, is the long, slow fall of England from the funeral of the warrior-king Henry V, through the erosion of his French conquests, the decline of royal power, and the resulting civil broils that spread to civil war. In depicting these events Shakespeare does not hammer so relentlessly as Hall on the theme that Henry's troubled reign was in expiation for Bullingbrook's usurpation of the throne in 1399; but none the less he deals in cause and consequence, relating circumstance to character and presenting not a random string of episodes but the moral consequences of disorder. "No simple man that sees / This jarring discord of nobility," says Exeter as events are moving inexorably towards Talbot's overthrow,

> This shouldering of each other in the court,
> This factious bandying of their favorites,
> But that it doth presage some ill event.
> 'Tis much, when sceptres are in children's hands;
> But more, when envy breeds unkind division:
> There comes the ruin, there begins confusion.
>
> (Part 1, IV.i.187–94)

To mould a theme like this requires a shaping hand, and therefore no one should read these plays to learn what really happened in the fifteenth century. Shakespeare manipulates his data in a way that no historian would approve; he telescopes, distorts, and rearranges "facts"; he even fabricates whole episodes to reinforce his own interpretation of the things he found in Hall and Holinshed. The reason for such license is apparent: beneath the busy, sometimes cluttered surface of the action he directs the movements of events to underscore his theme. This theme, which dominates the tetralogy, may be stated as the loss of national identity and national purpose through the evils of disorder and their restoration through the advent of the Tudors.

Even *1 Henry VI*, which is so loose and anecdotal that Bullough calls it "not so much a Chronicle play as a fantasia on historical themes," is adjusted to this end. At the very opening of the play the pageantry of Henry V's funeral is disrupted by the bickering of the dead king's brothers and by the news that Henry's French possessions—the trophies of his splendid reign —are slipping from control. The double motif thus proclaimed—internal dissension that dissipates the power of England—gains momentum as the play proceeds upon its sometimes helter-skelter way. At home, the rivalry of the Lord Protector Gloucester and the Bishop of Winchester, who exploit the weakness of the youthful Henry VI, is like "a viperous worm / That gnaws the bowels of the commonwealth" (III.i.72–73). Abroad, brave Talbot, once the terror of the French, is ill supported and betrayed by his allies, and so, unable to withstand the witch and strumpet Joan of Arc, he falls.

There are two main links between the bustling action of Part 1 and the plays that follow. First, in the famous Temple Garden scene (II.iv)—which many early scholars considered one of Shakespeare's contributions to the work that he had undertaken to revise—the fateful problem of succession is announced in the quarrel between Richard Plantagenet, Duke of York, and the Lancastrian Earl of Somerset. Warwick's choric comment on their altercation is prophetic of the ruin to come:

> this brawl to-day,
> Grown to this faction in the Temple Garden,
> Shall send between the Red Rose and the White
> A thousand souls to death and deadly night.
>
> (II.iv.124–27)

Second, although Henry VI's betrothal, through his unscrupulous agent Suffolk, to Margaret of Anjou provides a kind of cadence for Part 1, it also supplies both circumstance and motive for Part 2. Involving as it does the breach of Henry's contract with Joan of Armagnac and the surrender of yet more territory in France, it indicates the spreading moral blight that saps and finally destroys the royal power; by linking Henry with the she-wolf Margaret (who succeeds the fallen Joan of Arc as England's evil star) it portends new dangers for the throne; and by preparing for the intrigue between Margaret and Suffolk it generates a major motif of the plot in the succeeding play. As Part 1 closes with the prospects of a splendid royal wedding and a patched-up peace with France, Suffolk's declaration of his dark intentions suggests that mounting troubles are in store for England:

> Margaret shall now be Queen, and rule the King;
> But I will rule both her, the King, and realm.
>
> (V.v.107–8)

Part 2 is like its predecessor in its linear, episodic structure, but it is much more soundly built. For one thing, the lightly sketched but vivid episodes with which the play is dotted—the Duchess of Gloucester's incantation scene (I.iv), the spurious miracle of St. Albans (II.i), the contest between Horner and his man (III.i), Suffolk's execution (IV.i), and Iden's capture of Jack Cade (IV.x)—are, unlike the encounter between Talbot and the Countess of Auvergne in Part 1 (II.iii), not merely anecdotal but organic to the plot. For another, all the complicated strands of intrigue converge upon the rise of Richard, Duke of York, whose career gives shape and movement to the play. Thus such potentially disparate elements as Margaret's love affair with Suffolk, Cardinal Beaufort's hatred of his nephew Gloucester, the fall of Gloucester and his wife, and Cade's rebellion are brought into alignment and contribute to the one main thrust of action. Such unity, achieved through the most drastic rearrangement of historical data, is assisted by the bold, broad strokes with which the play unfolds. For example, in some two hundred fifty lines the opening scene moves from the pomp and glitter of the Queen's reception at the English court, to Gloucester's angry comments on King Henry's "shameful" league and "fatal" marriage, to Beaufort's and Buckingham's design to "hoise Duke Humphrey from his seat," to Salisbury's hope to save the realm by making peace between the warring factions, and so to York's soliloquy, with which the scene is closed. This soliloquy serves a triple function: it reveals York's brutal strength of purpose, it gives us his realistic views on politics, and it voices his intention

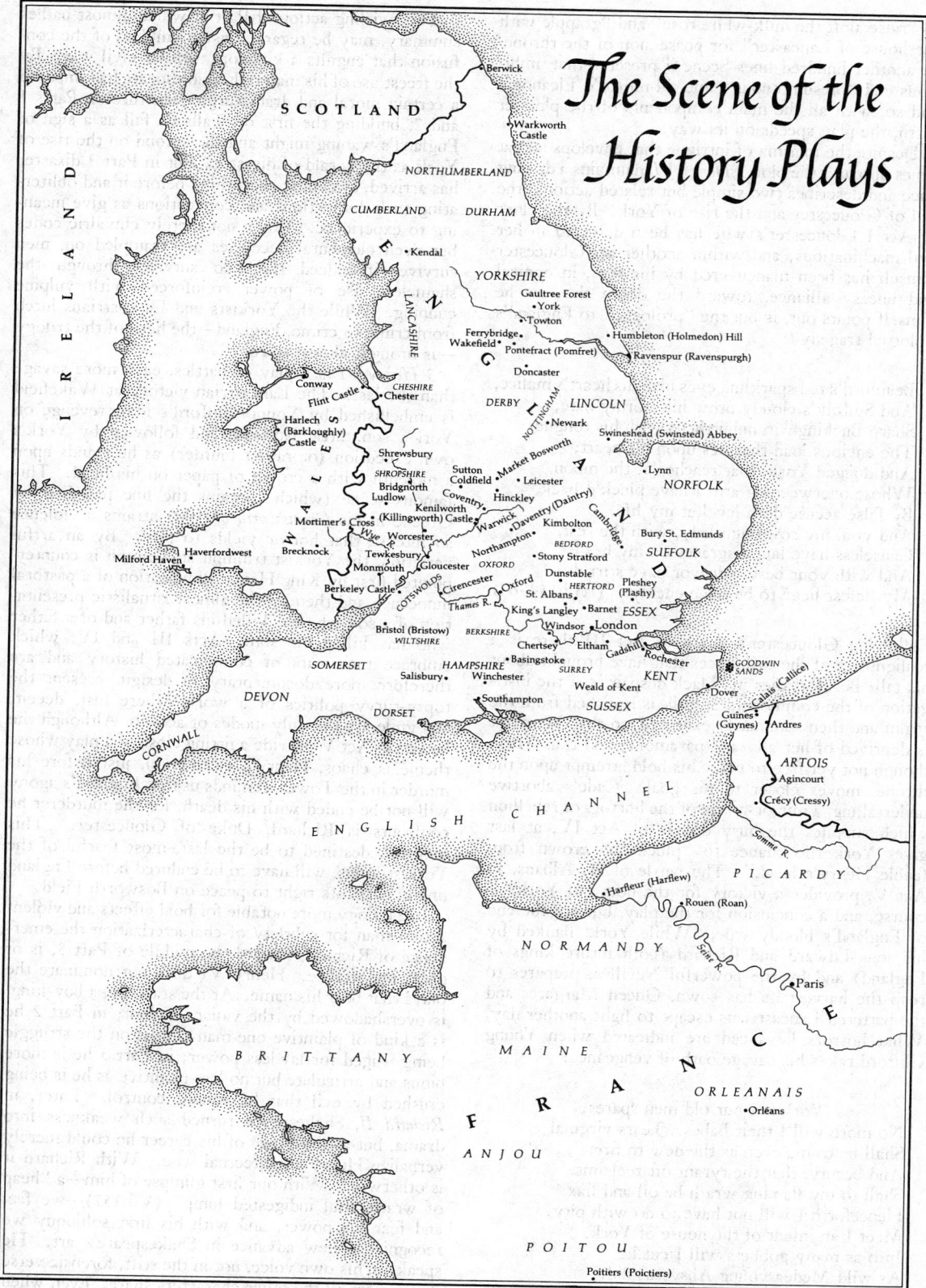

The Scene of the History Plays

SCOTLAND

Berwick

Warkworth
Castle

NORTHUMBERLAND

CUMBERLAND   DURHAM

Kendal

YORKSHIRE

Gaultree Forest
York
Towton

Ferrybridge   Humbleton (Holmedon) Hill
Wakefield   Pontefract (Pomfret)   Ravenspur (Ravenspurgh)

Doncaster

LANCASHIRE

Conway   CHESHIRE
Flint Castle   Chester   DERBY   LINCOLN

Harlech
(Barkloughly)   Newark
Castle   NOTTINGHAM

Shrewsbury   Swineshead (Swinsted) Abbey

SHROPSHIRE   Sutton   Market Bosworth
Coldfield   Leicester   Lynn
Bridgnorth   Coventry   Hinckley   NORFOLK
Ludlow   Kenilworth
(Killingworth) Castle   Daventry (Daintry)   Cambridge
Mortimer's Cross   Warwick   Kimbolton
Wye   Worcester   Northampton   BEDFORD   Bury St. Edmunds
Brecknock   Tewkesbury   OXFORD   Stony Stratford   SUFFOLK
Milford Haven   Monmouth   Gloucester   Dunstable
    Berkeley Castle   COTSWOLDS   Cirencester   Oxford   Pleshey
    Thames R.   St. Albans   HERTFORD   (Plashy)
    King's Langley   Barnet   ESSEX
    Bristol (Bristow)   Windsor   London
    WILTSHIRE   BERKSHIRE   Chertsey   Eltham   Gadshill
    SOMERSET   Basingstoke   Rochester   GOODWIN
    HAMPSHIRE   SURREY   SANDS
    Salisbury   Winchester   KENT   Dover   Calais (Callice)
    DEVON   Weald of Kent   Guines   Ardres
    DORSET   Southampton   SUSSEX   (Guynes)
    CORNWALL   ARTOIS
    Agincourt
    ENGLISH   CHANNEL   Somme R.   Crécy (Cressy)
    PICARDY
    Harfleur (Harflew)
    Rouen (Roan)
    NORMANDY   Seine R.
    Paris
    MAINE   Seine R.
    BRITTANY   F R A N C E
    ORLEANAIS
    ANJOU   Orléans
    POITOU
    Poitiers (Poictiers)

WALES

ENGLAND

IRELAND

Haverfordwest

to "raise aloft the milk-white rose" and "grapple with the house of Lancaster" for possession of the throne. In another hundred lines Scene ii presents that ambitious and "presumptuous dame, ill-nurtur'd Eleanor," and so, with all the main components of the plot set forth, the play speeds on its way.

Despite the miasma of intrigue that envelops and at times obscures the plot, *2 Henry VI* maintains a driving pace and describes two simple but related actions: the fall of Gloucester and the rise of York. By the close of Act I Gloucester's wife has been detected in her evil machinations; and within another act Gloucester himself has been maneuvered by his foes, in cynical and uneasy alliance, toward the doom that, as he himself points out, is but the "prologue" to England's "plotted tragedy":

> Beauford's red sparkling eyes blab his heart's malice,
> And Suffolk's cloudy brow his stormy hate;
> Sharp Buckingham unburthens with his tongue
> The envious load that lies upon his heart;
> And dogged York, that reaches at the moon,
> Whose overweening arm I have pluck'd back,
> By false accuse doth level at my life.
> And you, my sovereign lady, with the rest,
> Causeless have laid disgraces on my head,
> And with your best endeavor have stirr'd up
> My liefest liege to be mine enemy.   (III.i.154–64)

Following Gloucester's death in Act III there is a realignment of the evil forces that have brought about his fall: Beaufort dies in "black despair"; at the instigation of the commoners Suffolk is banished from the realm and then summarily executed, so that Margaret is deprived of her ally and paramour; and thus York, though not yet free to make his bold attempt upon the throne, moves closer to his goal. Cade's abortive undertaking, a mirror-image of the horrors of rebellion which supplies the busy doings of Act IV, at last gives York the chance to "pluck the crown from feeble Henry's head." The battle of St. Albans, in Act V, provides a victory for the house of York, of course, and a conclusion for the play, but not the end of England's bloody woe. While York, flanked by his sons Edward and Richard (both future kings of England) and by the powerful Nevilles, prepares to reap the harvest he has sown, Queen Margaret and the battered Lancastrians escape to fight another day. What horrors lie ahead are indicated when Young Clifford takes his savage oath of vengeance:

> York not our old men spares;
> No more will I their babes. Tears virginal
> Shall be to me even as the dew to fire,
> And beauty, that the tyrant oft reclaims,
> Shall to my flaming wrath be oil and flax.
> Henceforth I will not have to do with pity.
> Meet I an infant of the house of York,
> Into as many gobbets will I cut it
> As wild Medea young Absyrtus did;
> In cruelty will I seek out my fame.   (V.ii.51–60)

The swirling action of Part 3, which almost baffles summary, may be regarded as an emblem of the confusion that engulfs a kingdom torn by civil war. By the freest use of his materials Shakespeare had imposed a certain moral and dramaturgic structure on Parts 1 and 2, building the first on Talbot's fall as a sign of England's waning might and the second on the rise of York as the herald of disaster. But in Part 3 disaster has arrived, sweeping everything before it and obliterating such distinctions and conventions as give meaning to experience. When not merely chivalric codes but even elemental decencies are trampled on, men survive—if indeed they do survive—through the shameless use of power, reinforced with vulpine cunning. While the Yorkists and Lancastrians lurch from crime to crime, England—the hero of the trilogy —is brought almost to ruin.

3 Henry VI is a play of battles, each more savage than the last. The Lancastrian victory at Wakefield is embellished by Young Clifford's idiot revenge on York's son, little Rutland, and followed by York's own execution (or rather murder) as he stands upon a molehill with a crown of paper on his head. This famous scene (which contains the line parodied by Greene in his *Groatsworth of Wit*) attains a violence so intense that horror yields to pity. By an artful variation, the Yorkist triumph at Towton is counterpointed first by King Henry's invocation of a pastoral innocence and then by the almost ritualistic presentation of a son who has killed his father and of a father who has killed his son. Acts III and IV, which embrace ten years of complicated history and are therefore more documentary in design, present the topsy-turvy politics of a world where lust, deceit, and guile are the only modes of action. Although the battles in Act V provide a fitting close of a play whose theme is chaos, Henry's valediction, just before his murder in the Tower, reminds us that England's agony will not be ended with his death, for the murderer he confronts is Richard, Duke of Gloucester. This monster, destined to be the last, most fearful of the Yorkist kings, will have to be endured before England finally earns its right to peace on Bosworth Field.

In a trilogy more notable for bold effects and violent action than for subtlety of characterization the emergence of Richard, toward the middle of Part 3, is of great importance. Henry VI does not dominate the plays that bear his name. At the start, he, a boy-king, is overshadowed by the valiant Talbot; in Part 2 he is a kind of plaintive one-man chorus on the struggle being waged for lawless power; in Part 3 he is more pious and articulate but no less plaintive as he is being crushed by evil that he cannot control. Later, in *Richard II*, Shakespeare turned such weakness into drama, but at this stage of his career he could merely verbalize Henry's ineffectual woe. With Richard it is otherwise. With our first glimpse of him—a "heap of wrath, foul indigested lump" (V.i.157)—we feel and fear his power, and with his first soliloquy we recognize a new advance in Shakespeare's art. He speaks in his own voice, not in the stiff, forensic verse that almost all the other characters share. Even when

Margaret bids farewell to Suffolk and when York, weeping for his murdered son, denounces his tormentors, their language is contrived for declamation: it serves a public function, and in a sense it insulates the speakers within a web of rhetoric. When Richard comes upon the scene, however, the very movement of his speech, quite apart from what he says, reveals the man behind the voice: mocking, clever, cruel, and supple.

> Why, I can smile, and murther whiles I smile,
> And cry "Content" to that which grieves my heart,
> And wet my cheeks with artificial tears,
> And frame my face to all occasions.
> I'll drown more sailors than the mermaid shall,
> I'll slay more gazers than the basilisk,

> I'll play the orator as well as Nestor,
> Deceive more slily than Ulysses could,
> And, like a Sinon, take another Troy.
> I can add colors to the chameleon,
> Change shapes with Proteus for advantages,
> And set the murtherous Machevil to school.
> Can I do this, and cannot get a crown?
> Tut, were it farther off, I'll pluck it down.
>
> (III.ii.182–95)

Already, it is clear, *Richard III* was taking shape in Shakespeare's mind. If the Henry VI plays had served no other purpose, it would have been enough that they supplied him an apprenticeship and prepared him for that great event.

Herschel Baker

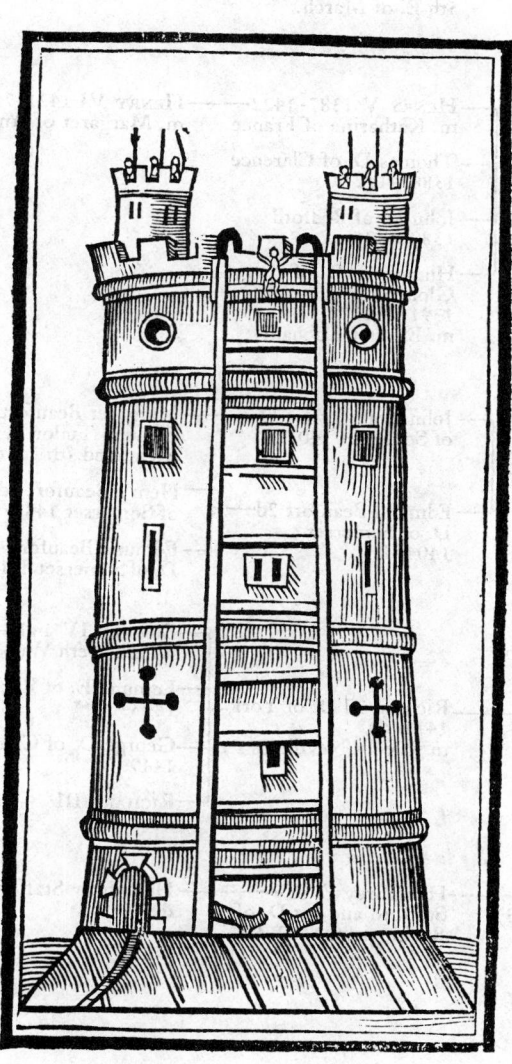

A scaling ladder. From Robert Ward, *Animadversions of War* (1639). This picture of a scaling ladder may be somewhat fanciful but it illustrates none the less the principle behind that "engine of war." Sheltered both within and behind the structure, a sizable force of besiegers could approach right up to the walls of a city, avoiding the shot, rocks, and molten lead directed at them by the city's defenders. The scaling ladders employed in *1 Henry VI* (II.i), when the English forces under Talbot surprise the city of Orleans and capture it from the French, were presumably of simpler form, probably nothing more than ordinary ladders. (*By permission of the Huntington Library, San Marino, California*)

"Edward's Sacred Blood"
The Descendants of Edward III

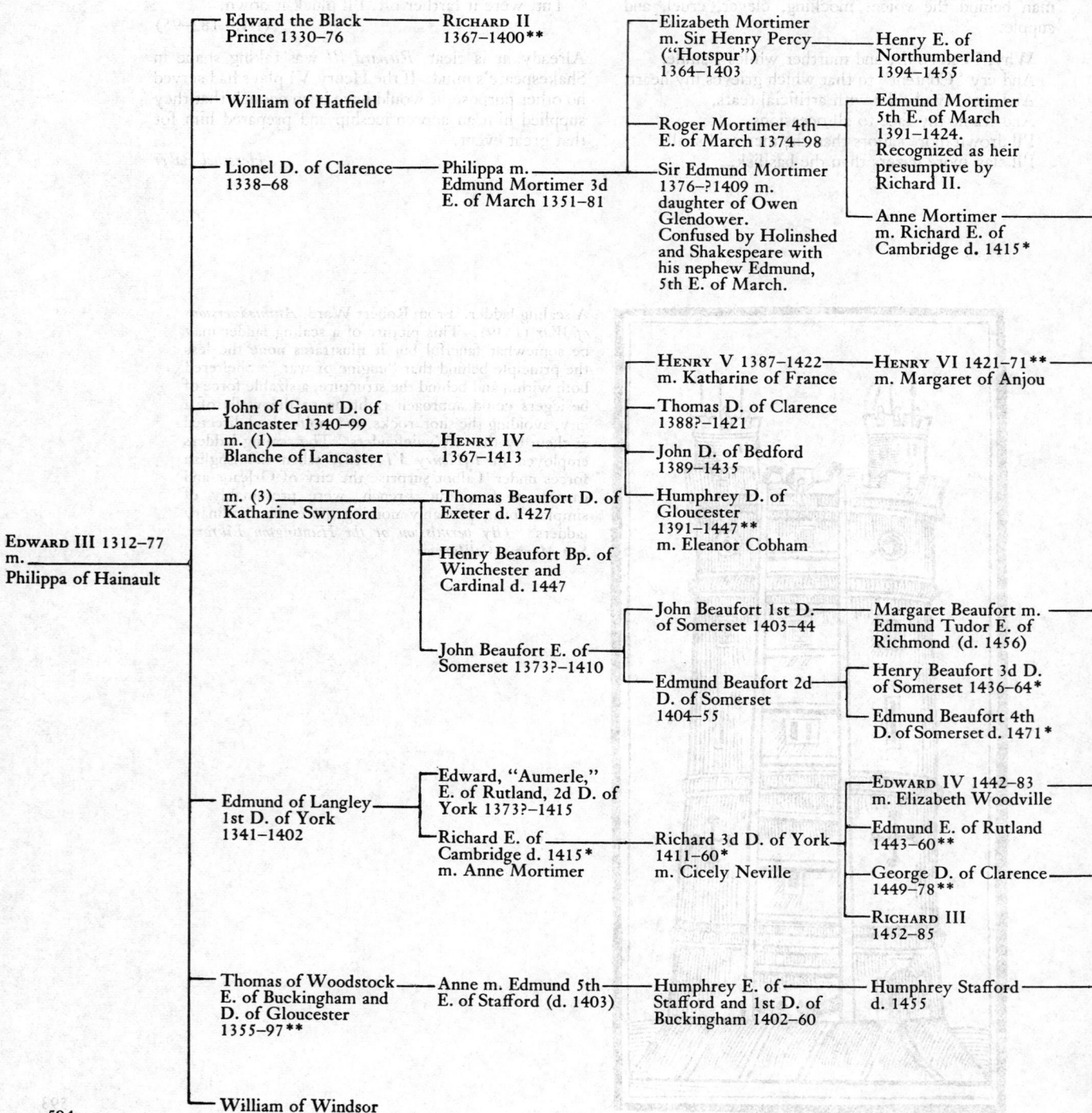

EDWARD III 1312–77
m.
Philippa of Hainault

- Edward the Black Prince 1330–76 — RICHARD II 1367–1400**

- William of Hatfield

- Lionel D. of Clarence 1338–68 — Philippa m. Edmund Mortimer 3d E. of March 1351–81
  - Elizabeth Mortimer m. Sir Henry Percy ("Hotspur") 1364–1403 — Henry E. of Northumberland 1394–1455
  - Roger Mortimer 4th E. of March 1374–98
    - Edmund Mortimer 5th E. of March 1391–1424. Recognized as heir presumptive by Richard II.
    - Anne Mortimer m. Richard E. of Cambridge d. 1415*
  - Sir Edmund Mortimer 1376–?1409 m. daughter of Owen Glendower. Confused by Holinshed and Shakespeare with his nephew Edmund, 5th E. of March.

- John of Gaunt D. of Lancaster 1340–99
  m. (1) Blanche of Lancaster — HENRY IV 1367–1413
    - HENRY V 1387–1422 m. Katharine of France — HENRY VI 1421–71** m. Margaret of Anjou
    - Thomas D. of Clarence 1388?–1421
    - John D. of Bedford 1389–1435
    - Humphrey D. of Gloucester 1391–1447** m. Eleanor Cobham
  m. (3) Katharine Swynford
    - Thomas Beaufort D. of Exeter d. 1427
    - Henry Beaufort Bp. of Winchester and Cardinal d. 1447
    - John Beaufort E. of Somerset 1373?–1410
      - John Beaufort 1st D. of Somerset 1403–44 — Margaret Beaufort m. Edmund Tudor E. of Richmond (d. 1456)
      - Edmund Beaufort 2d D. of Somerset 1404–55
        - Henry Beaufort 3d D. of Somerset 1436–64*
        - Edmund Beaufort 4th D. of Somerset d. 1471*

- Edmund of Langley 1st D. of York 1341–1402
  - Edward, "Aumerle," E. of Rutland, 2d D. of York 1373?–1415
  - Richard E. of Cambridge d. 1415* m. Anne Mortimer — Richard 3d D. of York 1411–60* m. Cicely Neville
    - EDWARD IV 1442–83 m. Elizabeth Woodville
    - Edmund E. of Rutland 1443–60**
    - George D. of Clarence 1449–78**
    - RICHARD III 1452–85

- Thomas of Woodstock E. of Buckingham and D. of Gloucester 1355–97** — Anne m. Edmund 5th E. of Stafford (d. 1403) — Humphrey E. of Stafford and 1st D. of Buckingham 1402–60 — Humphrey Stafford d. 1455

- William of Windsor

594

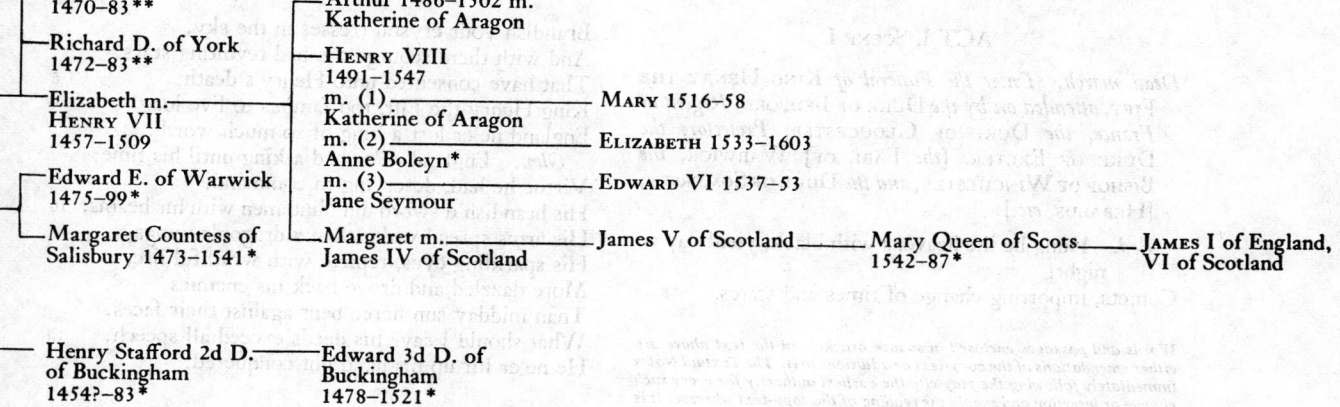

THE KINGS AND QUEENS OF ENGLAND	SOME PRINCIPAL EVENTS
Richard II 1377–99	1399 Deposition of Richard II
Henry IV 1399–1413	1403 Battle of Shrewsbury
Henry V 1413–22	1415 Battle of Agincourt
Henry VI 1422–61	1420 Treaty of Troyes
Edward IV 1461–83	1431 Execution of Joan of Arc
Richard III 1483–85	1450 Cade's Rebellion
Henry VII 1485–1509	1455 First Battle of St. Albans
Henry VIII 1509–47	1460 Battle of Wakefield
Edward VI 1547–53	1461 Second Battle of St. Albans
Mary 1553–58	1471 Battle of Tewkesbury
Elizabeth 1558–1603	1485 Battle of Bosworth Field
James I 1603–25	1520 Field of the Cloth of Gold

*Executed
**Murdered
Many persons of no significance to
Shakespeare's history plays are omitted.

Richard 3d D. of York
1411–60*; husband of
Cicely Neville and
father of EDWARD IV
and RICHARD III

Edward Prince of
Wales 1453–71**

Henry Tudor E. of
Richmond, HENRY VII
1457–1509

EDWARD V
1470–83**

Richard D. of York
1472–83**

Elizabeth m.
HENRY VII
1457–1509

Edward E. of Warwick
1475–99*

Margaret Countess of
Salisbury 1473–1541*

Arthur 1486–1502 m.
Katherine of Aragon

HENRY VIII
1491–1547
m. (1)
Katherine of Aragon — MARY 1516–58
m. (2)
Anne Boleyn* — ELIZABETH 1533–1603
m. (3)
Jane Seymour — EDWARD VI 1537–53

Margaret m.
James IV of Scotland — James V of Scotland — Mary Queen of Scots — JAMES I of England,
1542–87* VI of Scotland

Henry Stafford 2d D.
of Buckingham
1454?–83*

Edward 3d D. of
Buckingham
1478–1521*

595

The First Part of Henry the Sixth

ACT I, SCENE I

Dead march. Enter the Funeral of KING HENRY THE FIFT, *attended on by the* DUKE OF BEDFORD, *Regent of France, the* DUKE OF GLOUCESTER, *Protector, the* DUKE OF EXETER, [*the* EARL OF] WARWICK, *the* BISHOP OF WINCHESTER, *and the* DUKE OF SOMERSET; [HERALDS, *etc.*].

Bed. Hung be the heavens with black, yield day to night!
Comets, importing change of times and states,
Brandish your crystal tresses in the sky,
And with them scourge the bad revolting stars
That have consented unto Henry's death: 5
King Henry the Fift, too famous to live long!
England ne'er lost a king of so much worth.
  Glou. England ne'er had a king until his time:
Virtue he had, deserving to command;
His brandish'd sword did blind men with his beams; 10
His arms spread wider than a dragon's wings;
His sparkling eyes, replete with wrathful fire,
More dazzled and drove back his enemies
Than midday sun fierce bent against their faces.
What should I say? his deeds exceed all speech: 15
He ne'er lift up his hand but conquered.

Words and passages enclosed in square brackets in the text above are either emendations of the copy-text or additions to it. The Textual Notes immediately following the play cite the earliest authority for every such change or insertion and supply the reading of the copy-text wherever it is emended in this edition.

I.i. Location: Westminster Abbey.
o.s.d. **Dead march**: funeral march.   **Fift**: Fifth.
1. **Hung ... black**. Alluding to the fact that the "heavens"—a roof or canopy projecting over the stage—were draped in black for the presentation of a tragedy.   2. **importing**: signifying, foretelling.

3. **Brandish**: flourish, flash.   **crystal tresses**: i.e. shining tails.
4. **revolting**: rebelling, i.e. traitorous.
5. **consented unto**: i.e. conspired to bring about.
9. **Virtue**: merit, power.   10. **his**: its.
16. **lift**: lifted.   **but conquered**: without conquering.

Exe. We mourn in black, why mourn we not in
    blood?
Henry is dead, and never shall revive.
Upon a wooden coffin we attend,
And death's dishonorable victory   20
We with our stately presence glorify,
Like captives bound to a triumphant car.
What? shall we curse the planets of mishap
That plotted thus our glory's overthrow?
Or shall we think the subtile-witted French   25
Conjurers and sorcerers, that, afraid of him,
By magic verses have contriv'd his end?

Win. He was a king blest of the King of kings.
Unto the French the dreadful Judgment Day
So dreadful will not be as was his sight.   30
The battles of the Lord of hosts he fought;
The Church's prayers made him so prosperous.

Glou. The Church? where is it? Had not church-
    men pray'd,
His thread of life had not so soon decay'd.
None do you like but an effeminate prince,   35
Whom like a schoolboy you may overawe.

Win. Gloucester, what e'er we like, thou art
    Protector,
And lookest to command the Prince and realm.
Thy wife is proud, she holdeth thee in awe,
More than God or religious churchmen may.   40

Glou. Name not religion, for thou lov'st the flesh,
And ne'er throughout the year to church thou go'st
Except it be to pray against thy foes.

Bed. Cease, cease these jars and rest your minds in
    peace.
Let's to the altar. Heralds, wait on us.   45
In stead of gold, we'll offer up our arms,
Since arms avail not now that Henry's dead.
Posterity, await for wretched years,
When at their mothers' moist'ned eyes babes shall
    suck,
Our isle be made a nourish of salt tears,   50
And none but women left to wail the dead.
Henry the Fift, thy ghost I invocate:
Prosper this realm, keep it from civil broils,
Combat with adverse planets in the heavens!
A far more glorious star thy soul will make   55
Than Julius Caesar or bright—

Enter a MESSENGER.

Mess. My honorable lords, health to you all!
Sad tidings bring I to you out of France,
Of loss, of slaughter, and discomfiture:

19. wooden: i.e. insensible, useless.   22. car: chariot.
27. verses: incantations, spells.   32. prosperous: successful.
37. Protector. According to Hall (Bullough, III, 44), the dying Henry
V named his brother John, Duke of Bedford (together with Philip,
Duke of Burgundy), "regent of the realme of Fraunce" and his
brother Humphrey, Duke of Gloucester, "Protector of England
duryng the minoritie of my child." His heir, Henry VI, was nine
months old when he succeeded to the throne in 1422.
39. wife: Eleanor Cobham, first the mistress and then the second
wife of Gloucester, whom he married in 1428 after his first wife,
Jacqueline of Hainault, had been captured by Philip, Duke of Burgundy.   holdeth . . . awe: overawes you. Eleanor's pride and ambition are emphasized in *2 Henry VI.*   44. jars: discords.
48. await for: look out for, expect.
50. nourish: nurse (French *nourrice*).
52. invocate: call upon, invoke (as a saint).

Guienne, Champaigne, Rheims, Orleance,   60
Paris, Guysors, Poictiers, are all quite lost.

Bed. What say'st thou, man, before dead Henry's
    corse?
Speak softly, or the loss of those great towns
Will make him burst his lead and rise from death.

Glou. Is Paris lost? is Roan yielded up?   65
If Henry were recall'd to life again,
These news would cause him once more yield the
    ghost.

Exe. How were they lost? what treachery was us'd?

Mess. No treachery, but want of men and money.
Amongst the soldiers this is muttered,   70
That here you maintain several factions;
And whilst a field should be dispatch'd and fought,
You are disputing of your generals.
One would have ling'ring wars with little cost;
Another would fly swift, but wanteth wings;   75
A third thinks, without expense at all,
By guileful fair words peace may be obtain'd.
Awake, awake, English nobility!
Let not sloth dim your honors new begot.
Cropp'd are the flower-de-luces in your arms,   80
Of England's coat one half is cut away.   [*Exit.*]

Exe. Were our tears wanting to this funeral,
These tidings would call forth her flowing tides.

Bed. Me they concern, Regent I am of France.
Give me my steeled coat, I'll fight for France.   85
Away with these disgraceful wailing robes!
Wounds will I lend the French in stead of eyes,
To weep their intermissive miseries.

Enter to them another MESSENGER.

[2.] *Mess.* Lords, view these letters full of bad
    mischance.
France is revolted from the English quite,   90
Except some petty towns of no import.
The Dolphin Charles is crowned king in Rheims;
The Bastard of Orleance with him is join'd;

60–61. Guienne . . . Poictiers. One of many departures from historical
fact in this play. Two of the places named—Orleans and Poitiers—had
never been in English hands, and the others were not recaptured by
the French until long after the period represented.
60. Champaigne: Compiègne.   Orleance: Orleans.
62. corse: corpse.   64. lead: leaden coffin.
65. Roan: Rouen, the capital of Normandy.
71. several: separate, i.e. divisive.
72. field: (1) combat force; (2) battle.   73. of: about.
75. wanteth: lacks.
80. flower-de-luces: fleur-de-lis ("lily flower"), national emblem of
France. Through the marriage (1308) of Edward II with Isabella,
daughter of Philip IV of France, English sovereigns had claimed the
French throne for almost a hundred years, and by the Treaty of
Troyes (1420) Henry V at last secured the title "King of England and
Heir of France," leaving his father-in-law Charles VI in actual possession of the crown (see *Henry V*, V.ii). It was Charles VII's accession
to the throne of France in 1422, shortly after the death of Henry V,
that led to the renewed hostilities with England which are the subject
of this play.   80, 81. arms, coat: coat of arms.
86. wailing robes: mourning garments.
88. To weep: i.e. to weep blood (from the wounds, instead of tears
from the eyes).   intermissive: i.e. now resumed after an interval.
92. Dolphin: Dauphin, after 1349 the title of the heir apparent of
the French king; in this play, Charles (1403–61), who succeeded his
father in 1422. Actually, his coronation at Rheims (as Charles VII)
did not occur until 1429, seven years after the time represented in
this scene.
93. Bastard: Jean, Count Dunois (1403?–1468), illegitimate son of
Louis, Duke of Orleans, and thus nephew of King Charles VI; later
an associate of Joan of Arc in her spectacular campaign against the
English.

597

1 Henry VI [Reignier], Duke of Anjou, doth take his part;
I.i   The Duke of Alanson flieth to his side.   *Exit.* 95
       Exe.   The Dolphin crowned king? All fly to him?
       O, whither shall we fly from this reproach?
         Glou.   We will not fly but to our enemies' throats.
       Bedford, if thou be slack, I'll fight it out.
         Bed.   Gloucester, why doubt'st thou of my for-
                 wardness?   100
       An army have I muster'd in my thoughts,
       Wherewith already France is overrun.

                  Enter another MESSENGER.

         [3.] *Mess.*   My gracious lords, to add to your
                 laments,
       Wherewith you now bedew King Henry's hearse,
       I must inform you of a dismal fight   105
       Betwixt the stout Lord Talbot and the French.
         Win.   What? Wherein Talbot overcame, is't so?
         3. Mess.   O no; wherein Lord Talbot was o'er-
                 thrown.
       The circumstance I'll tell you more at large.
       The tenth of August last this dreadful lord,   110
       Retiring from the siege of Orleance,
       Having full scarce six thousand in his troop,
       By three and twenty thousand of the French
       Was round encompassed, and set upon.
       No leisure had he to enrank his men;   115
       He wanted pikes to set before his archers;
       In stead whereof sharp stakes pluck'd out of hedges
       They pitched in the ground confusedly,
       To keep the horsemen off from breaking in.
       More than three hours the fight continued,   120
       Where valiant Talbot above human thought
       Enacted wonders with his sword and lance:
       Hundreds he sent to hell, and none durst stand him;
       Here, there, and every where, enrag'd he slew.
       The French exclaim'd, the devil was in arms;   125
       All the whole army stood agaz'd on him.
       His soldiers, spying his undaunted spirit,
       "A Talbot! a Talbot!" cried out amain,
       And rush'd into the bowels of the battle.
       Here had the conquest fully been seal'd up,   130
       If Sir John Falstaff had not play'd the coward.

He, being in the vaward, plac'd behind
With purpose to relieve and follow them,
Cowardly fled, not having struck one stroke.
Hence grew the general wrack and massacre;   135
Enclosed were they with their enemies.
A base Wallon, to win the Dolphin's grace,
Thrust Talbot with a spear into the back,
Whom all France with their chief assembled strength
Durst not presume to look once in the face.   140
  Bed.   Is Talbot slain then? I will slay myself
For living idly here in pomp and ease,
Whilst such a worthy leader, wanting aid,
Unto his dastard foemen is betray'd.
  3. Mess.   O no, he lives, but is took prisoner, 145
And Lord Scales with him, and Lord Hungerford.
Most of the rest slaughter'd or took likewise.
  Bed.   His ransom there is none but I shall pay:
I'll hale the Dolphin headlong from his throne,
His crown shall be the ransom of my friend;   150
Four of their lords I'll change for one of ours.
Farewell, my masters, to my task will I.
Bonfires in France forthwith I am to make,
To keep our great Saint George's feast withal.
Ten thousand soldiers with me I will take,   155
Whose bloody deeds shall make all Europe quake.
  3. Mess.   So you had need, for Orleance is besieg'd;
The English army is grown weak and faint;
The Earl of Salisbury craveth supply,
And hardly keeps his men from mutiny,   160
Since they, so few, watch such a multitude.   [*Exit.*]
  Exe.   Remember, lords, your oaths to Henry sworn:
Either to quell the Dolphin utterly,
Or bring him in obedience to your yoke.
  Bed.   I do remember it, and here take my leave, 165
To go about my preparation.   *Exit Bedford.*
  Glou.   I'll to the Tower with all the haste I can,
To view th' artillery and munition,
And then I will proclaim young Henry king.
                                Exit Gloucester.
  Exe.   To Eltam will I, where the young King is, 170
Being ordain'd his special governor,
And for his safety there I'll best devise.   *Exit.*
  Win.   Each hath his place and function to attend:
I am left out; for me nothing remains.
But long I will not be Jack out of office.   175
The King from Eltam I intend to send,
And sit at chiefest stern of public weal.   *Exeunt.*

95. **Alanson:** Alençon.   105. **dismal:** unlucky.
106. **Lord Talbot:** John Talbot, first Earl of Shrewsbury (1388?–1453), the most celebrated English warrior of his day. After 1427 a valued associate of John, Duke of Bedford, he was captured by Joan of Arc in 1429 and imprisoned for two years. Following his release he became an ally of Philip of Burgundy, and his reputation mounted until he, together with his son, was killed in action at Castillon.
109. **at large:** in detail.
110–40. **The tenth . . .** This episode actually occurred at the battle of Patay, some six weeks after the siege of Orleans had been raised by Joan of Arc in May 1429.   112. **full scarce:** barely.
116. **pikes:** ironbound, sharpened stakes set in the earth before archers for protection against advancing horsemen.
126. **agaz'd on:** astounded at.   128. **amain:** strongly.
130. **seal'd up:** completed.
131. **Falstaff:** i.e. Sir John Fastolfe (c. 1378–1459), a Norfolk landowner who served with notable success under Henry V and then the Duke of Bedford, rose to the governorship of Anjou and Maine in 1423, and acquired great wealth and power after his return to England. Although he was esteemed by his contemporaries, here and elsewhere in the play Shakespeare, like the Tudor chroniclers whom he followed, depicts him as a coward. This unflattering and erroneous view of Fastolfe derived ultimately from the fifteenth-century *Chronique* of

Monstrelet. He is not to be confused with the Sir John Falstaff of the *Henry IV* plays (to whom Shakespeare originally gave the name Oldcastle).
132. **vaward:** vanguard.   135. **wrack:** destruction.
137. **Wallon:** Walloon, an inhabitant of what is now southern Belgium.
154. **Saint George's feast:** April 23. St. George was the patron saint of England and also of the Order of the Garter.
159. **Salisbury:** Thomas de Montacute, fourth Earl of Salisbury (1388–1428), a stalwart of the English who lost his life while leading the siege of Orleans (see I.iv).
167. **Tower:** Tower of London, long used as both a royal palace and an arsenal.
170. **Eltam:** Eltham, a town southeast of London, formerly the site of a royal palace.   175. **Jack . . . office:** i.e. an unemployed nobody.
177. **at chiefest stern:** in position of control.

[SCENE II]

Sound a flourish.   Enter CHARLES [*the Dolphin*],
ALANSON, *and* REIGNIER, *marching with Drum and
Soldiers.*

Char.   Mars his true moving, even as in the heavens,
So in the earth, to this day is not known.
Late did he shine upon the English side;
Now we are victors, upon us he smiles.
What towns of any moment but we have?   5
At pleasure here we lie near Orleance;
Otherwhiles the famish'd English, like pale ghosts,
Faintly besiege us one hour in a month.
Alan.   They want their porridge and their fat bull-
beeves:
Either they must be dieted like mules   10
And have their provender tied to their mouths,
Or piteous they will look, like drowned mice.
Reig.   Let's raise the siege; why live we idly here?
Talbot is taken, whom we wont to fear;
Remaineth none but mad-brain'd Salisbury,   15
And he may well in fretting spend his gall—
Nor men nor money hath he to make war.
Char.   Sound, sound alarum! We will rush on them.
Now for the honor of the forlorn French!
Him I forgive my death that killeth me,   20
When he sees me go back one foot or fly.   *Exeunt.*

*Here alarum; they are beaten back by the English with
great loss. Enter* CHARLES, ALANSON, *and* REIGNIER.

Char.   Who ever saw the like? What men have I!
Dogs! cowards! dastards! I would ne'er have fled,
But that they left me midst my enemies.
Reig.   Salisbury is a desperate homicide,   25
He fighteth as one weary of his life.
The other lords, like lions wanting food,
Do rush upon us as their hungry prey.
Alan.   Froissard, a countryman of ours, records
England all Olivers and Rolands bred   30
During the time Edward the Third did reign.
More truly now may this be verified,
For none but Samsons and Goliases
It sendeth forth to skirmish. One to ten!
Lean raw-bon'd rascals! who would e'er suppose   35
They had such courage and audacity?

Char.   Let's leave this town, for they are hare-
brain'd slaves,
And hunger will enforce them to be more eager.
Of old I know them; rather with their teeth
The walls they'll tear down than forsake the siege.   40
Reig.   I think by some odd gimmors or device
Their arms are set, like clocks, still to strike on;
Else ne'er could they hold out so as they do.
By my consent, we'll even let them alone.
Alan.   Be it so.   45

Enter the BASTARD *of* ORLEANCE.

Bast.   Where's the Prince Dolphin? I have news
for him.
Char.   Bastard of Orleance, thrice welcome to us.
Bast.   Methinks your looks are sad, your cheer
appal'd.
Hath the late overthrow wrought this offense?
Be not dismay'd, for succor is at hand: 50
A holy maid hither with me I bring,
Which by a vision sent to her from heaven
Ordained is to raise this tedious siege,
And drive the English forth the bounds of France.
The spirit of deep prophecy she hath,   55
Exceeding the nine sibyls of old Rome:
What's past and what's to come she can descry.
Speak, shall I call her in? Believe my words,
For they are certain and unfallible.
Char.   Go call her in. [*Exit Bastard.*] But first, to
try her skill,   60
Reignier, stand thou as Dolphin in my place;
Question her proudly, let thy looks be stern.
By this means shall we sound what skill she hath.

Enter JOAN [DE] PUCELLE [*and* BASTARD].

Reig.   Fair maid, is't thou wilt do these wondrous
feats?
Puc.   Reignier, is't thou that thinkest to beguile me?
Where is the Dolphin? Come, come from behind,   66
I know thee well, though never seen before.
Be not amaz'd, there's nothing hid from me;
In private will I talk with thee apart.
Stand back, you lords, and give us leave a while.   70
Reig.   She takes upon her bravely at first dash.
Puc.   Dolphin, I am by birth a shepherd's daughter,
My wit untrain'd in any kind of art.
Heaven and our Lady gracious hath it pleas'd
To shine on my contemptible estate.   75
Lo, whilest I waited on my tender lambs,
And to sun's parching heat display'd my cheeks,
God's Mother deigned to appear to me,
And in a vision full of majesty

I.ii. Location: France. Before Orleans.
o.s.d. **flourish:** fanfare of trumpets. **Reignier:** René (1409–80),
Duke of Anjou and Lorraine and titular King of Naples and Sicily,
whose daughter Margaret married (1445) Henry VI of England. His
appearance here (as well as at II.i and III.ii) is unhistorical. **Drum:**
drummer.
1–2. Mars . . . known. The notoriously eccentric orbit of the planet
Mars was not explained until Johannes Kepler published his *Astro-
nomia Nova de Motibus Stellae Martis* in 1609.
7. Otherwhiles: at times, from time to time.
14. wont: were accustomed.
16. spend his gall: exhaust his anger.   **17. Nor:** neither.
18. alarum: call to arms.   **19. forlorn:** lost (ironical).
28. their hungry prey: prey of their hunger.
29. Froissard: Jean Froissart (1333?–?1400), author of a splendid
Cronique that treats the history of France and England in the fourteenth century.
30. Olivers and Rolands. Oliver and Roland were the most renowned
of Charlemagne's twelve peers.
33. Samsons and Goliases. For the exploits of Samson and Goliath,
Biblical characters of legendary strength, see Judges 13–16 and 1
Samuel 17.   **35. rascals:** lean, inferior deer.

41. gimmors: gimmals, mechanical joints.
42. still: always, repeatedly.
48. cheer appal'd: countenance made pale.   **54. forth:** out of.
56. nine sibyls. The sibyls—inspired women revered by the ancients
for their alleged gift of prophecy—were often represented as five in
number (as by Michelangelo on the ceiling of the Sistine Chapel);
Shakespeare was perhaps confused by the story of the Cumaean sibyl's
offering nine books of oracular utterances to Tarquin, king of Rome.
63. sound: ascertain.
64 s.d. Pucelle: the Maid (of Orleans), Joan of Arc.
71. takes . . . dash: plays her part splendidly from the first.
73. wit: mind.

1 Henry VI
I.ii

Will'd me to leave my base vocation   80
And free my country from calamity.
Her aid she promis'd, and assur'd success;
In complete glory she reveal'd herself;
And whereas I was black and swart before,
With those clear rays which she infus'd on me   85
That beauty am I blest with which you may see.
Ask me what question thou canst possible,
And I will answer unpremeditated;
My courage try by combat, if thou dar'st,
And thou shalt find that I exceed my sex.   90
Resolve on this: thou shalt be fortunate
If thou receive me for thy warlike mate.
  Char.   Thou hast astonish'd me with thy high terms.
Only this proof I'll of thy valor make,
In single combat thou shalt buckle with me;   95
And if thou vanquishest, thy words are true,
Otherwise I renounce all confidence.
  Puc.   I am prepar'd; here is my keen-edg'd sword,
Deck'd with [five] flower-de-luces on each side,
The which at Touraine, in Saint Katherine's church-
       yard,   100
Out of a great deal of old iron I chose forth.
  Char.   Then come a' God's name, I fear no woman.
  Puc.   And while I live, I'll ne'er fly from a man.
       Here they fight, and Joan de Pucelle overcomes.
  Char.   Stay, stay thy hands! Thou art an Amazon,
And fightest with the sword of Deborah.   105
  Puc.   Christ's Mother helps me, else I were too
       weak.
  Char.   Whoe'er helps thee, 'tis thou that must help
       me:
Impatiently I burn with thy desire;
My heart and hands thou hast at once subdu'd.
Excellent Pucelle, if thy name be so,   110
Let me thy servant and not sovereign be.
'Tis the French Dolphin sueth to thee thus.
  Puc.   I must not yield to any rites of love,
For my profession's sacred from above.
When I have chased all thy foes from hence,   115
Then will I think upon a recompense.
  Char.   Mean time look gracious on thy prostrate
       thrall.
  Reig.   My lord, methinks, is very long in talk.
  Alan.   Doubtless he shrives this woman to her
       smock,
Else ne'er could he so long protract his speech.   120
  Reig.   Shall we disturb him, since he keeps no
       mean?
  Alan.   He may mean more than we poor men do
       know:
These women are shrewd tempters with their tongues.
  Reig.   My lord, where are you? What devise you
       on?

Shall we give o'er Orleance, or no?   125
  Puc.   Why, no, I say. Distrustful recreants,
Fight till the last gasp; I'll be your guard.
  Char.   What she says I'll confirm. We'll fight it
       out.
  Puc.   Assign'd am I to be the English scourge.
This night the siege assuredly I'll raise: 130
Expect Saint Martin's summer, halcyons' days,
Since I have entered into these wars.
Glory is like a circle in the water,
Which never ceaseth to enlarge itself,
Till by broad spreading it disperse to nought.   135
With Henry's death the English circle ends,
Dispersed are the glories it included.
Now am I like that proud insulting ship
Which Caesar and his fortune bare at once.
  Char.   Was Mahomet inspired with a dove?   140
Thou with an eagle art inspired then.
Helen, the mother of great Constantine,
Nor yet Saint Philip's daughters, were like thee.
Bright star of Venus, fall'n down on the earth,
How may I reverently worship thee enough?   145
  Alan.   Leave off delays, and let us raise the siege.
  Reig.   Woman, do what thou canst to save our
       honors;
Drive them from Orleance and be immortaliz'd.
  Char.   Presently we'll try; come, let's away about
       it.   149
No prophet will I trust, if she prove false.   *Exeunt.*

[Scene III]

Enter Gloucester *with his* Servingmen [*in blue coats*].

  Glou.   I am come to survey the Tower this day;
Since Henry's death, I fear, there is conveyance.
Where be these warders, that they wait not here?
Open the gates, 'tis Gloucester that calls.
  1. Warder.   [*Within.*] Who's there, that knocks so
       imperiously?   5
  1. Serv.   It is the noble Duke of Gloucester.
  2. Warder.   [*Within.*] Whoe'er he be, you may not
       be let in.
  1. Serv.   Villains, answer you so the Lord Pro-
       tector?

---

131. **Saint Martin's summer:** Indian summer. St. Martin's Day is November 11. **halcyons' days:** i.e. unseasonably fine weather. According to the ancients the sea became calm around the winter solstice so that the halcyon (kingfisher) could nest upon it.
138–39. **Now . . . once.** According to North's translation of Plutarch, when the timorous commander of a ship carrying Caesar, incognito, across the stormy Adriatic ordered the vessel to return to port, the distinguished passenger said, "Good fellow, be of good cheare, and forwardes hardily, feare not, for thou hast Caesar & his fortune with thee."   138. **insulting:** proudly exultant.
140. **Mahomet . . . dove.** The founder of Islam was said to have been inspired by a dove who whispered in his ear.
142. **Helen:** mother of the Emperor Constantine (who made Christianity the religion of the Roman Empire in 313) and reputedly the discoverer of the True Cross and the Holy Sepulchre.
143. **Saint Philip's daughters:** the four "virgins, which did prophesy," mentioned in Acts 21:9.   149. **Presently:** immediately.

I.iii. Location: London. Before the Tower gates.
o.s.d. **blue coats.** Customarily worn by servingmen.
2. **conveyance:** trickery.

---

85. **infus'd:** poured.   91. **Resolve on:** make up your mind to.
93. **high terms:** lofty claims.   94. **proof:** test.
95. **buckle:** contend.   102. **a':** in, by.
104. **Amazon:** one of a fabulous race of female warriors.
105. **Deborah:** Hebrew prophetess who successfully led her people against their Canaanite oppressors. See Judges 4, 5.
108. **thy desire:** desire for you.   111. **servant:** professed lover.
119. **shrives . . . smock:** i.e. makes love to her.
121. **mean:** moderation.   123. **shrewd:** malicious, mischievous.
124. **devise:** decide.

1. Warder.   [*Within.*] The Lord protect him! so we
answer him.
We do no otherwise than we are will'd.   10
   Glou.   Who willed you? or whose will stands but
mine?
There's none Protector of the realm but I.—
Break up the gates, I'll be your warrantize.
Shall I be flouted thus by dunghill grooms?

> *Gloucester's men rush at the Tower gates, and*
> *Woodvile the Lieutenant speaks within.*

   Woodv.   What noise is this? What traitors have we
here?   15
   Glou.   Lieutenant, is it you whose voice I hear?
Open the gates, here's Gloucester that would enter.
   Woodv.   Have patience, noble Duke, I may not
open,
The Cardinal of Winchester forbids.
From him I have express commandement   20
That thou nor none of thine shall be let in.
   Glou.   Faint-hearted Woodvile, prizest him 'fore
me?
Arrogant Winchester, that haughty prelate,
Whom Henry, our late sovereign, ne'er could brook?
Thou art no friend to God or to the King.   25
Open the gates, or I'll shut thee out shortly.
   Servingmen.   Open the gates unto the Lord Pro-
tector,
Or we'll burst them open, if that you come not quickly.

Enter to the Protector at the Tower gates Winchester
and his Men *in tawny coats.*

   Win.   How now, ambitious [Humphrey], what
means this?
   Glou.   Peel'd priest, dost thou command me to be
shut out?   30
   Win.   I do, thou most usurping proditor,
And not Protector, of the King or realm.
   Glou.   Stand back, thou manifest conspirator,
Thou that contrivedst to murther our dead lord,
Thou that giv'st whores indulgences to sin.   35
I'll canvass thee in thy broad cardinal's hat,
If thou proceed in this thy insolence.
   Win.   Nay, stand thou back, I will not budge a foot:
This be Damascus, be thou cursed Cain,
To slay thy brother Abel, if thou wilt.   40
   Glou.   I will not slay thee, but I'll drive thee back.

Thy scarlet robes as a child's bearing-cloth
I'll use to carry thee out of this place.
   Win.   Do what thou dar'st, I beard thee to thy face.
   Glou.   What? am I dar'd and bearded to my face?   45
Draw, men, for all this privileged place—
Blue coats to tawny coats! Priest, beware your beard,
I mean to tug it and to cuff you soundly.
Under my feet I stamp thy cardinal's hat;
In spite of Pope or dignities of church,   50
Here by the cheeks I'll drag thee up and down.
   Win.   Gloucester, thou wilt answer this before the
Pope.
   Glou.   Winchester goose, I cry, "A rope! a rope!"
Now beat them hence, why do you let them stay?
Thee I'll chase hence, thou wolf in sheep's array.   55
Out, tawny-coats! Out, scarlet hypocrite!

Here Gloucester's men beat out the Cardinal's men, and
enter in the hurly-burly the Mayor of London *and*
his Officers.

   May.   Fie, lords, that you, being supreme magis-
trates,
Thus contumeliously should break the peace!
   Glou.   Peace, Mayor, thou know'st little of my
wrongs.
Here's Beauford, that regards nor God nor king,   60
Hath here distrain'd the Tower to his use.
   Win.   Here's Gloucester, a foe to citizens,
One that still motions war and never peace,
O'ercharging your free purses with large fines;
That seeks to overthrow religion   65
Because he is Protector of the realm,
And would have armor here out of the Tower,
To crown himself king and suppress the Prince.
   Glou.   I will not answer thee with words, but blows.
                          Here they skirmish again.
   May.   Nought rests for me in this tumultuous strife
But to make open proclamation.   71
Come, officer, as loud as e'er thou canst,
Cry,
   [*Off.*] All manner of men assembled here in arms
this day against God's peace and the King's, we   75
charge and command you, in his Highness' name, to
repair to your several dwelling-places, and not to wear,
handle, or use any sword, weapon, or dagger, hence-
forward, upon pain of death.
   Glou.   Cardinal, I'll be no breaker of the law;   80
But we shall meet, and break our minds at large.
   Win.   Gloucester, we'll meet to thy cost, be sure:
Thy heart-blood I will have for this day's work.
   May.   I'll call for clubs, if you will not away.
This cardinal's more haughty than the devil.   85

---

10. **will'd:** commanded.   13. **warrantize:** guarantee.
14 s.d. **Woodvile:** Richard Woodville (died c. 1441), a loyal Lancastrian whose descendants rose to wealth and power as supporters of
the House of York after his granddaughter Elizabeth married Edward
IV in 1464.
19. **Cardinal of Winchester.** An apparent mistake. At III.i.53 and
in the opening stage direction of IV.i Beaufort is called a bishop,
and at V.i.28 ff. he is spoken of as a newly created cardinal. Actually
he received his red hat in 1427.   24. **brook:** endure.
28 s.d. **tawny coats.** Customarily worn by the attendants of a great
ecclesiastic.   30. **Peel'd:** shaven, tonsured.   31. **proditor:** traitor.
34–35. **Thou . . . sin.** In 1426 Gloucester charged Beaufort with various crimes, including a conspiracy against the late king when he was
Prince of Wales. As Bishop of Winchester Beaufort enjoyed the revenues from the brothels in Bankside, the disreputable area south of
the Thames where such theatres as the Rose and the Globe were
erected in Shakespeare's time.
36. **canvass:** toss in a canvas sheet, belabor.
39. **Damascus . . . Cain.** In medieval legend the site of Damascus
was thought to be the place where Cain had murdered Abel.

42. **bearing-cloth:** christening robe.   44. **beard:** openly defy.
46. **privileged place.** As a royal residence the Tower was one of the
places where the use of weapons was forbidden.
48. **tug.** To pull a man's beard was the deadliest of insults.
50. **dignities:** dignitaries.
53. **Winchester goose:** slang term for a venereal disease (see note to
lines 34–35 above).   **A rope:** a halter to hang him.
61. **distrain'd:** confiscated.   63. **still motions:** continually stirs up.
64. **your free purses:** your purses freely.
81. **break our minds:** disclose our intentions.
84. **clubs:** i.e. assistance. "Prentices and clubs" was the rallying cry
for the London apprentices.

1 Henry VI
I.iii

Glou. Mayor, farewell; thou dost but what thou
    mayst.
Win. Abominable Gloucester, guard thy head,
For I intend to have it ere long.

    *Exeunt, [several ways, Gloucester and Winchester
    with their Servingmen].*

May. See the coast clear'd, and then we will de-
    part.
Good God, these nobles should such stomachs bear! 90
I myself fight not once in forty year.   *Exeunt.*

[SCENE IV]

Enter the MASTER GUNNER *of Orleance and his* BOY.

M. Gun. Sirrah, thou know'st how Orleance is be-
    sieg'd,
And how the English have the suburbs won.
Boy. Father, I know, and oft have shot at them,
Howe'er unfortunate I miss'd my aim.
M. Gun. But now thou shalt not. Be thou rul'd
    by me.   5
Chief master gunner am I of this town,
Something I must do to procure me grace.
The Prince's espials have informed me
How the English, in the suburbs close intrench'd,
[Wont] through a secret grate of iron bars   10
In yonder tower to overpeer the city,
And thence discover how with most advantage
They may vex us with shot or with assault.
To intercept this inconvenience,
A piece of ord'nance 'gainst it I have plac'd,   15
And even these three days have I watch'd
If I could see them.
Now do they watch, for I can stay no longer.
If thou spy'st any, run and bring me word,
And thou shalt find me at the Governor's. *Exit.* 20
Boy. Father, I warrant you, take you no care,
I'll never trouble you, if I may spy them.   *Exit.*

Enter SALISBURY *and* TALBOT, [SIR WILLIAM GLANS-
DALE, SIR THOMAS GARGRAVE,] *on the turrets, with
others.*

Sal. Talbot, my life, my joy, again return'd?
How wert thou handled, being prisoner?
Or by what means gots thou to be releas'd?   25
Discourse, I prithee, on this turret's top.
Tal. The Earl of Bedford had a prisoner
Call'd the brave Lord Ponton de Santrailles,
For him was I exchang'd and ransomed.
But with a baser man of arms by far   30
Once in contempt they would have barter'd me;
Which I, disdaining, scorn'd, and craved death
Rather than I would be so pill'd esteem'd;
In fine, redeem'd I was as I desir'd.

But O, the treacherous Falstaff wounds my heart,   35
Whom with my bare fists I would execute,
If I now had him brought into my power.
Sal. Yet tell'st thou not how thou wert entertain'd.
Tal. With scoffs and scorns and contumelious
    taunts.
In open market-place produc'd they me   40
To be a public spectacle to all:
Here, said they, is the terror of the French,
The scarecrow that affrights our children so.
Then broke I from the officers that led me,
And with my nails digg'd stones out of the ground   45
To hurl at the beholders of my shame.
My grisly countenance made others fly,
None durst come near for fear of sudden death.
In iron walls they deem'd me not secure;
So great fear of my name 'mongst them were spread   50
That they suppos'd I could rend bars of steel,
And spurn in pieces posts of adamant;
Wherefore a guard of chosen shot I had
That walk'd about me every minute while;
And if I did but stir out of my bed,   55
Ready they were to shoot me to the heart.

Enter the BOY *with a linstock.*

Sal. I grieve to hear what torments you endur'd,
But we will be reveng'd sufficiently.
Now it is supper-time in Orleance:
Here, through this grate, I count each one,   60
And view the Frenchmen how they fortify.
Let us look in, the sight will much delight thee.
Sir Thomas Gargrave, and Sir William Glansdale,
Let me have your express opinions,
Where is best place to make our batt'ry next?   65
Gar. I think at the North Gate, for there stands
    lords.
Glan. And I here, at the bulwark of the bridge.
Tal. For aught I see, this city must be famish'd,
Or with light skirmishes enfeebled.

    *Here they shoot, and Salisbury falls down
    [together with Gargrave].*

Sal. O Lord, have mercy on us, wretched sinners!
Gar. O Lord, have mercy on me, woeful man!   71
Tal. What chance is this that suddenly hath cross'd
    us?
Speak, Salisbury; at least, if thou canst, speak.
How far'st thou, mirror of all martial men?
One of thy eyes and thy cheek's side struck off!   75
Accursed tower! accursed fatal hand
That hath contriv'd this woeful tragedy!
In thirteen battles Salisbury o'ercame;

---

90. **stomachs:** fighting dispositions.

I.iv. Location: France. Orleans.
1. **Sirrah:** customary term of address to an inferior.
7. **grace:** honor, distinction.   8. **espials:** spies.
14. **inconvenience:** mischief, harm.
15. **ord'nance:** ordnance (a sense only later differentiated by spelling
from *ordinance*).   25. **gots:** gottest.
33. **pill'd:** despoiled, impoverished.

38. **entertain'd:** treated.
52. **spurn:** kick.   **adamant:** i.e. the hardest substance imaginable.
53. **chosen shot:** selected musketeers.
54. **every minute while:** i.e. continually
56 s.d. **linstock:** stick to hold the gunner's match.
64. **express:** precise.
68. **must be famish'd:** will have to be starved out.
74. **mirror:** example.
75. **One . . . off.** A detail supplied by Hall (Bullough, III, 55): "the
sonne of the Master gonner, perceived men lokyng out at the wyn-
dowe, toke his matche, as his father had taught hym, whiche was
gone doune to dinner, and fired the gonne, whiche brake & shevered
the yron barres of the grate, whereof one strake therle so strongly on
the hed, that it stroke away one of his iyes and the side of his cheke."

Henry the Fift he first train'd to the wars;
Whilst any trump did sound, or drum struck up,   80
His sword did ne'er leave striking in the field.
Yet liv'st thou, Salisbury? Though thy speech doth
   fail,
One eye thou hast to look to heaven for grace;
The sun with one eye vieweth all the world.
Heaven, be thou gracious to none alive,   85
If Salisbury wants mercy at thy hands!
Bear hence his body, I will help to bury it.
Sir Thomas Gargrave, hast thou any life?
Speak unto Talbot, nay, look up to him.
Salisbury, cheer thy spirit with this comfort,   90
Thou shalt not die whiles—
He beckons with his hand and smiles on me,
As who should say, "When I am dead and gone,
Remember to avenge me on the French."
Plantagenet, I will, and like thee, [Nero,]   95
Play on the lute, beholding the towns burn;
Wretched shall France be only in my name.

Here an alarum, and it thunders and lightens.

What stir is this? what tumult's in the heavens?
Whence cometh this alarum, and the noise?

Enter a MESSENGER.

Mess. My lord, my lord, the French have gather'd
   head.   100
The Dolphin, with one Joan de Pucelle join'd,
A holy prophetess new risen up,
Is come with a great power to raise the siege.

Here Salisbury lifteth himself up and groans.

Tal. Hear, hear how dying Salisbury doth groan!
It irks his heart he cannot be reveng'd.   105
Frenchmen, I'll be a Salisbury to you.
Pucelle or puzzel, Dolphin or dogfish,
Your hearts I'll stamp out with my horse's heels,
And make a quagmire of your mingled brains.
Convey me Salisbury into his tent,   110
And then we'll try what these dastard Frenchmen dare.

Alarum. Exeunt [bearing out the bodies].

[SCENE V]

Here an alarum again, and TALBOT *pursueth the* DOLPHIN,
   and driveth him. Then enter JOAN DE PUCELLE,
   *driving Englishmen before her, [and exit after them].
   Then enter* TALBOT.

Tal. Where is my strength, my valor, and my
   force?
Our English troops retire, I cannot stay them;
A woman clad in armor chaseth them.

86. **wants:** lacks.   91. **whiles:** until.
95. **Plantagenet.** Salisbury's family name was Montacute, but he was distantly related to the royal family. See note to II.iv o.s.d. **Nero.** According to Suetonius, the emperor Nero ordered certain parts of Rome put to the torch, and as he watched the fire he sang of the sack of Ilium.   97. **only in:** at the very sound of.
100. **gather'd head:** assembled armed forces.   103. **power:** army.
107. **puzzel:** slut, drab. Note the pun with *Pucelle*, and also that between *Dolphin* and *dogfish* (small shark).

I.v. Location: Scene continues.

Enter PUCELLE.

Here, here she comes. I'll have a bout with thee;
Devil or devil's dam, I'll conjure thee.   5
Blood will I draw on thee—thou art a witch—
And straightway give thy soul to him thou serv'st.

Puc. Come, come, 'tis only I that must disgrace
   thee.   *Here they fight.*

Tal. Heavens, can you suffer hell so to prevail?
My breast I'll burst with straining of my courage,   10
And from my shoulders crack my arms asunder,
But I will chastise this high-minded strumpet.

They fight again.

Puc. Talbot, farewell, thy hour is not yet come.
I must go victual Orleance forthwith.

A short alarum: then enter the town with soldiers.

O'ertake me if thou canst, I scorn thy strength.   15
Go, go, cheer up thy hungry-starved men;
Help Salisbury to make his testament.
This day is ours, as many more shall be.   *Exit.*

Tal. My thoughts are whirled like a potter's wheel,
I know not where I am, nor what I do.   20
A witch by fear, not force, like Hannibal,
Drives back our troops and conquers as she lists:
So bees with smoke and doves with noisome stench
Are from their hives and houses driven away.
They call'd us for our fierceness English dogs,   25
Now, like to whelps, we crying run away.

A short alarum.

Hark, countrymen, either renew the fight,
Or tear the lions out of England's coat;
Renounce your soil, give sheep in lions' stead:
Sheep run not half so treacherous from the wolf,   30
Or horse or oxen from the leopard,
As you fly from your oft-subdued slaves.

Alarum. Here another skirmish.

It will not be, retire into your trenches.
You all consented unto Salisbury's death,
For none would strike a stroke in his revenge.   35
Pucelle is ent'red into Orleance
In spite of us, or aught that we could do.
O would I were to die with Salisbury!
The shame hereof will make me hide my head.

Exit Talbot. Alarum; retreat.

[SCENE VI]

Flourish. Enter on the walls PUCELLE, [CHARLES *the*]
   Dolphin, REIGNIER, ALANSON, *and Soldiers.*

Puc. Advance our waving colors on the walls,
Rescu'd is Orleance from the English!
Thus Joan de Pucelle hath perform'd her word.

12. **But I will:** if I do not.   **high-minded:** arrogant.
16. **hungry-starved:** dying of hunger.
21. **Hannibal.** According to Livy, the Carthaginian leader routed the Roman army by tying blazing faggots to the horns of oxen.
22. **lists:** pleases.   28. **coat:** coat of arms.
29. **soil:** native country.   **give:** display (as in a heraldic emblem).
35. **his revenge:** revenge of him.
39 s.d. **retreat:** trumpet signal to recall a pursuing force.

I.vi. Location: Scene continues.
1. **Advance:** raise.

1 Henry VI
I.vi

Char. Divinest creature, Astraea's daughter,
How shall I honor thee for this success?   5
Thy promises are like Adonis' garden,
That one day bloom'd and fruitful were the next.
France, triumph in thy glorious prophetess!
Recover'd is the town of Orleance.
More blessed hap did ne'er befall our state.   10
   Reig. Why ring not out the bells aloud throughout
      the town?
Dolphin, command the citizens make bonfires,
And feast and banquet in the open streets,
To celebrate the joy that God hath given us.   14
   Alan. All France will be replete with mirth and joy,
When they shall hear how we have play'd the men.
   Char. 'Tis Joan, not we, by whom the day is won;
For which I will divide my crown with her,
And all the priests and friars in my realm
Shall in procession sing her endless praise.   20
A statelier pyramis to her I'll rear
Than Rhodope's [of] Memphis ever was.
In memory of her when she is dead,
Her ashes, in an urn more precious
Than the rich-jewell'd coffer of Darius,   25
Transported shall be at high festivals
Before the kings and queens of France.
No longer on Saint Denis will we cry,
But Joan de Pucelle shall be France's saint.
Come in, and let us banquet royally,   30
After this golden day of victory.   *Flourish. Exeunt.*

ACT II, Scene I

Enter a [French] Sergeant *of a band, with two* Sentinels.

Serg. Sirs, take your places and be vigilant.
If any noise or soldier you perceive
Near to the walls, by some apparent sign
Let us have knowledge at the court of guard.
   [*1.*] *Sent.* Sergeant, you shall. [*Exit Sergeant.*]
      Thus are poor servitors,   5
When others sleep upon their quiet beds,
Constrain'd to watch in darkness, rain, and cold.

Enter Talbot, Bedford, *and* Burgundy, [*and forces*]
with scaling-ladders.

Tal. Lord Regent, and redoubted Burgundy,

By whose approach the regions of Artois,
Wallon, and Picardy are friends to us,   10
This happy night the Frenchmen are secure,
Having all day carous'd and banqueted:
Embrace we then this opportunity
As fitting best to quittance their deceit
Contriv'd by art and baleful sorcery.   15
   Bed. Coward of France, how much he wrongs his
      fame,
Despairing of his own arm's fortitude,
To join with witches and the help of hell!
   Bur. Traitors have never other company.
But what's that Pucelle whom they term so pure? 20
   Tal. A maid, they say.
   Bed.   A maid? and be so martial?
   Bur. Pray God she prove not masculine ere long,
If underneath the standard of the French
She carry armor as she hath begun.
   Tal. Well, let them practice and converse with
      spirits.   25
God is our fortress, in whose conquering name
Let us resolve to scale their flinty bulwarks.
   Bed. Ascend, brave Talbot, we will follow thee.
   Tal. Not all together. Better far, I guess,
That we do make our entrance several ways;   30
That, if it chance the one of us do fail,
The other yet may rise against their force.
   Bed. Agreed. I'll to yond corner.
   Bur.   And I to this.
   Tal. And here will Talbot mount, or make his
      grave.
Now, Salisbury, for thee, and for the right   35
Of English Henry, shall this night appear
How much in duty I am bound to both.
         Cry: "Saint George!" "A Talbot!"
      [*The English scale the walls.*]
   [*1.*] *Sent.* Arm, arm! the enemy doth make assault!

*The French leap o'er the walls in their shirts. Enter,
several ways,* Bastard, Alanson, Reignier, *half
ready and half unready.*

   Alan. How now, my lords? what, all unready so?
   Bast. Unready? Ay, and glad we scap'd so well.
   Reig. 'Twas time, I trow, to wake and leave our
      beds,   41
Hearing alarums at our chamber-doors.
   Alan. Of all exploits since first I follow'd arms,
Ne'er heard I of a warlike enterprise
More venturous or desperate than this.   45
   Bast. I think this Talbot is a fiend of hell.
   Reig. If not of hell, the heavens sure favor him.
   Alan. Here cometh Charles, I marvel how he sped.

Enter Charles *and* Joan [de Pucelle].

   Bast. Tut, holy Joan was his defensive guard.

---

4. **Astraea:** goddess of Justice, who forsook the world when it became corrupt.
6. **Adonis' garden:** mythical garden noted for fertility; perhaps an
allusion to a famous episode in Spenser's *Faerie Queene*, Book III,
Canto vi.   21. **pyramis:** pyramid.
22. **Rhodope:** renowned Greek courtesan alleged to have married the
king of Egypt, who built one of the most beautiful of the pyramids for
her.   **Memphis:** ancient city on the Nile.
25. **Darius:** Persian king whose jewelled treasure chest was used by
Alexander the Great to carry Homer's poems on his campaigns.
28. **Saint Denis:** patron saint of France.

II.i. Location: Before Orleans.
3. **apparent:** plain, unmistakable.   4. **court of guard:** guardroom.
7 s.d. **Burgundy:** Philip the Good, Duke of Burgundy (1396–1467),
who became an ally of the English by the Treaty of Troyes (1420) and
was named co-regent of France (together with John, Duke of Bedford)
by the dying Henry V (see note to I.i.37). After 1435 Philip shifted his
allegiance to Charles VII.

11. **secure:** unsuspecting, overconfident.
14. **quittance:** requite.   15. **art:** i.e. magic.
16. **Coward of France:** i.e. the Dauphin.   **fame:** reputation.
25. **practice:** plot, scheme.   30. **several:** different.
38 s.d. **ready:** dressed.   According to Hall (Bullough, III, 53–54),
the incident on which this scene is based actually occurred at Le Mans
in May 1428, a year before the siege of Orleans.   41. **trow:** believe.
48. **sped:** fared.

Char. Is this thy cunning, thou deceitful dame? 50
Didst thou at first, to flatter us withal,
Make us partakers of a little gain,
That now our loss might be ten times so much?
  Puc. Wherefore is Charles impatient with his
    friend?
At all times will you have my power alike? 55
Sleeping or waking, must I still prevail,
Or will you blame and lay the fault on me?
Improvident soldiers, had your watch been good,
This sudden mischief never could have fall'n.
  Char. Duke of Alanson, this was your default, 60
That, being captain of the watch to-night,
Did look no better to that weighty charge.
  Alan. Had all your quarters been as safely kept
As that whereof I had the government,
We had not been thus shamefully surpris'd. 65
  Bast. Mine was secure.
  Reig.   And so was mine, my lord.
  Char. And for myself, most part of all this night,
Within her quarter and mine own precinct
I was employ'd in passing to and fro,
About relieving of the sentinels. 70
Then how, or which way, should they first break in?
  Puc. Question, my lords, no further of the case,
How or which way. 'Tis sure they found some place
But weakly guarded, where the breach was made.
And now there rests no other shift but this, 75
To gather our soldiers, scatter'd and dispers'd,
And lay new platforms to endamage them.

Alarum. Enter [an English] Soldier *crying,* "A Talbot!
a Talbot!" *They fly, leaving their clothes behind.*

  Sold. I'll be so bold to take what they have left.
The cry of Talbot serves me for a sword,
For I have loaden me with many spoils, 80
Using no other weapon but his name.   *Exit.*

[Scene II]

Enter Talbot, Bedford, Burgundy, [*a Captain, and
others], their Drums beating a dead march.*

  Bed. The day begins to break, and night is fled,
Whose pitchy mantle over-veil'd the earth.
Here sound retreat, and cease our hot pursuit.

                                      Retreat.

  Tal. Bring forth the body of old Salisbury,
And here advance it in the market-place, 5
The middle centure of this cursed town.
Now have I paid my vow unto his soul;
For every drop of blood was drawn from him
There hath at least five Frenchmen died to-night.
And that hereafter ages may behold 10

What ruin happened in revenge of him,
Within their chiefest temple I'll erect
A tomb, wherein his corpse shall be interr'd;
Upon the which, that every one may read,
Shall be engrav'd the sack of Orleance, 15
The treacherous manner of his mournful death,
And what a terror he had been to France.
But, lords, in all our bloody massacre,
I muse we met not with the Dolphin's grace,
His new-come champion, virtuous Joan of [Aire], 20
Nor any of his false confederates.
  Bed. 'Tis thought, Lord Talbot, when the fight
    began,
Rous'd on the sudden from their drowsy beds,
They did amongst the troops of armed men
Leap o'er the walls for refuge in the field. 25
  Bur. Myself, as far as I could well discern
For smoke and dusky vapors of the night,
Am sure I scar'd the Dolphin and his trull,
When arm in arm they both came swiftly running,
Like to a pair of loving turtle-doves 30
That could not live asunder day or night.
After that things are set in order here,
We'll follow them with all the power we have.

Enter a Messenger.

  Mess. All hail, my lords! which of this princely
    train
Call ye the warlike Talbot, for his acts 35
So much applauded through the realm of France?
  Tal. Here is the Talbot, who would speak with
    him?
  Mess. The virtuous lady, Countess of Auvergne,
With modesty admiring thy renown,
By me entreats, great lord, thou wouldst vouchsafe 40
To visit her poor castle where she lies,
That she may boast she hath beheld the man
Whose glory fills the world with loud report.
  Bur. Is it even so? Nay, then I see our wars
Will turn unto a peaceful comic sport, 45
When ladies crave to be encount'red with.
You may not, my lord, despise her gentle suit.
  Tal. Ne'er trust me then; for when a world of men
Could not prevail with all their oratory,
Yet hath a woman's kindness overrul'd; 50
And therefore tell her I return great thanks,
And in submission will attend on her.
Will not your honors bear me company?
  Bed. No, truly, 'tis more than manners will;
And I have heard it said, unbidden guests 55
Are often welcomest when they are gone.
  Tal. Well then, alone (since there's no remedy)
I mean to prove this lady's courtesy.
Come hither, captain. (*Whispers.*) You perceive my
    mind?

---

50. **cunning:** skill (with magic).
61. **to-night:** last night.   68. **her:** i.e. Joan's.
75. **shift:** plan, device.   77. **platforms:** plans.

II.ii. Location: Within the town of Orleans.
o.s.d. **dead march.** For Salisbury.
3. **retreat:** trumpet signal for withdrawal of forces.
5. **advance:** raise (on a bier).   6. **centure:** cincture, belt.
8. **was:** that was.

12–13. **Within . . . interr'd.** Actually, as Hall records (Bullough, III, 56), Salisbury's body "was conveyed into England, with al funerall and pompe, and buried at Bissam by his progenitors."
19. **muse:** wonder.   28. **trull:** whore.   33. **power:** forces.
41. **lies:** lives.   47. **gentle:** courteous.
54. **manners will:** etiquette allows.   58. **prove:** test.

1 Henry VI
II.ii

Capt. I do, my lord, and mean accordingly. 60
                               Exeunt.

[SCENE III]

Enter COUNTESS [OF AUVERGNE *and her* PORTER].

Count. Porter, remember what I gave in charge,
And when you have done so, bring the keys to me.
  Port. Madam, I will.   *Exit.*
  Count. The plot is laid. If all things fall out right,
I shall as famous be by this exploit   5
As Scythian Tomyris by Cyrus' death.
Great is the rumor of this dreadful knight,
And his achievements of no less account;
Fain would mine eyes be witness with mine ears
To give their censure of these rare reports.   10

Enter MESSENGER *and* TALBOT.

  Mess. Madam,
According as your ladyship desir'd,
By message crav'd, so is Lord Talbot come.
    Count. And he is welcome. What? is this the man?
    Mess. Madam, it is.
    Count.   Is this the scourge of France?
Is this the Talbot, so much fear'd abroad   16
That with his name the mothers still their babes?
I see report is fabulous and false.
I thought I should have seen some Hercules,
A second Hector, for his grim aspect   20
And large proportion of his strong-knit limbs.
Alas, this is a child, a silly dwarf!
It cannot be this weak and writhled shrimp
Should strike such terror to his enemies.
  Tal. Madam, I have been bold to trouble you;   25
But since your ladyship is not at leisure,
I'll sort some other time to visit you.   [*Going.*]
  Count. What means he now? Go ask him whither
    he goes.
  Mess. Stay, my Lord Talbot, for my lady craves
To know the cause of your abrupt departure.   30
  Tal. Marry, for that she's in a wrong belief,
I go to certify her Talbot's here.

Enter PORTER *with keys.*

  Count. If thou be he, then art thou prisoner.
  Tal. Prisoner? to whom?
  Count.   To me, blood-thirsty lord;
And for that cause I train'd thee to my house.   35
Long time thy shadow hath been thrall to me,

For in my gallery thy picture hangs;
But now the substance shall endure the like,
And I will chain these legs and arms of thine,
That hast by tyranny these many years   40
Wasted our country, slain our citizens,
And sent our sons and husbands captivate.
  Tal. Ha, ha, ha!
  Count. Laughest thou, wretch? Thy mirth shall
    turn to moan.
  Tal. I laugh to see your ladyship so fond   45
To think that you have aught but Talbot's shadow
Whereon to practice your severity.
  Count. Why? art not thou the man?
  Tal.   I am indeed.
  Count. Then have I substance too.
  Tal. No, no, I am but shadow of myself.   50
You are deceiv'd, my substance is not here;
For what you see is but the smallest part
And least proportion of humanity.
I tell you, madam, were the whole frame here,
It is of such a spacious lofty pitch,   55
Your roof were not sufficient to contain't.
  Count. This is a riddling merchant for the nonce:
He will be here, and yet he is not here.
How can these contrarieties agree?
  Tal. That will I show you presently.   60
          Winds his horn. Drums strike up;
             a peal of ordinance.

Enter SOLDIERS.

How say you, madam? Are you now persuaded
That Talbot is but shadow of himself?
These are his substance, sinews, arms, and strength,
With which he yoketh your rebellious necks,
Razeth your cities, and subverts your towns,   65
And in a moment makes them desolate.
  Count. Victorious Talbot, pardon my abuse.
I find thou art no less than fame hath bruited,
And more than may be gathered by thy shape.
Let my presumption not provoke thy wrath,   70
For I am sorry that with reverence
I did not entertain thee as thou art.
  Tal. Be not dismay'd, fair lady, nor misconster
The mind of Talbot, as you did mistake
The outward composition of his body.   75
What you have done hath not offended me;
Nor other satisfaction do I crave,
But only, with your patience, that we may
Taste of your wine and see what cates you have,
For soldiers' stomachs always serve them well.   80
  Count. With all my heart, and think me honored
To feast so great a warrior in my house.   *Exeunt.*

---

60. **mean:** i.e. intend to act.

II.iii. Location: Auvergne. The Countess' castle.
1. **gave in charge:** commanded.
6. **Tomyris:** Scythian queen who killed Cyrus the Great in battle and preserved his head in a wineskin filled with blood.
10. **censure:** judgment, opinion.
19, 20. **Hercules, Hector.** Men of legendary strength.
21. **proportion:** size. 23. **writhled:** wrinkled. 27. **sort:** choose.
31. **Marry:** indeed (originally the name of the Virgin Mary used as an oath). **for that:** because. 32. **certify:** inform.
35. **train'd:** enticed.
36. **shadow . . . me:** i.e. I have held your picture prisoner.

42. **captivate:** taken captive. 45. **fond:** foolish.
53. **proportion of humanity:** part of the man. 55. **pitch:** height.
57. **riddling merchant:** dealer in riddles. **for the nonce:** for the occasion (a meaningless line-filler).
60. **presently:** immediately. s.d. **Winds:** sounds.
65. **subverts:** overturns. 67. **abuse:** deception.
68. **fame:** report. **bruited:** announced.
72. **entertain:** receive. 73. **misconster:** misconstrue.
78. **patience:** permission. 79. **cates:** delicacies.

[SCENE IV]

Enter RICHARD PLANTAGENET, WARWICK, SOMERSET,
    POLE [EARL OF SUFFOLK], *and others* [VERNON *and
    a* LAWYER].

Plan.   Great lords and gentlemen, what means this
        silence?
Dare no man answer in a case of truth?

Suf.   Within the Temple Hall we were too loud,
The garden here is more convenient.

Plan.   Then say at once if I maintain'd the truth;   5
Or else was wrangling Somerset in th' error?

Suf.   Faith, I have been a truant in the law,
And never yet could frame my will to it,
And therefore frame the law unto my will.

Som.   Judge you, my Lord of Warwick, then be-
        tween us.   10

War.   Between two hawks, which flies the higher
        pitch,
Between two dogs, which hath the deeper mouth,
Between two blades, which bears the better temper,
Between two horses, which doth bear him best,
Between two girls, which hath the merriest eye—   15
I have perhaps some shallow spirit of judgment;
But in these nice sharp quillets of the law,
Good faith, I am no wiser than a daw.

Plan.   Tut, tut, here is a mannerly forbearance.
The truth appears so naked on my side   20
That any purblind eye may find it out.

Som.   And on my side it is so well apparell'd,
So clear, so shining, and so evident,
That it will glimmer through a blindman's eye.

Plan.   Since you are tongue-tied and so loath to
        speak,   25
In dumb significants proclaim your thoughts:
Let him that is a true-born gentleman
And stands upon the honor of his birth,
If he suppose that I have pleaded truth,
From off this brier pluck a white rose with me.   30

Som.   Let him that is no coward nor no flatterer,
But dare maintain the party of the truth,
Pluck a red rose from off this thorn with me.

War.   I love no colors; and without all color
Of base insinuating flattery,   35
I pluck this white rose with Plantagenet.

Suf.   I pluck this red rose with young Somerset,
And say withal, I think he held the right.

Ver.   Stay, lords and gentlemen, and pluck no more,
Till you conclude that he upon whose side   40
The fewest roses are cropp'd from the tree
Shall yield the other in the right opinion.

Som.   Good Master Vernon, it is well objected;
If I have fewest, I subscribe in silence.

Plan.   And I.   45

Ver.   Then for the truth and plainness of the case,
I pluck this pale and maiden blossom here,
Giving my verdict on the white rose side.

Som.   Prick not your finger as you pluck it off,
Lest, bleeding, you do paint the white rose red,   50
And fall on my side so against your will.

Ver.   If I, my lord, for my opinion bleed,
Opinion shall be surgeon to my hurt,
And keep me on the side where still I am.

Som.   Well, well, come on, who else?   55

Law.   Unless my study and my books be false,
The argument you held was wrong in you;
                                [*To Somerset.*]
In sign whereof I pluck a white rose too.

Plan.   Now, Somerset, where is your argument?

Som.   Here in my scabbard, meditating that   60
Shall dye your white rose in a bloody red.

Plan.   Mean time your cheeks do counterfeit our
        roses;
For pale they look with fear, as witnessing
The truth on our side.

Som.   No, Plantagenet;
'Tis not for fear, but anger, that thy cheeks   65
Blush for pure shame to counterfeit our roses,
And yet thy tongue will not confess thy error.

Plan.   Hath not thy rose a canker, Somerset?

Som.   Hath not thy rose a thorn, Plantagenet?

Plan.   Ay, sharp and piercing, to maintain his truth,
Whiles thy consuming canker eats his falsehood.   71

Som.   Well, I'll find friends to wear my bleeding
        roses,
That shall maintain what I have said is true,
Where false Plantagenet dare not be seen.

Plan.   Now, by this maiden blossom in my hand,
I scorn thee and thy fashion, peevish boy.   76

Suf.   Turn not thy scorns this way, Plantagenet.

Plan.   Proud Pole, I will, and scorn both him and
        thee.

Suf.   I'll turn my part thereof into thy throat.

Som.   Away, away, good William de la Pole!   80
We grace the yeoman by conversing with him.

War.   Now, by God's will, thou wrong'st him,
        Somerset;
His grandfather was Lionel Duke of Clarence,
Third son to the third Edward, King of England.

II.iv. Location: London. The Temple Garden (in the precincts of the
Middle Temple and Inner Temple, two of the Inns of Court housing
the legal societies of London, so named because the buildings had
earlier belonged to the Knights Templars).
o.s.d. **Plantagenet:** nickname for Geoffrey of Anjou, father of
Henry II and thus founder of the dynasty that ruled England from
1154 until the advent of the Tudors in 1485. The name, later associated with all the members of this royal house, was apparently first
used by Richard, Duke of York, in order to emphasize his royal
lineage and thus bolster his claim to the throne against the Lancastrian branch of the family. **3. were:** would be.
11. pitch: flight (a term from falconry). **12. mouth:** voice.
14. bear him: carry himself.
17. nice: precise. **quillets:** subtleties. **18. daw:** jackdaw.
21. purblind: dim-sighted. **26. significants:** signs.
29. pleaded: argued (one of a number of legal terms in this scene).
32. party: side. **34. colors:** pretenses, pretexts.
38. withal: besides.

43. objected: urged.
44. subscribe: submit. **52. opinion:** judgment, conviction.
53. Opinion: public opinion, reputation, honor.
60. that: that which. **62. counterfeit:** imitate.
68. canker: cankerworm, grub. **70. his:** its.
76. fashion: kind, sort. **peevish boy:** sullen youngster.
78. Pole: family name of the Duke of Suffolk.
79. turn . . . throat: throw the slanders back into the throat from
which they came.
81. yeoman: freeholder below the rank of gentleman.
83–84. His . . . England. Lionel was actually Richard's maternal
great-great-grandfather; but Edward III's fifth son, Edmund, Duke
of York, was Richard's paternal grandfather. He could thus claim
descent from Edward III through both his parents.

1 Henry VI
II.iv

Spring crestless yeomen from so deep a root?   85
    Plan.   He bears him on the place's privilege,
Or durst not for his craven heart say thus.
    Som.   By Him that made me, I'll maintain my words
On any plot of ground in Christendom.
Was not thy father, Richard Earl of Cambridge,   90
For treason executed in our late king's days?
And by his treason, stand'st not thou attainted,
Corrupted, and exempt from ancient gentry?
His trespass yet lives guilty in thy blood,
And till thou be restor'd, thou art a yeoman.   95
    Plan.   My father was attached, not attainted,
Condemn'd to die for treason, but no traitor;
And that I'll prove on better men than Somerset,
Were growing time once ripened to my will.
For your partaker Pole, and you yourself,   100
I'll note you in my book of memory,
To scourge you for this apprehension.
Look to it well, and say you are well warn'd.
    Som.   Ah, thou shalt find us ready for thee still;
And know us by these colors for thy foes,   105
For these my friends in spite of thee shall wear.
    Plan.   And, by my soul, this pale and angry rose,
As cognizance of my blood-drinking hate,
Will I for ever and my faction wear,
Until it wither with me to my grave,   110
Or flourish to the height of my degree.
    Suf.   Go forward, and be chok'd with thy ambition!
And so farewell until I meet thee next.   *Exit.*
    Som.   Have with thee, Pole. Farewell, ambitious
        Richard.   *Exit.*
    Plan.   How I am brav'd, and must perforce endure
        it!   115
    War.   This blot that they object against your house
Shall be [wip'd] out in the next parliament,
Call'd for the truce of Winchester and Gloucester;
And if thou be not then created York,
I will not live to be accounted Warwick.   120
Mean time, in signal of my love to thee,
Against proud Somerset and William Pole,
Will I upon thy party wear this rose.
And here I prophesy: this brawl to-day,
Grown to this faction in the Temple Garden,   125
Shall send between the Red Rose and the White
A thousand souls to death and deadly night.
    Plan.   Good Master Vernon, I am bound to you
That you on my behalf would pluck a flower.
    Ver.   In your behalf still will I wear the same.   130

85. **crestless:** without a coat of arms.
86. **bears . . . privilege:** takes advantage of the fact that this is a privileged place, where weapons are forbidden. Actually, the Temple Garden, unlike the Tower (I.iii.46), enjoyed no such privilege.
91. **late king's:** i.e. Henry V's.   92. **attainted:** disgraced.
93. **exempt:** excluded.
96. **attached, not attainted:** arrested, not convicted. This is an important distinction, for normally the heirs of a nobleman attainted for treason were "exempt from ancient gentry" and stripped of all their rights. Richard's statement is true: his father, the Earl of Cambridge, had been summarily executed for treason without a bill of attainder (see *Henry V*, II.ii).
99. **Were . . . will:** if I ever have the chance.
100. **For:** as for.   **partaker:** supporter.
102. **apprehension:** opinion.   104. **still:** always.
108. **cognizance:** badge.   111. **degree:** rank.
114. **Have with thee:** let's go.   115. **brav'd:** defied, insulted.
116. **object:** allege.
118. **Call'd . . . of:** summoned to make peace between.

Law.   And so will I.
    Plan.   Thanks, [gentlemen].
Come, let us four to dinner. I dare say
This quarrel will drink blood another day.   *Exeunt.*

[SCENE V]

Enter MORTIMER, *brought in a chair, and* JAILERS.

    Mor.   Kind keepers of my weak decaying age,
Let dying Mortimer here rest himself.
Even like a man new haled from the rack,
So fare my limbs with long imprisonment;
And these grey locks, the pursuivants of death,   5
Nestor-like aged, in an age of care,
Argue the end of Edmund Mortimer.
These eyes, like lamps whose wasting oil is spent,
Wax dim, as drawing to their exigent;
Weak shoulders, overborne with burthening grief,   10
And pithless arms, like to a withered vine
That droops his sapless branches to the ground.
Yet are these feet, whose strengthless stay is numb
(Unable to support this lump of clay),
Swift-winged with desire to get a grave,   15
As witting I no other comfort have.
But tell me, keeper, will my nephew come?
    [*1.*] *Keeper.*   Richard Plantagenet, my lord, will
        come.
We sent unto the Temple, unto his chamber,
And answer was return'd that he will come.   20
    Mor.   Enough; my soul shall then be satisfied.
Poor gentleman, his wrong doth equal mine.
Since Henry Monmouth first began to reign,
Before whose glory I was great in arms,
This loathsome sequestration have I had;   25
And even since then hath Richard been obscur'd,
Depriv'd of honor and inheritance.
But now, the arbitrator of despairs,
Just Death, kind umpire of men's miseries,
With sweet enlargement doth dismiss me hence.   30
I would his troubles likewise were expir'd,
That so he might recover what was lost.

Enter RICHARD [PLANTAGENET].

    [*1.*] *Keeper.*   My lord, your loving nephew now is
        come.
    Mor.   Richard Plantagenet, my friend, is he come?
    Plan.   Ay, noble uncle, thus ignobly us'd,   35
Your nephew, late-despised Richard, comes.

II.v. **Location:** London. The Tower.
5. **pursuivants:** heralds.
6. **Nestor-like:** i.e. extremely old, like Nestor, one of the Grecian leaders at the siege of Troy.
7. **Argue:** indicate.   **Edmund Mortimer.** A mistake, adopted from the chroniclers, for Sir John Mortimer, who, after several years in prison, was executed in 1424 for urging his cousin Edmund Mortimer's claim to the throne. Edmund, fifth Earl of March and great-grandson of Lionel, Duke of Clarence, had been recognized as heir presumptive by Richard II in 1398. Although an object of suspicion during the early years of the Lancastrian revolution, he served honorably with Henry V in France and died in 1425 as Lord Lieutenant of Ireland.   9. **exigent:** end.   11. **pithless:** weak.
13. **stay:** support.   16. **witting:** knowing.
22. **his wrong:** the wrong done to him.
23. **Henry Monmouth:** i.e. Henry V.
25. **sequestration:** imprisonment.   30. **enlargement:** release.
36. **late-despised:** lately treated with contempt.

Mor. Direct mine arms I may embrace his neck,
And in his bosom spend my latter gasp.
O, tell me when my lips do touch his cheeks,
That I may kindly give one fainting kiss.   40
And now declare, sweet stem from York's great stock,
Why didst thou say, of late thou wert despis'd?
Plan. First, lean thine aged back against mine arm,
And in that ease, I'll tell thee my disease.
This day, in argument upon a case,   45
Some words there grew 'twixt Somerset and me;
Among which terms he us'd his lavish tongue
And did upbraid me with my father's death;
Which obloquy set bars before my tongue,
Else with the like I had requited him.   50
Therefore, good uncle, for my father's sake,
In honor of a true Plantagenet,
And for alliance sake, declare the cause
My father, Earl of Cambridge, lost his head.   54
Mor. That cause, fair nephew, that imprison'd me
And hath detain'd me all my flow'ring youth
Within a loathsome dungeon, there to pine,
Was cursed instrument of his decease.
Plan. Discover more at large what cause that was,
For I am ignorant and cannot guess.   60
Mor. I will, if that my fading breath permit
And death approach not ere my tale be done.
Henry the Fourth, grandfather to this king,
Depos'd his nephew Richard, Edward's son,
The first begotten, and the lawful heir   65
Of Edward king, the third of that descent;
During whose reign the Percies of the north,
Finding his usurpation most unjust,
Endeavor'd my advancement to the throne.
The reason mov'd these warlike lords to this   70
Was, for that (young Richard thus remov'd,
Leaving no heir begotten of his body)
I was the next by birth and parentage;
For by my mother I derived am
From Lionel Duke of Clarence, third son   75
To King Edward the Third; whereas he
From John of Gaunt doth bring his pedigree,
Being but fourth of that heroic line.
But mark: as in this haughty great attempt
They labored to plant the rightful heir,   80
I lost my liberty, and they their lives.
Long after this, when Henry the Fift
(Succeeding his father Bullingbrook) did reign,
Thy father, Earl of Cambridge then, deriv'd
From famous Edmund Langley, Duke of York,   85
Marrying my sister that thy mother was,
Again, in pity of my hard distress,
Levied an army, weening to redeem
And have install'd me in the diadem.
But as the rest, so fell that noble earl,   90
And was beheaded. Thus the Mortimers,
In whom the title rested, were suppress'd.

Plan. Of which, my lord, your honor is the last.
Mor. True; and thou seest that I no issue have,
And that my fainting words do warrant death.   95
Thou art my heir; the rest I wish thee gather;
But yet be wary in thy studious care.
Plan. Thy grave admonishments prevail with me.
But yet methinks, my father's execution
Was nothing less than bloody tyranny.   100
Mor. With silence, nephew, be thou politic.
Strong fixed is the house of Lancaster,
And like a mountain, not to be remov'd.
But now thy uncle is removing hence,
As princes do their courts, when they are cloy'd   105
With long continuance in a settled place.
Plan. O uncle, would some part of my young
          years
Might but redeem the passage of your age!
Mor. Thou dost then wrong me, as that slaughterer
          doth
Which giveth many wounds when one will kill.   110
Mourn not, except thou sorrow for my good,
Only give order for my funeral.
And so farewell, and fair be all thy hopes,
And prosperous be thy life in peace and war!   *Dies.*
Plan. And peace, no war, befall thy parting soul!
In prison hast thou spent a pilgrimage,   116
And like a hermit overpass'd thy days.
Well, I will lock his counsel in my breast,
And what I do imagine, let that rest.
Keepers, convey him hence, and I myself   120
Will see his burial better than his life.
          Exeunt [Keepers, bearing out the body of Mortimer].
Here dies the dusky torch of Mortimer,
Chok'd with ambition of the meaner sort;
And for those wrongs, those bitter injuries,
Which Somerset hath offer'd to my house,   125
I doubt not but with honor to redress.
And therefore haste I to the parliament,
Either to be restored to my blood,
Or make my will th' advantage of my good.   *Exit.*

ACT III, SCENE I

Flourish. Enter KING, EXETER, GLOUCESTER, WIN-
CHESTER, WARWICK, SOMERSET, SUFFOLK, RICHARD
PLANTAGENET, [*and others*]. *Gloucester offers to put
up a bill; Winchester snatches it, tears it.*

Win. Com'st thou with deep premeditated lines,
With written pamphlets studiously devis'd?
Humphrey of Gloucester, if thou canst accuse,
Or aught intend'st to lay unto my charge,
Do it without invention, suddenly,   5

---

1 Henry VI
III.i

---

38. **latter:** final.   44. **disease:** trouble, grievance.
53. **for alliance sake:** for the sake of our relationship. Richard's
mother, Anne, was Edmund's sister. 59. **Discover:** divulge.
64. **nephew:** kinsman (here, cousin).   67. **whose:** i.e. Henry IV's.
70. **mov'd:** which moved.   71. **for that:** because.
74. **mother.** Actually, his paternal grandmother (Philippa, daughter
of Lionel, Duke of Clarence).   88. **weening:** thinking.

95. **warrant:** certify.   96. **gather:** infer.
117. **overpass'd:** passed, spent.
123. **with:** by.   **meaner sort:** those of lower rank (i.e. the Lancastrians).   128. **blood:** hereditary rights.
129. **make . . . good:** make my desire the means whereby I'll reach
my goal.

III.i. Location: London. The Parliament House.
o.s.d. **bill:** written statement.   1. **lines:** i.e. of writing.
5. **invention:** deliberate preparation.   **suddenly:** extempore.

1 Henry VI
III.i

As I with sudden and extemporal speech
Purpose to answer what thou canst object.
   Glou. Presumptuous priest, this place commands
      my patience,
Or thou shouldst find thou hast dishonor'd me.
Think not, although in writing I preferr'd   10
The manner of thy vile outrageous crimes,
That therefore I have forg'd, or am not able
Verbatim to rehearse the method of my pen.
No, prelate, such is thy audacious wickedness,
Thy lewd, pestiferous, and dissentious pranks,   15
As very infants prattle of thy pride.
Thou art a most pernicious usurer,
Froward by nature, enemy to peace,
Lascivious, wanton, more than well beseems
A man of thy profession and degree;   20
And for thy treachery, what's more manifest?
In that thou laidst a trap to take my life,
As well at London Bridge as at the Tower.
Beside, I fear me, if thy thoughts were sifted,
The King, thy sovereign, is not quite exempt   25
From envious malice of thy swelling heart.
   Win. Gloucester, I do defy thee. Lords, vouchsafe
To give me hearing what I shall reply.
If I were covetous, ambitious, or perverse,
As he will have me, how am I so poor?   30
Or how haps it I seek not to advance
Or raise myself, but keep my wonted calling?
And for dissension, who preferreth peace
More than I do, except I be provok'd?
No, my good lords, it is not that offends,   35
It is not that that hath incens'd the Duke:
It is because no one should sway but he,
No one, but he, should be about the King;
And that engenders thunder in his breast,
And makes him roar these accusations forth.   40
But he shall know I am as good—
   Glou.   As good?
Thou bastard of my grandfather!
   Win. Ay, lordly sir; for what are you, I pray,
But one imperious in another's throne?
   Glou. Am I not Protector, saucy priest?   45
   Win. And am not I a prelate of the Church?
   Glou. Yes, as an outlaw in a castle keeps
And useth it to patronage his theft.
   Win. Unreverent Gloucester!
   Glou.   Thou art reverent
Touching thy spiritual function, not thy life.   50

   Win. Rome shall remedy this.
   [*Glou.*]   Roam thither then.
   War. My lord [*to Winchester*], it were your duty
     to forbear.
   Som. Ay, [so] the Bishop be not overborne.
Methinks my lord should be religious,
And know the office that belongs to such.   55
   War. Methinks his lordship should be humbler,
It fitteth not a prelate so to plead.
   Som. Yes, when his holy state is touch'd so near.
   War. State holy or unhallow'd, what of that?
Is not his Grace Protector to the King?   60
   Plan. [*Aside.*] Plantagenet, I see, must hold his
     tongue,
Lest it be said, "Speak, sirrah, when you should;
Must your bold verdict enter talk with lords?"
Else would I have a fling at Winchester.
   King. Uncles of Gloucester and of Winchester,
The special watchmen of our English weal,   66
I would prevail, if prayers might prevail,
To join your hearts in love and amity.
O, what a scandal is it to our crown
That two such noble peers as ye should jar!   70
Believe me, lords, my tender years can tell,
Civil dissension is a viperous worm
That gnaws the bowels of the commonwealth.
   A noise within, "Down with the tawny-coats!"
What tumult's this?
   War.   An uproar, I dare warrant,
Begun through malice of the Bishop's men.   75
      A noise again, "Stones! stones!"

Enter MAYOR [*OF LONDON, attended*].

   May. O my good lords, and virtuous Henry,
Pity the city of London, pity us!
The Bishop and the Duke of Gloucester's men,
Forbidden late to carry any weapon,
Have fill'd their pockets full of pebble stones;   80
And, banding themselves in contrary parts,
Do pelt so fast at one another's pate
That many have their giddy brains knock'd out;
Our windows are broke down in every street,
And we, for fear, compell'd to shut our shops.   85

Enter [SERVINGMEN *of both parties,*] *in skirmish, with
   bloody pates.*

   King. We charge you, on allegiance to ourself,
To hold your slaught'ring hands and keep the peace.
Pray, uncle Gloucester, mitigate this strife.
   1. Serv. Nay, if we be forbidden stones, we'll fall
to it with our teeth.   90
   2. Serv. Do what ye dare, we are as resolute.
                      Skirmish again.
   Glou. You of my household, leave this peevish
     broil,

---

7. object: urge in accusation.
8. this place: i.e. in Parliament, with the King presiding.
10. preferr'd: set forth, explained. At the Parliament that met at Leicester in 1426 Gloucester, according to Hall (Bullough, III, 49–50), brought against the Bishop of Winchester various charges of misconduct, including an attempted ambush of the Protector as he was journeying toward Eltham for consultation with the King.
13. Verbatim: orally.   **method:** summary of the contents of a document.   **15. lewd:** wicked.   **pestiferous:** deadly.   **16. As:** that.
31. haps: happens.   **35. that:** that which.
42. grandfather: John of Gaunt, from whose liaison with Katherine Swynford the mighty Beaufort family sprang. Following Gaunt's marriage to his mistress in 1396, their children were legitimized by an act of Parliament, and they and their descendants were powerful through the fifteenth century. Margaret Beaufort, daughter of Winchester's nephew John (the Duke of Somerset of this play), was the mother of Henry VII.   **47. keeps:** dwells.
48. patronage: protect.

58. when . . . near: i.e. when his position as a churchman is concerned.
63. bold verdict: insolent opinion.   **enter talk:** engage in discussion.   **66. weal:** common good.   **70. jar:** quarrel.
71. tender years: Actually, Henry VI was five years old at the time of the events represented.
77. London. Actually, the meeting of Parliament represented in this scene was at Leicester. See note to line 10 above.
92. peevish: childish.

And set this unaccustom'd fight aside.

　3. Serv.　My lord, we know your Grace to be a man
Just and upright; and, for your royal birth,　95
Inferior to none but to his Majesty;
And ere that we will suffer such a prince,
So kind a father of the commonweal,
To be disgraced by an inkhorn mate,
We and our wives and children all will fight,　100
And have our bodies slaught'red by thy foes.

　1. Serv.　Ay, and the very parings of our nails
Shall pitch a field when we are dead.　*Begin again.*

　Glou.　　　　　　　　　　Stay, stay, I say!
And if you love me, as you say you do,
Let me persuade you to forbear a while.　105

　King.　O, how this discord doth afflict my soul!
Can you, my Lord of Winchester, behold
My sighs and tears, and will not once relent?
Who should be pitiful, if you be not?
Or who should study to prefer a peace,　110
If holy churchmen take delight in broils?

　War.　Yield, my Lord Protector, yield, Win-
　　chester,
Except you mean with obstinate repulse
To slay your sovereign and destroy the realm.
You see what mischief, and what murther too,　115
Hath been enacted through your enmity.
Then be at peace, except ye thirst for blood.

　Win.　He shall submit, or I will never yield.

　Glou.　Compassion on the King commands me
　　stoop,
Or I would see his heart out ere the priest　120
Should ever get that privilege of me.

　War.　Behold, my Lord of Winchester, the Duke
Hath banish'd moody discontented fury,
As by his smoothed brows it doth appear.
Why look you still so stern and tragical?　125

　Glou.　Here, Winchester, I offer thee my hand.

　King.　Fie, uncle Beauford, I have heard you preach
That malice was a great and grievous sin;
And will not you maintain the thing you teach,
But prove a chief offender in the same?　130

　War.　Sweet King! the Bishop hath a kindly gird.
For shame, my Lord of Winchester, relent!
What, shall a child instruct you what to do?

　Win.　Well, Duke of Gloucester, I will yield to
　　thee;
Love for thy love and hand for hand I give.　135

　Glou.　[*Aside.*]　Ay, but, I fear me, with a hollow
　　heart.—
See here, my friends and loving countrymen,
This token serveth for a flag of truce
Betwixt ourselves and all our followers.
So help me God, as I dissemble not!　140

　Win.　[*Aside.*]　So help me God, as I intend it not!

　King.　O loving uncle, kind Duke of Gloucester,
How joyful am I made by this contract!
Away, my masters, trouble us no more,

But join in friendship, as your lords have done.　145

　1. Serv.　Content, I'll to the surgeon's.

　2. Serv.　　　　　　　　　　　And so will I.

　3. Serv.　And I will see what physic the tavern
　　affords.　　*Exeunt* [*Servingmen, Mayor, etc.*].

　War.　Accept this scroll, most gracious sovereign,
Which in the right of Richard Plantagenet
We do exhibit to your Majesty.　150

　Glou.　Well urg'd, my Lord of Warwick; for,
　　sweet prince,
And if your Grace mark every circumstance,
You have great reason to do Richard right,
Especially for those occasions
At Eltam Place I told your Majesty.　155

　King.　And those occasions, uncle, were of force:
Therefore, my loving lords, our pleasure is
That Richard be restored to his blood.

　War.　Let Richard be restored to his blood,
So shall his father's wrongs be recompens'd.　160

　Win.　As will the rest, so willeth Winchester.

　King.　If Richard will be true, not that alone
But all the whole inheritance I give
That doth belong unto the house of York,
From whence you spring by lineal descent.　165

　Plan.　Thy humble servant vows obedience
And humble service till the point of death.

　King.　Stoop then and set your knee against my
　　foot,
And in reguerdon of that duty done,
I girt thee with the valiant sword of York:　170
Rise, Richard, like a true Plantagenet,
And rise created princely Duke of York.

　Plan.　And so thrive Richard as thy foes may fall!
And as my duty springs, so perish they
That grudge one thought against your Majesty!　175

　All.　Welcome, high prince, the mighty Duke of
　　York!

　Som.　[*Aside.*]　Perish, base prince, ignoble Duke of
　　York!

　Glou.　Now will it best avail your Majesty
To cross the seas and to be crown'd in France.
The presence of a king engenders love　180
Amongst his subjects and his loyal friends,
As it disanimates his enemies.

　King.　When Gloucester says the word, King
　　Henry goes,
For friendly counsel cuts off many foes.

　Glou.　Your ships already are in readiness.　185
　　　　Sennet. Flourish. Exeunt. Manet Exeter.

　Exe.　Ay, we may march in England, or in France,
Not seeing what is likely to ensue.
This late dissension grown betwixt the peers

99. **inkhorn mate:** i.e. scribbler.
103. **pitch a field:** fight a battle.　110. **prefer:** propose.
121. **privilege:** advantage.　123. **moody:** haughty.
131. **kindly gird:** proper rebuke.　138. **This token:** i.e. handshake.
144. **masters:** here, a term of condescension.

147. **physic:** remedy.　150. **exhibit:** present.　152. **And if:** if.
154. **occasions:** reasons.　156. **of force:** strong, compelling.
158. **blood:** hereditary rights (as heir to the Earl of Cambridge).
169. **reguerdon:** reward.
170. **girt:** gird.　**York.** The King restores to Richard not only the
earldom of Cambridge (which he inherited from his father) but also
the dukedom of York (which he inherited from his father's elder
brother, who had been killed at Agincourt).
175. **grudge one thought:** i.e. harbor one grudging thought.
179. **cross the seas.** Actually, Henry VI did not go to France until
1430, four years after the events represented in this scene.
185 s.d. **Sennet:** trumpet notes to signal the arrival or departure of
a procession.

1 Henry VI
III.i

Burns under feigned ashes of forg'd love,
And will at last break out into a flame: 190
As fest'red members rot but by degree,
Till bones and flesh and sinews fall away,
So will this base and envious discord breed.
And now I fear that fatal prophecy
Which in the time of Henry nam'd the Fift 195
Was in the mouth of every sucking babe,
That Henry born at Monmouth should win all,
And Henry born at Windsor lose all:
Which is so plain that Exeter doth wish 199
His days may finish ere that hapless time. *Exit.*

SCENE II

Enter PUCELLE, *disguis'd, with four* SOLDIERS *with
sacks upon their backs.*

Puc. These are the city-gates, the gates of Roan,
Through which our policy must make a breach.
Take heed, be wary how you place your words,
Talk like the vulgar sort of market men
That come to gather money for their corn. 5
If we have entrance, as I hope we shall,
And that we find the slothful watch but weak,
I'll by a sign give notice to our friends,
That Charles the Dolphin may encounter them.
[1.] Sol. Our sacks shall be a mean to sack the city,
And we be lords and rulers over Roan, 11
Therefore we'll knock. *Knock.*
Watch. [*Within.*] Qui là?
Puc. Paysans, la pauvre gens de France,
Poor market folks that come to sell their corn. 15
Watch. Enter, go in, the market bell is rung.
Puc. Now, Roan, I'll shake thy bulwarks to the
ground. *Exeunt [to the town].*

Enter CHARLES, BASTARD, ALANSON, [REIGNIER, *and
forces*].

Char. Saint Denis bless this happy stratagem!
And once again we'll sleep secure in Roan.
Bast. Here ent'red Pucelle and her practisants. 20
Now she is there, how will she specify
Here is the best and safest passage in?
Reig. By thrusting out a torch from yonder tower,
Which once discern'd, shows that her meaning is,
No way to that, for weakness, which she ent'red. 25

Enter PUCELLE *on the top, thrusting out a torch burning.*

Puc. Behold, this is the happy wedding torch
That joineth Roan unto her countrymen,

But burning fatal to the Talbonites! [*Exit.*]
Bast. See, noble Charles, the beacon of our friend,
The burning torch in yonder turret stands. 30
Char. Now shine it like a comet of revenge,
A prophet to the fall of all our foes!
Reig. Defer no time, delays have dangerous ends,
Enter and cry "The Dolphin!" presently,
And then do execution on the watch. 35
Alarum. [Exeunt.]

An alarum. [Enter] TALBOT *in an excursion.*

Tal. France, thou shalt rue this treason with thy
tears,
If Talbot but survive thy treachery.
Pucelle, that witch, that damned sorceress,
Hath wrought this hellish mischief unawares,
That hardly we escap'd the pride of France. *Exit.* 40

An alarum. Excursions. BEDFORD *brought in sick in a
chair. Enter* TALBOT *and* BURGUNDY *without; within,*
PUCELLE, CHARLES, BASTARD, [ALANSON,] *and*
REIGNIER, *on the walls.*

Puc. Good morrow, gallants, want ye corn for
bread?
I think the Duke of Burgundy will fast
Before he'll buy again at such a rate.
'Twas full of darnel; do you like the taste?
Bur. Scoff on, vile fiend and shameless courtezan!
I trust ere long to choke thee with thine own, 46
And make thee curse the harvest of that corn.
Char. Your Grace may starve, perhaps, before that
time.
Bed. O, let no words, but deeds, revenge this
treason!
Puc. What will you do, good greybeard? Break
a lance, 50
And run a-tilt at Death within a chair?
Tal. Foul fiend of France, and hag of all despite,
Encompass'd with thy lustful paramours!
Becomes it thee to taunt his valiant age,
And twit with cowardice a man half dead? 55
Damsel, I'll have a bout with you again,
Or else let Talbot perish with this shame.
Puc. Are ye so hot, sir? Yet, Pucelle, hold thy
peace,
If Talbot do but thunder, rain will follow. 59
They [the English] whisper together in council.
God speed the parliament! Who shall be the speaker?
Tal. Dare ye come forth and meet us in the field?
Puc. Belike your lordship takes us then for fools,
To try if that our own be ours or no.
Tal. I speak not to that railing Hecate,
But unto thee, Alanson, and the rest. 65
Will ye, like soldiers, come and fight it out?

189. **forg'd:** false.
194. **fatal prophecy.** According to Hall (Bullough, III, 42–43), when Henry V was informed of the birth of his son at Windsor, "whether he fantasied some old blind prophesy, or had some foreknowledge, or els judged of his sonnes fortune, he sayd to the lord Fitzheugh his trusty Chamberlein these words. 'My lorde, I Henry borne at Monmoth shall small tyme reigne & much get, & Henry borne at Wyndsore shall long reigne and al lese, but as God will so be it.'"

III.ii. Location: France. Before Rouen. (The story of the capture of Rouen, as represented in this scene, is fictitious. The city was not relinquished by the English until 1449.) 2. **policy:** trickery. 5. **corn:** grain. 7. **that:** if. 10. **mean:** means. 13–14. **Qui...France:** "Who's there?" "Peasants, poor French folk." 20. **practisants:** fellow conspirators. 25. **to:** i.e. is comparable to.

31. **shine it:** may it shine. 34. **presently:** immediately.
35 s.d. **excursion:** sally, sortie. 39. **unawares:** unexpectedly.
40. **pride:** i.e. princes. 44. **darnel:** weeds.
46. **thine own:** i.e. your own bread.
50. **greybeard.** Actually, John, Duke of Bedford, did not die until 1435 (at the age of forty-five), some four years after he had presided over the execution of Joan of Arc.
51. **run...chair:** joust with Death from your invalid's chair.
52. **of all despite:** most despicable.
64. **Hecate:** goddess of witchcraft.

Alan. Signior, no.

Tal. Signior, hang! Base muleters of France!
Like peasant footboys do they keep the walls,
And dare not take up arms like gentlemen.   70

Puc. Away, captains, let's get us from the walls,
For Talbot means no goodness by his looks.
God buy, my lord, we came but to tell you
That we are here.   *Exeunt from the walls.*

Tal. And there will we be too, ere it be long,   75
Or else reproach be Talbot's greatest fame!
Vow, Burgundy, by honor of thy house,
Prick'd on by public wrongs sustain'd in France,
Either to get the town again, or die:
And I, as sure as English Henry lives   80
And as his father here was conqueror,
As sure as in this late-betrayed town
Great Cordelion's heart was buried,
So sure I swear to get the town, or die.   84

Bur. My vows are equal partners with thy vows.

Tal. But ere we go, regard this dying prince,
The valiant Duke of Bedford. Come, my lord,
We will bestow you in some better place,
Fitter for sickness and for crazy age.

Bed. Lord Talbot, do not so dishonor me: 90
Here will I sit before the walls of Roan
And will be partner of your weal or woe.

Bur. Courageous Bedford, let us now persuade you.

Bed. Not to be gone from hence; for once I read
That stout Pendragon in his litter sick   95
Came to the field and vanquished his foes.
Methinks I should revive the soldiers' hearts,
Because I ever found them as myself.

Tal. Undaunted spirit in a dying breast!
Then be it so. Heavens keep old Bedford safe!   100
And now no more ado, brave Burgundy,
But gather we our forces out of hand,
And set upon our boasting enemy.

Exit [*with Burgundy and forces into the town*].

An alarum. Excursions. Enter Sir John Falstaff *and
a* Captain.

Capt. Whither away, Sir John Falstaff, in such
haste?

Fal. Whither away? to save myself by flight.   105
We are like to have the overthrow again.

Capt. What? will you fly, and leave Lord Talbot?

Fal.   Ay,
All the Talbots in the world, to save my life.   *Exit.*

Capt. Cowardly knight, ill fortune follow thee!

Exit [*into the town*].

Retreat. Excursions. Pucelle, Alanson, *and* Charles
[*enter from the town and*] *fly.*

Bed. Now, quiet soul, depart when heaven please,

For I have seen our enemies' overthrow.   111
What is the trust or strength of foolish man?
They that of late were daring with their scoffs
Are glad and fain by flight to save themselves.

Bedford dies, and is carried in by two in his chair.

An alarum. Enter Talbot, Burgundy, *and the rest.*

Tal. Lost, and recovered in a day again!   115
This is a double honor, Burgundy;
Yet heavens have glory for this victory!

Bur. Warlike and martial Talbot, Burgundy
Enshrines thee in his heart, and there erects
Thy noble deeds as valor's monuments.   120

Tal. Thanks, gentle Duke. But where is Pucelle
now?
I think her old familiar is asleep.
Now where's the Bastard's braves, and Charles his
glikes?
What, all amort? Roan hangs her head for grief
That such a valiant company are fled.   125
Now will we take some order in the town,
Placing therein some expert officers,
And then depart to Paris to the King,
For there young Henry with his nobles lie.

Bur. What wills Lord Talbot pleaseth Burgundy.

Tal. But yet before we go, let's not forget   131
The noble Duke of Bedford late deceas'd,
But see his exequies fulfill'd in Roan.
A braver soldier never couched lance,
A gentler heart did never sway in court;   135
But kings and mightiest potentates must die,
For that's the end of human misery.   *Exeunt.*

Scene III

Enter Charles, Bastard, Alanson, Pucelle, [*and
forces*].

Puc. Dismay not, princes, at this accident,
Nor grieve that Roan is so recovered:
Care is no cure, but rather corrosive,
For things that are not to be remedied.
Let frantic Talbot triumph for a while,   5
And like a peacock sweep along his tail;
We'll pull his plumes and take away his train,
If Dolphin and the rest will be but rul'd.

Char. We have been guided by thee hitherto,
And of thy cunning had no diffidence;   10
One sudden foil shall never breed distrust.

Bast. Search out thy wit for secret policies,
And we will make thee famous through the world.

Alan. We'll set thy statue in some holy place,
And have thee reverenc'd like a blessed saint.   15

---

68. **muleters:** muleteers, mule drivers.
73. **God buy:** God be with you (good-by).
81. **father . . . conqueror.** Henry V had captured Rouen, after a long siege, in 1419.
83. **Cordelion's heart.** Holinshed records that Richard I, who died in 1199, requested that his heart be buried in Rouen as a token of his affection for that city. On his sobriquet *Coeur-de-Lion* see the note to *King John,* I.i.54.   89. **crazy:** broken, decrepit.
95. **Pendragon:** the legendary Uther Pendragon, father of King Arthur.   102. **out of hand:** immediately.

---

114. **fain:** eager.
121. **gentle:** noble.   122. **familiar:** attendant demon.
123. **braves:** boasts.   **glikes:** gleeks, scoffs.
124. **amort:** downcast, prostrated.   133. **exequies:** funeral rites.
134. **couched:** lowered to the position of attack.

III.iii. Location: Plains near Rouen.
1. **Dismay:** lose courage.
10. **diffidence:** distrust, suspicion.   11. **foil:** repulse.
12. **policies:** stratagems, tricks.

1 Henry VI
III.iii

Employ thee then, sweet virgin, for our good.
  Puc. Then thus it must be, this doth Joan devise:
By fair persuasions, mix'd with sug'red words,
We will entice the Duke of Burgundy
To leave the Talbot and to follow us.   20
  Char. Ay, marry, sweeting, if we could do that,
France were no place for Henry's warriors,
Nor should that nation boast it so with us,
But be extirped from our provinces.
  Alan. For ever should they be expuls'd from
      France,   25
And not have title of an earldom here.
  Puc. Your honors shall perceive how I will work
To bring this matter to the wished end.
                                    Drum sounds afar off.
Hark, by the sound of drum you may perceive
Their powers are marching unto Paris-ward.   30
                          Here sound an English march.
There goes the Talbot, with his colors spread,
And all the troops of English after him.
                                          French march.
Now in the rearward comes the Duke and his.
Fortune in favor makes him lag behind.
Summon a parley, we will talk with him.   35
                                Trumpets sound a parley.

[*Enter the* Duke of Burgundy *and forces*.]

  Char. A parley with the Duke of Burgundy!
  Bur. Who craves a parley with the Burgundy?
  Puc. The princely Charles of France, thy country-
      man.
  Bur. What say'st thou, Charles? for I am marching
      hence.
  Char. Speak, Pucelle, and enchant him with thy
      words.   40
  Puc. Brave Burgundy, undoubted hope of France,
Stay, let thy humble handmaid speak to thee.
  Bur. Speak on, but be not over-tedious.
  Puc. Look on thy country, look on fertile France,
And see the cities and the towns defac'd   45
By wasting ruin of the cruel foe.
As looks the mother on her lowly babe
When death doth close his tender-dying eyes,
See, see the pining malady of France!
Behold the wounds, the most unnatural wounds,   50
Which thou thyself hast given her woeful breast.
O, turn the edged sword another way,
Strike those that hurt, and hurt not those that help.
One drop of blood drawn from thy country's bosom
Should grieve thee more than streams of foreign gore.
Return thee therefore with a flood of tears,   56
And wash away thy country's stained spots.
  Bur. Either she hath bewitch'd me with her words,
Or nature makes me suddenly relent.
  Puc. Besides, all French and France exclaims on
      thee,   60
Doubting thy birth and lawful progeny.

Who join'st thou with, but with a lordly nation
That will not trust thee but for profit's sake?
When Talbot hath set footing once in France
And fashion'd thee that instrument of ill,   65
Who then but English Henry will be lord,
And thou be thrust out like a fugitive?
Call we to mind, and mark but this for proof:
Was not the Duke of Orleance thy foe?
And was he not in England prisoner?   70
But when they heard he was thine enemy,
They set him free without his ransom paid,
In spite of Burgundy and all his friends.
See then, thou fight'st against thy countrymen
And join'st with them will be thy slaughter-men.   75
Come, come, return; return, thou wandering lord!
Charles and the rest will take thee in their arms.
  Bur. [*Aside.*] I am vanquished. These haughty
      words of hers
Have batt'red me like roaring cannon-shot,
And made me almost yield upon my knees.—   80
Forgive me, country, and sweet countrymen,
And, lords, accept this hearty kind embrace.
My forces and my power of men are yours.
So farewell, Talbot, I'll no longer trust thee.
  Puc. [*Aside.*] Done like a Frenchman—turn and
      turn again!   85
  Char. Welcome, brave Duke, thy friendship makes
      us fresh.
  Bast. And doth beget new courage in our breasts.
  Alan. Pucelle hath bravely play'd her part in this,
And doth deserve a coronet of gold.
  Char. Now let us on, my lords, and join our
      powers,   90
And seek how we may prejudice the foe.   *Exeunt.*

Scene IV

Enter the King, Gloucester, Winchester, [*Richard
  Plantagenet, now* Duke of] York, Suffolk,
  Somerset, Warwick, Exeter, [Vernon, Basset,
  and others*]. *To them, with his Soldiers,* Talbot.

  Tal. My gracious prince, and honorable peers,
Hearing of your arrival in this realm,
I have a while given truce unto my wars,
To do my duty to my sovereign;
In sign whereof, this arm, that hath reclaim'd   5
To your obedience fifty fortresses,
Twelve cities, and seven walled towns of strength,
Beside five hundred prisoners of esteem,
Lets fall his sword before your Highness' feet,
And with submissive loyalty of heart   10

19–20. **We . . . us.** Actually, the Duke of Burgundy did not desert his English allies until 1435, four years after the death of Joan of Arc.
24. **extirped:** rooted out.   34. **favor:** i.e. to us (the French).
35. **Summon a parley:** sound a trumpet to request negotiations.
57. **country's stained spots:** stained country's spots.
60. **exclaims on:** denounces.   61. **progeny:** descent.

67. **fugitive:** renegade.
69. **Was . . . foe.** Actually, Charles, Duke of Orleans, who had been captured at Agincourt in 1415, was not released until 1440, five years after the Duke of Burgundy had shifted his allegiance to the French.
75. **them:** them who.
85. **Done . . . again.** Perhaps an allusion to the conversion, in 1593, of Henry of Navarre to Catholicism after he had long been aided by the English as a Protestant claimant to the throne of France.
91. **prejudice:** hurt.

III.iv. Location: Paris. The palace.
4. **duty:** homage.   8. **esteem:** i.e. exalted rank.

Ascribes the glory of his conquest got
First to my God and next unto your Grace. [*Kneels.*]
    King.   Is this the Lord Talbot, uncle Gloucester,
That hath so long been resident in France?
    Glou.   Yes, if it please your Majesty, my liege.   15
    King.   Welcome, brave captain and victorious lord!
When I was young (as yet I am not old),
I do remember how my father said
A stouter champion never handled sword.
Long since we were resolved of your truth,   20
Your faithful service, and your toil in war;
Yet never have you tasted our reward,
Or been reguerdon'd with so much as thanks,
Because till now we never saw your face.
Therefore stand up, and for these good deserts   25
We here create you Earl of Shrewsbury,
And in our coronation take your place.
               Sennet. Flourish. Exeunt. Manent
                     Vernon and Basset.
    Ver.   Now, sir, to you, that were so hot at sea,
Disgracing of these colors that I wear
In honor of my noble Lord of York,   30
Dar'st thou maintain the former words thou spak'st?
    Bas.   Yes, sir, as well as you dare patronage
The envious barking of your saucy tongue
Against my lord the Duke of Somerset.
    Ver.   Sirrah, thy lord I honor as he is.   35
    Bas.   Why, what is he? as good a man as York.
    Ver.   Hark ye; not so; in witness, take ye that.
                                        Strikes him.
    Bas.   Villain, thou knowest the law of arms is such
That whoso draws a sword, 'tis present death,
Or else this blow should broach thy dearest blood.   40
But I'll unto his Majesty, and crave
I may have liberty to venge this wrong,
When thou shalt see I'll meet thee to thy cost.
    Ver.   Well, miscreant, I'll be there as soon as you,
And after meet you, sooner than you would.   45
                                        Exeunt.

               ACT IV, SCENE I

Enter KING, GLOUCESTER, WINCHESTER, YORK,
SUFFOLK, SOMERSET, WARWICK, TALBOT, *and*
GOVERNOR [*of* PARIS,] EXETER, [*and others*].

    Glou.   Lord Bishop, set the crown upon his head.
    Win.   God save King Henry, of that name the sixt!
    Glou.   Now, Governor of Paris, take your oath:
                                        [*Governor kneels.*]

That you elect no other king but him;
Esteem none friends but such as are his friends,   5
And none your foes but such as shall pretend
Malicious practices against his state.
This shall ye do, so help you righteous God!
               [*Exeunt Governor and Train.*]

               Enter FALSTAFF.

    Fal.   My gracious sovereign, as I rode from Callice,
To haste unto your coronation,   10
A letter was deliver'd to my hands,
Writ to your Grace from th' Duke of Burgundy.
                                        [*Presents it.*]
    Tal.   Shame to the Duke of Burgundy and thee!
I vow'd, base knight, when I did meet thee next,
To tear the Garter from thy craven's leg,   15
                                        [*Plucking it off.*]
Which I have done, because (unworthily)
Thou wast installed in that high degree.
Pardon me, princely Henry, and the rest.
This dastard, at the battle of Poictiers,
When (but in all) I was six thousand strong   20
And that the French were almost ten to one,
Before we met, or that a stroke was given,
Like to a trusty squire did run away;
In which assault we lost twelve hundred men;
Myself and divers gentlemen beside   25
Were there surpris'd and taken prisoners.
Then judge, great lords, if I have done amiss;
Or whether that such cowards ought to wear
This ornament of knighthood, yea or no?
    Glou.   To say the truth, this fact was infamous   30
And ill beseeming any common man,
Much more a knight, a captain, and a leader.
    Tal.   When first this order was ordain'd, my lords,
Knights of the Garter were of noble birth,
Valiant and virtuous, full of haughty courage,   35
Such as were grown to credit by the wars;
Not fearing death, nor shrinking for distress,
But always resolute in most extremes.
He then, that is not furnish'd in this sort,
Doth but usurp the sacred name of knight,   40
Profaning this most honorable order,
And should (if I were worthy to be judge)
Be quite degraded, like a hedge-born swain
That doth presume to boast of gentle blood.
    King.   Stain to thy countrymen, thou hear'st thy
                                        doom!   45

---

15. **liege:** sovereign.
18–19. **I . . . sword.** Historically an impossibility, since Henry V
died when his son was nine months old.   20. **resolved:** convinced.
26–27. **We . . . place.** Actually, Talbot did not receive his earldom
until 1442, eleven years after Henry VI's coronation.
28–31. **Now . . . spak'st.** The circumstances of this quarrel are more
fully explained at IV.i.89–97.   32. **patronage:** uphold, defend.
39. **draws a sword:** i.e. in the king's court, which was a privileged
place.   **present:** immediate.
40. **broach . . . blood:** draw your life blood.

IV.i. Location: Paris. The palace. (Despite the Folio act break,
this scene seems to be continuous with III.iv.)
1. **set . . . head.** This scene, though dramatically effective, is historically grotesque. When Henry VI was crowned at Paris in 1431,
Talbot, who had been captured at Patay, was still a prisoner of the
French, Exeter was dead, and Gloucester was in England.

4. **elect:** accept, acknowledge.   6. **pretend:** intend.
13–47. **Shame . . . death.** Hall's account of this episode (Bullough,
III, 59–60) differs in significant detaill: "From this battaill [of Patay],
departed without any stroke striken, sir John Fastolffe, the same yere
for his valiauntnes elected into the ordre of the Garter. For whiche
cause the Duke of Bedford, in a great anger, toke from hym the Image
of sainct George, and his Garter, but afterward, by meane of frendes,
and apparant causes of good excuse by hym alledged, he was restored
to the order again, against the mynd of the lorde Talbot."
15. **Garter:** i.e. the badge of the Order of the Garter, a blue velvet
ribbon worn below the left knee.
19. **dastard:** coward.   **Poictiers.** Many editors emend to *Patay*.
30. **fact:** deed.   35. **haughty courage:** lofty spirit.
36. **credit:** fame, estimation.
38. **most extremes:** greatest extremities.
39. **furnish'd . . . sort:** thus endowed.
43. **degraded:** reduced in rank.   **hedge-born swain:** base-born rustic.
45. **doom:** judgment, sentence.

1 Henry VI
IV.i

Be packing therefore, thou that wast a knight;
Henceforth we banish thee, on pain of death.

                                                  [Exit Falstaff.]

And now, Lord Protector, view the letter
Sent from our uncle Duke of Burgundy.
    Glou. What means his Grace, that he hath chang'd
      his style?   50
No more but plain and bluntly "To the King"?
Hath he forgot he is his sovereign?
Or doth this churlish superscription
Pretend some alteration in good will?
What's here? *[Reads.]* "I have, upon especial cause,
Mov'd with compassion of my country's wrack, 56
Together with the pitiful complaints
Of such as your oppression feeds upon,
Forsaken your pernicious faction
And join'd with Charles, the rightful King of France."
O monstrous treachery! can this be so? 61
That in alliance, amity, and oaths,
There should be found such false dissembling guile?
    King. What? doth my uncle Burgundy revolt?
    Glou. He doth, my lord, and is become your foe. 65
    King. Is that the worst this letter doth contain?
    Glou. It is the worst, and all, my lord, he writes.
    King. Why then Lord Talbot there shall talk with
      him,
And give him chastisement for this abuse.
How say you, my lord? are you not content? 70
    Tal. Content, my liege? Yes. But that I am pre-
      vented,
I should have begg'd I might have been employ'd.
    King. Then gather strength and march unto him
      straight.
Let him perceive how ill we brook his treason,
And what offense it is to flout his friends. 75
    Tal. I go, my lord, in heart desiring still
You may behold confusion of your foes.   *[Exit.]*

           Enter VERNON *and* BASSET.

    Ver. Grant me the combat, gracious sovereign.
    Bas. And me, my lord, grant me the combat too.
    York. This is my servant, hear him, noble prince.
    Som. And this is mine, sweet Henry, favor him. 81
    King. Be patient, lords, and give them leave to
      speak.
Say, gentlemen, what makes you thus exclaim?
And wherefore crave you combat? or with whom?
    Ver. With him, my lord, for he hath done me
      wrong.   85
    Bas. And I with him, for he hath done me wrong.
    King. What is that wrong whereof you both
      complain?
First let me know, and then I'll answer you.
    Bas. Crossing the sea from England into France,

This fellow here, with envious carping tongue, 90
Upbraided me about the rose I wear,
Saying the sanguine color of the leaves
Did represent my master's blushing cheeks,
When stubbornly he did repugn the truth
About a certain question in the law 95
Argu'd betwixt the Duke of York and him;
With other vile and ignominious terms:
In confutation of which rude reproach,
And in defense of my lord's worthiness,
I crave the benefit of law of arms. 100
    Ver. And that is my petition, noble lord.
For though he seem with forged quaint conceit
To set a gloss upon his bold intent,
Yet know, my lord, I was provok'd by him,
And he first took exceptions at this badge, 105
Pronouncing that the paleness of this flower
Bewray'd the faintness of my master's heart.
    York. Will not this malice, Somerset, be left?
    Som. Your private grudge, my Lord of York, will
      out,
Though ne'er so cunningly you smother it. 110
    King. Good Lord, what madness rules in brain-
      sick men,
When for so slight and frivolous a cause
Such factious emulations shall arise!
Good cousins both, of York and Somerset,
Quiet yourselves, I pray, and be at peace. 115
    York. Let this dissension first be tried by fight,
And then your Highness shall command a peace.
    Som. The quarrel toucheth none but us alone,
Betwixt ourselves let us decide it then.
    York. There is my pledge, accept it, Somerset.
    Ver. Nay, let it rest where it began at first. 121
    Bas. Confirm it so, mine honorable lord.
    Glou. Confirm it so? Confounded be your strife,
And perish ye, with your audacious prate!
Presumptuous vassals, are you not asham'd 125
With this immodest clamorous outrage
To trouble and disturb the King and us?
And you, my lords, methinks you do not well
To bear with their perverse objections;
Much less to take occasion from their mouths 130
To raise a mutiny betwixt yourselves.
Let me persuade you take a better course.
    Exe. It grieves his Highness. Good my lords, be
      friends.
    King. Come hither, you that would be com-
      batants:
Henceforth I charge you, as you love our favor, 135
Quite to forget this quarrel, and the cause.
And you, my lords: remember where we are—

---

49. **uncle.** The houses of Lancaster and Burgundy were allied through the marriage (1423) of John, Duke of Bedford (Henry VI's uncle), and Anne of Burgundy (Duke Philip's sister).
50. **style:** form of address.
53. **churlish superscription:** insolent form of address (on the outside of the letter).   54. **Pretend:** indicate.
56. **wrack:** destruction.   69. **abuse:** deception.
71. **prevented:** forestalled.   76. **still:** always.
78. **combat:** i.e. permission to fight.

90. **envious:** malicious.   91. **rose:** i.e. the red rose of Lancaster.
92. **sanguine:** blood-red.   **leaves:** petals.   94. **repugn:** reject.
100. **law of arms:** right to defend one's honor in personal combat.
102. **forged quaint conceit:** false ingenious phrases.
103. **gloss:** good appearance.
106. **flower:** i.e. the white rose of York.   107. **Bewray'd:** showed.
111. **brainsick:** foolish.
113. **factious emulations:** partisan dissensions.
114. **cousins:** kinsmen.
120. **pledge:** the glove or gauntlet that York flings down as a gage.   123. **Confounded:** destroyed.
126. **immodest:** immoderate.   129. **objections:** accusations.

In France, amongst a fickle, wavering nation.
If they perceive dissension in our looks,
And that within ourselves we disagree,   140
How will their grudging stomachs be provok'd
To willful disobedience, and rebel!
Beside, what infamy will there arise,
When foreign princes shall be certified
That for a toy, a thing of no regard,   145
King Henry's peers and chief nobility
Destroy'd themselves, and lost the realm of France!
O, think upon the conquest of my father,
My tender years, and let us not forgo
That for a trifle that was bought with blood!   150
Let me be umpeer in this doubtful strife.
I see no reason, if I wear this rose,
                             [Putting on a red rose.]
That any one should therefore be suspicious
I more incline to Somerset than York:
Both are my kinsmen, and I love them both.   155
As well they may upbraid me with my crown,
Because, forsooth, the King of Scots is crown'd.
But your discretions better can persuade
Than I am able to instruct or teach;
And therefore, as we hither came in peace,   160
So let us still continue peace, and love.
Cousin of York, we institute your Grace
To be our regent in these parts of France;
And, good my Lord of Somerset, unite
Your troops of horsemen with his bands of foot,   165
And like true subjects, sons of your progenitors,
Go cheerfully together and digest
Your angry choler on your enemies.
Ourself, my Lord Protector, and the rest,
After some respite, will return to Callice;   170
From thence to England, where I hope ere long
To be presented, by your victories,
With Charles, Alanson, and that traitorous rout.
        *Flourish. Exeunt. Manent York, Warwick,
               Exeter, Vernon.*

War. My Lord of York, I promise you, the King
Prettily, methought, did play the orator.   175
York. And so he did, but yet I like it not,
In that he wears the badge of Somerset.
War. Tush, that was but his fancy, blame him not.
I dare presume, sweet prince, he thought no harm.
York. And if I [wist] he did—but let it rest,   180
Other affairs must now be managed.
                      Exeunt. Manet Exeter.
Exe. Well didst thou, Richard, to suppress thy
       voice;
For had the passions of thy heart burst out,
I fear we should have seen decipher'd there
More rancorous spite, more furious raging broils,   185
Than yet can be imagin'd or suppos'd.
But howsoe'er, no simple man that sees
This jarring discord of nobility,

This shouldering of each other in the court,
This factious bandying of their favorites,   190
But that it doth presage some ill event.
'Tis much, when sceptres are in children's hands;
But more, when envy breeds unkind division:
There comes the ruin, there begins confusion.   *Exit.*

[SCENE II]

Enter TALBOT *with Trump and Drum before Burdeaux.*

Tal. Go to the gates of Burdeaux, trumpeter,
Summon their general unto the wall.

[Trumpet] sounds. Enter GENERAL *[and others] aloft.*

English John Talbot, captains, [calls] you forth,
Servant in arms to Harry King of England,
And thus he would: Open your city-gates,   5
Be humble to us, call my sovereign yours,
And do him homage as obedient subjects,
And I'll withdraw me and my bloody power.
But if you frown upon this proffer'd peace,
You tempt the fury of my three attendants,   10
Lean famine, quartering steel, and climbing fire,
Who in a moment even with the earth
Shall lay your stately and air-braving towers,
If you forsake the offer of their love.
  [Gen.] Thou ominous and fearful owl of death, 15
Our nation's terror and their bloody scourge!
The period of thy tyranny approacheth.
On us thou canst not enter but by death;
For I protest we are well fortified,
And strong enough to issue out and fight.   20
If thou retire, the Dolphin, well appointed,
Stands with the snares of war to tangle thee.
On either hand thee there are squadrons pitch'd,
To wall thee from the liberty of flight;
And no way canst thou turn thee for redress,   25
But death doth front thee with apparent spoil,
And pale destruction meets thee in the face.
Ten thousand French have ta'en the sacrament
To rive their dangerous artillery
Upon no Christian soul but English Talbot.   30
Lo, there thou stand'st, a breathing valiant man,
Of an invincible unconquer'd spirit!
This is the latest glory of thy praise
That I thy enemy due thee withal;
For ere the glass, that now begins to run,   35
Finish the process of his sandy hour,
These eyes, that see thee now well colored,

---

190. **bandying**: contending.   **favorites**: followers.
191. **event**: outcome.   193. **envy**: malice.   **unkind**: unnatural.

IV.ii. Location: France. Before Bordeaux.
o.s.d. **Trump**: trumpeter.   **Burdeaux**: Bordeaux. Although in this act Talbot is shown dying in a vain attempt to take Bordeaux, he actually overran that city, as well as the whole Bordelais, before he fell at Castillon in 1453—twenty-two years after the coronation of Henry VI that is represented in the previous scene.
11. **quartering**: butchering.
13. **air-braving**: heaven-defying, i.e. lofty.   17. **period**: end.
21. **appointed**: equipped.
23. **either hand thee**: both sides of you.
26. **front**: confront.   **apparent spoil**: obvious destruction.
29. **rive**: cause to burst, discharge.   34. **due**: endue.
37. **well colored**: i.e. in health.

---

141. **grudging stomachs**: unruly tempers.
144. **certified**: informed.   145. **toy**: trifle.
150. **That . . . that**: for a trifle that which.   151. **umpeer**: umpire.
162–63. **Cousin . . . France**. Actually, John, Duke of Bedford, was regent at the time.   167. **digest**: dissipate.
170. **respite**: rest.   180. **And . . . wist**: if I knew.
184. **decipher'd**: displayed.

1 Henry VI
IV.ii

Shall see thee withered, bloody, pale, and dead.
Drum afar off.
Hark, hark, the Dolphin's drum, a warning bell,
Sings heavy music to thy timorous soul,	40
And mine shall ring thy dire departure out.
Exit [with others above].
Tal. He fables not, I hear the enemy.
Out, some light horsemen, and peruse their wings.
O negligent and heedless discipline!
How are we park'd and bounded in a pale,	45
A little herd of England's timorous deer,
Maz'd with a yelping kennel of French curs!
If we be English deer, be then in blood,
Not rascal-like, to fall down with a pinch,
But rather, moody-mad; and, desperate stags,	50
Turn on the bloody hounds with heads of steel,
And make the cowards stand aloof at bay.
Sell every man his life as dear as mine,
And they shall find dear deer of us, my friends.	54
God and Saint George, Talbot and England's right,
Prosper our colors in this dangerous fight!	[*Exeunt.*]

[SCENE III]

Enter a MESSENGER *that meets York. Enter* YORK *with Trumpet and many Soldiers.*

York. Are not the speedy scouts return'd again
That dogg'd the mighty army of the Dolphin?
Mess. They are return'd, my lord, and give it out
That he is march'd to Burdeaux with his power
To fight with Talbot. As he march'd along,	5
By your espials were discovered
Two mightier troops than that the Dolphin led,
Which join'd with him and made their march for
Burdeaux.	[*Exit.*]
York. A plague upon that villain Somerset,
That thus delays my promised supply	10
Of horsemen, that were levied for this siege!
Renowned Talbot doth expect my aid,
And I am louted by a traitor villain
And cannot help the noble chevalier.
God comfort him in this necessity!	15
If he miscarry, farewell wars in France!

Enter another Messenger [SIR WILLIAM LUCY].

[*Lucy.*] Thou princely leader of our English
strength,
Never so needful on the earth of France,
Spur to the rescue of the noble Talbot,
Who now is girdled with a waist of iron	20
And hemm'd about with grim destruction.
To Burdeaux, warlike Duke! to Burdeaux, York!
Else farewell Talbot, France, and England's honor!

York. O God, that Somerset, who in proud heart
Doth stop my cornets, were in Talbot's place!	25
So should we save a valiant gentleman
By forfeiting a traitor and a coward.
Mad ire and wrathful fury makes me weep,
That thus we die, while remiss traitors sleep.	29
[*Lucy.*] O, send some succor to the distress'd lord!
York. He dies, we lose; I break my warlike word;
We mourn, France smiles; we lose, they daily get;
All long of this vile traitor Somerset.
[*Lucy.*] Then God take mercy on brave Talbot's
soul,
And on his son young John, who two hours since	35
I met in travel toward his warlike father!
This seven years did not Talbot see his son,
And now they meet where both their lives are done.
York. Alas, what joy shall noble Talbot have
To bid his young son welcome to his grave?	40
Away! vexation almost stops my breath,
That sund'red friends greet in the hour of death.
Lucy, farewell, no more my fortune can,
But curse the cause I cannot aid the man.
Maine, Blois, Poictiers, and Tours, are won away,
Long all of Somerset and his delay.	46
Exit [with his Soldiers].
[*Lucy.*] Thus while the vulture of sedition
Feeds in the bosom of such great commanders,
Sleeping neglection doth betray to loss
The conquest of our scarce-cold conqueror,	50
That ever-living man of memory,
Henry the Fift. Whiles they each other cross,
Lives, honors, lands, and all, hurry to loss.

[SCENE IV]

Enter SOMERSET *with his army, [a* CAPTAIN *of Talbot's with him].*

Som. It is too late, I cannot send them now.
This expedition was by York and Talbot
Too rashly plotted. All our general force
Might with a sally of the very town
Be buckled with. The over-daring Talbot	5
Hath sullied all his gloss of former honor
By this unheedful, desperate, wild adventure.
York set him on to fight and die in shame,
That, Talbot dead, great York might bear the name.
Capt. Here is Sir William Lucy, who with me	10
Set from our o'ermatch'd forces forth for aid.
Som. How now, Sir William, whither were you
sent?
Lucy. Whither, my lord? from bought and sold
Lord Talbot,
Who, ring'd about with bold adversity,

41. **departure:** i.e. death.
43. **peruse their wings:** reconnoitre their flanks.
44. **discipline:** tactics.
45. **park'd . . . pale:** enclosed and fenced in.
47. **Maz'd:** dazed.   48. **in blood:** in good condition, vigorous.
49. **rascal-like:** like worthless deer.   **pinch:** bite, nip.
50. **moody-mad:** dangerously incensed.

IV.iii. Location: France. Plains in Gascony.
13. **louted:** made a fool of, mocked.

25. **stop my cornets:** hold back my squadrons of horse.
30. **distress'd:** in difficulties.   33. **long of:** on account of.
41. **vexation:** anguish.   43. **can:** is able to do.
50. **scarce-cold conqueror.** At the time represented in this scene
Henry V had been dead thirty-one years.
51. **ever-living . . . memory:** man of ever-living memory.

IV.iv. Location: Scene continues.
4. **the very town:** i.e. only the garrison (without additional military
support).   5. **buckled with:** successfully resisted.

Cries out for noble York and Somerset   15
To beat assailing death from his weak [legions];
And whiles the honorable captain there
Drops bloody sweat from his war-wearièd limbs,
And, in advantage ling'ring, looks for rescue,
You, his false hopes, the trust of England's honor,   20
Keep off aloof with worthless emulation.
Let not your private discord keep away
The levied succors that should lend him aid,
While he, renownèd noble gentleman,
Yield up his life unto a world of odds.   25
Orleance the Bastard, Charles, Burgundy,
Alanson, [Reignier], compass him about,
And Talbot perisheth by your default.
   Som.   York set him on, York should have sent him
       aid.
   Lucy.   And York as fast upon your Grace exclaims,
Swearing that you withhold his levied host,   31
Collected for this expedition.
   Som.   York lies; he might have sent, and had the
       horse.
I owe him little duty, and less love,
And take foul scorn to fawn on him by sending.   35
   Lucy.   The fraud of England, not the force of
       France,
Hath now entrapp'd the noble-minded Talbot:
Never to England shall he bear his life,
But dies, betray'd to fortune by your strife.
   Som.   Come go, I will dispatch the horsemen
       straight;   40
Within six hours they will be at his aid.
   Lucy.   Too late comes rescue, he is ta'en or slain;
For fly he could not, if he would have fled;
And fly would Talbot never, though he might.
   Som.   If he be dead, brave Talbot, then adieu!   45
   Lucy.   His fame lives in the world, his shame in
       you.   *Exeunt.*

[Scene V]

Enter Talbot *and his son* [John].

   Tal.   O young John Talbot, I did send for thee
To tutor thee in stratagems of war,
That Talbot's name might be in thee reviv'd,
When sapless age and weak unable limbs
Should bring thy father to his drooping chair.   5
But O malignant and ill-boding stars!
Now thou art come unto a feast of death,
A terrible and unavoided danger;
Therefore, dear boy, mount on my swiftest horse,
And I'll direct thee how thou shalt escape   10
By sudden flight. Come, dally not, be gone.
   John.   Is my name Talbot? and am I your son?
And shall I fly? O, if you love my mother,
Dishonor not her honorable name
To make a bastard and a slave of me!   15

19. **in advantage ling'ring**: trying to maintain such strength as the situation affords (?).   21. **worthless emulation**: unworthy rivalry.
35. **take foul scorn**: regard it as disgraceful.

IV.v. Location: France. A field of battle near Bordeaux.
8. **unavoided**: unavoidable.

The world will say, he is not Talbot's blood,
That basely fled when noble Talbot stood.
   Tal.   Fly, to revenge my death, if I be slain.
   John.   He that flies so will ne'er return again.
   Tal.   If we both stay, we both are sure to die.   20
   John.   Then let me stay, and, father, do you fly.
Your loss is great, so your regard should be;
My worth unknown, no loss is known in me.
Upon my death the French can little boast;
In yours they will, in you all hopes are lost.   25
Flight cannot stain the honor you have won,
But mine it will, that no exploit have done.
You fled for vantage, every one will swear;
But if I bow, they'll say it was for fear.
There is no hope that ever I will stay,   30
If the first hour I shrink and run away.
Here on my knee I beg mortality,
Rather than life preserv'd with infamy.
   Tal.   Shall all thy mother's hopes lie in one tomb?
   John.   Ay, rather than I'll shame my mother's
       womb.   35
   Tal.   Upon my blessing I command thee go.
   John.   To fight I will, but not to fly the foe.
   Tal.   Part of thy father may be sav'd in thee.
   John.   No part of him but will be shame in me.
   Tal.   Thou never hadst renown, nor canst not lose
       it.   40
   John.   Yes, your renownèd name. Shall flight
       abuse it?
   Tal.   Thy father's charge shall clear thee from that
       stain.
   John.   You cannot witness for me, being slain.
If death be so apparent, then both fly.
   Tal.   And leave my followers here to fight and die?
My age was never tainted with such shame.   46
   John.   And shall my youth be guilty of such blame?
No more can I be severed from your side
Than can yourself yourself in twain divide.
Stay, go, do what you will, the like do I;   50
For live I will not if my father die.
   Tal.   Then here I take my leave of thee, fair son,
Born to eclipse thy life this afternoon.
Come, side by side, together live and die,
And soul with soul from France to heaven fly.   55
                                              Exeunt.

[Scene VI]

Alarum.   Excursions, wherein Talbot's son [John] *is
hemm'd about, and* Talbot *rescues him.*

   Tal.   Saint George and victory! fight, soldiers,
       fight!
The Regent hath with Talbot broke his word,
And left us to the rage of France his sword.
Where is John Talbot? Pause, and take thy breath;
I gave thee life, and rescu'd thee from death.   5

22. **regard**: i.e. concern for yourself.
28. **vantage**: military advantage.   32. **mortality**: death.
41. **abuse**: dishonor.   46. **age**: lifetime.

IV.vi. Location: Scene continues.
2. **Regent**: i.e. the Duke of York (see IV.i.162-63).

1 Henry VI
IV.vi

John. O, twice my father, twice am I thy son!
The life thou gav'st me first was lost and done,
Till with thy warlike sword, despite of fate,
To my determin'd time thou gav'st new date.

Tal. When from the Dolphin's crest thy sword
    struck fire,   10
It warm'd thy father's heart with proud desire
Of bold-fac'd victory. Then leaden age,
Quicken'd with youthful spleen and warlike rage,
Beat down Alanson, Orleance, Burgundy,
And from the pride of Gallia rescued thee.   15
The ireful Bastard Orleance, that drew blood
From thee, my boy, and had the maidenhood
Of thy first fight, I soon encountered,
And interchanging blows I quickly shed
Some of his bastard blood, and in disgrace   20
Bespoke him thus: "Contaminated, base,
And misbegotten blood I spill of thine,
Mean and right poor, for that pure blood of mine
Which thou didst force from Talbot, my brave boy."
Here, purposing the Bastard to destroy,   25
Came in strong rescue. Speak, thy father's care:
Art thou not weary, John? How dost thou fare?
Wilt thou yet leave the battle, boy, and fly,
Now thou art seal'd the son of chivalry?
Fly, to revenge my death when I am dead;   30
The help of one stands me in little stead.
O, too much folly is it, well I wot,
To hazard all our lives in one small boat!
If I to-day die not with Frenchmen's rage,
To-morrow I shall die with mickle age.   35
By me they nothing gain and if I stay,
'Tis but the short'ning of my life one day.
In thee thy mother dies, our household's name,
My death's revenge, thy youth, and England's fame:
All these, and more, we hazard by thy stay;   40
All these are sav'd if thou wilt fly away.

John. The sword of Orleance hath not made me
    smart;
These words of yours draw life-blood from my heart.
On that advantage, bought with such a shame,
To save a paltry life and slay bright fame,   45
Before young Talbot from old Talbot fly
The coward horse that bears me fall and die!
And like me to the peasant boys of France,
To be shame's scorn and subject of mischance!
Surely, by all the glory you have won,   50
And if I fly, I am not Talbot's son.
Then talk no more of flight, it is no boot;
If son to Talbot, die at Talbot's foot.

Tal. Then follow thou thy desp'rate sire of Crete,
Thou Icarus; thy life to me is sweet.   55

If thou wilt fight, fight by thy father's side,
And commendable prov'd, let's die in pride. *Exeunt.*

[SCENE VII]

Alarum. Excursions. Enter old TALBOT *led* [*by a*
SERVANT].

Tal. Where is my other life? mine own is gone.
O, where's young Talbot? where is valiant John?
Triumphant Death, smear'd with captivity,
Young Talbot's valor makes me smile at thee.
When he perceiv'd me shrink and on my knee,   5
His bloody sword he brandish'd over me,
And like a hungry lion did commence
Rough deeds of rage and stern impatience;
But when my angry guardant stood alone,
Tend'ring my ruin and assail'd of none,   10
Dizzy-ey'd fury and great rage of heart
Suddenly made him from my side to start
Into the clust'ring battle of the French;
And in that sea of blood my boy did drench
His overmounting spirit; and there died   15
My Icarus, my blossom, in his pride.

Enter [SOLDIERS] *with* JOHN TALBOT *borne.*

Serv. O my dear lord, lo where your son is borne!

Tal. Thou antic Death, which laugh'st us here to
    scorn,
Anon, from thy insulting tyranny,
Coupled in bonds of perpetuity,   20
Two Talbots, winged through the lither sky,
In thy despite shall scape mortality.
O thou whose wounds become hard-favored Death,
Speak to thy father ere thou yield thy breath!
Brave Death by speaking, whether he will or no; 25
Imagine him a Frenchman, and thy foe.
Poor boy, he smiles, methinks, as who should say,
Had Death been French, then Death had died to-day.
Come, come, and lay him in his father's arms,
My spirit can no longer bear these harms.   30
Soldiers, adieu! I have what I would have,
Now my old arms are young John Talbot's grave.
    Dies.

Enter CHARLES, ALANSON, BURGUNDY, BASTARD, *and*
PUCELLE [*with forces*].

Char. Had York and Somerset brought rescue in,
We should have found a bloody day of this.

Bast. How the young whelp of Talbot's, raging
    wood,   35
Did flesh his puny sword in Frenchmen's blood!

Puc. Once I encount'red him, and thus I said:
"Thou maiden youth, be vanquish'd by a maid!"

9. **determin'd:** having a definite limit. **date:** limit.
13. **youthful spleen:** the eagerness of youth. 15. **Gallia:** France.
25. **purposing:** as I purposed. 29. **seal'd:** confirmed, certified.
32. **wot:** know. 35. **mickle:** great. 48. **like:** liken.
51. **And if:** if. 52. **boot:** advantage, profit.
54–55. **sire . . . Icarus.** Alluding to the desperate attempt of Daedalus
and his son Icarus to escape from King Minos of Crete by means of
wings that they had made. Daedalus got away in safety, but Icarus
flew so high that the wax with which the wings were fastened to his
shoulders was melted by the sun, and he fell into the sea and was
drowned.

IV.vii. Location: Scene continues.
3. **smear'd with captivity:** i.e. although (I am) stained by defeat (?).
9. **guardant:** guardian.
10. **Tend'ring my ruin:** anxiously protecting me in my fall.
13. **battle:** army, forces. 14. **drench:** drown.
18. **antic:** i.e. grinning like a clown, as in the pictorial representations of the *danse macabre.* 21. **lither:** yielding.
23. **become . . . Death:** make hideous Death attractive.
25. **Brave:** defy. 35. **wood:** mad.
36. **flesh:** use for the first time in battle.

But with a proud majestical high scorn
He answer'd thus: "Young Talbot was not born   40
To be the pillage of a giglot wench."
So rushing in the bowels of the French,
He left me proudly, as unworthy fight.
  Bur. Doubtless he would have made a noble knight.
See where he lies inhearsed in the arms   45
Of the most bloody nurser of his harms!
  Bast. Hew them to pieces, hack their bones asunder,
Whose life was England's glory, Gallia's wonder.
  Char. O no, forbear! for that which we have fled
During the life, let us not wrong it dead.   50

Enter LUCY [*attended,* HERALD *of the French preceding*].

  Lucy. Herald, conduct me to the Dolphin's tent,
To know who hath obtain'd the glory of the day.
  Char. On what submissive message art thou sent?
  Lucy. Submission, Dolphin? 'tis a mere French word;
We English warriors wot not what it means.   55
I come to know what prisoners thou hast ta'en,
And to survey the bodies of the dead.
  Char. For prisoners ask'st thou? Hell our prison is.
But tell me whom thou seek'st.
  Lucy. But where's the great Alcides of the field,   60
Valiant Lord Talbot, Earl of Shrewsbury,
Created, for his rare success in arms,
Great Earl of Washford, Waterford, and Valence,
Lord Talbot of Goodrig and Urchinfield,
Lord Strange of Blackmere, Lord Verdon of Alton,   65
Lord Cromwell of Wingfield, Lord Furnival of Sheffield,
The thrice-victorious Lord of Falconbridge,
Knight of the noble Order of Saint George,
Worthy Saint Michael, and the Golden Fleece,
Great marshal to Henry the Sixt   70
Of all his wars within the realm of France?
  Puc. Here's a silly stately style indeed!
The Turk, that two and fifty kingdoms hath,
Writes not so tedious a style as this.
Him that thou magnifi'st with all these titles   75
Stinking and fly-blown lies here at our feet.
  Lucy. Is Talbot slain, the Frenchmen's only scourge,
Your kingdom's terror and black Nemesis?
O, were mine eyeballs into bullets turn'd,
That I in rage might shoot them at your faces!   80
O, that I could but call these dead to life,
It were enough to fright the realm of France!
Were but his picture left amongst you here,

It would amaze the proudest of you all.
Give me their bodies, that I may bear them hence   85
And give them burial as beseems their worth.
  Puc. I think this upstart is old Talbot's ghost,
He speaks with such a proud commanding spirit.
For God's sake let him have ['em]; to keep them here,
They would but stink, and putrefy the air.   90
  Char. Go take their bodies hence.
  Lucy. I'll bear them hence; but from their ashes shall be rear'd
A phoenix that shall make all France afeard.
  Char. So we be rid of them, do with ['em] what thou wilt.
And now to Paris in this conquering vein,   95
All will be ours, now bloody Talbot's slain.   *Exeunt.*

[ACT V,] SCENE [I]

Sennet. Enter KING, GLOUCESTER, *and* EXETER.

  King. Have you perus'd the letters from the Pope,
The Emperor, and the Earl of Arminack?
  Glou. I have, my lord, and their intent is this:
They humbly sue unto your Excellence
To have a godly peace concluded of   5
Between the realms of England and of France.
  King. How doth your Grace affect their motion?
  Glou. Well, my good lord, and as the only means
To stop effusion of our Christian blood,
And stablish quietness on every side.   10
  King. Ay, marry, uncle, for I always thought
It was both impious and unnatural
That such immanity and bloody strife
Should reign among professors of one faith.
  Glou. Beside, my lord, the sooner to effect   15
And surer bind this knot of amity,
The Earl of Arminack, near knit to Charles,
A man of great authority in France,
Proffers his only daughter to your Grace
In marriage, with a large and sumptuous dowry.   20
  King. Marriage, uncle? Alas, my years are young;
And fitter is my study and my books
Than wanton dalliance with a paramour.
Yet call th' embassadors, and as you please,
So let them have their answers every one.   25

84. **amaze:** throw into confusion.
93. **phoenix:** fabulous bird that every five hundred years died upon a funeral pyre of its own construction and then was reborn from its ashes.

V.i. Location: London. The palace.
1–2. **Have . . . Arminack.** Another anachronism. The events alluded to here—the intervention (1435) of the Emperor Sigismund and the Pope in a futile effort to secure a truce, and the abortive negotiations (1442–43) for a marriage between Henry VI and the daughter of the Duke of Armagnac—occurred long before the death of Talbot (1453).
7. **affect their motion:** like their proposal.   13. **immanity:** ferocity.
20. **dowry.** According to Hall (Bullough, III, 70–71), Armagnac's offer of a princely dower for his daughter—including not only "silver hilles, and golden mountaines" but also "the whole duchie of Acquitayn or Guyen"—was so attractive that the agents of Henry VI "concluded the mariage, and by proxie affied the young Lady." The match was blocked, however, when Charles VII, in retaliation, seized Armagnac and his daughter.
21. **my . . . young.** Actually, Henry was twenty-one at the time.

41. **giglot:** wanton.   45. **inhearsed:** coffined.
46. **nurser . . . harms:** fosterer of his power to injure (the French).
60. **Alcides:** Hercules, who was descended from Alcaeus.
61–71. **Valiant . . . France.** This list of Talbot's titles, once thought to have been copied from the description of his tomb in Rouen in Richard Crompton's *Mansion of Magnanimity* (1599) and therefore to prove that Shakespeare had revised the play long after its original composition, appears also in Roger Cotton's *Armor of Proof* (1596). E. K. Chambers has suggested (*William Shakespeare,* I, 293) that it had perhaps been made long familiar by the tales of English travellers.
63. **Washford:** Wexford (in Ireland).   72. **style:** list of titles.
73. **The Turk:** the Grand Turk, the sultan.
78. **Nemesis:** goddess of retributive justice.

I shall be well content with any choice
Tends to God's glory and my country's weal.

Enter WINCHESTER [*in cardinal's habit*] *and three*
AMBASSADORS, [*one of them a* PAPAL LEGATE].

Exe. What, is my Lord of Winchester install'd,
And call'd unto a cardinal's degree?
Then I perceive that will be verified   30
Henry the Fift did sometime prophesy:
"If once he come to be a cardinal,
He'll make his cap co-equal with the crown."
King. My lords ambassadors, your several suits
Have been consider'd and debated on.   35
Your purpose is both good and reasonable;
And therefore are we certainly resolv'd
To draw conditions of a friendly peace,
Which by my Lord of Winchester we mean
Shall be transported presently to France.   40
Glou. [*To the Ambassador from Arminack.*] And
for the proffer of my lord your master,
I have inform'd his Highness so at large,
As liking of the lady's virtuous gifts,
Her beauty, and the value of her dower,
He doth intend she shall be England's queen.   45
King. In argument and proof of which contract,
Bear her this jewel, pledge of my affection.
And so, my Lord Protector, see them guarded
And safely brought to Dover, wherein shipp'd,
Commit them to the fortune of the sea.   50
Exeunt [*all but Winchester and Legate*].
Win. Stay, my lord legate, you shall first receive
The sum of money which I promised
Should be delivered to his Holiness
For clothing me in these grave ornaments.
Leg. I will attend upon your lordship's leisure.   55
[*Exit.*]
Win. Now Winchester will not submit, I trow,
Or be inferior to the proudest peer.
Humphrey of Gloucester, thou shalt well perceive
That neither in birth, or for authority,
The Bishop will be overborne by thee.   60
I'll either make thee stoop and bend thy knee,
Or sack this country with a mutiny.   *Exit.*

SCENE [II]

Enter CHARLES, BURGUNDY, ALANSON, BASTARD,
REIGNIER, *and* JOAN [DE PUCELLE, *with forces*].

Char. These news, my lords, may cheer our droop-
ing spirits:
'Tis said the stout Parisians do revolt,
And turn again unto the warlike French.
Alan. Then march to Paris, royal Charles of
France,
And keep not back your powers in dalliance.   5

Puc. Peace be amongst them if they turn to us,
Else ruin combat with their palaces!

Enter SCOUT.

Scout. Success unto our valiant general,
And happiness to his accomplices!
Char. What tidings send our scouts? I prithee
speak.   10
Scout. The English army, that divided was
Into two parties, is now conjoin'd in one,
And means to give you battle presently.
Char. Somewhat too sudden, sirs, the warning is,
But we will presently provide for them.   15
Bur. I trust the ghost of Talbot is not there.
Now he is gone, my lord, you need not fear.
Puc. Of all base passions, fear is most accurs'd.
Command the conquest, Charles, it shall be thine,
Let Henry fret, and all the world repine.   20
Char. Then on, my lords, and France be fortunate!
Exeunt.

[SCENE III]

Alarum. Excursions. Enter JOAN DE PUCELLE.

Puc. The Regent conquers, and the Frenchmen fly.
Now help, ye charming spells and periapts,
And ye choice spirits that admonish me
And give me signs of future accidents.   *Thunder.*
You speedy helpers, that are substitutes   5
Under the lordly Monarch of the North,
Appear, and aid me in this enterprise.

Enter FIENDS.

This speedy and quick appearance argues proof
Of your accustom'd diligence to me.
Now, ye familiar spirits, that are cull'd   10
Out of the powerful regions under earth,
Help me this once, that France may get the field.
They walk, and speak not.
O, hold me not with silence over-long!
Where I was wont to feed you with my blood,
I'll lop a member off and give it you   15
In earnest of a further benefit,
So you do condescend to help me now.
They hang their heads.
No hope to have redress? My body shall
Pay recompense, if you will grant my suit.
They shake their heads.
Cannot my body nor blood-sacrifice   20
Entreat you to your wonted furtherance?
Then take my soul—my body, soul, and all,
Before that England give the French the foil.
They depart.

7. **ruin combat with:** let ruin destroy.   9. **accomplices:** allies.

V.iii. **Location:** France. Before Angiers.
2. **periapts:** amulets.   3. **admonish:** warn.
4. **accidents:** events.   5. **substitutes:** agents.
6. **Monarch . . . North:** i.e. the devil, who, with his attendant demons, was thought to inhabit northern regions.   8. **quick:** in living form.
12. **get the field:** win the battle.   15. **member:** limb.
16. **earnest:** advance payment.
21. **wonted furtherance:** customary assistance.   23. **foil:** defeat.

27. **Tends:** which tends.   31. **sometime:** once.
40. **presently:** immediately.   49. **shipp'd:** embarked.
62. **mutiny:** open revolt.

V.ii. **Location:** France. Plains in Anjou.
5. **powers:** forces.   **dalliance:** idle delay.

See, they forsake me! Now the time is come
That France must vail her lofty-plumed crest 25
And let her head fall into England's lap.
My ancient incantations are too weak,
And hell too strong for me to buckle with:
Now, France, thy glory droopeth to the dust. *Exit.*

Excursions. BURGUNDY *and* YORK [*enter and*] *fight
hand to hand. French fly.* [PUCELLE *is brought in
captive.*]

York. Damsel of France, I think I have you fast: 30
Unchain your spirits now with spelling charms,
And try if they can gain your liberty.
A goodly prize, fit for the devil's grace!
See how the ugly witch doth bend her brows,
As if, with Circe, she would change my shape! 35
Puc. Chang'd to a worser shape thou canst not be.
York. O, Charles the Dolphin is a proper man,
No shape but his can please your dainty eye.
Puc. A plaguing mischief light on Charles and thee!
And may ye both be suddenly surpris'd 40
By bloody hands, in sleeping on your beds!
York. Fell banning hag, enchantress, hold thy
tongue!
Puc. I prithee give me leave to curse a while.
York. Curse, miscreant, when thou com'st to the
stake. *Exeunt.*

Alarum. Enter SUFFOLK *with* MARGARET *in his hand.*

Suf. Be what thou wilt, thou art my prisoner. 45
Gazes on her.
O fairest beauty, do not fear nor fly,
For I will touch thee but with reverend hands.
I kiss these fingers for eternal peace,
And lay them gently on thy tender side.
Who art thou? say, that I may honor thee. 50
Mar. Margaret my name, and daughter to a king,
The King of Naples, whosoe'er thou art.
Suf. An earl I am, and Suffolk am I call'd.
Be not offended, nature's miracle,
Thou art allotted to be ta'en by me; 55
So doth the swan her downy cygnets save,
Keeping them prisoner underneath [her] wings.
Yet, if this servile usage once offend,
Go, and be free again, as Suffolk's friend.
She is going.

O, stay! [*Aside.*] I have no power to let her pass,
My hand would free her, but my heart says no. 61
As plays the sun upon the glassy streams,
Twinkling another counterfeited beam,
So seems this gorgeous beauty to mine eyes.
Fain would I woo her, yet I dare not speak: 65
I'll call for pen and ink, and write my mind.
Fie, De la Pole, disable not thyself.
Hast not a tongue? Is she not here?
Wilt thou be daunted at a woman's sight?
Ay; beauty's princely majesty is such, 70
'Confounds the tongue and makes the senses rough.
Mar. Say, Earl of Suffolk—if thy name be so—
What ransom must I pay before I pass?
For I perceive I am thy prisoner.
Suf. [*Aside.*] How canst thou tell she will deny
thy suit, 75
Before thou make a trial of her love?
Mar. Why speak'st thou not? What ransom must
I pay?
Suf. [*Aside.*] She's beautiful; and therefore to be
wooed:
She is a woman; therefore to be won.
Mar. Wilt thou accept of ransom, yea or no? 80
Suf. [*Aside.*] Fond man, remember that thou hast
a wife,
Then how can Margaret be thy paramour?
Mar. I were best to leave him, for he will not hear.
Suf. [*Aside.*] There all is marr'd; there lies a cool-
ing card.
Mar. He talks at randon; sure the man is mad. 85
Suf. [*Aside.*] And yet a dispensation may be had.
Mar. And yet I would that you would answer me.
Suf. [*Aside.*] I'll win this Lady Margaret. For
whom?
Why, for my king. Tush, that's a wooden thing!
Mar. He talks of wood; it is some carpenter. 90
Suf. [*Aside.*] Yet so my fancy may be satisfied,
And peace established between these realms.
But there remains a scruple in that too;
For though her father be the King of Naples,
Duke of Anjou and Maine, yet is he poor, 95
And our nobility will scorn the match.
Mar. Hear ye, captain? Are you not at leisure?
Suf. [*Aside.*] It shall be so, disdain they ne'er so
much.
Henry is youthful and will quickly yield.—
Madam, I have a secret to reveal. 100
Mar. [*Aside.*] What though I be enthrall'd, he
seems a knight,
And will not any way dishonor me.
Suf. Lady, vouchsafe to listen what I say.

25. vail: lower.
31. spirits: i.e. attendant demons. spelling charms: charms that cast
a spell, incantations.
35. Circe: enchantress who, according to Homer, enticed her victims
into her palace and then transformed them into beasts.
37. proper: handsome. 38. dainty: fastidious.
40. surpris'd: captured. 42. Fell banning: fierce cursing.
44 s.d. Suffolk. William de la Pole, fourth Earl and first Duke of
Suffolk (1396–1450), served with such distinction in France that after
Salisbury's death he was named commander of the English forces;
but when Joan of Arc's successes led to his decline, he returned to
England (1431), married Salisbury's widow (who was perhaps Geoffrey
Chaucer's granddaughter), and emerged as leader of the group that,
in opposition to Gloucester, sought peace with France. In 1444 he
arranged Henry VI's marriage with Margaret of Anjou, and after
escorting her to England became her principal ally in contriving
Gloucester's fall. There is no historical foundation for his love affair
with Margaret, which Shakespeare makes one of the principal motifs
of *2 Henry VI.* 48. for: in token of.
52. King of Naples. This is the Reignier of earlier scenes; see note to
I.ii o.s.d. 55. allotted: destined. 59. friend: lover.

63. counterfeited: i.e. reflected. 67. disable: disparage.
69. a woman's sight: the sight of a woman.
71. 'Confounds: that it confounds. rough: dull.
78–79. She's . . . won. A quasi-proverbial expression; cf. *Titus
Andronicus,* II.i.82–83; *Richard III,* I.ii.227–28. 81. Fond: foolish.
84. cooling card: something that cools one's ardor or disappoints
one's hopes; a check, deterrent. 85. randon: random.
86. dispensation: special permission from the Pope.
89. wooden: useless, stupid (referring either to his scheme or to the
King). 91. fancy: love. 93. scruple: objection.
101. enthrall'd: captured, made prisoner.

623

1 Henry VI
V.iii

Mar. [*Aside.*] Perhaps I shall be rescu'd by the
French,
And then I need not crave his courtesy. 105
Suf. Sweet madam, give me hearing in a cause.
Mar. [*Aside.*] Tush, women have been captivate
ere now.
Suf. Lady, wherefore talk you so?
Mar. I cry you mercy, 'tis but *quid* for *quo.*
Suf. Say, gentle Princess, would you not suppose
Your bondage happy, to be made a queen? 111
Mar. To be a queen in bondage is more vile
Than is a slave in base servility;
For princes should be free.
Suf.　　　　　　　And so shall you,
If happy England's royal king be free. 115
Mar. Why, what concerns his freedom unto me?
Suf. I'll undertake to make thee Henry's queen,
To put a golden sceptre in thy hand,
And set a precious crown upon thy head,
If thou wilt condescend to be my—
Mar.　　　　　　　　　　　What? 120
Suf. His love.
Mar. I am unworthy to be Henry's wife.
Suf. No, gentle madam, I unworthy am
To woo so fair a dame to be his wife
And have no portion in the choice myself. 125
How say you, madam, are ye so content?
Mar. And if my father please, I am content.
Suf. Then call our captains and our colors forth,
And, madam, at your father's castle walls
We'll crave a parley, to confer with him. 130

　　　Sound [*a parley*]. *Enter* REIGNIER *on the walls.*

See, Reignier, see, thy daughter prisoner!
Reig. To whom?
Suf.　　　　　To me.
Reig.　　　　　　　Suffolk, what remedy?
I am a soldier, and unapt to weep,
Or to exclaim on fortune's fickleness.
Suf. Yes, there is remedy enough, my lord. 135
Consent, and for thy honor give consent,
Thy daughter shall be wedded to my king,
Whom I with pain have wooed and won thereto;
And this her easy-held imprisonment
Hath gain'd thy daughter princely liberty. 140
Reig. Speaks Suffolk as he thinks?
Suf.　　　　　　　　Fair Margaret knows
That Suffolk doth not flatter, face, or feign.
Reig. Upon thy princely warrant, I descend
To give thee answer of thy just demand.
　　　　　　　　　　　[*Exit from the walls.*]
Suf. And here I will expect thy coming. 145

　　　Trumpets sound. Enter REIGNIER [*below*].

Reig. Welcome, brave Earl, into our territories!
Command in Anjou what your honor pleases.

Suf. Thanks, Reignier, happy for so sweet a child,
Fit to be made companion with a king.
What answer makes your Grace unto my suit? 150
Reig. Since thou dost deign to woo her little worth
To be the princely bride of such a lord,
Upon condition I may quietly
Enjoy mine own, the country Maine and Anjou,
Free from oppression or the stroke of war, 155
My daughter shall be Henry's, if he please.
Suf. That is her ransom; I deliver her,
And those two counties I will undertake
Your Grace shall well and quietly enjoy.
Reig. And I again, in Henry's royal name, 160
As deputy unto that gracious king,
Give thee her hand, for sign of plighted faith.
Suf. Reignier of France, I give thee kingly thanks,
Because this is in traffic of a king. 164
[*Aside.*] And yet methinks I could be well content
To be mine own attorney in this case.—
I'll over then to England with this news,
And make this marriage to be solemniz'd.
So farewell, Reignier! set this diamond safe
In golden palaces, as it becomes. 170
Reig. I do embrace thee, as I would embrace
The Christian prince, King Henry, were he here.
Mar. Farewell, my lord! Good wishes, praise, and
prayers
Shall Suffolk ever have of Margaret.　　　*She is going.*
Suf. Farewell, sweet madam! But hark you,
Margaret, 175
No princely commendations to my king?
Mar. Such commendations as becomes a maid,
A virgin, and his servant, say to him.
Suf. Words sweetly plac'd and [modestly] directed.
But, madam, I must trouble you again, 180
No loving token to his Majesty?
Mar. Yes, my good lord, a pure unspotted heart,
Never yet taint with love, I send the King.
Suf. And this withal.　　　　　　*Kiss her.*
Mar. That for thyself; I will not so presume 185
To send such peevish tokens to a king.
　　　　　　　　[*Exeunt Reignier and Margaret.*]
Suf. O, wert thou for myself! but, Suffolk, stay,
Thou mayest not wander in that labyrinth,
There Minotaurs and ugly treasons lurk.
Solicit Henry with her wondrous praise; 190
Bethink thee on her virtues that surmount,
[And] natural graces that extinguish art;
Repeat their semblance often on the seas,
That, when thou com'st to kneel at Henry's feet, 194
Thou mayest bereave him of his wits with wonder.
　　　　　　　　　　　　　　　Exit.

---

107. **captivate:** taken prisoner.
109. **cry you mercy:** beg your pardon. **quid for quo:** tit for tat,
i.e. retaliation for Suffolk's muttering to himself.
111. **to be:** i.e. if you were to be.
142. **face:** pretend (i.e. show a false face). 145. **expect:** await.

148. **for:** in the possession of. 158. **counties:** domains of a count.
164. **in . . . king:** in a king's business.
166. **mine own attorney:** advocate on my own behalf.
170. **as it becomes:** as befits it. 176. **commendations:** greetings.
183. **taint:** tainted. 186. **peevish:** silly.
188. **labyrinth:** a maze built by Daedalus (see note to IV.vi.54–55)
for King Minos of Crete, who confined in it the Minotaur, a monster
born of the union of Queen Pasiphaë with a bull.
193. **Repeat their semblance:** recall their image.

[SCENE IV]

Enter YORK, WARWICK, SHEPHERD, PUCELLE [*guarded*].

York. Bring forth that sorceress condemn'd to burn.
Shep. Ah, Joan, this kills thy father's heart out-
 right!
Have I sought every country far and near,
And now it is my chance to find thee out,
Must I behold thy timeless cruel death?   5
Ah, Joan, sweet daughter Joan, I'll die with thee!
Puc. Decrepit miser! base ignoble wretch!
I am descended of a gentler blood.
Thou art no father nor no friend of mine.
Shep. Out, out! My lords, and please you, 'tis not
 so,   10
I did beget her, all the parish knows.
Her mother liveth yet, can testify
She was the first fruit of my bach'lorship.
War. Graceless, wilt thou deny thy parentage?
York. This argues what her kind of life hath been,
Wicked and vile, and so her death concludes. 16
Shep. Fie, Joan, that thou wilt be so obstacle!
God knows thou art a collop of my flesh,
And for thy sake have I shed many a tear.
Deny me not, I prithee, gentle Joan. 20
Puc. Peasant, avaunt!—You have suborn'd this
 man
Of purpose to obscure my noble birth.
Shep. 'Tis true, I gave a noble to the priest
The morn that I was wedded to her mother.
Kneel down and take my blessing, good my girl. 25
Wilt thou not stoop? Now cursed be the time
Of thy nativity! I would the milk
Thy mother gave thee, when thou suck'st her breast,
Had been a little ratsbane for thy sake!
Or else, when thou didst keep my lambs a-field, 30
I wish some ravenous wolf had eaten thee!
Dost thou deny thy father, cursed drab?
O, burn her, burn her! hanging is too good. *Exit.*
York. Take her away, for she hath liv'd too long,
To fill the world with vicious qualities. 35
Puc. First let me tell you whom you have con-
 demn'd:
Not me begotten of a shepherd swain,
But issued from the progeny of kings;
Virtuous and holy, chosen from above,
By inspiration of celestial grace, 40
To work exceeding miracles on earth.
I never had to do with wicked spirits.
But you, that are polluted with your lusts,
Stain'd with the guiltless blood of innocents,
Corrupt and tainted with a thousand vices, 45
Because you want the grace that others have,

You judge it straight a thing impossible
To compass wonders but by help of devils.
No, misconceived! Joan of Aire hath been
A virgin from her tender infancy, 50
Chaste, and immaculate in very thought,
Whose maiden blood, thus rigorously effus'd,
Will cry for vengeance at the gates of heaven.
York. Ay, ay; away with her to execution!
War. And hark ye, sirs: because she is a maid, 55
Spare for no faggots, let there be enow.
Place barrels of pitch upon the fatal stake,
That so her torture may be shortened.
Puc. Will nothing turn your unrelenting hearts?
Then, Joan, discover thine infirmity, 60
That warranteth by law to be thy privilege.
I am with child, ye bloody homicides!
Murther not then the fruit within my womb,
Although ye hale me to a violent death.
York. Now heaven forfend, the holy maid with
 child? 65
War. The greatest miracle that e'er ye wrought!
Is all your strict preciseness come to this?
York. She and the Dolphin have been juggling.
I did imagine what would be her refuge.
War. Well, go to, we'll have no bastards live, 70
Especially since Charles must father it.
Puc. You are deceiv'd, my child is none of his,
It was Alanson that enjoy'd my love.
York. Alanson, that notorious Machevile?
It dies, and if it had a thousand lives. 75
Puc. O, give me leave, I have deluded you,
'Twas neither Charles nor yet the duke I nam'd,
But Reignier, King of Naples, that prevail'd.
War. A married man! that's most intolerable.
York. Why, here's a girl! I think she knows not
 well 80
(There were so many) whom she may accuse.
War. It's sign she hath been liberal and free.
York. And yet forsooth she is a virgin pure.
Strumpet, thy words condemn thy brat and thee.
Use no entreaty, for it is in vain. 85
Puc. Then lead me hence; with whom I leave my
 curse:
May never glorious sun reflex his beams
Upon the country where you make abode;
But darkness and the gloomy shade of death
Environ you, till mischief and despair 90
Drive you to break your necks or hang yourselves!
         Exit [*guarded*].

47. **straight:** straightway, immediately.
49. **misconceived:** mistaken ones.
52. **rigorously effus'd:** cruelly shed. 56. **enow:** enough.
60–61. **discover . . . privilege:** reveal your pregnancy, which, by law, will save you from execution. A pregnant woman condemned to death could petition for a stay of execution until her child was born. Shakespeare could have found this detail in Holinshed (Bullough, III, 77).
67. **preciseness:** propriety. 68. **juggling:** i.e. misbehaving.
69. **refuge:** defense.
74. **Machevile:** Niccolò Machiavelli (1469–1527), Florentine writer and statesman who, as author of *Il Principe* (The Prince), became notorious for expounding political immorality and cynicism. The allusion to him here is of course anachronistic.
82. **liberal:** loose, wanton. 87. **reflex:** reflect.

V.iv. Location: France. Camp of the Duke of York in Anjou.
4. **now . . . out:** now that I have happened to discover you.
5. **timeless:** untimely. 7. **miser:** wretch.
8. **gentler:** nobler. 9. **friend:** relative.
13. **first . . . bach'lorship:** i.e. conceived out of wedlock.
15. **argues:** indicates, implies. 17. **obstacle:** obstinate.
18. **collop:** slice. 23. **noble:** gold coin worth 6*s.* 8*d.*
29. **ratsbane:** rat poison. 35. **qualities:** tricks (?).
46. **want:** lack.

1 Henry VI
V.iv

York. Break thou in pieces and consume to ashes,
Thou foul accursed minister of hell!

Enter [Winchester, now] CARDINAL [BEAUFORD, *attended*].

Car. Lord Regent, I do greet your Excellence
With letters of commission from the King.   95
For know, my lords, the states of Christendom,
Mov'd with remorse of these outrageous broils,
Have earnestly implor'd a general peace
Betwixt our nation and the aspiring French;
And here at hand the Dolphin and his train   100
Approacheth, to confer about some matter.

York. Is all our travail turn'd to this effect?
After the slaughter of so many peers,
So many captains, gentlemen, and soldiers,
That in this quarrel have been overthrown   105
And sold their bodies for their country's benefit,
Shall we at last conclude effeminate peace?
Have we not lost most part of all the towns,
By treason, falsehood, and by treachery,
Our great progenitors had conquered?   110
O Warwick, Warwick, I foresee with grief
The utter loss of all the realm of France.

War. Be patient, York. If we conclude a peace,
It shall be with such strict and severe covenants,
As little shall the Frenchmen gain thereby.   115

Enter CHARLES, ALANSON, BASTARD, REIGNIER, *[and others]*.

Char. Since, lords of England, it is thus agreed
That peaceful truce shall be proclaim'd in France,
We come to be informed by yourselves
What the conditions of that league must be.

York. Speak, Winchester, for boiling choler chokes
The hollow passage of my poison'd voice,   121
By sight of these our baleful enemies.

Car. Charles, and the rest, it is enacted thus:
That, in regard King Henry gives consent,
Of mere compassion and of lenity,   125
To ease your country of distressful war
And suffer you to breathe in fruitful peace,
You shall become true liegemen to his crown.
And, Charles, upon condition thou wilt swear
To pay him tribute and submit thyself,   130
Thou shalt be plac'd as viceroy under him,
And still enjoy thy regal dignity.

Alan. Must he be then as shadow of himself?
Adorn his temples with a coronet,
And yet, in substance and authority,   135
Retain but privilege of a private man?
This proffer is absurd and reasonless.

Char. 'Tis known already that I am possess'd
With more than half the Gallian territories,
And therein reverenc'd for their lawful king.   140
Shall I, for lucre of the rest unvanquish'd,
Detract so much from that prerogative
As to be call'd but viceroy of the whole?
No, lord ambassador, I'll rather keep
That which I have, than, coveting for more,   145
Be cast from possibility of all.

York. Insulting Charles, hast thou by secret means
Us'd intercession to obtain a league,
And, now the matter grows to compremise,
Stand'st thou aloof upon comparison?   150
Either accept the title thou usurp'st,
Of benefit proceeding from our king,
And not of any challenge of desert,
Or we will plague thee with incessant wars.

Reig. *[Aside to Charles.]* My lord, you do not well
in obstinacy   155
To cavil in the course of this contract.
If once it be neglected, ten to one
We shall not find like opportunity.

Alan. *[Aside to Charles.]* To say the truth, it is
your policy
To save your subjects from such massacre   160
And ruthless slaughters as are daily seen
By our proceeding in hostility,
And therefore take this compact of a truce,
Although you break it when your pleasure serves.

War. How say'st thou, Charles? Shall our condition stand?   165

Char. It shall;
Only reserv'd, you claim no interest
In any of our towns of garrison.

York. Then swear allegiance to his Majesty,
As thou art knight, never to disobey   170
Nor be rebellious to the crown of England,
Thou, nor thy nobles, to the crown of England.
[*Charles and his party give tokens of fealty.*]
So, now dismiss your army when ye please;
Hang up your ensigns, let your drums be still,
For here we entertain a solemn peace.   *Exeunt.*   175

[SCENE] V

Enter SUFFOLK *in conference with the* KING, GLOUCESTER, *and* EXETER.

King. Your wondrous rare description, noble Earl,
Of beauteous Margaret hath astonish'd me.
Her virtues, graced with external gifts,
Do breed love's settled passions in my heart,
And like as rigor of tempestuous gusts   5

---

93. **Thou . . . hell.** This represents the contemporary English view of Joan. Hall (Bullough, III, 61) describes her as "a shepherdes daughter, a chamberlein in an hostrie, and a beggers brat: whiche blindyng the wittes of the French nacion, by revelacions, dreames & phantasticall visions, made them beleve thyngs not to be supposed, and to geve faithe to thynges impossible. For surely, if credite maie be geven to the actes of the Clergie, openly done, and commonly shewed, this woman was not inspired with the holy ghoste, nor sent from God, (as the Frenchmen beleve) but an enchanteresse, an orgayne of the devill, sent from Sathan, to blind the people and brynge them in unbelife." 120. **choler:** anger. 124. **in regard:** since. 125. **Of:** out of. **mere:** pure. 128. **liegemen:** subjects. 134. **coronet:** small crown indicating a rank lower than sovereignty.

139. **Gallian:** French.
141-43. **Shall . . . whole:** i.e. to make sure that part of my domain is unmolested shall I be reduced to the status of viceroy for the whole. **lucre:** gain.
149. **grows to compremise:** is on the point of arbitration.
150. **comparison:** i.e. of the articles of the proposed truce.
152. **Of benefit:** as a favor. 159. **policy:** astute course.
168. **towns of garrison:** fortified towns.

V.v. Location: London. The palace.

Provokes the mightiest hulk against the tide,
So am I driven by breath of her renown,
Either to suffer shipwrack, or arrive
Where I may have fruition of her love.
  Suf. Tush, my good lord, this superficial tale   10
Is but a preface of her worthy praise.
The chief perfections of that lovely dame
(Had I sufficient skill to utter them)
Would make a volume of enticing lines,
Able to ravish any dull conceit;   15
And, which is more, she is not so divine,
So full replete with choice of all delights,
But with as humble lowliness of mind
She is content to be at your command—
Command, I mean, of virtuous chaste intents,   20
To love and honor Henry as her lord.
  King. And otherwise will Henry ne'er presume.
Therefore, my Lord Protector, give consent
That Marg'ret may be England's royal queen.
  Glou. So should I give consent to flatter sin.   25
You know, my lord, your Highness is betroth'd
Unto another lady of esteem.
How shall we then dispense with that contract,
And not deface your honor with reproach?
  Suf. As doth a ruler with unlawful oaths,   30
Or one that at a triumph, having vow'd
To try his strength, forsaketh yet the lists
By reason of his adversary's odds.
A poor earl's daughter is unequal odds,
And therefore may be broke without offense.   35
  Glou. Why, what, I pray, is Margaret more than
      that?
Her father is no better than an earl,
Although in glorious titles he excel.
  Suf. Yes, my lord, her father is a king,
The King of Naples and Jerusalem,   40
And of such great authority in France
As his alliance will confirm our peace,
And keep the Frenchmen in allegiance.
  Glou. And so the Earl of Arminack may do,
Because he is near kinsman unto Charles.   45
  Exe. Beside, his wealth doth warrant a liberal
      dower,
Where Reignier sooner will receive than give.
  Suf. A dow'r, my lords? disgrace not so your king,
That he should be so abject, base, and poor,
To choose for wealth and not for perfect love.   50
Henry is able to enrich his queen,
And not to seek a queen to make him rich:
So worthless peasants bargain for their wives,
As market men for oxen, sheep, or horse.
Marriage is a matter of more worth   55
Than to be dealt in by attorneyship.
Not whom we will, but whom his Grace affects,
Must be companion of his nuptial bed.

And therefore, lords, since he affects her most,
Most of all these reasons bindeth us   60
In our opinions she should be preferr'd.
For what is wedlock forced, but a hell,
An age of discord and continual strife?
Whereas the contrary bringeth bliss,
And is a pattern of celestial peace.   65
Whom should we match with Henry, being a king,
But Margaret, that is daughter to a king?
Her peerless feature, joined with her birth,
Approves her fit for none but for a king.
Her valiant courage and undaunted spirit   70
(More than in women commonly is seen)
Will answer our hope in issue of a king;
For Henry, son unto a conqueror,
Is likely to beget more conquerors,
If with a lady of so high resolve   75
(As is fair Margaret) he be link'd in love.
Then yield, my lords, and here conclude with me
That Margaret shall be Queen, and none but she.
  King. Whether it be through force of your report,
My noble Lord of Suffolk, or for that   80
My tender youth was never yet attaint
With any passion of inflaming [love],
I cannot tell; but this I am assur'd,
I feel such sharp dissension in my breast,
Such fierce alarums both of hope and fear,   85
As I am sick with working of my thoughts.
Take therefore shipping, post, my lord, to France,
Agree to any covenants, and procure
That Lady Margaret do vouchsafe to come
To cross the seas to England and be crown'd   90
King Henry's faithful and anointed queen.
For your expenses and sufficient charge,
Among the people gather up a tenth.
Be gone, I say, for till you do return,
I rest perplexed with a thousand cares.   95
And you, good uncle, banish all offense.
If you do censure me by what you were,
Not what you are, I know it will excuse
This sudden execution of my will.
And so conduct me where, from company,   100
I may revolve and ruminate my grief.   *Exit.*
  Glou. Ay, grief, I fear me, both at first and last.

Exit Gloucester [with Exeter].

  Suf. Thus Suffolk hath prevail'd, and thus he goes,
As did the youthful Paris once to Greece,
With hope to find the like event in love,   105
But prosper better than the Troyan did.
Margaret shall now be Queen, and rule the King;
But I will rule both her, the King, and realm.   *Exit.*

---

15. conceit: imagination.
27. another lady: i.e. the daughter of the Earl of Armagnac.
31. triumph: tournament.   32. lists: tournament ground.
42. As: that.   46. warrant: ensure.
56. attorneyship: proxy.   57. affects: desires.

59. since: i.e. the fact that.
65. pattern: model, example.   68. feature: figure.
80. for that: because.   81. attaint: infected.
87. post: hasten.   92. charge: money.
93. gather . . . tenth: levy a tax of ten percent on incomes.
97. censure . . . were: judge me as when you yourself were young
and passionate.   100. from company: i.e. alone.
104. Paris: a son of Priam, king of Troy, whose abduction of Helen,
wife of King Menelaus of Sparta, led to the Trojan war.
105. event: outcome.

The only authority for the text of *1 Henry VI* is the First Folio (1623); all later editions are derived from that source.

It seems highly probable that the copy for F1 was a transcript of the authors' (or author's) manuscript, and that either the transcript or the manuscript behind it bore sporadic notations by a reviser or the book-keeper. Judging, however, by the inconsistency in the use of speech-prefixes, the misplacing of some stage directions and the absence of others, and the possible implications of the confused act and scene division of the last two acts, it is most unlikely that the copy

for F1 ever served as a prompt-book.

The F2 text contains an unusually large number of variant readings. These, although they are without any claim to authority, are recorded in the Textual Notes.

For further information, see: J. D. Wilson, ed., New Cambridge *1–3 Henry VI* (Cambridge, 1952); W. W. Greg, *The Shakespeare First Folio* (Oxford, 1955); Philip Williams, "New Approaches to Textual Problems in Shakespeare," *SB*, VIII (1956), 3–13; A. S. Cairncross, ed., New Arden *1 Henry VI* (London, 1962).

TEXTUAL NOTES

Title: **Sixth**] Sixt *F1*
Dramatis personae: *subs. as first given in Rowe*
Act-scene division: *F1 designates I.i, II.i, III.i–iv, IV.i as in the present text, and then marks the present V.i, ii as IV.ii, iii and the present V.v as Act V; other act-scene divisions from Pope and Capell (see first note to each scene); present act-scene arrangement as a whole first established by Capell (in whose edition, however, the heading for IV.vi is erroneously repeated for IV.vii)*

I.i

Location: *Theobald*
o.s.d. **Gloucester**] *Rowe*; Gloster *F1 (see l. 37)*
o.s.d. **Heralds, etc.**] *Malone*
24 **glory's**] *Rowe*; Glories *F1*
37 **Gloucester**] *Cambridge*; Gloster *F1 (through III.i and at V.i.58; elsewhere Gloucester); Gloucester first used throughout text and s.pp. (as here) in Cambridge*
45 **Heralds,**] *Pope*; Heralds *F1*
48 **Posterity,**] *Capell*; Posteritie *F1*
76 **third**] third man *F2*
80 **arms,**] *Pope*; Armes *F1*
81 s.d. **Exit.**] *Wilson*
89 s.p. **2. Mess.**] *Rowe*; Mess. *F1*
94 **Reignier**] *Rowe*; Reynold *F1*
96 **crowned**] *Rowe*; crown'd *F1*
103 s.p. **3. Mess.**] *Rowe.* Mes. *F1*
121 **human**] *F4*; humane *F1*
131 **Falstaff**] Fastolfe *Theobald (and most eds.)*
132 **vaward**] *Rowe*; Vauward *F1*
161 s.d. **Exit.**] *Wilson*
176 **send**] steal *Mason conj.*
177 s.d. **Exeunt.**] *Cambridge*; Exit. *F1*

I.ii

Location: *Theobald (after Pope)*
o.s.d **Reignier**] *F4*; Reigneir *F1 (frequently through III.ii)*
29 **Froissard**] *Reed*; Froysard *F1*
30 **bred**] *Rowe*; breed *F1*
37 **hare-brain'd**] *Dyce*; hayre-brayn'd *F1*
47 s.p. **Char.**] *Capell*; Dolph. *F1 (throughout scene)*
60 s.d. **Exit Bastard.**] *Capell*
63 s.d. **de Pucelle**] *ed. (after Rowe)*; Puzel *F1 (the regular spelling through III.i)*
63 s.d. **and Bastard**] *Malone*
65 s.p. **Puc.**] *Rowe*; Puzel. *F1 (through III.i, except Ioane. at II.i.54, 72)*
99 **five**] *Steevens conj. (after Holinshed)*; fine *F1*
113 **rites**] *Pope*; rights *F1*
131 **halcyons'**] *ed.*; Halcyons *F1*; Halcyon *F3*
132 **entered**] *Malone*; entred *F1*

I.iii

Location: *Hanmer (after Pope, Theobald)*
o.s.d. **in blue coats**] *Malone (after Capell)*
4 **Gloucester**] *Rowe*; Gloster *F1 (trisyllabic form needed)*
5, 7, 9 s.dd. **Within.**] *Malone*

6, 8 s.pp. **1. Serv.**] *Malone (after Capell)*; Glost. 1. Man. *and* 1. Man. *F1*
6 **Gloucester**] *Pope*; Gloster *F1 (trisyllabic form needed)*
29 **Humphrey**] *Theobald*; Vmpheir *F1 (in italics)*
30 **Peel'd**] *Boswell*; Piel'd *F1*
62 **Gloucester**] *Cambridge*; Gloster *F1 (trisyllabic form needed)*
74 s.p. **Off.**] *Hanmer*
82 **cost**] deare cost *F2*
87 **Abominable**] *F3*; Abhominable *F1*
88 s.d. **several . . . Servingmen**] *Dyce (after Capell)*

I.iv

Location: *Pope*
10 **Wont**] *Tyrwhitt conj.*; Went *F1*
22 s.d. **Sir William . . . Gargrave**] *Capell*
28 **Santrailles**] *Capell*; Santrayle *F1*
29 **ransomed**] *Rowe*; ransom'd *F1*
33 **pill'd**] *Capell*; pil'd *F1*
69 s.d. **shoot**] *Rowe*; shot *F1*
69 s.d. **together with Gargrave**] *Hanmer (subs.)*
95 **like thee, Nero**] *Malone*; like thee *F1* Nero like will *F2*
101 **Pucelle**] *Rowe*; Puzel *F1*
107 **Pucelle**] *Theobald*; Puzel *F1*
107 **puzzel**] *Capell*; Pussel *F1*
111 s.d. **bearing . . . bodies**] *Theobald (subs.)*

I.v.

Location: *ed. (after Wilson)*
o.s.d. **and . . . them**] *Dyce (subs.)*
6 **thee— . . . witch—**] *Dyce*; thee, . . . Witch, *F1*

I.vi

Location: *ed. (after Wilson)*
o.s.d. **Flourish.**] *placed as in Collier; after retreat. I.v. 39 s.d., F1*
2 **English!**] English wolves: *F2*
4 s.p. **Char.**] *Capell*; Dolph. *F1 (throughout scene)*
4 **Astraea's**] *F2 (reading bright Astraea's)*; Astrea's *F1*
22 **of**] *Capell conj.*; or *F1*
26 **Transported**] *F4*; Transported, *F1*

II.i

Location: *Theobald (after Pope)*
o.s.d. **French**] *Capell*
5 s.p. **1. Sent.**] *Capell*; Sent. *F1*
5 s.d. **Exit Sergeant.**] *Johnson*
7 s.d. **and forces**] *Capell*
7 s.d. **scaling-ladders.**] *Wilson*; scaling Ladders: Their Drummes beating a Dead March. *F1 (see below, II.ii o.s.d.)*
17 **arm's**] *Johnson*; armes *F1*
29 **all together**] *Rowe*; altogether *F1*
37 s.d. **Cry . . . Talbot!"**] *placed subs. as in Capell; after l. 38, F1*
37 s.d. **The . . . walls.**] *Theobald (subs., after l. 38); placed as in Capell*

38 s.p. **1. Sent.**] *ed.*; Sent. *F1*
38 s.d. **ready**] *Pope*; ready, *F1*
48 s.d. **de Pucelle**] *ed. (after Capell)*
54, 72 s.pp. **Puc.**] *Rowe*; Ioane. *F1*
77 **them.**] *Capell*; them. / Exeunt. *F1*
77 s.d. **an English**] *Capell*; a *F1*

II.ii

II.ii] *Capell*
Location: *Capell (after Theobald)*
o.s.d. **a . . . others**] *Capell*
o.s.d. **their . . . march**] *placed as in Pelican (after Wilson conj.); end of s.d. at II.i.7 in F1*
20 **Aire**] *ed. conj., Cairncross*; Acre *F1 (Holinshed reads Are; cf. V.iv.49)*
38 **Auvergne**] *Rowe*; Ouergne *F1*
59 s.d. **Whispers.**] *placed as in Johnson; after l. 59, F1*
59 **mind?**] *Dyce*; minde. *F1*

II.iii

II.iii] *Capell*
Location: *Pope*
o.s.d. **and her Porter**] *Pope*
4 **laid.**] *Pope (subs.)*; layd, *F1*
16 **abroad**] *Johnson*; abroad? *F1*
27 s.d. **Going.**] *Capell*
44 **thou,**] *Theobald*; thou *F1*

II.iv

II.iv] *Capell*
Location: *Pope*
o.s.d. **Pole**] *Kittredge*; Poole *F1*
o.s.d. **Vernon**] *Hanmer*
o.s.d. **and a Lawyer**] *Ritson conj.*
1 s.p. **Plan.**] *Rowe*; Yorke. *F1 (throughout scene)*
57 s.d. **To Somerset.**] *Rowe*
78 **Pole**] *Hanmer*; Poole *F1 (throughout scene)*
117 **wip'd**] *F2*; whipt *F1*
126 **Red Rose**] *Rowe*; Red-Rose *F1*
131 **gentlemen**] *anon. conj. (in Cambridge)*; gentle *F1*; gentle Sir *F2*

II.v

II.v] *Capell*
Location: *Capell (subs.)*
3 **rack**] *Pope*; Wrack *F1*
18, 33 s.pp. **1. Keeper.**] *Capell*; Keeper. *F1*
35 s.p. **Plan.**] *Rowe*; Rich. *F1 (throughout scene)*
36 **late-despised**] *hyphen, Capell*
71 **Richard**] King Richard *F2*
75 **third**] the third *F2*
78 **fourth**] the fourth *F2*
84 **Cambridge then,**] *J. C. Maxwell conj. (privately)*; Cambridge, then *F1*
118 **counsel**] *F2*; Councell *F1*
121 s.d. **Exeunt . . . Mortimer.**] *Capell (subs.)*; Exit. *F1*
129 **my will**] my ill *Theobald*; mine ill *Cairncross*

III.i

Location: *Capell (after Pope)*
o.s.d. **and others**] *Malone (after Capell)*
41 **good—**] *F2*; good. *F1*

51 s.p. **Glou.**] *Hanmer*; Warw. *F1*
52 s.p. **War.**] *Hanmer*; *line continued to Warwick, F1 (see preceding note)*
52 s.d. **to Winchester**] *Hanmer*
53 **so**] *Cairncross; see F1*
61 s.d. **Aside.**] *Hanmer*
74 **What**] *Capell; King. What F1 (repeated s.p.)*
75 s.d. **of London attended**] *Capell*
80 **pebble**] *F3;* peeble *F1*
85 s.d. **Servingmen . . . parties**] *Capell (subs.)*
88 **Pray**] *F4;* Pray' *F1*
136 s.d. **Aside.**] *Collier*
141 s.d. **Aside.**] *Pope*
142 **Gloucester**] *Cambridge;* Gloster *F1 (trisyllabic form needed)*
147 s.d. **Servingmen, Mayor, etc.**] *Capell (subs.)*
162 **that**] *F2;* that all *F1*
177 s.d. **Aside.**] *Rowe*
198 **lose**] *F2 (reading should lose);* loose *F1*

III.ii

Location: *Capell (after Pope)*
o.s.d. **Pucelle**] *Rowe;* Pucell *F1 (throughout rest of play, except* Ione *in V.ii o.s.d.)*
10 s.p. **1. Sol.**] *Capell;* Souldier. *F1*
13 s.d. **Within.**] *Capell*
13 **Qui là?**] *Sisson;* Che la. *F1*
17 s.d. **to the town**] *Capell (subs.)*
17 s.d. **Reignier, and forces**] *Cambridge (after Capell)*
21–2 **specify . . . in?**] *Rowe (subs.);* specifie? . . . in. *F1*
28 s.d. **Exit.**] *Cambridge*
35 s.d. **Exeunt.**] *Cambridge (after Capell)*
35 s.d. **Enter**] *Capell*
40 s.d. **Burgundy**] *Rowe;* Burgonie *F1 (throughout scene)*
40 s.d. **Alanson**] *Hanmer (subs.; but om. Reignier from the s.d.)*
41 **Good**] *F3;* God *F1*
59 s.d. **the English**] *Cambridge (after Capell)*
59 s.d. **council**] *Theobald (1757);* counsell *F1*
82 **late-betrayed**] *hyphen, Theobald*
103 s.d. **with . . . forces**] *Capell (subs.)*
109 s.d. **into the town**] *Dyce*
109 s.d. **enter . . . and**] *Malone*
111 **enemies'**] *Theobald;* Enemies *F1*
137 **human**] *Rowe;* humane *F1*

III.iii

Location: *Dyce (after Capell)*
o.s.d. **and forces**] *Capell*
19 **Burgundy**] *Rowe;* Burgonie *F1 (throughout scene)*
35 s.d. **Enter . . . Burgundy**] *Rowe*
35 s.d. **and forces**] *Capell*
46 **foe.**] *Pope;* Foe, *F1*
48 **eyes,**] *F2;* Eyes. *F1*
78 s.d. **Aside.**] *Dyce*
85 s.d. **Aside.**] *Capell*

III.iv

Location: *Capell (after Pope)*
o.s.d. **Richard . . . of**] *ed. (after Kittredge)*
o.s.d. **Vernon . . . others**] *Capell*
12 s.d. **Kneels.**] *Cambridge*
27 s.d. **Manent**] *F2;* Manet *F1*
39 **whoso**] *Rowe;* who so *F1*

IV.i

Location: *Wilson (after Capell)*
o.s.d. **Governor . . . Exeter**] *Rowe (subs.);* Gouernor Exeter. *F1*
s.d. **and others**] *Malone (after Capell)*
3 s.d. **Governor kneels.**] *Capell*
8 s.d. **Exeunt . . . Train.**] *Capell*
12 s.d. **Presents it.**] *Capell (subs.)*
14 **thee**] *F2;* the *F1*
15 s.d. **Plucking it off.**] *Capell*
19 **Poictiers**] *Patay Capell conj. (from Holinshed; followed by most eds.)*
26 **there**] *F2;* thete *F1*
47 s.d. **Exit Falstaff.**] *Wilson (after F2)*
48 **Lord**] my Lord *F2*

55 s.d. **Reads.**] *Rowe*
77 s.d. **Exit.**] *Rowe*
77 s.d. **Basset**] *F2;* Bassit *F1*
93 **cheeks,**] *Capell;* cheekes: *F1*
112 **slight**] *F2;* slighr *F1*
151 **umpeer**] *ed.;* Vmper *F1*
152 s.d. **Putting . . . rose.**] *Johnson*
172 **presented.**] *Theobald;* presented *F1*
173 s.d. **Flourish.**] *placed as in Theobald; after l. 181, F1*
173 s.d. **Manent**] *F3;* Manet *F1*
180 **I wist**] *Capell;* I wish *F1; Wilson's* iwis (= indeed) *is tempting, and OED offers contemporary examples of* wis *corrupted to* wish, *but the emphatic position the word would be given in the present context seems false for this period and contrasts with Shakespeare's three acknowledged uses*
180 **did—**] *Pope;* did. *F1*

IV.ii

IV.ii] *Capell*
Location: *from F1 o.s.d.*
2 s.d. **Trumpet**] *Capell*
2 s.d. **and others**] *Malone*
3 **calls**] *F2;* call *F1*
12 **even**] *F2;* eeuen *F1*
15 s.p. **Gen.**] *Theobald;* Cap. *F1*
34 **due**] *Theobald;* dew *F1*
41 s.d. **with others above**] *ed. (after Malone)*
50 **moody-mad**] *hyphen, Capell*
56 s.d. **Exeunt.**] *F2*

IV.iii

IV.iii] *Capell*
Location: *Capell*
5 **Talbot. . . . along,**] *F2;* Talbot . . . along. *F1*
8 s.d. **Exit.**] *Cairncross*
16 s.d. **Sir William Lucy**] *Theobald*
17, 30, etc. s.pp. **Lucy.**] *Theobald;* 2. Mes. *or* Mes. *F1*
20 **waist**] *Steevens;* waste *F1*
36 **travel**] *F3;* trauaile *F1*
38 **lives**] *F1 not clear, possibly* lines; lives *F2*
46 s.d. **with his Soldiers**] *Cambridge (after Collier)*
49 **loss**] *Pope;* losse: *F1*

IV.iv

IV.iv] *Capell*
Location: *ed. (after Wilson)*
o.s.d. **a . . . him**] *Capell (subs.)*
13 **lord?**] *F3;* Lord, *F1*
16 **legions**] *Rowe;* Regions *F1*
26 **Burgundy**] and Burgundie *F2*
27 **Reignier**] *Rowe;* Reignard *F1*
46 **world,**] *F4;* world. *F1*

IV.v

IV.v] *Capell*
Location: *Theobald (after Pope)*
o.s.d. **John**] *Malone*
55 s.d. **Exeunt.**] *F2;* Exit. *F1*

IV.vi

IV.vi] *Capell*
Location: *ed. (after Wilson)*
18 **encountered**] *F3;* encountred *F1*
26 **Speak,**] *F4;* Speake *F1*
36 **gain**] *Knight;* gaine, *F1*
55 **Icarus**] *Capell (after Theobald);* Icarus, *F1*
57 s.d. **Exeunt.**] *Rowe;* Exit. *F1*

IV.vii

IV.vii] *Pope*
Location: *ed. (after Wilson)*
o.s.d. **by a Servant**] *Capell (subs.)*
16 s.d. **Soldiers**] *Capell*
18 **antic**] *F3;* antique *F1*
32] *Following this line F2 begins* Actus Quintus, Scaena Prima.
32 s.d. **with forces**] *Malone (after Capell)*
36 **puny sword**] *Rowe;* punie-sword *F1*
50 s.d. **attended . . . preceding**] *Capell*
67 **thrice-victorious**] *hyphen, Knight*

70 **Henry**] our King Henry *F2*
89 **'em**] *Theobald;* him *F1*
94 **'em**] *Malone;* him *F1;* them *F2*
96 s.d. **Exeunt.**] *Rowe;* Exit. *F1*

V.i

V.i] *Capell;* Scena secunda. *F1*
Location: *Capell (subs.)*
27 s.d. **in cardinal's habit**] *Capell*
27 s.d. **one . . . Legate**] *Kittredge (after Capell)*
41 s.d. **To . . . Arminack.**] *M. Edel (after Capell, at l. 47)*
50 s.d. **all . . . Legate**] *Cambridge (after Capell)*
55, 62 s.dd. **Exit.**] *Collier MS*

V.ii

V.ii] *Capell;* Scoena Tertia. *F1*
Location: *Capell (after Pope)*
s.d. **with forces**] *Capell (subs.)*

V.iii

V.iii] *Capell*
Location: *Malone (after Capell)*
13 **silence**] *F2;* silenee *F1*
25 **lofty-plumed**] *hyphen, Johnson*
29 s.d. **enter and**] *ed.*
29 s.d. **Pucelle . . . captive.**] *Malone (subs.)*
43 **a while**] *F3;* awhile *F1*
50 **thou? say**] *Pope;* thou, say? *F1*
57 **her**] *F2;* his *F1*
60, 84, 86, 98 s.dd. **Aside.**] *Dyce*
65 **woo**] *F2;* woe *F1 (throughout scene)*
75, 78, 81, 91 s.dd. **Aside.**] *Pope*
101, 104, 107 s.dd. **Aside.**] *Theobald*
130 s.d. **a parley**] *Capell*
139 **easy-held**] *hyphen, Rowe*
144 s.d. **Exit . . . walls.**] *Capell*
145 s.d. **below**] *Capell*
165 s.d. **Aside.**] *Rowe*
179 **modestly**] *F2;* modestie *F1*
186 s.d. **Exeunt . . . Margaret.**] *Capell*
190 **wondrous**] *F3;* wonderous *F1*
192 **And**] *Capell;* Mad *F1*

V.iv

V.iv] *Capell*
Location: *Capell*
o.s.d. **guarded**] *Capell*
10 **so,**] *F2;* so *F1*
28 **suck'st**] suck'dst *F2*
32 **Dost**] *F3;* Doest *F1*
49 **No, misconceived!**] *Steevens (comma, F4);* No misconceyued, *F1*
52 **maiden blood**] *Theobald;* Maiden-blood *F1*
58 **torture**] *F2;* tortute *F1*
58 **shortened**] *Pope;* shortned *F1*
60 **discover**] *F3;* discouet *F1*
61 **warranteth**] *F2;* wartanteth *F1*
91 s.d. **guarded**] *Theobald*
93 **Winchester, now**] *Pelican*
93 s.d. **Beauford, attended**] *Capell; s.d. placed as in Pope; after l. 91, F1*
102 **travail**] *Steevens;* trauell *F1*
102 **effect?**] *Rowe;* effect, *F1*
115 s.d. **and others**] *Capell*
123 s.p. **Car.**] *Capell;* Win. *F1*
145 **have than,**] *Cambridge;* haue, than *F1*
155 s.d. **Aside to Charles.**] *Capell*
159 s.d. **Aside to Charles.**] *Collier (after Capell)*
172 s.d. **Charles . . . fealty.**] *Johnson*

V.v

V.v] *Capell;* Actus Quintus. *F1*
Location: *Capell (subs.)*
39 **lord**] good Lord *F2*
55 **Marriage**] But marriage *F2*
62 **wedlock**] *F2;* wedloeke *F1*
62 **forced,**] *F2;* forced? *F1*
64 **bringeth**] bringeth forth *F2*
82 **love**] *F2;* Ioue *F1*
102 s.d. **with Exeter**] *Hanmer (subs.)*
108 s.d. **Exit.**] Exit / FINIS. *F1*

The Second Part of Henry the Sixth

[DRAMATIS PERSONAE

KING HENRY THE SIXTH
HUMPHREY, *Duke of Gloucester, his uncle*
CARDINAL BEAUFORD, *Bishop of Winchester, great-uncle to the King*
RICHARD PLANTAGENET, *Duke of York*
EDWARD *and* RICHARD, *his sons*
DUKE OF SOMERSET
DUKE OF SUFFOLK
DUKE OF BUCKINGHAM
LORD CLIFFORD
YOUNG CLIFFORD, *his son*
EARL OF SALISBURY
EARL OF WARWICK
LORD SCALES
LORD SAY
SIR HUMPHREY STAFFORD, *and* WILLIAM STAFFORD, *his brother*
SIR JOHN STANLEY
VAUX
MATTHEW GOFFE
ALEXANDER IDEN, *a Kentish gentleman*
LIEUTENANT, SHIPMASTER, *and* MASTER'S MATE, *and* WALTER WHITMORE

Two GENTLEMEN, *prisoners with Suffolk*
JOHN HUME *and* JOHN SOUTHWELL, *priests*
ROGER BOLINGBROOK, *a conjurer*
THOMAS HORNER, *an armorer*
PETER THUMP, *his man*
CLERK OF CHARTAM
MAYOR OF SAINT ALBONS
SIMPCOX, *an impostor*
JACK CADE, *a rebel*
GEORGE BEVIS, JOHN HOLLAND, DICK *the butcher,* SMITH *the weaver,* MICHAEL, *etc., followers of Cade*
Two MURDERERS

MARGARET, *Queen to King Henry*
ELEANOR, DUCHESS OF GLOUCESTER
MARGERY JORDAN, *a witch*
WIFE *to Simpcox*

SPIRIT

LORDS, LADIES, ATTENDANTS, PETITIONERS, ALDERMEN, HERALD, BEADLE, SHERIFF *and* OFFICERS, CITIZENS, PRENTICES, FALCONERS, GUARDS, SOLDIERS MESSENGERS, *etc.*

SCENE: *England*]

ACT I, SCENE I

Flourish of trumpets: then hoboys. Enter KING [HENRY], DUKE HUMPHREY [OF GLOUCESTER], SALISBURY, WARWICK, *and* [CARDINAL] BEAUFORD, *on the one side; the* QUEEN, SUFFOLK, YORK, SOMERSET, *and* BUCKINGHAM, *on the other.*

Suf. As by your high imperial Majesty
I had in charge at my depart for France,
As procurator to your Excellence,
To marry Princess Margaret for your Grace;
So in the famous ancient city Tours,   5

Words and passages enclosed in square brackets in the text above are either emendations of the copy-text or additions to it. The Textual Notes immediately following the play cite the earliest authority for every such change or insertion and supply the reading of the copy-text wherever it is emended in this edition.

I.i. Location: London. The palace.
o.s.d. Flourish: fanfare.   hoboys: oboes.
2. had in charge: was commissioned.
3. procurator: agent, deputy.

In presence of the Kings of France and Sicil,
The Dukes of Orleance, Calaber, Bretagne, and Alanson,
Seven earls, twelve barons, and twenty reverend bishops,
I have perform'd my task, and was espous'd;
And humbly now upon my bended knee,   10
In sight of England and her lordly peers,
Deliver up my title in the Queen
To your most gracious hands, that are the substance
Of that great shadow I did represent:
The happiest gift that ever marquess gave,   15
The fairest queen that ever king receiv'd.

King. Suffolk, arise. Welcome, Queen Margaret,
I can express no kinder sign of love
Than this kind kiss. O Lord, that lends me life,

6. Sicil: Sicily, of which René, Margaret's father, was titular king.
7. Orleance: Orleans.   Calaber: Calabria, a region in southern Italy.   Alanson: Alençon.   9. espous'd: betrothed (as your deputy).
18. kinder: more natural.   19. kind: affectionate.

Lend me a heart replete with thankfulness!   20
For thou hast given me in this beauteous face
A world of earthly blessings to my soul,
If sympathy of love unite our thoughts.
 Queen.   Great King of England, and my gracious
  lord,
The mutual conference that my mind hath had,   25
By day, by night, waking and in my dreams,
In courtly company, or at my beads,
With you, mine alder-liefest sovereign,
Makes me the bolder to salute my king
With ruder terms, such as my wit affords   30
And overjoy of heart doth minister.
 King.   Her sight did ravish, but her grace in speech,
Her words yclad with wisdom's majesty,
Makes me from wond'ring fall to weeping joys,
Such is the fullness of my heart's content.   35
Lords, with one cheerful voice welcome my love.
 All.   (*Kneel*.)   Long live Queen Margaret, Eng-
  land's happiness!   *Flourish*.
 Queen.   We thank you all.
 Suf.   My Lord Protector, so it please your Grace,
Here are the articles of contracted peace   40
Between our sovereign and the French King Charles,
For eighteen months concluded by consent.
 Glou.   (*Reads*.)   "Inprimis, It is agreed between the
French King Charles, and William de la Pole, Mar-
quess of Suffolk, ambassador for Henry King of   45
England, that the said Henry shall espouse the Lady
Margaret, daughter unto Reignier King of Naples,
Sicilia, and Jerusalem, and crown her Queen of
England ere the thirtieth of May next ensuing. *Item*,
[It is further agreed between them,] that the duchy 50
of Anjou and the county of Maine shall be releas'd and
deliver'd [over] to the King her father"—
     [*Duke Humphrey lets it fall*.]
 King.   Uncle, how now?
 Glou.   Pardon me, gracious lord,
Some sudden qualm hath struck me at the heart,
And dimm'd mine eyes, that I can read no further. 55
 King.   Uncle of Winchester, I pray read on.
 Car.   [*Reads*.]   "Item, It is further agreed between
them, that the [duchy] of Anjou and [the county of]
Maine shall be releas'd and deliver'd over to the King
her father, and she sent over of the King of England's   60
own proper cost and charges, without having any
dowry."   62
 King.   They please us well.   Lord Marquess,
  kneel down.
We here create thee the first Duke of Suffolk,
And girt thee with the sword.   Cousin of York,   65
We here discharge your Grace from being Regent
I' th' parts of France, till term of eighteen months

Be full expir'd.   Thanks, uncle Winchester,
Gloucester, York, Buckingham, Somerset,
Salisbury, and Warwick;   70
We thank you all for this great favor done
In entertainment to my princely queen.
Come, let us in, and with all speed provide
To see her coronation be perform'd.
  *Exeunt King, Queen, and Suffolk.   Manent
  the rest, [stayed by Gloucester]*.
 Glou.   Brave peers of England, pillars of the state,
To you Duke Humphrey must unload his grief,   76
Your grief, the common grief of all the land.
What? did my brother Henry spend his youth,
His valor, coin, and people, in the wars?
Did he so often lodge in open field,   80
In winter's cold and summer's parching heat,
To conquer France, his true inheritance?
And did my brother Bedford toil his wits,
To keep by policy what Henry got?
Have you yourselves, Somerset, Buckingham,   85
Brave York, Salisbury, and victorious Warwick,
Receiv'd deep scars in France and Normandy?
Or hath mine uncle Beauford and myself,
With all the learned Council of the realm,
Studied so long, sat in the Council-house   90
Early and late, debating to and fro
How France and Frenchmen might be kept in awe,
And hath his Highness in his infancy
Crowned in Paris in despite of foes?
And shall these labors and these honors die?   95
Shall Henry's conquest, Bedford's vigilance,
Your deeds of war, and all our counsel die?
O peers of England, shameful is this league,
Fatal this marriage, cancelling your fame,
Blotting your names from books of memory,   100
Rasing the characters of your renown,
Defacing monuments of conquer'd France,
Undoing all, as all had never been!
 Car.   Nephew, what means this passionate dis-
  course,
This peroration with such circumstance?   105
For France, 'tis ours; and we will keep it still.
 Glou.   Ay, uncle, we will keep it, if we can;
But now it is impossible we should.
Suffolk, the new-made duke that rules the roast,
Hath given the duchy of Anjou, and Maine,   110

---

25. **mutual conference:** intimate communication.
27. **at my beads:** i.e. while saying prayers with the rosary.
28. **alder-liefest:** dearest of all.   31. **minister:** supply.
33. **yclad:** clad.
39. **Protector:** i.e. Gloucester. Actually, his protectorship had been formally annulled in 1429, when Henry VI was crowned at Westminster at the age of eight.
43. **Inprimis:** imprimis, in the first place.   49. **Item:** also.
55. **that:** so that.   60. **of:** at.   61. **proper:** personal.
64. **We . . . Suffolk.** Actually, the title was conferred on Suffolk in 1448, four years after the time represented in this scene.
65. **girt:** gird.   **Cousin:** kinsman.

72. **entertainment to:** reception of.
75–146. **Brave . . . long.** When the terms of Henry's marriage were revealed, says Hall (Bullough, III, 103), they "semed to many, bothe infortunate, and unprofitable to the realme of England, and that for many causes. First the kyng with her [i.e. Margaret] had not one peny, and for the fetchyng of her, the Marques of Suffolke, demaunded a whole fiftene, in open parliament: also for her mariage, the Duchie of Anjow, the citee of Mauns, and the whole countie of Mayne, were delivered and released to Kyng Reyner her father, whiche countries were the very stayes, and backestandes to the Duchy of Normandy. Furthermore for this mariage, the Earle of Arminacke, toke suche great displeasure, that he became utter enemy to the realme of Englande and was the chief cause, that the Englishmen, wer expulsed out of the whole duchie of Acquitayne, and lost bothe the countreis of Gascoyn and Guyen."
78. **my brother Henry:** Henry V.
82. **inheritance.** For the English claim to the French throne see the note to *1 Henry VI*, I.i.80.   84. **policy:** administrative skill.
92. **awe:** obedience.   100. **books of memory:** i.e. chronicles.
101. **Rasing the characters:** erasing the records.
106. **still:** always.   109. **rules the roast:** domineers.

2 Henry VI
I.i

Unto the poor King Reignier, whose large style
Agrees not with the leanness of his purse.
   Sal. Now by the death of Him that died for all,
These counties were the keys of Normandy.
But wherefore weeps Warwick, my valiant son? 115
   War. For grief that they are past recovery;
For were there hope to conquer them again,
My sword should shed hot blood, mine eyes no tears.
Anjou and Maine? myself did win them both.
Those provinces these arms of mine did conquer, 120
And are the cities that I got with wounds
Deliver'd up again with peaceful words?
Mort Dieu!
   York. For Suffolk's duke, may he be suffocate,
That dims the honor of this warlike isle! 125
France should have torn and rent my very heart
Before I would have yielded to this league.
I never read but England's kings have had
Large sums of gold and dowries with their wives,
And our King Henry gives away his own, 130
To match with her that brings no vantages.
   Glou. A proper jest, and never heard before,
That Suffolk should demand a whole fifteenth
For costs and charges in transporting her!
She should have stay'd in France, and starv'd in France,
Before— 136
   Car. My Lord of Gloucester, now ye grow too
     hot:
It was the pleasure of my lord the King.
   Glou. My Lord of Winchester, I know your mind.
'Tis not my speeches that you do mislike, 140
But 'tis my presence that doth trouble ye;
Rancor will out. Proud prelate, in thy face
I see thy fury. If I longer stay,
We shall begin our ancient bickerings.
Lordings, farewell, and say, when I am gone, 145
I prophesied France will be lost ere long.
                    Exit Humphrey.
   Car. So, there goes our Protector in a rage.
'Tis known to you he is mine enemy;
Nay more, an enemy unto you all,
And no great friend, I fear me, to the King. 150
Consider, lords, he is the next of blood,
And heir-apparent to the English crown.
Had Henry got an empire by his marriage,
And all the wealthy kingdoms of the west,
There's reason he should be displeas'd at it. 155
Look to it, lords, let not his smoothing words
Bewitch your hearts. Be wise and circumspect.
What though the common people favor him,

Calling him "Humphrey, the good Duke of Glouces-
    ter,"
Clapping their hands, and crying with loud voice, 160
"Jesu maintain your royal Excellence!"
With "God preserve the good Duke Humphrey!"
I fear me, lords, for all this flattering gloss,
He will be found a dangerous Protector.
   Buck. Why should he then protect our sovereign,
He being of age to govern of himself? 166
Cousin of Somerset, join you with me,
And all together, with the Duke of Suffolk,
We'll quickly hoise Duke Humphrey from his seat.
   Car. This weighty business will not brook delay,
I'll to the Duke of Suffolk presently.   *Exit Cardinal.*
   Som. Cousin of Buckingham, though Humphrey's
     pride 172
And greatness of his place be grief to us,
Yet let us watch the haughty Cardinal;
His insolence is more intolerable 175
Than all the princes in the land beside.
If Gloucester be displac'd, he'll be Protector.
   Buck. Or thou or I, Somerset, will be [Protector],
Despite Duke Humphrey or the Cardinal.
             Exeunt Buckingham and Somerset.
   Sal. Pride went before, ambition follows him. 180
While these do labor for their own preferment,
Behooves it us to labor for the realm.
I never saw but Humphrey Duke of Gloucester
Did bear him like a noble gentleman.
Oft have I seen the haughty Cardinal, 185
More like a soldier than a man o' th' church,
As stout and proud as he were lord of all,
Swear like a ruffian, and demean himself
Unlike the ruler of a commonweal.
Warwick, my son, the comfort of my age, 190
Thy deeds, thy plainness, and thy house-keeping,
Hath won the greatest favor of the commons,
Excepting none but good Duke Humphrey;
And, brother York, thy acts in Ireland,
In bringing them to civil discipline, 195
Thy late exploits done in the heart of France
When thou wert Regent for our sovereign,
Have made thee fear'd and honor'd of the people;
Join we together, for the public good,
In what we can to bridle and suppress 200
The pride of Suffolk and the Cardinal,
With Somerset's and Buckingham's ambition;
And as we may, cherish Duke Humphrey's deeds
While they do tend the profit of the land.
   War. So God help Warwick, as he loves the land
And common profit of his country! 206

---

111. **large style:** imposing title.
119. **Anjou . . . both.** An inaccuracy. Richard Neville, Earl of Warwick and Salisbury (1428–71), "the Kingmaker," first saw military service at the battle of St. Albans (1455), the event with which this play concludes. He is probably confused here with his father-in-law Richard Beauchamp, Earl of Warwick, who died in 1439, and whose title, descending first to his own son, was not conferred upon Neville until 1449. 123. **Mort Dieu:** by God's (Christ's) death.
131. **vantages:** profit, i.e. dowry.
133. **whole fifteenth:** tax of fifteen percent on income from land. In *1 Henry VI*, V.v.93, Suffolk had been authorized by the King to "gather up a tenth." 145. **Lordings:** gentlemen.
151. **next of blood.** Gloucester was the eldest living uncle of the then childless king.
154. **wealthy . . . west.** Perhaps an anachronistic allusion to America.
155. **he:** i.e. Gloucester. 156. **smoothing:** flattering.

163. **flattering gloss:** attractive appearance.
166. **age.** At the time represented in this scene Henry VI was twenty-four and had long since assumed the royal power.
169. **hoise:** hoist. 170. **brook:** permit.
171. **presently:** immediately. 173. **grief:** grievance.
175. **insolence:** pride. 176. **all:** that of all. 178. **Or:** either.
180. **Pride:** i.e. the Cardinal. **ambition:** i.e. Buckingham and Somerset. 187. **as:** as if. 188. **demean:** behave.
191. **house-keeping:** hospitality.
193. **Excepting none but:** (greatest) except for their favor to.
194. **brother:** i.e. brother-in-law. York's wife was Salisbury's sister Cicely. **acts in Ireland.** An anachronism. York was appointed the King's lieutenant in Ireland in 1447, two years after the events represented in this scene. He did not return to England until 1450.

York. And so says York—[*aside*] for he hath greatest cause.

Sal. Then let's make haste away, and look unto
the main.

War. Unto the main? O father, Maine is lost!
That Maine which by main force Warwick did win,
And would have kept so long as breath did last! 211
Main chance, father, you meant, but I meant Maine,
Which I will win from France, or else be slain.

Exeunt Warwick and Salisbury. Manet York.

York. Anjou and Maine are given to the French,
Paris is lost, the state of Normandy   215
Stands on a tickle point now they are gone.
Suffolk concluded on the articles,
The peers agreed, and Henry was well pleas'd
To change two dukedoms for a duke's fair daughter.
I cannot blame them all, what is't to them?   220
'Tis thine they give away, and not their own.
Pirates may make cheap pennyworths of their pillage
And purchase friends and give to courtezans,
Still revelling like lords till all be gone;
While as the silly owner of the goods   225
Weeps over them, and wrings his hapless hands,
And shakes his head, and trembling stands aloof,
While all is shar'd and all is borne away,
Ready to starve, and dare not touch his own.
So York must sit, and fret, and bite his tongue, 230
While his own lands are bargain'd for and sold.
Methinks the realms of England, France, and Ireland
Bear that proportion to my flesh and blood
As did the fatal brand Althaea burnt
Unto the Prince's heart of Calydon.   235
Anjou and Maine both given unto the French!
Cold news for me; for I had hope of France,
Even as I have of fertile England's soil.
A day will come when York shall claim his own,
And therefore I will take the Nevils' parts,   240
And make a show of love to proud Duke Humphrey,
And, when I spy advantage, claim the crown,
For that's the golden mark I seek to hit.
Nor shall proud Lancaster usurp my right,
Nor hold the sceptre in his childish fist,   245
Nor wear the diadem upon his head,
Whose church-like humors fits not for a crown.
Then, York, be still awhile, till time do serve.
Watch thou, and wake when others be asleep,
To pry into the secrets of the state,   250
Till Henry, surfeiting in joys of love
With his new bride and England's dear-bought queen,
And Humphrey with the peers be fall'n at jars:
Then will I raise aloft the milk-white rose,
With whose sweet smell the air shall be perfum'd,
And in my standard bear the arms of York,   256
To grapple with the house of Lancaster;
And force perforce I'll make him yield the crown,
Whose bookish rule hath pull'd fair England down.

Exit York.

[SCENE II]

Enter Duke Humphrey [of Gloucester] *and his wife*
Eleanor [the Duchess].

Duch. Why droops my lord, like over-ripen'd corn
Hanging the head at Ceres' plenteous load?
Why doth the great Duke Humphrey knit his brows,
As frowning at the favors of the world?
Why are thine eyes fix'd to the sullen earth,   5
Gazing on that which seems to dim thy sight?
What seest thou there? King Henry's diadem,
Enchas'd with all the honors of the world?
If so, gaze on, and grovel on thy face,
Until thy head be circled with the same.   10
Put forth thy hand, reach at the glorious gold.
What, is't too short? I'll lengthen it with mine,
And having both together heav'd it up,
We'll both together lift our heads to heaven,
And never more abase our sight so low   15
As to vouchsafe one glance unto the ground.

Glou. O Nell, sweet Nell, if thou dost love thy
lord,
Banish the canker of ambitious thoughts!
And may that thought, when I imagine ill
Against my king and nephew, virtuous Henry,   20
Be my last breathing in this mortal world!
My troublous dreams this night doth make me sad.

Duch. What dream'd my lord? Tell me, and I'll
requite it
With sweet rehearsal of my morning's dream.

Glou. Methought this staff, mine office-badge in
court,   25
Was broke in twain (by whom I have forgot,
But, as I think, it was by th' Cardinal),
And on the pieces of the broken wand
Were plac'd the heads of Edmund Duke of Somerset,
And William de la Pole, first Duke of Suffolk.   30
This was my dream, what it doth bode God knows.

Duch. Tut, this was nothing but an argument
That he that breaks a stick of Gloucester's grove
Shall lose his head for his presumption.
But list to me, my Humphrey, my sweet duke: 35
Methought I sate in seat of majesty

---

207. **greatest cause:** i.e. as head of the rival house to Lancaster.
208. **main:** i.e. principal concern (with a pun on *main*, a term from
the dice game called hazard, and on *Maine,* the French province).
216. **tickle:** precarious.   217. **concluded on:** agreed to.
221. **thine:** i.e. York's.
222. **make . . . of:** i.e. sell for almost nothing.
225. **While as:** while.   **silly:** helpless.   233. **proportion:** relation.
234. **fatal brand.** Told by the Fates that her son Meleager would die
when a brand then burning in the fire was consumed, Althaea snatched
forth the brand and saved it until, years later, she caused his death
by throwing it back into the fire.
235. **Prince's . . . Calydon:** heart of the Prince of Calydon (Meleager).
240. **take . . . parts:** i.e. ally myself with Salisbury and his son.
242. **advantage:** opportunity.   243. **mark:** the center of a target.
244. **proud Lancaster:** i.e. Henry VI.
247. **church-like humors:** pious disposition.

253. **at jars:** into contention.
258. **force perforce:** by violent compulsion.
259. **bookish:** scholarly, i.e. tame.

I.ii. Location: London. The Duke of Gloucester's house.
2. **Ceres' plenteous load:** i.e. rich harvest. Ceres was the goddess of
agriculture.   8. **Enchas'd:** decorated.   18. **canker:** ulcer.
22. **this night:** i.e. last night.
24. **morning's dream.** It was an ancient superstition that morning
dreams were true.
25. **mine office-badge:** symbol of my authority as Protector.
32. **argument:** proof.   36. **sate:** sat.

2 Henry VI
I.ii

In the cathedral church of Westminster,
And in that chair where kings and queens were
    crown'd,
Where Henry and Dame Margaret kneel'd to me,
And on my head did set the diadem.   40
    Glou. Nay, Eleanor, then must I chide outright.
Presumptuous dame, ill-nurtur'd Eleanor,
Art thou not second woman in the realm?
And the Protector's wife, belov'd of him?
Hast thou not worldly pleasure at command   45
Above the reach or compass of thy thought?
And wilt thou still be hammering treachery,
To tumble down thy husband and thyself
From top of honor to disgrace's feet?
Away from me, and let me hear no more!   50
    Duch. What, what, my lord? are you so choleric
With Eleanor, for telling but her dream?
Next time I'll keep my dreams unto myself,
And not be check'd.
    Glou. Nay, be not angry, I am pleas'd again.   55

Enter MESSENGER.

    Mess. My Lord Protector, 'tis his Highness'
        pleasure
You do prepare to ride unto Saint Albons,
Where as the King and Queen do mean to hawk.
    Glou. I go. Come, Nell, thou wilt ride with us?
    Duch. Yes, my good lord, I'll follow presently. 60
                        Exit Humphrey [with Messenger].
Follow I must, I cannot go before
While Gloucester bears this base and humble mind.
Were I a man, a duke, and next of blood,
I would remove these tedious stumbling-blocks,
And smooth my way upon their headless necks;   65
And, being a woman, I will not be slack
To play my part in Fortune's pageant.
Where are you there? Sir John! Nay, fear not, man,
We are alone, here's none but thee and I.

Enter HUME.

    Hume. Jesus preserve your royal Majesty!   70
    Duch. What say'st thou? Majesty? I am but
        Grace.
    Hume. But, by the grace of God and Hume's ad-
        vice,
Your Grace's title shall be multiplied.
    Duch. What say'st thou, man? Hast thou as yet
        conferr'd
With Margery Jordan, the cunning witch,   75
With Roger Bolingbrook, the conjurer?
And will they undertake to do me good?
    Hume. This they have promised, to show your
        Highness
A spirit rais'd from depth of under ground,

That shall make answer to such questions   80
As by your Grace shall be propounded him.
    Duch. It is enough, I'll think upon the questions.
When from Saint Albons we do make return,
We'll see these things effected to the full.
Here, Hume, take this reward. Make merry, man,
With thy confederates in this weighty cause.   86
                                        Exit Eleanor.
    Hume. Hume must make merry with the Duchess'
        gold;
Marry, and shall. But how now, Sir John Hume?
Seal up your lips, and give no words but mum;
The business asketh silent secrecy.   90
Dame Eleanor gives gold to bring the witch;
Gold cannot come amiss, were she a devil.
Yet have I gold flies from another coast—
I dare not say from the rich Cardinal
And from the great and new-made Duke of Suffolk,
Yet I do find it so; for, to be plain,   96
They, knowing Dame Eleanor's aspiring humor,
Have hired me to undermine the Duchess,
And buzz these conjurations in her brain.
They say, "A crafty knave does need no broker," 100
Yet am I Suffolk and the Cardinal's broker.
Hume, if you take not heed, you shall go near
To call them both a pair of crafty knaves.
Well, so it stands; and thus, I fear, at last
Hume's knavery will be the Duchess' wrack,   105
And her attainture will be Humphrey's fall.
Sort how it will, I shall have gold for all.   *Exit.*

[SCENE III]

Enter three or four PETITIONERS, [PETER] *the Armorer's
man being one.*

    1. Petit. My masters, let's stand close. My Lord
Protector will come this way by and by, and then we
may deliver our supplications in the quill.
    2. Petit. Marry, the Lord protect him, for he's a
good man! Jesu bless him!   5

Enter SUFFOLK *and* QUEEN.

    Peter. Here 'a comes, methinks, and the Queen
with him. I'll be the first, sure.
    2. Petit. Come back, fool. This is the Duke of
Suffolk and not my Lord Protector.   9
    Suf. How now, fellow? wouldst any thing with me?
    1. Petit. I pray, my lord, pardon me, I took ye for
my Lord Protector.
    Queen. [*Reading.*] "To my Lord Protector"? Are
your supplications to his lordship? Let me see them.
What is thine?   15

---

38. **chair:** the coronation chair containing the ancient Stone of Scone,
which Edward I brought from Scotland in 1296.
42. **ill-nurtur'd:** ill-bred.   47. **hammering:** devising.
54. **check'd:** rebuked.
57. **Saint Albons:** St. Albans (the Roman Verulam), a town some
twenty miles north of London.   58. **Where as:** where.
60. **presently:** immediately.
70. **Majesty.** An anachronism. "Your Majesty" was a title first
used by the Tudors.

88. **Marry:** indeed (originally the name of the Virgin Mary used as an
oath).   93. **flies:** that flies.   **coast:** direction.
97. **aspiring humor:** ambitious nature.   100. **broker:** agent.
105. **wrack:** destruction.
106. **attainture:** conviction (and disgrace).   107. **Sort:** turn out.

I.iii. Location: London. The palace.
3. **in the quill:** i.e. all together.   6. **'a:** he.

1. Petit. Mine is, and't please your Grace, against John Goodman, my Lord Cardinal's man, for keeping my house, and lands, and wife and all, from me.

Suf. Thy wife too? that's some wrong indeed. What's yours? What's here? [*Reads.*] "Against the Duke of Suffolk, for enclosing the commons of Melford." How now, sir knave?   20

2. Petit. Alas, sir, I am but a poor petitioner of our whole township.   24

Peter. [*Giving his petition.*] Against my master, Thomas Horner, for saying that the Duke of York was rightful heir to the crown.

Queen. What say'st thou? Did the Duke of York say he was rightful heir to the crown?   29

Peter. That my [master] was? No, forsooth; my master said that he was, and that the King was an usurper.

Suf. Who is there? (*Enter Servant.*) Take this fellow in, and send for his master with a pursuivant 34 presently. We'll hear more of your matter before the King.   *Exit* [*Servant with Peter*].

Queen. And as for you, that love to be protected Under the wings of our Protector's grace, Begin your suits anew, and sue to him.

                          Tear the supplication.

Away, base cullions! Suffolk, let them go.   40

All [*Petitioners*]. Come, let's be gone.   *Exeunt.*

Queen. My Lord of Suffolk, say, is this the guise, Is this the fashions in the court of England? Is this the government of Britain's isle, And this the royalty of Albion's king?   45 What, shall King Henry be a pupil still Under the surly Gloucester's governance? Am I a queen in title and in style, And must be made a subject to a duke? I tell thee, Pole, when in the city Tours   50 Thou ran'st a-tilt in honor of my love And stol'st away the ladies' hearts of France, I thought King Henry had resembled thee In courage, courtship, and proportion; But all his mind is bent to holiness,   55 To number Ave-Maries on his beads; His champions are the prophets and apostles, His weapons holy saws of sacred writ, His study is his tilt-yard, and his loves Are brazen images of canonized saints.   60 I would the college of the Cardinals Would choose him Pope and carry him to Rome, And set the triple crown upon his head— That were a state fit for his holiness.

Suf. Madam, be patient. As I was cause   65 Your Highness came to England, so will I In England work your Grace's full content.

Queen. Beside the haughty Protector, have we Beauford The imperious churchman, Somerset, Buckingham, And grumbling York; and not the least of these 70 But can do more in England than the King.

Suf. And he of these that can do most of all Cannot do more in England than the Nevils: Salisbury and Warwick are no simple peers.   74

Queen. Not all these lords do vex me half so much As that proud dame, the Lord Protector's wife: She sweeps it through the court with troops of ladies, More like an empress than Duke Humphrey's wife. Strangers in court do take her for the Queen. She bears a duke's revenues on her back,   80 And in her heart she scorns our poverty. Shall I not live to be aveng'd on her? Contemptuous base-born callot as she is, She vaunted 'mongst her minions t' other day, The very train of her worst wearing gown   85 Was better worth than all my father's lands, Till Suffolk gave two dukedoms for his daughter.

Suf. Madam, myself have lim'd a bush for her, And plac'd a choir of such enticing birds That she will light to listen to the lays,   90 And never mount to trouble you again. So let her rest; and, madam, list to me, For I am bold to counsel you in this. Although we fancy not the Cardinal, Yet must we join with him and with the lords,   95 Till we have brought Duke Humphrey in disgrace. As for the Duke of York, this late complaint Will make but little for his benefit. So one by one we'll weed them all at last, And you yourself shall steer the happy helm.   100

Sound a sennet. Enter the KING, DUKE HUMPHREY [*of* GLOUCESTER], CARDINAL, BUCKINGHAM, YORK, [SOMERSET,] SALISBURY, WARWICK, *and the* DUCHESS [*of* GLOUCESTER].

King. For my part, noble lords, I care not which, Or Somerset or York, all's one to me.

York. If York have ill demean'd himself in France, Then let him be denay'd the regentship.

Som. If Somerset be unworthy of the place,   105 Let York be Regent, I will yield to him.

War. Whether your Grace be worthy, yea or no, Dispute not that; York is the worthier.

---

21. commons: common land, the enclosure of which by landlords was the cause of mounting complaint by their tenants.
22. Melford: Long Melford, town in the county of Suffolk.
26-27. for . . . crown. In Hall (Bullough, III, 105), from whom Shakespeare drew the episode of the armorer and his man, the question of York's loyalty is not raised at all.
34. **pursuivant:** junior official attendant on a herald, messenger.
40. **cullions:** wretches (Italian *coglioni*, testicles).
42. **guise:** custom.   48. **style:** title.
51. **ran'st a-tilt:** took part in a tournament. Hall reports (Bullough, I, 102) that when Suffolk went to France to arrange Henry's marriage with Margaret "there wer triumphaunt Justes, costly feastes, and delicate banquettes" to celebrate the nuptials.
54. **courtship:** courtliness of manner.   **proportion:** physical grace.
64. **state:** status.

74. **Salisbury . . . peers.** This remark anticipates the decisive part played by the powerful Neville family in the ensuing struggles between the Yorkists and Lancastrians. Salisbury was the son and Warwick ("the Kingmaker") the grandson of Sir Ralph Neville (created first Earl of Westmorland by Richard II in 1397) and his second wife Joan Beaufort (a daughter of John of Gaunt and a sister of the Cardinal). On the Beaufort family see note to *1 Henry VI*, III.i.42.
75-87. **Not . . . daughter.** Actually, Eleanor, Duchess of Gloucester, had been accused of witchcraft and banished from the court in 1441, four years before Queen Margaret came to England.
83. **Contemptuous:** contemptible.   **callot:** callet, strumpet.
88. **lim'd:** covered with birdlime, a sticky substance used to catch birds.   89. **enticing birds:** decoys.
97. **late complaint:** i.e. of Peter the armorer's man against his master.
100 s.d. **sennet:** trumpet call announcing a procession.
104. **denay'd:** refused.

2 Henry VI
I.iii

Car. Ambitious Warwick, let thy betters speak.

War. The Cardinal's not my better in the field.

Buck. All in this presence are thy betters, War-
wick.   111

War. Warwick may live to be the best of all.

Sal. Peace, son, and show some reason, Buckingham,
Why Somerset should be preferr'd in this.

Queen. Because the King, forsooth, will have it so.

Glou. Madam, the King is old enough himself 116
To give his censure. These are no women's matters.

Queen. If he be old enough, what needs your Grace
To be Protector of his Excellence?

Glou. Madam, I am Protector of the realm, 120
And at his pleasure will resign my place.

Suf. Resign it then and leave thine insolence.
Since thou wert king—as who is king but thou?—
The commonwealth hath daily run to wrack,
The Dolphin hath prevail'd beyond the seas, 125
And all the peers and nobles of the realm
Have been as bondmen to thy sovereignty.

Car. The commons hast thou rack'd, the clergy's
bags
Are lank and lean with thy extortions.

Som. Thy sumptuous buildings and thy wive's
attire   130
Have cost a mass of public treasury.

Buck. Thy cruelty in execution
Upon offenders hath exceeded law,
And left thee to the mercy of the law.

Queen. Thy sale of offices and towns in France,
If they were known, as the suspect is great, 136
Would make thee quickly hop without thy head.

Exit Humphrey. [*The Queen lets fall her fan.*]
Give me my fan. What, minion, can ye not?

                    She gives the Duchess a box on the ear.
I cry you mercy, madam; was it you?

Duch. Was't I? yea, I it was, proud Frenchwoman.
Could I come near your beauty with my nails, 141
I could set my ten commandements in your face.

King. Sweet aunt, be quiet, 'twas against her will.

Duch. Against her will, good king? Look to't in
time,
She'll hamper thee, and dandle thee like a baby. 145
Though in this place most master wear no breeches,
She shall not strike Dame Eleanor unreveng'd.

                                               Exit Eleanor.
Buck. Lord Cardinal, I will follow Eleanor,
And listen after Humphrey, how he proceeds.
She's tickled now; her fume needs no spurs, 150
She'll gallop far enough to her destruction.

                                         Exit Buckingham.

117. **censure:** judgment.
125. **Dolphin:** Dauphin, title of the heir apparent to the French throne. Charles VII is so called here because the English considered Henry VI the rightful king of France.
128. **rack'd:** impoverished by extortion.   130. **wive's:** wife's.
131. **treasury:** treasure.   136. **suspect:** suspicion.
139. **cry you mercy:** beg your pardon.
142. **ten commandements:** i.e. ten fingers.
144. **Against her will:** unintentional.
146. **most master:** the one most masterful, i.e. the Queen.
149. **listen after:** inquire about.
150. **tickled:** irritated.   **fume:** smoke, i.e. fury.

Enter HUMPHREY [OF GLOUCESTER].

Glou. Now, lords, my choler being overblown
With walking once about the quadrangle,
I come to talk of commonwealth affairs.
As for your spiteful false objections, 155
Prove them, and I lie open to the law;
But God in mercy so deal with my soul
As I in duty love my king and country!
But to the matter that we have in hand.
I say, my sovereign, York is meetest man 160
To be your Regent in the realm of France.

Suf. Before we make election, give me leave
To show some reason, of no little force,
That York is most unmeet of any man.

York. I'll tell thee, Suffolk, why I am unmeet: 165
First, for I cannot flatter thee in pride;
Next, if I be appointed for the place,
My Lord of Somerset will keep me here
Without discharge, money, or furniture,
Till France be won into the Dolphin's hands. 170
Last time, I danc'd attendance on his will
Till Paris was besieg'd, famish'd, and lost.

War. That can I witness, and a fouler fact
Did never traitor in the land commit.

Suf. Peace, headstrong Warwick! 175

War. Image of pride, why should I hold my peace?

Enter [HORNER *the*] *armorer and his man* [PETER,
guarded].

Suf. Because here is a man accused of treason.
Pray God the Duke of York excuse himself!

York. Doth any one accuse York for a traitor?

King. What mean'st thou, Suffolk? tell me, what
are these? 180

Suf. Please it your Majesty, this is the man
That doth accuse his master of high treason.
His words were these: that Richard Duke of York
Was rightful heir unto the English crown
And that your Majesty was an usurper. 185

King. Say, man, were these thy words?

Hor. And't shall please your Majesty, I never said
nor thought any such matter. God is my witness, I am
falsely accus'd by the villain. 189

Peter. By these ten bones, my lords [*holding up his
hands*], he did speak them to me in the garret one night,
as we were scouring my Lord of York's armor.

York. Base dunghill villain and mechanical,
I'll have thy head for this thy traitor's speech.
I do beseech your royal Majesty, 195
Let him have all the rigor of the law.

Hor. Alas, my lord, hang me if ever I spake the
words. My accuser is my prentice, and when I did
correct him for his fault the other day, he did vow upon
his knees he would be even with me. I have good 200
witness of this; therefore I beseech your Majesty, do
not cast away an honest man for a villain's accusation.

152. **overblown:** blown over, dissipated.   162. **election:** choice.
166. **for:** because.
169. **discharge:** financial settlement.   **furniture:** military equipment.
171. **Last time.** See *I Henry VI*, IV.iii.   173. **fact:** deed, crime.
193. **mechanical:** menial.   202. **cast away:** destroy.

King.   Uncle, what shall we say to this in law?
Glou.   This doom, my lord, if I may judge:
Let Somerset be Regent o'er the French,   205
Because in York this breeds suspicion;
And let these have a day appointed them
For single combat in convenient place,
For he hath witness of his servant's malice.
This is the law, and this Duke Humphrey's doom.
Som.   I humbly thank your royal Majesty.   211
Hor.   And I accept the combat willingly.
Peter.   Alas, my lord, I cannot fight; for God's sake
pity my case. The spite of man prevaileth against me.
O Lord, have mercy upon me! I shall never be able to
fight a blow. O Lord, my heart!   216
Glou.   Sirrah, or you must fight, or else be hang'd.
King.   Away with them to prison; and the day of
combat shall be the last of the next month. Come,
Somerset, we'll see thee sent away.   220

                Flourish. Exeunt.

[SCENE IV]

Enter the witch [MARGERY JORDAN], *the two priests*
[HUME *and* SOUTHWELL], *and* BOLINGBROOK.

Hume.   Come, my masters, the Duchess, I tell you,
expects performance of your promises.
Boling.   Master Hume, we are therefore provided.
Will her ladyship behold and hear our exorcisms?
Hume.   Ay, what else? fear you not her courage.   5
Boling.   I have heard her reported to be a woman of
an invincible spirit; but it shall be convenient, Master
Hume, that you be by her aloft, while we be busy be-
low; and so I pray you go in God's name, and leave
us. (*Exit Hume.*) Mother Jordan, be you prostrate   10
and grovel on the earth. [*She lies down upon her face.*]
John Southwell, read you; and let us to our work.

Enter ELEANOR [THE DUCHESS] *aloft*, [HUME *following*].

Duch.   Well said, my masters, and welcome all.
To this gear, the sooner the better.
Boling.   Patience, good lady, wizards know their
    times.   15
Deep night, dark night, the silent of the night,
The time of night when Troy was set on fire,
The time when screech-owls cry and ban-dogs howl,
And spirits walk, and ghosts break up their graves,
That time best fits the work we have in hand.   20
Madam, sit you and fear not. Whom we raise,
We will make fast within a hallow'd verge.

    Here do the ceremonies belonging, and make the
    circle; Bolingbrook or Southwell reads, "Conjuro
    te, etc." It thunders and lightens terribly; then
    the Spirit riseth.

Spir.   *Adsum.*
M. Jord.   Asmath,
By the eternal God, whose name and power   25
Thou tremblest at, answer that I shall ask;
For, till thou speak, thou shalt not pass from hence.
Spir.   Ask what thou wilt. That I had said, and
    done!
Boling.   "First of the King: what shall of him
    become?"   [*Reading out of a paper.*]
Spir.   The duke yet lives that Henry shall depose;
But him out-live, and die a violent death.   31
        [*As the Spirit speaks, Bolingbrook*
        writes the answer.]
Boling.   "[Tell me] what [fate awaits] the Duke of
    Suffolk?"
Spir.   By water shall he die, and take his end.
Boling.   "What shall [betide] the Duke of Somer-
    set?"
Spir.   Let him shun castles.   35
Safer shall he be upon the sandy plains
Than where castles mounted stand.
Have done, for more I hardly can endure.
Boling.   Descend to darkness and the burning lake!
False fiend, avoid!   40
        Thunder and lightning. Exit Spirit
        [*sinking down again*].

Enter the DUKE OF YORK *and the* DUKE OF BUCKINGHAM
with their GUARD, [SIR HUMPHREY STAFFORD *as*
Captain,] *and break in.*

York.   Lay hands upon these traitors and their
    trash.
Beldam, I think we watch'd you at an inch.
What, madam, are you there? The King and common-
weal
Are deeply indebted for this piece of pains.
My Lord Protector will, I doubt it not,   45
See you well guerdon'd for these good deserts.
Duch.   Not half so bad as thine to England's king,
Injurious duke, that threatest where's no cause.
Buck.   True, madam, none at all. What call you
    this?
Away with them, let them be clapp'd up close,   50
And kept asunder. You, madam, shall with us.
Stafford, take her to thee.
        [*Exeunt, above, Duchess and Hume guarded.*]
We'll see your trinkets here all forthcoming.
All away!   *Exit* [*Guard with Jordan, Southwell, etc.*].
York.   Lord Buckingham, methinks you watch'd
    her well.   55
A pretty plot, well chosen to build upon!
Now pray, my lord, let's see the devil's writ.
What have we here?   *Reads.*

---

204. **doom:** judgment.
217. **Sirrah:** customary form of address to an inferior.

I.iv. Location: London. Gloucester's garden.
4. **exorcisms:** conjurations.   13. **Well said:** well done.
14. **To this gear:** on with the business.
18. **ban-dogs:** dogs chained up, either to guard a house or because of
their ferocity.
22. **make . . . verge:** confine within a magic circle.   s.d. **ceremonies**
belonging: i.e. the ritual pertaining to the conjurations, such as drawing a magic circle and repeating formulas of incantation.   **Conjuro**
te: I conjure you.

23. **Adsum:** I am here.
24. **Asmath:** the name of the conjured fiend, perhaps a misprint for
Asnath, an anagram for *Sathan* (Satan).   26. **that:** what.
28. **That:** would that.   40. **False:** treacherous.   **avoid:** depart.
42. **Beldam:** hag.   **at an inch:** closely.
46. **guerdon'd:** rewarded.
50. **clapp'd up close:** imprisoned closely.
53. **trinkets:** trash.   **forthcoming:** given into legal custody.
56. **plot:** (1) trick; (2) plot of ground.

2 Henry VI
I.iv

"The duke yet lives that Henry shall depose;
But him out-live, and die a violent death." 60
Why, this is just
"*Aio* [*te,*] *Aeacida, Romanos vincere posse.*"
Well, to the rest:
"Tell me what fate awaits the Duke of Suffolk?"
"By water shall he die, and take his end." 65
"What shall betide the Duke of Somerset?"
"Let him shun castles;
Safer shall he be upon the sandy plains
Than where castles mounted stand."
Come, come, my lords, these oracles 70
Are hardly attain'd, and hardly understood.
The King is now in progress towards Saint Albons,
With him the husband of this lovely lady.
Thither goes these news, as fast as horse can carry
them—
A sorry breakfast for my Lord Protector. 75
   Buck. Your Grace shall give me leave, my Lord of
     York,
To be the post, in hope of his reward.
    York. At your pleasure, my good lord. Who's
     within there, ho?

Enter a SERVINGMAN.

Invite my Lords of Salisbury and Warwick 79
To sup with me to-morrow night. Away!   *Exeunt.*

[ACT II, SCENE I]

Enter the KING, QUEEN [*with her hawk on her fist*],
PROTECTOR [GLOUCESTER], CARDINAL, *and* SUFFOLK,
with FALC'NERS *hallowing.*

   Queen. Believe me, lords, for flying at the brook,
I saw not better sport these seven years' day;
Yet by your leave, the wind was very high,
And ten to one, old Joan had not gone out.
   King. But what a point, my lord, your falcon made,
And what a pitch she flew above the rest! 6
To see how God in all his creatures works!
Yea, man and birds are fain of climbing high.
   Suf. No marvel, and it like your Majesty,
My Lord Protector's hawks do tow'r so well; 10
They know their master loves to be aloft,
And bears his thoughts above his falcon's pitch.
   Glou. My lord, 'tis but a base ignoble mind
That mounts no higher than a bird can soar.
   Car. I thought as much, he would be above the
    clouds. 15

   Glou. Ay, my Lord Cardinal, how think you by
    that?
Were it not good your Grace could fly to heaven?
   King. The treasury of everlasting joy.
   Car. Thy heaven is on earth, thine eyes and
    thoughts
Beat on a crown, the treasure of thy heart, 20
Pernicious Protector, dangerous peer,
That smooth'st it so with king and commonweal!
   Glou. What, Cardinal? is your priesthood grown
    peremptory?
Tantaene animis caelestibus irae?
Churchmen so hot? Good uncle, hide such malice; 25
With such holiness can you do it?
   Suf. No malice, sir, no more than well becomes
So good a quarrel and so bad a peer.
   Glou. As who, my lord?
   Suf.   Why, as you, my lord,
An't like your lordly Lord's Protectorship. 30
   Glou. Why, Suffolk, England knows thine inso-
    lence.
   Queen. And thy ambition, Gloucester.
   King.   I prithee peace,
Good queen, and whet not on these furious peers,
For blessed are the peacemakers on earth.
   Car. Let me be blessed for the peace I make 35
Against this proud Protector with my sword!
   Glou. [*Aside to Cardinal.*] Faith, holy uncle,
    would't were come to that!
   Car. [*Aside to Gloucester.*] Marry, when thou dar'st.
   Glou. [*Aside to Cardinal.*] Make up no factious num-
    bers for the matter,
In thine own person answer thy abuse. 40
   Car. [*Aside to Gloucester.*] Ay, where thou dar'st
    not peep. And if thou dar'st,
This evening, on the east side of the grove.
   King. How now, my lords?
   Car.   Believe me, cousin Gloucester,
Had not your man put up the fowl so suddenly,
We had had more sport. [*Aside to Gloucester.*] Come
with thy two-hand sword. 45
   Glou. True, uncle.
[*Car.*] [*Aside to Gloucester.*] Are ye advis'd? The
    east side of the grove.
   Glou. [*Aside to Cardinal.*] Cardinal, I am with you.
   King.   Why, how now, uncle Gloucester?
   Glou. Talking of hawking; nothing else, my lord.
[*Aside to Cardinal.*] Now by God's Mother, priest,
    I'll shave your crown for this, 50
Or all my fence shall fail.
   Car.   [*Aside to Gloucester.*] *Medice, teipsum*—
Protector, see to't well, protect yourself.
   King. The winds grow high, so do your stomachs,
    lords.

---

61. **just:** precisely.
62. **Aio . . . posse:** "I say that you, descendant of Aeacus, the Romans can conquer," the ambiguous answer given by the Pythian Apollo to Pyrrhus.   71. **hardly attain'd:** with difficulty obtained.

II.i. Location: St. Albans.
1. **flying . . . brook:** hawking for waterfowl (a form of falconry favored by the nobility).
4. **old . . . out:** i.e. the old hawk (named Joan) would not have flown in such a high wind.
5. **point:** place from which to swoop upon the prey.
6. **pitch:** height.   8. **fain:** fond.
10. **My . . . hawks.** Gloucester's badge was a falcon with a maiden's head, which explains the gibes that follow.   **tow'r:** wheel and rise until the proper "point" is reached.

20. **Beat on:** i.e. ponder.
22. **smooth'st:** flatterest.
24. **Tantaene . . . irae:** "Is there such anger in heavenly minds" (*Aeneid*, i.11).   31. **insolence:** pride.
33. **whet:** sharpen, encourage.
39. **Make . . . matter:** i.e. do not involve your unruly supporters in the quarrel.   40. **abuse:** offense, insult.
44. **put . . . fowl:** i.e. raised the game.   47. **advis'd:** agreed.
51. **fence:** skill in fencing.   **Medice, teipsum:** "Physician, [heal] thyself" (Luke 4:23).   53. **stomachs:** angry tempers.

How irksome is this music to my heart!
When such strings jar, what hope of harmony? 55
I pray, my lords, let me compound this strife.

Enter one crying, "A miracle!"

Glou. What means this noise?
Fellow, what miracle dost thou proclaim?
One. A miracle, a miracle! 59
Suf. Come to the King and tell him what miracle.
One. Forsooth, a blind man at Saint Alban's shrine,
Within this half hour, hath receiv'd his sight,
A man that ne'er saw in his life before.
King. Now God be prais'd, that to believing souls
Gives light in darkness, comfort in despair! 65

Enter the Mayor of Saint Albons *and his* Brethren,
[with music,] bearing the man [Simpcox] *between two
in a chair,* [Simpcox's Wife *and others following*].

Car. Here comes the townsmen on procession,
To present your Highness with the man.
King. Great is his comfort in this earthly vale,
Although by his sight his sin be multiplied.
Glou. Stand by, my masters. Bring him near the
King, 70
His Highness' pleasure is to talk with him.
King. Good fellow, tell us here the circumstance,
That we for thee may glorify the Lord.
What, hast thou been long blind and now restor'd?
Simp. Born blind, and't please your Grace. 75
Wife. Ay indeed was he.
Suf. What woman is this?
Wife. His wife, and't like your worship.
Glou. Hadst thou been his mother, thou couldst
have better told.
King. Where wert thou born? 80
Simp. At Berwick in the north, and't like your
Grace.
King. Poor soul, God's goodness hath been great
to thee.
Let never day nor night unhallowed pass,
But still remember what the Lord hath done.
Queen. Tell me, good fellow, cam'st thou here by
chance 85
Or of devotion, to this holy shrine?
Simp. God knows, of pure devotion, being call'd
A hundred times and oft'ner, in my sleep,
By good Saint Alban, who said, "Simon, come;
Come offer at my shrine, and I will help thee." 90

Wife. Most true, forsooth; and many time and oft
Myself have heard a voice to call him so.
Car. What, art thou lame?
Simp.   Ay, God Almighty help me!
Suf. How cam'st thou so?
Simp.   A fall off of a tree.
Wife. A plum-tree, master.
Glou.   How long hast thou been blind? 95
Simp. O, born so, master.
Glou.   What, and wouldst climb a tree?
Simp. But that in all my life, when I was a youth.
Wife. Too true, and bought his climbing very dear.
Glou. Mass, thou lov'dst plums well, that wouldst
venture so.
Simp. Alas, good master, my wife desired some
damsons, 100
And made me climb, with danger of my life.
Glou. A subtile knave, but yet it shall not serve.
Let me see thine eyes. Wink now; now open them.
In my opinion yet thou seest not well.
Simp. Yes, master, clear as day, I thank God and
Saint Alban. 106
Glou. Say'st thou me so? What color is this cloak
of?
Simp. Red, master, red as blood.
Glou. Why, that's well said. What color is my
gown of?
Simp. Black, forsooth, coal-black as jet. 110
King. Why then, thou know'st what color jet is of?
Suf. And yet, I think, jet did he never see.
Glou. But cloaks and gowns, before this day, a
many.
Wife. Never, before this day, in all his life.
Glou. Tell me, sirrah, what's my name? 115
Simp. Alas, master, I know not.
Glou. What's his name?
Simp. I know not.
Glou. Nor his?
Simp. No indeed, master. 120
Glou. What's thine own name?
Simp. Saunder Simpcox, and if it please you,
master.
Glou. Then, Saunder, sit there, the lying'st knave
In Christendom. If thou hadst been born blind,
Thou mightst as well have known all our names, as thus
To name the several colors we do wear. 126
Sight may distinguish of colors; but suddenly
To nominate them all, it is impossible.
My lords, Saint Alban here hath done a miracle;
And would ye not think [his] cunning to be great, 130
That could restore this cripple to his legs again?
Simp. O master, that you could!
Glou. My masters of Saint Albons, have you not
Beadles in your town, and things call'd whips?
May. Yes, my lord, if it please your Grace. 135
Glou. Then send for one presently.
May. Sirrah, go fetch the beadle hither straight.

Exit [one].

56. compound: settle.
57–160. Shakespeare found the spurious miracle of St. Albans in John Foxe's *Acts and Monuments* (1583), where it is introduced (Bullough, III, 127) as "reported as well by the penne of syr Thomas More, as also by M. William Tindall, the true Apostle of these our latter dayes, to the intent to see and note, not only the craftye working of false miracles in the clergye, but also that the prudent discretion of this high and mighty prince, the fore sayd Duke Humfrey, may geve us better to understand what man he was."
61. Albon: Alban, allegedly the first British martyr, executed (304?) in the Roman town Verulam (later renamed St. Albans) for protecting Christian converts. 66. on: in.
69. by . . . multiplied: i.e. he will be subject to more temptation.
75. and: if. 78. like: please.
81. Berwick: town and fortress on the Scottish border at the mouth of the River Tweed. 83. unhallowed: unblessed.
84. still: always.

97. But that: i.e. only that one.
99. Mass: by the Mass. 103. Wink: close both eyes.
128. nominate: call by name.
134. Beadles: officers who administered corporal punishment.
136. presently: immediately.

639

2 Henry VI
II.i

Glou. Now fetch me a stool hither by and by. [A stool brought.] Now, sirrah, if you mean to save yourself from whipping, leap me over this stool and run away. 141

Simp. Alas, master, I am not able to stand alone; You go about to torture me in vain.

Enter a BEADLE *with whips.*

Glou. Well, sir, we must have you find your legs. Sirrah beadle, whip him till he leap over that same stool. 146

Bead. I will, my lord. Come on, sirrah, off with your doublet quickly.

Simp. Alas, master, what shall I do? I am not able to stand. 150

After the Beadle hath hit him once, he leaps over the stool and runs away; and they follow and cry, "A miracle!"

King. O God, seest thou this, and bearest so long?

Queen. It made me laugh to see the villain run.

Glou. Follow the knave, and take this drab away.

Wife. Alas, sir, we did it for pure need.

Glou. Let them be whipt through every market town, 155
Till they come to Berwick, from whence they came.

Exeunt [*Wife, Beadle, Mayor, etc.*].

Car. Duke Humphrey has done a miracle to-day.

Suf. True; made the lame to leap and fly away.

Glou. But you have done more miracles than I:
You made in a day, my lord, whole towns to fly. 160

Enter BUCKINGHAM.

King. What tidings with our cousin Buckingham?

Buck. Such as my heart doth tremble to unfold:
A sort of naughty persons, lewdly bent,
Under the countenance and confederacy
Of Lady Eleanor, the Protector's wife, 165
The ringleader and head of all this rout,
Have practic'd dangerously against your state,
Dealing with witches and with conjurers,
Whom we have apprehended in the fact,
Raising up wicked spirits from under ground, 170
Demanding of King Henry's life and death,
And other of your Highness' Privy Council,
As more at large your Grace shall understand.

Car. And so, my Lord Protector, by this means
Your lady is forthcoming yet at London. 175
[*Aside to Gloucester.*] This news, I think, hath turn'd
your weapon's edge;
'Tis like, my lord, you will not keep your hour.

Glou. Ambitious churchman, leave to afflict my
heart.
Sorrow and grief have vanquish'd all my powers;
And vanquish'd as I am, I yield to thee, 180

Or to the meanest groom.

King. O God, what mischiefs work the wicked
ones,
Heaping confusion on their own heads thereby!

Queen. Gloucester, see here the tainture of thy
nest,
And look thyself be faultless, thou wert best. 185

Glou. Madam, for myself, to heaven I do appeal,
How I have lov'd my king and commonweal;
And for my wife, I know not how it stands.
Sorry I am to hear what I have heard.
Noble she is; but if she have forgot 190
Honor and virtue, and convers'd with such
As, like to pitch, defile nobility,
I banish her my bed and company,
And give her as a prey to law and shame,
That hath dishonored Gloucester's honest name. 195

King. Well, for this night we will repose us here;
To-morrow toward London back again,
To look into this business thoroughly,
And call these foul offenders to their answers,
And poise the cause in justice' equal scales, 200
Whose beam stands sure, whose rightful cause prevails.

Flourish. Exeunt.

[SCENE II]

Enter YORK, SALISBURY, *and* WARWICK.

York. Now, my good Lords of Salisbury and
Warwick,
Our simple supper ended, give me leave
In this close walk to satisfy myself
In craving your opinion of my title,
Which is infallible, to England's crown. 5

Sal. My lord, I long to hear it at full.

War. Sweet York, begin; and if thy claim be good,
The Nevils are thy subjects to command.

York. Then thus:
Edward the Third, my lords, had seven sons: 10
The first, Edward the Black Prince, Prince of Wales;
The second, William of Hatfield; and the third,
Lionel Duke of Clarence; next to whom
Was John of Gaunt, the Duke of Lancaster;
The fift was Edmund Langley, Duke of York; 15
The sixt was Thomas of Woodstock, Duke of
Gloucester;
William of Windsor was the seventh and last.
Edward the Black Prince died before his father,
And left behind him Richard, his only son,
Who after Edward the Third's death reign'd as king 20
Till Henry Bullingbrook, Duke of Lancaster,
The eldest son and heir of John of Gaunt,
Crown'd by the name of Henry the Fourth,
Seiz'd on the realm, depos'd the rightful king,
Sent his poor queen to France, from whence she came,
And him to Pomfret; where, as all you know, 26
Harmless Richard was murthered traitorously.

---

140. me: for me, at my bidding.
160. You . . . fly. An ironic allusion to the Queen's dowry that Suffolk had arranged.
163. A sort . . . bent: a gang of disreputable people wickedly disposed.
164. Under . . . confederacy: with the protection and even the complicity. 167. practic'd: plotted. 169. fact: act.
175. forthcoming: in custody.
177. hour: appointment (for the duel previously arranged).

181. meanest: lowest.
191. convers'd: consorted. 200. poise: weigh.

II.ii. Location: London. The Duke of York's garden.
3. close walk: private path.

War. Father, the Duke hath told the truth;
Thus got the house of Lancaster the crown.

York. Which now they hold by force and not by
right; 30
For Richard, the first son's heir, being dead,
The issue of the next son should have reign'd.

Sal. But William of Hatfield died without an heir.

York. The third son, Duke of Clarence, from
whose line
I claim the crown, had issue, Philippe, a daughter, 35
Who married Edmund Mortimer, Earl of March;
Edmund had issue, Roger Earl of March;
Roger had issue, Edmund, Anne, and Eleanor.

Sal. This Edmund, in the reign of Bullingbrook,
As I have read, laid claim unto the crown, 40
And but for Owen Glendower, had been king,
Who kept him in captivity till he died.
But, to the rest.

York.　　His eldest sister, Anne,
My mother, being heir unto the crown,
Married Richard Earl of Cambridge, who was 45
To Edmund Langley, Edward the Third's fift [son,]
son.
By her I claim the kingdom. She was heir
To Roger Earl of March, who was the son
Of Edmund Mortimer, who married Philippe,
Sole daughter unto Lionel Duke of Clarence; 50
So, if the issue of the elder son
Succeed before the younger, I am king.

War. What plain proceedings is more plain than
this?
Henry doth claim the crown from John of Gaunt,
The fourth son, York claims it from the third; 55
Till Lionel's issue fails, his should not reign.
It fails not yet, but flourishes in thee,
And in thy sons, fair slips of such a stock.
Then, father Salisbury, kneel we together,
And in this private plot be we the first 60
That shall salute our rightful sovereign
With honor of his birthright to the crown.

Both. Long live our sovereign Richard, England's
king!

York. We thank you, lords. But I am not your king
Till I be crown'd, and that my sword be stain'd 65
With heart-blood of the house of Lancaster;
And that's not suddenly to be perform'd,
But with advice and silent secrecy.
Do you as I do in these dangerous days:
Wink at the Duke of Suffolk's insolence, 70
At Beauford's pride, at Somerset's ambition,
At Buckingham, and all the crew of them,
Till they have snar'd the shepherd of the flock,
That virtuous prince, the good Duke Humphrey.

'Tis that they seek; and they in seeking that 75
Shall find their deaths, if York can prophesy.

Sal. My lord, break we off; we know your mind
at full.

War. My heart assures me that the Earl of Warwick
Shall one day make the Duke of York a king.

York. And, Nevil, this I do assure myself, 80
Richard shall live to make the Earl of Warwick
The greatest man in England but the King. *Exeunt.*

[SCENE III]

Sound trumpets. Enter the KING *and State:* [*the* QUEEN,
GLOUCESTER, YORK, SUFFOLK, *and* SALISBURY,] *with*
GUARD, *to banish the Duchess.* [*Enter, guarded, the*
DUCHESS OF GLOUCESTER, MARGERY JORDAN,
SOUTHWELL, HUME, *and* BOLINGBROOK.]

King. Stand forth, Dame Eleanor Cobham,
Gloucester's wife:
In sight of God and us, your guilt is great;
Receive the sentence of the law for [sins]
Such as by God's book are adjudg'd to death.
You four, from hence to prison back again; 5
From thence, unto the place of execution.
The witch in Smithfield shall be burnt to ashes,
And you three shall be strangled on the gallows.
You, madam, for you are more nobly born,
Despoiled of your honor in your life, 10
Shall, after three days' open penance done,
Live in your country here in banishment,
With Sir John Stanley, in the Isle of Man.

Duch. Welcome is banishment, welcome were my
death.

Glou. Eleanor, the law, thou seest, hath judged
thee; 15
I cannot justify whom the law condemns.
[*Exeunt Duchess and other prisoners, guarded.*]
Mine eyes are full of tears, my heart of grief.
Ah, Humphrey, this dishonor in thine age
Will bring thy head with sorrow to the ground!
I beseech your Majesty give me leave to go; 20
Sorrow would solace, and mine age would ease.

King. Stay, Humphrey Duke of Gloucester! Ere
thou go,
Give up thy staff. Henry will to himself
Protector be, and God shall be my hope,
My stay, my guide, and lanthorn to my feet; 25
And go in peace, Humphrey, no less belov'd
Than when thou wert Protector to thy king.

39–42. **This . . . died.** Here, as in *1 Henry IV* (see note to I.i.38) and in the chroniclers whom Shakespeare followed, Edmund Mortimer, fifth Earl of March, who was named heir presumptive to the throne by Richard II, is confused with his uncle Edmund, brother of the fourth Earl, who married Glendower's daughter. The statement that Glendower kept Edmund "in captivity till he died" seems to be Shakespeare's own addition. 53. **proceedings:** succession.
56. **his:** i.e. John of Gaunt's 58. **slips:** cuttings.
60. **plot:** ground.
62. **birthright:** hereditary right by the law of primogeniture.
68. **advice:** deliberation. 70. **Wink at:** close your eyes to.

II.iii. Location: London. A hall of justice.
3–4. **sins . . . death.** A typical Old Testament injunction against witches is that in Exodus 22:18.
8. **strangled . . . gallows.** Hall's account (Bullough, III, 101–2) is somewhat different: "Margery Jordayne was brent in Smithfelde, & Roger Bolyngbroke was drawen & quartered at Tiborne, takyng upon his death, that there was never no suche thyng [as the alleged conspiracy] by theim ymagined, John Hum had his pardon, & Southwel died in the toure before execution: the duke of Gloucester, toke all these thynges paciently, and saied litle." 9. **for:** because.
13. **Sir John Stanley.** Actually, Sir Thomas Stanley. **Isle of Man:** island off the northwest coast of England. 21. **would:** would have.
25. **lanthorn:** lantern.

Queen. I see no reason why a king of years
Should be to be protected like a child.   30
God and King Henry govern England's realm.
Give up your staff, sir, and the King his realm.

Glou. My staff? Here, noble Henry, is my staff.
As willingly do I the same resign
As ere thy father Henry made it mine;
And even as willingly at thy feet I leave it   35
As others would ambitiously receive it.
Farewell, good King; when I am dead and gone,
May honorable peace attend thy throne!

Exit Gloucester.

Queen. Why, now is Henry king and Margaret
     queen,
And Humphrey Duke of Gloucester scarce himself, 40
That bears so shrewd a maim: two pulls at once—
His lady banish'd, and a limb lopp'd off.
This staff of honor raught, there let it stand,
Where it best fits to be, in Henry's hand.

Suf. Thus droops this lofty pine and hangs his
     sprays,   45
Thus Eleanor's pride dies in her youngest days.

York. Lords, let him go. Please it your Majesty,
This is the day appointed for the combat,
And ready are the appellant and defendant,
The armorer and his man, to enter the lists,   50
So please your Highness to behold the fight.

Queen. Ay, good my lord; for purposely therefore
Left I the court, to see this quarrel tried.

King. A' God's name see the lists and all things
     fit;
Here let them end it, and God defend the right!   55

York. I never saw a fellow worse bestead,
Or more afraid to fight, than is the appellant,
The servant of this armorer, my lords.

Enter at one door [HORNER] *the armorer and his* NEIGH-
BORS, *drinking to him so much that he is drunk;
and he enters with a Drum before him and his staff with
a sand-bag fastened to it; and at the other door* [PETER,]
his man, with a Drum and sand-bag, and PRENTICES
drinking to him.

1. Neigh. Here, neighbor Horner, I drink to you
in a cup of sack; and fear not, neighbor, you shall do
well enough.   61

2. Neigh. And here, neighbor, here's a cup of
charneco.

3. Neigh. And here's a pot of good double beer,
neighbor. Drink, and fear not your man.   65

Hor. Let it come, i' faith, and I'll pledge you all,
and a fig for Peter!

1. Pren. Here, Peter, I drink to thee, and be not
afraid.

2. Pren. Be merry, Peter, and fear not thy master.
Fight for credit of the prentices.   71

Peter. I thank you all. Drink, and pray for me, I
pray you, for I think I have taken my last draught in
this world. Here, Robin, and if I die, I give thee my
aporn; and, Will, thou shalt have my hammer;   75
and here, Tom, take all the money that I have. O Lord
bless me, I pray God, for I am never able to deal with
my master, he hath learnt so much fence already.

Sal. Come, leave your drinking, and fall to blows.
Sirrah, what's thy name?   80

Peter. Peter, forsooth.

Sal. Peter? What more?

Peter. Thump.

Sal. Thump? Then see thou thump thy master well.

Hor. Masters, I am come hither, as it were, upon
my man's instigation, to prove him a knave and   86
myself an honest man; and touching the Duke of York,
I will take my death, I never meant him any ill, nor the
King, nor the Queen; and therefore, Peter, have at thee
with a downright blow!   90

York. Dispatch. This knave's tongue begins to
double.

Sound, trumpets, alarum to the combatants!

*[Alarum.] They fight, and Peter [hits him on
the head and] strikes him down.*

Hor. Hold, Peter, hold! I confess, I confess
treason.   *[He dies.]*   94

York. Take away his weapon. Fellow, thank God,
and the good wine in thy master's way.

Peter. *[He kneels down.]* O God, have I overcome
mine enemies in this presence? O Peter, thou hast
prevail'd in right?

King. Go, take hence that traitor from our sight,
For by his death we do perceive his guilt,   101
And God in justice hath reveal'd to us
The truth and innocence of this poor fellow,
Which he had thought to have murther'd wrongfully.
Come, fellow, follow us for thy reward.   105

Sound a flourish. Exeunt.

[SCENE IV]

Enter DUKE HUMPHREY [OF GLOUCESTER] *and his*
MEN *in mourning cloaks.*

Glou. Thus sometimes hath the brightest day a
     cloud,
And after summer evermore succeeds
Barren winter, with his wrathful nipping cold;
So cares and joys abound, as seasons fleet.
Sirs, what's a' clock?

Servant.   Ten, my lord.   5

Glou. Ten is the hour that was appointed me
To watch the coming of my punish'd duchess.
Uneath may she endure the flinty streets,

28. **of years:** i.e. of legal age.
41. **bears . . . maim:** endures such a grievous mutilation.   **pulls:**
pluckings, loppings-off.   43. **raught:** snatched.
49. **appellant:** challenger.   52. **therefore:** therefor.   54. **A':** in.
56. **bestead:** prepared.   58 s.d. **Drum:** drummer.
60. **sack:** dry Spanish wine.
63. **charneco:** sweet Portuguese wine.
64. **double:** i.e. exceptionally strong.
66. **Let it come:** i.e. let the toast be drunk.
67. **fig:** sign of contempt made by thrusting the thumb between the
fingers.

75. **aporn:** apron.   78. **fence:** skill in fencing.
88. **take my death:** take my oath on pain of death.
91. **double:** speak thick, stammer.
92. **alarum:** call to arms, signal to begin fighting.
104. **Which:** whom.

II.iv. Location: London. A street.   8. **Uneath:** scarcely.

To tread them with her tender-feeling feet.
Sweet Nell, ill can thy noble mind abrook   10
The abject people gazing on thy face,
With envious looks laughing at thy shame,
That erst did follow thy proud chariot-wheels
When thou didst ride in triumph through the streets.
But soft, I think she comes, and I'll prepare   15
My tear-stain'd eyes to see her miseries.

Enter the DUCHESS [*of* GLOUCESTER, *barefoot*], *in a
white sheet,* [*and verses written on her back and pinned
on,*] *and a taper burning in her hand, with* [SIR JOHN
STANLEY,] *the* SHERIFF, *and* OFFICERS.

   Servant.   So please your Grace, we'll take her from
the sheriff.
   Glou.   No, stir not for your lives, let her pass by.
   Duch.   Come you, my lord, to see my open shame?
Now thou dost penance too. Look how they gaze!   20
See how the giddy multitude do point
And nod their heads, and throw their eyes on thee!
Ah, Gloucester, hide thee from their hateful looks,
And in thy closet pent up, rue my shame,
And ban thine enemies, both mine and thine.   25
   Glou.   Be patient, gentle Nell, forget this grief.
   Duch.   Ah, Gloucester, teach me to forget myself;
For whilest I think I am thy married wife,
And thou a prince, Protector of this land,
Methinks I should not thus be led along,   30
Mail'd up in shame, with papers on my back,
And follow'd with a rabble that rejoice
To see my tears and hear my deep-fet groans.
The ruthless flint doth cut my tender feet,
And when I start, the envious people laugh,   35
And bid me be advised how I tread.
Ah, Humphrey, can I bear this shameful yoke?
Trowest thou that e'er I'll look upon the world,
Or count them happy that enjoys the sun?
No; dark shall be my light, and night my day;   40
To think upon my pomp shall be my hell.
Sometime I'll say, I am Duke Humphrey's wife,
And he a prince, and ruler of the land;
Yet so he rul'd, and such a prince he was,
As he stood by, whilest I, his forlorn duchess,   45
Was made a wonder and a pointing-stock
To every idle rascal follower.
But be thou mild, and blush not at my shame,
Nor stir at nothing, till the axe of death
Hang over thee, as sure it shortly will;   50
For Suffolk, he that can do all in all
With her that hateth thee and hates us all,
And York and impious Beauford, that false priest,
Have all lim'd bushes to betray thy wings,
And fly thou how thou canst, they'll tangle thee.   55
But fear not thou, until thy foot be snar'd,
Nor never seek prevention of thy foes.

---

10. **abrook:** endure.
11. **abject:** low, common.   12. **envious:** spiteful.
23. **hateful:** full of hate.   24. **closet:** private apartment.
25. **ban:** curse.   31. **Mail'd:** wrapped.
33. **deep-fet:** deep-fetched.   35. **start:** flinch.
36. **advised:** careful.   38. **Trowest thou:** do you think.
46. **pointing-stock:** butt.
57. **seek prevention:** i.e. try to foil by anticipating.

   Glou.   Ah, Nell, forbear! thou aimest all awry.
I must offend before I be attainted;
And had I twenty times so many foes,   60
And each of them had twenty times their power,
All these could not procure me any scathe
So long as I am loyal, true, and crimeless.
Wouldst have me rescue thee from this reproach?
Why, yet thy scandal were not wip'd away,   65
But I in danger for the breach of law.
Thy greatest help is quiet, gentle Nell.
I pray thee sort thy heart to patience,
These few days' wonder will be quickly worn.

Enter a HERALD.

   Her.   I summon your Grace to his Majesty's
parliament,   70
Holden at Bury the first of this next month.
   Glou.   And my consent ne'er ask'd herein before?
This is close dealing. Well, I will be there.
                                       [*Exit Herald.*]
My Nell, I take my leave; and, Master Sheriff,
Let not her penance exceed the King's commission.   75
   Sher.   And't please your Grace, here my commis-
sion stays;
And Sir John Stanley is appointed now
To take her with him to the Isle of Man.
   Glou.   Must you, Sir John, protect my lady here?
   Stan.   So am I given in charge, may't please your
Grace.   80
   Glou.   Entreat her not the worse in that I pray
You use her well. The world may laugh again,
And I may live to do you kindness if
You do it her. And so, Sir John, farewell!
   Duch.   What, gone, my lord, and bid me not fare-
well?   85
   Glou.   Witness my tears, I cannot stay to speak.
                            Exit Gloucester [*with his Men*].
   Duch.   Art thou gone too? All comfort go with
thee,
For none abides with me. My joy is death;
Death, at whose name I oft have been afeard,
Because I wish'd this world's eternity.   90
Stanley, I prithee go, and take me hence,
I care not whither, for I beg no favor;
Only convey me where thou art commanded.
   Stan.   Why, madam, that is to the Isle of Man,
There to be us'd according to your state.   95
   Duch.   That's bad enough, for I am but reproach;
And shall I then be us'd reproachfully?
   Stan.   Like to a duchess, and Duke Humphrey's
lady,
According to that state you shall be us'd.
   Duch.   Sheriff, farewell, and better than I fare, 100
Although thou hast been conduct of my shame.
   Sher.   It is my office, and, madam, pardon me.

---

59. **attainted:** condemned for treason or felony.   62. **scathe:** harm.
68. **sort:** fit, adapt.   69. **worn:** i.e. forgotten.
71. **Bury:** Bury St. Edmunds, town in the county of Suffolk. The
Parliament at Bury did not actually meet until 1447, six years after
the Duchess of Gloucester's disgrace.   73. **close:** underhand.
81. **Entreat:** treat.
95. **state:** status, rank (but Eleanor quibbles on the sense "condition").   101. **conduct:** guide.

2 Henry VI
II.iv

Duch. Ay, ay, farewell, thy office is discharg'd.
Come, Stanley, shall we go?
　　Stan. Madam, your penance done, throw off this
　　　sheet,　　　　　　　　　　　　　　　105
And go we to attire you for our journey.
　　Duch. My shame will not be shifted with my sheet.
No, it will hang upon my richest robes,
And show itself, attire me how I can.　　　　109
Go, lead the way, I long to see my prison. *Exeunt.*

[ACT III, Scene I]

Sound a sennet. [*Enter two* HERALDS *before. Then*]
enter KING, QUEEN, CARDINAL, SUFFOLK, YORK,
BUCKINGHAM, SALISBURY, *and* WARWICK *to the*
parliament.

　　King. I muse my Lord of Gloucester is not come;
'Tis not his wont to be the hindmost man,
What e'er occasion keeps him from us now.
　　Queen. Can you not see? or will ye not observe
The strangeness of his alter'd countenance?　　　5
With what a majesty he bears himself,
How insolent of late he is become,
How proud, how peremptory, and unlike himself?
We know the time since he was mild and affable,
And if we did but glance a far-off look,　　　10
Immediately he was upon his knee,
That all the court admir'd him for submission;
But meet him now, and, be it in the morn,
When every one will give the time of day,
He knits his brow and shows an angry eye,　　　15
And passeth by with stiff unbowed knee,
Disdaining duty that to us belongs.
Small curs are not regarded when they grin,
But great men tremble when the lion roars,
And Humphrey is no little man in England.　　　20
First note that he is near you in descent,
And should you fall, he is the next will mount.
Me seemeth then it is no policy,
Respecting what a rancorous mind he bears
And his advantage following your decease,　　　25
That he should come about your royal person,
Or be admitted to your Highness' Council.
By flattery hath he won the commons' hearts;
And when he please to make commotion,
'Tis to be fear'd they all will follow him.　　　30
Now 'tis the spring, and weeds are shallow-rooted;
Suffer them now, and they'll o'ergrow the garden,
And choke the herbs for want of husbandry.
The reverent care I bear unto my lord
Made me collect these dangers in the Duke.　　　35
If it be fond, call it a woman's fear;
Which fear, if better reasons can supplant,

I will subscribe, and say I wrong'd the Duke.
My Lord of Suffolk, Buckingham, and York,
Reprove my allegation if you can,　　　　40
Or else conclude my words effectual.
　　Suf. Well hath your Highness seen into this duke;
And, had I first been put to speak my mind,
I think I should have told your Grace's tale.
The Duchess by his subornation,　　　45
Upon my life, began her devilish practices;
Or if he were not privy to those faults,
Yet, by reputing of his high descent,
As next the King he was successive heir,
And such high vaunts of his nobility,　　　50
Did instigate the bedlam brain-sick Duchess
By wicked means to frame our sovereign's fall.
Smooth runs the water where the brook is deep,
And in his simple show he harbors treason.
The fox barks not when he would steal the lamb.　　55
No, no, my sovereign, Gloucester is a man
Unsounded yet and full of deep deceit.
　　Car. Did he not, contrary to form of law,
Devise strange deaths for small offenses done?
　　York. And did he not, in his protectorship,　　60
Levy great sums of money through the realm
For soldiers' pay in France, and never sent it,
By means whereof the towns each day revolted?
　　Buck. Tut, these are petty faults to faults unknown,
Which time will bring to light in smooth Duke
　　Humphrey.　　　　　　　　65
　　King. My lords, at once: the care you have of us
To mow down thorns that would annoy our foot
Is worthy praise; but shall I speak my conscience,
Our kinsman Gloucester is as innocent
From meaning treason to our royal person　　　70
As is the sucking lamb or harmless dove.
The Duke is virtuous, mild, and too well given
To dream on evil or to work my downfall.
　　Queen. Ah, what's more dangerous than this fond
　　affiance!
Seems he a dove? his feathers are but borrow'd,　　75
For he's disposed as the hateful raven.
Is he a lamb? his skin is surely lent him,
For he's inclin'd as is the ravenous wolves.
Who cannot steal a shape that means deceit?
Take heed, my lord, the welfare of us all　　80
Hangs on the cutting short that fraudful man.

Enter SOMERSET.

　　Som. All health unto my gracious sovereign!
　　King. Welcome, Lord Somerset. What news from
　　France?
　　Som. That all your interest in those territories
Is utterly bereft you: all is lost.　　　85

---

107. **shifted:** changed.

III.i. Location: Bury St. Edmunds. The abbey.
1. **muse:** wonder.　9. **since:** when.　12. **That:** so that.
14. **give . . . day:** say good morning.
18. **grin:** show the teeth, snarl.
19. **lion.** Heraldic emblem of the kings of England.
23–24. **Me . . . bears:** i.e. I therefore think it not prudent, considering his rancor.　29. **make commotion:** i.e. lead an insurrection.
35. **collect:** perceive.　36. **fond:** foolish.

38. **subscribe:** concur.　40. **Reprove:** disprove.
41. **effectual:** decisive.　45. **subornation:** instigation.
48. **reputing:** boasting.　51. **bedlam:** crazy.
54. **simple show:** innocent appearance.
57. **Unsounded:** undisclosed.　64. **to:** compared to.
74. **affiance:** confidence.
76. **he's disposed as:** he has the nature of.
79. **that means deceit.** Modifies *Who.*
84–85. **That . . . lost.** Somerset's report, though accurate, is anachronistic, for it concerns events that occurred several years after the
time represented in this scene.

King. Cold news, Lord Somerset; but God's will
    be done!
York. [*Aside.*] Cold news for me; for I had hope
    of France
As firmly as I hope for fertile England.
Thus are my blossoms blasted in the bud,
And caterpillars eat my leaves away;   90
But I will remedy this gear ere long,
Or sell my title for a glorious grave.

       Enter GLOUCESTER.

Glou. All happiness unto my lord the King!
Pardon, my liege, that I have stay'd so long.
Suf. Nay, Gloucester, know that thou art come
    too soon,   95
Unless thou wert more loyal than thou art.
I do arrest thee of high treason here.
Glou. Well, Suffolk, thou shalt not see me blush
Nor change my countenance for this arrest;
A heart unspotted is not easily daunted.   100
The purest spring is not so free from mud
As I am clear from treason to my sovereign.
Who can accuse me? Wherein am I guilty?
York. 'Tis thought, my lord, that you took bribes
    of France,
And being Protector, stay'd the soldiers' pay,   105
By means whereof his Highness hath lost France.
Glou. Is it but thought so? What are they that
    think it?
I never robb'd the soldiers of their pay,
Nor ever had one penny bribe from France.
So help me God, as I have watch'd the night,   110
Ay, night by night, in studying good for England.
That doit that e'er I wrested from the King,
Or any groat I hoarded to my use,
Be brought against me at my trial day!
No; many a pound of mine own proper store,   115
Because I would not tax the needy commons,
Have I dispursed to the garrisons,
And never ask'd for restitution.
Car. It serves you well, my lord, to say so much.
Glou. I say no more than truth, so help me God!
York. In your protectorship you did devise   121
Strange tortures for offenders, never heard of,
That England was defam'd by tyranny.
Glou. Why, 'tis well known that, whiles I was
    Protector,
Pity was all the fault that was in me;   125
For I should melt at an offender's tears,
And lowly words were ransom for their fault.
Unless it were a bloody murtherer,
Or foul felonious thief that fleec'd poor passengers,
I never gave them condign punishment.   130

Murther indeed, that bloody sin, I tortur'd
Above the felon or what trespass else.
Suf. My lord, these faults are easy, quickly
    answer'd;
But mightier crimes are laid unto your charge,
Whereof you cannot easily purge yourself.   135
I do arrest you in his Highness' name,
And here commit you to my Lord Cardinal
To keep, until your further time of trial.
King. My Lord of Gloucester, 'tis my special hope
That you will clear yourself from all suspense.   140
My conscience tells me you are innocent.
Glou. Ah, gracious lord, these days are dangerous:
Virtue is chok'd with foul ambition,
And charity chas'd hence by rancor's hand;
Foul subornation is predominant,   145
And equity exil'd your Highness' land.
I know their complot is to have my life;
And if my death might make this island happy,
And prove the period of their tyranny,
I would expend it with all willingness.   150
But mine is made the prologue to their play;
For thousands more, that yet suspect no peril,
Will not conclude their plotted tragedy.
Beauford's red sparkling eyes blab his heart's malice,
And Suffolk's cloudy brow his stormy hate;   155
Sharp Buckingham unburthens with his tongue
The envious load that lies upon his heart;
And dogged York, that reaches at the moon,
Whose overweening arm I have pluck'd back,
By false accuse doth level at my life.   160
And you, my sovereign lady, with the rest,
Causeless have laid disgraces on my head,
And with your best endeavor have stirr'd up
My liefest liege to be mine enemy.
Ay, all of you have laid your heads together—   165
Myself had notice of your conventicles—
And all to make away my guiltless life.
I shall not want false witness to condemn me,
Nor store of treasons to augment my guilt.
The ancient proverb will be well effected: 170
"A staff is quickly found to beat a dog."
Car. My liege, his railing is intolerable.
If those that care to keep your royal person
From treason's secret knife and traitors' rage
Be thus upbraided, chid, and rated at,   175
And the offender granted scope of speech,
'Twill make them cool in zeal unto your Grace.
Suf. Hath he not twit our sovereign lady here
With ignominious words, though clerkly couch'd,
As if she had suborned some to swear   180
False allegations to o'erthrow his state?
Queen. But I can give the loser leave to chide.

---

91. **gear:** business.
94. **stay'd:** delayed.   105. **stay'd:** kept back.
110. **watch'd the night:** stayed awake all night.
112. **doit:** small coin of little value.
113. **groat:** coin worth fourpence.
115. **proper store:** personal funds.
117. **dispursed:** disbursed, paid out.   123. **That:** so that.
124. **whiles:** whilst.   126. **should:** would.
127. **their:** i.e. offenders'.   129. **passengers:** wayfarers.
130. **condign:** just, i.e. as severe as they deserved.

132. **Above . . . else:** i.e. more than any other crime.
133. **easy:** slight.
140. **suspense:** i.e. uncertainty as to your innocence.
145. **subornation:** instigation to perjury. 146. **exil'd:** exiled from.
149. **prove the period:** mark the end.
160. **accuse:** accusation.   **level:** aim.
164. **liefest liege:** dearest sovereign.
166. **conventicles:** secret meetings. 168. **want:** lack.
178. **twit:** twitted.
179. **clerkly couch'd:** cleverly phrased.

2 Henry VI
III.i

Glou. Far truer spoke than meant. I lose indeed;
Beshrew the winners, for they play'd me false!
And well such losers may have leave to speak.   185
    Buck. He'll wrest the sense and hold us here all day.
Lord Cardinal, he is your prisoner.
    Car. Sirs, take away the Duke, and guard him sure.
    Glou. Ah, thus King Henry throws away his crutch
Before his legs be firm to bear his body.   190
Thus is the shepherd beaten from thy side,
And wolves are gnarling who shall gnaw thee first.
Ah, that my fear were false, ah, that it were!
For, good King Henry, thy decay I fear.
                Exit Gloucester [with the Cardinal's Men].
    King. My lords, what to your wisdoms seemeth best,   195
Do or undo, as if ourself were here.
    Queen. What, will your Highness leave the parliament?
    King. Ay, Margaret; my heart is drown'd with grief,
Whose flood begins to flow within mine eyes;
My body round engirt with misery—   200
For what's more miserable than discontent?
Ah, uncle Humphrey, in thy face I see
The map of honor, truth, and loyalty;
And yet, good Humphrey, is the hour to come
That e'er I prov'd thee false or fear'd thy faith.   205
What low'ring star now envies thy estate,
That these great lords, and Margaret our queen,
Do seek subversion of thy harmless life?
Thou never didst them wrong, nor no man wrong;
And as the butcher takes away the calf,   210
And binds the wretch, and beats it when it strays,
Bearing it to the bloody slaughter-house,
Even so remorseless have they borne him hence;
And as the dam runs lowing up and down,
Looking the way her harmless young one went,   215
And can do nought but wail her darling's loss,
Even so myself bewails good Gloucester's case
With sad unhelpful tears, and with dimm'd eyes
Look after him, and cannot do him good,
So mighty are his vowed enemies.   220
His fortunes I will weep, and 'twixt each groan
Say, "Who's a traitor, Gloucester he is none."
                *Exit [with Buckingham, Salisbury,
                and Warwick].*
    Queen. Free lords, cold snow melts with the sun's hot beams;
Henry my lord is cold in great affairs,
Too full of foolish pity; and Gloucester's show   225
Beguiles him as the mournful crocodile
With sorrow snares relenting passengers;
Or as the snake roll'd in a flow'ring bank,
With shining checker'd slough, doth sting a child
That for the beauty thinks it excellent.   230
Believe me, lords, were none more wise than I—
And yet herein I judge mine own wit good—

This Gloucester should be quickly rid the world,
To rid us from the fear we have of him.
    Car. That he should die is worthy policy,   235
But yet we want a color for his death.
'Tis meet he be condemn'd by course of law.
    Suf. But, in my mind, that were no policy:
The King will labor still to save his life,
The commons haply rise, to save his life;   240
And yet we have but trivial argument,
More than mistrust, that shows him worthy death.
    York. So that, by this, you would not have him die.
    Suf. Ah, York, no man alive so fain as I!
    York. 'Tis York that hath more reason for his death.   245
But, my Lord Cardinal, and you, my Lord of Suffolk,
Say as you think, and speak it from your souls:
Were't not all one, an empty eagle were set
To guard the chicken from a hungry kite,   249
As place Duke Humphrey for the King's Protector?
    Queen. So the poor chicken should be sure of death.
    Suf. Madam, 'tis true; and were't not madness then,
To make the fox surveyor of the fold?
Who being accus'd a crafty murtherer,
His guilt should be but idly posted over,   255
Because his purpose is not executed.
No; let him die, in that he is a fox,
By nature prov'd an enemy to the flock,
Before his chaps be stain'd with crimson blood,
As Humphrey, prov'd by reasons, to my liege.   260
And do not stand on quillets how to slay him;
Be it by gins, by snares, by subtlety,
Sleeping, or waking, 'tis no matter how,
So he be dead; for that is good deceit
Which mates him first that first intends deceit.   265
    Queen. Thrice-noble Suffolk, 'tis resolutely spoke.
    Suf. Not resolute, except so much were done,
For things are often spoke and seldom meant;
But that my heart accordeth with my tongue,
Seeing the deed is meritorious,   270
And to preserve my sovereign from his foe,
Say but the word, and I will be his priest.
    Car. But I would have him dead, my Lord of Suffolk,
Ere you can take due orders for a priest.
Say you consent, and censure well the deed,   275
And I'll provide his executioner,
I tender so the safety of my liege.
    Suf. Here is my hand, the deed is worthy doing.
    Queen. And so say I.
    York. And I; and now we three have spoke it,   280
It skills not greatly who impugns our doom.

---

184. Beshrew: curse.
192. gnarling: snarling. **222. Who's:** whoever is.
223. Free: noble, magnanimous.
226. mournful crocodile. The crocodile was thought to lure its victims with its show of pretended grief. **229. slough:** skin.

236. color: pretext. **239. still:** continually.
240. haply: perhaps. **241. argument:** evidence.
242. mistrust: suspicion. **244. fain:** gladly.
248. empty: i.e. hungry. **249. kite:** scavenger bird, a kind of hawk.
255. idly posted over: foolishly ignored.
260. prov'd: i.e. an enemy. **261. quillets:** subtle disputes.
262. gins: traps. **265. mates:** subdues.
269. that: i.e. to show that.
272. be his priest: i.e. perform the last offices for him.
275. censure well: approve.
277. tender so: am so solicitous about.
281. It . . . doom: i.e. it does not much matter who questions our decision.

Enter a Post.

Post. Great lords, from Ireland am I come amain,
To signify that rebels there are up
And put the Englishmen unto the sword.
Send succors, lords, and stop the rage betime, 285
Before the wound do grow uncurable;
For being green, there is great hope of help. [*Exit.*]
Car. A breach that craves a quick expedient stop!
What counsel give you in this weighty cause?
York. That Somerset be sent as Regent thither:
'Tis meet that lucky ruler be employ'd— 291
Witness the fortune he hath had in France.
Som. If York, with all his far-fet policy,
Had been the Regent there in stead of me,
He never would have stay'd in France so long. 295
York. No, not to lose it all, as thou hast done.
I rather would have lost my life betimes
Than bring a burthen of dishonor home
By staying there so long till all were lost.
Show me one scar character'd on thy skin: 300
Men's flesh preserv'd so whole do seldom win.
Queen. Nay then, this spark will prove a raging fire,
If wind and fuel be brought to feed it with.
No more, good York; sweet Somerset, be still.
Thy fortune, York, hadst thou been Regent there, 305
Might happily have prov'd far worse than his.
York. What, worse than nought? nay, then a shame
take all!
Som. And, in the number, thee that wishest shame!
Car. My Lord of York, try what your fortune is.
Th' uncivil kerns of Ireland are in arms, 310
And temper clay with blood of Englishmen.
To Ireland will you lead a band of men,
Collected choicely, from each county some,
And try your hap against the Irishmen?
York. I will, my lord, so please his Majesty. 315
Suf. Why, our authority is his consent,
And what we do establish he confirms.
Then, noble York, take thou this task in hand.
York. I am content. Provide me soldiers, lords,
Whiles I take order for mine own affairs. 320
Suf. A charge, Lord York, that I will see per-
form'd.
But now return we to the false Duke Humphrey.
Car. No more of him; for I will deal with him
That henceforth he shall trouble us no more.
And so break off, the day is almost spent; 325
Lord Suffolk, you and I must talk of that event.
York. My Lord of Suffolk, within fourteen days
At Bristow I expect my soldiers,
For there I'll ship them all for Ireland.
Suf. I'll see it truly done, my Lord of York. 330
                    Exeunt. Manet York.
York. Now, York, or never, steel thy fearful
thoughts,

And change misdoubt to resolution;
Be that thou hop'st to be, or what thou art
Resign to death; it is not worth th' enjoying.
Let pale-fac'd fear keep with the mean-born man, 335
And find no harbor in a royal heart.
Faster than spring-time show'rs comes thought on
thought,
And not a thought but thinks on dignity.
My brain, more busy than the laboring spider,
Weaves tedious snares to trap mine enemies. 340
Well, nobles, well; 'tis politicly done,
To send me packing with an host of men:
I fear me you but warm the starved snake,
Who, cherish'd in your breasts, will sting your hearts.
'Twas men I lack'd, and you will give them me; 345
I take it kindly. Yet be well assur'd
You put sharp weapons in a madman's hands.
Whiles I in Ireland nourish a mighty band,
I will stir up in England some black storm
Shall blow ten thousand souls to heaven or hell; 350
And this fell tempest shall not cease to rage
Until the golden circuit on my head,
Like to the glorious sun's transparent beams,
Do calm the fury of this mad-bred flaw.
And for a minister of my intent, 355
I have seduc'd a headstrong Kentishman,
John Cade of Ashford,
To make commotion, as full well he can,
Under the title of John Mortimer.
In Ireland have I seen this stubborn Cade 360
Oppose himself against a troop of kerns,
And fought so long, till that his thighs with darts
Were almost like a sharp-quill'd porpentine;
And in the end being rescued, I have seen
Him caper upright like a wild Morisco, 365
Shaking the bloody darts as he his bells.
Full often, like a shag-hair'd crafty kern,
Hath he conversed with the enemy,
And undiscover'd come to me again,
And given me notice of their villainies. 370
This devil here shall be my substitute;
For that John Mortimer, which now is dead,
In face, in gait, in speech, he doth resemble.
By this I shall perceive the commons' mind,
How they affect the house and claim of York. 375
Say he be taken, rack'd, and tortured,
I know no pain they can inflict upon him
Will make him say I mov'd him to those arms.
Say that he thrive, as 'tis great like he will,
Why then from Ireland come I with my strength,
And reap the harvest which that rascal sow'd. 381
For Humphrey being dead, as he shall be,
And Henry put apart, the next for me. *Exit.*

281 s.d. **Post:** messenger.
282. **amain:** at full speed.   285. **betime:** promptly.
287. **green:** fresh.   293. **far-fet:** far-fetched, i.e. deep.
300. **character'd:** inscribed.   306. **happily:** haply, perhaps.
310. **uncivil kerns:** uncivilized light-armed Irish soldiers.
311. **temper:** moisten.   320. **take order for:** arrange.
328. **Bristow:** Bristol, city near the mouth of the Severn estuary, long
a major port.   331. **fearful:** timid.

340. **tedious:** intricate.   343. **starved:** stiff with cold.
350. **Shall:** that shall.   352. **circuit:** circlet, i.e. crown.
354. **mad-bred:** i.e. created by the mad mismanagement of affairs by
Henry.   **flaw:** squall.
359. **John Mortimer.** For Cade's absurd claim to descent from the
powerful house of Mortimer see IV.ii.136–46.
363. **porpentine:** porcupine.
365. **Morisco:** morris, a vigorous dance common in pageants and
May-day games.   366. **he:** i.e. the morris dancer.
372. **For that:** because.   375. **affect:** favor.
379. **great like:** very likely.

2 Henry VI
III.ii

Enter two or three [MURDERERS] *running over the stage, from the murther of Duke Humphrey.*

1. Mur. Run to my Lord of Suffolk; let him know
We have dispatch'd the Duke, as he commanded.

2. Mur. O that it were to do! What have we
done?
Didst ever hear a man so penitent?

Enter SUFFOLK.

1. Mur. Here comes my lord.   5
Suf. Now, sirs, have you dispatch'd this thing?
1. Mur. Ay, my good lord, he's dead.
Suf. Why, that's well said. Go, get you to my
house,
I will reward you for this venturous deed.
The King and all the peers are here at hand.   10
Have you laid fair the bed? Is all things well,
According as I gave directions?
1. Mur. 'Tis, my good lord.
Suf. Away, be gone.   *Exeunt.*

Sound trumpets. Enter the KING, *the* QUEEN, CARDINAL,
SUFFOLK, SOMERSET, *with* ATTENDANTS.

King. Go call our uncle to our presence straight.
Say we intend to try his Grace to-day,   16
If he be guilty, as 'tis published.
Suf. I'll call him presently, my noble lord.   *Exit.*
King. Lords, take your places; and I pray you all
Proceed no straiter 'gainst our uncle Gloucester   20
Than from true evidence of good esteem
He be approv'd in practice culpable.
Queen. God forbid any malice should prevail,
That faultless may condemn a nobleman!
Pray God he may acquit him of suspicion!   25
King. I thank thee, [Meg], these words content
me much.

Enter SUFFOLK.

How now? Why look'st thou pale? Why tremblest
thou?
Where is our uncle? What's the matter, Suffolk?
Suf. Dead in his bed, my lord; Gloucester is dead.
Queen. Marry, God forfend!   30
Car. God's secret judgment. I did dream to-night
The Duke was dumb and could not speak a word.
                                                    King sounds.
Queen. How fares my lord? Help, lords, the King
is dead.
Som. Rear up his body, wring him by the nose.
Queen. Run, go, help, help! O Henry, ope thine
eyes!   35
Suf. He doth revive again. Madam, be patient.
King. O heavenly God!
Queen.   How fares my gracious lord?

Suf. Comfort, my sovereign! gracious Henry,
comfort!
King. What, doth my Lord of Suffolk comfort me?
Came he right now to sing a raven's note,   40
Whose dismal tune bereft my vital pow'rs;
And thinks he that the chirping of a wren,
By crying comfort from a hollow breast,
Can chase away the first-conceived sound?
Hide not thy poison with such sug'red words.   45
Lay not thy hands on me; forbear, I say!
Their touch affrights me as a serpent's sting.
Thou baleful messenger, out of my sight!
Upon thy eyeballs murderous tyranny
Sits in grim majesty, to fright the world.   50
Look not upon me, for thine eyes are wounding.
Yet do not go away. Come, basilisk,
And kill the innocent gazer with thy sight;
For in the shade of death I shall find joy;
In life but double death, now Gloucester's dead.   55
Queen. Why do you rate my Lord of Suffolk thus?
Although the Duke was enemy to him,
Yet he most Christian-like laments his death;
And for myself, foe as he was to me,
Might liquid tears or heart-offending groans   60
Or blood-consuming sighs recall his life,
I would be blind with weeping, sick with groans,
Look pale as primrose with blood-drinking sighs,
And all to have the noble Duke alive.
What know I how the world may deem of me,   65
For it is known we were but hollow friends?
It may be judg'd I made the Duke away,
So shall my name with slander's tongue be wounded,
And princes' courts be fill'd with my reproach.
This get I by his death. Ay me, unhappy,   70
To be a queen, and crown'd with infamy!
King. Ah, woe is me for Gloucester, wretched
man!
Queen. Be woe for me, more wretched than he is.
What, dost thou turn away and hide thy face?
I am no loathsome leper, look on me.   75
What? art thou like the adder waxen deaf?
Be poisonous too, and kill thy forlorn queen.
Is all thy comfort shut in Gloucester's tomb?
Why then Dame [Margaret] was ne'er thy joy.
Erect his statuë and worship it,   80
And make my image but an alehouse sign.
Was I for this nigh wrack'd upon the sea,
And twice by awkward wind from England's bank
Drove back again unto my native clime?
What boded this, but well forewarning wind   85
Did seem to say, "Seek not a scorpion's nest,
Nor set no footing on this unkind shore"?
What did I then, but curs'd the gentle gusts,
And he that loos'd them forth their brazen caves,   89

---

40. **right now:** just now, a moment ago.
52. **basilisk:** fabulous serpent whose glance was alleged to cause death.
56. **rate:** upbraid.
61. **blood-consuming sighs.** It was long believed that each sigh drew a drop of blood from the heart; cf. *blood-drinking sighs* in line 63.
76. **like . . . deaf.** It was another ancient superstition that adders were deaf. See Psalms 58:4–5. **waxen:** grown.
83. **awkward:** contrary. **bank:** shore.
89. **he:** him, i.e. Aeolus, god of the winds. **forth:** out of.

III.ii. Location: Bury St. Edmunds. A room of state.
3. **to do:** still to be done, i.e. undone.
17. **published:** publicly proclaimed.
18. **presently:** immediately. 20. **straiter:** more rigorously.
21. **of good esteem:** i.e. creditable.
22. **approv'd in:** proved guilty of. 30. **forfend:** forbid.
31. **to-night:** last night. 32 s.d. **sounds:** swoons.

And bid them blow towards England's blessed shore,
Or turn our stern upon a dreadful rock?
Yet Aeolus would not be a murtherer,
But left that hateful office unto thee.
The pretty vaulting sea refus'd to drown me,   94
Knowing that thou wouldst have me drown'd on shore
With tears as salt as sea, through thy unkindness.
The splitting rocks cow'r'd in the sinking sands,
And would not dash me with their ragged sides,
Because thy flinty heart, more hard than they,
Might in thy palace perish [Margaret].   100
As far as I could ken thy chalky cliffs,
When from thy shore the tempest beat us back,
I stood upon the hatches in the storm;
And when the dusky sky began to rob
My earnest-gaping sight of thy land's view,   105
I took a costly jewel from my neck,
A heart it was, bound in with diamonds,
And threw it towards thy land. The sea receiv'd it,
And so I wish'd thy body might my heart.
And even with this I lost fair England's view,   110
And bid mine eyes be packing with my heart,
And call'd them blind and dusky spectacles,
For losing ken of Albion's wished coast.
How often have I tempted Suffolk's tongue
(The agent of thy foul inconstancy)   115
To sit and [witch] me, as Ascanius did
When he to madding Dido would unfold
His father's acts commenc'd in burning Troy!
Am I not witch'd like her? or thou not false like him?
Ay me, I can no more! Die, [Margaret!]   120
For Henry weeps that thou dost live so long.

Noise within. Enter WARWICK, [SALISBURY,] *and many*
COMMONS.

    War. It is reported, mighty sovereign,
That good Duke Humphrey traitorously is murd'red
By Suffolk and the Cardinal Beauford's means.
The commons, like an angry hive of bees   125
That want their leader, scatter up and down,
And care not who they sting in his revenge.
Myself have calm'd their spleenful mutiny,
Until they hear the order of his death.
    King. That he is dead, good Warwick, 'tis too
        true,   130
But how he died God knows, not Henry.
Enter his chamber, view his breathless corpse,
And comment then upon his sudden death.
    War. That shall I do, my liege. Stay, Salisbury,
With the rude multitude till I return.   135

[*Exit Warwick; then Salisbury with the Commons.*]
    King. O Thou that judgest all things, stay my
        thoughts,
My thoughts that labor to persuade my soul
Some violent hands were laid on Humphrey's life!
If my suspect be false, forgive me, God,
For judgment only doth belong to thee.   140
Fain would I go to chafe his paly lips
With twenty thousand kisses, and to drain
Upon his face an ocean of salt tears,
To tell my love unto his dumb deaf trunk,
And with my fingers feel his hand unfeeling.   145
But all in vain are these mean obsequies,

Bed put forth [*with the body of Gloucester in it. Enter*
WARWICK.]

And to survey his dead and earthy image,
What were it but to make my sorrow greater?
    War. Come hither, gracious sovereign, view this
        body.
    King. That is to see how deep my grave is made,
For with his soul fled all my worldly solace;   151
For seeing him, I see my life in death.
    War. As surely as my soul intends to live
With that dread King that took our state upon him,
To free us from his Father's wrathful curse,   155
I do believe that violent hands were laid
Upon the life of this thrice-famed duke.
    Suf. A dreadful oath, sworn with a solemn tongue!
What instance gives Lord Warwick for his vow?
    War. See how the blood is settled in his face.   160
Oft have I seen a timely-parted ghost,
Of ashy semblance, meagre, pale, and bloodless,
Being all descended to the laboring heart,
Who, in the conflict that it holds with death,
Attracts the same for aidance 'gainst the enemy,   165
Which with the heart there cools and ne'er returneth
To blush and beautify the cheek again.
But see, his face is black and full of blood,
His eyeballs further out than when he lived,
Staring full ghastly, like a strangled man;   170
His hair uprear'd, his nostrils stretch'd with strug-
        gling;
His hands abroad display'd, as one that grasp'd
And tugg'd for life, and was by strength subdu'd.
Look, on the sheets his hair, you see, is sticking,   174
His well-proportion'd beard made rough and rugged,
Like to the summer's corn by tempest lodged.
It cannot be but he was murd'red here,

---

94. **vaulting:** bounding.   100. **perish:** destroy.
101. **ken:** discern.   111. **be packing:** take flight.
112. **spectacles:** instruments of vision, i.e. eyes.
113. **Albion's:** England's.
115. **agent.** Suffolk had been Henry's "procurator" in arranging
Margaret's marriage.
116. **witch:** bewitch.   **Ascanius:** son of Aeneas, whose wooing of
Dido, Queen of Carthage, is related in Virgil's *Aeneid*, i.657–60. In
Virgil, however, it is Cupid in the form of Ascanius who stirs the
amorous queen.
117. **madding:** becoming frantic (with love).   126. **want:** lack.
127. **his revenge:** revenge for him.
128. **spleenful mutiny:** angry insurrection.   129. **order:** manner.
133. **comment . . . upon:** explain.

139. **suspect:** suspicion.
141. **paly:** pale.   146. **obsequies:** duties for the dead.
154. **King:** i.e. Christ.   **state:** condition (of humanity).
159. **instance:** proof.
161. **timely-parted ghost:** i.e. the corpse of one who has died a natural
death.   163. **Being all descended:** i.e. all the blood having descended.
165. **the same:** i.e. the blood.   **aidance:** aid.
170. **strangled man.** Hall (Bullough, III, 107) is less certain of the
cause of Gloucester's death: "The duke the night after his emprisone-
ment, was found dedde in his bed, and his body shewed to the lordes
and commons, as though he had died of a palsey or empostome: but
all indifferent persons well knewe, that he died of no natural death
but of some violent force: some judged hym to be strangled: some
affirme, that a hote spitte was put in at his foundement: other write,
that he was stiffeled or smoldered betwene twoo fetherbeddes."
172. **abroad display'd:** i.e. spread out.   176. **lodged:** beaten down.

2 Henry VI
III.ii

The least of all these signs were probable.

Suf. Why, Warwick, who should do the Duke to
death?
Myself and Beauford had him in protection,   180
And we, I hope, sir, are no murtherers.

War. But both of you were vowed Duke Hum-
phrey's foes,
And you [*to Cardinal*], forsooth, had the good Duke
to keep.
'Tis like you would not feast him like a friend,
And 'tis well seen he found an enemy.   185

Queen. Then you belike suspect these noblemen
As guilty of Duke Humphrey's timeless death.

War. Who finds the heifer dead and bleeding fresh,
And sees fast by a butcher with an axe,
But will suspect 'twas he that made the slaughter?
Who finds the partridge in the puttock's nest   191
But may imagine how the bird was dead,
Although the kite soar with unbloodied beak?
Even so suspicious is this tragedy.

Queen. Are you the butcher, Suffolk? where's
your knife?   195
Is Beauford term'd a kite? where are his talons?

Suf. I wear no knife to slaughter sleeping men,
But here's a vengeful sword, rusted with ease,
That shall be scoured in his rancorous heart
That slanders me with murther's crimson badge.   200
Say, if thou dar'st, proud Lord of Warwickshire,
That I am faulty in Duke Humphrey's death.

[*Exeunt Cardinal, Somerset, and others.*]

War. What dares not Warwick, if false Suffolk
dare him?

Queen. He dares not calm his contumelious spirit,
Nor cease to be an arrogant controller,   205
Though Suffolk dare him twenty thousand times.

War. Madam, be still—with reverence may I say—
For every word you speak in his behalf
Is slander to your royal dignity.

Suf. Blunt-witted lord, ignoble in demeanor!   210
If ever lady wrong'd her lord so much,
Thy mother took into her blameful bed
Some stern untutor'd churl; and noble stock
Was graft with crab-tree slip, whose fruit thou art
And never of the Nevils' noble race.   215

War. But that the guilt of murther bucklers thee,
And I should rob the deathsman of his fee,
Quitting thee thereby of ten thousand shames,
And that my sovereign's presence makes me mild,
I would, false murd'rous coward, on thy knee   220
Make thee beg pardon for thy passed speech,
And say it was thy mother that thou meant'st,
That thou thyself wast born in bastardy;
And after all this fearful homage done,
Give thee thy hire and send thy soul to hell,   225
Pernicious blood-sucker of sleeping men!

Suf. Thou shalt be waking while I shed thy blood,

If from this presence thou dar'st go with me.

War. Away even now, or I will drag thee hence.
Unworthy though thou art, I'll cope with thee,   230
And do some service to Duke Humphrey's ghost.

Exeunt [*Suffolk and Warwick*].

King. What stronger breastplate than a heart un-
tainted!
Thrice is he arm'd that hath his quarrel just;
And he but naked, though lock'd up in steel,
Whose conscience with injustice is corrupted.   235

A noise within.

Queen. What noise is this?

Enter Suffolk *and* Warwick *with their weapons drawn.*

King. Why, how now, lords? your wrathful
weapons drawn
Here in our presence? Dare you be so bold?
Why, what tumultuous clamor have we here?

Suf. The trait'rous Warwick, with the men of
Bury,   240
Set all upon me, mighty sovereign.

Enter Salisbury.

Sal. [*To the Commons within.*] Sirs, stand apart,
the King shall know your mind.—
Dread lord, the commons send you word by me,
Unless Lord Suffolk straight be done to death,
Or banished fair England's territories,   245
They will by violence tear him from your palace,
And torture him with grievous ling'ring death.
They say, by him the good Duke Humphrey died;
They say, in him they fear your Highness' death;
And mere instinct of love and loyalty,   250
Free from a stubborn opposite intent,
As being thought to contradict your liking,
Makes them thus forward in his banishment.
They say, in care of your most royal person,
That if your Highness should intend to sleep,   255
And charge that no man should disturb your rest
In pain of your dislike, or pain of death,
Yet notwithstanding such a strait edict,
Were there a serpent seen, with forked tongue,
That slily glided towards your Majesty,   260
It were but necessary you were wak'd,
Lest being suffer'd in that harmful slumber,
The mortal worm might make the sleep eternal.
And therefore do they cry, though you forbid,
That they will guard you, whe'er you will or no,   265
From such fell serpents as false Suffolk is;
With whose envenomed and fatal sting,
Your loving uncle, twenty times his worth,
They say is shamefully bereft of life.

Commons. (*Within.*) An answer from the King,
my Lord of Salisbury!   270

Suf. 'Tis like the commons, rude unpolish'd hinds,

---

178. **probable:** sufficient proof.   187. **timeless:** untimely.
191. **puttock's:** kite's.   202. **faulty:** guilty.
205. **controller:** censorious critic.   213. **stern:** rough.
214. **slip:** cutting.   216. **bucklers:** shields.
217. **deathsman:** executioner.   218. **Quitting:** ridding.
221. **passed:** uttered.   224. **fearful homage:** craven submission.
225. **hire:** reward.

230. **cope with:** encounter, i.e. fight.   250. **mere:** pure.
251. **Free . . . intent:** i.e. not prompted by mere antagonism.
258. **strait:** strict.
262. **being suffer'd:** if you were allowed to continue.
263. **mortal worm:** deadly serpent.   265. **whe'er:** whether.
266. **fell:** cruel.   268. **his:** i.e. Suffolk's.
271. **like:** probable (ironic).

Could send such message to their sovereign.
But you, my lord, were glad to be employ'd,
To show how quaint an orator you are;
But all the honor Salisbury hath won   275
Is, that he was the lord embassador
Sent from a sort of tinkers to the King.

    [Commons.] (Within.) An answer from the King,
        or we will all break in!

    King. Go, Salisbury, and tell them all from me,
I thank them for their tender loving care;   280
And had I not been cited so by them,
Yet did I purpose as they do entreat;
For sure, my thoughts do hourly prophesy
Mischance unto my state by Suffolk's means.
And therefore by His majesty I swear,   285
Whose far-unworthy deputy I am,
He shall not breathe infection in this air
But three days longer, on the pain of death.

                                    [Exit Salisbury.]

    Queen. O Henry, let me plead for gentle Suffolk!
    King. Ungentle queen, to call him gentle Suffolk!
No more, I say! If thou dost plead for him,   291
Thou wilt but add increase unto my wrath.
Had I but said, I would have kept my word;
But when I swear, it is irrevocable.
If after three days' space thou here be'st found 295
On any ground that I am ruler of,
The world shall not be ransom for thy life.
Come, Warwick, come, good Warwick, go with me,
I have great matters to impart to thee.

                            Exit [with Warwick].

    Queen. Mischance and sorrow go along with you!
Heart's discontent and sour affliction   301
Be playfellows to keep you company!
There's two of you, the devil make a third,
And threefold vengeance tend upon your steps!

    Suf. Cease, gentle queen, these execrations, 305
And let thy Suffolk take his heavy leave.
    Queen. Fie, coward woman and soft-hearted
        wretch!
Hast thou not spirit to curse thine enemy?
    Suf. A plague upon them! wherefore should I curse
        them?
Would curses kill, as doth the mandrake's groan, 310
I would invent as bitter searching terms,

As curst, as harsh, and horrible to hear,
Deliver'd strongly through my fixed teeth,
With full as many signs of deadly hate,
As lean-fac'd Envy in her loathsome cave.   315
My tongue should stumble in mine earnest words,
Mine eyes should sparkle like the beaten flint,
Mine hair be fix'd an end, as one distract;
Ay, every joint should seem to curse and ban;
And even now my burthen'd heart would break,   320
Should I not curse them. Poison be their drink!
Gall, worse than gall, the daintiest that they taste!
Their sweetest shade a grove of cypress trees!
Their chiefest prospect murd'ring basilisks!
Their softest touch as smart as lizards' stings! 325
Their music frightful as the serpent's hiss,
And boding screech-owls make the consort full!
All the foul terrors in dark-seated hell—
    Queen. Enough, sweet Suffolk, thou torment'st
        thyself,
And these dread curses, like the sun 'gainst glass, 330
Or like an overcharged gun, recoil,
And turns the force of them upon thyself.
    Suf. You bade me ban, and will you bid me leave?
Now by the ground that I am banish'd from,
Well could I curse away a winter's night,   335
Though standing naked on a mountain top,
Where biting cold would never let grass grow,
And think it but a minute spent in sport.
    Queen. O, let me entreat thee cease. Give me thy
        hand,
That I may dew it with my mournful tears;   340
Nor let the rain of heaven wet this place
To wash away my woeful monuments.
O, could this kiss be printed in thy hand,
That thou mightst think upon these by the seal,
Through whom a thousand sighs are breath'd for thee!
So get thee gone, that I may know my grief,   346
'Tis but surmis'd whiles thou art standing by,
As one that surfeits thinking on a want.
I will repeal thee, or, be well assur'd,
Adventure to be banished myself;   350
And banished I am, if but from thee.
Go, speak not to me; even now be gone.
O, go not yet! Even thus two friends condemn'd
Embrace, and kiss, and take ten thousand leaves,
Loather a hundred times to part than die.   355
Yet now farewell, and farewell life with thee!
    Suf. Thus is poor Suffolk ten times banished,
Once by the King, and three times thrice by thee.
'Tis not the land I care for, wert thou thence;
A wilderness is populous enough,   360
So Suffolk had thy heavenly company:
For where thou art, there is the world itself,
With every several pleasure in the world;

274. quaint: skillful.   277. sort: gang.
279–97. Go . . . life. In treating Suffolk's banishment Shakespeare
characteristically suppresses some of the details in Hall's account
(Bullough, III, 112): "When kyng Henry perceived, that the commons
wer thus stomacked and bent against the Quenes dearlynge William
Duke of Suffolke, he playnly sawe that neither glosyng wolde serve,
nor dissimulacion coulde appeace the continual clamor of the importunate commons: Wherfore to begyn a shorte pacificacion in so
long a broyle: Firste he sequestred the lord Say, beyng threasorer of
Englande, and other the Dukes adherentes, from theire offices, and
authoritie, and after banished and put in exile the duke of Suffolke, as
the abhorred tode, and common noysaunce of the Realme of Englande,
for the terme of .v. yeres: meanyng by this exile, to appease the
furious rage of the outragious people, and that pacified, to revocate
him into his olde estate, as the Quenes chefe frende & counsailer."
281. cited: incited, urged.   284. Mischance: disaster.
285. His: i.e. God's.   287. breathe infection in: infect.
289. gentle: noble.   293. but said: i.e. without oath.
306. heavy: mournful.
310. mandrake's groan. It was thought that the mandrake, an herb
with a forked root supposed to resemble a man, uttered a shriek when
uprooted which killed the hearer or drove him mad.

312. curst: malignant.   313. fixed: clenched.
318. an: on.   distract: mad.   319. ban: curse.
323. cypress: tree associated with graveyards and therefore regarded
as dismal.   324. prospect: view.   325. smart: sharp.
327. consort: group of musicians.   333. leave: cease.
342. woeful monuments: signs of grief, i.e. tearstains.
344. these: i.e. lips.   seal: imprint.
348. surfeits: gluts oneself.   want: famine.
349. repeal thee: obtain your recall.   350. Adventure: venture.
363. several: separate.

2 Henry VI
III.ii

And where thou art not, desolation.
I can no more: live thou to joy thy life;   365
Myself no joy in nought but that thou liv'st.

Enter VAUX.

Queen. Whither goes Vaux so fast? What news,
I prithee?
Vaux. To signify unto his Majesty
That Cardinal Beauford is at point of death;
For suddenly a grievous sickness took him,   370
That makes him gasp, and stare, and catch the air,
Blaspheming God and cursing men on earth.
Sometime he talks as if Duke Humphrey's ghost
Were by his side; sometime he calls the King,
And whispers to his pillow as to him   375
The secrets of his overcharged soul;
And I am sent to tell his Majesty
That even now he cries aloud for him.
Queen. Go tell this heavy message to the King.
                                        Exit [*Vaux*].
Ay me! what is this world! what news are these!   380
But wherefore grieve I at an hour's poor loss,
Omitting Suffolk's exile, my soul's treasure?
Why only, Suffolk, mourn I not for thee,
And with the southern clouds contend in tears,
Theirs for the earth's increase, mine for my sorrows?
Now get thee hence, the King, thou know'st, is
              coming.   386
If thou be found by me, thou art but dead.
Suf. If I depart from thee, I cannot live,
And in thy sight to die, what were it else
But like a pleasant slumber in thy lap?   390
Here could I breathe my soul into the air,
As mild and gentle as the cradle-babe
Dying with mother's dug between its lips;
Where, from thy sight, I should be raging mad,
And cry out for thee to close up mine eyes,   395
To have thee with thy lips to stop my mouth;
So shouldst thou either turn my flying soul,
Or I should breathe it so into thy body,
And then it liv'd in sweet Elysium.
To die by thee were but to die in jest,   400
From thee to die were torture more than death.
O, let me stay, befall what may befall!
Queen. Away! though parting be a fretful corrosive,
It is applied to a deathful wound.
To France, sweet Suffolk! Let me hear from thee;
For wheresoe'er thou art in this world's globe,   406
I'll have an Iris that shall find thee out.
Suf. I go.
Queen.   And take my heart with thee.
                                    [*She kisseth him.*]
Suf. A jewel, lock'd into the woefull'st cask
That ever did contain a thing of worth.   410
Even as a splitted bark, so sunder we;

This way fall I to death.
Queen.   This way for me. *Exeunt* [*severally*].

[SCENE III]

Enter the KING, SALISBURY, *and* WARWICK *to the*
CARDINAL *in bed,* [*raving and staring as if he were
mad*].

King. How fares my lord? Speak, Beauford, to thy
sovereign.
Car. If thou beest death, I'll give thee England's
treasure,
Enough to purchase such another island,
So thou wilt let me live, and feel no pain.
King. Ah, what a sign it is of evil life,   5
Where death's approach is seen so terrible!
War. Beauford, it is thy sovereign speaks to thee.
Car. Bring me unto my trial when you will.
Died he not in his bed? Where should he die?
Can I make men live, whe'er they will or no?   10
O, torture me no more, I will confess.
Alive again? Then show me where he is,
I'll give a thousand pound to look upon him.
He hath no eyes, the dust hath blinded them.
Comb down his hair; look, look, it stands upright,   15
Like lime-twigs set to catch my winged soul.
Give me some drink, and bid the apothecary
Bring the strong poison that I bought of him.
King. O thou eternal Mover of the heavens,
Look with a gentle eye upon this wretch!   20
O, beat away the busy meddling fiend
That lays strong siege unto this wretch's soul,
And from his bosom purge this black despair!
War. See how the pangs of death do make him grin!
Sal. Disturb him not, let him pass peaceably.   25
King. Peace to his soul, if God's good pleasure be!
Lord Card'nal, if thou think'st on heaven's bliss,
Hold up thy hand, make signal of thy hope.
                              [*The Cardinal dies.*]
He dies, and makes no sign. O God, forgive him!
War. So bad a death argues a monstrous life.   30
King. Forbear to judge, for we are sinners all.
Close up his eyes, and draw the curtain close,
And let us all to meditation.   *Exeunt.*

[ACT IV, SCENE I]

Alarum [*within*]. *Ord'nance goes off* [*like as it were a*]
fight at sea. Enter LIEUTENANT, [*a* SHIPMASTER *and
his* MATE, WALTER WHITMORE,] *and others;* [*with
them*] SUFFOLK, [*disguised, and other* GENTLEMEN,
prisoners].

Lieu. The gaudy, blabbing, and remorseful day

III.iii. Location: London. The Cardinal's bedchamber.
2. treasure: i.e. the wealth that Beaufort had accumulated through his
avarice and rapacity.   4. So: if.   9. he: i.e. Gloucester.
16. lime-twigs: twigs smeared with birdlime.

IV.i. Location: The coast of Kent.
o.s.d. Ord'nance: ordnance (a sense only later differentiated ortho-
graphically from *ordinance*).
1. blabbing: i.e. revealing secrets of the dark.

369. point of death. Actually, Beaufort died (April 1447) some six
weeks after Gloucester's murder and three years before Suffolk's
banishment.
381. at...loss: i.e. at Beaufort's death, since he was old and already near his end.   382. Omitting: ignoring.
403. fretful corrosive: painful remedy.
404. applied: suitable.   deathful: deadly.
407. Iris: Juno's messenger.   409. cask: casket.

Is crept into the bosom of the sea;
And now loud-howling wolves arouse the jades
That drag the tragic melancholy night;
Who with their drowsy, slow, and flagging wings   5
Cleep dead men's graves, and from their misty jaws
Breathe foul contagious darkness in the air.
Therefore bring forth the soldiers of our prize,
For whilst our pinnace anchors in the Downs,
Here shall they make their ransom on the sand,   10
Or with their blood stain this discolored shore.
Master, this prisoner freely give I thee,
And thou that art his mate, make boot of this;
The other, Walter Whitmore, is thy share.

   1. Gent. What is my ransom, master? Let me
know.   15

   Mast. A thousand crowns, or else lay down your
head.

   Mate. And so much shall you give, or off goes
yours.

   Lieu. What, think you much to pay two thousand
crowns,
And bear the name and port of gentlemen?
Cut both the villains' throats; for die you shall.   20
The lives of those which we have lost in fight
Be counterpois'd with such a petty sum!

   1. Gent. I'll give it, sir, and therefore spare my life.

   2. Gent. And so will I, and write home for it
straight.

   Whit. I lost mine eye in laying the prize aboard,
And therefore to revenge it shalt thou die,   26
                           [*To Suffolk.*]
And so should these, if I might have my will.

   Lieu. Be not so rash, take ransom, let him live.

   Suf. Look on my George, I am a gentleman:
Rate me at what thou wilt, thou shalt be paid.   30

   Whit. And so am I; my name is Walter Whitmore.
How now? why starts thou? What, doth death affright?

   Suf. Thy name affrights me, in whose sound is
death.
A cunning man did calculate my birth
And told me that by water I should die: 35
Yet let not this make thee be bloody-minded;
Thy name is Gaultier, being rightly sounded.

   Whit. Gaultier or Walter, which it is, I care not.
Never yet did base dishonor blur our name
But with our sword we wip'd away the blot;   40
Therefore, when merchant-like I sell revenge,
Broke be my sword, my arms torn and defac'd,
And I proclaim'd a coward through the world!

   Suf. Stay, Whitmore, for thy prisoner is a prince,

The Duke of Suffolk, William de la Pole.   45

   Whit. The Duke of Suffolk muffled up in rags?

   Suf. Ay, but these rags are no part of the duke;
[Jove sometime went disguis'd, and why not I?]

   Lieu. But Jove was never slain, as thou shalt be.

   [*Suf.*] Obscure and lousy swain, King Henry's
blood,   50
The honorable blood of Lancaster,
Must not be shed by such a jaded groom.
Hast thou not kiss'd thy hand and held my stirrup?
Bare-headed plodded by my foot-cloth mule
And thought thee happy when I shook my head?   55
How often hast thou waited at my cup,
Fed from my trencher, kneel'd down at the board,
When I have feasted with Queen Margaret?
Remember it, and let it make thee crestfall'n,
Ay, and allay this thy abortive pride: 60
How in our voiding lobby hast thou stood
And duly waited for my coming forth?
This hand of mine hath writ in thy behalf,
And therefore shall it charm thy riotous tongue.

   Whit. Speak, captain, shall I stab the forlorn
swain?   65

   Lieu. First let my words stab him, as he hath me.

   Suf. Base slave, thy words are blunt and so art
thou.

   Lieu. Convey him hence, and on our longboat's side
Strike off his head.

   Suf. Thou dar'st not, for thy own.

   [*Lieu.* Yes, Poole.

   Suf. Poole?]

   Lieu. Poole! Sir Poole! lord!
Ay, kennel, puddle, sink, whose filth and dirt   71
Troubles the silver spring where England drinks.
Now will I dam up this thy yawning mouth
For swallowing the treasure of the realm.
Thy lips that kiss'd the Queen shall sweep the ground,
And thou that smil'dst at good Duke Humphrey's
death   76
Against the senseless winds shall grin in vain,
Who in contempt shall hiss at thee again;
And wedded be thou to the hags of hell,
For daring to affy a mighty lord   80
Unto the daughter of a worthless king,
Having neither subject, wealth, nor diadem.
By devilish policy art thou grown great,
And like ambitious Sylla, overgorg'd
With gobbets of thy [mother's] bleeding heart.   85
By thee Anjou and Maine were sold to France.
The false revolting Normans thorough thee

---

3. **jades:** i.e. the dragons that draw the chariot of the night.
6. **Cleep:** clip, embrace.
8. **soldiers . . . prize:** i.e. those whom we have captured.
9. **pinnace:** small sailing vessel. **Downs:** roadstead off the Kentish coast.
11. **discolored shore:** i.e. shore that will be discolored with their blood.
13. **make . . . this:** i.e. take your profit from the ransom of this prisoner. 19. **port:** demeanor.
25. **laying . . . aboard:** boarding the captured vessel.
29. **George:** badge of the Order of the Garter. 30. **Rate:** assess.
33. **name.** *Walter* was pronounced *Water*.
34. **A cunning . . . birth:** an astrologer cast my horoscope.
35. **by . . . die.** See I.iv.33. 37. **Gaultier:** French form of *Walter*.
41. **sell revenge:** i.e. for ransom. 42. **arms:** coat of arms.

50. **lousy swain:** louse-infested rustic. **King Henry's blood.** A dubious claim, since Suffolk's connection with the house of Lancaster was at best exceedingly remote. 52. **jaded:** ignoble.
54. **foot-cloth:** ornamental trappings for the mounts of dignitaries, especially in ceremonial processions.
55. **shook:** nodded (in recognition). 57. **trencher:** platter.
60. **abortive:** monstrous. 61. **voiding lobby:** antechamber.
63. **writ . . . behalf:** i.e. letters of recommendation.
65. **forlorn:** lost.
71. **kennel:** gutter. **sink:** cesspool. 74. **For:** to prevent.
77. **senseless:** insensible. 80. **affy:** betroth. 83. **policy:** cunning.
84. **Sylla:** Lucius Cornelius Sulla (138–75 B.C.), Roman dictator notorious for his cruelty to his adversaries.
84–85. **overgorg'd . . . heart:** i.e. stuffed with pieces of raw flesh from the bleeding heart of your mother, England.
87. **revolting:** disloyal. **thorough:** through.

2 Henry VI
IV.i

Disdain to call us lord, and Picardy
Hath slain their governors, surpris'd our forts,
And sent the ragged soldiers wounded home.   90
The princely Warwick, and the Nevils all,
Whose dreadful swords were never drawn in vain,
As hating thee, [are] rising up in arms;
And now the house of York, thrust from the crown
By shameful murther of a guiltless king   95
And lofty, proud, encroaching tyranny,
Burns with revenging fire, whose hopeful colors
Advance our half-fac'd sun, striving to shine,
Under the which is writ, "Invitis nubibus."
The commons here in Kent are up in arms,   100
And to conclude, reproach and beggary
Is crept into the palace of our king,
And all by thee. Away, convey him hence.
    Suf. O that I were a god, to shoot forth thunder
Upon these paltry, servile, abject drudges!   105
Small things make base men proud. This villain here,
Being captain of a pinnace, threatens more
Than Bargulus the strong Illyrian pirate.
Drones suck not eagles' blood, but rob beehives.
It is impossible that I should die   110
By such a lowly vassal as thyself.
Thy words move rage and not remorse in me.
    [Lieu. Ay, but my deeds shall stay thy fury soon.]
    [Suf.] I go of message from the Queen to France;
I charge thee waft me safely cross the Channel.   115
    [Whit.] Come, Suffolk, I must waft thee to thy
        death.
    Suf. [Pene] gelidus timor occupat artus: it is thee I
        fear.
    Whit. Thou shalt have cause to fear before I leave
        thee.
What, are ye daunted now? Now will ye stoop?
    1. Gent. My gracious lord, entreat him, speak him
        fair.   120
    Suf. Suffolk's imperial tongue is stern and rough,
Us'd to command, untaught to plead for favor.
Far be it we should honor such as these
With humble suit. No, rather let my head
Stoop to the block than these knees bow to any   125
Save to the God of heaven and to my king;
And sooner dance upon a bloody pole
Than stand uncover'd to the vulgar groom.
True nobility is exempt from fear:
More can I bear than you dare execute.   130
    Lieu. Hale him away, and let him talk no more.
    [Suf.] Come, soldiers, show what cruelty ye can,
That this my death may never be forgot!
Great men oft die by vild besonians:
A Roman sworder and bandetto slave   135

Murder'd sweet Tully; Brutus' bastard hand
Stabb'd Julius Caesar; savage islanders
Pompey the Great; and Suffolk dies by pirates.
            Exit Walter [Whitmore] with Suffolk.
    Lieu. And as for these whose ransom we have set,
It is our pleasure one of them depart;   140
Therefore come you with us and let him go.
            Exeunt Lieutenant and the rest.
            Manet the First Gentleman.

Enter WALTER [WHITMORE] with the body [of Suffolk].

    Whit. There let his head and liveless body lie,
Until the Queen his mistress bury it.   Exit Walter.
    1. Gent. O barbarous and bloody spectacle!
His body will I bear unto the King.   145
If he revenge it not, yet will his friends;
So will the Queen, that living held him dear.
                        [Exit with the body.]

[SCENE II]

Enter [GEORGE] BEVIS and JOHN HOLLAND [with long
    staves].

    Bevis. Come and get thee a sword, though made of
a lath; they have been up these two days.
    Holl. They have the more need to sleep now, then.
    Bevis. I tell thee, Jack Cade the clothier means to
dress the commonwealth, and turn it, and set a new
nap upon it.   6
    Holl. So he had need, for 'tis threadbare. Well, I
say, it was never merry world in England since gentlemen came up.
    Bevis. O miserable age! virtue is not regarded in
handicrafts-men.   11
    Holl. The nobility think scorn to go in leather
aprons.
    Bevis. Nay more, the King's Council are no good
workmen.   15
    Holl. True; and yet it is said, labor in thy vocation;
which is as much to say as, let the magistrates be
laboring men; and therefore should we be magistrates.
    Bevis. Thou hast hit it; for there's no better sign
of a brave mind than a hard hand.   20
    Holl. I see them, I see them! There's Best's son,
the tanner of Wingham—

95. **guiltless king:** i.e. Richard II, to whose deposition and murder
Shakespeare and the Tudor chroniclers traced the political upheavals
of the fifteenth century.
98. **Advance:** display.   **half-fac'd sun.** The sun breaking through
the clouds had been the personal badge of Edward III.
99. **Invitis nubibus:** in spite of clouds.
108. **Bargulus:** a pirate (Bardulis) alluded to by Cicero (De Officiis,
II.xi).   109. **Drones:** beetles.   114. **of message:** as a messenger.
115. **waft:** convey.
117. **Pene . . . artus:** cold fear almost overpowers my joints.
131. **Hale:** haul.
134. **vild:** vile.   **besonians:** scoundrels (from Italian bisogno).
135. **sworder:** gladiator.   **bandetto:** bandit.

136. **Tully.** Marcus Tullius Cicero (106–43 B.C.) was actually hunted
down and executed by Mark Antony's soldiers.   **Brutus' bastard
hand.** Marcus Junius Brutus (78?–42 B.C.), one of the leaders in the
conspiracy against Julius Caesar, was erroneously thought to be the
illegitimate son of his victim.
138. **Pompey the Great.** Gnaeus Pompeius (106–48 B.C.) was actually
killed by King Ptolemy's soldiers in Egypt, where he had fled following his defeat at the battle of Pharsalia in Thessaly.
142. **liveless:** lifeless.

IV.ii. Location: Blackheath.
o.s.d. **George Bevis, John Holland.** Holland was an actor whose name
is recorded elsewhere in dramatic documents of the period, and Bevis
was no doubt one of his colleagues. Their names here probably derive
from a prompter's note.
2. **lath:** a strip of wood, commonly used as a sword by the Vice in
the morality plays.   **up:** up in arms.   9. **up:** i.e. into fashion.
20. **hard:** calloused by manual labor.
22. **Wingham:** village near Canterbury.

Bevis. He shall have the skins of our enemies, to make dog's-leather of.

Holl. And Dick the butcher— 25

Bevis. Then is sin struck down like an ox, and iniquity's throat cut like a calf.

Holl. And Smith the weaver—

Bevis. Argo, their thread of life is spun.

Holl. Come, come, let's fall in with them. 30

Drum. Enter CADE, DICK *butcher,* SMITH *the weaver, and a* SAWYER, *with infinite numbers,* [*with long staves*].

Cade. We John Cade, so term'd of our suppos'd father—

Dick. [*Aside.*] Or rather of stealing a cade of herrings. 34

Cade. For our enemies shall [fall] before us, inspir'd with the spirit of putting down kings and princes —command silence.

Dick. Silence!

Cade. My father was a Mortimer— 39

Dick. [*Aside.*] He was an honest man, and a good bricklayer.

Cade. My mother a Plantagenet—

Dick. [*Aside.*] I knew her well, she was a midwife.

Cade. My wife descended of the Lacies— 44

Dick. [*Aside.*] She was indeed a pedlar's daughter, and sold many laces.

Smith. [*Aside.*] But now of late, not able to travel with her furr'd pack, she washes bucks here at home.

Cade. Therefore am I of an honorable house. 49

Dick. [*Aside.*] Ay, by my faith, the field is honorable, and there was he born, under a hedge; for his father had never a house but the cage.

Cade. Valiant I am.

Smith. [*Aside.*] 'A must needs, for beggary is valiant. 55

Cade. I am able to endure much.

Dick. [*Aside.*] No question of that; for I have seen him whipt three market-days together.

Cade. I fear neither sword nor fire. 59

Smith. [*Aside.*] He need not fear the sword, for his coat is of proof.

Dick. [*Aside.*] But methinks he should stand in fear of fire, being burnt i' th' hand for stealing of sheep. 63

Cade. Be brave then, for your captain is brave, and vows reformation. There shall be in England seven halfpenny loaves sold for a penny; the three-hoop'd pot shall have ten hoops, and I will make it felony to drink small beer. All the realm shall be in common, and in Cheapside shall my palfrey go to grass; and when I am king, as king I will be— 70

All. God save your Majesty!

Cade. I thank you, good people—there shall be no money; all shall eat and drink on my score, and I will apparel them all in one livery, that they may agree like brothers, and worship me their lord. 75

Dick. The first thing we do, let's kill all the lawyers.

Cade. Nay, that I mean to do. Is not this a lamentable thing, that of the skin of an innocent lamb should be made parchment? that parchment, being 80 scribbled o'er, should undo a man? Some say the bee stings, but I say, 'tis the bee's wax; for I did but seal once to a thing, and I was never mine own man since. How now? Who's there? 84

Enter [*one with*] *a* CLERK.

Smith. The clerk of Chartam. He can write and read and cast accompt.

Cade. O monstrous!

Smith. We took him setting of boys' copies.

Cade. Here's a villain! 89

Smith. H'as a book in his pocket with red letters in't.

Cade. Nay, then he is a conjurer.

Dick. Nay, he can make obligations, and write court-hand. 94

Cade. I am sorry for't. The man is a proper man, of mine honor; unless I find him guilty, he shall not die. Come hither, sirrah, I must examine thee. What is thy name?

Clerk. Emmanuel. 99

Dick. They use to write it on the top of letters; 'twill go hard with you.

Cade. Let me alone. Dost thou use to write thy name? or hast thou a mark to thyself, like a honest plain-dealing man? 104

Clerk. Sir, I thank God, I have been so well brought up that I can write my name.

All. He hath confess'd! away with him! he's a villain and a traitor.

Cade. Away with him, I say! Hang him with his pen and inkhorn about his neck. 110

Exit one with the Clerk.

Enter MICHAEL.

Mich. Where's our general?

Cade. Here I am, thou particular fellow.

Mich. Fly, fly, fly! Sir Humphrey Stafford and his brother are hard by, with the King's forces. 114

Cade. Stand, villain, stand, or I'll fell thee down. He shall be encount'red with a man as good as himself. He is but a knight, is 'a?

Mich. No.

24. **dog's-leather.** Commonly used for making gloves.
29. **Argo:** i.e. ergo, therefore.   33. **cade:** cask.
35. **For:** because.   **fall.** With a play on Latin *cadere*, "to fall."
44. **Lacies.** Lacy was the family name of the earls of Lincoln.
48. **furr'd pack:** knapsack of skin with the hair turned outward.
bucks: soiled clothes.   52. **cage:** jail.
54. **'A must needs:** he has to be.   58. **whipt:** i.e. as a vagabond.
61. **of proof:** (1) impenetrable; (2) badly worn.
63. **burnt . . . hand:** i.e. branded with a *T* as a thief.
66. **three-hoop'd pot:** wooden drinking cup holding a quart.
68. **small:** weak.
69. **Cheapside:** the principal commercial street of London.

73. **on my score:** at my expense.
82. **bee's wax:** i.e. sealing wax (on legal documents).
82-83. **but . . . thing:** i.e. put my name only once to a bond.
85. **Chartam:** Chartham, a town in Kent.
86. **cast accompt:** i.e. do arithmetic.
88. **setting . . . copies:** i.e. teaching boys to write.
90. **book . . . letters:** textbook (probably the primer) with the capital letters in red.   93. **make obligations:** draw up bonds.
94. **court-hand:** type of writing used in legal documents.
99-100. **Emmanuel . . . letters.** *Emmanuel* ("God with us") was commonly prefixed to documents and letters as a kind of salutation.
112. **particular:** i.e. private (as opposed to *general*).
118. **No:** i.e. only a knight.

2 Henry VI
IV.ii

Cade. To equal him, I will make myself a knight presently. [*Kneels*.] Rise up Sir John Mortimer. [*Rises*.] Now have at him! 121

Enter SIR HUMPHREY STAFFORD *and his* BROTHER *with Drum and Soldiers.*

Staf. Rebellious hinds, the filth and scum of Kent,
Mark'd for the gallows, lay your weapons down,
Home to your cottages, forsake this groom:
The King is merciful, if you revolt. 125

Bro. But angry, wrathful, and inclin'd to blood,
If you go forward; therefore yield, or die.

Cade. As for these silken-coated slaves, I pass not,
It is to you, good people, that I speak,
Over whom, in time to come, I hope to reign, 130
For I am rightful heir unto the crown.

Staf. Villain, thy father was a plasterer,
And thou thyself a shearman, art thou not?

Cade. And Adam was a gardener.

Bro. And what of that? 135

Cade. Marry, this: Edmund Mortimer, Earl of March,
Married the Duke of Clarence' daughter, did he not?

Staf. Ay, sir.

Cade. By her he had two children at one birth.

Bro. That's false. 140

Cade. Ay, there's the question; but I say, 'tis true.
The elder of them, being put to nurse,
Was by a beggar-woman stol'n away,
And ignorant of his birth and parentage,
Became a bricklayer when he came to age. 145
His son am I, deny it if you can.

Dick. Nay, 'tis too true; therefore he shall be king.

Smith. Sir, he made a chimney in my father's house,
and the bricks are alive at this day to testify it; therefore deny it not. 150

Staf. And will you credit this base drudge's words,
That speaks he knows not what?

All. Ay, marry, will we; therefore get ye gone.

Bro. Jack Cade, the Duke of York hath taught you this. 154

Cade. [*Aside*.] He lies, for I invented it myself.—
Go to, sirrah, tell the King from me, that, for his father's sake, Henry the Fift (in whose time boys went to span-counter for French crowns), I am content he shall reign, but I'll be Protector over him. 159

Dick. And furthermore, we'll have the Lord Say's head for selling the dukedom of Maine.

Cade. And good reason; for thereby is England main'd, and fain to go with a staff, but that my puissance holds it up. Fellow kings, I tell you that that Lord Say hath gelded the commonwealth, and 165 made it an eunuch; and more than that, he can speak French, and therefore he is a traitor.

Staf. O gross and miserable ignorance!

Cade. Nay, answer if you can. The Frenchmen

are our enemies. Go to then, I ask but this: can he that speaks with the tongue of an enemy be a good counsellor, or no? 172

All. No, no, and therefore we'll have his head.

Bro. Well, seeing gentle words will not prevail,
Assail them with the army of the King. 175

Staf. Herald, away, and throughout every town
Proclaim them traitors that are up with Cade,
That those which fly before the battle ends
May, even in their wives' and children's sight,
Be hang'd up for example at their doors. 180
And you that be the King's friends, follow me.
Exit [*with his Brother and Men*].

Cade. And you that love the commons, follow me.
Now show yourselves men, 'tis for liberty.
We will not leave one lord, one gentleman;
Spare none but such as go in clouted shoon, 185
For they are thrifty honest men, and such
As would (but that they dare not) take our parts.

Dick. They are all in order, and march toward us.

Cade. But then are we in order when we are most
out of order. Come, march forward. [*Exeunt*.] 190

[SCENE III]

Alarums to the fight, wherein both the STAFFORDS *are slain. Enter* CADE *and the rest.*

Cade. Where's Dick, the butcher of Ashford?

Dick. Here, sir.

Cade. They fell before thee like sheep and oxen, and thou behavedst thyself as if thou hadst been in thine own slaughter-house; therefore thus will I 5 reward thee: the Lent shall be as long again as it is, and thou shalt have a license to kill for a hundred lacking one.

Dick. I desire no more. 9

Cade. And, to speak truth, thou deserv'st no less. This monument of the victory will I bear [*putting on Stafford's armor*], and the bodies shall be dragg'd at my horse heels till I do come to London, where we will have the Mayor's sword borne before us. 14

Dick. If we mean to thrive and do good, break open the jails and let out the prisoners.

Cade. Fear not that, I warrant thee. Come, let's march towards London. *Exeunt.*

[SCENE IV]

Enter the KING *with a supplication and the* QUEEN *with Suffolk's head, the* DUKE OF BUCKINGHAM *and the* LORD SAY.

Queen. Oft have I heard that grief softens the mind,
And makes it fearful and degenerate;

---

120. **presently:** immediately.   122. **hinds:** peasants.
125. **revolt:** turn again (to the King).   128. **pass:** care.
133. **shearman:** one who shears the nap on woollen cloth.
148. **he:** i.e. Cade's father.
158. **span-counter:** game in which the player tosses a coin or counter, trying to land it within a span (nine inches) of another.
163. **main'd:** maimed (with a pun on *Maine*).   **fain . . . staff:** forced to walk with a cane.

185. **clouted shoon:** hobnailed shoes.

IV.iii. Location: Scene continues.
6. **Lent.** In Elizabethan England butchers were allowed to kill beasts during Lent only if they had a license to supply those with special needs.   17. **Fear:** doubt.

IV.iv. Location: London. The palace.
o.s.d. **supplication:** petition.   2. **fearful:** full of fears.

Think therefore on revenge and cease to weep.
But who can cease to weep and look on this?
Here may his head lie on my throbbing breast;
But where's the body that I should embrace? 5

Buck. What answer makes your Grace to the
rebels' supplication?

King. I'll send some holy bishop to entreat;
For God forbid so many simple souls 10
Should perish by the sword! And I myself,
Rather than bloody war shall cut them short,
Will parley with Jack Cade their general.
But stay, I'll read it over once again.

Queen. Ah, barbarous villains! hath this lovely face
Rul'd like a wandering planet over me, 16
And could it not enforce them to relent,
That were unworthy to behold the same?

King. Lord Say, Jack Cade hath sworn to have thy
head.

Say. Ay, but I hope your Highness shall have his.

King. How now, madam? 21
Still lamenting and mourning for Suffolk's death?
I fear me, love, if that I had been dead,
Thou wouldst not have mourn'd so much for me.

Queen. No, my love, I should not mourn, but die
for thee. 25

Enter a MESSENGER.

King. How now? what news? why com'st thou in
such haste?

Mess. The rebels are in Southwark; fly, my lord!
Jack Cade proclaims himself Lord Mortimer,
Descended from the Duke of Clarence' house,
And calls your Grace usurper, openly, 30
And vows to crown himself in Westminster.
His army is a ragged multitude
Of hinds and peasants, rude and merciless.
Sir Humphrey Stafford and his brother's death
Hath given them heart and courage to proceed. 35
All scholars, lawyers, courtiers, gentlemen,
They call false caterpillars, and intend their death.

King. O graceless men! they know not what they
do.

Buck. My gracious lord, retire to Killingworth,
Until a power be rais'd to put them down. 40

Queen. Ah, were the Duke of Suffolk now alive,
These Kentish rebels would be soon appeas'd!

King. Lord Say, the traitors hateth thee,
Therefore away with us to Killingworth.

Say. So might your Grace's person be in danger. 45
The sight of me is odious in their eyes;
And therefore in this city will I stay
And live alone as secret as I may.

Enter another MESSENGER.

[2.] Mess. Jack Cade hath gotten London Bridge:
The citizens fly and forsake their houses; 50

The rascal people, thirsting after prey,
Join with the traitor, and they jointly swear
To spoil the city and your royal court.

Buck. Then linger not, my lord, away, take horse.

King. Come, Margaret, God, our hope, will succor us. 55

Queen. My hope is gone, now Suffolk is deceas'd.

King. Farewell, my lord, trust not the Kentish
rebels.

Buck. Trust nobody, for fear you [be] betray'd.

Say. The trust I have is in mine innocence,
And therefore am I bold and resolute. *Exeunt.* 60

[SCENE V]

Enter LORD SCALES *upon the Tower, walking. Then
enters two or three* CITIZENS *below.*

Scales. How now? is Jack Cade slain?

1. Cit. No, my lord, nor likely to be slain; for they
have won the Bridge, killing all those that withstand
them. The Lord Mayor craves aid of your honor from
the Tower to defend the city from the rebels. 5

Scales. Such aid as I can spare you shall command,
But I am troubled here with them myself;
The rebels have assay'd to win the Tower.
But get you to Smithfield and gather head,
And thither I will send you Matthew Goffe. 10
Fight for your king, your country, and your lives,
And so farewell, for I must hence again. *Exeunt.*

[SCENE VI]

Enter JACK CADE *and the rest, and strikes his staff on
London Stone.*

Cade. Now is Mortimer lord of this city. And
here, sitting upon London Stone, I charge and command that, of the city's cost, the pissing-conduit run
nothing but claret wine this first year of our reign.
And now henceforward it shall be treason for any that
calls me other than Lord Mortimer. 6

Enter a SOLDIER running.

Sold. Jack Cade! Jack Cade!

Cade. Knock him down there. *They kill him.*

[Smith.] If this fellow be wise, he'll never call ye
Jack Cade more. I think he hath a very fair warning.

Dick. My lord, there's an army gather'd together
in Smithfield. 12

Cade. Come, then, let's go fight with them. But
first go and set London Bridge on fire, and if you can,
burn down the Tower too. Come, let's away. 15
Exeunt omnes.

53. **spoil:** loot.

IV.v. Location: London. The Tower.
9. **Smithfield:** open area outside the city wall, northwest of St. Paul's.
head: a force.

16. **planet.** Astrologers held that a star in the ascendant controlled
the destinies of those born under it.
27. **Southwark:** section of London on the south bank of the Thames
at the end of London Bridge.
39. **Killingworth:** Kenilworth, a royal castle in Warwickshire.
40. **power:** army.

IV.vi. Location: London. Canwick Street (modern Cannon Street).
o.s.d. **London Stone:** ancient stone in Cannon Street, long famous as
a landmark.
3. **pissing-conduit:** conduit near the junction of Threadneedle Street
and Cornhill in the City of London.

[SCENE VII]

Alarums. MATTHEW GOFFE *is slain, and all the rest.*
Then enter JACK CADE *with his company.*

Cade. So, sirs. Now go some and pull down the
Savoy; others to th' Inns of Court; down with them all.
Dick. I have a suit unto your lordship.
Cade. Be it a lordship, thou shalt have it for that
word.   5
Dick. Only that the laws of England may come out
of your mouth.
Holland. [*Aside.*] Mass, 'twill be sore law then,
for he was thrust in the mouth with a spear, and 'tis
not whole yet.   10
Smith. [*Aside.*] Nay, John, it will be stinking law,
for his breath stinks with eating toasted cheese.
Cade. I have thought upon it, it shall be so. Away,
burn all the records of the realm, my mouth shall be
the parliament of England.   15
Holland. [*Aside.*] Then we are like to have biting
statutes, unless his teeth be pull'd out.
Cade. And henceforward all things shall be in
common.   19

Enter a MESSENGER.

Mess. My lord, a prize, a prize! Here's the Lord
Say, which sold the towns in France; he that made us
pay one and twenty fifteens, and one shilling to the
pound, the last subsidy.

Enter GEORGE [BEVIS] *with the* LORD SAY.

Cade. Well, he shall be beheaded for it ten times.
Ah, thou say, thou serge, nay, thou buckram lord!   25
now art thou within point-blank of our jurisdiction
regal. What canst thou answer to my Majesty for
giving up of Normandy unto Mounsieur Basimecu,
the Dolphin of France? Be it known unto thee by these
presence, even the presence of Lord Mortimer,   30
that I am the besom that must sweep the court clean of
such filth as thou art. Thou hast most traitorously
corrupted the youth of the realm in erecting a grammar
school; and whereas, before, our forefathers had no
other books but the score and the tally, thou hast   35
caus'd printing to be us'd, and, contrary to the King,
his crown, and dignity, thou hast built a paper-mill. It
will be prov'd to thy face that thou hast men about thee
that usually talk of a noun and a verb, and such
abominable words as no Christian ear can endure   40

IV.vii. Location: London. Smithfield.
2. Savoy: London palace, formerly the town seat of the dukes of
Lancaster.   **Inns of Court:** the legal centre of London.
22–23. one . . . subsidy. An exaggerated estimate of the customary
tax of one-fifteenth on income from land, frequently levied as a
"subsidy" for special purposes.
25. say, serge, buckram: kinds of fabric, the first of silk, the second
of wool, the third of linen.
28. Mounsieur Basimecu: contemptuous term for a Frenchman
(*baise mon cul*).
29–30. these presence: i.e. these presents, a legal term meaning "the
present document."   **31. besom:** broom.
35. score . . . tally: primitive device for keeping accounts; one half
of a stick notched to record the transactions was held by the debtor
and the other by the creditor.
36. printing. An anachronism, like the reference to paper-mills in
line 37. The first printing press in England was established by William
Caxton in 1477, twenty-seven years after Cade's rebellion; the first
paper-mill, not until 1588.   **39. usually:** habitually.

to hear. Thou hast appointed justices of peace, to call
poor men before them about matters they were not able
to answer. Moreover, thou hast put them in prison,
and because they could not read, thou hast hang'd them,
when, indeed, only for that cause they have been   45
most worthy to live. Thou dost ride in a foot-cloth,
dost thou not?
Say. What of that?
Cade. Marry, thou oughtst not to let thy horse
wear a cloak, when honester men than thou go in their
hose and doublets.   51
Dick. And work in their shirt too, as myself, for
example, that am a butcher.
Say. You men of Kent—
Dick. What say you of Kent?   55
Say. Nothing but this; 'tis "*bona terra, mala gens.*"
Cade. Away with him, away with him! he speaks
Latin.
Say. Hear me but speak, and bear me where you
will.
Kent, in the Commentaries Caesar writ,   60
Is term'd the civill'st place of all this isle:
Sweet is the country, because full of riches,
The people liberal, valiant, active, wealthy,
Which makes me hope you are not void of pity.
I sold not Maine, I lost not Normandy,   65
Yet to recover them would lose my life.
Justice with favor have I always done;
Pray'rs and tears have mov'd me, gifts could never.
When have I aught exacted at your hands,
[But] to maintain the King, the realm, and you?   70
Large gifts have I bestow'd on learned clerks,
Because my book preferr'd me to the King;
And seeing ignorance is the curse of God,
Knowledge the wing wherewith we fly to heaven,
Unless you be possess'd with devilish spirits   75
You cannot but forbear to murther me.
This tongue hath parley'd unto foreign kings
For your behoof—
Cade. Tut, when struck'st thou one blow in the
field?   80
Say. Great men have reaching hands; oft have I
struck
Those that I never saw, and struck them dead.
Bevis. O monstrous coward! What, to come behind
folks?
Say. These cheeks are pale for watching for your
good.   85
Cade. Give him a box o' th' ear, and that will make
'em red again.
Say. Long sitting to determine poor men's causes
Hath made me full of sickness and diseases.
Cade. Ye shall have a hempen [caudle] then, and the
help of hatchet.   91
Dick. Why dost thou quiver, man?

44. read: i.e. claim "benefit of clergy" by demonstrating their literacy.
46. foot-cloth. See note to IV.i.54.
51. hose and doublets: breeches and coats.
56. bona . . . gens: good land, bad people.
69. exacted: i.e. as Lord Treasurer.   **71. clerks:** scholars.
72. book: i.e. learning.
90–91. hempen . . . hatchet: executioner's rope and axe, i.e. hanging
and beheading.   **caudle:** a warm drink.

Say. The palsy, and not fear, provokes me.

Cade. Nay, he nods at us, as who should say, I'll be
even with you. I'll see if his head will stand steadier on
a pole, or no. Take him away, and behead him. 96

Say. Tell me: wherein have I offended most?
Have I affected wealth or honor? Speak.
Are my chests fill'd up with extorted gold?
Is my apparel sumptuous to behold? 100
Whom have I injur'd that ye seek my death?
These hands are free from guiltless blood-shedding,
This breast from harboring foul deceitful thoughts.
O, let me live! 104

Cade. [*Aside.*] I feel remorse in myself with his
words; but I'll bridle it. He shall die, and it be but for
pleading so well for his life.—Away with him, he has a
familiar under his tongue, he speaks not a' God's name.
Go, take him away I say, and strike off his head
presently, and then break into his son-in-law's house,
Sir James Cromer, and strike off his head, and bring
them both upon two poles hither. 112

All. It shall be done.

Say. Ah, countrymen! if when you make your
pray'rs,
God should be so obdurate as yourselves, 115
How would it fare with your departed souls?
And therefore yet relent, and save my life.

Cade. Away with him, and do as I command ye.
[*Exeunt some with the Lord Say.*] The proudest peer in
the realm shall not wear a head on his shoulders, 120
unless he pay me tribute. There shall not be a maid be
married, but she shall pay to me her maidenhead ere
they have it. Men shall hold of me *in capite*; and we
charge and command that their wives be as free as
heart can wish or tongue can tell. 125

Dick. My lord, when shall we go to Cheapside and
take up commodities upon our bills?

Cade. Marry, presently.

All. O, brave! 129

*Enter one with the heads [of Say and Cromer upon two
poles].*

Cade. But is not this braver? Let them kiss one
another, for they lov'd well when they were alive.
Now part them again, lest they consult about the giving up of some more towns in France. Soldiers, defer
the spoil of the city until night; for with these borne
before us, in stead of maces, will we ride through the
streets, and at every corner have them kiss. Away! 136
Exeunt.

[SCENE VIII]

Alarum and retreat. Enter again CADE *and all his rabble-
ment.*

98. **affected:** loved.
102. **guiltless blood-shedding:** shedding of guiltless blood.
108. **familiar:** attendant demon. **a':** in.
110. **presently:** immediately. 123. **in capite:** (as tenant) in chief, i.e.
by direct grant from the Crown. Note the bilingual pun on "maidenhead" (*capite* is the ablative case of *caput*, "head").
127. **take . . . bills:** secure merchandise on credit (with a pun on
bills = weapons). 135. **maces:** magistrates' symbols of office.

IV.viii. Location: Southwark.
o.s.d. **retreat:** signal to recall forces.

Cade. Up Fish Street! down Saint Magnus'
Corner! kill and knock down! throw them into
Thames! (*Sound a parley.*) What noise is this I hear?
Dare any be so bold to sound retreat or parley when I
command them kill? 5

Enter BUCKINGHAM *and old* CLIFFORD [*attended*].

Buck. Ay, here they be that dare and will disturb
thee.
Know, Cade, we come ambassadors from the King
Unto the commons, whom thou hast misled,
And here pronounce free pardon to them all
That will forsake thee and go home in peace. 10

Clif. What say ye, countrymen? will ye relent
And yield to mercy whilst 'tis offered you,
Or let a [rebel] lead you to your deaths?
Who loves the King, and will embrace his pardon,
Fling up his cap, and say, "God save his Majesty!" 15
Who hateth him and honors not his father,
Henry the Fift, that made all France to quake,
Shake he his weapon at us and pass by.

All. God save the King! God save the King! 19

Cade. What, Buckingham and Clifford, are ye so
brave? And you, base peasants, do ye believe him?
Will you needs be hang'd with your pardons about
your necks? Hath my sword therefore broke through
London gates, that you should leave me at the White
Hart in Southwark? I thought ye would never 25
have given out these arms till you had recover'd your
ancient freedom. But you are all recreants and dastards,
and delight to live in slavery to the nobility. Let them
break your backs with burthens, take your houses
over your heads, ravish your wives and daughters 30
before your faces. For me, I will make shift for one;
and so God's curse light upon you all!

All. We'll follow Cade, we'll follow Cade!

Clif. Is Cade the son of Henry the Fift,
That thus you do exclaim you'll go with him? 35
Will he conduct you through the heart of France,
And make the meanest of you earls and dukes?
Alas, he hath no home, no place to fly to;
Nor knows he how to live but by the spoil,
Unless by robbing of your friends and us. 40
Were't not a shame that, whilst you live at jar,
The fearful French, whom you late vanquished,
Should make a start o'er seas and vanquish you?
Methinks already in this civil broil
I see them lording it in London streets, 45
Crying "*Villiago!*" unto all they meet.
Better ten thousand base-born Cades miscarry
Than you should stoop unto a Frenchman's mercy.
To France, to France, and get what you have lost!
Spare England, for it is your native coast. 50
Henry hath money, you are strong and manly;
God on our side, doubt not of victory.

1–2. **Fish Street, Saint Magnus' Corner:** places at the north end of
London Bridge opposite Southwark.
3. **parley:** signal to request a conference. 21. **brave:** arrogant.
24–25. **White Hart:** ancient inn in Borough High Street, one of the
principal thoroughfares of Southwark. 26. **out:** up.
41. **at jar:** in discord. 42. **fearful:** timid.
46. **Villiago:** rascal (Italian). 47. **miscarry:** meet disaster.

All. A Clifford! a Clifford! we'll follow the King and Clifford.   54

Cade. [*Aside.*] Was ever feather so lightly blown to and fro as this multitude? The name of Henry the Fift hales them to an hundred mischiefs, and makes them leave me desolate. I see them lay their heads together to surprise me. My sword make way for me, for here is no staying.—In despite of the devils   60 and hell, have through the very middest of you! And heavens and honor be witness that no want of resolution in me, but only my followers' base and ignominious treasons, makes me betake me to my heels.

[*He runs through them with his sword and flies away.*] *Exit.*

Buck. What, is he fled? Go some, and follow him, And he that brings his head unto the King   66 Shall have a thousand crowns for his reward.

Exeunt some of them.

Follow me, soldiers, we'll devise a mean
To reconcile you all unto the King.   *Exeunt omnes.*

[SCENE IX]

Sound trumpets. Enter KING, QUEEN, *and* SOMERSET *on the tarras.*

King. Was ever king that joy'd an earthly throne
And could command no more content than I?
No sooner was I crept out of my cradle
But I was made a king, at nine months old.
Was never subject long'd to be a king   5
As I do long and wish to be a subject.

Enter BUCKINGHAM *and* [*old*] CLIFFORD.

Buck. Health and glad tidings to your Majesty!
King. Why, Buckingham, is the traitor Cade surpris'd?
Or is he but retir'd to make him strong?

Enter, [*below,*] *multitudes with halters about their necks.*

Clif. He is fled, my lord, and all his powers do yield,   10
And humbly thus, with halters on their necks,
Expect your Highness' doom, of life or death.
King. Then, heaven, set ope thy everlasting gates
To entertain my vows of thanks and praise!
Soldiers, this day have you redeem'd your lives,   15
And show'd how well you love your prince and country:
Continue still in this so good a mind,
And Henry, though he be infortunate,
Assure yourselves, will never be unkind.
And so with thanks and pardon to you all,   20
I do dismiss you to your several countries.
All. God save the King! God save the King!

Enter a MESSENGER.

Mess. Please it your Grace to be advertised

The Duke of York is newly come from Ireland,
And with a puissant and a mighty power   25
Of gallowglasses and stout kerns
Is marching hitherward in proud array,
And still proclaimeth, as he comes along,
His arms are only to remove from thee
The Duke of Somerset, whom he terms a traitor.   30
King. Thus stands my state, 'twixt Cade and York distress'd,
Like to a ship that, having scap'd a tempest,
Is straightway [calm'd] and boarded with a pirate.
But now is Cade driven back, his men dispers'd,
And now is York in arms to second him.   35
I pray thee, Buckingham, go and meet him,
And ask him what's the reason of these arms.
Tell him I'll send Duke Edmund to the Tower;
And, Somerset, we will commit thee thither,
Until his army be dismiss'd from him.   40
Som. My lord,
I'll yield myself to prison willingly,
Or unto death, to do my country good.
King. In any case, be not too rough in terms,
For he is fierce and cannot brook hard language.   45
Buck. I will, my lord, and doubt not so to deal
As all things shall redound unto your good.
King. Come, wife, let's in, and learn to govern better,
For yet may England curse my wretched reign.

Flourish. Exeunt.

[SCENE X]

Enter CADE.

Cade. Fie on ambitions! fie on myself, that have a sword, and yet am ready to famish! These five days have I hid me in these woods and durst not peep out, for all the country is laid for me; but now am I so hungry that, if I might have a lease of my life for a   5 thousand years, I could stay no longer. Wherefore, on a brick wall have I climb'd into this garden, to see if I can eat grass, or pick a sallet another while, which is not amiss to cool a man's stomach this hot weather. And I think this word "sallet" was born to do me   10 good; for many a time, but for a sallet, my brain-pan had been cleft with a brown bill; and many a time, when I have been dry and bravely marching, it hath serv'd me instead of a quart pot to drink in; and now the word "sallet" must serve me to feed on.   15

[*He lies down picking of herbs and eating them.*]

26. **gallowglasses:** heavy-armed Irish foot soldiers.   **kerns:** light-armed Irish foot soldiers.   28. **still:** continually.
44. **terms:** language.   45. **brook:** endure.   49. **yet:** until now.

IV.x. This famous scene is based upon a single sentence in Hall (Bullough, III, 118): "For after a Proclamacion made, that whosoever could apprehende thesaied Jac Cade, should have for his pain, a .M. markes, many sought for hym, but few espied hym, til one Alexander Iden, esquire of Kent found hym in a garden, and there in his defence, manfully slewe the caitife Cade, & brought his ded body to London, whose hed was set on London bridge."
Location: Kent. Iden's garden.
4. **laid:** set with snares.   6. **stay:** wait.
8. **sallet:** raw vegetable (play in line 11 on the meaning "helmet").
12. **brown:** bloodstained (?) or varnished to prevent rust (?).   **bill:** long weapon with an axe-like head.

57. **hales:** draws.   59. **surprise:** capture.

IV.ix. Location: Kenilworth Castle.
o.s.d. **on the tarras:** on the terrace, i.e. on an upper level.
1. **joy'd:** enjoyed.   12. **Expect:** await.   **doom:** judgment.
21. **countries:** localities.   23. **advertised:** informed.

Enter IDEN [*followed at a distance by his* SERVANTS].

Iden. Lord, who would live turmoiled in the court
And may enjoy such quiet walks as these?
This small inheritance my father left me
Contenteth me, and worth a monarchy.
I seek not to wax great by others' [waning],   20
Or gather wealth, I care not with what envy.
Sufficeth that I have maintains my state
And sends the poor well pleased from my gate.

Cade. [*Aside.*] Here's the lord of the soil come to
seize me for a stray, for entering his fee-simple 25
without leave.—Ah, villain, thou wilt betray me, and
get a thousand crowns of the King by carrying my
head to him, but I'll make thee eat iron like an ostridge,
and swallow my sword like a great pin, ere thou and
I part.   30

Iden. Why, rude companion, whatsoe'er thou be,
I know thee not, why then should I betray thee?
Is't not enough to break into my garden,
And like a thief to come to rob my grounds,
Climbing my walls in spite of me the owner,   35
But thou wilt brave me with these saucy terms?

Cade. Brave thee? Ay, by the best blood that ever
was broach'd, and beard thee too. Look on me well. I
have eat no meat these five days, yet come thou and
thy five men, and if I do not leave you all as dead as a
doornail, I pray God I may never eat grass more. 41

Iden. Nay, it shall ne'er be said, while England
    stands,
That Alexander Iden, an esquire of Kent,
Took odds to combat a poor famish'd man.
Oppose thy steadfast-gazing eyes to mine,   45
See if thou canst outface me with thy looks.
Set limb to limb, and thou art far the lesser;
Thy hand is but a finger to my fist,
Thy leg a stick compared with this truncheon;
My foot shall fight with all the strength thou hast, 50
And if mine arm be heaved in the air,
Thy grave is digg'd already in the earth.
As for words, whose greatness answers words,
Let this my sword report what speech forbears.   54

Cade. By my valor, the most complete champion
that ever I heard! Steel, if thou turn the edge, or cut
not out the burly-bon'd clown in chines of beef ere thou
sleep in thy sheath, I beseech [God] on my knees thou
mayst be turn'd to hobnails.   59

    Here they fight [*and Cade falls down*].
O, I am slain! Famine and no other hath slain me. Let
ten thousand devils come against me, and give me but
the ten meals I have lost, and I'd defy them all.
Wither, garden, and be henceforth a burying-place to
all that do dwell in this house, because the unconquer'd
soul of Cade is fled.   65

Iden. Is't Cade that I have slain, that monstrous
    traitor?

Sword, I will hallow thee for this thy deed,
And hang thee o'er my tomb when I am dead.
Ne'er shall this blood be wiped from thy point,
But thou shalt wear it as a herald's coat,   70
To emblaze the honor that thy master got.

Cade. Iden, farewell, and be proud of thy victory.
Tell Kent from me, she hath lost her best man, and
exhort all the world to be cowards; for I, that never
fear'd any, am vanquish'd by famine, not by valor. 75

    Dies.

Iden. How much thou wrong'st me, heaven be my
    judge.
Die, damned wretch, the curse of her that bare thee;
And as I thrust thy body in with my sword,
So wish I, I might thrust thy soul to hell.
Hence will I drag thee headlong by the heels   80
Unto a dunghill, which shall be thy grave,
And there cut off thy most ungracious head,
Which I will bear in triumph to the King,
Leaving thy trunk for crows to feed upon.   84

    Exit [*dragging out the body, with his* Servants].

[ACT V, SCENE I]

Enter YORK *and his army of Irish with Drum and Colors.*

York. From Ireland thus comes York to claim his
    right,
And pluck the crown from feeble Henry's head.
Ring bells, aloud, burn bonfires clear and bright
To entertain great England's lawful king!
Ah, *sancta majestas!* who would not buy thee dear? 5
Let them obey that knows not how to rule;
This hand was made to handle nought but gold.
I cannot give due action to my words,
Except a sword or sceptre balance it.
A sceptre shall it have, have I a soul,   10
On which I'll toss the flow'r-de-luce of France.

Enter BUCKINGHAM.

Whom have we here? Buckingham, to disturb me?
The King hath sent him sure; I must dissemble.

Buck. York, if thou meanest well, I greet thee well.

York. Humphrey of Buckingham, I accept thy
    greeting.   15
Art thou a messenger, or come of pleasure?

Buck. A messenger from Henry, our dread liege,
To know the reason of these arms in peace;
Or why thou, being a subject as I am,
Against thy oath and true allegiance sworn,   20
Should raise so great a power without his leave,
Or dare to bring thy force so near the court.

York. [*Aside.*] Scarce can I speak, my choler is so
    great.
O, I could hew up rocks and fight with flint,

---

16. **turmoiled:** harried, distraught.
22. **Sufficeth . . . state:** it suffices that what I have maintains my way of life.   25. **stray:** trespasser.   **fee-simple:** freehold property.
31. **rude companion:** base fellow.
36. **brave:** defy, taunt.   **saucy:** insolent.
38. **broach'd:** shed.   **beard:** defy.   39. **eat:** eaten.
44. **odds:** advantage.   49. **truncheon:** thick staff (i.e. Iden's leg).
53. **answers words:** matches your words.   57. **chines:** saddles, roasts.

71. **emblaze:** signify by a heraldic device.   77. **bare:** bore.
80. **headlong:** at full length.

V.i. Location: Fields near St. Albans; the Castle Inn at one side.
o.s.d. **Colors:** flagbearer.
4. **entertain:** receive.   5. **sancta majestas:** holy majesty.
11. **toss:** bear aloft.   **flow'r-de-luce:** fleur-de-lis, the national emblem of France.

2 Henry VI
V.i

I am so angry at these abject terms;   25
And now, like Ajax Telamonius,
On sheep or oxen could I spend my fury.
I am far better born than is the King;
More like a king, more kingly in my thoughts;
But I must make fair weather yet a while,   30
Till Henry be more weak and I more strong.—
Buckingham, I prithee pardon me,
That I have given no answer all this while;
My mind was troubled with deep melancholy.
The cause why I have brought this army hither   35
Is to remove proud Somerset from the King,
Seditious to his Grace and to the state.
    Buck. That is too much presumption on thy part;
But if thy arms be to no other end,
The King hath yielded unto thy demand: 40
The Duke of Somerset is in the Tower.
    York. Upon thine honor, is he prisoner?
    Buck. Upon mine honor, he is prisoner.
    York. Then, Buckingham, I do dismiss my pow'rs.
Soldiers, I thank you all; disperse yourselves.   45
Meet me to-morrow in Saint George's Field,
You shall have pay and every thing you wish.

                                         [*Exeunt Soldiers.*]

And let my sovereign, virtuous Henry,
Command my eldest son, nay, all my sons,
As pledges of my fealty and love;   50
I'll send them all as willing as I live.
Lands, goods, horse, armor, any thing I have
Is his to use, so Somerset may die.
    Buck. York, I commend this kind submission;
We twain will go into his Highness' tent.   55

                    Enter KING *and* ATTENDANTS.

    King. Buckingham, doth York intend no harm to us
That thus he marcheth with thee arm in arm?
    York. In all submission and humility
York doth present himself unto your Highness.
    King. Then what intends these forces thou dost
        bring?   60
    York. To heave the traitor Somerset from hence,
And fight against that monstrous rebel Cade,
Who since I heard to be discomfited.

                 Enter IDEN *with Cade's head.*

    Iden. If one so rude and of so mean condition
May pass into the presence of a king,   65
Lo, I present your Grace a traitor's head,
The head of Cade, whom I in combat slew.
    King. The head of Cade! Great God, how just art
        thou!
O, let me view his visage, being dead,
That living wrought me such exceeding trouble.   70
Tell me, my friend, art thou the man that slew him?
    Iden. I was, an't like your Majesty.

    King. How art thou call'd? and what is thy degree?
    Iden. Alexander Iden, that's my name,
A poor esquire of Kent, that loves his king.   75
    Buck. So please it you, my lord, 'twere not amiss
He were created knight for his good service.
    King. Iden, kneel down. [*He kneels.*] Rise up a
        knight.
We give thee for reward a thousand marks,
And will that thou henceforth attend on us.   80
    Iden. May Iden live to merit such a bounty,
And never live but true unto his liege!   [*Rises.*]

                    Enter QUEEN *and* SOMERSET.

    King. See, Buckingham, Somerset comes with th'
        Queen.
Go bid her hide him quickly from the Duke.
    Queen. For thousand Yorks he shall not hide his
        head,   85
But boldly stand and front him to his face.
    York. How now? is Somerset at liberty?
Then, York, unloose thy long-imprisoned thoughts,
And let thy tongue be equal with thy heart.
Shall I endure the sight of Somerset?   90
False king, why hast thou broken faith with me,
Knowing how hardly I can brook abuse?
King did I call thee? No; thou art not king;
Not fit to govern and rule multitudes,
Which dar'st not, no, nor canst not rule a traitor.   95
That head of thine doth not become a crown:
Thy hand is made to grasp a palmer's staff
And not to grace an aweful princely sceptre.
That gold must round engirt these brows of mine,
Whose smile and frown, like to Achilles' spear,   100
Is able with the change to kill and cure.
Here is a hand to hold a sceptre up,
And with the same to act controlling laws.
Give place! By heaven, thou shalt rule no more
O'er him whom heaven created for thy ruler.   105
    Som. O monstrous traitor! I arrest thee, York,
Of capital treason 'gainst the King and crown.
Obey, audacious traitor, kneel for grace.
    York. Wouldst have me kneel? First let me ask of
        [these]
If they can brook I bow a knee to man.   110
Sirrah, call in my [sons] to be my bail.

                                        [*Exit Attendant.*]

I know, ere they will have me go to ward,
They'll pawn their swords [for] my enfranchisement.
    Queen. Call hither Clifford, bid him come amain,
To say if that the bastard boys of York   115
Shall be the surety for their traitor father.

                                       [*Exit Buckingham.*]

    York. O blood-bespotted Neapolitan,

---

25. **abject terms:** insulting words.
26–27. **Ajax ... fury.** According to Homer, Ajax, a Greek warrior driven mad by his jealousy of Ulysses, killed the sheep and oxen which he mistook for his enemies.
30. **make fair weather:** be pleasant, equivocate.
46. **Saint George's Field:** open area opposite London on the south bank of the Thames.
49–50. **Command ... As pledges:** hold ... as hostages.
53. **so:** provided that.   64. **rude:** uncultivated.

80. **will:** command.   86. **front:** confront.
92. **brook abuse:** endure deception.   97. **palmer's:** pilgrim's.
99. **gold:** i.e. golden crown.
100–101. **Whose ... cure.** In Greek legend, Telephus, a son of Hercules, was not cured of a wound from Achilles' spear until rust from the weapon was applied to his injury.   103. **act:** enact.
111. **sons.** Actually, York's sons were children at the time (1452), Edward (later Edward IV) being ten and Richard (later Richard III) only a few months old.   112. **to ward:** into custody.
114. **amain:** at full speed.
117. **Neapolitan.** Margaret's father René (Reignier) was the titular king of Naples.

Outcast of Naples, England's bloody scourge!
The sons of York, thy betters in their birth,
Shall be their father's bail, and bane to those   120
That for my surety will refuse the boys!

Enter EDWARD *and* RICHARD [PLANTAGENET *with Drum
and Soldiers at one door*].

See where they come, I'll warrant they'll make it good.

Enter CLIFFORD [*and his son* YOUNG CLIFFORD *with
Drum and Soldiers at the other door*].

Queen.   And here comes Clifford to deny their bail.
Clif.   Health and all happiness to my lord the King!
                                              [*Kneels.*]
York.   I thank thee, Clifford. Say, what news with
          thee?   125
Nay, do not fright us with an angry look.
We are thy sovereign, Clifford, kneel again;
For thy mistaking so, we pardon thee.
Clif.   This is my king, York, I do not mistake,
But thou mistakes me much to think I do.   130
To Bedlam with him! is the man grown mad?
King.   Ay, Clifford, a bedlam and ambitious humor
Makes him oppose himself against his king.
Clif.   He is a traitor, let him to the Tower,
And chop away that factious pate of his.   135
Queen.   He is arrested, but will not obey.
His sons, he says, shall give their words for him.
York.   Will you not, sons?
Edw.   Ay, noble father, if our words will serve.
Rich.   And if words will not, then our weapons
          shall.   140
Clif.   Why, what a brood of traitors have we here!
York.   Look in a glass, and call thy image so.
I am thy king, and thou a false-heart traitor.
Call hither to the stake my two brave bears,
That with the very shaking of their chains   145
They may astonish these fell-lurking curs.
Bid Salisbury and Warwick come to me.

Enter the EARLS OF WARWICK *and* SALISBURY [*with
Drum and Soldiers*].

Clif.   Are these thy bears? We'll bait thy bears to
          death,
And manacle the bearard in their chains,
If thou dar'st bring them to the baiting-place. 150
Rich.   Oft have I seen a hot o'erweening cur
Run back and bite, because he was withheld,
Who, being suffer'd, with the bear's fell paw
Hath clapp'd his tail between his legs and cried;
And such a piece of service will you do,   155
If you oppose yourselves to match Lord Warwick.

Clif.   Hence, heap of wrath, foul indigested lump,
As crooked in thy manners as thy shape!
York.   Nay, we shall heat you thoroughly anon.
Clif.   Take heed, lest by your heat you burn your-
          selves.   160
King.   Why, Warwick, hath thy knee forgot to
          bow?
Old Salisbury, shame to thy silver hair,
Thou mad misleader of thy brain-sick son!
What, wilt thou on thy death-bed play the ruffian,
And seek for sorrow with thy spectacles?   165
O, where is faith? O, where is loyalty?
If it be banish'd from the frosty head,
Where shall it find a harbor in the earth?
Wilt thou go dig a grave to find out war,
And shame thine honorable age with blood?   170
Why art thou old, and want'st experience?
Or wherefore dost abuse it if thou hast it?
For shame, in duty bend thy knee to me
That bows unto the grave with mickle age.
Sal.   My lord, I have considered with myself   175
The title of this most renowned duke,
And in my conscience do repute his Grace
The rightful heir to England's royal seat.
King.   Hast thou not sworn allegiance unto me?
Sal.   I have.   180
King.   Canst thou dispense with heaven for such an
          oath?
Sal.   It is great sin to swear unto a sin,
But greater sin to keep a sinful oath.
Who can be bound by any solemn vow
To do a murd'rous deed, to rob a man,   185
To force a spotless virgin's chastity,
To reave the orphan of his patrimony,
To wring the widow from her custom'd right,
And have no other reason for this wrong
But that he was bound by a solemn oath?   190
Queen.   A subtle traitor needs no sophister.
King.   Call Buckingham, and bid him arm himself.
York.   Call Buckingham, and all the friends thou
          hast,
I am resolv'd for death [or] dignity.   194
Clif.   The first I warrant thee, if dreams prove true.
War.   You were best to go to bed and dream again,
To keep thee from the tempest of the field.
Clif.   I am resolv'd to bear a greater storm
Than any thou canst conjure up to-day;
And that I'll write upon thy burgonet,   200
Might I but know thee by thy [household] badge.
War.   Now, by my father's badge, old Nevil's crest,
The rampant bear chain'd to the ragged staff,
This day I'll wear aloft my burgonet,
As on a mountain top the cedar shows   205
That keeps his leaves in spite of any storm,

---

120. **bane:** destruction.
131. **Bedlam:** hospital of St. Mary of Bethlehem, an asylum for
lunatics in London.
132. **bedlam:** mad.   **humor:** temperament.
144. **two brave bears:** i.e. Salisbury and his son Warwick, so called
because Warwick's badge was a rampant bear chained to a staff.
See note to lines 202-3.
146. **astonish:** dismay.   **fell-lurking:** cruelly waiting.
149. **bearard:** bear-ward, keeper of bears. Throughout this passage
the imagery is derived from the savage Elizabethan sport of bear-
baiting.   150. **baiting-place:** bear pit.
153. **suffer'd:** i.e. permitted to attack.
156. **oppose yourselves:** undertake.

157. **indigested:** shapeless, misformed. On Richard's deformity see
Richard III, I.i.14-27.   165. **spectacles:** organs of sight.
171. **want'st:** lackest.   172. **abuse:** disgrace.   174. **mickle:** great.
181. **dispense with:** obtain dispensation from.
187. **reave:** bereave, rob.
188. **custom'd right:** i.e. of inheriting part of her husband's estate.
191. **sophister:** sophist, equivocator.   200. **burgonet:** helmet.
202-3. **my . . . staff.** Actually, the Neville badge was a bull. Warwick's famous badge of a bear chained to a staff was, like his earldom,
inherited from his father-in-law Richard Beauchamp.

2 Henry VI
V.i

Even to affright thee with the view thereof.

Clif. And from thy burgonet I'll rend thy bear,
And tread it under foot with all contempt,
Despite the bearard that protects the bear.   210

Y. Clif. And so to arms, victorious father,
To quell the rebels and their complices.

Rich. Fie! charity, for shame! speak not in spite,
For you shall sup with Jesu Christ to-night.

Y. Clif. Foul stigmatic, that's more than thou canst
tell.   215

Rich. If not in heaven, you'll surely sup in hell.

Exeunt [*severally*].

[SCENE II]

[*Alarums to the battle.*] *Enter* WARWICK.

War. Clifford of Cumberland, 'tis Warwick calls!
And if thou dost not hide thee from the bear,
Now when the angry trumpet sounds alarum,
And dead men's cries do fill the empty air,
Clifford, I say, come forth and fight with me.   5
Proud northern lord, Clifford of Cumberland,
Warwick is hoarse with calling thee to arms.

Enter YORK.

How now, my noble lord? what, all afoot?

York. The deadly-handed Clifford slew my steed;
But match to match I have encount'red him,   10
And made a prey for carrion kites and crows
Even of the bonny beast he lov'd so well.

Enter [*old*] CLIFFORD.

War. Of one or both of us the time is come.

York. Hold, Warwick; seek thee out some other
chase,
For I myself must hunt this deer to death.   15

War. Then nobly, York, 'tis for a crown thou
fight'st.
As I intend, Clifford, to thrive to-day,
It grieves my soul to leave thee unassail'd.

Exit Warwick.

Clif. What seest thou in me, York? Why dost thou
pause?

York. With thy brave bearing should I be in love,
But that thou art so fast mine enemy.   21

Clif. Nor should thy prowess want praise and
esteem,
But that 'tis shown ignobly and in treason.

York. So let it help me now against thy sword,
As I in justice and true right express it.   25

Clif. My soul and body on the action both!

York. A dreadful lay! Address thee instantly.

[*They fight, and Clifford falls.*]

Clif. La fin couronne les [*œuvres*].   [*Dies.*]

York. Thus war hath given thee peace, for thou art
still.   29
Peace with his soul, heaven, if it be thy will! [*Exit.*]

Enter YOUNG CLIFFORD.

Y. Clif. Shame and confusion! all is on the rout,
Fear frames disorder, and disorder wounds
Where it should guard. O war, thou son of hell,
Whom angry heavens do make their minister,
Throw in the frozen bosoms of our part   35
Hot coals of vengeance! Let no soldier fly.
He that is truly dedicate to war
Hath no self-love; nor he that loves himself
Hath not essentially but by circumstance
The name of valor. [*Sees his dead father.*] O, let the
vile world end,   40
And the premised flames of the last day
Knit earth and heaven together!
Now let the general trumpet blow his blast,
Particularities and petty sounds
To cease! Wast thou ordain'd, dear father,   45
To lose thy youth in peace, and to achieve
The silver livery of advised age,
And in thy reverence, and thy chair-days, thus
To die in ruffian battle? Even at this sight
My heart is turn'd to stone; and while 'tis mine,   50
It shall be stony. York not our old men spares;
No more will I their babes. Tears virginal
Shall be to me even as the dew to fire,
And beauty, that the tyrant oft reclaims,
Shall to my flaming wrath be oil and flax.   55
Henceforth I will not have to do with pity.
Meet I an infant of the house of York,
Into as many gobbets will I cut it
As wild Medea young Absyrtus did;
In cruelty will I seek out my fame.   60

[*He takes him up on his back.*]

Come, thou new ruin of old Clifford's house:
As did Aeneas old Anchises bear,
So bear I thee upon my manly shoulders;
But then Aeneas bare a living load—
Nothing so heavy as these woes of mine.   65

[*Exit bearing off his father.*]

Enter RICHARD *and* SOMERSET *to fight.* [*Somerset is
killed under the sign of the Castle Inn.*]

Rich. So lie thou there;
For underneath an alehouse' paltry sign,
The Castle in Saint Albans, Somerset
Hath made the wizard famous in his death.

---

207. **thereof:** i.e. of the burgonet.
215. **stigmatic:** literally, a branded person, hence one marked with
deformity (i.e. branded by God).

V.ii. Location: Scene continues.
14. **chase:** game.   21. **fast:** unchangeably.
27. **lay:** wager.   **Address thee:** prepare yourself.
28. **La fin ... œuvres:** the end crowns the work.

32. **frames:** makes, produces.
35. **frozen:** i.e. cowardly.   **part:** side.
37. **dedicate:** dedicated.   41. **premised:** preordained.
44. **Particularities:** trifles.   45. **ordain'd:** destined.
47. **advised:** deliberate, wise.
53. **dew to fire.** Dew was supposed to make fire burn more fiercely.
58. **gobbets:** pieces.
59. **As ... did.** In Greek legend, Medea, before fleeing from Colchos
with Jason, hacked her brother Absyrtus into small pieces in order to
delay pursuit by her father.
62. **As ... bear.** In Virgil's *Aeneid* Aeneas carried his aged father
Anchises on his back when he escaped from Troy.
65. **Nothing:** in no respect.
67–69. **underneath ... death:** i.e. by meeting death under the sign of
the Castle Inn Somerset has fulfilled the spirit's prophecy (I.iv.35–37).
69. **wizard:** spirit.

Sword, hold thy temper; heart, be wrathful still: 70
Priests pray for enemies, but princes kill.   [*Exit*.]

Fight. Excursions. Enter KING, QUEEN, *and others*.

Queen.   Away, my lord! you are slow, for shame, away!
King.   Can we outrun the heavens?   Good Margaret, stay.
Queen.   What are you made of?   You'll nor fight nor fly.
Now is it manhood, wisdom, and defense   75
To give the enemy way, and to secure us
By what we can, which can no more but fly.

Alarum afar off.

If you be ta'en, we then should see the bottom
Of all our fortunes; but if we haply scape
(As well we may, if not through your neglect),   80
We shall to London get, where you are lov'd,
And where this breach now in our fortunes made
May readily be stopp'd.

Enter [YOUNG] CLIFFORD.

Y. Clif.   But that my heart's on future mischief set,
I would speak blasphemy ere bid you fly.   85
But fly you must.   Uncurable discomfit
Reigns in the hearts of all our present parts.
Away, for your relief! and we will live
To see their day, and them our fortune give.
Away, my lord, away!   *Exeunt*.   90

[SCENE III]

Alarum. Retreat. Enter YORK, RICHARD, WARWICK,
and Soldiers with Drum and Colors.

York.   Of Salisbury, who can report of him,

---

71 s.d. **Excursions**: sallies, sorties.
73. **outrun**: escape from.   74. **nor . . . nor**: neither . . . nor.
77. **what**: whatever means.   **which**: (we) who.
80. **if not**: if we don't fail to do so.
86. **Uncurable discomfit**: irrevocable defeat.
87. **present parts**: remaining forces.
89. **To . . . give**: i.e. to see a day of victory like theirs and to give them our misfortune.

V.iii. Location: Scene continues.

That winter lion, who in rage forgets
Aged contusions and all brush of time;
And like a gallant in the brow of youth,
Repairs him with occasion?   This happy day   5
Is not itself, nor have we won one foot,
If Salisbury be lost.
Rich.   My noble father,
Three times to-day I holp him to his horse,
Three times bestrid him; thrice I led him off,
Persuaded him from any further act: 10
But still, where danger was, still there I met him,
And like rich hangings in a homely house,
So was his will in his old feeble body.
But noble as he is, look where he comes.

Enter SALISBURY.

Sal.   Now, by my sword, well hast thou fought to-day;   15
By th' mass, so did we all.   I thank you, Richard.
God knows how long it is I have to live,
And it hath pleas'd him that three times to-day
You have defended me from imminent death.
Well, lords, we have not got that which we have: 20
'Tis not enough our foes are this time fled,
Being opposites of such repairing nature.
York.   I know our safety is to follow them,
For, as I hear, the King is fled to London,
To call a present court of parliament.   25
Let us pursue him ere the writs go forth.
What says Lord Warwick? shall we after them?
War.   After them!   Nay, before them, if we can.
Now, by my [faith], lords, 'twas a glorious day.
Saint Albons battle won by famous York   30
Shall be eterniz'd in all age to come.
Sound drum and trumpets, and to London all,
And more such days as these to us befall!   *Exeunt*.

---

2. **winter**: aged.   3. **brush**: attack.
5. **Repairs . . . occasion**: i.e. restores himself with the opportunity of fresh encounters.   8. **holp**: helped.
9. **bestrid him**: i.e. defended him when he was down.
12. **homely**: modest.
22. **opposites . . . nature**: adversaries with such power of recovery.
26. **writs**: royal summons for a meeting of Parliament.
31. **eterniz'd**: immortalized.

NOTE ON THE TEXT

There is only one authoritative text of *2 Henry VI*, that in the First Folio (1623); all later texts are derived primarily from that source. There is also, however, a "bad" quarto, or memorially reported version, derived from essentially the same text (with theatrical cuts) as that printed in F1; it was published in 1594 with the title *The First part of the Contention betwixt the two famous Houses of Yorke and Lancaster*. This text (Q1) was reprinted in 1600 (Q2) and 1619 (Q3). Q3, based on Q1, makes a number of additions and changes which seem to anticipate the F1 text. Although Q1 has no basic authority, it occasionally helps to resolve textual difficulties in F1, and its stage directions (frequently included in the present edition) are especially valuable as giving us

some insight into at least one Elizabethan production of the play.   Recently C. T. Prouty has attempted to revive the old theory that Q1 is an original play upon which Shakespeare based his *2 Henry VI*, but the arguments he advances are not at all convincing.

The copy behind F1, it is generally agreed, was most probably some form of Shakespeare's autograph (or at least a manuscript in which Shakespeare had a considerable share) that had been used as a prompt-book. But in 1957 A. S. Cairncross, in his New Arden edition, extended the possibilities of corruption in the F1 text by arguing that substantial parts of F1 were set up from a copy of Q3 (with occasional use of Q2) corrected from a manuscript of the kind postulated above, and that only where Q copy was hopelessly corrupt or incomplete was recourse had directly to the manuscript by the compositor. If accepted, this theory presents a textual situation apparently similar to that found in *Richard III* and *Lear*: where F1 adopts a reading from a later quarto not found in Q1 (the readings of the later quartos being presumably without manuscript or any other kind of authority), an editor should adopt the reading of Q1. But in *2 Henry VI* (as also in *3 Henry VI*) the status of Q3 is unusual, since it cannot be described as a mere reprint of Q1 and the new readings it affords which link it with F1 may have been introduced by someone familiar with the play as acted. Hence it would be dangerous to apply the textual approach used in *Richard III* and *Lear*, particularly as a number of the unique links between Q3 and F1 present only similar, not identical, readings. The present edition, therefore, retains the readings of the F1 text, but a complete record of the significant links between F1 and Q3 (or Q2) may be found in the Textual Notes (see, for example, I.i.8, 186, I.ii.26–7, 29, 62–7, I.iii.80, II.i.10, 11–2, 14, 26, 50, 81, 108, II.ii.12–52, II.iii.34, 69, III.i.359, III.ii.19, IV.ii.149, IV.iii.6–7, IV.x.42, 83). Whatever view is taken of the exact nature of the copy for F1, it is generally agreed that IV.v and the first six lines of IV.vi were set directly from a slightly corrected copy of one of the quartos, probably Q2. Where only one or two of the three quartos are cited, agreement

of the uncited quarto (or quartos) with the lemma may be assumed.

The Textual Notes generally record the variants in Q1–3 only where they figure in a reading cited in connection with the F1 text. The absence of citation of Q1–3 among the sigla in any entry indicates that the reading of the lemma occurs in a passage which in Q1–3 is either omitted or so differently worded that it offers no recognizable equivalent. Some longer sections of Q1–3, where divergence from the F1 text is most noticeable, may be consulted in the Textual Notes at I.iv.22 s.d., 40 s.d., II.ii.12–52, IV.ii.21–8, 121, IV.vii.56–8, 125, IV.ix.1–22, 23–49, V.ii.1–7, 19–60, 65 s.d., V.iii.1–26.

For further information, see: Madeleine Doran, "*Henry VI, Parts II and III*": *Their Relation to the "Contention" and the "True Tragedy*," University of Iowa Studies (Humanistic), IV (1928); Peter Alexander, *Shakespeare's "Henry VI" and "Richard III"* (Cambridge, 1929); C. T. Prouty, "*The Contention*" *and Shakespeare's "2 Henry VI"* (New Haven, 1954) [for criticisms of Prouty's thesis, see: G. B. Evans, *JEGP*, LIII (1954), 628–37, and J. G. McManaway, "*The Contention* and *2 Henry VI*," *Studies in Language and Literature Presented to Karl Brunner* (1957), pp. 143–54]; W. W. Greg, *The Shakespeare First Folio* (Oxford, 1955); J. D. Wilson, ed., New Cambridge *1–3 Henry VI* (Cambridge, 1952); A. S. Cairncross, ed., New Arden *2 Henry VI* (London, 1957) and *3 Henry VI* (London, 1964).

TEXTUAL NOTES

Title: The Second . . . Sixth] The second Part of Henry the Sixt, with the death of the Good Duke Humfrey. *F1*; The First part of the Contention betwixt the two famous Houses of Yorke and Lancaster, with the death of the good Duke Humphrey: And the banishment and death of the Duke of Suffolke, and the Tragicall end of the proud Cardinall of Winchester, with the notable Rebellion of Iacke Cade: And the Duke of Yorkes first claime vnto the Crowne. *Q1 (title-page)*
Dramatis personae] *subs. as first given in Rowe*
Act-scene division: *none in Q1–3; F1 marks only I.i; other act-scene divisions from Pope and later editors (see first note to each scene); present act-scene arrangement as a whole first established by Steevens*

I.i
Location: *Capell, Theobald*
o.s.d. **Beauford]** Bewford *Q1–3 (throughout, indicating pronunciation); Q1–3 s.d. reads:* Enter at one doore, King Henry the sixt, and Humphrey Duke of Gloster, the Duke of Sommerset, the Duke of Buckingham, Cardinall Bewford, and others. Enter at the other doore, the Duke of Yorke, and the Marquesse of Suffolke, and Queene Margaret, and the Earle of Salisbury and Warwicke.
8 **twenty]** then the *Q1–2*
28 **alder-liefest]** *Pope;* Alder liefest *F1 (in italics)*
34 **wond'ring]** *Theobald;* Wondring, *F1*
37 s.d. **Flourish.]** *placed as in Cairncross; after l. 38, F1;* Sound Trumpets. *Q1–3 (after l. 38)*
43 **Inprimis]** Imprimis *Q1*
50 **It . . . them,]** *Q1–3*
52 **over]** *Q1–3*
52 **father"—]** *Malone (after Q3* fa—*);* father. *F1;* fa. *Q1*
52 s.d. **Duke . . . fall.]** *Q1–3*
57 s.p. **Car.]** *Q1–2;* Win. *F1;* Yorke. *Q3*
57 s.d. **Reads.]** *Capell (subs.)*
58 **duchy]** *Cairncross;* Dutchesse *F1, Q3;* Duches *Q1;* Dutches *Q2*
58 **the county of]** *Cairncross*

74 s.d. **Exeunt]** *F2;* Exit *F1, Q2–3;* Exet *Q1 (Q1 regularly reads* Exet *for Q2–3, F1* Exit; *this variation not hereafter noted)*
74 s.d. **Manent]** *F2;* Manet *F1*
74 s.d. **stayed by Gloucester]** *ed., from Q1–3 s.d.:* and Duke Humphrey staies all the rest.
89 **Council]** *F3;* Counsell *F1*
105 **peroration]** *F2;* preroration *F1*
110 **Anjou,]** *ed.;* Aniou *F1*
132, 139 s.pp. **Glou.]** *Rowe;* Hum. *F1 (occasionally throughout)*
142 **out.]** *Johnson;* out, *F1*
168 **all together]** *Rowe;* altogether *F1*
178 **Protector]** *Q1–3;* Protectors *F1*
179 s.d. **Exeunt]** *Hanmer;* Exit *F1, Q1–3*
186 **o' th']** of *Q1–2;* of the *Q3*
188 **ruffian]** Ruffin *Q1–2*
207 s.d. **aside]** *Alexander (Theobald at beginning of line)*
212 **Main chance]** *Theobald;* Main-chance *F1, Q1–3*
213 s.d. **Exeunt]** *Hanmer;* Exit *F1, Q1–3*
252 **dear-bought]** *hyphen, Theobald*
254 **milk-white rose]** *Q1–3;* Milke-white-Rose *F1*
256 **in]** *Q1–3;* in in *F1*
257 **grapple]** graffle *Q1–2*

I.ii
I.ii] *Capell*
Location: *Theobald*
o.s.d. **Eleanor]** *Rowe;* Elianor *F1 (throughout, except Elinor in l. 41 and III.ii.120);* Ellanor *Q1–3*
1 s.p. **Duch.]** *Capell;* Elia. *F1 (or Elianor, throughout scene);* Elnor. *Q1–3 (their usual form)*
26–7 **twain . . . Cardinal]** two *Q1–2;* twaine, by whom I cannot gesse: / But as I thinke by the Cardinall. What it bodes / God knowes; *Q3*
29 **Edmund Duke of Somerset]** the Cardinall of Winchester *Q1–2*
30 **Pole]** Poule *Q1;* Poole *Q2*
60 s.d. **Exit]** *Q1–3 (subs.);* Ex. *F1*
60 s.d. **with Messenger]** *Capell (subs.)*
62–7 **While . . . pageant.]** But ere it be long, Ile go before them all, / Despight of all that seeke to crosse me thus, *Q1–2;* As long as

Gloster beares this base and humble mind: / Were I a man, and Protector as he is, / I'de reach to'th Crowne, or make some hop headlesse. / And being but a woman, ile not behinde / For playing of my part, in spite of all that seeke to crosse me thus: *Q3*
69 s.d. **Hume]** Hum *Q1–3 (throughout)*
75 **witch]** Witch of Ely *Q1–2 (i.e. of Eie);* witch of Rye *Q3*

I.iii
I.iii] *Capell*
Location: *Hanmer (after Theobald)*
o.s.d. **Peter]** *Theobald*
1 **let's]** let vs *Q1–2;* lets *Q3*
5 s.d. **Enter . . . Queen.]** Enter the Duke of Suffolke with the Queene, and they take him for Duke Humphrey, and giues him their writings. *Q1–3*
13 s.d. **Reading.]** *Rowe*
20 s.d. **Reads.]** *Rowe*
25 s.d. **Giving his petition.]** *Capell*
27 **to]** vnto *Q1–2*
30 **master]** *Warburton;* Mistresse *F1*
31–2 **King . . . usurper.]** *Q1–3 vary this as follows:* King was an vsurer. / Queene. An vsurper thou wouldst say. / Peter. I forsooth an vsurper.
35 **your matter]** this *Q1–2;* this thing *Q3*
36 s.d. **Servant with Peter]** *Capell (Servants)*
39 s.d. **Tear the supplication.]** He teares the papers. *Q1–3*
41 s.p. **Petitioners]** *ed.*
41 s.d. **Exeunt.]** *Q2;* Exit. *F1;* Exet Petitioners. *Q1, Q3*
50 **Pole]** *Q3;* Poole *F1 (frequently throughout), Q2;* Poull *Q1*
80 **She . . . back,]** *om. Q1–2;* She beares a Dukes whole reuennewes on her backe. *Q3*
100 **helm.]** *Rowe;* Helme. Exit. *F1*
100 s.d. **Sound . . . Gloucester.]** *Q1–3 read:* Enter King Henry, and the Duke of Yorke and the Duke of Somerset on both sides of the King, whispering with him, and enter [Then entereth *Q3*] Duke Humphrey, Dame Elnor, the Duke of Buckingham, the Earle of Salsbury, the Earle of Warwicke, and the Cardinall of Winchester.
100 s.d. **Somerset]** *Hanmer*

108 **that;]** *Theobald;* that, *F1*
137 s.d. **The . . . fan.]** *Johnson (subs., after Q1–3* The Queene lets fall her gloue, . . .)*
150 **needs]** can neede *F2*
176 s.d. **Horner . . . guarded]** *Theobald;* Armorer and his Man. *F1,* (the Armourer) *Q1–3*
187 s.p. **Hor.]** *Malone;* Armorer. *F1, Q1–3 (throughout)*
190 s.d. **holding . . . hands]** *Steevens*
210 **doom.]** *following this line Theobald inserts from Q1–3:* King. Then be it so my Lord of Somerset. / We make your grace Regent ouer [ore *Q3*] the French,
214 **man]** my man *F2*

I.iv

I.iv] *Capell*
Location: *Capell*
o.s.d. **Bolingbrook]** *ed. (after Holinshed);* Bullingbrooke *F1 (throughout scene);* Bullenbrooke *Q1–3 (generally throughout)*
11 s.d. **She . . . face.]** *Q1–3*
12 s.d. **Hume following]** *Dyce (subs.); Q1–3 s.d. reads:* She goes vp to the Tower.
13 s.p. **Duch.]** *Capell;* Elianor. *F1 (throughout rest of play);* Elnor. *Q1–3*
16 **silent]** silence *Q1–3*
22 s.d. **Here . . . riseth.]** *Bullenbrooke makes a Cirkle. Q1–3 (before l. 16); after l. 16 Q1–3 read (in place of F1 ll. 17–27):* Wherein the Furies maske in hellish troupes, / Send vp I charge you from Sosetus lake, / The spirit Askalon to come to me, / To pierce the bowels of this Centricke earth, / And hither come in twinkling of an eye, / Askalon, Assenda, Assenda [Ascenda, Ascenda *Q2*]. / It thunders and lightens, and then the spirit riseth vp.
23 **Adsum]** *F2;* Ad sum *F1*
24 s.p. **M. Jord.]** *Rowe;* Witch. *F1*
29 s.d. **Reading . . . paper.]** *Capell*
31 s.d. **As . . . answer.]** *Rowe (subs.)*
32 **Tell me]** *Pope (on the basis of l. 64)*
32 **fate awaits]** *Q2–3;* fates await *F1;* fate awayt *Q1*
34 **betide]** *Q1–3;* befall *F1*
40 s.d. **sinking down again]** *Pelican, from Q1–3:* He sinkes downe againe.; *Q1–3 then add (in place of F1 ll. 39–40):* Bullen. Then downe I say, vnto the damned poule. / Where Pluto in his firie Waggon sits. / Ryding amidst the singde and parched smoakes, / The Rode of Dytas by the Riuer Stykes, / There howle and burne for euer in those flames, / Rise Iordaine rise, and staie thy charming Spels. / Sonnes [Zounds *Q3*], we are betraide.
40 s.d. **Sir . . . Captain]** *ed.*
52 s.d. **Exeunt . . . guarded.]** *Dyce (after Malone);* Exet Elnor aboue. *Q1–3*
54 s.d. **Guard . . . etc.]** *Rowe; Q1–3 s.d. reads:* Exet with them.
62 **te]** *Theobald*
62 **posse]** *F2;* posso *F1 (in italics)*

II.i

II.i] *Pope*
Location: *Pope*
o.s.d. **with . . . fist]** *Q1–3*
10 **hawks do]** Hawke done *Q1;* hawke doe *Q2*
11–2 **They . . . pitch.]** He knows his maister loues to be aloft. *Q1–2;* They know their master sores a Faulcons pitch. *Q3*
13 **'tis]** it is *Q1;* it's *Q3*
14 **That . . . soar.]** That can sore no higher then a Falkons pitch. *Q1–2;* That sores no higher then a bird can soule. *Q3*
26 **do it]** doate *Q1;* dote *Q2;* do't *Q3*
30 **An't like]** And it like *Q1–2;* and t'like *Q3*
37–51 s.dd. **Aside to Cardinal., Aside to Gloucester.]** *Rowe (subs.)*
38 **dar't]** darest *Q1–2*
47 s.p. **Car.]** *Theobald;* line continued to Gloucester, *F1; in Q1–3, which om. ll. 46–9, the first mention of the east side of the grove comes from Gloucester*

50 **God's Mother]** Faith *Q1–2*
51 **Medice, teipsum—]** *Cambridge (comma, Theobald);* Medice teipsum, *F1*
56 s.d. **"A miracle!"]** A miracle, a miracle. *Q1, Q3*
65 s.d. **with music]** *Q1–3*
65 s.d. **Simpcox's . . . following]** *Rowe*
72 **Good fellow]** *Theobald;* Good-fellow *F1*
81 s.p. **Simp.]** Poore man. *Q1–3 (throughout scene)*
81 **and't . . . Grace]** sir *Q1–2;* please your Maiesty *Q3* (*Q3 gives l. 80 to the King*)
85 **good fellow]** *Pope;* good-fellow *F1*
99–101 **Mass . . . life.]** *as verse, Pope; as prose, F1*
106 **Albon]** *F2;* Albones *F1*
108 **Red]** Why red *Q1–2*
125 **mightst]** mightest *Q1*
130 **his]** *Q1–3;* it, *F1*
137 s.d. **one]** *Q1–3*
139 s.d. **A stool brought.]** *Capell (subs.)*
147–8 **I . . . quickly.]** *as prose, Q1 (?), Q2–3; as verse, F1*
156 s.d. **Exeunt . . . etc.]** *Capell;* Exit. *F1;* Exet Mayor. *Q1–3 (after: Mayor.* It shall be done my Lord.)
176 s.d. **Aside to Gloucester]** *Sisson (Rowe after l. 174)*
184 **tainture]** *Rowe;* Taincture *F1*

II.ii

II.ii] *Capell*
Location: *Capell (after Pope)*
11, 18 **Black Prince]** *Q1–3;* Black-Prince *F1*
12–52 **The second . . . king.]** *these genealogical lines appear in a badly confused form in Q1–3, but Q3 makes an attempt, not very successful, to unscramble them and anticipates several details of the F1 version:* The second was Edmund of Langly, / Duke of York. / The third was Lyonell Duke of Clarence. / The fourth was Iohn of Gaunt, / The Duke of Lancaster. / The fifth was Roger Mortemor, Earle of March. / The sixt was sir Thomas of Woodstocke. / William of Winsore was the seuenth and last. / Now, Edward the blacke Prince he died before his father, / and left behinde him Richard, that afterwards was King, Crownde by the name of Richard the second, and he died without an heire. Edmund of Langly Duke of Yorke died, and left behind him two daughters, Anne and Elinor. / Lyonell Duke of Clarence died, and left behinde Alice, Anne, and Elinor, that was after married to my father, and by her I claime the Crowne, as the true heire to Lyonell Duke of Clarence, the third sonne to Edward the third. Now sir. In the time of Richards raigne, Henry of Bullingbrooke, sonne and heire to Iohn of Gaunt, the Duke of Lancanster fourth sonne to Edward the third, he claimde the Crowne, deposde the Merthfull King, and as both you [you both *Q2*] know, in Pomphret Castle harmelesse Richard was shamefully murthered, and so by Richards death came the house of Lancaster vnto the Crowne. / Sals. Sauing your tale my Lord, as I haue heard, in the raigne of Bullenbrooke, the Duke of Yorke did claime the Crowne, and but for Owin Glendor, had bene King. / Yorke. True. But so it fortuned then, by meanes of that mon- / strous rebel Glendor, the noble Duke of York was done to death, and so euer since the heires of Iohn of Gaunt haue possessed the Crowne. But if the issue of the elder should succeed before the is- / sue of the yonger, then am I lawfull heire vnto the kingdome. *Q1–2;* The second was William of Hatfield, / Who dyed young. / The third was Lyonell, Duke of Clarence. / The fourth was Iohn of Gaunt, / The Duke of Lancaster. / The fift was Edmund of Langley, / Duke of Yorke. The sixt was William of Windsore, / Who dyed young. / The

seauenth and last was Sir *Thomas* of *Woodstocke,* Duke of / *Yorke.* / Now *Edward* the blacke Prince dyed before his Father, leauing behinde him two sonnes, *Edward* borne at *Angolesme,* who died young, and *Richard* that was after crowned King, by the name of *Richard* the second, who dyed without an heyre. / *Lyonell* Duke of *Clarence* dyed, and left him one onely daugh- / ter, named *Phillip,* who was married to Edmund Mortimer earle of March and Vlster: and so by her I claime the Crowne, as the true heire to *Lyonell* Duke of *Clarence,* third sonne to Edward the third. Now sir, in time of *Richards* reigne, . . . [*the remaining lines are essentially the same as in Q1–2, except for* putte to / death *for* done to death] *Q3*
21 **Bullingbrook]** *ed.,* Bullingbrooke *F1 (throughout), Q1, Q3;* Bullenbrooke *Q2*
26 **Pomfret]** *Q3·* Pumfret *F1;* Pomphret *Q1–2*
35, 49 **Philippe]** *Hanmer;* Phillip *F1 (so Q3 in l. 35)*
38 **Eleanor]** *Rowe;* Elianor *F1;* Elinor *Q1–2; om. Q3*
41 **Glendower]** *Hanmer;* Glendour *F1, Q3;* Glendor *Q1–2*
46 **son, son.]** *Alexander;* Sonnes Sonne; *F1*

II.iii

II.iii] *Capell*
Location: *Capell*
o.s.d. **the . . . Salisbury]** *Capell*
o.s.d. **Enter . . . Bolingbrook.]** *Theobald (subs.); Q1–3 s.d. reads:* Enter King Henry, and the Queene, Duke Humphrey, the Duke of Suffolke, and the Duke of Buckingham, the Cardinall, and Dame Elnor Cobham, led with the Officers, and then enter to them the Duke of Yorke, and the Earles of Salsbury and Warwicke.
3 **sins]** *Theobald;* sinne *F1*
16 s.d. **Exeunt . . . guarded.]** *Theobald;* Exet some with Elnor. *Q1, Q3,* (exeunt) *Q2*
34 **ere]** erst *Q1–2*
58 s.d. **Horner . . . Peter]** *Malone*
64 **double beer]** *Q1–3;* Double-Beere *F1*
69 **afraid]** affeard *Q1–2*
90 *Following this line Warburton inserts from Q1–3:* as Beuys of South-hampton fell vpon Askapart.
92 s.d. **Alarum.]** *Capell;* Alarmes, *Q1, Q3;* Alarme: *Q2*
92 s.d. **hits . . . and]** *Q1–3*
94 s.d. **He dies.]** *Q1–3*
97 s.d. **He kneels down.]** *Q1–3*

II.iv

II.iv] *Capell*
Location: *Theobald*
16 s.d. **barefoot]** *Q1–3*
16 s.d. **and . . . on,]** *Q1–3*
16 s.d. **Sir John Stanley]** *Theobald*
20 **dost]** doest *Q1–2*
46 **pointing-stock]** *hyphen, Hanmer*
47 **rascal]** rascald *Q1–2*
55 **canst]** can *Q1–2*
69 s.d. **Herald]** Herald of Armes *Q1–3*
73 s.d. **Exit Herald.]** *Q1–3*
86 s.d. **with his Men]** *from Q1–3 s.d.* Exet [exeunt *Q2*] Humphrey and his men.

III.i

III.i] *Pope*
Location: *Steevens (after Theobald, Capell)*
o.s.d. **Enter . . . Then]** *Q1–3 (the Q1–3 s.d. reads:* Enter to the Parlament. Enter two Haralds before, then the Duke of Buckingham and [*Q3 om.* and] the Duke of Suffolke, and then the Duke of Yorke, and the Cardinall of Winchester, and then the King and the [*Q2 om.* the] Queene, and then the Earle of Salisbury, and the Earle of Warwicke.)
46 **life]** *Pope;* Life *F1*
87 s.d. **Aside.]** *Rowe*
174 **traitors']** *Capell;* Traytors *F1*
182 **But]** I but *Q1;* Yea but *Q2*

194 s.d. with . . . Men] *Q1–3*
218 dimm'd] *Rowe (subs.);* dimn'd *F1*
218 eyes] *Pope;* eyes; *F1*
222 traitor,] *Q1, Q3;* Traytor? *F1, Q2*
222 s.d. Exit] *om. in some copies of F1*
222 s.d. with . . . Warwick] *from Q1–3 King, Salsbury, and Warwicke (Buckingham added, Pelican after Cambridge)*
266 Thrice-noble] *hyphen, Theobald*
282 s.d. Post] Messenger *Q1–3*
287 s.d. Exit.] *ed.*
328 I] I wil *Q1–2;* I'le *Q3*
333–4 art . . . death;] *F4 (subs.);* art; . . . death, *F1*
359] *Following this line Q3 inserts:* (For he is like him euery kinde of way), *thus anticipating ll. 372–3 in F1 (lines om. in Q1–3)*
365 caper] *F2;* capre *F1*
382 Humphrey] *F3;* Humfrey, *F1*

III.ii

III.ii] *Capell*
Location: *Cambridge (after Theobald)*
o.s.d. Murderers] *Capell; Q1–3 s.d. reads:* Then the Curtaines being drawne, Duke Humphrey is discoured in his bed, and two men lying on his brest and smothering him in his bed. And then enter the Duke of Suffolke to them.
1 s.p. 1. Mur.] *Capell;* 1. *F1 (throughout scene);* One. *Q1–3*
3 s.p. 2. Mur.] *Capell;* 2. *F1*
14 s.d. Suffolk] *om. Q1–3; F1 re-enters Suffolk here after the Cardinal, since Theobald have adopted the Q1–3 arrangement, which leaves Suffolk on stage (Exet [exeunt Q2] murtherers.) after the Murderers exit)*
20 'gainst] against *Q1–2*
24 nobleman] *Rowe;* Noble man *F1*
26 Meg] *Capell;* Nell *F1 (almost certainly Shakespeare's slip; cf. note below on ll. 79, etc.)*
74 dost] doest *Q1*
75 leper] *F3;* Leaper *F1, Q2–3;* leoper *Q1*
79, 100, 120 Margaret] *Rowe;* Elianor (Elinor *l. 120) F1 (as in l. 26, Shakespeare seems to have confused the names of the Queen and Gloucester's wife)*
80 statuĕ] *Keightley;* Statue *F1*
105 earnest-gaping sight] *Pope;* earnest-gaping-sight *F1*
116 witch] *Theobald;* watch *F1*
121 s.d. Salisbury] *Q1, Q3;* Salsbury *Q2*
135 s.d. Exit . . . Commons.] *Alexander (after Theobald);* Exet Salbury *Q1,* (Salsbury) *Q2,* (Salisbury) *Q3*
146 s.d. with . . . Warwick] *Cambridge (subs., after Rowe); Q1–3 s.d. reads:* Warwicke drawes the curtaines and showes Duke Humphrey in his bed. *(Some eds. suppose that the curtains mentioned here and in the o.s.d. in Q1–3 refer to bed hangings, but the handling of the scene in Q1–3 makes it more likely that the curtains are those of some kind of inner room.)*
174 Look,] *Cambridge;* Looke *F1*
183 s.d. to Cardinal] *ed.*
189 fast by] *Rowe;* fast-by *F1;* hard-by *Q1;* hard by *Q2–3*
196 his talons] your talants *Q1–2;* his talents *Q3*
198 ease] case *Q1*
202 s.d. Exeunt . . . others.] *Capell;* Exet Cardinall. *Q1–3*
223 born] *F3;* borne *F1, Q1–3*
231 s.d. Suffolk and Warwick] *Hanmer; Q1–3 s.d. reads:* Warwicke puls him out. Exet Warwicke and Suffolke, and then all the Commons within, cries, downe with Suffolke, downe with Suffolke. And then enter againe, the Duke of Suffolke and Warwicke, with their weapons drawne. *(see l. 236 s.d.)*
241 s.d. Enter Salisbury] *Q1–3 s.d. reads:* The Commons againe cries, downe with Suffolke, downe with Suffolke. And then

enter from them, the Earle of Salbury [Salisbury *Q2–3*].
242 s.d. To . . . within.] *Kittredge (after Johnson)*
278 s.p. Commons.] *Capell*
288 s.d. Exit Salisbury.] *Q1,* (Salsbury) *Q2–3*
299 s.d. with Warwick] *from Q1–3 s.d.* Exet King and Warwicke, Manet Queene and Suffolke.
327 screech-owls] scrike-oules *Q1–2;* scritch-owles *Q3*
350 Adventure] *F2;* Aduenrure *F1;* Or venture *Q1–2;* Or venter *Q3*
359 thence] *Pope (subs.);* thence, *F1*
366 s.d. Vaux] Vawse *Q1–3 (indicating pronunciation)*
379 s.d. Vaux] *Pope*
408 s.d. She kisseth him.] *Q1–3*
410 worth.] *Theobald;* worth, *F1*
412 s.d. severally] *Rowe; Q1–3 s.dd. read:* Exet Suffolke. *after* death. *and* Exet Queene. *after* me.

III.iii

III.iii] *Capell*
Location: *Theobald*
o.s.d. raving . . . mad] *from Q1–3 s.d.* Enter King and Salsbury, and then the Curtaines be drawne, and the Cardinall is discoured in his bed, rauing and staring as if he were madde. *(note omission of Warwick)*
8 s.p. Car.] *Q1–3;* Beau. *F1*
28 s.d. The Cardinal dies.] *Q1–2;* Car. dies. *Q3*

IV.i

IV.i] *Pope*
Location: *Pope*
o.s.d. Alarum . . . sea.] *ed. (from F1, Q1–3);* Alarum. Fight at Sea. Ordnance goes off. *F1;* Alarmes within, and the chambers be discharged, like as it were a fight at sea. *Q1–3*
o.s.d. a Shipmaster . . . prisoners] *based on Q1–3, plus Rowe; Q1–3 s.d. reads:* And then enter the Captaine of the ship and the Maister, and the Maisters Mate, & the Duke of Suffolke disguised, and others with him, and Water Whickmore [Walter Whickmore *Q2*]. *F1 s.d. reads:* Enter Lieutenant, Suffolke, and others.
3 loud-howling] *hyphen, Capell*
14 Walter Whitmore] Water Whickmore *Q1, Q3 (throughout scene, except Walter in two s.pp. and one non-F1 passage in Q3);* Walter Whickmore *Q2 (throughout rest of scene); Q1, Q3 spelling makes the word-play in l. 35 clear; F1 has Water in s.d. at l. 138, and see l. 115 below*
22 sum!] *White;* summe. *F1*
26 s.d. To Suffolk.] *Rowe*
32 why starts thou?] *Q1–3 give s.d.* He starteth. *after first mention of Whitmore's name in l. 14*
32 What,] *Rowe;* What *F1*
37, 38 Gualtier] Gaulter *Q1–3*
48 . . . I?] *Q1–3*
50 s.p. Suf.] *Q1–3; line continued to Lieutenant in F1, with s.p. Suf. before l. 51*
70 Lieu. Yes . . . Poole?] *Q1–3 (subs., with Q2 spelling Poole, as in last half of line in F1; Q1 reads Poull and Q3 Pole; Q1–3 give the first speech to Cap.; s.p. Lieu. Neilson)*
77 shall] shalt *Q1–3, F2*
84 Sylla, overgorg'd] *Pope;* Sylla ouer-gorg'd, *F1*
85 mother's bleeding] *Rowe;* Mother-bleeding *F1*
93 are] *Rowe;* and *F1*
113 Lieu. Ay . . . soon.] *Q1–3 (spoken by Cap.); first added by Cairncross*
114 s.p. Suf.] *Cairncross*
115] *Following this line F1 reads:* Lieu. Water: W. *followed by l. 116; Cairncross suggests that Lieu. is the s.p. for the*

accidentally omitted l. 113 above and that Water: W. *should be taken as the s.p. for l. 116*
116 s.p. Whit.] *Rowe*
117 Pene] *Malone;* Pine *F1*
118, 142 s.pp. Whit.] *Rowe;* Wal. *F1*
119 daunted] *F3;* danted *F1*
132 s.p. Suf.] *Hanmer; line continued to Lieutenant, F1, with s.p. Suf. before l. 133*
136 Brutus] *Q1–3 (subs.);* Brutsn *F1*
138 s.d. Walter] *Q2;* Water *F1, Q1, Q3*
141 s.d. Exeunt] *Capell;* Exit *F1;* Exet omnes. *Q1, Q3;* exeunt omnes. *Q2*
141 s.d. of Suffolk] *Capell*
147 s.d. Exit . . . body.] *Capell (after Exit. F2)*

IV.ii

IV.ii] *Pope*
Location: *Capell*
o.s.d. George] *Capell; Q1–3 s.d. reads:* Enter two of the Rebels with long staues. *(the s.pp. for these two characters being George. and Nicke.; Holland and Bevis are actors' names)*
o.s.d. with long staves] *Q1–3*
17 say as,] *Capell (subs.);* say, as *F1*
21–8] *Q1–3 offer a larger list of Cade's followers:* Why theres Dicke the Butcher, and Robin the Sadler, and Will that came a wooing to our Nan last Sunday, and Harry and Tom, and Gregory that should haue your Parnill, and a great sort more is come from Rochester, and from Maydstone, and Canterbury, and all the Townes here abouts, and we must all be [be al *Q3*] Lords or squires, assoone as Iacke Cade is King.
30 s.d. with long staves] *from Q1–3 s.d.* Enter Iacke Cade, Dicke Butcher, Robin, Will, Tom, Harry and the rest, with long staues.
33 s.p. Dick.] *Q1–3;* But. *F1 (throughout scene)*
33–62 s.dd. Aside.] *Capell*
35 fall] *F4;* faile *F1*
36–7 princes—command] *Alexander;* Princes. Command *F1;* Proclaime *Q1–3*
38 s.p. Dick.] All. *Q1–3*
40 s.p. Dick.] Nicke. *Q1–2*
44 Lacies] Brases *Q1–2*
45 s.p. Dick.] Will. *Q1–2;* Nicke. *Q3*
47 s.p. Smith.] *Steevens;* Weauer. *F1 (throughout scene);* Robin. *Q1–3*
50 s.p. Dick.] Harry. *Q1–3*
57 s.p. Dick.] George. *Q1–3*
60 s.p. Smith.] *Steevens;* Wea. *F1;* Will. *Q1–3*
80 should . . . parchment] should parchment be made *Q1–2;* parchment should be made *Q3*
84 s.d. one with] *ed. (after F1, Q1–3 s.d. at l. 110);* Enter Will with the Clarke of Chattam.
85 s.p. Smith.] *Steevens;* Weauer. *F1;* Will. *Q1–3*
85 Chartam] Chattam *Q1–3*
90 H'as] *Rowe;* Ha's *F1;* hee has *Q1–3*
110 pen and inkhorn] penny inckehorne *Q2*
110 s.d. Michael] Tom *Q1–3 (Michael's speeches given to Tom in Q1–3)*
120 s.d. Kneels.] *Collier*
121 s.d. Rises.] *Collier*
121 him!] *following this word Theobald inserts from Q1–3:* Is there any more of them that be Knights? / *Tom.* I his brother. / He Knights *Dicke Butcher* [him *Q3 (s.d. after next line)*]. / *Cade.* Then kneele downe Dicke Butcher, / Rise vp sir Dicke Butcher. / Now stand vp the Drumme. *(the final s.d. being part of Cade's speech in Q3)*
136–7 Marry . . . not?] *as verse, Capell (Q1–3); as prose, F1*
136 this:] *Theobald (subs.);* this *F1*
147–50 Nay . . . not.] *Q1–3 give these lines to Nicke.*
149 testify it] testifie *Q1–2*

151-2 And . . . what?] *as verse, Pope; as prose, F1*
155 s.d. Aside.] *Capell*
164 Fellow kings] *Capell;* Fellow-Kings *F1*
172 counsellor] *Pope;* Councellour *F1*
181 s.d. with . . . Men] *ed. (after Steevens) from Q1-3* Stafford and his men
190 s.d. Exeunt.] *Q2 (*exeunt omnes.*);* Exet omnes. *Q1, Q3*

IV.iii

IV.iii] *Capell*
Location: *ed. (after Wilson)*
2 s.p. Dick.] *Rowe;* But. *F1 (throughout scene)*
6-7 and thou] Thou *Q1-2*
11-2 s.d. putting . . . armor] *Collier*

IV.iv

IV.iv] *Pope*
Location: *Capell*
s.d. with a supplication] reading of a Letter *Q1-3 (Q1-3 s.d. adds* with others. *after* Lord Say)
19 have] *Q1-3;* huae *F1*
49 s.p. 2. Mess.] *Rowe;* Mess. *F1*
58 be] *F2*

IV.v

IV.v] *Pope*
Location: *Capell (after Pope)*
o.s.d. two or three] three or foure *Q1-3*
2-5 No . . . rebels.] *as prose, Pope; as verse, F1, Q1-3*

IV.vi

IV.vi] *Capell*
Location: *ed. (after Theobald)*
s.d. staff] sword *Q1-3*
1-6 Now . . . Mortimer.] *as prose, Pope; as verse, F1, Q1-3*
9 s.p. Smith.] *Rowe (Weav.);* But. *F1*
13-5 Come . . . away.] *as prose, Pope; as verse, F1, Q1-3*

IV.vii

IV.vii] *Capell*
Location: *Theobald*
2 Court] the Court *Q1-2*
3, 6 s.pp. Dick.] *Q1-3 (second speech given earlier to Cade);* Hut. *and* But. *F1*
8, 16 s.pp. Holland.] *Cambridge;* Iohn. *F1;* Dicke. *Q1-3 (om. second speech)*
8, 11, 16 s.dd. Aside.] *Capell*
11 s.p. Smith.] George. *Q1-3*
16-7 Then . . . out.] *as prose, Pope; as verse, F1*
19 s.d. Messenger.] George. *Q1-3*
23 s.d. Bevis] *Steevens*
25 serge] *Rowe;* Surge *F1;* George *Q1-3*
40 abominable] *Q2;* abhominable *F1, Q1, Q3*
47 dost] doest *Q1*
56-8 Nothing . . . Latin.] *Q1-3 read:* Nothing but bona, terra [terra bona *Q2*]. / *Cade.* Bonum terum, sounds [zwounds *Q3*] whats that? / *Dicke.* He speakes French. / *Will.* No tis Dutch. / *Nicke.* No tis outtalian [Outalian *Q3*], I know it well inough.
59 where] *F3;* wher'e *F1*
69-70 hands . . . you?] *hands? / Kent to maintaine, . . . you, F1*
90 caudle] *F4;* Candle *F1*
105 s.d. Aside.] *Capell*
109 strike off] chop of *Q1-2* choppe off *Q3*
119 s.d. Exeunt . . . Say.] *Hanmer*
125] *Following the speech that ends with this line, Q1-3 have a scene fragment not found in F1:* Enter Robin. / *Robin.* O Captaine, London bridge is a fire. / *Cade.* Runne to Billingsgate, and fetch pitch and flaxe and squench [quench *Q3*] it. / Enter *Dicke* and a Sargiant. / *Sargiant.* Iustice, iustice, I pray you sir, let me haue iustice of this fellow here. / *Cade.* Why what has he done? / *Sarg.* Alasse sir he has rauisht my wife. / *Dicke.* Why my Lord he would haue rested me, / And I went and entred my Action in his wiues paper house. / *Cade.* Dicke follow thy sute in her common place, / You horson villaine, you are a Sargiant, [sergeant, youle *Q2-3*] / Take any man by the throate for twelue pence, / And rest a man when hees [he is *Q3*] at dinner, / And haue him to prison ere the meate be out of his [on's *Q3*] mouth. / Go Dicke take him hence, cut [and cut *Q3*] out his toong for cogging, / Hough him for running, and to conclude, / Braue him with his owne mace. / *Exet with the Sargiant.*
126 s.p. Dick.] Nicke. *Q1-3*
129 s.d. of . . . poles] *from Q1-3 s.d.* Enter two with the Lord Sayes head, and sir Iames Cromers, vpon two poles.
130-6 But . . . Away!] *as prose, Theobald (last two-and-a-half lines prose, Q1-3); as verse, F1*
136 s.d. Exeunt.] *Rowe;* Exit *F1*

IV.viii

IV.viii] *Capell*
Location: *Theobald*
1 Magnus'] *Theobald;* Magnes *F1*
3-5 What . . . kill?] *as prose, Capell; as verse, F1*
5 s.d. old Clifford] Lord Clifford the Earle of Cumberland *Q1-3*
5 s.d. attended] *Theobald*
13 rebel] *Singer (after Q1-3* Traitor*);* rabble *F1*
19] *At the equivalent of this point Q1-3 insert s.d.:* They forsake Cade.
24-5 White Hart] *F4 (subs.);* White-heart *F1*
33] *At the equivalent of this point Q1-3 insert s.d.:* They runne to Cade againe.
43 o'er seas] *F3;* ore-seas *F1*
55 s.d. Aside.] *Dyce*
59 sword] staffe *Q1-3*
64 s.d. He . . . away.] *ed., after Q1-3 s.d.* He runs through them with his staffe, and flies away. *(but cf. IV.vi o.s.d. in F1, Q1-3)*

IV.ix

IV.ix] *Capell*
Location: *Theobald (subs.)*
1-22] *Q1-3 offer an essentially different version of these lines (see below, ll. 23-49, for the remainder of the scene in Q1-3):* King. Lord Somerset, what newes here [heare *Q2-3*] you of the Rebell Cade? / *Som.* This, my gratious Lord, that the Lord Say is don to death, / And the Citie is almost sackt. / *King.* Gods will be done, for as he hath decreede, so must it [it must *Q2*] be: / And be it [it *om. Q3*] as he please, to stop the pride of those rebellious men. / *Queene.* Had the noble Duke of Suffolke bene aliue, / The Rebell Cade had bene supprest ere this, [*cf. IV.iv.41-2*] / And all the rest that do take part with him. / Enter the Duke of Buckingham and *Clifford*, with the Rebels, with halters about their necks. / *Cliff.* Long liue King Henry, Englands lawfull King, / Loe here my Lord, these Rebels are subdude, / And offer their liues before your highnesse feete. / *King.* But tell me Clifford, is there [their *Q2-3*] Captaine here. / *Cliff.* No, my gratious Lord, he is fled away, but proclamations are sent forth, that he that can bring his head, shall haue a thou- / sand crownes. But may it please your Maiestie, to pardon these their faults, that by that [these *Q3*] traitors meanes were thus misled. / *King.* Stand vp you simple men, and giue God praise, / For you did take in hand you know not what, / And go in peace obedient to your King, / And liue as subiects, and you shall not want, / Whilst Henry liues, and weares the English Crowne. / *All.* God saue the King, God saue the King.
6 s.d. old] *Capell*
9 s.d. below] *Capell*

23-49 Mess. Please . . . reign.] *Q1-3 omit the announcement of York's return with an army and substitute the following lines:* King. Come let vs hast to London now with speed, / That solemne prosessions may be sung, / In laud and honour of the God of heauen, / And triumphs of this happie victorie.
33 calm'd] *F4;* calme *F1*

IV.x

IV.x] *Steevens*
Location: *Capell (after Pope)*
15 s.d. He . . . them.] *Q1-3 (see second note below)*
15 s.d. Iden] Eyden *Q1-3 (indicates pronunciation)*
15 s.d. followed . . . Servants] *ed. (after Steevens); Q1-3 s.d. reads:* Enter Iacke Cade at one doore, and at the other, maister Alexander Eyden and his men, and Jack Cade lies downe picking of hearbes and eating them. *(Q1-3 begin the scene at this point)*
20 waning] *Rowe;* warning *F1*
24 s.d. Aside.] *Dyce*
26 Ah] *F3;* A *F1;* Stand *Q1-3*
40 and if I] and I *Q1-2;* if do *Q3*
42 shall ne'er] neuer shall *Q1-2;* shall neuer *Q3*
42 stands] doth stand *Q1-2*
45 steadfast-gazing] *hyphen, Capell*
57 burly-bon'd] *hyphen, Q1, Q3*
58 God] *Q1-2;* Ioue *F1; om. Q3*
59 s.d. and . . . down] *Q1-3*
83 to the King] *om. Q1;* with me *Q2*
84 s.d. dragging . . . Servants] *Dyce (subs.)*

V.i

V.i] *Pope*
Location: *ed. (after Capell); eds. usually read* Fields between Dartford and Blackheath. *following Malone, which is historically accurate but ignores the obvious continuity between Scenes i and ii*
11 flow'r-de-luce] *ed. (after F3);* Fleure-de-Luce *F1*
23 s.d. Aside.] *Rowe*
47 s.d. Exeunt Soldiers.] *Q2;* Exet souldiers. *Q1, Q3*
55] *Following this line Q1-3 read:* But see, his grace is comming to meete with vs. *(a line which clarifies the stage business here)*
78 s.d. He kneels.] *Johnson*
82 s.d. Rises.] *Collier MS*
109 these] *Theobald;* thee *F1*
111 sons] *Q1-3;* sonne *F1*
111 bail] *Q1-3;* bale *F1*
111 s.d. Exit Attendant.] *Capell*
113 for] *F2;* of *F1*
116 s.d. Exit Buckingham.] *Capell*
121 s.d. Plantagenet . . . door] *from Q1-3 s.d.:* Enter the Duke of Yorkes sonnes, Edward the Earle of March, and crook-backe Richard, at the one doore, with Drumme and soldiers, and at the other doore, enter Clifford and his sonne, with Drumme and souldiers, and Clifford kneeles to Henry, and speakes.
122 s.d. and . . . door] *Q1-3 (subs.; see preceding note)*
124 s.d. Kneels.] *Johnson (after Q1-3)*
136 arrested] *Q1-3;* arrested *F1*
147 s.d. with . . . Soldiers] *from Q1-3 s.d.* Enter at one doore, the Earles [Earle *Q2*] of Salsbury and Warwicke, with Drumme and souldiers. And at the other [other *Q3*] doore, the Duke of Buckingham, with Drumme and souldiers.
153 suffer'd,] *Vaughan conj.;* suffer'd *F1*
172 dost] *F4;* doest *F1*
193] *Following this line Cairncross inserts from Q1-3:* Both thou and they, shall curse this fatall houre.
194 or] *Rowe;* and *F1*
195 s.p. Clif.] *Malone;* Old Clif. *F1 (throughout rest of scene)*

201 household] *Q1–3*; housed *F1*
207 to] *Q1–3*; io *F1*; so *F2*
213 Fie! charity,] *Capell*; Fɪe, Charitie *F1, Q1–3*
216 s.d. severally] *Theobald*

V.ii

V.ii] *Steevens*
Location: *ed. (after Wilson)*
o.s.d. **Alarums . . . battle.]** *Q1–3* (Alarmes)
1–7 Clifford . . . arms.] *Following an almost identical version of these lines, Q1–3 add:* Clifford speakes within. / Warwicke stand still, and view the way that Clifford hewes with / his murthering Curtelaxe, through the fainting troopes to finde / thee out. / Warwicke stand still, and stir not till I come.
8 How] *Johnson; War.* How *F1 (repeated s.p.)*
9 deadly-handed] *hyphen, Pope*
12 lov'd] *Q1–3;* loued *F1*
12 s.d. old] *Dyce*
19–60 What . . . fame.] *Q1–3 offer an essentially different version of these lines:* Yorke. Now Clifford, since we are singled here alone, / Be this the day of doome to one of vs, / For now my heart hath sworne immortall hate / To thee and all the house of Lancaster. / Cliffood. And here I stand, and pitch my foot to thine, / Vowing neuer to stir, till thou or I be slaine. / For neuer shall my heart be safe at rest, / Till I haue spoyld the hatefull house of Yorke. / Alarmes, and they fight, and Yorke kils Clifford. / Yorke. Now Lancaster sit sure, thy sinowes [sinewes *Q2–3*] shrinke, / Come fearefull Henry grouelling on thy face, / Yeeld vp thy Crowne vnto the Prince of Yorke. / Exet Yorke. / Alarmes, then enter yoong Clifford alone, / Yoong Clifford. Father of Comberland, / Where may I [I may *Q3*] seeke my aged father forth? / O! [Oh *Q3*] dismall sight, see where he breathlesse lies, / All smeard and weltred in his luke-warme blood, / Ah,

aged pillar of all Comberlands true house, / Sweete father, to thy murthred ghoast I sweare, / Immortall hate vnto the house of Yorke, / Nor neuer shall I sleepe secure one night, / Till I haue furiously reuengde thy death, / And left not one of them to breath on earth.
27 s.d. They . . . falls.] *Capell; Q1–3 s.d. reads:* Alarmes, and they fight, and Yorke kils Clifford.
28 œuvres] *F2;* eumenes *F1*
28 s.d. Dies.] *F2*
30 s.d. Exit.] *Q1–3*
31 confusion!] *Pope (after Rowe);* Confusion *F1*
40 s.d. Sees . . . father.] *Theobald (subs.)*
52 babes. Tears virginal] *Pope (subs.);* Babes, Teares Virginall, *F1*
59 Absyrtus] *Theobald;* Absirtis *F1*
60 s.d. He . . . back.] *Q1–3*
65 s.d. Exit . . . father.] *Pope (after Q1–3 s.d.* Exet yoong Clifford with his father.)*; following the equivalent of F1 ll. 61–5, Q1–3 add:* But staie, heres one of them, / To whom my soule hath sworne immortall hate. / Enter Richard, and then Clifford laies downe his father, / fights with him, and Richard flies away againe. / Out crooktbacke [crook'd-backe *Q3*] villaine, get thee from my sight, / But I will after thee, and once againe / When I haue borne my father to his Tent, / Ile trie my fortune better with thee yet [*Q2 om.* yet]. / Exet yoong Clifford with his father. / Alarmes againe, and then enter three or foure, bearing the Duke / of Buckingham wounded to his Tent.
65 s.d. Somerset . . . Inn] *from Q1–3 s.d.* Alarmes to the battaile, and then enter the Duke of Somerset and Richard fighting, and [*om. Q2*] Richard kils him vnder the signe of the Castle in saint Albones.
66 there;] there, and breathe thy last. *Q1–2;* there, and tumble in thy blood, *Q3*
71 s.d. Exit.] *Theobald*

83 s.d. Young] *Capell*
84 s.p. Y. Clif.] *Capell;* Clif. *F1*

V.iii

V.iii] *Steevens*
Location: *ed. (after Wilson)*
o.s.d. **Alarum. . . . Colors.]** Alarmes, and then a flourish, and enter the Duke of Yorke and Richard [Yorke, Edward, and Richard *Q3*]. *Q1–3*
1–26] *Q1–3 offer an essentially different version of these lines:* Yorke. How now boys, fortunate this fight hath bene, / I hope to vs and ours, for Englands good, / And our great honour, that so long we lost, / Whilst faint-heart Henry did vsurpe our rights: / But did you see old Salsbury, since we / With bloodie mindes did buckle with the foe, / I would not for the losse of this right hand, / That ought but well betide that good old man. / Rich. My Lord, I saw him in the thickest throng, / Charging his Lance with his old weary armes, / And thrise I saw him beaten from his horse, / And thrise this hand did set him vp againe, / And still he fought with courage gainst his foes, / The boldest sprited [spirited *Q3*] man that ere mine eyes beheld. / Enter Salsbury and Warwicke. / Edward. See noble father, where they both do come, / The onely props vnto the house of Yorke. / Sals. Well hast thou fought this day, thou valiant Duke, / And thou braue bud of Yorkes encreasing house, / The small remainder of my weary life, / I hold for thee, for with thy warlike arme, / Three times this day thou hast preseru'd my life. / Yorke. What say you Lords, the King is fled to London? / There as I here [heare *Q2,* heere *Q3*] to hold a Parlament [Parliament *Q3*].
1 Of] *Old Q1–3*
29 faith] *Q1–3;* hand *F1*
33 s.d. Exeunt.] Exeunt. / FINIS. *F1;* Exet [exeunt *Q2*] omnes. / FINIS. *Q1–3*

The "fearful porpentine." From Edward Topsell, *The History of Four-footed Beasts* (1607). Although the "sharp-quill'd porpentine" (i.e. porcupine) is mentioned in *2 Henry VI* (III.i.363), Shakespeare's most famous reference to this prickly rodent occurs in *Hamlet* (I.v.17–20): "Make . . . each particular hair to stand an end, / Like quills upon the fearful porpentine." When alarmed ("fearful"), the porpentine erected its quills and, according to the belief of the time, shot them at its enemy. (*By permission of the Harvard College Library*)

The Third Part of Henry the Sixth

[DRAMATIS PERSONAE

KING HENRY THE SIXTH
EDWARD, *Prince of Wales, his son*
LEWIS THE ELEVENTH, *King of France*
DUKE OF SOMERSET
DUKE OF EXETER
EARL OF OXFORD
EARL OF NORTHUMBERLAND
EARL OF WESTMERLAND
LORD CLIFFORD
RICHARD PLANTAGENET, *Duke of York*
EDWARD, *Earl of March, afterwards* KING
  EDWARD IV
EDMUND, *Earl of Rutland*
GEORGE, *afterwards Duke of Clarence* } *his sons*
RICHARD, *afterwards Duke of Gloucester*
DUKE OF NORFOLK
MARQUESS OF MONTAGUE
EARL OF WARWICK
EARL OF PEMBROKE
LORD HASTINGS
LORD STAFFORD

SIR JOHN MORTIMER }
SIR HUGH MORTIMER } *uncles to the Duke of York*
HENRY, *Earl of Richmond, a youth*
LORD RIVERS, *brother to Lady Grey*
SIR WILLIAM STANLEY
SIR JOHN MONTGOMERY
SIR JOHN SOMERVILE
TUTOR, *to Rutland*
MAYOR OF YORK, MAYOR OF COVENTRY
LIEUTENANT OF THE TOWER
NOBLEMAN
Two KEEPERS
HUNTSMAN
SON *that has killed his father*
FATHER *that has killed his son*

QUEEN MARGARET
LADY GREY, *afterwards Queen to Edward IV*
BONA, *sister to the French Queen*

SOLDIERS, ATTENDANTS, ALDERMEN, MESSENGERS,
  WATCHMEN, *etc.*

SCENE: *England and France*]

ACT I, SCENE I

Alarum. Enter [RICHARD] PLANTAGENET [THE DUKE
OF YORK], EDWARD, RICHARD, NORFOLK, MON-
TAGUE, WARWICK, [*with Drum*] *and Soldiers,* [*with
white roses in their hats*].

War. I wonder how the King escap'd our hands.
York. While we pursu'd the horsemen of the north,
He slily stole away and left his men;
Whereat the great Lord of Northumberland,
Whose warlike ears could never brook retreat, 5
Cheer'd up the drooping army, and himself,
Lord Clifford, and Lord Stafford, all abreast,

Charg'd our main battle's front; and breaking in,
Were by the swords of common soldiers slain.
  Edw. Lord Stafford's father, Duke of Buckingham,
Is either slain or wounded dangerous; 11
I cleft his beaver with a downright blow.
That this is true, father, behold his blood.
  Mont. And, brother, here's the Earl of Wiltshire's
    blood,
Whom I encount'red as the battles join'd. 15
  Rich. Speak thou for me and tell them what I did.
    [*Showing the Duke of Somerset's head.*]
  York. Richard hath best deserv'd of all my sons.
But is your Grace dead, my Lord of Somerset?
  Norf. Such hope have all the line of John of Gaunt!
  Rich. Thus do I hope to shake King Henry's head.
  War. And so do I, victorious prince of York. 21

---

*Words and passages enclosed in square brackets in the text above are
either emendations of the copy-text or additions to it. The Textual Notes
immediately following the play cite the earliest authority for every such
change or insertion and supply the reading of the copy-text wherever it is
emended in this edition.*

I.i. Location: London. The Parliament House.
o.s.d. Alarum: call to arms.   Drum: drummer.
1. I . . . hands. Actually, Henry VI, slightly wounded, was captured
by the Yorkists after the first battle of St. Albans (1455).
5. brook: endure.   retreat: trumpet call for withdrawal of forces.
7–9. Clifford . . . slain. In *2 Henry VI* (V.ii) Clifford is killed by York,
a fact alluded to several times in the present play.

8. main battle: main body of the army.
12. beaver: here, helmet. The word usually refers to the face-guard
or visor of a helmet.
14. brother. Actually, John Neville, Marquis of Montague, was
Warwick's brother and York's nephew. He did not secure his title
until 1461, several years after the events represented in this scene.
17. Richard . . . sons. Actually, Richard was three years old when
the first battle of St. Albans was fought in 1455.

3 Henry VI
I.i

Before I see thee seated in that throne
Which now the house of Lancaster usurps,
I vow by heaven these eyes shall never close.
This is the palace of the fearful king,   25
And this the regal seat. Possess it, York,
For this is thine and not King Henry's heirs'.
  York. Assist me then, sweet Warwick, and I will,
For hither we have broken in by force.
  Norf. We'll all assist you; he that flies shall die.
  York. Thanks, gentle Norfolk. Stay by me, my
    lords,   31
And, soldiers, stay and lodge by me this night.
                                             They go up.
  War. And when the King comes, offer him no
    violence,
Unless he seek to thrust you out perforce.
  York. The Queen this day here holds her parlia-
    ment,   35
But little thinks we shall be of her council.
By words or blows here let us win our right.
  Rich. Arm'd as we are, let's stay within this house.
  War. The bloody parliament shall this be call'd,
Unless Plantagenet, Duke of York, be king,   40
And bashful Henry depos'd, whose cowardice
Hath made us by-words to our enemies.
  York. Then leave me not, my lords, be resolute,
I mean to take possession of my right.
  War. Neither the King, nor he that loves him best,
The proudest he that holds up Lancaster,   46
Dares stir a wing if Warwick shake his bells.
I'll plant Plantagenet, root him up who dares.
Resolve thee, Richard, claim the English crown.
                               [*York takes the throne.*]

Flourish. Enter KING HENRY, CLIFFORD, NORTH-
UMBERLAND, WESTMERLAND, EXETER, *and the rest,*
[*with red roses in their hats*].

  K. Hen. My lords, look where the sturdy rebel
    sits,   50
Even in the chair of state. Belike he means,
Back'd by the power of Warwick, that false peer,
To aspire unto the crown and reign as king.
Earl of Northumberland, he slew thy father,
And thine, Lord Clifford, and you both have vow'd
    revenge   55
On him, his sons, his favorites, and his friends.
  North. If I be not, heavens be reveng'd on me!
  Clif. The hope thereof makes Clifford mourn in
    steel.
  West. What, shall we suffer this? Let's pluck him
    down.
My heart for anger burns, I cannot brook it.   60
  K. Hen. Be patient, gentle Earl of Westmerland.
  Clif. Patience is for poltroons, such as he.
He durst not sit there, had your father liv'd.

My gracious lord, here in the parliament
Let us assail the family of York.   65
  North. Well hast thou spoken, cousin, be it so.
  K. Hen. Ah, know you not the city favors them,
And they have troops of soldiers at their beck?
  [*Exe.*] But when the Duke is slain, they'll quickly
    fly.
  K. Hen. Far be the thought of this from Henry's
    heart,   70
To make a shambles of the parliament house!
Cousin of Exeter, frowns, words, and threats
Shall be the war that Henry means to use.
Thou factious Duke of York, descend my throne,
And kneel for grace and mercy at my feet: 75
I am thy sovereign.
  York.   I am thine.
  Exe. For shame, come down. He made thee Duke
    of York.
  York. It was my inheritance, as the earldom was.
  Exe. Thy father was a traitor to the crown.
  War. Exeter, thou art a traitor to the crown,   80
In following this usurping Henry.
  Clif. Whom should he follow but his natural king?
  War. True, Clifford, that's Richard Duke of York.
  K. Hen. And shall I stand, and thou sit in my
    throne?
  York. It must and shall be so. Content thyself.   85
  War. Be Duke of Lancaster, let him be King.
  West. He is both King and Duke of Lancaster,
And that the Lord of Westmerland shall maintain.
  War. And Warwick shall disprove it. You forget
That we are those which chas'd you from the field,   90
And slew your fathers, and with colors spread
March'd through the city to the palace gates.
  North. Yes, Warwick, I remember it to my grief,
And by his soul, thou and thy house shall rue it.
  West. Plantagenet, of thee and these thy sons,   95
Thy kinsmen and thy friends, I'll have more lives
Than drops of blood were in my father's veins.
  Clif. Urge it no more, lest that, in stead of words,
I send thee, Warwick, such a messenger
As shall revenge his death before I stir.   100
  War. Poor Clifford, how I scorn his worthless
    threats!
  York. Will you we show our title to the crown?
If not, our swords shall plead it in the field.
  K. Hen. What title hast thou, traitor, to the crown?
[Thy] father was, as thou art, Duke of York,   105
Thy grandfather, Roger Mortimer, Earl of March:
I am the son of Henry the Fift,
Who made the Dolphin and the French to stoop,
And seiz'd upon their towns and provinces.   109
  War. Talk not of France, sith thou hast lost it all.

---

25. **fearful:** full of fears.
32 s.d. **They go up.** The "chair of state" (line 51) is elevated, prob-ably on a platform.   34. **perforce:** by force.
42. **by-words:** objects of derision.   46. **holds up:** supports.
47. **shake his bells:** i.e. like a falcon with bells attached to its legs.
49 s.d. **Flourish:** trumpet fanfare.
57. **be not:** i.e. be not revenged.
58. **in steel:** i.e. armed, instead of in conventional mourning clothes.

67. **city:** i.e. London, which was sympathetic to the Yorkists.
74. **factious:** rebellious.
78. **earldom:** i.e. the earldom of March, which York inherited from his mother and through which he claimed the throne. See *2 Henry VI*, II.ii.9–52.
79. **Thy . . . crown.** Richard, Earl of Cambridge, was executed for treason by Henry V. See *Henry V*, II.ii.   91. **colors:** flags.
105. **Thy . . . York.** Actually, York inherited the title from his father's elder brother, Edward, second Duke of York, who fell at Agincourt.
108. **Dolphin:** i.e. the Dauphin Charles, who succeeded his father as King of France in 1422, a few months after Henry V's death.
110. **sith:** since.

K. Hen. The Lord Protector lost it, and not I;
When I was crown'd I was but nine months old.

Rich. You are old enough now, and yet methinks
you lose.

Father, tear the crown from the usurper's head.

Edw. Sweet father, do so, set it on your head. 115

Mont. Good brother, as thou lov'st and honorest
arms,
Let's fight it out, and not stand cavilling thus.

Rich. Sound drums and trumpets, and the King will
fly.

York. Sons, peace!

K. Hen. Peace thou! and give King Henry leave to
speak. 120

War. Plantagenet shall speak first. Hear him,
lords,
And be you silent and attentive too,
For he that interrupts him shall not live.

K. Hen. Think'st thou that I will leave my kingly
throne,
Wherein my grandsire and my father sat? 125
No; first shall war unpeople this my realm;
Ay, and their colors, often borne in France,
And now in England to our heart's great sorrow,
Shall be my winding-sheet. Why faint you, lords?
My title's good, and better far than his. 130

War. Prove it, Henry, and thou shalt be King.

K. Henry. Henry the Fourth by conquest got the
crown.

York. 'Twas by rebellion against his king.

K. Hen. [*Aside.*] I know not what to say, my
title's weak.—
Tell me, may not a king adopt an heir? 135

York. What then?

K. Hen. And if he may, then am I lawful king;
For Richard, in the view of many lords,
Resign'd the crown to Henry the Fourth,
Whose heir my father was, and I am his. 140

York. He rose against him, being his sovereign,
And made him to resign his crown perforce.

War. Suppose, my lords, he did it unconstrain'd,
Think you 'twere prejudicial to his crown?

Exe. No; for he could not so resign his crown 145
But that the next heir should succeed and reign.

K. Hen. Art thou against us, Duke of Exeter?

Exe. His is the right, and therefore pardon me.

York. Why whisper you, my lords, and answer
not?

Exe. My conscience tells me he is lawful king. 150

K. Hen. [*Aside.*] All will revolt from me and turn
to him.

North. Plantagenet, for all the claim thou lay'st,
Think not that Henry shall be so depos'd.

War. Depos'd he shall be, in despite of all.

North. Thou art deceiv'd. 'Tis not thy southern
power 155

111. **Lord Protector:** i.e. Humphrey, Duke of Gloucester, whose
downfall is treated in *2 Henry VI.*
129. **faint:** grow fainthearted.   137. **And if:** if.
139. **Resign'd the crown.** For Shakespeare's account of Richard II's
deposition see *Richard II*, IV.i.
141. **him, being:** i.e. Richard, who was.
144. **his crown:** i.e. his legal claim to the crown.
154. **despite:** spite.   155. **deceiv'd:** mistaken.

Of Essex, Norfolk, Suffolk, nor of Kent,
Which makes thee thus presumptuous and proud,
Can set the Duke up in despite of me.

Clif. King Henry, be thy title right or wrong,
Lord Clifford vows to fight in thy defense. 160
May that ground gape, and swallow me alive,
Where I shall kneel to him that slew my father!

K. Hen. O Clifford, how thy words revive my
heart!

York. Henry of Lancaster, resign thy crown.
What mutter you, or what conspire you, lords? 165

War. Do right unto this princely Duke of York,
Or I will fill the house with armed men,
And over the chair of state, where now he sits,
Write up his title with usurping blood.

> *He stamps with his foot, and the*
> *Soldiers show themselves.*

K. Hen. My Lord of Warwick, hear but one
word: 170
Let me for this my life-time reign as king.

York. Confirm the crown to me and to mine heirs,
And thou shalt reign in quiet while thou liv'st.

K. Hen. I am content: Richard Plantagenet,
Enjoy the kingdom after my decease. 175

Clif. What wrong is this unto the Prince your son!

War. What good is this to England and himself!

West. Base, fearful, and despairing Henry!

Clif. How hast thou injur'd both thyself and us!

West. I cannot stay to hear these articles. 180

North. Nor I.

Clif. Come, cousin, let us tell the Queen these
news.

West. Farewell, faint-hearted and degenerate king,
In whose cold blood no spark of honor bides. [*Exit.*]

North. Be thou a prey unto the house of York,
And die in bands for this unmanly deed! [*Exit.*] 186

Clif. In dreadful war mayst thou be overcome,
Or live in peace abandon'd and despis'd! [*Exit.*]

War. Turn this way, Henry, and regard them not.

Exe. They seek revenge, and therefore will not
yield. 190

K. Hen. Ah, Exeter!

War.   Why should you sigh, my lord?

K. Hen. Not for myself, Lord Warwick, but my
son,
Whom I unnaturally shall disinherit.
But be it as it may. [*To York.*] I here entail
The crown to thee and to thine heirs for ever, 195
Conditionally that here thou take an oath
To cease this civil war, and whilst I live
To honor me as thy king and sovereign,
And neither by treason nor hostility
To seek to put me down and reign thyself. 200

York. This oath I willingly take and will perform.

War. Long live King Henry! Plantagenet, embrace him.

K. Hen. And long live thou, and these thy forward
sons! 203

York. Now York and Lancaster are reconcil'd.

180. **articles:** terms of agreement.   186. **bands:** bonds.
203. **forward:** precocious.

3 Henry VI
I.i

Exe.   Accurs'd be he that seeks to make them foes!
                                Sennet. Here they come down.
York.   Farewell, my gracious lord, I'll to my castle.
                    [*Exeunt York and his sons with Soldiers.*]
War.   And I'll keep London with my soldiers.
                                        [*Exit with Soldiers.*]
Norf.   And I to Norfolk with my followers.   208
                                        [*Exit with Soldiers.*]
Mont.   And I unto the sea, from whence I came.
                                        [*Exit with Soldiers.*]
K. Hen.   And I with grief and sorrow to the court.

Enter the QUEEN [MARGARET *and* PRINCE EDWARD].

Exe.   Here comes the Queen, whose looks bewray
       her anger.   211
I'll steal away.
K. Hen.   Exeter, so will I.
Q. Mar.   Nay, go not from me, I will follow thee.
K. Hen.   Be patient, gentle queen, and I will stay.
Q. Mar.   Who can be patient in such extremes?
Ah, wretched man, would I had died a maid   216
And never seen thee, never borne thee son,
Seeing thou hast prov'd so unnatural a father!
Hath he deserv'd to lose his birthright thus?
Hadst thou but lov'd him half so well as I,   220
Or felt that pain which I did for him once,
Or nourish'd him as I did with my blood,
Thou wouldst have left thy dearest heart-blood there
Rather than have made that savage duke thine heir,
And disinherited thine only son.   225
Prince.   Father, you cannot disinherit me.
If you be king, why should not I succeed?
K. Hen.   Pardon me, Margaret, pardon me, sweet
       son,
The Earl of Warwick and the Duke enforc'd me.
Q. Mar.   Enforc'd thee? Art thou king, and wilt
       be forc'd?   230
I shame to hear thee speak. Ah, timorous wretch,
Thou hast undone thyself, thy son, and me,
And giv'n unto the house of York such head
As thou shalt reign but by their sufferance.
To entail him and his heirs unto the crown,   235
What is it, but to make thy sepulchre,
And creep into it far before thy time?
Warwick is chancellor and the lord of Callice,
Stern Falconbridge commands the Narrow Seas,
The Duke is made Protector of the realm,   240
And yet shalt thou be safe? Such safety finds
The trembling lamb environed with wolves.
Had I been there, which am a silly woman,
The soldiers should have toss'd me on their pikes,
Before I would have granted to that act.   245
But thou prefer'st thy life before thine honor;

205 s.d. **Sennet:** trumpet notes to signal a procession.
211. **bewray:** reveal.
226–27. **Father . . . succeed.** At the time represented by this scene
(1460) Prince Edward was seven years old.
233. **head:** freedom of action (a term from horsemanship).
238. **Callice:** Calais.
239. **Falconbridge:** perhaps Thomas Neville, a bastard son of William
Neville, Baron Fauconberg (d. 1463), and thus a kinsman of the Earl
of Warwick.   **Narrow Seas:** English Channel.
240. **Duke:** i.e. the Duke of York.   243. **silly:** feeble.
244. **pikes:** weapons with axe-like heads.
245. **granted:** submitted.

And seeing thou dost, I here divorce myself
Both from thy table, Henry, and thy bed,
Until that act of parliament be repeal'd
Whereby my son is disinherited.   250
The northern lords that have forsworn thy colors
Will follow mine, if once they see them spread;
And spread they shall be, to thy foul disgrace,
And utter ruin of the house of York.
Thus do I leave thee. Come, son, let's away.   255
Our army is ready; come, we'll after them.
K. Hen.   Stay, gentle Margaret, and hear me speak.
Q. Mar.   Thou hast spoke too much already; get
       thee gone.
K. Hen.   Gentle son Edward, thou wilt stay [with]
       me?
Q. Mar.   Ay, to be murther'd by his enemies.   260
Prince.   When I return with victory [from] the field
I'll see your Grace; till then, I'll follow her.
Q. Mar.   Come, son, away, we may not linger thus.
                    [*Exeunt Queen Margaret and the Prince.*]
K. Hen.   Poor queen, how love to me and to her son
Hath made her break out into terms of rage!   265
Reveng'd may she be on that hateful duke,
Whose haughty spirit, winged with desire,
Will cost my crown, and like an empty eagle
Tire on the flesh of me and of my son!
The loss of those three lords torments my heart;   270
I'll write unto them and entreat them fair;
Come, cousin, you shall be the messenger.
Exe.   And I, I hope, shall reconcile them all.
                                        Flourish. Exeunt.

[SCENE II]

Enter RICHARD, EDWARD, *and* MONTAGUE.

Rich.   Brother, though I be youngest, give me leave.
Edw.   No, I can better play the orator.
Mont.   But I have reasons strong and forcible.

Enter the DUKE OF YORK.

York.   Why, how now, sons and brother, at a strife?
What is your quarrel? how began it first?   5
Edw.   No quarrel, but a slight contention.
York.   About what?
Rich.   About that which concerns your Grace and
       us:
The crown of England, father, which is yours.   9
York.   Mine, boys? not till King Henry be dead.
Rich.   Your right depends not on his life or death.
Edw.   Now you are heir, therefore enjoy it now.
By giving the house of Lancaster leave to breathe,
It will outrun you, father, in the end.   14
York.   I took an oath that he should quietly reign.
Edw.   But for a kingdom any oath may be broken:
I would break a thousand oaths to reign one year.
Rich.   No; God forbid your Grace should be for-
       sworn.

268. **cost:** i.e. rob me of.   **empty:** i.e. hungry.
269. **Tire:** feed ravenously.   271. **fair:** courteously.

I.ii. Location: Sandal Castle, near Wakefield, in Yorkshire.
13. **breathe:** rest.

York. I shall be, if I claim by open war.

Rich. I'll prove the contrary, if you'll hear me
speak. 20

York. Thou canst not, son; it is impossible.

Rich. An oath is of no moment, being not took
Before a true and lawful magistrate
That hath authority over him that swears.
Henry had none, but did usurp the place. 25
Then seeing 'twas he that made you to depose,
Your oath, my lord, is vain and frivolous.
Therefore to arms! And, father, do but think
How sweet a thing it is to wear a crown,
Within whose circuit is Elysium 30
And all that poets feign of bliss and joy.
Why do we linger thus? I cannot rest
Until the white rose that I wear be dy'd
Even in the lukewarm blood of Henry's heart.

York. Richard, enough; I will be king, or die. 35
Brother, thou shalt to London presently,
And whet on Warwick to this enterprise.
Thou, Richard, shalt to the Duke of Norfolk,
And tell him privily of our intent.
You, Edward, shall unto my Lord Cobham, 40
With whom the Kentishmen will willingly rise;
In them I trust, for they are soldiers,
Witty, courteous, liberal, full of spirit.
While you are thus employ'd, what resteth more,
But that I seek occasion how to rise, 45
And yet the King not privy to my drift,
Nor any of the house of Lancaster?

Enter [a Messenger*].*

But stay, what news? Why com'st thou in such post?

[*Mess.*] The Queen with all the northern earls and
lords
Intend here to besiege you in your castle. 50
She is hard by with twenty thousand men;
And therefore fortify your hold, my lord.

York. Ay, with my sword. What? think'st thou
that we fear them?
Edward and Richard, you shall stay with me,
My brother Montague shall post to London. 55
Let noble Warwick, Cobham, and the rest,
Whom we have left protectors of the King,
With pow'rful policy strengthen themselves,
And trust not simple Henry nor his oaths.

Mont. Brother, I go; I'll win them, fear it not. 60
And thus most humbly I do take my leave.

Exit Montague.

*Enter [*Sir John*] Mortimer and his brother [*Sir Hugh
Mortimer*].*

York. Sir John and Sir Hugh Mortimer, mine
uncles,
You are come to Sandal in a happy hour;
The army of the Queen mean to besiege us.

Sir John. She shall not need, we'll meet her in the
field. 65

York. What, with five thousand men?

Rich. Ay, with five hundred, father, for a need.
A woman's general: what should we fear?

A march afar off.

Edw. I hear their drums. Let's set our men in
order,
And issue forth and bid them battle straight. 70

York. Five men to twenty! Though the odds be
great,
I doubt not, uncle, of our victory.
Many a battle have I won in France
When as the enemy hath been ten to one;
Why should I not now have the like success? 75

Alarum. Exeunt.

[Scene III]

[Alarums.] Enter Rutland *and his* Tutor.

Rut. Ah, whither shall I fly to scape their hands?
Ah, tutor, look where bloody Clifford comes!

Enter Clifford *[and Soldiers].*

Clif. Chaplain, away, thy priesthood saves thy life.
As for the brat of this accursed duke,
Whose father slew my father, he shall die. 5

Tut. And I, my lord, will bear him company.

Clif. Soldiers, away with him!

Tut. Ah, Clifford, murther not this innocent child,
Lest thou be hated both of God and man.

Exit [dragged off by Soldiers].

Clif. How now? is he dead already? Or is it fear
That makes him close his eyes? I'll open them. 11

Rut. So looks the pent-up lion o'er the wretch
That trembles under his devouring paws;
And so he walks, insulting o'er his prey,
And so he comes, to rend his limbs asunder. 15
Ah, gentle Clifford, kill me with thy sword
And not with such a cruel threat'ning look.
Sweet Clifford, hear me speak before I die:
I am too mean a subject for thy wrath,
Be thou reveng'd on men, and let me live. 20

Clif. In vain thou speak'st, poor boy; my father's
blood
Hath stopp'd the passage where thy words should
enter.

Rut. Then let my father's blood open it again,
He is a man, and, Clifford, cope with him. 24

Clif. Had I thy brethren here, their lives and thine
Were not revenge sufficient for me;
No, if I digg'd up thy forefathers' graves
And hung their rotten coffins up in chains,
It could not slake mine ire nor ease my heart.
The sight of any of the house of York 30
Is as a fury to torment my soul;
And till I root out their accursed line,
And leave not one alive, I live in hell.

---

22. moment: force.
26. depose: swear an oath. 36. presently: at once.
44. what resteth more: what else remains.
46. And ... drift: without the King's discovering what I am up to.
48. post: haste. 52. hold: castle. 58. policy: cunning.
62. uncles. They were brothers of his mother Anne.

67. for a need: if necessary. 70. straight: at once.
74. When as: when.

I.iii. Location: A field of battle between Sandal Castle and Wakefield.

3 Henry VI   Therefore—
I.iii

  Rut. O, let me pray before I take my death!   35
To thee I pray; sweet Clifford, pity me!
  Clif. Such pity as my rapier's point affords.
  Rut. I never did thee harm; why wilt thou slay me?
  Clif. Thy father hath.
  Rut.   But 'twas ere I was born.
Thou hast one son, for his sake pity me,   40
Lest in revenge thereof, sith God is just,
He be as miserably slain as I.
Ah, let me live in prison all my days,
And when I give occasion of offense,
Then let me die, for now thou hast no cause.   45
  Clif. No cause?
Thy father slew my father; therefore die.
                            [Stabs him.]
  Rut. *Dii faciant laudis summa sit ista tuae!* *[Dies.]*
  Clif. Plantagenet, I come, Plantagenet!
And this thy son's blood cleaving to my blade   50
Shall rust upon my weapon, till thy blood,
Congeal'd with this, do make me wipe off both.
                                Exit.

[Scene IV]

Alarum. Enter Richard Duke of York.

  York. The army of the Queen hath got the field:
My uncles both are slain in rescuing me;
And all my followers to the eager foe
Turn back and fly, like ships before the wind,
Or lambs pursu'd by hunger-starved wolves.   5
My sons, God knows what hath bechanced them;
But this I know, they have demean'd themselves
Like men born to renown by life or death.
Three times did Richard make a lane to me,
And thrice cried, "Courage, father! fight it out!"   10
And full as oft came Edward to my side
With purple falchion, painted to the hilt
In blood of those that had encount'red him.
And when the hardiest warriors did retire,
Richard cried, "Charge! and give no foot of ground!"
And cried, "A crown, or else a glorious tomb!   16
A sceptre, or an earthly sepulchre!"
With this we charg'd again; but out, alas,
We bodg'd again, as I have seen a swan
With bootless labor swim against the tide,   20
And spend her strength with overmatching waves.
                   A short alarum within.
Ah, hark, the fatal followers do pursue,
And I am faint, and cannot fly their fury;
And were I strong, I would not shun their fury.
The sands are numb'red that makes up my life,   25
Here must I stay, and here my life must end.

Enter the Queen [Margaret], Clifford, Northumberland, *the young* Prince [Edward], *and Soldiers.*

Come, bloody Clifford, rough Northumberland,
I dare your quenchless fury to more rage.
I am your butt, and I abide your shot.
  North. Yield to our mercy, proud Plantagenet.   30
  Clif. Ay, to such mercy as his ruthless arm
With downright payment show'd unto my father.
Now Phaëton hath tumbled from his car,
And made an evening at the noontide prick.
  York. My ashes, as the phoenix, may bring forth
A bird that will revenge upon you all;   36
And in that hope I throw mine eyes to heaven,
Scorning what e'er you can afflict me with.
Why come you not? What, multitudes, and fear?
  Clif. So cowards fight when they can fly no
     further,   40
So doves do peck the falcon's piercing talons,
So desperate thieves, all hopeless of their lives,
Breathe out invectives 'gainst the officers.
  York. O Clifford, but bethink thee once again,
And in thy thought o'errun my former time;   45
And if thou canst for blushing, view this face,
And bite thy tongue, that slanders him with cowardice
Whose frown hath made thee faint and fly ere this!
  Clif. I will not bandy with thee word for word,
But buckler with thee blows, twice two for one.   50
  Q. Mar. Hold, valiant Clifford! for a thousand
     causes
I would prolong a while the traitor's life.
Wrath makes him deaf; speak thou, Northumberland.
  North. Hold, Clifford, do not honor him so much
To prick thy finger, though to wound his heart.   55
What valor were it, when a cur doth grin,
For one to thrust his hand between his teeth,
When he might spurn him with his foot away?
It is war's prize to take all vantages,
And ten to one is no impeach of valor.   60
      [They lay hands on York, who struggles.]
  Clif. Ay, ay, so strives the woodcock with the gin.
  North. So doth the cony struggle in the net.
  York. So triumph thieves upon their conquer'd
     booty,
So true men yield, with robbers so o'ermatch'd.
  North. What would your Grace have done unto
     him now?   65
  Q. Mar. Brave warriors, Clifford and Northum-
     berland,
Come make him stand upon this molehill here
That raught at mountains with outstretched arms,
Yet parted but the shadow with his hand.
What, was it you that would be England's king?   70
Was't you that revell'd in our parliament,
And made a preachment of your high descent?

---

39. ere . . . born. Actually, Edmund, Earl of Rutland, York's
second son, was twelve years old at the time of the elder Clifford's
death in 1455. **41. sith:** since.
48. Dii . . . tuae: "the gods grant that this be the summit of thy
glory" (Ovid, *Heroides,* ii.66).

I.iv. Location: Scene continues.
2. uncles: i.e. Sir John and Sir Hugh Mortimer.
4. Turn back: turn their backs.   **7. demean'd:** behaved.
12. falchion: curved sword.   **19. bodg'd:** budged, gave way.

29. butt: target.
33. Phaëton: Phaëthon, son of Apollo, the sun-god, who, when he
tried to drive his father's chariot (*car*), was thrown from it and killed.
34. noontide prick: point on the sundial marking noon.
35. phoenix: fabulous bird that was reborn from its own ashes.
36. bird: young one.   **45. o'errun:** survey, review.
46. for: on account of.   **50. buckler:** catch or ward off (blows).
56. grin: show teeth.   **60. impeach:** reproach.   **61. gin:** snare.
62. cony: rabbit.   **64. true:** honest.   **68. raught:** reached.
71. revell'd: rioted.

Where are your mess of sons to back you now,
The wanton Edward, and the lusty George?
And where's that valiant crook-back prodigy,   75
Dicky, your boy, that with his grumbling voice
Was wont to cheer his dad in mutinies?
Or with the rest, where is your darling, Rutland?
Look, York, I stain'd this napkin with the blood
That valiant Clifford with his rapier's point   80
Made issue from the bosom of the boy;
And if thine eyes can water for his death,
I give thee this to dry thy cheeks withal.
Alas, poor York, but that I hate thee deadly,
I should lament thy miserable state.   85
I prithee grieve, to make me merry, York.
What, hath thy fiery heart so parch'd thine entrails
That not a tear can fall for Rutland's death?
Why art thou patient, man? Thou shouldst be mad;
And I, to make thee mad, do mock thee thus.   90
Stamp, rave, and fret, that I may sing and dance.
Thou wouldst be fee'd, I see, to make me sport:
York cannot speak unless he wear a crown.
A crown for York! and, lords, bow low to him;
Hold you his hands whilest I do set it on.   95
          [*Putting a paper crown on his head.*]
Ay, marry, sir, now looks he like a king!
Ay, this is he that took King Henry's chair,
And this is he was his adopted heir.
But how is it that great Plantagenet
Is crown'd so soon, and broke his solemn oath?   100
As I bethink me, you should not be king
Till our King Henry had shook hands with death.
And will you pale your head in Henry's glory,
And rob his temples of the diadem,
Now in his life, against your holy oath?   105
O, 'tis a fault too too unpardonable!
Off with the crown; and, with the crown, his head,
And whilest we breathe, take time to do him dead.
     Clif. That is my office, for my father's sake.
     Q. Mar. Nay, stay, let's hear the orisons he makes.
     York. She-wolf of France, but worse than wolves
          of France,   111
Whose tongue more poisons than the adder's tooth!
How ill-beseeming is it in thy sex
To triumph like an Amazonian trull
Upon their woes whom fortune captivates!   115
But that thy face is vizard-like, unchanging,
Made impudent with use of evil deeds,
I would assay, proud queen, to make thee blush.
To tell thee whence thou cam'st, of whom deriv'd,
Were shame enough to shame thee, wert thou not
          shameless.   120
Thy father bears the type of King of Naples,

Of both the Sicils and Jerusalem,
Yet not so wealthy as an English yeoman.
Hath that poor monarch taught thee to insult?
It needs not, nor it boots thee not, proud queen,   125
Unless the adage must be verified,
That beggars mounted run their horse to death.
'Tis beauty that doth oft make women proud,
But God he knows thy share thereof is small.
'Tis virtue that doth make them most admir'd,   130
The contrary doth make thee wond'red at.
'Tis government that makes them seem divine,
The want thereof makes thee abominable.
Thou art as opposite to every good
As the antipodes are unto us,   135
Or as the south to the septentrion.
O tiger's heart wrapp'd in a woman's hide!
How couldst thou drain the life-blood of the child,
To bid the father wipe his eyes withal,
And yet be seen to wear a woman's face?   140
Women are soft, mild, pitiful, and flexible;
Thou stern, obdurate, flinty, rough, remorseless.
Bid'st thou me rage? why, now thou hast thy wish:
Wouldst have me weep? why, now thou hast thy will:
For raging wind blows up incessant showers,   145
And when the rage allays, the rain begins.
These tears are my sweet Rutland's obsequies,
And every drop cries vengeance for his death
'Gainst thee, fell Clifford, and thee, false French-
          woman.
     North. Beshrew me, but his passions moves me so
That hardly can I check my eyes from tears.   151
     York. That face of his the hungry cannibals
Would not have touch'd, would not have stain'd with
          blood;
But you are more inhuman, more inexorable,
O, ten times more, than tigers of Hyrcania.   155
See, ruthless queen, a hapless father's tears!
This cloth thou dipp'dst in blood of my sweet boy,
And I with tears do wash the blood away.
Keep thou the napkin and go boast of this,
And if thou tell'st the heavy story right,   160
Upon my soul, the hearers will shed tears;
Yea, even my foes will shed fast-falling tears,
And say, "Alas, it was a piteous deed!"
There, take the crown, and with the crown, my curse,
And in thy need such comfort come to thee   165
As now I reap at thy too cruel hand!
Hard-hearted Clifford, take me from the world,
My soul to heaven, my blood upon your heads!
     North. Had he been slaughter-man to all my kin,
I should not for my life but weep with him,   170
To see how inly sorrow gripes his soul.
     Q. Mar. What, weeping-ripe, my Lord North-
          umberland?
Think but upon the wrong he did us all,

---

73. **mess:** set of four.
75. **prodigy:** monster.   79. **napkin:** handkerchief.
92. **fee'd:** paid.
96. **marry:** indeed (originally the name of the Virgin Mary used as
an oath).   103. **pale:** enclose.
108. **breathe:** rest.   **do him dead:** kill him.
110. **orisons:** prayers.
114. **Amazonian:** resembling the Amazons, a race of legendary female
warriors.   115. **captivates:** subdues.
116. **vizard-like:** masklike.   118. **assay:** essay, try.
121. **type:** title.

122. **both the Sicils:** the Kingdom of the Two Sicilies, of which
Margaret's father René (Reignier) was titular king.
125. **boots:** profits.   132. **government:** discipline, self-control.
135. **antipodes:** the opposite side of the globe.
136. **septentrion:** north.
141. **pitiful:** full of pity, compassionate.   146. **allays:** abates.
149. **fell:** cruel.   150. **Beshrew:** curse.
155. **Hyrcania:** region near the Caspian Sea noted for its tigers.
171. **inly:** inward.

3 Henry VI
I.iv

Clif. Here's for my oath, here's for my father's
       death.   [Stabbing him.] 175
Q. Mar. And here's to right our gentle-hearted
         king.   [Stabbing him.]
York. Open thy gate of mercy, gracious God!
My soul flies through these wounds to seek out thee.
                                         [Dies.]
Q. Mar. Off with his head, and set it on York
         gates,
So York may overlook the town of York.   180
                               Flourish. Exeunt.

[ACT II, Scene I]

A march. Enter EDWARD, RICHARD, and their power.

Edw. I wonder how our princely father scap'd;
Or whether he be scap'd away or no
From Clifford's and Northumberland's pursuit.
Had he been ta'en, we should have heard the news;
Had he been slain, we should have heard the news; 5
Or had he scap'd, methinks we should have heard
The happy tidings of his good escape.
How fares my brother? Why is he so sad?
Rich. I cannot joy, until I be resolv'd
Where our right valiant father is become.   10
I saw him in the battle range about,
And watch'd him how he singled Clifford forth.
Methought he bore him in the thickest troop
As doth a lion in a herd of neat,
Or as a bear, encompass'd round with dogs,   15
Who having pinch'd a few and made them cry,
The rest stand all aloof and bark at him.
So far'd our father with his enemies,
So fled his enemies my warlike father;
Methinks 'tis prize enough to be his son.   20
                      [Three suns appear in the air.]
See how the morning opes her golden gates,
And takes her farewell of the glorious sun!
How well resembles it the prime of youth,
Trimm'd like a younker prancing to his love!   24
Edw. Dazzle mine eyes, or do I see three suns?
Rich. Three glorious suns, each one a perfect sun,
Not separated with the racking clouds,
But sever'd in a pale clear-shining sky.
See, see, they join, embrace, and seem to kiss,
As if they vow'd some league inviolable.   30
Now are they but one lamp, one light, one sun.
In this the heaven figures some event.
Edw. 'Tis wondrous strange, the like yet never
      heard of.
I think it cites us, brother, to the field,

II.i. Location: A plain near Mortimer's Cross in Herefordshire.
10. Where . . . become: i.e. what has happened to him.
14. neat: cattle.   24. younker: stripling.
25. three suns. According to Hall (Bullough, III, 179), when Edward,
before the battle of Mortimer's Cross (which Shakespeare does not
represent), saw three suns "sodainly joined all together in one," he
"toke suche courage, that he fiercely set on his enemies, & them
shortly discomfited: for which cause, men imagined, that he gave the
sunne in his full brightnes for his cognisaunce or badge."
27. racking: scudding, drifting.   32. figures: reveals, portends.
34. cites: urges.

That we, the sons of brave Plantagenet,   35
Each one already blazing by our meeds,
Should notwithstanding join our lights together,
And over-shine the earth as this the world.
What e'er it bodes, henceforward will I bear
Upon my target three fair shining suns.   40
Rich. Nay, bear three daughters; by your leave I
       speak it,
You love the breeder better than the male.

Enter one [a MESSENGER] blowing.

But what art thou, whose heavy looks foretell
Some dreadful story hanging on thy tongue?
Mess. Ah, one that was a woeful looker-on   45
When as the noble Duke of York was slain,
Your princely father and my loving lord!
Edw. O, speak no more, for I have heard too much.
Rich. Say how he died, for I will hear it all.
Mess. Environed he was with many foes,   50
And stood against them, as the hope of Troy
Against the Greeks that would have ent'red Troy.
But Hercules himself must yield to odds;
And many strokes, though with a little axe,
Hews down and fells the hardest-timber'd oak.   55
By many hands your father was subdu'd,
But only slaught'red by the ireful arm
Of unrelenting Clifford and the Queen;
Who crown'd the gracious Duke in high despite,
Laugh'd in his face; and when with grief he wept, 60
The ruthless Queen gave him to dry his cheeks
A napkin steeped in the harmless blood
Of sweet young Rutland, by rough Clifford slain.
And after many scorns, many foul taunts,
They took his head, and on the gates of York   65
They set the same, and there it doth remain,
The saddest spectacle that e'er I view'd.
Edw. Sweet Duke of York, our prop to lean upon,
Now thou art gone we have no staff, no stay.
O Clifford, boist'rous Clifford, thou hast slain 70
The flow'r of Europe for his chevalry,
And treacherously hast thou vanquish'd him,
For hand to hand he would have vanquish'd thee.
Now my soul's palace is become a prison;
Ah, would she break from hence, that this my body
Might in the ground be closed up in rest!   76
For never henceforth shall I joy again,
Never, O never, shall I see more joy!
Rich. I cannot weep; for all my body's moisture
Scarce serves to quench my furnace-burning heart; 80
Nor can my tongue unload my heart's great burthen,
For self-same wind that I should speak withal
Is kindling coals that fires all my breast,
And burns me up with flames that tears would quench.
To weep is to make less the depth of grief: 85
Tears then for babes; blows and revenge for me.
Richard, I bear thy name, I'll venge thy death,
Or die renowned by attempting it.

36. meeds: deserts, merits.
40. target: targe, shield.   51. hope of Troy: i.e. Hector.
70. boist'rous: savage.   71. chevalry: chivalry, knightly qualities.
78. see more joy: see joy again.

Edw. His name that valiant duke hath left with
thee;
His dukedom and his chair with me is left.   90
Rich. Nay, if thou be that princely eagle's bird,
Show thy descent by gazing 'gainst the sun;
For chair and dukedom, throne and kingdom say,
Either that is thine, or else thou wert not his.

March. Enter WARWICK, MARQUESS MONTAGUE, *and
their army.*

War. How now, fair lords? What fare? What
news abroad?   95
Rich. Great Lord of Warwick, if we should re-
compt
Our baleful news, and at each word's deliverance
Stab poniards in our flesh till all were told,
The words would add more anguish than the wounds.
O valiant lord, the Duke of York is slain!   100
Edw. O Warwick, Warwick, that Plantagenet,
Which held thee dearly as his soul's redemption,
Is by the stern Lord Clifford done to death.
War. Ten days ago I drown'd these news in tears;
And now, to add more measure to your woes,   105
I come to tell you things sith then befall'n.
After the bloody fray at Wakefield fought,
Where your brave father breath'd his latest gasp,
Tidings, as swiftly as the posts could run,
Were brought me of your loss and his depart.   110
I, then in London, keeper of the King,
Muster'd my soldiers, gathered flocks of friends,
[And very well appointed, as I thought,]
March'd toward Saint Albons to intercept the Queen,
Bearing the King in my behalf along;   115
For by my scouts I was advertised
That she was coming with a full intent
To dash our late decree in parliament
Touching King Henry's oath and your succession.
Short tale to make, we at Saint Albons met,   120
Our battles join'd, and both sides fiercely fought;
But whether 'twas the coldness of the King,
Who look'd full gently on his warlike queen,
That robb'd my soldiers of their heated spleen;
Or whether 'twas report of her success,   125
Or more than common fear of Clifford's rigor,
Who thunders to his captives blood and death,
I cannot judge: but, to conclude with truth,
Their weapons like to lightning came and went;
Our soldiers', like the night-owl's lazy flight,   130
Or like [an idle] thresher with a flail,
Fell gently down, as if they struck their friends.
I cheer'd them up with justice of our cause,
With promise of high pay and great rewards;
But all in vain, they had no heart to fight,   135
And we, in them, no hope to win the day,
So that we fled: the King unto the Queen;
Lord George your brother, Norfolk, and myself,
In haste, post-haste, are come to join with you;

For in the marches here we heard you were,   140
Making another head to fight again.
Edw. Where is the Duke of Norfolk, gentle War-
wick?
And when came George from Burgundy to England?
War. Some six miles off the Duke is with the
soldiers,
And for your brother, he was lately sent   145
From your kind aunt, Duchess of Burgundy,
With aid of soldiers to this needful war.
Rich. 'Twas odds, belike, when valiant Warwick
fled:
Oft have I heard his praises in pursuit,
But ne'er till now his scandal of retire.   150
War. Nor now my scandal, Richard, dost thou
hear;
For thou shalt know this strong right hand of mine
Can pluck the diadem from faint Henry's head,
And wring the aweful sceptre from his fist,
Were he as famous and as bold in war   155
As he is fam'd for mildness, peace, and prayer.
Rich. I know it well, Lord Warwick, blame me
not.
'Tis love I bear thy glories make me speak.
But in this troublous time what's to be done?
Shall we go throw away our coats of steel,   160
And wrap our bodies in black mourning gowns,
Numb'ring our Ave-Maries with our beads?
Or shall we on the helmets of our foes
Tell our devotion with revengeful arms?
If for the last, say ay, and to it, lords.   165
War. Why, therefore Warwick came to seek you
out,
And therefore comes my brother Montague.
Attend me, lords: the proud insulting Queen,
With Clifford and the haught Northumberland,
And of their feather many moe proud birds,   170
Have wrought the easy-melting King like wax.
He swore consent to your succession,
His oath enrolled in the parliament;
And now to London all the crew are gone
To frustrate both his oath and what beside   175
May make against the house of Lancaster.
Their power, I think, is thirty thousand strong.
Now, if the help of Norfolk and myself,
With all the friends that thou, brave Earl of March,
Amongst the loving Welshmen canst procure,   180
Will but amount to five and twenty thousand,
Why, *via!* to London will we march,

---

90. **chair:** i.e. the throne that he had claimed.
92. **'gainst the sun.** The eagle was supposedly able to look at the sun without blinking. 108. **latest:** last. 110. **depart:** death.
116. **advertised:** informed. 118. **dash:** overturn.
121. **battles:** armies. 124. **spleen:** spirit.
138. **Lord George:** i.e. the Duke of Clarence.

140. **marches:** border country.
141. **Making another head:** raising another force.
146. **Duchess of Burgundy:** i.e. Isabel, wife of Philip, Duke of Burgundy, and a granddaughter of John of Gaunt. According to Hall (Bullough, III, 180), York's widow sent George and Richard, her two surviving younger sons, to Philip's court in Utrecht, "and so there thei remayned, till their brother Edwarde had obteyned the Realme, and gotten the regiment [rule]."
148. **odds:** i.e. heavy odds, very likely.
149–50. **Oft . . . retire:** i.e. I have often heard him praised for his eagerness in pursuit but never until now condemned for his disgrace in retreat. 162. **beads:** rosary.
164. **Tell our devotion:** count off our prayers.
169. **haught:** haughty. 170. **moe:** more.
171. **wrought:** worked, manipulated.
179. **Earl of March:** i.e. Edward. 182. **via:** onward.

3 Henry VI
II.i

And once again bestride our foaming steeds,
And once again cry "Charge!" upon our foes,
But never once again turn back and fly.   185
   Rich. Ay, now methinks I hear great Warwick
    speak.
Ne'er may he live to see a sunshine day
That cries "Retire!" if Warwick bid him stay.
   Edw. Lord Warwick, on thy shoulder will I lean,
And when thou fail'st (as God forbid the hour!)   190
Must Edward fall, which peril heaven forefend!
   War. No longer Earl of March, but Duke of York;
The next degree is England's royal throne;
For King of England shalt thou be proclaim'd
In every borough as we pass along,   195
And he that throws not up his cap for joy
Shall for the fault make forfeit of his head.
King Edward, valiant Richard, Montague,
Stay we no longer, dreaming of renown,
But sound the trumpets, and about our task.   200
   Rich. Then, Clifford, were thy heart as hard as
    steel,
As thou hast shown it flinty by thy deeds,
I come to pierce it, or to give thee mine.
   Edw. Then strike up drums. God and Saint
    George for us!

Enter a MESSENGER.

   War. How now? what news?   205
   Mess. The Duke of Norfolk sends you word by me
The Queen is coming with a puissant host,
And craves your company for speedy counsel.
   War. Why then it sorts, brave warriors. Let's
    away.   *Exeunt omnes.*

[SCENE II]

Flourish.   Enter the KING [HENRY], *the* QUEEN
[MARGARET], CLIFFORD, NORTHUMBERLAND, *and
young* PRINCE [EDWARD], *with Drum and Trumpets.*

   Q. Mar. Welcome, my lord, to this brave town of
    York.
Yonder's the head of that arch-enemy
That sought to be encompass'd with your crown.
Doth not the object cheer your heart, my lord?
   K. Hen. Ay, as the rocks cheer them that fear
    their wrack: 5
To see this sight, it irks my very soul.
Withhold revenge, dear God! 'tis not my fault,
Nor wittingly have I infring'd my vow.
   Clif. My gracious liege, this too much lenity
And harmful pity must be laid aside.   10
To whom do lions cast their gentle looks?
Not to the beast that would usurp their den.
Whose hand is that the forest bear doth lick?

Not his that spoils her young before her face.
Who scapes the lurking serpent's mortal sting?   15
Not he that sets his foot upon her back.
The smallest worm will turn, being trodden on,
And doves will peck in safeguard of their brood.
Ambitious York did level at thy crown,
Thou smiling while he knit his angry brows: 20
He, but a duke, would have his son a king,
And raise his issue like a loving sire;
Thou, being a king, blest with a goodly son,
Didst yield consent to disinherit him,
Which argued thee a most unloving father.   25
Unreasonable creatures feed their young,
And though man's face be fearful to their eyes,
Yet in protection of their tender ones,
Who hath not seen them, even with those wings
Which sometime they have us'd with fearful flight,   30
Make war with him that climb'd unto their nest,
Offering their own lives in their young's defense?
For shame, my liege, make them your president!
Were it not pity that this goodly boy
Should lose his birthright by his father's fault,   35
And long hereafter say unto his child,
"What my great-grandfather and grandsire got,
My careless father fondly gave away"?
Ah, what a shame were this! Look on the boy,
And let his manly face, which promiseth   40
Successful fortune, steel thy melting heart
To hold thine own and leave thine own with him.
   K. Hen. Full well hath Clifford play'd the orator,
Inferring arguments of mighty force.
But, Clifford, tell me, didst thou never hear   45
That things ill got had ever bad success?
And happy always was it for that son
Whose father for his hoarding went to hell?
I'll leave my son my virtuous deeds behind,
And would my father had left me no more!   50
For all the rest is held at such a rate
As brings a thousandfold more care to keep
Than in possession any jot of pleasure.
Ah, cousin York, would thy best friends did know
How it doth grieve me that thy head is here!   55
   Q. Mar. My lord, cheer up your spirits, our foes
    are nigh,
And this soft courage makes your followers faint.
You promis'd knighthood to our forward son,
Unsheathe your sword, and dub him presently.
Edward, kneel down.   60
   K. Hen. Edward Plantagenet, arise a knight,
And learn this lesson: Draw thy sword in right.
   Prince. My gracious father, by your kingly leave,
I'll draw it as apparent to the crown,
And in that quarrel use it to the death.   65
   Clif. Why, that is spoken like a toward prince.

---

191. **forefend:** forfend, forbid.   193. **degree:** step.
209. **sorts:** fits.

II.ii. *Location: Before York.*
o.s.d. **Trumpets:** trumpeters.
2. **Yonder:** i.e. on the gate of the city, where Margaret had ordered
York's head placed.   5. **wrack:** destruction.
8. **wittingly:** intentionally.   9. **liege:** sovereign.

14. **spoils:** destroys.   19. **level:** aim.
26. **Unreasonable creatures:** i.e. animals.
33. **president:** precedent, model.
37. **great-grandfather and grandsire:** i.e. Henry IV and Henry V.
38. **fondly:** foolishly.   44. **Inferring:** adducing.
46. **success:** outcome.   57. **faint:** lose heart.
59. **presently:** at once.   64. **apparent:** heir.   66. **toward:** bold.

Enter a MESSENGER.

Mess. Royal commanders, be in readiness,
For with a band of thirty thousand men
Comes Warwick, backing of the Duke of York,
And in the towns, as they do march along, 70
Proclaims him king, and many fly to him.
Darraign your battle, for they are at hand.

Clif. I would your Highness would depart the field,
The Queen hath best success when you are absent.

Q. Mar. Ay, good my lord, and leave us to our
fortune. 75

K. Hen. Why, that's my fortune too, therefore
I'll stay.

North. Be it with resolution then to fight.

Prince. My royal father, cheer these noble lords,
And hearten those that fight in your defense.
Unsheathe your sword, good father; cry "Saint
George!" 80

March. Enter EDWARD, WARWICK, RICHARD, [GEORGE
OF] CLARENCE, NORFOLK, MONTAGUE, *and Soldiers.*

Edw. Now, perjur'd Henry, wilt thou kneel for
grace,
And set thy diadem upon my head,
Or bide the mortal fortune of the field?

Q. Mar. Go rate thy minions, proud insulting boy!
Becomes it thee to be thus bold in terms 85
Before thy sovereign and thy lawful king?

Edw. I am his king, and he should bow his knee.
I was adopted heir by his consent.
Since when, his oath is broke; for, as I hear,
You that are king, though he do wear the crown, 90
Have caus'd him, by new act of parliament,
To blot out me, and put his own son in.

Clif. And reason too:
Who should succeed the father but the son? 94

Rich. Are you there, butcher? O, I cannot speak!

Clif. Ay, crook-back, here I stand to answer thee,
Or any he the proudest of thy sort.

Rich. 'Twas you that kill'd young Rutland, was it
not?

Clif. Ay, and old York, and yet not satisfied.

Rich. For God's sake, lords, give signal to the
fight. 100

War. What say'st thou, Henry, wilt thou yield the
crown?

Q. Mar. Why, how now, long-tongu'd Warwick,
dare you speak?
When you and I met at Saint Albons last,
Your legs did better service than your hands.

War. Then 'twas my turn to fly, and now 'tis
thine. 105

Clif. You said so much before, and yet you fled.

War. 'Twas not your valor, Clifford, drove me
thence.

North. No, nor your manhood that durst make you
stay.

Rich. Northumberland, I hold thee reverently.

Break off the parley, for scarce I can refrain 110
The execution of my big-swoll'n heart
Upon that Clifford, that cruel child-killer.

Clif. I slew thy father, call'st thou him a child?

Rich. Ay, like a dastard and a treacherous coward,
As thou didst kill our tender brother Rutland, 115
But ere sunset I'll make thee curse the deed.

K. Hen. Have done with words, my lords, and
hear me speak.

Q. Mar. Defy them then, or else hold close thy
lips.

K. Hen. I prithee give no limits to my tongue,
I am a king, and privileg'd to speak. 120

Clif. My liege, the wound that bred this meeting
here
Cannot be cur'd by words; therefore be still.

Rich. Then, executioner, unsheathe thy sword.
By Him that made us all, I am resolv'd
That Clifford's manhood lies upon his tongue. 125

Edw. Say, Henry, shall I have my right, or no?
A thousand men have broke their fasts to-day
That ne'er shall dine unless thou yield the crown.

War. If thou deny, their blood upon thy head,
For York in justice puts his armor on. 130

Prince. If that be right which Warwick says is
right,
There is no wrong, but every thing is right.

[*Rich.*] Whoever got thee, there thy mother
stands,
For well I wot, thou hast thy mother's tongue.

Q. Mar. But thou art neither like thy sire nor dam,
But like a foul misshapen stigmatic, 136
Mark'd by the destinies to be avoided,
As venom toads, or lizards' dreadful stings.

Rich. Iron of Naples hid with English gilt,
Whose father bears the title of a king 140
(As if a channel should be call'd the sea),
Sham'st thou not, knowing whence thou art extraught,
To let thy tongue detect thy base-born heart?

Edw. A wisp of straw were worth a thousand
crowns
To make this shameless callet know herself. 145
Helen of Greece was fairer far than thou,
Although thy husband may be Menelaus;
And ne'er was Agamemnon's brother wrong'd
By that false woman as this king by thee.
His father revell'd in the heart of France, 150
And tam'd the King and made the Dolphin stoop;
And had he match'd according to his state,
He might have kept that glory to this day.
But when he took a beggar to his bed,
And grac'd thy poor sire with his bridal day, 155

69. **Duke of York:** i.e. Edward.
72. **Darraign your battle:** draw up your army.
84. **rate thy minions:** scold your favorites.
85. **terms:** language.   97. **sort:** gang.

110. **refrain:** give up.   111. **execution:** exercise (of powers).
124. **resolv'd:** convinced.   133. **got:** begot.   134. **wot:** know.
136. **stigmatic:** one marked with deformity.
138. **venom:** poisonous.   141. **channel:** gutter.
142. **extraught:** extracted, derived.   143. **detect:** expose.
144. **wisp of straw.** Mark of disgrace for a scold.
145. **callet:** strumpet.
146–49. **Helen . . . thee.** The abduction of Helen, wife of Menelaus,
king of Sparta, eventuated in the Trojan war, in which the Greeks
were led by Menelaus' brother Agamemnon, king of Mycenae.
152. **he:** i.e. Henry VI.   **match'd:** married.
154–55. **when . . . day.** An allusion to the overgenerous marriage
contract that Suffolk had arranged. See *2 Henry VI,* I.i.57–62.

3 Henry VI
II.ii

Even then that sunshine brew'd a show'r for him,
That wash'd his father's fortunes forth of France,
And heap'd sedition on his crown at home.
For what hath broach'd this tumult but thy pride?
Hadst thou been meek, our title still had slept, 160
And we, in pity of the gentle king,
Had slipp'd our claim until another age.

Geo. But when we saw our sunshine made thy
    spring,
And that thy summer bred us no increase,
We set the axe to thy usurping root; 165
And though the edge hath something hit ourselves,
Yet know thou, since we have begun to strike,
We'll never leave till we have hewn thee down,
Or bath'd thy growing with our heated bloods.

Edw. And in this resolution, I defy thee, 170
Not willing any longer conference,
Since thou deniedst the gentle king to speak.
Sound trumpets! Let our bloody colors wave!
And either victory, or else a grave.

Q. Mar. Stay, Edward. 175

Edw. No, wrangling woman, we'll no longer stay,
These words will cost ten thousand lives this day.

Exeunt omnes.

[SCENE III]

Alarum. Excursions. Enter WARWICK.

War. Forespent with toil, as runners with a race,
I lay me down a little while to breathe;
For strokes receiv'd and many blows repaid
Have robb'd my strong-knit sinews of their strength,
And spite of spite needs must I rest awhile. 5

Enter EDWARD *running.*

Edw. Smile, gentle heaven! or strike, ungentle
    death!
For this world frowns, and Edward's sun is clouded.

War. How now, my lord, what hap? what hope of
    good?

Enter [GEORGE OF] CLARENCE.

Geo. Our hap is loss, our hope but sad despair,
Our ranks are broke, and ruin follows us. 10
What counsel give you? Whither shall we fly?

Edw. Bootless is flight, they follow us with wings,
And weak we are and cannot shun pursuit.

Enter RICHARD [*running*].

Rich. Ah, Warwick, why hast thou withdrawn
    thyself?

Thy brother's blood the thirsty earth hath drunk, 15
Broach'd with the steely point of Clifford's lance;
And in the very pangs of death he cried,
Like to a dismal clangor heard from far,
"Warwick, revenge! brother, revenge my death!"
So underneath the belly of their steeds, 20
That stain'd their fetlocks in his smoking blood,
The noble gentleman gave up the ghost.

War. Then let the earth be drunken with our blood!
I'll kill my horse, because I will not fly.
Why stand we like soft-hearted women here, 25
Wailing our losses, whiles the foe doth rage,
And look upon, as if the tragedy
Were play'd in jest by counterfeiting actors?
Here on my knee I vow to God above
I'll never pause again, never stand still, 30
Till either death hath clos'd these eyes of mine
Or fortune given me measure of revenge.

Edw. O Warwick, I do bend my knee with thine,
And in this vow do chain my soul to thine!
And ere my knee rise from the earth's cold face, 35
I throw my hands, mine eyes, my heart to Thee,
Thou setter-up and plucker-down of kings,
Beseeching thee (if with thy will it stands)
That to my foes this body must be prey,
Yet that thy brazen gates of heaven may ope 40
And give sweet passage to my sinful soul!
Now, lords, take leave until we meet again,
Where e'er it be, in heaven or in earth.

Rich. Brother, give me thy hand, and gentle
    Warwick,
Let me embrace thee in my weary arms. 45
I, that did never weep, now melt with woe
That winter should cut off our spring-time so.

War. Away, away! Once more, sweet lords,
    farewell.

Geo. Yet let us all together to our troops,
And give them leave to fly that will not stay; 50
And call them pillars that will stand to us;
And if we thrive, promise them such rewards
As victors wear at the Olympian games.
This may plant courage in their quailing breasts,
For yet is hope of life and victory. 55
Foreslow no longer, make we hence amain. *Exeunt.*

[SCENE IV]

Excursions. Enter RICHARD [*at one door*] *and* CLIFFORD
[*at the other*].

Rich. Now, Clifford, I have singled thee alone:
Suppose this arm is for the Duke of York,
And this for Rutland, both bound to revenge,
Wert thou environ'd with a brazen wall.

159. **broach'd:** set flowing.   160. **title:** legal claim to the throne.
162. **slipp'd:** let slide, postponed.   164. **increase:** harvest.
166. **something:** somewhat.

II.iii. Location: Scene continues. (Scenes iii–vi represent the so-called
battle of Towton, which took place in the area between Towton and
Saxton, near York, but Shakespeare does not specify any change of
locale or passage of time between Scene ii [*Before York.*] and Scene iii,
and clearly thinks of Scene iii as following immediately in the same
general area as Scene ii.) o.s.d. **Excursions:** sallies, sorties.   1. **Forespent:** exhausted.
5. **spite of spite:** i.e. no matter what happens.

15. **Thy . . . drunk.** Warwick's illegitimate half-brother, the so-called
Bastard of Salisbury, was killed in a skirmish at Ferrybridge two days
before the battle of Towton (March 29, 1461). Hall (Bullough, III,
181), who describes him as "a valeaunt yong gentelman, and of great
audacitie," says that in his rage and grief Warwick was "like a man
desperate." 26. **whiles:** while.
27. **look upon:** look on, be spectators.   56. **Foreslow:** delay.

II.iv. Location: Scene continues.
1. **singled:** chosen.

Clif. Now, Richard, I am with thee here alone: 5
This is the hand that stabb'd thy father York,
And this the hand that slew thy brother Rutland,
And here's the heart that triumphs in their death,
And cheers these hands that slew thy sire and brother
To execute the like upon thyself— 10
And so have at thee!

[*Alarums.*] *They fight.* WARWICK *comes;* Clifford *flies.*

Rich. Nay, Warwick, single out some other chase,
For I myself will hunt this wolf to death. *Exeunt.*

[SCENE V]

Alarum. Enter KING HENRY *alone.*

K. Hen. This battle fares like to the morning's
war,
When dying clouds contend with growing light,
What time the shepherd, blowing of his nails,
Can neither call it perfect day nor night.
Now sways it this way, like a mighty sea 5
Forc'd by the tide to combat with the wind;
Now sways it that way, like the self-same sea
Forc'd to retire by fury of the wind.
Sometime the flood prevails, and then the wind;
Now one the better, then another best; 10
Both tugging to be victors, breast to breast,
Yet neither conqueror nor conquered;
So is the equal poise of this fell war.
Here on this molehill will I sit me down.
To whom God will, there be the victory! 15
For Margaret my queen, and Clifford too,
Have chid me from the battle; swearing both
They prosper best of all when I am thence.
Would I were dead, if God's good will were so;
For what is in this world but grief and woe? 20
O God! methinks it were a happy life
To be no better than a homely swain,
To sit upon a hill, as I do now,
To carve out dials quaintly, point by point,
Thereby to see the minutes how they run: 25
How many makes the hour full complete,
How many hours brings about the day,
How many days will finish up the year,
How many years a mortal man may live.
When this is known, then to divide the times: 30
So many hours must I tend my flock,
So many hours must I take my rest,
So many hours must I contemplate,
So many hours must I sport myself,
So many days my ewes have been with young, 35
So many weeks ere the poor fools will ean,
So many years ere I shall shear the fleece:
So minutes, hours, days, months, and years,
Pass'd over to the end they were created,

Would bring white hairs unto a quiet grave. 40
Ah! what a life were this! how sweet! how lovely!
Gives not the hawthorn bush a sweeter shade
To shepherds looking on their silly sheep
Than doth a rich embroider'd canopy
To kings that fear their subjects' treachery? 45
O yes, it doth; a thousandfold it doth.
And to conclude, the shepherd's homely curds,
His cold thin drink out of his leather bottle,
His wonted sleep under a fresh tree's shade,
All which secure and sweetly he enjoys, 50
Is far beyond a prince's delicates—
His viands sparkling in a golden cup,
His body couched in a curious bed,
When care, mistrust, and treason waits on him.

Alarum. Enter a SON *that hath kill'd his father, at one
door,* [*dragging in the dead body*].

Son. Ill blows the wind that profits nobody. 55
This man whom hand to hand I slew in fight
May be possessed with some store of crowns,
And I that, haply, take them from him now,
May yet, ere night, yield both my life and them
To some man else, as this dead man doth me. 60
Who's this? O God! it is my father's face,
Whom in this conflict I, unwares, have kill'd.
O heavy times, begetting such events!
From London by the King was I press'd forth;
My father, being the Earl of Warwick's man, 65
Came on the part of York, press'd by his master;
And I, who at his hands receiv'd my life,
Have by my hands of life bereaved him.
Pardon me, God, I knew not what I did!
And pardon, father, for I knew not thee! 70
My tears shall wipe away these bloody marks;
And no more words till they have flow'd their fill.

K. Hen. O piteous spectacle! O bloody times!
Whiles lions war and battle for their dens,
Poor harmless lambs abide their enmity. 75
Weep, wretched man; I'll aid thee tear for tear,
And let our hearts and eyes, like civil war,
Be blind with tears, and break o'ercharg'd with grief.

Enter [a] FATHER *that hath kill'd his son, at another door,
bearing of his son.*

Fath. Thou that so stoutly hath resisted me,
Give me thy gold—if thou hast any gold— 80
For I have bought it with an hundred blows.
But let me see: is this our foeman's face?
Ah, no, no, no, it is mine only son!
Ah, boy, if any life be left in thee,
Throw up thine eye! See, see what show'rs arise, 85
Blown with the windy tempest of my heart
Upon thy wounds, that kills mine eye and heart!
O, pity, God, this miserable age!
What stratagems! how fell! how butcherly!
Erroneous, mutinous, and unnatural, 90

---

12. chase: game, prey.

II.v. Location: Scene continues.
3. of: on.   13. poise: balance.
22. homely swain: simple shepherd.
24. dials: sundials.   quaintly: carefully.   34. sport: amuse.
36. ean: yean, bring forth.

43. silly: feeble, helpless.
51. delicates: luxuries.   53. curious: elaborate.
58. haply: perhaps.
64. press'd forth: impressed, conscripted.   66. part: side.
75. abide: pay the penalty for.
89. stratagems: wicked deeds.   90. Erroneous: criminal.

3 Henry VI
II.v

This deadly quarrel daily doth beget!
O boy! thy father gave thee life too soon,
And hath bereft thee of thy life too late.
    K. Hen. Woe above woe! grief more than common grief!
O that my death would stay these ruthful deeds!   95
O, pity, pity, gentle heaven, pity!
The red rose and the white are on his face,
The fatal colors of our striving houses;
The one his purple blood right well resembles,
The other his pale cheeks, methinks, presenteth.   100
Wither one rose, and let the other flourish;
If you contend, a thousand lives must wither.
    Son. How will my mother for a father's death
Take on with me, and ne'er be satisfied!
    Fath. How will my wife for slaughter of my son
Shed seas of tears, and ne'er be satisfied!   106
    K. Hen. How will the country for these woeful chances
Misthink the King, and not be satisfied!
    Son. Was ever son so ru'd a father's death?
    Fath. Was ever father so bemoan'd his son?   110
    K. Hen. Was ever king so griev'd for subjects' woe?
Much is your sorrow; mine ten times so much.
    Son. I'll bear thee hence, where I may weep my fill.
                                        [*Exit with his father.*]
    Fath. These arms of mine shall be thy winding-sheet;
My heart, sweet boy, shall be thy sepulchre,   115
For from my heart thine image ne'er shall go;
My sighing breast shall be thy funeral bell;
And so obsequious will thy father be,
[E'en] for the loss of thee, having no more,
As Priam was for all his valiant sons.   120
I'll bear thee hence, and let them fight that will,
For I have murthered where I should not kill.
                                        Exit [*with his son*].
    K. Hen. Sad-hearted men, much overgone with care,
Here sits a king more woeful than you are.

Alarums. Excursions. Enter the QUEEN [MARGARET],
the PRINCE [EDWARD], *and* EXETER.

    Prince. Fly, father, fly! for all your friends are fled,
And Warwick rages like a chafed bull.   126
Away! for death doth hold us in pursuit.
    Q. Mar. Mount you, my lord, towards Berwick post amain.
Edward and Richard, like a brace of greyhounds
Having the fearful flying hare in sight,   130
With fiery eyes sparkling for very wrath,
And bloody steel grasp'd in their ireful hands,
Are at our backs, and therefore hence amain.
    Exe. Away! for vengeance comes along with them.
Nay, stay not to expostulate, make speed,   135

Or else come after. I'll away before.
    K. Hen. Nay, take me with thee, good sweet Exeter;
Not that I fear to stay, but love to go
Whither the Queen intends. Forward, away!
                                        Exeunt.

[SCENE VI]

A loud alarum. Enter CLIFFORD *wounded* [*with an arrow in his neck*].

    Clif. Here burns my candle out; ay, here it dies,
Which whiles it lasted, gave King Henry light.
O Lancaster! I fear thy overthrow
More than my body's parting with my soul.
My love and fear glu'd many friends to thee,   5
And now I fall, thy tough commixtures melts,
Impairing Henry, strength'ning misproud York.
[The common people swarm like summer flies,]
And whither fly the gnats but to the sun?
And who shines now but Henry's enemies?   10
O Phoebus! hadst thou never given consent
That Phaëton should check thy fiery steeds,
Thy burning car never had scorch'd the earth.
And, Henry, hadst thou sway'd as kings should do,
Or as thy father and his father did,   15
Giving no ground unto the house of York,
They never then had sprung like summer flies;
I and ten thousand in this luckless realm
Had left no mourning widows for our death,
And thou this day hadst kept thy chair in peace.   20
For what doth cherish weeds but gentle air?
And what makes robbers bold but too much lenity?
Bootless are plaints, and cureless are my wounds;
No way to fly, nor strength to hold out flight.
The foe is merciless, and will not pity;   25
For at their hands I have deserv'd no pity.
The air hath got into my deadly wounds,
And much effuse of blood doth make me faint.
Come, York and Richard, Warwick and the rest,
I stabb'd your fathers' bosoms, split my breast.   30
                                        [*He faints.*]

Alarum and retreat. Enter EDWARD, WARWICK,
RICHARD, *and Soldiers,* MONTAGUE, *and* [GEORGE
OF] CLARENCE.

    Edw. Now breathe we, lords, good fortune bids us pause
And smooth the frowns of war with peaceful looks.
Some troops pursue the bloody-minded queen,
That led calm Henry, though he were a king,
As doth a sail, fill'd with a fretting gust,   35

---

93. **late:** recently.   104. **satisfied:** comforted.
108. **Misthink:** think ill of.
118. **obsequious:** dutiful in showing respect for the dead.
120. **Priam:** king of Troy whose fifty sons were killed in the war with the Greeks.   123. **overgone:** overpowered.   126. **chafed:** enraged.
128. **Berwick:** town and fortress on the Scottish border at the mouth of the River Tweed.   **amain:** at full speed.

II.vi. Location: Scene continues.
o.s.d. **Clifford.** Actually, Clifford was killed in the skirmish at Ferrybridge where Warwick's half-brother fell. According to Hall (Bullough, III, 181–82), he was struck in the neck by an arrow and "incontinent [forthwith] rendered hys spirite."
5. **My . . . fear:** love and fear of me.
6. **commixtures:** i.e. the compound of "love and fear."
7. **misproud:** arrogant.
11–13. O . . . **earth.** See note to I.iv.33. Phaëton was so little able to control (*check*) his father's horses that they drew the sun-chariot too close to the earth and scorched it.   14. **sway'd:** ruled.
20. **chair:** throne.   28. **effuse:** effusion.
35. **fretting:** blowing in gusts.

Command an argosy to stem the waves.
But think you, lords, that Clifford fled with them?
War. No, 'tis impossible he should escape;
For (though before his face I speak the words)
Your brother Richard mark'd him for the grave, 40
And wheresoe'er he is, he's surely dead.
    Clifford groans [and then dies].
Rich. Whose soul is that which takes her heavy
 leave?
A deadly groan, like life and death's departing.
See who it is.
Edw.   And, now the battle's ended,
If friend or foe, let him be gently used. 45
Rich. Revoke that doom of mercy, for 'tis Clifford,
Who, not contented that he lopp'd the branch
In hewing Rutland when his leaves put forth,
But set his murth'ring knife unto the root
From whence that tender spray did sweetly spring, 50
I mean our princely father, Duke of York.
War. From off the gates of York fetch down the
 head,
Your father's head, which Clifford placed there;
In stead whereof let this supply the room:
Measure for measure must be answered. 55
Edw. Bring forth that fatal screech-owl to our
 house
That nothing sung but death to us and ours.
Now death shall stop his dismal threat'ning sound,
And his ill-boding tongue no more shall speak.
War. I think [his] understanding is bereft. 60
Speak, Clifford, dost thou know who speaks to thee?
Dark cloudy death o'ershades his beams of life,
And he nor sees nor hears us what we say.
Rich. O would he did! and so, perhaps, he doth;
'Tis but his policy to counterfeit, 65
Because he would avoid such bitter taunts
Which in the time of death he gave our father.
Geo. If so thou think'st, vex him with eager words.
Rich. Clifford, ask mercy and obtain no grace.
Edw. Clifford, repent in bootless penitence. 70
War. Clifford, devise excuses for thy faults.
Geo. While we devise fell tortures for thy faults.
Rich. Thou didst love York, and I am son to York.
Edw. Thou pitiedst Rutland, I will pity thee.
Geo. Where's Captain Margaret, to fence you now?
War. They mock thee, Clifford, swear as thou
 wast wont. 76
Rich. What, not an oath? Nay, then the world
 goes hard
When Clifford cannot spare his friends an oath.
I know by that he's dead, and by my soul,
If this right hand would buy two hours' life 80
That I, in all despite, might rail at him,
This hand should chop it off; and with the issuing
 blood
Stifle the villain whose unstanched thirst
York and young Rutland could not satisfy.

War. Ay, but he's dead. Off with the traitor's
 head, 85
And rear it in the place your father's stands.
And now to London with triumphant march,
There to be crowned England's royal king;
From whence shall Warwick cut the sea to France,
And ask the Lady Bona for thy queen. 90
So shalt thou sinow both these lands together,
And having France thy friend, thou shalt not dread
The scatt'red foe that hopes to rise again;
For though they cannot greatly sting to hurt,
Yet look to have them buzz to offend thine ears. 95
First will I see the coronation,
And then to Brittany I'll cross the sea
To effect this marriage, so it please my lord.
Edw. Even as thou wilt, sweet Warwick, let it be;
For in thy shoulder do I build my seat, 100
And never will I undertake the thing
Wherein thy counsel and consent is wanting.
Richard, I will create thee Duke of Gloucester,
And George, of Clarence. Warwick, as ourself,
Shall do and undo as him pleaseth best. 105
Rich. Let me be Duke of Clarence, George of
 Gloucester,
For Gloucester's dukedom is too ominous.
War. Tut, that's a foolish observation.
Richard, be Duke of Gloucester. Now to London
To see these honors in possession. *Exeunt.* 110

[ACT III, Scene I]

Enter [two Keepers] *with cross-bows in their hands.*

[*1. Keep.*] Under this thick-grown brake we'll
 shroud ourselves,
For through this laund anon the deer will come,
And in this covert will we make our stand,
Culling the principal of all the deer.
[*2. Keep.*] I'll stay above the hill, so both may
 shoot. 5
[*1. Keep.*] That cannot be, the noise of thy cross-
 bow
Will scare the herd, and so my shoot is lost.
Here stand we both and aim we at the best;
And for the time shall not seem tedious,
I'll tell thee what befell me on a day 10
In this self place where now we mean to stand.

36. **argosy:** large merchant ship. 43. **departing:** parting.
44-45. **And . . . used.** Actually, Edward was so implacable against
the defeated Lancastrians that he ordered the execution of all captives
of rank. 46. **doom:** judgment. 60. **bereft:** destroyed.
63. **nor . . . nor:** neither . . . nor. 68. **eager:** bitter.
75. **fence:** protect. 83. **unstanched:** insatiable.

90. **Lady Bona:** daughter of Louis, Duke of Savoy, and sister-in-law
of Louis XI of France. 91. **sinow:** sinew, tie firmly.
107. **Gloucester's . . . ominous.** Three earlier dukes of Gloucester—
including Richard II's uncle Thomas of Woodstock and Henry VI's
uncle Humphrey—had met violent deaths. Shakespeare apparently
remembered Hall, who, commenting on Humphrey of Gloucester's
murder, remarked (Bullough, III, 108) "that the name and title of
Gloucester, hath been unfortunate and unluckie to diverse, whiche
for their honor, have been erected by creacion of princes, to that stile
and dignitie, as Hugh Spencer, Thomas of Woodstocke, sonne to
kyng Edward the third, and this duke Humfrey, which thre persones,
by miserable death finished their daies, and after them kynge Richard
the .III. also, duke of Gloucester, in civill warre was slain and confounded: so that this name of Gloucester, is taken for an unhappie
and unfortunate stile."

III.i. Location: A forest in the north of England.
o.s.d. **Keepers:** gamekeepers. 1. **brake:** thicket.
2. **laund:** glade. 8. **at the best:** as well as we can.
9. **for:** in order that. 11. **self:** same.

3 Henry VI
III.i

[*2. Keep.*] Here comes a man, let's stay till he be past.

Enter the KING [HENRY, *disguised,*] *with a prayer-book.*

K. Hen. From Scotland am I stol'n, even of pure love,
To greet mine own land with my wishful sight.
No, Harry, Harry, 'tis no land of thine;   15
Thy place is fill'd, thy sceptre wrung from thee,
Thy balm wash'd off wherewith thou was anointed.
No bending knee will call thee Caesar now,
No humble suitors press to speak for right,
No, not a man comes for redress of thee;   20
For how can I help them and not myself?
  [*1. Keep.*] Ay, here's a deer whose skin's a keeper's fee:
This is the quondam king; let's seize upon him.
  K. Hen. Let me embrace [thee,] sour [adversities],
For wise men say it is the wisest course.   25
  [*2. Keep.*] Why linger we? Let us lay hands upon him.
  [*1. Keep.*] Forbear awhile, we'll hear a little more.
  K. Hen. My queen and son are gone to France for aid;
And, as I hear, the great commanding Warwick
[Is] thither gone to crave the French king's sister   30
To wife for Edward. If this news be true,
Poor queen and son, your labor is but lost;
For Warwick is a subtle orator,
And Lewis a prince soon won with moving words.
By this account then, Margaret may win him,   35
For she's a woman to be pitied much.
Her sighs will make a batt'ry in his breast,
Her tears will pierce into a marble heart;
The tiger will be mild whiles she doth mourn;
And Nero will be tainted with remorse   40
To hear and see her plaints, her brinish tears.
Ay, but she's come to beg; Warwick, to give:
She, on his left side, craving aid for Henry;
He, on his right, asking a wife for Edward.
She weeps, and says her Henry is depos'd;   45
He smiles, and says his Edward is install'd;
That she, poor wretch, for grief can speak no more;
Whiles Warwick tells his title, smooths the wrong,
Inferreth arguments of mighty strength,
And in conclusion wins the King from her   50
With promise of his sister and what else,
To strengthen and support King Edward's place.
O Margaret, thus 'twill be, and thou, poor soul,
Art then forsaken, as thou went'st forlorn!
  [*2. Keep.*] Say, what art thou talk'st of kings and queens?   55
  K. Hen. More than I seem, and less than I was born to;
A man at least, for less I should not be;
And men may talk of kings, and why not I?
  [*2. Keep.*] Ay, but thou talk'st as if thou wert a king.

K. Hen. Why, so I am—in mind, and that's enough.
  [*2. Keep.*] But if thou be a king, where is thy crown?   61
  K. Hen. My crown is in my heart, not on my head;
Not deck'd with diamonds and Indian stones,
Nor to be seen. My crown is call'd content,
A crown it is that seldom kings enjoy.   65
  [*2. Keep.*] Well, if you be a king crown'd with content,
Your crown content and you must be contented
To go along with us; for, as we think,
You are the king King Edward hath depos'd;
And we his subjects, sworn in all allegiance,   70
Will apprehend you as his enemy.
  K. Hen. But did you never swear and break an oath?
  [*2. Keep.*] No, never such an oath, nor will not now.
  K. Hen. Where did you dwell when I was King of England?
  [*2. Keep.*] Here in this country where we now remain.   75
  K. Hen. I was anointed king at nine months old,
My father and my grandfather were kings;
And you were sworn true subjects unto me;
And tell me then, have you not broke your oaths?
  [*1. Keep.*] No,   80
For we were subjects but while you were king.
  K. Hen. Why? Am I dead? Do I not breathe a man?
Ah, simple men, you know not what you swear!
Look, as I blow this feather from my face,
And as the air blows it to me again,   85
Obeying with my wind when I do blow,
And yielding to another when it blows,
Commanded always by the greater gust,
Such is the lightness of you common men.
But do not break your oaths, for of that sin   90
My mild entreaty shall not make you guilty.
Go where you will, the King shall be commanded;
And be you kings: command, and I'll obey.
  [*1. Keep.*] We are true subjects to the King, King Edward.
  K. Hen. So would you be again to Henry,   95
If he were seated as King Edward is.
  [*1. Keep.*] We charge you, in God's name and the King's,
To go with us unto the officers.
  K. Hen. In God's name lead; your king's name be obey'd;
And what God will, that let your king perform;   100
And what he will, I humbly yield unto.   *Exeunt.*

[SCENE II]

Enter KING EDWARD, GLOUCESTER, CLARENCE, LADY GREY.

  K. Edw. Brother of Gloucester, at Saint Albons field

---

14. **wishful:** longing.   19. **speak for right:** ask for justice.
20. **of:** from.   37. **batt'ry:** breach, bruise.
40. **Nero.** A byword for cruelty.   **tainted:** touched.
48. **his title:** i.e. Edward's claim.   49. **Inferreth:** adduces.

71. **apprehend:** arrest.   81. **but:** only.

III.ii. Location: London. The palace.

This lady's husband, Sir Richard Grey, was slain,
His land then seiz'd on by the conqueror.
Her suit is now to repossess those lands,
Which we in justice cannot well deny, 5
Because in quarrel of the house of York
The worthy gentleman did lose his life.
  Glou. Your Highness shall do well to grant her suit;
It were dishonor to deny it her.
  K. Edw. It were no less, but yet I'll make a pause.
  Glou. [*Aside to Clarence.*] Yea, is it so? 11
I see the lady hath a thing to grant,
Before the King will grant her humble suit.
  Clar. [*Aside to Gloucester.*] He knows the game;
    how true he keeps the wind!
  Glou. [*Aside to Clarence.*] Silence! 15
  K. Edw. Widow, we will consider of your suit,
And come some other time to know our mind.
  L. Grey. Right gracious lord, I cannot brook delay.
May it please your Highness to resolve me now,
And what your pleasure is shall satisfy me. 20
  Glou. [*Aside to Clarence.*] Ay, widow? Then I'll
    warrant you all your lands,
And if what pleases him shall pleasure you.
Fight closer or, good faith, you'll catch a blow.
  Clar. [*Aside to Gloucester.*] I fear her not, unless she
    chance to fall.
  Glou. [*Aside to Clarence.*] God forbid that, for he'll
    take vantages. 25
  K. Edw. How many children hast thou, widow?
    tell me.
  Clar. [*Aside to Gloucester.*] I think he means to beg
    a child of her.
  Glou. [*Aside to Clarence.*] Nay then whip me; he'll
    rather give her two.
  L. Grey. Three, my most gracious lord.
  Glou. [*Aside to Clarence.*] You shall have four [and]
    you'll be rul'd by him. 30
  K. Edw. 'Twere pity they should lose their
    father's lands.
  L. Grey. Be pitiful, dread lord, and grant it then.
  K. Edw. Lords, give us leave. I'll try this widow's
    wit.
  Glou. [*Aside to Clarence.*] Ay, good leave have you,
    for you will have leave
Till youth take leave and leave you to the crutch. 35
    [*Gloucester and Clarence retire.*]
  K. Edw. Now tell me, madam, do you love your
    children?
  L. Grey. Ay, full as dearly as I love myself.
  K. Edw. And would you not do much to do them
    good?
  L. Grey. To do them good I would sustain some
    harm.

  K. Edw. Then get your husband's lands, to do
    them good. 40
  L. Grey. Therefore I came unto your Majesty.
  K. Edw. I'll tell you how these lands are to be got.
  L. Grey. So shall you bind me to your Highness'
    service.
  K. Edw. What service wilt thou do me if I give
    them?
  L. Grey. What you command that rests in me to
    do. 45
  K. Edw. But you will take exceptions to my boon.
  L. Grey. No, gracious lord, except I cannot do it.
  K. Edw. Ay, but thou canst do what I mean to ask.
  L. Grey. Why then I will do what your Grace
    commands.
  Glou. [*Aside to Clarence.*] He plies her hard, and
    much rain wears the marble. 50
  Clar. [*Aside to Gloucester.*] As red as fire? nay then,
    her wax must melt.
  L. Grey. Why stops my lord? shall I not hear my
    task?
  K. Edw. An easy task, 'tis but to love a king.
  L. Grey. That's soon perform'd, because I am a
    subject.
  K. Edw. Why then, thy husband's lands I freely
    give thee. 55
  L. Grey. I take my leave with many thousand
    thanks.
  Glou. [*Aside to Clarence.*] The match is made, she
    seals it with a cur'sy.
  K. Edw. But stay thee, 'tis the fruits of love I
    mean.
  L. Grey. The fruits of love I mean, my loving
    liege.
  K. Edw. Ay, but I fear me in another sense. 60
What love, think'st thou, I sue so much to get?
  L. Grey. My love till death, my humble thanks,
    my prayers—
That love which virtue begs and virtue grants.
  K. Edw. No, by my troth, I did not mean such
    love.
  L. Grey. Why then you mean not as I thought you
    did. 65
  K. Edw. But now you partly may perceive my
    mind.
  L. Grey. My mind will never grant what I perceive
Your Highness aims at, if I aim aright.
  K. Edw. To tell thee plain, I aim to lie with thee.
  L. Grey. To tell you plain, I had rather lie in
    prison. 70
  K. Edw. Why then thou shalt not have thy hus-
    band's lands.
  L. Grey. Why then mine honesty shall be my
    dower,
For by that loss I will not purchase them.
  K. Edw. Therein thou wrong'st thy children
    mightily.
  L. Grey. Herein your Highness wrongs both them
    and me. 75

2–7. **This ... life.** Actually, Sir John—not Richard—Grey lost his life while fighting for Margaret and the Lancastrians at the second battle of St. Albans in 1461. In *Richard III* (I.iii.126–29) the facts are given accurately.
14. **keeps the wind:** i.e. so that the game will not catch the scent and be alarmed. 21. **warrant:** guarantee.
24. **fear:** i.e. fear for. 25. **vantages:** opportunities. 30. **and:** if.
33. **give us leave:** pardon us, i.e. leave us alone.
34. **Ay ... have leave:** yes, may you have pardon, for you will take liberties.

46. **boon:** request for a favor. 47. **except:** unless.
57. **cur'sy:** curtsy. 68. **aim:** guess. 72. **honesty:** chastity.

687

3 Henry VI
III.ii

But, mighty lord, this merry inclination
Accords not with the sadness of my suit.
Please you dismiss me, either with ay or no.

K. Edw. Ay, if thou wilt say ay to my request;
No, if thou dost say no to my demand. 80

L. Grey. Then no, my lord. My suit is at an end.

Glou. [*Aside to Clarence.*] The widow likes him
not, she knits her brows.

Clar. [*Aside to Gloucester.*] He is the bluntest wooer
in Christendom.

K. Edw. [*Aside.*] Her looks doth argue her re-
plete with modesty,
Her words doth show her wit incomparable, 85
All her perfections challenge sovereignty:
One way or other, she is for a king,
And she shall be my love or else my queen.—
Say that King Edward take thee for his queen?

L. Grey. 'Tis better said than done, my gracious
lord. 90
I am a subject fit to jest withal,
But far unfit to be a sovereign.

K. Edw. Sweet widow, by my state I swear to
thee
I speak no more than what my soul intends,
And that is, to enjoy thee for my love. 95

L. Grey. And that is more than I will yield unto.
I know I am too mean to be your queen,
And yet too good to be your concubine.

K. Edw. You cavil, widow, I did mean my queen.

L. Grey. 'Twill grieve your Grace my sons should
call you father. 100

K. Edw. No more than when my daughters call
thee mother.
Thou art a widow, and thou hast some children,
And by God's Mother, I, being but a bachelor,
Have other some. Why, 'tis a happy thing
To be the father unto many sons. 105
Answer no more, for thou shalt be my queen.

Glou. [*Aside to Clarence.*] The ghostly father now
hath done his shrift.

Clar. [*Aside to Gloucester.*] When he was made a
shriver, 'twas for shift.

K. Edw. Brothers, you muse what chat we two
have had.

Glou. The widow likes it not, for she looks very
sad. 110

K. Edw. You'ld think it strange if I should marry
her.

Clar. To who, my lord?

K. Edw. Why, Clarence, to myself.

Glou. That would be ten days' wonder at the least.

Clar. That's a day longer than a wonder lasts.

Glou. By so much is the wonder in extremes. 115

K. Edw. Well, jest on, brothers. I can tell you
both
Her suit is granted for her husband's lands.

Enter a NOBLEMAN.

Nob. My gracious lord, Henry your foe is taken,
And brought your prisoner to your palace gate.

K. Edw. See that he be convey'd unto the Tower;
And go we, brothers, to the man that took him, 121
To question of his apprehension.
Widow, go you along. Lords, use her [honorably].
Exeunt. Manet Richard [of Gloucester].

Glou. Ay, Edward will use women honorably.
Would he were wasted, marrow, bones, and all, 125
That from his loins no hopeful branch may spring,
To cross me from the golden time I look for!
And yet, between my soul's desire and me—
The lustful Edward's title buried—
Is Clarence, Henry, and his son young Edward, 130
And all the unlook'd-for issue of their bodies
To take their rooms, ere I can place myself:
A cold premeditation for my purpose!
Why then I do but dream on sovereignty,
Like one that stands upon a promontory 135
And spies a far-off shore where he would tread,
Wishing his foot were equal with his eye,
And chides the sea that sunders him from thence,
Saying, he'll lade it dry to have his way:
So do I wish the crown, being so far off, 140
And so I chide the means that keeps me from it,
And so, I say, I'll cut the causes off,
Flattering me with impossibilities.
My eye's too quick, my heart o'erweens too much,
Unless my hand and strength could equal them. 145
Well, say there is no kingdom then for Richard;
What other pleasure can the world afford?
I'll make my heaven in a lady's lap,
And deck my body in gay ornaments,
And witch sweet ladies with my words and looks.
O miserable thought! and more unlikely 151
Than to accomplish twenty golden crowns!
Why, love forswore me in my mother's womb;
And for I should not deal in her soft laws,
She did corrupt frail nature with some bribe, 155
To shrink mine arm up like a wither'd shrub,
To make an envious mountain on my back,
Where sits deformity to mock my body;
To shape my legs of an unequal size,
To disproportion me in every part, 160
Like to a chaos, or an unlick'd bear-whelp
That carries no impression like the dam.
And am I then a man to be belov'd?
O monstrous fault, to harbor such a thought!
Then since this earth affords no joy to me 165
But to command, to check, to o'erbear such
As are of better person than myself,
I'll make my heaven to dream upon the crown,
And whiles I live, t' account this world but hell,
Until my misshap'd trunk that bears this head 170

77. sadness: seriousness.   93. state: i.e. royalty.
104. other some: some others.
107. ghostly father: spiritual father, confessor.   done his shrift:
heard her confession and given absolution.
108. shift: trick, shifty purpose.   109. muse: wonder.
114. That's . . . lasts. A "nine days' wonder" is still proverbial.

129. buried: i.e. eliminated.   131. unlook'd for: unforeseeable.
133. cold premeditation: i.e. chilly prospect.
139. lade: empty.   141. means: obstacles.   143. me: myself.
144. o'erweens: presumes.   150. witch: bewitch.
154. for . . . not: lest I.   157. envious: hateful.
161. unlick'd bear-whelp. Bear cubs were supposedly born as shapeless lumps of flesh and licked into shape by the mother.
166. check: control.   o'erbear: dominate.

Be round impaled with a glorious crown.
And yet I know not how to get the crown,
For many lives stand between me and home;
And I—like one lost in a thorny wood,
That rents the thorns, and is rent with the thorns,
Seeking a way, and straying from the way,   176
Not knowing how to find the open air,
But toiling desperately to find it out—
Torment myself to catch the English crown;
And from that torment I will free myself,   180
Or hew my way out with a bloody axe.
Why, I can smile, and murther whiles I smile,
And cry "Content" to that which grieves my heart,
And wet my cheeks with artificial tears,
And frame my face to all occasions.   185
I'll drown more sailors than the mermaid shall,
I'll slay more gazers than the basilisk,
I'll play the orator as well as Nestor,
Deceive more slily than Ulysses could,
And like a Sinon, take another Troy.   190
I can add colors to the chameleon,
Change shapes with Proteus for advantages,
And set the murtherous Machevil to school.
Can I do this, and cannot get a crown?   194
Tut, were it farther off, I'll pluck it down.   *Exit.*

[SCENE III]

Flourish. Enter LEWIS *the French King, his sister* BONA,
his Admiral, call'd BOURBON, PRINCE EDWARD,
QUEEN MARGARET, *and the* EARL OF OXFORD.
Lewis sits, and riseth up again.

   K. Lew.   Fair Queen of England, worthy Mar-
      garet,
Sit down with us. It ill befits thy state
And birth that thou shouldst stand while Lewis doth
   sit.
   Q. Mar.   No, mighty King of France; now Mar-
      garet
Must strike her sail and learn a while to serve   5
Where kings command. I was, I must confess,
Great Albion's queen in former golden days;
But now mischance hath trod my title down,
And with dishonor laid me on the ground,
Where I must take like seat unto my fortune,   10
And to my humble seat conform myself.
   K. Lew.   Why, say, fair queen, whence springs this
      deep despair?
   Q. Mar.   From such a cause as fills mine eyes with
      tears   13

And stops my tongue, while heart is drown'd in cares.
   K. Lew.   What e'er it be, be thou still like thyself,
And sit thee by our side. (*Seats her by him.*) Yield not
      thy neck   16
To fortune's yoke, but let thy dauntless mind
Still ride in triumph over all mischance.
Be plain, Queen Margaret, and tell thy grief;
It shall be eas'd if France can yield relief.   20
   Q. Mar.   Those gracious words revive my droop-
      ing thoughts
And give my tongue-tied sorrows leave to speak.
Now therefore be it known to noble Lewis,
That Henry, sole possessor of my love,
Is, of a king, become a banish'd man,   25
And forc'd to live in Scotland a forlorn;
While proud ambitious Edward, Duke of York,
Usurps the regal title and the seat
Of England's true-anointed lawful king.
This is the cause that I, poor Margaret,   30
With this my son, Prince Edward, Henry's heir,
Am come to crave thy just and lawful aid;
And if thou fail us, all our hope is done.
Scotland hath will to help, but cannot help;
Our people and our peers are both misled,   35
Our treasure seiz'd, our soldiers put to flight,
And as thou seest, ourselves in heavy plight.
   K. Lew.   Renowned queen, with patience calm the
      storm,
While we bethink a means to break it off.
   Q. Mar.   The more we stay, the stronger grows
      our foe.   40
   K. Lew.   The more I stay, the more I'll succor thee.
   Q. Mar.   O, but impatience waiteth on true sorrow.
And see where comes the breeder of my sorrow!

Enter WARWICK.

   K. Lew.   What's he approacheth boldly to our
      presence?
   Q. Mar.   Our Earl of Warwick, Edward's greatest
      friend.   45
   K. Lew.   Welcome, brave Warwick! What brings
      thee to France?   *He descends. She ariseth.*
   Q. Mar.   Ay, now begins a second storm to rise,
For this is he that moves both wind and tide.
   War.   From worthy Edward, King of Albion,
My lord and sovereign and thy vowed friend,   50
I come, in kindness and unfeigned love,
First, to do greetings to thy royal person,
And then to crave a league of amity,
And lastly, to confirm that amity
With nuptial knot, if thou vouchsafe to grant   55
That virtuous Lady Bona, thy fair sister,
To England's king in lawful marriage.
   Q. Mar.   [*Aside.*] If that go forward, Henry's
      hope is done.
   War.   And, gracious madam (*speaking to Bona*), in
      our king's behalf
I am commanded, with your leave and favor,   60
Humbly to kiss your hand, and with my tongue

---

171. **impaled:** enclosed.   173. **home:** i.e. his goal.
175. **rents:** rends.   184. **artificial:** feigned.
186. **mermaid.** Thought to lure mariners to their death.
187. **basilisk:** fabulous serpent whose look was thought to cause
death.   188, 189. **Nestor, Ulysses:** Greek leaders in the Trojan war.
190. **Sinon:** Greek warrior who contrived the ruse of the wooden
horse by which Troy was taken.
192. **Proteus:** the "Old Man of the Sea" who could change his shape
when captured.
193. **set . . . school:** i.e. to teach Machiavelli himself about murder. See
note to *1 Henry VI*, V.iv.74.

III.iii. **Location:** France. The King's palace.
2. **state:** rank.   5. **strike her sail:** humble herself.
7. **Albion's:** England's.

20. **France:** i.e. the King of France.
25. **of a king:** from being a king.   26. **forlorn:** outcast.
40. **stay:** delay.   56. **sister:** i.e. sister-in-law.

3 Henry VI
III.iii

To tell the passion of my sovereign's heart,
Where fame, late ent'ring at his heedful ears,
Hath plac'd thy beauty's image and thy virtue.
 Q. Mar. King Lewis and Lady Bona, hear me
  speak   65
Before you answer Warwick. His demand
Springs not from Edward's well-meant honest love,
But from deceit bred by necessity;
For how can tyrants safely govern home,
Unless abroad they purchase great alliance? 70
To prove him tyrant this reason may suffice,
That Henry liveth still; but were he dead,
Yet here Prince Edward stands, King Henry's son.
Look therefore, Lewis, that by this league and mar-
 riage
Thou draw not on thy danger and dishonor; 75
For though usurpers sway the rule a while,
Yet heav'ns are just, and time suppresseth wrongs.
 War. Injurious Margaret!
 Prince.   And why not Queen?
 War. Because thy father Henry did usurp,
And thou no more art prince than she is queen. 80
 Oxf. Then Warwick disannuls great John of
 Gaunt,
Which did subdue the greatest part of Spain;
And after John of Gaunt, Henry the Fourth,
Whose wisdom was a mirror to the wisest;
And after that wise prince, Henry the Fift, 85
Who by his prowess conquered all France:
From these our Henry lineally descends.
 War. Oxford, how haps it in this smooth discourse
You told not how Henry the Sixt hath lost
All that which Henry the Fift had gotten? 90
Methinks these peers of France should smile at that.
But for the rest: you tell a pedigree
Of threescore and two years—a silly time
To make prescription for a kingdom's worth.
 Oxf. Why, Warwick, canst thou speak against thy
 liege,   95
Whom thou obey'dst thirty and six years,
And not bewray thy treason with a blush?
 War. Can Oxford, that did ever fence the right,
Now buckler falsehood with a pedigree?
For shame, leave Henry, and call Edward king. 100
 Oxf. Call him my king by whose injurious doom
My elder brother, the Lord Aubrey Vere,
Was done to death? and more than so, my father,
Even in the downfall of his mellow'd years,
When nature brought him to the door of death? 105
No, Warwick, no; while life upholds this arm,
This arm upholds the house of Lancaster.
 War. And I the house of York.

78. Injurious: insulting. **81. disannuls:** cancels.
93. Of . . . years: i.e. from the deposition of Richard II by Henry IV (1399). The time represented here is thus 1461, but Warwick's marriage embassy actually took place in 1463.
94. prescription: a claim founded upon *de facto* possession.
96. thirty . . . years: i.e. the time between Henry VI's accession in 1422 and his open break with Warwick in 1458 (?). Warwick, however, was in fact only thirty in the latter year. **98. fence:** defend.
99. buckler: protect.
101–5. Call . . . death. John de Vere, twelfth Earl of Oxford, and his eldest son Aubrey were attainted and executed as Lancastrian agitators in 1462.

690

 K. Lew. Queen Margaret, Prince Edward, and
 Oxford,
Vouchsafe, at our request, to stand aside, 110
While I use further conference with Warwick.
          They stand aloof.
 Q. Mar. Heavens grant that Warwick's words
 bewitch him not!
 K. Lew. Now, Warwick, tell me, even upon thy
 conscience,
Is Edward your true king? for I were loath
To link with him that were not lawful chosen. 115
 War. Thereon I pawn my credit and mine honor.
 K. Lew. But is he gracious in the people's eye?
 War. The more that Henry was unfortunate.
 K. Lew. Then further: all dissembling set aside,
Tell me for truth the measure of his love 120
Unto our sister Bona.
 War.   Such it seems
As may beseem a monarch like himself.
Myself have often heard him say, and swear,
That this his love was an [eternal] plant,
Whereof the root was fix'd in virtue's ground, 125
The leaves and fruit maintain'd with beauty's sun,
Exempt from envy, but not from disdain,
Unless the Lady Bona quit his pain.
 K. Lew. Now, sister, let us hear your firm resolve.
 Bona. Your grant, or your denial, shall be mine. 130
Yet I confess that often ere this day,
         Speaks to Warwick.
When I have heard your king's desert recounted,
Mine ear hath tempted judgment to desire.
 K. Lew. Then, Warwick, thus: our sister shall be
 Edward's.
And now forthwith shall articles be drawn 135
Touching the jointure that your king must make,
Which with her dowry shall be counterpois'd.
Draw near, Queen Margaret, and be a witness
That Bona shall be wife to the English king. 139
 Prince. To Edward, but not to the English king.
 Q. Mar. Deceitful Warwick, it was thy device
By this alliance to make void my suit.
Before thy coming, Lewis was Henry's friend.
 K. Lew. And still is friend to him and Margaret.
But if your title to the crown be weak, 145
As may appear by Edward's good success,
Then 'tis but reason that I be releas'd
From giving aid which late I promised.
Yet shall you have all kindness at my hand
That your estate requires and mine can yield. 150
 War. Henry now lives in Scotland at his ease;
Where having nothing, nothing can he lose.
And as for you yourself, our quondam queen,
You have a father able to maintain you,
And better 'twere you troubled him than France. 155
 Q. Mar. Peace, impudent and shameless Warwick,
Proud setter-up and puller-down of kings!
I will not hence, till with my talk and tears
(Both full of truth) I make King Lewis behold

127. envy: malice. **disdain:** contempt.
128. quit his pain: i.e. relieve his passion with her love.
136. jointure: marriage settlement.
137. counterpois'd: balanced.

Thy sly conveyance and thy lord's false love,　160
For both of you are birds of self-same feather.

Post blowing a horn within.

K. Lew.　Warwick, this is some post to us or thee.

Enter the Post.

Post.　My lord ambassador, these letters are for you,
Speaks to Warwick.
Sent from your brother, Marquess Montague.　164
These from our king unto your Majesty.　*To Lewis.*
And, madam, these for you; from whom I know not.
To Margaret.
They all read their letters.

Oxf.　I like it well that our fair queen and mistress
Smiles at her news, while Warwick frowns at his.

Prince.　Nay, mark how Lewis stamps as he were
nettled.
I hope all's for the best.　170

K. Lew.　Warwick, what are thy news?　And
yours, fair queen?

Q. Mar.　Mine such as fill my heart with unhop'd
joys.

War.　Mine full of sorrow and heart's discontent.

K. Lew.　What? has your king married the Lady
Grey?
And now to soothe your forgery and his,　175
Sends me a paper to persuade me patience?
Is this th' alliance that he seeks with France?
Dare he presume to scorn us in this manner?

Q. Mar.　I told your Majesty as much before:　179
This proveth Edward's love and Warwick's honesty.

War.　King Lewis, I here protest in sight of heaven,
And by the hope I have of heavenly bliss,
That I am clear from this misdeed of Edward's;
No more my king, for he dishonors me,
But most himself if he could see his shame.　185
Did I forget that by the house of York
My father came untimely to his death?
Did I let pass th' abuse done to my niece?
Did I impale him with the regal crown?
Did I put Henry from his native right?　190
And am I guerdon'd at the last with shame?
Shame on himself! for my desert is honor;
And to repair my honor lost for him,
I here renounce him and return to Henry.
My noble queen, let former grudges pass,　195
And henceforth I am thy true servitor.
I will revenge his wrong to Lady Bona,
And replant Henry in his former state.

Q. Mar.　Warwick, these words have turn'd my
hate to love,
And I forgive and quite forget old faults,　200
And joy that thou becom'st King Henry's friend.

War.　So much his friend, ay, his unfeigned friend,

That if King Lewis vouchsafe to furnish us
With some few bands of chosen soldiers,
I'll undertake to land them on our coast,　205
And force the tyrant from his seat by war.
'Tis not his new-made bride shall succor him,
And as for Clarence, as my letters tell me,
He's very likely now to fall from him,
For matching more for wanton lust than honor,　210
Or than for strength and safety of our country.

Bona.　Dear brother, how shall Bona be reveng'd
But by thy help to this distressed queen?

Q. Mar.　Renowned prince, how shall poor Henry
live,
Unless thou rescue him from foul despair?　215

Bona.　My quarrel and this English queen's are one.

War.　And mine, fair Lady Bona, joins with yours.

K. Lew.　And mine with hers, and thine, and
Margaret's.
Therefore, at last, I firmly am resolv'd
You shall have aid.　220

Q. Mar.　Let me give humble thanks for all at once.

K. Lew.　Then, England's messenger, return in
post,
And tell false Edward, thy supposed king,
That Lewis of France is sending over masquers
To revel it with him and his new bride.　225
Thou seest what's pass'd, go fear thy king withal.

Bona.　Tell him, in hope he'll prove a widower
shortly,
I wear the willow garland for his sake.

Q. Mar.　Tell him, my mourning weeds are laid
aside,
And I am ready to put armor on.　230

War.　Tell him from me that he hath done me
wrong,
And therefore I'll uncrown him ere't be long.
There's thy reward, be gone.　*Exit Post.*

K. Lew.　　　　　　　　But, Warwick,
Thou and Oxford, with five thousand men,
Shall cross the seas and bid false Edward battle;　235
And as occasion serves, this noble queen
And prince shall follow with a fresh supply.
Yet ere thou go, but answer me one doubt:
What pledge have we of thy firm loyalty?

War.　This shall assure my constant loyalty,　240
That if our queen and this young prince agree,
I'll join mine eldest daughter, and my joy,
To him forthwith in holy wedlock bands.

Q. Mar.　Yes, I agree, and thank you for your
motion.
Son Edward, she is fair and virtuous,　245
Therefore delay not, give thy hand to Warwick,
And with thy hand, thy faith irrevocable

---

160. **conveyance:** deceit.　161 s.d. **Post:** messenger.
175. **soothe your forgery:** palliate your deceit.
176. **persuade:** advise.
186–87. **Did . . . death.** Actually, Warwick's father—the Earl of Salisbury of *2 Henry VI*—had been captured at the battle of Wakefield (1460) and executed by the victorious Lancastrians.
188. **th' abuse . . . niece.** According to Hall (Bullough, III, 188), the notoriously lecherous Edward, while a guest in Warwick's house, "woulde have deflowred his doughter or his nece."
189. **impale him:** encircle his head.　191. **guerdon'd:** rewarded.

205–6. **I'll . . . war.** Another anachronism. Warwick did not seek Henry VI's restoration until 1470.　210. **matching:** marrying.
226. **fear:** frighten.　**withal:** with this.
228. **willow garland.** Token of a forsaken lover.
242. **eldest daughter.** Warwick's eldest daughter was Isabella, who married George, Duke of Clarence, in 1469. It was Anne (1456–85), Warwick's second daughter, to whom Prince Edward was betrothed the following year, but his capture and murder at the hands of the Yorkists after the battle of Tewkesbury in 1471 (see V.v) occurred before they could be married. In 1474 she married Richard, Duke of Gloucester (later Richard III).　244. **motion:** offer.

3 Henry VI
III.iii

That only Warwick's daughter shall be thine.

Prince. Yes, I accept her, for she well deserves it,
And here, to pledge my vow, I give my hand. 250
    He gives his hand to Warwick.

K. Lew. Why stay we now? These soldiers shall
    be levied,
And thou, Lord Bourbon, our High Admiral,
Shall waft them over with our royal fleet.
I long till Edward fall by war's mischance,
For mocking marriage with a dame of France. 255
    Exeunt. Manet Warwick.

War. I came from Edward as ambassador,
But I return his sworn and mortal foe.
Matter of marriage was the charge he gave me,
But dreadful war shall answer his demand.
Had he none else to make a stale but me? 260
Then none but I shall turn his jest to sorrow.
I was the chief that rais'd him to the crown,
And I'll be chief to bring him down again;
Not that I pity Henry's misery,
But seek revenge on Edward's mockery. *Exit.* 265

[ACT IV, SCENE I]

Enter RICHARD [OF GLOUCESTER], CLARENCE, SOM-
ERSET, *and* MONTAGUE.

Glou. Now tell me, brother Clarence, what think
    you
Of this new marriage with the Lady Grey?
Hath not our brother made a worthy choice?

Clar. Alas, you know, 'tis far from hence to France;
How could he stay till Warwick made return? 5

Som. My lords, forbear this talk; here comes the
    King.

Flourish. Enter KING EDWARD, *Lady Grey,* [*now*
QUEEN ELIZABETH,] PEMBROKE, STAFFORD, HAS-
TINGS, [*and others*]. *Four stand on one side and four
on the other.*

Glou. And his well-chosen bride.

Clar. I mind to tell him plainly what I think.

K. Edw. Now, brother of Clarence, how like you
    our choice,
That you stand pensive as half malecontent? 10

Clar. As well as Lewis of France or the Earl of
    Warwick,
Which are so weak of courage and in judgment
That they'll take no offense at our abuse.

K. Edw. Suppose they take offense without a
    cause;
They are but Lewis and Warwick, I am Edward, 15
Your king and Warwick's, and must have my will.

Glou. And shall have your will, because our king.
Yet hasty marriage seldom proveth well.

K. Edw. Yea, brother Richard, are you offended
    too?

Glou. Not I. 20
No; God forbid that I should wish them sever'd
Whom God hath join'd together; ay, and 'twere pity
To sunder them that yoke so well together.

K. Edw. Setting your scorns and your mislike
    aside,
Tell me some reason why the Lady Grey 25
Should not become my wife and England's queen.
And you too, Somerset and Montague,
Speak freely what you think.

Clar. Then this is mine opinion: that King Lewis
Becomes your enemy, for mocking him 30
About the marriage of the Lady Bona.

Glou. And Warwick, doing what you gave in
    charge,
Is now dishonored by this new marriage.

K. Edw. What if both Lewis and Warwick be
    appeas'd
By such invention as I can devise? 35

Mont. Yet, to have join'd with France in such
    alliance
Would more have strength'ned this our common-
    wealth
'Gainst foreign storms than any home-bred marriage.

Hast. Why, knows not Montague that of itself
England is safe, if true within itself? 40

Mont. But the safer when 'tis back'd with France.

Hast. 'Tis better using France than trusting France.
Let us be back'd with God, and with the seas,
Which he hath giv'n for fence impregnable,
And with their helps only defend ourselves: 45
In them, and in ourselves, our safety lies.

Clar. For this one speech Lord Hastings well
    deserves
To have the heir of the Lord Hungerford.

K. Edw. Ay, what of that? It was my will and
    grant,
And for this once my will shall stand for law. 50

Glou. And yet methinks your Grace hath not done
    well
To give the heir and daughter of Lord Scales
Unto the brother of your loving bride.
She better would have fitted me or Clarence;
But in your bride you bury brotherhood. 55

Clar. Or else you would not have bestow'd the heir
Of the Lord Bonville on your new wive's son,
And leave your brothers to go speed elsewhere.

K. Edw. Alas, poor Clarence! is it for a wife
That thou art malecontent? I will provide thee. 60

32. **gave in charge:** commissioned.
35. **invention:** design, plan.
47–58. **For . . . elsewhere.** These allusions to the profitable marriages arranged for the Queen's upstart relatives are probably derived from Hall (Bullough, III, 186–87): "Her father also was created erle Ryvers, and made high Constable of Englande: her brother lorde Anthony, was maried to the sole heyre of Thomas lord Scales, & by her he was lord Scales. Syr Thomas Grey, sonne of syr John Grey, the quenes fyrst husband, was created Marques Dorset, and maried to Cicilie, heyre to the lord Bonvile. Albeit this mariage, at the first apparaunce was very pleasaunt to the king, but more joyous to the quene & profitable to her bloud, which were so highly exalted, yea, & so sodainly promoted, that all the nobilitie more marvayled then allowed this sodayne risyng and swift elevacion." 57. **wive's:** wife's.
58. **speed:** achieve success (in seeking wives for themselves).

253. **waft:** convey by water. 260. **stale:** laughingstock.

IV.i. Location: London. The palace.
10. **malecontent:** malcontent. 13. **abuse:** insult.
16. **will:** determination (with following play on the sense "lust").

Clar. In choosing for yourself, you show'd your
judgment;
Which being shallow, you shall give me leave
To play the broker in mine own behalf;
And to that end I shortly mind to leave you.

K. Edw. Leave me, or tarry, Edward will be king,
And not be tied unto his brother's will.   66

Q. Eliz. My lords, before it pleas'd his Majesty
To raise my state to title of a queen,
Do me but right, and you must all confess
That I was not ignoble of descent,   70
And meaner than myself have had like fortune.
But as this title honors me and mine,
So your dislikes, to whom I would be pleasing,
Doth cloud my joys with danger and with sorrow.

K. Edw. My love, forbear to fawn upon their
frowns.   75
What danger or what sorrow can befall thee
So long as Edward is thy constant friend
And their true sovereign whom they must obey?
Nay, whom they shall obey, and love thee too,
Unless they seek for hatred at my hands;   80
Which if they do, yet will I keep thee safe,
And they shall feel the vengeance of my wrath.

Glou. [*Aside.*] I hear, yet say not much, but think
the more.

Enter a Post.

K. Edw. Now, messenger, what letters or what
news
From France?   85

Post. My sovereign liege, no letters, and few
words,
But such as I (without your special pardon)
Dare not relate.

K. Edw. Go to, we pardon thee; therefore, in brief,
Tell me their words as near as thou canst guess them.
What answer makes King Lewis unto our letters?   91

Post. At my depart, these were his very words:
"Go tell false Edward, the supposed king,
That Lewis of France is sending over masquers
To revel it with him and his new bride."   95

K. Edw. Is Lewis so brave? belike he thinks me
Henry.
But what said Lady Bona to my marriage?

Post. These were her words, utt'red with mild dis-
dain:
"Tell him, in hope he'll prove a widower shortly,
I'll wear the willow garland for his sake."   100

K. Edw. I blame not her: she could say little less;
She had the wrong. But what said Henry's queen?
For I have heard that she was there in place.

Post. "Tell him," quoth she, "my mourning weeds
are done,
And I am ready to put armor on."   105

K. Edw. Belike she minds to play the Amazon.
But what said Warwick to these injuries?

Post. He, more incens'd against your Majesty
Than all the rest, discharg'd me with these words:
"Tell him from me that he hath done me wrong,   110
And therefore I'll uncrown him ere't be long."

K. Edw. Ha? durst the traitor breathe out so
proud words?
Well, I will arm me, being thus forewarn'd.
They shall have wars, and pay for their presumption.
But say, is Warwick friends with Margaret?   115

Post. Ay, gracious sovereign, they are so link'd in
friendship
That young Prince Edward marries Warwick's
daughter.

Clar. Belike the elder; Clarence will have the
younger.
Now, brother king, farewell, and sit you fast,
For I will hence to Warwick's other daughter,   120
That though I want a kingdom, yet in marriage
I may not prove inferior to yourself.
You that love me and Warwick, follow me.

Exit Clarence, and Somerset follows.

Glou. [*Aside.*] Not I;
My thoughts aim at a further matter: I   125
Stay not for the love of Edward, but the crown.

K. Edw. Clarence and Somerset both gone to
Warwick?
Yet am I arm'd against the worst can happen;
And haste is needful in this desp'rate case.
Pembroke and Stafford, you in our behalf   130
Go levy men, and make prepare for war;
They are already or quickly will be landed.
Myself in person will straight follow you.

Exeunt Pembroke and Stafford.

But ere I go, Hastings and Montague,
Resolve my doubt. You twain, of all the rest,   135
Are near to Warwick by blood and by alliance:
Tell me if you love Warwick more than me?
If it be so, then both depart to him;
I rather wish you foes than hollow friends.
But if you mind to hold your true obedience,   140
Give me assurance with some friendly vow,
That I may never have you in suspect.

Mont. So God help Montague as he proves true!

Hast. And Hastings as he favors Edward's cause!

K. Edw. Now, brother Richard, will you stand by
us?   145

Glou. Ay, in despite of all that shall withstand you.

K. Edw. Why, so! then am I sure of victory.
Now therefore let us hence, and lose no hour,
Till we meet Warwick with his foreign pow'r.

Exeunt.

[SCENE II]

Enter WARWICK *and* OXFORD *in England, with French
Soldiers.*

War. Trust me, my lord, all hitherto goes well,

---

63. **broker**: agent.
70. **I . . . descent.** Elizabeth, the first commoner to become a queen of
England, was the daughter of Sir Richard Woodville (later Lord
Rivers) and Jacquetta of Luxemburg, widow of John, Duke of Bedford.   90. **guess**: i.e. approximate.
104. **done**: i.e. no longer needed.

118. **Belike . . . younger.** See note to III.iii.242.   121. **want**: lack.
131. **prepare**: preparation.   142. **suspect**: suspicion.

IV.ii. Location: A plain in Warwickshire.

3 Henry VI The common people by numbers swarm to us.
IV.ii

Enter CLARENCE *and* SOMERSET.

But see where Somerset and Clarence comes!
Speak suddenly, my lords, are we all friends?
  Clar. Fear not that, my lord.   5
  War. Then, gentle Clarence, welcome unto War-
        wick,
And welcome, Somerset! I hold it cowardice
To rest mistrustful where a noble heart
Hath pawn'd an open hand in sign of love;
Else might I think that Clarence, Edward's brother, 10
Were but a feigned friend to our proceedings.
But welcome, sweet Clarence, my daughter shall be
        thine.
And now what rests but, in night's coverture,
Thy brother being carelessly encamp'd,
His soldiers lurking in the town about,   15
And but attended by a simple guard,
We may surprise and take him at our pleasure?
Our scouts have found the adventure very easy;
That as Ulysses and stout Diomede
With sleight and manhood stole to Rhesus' tents   20
And brought from thence the Thracian fatal steeds,
So we, well cover'd with the night's black mantle,
At unawares may beat down Edward's guard,
And seize himself; I say not, slaughter him,
For I intend but only to surprise him.   25
You that will follow me to this attempt,
Applaud the name of Henry with your leader.
                            They all cry, "Henry!"
Why then, let's on our way in silent sort.
For Warwick and his friends, God and Saint George!
                                        Exeunt.

[SCENE III]

Enter three WATCHMEN *to guard the King's tent.*

  1. Watch. Come on, my masters, each man take
        his stand,
The King by this is set him down to sleep.
  2. Watch. What, will he not to bed?
  1. Watch. Why, no; for he hath made a solemn vow
Never to lie and take his natural rest   5
Till Warwick or himself be quite suppress'd.
  2. Watch. To-morrow then belike shall be the day,
If Warwick be so near as men report.
  3. Watch. But say, I pray, what nobleman is that
That with the King here resteth in his tent?   10
  1. Watch. 'Tis the Lord Hastings, the King's
        chiefest friend.
  3. Watch. O, is it so? But why commands the
        King

That his chief followers lodge in towns about him,
While he himself keeps in the cold field?
  2. Watch. 'Tis the more honor, because more
        dangerous.   15
  3. Watch. Ay, but give me worship and quietness,
I like it better than a dangerous honor.
If Warwick knew in what estate he stands,
'Tis to be doubted he would waken him.
  1. Watch. Unless our halberds did shut up his
        passage.   20
  2. Watch. Ay; wherefore else guard we his royal
        tent
But to defend his person from night-foes?

Enter WARWICK, CLARENCE, OXFORD, SOMERSET, *and*
  French Soldiers, silent all.

  War. This is his tent, and see where stand his
        guard.
Courage, my masters! honor now or never!
But follow me, and Edward shall be ours.   25
  1. Watch. Who goes there?
  2. Watch. Stay, or thou diest!
        Warwick and the rest cry all, "Warwick!
        Warwick!" *and set upon the Guard, who
        fly, crying,* "Arm! arm!", *Warwick and the
        rest following them.*

The Drum playing and Trumpet sounding, enter
WARWICK, SOMERSET, *and the rest, bringing the* KING
[EDWARD] *out in his gown, sitting in a chair.* RICHARD
[OF GLOUCESTER] *and* HASTINGS *flies over the stage.*

  Som. What are they that fly there?
  War. Richard and Hastings. Let them go, here is
The Duke.
  K. Edw.   The Duke? Why, Warwick, when we
        parted,   30
Thou call'dst me King.
  War.   Ay, but the case is alter'd.
When you disgrac'd me in my embassade,
Then I degraded you from being king,
And come now to create you Duke of York.
Alas, how should you govern any kingdom,   35
That know not how to use embassadors,
Nor how to be contented with one wife,
Nor how to use your brothers brotherly,
Nor how to study for the people's welfare,
Nor how to shroud yourself from enemies?   40
  K. Edw. Yea, brother of Clarence, art thou here
        too?
Nay then I see that Edward needs must down.
Yet, Warwick, in despite of all mischance,
Of thee thyself and all thy complices,
Edward will always bear himself as king.   45
Though Fortune's malice overthrow my state,
My mind exceeds the compass of her wheel.
  War. Then for his mind, be Edward England's
        king,   *Takes off his crown.*

4. **suddenly:** quickly.   9. **pawn'd:** pledged.
13. **rests:** remains.   **coverture:** shadow.
15. **lurking:** lodging.   18. **adventure:** venture.
19–21. **That ... steeds.** After an oracle had said that Troy was safe
so long as the horses of Rhesus, king of Thrace, grazed on the Trojan
plain, Ulysses and Diomedes, in a daring raid by night, killed Rhesus
and captured his horses. See *Iliad*, Book X.
23. **At unawares:** suddenly.   25. **surprise:** capture.
28. **sort:** fashion.   29. **Saint George:** patron saint of England.

13. **lodge:** sleep.   16. **worship:** ease and dignity.
18. **estate:** condition.   19. **doubted:** feared.
20. **halberds:** halberdiers, guards bearing long weapons with axe-like
heads.   32. **embassade:** embassy.

IV.iii. Location: King Edward's camp, near Warwick.

But Henry now shall wear the English crown,
And be true king indeed, thou but the shadow. 50
My Lord of Somerset, at my request,
See that forthwith Duke Edward be convey'd
Unto my brother, Archbishop of York.
When I have fought with Pembroke and his fellows,
I'll follow you, and tell what answer 55
Lewis and the Lady Bona send to him.
Now for awhile farewell, good Duke of York.
They lead him out forcibly.
K. Edw. What fates impose, that men must needs
abide;
It boots not to resist both wind and tide. 59
Exit [guarded, with Somerset].
Oxf. What now remains, my lords, for us to do
But march to London with our soldiers?
War. Ay, that's the first thing that we have to do,
To free King Henry from imprisonment,
And see him seated in the regal throne. *Exeunt.*

[SCENE IV]

Enter RIVERS *and Lady Grey, [now* QUEEN ELIZABETH].

Riv. Madam, what makes you in this sudden
change?
Q. Eliz. Why, brother Rivers, are you yet to learn
What late misfortune is befall'n King Edward?
Riv. What? loss of some pitch'd battle against
Warwick?
Q. Eliz. No, but the loss of his own royal person.
Riv. Then is my sovereign slain? 6
Q. Eliz. Ay, almost slain, for he is taken prisoner,
Either betray'd by falsehood of his guard
Or by his foe surpris'd at unawares;
And as I further have to understand, 10
Is new committed to the Bishop of York,
Fell Warwick's brother, and by that our foe.
Riv. These news I must confess are full of grief,
Yet, gracious madam, bear it as you may:
Warwick may lose, that now hath won the day. 15
Q. Eliz. Till then fair hope must hinder live's
decay;
And I the rather wain me from despair
For love of Edward's offspring in my womb.
This is it that makes me bridle passion,
And bear with mildness my misfortune's cross; 20
Ay, ay, for this I draw in many a tear,
And stop the rising of blood-sucking sighs,
Lest with my sighs or tears I blast or drown
King Edward's fruit, true heir to th' English crown.
Riv. But, madam, where is Warwick then be-
come? 25
Q. Eliz. I am inform'd that he comes towards
London

To set the crown once more on Henry's head.
Guess thou the rest; King Edward's friends must
down.
But to prevent the tyrant's violence
(For trust not him that hath once broken faith), 30
I'll hence forthwith unto the sanctuary,
To save, at least, the heir of Edward's right;
There shall I rest secure from force and fraud.
Come therefore, let us fly while we may fly,
If Warwick take us we are sure to die. *Exeunt.* 35

[SCENE V]

Enter RICHARD [OF GLOUCESTER], LORD HASTINGS, *and*
SIR WILLIAM STANLEY.

Glou. Now, my Lord Hastings and Sir William
Stanley,
Leave off to wonder why I drew you hither
Into this chiefest thicket of the park.
Thus [stands] the case: you know our king, my
brother,
Is prisoner to the Bishop here, at whose hands 5
He hath good usage and great liberty,
And often but attended with weak guard,
[Comes] hunting this way to disport himself.
I have advertis'd him by secret means
That if about this hour he make this way, 10
Under the color of his usual game,
He shall here find his friends with horse and men
To set him free from his captivity.

Enter KING EDWARD, *and a* HUNTSMAN *with him.*

Hunt. This way, my lord, for this way lies the
game.
K. Edw. Nay, this way, man, see where the
huntsmen stand. 15
Now, brother of Gloucester, Lord Hastings, and the
rest,
Stand you thus close to steal the Bishop's deer?
Glou. Brother, the time and case requireth haste,
Your horse stands ready at the park-corner.
K. Edw. But whither shall we then?
Hast. To Lynn, my lord— 20
[*To Gloucester.*] And shipp'd from thence to Flanders?
Glou. Well guess'd, believe me, for that was my
meaning.
K. Edw. Stanley, I will requite thy forwardness.
Glou. But wherefore stay we? 'tis no time to talk.
K. Edw. Huntsman, what say'st thou? Wilt thou
go along? 25
Hunt. Better do so than tarry and be hang'd.
Glou. Come then away, let's ha' no more ado.
K. Edw. Bishop, farewell! shield thee from War-
wick's frown,
And pray that I may repossess the crown. *Exeunt.*

---

53. **brother:** i.e. George Neville (1433?–1476), a notable ecclesiastic and politician who was named chancellor of England in 1460 and again in 1470. 59. **boots:** helps.

IV.iv. Location: London. The palace.
16. **live's:** life's. 17. **wain:** wean.
22. **blood-sucking sighs.** Each sigh was thought to draw a drop of blood from the heart.

29. **prevent:** forestall. 32. **right:** claim to the throne.
IV.v. Location: A park near Middleham Castle, in Yorkshire.
3. **chiefest thicket:** thickest section.
9. **advertis'd:** informed. 11. **color:** pretext.
17. **close:** hidden. 18. **case:** circumstances.
20. **Lynn:** seaport in Norfolk. 23. **forwardness:** zeal.

[SCENE VI]

Flourish. Enter KING HENRY THE SIXT, CLARENCE,
WARWICK, SOMERSET, *young* HENRY [RICHMOND],
OXFORD, MONTAGUE, *and* LIEUTENANT [OF THE
TOWER].

    K. Hen. Master Lieutenant, now that God and
        friends
Have shaken Edward from the regal seat,
And turn'd my captive state to liberty,
My fear to hope, my sorrows unto joys,
At our enlargement what are thy due fees?   5
    Lieu. Subjects may challenge nothing of their
        sov'reigns,
But if an humble prayer may prevail,
I then crave pardon of your Majesty.
    K. Hen. For what, Lieutenant? For well using me?
Nay, be thou sure, I'll well requite thy kindness,   10
For that it made my imprisonment a pleasure;
Ay, such a pleasure as incaged birds
Conceive, when, after many moody thoughts,
At last by notes of household harmony
They quite forget their loss of liberty.   15
But, Warwick, after God, thou set'st me free,
And chiefly therefore I thank God and thee.
He was the author, thou the instrument.
Therefore that I may conquer fortune's spite
By living low, where fortune cannot hurt me,   20
And that the people of this blessed land
May not be punish'd with my thwarting stars,
Warwick, although my head still wear the crown,
I here resign my government to thee,
For thou art fortunate in all thy deeds.   25
    War. Your Grace hath still been fam'd for vir-
        tuous,
And now may seem as wise as virtuous
By spying and avoiding fortune's malice,
For few men rightly temper with the stars;
Yet in this one thing let me blame your Grace,   30
For choosing me when Clarence is in place.
    Clar. No, Warwick, thou art worthy of the sway,
To whom the heav'ns in thy nativity
Adjudg'd an olive branch and laurel crown,
As likely to be blest in peace and war;   35
And therefore I yield thee my free consent.
    War. And I choose Clarence only for Protector.
    K. Hen. Warwick and Clarence, give me both
        your hands.
Now join your hands, and with your hands your hearts,
That no dissension hinder government.   40
I make you both Protectors of this land,
While I myself will lead a private life,
And in devotion spend my latter days,
To sin's rebuke and my Creator's praise.
    War. What answers Clarence to his sovereign's
        will?   45
    Clar. That he consents, if Warwick yield consent,

For on thy fortune I repose myself.
    War. Why then, though loath, yet must I be con-
        tent.
We'll yoke together like a double shadow
To Henry's body, and supply his place;   50
I mean, in bearing weight of government,
While he enjoys the honor and his ease.
And, Clarence, now then it is more than needful
Forthwith that Edward be pronounc'd a traitor,
And all his lands and goods confiscate.   55
    Clar. What else? and that succession be deter-
        mined.
    War. Ay, therein Clarence shall not want his part.
    K. Hen. But with the first of all your chief affairs,
Let me entreat (for I command no more)
That Margaret your queen and my son Edward   60
Be sent for, to return from France with speed;
For till I see them here, by doubtful fear
My joy of liberty is half eclips'd.
    Clar. It shall be done, my sovereign, with all speed.
    K. Hen. My Lord of Somerset, what youth is that
Of whom you seem to have so tender care?   66
    Som. My liege, it is young Henry, Earl of Rich-
        mond.
    K. Hen. Come hither, England's hope. (*Lays his
        hand on his head.*) If secret powers
Suggest but truth to my divining thoughts,
This pretty lad will prove our country's bliss.   70
His looks are full of peaceful majesty,
His head by nature fram'd to wear a crown,
His hand to wield a sceptre, and himself
Likely in time to bless a regal throne.
Make much of him, my lords, for this is he   75
Must help you more than you are hurt by me.

Enter a POST.

    War. What news, my friend?
    Post. That Edward is escaped from your brother,
And fled (as he hears since) to Burgundy.
    War. Unsavory news! but how made he escape?
    Post. He was convey'd by Richard, Duke of
        Gloucester,   81
And the Lord Hastings, who attended him
In secret ambush on the forest side,
And from the Bishop's huntsmen rescu'd him;
For hunting was his daily exercise.   85
    War. My brother was too careless of his charge.
But let us hence, my sovereign, to provide
A salve for any sore that may betide.
    Exeunt. Manent SOMERSET, RICHMOND, *and* OXFORD.
    Som. My lord, I like not of this flight of Edward's;
For doubtless Burgundy will yield him help,   90
And we shall have more wars before't be long.
As Henry's late presaging prophecy
Did glad my heart with hope of this young Richmond,
So doth my heart misgive me, in these conflicts
What may befall him, to his harm and ours.   95
Therefore, Lord Oxford, to prevent the worst,
Forthwith we'll send him hence to Brittany,

IV.vi. Location: London. The Tower.
5. enlargement: setting free.
22. thwarting stars: i.e. evil fortune.   26. still: always.
29. rightly . . . stars: adjust themselves to their destiny.
43. latter: last.

67. Henry . . . Richmond: Henry Tudor (1457–1509), later Henry VII,
founder of the Tudor dynasty. See note to *Richard III*, I.iii.20.
82. attended: awaited. 88. betide: occur, come about.

Till storms be past of civil enmity.

Oxf. Ay; for if Edward repossess the crown,
'Tis like that Richmond with the rest shall down. 100

Som. It shall be so; he shall to Brittany.
Come therefore, let's about it speedily.　　*Exeunt.*

[SCENE VII]

Flourish. Enter [KING] EDWARD, RICHARD [OF
GLOUCESTER], HASTINGS, *and Soldiers* [*a troop
of Hollanders*].

K. Edw. Now, brother Richard, Lord Hastings,
　　and the rest,
Yet thus far fortune maketh us amends,
And says that once more I shall interchange
My waned state for Henry's regal crown.
Well have we pass'd and now repass'd the seas, 5
And brought desired help from Burgundy.
What then remains, we being thus arriv'd
From Ravenspurgh haven before the gates of York,
But that we enter as into our dukedom?

Glou. The gates made fast? Brother, I like not
　　this; 10
For many men that stumble at the threshold
Are well foretold that danger lurks within.

K. Edw. Tush, man, abodements must not now
　　affright us.
By fair or foul means we must enter in,
For hither will our friends repair to us. 15

Hast. My liege, I'll knock once more to summon
　　them.

Enter on the walls the MAYOR OF YORK *and his brethren*
[*the* ALDERMEN].

May. My lords, we were forewarned of your
　　coming,
And shut the gates for safety of ourselves;
For now we owe allegiance unto Henry.

K. Edw. But, Master Mayor, if Henry be your
　　king, 20
Yet Edward, at the least, is Duke of York.

May. True, my good lord, I know you for no less.

K. Edw. Why, and I challenge nothing but my
　　dukedom,
As being well content with that alone.

Glou. [*Aside.*] But when the fox hath once got in
　　his nose, 25
He'll soon find means to make the body follow.

Hast. Why, Master Mayor, why stand you in a
　　doubt?
Open the gates, we are King Henry's friends.

May. Ay, say you so? The gates shall then be
　　opened. 　　*He descends* [*with the Aldermen*].

Glou. A wise stout captain, and soon persuaded!

Hast. The good old man would fain that all were
　　well, 31
So 'twere not long of him; but being ent'red,

I doubt not, I, but we shall soon persuade
Both him and all his brothers unto reason.

Enter the MAYOR *and two* ALDERMEN [*below*].

K. Edw. So, Master Mayor; these gates must not
　　be shut, 35
But in the night, or in the time of war.
What, fear not, man, but yield me up the keys,
　　　　　　Takes his keys.
For Edward will defend the town and thee,
And all those friends that deign to follow me.

March. Enter MONTGOMERY *with Drum and Soldiers.*

Glou. Brother, this is Sir John Montgomery, 40
Our trusty friend, unless I be deceiv'd.

K. Edw. Welcome, Sir John! but why come you in
　　arms?

Montg. To help King Edward in his time of storm,
As every loyal subject ought to do.

K. Edw. Thanks, good Montgomery; but we now
　　forget 45
Our title to the crown, and only claim
Our dukedom, till God please to send the rest.

Montg. Then fare you well, for I will hence again,
I came to serve a king and not a duke.
Drummer, strike up, and let us march away. 50
　　　　　　The Drum begins to march.

K. Edw. Nay, stay, Sir John, a while, and we'll
　　debate
By what safe means the crown may be recover'd.

Montg. What talk you of debating? In few words,
If you'll not here proclaim yourself our king,
I'll leave you to your fortune, and be gone 55
To keep them back that come to succor you.
Why shall we fight if you pretend no title?

Glou. Why, brother, wherefore stand you on nice
　　points?

K. Edw. When we grow stronger, then we'll make
　　our claim;
Till then, 'tis wisdom to conceal our meaning. 60

Hast. Away with scrupulous wit! now arms must
　　rule.

Glou. And fearless minds climb soonest unto
　　crowns.
Brother, we will proclaim you out of hand,
The bruit thereof will bring you many friends.

K. Edw. Then be it as you will; for 'tis my right,
And Henry but usurps the diadem. 66

Montg. Ay, now my sovereign speaketh like him-
　　self,
And now will I be Edward's champion.

Hast. Sound trumpet, Edward shall be here pro-
　　claim'd.
Come, fellow soldier, make thou proclamation. 70
　　　　　　[*Gives him a paper.*] *Flourish. Sound.*

Sold. [*Reads.*] "Edward the Fourth, by the grace
of God, King of England and France, and Lord of
Ireland, etc."

IV.vii. Location: Before York.
8. **Ravenspurgh:** i.e. Ravenspur, former seaport on the coast of
Yorkshire. 13. **abodements:** evil omens.
23. **challenge:** claim. 31. **fain:** be glad.
32. **long of him:** owing to him, i.e. his responsibility.

39. **deign:** are willing. 57. **pretend:** claim.
58. **nice:** meticulous. 61. **scrupulous wit:** prudent wisdom.
64. **bruit:** report.

3 Henry VI
IV.vii

Montg.   And whosoe'er gainsays King Edward's
     right,
By this I challenge him to single fight.   75
          Throws down his gauntlet.
All.   Long live Edward the Fourth!
K. Edw.   Thanks, brave Montgomery, and thanks
     unto you all.
If fortune serve me, I'll requite this kindness.
Now for this night, let's harbor here in York;
And when the morning sun shall raise his car   80
Above the border of this horizon,
We'll forward towards Warwick and his mates;
For well I wot that Henry is no soldier.
Ah, froward Clarence, how evil it beseems thee
To flatter Henry and forsake thy brother!   85
Yet as we may, we'll meet both thee and Warwick.
Come on, brave soldiers; doubt not of the day,
And that once gotten, doubt not of large pay.
                              Exeunt.

[SCENE VIII]

Flourish. Enter the KING [HENRY], WARWICK, MON-
TAGUE, CLARENCE, OXFORD, *and* [EXETER].

War.   What counsel, lords? Edward from Belgia,
With hasty Germans and blunt Hollanders,
Hath pass'd in safety through the Narrow Seas,
And with his troops doth march amain to London,
And many giddy people flock to him.   5
K. Hen.   Let's levy men, and beat him back again.
Clar.   A little fire is quickly trodden out,
Which being suffer'd, rivers cannot quench.
War.   In Warwickshire I have true-hearted friends,
Not mutinous in peace, yet bold in war;   10
Those will I muster up; and thou, son Clarence,
Shalt stir up in Suffolk, Norfolk, and in Kent,
The knights and gentlemen to come with thee.
Thou, brother Montague, in Buckingham,
Northampton, and in Leicestershire, shalt find   15
Men well inclin'd to hear what thou command'st;
And thou, brave Oxford, wondrous well belov'd,
In Oxfordshire shalt muster up thy friends.
My sovereign, with the loving citizens,
Like to his island, girt in with the ocean,   20
Or modest Dian, circled with her nymphs,
Shall rest in London till we come to him.
Fair lords, take leave and stand not to reply.
Farewell, my sovereign.
K. Hen.   Farewell, my Hector, and my Troy's true
     hope.   25
Clar.   In sign of truth, I kiss your Highness' hand.
K. Hen.   Well-minded Clarence, be thou fortunate!
Mont.   Comfort, my lord! and so I take my leave.
Oxf.   And thus [*kissing Henry's hand*] I seal my
     truth, and bid adieu.
K. Hen.   Sweet Oxford, and my loving Montague,
And all at once, once more a happy farewell.   31

War.   Farewell, sweet lords, let's meet at Coventry.
          Exeunt [all but King Henry and Exeter].
K. Hen.   Here at the palace will I rest a while.
Cousin of Exeter, what thinks your lordship?
Methinks the power that Edward hath in field   35
Should not be able to encounter mine.
Exe.   The doubt is that he will seduce the rest.
K. Hen.   That's not my fear, my meed hath got me
     fame:
I have not stopp'd mine ears to their demands,
Nor posted off their suits with slow delays;   40
My pity hath been balm to heal their wounds,
My mildness hath allay'd their swelling griefs,
My mercy dried their water-flowing tears;
I have not been desirous of their wealth,
Nor much oppress'd them with great subsidies,   45
Nor forward of revenge, though they much err'd.
Then why should they love Edward more than me?
No, Exeter, these graces challenge grace;
And when the lion fawns upon the lamb,
The lamb will never cease to follow him.   50
          Shout within, "A Lancaster! A Lancaster!"
Exe.   Hark, hark, my lord, what shouts are these?

Enter [KING] EDWARD *and his Soldiers* [*with* GLOUCES-
TER *and others*].

K. Edw.   Seize on the shame-fac'd Henry, bear
     him hence,
And once again proclaim us King of England.
You are the fount that makes small brooks to flow;
Now stops thy spring, my sea shall suck them dry,
And swell so much the higher by their ebb.   56
Hence with him to the Tower, let him not speak.
          Exit [Exeter] with King Henry [guarded].
And, lords, towards Coventry bend we our course,
Where peremptory Warwick now remains.
The sun shines hot, and, if we use delay,   60
Cold biting winter mars our hop'd-for hay.
Glou.   Away betimes, before his forces join,
And take the great-grown traitor unawares.
Brave warriors, march amain towards Coventry.
                              Exeunt.

[ACT V, SCENE I]

Enter WARWICK, *the* MAYOR OF COVENTRY, *two*
MESSENGERS, *and others, upon the walls.*

War.   Where is the post that came from valiant
     Oxford?
How far hence is thy lord, mine honest fellow?
1. Mess.   By this at Dunsmore, marching hither-
     ward.
War.   How far off is our brother Montague?
Where is the post that came from Montague?   5

IV.viii. Location: London. The Bishop of London's palace.
1. **Belgia:** i.e. the Low Countries.
2. **hasty:** quick-tempered.   **blunt:** harsh.
4. **amain:** with full speed.   11. **son:** i.e. son-in-law.
21. **Dian:** Diana, the moon-goddess.
25. **Hector:** i.e. protector.   31. **at once:** together.

37. **doubt:** fear.
38. **my . . . fame:** my merits (for dealing justly) have secured my
reputation.   40. **posted off:** postponed.
45. **subsidies:** special taxes.   46. **forward of:** eager for.
48. **challenge grace:** claim favor.   52. **shame-fac'd:** shy.
59. **peremptory:** overbearing.

V.i. Location: Coventry.
3. **Dunsmore:** hamlet in eastern Warwickshire.

2. *Mess.*   By this at Daintry, with a puissant troop.

Enter [Sir John] Somervile.

War.   Say, Somervile, what says my loving son?
And, by thy guess, how nigh is Clarence now?
Som.   At Southam I did leave him with his forces,
And do expect him here some two hours hence.   10

[*Drum heard.*]

War.   Then Clarence is at hand, I hear his drum.
Som.   It is not his, my lord, here Southam lies;
The drum your honor hears marcheth from Warwick.
War.   Who should that be? belike unlook'd-for
friends.
Som.   They are at hand, and you shall quickly know.

March. Flourish. Enter [King] Edward, Richard
[of Gloucester], *and Soldiers.*

K. Edw.   Go, trumpet, to the walls, and sound a
parle.   16
Glou.   See how the surly Warwick mans the wall!
War.   O unbid spite, is sportful Edward come?
Where slept our scouts, or how are they seduc'd,
That we could hear no news of his repair?   20
K. Edw.   Now, Warwick, wilt thou ope the city-
gates,
Speak gentle words and humbly bend thy knee,
Call Edward king and at his hands beg mercy?
And he shall pardon thee these outrages.   24
War.   Nay rather, wilt thou draw thy forces hence,
Confess who set thee up and pluck'd thee down,
Call Warwick patron, and be penitent?
And thou shalt still remain the Duke of York.
Glou.   I thought, at least, he would have said the
King,
Or did he make the jest against his will?   30
War.   Is not a dukedom, sir, a goodly gift?
Glou.   Ay, by my faith, for a poor earl to give.
I'll do thee service for so good a gift.
War.   'Twas I that gave the kingdom to thy
brother.
K. Edw.   Why then 'tis mine, if but by Warwick's
gift.   35
War.   Thou art no Atlas for so great a weight;
And, weakling, Warwick takes his gift again,
And Henry is my king, Warwick his subject.
K. Edw.   But Warwick's king is Edward's pris-
oner.
And, gallant Warwick, do but answer this: 40
What is the body when the head is off?
Glou.   Alas, that Warwick had no more forecast,
But, whiles he thought to steal the single ten,
The king was slily finger'd from the deck!
You left poor Henry at the Bishop's palace,   45
And ten to one you'll meet him in the Tower.

K. Edw.   'Tis even so, yet you are Warwick still.
Glou.   Come, Warwick, take the time, kneel down,
kneel down.
Nay, when? strike now, or else the iron cools.
War.   I had rather chop this hand off at a blow,   50
And with the other fling it at thy face,
Than bear so low a sail to strike to thee.
K. Edw.   Sail how thou canst, have wind and tide
thy friend,
This hand, fast wound about thy coal-black hair,
Shall, whiles thy head is warm and new cut off,   55
Write in the dust this sentence with thy blood:
"Wind-changing Warwick now can change no more."

Enter Oxford *with Drum and Colors.*

War.   O cheerful colors! see where Oxford comes!
Oxf.   Oxford, Oxford, for Lancaster!

[*He and his forces enter the city.*]

Glou.   The gates are open, let us enter too.   60
K. Edw.   So other foes may set upon our backs.
Stand we in good array; for they no doubt
Will issue out again and bid us battle.
If not, the city being but of small defense,
We'll quickly rouse the traitors in the same.   65
War.   O, welcome, Oxford, for we want thy help.

Enter Montague *with Drum and Colors.*

Mont.   Montague, Montague, for Lancaster!

[*He and his forces enter the city.*]

Glou.   Thou and thy brother both shall buy this
treason
Even with the dearest blood your bodies bear.
K. Edw.   The harder match'd, the greater victory:
My mind presageth happy gain and conquest.   71

Enter Somerset *with Drum and Colors.*

Som.   Somerset, Somerset, for Lancaster!

[*He and his forces enter the city.*]

Glou.   Two of thy name, both Dukes of Somerset,
Have sold their lives unto the house of York,
And thou shalt be the third, [and] this sword hold.   75

Enter Clarence *with Drum and Colors.*

War.   And lo, where George of Clarence sweeps
along,
Of force enough to bid his brother battle;
With whom [an] upright zeal to right prevails
More than the nature of a brother's love!

[*Gloucester and Clarence whisper together.*]

Come, Clarence, come; thou wilt, if Warwick call.   80
Clar.   Father of Warwick, know you what this
means?
Look here, I throw my infamy at thee.

[*Clarence takes his red rose out of
his hat and throws it at Warwick.*]

6. **Daintry:** i.e. Daventry, a town in Northamptonshire.
9. **Southam:** hamlet in Gloucestershire.
13. **Warwick:** town south of Coventry.
16. **parle:** signal for a parley.
18. **unbid:** uninvited, i.e. unwelcome.   **sportful:** lascivious.
20. **repair:** approach.
36. **Atlas:** in classical mythology, the Titan who upheld the heavens with his hands and shoulders.
43. **single ten:** mere ten-card.   44. **finger'd:** stolen.

48. **take the time:** seize the opportunity.
52. **strike:** lower sail (in token of submission).
57 s.d. **Colors:** flagbearers.   61. **backs:** rear (of army).
65. **rouse . . . in:** drive . . . from.
73–74. **Two . . . York.** Edmund Beaufort, second Duke of Somerset, was killed while fighting for the Lancastrians at the first battle of St. Albans in 1455, and his son and heir Henry was executed by the Yorkists in 1464.   75. **and:** if.

I will not ruinate my father's house,
Who gave his blood to lime the stones together,
And set up Lancaster. Why, trowest thou, Warwick,
That Clarence is so harsh, so blunt, unnatural,   86
To bend the fatal instruments of war
Against his brother and his lawful king?
Perhaps thou wilt object my holy oath:
To keep that oath were more impiety   90
Than Jephthah when he sacrific'd his daughter.
I am so sorry for my trespass made
That to deserve well at my brother's hands,
I here proclaim myself thy mortal foe;
With resolution, wheresoe'er I meet thee   95
(As I will meet thee, if thou stir abroad),
To plague thee for thy foul misleading me.
And so, proud-hearted Warwick, I defy thee,
And to my brother turn my blushing cheeks.
Pardon me, Edward, I will make amends;   100
And, Richard, do not frown upon my faults,
For I will henceforth be no more unconstant.
    K. Edw. Now welcome more, and ten times more
      belov'd,
Than if thou never hadst deserv'd our hate.
    Glou. Welcome, good Clarence, this is brother-like.
    War. O passing traitor, perjur'd and unjust!   106
    K. Edw. What, Warwick, wilt thou leave the
      town, and fight?
Or shall we beat the stones about thine ears?
    War. Alas, I am not coop'd here for defense!
I will away towards Barnet presently,   110
And bid thee battle, Edward, if thou dar'st.
    K. Edw. Yes, Warwick, Edward dares, and leads
      the way.
Lords, to the field! Saint George and victory!
    *Exeunt [King Edward and his company]. March.
    Warwick and his company follows.*

[SCENE II]

Alarum and excursions. Enter [KING] EDWARD, *bringing forth* WARWICK *wounded.*

    K. Edw. So, lie thou there. Die thou, and die our
      fear,
For Warwick was a bug that fear'd us all.
Now, Montague, sit fast, I seek for thee,
That Warwick's bones may keep thine company.
                      Exit.

    War. Ah, who is nigh? Come to me, friend or foe,
And tell me who is victor, York or Warwick?   6
Why ask I that? My mangled body shows,
My blood, my want of strength, my sick heart shows,
That I must yield my body to the earth,
And by my fall, the conquest to my foe.   10
Thus yields the cedar to the axe's edge,

---

84. lime: cement.   85. trowest: thinkest.   89. object: urge.
91. Jephthah: a judge of Israel who sacrificed his daughter to Jehovah in fulfillment of a vow that if victorious in battle he would offer up whoever met him first on his return. See Judges 11:30–40.
106. passing: surpassing.
110. Barnet: town in Hertfordshire.   presently: immediately.

V.ii. Location: A field of battle near Barnet.
2. bug: bugbear.   fear'd: frightened.

Whose arms gave shelter to the princely eagle,
Under whose shade the ramping lion slept,
Whose top-branch overpeer'd Jove's spreading tree,
And kept low shrubs from winter's pow'rful wind.   15
These eyes, that now are dimm'd with death's black
    veil,
Have been as piercing as the midday sun
To search the secret treasons of the world.
The wrinkles in my brows, now fill'd with blood,
Were lik'ned oft to kingly sepulchres;   20
For who liv'd king, but I could dig his grave?
And who durst smile when Warwick bent his brow?
Lo, now my glory smear'd in dust and blood!
My parks, my walks, my manors that I had,
Even now forsake me; and of all my lands   25
Is nothing left me but my body's length.
Why, what is pomp, rule, reign, but earth and dust?
And live we how we can, yet die we must.

Enter OXFORD *and* SOMERSET.

    Som. Ah, Warwick, Warwick, wert thou as we are,
We might recover all our loss again.   30
The Queen from France hath brought a puissant
    power;
Even now we heard the news. Ah, couldst thou fly!
    War. Why then I would not fly. Ah, Montague,
If thou be there, sweet brother, take my hand,
And with thy lips keep in my soul a while.   35
Thou lov'st me not; for, brother, if thou didst,
Thy tears would wash this cold congealed blood
That glues my lips and will not let me speak.
Come quickly, Montague, or I am dead.
    Som. Ah, Warwick, Montague hath breath'd his
      last,   40
And to the latest gasp cried out for Warwick,
And said, "Commend me to my valiant brother."
And more he would have said, and more he spoke,
Which sounded like a cannon in a vault,
That mought not be distinguish'd; but at last   45
I well might hear, delivered with a groan,
"O, farewell, Warwick!"
    War. Sweet rest his soul! Fly, lords, and save
     yourselves,
For Warwick bids you all farewell, to meet in
     heaven.   *[He dies.]*   49
    Oxf. Away, away, to meet the Queen's great
     power! *Here they bear away his body. Exeunt.*

[SCENE III]

Flourish. Enter KING EDWARD *in triumph, with*
RICHARD [OF GLOUCESTER], CLARENCE, *and the
rest.*

    K. Edw. Thus far our fortune keeps an upward
     course,
And we are grac'd with wreaths of victory.
But in the midst of this bright-shining day,

---

13. ramping: upreared, rampant.
14. Jove's spreading tree: i.e. the oak.   41. latest: last.
45. mought: might.

V.iii. Location: Scene continues.

I spy a black, suspicious, threat'ning cloud,
That will encounter with our glorious sun,   5
Ere he attain his easeful western bed:
I mean, my lords, those powers that the Queen
Hath rais'd in Gallia have arriv'd our coast,
And as we hear, march on to fight with us.
  Clar. A little gale will soon disperse that cloud,   10
And blow it to the source from whence it came;
Thy very beams will dry those vapors up,
For every cloud engenders not a storm.
  Glou. The Queen is valued thirty thousand strong,
And Somerset, with Oxford, fled to her;   15
If she have time to breathe, be well assur'd
Her faction will be full as strong as ours.
  K. Edw. We are advertis'd by our loving friends
That they do hold their course toward Tewksbury.
We, having now the best at Barnet field,   20
Will thither straight, for willingness rids way,
And as we march, our strength will be augmented
In every county as we go along.
Strike up the drum, cry "Courage!" and away.
                                          Exeunt.

[SCENE IV]

Flourish. March. Enter the QUEEN [MARGARET], *young*
[PRINCE] EDWARD, SOMERSET, OXFORD, *and Soldiers.*

  Q. Mar. Great lords, wise men ne'er sit and wail
        their loss,
But cheerly seek how to redress their harms.
What though the mast be now blown overboard,
The cable broke, the holding-anchor lost,
And half our sailors swallow'd in the flood?   5
Yet lives our pilot still. Is't meet that he
Should leave the helm and, like a fearful lad,
With tearful eyes add water to the sea,
And give more strength to that which hath too much,
Whiles, in his moan, the ship splits on the rock,   10
Which industry and courage might have sav'd?
Ah, what a shame, ah, what a fault were this!
Say Warwick was our anchor; what of that?
And Montague our topmast; what of him?
Our slaught'red friends the tackles; what of these?   15
Why, is not Oxford here another anchor?
And Somerset another goodly mast?
The friends of France our shrouds and tacklings?
And though unskillful, why not Ned and I
For once allow'd the skillful pilot's charge?   20
We will not from the helm to sit and weep,
But keep our course (though the rough wind say no)
From shelves and rocks that threaten us with wrack.
As good to chide the waves as speak them fair.
And what is Edward but a ruthless sea?   25
What Clarence but a quicksand of deceit?
And Richard but a [ragged] fatal rock?

8. Gallia: France.   16. breathe: i.e. collect her strength.
18. advertis'd: informed.
19. Tewksbury: Tewkesbury, a town at the confluence of the Avon
and the Severn in Gloucestershire.
21. rids way: makes for rapid progress.

V.iv. Location: Plains near Tewkesbury.
18. shrouds: sails.   20. charge: responsibility.
23. shelves: shoals.   wrack: destruction.

All these the enemies to our poor bark.
Say you can swim, alas, 'tis but a while;
Tread on the sand, why, there you quickly sink;   30
Bestride the rock, the tide will wash you off,
Or else you famish—that's a threefold death.
This speak I, lords, to let you understand,
If case some one of you would fly from us,
That there's no hop'd-for mercy with the brothers   35
More than with ruthless waves, with sands and rocks.
Why, courage then! what cannot be avoided,
'Twere childish weakness to lament or fear.
  Prince. Methinks a woman of this valiant spirit
Should, if a coward heard her speak these words,   40
Infuse his breast with magnanimity,
And make him, naked, foil a man at arms.
I speak not this as doubting any here;
For did I but suspect a fearful man,
He should have leave to go away betimes,   45
Lest in our need he might infect another,
And make him of like spirit to himself.
If any such be here—as God forbid!—
Let him depart before we need his help.
  Oxf. Women and children of so high a courage,
And warriors faint! why, 'twere perpetual shame.   51
O brave young prince! thy famous grandfather
Doth live again in thee. Long mayst thou live
To bear his image and renew his glories!
  Som. And he that will not fight for such a hope   55
Go home to bed, and like the owl by day,
If he arise, be mock'd and wond'red at.
  Q. Mar. Thanks, gentle Somerset, sweet Oxford,
        thanks.
  Prince. And take his thanks that yet hath nothing
        else.

Enter a MESSENGER.

  Mess. Prepare you, lords, for Edward is at hand,   60
Ready to fight; therefore be resolute.
  Oxf. I thought no less; it is his policy
To haste thus fast, to find us unprovided.
  Som. But he's deceiv'd, we are in readiness.
  Q. Mar. This cheers my heart, to see your for-
        wardness.   65
  Oxf. Here pitch our battle, hence we will not
        budge.

Flourish and march. Enter [KING] EDWARD, RICHARD
[OF GLOUCESTER], CLARENCE, *and Soldiers.*

  K. Edw. Brave followers, yonder stands the
        thorny wood,
Which by the heavens' assistance and your strength,
Must by the roots be hewn up yet ere night.
I need not add more fuel to your fire,   70
For well I wot ye blaze to burn them out.
Give signal to the fight, and to it, lords!
  Q. Mar. Lords, knights, and gentlemen, what I
        should say
My tears gainsay; for every word I speak,
Ye see I drink the water of my eye.   75

34. If case: in case.   42. foil: overcome.
54. image: likeness.   63. unprovided: unprepared.
66. pitch our battle: draw up our forces.

3 Henry VI
V.iv

Therefore no more but this: Henry, your sovereign,
Is prisoner to the foe, his state usurp'd,
His realm a slaughter-house, his subjects slain,
His statutes cancell'd, and his treasure spent;
And yonder is the wolf that makes this spoil.   80
You fight in justice; then in God's name, lords,
Be valiant, and give signal to the fight.

*Alarum [to the battle]. Retreat. [King Edward,
with his followers, flies]. Excursions; [the
chambers be discharged. Then enter King
Edward, Clarence, Gloucester, and the rest of the
King's followers and make a great shout, and
cry, "For York! for York!"; and then Queen
Margaret is taken, and Prince Edward and
Oxford and Somerset.] Exeunt.*

[SCENE V]

Flourish. Enter [KING] EDWARD, RICHARD [OF
GLOUCESTER *with*] QUEEN [MARGARET *prisoner*],
CLARENCE, [*and Soldiers with*] OXFORD, SOMERSET
[*prisoners*].

K. Edw.   Now here a period of tumultuous broils.
Away with Oxford to Hames Castle straight;
For Somerset, off with his guilty head.
Go bear them hence, I will not hear them speak.   4
Oxf.   For my part, I'll not trouble thee with words.
Som.   Nor I, but stoop with patience to my fortune.
Exeunt [Oxford and Somerset, guarded].
Q. Mar.   So part we sadly in this troublous world,
To meet with joy in sweet Jerusalem.
K. Edw.   Is proclamation made, that who finds
          Edward
Shall have a high reward, and he his life?   10
Glou.   It is, and lo where youthful Edward comes!

Enter [Soldiers with] the PRINCE [EDWARD].

K. Edw.   Bring forth the gallant, let us hear him
          speak.
What? can so young a thorn begin to prick?
Edward, what satisfaction canst thou make
For bearing arms, for stirring up my subjects,   15
And all the trouble thou hast turn'd me to?
Prince.   Speak like a subject, proud ambitious York!
Suppose that I am now my father's mouth:
Resign thy chair, and where I stand kneel thou,
Whilst I propose the self-same words to thee,   20
Which, traitor, thou wouldst have me answer to.
Q. Mar.   Ah, that thy father had been so resolv'd!
Glou.   That you might still have worn the petticoat,
And ne'er have stol'n the breech from Lancaster.
Prince.   Let Aesop fable in a winter's night,   25
His currish riddles sorts not with this place.

82 s.d. **chambers:** short cannon.

V.v. Location: Scene continues.
1. **period:** end.
2. **Hames Castle:** i.e. Hanmes, a castle near Calais. Actually, Oxford, who did not fight at Tewkesbury, was not apprehended and imprisoned until 1474, three years after the time represented in this scene.
24. **breech:** breeches.
25. **Aesop:** Greek fabulist who (like Gloucester) was deformed.
26. **sorts:** agree.

Glou.   By heaven, brat, I'll plague ye for that word.
Q. Mar.   Ay, thou wast born to be a plague to men.
Glou.   For God's sake, take away this captive scold.
Prince.   Nay, take away this scolding crook-back,
          rather.   30
K. Edw.   Peace, willful boy, or I will charm your
          tongue.
Clar.   Untutor'd lad, thou art too malapert.
Prince.   I know my duty, you are all undutiful.
Lascivious Edward, and thou perjur'd George,
And thou misshapen Dick, I tell ye all   35
I am your better, traitors as ye are,
And thou usurp'st my father's right and mine.
K. Edw.   Take that, the likeness of this railer here.
          Stabs him.
Glou.   Sprawl'st thou? take that, to end thy agony.
          Richard stabs him.
Clar.   And there's for twitting me with perjury.
          Clarence stabs him.
Q. Mar.   O, kill me too!   41
Glou.   Marry, and shall.   *Offers to kill her.*
K. Edw.   Hold, Richard, hold, for we have done
          too much.
Glou.   Why should she live, to fill the world with
          words?
K. Edw.   What? doth she swoun? Use means for
          her recovery.   45
Glou.   Clarence, excuse me to the King my brother;
I'll hence to London on a serious matter.
Ere ye come there, be sure to hear some news.
Clar.   What? what?
Glou.   [The] Tower, the Tower.   *Exit.*
Q. Mar.   O Ned, sweet Ned, speak to thy mother,
          boy!   51
Canst thou not speak? O traitors, murtherers!
They that stabb'd Caesar shed no blood at all,
Did not offend, nor were not worthy blame,
If this foul deed were by to equal it.   55
He was a man; this, in respect, a child,
And men ne'er spend their fury on a child.
What's worse than murtherer, that I may name it?
No, no, my heart will burst and if I speak,
And I will speak, that so my heart may burst.   60
Butchers and villains! bloody cannibals!
How sweet a plant have you untimely cropp'd!
You have no children, butchers; if you had,
The thought of them would have stirr'd up remorse,
But if you ever chance to have a child,   65
Look in his youth to have him so cut off
As, deathsmen, you have rid this sweet young prince!
K. Edw.   Away with her, go bear her hence per-
          force.
Q. Mar.   Nay, never bear me hence, dispatch me
          here;
Here sheathe thy sword, I'll pardon thee my death.   70
What? wilt thou not? Then, Clarence, do it thou.
Clar.   By heaven, I will not do thee so much ease.

31. **charm:** cast a spell upon, silence.
32. **malapert:** impudent.   38. **this railer:** i.e. Margaret.
39. **Sprawl'st:** i.e. twitching in the agony of death.
45. **swoun:** swoon.   48. **be sure:** expect.
56. **in respect:** by comparison.   67. **rid:** removed.

Q. Mar.   Good Clarence, do; sweet Clarence, do
 thou do it.

Clar.   Didst thou not hear me swear I would not do
 it?

Q. Mar.   Ay, but thou usest to forswear thyself.
'Twas sin before, but now 'tis charity.   76
What, wilt thou not? Where is that devil's butcher,
Hard-favor'd Richard? Richard, where art thou?
Thou art not here. Murther is thy alms-deed;
Petitioners for blood thou ne'er put'st back.   80

K. Edw.   Away I say, I charge ye bear her hence.

Q. Mar.   So come to you, and yours, as to this
 prince! *Exit Queen* [*Margaret, led out forcibly*].

K. Edw.   Where's Richard gone?

Clar.   To London, all in post, and as I guess,
To make a bloody supper in the Tower.   85

K. Edw.   He's sudden, if a thing comes in his head.
Now march we hence. Discharge the common sort
With pay and thanks, and let's away to London
And see our gentle queen how well she fares.
By this, I hope, she hath a son for me.   *Exeunt.* 90

[SCENE VI]

Enter HENRY THE SIXT *and* RICHARD [OF GLOUCESTER]
with the LIEUTENANT, *on the walls.*

Glou.   Good day, my lord. What, at your book so
 hard?

K. Hen.   Ay, my good lord—my lord, I should
 say rather.
'Tis sin to flatter, "good" was little better:
"Good Gloucester" and "good devil" were alike,
And both preposterous; therefore, not "good lord." 5

Glou.   Sirrah, leave us to ourselves, we must confer.
                                    [*Exit Lieutenant.*]

K. Hen.   So flies the reakless shepherd from the
 wolf;
So first the harmless sheep doth yield his fleece,
And next his throat unto the butcher's knife.
What scene of death hath Roscius now to act?   10

Glou.   Suspicion always haunts the guilty mind;
The thief doth fear each bush an officer.

K. Hen.   The bird that hath been limed in a bush,
With trembling wings misdoubteth every bush;
And I, the hapless male to one sweet bird,   15
Have now the fatal object in my eye
Where my poor young was lim'd, was caught, and
 kill'd.

Glou.   Why, what a peevish fool was that of Crete
That taught his son the office of a fowl!
And yet, for all his wings, the fool was drown'd. 20

---

75. **thou . . . forswear:** you make a habit of swearing falsely.
87. **common sort:** ordinary soldiers.
90. **a son.** Actually, Edward's son had been born in November 1470, some six months before the battle of Tewkesbury.

V.vi. **Location:** London. The Tower.
6. **Sirrah:** customary form of address to an inferior.
7. **reakless:** reckless, heedless.
10. **What . . . act:** i.e. what tragic role have you in mind for me. Roscius was a Roman actor much admired by Cicero.
13. **limed:** snared with birdlime.   15. **male . . . bird:** father . . . son.
18–25. **Why . . . life.** For the myth of Daedalus and Icarus see note to *1 Henry VI*, IV.vi.54–55.   18. **peevish:** silly.

K. Hen.   I, Daedalus; my poor boy, Icarus;
Thy father, Minos, that denied our course;
The sun that sear'd the wings of my sweet boy,
Thy brother Edward; and thyself, the sea
Whose envious gulf did swallow up his life.   25
Ah, kill me with thy weapon, not with words!
My breast can better brook thy dagger's point
Than can my ears that tragic history.
But wherefore dost thou come? Is't for my life?

Glou.   Think'st thou I am an executioner?   30

K. Hen.   A persecutor I am sure thou art.
If murthering innocents be executing,
Why then thou art an executioner.

Glou.   Thy son I kill'd for his presumption.

K. Hen.   Hadst thou been kill'd when first thou
 didst presume,   35
Thou hadst not liv'd to kill a son of mine.
And thus I prophesy, that many a thousand
Which now mistrust no parcel of my fear,
And many an old man's sigh and many a widow's,
And many an orphan's water-standing eye—   40
Men for their sons, wives for their husbands,
Orphans for their parents' timeless death—
Shall rue the hour that ever thou wast born.
The owl shriek'd at thy birth, an evil sign;
The night-crow cried, aboding luckless time;   45
Dogs howl'd, and hideous tempest shook down trees;
The raven rook'd her on the chimney's top,
And chatt'ring pies in dismal discords sung;
Thy mother felt more than a mother's pain,
And yet brought forth less than a mother's hope, 50
To wit, an indigested and deformed lump,
Not like the fruit of such a goodly tree.
Teeth hadst thou in thy head when thou wast born,
To signify thou cam'st to bite the world;
And if the rest be true which I have heard,   55
Thou cam'st—

Glou.   I'll hear no more; die, prophet, in thy
 speech: *Stabs him.*
For this, amongst the rest, was I ordain'd.

K. Hen.   Ay, and for much more slaughter after
 this.
O God forgive my sins, and pardon thee!   *Dies.* 60

Glou.   What? will the aspiring blood of Lancaster
Sink in the ground? I thought it would have mounted.
See how my sword weeps for the poor king's death!
O may such purple tears be alway shed
From those that wish the downfall of our house!   65
If any spark of life be yet remaining,
Down, down to hell, and say I sent thee thither—
                                    Stabs him again.
I, that have neither pity, love, nor fear.
Indeed 'tis true that Henry told me of,
For I have often heard my mother say   70
I came into the world with my legs forward.
Had I not reason, think ye, to make haste,
And seek their ruin that usurp'd our right?

---

38. **mistrust . . . fear:** i.e. feel none of the apprehension that I feel.
40. **water-standing:** i.e. tear-flooded.   42. **timeless:** untimely.
45. **aboding:** foreboding.
47. **rook'd:** rucked, i.e. squatted, crouched.
48. **pies:** magpies (birds of ill omen).
64. **purple tears:** i.e. drops of blood.

3 Henry VI
V.vi

The midwife wonder'd and the women cried,
"O, Jesus bless us, he is born with teeth!"   75
And so I was, which plainly signified
That I should snarl, and bite, and play the dog.
Then since the heavens have shap'd my body so,
Let hell make crook'd my mind to answer it.
I have no brother, I am like no brother;   80
And this word "love," which greybeards call divine,
Be resident in men like one another,
And not in me: I am myself alone.
Clarence, beware! thou [keep'st] me from the light,
But I will sort a pitchy day for thee;   85
For I will buzz abroad such prophecies
That Edward shall be fearful of his life,
And then to purge his fear, I'll be thy death.
King Henry and the Prince his son are gone;
Clarence, thy turn is next, and then the rest,   90
Counting myself but bad till I be best.
I'll throw thy body in another room,
And triumph, Henry, in thy day of doom.
                                        Exit [*with the body*].

[SCENE VII]

Flourish. Enter KING [EDWARD], QUEEN [ELIZABETH],
    CLARENCE, RICHARD [OF GLOUCESTER], HASTINGS,
    NURSE [*with the young Prince*], *and* ATTENDANTS.

    K. Edw. Once more we sit in England's royal
        throne,
Repurchas'd with the blood of enemies.
What valiant foemen, like to autumn's corn,
Have we mow'd down in tops of all their pride!
Three Dukes of Somerset, threefold [renown'd]   5
For hardy and undoubted champions;
Two Cliffords, as the father and the son,
And two Northumberlands—two braver men
Ne'er spurr'd their coursers at the trumpet's sound;
With them, the two brave bears, Warwick and
        Montague,   10

79. answer: match. 85. sort: pick. 91. bad: lowly.

V.vii. Location: London. The palace.
3. corn: grain. 4. in tops: at the height.
6. undoubted: fearless. 7. as: namely.
10. bears. An allusion to the rampant bear chained to a staff, the
badge of the House of Warwick. See note on *2 Henry VI*, v.i.202–3.

That in their chains fetter'd the kingly lion,
And made the forest tremble when they roar'd.
Thus have we swept suspicion from our seat,
And made our footstool of security.
Come hither, Bess, and let me kiss my boy.   15
Young Ned, for thee, thine uncles and myself
Have in our armors watch'd the winter's night,
Went all afoot in summer's scalding heat,
That thou mightst repossess the crown in peace,
And of our labors thou shalt reap the gain.   20
    Glou. [*Aside.*] I'll blast his harvest, [and] your
        head were laid,
For yet I am not look'd on in the world.
This shoulder was ordain'd so thick to heave,
And heave it shall some weight, or break my back:
Work thou the way—and that [shall] execute.   25
    K. Edw. Clarence and Gloucester, love my lovely
        queen,
And kiss your princely nephew, brothers both.
    Clar. The duty that I owe unto your Majesty
I seal upon the lips of this sweet babe.
    [*Q. Eliz.*] [Thanks], noble Clarence, worthy
        brother, thanks.   30
    Glou. And that I love the tree from whence thou
        sprang'st,
Witness the loving kiss I give the fruit.
[*Aside.*] To say the truth, so Judas kiss'd his master,
And cried "All hail!" when as he meant all harm.
    K. Edw. Now am I seated as my soul delights,   35
Having my country's peace and brothers' loves.
    Clar. What will your Grace have done with
        Margaret?
[Reignier], her father, to the King of France
Hath pawn'd the Sicils and Jerusalem,
And hither have they sent it for her ransom.   40
    K. Edw. Away with her, and waft her hence to
        France.
And now what rests but that we spend the time
With stately triumphs, mirthful comic shows,
Such as befits the pleasure of the court?
Sound drums and trumpets! Farewell sour annoy!   45
For here I hope begins our lasting joy. *Exeunt omnes.*

13. suspicion: anxiety. 21. and . . . laid: i.e. if you were dead.
25. thou . . . that: i.e. my head . . . my hand (indicated by gestures).
40. it: i.e. the money thus raised.

NOTE ON THE TEXT

The First Folio (1623) affords the only authoritative text of *3 Henry VI*; all later editions are derived primarily from that source. Again, however, as with *2 Henry VI*, there is a "bad" quarto (actually an octavo). This memorially reported text, which is based on essentially the same text as that printed in F1, was published in 1595 under the title *The true Tragedie of Richard Duke of Yorke* (see Textual Notes for the full descriptive title). This version (called hereafter Q1 for convenience, rather than O1) was reprinted in 1600 (Q2) and 1619 (Q3). Q3, printed from Q1, like Q3 of *2 Henry VI*, makes a number of changes and one addition

(see Textual Notes, V.vi.89–90) that appear to anticipate the F1 text.

The problems of the F1 text seem in all essentials to be similar to those outlined for *2 Henry VI* (see "Note on the Text"). For the reason there suggested, the readings in which F1 agrees with Q3 readings (or, in a few cases, Q2) as against the other two quartos have been retained in the present text (see, for example, Textual Notes, I.i.24, 78, 83, 196, I.iv.63, 75, 166, II.i.104, 123, II.ii.46, 101, 107, 116, II.vi.59, III.ii.183, III.iii.243, IV.i.22, 29, 136, V.i.111, V.v.88, V.vi.71, V.vii.21, 38), except at III.ii.30, V.i.75, and

V.vii.21, where Q1–2 *and* has been substituted for F1, Q3 *if*. It is believed that at least one passage (IV.ii.1–18) was set directly from one of the quartos (probably Q3). Where only one or two of the three quartos are cited, agreement of the uncited quarto (or quartos) with the lemma may be assumed.

The Textual Notes generally record the variants in Q1–3 only where they figure in a reading cited in connection with the F1 text. The absence of citation of Q1–3 among the sigla in any entry indicates that the reading of the lemma occurs in a passage which in Q1–3 is either missing or so differently worded that it offers no recognizable equivalent. Some longer sections of Q1–3, where divergence from the F1 text is most noticeable, may be consulted in the Textual Notes at I.iv.1–6, II.iii.7–13, 15–22, III.iii.1–43, IV.iv, V.i.77, V.ii.50, V.iv.1–50, V.vi.89–90.

For further information, see the works cited in the "Note on the Text" to *2 Henry VI*.

TEXTUAL NOTES

Title: The Third . . . Sixt] The third Part of Henry the Sixt, with the death of the Duke of Yorke. *F1;* The true Tragedie of Richard Duke of Yorke, and the death of good King Henrie the Sixt, with the whole contention betweene the two Houses Lancaster and Yorke, as it was sundrie times acted by the Right Honourable the Earle of Pembrooke his seruants. *Q1 (title-page)*

Dramatis personae: *subs. as first given by Rowe*

Act-scene division: *none in Q1–3; F1 marks only I.i; other act-scene divisions from Rowe and later editors (see first note to each scene); present act-scene arrangement as a whole first established by Capell*

I.i

Location: *Theobald, Capell (after Hanmer)*
o.s.d. Montague] *Q1–2;* Mountague *F1 (throughout), Q3 (here only)*
o.s.d. with Drum] *Q1–3 (Q1–3 include the yong Earle of Rutland in the entry)*
o.s.d. with white . . . hats] *Q1–3*
2 s.p. York.] *Q1–3;* P1. *F1 (or Plant. through l. 43)*
6 himself,] *Rowe;* himselfe. *F1*
16 s.d. Showing . . . head.] *Hanmer (after Theobald)*
24 heaven] heauens *Q1–2*
27 heirs'] *Warburton;* Heires *F1, Q1–3*
36 council] *Pope;* counsaile *F1*
49 s.d. York . . . throne.] *Collier MS (after Johnson, but following l. 32); placed as in Johnson*
49 s.d. with . . . hats] *Q1–3*
66 cousin] *Q1–3;* Cousin *F1*
69 s.p. Exe.] *Q1–3;* Westm. *F1*
78 my] mine *Q1–2*
83 that's] and that is *Q1–2;* and that's *Q3, F2*
93 Yes] No *Q1–3*
102 s.p. York.] *Q1–3;* Plant. *F1 (throughout scene)*
105 Thy] *Q1–3;* My *F1*
120 s.p. K. Hen.] Northum. *Q1–3 (better perhaps)*
134, 151 s.dd. Aside.] *Capell*
170 hear . . . word] heare me speake *Q1–3 (some eds. insert me after F1 hear)*
184, 186, 188 s.dd. Exit.] *Q1–3*
186 unmanly] vnkingly *Q1–2;* vnkindly *Q3*
194 s.d. To York.] *Collier MS*
196 an] thine *Q1–3*
206 s.d. Exeunt . . . Soldiers.] *ed. (after Q1–3 Exit Yorke and [with Q3] his sonnes.)*
207, 208, 209 s.dd. Exit with Soldiers.] *ed. (after Q1–3 Exit.)*
210 s.d. and Prince Edward] *from Q1–3 s.d. (and the Prince)*
213 s.p. Q. Mar.] *Malone;* Queene. *F1 (through II.iv), Q1–3 (throughout)*
213 I will] I *Q1–2;* Ile *Q3*
251 northern] Northen *Q1–2*
259 with] *Q1–3*
261 from] *Q1–3;* to *F1*
263 s.d. Exeunt . . . Prince.] *Rowe; Q1–3 (omitting l. 263) give them separate exits after ll. 260 and 262*
273 s.d. Flourish.] *placed as in Wilson; part of entry for next scene, F1*

273 s.d. Exeunt.] *Pope;* Exit *F1*

I.ii

I.ii] *Capell*
Location: *Theobald (after Pope)*
47 s.d. a Messenger] *Q1–3;* Gabriel *F1 (probably Gabriel Spencer, who played the role)*
49 s.p. Mess.] *Q1–3;* Gabriel. *F1*
51 twenty] thirtie *Q1–3*
55 brother] cosen *Q1–3*
61 s.d. Enter . . . Mortimer.] *F1, adjusted after Q1–3* Enter sir Iohn and sir Hugh Mortimer.
75 s.d. Exeunt.] *Q2;* Exit. *F1, Q1, Q3*

I.iii

I.iii] *Capell*
Location: *Theobald*
o.s.d. Alarums] *Q1–3* (Alarmes)
2 s.d. and Soldiers] *Theobald*
9 s.d. dragged . . . Soldiers] *Theobald; Q1–3 s.d. reads:* Exit the Chaplein.
14 o'er] ouer *Q1–2*
47 s.d. Stabs him.] *Rowe*
48 s.d. Dies.] *Theobald*

I.iv

I.iv] *Capell*
Location: *ed. (after Pelican)*
1–6 The . . . them;] *Q1–3 give a different version of these lines:* Ah Yorke, post to thy castell, saue thy life, / The goale is lost thou house of *Lancaster,* / Thrise happie chance is it for thee and thine, / That heauen abridgde my daies and cals me hence, / But God knowes what chance hath betide my sonnes.
26 s.d.] *Q1–3 om.* Prince Edward
60 s.d. They . . . struggles.] *Johnson;* Fight and take him. *Q1–3*
63 conquer'd] conquered *Q1–2*
64 yield, with robbers] *F2;* yeeld with Robbers, *F1*
75 where's] where is *Q1–2*
75 crook-back] Crookbackt *Q1–2;* crookt-backt *Q3*
87 What,] What *Q1–2*
95 s.d. Putting . . . head.] *Rowe*
112 tongue more poisons] tongue more poison'd *Q1–2;* tongue's more poison'd *Q3*
112 than] *Q1–2;* then *F1, Q3*
117 deeds,] *F2;* deedes. *F1;* deedes: *Q1–2;* deeds; *Q3*
133 abominable] *F3;* abhominable *F1*
137 tiger's] *Q1–3* (Tygers); Tygres *F1*
153 stain'd] (*Q1–3*); stayn'd the roses just *F2*
154 inhuman] *Rowe;* inhumane *F1, Q3;* in-humaine *Q1–2*
166 too] two *Q1–2*
172 weeping-ripe] *hyphen, Theobald*
175 s.d. Stabbing him.] *Pope*
176 s.d. Stabbing him.] *Rowe*
178 s.d. Dies.] *Rowe*
180 s.d. Exeunt.] *Q1–3* (Exeunt omnes.); Exit. *F1*

II.i

II.i] *Rowe*
Location: *Capell (after Theobald)*
o.s.d. and their power] with drum and Souldiers *Q1–3*

20 s.d. Three . . . air.] *Q1–3*
25 Dazzle] Dasell *Q1–2*
40 target] *Q1–3;* Targuet *F1*
42 s.d. a Messenger] *from Q3 s.d.:* Enter a Messenger.; *s.d. om. Q1–2*
45 looker-on] *hyphen, Capell*
94 s.d. Montague] *Q1–3;* Mountacute *F1*
95 fare] *Q1–3;* faire *F1*
96 recompt] *F2;* tecompt *F1;* recount *F3;* report *Q1, Q3;* but reporte *Q2*
104 news] things *Q1–2*
113 And . . . thought,] *Q1–3*
123 Who] He *Q1, Q3*
127 captives] *Rowe;* Captiues, *F1;* captaines *Q1–3*
130 soldiers'] *Capell;* Souldiers *F1, Q1–3*
131 an idle] *Q1–3;* a lazie *F1 (lazie presumably caught from l. 130)*
177 thirty] fifty *Q1–3*
181 five and twenty] 48. *Q1–2;* eight and forty *Q3*
182 march,] march amaine *Q1–3*
184 "Charge!" . . . foes] *Staunton;* Charge vpon our Foes *F1,* (the foe) *Q1–3 (many eds. read "Charge . . . foes")*
190 fail'st] faints *Q1, Q3;* faint'st *Q2*
198 Richard, Montague] *Q1–3;* Richard Mountague *F1*
209 warriors. Let's] *Capell (subs., after Q1–3* Lordes. Lets); Warriors, let's *F1*

II.ii

II.ii] *Capell*
Location: *Capell (after Pope)*
o.s.d. Northumberland] *F2;* Northum- *F1 (Q1–3 give Northerne Earles for Clifford and Northumberland)*
o.s.d. Trumpets] Soldiers *Q1–3*
37 great-grandfather] *hyphen, Capell*
46 ill] euill *Q1–2*
48 hell?] *Q1–3;* hell: *F1*
62 lesson:] lesson boy, *Q1–2*
89 Since] *F2 (continuing the speech to Edward);* Cla. Since *F1;* George. Since *Q1–3*
92 out me] our brother out *Q1–3*
100 signal] synald *Q1–2*
101 fly] flee *Q1–2*
107 Clifford,] Clifford, That *Q1–2*
116 sunset] sunne set *Q1–2;* sun-set *Q3*
133 s.p. Rich.] *Q1–3;* War. *F1*
142 Sham'st] Shames *Q1–2*
163 s.p. Geo.] *Q1–3;* Cla. *F1 (or Clar., Clarence. throughout)*

II.iii

II.iii] *Capell*
Location: *ed.*
1 Forespent] Sore spent *Q1–3*
7–13 For . . . pursuit.] *Q1–3 give a different version of these lines:* That we maie die vnlesse we gaine the daie: / What fatall starre malignant frownes from heauen / Vpon the harmelesse line of *Yorkes* true house? / Enter George. / *George.* Come brother, come, lets to the field againe, / For yet theres hope inough to win the daie: / Then let vs backe to cheere our fainting Troupes, / Lest they retire now we haue left the field. / *War.* How now my lords: what hap, what hope of good?

13 s.d. **running]** *Q1–3*

15–22 **Thy . . . ghost.]** *Q1–3 give a different version of these lines:* Thy noble father in the thickest thronges, / Cride still for *Warwike* his thrise valiant son, / Vntill with thousand swords he was beset, / And manie wounds made in his aged brest, / And as he tottering [tottring *Q3*] sate vpon his steede, / He waft his hand to me and cride aloud: / *Richard,* commend me to my valiant sonne, [*cf. V.ii.42*] / And still he cride *Warwike* reuenge my death, / And with those words he tumbled off his horse, / And so the noble *Salsbury* gaue vp the ghost.

37 **setter-up and plucker-down]** *hyphens, Dyce*

49 **all together]** *Rowe;* altogether *F1*

II.iv

II.iv] *Capell*

Location: *ed. (after Wilson)*

o.s.d. **at one door . . . at the other]** *Q1–3*

1] *Preceding this line, Q1–2, give:* Rich. A Clifford a Clifford. / Clif. A Richard a Richard.

8 **death]** deathes *Q1–3 (perhaps a better reading)*

11 s.d. **Alarums.]** *from Q1–3 s.d.:* Alarmes. They fight, and then enters Warwike and rescues Richard, & then exeunt omnes.

II.v

II.v] *Capell*

Location: *ed. (after Wilson)*

54 s.d. **dragging . . . body]** *Capell; Q1–3 s.d. reads:* Enter a souldier with a dead man in his armes.

78 s.d. **that . . . door]** *F1 (from s.d. at l. 54, where F1 anticipates the Father's entry); Q1–3 s.d. reads:* Enter an other souldier, with a dead man.

89 **stratagems]** *F3;* Stragems *F1*

90 **Erroneous]** *F2;* Erreoneous *F1;* ironious *Q1–2;* ironous *Q3*

92–3 **soon . . . late]** . . . sone *Q1–3*

113 s.d. **Exit . . . father.]** *Q1–3*

119 **E'en]** *Collier MS;* Men *F1*

122 s.d. **with his son]** *Q1–3*

123 **Sad-hearted men]** *F3;* Sad-hearted-men *F1*

124 s.d. **Enter . . . Exeter.]** *in Q1–3 the three characters enter separately, each immediately before speaking, the Queen's entry and speech preceding Prince Edward's*

II.vi

II.vi] *Capell*

Location: *ed. (after Wilson)*

o.s.d. **with . . . neck]** *Q1–3*

6 **fall, thy]** *Rowe;* fall. Thy *F1;* die, that *Q1–3*

8 **The . . . flies,]** *Q1–3 (first inserted by Theobald)*

19 **Had]** *Q1–3;* Hed *F1*

19 **death]** deathes *Q1–3 (perhaps a better reading)*

30 s.d. **He faints.]** *Rowe*

39 **For (though]** *Capell (subs.);* (For though *F1;* For though *Q1–3*

41 s.d. **and then dies]** *Q1–3*

44 **See . . . is.]** *given to Edward, Q1–3*

59 **ill-boding]** euill boding *Q1, Q3;* yll boding *Q2*

60 **his]** *Q1–3;* is *F1*

85 **Off]** *Q1–3;* Of *F1*

III.i

III.i] *Rowe*

Location: *Hanmer (after Theobald)*

o.s.d. **two Keepers]** *Q1–3;* Sinklo, and Humfrey *F1 (actors' names;* Humfrey *is probably Humphrey Jeaffes)*

o.s.d. **cross-bows]** bow and arrowes *Q1–3*

1 s.p. **1. Keep.]** *Malone;* Sink. *F1 (or Sinklo. throughout scene);* Keeper. *Q1–3*

1 **thick-grown]** *hyphen, Pope*

5 s.p. **2. Keep.]** *Malone;* Hum. *F1 (throughout scene);* Keeper. *Q1–3*

---

7 **scare]** *F3;* scarre *F1*

11 **self place]** *Capell;* selfe-place *F1*

12 s.d. **disguised]** *Q1–3*

24 **thee]** *Dyce conj.;* the *F1*

24 **adversities]** *Pope;* Aduersaries *F1*

30 **I]** *F2;* I: *F1*

55 **thou talk'st]** thou that talkes *Q1–3*

56 s.p. **K. Hen.]** *Rowe;* King. *F1 (throughout rest of scene);* Hen. *Q1–3*

III.ii

III.ii] *Pope*

Location: *Hanmer (after Theobald)*

8 s.p. **Glou.]** *Q1–3;* Rich. *F1 (throughout)*

11, 15, 25, 28 s.dd. **Aside to Clarence.]** *Capell*

14, 24, 27 s.dd. **Aside to Gloucester.]** *Capell*

18 s.p. **L. Grey.]** *Rowe;* Wid. *F1 (throughout scene)*

21, 30, 34, 57 s.dd. **Aside to Clarence.]** *Cambridge*

25 **God forbid]** Marie godsforbot *Q1;* Marie gods-forbot *Q2;* Marry gods-forbot *Q3*

30 **and]** *Q1–2;* if *F1, Q3*

31 **'Twere]** Were it *Q1–2;* Wer't *Q3*

35 s.d. **Gloucester . . . retire.]** *Johnson*

50, 82, 107 s.dd. **Aside to Clarence.]** *Dyce*

51, 83, 108 s.dd. **Aside to Gloucester.]** *Dyce*

84 s.d. **Aside.]** *Johnson*

104 **other some]** *Q1–3;* other-some *F1*

117 s.d. **Nobleman]** *Rowe;* Noble man *F1;* Messenger *Q1–3*

123 **honorably]** *Q1–3;* honourable *F1*

144 **eye's]** *F3;* Eyes *F1*

150 **witch]** *Q1–3;* 'witch *F1*

183 **that which]** that that *Q1;* that, that *Q2*

III.iii

III.iii] *Capell*

Location: *Pope, Cambridge (after Capell)*

o.s.d. **Bourbon]** *Q1–3 om. this character, but add* and others *after Oxford*

1–43 **Fair . . . sorrow!]** *Q1–3 give a different and reduced version of these lines:* Welcome Queene Margaret to the Court of *France,* / It fits not *Lewis* to sit while thou dost stand. / Sit by my side, and here I vow to thee, / Thou shalt haue aide to repossesse thy right, / And beat proud Edward from his vsurped seat. / And place king *Henry* in his former rule. / *Queen.* I humblie thanke your royall maiestie. / And pray the God of heauen to blesse thy state, / Great king of *France,* that thus regards our wrongs.

29 **true-anointed]** *hyphen, Theobald*

58 s.d. **Aside.]** *Capell*

78 s.p. **Prince.]** *Rowe;* Edw. *F1;* Prince Ed. *Q1–3*

124 **eternal]** *Q1–3;* externall *F1*

156 **Peace, impudent]** *Theobald;* Peace impudent, *F1*

156 **Warwick,]** Warwicke, Peace, *F2*

157 **setter-up and puller-down]** *hyphens, Dyce*

161 s.d. **Post . . . within.]** *placed as in Capell (who reads:* Tucket heard.); *after l. 160, F1;* Sound for a post within. *Q1–3 (after l. 155; Q1–3 here om. ll. 156–61)*

169–70 **Nay . . . best.]** *as verse, Rowe; as prose, F1 (Q1–3 om. l.170)*

226 **pass'd]** *Wilson;* past *F1*

233 **Exit Post.]** *om. Q1–2;* Exit Mes. *Q3*

243 **wedlock]** wedlockes *Q1–2*

IV.i

IV.i] *Rowe*

Location: *Capell (after Pope)*

6 s.d. **now Queen Elizabeth]** *Rowe (subs.);* the Queene *Q1–3 (om. Lady Grey)*

6 s.d. **Pembroke]** *F2 (subs.);* Penbrooke *F1, Q1–3*

6 s.d. **and others]** *Capell (subs.); s.d. in Q1–3, which begin the scene here, reads:* Enter king Edward, the Queene and Clarence, and Gloster, and Montague, and Hastings, and Penbrooke, with souldiers. (*Q3 om. the first four* and's)

22 **pitty]** a pittie *Q1–2*

29 **mine]** my *Q1–2*

---

34 **What]** *Dyce;* What, *F1*

41 **But]** Yes, but *F2*

60 **malecontent]** mal-content *Q1–2*

66 **brother's will]** *Rowe;* Brothers will *F1;* brothers wils *Q1–3*

67 s.p. **Q. Eliz.]** *Q1–3 (Queen.);* Lady Grey. *F1*

83 s.d. **Aside.]** *Johnson*

84–5 **Now . . . France?]** *as verse, Capell (after Pope); as prose, F1 (Q1–3 give subs. l. 84 and om. ll. 81–3, replacing them with a line by Montague:* My Lord, heere is the messenger returnd from France.)

116 **they are]** theare *Q1*

124 s.d. **Aside.]** *Rowe*

136 **near]** neerest *Q1–2*

IV.ii

IV.ii] *Capell*

Location: *Capell (after Theobald)*

IV.iii

IV.iii] *Capell*

Location: *Capell*

9 **nobleman]** *F4;* Noble man *F1 (Q1–3 om. ll. 1–22)*

29–30 **Richard . . . Duke.]** *as verse, Pope; as prose, F1, Q1–3*

55–6 **I'll . . . him.]** Ile come and tell thee what the ladie *Bona* saies, *Q1–3*

57 s.d. **out]** *F2;* ont *F1*

59 s.d. **Exit . . . Somerset.]** *Cambridge, Capell;* Exeunt. *F1;* Exeunt some with Edward. *Q1–2,* (Exit) *Q3 (Q1–3 om. ll. 58–9)*

64 s.d. **Exeunt.]** *Q1–3 (*Exeunt omnes.); exit. *F1*

IV.iv

IV.iv] *Capell*

Q1–3 reverse the order of Scenes iv and v; cf. the essentially variant version of this scene in Q1–3: Enter the *Queene* and the Lord *Riuers.* / *Riuers.* Tel me good maddam, why is your grace / So passionate of late? / *Queen.* Why brother *Riuers,* heare you [ye *Q3*] not the newes, / Of that successe king *Edward* had of late? / *Riu.* What? losse of some pitcht battaile against *Warwike,* / Tush, feare not faire *Queen,* but cast those cares aside. / King *Edwards* noble mind his honours doth display: / And *Warwike* maie loose, though then he got the day. / *Queen.* If that were all, my griefes were at an end: / But greater troubles will I feare befall. / *Riu.* What, is he taken prisoner by the foe, / To the danger of his royall person then? / *Queen.* I, thears my griefe, king *Edward* is surprisde, / And led awaie, as prisoner [prison *Q2*] vnto *Yorke.* / *Riu.* The newes is passing strange, I must confesse: / Yet comfort your selfe, for *Edward* hath more friends, / Then *Lancaster* at this time must perceiue, / That some will set him in his throne againe. / *Queen.* God grant they maie, but gentle brother come, / And let me leane vpon thine arme a while, / Vntill I come vnto the sanctuarie, / There to preserue the fruit within my wombe, / K. *Edwards* seed true heire to *Englands* crowne. *Exit.*

Location: *Capell, Theobald*

o.s.d. **now Queen Elizabeth]** *Theobald (subs.);* the Queene *Q1–3 (om. Lady Grey)*

2 s.p. **Q. Eliz.]** *Q1–3 (Queen.);* Gray. *F1 (throughout scene)*

4 **What?]** *Q1–3;* What *F1*

20 **misfortune's]** *Pope;* misfortunes *F1*

IV.v

IV.v] *Capell*

Location: *Theobald (after Pope)*

4 **stands]** *F2;* stand *F1*

8 **Comes]** *F2;* Come *F1*

20–1 **lord— . . . Flanders?]** *ed.;* Lord, . . . Flanders. *F1*

21 s.d. **To Gloucester.]** *ed.*

IV.vi

IV.vi] *Capell*

Q1–3 reverse the order of Scenes vi and vii and om. ll. 3–37, 48–64, 77–102 of this scene
Location: *Pope, Theobald*
o.s.d. **Enter . . . Tower.]** Enter Warwike and Clarence, with the Crowne, and then enter Henry, and Oxford, and Summerset, and the yong Earle of Richmond. *Q1–3* (*Q3 om. the third and fourth and's*)
o.s.d. **of the Tower]** *Rowe*
88 s.d. **Manent]** *F2*; Manet *F1*

IV.vii

IV.vii] *Capell*
Location: *Capell (after Pope)*
o.s.d. **a . . . Hollanders]** *Q1–3*
4 **waned]** *Steevens;* wained *F1*
8 **Ravenspurgh]** *F2;* Rauenspurre *F1;* Raunspur *Q1, Q3;* Rounspur *Q2*
16 s.d. **the Aldermen]** *Dyce (subs.)*
25 s.d. **Aside.]** *Rowe*
29 s.d. **He descends]** Exit Maire. *Q1–3*
29 s.d. **with the Aldermen]** *Dyce (after Malone)*
34 s.d. **below]** *Capell; Q1–3 s.d. reads:* The Maire opens the dore, and brings the keies in his hand.
70 s.d. **Gives . . . paper.]** *Capell (subs.)*
71 s.d. **Reads.]** *Capell*

IV.viii

IV.viii] *Capell*
Location: *Pope, Kittredge (from Wright conj.)*
o.s.d. **Exeter]** *Capell;* Somerset *F1; Q1–3 s.d. reads:* Enter one with a letter to Warwike. (*as continuation of IV.vi, which precedes this scene in Q1–3*)
29 s.d. **kissing Henry's hand]** *Johnson*
32 s.d. **all . . . Exeter]** *Capell (subs.); Wilson, following P. A. Daniel's suggestion, marks a new scene here; Q1–3 s.d. reads:* Exeunt omnes. (*following All. Agreed., a speech found only in Q1–3*)
51 s.d. **with Gloucester]** *Hanmer (subs.)*
51 s.d. **and others]** *ed., from Q1–3 s.d.:* Enter Edward and his traine.
57 s.d. **Exeter]** *ed. (after Pelican)*
57 s.d. **guarded]** *ed. (after Pelican)*

V.i

V.i] *Pope*
Location: *Theobald (subs.)*
o.s.d. **Enter . . . walles.]** Enter Warwike on the walles. *Q1–3*
3 **Dunsmore]** Daintrie *Q1–3*
6 **Daintry]** Donsmore *Q1–3*
6 s.d. **Sir John]** *Capell*
10 s.d. **Drum heard.]** *Capell*
14 **unlook'd-for]** *hyphen, Pope*
24 **outrages.]** *Pope;* Outrages? *F1*
57 s.d. **Colors.]** souldiers & al crie, *Q1; Q2 makes l. 59 part of the s.d. following* all crie: *Q3 om.* & al crie *and restores l. 59 to* Oxford (*the s.d. follows l. 58 in Q1–3*)
59 s.d. **He . . . city.]** *Capell;* Exit. *Q1, Q3;* Exeunt. *Q2*
66, 71, 75 s.dd. **Colors]** souldiers *Q1–3* (*Somerset precedes Montague in Q1–3*)
67, 72 s.dd. **He . . . city.]** *Malone (after Capell);* Exit. *Q1, Q3;* Exeunt. *Q2*
75 **and]** *Q1–2;* if *F1, Q3*
77] *After this line, and omitting ll. 78–9, Q1–3 read:* Cla. Clarence, Clarence, for Lancaster. [*Exeunt. Q2*] / *Edw.* [*om. Q2*] Et tu Brute, wilt thou stab Caesar too? / A parlie sirra to George of Clarence.
78 **an]** *F2;* in *F1*
79 s.d. **Gloucester . . . together.]** *Collier, from Q1–3 s.d.:* Sound a Parlie, and Richard and Clarence whispers togither, and then

Clarence takes his red Rose out of his hat, and throwes it at Warwike.
82 s.d. **Clarence . . . Warwick.]** *Q1–3* (*see preceding note*)
91 **Jephthah]** *F3 (subs.);* Iephah *F1*
111 **dar'st]** darest *Q1–2*
113 s.d. **King . . . company]** *Cambridge*

V.ii

V.ii] *Capell*
Location: *Theobald (after Pope)*
o.s.d. **King Edward]** *Q1–3 om. the King from this scene*
44 **cannon]** clamor *Q1–3*
49 s.d. **He dies.]** *Q1–3*
50 **Away . . . power!]** *Q1–3 expand Oxford's single line to six:* Come noble *Summerset,* lets take our horse, / And cause retrait [retreate *Q3*] be sounded through the campe, / That all our friends that yet remaine aliue, / Maie be awarn'd [forwarn'd *Q3*] and saue themselues by flight. / That done, with them weele post vnto the *Queene,* / And once more trie our fortune in the field *Ex.* [*Exit Q3*] *ambo.*

V.iii

V.iii] *Capell*
Location: *ed. (after Wilson)*
8 **arriv'd]** *Rowe;* arriued *F1*
22–3 **augmented . . . along.]** *pointing based on sense of Q1–3* (And in euerie countie [country *Q3*] as we passe along / Our strengthes shall be augmented.); augmented: . . . along, *F1*

V.iv

V.iv] *Capell*
Location: *Theobald (after Pope)*
o.s.d. **and Soldiers]** with drum and souldiers *Q1–3*
1–50 **Great . . . help.]** *Q1–3 give an essentially different and reduced version of these lines:* Welcome to *England* my louing friends of *France,* / And welcome *Summerset,* and *Oxford* too. / Once more haue we spread our sailes abroad, / And though our tackling be almost consumde, / And *Warwike* as our maine mast ouerthrowne, / Yet warlike Lords raise you that sturdie post, / That beares the sailes to bring vs vnto rest, / And *Ned* and *I* as willing Pilots should / For once with carefull mindes guide on the sterne, / To beare vs throngh [through *Q2–3*] that dangerous gulfe / That heretofore hath swallowed vp our friends. / *Prince.* And if there be, as God forbid there should, / Amongst vs a timorous or fearefull man, / Let him depart before the battels ioine, / Least he in time of need intise another, / And so withdraw the souldiers harts from vs. / I will not stand alone and bid you fight, / But with my sword presse in the thickest thronges, / And single *Edward* from his strongest guard, / And hand to hand enforce him for to yeeld, / Or leaue my bodie as witnesse of my thoughts.
27 **ragged]** *Rowe;* raged *F1*
66 s.d. **Richard of Gloucester]** Glo. Hast. *Q1–3*
82 s.d. **Alarum . . . Somerset.]** *ed. (after Pelican) from Q1–3 and F1:* Alarmes to the battell, Yorke flies, then the chambers be discharged. Then enter the king, Cla & Glo. & the rest, & make a great shout and crie, for Yorke, for Yorke, and then the Queene is taken, & the prince, & Oxf. & Sum. and then sound and enter all againe. *Q1–3* (*Q3 rephrases slightly*); Alarum, Retreat, Excursions. Exeunt. *F1*

V.v

V.v] *Capell*
Location: *ed. (after Wilson)*
o.s.d. **prisoner]** *Pelican*
o.s.d. **and Soldiers with]** *Capell (subs.)*
o.s.d. **prisoners]** *Rowe (see Q1–3 s.d. at V.iv.82)*
6 s.d. **Oxford . . . guarded]** *Capell; Q1–3 read* Exit Oxford. *after l. 5 and* Exit Sum. *after l. 6*
11 s.d. **Soldiers with]** *Capell*
30 **crook-back]** Crooktbacke *Q1–2*
38 **the likeness]** the litnes *Q1;* the lightnes *Q2;* thou likenesse *F1*
38 s.d. **Stabs him.]** *om. Q1–2*
50 **The]** *Q1–3*
66 **off,]** *Q1–3;* off. *F1*
77 **butcher,]** *Q1, Q3;* butcher Richard? *F1;* butcher? *Q2*
82 s.d. **Margaret . . . forcibly]** *Capell*
88 **let's]** let vs *Q1–2*
90 s.d. **Exeunt.]** *Q1–3* (Exeunt Omnes.); Exit. *F1*

V.vi

V.vi] *Capell*
Location: *Pope (after Q1–3)*
o.s.d. **Enter . . . walls.]** Enter Gloster to king Henry in the Tower. *Q1–3*
6 s.d. **Exit Lieutenant.]** *Rowe*
7 **reakless]** *ed.;* wreaklesse *F1*
10 **Roscius]** *Pope;* Rossius *F1;* Rosius *Q1–3*
22–3 **course; . . . boy,]** *Rowe; pointing follows sense of Q1–3* (course, / Thy brother *Edward,* the sunne that searde his wings,); course, . . . Boy. *F1*
40 **water-standing eye]** *Rowe;* water-standing-eye *F1;* water standing eie *Q1–3*
41 **husbands,]** (*Q1–3*); Husbands fate, / And *F2*
57 s.d. **Stabs him.]** He stabs him. *Q1–2*
71 **I]** That I *Q1–2*
79] *Following this line Theobald inserts from Q1–3:* I had no father, I am like no father, / I have no brother, have no brothers *Q1, Q3*
81 **"love"]** [Loue] *F1;* Loue *Q1–3* (*in italics*)
84 **keep'st]** *F3;* keept'st *F1;* keptst *Q1–3*
86] *Following this line Q3 adds:* Vnder pretence of outward seeming ill.
89–90 **King . . . rest,]** *Henry* and his sonne are gone, thou *Clarence* next, / And one by one ile dispatch the rest, *Q1–2;* King *Henry,* and the Prince his sonne are gone, / And *Clarence* thou art next must follow them, / So by one and one dispatching all the rest, *Q3*
93 s.d. **with the body]** *Capell*

V.vii

V.vii] *Capell*
Location: *Theobald*
o.s.d. **Elizabeth]** *Q1–3*
o.s.d. **Richard of Gloucester]** *om. Q1–2*
o.s.d. **with . . . Prince]** *Capell*
5 **renown'd]** *Q3;* Renowne *F1;* renowmd *Q1–2*
21, 33 s.dd. **Aside.]** *Rowe*
21 **and]** *Q1–2;* if *F1, Q3*
25 **way—]** *F3;* way, *F1, Q1–3*
25 **that shall]** *F3;* that shalt *F1;* thou shalt *Q1–3*
26 **Clarence . . . queen,]** Brothers of Clarence and of Gloster, / Pray loue my louely Queene, *Q3* (*om. brothers in l. 27*)
30 s.p. **Q. Eliz.]** *Q1–3* (Queen.); Cla. *F1*
30 **Thanks]** *Q1–3;* Thanke *F1*
31 **sprang'st,]** *Q1–3;* sprang'st: *F1*
38 **Reignier]** *Rowe;* Reynard *F1, Q3;* Ranard *Q1–2*
46 s.d. **Exeunt omnes.]** Exeunt omnes / FINIS. *F1, Q1–3*

Richard III

THE EARLY SUCCESS OF *Richard III*, one of the perennial favorites of English dramatic literature, is indicated by the history of its publication. Written probably about 1592, and in any event not long after *3 Henry VI* (to which it forms a sequel), the work appeared in print anonymously in 1597 in a version apparently put together as a memorial reconstruction by actors who no longer had their prompt-book to consult. The text of this "bad" quarto was reprinted in 1598 (with "William Shake-speare" on the title-page), 1602, 1605, 1612 ("As it hath beene lately Acted by the Kings Maiesties seruants"), and 1622; and even after its inclusion, in a better version, in the Folio of 1623, the play was reprinted twice more as a quarto, in 1629 and 1634. Only *1 Henry IV* can show a longer list of early reprints.

Since King Richard III had been an object of stylized abuse and of morbid fascination for a hundred years or more, there was a small library that Shakespeare could have drawn upon for sources. The account of the last and most evil of the Yorkist kings in Polydore Vergil's *Historia Anglica* (1534 ff.), a work that Henry VII had commissioned, did much to establish Richard's reputation as a villain; but even more important was Thomas More's *History of King Richard the Third*. This fragment, an authentic masterpiece of biography, was written about 1513 and survives in both an English and a Latin version that differ in details. The Latin, it has been suggested, was perhaps the work of John Morton, a supporter of the Earl of Richmond who, after his master's accession as Henry VII in 1485, became a stalwart Tudor politician (the Ely of the present play), a cardinal, and a patron of young Thomas More. Even if Morton did not compose the life of Richard, he no doubt provided More

with much of the vivid, first-hand information that gives the work distinction. The English version, first printed in a sadly mutilated form in Grafton's continuation of Hardyng's *Chronicle* (1543), was followed almost word for word by Hall in his *Union . . . of Lancaster and York* (1548) and thereafter, in the accommodating fashion of the age, by most of his successors. Although the authentic English text was given in William Rastell's 1557 printing of his famous uncle's *Works* and the Latin in the *Omnia Opera* of 1566, Shakespeare seems to have used Hall and (as the detail about the bleeding corpse at I.ii.55–56 shows) either Holinshed or Stow.

Meanwhile Richard had entered the domain of more or less belletristic literature. The first two editions of *A Mirror for Magistrates* (1559 and 1563) contain some eight "tragedies"—among others, those of Henry VI, George Duke of Clarence, Hastings, Buckingham, and Jane Shore—in which Richard comes off very badly. About 1579 Thomas Legge, Master of Caius College, Cambridge, wrote the Latin *Richardus Tertius*, a three-part Senecan tragedy, based largely on Hall, that depicts Richard as a tyrant. The anonymous *True Tragedy of Richard III*, which was probably written three or four years before its publication in 1594, is a crude but not wholly unsuccessful effort to combine the motif of Senecan revenge with the English history play. If Shakespeare knew this work (as is not unlikely, for he later quotes from it in Hamlet's line about the croaking raven that doth bellow for revenge) he may have been impressed by its use of a central, dominating character (in the style of Marlowe's Tamburlaine); moreover, he could have got from it a few details of plot.

It was More, however, who supplied the main outlines as well as most of the details for Shakespeare's portrait of the tyrant-king. Thus *The History of King*

Richard the Third must be accounted one of the most persistent triumphs in English historical literature, for thanks to Shakespeare's use of it—and despite modern efforts to salvage Richard's reputation—it has lasted to this day. "Little of stature, ill-featured of limbs, crook-backed, his left shoulder much higher than his right," says More in devastating and unforgettable detail, Richard was

> hard-favored of visage, and such as is in states [i.e. rulers] called warly [i.e. warlike], in other men otherwise; he was malicious, wrathful, envious, and, from afore his birth, ever froward. It is for truth reported that the duchess, his mother, had so much ado in her travail that she could not be delivered of him uncut, and that he came into the world with the feet forward, as men be borne outward, and (as the fame runneth) also not untoothed .... He was close and secret, a deep dissimuler, lowly of countenance, arrogant of heart, outwardly coumpinable [i.e. companionable] where he inwardly hated, not letting to kiss [i.e. abstaining from kissing] whom he thought to kill; dispitious and cruel, not for evil will alway, but ofter for ambition, and either for the surety or increase of his estate. Friend and foe was muchwhat indifferent; where his advantage grew he spared no man's death whose life withstood his purpose.

As the final unit in the first tetralogy, *Richard III* both closes Shakespeare's long survey of England's troubles in the fifteenth century and completes his exposition of the providential theme that he had got from Hall. Here we see the death-throes of the house of York, and here the little Richmond whom Henry VI had hailed as "England's hope" (*3 Henry VI*, IV.vi.78) fulfills his destiny on Bosworth Field, unites the white rose and the red, and inaugurates the Tudor peace. "England hath long been mad and scarr'd herself," he says in formal valediction,

> The brother blindly shed the brother's blood,
> The father rashly slaughter'd his own son,
> The son, compell'd, been butcher to the sire.
> All this divided York and Lancaster,
> Divided in their dire division,
> O now let Richmond and Elizabeth,
> The true succeeders of each royal house,
> By God's fair ordinance conjoin together!
> And let their heirs (God, if thy will be so)
> Enrich the time to come with smooth-fac'd peace,
> With smiling plenty, and fair prosperous days!
>
> (V.v.23–34)

But if *Richard III* closes on this apocalyptic note, it is more than Shakespeare's final step in his demonstration of a consoling commonplace. He accepts the Tudor party line and the standard view of Richard, but he adapts and deepens them to serve his purpose. Here, the accredited slogans, the politics and history, are used for more than propaganda. They provide the base for Shakespeare's explorations of the fact of evil and the means by which he shows its strength and

limitations. With the earlier villains—Queen Margaret and Beaufort, for example, to say nothing of the witch and strumpet Joan—he had been content to slap his primary colors on in strong, clear lines, and consequently these characters are as simple and sometimes as vulgar as cartoons. But the tyrant that he draws in Richard is more than just a villain: sometimes gay and debonair, sometimes coarse and even brutal, he is a man so driven by the lust for power that despite his wit and charm and intellect—which he possesses in abundance—he becomes the agent of his own destruction. "I am myself alone," Richard had declared when young (*3 Henry VI*, V.vi.83), and although he makes the same bizarre assertion as he prepared for Bosworth Field, he knows that "if I die no soul shall pity me" (V.iii.201). Therefore he can sport and frolic with his victims, and except for that one appalling moment at the end he can contemplate his crimes with dreadful satisfaction. The result is melodrama, to be sure, but melodrama that suggests the more subtle splendors of *Macbeth*. In both plays, Shakespeare's hero is a blood-stained tyrant, but, as Hazlitt pointed out, Richard's cruelty is rooted in his nature, Macbeth's in "accidental circumstances" that do not obliterate his claim upon us as a man.

Although a work of real if intermittent power, *Richard III* is very formal in its language and its structure. The balance of such a line as "If you will live, lament; if die, be brief" attests to the relentless artifice that pervades the language of a play where everything is shaped and planned. Richard's opening soliloquy, for instance, reveals a virtuoso wit, but it is made to serve a triple function of characterizing the speaker, disclosing his motives, and announcing the course of action to be followed; and thus its great creative energy is controlled by Senecan conventions. Even in the scenes of private woe, as when the Lady Anne laments the murder of the last Lancastrian king, the style is tailored to a rhetoric:

> O, cursed be the hand that made these holes!
> Cursed the heart that had the heart to do it!
> Cursed the blood that let this blood from hence!
>
> (I.ii.14–16)

and in the public, choric lamentations the antiphonal exchanges are so stiff and patterned that grief assumes the form of ritual:

> *Q. Elizabeth.* What stay had I but Edward? and he's gone.
> *Children.* What stay had we but Clarence? and he's gone.
> *Duchess.* What stays had I but they? and they are gone.
> *Q. Elizabeth.* Was never widow had so dear a loss.
> *Children.* Were never orphans had so dear a loss.
> *Duchess.* Was never mother had so dear a loss.
> Alas! I am the mother of these griefs:
> Their woes are parcell'd, mine is general.
> She for an Edward weeps, and so do I;

I for a Clarence weep, so doth not she;
These babes for Clarence weep, and so do I;
I for an Edward weep, so do not they.
Alas! you three on me, threefold distress'd,
Pour all your tears. I am your sorrow's nurse,
And I will pamper it with lamentation.

(II.ii.74–88)

The style of Richard's wooing (I.ii) is more brisk, of course, but no less formal in its stichomythic pattern, and that of such set pieces as Clarence's dream is merely formal in a different way—in its symbolic implications and its dazzling use of sound and color:

O Lord, methought what pain it was to drown!
What dreadful noise of waters in my ears!
What sights of ugly death within my eyes!
Methoughts I saw a thousand fearful wracks;
A thousand men that fishes gnaw'd upon;
Wedges of gold, great anchors, heaps of pearl,
Inestimable stones, unvalued jewels,
All scatt'red in the bottom of the sea:
Some lay in dead men's skulls, and in the holes
Where eyes did once inhabit, there were crept
(As 'twere in scorn of eyes) reflecting gems,
That woo'd the slimy bottom of the deep,
And mock'd the dead bones that lay scatt'red by.

(I.iv.21–33)

In certain massive block-like scenes—for instance, the lamentation of the three queens at IV.iv and the stylized procession of the ghosts of Richard's victims at V.iii—almost the only action is provided by the formal movement of the verse. Even the low language of Clarence's murderers (I.iv) and the commonplaces of the prudent citizens (II.iii), which seem to echo living speech, are shaped into a kind of choric comment on the moral climate of the play:

1. Citizen. Come, come, we fear the worst; all will be well.
3. Citizen. When clouds are seen, wise men put on their cloaks;
When great leaves fall, then winter is at hand;
When the sun sets, who doth not look for night?
Untimely storms makes men expect a dearth.
All may be well; but if God sort it so,
'Tis more than we deserve or I expect.

(II.iii.31–37)

Despite such persistent formality of language, the plot, except for scenes like that of Richard's second wooing (IV.iv), moves very fast. Its velocity depends in part upon the precision and economy with which Shakespeare handles his materials. Unlike *3 Henry VI*, with its sprawling, sometimes ill-articulated action, *Richard III* pulses with a beat that quickens as the play proceeds. Even such surcharged moments as Richard's "Off with his head" when he sends Hastings to the block (III.iv) and his "A horse, a horse! my kingdom for a horse!" when he sees death appear (V.iv) are adjusted to the rising movement of the

scenes where they occur; and the many *coups de théâtre* with which the play is dotted—like Richard's offer of his dagger to the Lady Anne (I.ii) and his break with Buckingham (IV.iii)—accelerate but do not punctuate the action. As usual in the histories, Shakespeare preserves the linear contour of events; but here the events are notably compressed and rearranged to maintain the rapid tempo of the plot. Propelled by Richard's stunning initial soliloquy, in Act I we sweep from Clarence's arrest (which occurred in 1477) and the report of Edward's final illness (1483), to a scene that conflates Henry VI's funeral (1471) and Richard's wooing of the Lady Anne, to Richard's appointment as Protector (1483), to the reappearance of old Margaret of Anjou (who had died in France in 1482), to Clarence's death by drowning in the malmsey-butt (1478). Such foreshortening and distortion do great violence to the facts, of course, but as A. P. Rossiter said of *Woodstock* (an anonymous play about the early reign of Richard II), the technique is very useful to a writer more concerned with moral meanings than with the recording of events.

Next to Richard's compelling central role it is Shakespeare's presentation of such moral meanings that most surely shapes the play. If its rather old-fashioned Senecan devices and its swift but episodic action mark *Richard III* as one of Shakespeare's early works, so does its debt to the tradition of the morality play, that remnant of an age when the struggle between good and evil for possession of man's soul was the main concern of drama. Although Shakespeare pointed to the debt himself—after all, the role of Richard, that consummate actor, is "the formal Vice, Iniquity" (III.i.82)—he goes far beyond the didactic crudities of such plays as Bale's *King John*. There can be no question of Richard's being saved like Everyman, of course, but he does epitomize the fact of evil, and his downfall, like that of Marlowe's *Doctor Faustus*, takes the form of retribution. The world he bustles in is one, despite "the grossness of the age," where effect is linked to cause in moral sequence, and where what happens to a man depends upon the kind of man he is. On one level this moral pattern is made to serve the use of Tudor propaganda, but it also, and more significantly, exemplifies the notion of retributive justice—or Nemesis, as R. G. Moulton called it.

As a Machiavel who takes evil for his good, and whose twisted body signifies his moral nihilism, Richard is a freak. He is not a good man who, when tempted, falls, and who, when fallen, hopes to find redemption. He is a "poisonous bunch-back'd toad," a "bottled spider," an "abortive, rooting hog," who sins with such bravado and exhilaration that E. K. Chambers decided Shakespeare really had no interest in the moral implications of his rise and fall. One finds it hard to follow this interpretation. Admittedly, this play does not unfold the cosmic evil that imparts such terror to *King Lear*: there is a sportive streak in Richard, and his crimes reveal a kind of antic cunning that both he and we enjoy. But that they are crimes is clear, and finally we recoil. Despite his string of quick successes, which seem to sweep the kingdom up into a spiral of corruption, the play is built upon a mounting sequence of crime and retribution—Clarence's, the Woodvilles', Hastings', Buckingham's—that finds its climax in the master-villain's death. The rhythm of this sequence not only confers a moral pattern on the action; it also underscores the words that Richmond, that paragon of sanity and order, addresses to his men as they prepare to meet and overcome their foe:

> Truly, gentlemen,
> A bloody tyrant and a homicide;
> One rais'd in blood, and one in blood established;
> One that made means to come by what he hath,

> And slaughtered those that were the means to help him;
> A base foul stone, made precious by the foil
> Of England's chair, where he is falsely set;
> One that hath ever been God's enemy.
>
> (V.iii.245–52)

In short, there are few if any moral ambiguities in Shakespeare's presentation of this "abortive, rooting hog," and it is not surprising that Colley Cibber's mangled version of the play (1700), which crudely underscored the fact of Richard's evil, terrified and titillated audiences on both sides of the Atlantic for nearly two centuries.

Herschel Baker

Sword and buckler

Sword and square target

From *Di Grassi His True Art of Defence*, trans. I. G. (1594). (*By permission of the Harvard College Library*)

The Tragedy of Richard the Third

ACT I, SCENE I

Enter RICHARD DUKE OF GLOUCESTER *solus.*

[*Glou.*]   Now is the winter of our discontent
Made glorious summer by this son of York;
And all the clouds that low'r'd upon our house
In the deep bosom of the ocean buried.
Now are our brows bound with victorious wreaths, 5

Our bruised arms hung up for monuments,
Our stern alarums chang'd to merry meetings,
Our dreadful marches to delightful measures.
Grim-visag'd War hath smooth'd his wrinkled front;
And now, in stead of mounting barbed steeds   10
To fright the souls of fearful adversaries,
He capers nimbly in a lady's chamber
To the lascivious pleasing of a lute.
But I, that am not shap'd for sportive tricks,
Nor made to court an amorous looking-glass;   15
I, that am rudely stamp'd, and want love's majesty
To strut before a wanton ambling nymph;
I, that am curtail'd of this fair proportion,

Words and passages enclosed in square brackets in the text above are
either emendations of the copy-text or additions to it. The Textual Notes
immediately following the play cite the earliest authority for every such
change or insertion and supply the reading of the copy-text wherever it is
emended in this edition.

I.i. Location: London. A street.
o.s.d. **solus:** alone.
2. **son.** With a pun on *sun* (the badge of Edward IV). For the origin
of the sun-badge see *3 Henry VI*, II.i.25–40.

6. **arms:** armor.   **monuments:** trophies.
7. **alarums:** calls to arms.   8. **measures:** dances.
9. **wrinkled front:** frowning brow.   10. **barbed:** armored.
11. **fearful:** frightened.   18. **proportion:** shape.

Cheated of feature by dissembling nature,
Deform'd, unfinish'd, sent before my time   20
Into this breathing world, scarce half made up,
And that so lamely and unfashionable
That dogs bark at me as I halt by them—
Why, I, in this weak piping time of peace,
Have no delight to pass away the time,   25
Unless to see my shadow in the sun
And descant on mine own deformity.
And therefore, since I cannot prove a lover
To entertain these fair well-spoken days,
I am determined to prove a villain   30
And hate the idle pleasures of these days.
Plots have I laid, inductions dangerous,
By drunken prophecies, libels, and dreams,
To set my brother Clarence and the King
In deadly hate the one against the other;   35
And if King Edward be as true and just
As I am subtle, false, and treacherous,
This day should Clarence closely be mew'd up
About a prophecy, which says that G
Of Edward's heirs the murtherer shall be.   40
Dive, thoughts, down to my soul, here Clarence
    comes!

Enter CLARENCE, *guarded, and* BRAKENBURY, [*Lieu-*
tenant of the Tower].

Brother, good day. What means this armed guard
That waits upon your Grace?
    Clar.   His Majesty,
Tend'ring my person's safety, hath appointed
This conduct to convey me to the Tower.   45
    Glou. Upon what cause?
    Clar.   Because my name is George.
    Glou. Alack, my lord, that fault is none of yours;
He should for that commit your godfathers.
O, belike his Majesty hath some intent
That you should be new christ'ned in the Tower.   50
But what's the matter, Clarence, may I know?
    Clar. Yea, Richard, when I know; but I protest
As yet I do not. But, as I can learn,
He hearkens after prophecies and dreams,
And from the cross-row plucks the letter G,   55
And says a wizard told him that by G
His issue disinherited should be;
And for my name of George begins with G,
It follows in his thought that I am he.
These (as I learn) and such-like toys as these   60
Hath mov'd his Highness to commit me now.

    Glou. Why, this it is, when men are rul'd by
        women:
'Tis not the King that sends you to the Tower;
My Lady Grey his wife, Clarence, 'tis she
That [tempers] him to this extremity.   65
Was it not she, and that good man of worship,
Anthony Woodvile, her brother there,
That made him send Lord Hastings to the Tower,
From whence this present day he is delivered?
We are not safe, Clarence, we are not safe.   70
    Clar. By heaven, I think there is no man [is] secure
But the Queen's kindred, and night-walking heralds
That trudge betwixt the King and Mistress Shore.
Heard you not what an humble suppliant
Lord Hastings was [to her for his] delivery?   75
    Glou. Humbly complaining to her deity
Got my Lord Chamberlain his liberty.
I'll tell you what, I think it is our way,
If we will keep in favor with the King,
To be her men and wear her livery.   80
The jealous o'erworn widow and herself,
Since that our brother dubb'd them gentlewomen,
Are mighty gossips in our monarchy.
    Brak. I beseech your Graces both to pardon me:
His Majesty hath straitly given in charge   85
That no man shall have private conference
(Of what degree soever) with your brother.
    Glou. Even so? And please your worship, Braken-
        bury,
You may partake of any thing we say:
We speak no treason, man. We say the King   90
Is wise and virtuous, and his noble queen
Well strook in years, fair, and not jealous;
We say that Shore's wife hath a pretty foot,
A cherry lip, a bonny eye, a passing pleasing tongue;
And that the Queen's kindred are made gentlefolks.
How say you, sir? Can you deny all this?   96
    Brak. With this, my lord, myself have nought to do.
    Glou. Naught to do with Mistress Shore? I tell
        thee, fellow,
He that doth naught with her (excepting one)
Were best to do it secretly alone.   100
    Brak. What one, my lord?
    Glou. Her husband, knave. Wouldst thou betray
        me?

---

64. **Lady Grey.** Queen Elizabeth's first husband was Sir John Grey.
65. **tempers:** moulds.
67. **Anthony Woodvile.** Woodvil(l)e succeeded his father as Earl Rivers in 1469. Richard sarcastically strips him and his sister, Queen Elizabeth, of their titles.
68. **send . . . Tower.** The chroniclers record no such imprisonment for William, Baron Hastings (1430?–1483), who had long and loyally served the House of York.
72. **night-walking heralds:** i.e. secret emissaries.
73. **Mistress Shore:** Jane Shore, wife of a London goldsmith and mistress of Edward IV. She long survived her early triumphs, not dying until about 1527. In Elizabethan usage *Mistress* was a title of respect for any woman, married or unmarried.
76. **her deity:** i.e. Jane Shore.
77. **Lord Chamberlain:** i.e. Lord Hastings, who served Edward IV in this capacity from 1461 to 1483.
81. **widow:** i.e. Queen Elizabeth, who was a widow when Edward married her.   83. **mighty gossips:** powerful busybodies.
85. **straitly:** strictly.
87. **degree:** rank. (*Of what degree* modifies *man*.)
92. **Well strook:** well struck, i.e. advanced. Elizabeth was about forty at the time.   **jealous:** jealous.   94. **passing:** exceedingly.
97. **nought:** nothing.   98. **Naught:** wickedness.

---

19. **feature:** general appearance.   **dissembling:** deceiving.
22. **unfashionable:** badly fashioned.   23. **halt:** limp.
27. **descant:** comment, discourse.   32. **inductions:** preparations.
36. **true and just:** i.e. naively unsuspecting.
38. **mew'd up:** caged (like a hawk).
39–40. **a prophecy . . . be.** According to Hall (Bullough, III, 249), "the fame was that the king or the Quene, or bothe [were] sore troubled with a folysh Prophesye, and by reason thereof began to stomacke & grevously to grudge agaynst the duke [of Clarence]. The effect of which was, after king Edward should reigne, one whose first letter of hys name shoulde be a G."   44. **Tend'ring:** caring for.
45. **conduct:** escort.   49. **belike:** probably.
55. **cross-row:** Christ- (or criss-)cross-row, i.e. the alphabet, so called from the figure of the cross usually prefixed to it in primers.
56. **wizard:** wise man, prophet.   58. **for:** because.
60. **toys:** trifles.

Richard III
I.i

Brak. I do beseech your Grace to pardon me, and withal
Forbear your conference with the noble Duke.
   Clar. We know thy charge, Brakenbury, and will obey.   105
   Glou. We are the Queen's abjects, and must obey.
Brother, farewell, I will unto the King,
And whatsoe'er you will employ me in,
Were it to call King Edward's widow sister,
I will perform it to enfranchise you.   110
Mean time, this deep disgrace in brotherhood
Touches me deeper than you can imagine.
   Clar. I know it pleaseth neither of us well.
   Glou. Well, your imprisonment shall not be long,
I will deliver you, or else lie for you.   115
Mean time, have patience.
   Clar.   I must perforce. Farewell.
         Exit Clarence [with Brakenbury and Guard].
   Glou. Go tread the path that thou shalt ne'er return:
Simple plain Clarence, I do love thee so
That I will shortly send thy soul to heaven,
If heaven will take the present at our hands.   120
But who comes here? the new-delivered Hastings?

      Enter Lord Hastings.

   Hast. Good time of day unto my gracious lord!
   Glou. As much unto my good Lord Chamberlain!
Well are you welcome to [the] open air.
How hath your lordship brook'd imprisonment?   125
   Hast. With patience, noble lord, as prisoners must;
But I shall live, my lord, to give them thanks
That were the cause of my imprisonment.
   Glou. No doubt, no doubt, and so shall Clarence too,
For they that were your enemies are his,   130
And have prevail'd as much on him as you.
   Hast. More pity that the eagles should be mew'd,
Whiles kites and buzzards [prey] at liberty.
   Glou. What news abroad?
   Hast. No news so bad abroad as this at home: 135
The King is sickly, weak, and melancholy,
And his physicians fear him mightily.
   Glou. Now by Saint John, that news is bad indeed!
O, he hath kept an evil diet long,
And overmuch consum'd his royal person: 140
'Tis very grievous to be thought upon.
Where is he? in his bed?
   Hast. He is.
   Glou. Go you before, and I will follow you.
               Exit Hastings.
He cannot live, I hope, and must not die   145
Till George be pack'd with post-horse up to heaven.
I'll in, to urge his hatred more to Clarence
With lies well steel'd with weighty arguments,

And if I fail not in my deep intent,
Clarence hath not another day to live: 150
Which done, God take King Edward to his mercy,
And leave the world for me to bustle in!
For then I'll marry Warwick's youngest daughter.
What though I kill'd her husband and her father?
The readiest way to make the wench amends   155
Is to become her husband and her father:
The which will I, not all so much for love
As for another secret close intent
By marrying her which I must reach unto.
But yet I run before my horse to market: 160
Clarence still breathes, Edward still lives and reigns;
When they are gone, then must I count my gains.
                    Exit.

              Scene II

Enter the corse of Henry the Sixt, *with Halberds to guard it,* Lady Anne *being the mourner, [attended by* Tressel *and* Berkeley].

   Anne. Set down, set down your honorable load,
If honor may be shrouded in a hearse,
Whilst I awhile obsequiously lament
Th' untimely fall of virtuous Lancaster.
Poor key-cold figure of a holy king,   5
Pale ashes of the house of Lancaster,
Thou bloodless remnant of that royal blood,
Be it lawful that I invocate thy ghost
To hear the lamentations of poor Anne,
Wife to thy Edward, to thy slaught'red son,   10
Stabb'd by the self-same hand that made these wounds!
Lo, in these windows that let forth thy life
I pour the helpless balm of my poor eyes.
O, cursed be the hand that made these holes!
Cursed the heart that had the heart to do it!   15
Cursed the blood that let this blood from hence!
More direful hap betide that hated wretch
That makes us wretched by the death of thee
Than I can wish to wolves—to spiders, toads,
Or any creeping venom'd thing that lives!   20
If ever he have child, abortive be it,
Prodigious, and untimely brought to light,
Whose ugly and unnatural aspect
May fright the hopeful mother at the view,
And that be heir to his unhappiness!   25
If ever he have wife, let her be made
More miserable by the [life] of him
Than I am made by my young lord and thee!

---

103. **withal:** at the same time.   106. **abjects:** servile subjects.
110. **enfranchise:** liberate.
115. **lie for you:** i.e. take your place in prison (with a pun on *lie* as "prevaricate").   125. **brook'd:** endured.
133. **kites:** scavenger birds, a kind of hawk.
137. **fear:** fear for.   139. **diet:** course of life.
146. **with post-horse:** i.e. as quickly as possible.
148. **steel'd:** hardened, strengthened.

153. **Warwick's youngest daughter:** Anne Neville, daughter of the famous "Kingmaker," who had been betrothed (but not married) to Prince Edward, son of Henry VI. Shakespeare assumes throughout that Anne was Prince Edward's widow.   158. **intent:** design.

I.ii. **Location:** London. Another street.
o.s.d. **corse:** corpse.   **Sixt:** Sixth.   **Halberds:** halberdiers, guards bearing long weapons with axe-like heads.
2. **hearse:** a coffin on a bier.
3. **obsequiously:** mournfully, in a manner appropriate to a funeral.
5. **key-cold:** i.e. cold as a key, a proverbial expression for "cold as death."   13. **helpless:** useless.   17. **hap betide:** fortune befall.
21. **abortive:** unnatural.   22. **Prodigious:** monstrous.
25. **unhappiness:** evil nature.
28. **by . . . thee:** i.e. by the deaths of Prince Edward and Henry VI.

Come now towards Chertsey with your holy load,
Taken from Paul's to be interred there;   30
And still as you are weary of this weight,
Rest you, whiles I lament King Henry's corse.

Enter RICHARD DUKE OF GLOUCESTER.

Glou.   Stay, you that bear the corse, and set it down.
Anne.   What black magician conjures up this fiend
To stop devoted charitable deeds?   35
Glou.   Villains, set down the corse, or, by Saint
    Paul,
I'll make a corse of him that disobeys.
Gentleman.   My lord, stand back, and let the coffin
    pass.
Glou.   Unmanner'd dog, [stand] thou when I com-
    mand.
Advance thy halberd higher than my breast,   40
Or by Saint Paul I'll strike thee to my foot,
And spurn upon thee, beggar, for thy boldness.
Anne.   What do you tremble? are you all afraid?
Alas, I blame you not, for you are mortal,
And mortal eyes cannot endure the devil.—   45
Avaunt, thou dreadful minister of hell!
Thou hadst but power over his mortal body,
His soul thou canst not have. Therefore be gone.
Glou.   Sweet saint, for charity, be not so curst.
Anne.   Foul devil, for God's sake hence, and
    trouble us not,   50
For thou hast made the happy earth thy hell,
Fill'd it with cursing cries and deep exclaims.
If thou delight to view thy heinous deeds,
Behold this pattern of thy butcheries.
O gentlemen, see, see dead Henry's wounds   55
Open their congeal'd mouths and bleed afresh!
Blush, blush, thou lump of foul deformity;
For 'tis thy presence that exhales this blood
From cold and empty veins where no blood dwells.
Thy deeds inhuman and unnatural   60
Provokes this deluge most unnatural.
O God! which this blood mad'st, revenge his death!
O earth! which this blood drink'st, revenge his death!
Either heav'n with lightning strike the murth'rer dead;
Or earth gape open wide and eat him quick,   65
As thou dost swallow up this good king's blood,
Which his hell-govern'd arm hath butchered!
Glou.   Lady, you know no rules of charity,
Which renders good for bad, blessings for curses.
Anne.   Villain, thou know'st nor law of God nor
    man: 70
No beast so fierce but knows some touch of pity.

---

29. **Chertsey:** monastery near London on the south side of the Thames. Although the main contents of this scene (such as Anne's presence at Henry VI's funeral) are unhistorical, Holinshed (Bullough, III, 249n.) supplies the detail that when Henry's corpse was exposed in St. Paul's "the same in the presence of the beholders did bleed" (cf. lines 55–56).
30. **Paul's:** St. Paul's Cathedral in London.
31. **still, as:** whenever.   39. **stand:** halt.
40. **Advance . . . breast:** i.e. keep your weapon upright.
42. **spurn:** trample.   43. **What:** why.   46. **Avaunt:** be gone.
49. **curst:** shrewish.   52. **exclaims:** exclamations.
54. **pattern:** example.
55–56. **dead . . . afresh.** It was popularly believed that a murdered person's wounds would bleed afresh in the presence of the murderer.
58. **exhales:** draws out.   65. **quick:** alive.
70. **nor . . . nor:** neither . . . nor.

Glou.   But I know none, and therefore am no beast.
Anne.   O wonderful, when devils tell the [troth]!
Glou.   More wonderful, when angels are so angry.
Vouchsafe, divine perfection of a woman,   75
Of these supposed crimes, to give me leave
By circumstance but to acquit myself.
Anne.   Vouchsafe, defus'd infection of [a] man,
Of these known evils, but to give me leave
By circumstance [t' accuse] thy cursed self.   80
Glou.   Fairer than tongue can name thee, let me
    have
Some patient leisure to excuse myself.
Anne.   Fouler than heart can think thee, thou canst
    make
No excuse current but to hang thyself.
Glou.   By such despair I should accuse myself.   85
Anne.   And by despairing shalt thou stand excused
For doing worthy vengeance on thyself,
That didst unworthy slaughter upon others.
Glou.   Say that I slew them not?
Anne.   Then say they were not slain.
But dead they are, and, devilish slave, by thee. 90
Glou.   I did not kill your husband.
Anne.   Why then he is alive.
Glou.   Nay, he is dead, and slain by Edward's hands.
Anne.   In thy foul throat thou li'st! Queen
    Margaret saw
Thy murd'rous falchion smoking in his blood;
The which thou once didst bend against her breast, 95
But that thy brothers beat aside the point.
Glou.   I was provoked by her sland'rous tongue,
That laid their guilt upon my guiltless shoulders.
Anne.   Thou wast provoked by thy bloody mind,
That never dream'st on aught but butcheries.   100
Didst thou not kill this king?
Glou.   I grant ye.
Anne.   Dost grant me, hedgehog? Then God grant
    me too
Thou mayst be damned for that wicked deed!
O, he was gentle, mild, and virtuous!
Glou.   The better for the King of Heaven that hath
    him.   105
Anne.   He is in heaven, where thou shalt never
    come.
Glou.   Let him thank me that holp to send him
    thither;
For he was fitter for that place than earth.
Anne.   And thou unfit for any place, but hell.
Glou.   Yes, one place else, if you will hear me name
    it.   110
Anne.   Some dungeon.
Glou.   Your bedchamber.
Anne.   Ill rest betide the chamber where thou liest!
Glou.   So will it, madam, till I lie with you.
Anne.   I hope so.
Glou.   I know so. But, gentle Lady Anne,

---

77. **circumstance:** detailed argument.
78. **defus'd:** diffused, i.e. misshapen.
84. **current:** acceptable, i.e. genuine (a term from coinage).
93–98. **Queen . . . shoulders.** See *3 Henry VI*, V.v.38–43.
94. **falchion:** curved sword.
102. **hedgehog.** Perhaps with an allusion to Richard's badge, a wild boar (hog).   107. **holp:** helped.

Richard III
I.ii

To leave this keen encounter of our wits   115
And fall something into a slower method:
Is not the causer of the timeless deaths
Of these Plantagenets, Henry and Edward,
As blameful as the executioner?

    Anne.   Thou wast the cause, and most accurs'd
    effect.   120

    Glou.   Your beauty was the cause of that effect—
Your beauty, that did haunt me in my sleep
To undertake the death of all the world,
So I might live one hour in your sweet bosom.

    Anne.   If I thought that, I tell thee, homicide,   125
These nails should rent that beauty from my cheeks.

    Glou.   These eyes could not endure that beauty's
    wrack;
You should not blemish it, if I stood by:
As all the world is cheered by the sun,
So I by that; it is my day, my life.   130

    Anne.   Black night o'ershade thy day, and death thy
    life!

    Glou.   Curse not thyself, fair creature—thou art
    both.

    Anne.   I would I were, to be reveng'd on thee.

    Glou.   It is a quarrel most unnatural,
To be reveng'd on him that loveth thee.   135

    Anne.   It is a quarrel just and reasonable,
To be reveng'd on him that kill'd my husband.

    Glou.   He that bereft thee, lady, of thy husband,
Did it to help thee to a better husband.   139

    Anne.   His better doth not breathe upon the earth.

    Glou.   He lives, that loves thee better than he could.

    Anne.   Name him.

    Glou.   Plantagenet.

    Anne.   Why, that was he.

    Glou.   The self-same name, but one of better nature.

    Anne.   Where is he?

    Glou.   Here. ([*She*] *spits at him.*) Why
    dost thou spit at me?   144

    Anne.   Would it were mortal poison for thy sake!

    Glou.   Never came poison from so sweet a place.

    Anne.   Never hung poison on a fouler toad.
Out of my sight, thou dost infect mine eyes!

    Glou.   Thine eyes, sweet lady, have infected mine.

    Anne.   Would they were basilisks, to strike thee
    dead!   150

    Glou.   I would they were, that I might die at once;
For now they kill me with a living death.
Those eyes of thine from mine have drawn salt tears,
Sham'd their aspects with store of childish drops:
These eyes, which never shed remorseful tear—   155
No, when my father York and Edward wept
To hear the piteous moan that Rutland made
When black-fac'd Clifford shook his sword at him;
Nor when thy warlike father, like a child,
Told the sad story of my father's death,   160

117. **timeless:** untimely.
120. **effect:** agent.   121. **effect:** result.
125. **homicide:** murderer.   126. **rent:** rend.
127. **wrack:** destruction.
141. **He lives:** i.e. there is a man.   **he:** i.e. Prince Edward.
150. **basilisks:** fabulous serpents whose glance was alleged to cause
death.   154. **aspects:** appearance.
156–58. **when . . . him.** See *3 Henry VI*, I.iii.

716

And twenty times made pause to sob and weep,
That all the standers-by had wet their cheeks
Like trees bedash'd with rain—in that sad time
My manly eyes did scorn an humble tear;
And what these sorrows could not thence exhale,   165
Thy beauty hath, and made them blind with weeping.
I never sued to friend nor enemy;
My tongue could never learn sweet smoothing word;
But now thy beauty is propos'd my fee,   169
My proud heart sues, and prompts my tongue to speak.

                    She looks scornfully at him.
Teach not thy lip such scorn; for it was made
For kissing, lady, not for such contempt.
If thy revengeful heart cannot forgive,
Lo here I lend thee this sharp-pointed sword,
Which if thou please to hide in this true breast,   175
And let the soul forth that adoreth thee,
I lay it naked to the deadly stroke,
And humbly beg the death upon my knee.

         *He lays his breast open: she offers
             at [it] with his sword.*
Nay, do not pause: for I did kill King Henry—
But 'twas thy beauty that provoked me.   180
Nay, now dispatch: 'twas I that stabb'd young
    Edward—
But 'twas thy heavenly face that set me on.

                     She falls the sword.
Take up the sword again, or take up me.

    Anne.   Arise, dissembler! Though I wish thy death,
I will not be thy executioner.   185

    Glou.   Then bid me kill myself, and I will do it.

    Anne.   I have already.

    Glou.   That was in thy rage.
Speak it again, and even with the word
This hand, which for thy love did kill thy love,
Shall for thy love kill a far truer love;   190
To both their deaths shalt thou be accessary.

    Anne.   I would I knew thy heart.

    Glou.   'Tis figur'd in my tongue.

    Anne.   I fear me both are false.

    Glou.   Then never [was man] true.   195

    Anne.   Well, well, put up your sword.

    Glou.   Say then my peace is made.

    Anne.   That shalt thou know hereafter.

    Glou.   But shall I live in hope?

    Anne.   All men, I hope, live so.   200

    [*Glou.*]   Vouchsafe to wear this ring.

    [*Anne.*   To take is not to give.]

             [Gloucester slips the ring on her finger.]

    Glou.   Look how my ring encompasseth thy finger,
Even so thy breast encloseth my poor heart:
Wear both of them, for both of them are thine.   205
And if thy poor devoted servant may
But beg one favor at thy gracious hand,
Thou dost confirm his happiness for ever.

    Anne.   What is it?

    Glou.   That it may please you leave these sad de-
    signs   210

162. **That:** so that.   168. **smoothing:** flattering.
169. **propos'd my fee:** held forth as my reward.
178 s.d. **offers:** thrusts.   182 s.d. **falls:** lets fall.
191. **accessary:** accessory.   193. **figur'd:** expressed.
201. **Vouchsafe:** consent.   206. **servant:** (1) menial; (2) lover.

To him that hath most cause to be a mourner,
And presently repair to Crosby House;
Where (after I have solemnly interr'd
At Chertsey monast'ry this noble king,
And wet his grave with my repentant tears)   215
I will with all expedient duty see you.
For divers unknown reasons, I beseech you,
Grant me this boon.
   Anne. With all my heart, and much it joys me too,
To see you are become so penitent.   220
Tressel and Berkeley, go along with me.
   Glou. Bid me farewell.
   Anne.   'Tis more than you deserve;
But since you teach me how to flatter you,
Imagine I have said farewell already.   224
     Exeunt two, [Tressel and Berkeley,] with Anne.
   [*Glou.* Sirs, take up the corse.]
   Gent.   Towards Chertsey, noble lord?
   Glou. No; to White-Friars, there attend my com-
     ing.   *Exit corse [with Halberds].*
Was ever woman in this humor woo'd?
Was ever woman in this humor won?
I'll have her, but I will not keep her long.
What? I, that kill'd her husband and his father,   230
To take her in her heart's extremest hate,
With curses in her mouth, tears in her eyes,
The bleeding witness of my hatred by,
Having God, her conscience, and these bars against me,
And I no friends to back my suit [at all]   235
But the plain devil and dissembling looks?
And yet to win her! All the world to nothing!
Hah!
Hath she forgot already that brave prince,   239
Edward, her lord, whom I, some three months since,
Stabb'd in my angry mood at Tewksbury?
A sweeter and a lovelier gentleman,
Fram'd in the prodigality of nature—
Young, valiant, wise, and (no doubt) right royal—
The spacious world cannot again afford.   245
And will she yet abase her eyes on me,
That cropp'd the golden prime of this sweet prince
And made her widow to a woeful bed?
On me, whose all not equals Edward's moi'ty?
On me, that halts and am misshapen thus?   250
My dukedom to a beggarly denier,
I do mistake my person all this while!
Upon my life, she finds (although I cannot)
Myself to be a marv'llous proper man.
I'll be at charges for a looking-glass,   255
And entertain a score or two of tailors
To study fashions to adorn my body:
Since I am crept in favor with myself,
I will maintain it with some little cost.

But first I'll turn yon fellow in his grave,   260
And then return lamenting to my love.
Shine out, fair sun, till I have bought a glass,
That I may see my shadow as I pass.   *Exit.*

Scene III

Enter the Queen Mother [Elizabeth], Lord Rivers,
[Marquess of Dorset,] *and* Lord Grey.

   Riv. Have patience, madam, there's no doubt his
     Majesty
Will soon recover his accustom'd health.
   Grey. In that you brook it ill, it makes him worse;
Therefore for God's sake entertain good comfort,
And cheer his Grace with quick and merry eyes.   5
   Q. Eliz. If he were dead, what would betide on me?
   Grey. No other harm but loss of such a lord.
   Q. Eliz. The loss of such a lord includes all harms.
   Grey. The heavens have blest you with a goodly
     son
To be your comforter when he is gone.   10
   Q. Eliz. Ah! he is young; and his minority
Is put unto the trust of Richard Gloucester,
A man that loves not me, nor none of you.
   Riv. Is it concluded he shall be Protector?
   Q. Eliz. It is determin'd, not concluded yet;   15
But so it must be, if the King miscarry.

Enter Buckingham *and* [Lord Stanley, *Earl of*]
Derby.

   Grey. Here [come] the [lords] of Buckingham and
     Derby.
   Buck. Good time of day unto your royal Grace!
   Stan. God make your Majesty joyful, as you have
     been!
   Q. Eliz. The Countess Richmond, good my Lord
     of Derby,   20
To your good prayer will scarcely say amen.
Yet, Derby, notwithstanding she's your wife
And loves not me, be you, good lord, assur'd
I hate not you for her proud arrogance.
   Stan. I do beseech you, either not believe   25
The envious slanders of her false accusers;
Or if she be accus'd on true report,
Bear with her weakness, which I think proceeds
From wayward sickness and no grounded malice.
   Q. Eliz. Saw you the King to-day, my Lord of
     Derby?   30

---

212. **presently:** immediately.   **Crosby House:** one of Richard's London residences.   216. **expedient:** speedy.
217. **unknown:** secret.
226. **White-Friars:** Carmelite priory in London.   **attend:** await.
227–28. **Was . . . won.** Cf. *Titus Andronicus*, II.i.82–83; *1 Henry VI*, V.iii.78–79.
240. **three months since.** Henry's funeral occurred on May 23, 1471, some three weeks after Prince Edward's death at Tewkesbury.
249. **Edward's moi'ty:** half of Edward.
251. **denier:** a small copper coin.   254. **proper:** handsome.
255. **be . . . for:** buy.   256. **entertain:** employ.

260. **in:** into.
I.iii. Location: London. The palace.
6. **betide on:** happen to.
14–15. **Is . . . yet.** Richard was named Protector by the council on May 4, 1483, almost a month after Edward's death.
14. **concluded:** officially decreed.   16. **miscarry:** i.e. die.
20. **Countess Richmond:** Margaret Beaufort, great-granddaughter of John of Gaunt and daughter of John Beaufort, Duke of Somerset, to whose marriage with Edmund Tudor, Earl of Richmond, was born (1456) the son whom Henry VI called "England's hope" (*3 Henry VI*, IV.vi.68) and who came to the throne in 1485 as Henry VII. Margaret's second husband was Lord Henry Stafford; her third (who appears throughout this play) was Thomas, Lord Stanley (later Earl of Derby).   24. **arrogance:** i.e. ambition for her son.
29. **wayward:** erratic.

Richard III
I.iii

Stan. But now the Duke of Buckingham and I
Are come from visiting his Majesty.
  Q. Eliz. What likelihood of his amendment, lords?
  Buck. Madam, good hope, his Grace speaks cheer-
      fully.
  Q. Eliz. God grant him health! Did you confer
      with him?   35
  Buck. Ay, madam, he desires to make atonement
Between the Duke of Gloucester and your brothers,
And between them and my Lord Chamberlain,
And sent to warn them to his royal presence.
  Q. Eliz. Would all were well! but that will never
      be: 40
I fear our happiness is at the height.

Enter RICHARD [DUKE OF GLOUCESTER *and* LORD
HASTINGS].

  Glou. They do me wrong, and I will not endure it!
Who is it that complains unto the King
That I, forsooth, am stern, and love them not?
By holy Paul, they love his Grace but lightly   45
That fill his ears with such dissentious rumors.
Because I cannot flatter and look fair,
Smile in men's faces, smooth, deceive, and cog,
Duck with French nods and apish courtesy,
I must be held a rancorous enemy.   50
Cannot a plain man live and think no harm,
But thus his simple truth must be abus'd
With silken, sly, insinuating Jacks?
  Grey. To who in all this presence speaks your
      Grace?   54
  Glou. To thee, that hast nor honesty nor grace:
When have I injur'd thee? When done thee wrong?
Or thee? or thee? or any of your faction?
A plague upon you all! His royal Grace
(Whom God preserve better than you would wish!)
Cannot be quiet scarce a breathing while   60
But you must trouble him with lewd complaints.
  Q. Eliz. Brother of Gloucester, you mistake the
      matter:
The King, on his own royal disposition
(And not provok'd by any suitor else),
Aiming, belike, at your interior hatred,   65
That in your outward action shows itself
Against my children, brothers, and myself,
Makes him to send, that he may learn the ground.
  Glou. I cannot tell, the world is grown so bad   69
That wrens make prey where eagles dare not perch.
Since every Jack became a gentleman,
There's many a gentle person made a Jack.
  Q. Eliz. Come, come, we know your meaning,
      brother Gloucester;
You envy my advancement and my friends'.
God grant we never may have need of you!   75
  Glou. Mean time, God grants that I have need of
      you.

Our brother is imprison'd by your means,
Myself disgrac'd, and the nobility
Held in contempt, while great promotions
Are daily given to ennoble those   80
That scarce some two days since were worth a noble.
  Q. Eliz. By Him that rais'd me to this careful
      height
From that contented hap which I enjoy'd,
I never did incense his Majesty
Against the Duke of Clarence, but have been   85
An earnest advocate to plead for him.
My lord, you do me shameful injury
Falsely to draw me in these vile suspects.
  Glou. You may deny that you were not the mean
Of my Lord Hastings' late imprisonment.   90
  Riv. She may, my lord, for—
  Glou. She may, Lord Rivers! Why, who knows
      not so?
She may do more, sir, than denying that:
She may help you to many fair preferments,
And then deny her aiding hand therein   95
And lay those honors on your high desert.
What may she not, she may, ay, marry, may she.
  Riv. What, marry, may she?
  Glou. What, marry, may she? Marry with a king,
A bachelor, and a handsome stripling too: 100
Iwis your grandam had a worser match.
  Q. Eliz. My Lord of Gloucester, I have too long
      borne
Your blunt upbraidings and your bitter scoffs.
By heaven, I will acquaint his Majesty
Of those gross taunts that oft I have endur'd.   105
I had rather be a country servant maid
Than a great queen with this condition,
To be so baited, scorn'd, and stormed at.

Enter old QUEEN MARGARET [*behind*].

Small joy have I in being England's queen.
  Q. Mar. [*Aside.*] And less'ned be that small, God
      I beseech him!   110
Thy honor, state, and seat is due to me.
  Glou. What? threat you me with telling of the
      King?
[Tell him, and spare not. Look what I have said,]
I will avouch't in presence of the King.
I dare adventure to be sent to th' Tow'r.   115
'Tis time to speak, my pains are quite forgot.
  Q. Mar. [*Aside.*] Out, devil! I do remember them
      too well:
Thou kill'dst my husband Henry in the Tower,
And Edward, my poor son, at Tewksbury.

---

77. **Our brother:** i.e. George, Duke of Clarence.
81. **noble:** (1) a gold coin; (2) nobleman.
82. **careful:** full of care, uneasy.
88. **in:** into. **suspects:** suspicions.
97. **What . . . she may:** what she may (i.e. should) not do, she does.
marry: indeed (originally the name of the Virgin Mary used as an oath); with following pun on "wed." 101. **Iwis:** certainly.
108. **baited:** harassed. s.d. **Queen Margaret.** The appearance here of Henry VI's widow—the embodiment of the Lancastrians' blasted hopes—is entirely fictitious. Following the battle of Tewkesbury (1471) she was imprisoned in England for five years and then sent to France, where she lived until 1482 as an unwelcome pensioner of Louis XI.
111. **state:** rank. **seat:** throne. 115. **adventure:** venture, risk.

---

36. **atonement:** reconciliation. 39. **warn:** summon.
41. **height:** i.e. of Fortune's whirling wheel. 48. **cog:** cheat.
49. **Duck:** bow. 53. **Jacks:** worthless fellows.
55. **grace:** sense of duty or propriety.
60. **breathing while:** i.e. the length of a breath.
61. **lewd:** base. 63. **disposition:** inclination.

Glou.   Ere you were queen, ay, or your husband
            king,   120
I was a pack-horse in his great affairs:
A weeder-out of his proud adversaries,
A liberal rewarder of his friends;
To royalize his blood I spent mine own.
      Q. Mar.   [*Aside.*] Ay, and much better blood than
            his or thine.   125
      Glou.   In all which time you and your husband
            Grey
Were factious for the house of Lancaster;
And, Rivers, so were you. Was not your husband
In Margaret's battle at Saint Albons slain?
Let me put in your minds, if you forget,   130
What you have been ere this, and what you are;
Withal, what I have been, and what I am.
      Q. Mar.   [*Aside.*] A murth'rous villain, and so still
            thou art.
      Glou.   Poor Clarence did forsake his father, War-
            wick,
Ay, and forswore himself—which Jesu pardon!— 135
      Q. Mar.   [*Aside.*] Which God revenge!
      Glou.   To fight on Edward's party for the crown,
And for his meed, poor lord, he is mewed up.
I would to God my heart were flint, like Edward's,
Or Edward's soft and pitiful, like mine: 140
I am too childish-foolish for this world.
      Q. Mar.   [*Aside.*] Hie thee to hell for shame, and
            leave this world,
Thou cacodemon, there thy kingdom is.
      Riv.   My Lord of Gloucester, in those busy days,
Which here you urge to prove us enemies,   145
We follow'd then our lord, our sovereign king.
So should we you, if you should be our king.
      Glou.   If I should be? I had rather be a pedlar:
Far be it from my heart, the thought thereof!   149
      Q. Eliz.   As little joy, my lord, as you suppose
You should enjoy, were you this country's king—
As little joy you may suppose in me
That I enjoy, being the queen thereof.
      Q. Mar.   [*Aside.*] A little joy enjoys the queen
            thereof,
For I am she, and altogether joyless.   155
I can no longer hold me patient.   [*Comes forward.*]
Hear me, you wrangling pirates, that fall out
In sharing that which you have pill'd from me!
Which of you trembles not that looks on me?
If not, that I am queen, you bow like subjects,   160
Yet that, by you depos'd, you quake like rebels?
Ah, gentle villain, do not turn away!
      Glou.   Foul wrinkled witch, what mak'st thou in my
            sight?
      Q. Mar.   But repetition of what thou hast marr'd,
That will I make before I let thee go.   165

Glou.   Wert thou not banished on pain of death?
      Q. Mar.   I was; but I do find more pain in banish-
            ment
Than death can yield me here by my abode.
A husband and a son thou ow'st to me—
And thou a kingdom—all of you allegiance.   170
This sorrow that I have, by right is yours,
And all the pleasures you usurp are mine.
      Glou.   The curse my noble father laid on thee
When thou didst crown his warlike brows with paper,
And with thy scorns drew'st rivers from his eyes, 175
And then, to dry them, gav'st the Duke a clout
Steep'd in the faultless blood of pretty Rutland—
His curses then, from bitterness of soul
Denounc'd against thee, are all fall'n upon thee;
And God, not we, hath plagu'd thy bloody deed.   180
      Q. Eliz.   So just is God, to right the innocent.
      Hast.   O, 'twas the foulest deed to slay that babe,
And the most merciless, that e'er was heard of!
      Riv.   Tyrants themselves wept when it was re-
            ported.
      Dor.   No man but prophesied revenge for it.   185
      Buck.   Northumberland, then present, wept to see
            it.
      Q. Mar.   What? were you snarling all before I
            came,
Ready to catch each other by the throat,
And turn you all your hatred now on me?
Did York's dread curse prevail so much with heaven
That Henry's death, my lovely Edward's death,   191
Their kingdom's loss, my woeful banishment,
Should all but answer for that peevish brat?
Can curses pierce the clouds and enter heaven?
Why then give way, dull clouds, to my quick curses!
Though not by war, by surfeit die your king,   196
As ours by murther, to make him a king!
Edward thy son, that now is Prince of Wales,
For Edward our son, that was Prince of Wales,
Die in his youth by like untimely violence!   200
Thyself a queen, for me that was a queen,
Outlive thy glory like my wretched self!
Long mayst thou live to wail thy children's death,
And see another, as I see thee now,
Deck'd in thy rights as thou art stall'd in mine! 205
Long die thy happy days before thy death,
And after many length'ned hours of grief,
Die neither mother, wife, nor England's queen!
Rivers and Dorset, you were standers-by,
And so wast thou, Lord Hastings, when my son   210
Was stabb'd with bloody daggers: God, I pray him
That none of you may live his natural age,
But by some unlook'd accident cut off!

---

121. **pack-horse:** workhorse, i.e. drudge.
127. **factious for:** i.e. a party to the agitation of.
134. **father:** i.e. father-in-law. Clarence had married Warwick's daughter Isabella, sister of the Lady Anne of this play, and for a time supported the Lancastrians, until he "forswore himself" by returning to the Yorkist side. 137. **party:** side. 138. **meed:** reward.
143. **cacodemon:** evil spirit. 145. **urge:** cite.
152. **in:** as regards. 158. **pill'd:** pillaged.
160–61. **If . . . rebels:** i.e. even if you do not bow before me as your queen, you quake because you have deposed me. 164. **But:** only.

169. **thou:** i.e. Richard. 170. **thou:** i.e. Queen Elizabeth.
173–77. **The curse . . . Rutland.** See *3 Henry VI*, I.iv.
176. **clout:** cloth, i.e. handkerchief.
182. **babe:** i.e. Rutland. 193. **but answer for:** merely equal.
195. **quick:** animated. 196. **surfeit:** dissipation.
201. **for:** in place of. 205. **stall'd:** installed.
209–11. **Rivers . . . daggers.** Although Hall (Bullough, III, 206) names King Edward and his two brothers, Dorset, and Hastings as parties to Prince Edward's murder, Shakespeare includes only the King and his brothers in his version of the crime at Tewkesbury (*3 Henry VI*, V.v). 213. **unlook'd:** unexpected.

Richard III
I.iii

Glou. Have done thy charm, thou hateful with'red
   hag.
  Q. Mar. And leave out thee? Stay, dog, for thou
   shalt hear me.   215
If heaven have any grievous plague in store
Exceeding those that I can wish upon thee,
O, let them keep it till thy sins be ripe,
And then hurl down their indignation
On thee, the troubler of the poor world's peace!   220
The worm of conscience still begnaw thy soul!
Thy friends suspect for traitors while thou liv'st,
And take deep traitors for thy dearest friends!
No sleep close up that deadly eye of thine,
Unless it be while some tormenting dream   225
Affrights thee with a hell of ugly devils!
Thou elvish-mark'd, abortive, rooting hog!
Thou that wast seal'd in thy nativity
The slave of nature and the son of hell!
Thou slander of thy heavy mother's womb!   230
Thou loathed issue of thy father's loins!
Thou rag of honor! thou detested—
  Glou. Margaret.
  Q. Mar.   Richard!
  Glou.   Ha!
  Q. Mar.   I call thee not.
  Glou. I cry thee mercy then; for I did think
That thou hadst call'd me all these bitter names.   235
  Q. Mar. Why, so I did, but look'd for no reply.
O, let me make the period to my curse!
  Glou. 'Tis done by me, and ends in "Margaret."
  Q. Eliz. Thus have you breath'd your curse against
   yourself.
  Q. Mar. Poor painted queen, vain flourish of my
   fortune!   240
Why strew'st thou sugar on that bottled spider
Whose deadly web ensnareth thee about?
Fool, fool, thou whet'st a knife to kill thyself.
The day will come that thou shalt wish for me
To help thee curse this poisonous bunch-back'd toad.
  Hast. False-boding woman, end thy frantic curse,
Lest to thy harm thou move our patience.   247
  Q. Mar. Foul shame upon you, you have all mov'd
   mine.
  Riv. Were you well serv'd, you would be taught
   your duty.
  Q. Mar. To serve me well, you all should do me
   duty,   250
Teach me to be your queen, and you my subjects:
O, serve me well, and teach yourselves that duty!
  Dor. Dispute not with her, she is lunatic.
  Q. Mar. Peace, Master Marquess, you are mala-
   pert,

Your fire-new stamp of honor is scarce current.   255
O that your young nobility could judge
What 'twere to lose it and be miserable!
They that stand high have many blasts to shake them,
And if they fall, they dash themselves to pieces.
  Glou. Good counsel, marry! Learn it, learn it,
   Marquess.   260
  Dor. It touches you, my lord, as much as me.
  Glou. Ay, and much more; but I was born so high,
Our aery buildeth in the cedar's top
And dallies with the wind and scorns the sun.
  Q. Mar. And turns the sun to shade—alas, alas!
Witness my son, now in the shade of death,   266
Whose bright out-shining beams thy cloudy wrath
Hath in eternal darkness folded up.
Your aery buildeth in our aery's nest:
O God that seest it, do not suffer it!   270
As it is won with blood, lost be it so!
  Buck. Peace, peace, for shame! if not, for charity.
  Q. Mar. Urge neither charity nor shame to me.
               [*Turning to the others.*]
Uncharitably with me have you dealt,
And shamefully my hopes, by you, are butcher'd.   275
My charity is outrage, life my shame,
And in that shame still live my sorrow's rage!
  Buck. Have done, have done.
  Q. Mar. O princely Buckingham, I'll kiss thy hand
In sign of league and amity with thee.   280
Now fair befall thee and thy noble house!
Thy garments are not spotted with our blood;
Nor thou within the compass of my curse.
  Buck. Nor no one here; for curses never pass
The lips of those that breathe them in the air.   285
  Q. Mar. I will not think but they ascend the sky,
And there awake God's gentle-sleeping peace.
O Buckingham, take heed of yonder dog!
Look when he fawns he bites; and when he bites,
His venom tooth will rankle to the death.   290
Have not to do with him, beware of him;
Sin, death, and hell have set their marks on him,
And all their ministers attend on him.
  Glou. What doth she say, my Lord of Buckingham?
  Buck. Nothing that I respect, my gracious lord.
  Q. Mar. What, dost thou scorn me for my gentle
   counsel?   296
And soothe the devil that I warn thee from?
O but remember this another day,
When he shall split thy very heart with sorrow,
And say poor Margaret was a prophetess!   300
Live each of you the subjects to his hate,
And he to yours, and all of you to God's!   *Exit.*
  Buck. My hair doth stand an end to hear her curses.
  Riv. And so doth mine. I muse why she's at
   liberty.
  Glou. I cannot blame her; by God's holy Mother,

---

214. **charm:** incantation, curse.
221. **still begnaw:** continually gnaw.
227. **elvish-mark'd:** deformed by elves. **hog.** See note to I.ii.102.
228. **seal'd:** stamped, confirmed.
229. **slave of nature:** i.e. because he was congenitally deformed.
230. **heavy:** sorrowful. 234. **cry thee mercy:** beg your pardon.
237. **period:** conclusion.
240. **painted:** counterfeit. **vain . . . fortune:** empty ornament of the position that belongs to me.
241. **bottled:** swollen, big-bellied.
245. **bunch-back'd:** hunchbacked.
246. **False-boding:** falsely prophesying. 250. **duty:** obeisance.
254. **malapert:** impudent.

255. **Your . . . current:** i.e. your title is so recently minted that it is hardly accepted yet as genuine. Actually, Sir Thomas Grey, Queen Elizabeth's eldest son by her first marriage, had been raised to the peerage as the Earl of Dorset in 1475, eight years before the time represented in this scene. 263. **aery:** eagle's brood.
281. **fair befall:** good luck to.
290. **venom:** venomous. **rankle:** cause a festering wound.
303. **an:** on. 304. **muse:** wonder.

She hath had too much wrong, and I repent   306
My part thereof that I have done to her.
  [*Q. Eliz.*] I never did her any to my knowledge.
  Glou. Yet you have all the vantage of her wrong.
I was too hot to do somebody good   310
That is too cold in thinking of it now.
Marry, as for Clarence, he is well repaid;
He is frank'd up to fatting for his pains—
God pardon them that are the cause thereof!
  Riv. A virtuous and a Christian-like conclusion—
To pray for them that have done scathe to us.   316
  Glou. So do I ever—(*speaks to himself*) being well
    advis'd;
For had I curs'd now, I had curs'd myself.

Enter CATESBY.

  Cate. Madam, his Majesty doth call for you,   319
And for your Grace, and yours, my gracious lord.
  Q. Eliz. Catesby, I come. Lords, will you go with
    me?
  Riv. We wait upon your Grace.
                    Exeunt all but Gloucester.
  Glou. I do the wrong, and first begin to brawl.
The secret mischiefs that I set abroach
I lay unto the grievous charge of others.   325
Clarence, who I indeed have cast in darkness,
I do beweep to many simple gulls—
Namely, to Derby, Hastings, Buckingham—
And tell them 'tis the Queen and her allies
That stir the King against the Duke my brother.   330
Now they believe it, and withal whet me
To be reveng'd on Rivers, Dorset, Grey.
But then I sigh, and, with a piece of scripture,
Tell them that God bids us do good for evil:
And thus I clothe my naked villainy   335
With odd old ends stol'n forth of holy writ,
And seem a saint, when most I play the devil.

Enter two MURTHERERS.

But soft, here come my executioners.
How now, my hardy, stout, resolved mates,
Are you now going to dispatch this thing?   340
  [*1. Mur.*] We are, my lord, and come to have the
    warrant,
That we may be admitted where he is.
  Glou. Well thought upon, I have it here about me.
                     [*Gives the warrant.*]
When you have done, repair to Crosby Place.
But, sirs, be sudden in the execution,   345
Withal obdurate, do not hear him plead;
For Clarence is well-spoken, and perhaps
May move your hearts to pity if you mark him.
  [*1. Mur.*] Tut, tut, my lord, we will not stand to
    prate;
Talkers are no good doers. Be assur'd;   350
We go to use our hands, and not our tongues.

  Glou. Your eyes drop millstones, when fools' eyes
    fall tears.
I like you, lads, about your business straight.
Go, go, dispatch.
  [*1. Mur.*]   We will, my noble lord. [*Exeunt.*]

SCENE IV

Enter CLARENCE *and* KEEPER.

  Keep. Why looks your Grace so heavily to-day?
  Clar. O, I have pass'd a miserable night,
So full of fearful dreams, of ugly sights,
That, as I am a Christian faithful man,
I would not spend another such a night   5
Though 'twere to buy a world of happy days—
So full of dismal terror was the time.
  Keep. What was your dream, my lord? I pray you
    tell me.
  Clar. Methoughts that I had broken from the
    Tower
And was embark'd to cross to Burgundy,   10
And in my company my brother Gloucester,
Who from my cabin tempted me to walk
Upon the hatches. [Thence] we look'd toward Eng-
    land,
And cited up a thousand heavy times,
During the wars of York and Lancaster,   15
That had befall'n us. As we pac'd along
Upon the giddy footing of the hatches,
Methought that Gloucester stumbled, and in falling
Strook me (that thought to stay him) overboard
Into the tumbling billows of the main.   20
O Lord, methought what pain it was to drown!
What dreadful noise of [waters] in [my] ears!
What sights of ugly death within [my] eyes!
Methoughts I saw a thousand fearful wracks;
A thousand men that fishes gnaw'd upon;   25
Wedges of gold, great anchors, heaps of pearl,
Inestimable stones, unvalued jewels,
All scatt'red in the bottom of the sea:
Some lay in dead men's skulls, and in the holes
Where eyes did once inhabit, there were crept   30
(As 'twere in scorn of eyes) reflecting gems,
That woo'd the slimy bottom of the deep,
And mock'd the dead bones that lay scatt'red by.
  Keep. Had you such leisure in the time of death
To gaze upon these secrets of the deep?   35
  Clar. Methought I had, and often did I strive
To yield the ghost; but still the envious flood
Stopp'd in my soul, and would not let it forth
To find the empty, vast, and wand'ring air,
But smother'd it within my panting bulk,   40
Who almost burst to belch it in the sea.

352. fall: let fall.

I.iv. Location: London. The Tower.
10. Burgundy. Where, following their father's death, he and his
brother Richard had been sent for safety.
13. hatches: movable planks forming a deck.
14. cited up: recalled.   19. stay: steady.
24. Methoughts: it seemed to me.   wracks: wrecks.
27. Inestimable: invaluable (?) or numberless (?).   unvalued: price-
less.   37. envious: malicious.   40. bulk: body.

309. vantage of: benefits derived from.
313. frank'd up: penned (as in a sty).   316. scathe: harm.
322. wait upon: attend.   324. set abroach: set flowing.
327. gulls: credulous fools.   331. whet: urge.
339. resolved: resolute.   345. sudden: quick.

Richard III
I.iv

Keep. Awak'd you not in this sore agony?

Clar. No, no, my dream was lengthen'd after life.
O then began the tempest to my soul!
I pass'd (methought) the melancholy flood, 45
With that sour ferryman which poets write of,
Unto the kingdom of perpetual night.
The first that there did greet my stranger soul
Was my great father-in-law, renowned Warwick,
Who spake aloud, "What scourge for perjury 50
Can this dark monarchy afford false Clarence?"
And so he vanish'd. Then came wand'ring by
A shadow like an angel, with bright hair
Dabbled in blood, and he shriek'd out aloud,
"Clarence is come—false, fleeting, perjur'd Clarence,
That stabb'd me in the field by Tewksbury: 56
Seize on him, Furies, take him unto torment!"
With that ([methoughts]) a legion of foul fiends
Environ'd me, and howled in mine ears
Such hideous cries that with the very noise 60
I, trembling, wak'd, and for a season after
Could not believe but that I was in hell,
Such terrible impression made my dream.

Keep. No marvel, lord, though it affrighted you;
I am afraid (methinks) to hear you tell it.

Clar. Ah, Keeper, Keeper, I have done these things
(That now give evidence against my soul)
For Edward's sake, and see how he requites me!
O God! if my deep pray'rs cannot appease thee,
But thou wilt be aveng'd on my misdeeds, 70
Yet execute thy wrath in me alone!
O, spare my guiltless wife and my poor children!
Keeper, I prithee sit by me awhile.
My soul is heavy, and I fain would sleep.

Keep. I will, my lord. God give your Grace good
rest! [*Clarence sleeps.*] 75

Enter BRAKENBURY, *the Lieutenant.*

Brak. Sorrow breaks seasons and reposing hours,
Makes the night morning and the noontide night:
Princes have but their titles for their glories,
An outward honor for an inward toil,
And for unfelt imaginations 80
They often feel a world of restless cares;
So that between their titles and low name
There's nothing differs but the outward fame.

Enter two MURTHERERS.

1. Mur. Ho, who's here?

Brak. What wouldst thou, fellow? and how cam'st
thou hither?

[1.] Mur. I would speak with Clarence, and I
came hither on my legs.

Brak. What, so brief?

[2.] Mur. 'Tis better, sir, than to be tedious. Let
him see our commission, and talk no more. 90

[*Brakenbury*] *reads* [*it*].

Brak. I am in this commanded to deliver

The noble Duke of Clarence to your hands.
I will not reason what is meant hereby,
Because I will be guiltless from the meaning.
There lies the Duke asleep, and there the keys. 95
I'll to the King and signify to him
That thus I have resign'd to you my charge.

1. Mur. You may, sir, 'tis a point of wisdom.
Fare you well. *Exit* [*Brakenbury with Keeper*].

2. Mur. What, shall [I] stab him as he sleeps? 100

1. Mur. No, he'll say 'twas done cowardly when
he wakes.

2. Mur. Why, he shall never wake until the great
Judgment Day.

1. Mur. Why, then he'll say we stabb'd him sleeping.
106

2. Mur. The urging of that word "judgment" hath
bred a kind of remorse in me.

1. Mur. What? art thou afraid?

2. Mur. Not to kill him, having a warrant, but to
be damn'd for killing him, from the which no warrant
can defend me. 112

1. Mur. I thought thou hadst been resolute.

2. Mur. So I am—to let him live.

1. Mur. I'll back to the Duke of Gloucester and
tell him so. 116

2. Mur. Nay, I prithee stay a little. I hope this
passionate humor of mine will change. It was wont to
hold me but while one tells twenty.

1. Mur. How dost thou feel thyself now? 120

2. Mur. [Faith,] some certain dregs of conscience
are yet within me.

1. Mur. Remember our reward when the deed's
done. 124

2. Mur. ['Zounds], he dies! I had forgot the
reward.

1. Mur. Where's thy conscience now?

2. Mur. O, in the Duke of Gloucester's purse.

1. Mur. When he opens his purse to give us our
reward, thy conscience flies out. 130

2. Mur. 'Tis no matter, let it go. There's few or
none will entertain it.

1. Mur. What if it come to thee again?

2. Mur. I'll not meddle with it, it makes a man a
coward. A man cannot steal, but it accuseth him; 135
a man cannot swear, but it checks him; a man cannot
lie with his neighbor's wife, but it detects him. 'Tis a
blushing shame-fac'd spirit that mutinies in a man's
bosom. It fills a man full of obstacles. It made me once
restore a purse of gold that (by chance) I found. 140
It beggars any man that keeps it. It is turn'd out of
towns and cities for a dangerous thing, and every man
that means to live well endeavors to trust to himself
and live without it.

1. Mur. ['Zounds,] 'tis even now at my elbow,
persuading me not to kill the Duke. 146

2. Mur. Take the devil in thy mind, and believe
him not; he would insinuate with thee but to make thee
sigh.

---

45. **melancholy flood:** the river Styx, across which Charon rowed the spirits of the dead to the underworld.
53. **shadow:** i.e. Prince Edward, son of Henry VI.
74. **fain:** gladly.
80. **unfelt imaginations:** i.e. glories imagined but not experienced.

94. **will be:** will to be.
118. **passionate humor:** compassionate mood.
119. **tells:** counts.   125. **'Zounds:** by God's (Christ's) wounds.
147. **Take . . . mind:** i.e. subdue the promptings of your conscience.
148. **him:** the devil, i.e. conscience.   **insinuate:** ingratiate himself.

1. Mur. I am strong-fram'd, he cannot prevail with me.   151

2. Mur. Spoke like a tall man that respects thy reputation. Come, shall we fall to work?

1. Mur. Take him on the costard with the hilts of thy sword, and then throw him into the malmsey-butt in the next room.   156

2. Mur. O excellent device! and make a sop of him.

1. Mur. Soft, he wakes.

2. Mur. Strike!

1. Mur. No, we'll reason with him.   160

Clar. Where art thou, Keeper? Give me a cup of wine.

2. Mur. You shall have wine enough, my lord, anon.

Clar. In God's name, what art thou?

1. Mur. A man, as you are.

Clar. But not, as I am, royal.   165

[2.] Mur. Nor you, as we are, loyal.

Clar. Thy voice is thunder, but thy looks are humble.

1. Mur. My voice is now the King's, my looks mine own.

Clar. How darkly and how deadly dost thou speak! Your eyes do menace me. Why look you pale?   170 Who sent you hither? Wherefore do you come?

[Both.] To, to, to—

Clar. To murther me?

Both. Ay, ay.   174

Clar. You scarcely have the hearts to tell me so, And therefore cannot have the hearts to do it. Wherein, my friends, have I offended you?

1. Mur. Offended us you have not, but the King.

Clar. I shall be reconcil'd to him again.   179

2. Mur. Never, my lord, therefore prepare to die.

Clar. Are you drawn forth among a world of men To slay the innocent? What is my offense? Where is the evidence that doth accuse me? What lawful quest have given their verdict up Unto the frowning judge? or who pronounc'd   185 The bitter sentence of poor Clarence' death? Before I be convict by course of law, To threaten me with death is most unlawful. I charge you, as you hope [to have redemption By Christ's dear blood shed for our grievous sins,] That you depart, and lay no hands on me.   191 The deed you undertake is damnable.

1. Mur. What we will do, we do upon command.

2. Mur. And he that hath commanded is our King.

Clar. Erroneous vassals, the great King of kings Hath in the table of his law commanded   196 That thou shalt do no murther. Will you then Spurn at his edict, and fulfill a man's? Take heed; for he holds vengeance in his hand, To hurl upon their heads that break his law.   200

2. Mur. And that same vengeance doth he hurl on thee

For false forswearing and for murther too. Thou didst receive the sacrament to fight In quarrel of the house of Lancaster.

1. Mur. And like a traitor to the name of God   205 Didst break that vow, and with thy treacherous blade Unrip'st the bowels of thy sov'reign's son.

2. Mur. Whom thou wast sworn to cherish and defend.

1. Mur. How canst thou urge God's dreadful law to us, When thou hast broke it in such dear degree?   210

Clar. Alas! for whose sake did I that ill deed? For Edward, for my brother, for his sake. He sends you not to murther me for this, For in that sin he is as deep as I. If God will be avenged for the deed,   215 O, know you yet he doth it publicly. Take not the quarrel from his pow'rful arm; He needs no indirect or lawless course To cut off those that have offended him.

1. Mur. Who made thee then a bloody minister, When gallant-springing brave Plantagenet,   221 That princely novice, was struck dead by thee?

Clar. My brother's love, the devil, and my rage.

1. Mur. Thy brother's love, our duty, and thy faults Provoke us hither now to slaughter thee.   225

Clar. [O,] if you love my brother, hate not me! I am his brother and I love him well. If you are hir'd for meed, go back again, And I will send you to my brother Gloucester, Who shall reward you better for my life   230 Than Edward will for tidings of my death.

2. Mur. You are deceiv'd, your brother Gloucester hates you.

Clar. O no; he loves me and he holds me dear. Go you to him from me.

1. Mur.   Ay, so we will.

Clar. Tell him, when that our princely father York Blest his three sons with his victorious arm,   236 [And charg'd us from his soul to love each other,] He little thought of this divided friendship. Bid Gloucester think [of] this, and he will weep.

1. Mur. Ay, millstones, as he lesson'd us to weep.

Clar. O, do not slander him, for he is kind.   241

1. Mur. Right, as snow in harvest. Come, you deceive yourself, 'Tis he that sends us to destroy you here.

Clar. It cannot be, for he bewept my fortune, And hugg'd me in his arms, and swore with sobs   245 That he would labor my delivery.

1. Mur. Why, so he doth, when he delivers you From this earth's thralldom to the joys of heaven.

2. Mur. Make peace with God, for you must die, my lord.

Clar. Have you that holy feeling in your souls   250 To counsel me to make my peace with God,

---

152. **tall:** brave.   154. **costard:** kind of apple, i.e. head.
155. **malmsey-butt:** i.e. wine cask. Malmsey was a sweet, aromatic wine.   157. **sop:** cake soaked in wine.   160. **reason:** talk.
184. **quest:** inquest, i.e. jury.   187. **convict:** convicted.
195. **Erroneous vassals:** criminal wretches.

207. **Unrip'st:** i.e. unrippedst.   210. **dear:** grievous.
221. **gallant-springing:** i.e. gallant and aspiring.
222. **novice:** youth.
223. **My brother's love:** i.e. my love for my brother.
240. **lesson'd:** taught.   246. **labor:** work for.

Richard III
I.iv

And are you yet to your own souls so blind
That you will war with God by murd'ring me?
O, sirs, consider, they that set you on
To do this deed will hate you for the deed.   255
  2. Mur. What shall we do?
  Clar.   Relent, and save your souls.
Which of you, if you were a prince's son,
Being pent from liberty, as I am now,
If two such murtherers as yourselves came to you,
Would not entreat for life?   260
  1. Mur. Relent? No: 'tis cowardly and womanish.
  Clar. Not to relent is beastly, savage, devilish.
My friend [*to Second Murderer*], I spy some pity in thy
          looks.
O, if thine eye be not a flatterer,
Come thou on my side, and entreat for me,   265
As you would beg, were you in my distress.
A begging prince what beggar pities not?
  2. Mur. Look behind you, my lord.
  1. Mur. Take that! and that! (*Stabs him.*) If all
          this will not do,
I'll drown you in the malmsey-butt within.   270
                    Exit [with the body].
  2. Mur. A bloody deed, and desperately dis-
          patch'd!
How fain, like Pilate, would I wash my hands
Of this most grievous murther!

                    Enter First Murtherer.

  1. Mur. How now? what mean'st thou, that thou
          help'st me not?
By [heavens], the Duke shall know how slack you have
          been!   275
  2. Mur. I would he knew that I had sav'd his
          brother!
Take thou the fee and tell him what I say,
For I repent me that the Duke is slain.   *Exit.*
  1. Mur. So do not I. Go, coward as thou art.
Well, I'll go hide the body in some hole   280
Till that the Duke give order for his burial;
And when I have my meed, I will away,
For this will out, and then I must not stay.   *Exit.*

ACT II, Scene I

Flourish. Enter the King [Edward] *sick, the* Queen
[Elizabeth], Lord Marquess Dorset, Rivers,
Hastings, Catesby, Buckingham, [Grey, *and
others*].

  K. Edw. Why, so: now have I done a good day's
          work.
You peers, continue this united league.
I every day expect an embassage
From my Redeemer to redeem me hence;
And more [in] peace my soul shall part to heaven,   5
Since I have made my friends at peace on earth.
[Hastings] and Rivers, take each other's hand,

258. pent: shut up.

II.i. Location: London. The palace.
o.s.d. Flourish: fanfare of trumpets to announce the arrival of an
illustrious person.

Dissemble not your hatred, swear your love.
  Riv. By heaven, my soul is purg'd from grudging
          hate,
And with my hand I seal my true heart's love.   10
  Hast. So thrive I, as I truly swear the like!
  K. Edw. Take heed you dally not before your
          king,
Lest He that is the supreme King of kings
Confound your hidden falsehood and award
Either of you to be the other's end.   15
  Hast. So prosper I, as I swear perfect love!
  Riv. And I, as I love Hastings with my heart!
  K. Edw. Madam, yourself is not exempt from
          this;
Nor you, son Dorset; Buckingham, nor you;
You have been factious one against the other.   20
Wife, love Lord Hastings, let him kiss your hand,
And what you do, do it unfeignedly.
  Q. Eliz. There, Hastings, I will never more re-
          member
Our former hatred, so thrive I and mine!
  K. Edw. Dorset, embrace him; Hastings, love
          Lord Marquess.   25
  Dor. This interchange of love, I here protest,
Upon my part shall be inviolable.
  Hast. And so swear I.   [*They embrace.*]
  K. Edw. Now, princely Buckingham, seal thou
          this league
With thy embracements to my wive's allies,   30
And make me happy in your unity.
  Buck. When ever Buckingham doth turn his hate
Upon your Grace [*to the Queen*], but with all duteous
          love
Doth cherish you and yours, God punish me
With hate in those where I expect most love!   35
When I have most need to employ a friend,
And most assured that he is a friend,
Deep, hollow, treacherous, and full of guile
Be he unto me! This do I beg of [God],
When I am cold in love to you or yours.   40
                    [*They*] *embrace.*
  K. Edw. A pleasing cordial, princely Buckingham,
Is this thy vow unto my sickly heart.
There wanteth now our brother Gloucester here
To make the blessed period of this peace.
  Buck. And in good time,   45
Here comes Sir Richard Ratcliffe and the Duke.

                    Enter Ratcliffe *and* Gloucester.

  Glou. Good morrow to my sovereign king and
          queen,
And, princely peers, a happy time of day!
  K. Edw. Happy indeed, as we have spent the day.
Gloucester, we have done deeds of charity,   50
Made peace of enmity, fair love of hate,

8. Dissemble: disguise (under the appearance of affection).
12. dally: trifle.
14–15. award . . . end: i.e. cause each of you to be the means by which
the other dies. 20. factious: quarrelsome.
33. but. Apparently a corruption. The sense of the passage requires
nor. 41. cordial: restorative. 43. wanteth: lacks.

Between these swelling wrong-incensed peers.
    Glou. A blessed labor, my most sovereign lord.
Among this princely heap, if any here
By false intelligence or wrong surmise   55
Hold me a foe—
If I [unwittingly], or in my rage,
Have aught committed that is hardly borne
[By] any in this presence, I desire
To reconcile me to his friendly peace.   60
'Tis death to me to be at enmity;
I hate it, and desire all good men's love.
First, madam, I entreat true peace of you,
Which I will purchase with my duteous service;
Of you, my noble cousin Buckingham,   65
If ever any grudge were lodg'd between us;
Of you, and you, Lord Rivers, and of Dorset,
That all without desert have frown'd on me;
Dukes, earls, lords, gentlemen—indeed of all.
I do not know that Englishman alive   70
With whom my soul is any jot at odds
More than the infant that is born to-night.
I thank my God for my humility.
    Q. Eliz. A holy day shall this be kept hereafter.
I would to God all strifes were well compounded. 75
My sovereign lord, I do beseech your Highness
To take our brother Clarence to your grace.
    Glou. Why, madam, have I off'red love for this,
To be so flouted in this royal presence?
Who knows not that the gentle Duke is dead?   80
                                 They all start.
You do him injury to scorn his corse.
    K. Edw. Who knows not he is dead? Who knows
        he is?
    Q. Eliz. All-seeing heaven, what a world is this!
    Buck. Look I so pale, Lord Dorset, as the rest?
    Dor. Ay, my good lord, and no man in the presence
But his red color hath forsook his cheeks.   86
    K. Edw. Is Clarence dead? The order was re-
        vers'd.
    Glou. But he, poor man, by your first order died,
And that a winged Mercury did bear;
Some tardy cripple bare the countermand,   90
That came too lag to see him buried.
God grant that some, less noble and less loyal,
Nearer in bloody thoughts, [but] not in blood,
Deserve not worse than wretched Clarence did,
And yet go current from suspicion!   95

            Enter [STANLEY,] *Earl of Derby.*

    Stan. A boon, my sovereign, for my service done!
                                         [*Kneels.*]

    K. Edw. I prithee peace, my soul is full of sorrow.
    Stan. I will not rise, unless your Highness hear me.
    K. Edw. Then say at once what is it thou requests.
    Stan. The forfeit, sovereign, of my servant's life,
Who slew to-day a riotous gentleman   101
Lately attendant on the Duke of Norfolk.
    K. Edw. Have I a tongue to doom my brother's
        death,
And shall that tongue give pardon to a slave?
My brother kill'd no man, his fault was thought, 105
And yet his punishment was bitter death.
Who sued to me for him? Who (in my wrath)
Kneel'd [at] my feet and bid me be advis'd?
Who spoke of brotherhood? Who spoke of love?
Who told me how the poor soul did forsake   110
The mighty Warwick and did fight for me?
Who told me, in the field at Tewksbury,
When Oxford had me down, he rescued me,
And said, "Dear brother, live, and be a king"?
Who told me, when we both lay in the field   115
Frozen (almost) to death, how he did lap me
Even in his [own] garments, and did give himself
(All thin and naked) to the numb cold night?
All this from my remembrance brutish wrath
Sinfully pluck'd, and not a man of you   120
Had so much grace to put it in my mind.
But when your carters or your waiting vassals
Have done a drunken slaughter, and defac'd
The precious image of our dear Redeemer,   124
You straight are on your knees for pardon, pardon,
And I (unjustly too) must grant it you. [*Stanley rises.*]
But for my brother not a man would speak,
Nor I (ungracious)speak unto myself
For him, poor soul. The proudest of you all
Have been beholding to him in his life;   130
Yet none of you would once beg for his life.
O God! I fear thy justice will take hold
On me and you, and mine and yours, for this.
Come, Hastings, help me to my closet. Ah, poor
        Clarence!   *Exeunt some with King and Queen.*
    Glou. This is the fruits of rashness! Mark'd you
        not   135
How that the guilty kindred of the Queen
Look'd pale when they did hear of Clarence' death?
O, they did urge it still unto the King!
God will revenge it. Come, lords, will you go
To comfort Edward with our company.   140
    Buck. We wait upon your Grace.   *Exeunt.*

SCENE II

Enter the old DUCHESS OF YORK *with the two children of*
Clarence [EDWARD *and* MARGARET PLANTAGENET].

    Boy. Good grandam, tell us, is our father dead?
    Duch. No, boy.

---

52. **swelling:** i.e. with anger.   54. **heap:** band.
55. **intelligence:** information.   58. **hardly borne:** resented.
68. **all without desert:** entirely without my having deserved it.
75. **compounded:** settled.
81. **scorn his corse:** i.e. be facetious about the dead.
85. **presence:** i.e. of the King.
87. **Is . . . revers'd.** According to Hall (Bullough, III, 252), Clarence
was charged with "heinous treason," and so, "were he in faulte or
wer he faultelesse, attainted was he by parliament and judged to death,
and there upon hastely drowned in a butte of malmesey within the
towre of London. Whose death kynge Edwarde (although he com-
maunded it) when he wiste it was doen piteously he bewayled and
sorowfully repented it."
90. **bare:** bore.   91. **lag:** late.   93. **blood:** kinship.
95. **go current:** pass at face value.   **from:** i.e. without.

100. **forfeit:** i.e. remission of the forfeit.   103. **doom:** decree.
108. **be advis'd:** take careful thought.
113. **When . . . down.** See note to *3 Henry VI,* V.v.2.
122. **carters:** draymen.   134. **closet:** private quarters.

II.ii. Location: London. The palace.

Richard III
II.ii

Girl. Why do [you] weep so oft, and beat your
       breast,
And cry, "O Clarence, my unhappy son!"?
    Boy. Why do you look on us, and shake your head,
And call us orphans, wretches, castaways,   6
If that our noble father were alive?
    Duch. My pretty cousins, you mistake me both:
I do lament the sickness of the King,
As loath to lose him, not your father's death;   10
It were lost sorrow to wail one that's lost.
    Boy. Then you conclude, my grandam, he is dead.
The King mine uncle is to blame for it.
God will revenge it, whom I will importune
With earnest prayers all to that effect.   15
    Girl. And so will I.
    Duch. Peace, children, peace, the King doth love
       you well.
Incapable and shallow innocents,
You cannot guess who caus'd your father's death.
    Boy. Grandam, we can; for my good uncle
       Gloucester   20
Told me the King, provok'd to it by the Queen,
Devis'd impeachments to imprison him;
And when my uncle told me so, he wept,
And pitied me, and kindly kiss'd my cheek;
Bade me rely on him as on my father,   25
And he would love me dearly as a child.
    Duch. Ah! that deceit should steal such gentle
       shape,
And with a virtuous visor hide deep vice!
He is my son—ay, and therein my shame,
Yet from my dugs he drew not this deceit.   30
    Boy. Think you my uncle did dissemble, grandam?
    Duch. Ay, boy.
    Boy. I cannot think it. Hark, what noise is this?

Enter the QUEEN [ELIZABETH] *with her hair about her*
ears; RIVERS *and* DORSET *after her.*

    Q. Eliz. Ah! who shall hinder me to wail and weep,
To chide my fortune, and torment myself?   35
I'll join with black despair against my soul,
And to myself become an enemy.
    Duch. What means this scene of rude impatience?
    Q. Eliz. To make an act of tragic violence.
Edward, my lord, thy son, our king, is dead!   40
Why grow the branches when the root is gone?
Why wither not the leaves that want their sap?
If you will live, lament; if die, be brief,
That our swift-winged souls may catch the King's,
Or like obedient subjects follow him   45
To his new kingdom of ne'er-changing night.
    Duch. Ah, so much interest have [I] in thy sorrow
As I had title in thy noble husband!
I have bewept a worthy husband's death,
And liv'd with looking on his images;   50
But now two mirrors of his princely semblance

Are crack'd in pieces by malignant death,
And I for comfort have but one false glass,
That grieves me when I see my shame in him.
Thou art a widow; yet thou art a mother,   55
And hast the comfort of thy children left;
But death hath snatch'd my husband from mine arms,
And pluck'd two crutches from my feeble hands,
Clarence and Edward. O, what cause have I
(Thine being but a moi'ty of my moan)   60
To overgo thy woes and drown thy cries!
    Boy. Ah, aunt! you wept not for our father's death;
How can we aid you with our kindred tears?
    Girl. Our fatherless distress was left unmoan'd,
Your widow-dolor likewise be unwept!   65
    Q. Eliz. Give me no help in lamentation,
I am not barren to bring forth complaints.
All springs reduce their currents to mine eyes,
That I being govern'd by the watery moon,
May send forth plenteous tears to drown the world! 70
Ah for my husband, for my dear Lord Edward!
    Chil. Ah for our father, for our dear Lord Clarence!
    Duch. Alas for both, both mine, Edward and
       Clarence!
    Q. Eliz. What stay had I but Edward? and he's
       gone.
    Chil. What stay had we but Clarence? and he's
       gone.   75
    Duch. What stays had I but they? and they are
       gone.
    Q. Eliz. Was never widow had so dear a loss.
    Chil. Were never orphans had so dear a loss.
    Duch. Was never mother had so dear a loss.
Alas! I am the mother of these griefs: 80
Their woes are parcell'd, mine is general.
She for an Edward weeps, and so do I;
I for a Clarence [weep], so doth not she;
These babes for Clarence weep, [and so do I;
I for an Edward weep,] so do not they.   85
Alas! you three on me, threefold distress'd,
Pour all your tears. I am your sorrow's nurse,
And I will pamper it with lamentation.
    Dor. Comfort, dear mother, God is much displeas'd
That you take with unthankfulness his doing.   90
In common worldly things 'tis call'd ungrateful
With dull unwillingness to repay a debt,
Which with a bounteous hand was kindly lent;
Much more to be thus opposite with heaven,
For it requires the royal debt it lent you.   95
    Riv. Madam, bethink you like a careful mother
Of the young Prince your son. Send straight for him,
Let him be crown'd, in him your comfort lives.
Drown desperate sorrow in dead Edward's grave,
And plant your joys in living Edward's throne.   100

Enter RICHARD [OF GLOUCESTER], BUCKINGHAM,
[STANLEY, *Earl of*] DERBY, HASTINGS, *and* RAT-
CLIFFE.

---

8. cousins: kinsmen.   18. Incapable: not able to understand.
22. impeachments: accusations.
27. gentle shape: appearance of gentleness.
28. virtuous visor: mask of pretended virtue.
40. Edward . . . dead. A characteristic telescoping of events. Clarence's death (1478) preceded that of Edward IV by some five years.
48. title: legal right.   50. images: i.e. sons.

60. moi'ty: part.   61. overgo: exceed.
63. kindred tears: i.e. tears of kinsmen.
68. All springs reduce: let all springs lead.   77. dear: grievous.
81. parcell'd: i.e. distributed to each separately.   general: inclusive.
94. opposite with: in opposition to.   95. For: because.

Glou. Sister, have comfort. All of us have cause
To wail the dimming of our shining star;
But none can help our harms by wailing them.
Madam, my mother, I do cry you mercy,
I did not see your Grace. Humbly on my knee　105
I crave your blessing.
Duch. God bless thee, and put meekness in thy
　　breast,
Love, charity, obedience, and true duty!
Glou. Amen!—[*aside*] and make me die a good old
　　man!
That is the butt-end of a mother's blessing.　110
I marvel that her Grace did leave it out.
Buck. You cloudy princes and heart-sorrowing
　　peers
That bear this heavy mutual load of moan,
Now cheer each other in each other's love.
Though we have spent our harvest of this king,　115
We are to reap the harvest of his son.
The broken rancor of your high-swoll'n hates,
But lately splinter'd, knit, and join'd together,
Must gently be preserv'd, cherish'd, and kept.
Me seemeth good that, with some little train,　120
Forthwith from Ludlow the young Prince be fet
Hither to London, to be crown'd our king.
Riv. Why with some little train, my Lord of
　　Buckingham?
Buck. Marry, my lord, lest by a multitude
The new-heal'd wound of malice should break out,
Which would be so much the more dangerous,　126
By how much the estate is green and yet ungovern'd.
Where every horse bears his commanding rein
And may direct his course as please himself,
As well the fear of harm, as harm apparent,　130
In my opinion, ought to be prevented.
Glou. I hope the King made peace with all of us,
And the compact is firm and true in me.
Riv. And so in me, and so (I think) in all.
Yet since it is but green, it should be put　135
To no apparent likelihood of breach,
Which haply by much company might be urg'd;
Therefore I say with noble Buckingham,
That it is meet so few should fetch the Prince.
Hast. And so say I.　140
Glou. Then be it so, and go we to determine
Who they shall be that straight shall post to [Ludlow].
Madam, and you, my sister, will you go
To give your censures in this business?
[*Q. Eliz., Duch.* With all our hearts.]　145
　　　Exeunt. Manent Buckingham and Richard.
Buck. My lord, whoever journeys to the Prince,
For God sake let not us two stay at home;
For by the way, I'll sort occasion,
As index to the story we late talk'd of,

To part the Queen's proud kindred from the Prince.　150
Glou. My other self, my counsel's consistory,
My oracle, my prophet, my dear cousin,
I, as a child, will go by thy direction.
Toward [Ludlow] then, for we'll not stay behind.
　　　　　　　　　　　　　　　Exeunt.

SCENE III

Enter one CITIZEN *at one door and another at the other.*

1. Cit. Good morrow, neighbor, whither away so
　　fast?
2. Cit. I promise you, I scarcely know myself.
Hear you the news abroad?
1. Cit. 　　　　　　　　Yes, that the King is dead.
2. Cit. Ill news, by'r lady—seldom comes the
　　better.
I fear, I fear 'twill prove a giddy world.　5

Enter another CITIZEN.

3. Cit. Neighbors, God speed!
1. Cit. 　　　　　　　Give you good morrow, sir.
3. Cit. Doth the news hold of good King Edward's
　　death?
2. Cit. Ay, sir, it is too true, God help the while!
3. Cit. Then, masters, look to see a troublous
　　world.
1. Cit. No, no, by God's good grace his son shall
　　reign.　10
3. Cit. Woe to that land that's govern'd by a child!
2. Cit. In him there is a hope of government,
Which in his nonage, council under him,
And in his full and ripened years, himself,
No doubt shall then, and till then, govern well.　15
1. Cit. So stood the state when Henry the Sixt
Was crown'd in Paris but at nine months old.
3. Cit. Stood the state so? No, no, good friends,
　　God wot,
For then this land was famously enrich'd
With politic grave counsel; then the King　20
Had virtuous uncles to protect his Grace.
1. Cit. Why, so hath this, both by his father and
　　mother.
3. Cit. Better it were they all came by his father,
Or by his father there were none at all;
For emulation who shall now be nearest　25
Will touch us all too near, if God prevent not.
O, full of danger is the Duke of Gloucester,
And the Queen's sons and brothers haught and proud!
And were they to be rul'd, and not to rule,
This sickly land might solace as before.　30
1. Cit. Come, come, we fear the worst; all will be
　　well.
3. Cit. When clouds are seen, wise men put on
　　their cloaks;
When great leaves fall, then winter is at hand;
When the sun sets, who doth not look for night?

---

112. **cloudy:** gloomy. 118. **splinter'd:** bound in splints.
120. **Me seemeth:** it seems to me. **little train:** small entourage.
121. **Ludlow:** castle in Shropshire, Prince Edward's seat in his capacity as justicer of Wales, an office he had held since 1476. **fet:** fetched.
124. **multitude:** i.e. large entourage.
127. **the estate is green:** i.e. the government is newly established.
128. **bears:** controls. 137. **haply:** perhaps. **urg'd:** provoked.
142. **post:** hasten. 144. **censures:** opinions. 148. **sort:** find.
149. **index:** introduction.

151. **consistory:** council chamber, i.e. source of wisdom.

II.iii. Location: London. A street.
4. **by'r lady:** by Our Lady. 13. **nonage:** minority.
18. **wot:** knows. 20. **politic:** sagacious. 28. **haught:** haughty.
30. **solace:** be happy.

Richard III
II.iii

Untimely storms makes men expect a dearth.   35
All may be well; but if God sort it so,
'Tis more than we deserve or I expect.
    2. Cit.   Truly, the hearts of men are full of fear.
You cannot reason (almost) with a man
That looks not heavily and full of dread.   40
    3. Cit.   Before the days of change, still is it so.
By a divine instinct men's minds mistrust
Ensuing danger; as by proof we see
The water swell before a boist'rous storm.
But leave it all to God. Whither away?   45
    2. Cit.   Marry, we were sent for to the justices.
    3. Cit.   And so was I. I'll bear you company.
                                                Exeunt.

SCENE IV

Enter ARCHBISHOP [OF YORK, the] young [DUKE OF]
YORK, the QUEEN [ELIZABETH], and the DUCHESS
[OF YORK].

    Arch.   Last night, I [hear], they lay at Stony-
        Stratford,
And at Northampton they do rest to-night.
To-morrow, or next day, they will be here.
    Duch.   I long with all my heart to see the Prince.
I hope he is much grown since last I saw him.   5
    Q. Eliz.   But I hear no; they say my son of York
Has almost overta'en him in his growth.
    York.   Ay, mother, but I would not have it so.
    Duch.   Why, my good cousin, it is good to grow.
    York.   Grandam, one night as we did sit at supper,
My uncle Rivers talk'd how I did grow   11
More than my brother. "Ay," quoth my uncle
        Gloucester,
"Small herbs have grace, great weeds do grow apace."
And since, methinks I would not grow so fast,
Because sweet flow'rs are slow and weeds make haste.
    Duch.   Good faith, good faith, the saying did not
        hold   16
In him that did object the same to thee:
He was the wretched'st thing when he was young,
So long a-growing and so leisurely
That if his rule were true, he should be gracious.   20
    [Arch.]   And so no doubt he is, my gracious
        madam.
    Duch.   I hope he is, but yet let mothers doubt.
    York.   Now by my troth, if I had been remem'bred,
I could have given my uncle's Grace a flout,
To touch his growth nearer than he touch'd mine.   25
    Duch.   How, my young York? I prithee let me
        hear it.

    York.   Marry (they say) my uncle grew so fast
That he could gnaw a crust at two hours old;
'Twas full two years ere I could get a tooth.
Grandam, this would have been a biting jest.   30
    Duch.   I prithee, pretty York, who told thee this?
    York.   Grandam, his nurse.
    Duch.   His nurse? why, she was dead ere thou wast
        born.
    York.   If 'twere not she, I cannot tell who told me.
    Q. Eliz.   A parlous boy! Go to, you are too shrewd.
    Duch.   Good madam, be not angry with the child.
    Q. Eliz.   Pitchers have ears.   37

        Enter a MESSENGER.

    Arch.   Here comes a messenger. What news?
    Mess.   Such news, my lord, as grieves me to report.
    Q. Eliz.   How doth the Prince?
    Mess.   Well, madam, and in health.
    Duch.   What is thy news?   41
    Mess.   Lord Rivers and Lord Grey are sent to
        Pomfret,
And with them Sir Thomas Vaughan, prisoners.
    Duch.   Who hath committed them?
    Mess.   The mighty dukes,
Gloucester and Buckingham.
    Arch.   For what offense?   45
    Mess.   The sum of all I can I have disclos'd.
Why, or for what, the nobles were committed
Is all unknown to me, my gracious lord.
    Q. Eliz.   Ay me! I see the ruin of my house:
The tiger now hath seiz'd the gentle hind;   50
Insulting tyranny begins to jut
Upon the innocent and aweless throne.
Welcome destruction, blood, and massacre!
I see (as in a map) the end of all.
    Duch.   Accursed and unquiet wrangling days,   55
How many of you have mine eyes beheld!
My husband lost his life to get the crown,
And often up and down my sons were toss'd
For me to joy and weep their gain and loss;
And being seated, and domestic broils   60
Clean overblown, themselves, the conquerors,
Make war upon themselves, brother to brother,
Blood to blood, self against self. O, preposterous
And frantic outrage, end thy damned spleen,
Or let me die, to look on [death] no more!   65
    Q. Eliz.   Come, come, my boy, we will to sanctuary.
Madam, farewell.
    Duch.   Stay, I will go with you.
    Q. Eliz.   You have no cause.
    Arch.   [To the Queen.] My gracious lady, go,

36. sort: arrange, dispose.
39. reason: talk.   42. mistrust: suspect.

II.iv. Location: London. The palace.
1. Stony-Stratford: town in Buckinghamshire.
2. Northampton: town in Northamptonshire.
6–7. But . . . growth. Edward, Prince of Wales, was thirteen and his
brother Richard, Duke of York, eleven when their father died.
16. did not hold: was not exemplified.
17. object . . . to: urge . . . against, i.e. apply . . . to.
23. troth: truth, faith.   been remem'bred: recollected, considered.
24. my uncle's Grace: his Grace, my uncle.   flout: gibe.
25. touch . . . mine: i.e. taunt him about his growth more tellingly
than he taunted me about mine.

35. parlous: clever, precocious.   shrewd: bitter.
42. Pomfret: Pontefract, in Yorkshire, site of the castle in which
Richard II met his death in 1400.   46. can: know.
50. hind: female deer.   51. jut: encroach.
52. aweless: inspiring no awe (because of its occupant's youth).
54. as . . . map: i.e. graphically epitomized.
60. seated: enthroned.   64. spleen: malevolence.
66. sanctuary: a place of refuge (generally a church) for those in
danger of their lives. According to More (Bullough, III, 257), as soon
as Queen Elizabeth heard the "heavy tidynges" of her son and kinsmen
"she toke her younger sonne the duke of Yorke and her doughters
and went out of the palays of Westminster into the sanctuary, and
there lodged in the abbotes place, and she and all her chyldren and
compaignie were regestred for sanctuarye persons."

And thither bear your treasure and your goods.
For my part, I'll resign unto your Grace
The seal I keep, and so betide to me　　　　　　70
As well I tender you and all of yours!
Go, I'll conduct you to the sanctuary.　　　*Exeunt.*

ACT III, SCENE I

The trumpets sound. Enter young PRINCE [EDWARD], *the*
DUKES OF GLOUCESTER *and* BUCKINGHAM, [LORD]
CARDINAL [BOURCHIER, CATESBY, *with others*].

Buck.　Welcome, sweet Prince, to London, to your
　chamber.
Glou.　Welcome, dear cousin, my thoughts' sover-
　eign,
The weary way hath made you melancholy.
Prince.　No, uncle, but our crosses on the way
Have made it tedious, wearisome, and heavy.　　5
I want more uncles here to welcome me.
Glou.　Sweet Prince, the untainted virtue of your
　years
Hath not yet div'd into the world's deceit;
Nor more can you distinguish of a man
Than of his outward show, which, God he knows,　10
Seldom or never jumpeth with the heart.
Those uncles which you want were dangerous;
Your Grace attended to their sug'red words,
But look'd not on the poison of their hearts.　　14
God keep you from them, and from such false friends!
Prince.　God keep me from false friends!—but they
　were none.
Glou.　My lord, the Mayor of London comes to
　greet you.

Enter LORD MAYOR [*and his* TRAIN].

May.　God bless your Grace with health and happy
　days!
Prince.　I thank you, good my lord, and thank you
　all.　　　　　　[*Mayor and Train stand aside.*]
I thought my mother and my brother York　　20
Would long ere this have met us on the way.
Fie, what a slug is Hastings, that he comes not
To tell us whether they will come or no!

Enter LORD HASTINGS.

Buck.　And in good time, here comes the sweating
　lord.
Prince.　Welcome, my lord.　What, will our
　mother come?　　25
Hast.　On what occasion, God he knows, not I,
The Queen your mother and your brother York
Have taken sanctuary. The tender Prince
Would fain have come with me to meet your Grace,
But by his mother was perforce withheld.　　30
Buck.　Fie, what an indirect and peevish course

Is this of hers! Lord Cardinal, will your Grace
Persuade the Queen to send the Duke of York
Unto his princely brother presently?
If she deny, Lord Hastings, go with him,　　35
And from her jealous arms pluck him perforce.
Card.　My Lord of Buckingham, if my weak ora-
　tory
Can from his mother win the Duke of York,
Anon expect him here; but if she be obdurate
To mild entreaties, God in heaven forbid　　40
We should infringe the holy privilege
Of blessed sanctuary! Not for all this land
Would I be guilty of so deep a sin.
Buck.　You are too senseless-obstinate, my lord,
Too ceremonious and traditional.　　45
Weigh it but with the grossness of this age,
You break not sanctuary in seizing him.
The benefit thereof is always granted
To those whose dealings have deserv'd the place
And those who have the wit to claim the place.　　50
This prince hath neither claim'd it nor deserv'd it,
And therefore, in mine opinion, cannot have it.
Then taking him from thence that is not there,
You break no privilege nor charter there.
Oft have I heard of sanctuary men,　　55
But sanctuary children never till now.
Card.　My lord, you shall overrule my mind for
　once.
Come on, Lord Hastings, will you go with me?
Hast.　I go, my lord.
Prince.　Good lords, make all the speedy haste you
　may.　　　　　[*Exeunt Cardinal and Hastings.*]
Say, uncle Gloucester, if our brother come,　　61
Where shall we sojourn till our coronation?
Glou.　Where it seems best unto your royal self.
If I may counsel you, some day or two
Your Highness shall repose you at the Tower;　　65
Then where you please, and shall be thought most fit
For your best health and recreation.
Prince.　I do not like the Tower, of any place.
Did Julius Caesar build that place, my lord?
Buck.　He did, my gracious lord, begin that place,
Which, since, succeeding ages have re-edified.　　71
Prince.　Is it upon record, or else reported
Successively from age to age, he built it?
Buck.　Upon record, my gracious lord.
Prince.　But say, my lord, it were not regist'red,　75
Methinks the truth should live from age to age,
As 'twere retail'd to all posterity,
Even to the general all-ending day.
Glou.　[*Aside.*]　So wise so young, they say do
　never live long.
Prince.　What say you, uncle?　　80
Glou.　I say, without characters fame lives long.
[*Aside.*] Thus, like the formal Vice, Iniquity,

III.i. Location: London. A street.
1. **chamber.** London was known as "the King's Chamber" (*camera regis*). 4. **crosses:** unfortunate events, i.e. the arrests.
6. **want:** (1) lack; (2) desire. 11. **jumpeth:** accords.
22. **slug:** sluggard. 26. **On what occasion:** for what reason.
30. **perforce:** forcibly.
31. **indirect and peevish:** irregular and perverse.

34. **presently:** immediately.
45. **ceremonious:** bound by formalities.
46. **grossness:** coarseness, lack of (moral) refinement.
68. **of any place:** of all places.
75. **regist'red:** written down. 77. **retail'd:** handed down.
81. **characters:** (1) written records; (2) moral qualities.
82. **formal Vice:** i.e. the stock character called Iniquity, who in six-teenth-century morality plays represented all the vices.

Richard III
III.i

I moralize two meanings in one word.

Prince. That Julius Caesar was a famous man;
With what his valor did enrich his wit,   85
His wit set down to make his valure live.
Death makes no conquest of this conqueror,
For now he lives in fame though not in life.
I'll tell you what, my cousin Buckingham—

Buck. What, my gracious lord?   90

Prince. And if I live until I be a man,
I'll win our ancient right in France again,
Or die a soldier as I liv'd a king.

Glou. [*Aside.*] Short summers lightly have a forward spring.

Enter young YORK, HASTINGS, CARDINAL [BOURCHIER].

Buck. Now in good time, here comes the Duke of
York.   95

Prince. Richard of York, how fares our loving
brother?

York. Well, my dread lord—so must I call you
now.

Prince. Ay, brother, to our grief, as it is yours.
Too late he died that might have kept that title,
Which by his death hath lost much majesty.   100

Glou. How fares our cousin, noble Lord of York?

York. I thank you, gentle uncle. O my lord,
You said that idle weeds are fast in growth:
The Prince my brother hath outgrown me far.

Glou. He hath, my lord.

York.   And therefore is he idle?   105

Glou. O my fair cousin, I must not say so.

York. Then he is more beholding to you than I.

Glou. He may command me as my sovereign,
But you have power in me as in a kinsman.

York. I pray you, uncle, give me this dagger.   110

Glou. My dagger, little cousin? with all my heart.

Prince. A beggar, brother?

York. Of my kind uncle, that I know will give,
And being but a toy, which is no grief to give.   114

Glou. A greater gift than that I'll give my cousin.

York. A greater gift? O, that's the sword to it.

Glou. Ay, gentle cousin, were it light enough.

York. O then I see you will part but with light
gifts!
In weightier things you'll say a beggar nay.

Glou. It is too heavy for your Grace to wear.   120

York. I weigh it lightly, were it heavier.

Glou. What, would you have my weapon, little
lord?

York. I would, that I might thank you as you call
me.

Glou. How?

York. Little.   125

Prince. My Lord of York will still be cross in talk.

Uncle, your Grace knows how to bear with him.

York. You mean, to bear me, not to bear with me.
Uncle, my brother mocks both you and me:
Because that I am little, like an ape,   130
He thinks that you should bear me on your shoulders.

Buck. [*Aside to Hastings.*] With what a sharp-
provided wit he reasons!
To mitigate the scorn he gives his uncle,
He prettily and aptly taunts himself:
So cunning and so young is wonderful.   135

Glou. My lord, will't please you pass along?
Myself and my good cousin Buckingham
Will to your mother, to entreat of her
To meet you at the Tower and welcome you.   139

York. What, will you go unto the Tower, my lord?

Prince. My Lord Protector needs will have it so.

York. I shall not sleep in quiet at the Tower.

Glou. Why, what should you fear?

York. Marry, my uncle Clarence' angry ghost.
My grandam told me he was murd'red there.   145

Prince. I fear no uncles dead.

Glou. Nor none that live, I hope.

Prince. And if they live, I hope I need not fear.
But come, my lord; with a heavy heart,
Thinking on them, go I unto the Tower.   150

[*A sennet.*] *Exeunt Prince* [*Edward*], *York, Hastings,* [*Cardinal Bourchier, and others*]. *Manent
Richard, Buckingham,* [*and Catesby*].

Buck. Think you, my lord, this little prating York
Was not incensed by his subtile mother
To taunt and scorn you thus opprobriously?

Glou. No doubt, no doubt. O, 'tis a perilous boy,
Bold, quick, ingenious, forward, capable: 155
He is all the mother's, from the top to toe.

Buck. Well, let them rest. Come hither, Catesby.
Thou art sworn as deeply to effect what we intend
As closely to conceal what we impart.
Thou know'st our reasons urg'd upon the way;   160
What think'st thou? Is it not an easy matter
To make William Lord Hastings of our mind
For the installment of this noble Duke
In the seat royal of this famous isle?

Cate. He for his father's sake so loves the Prince
That he will not be won to aught against him.   166

Buck. What think'st thou then of Stanley? Will
not he?

Cate. He will do all in all as Hastings doth.

Buck. Well then, no more but this: go, gentle
Catesby,
And as it were far off, sound thou Lord Hastings   170
How he doth stand affected to our purpose,
And summon him to-morrow to the Tower
To sit about the coronation.

---

83. **moralize . . . word:** play upon the double meaning of a phrase
(i.e. *live long*). 86. **valure:** valor.
92. **right:** i.e. the English sovereign's legal claim to the French throne.
See note in *1 Henry VI*, I.i.80.
94. **Short . . . spring:** i.e. those who die young are usually precocious.
97. **dread:** to be held in reverential fear (as king).
99. **late:** recently. 103. **idle:** useless. 114. **toy:** trifle.
116. **to it:** i.e. to match the dagger. 118. **light:** trivial.
121. **lightly:** as a trifle.
126. **cross:** perverse, i.e. twisting words.

130–31. **Because . . . shoulders.** Court jesters and bears (at fairs and
carnivals) sometimes carried an ape upon their backs. A slur on
Richard's hunchback. 132. **sharp-provided:** keenly reasoned.
148. **And if:** if. **they:** i.e. Rivers and Grey, who had been arrested.
Actually, Grey was Prince Edward's stepbrother.
150 s.d. **sennet:** trumpet notes to signal the arrival or departure of
a procession. 152. **incensed:** incited.
154. **perilous:** (1) clever, precocious (cf. *parlous*, II.iv.35); (2) dangerous. 160. **way:** i.e. from Ludlow Castle.
163. **installment:** installation.
171. **doth stand affected:** is disposed. 173. **sit about:** discuss.

If thou dost find him tractable to us,
Encourage him, and tell him all our reasons;　　175
If he be leaden, icy, cold, unwilling,
Be thou so too, and so break off the talk,
And give us notice of his inclination;
For we to-morrow hold divided Councils,
Wherein thyself shalt highly be employ'd.　　180
　　Glou. Commend me to Lord William. Tell him,
　　　Catesby,
His ancient knot of dangerous adversaries
To-morrow are let blood at Pomfret Castle,
And bid my lord, for joy of this good news,
Give Mistress Shore one gentle kiss the more.　　185
　　Buck. Good Catesby, go effect this business
　　　soundly.
　　Cate. My good lords both, with all the heed I can.
　　Glou. Shall we hear from you, Catesby, ere we
　　　sleep?
　　Cate. You shall, my lord.
　　Glou. At Crosby House, there shall you find us
　　　both.　　　　　　　　　　　*Exit Catesby.*　　190
　　Buck. Now, my lord, what shall we do if we per-
　　　ceive
Lord Hastings will not yield to our complots?
　　Glou. Chop off his head! Something we will de-
　　　termine.
And look when I am king, claim thou of me
The earldom of Herford, and all the moveables　　195
Whereof the King my brother was possess'd.
　　Buck. I'll claim that promise at your Grace's hand.
　　Glou. And look to have it yielded with all kindness.
Come, let us sup betimes, that afterwards　　199
We may digest our complots in some form.　　*Exeunt.*

SCENE II

Enter a MESSENGER *to the door of Hastings.*

　　Mess. My lord! my lord!
　　Hast. [*Within.*] Who knocks?
　　Mess. One from the Lord Stanley.
　　Hast. [*Within.*] What is't a' clock?
　　Mess. Upon the stroke of four.　　5

Enter LORD HASTINGS.

　　Hast. Cannot my Lord Stanley sleep these tedious
　　　nights?
　　Mess. So it appears by that I have to say:
First, he commends him to your noble self.
　　Hast. What then?

　　Mess. Then certifies your lordship that this night　10
He dreamt the boar had rased off his helm.
Besides, he says there are two Councils kept;
And that may be determin'd at the one
Which may make you and him to rue at th' other.
Therefore he sends to know your lordship's pleasure,
If you will presently take horse with him,　　16
And with all speed post with him toward the north,
To shun the danger that his soul divines.
　　Hast. Go, fellow, go, return unto thy lord,
Bid him not fear the separated Council:　　20
His honor and myself are at the one,
And at the other is my good friend Catesby;
Where nothing can proceed that toucheth us
Whereof I shall not have intelligence.
Tell him his fears are shallow, without instance;　　25
And for his dreams, I wonder he's so simple
To trust the mock'ry of unquiet slumbers.
To fly the boar before the boar pursues
Were to incense the boar to follow us,
And make pursuit where he did mean no chase.　　30
Go, bid thy master rise and come to me,
And we will both together to the Tower,
Where he shall see the boar will use us kindly.
　　Mess. I'll go, my lord, and tell him what you say.
　　　　　　　　　　　　　　　　　Exit.

Enter CATESBY.

　　Cate. Many good morrows to my noble lord!　　35
　　Hast. Good morrow, Catesby, you are early stir-
　　　ring.
What news, what news, in this our tott'ring state?
　　Cate. It is a reeling world indeed, my lord,
And I believe will never stand upright
Till Richard wear the garland of the realm.　　40
　　Hast. How? wear the garland? Dost thou mean the
　　　crown?
　　Cate. Ay, my good lord.
　　Hast. I'll have this crown of mine cut from my
　　　shoulders
Before I'll see the crown so foul misplac'd.
But canst thou guess that he doth aim at it?　　45
　　Cate. Ay, on my life, and hopes to find you for-
　　　ward
Upon his party for the gain thereof;
And thereupon he sends you this good news,
That this same very day your enemies,
The kindred of the Queen, must die at Pomfret.　　50
　　Hast. Indeed I am no mourner for that news,
Because they have been still my adversaries;
But that I'll give my voice on Richard's side
To bar my master's heirs in true descent,
God knows I will not do it, to the death!　　55
　　Cate. God keep your lordship in that gracious mind!
　　Hast. But I shall laugh at this a twelvemonth
　　　hence,
That they which brought me in my master's hate,

---

179. **divided:** separate. More (Bullough, III, 262) explained that Richard "caused all the lordes whiche he knewe to bee faithfull to the kyng to assemble at Baynardes castle to commen [confer] of the ordre of the coronacion, whyle he and other of his complices & of his affinitee at Crosbies place contrived the contrary and to make the protectour kyng: to which counsail there were adhibite [admitted] very fewe, and they very secrete."
181. **Lord William:** i.e. Hastings.
183. **are let blood:** bleed, i.e. will be executed.
185. **Mistress Shore.** According to More (Bullough, III, 264), Hastings "from the death of kyng Edward kept Shores wife."
192. **complots:** conspiracies.　195. **moveables:** personal property.
199. **betimes:** soon.

III.ii. Location: Before Lord Hastings' house.

10. **certifies:** informs.
11. **boar:** i.e. Richard (see note to I.ii.102).　**rased . . . helm:** torn off his helmet.　25. **instance:** grounds.　27. **To:** as to.
43. **crown:** i.e. head.
46–47. **forward . . . party:** eager to his cause.
56. **gracious:** righteous.

Richard III
III.ii

I live to look upon their tragedy.
Well, Catesby, ere a fortnight make me older,   60
I'll send some packing that yet think not on't.
    Cate. 'Tis a vile thing to die, my gracious lord,
When men are unprepar'd and look not for it.
    Hast. O monstrous, monstrous! and so falls it out
With Rivers, Vaughan, Grey; and so 'twill do   65
With some men else, that think themselves as safe
As thou and I, who (as thou know'st) are dear
To princely Richard and to Buckingham.   68
    Cate. The princes both make high account of you—
[*Aside.*] For they account his head upon the bridge.
    Hast. I know they do, and I have well deserv'd it.

Enter LORD STANLEY.

Come on, come on, where is your boar-spear, man?
Fear you the boar, and go so unprovided?
    Stan. My lord, good morrow, good morrow,
        Catesby.
You may jest on, but, by the holy rood,   75
I do not like these several Councils, I.
    Hast. My lord,
I hold my life as dear as [you do] yours,
And never in my days, I do protest,
Was it so precious to me as 'tis now.   80
Think you, but that I know our state secure,
I would be so triumphant as I am?
    Stan. The lords at Pomfret, when they rode from
        London,
Were jocund, and suppos'd their states were sure,
And they indeed had no cause to mistrust;   85
But yet you see how soon the day o'ercast.
This sudden stab of rancor I misdoubt;
Pray God, I say, I prove a needless coward!
What, shall we toward the Tower? the day is spent.
    Hast. Come, come, have with you. Wot you what,
        my lord?   90
To-day the lords you [talk'd] of are beheaded.
    Stan. They, for their truth, might better wear their
        heads
Than some that have accus'd them wear their hats.
But come, my lord, let's away.   94

Enter a PURSUIVANT [*also named Hastings*].

    Hast. Go on before, I'll talk with this good fellow.
                    Exeunt Lord Stanley and Catesby.
How now, sirrah? how goes the world with thee?
    Purs. The better that your lordship please to ask.
    Hast. I tell thee, man, 'tis better with me now
Than when thou met'st me last where now we meet.
Then was I going prisoner to the Tower,   100
By the suggestion of the Queen's allies;
But now I tell thee (keep it to thyself)

This day those enemies are put to death,
And I in better state than e'er I was.   104
    Purs. God hold it, to your honor's good content!
    Hast. Gramercy, fellow. There, drink that for me.
                                Throws him his purse.
    Purs. I thank your honor.   *Exit Pursuivant.*

Enter a PRIEST.

    Priest. Well met, my lord, I am glad to see your
        honor.
    Hast. I thank thee, good Sir John, with all my heart.
I am in your debt for your last exercise;   110
Come the next Sabbath, and I will content you.
                            [*He whispers in his ear.*]
    Priest. I'll wait upon your lordship.

Enter BUCKINGHAM.

    Buck. What, talking with a priest, Lord Chamber-
        lain?
Your friends at Pomfret, they do need the priest,
Your honor hath no shriving work in hand.   115
    Hast. Good faith, and when I met this holy man
The men you talk of came into my mind.
What, go you toward the Tower?
    Buck. I do, my lord, but long I cannot stay there.
I shall return before your lordship thence.   120
    Hast. Nay, like enough, for I stay dinner there.
    Buck. [*Aside.*] And supper too, although thou
        know'st it not.—
Come, will you go?
    Hast.   I'll wait upon your lordship. *Exeunt.*

SCENE III

Enter SIR RICHARD RATCLIFFE *with Halberds, carrying
    the nobles* [RIVERS, GREY, *and* VAUGHAN] *to death at
    Pomfret.*

    [*Rat.* Come, bring forth the prisoners.]
    Riv. Sir Richard Ratcliffe, let me tell thee this:
To-day shalt thou behold a subject die
For truth, for duty, and for loyalty.
    Grey. God bless the Prince from all the pack of
        you!   5
A knot you are of damned blood-suckers.
    Vaug. You live that shall cry woe for this here-
        after.
    Rat. Dispatch, the limit of your lives is out.
    Riv. O Pomfret, Pomfret! O thou bloody prison!
Fatal and ominous to noble peers!   10
Within the guilty closure of thy walls
Richard the Second here was hack'd to death;
And for more slander to thy dismal seat,
We give to thee our guiltless blood to drink.

69. **make . . . you**: esteem you highly.
70. **account**: expect. **bridge**: i.e. London Bridge, where the heads
of traitors were exhibited.   75. **rood**: cross.
76. **several**: separate.   82. **triumphant**: exultant.
86. **o'ercast**: became overcast. 87. **misdoubt**: suspect.
89. **spent**: i.e. well advanced. The scene had opened at 4 a.m.
90. **have with you**: I'll accompany you.
94 s.d. **Pursuivant**: an official, attendant on a herald, empowered to
serve warrants.
96. **sirrah**: customary form of address to an inferior.
101. **suggestion**: instigation.

105. **hold it**: i.e. preserve things as they are.
106. **Gramercy**: thank you.
109. **Sir**: a common title of respect for clergymen.
110. **exercise**: sermon.
115. **shriving work**: confession and absolution, i.e. ministrations for
those about to die.

III.iii. Location: Pomfret Castle.
6. **knot**: group.   11. **closure**: enclosure.
13. **for . . . seat**: i.e. to add to your evil reputation.

Grey. Now Margaret's curse is fall'n upon our
     heads,   15
When she exclaim'd on Hastings, you, and I,
For standing by when Richard stabb'd her son.
     Riv. Then curs'd she Richard, then curs'd she
     Buckingham,
Then curs'd she Hastings. O, remember, God,
To hear her prayer for them, as now for us!   20
And for my sister and her princely sons,
Be satisfied, dear God, with our true blood,
Which, as thou know'st, unjustly must be spilt.
     Rat. Make haste, the hour of death is expiate.
     Riv. Come, Grey, come, Vaughan, let us here
     embrace.   25
Farewell, until we meet again in heaven.   *Exeunt.*

SCENE IV

Enter BUCKINGHAM, [STANLEY, *Earl of*] *Derby*, HAS-
TINGS, BISHOP OF ELY, NORFOLK, RATCLIFFE, LOVEL,
with others, at a table.

     Hast. Now, noble peers, the cause why we are met
Is to determine of the coronation.
In God's name speak, when is the royal day?
     Buck. Is all things ready for the royal time?
     Stan. It is, and wants but nomination.   5
     Ely. To-morrow then I judge a happy day.
     Buck. Who knows the Lord Protector's mind
     herein?
Who is most inward with the noble Duke?
     Ely. Your Grace, we think, should soonest know
     his mind.
     Buck. We know each other's faces; for our hearts,
He knows no more of mine than I of yours,   11
Or I of his, my lord, than you of mine.
Lord Hastings, you and he are near in love.
     Hast. I thank his Grace, I know he loves me well;
But for his purpose in the coronation,   15
I have not sounded him, nor he deliver'd
His gracious pleasure any way therein.
But you, my honorable lords, may name the time,
And in the Duke's behalf I'll give my voice,
Which I presume he'll take in gentle part.   20

Enter GLOUCESTER.

     Ely. In happy time, here comes the Duke himself.
     Glou. My noble lords and cousins all, good mor-
     row.
I have been long a sleeper; but I trust
My absence doth neglect no great design,   24
Which by my presence might have been concluded.
     Buck. Had you not come upon your cue, my lord,
William Lord Hastings had pronounc'd your part,
I mean your voice for crowning of the King.

     Glou. Than my Lord Hastings no man might be
     bolder,
His lordship knows me well and loves me well.   30
My Lord of Ely, when I was last in Holborn,
I saw good strawberries in your garden there.
I do beseech you send for some of them.
     Ely. Marry, and will, my lord, with all my heart.
                                        Exit Bishop.
     Glou. Cousin of Buckingham, a word with you. 35
                              [*Drawing him aside.*]
Catesby hath sounded Hastings in our business,
And finds the testy gentleman so hot
That he will lose his head ere give consent
His master's child, as worshipfully he terms it,
Shall lose the royalty of England's throne.   40
     Buck. Withdraw yourself a while, I'll go with you.
                    Exeunt [*Gloucester and Buckingham*].
     Stan. We have not yet set down this day of triumph.
To-morrow, in my judgment, is too sudden,
For I myself am not so well provided
As else I would be, were the day prolong'd.   45

Enter the BISHOP OF ELY.

     Ely. Where is my lord the Duke of Gloucester?
I have sent for these strawberries.
     Hast. His Grace looks cheerfully and smooth this
     morning;
There's some conceit or other likes him well,
When that he bids good morrow with such spirit.   50
I think there's never a man in Christendom
Can lesser hide his love or hate than he,
For by his face straight shall you know his heart.
     Stan. What of his heart perceive you in his face
By any livelihood he show'd to-day?   55
     Hast. Marry, that with no man here he is offended;
For were he, he had shown it in his looks.
[*Stan.* I pray God he be not, I say.]

Enter RICHARD [OF GLOUCESTER] *and* BUCKINGHAM

     Glou. I pray you all, tell me what they deserve
That do conspire my death with devilish plots   60
Of damned witchcraft, and that have prevail'd
Upon my body with their hellish charms?
     Hast. The tender love I bear your Grace, my lord,
Makes me most forward in this princely presence
To doom th' offenders, whosoe'er they be: 65
I say, my lord, they have deserved death.
     Glou. Then be your eyes the witness of their evil.
Look how I am bewitch'd; behold, mine arm
Is like a blasted sapling, wither'd up;
And this is Edward's wife, that monstrous witch,   70
Consorted with that harlot, strumpet Shore,
That by their witchcraft thus have marked me.
     Hast. If they have done this deed, my noble lord—
     Glou. If? Thou protector of this damned strumpet,
Talk'st thou to me of "ifs"? Thou art a traitor.   75
Off with his head! Now by Saint Paul I swear

15–18. **Now . . . Buckingham.** Actually, Margaret had not included
Grey and Vaughan in her execrations, and Buckingham had received
not her curse but her prophecy of disaster (I.iii).
24. **expiate:** fully come.

III.iv. Location: London. The Tower.
2. **determine of:** decide about. 5. **nomination:** setting the date.
8. **inward:** intimate. 10. **for:** as for. 19. **voice:** vote.
24. **neglect . . . design:** i.e. cause no important matter to be neglected.

31. **Holborn:** district in London where the Bishop of Ely had his
residence. 40. **royalty:** sovereignty. 45. **prolong'd:** postponed.
49. **conceit:** fancy. **likes:** pleases.
53. **straight:** straightway. 55. **livelihood:** animation.
71. **Consorted:** associated.

Richard III
III.iv

I will not dine until I see the same.
Lovel and Ratcliffe, look that it be done:
The rest that love me, rise, and follow me.
Exeunt. Manent Lovel and Ratcliffe
with the Lord Hastings.

Hast. Woe, woe for England, not a whit for me!
For I, too fond, might have prevented this.   81
Stanley did dream the boar did [rase] our helms,
And I did scorn it and disdain to fly.
Three times to-day my foot-cloth horse did stumble,
And started when he look'd upon the Tower,   85
As loath to bear me to the slaughter-house.
O now I need the priest that spake to me!
I now repent I told the pursuivant,
As too triumphing, how mine enemies
To-day at Pomfret bloodily were butcher'd,   90
And I myself secure, in grace and favor.
O Margaret, Margaret, now thy heavy curse
Is lighted on poor Hastings' wretched head!
Rat. Come, come, dispatch, the Duke would be at
dinner.
Make a short shrift, he longs to see your head.   95
Hast. O momentary grace of mortal men,
Which we more hunt for than the grace of God!
Who builds his hope in air of your good looks
Lives like a drunken sailor on a mast,
Ready with every nod to tumble down   100
Into the fatal bowels of the deep.
Lov. Come, come, dispatch, 'tis bootless to ex-
claim.
Hast. O bloody Richard! Miserable England!
I prophesy the fearfull'st time to thee
That ever wretched age hath look'd upon.   105
Come, lead me to the block; bear him my head.
They smile at me who shortly shall be dead.   *Exeunt.*

[SCENE V]

Enter RICHARD [OF GLOUCESTER] *and* BUCKINGHAM *in*
rotten armor, marvellous ill-favored.

Glou. Come, cousin, canst thou quake and change
thy color,
Murther thy breath in middle of a word,
And then again begin, and stop again,
As if thou were distraught and mad with terror?
Buck. Tut, I can counterfeit the deep tragedian,   5
Speak and look back, and pry on every side,
Tremble and start at wagging of a straw;
Intending deep suspicion, ghastly looks
Are at my service, like enforced smiles;
And both are ready in their offices   10
At any time to grace my stratagems.
But what, is Catesby gone?
Glou. He is, and see, he brings the Mayor along.

Enter the MAYOR *and* CATESBY.

Buck. Lord Mayor—
Glou. Look to the drawbridge there!   15
Buck. Hark, a drum!
Glou. Catesby, o'erlook the walls.
Buck. Lord Mayor, the reason we have sent—
Glou. Look back, defend thee, here are enemies!
Buck. God and our [innocence] defend and guard
us!   20

Enter LOVEL *and* RATCLIFFE *with Hastings' head.*

Glou. Be patient, they are friends—Ratcliffe and
Lovel.
Lov. Here is the head of that ignoble traitor,
The dangerous and unsuspected Hastings.
Glou. So dear I lov'd the man that I must weep.
I took him for the plainest harmless creature   25
That breath'd upon the earth a Christian;
Made him my book, wherein my soul recorded
The history of all her secret thoughts.
So smooth he daub'd his vice with show of virtue
That, his apparent open guilt omitted—   30
I mean, his conversation with Shore's wife—
He liv'd from all attainder of suspects.
Buck. Well, well, he was the covert'st shelt'red
traitor
That ever liv'd. [Look ye, my Lord Mayor,]
Would you imagine, or almost believe,   35
Were't not that by great preservation
We live to tell it, that the subtile traitor
This day had plotted, in the Council-house,
To murther me and my good Lord of Gloucester?
May. Had he done so?   40
Glou. What? think you we are Turks or infidels?
Or that we would, against the form of law,
Proceed thus rashly in the villain's death,
But that the extreme peril of the case,
The peace of England, and our persons' safety,   45
Enforc'd us to this execution?
May. Now fair befall you! he deserv'd his death,
And your good Graces both have well proceeded,
To warn false traitors from the like attempts.
Buck. I never look'd for better at his hands   50
After he once fell in with Mistress Shore.
Yet had we not determin'd he should die
Until your lordship came to see his end,
Which now the loving haste of these our friends,
Something against our meanings, have prevented;   55
Because, my lord, I would have had you heard
The traitor speak, and timorously confess
The manner and the purpose of his treasons,
That you might well have signified the same
Unto the citizens, who haply may   60
Misconster us in him and wail his death.

81. **fond:** foolish.
84. **foot-cloth:** wearing ornamental trappings (as the mount of a
dignitary). 95. **shrift:** confession.
98. **in . . . looks:** on your favorable external seeming.
102. **bootless:** useless.
III.v. Location: London. The Tower walls.
o.s.d. **rotten:** rusty. **ill-favored:** ugly. 8. **Intending:** pretending.
10. **offices:** functions.

17. **o'erlook:** inspect.
25. **harmless:** i.e. most harmless. (Cf., in line 33, *shelt'red* = most
concealed.) 30. **apparent:** manifest.
31. **conversation:** intercourse.
32. **from . . . suspects:** free from all taint of suspicion.
48. **proceeded:** done.
55. **Something . . . meanings:** somewhat contrary to our intentions.
prevented: anticipated.
61. **Misconster . . . him:** i.e. misconstrue our handling of this business.

May.   But, my good lord, your Grace's words shall
      serve
As well as I had seen, and heard him speak;
And do not doubt, right noble princes both,
But I'll acquaint our duteous citizens   65
With all your just proceedings in this [cause].
   Glou.   And to that end we wish'd your lordship here,
T' avoid the censures of the carping world.
   Buck.   Which since you come too late of our intent,
Yet witness what you hear we did intend.   70
And so, my good Lord Mayor, we bid farewell.
                                        Exit Mayor.
   Glou.   Go after, after, cousin Buckingham.
The Mayor towards Guildhall hies him in all post.
There, at your meet'st [advantage] of the time,
Infer the bastardy of Edward's children.   75
Tell them how Edward put to death a citizen
Only for saying he would make his son
Heir to the Crown—meaning indeed his house,
Which by the sign thereof was termed so.
Moreover, urge his hateful luxury   80
And bestial appetite in change of lust,
Which stretch'd unto their servants, daughters, wives,
Even where his raging eye or savage heart,
Without control, lusted to make a prey.
Nay, for a need, thus far come near my person: 85
Tell them, when that my mother went with child
Of that insatiate Edward, noble York,
My princely father, then had wars in France,
And by true computation of the time,
Found that the issue was not his begot;   90
Which well appeared in his lineaments,
Being nothing like the noble Duke my father.
Yet touch this sparingly, as 'twere far off,
Because, my lord, you know my mother lives.
   Buck.   Doubt not, my lord, I'll play the orator   95
As if the golden fee for which I plead
Were for myself—and so, my lord, adieu.
   Glou.   If you thrive well, bring them to Baynard's
      Castle,
Where you shall find me well accompanied
With reverend fathers and well-learned bishops.   100
   Buck.   I go, and towards three or four a' clock
Look for the news that the Guildhall affords.
                                        Exit Buckingham.
   Glou.   Go, Lovel, with all speed to Doctor Shaw;
[*To Catesby.*]   Go thou to Friar [Penker]; bid them
      both

Meet me within this hour at Baynard's Castle.   105
                               Exeunt [*Lovel and Catesby*].
[*To Ratcliffe.*] Now will I go to take some privy
      order
To draw the brats of Clarence out of sight,
And to give order that no manner person
Have any time recourse unto the Princes.   *Exeunt.*

[SCENE VI]

Enter a SCRIVENER [*with a paper in his hand*].

   Scriv.   Here is the indictment of the good Lord
      Hastings,
Which in a set hand fairly is engross'd
That it may be to-day read o'er in Paul's.
And mark how well the sequel hangs together:
Eleven hours I have spent to write it over,   5
For yesternight by Catesby was it sent me;
The precedent was full as long a-doing,
And yet within these five hours Hastings liv'd,
Untainted, unexamin'd, free, at liberty.
Here's a good world the while! Who is so gross   10
That cannot see this palpable device?
Yet who['s] so bold but says he sees it not?
Bad is the world, and all will come to nought,
When such ill dealing must be seen in thought.   *Exit.*

[SCENE VII]

Enter RICHARD [OF GLOUCESTER] *and* BUCKINGHAM
at several doors.

   Glou.   How now, how now, what say the cit-
      izens?
   Buck.   Now, by the holy Mother of our Lord,
The citizens are mum, say not a word.
   Glou.   Touch'd you the bastardy of Edward's
      children?
   Buck.   I did, with his contract with Lady Lucy,   5
And his contract by deputy in France,
Th' unsatiate greediness of his desire,
And his enforcement of the city wives,

---

69. **of our intent:** i.e. for things to proceed as we intended.
70. **witness:** bear witness to.
73. **Guildhall:** seat of municipal government in London.   **post:** haste.
74. **meet'st . . . time:** most favorable opportunity.
75. **Infer:** assert.
76–79. **Tell . . . so.** According to More (Bullough, III, 273), when a merchant named Burdet, "dwellyng in Chepesyd[e] at the signe of the Croune," told his son that "he would make hym inheritor of the Croune, meanyng his awne house," King Edward, misconstruing the remark, had him promptly "apprehended, judged, drawen and quartered."   80. **luxury:** sensuality.
81. **change of lust:** i.e. fickleness in shifting from one woman to another.   85. **for a need:** if necessary.
86–87. **went . . . Of:** was pregnant with.
96. **golden fee:** i.e. the crown.
98. **Baynard's Castle:** one of Richard's London residences.
103, 104. **Shaw, Penker.** Among Richard's creatures, says More (Bullough, III, 269–70), were "Raffe Shaa [i.e. Shaw] clerke brother

to the Mayre, & Freer Pynkie [i.e. Penker] provinciall of the Augustine Freers," one of whom "made a sermonde in prayse of the Protectour before the coronacion" and the other a similar sermon after the ceremony, "bothe so full of tedious flattery, that no good mans eares coulde abyde them."
106. **take . . . order:** make some private arrangement.
108–9. **that . . . Princes:** that no person whatever at any time have access to the Princes.

III.vi. Location: London. A street.
2. **set hand:** style of script used in legal documents.
7. **precedent:** first draft.   10. **gross:** stupid.
14. **seen in thought:** i.e. perceived but not spoken of.

III.vii. Location: London. Baynard's Castle.
o.s.d. **several:** different.
4–6. **Touch'd . . . France.** As Buckingham argues later in the scene (lines 177–91), Edward's alleged betrothal to Elizabeth Lucy (by whom he had had a child) and his offer of marriage to Bona of Savoy invalidated his marriage with Elizabeth Grey, and thus their children—seven of whom survived infancy—were bastards. On the negotiations with Bona of Savoy see *3 Henry VI*, III.iii.
5. **contract:** betrothal.   7. **unsatiate:** insatiable.
8. **enforcement:** forcible seduction.

Richard III
III.vii

His tyranny for trifles, his own bastardy,
As being got, your father then in France, 10
And his resemblance, being not like the Duke.
Withal I did infer your lineaments,
Being the right idea of your father,
Both in your form and nobleness of mind;
Laid open all your victories in Scotland, 15
Your discipline in war, wisdom in peace,
Your bounty, virtue, fair humility;
Indeed, left nothing fitting for your purpose
Untouch'd or slightly handled in discourse.
And when [mine] oratory drew [to an] end, 20
I bid them that did love their country's good
Cry, "God save Richard, England's royal king!"
   Glou. And did they so?
   Buck. No, so God help me, they spake not a word,
But like dumb statuës, or breathing stones, 25
Star'd each on other, and look'd deadly pale;
Which when I saw, I reprehended them,
And ask'd the Mayor what meant this willful silence.
His answer was, the people were not used
To be spoke to but by the Recorder. 30
Then he was urg'd to tell my tale again:
"Thus saith the Duke, thus hath the Duke inferr'd"—
But nothing [spake] in warrant from himself.
When he had done, some followers of mine own,
At lower end of the hall, hurl'd up their caps, 35
And some ten voices cried, "God save King Richard!"
And thus I took the vantage of those few:
"Thanks, gentle citizens and friends," quoth I,
"This general applause and cheerful shout
Argues your [wisdoms] and your love to Richard"—
And even here brake off, and came away. 41
   Glou. What tongueless blocks were they! Would
     they not speak?
   [*Buck.* No, by my troth, my lord.]
   [*Glou.*] Will not the Mayor then and his brethren
     come?
   Buck. The Mayor is here at hand. Intend some
     fear, 45
Be not you spoke with but by mighty suit;
And look you get a prayer-book in your hand,
And stand between two churchmen, good my lord—
For on that ground I'll make a holy descant—
And be not easily won to our requests: 50
Play the maid's part, still answer nay, and take it.
   Glou. I go; and if you plead as well for them
As I can say nay to thee for myself,
No doubt we bring it to a happy issue.
   Buck. Go, go up to the leads, the Lord Mayor
     knocks.   [*Exit Gloucester.*]

Enter the MAYOR, [ALDERMEN,] *and* CITIZENS.

Welcome, my lord! I dance attendance here; 56
I think the Duke will not be spoke withal.

Enter CATESBY.

Now, Catesby, what says your lord to my request?
   Cate. He doth entreat your Grace, my noble lord,
To visit him to-morrow or next day. 60
He is within, with two right reverend fathers,
Divinely bent to meditation,
And in no worldly suits would he be mov'd,
To draw him from his holy exercise.
   Buck. Return, good Catesby, to the gracious Duke,
Tell him, myself, the Mayor and Aldermen, 66
In deep designs, in matter of great moment,
No less importing than our general good,
Are come to have some conference with his Grace.
   Cate. I'll signify so much unto him straight. *Exit.*
   Buck. Ah ha, my lord, this prince is not an
     Edward! 71
He is not lulling on a lewd love-bed,
But on his knees at meditation;
Not dallying with a brace of courtezans,
But meditating with two deep divines; 75
Not sleeping, to engross his idle body,
But praying, to enrich his watchful soul.
Happy were England, would this virtuous prince
Take on his Grace the sovereignty thereof,
But sure I fear we shall not win him to it. 80
   May. Marry, God defend his Grace should say us
     nay!
   Buck. I fear he will. Here Catesby comes again.

Enter CATESBY.

Now, Catesby, what says his Grace?
   Cate.   [My lord,]
He wonders to what end you have assembled
Such troops of citizens to come to him, 85
His Grace not being warn'd thereof before:
He fears, my lord, you mean no good to him.
   Buck. Sorry I am my noble cousin should
Suspect me that I mean no good to him.
By heaven, we come to him in perfit love, 90
And so once more return and tell his Grace.
                 Exit [*Catesby*].
When holy and devout religious men
Are at their beads, 'tis much to draw them thence,
So sweet is zealous contemplation.

Enter RICHARD [OF GLOUCESTER] *aloft, between two*
BISHOPS. [CATESBY *returns.*]

   May. See where his Grace stands, 'tween two
     clergymen! 95
   Buck. Two props of virtue for a Christian prince,
To stay him from the fall of vanity;
And see, a book of prayer in his hand—
True ornaments to know a holy man.
Famous Plantagenet, most gracious prince, 100

9. **tyranny for trifles:** harshness toward trifling offenses.
11. **resemblance:** appearance.
12. **infer your lineaments:** comment on your features.
13. **right idea:** very image.
15. **victories in Scotland.** As leader of an expedition against the Scots in 1482 Richard had advanced as far as Edinburgh.
30. **Recorder:** a city official.   32. **inferr'd:** asserted.
33. **in . . . himself:** on his own authority.   41. **brake:** broke.
45. **Intend:** pretend.   46. **mighty suit:** urgent entreaty.
49. **ground:** plain-song or bass.   **descant:** variation.
55. **leads:** i.e. roof (so called from the sheets of metal used for covering).

57. **spoke withal:** spoken with.
68. **No less importing:** relating to nothing less.
72. **lulling:** lolling.   76. **engross:** fatten.   81. **defend:** forbid.
90. **perfit:** perfect.   93. **beads:** prayers.
97. **stay:** prevent.   **of:** caused by.

Lend favorable ear to our requests,
And pardon us the interruption
Of thy devotion and right Christian zeal.
  Glou. My lord, there needs no such apology.
I do beseech your Grace to pardon me,   105
Who, earnest in the service of my God,
Deferr'd the visitation of my friends.
But leaving this, what is your Grace's pleasure?
  Buck. Even that (I hope) which pleaseth God above
And all good men of this ungovern'd isle.   110
  Glou. I do suspect I have done some offense
That seems disgracious in the city's eye,
And that you come to reprehend my ignorance.
  Buck. You have, my lord. Would it might please
    your Grace,
On our entreaties, to amend your fault!   115
  Glou. Else wherefore breathe I in a Christian land?
  Buck. Know then, it is your fault that you resign
The supreme seat, the throne majestical,
The sceptred office of your ancestors,
Your state of fortune, and your due of birth,   120
The lineal glory of your royal house,
To the corruption of a blemish'd stock;
Whiles in the mildness of your sleepy thoughts,
Which here we waken to our country's good,
The noble isle doth want [her] proper limbs;   125
[Her] face defac'd with scars of infamy,
[Her] royal stock graft with ignoble plants,
And almost should'red in the swallowing gulf
Of dark forgetfulness and deep oblivion.
Which to recure, we heartily solicit   130
Your gracious self to take on you the charge
And kingly government of this your land:
Not as protector, steward, substitute,
Or lowly factor for another's gain;
But as successively, from blood to blood,   135
Your right of birth, your empery, your own.
For this, consorted with the citizens,
Your very worshipful and loving friends,
And by their vehement instigation,
In this just cause come I to move your Grace.   140
  Glou. I cannot tell if to depart in silence,
Or bitterly to speak in your reproof,
Best fitteth my degree or your condition.
If not to answer, you might haply think
Tongue-tied ambition, not replying, yielded   145
To bear the golden yoke of sovereignty,
Which fondly you would here impose on me.
If to reprove you for this suit of yours,
So season'd with your faithful love to me,
Then on the other side, I check'd my friends.   150
Therefore—to speak, and to avoid the first,
And then, in speaking, not to incur the last—
Definitively thus I answer you:
Your love deserves my thanks, but my desert

Unmeritable shuns your high request.   155
First, if all obstacles were cut away,
And that my path were even to the crown,
As the ripe revenue and due of birth,
Yet so much is my poverty of spirit,
So mighty and so many my defects,   160
That I would rather hide me from my greatness—
Being a bark to brook no mighty sea—
Than in my greatness covet to be hid
And in the vapor of my glory smother'd.
But God be thank'd, there is no need of me,   165
And much I need to help you, were there need:
The royal tree hath left us royal fruit,
Which mellow'd by the stealing hours of time,
Will well become the seat of majesty,
And make (no doubt) us happy by his reign.   170
On him I lay that you would lay on me,
The right and fortune of his happy stars,
Which God defend that I should wring from him!
  Buck. My lord, this argues conscience in your
    Grace,
But the respects thereof are nice and trivial,   175
All circumstances well considered.
You say that Edward is your brother's son:
So say we too, but not by Edward's wife;
For first was he contract to Lady Lucy—
Your mother lives a witness to his vow—   180
And afterward by substitute betroth'd
To Bona, sister to the King of France.
These both put off, a poor petitioner,
A care-craz'd mother to a many sons,
A beauty-waning and distressed widow,   185
Even in the afternoon of her best days,
Made prize and purchase of his wanton eye,
Seduc'd the pitch and height of his degree
To base declension and loath'd bigamy.
By her, in his unlawful bed, he got   190
This Edward, whom our manners call the Prince.
More bitterly could I expostulate,
Save that for reverence to some alive,
I give a sparing limit to my tongue.
Then, good my lord, take to your royal self   195
This proffer'd benefit of dignity;
If not to bless us and the land withal,
Yet to draw forth your noble ancestry
From the corruption of abusing times
Unto a lineal true-derived course.   200

---

112. **disgracious:** displeasing.
123. **sleepy:** i.e. conducive to repose and meditation.
125. **want:** lack.   **proper:** own.   127. **graft:** engrafted.
128. **should'red in:** plunged into.   130. **recure:** remedy.
134. **factor:** agent.   135. **successively:** in order of succession.
136. **empery:** realm to be ruled.   143. **condition:** rank.
147. **fondly:** foolishly.   149. **season'd:** i.e. made palatable.
150. **check'd:** rebuked.

157. **even:** unimpeded.
158. **revenue:** possession ready for enjoyment.
163. **in . . . hid:** i.e. wish to be protected by my greatness.
166. **much I need:** I am greatly lacking (in ability).
175. **respects:** the reasons you advance.   **nice:** overscrupulous.
180. **Your . . . vow.** According to Hall (Bullough, III, 271), Edward's
mother was so much troubled by his liaison with Elizabeth Lucy "that
either the bishoppe durste not, or the kynge would not proceade to
the solemnisacion of the mariage [with Elizabeth Grey] til his fame
were clerely purged, and the truth well and openly testified."
183-89. **a poor . . . bigamy.** For the circumstances of Edward's match
with Elizabeth Grey see *3 Henry VI*, III.ii.
187. **purchase:** booty.
188. **Seduc'd:** debased.   **pitch:** height (a term from falconry).
189. **declension:** decline.
191. **our manners:** i.e. we, in mere politeness.
192. **expostulate:** discuss.
195. **good my lord:** my good lord.
199. **of abusing times:** caused by the abuses of the times.

Richard III
III.vii

May. Do, good my lord, your citizens entreat you.
Buck. Refuse not, mighty lord, this proffer'd love.
Cate. O, make them joyful, grant their lawful suit!
Glou. Alas, why would you heap this care on me?
I am unfit for state and majesty.   205
I do beseech you take it not amiss,
I cannot nor I will not yield to you.
Buck. If you refuse it—as, in love and zeal,
Loath to depose the child, your brother's son;
As well we know your tenderness of heart   210
And gentle, kind, effeminate remorse,
Which we have noted in you to your kindred
And egally indeed to all estates—
Yet know, whe'er you accept our suit or no,
Your brother's son shall never reign our king,   215
But we will plant some other in the throne,
To the disgrace and downfall of your house;
And in this resolution here we leave you.
Come, citizens. ['Zounds, I'll] entreat no more.
    [*Glou.* O, do not swear, my Lord of Buckingham.]
                Exeunt [*Buckingham, Mayor,*
                    Aldermen, and Citizens].
Cate. Call him again, sweet prince, accept their
    suit.   221
If you deny them, all the land will rue it.
Glou. Will you enforce me to a world of cares?
Call them again, I am not made of stones,
But penetrable to your kind entreaties,   225
Albeit against my conscience and my soul.

Enter BUCKINGHAM *and the rest.*

Cousin of Buckingham, and sage grave men,
Since you will buckle Fortune on my back,
To bear her burthen whe'er I will or no,
I must have patience to endure the load;   230
But if black scandal or foul-fac'd reproach
Attend the sequel of your imposition,
Your mere enforcement shall acquittance me
From all the impure blots and stains thereof;
For God doth know, and you may partly see,   235
How far I am from the desire of this.
May. God bless your Grace! we see it and will say
    it.
Glou. In saying so you shall but say the truth.
Buck. Then I salute you with this royal title—
Long live Richard, England's worthy king!   240
All. Amen.
Buck. To-morrow may it please you to be crown'd?
Glou. Even when you please, for you will have it
    so.
Buck. To-morrow then we will attend your Grace,
And so most joyfully we take our leave.   245
Glou. [*To the Bishops.*] Come, let us to our holy
    work again.—
Farewell, my [cousin], farewell, gentle friends.
                                                      Exeunt.

ACT IV, SCENE I

Enter the QUEEN [ELIZABETH], *the* DUCHESS OF YORK,
and MARQUESS DORSET [*at one door*]; ANNE DUCHESS
OF GLOUCESTER [*leading* LADY MARGARET PLAN-
TAGENET, *Clarence's young daughter, at another door*].

Duch. Who meets us here? My niece Plantagenet,
Led in the hand of her kind aunt of Gloucester?
Now, for my life, she's wand'ring to the Tower,
On pure heart's love, to greet the tender Prince.
Daughter, well met.
Anne.   God give your Graces both   5
A happy and a joyful time of day!
Q. Eliz. As much to you, good sister! Whither
    away?
Anne. No farther than the Tower, and as I guess,
Upon the like devotion as yourselves,
To gratulate the gentle Princes there.   10
Q. Eliz. Kind sister, thanks, we'll enter all to-
    gether.

Enter the Lieutenant [BRAKENBURY].

And in good time, here the Lieutenant comes.
Master Lieutenant, pray you, by your leave,
How doth the Prince and my young son of York?
Brak. Right well, dear madam. By your patience,
I may not suffer you to visit them,   16
The King hath strictly charg'd the contrary.
Q. Eliz. The King? who's that?
Brak.   I mean the Lord Protector.
Q. Eliz. The Lord protect him from that kingly
    title!
Hath he set bounds between their love and me?   20
I am their mother, who shall bar me from them?
Duch. I am their father's mother, I will see them.
Anne. Their aunt I am in law, in love their mother;
Then bring me to their sights. I'll bear thy blame,
And take thy office from thee on my peril.   25
Brak. No, madam, no; I may not leave it so:
I am bound by oath, and therefore pardon me.
                                            Exit Lieutenant.

Enter STANLEY.

Stan. Let me but meet you, ladies, [an] hour hence,
And I'll salute your Grace of York as mother
And reverend looker-on of two fair queens.   30
[*To Anne.*] Come, madam, you must straight to
    Westminster,
There to be crowned Richard's royal queen.
Q. Eliz. Ah, cut my lace asunder,
That my pent heart may have some scope to beat,
Or else I swoon with this dead-killing news!   35
Anne. Despiteful tidings, O unpleasing news!

IV.i. Location: London. Before the Tower.
1. niece: i.e. granddaughter.   4. On: out of.
5. Daughter: i.e. daughter-in-law.
7. sister: i.e. sister-in-law.   10. gratulate: greet.
20. bounds: barriers.
25. take . . . peril: i.e. be responsible for relieving you of your duties.
26. it: i.e. his office.   29. mother: i.e. mother-in-law.
30. queens: i.e. Elizabeth (consort of Edward IV) and Anne (consort
of Richard III).   33. cut . . . asunder: i.e. loosen my bodice.
36. Despiteful: cruel.

---

211. kind, effeminate remorse: natural, tender pity.
213. egally: equally.   estates: ranks.
232. imposition: charge (of kingship).
233. mere: downright.   acquittance: acquit.

Dor. Be of good cheer. Mother, how fares your
Grace?

Q. Eliz. O Dorset, speak not to me, get thee gone!
Death and destruction dogs thee at thy heels;
Thy mother's name is ominous to children.   40
If thou wilt outstrip death, go cross the seas,
And live with Richmond, from the reach of hell.
Go hie thee, hie thee from this slaughter-house,
Lest thou increase the number of the dead,
And make me die the thrall of Margaret's curse,   45
Nor mother, wife, nor England's counted queen.

Stan. Full of wise care is this your counsel,
madam;
Take all the swift advantage of the hours.
You shall have letters from me to my son
In your behalf, to meet you on the way.   50
Be not ta'en tardy by unwise delay.

Duch. O ill-dispersing wind of misery!
O my accursed womb, the bed of death!
A cockatrice hast thou hatch'd to the world,
Whose unavoided eye is murtherous.   55

Stan. Come, madam, come, I in all haste was sent.

Anne. And I with all unwillingness will go.
O would to God that the inclusive verge
Of golden metal that must round my brow
Were red-hot steel, to sear me to the brains!   60
Anointed let me be with deadly venom,
And die ere men can say, "God save the Queen!"

Q. Eliz. Go, go, poor soul, I envy not thy glory,
To feed my humor wish thyself no harm.   64

Anne. No! why? When he that is my husband now
Came to me as I follow'd Henry's corse,
When scarce the blood was well wash'd from his hands
Which issued from my other angel husband,
And that dear saint which then I weeping follow'd—
O, when, I say, I look'd on Richard's face,   70
This was my wish: "Be thou," quoth I, "accurs'd
For making me, so young, so old a widow!
And when thou wed'st, let sorrow haunt thy bed;
And be thy wife—if any be so mad—
More miserable by the life of thee   75
Than thou hast made me by my dear lord's death!"
Lo, ere I can repeat this curse again,
Within so small a time, my woman's heart
Grossly grew captive to his honey words,
And prov'd the subject of mine own soul's curse,   80
Which hitherto hath held [my] eyes from rest;
For never yet one hour in his bed
Did I enjoy the golden dew of sleep,
But with his timorous dreams was still awak'd.
Besides, he hates me for my father Warwick,   85
And will, no doubt, shortly be rid of me.

Q. Eliz. Poor heart, adieu, I pity thy complaining.

Anne. No more than with my soul I mourn for
yours.

Dor. Farewell, thou woeful welcomer of glory!

Anne. Adieu, poor soul, that tak'st thy leave of it!

Duch. [*To Dorset.*] Go thou to Richmond, and
good fortune guide thee!   91
[*To Anne.*] Go thou to Richard, and good angels tend
thee!
[*To Queen Elizabeth.*] Go thou to sanctuary, and good
thoughts possess thee!
I to my grave, where peace and rest lie with me!
Eighty odd years of sorrow have I seen,   95
And each hour's joy wrack'd with a week of teen.

Q. Eliz. Stay, yet look back with me unto the
Tower.
Pity, you ancient stones, those tender babes
Whom envy hath immur'd within your walls—
Rough cradle for such little pretty ones!   100
Rude ragged nurse, old sullen playfellow
For tender princes—use my babies well!
So foolish sorrows bids your stones farewell. *Exeunt.*

SCENE II

Sound a sennet. Enter RICHARD *in pomp,* [*crowned*];
BUCKINGHAM, CATESBY, RATCLIFFE, LOVEL, [*a* PAGE,
and others].

K. Rich. Stand all apart. Cousin of Buckingham—

Buck. My gracious sovereign?

K. Rich. Give me thy hand.
[*Here he ascendeth the throne.*] *Sound.*
Thus high, by thy advice
And thy assistance, is King Richard seated;
But shall we wear these glories for a day?   5
Or shall they last, and we rejoice in them?

Buck. Still live they, and for ever let them last!

K. Rich. Ah, Buckingham, now do I play the touch,
To try if thou be current gold indeed.
Young Edward lives: think now what I would speak.

Buck. Say on, my loving lord.   11

K. Rich. Why, Buckingham, I say I would be
king.

Buck. Why, so you are, my thrice-renowned lord.

K. Rich. Ha? am I king? 'Tis so—but Edward
lives.

Buck. True, noble prince.

K. Rich.   O bitter consequence,
That Edward still should live true noble prince!   16
Cousin, thou wast not wont to be so dull.
Shall I be plain? I wish the bastards dead,
And I would have it suddenly perform'd.
What say'st thou now? Speak suddenly, be brief.   20

Buck. Your Grace may do your pleasure.

K. Rich. Tut, tut, thou art all ice, thy kindness
freezes.
Say, have I thy consent that they shall die?

---

42. **Richmond.** Henry Tudor, Earl of Richmond (later Henry VII),
had been a refugee in Brittany during the reign of Edward IV.
46. **counted:** esteemed.   49. **son:** i.e. stepson.
51. **ta'en:** taken, i.e. caught.
52. **ill-dispersing:** i.e. scattering misfortune.
54. **cockatrice:** basilisk (see note to I.ii.150).
58. **inclusive verge:** enclosing rim (of the crown).
72. **so . . . widow:** i.e. because she would have so long to live widowed.
79. **Grossly:** stupidly.   84. **timorous:** fearful.
87. **complaining:** lament.

95. **Eighty odd years.** Actually the Duchess of York was sixty-eight
at Richard's accession in 1483.
96. **wrack'd:** destroyed.   **teen:** sorrow.

IV.ii. Location: London. The palace.
8. **play the touch:** assume the function of a touchstone (which was
used for testing the quality of gold).   9. **current:** genuine.
15. **consequence:** retort (to Richard's assertion, "Edward lives").

Richard III
IV.ii

Buck. Give me some little breath, some pause, dear lord,
Before I positively speak in this.   25
I will resolve you herein presently. *Exit Buckingham.*
Cate. [*Aside to a stander-by.*] The King is angry,
        see, he gnaws his lip.
K. Rich. I will converse with iron-witted fools
And unrespective boys; none are for me
That look into me with considerate eyes.   30
High-reaching Buckingham grows circumspect.
Boy!
        Page. My lord?
        K. Rich. Know'st thou not any whom corrupting
        gold
Will tempt unto a close exploit of death?   35
Page. I know a discontented gentleman
Whose humble means match not his haughty spirit.
Gold were as good as twenty orators,
And will, no doubt, tempt him to any thing.   39
        K. Rich. What is his name?
        Page.   His name, my lord, is Tyrrel.
        K. Rich. I partly know the man; go call him
        hither, boy.   *Exit* [*Page.*]
The deep-revolving witty Buckingham
No more shall be the neighbor to my counsels.
Hath he so long held out with me untir'd,
And stops he now for breath? Well, be it so.   45

Enter STANLEY.

How now, Lord Stanley, what's the news?
        Stan. Know, my loving lord,
The Marquess Dorset, as I hear, is fled
To Richmond, in the parts where he abides.   49
                                [*Stands apart.*]
        K. Rich. Come hither, Catesby. Rumor it abroad
That Anne, my wife, is very grievous sick;
I will take order for her keeping close.
Inquire me out some mean poor gentleman,
Whom I will marry straight to Clarence' daughter;
The boy is foolish, and I fear not him.   55
Look how thou dream'st! I say again, give out
That Anne, my queen, is sick and like to die.
About it, for it stands me much upon
To stop all hopes whose growth may damage me.
                                [*Exit Catesby.*]
I must be married to my brother's daughter,   60
Or else my kingdom stands on brittle glass.
Murther her brothers and then marry her—
Uncertain way of gain! But I am in
So far in blood that sin will pluck on sin.
Tear-falling pity dwells not in this eye.   65

---

26. **resolve:** inform.   29. **unrespective:** thoughtless.
30. **considerate:** thoughtful, reflective.
35. **close exploit:** secret undertaking.   42. **witty:** cunning.
52. **take:** give.   **close:** confined, i.e. imprisoned.
55. **boy:** i.e. Clarence's eldest son Edward, Earl of Warwick (1475–99), whom Henry VII executed, after long imprisonment, on a trumped-up charge of treason.
58. **stands . . . upon:** is of great concern to me.
60. **my brother's daughter:** i.e. Edward's daughter Elizabeth (1465–1503), whom Richard sought to marry, said Hall (Bullough, III, 286), "so by that meanes the erle of Richemonde of the affinite of his nece should be utterly defrauded and beguyled." Richard's plan did not succeed, and in 1486 the marriage of Elizabeth and Henry VII finally united the houses of York and Lancaster.

Enter [PAGE *with* SIR JAMES] TYRREL.

Is thy name Tyrrel?
        Tyr. James Tyrrel, and your most obedient sub-
        ject.
        K. Rich. Art thou indeed?
        Tyr.   Prove me, my gracious lord.
        K. Rich. Dar'st thou resolve to kill a friend of
        mine?
Tyr. Please you;   70
But I had rather kill two enemies.
        K. Rich. Why, [there] thou hast it; two deep
        enemies,
Foes to my rest and my sweet sleep's disturbers,
Are they that I would have thee deal upon:
Tyrrel, I mean those bastards in the Tower.   75
        Tyr. Let me have open means to come to them,
And soon I'll rid you from the fear of them.
        K. Rich. Thou sing'st sweet music. Hark, come
        hither, Tyrrel.
Go, by this token. Rise, and lend thine ear. *Whispers.*
There is no more but so; say it is done,   80
And I will love thee and prefer thee for it.
Tyr. I will dispatch it straight.   *Exit.*

Enter BUCKINGHAM.

Buck. My lord, I have consider'd in my mind
The late request that you did sound me in.
        K. Rich. Well, let that rest. Dorset is fled to
        Richmond.   85
Buck. I hear the news, my lord.
        K. Rich. Stanley, he is your wive's son: well, look
        unto it.
Buck. My lord, I claim the gift, my due by promise,
For which your honor and your faith is pawn'd,
Th' earldom of [Herford], and the moveables,   90
Which you have promised I shall possess.
        K. Rich. Stanley, look to your wife. If she convey
Letters to Richmond, you shall answer it.
Buck. What says your Highness to my just request?
        K. Rich. I do remember me, Henry the Sixt   95
Did prophesy that Richmond should be king,
When Richmond was a little peevish boy.
A king—perhaps—[perhaps—
Buck. My lord—
        K. Rich. How chance the prophet could not at that
        time   100
Have told me, I being by, that I should kill him?
Buck. My lord, your promise for the earldom—
        K. Rich. Richmond! When last I was at Exeter,
The mayor in courtesy show'd me the castle,   104
And call'd it Rouge-mount, at which name I started,
Because a bard of Ireland told me once
I should not live long after I saw Richmond.
        Buck. My lord—

---

68. **Prove:** test.   76. **open:** unimpeded.
81. **prefer:** advance.   84. **sound me in:** ask me about.
87. **he:** i.e. Richmond.   **wive's:** wife's.   89. **pawn'd:** pledged.
93. **answer:** answer for.
95–97. **Henry . . . boy.** See *3 Henry VI*, IV.vi.67–76.
103–7. **When . . . Richmond.** Although the play on *Rougemont* (Red Mountain) and *Richmond* is forced, the incident is historical.
106. **bard of Ireland.** Irish bards were credited with prophetic powers.

K. Rich. Ay, what's a' clock?   109
Buck. I am thus bold to put your Grace in mind
Of what you promis'd me.
K. Rich.   Well, but what's a' clock?
Buck. Upon the stroke of ten.
K. Rich.   Well, let it strike.
Buck. Why let it strike?
K. Rich. Because that like a Jack thou keep'st the
    stroke
Betwixt thy begging and my meditation.   115
I am not in the giving vein to-day.]
Buck. May it please you to resolve me in my suit.
K. Rich. Thou troublest me, I am not in the vein.
                              Exit [with all but Buckingham].
Buck. And is it thus? repays he my deep service
With such contempt? Made I him king for this?   120
O, let me think on Hastings, and be gone
To Brecknock while my fearful head is on!   *Exit.*

[SCENE III]

Enter TYRREL.

Tyr. The tyrannous and bloody act is done,
The most arch deed of piteous massacre
That ever yet this land was guilty of.
Dighton and Forrest, who I did suborn
To do this piece of [ruthless] butchery,   5
Albeit they were flesh'd villains, bloody dogs,
Melted with tenderness and [kind] compassion,
Wept like [two] children in their deaths' sad story.
"O, thus," quoth Dighton, "lay the gentle babes."
"Thus, thus," quoth Forrest, "girdling one another 10
Within their alablaster innocent arms.
Their lips were four red roses on a stalk,
[Which] in their summer beauty kiss'd each other.
A book of prayers on their pillow lay,
Which [once]," quoth Forrest, "almost chang'd my
    mind;   15
But O! the devil"—there the villain stopp'd;
When Dighton thus told on, "We smothered
The most replenished sweet work of Nature
That from the prime creation e'er she framed."

Hence both are gone with conscience and remorse 20
They could not speak; and so I left them both,
To bear this tidings to the bloody King.

Enter [KING] RICHARD.

And here he comes. All health, my sovereign lord!
K. Rich. Kind Tyrrel, am I happy in thy news?
Tyr. If to have done the thing you gave in charge
Beget your happiness, be happy then,   26
For it is done.
K. Rich.   But didst thou see them dead?
Tyr. I did, my lord.
K. Rich.   And buried, gentle Tyrrel?
Tyr. The chaplain of the Tower hath buried them,
But where (to say the truth) I do not know.   30
K. Rich. Come to me, Tyrrel, soon, [at] after-
    supper,
When thou shalt tell the process of their death.
Mean time, but think how I may do thee good,
And be inheritor of thy desire.   34
Farewell till then.
Tyr.   I humbly take my leave. [*Exit.*]
K. Rich. The son of Clarence have I pent up close,
His daughter meanly have I match'd in marriage,
The sons of Edward sleep in Abraham's bosom,
And Anne my wife hath bid this world good night.
Now for I know the Britain Richmond aims   40
At young Elizabeth, my brother's daughter,
And by that knot looks proudly on the crown,
To her go I, a jolly thriving wooer.

Enter RATCLIFFE.

Rat. My lord—
K. Rich. Good or bad news, that thou com'st in so
    bluntly?   45
Rat. Bad news, my lord. Morton is fled to Rich-
    mond,
And Buckingham, back'd with the hardy Welshmen,
Is in the field, and still his power increaseth.
K. Rich. Ely with Richmond troubles me more
    near

109–15. Ay . . . meditation. The general sense is that Buckingham, obviously on the point of making a request but still not making it, is like a Jack (the manikin in old clocks that strikes the bell) poised for action. Thus he interferes with Richard's "meditation."
117. resolve me in: satisfy me about.
119. deep: i.e. full of danger to oneself.
122. Brecknock: mansion house in Wales. **fearful:** full of fears. According to More (Bullough, III, 281), Buckingham was so much appalled by Richard's murder of the princes ("to the whiche," he told John Morton, Bishop of Ely, "God be my judge I never agreed nor condiscended") that he "abhorred the sighte and much more the compaignie of hym" and so retired to Brecknock.

IV.iii. Location: London. The palace.
2. arch: i.e. heinous.
4. Dighton and Forrest. For the murder of the princes, according to More (Bullough, III, 279), Tyrrel "appointed Myles Forest one of the foure that before kepte them, a felowe fleshe bred in murther before tyme: and to him he joyned one John Dighton his awne horsekeper, a bygge broade square and strong knave."
6. flesh'd: accustomed to slaughter (a term applied to hounds after they had eaten of the first game they had killed).
11. alablaster: alabaster, marble-white.
18. replenished: complete. **19. prime:** first.

20. gone: overwhelmed. **21. speak:** express, utter.
25. gave in charge: commissioned. **31. after-supper:** dessert.
32. process: story. **34. inheritor:** possessor.
36–37. The son . . . marriage. On Clarence's son Edward, Earl of Warwick, see note to IV.ii.55. Perhaps Shakespeare confused the daughter "meanly" matched in marriage with Lady Cicely, one of Edward IV's children, who, according to Hall (Bullough, III, 254), "not so fortunate as faire, firste wedded to the viscounte Welles, after to one Kyne and lived not in greate wealthe."
38. Abraham's bosom: i.e. heaven (see Luke 16:22 ff.).
39. Anne . . . good night. According to Hall (Bullough, III, 287–88), Richard spread the rumor of his wife's death "to thentent that she takyng some conceipte of this straung fame, should fall into some sodayne sicknes or grevous maladye." As a consequence, "either by inward thought and pensyvenes of hearte, or by intoxicacion of poyson (which is affirmed to be most likely) within a few daies after, the quene departed oute of this transitorie lyfe, and was with dewe solempnite buried in the churche of seint Peter at Westminster." She died in March 1485, less than a year after her only son.
40. for: because. **Britain:** Breton. **42. knot:** alliance.
46. Morton. John Morton (1420?–1500), Bishop of Ely, an associate of Buckingham who ultimately escaped to Flanders, was recalled by Henry VII, and thereafter became one of the new king's most trusted advisers. Named Archbishop of Canterbury in 1486 and cardinal in 1493, he was an early patron of Thomas More and perhaps the author of the Latin version of More's hostile biography of Richard III that Hall and Grafton and others incorporated into their chronicles and that Shakespeare followed closely in the writing of this play.

Richard III
IV.iii

Than Buckingham and his rash-levied strength. 50
Come, I have learn'd that fearful commenting
Is leaden servitor to dull delay;
Delay [leads] impotent and snail-pac'd beggary.
Then fiery expedition be my wing,
Jove's Mercury, and herald for a king! 55
Go muster men. My counsel is my shield;
We must be brief when traitors brave the field.

Exeunt.

SCENE [IV]

Enter old QUEEN MARGARET.

Q. Mar. So now prosperity begins to mellow
And drop into the rotten mouth of death.
Here in these confines slily have I lurk'd,
To watch the waning of mine enemies.
A dire induction am I witness to, 5
And will to France, hoping the consequence
Will prove as bitter, black, and tragical.
Withdraw thee, wretched Margaret; who comes here?

[Retires.]

Enter DUCHESS [OF YORK] *and* QUEEN [ELIZABETH].

Q. Eliz. Ah, my poor princes! ah, my tender
babes!
My [unblown] flow'rs, new-appearing sweets! 10
If yet your gentle souls fly in the air
And be not fix'd in doom perpetual,
Hover about me with your aery wings
And hear your mother's lamentation!
Q. Mar. [Aside.] Hover about her; say that right
for right 15
Hath dimm'd your infant morn to aged night.
Duch. So many miseries have craz'd my voice
That my woe-wearied tongue is still and mute.
Edward Plantagenet, why art thou dead?
Q. Mar. [Aside.] Plantagenet doth quit Plantagenet,
Edward for Edward pays a dying debt. 21
Q. Eliz. Wilt thou, O God, fly from such gentle
lambs,
And throw them in the entrails of the wolf?
When didst thou sleep when such a deed was done?
Q. Mar. [Aside.] When holy Harry died, and my
sweet son. 25
Duch. Dead life, blind sight, poor mortal-living
ghost,
Woe's scene, world's shame, grave's due by life
usurp'd,

---

50. **rash-levied:** hastily recruited.
51. **fearful commenting:** timorous discussion.
53. **leads:** leads to.   54. **expedition:** haste.
55. **Mercury:** messenger of the gods.   57. **brave:** challenge.

IV.iv. Location: London. Before the palace.
5. **induction:** beginning (as of a play).
6. **will to France.** Actually, Margaret had left England for the last time in 1476, some nine years before the time represented in this scene.   **consequence:** conclusion (as of a play).
10. **sweets:** flowers.   15. **right for right:** i.e. avenging justice.
17. **craz'd:** cracked.   20. **quit:** requite.
21. **Edward for Edward:** i.e. Edward V for Prince Edward, Margaret's son.   **dying debt:** i.e. a debt to be paid with death.
25. **holy Harry:** i.e. Henry VI.
26. **mortal-living ghost:** i.e. a ghost doomed to life.
27. **grave's . . . usurp'd:** i.e. one who by being still alive is depriving the grave of its due.

Brief abstract and record of tedious days,
Rest thy unrest on England's lawful earth,

[Sitting down.]

Unlawfully made drunk with innocent blood! 30
Q. Eliz. Ah, that thou wouldst as soon afford a
grave
As thou canst yield a melancholy seat!
Then would I hide my bones, not rest them here.
Ah, who hath any cause to mourn but we?

[Sitting down by her.]

Q. Mar. [Coming forward.] If ancient sorrow be
most reverent, 35
Give mine the benefit of seniory,
And let my griefs frown on the upper hand.
If sorrow can admit society,

[Sitting down with them.]

[Tell over your woes again by viewing mine:]
I had an Edward, till a Richard kill'd him; 40
I had a [Harry], till a Richard kill'd him:
Thou hadst an Edward, till a Richard kill'd him;
Thou hadst a Richard, till a Richard kill'd him.
Duch. I had a Richard too, and thou didst kill him;
I had a Rutland too, thou [holp'st] to kill him. 45
Q. Mar. Thou hadst a Clarence too, and Richard
kill'd him.
From forth the kennel of thy womb hath crept
A hell-hound that doth hunt us all to death:
That dog, that had his teeth before his eyes
To worry lambs and lap their gentle blood, 50
That foul defacer of God's handiwork,
That excellent grand tyrant of the earth
That reigns in galled eyes of weeping souls,
Thy womb let loose to chase us to our graves.
O upright, just, and true-disposing God, 55
How do I thank thee that this carnal cur
Preys on the issue of his mother's body,
And makes her pew-fellow with others' moan!
Duch. O Harry's wife, triumph not in my woes!
God witness with me, I have wept for thine. 60
Q. Mar. Bear with me; I am hungry for revenge,
And now I cloy me with beholding it.
Thy Edward he is dead, that kill'd my Edward;
[Thy] other Edward dead, to quit my Edward;
Young York he is but boot, because both they 65
Match'd not the high perfection of my loss.
Thy Clarence he is dead that stabb'd my Edward,
And the beholders of this frantic play,
Th' adulterate Hastings, Rivers, Vaughan, Grey,
Untimely smoth'red in their dusky graves. 70
Richard yet lives, hell's black intelligencer,
Only reserv'd their factor to buy souls
And send them thither; but at hand, at hand,
Ensues his piteous and unpitied end.
Earth gapes, hell burns, fiends roar, saints pray, 75

---

28. **abstract:** epitome.
36. **seniory:** seniority.   37. **on . . . hand:** in place of precedence.
42, 43. **Thou:** i.e. Queen Elizabeth.
44. **Richard:** i.e. her husband.   50. **worry:** pull to pieces.
53. **galled:** sore (with weeping).   56. **carnal:** carnivorous.
58. **pew-fellow:** companion.   63. **Thy Edward:** i.e. Edward IV.
64. **Thy other Edward:** i.e. Edward V.   **quit:** pay for (as a penalty).
65. **but boot:** is merely something given in addition.
69. **adulterate:** adulterous.   71. **intelligencer:** spy, agent.
72. **reserv'd their factor:** retained as (hell's) agent.

To have him suddenly convey'd from hence.
Cancel his bond of life, dear God, I pray,
That I may live and say, "The dog is dead."
    Q. Eliz. O, thou didst prophesy the time would
      come
That I should wish for thee to help me curse   80
That bottled spider, that foul bunch-back'd toad!
    Q. Mar. I call'd thee then vain flourish of my
      fortune;
I call'd thee then poor shadow, painted queen,
The presentation of but what I was;
The flattering index of a direful pageant;   85
One heav'd a-high, to be hurl'd down below;
A mother only mock'd with two fair babes;
A dream of what thou wast, a garish flag
To be the aim of every dangerous shot;
A sign of dignity, a breath, a bubble;   90
A queen in jest, only to fill the scene.
Where is thy husband now? Where be thy brothers?
Where be thy two sons? Wherein dost thou joy?
Who sues, and kneels, and says, "God save the
    Queen"?
Where be the bending peers that flattered thee?   95
Where be the thronging troops that followed thee?
Decline all this, and see what now thou art:
For happy wife, a most distressed widow;
For joyful mother, one that wails the name;
For one being sued to, one that humbly sues;   100
For queen, a very caitiff crown'd with care;
For she that scorn'd at me, now scorn'd of me;
For she being feared of all, now fearing one;
For she commanding all, obey'd of none.
Thus hath the course of justice whirl'd about,   105
And left thee but a very prey to time,
Having no more but thought of what thou wast,
To torture thee the more, being what thou art.
Thou didst usurp my place, and dost thou not
Usurp the just proportion of my sorrow?   110
Now thy proud neck bears half my burthen'd yoke,
From which even here I slip my [weary] head,
And leave the burthen of it all on thee.
Farewell, York's wife, and queen of sad mischance,
These English woes shall make me smile in France.
    Q. Eliz. O thou well skill'd in curses, stay awhile,
And teach me how to curse mine enemies!   117
    Q. Mar. Forbear to sleep the [nights], and fast the
    [days];
Compare dead happiness with living woe;
Think that thy babes were sweeter than they were,
And he that slew them fouler than he is.   121
Bett'ring thy loss makes the bad causer worse;
Revolving this will teach thee how to curse.
    Q. Eliz. My words are dull, O, quicken them with
    thine!
    Q. Mar. Thy woes will make them sharp and
    pierce like mine. *Exit [Queen] Margaret.*   125

    Duch. Why should calamity be full of words?
    Q. Eliz. Windy attorneys to their client's woes,
Aery succeeders of [intestate] joys,
Poor breathing orators of miseries,
Let them have scope! though what they will impart
Help nothing else, yet do they ease the heart.   131
    Duch. If so then, be not tongue-tied; go with me,
And in the breath of bitter words let's smother
My damned son that thy two sweet sons smother'd.
The trumpet sounds, be copious in exclaims.   135

Enter KING RICHARD *and his* TRAIN [*marching, with
Drums and Trumpets*].

    K. Rich. Who intercepts me in my expedition?
    Duch. O, she that might have intercepted thee,
By strangling thee in her accursed womb,
From all the slaughters, wretch, that thou hast done!
    Q. Eliz. Hid'st thou that forehead with a golden
    crown   140
Where should be branded, if that right were right,
The slaughter of the prince that ow'd that crown,
And the dire death of my poor sons and brothers?
Tell me, thou villain-slave, where are my children?
    Duch. Thou toad, thou toad, where is thy brother
    Clarence?   145
And little Ned Plantagenet, his son?
    Q. Eliz. Where is the gentle Rivers, Vaughan,
    Grey?
    Duch. Where is kind Hastings?
    K. Rich. A flourish, trumpets! strike alarum,
    drums!
Let not the heavens hear these tell-tale women   150
Rail on the Lord's anointed. Strike, I say!
                  Flourish. Alarums.
Either be patient and entreat me fair,
Or with the clamorous report of war
Thus will I drown your exclamations.
    Duch. Art thou my son?   155
    K. Rich. Ay, I thank God, my father, and yourself.
    Duch. Then patiently hear my impatience.
    K. Rich. Madam, I have a touch of your condition,
That cannot brook the accent of reproof.
    Duch. O, let me speak!
    K. Rich.   Do then, but I'll not hear.
    Duch. I will be mild and gentle in my words.   161
    K. Rich. And brief, good mother, for I am in haste.
    Duch. Art thou so hasty? I have stay'd for thee,
God knows, in torment and in agony.
    K. Rich. And came I not at last to comfort you?   165
    Duch. No, by the holy rood, thou know'st it well,
Thou cam'st on earth to make the earth my hell.
A grievous burthen was thy birth to me,
Tetchy and wayward was thy infancy;
Thy school-days frightful, desp'rate, wild, and furious,
Thy prime of manhood daring, bold, and venturous;   171

---

85. **index:** table of contents prefixed to a book, hence prologue.
88–89. **garish . . . shot:** i.e. gaudy or conspicuous standard-bearer
who draws the enemy fire.   90. **sign:** (mere) token.
97. **Decline:** recite in order.   101. **caitiff:** pitiful wretch.
102, 103, 104. **of:** by.   111. **burthen'd:** burdensome.
122. **Bett'ring:** magnifying.   124. **quicken:** put life into.

128. **intestate:** dead without bequeathing anything.
135 s.d. **Drums and Trumpets:** drummers and trumpeters.
136. **expedition:** (1) haste; (2) march.   142. **ow'd:** owned.
146. **Ned Plantagenet.** Actually, he was not one of Richard's victims.
See note to IV.ii.55.   152. **entreat me fair:** treat me courteously.
158. **condition:** disposition.   169. **Tetchy:** fretful.
170. **frightful:** full of fears.   171. **prime of:** early.

Richard III
IV.iv

Thy age confirm'd, proud, subtle, sly, and bloody,
More mild, but yet more harmful—kind in hatred.
What comfortable hour canst thou name
That ever grac'd me with thy company?   175
 K. Rich. Faith, none, but Humphrey Hour, that
  call'd your Grace
To breakfast once, forth of my company.
If I be so disgracious in your eye,
Let me march on and not offend you, madam.
Strike up the drum.
 Duch.   I prithee hear me speak.   180
 K. Rich. You speak too bitterly.
 Duch.   Hear me a word;
For I shall never speak to thee again.
 K. Rich. So.
 Duch. Either thou wilt die by God's just ordinance
Ere from this war thou turn a conqueror,   185
Or I with grief and extreme age shall perish
And never more behold thy face again.
Therefore take with thee my most grievous curse,
Which in the day of battle tire thee more
Than all the complete armor that thou wear'st!   190
My prayers on the adverse party fight,
And there the little souls of Edward's children
Whisper the spirits of thine enemies
And promise them success and victory.
Bloody thou art, bloody will be thy end;   195
Shame serves thy life and doth thy death attend. *Exit.*
 Q. Eliz. Though far more cause, yet much less
  spirit to curse
Abides in me; I say amen to her.
 K. Rich. Stay, madam, I must talk a word with
  you.
 Q. Eliz. I have no moe sons of the royal blood 200
For thee to slaughter. For my daughters, Richard,
They shall be praying nuns, not weeping queens;
And therefore level not to hit their lives.
 K. Rich. You have a daughter call'd Elizabeth,
Virtuous and fair, royal and gracious.   205
 Q. Eliz. And must she die for this? O, let her live!
And I'll corrupt her manners, stain her beauty,
Slander myself as false to Edward's bed,
Throw over her the veil of infamy.
So she may live unscarr'd of bleeding slaughter,   210
I will confess she was not Edward's daughter.
 K. Rich. Wrong not her birth, she is a royal
  princess.
 Q. Eliz. To save her life, I'll say she is not so.
 K. Rich. Her life is safest only in her birth.   214
 Q. Eliz. And only in that safety died her brothers.
 K. Rich. Lo at their birth good stars were op-
  posite.
 Q. Eliz. No, to their lives ill friends were contrary.
 K. Rich. All unavoided is the doom of destiny.

 Q. Eliz. True—when avoided grace makes destiny:
My babes were destin'd to a fairer death,   220
If grace had blest thee with a fairer life.
 K. Rich. You speak as if that I had slain my
  cousins!
 Q. Eliz. Cousins indeed, and by their uncle
  cozen'd
Of comfort, kingdom, kindred, freedom, life.
Whose hand soever lanch'd their tender hearts,   225
Thy head (all indirectly) gave direction.
No doubt the murd'rous knife was dull and blunt
Till it was whetted on thy stone-hard heart
To revel in the entrails of my lambs.
But that still use of grief makes wild grief tame,   230
My tongue should to thy ears not name my boys
Till that my nails were anchor'd in thine eyes;
And I, in such a desp'rate bay of death,
Like a poor bark of sails and tackling reft,
Rush all to pieces on thy rocky bosom.   235
 K. Rich. Madam, so thrive I in my enterprise
And dangerous success of bloody wars,
As I intend more good to you and yours
Than ever you [or] yours by me were harm'd!
 Q. Eliz. What good is cover'd with the face of
  heaven,   240
To be discover'd, that can do me good?
 K. Rich. Th' advancement of your children, gentle
  lady.
 Q. Eliz. Up to some scaffold, there to lose their
  heads.
 K. Rich. Unto the dignity and height of fortune,
The high imperial type of this earth's glory.   245
 Q. Eliz. Flatter my sorrow with report of it;
Tell me, what state, what dignity, what honor,
Canst thou demise to any child of mine?
 K. Rich. Even all I have—ay, and myself and all—
Will I withal endow a child of thine;   250
So in the Lethe of thy angry soul
Thou drown the sad remembrance of those wrongs
Which thou supposest I have done to thee.
 Q. Eliz. Be brief, lest that the process of thy kind-
  ness
Last longer telling than thy kindness' date.   255
 K. Rich. Then know that from my soul I love thy
  daughter.
 Q. Eliz. My daughter's mother thinks it with her
  soul.
 K. Rich. What do you think?
 Q. Eliz. That thou dost love my daughter from thy
  soul;
So from thy soul's love didst thou love her brothers, 260
And from my heart's love I do thank thee for it.

219. **avoided grace:** one who rejects God's grace, i.e. Richard.
223. **cozen'd:** cheated.
225. **Whose . . . lanch'd:** whatever hand pierced.
226. **all:** although. 230. **But:** except. **still:** continual.
233. **bay:** inlet. 234. **reft:** bereft.
236–39. **so . . . harm'd:** i.e. may the success of my hazardous endeavors be as certain as my determination to do more good to you and your children than I have done harm in the past.
245. **type:** symbol, i.e. the crown. 248. **demise:** transmit.
251. **Lethe:** river of oblivion in the underworld.
254. **process:** story. 256. **from:** with.
259. 260, 261. **from:** apart from.

172. **age confirm'd:** settled maturity. Richard died at thirty-three.
173. **kind in hatred:** vindictive under a pretense of kindness.
176. **Humphrey Hour.** An unexplained sarcasm. Proverbially, "to dine with Duke Humphrey" was to go hungry.
178. **disgracious:** displeasing. 191. **party:** side.
196. **serves:** attends. 200. **moe:** more. 203. **level:** aim.
204. **Elizabeth.** See note to IV.ii.60. 207. **manners:** morals.
210. **So:** provided. 216. **opposite:** adverse.
218. **unavoided:** unavoidable.

K. Rich. Be not so hasty to confound my meaning:
I mean that with my soul I love thy daughter,
And do intend to make her Queen of England.

Q. Eliz. Well then, who dost thou mean shall be
her king? 265

K. Rich. Even he that makes her queen. Who
[should be else]?

Q. Eliz. What, thou?

K. Rich. Even so. How think you of it?

Q. Eliz. How canst thou woo her?

K. Rich. That [would I] learn of you,
As one being best acquainted with her humor.

Q. Eliz. And wilt thou learn of me?

K. Rich. Madam, with all my heart.

Q. Eliz. Send to her by the man that slew her
brothers 271
A pair of bleeding hearts; thereon engrave
"Edward" and "York"; then haply will she weep.
Therefore present to her—as [sometimes] Margaret
Did to thy father, steep'd in Rutland's blood— 275
A [handkercher], which, say to her, did drain
The purple sap from her sweet brother's body,
And bid her wipe her weeping eyes withal.
If this inducement move her not to love,
Send her a letter of thy noble deeds: 280
Tell her thou mad'st away her uncle Clarence,
Her uncle Rivers, ay (and for her sake!),
Mad'st quick conveyance with her good aunt Anne.

K. Rich. You mock me, madam, this [is] not the
way
To win your daughter.

Q. Eliz. There is no other way, 285
Unless thou couldst put on some other shape
And not be Richard that hath done all this.

K. Rich. Say that I did all this for love of her.

Q. Eliz. Nay then indeed she cannot choose but
hate thee,
Having bought love with such a bloody spoil. 290

K. Rich. Look what is done cannot be now
amended:
Men shall deal unadvisedly sometimes,
Which after-hours gives leisure to repent.
If I did take the kingdom from your sons,
To make amends I'll give it to your daughter; 295
If I have kill'd the issue of your womb,
To quicken your increase, I will beget
Mine issue of your blood upon your daughter.
A grandam's name is little less in love
Than is the doting title of a mother; 300
They are as children but one step below,
Even of your metal, of your very blood;
Of all one pain, save for a night of groans
Endur'd of her, for whom you bid like sorrow.
Your children were vexation to your youth, 305
But mine shall be a comfort to your age.
The loss you have is but a son being king,
And by that loss your daughter is made queen.

I cannot make you what amends I would,
Therefore accept such kindness as I can. 310
Dorset your son, that with a fearful soul
Leads discontented steps in foreign soil,
This fair alliance quickly shall call home
To high promotions and great dignity.
The King, that calls your beauteous daughter wife,
Familiarly shall call thy Dorset brother; 316
Again shall you be mother to a king;
And all the ruins of distressful times
Repair'd with double riches of content.
What? we have many goodly days to see: 320
The liquid drops of tears that you have shed
Shall come again, transform'd to orient pearl,
Advantaging their love with interest
Of ten times double gain of happiness.
Go then, my mother, to thy daughter go, 325
Make bold her bashful years with your experience;
Prepare her ears to hear a wooer's tale;
Put in her tender heart th' aspiring flame
Of golden sovereignty; acquaint the Princess
With the sweet silent hours of marriage joys; 330
And when this arm of mine hath chastised
The petty rebel, dull-brain'd Buckingham,
Bound with triumphant garlands will I come
And lead thy daughter to a conqueror's bed;
To whom I will retail my conquest won, 335
And she shall be sole victoress, Caesar's Caesar.

Q. Eliz. What were I best to say? Her father's
brother
Would be her lord? Or shall I say her uncle?
Or he that slew her brothers and her uncles?
Under what title shall I woo for thee, 340
That God, the law, my honor, and her love
Can make seem pleasing to her tender years?

K. Rich. Infer fair England's peace by this alliance.

Q. Eliz. Which she shall purchase with still-lasting
war.

K. Rich. Tell her the King, that may command,
entreats. 345

Q. Eliz. That at her hands which the King's King
forbids.

K. Rich. Say she shall be a high and mighty queen.

Q. Eliz. To vail the title, as her mother doth.

K. Rich. Say I will love her everlastingly. 349

Q. Eliz. But how long shall that title "ever" last?

K. Rich. Sweetly in force unto her fair live's end.

Q. Eliz. But how long fairly shall her sweet life
last? 352

K. Rich. As long as heaven and nature lengthens it.

Q. Eliz. As long as hell and Richard likes of it.

K. Rich. Say I, her sovereign, am her subject low.

---

269. **humor:** mood.
274–275. **as ... blood.** See *3 Henry VI*, I.iv.79–83.
283. **conveyance with:** riddance of.
290. **spoil:** slaughter (a term from hunting).
297. **quicken your increase:** i.e. give (new) life to your progeny.
302. **metal:** substance.　304. **of:** by.　**bid:** bided, endured.

310. **can:** i.e. can provide.
311–12. **Dorset ... soil.** When, on his mother's urging (IV.i.38–46), Dorset fled from Richard's terror he first went to Yorkshire, then took part in Buckingham's unsuccessful uprising (1483), and thereafter made his way to Brittany, where he joined Richmond. Although Shakespeare places him at the battle of Bosworth Field (V.iii), he did not in fact return to England until recalled by the new king in 1486.　311. **fearful:** full of fears.　322. **orient:** shining.
323. **Advantaging:** adding to the value of.　335. **retail:** relate.
343. **Infer:** allege.
348. **vail:** lower, yield (in token of submission).
351. **live's:** life's.

Richard III
IV.iv

Q. Eliz.   But she, your subject, loathes such sover-
eignty.   356
K. Rich.   Be eloquent in my behalf to her.
Q. Eliz.   An honest tale speeds best being plainly
told.
K. Rich.   Then plainly to her tell my loving tale.
Q. Eliz.   Plain and not honest is too harsh a style.
K. Rich.   Your reasons are too shallow and too
quick.   361
Q. Eliz.   O no, my reasons are too deep and dead—
Too deep and dead, poor infants, in their graves.
K. Rich.   Harp not on that string, madam, that is
past.
[*Q. Eliz.*]   Harp on it still shall I till heart-strings
break.   365
[*K. Rich.*]   Now by my George, my Garter, and
my crown—
Q. Eliz.   Profan'd, dishonor'd, and the third
usurp'd.
K. Rich.   I swear—
Q. Eliz.   By nothing, for this is no oath:
Thy George, profan'd, hath lost his lordly honor;
Thy Garter, blemish'd, pawn'd his knightly virtue; 370
Thy crown, usurp'd, disgrac'd his kingly glory.
If something thou wouldst swear to be believ'd,
Swear then by something that thou hast not wrong'd.
K. Rich.   Then by myself—
Q. Eliz.   Thyself is self-misus'd.
K. Rich.   Now by the world—
Q. Eliz.   'Tis full of thy foul wrongs.   375
K. Rich.   My father's death—
Q. Eliz.   Thy life hath it dishonor'd.
K. Rich.   Why then, by [God]—
Q. Eliz.   [God's] wrong is most of all:
If thou didst fear to break an oath with him,
The unity the King my husband made
Thou hadst not broken, nor my brothers died.   380
If thou hadst fear'd to break an oath by him,
Th' imperial metal, circling now thy head,
Had grac'd the tender temples of my child,
And both the Princes had been breathing here,
Which now, two tender bedfellows for dust,   385
Thy broken faith hath made the prey for worms.
What canst thou swear by now?
K. Rich.   The time to come.
Q. Eliz.   That thou hast wronged in the time
o'erpast;
For I myself have many tears to wash
Hereafter time, for time past wrong'd by thee.   390
The children live whose fathers thou hast slaughter'd,
Ungovern'd youth, to wail it [in] their age;
The parents live whose children thou hast butcher'd,
Old barren plants, to wail it with their age.
Swear not by time to come, for that thou hast   395
Misus'd ere us'd, by times ill-us'd [o'erpast].
K. Rich.   As I intend to prosper and repent,
So thrive I in my dangerous affairs

Of hostile arms! Myself myself confound!
Heaven and fortune bar me happy hours!   400
Day, yield me not thy light, nor, night, thy rest!
Be opposite all planets of good luck
To my proceeding, if with dear heart's love,
Immaculate devotion, holy thoughts,
I tender not thy beauteous princely daughter!   405
In her consists my happiness and thine;
Without her, follows to myself and thee,
Herself, the land, and many a Christian soul,
Death, desolation, ruin, and decay.
It cannot be avoided but by this;   410
It will not be avoided but by this.
Therefore, dear mother—I must call you so—
Be the attorney of my love to her.
Plead what I will be, not what I have been;
Not my deserts, but what I will deserve.   415
Urge the necessity and state of times,
And be not peevish[-fond] in great designs.
Q. Eliz.   Shall I be tempted of the devil thus?
K. Rich.   Ay, if the devil tempt you to do good.
Q. Eliz.   Shall I forget myself to be myself?   420
K. Rich.   Ay, if yourself's remembrance wrong
yourself.
Q. Eliz.   Yet thou didst kill my children.
K. Rich.   But in your daughter's womb I bury
them;
Where in that nest of spicery they will breed
Selves of themselves, to your recomfortture.   425
Q. Eliz.   Shall I go win my daughter to thy will?
K. Rich.   And be a happy mother by the deed.
Q. Eliz.   I go. Write to me very shortly,
And you shall understand from me her mind.
K. Rich.   Bear her my true love's kiss; and so
farewell.   *Exit Queen* [*Elizabeth*].
Relenting fool, and shallow, changing woman!   431

Enter RATCLIFFE, [CATESBY *following*].

How now? what news?
Rat.   Most mighty sovereign, on the western coast
Rideth a puissant navy; to our shores
Throng many doubtful hollow-hearted friends,   435
Unarm'd, and unresolv'd to beat them back.
'Tis thought that Richmond is their admiral;
And there they hull, expecting but the aid
Of Buckingham to welcome them ashore.
K. Rich.   Some light-foot friend post to the Duke of
Norfolk;   440
Ratcliffe, thyself—or Catesby—where is he?
Cate.   Here, my good lord.
K. Rich.   Catesby, fly to the Duke.
Cate.   I will, my lord, with all convenient haste.
K. Rich.   [Ratcliffe], come hither. Post to Salis-
bury;
When thou com'st thither— [*To Catesby.*] Dull un-
mindful villain,   445
Why stay'st thou here, and go'st not to the Duke?

---

358. **speeds**: succeeds.   361. **quick**: hasty.
366. **George**: pendant with figures of St. George and the Dragon,
worn by members of the Order of the Garter. **Garter**: the badge
of the Order of the Garter, a blue velvet ribbon worn below the left
knee.   390. **Hereafter time**: the future.
392. **Ungovern'd**: i.e. without parents to guide them.

405. **tender**: cherish.   417. **peevish-fond**: perversely foolish.
424. **nest of spicery.** A nest of spices was both the funeral pyre and
the birthplace of the phoenix, the fabulous bird who, every five
hundred years, was consumed by fire and then rose from its own ashes.
425. **recomfortture**: consolation.   434. **puissant**: mighty.
438. **hull**: drift.   444. **Salisbury**: a town in Wiltshire.

Cate. First, mighty liege, tell me your Highness'
pleasure,
What from your Grace I shall deliver to him.

K. Rich. O, true, good Catesby. Bid him levy
straight
The greatest strength and power that he can make, 450
And meet me suddenly at Salisbury.

Cate. I go.   *Exit.*

Rat. What, may it please you, shall I do at
Salisbury?

K. Rich. Why, what wouldst thou do there before
I go?   454

Rat. Your Highness told me I should post before.

K. Rich. My mind is chang'd.

Enter LORD STANLEY.

Stanley, what news with you?

Stan. None good, my liege, to please you with the
hearing,
Nor none so bad but well may be reported.

K. Rich. Hoy-day, a riddle! neither good nor bad!
What need'st thou run so many miles about, 460
When thou mayest tell thy tale the nearest way?
Once more, what news?

Stan.   Richmond is on the seas.

K. Rich. There let him sink, and be the seas on
him!
White-liver'd runagate, what doth he there?

Stan. I know not, mighty sovereign, but by guess.

K. Rich. Well, as you guess?   466

Stan. Stirr'd up by Dorset, Buckingham, and
Morton,
He makes for England, here to claim the crown.

K. Rich. Is the chair empty? is the sword un-
sway'd?
Is the King dead? the empire unpossess'd?   470
What heir of York is there alive but we?
And who is England's king but great York's heir?
Then tell me, what makes he upon the seas?

Stan. Unless for that, my liege, I cannot guess.

K. Rich. Unless for that he comes to be your liege,
You cannot guess wherefore the Welshman comes. 476
Thou wilt revolt and fly to him, I fear.

Stan. No, my good lord, therefore mistrust me not.

K. Rich. Where is thy power then, to beat him
back?
Where be thy tenants and thy followers?   480
Are they not now upon the western shore,
Safe-conducting the rebels from their ships?

Stan. No, my good lord, my friends are in the
north.

K. Rich. Cold friends to me! What do they in the
north,
When they should serve their sovereign in the west?

Stan. They have not been commanded, mighty
King.   486

Pleaseth your Majesty to give me leave,
I'll muster up my friends and meet your Grace
Where and what time your Majesty shall please.

K. Rich. Ay, thou wouldst be gone to join with
Richmond;   490
But I'll not trust thee.

Stan.   Most mighty sovereign,
You have no cause to hold my friendship doubtful.
I never was nor never will be false.

K. Rich. Go then, and muster men; but leave be-
hind
Your son, George Stanley. Look your heart be firm,
Or else his head's assurance is but frail.   496

Stan. So deal with him as I prove true to you.

Exit Stanley.

Enter a MESSENGER.

[1.] Mess. My gracious sovereign, now in Devon-
shire,
As I by friends am well advertised,
Sir Edward Courtney and the haughty prelate,   500
Bishop of Exeter, his elder brother,
With many moe confederates, are in arms.

Enter another MESSENGER.

[2.] Mess. In Kent, my liege, the Guilfords are in
arms,
And every hour more competitors
Flock to the rebels, and their power grows strong.

Enter another MESSENGER.

[3.] Mess. My lord, the army of great Buckingham—   506

K. Rich. Out on [you], owls! nothing but songs of
death?   *He striketh him.*
There, take thou that, till thou bring better news.

[3.] Mess. The news I have to tell your Majesty
Is that by sudden floods and fall of waters   510
Buckingham's army is dispers'd and scatter'd,
And he himself wand'red away alone,
No man knows whither.

K. Rich.   I cry thee mercy;
There is my purse to cure that blow of thine.
Hath any well-advised friend proclaim'd   515
Reward to him that brings the traitor in?

[3.] Mess. Such proclamation hath been made, my
lord.

Enter another MESSENGER.

[4.] Mess. Sir Thomas Lovel and Lord Marquess
Dorset,
'Tis said, my liege, in Yorkshire are in arms.
But this good comfort bring I to your Highness: 520
The Britain navy is dispers'd by tempest.

447. **liege:** sovereign.   451. **suddenly:** promptly.
459. **Hoy-day:** an exclamation of impatience.
464. **White-liver'd runagate:** cowardly fugitive.
470. **empire:** kingdom.   473. **makes he:** is he doing.
476. **Welshman.** Richmond was the grandson of Owen Tudor, a
Welshman to whom Katherine of Valois, widow of Henry V, bore
three sons and a daughter. It is uncertain that they were ever married.

496. **assurance:** safety.
498–538. **My . . . me.** Shakespeare telescopes Hall's accounts (Bullough, III, 283–85, 288–89) of Richmond's abortive attempt to invade
England and join forces with Buckingham and his associates in October 1483 and his successful invasion in August 1485.
499. **advertised:** informed.
500–502. **Sir . . . arms.** One of the many details that Shakespeare
got from Hall (Bullough, III, 283): "Sir Edward Courtney and Peter
his brother bishop of Exsetter, reised another army in devonshire and
cornewall." Actually, Sir Edward and Peter Courtney were cousins.
504. **competitors:** associates.   521. **Britain:** Breton.

Richard III
IV.iv

Richmond in Dorsetshire sent out a boat
Unto the shore, to ask those on the banks
If they were his assistants, yea or no;
Who answer'd him, they came from Buckingham 525
Upon his party. He, mistrusting them,
Hois'd sail, and made his course again for Britain.

   K. Rich. March on, march on, since we are up in
     arms,
If not to fight with foreign enemies,
Yet to beat down these rebels here at home. 530

Enter CATESBY.

   Cate. My liege, the Duke of Buckingham is taken—
That is the best news. That the Earl of Richmond
Is with a mighty power landed at Milford
Is colder [tidings], yet they must be told.

   K. Rich. Away towards Salisbury! while we reason
     here, 535
A royal battle might be won and lost.
Some one take order Buckingham be brought
To Salisbury, the rest march on with me.

                Flourish. Exeunt.

SCENE [V]

Enter [STANLEY, *Earl of*] *Derby, and* SIR CHRISTOPHER
[URSWICK, *a priest*].

   Stan. Sir Christopher, tell Richmond this from me:
That in the sty of the most deadly boar
My son George Stanley is frank'd up in hold;
If I revolt, off goes young George's head;
The fear of that holds off my present aid. 5
So get thee gone; commend me to thy lord.
Withal say that the Queen hath heartily consented
He should espouse Elizabeth her daughter.
But tell me, where is princely Richmond now?

   Chris. At Pembroke or at [Ha'rford-]West in
     Wales. 10

   Stan. What men of name resort to him?

   Chris. Sir Walter Herbert, a renowned soldier,
Sir Gilbert Talbot, Sir William Stanley,
Oxford, redoubted Pembroke, Sir James Blunt,
And Rice ap Thomas, with a valiant crew, 15
And many other of great name and worth;
And towards London do they bend their power,
If by the way they be not fought withal.

   Stan. Well, hie thee to thy lord; I kiss his hand.
My letter will resolve him of my mind. 20
Farewell.   *Exeunt.*

ACT V, SCENE I

Enter BUCKINGHAM, *with Halberds* [*and the* SHERIFF],
led to execution.

   Buck. Will not King Richard let me speak with
     him?

   Sher. No, my good lord, therefore be patient.

   Buck. Hastings, and Edward's children, Grey and
     Rivers,
Holy King Henry and thy fair son Edward,
Vaughan, and all that have miscarried 5
By underhand corrupted foul injustice,
If that your moody discontented souls
Do through the clouds behold this present hour,
Even for revenge mock my destruction!
This is All-Souls' day, fellow, is it not? 10

   Sher. It is, [my lord].

   Buck. Why then All-Souls' day is my body's
     doomsday.
This is the day which, in King Edward's time,
I wish'd might fall on me when I was found
False to his children and his wive's allies; 15
This is the day wherein I wish'd to fall
By the false faith of him whom most I trusted;
This, this All-Souls' day to my fearful soul,
Is the determin'd respite of my wrongs.
That high All-Seer, which I dallied with, 20
Hath turn'd my feigned prayer on my head,
And given in earnest what I begg'd in jest.
Thus doth he force the swords of wicked men
To turn their own points in their masters' bosoms;
Thus Margaret's curse falls heavy on my neck: 25
"When he," quoth she, "shall split thy heart with
     sorrow,
Remember Margaret was a prophetess."
Come lead me, officers, to the block of shame;
Wrong hath but wrong, and blame the due of blame.

     Exeunt Buckingham [*and Sheriff*] *with Officers.*

SCENE II

Enter RICHMOND, OXFORD, [SIR JAMES] BLUNT,
[SIR WALTER] HERBERT, *and others, with Drum
and Colors.*

   Richm. Fellows in arms, and my most loving
     friends,
Bruis'd underneath the yoke of tyranny,
Thus far into the bowels of the land

---

527. **Hois'd:** hoisted. **Britain:** Brittany.

IV.v. Location: London. Lord Stanley's house.
o.s.d. **Sir:** courtesy title for a clergyman.
3. **frank'd . . . hold:** penned in custody (as a hostage).
10. **Pembroke:** county in Wales. **Ha'rford-West:** Haverfordwest, a
town in Pembrokeshire. 11. **name:** rank.
14. **redoubted:** dreaded. **Pembroke:** i.e. Jasper Tudor, Earl of
Pembroke, second son of Owen Tudor and thus Richmond's uncle.
He helped his nephew escape to Brittany after the Yorkist victory at
Tewkesbury in 1471 and fourteen years later provided great assistance
to the invasion that led to Richard's overthrow and Richmond's accession as Henry VII.
20. **resolve . . . mind:** inform him of my intentions.

V.i. Location: Salisbury. An open place.
5. **miscarried:** perished.
7. **moody:** angry. **discontented:** i.e. because their deaths were un-
avenged.
10. **All-Souls' day:** November 2. According to Hall (Bullough, III,
284), when Buckingham, after his capture and transference to Salisbury, "had confessed the whole facte and conspiracye upon Allsoulen
day without arreignemente or judgemente he was at Salsburye in the
open merket place on a newe skaffolde behedded and put to death."
13–15. **This . . . allies.** See II.i.32–40.
19. **determin'd . . . wrongs:** i.e. the date fixed to answer for my wrongdoing. *Respite* = day to which something is postponed.
20. **dallied:** trifled.
25–27. **Thus . . . prophetess.** See I.iii.296–300.

V.ii. Location: A camp near Tamworth.
o.s.d. **Colors:** flagbearer.

Have we march'd on without impediment;
And here receive we from our father Stanley   5
Lines of fair comfort and encouragement.
The wretched, bloody, and usurping boar,
That spoil'd your summer fields and fruitful vines,
Swills your warm blood like wash and makes his
    trough
In your embowell'd bosoms—this foul swine   10
Is now even in the centry of this isle,
Near to the town of Leicester, as we learn.
From Tamworth thither is but one day's march.
In God's name cheerly on, courageous friends,
To reap the harvest of perpetual peace   15
By this one bloody trial of sharp war.
    Oxf. Every man's conscience is a thousand men,
To fight against this guilty homicide.
    Herb. I doubt not but his friends will turn to us.
    Blunt. He hath no friends but what are friends for
    fear,   20
Which in his dearest need will fly from him.
    Richm. All for our vantage. Then in God's name
    march!
True hope is swift and flies with swallow's wings,
Kings it makes gods, and meaner creatures kings.
                                    Exeunt omnes.

[Scene III]

Enter [at one door] King Richard, *in arms, with*
Norfolk, Ratcliffe, *and the* Earl of Surrey,
[*with others*].

    K. Rich. Here pitch our tent, even here in Bos-
    worth field.
My Lord of Surrey, why look you so sad?
    Sur. My heart is ten times lighter than my looks.
    K. Rich. My Lord of Norfolk—
    Nor.   Here, most gracious liege.
    K. Rich. Norfolk, we must have knocks. Ha,
    must we not?   5
    Nor. We must both give and take, my loving lord.
    K. Rich. Up with my tent! Here will I lie to-
    night—

    [*Soldiers begin to set up the King's tent.*]
But where to-morrow? Well, all's one for that.
Who hath descried the number of the traitors?   9
    Nor. Six or seven thousand is their utmost power.
    K. Rich. Why, our battalia trebles that account;
Besides, the King's name is a tower of strength,
Which they upon the adverse faction want.
Up with the tent! Come, noble gentlemen,
Let us survey the vantage of the ground.   15
Call for some men of sound direction:
Let's lack no discipline, make no delay,
For, lords, to-morrow is a busy day.   *Exeunt.*

Enter [at the other door] Richmond, Sir William
Brandon, Oxford, *and* Dorset, [Blunt, Herbert,
and others. Some of the soldiers pitch Richmond's tent].

    Richm. The weary sun hath made a golden set,
And by the bright tract of his fiery car   20
Gives token of a goodly day to-morrow.
Sir William Brandon, you shall bear my standard.
Give me some ink and paper in my tent;
I'll draw the form and model of our battle,
Limit each leader to his several charge,   25
And part in just proportion our small power.
My Lord of Oxford—you, Sir William Brandon—
And [you], Sir Walter Herbert—stay with me.
The Earl of Pembroke keeps his regiment;
Good Captain Blunt, bear my good-night to him,   30
And by the second hour in the morning
Desire the Earl to see me in my tent.
Yet one thing more, good captain, do for me—
Where is Lord Stanley quarter'd, do you know?
    Blunt. Unless I have mista'en his colors much   35
(Which well I am assur'd I have not done),
His regiment lies half a mile at least
South from the mighty power of the King.
    Richm. If without peril it be possible,
Sweet Blunt, make some good means to speak with
    him,   40
And give him from me this most needful note.
    Blunt. Upon my life, my lord, I'll undertake it,
And so God give you quiet rest to-night!
    Richm. Good night, good Captain Blunt. [*Exit
    Blunt.*] Come, gentlemen,
Let us consult upon to-morrow's business.   45
In to my tent, the dew is raw and cold.
                        They withdraw into the tent.

Enter [to his tent King] Richard, Ratcliffe, Norfolk, *and* Catesby.

    K. Rich. What is't a' clock?
    Cate.   It's supper-time, my lord,
It's nine a' clock.
    K. Rich.   I will not sup to-night.
Give me some ink and paper.
What? is my beaver easier than it was?   50
And all my armor laid into my tent?
    Cate. It is, my liege, and all things are in readiness.
    K. Rich. Good Norfolk, hie thee to thy charge,
Use careful watch, choose trusty [sentinels].
    Nor. I go, my lord.   55
    K. Rich. Stir with the lark to-morrow, gentle
    Norfolk.
    Nor. I warrant you, my lord.   [*Exit.*]
    K. Rich. Catesby!
[*Cate.*] My lord?
    K. Rich.   Send out a pursuivant-at-arms

5. **father:** i.e. stepfather.
8. **spoil'd:** despoiled.   9. **wash:** swill.
10. **embowell'd:** disembowelled.   11. **centry:** centre.
13. **Tamworth:** town in Staffordshire.   21. **dearest:** most crucial.

V.iii. Location: Bosworth Field.
1. **Bosworth:** Market Bosworth, town in Leicestershire.
11. **battalia:** forces.
15. **vantage:** features likely to give superiority.
16. **direction:** military judgment.

18 s.d. **Dorset.** See note to IV.iv.311–12.   19. **set:** setting.
20. **tract:** trace, course.   **car:** chariot.
24. **form and model:** military formation and plan.
25. **Limit:** appoint.   **several charge:** separate command.
29. **keeps:** stays with.
50. **beaver:** visor or face-guard of a helmet.
59. **pursuivant-at-arms:** attendant on a herald.

Richard III
V.iii

To Stanley's regiment, bid him bring his power   60
Before sunrising, lest his son George fall
Into the blind cave of eternal night.   [*Exit Catesby.*]
Fill me a bowl of wine. Give me a watch.
Saddle white Surrey for the field to-morrow.
Look that my staves be sound, and not too heavy.   65
Ratcliffe!
    Rat.   My lord?
    K. Rich.   Saw'st thou the melancholy Lord North-
umberland?
    Rat.   Thomas the Earl of Surrey and himself,
Much about cock-shut time, from troop to troop   70
Went through the army, cheering up the soldiers.
    K. Rich.   So, I am satisfied. Give me a bowl of
wine.
I have not that alacrity of spirit
Nor cheer of mind that I was wont to have.
                                        [*Wine brought.*]
Set it down. Is ink and paper ready?   75
    Rat.   It is, my lord.
    K. Rich.   Bid my guard watch; leave me.
Ratcliffe, about the mid of night come to my tent
And help to arm me. Leave me, I say.
                        Exit Ratcliffe. [*Richard sleeps.*]

Enter [STANLEY, *Earl of*] *Derby, to* RICHMOND *in his
tent,* [LORDS *and others attending*].

    Stan.   Fortune and victory sit on thy helm!
    Richm.   All comfort that the dark night can afford
Be to thy person, noble father-in-law!   81
Tell me, how fares our loving mother?
    Stan.   I, by attorney, bless thee from thy mother,
Who prays continually for Richmond's good.
So much for that. The silent hours steal on,   85
And flaky darkness breaks within the east.
In brief—for so the season bids us be—
Prepare thy battle early in the morning,
And put thy fortune to the arbitrement
Of bloody strokes and mortal-staring war.   90
I, as I may—that which I would I cannot—
With best advantage will deceive the time,
And aid thee in this doubtful shock of arms;
But on thy side I may not be too forward,
Lest being seen, thy brother, tender George,   95
Be executed in his father's sight.
Farewell! the leisure and the fearful time
Cuts off the ceremonious vows of love
And ample interchange of sweet discourse
Which so long sund'red friends should dwell upon.
God give us leisure for these rites of love!   101
Once more, adieu! Be valiant, and speed well!

    Richm.   Good lords, conduct him to his regiment.
I'll strive with troubled thoughts to take a nap,
Lest leaden slumber peize me down to-morrow,   105
When I should mount with wings of victory.
Once more, good night, kind lords and gentlemen.
                        Exeunt. [*Manet Richmond.*]
O Thou whose captain I account myself,
Look on my forces with a gracious eye;
Put in their hands thy bruising irons of wrath,   110
That they may crush down with a heavy fall
The usurping helmets of our adversaries;
Make us thy ministers of chastisement,
That we may praise thee in the victory!
To thee I do commend my watchful soul   115
Ere I let fall the windows of mine eyes:
Sleeping and waking, O, defend me still!   [*Sleeps.*]

Enter *the Ghost of young* PRINCE EDWARD, *son* [*to*]
Henry the Sixt, to Richard.

    Ghost.   (*To Richard.*) Let me sit heavy on thy soul
to-morrow!
Think how thou stab'st me in my prime of youth
At Tewksbury. Despair therefore and die!   120
(*To Richmond.*) Be cheerful, Richmond, for the
wronged souls
Of butchered princes fight in thy behalf.
King Henry's issue, Richmond, comforts thee.

Enter *the Ghost of* HENRY THE SIXT.

    Ghost.   (*To Richard.*) When I was mortal, my
anointed body
By thee was punched full of deadly holes.   125
Think on the Tower and me. Despair and die!
Harry the Sixt bids thee despair and die.
(*To Richmond.*) Virtuous and holy, be thou con-
queror!
Harry, that prophesied thou shouldst be king,
Doth comfort thee in thy sleep. Live and flourish!

Enter *the Ghost of* CLARENCE.

    Ghost.   [*To Richard.*] Let me sit heavy in thy soul
to-morrow,   131
I that was wash'd to death with fulsome wine,
Poor Clarence, by thy guile betray'd to death!
To-morrow in the battle think on me,
And fall thy edgeless sword. Despair and die!   135
(*To Richmond.*) Thou offspring of the house of Lan-
caster,
The wronged heirs of York do pray for thee.
Good angels guard thy battle! Live and flourish!

Enter *the Ghosts of* RIVERS, GREY, VAUGHAN.

    [*Ghost of R.*]   [*To Richard.*] Let me sit heavy in thy
soul to-morrow,
Rivers, that died at Pomfret! Despair and die!   140
    [*Ghost of*] G.   [*To Richard.*] Think upon Grey, and
let thy soul despair!

---

60. **power:** forces.
63. **watch:** watch-light (?) or sentinel (?).
64. **Surrey.** The chroniclers speak of Richard's great white horse but the name was apparently Shakespeare's own invention.
65. **staves:** lance-staffs.   70. **cock-shut time:** sunset.
81. **father-in-law:** i.e. stepfather.   83. **attorney:** deputy.
86. **flaky:** streaked with light (?).   88. **battle:** army.
89. **arbitrement:** decision.   90. **mortal-staring:** deadly glaring.
91–92. **I, as . . . time.** The general sense is that Stanley, although unable to fight openly for Richmond, will mislead the enemy as best he can (by pretending loyalty to Richard).   **time:** the people around one, i.e. Richard's soldiers.   95. **brother:** i.e. stepbrother.
97. **leisure:** lack of leisure, i.e. urgency.   **fearful:** full of fears.
102. **speed well:** good luck.

104. **with:** i.e. despite.
105. **peize:** weigh.   116. **windows:** i.e. eyelids.
119. **stab'st:** i.e. stabbedst.   124. **mortal:** alive.
129. **Harry . . . king.** See *3 Henry VI*, IV.vi.68–76.
132. **fulsome:** cloying.

[Ghost of] V. *[To Richard.]* Think upon Vaughan,
  and with guilty fear
Let fall thy lance. Despair and die!
  All. *(To Richmond.)*   Awake and think our
    wrongs in Richard's bosom
[Will] conquer him! Awake and win the day!   145

Enter the Ghosts of the two young PRINCES.

  Ghosts. *(To Richard.)*   Dream on thy cousins
    smothered in the Tower.
Let us be lead within thy bosom, Richard,
And weigh thee down to ruin, shame, and death!
Thy nephews' souls bid thee despair and die!
(To Richmond.) Sleep, Richmond, sleep in peace and
  wake in joy.   150
Good angels guard thee from the boar's annoy!
Live and beget a happy race of kings!
Edward's unhappy sons do bid thee flourish.

Enter the Ghost of HASTINGS.

  Ghost. *[To Richard.]* Bloody and guilty, guiltily
    awake,
And in a bloody battle end thy days!   155
Think on Lord Hastings. Despair and die!
(To Richmond.) Quiet untroubled soul, awake,
  awake!
Arm, fight, and conquer for fair England's sake!

Enter the Ghost of LADY ANNE, *his wife.*

  [Ghost.] *[To Richard.]* Richard, thy wife, that
    wretched Anne thy wife,
That never slept a quiet hour with thee,   160
Now fills thy sleep with perturbations.
To-morrow in the battle think on me,
And fall thy edgeless sword. Despair and die!
(To Richmond.) Thou quiet soul, sleep thou a quiet
  sleep,
Dream of success and happy victory!   165
Thy adversary's wife doth pray for thee.

Enter the Ghost of BUCKINGHAM.

  [Ghost.] *[To Richard.]* The first was I that help'd
    thee to the crown;
The last was I that felt thy tyranny.
O, in the battle think on Buckingham,
And die in terror of thy guiltiness!   170
Dream on, dream on, of bloody deeds and death;
Fainting, despair; despairing, yield thy breath!
(To Richmond.) I died for hope ere I could lend thee
  aid,
But cheer thy heart, and be thou not dismay'd.
God and good angels fight on Richmond's side,   175
And Richard falls in height of all his pride!

  [The Ghosts vanish.] *Richard starteth up
    out of a dream.*
  K. Rich. Give me another horse! Bind up my
    wounds!
Have mercy, Jesu! Soft, I did but dream.
O coward conscience, how dost thou afflict me!

151. **boar's annoy:** i.e. injury from Richard.
173. **for hope:** hoping I could aid you.

The lights burn blue. It is now dead midnight.   180
Cold fearful drops stand on my trembling flesh.
What do I fear? Myself? There's none else by.
Richard loves Richard, that is, I [am] I.
Is there a murtherer here? No. Yes, I am.
Then fly. What, from myself? Great reason why—
Lest I revenge. What, myself upon myself?   186
Alack, I love myself. Wherefore? For any good
That I myself have done unto myself?
O no! Alas, I rather hate myself
For hateful deeds committed by myself.   190
I am a villain; yet I lie, I am not.
Fool, of thyself speak well; fool, do not flatter:
My conscience hath a thousand several tongues,
And every tongue brings in a several tale,
And every tale condemns me for a villain.   195
Perjury, perjury, in the highest degree;
Murther, stern murther, in the direst degree;
All several sins, all us'd in each degree,
Throng to the bar, crying all, "Guilty! guilty!"
I shall despair; there is no creature loves me,   200
And if I die no soul will pity me.
And wherefore should they, since that I myself
Find in myself no pity to myself?
Methought the souls of all that I had murther'd
Came to my tent, and every one did threat   205
To-morrow's vengeance on the head of Richard.

Enter RATCLIFFE.

  Rat. My lord!
  K. Rich. 'Zounds, who is there?
  Rat. Ratcliffe, my lord, 'tis I. The early village
    cock
Hath twice done salutation to the morn,   210
Your friends are up and buckle on their armor.
  K. Rich. O Ratcliffe, I have dream'd a fearful
    dream!
What think'st thou—will our friends prove all true?
  Rat. No doubt, my lord.
  K. Rich.   O Ratcliffe, I fear, I fear!
  Rat. Nay, good my lord, be not afraid of shadows.
  K. Rich. By the apostle Paul, shadows to-night   216
Have strook more terror to the soul of Richard
Than can the substance of ten thousand soldiers
Armed in proof and led by shallow Richmond.
'Tis not yet near day. Come, go with me,   220
Under our tents I'll play the ease-dropper,
To see if any mean to shrink from me.   *Exeunt.*

Enter the LORDS *to* RICHMOND *[sitting in his tent].*

  Lords. Good morrow, Richmond!
  Richm. Cry mercy, lords and watchful gentlemen,
That you have ta'en a tardy sluggard here.   225
  Lords. How have you slept, my lord?
  Richm. The sweetest sleep and fairest-boding
    dreams
That ever ent'red in a drowsy head

180. **lights burn blue.** A sign that ghosts are present.
198. **us'd:** committed.   **degree:** i.e. of infamy (bad, worse, worst).
219. **proof:** impenetrable armor.
221. **ease-dropper:** eavesdropper.
224. **Cry mercy:** I beg your pardon.
227. **fairest-boding:** most happily prophetic.

751

Richard III
V.iii

Have I since your departure had, my lords.
Methought their souls whose bodies Richard murther'd
Came to my tent and cried on victory.   231
I promise you, my soul is very jocund
In the remembrance of so fair a dream.
How far into the morning is it, lords?
   Lords. Upon the stroke of four.   235
   Richm. Why, then 'tis time to arm and give
      direction.

His oration to his Soldiers.

More than I have said, loving countrymen,
The leisure and enforcement of the time
Forbids to dwell upon, yet remember this:
God and our good cause fight upon our side;   240
The prayers of holy saints and wronged souls,
Like high-rear'd bulwarks, stand before our faces.
Richard except, those whom we fight against
Had rather have us win than him they follow:
For what is he they follow? Truly, gentlemen,   245
A bloody tyrant and a homicide;
One rais'd in blood, and one in blood established;
One that made means to come by what he hath,
And slaughtered those that were the means to help him;
A base foul stone, made precious by the foil   250
Of England's chair, where he is falsely set;
One that hath ever been God's enemy.
Then if you fight against God's enemy,
God will in justice ward you as his soldiers;
If you do sweat to put a tyrant down,   255
You sleep in peace, the tyrant being slain;
If you do fight against your country's foes,
Your country's fat shall pay your pains the hire;
If you do fight in safeguard of your wives,
Your wives shall welcome home the conquerors;   260
If you do free your children from the sword,
Your children's children quits it in your age.
Then in the name of God and all these rights,
Advance your standards, draw your willing swords.
For me, the ransom of my bold attempt   265
Shall be this cold corpse on the earth's cold face;
But if I thrive, the gain of my attempt
The least of you shall share his part thereof.
Sound drums and trumpets boldly and cheerfully.
God and Saint George! Richmond and victory!   270
                                                                [Exeunt.]

Enter King Richard, Ratcliffe, [Attendants, *and*
   forces].

   K. Rich. What said Northumberland as touching
      Richmond?
   Rat. That he was never trained up in arms.
   K. Rich. He said the truth, and what said Surrey
      then?
   Rat. He smil'd and said, "The better for our
      purpose."   274

   K. Rich. He was in the right, and so indeed it is.
                                                       The clock striketh.
Tell the clock there. Give me a calendar.
Who saw the sun to-day?
   Rat.   Not I, my lord.
   K. Rich. Then he disdains to shine, for by the book
He should have brav'd the east an hour ago.
A black day will it be to somebody.   280
Ratcliffe!
   Rat. My lord?
   K. Rich.   The sun will not be seen to-day,
The sky doth frown and low'r upon our army.
I would these dewy tears were from the ground.
Not shine to-day? Why, what is that to me   285
More than to Richmond? for the self-same heaven
That frowns on me looks sadly upon him.

Enter Norfolk.

   Nor. Arm, arm, my lord, the foe vaunts in the field.
   K. Rich. Come, bustle, bustle! Caparison my
      horse!
Call up Lord Stanley, bid him bring his power.   290
I will lead forth my soldiers to the plain,
And thus my battle shall be ordered:
My foreward shall be drawn out all in length,
Consisting equally of horse and foot;
Our archers shall be placed in the midst;   295
John Duke of Norfolk, Thomas Earl of Surrey,
Shall have the leading of this foot and horse.
They thus directed, we will follow
In the main battle, whose puissance on either side
Shall be well winged with our chiefest horse.   300
This, and Saint George to [boot]! What think'st thou,
      Norfolk?
   Nor. A good direction, warlike sovereign.
                                                  He sheweth him a paper.
This found I on my tent this morning.
[*Reads.*] "Jockey of Norfolk, be not so bold,
      For Dickon thy master is bought and sold."
   K. Rich. A thing devised by the enemy.   306
Go, gentlemen, every man unto his charge.
Let not our babbling dreams affright our souls;
Conscience is but a word that cowards use,
Devis'd at first to keep the strong in awe: 310
Our strong arms be our conscience, swords our law!
March on, join bravely, let us to it pell-mell;
If not to heaven, then hand in hand to hell.

His oration to his Army.

What shall I say more than I have inferr'd?
Remember whom you are to cope withal: 315
A sort of vagabonds, rascals, and runaways,
A scum of Britains and base lackey peasants,

231. cried on: yelped on the scent (a term from hunting); here, urged
on to.   243. except: excepted.
250. foil: thin sheet of metal used to set off a jewel to advantage.
254. ward: guard.   258. fat: abundance.   hire: reward.
262. quits: requite.   265. ransom: penalty (in case of failure).
270. Saint George: patron saint of England.

276. Tell: count the strokes of.   calendar: almanac.
279. brav'd: made splendid.   283. low'r: lour.
289. Caparison: cover with trappings.   293. foreward: vanguard.
298. directed: deployed.   299. battle: army.
300. winged: flanked.
304-6. Jockey...enemy. According to Hall (Bullough, III, 297),
John, Duke of Norfolk, had been "warned by dyvers to refrayne
from the felde, in so much that the nyghte before he shoulde set
forwarde towarde the kynge, one wrote on his gate" the doggerel
that Shakespeare quotes. (*Jockey* = Jack; *Dickon* = Dick.)
312. pell-mell: with vehement onset.   314. inferr'd: stated.
316. sort: gang.   317. Britains: Bretons.

Whom their o'ercloyed country vomits forth
To desperate adventures and assur'd destruction.
You sleeping safe, they bring to you unrest;   320
You having lands, and blest with beauteous wives,
They would restrain the one, distain the other.
And who doth lead them but a paltry fellow,
Long kept in Britain at our mother's cost?
A milksop, one that never in his life   325
Felt so much cold as over shoes in snow?
Let's whip these stragglers o'er the seas again;
Lash hence these overweening rags of France,
These famish'd beggars weary of their lives,
Who (but for dreaming on this fond exploit)   330
For want of means, poor rats, had hang'd themselves.
If we be conquered, let men conquer us,
And not these bastard Britains, whom our fathers
Have in their own land beaten, bobb'd, and thump'd,
And in record left them the heirs of shame.   335
Shall these enjoy our lands? lie with our wives?
Ravish our daughters? [Drum afar off.] Hark, I hear
    their drum.
Fight, gentlemen of England! fight, bold yeomen!
Draw, archers, draw your arrows to the head!
Spur your proud horses hard, and ride in blood;   340
Amaze the welkin with your broken staves!

[Enter a MESSENGER.]

What says Lord Stanley? Will he bring his power?
    Mess.   My lord, he doth deny to come.
    K. Rich.   Off with his son George's head!
    Nor.   My lord, the enemy is past the marsh,   345
After the battle let George Stanley die.
    K. Rich.   A thousand hearts are great within my
    bosom.
Advance our standards, set upon our foes.
Our ancient word of courage, fair Saint George,
Inspire us with the spleen of fiery dragons!   350
Upon them! Victory sits on our helms.   Exeunt.

[SCENE IV]

Alarum. Excursions. Enter [NORFOLK and forces fight-
    ing; to him] CATESBY.

    Cate.   Rescue, my Lord of Norfolk, rescue, rescue!
The King enacts more wonders than a man,
Daring an opposite to every danger.
His horse is slain, and all on foot he fights,
Seeking for Richmond in the throat of death.   5

Rescue, fair lord, or else the day is lost!

[Alarums.] Enter [KING] RICHARD.

    K. Rich.   A horse, a horse! my kingdom for a
    horse!
    Cate.   Withdraw, my lord, I'll help you to a horse.
    K. Rich.   Slave, I have set my life upon a cast,
And I will stand the hazard of the die.   10
I think there be six Richmonds in the field;
Five have I slain to-day in stead of him.
A horse, a horse! my kingdom for a horse! [Exeunt.]

[SCENE V]

Alarum. Enter [KING] RICHARD and RICHMOND; they
fight; Richard is slain. Then, retrait being sounded,
[flourish, and] enter RICHMOND, [STANLEY, Earl of]
Derby, bearing the crown, with other LORDS, etc.

    Richm.   God and your arms be prais'd, victorious
    friends,
The day is ours, the bloody dog is dead.
    Stan.   Courageous Richmond, well hast thou acquit
    thee.
Lo here this long-usurped royalty
From the dead temples of this bloody wretch   5
Have I pluck'd off to grace thy brows withal.
Wear it, enjoy it, and make much of it.
    Richm.   Great God of heaven, say amen to all!
But tell me, is young George Stanley living?   9
    Stan.   He is, my lord, and safe in Leicester town,
Whither, if it please you, we may now withdraw us.
    Richm.   What men of name are slain on either side?
    [Stan.]   John Duke of Norfolk, Walter Lord
    [Ferrers],
Sir Robert Brakenbury, and Sir William Brandon.
    Richm.   Inter their bodies as become their births.   15
Proclaim a pardon to the soldiers fled
That in submission will return to us,
And then as we have ta'en the sacrament,
We will unite the White Rose and the Red.
Smile heaven upon this fair conjunction,   20
That long have frown'd upon their enmity!
What traitor hears me, and says not amen?
England hath long been mad and scarr'd herself:
The brother blindly shed the brother's blood,
The father rashly slaughter'd his own son,   25
The son, compell'd, been butcher to the sire.
All this divided York and Lancaster,
Divided in their dire division,
O now let Richmond and Elizabeth,
The true succeeders of each royal house,   30
By God's fair ordinance conjoin together!
And let their heirs (God, if thy will be so)
Enrich the time to come with smooth-fac'd peace,
With smiling plenty, and fair prosperous days!

---

322. **restrain:** deprive you of.   **distain:** outrage.
324. **mother's.** In Holinshed's recension of Hall, which Shakespeare
followed, there appears this misprint for *brother's*, i.e. Burgundy's.
Despite the fact that he was Richard's brother-in-law (the husband
of his sister Margaret), Charles, Duke of Burgundy, had long supported Richmond in exile. In Hall (Bullough, III, 293) the passage
reads as follows: "And to begyn with the earle of Richmond Captaine
of this rebellion, he is a Welsh mylkesoppe, a man of small courage
and of lesse experience in marcyall actes and feates of warr, brought
up by my brothers meanes and myne like a captive in a close cage in
the court of Fraunces duke of Britaine."
334. **bobb'd:** thrashed.   341. **Amaze the welkin:** terrify the sky.
349. **word of courage:** battle-cry.   350. **spleen:** wrath.

V.iv. **Location:** Scene continues.
o.s.d. **Excursions:** sallies, sorties.
3. **an opposite:** i.e. to oppose himself.

9. **cast:** throw of the dice.   10. **die.** Singular of *dice*.
11. **six Richmonds:** i.e. Richmond and five men dressed like him (a
common stratagem in battle).

V.v. **Location:** Scene continues.
o.s.d. **retrait:** retreat, trumpet call for withdrawal of forces.
20. **conjunction:** union.

Richard III
V.v

Abate the edge of traitors, gracious Lord,   35
That would reduce these bloody days again,
And make poor England weep in streams of blood!

35. **Abate:** blunt.
36. **reduce:** bring back.

Let them not live to taste this land's increase
That would with treason wound this fair land's peace!
Now civil wounds are stopp'd, peace lives again;   40
That she may long live here, God say amen!

[*Exeunt.*]

NOTE ON THE TEXT

Richard III presents a difficult textual problem. The play first appeared in quarto (Q1) in 1597, and five more quarto editions, Q2 (1598), Q3 (1602), Q4 (1605), Q5 (1612), Q6 (1622), were printed before the publication of the First Folio (1623) text. Each of the quartos after Q1 was printed from the immediately preceding edition (Q5 from both Q3 and Q4), each new edition compounding the errors of its predecessor and adding new ones of its own. Two later quartos, published in 1629 (Q7) and 1634 (Q8), are textually of no concern here.

Q1, it is now generally agreed, must be considered to fall into the category of "bad" quartos (i.e. reported or memorially contaminated texts), even though it is an unusually "good" bad quarto. Its textual authority is, therefore, extremely dubious. F1 offers a similarly ambiguous authority, since it was printed partly from Q3 and partly from Q6, the copy of Q6 having been corrected against an independent manuscript, possibly Shakespeare's "foul papers," but in any case almost certainly not a manuscript with theatrical connections. Those stretches of text for which Q3 served as copy (III.i.1–158, V.iii.48 to end of play) show no evidence of correction against this manuscript. It may thus be readily seen that, except for some 190 lines found only in F1, lines which probably bring us closer to Shakespeare's actual text than any others in the play, the authority of the greater part of the F1 text rests heavily on the accuracy with which the corrector who collated the Q6 text with the manuscript performed his work. That this corrector carried out his task with some degree of intelligence and care seems borne out by the F1 text in general, but that he was not always careful about single substantive and semi-substantive variants between Q6 and the manuscript is proved by the some 43 times F1 agrees with the reading of Q6 against the reading of Q1 and the some 19 other occasions on which F1 readings seem to have been influenced by Q6 readings. Such agreement or influence is damaging because these Q6 readings are all the result of unauthorized changes introduced into the text during the several reprintings between Q1 and Q6; since the corrector failed to correct Q6 at these points, it seems in the highest degree likely that he was similarly guilty at other places in the text where, unfortunately, we have no means of checking his accuracy. Consequently, no reading in those sections of F1 printed from Q6 which agrees with Q1 is entirely above suspicion.

The present text uses F1 as copy-text, except in the two sections set directly from an uncorrected copy of Q3. For these sections (III.i.1–158, V.iii.48 to end of play) the copy-text must necessarily be Q1, since Q3 is essentially nothing but a twice-removed reprint of Q1 and such slight changes as appear in it can claim no independent manuscript authority. Where F1, as noticed above, follows a reading originating in Q2–6, except for the additional two lines appearing first in Q2 at I.i.101–2 or where such a reading represents an obvious correction of the Q1 text (e.g. I.iii.33), the present text returns to the reading of Q1. Further, twenty-nine lines or part-lines from Q1, generally accepted as Shakespeare's but missing in F1 for one reason or another, notably the famous "clock" episode (IV.ii.98–116), have also been included.

In view of the extremely complicated relationship between the F1 text and the quartos, the Textual Notes, in addition to providing the usual documentation of the present text, record all significant variants in Q1, together with the readings of Q2–6 for these variants.

For further information, see: Peter Alexander, *Shakespeare's "Henry VI" and "Richard III"* (Cambridge, 1929); D. L. Patrick, *The Textual History of "Richard III"* (Stanford, 1936); Alice Walker, *Textual Problems of the First Folio* (Cambridge, 1953); J. D. Wilson, ed., New Cambridge *Richard III* (Cambridge, 1954); W. W. Greg, *The Shakespeare First Folio* (Oxford, 1955); J. K. Walton, *The Copy for the Folio Text of "Richard III"* (Auckland, 1955), and "The Quarto Copy for the Folio *Richard III*," *RES*, n.s. X (1959), 127–40 [both studies attempt to discredit Q6 as copy-text for F1 in favor of Q3 throughout]; A. S. Cairncross, "The Quartos and the Folio Text of *Richard III*," *RES*, n.s. VIII (1957), 225–33 [argues, not successfully on the whole, for inclusion of Q1 as well as Q6 and Q3 among the copy-texts used for F1]; Fredson Bowers, "The Copy for the Folio *Richard III*," *SQ*, X (1959), 541–4; Kristian Smidt, *Iniurious Impostors and "Richard III"* (Oslo, 1964) [an attempt to disprove Patrick's view of Q1 as a "bad" quarto; makes some interesting points but does not alter the status of Q1 in its relation to F1], and ed., *The Tragedy of King Richard the Third* (Oslo, 1969) [a Q1-F1 parallel-text, old-spelling edition, with helpful collations of the quartos].

TEXTUAL NOTES

Title: The . . . Third] The Tragedy of Richard the Third: with the Landing of Earle Richmond, and the Battell at Bosworth Field. *F1;* The Tragedy of King Richard the third. Containing, His treacherous Plots against his brother Clarence: the pittiefull murther of his iunocent [*sic*] nephewes: his tyrannicall vsurpation: with the whole course of his detested life, and most deserued death. As it hath beene

lately Acted by the Right honourable the Lord Chamberlaine his seruants. *Q1* (title-page)
Dramatis personae: subs. *as first given by* Rowe
Act-scene division: none in Q1–6; from F1, *with the following exceptions:* III.v–vii *(no scene divisions in F1);* IV.iii *(no scene division in F1);* IV.iv, v *(numbered IV.iii, iv in F1);* V.iii–v *(no scene divisions in F1);*

see first note to each scene; present act-scene arrangement as a whole first established by Dyce

I.i

Location: *Capell*
1 s.p. Glou.] *Capell*
7 alarums] alarmes *Q1*
13 lute] loue *Q1–6*
26 see] spie *Q1–6*

32 **inductions**] inductious *Q1–2*
38 **mew'd**] mewed *Q1–3*
38 **up**] *Q1–6* (vp,); vp: *F1*
40 **murtherer**] murtherers *Q1–2*
41 s.d. **Clarence . . . Brakenbury**] *Rowe;* Clarence, and Brakenbury, guarded. *F1;* Clarence with a gard of men. *Q1–6 (after soul, l. 41)*
41 s.d. **Lieutenant . . . Tower**] *Wilson*
42 **day**] dayes *Q1–6*
44 **Tend'ring**] tendering *Q1–6*
45 **the**] *Q1–6;* th' *F1 (line very crowded and final period om.)*
46 s.p. **Glou.**] *Q1–6 (throughout);* Rich. *F1 (generally throughout)*
50 **should be**] shalbe *Q1–6*
50 **christ'ned**] christened *Q1, Q6*
52 **but**] for *Q1–6*
61 **Hath**] Haue *Q1–6*
64 **she**] *Q4–6;* shee. *F1;* she, *Q1–3*
65 **tempers . . . this**] *Q1;* tempts him to this harsh *F1;* tempts him to this *Q2–6*
67 **Woodvile**] *Q1–6;* Woodeulle *F1;* Woodville *F2;* Woodvil *F4*
71 **is secure**] *Capell;* secure *F1;* is securde *Q1–3;* securde *Q4–5;* secur'd *Q6*
74 **you**] ye *Q1–6*
75 **was . . . his**] *Q1–6;* was, for her *F1*
83 **our**] this *Q1–6*
84 s.p. **Brak.**] Bro. *Q1–6 (throughout)*
87 **your**] his *Q1–6*
88 **Brakenbury**] Brokenbury *Q1–6 (throughout, except Brookenbury at V.v.14 in Q1–2)*
88 **so?**] *Capell;* so, *F1;* so *Q1–6*
92 **jealious**] iealous *Q1–6*
95 **gentlefolks**] *Q1;* gentle Folkes *F1;* gentle folkes *Q2–6*
100 **to**] he *Q1–6*
101–2 **Brak. What . . . me?**] *these lines first appear in Q2; retained in Q3–6, F1*
103 **do**] om. *Q1–6*
108 **whatsoe'er**] whatsoeuer *Q1–6*
115 **else**] om. *Q1–6*
116 s.d. **with . . . Guard**] *Capell*
124 **the**] *Q1–2;* this *F1, Q3–6*
132 **eagles**] Eagle *Q1–6*
133 **Whiles**] While *Q1–6*
133 **buzzards**] bussards *Q1–2;* buzars *Q3–5*
133 **prey**] *Q1–6;* play *F1*
138 **Saint John**] Saint Paul *Q1–6*
138 **that**] this *Q1–6*
142 **Where**] What *Q1–6*
152 **bustle**] *F4;* bussle *F1;* bussell *Q1–6*

I.ii

Location: *Capell (after Theobald)*
o.s.d. **Enter . . . mourner**] Enter Lady Anne with the hearse of Harry the 6. *Q1–6*
o.s.d. **attended . . . Berkeley**] *Alexander*
1 **load,**] lo *Q1;* lord *Q2;* Lord, *Q3–6*
2 **hearse,**] *Q1–6;* hearse; *F1*
4 **Th'**] The *Q1–6*
10 **slaught'red**] slaughtered *Q1–2, Q6*
11 **hand**] hands *Q1–6*
11 **wounds**] holes *Q1–6*
12 **these**] those *Q1–6*
14 **O, cursed**] Curst *Q1–6*
14 **these**] these fatall *Q1–2;* the fatall *Q3–6*
15 **Cursed**] Curst be *Q1–6*
16 **Cursed . . . hence!**] om. *Q1–6 (F1 reads* Cnrsed)
19 **wolves—to**] *Kittredge;* Wolues, to *F1;* adders, *Q1–6*
25 **And . . . unhappiness!**] om. *Q1–6*
27 **More**] As *Q1–6*
27 **life**] *Cibber, Blackstone conj.;* death *F1, Q1–6*
28 **Than**] As *Q1–6*
28 **young**] poore *Q1–6*
31 **this**] the *Q1–6*
34 s.p. **Anne.**] La. (*or* Lady) *Q1–6 (throughout scene)*
36 **Villains**] Villaine *Q1–6*
39 **stand**] *Q1–6;* Stand'st *F1*
60 **deeds**] deed *Q1–6*
60 **inhuman**] *Rowe;* inhumane *F1, Q1–5;* inhumaine *Q6*

62 **mad'st**] madest *Q1–3*
64 **heav'n**] heauen *Q1–6*
64 **murth'rer**] murtherer *Q1–6*
66 **dost**] doest *Q1–5 (frequent, not hereafter recorded);* didst *Q6*
70 **know'st**] knowest *Q1–2*
70 **nor**] no *Q1–6*
73 **troth**] *Q1;* truth *F1, Q2–6*
75 **Vouchsafe**] Voutsafe *Q1;* Vouchafe *Q2*
76 **crimes**] euils *Q1–6*
78 **a**] *Q1–6*
79 **Of**] For *Q1–6*
80 **t' accuse**] *ed. (after Spedding conj. to* accuse)*;* to curse *F1, Q1–6*
86 **shalt**] shouldst *Q1–6*
88 **That**] Which *Q1–6*
89 **Then . . . slain**] Why then they are not dead *Q1–6*
92 **hands**] hand *Q1–6*
93 **li'st**] liest *Q1–6*
94 **murd'rous**] bloudy *Q1–2;* bloodly *Q3–6*
97 **sland'rous**] slaunderous *Q1–6*
98 **That**] Which *Q1–6*
99 **wast**] *Q1–6;* was't *F1*
100 **That**] Which *Q1–6*
100 **dream'st**] dreamt *Q1–6*
101 **ye**] yea *Q1–2*
102 **hedgehog?**] *Pope;* Hedge-hogge, *F1;* hedghogge *Q1;* hedgehog *Q2–6*
103 **mayst**] maiest *Q1–6*
103 **damned**] damnd *Q1–2*
105 **better**] fitter *Q1–6*
116 **something**] somewhat *Q1–6*
116 **method:**] *Q1–6;* method. *F1*
120 **wast**] *F4;* was't *F1;* art *Q1–6*
122 **that**] which *Q1–6*
124 **live**] rest *Q1–6*
126 **rent**] rend *Q1–6*
127 **not . . . that**] neuer indure sweet *Q1–6*
128 **it**] them *Q1–6*
131 **o'ershade**] ouershade *Q1–6*
133 **reveng'd**] reuenged *Q1–2, Q6*
135 **thee**] you *Q1–6*
137 **kill'd**] slew *Q1–6*
138 **thee**] *Q1–6;* the *F1*
141 **He**] Go to, he *Q1–2;* Go too, he *Q3–6*
141 **thee**] you *Q1–6*
144 s.d. **She**] *Q1 (Q1 s.d. follows* he? *l. 144)*
144 s.d. **spits**] spitteth *Q1–6*
148 **dost infect mine**] doest infect my *Q1–6*
153 **drawn**] drawen *Q1*
153] *Following this line F1 has catchword* For, *(first word of next line is* Sham'd *in F1,* Shamd *in Q1,* Shamed *in Q2–6), either picked up from beginning of l. 152 or indicating an omitted line (or lines) in F1, Q1–6*
154 **aspects**] aspect *Q1–6*
155–66 **These . . . weeping.**] om. *Q1–6*
162 **standers-by**] *hyphen, Rowe*
168 **smoothing word**] soothing words *Q1–6*
170 s.d. **She . . . him.**] om. *Q1–6*
171 **lip . . . it was**] lips . . . they were *Q1–6*
175 **breast**] bosome *Q1–6*
178 s.d. **He . . . sword.**] om. *Q1–6*
178 s.d. **it**] *F2*
179 **for . . . Henry**] 'twas I that kild your husband *Q1–6*
181 **stabb'd young Edward**] kild King Henry *Q1–6*
182 s.d. **She falls**] Here she lets fall *Q1–6*
185 **thy**] the *Q1–6*
187 **That**] Tush that *Q1–6*
189 **This**] That *Q1–6*
195 **was man**] *Q1–2;* Man was *F1, Q3–6*
198 **shalt thou**] shall you *Q1–6*
201 s.p. **Glou.**] *Q1–6;* line continued to Anne, *F1*
201 **Vouchsafe**] Voutsafe *Q1*
202 **Anne. To . . . give.**] *Q1–6*
202 s.d. **Gloucester . . . finger.**] *Sisson*
203 **my**] this *Q1–6*
206 **servant**] suppliant *Q1–6*
210 **may please you**] would please thee *Q1–6*
211 **most**] more *Q1–6*
212 **House**] place *Q1–6*
214 **monast'ry**] monastery *Q1–6*
216 **you.**] *Q1–6 (you:);* you, *F1*

221 **Tressel**] Tressill *Q1–6*
224 s.d. **Exeunt**] *Rowe;* Exit *F1; Q1–6 s.d. reads:* Exit.
224 s.d. **Tressel and Berkeley**] *Steevens (after Capell); Q1–6 s.d. reads:* Exit.
225 **Glou. Sirs . . . corse.**] *Q1–6*
226 s.d. **with Halberds**] *ed.; Q1–6 s.d. reads:* Exeunt. manet Gl.
230 **What? I**] What I *Q1–2, Q4–6;* What I? *Q3*
233 **my**] her *Q1–6*
235 **no friends**] nothing *Q1–6*
235 **at all**] *Q1–2;* withall *F1, Q3–6*
237 **her!**] *Wilson;* her? *F1;* her *Q1–6*
241 **Tewksbury**] *F3;* Tewkesbury *F1 (throughout);* Tewxbery *Q1;* Tewxbury *Q2–6*
246 **abase**] debase *Q1–6*
250 **halts . . . misshapen**] halt . . . vnshapen *Q1–6*
254 **marv'llous**] merueilous *Q1;* maruailous *Q2–6*
256 **a**] some *Q1–6*

I.iii

Location: *Theobald*
o.s.d. **Marquess of Dorset**] *Hanmer*
5 **with**] om. *Q1*
5 **eyes**] words *Q1–6*
6 s.p. **Q. Eliz.**] *Malone;* Qu. *or* Que. *F1, Q1–6 (throughout scene)*
6 **on**] of *Q1–6 (F1 repeats l. 6 at the beginning of the next page, though the catchword* Gray. *is correct following l. 6)*
7 s.p. **Grey.**] Ry. *Q1–6*
8 **harms**] harme *Q1–6*
11 **Ah**] Oh *Q1–6*
17 **come the lords**] *Q1–2;* comes the Lord *F1;* comes the Lords *Q3–6*
19, 25, 31 s.pp. **Stan.**] *Theobald;* Der. *F1;* Dar. *Q1–6*
20 **Derby,**] *Q1–6 (Darby,);* Derby. *F1*
21 **prayer**] praiers *Q1–6*
27 **on**] in *Q1–6*
30 s.p. **Q. Eliz.**] Ry. *Q1–6*
32 **Are come**] Came *Q1–6*
33 **What**] With *Q1–2*
36 **Ay, Madam**] Madame we did *Q1–6*
37–8 **Between . . . between**] Betwixt . . . betwixt *Q1–6*
41 **height**] highest *Q1–6*
41 s.d. **Lord Hastings**] *Hanmer*
43 **is it**] are they *Q1–6*
44 **That**] *Q1–6;* Thar *F1*
47 **look**] speake *Q1–6*
53 **With**] By *Q1–6*
54 s.p. **Grey.**] Ry. *Q1–6*
54 **who**] whom *Q1–5;* home *Q6*
54 **all**] om. *Q6*
58 **Grace**] person *Q1–6*
63 **on**] of *Q1–6*
66 **That . . . action**] Which . . . actions *Q1–6*
67 **children, brothers**] kindred, brother *Q1, Q6;* kinred, brother *Q2–5*
68 **he . . . ground.**] thereby he may gather / The ground of your ill will and to remoue it. *Q1–5,* (grounds) *Q6*
69 **grown**] growen *Q1*
70 **perch.**] pearch. *Q1–6*
71 **gentleman,**] Gentleman: *Q1–2;* Gentleman *Q6*
74 **friends'**] *Knight;* friends *F1, Q1–6*
76 **I**] we *Q1–6*
79 **while great**] whilst many faire *Q1–6*
89 **mean**] cause *Q1–6*
91 **for—**] om. *Q1–6*
96 **desert**] deserts *Q1–6*
97 **ay**] yea *Q1–6*
98 **she?**] she. *Q1*
100 **and**] om. *Q1–6*
101 **Iwis**] *Q1–3;* I wis *F1, Q4–6*
105 **Of . . . that oft . . . endur'd**] With . . . I often . . . endured *Q1–6*
108 **so . . . stormed**] thus taunted, scorned, and baited *Q1–6*
108 **at.**] *Q1–3* (at:); at, *F1, Q6;* at *Q4–5*
108 s.d. **behind**] *Steevens; s.d. placed as in Q1–6; after l. 109, F1*

110, 117, 125, 133, 136, 142, 154 s.dd. **Aside.**] *Collier*
110 **him**] thee *Q1–6*
113 **Tell . . . said**] *Q1–2, (om.* have) *Q3–6*
114 **avouch't**] auouch *Q1–6*
115 **I . . . Tow'r.**] *om. Q1–6*
117 **do**] *om. Q1–6*
118 **kill'dst**] slewest *Q1–6*
120 **ay**] yea *Q1–6*
122 **weeder-out**] *hyphen, Capell*
124 **spent**] spilt *Q1–6*
124 **own**] *Q1–6;* owue *F1*
125 **Ay**] Yea *Q1–6*
129 **Albons**] Albones *Q1*
130 **you**] yours *Q1–6*
131 **this**] now *Q1–6*
133 **murth'rous**] murtherous *Q1–6*
135 **Ay**] Yea *Q1–6*
141 **childish-foolish**] *Theobald;* childish foolish *F1, Q3–6;* childish, foolish *Q1–2*
142 **Hie**] *Q1–6;* High *F1*
142 **this**] the *Q1–6*
146 **sovereign**] lawfull *Q1–6*
149 **thereof**] of it *Q1–6*
152 **you may**] may you *Q1–6*
156 s.d. **Comes forward.**] *Capell (subs.)*
158 **pill'd**] pild *Q1–6*
159 **of**] *Q1–6;* off *F1*
160 **am**] being *Q1–6*
161 **rebels?**] *Theobald;* Rebells. *F1;* rebels: *Q1–6*
162 **Ah**] O *Q1–6*
166–8 **Glou. Wert . . . abode.**] *om. Q1–6*
169 **ow'st**] owest *Q1–6*
171 **This**] The *Q1–6*
175 **scorns**] scorne *Q1–6*
179 **fall'n**] fallen *Q1–6*
183 **e'er**] euer *Q1–6*
193 **Should**] Could *Q1–6*
196 **Though**] If *Q1–6*
198 **that**] which *Q1–6*
199 **our son, that**] my sonne which *Q1–6*
203 **mayst**] maiest *Q1*
203 **death**] losse *Q1–6*
207 **length'ned**] lengthened *Q1–6*
209 **standers-by**] *hyphen, Rowe*
212 **his**] your *Q1–6*
214 **with'red**] *Q1;* wither'd *F1;* withered *Q2–6*
215 **thee? Stay**] the stay *Q1–2*
225 **while**] whilest *Q1–5;* whilst *Q6*
227 **elvish-mark'd**] *hyphen, Pope*
230 **heavy mother's**] mothers heauy *Q1–6*
232 **detested—**] detested, &c. *Q1–6*
234 **I . . . think**] Then I crie thee mercy, for I had thought *Q1–6*
244 **day**] time *Q1–6*
245 **this**] that *Q1–6*
258 **blasts**] blast *Q1*
261 **touches**] toucheth *Q1–6*
262 **Ay**] Yea *Q1–6*
262 **high,**] *Q1–6;* High: *F1*
271 **is**] was *Q1–6*
272 **Peace, peace,**] Haue done *Q1–6*
273 s.d. **Turning . . . others.**] *ed.*
275 **my . . . you**] by you my hopes *Q1–6*
277 **that**] my *Q1–6*
278 **have done**] *om. Q1–6*
279 **I'll**] I will *Q1–6*
281 **noble**] Princely *Q1–6*
286 **I . . . think**] Ile not beleeue *Q1–6*
287 **gentle-sleeping**] *hyphen, Theobald*
288 **take heed**] beware *Q1–6*
290 **rankle**] rackle *Q1*
290 **to the**] thee to *Q1–6*
297 **soothe**] *Q3, Q5;* sooth *F1, Q1–2, Q4;* soothd *Q6*
300 **poor Margaret**] *Q1–6;* (poore Margaret) *F1*
301 **to**] of *Q1–6*
302 **yours**] your *Q1–2;* you *Q3–6*
303 s.p. **Buck.**] Hast. *Q1–6*
303 **an**] on *Q1–6*
304 **muse why**] wonder *Q1–6*
305 **her;**] *Collier;* her, *F1;* her *Q1–6*
307 **to her**] *om. Q1–6*
308 s.p. **Q. Eliz.**] *Q1–5* (Qu.), *Capell (subs.);* Mar. *F1;* Hast. *Q6;* Der. *F3*

309 **Yet . . . her**] But . . . this *Q1–6*
312 **repaid**] *Q1–6;* repayed *F1*
314 **thereof**] of it *Q1–6*
316 **scathe**] *Q1–5;* scath *F1, Q6*
317 s.d. **speaks to himself**] *placed as in Walker conj.; after* advis'd; *l.* 317, *F1; om. Q1–6*
318 **curs'd now,**] curst, now *Q1–3, Q5–6*
318 s.d. **Enter Catesby.**] *om. Q1–6*
320 **Grace**] noble Grace *Q3–6*
320 **yours, my gracious lord.**] *(comma, F4);* you my noble Lo: *Q1–2;* you my noble Lord. *Q3–6*
321 **I . . . me**] we . . . vs *Q1–6*
322 **We wait upon**] Madame we will attend *Q1–6*
322 s.d. **all but Gloucester**] man. Ri. *Q1–2;* ma. Clo. *Q3, Q5–6;* ma. Glo. *Q4*
323 **begin**] began *Q1–6*
324 **abroach**] *Q1–6;* abroaeh *F1*
326 **who . . . cast**] whom . . . laid *Q1–6*
328 **Derby, Hastings**] Hastings, Darby *Q1–6*
329 **tell them 'tis**] say it is *Q1–6*
331 **it**] me *Q1–6*
332 **Dorset**] Vaughan *Q1–6*
336 **odd old**] old odde *Q1–6*
336 **forth**] out *Q1–6*
337 s.d. **Enter two Murtherers.**] Enter Executioners. *Q1–6 (after l. 338)*
340 **thing**] deede *Q1–6*
341, 349 s.pp. **1. Mur.**] *Capell;* Vil. *F1;* Execu. *Q1–6*
343 **Well**] It was well *Q1–6*
343 s.d. **Gives the warrant.**] *Capell*
344 **done,**] done *Q1*
349 **Tut, tut**] Tush feare not *Q1–6*
350 **doers. Be assur'd**] *F4 (subs.);* dooers, be assur'd *F1;* doers, be assured *Q1, Q3–6;* doers, be assured *Q2*
351 **go**] come *Q1–6*
352 **fall**] drop *Q1–6*
353–4 **straight. . . . lord.**] *om. Q1–6*
354 s.p. **1. Mur.**] *Capell;* Vil. *F1; speech om. Q1–6*
354 s.d. **Exeunt.**] *Q1–6*

I.iv

Location: *Pope*
o.s.d. **Keeper**] *Q1–6 give the Keeper's role to Brakenbury*
3 **fearful . . . sights**] vgly sights, of gastly dreames *Q1–6*
8 **my lord**] *om. Q1–6*
8 **pray . . . me**] long to heare you tell it *Q1–6*
9–10 **that . . . cross to**] I was imbarkt for *Q1–6*
13 **Thence**] *Q1–5;* There *F1, Q6*
14 **heavy**] fearefull *Q1–6*
16 **pac'd**] pact *Q1;* past *Q2–6*
18 **falling**] stumbling *Q1–6*
19 **Strook**] Stroke *Q1–4*
21 **O Lord**] Lord, Lord *Q1–6*
22 **waters**] *Q1–5;* water *F1, Q6*
22 **my**] *Q1;* mine *F1, Q2–6*
23 **sights of ugly**] vgly sights of *Q1–6*
23 **my**] *Q1;* mine *F1, Q2–6*
24 **Methoughts**] Me thought *Q1–6*
25 **A**] Ten *Q1–6*
28 **All . . . sea:**] *om. Q1–6*
29 **dead men's**] *Q1–3, Q5–6 (subs.);* dead-mens *F1;* deadmens *Q4*
29 **the**] those *Q1–6*
32 **That**] Which *Q1–6*
32 **woo'd**] woed *Q1–4;* wade *Q5–6*
35 **these**] the *Q1–6*
36–7 **and . . . ghost;**] *om. Q1–6*
37 **but**] for *Q1–6*
38 **Stopp'd**] Kept *Q1–6*
39 **find**] seeke *Q1–2;* keepe *Q3–6*
39 **wand'ring**] wandering *Q1–2*
41 **Who**] Which *Q1–6*
42 **in**] with *Q1–6*
43 **No**] O *Q1–6*
45 **I**] Who *Q1–6*
46 **sour**] grim *Q1–6*
48 **stranger soul**] *Q1–6;* Stranger-soule *F1*
49 **renowned**] renowmed *Q1–5*
50 **spake**] cried *Q1–6*

50 **perjury**] *Q3–6;* Periurie, *F1;* periury. *Q1–2*
53 **with**] in *Q1–6*
54 **Dabbled**] *Q1–5* (Dabled); Dabbel'd *F1;* Dadled *Q6*
54 **shriek'd**] squakt *Q1;* squeakt *Q2–6*
57 **unto torment**] to your torments *Q1–6*
58 **methoughts**] *Q1;* me thought *F1, Q2–6*
59 **me**] me about *Q1–6*
63 **my**] the *Q1–6*
64 **lord**] my Lo: *Q1–6*
65 **I . . . methinks**] I promise you, I am afraid *Q1–6*
66 **Ah, Keeper, Keeper**] O Brokenbury *Q1–6*
66 **these**] those *Q1–6*
67 **(That)**] Which *Q1–6*
67 **give**] beare *Q1–6*
68 **requites**] *Q1–6;* requits *F1*
69–72 **O . . . children!**] *om. Q1–6*
73 **Keeper . . . awhile**] I pray thee gentle keeper stay by me *Q1–6*
75 s.d. **Clarence sleeps.**] *Johnson*
75 s.d. **Enter . . . Lieutenant.**] *om. Q1–6 (ll. 76–83 being assigned to Brakenbury)*
76 **breaks**] breake *Q1*
76 **hours,**] howers *Q1–6*
80 **imaginations**] imagination *Q1–6*
82 **between**] betwixt *Q1–6*
82 **name**] names *Q1–6*
83 s.d. **Enter two Murtherers.**] The murtherers enter. *Q1–6*
84 **1. Mur. Ho, who's here?**] *om. Q1–6*
85 **What . . . thou**] In Gods name what are you, and how came you *Q1–6*
86 s.p. **1 Mur.**] *Capell;* 2. Mur. *F1;* Execu. *Q1–6*
88 **What**] Yea, are you *Q1–2;* Yea, are ye *Q3–6*
89 s.p. **2. Mur.**] *Capell;* 1. *F1 (from here F1 designates the Murderers as simply 1 and 2 until l. 276);* 2 Exe. *Q1–6*
89–90 **'Tis . . . more.**] *as prose, Pope; as verse, F1, Q1–6 (Q1–6 print all the Murderers' speeches as rough verse)*
89 **'Tis . . . be**] O sir, it is better to be briefe then *Q1–6 (to om. Q3–6)*
89–90 **Let . . . and**] Shew him our commission, *Q1–6*
90 s.d. **Brakenbury reads it.**] *Pope (subs.);* Reads *F1;* He readeth it. *Q1–6*
94 **from**] of *Q1–6*
95 **There . . . keys**] Here are the keies, there sits the Duke a sleepe *Q1–6*
96 **the King . . . him**] his Maiesty, and certifie his Grace *Q1–6*
97 **to . . . charge**] my charge to you *Q1–2;* my place to you *Q3–6*
98–9 **You . . . well.**] *as prose, Pope; as verse, F1, (?) Q1–6 (see below, ll. 98, 99)*
98 **You . . . 'tis**] Doe so, it is *Q1–6*
99 **Fare you well**] *om. Q1–6*
99 s.d. **Exit . . . Keeper.**] *Collier MS;* Exit. *F1 (after l. 97); om. Q1–6*
100 s.p. **2. Mur.**] *from here Q1–6 designate the Murderers as simply 1 and 2*
100 **I**] *Q1–2;* we *F1, Q3–6*
101 **he'll**] then he will *Q1–6*
103 **Why . . . great**] When he wakes, / Why foole he shall neuer wake till the *Q1–6*
105 **he'll**] he will *Q1–6*
108 **What?**] What *Q1–6*
110–2 **Not . . . me.**] *as prose, Pope; as verse, F1, Q1–6*
110 **warrant**] warrant for it *Q1–6*
111 **damn'd**] dānd *Q1;* damd *Q3*
111 **the**] *om. Q1–6*
112 **me**] vs *Q1–6*
113–4 **1. Mur. I . . . live.**] *om. Q1–6*
115 **I'll**] *om. Q1–6*
115 **and**] *om. Q1–6*
117 **Nay . . . little**] I pray thee stay a whiel *Q1–6*
117–9 **Nay . . . twenty.**] *as prose, Pope; as verse, F1, Q1–6*
117–8 **this . . . mine**] my holy humor *Q1–6*
118–9 **It was . . . tells**] twas . . . would tel *Q1–6*
121 **Faith**] *Q1–6*

123 **deed's]** deede is *Q1–6*
125 **'Zounds]** *Q1–6;* Come *F1*
127 **Where's]** Where is *Q1–6*
128 **O]** om. *Q1–6*
129 **When]** So when *Q1–6*
131 **'Tis no matter]** om. *Q1–6*
133 **What]** How *Q1–6*
134 **with it]** with it, it is a dangerous thing, *Q1–6*
136 **a man . . . a man]** he . . . He *Q1–6*
137 **'Tis]** It is *Q1–6*
138 **shame-fac'd]** shamefast *Q1–6*
139 **a man]** one *Q1–6*
140 **by chance]** om. *Q1–6*
141 **turn'd]** turned *Q1*
142 **towns]** all Townes *Q1–6*
143 **trust to]** trust to / To *Q1*
144 **live]** to liue *Q1–6*
145 **'Zounds]** *Q1–6*
145 **'tis]** it is *Q1–6*
146 **Duke]** *Q1–6;* Dkue *F1*
147–9 **Take . . . sigh.]** *as prose, Pope; as verse, F1, Q1–6*
148 **but]** om. *Q1–6*
150 **I]** Tut, I *Q1–6*
150 **strong-fram'd]** *Capell;* strong fram'd *F1;* strong in fraud *Q1–6*
151 **me.]** me, I warrant thee. *Q1–6*
152 **man . . . thy]** fellow . . . his *Q1–6*
153 **fall to work]** to this geere *Q1–6*
154 **on]** ouer *Q1–6*
155 **throw him into]** we wil chop him in *Q1–6*
157 **and]** om. *Q1–6*
158–9 **Soft . . . Strike!]** Harke he stirs, shall I strike. *Q1–6*
160 **s.p. 1. Mur.]** *2 Q1–6*
160 **we'll]** first lets *Q1–6*
160] *Following this line Q3–6 read:* Cla. awaketh.
163 **s.p. 2. Mur.]** *1 Q1–6*
164, 168 **s.pp. 1. Mur.]** *2 Q1–6*
165 **am,]** *Q1–6;* am *F1*
166 **s.p. 2. Mur.]** *Q1–4;* 1 *F1, Q5–6*
170 **Your . . . pale?]** om. *Q1–6*
171 **Who . . . come?]** Tell me who are you, wherefore come you hither? *Q1–6*
172 **s.p. Both.]** *from Q1–6* Am. (= Ambo.); *2 F1*
172 **to—]** to. *Q1–6*
174 **s.p. Both.]** Am. *Q1–6*
174 **Ay, ay]** *F1* (I, I); I *Q1–6*
181 **drawn forth among]** cald foorth from out *Q1–6*
183 **is . . . doth]** are . . . doe *Q1–2;* are . . . to *Q3–6*
186–7 **death? . . . law,]** *F2;* death, . . . Law? *F1, Q1–6*
189–90 **to . . . sins,]** *Q1–6;* for any goodnesse *F1*
194 **our]** the *Q1–6*
195 **vassals]** Vassaile *Q1–6*
196 **table]** tables *Q1–6*
197 **Will you]** and wilt thou *Q1–6*
199 **hand]** hands *Q1–6*
201 **hurl]** throw *Q1–6*
203 **sacrament]** holy sacrament *Q1–6*
207 **sov'reign's]** soueraignes *Q1–6*
208 **wast]** *Rowe;* was't *F1;* wert *Q1–6*
210 **such]** so *Q1–6*
213 **He]** Why sirs, he *Q1–6*
213 **you]** ye *Q1–6*
214 **that]** this *Q1–6*
215 **avenged]** reuenged *Q1–6*
215 **the]** this *Q1–6*
216 **O . . . publicly.]** om. *Q1–6*
218 **or lawless]** nor lawlesse *Q1;* nor lawfull *Q2–6*
221 **gallant-springing]** *hyphen, Pope*
222 **struck]** stroke *Q1;* strooke *Q2–6*
224 **our duty . . . faults]** the diuell . . . fault *Q1–6*
225 **Provoke . . . slaughter]** Haue brought vs hither now to murder *Q1–6*
226 **O . . . my]** *Q1–3;* If you do loue my *F1;* Oh, if you loue *Q4–6*
228 **are]** be *Q1–6*
230 **shall]** will *Q1–6*
234, 240 **s.pp. 1. Mur.]** Am. *Q1–6*
237 **And . . . other,]** *Q1–6*

239 **of]** *Q1–5;* on *F1, Q6*
240 **lesson'd]** *Q1–5;* lessoned *F1, Q6*
242 **Come . . . yourself]** thou deceiu'st thy selfe *Q1–6*
243 **that . . . here]** hath sent vs hither now to slaughter thee *Q1,* (murder) *Q2–5,* (murther) *Q6*
244–5 **he . . . And]** when I parted with him, / He *Q1–6*
247, 249 **s.pp. 1. Mur. . . . 2. Mur.]** 2 . . . 1 *Q1–6*
247–8 **when . . . you . . . earth's]** now . . . thee . . . worlds *Q1–6*
249 **Make]** Makes *Q1*
250 **Have you . . . your souls]** Hast thou . . . thy soule *Q1–6*
252 **are you . . . your own souls]** art thou . . . thy owne soule *Q1–6*
253 **you will]** thou wilt *Q1–6*
254 **O]** Ah *Q1–6*
254 **they]** he *Q1–6*
255 **the]** this *Q1–6*
257–60 **Which . . . life?]** om. *Q1–6*
261 **No]** om. *Q1–6*
263 **s.d. to Second Murderer]** *Sisson*
264 **thine]** thy *Q1–6*
266 **As . . . distress.]** *line placed as in Tyrwhitt conj.; after l. 260, F1;* om. *Q1–6*
268 **2. Mur. Look . . . lord.]** om. *Q1–6*
269 **Take . . . do]** I thus, and thus: if this wil not serue *Q1–6*
269 **s.d. Stabs]** He stabs *Q1–6; s.d. after l. 269, F1, Q1–6; placed as in Capell*
270 **drown . . . within.]** chop thee in the malmesey But, in the next roome. *Q1–6*
270 **s.d. with the body]** *Malone* (s.d. om. *Q1–6*)
271 **dispatch'd]** performd *Q1–6*
272 **hands]** hand *Q1–6*
273 **murther]** guilty murder done *Q1–6*
273 **s.d. Enter First Murtherer]** *Capell*
274–5 **How . . . been!]** *as verse, Rowe, Q1–6; as prose, F1*
274 **How . . . not]** Why doest thou not helpe me *Q1–6*
275 **heavens]** *Q1–5;* Heauen *F1, Q6*
275 **you have been]** thou art *Q1–6*
280 **Well . . . the]** Now must I hide his *Q1–6*
281 **Till . . . give]** Vntill . . . take *Q1–6*
282 **will]** must *Q1–6*
283 **then]** here *Q1–6*
283 **s.d. Exit.]** Exeunt. *Q1–6*

II.i

Location: *Capell*
o.s.d. Flourish.] om. *Q1–6*
o.s.d. Rivers] *F1 also includes* Woodvill *in s.d., simply another name for Rivers; Q1–2 s.d. reads:* Enter King, Queene, Hastings, Ryuers, Dorcet, &c. (Q3–6 om. Dorset)
o.s.d. Grey, and others] *Capell*
1 **Why, so:]** So, *Q1–6*
1 **have I]** I haue *Q1–6*
5 **more]** now *Q1–6*
5 **in]** *Q1–6;* to *F1*
5 **to]** from *Q1* (u), *Q2*
6 **made]** set *Q1–6*
7 **Hastings and Rivers]** *Rowe;* Dorset and Riuers *F1;* Riuers and Hastings *Q1–6*
9 **soul]** heart *Q1–6*
18 **from]** in *Q1–6*
19 **you]** your *Q1–6*
23 **There]** Here *Q1–6*
25 **K. Edw. Dorset . . . Marquess.]** om. *Q1–6*
28 **I.]** I my Lord. *Q1–6*
28 **s.d. They embrace.]** *Capell*
33 **Upon your Grace]** On you or yours *Q1–6*
33 **s.d. to the Queen]** *Rowe*
39 **God]** *Q1–6;* heauen *F1*
40 **love]** zeale *Q1–6*
40 **s.d. They]** *Capell* (s.d. om. *Q1–6*)
44 **blessed]** perfect *Q1–6*
46 **comes . . . the]** comes the noble *Q1–6*
46 **s.d. Enter . . . Gloucester.]** Enter Glocest. *Q1–6* (after l. 44)
50 **Gloucester]** Brother *Q1–6*
52 **wrong-incensed]** *hyphen, Rowe*

53 **lord]** liege *Q1–6*
54 **Among]** Amongst *Q1–6*
57 **unwittingly]** *Q1–6;* vnwillingly *F1*
59 **By]** *Q1–6;* To *F1*
67 **Of . . . Dorset]** Of you Lo: Riuers, and Lord Gray of you *Q1–4,* (you my Lord Riuers) *Q5–6*
68 **me;]** me: / Of you Lord Wooduill, and Lord Scales of you, *F1 (both names are titles of Rivers, already referred to in l. 67)*
76 **lord]** liege *Q1–6*
79 **so flouted]** thus scorned *Q1–4;* thus scornde *Q5–6*
80 **gentle]** noble *Q1–6*
82 **s.p. K. Edw.]** Ryu. *Q1–6*
85 **man in the]** one in this *Q1–6*
88 **man]** soule *Q1–6*
89 **winged]** wingled *Q1*
90 **bare]** bore *Q1–6*
93 **but]** *Q1–6;* and *F1*
96, 98, 100 **s.pp. Stan.]** *Theobald;* Der. *F1;* Dar. *Q1–6*
96 **s.d. Kneels.]** *Furnivall conj.*
97 **prithee]** pray thee *Q1–6*
98 **hear me]** grant *Q1–6*
99 **say . . . requests]** speake . . . demaundst *Q1–5,* (demaundest) *Q6*
104 **that tongue]** the same *Q1–6*
105 **kill'd]** slew *Q1–6*
106 **bitter]** cruell *Q1–6*
107 **wrath]** rage *Q1–6*
108 **at]** *Q1–6;* and *F1*
108 **bid]** bad *Q1–6*
109 **spoke . . . spoke]** spake . . . who *Q1–6*
112 **at]** by *Q1–6*
113 **me,]** *Q1–6;* me: *F1*
117 **his own garments]** *Q1–5;* his Garments *F1;* his owne armes *Q6*
117 **did give]** gaue *Q1–6*
118 **numb cold]** numbcold *Q1–2*
123 **defac'd]** defaste *Q1–3*
126 **s.d. Stanley rises.]** *Wilson (after Furnivall conj.)*
131 **beg]** pleade *Q1–6*
134 **Ah]** oh *Q1–6*
134 **s.d. Exeunt . . . Queen.]** Exit. *Q1–6* (after l. 133)
135 **fruits]** fruit *Q1–6*
139 **Come . . . go]** But come lets in *Q1–6*
141 **Buck. We . . . Grace.]** om. *Q1–6*

II.ii

Location: *Capell*
o.s.d. the two . . . Clarence] Clarence Children *Q1–6*
o.s.d. Edward . . . Plantagenet] *Sisson*
1 **s.p. Boy.]** *Q1–6;* Edw. *F1*
1 **Good . . . us]** Tell me good Granam *Q1–6* (Granam *throughout Q1–6, except* Grandam *at II.iv.10 in Q1–2*)
3 **s.p. Girl.]** *Neilson;* Daugh. *F1 (throughout);* Boy. *F1*
3 **Why . . . oft]** Why doe you wring your hands *Q1–6*
3 **you]** *Q1–6*
5 **s.p. Boy.]** Gerl. *Q1–6*
6 **orphans, wretches]** wretches, Orphanes *Q1–6*
7 **were]** be *Q1–6*
8 **both]** much *Q1–6*
11 **sorrow . . . wail]** labour, to weep for *Q1–6*
12 **you . . . grandam]** Granam you conclude that *Q1–6*
13 **mine]** my *Q1–6*
13 **it]** this *Q1–6*
15 **earnest]** daily *Q1–6*
16 **Girl. And so will I.]** om. *Q1–6*
21 **provok'd to it]** prouoked *Q1–6*
23 **my uncle]** he *Q1–6*
24 **pitied me]** hugd me in his arme *Q1–6*
24 **cheek]** checke *Q1;* cheekes *Q6*
25 **Bade]** And bad *Q1–6*
26 **a]** his *Q1–6*
27 **Ah]** Oh *Q1–6*
27 **shape]** shapes *Q1–6*
28 **visor]** visard *Q1–2;* vizard *Q3–6*
28 **deep vice]** foule guile *Q1–6*
29 **ay]** *F1* (I); yea *Q1–6*

33 s.d. **Enter . . . her.**] Enter the Quee. *Q1–6*
34 **Ah**] Oh *Q1–2*; Wh *Q3–4*; *om.* *Q5–6*
40 **thy**] your *Q1–6*
41 **when . . . gone**] now . . . witherd *Q1–2*, (withred) *Q3–6*
42 **that . . . sap**] the sap being gone *Q1–6*
46 **ne'er-changing night**] perpetuall rest *Q1–6*
47 **I**] *Q1–6*
50 **with**] by *Q1–6*
54 **That**] Which *Q1–6*
56 **left**] left thee *Q1–6*
57 **husband**] children *Q1–6*
58 **hands**] limmes *Q1–6*
59 **Clarence and Edward**] Edward and Clarence *Q1–6*
60 **Thine**] Then *Q1–6*
60 **a moi'ty**] moity *Q1–5*; motitie *Q6*
60 **moan**] griefe *Q1–5*; selfe *Q6*
61 **woes**] plaints *Q1–6*
62 **Ah**] Good *Q1–6*
63 **kindred**] kindreds *Q1–6*
65 **widow-dolor**] widdowes dolours *Q1–6*
67 **complaints**] laments *Q1–6*
69 **watery moon**] watry moane *Q1–6*
71 **Ah**] Oh *Q1–6*
71 **dear**] eire *Q1*; eyre *Q2*; heire *Q3–6*
72 s.p. **Chil.**] Ambo *or* Am. *Q1–6* (*throughout scene*)
72 **Ah**] Oh *Q1–6*
74, 75 **he's**] he is *Q1–5*; is he *Q6*
78 **Were**] Was *Q1–6*
78, 79 **so dear a**] a dearer *Q1–6*
80 **griefs**] moans *Q1–6*
81 **is**] are *Q1–6*
82 **an**] *om.* *Q1–6*
83 **weep**] *Q1–6*; weepes *F1*
84–5 **and . . . weep,**] *Q1–6* (weep *om.* *Q4*)
86 **distress'd,**] *Q1–2, Q4* (distress,); distrest *F1*; distrest. *Q3, Q5–6*
87 **Pour**] *Q1*; Proue *Q2*; Powre *Q3–6*; Power *F1*
88 **lamentation**] lamentations *Q1–6*
89–100 **Dor. Comfort . . . throne.**] *om.* *Q1–6*
100 s.d. **Enter . . . Ratcliffe.**] Enter Glocest. with others. *Q1–6*
101 **Sister**] Madame *Q1–6*
103 **help our**] cure their *Q1–6*
107 **breast**] minde *Q1–6*
109 s.d. **aside**] *Collier*
110 **That is**] Thats *Q1–6*
111 **that**] why *Q1–6*
112 **cloudy princes**] *Q1–6*; clowdy-Princes *F1*
112 **heart-sorrowing peers**] *Q1–6*; hart-sorowing-Peeres *F1*
113 **heavy mutual**] mutuall heauy *Q1–6*
117 **hates**] hearts *Q1–6*
121 **fet**] fetcht *Q1–6*
123–40 **Riv. Why . . . I.**] *om.* *Q1–6*
142, 154 **Ludlow**] *Q1–6*; London *F1*
143 **sister**] mother *Q1–6*
144 **business**] waighty busines *Q1–6*
145 s.p. **Q. Eliz., Duch.**] *Staunton* (*subs.*); Ans. *Q1–6*; *om.* *F1*
145 **With . . . hearts.**] *Q1–6*
145 s.d. **Manent**] *F2*; Manet *F1, Q3–6*; man. *Q1–2*
147 **stay at home**] stay behinde *Q1*; be behinde *Q2–6*
150 **Prince**] King *Q1–6*
153 **as**] like *Q1–6*
154 **we'll**] we will *Q1–6*
154 **Exeunt.**] *om.* *Q1–2*; Exit. *Q3–6*

II.iii

Location: *Theobald* (*subs.*)
o.s.d. **Enter . . . other.**] Enter two Citizens. *Q1–6*
1 **Good morrow, neighbor**] Neighbour well met *Q1–6*
3 **Hear**] 1 Heare *Q1–6*
3 s.p. **1. Cit.**] 2 *Q1–6* (*beginning with this speech F1 designates the Citizens as 1., 2., 3.; so too Q1–6, except for 3 Cit. at l. 6*)
3 **Yes**] I *Q1–6*
4, 38 s.pp. **2. Cit.**] 1 *Q1–6*
4 **Ill**] Bad *Q1–6*
5 **giddy**] troublous *Q1*; troublesome *Q2–6*

6 **Neighbors, God speed**] Good morrow neighbours *Q1–6*
6 **1. Cit. Give . . . sir.**] *om.* *Q1–6*
7 **the**] this *Q1–6*
8 **2. Cit. Ay . . . while!**] 1 It doth. *Q1–6*
13 **Which**] That *Q1–6*
13 **council**] *Johnson;* counsell *F1, Q1–6*
16 **Henry**] Harry *Q1–6*
17 **in**] at *Q1–6*
18 **No . . . wot**] no good my friend not so *Q1–6*
22, 31 s.pp. **1. Cit.**] 2 *Q1–6*
22 **Why**] *om.* *Q1–6*
22, 23, 24 **his**] the *Q1–6*
25 **who shall now**] now, who shall *Q1–6*
28 **sons . . . haught**] kindred hauty *Q1–6*
31 **will be**] shalbe *Q1–6*
32 **are seen**] appeare *Q1–6*
32 **wise men**] *Q1–6*; wisemen *F1*
33 **then**] the *Q1–6*
35 **makes**] make *Q1–6*
38 **fear**] bread *Q1–2*; dread *Q3–6*
39 **You**] Yee *Q1–6*
39 **reason (almost)**] almost reason *Q1–6*
40 **dread**] feare *Q1–6*
41 **days**] times *Q1–6*
41 **so.**] *Q1–6* (so:); so, *F1*
43 **Ensuing**] *F1* (*catchword*), *Q1–6*; Pursuing *F1*
43 **danger**] dangers *Q1–6*
44 **water**] waters *Q1–6*
46 **Marry, we were**] We are *Q1–6*
46 **justices**] Iustice *Q1–6*

II.iv

Location: *Capell* (*after Theobald*)
o.s.d. **Archbishop**] Cardinall *Q1–6* (*with Car. for* s.pp.)
1 **hear**] *Q1–2*; heard *F1, Q3–6*
1 **Stony-Stratford**] Northhampton *Q1–6*
2 **And . . . rest**] At Stonistratford will they be *Q1–6*
6 s.p. **Q. Eliz.**] *Malone;* Qu. *F1, Q1–6* (*throughout scene*)
9 **my good**] my young *Q1–6*
12 **uncle**] Nnckle *Q1*
13 **do**] *om.* *Q1–6*
20 **his . . . true**] this were a true rule *Q1–2*; this were a rule *Q3–6*
21 s.p. **Arch.**] *Capell;* Yor. *F1;* Car. *Q1–6*
21 **And . . . Madam**] Why Madame, so no doubt he is *Q1–6*
22 **he . . . yet**] so too, but yer *Q1*, (yet) *Q2–6*
25 **To . . . touch'd**] That should haue neerer toucht his growth then he did *Q1–6*
26 **young . . . prithee**] prety Yorke? I pray thee *Q1–6*
31 **prithee**] pray thee *Q1–6*
31 **this**] so *Q1–6*
33 **wast**] wert *Q1–6*
35 **parlous**] perilous *Q1–6*
36 s.p. **Duch.**] Car. *Q1–6*
37 s.d. **Enter a Messenger.**] Enter Dorset. *Q1–6* (*with Messenger's lines given to Dorset*)
38 **Arch. Here . . . news?**] *Car.* Here comes your sonne, Lo: M. Dorset. / What newes Lo: Marques? *Q1–6*
39 **report**] vnfold *Q1–6*
40 **doth**] fares *Q1–6*
41 **news**] newes then *Q1–6*
43 **And**] *om.* *Q1–6*
47 **the**] these *Q1–6*
48 **lord**] Lady *Q1–6*
49 **ruin of my**] downfall of our *Q1–6*
51 **jut**] iet *Q1–6*
52 **aweless**] lawlesse *Q1–6*
53 **blood**] death *Q1–6*
60–1 **broils . . . themselves,**] broiles, / Cleane ouerblowne themselues, *Q1*
62 **brother to brother**] *om.* *Q1–6*
63 **to**] against *Q1–6*
65 **death**] *Q1–6*; earth *F1*
67 **Madam, farewell.**] *om.* *Q1–6*
67 **Stay . . . go**] Ile go along *Q1–6*
68 s.p. **Arch.**] Car. *Q1–6*
68 s.d. **To the Queen.**] *Malone*
73 **Go**] Come *Q1–6*

III.i

Location: *Pope, Capell*
o.s.d. **Lord**] *F1* (*Q1 is the basic text for ll. 1–158*)
o.s.d. **Catesby**] *Capell*
o.s.d. **with others**] *F1;* &c. *Q1–6*
8 **div'd**] *F1;* diued *Q1–6*
9 **Nor**] No *F1*
17 s.d. **and his train**] *Capell*
19 s.d. **Mayor . . . aside.**] *Capell* (*subs.*)
40 **in heaven**] *om.* *Q3–6, F1*
43 **deep**] great *Q3–6, F1*
44 **senseless-obstinate**] *hyphen, Theobald*
49 **deserv'd**] deserued *Q2–6*
51 **claim'd . . . deserv'd**] *F1;* claimed . . . deserued *Q1–6*
56 **never**] ne're *F1*
57 **overrule**] o're-rule *F1*
60 s.d. **Exeunt . . . Hastings.**] *Q3–6* (Exit), *F1*
63 **seems**] thinkst *Q3–6, F1*
71 **since,**] *F1;* since *Q1–6*
73 **age,**] *F1;* age *Q1–6*
78 **all-ending**] ending *Q2–6, F1*
79, 94 s.dd. **Aside.**] *Johnson*
82 s.d. **Aside.**] *F2*
82 **Vice, Iniquity**] *F1;* vice iniquity *Q1–4;* vice, iniquitie *Q5–6*
86 **valure**] valour *Q3–6, F1*
87 **this**] his *Q2–6, F1*
96 **loving**] noble *Q3–6, F1*
97 **dread**] deare *Q3–6, F1*
98 **brother,**] *F1;* brother *Q1–6*
104 **outgrown**] *Q2–6, F1;* outgrowen *Q1*
111 **cousin**] *F1;* Coscn *Q1;* Cousen *Q2–6*
111 **with all**] *Q3–6, F1;* withall *Q1–2*
120 **heavy**] weightie *Q2–6, F1*
123 **as**] as as *Q3;* as, as, *F1*
132 s.d. **Aside to Hastings.**] *Capell*
132 **sharp-provided**] *hyphen, Theobald*
132–3 **reasons!**] *Q1–6* (subs.); reasons, . . . Vnckle: *Q1;* reasons . . . Vnckle: *Q2;* reasons, . . . vncle, *Q3–6*
134 **himself:**] *Q3–6, F1;* himselfe, *Q1–2*
136 **will't**] *Pope;* wilt *Q1–6, F1*
141 **needs**] *om.* *Q2–6, F1*
144 **Marry**] *F1;* Mary *Q1–6*
145 **grandam**] *F1;* Granam *Q1–6*
145 **murd'red**] murther'd *F1*
149 **with**] and with *F1*
150 s.d. **A Sennet.**] *F1*
150 s.d. **Hastings**] *Hanmer;* Hast. Dors. *Q1–6;* Hastings, and Dorset *F1* (*Dorset has not appeared in the scene*)
150 s.d. **Cardinal . . . others**] *Capell* (subs.)
150 s.d. **Manent**] *F2;* Manet *Q1–6, F1*
150 s.d. **and Catesby**] *F1*
159] *With this line F1 becomes again the basic text*
167 **think'st**] thinkest *Q1–6*
167 **Will not he**] what will he *Q1–6*
170 **far**] a farre *Q1–6*
171 **doth stand**] stands *Q1–6*
171 **to**] vnto *Q1–6*
171–4 **purpose . . . us,**] purpose, if he be willing, *Q1–6*
175 **tell**] shew *Q1–6*
177 **the**] your *Q1–6*
184 **lord**] friend *Q1–5;* friends *Q6*
186 **go**] *om.* *Q1–6*
187 **lords**] Lo: *Q1–2*
187 **can**] may *Q1–6*
190 **House**] place *Q1–6*
190 s.d. **Exit Catesby.**] *om.* *Q1–2; after l. 189, Q3–6*
192 **Lord**] William Lo: *Q1–6*
193 **head . . . determine**] head man, somewhat we will doe *Q1–6*
195 **Herford**] *Q3–5;* Hereford *F1, Q1–2;* Hertford *Q6*
195 **all**] *om.* *Q1–6*
196 **was**] stood *Q1–6*
197 **hand**] hands *Q1–6*
198 **kindness**] willingnes *Q1–6*

III.ii

Location: *Theobald*
o.s.d. **the door of**] Lo: *Q1–6*
1 **My lord! my lord!**] What ho my Lord. *Q1–6*

2, 4 s.dd. **Within.**] *Theobald (the second Within. implied)*; *Q1–6 enter Lord Hastings after l. 3*

2 **knocks?**] knockes at the dore. *Q1–6*

3 **One**] A messenger *Q1–6*

4 **What is't**] Whats *Q1–6*

4 **my Lord Stanley**] thy Master *Q1–6*

7 **appears**] should seeme *Q1–6*

8 **self**] Lordship *Q1–6*

9 **What**] And *Q1–6*

10–11 **Then . . . off**] And then he sends you word. / He dreamt to night the beare had raste *Q1*, (word), *Q2–4*, *Q5* (caste); And then he sends you word, / He dreamt to night, the Boare had cast *Q6*

12 **kept**] held *Q1–6*

14 **th'**] the *Q1–6*

16 **you will presently**] presently you will *Q1–6*

17 **with him toward**] into *Q1–6*

20 **Council**] counsells *Q1–6*

22 **good friend**] seruant *Q1–6*

26 **he's so simple**] he is so fond *Q1–6* (so om. *Q4*)

27 **mock'ry**] mockery *Q1–6*

28 **pursues**] pursues vs *Q1–2*; pursue vs *Q3–6*

34 **I'll . . . and**] My gratious Lo: Ile *Q1–6*

34 s.d. **Exit.**] om. *Q1–2*

37 **tott'ring**] tottering *Q1–6*

39 **will**] it will *Q1–2*; twill *Q3–6*

41 **How?**] *Q1–2*; How *F1*; Who? *Q3–6*

41 **Dost**] *F3*; Doest *F1*, *Q1–6*

44 **Before I'll**] Ere I will *Q1–6*

46 **Ay, . . . life**] Vpon my life my Lo: *Q1–6*

52 **my adversaries**] mine enemies *Q1–6*

55 **it,**] it *Q1–6*

58 **which**] who *Q1–6*

60 **Well . . . older,**] I tell thee Catesby. *Cat.* What my Lord? / *Hast.* Ere a fort-night make me elder, *Q1–6*

61 **on't**] on it *Q1–6*

66 **that**] who *Q1–6*

67 **know'st**] knowest *Q1–2*

70 s.d. **Aside.**] *F4*

72 **Come on, come on**] What my Lo: *Q1–6*

78 **you do**] do *Q1–6*

79 **days**] life *Q1–6*

80 **so . . . as 'tis**] mòre . . . then it is *Q1–6*

84 **were**] was *Q1–6*

86 **o'ercast**] ouercast *Q1–2*

87 **stab**] scab *Q1–6*

89–91 **What . . . lords**] But come my Lo: shall we to your tower? / *Hast.* I go: but stay, heare you not the newes, / This day those men *Q1–6*

91 **talk'd**] *Q1–2*; talke *F1*, *Q3–6*

94 **let's**] let vs *Q1–6*

94 s.d. **also named Hastings**] *ed.*, *from Q1–6 s.d.*: Hastin. a Purssuant.

95 **Go . . . fellow.**] Go you before, Ile follow presently. *Q1–6*

95 s.d. **Exeunt**] *Rowe*; Exit *F1*, *Q3–6* (after l. 94)

96 **How now, sirrah?**] Well met Hastings, *Q1–6* (with repeated s.p.)

97 **your . . . ask**] it please your Lo: to aske *Q1–2*; it please your good Lordship to ask *Q3–6*

98 **man**] fellow *Q1–6*

99 **thou met'st me**] I met thee *Q1–6*

104 **e'er**] euer *Q1–6*

106 **fellow . . . me**] Hastings hold spend thou that *Q1*, (Hastings,) *Q2–6*

106 s.d. **Throws**] He giues *Q1–6*

107 **I . . . honor**] God saue your Lordship *Q1–6*

107 s.d. **Exit Pursuivant.**] om. *Q1–2*

108–9 **Priest. Well . . , heart.**] *Hast.* What Sir Iohn, you are wel met. *Q1–6*

110 **in . . . last**] beholding to you for your last daies *Q1–6*

111 **Sabbath**] *Q8*; Sabboth *F1*, *Q3–6*; sabaoth *Q1–2*

111 s.d. **He . . . ear.**] *Q1–6*

112 **Priest. I'll . . . lordship.**] om. *Q1–6*

113 **What . . . Chamberlain**] How now Lo: Chamberlaine, what talking with a priest *Q1–6*

---

117 **The**] Those *Q1–6*

118 **toward the Tower**] to the tower my Lord *Q1–6*

119 **my lord**] om. *Q1–6*

119 **cannot stay there**] shall not stay *Q1–6*

121 **Nay**] Tis *Q1–6*

122 s.d. **Aside.**] *Rowe*

122 **know'st**] knowest *Q1–2*; knowh *Q6*

123 **will you go**] shall we go along *Q1–6*

123 **Hast. I'll . . . lordship.**] om. *Q1–6*

III.iii

Location: *Theobald*

o.s.d. **Rivers . . . Vaughan**] *from Q1–6 s.d.*: Enter Sir Rickard Ratliffe, with the Lo: Riuers, Gray, and Vaughan, prisoners.

1 **Rat. Come . . . prisoners.**] *Q1–6*

2 **Ratcliffe**] Ratliffe *Q1–6*

5 **bless**] keepe *Q1–6*

7–8 **Vaug. You . . . out.**] om. *Q1–6* (but l. 8 appears as Come come dispatch, the limit of your linea [lines *Q2*; liues *Q3–6*] is out., replacing l. 24 of *F1*)

13 **seat**] soule *Q1–6*

14 **to thee . . . blood**] thee vp . . . blouds *Q1–6*

16 **When . . . I,**] om. *Q1–6*

18 **Richard**] Hastings *Q1–6*

19 **Hastings**] Richard *Q1*

20 **prayer**] praiers *Q1–6*

21 **sons**] sonne *Q1–6*

22 **blood**] blouds *Q1–6*

23 **know'st**] knowest *Q1–6*

24] *See above, ll. 7–8*

25 **here**] all *Q1–6*

26 **Farewell . . . again**] And take our leaue vntill we meete *Q1–5*, (leaues) *Q6*

III.iv

Location: *Pope*

o.s.d. **Enter . . . table.**] Enter the Lords to Councell. *Q1–6*

1 **Now, noble peers**] My lords at once *Q1–6*

3 **speak . . . the**] say . . . this *Q1–6*

4 **Is . . . ready . . . the**] Are . . . fitting . . . that *Q1–6*

5 s.p. **Stan.**] *Theobald*; Darb. *F1* (throughout scene); Dar. *Q1–6*

6 s.p. **Ely.**] Ryu. *Q1*; Riu. *Q2*; Bish. *Q3–6*

6 **judge . . . day**] guesse . . . time *Q1–6*

7 **Your . . . think**] Why you my Lo: me thinkes you *Q1–6*

10 **We**] Who I my Lo? we *Q1–6*

10 **for**] But for *Q1–6*

12 **Or . . . lord**] nor I no more of his *Q1–6*

17 **gracious**] Graces *Q1–6*

18 **honorable lords**] noble Lo: *Q1–2*; L. *Q3–6*

20 **he'll**] he will *Q1–6*

20 s.d. **Enter Gloucester.**] after l. 21, *Q1–6*

21 **In happy**] Now in good *Q1–6*

22 **lords**] L. *Q1–6*

23 **trust**] hope *Q1–6*

24 **design**] designes *Q1–6*

26 **you not**] not you *Q1–6*

26 **cue**] *Q1–6* (kew); Q *F1*

27 **had**] had now *Q1–6*

31 **My . . . when,**] *Hast.* I thanke you my Grace. / *Glo.* My Lo: of Elie, *Bish.* My Lo: / *Glo.* When *Q1–6*

34 **Marry . . . heart.**] I go my Lord. *Q1–6*

34 **Marry**] *F3*; Mary *F1*

34 s.d. **Exit Bishop.**] om. *Q1–6*

35 **of**] om. *Q1–6*

35 s.d. **Drawing him aside.**] *Capell*

38 **That**] As *Q1–6*

39 **child, as worshipfully**] sonne as worshipful *Q1–5*, (wotshipfull) *Q6*

41 **yourself . . . with**] you hence my Lo: Ile follow *Q1–6*

41 s.d. **Gloucester and Buckingham**] *Pope*; *Q1–6 s.d. reads:* Ex. Gl.

43 **my judgment**] mine opinion *Q1–6*

46 **lord . . . Gloucester**] L. protector *Q1–6*

48 **this morning**] to day *Q1–6*

50 **that he bids . . . such**] he doth bid . . . such a *Q1–6*

51 **there's**] there is *Q1–6*

52 **Can**] That can *Q1–6*

---

55 **livelihood**] likelihood *Q1–6*

56 **Marry**] *Q6*; Mary *F1*, *Q1–5*

57 **For . . . had**] For if he were, he would haue *Q1–6*

57 **shown**] shewen *Q1–5*

58 **Stan. I . . . say.**] *Q1–6* (with s.p. Dar.)

58 s.d. **and Buckingham**] om. *Q1–6*

59 **tell me what**] what do *Q1–6*

64 **princely**] noble *Q1–6*

65 **th' offenders, whosoe'er**] the offenders whatsoeuer *Q1–6*

67 **their evil**] this ill *Q1–6*

68 **Look**] See *Q1–6*

70 **And this is**] This is that *Q1–6*

73 **deed, my noble**] thing my gratious *Q1–6*

75 **Talk'st thou to**] Telst thou *Q1–6*

76 **I swear**] om. *Q1–6*

77 **dine**] dine to day I sweare *Q1–6*

78 **Lovel . . . done**] some see it done *Q1–6*

79 **rise**] come *Q1–6*

79 s.d. **Exeunt.**] placed as in *Q1–6*; after l. 78, *F1*

79 s.d. **Manent**] *F2*; Manet *F1*, *Q1–6*

79 s.d. **Lovel . . . Hastings**] Cat. with Ha. *Q1–6*

82 **rase**] *Q1–6* (race); rowse *F1*

82 **our helms**] his helme *Q1–6* (perhaps correctly)

83 **And . . . disdain**] But I disdaind it, and did scorne *Q1–6*

84 **foot-cloth horse**] *Rowe*; Foot-Cloth-Horse *F1*; footecloth horse *Q1–6*

85 **started**] startled *Q1–6* (perhaps the better reading)

87 **need**] want *Q1–6*

89 **too . . . how**] twere . . . at *Q1–6*

90 **To-day**] How they *Q1–6*

94 s.p. **Rat.**] Cat. *Q1–6*

94 **Come, come, dispatch**] Dispatch my Lo: *Q1–6*

96 **grace of mortal**] state of worldly *Q1–6*

97 **God**] heauen *Q1–6*

98 **hope . . . good**] hopes . . . faire *Q1–6*

102–5 **Lov. Come . . . upon.**] om. *Q1–6*

III.v

III.v] *Capell*

Location: *Theobald*

o.s.d. **Enter . . . ill-favored.**] Enter Duke of Glocester and Buckingham in armonr. *Q1*, (armour) *Q1–6*

3 **again begin**] beginne againe *Q1–6*

4 **were**] wert *Q1–6*

5 **Tut,**] Tut feare not me. *Q1–6*

7 **Tremble . . . straw;**] om. *Q1–6*

11 **At any time**] om. *Q1–6*

12–4 **But . . . Mayor—**] *Glo.* Here comes the Maior. / *Buc.* Let me alone to entertaine him. Lo: Maior, *Q1–6*

13 s.d. **Enter . . . Catesby.**] Enter Maior. *Q1–6* (after l. 11)

16, 17] *These lines, in reverse order, follow l. 18 in Q1–6*

16 **Hark,**] Harke, I heare *Q1–6*

17 **o'erlook**] ouerlooke *Q1–6*

18 **Lord . . . sent—**] The reason we haue sent for you. *Q1–6*

20 **innocence**] *Q1*; Innocencie *F1*, *Q2–6*

20 **and guard**] om. *Q1–6*

20 s.d. **Enter . . . head.**] Enter Catesby with Hast. Head. *Q1–6* (after l. 21, *Q3–6*)

21 **Be . . . Lovel.**] O, O, be quiet, it is Catesby. *Q1–6*

22 s.p. **Lov.**] Cat. *Q1–6*

25 **creature**] man *Q1–6*

26 **the**] this *Q1–6*

32 **liv'd . . . suspects**] laid . . . suspect *Q1–6*

34 **Look . . . Mayor,**] *Q1–6* (after l. 26); placed as in Capell

35 **you imagine**] you haue imagined *Q1–6*

36 **Were't**] *F3*; Wert *F1*, *Q1–5*; were *Q6*

36 **that**] om. *Q1–6*

37 **it, that the**] it you? The *Q1–6*

38 **This . . . plotted**] Had this day plotted *Q1–6*

39 **murther**] murder *Q1–6*

40 **Had he done**] What, had he *Q1–6*

43 **in**] to *Q1–6*

48 **your good Graces**] you my good Lords *Q1–6*

50–1 **Buck. I . . . Shore.**] *continued to Mayor, Q1–6*

52–61 **Yet . . . death.**] *given to Dut. Q1–2 (perhaps a misreading for Buc.); to Clo. Q3, Q5; to Glo. Q4, Q6*

52 **we not determin'd**] not we determined *Q1–6*

53 **end**] death *Q1–6*

54 **loving**] longing *Q1–6*

55 **Something . . . meanings**] Somewhat . . . meaning *Q1–6*

56 **I**] we *Q1–6*

58 **treasons**] treason *Q1–6*

60 **haply**] happily *Q1–6*

62 **Grace's**] *F4;* Graces *F1, Q1–6*

62 **words**] word *Q1–6*

63 **and**] or *Q1–6*

64 **do not doubt**] doubt you not *Q1–6*

65 **our**] your *Q1–6*

66 **cause**] *Q1–5;* case *F1;* ease *Q6*

68 **T' avoid . . .**] To auoyde the carping censures of the *Q1–6*

69 **Which . . . intent**] But . . . intents *Q1–6*

70 **you hear**] *om. Q1–6*

71 **my . . . farewell**] my Lord adue *Q1–6*

71 s.d. **Exit Mayor.**] *after l. 72, Q1–6*

72 **Go**] *om. Q1–6*

74 **meet'st advantage**] *Q1–5;* meetest vantage *F1;* meetest aduantage *Q6*

81 **bestial**] *Q1–5;* beastiall *F1, Q6*

82 **stretch'd unto**] stretched to *Q1–6*

83 **raging**] lustfull *Q1–6*

84 **lusted . . . a**] listed . . . his *Q1–6*

85 **need, thus far**] neede thus farre, *Q1–2;* need thus farre *Q3–6*

87 **insatiate**] vnsatiate *Q1–6*

89 **true**] iust *Q1–6*

93 **Yet . . . 'twere**] But . . . it were *Q1–6*

94 **my . . . know**] you know, my Lord, *Q1–6*

95 **Doubt**] Feare *Q1–6*

97 **and . . . adieu.**] *om. Q1–6 (but see l. 102)*

101–2 **I . . . affords.**] About three or foure a clocke look to heare / What news Guildhall affordeth, and so my Lord farewell. *Q1–6*

103–5 **Go . . . Castle.**] *om. Q1–6*

104 s.d. **To Catesby.**] *Capell*

104 **Penker**] *Capell;* Peuker *F1*

105 s.d. **Exeunt . . . Catesby.**] *ed.;* Exit. *F1*

106 s.d. **To Ratcliffe.**] *ed. (eds. make Ratcliffe exit with Lovel and Catesby, but there is nothing to suggest he does so, and F1 has Exeunt. at l. 109;* Exit., *however, Q1–6*

106 **go**] in *Q1–6*

108 **order . . . manner**] notice, . . . maner of *Q1–6*

109 **Have any time**] At any tyme haue *Q1–6*

III.vi

III.vi] *Capell*

Location: *Capell*

o.s.d. **with . . . hand**] *Q1–6*

1 **Here**] This *Q1–6*

3 **to-day**] this day *Q1–6*

3 **o'er**] ouer *Q1–6*

5 **have**] *om. Q1–6*

6 **sent**] brought *Q1–6*

7 **precedent**] president *Q1–6 (Shakespeare's usual form)*

8 **Hastings liv'd**] liued Lord Hastings *Q1–6*

10 **Who is**] Why whoes *Q1–2;* Why, who's *Q3–6*

11 **cannot see**] sees not *Q1–6*

12 **who's**] *Q1–2;* who *F1, Q3–6*

12 **bold**] blinde *Q1–6*

14 **ill**] bad *Q1–6*

III.vii

III.vii] *Pope*

Location: *Theobald*

o.s.d. **Richard . . . doors**] Glocester at one doore, Buckingham at another *Q1–6*

1 **how now**] my Lord *Q1–6*

3 **say**] and speake *Q1–6*

5–6 **his . . . France,**] *om. Q1–6*

7 **Th' unsatiate**] the insatiate *Q1–6*

7 **desire**] desires *Q1–6*

8 **And . . . wives,**] *om. Q1–6*

11 **And . . . Duke.**] *om. Q1–6*

13 **idea**] Idea *F1 (in italics)*

18 **your**] the *Q1–6*

20 **mine**] *Q1–2;* my *F1, Q3–6*

20 **drew**] grew *Q1–6*

20 **to an**] *Q1–2, Q4;* toward *F1;* to *Q3, Q5–6*

23 **And**] A and *Q1;* A, and *Q2–6*

24 **they . . . word,**] *om. Q1–6*

25 **statues**] *Keightley;* Statues *F1, Q1–6*

26 **Star'd**] Gazde *Q1–6*

29 **used**] wont *Q1–6*

33 **spake**] *Q1–5;* spoke *F1;* speake *Q6*

37 **And . . . few:**] *om. Q1–6*

38 **gentle**] louing *Q1–6*

39 **cheerful**] louing *Q1–6*

40 **wisdoms**] *Q1–2;* wisdome *F1, Q3–6*

41 **even here**] so *Q1–6*

43 **Buck. No . . . lord.**] *Q1–6*

44 s.p. **Glou.**] *Q1–6*

46 **you . . . by**] spoken withall, but with *Q1–6*

48 **between**] betwixt *Q1–6*

49 **make**] build *Q1–6*

50 **And be . . . requests**] Be . . . request *Q1–6*

51 **still . . . and**] say no, but *Q1–6*

52 **I . . . plead**] Feare not me, if thou canst pleade *Q1–6*

54 **we**] weele *Q1–6*

55–6 **Go . . . lord!**] You shal see what I can do, get you vp to the leads. *Exit.* / Now my L. Maior. *Q1–6*

55 s.d. **Exit Gloucester.**] *Rowe (after l. 54; here placed as in Capell);* Exit. *Q1–6 (after leads, l. 55)*

55 s.d. **Aldermen**] *Capell*

58 **Now . . . request?**] Here comes his seruant: how now *Catesby* what saies he. *Q1–6*

59 **He . . . lord**] My Lord, he doth intreat your grace *Q1–6*

63 **suits**] suite *Q1–6*

65 **the gracious Duke**] thy Lord againe *Q1–6*

66 **Aldermen**] Cittizens *Q1–6*

67 **in matter**] and matters *Q1–6*

70 **signify . . . straight**] tell him what you say my Lord *Q1–6*

71 **Ah**] A *Q1–6*

72 **love-bed**] day bed *Q1–6*

78 **virtuous**] gracious *Q1–6*

79 **his Grace . . . thereof**] himselfe . . . thereon *Q1–6*

80 **not**] neuer *Q1–6*

81 **defend**] forbid *Q1–6*

82 **Here . . . again.**] *om. Q1–6*

83 **Now . . . Grace?**] how now Catesby, / What saies your Lord? *Q1–6*

83 **My lord,**] *Q1–6*

85 **come to**] speake with *Q1–6*

87 **He . . . lord**] My Lord, he feares *Q1–6*

90 **we . . . love**] I come in perfect loue to him *Q1–6*

91 s.d. **Catesby**] *Q1–6*

93 **much**] hard *Q1–6*

94 s.d. **aloft . . . Bishops**] with two bishops a loste *Q1,* (aloft) *Q2–6*

94 s.d. **Catesby returns.**] *Theobald*

95 **his . . . 'tween**] he stands between *Q1–6*

98–9 **And . . . man.**] *om. Q1–6*

101 **ear**] eares *Q1–6*

101 **our requests**] our request *Q1;* my request *Q2–6*

105 **do . . . to**] rather do beseech you *Q1–6*

107 **Deferr'd**] Neglect *Q1–6*

110 **ungovern'd**] vngouerned *Q1–4*

112 **eye**] eies *Q1–6*

114 **might**] *om. Q1–6*

115 **On**] At *Q1–6*

115 **your**] that *Q1–6*

117 **Know then**] Then know *Q1–6*

120 **Your . . . birth,**] *om. Q1–6*

123 **Whiles**] Whilst *Q1;* Whilest *Q2–6*

125 **The**] This *Q1–6*

125 **her**] *Q1–2;* his *F1, Q3–6*

126 **Her**] *Q1–6;* His *F1*

127 **Her . . . plants,**] *om. Q1–6*

127 **Her**] *Pope;* His *F1*

129 **dark . . . deep**] blind . . . darke *Q1–6*

131–2 **charge . . . land:**] soueraingtie thereof,

Q1–6

140 **cause**] suite *Q1–6*

141 **cannot tell if**] know not whether *Q1–4;* know whither *Q5–6*

144–53 **If . . . you:**] *om. Q1–6*

158 **the . . . of**] my . . . by *Q1–6*

161 **That**] As *Q1–6*

161 **would**] had *Q1–6*

165 **thank'd, there is**] thanked there's *Q1–6*

166 **were there need**] if need were *Q1–6*

171 **that**] what *Q1–6*

179 **was he**] he was *Q1–6*

180 **his**] that *Q1–6*

183 **off**] by *Q1–6*

184 **to . . . sons**] of a many children *Q1;* of many children *Q2–6*

187 **prize**] prise *Q1–3, Q5–6*

187 **wanton**] lustfull *Q1–6*

188 **his degree**] al his thoughts *Q1–6*

191 **call**] terme *Q1–6*

195 **good**] *Q1–6;* good, *F1*

198 **forth . . . ancestry**] out your royall stocke *Q1–6*

199 **times**] time *Q1–6*

200 **true-derived**] *hyphen, Theobald*

201 **Do,**] *F4;* Do *F1, Q1–6*

202 **Buck. Refuse . . . love.**] *om. Q1–6*

204 **this care**] these cares *Q1;* those cares *Q2–6*

205 **majesty**] dignitie *Q1–6*

212 **kindred**] kin *Q1–6*

214 **know, whe'er**] *Theobald;* know, where *F1;* whether *Q1–6*

219 **'Zounds, I'll**] *Q1–6;* we will *F1*

220 **Glou. O . . . Buckingham.**] *Q1–6*

220 s.d. **Buckingham . . . Citizens**] *Dyce (s.d. om. Q1–6)*

221 **him . . . prince**] them againe, my lord *Q1–6*

222 **If . . . will**] *Ano.* Doe, good my lord, least all the land do *Q1–6*

223 **Will . . . cares**] Would . . . care *Q1–6*

224 **Call**] Well, call *Q1–6*

225 **entreaties**] intreates *Q1–6*

226 s.d. **Enter . . . rest.**] *om. Q1–6*

227 **sage**] you sage *Q1–6*

229 **whe'er**] *Steevens;* where *F1;* whether *Q1–6*

229 **no,**] *Q1–6;* no. *F1*

231 **foul-fac'd**] soule-fac't *Q1–2;* so foule fac't *Q3–6*

235 **doth know**] he knowes *Q1–6*

236 **of this**] thereof *Q1–6*

239 **royal**] kingly *Q1–6*

240 **Richard**] *Q1–2;* King Richard *F1, Q3–6*

240 **worthy**] royall *Q1–6*

241 s.p. **All.**] Mayor. *Q1–6*

242 **may**] will *Q1–6*

243 **please, for**] will, since *Q1–6*

245 **And . . . leave.**] *om. Q1–6*

246 s.d. **To the Bishops.**] *Johnson (subs.)*

246 **work**] taske *Q1–6*

247 **my**] good *Q1–6*

247 **cousin**] *Q1–6;* Cousins *F1*

IV.i

Location: *Theobald (after Pope)*

o.s.d. **at one door . . . at another door**] *Q1–6 (the order of entry is taken from Q1–6 s.d.:* Enter Quee. mother, Duchesse of Yorke, Marques Dorset, at one doore, Duchesse of Glocest. at another doore.; *F1 s.d. reads:* Enter the Queene, Anne Duchesse of Gloucester, the Duchesse of Yorke, and Marquesse Dorset.)

o.s.d. **leading . . . daughter**] *Johnson*

2–7 **Led . . . away?**] *Qu.* Sister well met, whether awaie so fast? *Q1–6*

8 s.p. **Anne.**] Duch. *Q1–2;* Dut. Glo. *Q3–6*

10 **gentle**] tender *Q1–6*

11 s.d. **the Lieutenant**] Lieutenant *Q1–2;* the Lieutenant of the Tower *Q3–6*

14 **doth . . . York?**] fares the Prince? *Q1–6 (see also l. 16)*

15 s.p. **Brak.**] *Capell;* Lieu. *F1, Q1–6 (throughout scene)*

15 **Right . . . patience**] Wel Madam, and in health, but by your leaue *Q1–6*

16 them] him Q1–6
17 strictly] straightlie Q1–6
18 King?] King? whie Q1–6
18 I mean] I crie you mercie, I meane Q1–6
20 between] betwixt Q1–6
21 shall bar] should keepe Q1–6
24 bring . . . sights] feare not thou Q1–6
26 No . . . so] I doe beseech your graces all to pardon me Q1–6
27 and . . . me] I may not doe it Q1–6
27 s.d. Exit Lieutenant.] om. Q1–6
28 an] Q1–4; one F1; at an Q5–6
30 reverend] reuerente Q1–6
30 looker-on] hyphen, Capell
31 s.d. To Anne.] Capell
31 straight] go with me Q1–6
33 Ah . . . asunder] O . . . in sunder Q1–6
35 swoon] sound Q1–6
36 Anne. Despiteful . . . news!] om. Q1–6
37 Be . . . Mother] Madam, haue comfort Q1–6
38 gone] hence Q1–6
39 dogs . . . thy] dogge . . . the Q1–6
48 hours] time Q1–6
50 In . . . way] To meete you on the way, and welcome you Q1–6
52 ill-dispersing] hyphen, Theobald
54 hatch'd] hatch Q1
56 come] om. Q1–6 (Q3–6 add for after sent)
57 s.p. Anne.] Duch. Q1–6
57 with] in Q1–6
58 O] I Q1–6
60 brains] braine Q1–6
61 venom] poyson Q1–6
63 Go, go] Alas Q1–6
65 why] om. Q1–6
69 dear] dead Q1–6
75 More . . . life] As . . . death Q1–6
76 Than] As Q1–6
78 Within . . . time] Euen in so short a space Q1–6
80 mine] my Q1–6
81 hitherto hath held] euer since hath kept Q1–6
81 my] Q1–5; mine F1, Q6
81 rest] sleepe Q1–6
83 Did I enjoy] Haue I enioyed Q1–6
84 with . . . awak'd] haue bene waked by his timerous dreames Q1–6
87 Poor . . . complaining] Alas poore soule, I pittie thy complaints Q1–6
88 with] from Q1–6
90 that] thou Q1–6
91 s.d. To Dorset.] F2 (subs.)
92 s.d. To Anne.] F2 (subs.)
92 tend] garde Q1–6
93 s.d. To Queen Elizabeth.] F2 (subs.)
93 and] om. Q1–6
97–103 Q. Eliz. Stay . . . farewell.] om. Q1–6
103 s.d. Exeunt.] om. Q1–6

IV.ii

Location: *Capell (after Pope)*
o.s.d. Sound a sennet.] The Trumpets sound, Q1–6
o.s.d. in pomp] om. Q1–6
o.s.d. crowned] Q2–6; crownd Q1
o.s.d. Ratcliffe] om. Q1–6
o.s.d. a Page, and others] Capell; with other Nobles Q1–6
2 Buck. My gracious sovereign?] om. Q1–6
3 s.d. Here . . . the throne.] Q1–2; Here . . . throne. Q3; Here . . . his throne Q4–6
3 s.d. Sound.] om. Q1–6
5 glories] honours Q1–6
7 let them] may they Q1–6
8 Ah] O Q1–6
10 speak] say Q1–6
11 loving lord] gracious soueraigne Q1–6
13 lord] liege Q1–6
17 wast] wert Q1–6
20 now] om. Q1–6
22 freezes] freezeth Q1–6
24 little breath, some] breath, some little Q1–6
24 dear] my Q1–6
25 in this] herein Q1–6

26 you herein presently] your grace immediatlie Q1–6
27 s.d. Aside . . . by.] Capell (after Hanmer)
27 gnaws his] bites the Q1–6
32 Boy!] at beginning of l. 31, Q1–6
33 s.p. Page.] Boy. Q1–6 (throughout scene)
35 Will] Would Q1–6
36 I] My lord, I Q1–6
37 spirit] mind Q1–6
41 I . . . man;] om. Q1–6
41 boy] presentlie Q1–6
41 s.d. Page] Pope (subs.); s.d. om. Q1–6
42 deep-revolving] hyphen, Pope
43 counsels] counsell Q1–6
45 Well, be it so.] om. Q1–6
46 Lord . . . news] What neewes with you Q1–6
47–8 Know . . . hear] My Lord, I heare the Marques Dorset Q1–6
49 the parts] those partes beyond the seas Q1–6
49 s.d. Stands apart.] Cambridge
50 Come hither, Catesby.] Catesby. *Cat.* My Lord. Q1–6
51 very grievous sick] sicke and like to die Q1–6
53 poor] borne Q1–6
59 s.d. Exit Catesby.] Capell
65 s.d. Page, with] Capell
65 s.d. Sir James] Neilson
68 lord] soueraigne Q1–6
70 Please you] I my Lord Q1–6
72 there] Q1–6; then F1
73 disturbers] disturbs Q1–6
78 Hark,] om. Q1–6
79 this] that Q1–6
79 s.d. Whispers.] he wispers in his eare. Q1, (whispers) Q2–6
80 There is] Tis Q1–6
81 for it] too Q1–6
82 I . . . straight.] Tis done my gracious lord. / *King* Shal we heare from thee *Tirrel* ere we sleep? *Enter Buc. / Tir.* Ye shall my lord, Q1–5 (apparently a memorial slip repeating III.i.188–9; so Q6, except that it reads Tyrrel's second speech as Yea my good Lord.)
84 request] demand Q1–6
85 rest] passe Q1–6
86 the] that Q1–6
87 wive's] wifes Q1 (wive's is Shakespeare's usual form)
87 son] sonnes Q1–3
87 unto it] to it Q1–6
88 the] your Q1–6
90 Herford] Q1–3, Q5–6; Hertford F1; Herfort Q4
91 Which . . . shall] The which you promised I should Q1–6
94 request] demand Q1–6
95 I . . . me] As I remember Q1–6
98–116 perhaps . . . to-day.] Q1–6
105 call'd] Pope; called Q1–6
117 May . . . suit.] Whie then resolue me whether you wil or no? Q1–6
118 Thou] Tut, tut, thou Q1–6
118 s.d. with . . . Buckingham] Cambridge (subs.)
119 And . . . deep] Is it euen so, rewardst he my true Q1, (rewards) Q2–6
120 such] such deepe Q1–6

IV.iii

IV.iii] *Pope*
Location: *Capell*
o.s.d. Tyrrel] Sir Francis Tirrell Q1–6
1 act] deed Q1–6
2 arch deed] arch-act Q1–3, Q5–6; arch act Q4
4 who] whom Q1–6
5 piece of ruthless] Pope; peece of ruthfull F1; ruthles peece of Q1–2; ruthfull peece of Q3–6
6 Albeit] Although Q1–6
7 Melted] Melting Q1–6
7 kind] Q1–5; milde F1; om. Q6
8 two] Q1–6; to F1

8 deaths'] Theobald; deaths F1, Q1–3, Q5–6; death Q4
8 story] stories Q1–6
9 O] Lo Q1–6
9 the gentle] those tender Q1–5; these tender Q6
10 one] on Q1–2
11 alablaster innocent] innocent alablaster Q1–6
13 Which] Q1–5; And F1; When Q6
15 once] Q1–6; one F1
16 But . . . there] Theobald (after Rowe); But oh the Diuell, there F1; But ô the Diuell their Q1; But ô the diuel: their Q2; But O the diuel: there Q3–4; But O the diuel! there Q5–6
17 When] Whilst Q1, Q3–6; Whilest Q2
17 on,] on Q1–6
19 e'er she] euer he Q1–6
20 Hence] Thus Q1–2 (line om. Q3–6)
20 remorse] Kittredge; Remorse, F1, Q1–2 (line om. Q3–6)
22 bear] bring Q1–6
23 health] haile Q1–6
25 gave] giue Q1–2
27 done] done my Lord Q1–6
30 where . . . truth]] how or in what place Q1–6
31 at] Q1–6; and F1
32 When] And Q1–6
33 thee] Q1–6; the F1
35 then] soone F1
35 Tyr. I . . . leave.] om. Q1–6
35 s.d. Exit.] Q1–6 (Exit Tirrel. after l. 34; see preceding note); placed as in Pope
39 this] the Q1–6
39 good night] godnight Q1–2; goodnight Q3–6
42 on] ore Q1–6
43 go I] I go Q1–6
43 s.d. Enter Ratcliffe.] Enter Catesby. Q1–6 (with Ratcliffe's speeches given to Catesby)
45 or bad news] newes or bad Q1–6
46 Morton] Rowe; Mourton F1; Ely Q1–6
50 rash-levied] hyphen, Pope
50 strength] armie Q1–6
51 learn'd] heard Q1–6
53 leads] Q1–6; leds F1
56 Go] Come Q1–6

IV.iv

IV.iv] *Pope*; Scena Tertia. F1
Location: *Capell*
o.s.d. Enter . . . Margaret.] Enter Queene Margaret sola. Q1–6
4 enemies] aduersaries Q1–6
8 s.d. Retires.] Collier (subs.)
8 s.d. Enter . . . Elizabeth.] Enter the Qu. and the Duchesse of Yorke. Q1–6
9 poor] young Q1–6
10 unblown] Q1–6; vnblowed F1
10 new-appearing] hyphen, Pope
15, 20, 25 s.dd. Aside.] Collier
17–9 Duch. So . . . dead?] after l. 34, Q1–6
18 still and mute] mute and dumbe Q1–6
20–1 Q. Mar. Plantagenet . . . debt.] om. Q1–6
26 Dead . . . sight] Blind sight, dead life Q1–6
26 mortal-living] hyphen, Vaughan conj.
27 due by] Q1–6; due, by F1
28 Brief . . . days,] om. Q1–6
29 s.d. Sitting down.] Capell (subs.)
30 innocent] innocents Q1–6
31 Ah . . . as soon] O . . . aswel Q1–6
34 Ah . . . we] O . . . I Q1–6
34 s.d. Sitting . . . her.] Hanmer (subs.)
35 s.d. Coming forward.] Collier
36 seniory] Capell; signeurie F1; signorie Q1–5; signiorie Q6
37 griefs] woes Q1–6
37–8 hand. . . . society,] Warburton; hand . . . Society. F1; hand, . . . societie, Q1–6
38 s.d. Sitting . . . them.] Capell (subs.)
39 Tell . . . mine:] om. Q1–6
41 Harry] Cambridge; Husband F1; Richard Q1–6
45 holp'st] Q3–6; hop'st F1; hopst Q1–2

48 **doth**] doeth *Q1*
50 **blood**] blouds *Q1–6*
52, 53] *Order as in Capell; lines transposed in
F1; om. Q1–6*
59 **wife**] wifes *Q1*
63 **kill'd**] stabd *Q1–6*
64 **Thy**] *Q1–6; The F1*
66 **Match'd**] Match *Q1–6*
67 **stabb'd**] kild *Q1–6*
68 **frantic**] tragicke *Q1–6*
69 **Th'**] The *Q1–6*
70 **smoth'red**] *Q1–5; smother'd F1; smooth-
ered Q6*
73 **hand, at hand**] hand at handes *Q1*
74 **Ensues**] *Q1–6; Issues F1*
76 **convey'd from hence**] conueied away
Q1–6
78 **and**] to *Q1–6*
86 **heav'd**] heaued *Q1–2*
86 **a-high**] *hyphen, Dyce*
87 **fair**] sweete *Q1–6*
88 **wast . . . flag**] wert a breath, a bubble
Q1–6
89, 90] *Lines transposed, Q1–6*
90 **a . . . bubble**] a garish flagge *Q1–6*
93 **be . . . sons**] are thy children *Q1–2;* be
thy children *Q3–6 (we should perhaps read:
are thy two sons)*
94 **and . . . says**] to thee, and cries *Q1–6*
100–4] *Q1–6 om. l. 103 and read the others
in the order 101, 100, 104, 102*
102, 104 **she**] one *Q1–6*
105 **whirl'd**] whe'eld *Q1;* wheel'd *Q2–6*
107–8 **wast . . . art.**] *F4;* wast. . . . art, *F1;*
wert, . . . art, *Q1–2;* art, . . . art. *Q3–6*
112 **weary**] *Q1–5;* wearied *F1, Q6*
112 **head**] necke *Q1–6*
115 **shall**] will *Q1–6*
118 **nights . . . days**] *Q1–2;* night . . . day *F1,
Q3–6*
120 **sweeter**] fairer *Q1–6*
125 s.d. **Exit Queen Margaret.**] *after l. 26,
Q1–6*
127 **their client's**] *Pope (reading your);* their
Clients *F1;* your Client *Q1–3, Q5–6;*
your clients *Q4*
128 **intestate**] *Q1–6;* intestine *F1 (possibly
the correct reading)*
130 **will**] do *Q1–6*
131 **nothing else**] not at al *Q1–6*
132 **so then,**] so, then *Q1–6*
134 **that**] which *Q1–6*
135 **The trumpet sounds**] I heare his drum
Q1–6
135 s.d. **marching . . . Trumpets**] *om. Q1–6*
136 **me in**] *om. Q1–6*
137 **O**] A *Q1–6*
138 **accursed**] *Q1–6;* acursed *F1*
141 **Where**] *Q1–6;* Where't *F1*
141 **branded**] grauen *Q1–6*
141 **right,**] *Q1–6;* right? *F1*
142 **ow'd**] owed *Q1–2*
143 **poor**] two *Q1–6*
147–8 **Where . . . Hastings?**] Where is kind
Hastings, Riuers, Vaughan, Gray? Q1–6
149 **alarum,**] *F4;* Alarum *F1, Q1–6*
151 s.d. **Flourish. Alarums.**] The trumpets
Q1; The trumpets sound. *Q2;* The trumpets
sounds. *Q3–6*
159 **That**] Which *Q1–6*
160 **Duch. O . . . hear.**] *om. Q1–6*
161 **words**] speach *Q1–6*
164 **torment and in**] anguish, paine and *Q1–6*
170 **desp'rate**] desperate *Q1–6*
172 **confirm'd**] confirmed *Q1–4*
172 **sly, and bloody**] bloudie, trecherous *Q1–6*
173 **More . . . hatred.**] *om. Q1–6*
175 **with**] in *Q1–6*
177 **breakfast**] breake fast *Q1*
178 **eye**] sight *Q1–6*
179 **you, madam**] your grace *Q1–6*
180–3 **Strike . . . So.**] *Du.* O heare me
speake for I shal neuer see thee more. /
King. Come, come, you art too bitter.
Q1, (are) *Q2–6*
187 **more behold**] looke vpon *Q1–6*
188 **grievous**] heauy *Q1–6*
198 **her**] all *Q1–6*

199 **talk**] speake *Q1–6*
200 **moe**] *Q1;* more *F1, Q2–6*
201 **slaughter.**] murther *Q1;* murther, *Q2–6*
205 **gracious.**] *Q1–6;* Gracious? *F1*
206 **live!**] *Q1–2;* liue? *Q3–5;* liue, *F1, Q6*
208–9 **bed, . . . infamy.**] *Pope;* bed: . . .
Infamy, *F1;* bed . . . infamie, *Q1;* bed, . . .
infamie *Q2–6*
210 **of**] from *Q1–6*
212 **a royal princess**] of roiall bloud *Q1–6*
214 **safest only**] onlie safest *Q1–6*
215 **died**] dyed *F1*
216 **birth**] births *Q1–6 (perhaps a preferable
reading)*
217 **ill**] bad *Q1–6*
222–35 **K. Rich. You . . . bosom.**] *om. Q1–6*
236–7 **enterprise . . . wars**] dangerous attempt
of hostile armes *Q1–6*
239 **or**] *Q1–5;* and *F1, Q6*
239 **by . . . harm'd**] were by me wrongd *Q1–6*
241 **discover'd**] *Q1–5;* discoured *F1, Q6*
242 **Th'**] The *Q1–6*
242 **gentle**] mightie *Q1–6*
244 **Unto**] No to *Q1–6*
244 **fortune**] honor *Q1–6*
246 **sorrow**] sorrowes *Q1–6*
249 **ay**] *F1* (I); yea *Q1–6*
255 **kindness' date**] *Capell;* kindnesse date
F1; kindnes doe *Q1–6*
259 **soul;**] *F4 (subs.);* soule *F1;* soule, *Q1–6*
264 **do intend**] meane *Q1–6*
265 **Well**] Saie *Q1–6*   266 **Who**] how *Q5*
266 **should be else?**] *Q1;* else should bee? *F1;*
should else? *Q2–6*
267 **Even . . . it**] I euen I, what thinke you of
it Maddame *Q1–6*
268 **would I**] *Q1–2;* I would *F1, Q3–6*
269 **that are**] *Q1–2;* that were *Q3–6*
273 **haply**] happelie *Q1–2;* happily *Q3–6*
273 **will she**] she wil *Q1–6*
274 **sometimes**] *Q1–2;* sometime *F1, Q3–6*
275 **steep'd**] a handkercher steept *Q1;* a
handkercheffe steept *Q2–6*
276 **handkercher**] *Q1;* hand-kercheefe *F1,
Q2–6 (see l. 275)*
276–7 **which . . . body,**] *om. Q1–6*
278 **wipe . . . withal**] drie . . . therewith *Q1–6*
279 **move**] force *Q1–6*
280 **letter . . . deeds**] storie . . . acts *Q1–6*
282 **ay**] *F1* (I); yea *Q1–6*
284 **You . . . madam**] Come, come, you
mocke me *Q1–2,* (ye) *Q3–6*
284 **is**] *Q1–6*
288–342 **K. Rich. Say . . . years?**] *om. Q1–6*
324 **Of ten times**] *Theobald;* Of ten-times *F1;*
Often-times *F2*
345 **Tell her . . . that**] Saie that . . . which
Q1–6
348 **vail**] waile *Q1–6*
351 **in force**] inforce *Q1–6*
353, 354 **As**] So *Q1–6*
355 **low**] loue *Q1;* lone *Q2–6*
359 **plainly . . . tell**] in plaine termes tell her
Q1–6
361 **Your**] Madame your *Q1–6*
364 **K. Rich. Harp . . . past.**] *placed as in Q1;
after l. 365, F1; om. Q1–6*
364 **on**] one *Q1*
365 s.p. **Q. Eliz.**] *Q1* (Qu.); King. *Q2;
continued, with omission of l. 364, to Queen
Elizabeth, Q3–6*
366 s.p. **K. Rich.**] *Q1–6* (King)
368 **swear—**] *Collier;* sweare. *F1;* sweare by
nothing. *Q1–6*
369, 370, 371 **Thy**] The *Q1–6*
369 **lordly**] holie *Q1–6*
371 **glory**] dignity *Q1–6*
372 **wouldst**] wilt *Q1–6*
374 **K. Rich. Then . . . self-misus'd.**] *after
l. 376, Q1–6*
374 **is self-misus'd**] thy selfe misusest *Q1–6*
376 **it**] that *Q1–6*
377 **God . . . God's**] *Q1–6;* Heauen . . .
Heanens *F1*
378 **didst fear . . . with**] hadst feard . . . by
Q1–6
379 **husband**] brother *Q1–6*
380 **Thou . . . died**] Had not bene broken, nor

my brother slaine *Q1–6*
382 **Th'**] The *Q1–6*
382 **head**] brow *Q1–6*
385 **bedfellows**] plaie-fellows *Q1–6*
386 **the**] a *Q1–6*
387 **What . . . now?**] *om. Q1–6*
387 **The**] By the *Q1–6*
388 **wronged in the**] wrongd in *Q1–6*
390 **time, for . . . thee.**] time, for time, by the
past wrongd, *Q1–2;* time for time, by the
past wrongd, *Q3–4;* time for time, by thee
past wrongd, *Q5–6 (F1 may be only an
unauthoritative sophistication of the Q1
reading, if* the *is understood as* thee, *under
the influence of Q5–6)*
391 **fathers**] parents *Q1–6*
392 **in**] *Q1–4;* with *F1, Q5–6*
394 **barren**] withered *Q1–6*
396 **times ill-us'd**] time misused *Q1–6*
396 **o'erpast**] *Q1–6;* repast *F1*
398 **affairs**] attempt *Q1–6*
400 **Heaven . . . hours!**] *om. Q1–6*
403 **proceeding . . . dear**] proceedings . . . pure
Q1–6
407–8 **myself . . . land**] this land and me, /
To thee her selfe *Q1–6*
409 **Death**] Sad *Q1–6*
411 **by**] *om. Q1*
412 **dear**] good *Q1–6*
415 **my**] by *Q1–6*
417 **peevish-fond**] *Q3–6 (hyphen, Malone
conj.);* peeuish found *F1;* pieuish, fond
Q1–2
419 **you**] thee *Q1–6*
422 **Yet**] But *Q1–6*
423 **I bury**] I buried *Q1–2;* Ile burie *Q4–6*
424 **will**] shall *Q1–6*
425 **Selves**] Selfes *Q1–6*
425 **recomforture**] recomfiture *Q1–6*
429 **And . . . mind.**] *om. Q1–6*
430 **and so**] *om. Q1–6*
430 s.d. **Exit Queen Elizabeth.**] *placed as in
Q1–6* (Exit. *Q1–2;* Exit Qu. *Q3–6); after
l. 429, F1* (Exit. Q.)
431 **shallow, changing**] *Theobald;* shallow-
changing *F1;* shallow changing *Q1–6*
431 s.d. **Enter Ratcliffe**] *placed as in Q1–6;
after l. 432, F1*
431 s.d. **Catesby following**] *Capell*
432 **How . . . news?**] *om. Q1–6*
433 **Most mighty**] My gracious *Q1–6*
434 **our shores**] the shore *Q1–6*
435 **hollow-hearted**] hollow harted *Q1–4*
440 **Norfolk**] Norff. *Q1–5*
442 **good**] *om. Q1–6*
442 **Catesby**] *om. Q1–6*
443–4 **Cate. I . . . hither.**] *om. Q1–6*
444 **Ratcliffe**] *Rowe;* Catesby *F1*
444 **Post**] post thou *Q1–6*
445 **thither**] there *Q1–6*
445 s.d. **To Catesby.**] *Rowe*
446 **stay'st thou here**] standst thou still
Q1–3, Q5–6, (stands) *Q4*
447 **liege . . . pleasure**] Soueraigne, let me
know your minde *Q1–6*
448 **to him**] them *Q1–2;* him *Q3–6*
450 **that**] *om. Q1–6*
451 **suddenly**] presentlie *Q1–6*
452 **Cate. I go.**] *om. Q1–6*
452 s.d. **Exit.**] *om. Q1–6*
453 **may . . . I**] is it your highnes pleasure I
shall *Q1–4;* it is your highnes pleasure I
shall *Q5;* is your highnesse pleasure I
shall *Q6*
456 **My mind**] My mind is changd sir, my
minde *Q1–6*
456 s.d. **Stanley**] Darbie *Q1–6 (s.d. after
you? l. 456)*
456 **Stanley**] How now *Q1–6*
457 **None good,**] *F4;* None, good *F1;* None
good *Q1–6*
457 **liege**] Lord *Q1–6*
458 **well . . . reported**] it may well be told
Q1–6
460 **needst . . . miles**] doest . . . mile *Q1–2;*
doost . . . mile *Q3–6*
461 **mayest . . . the nearest**] maist . . . a
neerer *Q1–6*

464 **doth**] doeth *Q1*
466 **as you guess**] sir, as you guesse, as you guesse *Q1–6*
467 **Morton**] Elie *Q1–6*
468 **here**] there *Q1–6*
469 **unsway'd**] vnswaied *Q1–2*
473 **makes . . . seas**] doeth . . . sea *Q1–2*; doth . . . sea *Q3–6*
478 **my good lord**] mightie liege *Q1–6*
480 **be**] are *Q1–6*
482 **Safe-conducting**] Safe conducting *Q1–6*
484 **me**] Richard *Q1–6*
486 **King**] soueraigne *Q1–6*
487 **Pleaseth**] Please it *Q1–6*
490 **Ay**] *F1* (I); I, I *Q1–6*
490 **wouldst**] wouldest *Q1*
491 **But . . . thee**] I will not trust you Sir *Q1–6*
494 **Go . . . but**] Well, go muster men, but heare you *Q1–6*
495 **heart**] faith *Q1–6*
497 s.d. **Exit Stanley.**] *om. Q1–2*; Exit Dar. *Q3–5*; Exit. *Q6*
498 s.p. **1. Mess.**] *Capell*; Mess. *F1, Q1–6*
500 **Edward**] William *Q1–6*
501 **elder brother**] brother there *Q1–6*
503 s.p. **2. Mess.**] *Capell*; Mess. *F1, Q1–6*
503 **In . . . liege**] My Liege, in Kent *Q1–6*
505 **the . . . strong**] their aide, and still their power increaseth *Q1–6*
506, 509, 517 s.pp. **3. Mess.**] *Capell*; Mess. *F1, Q1–6*
506 **great**] the Duke of *Q1–6*
507 **you**] *Q1–5*; ye *F1, Q6*
507 **death?**] *Pope*; Death, *F1*; death. *Q1–6*
507 s.d. **He striketh him.**] *after l. 506, Q1–6*
508 **There . . . bring**] Take that vntill thou bring me *Q1–5*, (you) *Q6*
509–10 **The news . . . waters**] Your grace mistakes, the newes I bring is good, / My newes is that by sudden floud, and fall of water, *Q1–6*
511 **Buckingham's**] The Duke of Buckinghams *Q1–6*
512 **wand'red away alone**] fled *Q1–6*
513–4 **I . . . thine.**] O I crie you mercie, I did mistake, / Ratcliffe reward him, for the blow I gaue him, *Q1–6*
515 **well-advised friend proclaim'd**] well aduised friend giuen out *Q1–6*
516 **Reward . . . in**] Rewardes for him that brings in Buckingham *Q1–6*
517 **lord**] liege *Q1–6*
518 s.p. **4. Mess.**] *Capell*; Mess. *F1, Q1–6*
519 **in Yorkshire are**] are vp *Q1–6*
520 **But . . . Highness**] Yet . . . grace *Q1–6*
521 **by tempest**] *om. Q1–6*
522 **Dorsetshire**] Dorshire *Q1–5*
523 **Unto . . . banks**] to aske them on the shore *Q1–6*
527 **Hois'd . . . his course again**] Hoist . . . away *Q1–6*
534 **tidings,**] *Q1–5*; Newes, but *F1*; newes, *Q6*
538 s.d. **Flourish.**] *om. Q1–6*

IV.v

IV.v] *Capell*; Scena Quarta. *F1*
Location: *Hanmer*
o.s.d. **Urswick, a priest**] *Theobald, ed.*
1 s.p. **Stan.**] *Pope*; Der. *F1* (*throughout scene*); Dar. *Q1–6* (*throughout scene*)
2 **the most deadly**] this most bloudie *Q1–6*
5 **holds off**] with holds *Q1*; withholds *Q2–5*; with-holds *Q6*
6–7 **So . . . say**] Retourne vnto thy Lord, commend me to him, / Tell him *Q1–6*
6–8 **So . . . daughter.**] *in Q1–6 these lines* (*subs.*) *follow l. 18, replacing l. 19 of F1*
8 **should**] shall *Q1–6*
10 **Pembroke**] *Q1–2*; Penbroke *F1*; Pembrooke *Q3–6*
10 **Ha'rford-West**] *Q1* (Harford-west); Hertford West *F1*; Herford-west *Q2, Q5*; Hertford-west *Q3, Q4*; Hertford west *Q6*
15 **And**] *om. Q1–6*
15 **ap**] vp *Q1–5*
16 **And . . . name**] With many moe of noble fame *Q1–6*

17 **do they**] they do *Q1–6*
17 **power**] course *Q1–6*
19 **Well . . . hand.**] *om. Q1–6*
20 **My letter**] These letters *Q1–6*

V.i

Location: *Capell (after Pope)*
o.s.d. **with Halberds . . . led**] *om. Q1–6*
o.s.d. **and the Sheriff**] *Rowe* (*subs.*)
2, 11 s.pp. **Sher.**] Rat. *Q1–6* (*throughout scene*)
2 **good**] *om. Q1–6*
3 **Grey and Rivers**] Riuers, Gray *Q1–6*
10 **fellow**] fellowes *Q1–6*
11 **my lord**] *om. Q1–6*
12 **doomsday.**] *Q1–6* (*subs.*); doomsday *F1*
13 **which**] that *Q1–6*
17 **whom . . . trusted**] I trusted most *Q1–6*
20 **which**] that *Q1–6*
23 **doth**] doeth *Q1–5*
24 **in . . . bosoms**] on . . . bosome *Q1–6*
25 **Thus . . . neck**] Now Margarets curse, is fallen vpon my head *Q1–6*
28 **lead me, officers**] sirs, conuey me *Q1–6*
29 s.d. **and Sheriff**] *Theobald* (*subs.*); s.d. om. *Q1–6*

V.ii

Location: *Hanmer*
o.s.d. **Enter . . . Colors.**] Enter Richmond with drums and trumpets. *Q1–6*
10 **embowell'd**] inboweld *Q1–5*; imboweld *Q6*
11 **Is**] Lies *Q1–6*
11 **centry**] center *Q1–6*
12 **Near**] *Q1–5*; Ne're *F1*; Neere *Q6*
14 **cheerly**] *F4*; cheerely *F1*; cheerelie *Q1*; cheere *Q2–6*
17 s.p. **Oxf.**] 1 Lo. *Q1–6*
17 **men**] swordes *Q1–6*
18 **this guilty**] that bloudie *Q1–6*
19 s.p. **Herb.**] 2 Lo. *Q1–6*
19 **turn**] flie *Q1–6*
20 s.p. **Blunt.**] 3 Lo. *Q1–6*
20 **what**] who *Q1–6*
21 **dearest . . . fly**] greatest . . . shrinke *Q1–6*
24 s.d. **Exeunt omnes.**] Exit. *Q1*; *om. Q2–6*

V.iii

V.iii] *Pope*
Location: *Pope*
o.s.d. **at one door**] *Sisson*
o.s.d. **in arms**] *om. Q1–6*
o.s.d. **with others**] *Q1–6* (*Q1–6 enter Catesby here in place of Surrey*)
1 **tent**] tentes *Q1–6*
2 **My . . . sad**] Whie, how now Catesbie, whie lookst thou so bad *Q1*, (sad) *Q2–6*
3 s.p. **Sur.**] Cat. *Q1–6*
4 **My . . . liege.**] Norffolke, come hether. *Q1–6*
6 **loving**] gracious *Q1–6*
7 **tent**] tent there *Q1–6*
7 s.d. **Soldiers . . . tent.**] *ed.* (*after Capell*)
8 **all's**] all is *Q1–6*
9 **traitors**] foe *Q1–6*
10 **power**] number *Q1–6*
11 **battalia**] battalion *Q1–6*
13 **faction**] partie *Q1–6*
14 **the . . . noble**] my tent there, valiant *Q1–6*
15 **ground**] field *Q1–6*
17 **lack**] want *Q1–6*
18 s.d. **at . . . door**] *Sisson*; *Q1–2 s.d. reads:* Enter Richmond with the Lordes, &c.; *Q3–6 om.* &c.
18 s.d. **Blunt . . . tent**] *Capell*
18 **set**] sete *Q2–6*
20 **tract**] tracke *Q1–6*
21 **token**] signall *Q1–6*
22 **Sir . . . you**] Where is Sir William Brandon, he *Q1–6*
23–8 **Give . . . me.**] *Q1–6 shift ll. 23–6 to follow* Blunt. *l. 44 and om. ll. 27–8*
26 **power**] strength *Q1–6*
28 **you**] *F2*; your *F1*
29 **keeps**] keepe *Q1–6*
33 **captain . . . me**] Blunt before thou goest *Q1–6*

34 **Stanley . . . you**] Stanlie quarterd, doest thou *Q1–6*
40 **Sweet . . . him**] Good captaine Blunt beare my good night to him *Q1–6* (*cf. l. 30*)
41 **note**] scrowle *Q1–6*
43 **And . . . to-night.**] *om. Q1–6*
44 **Good . . . Blunt.**] Farewell good Blunt. *Q1–6*
44 s.d. **Exit Blunt.**] *Capell*
44 **gentlemen**] *om. Q1–6*
46 **In to**] *Q1–5*; Into *F1, Q6*
46 **my . . . dew**] our . . . aire *Q1–6*
46 s.d. **They . . . tent.**] *om. Q1–6*
46 s.d. **to his tent**] *Capell*
46 s.d. **and Catesby**] Catesbie, &c. *Q1–2*
47 **is't**] is *Q1–6*
47–8 **It's . . . a' clock.**] It is sixe of clocke, full supper time. *Q1–2*, (of the) *Q3–6*
48 **I . . . to-night.**] *beginning at this half-line, the basic text for the remainder of the play is* Q1
54 **sentinels**] *F1*; centinell *Q1–6*
57 s.d. **Exit.**] *F1*
58 **Catesby**] Ratcliffe *F1*
59 s.p. **Cate.**] *Pope*; Rat. *Q1–6, F1*
61 **sunrising**] *Q6, F1* (Sun-rising); sun rising *Q1–5*
62 s.d. **Exit Catesby.**] *Cambridge*
65–6 **heavy. Ratcliffe!**] *F1* (subs.); heauy Ratliffe. *Q1–5*; heauy Ratcliffe. *Q6*
68 **thou**] *om. F1*
74 s.d. **Wine brought.**] *Capell*
77 **Ratcliffe**] *Q3, Q5–6, F1*; Ratliffe *Q1–2, Q4*
78 s.d. **Richard sleeps.**] *Neilson*
78 s.d. **Ratcliff**] *Q6, F1*; Ratliffe *Q1–5*
78 s.d. **Lords . . . attending**] *Cambridge*
79 s.p. **Stan.**] *Pope*; Dar. *Q1* (*throughout scene*); Der. *F1* (*throughout scene*)
79 **sit**] *Q2–6, F1*; set *Q1*
82 **loving**] noble *Q3–6, F1* (*picked up from l.81*)
85 **that.**] *F1*; that *Q1–2*; that: *Q3–6*
89 **the**] th' *F1*
90 **mortal-staring**] *hyphen, Steevens*
95 **brother, tender**] *F1*; brother tender *Q1–5*; tender brother *Q6*
100 **sund'red**] *F1*; sundried *Q1–2*; sundired *Q3–4*; sundered *Q5–6*
101 **rites**] *F1*; rights *Q1–6*
104 **thoughts**] noise *F1*
107 s.d. **Exeunt.**] *Q3–6, F1*; Exunt. *Q1–2*
107 s.d. **Manet Richmond.**] *F1*
112 **The**] Th' *F1*
114 **the**] thy *Q3–5, F1*
117 s.d. **Sleeps.**] *F1*
117 s.d. **young**] *om. Q3–6, F1*
117 s.d. **to**] *Q2–6, F1*
117 s.d. **Henry**] *Q2–6, F1*; Harry *Q1*
117 s.d. **to Richard**] *om. Q3–6, F1*
122 **butchered**] butcher'd *F1*; butchred *Q3–5*
125 **deadly**] *om. F1*
130 **thy**] *om. F1*
131, 139, 141, 142, 154 s.dd. **To Richard.**] *Rowe*
131 **sit**] *Q2–6, F1*; set *Q1*
139 s.p. **Ghost of R.**] *Dyce*; King *Q1*; Riu. *Q2–6, F1*
141, 142 s.pp. **Ghost of**] *Dyce*
145 **Will**] *Q2–6, F1*; Wel *Q1*
145 s.d., 146–53 **Enter . . . flourish.**] *these lines follow l. 158 in Q3–6, F1* (*this gives a chronological order based on the time of death*)
146 s.p. **Ghosts.**] *F1*; Ghost *Q1–2, 6*; Gho. *Q3–5*
147 **lead**] laid *Q2–6, F1*
149 **souls bid**] soule bids *F1*
153 s.d. **Hastings**] Lord Hastings *Q3–6, F1*
158 s.d. **Lady Anne**] Queene Anne *Q3–6*; Anne *F1*
159, 167 s.pp., s.dd. **Ghost. To Richard.**] *F1*
161 **perturbations**] *Q2–6, F1*; preturbations *Q1*
175 **Richmond's**] *Q2–6, F1*; Richmons *Q1*
176 **falls**] fall *F1*
176 s.d. **The Ghosts vanish.**] *Rowe*
176 s.d. **starteth . . . a**] starteth out of a *Q3–6*; starts out of his *F1*

180 now] not *Q2–6, F1*
182 What . . . Myself?] What do I feare my selfe? *Q2–6*; What? do I feare my Selfe? *F1*
183 am] *Q2–6, F1*; and *Q1* (*though Q1 and makes possible sense, all eds. accept Q2 am*)
185 reason why—] *Dyce*; reason whie? *Q1–2*; reason why, *Q3–6*; reason: why? *F1*
196 Perjury, perjury] Periurie *Q3–6, F1*
196 highest] high'st *F1*
197 direst] dyr'st *F1*
199 Throng] Throng all *Q3–6, F1*
199 the] th' *F1*
199 all,] *Q2–6, F1*; all *Q1*
201 will] shall *Q3–6, F1*
202 And] Nay *F1*
208 'Zounds, who is] Who's *F1*
212–4 K. Rich. O . . . lord.] *om. F1*
217 strook] *Q2–6*; stroke *Q1, F1*
221 ease-dropper] *F1*; ease dropper *Q1*; ewse dropper *Q2*; ewse-dropper *Q3*; eawse-dropper *Q4*; ewese-dropper *Q5–6*
222 see] heare *Q3–6, F1*
222 s.d. Exeunt.] Exeunt Richard & Ratliffe. *F1*
222 s.d. sitting . . . tent] *F1*
223 s.p. Lords.] *Q3–6*; Lo. *Q1*; Lor. *Q2*; Richm. *F1*
226 s.p. Lords.] *F1*; Lo. *Q1*; Lor. *Q2–6*
227 fairest-boding] *hyphen, Theobald*
229 departure] *Q2–6, F1*; depature *Q1*
232 soul] Heart *F1*
235 s.p. Lords.] *F4*; Lo. *Q1–2*; Lor. *Q3–6, F1*
242 high-rear'd] *hyphen, Pope*
243 Richard except,] *Q3–6*; Richard, except *Q1–2*; (Richard except) *F1*
247 established] establish'd *F1*
249 slaughtered] slaugtered *Q3*; slandered *Q4*; slaughter'd *F1*

250 foil] soile *Q3–6, F1*
254 in] *Q2–6, F1*; ln *Q1*
255 sweat] sweare *Q3–6, F1*
270 s.d. Exeunt.] *Capell*
270 s.d. Attendants, and forces] *Capell*; &c. *Q1–6*; and Catesby *F1*
274 smil'd] *F1*; smiled *Q1–6*
275 s.d. The clock striketh.] Clocke strikes. *F1*
280–1 somebody. Ratcliffe!] *F1*; some bodie Rat. *Q1–6*
283 doth] *Q2–6, F1*; doeth *Q1*
290 Stanley] *Q2–6, F1*; Standlie *Q1*
292 ordered] ordred *F1*
293 drawn] *Q2–6, F1*; drawen *Q1*
293 out am] *om. Q2–6, F1*
297 this] the *Q3–6, F1*
299 main] *Q2–6, F1*; matne *Q1*
300 well winged] well-winged *F1*
301 boot] *Q3–6, F1*; bootes *Q1–2*
302 s.d. He . . . paper.] *om. F1*
304 s.d. Reads.] *Rowe*
307 unto] to *F1*
309 Conscience is but] Conscience is *Q3–6*; For Conscience is *F1*
311 conscience, swords] *Q2–6, F1*; conscience swords, *Q1*
312 to it] too't *F1*
313 s.d. His . . . Army.] *om. F1*
320 to you] you to *Q2–6, F1*
321 wives] *Q2–6, F1*; wifes *Q1*
325 milksop] *Q6, F1*; milkesopt *Q1–5*
335 in] on *Q3–6, F1*
337 s.d. Drum afar off.] *F1*
338 Fight] Right *Q3–6, F1*
338 bold] boldly *Q2–6, F1*
341 s.d. Enter a Messenger.] *F1*
351 them! Victory] *Pope*; them victorie *Q1*; them, Victorie *Q2–6, F1*
351 helms] helpes *Q3, Q5–6, F1*

351 s.d. Exeunt.] *om. Q3–6, F1*

V.iv

V.iv] *Capell*
Location: *ed.* (*after Rowe*)
o.s.d. Norfolk . . . him] *Capell*
6 s.d. Alarums.] *F1*
13 s.d. Exeunt.] *Theobald*

V.v

V.v] *Dyce*
Location: *ed.* (*after Rowe*)
o.s.d. Then . . . sounded,] Retreat *F1*
o.s.d. flourish, and] *ed.* (*from F1 and Flourish*)
o.s.d. other] diuers other *F1*
o.s.d. etc.] *om. Q3–6, F1*
3, 10 s.pp. Stan.] *Pope*; Dar. *Q1–6*; Der. *F1*
4 Lo . . . royalty] Loe here this long vsurped royalties *Q2–6*; Loe, / Heere these long vsurped Royalties *F1*
7 enjoy it] *om. Q3–6, F1*
11 it . . . now] you please) we may *F1*
13 s.p. Stan.] *F1* (Der.)
13 Walter Lord Ferrers] *Capell* (*after Holinshed*); Water Lord Ferris *Q1–5*; Walter Lord Ferris *Q6, F1*
14 Brakenbury] *F4*; Brookenbury *Q1–2*; Brokenbury *Q3–6, F1*
23 scarr'd] *F1*; scard *Q1–6*
25 slaughter'd] slaughtered *Q2–6, F1*
28 division,] *Johnson conj.*; deuision. *Q1*; Diuision. *Q2–6, F1*
32 their] thy *Q3–6, F1*
33 smooth-fac'd] *F1*; smooth-faste *Q1–3, Q5*; smooth fast *Q4*; smooth-fac't *Q6*
41 here] *F1*; heare *Q1–6*
41 s.d. Exeunt.] *F1* (Exeunt / FINIS.); FINIS. *Q1–6*

Halberds and bills

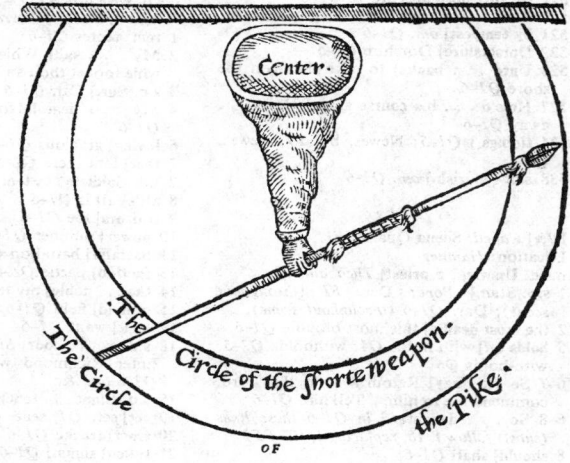

The pike

From *Di Grassi His True Art of Defence*, trans. I. G. (1594). (*By permission of the Harvard College Library*)

King John

THE DATE OF *King John*, a play noted by Francis Meres in 1598 and, so far as we know, first printed in the Folio of 1623, is difficult to fix. Although 1594–95 would seem to be the safest guess, external evidence is altogether lacking and internal evidence is, as usual, oblique and inconclusive. "Basilisco-like" (I.i.244) no doubt derives from the name of a character in *Soliman and Perseda*, a play written between 1589 and 1592 and perhaps subsequently revived. The action of *King John*, about an English monarch who is plagued by a rival with a better claim, by the enmity of Rome, and by a strong invading power, suggests the tangled relationships between Elizabeth, her cousin Mary Stuart, and the King of Spain; but to construe the play as an allegory of the Armada years is to press the case too hard. Moreover, attempts to fix a date from alleged topical allusions to the defeat of the Armada (1588) in the loss of the French fleet, to Henry IV's apostasy (1593) in the vacillation of King Philip and the Dauphin Lewis, and to the death of Shakespeare's son Hamnet (1596) in Constance's laments for Arthur do not impart conviction.

The Troublesome Reign of John, King of England—an anonymous play published in two parts in 1591, ascribed to "W. Sh." on the title-page of the second quarto in 1611, to "W. Shakespeare" in the third quarto in 1622, and subsequently to almost everyone who was writing for the stage in the early 1590's—poses special problems about the source and date of Shakespeare's play and has therefore prompted much conjecture. That *The Troublesome Reign* and *King John* are somehow intimately related is not open to

dispute; indeed, the close parallelism of their plots, which, although Shakespeare's play is some three hundred lines shorter than its companion piece, exhibit virtually the same episodes in the same order, makes it clear that one play is based upon the other, unless a common source, now lost, is postulated. This kinship is confirmed by smaller details as well, as when both confusingly identify Widomar, Viscount of Limoges, with Leopold, Archduke of Austria (II.i.5), or deprive Constance of her third husband in order to present her as a strident widow (II.i.32), or show scores of verbal similarities, though only two that extend to as much as a whole line of verse (II.i.528, V.iv.42). *The Troublesome Reign* has long been held a source—in Dover Wilson's opinion, indeed, the only source—of *King John*; but Peter Alexander and E. A. J. Honigmann have separately advanced the theory that *King John* was written first (about 1590–91) and that *The Troublesome Reign* should be regarded as a reported text, or "bad" quarto, of Shakespeare's play. However, the data cited to support this view are at best tangential, and in the absence of more compelling evidence most scholars still prefer to think that Shakespeare wrote *King John*, as E. K. Chambers said, with a copy of *The Troublesome Reign* at hand.

It is most unlikely that Shakespeare knew of John Bale's *King John*, a virulently anti-Catholic play of the 1530's, but he certainly used Holinshed's *Chronicles* and probably Foxe's *Acts and Monuments* for details not included in *The Troublesome Reign*, and he may also have looked at Matthew Paris' *Chronica Majora*. Mr. Honigmann thinks that he got the date of Queen Elinor's death (IV.ii.120)—which was apparently unavailable in any printed source—from the Latin manuscript Wakefield chronicle and that for the great scene (IV.i) between Hubert and Arthur he followed the Latin chronicle of Ralph Coggeshall.

Stylistically, *King John* is marked by tumid rhetoric. It is filled with violent action, but the action often serves as the occasion for debate or disputation, and consequently the play is very verbal. For example, in a wryly comic scene almost at the beginning Faulconbridge and his puny brother contest their patrimony; and the second act presents a sequence of debates—or at any rate of declamations—with John opposed to Philip, Elinor to Constance, the French and English heralds before the city of Angiers, Faulconbridge and Hubert, each advancing his proposal. Elsewhere the action hovers on such forensic exhibitions as Pandulph's equivocating defense of oath-breaking (III.i.253–97), Arthur's moving plea to Hubert for his life (IV.i.253 ff.), and the Dauphin's explanation of his plan to conquer England (V.ii.78–108). Most conspicuous of all are Constance's lamentations, in Acts II and III, for the injuries to her son. "I defy all counsel, all redress," she says when he is captured,

> But that which ends all counsel, true redress:
> Death, death. O amiable lovely death!
> Thou odoriferous stench! sound rottenness!
> Arise forth from the couch of lasting night,
> Thou hate and terror to prosperity,
> And I will kiss thy detestable bones,
> And put my eyeballs in thy vaulty brows,
> And ring these fingers with thy household worms,
> And stop this gap of breath with fulsome dust,
> And be a carrion monster like thyself.
> Come, grin on me, and I will think thou smil'st,
> And buss thee as thy wife. Misery's love,
> O, come to me! (III.iv.23–36)

Philip's comment on this appalling woman's rhetoric (which has endeared the role to many actresses) is one that every reader will endorse: "You are as fond of grief as of your child." On the other hand, such scenes as John's exchange with Hubert (III.iii.64–66) about getting rid of Arthur are so tight and so alive with drama that they mark a new advance in Shakespeare's style:

> *K. John.* Thou art his keeper.
> *Hubert.* And I'll keep him so,
> That he shall not offend your Majesty.
> *K. John.* Death.
> *Hubert.* My lord?
> *K. John.* A grave.
> *Hubert.* He shall not live.
> *K. John.* Enough.

A puzzling and uneven play, *King John* is a daring exploration into the murky depths of *Realpolitik*. In Shakespeare's earlier history plays—the *Henry VI* trilogy and *Richard III*—politics is treated as a branch of morals. The course of events, apparently so jagged and complex, is shown to have a pattern and a direction that reveal a moral purpose coextensive with the will of God. Even if evil seems to triumph over good,

as when the tyrant Richard wades through blood to reach the throne, we know that God directs events—the convulsions of dynastic struggle no less than the fall of a sparrow—and that His intentions are benign. This doctrine of providential history, which St. Augustine devised and which most Tudor chroniclers thriftily converted into a tool of party politics, begins to yield to something darker and more subtle in *King John*. Shakespeare is still concerned with politics, of course, but in tracing the link between politics and morals he is less cocksure and doctrinaire. Slogans no longer serve his purpose, nor do the inert, reassuring commonplaces of Hall and Holinshed supply the need for explanation. Instead, the ambiguities of character assert themselves, and history is presented not as a paradigm of moral purpose but as a tangled skein of good and evil, where mixed motives are revealed in indecisive actions, and where even a good man fears to lose his way.

This being a history play, the dynastic situation itself (which Shakespeare, as usual, distorts for his own purpose) exemplifies equivocation. In John, Arthur, and Faulconbridge we are presented, as it were, with three aspects of kingship: a sovereign whose very title is suspect, his youthful rival whose better claim is made the pawn of scheming politicians, and a bastard son of royalty who, finding his identity, is compelled to exercise the awful functions wherein the other two have failed. In other words, the bad, weak man in possession of the throne flouts the helpless rightful heir, brings his kingdom to distraction, and dies as the very "module of confounded royalty" while the Bastard rises to assume the kingly burden that the King himself could not sustain. By juxtaposing these contrapuntal ambiguities Shakespeare does great violence to the notion that might and right are always intertwined, but he makes us look anew at what Edmund Burke called the solemn plausibilities whereby we order our existence.

One such solemn plausibility is the moral authority of kingship, which is scrutinized relentlessly. In this play the eponymous hero is in fact an anti-hero whom we cannot admire and whom we find it easy to detest. Whereas the author of *The Troublesome Reign*, like virtually all the Tudor chroniclers, presents John as a Protestant martyr, a "warlike Christian" who

> set himself against the Man of Rome,
> Until base treason (by a damned wight)
> Did all his former triumphs put to flight,

Shakespeare, subordinating this facile chauvinistic theme, makes him unstable, treacherous, and cruel—an adventurer who has grasped a crown too big for him to wear. He is a king *de facto*, not *de jure*, whose "strong possession," not his "right," is all that he can claim. Even weaker than his title, however, is his conception of what a king should be and do, for he soils everything he touches. At three important junctures of his reign—his accession (which leads to such ignoble consequences), his humiliation and defeat by Rome, and the rebellion of the nobles who were pledged to his protection—he is shown to be a failure; and therefore it remains for his successor

> To set a form upon that indigest
> Which he hath left so shapeless and so rude.

John typifies the world in which he lives, which is a moral swamp and has the "smell of sin." He himself, abetted by his wolfish mother, moves from one betrayal to another; Lady Faulconbridge, accused by her own son of adultery, admits that she has been unfaithful to her husband; Philip of France, adept at power politics, forsakes the helpless Constance to make common cause with John and then betrays his new ally at papal instigation; Salisbury, citing the "infection of the time," deserts his hard-pressed king and then deserts the French when the traitorous Melun reveals their schemes; for all his unctuous piety, Pandulph is a savage papal politician; John, a royal guest, is poisoned by his host. It is therefore not surprising that the Bastard, instructed by his betters, declares that everyone is "mad" and concludes that "tickling commodity," a sly or ruthless sense of self-advantage, is

> the bias of the world—
> The world, who of itself is peized well,
> Made to run even upon even ground,
> Till this advantage, this vile-drawing bias,
> This sway of motion, this commodity,
> Makes it take head from all indifferency,
> From all direction, purpose, course, intent.
> (II.i.574–80)

It is significant, however, that this famous soliloquy (II.i) occurs so early in the play, for it is the start and not the end of the Bastard's hard-bought worldly knowledge. As John, initially so brisk and bold and callous, sinks through moral torpor to defeat, Faulconbridge grows strong in self-awareness. In a world of knaves and fools that is governed by "Commodity" he alone cuts through fraud and privileged error to assert the claims of valor, truth, and loyalty. With neither John's "possession" of the throne nor Arthur's "right" to it, he exemplifies the true regality of character, for in him there shines "the very spirit of Plantagenet."

He is therefore one of Shakespeare's grand creations. In him, as Johnson said, levity and greatness are united. One sign of his distinction is a superb vitality, which has a language all its own. Most of the other characters are insulated, as it were, in a rhetoric appropriate to their rank and function, and therefore it is hard to distinguish, say, Constance from the wailing woman or Pandulph from the papal legate; but Faulconbridge is nothing but himself. Slangy, coarse, and impudent, his language throbs with life; and whether mocking the pretensions of his brother or pointing to the "bare-pick'd bone of majesty" or rousing John to action he speaks in his own voice. As Mark Van Doren has observed, poetry works like yeast in every line he utters. Thus his comment on Hubert's brand of oratory:

> Here's a stay
> That shakes the rotten carcass of old Death
> Out of his rags! Here's a large mouth indeed,
> That spits forth death and mountains, rocks and seas,
> Talks as familiarly of roaring lions
> As maids of thirteen do of puppy-dogs!
> What cannoneer begot this lusty blood?
> He speaks plain cannon-fire, and smoke, and bounce,
> He gives the bastinado with his tongue;
> Our ears are cudgell'd—not a word of his
> But buffets better than a fist of France.
> 'Zounds, I was never so bethump'd with words
> Since I first call'd my brother's father dad.
> (II.i.455–67)

As a stylist, then, Faulconbridge ridicules and undercuts the fustian of the play; as a man of action he provides a contrast to the moral stupefaction of King John and all the others. His own position made uncertain by virtue of his birth, he is in a sense an uncommitted man; he has no dynastic aspirations of his own; and he stands outside the "tug and scamble" of dirty politics. A kind of Machiavel, as J. F. Danby has suggested, he is sometimes witty, saucy, and detached, sometimes blunt and crude, but we cannot resist his candor. As a "beggar," he remarks, he will rail upon the rich, but being rich himself he will "say there is no vice but beggary," for he is an opportunist who, instructed by his betters, is determined to survive at any cost.

> Since kings break faith upon commodity,
> Gain, be my lord, for I will worship thee.
> (II.i.597–98)

And yet Faulconbridge becomes the hero of the play, for he represents a kind of truth that bears the stamp of knowledge. This enables him to root his actions in belief, or at any rate in loyalties that he has tested by experience. He is true to England, which he would save at any cost, and also to his king; and although he does not formulate his politics in systematic terms, his instinct is unerring. Thus the nobles, when they come on Arthur's broken body, vent their wordy grief in rhetoric:

> This is the very top,
> The heighth, the crest, or crest unto the crest,
> Of murther's arms, (IV.iii.45–47)

and then slip into rebellion; but Faulconbridge, no less appalled than they, shows the loyalty and valor that mark him as a special man. Like most people of good will and elemental decency he is lost "among the thorns and dangers of this world," but when action is required, he acts. "Wherefore do you droop?" he asks the spineless, wicked king whom misfortune overwhelms,

> why look you sad?
> Be great in act, as you have been in thought.
> Let not the world see fear and sad distrust
> Govern the motion of a kingly eye.
> Be stirring as the time, be fire with fire,
> Threaten the threat'ner, and outface the brow

King John

Of dragging horror; so shall inferior eyes,
That borrow their behaviors from the great,
Grow great by your example, and put on
The dauntless spirit of resolution.
Away, and glister like the god of war
When he intendeth to become the field.
Show boldness and aspiring confidence.

(V.i.44–56)

Wisely, John gives to Faulconbridge "the ordering of this present time," and Shakespeare gives to him the

speech wherein, beneath the clatter of what some have called "Armada rhetoric," lies the final wisdom of the play:

This England never did, nor never shall,
Lie at the proud foot of a conqueror,
But when it first did help to wound itself.
Now these her princes are come home again,
Come the three corners of the world in arms,
And we shall shock them. Nought shall make us rue,
If England to itself do rest but true.

Herschel Baker

THE DESCENDANTS OF HENRY II

Henry II m. Eleanor of Aquitaine
reigned 1154–89

Henry
d. 1183

Richard I
Coeur-de-Lion
reigned 1189–99

Geoffrey m. Constance of
d. 1186　　　Brittany

Arthur
1187–1203

John
reigned 1199–1216

Henry III
reigned 1216–72

Elinor m. Alfonso VIII
d. 1214　　of Castile

Blanch of Castile
1187?–1252

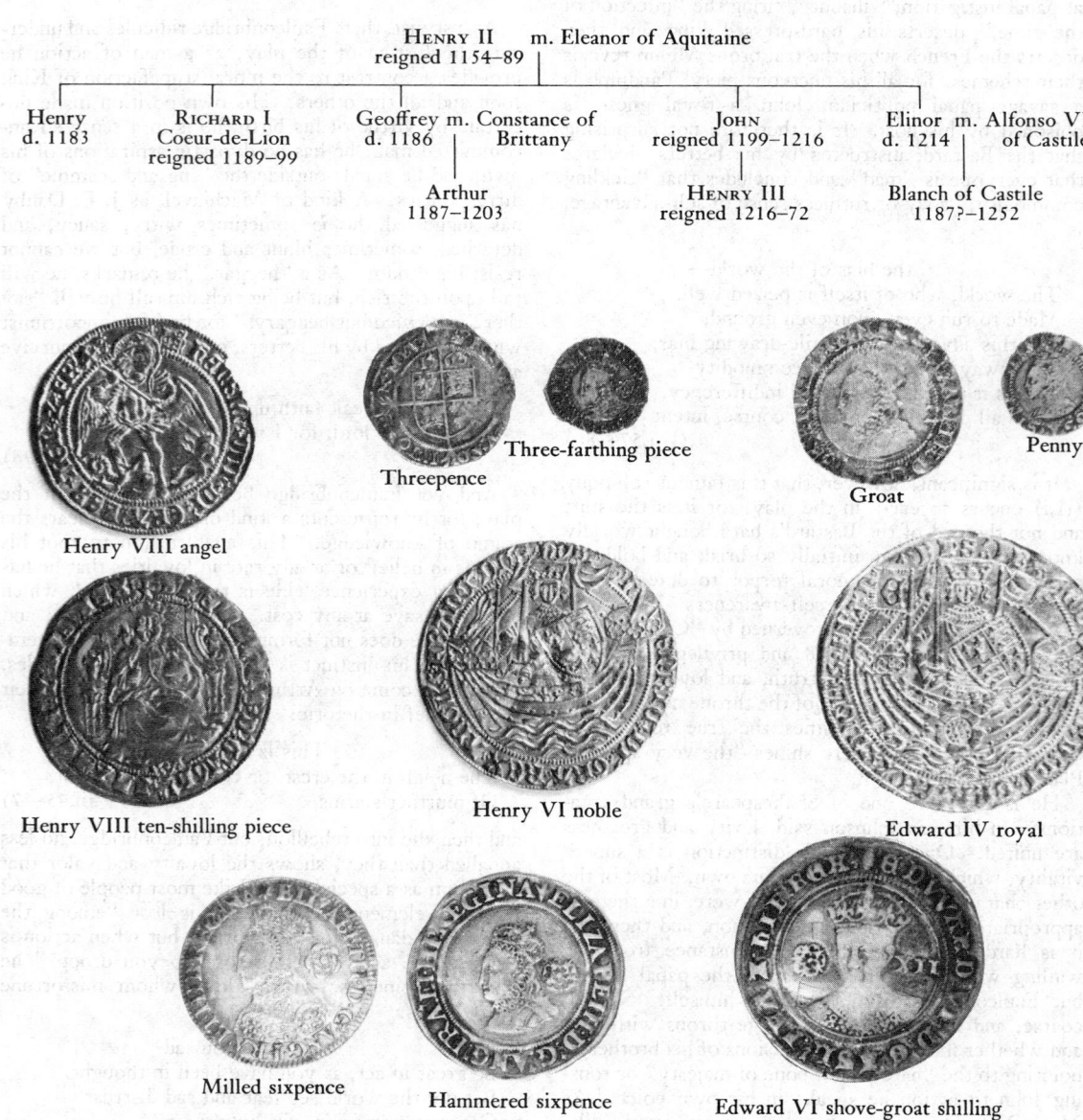

Henry VIII angel

Threepence

Three-farthing piece

Groat

Penny

Henry VIII ten-shilling piece

Henry VI noble

Edward IV royal

Milled sixpence

Hammered sixpence

Edward VI shove-groat shilling

From the collection of John Ford Clapp, Jr., Boston; photograph by Mark Silber

768

The Life and Death of King John

[Dramatis Personae

KING JOHN
PRINCE HENRY, *son to the King*
ARTHUR, *Duke of Britain, nephew to the King*
EARL OF PEMBROKE
EARL OF ESSEX
EARL OF SALISBURY
LORD BIGOT
HUBERT DE BURGH
ROBERT FAULCONBRIDGE, *son of Sir Robert Faulconbridge*
PHILIP THE BASTARD, *his half-brother (also called RICHARD)*
JAMES GURNEY, *servant to Lady Faulconbridge*
PETER OF POMFRET, *a prophet*

PHILIP, *King of France*
LEWIS, *the Dolphin*

LYMOGES, *Duke of Austria*
CARDINAL PANDULPH, *the Pope's legate*
MELUNE, *a French lord*
CHATILLION, *ambassador from France to King John*

QUEEN ELINOR, *widow of Henry II, mother to King John*
CONSTANCE, *widow of Geffrey, John's elder brother, mother to Arthur*
BLANCH OF SPAIN, *daughter to the King of Castile, niece to King John*
LADY FAULCONBRIDGE, *widow of Sir Robert Faulconbridge*

LORDS, CITIZENS *of Angiers*, SHERIFF, HERALDS, OFFICERS, SOLDIERS, EXECUTIONERS, MESSENGERS, *and* ATTENDANTS

SCENE: *Partly in England, and partly in France*]

ACT I, SCENE I

Enter KING JOHN, QUEEN ELINOR, PEMBROKE, ESSEX, *and* SALISBURY, *with the* CHATILLION *of France.*

K. John. Now say, Chatillion, what would France
　　with us?
Chat. Thus, after greeting, speaks the King of
　　France
In my behavior to the majesty,
The borrowed majesty, of England here.
El. A strange beginning: "borrowed majesty"! 5
K. John. Silence, good mother, hear the embassy.
Chat. Philip of France, in right and true behalf

Of thy deceased brother Geffrey's son,
Arthur Plantagenet, lays most lawful claim
To this fair island and the territories, 　　　10
To Ireland, Poictiers, Anjou, Touraine, Maine,
Desiring thee to lay aside the sword
Which sways usurpingly these several titles,
And put the same into young Arthur's hand,
Thy nephew and right royal sovereign. 　　　15
K. John. What follows if we disallow of this?
Chat. The proud control of fierce and bloody war,
To enforce these rights so forcibly withheld.
K. John. Here have we war for war and blood for
　　blood,
Controlment for controlment: so answer France. 20
Chat. Then take my King's defiance from my
　　mouth,
The farthest limit of my embassy.
K. John. Bear mine to him, and so depart in peace.
Be thou as lightning in the eyes of France;
For ere thou canst report, I will be there; 　　25
The thunder of my cannon shall be heard.

Words and passages enclosed in square brackets in the text above are either emendations of the copy-text or additions to it. The Textual Notes immediately following the play cite the earliest authority for every such change or insertion and supply the reading of the copy-text wherever it is emended in this edition.

I.i. Location: England. King John's palace.
1. **France:** King of France.
3. **In my behavior:** in my words and deeds, i.e. through me.
4. **borrowed:** stolen, i.e. spurious. 6. **embassy:** message.
7–15. **Philip . . . sovereign.** Just before the death of King Richard I, says Holinshed (Bullough, IV, 25), he had "assigned the crowne of England, and all other his lands and dominions" to his youngest brother John, who was duly crowned in May 1199. On the other hand John's nephew Arthur, posthumous son of Geoffrey of Brittany, inherited from his father the duchies of Anjou, Maine, and Touraine, and was recognized as their "liege and sovereigne lord." There is no evidence for Philip II's bellicose assertion of Arthur's claim to England as Shakespeare represents it here.

9. **Plantagenet:** family name of members of the royal family. See note to *1 Henry VI*, II.iv o.s.d. 13. **titles:** possessions.
14. **young Arthur's hand.** Depicted in this play as a gentle child of eight or so, Arthur was sixteen when he was murdered, probably at John's instigation, in 1203. Holinshed (Bullough, IV, 26) calls him "but a babe to speake of." 17. **control:** compulsion.
26. **cannon.** An anachronism; gunpowder was not used in western Europe until the fourteenth century.

King John
I.i

So hence! Be thou the trumpet of our wrath,
And sullen presage of your own decay.
An honorable conduct let him have.
Pembroke, look to't. Farewell, Chatillion.   30

Exeunt Chatillion and Pembroke.

El.   What now, my son, have I not ever said
How that ambitious Constance would not cease
Till she had kindled France, and all the world,
Upon the right and party of her son?
This might have been prevented and made whole   35
With very easy arguments of love,
Which now the manage of two kingdoms must
With fearful bloody issue arbitrate.

K. John.   Our strong possession and our right for
us.

El.   Your strong possession much more than your
right,   40
Or else it must go wrong with you and me;
So much my conscience whispers in your ear,
Which none but heaven, and you, and I, shall hear.

Enter a Sheriff [*and whispers Essex in the ear*].

Essex.   My liege, here is the strangest controversy
Come from the country to be judg'd by you   45
That e'er I heard. Shall I produce the men?

K. John.   Let them approach.   [*Exit Sheriff.*]
Our abbeys and our priories shall pay
This [expedition's] charge.

Enter Robert Faulconbridge *and* Philip [the Bas-
tard].

What men are you?

Bast.   Your faithful subject I, a gentleman,   50
Born in Northamptonshire, and eldest son,
As I suppose, to Robert Faulconbridge,
A soldier, by the honor-giving hand
Of Cordelion knighted in the field.

K. John.   What art thou?   55

Rob.   The son and heir to that same Faulconbridge.

K. John.   Is that the elder, and art thou the heir?
You came not of one mother then, it seems.

Bast.   Most certain of one mother, mighty King—
That is well known—and, as I think, one father;   60
But for the certain knowledge of that truth
I put you o'er to heaven and to my mother.
Of that I doubt, as all men's children may.

El.   Out on thee, rude man, thou dost shame thy
mother,
And wound her honor with this diffidence.   65

Bast.   I, madam? No, I have no reason for it;
That is my brother's plea and none of mine,
The which if he can prove, 'a pops me out
At least from fair five hundred pound a year.
Heaven guard my mother's honor, and my land!   70

K. John.   A good blunt fellow. Why, being
younger born,
Doth he lay claim to thine inheritance?

Bast.   I know not why, except to get the land;
But once he slander'd me with bastardy.
But whe'er I be as true begot or no,   75
That still I lay upon my mother's head,
But that I am as well begot, my liege
(Fair fall the bones that took the pains for me!),
Compare our faces, and be judge yourself.
If old Sir Robert did beget us both,   80
And were our father, and this son like him,
O old Sir Robert, father, on my knee
I give heaven thanks I was not like to thee!

K. John.   Why, what a madcap hath heaven lent us
here!

El.   He hath a trick of Cordelion's face,   85
The accent of his tongue affecteth him.
Do you not read some tokens of my son
In the large composition of this man?

K. John.   Mine eye hath well examined his parts,
And finds them perfect Richard. Sirrah, speak,   90
What doth move you to claim your brother's land?

Bast.   Because he hath a half-face like my father!
With half that face would he have all my land—
A half-fac'd groat five hundred pound a year!

Rob.   My gracious liege, when that my father liv'd,
Your brother did employ my father much—   96

Bast.   Well, sir, by this you cannot get my land;
Your tale must be how he employ'd my mother.

Rob.   And once dispatch'd him in an embassy
To Germany, there with the Emperor   100
To treat of high affairs touching that time.
Th' advantage of his absence took the King,
And in the mean time sojourn'd at my father's;
Where how he did prevail I shame to speak.
But truth is truth. Large lengths of seas and shores
Between my father and my mother lay,   106
As I have heard my father speak himself,
When this same lusty gentleman was got.
Upon his death-bed he by will bequeath'd
His lands to me, and took it on his death   110
That this my mother's son was none of his;
And if he were, he came into the world
Full fourteen weeks before the course of time.
Then, good my liege, let me have what is mine,
My father's land, as was my father's will.   115

K. John.   Sirrah, your brother is legitimate,
Your father's wife did after wedlock bear him;
And if she did play false, the fault was hers,
Which fault lies on the hazards of all husbands
That marry wives. Tell me, how if my brother,   120

---

28. **sullen presage:** dismal portent.   **decay:** destruction.
34. **Upon:** in support of.   36. **arguments of love:** friendly negotiation.
37. **manage:** government.   38. **issue:** consequence.
44. **liege:** sovereign.
54. **Cordelion:** Coeur-de-Lion (Lionheart), i.e. Richard I, who reputedly earned the sobriquet when, pitted against a lion by his captor
Leopold, Archduke of Austria, he thrust his hand into the creature's
mouth and tore out its heart.   62. **put you o'er:** refer you.
64. **rude:** coarse.   65. **diffidence:** mistrust.   68. **'a:** he.

74. **once:** in short.   75. **true:** legitimately.
76. **lay . . . head:** leave it to my mother to say.
78. **Fair fall:** may good befall.   81. **this son:** i.e. Robert.
85. **trick:** characteristic expression.   86. **affecteth:** resembles.
88. **large:** general.
90. **Sirrah:** customary form of address to an inferior.
92. **half-face:** (1) profile; (2) pinched face.
94. **half-fac'd groat:** thin silver coin (worth fourpence) bearing the
sovereign's head in profile.   96. **Your brother:** i.e. King Richard.
108. **got:** begotten.
110. **took . . . death:** i.e. took a solemn oath, swore.
113. **course:** due course.   119. **lies on:** is one of.

Who, as you say, took pains to get this son,
Had of your father claim'd this son for his?
In sooth, good friend, your father might have kept
This calf, bred from his cow, from all the world;
In sooth he might; then if he were my brother's,   125
My brother might not claim him, nor your father,
Being none of his, refuse him. This concludes:
My mother's son did get your father's heir;
Your father's heir must have your father's land.

  Rob. Shall then my father's will be of no force
To dispossess that child which is not his?   131

  Bast. Of no more force to dispossess me, sir,
Than was his will to get me, as I think.

  El. Whether hadst thou rather be a Faulconbridge,
And like thy brother, to enjoy thy land;   135
Or the reputed son of Cordelion,
Lord of thy presence and no land beside?

  Bast. Madam, and if my brother had my shape
And I had his, Sir Robert's his, like him,
And if my legs were two such riding-rods,   140
My arms such eel-skins stuff'd, my face so thin
That in mine ear I durst not stick a rose
Lest men should say, "Look where three-farthings
          goes!"
And to his shape were heir to all this land,
Would I might never stir from off this place,   145
I would give it every foot to have this face;
It would not be Sir Nob in any case.

  El. I like thee well. Wilt thou forsake thy fortune,
Bequeath thy land to him, and follow me?
I am a soldier, and now bound to France.   150

  Bast. Brother, take you my land, I'll take my
          chance.
Your face hath got five hundred pound a year,
Yet sell your face for five pence and 'tis dear.
Madam, I'll follow you unto the death.   154

  El. Nay, I would have you go before me thither.

  Bast. Our country manners give our betters way.

  K. John. What is thy name?

  Bast. Philip, my liege, so is my name begun,
Philip, good old Sir Robert's wive's eldest son.

  K. John. From henceforth bear his name whose
          form thou bearest: 160
Kneel thou down Philip, but rise more great,
Arise Sir Richard, and Plantagenet.

  Bast. Brother by th' mother's side, give me your
          hand;
My father gave me honor, yours gave land.
Now blessed be the hour by night or day   165
When I was got, Sir Robert was away!

  El. The very spirit of Plantagenet!
I am thy grandame, Richard, call me so.

  Bast. Madam, by chance, but not by truth; what
          though?
Something about, a little from the right,   170
In at the window, or else o'er the hatch.
Who dares not stir by day must walk by night,
And have is have, however men do catch.
Near or far off, well won is still well shot,
And I am I, howe'er I was begot.   175

  K. John. Go, Faulconbridge, now hast thou thy
          desire,
A landless knight makes thee a landed squire.
Come, madam, and come, Richard, we must speed
For France, for France, for it is more than need.   179

  Bast. Brother, adieu, good fortune come to thee!
For thou wast got i' th' way of honesty.

          Exeunt all but Bastard.

A foot of honor better than I was,
But many a many foot of land the worse.
Well, now can I make any Joan a lady.   184
"Good den, Sir Richard!" "God-a-mercy, fellow!"
And if his name be George, I'll call him Peter;
For new-made honor doth forget men's names;
'Tis too respective and too sociable
For your conversion. Now your traveller,
He and his toothpick at my worship's mess,   190
And when my knightly stomach is suffic'd,
Why then I suck my teeth, and catechize
My picked man of countries. "My dear sir,"
Thus, leaning on mine elbow, I begin,
"I shall beseech you"—that is question now;   195
And then comes answer like an Absey book:
"O sir," says answer, "at your best command,
At your employment, at your service, sir."
"No, sir," says question, "I, sweet sir, at yours";
And so ere answer knows what question would,   200
Saving in dialogue of compliment,
And talking of the Alps and Apennines,
The Pyrenean and the river Po,
It draws toward supper in conclusion so.
But this is worshipful society,   205
And fits the mounting spirit like myself;
For he is but a bastard to the time
That doth not [smack] of observation—
And so am I, whether I smack or no;
And not alone in habit and device,   210
Exterior form, outward accoutrement,
But from the inward motion to deliver

---

169. **truth:** virtue.   170. **Something about:** rather indirectly.
171. **o'er the hatch:** conceived out of wedlock (proverbial). A hatch
is the lower half of a door opening in two parts.
182. **foot:** footing, status.
184. **lady:** title appropriate for the wife of a knight.
185. **Good den:** good even. (The Bastard imagines an encounter between himself and a rustic.)   **God-a-mercy:** God reward you, i.e.
thank you.
188–89. **'Tis . . . conversion:** it is showing too much respect and so-
ciability for one just promoted.
190. **toothpick.** A common affectation with travellers.   **my worship's
mess:** i.e. my dinner table. A knight was commonly addressed as
"your worship."   193. **picked:** (1) spruce; (2) with picked teeth.
196. **Absey book:** ABC book, primer. Such books were often cast in
the form of a dialogue between master and pupil.
207. **bastard . . . time:** no true son of the age, unfashionable.
208. **doth . . . observation:** is not somewhat given to obsequiousness.
209. **so am I:** i.e. not a true child of the time.
210. **habit:** attire.   **device:** knightly insignia.
212. **from:** lacking.   **inward motion:** inclination.

---

127. **refuse:** disclaim.   **concludes:** resolves the problem.
137. **Lord . . . presence:** i.e. your own master (as having royal blood)
(?). Cf. II.i.367.   138. **and if:** if
139. **Sir Robert's his.** An archaic double genitive.
140. **riding-rods:** switches.
143. **three-farthings.** Certain coins of small value were stamped with
a rose behind the Queen's head.
144. **to his shape:** in addition to inheriting his physique.
147. **Nob:** nickname for Robert.
156. **give . . . way:** require that our betters precede us.
159. **wive's:** wife's.

King John
I.i

Sweet, sweet, sweet poison for the age's tooth,
Which though I will not practice to deceive,
Yet to avoid deceit, I mean to learn;   215
For it shall strew the footsteps of my rising.
But who comes in such haste in riding-robes?
What woman-post is this? Hath she no husband
That will take pains to blow a horn before her?

Enter LADY FAULCONBRIDGE *and* JAMES GURNEY.

O me, 'tis my mother. How now, good lady,   220
What brings you here to court so hastily?
    Lady F. Where is that slave, thy brother? Where
      is he,
That holds in chase mine honor up and down?
    Bast. My brother Robert, old Sir Robert's son?
Colbrand the giant, that same mighty man?   225
Is it Sir Robert's son that you seek so?
    Lady F. Sir Robert's son! Ay, thou unreverend
      boy,
Sir Robert's son! Why scorn'st thou at Sir Robert?
He is Sir Robert's son, and so art thou.
    Bast. James Gurney, wilt thou give us leave a
      while?   230
    Gur. Good leave, good Philip.
    Bast.   Philip? sparrow! James,
There's toys abroad; anon I'll tell thee more.
                     Exit James [*Gurney*].
Madam, I was not old Sir Robert's son;
Sir Robert might have eat his part in me
Upon Good Friday and ne'er broke his fast.   235
Sir Robert could do well—marry, to confess—
Could [he] get me. Sir Robert could not do it;
We know his handiwork. Therefore, good mother,
To whom am I beholding for these limbs?
Sir Robert never holp to make this leg.   240
    Lady F. Hast thou conspired with thy brother too,
That for thine own gain shouldst defend mine honor?
What means this scorn, thou most untoward knave?
    Bast. Knight, knight, good mother, Basilisco-
      like.
What, I am dubb'd! I have it on my shoulder.   245
But, mother, I am not Sir Robert's son,
I have disclaim'd Sir Robert and my land,
Legitimation, name, and all is gone;
Then, good my mother, let me know my father;
Some proper man, I hope. Who was it, mother?   250

    Lady F. Hast thou denied thyself a Faulcon-
      bridge?
    Bast. As faithfully as I deny the devil.
    Lady F. King Richard Cordelion was thy father.
By long and vehement suit I was seduc'd
To make room for him in my husband's bed.   255
Heaven! lay not my transgression to my charge,
That art the issue of my dear offense,
Which was so strongly urg'd past my defense.
    Bast. Now by this light, were I to get again,
Madam, I would not wish a better father.   260
Some sins do bear their privilege on earth,
And so doth yours: your fault was not your folly;
Needs must you lay your heart at his dispose,
Subjected tribute to commanding love,
Against whose fury and unmatched force   265
The aweless lion could not wage the fight,
Nor keep his princely heart from Richard's hand.
He that perforce robs lions of their hearts
May easily win a woman's. Ay, my mother,
With all my heart I thank thee for my father!   270
Who lives and dares but say thou didst not well
When I was got, I'll send his soul to hell.
Come, lady, I will show thee to my kin,
And they shall say, when Richard me begot,
If thou hadst said him nay, it had been sin.   275
Who says it was, he lies, I say 'twas not.   *Exeunt.*

[ACT II,] SCENE [I]

Enter, before Angiers, PHILIP, *King of France,* LEWIS
[*the*] *Dolphin,* CONSTANCE, ARTHUR, [*with forces, at
one door; at the other,*] AUSTRIA [*with forces*].

    [*K. Phi.*] Before Angiers well met, brave Austria.
Arthur, that great forerunner of thy blood,
Richard, that robb'd the lion of his heart,
And fought the holy wars in Palestine,
By this brave duke came early to his grave;   5
And for amends to his posterity,
At our importance hither is he come
To spread his colors, boy, in thy behalf,
And to rebuke the usurpation
Of thy unnatural uncle, English John.   10
Embrace him, love him, give him welcome hither.
    Arth. God shall forgive you Cordelion's death
The rather that you give his offspring life,
Shadowing their right under your wings of war.
I give you welcome with a powerless hand.   15

213. **poison:** i.e. flattery. **tooth:** appetite.
215. **deceit:** being deceived.
218. **woman-post:** female messenger.
219. **horn.** Alluding to the cuckold's horns.
223. **holds in chase:** pursues.
225. **Colbrand:** Danish giant overcome by Guy in the popular romance *Guy of Warwick*. 227. **unreverend:** disrespectful.
230. **give us leave:** leave us alone.
231. **Philip? sparrow!** i.e. use that name for sparrows (which were commonly called Philip), not for me.
232. **There's toys abroad.** Another jocular hint that interesting things have been happening.
236. **do:** copulate. **marry:** indeed (originally the name of the Virgin Mary used as an oath). 239. **beholding:** beholden, indebted.
240. **holp:** helped. 243. **untoward:** unmannerly.
244. **Knight . . . Basilisco-like.** An allusion to the contemporary play *Soliman and Perseda,* in which the braggart knight Basilisco is called a knave by his servant.
245. **dubb'd:** formally created a knight with a sword-tap on the shoulder. 250. **proper:** handsome.

256. **lay.** The implied subject is *thou* (i.e. the Bastard).
257. **dear:** grievous. 259. **get:** be conceived.
261. **do . . . privilege:** i.e. are venial. 263. **dispose:** disposal.

II.i. o.s.d. **Angiers:** Angers, city in northwestern France, capital of the duchy of Anjou. **Dolphin:** Dauphin, title of the heir apparent of the King of France.
4. **fought . . . Palestine.** With his allies Philip II of France and Emperor Frederick I (Barbarossa), Richard had been a leader of the Third Crusade (1190–92).
5. **By . . . grave.** Like the author of *The Troublesome Reign of King John* (Bullough, IV, 83–84), Shakespeare confusingly identifies Widomar, Viscount of Limoges, with Leopold, Archduke of Austria. Richard had been imprisoned briefly by Leopold in 1193–94, and was fatally wounded while besieging Widomar's castle in 1199.
7. **importance:** importunity. 8. **colors:** flags.
13. **offspring:** descendants. 14. **Shadowing:** protecting.

But with a heart full of unstained love.
Welcome before the gates of Angiers, Duke.
    [*K. Phi.*] A noble boy! Who would not do thee
        right?
    Aust. Upon thy cheek lay I this zealous kiss
As seal to this indenture of my love: 20
That to my home I will no more return
Till Angiers, and the right thou hast in France,
Together with that pale, that white-fac'd shore,
Whose foot spurns back the ocean's roaring tides
And coops from other lands her islanders,   25
Even till that England, hedg'd in with the main,
That water-walled bulwark, still secure
And confident from foreign purposes,
Even till that utmost corner of the west
Salute thee for her king; till then, fair boy,   30
Will I not think of home, but follow arms.
    Const. O, take his mother's thanks, a widow's
        thanks,
Till your strong hand shall help to give him strength
To make a more requital to your love!
    Aust. The peace of heaven is theirs that lift their
        swords   35
In such a just and charitable war.
    K. Phi. Well, then to work! Our cannon shall be
        bent
Against the brows of this resisting town.
Call for our chiefest men of discipline
To cull the plots of best advantages.   40
We'll lay before this town our royal bones,
Wade to the market-place in Frenchmen's blood,
But we will make it subject to this boy.
    Const. Stay for an answer to your embassy,
Lest unadvis'd you stain your swords with blood.   45
My Lord Chatillion may from England bring
That right in peace which here we urge in war,
And then we shall repent each drop of blood
That hot rash haste so indirectly shed.

                  Enter CHATILLION.

    K. Phi. A wonder, lady! Lo upon thy wish   50
Our messenger Chatillion is arriv'd!
What England says, say briefly, gentle lord,
We coldly pause for thee; Chatillion, speak.
    Chat. Then turn your forces from this paltry siege,
And stir them up against a mightier task.   55
England, impatient of your just demands,
Hath put himself in arms. The adverse winds,
Whose leisure I have stay'd, have given him time
To land his legions all as soon as I;
His marches are expedient to this town,   60
His forces strong, his soldiers confident.
With him along is come the mother-queen,
An [Ate,] stirring him to blood and strife;

With her her niece, the Lady Blanch of Spain;
With them a bastard of the king's deceas'd,   65
And all th' unsettled humors of the land,
Rash, inconsiderate, fiery voluntaries,
With ladies' faces and fierce dragons' spleens,
Have sold their fortunes at their native homes,
Bearing their birthrights proudly on their backs,   70
To make a hazard of new fortunes here.
In brief, a braver choice of dauntless spirits
Than now the English bottoms have waft o'er
Did never float upon the swelling tide
To do offense and scathe in Christendom.   75
The interruption of their churlish drums
Cuts off more circumstance. They are at hand,
                                      Drum beats.
To parley or to fight, therefore prepare.
    K. Phi. How much unlook'd for is this expedition!
    Aust. By how much unexpected, by so much   80
We must awake endeavor for defense,
For courage mounteth with occasion.
Let them be welcome then, we are prepar'd.

Enter [JOHN,] *King of England*, BASTARD, QUEEN
[ELINOR], BLANCH, PEMBROKE, *and others.*

    K. John. Peace be to France—if France in peace
        permit
Our just and lineal entrance to our own;   85
If not, bleed France, and peace ascend to heaven,
Whiles we, God's wrathful agent, do correct
Their proud contempt that beats his peace to heaven.
    K. Phi. Peace be to England, if that war return
From France to England, there to live in peace.   90
England we love, and for that England's sake
With burden of our armor here we sweat.
This toil of ours should be a work of thine;
But thou from loving England art so far
That thou hast under-wrought his lawful king,   95
Cut off the sequence of posterity,
Outfaced infant state, and done a rape
Upon the maiden virtue of the crown.
Look here upon thy brother Geffrey's face:
These eyes, these brows, were moulded out of his;
This little abstract doth contain that large   101
Which died in Geffrey; and the hand of time
Shall draw this brief into as huge a volume.
That Geffrey was thy elder brother born,
And this his son; England was Geffrey's right,   105

---

64. **niece:** i.e. granddaughter (a common Elizabethan usage). One of Elinor's daughters by Henry II married King Alfonso of Castile.
65. **of . . . deceas'd:** of the dead king (a double genitive).
66. **unsettled humors:** unruly, disaffected men.
67. **voluntaries:** volunteers.
68. **spleens.** In Elizabethan psychology the spleen was the seat of passion.
70. **Bearing . . . backs:** i.e. having squandered everything they possessed on armor.   73. **bottoms:** ships.   **waft:** wafted.
75. **scathe:** injury.   76. **churlish:** rough.
77. **circumstance:** detail.   79. **expedition:** speed.
82. **occasion:** emergency.   85. **lineal:** due by hereditary right.
91. **England's:** i.e. Arthur's, for he, as Philip thinks, is the lawful king of England.   95. **under-wrought his:** undermined its.
96. **posterity:** lineal descent.
97. **Outfaced infant state:** defied the authority of the child-king.
101. **little abstract:** epitome.   101–2. **that large Which:** that which large (=complete, in full).
103. **draw this brief:** expand this summasy.

---

25. **coops:** encloses for protection or defense.   27. **still:** always.
32. **a widow's thanks.** Another error copied from *The Troublesome Reign* (Bullough, IV, 95). At the time represented, Constance was married to her third husband, Guy de Thouars.   34. **more:** greater.
37. **bent:** aimed.   39. **discipline:** i.e. military science.
40. **cull . . . advantages:** select the most suitable positions.
43. **But:** unless.   45. **unadvis'd:** unwisely.   49. **indirectly:** unjustly.
52. **England:** the King of England.
53. **coldly:** calmly, dispassionately.   60. **expedient:** speedy.
63. **Ate:** Greek goddess of discord.

King John
II.i

And this is Geffrey's in the name of God.
How comes it then that thou art call'd a king,
When living blood doth in these temples beat,
Which owe the crown that thou o'ermasterest?

K. John.   From whom hast thou this great com-
    mission, France,   110
To draw my answer from thy articles?

K. Phi.   From that supernal judge that stirs good
    thoughts
In any [breast] of strong authority,
To look into the blots and stains of right.
That judge hath made me guardian to this boy,   115
Under whose warrant I impeach thy wrong,
And by whose help I mean to chastise it.

K. John.   Alack, thou dost usurp authority.

K. Phi.   Excuse it is to beat usurping down.

El.   Who is it thou dost call usurper, France?   120

Const.   Let me make answer: thy usurping son.

El.   Out, insolent, thy bastard shall be king
That thou mayst be a queen, and check the world!

Const.   My bed was ever to thy son as true
As thine was to thy husband, and this boy   125
Liker in feature to his father Geffrey
Than thou and John in manners, being as like
As rain to water, or devil to his dam.
My boy a bastard? By my soul I think
His father never was so true begot—   130
It cannot be, and if thou wert his mother.

El.   There's a good mother, boy, that blots thy
    father.

Const.   There's a good grandame, boy, that would
    blot thee.

Aust.   Peace!

Bast.   Hear the crier.

Aust.   What the devil art thou?

Bast.   One that will play the devil, sir, with you,
And 'a may catch your hide and you alone.   136
You are the hare of whom the proverb goes,
Whose valor plucks dead lions by the beard;
I'll smoke your skin-coat and I catch you right.
Sirrah, look to't, i' faith I will, i' faith.   140

Blanch.   O, well did he become that lion's robe,
That did disrobe the lion of that robe!

Bast.   It lies as sightly on the back of him
As great Alcides' [shows] upon an ass.
But, ass, I'll take that burthen from your back,   145
Or lay on that shall make your shoulders crack.

Aust.   What cracker is this same that deafs our ears
With this abundance of superfluous breath?
King [Philip], determine what we shall do straight.

[K. Phi.]   Women and fools, break off your con-
    ference.   150
King John, this is the very sum of all:
England and Ireland, [Anjou], Touraine, Maine,
In right of Arthur do I claim of thee.
Wilt thou resign them and lay down thy arms?

K. John.   My life as soon. I do defy thee, France.
Arthur of Britain, yield thee to my hand,   156
And out of my dear love I'll give thee more
Than e'er the coward hand of France can win.
Submit thee, boy.

El.   Come to thy grandame, child.

Const.   Do, child, go to it grandame, child,   160
Give grandame kingdom, and it grandame will
Give it a plum, a cherry, and a fig.
There's a good grandame.

Arth.   Good my mother, peace.
I would that I were low laid in my grave,
I am not worth this coil that's made for me.   165

El.   His mother shames him so, poor boy, he weeps.

Const.   Now shame upon you, whe'er she does or
    no!
His grandame's wrongs, and not his mother's shames,
Draws those heaven-moving pearls from his poor eyes,
Which heaven shall take in nature of a fee;   170
Ay, with these crystal beads heaven shall be brib'd
To do him justice, and revenge on you.

El.   Thou monstrous slanderer of heaven and earth!

Const.   Thou monstrous injurer of heaven and earth,
Call not me slanderer! Thou and thine usurp   175
The dominations, royalties, and rights
Of this oppressed boy. This is thy eldest son's son,
Infortunate in nothing but in thee.
Thy sins are visited in this poor child,
The canon of the law is laid on him,   180
Being but the second generation
Removed from thy sin-conceiving womb.

K. John.   Bedlam, have done.

Const.   I have but this to say,
That he is not only plagued for her sin,
But God hath made her sin and her the plague   185
On this removed issue, plagued for her,
And with her plague, her sin; his injury
Her injury, the beadle to her sin—
All punish'd in the person of this child,
And all for her. A plague upon her!   190

---

106. **this:** i.e. the city of Angers, to which King Philip points (?)'
Depending on the actor's gesture, it might instead mean Arthur or
John's crown.   109. **owe:** own.   110. **commission:** warrant.
111. **articles:** items in a formal indictment.
116. **impeach:** formally accuse.
119. **Excuse . . . down:** the excuse (for my usurpation of authority)
is that I am resisting usurpation.   123. **check:** control.
132. **blots:** slanders.
136. **hide:** the lion's skin that Austria wears to commemorate his
victory over Richard I.   139. **smoke:** beat.
140. **Sirrah:** customary form of address to an inferior (hence an
insult here).   143. **sightly:** appropriately.
144. **Alcides:** Hercules, who wore the skin of the Nemean lion that
he had slain.   146. **that:** that which, i.e. a club.
147. **cracker:** boaster.

150. **fools:** children.   156. **Britain:** Brittany.
160-63. **Do . . . grandame.** Contemptuous baby talk.
165. **coil:** turmoil.
176. **dominations:** dominions.   **royalties:** royal prerogatives and
dignities.
177. **eldest son's son:** eldest grandson (not "son of your eldest son").
178. **Infortunate:** unfortunate.   179. **visited:** punished.
180. **canon . . . law:** Exodus 20:5, which asserts that God is jealous,
"visiting the iniquity of the fathers upon the children unto the third
and fourth generation of them that hate me."   183. **Bedlam:** lunatic.
184-90. **That . . . upon her.** The sense of this obscurely worded
passage is clear: Arthur is being chastised for his grandmother's
wickedness, and she and John—himself the product of her sin—are
sent to punish him unjustly.
184. **sin:** i.e. in conceiving John out of wedlock (as Constance had
implied in lines 129-31).   185. **her sin:** i.e. John.
186. **removed issue:** distant descendant, i.e. Arthur.
187. **his injury:** i.e. the wrong done to Arthur.
188. **Her . . . sin:** i.e. the wrong she has done lashes John (*her sin*) on
to further wrongs.   **beadle:** parish official who administers corporal
punishment.

El. Thou unadvised scold, I can produce
A will that bars the title of thy son.

Const. Ay, who doubts that? A will! a wicked will,
A woman's will, a cank'red grandam's will!

K. Phi. Peace, lady, pause, or be more temperate.
It ill beseems this presence to cry aim   196
To these ill-tuned repetitions.
Some trumpet summon hither to the walls
These men of Angiers; let us hear them speak
Whose title they admit, Arthur's or John's.   200

Trumpet sounds. Enter [HUBERT *and other* CITIZENS]
upon the walls.

[*Hub.*] Who is it that hath warn'd us to the walls?
K. Phi. 'Tis France, for England.
K. John.   England for itself.
You men of Angiers, and my loving subjects—
K. Phi. You loving men of Angiers, Arthur's sub-
   jects,
Our trumpet call'd you to this gentle parle—   205
K. John. For our advantage—therefore hear us
   first:
These flags of France, that are advanced here
Before the eye and prospect of your town,
Have hither march'd to your endamagement.
The cannons have their bowels full of wrath,   210
And ready mounted are they to spit forth
Their iron indignation 'gainst your walls;
All preparation for a bloody siege
And merciless proceeding by these French
[Confronts your] city's eyes, your winking gates; 215
And but for our approach those sleeping stones,
That as a waist doth girdle you about,
By the compulsion of their ordinance
By this time from their fixed beds of lime
Had been dishabited, and wide havoc made   220
For bloody power to rush upon your peace.
But on the sight of us, your lawful King,
Who painfully with much expedient march
Have brought a countercheck before your gates,
To save unscratch'd your city's threat'ned cheeks,
Behold, the French amaz'd vouchsafe a parle,   226
And now instead of bullets wrapp'd in fire,
To make a shaking fever in your walls,
They shoot but calm words folded up in smoke,
To make a faithless error in your ears;   230
Which trust accordingly, kind citizens,
And let us in—your King, whose labor'd spirits,
Forewearied in this action of swift speed,
Craves harborage within your city walls.
K. Phi. When I have said, make answer to us both.
Lo in this right hand, whose protection   236
Is most divinely vow'd upon the right
Of him it holds, stands young Plantagenet,
Son to the elder brother of this man,
And king o'er him and all that he enjoys.   240
For this down-trodden equity, we tread
In warlike march these greens before your town,
Being no further enemy to you
Than the constraint of hospitable zeal
In the relief of this oppressed child   245
Religiously provokes. Be pleased then
To pay that duty which you truly owe
To him that owes it, namely this young prince,
And then our arms, like to a muzzled bear,
Save in aspect, hath all offense seal'd up;   250
Our cannons' malice vainly shall be spent
Against th' [invulnerable] clouds of heaven,
And with a blessed and unvex'd retire,
With unhack'd swords, and helmets all unbruis'd,
We will bear home that lusty blood again   255
Which here we came to spout against your town,
And leave your children, wives, and you in peace.
But if you fondly pass our proffer'd offer,
'Tis not the rounder of your old-fac'd walls
Can hide you from our messengers of war,   260
Though all these English and their discipline
Were harbor'd in their rude circumference.
Then tell us, shall your city call us lord,
In that behalf which we have challeng'd it?
Or shall we give the signal to our rage,   265
And stalk in blood to our possession?
[*Hub.*] In brief, we are the King of England's sub-
   jects:
For him, and in his right, we hold this town.
K. John. Acknowledge then the King, and let me
   in.
[*Hub.*] That can we not; but he that proves the
   King,   270
To him will we prove loyal. Till that time
Have we ramm'd up our gates against the world.
K. John. Doth not the crown of England prove the
   King?
And if not that, I bring you witnesses,   274
Twice fifteen thousand hearts of England's breed—
Bast. Bastards, and else.
K. John. To verify our title with their lives.
K. Phi. As many and as well-born bloods as
   those—
Bast. Some bastards too.   279
K. Phi. Stand in his face to contradict his claim.
[*Hub.*] Till you compound whose right is worthiest,
We for the worthiest hold the right from both.
K. John. Then God forgive the sin of all those
   souls
That to their everlasting residence,
Before the dew of evening fall, shall fleet   285
In dreadful trial of our kingdom's king!

---

191. **unadvised:** rash.   192. **A will.** See note to I.i.7–15.
196–97. **cry aim To:** encourage (a term from archery).
198. **trumpet:** trumpeter.   205. **parle:** parley.
207. **advanced:** raised.   215. **winking:** shut.
218. **ordinance:** ordnance.
220. **dishabited:** dislodged.   223. **havoc:** i.e. breach.
223. **expedient:** speedy.   226. **amaz'd:** stunned.
227. **bullets:** cannon balls.   229. **smoke:** i.e. breath.
230. **faithless error:** disloyal lie.   233. **Forewearied in:** exhausted by.
237. **divinely:** piously.   **upon:** i.e. to defend.

241. **down-trodden equity:** flouted right.
244. **constraint:** necessity.   248. **owes:** owns, has a right to.
250. **Save in aspect:** except in appearance.
253. **unvex'd retire:** orderly withdrawal.
258. **fondly pass:** foolishly reject.
259. **rounder:** roundure, i.e. circle, circumference.
264. **In . . . which:** on behalf of him for whom.
270. **proves:** proves to be.   276. **else:** others.
278. **bloods:** men of spirit and good families.
281. **compound:** determine.   285. **fleet:** leave their bodies.

King John
II.i

K. Phi. Amen, amen! Mount, chevaliers! To arms!
Bast. Saint George, that swing'd the dragon, and
      e'er since
Sits on 's horseback at mine hostess' door,
Teach us some fence! [*To Austria.*] Sirrah, were I at
      home,   290
At your den, sirrah, with your lioness,
I would set an ox-head to your lion's hide,
And make a monster of you.
      Aust.   Peace, no more.
      Bast. O, tremble! for you hear the lion roar.
      K. John. Up higher to the plain, where we'll set
            forth   295
In best appointment all our regiments.
      Bast. Speed then to take advantage of the field.
      K. Phi. It shall be so, and at the other hill
Command the rest to stand. God and our right!
                    Exeunt. [*Hubert and Citizens remain above.*]

Here, after excursions, enter the HERALD OF FRANCE *with
      Trumpets to the gates.*

      F. Her. You men of Angiers, open wide your
            gates,   300
And let young Arthur Duke of Britain in,
Who by the hand of France this day hath made
Much work for tears in many an English mother,
Whose sons lie scattered on the bleeding ground.
Many a widow's husband grovelling lies,   305
Coldly embracing the discolored earth,
And victory with little loss doth play
Upon the dancing banners of the French,
Who are at hand, triumphantly displayed,
To enter conquerors, and to proclaim   310
Arthur of Britain England's King and yours.

      Enter ENGLISH HERALD *with Trumpet.*

      E. Her. Rejoice, you men of Angiers, ring your
            bells,
King John, your King and England's, doth approach,
Commander of this hot malicious day.
Their armors, that march'd hence so silver-bright,
Hither return all gilt with Frenchmen's blood.   316
There stuck no plume in any English crest
That is removed by a staff of France;
Our colors do return in those same hands
That did display them when we first march'd forth;
And like a jolly troop of huntsmen come   321
Our lusty English, all with purpled hands,
Dy'd in the dying slaughter of their foes.
Open your gates and give the victors way.
      Hub. Heralds, from off our tow'rs we might be-
            hold,   325
From first to last, the onset and retire
Of both your armies, whose equality

By our best eyes cannot be censured.
Blood hath bought blood, and blows have answer'd
      blows;
Strength match'd with strength, and power con-
      fronted power: 330
Both are alike, and both alike we like.
One must prove greatest. While they weigh so even,
We hold our town for neither; yet for both.

Enter the two KINGS *with their powers at several doors.*

      K. John. France, hast thou yet more blood to cast
            away?
Say, shall the current of our right roam on?   335
Whose passage, vex'd with thy impediment,
Shall leave his native channel and o'erswell
With course disturb'd even thy confining shores,
Unless thou let his silver water keep
A peaceful progress to the ocean.   340
      K. Phi. England, thou hast not sav'd one drop of
            blood
In this hot trial more than we of France,
Rather lost more. And by this hand I swear,
That sways the earth this climate overlooks,
Before we will lay down our just-borne arms   345
We'll put thee down, 'gainst whom these arms we bear,
Or add a royal number to the dead,
Gracing the scroll that tells of this war's loss
With slaughter coupled to the name of kings.
      Bast. Ha, majesty! how high thy glory tow'rs   350
When the rich blood of kings is set on fire!
O now doth Death line his dead chaps with steel,
The swords of soldiers are his teeth, his fangs,
And now he feasts, mousing the flesh of men,
In undetermin'd differences of kings.   355
Why stand these royal fronts amazed thus?
Cry "havoc," kings! back to the stained field,
You equal potents, fiery kindled spirits!
Then let confusion of one part confirm   359
The other's peace. Till then, blows, blood, and death!
      K. John. Whose party do the townsmen yet admit?
      K. Phi. Speak, citizens, for England. Who's your
            king?
      Hub. The King of England, when we know the
            King.
      K. Phi. Know him in us, that here hold up his right.
      K. John. In us, that are our own great deputy,   365
And bear possession of our person here,
Lord of our presence, Angiers, and of you.
      [*Hub.*] A greater pow'r than we denies all this,
And till it be undoubted, we do lock
Our former scruple in our strong-barr'd gates,   370
Kings of our fear, until our fears, resolv'd,
Be by some certain king purg'd and depos'd.

288–89. **Saint George . . . door.** The figure of St. George, the patron
saint of England, reputed to have slain a dragon, was often represented
on inn signs. **swing'd:** thrashed (past tense of *swinge*).
290. **fence:** swordsmanship.   291. **lioness:** i.e. harlot.
292. **set an ox-head:** i.e. give you horns, make you a cuckold.
299 s.d. **excursions:** sallies, sorties.
316. **gilt.** Blood was often called golden.   318. **staff:** spear.
323. **Dy'd . . . foes:** i.e. like hunters who, by custom, celebrated a
successful chase by dipping their hands in the blood of the slain deer.

328. **censured:** impugned, denied (?).
333 s.d. **powers:** armies.   **several:** separate.
338. **thy confining shores:** i.e. the fealty owed to you (as feudal
sovereign of the duchy of Anjou) (?).   344. **climate:** part of the sky.
350. **glory:** vainglory.   352. **chaps:** jaws.   354. **mousing:** gnawing.
355. **undetermin'd differences:** unresolved conflicts.
356. **fronts:** foreheads, i.e. faces.
357. **Cry "havoc":** proclaim a general slaughter.
358. **potents:** potentates.   359. **confusion:** defeat.   361. **yet:** now.
366. **bear . . . person:** symbolize the rights of sovereignty in our own
person.   367. **Lord . . . presence.** See note to I.i.137.

Bast. By heaven, these scroyles of Angiers flout
you, kings,
And stand securely on their battlements
As in a theatre, whence they gape and point   375
At your industrious scenes and acts of death.
Your royal presences be rul'd by me:
Do like the mutines of Jerusalem,
Be friends awhile, and both conjointly bend
Your sharpest deeds of malice on this town.   380
By east and west let France and England mount
Their battering cannon charged to the mouths,
Till their soul-fearing clamors have brawl'd down
The flinty ribs of this contemptuous city.
I'd play incessantly upon these jades,   385
Even till unfenced desolation
Leave them as naked as the vulgar air.
That done, dissever your united strengths,
And part your mingled colors once again,
Turn face to face and bloody point to point;   390
Then, in a moment, Fortune shall cull forth
Out of one side her happy minion,
To whom in favor she shall give the day,
And kiss him with a glorious victory.
How like you this wild counsel, mighty states?   395
Smacks it not something of the policy?
    K. John. Now, by the sky that hangs above our
heads,
I like it well. France, shall we knit our pow'rs,
And lay this Angiers even with the ground,
Then after fight who shall be king of it?   400
    Bast. And if thou hast the mettle of a king,
Being wrong'd as we are by this peevish town,
Turn thou the mouth of thy artillery,
As we will ours, against these saucy walls,
And when that we have dash'd them to the ground,
Why then defy each other, and pell-mell   406
Make work upon ourselves, for heaven or hell.
    K. Phi. Let it be so. Say, where will you assault?
    K. John. We from the west will send destruction
Into this city's bosom.   410
    Aust. I from the north.
    K. Phi.   Our thunder from the south
Shall rain their drift of bullets on this town.
    Bast. [*Aside.*] O prudent discipline! From north to
south—
Austria and France shoot in each other's mouth.
I'll stir them to it.—Come, away, away!   415
    Hub. Hear us, great kings! Vouchsafe awhile to
stay,
And I shall show you peace and fair-fac'd league;
Win you this city without stroke or wound,
Rescue those breathing lives to die in beds,
That here come sacrifices for the field.   420
Persever not, but hear me, mighty kings.

K. John. Speak on with favor, we are bent to hear.
    Hub. That daughter there of Spain, the Lady
Blanch,
Is near to England. Look upon the years
Of Lewis the Dolphin and that lovely maid.   425
If lusty love should go in quest of beauty,
Where should he find it fairer than in Blanch?
If zealous love should go in search of virtue,
Where should he find it purer than in Blanch?
If love ambitious sought a match of birth,   430
Whose veins bound richer blood than Lady Blanch?
Such as she is, in beauty, virtue, birth,
Is the young Dolphin every way complete:
If not complete of, say he is not she,
And she again wants nothing, to name want,   435
If want it be not that she is not he.
He is the half part of a blessed man,
Left to be finished by such as she,
And she a fair divided excellence,
Whose fullness of perfection lies in him.   440
O, two such silver currents when they join
Do glorify the banks that bound them in;
And two such shores to two such streams made one,
Two such controlling bounds shall you be, kings,
To these two princes, if you marry them.   445
This union shall do more than battery can
To our fast-closed gates; for at this match,
With swifter spleen than powder can enforce,
The mouth of passage shall we fling wide ope,
And give you entrance; but without this match,   450
The sea enraged is not half so deaf,
Lions more confident, mountains and rocks
More free from motion, no, not Death himself
In mortal fury half so peremptory,
As we to keep this city.
    Bast.   Here's a stay   455
That shakes the rotten carcass of old Death
Out of his rags! Here's a large mouth indeed,
That spits forth death and mountains, rocks and seas,
Talks as familiarly of roaring lions
As maids of thirteen do of puppy-dogs!   460
What cannoneer begot this lusty blood?
He speaks plain cannon-fire, and smoke, and bounce,
He gives the bastinado with his tongue;
Our ears are cudgell'd—not a word of his
But buffets better than a fist of France.   465
'Zounds, I was never so bethump'd with words
Since I first call'd my brother's father dad.
    El. Son, list to this conjunction, make this match,
Give with our niece a dowry large enough,
For by this knot thou shalt so surely tie   470
Thy now unsur'd assurance to the crown,

373. **scroyles:** scurvy fellows.
378. **mutines:** mutineers. The reference is to John of Gischala and
Simon bar Giora, who combined their factions against the Romans
under Titus when Jerusalem was besieged and taken (A.D. 70).
383. **fearing:** frightening.
385. **play . . . upon:** cannonade. **jades:** wretches.
387. **vulgar:** common. 392. **minion:** favorite.
395. **states:** monarchs. 396. **the policy:** i.e. the proper policy.
401. **mettle:** spirit. 402. **peevish:** troublesome.
406. **pell-mell:** headlong. 412. **drift:** shower.

422. **favor:** permission. **bent:** inclined.
424. **near to England:** closely related to the King of England. Blanch
was John's niece (see note to II.i.64).
430. **match of birth:** i.e. dynastic marriage. 431. **bound:** contain.
433. **complete:** perfect.
434. **If . . . she:** if he is not perfect it is only because he lacks her.
of: therein. 435. **wants:** lacks. 446. **battery:** artillery.
447. **match:** (1) marriage; (2) means of firing a charge of gunpowder.
448. **spleen:** eagerness. 454. **peremptory:** determined.
455. **stay:** check (a term from horsemanship). 462. **bounce:** boom.
463. **bastinado:** cudgelling.
466. **'Zounds:** by God's (Christ's) wounds. 468. **list:** listen.

King John
II.i

That yon green boy shall have no sun to ripe
The bloom that promiseth a mighty fruit.
I see a yielding in the looks of France;
Mark how they whisper. Urge them while their souls
Are capable of this ambition,   476
Lest zeal, now melted by the windy breath
Of soft petitions, pity, and remorse,
Cool and congeal again to what it was.
    Hub. Why answer not the double majesties   480
This friendly treaty of our threat'ned town?
    K. Phi. Speak England first, that hath been for-
        ward first
To speak unto this city: what say you?
    K. John. If that the Dolphin there, thy princely
        son,
Can in this book of beauty read, "I love,"   485
Her dowry shall weigh equal with a queen;
For [Anjou] and fair Touraine, Maine, Poictiers,
And all that we upon this side the sea
(Except this city now by us besieg'd)
Find liable to our crown and dignity,   490
Shall gild her bridal bed and make her rich
In titles, honors, and promotions,
As she in beauty, education, blood,
Holds hand with any princess of the world.
    K. Phi. What say'st thou, boy? Look in the lady's
        face.   495
    Lew. I do, my lord, and in her eye I find
A wonder, or a wondrous miracle,
The shadow of myself form'd in her eye,
Which being but the shadow of your son,
Becomes a sun and makes your son a shadow.   500
I do protest I never lov'd myself
Till now infixed I beheld myself
Drawn in the flattering table of her eye.
                                        Whispers with Blanch.
    Bast. [*Aside.*] Drawn in the flattering table of her
        eye!
Hang'd in the frowning wrinkle of her brow!   505
And quarter'd in her heart! he doth espy
Himself love's traitor. This is pity now,
That hang'd and drawn and quarter'd there should be
In such a love so vile a lout as he.
    Blanch. My uncle's will in this respect is mine.
If he see aught in you that makes him like,   511
That any thing he sees, which moves his liking,
I can with ease translate it to my will;
Or if you will, to speak more properly,
I will enforce it eas'ly to my love.   515
Further I will not flatter you, my lord,
That all I see in you is worthy love,

472. **green:** young.   **boy:** i.e. Arthur.
476. **capable of:** susceptible to.
477. **zeal:** i.e. the zeal that Philip has shown in Arthur's cause.
481. **treaty:** proposal.   490. **liable:** subject.
494. **Holds hand with:** equals.   498. **shadow:** reflection.
500. **Becomes a sun:** i.e. because the lady's eyes are so bright.
503. **table:** board or surface on which a picture is painted.
504–9. **Drawn . . . he.** In *The Troublesome Reign* (Bullough, IV, 93) the Bastard says that Elinor had given him "halfe a promise" to Blanch's hand. This fact, although suppressed by Shakespeare, helps us understand these disgruntled comments on a rival.
504–7. **Drawn, Hang'd, quarter'd, traitor.** The Bastard's puns relate to the punishment of traitors, who were hanged, cut down while still alive, disembowelled (*drawn*), and quartered.   509. **love:** lover.
513. **will:** desire.   514. **properly:** precisely.

Than this: that nothing do I see in you,
Though churlish thoughts themselves should be your
        judge,
That I can find should merit any hate.   520
    K. John. What say these young ones? What say
        you, my niece?
    Blanch. That she is bound in honor still to do
What you in wisdom still vouchsafe to say.
    K. John. Speak then, Prince Dolphin, can you love
        this lady?
    Lew. Nay, ask me if I can refrain from love,   525
For I do love her most unfeignedly.
    K. John. Then do I give Volquessen, Touraine,
        Maine,
Poictiers, and Anjou, these five provinces,
With her to thee, and this addition more,
Full thirty thousand marks of English coin.   530
Philip of France, if thou be pleas'd withal,
Command thy son and daughter to join hands.
    K. Phi. It likes us well, young princes; close your
        hands.
    Aust. And your lips too, for I am well assur'd
That I did so when I was first assur'd.   535
    K. Phi. Now, citizens of Angiers, ope your gates,
Let in that amity which you have made,
For at Saint Mary's Chapel presently
The rites of marriage shall be solemniz'd.
Is not the Lady Constance in this troop?   540
I know she is not, for this match made up
Her presence would have interrupted much.
Where is she and her son? tell me, who knows.
    Lew. She is sad and passionate at your Highness'
        tent.
    K. Phi. And by my faith, this league that we have
        made   545
Will give her sadness very little cure.
Brother of England, how may we content
This widow lady? In her right we came,
Which we, God knows, have turn'd another way,
To our own vantage.
    K. John.   We will heal up all,   550
For we'll create young Arthur Duke of Britain
And Earl of Richmond, and this rich fair town
We make him lord of. Call the Lady Constance;
Some speedy messenger bid her repair
To our solemnity. I trust we shall,   555
If not fill up the measure of her will,
Yet in some measure satisfy her so
That we shall stop her exclamation.
Go we, as well as haste will suffer us,
To this unlook'd-for, unprepared pomp.   560
                          Exeunt [all but the Bastard].
    Bast. Mad world, mad kings, mad composition!
John, to stop Arthur's title in the whole,
Hath willingly departed with a part,

519. **churlish:** grudging.   522. **still:** always.
530. **thirty thousand marks:** i.e. twenty thousand pounds (since a mark amounted to 13s. 4d.).   533. **likes:** pleases.   **close:** clasp.
535. **assur'd:** betrothed.   538. **presently:** at once.
544. **passionate:** disturbed.
555. **our solemnity:** i.e. the marriage ceremony.
556. **fill . . . will:** gratify her desires completely.
557. **so:** sufficiently.   558. **exclamation:** complaint.
561. **composition:** agreement.   563. **departed:** parted.

And France, whose armor conscience buckled on,
Whom zeal and charity brought to the field   565
As God's own soldier, rounded in the ear
With that same purpose-changer, that sly devil,
That broker that still breaks the pate of faith,
That daily break-vow, he that wins of all,
Of kings, of beggars, old men, young men, maids,   570
Who having no external thing to lose
But the word "maid," cheats the poor maid of that,
That smooth-fac'd gentleman, tickling commodity,
Commodity, the bias of the world—
The world, who of itself is peized well,   575
Made to run even upon even ground,
Till this advantage, this vile-drawing bias,
This sway of motion, this commodity,
Makes it take head from all indifferency,
From all direction, purpose, course, intent—   580
And this same bias, this commodity,
This bawd, this broker, this all-changing word,
Clapp'd on the outward eye of fickle France,
Hath drawn him from his own determin'd aid,
From a resolv'd and honorable war   585
To a most base and vile-concluded peace.
And why rail I on this commodity?
But for because he hath not woo'd me yet:
Not that I have the power to clutch my hand
When his fair angels would salute my palm,   590
But for my hand, as unattempted yet,
Like a poor beggar, raileth on the rich.
Well, whiles I am a beggar, I will rail,
And say there is no sin but to be rich;
And being rich, my virtue then shall be   595
To say there is no vice but beggary.
Since kings break faith upon commodity,
Gain, be my lord, for I will worship thee.   *Exit.*

ACT [III, Scene I]

Enter Constance, Arthur, *and* Salisbury.

Const. Gone to be married? Gone to swear a
        peace?
False blood to false blood join'd! Gone to be friends?
Shall Lewis have Blanch, and Blanch those provinces?
It is not so, thou hast misspoke, misheard;
Be well advis'd, tell o'er thy tale again.   5
It cannot be, thou dost but say 'tis so.
I trust I may not trust thee, for thy word
Is but the vain breath of a common man.
Believe me, I do not believe thee, man,

I have a king's oath to the contrary.   10
Thou shalt be punish'd for thus frighting me,
For I am sick and capable of fears,
Oppress'd with wrongs, and therefore full of fears,
A widow, husbandless, subject to fears,
A woman, naturally born to fears;   15
And though thou now confess thou didst but jest,
With my vex'd spirits I cannot take a truce,
But they will quake and tremble all this day.
What dost thou mean by shaking of thy head?
Why dost thou look so sadly on my son?   20
What means that hand upon that breast of thine?
Why holds thine eye that lamentable rheum,
Like a proud river peering o'er his bounds?
Be these sad signs confirmers of thy words?
Then speak again, not all thy former tale,   25
But this one word, whether thy tale be true.
  Sal. As true as I believe you think them false
That give you cause to prove my saying true.
  Const. O, if thou teach me to believe this sorrow,
Teach thou this sorrow how to make me die,   30
And let belief and life encounter so
As doth the fury of two desperate men,
Which in the very meeting fall, and die.
Lewis marry Blanch? O boy, then where art thou?
France friend with England, what becomes of me?   35
Fellow, be gone! I cannot brook thy sight,
This news hath made thee a most ugly man.
  Sal. What other harm have I, good lady, done,
But spoke the harm that is by others done?
  Const. Which harm within itself so heinous is   40
As it makes harmful all that speak of it.
  Arth. I do beseech you, madam, be content.
  Const. If thou that bid'st me be content wert grim,
Ugly, and sland'rous to thy mother's womb,
Full of unpleasing blots and sightless stains,   45
Lame, foolish, crooked, swart, prodigious,
Patch'd with foul moles and eye-offending marks,
I would not care, I then would be content,
For then I should not love thee; no, nor thou
Become thy great birth nor deserve a crown.   50
But thou art fair, and at thy birth, dear boy,
Nature and Fortune join'd to make thee great.
Of Nature's gifts thou mayst with lilies boast,
And with the half-blown rose. But Fortune, O,
She is corrupted, chang'd, and won from thee;   55
Sh' adulterates hourly with thine uncle John,
And with her golden hand hath pluck'd on France
To tread down fair respect of sovereignty,
And made his majesty the bawd to theirs.
France is a bawd to Fortune and King John,   60
That strumpet Fortune, that usurping John!
Tell me, thou fellow, is not France forsworn?
Envenom him with words, or get thee gone,
And leave those woes alone, which I alone

566. **rounded:** whispered.   567. **With:** by.
568. **broker:** agent.   571. **Who:** i.e. the maids.
573. **tickling:** flattering.   **commodity:** self-interest, expediency.
574. **bias:** in the game of bowls, a piece of lead in the side of a bowl,
making it take a curved course.   575. **peized:** balanced.
577. **vile-drawing:** attracting to evil.   578. **sway:** control.
579. **take head:** rush away.   **indifferency:** evenness, inclining neither
to one side nor to the other.
583. **Clapp'd on:** presented to.   **France:** i.e. Philip.
588. **But for because:** merely because.
589. **clutch:** close up (in refusal).
590. **angels:** coins, worth ten shillings, stamped with the figure of an
angel.   591. **unattempted:** untempted.   597. **upon:** on account of.

III.i. Location: France. The French King's pavilion.

12. **capable of:** susceptible to.
16. **jest.** With a pun on *joust*, leading to the *truce* of line 17.
17. **take a truce:** make peace.
22. **lamentable:** sad.   **rheum:** moisture, i.e. tears.
27. **them:** i.e. the French.   42. **content:** calm.
44. **sland'rous:** disgraceful.   45. **sightless:** unsightly.
46. **swart:** swarthy.   **prodigious:** monstrous.
54. **half-blown:** half-opened.   56. **adulterates:** commits adultery.
57. **pluck'd on:** induced.   63. **Envenom:** poison.

King John
III.i

Am bound to underbear.

Sal.   Pardon me, madam,   65
I may not go without you to the kings.

Const. Thou mayst, thou shalt, I will not go with
thee.
I will instruct my sorrows to be proud,
For grief is proud and makes his owner stoop.
To me and to the state of my great grief   70
Let kings assemble; for my grief's so great
That no supporter but the huge firm earth
Can hold it up. [*Throws herself on the ground.*] Here
I and sorrows sit;
Here is my throne, bid kings come bow to it.

Enter KING JOHN, [KING PHILIP *of*] France, [LEWIS
the] *Dolphin*, BLANCH, ELINOR, PHILIP [THE BAS-
TARD], AUSTRIA, [*and* ATTENDANTS].

K. Phi. 'Tis true, fair daughter, and this blessed
day   75
Ever in France shall be kept festival.
To solemnize this day the glorious sun
Stays in his course and plays the alchymist,
Turning with splendor of his precious eye
The meagre cloddy earth to glittering gold.   80
The yearly course that brings this day about
Shall never see it but a holy day.

Const. A wicked day, and not a holy day!
[*Rising.*]
What hath this day deserv'd? what hath it done,
That it in golden letters should be set   85
Among the high tides in the calendar?
Nay, rather turn this day out of the week,
This day of shame, oppression, perjury.
Or if it must stand still, let wives with child
Pray that their burthens may not fall this day,   90
Lest that their hopes prodigiously be cross'd;
But on this day let seamen fear no wrack;
No bargains break that are not this day made:
This day all things begun come to ill end,
Yea, faith itself to hollow falsehood change!   95

K. Phi. By heaven, lady, you shall have no cause
To curse the fair proceedings of this day.
Have I not pawn'd to you my majesty?

Const. You have beguil'd me with a counterfeit
Resembling majesty, which being touch'd and tried,
Proves valueless. You are forsworn, forsworn!   101
You came in arms to spill mine enemies' blood,
But now in arms you strengthen it with yours.
The grappling vigor and rough frown of war
Is cold in amity and painted peace,   105
And our oppression hath made up this league.
Arm, arm, you heavens, against these perjur'd kings!
A widow cries; be husband to me, heavens!
Let not the hours of this ungodly day
Wear out the [day] in peace; but ere sunset,   110

Set armed discord 'twixt these perjur'd kings!
Hear me, O, hear me!

Aust.   Lady Constance, peace!

Const. War, war, no peace! Peace is to me a war.
O Lymoges, O Austria! thou dost shame
That bloody spoil. Thou slave, thou wretch, thou
coward!   115
Thou little valiant, great in villainy!
Thou ever strong upon the stronger side!
Thou Fortune's champion that dost never fight
But when her humorous ladyship is by
To teach thee safety! thou art perjur'd too,   120
And sooth'st up greatness. What a fool art thou,
A ramping fool, to brag and stamp and swear
Upon my party! Thou cold-blooded slave,
Hast thou not spoke like thunder on my side?
Been sworn my soldier, bidding me depend   125
Upon thy stars, thy fortune, and thy strength,
And dost thou now fall over to my foes?
Thou wear a lion's hide! Doff it for shame,
And hang a calve's-skin on those recreant limbs.

Aust. O, that a man should speak those words to
me!   130

Bast. And hang a calve's-skin on those recreant
limbs.

Aust. Thou dar'st not say so, villain, for thy life.

Bast. And hang a calve's-skin on those recreant
limbs.

K. John. We like not this, thou dost forget thyself.

Enter PANDULPH.

K. Phi. Here comes the holy legate of the Pope.

Pand. Hail, you anointed deputies of heaven!   136
To thee, King John, my holy errand is:
I Pandulph, of fair Milan cardinal,
And from Pope Innocent the legate here,
Do in his name religiously demand   140
Why thou against the Church, our holy mother,
So willfully dost spurn; and force perforce
Keep Stephen Langton, chosen Archbishop
Of Canterbury, from that holy see?
This, in our foresaid Holy Father's name,   145
Pope Innocent, I do demand of thee.

K. John. What earthy name to interrogatories
Can taste the free breath of a sacred king?

65. **underbear:** endure.   70. **state:** pomp.
86. **high tides:** great festivals.
91. **prodigiously be cross'd:** be thwarted by the birth of a monster (?).
92. **But:** except.   **wrack:** shipwreck.   98. **pawn'd:** pledged.
100. **touch'd:** tested (as gold is with a touchstone).
102. **in arms:** armed.   103. **in arms:** embracing.
105. **painted:** i.e. unreal.
106. **our oppression:** i.e. your oppression of us.

114. **Lymoges, Austria.** See note to II.i.5.
115. **bloody spoil:** i.e. Richard's lion-skin that Austria wears.
119. **humorous:** whimsical.
121. **sooth'st up greatness:** flatterest powerful men.
123. **Upon my party:** in my support.
129. **calve's-skin.** Often worn by domestic fools and jesters.   **recreant:** cowardly.
138–46. **I . . . thee.** John's famous defiance of Rome—which made him a Protestant hero to most Elizabethans—was prompted by Innocent III's consecrating Stephen Langton as Archbishop of Canterbury (1207) after the King and the clergy had been unable to agree upon a candidate. John's rejection of Langton led to a papal interdict against England (1208) and, after prolonged bickering, to a papal bull deposing him (1212). The issue was resolved (1213) only after John had been forced to accept his kingdom as a papal fief (V.i) and to agree to pay an annual tribute to the Pope. In this scene, as elsewhere in the play, chronology is violently distorted. The betrothal of Lewis and Blanch and Pandulph's protest about John's intransigence, which are represented as almost simultaneous events, occurred respectively in 1200 and 1211.
142. **spurn:** kick.   **force perforce:** i.e. through violence.
147. **name to interrogatories:** title (or right) to demand answers to interrogations.   148. **taste:** test.

Thou canst not, Cardinal, devise a name
So slight, unworthy, and ridiculous, 150
To charge me to an answer, as the Pope.
Tell him this tale, and from the mouth of England
Add thus much more, that no Italian priest
Shall tithe or toll in our dominions;
But as we, under [God], are supreme head, 155
So under Him that great supremacy,
Where we do reign, we will alone uphold
Without th' assistance of a mortal hand.
So tell the Pope, all reverence set apart
To him and his usurp'd authority. 160
   K. Phi. Brother of England, you blaspheme in this.
   K. John. Though you and all the kings of Christen-
dom
Are led so grossly by this meddling priest,
Dreading the curse that money may buy out,
And by the merit of vild gold, dross, dust, 165
Purchase corrupted pardon of a man
Who in that sale sells pardon from himself;
Though you, and all the rest so grossly led,
This juggling witchcraft with revenue cherish,
Yet I alone, alone do me oppose 170
Against the Pope, and count his friends my foes.
   Pand. Then, by the lawful power that I have,
Thou shalt stand curs'd and excommunicate,
And blessed shall he be that doth revolt
From his allegiance to an heretic, 175
And meritorious shall that hand be call'd,
Canonized and worshipp'd as a saint,
That takes away by any secret course
Thy hateful life.
   Const.   O, lawful let it be
That I have room with Rome to curse a while! 180
Good father Cardinal, cry thou amen
To my keen curses; for without my wrong
There is no tongue hath power to curse him right.
   Pand. There's law and warrant, lady, for my curse.
   Const. And for mine too: when law can do no right,
Let it be lawful that law bar no wrong; 186
Law cannot give my child his kingdom here,
For he that holds his kingdom holds the law;
Therefore since law itself is perfect wrong,
How can the law forbid my tongue to curse? 190
   Pand. Philip of France, on peril of a curse,
Let go the hand of that arch-heretic,
And raise the power of France upon his head,
Unless he do submit himself to Rome.
   El. Look'st thou pale, France? Do not let go thy
hand. 195

152–60. **Tell . . . authority.** In Holinshed (Bullough, IV, 35–36) John
expresses his defiance in a letter, asserting "that he would never
consent that Stephan which had beene brought up & alwaies conversant with his enimies the Frenchmen, should now enjoy the rule
of the bishoprike and dioces of Canturburie. Moreover, he declared
in the same letters, that he marvelled not a little what the pope ment,
in that he did not consider how necessarie the freendship of the king
of England was to the see of Rome, sith there came more gains to the
Romane church out of that kingdome, than out of any other realme
on this side the mountaines. He added hereto, that for the liberties
of his crowne he would stand to the death, if the matter so required."
154. **tithe:** impose tithes. **toll:** collect taxes.
165. **vild:** vile, base. 167. **sells pardon from:** i.e. damns.
180. **room with Rome.** A homophonic pun for the Elizabethans.
182. **without my wrong:** i.e. without the motive that the wrong done
to me has provided.

   Const. Look to that, devil, lest that France repent,
And by disjoining hands hell lose a soul.
   Aust. King Philip, listen to the Cardinal.
   Bast. And hang a calve's-skin on his recreant limbs.
   Aust. Well, ruffian, I must pocket up these wrongs,
Because—
   Bast.   Your breeches best may carry them. 201
   K. John. Philip, what say'st thou to the Cardinal?
   Const. What should he say, but as the Cardinal?
   Lew. Bethink you, father, for the difference
Is purchase of a heavy curse from Rome, 205
Or the light loss of England for a friend.
Forgo the easier.
   Blanch.   That's the curse of Rome.
   Const. O Lewis, stand fast! the devil tempts thee
here
In likeness of a new untrimmed bride.
   Blanch. The Lady Constance speaks not from her
faith, 210
But from her need.
   Const.   O, if thou grant my need,
Which only lives but by the death of faith,
That need must needs infer this principle,
That faith would live again by death of need.
O then tread down my need, and faith mounts up;
Keep my need up, and faith is trodden down! 216
   K. John. The King is mov'd, and answers not to
this.
   Const. O, be remov'd from him, and answer well!
   Aust. Do so, King Philip, hang no more in doubt.
   Bast. Hang nothing but a calve's-skin, most sweet
lout. 220
   K. Phi. I am perplex'd, and know not what to say.
   Pand. What canst thou say but will perplex thee
more,
If thou stand excommunicate and curs'd?
   K. Phi. Good reverend father, make my person
yours,
And tell me how you would bestow yourself. 225
This royal hand and mine are newly knit,
And the conjunction of our inward souls
Married in league, coupled, and link'd together
With all religious strength of sacred vows.
The latest breath that gave the sound of words 230
Was deep-sworn faith, peace, amity, true love
Between our kingdoms and our royal selves,
And even before this truce, but new before,
No longer than we well could wash our hands
To clap this royal bargain up of peace, 235
Heaven knows they were besmear'd and over-stain'd
With slaughter's pencil—where revenge did paint
The fearful difference of incensed kings—
And shall these hands, so lately purg'd of blood,
So newly join'd in love, so strong in both, 240
Unyoke this seizure and this kind regreet?
Play fast and loose with faith? so jest with heaven?
Make such unconstant children of ourselves,

209. **untrimmed:** i.e. with flowing locks. 213. **infer:** imply.
224. **make . . . yours:** put yourself in my place.
225. **bestow:** conduct.
233. **even before:** just before. **new:** immediately.
238. **difference:** quarrel. 240. **both:** i.e. battle and love.
241. **seizure:** handclasp. **regreet:** salutation of friendship.

King John
III.i

As now again to snatch our palm from palm,
Unswear faith sworn, and on the marriage-bed 245
Of smiling peace to march a bloody host,
And make a riot on the gentle brow
Of true sincerity? O holy sir,
My reverend father, let it not be so!
Out of your grace devise, ordain, impose 250
Some gentle order, and then we shall be blest
To do your pleasure and continue friends.
    Pand. All form is formless, order orderless,
Save what is opposite to England's love.
Therefore to arms! be champion of our Church, 255
Or let the Church, our mother, breathe her curse,
A mother's curse, on her revolting son.
France, thou mayst hold a serpent by the tongue,
A cased lion by the mortal paw,
A fasting tiger safer by the tooth, 260
Than keep in peace that hand which thou dost hold.
    K. Phi. I may disjoin my hand, but not my faith.
    Pand. So mak'st thou faith an enemy to faith,
And like a civil war set'st oath to oath,
Thy tongue against thy tongue. O, let thy vow 265
First made to heaven, first be to heaven perform'd,
That is, to be the champion of our Church,
What since thou swor'st is sworn against thyself,
And may not be performed by thyself,
For that which thou hast sworn to do amiss 270
Is not amiss when it is truly done;
And being not done, where doing tends to ill,
The truth is then most done not doing it.
The better act of purposes mistook
Is to mistake again; though indirect, 275
Yet indirection thereby grows direct,
And falsehood falsehood cures, as fire cools fire
Within the scorched veins of one new burn'd.
It is religion that doth make vows kept,
But thou hast sworn against religion, 280
By what thou swear'st against the thing thou swear'st,
And mak'st an oath the surety for thy truth
Against an oath; the truth thou art unsure
To swear, swears only not to be forsworn,
Else what a mockery should it be to swear! 285
But thou dost swear only to be forsworn,
And most forsworn, to keep what thou dost swear;
Therefore thy later vows, against thy first,
Is in thyself rebellion to thyself;
And better conquest never canst thou make 290
Than arm thy constant and thy nobler parts
Against these giddy loose suggestions;
Upon which better part our pray'rs come in,
If thou vouchsafe them. But if not, then know
The peril of our curses light on thee 295
So heavy as thou shalt not shake them off,
But in despair die under their black weight.
    Aust. Rebellion, flat rebellion!
    Bast.   Will't not be?
Will not a calve's-skin stop that mouth of thine?
    Lew. Father, to arms!
    Blanch.   Upon thy wedding-day? 300

259. **cased:** caged. **mortal:** deadly.
271. **truly:** i.e. as explained by the *truth* of line 273.
292. **suggestions:** temptations. 296. **as:** that.

782

Against the blood that thou hast married?
What, shall our feast be kept with slaughtered men?
Shall braying trumpets and loud churlish drums,
Clamors of hell, be measures to our pomp?
O husband, hear me! ay, alack, how new 305
Is "husband" in my mouth! even for that name,
Which till this time my tongue did ne'er pronounce,
Upon my knee I beg, go not to arms
Against mine uncle.
    Const.   O, upon my knee,
Made hard with kneeling, I do pray to thee, 310
Thou virtuous Dolphin, alter not the doom
Forethought by heaven!
    Blanch. Now shall I see thy love. What motive
      may
Be stronger with thee than the name of wife?
    Const. That which upholdeth him that thee up-
      holds, 315
His honor. O, thine honor, Lewis, thine honor!
    Lew. I muse your Majesty doth seem so cold,
When such profound respects do pull you on.
    Pand. I will denounce a curse upon his head.
    K. Phi. Thou shalt not need. England, I will fall
      from thee. 320
    Const. O fair return of banish'd majesty!
    El. O foul revolt of French inconstancy!
    K. John. France, thou shalt rue this hour within
      this hour.
    Bast. Old Time the clock-setter, that bald sexton
      Time!
Is it as he will? Well then, France shall rue. 325
    Blanch. The sun's o'ercast with blood; fair day,
      adieu!
Which is the side that I must go withal?
I am with both, each army hath a hand,
And in their rage, I having hold of both,
They whirl asunder and dismember me. 330
Husband, I cannot pray that thou mayst win;
Uncle, I needs must pray that thou mayst lose;
Father, I may not wish the fortune thine;
Grandam, I will not wish thy wishes thrive:
Whoever wins, on that side shall I lose; 335
Assured loss before the match be play'd.
    Lew. Lady, with me, with me thy fortune lies.
    Blanch. There where my fortune lives, there my
      life dies.
    K. John. Cousin, go draw our puissance together.
                         [*Exit Bastard.*]
France, I am burn'd up with inflaming wrath, 340
A rage whose heat hath this condition,
That nothing can allay, nothing but blood,
The blood and dearest-valued blood of France.
    K. Phi. Thy rage shall burn thee up, and thou
      shalt turn
To ashes, ere our blood shall quench that fire. 345
Look to thyself, thou art in jeopardy.

304. **measures . . . pomp:** music for our wedding.
312. **Forethought:** destined. 317. **muse:** wonder.
318. **respects:** considerations. 319. **denounce:** call down.
333. **Father:** i.e. father-in-law, King Philip.
339. **Cousin:** kinsman. **puissance:** army.
341. **hath this condition:** is such.

K. John. No more than he that threats. To arms
let's hie!   *Exeunt.*

SCENE II

Alarums, excursions. Enter BASTARD *with Austria's
head.*

Bast. Now by my life, this day grows wondrous
hot;
Some aery devil hovers in the sky
And pours down mischief. Austria's head lie there,
While Philip breathes.

       Enter [KING] JOHN, ARTHUR, HUBERT.

K. John. Hubert, keep this boy. Philip, make up.
My mother is assailed in our tent,   5
And ta'en, I fear.
Bast.   My lord, I rescued her;
Her Highness is in safety, fear you not.
But on, my liege, for very little pains
Will bring this labor to an happy end. *Exeunt.* 10

[SCENE III]

Alarums, excursions, retreat. Enter [KING] JOHN, ELI-
NOR, ARTHUR, BASTARD, HUBERT, LORDS.

K. John. [*To Elinor.*] So shall it be; your Grace
shall stay behind
So strongly guarded. [*To Arthur.*] Cousin, look not
sad,
Thy grandame loves thee, and thy uncle will
As dear be to thee as thy father was.
Arth. O, this will make my mother die with grief!
K. John. [*To the Bastard.*] Cousin, away for
England! haste before,   6
And ere our coming see thou shake the bags
Of hoarding abbots, imprisoned angels
Set at liberty. The fat ribs of peace
Must by the hungry now be fed upon.   10
Use our commission in his utmost force.
Bast. Bell, book, and candle shall not drive me back,
When gold and silver becks me to come on.
I leave your Highness. Grandame, I will pray
(If ever I remember to be holy)   15
For your fair safety; so I kiss your hand.
El. Farewell, gentle cousin.
K. John.   Coz, farewell. [*Exit Bastard.*]
El. Come hither, little kinsman, hark, a word.
                          [*Takes Arthur aside.*]
K. John. Come hither, Hubert. O my gentle
Hubert,
We owe thee much! Within this wall of flesh   20

III.ii. Location: France. Plains near Angiers.
o.s.d. *Alarums*: calls to arms.
2. **aery devil.** Thought to be the cause of thunderstorms.
4. **breathes**: catches his breath, rests.   5. **make up**: hasten.

III.iii. Location: Scene continues.
o.s.d. *retreat*: trumpet signal for withdrawal of forces.
11. **commission**: warrant.   **his**: its.
12. **Bell . . . candle.** Used in the ritual of excommunication.
17. **Coz**: cousin, i.e. kinsman.
20. **We . . . much**: i.e. for proposing the match between Lewis and
Blanch (?).

There is a soul counts thee her creditor,
And with advantage means to pay thy love;
And, my good friend, thy voluntary oath
Lives in this bosom, dearly cherished.
Give me thy hand. I had a thing to say,   25
But I will fit it with some better [time].
By heaven, Hubert, I am almost asham'd
To say what good respect I have of thee.
Hub. I am much bounden to your Majesty.
K. John. Good friend, thou hast no cause to say
so yet,   30
But thou shalt have; and creep time ne'er so slow,
Yet it shall come for me to do thee good.
I had a thing to say, but let it go.
The sun is in the heaven, and the proud day,
Attended with the pleasures of the world,   35
Is all too wanton and too full of gawds
To give me audience. If the midnight bell
Did with his iron tongue and brazen mouth
Sound on into the drowsy race of night;
If this same were a churchyard where we stand, 40
And thou possessed with a thousand wrongs;
Or if that surly spirit, melancholy,
Had bak'd thy blood and made it heavy, thick,
Which else runs tickling up and down the veins,
Making that idiot, laughter, keep men's eyes   45
And strain their cheeks to idle merriment—
A passion hateful to my purposes;
Or if that thou couldst see me without eyes,
Hear me without thine ears, and make reply
Without a tongue, using conceit alone,   50
Without eyes, ears, and harmful sound of words—
Then, in despite of brooded watchful day,
I would into thy bosom pour my thoughts.
But, ah, I will not! yet I love thee well,
And by my troth I think thou lov'st me well.   55
Hub. So well, that what you bid me undertake,
Though that my death were adjunct to my act,
By heaven, I would do it.
K. John.   Do not I know thou wouldst?
Good Hubert, Hubert, Hubert, throw thine eye
On yon young boy. I'll tell thee what, my friend, 60
He is a very serpent in my way,
And wheresoe'er this foot of mine doth tread,
He lies before me. Dost thou understand me?
Thou art his keeper.
Hub.   And I'll keep him so,
That he shall not offend your Majesty.
K. John.   Death.   65
Hub. My lord?
K. John.   A grave.
Hub.   He shall not live.
K. John.   Enough.
I could be merry now. Hubert, I love thee.
Well, I'll not say what I intend for thee.
Remember. Madam, fare you well,
I'll send those powers o'er to your Majesty.   70

22. **advantage**: interest.   28. **respect**: opinion.
36. **gawds**: toys, gay trifles.   39. **race**: course.
44. **tickling**: tingling.   45. **idiot**: jester.   47. **passion**: emotion.
50. **conceit**: thought.   52. **brooded**: brooding, i.e. observing (?).
55. **troth**: truth, faith.   57. **adjunct to**: consequent upon.
70. **powers**: troops.

King John
III.iii

El. My blessing go with thee!
K. John.   For England, cousin, go.
Hubert shall be your man, attend on you
With all true duty. On toward Callice, ho! *Exeunt.*

Scene [IV]

Enter [King Philip *of*] *France,* [Lewis *the*] *Dolphin,*
Pandulpho, Attendants.

K. Phi. So by a roaring tempest on the flood,
A whole armado of convicted sail
Is scattered and disjoin'd from fellowship.
Pand. Courage and comfort! all shall yet go well.
K. Phi. What can go well, when we have run so
       ill?   5
Are we not beaten? Is not Angiers lost?
Arthur ta'en prisoner? Divers dear friends slain?
And bloody England into England gone,
O'erbearing interruption, spite of France?
Lew. What he hath won, that hath he fortified.
So hot a speed with such advice dispos'd,   11
Such temperate order in so fierce a cause,
Doth want example. Who hath read or heard
Of any kindred action like to this?
K. Phi. Well could I bear that England had this
       praise,   15
So we could find some pattern of our shame.

Enter Constance.

Look who comes here! a grave unto a soul,
Holding th' eternal spirit, against her will,
In the vild prison of afflicted breath.
I prithee, lady, go away with me.   20
Const. Lo! now! now see the issue of your peace.
K. Phi. Patience, good lady, comfort, gentle Con-
       stance!
Const. No, I defy all counsel, all redress,
But that which ends all counsel, true redress:
Death, death. O amiable lovely death!   25
Thou odoriferous stench! sound rottenness!
Arise forth from the couch of lasting night,
Thou hate and terror to prosperity,
And I will kiss thy detestable bones,
And put my eyeballs in thy vaulty brows,   30

And ring these fingers with thy household worms,
And stop this gap of breath with fulsome dust,
And be a carrion monster like thyself.
Come, grin on me, and I will think thou smil'st,
And buss thee as thy wife. Misery's love,   35
O, come to me!
K. Phi.   O fair affliction, peace!
Const. No, no, I will not, having breath to cry.
O that my tongue were in the thunder's mouth!
Then with a passion would I shake the world,
And rouse from sleep that fell anatomy   40
Which cannot hear a lady's feeble voice,
Which scorns a modern invocation.
Pand. Lady, you utter madness, and not sorrow.
Const. Thou art [not] holy to belie me so,
I am not mad. This hair I tear is mine,   45
My name is Constance, I was Geffrey's wife,
Young Arthur is my son, and he is lost.
I am not mad, I would to heaven I were!
For then 'tis like I should forget myself.
O, if I could, what grief should I forget!   50
Preach some philosophy to make me mad,
And thou shalt be canoniz'd, Cardinal;
For, being not mad, but sensible of grief,
My reasonable part produces reason
How I may be deliver'd of these woes,   55
And teaches me to kill or hang myself.
If I were mad, I should forget my son,
Or madly think a babe of clouts were he.
I am not mad; too well, too well I feel
The different plague of each calamity.   60
K. Phi. Bind up those tresses. O, what love I note
In the fair multitude of those her hairs!
Where but by chance a silver drop hath fall'n,
Even to that drop ten thousand wiry [friends]
Do glue themselves in sociable grief,   65
Like true, inseparable, faithful loves,
Sticking together in calamity.
Const. To England, if you will.
K. Phi.   Bind up your hairs.
Const. Yes, that I will; and wherefore will I do it?
I tore them from their bonds, and cried aloud,   70
"O that these hands could so redeem my son
As they have given these hairs their liberty!"
But now I envy at their liberty,
And will again commit them to their bonds,
Because my poor child is a prisoner.   75
And, father Cardinal, I have heard you say
That we shall see and know our friends in heaven.
If that be true, I shall see my boy again;
For since the birth of Cain, the first male child,
To him that did but yesterday suspire,   80
There was not such a gracious creature born.
But now will canker-sorrow eat my bud,

---

71. **For England.** Actually, Arthur was never sent to England.
Following the lucky stroke in capturing him at Mirebeau in 1202,
John at first tried to woo him from his French allies, says Holinshed
(Bullough, IV, 31–32); but when Arthur—by no means the docile
boy whom Shakespeare represents—haughtily demanded the English
crown as well as "all those other lands and possessions which king
Richard had in his hand at the houre of his death," John was so
"sore mooved" by his nephew's attitude that he had him "straitlie
kept in prison, as first in Falais, and after at Roan within the new
castell there." The abortive plan to "put out the yoong gentlemans
eies" (IV.i) was hatched while Arthur was incarcerated at Falaise,
and his death (IV.iii) occurred at Rouen. 73. **Callice:** Calais.

III.iv. Location: France. The French King's pavilion.
2. **convicted:** doomed (?) or defeated (?).
11. **with . . . dispos'd:** disciplined by such judgment.
12. **cause:** quarrel.   13. **Doth want example:** lacks precedent.
14. **kindred:** similar.
16. **So:** provided.   **pattern of:** precedent for. 21. **issue:** outcome.
23. **defy:** renounce.   **redress:** relief from trouble.
25. **lovely:** lovable.   30. **vaulty:** arched.

32. **fulsome:** repulsive.   35. **buss:** kiss amorously.
40. **fell anatomy:** cruel skeleton.   42. **modern:** ordinary.
53. **sensible:** capable.
58. **babe of clouts:** rag doll (*clout* = cloth).
63. **silver drop:** i.e. tear.   64. **wiry friends:** i.e. hairs.
68. **To . . . will.** Since this appears to be irrelevant it has been cited
as proof of revision in this scene, but perhaps it is a delayed response
to Philip's invitation in line 20.   80. **suspire:** breathe.

And chase the native beauty from his cheek,
And he will look as hollow as a ghost,
As dim and meagre as an ague's fit,   85
And so he'll die; and rising so again,
When I shall meet him in the court of heaven
I shall not know him: therefore never, never
Must I behold my pretty Arthur more.
   Pand.   You hold too heinous a respect of grief. 90
   Const.   He talks to me that never had a son.
   K. Phi.   You are as fond of grief as of your child.
   Const.   Grief fills the room up of my absent child,
Lies in his bed, walks up and down with me,
Puts on his pretty looks, repeats his words,   95
Remembers me of all his gracious parts,
Stuffs out his vacant garments with his form;
Then, have I reason to be fond of grief?
Fare you well! Had you such a loss as I,
I could give better comfort than you do.   100
I will not keep this form upon my head
                                  [*Tearing her hair.*]
When there is such disorder in my wit.
O Lord, my boy, my Arthur, my fair son!
My life, my joy, my food, my all the world!   104
My widow-comfort, and my sorrows' cure!   *Exit.*
   K. Phi.   I fear some outrage, and I'll follow her.
                                       Exit.
   Lew.   There's nothing in this world can make me
     joy:
Life is as tedious as a twice-told tale
Vexing the dull ear of a drowsy man;   109
And bitter shame hath spoil'd the sweet word's taste,
That it yields nought but shame and bitterness.
   Pand.   Before the curing of a strong disease,
Even in the instant of repair and health,
The fit is strongest; evils that take leave,
On their departure most of all show evil.   115
What have you lost by losing of this day?
   Lew.   All days of glory, joy, and happiness.
   Pand.   If you had won it, certainly you had.
No, no; when Fortune means to men most good,
She looks upon them with a threat'ning eye.   120
'Tis strange to think how much King John hath lost
In this which he accounts so clearly won.
Are not you griev'd that Arthur is his prisoner?
   Lew.   As heartily as he is glad he hath him.
   Pand.   Your mind is all as youthful as your blood.
Now hear me speak with a prophetic spirit;   126
For even the breath of what I mean to speak
Shall blow each dust, each straw, each little rub,
Out of the path which shall directly lead
Thy foot to England's throne. And therefore mark:
John hath seiz'd Arthur, and it cannot be   131
That whiles warm life plays in that infant's veins,
The misplac'd John should entertain an hour,
One minute, nay, one quiet breath of rest.

A sceptre snatch'd with an unruly hand   135
Must be as boisterously maintain'd as gain'd;
And he that stands upon a slipp'ry place
Makes nice of no vild hold to stay him up.
That John may stand, then Arthur needs must fall:
So be it, for it cannot be but so.   140
   Lew.   But what shall I gain by young Arthur's fall?
   Pand.   You, in the right of Lady Blanch your wife,
May then make all the claim that Arthur did.
   Lew.   And lose it, life and all, as Arthur did.
   Pand.   How green you are and fresh in this old
     world!   145
John lays you plots; the times conspire with you,
For he that steeps his safety in true blood
Shall find but bloody safety, and untrue.
This act so evilly borne shall cool the hearts
Of all his people, and freeze up their zeal,   150
That none so small advantage shall step forth
To check his reign, but they will cherish it;
No natural exhalation in the sky,
No scope of nature, no distemper'd day,
No common wind, no customed event,   155
But they will pluck away his natural cause
And call them meteors, prodigies, and signs,
Abortives, presages, and tongues of heaven,
Plainly denouncing vengeance upon John.   159
   Lew.   May be he will not touch young Arthur's life,
But hold himself safe in his prisonment.
   Pand.   O sir, when he shall hear of your approach,
If that young Arthur be not gone already,
Even at that news he dies; and then the hearts
Of all his people shall revolt from him,   165
And kiss the lips of unacquainted change,
And pick strong matter of revolt and wrath
Out of the bloody fingers' ends of John.
Methinks I see this hurly all on foot;
And O, what better matter breeds for you   170
Than I have nam'd! The bastard Faulconbridge
Is now in England ransacking the Church,
Offending charity. If but a dozen French
Were there in arms, they would be as a call
To train ten thousand English to their side,   175
Or as a little snow, tumbled about,
Anon becomes a mountain. O noble Dolphin,
Go with me to the King. 'Tis wonderful
What may be wrought out of their discontent,
Now that their souls are topful of offense.   180
For England go; I will whet on the King.
   Lew.   Strong reasons makes strange actions. Let us
     go;
If you say ay, the King will not say no.   *Exeunt.*

---

90. **heinous a respect:** terrible a notion.   96. **Remembers:** reminds.
101. **form:** coiffure.   102. **wit:** i.e. brain.
110. **bitter . . . taste:** i.e. the recognition of my failure obliterates even my delight in praise (*sweet word*) for my success (?). Most editors have followed Pope in emending *word's* to *world's.*
128. **rub:** obstruction.   132. **whiles:** while.
133. **misplac'd:** i.e. usurping.

136. **boisterously:** violently.
138. **Makes nice of:** is fastidious about.
146. **lays you plots:** i.e. lays plots by which you may benefit.
149. **borne:** executed.
151. **none . . . advantage:** no opportunity, however small.
153. **exhalation:** meteor.   154. **scope:** freak (?).
156. **his:** its.   158. **Abortives:** abnormalities.
159. **denouncing:** calling down.   161. **hold:** consider.
166. **unacquainted:** unfamiliar.   169. **hurly:** tumult. **on foot:** begun.
174. **call:** decoy.   175. **train:** draw, entice.
180. **topful:** brimful. **offense:** grievance.

ACT IV, Scene I

Enter Hubert *and* Executioners.

Hub. Heat me these irons hot, and look thou stand
Within the arras. When I strike my foot
Upon the bosom of the ground, rush forth
And bind the boy which you shall find with me
Fast to the chair. Be heedful. Hence, and watch.   5
    [*1.*] *Exec.* I hope your warrant will bear out the
        deed.
    Hub. Uncleanly scruples! fear not you. Look to't.
                                [*Exeunt Executioners.*]
Young lad, come forth; I have to say with you.

Enter Arthur.

Arth. Good morrow, Hubert.
Hub.   Good morrow, little prince.
Arth. As little prince, having so great a title   10
To be more prince, as may be. You are sad.
Hub. Indeed I have been merrier.
Arth.   Mercy on me!
Methinks nobody should be sad but I.
Yet I remember, when I was in France,
Young gentlemen would be as sad as night,   15
Only for wantonness. By my christendom,
So I were out of prison and kept sheep,
I should be as merry as the day is long;
And so I would be here, but that I doubt
My uncle practices more harm to me.   20
He is afraid of me and I of him.
Is it my fault that I was Geffrey's son?
No indeed is't not; and I would to heaven
I were your son, so you would love me, Hubert.
Hub. [*Aside.*] If I talk to him, with his innocent
        prate   25
He will awake my mercy, which lies dead;
Therefore I will be sudden, and dispatch.
Arth. Are you sick, Hubert? You look pale to-day.
In sooth, I would you were a little sick,
That I might sit all night and watch with you.   30
I warrant I love you more than you do me.
Hub. [*Aside.*] His words do take possession of
        my bosom.—
Read here, young Arthur.   [*Showing a paper.*]
                [*Aside.*] How now, foolish rheum?
Turning dispiteous torture out of door?
I must be brief, lest resolution drop   35
Out at mine eyes in tender womanish tears.—
Can you not read it? Is it not fair writ?
Arth. Too fairly, Hubert, for so foul effect.
Must you with hot irons burn out both mine eyes?
Hub. Young boy, I must.
Arth.   And will you?
Hub.   And I will.

Arth. Have you the heart? When your head did
        but ache,   41
I knit my handkercher about your brows
(The best I had, a princess wrought it me)
And I did never ask it you again;
And with my hand at midnight held your head;   45
And like the watchful minutes to the hour,
Still and anon cheer'd up the heavy time,
Saying, "What lack you?" and "Where lies your
        grief?"
Or "What good love may I perform for you?"
Many a poor man's son would have lien still,   50
And ne'er have spoke a loving word to you;
But you at your sick service had a prince.
Nay, you may think my love was crafty love,
And call it cunning. Do, and if you will;
If heaven be pleas'd that you must use me ill,   55
Why then you must. Will you put out mine eyes,
These eyes that never did nor never shall
So much as frown on you?
Hub.   I have sworn to do it;
And with hot irons must I burn them out.
Arth. Ah, none but in this iron age would do it!   60
The iron of itself, though heat red-hot,
Approaching near these eyes, would drink my tears,
And quench [his] fiery indignation
Even in the matter of mine innocence;
Nay, after that, consume away in rust,   65
But for containing fire to harm mine eye.
Are you more stubborn-hard than hammer'd iron?
And if an angel should have come to me
And told me Hubert should put out mine eyes,
I would not have believ'd him—no tongue but Hubert's.
Hub. Come forth.   [*Stamps.*]

[*Enter* Executioners *with a cord, irons, etc.*]

                Do as I bid you do.   71
Arth. O, save me, Hubert, save me! My eyes are
        out
Even with the fierce looks of these bloody men.
Hub. Give me the iron, I say, and bind him here.
Arth. Alas, what need you be so boist'rous-rough?
I will not struggle, I will stand stone-still.   76
For heaven sake, Hubert, let me not be bound!
Nay, hear me, Hubert, drive these men away,
And I will sit as quiet as a lamb;
I will not stir, nor winch, nor speak a word,   80
Nor look upon the iron angerly.
Thrust but these men away, and I'll forgive you,
What ever torment you do put me to.
Hub. Go stand within; let me alone with him.   84
    [*1.*] *Exec.* I am best pleas'd to be from such a deed.
                                [*Exeunt Executioners.*]
Arth. Alas, I then have chid away my friend!
He hath a stern look, but a gentle heart.

IV.i. Location: England. A castle.
1. me: for me.   2. Within the arras: behind the wall-hangings.
7. Uncleanly: unbecoming.
10–11. As . . . be: i.e. despite my great title I am as little a prince as
it is possible to be.
16. wantonness: affectation.   By my christendom: as I am a Christian.
17. So: if.   19. doubt: fear.   20. practices: plots.
25. prate: prattle.   29. sooth: truth.   34. dispiteous: pitiless.
37. fair: legibly.   38. effect: meaning.

42. knit: bound.   43. wrought: worked, embroidered.
46. watchful . . . hour: minutes that mark the progress of the hour.
47. Still and anon: continually.   heavy: dreary.
48. grief: pain.   49. love: loving service.   50. lien: lain.
52. your sick service: your service when you were sick.
61. heat: heated.   64. matter . . . innocence: i.e. my tears.
66. But for containing: only because it contains.   75. what: why.
80. winch: wince.   85. from: away from.

Let him come back, that his compassion may
Give life to yours.
    Hub.   Come, boy, prepare yourself.   89
    Arth.   Is there no remedy?
    Hub.   None, but to lose your eyes.
    Arth.   O heaven! that there were but a mote in
          yours,
A grain, a dust, a gnat, a wandering hair,
Any annoyance in that precious sense!
Then feeling what small things are boisterous there,
Your vild intent must needs seem horrible.   95
    Hub.   Is this your promise?   Go to, hold your
          tongue.
    Arth.   Hubert, the utterance of a brace of tongues
Must needs want pleading for a pair of eyes.
Let me not hold my tongue, let me not, Hubert;
Or, Hubert, if you will, cut out my tongue,   100
So I may keep mine eyes.   O, spare mine eyes,
Though to no use but still to look on you!
Lo, by my troth, the instrument is cold,
And would not harm me.
    Hub.   I can heat it, boy.
    Arth.   No, in good sooth; the fire is dead with grief,
Being create for comfort, to be us'd   106
In undeserv'd extremes. See else yourself,
There is no malice in this burning coal;
The breath of heaven hath blown his spirit out,
And strew'd repentant ashes on his head.   110
    Hub.   But with my breath I can revive it, boy.
    Arth.   And if you do, you will but make it blush
And glow with shame of your proceedings, Hubert.
Nay, it perchance will sparkle in your eyes;
And, like a dog that is compell'd to fight,   115
Snatch at his master that doth tarre him on.
All things that you should use to do me wrong
Deny their office; only you do lack
That mercy which fierce fire and iron extends,
Creatures of note for mercy-lacking uses.   120
    Hub.   Well, see to live; I will not touch thine eye
For all the treasure that thine uncle owes.
Yet am I sworn, and I did purpose, boy,
With this same very iron to burn them out.   124
    Arth.   O now you look like Hubert! All this while
You were disguis'd.
    Hub.   Peace; no more. Adieu.
Your uncle must not know but you are dead.
I'll fill these dogged spies with false reports;
And, pretty child, sleep doubtless and secure
That Hubert, for the wealth of all the world,   130
Will not offend thee.
    Arth.   O heaven! I thank you, Hubert.
    Hub.   Silence, no more. Go closely in with me;
Much danger do I undergo for thee.   *Exeunt.*

---

93. **precious sense:** i.e. sight.   94. **boisterous:** painful.
98. **want pleading:** lack pleading, i.e. plead inadequately.
99. **Let me not:** i.e. don't hold me to my promise to.
106. **create:** created.
107. **In undeserv'd extremes:** in (inflicting) undeserved torments.
114. **sparkle:** throw sparks into.   116. **Snatch:** snap. **tarre:** urge.
118. **office:** function, duty.
120. **Creatures of note:** objects notorious.   122. **owes:** owns.
128. **dogged:** fierce.   129. **doubtless:** fearless.   **secure:** confident.
131. **offend:** harm.   132. **closely:** secretly.

SCENE II

Enter [KING] JOHN, PEMBROKE, SALISBURY, *and other*
LORDS.

    K. John.   Here once again we sit; once [again]
          crown'd,
And look'd upon, I hope, with cheerful eyes.
    Pem.   This "once again" (but that your Highness
          pleas'd)
Was once superfluous. You were crown'd before,
And that high royalty was ne'er pluck'd off;   5
The faiths of men ne'er stained with revolt;
Fresh expectation troubled not the land
With any long'd-for change or better state.
    Sal.   Therefore, to be possess'd with double pomp,
To guard a title that was rich before,   10
To gild refined gold, to paint the lily,
To throw a perfume on the violet,
To smooth the ice, or add another hue
Unto the rainbow, or with taper-light
To seek the beauteous eye of heaven to garnish,   15
Is wasteful and ridiculous excess.
    Pem.   But that your royal pleasure must be done,
This act is as an ancient tale new told,
And, in the last repeating, troublesome,
Being urged at a time unseasonable.   20
    Sal.   In this the antique and well-noted face
Of plain old form is much disfigured,
And like a shifted wind unto a sail,
It makes the course of thoughts to fetch about,
Startles and frights consideration,   25
Makes sound opinion sick, and truth suspected,
For putting on so new a fashion'd robe.
    Pem.   When workmen strive to do better than well,
They do confound their skill in covetousness,
And oftentimes excusing of a fault   30
Doth make the fault the worse by th' excuse:
As patches set upon a little breach
Discredit more in hiding of the fault
Than did the fault before it was so patch'd.   34
    Sal.   To this effect, before you were new crown'd,
We breath'd our counsel; but it pleas'd your Highness
To overbear it, and we are all well pleas'd,
Since all and every part of what we would
Doth make a stand at what your Highness will.   39
    K. John.   Some reasons of this double coronation
I have possess'd you with, and think them strong;
And more, more strong than lesser is my fear,
I shall indue you with. Mean time but ask

IV.ii. Location: England. King John's palace.
1. **once again crown'd.** John had been proclaimed king and was
duly crowned at Westminster in May 1199, shortly after Richard's
death, but in October 1200, reports Holinshed (Bullough, IV, 31–32),
he returned from France to England and "caused himselfe to be
crowned againe at Canturburie." In March 1201 he was crowned
for the third time.   10. **guard:** adorn.
21. **well-noted:** well-known.   22. **form:** order, customary procedure.
24. **fetch about:** change direction.
25. **frights consideration:** i.e. prompts re-examination of John's title
to the throne (?).   29. **confound:** destroy.
32. **breach:** hole.   33. **fault:** defect.   37. **overbear:** ignore.
39. **make a stand:** stop short.
41. **possess'd you with:** informed you of.
42–43. **more . . . with:** i.e. I shall provide you with other reasons
which will be strong in proportion as the object of my fear (i.e.
Arthur) is lesser.

King John
IV.ii

What you would have reform'd that is not well,
And well shall you perceive how willingly   45
I will both hear and grant you your requests.
    Pem. Then I, as one that am the tongue of these
To sound the purposes of all their hearts,
Both for myself and them—but, chief of all,
Your safety, for the which myself and them   50
Bend their best studies—heartily request
Th' enfranchisement of Arthur, whose restraint
Doth move the murmuring lips of discontent
To break into this dangerous argument:
If what in rest you have in right you hold,   55
Why then your fears, which (as they say) attend
The steps of wrong, should move you to mew up
Your tender kinsman, and to choke his days
With barbarous ignorance, and deny his youth
The rich advantage of good exercise.   60
That the time's enemies may not have this
To grace occasions, let it be our suit
That you have bid us ask his liberty,
Which for our goods we do no further ask
Than whereupon our weal, on you depending,   65
Counts it your weal he have his liberty.

Enter HUBERT.

    K. John. Let it be so; I do commit his youth
To your direction. Hubert, what news with you?
                                     [Taking him aside.]
    Pem. This is the man should do the bloody deed;
He show'd his warrant to a friend of mine.   70
The image of a wicked heinous fault
Lives in his eye; that close aspect of his
[Doth] show the mood of a much troubled breast,
And I do fearfully believe 'tis done,
What we so fear'd he had a charge to do.   75
    Sal. The color of the King doth come and go
Between his purpose and his conscience,
Like heralds 'twixt two dreadful battles set:
His passion is so ripe, it needs must break.
    Pem. And when it breaks, I fear will issue thence
The foul corruption of a sweet child's death.   81
    K. John. We cannot hold mortality's strong hand.
Good lords, although my will to give is living,
The suit which you demand is gone and dead.
He tells us Arthur is deceas'd to-night.   85
    Sal. Indeed we fear'd his sickness was past cure.
    Pem. Indeed we heard how near his death he was
Before the child himself felt he was sick.
This must be answer'd either here or hence.
    K. John. Why do you bend such solemn brows on
        me?   90
Think you I bear the shears of destiny?
Have I commandement on the pulse of life?

    Sal. It is apparent foul play, and 'tis shame
That greatness should so grossly offer it.
So thrive it in your game! and so farewell.   95
    Pem. Stay yet, Lord Salisbury, I'll go with thee,
And find th' inheritance of this poor child,
His little kingdom of a forced grave.
That blood which ow'd the breadth of all this isle,
Three foot of it doth hold; bad world the while!   100
This must not be thus borne. This will break out
To all our sorrows, and ere long I doubt.
                                     Exeunt [Lords].
    K. John. They burn in indignation. I repent.

Enter MESSENGER.

There is no sure foundation set on blood;
No certain life achiev'd by others' death.   105
A fearful eye thou hast. Where is that blood
That I have seen inhabit in those cheeks?
So foul a sky clears not without a storm,
Pour down thy weather. How goes all in France?
    Mess. From France to England. Never such a
        pow'r   110
For any foreign preparation
Was levied in the body of a land.
The copy of your speed is learn'd by them;
For when you should be told they do prepare,
The tidings comes that they are all arriv'd.   115
    K. John. O, where hath our intelligence been
        drunk?
Where hath it slept? Where is my mother's care,
That such an army could be drawn in France,
And she not hear of it?
    Mess.   My liege, her ear
Is stopp'd with dust: the first of April died   120
Your noble mother; and as I hear, my lord,
The Lady Constance in a frenzy died
Three days before; but this from rumor's tongue
I idly heard—if true or false I know not.   124
    K. John. Withhold thy speed, dreadful occasion!
O, make a league with me, till I have pleas'd
My discontented peers! What? mother dead?
How wildly then walks my estate in France!
Under whose conduct came those pow'rs of France
That thou for truth giv'st out are landed here?   130
    Mess. Under the Dolphin.

Enter BASTARD *and* PETER OF POMFRET.

    K. John.   Thou hast made me giddy

---

48. **sound:** give voice to.   51. **studies:** efforts.
55. **rest:** peace, tranquillity.
56–57. **your fears . . . should move:** should your fears . . . move.
57. **mew up:** confine, cage (a term from falconry).
61. **the time's enemies:** those hostile to the present state of affairs.
62. **grace occasions:** i.e. justify their disaffection (?).
64. **our goods:** our own benefit.
65. **whereupon:** so far as.   **weal:** welfare.
72. **close:** furtive.   75. **had a charge:** was commissioned.
78. **battles:** armies drawn up in readiness for battle.
89. **answer'd:** answered for, atoned.   **hence:** i.e. in heaven.

93. **apparent:** obvious.   94. **grossly offer:** flagrantly attempt.
95. **So . . . game:** may you have the same ill fortune.
98. **forced:** (1) involuntary; (2) imposed through violence.
99. **ow'd:** owned.   106. **fearful:** full of fear.
111. **preparation:** expedition.
113. **copy:** example.   **your speed.** See II.i.56–61.
116. **intelligence:** information service, spies.
118. **drawn:** levied.
119–59. **My . . . thee.** Chronology here, as throughout the play, is freely violated. Whereas the day and month of Elinor's death is, surprisingly, correct, Constance predeceased her mother-in-law by three years (in 1201); and whereas the episode of Peter the Hermit is assigned by Holinshed (Bullough, IV, 41) to 1212, that of the five moons (lines 182–84) must be dated twelve years earlier (Bullough, IV, 29).   124. **idly:** by chance.   125. **occasion:** course of events.
128. **wildly . . . walks:** staggers, totters.   **estate:** power.
129. **conduct:** command.

With these ill tidings.—Now! what says the world
To your proceedings? Do not seek to stuff
My head with more ill news, for it is full.
　　Bast. But if you be afeard to hear the worst,　135
Then let the worst unheard fall on your head.
　　K. John. Bear with me, cousin, for I was amaz'd
Under the tide; but now I breathe again
Aloft the flood, and can give audience
To any tongue, speak it of what it will.　140
　　Bast. How I have sped among the clergymen
The sums I have collected shall express.
But as I travell'd hither through the land,
I find the people strangely fantasied,
Possess'd with rumors, full of idle dreams,　145
Not knowing what they fear, but full of fear.
And here's a prophet that I brought with me
From forth the streets of Pomfret, whom I found
With many hundreds treading on his heels;
To whom he sung, in rude harsh-sounding rhymes,
That, ere the next Ascension-day at noon,　151
Your Highness should deliver up your crown.
　　K. John. Thou idle dreamer, wherefore didst thou
　　　so?
　　Peter. Foreknowing that the truth will fall out so.
　　K. John. Hubert, away with him; imprison him;
And on that day at noon, whereon he says　156
I shall yield up my crown, let him be hang'd.
Deliver him to safety, and return,
For I must use thee.　　　[*Exit Hubert with Peter.*]
　　　　　　　　O my gentle cousin,
Hear'st thou the news abroad, who are arriv'd?　160
　　Bast. The French, my lord; men's mouths are full
　　　of it.
Besides, I met Lord Bigot and Lord Salisbury,
With eyes as red as new-enkindled fire,
And others more, going to seek the grave
Of Arthur, whom they say is kill'd to-night　165
On your suggestion.
　　K. John.　　　　Gentle kinsman, go
And thrust thyself into their companies;
I have a way to win their loves again.
Bring them before me.
　　Bast.　　　　I will seek them out.
　　K. John. Nay, but make haste; the better foot
　　　before.　170
O, let me have no subject enemies
When adverse foreigners affright my towns
With dreadful pomp of stout invasion!
Be Mercury, set feathers to thy heels,
And fly, like thought, from them to me again.　175
　　Bast. The spirit of the time shall teach me speed.
　　　　　　　　　　　　　　　　　　Exit.

　　K. John. Spoke like a sprightful noble gentleman.
Go after him; for he perhaps shall need
Some messenger betwixt me and the peers,
And be thou he.
　　Mess.　　　　With all my heart, my liege. [*Exit.*]
　　K. John. My mother dead!　181

Enter HUBERT.

　　Hub. My lord, they say five moons were seen
　　　to-night;
Four fixed, and the fift did whirl about
The other four in wondrous motion.
　　K. John. Five moons?
　　Hub.　　　　Old men and beldames in the streets
Do prophesy upon it dangerously.　186
Young Arthur's death is common in their mouths,
And when they talk of him, they shake their heads,
And whisper one another in the ear;
And he that speaks doth gripe the hearer's wrist,　190
Whilst he that hears makes fearful action
With wrinkled brows, with nods, with rolling eyes.
I saw a smith stand with his hammer, thus,
The whilst his iron did on the anvil cool,
With open mouth swallowing a tailor's news,　195
Who, with his shears and measure in his hand,
Standing on slippers, which his nimble haste
Had falsely thrust upon contrary feet,
Told of a many thousand warlike French
That were embattailed and rank'd in Kent.　200
Another lean unwash'd artificer
Cuts off his tale and talks of Arthur's death.
　　K. John. Why seek'st thou to possess me with
　　　these fears?
Why urgest thou so oft young Arthur's death?　204
Thy hand hath murd'red him. I had a mighty cause
To wish him dead, but thou hadst none to kill him.
　　Hub. No had, my lord? Why, did you not provoke
　　　me?
　　K. John. It is the curse of kings to be attended
By slaves that take their humors for a warrant
To break within the bloody house of life,　210
And on the winking of authority
To understand a law; to know the meaning
Of dangerous majesty, when perchance it frowns
More upon humor than advis'd respect.
　　Hub. Here is your hand and seal for what I did.
　　K. John. O, when the last accompt 'twixt heaven
　　　and earth　216
Is to be made, then shall this hand and seal
Witness against us to damnation!

---

133. **proceedings**: i.e. in looting the monasteries, as John had ordered
at III.iii.6–11.　137. **amaz'd**: stunned.
141. **sped**: succeeded.
147–57. **And . . . hang'd.** Holinshed (Bullough, IV, 41), who identifies
Peter as a hermit "dwelling about Yorke," says that when the day
that he had predicted as ominous for John passed without "notable
damage" he, "togither with his sonne," was hanged.
148. **Pomfret**: Pontefract, a town in Yorkshire.
151. **Ascension-day**: the Thursday forty days after Easter.
158. **safety**: custody.　159. **gentle**: noble.
166. **suggestion**: instigation.
174. **Mercury**: messenger of the gods, often depicted as wearing
winged sandals.

177. **sprightful**: high-spirited.
182. **five moons.** "About the moneth of December [1200]," says
Holinshed (Bullough, IV, 29), "there were seene in the province of
Yorke five moones, one in the east, the second in the west, the third
in the north, the fourth in the south, and the fift as it were set in the
middest of the other, having manie stars about it."
185. **beldames**: old women, crones.
186. **prophesy upon it**: i.e. expound its significance.
190. **gripe**: grasp.　191. **action**: gestures.
200. **embattailed**: drawn up in line of battle.
201. **artificer**: artisan.
207. **No had**: did I not have.　**provoke**: incite.
209. **humors**: moods.　211. **winking**: closing both eyes.
214. **upon humor**: by caprice.　**advis'd respect**: deliberate consideration.

King John
IV.ii

How oft the sight of means to do ill deeds
Make deeds ill done! Hadst not thou been by,   220
A fellow by the hand of nature mark'd,
Quoted, and sign'd to do a deed of shame,
This murther had not come into my mind;
But taking note of thy abhorr'd aspect,
Finding thee fit for bloody villainy,   225
Apt, liable to be employ'd in danger,
I faintly broke with thee of Arthur's death;
And thou, to be endeared to a king,
Made it no conscience to destroy a prince.

   Hub. My lord—   230

   K. John. Hadst thou but shook thy head or made a
      pause
When I spake darkly what I purposed,
Or turn'd an eye of doubt upon my face,
As bid me tell my tale in express words,   234
Deep shame had struck me dumb, made me break off,
And those thy fears might have wrought fears in me.
But thou didst understand me by my signs,
And didst in signs again parley with sin,
Yea, without stop, didst let thy heart consent,
And consequently thy rude hand to act   240
The deed, which both our tongues held vild to name.
Out of my sight, and never see me more!
My nobles leave me, and my state is braved,
Even at my gates, with ranks of foreign pow'rs;
Nay, in the body of this fleshly land,   245
This kingdom, this confine of blood and breath,
Hostility and civil tumult reigns
Between my conscience and my cousin's death.

   Hub. Arm you against your other enemies,
I'll make a peace between your soul and you.   250
Young Arthur is alive. This hand of mine
Is yet a maiden and an innocent hand,
Not painted with the crimson spots of blood.
Within this bosom never ent'red yet
The dreadful motion of a murderous thought,   255
And you have slander'd nature in my form,
Which howsoever rude exteriorly,
Is yet the cover of a fairer mind
Than to be butcher of an innocent child.

   K. John. Doth Arthur live? O, haste thee to the
      peers,   260
Throw this report on their incensed rage,
And make them tame to their obedience!
Forgive the comment that my passion made
Upon thy feature, for my rage was blind,
And foul imaginary eyes of blood   265
Presented thee more hideous than thou art.
O, answer not! but to my closet bring
The angry lords with all expedient haste.
I conjure thee but slowly; run more fast.   *Exeunt.*

222. **Quoted, and sign'd:** designated and marked.
223. **murther:** murder.   226. **liable:** suitable.
227. **faintly:** hintingly, indirectly.   **broke with thee:** broached to
you the subject.   229. **Made . . . conscience:** did not scruple.
234. **As:** as if to.   **express:** explicit.   240. **act:** perform.
243. **state is braved:** government is challenged.
245. **this fleshly land:** i.e. John's own body.
246. **confine:** (1) region; (2) prison.   255. **motion:** impulse.
256. **nature . . . form:** humanity in my person.
264. **feature:** physical appearance.   265. **imaginary:** imagined.
267. **closet:** chamber.   269. **conjure:** adjure.

Scene III

Enter Arthur *on the walls.*

   Arth. The wall is high, and yet will I leap down.
Good ground, be pitiful and hurt me not!
There's few or none do know me; if they did,
This ship-boy's semblance hath disguis'd me quite.
I am afraid, and yet I'll venture it.   5
If I get down, and do not break my limbs,
I'll find a thousand shifts to get away.
As good to die and go, as die and stay. [*Leaps down.*]
O me, my uncle's spirit is in these stones.
Heaven take my soul, and England keep my bones!   10
                       Dies.

Enter Pembroke, Salisbury, *and* Bigot.

   Sal. Lords, I will meet him at Saint Edmundsbury.
It is our safety, and we must embrace
This gentle offer of the perilous time.

   Pem. Who brought that letter from the Cardinal?

   Sal. The Count Melune, a noble lord of France,
Whose private with me of the Dolphin's love   16
Is much more general than these lines import.

   Big. To-morrow morning let us meet him then.

   Sal. Or rather then set forward, for 'twill be
Two long days' journey, lords, or ere we meet.   20

Enter Bastard.

   Bast. Once more to-day well met, distemper'd
      lords!
The King by me requests your presence straight.

   Sal. The King hath dispossess'd himself of us.
We will not line his thin bestained cloak
With our pure honors, nor attend the foot   25
That leaves the print of blood where e'er it walks.
Return, and tell him so. We know the worst.

   Bast. What e'er you think, good words I think
      were best.

   Sal. Our griefs, and not our manners, reason now.

   Bast. But there is little reason in your grief;   30
Therefore 'twere reason you had manners now.

   Pem. Sir, sir, impatience hath his privilege.

   Bast. 'Tis true—to hurt his master, no [man] else.

   Sal. This is the prison. [*Seeing Arthur.*] What is
      he lies here?

   Pem. O death, made proud with pure and princely
      beauty!   35
The earth had not a hole to hide this deed.

IV.iii. Location: England. Before the castle.
1–10. **The wall . . . bones.** Some historians, says Holinshed (Bullough, IV, 33), think that as Arthur "assaied to have escaped out of prison, and prooving to clime over the wals of the castell [of Rouen], he fell into the river of Saine, and so was drowned. Other write, that through verie greefe and languor he pined awaie, and died of naturall sicknesse. But some affirme, that king John secretlie caused him to be murthered and made awaie, so as it is not throughlie agreed upon, in what sort he finished his daies: but verelie king John was had in great suspicion, whether worthilie or not, the lord knoweth."   4. **semblance:** disguise.
7. **shifts:** (1) contrivances; (2) changes of clothing.
11. **him:** i.e. Lewis.   **Saint Edmundsbury:** Bury St. Edmunds, ancient town in Suffolk.   16. **private:** private communication.
17. **general:** comprehensive.   20. **or ere:** before.
21. **distemper'd:** disturbed, out of temper.
29. **griefs:** grievances.   **reason:** speak.

Sal. Murther, as hating what himself hath done,
Doth lay it open to urge on revenge.
　Big. Or when he doom'd this beauty to a grave,
Found it too precious-princely for a grave. 40
　Sal. Sir Richard, what think you? [Have you] beheld,
Or have you read, or heard, or could you think?
Or do you almost think, although you see,
That you do see? Could thought, without this object,
Form such another? This is the very top, 45
The heighth, the crest, or crest unto the crest,
Of murther's arms. This is the bloodiest shame,
The wildest savagery, the vildest stroke,
That ever wall-ey'd wrath or staring rage
Presented to the tears of soft remorse. 50
　Pem. All murthers past do stand excus'd in this;
And this, so sole and so unmatchable,
Shall give a holiness, a purity,
To the yet unbegotten sin of times;
And prove a deadly bloodshed but a jest, 55
Exampled by this heinous spectacle.
　Bast. It is a damned and a bloody work,
The graceless action of a heavy hand—
If that it be the work of any hand.
　Sal. If that it be the work of any hand? 60
We had a kind of light what would ensue.
It is the shameful work of Hubert's hand,
The practice and the purpose of the King;
From whose obedience I forbid my soul,
Kneeling before this ruin of sweet life, 65
And breathing to his breathless excellence
The incense of a vow, a holy vow,
Never to taste the pleasures of the world,
Never to be infected with delight,
Nor conversant with ease and idleness, 70
Till I have set a glory to this hand,
By giving it the worship of revenge.
　Pem., Big. Our souls religiously confirm thy words.

Enter HUBERT.

　Hub. Lords, I am hot with haste in seeking you.
Arthur doth live, the King hath sent for you. 75
　Sal. O, he is bold, and blushes not at death.
Avaunt, thou hateful villain, get thee gone!
　Hub. I am no villain.
　Sal. 　　　　　　　　Must I rob the law?
　　　　　　　　　　　　　　　[*Drawing his sword.*]
　Bast. Your sword is bright, sir, put it up again.
　Sal. Not till I sheathe it in a murtherer's skin. 80
　Hub. Stand back, Lord Salisbury, stand back, I say;
By heaven, I think my sword's as sharp as yours.
I would not have you, lord, forget yourself,
Nor tempt the danger of my true defense,
Lest I, by marking of your rage, forget 85

41. **Sir Richard:** i.e. the Bastard. 43. **almost:** even.
44. **That:** that which. 46. **heighth:** height.
49. **wall-ey'd:** i.e. glaring. 50. **remorse:** compassion.
54. **times:** the future. 56. **Exampled:** compared with.
58. **graceless:** impious. **heavy:** wicked.
61. **light:** premonition. 63. **practice:** scheming.
72. **worship:** honor. 77. **Avaunt:** be gone. 84. **tempt:** test.

Your worth, your greatness, and nobility.
　Big. Out, dunghill! dar'st thou brave a nobleman?
　Hub. Not for my life; but yet I dare defend
My innocent life against an emperor.
　Sal. Thou art a murtherer.
　Hub. 　　　　　　　　Do not prove me so;
Yet I am none. Whose tongue soe'er speaks false, 91
Not truly speaks; who speaks not truly, lies.
　Pem. Cut him to pieces.
　Bast. 　　　　　　　Keep the peace, I say.
　Sal. Stand by, or I shall gall you, Faulconbridge.
　Bast. Thou wert better gall the devil, Salisbury.
If thou but frown on me, or stir thy foot, 96
Or teach thy hasty spleen to do me shame,
I'll strike thee dead. Put up thy sword betime,
Or I'll so maul you and your toasting-iron
That you shall think the devil is come from hell. 100
　Big. What wilt thou do, renowned Faulconbridge?
Second a villain and a murtherer?
　Hub. Lord Bigot, I am none.
　Big. 　　　　　　　Who kill'd this prince?
　Hub. 'Tis not an hour since I left him well.
I honor'd him, I lov'd him, and will weep 105
My date of life out for his sweet live's loss.
　Sal. Trust not those cunning waters of his eyes,
For villainy is not without such rheum,
And he, long traded in it, makes it seem
Like rivers of remorse and innocency. 110
Away with me, all you whose souls abhor
Th' uncleanly savors of a slaughter-house,
For I am stifled with this smell of sin.
　Big. Away toward Bury, to the Dolphin there!
　Pem. There, tell the King, he may inquire us out.
　　　　　　　　　　　　　　　Exeunt Lords.
　Bast. Here's a good world! Knew you of this fair work? 116
Beyond the infinite and boundless reach
Of mercy, if thou didst this deed of death,
Art thou damn'd, Hubert.
　Hub. 　　　　　　Do but hear me, sir.
　Bast. Ha? I'll tell thee what; 120
Thou'rt damn'd as black—nay, nothing is so black—
Thou art more deep damn'd than Prince Lucifer.
There is not yet so ugly a fiend of hell
As thou shalt be, if thou didst kill this child.
　Hub. Upon my soul—
　Bast. 　　　　　　If thou didst but consent
To this most cruel act, do but despair, 126
And if thou want'st a cord, the smallest thread
That ever spider twisted from her womb
Will serve to strangle thee; a rush will be a beam
To hang thee on; or wouldst thou drown thyself, 130
Put but a little water in a spoon,
And it shall be as all the ocean,
Enough to stifle such a villain up.
I do suspect thee very grievously.
　Hub. If I in act, consent, or sin of thought 135
Be guilty of the stealing that sweet breath
Which was embounded in this beauteous clay,

90. **prove me so:** i.e. by forcing me to kill you.
94. **gall:** injure. 97. **spleen:** anger. 106. **live's:** life's.
109. **traded:** experienced. 112. **savors:** odors.

King John
IV.iii

Let hell want pains enough to torture me.
I left him well.
    Bast.   Go, bear him in thine arms.
I am amaz'd, methinks, and lose my way   140
Among the thorns and dangers of this world.
How easy dost thou take all England up
From forth this morsel of dead royalty!
The life, the right, and truth of all this realm
Is fled to heaven; and England now is left   145
To tug and scamble, and to part by th' teeth
The unowed interest of proud swelling state.
Now for the bare-pick'd bone of majesty
Doth dogged war bristle his angry crest,
And snarleth in the gentle eyes of peace;   150
Now powers from home and discontents at home
Meet in one line; and vast confusion waits,
As doth a raven on a sick-fall'n beast,
The imminent decay of wrested pomp.
Now happy he whose cloak and center can   155
Hold out this tempest. Bear away that child,
And follow me with speed. I'll to the King.
A thousand businesses are brief in hand,
And heaven itself doth frown upon the land.   *Exeunt.*

ACT [V], SCENE I

Enter KING JOHN *and* PANDULPH, ATTENDANTS.

    K. John.   Thus have I yielded up into your hand
The circle of my glory.   [*Giving the crown.*]
    Pand.   Take again
From this my hand, as holding of the Pope,
Your sovereign greatness and authority.
    K. John.   Now keep your holy word, go meet the
      French,   5
And from his Holiness use all your power
To stop their marches 'fore we are inflam'd.
Our discontented counties do revolt;
Our people quarrel with obedience,
Swearing allegiance and the love of soul   10
To stranger blood, to foreign royalty.
This inundation of mistemp'red humor
Rests by you only to be qualified.
Then pause not; for the present time's so sick,
That present med'cine must be minist'red,   15
Or overthrow incurable ensues.
    Pand.   It was my breath that blew this tempest up,
Upon your stubborn usage of the Pope;

But since you are a gentle convertite,
My tongue shall hush again this storm of war,   20
And make fair weather in your blust'ring land.
On this Ascension-day, remember well,
Upon your oath of service to the Pope,
Go I to make the French lay down their arms.   *Exit.*
    K. John.   Is this Ascension-day?   Did not the
      prophet   25
Say that before Ascension-day at noon
My crown I should give off? Even so I have.
I did suppose it should be on constraint,
But (heav'n be thank'd!) it is but voluntary.

Enter BASTARD.

    Bast.   All Kent hath yielded; nothing there holds
      out   30
But Dover castle. London hath receiv'd,
Like a kind host, the Dolphin and his powers.
Your nobles will not hear you, but are gone
To offer service to your enemy;
And wild amazement hurries up and down   35
The little number of your doubtful friends.
    K. John.   Would not my lords return to me again
After they heard young Arthur was alive?
    Bast.   They found him dead and cast into the streets,
An empty casket, where the jewel of life   40
By some damn'd hand was robb'd and ta'en away.
    K. John.   That villain Hubert told me he did live.
    Bast.   So, on my soul, he did, for aught he knew.
But wherefore do you droop? why look you sad?
Be great in act, as you have been in thought.   45
Let not the world see fear and sad distrust
Govern the motion of a kingly eye.
Be stirring as the time, be fire with fire,
Threaten the threat'ner, and outface the brow
Of bragging horror; so shall inferior eyes,   50
That borrow their behaviors from the great,
Grow great by your example and put on
The dauntless spirit of resolution.
Away, and glister like the god of war
When he intendeth to become the field.   55
Show boldness and aspiring confidence.
What, shall they seek the lion in his den,
And fright him there? and make him tremble there?
O, let it not be said! Forage, and run
To meet displeasure farther from the doors,   60
And grapple with him ere he come so nigh.
    K. John.   The legate of the Pope hath been with me,
And I have made a happy peace with him,
And he hath promis'd to dismiss the powers
Led by the Dolphin.
    Bast.   O inglorious league!   65
Shall we, upon the footing of our land,
Send fair-play orders and make comprise,
Insinuation, parley, and base truce
To arms invasive? Shall a beardless boy,
A cock'red silken wanton, brave our fields,   70

---

140. **amaz'd:** stunned.   146. **scamble:** scramble.
147. **unowed:** of uncertain ownership.
151. **powers from home:** foreign troops.
154. **wrested pomp:** usurped authority.   155. **center:** cincture, belt.
158. **brief in hand:** i.e. demanding prompt action.

V.i. Location: England. King John's palace.
1–4. **Thus . . . authority.** After long defiance of the Pope, says Holinshed (Bullough, IV, 40), John was finally (1213) obliged to come to terms with him. "Wherefore shortlie after (in like manner as pope Innocent had commanded) he tooke the crowne from his owne head, and delivered the same to Pandulph the legat, neither he, nor his heires at anie time thereafter to receive the same, but at the popes hands."   11. **stranger:** foreign.
12. **mistemp'red:** unbalanced (referring to the excess of one of the four bodily humors, a condition that, in Elizabethan physiology, was thought to cause ill health).   13. **qualified:** abated.
15. **present:** immediate.   18. **Upon:** following.

36. **doubtful:** anxious.   55. **become:** adorn.   59. **Forage:** raven.
66. **upon . . . land:** standing on our own soil.
67. **fair-play:** chivalric.   **comprise:** compromise.
69. **invasive:** invading.
70. **cock'red:** pampered.   **brave:** make a splendid show of force in.

And flesh his spirit in a warlike soil,
Mocking the air with colors idly spread,
And find no check? Let us, my liege, to arms.
Perchance the Cardinal cannot make your peace;
Or if he do, let it at least be said,   75
They saw we had a purpose of defense.
  K. John. Have thou the ordering of this present
    time.
  Bast. Away then with good courage! Yet I know
Our party may well meet a prouder foe.   *Exeunt.*

SCENE II

Enter, *in arms*, [LEWIS *the*] *Dolphin*, SALISBURY,
MELUNE, PEMBROKE, BIGOT, SOLDIERS.

  Lew. My Lord Melune, let this be copied out,
And keep it safe for our remembrance.
Return the president to these lords again,
That having our fair order written down,
Both they and we, perusing o'er these notes,   5
May know wherefore we took the sacrament,
And keep our faiths firm and inviolable.
  Sal. Upon our sides it never shall be broken.
And, noble Dolphin, albeit we swear
A voluntary zeal and an unurg'd faith   10
To your proceedings, yet believe me, Prince,
I am not glad that such a sore of time
Should seek a plaster by contemn'd revolt,
And heal the inveterate canker of one wound
By making many. O, it grieves my soul,   15
That I must draw this metal from my side
To be a widow-maker! O, and there
Where honorable rescue and defense
Cries out upon the name of Salisbury!
But such is the infection of the time,   20
That for the health and physic of our right,
We cannot deal but with the very hand
Of stern injustice and confused wrong.
And is't not pity, O my grieved friends,
That we, the sons and children of this isle,   25
[Were] born to see so sad an hour as this,
Wherein we step after a stranger, march
Upon her gentle bosom, and fill up
Her enemies' ranks—I must withdraw and weep
Upon the spot of this enforced cause—   30
To grace the gentry of a land remote,
And follow unacquainted colors here?
What, here? O nation, that thou couldst remove!

71. **flesh**: initiate into slaughter. 72. **idely**: idly, carelessly.
76. **purpose of defense**: intention of defending ourselves.

V.ii. Location: England. The Dolphin's camp at Saint Edmundsbury.
3. **president**: precedent, i.e. first draft.
4. **order**: arrangement, proposal.
6. **took the sacrament.** Holinshed records (Bullough, IV, 42) that in
1214 the disaffected nobles assembled at Bury St. Edmunds and took
a "solemne oth" to oppose the King until he restored to them the
ancient "liberties" that he had stripped away. This event, a prologue
to the signing of Magna Carta in the following year, was historically
unrelated to the French invasion in 1216.
18–19. **Where ... Salisbury:** where those who are honorably defending their country exclaim against Salisbury. 21. **physic**: remedy.
27. **step after**: follow. **stranger**: alien. 30. **spot**: stain.
32. **unacquainted colors**: unfamiliar flags.

That Neptune's arms, who clippeth thee about,
Would bear thee from the knowledge of thyself,   35
And [gripple] thee unto a pagan shore,
Where these two Christian armies might combine
The blood of malice in a vein of league,
And not to spend it so unneighborly!
  Lew. A noble temper dost thou show in this,   40
And great affections wrastling in thy bosom
Doth make an earthquake of nobility.
O, what a noble combat hast [thou] fought
Between compulsion and a brave respect!
Let me wipe off this honorable dew,   45
That silverly doth progress on thy cheeks.
My heart hath melted at a lady's tears,
Being an ordinary inundation;
But this effusion of such manly drops,
This show'r, blown up by tempest of the soul,   50
Startles mine eyes, and makes me more amaz'd
Than had I seen the vaulty top of heaven
Figur'd quite o'er with burning meteors.
Lift up thy brow, renowned Salisbury,
And with a great heart heave away this storm.   55
Commend these waters to those baby eyes
That never saw the giant world enrag'd,
Nor met with fortune other than at feasts,
Full warm of blood, of mirth, of gossiping.
Come, come; for thou shalt thrust thy hand as deep
Into the purse of rich prosperity   61
As Lewis himself; so, nobles, shall you all,
That knit your sinews to the strength of mine.

Enter PANDULPHO.

And even there, methinks an angel spake.
Look where the holy legate comes apace,   65
To give us warrant from the hand of heaven,
And on our actions set the name of right
With holy breath.
  Pand.   Hail, noble Prince of France!
The next is this: King John hath reconcil'd
Himself to Rome, his spirit is come in,   70
That so stood out against the holy Church,
The great metropolis and see of Rome;
Therefore thy threat'ning colors now wind up,
And tame the savage spirit of wild war,
That like a lion fostered up at hand,   75
It may lie gently at the foot of peace,
And be no further harmful than in show.
  Lew. Your Grace shall pardon me, I will not back.
I am too high-born to be propertied,
To be a secondary at control,   80
Or useful servingman and instrument
To any sovereign state throughout the world.
Your breath first kindled the dead coal of wars
Between this chastis'd kingdom and myself,
And brought in matter that should feed this fire;   85

36. **gripple**: grapple.
37–38. **combine ... league**: i.e. spend their blood in a united effort
(against a common foe).
41. **affections**: passions. **wrastling**: wrestling.
44. **brave respect**: gallant regard (for your country).
53. **Figur'd**: adorned. 70. **is come in**: has submitted.
73. **wind**: furl. 78. **back**: go back.
79. **propertied**: made a chattel of.

King John
V.ii

And now 'tis far too huge to be blown out
With that same weak wind which enkindled it.
You taught me how to know the face of right,
Acquainted me with interest to this land,
Yea, thrust this enterprise into my heart,   90
And come ye now to tell me John hath made
His peace with Rome? What is that peace to me?
I, by the honor of my marriage-bed,
After young Arthur, claim this land for mine,
And now it is half conquer'd, must I back   95
Because that John hath made his peace with Rome?
Am I Rome's slave? What penny hath Rome borne?
What men provided? what munition sent,
To underprop this action? Is't not I
That undergo this charge? Who else but I,   100
And such as to my claim are liable,
Sweat in this business and maintain this war?
Have I not heard these islanders shout out
"*Vive le roi!*" as I have bank'd their towns?
Have I not here the best cards for the game,   105
To win this easy match play'd for a crown?
And shall I now give o'er the yielded set?
No, no, on my soul, it never shall be said.

   Pand. You look but on the outside of this work.
   Lew. Outside or inside, I will not return   110
Till my attempt so much be glorified
As to my ample hope was promised
Before I drew this gallant head of war,
And cull'd these fiery spirits from the world,
To outlook conquest and to win renown   115
Even in the jaws of danger and of death.

              [*Trumpet sounds.*]
What lusty trumpet thus doth summon us?

Enter BASTARD.

   Bast. According to the fair play of the world,
Let me have audience. I am sent to speak:
My holy Lord of Milan, from the King   120
I come to learn how you have dealt for him;
And, as you answer, I do know the scope
And warrant limited unto my tongue.

   Pand. The Dolphin is too willful-opposite,
And will not temporize with my entreaties.   125
He flatly says he'll not lay down his arms.

   Bast. By all the blood that ever fury breath'd,
The youth says well. Now hear our English King,
For thus his royalty doth speak in me:
He is prepar'd, and reason too he should—   130
This apish and unmannerly approach,
This harness'd masque and unadvised revel,
This [unhair'd] sauciness and boyish troops,
The King doth smile at, and is well prepar'd

To whip this dwarfish war, this pigmy arms,   135
From out the circle of his territories.
That hand which had the strength, even at your door,
To cudgel you and make you take the hatch,
To dive like buckets in concealed wells,
To crouch in litter of your stable planks,   140
To lie like pawns lock'd up in chests and trunks,
To hug with swine, to seek sweet safety out
In vaults and prisons, and to thrill and shake
Even at the crying of your nation's crow,
Thinking this voice an armed Englishman;   145
Shall that victorious hand be feebled here,
That in your chambers gave you chastisement?
No! Know the gallant monarch is in arms,
And like an eagle o'er his aery tow'rs,
To souse annoyance that comes near his nest;   150
And you degenerate, you ingrate revolts,
You bloody Neroes, ripping up the womb
Of your dear mother England, blush for shame;
For your own ladies and pale-visag'd maids
Like Amazons come tripping after drums,   155
Their thimbles into armed gauntlets change,
Their needl's to lances, and their gentle hearts
To fierce and bloody inclination.

   Lew. There end thy brave, and turn thy face in
     peace;
We grant thou canst outscold us. Fare thee well! 160
We hold our time too precious to be spent
With such a brabbler.

   Pand.   Give me leave to speak.
   Bast. No, I will speak.
   Lew.   We will attend to neither.
Strike up the drums, and let the tongue of war
Plead for our interest and our being here.   165

   Bast. Indeed your drums, being beaten, will cry
     out;
And so shall you, being beaten. Do but start
An echo with the clamor of thy drum,
And even at hand a drum is ready brac'd
That shall reverberate all as loud as thine.   170
Sound but another, and another shall
(As loud as thine) rattle the welkin's ear,
And mock the deep-mouth'd thunder; for at hand
(Not trusting to this halting legate here,
Whom he hath us'd rather for sport than need)   175
Is warlike John; and in his forehead sits
A bare-ribb'd death, whose office is this day
To feast upon whole thousands of the French.

   Lew. Strike up our drums, to find this danger out.
   Bast. And thou shalt find it, Dolphin, do not doubt.

                   Exeunt.

---

89. **interest:** i.e. my claim.   101. **liable:** subject.
104. **Vive le roi:** long live the king; perhaps alluding also to the name of a playing card (like the king or queen in modern decks), which suggests the figure in the following lines.   **bank'd:** sailed past; perhaps with play on another card term, designating the taking of a card.
107. **yielded set:** game already won.   113. **head of war:** army.
115. **outlook:** outstare, defy.
118. **fair play:** i.e. chivalric code.   123. **limited:** appointed.
124. **willful-opposite:** stubbornly opposed.
125. **temporize:** make terms.
132. **harness'd masque:** masque in armor.   **unadvised:** ill-considered.
133. **unhair'd:** beardless, i.e. youthful.

138. **take the hatch:** leap over the lower half of the door in haste.
141. **pawns:** articles in pawnshops.   143. **thrill:** shiver.
144. **crying . . . crow:** i.e. crowing of the cocks (?).
149. **aery:** nest.   **tow'rs:** soars.
150. **souse:** swoop down on.   151. **revolts:** rebels.
152. **Neroes:** i.e. unfilial wretches (alluding to the Roman emperor Nero, who reputedly murdered and then disembowelled his mother).
155. **Amazons:** legendary race of female warriors.
157. **needl's:** needles (monosyllabic, as often).
159. **brave:** swaggering.
163. **attend:** listen.   169. **brac'd:** tightened.

SCENE III

Alarums. Enter [KING] JOHN *and* HUBERT.

K. John. How goes the day with us? O, tell me,
   Hubert.
Hub. Badly, I fear. How fares your Majesty?
K. John. This fever, that hath troubled me so long,
Lies heavy on me. O, my heart is sick!

Enter a MESSENGER.

Mess. My lord, your valiant kinsman, Faulcon-
   bridge,   5
Desires your Majesty to leave the field,
And send him word by me which way you go.
K. John. Tell him toward Swinstead, to the abbey
   there.
Mess. Be of good comfort; for the great supply,
That was expected by the Dolphin here,   10
Are wrack'd three nights ago on Goodwin Sands;
This news was brought to Richard but even now.
The French fight coldly, and retire themselves.
K. John. Ay me, this tyrant fever burns me up,
And will not let me welcome this good news.   15
Set on toward Swinstead. To my litter straight,
Weakness possesseth me, and I am faint.   *Exeunt.*

SCENE IV

Enter SALISBURY, PEMBROKE, *and* BIGOT.

Sal. I did not think the King so stor'd with friends.
Pem. Up once again! Put spirit in the French;
If they miscarry, we miscarry too.
Sal. That misbegotten devil Faulconbridge,
In spite of spite, alone upholds the day.   5
Pem. They say King John, sore sick, hath left the
   field.

Enter MELUNE *wounded.*

Mel. Lead me to the revolts of England here.
Sal. When we were happy we had other names.
Pem. It is the Count Melune.
Sal.   Wounded to death.
Mel. Fly, noble English, you are bought and sold!
Unthread the rude eye of rebellion,   11
And welcome home again discarded faith.
Seek out King John and fall before his feet;
For if the French be lords of this loud day,
He means to recompense the pains you take   15
By cutting off your heads. Thus hath he sworn,
And I with him, and many moe with me,
Upon the altar at Saint Edmundsbury,

Even on that altar where we swore to you
Dear amity and everlasting love.   20
Sal. May this be possible? May this be true?
Mel. Have I not hideous death within my view,
Retaining but a quantity of life,
Which bleeds away even as a form of wax
Resolveth from his figure 'gainst the fire?   25
What in the world should make me now deceive,
Since I must lose the use of all deceit?
Why should I then be false, since it is true
That I must die here and live hence by truth?
I say again, if Lewis do win the day,   30
He is forsworn if e'er those eyes of yours
Behold another day break in the east;
But even this night, whose black contagious breath
Already smokes about the burning crest
Of the old, feeble, and day-wearied sun,   35
Even this ill night your breathing shall expire,
Paying the fine of rated treachery
Even with a treacherous fine of all your lives,
If Lewis by your assistance win the day.
Commend me to one Hubert with your king;   40
The love of him, and this respect besides,
For that my grandsire was an Englishman,
Awakes my conscience to confess all this.
In lieu whereof, I pray you bear me hence
From forth the noise and rumor of the field,   45
Where I may think the remnant of my thoughts
In peace, and part this body and my soul
With contemplation and devout desires.
Sal. We do believe thee, and beshrew my soul
But I do love the favor and the form   50
Of this most fair occasion, by the which
We will untread the steps of damned flight,
And like a bated and retired flood,
Leaving our rankness and irregular course,
Stoop low within those bounds we have o'erlook'd,
And calmly run on in obedience   56
Even to our ocean, to our great King John.
My arm shall give thee help to bear thee hence,
For I do see the cruel pangs of death
Right in thine eye. Away, my friends! New flight,
And happy newness, that intends old right.   61
             Exeunt [*leading off Melune*].

SCENE V

Enter [LEWIS *the*] *Dolphin and his* TRAIN.

Lew. The sun of heaven, methought, was loath to
   set,
But stay'd and made the western welkin blush,

V.iii. Location: England. The field of battle.
8. Swinstead. Shakespeare's mistake (perhaps derived from Foxe's *Acts and Monuments*) for Swineshead, site of an abbey in Lincolnshire.
9. supply: reinforcement.
11. wrack'd: shipwrecked. **Goodwin Sands:** dangerous shoal in the English Channel off the coast of Kent.

V.iv. Location: Scene continues.
5. In spite of spite: i.e. in spite of everything.
7. revolts: rebellious nobles. **10. bought and sold:** i.e. betrayed.
11. Unthread . . . rebellion: i.e. withdraw from rebellion, into which you have been drawn as thread into a needle's eye.
15. He: i.e. Lewis. **17. moe:** more.

23. quantity: i.e. small quantity. **25. Resolveth:** melts. **his:** its.
27. use: benefit. **29. hence:** i.e. to heaven.
34. smokes: grows misty. **crest:** helmet.
37. fine: penalty. **rated:** correctly estimated. **38. fine:** end.
41. respect: consideration.
44. In lieu whereof: i.e. in requital of which information.
45. rumor: noise. **49. beshrew:** curse.
50. But: unless. **favor . . . form:** i.e. appearance.
53. bated: checked. **54. rankness:** flooding.
55. o'erlook'd: overflowed. **60. Right:** unmistakable.
61. intends old right: has as its goal the restoration of ancient right.

V.v. Location: England. The French camp.

795

King John
V.v

When English measure backward their own ground
In faint retire. O, bravely came we off,
When with a volley of our needless shot,   5
After such bloody toil, we bid good night,
And wound our tott'ring colors clearly up,
Last in the field, and almost lords of it!

Enter a MESSENGER.

Mess. Where is my prince, the Dolphin?
Lew.   Here: what news?
Mess. The Count Melune is slain; the English lords
By his persuasion are again fall'n off,   11
And your supply, which you have wish'd so long,
Are cast away, and sunk on Goodwin Sands.
Lew. Ah, foul shrewd news! Beshrew thy very
    heart!
I did not think to be so sad to-night   15
As this hath made me. Who was he that said
King John did fly an hour or two before
The stumbling night did part our weary pow'rs?
Mess. Whoever spoke it, it is true, my lord.
Lew. Well; keep good quarter and good care to-
    night;   20
The day shall not be up so soon as I,
To try the fair adventure of to-morrow.   *Exeunt.*

SCENE VI

Enter BASTARD *and* HUBERT *severally.*

Hub. Who's there? Speak ho! speak quickly, or
    I shoot.
Bast. A friend. What art thou?
Hub.   Of the part of England.
Bast. Whither dost thou go?
Hub. What's that to thee? Why may not I demand
Of thine affairs, as well as thou of mine?   5
Bast. Hubert, I think.
Hub.   Thou hast a perfect thought.
I will upon all hazards well believe
Thou art my friend that know'st my tongue so well.
Who art thou?
Bast.   Who thou wilt; and if thou please,
Thou mayst befriend me so much as to think   10
I come one way of the Plantagenets.
Hub. Unkind remembrance! thou and endless night
Have done me shame. Brave soldier, pardon me
That any accent breaking from thy tongue
Should scape the true acquaintance of mine ear.   15
Bast. Come, come; sans compliment, what news
    abroad?
Hub. Why, here walk I in the black brow of night,
To find you out.
Bast.   Brief then; and what's the news?
Hub. O my sweet sir, news fitting to the night,

7. **tott'ring:** flying in tatters.   14. **shrewd:** bad.
18. **stumbling:** i.e. causing to stumble.   20. **quarter:** watch.
22. **adventure:** hazard.

V.vi. Location: England. An open place near Swinstead Abbey.
2. **Of the part:** on the side.   6. **perfect:** correct.
12. **Unkind remembrance:** i.e. what a bad memory I have.
14. **accent:** speech.
16. **sans compliment:** without the customary civilities.

Black, fearful, comfortless, and horrible.   20
Bast. Show me the very wound of this ill news;
I am no woman, I'll not swound at it.
Hub. The King, I fear, is poison'd by a monk.
I left him almost speechless, and broke out
To acquaint you with this evil, that you might   25
The better arm you to the sudden time
Than if you had at leisure known of this.
Bast. How did he take it? Who did taste to him?
Hub. A monk, I tell you, a resolved villain,
Whose bowels suddenly burst out. The King   30
Yet speaks, and peradventure may recover.
Bast. Who didst thou leave to tend his Majesty?
Hub. Why, know you not? the lords are all come
    back,
And brought Prince Henry in their company,
At whose request the King hath pardon'd them,   35
And they are all about his Majesty.
Bast. Withhold thine indignation, mighty heaven,
And tempt us not to bear above our power!
I'll tell thee, Hubert, half my power this night,
Passing these flats, are taken by the tide—   40
These Lincoln Washes have devoured them;
Myself, well mounted, hardly have escap'd.
Away before; conduct me to the King;
I doubt he will be dead or ere I come.   *Exeunt.*

SCENE VII

Enter PRINCE HENRY, SALISBURY, *and* BIGOT.

P. Hen. It is too late, the life of all his blood
Is touch'd corruptibly; and his pure brain
(Which some suppose the soul's frail dwelling-house)
Doth by the idle comments that it makes
Foretell the ending of mortality.   5

22. **swound:** swoon.
23. **poison'd ... monk.** Pursued by his enemies, says Holinshed
(Bullough, IV, 46–47), John ruthlessly ravaged the country as he
marched north from Winchester. Disheartened by the loss of "a
great part of his armie, with horsses and carriages" while crossing the
Welland in Lincolnshire, he "fell into an ague" that grew worse when
he gorged himself on raw peaches and cider at Swineshead Abbey,
and after being carried on a litter to Newark he died in great agony
on October 19, 1216. By Shakespeare's time it was widely thought
that he had died of poison, administered perhaps by a monk resentful
of his depredations or perhaps by one of his own servants, who, in
collusion with a "convert" of Swineshead Abbey, prepared for him
a dish of poisoned pears.   26. **sudden time:** emergency.
27. **at leisure:** i.e. later.
28. **it:** i.e. the poison.   **taste:** act as the taster (who ate of every dish
offered the king, to detect poison).
29–30. **A monk ... out.** In his *Acts and Monuments* John Foxe,
sharing none of Holinshed's reserve, asserts (Bullough, IV, 52–53)
that John was "most traiterously poisoned" by a monk named Simon.
Having told the abbot of his plan and receiving absolution, Simon
prepared the poison from "a most venemous Toad," put it in a cup
of wine, "and with a smiling and flattering countenance, he sayde
thus to the King: If it shall like your Princely majestie, here is such a
cuppe of wine, as yee never dronke a better before in all your life
time. I trust this Wassall shal make al England glad. And with that
he dranke a great draught thereof, the king pledging him. The Monke
anone after went to the farmerye, and there died (his guts gushing out
of his belly) and had continually from thenceefoorth three Monkes to
sing Masse for his soule, confirmed by theyr generall chapter."
34. **Prince Henry:** John's son and heir, the future Henry III (1207–72).
38. **bear ... power:** suffer beyond our capacity for endurance.
42. **hardly:** with difficulty.   44. **doubt:** fear.

V.vii. Location: England. The orchard at Swinstead Abbey.
2. **pure:** i.e. normally clear (?).
4. **idle comments:** i.e. babble.   5. **mortality:** life.

Enter PEMBROKE.

Pem. His Highness yet doth speak, and holds belief
That being brought into the open air,
It would allay the burning quality
Of that fell poison which assaileth him. 9
P. Hen. Let him be brought into the orchard here.
Doth he still rage? [*Exit Bigot.*]
Pem. He is more patient
Than when you left him; even now he sung.
P. Hen. O vanity of sickness! fierce extremes
In their continuance will not feel themselves.
Death, having prey'd upon the outward parts, 15
Leaves them invisible, and his siege is now
Against the [mind], the which he pricks and wounds
With many legions of strange fantasies,
Which in their throng and press to that last hold,
Confound themselves. 'Tis strange that death should
sing. 20
I am the [cygnet] to this pale faint swan
Who chaunts a doleful hymn to his own death,
And from the organ-pipe of frailty sings
His soul and body to their lasting rest.
Sal. Be of good comfort, Prince, for you are born
To set a form upon that indigest 26
Which he hath left so shapeless and so rude.

[KING] JOHN *brought in.*

K. John. Ay, marry, now my soul hath elbow-
room,
It would not out at windows nor at doors.
There is so hot a summer in my bosom 30
That all my bowels crumble up to dust.
I am a scribbled form, drawn with a pen
Upon a parchment, and against this fire
Do I shrink up.
P. Hen. How fares your Majesty?
K. John. Poison'd—ill fare! dead, forsook, cast off,
And none of you will bid the winter come 36
To thrust his icy fingers in my maw,
Nor let my kingdom's rivers take their course
Through my burn'd bosom, nor entreat the north
To make his bleak winds kiss my parched lips 40
And comfort me with cold. I do not ask you much,
I beg cold comfort; and you are so strait
And so ingrateful, you deny me that.
P. Hen. O that there were some virtue in my tears,
That might relieve you!
K. John. The salt in them is hot. 45
Within me is a hell, and there the poison
Is as a fiend confin'd to tyrannize
On unreprievable condemned blood.

Enter BASTARD.

Bast. O, I am scalded with my violent motion
And spleen of speed to see your Majesty! 50
K. John. O cousin, thou art come to set mine eye.
The tackle of my heart is crack'd and burn'd,

And all the shrouds wherewith my life should sail
Are turned to one thread, one little hair.
My heart hath one poor string to stay it by, 55
Which holds but till thy news be uttered,
And then all this thou seest is but a clod
And module of confounded royalty.
Bast. The Dolphin is preparing hitherward,
Where [God] he knows how we shall answer him;
For in a night the best part of my pow'r, 61
As I upon advantage did remove,
Were in the Washes all unwarily
Devoured by the unexpected flood. [*The King dies.*]
Sal. You breathe these dead news in as dead an ear.
My liege, my lord! but now a king, now thus. 66
P. Hen. Even so must I run on, and even so stop.
What surety of the world, what hope, what stay,
When this was now a king, and now is clay?
Bast. Art thou gone so? I do but stay behind 70
To do the office for thee of revenge,
And then my soul shall wait on thee to heaven,
As it on earth hath been thy servant still.
Now, now, you stars, that move in your right spheres,
Where be your pow'rs? Show now your mended
faiths, 75
And instantly return with me again
To push destruction and perpetual shame
Out of the weak door of our fainting land.
Straight let us seek, or straight we shall be sought;
The Dolphin rages at our very heels. 80
Sal. It seems you know not then so much as we.
The Cardinal Pandulph is within at rest,
Who half an hour since came from the Dolphin,
And brings from him such offers of our peace
As we with honor and respect may take, 85
With purpose presently to leave this war.
Bast. He will the rather do it when he sees
Ourselves well sinewed to our defense.
Sal. Nay, 'tis in a manner done already,
For many carriages he hath dispatch'd 90
To the sea-side, and put his cause and quarrel
To the disposing of the Cardinal,
With whom yourself, myself, and other lords,
If you think meet, this afternoon will post
To consummate this business happily. 95
Bast. Let it be so, and you, my noble Prince,
With other princes that may best be spar'd,
Shall wait upon your father's funeral.
P. Hen. At Worcester must his body be interr'd,
For so he will'd it.
Bast. Thither shall it then; 100

53. shrouds: ropes. 55. stay it: sustain itself.
58. module: image. confounded: shattered.
59. preparing: repairing. 60. answer: resist.
62. upon advantage: taking advantage of a good opportunity.
65. dead news: deadly news. 72. wait on: attend.
74. stars: i.e. the revolted nobles who had returned to John. right: proper. 75. faiths: loyalties. 86. presently: immediately.
90. carriages: baggage vehicles. 94. post: hasten.
99. Worcester. John's body was taken to Worcester by his "men of warre," says Holinshed (Bullough, IV, 47–48), "each man with his armour on his backe, in warlike order," and there "pompouslie buried in the cathedrall church before the high altar; not for that he had so appointed (as some write) but bicause it was thought to be a place of most suertie for the lords and other of his freends there to assemble, and to take order in their businesse now after his decease."

11. rage: rave.
16. invisible: imperceptibly (?). Some editors emend to *insensible*.
20. Confound: destroy. 26. indigest: formless confusion.
27. rude: crude. 42. strait: niggardly. 44. virtue: power.
50. spleen: eagerness. 51. set: close.

King John
V.vii

And happily may your sweet self put on
The lineal state and glory of the land!
To whom with all submission, on my knee,
I do bequeath my faithful services
And true subjection everlastingly.   105

   Sal. And the like tender of our love we make,
To rest without a spot for evermore.

   P. Hen. I have a kind soul that would give thanks,
And knows not how to do it but with tears.

101. **happily**: propitiously.   102. **lineal state**: hereditary royalty.
104. **bequeath**: give.   106. **tender**: offer.

   Bast. O, let us pay the time but needful woe,   110
Since it hath been beforehand with our griefs.
This England never did, nor never shall,
Lie at the proud foot of a conqueror,
But when it first did help to wound itself.
Now these her princes are come home again,   115
Come the three corners of the world in arms,
And we shall shock them. Nought shall make us rue,
If England to itself do rest but true.   *Exeunt.*

116. **three . . . world**: i.e. all the rest of the world (England being the
fourth corner).   117. **shock**: meet with force.

NOTE ON THE TEXT

The First Folio (1623) is the only authority for *King John*; all later texts are derived from that source. Opinion is divided over the exact nature of the copy-text underlying F1. Some scholars have argued for a prompt-book provenience; others for a direct use of Shakespeare's "foul papers." The most recent discussion (by E. A. J. Honigmann) favors "foul papers," and there is nothing in the F1 text which can be said to point unmistakably to the hand of a prompter. The confusion in character names (between King Philip and Lewis the Dolphin, the Citizen and Hubert), the Philip-Richard designation for Faulconbridge, and the inconsistency in certain speech-prefixes (for Lewis and Queen Elinor; see the Textual Notes) are characteristic of "foul papers." On the other hand, these irregularities do not seem serious enough to exclude the possibility that the manuscript underlying F1 had served as a prompt-book, and the difficulty in the F1 act-scene division in what is designated in modern texts (since Theobald) as III.i may perhaps be the result of markings in the manuscript which involved the cutting of the first seventy-four lines. Moreover, the almost complete absence of what may be called Shakespearean

spellings in the F1 text (note, however, *moth* for *mote* in IV.i.91) makes it somewhat difficult to believe that the compositors (identified as B and C) were setting directly from Shakespeare's autograph.

Fortunately, it is unnecessary to become entangled here in the knotty problem of the date of *King John* and its relation to the anonymous two-part play called *The Troublesome Raigne of Iohn King of England* (*T. R.*) published in 1591, except to notice that there has recently been a disposition (notably on the part of Alexander and Honigmann) to consider *T. R.* as a "bad" quarto based on Shakespeare's play, a view in sharp opposition to the orthodox opinion which takes *T. R.* as Shakespeare's principal source. Whatever the merits of the "bad" quarto view, *T. R.* itself is of no significant value in dealing with specifically textual problems in the F1 text.

For further information, see: J. D. Wilson, ed., New Cambridge *King John* (Cambridge, 1936); Peter Alexander, *Shakespeare's Life and Art* (London, 1939); E. A. J. Honigmann, ed., New Arden *King John* (London, 1954); W. W. Greg, *The Shakespeare First Folio* (Oxford, 1955).

TEXTUAL NOTES

Dramatis personae: *subs. as first given by Rowe*
Act-scene division: *from F1, with the following exceptions: II.i (I.ii in F1); III.i (headed as Act II in F1, which then marks III.i after III.i.74 in the present text); III.iii (no scene division in F1); III.iv (III.iii in F1); V.i (by error numbered IV.i in F1); see first note to each scene; present act-scene arrangement as a whole first established by Dyce*

I.i

Location: *Cambridge*
o.s.d. **Chatillion**] *Rowe (subs.);* Chattylion *F1*
8 **brother**] *F4;* brother, *F1*
11 **Anjou, Touraine**] *Rowe;* Aniowe, Torayne *F1*
30 s.d. **Exeunt**] *Warburton;* Exit *F1*
41 **me;**] *Pope;* me, *F1*
43 s.d. **and . . . ear**] *Capell (after T. R. & whispers the Earle of Sals in the eare.)*
47 s.d. **Exit Sheriff.**] *Capell*
49 **expedition's**] *F2 (subs.);* expeditious *F1*
49 s.d. **Enter . . . Philip**] *placed as in Dyce; after l. 49, F1*
50 s.p. **Bast.**] Philip. *F1 (until l. 138)*
50 **subject I,**] *Capell;* subiect, *F1*
53 **honor-giving hand**] *Rowe;* Honor-giuing-hand *F1*
79 **yourself.**] *Rowe;* your selfe *F1*
81 **him,**] *Collier;* him: *F1*

122 **his?**] *Theobald;* his, *F1*
139 **his,**] *Rowe;* his *F1*
140 **riding-rods**] *hyphen, Capell*
147 **Sir Nob**] *Capell;* sir nobbe *F1*
170 **about,**] *F4;* about *F1*
182 **A foot**] *Rowe;* Bast. A foot *F1 (repeated s.p.)*
189 **conversion.**] *Capell;* conuersion, *F1*
201 **compliment**] *Rowe;* Complement *F1*
203 **Pyrenean**] *Pope;* Perennean *F1*
208 **smack**] *Theobald;* smoake *F1*
218 **woman-post**] *hyphen, F4*
219 s.d. **Enter . . . Gurney.**] *placed as in Capell; after l. 221, F1*
222 s.p. **Lady F.**] *Malone;* Lady. *F1 (throughout scene)*
231 **Philip? sparrow!**] *Upton conj.;* Philip, sparrow, *F1*
236 **well— . . . confess—**] *Vaughan conj.;* well, marrie to confesse *F1*
237 **he**] *Pope; om. F1*
237 **me. Sir**] *Vaughan conj.;* me sir *F1*
256 **Heaven!**] *Knight;* Heauen *F1*
269 **Ay**] *Rowe;* aye *F1*

II.i

II.i] *Rowe;* Scaena Secunda. *F1*
o.s.d. **Enter . . . forces.**] *Kittredge (after Capell);* Enter before Angiers, Philip King of France, Lewis, Daulphin Austria, Constance, Arthur. *F1*

1, 18 s.pp. **K. Phi.**] *Theobald conj.;* Lewis. *F1*
37 s.p. **K. Phi.**] *Rowe;* King. *F1 (until l. 89);*
37 **work! Our**] *Collier (after Theobald)* worke our *F1*
59 **I;**] *F2 (subs.);* I *F1*
62 **mother-queen**] *hyphen, F4*
63 **Ate**] *Rowe;* Ace *F1*
89 s.p. **K. Phi.**] *Rowe;* Fran. *F1 (throughout rest of scene)*
113 **breast**] *F2;* beast *F1*
120 s.p. **El.**] *Rowe;* Queen. *F1 (throughout scene, except as noted)*
127 **John in manners,**] *Vaughan conj. (after Capell);* Iohn, in manners *F1*
144 **shows**] *Theobald;* shooes *F1*
149 **Philip**] *Theobald;* Lewis *F1*
150 s.p. **K. Phi.**] *Theobald;* Lew. *F1*
152 **Anjou**] *Theobald;* Angiers *F1*
166 s.p. **El.**] *Rowe;* Qu. Mo. *F1*
193 **that? A will!**] *Rowe;* that, a Will: *F1*
200 s.d. **Hubert**] *Honigmann (after a suggestion by Wilson);* a Citizen *F1*
200 s.d. **and other Citizens**] *ed. (after Capell)*
201, 267, 270, 281 s.pp. **Hub.**] *Honigmann;* Cit. *F1*
214 **French**] *Rowe (subs.);* French. *F1*
215 **Confronts**] *Capell (after Rowe);* Comfort *F1*
215 **your**] *F3;* yours *F1*
217 **waist**] *F4;* waste *F1*
252 **invulnerable**] *F2;* involuerable *F1*

267 **subjects:**] *Theobald* (*subs.*); subiects *F1*
287 **chevaliers! To**] *Capell*; Cheualiers to *F1*
290 s.d. **To Austria.**] *Pope*
299 s.d. **Hubert . . . above.**] *ed.*
306 **earth**] *F2*; earrh *F1*
327 **your**] *F2*; yonr *F1*
335 **on?**] *Pope*; on, *F1*
368 s.p. **Hub.**] *Honigmann*; Fra. *F1*
413 s.d. **Aside.**] *Capell*
468 s.p. **El.**] *Rowe*; Old Qu. *F1*
468 **match,**] *F2*; match *F1*
478 **pity,**] *Theobald*; pittie *F1*
487 **Anjou**] *Pope*; Angiers *F1*
496 s.p. **Lew.**] *Rowe*; Dol. *F1* (*throughout scene*)
500 **sun**] *Rowe*; sonne *F1*
504 s.d. **Aside.**] *Dyce*
507 **traitor. . . . now,**] *F4* (*subs.*); traytor, . . . now; *F1*
521 **young ones**] *Rowe*; yong-ones *F1*
536 **Angiers**] *F2*; Angires *F1*
539 **rites**] *F4*; rights *F1*
541 **not,**] *F3*; not *F1*
560 **unlook'd-for**] *hyphen, Warburton*
560 s.d. **all . . . Bastard**] *Rowe*
577 **vile-drawing**] *hyphen, Pope*
582 **all-changing word**] *Pope*; all-changing-word *F1*
588 **woo'd**] *Theobald*; wooed *F1*

III.i

III.i] *Pope*; Actus Secundus *F1*
Location: *Theobald*
3 **Blanch**] *F4*; Blaunch *F1* (*throughout scene*)
16–7 **jest, . . . spirits**] *Rowe*; iest . . . spirits, *F1*
63 **Envenom**] *F2*; Euuenom *F1*
73 s.d. **Throws . . . ground.**] *Steevens* (*after Theobald, Capell; following l. 74); placed as in Kittredge*
74] *Following this line F1 inserts* Actus Tertius, Scaena prima. (*suggests that ll. 1–74 may have been cut in performance); Theobald first continued the scene unbroken*
74 s.d. **Elinor**] *Rowe*; Elianor *F1*
74 s.d. **Austria,**] *Theobald*; Austria, Constance *F1*
83 s.d. **Rising.**] *Theobald*
92 **But . . . day**] *Dyce* (*after Rowe*); But (on this day) *F1*
102 **enemies'**] *Capell*; enemies *F1*
107 **kings!**] *Capell* (*after Rowe*); Kings, *F1*
108 **cries;**] *Capell*; cries, *F1*
110 **day**] *Theobald*; daies *F1*
144 **see**] *F4*; Sea *F1*
148 **taste**] *F3*; tast *F1*
155 **God**] *Collier MS* (*after T. R.*); heauen *F1*
185 **too: . . . right,**] *Rowe* (*subs.*); too, . . . right. *F1*
196 **that,**] *Pope*; that *F1*
242 **heaven?**] *ed.*; heauen, *F1*
243 **ourselves**] *F2* (*subs.*); onr selues *F1*
275 **again;**] *Theobald*; again, *F1*
280 **religion**] *Collier* (*after Knight*); religion: *F1*
282–3 **truth . . . oath;**] *Steevens* (*subs., after Heath conj.*); truth, . . . oath *F1*
300, 317, 337 s.pp. **Lew.**] *Rowe*; Daul. or Dolph. *F1*
324 **clock-setter**] *hyphen, F3*
330 **whirl**] *Rowe*; whurle *F1*
339 s.d. **Exit Bastard.**] *Pope*
347 **let's**] *F3*; le'ts *F1*

III.ii

Location: *Malone*
4 s.d. **Enter . . . Hubert.**] *placed as in Capell; after l. 3, F1* (*Pope, omitting l. 4, here inserts from T. R.:* Thus hath K. Richards Sonne performde his vowes. / And offred Austrias bloud for sacrifice / Unto his fathers euerliuing soule.)
10 s.d. **Exeunt.**] *Rowe*; Exit. *F1*

III.iii

III.iii] *Capell*
Location: *ed.* (*after Wilson*)
o.s.d. **Elinor**] *Rowe*; Eleanor *F1*

1 s.d. **To Elinor.**] *Hanmer*
2 s.d. **To Arthur.**] *Pope*
6 s.d. **To Bastard.**] *Pope*
17 s.d. **Exit Bastard.**] *Pope*
18 s.d. **Takes Arthur aside.**] *Pope* (*subs.*)
26 **time**] *Pope*; tune *F1*
66 **lord?**] *Rowe*; Lord. *F1*
67 **now.**] *Rowe*; now, *F1*

III.iv

III.iv] *Capell*; Scena Tertia. *F1*
Location: *Malone* (*subs.*)
1 s.p. **K. Phi.**] *Rowe*; Fra. *F1* (*throughout scene*)
10 s.p. **Lew.**] *Rowe*; Dol. *F1* (*throughout scene*)
14 **kindred action**] *Theobald*; kindred-action *F1*
25 **death.**] *Theobald* (*subs.*); death, *F1*
35 **Misery's**] *Rowe*; Miseries *F1*
44 **not**] *F4*
64 **friends**] *Rowe*; fiends *F1*
79 **male child**] *Pope*; male-childe *F1*
101 s.d. **Tearing her hair.**] *Collier MS*
105 **sorrows'**] *Capell*; sorrowes *F1*
114–5 **leave, . . . departure**] *Capell*; leaue . . . departure, *F1*
133 **misplac'd John**] *Rowe*; mis-plac'd-Iohn *F1*
180 **offense.**] *Knight*; offence, *F1*

IV.i

Location: *Capell* (*subs.*)
6, 85 s.pp. **1. Exec.**] *Cambridge* (*after Capell*); Exec. *F1*
7 **scruples!**] *Rowe*; scruples *F1*
7 s.d. **Exeunt Executioners.**] *Cambridge* (*after Capell*)
23 **indeed**] *F2*; in deede *F1*
25, 33 s.dd. **Aside.**] *Rowe*
29 **In sooth**] *Pope*; Insooth *F1*
32 s.d. **Aside.**] *Capell*
33 s.d. **Showing a paper.**] *Rowe*
38 **effect.**] *Rowe*; effect, *F1*
46 **minutes**] *Rowe*; minutes, *F1*
63 **his**] *Capell*; this *F1*
67 **stubborn-hard**] *hyphen, Theobald*
71 s.d. **Stamps.**] *Pope*
71 s.d. **Enter . . . etc.**] *Cambridge* (*after Pope, Capell*)
75 **boist'rous-rough**] *hyphen, Theobald*
85 s.d. **Exeunt Executioners.**] *Cambridge* (*after Pope, Capell*)
91 **mote**] *Steevens*; moth *F1*
100 **will,**] *Rowe*; will *F1*
107 **undeserv'd**] *Rowe*; vndeserued *F1*
120 **mercy-lacking**] *Pope*; mercy, lacking *F1*

IV.ii

Location: *Pope, Capell*
1 **again crown'd**] *F3*; against crown'd *F1*
8 **long'd-for change**] *Rowe*; long'd-for-change *F1*
21 **antique**] *Pope*; Anticke *F1*
21 **well-noted**] *hyphen, Pope*
42 **strong**] *Collier*; strong, *F1*
50 **safety,**] *Johnson*; safety: *F1*
51 **studies—**] *Rowe* (*subs.*); studies, *F1*
60 **exercise.**] *Rowe*; exercise, *F1*
61 **time's**] *Pope*; times *F1*
65 **Than . . . weal,**] *Pope*; Then, . . . weale *F1*
66 **weal**] *Rowe*; weale: *F1*
68 s.d. **Taking him aside.**] *Capell* (*subs. after Hanmer*)
73 **Doth**] *Dyce*; Do *F1*
102 s.d. **Lords**] *Capell*
110 **England.**] *Roderick conj.*; England, *F1*
143 **travell'd**] *F4*; trauail'd *F1*
159 s.d. **Exit . . . Peter.**] *Theobald*
180 s.d. **Exit.**] *Rowe*
246 **breath,**] *F4* (breath *F3*); breathe *F1*

IV.iii

Location: *Capell*
8 s.d. **Leaps down.**] *Rowe* (*T. R. gives the following s.d.:* He leapes, and brusing his bones, after he was from his traunce, speakes thus;)

15 **Melune**] *ed.*; Meloone *F1* (*or* Meloon *throughout*)
16 **love**] *Rowe*; loue, *F1*
24 **thin bestained**] *Rowe*; thin-bestained *F1*
33 **man**] *F2*; mans *F1*
34 s.d. **Seeing Arthur.**] *Pope*
40 **precious-princely**] *hyphen, Capell*
41 **Have you**] *F3*; you haue *F1*
78 s.d. **Drawing his sword.**] *Pope*
115 **There,**] *Theobald*; There *F1*
115 s.d. **Exeunt Lords.**] *Rowe*; Ex. *F1*
159 **Exeunt.**] *Rowe*; Exit. *F1*

V.i

V.i] *Rowe*; Actus Quartus, Scaena prima. *F1*
Location: *Pope, Capell*
2. s.d. **Giving the crown.**] *Pope*
11 **stranger blood**] *Theobald*; stranger-bloud *F1*
67 **fair-play orders**] *Capell*; fayre-play-orders *F1*
67 **comprimise**] *ed.*; comprimise *F1*
70 **cock'red silken**] *Fleay* (*after Pope*); cockred-silken *F1*

V.ii

Location: *Pope, Theobald*
1 s.p. **Lew.**] *Rowe*; Dol. *F1* (*throughout scene*)
16 **metal**] *Rowe*; mettle *F1*
26 **Were**] *F2*; Was *F1*
29–32 **ranks— . . . here?**] *Theobald* (*subs.*); ranks? . . . cause, . . . heere! *F1*
36 **gripple**] *Steevens conj.*; cripple *F1*
43 **thou**] *F4*
56 **baby eyes**] *Capell*; baby-eyes *F1*
57 **giant world**] *Theobald*; giant-world *F1*
72 **see**] *F4*; Sea *F1*
79 **propertied,**] *F4* (propertied *F2*); propor-tied *F1*
116 s.d. **Trumpet sounds.**] *Rowe*
124 **willful-opposite**] *hyphen, Theobald*
133 **unhair'd**] *Theobald*; vn-heard *F1*
153 **mother England**] *Theobald*; Mother-England *F1*
170 **all**] *Pope*; all, *F1*

V.iii

Location: *Pope*
11 **Sands;**] *Collier* (*subs.*); sands. *F1*
12 **now.**] *Johnson*; now, *F1*
14 **Ay**] *Rowe*; Aye *F1*

V.iv

Location: *ed.* (*after Wilson*)
2–3 **French; . . . miscarry,**] *Rowe* (*subs.*); French, . . . miscarry *F1*
61 s.d. **leading off Melune**] *Theobald*

V.v

Location: *Hanmer*
7 **wound**] *Rowe*; woon'd *F1*

V.vi

Location: *Theobald*
3 **dost**] *F2*; doest *F1*
16 **compliment**] *Warburton* (*in italics*); compliment *F1*
41 **Lincoln Washes**] *Pope*; Lincolne-Washes *F1*

V.vii

Location: *Theobald*
11 s.d. **Exit Bigot.**] *Capell*
17 **mind**] *Rowe*; winde *F1*
19 **throng**] *F2*; throng, *F1*
21 **cygnet**] *Rowe*; Symet *F1* (*possibly a misprint for Synet, a variant spelling of signet, in its turn a spelling of cygnet*)
29 **doors.**] *Pope*; doores. *F1*
35 **Poison'd—**] *Capell*; Poyson'd, *F1*
60 **God**] *S. Walker conj.*; heauen *F1* (*cf. III.i.155*)
64 s.d. **The King dies.**] *Rowe*
65 **ear.**] *F4* (*subs.*); eare *F1*
88 **sinewed**] *Rowe*; sinew'd *F1*
110 **time**] *Rowe*; time: *F1*

Richard II

UNLIKE SHAKESPEARE's earlier history plays—the Henry VI trilogy, whose authorship and date lie buried under mountains of conjecture; *Richard III*, whose text is such a challenge; and *King John*, whose connection with *The Troublesome Reign* is still a topic of debate—*Richard II* is fairly free of problems. Several pieces of evidence converge to indicate the mid-1590's as the most likely date of composition: the general lyricism of the work, which would put it near the sonnets, *A Midsummer Night's Dream*, and *Romeo and Juliet*; the publication in 1595 of the first installment of Daniel's *Civil Wars*, which most scholars now regard as a source; and an invitation from Sir Edward Hoby to Sir Robert Cecil to what sounds like a private showing of the play at Hoby's house in Canon Row, Westminster, on December 9, 1595 (see Appendix B, Number 15). If the "K. Richard" there presented was indeed Shakespeare's, and if Daniel's poem was indeed a source, *Richard II* can be dated within the limits of a single year, 1595. The piece was entered in the Stationers' Register on August 29, 1597, and published soon thereafter; a string of reprints (see the "Note on the Text" following the play) bear witness to its popularity.

Johnson's flat assertion that the play was "extracted" from Holinshed's *Chronicles* "with very little alteration" has not deterred research, and inevitably the research has complicated what appeared to be a simple problem. Although Shakespeare's debt to the second (1587) edition of Holinshed is clear, not only for the record of the main events of Richard's later reign but sometimes (as in II.iv) for the very language of a scene, several other alleged sources have been put forward. For example, the view of John of Gaunt

as a sage and patriotic elder statesman—not a trace of which appears in Holinshed—may reveal a knowledge of Froissart, but A. P. Rossiter has urged the claims of *Woodstock*, an anonymous play about the early reign of Richard II in which the young king's uncle, Thomas of Woodstock, Duke of Gloucester, fills a similar role. If, as seems probable, *Woodstock* is the earlier play, then Gaunt's allusion to "My brother Gloucester, plain well-meaning soul" (II.i.128) and to the old man's murder at Calais (I.ii.3) may be construed as further links, as may many verbal parallels about Richard's misbehavior as a king. *A Mirror for Magistrates* (with its examplary "tragedies" of Woodstock, Mowbray, Northumberland, and Richard II) and Marlowe's *Edward II* (another play about the downfall of a weak and unsuccessful king) do not provide such striking verbal echoes (or perhaps parallels deriving from a common source), but it can hardly be supposed that Shakespeare was uninfluenced by these works. The anonymous *Chronicque de la Traïson et Mort de Richart Deux* and Jean Créton's metrical *Histoire du Roy d'Angleterre Richard*, two anti-Lancastrian accounts of Richard's deposition, were still in manuscript in the later sixteenth century, but they were known to Stow and Holinshed, and Shakespeare may have drawn on them for certain sympathetic touches in his treatment of Richard, especially in the last two acts. His use of Daniel's *Civil Wars*, as Peter Ure and other scholars think, is more direct and therefore more important; also, it helps us date the composition of the play. Such alleged resemblances as those in Carlisle's speech about the horrors of rebellion (IV.i.121–29) may reflect a common Tudor attitude, and others may be merely coincidental; but Richard's entrance into London after he has given up the crown and the parting of the royal lovers (V.i) seems to draw on Daniel's touching treatment of the scene (Book I, Stanzas 66–98), not merely in its language but also in its pathos and intention. In short, Holinshed, whom Johnson took to be the only source, has now been joined by many rivals. Indeed, Dover Wilson, doubting that Shakespeare would have read so many books in preparation for his task, thought that *Richard II* may have had a single source in a now lost play by someone "soaked" in English history.

Shakespeare's eight plays on fifteenth-century history record the rise and fall of the Lancastrian line. In the so-called first tetralogy—the three *Henry VI* plays and *Richard III*, which were written near the start of his career—he traced its long decline through the crooked course of English politics between the death of Henry V in 1422 and the advent of the Tudors in 1485. In the second sequence—*Richard II, 1 and 2 Henry IV*, and *Henry V*—he treats its hard-fought rise to power in the early fifteenth century. Here his subject is the Lancastrian Bullingbrook's usurpation of his cousin Richard's throne, his misadventures as a king and his problems as the father of a wayward son, the accession of that son as Henry V and his victory in the foreign wars that brought such glory to his realm and such honor to his line. Whether or not Shakespeare conceived this second series of histories as a unit, these plays are made to serve a quasi-documentary function, for with the customary distortion and rearrangement of events they set forth the main facts of English history between 1398 and 1420. Also, starting as they do with such a dread event as the deposition of a lawful king, passing to its consequences in what Edward Hall in his *Union of . . . Lancaster and York* (1548) termed "the unquiet time" of Henry IV, and ending with "the victorious acts" of Henry V, they define a moral pattern of sin and retribution crowned by expiation and success. On one level, at least, the theme is that which Hall and many other Tudors held so dear: that rebellion is both a crime and a sin, and is bound to lead to trouble until the curse is lifted. Daniel's comment in the preface to his *Civil Wars* (which treats the same materials that Shakespeare treated in the two tetralogies) reflects the widely shared opinion that fifteenth-century history is both appalling and instructive because it shows

the deformities of civil dissension and the miserable events of rebellions, conspiracies, and bloody revengements which followed (as in a circle) upon that break of the due course of succession by the usurpation of Henry IV; [and because it makes] the blessings of peace and the happiness of an established government (in a direct line) the better to appear.

This motif is very strong in *Richard II*. When urged to seek revenge upon the King for the murder of Gloucester, Gaunt—the very embodiment of political morality and the speaker of the most stirring paean to England ever written (II.i.40–58)—says that he could "never lift / An angry arm" against the Lord's anointed. Later, Gaunt's brother York,

though dismayed by Richard's crimes, denounces any show of force as "gross rebellion and detested treason." Inevitably, the weak and foolish king himself, when he confronts disaster, takes comfort in the knowledge that

Not all the water in the rough rude sea
Can wash the balm off from an anointed king;
The breath of worldly men cannot depose
The deputy elected by the Lord.   (III.ii.54–57)

Even after Richard's deposition, Carlisle berates the usurper Bullingbrook for a crime so "heinous, black, obscene," and then he prophesies—what the first tetralogy had already shown—an age of woeful retribution. If Bullingbrook is crowned, he warns,

The blood of English shall manure the ground,
And future ages groan for this foul act.
Peace shall go sleep with Turks and infidels,
And in this seat of peace tumultuous wars
Shall kin with kin and kind with kind confound.
Disorder, horror, fear, and mutiny
Shall here inhabit, and this land be call'd
The fields of Golgotha and dead men's skulls.

(IV.i.137–44)

For his pains, however, Carlisle is promptly (and with flagrant illegality) arrested on a charge of treason, the king whose lost cause he defends is murdered, and Bullingbrook ascends the throne. In short, *Richard II* records with indignation the course and outcome of a successful insurrection.

Also, it records the deposition of a king who shows himself unfit to rule. To regard Richard as sentimentally as he regards himself is to ignore what Shakespeare is at pains to underscore: that whereas rebellion is a crime, kingship is a sacred burden which one must earn the right to bear. An "unstaid youth" burning in a "rash fierce blaze of riot," Richard has nothing but his royal birth and title to justify the misbehavior, and these are not enough to save him from the consequences of his crimes and follies. He acts flippantly toward Bullingbrook and Mowbray, insolently toward his uncles Gaunt and York, and illegally toward his banished cousin. Dissolute and avaricious, and "basely led / By flatterers," he converts his "sceptred isle" into a "pelting farm" and himself into the "landlord" of the realm. Delighting in the ceremonies and symbols of his station but unwilling—or perhaps unable—to assume its obligations, he betrays the trust of greatness. As the head and centre of the state—that delicate equipoise of reciprocal obligations—he should be wise and brave and just; but as the Gardener's servant recognizes, he is in fact the very emblem of disorder:

Why should we in the compass of a pale
Keep law and form and due proportion,
Showing, as in a model, our firm estate,
When our sea-walled garden, the whole land,
Is full of weeds, her fairest flowers chok'd up,
Her fruit-trees all unprun'd, her hedges ruin'd,
Her knots disordered and her wholesome herbs
Swarming with caterpillars?   (III.iv.40–47)

At last obliged to deal with the realities of his desperate situation, he turns to his own false image of himself —and it shatters like the glass wherein he views his "brittle glory." Therefore Richard's fall, however moving to himself and us as he verbalizes his despair, must be referred as much to his defects of character as to Bullingbrook's ambition.

Since Richard abdicates his royal function before he abdicates the throne, he creates a vacuum that Bullingbrook's ambition enables him to fill. If what he does is criminal, at any rate he saves the state. He is not, like Richard III, a moral monster, and Shakespeare makes it clear that he is not a fool. Lacking his cousin's delicacy of perception and his dazzling skill with words, he also lacks his fatal self-absorption, and in that regard at least he is more fit to be a king. He is verbal when he needs to be (as in the ritual of the lists at Coventry), so adept at politics that he stirs his cousin's envy, angry in a righteous cause, brave and energetic as a leader, and judicious in his use of power. Most important, he is a man of action rather than reflection, and as such the natural foil to Richard, who makes poetry of the fact:

> Here, cousin, seize the crown;
> Here, cousin,
> On this side my hand, and on that side thine.
> Now is this golden crown like a deep well
> That owes two buckets, filling one another,
> The emptier ever dancing in the air,
> The other down, unseen, and full of water:
> That bucket down and full of tears am I,
> Drinking my griefs, whilst you mount up on high.
>
> (IV.i.181–89)

To which Bullingbrook laconically replies, "I thought you had been willing to resign." This essential difference in their characters not only defines the basic movement of the plot, with Richard's fall producing Bullingbrook's ascent; it also enables Shakespeare to carry on his study of the proper use of power that he had started in the first tetralogy and that would occupy him deeply in the later history plays.

But there is more to *Richard II* than politics and history. Here as in *King John* (which was no doubt close in date of composition) Shakespeare goes beyond the Tudor slogans that had stocked the first tetralogy, and he expands the theme of providential history to such subtle and related questions as the source of political authority and the moral force of one's commitments. Here he uses history not just to prop a dogma or adorn a moral, but to see how men conduct themselves, and why. The Bastard Faulconbridge, almost alone among the swarms of men and women in the earlier history plays, achieves the status of a character, with an identity beyond his dramaturgic and thematic function. Except for moments now and then, we see the others only in their proper roles: Talbot as the man of patriotic valor, Beaufort (or Beauford, in Shakespeare's spelling) as the proud, ambitious prelate, Margaret as the fiend of France, King Henry as the pious weakling, Suffolk as the crafty politician, even Richard of Gloucester (despite

his virtuoso skill in acting) as the Yorkist villain. However boldly drawn, they are usually seen in only two dimensions, like the personified abstractions of the old morality plays. Conceived as means instead of ends, they exist to serve a function—to articulate a line of action or represent a type or exemplify a theme—and they wear their function like a badge.

With Richard it is otherwise. He typifies the unsuccessful king, of course, and to that extent instructs us; but it is as a man that he engages and retains our interest. Whereas we learn almost all we need to know about Richard of York from his first soliloquy (*2 Henry VI*, I.i.214–59), we continue to enlarge and modify our view of King Richard as the play proceeds, so that not until the final scene is our response to him complete. As in *King Lear*, this progressive illumination of the regal character is counterpointed with the decline of regal power: from the ceremonial if meretricious splendor of Act I through Richard's brutal treatment of his uncle Gaunt, his ineffectual posturing at Bullingbrook's invasion, and the pathos of his abdication, to the last indignity at Pomfret. Moreover, we can check our progressive recognition of Richard's complicated character by his own assessment of himself. An incorrigible egotist, he contemplates himself with endless fascination, and—poet that he is—he records his findings in poetry so persuasive that we almost think it true. His imperial rhetoric at the start is fitting for his image of himself as king and judge, but on his return from Ireland he assumes the role of king as loving parent, which he plays with ample self-esteem:

> As a long-parted mother with her child
> Plays fondly with her tears and smiles in meeting,
> So weeping, smiling, greet I thee, my earth,
> And do thee favors with my royal hands.
>
> (III.ii.8–11)

Then, as he learns the facts about his perilous situation, he depicts himself, with subtly modulated irony, as the royal victim of ingratitude:

> throw away respect,
> Tradition, form, and ceremonious duty,
> For you have but mistook me all this while.
> I live with bread like you, feel want,
> Taste grief, need friends: subjected thus,
> How can you say to me I am a king?
>
> (III.ii.172–77)

He undergoes the same swift change of mood, again expressed in words instead of deeds, when he yields to Bullingbrook at Flint; and in the deposition scene his rhetoric is so adroitly fitted to his fantasies—as when he compares himself to Christ—that the "woeful pageant" of his fall is turned into a play that he himself has staged. He is willing to resign his crown, he says,

> but still my griefs are mine.
> You may my glories and my state depose,
> But not my griefs; still am I king of those.
>
> (IV.i.191–93)

Even in the tearful parting from his queen he does not cease to dramatize himself, and then to contemplate his own sad image with a certain satisfaction. Finally, in the great aria-like soliloquy at Pomfret, his fantasies take so many shapes, and are expressed in language so complex, that he populates his "little world" with the products of his own "still-breeding thoughts."

It is fitting that a play about a poet-king so much enchanted by the resources, limitations, and ambiguities of language should never stoop to prose. In *Richard II* poetry approaches the condition of music, as Pater noted long ago, and the music lends a heightened function to the style. Limpid, clanging, or sonorous, the intensely musical idiom is so steady through the play—as in Bullingbrook's farewell (I.iii), the famous garden scene (III.iv), and York's account of Richard's entrance into London (V.ii)—that the doggerel in V.iii and V.vi has troubled certain critics. Richard himself is such a virtuoso in the arts of speech that when he fondles words and tropes he seems to listen to himself, tuning his language not merely to the situation but also to his mood, and rejoicing in his skill. Thus he can go from the bold, rhythmically assertive declamation of

> Face to face,
> And frowning brow to brow, ourselves will hear
> The accuser and the accused freely speak
>
> (I.i.15–17)

to jaunty ease and rancor toward the dying Gaunt, and then, within the compass of a single scene (III.ii), to the soft, caressing music of his salutation to the English earth, the deep-toned splendor of his hymn to royal power, the cacophony of his diatribe on the "three Judases," and finally to his lovely song about the death of kings. Even when he falls into "the mighty hold of Bullingbrook" he is more concerned with style than with emotion as he articulates his grief:

> I'll give my jewels for a set of beads,
> My gorgeous palace for a hermitage,
> My gay apparel for an almsman's gown,
> My figur'd goblets for a dish of wood,
> My sceptre for a palmer's walking-staff,
> My subjects for a pair of carved saints,
> And my large kingdom for a little grave,
> A little little grave, an obscure grave.
>
> (III.iii.147–54)

The earlier history plays, and notably *Richard III*, are also very formal in their language, but in *Richard II* the verse is more than just a mode of stately utterance: it serves to set the tone and underscore the theme. Richard's tendency to deal in simile and metaphor, for instance, reveals a man who prefers to excogitate and analyze a situation rather than to act, and whose attempts to verbalize his complicated states of mind— as in the deposition scene or in his solitude at Pomfret —engross his whole attention. A born poet, he almost always speaks in tropes (for example, of the sun as symbol of his kingly status, of grief expressed in tears, of England as a blessed plot of earth, of rebellion as a stain), and these tropes state, restate, and amplify the major motifs of the action in ways almost symphonic. Bullingbrook also knows the force of language and bends it to his purpose, but he does not confuse his mental constructs, however deftly verbalized, with hard, unyielding fact; and he does not permit mere words, however sacrosanct and laden with association, to take the place of swift, incisive action.

> O, who can hold a fire in his hand
> By thinking on the frosty Caucasus?
> Or cloy the hungry edge of appetite
> By bare imagination of a feast?
> Or wallow naked in December snow
> By thinking on fantastic summer's heat?
>
> (I.iii.294–99)

On the other hand, Richard has immense respect for words conceived as symbols; and it is symbols, rather than the things they represent, that govern his behavior. His crown as emblem of the royal power (and as a fertile source of metaphor) is of more concern to him than his duties as a king. His inability to distinguish the external sign or symbol—his royal title, for example, or his sceptre, or a gesture, or the ceremonies of his office—from what the symbol represents is as much a factor in his fall as his abuse of office. "Am I not king?" he says on his return from Ireland (when his cause is clearly hopeless);

> Is not the king's name twenty thousand names?
> Arm, arm, my name! (III.ii.83, 85–86)

The structure of the play is as formal as its language. Its double, complementary plot—the fall of Richard and the rise of Bullingbrook—holds no shock or terror; it is simple, grand, and elemental, like some ancient rite whose progress is prescribed and whose outcome is foreknown. Events are rarely shown directly, with the fresh impact of things as they occur; they come to us not as the realistic imitation of an action but as the ritual presentation of a form or type of action that is framed in ceremony, encased in rhetoric, and draped with rich symbolic implications. Thus we have the protocol of knightly jousts, but not the clash of armed encounter; the circumstances of an armed rebellion, but not the heat and dust of battle; the transaction of an actual deposition, but a deposition that becomes a sacrificial rite. In the light of Rossiter's definition of ritual as "the offering, or the hinting of an offering, of a gesture of regard or respect for something which goes beyond the state-of-affairs or the EVENT," even Richard's death is less a deed of violence than the conclusion of a "woeful pageant" whose subject is the failure of a high ideal.

In addition to the presumed private showing at Sir Edward Hoby's house in 1595, the early theatrical history of *Richard II* is enlivened by the account of a performance at the Globe on February 7, 1601. If this revival, arranged by friends of the Earl of Essex for the very eve of his ill-starred rebellion, was designed as propaganda, it must be regarded as a failure, for it did not lead Londoners to rally to his desperate undertaking. None the less, Elizabeth, a few months later, remarked that she herself was Richard, and she added tartly that the play had been presented forty times "in open streets and houses." Allowing for the Queen's exaggeration, we may infer from her remark and from the play's lively history of quarto publication that the work was widely known, and that the absence of the deposition scene in the earliest printed versions (see the "Note on the Text"), doubtless reflecting a theatrical cut, stemmed from her reluctance to have such lawless doings publicized. That she was not peculiarly sensitive on the subject is indicated by the fact that during the tumults of the late 1670's, when the problem of succession had reached a stage of crisis, Nahum Tate's adaptation of the play was twice suppressed.

Herschel Baker

Rapier and dagger

Rapier and cloak

A "case of rapiers"

The two-hand broadsword

From *Di Grassi His True Art of Defence*, trans. I. G. (1594). (*By permission of the Harvard College Library*)

The Tragedy of King Richard the Second

[DRAMATIS PERSONAE

KING RICHARD THE SECOND
JOHN OF GAUNT, *Duke of Lancaster* } *uncles to the*
EDMUND OF LANGLEY, *Duke of York* } *King*
HENRY, *surnamed* BULLINGBROOK, *Duke of Herford, son
to John of Gaunt; afterwards* KING HENRY IV
DUKE OF AUMERLE, *son to the Duke of York*
THOMAS MOWBRAY, *Duke of Norfolk*
DUKE OF SURREY
EARL OF SALISBURY
LORD BERKELEY
SIR JOHN BUSHY }
SIR JOHN BAGOT } *favorites to King Richard*
SIR HENRY GREEN }
EARL OF NORTHUMBERLAND
HENRY PERCY, *surnamed* HOTSPUR, *his son*
LORD ROSS
LORD WILLOUGHBY

LORD FITZWATER
BISHOP OF CARLISLE
ABBOT OF WESTMINSTER
LORD MARSHAL
SIR STEPHEN SCROOP
SIR PIERCE *of Exton*
CAPTAIN *of a band of Welshmen*
Two GARDENERS

QUEEN *to King Richard*
DUCHESS OF YORK
DUCHESS OF GLOUCESTER, *widow of Thomas of
Woodstock, Duke of Gloucester*
LADY *attending on the Queen*

LORDS, HERALDS, OFFICERS, SOLDIERS, KEEPER,
MESSENGER, GROOM, SERVINGMAN, *and other* AT-
TENDANTS

SCENE: *England and Wales*]

[ACT I, SCENE I]

Enter KING RICHARD, JOHN OF GAUNT, *with other*
NOBLES *and* ATTENDANTS.

K. Rich. Old John of Gaunt, time-honored Lan-
caster,
Hast thou, according to thy oath and band,
Brought hither Henry Herford thy bold son,
Here to make good the boist'rous late appeal,

*Words and passages enclosed in square brackets in the text above are
either emendations of the copy-text or additions to it. The Textual Notes
immediately following the play cite the earliest authority for every such
change or insertion and supply the reading of the copy-text wherever it is
emended in this edition.*

I.i. Location: Windsor. The castle.
1. **Old . . . Gaunt.** Gaunt (so called from his birthplace, Ghent in
Flanders) was fifty-eight at the time.   2. **band:** bond.
3. **Herford:** i.e. Hereford; probably pronounced *Harford.* Henry's
designation Bullingbrook (derived from the name of his birthplace
in Leicestershire) is pronounced without the *g* (and is sometimes
spelled so in the early texts). The form *Bolingbroke,* common in modern editions, never occurs in the early texts; it was first employed by
Pope in the early eighteenth century. Its adoption by succeeding editors has led to a good deal of uncertainty about the pronunciation.
4. **late appeal:** recent accusation. According to Holinshed (Bullough,
III, 387–89), the trouble between Bullingbrook and Mowbray had
started at the parliament that met in Shrewsbury in January 1398,
when Bullingbrook accused Mowbray of having uttered certain things
"sounding highlie to the kings dishonour." Summoned before the
council, the two men traded the accusations that are rehearsed later
in this scene. After further interrogations the case was adjourned until
the following April, when the King would be at Windsor. Other
accounts—including those by Hall (Bullough, III, 383), Froissart,

Which then our leisure would not let us hear,   5
Against the Duke of Norfolk, Thomas Mowbray?
  Gaunt. I have, my liege.
  K. Rich. Tell me, moreover, hast thou sounded
him,
If he appeal the Duke on ancient malice,
Or worthily, as a good subject should,   10
On some known ground of treachery in him?
  Gaunt. As near as I could sift him on that argument,
On some apparent danger seen in him
Aim'd at your Highness, no inveterate malice.
  K. Rich. Then call them to our presence; face to
face,   15
And frowning brow to brow, ourselves will hear
The accuser and the accused freely speak.
High-stomach'd are they both and full of ire,
In rage, deaf as the sea, hasty as fire.

and Daniel—have Mowbray begin the altercation by repeating to the
King certain complaints about Richard's misrule that Bullingbrook
had expressed "more for dolour and lamentacion, then for malice or
displeasure." For an authoritative discussion of the quarrel see
Charles Oman, *The History of England from the Accession of Richard
II to the Death of Richard III* (1910), pp. 141–43.
5. **our, us.** The royal plural (like *ourselves* in line 16).   **leisure:** i.e.
lack of leisure.   7. **liege:** sovereign.   8. **sounded:** questioned.
9. **appeal:** accuse.   **on ancient malice:** because of some old grudge.
12. **sift him:** ascertain his motives through indirect questions.   **argument:** topic.   13. **apparent:** manifest.
18. **High-stomach'd:** haughty.

805

Richard II
I.i

Enter BULLINGBROOK *and* MOWBRAY [*with* ATTEND-
ANTS].

Bull.   Many years of happy days befall   20
My gracious sovereign, my most loving liege!
Mow.   Each day still better other's happiness,
Until the heavens, envying earth's good hap,
Add an immortal title to your crown!
K. Rich.   We thank you both, yet one but flatters
us,   25
As well appeareth by the cause you come:
Namely, to appeal each other of high treason.
Cousin of Herford, what dost thou object
Against the Duke of Norfolk, Thomas Mowbray?
Bull.   First, heaven be the record to my speech,
In the devotion of a subject's love,   31
Tend'ring the precious safety of my prince,
And free from other misbegotten hate,
Come I appellant to this princely presence.
Now, Thomas Mowbray, do I turn to thee,   35
And mark my greeting well; for what I speak
My body shall make good upon this earth,
Or my divine soul answer it in heaven.
Thou art a traitor and a miscreant,
Too good to be so, and too bad to live,   40
Since the more fair and crystal is the sky,
The uglier seem the clouds that in it fly.
Once more, the more to aggravate the note,
With a foul traitor's name stuff I thy throat,
And wish (so please my sovereign) ere I move,   45
What my tongue speaks, my right drawn sword may
prove.
Mow.   Let not my cold words here accuse my zeal.
'Tis not the trial of a woman's war,
The bitter clamor of two eager tongues,
Can arbitrate this cause betwixt us twain;   50
The blood is hot that must be cool'd for this.
Yet can I not of such tame patience boast
As to be hush'd and nought at all to say.
First, the fair reverence of your Highness curbs me
From giving reins and spurs to my free speech,   55
Which else would post until it had return'd
These terms of treason doubled down his throat.
Setting aside his high blood's royalty,
And let him be no kinsman to my liege,
I do defy him, and I spit at him,   60
Call him a slanderous coward, and a villain,
Which to maintain I would allow him odds
And meet him, were I tied to run afoot
Even to the frozen ridges of the Alps,
Or any other ground inhabitable   65
Where ever Englishman durst set his foot.
Mean time, let this defend my loyalty:
By all my hopes, most falsely doth he lie.

23. **hap:** fortune.
24. **Add . . . crown:** i.e. change your earthly crown to a heavenly one.
28. **what . . . object:** on what grounds do you bring the charge (of treason).   32. **Tend'ring:** dutifully regarding.
38. **divine:** immortal.   43. **note:** stigma, i.e. charge of treason.
46. **right:** justly, i.e. in a righteous cause.
47. **accuse my zeal:** impugn my loyalty.
49. **eager:** sharp (French *aigre*).   50. **Can:** that can.
56. **post:** ride at high speed.
58. **his . . . royalty.** Bullingbrook, like Richard, was a grandson of
Edward III.   63. **tied:** obliged.   65. **inhabitable:** uninhabitable.

806

Bull.   Pale trembling coward, there I throw my
gage,
Disclaiming here the kinred of the King,   70
And lay aside my high blood's royalty,
Which fear, not reverence, makes thee to except.
If guilty dread have left thee so much strength
As to take up mine honor's pawn, then stoop.
By that, and all the rites of knighthood else,   75
Will I make good against thee, arm to arm,
What I have spoke, or thou canst worse devise.
Mow.   I take it up, and by that sword I swear
Which gently laid my knighthood on my shoulder,
I'll answer thee in any fair degree   80
Or chivalrous design of knightly trial;
And when I mount, alive may I not light,
If I be traitor or unjustly fight!
K. Rich.   What doth our cousin lay to Mowbray's
charge?
It must be great that can inherit us   85
So much as of a thought of ill in him.
Bull.   Look what I speak, my life shall prove it
true:
That Mowbray hath receiv'd eight thousand nobles
In name of lendings for your Highness' soldiers,
The which he hath detain'd for lewd employments, 90
Like a false traitor and injurious villain;
Besides I say, and will in battle prove,
Or here or elsewhere to the furthest verge
That ever was surveyed by English eye,
That all the treasons for these eighteen years, 95
Complotted and contrived in this land,
Fetch from false Mowbray their first head and spring.
Further I say, and further will maintain
Upon his bad life to make all this good,
That he did plot the Duke of Gloucester's death, 100
Suggest his soon-believing adversaries,
And consequently, like a traitor coward,
Sluic'd out his innocent soul through streams of blood,

69. **gage:** pledge (here, probably a glove or gauntlet).
70. **kinred:** kinship.   72. **except:** allege as an excuse.
74. **mine honor's pawn:** i.e. the gage flung down.
80–81. **any . . . trial:** any way sanctioned by the laws of chivalry.
85. **inherit us:** put us in possession of.   87. **Look what:** whatever.
88–103. **That . . . blood.**   Bullingbrook's charges against Mowbray
rake up the scandals of some ten years earlier (1387–88), when the
so-called Lords Appellant—a band of conservative peers including
the Duke of Gloucester (Thomas of Woodstock), the Earl of Arundel,
the Earl of Warwick, Mowbray, and Bullingbrook—brought about
the downfall of the young king's favorites and, installed as members
of the council, usurped almost all of his executive powers.   By 1389
Richard was strong enough to end this humiliating state of affairs and
dismiss the Lords Appellant, but it was not until 1397 that he began
to pay off his old scores with the arrest, for treason, of Warwick,
Arundel, and Gloucester.   One of them was banished and another
executed, but Gloucester was imprisoned at Calais in the custody of
Mowbray and there murdered, almost surely at the King's own
instigation (as is implied at I.ii.37–41).   These events are treated in
the anonymous play *Woodstock*, which some scholars regard as a
sort of prologue to *Richard II.*
88. **nobles:** gold coins worth 6s. 8d.
89. **lendings:** money advanced to soldiers when regular pay is not
available.   90. **lewd:** base, improper.
91. **injurious:** malicious.   93. **Or:** either.
95. **these eighteen years.**   According to Holinshed (Bullough, III,
390), Bullingbrook told the King that Mowbray "hath beene the
occasion of all the treason that hath beene contrived in your realme
for the space of these eighteene yeares," that is, since the Peasants' Revolt of 1381.   97. **head:** source.
101. **Suggest:** incite.   **soon-believing:** overcredulous.
102. **consequently:** subsequently.

Which blood, like sacrificing Abel's, cries,
Even from the tongueless caverns of the earth, 105
To me for justice and rough chastisement;
And, by the glorious worth of my descent,
This arm shall do it, or this life be spent.
    K. Rich.   How high a pitch his resolution soars!
Thomas of Norfolk, what say'st thou to this? 110
    Mow.   O, let my sovereign turn away his face,
And bid his ears a little while be deaf,
Till I have told this slander of his blood
How God and good men hate so foul a liar.
    K. Rich.   Mowbray, impartial are our eyes and
    ears. 115
Were he my brother, nay, my kingdom's heir,
As he is but my father's brother's son,
Now by [my] sceptre's awe I make a vow,
Such neighbor nearness to our sacred blood
Should nothing privilege him nor partialize 120
The unstooping firmness of my upright soul.
He is our subject, Mowbray; so art thou.
Free speech and fearless I to thee allow.
    Mow.   Then, Bullingbrook, as low as to thy heart
Through the false passage of thy throat thou liest.
Three parts of that receipt I had for Callice 126
Disburs'd I duly to his Highness' soldiers;
The other part reserv'd I by consent,
For that my sovereign liege was in my debt,
Upon remainder of a dear account, 130
Since last I went to France to fetch his queen.
Now swallow down that lie. For Gloucester's death,
I slew him not, but to my own disgrace
Neglected my sworn duty in that case.
For you, my noble Lord of Lancaster, 135
The honorable father to my foe,
Once did I lay an ambush for your life,
A trespass that doth vex my grieved soul;
But ere I last receiv'd the sacrament
I did confess it, and exactly begg'd 140
Your Grace's pardon, and I hope I had it.
This is my fault. As for the rest appeal'd,
It issues from the rancor of a villain,
A recreant and most degenerate traitor,
Which in myself I boldly will defend, 145
And interchangeably hurl down my gage
Upon this overweening traitor's foot,
To prove myself a loyal gentleman
Even in the best blood chamber'd in his bosom,

In haste whereof, most heartily I pray 150
Your Highness to assign our trial day.
    K. Rich.   Wrath-kindled [gentlemen], be rul'd by
    me,
Let's purge this choler without letting blood.
This we prescribe, though no physician;
Deep malice makes too deep incision. 155
Forget, forgive, conclude and be agreed,
Our doctors say this is no month to bleed.
Good uncle, let this end where it begun;
We'll calm the Duke of Norfolk, you your son. 159
    Gaunt.   To be a make-peace shall become my age.
Throw down, my son, the Duke of Norfolk's gage.
    K. Rich.   And, Norfolk, throw down his.
    Gaunt.   When, Harry? when?
Obedience bids I should not bid again.
    K. Rich.   Norfolk, throw down, we bid, there is no
    boot. 164
    Mow.   Myself I throw, dread sovereign, at thy
    foot, 165
My life thou shalt command, but not my shame:
The one my duty owes, but my fair name,
Despite of death that lives upon my grave,
To dark dishonor's use thou shalt not have.
I am disgrac'd, impeach'd, and baffled here, 170
Pierc'd to the soul with slander's venom'd spear,
The which no balm can cure but his heart-blood
Which breath'd this poison.
    K. Rich.   Rage must be withstood,
Give me his gage. Lions make leopards tame.
    Mow.   Yea, but not change his spots. Take but my
    shame, 175
And I resign my gage. My dear dear lord,
The purest treasure mortal times afford
Is spotless reputation; that away,
Men are but gilded loam or painted clay.
A jewel in a ten-times-barr'd-up chest 180
Is a bold spirit in a loyal breast.
Mine honor is my life, both grow in one,
Take honor from me, and my life is done.
Then, dear my liege, mine honor let me try;
In that I live, and for that will I die. 185
    K. Rich.   Cousin, throw up your gage, do you
    begin.
    Bull.   O, God defend my soul from such deep sin!
Shall I seem crestfallen in my father's sight?
Or with pale beggar-fear impeach my height
Before this outdar'd dastard? Ere my tongue 190

---

104. **like sacrificing Abel's.** See Genesis 4:4, 8–10.
109. **pitch:** highest point of a falcon's flight.
113. **slander . . . blood:** disgrace to the royal family.
118. **my sceptre's awe:** the reverence due to my sceptre.
120. **nothing:** not at all.   **partialize:** render partial.
126. **receipt:** money received.   **Callice:** Calais.
129. **For that:** because.
130. **Upon . . . account:** for the balance of a heavy debt.
131. **fetch his queen.** Mowbray had negotiated Richard's second marriage (1396) with Isabella, daughter of Charles VI of France.
135–41. **For . . . it.** "Marie true it is," Holinshed reports Mowbray as confessing (Bullough, III, 391), "that once I laid an ambush to have slaine the duke of Lancaster, that there sitteth: but neverthelesse he hath pardoned me thereof, and there was good peace made betwixt us, for the which I yeeld him my hartie thankes."
140. **exactly:** expressly and fully.
142. **appeal'd:** charged against me.   144. **recreant:** faithless.
146. **interchangeably:** in turn.

150. **In haste whereof:** to hasten which, i.e. to prove my innocence as soon as possible.
153. **Let's . . . blood:** i.e. let us relieve this wrath (resulting from excess of bile) by a purgative rather than by bleeding the patient.
155. **malice:** enmity.   156. **conclude:** come to terms.
164. **boot:** help for it.
170. **impeach'd:** accused.   **baffled:** dishonored (literally, stripped of knighthood).   173. **Which breath'd:** who uttered.
174. **Lions . . . tame.** Lions were the emblem of the English kings; Mowbray's emblem was a leopard.
177. **mortal times:** our earthly lives.   184. **try:** test in combat.
186. **throw . . . gage:** i.e. as a gesture of conciliation throw your gage up to me. The King is probably seated on a high dais. Holinshed records (Bullough, III, 389) that "there was a great scaffold erected within the castell of Windsor for the king to sit with the lords and prelats of his realme."
189. **impeach my height:** discredit my lofty rank.
190. **outdar'd:** cowed.

Richard II
I.i

Shall wound my honor with such feeble wrong,
Or sound so base a parley, my teeth shall tear
The slavish motive of recanting fear,
And spit it bleeding in his high disgrace,
Where shame doth harbor, even in Mowbray's face.
[*Exit Gaunt.*]

K. Rich. We were not born to sue, but to command,   196
Which since we cannot do to make you friends,
Be ready, as your lives shall answer it,
At Coventry upon Saint Lambert's day.
There shall your swords and lances arbitrate   200
The swelling difference of your settled hate.
Since we cannot atone you, we shall see
Justice design the victor's chivalry.
Lord Marshal, command our officers-at-arms
Be ready to direct these home alarms. *Exeunt.* 205

[SCENE II]

Enter JOHN OF GAUNT *with the* DUCHESS OF GLOUCESTER.

Gaunt. Alas, the part I had in Woodstock's blood
Doth more solicit me than your exclaims
To stir against the butchers of his life!
But since correction lieth in those hands
Which made the fault that we cannot correct,   5
Put we our quarrel to the will of heaven,
Who, when they see the hour's ripe on earth,
Will rain hot vengeance on offenders' heads.
Duch. Finds brotherhood in thee no sharper spur?
Hath love in thy old blood no living fire?   10
Edward's seven sons, whereof thyself art one,
Were as seven vials of his sacred blood,
Or seven fair branches springing from one root.
Some of those seven are dried by nature's course,
Some of those branches by the Destinies cut;   15

191. **feeble wrong**: false submission.
192. **sound . . . parley**: i.e. negotiate such a shameful truce. The trumpet signal for a conference was called a parley (or parle).
193. **motive**: instrument, i.e. tongue.   194. **his**: its, i.e. the tongue's.
195 s.d. **Exit Gaunt**. This exit (from F1) satisfies the stage convention that a character may not leave the stage at the end of one scene and immediately re-enter at the beginning of the next.
199. **Saint Lambert's day.** "Writers disagree about the daie that was appointed," says Holinshed judiciously (Bullough, III, 391), "for some saie, it was upon a mondaie in August; other upon saint Lamberts daie, being the seventeenth of September, other on the eleventh of September: but true it is, that the king assigned them not onlie the daie, but also appointed them listes and place for the combat, and thereupon great preparation was made, as to such a matter apperteined."   202 **atone**: reconcile.
203. **design . . . chivalry**: determine the victor in a chivalric encounter.
205. **home**: domestic.   **alarms**: calls to arms, i.e. combats.

I.ii. Location: London. The Duke of Lancaster's palace.
1. **the part . . . blood**: my relationship to Woodstock. John of Gaunt was the fourth and Thomas of Woodstock the sixth of Edward III's seven sons (who are itemized in *2 Henry VI*, II.ii.10–17).
4. **those**: i.e. Richard's.
14–15. **Some . . . cut.** Of Edward III's seven sons, two (William of Hatfield and William of Windsor) did not survive their youth; Lionel, Duke of Clarence, died in Italy in 1368; Edward the Black Prince, the heir apparent, predeceased his father by a year in 1376; and Thomas of Woodstock, Duke of Gloucester, was murdered at Calais in 1387. At the time represented in this scene—for which, incidentally, Shakespeare had no source in the chronicles—only John of Gaunt, Duke of Lancaster, and Edmund de Langley, Duke of York, were left, but their lives were nearly done, Gaunt dying in 1399 and York in 1402.

But Thomas, my dear lord, my life, my Gloucester,
One vial full of Edward's sacred blood,
One flourishing branch of his most royal root,
Is crack'd, and all the precious liquor spilt,
Is hack'd down, and his summer leaves all faded,   20
By envy's hand and murder's bloody axe.
Ah, Gaunt, his blood was thine! That bed, that womb,
That mettle, that self mould, that fashioned thee
Made him a man; and though thou livest and breathest,
Yet art thou slain in him. Thou dost consent   25
In some large measure to thy father's death,
In that thou seest thy wretched brother die,
Who was the model of thy father's life.
Call it not patience, Gaunt, it is despair.
In suff'ring thus thy brother to be slaught'red,   30
Thou showest the naked pathway to thy life,
Teaching stern murder how to butcher thee.
That which in mean men we entitle patience
Is pale cold cowardice in noble breasts.
What shall I say? To safeguard thine own life   35
The best way is to venge my Gloucester's death.
Gaunt. God's is the quarrel, for God's substitute,
His deputy anointed in His sight,
Hath caus'd his death, the which if wrongfully,
Let heaven revenge, for I may never lift   40
An angry arm against His minister.
Duch. Where then, alas, may I complain myself?
Gaunt. To God, the widow's champion and defense.
Duch. Why then I will. Farewell, old Gaunt!
Thou goest to Coventry, there to behold   45
Our cousin Herford and fell Mowbray fight.
O, [sit] my husband's wrongs on Herford's spear,
That it may enter butcher Mowbray's breast!
Or if misfortune miss the first career,
Be Mowbray's sins so heavy in his bosom   50
That they may break his foaming courser's back,
And throw the rider headlong in the lists,
A caitive recreant to my cousin Herford!
Farewell, old Gaunt! thy sometimes brother's wife
With her companion, grief, must end her life.   55
Gaunt. Sister, farewell, I must to Coventry.
As much good stay with thee as go with me!
Duch. Yet one word more! Grief boundeth where
[it] falls,
Not with the empty hollowness, but weight.
I take my leave before I have begun,   60
For sorrow ends not when it seemeth done.
Commend me to thy brother, Edmund York.
Lo this is all—nay, yet depart not so;
Though this be all, do not so quickly go;
I shall remember more. Bid him—ah, what?—   65
With all good speed at Plashy visit me.
Alack, and what shall good old York there see

21. **envy's**: malice's.   23. **mettle**: substance.   **self**: same.
25–26. **consent . . . to**: be an accomplice . . . in.
28. **model**: copy, image.   33. **mean**: lowly.
39. **his**: i.e. Gloucester's.   41. **minister**: agent.
46. **cousin**: kinsman.   **fell**: fierce.
49. **if . . . career**: if disaster for Mowbray does not come at the first charge.   53. **caitive**: caitiff, base.
54. **thy . . . wife**: your brother's former wife (now his widow).
66. **Plashy**: Pleshey, Gloucester's residence in Essex.

But empty lodgings and unfurnish'd walls,
Unpeopled offices, untrodden stones?
And what hear there for welcome but my groans? 70
Therefore commend me; let him not come there
To seek out sorrow that dwells every where.
Desolate, desolate, will I hence and die:
The last leave of thee takes my weeping eye. *Exeunt.*

[Scene III]

Enter Lord Marshal *and the* Duke Aumerle.

Mar. My Lord Aumerle, is Harry Herford arm'd?
Aum. Yea, at all points, and longs to enter in.
Mar. The Duke of Norfolk, sprightfully and bold,
Stays but the summons of the appellant's trumpet.
Aum. Why then the champions are prepar'd, and
     stay 5
For nothing but his Majesty's approach.

The trumpets sound, and the King *enters with his nobles*
     [Gaunt, Bushy, Bagot, Green, *and others*].
     When they are set, enter [Mowbray,] *the Duke of*
     Norfolk, in arms, defendant, [*with a* Herald].

K. Rich. Marshal, demand of yonder champion
The cause of his arrival here in arms;
Ask him his name, and orderly proceed
To swear him in the justice of his cause. 10
Mar. In God's name and the King's, say who
     thou art
And why thou comest thus knightly clad in arms,
Against what man thou com'st, and what thy quarrel.
Speak truly on thy knighthood and thy oath,
As so defend thee heaven and thy valor! 15
Mow. My name is Thomas Mowbray, Duke of
     Norfolk,
Who hither come engaged by my oath
(Which God defend a knight should violate!)
Both to defend my loyalty and truth
To God, my king, and my succeeding issue, 20
Against the Duke of Herford that appeals me,
And by the grace of God, and this mine arm,
To prove him, in defending of myself,
A traitor to my God, my king, and me—
And as I truly fight, defend me heaven! 25

The trumpets sound. Enter [Bullingbrook,] *Duke of*
     Herford, appellant, in armor, [*with a* Herald].

K. Rich. Marshal, ask yonder knight in arms,
Both who he is and why he cometh hither
Thus plated in habiliments of war,
And formally, according to our law,
Depose him in the justice of his cause. 30
Mar. What is thy name? and wherefore com'st
     thou hither

Before King Richard in his royal lists?
Against whom [com'st] thou? and what's thy quarrel?
Speak like a true knight, so defend thee heaven!
Bull. Harry of Herford, Lancaster, and Derby 35
Am I, who ready here do stand in arms
To prove by God's grace, and my body's valor,
In lists, on Thomas Mowbray, Duke of Norfolk,
That he is a traitor, foul and dangerous,
To God of heaven, King Richard, and to me— 40
And as I truly fight, defend me heaven!
Mar. On pain of death, no person be so bold
Or daring-hardy as to touch the lists,
Except the Marshal and such officers
Appointed to direct these fair designs. 45
Bull. Lord Marshal, let me kiss my sovereign's
     hand
And bow my knee before his Majesty,
For Mowbray and myself are like two men
That vow a long and weary pilgrimage.
Then let us take a ceremonious leave 50
And loving farewell of our several friends.
Mar. The appellant in all duty greets your High-
     ness,
And craves to kiss your hand and take his leave.
K. Rich. We will descend and fold him in our arms.
Cousin of Herford, as thy cause is right, 55
So be thy fortune in this royal fight!
Farewell, my blood, which if to-day thou shed,
Lament we may, but not revenge [thee] dead.
Bull. O, let no noble eye profane a tear
For me, if I be gor'd with Mowbray's spear. 60
As confident as is the falcon's flight
Against a bird, do I with Mowbray fight.
My loving lord, I take my leave of you;
Of you, my noble cousin, Lord Aumerle;
Not sick, although I have to do with death, 65
But lusty, young, and cheerly drawing breath.
Lo, as at English feasts, so I regreet
The daintiest last, to make the end most sweet:
O thou, the earthly author of my blood,
Whose youthful spirit, in me regenerate, 70
Doth with a twofold vigor lift me up
To reach at victory above my head,
Add proof unto mine armor with thy prayers,
And with thy blessings steel my lance's point,
That it may enter Mowbray's waxen coat, 75
And furbish new the name of John a' Gaunt,
Even in the lusty havior of his son.
Gaunt. God in thy good cause make thee prosper-
     ous!
Be swift like lightning in the execution,
And let thy blows, doubly redoubled, 80
Fall like amazing thunder on the casque
Of thy adverse pernicious enemy.
Rouse up thy youthful blood, be valiant and live.

Richard II
I.iii

---

68. **unfurnish'd:** bare.   69. **offices:** service quarters.
I.iii. Location: The lists at Coventry.
o.s.d. According to Holinshed (Bullough, III, 392), the Duke of Surrey served as high marshal and the Duke of Aumerle as high constable
at the lists in Coventry.   2. **in:** i.e. into the lists.
3. **sprightfully and bold:** spiritedly and boldly.
4. **Stays:** awaits.   18. **defend:** forbid.   28. **plated:** armored.
30. **Depose him:** take his sworn deposition.

45. **fair designs:** orderly proceedings.
59. **profane a tear:** i.e. weep for one proved to be a traitor.
66. **lusty:** vigorous, spirited.   **young.** Bullingbrook was thirty-one
at the time represented in this scene.
67. **regreet:** salute.   68. **The daintiest:** i.e. the best thing.
70. **regenerate:** reborn.   73. **proof:** impenetrability.
75. **enter . . . coat:** pierce Mowbray's coat of mail as if it were made
of wax.   76. **a':** of.   77. **havior:** conduct.
81. **amazing:** bewildering, astounding.   **casque:** helmet.

Richard II
I.iii

Bull. Mine innocence and Saint George to thrive!

Mow. However God or fortune cast my lot, 85
There lives or dies, true to King Richard's throne,
A loyal, just, and upright gentleman.
Never did captive with a freer heart
Cast off his chains of bondage, and embrace
His golden uncontroll'd enfranchisement, 90
More than my dancing soul doth celebrate
This feast of battle with mine adversary.
Most mighty liege, and my companion peers,
Take from my mouth the wish of happy years.
As gentle and as jocund as to jest 95
Go I to fight: truth hath a quiet breast.

K. Rich. Farewell, my lord, securely I espy
Virtue with valor couched in thine eye.
Order the trial, Marshal, and begin.

Mar. Harry of Herford, Lancaster, and Derby,
Receive thy lance, and God defend the right! 101

Bull. Strong as a tower in hope, I cry amen.

Mar. [*To an Officer.*]   Go bear this lance to
Thomas Duke of Norfolk.

[*1.*] *Her.* Harry of Herford, Lancaster, and Derby
Stands here for God, his sovereign, and himself, 105
On pain to be found false and recreant,
To prove the Duke of Norfolk, Thomas Mowbray,
A traitor to his God, his king, and him,
And dares him to set forward to the fight.

2. Her. Here standeth Thomas Mowbray, Duke of
Norfolk, 110
On pain to be found false and recreant,
Both to defend himself and to approve
Henry of Herford, Lancaster, and Derby
To God, his sovereign, and to him disloyal,
Courageously, and with a free desire, 115
Attending but the signal to begin.

Mar. Sound, trumpets, and set forward, combatants.   [*A charge sounded.*]
Stay, the King hath thrown his warder down.

K. Rich. Let them lay by their helmets and their
spears,
And both return back to their chairs again. 120
Withdraw with us, and let the trumpets sound
While we return these dukes what we decree.
                                    [*A long flourish.*]
Draw near,
And list what with our Council we have done:
For that our kingdom's earth should not be soil'd 125
With that dear blood which it hath fostered;
And for our eyes do hate the dire aspect
Of civil wounds plough'd up with neighbors' sword;
And for we think the eagle-winged pride

Of sky-aspiring and ambitious thoughts, 130
With rival-hating envy, set on you
To wake our peace, which in our country's cradle
Draws the sweet infant breath of gentle sleep;
Which so rous'd up with boist'rous untun'd drums,
With harsh-resounding trumpets' dreadful bray, 135
And grating shock of wrathful iron arms,
Might from our quiet confines fright fair peace,
And make us wade even in our kinred's blood:
Therefore we banish you our territories.
You, cousin Herford, upon pain of life, 140
Till twice five summers have enrich'd our fields
Shall not regreet our fair dominions,
But tread the stranger paths of banishment.

Bull. Your will be done. This must my comfort be,
That sun that warms you here shall shine on me, 145
And those his golden beams to you here lent
Shall point on me and gild my banishment.

K. Rich. Norfolk, for thee remains a heavier doom,
Which I with some unwillingness pronounce:
The sly, slow hours shall not determinate 150
The dateless limit of thy dear exile;
The hopeless word of "never to return"
Breathe I against thee, upon pain of life.

Mow. A heavy sentence, my most sovereign liege,
And all unlook'd for from your Highness' mouth. 155
A dearer merit, not so deep a maim
As to be cast forth in the common air,
Have I deserved at your Highness' hands.
The language I have learnt these forty years,
My native English, now I must forgo, 160
And now my tongue's use is to me no more
Than an unstringed viol or a harp,
Or like a cunning instrument cas'd up,
Or being open, put into his hands
That knows no touch to tune the harmony. 165
Within my mouth you have enjail'd my tongue,
Doubly portcullis'd with my teeth and lips,
And dull unfeeling barren ignorance
Is made my jailer to attend on me.
I am too old to fawn upon a nurse, 170
Too far in years to be a pupil now.
What is thy sentence [then] but speechless death,
Which robs my tongue from breathing native breath?

K. Rich. It boots thee not to be compassionate,
After our sentence plaining comes too late. 175

Mow. Then thus I turn me from my country's
light,
To dwell in solemn shades of endless night.

---

84. **Saint George:** patron saint of England.
95. **jest:** take part in a masque.
97. **securely:** confidently (modifies *couched* in line 98).
98. **couched:** expressed.   112. **approve:** prove.
116. **Attending:** awaiting.
118. **warder:** baton (which Richard held as umpire of the trial by combat).
121. **Withdraw with us.** Addressed to members of the council.
122. **While we return:** until we inform.   s.d. **A long flourish:** an extended trumpet call (to suggest the passage of time). Holinshed records (Bullough, III, 393) that the combatants waited "two long houres" while Richard and his council discussed the situation.
125. **For that:** in order that.   127. **for:** because.
129-38. **And . . . blood.** There is some confusion in this passage (in

which the *peace* of line 132 frights the *fair peace* of line 137). Kittredge paraphrases it thus: "And this disturbance of the King's peace might drive peace out of the realm."
131. **envy:** enmity.   **set on you:** set you on.
138. **kinred's:** kindred's.   143. **stranger:** alien.
150. **determinate:** bring to an end.
151. **dateless limit:** limitless term.   **dear:** grievous.
155. **unlook'd for.** According to Holinshed (Bullough, III, 394), Mowbray hoped "that he shoulde have beene borne out in the matter by the king, which when it fell out otherwise, it greeved him not a little."
156. **dearer merit:** more valued reward.
163. **cunning:** skillfully made.   164. **open:** uncased.
173. **Which:** i.e. the sentence.
174. **boots:** helps.   **compassionate:** self-pitying.
175. **plaining:** complaining.

K. Rich.   Return again, and take an oath with thee.
Lay on our royal sword your banish'd hands;
Swear by the duty that y' owe to God   180
(Our part therein we banish with yourselves)
To keep the oath that we administer:
You never shall, so help you truth and God,
Embrace each other's love in banishment,
Nor never look upon each other's face,   185
Nor never write, regreet, nor reconcile
This low'ring tempest of your home-bred hate,
Nor never by advised purpose meet
To plot, contrive, or complot any ill
'Gainst us, our state, our subjects, or our land.   190
    Bull.   I swear.
    Mow.   And I, to keep all this.
    Bull.   Norfolk, so fare as to mine enemy:
By this time, had the King permitted us,
One of our souls had wand'red in the air,   195
Banish'd this frail sepulchre of our flesh,
As now our flesh is banish'd from this land;
Confess thy treasons ere thou fly the realm;
Since thou hast far to go, bear not along
The clogging burthen of a guilty soul.   200
    Mow.   No, Bullingbrook, if ever I were traitor,
My name be blotted from the book of life,
And I from heaven banish'd as from hence!
But what thou art, God, thou, and I do know,
And all too soon, I fear, the King shall rue.   205
Farewell, my liege, now no way can I stray;
Save back to England, all the world's my way.   Exit.
    K. Rich.   Uncle, even in the glasses of thine eyes
I see thy grieved heart. Thy sad aspect
Hath from the number of his banish'd years   210
Pluck'd four away. [To Bullingbrook.] Six frozen win-
        ters spent,
Return with welcome home from banishment.
    Bull.   How long a time lies in one little word!
Four lagging winters and four wanton springs
End in a word: such is the breath of kings.   215
    Gaunt.   I thank my liege that in regard of me
He shortens four years of my son's exile,
But little vantage shall I reap thereby;
For ere the six years that he hath to spend   219
Can change their moons and bring their times about,
My oil-dried lamp and time-bewasted light
Shall be extinct with age and endless [night];
My inch of taper will be burnt and done,
And blindfold Death not let me see my son.   224
    K. Rich.   Why, uncle, thou hast many years to live.
    Gaunt.   But not a minute, King, that thou canst give.
Shorten my days thou canst with sullen sorrow,
And pluck nights from me, but not lend a morrow;
Thou canst help time to furrow me with age,

But stop no wrinkle in his pilgrimage;   230
Thy word is current with him for my death,
But dead, thy kingdom cannot buy my breath.
    K. Rich.   Thy son is banish'd upon good advice,
Whereto thy tongue a party-verdict gave.
Why at our justice seem'st thou then to low'r?   235
    Gaunt.   Things sweet to taste prove in digestion
        sour.
You urg'd me as a judge, but I had rather
You would have bid me argue like a father.
O, had't been a stranger, not my child,
To smooth his fault I should have been more mild.
A partial slander sought I to avoid,   241
And in the sentence my own life destroyed.
Alas, I look'd when some of you should say
I was too strict to make mine own away;
But you gave leave to my unwilling tongue   245
Against my will to do myself this wrong.
    K. Rich.   Cousin, farewell; and, uncle, bid him so.
Six years we banish him, and he shall go.
        [Flourish.] Exit [with his Train].
    Aum.   Cousin, farewell! What presence must not
        know,
From where you do remain let paper show.   250
    Mar.   My lord, no leave take I, for I will ride,
As far as land will let me, by your side.
    Gaunt.   O, to what purpose dost thou hoard thy
        words,
That thou returnest no greeting to thy friends?
    Bull.   I have too few to take my leave of you,   255
When the tongue's office should be prodigal
To breathe the abundant dolor of the heart.
    Gaunt.   Thy grief is but thy absence for a time.
    Bull.   Joy absent, grief is present for that time.   259
    Gaunt.   What is six winters? they are quickly gone.
    Bull.   To men in joy, but grief makes one hour ten.
    Gaunt.   Call it a travel that thou tak'st for pleasure.
    Bull.   My heart will sigh when I miscall it so,
Which finds it an enforced pilgrimage.
    Gaunt.   The sullen passage of thy weary steps   265
Esteem as foil wherein thou art to set
The precious jewel of thy home return.
    Bull.   Nay rather, every tedious stride I make
Will but remember me what a deal of world
I wander from the jewels that I love.   270
Must I not serve a long apprenticehood
To foreign passages, and in the end,
Having my freedom, boast of nothing else
But that I was a journeyman to grief?
    Gaunt.   All places that the eye of heaven visits   275
Are to a wise man ports and happy havens.

181. Our part therein: i.e. your duty to me as king.
193. as . . . enemy: as I would wish my enemy to fare.
206. stray: take the wrong road.   208. glasses: mirrors.
209–11. Thy . . . away. According to Holinshed (Bullough, III, 394), Bullingbrook "tooke his leave of the king at Eltham [a castle near London], who there released foure yeares of his banishment." Froissart (Bullough, III, 426) says that the King reduced Bulling-brook's sentence "to please the people withall."
216. regard: consideration.   218. vantage: profit, advantage.
222. extinct: extinguished.

231. current: authoritative, decisive.
234. thy . . . gave: i.e. you concurred in the verdict of the council.
240. smooth: extenuate.
241. A partial slander: the reproach of being partial (to my own son).
243. look'd when: expected that.
244. to . . . away: in making away with my own son.
249. What . . . know: i.e. that which I will be unable to learn from personal contact.   256. office: duty.
266. foil: thin metal leaf set behind a jewel to enhance its brilliance.
269. remember: remind.
271–74. Must . . . grief: i.e. having served my apprenticeship as an exile and thus earned my privileges (freedom), must I remain a journey-man (one who works for daily wages under a master) to grief and know only how to suffer.

Richard II
I.iii

Teach thy necessity to reason thus:
There is no virtue like necessity.
Think not the King did banish thee,
But thou the King. Woe doth the heavier sit   280
Where it perceives it is but faintly borne.
Go, say I sent thee forth to purchase honor,
And not the King exil'd thee; or suppose
Devouring pestilence hangs in our air,
And thou art flying to a fresher clime.   285
Look what thy soul holds dear, imagine it
To lie that way thou goest, not whence thou com'st.
Suppose the singing birds musicians,
The grass whereon thou tread'st the presence strow'd,
The flowers fair ladies, and thy steps no more   290
Than a delightful measure or a dance,
For gnarling sorrow hath less power to bite
The man that mocks at it and sets it light.
    Bull. O, who can hold a fire in his hand
By thinking on the frosty Caucasus?   295
Or cloy the hungry edge of appetite
By bare imagination of a feast?
Or wallow naked in December snow
By thinking on fantastic summer's heat?
O no, the apprehension of the good   300
Gives but the greater feeling to the worse.
Fell Sorrow's tooth doth never rankle more
Than when he bites, but lanceth not the sore.
    Gaunt. Come, come, my son, I'll bring thee on thy
            way;
Had I thy youth and cause, I would not stay.   305
    Bull. Then England's ground, farewell, sweet soil,
            adieu;
My mother, and my nurse, that bears me yet!
Where e'er I wander, boast of this I can,
Though banish'd, yet a true-born Englishman. *Exeunt.*

[SCENE IV]

Enter the KING *with* [GREEN *and* BAGOT] *at one door
and the* LORD AUMERLE *at another.*

    K. Rich. We did observe. Cousin Aumerle,
How far brought you high Herford on his way?
    Aum. I brought high Herford, if you call him so,
But to the next high way, and there I left him.
    K. Rich. And say, what store of parting tears were
            shed?   5
    Aum. Faith, none for me, except the northeast
            wind,
Which then blew bitterly against our faces,
Awak'd the sleeping rheum, and so by chance
Did grace our hollow parting with a tear.

    K. Rich. What said our cousin when you parted
            with him?   10
    Aum. "Farewell!"
And for my heart disdained that my tongue
Should so profane the word, that taught me craft
To counterfeit oppression of such grief
That words seem'd buried in my sorrow's grave.   15
Marry, would the word "farewell" have length'ned
            hours
And added years to his short banishment,
He should have had a volume of farewells;
But since it would not, he had none of me.   19
    K. Rich. He is our cousin's cousin, but 'tis doubt,
When time shall call him home from banishment,
Whether our kinsman come to see his friends.
Ourself and Bushy, [Bagot here and Green,]
Observ'd his courtship to the common people,
How he did seem to dive into their hearts   25
With humble and familiar courtesy,
What reverence he did throw away on slaves,
Wooing poor craftsmen with the craft of smiles
And patient underbearing of his fortune,
As 'twere to banish their affects with him.   30
Off goes his bonnet to an oyster-wench,
A brace of draymen bid God speed him well,
And had the tribute of his supple knee,
With "Thanks, my countrymen, my loving friends,"
As were our England in reversion his,   35
And he our subjects' next degree in hope.
    Green. Well, he is gone, and with him go these
            thoughts.
Now for the rebels which stand out in Ireland,
Expedient manage must be made, my liege,
Ere further leisure yield them further means   40
For their advantage and your Highness' loss.
    K. Rich. We will ourself in person to this war,
And for our coffers, with too great a court
And liberal largess, are grown somewhat light,
We are enforc'd to farm our royal realm,   45
The revenue whereof shall furnish us
For our affairs in hand. If that come short,
Our substitutes at home shall have blank charters,
Whereto, when they shall know what men are rich,
They shall subscribe them for large sums of gold,   50

281. **faintly**: faintheartedly.   282. **purchase**: acquire.
289. **the presence strow'd**: the royal presence-chamber strewed with
rushes.   291. **measure**: stately dance.
292. **gnarling**: snarling.   299. **fantastic**: imaginary.
303. **lanceth**: probes and opens (in order to afford relief).
304. **bring**: escort.   305. **stay**: linger.

I.iv. Location: London. The palace.
1. **We did observe.** As he enters, the King replies to a remark (probably about Bullingbrook's popularity with the "common people":
see lines 23 ff.) made by Bagot or Green.
6. **for me**: on my part.   8. **rheum**: moisture, i.e. tears.

12. **for**: because.   13. **that**: i.e. my disdain.
16. **Marry**: indeed (originally the name of the Virgin Mary used as
an oath).
20. **cousin's cousin.** Richard, Aumerle, and Bullingbrook, the sons
of three brothers, were cousins.
23–36. **Ourself . . . hope.** Holinshed (Bullough, III, 394) records of
Bullingbrook's departure that "a woonder it was to see what a
number of people ran after him in everie towne and street where he
came, before he tooke the sea, lamenting and bewailing his departure,
as who would saie, that when he departed, the onelie shield, defense,
and comfort of the commonwealth was vaded and gone."
29. **underbearing**: endurance.   30. **affects**: affections.
35. **in reversion**: by right of legal succession.
36. **next . . . hope**: i.e. heir presumptive to the throne.
38. **stand out**: rise in insurrection.
39. **Expedient manage**: swift handling (to cope with them).
42. **to**: go to.   45. **farm**: lease the revenues of.
48. **substitutes**: deputies.   **charters**: writs authorizing the collection
of revenues by agents of the king. These charters, says Holinshed
(Bullough, III, 394), produced "great grudge and murmuring" because "the kings officers wrote in the same what liked them [what
they pleased], as well for charging the parties with paiment of monie,
as otherwise."

[625–666]   [667–715]

II.i

And send them after to supply our wants,
For we will make for Ireland presently.

        Enter BUSHY.

[Bushy, what news?]
  Bushy. Old John of Gaunt is grievous sick, my
      lord,
Suddenly taken, and hath sent post-haste   55
To entreat your Majesty to visit him.
  K. Rich. Where lies he?
  Bushy. At Ely House.
  K. Rich. Now put it, God, in the physician's mind
To help him to his grave immediately!   60
The lining of his coffers shall make coats
To deck our soldiers for these Irish wars.
Come, gentlemen, let's all go visit him.
Pray God we may make haste and come too late!
  [*All.*] Amen.   *Exeunt.* 65

[ACT II, SCENE I]

Enter JOHN OF GAUNT, *sick, with the* DUKE OF YORK, *etc.*

  Gaunt. Will the King come, that I may breathe my
      last
In wholesome counsel to his unstayed youth?
  York. Vex not yourself, nor strive not with your
      breath,
For all in vain comes counsel to his ear.   4
  Gaunt. O but they say the tongues of dying men
Enforce attention like deep harmony.
Where words are scarce, they are seldom spent in vain,
For they breathe truth that breathe their words in pain.
He that no more must say is listened more   9
Than they whom youth and ease have taught to glose.
More are men's ends mark'd than their lives before.
The setting sun, and music at the close,
As the last taste of sweets, is sweetest last,
Writ in remembrance more than things long past.
Though Richard my live's counsel would not hear, 15
My death's sad tale may yet undeaf his ear.
  York. No, it is stopp'd with other flattering sounds,
As praises, of whose taste the wise are [fond],
Lascivious metres, to whose venom sound
The open ear of youth doth always listen;   20
Report of fashions in proud Italy,
Whose manners still our tardy, apish nation
Limps after in base imitation.
Where doth the world thrust forth a vanity—
So it be new, there's no respect how vile—   25

That is not quickly buzz'd into his ears?
Then all too late comes counsel to be heard,
Where will doth mutiny with wit's regard.
Direct not him whose way himself will choose,
'Tis breath thou lack'st, and that breath wilt thou lose.
  Gaunt. Methinks I am a prophet new inspir'd,   31
And thus expiring do foretell of him:
His rash fierce blaze of riot cannot last,
For violent fires soon burn out themselves;
Small show'rs last long, but sudden storms are short; 35
He tires betimes that spurs too fast betimes;
With eager feeding food doth choke the feeder;
Light vanity, insatiate cormorant,
Consuming means, soon preys upon itself.
This royal throne of kings, this sceptred isle,   40
This earth of majesty, this seat of Mars,
This other Eden, demi-paradise,
This fortress built by Nature for herself
Against infection and the hand of war,
This happy breed of men, this little world,   45
This precious stone set in the silver sea,
Which serves it in the office of a wall,
Or as [a] moat defensive to a house,
Against the envy of less happier lands;
This blessed plot, this earth, this realm, this England,
This nurse, this teeming womb of royal kings,   51
Fear'd by their breed, and famous by their birth,
Renowned for their deeds as far from home,
For Christian service and true chivalry,
As is the sepulchre in stubborn Jewry   55
Of the world's ransom, blessed Mary's Son;
This land of such dear souls, this dear dear land,
Dear for her reputation through the world,
Is now leas'd out—I die pronouncing it—
Like to a tenement or pelting farm.   60
England, bound in with the triumphant sea,
Whose rocky shore beats back the envious siege
Of wat'ry Neptune, is now bound in with shame,
With inky blots and rotten parchment bonds;
That England, that was wont to conquer others,   65
Hath made a shameful conquest of itself.
Ah, would the scandal vanish with my life,
How happy then were my ensuing death!

Enter KING *and* QUEEN, *etc.* [AUMERLE, BUSHY,
    GREEN, BAGOT, ROSS, *and* WILLOUGHBY].

  York. The King is come. Deal mildly with his
      youth,
For young hot colts being rag'd do rage the more. 70
  Queen. How fares our noble uncle Lancaster?
  K. Rich. What comfort, man? how is't with aged
      Gaunt?

---

52. presently: immediately.
58. Ely House: the Bishop of Ely's residence in Holborn, a district
north of St. Paul's Cathedral.
61. lining of his coffers: i.e. his treasure. **coats:** coats of mail, armor.

II.i. Location: London. Ely House.
2. unstayed: (1) unsupported (by wise counsellors); (2) unchecked.
10. glose: talk glibly, flatter. **12. close:** harmonic close, cadence.
15. my live's counsel: my advice while I lived.
16. My . . . tale: the grave words that I speak while dying. **undeaf.**
One of several such negative words in the play. See *unhappied* (III.i.
10), *uncurse* (III.ii.137), *unsay* (IV.i.9), *undo* (IV.i.203), *unking* (IV.
i.220, V.v.37), *undeck* (IV.i.250), *unkiss* (V.i.74).
21. proud: splendid, lavish.
22. still: always. **apish:** imitative.
25. there's no respect: it makes no difference.

28. will . . . regard: inclination rebels against judgment.
33. riot: dissipation. **36. betimes:** early.
38. Light vanity: heedless extravagance. **cormorant:** voracious bird
of prey; here, a glutton. **39. means:** i.e. means of sustaining life.
42. demi-paradise: little paradise.
44. infection: (1) pestilence; (2) moral contamination.
47. office: function.
52. Fear'd . . . breed: i.e. held in awe for their hereditary valor.
55. Jewry: Judea.
60. tenement: property held by a tenant. **pelting:** paltry.
64. bonds: i.e. the "blank charters" of I.iv.47–51.
70. rag'd: enraged through rough treatment (?).

Richard II
II.i

Gaunt. O how that name befits my composition!
Old Gaunt indeed, and gaunt in being old.
Within me grief hath kept a tedious fast;   75
And who abstains from meat that is not gaunt?
For sleeping England long time have I watch'd,
Watching breeds leanness, leanness is all gaunt.
The pleasure that some fathers feed upon
Is my strict fast—I mean, my children's looks;   80
And therein fasting, hast thou made me gaunt.
Gaunt am I for the grave, gaunt as a grave,
Whose hollow womb inherits nought but bones.
    K. Rich. Can sick men play so nicely with their
    names?
    Gaunt. No, misery makes sport to mock itself: 85
Since thou dost seek to kill my name in me,
I mock my name, great King, to flatter thee.
    K. Rich. Should dying men flatter with those that
    live?
    Gaunt. No, no, men living flatter those that die.
    K. Rich. Thou, now a-dying, sayest thou flatterest
    me.   90
    Gaunt. O no, thou diest, though I the sicker be.
    K. Rich. I am in health, I breathe, and see thee ill.
    Gaunt. Now He that made me knows I see thee ill,
Ill in myself to see, and in thee, seeing ill.
Thy death-bed is no lesser than thy land,   95
Wherein thou liest in reputation sick,
And thou, too careless patient as thou art,
Commit'st thy anointed body to the cure
Of those physicians that first wounded thee.
A thousand flatterers sit within thy crown,   100
Whose compass is no bigger than thy head,
And yet, [incaged] in so small a verge,
The waste is no whit lesser than thy land.
O had thy grandsire with a prophet's eye
Seen how his son's son should destroy his sons,   105
From forth thy reach he would have laid thy shame,
Deposing thee before thou wert possess'd,
Which art possess'd now to depose thyself.
Why, cousin, wert thou regent of the world,
It were a shame to let this land by lease;   110
But for thy world enjoying but this land,
Is it not more than shame to shame it so?
Landlord of England art thou now, not king,
Thy state of law is bond-slave to the law,
And thou—
    K. Rich. A lunatic lean-witted fool,   115
Presuming on an ague's privilege,
Darest with thy frozen admonition
Make pale our cheek, chasing the royal blood
With fury from his native residence.

Now by my seat's right royal majesty,   120
Wert thou not brother to great Edward's son,
This tongue that runs so roundly in thy head
Should run thy head from thy unreverent shoulders.
    Gaunt. O, spare me not, my [brother] Edward's
    son,
For that I was his father Edward's son,   125
That blood already, like the pelican,
Hast thou tapp'd out and drunkenly carous'd.
My brother Gloucester, plain well-meaning soul,
Whom fair befall in heaven 'mongst happy souls,
May be a president and witness good   130
That thou respect'st not spilling Edward's blood.
Join with the present sickness that I have,
And thy unkindness be like crooked age,
To crop at once a too long withered flower.
Live in thy shame, but die not shame with thee!   135
These words hereafter thy tormentors be!
Convey me to my bed, then to my grave;
Love they to live that love and honor have.
          Exit [borne off by his Attendants].
    K. Rich. And let them die that age and sullens
    have,
For both hast thou, and both become the grave.   140
    York. I do beseech your Majesty, impute his words
To wayward sickliness and age in him.
He loves you, on my life, and holds you dear
As Harry Duke of Herford, were he here.
    K. Rich. Right, you say true: as Herford's love, so
    his,   145
As theirs, so mine, and all be as it is.

          [*Enter* NORTHUMBERLAND.]

    North. My liege, old Gaunt commends him to your
Majesty.
    K. Rich. What says he?
    North.   Nay, nothing, all is said.
His tongue is now a stringless instrument,
Words, life, and all, old Lancaster hath spent.   150
    York. Be York the next that must be bankrout so!
Though death be poor, it ends a mortal woe.
    K. Rich. The ripest fruit first falls, and so doth he;
His time is spent, our pilgrimage must be.
So much for that. Now for our Irish wars: 155
We must supplant those rough rug-headed kerns,
Which live like venom where no venom else
But only they have privilege to live.
And, for these great affairs do ask some charge,
Towards our assistance we do seize to us   160
The plate, coin, revenues, and moveables

---

73. **composition:** condition, constitution.
77. **watch'd:** stayed awake.   83. **inherits:** possesses.
84. **nicely:** (1) subtly; (2) trivially.
86. **kill my name:** i.e. by banishing Bullingbrook, my heir.
99. **physicians:** i.e. the King's dissolute favorites.
102. **verge:** (1) rim of the crown; (2) distance of twelve miles from
wherever the king happened to be.   104. **grandsire:** i.e. Edward III.
107. **possess'd:** put in possession of the crown.
108. **possess'd:** seized by an evil spirit, therefore mad.
109. **regent:** ruler.   111. **world:** domain.
114. **Thy . . . the law:** i.e. your legal status is no longer that of a ruler
by divine right but that of a subject under law.
117. **frozen:** (1) stylistically inept; (2) caused by a chill or ague.

120. **seat's:** throne's.   122. **roundly:** freely and bluntly.
125. **For that:** because.
126. **pelican.** Popularly thought to feed its young with blood from
its own bosom.
127. **tapp'd out:** i.e. in the murder of Gloucester.   **carous'd:** drunk
in gulps.   129. **Whom fair befall:** to whom good fortune.
130. **president:** precedent, example.
131. **respect'st not:** hast no scruples in.
139. **sullens:** sulks.   140. **become:** are appropriate for.
151. **bankrout:** bankrupt.
156. **supplant:** expel.   **kerns:** light-armed Irish foot-soldiers.
157–58. **where . . . live.** An allusion to St. Patrick's allegedly banishing all snakes from Ireland.   **venom:** venomous snakes.
159. **for:** because.   **do . . . charge:** require some outlay, i.e. are expensive.   161. **moveables:** personal property.

Whereof our uncle Gaunt did stand possess'd.

York. How long shall I be patient? ah, how long
Shall tender duty make me suffer wrong? **164**
Not Gloucester's death, nor Herford's banishment,
Not Gaunt's rebukes, nor England's private wrongs,
Nor the prevention of poor Bullingbrook
About his marriage, nor my own disgrace,
Have ever made me sour my patient cheek,
Or bend one wrinkle on my sovereign's face. **170**
I am the last of noble Edward's sons,
Of whom thy father, Prince of Wales, was first.
In war was never lion rag'd more fierce,
In peace was never gentle lamb more mild,
Than was that young and princely gentleman. **175**
His face thou hast, for even so look'd he,
Accomplish'd with [the] number of thy hours;
But when he frowned it was against the French,
And not against his friends. His noble hand
Did win what he did spend, and spent not that **180**
Which his triumphant father's hand had won.
His hands were guilty of no kinred blood,
But bloody with the enemies of his kin.
O Richard! York is too far gone with grief,
Or else he never would compare between. **185**

K. Rich. Why, uncle, what's the matter?
York.   O my liege,
Pardon me, if you please; if not, I, pleas'd
Not to be pardoned, am content withal.
Seek you to seize and gripe into your hands
The royalties and rights of banish'd Herford? **190**
Is not Gaunt dead? and doth not Herford live?
Was not Gaunt just? and is not Harry true?
Did not the one deserve to have an heir?
Is not his heir a well-deserving son?
Take Herford's rights away, and take from Time **195**
His charters and his customary rights;
Let not to-morrow then ensue to-day;
Be not thyself; for how art thou a king
But by fair sequence and succession?
Now afore God—God forbid I say true!— **200**
If you do wrongfully seize Herford's rights,
Call in the letters-patents that he hath
By his attorneys-general to sue
His livery, and deny his off'red homage,
You pluck a thousand dangers on your head, **205**
You lose a thousand well-disposed hearts,

And prick my tender patience to those thoughts
Which honor and allegiance cannot think.
K. Rich. Think what you will, we seize into our
hands
His plate, his goods, his money, and his lands. **210**
York. I'll not be by the while. My liege, farewell!
What will ensue hereof, there's none can tell;
But by bad courses may be understood
That their events can never fall out good. *Exit.*
K. Rich. Go, Bushy, to the Earl of Wiltshire
straight, **215**
Bid him repair to us to Ely House
To see this business. To-morrow next
We will for Ireland, and 'tis time, I trow.
And we create, in absence of ourself,
Our uncle York lord governor of England; **220**
For he is just and always loved us well.
Come on, our queen, to-morrow must we part.
Be merry, for our time of stay is short.
[*Flourish.*] *Exeunt King and Queen* [*with others*].
Manet Northumberland [*with Willoughby and
Ross*].
North. Well, lords, the Duke of Lancaster is dead.
Ross. And living too, for now his son is Duke.
Willo. Barely in title, not in revenues. **226**
North. Richly in both, if justice had her right.
Ross. My heart is great, but it must break with
silence,
Ere't be disburdened with a liberal tongue.
North. Nay, speak thy mind, and let him ne'er
speak more **230**
That speaks thy words again to do thee harm!
Willo. Tends that thou wouldst speak to the Duke
of Herford?
If it be so, out with it boldly, man,
Quick is mine ear to hear of good towards him.
Ross. No good at all that I can do for him, **235**
Unless you call it good to pity him,
Bereft and gelded of his patrimony.
North. Now, afore God, 'tis shame such wrongs
are borne
In him, a royal prince, and many moe
Of noble blood in this declining land. **240**
The King is not himself, but basely led
By flatterers, and what they will inform,
Merely in hate, 'gainst any of us all,
That will the King severely prosecute
'Gainst us, our lives, our children, and our heirs. **245**
Ross. The commons hath he pill'd with grievous
taxes,
And quite lost their hearts; the nobles hath he fin'd
For ancient quarrels, and quite lost their hearts.
Willo. And daily new exactions are devis'd,

164. tender duty: scrupulous regard (for the King).
166. Gaunt's rebukes: i.e. Richard's rebukes to Gaunt.
167–68. prevention . . . marriage. Richard had blocked Bullingbrook's projected match with the Duc de Berri's daughter, a cousin of Charles VI of France.
170. bend one wrinkle: i.e. frown in the slightest degree.
172. Prince of Wales: Edward the Black Prince, eldest son of Edward III. **173. rag'd more fierce:** more fiercely enraged.
177. Accomplish'd . . . hours: at your age.
182. kinred blood: blood of his kindred.
190. royalties: privileges and perquisites granted by the king (through the "letters-patents" of line 202).
195–96. Take . . . rights: i.e. if you deprive Herford of his inheritance you flout the ancient law of succession, by which "customary rights" descend from father to son. **197. ensue:** follow.
202–4. Call . . . livery: i.e. revoke the royal grant that enables him to bring suit through his attorneys for possession of his hereditary rights.
204. deny . . . homage: i.e. refuse the ceremony of swearing allegiance as required by law for a legatee to secure his inheritance.
205. pluck: pull down.

214. events: results.
215. Earl of Wiltshire: William le Scrope or Scroop, treasurer of the realm and one of the King's notorious favorites. See note to III.ii.122–23.
217. see: see to, superintend. **To-morrow next:** to-morrow.
218. will: will set forth. **trow:** believe. **228. great:** i.e. heavy.
232. Tends . . . speak: does what you want to say concern.
239. moe: more. **243. Merely in hate:** out of pure hatred.
246. pill'd: peeled, stripped bare.

Richard II   As blanks, benevolences, and I wot not what.   250
II.i   But what a' God's name doth become of this?
             North.   Wars hath not wasted it, for warr'd he hath
                   not,
             But basely yielded upon compromise
             That which his noble ancestors achiev'd with blows.
             More hath he spent in peace than they in wars.   255
             Ross.   The Earl of Wiltshire hath the realm in farm.
             Willo.   The [King's] grown bankrout, like a broken
                   man.
             North.   Reproach and dissolution hangeth over him.
             Ross.   He hath not money for these Irish wars,
             His burthenous taxations notwithstanding,   260
             But by the robbing of the banish'd Duke.
             North.   His noble kinsman—most degenerate king!
             But, lords, we hear this fearful tempest sing,
             Yet seek no shelter to avoid the storm;
             We see the wind sit sore upon our sails,   265
             And yet we strike not, but securely perish.
             Ross.   We see the very wrack that we must suffer,
             And unavoided is the danger now,
             For suffering so the causes of our wrack.
             North.   Not so, even through the hollow eyes of
                   death   270
             I spy life peering, but I dare not say
             How near the tidings of our comfort is.
             Willo.   Nay, let us share thy thoughts, as thou dost
                   ours.
             Ross.   Be confident to speak, Northumberland:
             We three are but thyself, and, speaking so,   275
             Thy words are but as thoughts, therefore be bold.
             North.   Then thus: I have from Le Port Blanc,
             A bay in Britain, receiv'd intelligence
             That Harry Duke of Herford, Rainold Lord Cobham,
             [Thomas, son and heir to th' Earl of Arundel,]   280
             That late broke from the Duke of Exeter,
             His brother, Archbishop late of Canterbury,
             Sir Thomas Erpingham, Sir John Ramston,
             Sir John Norbery, Sir Robert Waterton, and Francis
                   [Coint]—
             All these, well furnished by the Duke of Britain   285
             With eight tall ships, three thousand men of war,

             Are making hither with all due expedience,
             And shortly mean to touch our northern shore.
             Perhaps they had ere this, but that they stay
             The first departing of the King for Ireland.   290
             If then we shall shake off our slavish yoke,
             Imp out our drooping country's broken wing,
             Redeem from broking pawn the blemish'd crown,
             Wipe off the dust that hides our sceptre's gilt,
             And make high majesty look like itself,   295
             Away with me in post to Ravenspurgh;
             But if you faint, as fearing to do so,
             Stay, and be secret, and myself will go.
             Ross.   To horse, to horse! urge doubts to them that
                   fear.   299
             Willo.   Hold out my horse, and I will first be there.
                                                           Exeunt.

                         [SCENE II]

                   Enter the QUEEN, BUSHY, BAGOT.

             Bushy.   Madam, your Majesty is too much sad.
             You promis'd, when you parted with the King,
             To lay aside life-harming heaviness
             And entertain a cheerful disposition.
             Queen.   To please the King I did, to please myself
             I cannot do it; yet I know no cause   6
             Why I should welcome such a guest as grief,
             Save bidding farewell to so sweet a guest
             As my sweet Richard. Yet again methinks
             Some unborn sorrow, ripe in fortune's womb,   10
             Is coming towards me, and my inward soul
             With nothing trembles; at some thing it grieves,
             More than with parting from my lord the King.
             Bushy.   Each substance of a grief hath twenty
                   shadows,
             Which shows like grief itself, but is not so;   15
             For sorrow's eyes, glazed with blinding tears,
             Divides one thing entire to many objects,
             Like perspectives, which rightly gaz'd upon
             Show nothing but confusion; ey'd awry
             Distinguish form; so your sweet Majesty,   20
             Looking awry upon your lord's departure,
             Find shapes of grief, more than himself, to wail,
             Which, look'd on as it is, is nought but shadows
             Of what it is not; then, thrice-gracious Queen,
             More than your lord's departure weep not—more is
                   not seen,   25

---

250. **blanks:** i.e. the "blank charters" of I.iv.47–51. **benevolences:**
forced loans levied with legal authority by the king. This allusion is
anachronistic, for they were first employed by Edward IV in 1473.
wot: know. 251. **a':** in. **this:** i.e. the money illegally collected.
256. **in farm:** on lease.
266. **strike:** (1) lower the sails; (2) strike a blow. **securely:** heedlessly, overconfidently. 268. **unavoided:** unavoidable.
269. **For suffering so:** as a result of permitting.
270. **eyes of death:** eye-sockets of a skull. 278. **Britain:** Brittany.
281. **broke from:** escaped from the custody of.
282. **His:** i.e. the Earl of Arundel's. **late:** until recently.
285–90. **All . . . Ireland.** Holinshed's account of Bullingbrook's expedition (Bullough, III, 397)—which, as the list of names in lines
279–84 indicates, Shakespeare had before him as he wrote—is somewhat less assured. Whereas some sources record that Bullingbrook
was supplied by the Duke of Brittany with three thousand men and
eight ships, Holinshed points out that "Froissard yet speaketh but of
three. Moreover, where *Froissard* and also the chronicles of Britaine
avouch, that he should land at Plimmouth, by our English writers it
seemeth otherwise: for it appeareth by their assured report, that he
approching to the shore, did not streight take land, but lay hovering
aloofe, and shewed himselfe now in this place, and now in that, to see
what countenance was made by the people, whether they meant
enviouslie to resist him, or freendlie to receive him." Henry actually
landed near Ravenspur (the Ravenspurgh of line 296), a village on
the Yorkshire coast, in July 1399. 286. **tall:** stately.

287. **expedience:** speed.
292. **Imp out:** graft new feathers on (a term from falconry).
293. **broking pawn:** i.e. pawnbrokers to whom the realm was pledged.
296. **post:** haste. 297. **faint:** are fainthearted.
300. **Hold . . . and:** if my horse holds out.

II.ii. Location: Windsor Castle.
o.s.d. **Queen.** Isabella, daughter of Charles VI of France, had become Richard's second wife in 1396, when she was seven. She was
therefore ten at the time represented in this scene.
3. **heaviness:** melancholy. 4. **entertain:** assume. 12. **With:** at.
14. **Each . . . shadows:** i.e. for each real grief there are twenty imaginary griefs.
16–20. **For . . . form.** Bushy somewhat confusingly compares the
Queen's tear-glazed eyes first (lines 16–17) to perspective glasses
whose multi-faceted lenses multiply a single object into various
images, and then (lines 18–20) to perspective pictures or figures that,
though seemingly distorted, present a normal appearance (*distinguish
form*) when viewed obliquely (*ey'd awry*).

Or if it be, 'tis with false sorrow's eye,
Which for things true weeps things imaginary.
   Queen.   It may be so; but yet my inward soul
Persuades me it is otherwise. Howe'er it be,
I cannot but be sad; so heavy sad,   30
As, [though] on thinking on no thought I think,
Makes me with heavy nothing faint and shrink.
   Bushy.   'Tis nothing but conceit, my gracious lady.
   Queen.   'Tis nothing less: conceit is still deriv'd
From some forefather grief; mine is not so,   35
For nothing hath begot my something grief,
Or something hath the nothing that I grieve—
'Tis in reversion that I do possess—
But what it is that is not yet known what,
I cannot name; 'tis nameless woe, I wot.   40

[Enter GREEN.]

   Green.   God save your Majesty! and well met,
          gentlemen.
I hope the King is not yet shipp'd for Ireland.
   Queen.   Why hopest thou so? 'Tis better hope he is,
For his designs crave haste, his haste good hope.
Then wherefore dost thou hope he is not shipp'd?   45
   Green.   That he, our hope, might have retir'd his
          power,
And driven into despair an enemy's hope,
Who strongly hath set footing in this land:
The banish'd Bullingbrook repeals himself,
And with uplifted arms is safe arriv'd   50
At Ravenspurgh.
   Queen.   Now God in heaven forbid!
   Green.   Ah, madam! 'tis too true, and that is worse,
The Lord Northumberland, his son young Harry
          Percy,
The Lords of Ross, Beaumond, and Willoughby,
With all their powerful friends, are fled to him.   55
   Bushy.   Why have you not proclaim'd Northumber-
          land
And all the rest revolted faction traitors?
   Green.   We have, whereupon the Earl of Worcester
Hath broken his staff, resign'd his stewardship,
And all the household servants fled with him   60
To Bullingbrook.
   Queen.   So, Green, thou art the midwife to my woe,
And Bullingbrook my sorrow's dismal heir.
Now hath my soul brought forth her prodigy,
And I, a gasping new-deliver'd mother,   65
Have woe to woe, sorrow to sorrow join'd.
   Bushy.   Despair not, madam.
   Queen.   Who shall hinder me?
I will despair, and be at enmity

With cozening hope. He is a flatterer,
A parasite, a keeper-back of death,   70
Who gently would dissolve the bands of life,
Which false hope lingers in extremity.

[Enter YORK.]

   Green.   Here comes the Duke of York.
   Queen.   With signs of war about his aged neck.
O, full of careful business are his looks!   75
Uncle, for God's sake speak comfortable words.
   York.   Should I do so, I should belie my thoughts.
Comfort's in heaven, and we are on the earth,
Where nothing lives but crosses, cares, and grief.
Your husband, he is gone to save far off,   80
Whilst others come to make him lose at home.
Here am I left to underprop his land,
Who, weak with age, cannot support myself.
Now comes the sick hour that his surfeit made,
Now shall he try his friends that flatter'd him.   85

[Enter a SERVINGMAN.]

   Serv.   My lord, your son was gone before I came.
   York.   He was—why, so go all which way it will!
The nobles they are fled, the commons they are cold,
And will, I fear, revolt on Herford's side.   89
Sirrah, get thee to Plashy, to my sister Gloucester,
Bid her send me presently a thousand pound.
Hold, take my ring.
   Serv.   My lord, I had forgot to tell your lordship:
To-day, as I came by, I called there—
But I shall grieve you to report the rest.   95
   York.   What is't, knave?
   Serv.   An hour before I came, the Duchess died.
   York.   God for his mercy, what a tide of woes
Comes rushing on this woeful land at once!
I know not what to do. I would to God   100
(So my untruth had not provok'd him to it)
The King had cut off my head with my brother's.
What, are there no posts dispatch'd for Ireland?
How shall we do for money for these wars?
Come, sister—cousin, I would say—pray pardon me.
Go, fellow, get thee home, provide some carts,   106
And bring away the armor that is there.
                              [Exit Servingman.]
Gentlemen, will you go muster men? If I
Know how or which way to order these affairs
Thus disorderly thrust into my hands,   110
Never believe me. Both are my kinsmen:
T' one is my sovereign, whom both my oath

---

33. **conceit:** imagination.
34. **'Tis nothing less:** i.e. it is anything but that.   **still:** always.
36. **something:** i.e. real, substantial.
38–40. **'Tis . . . name:** i.e. my grief is like my expectation of a legacy, the nature of which is as yet unknown.
38. **reversion:** legal right of future possession.
46. **retir'd his power:** drawn back his forces.
49. **repeals:** recalls (from exile).
50. **uplifted arms:** brandished weapons.   52. **that:** what.
57. **rest revolted faction:** rest of the rebellious clique.
59. **staff:** badge of office.   **stewardship.** In 1394 Northumberland's brother Thomas Percy, Earl of Worcester, had been appointed steward of the royal household, a post of great honor and importance.
63. **dismal heir:** ill-omened offspring.
64. **prodigy:** monstrous birth.

69. **cozening:** deceitful.   71. **bands:** bonds.
72. **Which . . . extremity:** i.e. the dissolving of "the bands of life" which false hope postpones, thus delaying the relief that death will bring.
74. **signs . . . neck.** Perhaps he wears a gorget, a piece of mail covering the throat.   75. **careful business:** anxious preoccupation.
76. **comfortable:** comforting.   79. **crosses:** vexations.
84. **surfeit:** dissipation.   85. **try:** test.
86. **son:** i.e. the Duke of Aumerle.
90. **Sirrah:** customary form of address to an inferior.
91. **presently:** immediately.
92. **take my ring:** i.e. as a sign that you are authorized by me.
96. **knave:** fellow.   101. **untruth:** disloyalty.
102. **brother's:** i.e. the Duke of Gloucester's.
105. **sister—cousin.** In his perturbation York momentarily confuses the Queen with the Duchess of Gloucester, who is uppermost in his mind.

Richard II
II.ii

And duty bids defend; t' other again
Is my kinsman, whom the King hath wrong'd,
Whom conscience and my kinred bids to right.   115
Well, somewhat we must do.
Come, cousin, I'll dispose of you.
Gentlemen, go muster up your men,
And meet me presently at Berkeley.
I should to Plashy too,   120
But time will not permit. All is uneven,
And every thing is left at six and seven.

*Exeunt Duke [of York], Queen. Manent Bushy,
Green, [Bagot].*

Bushy. The wind sits fair for news to go for
     Ireland,
But none returns. For us to levy power
Proportionable to the enemy   125
Is all unpossible.
Green. Besides, our nearness to the King in love
Is near the hate of those love not the King.
Bagot. And that is the wavering commons, for their
     love
Lies in their purses, and whoso empties them   130
By so much fills their hearts with deadly hate.
Bushy. Wherein the King stands generally con-
     demn'd.
Bagot. If judgment lie in them, then so do we,
Because we ever have been near the King.
Green. Well, I will for refuge straight to Bristow
     castle: 135
The Earl of Wiltshire is already there.
Bushy. Thither will I with you, for little office
Will the hateful commons perform for us,
Except like curs to tear us all to pieces.
Will you go along with us?   140
Bagot. No, I will to Ireland to his Majesty.
Farewell! If heart's presages be not vain,
We three here part that ne'er shall meet again.
Bushy. That's as York thrives to beat back
     Bullingbrook.
Green. Alas, poor duke, the task he undertakes
Is numb'ring sands and drinking oceans dry;   146
Where one on his side fights, thousands will fly.
Farewell at once, for once, for all, and ever.
Bushy. Well, we may meet again.
Bagot.   I fear me, never. [*Exeunt.*]

[SCENE III]

*Enter [*BULLINGBROOK, *Duke of*] *Herford,* NORTHUM-
BERLAND, [*and forces*].*

Bull. How far is it, my lord, to Berkeley now?
North. Believe me, noble lord,
I am a stranger here in Gloucestershire.
These high wild hills and rough uneven ways

Draws out our miles and makes them wearisome,   5
And yet your fair discourse hath been as sugar,
Making the hard way sweet and delectable.
But I bethink me what a weary way
From Ravenspurgh to Cotshall will be found
In Ross and Willoughby, wanting your company,   10
Which, I protest, hath very much beguil'd
The tediousness and process of my travel.
But theirs is sweet'ned with the hope to have
The present benefit which I possess,
And hope to joy is little less in joy   15
Than hope enjoyed. By this the weary lords
Shall make their way seem short, as mine hath done
By sight of what I have, your noble company.
Bull. Of much less value is my company
Than your good words. But who comes here?   20

Enter HARRY PERCY.

North. It is my son, young Harry Percy,
Sent from my brother Worcester, whencesoever.
Harry, how fares your uncle?
Percy. I had thought, my lord, to have learn'd his
     health of you.
North. Why, is he not with the Queen?   25
Percy. No, my good lord, he hath forsook the
     court,
Broken his staff of office, and dispers'd
The household of the King.
North.   What was his reason?
He was not so resolv'd when last we spake together.
Percy. Because your lordship was proclaimed
     traitor.   30
But he, my lord, is gone to Ravenspurgh
To offer service to the Duke of Herford,
And sent me over by Berkeley, to discover
What power the Duke of York had levied there,
Then with directions to repair to Ravenspurgh. 35
North. Have you forgot the Duke of [Herford],
     boy?
Percy. No, my good lord, for that is not forgot
Which ne'er I did remember. To my knowledge,
I never in my life did look on him.
North. Then learn to know him now, this is the
     Duke.   40
Percy. My gracious lord, I tender you my service,
Such as it is, being tender, raw, and young,
Which elder days shall ripen and confirm
To more approved service and desert.
Bull. I thank thee, gentle Percy, and be sure 45
I count myself in nothing else so happy
As in a soul rememb'ring my good friends,
And as my fortune ripens with thy love,
It shall be still thy true love's recompense.
My heart this covenant makes, my hand thus seals it. 50
North. How far is it to Berkeley? and what stir
Keeps good old York there with his men of war?

---

117. **dispose of:** make arrangements for.
119. **Berkeley:** castle between Bristol and Gloucester, the scene of
Edward II's murder in 1327.   124. **power:** forces.
128. **Is near:** involves.   **those:** those who.
133. **If . . . we:** if the power to pass judgment is lodged in them, then
we too stand condemned.   137. **office:** service.
138. **hateful:** full of hatred, i.e. hostile.

818   II.iii. Location: Wilds in Gloucestershire.

9. **Cotshall:** Cotswold, a range of hills in Gloucestershire.
10. **wanting:** lacking.   12. **tediousness and process:** tedious course.
16. **this:** i.e. the expectation of enjoying Bullingbrook's company.
21. **young Harry Percy.** Actually, young Percy—the Hotspur of
1 Henry IV—was thirty-five years old at the time. Bullingbrook was
thirty-two.
22. **whencesoever:** from somewhere or other (wherever he may be).

Percy. There stands the castle, by yon tuft of trees,
Mann'd with three hundred men, as I have heard,
And in it are the Lords of York, Berkeley, and
　　Seymour,
None else of name and noble estimate.　　　55

[*Enter* Ross *and* WILLOUGHBY.]

North. Here come the Lords of Ross and Wil-
　　loughby,
Bloody with spurring, fiery-red with haste.
Bull. Welcome, my lords. I wot your love pursues
A banish'd traitor. All my treasury　　　60
Is yet but unfelt thanks, which more enrich'd
Shall be your love and labor's recompense.
Ross. Your presence makes us rich, most noble
　　lord.
Willo. And far surmounts our labor to attain it.
Bull. Evermore thank's the exchequer of the poor,
Which, till my infant fortune comes to years,　　　66
Stands for my bounty. But who comes here?
North. It is my Lord of Berkeley, as I guess.

[*Enter* BERKELEY.]

Berk. My Lord of Herford, my message is to you.
Bull. My lord, my answer is to Lancaster,　　　70
And I am come to seek that name in England,
And I must find that title in your tongue,
Before I make reply to aught you say.
Berk. Mistake me not, my lord, 'tis not my mean-
　　ing
To rase one title of your honor out.　　　75
To you, my lord, I come, what lord you will,
From the most gracious regent of this land,
The Duke of York, to know what pricks you on
To take advantage of the absent time,
And fright our native peace with self-borne arms.　　　80

[*Enter* YORK *attended.*]

Bull. I shall not need transport my words by you,
Here comes his Grace in person. My noble uncle!

[*Kneels.*]

York. Show me thy humble heart, and not thy
　　knee,
Whose duty is deceivable and false.
Bull. My gracious uncle—　　　85
York. Tut, tut!
Grace me no grace, nor uncle me no uncle.
I am no traitor's uncle, and that word "grace"
In an ungracious mouth is but profane.
Why have those banish'd and forbidden legs　　　90

Dar'd once to touch a dust of England's ground?
But then more "why?"—why have they dar'd to
　　march
So many miles upon her peaceful bosom,
Frighting her pale-fac'd villages with war
And ostentation of despised arms?　　　95
Com'st thou because the anointed King is hence?
Why, foolish boy, the King is left behind,
And in my loyal bosom lies his power.
Were I but now lord of such hot youth
As when brave Gaunt, thy father, and myself　　　100
Rescued the Black Prince, that young Mars of men,
From forth the ranks of many thousand French,
O then how quickly should this arm of mine,
Now prisoner to the palsy, chastise thee,
And minister correction to thy fault!　　　105
Bull. My gracious uncle, let me know my fault,
On what condition stands it and wherein?
York. Even in condition of the worst degree,
In gross rebellion and detested treason.
Thou art a banish'd man, and here art come,　　　110
Before the expiration of thy time,
In braving arms against thy sovereign.
Bull. As I was banish'd, I was banish'd Herford,
But as I come, I come for Lancaster.
And, noble uncle, I beseech your Grace　　　115
Look on my wrongs with an indifferent eye.
You are my father, for methinks in you
I see old Gaunt alive. O then, my father,
Will you permit that I shall stand condemn'd
A wandering vagabond, my rights and royalties　　　120
Pluck'd from my arms perforce—and given away
To upstart unthrifts? Wherefore was I born?
If that my cousin king be King in England,
It must be granted I am Duke of Lancaster.
You have a son, Aumerle, my noble cousin,　　　125
Had you first died, and he been thus trod down,
He should have found his uncle Gaunt a father
To rouse his wrongs and chase them to the bay.
I am denied to sue my livery here,
And yet my letters-patents give me leave.　　　130
My father's goods are all distrain'd and sold,
And these, and all, are all amiss employed.
What would you have me do? I am a subject,
And I challenge law. Attorneys are denied me,
And therefore personally I lay my claim　　　135
To my inheritance of free descent.
North. The noble Duke hath been too much abused.
Ross. It stands your Grace upon to do him right.
Willo. Base men by his endowments are made
　　great.

56. estimate: rank.
57 s.d. Ross and Willoughby. According to Holinshed (Bullough,
III, 398), Ross and Willoughby had been the first to join Bullingbrook
when he came ashore at Ravenspur, and the Percies had thrown their
support to him at Doncaster, on his march to Gloucestershire. See
note to *1 Henry IV*, V.i.42.　59. wot: know.
61. unfelt: i.e. expressed by words, not things.
65. Evermore . . . poor: gratitude is always the treasury of the poor
(because they can make no other kind of payment in return for favors).
70. my . . . Lancaster: i.e. I answer only to my proper title, which is
Duke of Lancaster.
75. rase: erase.　title. With perhaps a pun on *tittle*.
79. absent time: i.e. time of the King's absence in Ireland.
80. self-borne: borne in one's own selfish interests (rather than in the
public good).
84. duty: function (of bowing in allegiance).　deceivable: deceitful.

95. ostentation: display.　despised: despicable.
100-102. As . . . French. The incident is unrecorded by the chroniclers.　105. minister: administer.
107. On . . . wherein: i.e. on what defect of character is it based and
in what does it consist.　112. braving: defiant.　114. for: as.
116. indifferent: impartial.　120. royalties. See note to II.i.190.
122. unthrifts: spendthrifts.　born: i.e. as heir to the Duke of Lancaster.　126. first: i.e. before Gaunt.
128. rouse: expose; literally, startle from the lair (a term from hunting).　bay: last stand (a term from hunting).
131. distrain'd: confiscated.
134. challenge law: claim my legal rights.
136. of free descent: through legitimate succession.
138. stands . . . upon: is incumbent upon your Grace.
139. his endowments: i.e. property and revenues that belong to him.

Richard II
II.iii

York. My lords of England, let me tell you this:
I have had feeling of my cousin's wrongs,   141
And labor'd all I could to do him right;
But in this kind to come, in braving arms,
Be his own carver and cut out his way,
To find out right with wrong—it may not be;   145
And you that do abet him in this kind
Cherish rebellion and are rebels all.

North. The noble Duke hath sworn his coming is
But for his own; and for the right of that
We all have strongly sworn to give him aid;   150
And let him never see joy that breaks that oath!

York. Well, well, I see the issue of these arms.
I cannot mend it, I must needs confess,
Because my power is weak and all ill left;
But if I could, by Him that gave me life,   155
I would attach you all, and make you stoop
Unto the sovereign mercy of the King;
But since I cannot, be it known unto you
I do remain as neuter. So fare you well,
Unless you please to enter in the castle,   160
And there repose you for this night.

Bull. An offer, uncle, that we will accept,
But we must win your Grace to go with us
To Bristow castle, which they say is held
By Bushy, Bagot, and their complices,   165
The caterpillars of the commonwealth,
Which I have sworn to weed and pluck away.

York. It may be I will go with you, but yet I'll
     pause,
For I am loath to break our country's laws.
Nor friends, nor foes, to me welcome you are: 170
Things past redress are now with me past care.

Exeunt.

[SCENE IV]

Enter EARL OF SALISBURY *and a* WELSH CAPTAIN.

Cap. My Lord of Salisbury, we have stay'd ten
     days,
And hardly kept our countrymen together,
And yet we hear no tidings from the King,
Therefore we will disperse ourselves. Farewell!

Sal. Stay yet another day, thou trusty Welshman.
The King reposeth all his confidence in thee.   6

Cap. 'Tis thought the King is dead; we will not
     stay.
The bay-trees in our country are all wither'd,
And meteors fright the fixed stars of heaven,

The pale-fac'd moon looks bloody on the earth,   10
And lean-look'd prophets whisper fearful change,
Rich men look sad, and ruffians dance and leap,
The one in fear to lose what they enjoy,
The other to enjoy by rage and war.
These signs forerun the death or fall of kings.   15
Farewell! Our countrymen are gone and fled,
As well assured Richard their king is dead.   [*Exit.*]

Sal. Ah, Richard! with the eyes of heavy mind
I see thy glory like a shooting star
Fall to the base earth from the firmament.   20
Thy sun sets weeping in the lowly west,
Witnessing storms to come, woe, and unrest.
Thy friends are fled to wait upon thy foes,
And crossly to thy good all fortune goes.   [*Exit.*]

[ACT III, SCENE I]

Enter [BULLINGBROOK,] *Duke of* HERFORD, YORK,
NORTHUMBERLAND, [ROSS, PERCY, WILLOUGHBY,
with] BUSHY *and* GREEN *prisoners.*

Bull. Bring forth these men.
Bushy and Green, I will not vex your souls—
Since presently your souls must part your bodies—
With too much urging your pernicious lives,
For 'twere no charity; yet, to wash your blood   5
From off my hands, here in the view of men
I will unfold some causes of your deaths:
You have misled a prince, a royal king,
A happy gentleman in blood and lineaments,
By you unhappied and disfigured clean;   10
You have in manner with your sinful hours
Made a divorce betwixt his queen and him,
Broke the possession of a royal bed,
And stain'd the beauty of a fair queen's cheeks
With tears drawn from her eyes by your foul wrongs;
Myself, a prince by fortune of my birth,   16
Near to the King in blood, and near in love
Till you did make him misinterpret me,
Have stoop'd my neck under your injuries,
And sigh'd my English breath in foreign clouds,   20
Eating the bitter bread of banishment,
Whilst you have fed upon my signories,
Dispark'd my parks and fell'd my forest woods,

---

143. **kind:** manner.
144. **Be . . . carver:** serve his own portion, i.e. indulge himself.
149. **for his own.** Bullingbrook had won the Percies' support, says Holinshed (Bullough, III, 398), when he swore to them "that he would demand no more, but the lands that were to him descended by inheritance from his father, and in right of his wife" (Mary Bohun, co-heiress of Hereford).   **right:** legality.
152. **issue . . . arms:** outcome of this resort to force.
154. **all ill left:** entirely inadequate.   156. **attach:** arrest.
159. **neuter:** neutral.   164. **Bristow:** Bristol.
165. **complices:** accomplices.
170. **Nor . . . nor:** neither as . . . nor as.

II.iv. **Location:** A camp in Wales.
2. **hardly:** with difficulty.
7–9. **'Tis . . . heaven.** In this short scene Shakespeare draws on two widely separated passages in Holinshed. In one it is reported (Bul-

lough, III, 400) that Richard, prevented by bad weather from returning to England as soon as he learned of Bullingbrook's invasion, sent the Earl of Salisbury to raise the Welsh in his support. However, the newly mustered troops grew impatient at the King's delay, decided that he was "suerlie dead," and after fourteen (not ten) days "scaled & departed awaie." Earlier, in an account of the general disaffection with Richard's extortions and misrule before he went to Ireland, Holinshed records (Bullough, III, 396) that "throughout all the realme of England, old baie trees withered, and afterwards, contrarie to all mens thinking, grew greene againe, a strange sight, and supposed to import some unknowne event."   22. **Witnessing:** signifying.
23. **wait upon:** offer allegiance to.   24. **crossly:** adversely.

III.i. **Location:** Bristol. Before the castle.
3. **presently:** immediately.   **part:** leave.
4. **urging:** dwelling on (in order to justify the summary execution).
9. **blood:** descent.
10. **unhappied.** See note to II.i.16.   **clean:** completely.
11. **in manner:** so to speak, as it were.
20. **foreign clouds:** i.e. the air of foreign lands.
22. **signories:** properties.
23. **Dispark'd:** i.e. put to uses unrelated to forestry and hunting.

From my own windows torn my household coat,
Ras'd out my imprese, leaving me no sign,   25
Save men's opinions and my living blood,
To show the world I am a gentleman.
This and much more, much more than twice all this,
Condemns you to the death. See them delivered over
To execution and the hand of death.   30

 Bushy. More welcome is the stroke of death to me
Than Bullingbrook to England. Lords, farewell!

 Green. My comfort is, that heaven will take our
   souls,
And plague injustice with the pains of hell.

 Bull. My Lord Northumberland, see them dispatch'd.   35

     [*Exeunt Northumberland and others
      with the prisoners.*]

Uncle, you say the Queen is at your house,
For God's sake fairly let her be entreated.
Tell her I send to her my kind commends;
Take special care my greetings be delivered.

 York. A gentleman of mine I have dispatch'd   40
With letters of your love to her at large.

 Bull. Thanks, gentle uncle. Come, lords, away,
To fight with Glendower and his complices.
A while to work, and after holiday.   *Exeunt.*

[SCENE II]

[*Drums: flourish and colors.*] *Enter the* KING, AUMERLE,
[*the* BISHOP OF] CARLISLE, *and* [SOLDIERS].

 K. Rich. Barkloughly castle call they this at hand?

 Aum. Yea, my lord. How brooks your Grace the
   air
After your late tossing on the breaking seas?

 K. Rich. Needs must I like it well; I weep for joy
To stand upon my kingdom once again.   5
Dear earth, I do salute thee with my hand,
Though rebels wound thee with their horses' hoofs.
As a long-parted mother with her child
Plays fondly with her tears and smiles in meeting,
So weeping, smiling, greet I thee, my earth,   10
And do thee favors with my royal hands.
Feed not thy sovereign's foe, my gentle earth,

Nor with thy sweets comfort his ravenous sense,
But let thy spiders, that suck up thy venom,
And heavy-gaited toads lie in their way,   15
Doing annoyance to the treacherous feet,
Which with usurping steps do trample thee.
Yield stinging nettles to mine enemies;
And when they from thy bosom pluck a flower,
Guard it, I pray thee, with a lurking adder,   20
Whose double tongue may with a mortal touch
Throw death upon thy sovereign's enemies.
Mock not my senseless conjuration, lords,
This earth shall have a feeling, and these stones
Prove armed soldiers, ere her native king   25
Shall falter under foul rebellion's arms.

 Car. Fear not, my lord, that Power that made you
   king
Hath power to keep you king in spite of all.
The means that heavens yield must be embrac'd,
And not neglected; else heaven would,   30
And we will not. Heaven's offer we refuse,
The proffered means of succors and redress.

 Aum. He means, my lord, that we are too remiss,
Whilst Bullingbrook, through our security,   34
Grows strong and great in substance and in power.

 K. Rich. Discomfortable cousin, know'st thou not
That when the searching eye of heaven is hid
Behind the globe, that lights the lower world,
Then thieves and robbers range abroad unseen
In murthers and in outrage [boldly] here,   40
But when from under this terrestrial ball
He fires the proud tops of the eastern pines
And darts his light through every guilty hole,
Then murthers, treasons, and detested sins,
The cloak of night being pluck'd from off their backs,
Stand bare and naked, trembling at themselves?   46
So when this thief, this traitor Bullingbrook,
Who all this while hath revell'd in the night,
Whilst we were wand'ring with the antipodes,
Shall see us rising in our throne, the east,   50
His treasons will sit blushing in his face,
Not able to endure the sight of day,
But self-affrighted tremble at his sin.
Not all the water in the rough rude sea
Can wash the balm off from an anointed king;   55
The breath of worldly men cannot depose
The deputy elected by the Lord;
For every man that Bullingbrook hath press'd
To lift shrewd steel against our golden crown,
God for his Richard hath in heavenly pay   60
A glorious angel; then if angels fight,
Weak men must fall, for heaven still guards the right.

---

24. **coat:** coat of arms.
25. **Ras'd:** erased. **imprese:** heraldic device consisting of an allegorical picture and a motto (Italian *impresa*, plural *imprese*).
37. **entreated:** treated. 38. **commends:** regards.
41. **at large:** in full.
43. **Glendower.** An unhistorical detail. Although Owen Glendower,
the fiery Welsh rebel of *1 Henry IV*, resisted Henry IV so strenuously
that the newly crowned king launched a campaign against him in
1400, there is no record of a clash between them at the time represented in this scene. This is the only mention of Glendower in the
play, unless, as some editors have suggested, he is the "Welsh Captain"
of II.iv.

III.ii. Location: The coast of Wales.
o.s.d. **flourish and colors:** fanfare and (a show of) flags.
1. **Barkloughly:** Shakespeare's version of Holinshed's *Barclowlie*, itself
an error for *Hertlowi*, i.e. Harlech, a castle in northern Wales built by
Edward I in 1285. Actually, when Richard returned from Ireland in
July 1399 he landed at Milford Haven in southern Wales.
2. **brooks:** likes.
6. **with my hand:** i.e. with a gesture of salutation. See line 11.
8. **a long-parted mother with:** a mother long parted from.
9. **fondly:** (1) foolishly; (2) dotingly.

13. **with . . . sense:** gratify his voracious appetite with your bounty.
21. **double:** forked. 22. **Throw:** inflict.
23. **senseless conjuration:** solemn injunction to things that cannot
understand it.
25. **native:** i.e. legitimate. Richard was born in Bordeaux.
30–31. **else . . . not:** i.e. otherwise we ignore the will of heaven.
34. **security:** overconfidence. 35. **power:** troops.
36. **Discomfortable:** discouraging.
38. **globe:** i.e. the earth. **that:** i.e. the "eye of heaven."
49. **antipodes:** people on the other side of the earth; here, the Irish.
55. **balm:** the oil used to anoint a king at his coronation.
56. **worldly:** earthly. 58. **press'd:** conscripted.
59. **shrewd:** harmful. 62. **still:** always.

Enter SALISBURY.

Richard II
III.ii

Welcome, my lord. How far off lies your power?

Sal. Nor near nor farther off, my gracious lord,
Than this weak arm. Discomfort guides my tongue 65
And bids me speak of nothing but despair.
One day too late, I fear me, noble lord,
Hath clouded all thy happy days on earth.
O, call back yesterday, bid time return,
And thou shalt have twelve thousand fighting men! 70
To-day, to-day, unhappy day, too late,
Overthrows thy joys, friends, fortune, and thy state,
For all the Welshmen, hearing thou wert dead,
Are gone to Bullingbrook, dispers'd and fled.

Aum. Comfort, my liege, why looks your Grace
so pale? 75

K. Rich. But now the blood of twenty thousand
men
Did triumph in my face, and they are fled;
And till so much blood thither come again,
Have I not reason to look pale and dead?
All souls that will be safe, fly from my side, 80
For time hath set a blot upon my pride.

Aum. Comfort, my liege, remember who you are.

K. Rich. I had forgot myself, am I not king?
Awake, thou coward majesty! thou sleepest.
Is not the king's name twenty thousand names? 85
Arm, arm, my name! a puny subject strikes
At thy great glory. Look not to the ground,
Ye favorites of a king, are we not high?
High be our thoughts. I know my uncle York
Hath power enough to serve our turn. But who comes
here? 90

Enter SCROOP.

Scroop. More health and happiness betide my liege
Than can my care-tun'd tongue deliver him!

K. Rich. Mine ear is open, and my heart prepar'd,
The worst is worldly loss thou canst unfold.
Say, is my kingdom lost? Why, 'twas my care, 95
And what loss is it to be rid of care?
Strives Bullingbrook to be as great as we?
Greater he shall not be; if he serve God,
We'll serve Him too, and be his fellow so.
Revolt our subjects? That we cannot mend, 100
They break their faith to God as well as us.
Cry woe, destruction, ruin, and decay:
The worst is death, and death will have his day.

Scroop. Glad am I that your Highness is so arm'd
To bear the tidings of calamity. 105
Like an unseasonable stormy day,
Which makes the silver rivers drown their shores,
As if the world were all dissolv'd to tears,
So high above his limits swells the rage

Of Bullingbrook, covering your fearful land 110
With hard bright steel, and hearts harder than steel.
White-beards have arm'd their thin and hairless scalps
Against thy majesty; boys, with women's voices,
Strive to speak big, and clap their female joints
In stiff unwieldy arms against thy crown; 115
Thy very beadsmen learn to bend their bows
Of double-fatal yew against thy state;
Yea, distaff-women manage rusty bills
Against thy seat: both young and old rebel,
And all goes worse than I have power to tell. 120

K. Rich. Too well, too well thou tell'st a tale so ill.
Where is the Earl of Wiltshire? Where is Bagot?
What is become of Bushy? Where is Green?
That they have let the dangerous enemy
Measure our confines with such peaceful steps? 125
If we prevail, their heads shall pay for it.
I warrant they have made peace with Bullingbrook.

Scroop. Peace have they made with him indeed, my
lord.

K. Rich. O villains, vipers, damn'd without re-
demption!
Dogs, easily won to fawn on any man! 130
Snakes, in my heart-blood warm'd, that sting my heart!
Three Judases, each one thrice worse than Judas!
Would they make peace? Terrible hell
Make war upon their spotted souls for this!

Scroop. Sweet love, I see, changing his property,
Turns to the sourest and most deadly hate. 136
Again uncurse their souls, their peace is made
With heads, and not with hands. Those whom you
curse
Have felt the worst of death's destroying wound,
And lie full low, grav'd in the hollow ground. 140

Aum. Is Bushy, Green, and the Earl of Wiltshire
dead?

Scroop. Ay, all of them at Bristow lost their heads.

Aum. Where is the Duke my father with his
power?

K. Rich. No matter where—of comfort no man
speak:
Let's talk of graves, of worms, and epitaphs, 145
Make dust our paper, and with rainy eyes
Write sorrow on the bosom of the earth.
Let's choose executors and talk of wills;
And yet not so, for what can we bequeath

---

112. **thin:** sparsely covered with hair.
114. **female:** i.e. weak (like those of women).
116. **beadsmen:** aged pensioners whose function was to pray for their benefactors.
117. **double-fatal:** i.e. because its foliage is poisonous and its wood was used for making bows.
118–19. **distaff-women . . . seat:** spinning-women wield rusty pikes against your throne.
122–23. **Where . . . Green.** Of the four notorious favorites whom Richard asks about, the Earl of Wiltshire, although reported by Holinshed (Bullough, III, 399), by Scroop in line 142, and by the Gardener in a later scene (III.iv.53) to have been captured and executed with Bushy and Green at Bristol (III.i), does not appear in this play. Bagot, last seen in II.ii, eluded Bullingbrook and reappears in IV.i; but since Richard could not have known of his escape his allusion in line 132 to "three Judases" is puzzling, like Aumerle's omission of Bagot's name in line 141.
125. **Measure our confines:** travel through our realm.
134. **spotted:** i.e. with treason. 135. **his property:** its quality.
137. **uncurse.** See note to II.i.16.

63 s.d. **Enter Salisbury.** In Holinshed's account (Bullough, III, 400–401), Richard, so "greatlie discomforted" at the news of Bullingbrook's success that he has already discharged his troops, meets Salisbury at Conway after a sorrowful march from "Barclowlie."
64. **near:** nearer. 72. **state:** regal power. 77. **triumph:** shine forth.
91 s.d. **Scroop:** presumably Sir Stephen Scroop (brother of Sir William Scroop, Earl of Wiltshire, whom Holinshed mentions (Bullough, III, 401) as one of Richard's attendants at Conway.
92. **care-tun'd:** tuned to the sounds of sorrow. **deliver:** report to.
109. **his:** its.

Save our deposed bodies to the ground?   150
Our lands, our lives, and all are Bullingbrook's,
And nothing can we call our own but death,
And that small model of the barren earth
Which serves as paste and cover to our bones.
For God's sake let us sit upon the ground   155
And tell sad stories of the death of kings:
How some have been depos'd, some slain in war,
Some haunted by the ghosts they have deposed,
Some poisoned by their wives, some sleeping kill'd,
All murthered—for within the hollow crown   160
That rounds the mortal temples of a king
Keeps Death his court, and there the antic sits,
Scoffing his state and grinning at his pomp,
Allowing him a breath, a little scene,
To monarchize, be fear'd, and kill with looks,   165
Infusing him with self and vain conceit,
As if this flesh which walls about our life
Were brass impregnable; and humor'd thus,
Comes at the last and with a little pin
Bores thorough his castle wall, and farewell king! 170
Cover your heads, and mock not flesh and blood
With solemn reverence, throw away respect,
Tradition, form, and ceremonious duty,
For you have but mistook me all this while.
I live with bread like you, feel want,   175
Taste grief, need friends: subjected thus,
How can you say to me I am a king?
    Car. My lord, wise men ne'er sit and wail their
        woes,
But presently prevent the ways to wail;
To fear the foe, since fear oppresseth strength,   180
Gives in your weakness strength unto your foe,
And so your follies fight against yourself.
Fear, and be slain—no worse can come to fight,
And fight and die is death destroying death,
Where fearing dying pays death servile breath.   185
    Aum. My father hath a power, inquire of him,
And learn to make a body of a limb.
    K. Rich. Thou chid'st me well. Proud Bulling-
        brook, I come
To change blows with thee for our day of doom.
This ague fit of fear is overblown,   190
An easy task it is to win our own.
Say, Scroop, where lies our uncle with his power?
Speak sweetly, man, although thy looks be sour.

    Scroop. Men judge by the complexion of the sky
The state and inclination of the day;   195
So may you by my dull and heavy eye:
My tongue hath but a heavier tale to say.
I play the torturer by small and small
To lengthen out the worst that must be spoken:
Your uncle York is join'd with Bullingbrook,   200
And all your northern castles yielded up,
And all your southern gentlemen in arms
Upon his party.
    K. Rich.   Thou hast said enough.
[*To Aumerle.*] Beshrew thee, cousin, which didst lead
        me forth
Of that sweet way I was in to despair!   205
What say you now? What comfort have we now?
By heaven, I'll hate him everlastingly
That bids me be of comfort any more.
Go to Flint castle, there I'll pine away—
A king, woe's slave, shall kingly woe obey.   210
That power I have, discharge, and let them go
To ear the land that hath some hope to grow,
For I have none. Let no man speak again
To alter this, for counsel is but vain.
    Aum. My liege, one word.
    K. Rich.   He does me double wrong 215
That wounds me with the flatteries of his tongue.
Discharge my followers, let them hence away,
From Richard's night to Bullingbrook's fair day.
                                          [*Exeunt.*]

                [SCENE III]

Enter, [with Drum and Colors,] BULLINGBROOK, YORK,
NORTHUMBERLAND, [ATTENDANTS, *and forces*].

    Bull. So that by this intelligence we learn
The Welshmen are dispers'd, and Salisbury
Is gone to meet the King, who lately landed
With some few private friends upon this coast.
    North. The news is very fair and good, my lord:
Richard not far from hence hath hid his head.   6
    York. It would beseem the Lord Northumberland
To say King Richard. Alack the heavy day
When such a sacred king should hide his head!
    North. Your Grace mistakes; only to be brief 10
Left I his title out.
    York.   The time hath been,
Would you have been so brief with him, he would
Have been so brief [with you] to shorten you,
For taking so the head, your whole head's length.   14
    Bull. Mistake not, uncle, further than you should.
    York. Take not, good cousin, further than you
        should,
Lest you mistake the heavens are over our heads.

---

153. **model:** mould, shape.
154. **paste:** pie crust. Dr. Johnson remarked that the metaphor is
"not of the most sublime kind."   158. **ghosts:** i.e. of kings.
161. **rounds:** encircles.
162–63. **the antic . . . pomp:** the jester sits, mocking the king's regality
and grinning at his splendor.
165. **monarchize:** play the monarch.
166. **self . . . conceit:** foolish fancies about himself.
168. **humor'd.** To make Death, rather than the king, subject of the
participle would seem to yield the better sense: "having thus amused
himself (by his antics with the king), Death comes," etc.
176. **subjected:** (1) liable (to common human needs); (2) made a
subject.
179. **presently . . . wail:** immediately block the paths that lead to
grief.   183. **to fight:** by fighting.
184–85. **fight . . . breath:** to die fighting is to conquer death by dying,
whereas to die in fear is to pay death the tribute of our cowardice.
186. **power:** troop of soldiers.
187. **learn . . . limb:** i.e. augment it by fresh recruits.
189. **for . . . doom:** i.e. to determine which of us will die.

197. **heavier:** more sorrowful.
198. **by small and small:** little by little (like the torturer who prolongs
the victim's agony on the rack).   203. **Upon his party:** on his side.
204. **Beshrew:** confound.   **forth:** out.
209. **Flint:** fortress near Chester.   212. **ear:** plough.

III.iii. Location: Wales. Before Flint Castle.
o.s.d. **Drum and Colors:** drummer and flagbearer.
1. **intelligence:** information.   13. **to:** as to.
14. **taking so the head:** i.e. being so presumptuous as to omit his title.
17. **mistake:** fail to understand that.

Richard II
III.iii

Bull. I know it, uncle, and oppose not myself
Against their will. But who comes here?

Enter [HARRY] PERCY.

Welcome, Harry. What, will not this castle yield? 20
    Percy. The castle royally is mann'd, my lord,
Against thy entrance.
    Bull. Royally?
Why, it contains no king.
    Percy.   Yes, my good lord,
It doth contain a king. King Richard lies 25
Within the limits of yon lime and stone,
And with him are the Lord Aumerle, Lord Salisbury,
Sir Stephen Scroop, besides a clergyman
Of holy reverence, who, I cannot learn.
    North. O, belike it is the Bishop of Carlisle. 30
    Bull. [*To Northumberland.*] Noble [lord],
Go to the rude ribs of that ancient castle;
Through brazen trumpet send the breath of parley
Into his ruin'd ears, and thus deliver:
Henry Bullingbrook 35
On both his knees doth kiss King Richard's hand,
And sends allegiance and true faith of heart
To his most royal person; hither come
Even at his feet to lay my arms and power,
Provided that my banishment repeal'd 40
And lands restor'd again be freely granted.
If not, I'll use the advantage of my power,
And lay the summer's dust with show'rs of blood
Rain'd from the wounds of slaughtered Englishmen,
The which, how far off from the mind of Bullingbrook
It is, such crimson tempest should bedrench 46
The fresh green lap of fair King Richard's land,
My stooping duty tenderly shall show.
Go signify as much, while here we march
Upon the grassy carpet of this plain. 50

                    [*Northumberland advances to the
                    castle, with a Trumpet.*]

Let's march without the noise of threat'ning drum,
That from this castle's tottered battlements
Our fair appointments may be well perus'd.
Methinks King Richard and myself should meet
With no less terror than the elements 55
Of fire and water, when their thund'ring shock
At meeting tears the cloudy cheeks of heaven.
Be he the fire, I'll be the yielding water;
The rage be his, whilst on the earth I rain
My waters—on the earth, and not on him. 60
March on, and mark King Richard how he looks.

The trumpets sound [*parle without and answer within;
then a flourish*]. RICHARD *appeareth on the walls* [*with*
CARLISLE, AUMERLE, SCROOP, SALISBURY].

See, see, King Richard doth himself appear,
As doth the blushing discontented sun
From out the fiery portal of the east,
When he perceives the envious clouds are bent 65
To dim his glory and to stain the track
Of his bright passage to the occident.
    York. Yet looks he like a king! Behold, his eye,
As bright as is the eagle's, lightens forth
Controlling majesty. Alack, alack for woe, 70
That any harm should stain so fair a show!
    K. Rich. [*To Northumberland.*] We are amaz'd,
        and thus long have we stood
To watch the fearful bending of thy knee,
Because we thought ourself thy lawful king;
And if we be, how dare thy joints forget 75
To pay their aweful duty to our presence?
If we be not, show us the hand of God
That hath dismiss'd us from our stewardship,
For well we know no hand of blood and bone
Can gripe the sacred handle of our sceptre, 80
Unless he do profane, steal, or usurp.
And though you think that all, as you have done,
Have torn their souls by turning them from us,
And we are barren and bereft of friends,
Yet know, my master, God omnipotent, 85
Is mustering in his clouds on our behalf
Armies of pestilence, and they shall strike
Your children yet unborn and unbegot,
That lift your vassal hands against my head,
And threat the glory of my precious crown. 90
Tell Bullingbrook—for yon methinks he stands—
That every stride he makes upon my land
Is dangerous treason. He is come to open
The purple testament of bleeding war;
But ere the crown he looks for live in peace, 95
Ten thousand bloody crowns of mothers' sons
Shall ill become the flower of England's face,
Change the complexion of her maid-pale peace
To scarlet indignation, and bedew
Her pasters' grass with faithful English blood. 100
    North. The King of heaven forbid our lord the
        King
Should so with civil and uncivil arms
Be rush'd upon! Thy thrice-noble cousin,
Harry Bullingbrook, doth humbly kiss thy hand,
And by the honorable tomb he swears 105
That stands upon your royal grandsire's bones,
And by the royalties of both your bloods,
Currents that spring from one most gracious head,
And by the buried hand of warlike Gaunt,
And by the worth and honor of himself, 110
Comprising all that may be sworn or said,
His coming hither hath no further scope

23–24. **Royally . . . king.** Actually, Richard, having left Conway in
despair, had been ambushed by Northumberland and "constrained"
to go to Flint. Hence Bullingbrook's surprise at his presence there is
unhistorical.   30. **belike:** probably.
34. **his ruin'd ears:** its (the castle's) ruinous loopholes.
40. **repeal'd:** revoked.   45. **The which:** as to which.
48. **stooping duty:** i.e. kneeling in submission.
50 s.d. **Trumpet:** trumpeter.
52. **tottered:** tattered, i.e. crenellated.
53. **appointments:** equipment.
61 s.d. **parle:** trumpet call sounded to request a conference.

63. **blushing:** i.e. red (like Richard's flushed and angry face). A red
sunrise was thought to indicate a stormy day.
65. **envious:** spiteful.   69. **lightens:** flashes.
71. **show:** appearance.   76. **aweful duty:** reverential homage.
77. **hand:** i.e. written hand, signature.   80. **gripe:** seize.
83. **torn . . . us:** i.e. lacerated their souls through the perjury of transferring their allegiance.   89. **vassal:** subject.
94. **purple testament:** blood-red will.   96. **crowns:** heads.
100. **pasters':** pastures'.
102. **civil:** employed in civil war.   **uncivil:** rude, barbarous.
106. **royal grandsire:** Edward III, whose "honorable tomb" is in
Westminster Abbey.   112. **scope:** aim, intention.

Than for his lineal royalties, and to beg
Enfranchisement immediate on his knees,
Which on thy royal party granted once,   115
His glittering arms he will commend to rust,
His barbed steeds to stables, and his heart
To faithful service of your Majesty.
This swears he, as he is [a prince, is] just,
And as I am a gentleman I credit him.   120
   K. Rich. Northumberland, say thus the King
    returns:
His noble cousin is right welcome hither,
And all the number of his fair demands
Shall be accomplish'd without contradiction.
With all the gracious utterance thou hast   125
Speak to his gentle hearing kind commends.
   [*Northumberland withdraws to Bullingbrook.*]
[*To Aumerle.*] We do debase ourselves, cousin, do
    we not,
To look so poorly and to speak so fair?
Shall we call back Northumberland, and send
Defiance to the traitor, and so die?   130
   Aum. No, good my lord, let's fight with gentle
    words,
Till time lend friends, and friends their helpful swords.
   K. Rich. O God, O God, that e'er this tongue of
    mine
That laid the sentence of dread banishment
On yon proud man should take it off again   135
With words of sooth! O that I were as great
As is my grief, or lesser than my name!
Or that I could forget what I have been!
Or not remember what I must be now!
Swell'st thou, proud heart? I'll give thee scope to beat,
Since foes have scope to beat both thee and me.   141
   Aum. Northumberland comes back from Bulling-
    brook.
   K. Rich. What must the King do now? Must he
    submit?
The King shall do it. Must he be depos'd?
The King shall be contented. Must he lose   145
The name of king? a' God's name let it go.
I'll give my jewels for a set of beads,
My gorgeous palace for a hermitage,
My gay apparel for an almsman's gown,
My figur'd goblets for a dish of wood,   150
My sceptre for a palmer's walking-staff,
My subjects for a pair of carved saints,
And my large kingdom for a little grave,
A little little grave, an obscure grave—
Or I'll be buried in the king's high way,   155
Some way of common trade, where subjects' feet
May hourly trample on their sovereign's head;

For on my heart they tread now whilst I live,
And buried once, why not upon my head?
Aumerle, thou weep'st, my tender-hearted cousin!   160
We'll make foul weather with despised tears;
Our sighs and they shall lodge the summer corn,
And make a dearth in this revolting land.
Or shall we play the wantons with our woes
And make some pretty match with shedding tears?
As thus to drop them still upon one place,   166
Till they have fretted us a pair of graves
Within the earth, and, therein laid—there lies
Two kinsmen digg'd their graves with weeping eyes.
Would not this ill do well? Well, well, I see   170
I talk but idlely, and you laugh at me.
Most mighty prince, my Lord Northumberland,
What says King Bullingbrook? Will his Majesty
Give Richard leave to live till Richard die?
You make a leg, and Bullingbrook says ay.   175
   North. My lord, in the base court he doth attend
To speak with you, may it please you to come down.
   K. Rich. Down, down I come, like glist'ring
    Phaëton,
Wanting the manage of unruly jades.
In the base court? Base court, where kings grow base,
To come at traitors' calls and do them grace.   181
In the base court, come down? Down court! down
    king!
For night-owls shriek where mounting larks should
    sing.   [*Exeunt above.*]
   Bull. What says his Majesty?
   North.   Sorrow and grief of heart
Makes him speak fondly like a frantic man,   185
Yet he is come.

[*Enter* King Richard *and his* Attendants *below.*]

   Bull. Stand all apart,
And show fair duty to his Majesty.   *He kneels down.*
My gracious lord—
   K. Rich. Fair cousin, you debase your princely
    knee   190
To make the base earth proud with kissing it.
Me rather had my heart might feel your love
Than my unpleased eye see your courtesy.
Up, cousin, up, your heart is up, I know,
Thus high at least [*touching his crown*], although your
    knee be low.   195
   Bull. My gracious lord, I come but for mine own.
   K. Rich. Your own is yours, and I am yours, and
    all.

---

113. **lineal royalties:** hereditary rights as a member of the royal family.
114. **Enfranchisement:** freedom (from banishment).
115. **party:** part.   116. **commend:** commit.
117. **barbed:** armored.   121. **returns:** replies.
124. **accomplish'd:** fulfilled.   126. **commends:** regards.
136. **sooth:** blandishment.   137. **name:** title.   146. **a':** in.
147. **set of beads:** rosary.
149. **almsman's gown:** i.e. the mean garb of one who lives on alms or charity.   150. **figur'd:** ornamented.
151. **palmer's:** pilgrim's. Palmers originally carried palm leaves to show that they had been to Jerusalem.   156. **trade:** passage.

162. **lodge:** beat down.   **corn:** wheat.
163. **dearth:** famine.   **revolting:** rebelling.
164. **play the wantons:** frolic.   165. **match:** game.
167. **fretted us:** eroded for us.   169. **digg'd:** who dug.
171. **idlely:** foolishly.   175. **make a leg:** curtsy.
176. **base court:** lower and outer courtyard of a castle (French *basse cour*).
178. **glist'ring:** glittering.   **Phaëton:** Phaëthon, son of Apollo, the sun-god; he attempted to drive his father's chariot across the sky and was hurled down to his death.
179. **Wanting . . . jades:** lacking the horsemanship to control unruly nags.   *Manage* = manège, the art of horsemanship.
183. **night-owls shriek.** An omen of disaster.
185. **speak fondly:** talk nonsense.   **frantic:** mad.
187. **duty:** obeisance.   192. **Me rather had:** I had rather.
193. **courtesy:** (1) civility; (2) curtsy.

Richard II
III.iii

Bull. So far be mine, my most redoubted lord,
As my true service shall deserve your love.
　　K. Rich. Well you deserve; they well deserve to
　　　　have　　　　　　　　　　　　　　　　200
That know the strong'st and surest way to get.
Uncle, give me your hands; nay, dry your eyes—
Tears show their love, but want their remedies.
Cousin, I am too young to be your father,
Though you are old enough to be my heir.　　205
What you will have, I'll give, and willing too,
For do we must what force will have us do.
Set on towards London, cousin, is it so?
　　Bull. Yea, my good lord.
　　K. Rich.　　　　　　Then I must not say no.
　　　　　　　　　　　　　　　[*Flourish. Exeunt.*]

[SCENE IV]

Enter the QUEEN *with* [*two* LADIES,] *her attendants.*

Queen. What sport shall we devise here in this
　　garden
To drive away the heavy thought of care?
　　[*1.*] *Lady.* Madam, we'll play at bowls.
　　Queen. 'Twill make me think the world is full of
　　rubs,
And that my fortune runs against the bias.　　5
　　[*1.*] *Lady.* Madam, we'll dance.
　　Queen. My legs can keep no measure in delight,
When my poor heart no measure keeps in grief;
Therefore no dancing, girl, some other sport.
　　[*1.*] *Lady.* Madam, we'll tell tales.　　10
　　Queen. Of sorrow or of [joy]?
　　[*1.*] *Lady.*　　　　　　Of either, madam.
　　Queen. Of neither, girl;
For if of joy, being altogether wanting,
It doth remember me the more of sorrow;
Or if of grief, being altogether had,　　15
It adds more sorrow to my want of joy;
For what I have I need not to repeat,
And what I want it boots not to complain.
　　[*1.*] *Lady.* Madam, I'll sing.
　　Queen.　　　　　　'Tis well that thou hast cause,
But thou shouldst please me better wouldst thou weep.
　　[*1.*] *Lady.* I could weep, madam, would it do you
　　good.　　　　　　　　　　　　　　　　21
　　Queen. And I could sing, would weeping do me
　　good,
And never borrow any tear of thee.

Enter [*a* GARDENER *and two of his* MEN].

But stay, here come the gardeners.
Let's step into the shadow of these trees.　　25

My wretchedness unto a row of [pins],
They will talk of state, for every one doth so
Against a change; woe is forerun with woe.
　　　　　　　　　　　[*Queen and Ladies retire.*]
　　Gard. Go bind thou up young dangling apricocks,
Which like unruly children make their sire　　30
Stoop with oppression of their prodigal weight;
Give some supportance to the bending twigs.
Go thou, and like an executioner
Cut off the heads of [too] fast growing sprays,
That look too lofty in our commonwealth:　　35
All must be even in our government.
You thus employed, I will go root away
The noisome weeds which without profit suck
The soil's fertility from wholesome flowers.
　　[*1.*] *Man.* Why should we in the compass of a pale
Keep law and form and due proportion,　　41
Showing as in a model our firm estate,
When our sea-walled garden, the whole land,
Is full of weeds, her fairest flowers chok'd up,
Her fruit-trees all unprun'd, her hedges ruin'd,　　45
Her knots disordered, and her wholesome herbs
Swarming with caterpillars?
　　Gard.　　　　　　Hold thy peace.
He that hath suffered this disordered spring
Hath now himself met with the fall of leaf.
The weeds which his broad-spreading leaves did
　　shelter,　　　　　　　　　　　　　　　50
That seem'd in eating him to hold him up,
Are pluck'd up root and all by Bullingbrook,
I mean the Earl of Wiltshire, Bushy, Green.
　　[*1.*] *Man.* What, are they dead?
　　Gard.　　　　　　They are; and Bullingbrook
Hath seiz'd the wasteful King. O, what pity is it　　55
That he had not so trimm'd and dress'd his land
As we this garden! [We] at time of year
Do wound the bark, the skin of our fruit-trees,
Lest being over-proud in sap and blood,
With too much riches it confound itself;　　60
Had he done so to great and growing men,
They might have liv'd to bear and he to taste
Their fruits of duty. Superfluous branches
We lop away, that bearing boughs may live;
Had he done so, himself had borne the crown,　　65
Which waste of idle hours hath quite thrown down.
　　[*1.*] *Man.* What, think you the King shall be de-
　　posed?
　　Gard. Depress'd he is already, and depos'd
'Tis doubt he will be. Letters came last night
To a dear friend of the good Duke of York's　　70
That tell black tidings.
　　Queen. O, I am press'd to death through want of
　　speaking!　　　　　　　[*Coming forward.*]

198. **redoubted:** dreaded.
202. **Uncle:** i.e. York.　203. **want:** lack.
204–5. **Cousin . . . heir.** Richard and Bullingbrook were in fact both born in 1367.

III.iv. Location: Langley. The Duke of York's garden.
4. **rubs:** impediments (a term from bowling).
5. **against the bias:** i.e. unnaturally crooked. In the game of bowls, *bias* = the desirable swerve or curving course of a bowl in motion.
7. **measure:** stately dance.　8. **measure:** moderation.
13. **wanting:** lacking.　14. **remember:** remind.
18. **boots not:** does no good.

26. **My wretchedness unto:** i.e. I wager my wretchedness against.
27. **state:** politics.　28. **Against:** in anticipation of.
29. **apricocks:** apricots.　36. **even:** equal.
40. **pale:** enclosure, i.e. walled garden.
46. **knots:** flower beds laid out in patterns.
48. **suffered:** permitted.
57. **time of year:** i.e. the proper season.
59. **over-proud:** too luxuriant.　68. **Depress'd:** humbled.
69. **doubt:** fear.
72. **press'd to death.** Customary penalty in England for refusing to plead guilty or not guilty before a court, i.e. for remaining silent.

Thou old Adam's likeness, set to dress this garden,
How dares thy harsh rude tongue sound this unpleas-
ing news?
What Eve, what serpent, hath suggested thee   75
To make a second fall of cursed man?
Why dost thou say King Richard is depos'd?
Dar'st thou, thou little better thing than earth,
Divine his downfall? Say, where, when, and how,
[Cam'st] thou by this ill tidings? Speak, thou wretch.
    Gard. Pardon me, madam, little joy have I   81
To breathe this news, yet what I say is true:
King Richard, he is in the mighty hold
Of Bullingbrook; their fortunes both are weigh'd.
In your lord's scale is nothing but himself,   85
And some few vanities that make him light;
But in the balance of great Bullingbrook,
Besides himself, are all the English peers,
And with that odds he weighs King Richard down.
Post you to London and you will find it so,   90
I speak no more than every one doth know.
    Queen. Nimble mischance, that art so light of foot,
Doth not thy embassage belong to me,
And am I last that knows it? O, thou thinkest
To serve me last that I may longest keep   95
Thy sorrow in my breast. Come, ladies, go
To meet at London London's king in woe.
What, was I born to this, that my sad look
Should grace the triumph of great Bullingbrook?
Gard'ner, for telling me these news of woe,   100
Pray God the plants thou graft'st may never grow.
                                Exit [*with Ladies*].
    Gard. Poor queen, so that thy state might be no
        worse,
I would my skill were subject to thy curse.
Here did she fall a tear, here in this place
I'll set a bank of rue, sour herb of grace.   105
Rue, even for ruth, here shortly shall be seen,
In the remembrance of a weeping queen.   *Exeunt.*

[ACT IV, Scene I]

Enter Bullingbrook *with the Lords* [Aumerle,
Northumberland, Percy, Fitzwater, Surrey,
the Bishop of Carlisle, *the* Abbot of Westminster, *and another* Lord] *to parliament;* [Herald].

    Bull. Call forth Bagot.

Enter [Officers *with*] Bagot.

Now, Bagot, freely speak thy mind,
What thou dost know of noble Gloucester's death,
Who wrought it with the King, and who perform'd
The bloody office of his timeless end.   5
    Bagot. Then set before my face the Lord Aumerle.
    Bull. Cousin, stand forth, and look upon that man.
    Bagot. My Lord Aumerle, I know your daring
        tongue
Scorns to unsay what once it hath delivered.
In that dead time when Gloucester's death was plotted,
I heard you say, "Is not my arm of length,   11
That reacheth from the restful English court
As far as Callice, to mine uncle's head?"
Amongst much other talk, that very time,
I heard you say that you had rather refuse   15
The offer of an hundred thousand crowns
Than Bullingbrook's return to England,
Adding withal, how blest this land would be
In this your cousin's death.
    Aum.   Princes and noble lords,
What answer shall I make to this base man?   20
Shall I so much dishonor my fair stars
On equal terms to give [him] chastisement?
Either I must, or have mine honor soil'd
With the attainder of his slanderous lips.
There is my gage, the manual seal of death,   25
That marks thee out for hell. I say thou liest,
And will maintain what thou hast said is false
In thy heart-blood, though being all too base
To stain the temper of my knightly sword.
    Bull. Bagot, forbear, thou shalt not take it up.   30
    Aum. Excepting one, I would he were the best
In all this presence that hath mov'd me so.
    Fitz. If that thy valure stand on sympathy,
There is my gage, Aumerle, in gage to thine.
By that fair sun which shows me where thou stand'st,
I heard thee say, and vauntingly thou spak'st it,   36
That thou wert cause of noble Gloucester's death.
If thou deniest it twenty times, thou liest,
And I will turn thy falsehood to thy heart,
Where it was forged, with my rapier's point.   40
    Aum. Thou dar'st not, coward, live to see that day.
    Fitz. Now by my soul, I would it were this hour.
    Aum. Fitzwater, thou art damn'd to hell for this.
    Percy. Aumerle, thou liest, his honor is as true
In this appeal as thou art all unjust,   45

4-5. **Who . . . end:** i.e. who persuaded the King to order the murder
and who did the deed itself.
5. **office:** service, duty.   **timeless:** untimely.
9. **unsay.** See note to II.i.16.   10. **dead:** i.e. dark.
11. **of length:** long.   12. **restful:** i.e. untroubled by Gloucester.
14. **that very time.** The chronology is confused. Gloucester's murder
occurred in 1387, eleven years before Bullingbrook's exile.
16. **an hundred thousand crowns.** Holinshed, who places Bagot's
accusations after Richard's deposition (Bullough, III, 409-10), gives
the sum as twenty thousand pounds. A crown was worth five shillings.
17. **Than Bullingbrook's return:** than have Bullingbrook return.
18. **withal:** besides.   21. **fair stars:** i.e. noble rank.
22. **On equal terms:** i.e. in formal combat.
24. **attainder:** foul accusation.
25. **gage:** pledge (here, a glove, as implied by the following phrase).
manual . . . death: death warrant sealed by my hand.
31. **one:** i.e. Bullingbrook.
33. **valure:** valor.   **stand on sympathy:** i.e. requires an opponent of
equal rank.
40. **rapier's point.** An anachronism (as Dr. Johnson noted in disapproval), for rapiers were not in use at the end of the fourteenth
century.
45. **appeal:** accusation.   **all unjust:** entirely false.

73. **old Adam's likeness:** i.e. because Adam was the first gardener.
dress: cultivate.   75. **suggested:** prompted.
76. **cursed:** under a curse (like Adam after his fall from grace).
79. **Divine:** prophesy.   83. **hold:** grip, custody.
85. **scale:** pan of the balance.   90. **Post:** hasten.
93. **embassage:** message, report.
96. **Thy sorrow:** the sorrow that you report.
102. **so that:** provided.   104. **fall:** drop.
105. **sour . . . grace:** bitter herb of repentance (which comes through
the grace of God).

IV.i. Location: Westminster Hall.

Richard II
IV.i

And that thou art so, there I throw my gage,
To prove it on thee to the extremest point
Of mortal breathing. Seize it, if thou dar'st.
   Aum. And if I do not, may my hands rot off,
And never brandish more revengeful steel   50
Over the glittering helmet of my foe!
   Another Lord. I task the earth to the like, for-
     sworn Aumerle,
And spur thee on with full as many lies
As may be hollowed in thy treacherous ear
From [sun] to [sun]. There is my honor's pawn,   55
Engage it to the trial, if thou darest.
   Aum. Who sets me else? By heaven, I'll throw at
     all!
I have a thousand spirits in one breast,
To answer twenty thousand such as you.
   Surrey. My Lord Fitzwater, I do remember well
The very time Aumerle and you did talk.   61
   Fitz. 'Tis very true, you were in presence then,
And you can witness with me this is true.
   Surrey. As false, by heaven, as heaven itself is true.
   Fitz. Surrey, thou liest.
   Surrey.   Dishonorable boy!   65
That lie shall lie so heavy on my sword,
That it shall render vengeance and revenge
Till thou the lie-giver and that lie do lie
In earth as quiet as thy father's skull;
In proof whereof, there is my honor's pawn,   70
Engage it to the trial, if thou dar'st.
   Fitz. How fondly dost thou spur a forward horse!
If I dare eat, or drink, or breathe, or live,
I dare meet Surrey in a wilderness,
And spit upon him whilst I say he lies,   75
And lies, and lies. There is [my] bond of faith,
To tie thee to my strong correction.
As I intend to thrive in this new world,
Aumerle is guilty of my true appeal;
Besides, I heard the banished Norfolk say   80
That thou, Aumerle, didst send two of thy men
To execute the noble Duke at Callice.
   Aum. Some honest Christian trust me with a gage—
That Norfolk lies, here do I throw down this,
If he may be repeal'd to try his honor.   85
   Bull. These differences shall all rest under gage
Till Norfolk be repeal'd. Repeal'd he shall be,
And though mine enemy, restor'd again
To all his lands and signories. When he is return'd,
Against Aumerle we will enforce his trial.   90
   Car. That honorable day shall never be seen.
Many a time hath banish'd Norfolk fought
For Jesu Christ in glorious Christian field,
Streaming the ensign of the Christian cross
Against black pagans, Turks, and Saracens,   95

50. **revengeful:** avenging.
52. **I . . . like:** i.e. I too fling my gage upon the ground.
53. **lies:** accusations of lying.
57. **sets:** puts up a stake in wager, i.e. challenges (a term from dicing, as is *throw*).
62. **in presence:** in the king's presence-chamber.
72. **fondly:** foolishly.   76. **bond of faith:** i.e. gage.
78. **in . . . world:** i.e. under the new king.
85. **repeal'd:** recalled home.
86. **under gage:** as standing challenges.
89. **signories:** properties.   90. **trial:** i.e. trial by combat.
94. **Streaming:** flying.

And toil'd with works of war, retir'd himself
To Italy, and there at Venice gave
His body to that pleasant country's earth,
And his pure soul unto his captain Christ,
Under whose colors he had fought so long.   100
   Bull. Why, Bishop, is Norfolk dead?
   Car. As surely as I live, my lord.
   Bull. Sweet peace conduct his sweet soul to the
     bosom
Of good old Abraham! Lords appellants,
Your differences shall all rest under gage   105
Till we assign you to your days of trial.

Enter YORK *[attended].*

   York. Great Duke of Lancaster, I come to thee
From plume-pluck'd Richard, who with willing soul
Adopts [thee] heir, and his high sceptre yields
To the possession of thy royal hand.   110
Ascend his throne, descending now from him,
And long live Henry, fourth of that name!
   Bull. In God's name I'll ascend the regal throne.
   Car. Marry, God forbid!
Worst in this royal presence may I speak,   115
Yet best beseeming me to speak the truth.
Would God that any in this noble presence
Were enough noble to be upright judge
Of noble Richard! Then true noblesse would
Learn him forbearance from so foul a wrong.   120
What subject can give sentence on his king?
And who sits here that is not Richard's subject?
Thieves are not judg'd but they are by to hear,
Although apparent guilt be seen in them,
And shall the figure of God's majesty,   125
His captain, steward, deputy, elect,
Anointed, crowned, planted many years,
Be judg'd by subject and inferior breath,
And he himself not present? O, forfend it, God,
That in a Christian climate souls refin'd   130
Should show so heinous, black, obscene a deed!
I speak to subjects, and a subject speaks,
Stirr'd up by God, thus boldly for his king.
My Lord of Herford here, whom you call king,
Is a foul traitor to proud Herford's king,   135
And if you crown him, let me prophesy,
The blood of English shall manure the ground,
And future ages groan for this foul act.

96. **toil'd:** exhausted.
103–4. **bosom . . . Abraham:** i.e. heaven. See Luke 16:22.
104. **appellants:** accusers.
107–12. **Great . . . name.** Here as elsewhere in this crowded scene Shakespeare rearranges and compresses the data as given by Holinshed (Bullough, III, 405–12), his principal source. Richard, "committed to safe custodie" in the Tower, "renounced and voluntarilie was deposed from his royall crowne and kinglie dignitie" on September 29, 1399. The next day, Bullingbrook, with the assent of Parliament, ascended the throne as Henry IV, and on October 13 he was duly crowned. Of the other episodes, the challenge to Aumerle and the protest of Thomas Merke, Bishop of Carlisle, occurred within ten days of Henry's coronation, but the Abbot of Westminster's conspiracy was not hatched until December.
115–16. **Worst . . . truth:** i.e. although in this royal presence I am the least worthy to speak, yet because of my sacred office it best becomes me to speak the truth.   119. **noblesse:** nobility.
120. **Learn him forbearance:** teach him to refrain.
123. **judg'd . . . by:** condemned except when they are present.
124. **apparent:** obvious.   126. **elect:** chosen one.
129. **forfend:** forbid.

Peace shall go sleep with Turks and infidels,
And in this seat of peace tumultuous wars　　140
Shall kin with kin and kind with kind confound.
Disorder, horror, fear, and mutiny
Shall here inhabit, and this land be call'd
The field of Golgotha and dead men's skulls.
O, if you raise this house against this house,　　145
It will the woefullest division prove
That ever fell upon this cursed earth.
Prevent it, resist it, let it not be so,
Lest child, child's children, cry against you "woe!"
　　North.　Well have you argued, sir, and, for your
　　　　pains,　　150
Of capital treason we arrest you here.
My Lord of Westminster, be it your charge
To keep him safely till his day of trial.
[May it please you, lords, to grant the commons' suit?
　　Bull.　Fetch hither Richard, that in common view
He may surrender; so we shall proceed　　156
Without suspicion.
　　York.　　　　　I will be his conduct.　　*Exit.*
　　Bull.　Lords, you that here are under our arrest,
Procure your sureties for your days of answer.
Little are we beholding to your love,　　160
And little look'd for at your helping hands.

Enter RICHARD *and* YORK [*with* OFFICERS *bearing the
crown and sceptre*].

　　K. Rich.　Alack, why am I sent for to a king
Before I have shook off the regal thoughts
Wherewith I reign'd? I hardly yet have learn'd
To insinuate, flatter, bow, and bend my knee.　　165
Give sorrow leave a while to tutor me
To this submission. Yet I well remember
The favors of these men. Were they not mine?
Did they not [sometimes] cry "All hail!" to me?
So Judas did to Christ; but He, in twelve,　　170
Found truth in all but one; I, in twelve thousand, none.
God save the King! Will no man say amen?
Am I both priest and clerk? Well then, amen.
God save the King! although I be not he,
And yet amen, if heaven do think him me.　　175
To do what service am I sent for hither?
　　York.　To do that office of thine own good will
Which tired majesty did make thee offer:
The resignation of thy state and crown
To Henry Bullingbrook.　　180
　　K. Rich.　Give me the crown. Here, cousin, seize
　　　　the crown;

Here, cousin,
On this side my hand, [and] on that side thine.
Now is this golden crown like a deep well
That owes two buckets, filling one another,　　185
The emptier ever dancing in the air,
The other down, unseen, and full of water:
That bucket down and full of tears am I,
Drinking my griefs, whilst you mount up on high.
　　Bull.　I thought you had been willing to resign.
　　K. Rich.　My crown I am, but still my griefs are
　　　　mine.　　191
You may my glories and my state depose,
But not my griefs; still am I king of those.
　　Bull.　Part of your cares you give me with your
　　　　crown.
　　K. Rich.　Your cares set up do not pluck my cares
　　　　down:　　195
My care is loss of care, by old care done,
Your care is gain of care, by new care won;
The cares I give I have, though given away,
They tend the crown, yet still with me they stay.
　　Bull.　Are you contented to resign the crown?　200
　　K. Rich.　Ay, no, no ay; for I must nothing be;
Therefore no no, for I resign to thee.
Now mark me how I will undo myself:
I give this heavy weight from off my head,
And this unwieldy sceptre from my hand,　　205
The pride of kingly sway from out my heart;
With mine own tears I wash away my balm,
With mine own hands I give away my crown,
With mine own tongue deny my sacred state,
With mine own breath release all duteous oaths;　210
All pomp and majesty I do forswear;
My manors, rents, revenues I forgo;
My acts, decrees, and statutes I deny;
God pardon all oaths that are broke to me!
God keep all vows unbroke are made to thee!　　215
Make me, that nothing have, with nothing griev'd,
And thou with all pleas'd, that hast all achiev'd!
Long mayst thou live in Richard's seat to sit,
And soon lie Richard in an earthy pit!
God save King Henry, unking'd Richard says,　　220
And send him many years of sunshine days!
What more remains?
　　North.　　　　　No more, but that you read
　　　　　　　　[*Presenting a paper.*]
These accusations, and these grievous crimes

---

141. **with:** by means of.　**confound:** destroy.
145. **this house . . . this house:** i.e. Lancaster . . . York.
151. **Of:** on a charge of.
154. **the commons' suit.** Holinshed reports (Bullough, III, 410–11) that Commons, shortly after Henry's coronation, requested a formal trial for Richard so that "he might have judgment decreed against him" for his crimes against the state. It was then that Thomas Merke, Bishop of Carlisle, "a man both learned, wise, and stout of stomach, boldlie shewed foorth his opinion concerning that demand," and as a consequence was charged with treason. Richard's abdication had occurred almost a month before.　156. **surrender:** abdicate.
157. **conduct:** escort.　160. **beholding:** beholden, indebted.
168. **favors:** (1) countenances; (2) benefits.
179. **state:** kingship.
181. **Give . . . seize the crown.** Although Holinshed (Bullough, III, 406–7) has Richard merely sign an instrument of abdication in the presence of commissioners, the more colorful accounts of Froissart, Hall, and Daniel have him hand his crown to Bullingbrook.

185. **owes:** owns, has.
195–99. **Your . . . stay.** The elaborate play on *care* as (1) grief and (2) responsibility may be paraphrased as follows: "The fact that you have taken on the cares of state does not relieve my sorrow. I lament the loss of kingly cares, whereas you are concerned about the new responsibilities that you were so eager to assume. I retain the anxieties that I now transfer to you, for although they accompany the crown they none the less remain with me."
201–2. **Ay . . . thee.** The pun is on *ay* and *I*, which were pronounced alike; moreover, *ay* was often written *I*. Richard says that he cannot answer either "ay" or "no," for with his kingship stripped from him there is no "I," but without an "I" a "no" has no force.
203. **undo:** i.e. annihilate my royal identity. See note to II.i.16.
209. **my sacred state:** my status as a ruler by divine right.
213. **deny:** cancel.
214. **oaths:** i.e. oaths of allegiance.　215. **are:** that are.
218. **seat:** throne.　220. **unking'd.** See note to II.i.16.
221. **sunshine:** sunny.
223. **accusations:** i.e. the formal charges brought against Richard at the request of Commons. See note to line 154.

Richard II
IV.i

Committed by your person and your followers
Against the state and profit of this land;   225
That by confessing them, the souls of men
May deem that you are worthily depos'd.
    K. Rich.   Must I do so? and must I ravel out
My weav'd-up follies? Gentle Northumberland,
If thy offenses were upon record,   230
Would it not shame thee in so fair a troop
To read a lecture of them? If thou wouldst,
There shouldst thou find one heinous article,
Containing the deposing of a king,
And cracking the strong warrant of an oath,   235
Mark'd with a blot, damn'd in the book of heaven.
Nay, all of you that stand and look upon me
Whilst that my wretchedness doth bait myself,
Though some of you, with Pilate, wash your hands,
Showing an outward pity, yet you Pilates   240
Have here deliver'd me to my sour cross,
And water cannot wash away your sin.
    North.   My lord, dispatch, read o'er these articles.
    K. Rich.   Mine eyes are full of tears, I cannot see;
And yet salt water blinds them not so much   245
But they can see a sort of traitors here.
Nay, if I turn mine eyes upon myself,
I find myself a traitor with the rest;
For I have given here my soul's consent
T' undeck the pompous body of a king;   250
Made glory base, [and] sovereignty a slave;
Proud majesty a subject, state a peasant.
    North.   My lord—
    K. Rich.   No lord of thine, thou haught insulting
          man,
Nor no man's lord. I have no name, no title,   255
No, not that name was given me at the font,
But 'tis usurp'd. Alack the heavy day,
That I have worn so many winters out
And know not now what name to call myself!
O that I were a mockery king of snow,   260
Standing before the sun of Bullingbrook,
To melt myself away in water-drops!
Good king, great king, and yet not greatly good,
And if my word be sterling yet in England,
Let it command a mirror hither straight,   265
That it may show me what a face I have
Since it is bankrout of his majesty.
    Bull.   Go some of you and fetch a looking-glass.
          [Exit an Attendant.]
    North.   Read o'er this paper while the glass doth
          come.
    K. Rich.   Fiend, thou torments me ere I come to
          hell!   270
    Bull.   Urge it no more, my Lord Northumberland.
    North.   The commons will not then be satisfied.

225. state and profit: settled prosperity.
226. by confessing: by your confessing.   227. worthily: justly.
232. read . . . them: i.e. read them out publicly.
233. article: item.
238. Whilst . . . myself: i.e. while I, in my wretchedness, torment
myself.   bait: attack, harass (a term from bearbaiting).
241. sour: bitter.   246. sort: gang.
250. undeck. See note to II.i.16.   pompous: splendid.
252. state: royalty.   254. haught: haughty.
256-57. not . . . usurp'd.   Perhaps an allusion to the Lancastrian
slander that Richard was illegitimate.
264. sterling: valid (a term from coinage).   269. while: until.

    K. Rich.   They shall be satisfied. I'll read enough,
When I do see the very book indeed
Where all my sins are writ, and that's myself.   275

          Enter one with a glass.

Give me that glass, and therein will I read.
No deeper wrinkles yet? Hath sorrow struck
So many blows upon this face of mine,
And made no deeper wounds? O flatt'ring glass,
Like to my followers in prosperity,   280
Thou dost beguile me! Was this face the face
That every day under his household roof
Did keep ten thousand men? Was this the face
That like the sun, did make beholders wink?
Is this the face which fac'd so many follies,   285
That was at last out-fac'd by Bullingbrook?
A brittle glory shineth in this face,
As brittle as the glory is the face,
          [Dashes the glass against the ground.]
For there it is, crack'd in an hundred shivers.
Mark, silent king, the moral of this sport,   290
How soon my sorrow hath destroy'd my face.
    Bull.   The shadow of your sorrow hath destroy'd
The shadow of your face.
    K. Rich.   Say that again.
The shadow of my sorrow! Ha, let's see.
'Tis very true, my grief lies all within,   295
And these external [manners] of laments
Are merely shadows to the unseen grief
That swells with silence in the tortur'd soul.
There lies the substance; and I thank thee, King,
For thy great bounty, that not only giv'st   300
Me cause to wail, but teachest me the way
How to lament the cause. I'll beg one boon,
And then be gone and trouble you no more.
Shall I obtain it?
    Bull.   Name it, fair cousin.
    K. Rich.   "Fair cousin"? I am greater than a king;
For when I was a king my flatterers   306
Were then but subjects; being now a subject,
I have a king here to my flatterer.
Being so great, I have no need to beg.
    Bull.   Yet ask.   310
    K. Rich.   And shall I have?
    Bull.   You shall.
    K. Rich.   Then give me leave to go.
    Bull.   Whither?
    K. Rich.   Whither you will, so I were from your
          sights.   315
    Bull.   Go some of you, convey him to the Tower.
    K. Rich.   O, good! convey! Conveyers are you all,
That rise thus nimbly by a true king's fall.]
          [Exeunt Richard, some Lords, and a Guard.]
    Bull.   On Wednesday next we solemnly proclaim
Our coronation. Lords, be ready all.   320
    Exeunt. Manent [Abbot of] Westminster, Carlisle,
          Aumerle.

284. wink: close the eyes.   285. fac'd: countenanced.
292-93. The shadow . . . face: i.e. the sorrow that overshadows you
has destroyed the reflection of your face in the mirror.
296. manners of laments: forms of grief.
300. that: i.e. Bullingbrook.   316. convey: escort.
317. convey: steal.   Conveyers: thieves.

Abbot. A woeful pageant have we here beheld.

Car. The woe's to come; the children yet unborn
Shall feel this day as sharp to them as thorn.

Aum. You holy clergymen, is there no plot
To rid the realm of this pernicious blot? 325

Abbot. My lord,
Before I freely speak my mind herein,
You shall not only take the sacrament
To bury mine intents, but also to effect
What ever I shall happen to devise. 330
I see your brows are full of discontent,
Your hearts of sorrow, and your eyes of tears.
Come home with me to supper, I'll lay
A plot shall show us all a merry day. *Exeunt.*

[ACT V, SCENE I]

Enter the QUEEN *with her* ATTENDANTS.

Queen. This way the King will come, this is the way
To Julius Caesar's ill-erected tower,
To whose flint bosom my condemned lord
Is doom'd a prisoner by proud Bullingbrook.
Here let us rest, if this rebellious earth 5
Have any resting for her true king's queen.

Enter RICHARD [*and* GUARD].

But soft, but see, or rather do not see,
My fair rose wither; yet look up, behold,
That you in pity may dissolve to dew
And wash him fresh again with true-love tears. 10
Ah, thou, the model where old Troy did stand,
Thou map of honor, thou King Richard's tomb,
And not King Richard; thou most beauteous inn,
Why should hard-favor'd grief be lodg'd in thee,
When triumph is become an alehouse guest? 15

K. Rich. Join not with grief, fair woman, do not so,
To make my end too sudden. Learn, good soul,
To think our former state a happy dream,
From which awak'd, the truth of what we are
Shows us but this. I am sworn brother, sweet, 20
To grim Necessity, and he and I
Will keep a league till death. Hie thee to France,
And cloister thee in some religious house.
Our holy lives must win a new world's crown,
Which our profane hours here have thrown down. 25

Queen. What, is my Richard both in shape and mind
Transform'd and weak'ned? Hath Bullingbrook depos'd
Thine intellect? Hath he been in thy heart?

The lion dying thrusteth forth his paw,
And wounds the earth, if nothing else, with rage 30
To be o'erpow'r'd, and wilt thou, pupil-like,
Take the correction, mildly kiss the rod,
And fawn on rage with base humility,
Which art a lion and the king of beasts?

K. Rich. A king of beasts indeed—if aught but beasts, 35
I had been still a happy king of men.
Good sometimes queen, prepare thee hence for France.
Think I am dead, and that even here thou takest,
As from my death-bed, thy last living leave.
In winter's tedious nights sit by the fire 40
With good old folks and let them tell [thee] tales
Of woeful ages long ago betid;
And ere thou bid good night, to quite their griefs,
Tell thou the lamentable tale of me,
And send the hearers weeping to their beds. 45
For why, the senseless brands will sympathize
The heavy accent of thy moving tongue,
And in compassion weep the fire out,
And some will mourn in ashes, some coal-black,
For the deposing of a rightful king. 50

Enter NORTHUMBERLAND [*and others*].

North. My lord, the mind of Bullingbrook is chang'd,
You must to Pomfret, not unto the Tower.
And, madam, there is order ta'en for you,
With all swift speed you must away to France.

K. Rich. Northumberland, thou ladder wherewithal 55
The mounting Bullingbrook ascends my throne,
The time shall not be many hours of age
More than it is, ere foul sin gathering head
Shall break into corruption. Thou shalt think,
Though he divide the realm and give thee half, 60
It is too little, helping him to all;
He shall think that thou, which knowest the way
To plant unrightful kings, wilt know again,
Being ne'er so little urg'd, another way
To pluck him headlong from the usurped throne. 65
The love of wicked men converts to fear,
That fear to hate, and hate turns one or both
To worthy danger and deserved death.

North. My guilt be on my head, and there an end.
Take leave and part, for you must part forthwith. 70

K. Rich. Doubly divorc'd! Bad men, you violate
A twofold marriage—'twixt my crown and me,
And then betwixt me and my married wife.—
Let me unkiss the oath 'twixt thee and me;
And yet not so, for with a kiss 'twas made. 75
Part us, Northumberland: I towards the north,

329. To . . . intents: not to reveal my plans.

V.i. Location: London. A street leading to the Tower.
2. Caesar's . . . tower: the Tower of London, popularly believed to have been built by Julius Caesar. ill-erected: built with evil consequences (because it had been the scene of so many crimes).
3. flint: flinty. 6. resting: resting-place.
11. model . . . stand: i.e. pattern of fallen greatness, like the ruins of Troy. 12. map of honor: mere outline of (former) glory.
13–15. thou . . . guest: i.e. why should grief reside in such a stately mansion (as Richard) when triumph is lodged in such an ugly tavern (as Bullingbrook). 24. new world's: heavenly.

31. To be: at being. 37. sometimes: sometime, former.
41–42. tales . . . betid: tales of woe that happened long ago.
43. quite their griefs: requite their sad tales.
46. For why: because. sympathize: be moved by.
52. Pomfret: Pontefract in Yorkshire, site of a Norman castle.
53. there . . . ta'en: arrangements have been made.
66. converts: changes.
67. one or both: i.e. the "unrightful" king or his sponsor or both.
68. worthy: well-merited.
74. unkiss the oath: i.e. cancel the marriage vow. On unkiss, see note to II.i.16.

831

Richard II
V.i

Where shivering cold and sickness pines the clime;
My wife to France, from whence set forth in pomp
She came adorned hither like sweet May,
Sent back like Hollowmas or short'st of day.   80
　　Queen.　And must we be divided? must we part?
　　K. Rich.　Ay, hand from hand, my love, and heart
　　　from heart.
　　Queen.　Banish us both, and send the King with me.
　　[*North.*]　That were some love, but little policy.   84
　　Queen.　Then whither he goes, thither let me go.
　　K. Rich.　So two together weeping make one woe.
Weep thou for me in France, I for thee here;
Better far off than, near, be ne'er the near.
Go count thy way with sighs, I mine with groans.
　　Queen.　So longest way shall have the longest
　　　moans.   90
　　K. Rich.　Twice for one step I'll groan, the way
　　　being short,
And piece the way out with a heavy heart.
Come, come, in wooing sorrow let's be brief,
Since wedding it, there is such length in grief.
One kiss shall stop our mouths, and dumbly part;   95
Thus give I mine, and thus take I thy heart.
　　Queen.　Give me mine own again, 'twere no good
　　　part
To take on me to keep and kill thy heart.
So now I have mine own again, be gone,
That I may strive to kill it with a groan.   100
　　K. Rich.　We make woe wanton with this fond
　　　delay,
Once more, adieu, the rest let sorrow say.　　*Exeunt.*

[SCENE II]

Enter DUKE OF YORK *and the* DUCHESS.

Duch.　My lord, you told me you would tell the
　　rest,
When weeping made you break the story [off,]
Of our two cousins coming into London.
　　York.　Where did I leave?
　　Duch.　　　　　　　　　At that sad stop, my lord,
Where rude misgoverned hands from windows' tops
Threw dust and rubbish on King Richard's head.   6
　　York.　Then, as I said, the Duke, great Bulling-
　　　brook,
Mounted upon a hot and fiery steed,
Which his aspiring rider seem'd to know,
With slow but stately pace kept on his course,   10
Whilst all tongues cried, "God save [thee], Bulling-
　　brook!"
You would have thought the very windows spake,
So many greedy looks of young and old

Through casements darted their desiring eyes
Upon his visage, and that all the walls   15
With painted imagery had said at once,
"Jesu preserve [thee]! Welcome, Bullingbrook!"
Whilst he, from the one side to the other turning,
Bare-headed, lower than his proud steed's neck,
Bespake them thus: "I thank you, countrymen."   20
And thus still doing, thus he pass'd along.
　　Duch.　Alack, poor Richard, where rode he the
　　　whilst?
　　York.　As in a theatre the eyes of men,
After a well-graced actor leaves the stage,
Are idly bent on him that enters next,   25
Thinking his prattle to be tedious,
Even so, or with much more contempt, men's eyes
Did scowl on gentle Richard. No man cried "God
　　save him!"
No joyful tongue gave him his welcome home,
But dust was thrown upon his sacred head,   30
Which with such gentle sorrow he shook off,
His face still combating with tears and smiles,
The badges of his grief and patience,
That had not God, for some strong purpose, steel'd
The hearts of men, they must perforce have melted,
And barbarism itself have pitied him.   36
But heaven hath a hand in these events,
To whose high will we bound our calm contents.
To Bullingbrook are we sworn subjects now,
Whose state and honor I for aye allow.   40
　　Duch.　Here comes my son Aumerle.

[*Enter* AUMERLE.]

　York.　　　　　　　　　Aumerle that was,
But that is lost for being Richard's friend;
And, madam, you must call him Rutland now.
I am in parliament pledge for his truth
And lasting fealty to the new-made king.   45
　　Duch.　Welcome, my son! Who are the violets now
That strew the green lap of the new-come spring?
　　Aum.　Madam, I know not, nor I greatly care not,
God knows I had as lief be none as one.
　　York.　Well, bear you well in this new spring of
　　　time,   50
Lest you be cropp'd before you come to prime.
What news from Oxford? Do these justs and triumphs
　　hold?
　　Aum.　For aught I know, my lord, they do.
　　York.　You will be there, I know.
　　Aum.　If God prevent not, I purpose so.   55

77. **pines the clime:** afflicts the region.
80. **Hollowmas:** Hallowmas, All Saints' Day (November 1).
84. **policy:** astuteness.
88. **Better...the near:** i.e. it is better to be widely separated than, though close together, to be never nearer.
101. **make woe wanton:** make a sport of grief.　**fond:** (1) affectionate; (2) foolish.

V.ii. **Location:** London. The Duke of York's palace.
4. **leave:** leave off.　5. **windows' tops:** high windows.

15–16. **walls ... imagery:** i.e. walls so thick with people that they looked like the painted hangings or tapestries commonly used for pageants and processions.　20. **Bespake:** addressed.
25. **idly:** indifferently.　33. **badges:** signs.　38. **bound:** limit.
40. **allow:** accept.
41–43. **Aumerle ... now.** As a result of his alleged complicity in the murder of Gloucester (IV.i) Aumerle had lost his ducal status, although he retained the title Earl of Rutland.
46. **violets:** i.e. the new king's favorites.
52. **Do ... hold:** i.e. are these jousts and pageants going forward as planned. According to Holinshed (Bullough, III, 411–12), the Abbot of Westminster and his accomplices planned to invite the new king to attend a joust at Oxford, where "when he should be most busilie marking the martiall pastime, he suddenlie should be slaine and destroied, and so by that means king Richard, who as yet lived, might be restored to libertie, and have his former estate & dignitie."

York. What seal is that, that hangs without thy
 bosom?
Yea, look'st thou pale? Let me see the writing.
 Aum. My lord, 'tis nothing.
 York.   No matter then who see it.
I will be satisfied, let me see the writing.
 Aum. I do beseech your Grace to pardon me. 60
It is a matter of small consequence,
Which for some reasons I would not have seen.
 York. Which for some reasons, sir, I mean to see.
I fear, I fear—
 Duch.   What should you fear?
'Tis nothing but some band that he is ent'red into 65
For gay apparel 'gainst the triumph day.
 York. Bound to himself! What doth he with a bond
That he is bound to? Wife, thou art a fool.
Boy, let me see the writing.
 Aum. I do beseech you pardon me, I may not
 show it. 70
 York. I will be satisfied, let me see it, I say.
    He plucks it out of his bosom and reads it.
Treason, foul treason! Villain, traitor, slave!
 Duch. What is the matter, my lord?
 York. Ho, who is within there?

     [Enter a SERVANT.]

          Saddle my horse.
God for his mercy! what treachery is here! 75
 Duch. Why, what is it, my lord?
 York. Give me my boots, I say, saddle my horse.
           [Exit Servant.]
Now by mine honor, by my life, by my troth,
I will appeach the villain.
 Duch.   What is the matter?
 York. Peace, foolish woman. 80
 Duch. I will not peace. What is the matter,
 Aumerle?
 Aum. Good mother, be content, it is no more
Than my poor life must answer.
 Duch.   Thy life answer?
 York. Bring me my boots, I will unto the King.

   His MAN enters with his boots.

 Duch. Strike him, Aumerle. Poor boy, thou art
 amaz'd. 85
—Hence, villain! never more come in my sight.
 York. Give me my boots, I say.
   [His Man helps him on with his boots and exit.]
 Duch. Why, York, what wilt thou do?
Wilt thou not hide the trespass of thine own?
Have we more sons? or are we like to have? 90
Is not my teeming date drunk up with time?
And wilt thou pluck my fair son from mine age,
And rob me of a happy mother's name?

Is he not like thee? is he not thine own?
 York. Thou fond mad woman, 95
Wilt thou conceal this dark conspiracy?
A dozen of them here have ta'en the sacrament,
And interchangeably set down their hands,
To kill the King at Oxford.
 Duch.   He shall be none,
We'll keep him here, then what is that to him? 100
 York. Away, fond woman, were he twenty times
 my son,
I would appeach him.
 Duch.   Hadst thou groan'd for him
As I have done, thou wouldst be more pitiful.
But now I know thy mind, thou dost suspect
That I have been disloyal to thy bed, 105
And that he is a bastard, not thy son.
Sweet York, sweet husband, be not of that mind,
He is as like thee as a man may be,
Not like to me, or any of my kin,
And yet I love him.
 York.   Make way, unruly woman! *Exit.* 110
 Duch. After, Aumerle! mount thee upon his horse,
Spur post, and get before him to the King,
And beg thy pardon ere he do accuse thee.
I'll not be long behind; though I be old,
I doubt not but to ride as fast as York. 115
An' never will I rise up from the ground
Till Bullingbrook have pardoned thee. Away, be gone!
            [Exeunt.]

      [SCENE III]

Enter the KING [HENRY] *with his nobles* [PERCY *and
 other* LORDS].

 K. Hen. Can no man tell me of my unthrifty son?
'Tis full three months since I did see him last.
If any plague hang over us, 'tis he.
I would to God, my lords, he might be found.
Inquire at London, 'mongst the taverns there, 5
For there, they say, he daily doth frequent,
With unrestrained loose companions,
Even such, they say, as stand in narrow lanes
And beat our watch and rob our passengers,
Which he, young wanton and effeminate boy, 10
Takes on the point of honor to support
So dissolute a crew.
 Percy. My lord, some two days since I saw the
 Prince,
And told him of those triumphs held at Oxford.
 K. Hen. And what said the gallant? 15

---

56. **seal . . . bosom.** Instead of being placed directly on a document,
a seal was often affixed to a strip of parchment hanging from the
border of the document. 65. **band:** bond.
66. **'gainst:** in anticipation of. 75. **God:** i.e. I pray God.
79. **appeach:** publicly accuse. 83. **answer:** answer for.
85. **him:** i.e. the servant. **amaz'd:** stupefied.
86. **villain:** i.e. the servant.
90–93. **Have . . . name.** Actually, Aumerle (who had a brother and
a sister) was the Duchess' stepson. All of York's children were by
his first wife, Isabel of Castile, who died in 1393.
91. **teeming date:** time of childbearing.

95. **fond:** foolish.
97–99. **A dozen . . . Oxford.** According to Holinshed (Bullough,
III, 412), the conspirators headed by the Abbot of Westminster had
"an indenture sextipartite made, sealed with their seales, and signed
with their hands, in the which each stood bound to other, to do their
whole indevour for the accomplishing of their purposed exploit."
100. **that:** i.e. the plot against the King.
111. **his horse:** one of his horses.
112. **post:** posthaste, i.e. as fast as possible. 116. **An':** and.

V.iii. Location: Windsor Castle.
1. **unthrifty:** profligate. 6. **frequent:** resort.
9. **watch:** watchmen. **passengers:** wayfarers.
10. **Which.** A loose connective here. **young . . . boy:** undisciplined
and self-indulgent boy. 14. **held:** planned.

Richard II
V.iii

Percy. His answer was, he would unto the stews,
And from the common'st creature pluck a glove
And wear it as a favor, and with that
He would unhorse the lustiest challenger.　19
　　K. Hen. As dissolute as desperate, yet through both
I see some sparks of better hope, which elder years
May happily bring forth. But who comes here?

Enter AUMERLE *amazed.*

　　Aum. Where is the King?
　　K. Hen. What means our cousin, that he stares and looks
So wildly?　25
　　Aum. God save your Grace! I do beseech your Majesty,
To have some conference with your Grace alone.
　　K. Hen. Withdraw yourselves, and leave us here alone.　　　　*[Exeunt Percy and Lords.]*
What is the matter with our cousin now?　29
　　Aum. For ever may my knees grow to the earth,
　　　　　　　　　　　　　　　　　[Kneels.]
My tongue cleave to my roof within my mouth,
Unless a pardon ere I rise or speak.
　　K. Hen. Intended, or committed, was this fault?
If on the first, how heinous e'er it be,
To win thy after-love I pardon thee.　35
　　Aum. Then give me leave that [I] may turn the key,
That no man enter till my tale be done.
　　K. Hen. Have thy desire.
　　　[Aumerle locks the door.] *The Duke of York knocks at the door and crieth.*
　　York. *[Within.]* My liege, beware! Look to thyself,
Thou hast a traitor in thy presence there.　40
　　K. Hen. Villain, I'll make thee safe.　*[Draws.]*
　　Aum. Stay thy revengeful hand, thou hast no cause to fear.
　　York. *[Within.]* Open the door, secure foolhardy King!
Shall I for love speak treason to thy face?
Open the door, or I will break it open.　45
　　　　　　　[King Henry unlocks the door.]

[Enter YORK.*]*

　　K. Hen. What is the matter, uncle? Speak,
Recover breath, tell us how near is danger
That we may arm us to encounter it.
　　York. Peruse this writing here, and thou shalt know
The treason that my haste forbids me show.　50
　　Aum. Remember, as thou read'st, thy promise pass'd.
I do repent me, read not my name there,
My heart is not confederate with my hand.

York. It was, villain, ere thy hand did set it down.
I tore it from the traitor's bosom, King;　55
Fear, and not love, begets his penitence.
Forget to pity him, lest thy pity prove
A serpent that will sting thee to the heart.
　　K. Hen. O heinous, strong, and bold conspiracy!
O loyal father of a treacherous son!　60
Thou sheer, immaculate, and silver fountain,
From whence this stream through muddy passages
Hath held his current and defil'd himself!
Thy overflow of good converts to bad,
And thy abundant goodness shall excuse　65
This deadly blot in thy digressing son.
　　York. So shall my virtue be his vice's bawd,
An' he shall spend mine honor with his shame,
As thriftless sons their scraping fathers' gold.
Mine honor lives when his dishonor dies,　70
Or my sham'd life in his dishonor lies:
Thou kill'st me in his life; giving him breath,
The traitor lives, the true man's put to death.
　　Duch. *[Within.]* What ho, my liege! for God's sake let me in.
　　K. Hen. What shrill[-voic'd] suppliant makes this eager cry?　75
　　Duch. *[Within.]* A woman, and thy aunt, great King, 'tis I.
Speak with me, pity me, open the door!
A beggar begs that never begg'd before.
　　K. Hen. Our scene is alt'red from a serious thing,
And now chang'd to "The Beggar and the King."　80
My dangerous cousin, let your mother in,
I know she is come to pray for your foul sin.
　　York. If thou do pardon, whosoever pray,
More sins for this forgiveness prosper may.
This fest'red joint cut off, the rest rest sound,　85
This let alone will all the rest confound.

[Enter DUCHESS.*]*

　　Duch. O King, believe not this hard-hearted man!
Love loving not itself, none other can.
　　York. Thou frantic woman, what dost thou make here?
Shall thy old dugs once more a traitor rear?　90
　　Duch. Sweet York, be patient. Hear me, gentle liege.　　　　　　　　　　*[Kneels.]*
　　K. Hen. Rise up, good aunt.
　　Duch.　　　　　　　Not yet, I thee beseech.
For ever will I walk upon my knees,
And never see day that the happy sees,
Till thou give joy, until thou bid me joy　95
By pardoning Rutland, my transgressing boy.
　　Aum. Unto my mother's prayers I bend my knee.
　　　　　　　　　　　　　　　　　[Kneels.]

16. **stews:** brothels.　23 s.d. **amazed:** distraught.
41. **safe:** harmless.　42. **revengeful:** avenging.
43. **secure:** heedless, unsuspecting.
44. **speak . . . face:** i.e. use such disrespectful language.
50. **my . . . show:** my breathlessness prevents my relating in detail.
51. **pass'd:** already given.

61. **sheer:** pure.　**fountain:** spring.
64. **converts:** changes.　66. **digressing:** wayward.
70. **lives:** comes to life, revives.
79–80. **Our . . . King:** i.e. we have now moved from a serious play to a comedy that could be called "The Beggar and the King" (perhaps with an allusion to "King Cophetua and the Beggar Maid," a ballad to which Shakespeare refers several times).
88. **Love . . . can:** i.e. he who does not love his own children can love no one, not even his king.　89. **make:** do.

York. Against them both my true joints bended be.
　　　　　　　　　　　　　　　　　　　　[*Kneels*.]
Ill mayst thou thrive if thou grant any grace! 99
Duch. Pleads he in earnest? Look upon his face:
His eyes do drop no tears, his prayers are in jest,
His words come from his mouth, ours from our breast;
He prays but faintly, and would be denied,
We pray with heart and soul, and all beside;
His weary joints would gladly rise, I know, 105
Our knees still kneel till to the ground they grow;
His prayers are full of false hypocrisy,
Ours of true zeal and deep integrity;
Our prayers do outpray his, then let them have
That mercy which true prayer ought to have. 110
　　[*K. Hen.*] Good aunt, stand up.
　　Duch.　　　　　　Nay, do not say "stand up";
Say "pardon" first, and afterwards "stand up."
And if I were thy nurse, thy tongue to teach,
"Pardon" should be the first word of thy speech.
I never long'd to hear a word till now, 115
Say "pardon," King, let pity teach thee how.
The word is short, but not so short as sweet,
No word like "pardon" for kings' mouths so meet.
　　York. Speak it in French, King, say "*pardonne
　　　moy.*"
　　Duch. Dost thou teach pardon pardon to destroy?
Ah, my sour husband, my hard-hearted lord, 121
That sets the word itself against the word!
Speak "pardon" as 'tis current in our land,
The chopping French we do not understand.
Thine eye begins to speak, set thy tongue there; 125
Or in thy piteous heart plant thou thine ear,
That hearing how our plaints and prayers do pierce,
Pity may move thee "pardon" to rehearse.
　　K. Hen. Good aunt, stand up.
　　Duch.　　　　　　　I do not sue to stand;
Pardon is all the suit I have in hand. 130
　　K. Hen. I pardon him as God shall pardon me.
　　Duch. O happy vantage of a kneeling knee!
Yet am I sick for fear, speak it again,
Twice saying "pardon" doth not pardon twain,
But makes one pardon strong.
　　K. Hen.　　　　　With all my heart 135
I pardon him.
　　Duch.　　　A god on earth thou art.
　　K. Hen. But for our trusty brother-in-law and the
　　　abbot,
With all the rest of that consorted crew,
Destruction straight shall dog them at the heels.
Good uncle, help to order several powers 140
To Oxford, or where e'er these traitors are.
They shall not live within this world, I swear,

But I will have them if I once know where.
Uncle, farewell, and, cousin, adieu! 144
Your mother well hath pray'd, and prove you true.
　　Duch. Come, my old son, I pray God make thee
　　　new.　　　　　　　　　*Exeunt.*

[SCENE IV]

[*Enter*] SIR PIERCE EXTON [*and* SERVANTS].

　　Exton. Didst thou not mark the King, what words
　　　he spake?
"Have I no friend will rid me of this living fear?"
Was it not so?
　　[*1.*] *Man.*　　These were his very words.
　　Exton. "Have I no friend?" quoth he. He spake it
　　　twice,
And urg'd it twice together, did he not? 5
　　[*1.*] *Man.* He did.
　　Exton. And speaking it, he wishtly look'd on me
As who should say, "I would thou wert the man
That would divorce this terror from my heart"—
Meaning the king at Pomfret. Come let's go. 10
I am the King's friend, and will rid his foe. [*Exeunt.*]

[SCENE V]

Enter RICHARD *alone.*

　　K. Rich. I have been studying how I may compare
This prison where I live unto the world;
And for because the world is populous,
And here is not a creature but myself,
I cannot do it; yet I'll hammer it out. 5
My brain I'll prove the female to my soul,
My soul the father, and these two beget
A generation of still-breeding thoughts;
And these same thoughts people this little world,
In humors like the people of this world: 10
For no thought is contented. The better sort,
As thoughts of things divine, are intermix'd
With scruples and do set the word itself
Against the word,
As thus: "Come, little ones," and then again, 15
"It is as hard to come as for a camel
To thread the postern of a small needle's eye."
Thoughts tending to ambition, they do plot
Unlikely wonders: how these vain weak nails
May tear a passage thorough the flinty ribs 20
Of this hard world, my ragged prison walls;
And for they cannot, die in their own pride.

---

106. **still:** will continue to.
119. **pardonne moy:** excuse me (a courteous refusal).
124. **chopping:** shifting in meaning.　125. **speak:** i.e. express pity.
137-39. **But . . . heels.** The King's "trusty brother-in-law" was his sister Elizabeth's husband John Holland, Duke of Exeter and Earl of Huntington, who, like Aumerle, had been degraded from his dukedom for his alleged part in Gloucester's murder. Despite the disclosure of their plot, he and his accomplices (including his nephew Thomas, Duke of Surrey and Earl of Kent) made an abortive effort to kill Henry at Windsor, but as they fled before the King they were trapped at Cirencester, and virtually all of the "consorted crew" were hunted down and executed. See V.vi.　140. **powers:** forces.

V.iv. Location: Windsor Castle.
7. **wishtly:** intently.　11. **rid:** rid him of.

V.v. Location: Pomfret Castle. A dungeon.
3. **for because:** because.　8. **still:** continually.
10. **humors:** temperaments.　13. **scruples:** doubts.
13-14. **do . . . word:** i.e. oppose Scriptural passages that seem to contradict each other.
15-17. **Come . . . eye.** See Matthew 19:14, 24.
17. **postern:** small gate.　**needle.** A monosyllable (pronounced *neeld* or *neele*).　21. **ragged:** rugged, rough.
22. **for:** because.　**pride:** prime.

Richard II
V. v

Thoughts tending to content flatter themselves
That they are not the first of fortune's slaves,
Nor shall not be the last—like seely beggars,   25
Who sitting in the stocks refuge their shame,
That many have and others must [sit] there;
And in this thought they find a kind of ease,
Bearing their own misfortunes on the back
Of such as have before endur'd the like.   30
Thus play I in one person many people,
And none contented. Sometimes am I king;
Then treasons make me wish myself a beggar,
And so I am. Then crushing penury
Persuades me I was better when a king;   35
Then am I king'd again, and by and by
Think that I am unking'd by Bullingbrook,
And straight am nothing. But what e'er I be,
Nor I, nor any man that but man is,
With nothing shall be pleas'd, till he be eas'd   40
With being nothing. (*The music plays.*) Music do I
    hear?
Ha, ha, keep time! How sour sweet music is
When time is broke, and no proportion kept!
So is it in the music of men's lives.
And here have I the daintiness of ear   45
To check time broke in a disordered string;
But for the concord of my state and time
Had not an ear to hear my true time broke.
I wasted time, and now doth time waste me;
For now hath time made me his numb'ring clock: 50
My thoughts are minutes, and with sighs they jar
Their watches on unto mine eyes, the outward watch,
Whereto my finger, like a dial's point,
Is pointing still, in cleansing them from tears.
Now, sir, the sound that tells what hour it is   55
Are clamorous groans, which strike upon my heart,
Which is the bell. So sighs, and tears, and groans
Show minutes, times, and hours; but my time
Runs posting on in Bullingbrook's proud joy,
While I stand fooling here, his Jack of the clock.   60
This music mads me, let it sound no more,
For though it have holp mad men to their wits,
In me it seems it will make wise men mad.
Yet blessing on his heart that gives it me!
For 'tis a sign of love; and love to Richard   65
Is a strange brooch in this all-hating world.

Enter a GROOM OF THE STABLE.

Groom. Hail, royal prince!
K. Rich.   Thanks, noble peer!
The cheapest of us is ten groats too dear.

What art thou? and how comest thou hither,
Where no man never comes, but that sad dog   70
That brings me food to make misfortune live?
    Groom. I was a poor groom of thy stable, King,
When thou wert king; who, travelling towards York,
With much ado (at length) have gotten leave
To look upon my sometimes royal master's face.   75
O how it ern'd my heart when I beheld
In London streets, that coronation-day,
When Bullingbrook rode on roan Barbary,
That horse that thou so often hast bestrid,
That horse that I so carefully have dress'd!   80
    K. Rich. Rode he on Barbary? Tell me, gentle
        friend,
How went he under him?
    Groom. So proudly as if he disdain'd the ground.
    K. Rich. So proud that Bullingbrook was on his
        back!
That jade hath eat bread from my royal hand,   85
This hand hath made him proud with clapping him.
Would he not stumble? Would he not fall down,
Since pride must have a fall, and break the neck
Of that proud man that did usurp his back?
Forgiveness, horse! why do I rail on thee,   90
Since thou, created to be aw'd by man,
Wast born to bear? I was not made a horse,
And yet I bear a burthen like an ass,
Spurr'd, gall'd, and tir'd by jauncing Bullingbrook.

Enter one [the KEEPER*] to Richard with meat.*

    Keep. Fellow, give place, here is no longer stay.
    K. Rich. If thou love me, 'tis time thou wert
        away.   96
    Groom. What my tongue dares not, that my heart
        shall say.   *Exit Groom.*
    Keep. My lord, will't please you to fall to?
    K. Rich. Taste of it first, as thou art wont to do.
    Keep. My lord, I dare not. Sir Pierce of Exton, who
Lately came from the King, commands the contrary.
    K. Rich. The devil take Henry of Lancaster and
        thee!   102
Patience is stale, and I am weary of it.
                              [*Beats the Keeper.*]
    Keep. Help, help, help!

*The murderers [*EXTON *and* SERVANTS*] rush in [armed].*

    K. Rich. How now, what means death in this rude
        assault?   105
Villain, thy own hand yields thy death's instrument,
        [*Snatches an axe from a Servant and kills him.*]
Go thou and fill another room in hell.
        [*Kills another.*] *Here Exton strikes him down.*
That hand shall burn in never-quenching fire
That staggers thus my person. Exton, thy fierce hand

---

25. **seely:** silly, i.e. simple.
26. **refuge their shame:** seek refuge for their disgrace.
37. **unking'd.** See note to II.i.16.
46. **check:** rebuke, i.e. be offended by.
51–54. **My . . . tears:** i.e. my (sad) thoughts are minutes, and my sighs, like the ticking of a clock, record or tick off (*jar*) their periods (*watches*) in my eyes—the clock face at which my finger, like the minute hand (*dial's point*), is always pointing as it wipes away my tears.
59. **posting:** with speed.
60. **Jack . . . clock:** manikin in old clocks that struck the bell.
61. **mads:** maddens.   62. **holp:** helped.   63. **wise:** sane.
66. **strange brooch:** rare ornament.   **this all-hating world:** this world in which all hate Richard.
67–68. **Hail . . . dear.** An elaborate play on coinage. The difference between a *royal* (worth 10s.) and a *noble* (worth 6s. 8d.) was ten

groats (40 pence), and since Richard says that the "cheapest of us" (i.e. himself, a prisoner) is "ten groats too dear," he estimates his value no higher than the groom's.   75. **sometimes:** former.
76. **ern'd:** grieved.   85. **eat:** eaten.
86. **with clapping:** by patting.
94. **jauncing:** making the horse prance.
99. **Taste:** i.e. to see that it was not poisoned.
107. **room:** place.   108. **never-quenching:** never-quenched.

Hath with the King's blood stain'd the King's own
    land.   110
Mount, mount, my soul! thy seat is up on high,
Whilst my gross flesh sinks downward, here to die.
                                  [*Dies.*]

   Exton.   As full of valure as of royal blood!
Both have I spill'd; O would the deed were good!
For now the devil that told me I did well   115
Says that this deed is chronicled in hell.
This dead king to the living king I'll bear;
Take hence the rest, and give them burial here.
                               [*Exeunt.*]

[SCENE VI]

[*Flourish.*] *Enter* Bullingbrook, [*now* KING HENRY,]
with the DUKE OF YORK [*with other* LORDS *and*
ATTENDANTS].

   K. Hen.   Kind uncle York, the latest news we hear
Is that the rebels have consum'd with fire
Our town of Ciceter in Gloucestershire,
But whether they be ta'en or slain we hear not.

            Enter NORTHUMBERLAND.

Welcome, my lord, what is the news?   5
   North.   First, to thy sacred state wish I all happi-
    ness.
The next news is, I have to London sent
The heads of Salisbury, [Spencer], Blunt, and Kent.
The manner of their taking may appear
At large discoursed in this paper here.   10
   K. Hen.   We thank thee, gentle Percy, for thy
    pains,
And to thy worth will add right worthy gains.

           Enter LORD FITZWATER.

   Fitz.   My lord, I have from Oxford sent to London
The heads of Brocas and Sir Bennet Seely,
Two of the dangerous consorted traitors   15
That sought at Oxford thy dire overthrow.
   K. Hen.   Thy pains, Fitzwater, shall not be forgot,
Right noble is thy merit, well I wot.

113. valure: valor.

V.vi. Location: Windsor Castle.
3. Ciceter: Cirencester.   6. state: royalty.
9. taking: capture.   12. worth: (1) assets; (2) deserts.

Enter HARRY PERCY [*and the* BISHOP OF CARLISLE].

   Percy.   The grand conspirator, Abbot of West-
    minster,
With clog of conscience and sour melancholy   20
Hath yielded up his body to the grave;
But here is Carlisle living, to abide
Thy kingly doom and sentence of his pride.
   K. Hen.   Carlisle, this is your doom:
Choose out some secret place, some reverent room,
More than thou hast, and with it joy thy life.   26
So as thou liv'st in peace, die free from strife,
For though mine enemy thou hast ever been,
High sparks of honor in thee have I seen.

 Enter EXTON *with* [ATTENDANTS *bearing*] *the coffin.*

   Exton.   Great King, within this coffin I present   30
Thy buried fear. Herein all breathless lies
The mightiest of thy greatest enemies,
Richard of Burdeaux, by me hither brought.
   K. Hen.   Exton, I thank thee not, for thou hast
    wrought
A deed of slander with thy fatal hand   35
Upon my head and all this famous land.
   Exton.   From your own mouth, my lord, did I this
    deed.
   K. Hen.   They love not poison that do poison need,
Nor do I thee. Though I did wish him dead,
I hate the murtherer, love him murthered.   40
The guilt of conscience take thou for thy labor,
But neither my good word nor princely favor.
With Cain go wander thorough shades of night,
And never show thy head by day nor light.
Lords, I protest my soul is full of woe   45
That blood should sprinkle me to make me grow.
Come mourn with me for what I do lament,
And put on sullen black incontinent.
I'll make a voyage to the Holy Land,
To wash this blood off from my guilty hand.   50
March sadly after, grace my mournings here,
In weeping after this untimely bier.   [*Exeunt.*]

20. clog: burden.   23. doom: judgment.
25. secret: retired.   reverent room: i.e. spot appropriate for a religious life.   26. joy: enjoy.   31. fear: object of fear.
33. Burdeaux: Bordeaux (Richard's birthplace).
35. of slander: i.e. grave enough to bring disgrace.
43. thorough: through.   48. incontinent: immediately.
51. grace: dignify.

NOTE ON THE TEXT

   Richard II was first published in quarto in 1597 (Q1); two
other quarto editions appeared in 1598 (Q2, Q3), and two
more (Q4, Q5) in 1608 and 1615 respectively, each reprinted
from the quarto immediately preceding. The play was, of
course, included in the First Folio (1623), and a sixth quarto
(Q6) was issued in 1634, its text derived from the Second
Folio (1632).

   It has generally been believed that Q1, which here serves
as copy-text (except for IV.i.154–318: see below), was set up
directly from Shakespeare's "foul papers," a view still supported by Charlton Hinman in the most recent study of the
Q1 text. There is, however, some support for the theory that
a transcript of the "foul papers" rather than the "foul
papers" themselves furnished the printer's copy. Such a view
would at least help to explain why so little in the way of
characteristic Shakespearean spellings can be detected in Q1.

   Q1 does not contain the so-called "deposition scene"
(IV.i.154–318). This part of the scene first appeared in Q4,
but in a version which strongly suggests a memorially contaminated text. F1 gives an obviously superior text and has

therefore been used as copy-text for these lines, although the lighter punctuation of Q4, as more in keeping with that of Q1, has been followed wherever possible. All Q4 substantive variants for the passage are recorded in the Textual Notes.

Aside from its importance for the "deposition scene," the F1 text requires some respectful notice. It was printed, according to R. E. Hasker (following a suggestion of A. W. Pollard's), from a composite copy made up from Q3 (for I.i.1–V.v.18, except for IV.i.154–318) and Q5 (for IV.i.154–318, V.v.19–V.vi.52), both sporadically corrected at some stage against an official prompt-book. Whether this composite copy had itself served as a prompt-book (as Hasker believes) or had been specially prepared as copy-text for F1 (as Peter Ure holds to be more likely), we cannot be sure, although the consistency with which Q1 *God* is softened to *heaven* and, perhaps, the omission of some lines in F1, presumably reflecting theatrical cuts, would seem to suggest the hand of the prompter. The significant point, however, is that the F1 text shows evidence, if only of a rather spotty kind, of having been checked against an independent manuscript (the improved text of the "deposition scene" certainly supports such a view), and it follows that substantive readings which appear for the first time in F1 deserve some consideration as possible Shakespearean second thoughts. Nevertheless, since we cannot be sure that such new readings are not due to other hands (the prompter's, the actors', the compositor's, or even the hypothetical collator's), very few F1 readings which do not correct obvious errors have been admitted in the present text. All significant readings and omissions originating in F1 are, however, recorded in the Textual Notes.

For further information, see: A. W. Pollard, "*King Richard II*": *A New Quarto* (London, 1916); R. E. Hasker, "The Copy for the First Folio *Richard II*," *SB*, V (1952–53), 53–72; W. W. Greg, *The Shakespeare First Folio* (Oxford, 1955); M. W. Black, ed., New Variorum *Richard II* (Philadelphia, 1955); Peter Ure, ed., New Arden *Richard II* (London, 1956); Charlton Hinman (and W. W. Greg), eds., *Richard the Second* (1597), facsimile of Q1 (Oxford, 1966).

TEXTUAL NOTES

Title: The . . . Second] The Tragedie of King Richard the second. As it hath beene publikely acted by the right Honourable the Lorde Chamberlaine his Seruants. *Q1 (title-page)*; The life and death of King Richard the Second. *F1*
Act-scene division: *none in Q1–5; from F1, with the following exceptions: V.iv (no scene division in F1); V.v, vi (numbered V.iv, v in F1); see first note to each scene; present act-scene arrangement as a whole first established by Steevens*

I.i

I.i] *F1*
Location: *Wilson*
3 **Herford]** *see note on I.ii.46*
15 **presence;]** *Pope*; presence *Q1–5, F1*
19 s.d. **with Attendants]** *Collier (after Capell)*
46 **drawn]** *Q2–5, F1*; drawen *F1*
53 **hush'd]** *Q2–5, F1*; huisht *Q1*
57 **doubled]** doubly *F1*
96 **land,]** *Q3–5, F1*; land: *Q1–2*
101 **soon-believing]** *hyphen, Pope*
102 **traitor]** *Q2–5, F1*; taitour *Q1*
104 **Abel's,]** *Q4–5 (subs.)*; Abels *Q1–3, F1*
118 **my]** *F1*
122 **Mowbray;]** *Collier*; Mowbray *Q1*; Mowbray, *Q2–5*; (Mowbray) *F1*
129–30 **debt, . . . account,]** *Q2–5, F1*; debt. / . . . account: *Q1*
133 **not,]** *Q2–5*; not *Q1*; not; *F1*
139 **But]** *so two copies of Q1; the other two extant copies read* Ah but *(it is not certain which reading represents the corrected state)*; Ah but *Q2–3*; Ah, but *Q4–5*
152 **Wrath-kindled]** *hyphen, Capell*
152 **gentlemen]** *F1*; gentleman *Q1–5*
152 **rul'd]** *F1*; ruled *Q1–5*
157 **month]** time *F1*
162 **when?]** *Q2–5, F1*; when *Q1*
163 **Obedience bids]** obedience bids, / Obedience bids *Q1–5, F1*; *Pope first om. the repetition, but reads* bids, *(followed by later eds. until White)*
170 **baffled]** *Rowe*; baffuld *Q1–5*; baffel'd *F1*
172 **heart-blood]** *hyphen, Pope*
176 **gage.]** *F1*; gage, *Q1, Q4–5*; gage *Q2–3*
177–8 **afford . . . reputation;]** *F1 (subs.)*; afford, / . . . Reputation *Q1*; affoord, / . . . reputation, *Q2–5*
180 **ten-times-barr'd-up]** *hyphens, Capell*
186 **up]** downe *F1*
187 **God]** heauen *F1*
192 **parley]** *ed.*; parlee *Q1–5*; parle *F1*
195 s.d. **Exit Gaunt.]** *F1*
201 **hate.]** *Q4–5, F1 (subs.)*; hate, *Q1–3*

204 **officers-at-arms]** *hyphens, Delius*
205 s.d. **Exeunt.]** *F1*; Exit. *Q1–5*

I.ii

I.ii] *F1*
Location: *Theobald*
1 **Woodstock's]** Glousters *F1*
7 **hour's]** *Q4–5 (hower's)*; houres *Q1–3, F1*
12, 17 **vials . . . vial]** *F2*; viols . . . violl *Q1–5, F1*
23 **mettle]** *F1*; mettall *Q1–5*
37 **God's . . . God's]** Heauens . . . heauens] *F1*
37 **quarrel,]** *Q3–5*; quarrell *Q1–2*; quarrell: *F1*
43 **God]** heauen *F1*
43 **and]** to *F1*
46 **Herford]** *Q2–5, F1*; Hereford *Q1 (Q1 uses both spellings,* Hereford *more frequently, but since a disyllable seems generally called for,* Herford *has been adopted throughout)*
47 **sit]** *F1*; set *Q1–5*
49 **career]** *F1 (carreere)*; carier *Q1–2*; carriere *Q3*; carrier *Q4–5*
58 **it]** *Q2–5, F1*; is *Q1*
60 **begun]** *Q2–5, F1*; begone *Q1*
70 **hear]** cheere *Q1 (u)*

I.iii

I.iii] *F1*
Location: *Pope*
6 s.d. **Gaunt . . . others]** *F1*
6 s.d. **with a Herald]** *from F1 and Harrold*
15 **thee]** *Q2–5, F1*; the *Q1*
18 **God]** heauen *F1*
20 **and my]** and his *F1*
25 s.d. **with a Herald]** *from F1 and Harold*
28 **plated]** placed *F1*
33 **com'st]** *F1*; comes *Q1–4*; comest *Q5*
37 **God's]** heauens *F1*
43 **daring-hardy]** *Theobald*; daring, hardy *Q1–5*; daring hardie *F1*
44, 46, 99 **Marshal]** *Q5, F1*; Martiall *Q1–4*
55 **right]** iust *F1*
58 **thee]** *Q3–5, F1*; the *Q1–2*
66 **cheerly]** *F3*; cheerely *Q1–5, F1*
69 **earthly]** earthy *F1*
71 **vigor]** rigor *F1*
76 **furbish]** furnish *F1*
78, 85, 101 **God]** Heauen *or* heauen *F1*
82 **adverse]** amaz'd *F1*
102 **hope, I cry]** *F1*; hope I cry, *Q1–5*
103 s.d. **To an Officer.]** *Capell*
104 s.p. **1. Her.]** *F1 (subs.)*; Herald *Q1–5*
117 s.d. **A charge sounded.]** *F1 (after l. 116); placed as in Malone*
118 **thrown]** *Q2–5, F1*; throwen *Q1*
122 s.d. **A long flourish.]** *F1*

124 **Council]** *F1*; counsell *Q1–5*
128 **civil]** cruell *Q1 (u)*
128 **neighbors']** *Hanmer*; neighbours *Q1–5, F1*
128 **sword]** swords *F1*
129–33 **And . . . sleep;]** *om. F1*
133 **sleep;]** *Pope*; sleepe *Q1*; sleepe, *Q2–5*
135 **harsh-resounding]** *hyphen, Theobald*
140 **life]** death *F1*
172 **then]** *F1*
180 **y' owe]** you owe *F1*
180, 183, 204 **God]** heauen *or* Heauen *F1*
206 **stray;]** *Roderick conj.*; stray, *Q1–5, F1*
211 s.d. **To Bullingbrook.]** *Steevens (subs., after Capell)*
221 **time-bewasted]** *hyphen, F1*
222 **extinct]** *Q2–5, F1*; extint *Q1*
222 **night]** *Q4–5, F1*; nightes *Q1–3*
223 **inch]** *Q3–5, F1*; intch *Q1–2*
227 **sullen]** sudden *F1*
233 **advice]** *F1*; aduise *Q1–5*
234 **party-verdict]** *hyphen, F1*
239–42 **O . . . destroyed.]** *om. F1*
248 s.d. **Flourish.]** *F1 (after F1 Exit.); placed as in Pope*
248 s.d. **with his Train]** *Capell (subs.)*
253 **dost]** *Q5, F1*; doest *Q1–4*
262 **travel]** *F1*; trauaile *Q1–5*
266 **as foil]** a foyle *Q2*; a soyle *Q3–5, F1*
268–93 **Bull. Nay . . . light.]** *om. F1*
269 **world]** *Q2 (c), Q3–5*; world: *Q1, Q2 (u)*
276 **wise man]** *Q3–5*; wiseman *Q1–2*
307 **that]** which *F1*
309 **true-born]** *F1 (true-borne)*; true borne *Q1–5*
309 **Englishman]** *Q2–5, F1*; English man *Q1*

I.iv

I.iv] *F1*
Location: *Sisson (after Theobald)*
o.s.d. **Green and Bagot]** *F1*; Bushie, &c *Q1–5 (Q1–5 later enter Bushy at l. 52)*
7 **blew]** grew *F1*
13 **word, . . . craft]** *F1*; word . . . craft, *Q1–5*
15 **words]** word *F1*
20 **cousin's cousin]** *Wilson*; Coosens Coosin *Q1–5*; Cosin (Cosin) *F1*
23 **Bagot . . . Green,]** *Q6*; heere Bagot and Greene *F1*; om. *Q1–5*
24 **Observ'd]** *F1*; Obserued *Q1–5*
28 **smiles]** soules *F1*
30 **him.]** *F1*; him, *Q1–5*
44 **grown]** *Q2–5, F1*; growen *Q1*
47 **hand.]** *F1 (subs.)*; hand *Q1–5*
52 s.d. **Enter Bushy.]** *F1*; Enter Bushie with newes. *Q1–5*
53 **Bushy, what news?]** *F1 (note Q1–5 s.d. at l. 52)*

54 **grievous**] verie *F1*
59, 64 **God**] heauen *F1*
64–5 **late! All. Amen.**] Staunton; late, / Amen *Q1*; late, / Amen. *Q2–3*; late: / Amen. *Q4–5*; late. *F1*
65 s.d. **Exeunt.**] Exit. *F1*

II.i

II.i] *F1*
Location: *Theobald*
12 **at**] is *F1*
18 **whose . . . wise**] whose state the wise *Q2*; of his state: then there *Q3–5*, *F1*
18 **fond**] *Collier conj.*; found *Q1–5*; sound *F1*
27 **Then**] That *F1*
33 **last**,] last; *F1*
36 **betimes;**] *F1*; betimes *Q1*; betimes, *Q2*; betimes. *Q3–5*
48 **a**] *Q4–5*, *F1*
68 s.d. **Aumerle . . . Willoughby**] *F1* (*s.d. after l. 70*)
85 **No,**] *Q3–5*, *F1*; No *Q1–2*
102 **incaged**] *F1*; inraged *Q1–5*
113 **now, not**] *Theobald*; now not, not *Q1–4*; now not, nor *Q5*; and not *F1*
115 **And thou— K. Rich. A**] *Capell*; And thou / *King. A Q1*; And thou. / *King. A Q2*; And thou. / *King. Ah Q3–5*; And— / *Rich. And thou, a F1*
118 **chasing**] chafing *F1*
124 **brother**] *Q2–5*; brothers *Q1*, *F1*
138 s.d. **borne . . . Attendants**] *Capell*
146 s.d. **Enter Northumberland.**] *F1*
172 **first.**] *Q2–5*; first *Q1*; first, *F1*
177 **the**] *F1*; a *Q1–5*
188 **withal**] *Q2*, *Q5*; with all *Q1*, *Q3–4*, *F1*
203 **attorneys-general**] *hyphen*, *Rowe*
209 **seize**] *Q3–5*; cease *Q1*; ceaze *Q2*; seise *F1*
218 **trow.**] *Q3–5*, *F1* (*subs.*); trow, *Q1–2*
223 s.d. **Flourish.**] *F1*
223 s.d. **with others**] *Rowe* (*&c.*); *F1 om. the whole exeunt part of the s.d.*
223 s.d. **with . . . Ross**] *F1* (*subs.*)
229 **Ere't**] *Rowe*; Eart *Q1*; Ert *Q2*; Er't *Q3–5*, *F1*
238 **God**] heauen *F1*
254 **noble**] *om. F1*
254 **achiev'd**] *F1*; atchiued *Q1*; atchiude *Q2–4*; atchieud *Q5*
257 **King's**] *Q3–5*; King *Q1–2*; Kings *F1*
257 **grown**] *Q2–5*, *F1*; growen *Q1*
262 **kinsman—**] *Rowe*; kinsman *Q1–5*; Kinsman, *F1*
277 **Le Port Blanc**] *Cambridge* (*after Holinshed and Pope*); le Port Blan *Q1–5*; Port le Blan *F1*
280 **Thomas . . . Arundel,**] *Hudson* (*based on Holinshed*)
283 **Ramston**] Rainston *F1*
284 **Coint**] *Halliwell* (*after Holinshed*); Coines *Q1–5*; Quoint *F1*
294 **gilt**] *F1*; guilt *Q1–5*

II.ii

II.ii] *F1*
Location: *Clarendon eds.*
3 **life-harming**] life harming *Q2*; halfe-harming *Q3–5*; selfe-harming *F1*
11–2 **soul . . . trembles;**] *Rowe*; soule, . . . trembles, *Q1–5*; soule . . . trembles, *F1*
12 **some thing**] *Q2–5*; something *Q1*, *F1*
16 **eyes**] eye *F1*
24 **thrice-gracious Queen**] *F1*; thrice (gracious Queene) *Q1–5*
25 **more is**] more's *F1*
31 **though**] *Q2–5*, *F1*; thought *Q1*
37–8 **grieve— . . . possess—**] *Wilson* (*after Theobald*); grieue, . . . possesse, *Q1–3*, *F1*; grieue, . . . possesse: *Q4–5*
39 **known what,**] *Q1* (knowen what,); knowne, what *Q2–5*, *F1*
40 s.d. **Enter Green.**] *F1*
41 **God**] Heauen *F1*
52 **Ah**] O *F1*
52 **worse**,] *F1*; worse; *Q1–5*
53 **son young Harry**] *ed.* (*after Q1* son yong H.); yong sonne H. *Q2–5*; yong sonne

---

Henrie *F1*
70 **keeper-back**] *hyphen*, *Capell*
72 s.d. **Enter York.**] *F1*
76 **God's**] heauens *F1*
77 **Should . . . thoughts.**] *om. F1*
85 s.d. **Enter a Servingman.**] *Kittredge* (*after F1* Enter a seruant.); *Q1–5 s.pp. are* Seruingman
87 **was—**] *Johnson*; was; *Q1*; was, *Q2–5*; was: *F1*
98, 100 **God**] Heau'n *and* heauen *F1*
103 **no**] two *Q2–5*; *om. F1*
107 s.d. **Exit Servingman.**] *Kittredge* (*after Capell*)
108 **go**] *om. F1*
119 **Berkeley**] *Theobald* (*subs.*); Barkly *Q1–2*; Barckly *Q3–5*; Barkley Castle *F1*
122 s.d. **Exeunt . . . Bagot.**] *ed* (*from Q1–5* Exeunt Duke, Qu. man. Bush, Green.); Exit *F1*
123 **for**] to *F1*
127 **Besides,**] *Q4–5*; Besides *Q1–3*, *F1*
129 **that is**] that's *F1*
130 **whoso**] *Q6*; who so *Q1–5*, *F1*
135 **Bristow**] *Kittredge*; Brist. *Q1–5*; Bristoll *F1*
142 **Farewell! If**] *Rowe* (*subs.*); Farewell if *Q1–2*; Farewell, if *Q3–5*
149 s.d. **Exeunt.**] *Rowe*; Exit. *F1*

II.iii

II.iii] *F1*
Location: *Theobald* (*subs.*)
o.s.d. **and forces**] *Capell* (*subs.*)
6 **your**] our *F1*
24 **learn'd**] *F1*; learned *Q1–5*
25 **Why,**] *F1*; Why *Q1–2*; Why? *Q3–5*
30 **lordship**] *Q2–5*, *F1*; Lo: *Q1*
36 **Herford, boy?**] *Q4–5*; Herfords boy? *Q1–2*: Hereford, boy? *Q3*; Hereford (Boy.) *F1*
55 **Seymour**] *F3*; Seymer *Q1*; Seymor *Q2–5*, *F1*
56 s.d. **Enter . . . Willoughby.**] *F1*
58 **fiery-red**] *hyphen*, *Theobald*
65 **thank's**] thankes, *Q5*, *F1*
68 s.d. **Enter Berkeley.**] *F1* (Barkely; *after l. 67*); *placed as in Dyce*
75 **rase**] *Valpy*; raze *Q1–5*, *F1*
80 s.d. **Enter York attended.**] *F1* (Enter Yorke.) *and Capell*
82 **person.**] *F1*; person, *Q1*; person: *Q2–5*
82 s.d. **Kneels.**] *Rowe*
87 **no uncle**] *om. F1*
92 **"why?"**] *quotes*, *Cambridge*
101 **men,**] *Q3–5*, *F1*; men. *Q1–2*
125 **cousin**] Kinsman *F1*
134 **I**] *om. F1*
145 **wrong—**] *Capell*; wrong *Q1*; wrong, *Q2*, *Q4–5*; wrong; *Q3*; Wrongs, *F1*
158 **known unto**] *Collier*; knowen vnto *Q1*; knowne to *Q2–5*, *F1*
170 **foes,**] *Q2–5*, *F1*; foes *Q1*

II.iv

II.iv] *F1*
Location: *Capell* (*after Theobald*)
1, 7 s.pp. Cap.] *F1*; Welch. *Q1–5*
1 **stay'd**] *Q3–5*, *F1*; stayed *Q1–2*
17 s.d. **Exit.**] *F1*
24 s.d. **Exit.**] *F1*

III.i

III.i] *F1*
Location: *Theobald*, *Capell*
o.s.d. **Ross . . . with**] *F1*
3 **bodies—**] *F1* (*subs.*); bodies *Q1*; bodyes, *Q2–5*
15 **drawn**] *Q2–5*, *F1*; drawen *Q1*
22 **signories**] *Capell*; segniories *Q1–5*; Seigniories *F1*
25 **Ras'd**] *Capell* (*sub.*); Rac't *Q1–5*; Raz'd *F1*
25 **imprese**] *Q5*, *F1*; impreese *Q1–4*
35 s.d. **Exeunt . . . prisoners.**] *Capell*
37 **God's**] Heauens *F1*
43 **Glendower**] *Rowe*; Glendor *Q1–5*; Glendoure *F1*

III.ii

III.ii] *F1*
Location: *Capell* (*after Pope*)
o.s.d. **Drums . . . Colors.**] *F1*
o.s.d. **and Soldiers**] *F1*; &c. *Q1–5*
29–32 **The . . . redress.**] *om. F1*
30 **neglected.**] *Pope* (*subs.*); neglected. *Q1–5*
31 **not.**] *Sisson*; not, *Q1–2*; not; *Q3–5*
35 **power**] friends *F1*
37–8 **hid . . . globe,**] *F1*; hid, . . . globe *Q1*; hid . . . globe *Q2–5*
40 **boldly**] *Collier conj.*; bouldy *Q1* (*possibly a form of* boldly); bloudy *Q2–5*, *F1*
49 **Whilst . . . antipodes,**] *om. F1*
55 **off**] *om. F1*
60 **God**] Heauen *F1*
63 **Welcome**] *F1*; King Welcome *Q1–5* (*repeated s.p.*)
72 **Overthrows**] Orethrowes *F1*
84 **coward**] sluggard *F1*
85 **twenty**] fortie *F1*
92 **care-tun'd**] *hyphen*, *F1*
98 **be;**] *Q3–5*, *F1* (*subs.*); be, *Q1–2*
102 **and**] Losse *F1*
105 **calamity.**] *F1*; calamity, *Q1–5*
112 **White-beards**] *hyphen*, *Reed*
115 **crown;**] *Rowe*; crowne, *Q1–5*; Crowne *F1*
117 **double-fatal**] *hyphen*, *Warburton*
117 **yew**] *Hanmer*; ewe *Q1–2*; wo *Q3–5*; Eugh *F1*
118 **distaff-women**] *hyphen*, *F1*
130 **won**] *Q3–5*; woon *Q1*, *F1*; woonne *Q2*
131 **heart-blood**] *hyphen*, *F3*
134 **this!**] this Offence. *F1*
139 **wound**] hand *F1*
155 **God's**] Heauens *F1*
162 **antic**] *Pope*; antique *Q1–5*, *F1*
178 **wise men**] *F1*; wisemen *Q1–5*
178 **sit . . . their**] waile their present *F1*
182 **And . . . yourself.**] *om. F1*
188 **well.**] *Q4–5*, *F1* (*subs.*); well, *Q1–3*
197 **say.**] *F1* (*subs.*); say, *Q1–5*
203 **party**] Faction *F1*
204 s.d. **To Aumerle.**] *Theobald*
218 s.d. **Exeunt.**] *F1*

III.iii

III.iii] *F1*
Location: *Capell* (*after Theobald*)
o.s.d. **with . . . Colors**] *F1*
o.s.d. **Attendants**] *F1*
o.s.d. **and forces**] *Capell*
13 **with you**] *F1*
23 **Royally?**] *F1*; Royally, *Q1–5*
24 **king.**] King? *F1*
31 **lord**] *F1*; Lords *Q1–5*
31 s.d. **To Northumberland.**] *Rowe*
36 **On both**] vpon *F1*
41 **restor'd**] *F1*; restored *Q1–5*
44 **Englishmen**] *Q2–5*, *F1*; English men *Q1*
50 s.d. **Northumberland . . . Trumpet.**] *Malone* (*after Capell*)
59 **rain**] *F1*; raigne. *Q1–2*; raigne *Q3–5*
60 **waters—**] *Kittredge* (*after Rowe*); water's *Q1–5*; Waters *F1*
61 s.d. **parle . . . flourish**] *F1*
61 s.d. **Richard . . . walls**] Enter on the Walls, Richard *F1*
61 s.d. **with . . . Salisbury**] *F1* (*except for* with)
62 **See**] *F1*; Bull. See *Q1–5* (*repeated s.p.*)
72 s.d. **To Northumberland.**] *Rowe* (*after l. 73*); *placed as in Hudson*
91 **stands**] is *F1*
100 **pasters'**] *ed.*; pastors *Q1–5*, *F1* (*a form representing Shakespeare's pronunciation; cf.* Timon of Athens, *IV.iii.12*)
101 **forbid**] *F1*; forbid: *Q1–3*; forbid, *Q4–5*
119 **a prince, is**] *F1*; princesse *Q1–2*; a Prince *Q3–5*
121 **thus . . . returns:**] *Rowe*; thus, . . . returnes, *Q1*; thus . . . returnes, *Q2*; thus: . . . returnes, *Q3–4*, *F1*; thus: . . . returnes *Q5*
126 s.d. **Northumberland . . . Bullingbrook.**] *Collier* (*subs.*)
127 s.d. **To Aumerle.**] *Rowe*

127 We] Q4–5, F1; King We Q1–3 (repeated s.p.)
171 laugh] mock F1
180 court?] F1; court, Q1–5
183 s.d. Exeunt above.] Capell (subs.)
186 s.d. Enter . . . below.] Capell
195 s.d. touching his crown] Hudson (after Johnson)
202 hands] Hand F1
206 too] Q4–5; to Q1–3, F1
209 s.d. Flourish.] F1
209 s.d. Exeunt.] Q4–5, F1

III.iv

III.iv] F1
Location: Capell
o.s.d. **two Ladies]** F1
3, 6, etc. s.pp. 1. Lady.] Capell; Lady Q1–5, F1
11 joy] Rowe; griefe Q1–5, F1
21 weep, . . . good.] F1; weepe; . . . good? Q1; weepe . . . good. Q2–5
23 s.d. a Gardener . . . Men] ed. (from F1 a Gardiner, and two Seruants); Gardeners Q1–5
26 pins] F1; pines Q1–5
28 change;] F1; change Q1–5
28 s.d. Queen . . . retire.] Pope
29 young] yon Q2–5; yond F1
29 apricocks] Q3–5, F1; Aphricokes Q1–2
34 too] F1; two Q1–5
40, 54, 67 s.pp. 1. Man.] ed. (after Capell); Man. Q1–5; Ser. F1
48 hath] Q2–5, F1; htah Q1
50 broad-spreading] hyphen, F1
55 seiz'd] Q3–5, F1; ceasde Q1–2
57 garden! We] Capell; garden Q1–5; Garden, F1
59 over-proud] hyphen, Q2–5, F1
63 duty] Q2–3, F1; duety Q1, Q4–5; dutie. All F2
72 s.d. Coming forward.] Capell (subs.)
80 Cam'st . . . tidings?] Q2–5, F1; Canst . . . tidings Q1
84 weigh'd] Q3–5 (weyde.); weyde Q1–2; weigh'd F1
85 lord's] F1; Lo. Q1–5
101 Pray God] I would F1
101 s.d. with Ladies] Pope (subs.)

IV.i

IV.i] F1
Location: Pope, Malone
o.s.d. **Aumerle . . . Westminster]** F1; Aumerle and others Q4–5
o.s.d. **and another Lord]** Capell
o.s.d. **to]** as to the F1
o.s.d. **Herald]** from F1 Herauld, Officers, and Bagot
1 s.d. Officers with] Halliwell (from F1 o.s.d.)
3 dost] Q3–5; doest Q1–2; do'st F1
22 him] Q3–5, F1; them Q1; my Q2
28 heart-blood] hyphen, Theobald
40 forged,] Q4–5; forged Q1–3, F1
43 Fitzwater] F1; Fitzwaters Q1–5
48 Seize] Q3–5; ceaze Q1–2
52–9 Another Lord. I . . . you.] om. F1
54 As] Johnson; As it Q1–5
55 sun to sun] Capell; sinne to sinne Q1–5
61 Aumerle] Q2–5, F1; (Aumerle) Q1
62 'Tis] My Lord, / 'Tis F1
72 dost] Q2–5; doest Q1; do'st F1
76 my] Q3–5, F1; om. Q1; the Q2
83–4 gage— . . . lies.] Collier (subs.); gage, . . . lies, Q1–5; Gage, . . . lyes: F1
101 Bishop] Q3–5, F1; B. Q1–2
106 s.d. attended] Capell
109 thee] Q2–5, F1; the Q1
114 Marry] F3; Mary Q1–5, F1
114 God] Heauen F1
115 speak,] F1; speake. Q1–2; speake: Q3–5
126 deputy,] Deputie F1
127 planted many years,] Q3–5, F1; planted, many yeares Q1; planted many yeares Q2
129 forfend] forbid F1
133 God] Heauen F1
145 you] Q2–5, F1; yon Q1

154–318 May . . . fall.] om. Q1–Q3 (the copy-text for these lines is F1; Q4–5 present an inferior, probably reported, text)
154 commons] common Q4–5
155 s.p. Bull.] speech continued to Northumberland, Q4–5
158 here] are heere, Q4–5
161 look'd] looke Q4–5
161 s.d. Richard and York] king Richard ' Q4–5
161 s.d. with . . . sceptre] Capell (subs.)
165 knee.] limbes? Q4–5
166 tutor] Q4–5; tuture F1
169 sometimes] Q4–5; sometime F1
180, 220 Henry] Harry Q4–5
181 Give . . . cousin,] om. Q4–5
183 and] Q4–5
183 thine] yours Q4–5
189 griefs] griefe Q4–5
199 tend] Q4–5; 'tend F1
201 Ay, no, no ay;] ed. (Ay . . . ay Theobald); I, no; no, I: F1; I, no no I; Q4–5
202 no no] Q4–5; no, no F1
210 duteous oaths] duties rites Q4–5
212 manors] Manners Q4; Mannors Q5
215 are made] that sweare Q4–5
222 s.d. Presenting a paper.] Capell
229 follies? Gentle Northumberland,] Folly, gentle Northumberland? Q4–5
237 all . . . me] these two words om. Q4–5
238 bait] bate Q4–5
241 deliver'd] deliuer Q4; deliuered Q5
245 salt water] Q4–5; salt-Water F1
250 T' undeck] To vndecke Q4–5
251 and] Q4–5; a F1
254 haught insulting] Q4–5; haught-insulting F1
255 Nor no] Q4–5; No, nor F1
260 mockery] Q4–5; Mockerie, F1
264 word] name Q4–5
267 bankrout] Q4–5; Bankrupt F1
268 s.d. Exit an Attendant.] Capell
276 that] the Q4–5
276 and . . . read.] om. Q4–5
277 struck] stroke Q4–5
281 Thou . . . me!] om. Q4–5
281 this face] this Q4–5
283–4 Was . . . wink?] om. Q4–5
285 Is . . . which] Was . . . that Q4–5
286 That] And Q4–5
288 s.d. Dashes . . . ground.] Theobald
289 an] a Q4–5
296 manners] Q4–5; manner F1
299 There . . . substance;] om. Q4–5
300 For . . . bounty,] om. Q4–5
304 Shall . . . it?] om. Q4–5
305 cousin"?] Coose, why? Q4–5
311 have?] haue it? Q4–5
313 Then] Why then Q4–5
318 s.d. Exeunt . . . Guard.] Capell (subs.)
319 On Wednesday] Q4–5, F1; Let it be so, and loe on wednesday Q1–3
320 s.d. Carlisle] Q2–5; Caleil Q1; F1 om. Manent . . . Aumerle.
326 My lord] om. Q3–5, F1

V.i

V.i] F1
Location: Pope, Capell
2 ill-erected] hyphen, F1
3 whose] Q3–4, F1; whose Q1
6 s.d. and Guard] F1
10 true-love] hyphen, F1
14 lodg'd] F1; lodged Q1–5
17 sudden.] F1 (subs.); sudden, Q1–5
25 thrown] stricken F1
41 thee] Q2–5, F1; the Q1 (possibly the correct reading)
43 night] Q3–4, F1; night Q1–2; om. Q5
43 quite] quit F1
44 tale] fall F1
50 s.d. and others] F1
64 urg'd,] F2; vrgde Q1–5, F1
64 way] Pope; way, Q1–5, F1
66 men] friends F1
72 marriage—] Dyce (after F1 Marriage;); marriage Q1; marriage, Q2–5

---

78 wife] Queene F1
84 s.p. North.] F1; King Q1–5
88 than, near,] Ure; than neere Q1; then neere Q2–5; then neere, F1

V.ii

V.ii] F1
Location: Pope
2 off,] F1; of Q1; om. Q2–5
11 thee] F1; the Q1–5
17 thee! Welcome,] Theobald (from F1 thee, welcom); the welcome Q1–5
18 the one] one F1
22 Alack] Q2–5; Alac Q1; Alas F1
28 gentle] om. F1
28 Richard] Q2–5, F1; Ric. Q1
30 thrown] Q2–5, F1; throwen Q1
41 s.d. Enter Aumerle.] Q4–5, F1 (after l. 40, F1)
71 s.d. He . . . it.] Snatches it F1
72 Treason] Q4–5, F1; Yorke Treason Q1–3 (repeated s.p.)
74 s.d. Enter a Servant.] Malone (after Capell)
75 God] Heauen F1
77 s.d. Exit Servant.] Capell
81 Aumerle] Sonne F1
87 s.d. His . . . exit.] ed. (after Wilson and Kittredge)
94 thee] Q2–5, F1; the Q1
104 thy] Q2–5, F1; rhy Q1
104 dost] Q2–5; doest Q1; do'st F1
112 Spur] F1; Spur, Q1–5
116 An'] ed.; An Q1; And Q2–5, F1
117 s.d. Exeunt.] Rowe; Exit F1

V.iii

V.iii] F1
Location: Theobald
o.s.d. **the King]** Bullingbrooke F1
o.s.d. **Percy . . . Lords]** F1
1 s.p. K. Hen.] Bul. F1 (throughout rest of play)
4 God] heauen F1
21 years] dayes F1
28 s.d. Exeunt . . . Lords.] Capell (after Hanmer)
30 s.d. Kneels.] Rowe
35 after-love] hyphen, F2
36 I] Q2–5, F1
38 s.d. Aumerle . . . door.] Capell (subs.)
39 s.d. Within.] F1
41 s.d. Draws.] Johnson (subs.)
43 s.d. Within.] Capell
43 foolhardy] F1 (foole-hardy); foole, hardie Q1–5
45 s.d. King . . . door.] Johnson (subs.)
45 s.d. Enter York.] F1
50 treason] reason F1
51 pass'd] Dyce; past Q1–5, F1
68 An'] ed.; An Q1; And Q2–5, F1
72 life;] Theobald; life Q1–5; life, F1
74 s.d. Within.] F1
74 God's] heauens F1
75 shrill-voic'd] Q3–5, F1 (hyphen, F1); shril voice Q1–5
76 s.d. Within.] Capell
83 pardon,] F1; pardon Q1–5
86 s.d. Enter Duchess.] F1
91, 97, 98 s.dd. Kneels.] Rowe
93 walk] kneele F1
99 Ill . . . grace!] om. F1
102 mouth] Q2–5, F1; month Q1
106 still] shall F1
111 s.p. K. Hen.] Q2–5, F1 (subs.); yorke Q1
112 Say] But F1
119 King, say] F1 (subs.); King say, Q1–5
119 pardonne] Pardon'ne F1
131 God] heauen F1
135–6 With . . . him.] Pope; I pardon him with al my heart. Q1–5, F1
139 heels.] Q3; heeles Q1–2, Q4–5; heeles: F1
144 cousin] Cosin too Q6
145 pray'd] F1; prayed Q1–5
146 God] heauen F1

V.iv

V.iv] *Steevens*
Location: *Capell (after Theobald)*
o.s.d. **Enter . . . Servants.**] *F1 (subs.); Manet sir Pierce Exton, &c. Q1–5 (no scene break in Q1–5, F1)*
3, 6 s.pp. **1. Man.**] *ed.*; Man *Q1–5*; Ser. *F1*
7 **wishtly**] wistly *Q3–5, F1*
11 s.d. **Exeunt.**] *Q4–5*; Exit. *F1*

V.v

V.v] *Steevens*; Scaena Quarta. *F1*
Location: *Pope (subs.)*
3 **for because**] *Q2, Q4–5, F1*; forbecause *Q1, Q3*
13–4 **word . . . word**] Faith . . . Faith *F1*
17 **small**] *om. F1*
18 **ambition, . . . plot**] *F1*; ambition . . . plot, *Q1*; ambition . . . plot *Q2–5*
22 **cannot, . . . pride.**] *F1*; cannot . . . pride, *Q1–5*
25 **last—**] *Theobald (subs.)*; last *Q1–2*; last, *Q3–5*; last. *F1*
27 **sit**] *Q3–5, F1*; set *Q1–2*
38 **be**] am *F1*

41 s.d. **The music plays.**] *placed as in Buell, Yale Shakespeare; after* hear? *l. 41, Q1–5; Musick F1 (after l. 38)*
41 **hear?**] *F1*; heare, *Q1–3*; heare; *Q4–5*
46 **check**] heare *F1*
73 **travelling**] *Q3–5, F1*; trauailling *Q1–2*
79 **bestrid**] *F1*; bestride *Q1–5*
83 **he**] he had *F1*
89 **proud**] *Q2–5, F1*; prond *Q1*
90 **horse!**] *F1* (horse:); horse *Q1–2*, horse, *Q3–5*
91 **aw'd**] *Q3–5, F1*; awed *Q1–2*
94 **Spurr'd, gall'd**] Spur-gall'd *F1*
94 s.d. **Enter . . . meat.**] Enter Keeper with a Dish. *F1*
103 s.d. **Beats the Keeper.**] *Rowe*
104 s.d. **Exton and Servants**] *F1*
104 s.d. **armed**] *Capell*
106 s.d. **Snatches . . . him.**] *Capell (subs., after Pope, Hanmer)*
107 s.d. **Kills another.**] *Pope*
108 **That**] *F1; Rich.* That *Q1–5 (repeated s.p.)*
112 **downward,**] *F1*; downeward *Q1–5*
112 s.d. **Dies.**] *Rowe*

118 s.d. **Exeunt.**] *Rowe*; Exit. *F1*

V.vi

V.vi] *Steevens*; Scaena Quinta. *F1*
Location: *Theobald (subs.)*
o.s.d. **Flourish.**] *F1*
o.s.d. **now King Henry**] *ed. (after Dyce)*
o.s.d. **with . . . Attendants**] *F1*
2 **consum'd**] *F1*; consumed *Q1–5*
8 **Salisbury, Spencer**] *F1* (Salsbury); Oxford, Salisbury *Q1–5*
12 s.d. **Fitzwater**] *Q6*; Fitzwaters *Q1–5, F1*
17 **Fitzwater**] *Q6*; Fitz. *Q1–5*; Fitzwaters *F1*
18 s.d. **Harry Percy**] *ed.*, H. Percie. *Q1–2*; Henry Percy. *Q3–5*; Percy *F1*
18 s.d. **and . . . Carlisle**] *F1* (and Carlisle)
29 s.d. **Attendants bearing**] *Malone (after Capell)*
43 **thorough shades**] *Cambridge;* through shades *Q1*; through the shade *Q2–5, F1*
47 **what**] that *F1*
51 **mournings**] mourning *F1*
52 s.d. **Exeunt.**] *F1* (Exeunt / FINIS.); FINIS. *Q1–6*

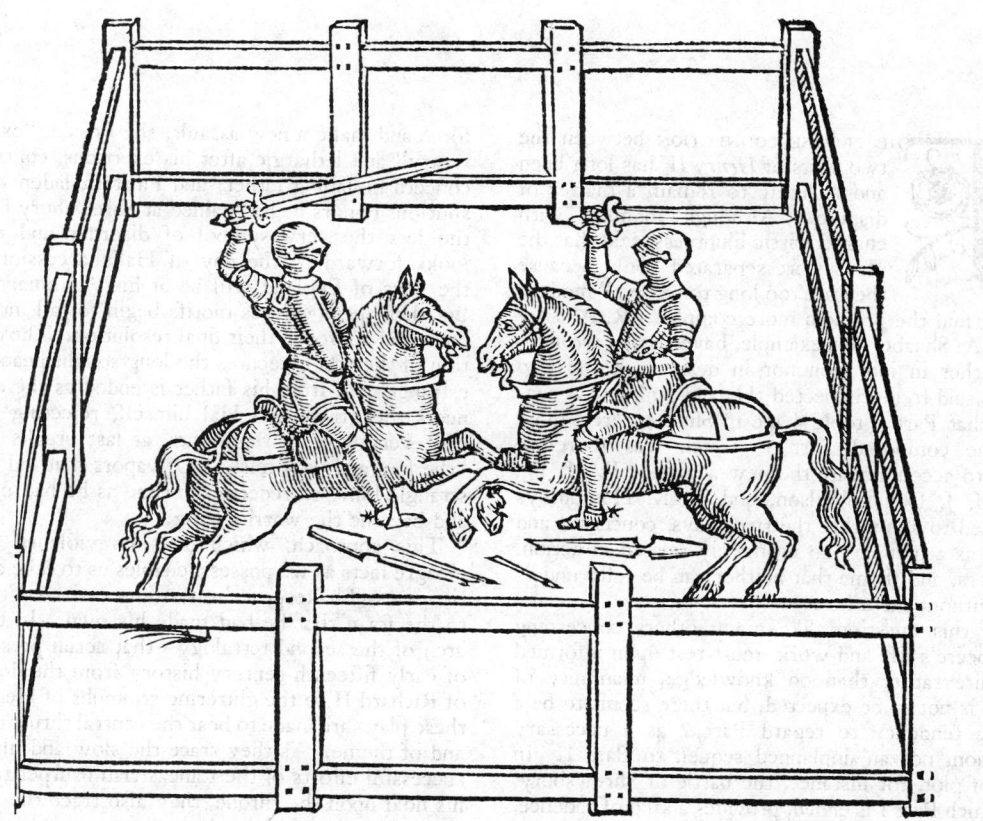

Knightly combat in the lists. From William Segar, *The Book of Honor and Arms* (1590), sig. M3. Two horsed knights in full armor here attack each other with broadswords. As the pair of shattered lances indicates, they have already run a-tilt, as the order of this kind of knightly combat dictated. A similar order of combat would have been followed in the abortive challenge scene in *Richard II*, I.iii. Mounted combat was, of course, impossible within the confines of an Elizabethan stage. Such combat is reported while in progress off-stage in *Pericles*, II.ii, and *The Two Noble Kinsmen*, V.iii. (*By permission of the Huntington Library, San Marino, California*)

Henry IV, Parts 1 and 2

HE PRECISE CONNECTION between the two parts of *Henry IV* has long been and is likely to remain a matter of dispute. Although Johnson, with characteristic bluntness, said that the plays were separated "only because they are too long to be one," modern scholars find the problem more complex. R. A. Law and M. A. Shaaber, for example, have argued strongly that neither in intention nor in design can the two parts be said to be connected; Harold Jenkins has suggested that Part 2 took shape in Shakespeare's mind while he composed Part 1, which was therefore altered to accommodate the new addition; E. M. W. Tillyard, J. Dover Wilson, and A. R. Humphreys have tried to show that the two plays, conceived and written as a unit, are so intimately related in action, characters, and theme that neither can be fully understood without the other.

Since this question, like many others concerning Shakespeare's life and work, must rest upon informed conjecture rather than on knowledge, unanimity of opinion is not to be expected, but there seems to be a growing tendency to regard Part 2 as a necessary conclusion, not an unplanned sequel, to Part 1. In terms of plot, for instance, the battle of Shrewsbury, with which Part 1 is ended, provides a kind of cadence, but it by no means tidies up the action. King Henry has checked but not destroyed his adversaries, and Hal has won his spurs; but with Northumberland and Archbishop Scroop at large there remains the danger of rebellion, and the Prince, despite his unexpected show of valor, has not resolved his father's doubts or achieved the "reformation" that he promised in Act I. Conversely, Part 2 picks up from its predecessor with no break in time or action: the scattered rebels gather

force and make a new assault; the Prince, "exceeding weary" and lethargic after his exertions, continues to concern his ailing father; and Falstaff, laden with the spurious honors he had gained at Shrewsbury but none the less the very symbol of disorder and misrule, looks forward to the day of Hal's accession, when the laws of England will be at his "commandment." But then these various motifs begin to fall into alignment and approach their final resolution. The destruction of the rebels secures the long-sought peace, Hal's estrangement from his father is ended as the old king nears the grave, and Hal himself, rejecting Falstaff and everything he represents, at last breaks through "the foul and ugly mists / Of vapors that did seem to strangle him" to redeem the time as he had promised and become the warrior-king.

This approach, which does no violence to such meagre facts as we possess, enables us to take a synoptic view of Shakespeare's most impressive contribution to the form that he had made his own. In the long arch of the second tetralogy—that serial presentation of early fifteenth-century history from the deposition of Richard II to the glittering triumphs of Henry V—these plays are made to bear the central thrust of action and of theme. As they trace the slow and ultimately successful efforts of the Lancastrian usurper to secure his hold upon the throne, they also trace the preparation of his son for the duties he must learn to bear, and these two lines of plot converge to underscore the massive central theme: the sources, uses, and responsibilities of power.

As the history of their publication shows, Part 1 was by far the more successful. Entered in the Stationers' Register on February 25, 1598, it was printed anonymously as *The History of Henry the Fourth* in two editions (the first surviving as a fragment) before the year was out; and there were five more reprints before it appeared in the Folio of 1623 as *The First Part of Henry the Fourth.* This play was presumably the "Henry the 4." that Francis Meres, in 1598, had cited in his list of Shakespeare's tragedies. Part 2 has no such record of popularity. Following its entry in the Stationers' Register on August 23, 1600, and its quarto publication soon thereafter, *The Second Part of Henry the Fourth* was not reprinted until the Folio of 1623. Whether the notion of a sequel was suggested by the immediate success of the first play or had been conceived earlier, Parts 1 and 2 were no doubt close in composition, and they are generally assigned to 1596–97 and 1598 respectively.

Evidence of one species of revision may be discerned in Hal's allusion (Part 1, I.ii.41) to "my old lad of the castle" and in the speech-prefix "*Old.*" (Part 2, I.ii.120), which show that Falstaff was originally called Oldcastle after the corresponding character in *The Famous Victories of Henry the Fifth,* an old play that was one of Shakespeare's sources. In what seems to be an addition to the epilogue of Part 2 (lines 26–34) Shakespeare is careful to dissociate the historical Sir John Oldcastle, Lord Cobham—a notorious Lollard who had been executed for heresy in 1417 and had come to be regarded as a martyr—from the fat knight of the play. Already, however, Shakespeare's distortion of the real Lord Cobham's character had been alluded to with disapproval in the prologue to *Sir John Oldcastle,* a collaboration by Drayton, Munday, Wilson, and Hathaway that was acted in 1599 and printed in 1600. "It is no pampered glutton we present," the authors of this rival play explained,

Nor aged counsellor to youthful sin,
But one whose virtue shone above the rest,
A valiant martyr and a virtuous peer.

It is likely that Shakespeare made the change from Oldcastle to Falstaff in deference to the powerful Sir William Brooke, seventh Baron Cobham, and that he changed the names Harvey and Russell (preserved in the quartos at Part 1, I.ii.162, and Part 2, II.ii o.s.d.) to Peto and Bardolph for a similar reason. The suggestion, made by A. E. Morgan and endorsed by Dover Wilson, that the Oldcastle scenes were originally written in verse has not gained wide support.

For the Henry IV plays Shakespeare supplemented Holinshed, his basic source, with certain collateral materials that he treated very freely. From the second (1587) edition of the *Chronicles* he got not only most of the details of Henry's troubled reign but also several errors (cited in the notes below) that show how closely he relied on Holinshed. As in his other history plays, however, the so-called facts were artfully or ruthlessly deployed to tighten up the action and reinforce the theme. An example is afforded by his treatment of the four main crises punctuating Henry's reign (1399–1413): the Abbot's conspiracy in 1399, the Percies' revolt in 1403, Archbishop Scroop's rebellion in 1405, and Northumberland's uprising in 1408. The first of these was used in *Richard II* (Act V) to show how the new king, unlike his predecessor, exemplified the regal use of power; and the other three, which provide the spine of plot for the two Henry IV plays, are so tightly squeezed together that they appear not widely spaced events but phases of a continuous and accelerating action. Historically, the battle of Shrewsbury, which forms the climax of Part 1, followed Henry's accession by four years and preceded his demise by ten, but in Shakespeare's rearrangement the King, remorseful over Richard's deposition, is found preparing for this battle when he had been but "twelve month" on the throne; the battle itself occurs a few months later; and Scroop's rebellion, with which Part 2 begins, is made to follow very soon, although in fact its date was 1405, eight years before the events with which Part 2 is closed. As for Northumberland's incursion of 1408, it is merely reported as a kind of epilogue to Scroop's abortive undertaking (Part 2, IV.iv.94–101).

As in Daniel's *Civil Wars* (1595 ff.), which Shakespeare almost surely knew and drew upon, these telescopings and distortions give shape and speed and moral meaning to Holinshed's inept narration; and just as they lead us to view Henry's reign as one of urgent and successive perils and as a drawn-out act of penance for the crime of usurpation, so Shakespeare's juggling with the ages and the motives of his characters serves the other, cognate theme of Prince Hal's preparation for the awful burden of the crown. King Henry, who is shown at the beginning as so "shaken" and so "wan with care" that his fatal illness in Part 2 occasions no surprise, was actually only thirty-six when he overcame his foes at Shrewsbury and ten years older when he died. Similarly, his "unthrifty son"—a lad of sixteen at Shrewsbury—is made coeval with Hotspur, who, though depicted as a splendid youth, was actually thirty-nine in 1403 and thus a generation older than the wayward prince to whom he stands, "amongst a grove the very straightest plant," as foil and rival. Among the many other readjustments of motive, circumstance, and chronology are the valor of Prince John at Shrewsbury, the remorseful Henry's hope of leading a crusade to the Holy Land to ease his guilty soul, and the brief but brilliant portraits of the uxorious Mortimer and his lovesick wife, the incisive Lady Percy, and the "extraordinary" Glendower, all of whom were worked up from the merest hints in Holinshed.

For the transformation of the madcap prince into a wise and splendid king, the favorite Elizabethan version of the Prodigal Son story, Shakespeare tapped a very old tradition. Launched shortly after Henry V's death in Tito Livio's quasi-official *Vita Henrici Quinti* (which was translated with additions in the early sixteenth century) and thereafter expanded and embellished, by Shakespeare's time the legend had worked its way into the chronicles and had perhaps inspired some now lost plays. Shakespeare's most important source for this material was *The Famous Victories of Henry the Fifth,* a crude comedy-history in rough-hewn prose which, though acted at least as early as 1588 and licensed six years later, survives only in an edition of 1598 that seems to be a corrupt reported version of a more substantial two-part play. This knockabout farce presents the basic plot and almost all the episodes that Shakespeare reconstructed for his vastly different purposes: the wild young prince who, in consort with a pack of low companions named Sir John Oldcastle, Tom, and Ned, commits a robbery at Gadshill, frequents an Eastcheap dive, and runs afoul the Lord Chief Justice before he is reconciled with his dying father, rejects his former cronies, and emerges as the valiant king who conquers France and takes its princess as his bride.

Shakespeare's use of this material in a work ostensibly devoted to the politics of Henry IV's reign was a stunning innovation, for by the introduction of a low-life comic element he achieved a counterpoint in action, style, and theme that is the glory of these plays. We move back and forth from court to tavern, from the cares of state to bawds and leaping-houses, from the urgency of great events that cut "athwart" the plans of kings and would-be kings to the sloth and heedless self-indulgence of Falstaff and his sleazy crew, from the gravity of a careworn ruler to the irreverent wit of Hal and his fat friend, from bold exploits and valor to chicanery and crime, from verse to prose, from honor to disgrace. This continual oscillation is the most conspicuous feature of these plays. Not all the earlier histories are so gravely uniform as *Richard II*, which contains no prose at all, but they are pitched upon a high and stately plane, and even when they do descend to common men—as in Horner's fight with Peter and in the Jack Cade scenes of *2 Henry VI*—the talk is anything but gay. In the Henry IV plays, however, the double theme of Henry's hard-fought rise to uncontested power and Hal's probation for the throne requires a universe of action that Shakespeare had not touched before. A single style or mood or plot could no longer serve his purpose. Here the brassy declamation and the facile patriotism of *Henry VI*, the dark, pervasive evil of *Richard III*, the rhetorical excesses of *King John*, and the univocal lyricism of *Richard II* yield to life itself, and as a result *Henry IV*, in its vitality and variety, is unmatched by any other history play. It is the triumph of the form.

For all their throbbing sense of life, their profusion of episode and character, and the pressures generated by their complex double plot, where each scene pushes hard upon the next, these plays are built with great precision. A persistent duality is the basic principle of organization. In structure this reveals itself most clearly through the artful alternation of politics and folly, the first centred in the King and the court, the second in the Prince and the tavern. Shuttling from scenes of state and grave affairs to scenes of bawdy wit and dissipation, Shakespeare weaves a rich design where each detail is set against its complementary and contrasting opposite so that they may sharpen one another. In the grouping of the characters the same device is seen. The King and Falstaff are aligned, for instance, through their relationship to Hal, the father standing for convention, duty, and control and his surrogate for disorder, crime, and license. Similarly,

Hal and Hotspur form another pair of corresponding but contrasting types, and so do Hal and Henry (as representing youth and age), Falstaff and the Lord Chief Justice (who stand for "riot" and law), Hotspur and Falstaff (who show excess of "honor" and total lack of it).

Also, the comic and the serious elements, contrived not merely to provide relief or to effect changes in pace and style, bear upon and reinforce each other in many subtle ways. They are sometimes parallel, as when King Henry's scheme to meet the troubles in the north (Part 1, I.i) is matched by Hal's and Falstaff's preparations for the Gadshill escapade (Part 1, I.ii); sometimes antithetical, as when the Prince's lethargy and indecision (Part 1, I.ii) are set against the fiery Hotspur's zeal "to pluck bright Honor from the pale-fac'd moon" (Part 1, I.iii); sometimes in parodic contrast, as when Falstaff, with a joint-stool for a throne, a leaden dagger for a sceptre, and a pillow for his crown, plays the part of Prince Hal's father and chides the erring youth (Part 1, II.iv) just as King Henry, though in a very different style, reproves him later in a pair of crucial scenes (Part 1, III.ii; Part 2, IV.v). Sometimes the contrasting elements are almost juxtaposed, sometimes widely spaced. Within fifty lines of Vernon's stirring news about King Henry's forces as they advance upon the foe

> All furnish'd, all in arms;
> All plum'd like estridges that with the wind
> Bated, like eagles having lately bath'd;
> Glittering in golden coats, like images;
> As full of spirit as the month of May
> And gorgeous as the sun at midsummer;
> Wanton as youthful goats, wild as young bulls,
>
> (Part 1, IV.i.97–103)

we hear Falstaff describe his ragged troop as "a commodity of warm slaves" so disreputable that he cannot bring himself to march with them. The ceremonial parley before Shrewsbury (Part 1, V.i), where Hal, "to save the blood on either side," proposes a chivalric encounter between Hotspur and himself, is ended with Falstaff left alone upon the stage to jeer at honor as a "mere scutcheon"; and the heroic feats in battle, capped by the Prince's valediction to the "great heart" he has slain, yield to the sight of Falstaff stabbing Hotspur's corpse and claiming credit for the crime. A much greater interval lies between the rebels' high-flown quarrel about the booty they expect to share when the kingdom is divided (Part 1, II.i) and Falstaff's fracas with the Hostess over unpaid bills (Part 2, II.i), or Hotspur's farewell to his lively Kate (Part 1, II.i) and Falstaff's to his drunken Doll (Part 2, II.iv) as they go off to war; but even such widely separated complementary scenes, reverberating one against the other, contribute to the polyphonic structure.

These various techniques of juxtaposition, inversion, and antithesis enable us to watch the action from many points of view. As we first see Henry in Act I, for instance, he is every inch a king. When he talks about his hope

To chase these pagans in those holy fields,
Over whose acres walk'd those blessed feet
Which fourteen hundred years ago were nail'd
For our advantage on the bitter cross,   (I.i.24–27)

he speaks in the splendid, spacious verse appropriate
to his station; and he maintains but subtly modulates
this style in discussing with his "gentle cousin Westmerland" and with Sir Walter Blunt, "a dear, a true
industrious friend," the "heavy news" from Wales.
But he will not tolerate "the moody frontier of a
servant brow," and he checks young Hotspur's insubordination in words so clipped that they admit of no
reply:

But, sirrah, henceforth
Let me not hear you speak of Mortimer.
Send me your prisoners with the speediest means,
Or you shall hear in such a kind from me
As will displease you. My Lord Northumberland:
We license your departure with your son.
Send us your prisoners, or you will hear of it.
(I.iii.118–24)

Viewed from Eastcheap, however, Henry is a different
man: the querulous, demanding father, the formalist,
and the very emblem of an ethic based on duty, honor,
and convention that Hal and Falstaff flout. To enlarge our vision further, Hotspur sees him as "this
thorn, this canker," and "this vile politician" whose
destruction is a point of honor, whereas the King
himself, sleepless with the cares of state, soliloquizes
on his office as a burden he can scarcely bear (Part 2,
III.i). All these partial truths converge when Henry,
with the candor of a dying man, assesses his career
(Part 2, IV.v), and so our knowledge of this able,
ambitious, remorseful, careworn ruler is finally
brought into focus.

Hal and Hotspur are subjected to the same incessant
contrapuntal presentation. To his father, Hal is the
"hot vengeance, and the rod of heaven," sent to
punish his "mistreadings"; to Falstaff, the "sweet
wag" who, as king, will not let "resolution" be
"fubb'd as it is with the rusty curb of old father antic
the law"; to Hotspur, a "sword-and-buckler Prince
of Wales" whom he would like to poison with a pot
of ale; and to himself, a man resolved to "pay the
debt I never promised" by shaking off his "loose
behavior" and "redeeming time when men think least
I will." Opposed to him—in valor and esteem—
stands Hotspur, and he provides a gauge whereby to
test the shabby prince. Hotspur is introduced (in
Henry's words) as "the theme of honor's tongue,"
and he goes far to justify the appellation. One of
Shakespeare's most engaging characters, he is generous, brave, and witty, and so superbly vocal—as when
he explains his conduct to the King (Part 1, I.iii) or
twits Glendower's pretensions (Part 1, III.i)—that,
like Mercutio in *Romeo and Juliet*, he dominates each
scene that he is in. But as the play proceeds, we,
instructed by his own behavior no less than by what
others say of him, begin to modify our view. A
willing victim of his own emotions, he is, as his own

father says, "a wasp-stung and impatient fool." So
much incensed at Henry that his anger turns to rage
and his vaunted honor to gesticulation, he is as willing
to carve up the realm as to cavil on the ninth part of
a hair. Hal, as always, understands the situation, and
so, as he assures the anxious King, the day will come

That this same child of honor and renown,
This gallant Hotspur, this all-praised knight,
And your unthought-of Harry chance to meet.
For every honor sitting on his helm,
Would they were multitudes, and on my head
My shames redoubled! For the time will come
That I shall make this northren youth exchange
His glorious deeds for my indignities.
(Part 1, III.ii.139–46)

The fact is, of course, that Hotspur, for all his bravado, wit, and charm, reveals a lack of mental poise.
He is a danger to the state and to the heir apparent,
and therefore his destruction at the hands of Hal—the
seeming wastrel whose temperance, courage, and icy
self-control will fit him for the crown that he was
born to wear—is more than just a turn of plot: it is a
judgment on two basic types of men. Hotspur is so
dazzling and bewitching that we endorse Hal's tribute
to his fallen foe (Part 1, V.iv) and Kate's assessment
of her "wondrous him" (Part 2, II.iii), but we realize,
to our sorrow, that the safety of the realm required
his death and that he was vanquished by a better man.

As for Falstaff, that authentic triumph of the literary imagination, Hazlitt may have thought of him
when he remarked, "If we wish to see the force of
human genius, we should read Shakespeare. If we
wish to see the insignificance of human learning, we
may study his commentators." Falstaff is so various,
so equivocal, and so overwhelming that he would
seem to baffle judgment, but since the eighteenth
century he has probably prompted more discussion
than anyone but Hamlet—and, like Hamlet's, his
mystery is secure. An amalgam of the Vice of the
morality play, the braggart soldier of Roman comedy,
the witty parasite, and the Fool as liberator from
convention and restraint, he has a complex genealogy,
but he transcends the jargon and the categories of the
literary historian as easily as he gulls poor Justice
Shallow. Although he is a sluggard, liar, glutton,
lecher, knave, and cheat, he is so superbly funny—
"not only witty in myself, but the cause that wit is in
other men" (Part 2, I.ii.9–10)—that as he lumbers
through these plays with his tatterdemalion crew of
ruffians, whores, and sycophants he seems to shed a
flood of light.

One ingredient of his charm is his dazzling intellect.
A virtuoso in the arts of language, he can hardly
speak a line that does not, like all great literature,
sharpen our response and jolt us into new perceptions.
He throws us from our stance and makes us look at
things afresh. When he trades indecent puns with
Hal, parodies the bombast circumstance of old-
fashioned drama, makes complicated fun of Bardolph's
nose, cites Scripture for his purpose, or mocks the
bumbling style of Justice Shallow he shows that

language is a tool of intellect which he uses with complete control. He never muffles his own tone of voice or blunts the cutting edge of wit, and even at his most outrageous he continues to instruct, astonish, and delight us by the thrust and vigor of his mind and by his uncanny way with words.

However, he is more than merely witty. His verbal skill is but a function of his complex comic vision, and this vision, if it can be defined at all, may perhaps be said to rest upon a tonic or corrosive disrespect not only for the slogans and the solemn plausibilities to which most men yield assent but also for the values—moral, social, and political—whereby most men organize experience and whereon the social structure rests. Therein lie his fascination and his peril. If Falstaff, incapable of intellectual torpor and indifferent to the curbs that shackle most of us, represents the lawless ease and freedom that every man desires and most men never find, he also represents destruction. An example of the way that Shakespeare forces us to trade our routine, clear-cut misconceptions for the interlocking ambiguities of knowledge, he is both wholesome and malign: he amuses and instructs us by exposing fraud and folly, but he appalls us by annihilating all sense of order. He flouts not merely the civilities, but man's most rooted need—that responsible commitment to his own ideals which gives shape and purpose to existence.

Like Hotspur, then, for a very different reason,

Falstaff is a threat that Hal must meet and overcome before he earns the right to power, and therefore his rejection, so necessary and painful, is the moral climax of these plays. When the dying Henry, just before his final reconciliation with his son, foretold what kind of king he feared the Prince would be if Falstaff were his guide, he underscored the central fact:

> Harry the Fift is crown'd! Up, vanity!
> Down, royal state! All you sage counsellors,
>   hence! . . .
> For the fift Harry from curb'd license plucks
> The muzzle of restraint, and the wild dog
> Shall flesh his tooth on every innocent.
> O my poor kingdom, sick with civil blows!
> When that my care could not withhold thy riots,
> What wilt thou do when riot is thy care?
> O, thou wilt be a wilderness again,
> Peopled with wolves, thy old inhabitants!
>   (Part 2, IV.v.119–20, 130–37)

Hal, of course, had seen the danger too. His "reformation" would perhaps have greater force if he himself had not foretold it from the start (Part 1, I.ii.195–217), but even though we know that Falstaff, "the tutor and the feeder of my riots," is just one aspect of the Prince's test and preparation for the crown, his rejection wrings our heart. It is the price that greatness pays for power.

Herschel Baker

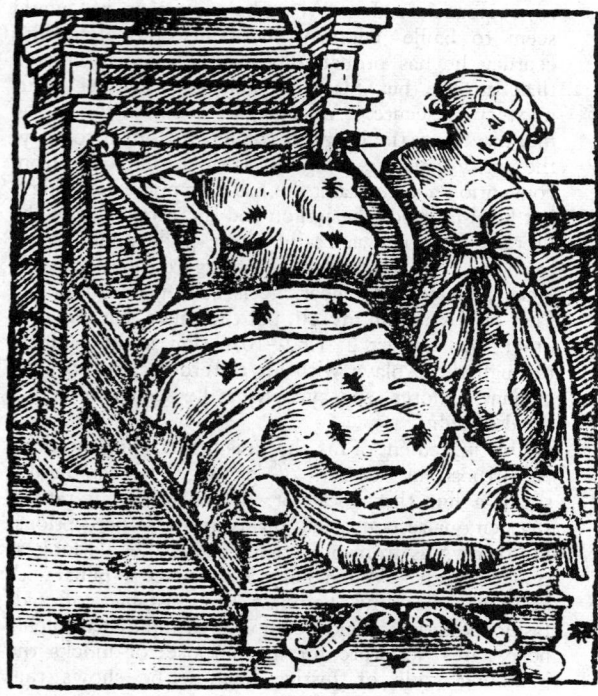

A bed full of fleas. From *Hortus Sanitatis* (1563). In an age when personal cleanliness was not stressed (in fact bathing was considered dangerous to health), travellers were often confronted with the situation in which the good woman in this picture finds herself. As the Second Carrier complains in *1 Henry IV*, after a night in the inn at Rochester, it is "the most villainous house in all London road for fleas," and the First Carrier agrees that "ne'er a king christen could be better bit than I have been since the first cock" (II.i.14–18). (*The Folger Shakespeare Library*)

The First Part of Henry the Fourth

[DRAMATIS PERSONAE

KING HENRY THE FOURTH
HENRY, PRINCE OF WALES
PRINCE JOHN OF LANCASTER } *sons to the King*
EARL OF WESTMERLAND
SIR WALTER BLUNT
THOMAS PERCY, *Earl of Worcester*
HENRY PERCY, *Earl of Northumberland*
HENRY PERCY, *surnamed* HOTSPUR, *his son*
EDMUND MORTIMER, *Earl of March*
RICHARD SCROOP, *Archbishop of York*
ARCHIBALD, *Earl of Douglas*
OWEN GLENDOWER
SIR RICHARD VERNON
SIR JOHN FALSTAFF

SIR MICHAEL, *of the household of the Archbishop of York*
EDWARD POINS, *gentleman-in-waiting to Prince Henry*
GADSHILL
PETO
BARDOLPH

LADY PERCY, *wife to Hotspur, and sister to Mortimer*
LADY MORTIMER, *daughter to Glendower, and wife to Mortimer*
MISTRESS QUICKLY, *hostess of the Boar's Head Tavern in Eastcheap*

LORDS, OFFICERS, SHERIFF, VINTNER, CHAMBERLAIN, OSTLER, DRAWERS, *two* CARRIERS, TRAVELLERS, *and* ATTENDANTS

SCENE: *England and Wales*]

[ACT I, SCENE I]

Enter the KING [HENRY], LORD JOHN OF LANCASTER,
EARL OF WESTMERLAND, [SIR WALTER BLUNT,]
with others.

King. So shaken as we are, so wan with care,
Find we a time for frighted peace to pant
And breathe short-winded accents of new broils
To be commenc'd in stronds afar remote.
No more the thirsty entrance of this soil 5
Shall daub her lips with her own children's blood,
No more shall trenching war channel her fields,
Nor bruise her flow'rets with the armed hoofs
Of hostile paces. Those opposed eyes,
Which, like the meteors of a troubled heaven, 10
All of one nature, of one substance bred,
Did lately meet in the intestine shock
And furious close of civil butchery,

Shall now, in mutual well-beseeming ranks,
March all one way and be no more oppos'd 15
Against acquaintance, kindred, and allies.
The edge of war, like an ill-sheathed knife,
No more shall cut his master. Therefore, friends,
As far as to the sepulchre of Christ—
Whose soldier now, under whose blessed cross 20
We are impressed and engag'd to fight—
Forthwith a power of English shall we levy,
Whose arms were moulded in their mother's womb,
To chase these pagans in those holy fields,
Over whose acres walk'd those blessed feet 25
Which fourteen hundred years ago were nail'd
For our advantage on the bitter cross.
But this our purpose now is twelve month old,
And bootless 'tis to tell you we will go;
Therefore we meet not now. Then let me hear 30
Of you, my gentle cousin Westmerland,
What yesternight our Council did decree
In forwarding this dear expedience.
West. My liege, this haste was hot in question.

Words and passages enclosed in square brackets in the text above are either emendations of the copy-text or additions to it. The Textual Notes immediately following the play cite the earliest authority for every such change or insertion and supply the reading of the copy-text wherever it is emended in this edition.

I.i. Location: London. The palace.
2. **Find we**: let us find. 3. **accents**: words.
3–4. **new . . . remote.** At the close of *Richard II* (V.vi.49–50) the newly crowned Henry IV, remorseful for the death of Richard, had promised to "make a voyage to the Holy Land / To wash this blood off from my guilty hand." 4. **stronds**: strands, shores.
5. **thirsty entrance**: parched mouth. 7. **trenching**: cutting.
8–9. **armed . . . paces**: tread of armed horses in combat.
12. **intestine**: internal. 13. **close**: hand-to-hand combat.

14. **mutual**: united for a common purpose. 18. **his**: its.
21. **impressed**: conscripted. **engag'd**: pledged.
22. **power**: force, army.
28. **twelve month old.** Actually, two years separated Richard II's death (1400) and the battle of Homildon (Shakespeare's Holmedon), news of which reaches the King at lines 52 ff.
29. **bootless**: useless.
30. **Therefore . . . now**: it is not for this purpose that we meet now.
31. **gentle cousin**: noble kinsman.
33. **dear expedience**: urgent undertaking.
34. **liege**: sovereign. **hot in question**: under urgent discussion.

And many limits of the charge set down 35
But yesternight, when all athwart there came
A post from Wales loaden with heavy news,
Whose worst was that the noble Mortimer,
Leading the men of [Herfordshire] to fight
Against the irregular and wild Glendower, 40
Was by the rude hands of that Welshman taken,
A thousand of his people butchered,
Upon whose dead corpse' there was such misuse,
Such beastly shameless transformation,
By those Welshwomen done as may not be 45
Without much shame retold or spoken of.
    King. It seems then that the tidings of this broil
Brake off our business for the Holy Land.
    West. This match'd with other did, my gracious
        lord,
For more uneven and unwelcome news 50
Came from the north, and thus it did import:
On Holy-rood day, the gallant Hotspur there,
Young Harry Percy, and brave Archibald,
That ever-valiant and approved Scot,
At Holmedon met, 55
Where they did spend a sad and bloody hour,
As by discharge of their artillery
And shape of likelihood the news was told;
For he that brought them, in the very heat
And pride of their contention did take horse, 60
Uncertain of the issue any way.
    King. Here is [a] dear, a true industrious friend,
Sir Walter Blunt, new lighted from his horse,
Stain'd with the variation of each soil
Betwixt that Holmedon and this seat of ours; 65
And he hath brought us smooth and welcome news.
The Earl of Douglas is discomfited:
Ten thousand bold Scots, two and twenty knights,

Balk'd in their own blood, did Sir Walter see
On Holmedon's plains. Of prisoners, Hotspur took
Mordake Earl of Fife and eldest son 71
To beaten Douglas, and the Earl of Athol,
Of Murray, Angus, and Menteith.
And is not this an honorable spoil?
A gallant prize? Ha, cousin, is it not? 75
    West. In faith,
It is a conquest for a prince to boast of.
    King. Yea, there thou mak'st me sad, and mak'st
        me sin
In envy that my Lord Northumberland
Should be the father to so blest a son— 80
A son who is the theme of honor's tongue,
Amongst a grove the very straightest plant,
Who is sweet Fortune's minion and her pride,
Whilst I, by looking on the praise of him,
See riot and dishonor stain the brow 85
Of my young Harry. O that it could be prov'd
That some night-tripping fairy had exchang'd
In cradle-clothes our children where they lay,
And call'd mine Percy, his Plantagenet!
Then would I have his Harry and he mine. 90
But let him from my thoughts. What think you, coz,
Of this young Percy's pride? The prisoners
Which he in this adventure hath surpris'd
To his own use he keeps, and sends me word
I shall have none but Mordake Earl of Fife. 95
    West. This is his uncle's teaching; this is
        Worcester,
Malevolent to you in all aspects,
Which makes him prune himself, and bristle up
The crest of youth against your dignity.
    King. But I have sent for him to answer this; 100
And for this cause a while we must neglect
Our holy purpose to Jerusalem.
Cousin, on Wednesday next our Council we
Will hold at Windsor, so inform the lords.
But come yourself with speed to us again, 105
For more is to be said and to be done
Than out of anger can be uttered.
    West. I will, my liege.   *Exeunt.*

---

35. **limits . . . down:** specific military responsibilities assigned.
36. **athwart:** across (the plans).
37. **post:** messenger.   **heavy:** sad, depressing.
38. **Mortimer.** Shakespeare, like Holinshed, had trouble keeping the Mortimers straight. By marrying (1368) Philippa, daughter of Lionel, Duke of Clarence, third son of Edward III, Edmund Mortimer, third Earl of March, raised his family to a place of great importance. In 1385 his son Roger, fourth Earl of March, was recognized by Richard II as heir presumptive to the throne. In the present scene Shakespeare confuses Glendower's captive Sir Edmund Mortimer (1376–?1409), Roger's younger brother, with Roger's son Edmund (1391–1425), fifth and last Earl of March, who had been named heir presumptive by Richard II in 1398 after the death of the fourth earl. See the genealogical table, pp. 594–95.
40. **irregular:** i.e. because he resorted to guerrilla warfare.
43. **corpse':** corpses.
44. **transformation:** mutilation. According to Holinshed (Bullough, IV, 182), "the shamefull villanie used by the Welsh-women towards the dead carcasses [of the English], was such, as honest eares would be ashamed to heare, and continent toongs to speake thereof."
48. **Brake:** broke.
49. **other:** i.e. other tidings. Actually, the battle at Homildon (or Humbleton) Hill in Northumberland (September 1402) occurred three months after Mortimer's capture by Glendower.
50. **uneven:** disturbing.
52. **Holy-rood day:** September 14.
53. **Young Harry Percy.** Although here and elsewhere (for example, III.ii.103) Shakespeare implies that Sir Henry Percy, eldest son of the first Earl of Northumberland, was a high-spirited youth, he was in fact thirty-eight years old in 1402, twenty-three years the senior of Prince Hal, his rival and presumed contemporary in this play.   **brave Archibald:** Archibald Douglas (1369?–1424), fourth Earl of Douglas and first Duke of Touraine, a Scot noted for his valor.
58. **shape of likelihood:** apparent probability.
59. **them:** i.e. the news.   60. **pride:** height.
62. **true industrious:** truly devoted.

69. **Balk'd:** heaped up in balks or ridges.
71. **Mordake.** Murdac Stewart, son of Robert Stewart, first Earl of Albany and "governor" of Scotland. Shakespeare's erroneously calling him the son of Archibald Douglas results from the faulty punctuation in Holinshed (Bullough, IV, 183): "of prisoners among other were these, Mordacke earle of Fife, son to the governour Archembald earle Dowglas, which in the fight lost one of his eies, Thomas erle of Murrey, Robert earle of Angus (and as some writers have) the earles of Atholl & Menteith, with five hundred other of meaner degrees."   82. **plant:** tree.   83. **minion:** darling.
87. **Some . . . fairy.** It was popularly believed that defective children were "changelings" left by fairies in exchange for babies whom they had abducted.
89. **Plantagenet:** family name of the English royal family. See note to *1 Henry VI*, II.iv o.s.d.
91. **from:** go from.   **coz:** cousin, i.e. kinsman.
93. **surpris'd:** captured.
94. **To . . . use:** i.e. for purpose of ransom.
95. **none but Mordake.** Although Hotspur could legitimately hold the other prisoners he had taken, the law of arms required that Murdac, being of royal blood, be surrendered to the King.
97. **Malevolent . . . aspects:** i.e. habitually hostile (a metaphor from astrology).
98. **Which:** i.e. Worcester's "teaching."   **prune:** preen, trim (a term from falconry).   101. **neglect:** put aside.
107. **uttered:** said in public.

848

[SCENE II]

Enter PRINCE OF WALES *and* SIR JOHN FALSTAFF.

Fal. Now, Hal, what time of day is it, lad?

Prince. Thou art so fat-witted with drinking of old
sack, and unbuttoning thee after supper, and sleeping
upon benches after noon, that thou hast forgotten to
demand that truly which thou wouldest truly know.   5
What a devil hast thou to do with the time of the day?
unless hours were cups of sack, and minutes capons,
and clocks the tongues of bawds, and dials the signs of
leaping-houses, and the blessed sun himself a fair hot
wench in flame-color'd taffata; I see no reason why
thou shouldst be so superfluous to demand the time
of the day.   12

Fal. Indeed you come near me now, Hal, for we
that take purses go by the moon and the seven stars,
and not by Phoebus, he, "that wand'ring knight   15
so fair." And I prithee, sweet wag, when thou art a
king, as, God save thy Grace—Majesty I should say,
for grace thou wilt have none—

Prince. What, none?   19

Fal. No, by my troth, not so much as will serve to
be prologue to an egg and butter.

Prince. Well, how then? Come, roundly, roundly.

Fal. Marry, then, sweet wag, when thou art king,
let not us that are squires of the night's body be call'd
thieves of the day's beauty. Let us be Diana's   25
foresters, gentlemen of the shade, minions of the moon,
and let men say we be men of good government, being
govern'd, as the sea is, by our noble and chaste mistress
the moon, under whose countenance we steal.   29

Prince. Thou sayest well, and it holds well too, for
the fortune of us that are the moon's men doth ebb and
flow like the sea, being govern'd, as the sea is, by the
moon. As, for proof, now: a purse of gold most
resolutely snatch'd on Monday night and most dissolutely spent on Tuesday morning; got with   35
swearing "Lay by," and spent with crying "Bring in";
now in as low an ebb as the foot of the ladder, and by
and by in as high a flow as the ridge of the gallows.

Fal. 'By the Lord, thou say'st true, lad. And is not
my hostess of the tavern a most sweet wench?   40

Prince. As the honey of Hybla, my old lad of the

castle. And is not a buff jerkin a most sweet robe of
durance?

Fal. How now, how now, mad wag? What, in thy
quips and thy quiddities? What a plague have I to do
with a buff jerkin?   46

Prince. Why, what a pox have I to do with my
hostess of the tavern?

Fal. Well, thou hast call'd her to a reckoning many
a time and oft.   50

Prince. Did I ever call for thee to pay thy part?

Fal. No, I'll give thee thy due, thou hast paid all
there.

Prince. Yea, and elsewhere, so far as my coin
would stretch, and where it would not, I have us'd my
credit.   56

Fal. Yea, and so us'd it that, were it not here
apparent that thou art heir apparent—But I prithee,
sweet wag, shall there be gallows standing in England
when thou art king? and resolution thus fubb'd as   60
it is with the rusty curb of old father antic the law?
Do not thou, when thou art king, hang a thief.

Prince. No, thou shalt.

Fal. Shall I? O rare! By the Lord, I'll be a brave
judge.   65

Prince. Thou judgest false already. I mean thou
shalt have the hanging of the thieves, and so become a
rare hangman.

Fal. Well, Hal, well, and in some sort it jumps with
my humor as well as waiting in the court, I can tell you.

Prince. For obtaining of suits?   71

Fal. Yea, for obtaining of suits, whereof the hangman hath no lean wardrobe. 'Sblood, I am as melancholy as a gib cat or a lugg'd bear.

Prince. Or an old lion, or a lover's lute.   75

Fal. Yea, or the drone of a Lincolnshire bagpipe.

Prince. What sayest thou to a hare, or the melancholy of Moor-ditch?

Fal. Thou hast the most unsavory [similes] and
art indeed the most comparative, rascalliest, sweet   80
young prince. But, Hal, I prithee trouble me no more
with vanity; I would to God thou and I knew where a
commodity of good names were to be bought. An old
lord of the Council rated me the other day in the street
about you, sir, but I mark'd him not, and yet he   85
talk'd very wisely, but I regarded him not, and yet he
talk'd wisely, and in the street too.

Prince. Thou didst well, for wisdom cries out in
the streets, and no man regards it.   89

I.ii. Location: London. Prince Henry's house.
3. **sack:** dry Spanish wine.   8. **dials:** clocks.
9. **leaping-houses:** brothels.
10. **taffata:** taffeta (often worn by prostitutes).
14. **seven stars:** constellation of the Pleiades.
15–16. **Phoebus . . . fair.** Falstaff identifies Phoebus, the sun-god or
knight of the sun, with the knight errant ("wand'ring knight") of a
popular romance.   16. **wag:** rogue.
18. **grace:** virtue, sense of propriety.   20. **troth:** faith.
21. **prologue . . . butter:** i.e. a short grace before a skimpy meal.
22. **roundly:** directly.
23. **Marry:** indeed (originally the name of the Virgin Mary used as an
oath).
25–26. **Diana's foresters:** i.e. thieves (Diana being the moon-goddess).
26. **minions:** darlings.   27. **government:** behavior.
29. **countenance:** (1) face; (2) protection, patronage.
30. **holds well:** is apt.   36. **Lay by:** hands up.
37. **ladder:** i.e. to the gallows.
41. **Hybla:** region of Sicily noted for its honey.
41–42. **old . . . castle:** (1) cant phrase for roisterer; (2) an allusion to
Sir John Oldcastle, the name that Shakespeare originally intended
for Falstaff (see the introduction).

42. **buff jerkin:** leather jacket (often worn by jailers).
42–43. **of durance:** (1) durable, serviceable; (2) of imprisonment.
45. **quiddities:** subtle jests.   49. **reckoning:** settling of the bill.
60. **resolution:** i.e. the valor of thieves.   **fubb'd:** fobbed, thwarted.
61. **antic:** clown, buffoon.   64. **brave:** fine.
69–70. **in . . . humor:** in some ways it suits my temperament.
71. **suits:** petitions (but Falstaff plays on another sense: the clothing
of an executed person that was claimed by the hangman).
73. **'Sblood:** by God's (Christ's) blood.
74. **gib cat:** tomcat.   **lugg'd:** led (as with a chain).
77. **hare:** i.e. because of its melancholy appearance.
78. **Moor-ditch:** open sewer or drainage ditch outside the walls of
London.
80. **comparative:** i.e. given to (unflattering) comparisons.
83. **commodity:** supply.   84. **rated:** berated.
88–89. **wisdom . . . it.** An echo of Proverbs 1:23, 24.

1 Henry IV
I.ii

Fal. O, thou hast damnable iteration, and art indeed able to corrupt a saint. Thou hast done much harm upon me, Hal, God forgive thee for it! Before I knew thee, Hal, I knew nothing, and now am I, if a man should speak truly, little better than one of the wicked. I must give over this life, and I will give 95 it over. By the Lord, and I do not, I am a villain, I'll be damn'd for never a king's son in Christendom.

Prince. Where shall we take a purse to-morrow, Jack?   99

Fal. 'Zounds, where thou wilt, lad, I'll make one, an' I do not, call me villain and baffle me.

Prince. I see a good amendment of life in thee, from praying to purse-taking.

Fal. Why, Hal, 'tis my vocation, Hal, 'tis no sin for a man to labor in his vocation.   105

Enter POINS.

Poins! Now shall we know if Gadshill have set a match. O, if men were to be sav'd by merit, what hole in hell were hot enough for him? This is the most omnipotent villain that ever cried "Stand!" to a true man.   110

Prince. Good morrow, Ned.

Poins. Good morrow, sweet Hal. What says Monsieur Remorse? What says Sir John Sack and Sugar? Jack, how agrees the devil and thee about thy soul that thou soldest him on Good Friday last, for a cup of Madeira and a cold capon's leg?   116

Prince. Sir John stands to his word, the devil shall have his bargain, for he was never yet a breaker of proverbs. He will give the devil his due.

Poins. Then art thou damn'd for keeping thy word with the devil.   121

Prince. Else he had been damn'd for cozening the devil.

Poins. But, my lads, my lads, to-morrow morning by four a' clock early, at Gadshill, there are 125 pilgrims going to Canterbury with rich offerings, and traders riding to London with fat purses. I have vizards for you all; you have horses for yourselves. Gadshill lies to-night in Rochester. I have bespoke supper to-morrow night in Eastcheap. We may do 130 it as secure as sleep. If you will go, I will stuff your purses full of crowns; if you will not, tarry at home and be hang'd.

Fal. Hear ye, Yedward, if I tarry at home and go not, I'll hang you for going.   135

Poins. You will, chops?

Fal. Hal, wilt thou make one?

Prince. Who, I rob? I a thief? Not I, by my faith.

Fal. There's neither honesty, manhood, nor good fellowship in thee, nor thou cam'st not of the blood royal, if thou darest not stand for ten shillings.   141

Prince. Well then, once in my days I'll be a madcap.

Fal. Why, that's well said.

Prince. Well, come what will, I'll tarry at home.

Fal. By the Lord, I'll be a traitor then, when thou art king.   147

Prince. I care not.

Poins. Sir John, I prithee leave the Prince and me alone, I will lay him down such reasons for this adventure that he shall go.   151

Fal. Well, God give thee the spirit of persuasion and him the ears of profiting, that what thou speakest may move and what he hears may be believ'd, that the true prince may (for recreation sake) prove a false thief, for the poor abuses of the time want countenance. Farewell, you shall find me in Eastcheap.   157

Prince. Farewell, the latter spring! Farewell, Allhallown summer!   [*Exit Falstaff.*]

Poins. Now, my good sweet honey lord, ride with us to-morrow. I have a jest to execute that I 161 cannot manage alone. Falstaff, [Bardolph, Peto], and Gadshill shall rob those men that we have already waylaid; yourself and I will not be there; and when they have the booty, if you and I do not rob them, cut this head off from my shoulders.   166

Prince. How shall we part with them in setting forth?

Poins. Why, we will set forth before or after them and appoint them a place of meeting, wherein it is at our pleasure to fail; and then will they adventure 171 upon the exploit themselves, which they shall have no sooner achiev'd but we'll set upon them.

Prince. Yea, but 'tis like that they will know us by our horses, by our habits, and by every other appointment to be ourselves.   176

Poins. Tut, our horses they shall not see—I'll tie them in the wood; our vizards we will change after we leave them; and, sirrah, I have cases of buckrom for the nonce, to immask our noted outward garments.

Prince. Yea, but I doubt they will be too hard for us.   182

Poins. Well, for two of them, I know them to be as true-bred cowards as ever turn'd back; and for the third, if he fight longer than he sees reason, I'll forswear arms. The virtue of this jest will be the 186 incomprehensible lies that this same fat rogue will tell

---

90. iteration: i.e. trick of repeating Biblical texts (with a satirical twist).   **96. and:** if.
100. 'Zounds: by God's (Christ's) wounds.   **make one:** be one of the party.
101. an': and, i.e. if.   **baffle:** disgrace (literally, deprive a perjured knight of his rank).
106. Gadshill: the name of one of the thieves.
106–7. set a match: planned a robbery.   **109. true:** honest.
115. Good Friday: i.e. the most solemn of fast days.
117. stands to: keeps.   **119. his due:** i.e. Falstaff's soul.
122. cozening: cheating.
125. Gadshill: hill near Rochester on the road from London to Canterbury, notorious for its robberies.
128. vizards: masks.   **129. lies:** lodges.
130. Eastcheap: thoroughfare in London, site of the tavern of line 40.
136. chops: fat-face.

141. royal. With a pun on *royal* = a gold coin worth ten shillings.   **stand for:** (1) make a fight for; (2) be worth.
156. want countenance: lack encouragement (from men of rank like the Prince).
158. latter spring: i.e. old man with youthful impulses.
158–59. All-hallown summer: i.e. Indian summer. All-hallows (or All Saints') Day is November 1.
163–64. waylaid: set an ambush for.   **175. habits:** clothes.
175–76. appointment: accoutrement.
179. sirrah: customarily a form of address to an inferior; here, a term of comradeship.
179–80. cases . . . nonce: garments of buckram (stiff, coarse cloth) suitable for the occasion.   **180. noted:** well-known.
181. doubt: fear.   **too hard:** i.e. too many.

us when we meet at supper, how thirty at least he
fought with, what wards, what blows, what extremities
he endur'd, and in the reproof of this lives the jest. 190
 Prince. Well, I'll go with thee. Provide us all
things necessary, and meet me to-morrow night in
Eastcheap, there I'll sup. Farewell.
 Poins. Farewell, my lord.   *Exit Poins.*
 Prince. I know you all, and will a while uphold
The unyok'd humor of your idleness,   196
Yet herein will I imitate the sun,
Who doth permit the base contagious clouds
To smother up his beauty from the world,
That when he please again to be himself, 200
Being wanted, he may be more wond'red at
By breaking through the foul and ugly mists
Of vapors that did seem to strangle him.
If all the year were playing holidays,
To sport would be as tedious as to work; 205
But when they seldom come, they wish'd for come,
And nothing pleaseth but rare accidents.
So when this loose behavior I throw off
And pay the debt I never promised,
By how much better than my word I am, 210
By so much shall I falsify men's hopes,
And like bright metal on a sullen ground,
My reformation, glitt'ring o'er my fault,
Shall show more goodly and attract more eyes
Than that which hath no foil to set it off. 215
I'll so offend, to make offense a skill,
Redeeming time when men think least I will. *Exit.*

[Scene III]

Enter the King, Northumberland, Worcester,
Hotspur, Sir Walter Blunt, *with others.*

 King. My blood hath been too cold and temperate,
Unapt to stir at these indignities,
And you have found me, for accordingly
You tread upon my patience; but be sure
I will from henceforth rather be myself, 5
Mighty and to be fear'd, than my condition,
Which hath been smooth as oil, soft as young down,
And therefore lost that title of respect
Which the proud soul ne'er pays but to the proud.
 Wor. Our house, my sovereign liege, little deserves
The scourge of greatness to be us'd on it, 11
And that same greatness too which our own hands

Have holp to make so portly.
 North. My lord—
 King. Worcester, get thee gone, for I do see 15
Danger and disobedience in thine eye.
O, sir, your presence is too bold and peremptory,
And majesty might never yet endure
The moody frontier of a servant brow.
You have good leave to leave us. When we need 20
Your use and counsel, we shall send for you.
           Exit Worcester.
You were about to speak.
 North.   Yea, my good lord.
Those prisoners in your Highness' name demanded,
Which Harry Percy here at Holmedon took,
Were, as he says, not with such strength denied 25
As is delivered to your Majesty.
Either envy, therefore, or misprision
Is guilty of this fault, and not my son.
 Hot. My liege, I did deny no prisoners,
But I remember, when the fight was done, 30
When I was dry with rage and extreme toil,
Breathless and faint, leaning upon my sword,
Came there a certain lord, neat, and trimly dress'd,
Fresh as a bridegroom, and his chin new reap'd
Show'd like a stubble-land at harvest-home. 35
He was perfumed like a milliner,
And 'twixt his finger and his thumb he held
A pouncet-box, which ever and anon
He gave his nose and took't away again,
Who therewith angry, when it next came there, 40
Took it in snuff—and still he smil'd and talk'd:
And as the soldiers bore dead bodies by,
He call'd them untaught knaves, unmannerly,
To bring a slovenly unhandsome corse
Betwixt the wind and his nobility.   45
With many holiday and lady terms
He questioned me, amongst the rest demanded
My prisoners in your Majesty's behalf.
I then, all smarting with my wounds being cold,
To be so pest'red with a popingay,   50
Out of my grief and my impatience
Answer'd neglectingly, I know not what—
He should, or he should not—for he made me mad
To see him shine so brisk and smell so sweet,
And talk so like a waiting-gentlewoman 55
Of guns, and drums, and wounds, God save the
   mark!
And telling me the sovereignest thing on earth
Was parmaciti for an inward bruise,

---

189. **wards:** postures of defense, parries. 190. **reproof:** disproof.
196. **unyok'd . . . idleness:** undisciplined tendency of your frivolity.
198. **contagious:** noxious (because fogs were thought to breed pestilence). 200. **That:** so that. 201. **wanted:** missed.
207. **rare accidents:** exceptional events.
211. **hopes:** expectations.
212. **sullen ground:** dark background.
215. **foil:** thin sheet of metal set behind a jewel to enhance its brilliance. 216. **to:** as to. **skill:** i.e. something good and clever.
217. **Redeeming time:** making up for misspent time.

I.iii. Location: London. The palace.
2. **Unapt:** slow. 3. **found me:** i.e. found me so mild.
5. **myself:** i.e. my kingly self.
6. **my condition:** my (naturally mild) disposition.
10. **Our house:** i.e. the Percy family, which had thrown its powerful
support to Bullingbrook on his return from exile. Worcester was
Northumberland's brother and thus Hotspur's uncle.

13. **holp:** helped. **portly:** stately. 16. **Danger:** defiance.
17. **peremptory:** imperious.
19. **moody frontier:** i.e. frowning forehead.
25. **strength:** vehemence. 26. **delivered:** reported.
27. **envy:** malice. **misprision:** misunderstanding.
34. **chin new reap'd:** i.e. beard freshly clipped.
35. **Show'd:** looked. 38. **pouncet-box:** pomander, perfume box.
40. **Who:** which (i.e. his nose).
41. **Took . . . snuff:** (1) snuffed it up; (2) was offended. **still:** continually. 44. **corse:** corpse.
46. **many . . . terms:** much dainty and effeminate language.
47. **questioned:** prattled to. **the rest:** other things.
50. **popingay:** popinjay, parrot. 51. **grief:** pain.
52. **neglectingly:** without considering.
56. **God . . . mark:** God forbid.
57. **sovereignest thing:** most efficacious remedy.
58. **parmaciti:** ointment made of spermaceti or whale sperm.

1 Henry IV
I.iii

And that it was great pity, so it was,
This villainous saltpetre should be digg'd   60
Out of the bowels of the harmless earth,
Which many a good tall fellow had destroyed
So cowardly, and but for these vile guns
He would himself have been a soldier.
This bald unjointed chat of his, my lord,   65
I answered indirectly, as I said,
And I beseech you, let not his report
Come current for an accusation
Betwixt my love and your high Majesty.
    Blunt.   The circumstance considered, good my lord,
What e'er Lord Harry Percy then had said   71
To such a person, and in such a place,
At such a time, with all the rest retold,
May reasonably die, and never rise
To do him wrong, or any way impeach   75
What then he said, so he unsay it now.
    King.   Why, yet he doth deny his prisoners,
But with proviso and exception,
That we at our own charge shall ransom straight
His brother-in-law, the foolish Mortimer,   80
Who, on my soul, hath willfully betray'd
The lives of those that he did lead to fight
Against that great magician, damn'd Glendower,
Whose daughter, as we hear, that Earl of March
Hath lately married. Shall our coffers then   85
Be emptied to redeem a traitor home?
Shall we buy treason? and indent with fears,
When they have lost and forfeited themselves?
No, on the barren mountains let him starve;
For I shall never hold that man my friend   90
Whose tongue shall ask me for one penny cost
To ransom home revolted Mortimer.
    Hot.   Revolted Mortimer!
He never did fall off, my sovereign liege,
But by the chance of war; to prove that true   95
Needs no more but one tongue for all those wounds,
Those mouthed wounds, which valiantly he took,
When on the gentle Severn's sedgy bank,
In single opposition hand to hand,
He did confound the best part of an hour   100
In changing hardiment with great Glendower.

62. **tall**: brave.   63. **but**: except.   65. **bald**: trivial.
68. **Come current**: be accepted as valid.   71. **had**: may have.
75. **impeach**: discredit.   76. **so**: provided that.
78. **But . . . exception**: unless on the condition.
79. **charge**: expense.   **straight**: immediately.
80. **brother-in-law**. Hotspur's wife Elizabeth (called Kate in this play) was the sister of Roger, fourth Earl of March, and of Sir Edmund Mortimer (who married Glendower's daughter).
83. **magician**.   Following Mortimer's capture, reports Holinshed (Bullough, IV, 182–83), Henry himself led an expedition to take Glendower, but the Welshman "conveied himself out of the waie, into his knowen lurking places, and (as was thought) through art magike, he caused such foule weather of winds, tempest, raine, snow, and haile to be raised, for the annoiance of the kings armie, that the like had not been heard of."
84–85. **Whose . . . married**. Once Mortimer had been captured, says Holinshed (Bullough, IV, 184), he, "whether for irkesomnesse of cruell captivitie, or feare of death, or for what other cause, it is un-certeine, agreed to take part with Owen [Glendower], against the king of England, and tooke to wife the daughter of the said Owen."
87. **indent with fears**: i.e. come to terms with persons who have given us cause to fear them.   92. **revolted**: rebellious.
97. **mouthed**: gaping.   100. **confound**: consume.
101. **changing hardiment**: matching valor.

Three times they breath'd and three times did they
    drink,
Upon agreement, of swift Severn's flood,
Who then affrighted with their bloody looks,
Ran fearfully among the trembling reeds,   105
And hid his crisp head in the hollow bank,
Blood-stained with these valiant combatants.
Never did bare and rotten policy
Color her working with such deadly wounds,
Nor never could the noble Mortimer   110
Receive so many, and all willingly.
Then let not him be slandered with revolt.
    King.   Thou dost belie him, Percy, thou dost belie
    him;
He never did encounter with Glendower.
I tell thee,   115
He durst as well have met the devil alone
As Owen Glendower for an enemy.
Art thou not asham'd? But, sirrah, henceforth
Let me not hear you speak of Mortimer.
Send me your prisoners with the speediest means,   120
Or you shall hear in such a kind from me
As will displease you. My Lord Northumberland:
We license your departure with your son.
Send us your prisoners, or you will hear of it.
                         Exit King [with Blunt and Train].
    Hot.   And if the devil come and roar for them,   125
I will not send them. I will after straight
And tell him so, for I will ease my heart,
Albeit I make a hazard of my head.
    North.   What? drunk with choler? Stay, and pause
    a while.
Here comes your uncle.

                    Enter WORCESTER.

    Hot.   Speak of Mortimer!   130
'Zounds, I will speak of him, and let my soul
Want mercy if I do not join with him.
Yea, on his part I'll empty all these veins,
And shed my dear blood drop by drop in the dust,
But I will lift the down-trod Mortimer   135
As high in the air as this unthankful king,
As this ingrate and cank'red Bullingbrook.
    North.   Brother, the King hath made your nephew
    mad.
    Wor.   Who strook this heat up after I was gone?
    Hot.   He will, forsooth, have all my prisoners,   140
And when I urg'd the ransom once again
Of my wive's brother, then his cheek look'd pale,
And on my face he turn'd an eye of death,
Trembling even at the name of Mortimer.   144
    Wor.   I cannot blame him: was not he proclaim'd
By Richard, that dead is, the next of blood?

102. **breath'd**: stopped to get their breath.
106. **crisp head**: curled head, i.e. rippled surface.
108. **policy**: cunning, trickery.
112. **revolt**: i.e. accusation of rebellion.
113. **belie**: not tell the truth about.
126. **after straight**: go after him at once.
129. **choler**: anger.   132. **Want**: lack.
133. **on his part**: in his behalf.   137. **cank'red**: malignant.
140. **forsooth**: indeed.   142. **wive's**: wife's.

North.   He was, I heard the proclamation.
And then it was when the unhappy king
(Whose wrongs in us God pardon!) did set forth
Upon his Irish expedition;   150
From whence he intercepted did return
To be depos'd, and shortly murdered.
Wor.   And for whose death we in the world's wide
          mouth
Live scandaliz'd and foully spoken of.
Hot.   But soft, I pray you, did King Richard then
Proclaim my brother Edmund Mortimer   156
Heir to the crown?
North.   He did, myself did hear it.
Hot.   Nay, then I cannot blame his cousin king,
That wish'd him on the barren mountains starve.
But shall it be that you, that set the crown   160
Upon the head of this forgetful man,
And for his sake wear the detested blot
Of murtherous subornation—shall it be
That you a world of curses undergo,
Being the agents or base second means,   165
The cords, the ladder, or the hangman rather?
O, pardon me that I descend so low
To show the line and the predicament
Wherein you range under this subtile king!
Shall it for shame be spoken in these days,   170
Or fill up chronicles in time to come,
That men of your nobility and power
Did gage them both in an unjust behalf
(As both of you—God pardon it!—have done)
To put down Richard, that sweet lovely rose,   175
And plant this thorn, this canker, Bullingbrook?
And shall it in more shame be further spoken,
That you are fool'd, discarded, and shook off
By him for whom these shames ye underwent?
No, yet time serves wherein you may redeem   180
Your banish'd honors and restore yourselves
Into the good thoughts of the world again;
Revenge the jeering and disdain'd contempt
Of this proud king, who studies day and night
To answer all the debt he owes to you   185
Even with the bloody payment of your deaths.
Therefore I say—
Wor.   Peace, cousin, say no more.
And now I will unclasp a secret book,
And to your quick-conceiving discontents
I'll read you matter deep and dangerous,   190
As full of peril and adventerous spirit
As to o'erwalk a current roaring loud
On the unsteadfast footing of a spear.
Hot.   If he fall in, good night, or sink or swim.

Send danger from the east unto the west,   195
So honor cross it from the north to south,
And let them grapple. O, the blood more stirs
To rouse a lion than to start a hare!
North.   Imagination of some great exploit
Drives him beyond the bounds of patience.   200
[*Hot.*]   By heaven, methinks it were an easy leap,
To pluck bright honor from the pale-fac'd moon,
Or dive into the bottom of the deep,
Where fadom-line could never touch the ground,
And pluck up drowned honor by the locks,   205
So he that doth redeem her thence might wear
Without corrival all her dignities;
But out upon this half-fac'd fellowship!
Wor.   He apprehends a world of figures here,
But not the form of what he should attend.   210
Good cousin, give me audience for a while.
Hot.   I cry you mercy.
Wor.   Those same noble Scots
That are your prisoners—
Hot.   I'll keep them all!
By God, he shall not have a Scot of them,
No, if a Scot would save his soul, he shall not!   215
I'll keep them, by this hand.
Wor.   You start away,
And lend no ear unto my purposes.
Those prisoners you shall keep.
Hot.   Nay, I will; that's flat.
He said he would not ransom Mortimer,
Forbade my tongue to speak of Mortimer,   220
But I will find him when he lies asleep,
And in his ear I'll hollow "Mortimer!"
Nay,
I'll have a starling shall be taught to speak
Nothing but "Mortimer," and give it him   225
To keep his anger still in motion.
Wor.   Hear you, cousin, a word.
Hot.   All studies here I solemnly defy,
Save how to gall and pinch this Bullingbrook,
And that same sword-and-buckler Prince of Wales,
But that I think his father loves him not   231
And would be glad he met with some mischance,
I would have him poisoned with a pot of ale.
Wor.   Farewell, kinsman! I'll talk to you
When you are better temper'd to attend.   235
North.   Why, what a wasp-stung and impatient fool
Art thou to break into this woman's mood,
Tying thine ear to no tongue but thine own!
Hot.   Why, look you, I am [whipt] and scourg'd
          with rods,
Nettled and stung with pismires, when I hear   240
Of this vile politician, Bullingbrook.

147–50. I . . . expedition. Shakespeare again confuses the Mortimers;
see note to I.i.38.
149. Whose . . . us: i.e. the wrongs that we did to him (by supporting Bullingbrook).
151. intercepted: interrupted (by Bullingbrook's return from exile).
154. scandaliz'd: defamed.   162. detested: detestable.
163. murtherous subornation: inciting to murder.
168. predicament: category.   169. range: i.e. are classified.
173. gage: pledge.   them both: i.e. nobility and power.
176. canker: (1) wild rose; (2) ulcer.
183. disdain'd: disdainful.   185. answer: discharge.
189. to . . . discontents: i.e. to you, who in your disaffection will be
quick to understand me.   191. adventerous: adventurous.
194. he: i.e. the man attempting such a crossing.   good . . . swim: i.e.
he's done for, whether he sinks or stays afloat (for a time).

196. So: provided that.   200. patience: self-control.
206. redeem: rescue.   207. corrival: partner.
208. half-fac'd: thin, meagre.   fellowship: i.e. sharing of honors.
209. apprehends: seizes on.   figures: figures of speech (an allusion
to Hotspur's highly figurative language).
210. attend: be intent upon.
212. cry you mercy: beg your pardon.
228. studies: concerns, pursuits.   defy: renounce.
230. sword-and-buckler. Like the vulgar "pot of ale" in line 233, an
allusion to the Prince's disreputable associates, for in Shakespeare's
time swords and bucklers were used only by the lowest class of
soldiers.   240. pismires: ants.
241. vile politician: contemptible schemer.

1 Henry IV
I.iii

In Richard's time—what do you call the place?—
A plague upon it, it is in Gloucestershire—
'Twas where the madcap duke his uncle kept—
His uncle York—where I first bow'd my knee   245
Unto this king of smiles, this Bullingbrook—
'Sblood!
When you and he came back from Ravenspurgh—
   North. At Berkeley castle.
   Hot. You say true.   250
Why, what a candy deal of courtesy
This fawning greyhound then did proffer me!
"Look when his infant fortune came to age"
And "gentle Harry Percy" and "kind cousin"—
O, the devil take such cozeners!—God forgive me!
Good uncle, tell your tale—I have done.   256
   Wor. Nay, if you have not, to it again,
We will stay your leisure.
   Hot.   I have done, i' faith.
   Wor. Then once more to your Scottish prisoners:
Deliver them up without their ransom straight,   260
And make the Douglas' son your only mean
For powers in Scotland, which, for divers reasons
Which I shall send you written, be assur'd
Will easily be granted. [*To Northumberland.*] You,
   my lord,
Your son in Scotland being thus employed,   265
Shall secretly into the bosom creep
Of that same noble prelate well belov'd,
The Archbishop.
   Hot. Of York, is it not?
   Wor. True, who bears hard   270
His brother's death at Bristow, the Lord Scroop.
I speak not this in estimation,
As what I think might be, but what I know
Is ruminated, plotted, and set down,
And only stays but to behold the face   275
Of that occasion that shall bring it on.
   Hot. I smell it. Upon my life, it will do well.
   North. Before the game is afoot thou still let'st slip.
   Hot. Why, it cannot choose but be a noble plot.
And then the power of Scotland, and of York,   280
To join with Mortimer, ha?
   Wor.   And so they shall.
   Hot. In faith, it is exceedingly well aim'd.
   Wor. And 'tis no little reason bids us speed,

To save our heads by raising of a head,
For bear ourselves as even as we can,   285
The King will always think him in our debt,
And think we think ourselves unsatisfied,
Till he hath found a time to pay us home.
And see already how he doth begin
To make us strangers to his looks of love.   290
   Hot. He does, he does, we'll be reveng'd on him.
   Wor. Cousin, farewell! No further go in this
Than I by letters shall direct your course.
When time is ripe, which will be suddenly,
I'll steal to Glendower and Lord Mortimer,   295
Where you and Douglas and our powers at once,
As I will fashion it, shall happily meet
To bear our fortunes in our own strong arms,
Which now we hold at much uncertainty.
   North. Farewell, good brother, we shall thrive, I
   trust.   300
   Hot. Uncle, adieu! O, let the hours be short,
Till fields, and blows, and groans applaud our sport!
                         Exeunt.

[ACT II, Scene I]

Enter a Carrier *with a lantern in his hand.*

   1. Car. Heigh-ho! an' it be not four by the day, I'll
be hang'd. Charles' wain is over the new chimney, and
yet our horse not pack'd. What, ostler!
   Ost. [*Within.*] Anon, anon.   4
   1. Car. I prithee, Tom, beat Cut's saddle, put a few
flocks in the point. Poor jade is wrung in the withers,
out of all cess.

Enter another Carrier.

   2. Car. Peas and beans are as dank here as a dog,
and that is the next way to give poor jades the   9
bots. This house is turn'd upside down since Robin
ostler died.
   1. Car. Poor fellow never joy'd since the price of
oats rose, it was the death of him.
   2. Car. I think this be the most villainous house in
all London road for fleas. I am stung like a tench.   15
   1. Car. Like a tench? by the mass, there is ne'er a
king christen could be better bit than I have been since
the first cock.
   2. Car. Why, they will allow us ne'er a jordan, and
then we leak in your chimney, and your chamber-lye

---

244. **kept:** resided.
245–46. **where . . . Bullingbrook.** See *Richard II*, II.iii.
248. **Ravenspurgh:** Ravenspur, at the mouth of the Humber in Yorkshire, where Henry landed on his return from exile.
251. **candy deal:** sugary lot.
253–54. **Look . . . cousin.** See *Richard II*, II.iii.45–49.
255. **cozeners:** cheats (with obvious pun).
258. **stay your leisure:** wait until you have time to listen.
260. **Deliver them up:** liberate them.   **straight:** at once.
261. **the Douglas' son:** i.e. Murdac Stewart. See note to I.i.71. Then as now the head of a prominent Scottish family was designated by his surname preceded by the definite article.
261–62. **mean For powers:** agent for raising troops.
268. **The Archbishop:** Richard le Scrope or Scroop (1350?–1405), one of the most prominent of the Percies' allies in their insurrection. In line 271 Shakespeare repeats Holinshed's error in calling him the brother, instead of the cousin, of William Scroop, Earl of Wiltshire (on whom see the notes to *Richard II*, II.i.215, III.ii.122–23).
270. **bears hard:** greatly resents.   271. **Bristow:** Bristol.
272. **estimation:** (mere) conjecture.   276. **occasion:** opportunity.
278. **thou . . . slip:** you always loose the dogs.
282. **aim'd:** planned.

284. **head:** army.
285. **even:** prudently, carefully.   286. **him:** himself.
288. **home:** fully.   294. **suddenly:** soon.
296. **powers at once:** united forces.   302. **fields:** battlefields.

II.i. Location: Rochester. An innyard.
1. **by the day:** in the morning.
2. **Charles' wain:** Charlemagne's wagon, i.e. the constellation of the Great Bear (*Ursa Major*).   3. **horse:** horses.
4. **Anon:** at once, i.e. coming.
6. **flocks . . . point:** tufts of wool in the pommel (to make it more comfortable for the horse).
6. **Poor . . . withers:** the nag is chafed (by the saddle) along the ridge between its shoulders.   **cess:** measure.
9. **next:** nearest, i.e. quickest.
10. **bots:** intestinal worms.   14. **house:** inn.
16. **tench:** spotted fish.   17. **king christen:** Christian king.
18. **first cock:** i.e. midnight.   19. **jordan:** chamber pot.
20. **chamber-lye:** urine.

breeds fleas like a loach.   21

1. Car. What, ostler! come away and be hang'd! come away.

2. Car. I have a gammon of bacon and two razes of ginger, to be deliver'd as far as Charing-cross.   25

1. Car. God's body, the turkeys in my pannier are quite starv'd. What, ostler! A plague on thee! hast thou never an eye in thy head? Canst not hear? And 'twere not as good deed as drink to break the   29 pate on thee, I am a very villain. Come, and be hang'd! hast no faith in thee?

Enter GADSHILL.

Gads. Good morrow, carriers, what's a' clock?

[*1.*] *Car.* I think it be two a' clock.

Gads. I prithee lend me thy lantern, to see my gelding in the stable.   35

1. Car. Nay, by God, soft, I know a trick worth two of that, i' faith.

Gads. I pray thee lend me thine.

2. Car. Ay, when, canst tell? Lend me thy lantern, quoth he! Marry, I'll see thee hang'd first.   40

Gads. Sirrah carrier, what time do you mean to come to London?

2. Car. Time enough to go to bed with a candle, I warrant thee. Come, neighbor Mugs, we'll call   44 up the gentlemen. They will along with company, for they have great charge.   *Exeunt* [*Carriers*].

Gads. What ho! chamberlain!

Enter CHAMBERLAIN.

Cham. At hand, quoth pick-purse.   48

Gads. That's even as fair as—at hand, quoth the chamberlain; for thou variest no more from picking of purses than giving direction doth from laboring: thou layest the plot how.

Cham. Good morrow, Master Gadshill. It holds current that I told you yesternight: there's a   54 franklin in the Wild of Kent hath brought three hundred marks with him in gold. I heard him tell it to one of his company last night at supper, a kind of auditor, one that hath abundance of charge too—God knows what. They are up already, and call for eggs and butter. They will away presently.   60

Gads. Sirrah, if they meet not with Saint Nicholas' clerks, I'll give thee this neck.

Cham. No, I'll none of it, I pray thee keep that for the hangman, for I know thou worshippest Saint Nicholas as truly as a man of falsehood may.   65

Gads. What talkest thou to me of the hangman? If I hang, I'll make a fat pair of gallows; for if I hang, old Sir John hangs with me, and thou knowest he is no starveling. Tut, there are other Troyans that   69 thou dream'st not of, the which for sport sake are content to do the profession some grace, that would (if matters should be look'd into) for their own credit sake make all whole. I am join'd with no foot land-rakers, no long-staff sixpenny strikers, none of these mad   74 mustachio purple-hu'd malt-worms, but with nobility and tranquility, burgomasters and great oney'rs, such as can hold in, such as will strike sooner than speak, and speak sooner than drink, and drink sooner than pray; and yet, 'zounds, I lie, for they pray   79 continually to their saint, the commonwealth, or rather, not pray to her, but prey on her, for they ride up and down on her, and make her their boots.

Cham. What, the commonwealth their boots? Will she hold out water in foul way?   84

Gads. She will, she will, justice hath liquor'd her. We steal as in a castle, cock-sure; we have the receipt of fern-seed, we walk invisible.

Cham. Nay, by my faith, I think you are more beholding to the night than to fern-seed for your walking invisible.   90

Gads. Give me thy hand. Thou shalt have a share in our purchase, as I am a true man.

Cham. Nay, rather let me have it as you are a false thief.   94

Gads. Go to, *homo* is a common name to all men. Bid the ostler bring my gelding out of the stable. Farewell, you muddy knave.   [*Exeunt.*]

[SCENE II]

Enter PRINCE, PETO, *and* [BARDOLPH, *with*] POINS [*following just behind*].

Poins. Come, shelter, shelter! I have remov'd Falstaff's horse, and he frets like a gumm'd velvet.

Prince. Stand close.   [*They retire.*]

---

63. **I'll ... it:** i.e. I don't want your neck.
69. **Troyans:** Trojans, i.e. roisterers.
71. **profession:** i.e. robbery.
73. **join'd:** associated.   **foot land-rakers:** footpads.
74. **long-staff sixpenny strikers:** those who, armed only with cudgels, will rob a man of sixpence; i.e. petty thieves.
74–75. **mad ... malt-worms:** topers whose mustaches are stained with ale.   76. **oney'rs:** ones (?).   77. **hold in:** retain secrets.
82. **boots:** booty.
84. **hold ... way:** keep one dryshod in muddy roads, i.e. protect one.
85. **liquor'd:** (1) greased; (2) bribed.
86. **as ... castle:** i.e. in security (with an allusion to Sir John Oldcastle, the name originally given to Falstaff in this play).
87. **receipt of fern-seed:** procedure for finding fern-seed, which, almost invisible itself, was thought to confer invisibility on whoever carried it.   89. **beholding:** beholden, indebted.
92. **purchase:** booty.   **true:** honest.
95. **homo:** man. Gadshill implies that a generic term, without such adjectives as *true* or *false*, will suffice.   97. **muddy:** stupid.

II.ii. Location: The highway near Gadshill.
2. **frets:** (1) complains; (2) frays.   **gumm'd:** stiffened with gum.
3. **close:** concealed.

---

21. **like a loach:** i.e. as fast as a loach (a kind of fish) spawns loaches.
22. **come away:** come along, hurry up.
24. **gammon of bacon:** ham.   **razes:** roots.
25. **Charing-cross:** village between London and Westminster.
28–30. **And ... thee:** if it were not as good to clout you on the head as to take a drink.   39. **Ay ... tell:** i.e. never.
45–46. **They ... charge:** they will want to travel in a group because of the valuables they are carrying.
47. **chamberlain:** servant who tended the rooms of an inn.
48. **At ... pick-purse:** here I am right beside you, as the pickpocket said.   49. **fair:** apt. Inn servants were notoriously dishonest.
50–52. **thou ... how:** i.e. you stand in the same relation to pickpockets as a foreman does to workmen, for you make the plans that others carry out.   53–54. **holds current:** proves to be true.
54. **that:** what.
55. **franklin:** small landowner.   **Wild:** Weald (forest).
55–56. **three hundred marks:** two hundred pounds.
57. **auditor:** accountant.   60. **presently:** at once.
61–62. **Saint Nicholas' clerks:** highwaymen. In Elizabethan slang St. Nicholas was regarded as the patron of thieves.

1 Henry IV
II.ii

Enter FALSTAFF.

Fal. Poins! Poins, and be hang'd! Poins!   4

Prince. [*Coming forward.*] Peace, ye fat-kidney'd rascal! what a brawling dost thou keep!

Fal. Where's Poins, Hal?

Prince. He is walk'd up to the top of the hill, I'll go seek him.   [*Retires.*]   9

Fal. I am accurs'd to rob in that thieve's company. The rascal hath remov'd my horse, and tied him I know not where. If I travel but four foot by the squier further afoot, I shall break my wind. Well, I doubt not but to die a fair death for all this, if I scape hanging for killing that rogue. I have forsworn his   15 company hourly any time this two and twenty years, and yet I am bewitch'd with the rogue's company. If the rascal have not given me medicines to make me love him, I'll be hang'd. It could not be else, I have drunk medicines. Poins! Hal! a plague upon you   20 both! Bardolph! Peto! I'll starve ere I'll rob a foot further. And 'twere not as good a deed as drink to turn true man and to leave these rogues, I am the veriest varlet that ever chew'd with a tooth. Eight yards of uneven ground is threescore and ten miles   25 afoot with me, and the stony-hearted villains know it well enough. A plague upon it when thieves cannot be true one to another! (*They whistle.*) Whew! a plague upon you all! Give me my horse, you rogues, give me my horse, and be hang'd!   30

Prince. [*Coming forward.*] Peace, ye fat-guts, lie down. Lay thine ear close to the ground, and list if thou canst hear the tread of travellers.

Fal. Have you any levers to lift me up again, being down? 'Sblood, I'll not bear my own flesh   35 so far afoot again for all the coin in thy father's exchequer. What a plague mean ye to colt me thus?

Prince. Thou liest, thou art not colted, thou art uncolted.   39

Fal. I prithee, good prince—Hal!—help me to my horse, good king's son.

Prince. Out, ye rogue! shall I be your ostler?

Fal. Hang thyself in thine own heir-apparent garters! If I be ta'en, I'll peach for this. And I have not ballads made on you all and sung to filthy   45 tunes, let a cup of sack be my poison. When a jest is so forward, and afoot too! I hate it.

Enter GADSHILL.

Gads. Stand.

Fal. So I do, against my will.   49

Poins. [*Coming forward with Bardolph and Peto.*] O, 'tis our setter, I know his voice.

[*Bard.*] What news?

[*Gads.*] Case ye, case ye, on with your vizards. There's money of the King's coming down the hill, 'tis going to the King's exchequer.   55

Fal. You lie, ye rogue, 'tis going to the King's tavern.

Gads. There's enough to make us all.

Fal. To be hang'd.   59

Prince. Sirs, you four shall front them in the narrow lane; Ned Poins and I will walk lower. If they scape from your encounter, then they light on us.

Peto. How many be there of them?

Gads. Some eight or ten.

Fal. 'Zounds, will they not rob us?   65

Prince. What, a coward, Sir John Paunch?

Fal. Indeed I am not John of Gaunt, your grandfather, but yet no coward, Hal.

Prince. Well, we leave that to the proof.   69

Poins. Sirrah Jack, thy horse stands behind the hedge; when thou need'st him, there thou shalt find him. Farewell, and stand fast.

Fal. Now cannot I strike him, if I should be hang'd.

Prince. [*Aside.*] Ned, where are our disguises?

Poins. [*Aside.*] Here, hard by. Stand close.   75
        [*Exeunt Prince and Poins.*]

Fal. Now, my masters, happy man be his dole, say I, every man to his business.

Enter the TRAVELLERS.

[*1.*] *Trav.* Come, neighbor, the boy shall lead our horses down the hill. We'll walk afoot a while, and ease our legs.   80

Thieves. Stand!

Travellers. Jesus bless us!

Fal. Strike! down with them! cut the villains' throats! Ah, whoreson caterpillars! bacon-fed knaves! they hate us youth. Down with them! fleece them!   85

[*1.*] *Trav.* O, we are undone, both we and ours for ever!

Fal. Hang ye, gorbellied knaves, are ye undone? No, ye fat chuffs, I would your store were here! On, bacons, on! What, ye knaves, young men must   90 live! You are grandjurors, are ye? We'll jure ye, faith.   *Here they rob them and bind them. Exeunt.*

Enter the PRINCE *and* POINS [*in buckram*].

Prince. The thieves have bound the true men. Now could thou and I rob the thieves and go merrily to London, it would be argument for a week, laughter for a month, and a good jest for ever.   96

Poins. Stand close, I hear them coming.

Enter the THIEVES *again.*

Fal. Come, my masters, let us share, and then to horse before day. And the Prince and Poins be not two arrant cowards, there's no equity stirring.   100

---

6. keep: keep up.
10. thieve's: thief's.   12. squier: square, foot rule.
14. for: despite.   18. medicines: potions.   37. colt: trick.
39. uncolted: i.e. deprived of your horse.
43–44. heir-apparent garters. An allusion to the Order of the Garter, in which the Prince, as heir apparent, had been installed as a knight.
44. peach: turn informer.   46–47. is so forward: goes so far.
51. setter. See note to I.ii.106–7.   53. Case ye: mask yourselves.

58. make us all: i.e. make our fortunes.
67. John of Gaunt. A punning allusion to Hal's thinness (on which see II.iv.244–48). John of Gaunt was so called from his birthplace, Ghent in Flanders.   69. proof: test.
76. happy . . . dole: i.e. may each man be fortunate; good luck to you. *Dole* = that which is dealt (by fate).
84. caterpillars: parasites.   88. gorbellied: potbellied.
89. chuffs: misers.   your store: all your possessions.
90. bacons: fat men.
91. grandjurors: i.e. affluent citizens (eligible for jury duty).
93. true: honest.   95. argument: topic of conversation.
100. equity: judgment, discrimination.

There's no more valor in that Poins than in a wild duck.

*As they are sharing, the
Prince and Poins set upon
them; they all run away,
and Falstaff, after a blow
or two, runs away too,
leaving the booty behind
them.*

Prince.   Your money!
Poins.   Villains!

Prince.   Got with much ease.   Now merrily to
   horse.
The thieves are all scatter'd, and possess'd with fear
So strongly that they dare not meet each other;   106
Each takes his fellow for an officer.
Away, good Ned.   Falstaff sweats to death,
And lards the lean earth as he walks along.
Were't not for laughing, I should pity him.   110
Poins.   How the fat rogue roar'd!   *Exeunt.*

[SCENE III]

Enter HOTSPUR *solus, reading a letter.*

[*Hot.*]   "But, for mine own part, my lord, I could be
well contented to be there, in respect of the love I bear
your house."   He could be contented: why is he not
then?   In the respect of the love he bears our house:
he shows in this, he loves his own barn better than   5
he loves our house.   Let me see some more.   "The
purpose you undertake is dangerous"—why, that's
certain.   'Tis dangerous to take a cold, to sleep, to
drink, but I tell you, my lord fool, out of this nettle,
danger, we pluck this flower, safety.   "The pur-   10
pose you undertake is dangerous, the friends you
have nam'd uncertain, the time itself unsorted, and your
whole plot too light for the counterpoise of so great an
opposition."   Say you so, say you so?   I say unto you
again, you are a shallow, cowardly hind, and   15
you lie.   What a lack-brain is this!   By the Lord, our
plot is a good plot as ever was laid, our friends true
and constant: a good plot, good friends, and full of
expectation; an excellent plot, very good friends.
What a frosty-spirited rogue is this!   Why, my   20
Lord of York commends the plot and the general
course of the action.   'Zounds, and I were now by this
rascal, I could brain him with his lady's fan.   Is there
not my father, my uncle, and myself?   Lord Edmund
Mortimer, my Lord of York, and Owen Glen-   25
dower?   is there not besides the Douglas?   have I not
all their letters to meet me in arms by the ninth of the
next month?   and are they not some of them set forward
already?   What a pagan rascal is this!   an infidel!   Ha,
you shall see now in very sincerity of fear and cold   30
heart will he to the King, and lay open all our proceedings.   O, I could divide myself and go to buffets, for

moving such a dish of skim-milk with so honorable an
action!   Hang him!   let him tell the King: we are
prepar'd.   I will set forward to-night.   35

Enter his LADY.

How now, Kate?   I must leave you within these two
hours.
   Lady.   O my good lord, why are you thus alone?
For what offense have I this fortnight been
A banish'd woman from my Harry's bed?
Tell me, sweet lord, what is't that takes from thee   40
Thy stomach, pleasure, and thy golden sleep?
Why dost thou bend thine eyes upon the earth,
And start so often when thou sit'st alone?
Why hast thou lost the fresh blood in thy cheeks,
And given my treasures and my rights of thee   45
To thick-ey'd musing and curst melancholy?
In thy faint slumbers I by thee have watch'd,
And heard thee murmur tales of iron wars,
Speak terms of manage to thy bounding steed,
Cry "Courage! to the field!"   And thou hast talk'd   50
Of sallies and retires, of trenches, tents,
Of palisadoes, frontiers, parapets,
Of basilisks, of cannon, culverin,
Of prisoners' ransom, and of soldiers slain,
And all the currents of a heady fight;   55
Thy spirit within thee hath been so at war,
And thus hath so bestirr'd thee in thy sleep,
That beads of sweat have stood upon thy brow,
Like bubbles in a late-disturbed stream,
And in thy face strange motions have appear'd,   60
Such as we see when men restrain their breath
On some great sudden hest.   O, what portents are
   these?
Some heavy business hath my lord in hand,
And I must know it, else he loves me not.
   Hot.   What ho!

[*Enter* SERVANT.]

   Is Gilliams with the packet gone?
   Serv.   He is, my lord, an hour ago.   66
   Hot.   Hath Butler brought those horses from the
   sheriff?
   Serv.   One horse, my lord, he brought even now.
   Hot.   What horse?   Roan?   a crop-ear, is it not?
   Serv.   It is, my lord.
   Hot.   That roan shall be my throne.
Well, I will back him straight.   O *Esperance!*   71
Bid Butler lead him forth into the park.

   [*Exit Servant.*]

   Lady.   But hear you, my lord.
   Hot.   What say'st thou, my lady?
   Lady.   What is it carries you away?   75
   Hot.   Why, my horse, my love, my horse.
   Lady.   Out, you mad-headed ape!
A weasel hath not such a deal of spleen

109. lards: bastes.

II.iii. Location: Warkworth Castle (stronghold of the Percies in
Northumberland).   o.s.d. solus: alone.
3. house: family.   He. The writer of the letter is never identified.
12. unsorted: unsuitable.
21. Lord of York: i.e. Archbishop Scroop.
29. pagan: unbelieving.   30. very: veritable.
32. divide . . . buffets: split in two and have a boxing-match with
myself (cf. "I could kick myself").

41. stomach: appetite.
47. faint: light.   49. manage: manège, horsemanship.
52. palisadoes: stakes set for defense.   frontiers: ramparts.
53. basilisks: heavy ordnance.   culverin: light ordnance.
55. heady: headlong.   62. hest: behest, command.
63. heavy: (1) weighty; (2) sorrowful.
71. Esperance: Hope (the motto of the house of Percy).
78. spleen: nervous energy, impulsiveness.

As you are toss'd with. In faith,
I'll know your business, Harry, that I will. 80
I fear my brother Mortimer doth stir
About his title, and hath sent for you
To line his enterprise, but if you go—
 Hot. So far afoot, I shall be weary, love.
 Lady. Come, come, you paraquito, answer me 85
Directly unto this question that I ask.
In faith, I'll break thy little finger, Harry,
And if thou wilt not tell me all things true.
 Hot. Away,
Away, you trifler! Love, I love thee not, 90
I care not for thee, Kate. This is no world
To play with mammets and to tilt with lips.
We must have bloody noses and crack'd crowns,
And pass them current too. God's me, my horse!
What say'st thou, Kate? What wouldst thou have
   with me? 95
 Lady. Do you not love me? do you not indeed?
Well, do not then, for since you love me not,
I will not love myself. Do you not love me?
Nay, tell me if you speak in jest or no.
 Hot. Come, wilt thou see me ride? 100
And when I am a' horseback, I will swear
I love thee infinitely. But hark you, Kate,
I must not have you henceforth question me
Whither I go, nor reason whereabout.
Whither I must, I must, and to conclude, 105
This evening must I leave you, gentle Kate.
I know you wise, but yet no farther wise
Than Harry Percy's wife; constant you are,
But yet a woman, and for secrecy,
No lady closer, for I well believe 110
Thou wilt not utter what thou dost not know,
And so far will I trust thee, gentle Kate.
 Lady. How! so far?
 Hot. Not an inch further. But hark you, Kate,
Whither I go, thither shall you go too; 115
To-day will I set forth, to-morrow you.
Will this content you, Kate?
 Lady.   It must of force. *Exeunt.*

[SCENE IV]

Enter PRINCE *and* POINS.

 Prince. Ned, prithee come out of that fat room,
and lend me thy hand to laugh a little.
 Poins. Where hast been, Hal?
 Prince. With three or four loggerheads amongst
three or four score hogsheads. I have sounded the 5
very base-string of humility. Sirrah, I am sworn
brother to a leash of drawers, and can call them all by
their christen names, as Tom, Dick, and Francis.
They take it already upon their salvation, that though
I be but Prince of Wales, yet I am the king of 10
courtesy, and tell me flatly I am no proud Jack like
Falstaff, but a Corinthian, a lad of mettle, a good boy
(by the Lord, so they call me!), and when I am King of
England I shall command all the good lads in Eastcheap. They call drinking deep, dyeing scarlet, 15
and when you breathe in your watering, they cry
"hem!" and bid you play it off. To conclude, I am so
good a proficient in one quarter of an hour, that I can
drink with any tinker in his own language during my
life. I tell thee, Ned, thou hast lost much honor 20
that thou wert not with me in this action. But, sweet
Ned—to sweeten which name of Ned, I give thee this
pennyworth of sugar, clapp'd even now into my hand
by an under-skinker, one that never spake other English in his life than "Eight shillings and sixpence,"
and "You are welcome," with this shrill addition, 26
"Anon, anon, sir! Score a pint of bastard in the Half-
moon," or so. But, Ned, to drive away the time till
Falstaff come, I prithee do thou stand in some by- 29
room, while I question my puny drawer to what end
he gave me the sugar, and do thou never leave calling "Francis," that his tale to me may be nothing but
"Anon." Step aside, and I'll show thee a [president].
         [*Exit Poins.*]
 Poins. [*Within.*] Francis!
 Prince. Thou art perfect. 35
 [*Poins.*] [*Within.*] Francis!

Enter Drawer [FRANCIS].

 Fran. Anon, anon, sir. Look down into the
Pomgarnet, Ralph.
 Prince. Come hither, Francis.
 Fran. My lord? 40
 Prince. How long hast thou to serve, Francis?
 Fran. ·Forsooth, five years, and as much as to—
 Poins. [*Within.*] Francis!
 Fran. Anon, anon, sir. 44
 Prince. Five year! by'r lady, a long lease for the
clinking of pewter. But, Francis, darest thou be so
valiant as to play the coward with thy indenture, and
show it a fair pair of heels and run from it?
 Fran. O Lord, sir, I'll be sworn upon all the books
in England, I could find in my heart— 50
 Poins. [*Within.*] Francis!
 Fran. Anon, sir.
 Prince. How old art thou, Francis?
 Fran. Let me see—about Michaelmas next I shall
be— 55

82. **title:** claim to the throne. 83. **line:** support.
92. **mammets:** dolls (like you). 94. **loggerheads:** blockheads.
94. **pass them current:** cause them to circulate as legal tender, i.e. give them in exchange. Hotspur is playing on two senses of *crowns:* (1) heads; (2) coins worth five shillings. Cracked coins were not normally accepted as currency. **God's me:** God save me. 101. **a':** on.
104. **whereabout:** about what. 109. **for:** as for.
117. **of force:** of necessity.

II.iv. **Location:** London. The Boar's Head Tavern in Eastcheap.
1. **fat:** vat (?) or stuffy (?). 4. **loggerheads:** blockheads.
7. **leash:** set of three. **drawers:** tapsters (who sometimes invited favored guests to have their drinks in the cellar).

11. **Jack:** fellow. 12. **Corinthian:** gay blade.
15. **dyeing scarlet.** Perhaps an allusion to the complexion of hard drinkers. 16. **breathe . . . watering:** stop for breath while drinking.
17. **play:** drink. 23. **sugar.** Used to sweeten certain wines, especially sack.
24. **under-skinker:** waiter's assistant.
27. **Anon:** at once, coming. **Score:** i.e. chalk up, charge. **bastard:** sweet Spanish wine.
27–28. **Half-moon.** Rooms in inns were often given special names.
30. **puny:** inexperienced. 33. **president:** precedent, example.
38. **Pomgarnet:** Pomegranate, another room in the tavern.
45. **by'r lady:** by Our Lady (i.e. the Virgin).
47. **indenture:** apprentice's contract (which was normally for seven years). 49. **books:** i.e. Bibles. 54. **Michaelmas:** September 29.

Poins. [*Within.*] Francis!

Fran. Anon, sir. Pray stay a little, my lord.

Prince. Nay, but hark you, Francis: for the sugar thou gavest me, 'twas a pennyworth, was't not?

Fran. O Lord, I would it had been two!   60

Prince. I will give thee for it a thousand pound. Ask me when thou wilt, and thou shalt have it.

Poins. [*Within.*] Francis!

Fran. Anon, anon.

Prince. Anon, Francis? No, Francis; but to- 65 morrow, Francis; or, Francis, a' Thursday; or indeed, Francis, when thou wilt. But, Francis!

Fran. My lord?

Prince. Wilt thou rob this leathern-jerkin, crystal-button, not-pated, agate-ring, puke-stocking, caddis-garter, smooth-tongue, Spanish-pouch—   71

Fran. O Lord, sir, who do you mean?

Prince. Why then your brown bastard is your only drink! for look you, Francis, your white canvas doublet will sully. In Barbary, sir, it cannot come to so much.

Fran. What, sir?   76

Poins. [*Within.*] Francis!

Prince. Away, you rogue, dost thou not hear them call?   79

> *Here they both call him; the drawer stands amazed, not knowing which way to go.*

Enter VINTNER.

Vint. What, stand'st thou still, and hear'st such a calling? Look to the guests within. [*Exit Francis.*] My lord, old Sir John with half a dozen more are at the door, shall I let them in?

Prince. Let them alone awhile, and then open the door. [*Exit Vintner.*] Poins!   85

Poins. [*Within.*] Anon, anon, sir.

Enter POINS.

Prince. Sirrah, Falstaff and the rest of the thieves are at the door; shall we be merry?

Poins. As merry as crickets, my lad. But hark ye, what cunning match have you made with this jest of the drawer? Come, what's the issue?   91

Prince. I am now of all humors that have show'd themselves humors since the old days of goodman Adam to the pupil age of this present twelve a' clock at midnight.

[*Enter FRANCIS hurrying across the stage with wine.*]

What's a' clock, Francis?

Fran. Anon, anon, sir.   [*Exit.*] 97

Prince. That ever this fellow should have fewer words than a parrot, and yet the son of a woman! His industry is up stairs and down stairs, his eloquence the parcel of a reckoning. I am not yet of Percy's mind, the Hotspur of the north, he that kills me some six or seven dozen of Scots at a breakfast, 103 washes his hands, and says to his wife, "Fie upon this quiet life! I want work." "O my sweet Harry," says she, "how many hast thou kill'd to-day?" "Give my roan horse a drench," says he, and answers, "Some fourteen," an hour after; "a trifle, a trifle." I 108 prithee call in Falstaff. I'll play Percy, and that damn'd brawn shall play Dame Mortimer his wife. "*Rivo!*" says the drunkard. Call in ribs, call in tallow.   112

Enter FALSTAFF, [GADSHILL, BARDOLPH, *and* PETO, FRANCIS *following with wine*].

Poins. Welcome, Jack, where hast thou been?

Fal. A plague of all cowards, I say, and a vengeance too! marry and amen! Give me a cup of sack, boy. Ere I lead this life long, I'll sew nether-stocks, and mend them and foot them too. A plague of all cowards! Give me a cup of sack, rogue. Is there no virtue extant?   *He drinketh.* 119

Prince. Didst thou never see Titan kiss a dish of butter, pitiful-hearted Titan, that melted at the sweet tale of the sun's? If thou didst, then behold that compound.   123

Fal. You rogue, here's lime in this sack too. There is nothing but roguery to be found in villainous man, yet a coward is worse than a cup of sack with lime in it. A villainous coward! Go thy ways, old Jack, die when thou wilt; if manhood, good manhood, be 128 not forgot upon the face of the earth, then am I a shotten herring. There lives not three good men unhang'd in England, and one of them is fat and grows old, God help the while! a bad world, I say. I would I were a weaver, I could sing psalms, or any thing. A plague of all cowards, I say still. 134

Prince. How now, wool-sack, what mutter you?

Fal. A king's son! If I do not beat thee out of thy kingdom with a dagger of lath, and drive all thy subjects afore thee like a flock of wild geese, I'll never wear hair on my face more. You, Prince of Wales!

Prince. Why, you whoreson round man, what's the matter?   141

Fal. Are not you a coward? Answer me to that; and Poins there?

Poins. 'Zounds, ye fat paunch, and ye call me coward, by the Lord, I'll stab thee.   145

69–71. **Wilt . . . pouch.** The Prince describes Francis' master, the vintner.
70. **not-pated:** close-cropped. **puke:** dark woollen. **caddis:** worsted.
71. **Spanish:** of Spanish leather.
74–75. **your . . . sully:** your costume (as an apprentice) will get dirty (in Barbary), i.e. you'd better stay here.   75. **it:** i.e. sugar.
79 s.d. **amazed:** thoroughly confused.
90–91. **what . . . issue:** i.e. what's the point of your teasing the servant.
92–95. **I . . . midnight:** i.e. as a consequence of my foolery with the servant I am now in the mood for anything.
93. **goodman:** occupational title for a farmer or yeoman.
94. **pupil:** youthful.

101. **parcel . . . reckoning:** items of a bill.
107. **drench:** medicinal drink.   110. **brawn:** pig.
111. **Rivo:** reveller's exclamation (of uncertain origin and meaning).
114. **of:** on.   116. **nether-stocks:** stockings.
119. **virtue:** manliness.   120. **Titan:** the sun.
121. **that:** i.e. the butter.
123. **compound:** melting butter, i.e. Falstaff.
124. **lime.** Sometimes used as an additive to wine to increase its sparkle.
130. **shotten herring:** (as thin as) a herring that has spawned.
132. **the while:** in these (bad) times.
133. **sing psalms.** Elizabethan weavers, many of whom were immigrants from the Low Countries and dissenters, were notorious for psalm-singing.
137. **dagger of lath:** wooden stick (commonly used by the Vice, the mischievously comic stock character in morality plays).

1 Henry IV
II.iv

Fal. I call thee coward! I'll see thee damn'd ere I call thee coward, but I would give a thousand pound I could run as fast as thou canst. You are straight 148 enough in the shoulders, you care not who sees your back. Call you that backing of your friends? A plague upon such backing! give me them that will face me. Give me a cup of sack. I am a rogue if I drunk to-day.

Prince. O villain, thy lips are scarce wip'd since thou drunk'st last. 154

Fal. All is one for that. (*He drinketh.*) A plague of all cowards, still say I.

Prince. What's the matter?

Fal. What's the matter! There be four of us here have ta'en a thousand pound this day morning.

Prince. Where is it, Jack? where is it? 160

Fal. Where is it? taken from us it is: a hundred upon poor four of us.

Prince. What, a hundred, man? 163

Fal. I am a rogue if I were not at half-sword with a dozen of them two hours together. I have scap'd by miracle. I am eight times thrust through the doublet, four through the hose, my buckler cut through and through, my sword hack'd like a hand-saw— 168 *ecce signum!* I never dealt better since I was a man; all would not do. A plague of all cowards! Let them speak; if they speak more or less than truth, they are villains and the sons of darkness.

[*Prince.*] Speak, sirs, how was it?

[*Gads.*] We four set upon some dozen—

Fal. Sixteen at least, my lord. 175

[*Gads.*] And bound them.

Peto. No, no, they were not bound.

Fal. You rogue, they were bound, every man of them, or I am a Jew else, an Ebrew Jew. 179

[*Gads.*] As we were sharing, some six or seven fresh men set upon us—

Fal. And unbound the rest, and then come in the other.

Prince. What, fought you with them all? 184

Fal. All? I know not what you call all, but if I fought not with fifty of them, I am a bunch of radish. If there were not two or three and fifty upon poor old Jack, then am I no two-legg'd creature.

Prince. Pray God you have not murd'red some of them. 190

Fal. Nay, that's past praying for, I have pepper'd two of them. Two I am sure I have paid, two rogues in buckrom suits. I tell thee what, Hal, if I tell 193 thee a lie, spit in my face, call me horse. Thou knowest my old ward: here I lay, and thus I bore my point. Four rogues in buckrom let drive at me—

Prince. What, four? Thou saidst but two even now.

Fal. Four, Hal, I told thee four. 198

Poins. Ay, ay, he said four.

Fal. These four came all afront, and mainly thrust

at me. I made me no more ado but took all their seven points in my target, thus.

Prince. Seven? why, there were but four even now.

Fal. In buckrom?

Poins. Ay, four, in buckrom suits. 205

Fal. Seven, by these hilts, or I am a villain else.

Prince. Prithee let him alone, we shall have more anon.

Fal. Dost thou hear me, Hal?

Prince. Ay, and mark thee too, Jack. 210

Fal. Do so, for it is worth the list'ning to. These nine in buckrom that I told thee of—

Prince. So, two more already.

Fal. Their points being broken—

Poins. Down fell their hose. 215

Fal. Began to give me ground; but I follow'd me close, came in, foot and hand, and with a thought seven of the eleven I paid.

Prince. O monstrous! eleven buckrom men grown out of two. 220

Fal. But, as the devil would have it, three misbegotten knaves in Kendal green came at my back and let drive at me, for it was so dark, Hal, that thou couldest not see thy hand. 224

Prince. These lies are like their father that begets them, gross as a mountain, open, palpable. Why, thou clay-brain'd guts, thou knotty-pated fool, thou whoreson, obscene, greasy tallow-catch—

Fal. What, art thou mad? art thou mad? is not the truth the truth? 230

Prince. Why, how couldst thou know these men in Kendal green when it was so dark thou couldst not see thy hand? Come, tell us your reason; what sayest thou to this?

Poins. Come, your reason, Jack, your reason. 235

Fal. What, upon compulsion? 'Zounds, and I were at the strappado, or all the racks in the world, I would not tell you on compulsion. Give you a reason on compulsion? if reasons were as plentiful as blackberries, I would give no man a reason upon compulsion, I. 240

Prince. I'll be no longer guilty of this sin. This sanguine coward, this bed-presser, this horse-back-breaker, this huge hill of flesh— 243

Fal. 'Sblood, you starveling, you [eel-]skin, you dried neat's tongue, you bull's pizzle, you stock-fish! O for breath to utter what is like thee! you tailor's yard, you sheath, you bowcase, you vile standing tuck— 248

Prince. Well, breathe a while, and then to it again, and when thou hast tir'd thyself in base comparisons, hear me speak but this—

Poins. Mark, Jack. 252

202. **target:** shield.
206. **these hilts:** i.e. the pommel, haft, etc. of a sword (a common oath).   **villain:** i.e. no gentleman.
214. **points:** sword points (but Poins takes the word in a second sense: tagged laces for holding garments together).
217. **with a thought:** as quick as thought.
222. **Kendal:** town in Westmorland noted for its textiles.
226. **gross:** obvious.   227. **knotty-pated:** thick-headed.
228. **tallow-catch:** tallow-tub.
237. **strappado:** a form of torture.
239. **reasons.** Pronounced *raisins* (hence the pun with *blackberries*).
242. **sanguine:** ruddy.   245. **neat's:** ox's.
245. **stock-fish:** dried cod.   248. **tuck:** rapier.

155. **All . . . that:** i.e. no matter.
164. **at half-sword:** i.e. at close quarters.
167. **hose:** breeches.   **buckler:** shield.
169. **ecce signum:** behold the proof.   **dealt:** i.e. fought.
179. **Ebrew:** Hebrew.   183. **other:** others.
192. **paid:** i.e. killed.   194. **horse:** i.e. a stupid animal.
195. **ward:** parry.   **lay:** stood.
200. **afront:** abreast.   **mainly:** powerfully.

Prince. We two saw you four set on four and bound them, and were masters of their wealth. Mark now how a plain tale shall put you down. Then did we two set on you four, and with a word, outfac'd you from your prize, and have it, yea, and can show it you here in the house; and, Falstaff, you carried your guts 258 away as nimbly, with as quick dexterity, and roar'd for mercy, and still run and roar'd, as ever I heard bull-calf. What a slave art thou to hack thy sword as thou hast done, and then say it was in fight! What trick? what device? what starting-hole? canst thou now 263 find out to hide thee from this open and apparent shame?

Poins. Come, let's hear, Jack, what trick hast thou now?

Fal. By the Lord, I knew ye as well as he that made ye. Why, hear you, my masters, was it 268 for me to kill the heir-apparent? Should I turn upon the true prince? Why, thou knowest I am as valiant as Hercules; but beware instinct—the lion will not touch the true prince. Instinct is a great matter; I was now a coward on instinct. I shall think the better 273 of myself, and thee, during my life; I for a valiant lion, and thou for a true prince. But by the Lord, lads, I am glad you have the money. Hostess, clap to the doors! Watch to-night, pray to-morrow. Gallants, lads, boys, hearts of gold, all the titles of good fellowship 278 come to you! What, shall we be merry, shall we have a play extempore?

Prince. Content, and the argument shall be thy running away.

Fal. Ah, no more of that, Hal, and thou lovest me!

Enter HOSTESS.

Host. O Jesu, my lord the Prince! 284

Prince. How now, my lady the hostess! what say'st thou to me?

Host. Marry, my lord, there is a nobleman of the court at door would speak with you. He says he comes from your father. 289

Prince. Give him as much as will make him a royal man, and send him back again to my mother.

Fal. What manner of man is he?

Host. An old man.

Fal. What doth gravity out of his bed at midnight? Shall I give him his answer? 295

Prince. Prithee do, Jack.

Fal. Faith, and I'll send him packing. *Exit.*

Prince. Now, sirs, by'r lady, you fought fair, so did you, Peto, so did you, Bardolph. You are lions too, you ran away upon instinct, you will not touch the true prince, no, fie! 301

Bard. Faith, I ran when I saw others run.

Prince. Faith, tell me now in earnest, how came Falstaff's sword so hack'd?

Peto. Why, he hack'd it with his dagger, and said

he would swear truth out of England but he would make you believe it was done in fight, and persuaded us to do the like. 308

Bard. Yea, and to tickle our noses with speargrass to make them bleed, and then to beslubber our garments with it and swear it was the blood of true men. I did that I did not this seven year before, I blush'd to hear his monstrous devices. 313

Prince. O villain, thou stolest a cup of sack eighteen years ago, and wert taken with the manner, and ever since thou hast blush'd extempore. Thou hadst fire and sword on thy side, and yet thou ran'st away; what instinct hadst thou for it? 318

Bard. My lord, do you see these meteors? do you behold these exhalations? [*Pointing to his own face.*]

Prince. I do.

Bard. What think you they portend?

Prince. Hot livers and cold purses. 323

Bard. Choler, my lord, if rightly taken.

Enter FALSTAFF.

Prince. No, if rightly taken, halter. Here comes lean Jack, here comes bare-bone. How now, my sweet creature of bumbast, how long is't ago, Jack, since thou sawest thine own knee? 328

Fal. My own knee? When I was about thy years, Hal, I was not an eagle's talent in the waist, I could have crept into any alderman's thumb-ring. A plague of sighing and grief, it blows a man up like a bladder. There's villainous news abroad. Here 333 was Sir John Bracy from your father; you must to the court in the morning. That same mad fellow of the north, Percy, and he of Wales that gave Amamon the bastinado and made Lucifer cuckold and swore the devil his true liegeman upon the cross of a Welsh hook—what a plague call you him?

Poins. O, Glendower. 340

Fal. Owen, Owen, the same; and his son-in-law Mortimer, and old Northumberland, and that sprightly Scot of Scots, Douglas, that runs a' horseback up a hill perpendicular— 344

Prince. He that rides at high speed and with his pistol kills a sparrow flying.

256. **with a word:** to be brief.　**outfac'd:** frightened, bluffed.
263. **starting-hole:** refuge, loophole; i.e. excuse.
264. **apparent:** obvious.　281. **argument:** subject.
290–91. **as much ... man:** i.e. 3*s.* 4*d.*, the difference between a noble (6*s.* 8*d.*) and a royal (10*s.*).
291. **send ... mother:** i.e. get rid of him permanently. The Prince's mother, Mary de Bohun, had died in 1394.　298. **fair:** well.

306. **swear ... England:** i.e. vanquish truth by the force of his lies. **but he would:** if he did not.
312. **that ... not:** what I hadn't done.
315. **taken ... manner:** caught in the act.
317. **fire.** An allusion to Bardolph's ruddy complexion, the subject of the jests and pun that follow.
319, 320. **meteors, exhalations:** i.e. the red blotches and carbuncles on Bardolph's face.
322. **portend:** threaten, presage (continuing the astronomical imagery of *meteors* and *exhalations*).
323. **Hot ... purses:** i.e. livers inflamed by liquor and purses emptied to pay for it.
324. **Choler ... taken:** i.e. my fiery complexion, if properly understood, indicates a choleric temperament (which makes me quick to anger and dangerous).
325. **No ... halter:** i.e. no, if you're arrested as you deserve, you'll get the hangman's noose. Behind *halter* lies a pun on *choler* and *collar*.
327. **bumbast:** bombast, cotton padding.　330. **talent:** talon.
334. **Sir John Bracy.** Apparently unhistorical.
336. **Amamon:** the name of a fiend.
337. **bastinado:** beating on the soles of the feet.　**made Lucifer cuckold:** i.e. gave Lucifer his horns (the sign of a cuckold).
338. **liegeman:** subject.
338–39. **Welsh hook:** pike with a curved blade.

1 Henry IV
II.iv

Fal. You have hit it.

Prince. So did he never the sparrow.

Fal. Well, that rascal hath good mettle in him, he will not run. 350

Prince. Why, what a rascal art thou then, to praise him so for running!

Fal. A' horseback, ye cuckoo, but afoot he will not budge a foot.

Prince. Yes, Jack, upon instinct. 355

Fal. I grant ye, upon instinct. Well, he is there too, and one Mordake, and a thousand blue-caps more. Worcester is stol'n away to-night. Thy father's beard is turn'd white with the news. You may buy land now as cheap as stinking mack'rel. 360

Prince. Why then, it is like, if there come a hot June and this civil buffeting hold, we shall buy maiden-heads as they buy hobnails, by the hundreds.

Fal. By the mass, lad, thou sayest true, it is like we shall have good trading that way. But tell me, 365 Hal, art not thou horrible afeard? Thou being heir-apparent, could the world pick thee out three such enemies again as that fiend Douglas, that spirit Percy, and that devil Glendower? Art thou not horribly afraid? Doth not thy blood thrill at it? 370

Prince. Not a whit, i' faith, I lack some of thy instinct.

Fal. Well, thou wilt be horribly chid to-morrow when thou comest to thy father. If thou love me, practice an answer. 375

Prince. Do thou stand for my father and examine me upon the particulars of my life.

Fal. Shall I? Content. This chair shall be my state, this dagger my sceptre, and this cushion my crown.

Prince. Thy state is taken for a join'd-stool, thy golden sceptre for a leaden dagger, and thy precious rich crown for a pitiful bald crown! 382

Fal. Well, and the fire of grace be not quite out of thee, now shalt thou be mov'd. Give me a cup of sack to make my eyes look red, that it may be thought I have wept, for I must speak in passion, and I will do it in King Cambyses' vein. 387

Prince. Well, here is my leg.

Fal. And here is my speech. Stand aside, nobility.

Host. O Jesu, this is excellent sport, i' faith! 390

Fal. Weep not, sweet queen, for trickling tears are vain.

Host. O, the father, how he holds his countenance!

Fal. For God's sake, lords, convey my [tristful] queen,
For tears do stop the flood-gates of her eyes. 394

Host. O Jesu, he doth it as like one of these harlotry players as ever I see!

Fal. Peace, good pint-pot, peace, good ticklebrain. Harry, I do not only marvel where thou spendest thy

time, but also how thou art accompanied; for 399 though the camomile, the more it is trodden on, the faster it grows, [yet] youth, the more it is wasted, the sooner it wears. That thou art my son I have partly thy mother's word, partly my own opinion, but chiefly a villainous trick of thine eye, and a foolish hang- 404 ing of thy nether lip, that doth warrant me. If then thou be son to me, here lies the point: why being son to me, art thou so pointed at? Shall the blessed sun of heaven prove a micher and eat blackberries? a question not to be ask'd. Shall the son of England prove a 409 thief and take purses? a question to be ask'd. There is a thing, Harry, which thou hast often heard of, and it is known to many in our land by the name of pitch. This pitch (as ancient writers do report) doth defile, so doth the company thou keepest; for, Harry, now I do 414 not speak to thee in drink, but in tears; not in pleasure, but in passion; not in words only, but in woes also. And yet there is a virtuous man whom I have often noted in thy company, but I know not his name. 419

Prince. What manner of man, and it like your Majesty?

Fal. A goodly portly man, i' faith, and a corpulent, of a cheerful look, a pleasing eye, and a most noble carriage, and as I think, his age some fifty, or, by'r lady, inclining to threescore; and now I remem- 425 ber me, his name is Falstaff. If that man should be lewdly given, he deceiveth me; for, Harry, I see virtue in his looks. If then the tree may be known by the fruit, as the fruit by the tree, then peremptorily I speak it, there is virtue in that Falstaff; him keep 430 with, the rest banish. And tell me now, thou naughty varlet, tell me, where hast thou been this month?

Prince. Dost thou speak like a king? Do thou stand for me, and I'll play my father. 434

Fal. .Depose me? If thou dost it half so gravely, so majestically, both in word and matter, hang me up by the heels for a rabbit-sucker or a poulter's hare.

Prince. Well, here I am set.

Fal. And here I stand. Judge, my masters.

Prince. Now, Harry, whence come you? 440

Fal. My noble lord, from Eastcheap.

Prince. The complaints I hear of thee are grievous.

Fal. 'Sblood, my lord, they are false.—Nay, I'll tickle ye for a young prince, i' faith. 444

Prince. Swearest thou, ungracious boy? henceforth ne'er look on me. Thou art violently carried away from grace, there is a devil haunts thee in the likeness of an old fat man, a tun of man is thy companion. Why

357. **blue-caps:** blue bonnets, i.e. Scots.   362. **hold:** continue.
370. **thrill:** run cold.   378. **state:** chair of state, i.e. throne.
380. **join'd-stool:** stool of joiner's work.
382. **bald crown:** bald pate.   386. **in passion:** with deep emotion.
387. **in . . . vein:** i.e. in a style of ludicrous and old-fashioned rant (like that of Thomas Preston's *Cambyses,* an early Elizabethan play).
388. **leg:** elaborate bow.
392. **holds his countenance:** keeps a straight face.
393. **convey:** escort hence.   **tristful:** sorrowful.
395–96. **harlotry:** knavish.   397. **ticklebrain:** strong drink.

400. **camomile:** plant of the aster family.   405. **warrant:** assure.
407. **pointed at:** i.e. in derision and disapproval.
408. **micher:** truant.   409. **England:** i.e. the King of England.
413. **ancient writers.** For one, the writer of the Apocryphal book Ecclesiasticus (13:1).   416. **passion:** sorrow.
422. **portly:** stately, imposing.   **corpulent:** full-fleshed.
427. **lewdly given:** wickedly inclined.
428–29. **If . . . by the fruit.** See Matthew 12:33.
429. **peremptorily:** decisively.
431–32. **naughty varlet:** ill-behaved boy.
437. **rabbit-sucker:** unweaned rabbit.   **poulter's:** poulterer's.
438. **set:** seated (i.e. on the "throne").
443–44. **I'll . . . prince:** I'll play the role of a young prince so as to delight you.   445. **ungracious:** graceless.

dost thou converse with that trunk of humors, that
bolting-hutch of beastliness, that swoll'n parcel   450
of dropsies, that huge bombard of sack, that stuff'd
cloak-bag of guts, that roasted Manningtree ox with
the pudding in his belly, that reverent Vice, that grey
Iniquity, that father ruffian, that vanity in years?
Wherein is he good, but to taste sack and drink   455
it? wherein neat and cleanly, but to carve a capon and
eat it? wherein cunning, but in craft? wherein crafty,
but in villainy? wherein villainous, but in all things?
wherein worthy, but in nothing?

Fal. I would your Grace would take me with you.
Whom means your Grace?   461

Prince. That villainous abominable misleader of
youth, Falstaff, that old white-bearded Sathan.

Fal. My lord, the man I know.

Prince. I know thou dost.   465

Fal. But to say I know more harm in him than in
myself, were to say more than I know. That he is old,
the more the pity, his white hairs do witness it, but that
he is, saving your reverence, a whoremaster, that I
utterly deny. If sack and sugar be a fault, God   470
help the wicked! If to be old and merry be a sin, then
many an old host that I know is damn'd. If to be fat
be to be hated, then Pharaoh's [lean] kine are to be
lov'd. No, my good lord, banish Peto, banish Bardolph,
banish Poins, but for sweet Jack Falstaff, kind   475
Jack Falstaff, true Jack Falstaff, valiant Jack Falstaff,
and therefore more valiant, being as he is old Jack
Falstaff, banish not him thy Harry's company, banish
not him thy Harry's company—banish plump Jack,
and banish all the world.   480

Prince. I do, I will.

[*A knocking heard. Exeunt Hostess,
Francis, and Bardolph.*]

Enter BARDOLPH *running.*

Bard. O my lord, my lord, the sheriff with a most
monstrous watch is at the door.

Fal. Out, ye rogue, play out the play, I have much
to say in the behalf of that Falstaff.   485

Enter the HOSTESS.

Host. O Jesu, my lord, my lord!

Prince. Heigh, heigh! the devil rides upon a fiddlestick. What's the matter?

Host. The sheriff and all the watch are at the door,
they are come to search the house. Shall I let them in?

Fal. Dost thou hear, Hal? Never call a true piece

of gold a counterfeit. Thou art essentially made,
without seeming so.   493

Prince. And thou a natural coward, without instinct.

Fal. I deny your major. If you will deny the
sheriff, so, if not, let him enter. If I become not a cart
as well as another man, a plague on my bringing up!
I hope I shall as soon be strangled with a halter as
another.   499

Prince. Go hide thee behind the arras, the rest walk
up above. Now, my masters, for a true face and good
conscience.

Fal. Both which I have had, but their date is out,
and therefore I'll hide me.   [*Exit.*]

Prince. Call in the sheriff.   505

[*Exeunt all except the Prince and Peto.*]

Enter SHERIFF *and the* CARRIER.

Now, Master Sheriff, what is your will with me?

Sher. First, pardon me, my lord. A hue and cry
Hath followed certain men unto this house.

Prince. What men?

Sher. One of them is well known, my gracious lord,
A gross fat man.

Car.   As fat as butter.   511

Prince. The man I do assure you is not here,
For I myself at this time have employ'd him.
And, sheriff, I will engage my word to thee
That I will by to-morrow dinner-time   515
Send him to answer thee, or any man,
For any thing he shall be charg'd withal,
And so let me entreat you leave the house.

Sher. I will, my lord. There are two gentlemen
Have in this robbery lost three hundred marks.   520

Prince. It may be so. If he have robb'd these men,
He shall be answerable, and so farewell.

Sher. Good night, my noble lord.

Prince. I think it is good morrow, is it not?   524

Sher. Indeed, my lord, I think it be two a' clock.

Exit [*with Carrier*].

Prince. This oily rascal is known as well as Paul's.
Go call him forth.

Peto. Falstaff!—Fast asleep behind the arras, and
snorting like a horse.   529

Prince. Hark how hard he fetches breath. Search
his pockets. (*He searcheth his pocket, and findeth certain
papers.*) What hast thou found?

Peto. Nothing but papers, my lord.

Prince. Let's see what they be. Read them.   534

[*Peto.*] [*Reads.*]

Item, a capon	.	.	.	.	2s. 2d.
Item, sauce	.	.	.	.	4d.
Item, sack, two gallons	.	.	.	.	5s. 8d.
Item, anchoves and sack after supper	.	.	2s. 6d.
Item, bread	.	.	.	.	ob.

449. **converse:** associate.   **humors:** secretions in the body, diseases.
450. **bolting-hutch:** miller's bin.
451. **bombard:** large leathern vessel.
452. **Manningtree:** town in Essex, a region noted for fat oxen.
453. **pudding:** stuffing.   **Vice:** mischievously comic stock character
in morality plays who served chiefly as a "misleader of youth" (lines
462-63). *Iniquity* (line 454) is another name for him.
456. **cleanly:** adroit, dextrous.   457. **cunning:** skillful.
460. **take ... you:** i.e. go more slowly (so I can keep up with you).
469. **saving your reverence:** i.e. excuse me for using an offensive term.
473. **Pharaoh's lean kine.** See Genesis 41:1-4.
483. **watch:** body of constables.
487-88. **the devil ... fiddlestick:** i.e. the Hostess is going to report
some astounding event.
491-93. **Never ... so.** A much disputed passage. Perhaps Falstaff
means that the Prince should not turn him—a true piece of gold—

over to the law as a counterfeit coin, for Hal himself, despite misleading appearances, is a true prince (*essentially made*).
495. **major:** major premise.
495-96. **deny the sheriff:** i.e. refuse to admit him.
496. **cart:** i.e. hangman's cart.
500. **arras:** tapestry wall-hangings.   501. **true:** honest.
514. **engage:** pledge.   517. **withal:** with.
524. **good morrow:** i.e. past midnight.
526. **Paul's:** St. Paul's Cathedral.   538. **anchoves:** anchovies.
539. **ob.:** obolus; here, halfpenny.

1 Henry IV
II.iv

[*Prince.*] O monstrous! but one half-penny- 540
worth of bread to this intolerable deal of sack! What
there is else, keep close, we'll read it at more advantage. There let him sleep till day. I'll to the court in
the morning. We must all to the wars, and thy place
shall be honorable. I'll procure this fat rogue a 545
charge of foot, and I know his death will be a march of
twelve score. The money shall be paid back again with
advantage. Be with me betimes in the morning, and so
good morrow, Peto. 549

Peto. Good morrow, good my lord.   *Exeunt.*

[ACT III, Scene I]

Enter Hotspur, Worcester, Lord Mortimer, Owen
    Glendower.

Mort. These promises are fair, the parties sure,
And our induction full of prosperous hope.
Hot. Lord Mortimer, and cousin Glendower,
Will you sit down?
And uncle Worcester—a plague upon it! 5
I have forgot the map.
Glend.   No, here it is.
Sit, cousin Percy, sit, good cousin Hotspur,
For by that name as oft as Lancaster
Doth speak of you, his cheek looks pale, and with
A rising sigh he wisheth you in heaven. 10
Hot. And you in hell, as oft as he hears
Owen Glendower spoke of.
Glend. I cannot blame him. At my nativity
The front of heaven was full of fiery shapes
Of burning cressets, and at my birth 15
The frame and huge foundation of the earth
Shak'd like a coward.
Hot.   Why, so it would have done
At the same season if your mother's cat had
But kitten'd, though yourself had never been born. 19
Glend. I say the earth did shake when I was born.
Hot. And I say the earth was not of my mind,
If you suppose as fearing you it shook.
Glend. The heavens were all on fire, the earth did
    tremble.
Hot. O then the earth shook to see the heavens on
    fire,
And not in fear of your nativity. 25
Diseased nature oftentimes breaks forth
In strange eruptions; oft the teeming earth
Is with a kind of colic pinch'd and vex'd
By the imprisoning of unruly wind 29
Within her womb, which, for enlargement striving,
Shakes the old beldame earth, and topples down

Steeples and moss-grown towers. At your birth
Our grandam earth, having this distemp'rature,
In passion shook.
Glend.   Cousin, of many men
I do not bear these crossings. Give me leave 35
To tell you once again that at my birth
The front of heaven was full of fiery shapes,
The goats ran from the mountains, and the herds
Were strangely clamorous to the frighted fields.
These signs have mark'd me extraordinary, 40
And all the courses of my life do show
I am not in the roll of common men.
Where is he living, clipt in with the sea
That chides the banks of England, Scotland, Wales,
Which calls me pupil or hath read to me? 45
And bring him out that is but woman's son
Can trace me in the tedious ways of art,
And hold me pace in deep experiments.
Hot. I think there's no man speaks better Welsh.
I'll to dinner. 50
Mort. Peace, cousin Percy, you will make him
    mad.
Glend. I can call spirits from the vasty deep.
Hot. Why, so can I, or so can any man,
But will they come when you do call for them?
Glend. Why, I can teach you, cousin, to command
The devil. 56
Hot. And I can teach thee, coz, to shame the devil
By telling truth: tell truth and shame the devil.
If thou have power to raise him, bring him hither,
And I'll be sworn I have power to shame him hence. 60
O, while you live, tell truth and shame the devil!
Mort. Come, come, no more of this unprofitable
    chat.
Glend. Three times hath Henry Bullingbrook made
    head
Against my power; thrice from the banks of Wye
And sandy-bottom'd Severn have I sent him 65
Bootless home and weather-beaten back.
Hot. Home without boots, and in foul weather too!
How scapes he agues, in the devil's name?
Glend. Come, here is the map. Shall we divide our
    right
According to our threefold order ta'en? 70
Mort. The Archdeacon hath divided it
Into three limits very equally:
England, from Trent and Severn hitherto,
By south and east is to my part assign'd;

34. **passion:** pain.   35. **crossings:** contradictions.
43. **clipt in with:** enclosed by.   45. **read to:** i.e. taught.
47. **trace . . . art:** follow me in the laborious ways of magic.
48. **hold me pace:** keep up with me.   **deep:** occult.
49. **better Welsh:** i.e. more boastfully and incomprehensibly.
52. **vasty deep:** lower world.   63. **made head:** raised a force.
64. **power:** armed followers.
66. **Bootless:** without advantage, i.e. unsuccessful.
69. **right:** rightful possessions.
71–78. **The Archdeacon . . . Trent.** According to Holinshed (Bullough,
IV, 185), the rebels "by their deputies in the house of the archdeacon
of Bangor, divided the realme amongst them, causing a tripartite
indenture to be made and sealed with their seales, by the covenants
whereof, all England from Severne and Trent, south and eastward,
was assigned to the earle of March: all Wales, & the lands beyond
Severne westward, were appointed to Owen Glendouer: and all the
remnant from Trent northward, to the lord Persie."
72. **limits:** regions defined by a boundary.
73. **hitherto:** to this point.

542. **close:** secret.   542–43. **more advantage:** a more opportune time.
546. **charge of foot:** command of a troop of infantry.
546–47. **death . . . score:** i.e. a march of 240 yards will kill him.
548. **advantage:** interest.

III.i. Location: Wales. Glendower's castle. (Holinshed places the
events of this scene in the house of the Archdeacon of Bangor [see the
note to lines 71–78], but the Archdeacon is not present in the scene and
Glendower acts throughout as host.)
2. **induction:** beginning.   **prosperous hope:** hope of prospering.
8. **Lancaster:** i.e. King Henry.   14. **front:** forehead.
15. **cressets:** fire-baskets mounted on poles; here, meteors.
30. **enlargement:** release.
31. **beldame:** grandmother, aged woman.

All westward, Wales beyond the Severn shore,   75
And all the fertile land within that bound,
To Owen Glendower; and, dear coz, to you
The remnant northward lying off from Trent.
And our indentures tripartite are drawn,
Which being sealed interchangeably   80
(A business that this night may execute),
To-morrow, cousin Percy, you and I
And my good Lord of Worcester will set forth
To meet your father and the Scottish power,
As is appointed us, at Shrewsbury.   85
My father Glendower is not ready yet,
Nor shall we need his help these fourteen days.
Within that space you may have drawn together
Your tenants, friends, and neighboring gentlemen. 89
　　Glend. A shorter time shall send me to you, lords,
And in my conduct shall your ladies come,
From whom you now must steal and take no leave,
For there will be a world of water shed
Upon the parting of your wives and you.
　　Hot. Methinks my moi'ty, north from Burton here,   95
In quantity equals not one of yours.
See how this river comes me cranking in,
And cuts me from the best of all my land
A huge half-moon, a monstrous [cantle] out.
I'll have the current in this place damm'd up,   100
And here the smug and silver Trent shall run
In a new channel fair and evenly.
It shall not wind with such a deep indent,
To rob me of so rich a bottom here.
　　Glend. Not wind? It shall, it must, you see it doth.
　　Mort. Yea, but   106
Mark how he bears his course, and runs me up
With like advantage on the other side,
Gelding the opposed continent as much
As on the other side it takes from you.   110
　　Wor. Yea, but a little charge will trench him here,
And on this north side win this cape of land,
And then he runs straight and even.
　　Hot. I'll have it so, a little charge will do it.
　　Glend. I'll not have it alt'red.
　　Hot.   Will not you?   115
　　Glend. No, nor you shall not.
　　Hot.   Who shall say me nay?
　　Glend. Why, that will I.
　　Hot.   Let me not understand you then,
Speak it in Welsh.
　　Glend. I can speak English, lord, as well as you,
For I was train'd up in the English court,   120

Where being but young I framed to the harp
Many an English ditty lovely well,
And gave the tongue a helpful ornament,
A virtue that was never seen in you.
　　Hot. Marry,   125
And I am glad of it with all my heart.
I had rather be a kitten and cry mew
Than one of these same metre ballet-mongers.
I had rather hear a brazen canstick turn'd,
Or a dry wheel grate on the axle-tree,   130
And that would set my teeth nothing an edge,
Nothing so much as mincing poetry.
'Tis like the forc'd gait of a shuffling nag.
　　Glend. Come, you shall have Trent turn'd.   134
　　Hot. I do not care. I'll give thrice so much land
To any well-deserving friend;
But in the way of bargain, mark ye me,
I'll cavil on the ninth part of a hair.
Are the indentures drawn? Shall we be gone?
　　Glend. The moon shines fair, you may away by night. 140
I'll haste the writer, and withal
Break with your wives of your departure hence.
I am afraid my daughter will run mad,
So much she doteth on her Mortimer.   *Exit.* 144
　　Mort. Fie, cousin Percy, how you cross my father!
　　Hot. I cannot choose. Sometime he angers me
With telling me of the moldwarp and the ant,
Of the dreamer Merlin and his prophecies,
And of a dragon and a finless fish,
A clip-wing'd griffin and a moulten raven,   150
A couching lion and a ramping cat,
And such a deal of skimble-skamble stuff
As puts me from my faith. I tell you what:
He held me last night at least nine hours
In reckoning up the several devils' names   155
That were his lackeys. I cried "hum," and "well, go to,"
But mark'd him not a word. O, he is as tedious
As a tired horse, a railing wife,
Worse than a smoky house. I had rather live
With cheese and garlic in a windmill, far,   160
Than feed on cates and have him talk to me
In any summer house in Christendom.
　　Mort. In faith, he is a worthy gentleman,

---

79. **our . . . drawn:** our agreement is now drawn up in triplicate.
86. **father:** i.e. father-in-law.　91. **conduct:** escort.
95. **moi'ty:** share.　97. **cranking:** winding.
99. **cantle:** piece, segment.　101. **smug:** smooth.
102. **fair and evenly:** i.e. in a straight course.
104. **bottom:** valley.
109. **Gelding . . . continent:** cutting off from the opposite bank.
111. **charge:** expense.
120. **For . . . court.** According to Holinshed (Bullough, IV, 180), Glendower "was first set to studie the lawes of the realme, and became an utter barrester, or an apprentise of the law (as they terme him) and served king Richard at Flint castell, when he was taken by Henrie duke of Lancaster, though other have written that he served this king Henry the fourth, before he came to atteine the crowne, in roome of an esquier."

123. **gave . . . ornament:** i.e. not only adorned the words with music but also enriched the language with poetry.
124. **virtue:** accomplishment.　128. **ballet:** ballad.
129. **canstick turn'd:** candlestick turned on a lathe.
133. **shuffling:** hobbled.　141. **withal:** also.
142. **Break with:** inform.
146–53. **Sometimes . . . faith.** According to Holinshed (Bullough, IV, 185), the rebels laid their plans "through a foolish credit given to a vaine prophesie, as though king Henrie was the moldwarpe, cursed of Gods owne mouth, and they three were the dragon, the lion, and the woolfe, which should divide this realme betweene them. Such is the deviation (saith *Hall*) and not divination of those blind and fantasticall dreames of the Welsh prophesiers."
147. **moldwarp:** mole.
148. **Merlin:** famous prophet and magician of Arthurian legend.
150. **griffin:** fabulous beast, half lion and half eagle.
151. **couching, ramping:** parodies of the heraldic terms *couchant* (lying down with the head raised) and *rampant* (rearing).
152. **skimble-skamble:** nonsensical.
153. **puts . . . faith:** i.e. kills my confidence (in Glendower).
155. **several:** various.　161. **cates:** delicacies.

1 Henry IV
III.i

Exceedingly well read, and profited
In strange concealments, valiant as a lion,   165
And wondrous affable, and as bountiful
As mines of India. Shall I tell you, cousin?
He holds your temper in a high respect,
And curbs himself even of his natural scope
When you come 'cross his humor, faith, he does.   170
I warrant you, that man is not alive
Might so have tempted him as you have done,
Without the taste of danger and reproof.
But do not use it oft, let me entreat you.   174

Wor.   In faith, my lord, you are too willful-blame,
And since your coming hither have done enough
To put him quite besides his patience.
You must needs learn, lord, to amend this fault;
Though sometimes it show greatness, courage, blood—
And that's the dearest grace it renders you—   180
Yet oftentimes it doth present harsh rage,
Defect of manners, want of government,
Pride, haughtiness, opinion, and disdain,
The least of which haunting a nobleman
Loseth men's hearts and leaves behind a stain   185
Upon the beauty of all parts besides,
Beguiling them of commendation.

Hot.   Well, I am school'd: good manners be your
speed!
Here come our wives, and let us take our leave.

Enter GLENDOWER *with the* LADIES.

Mort.   This is the deadly spite that angers me:
My wife can speak no English, I no Welsh.   191

Glend.   My daughter weeps, she'll not part with
you,
She'll be a soldier too, she'll to the wars.

Mort.   Good father, tell her that she and my aunt
Percy
Shall follow in your conduct speedily.   195

*Glendower speaks to her in Welsh, and
she answers him in the same.*

Glend.   She is desperate here, a peevish self-will'd
harlotry,
One that no persuasion can do good upon.

The lady speaks in Welsh.

Mort.   I understand thy looks. That pretty Welsh
Which thou pourest down from these swelling heavens
I am too perfect in, and but for shame,   200
In such a parley should I answer thee.

The lady again in Welsh.

I understand thy kisses, and thou mine,
And that's a feeling disputation,

But I will never be a truant, love,
Till I have learn'd thy language, for thy tongue   205
Makes Welsh as sweet as ditties highly penn'd,
Sung by a fair queen in a summer's bow'r,
With ravishing division, to her lute.

Glend.   Nay, if you melt, then will she run mad.

The lady speaks again in Welsh.

Mort.   O, I am ignorance itself in this!   210

Glend.   She bids you on the wanton rushes lay you
down,
And rest your gentle head upon her lap,
And she will sing the song that pleaseth you,
And on your eyelids crown the god of sleep,
Charming your blood with pleasing heaviness,   215
Making such difference 'twixt wake and sleep
As is the difference betwixt day and night
The hour before the heavenly-harness'd team
Begins his golden progress in the east.

Mort.   With all my heart I'll sit and hear her sing.
By that time will our book, I think, be drawn.   221

Glend.   Do so,
And those musicians that shall play to you
Hang in the air a thousand leagues from hence,
And straight they shall be here. Sit and attend.   225

Hot.   Come, Kate, thou art perfect in lying down.
Come, quick, quick, that I may lay my head in thy lap.

Lady P.   Go, ye giddy goose.   *The music plays.*

Hot.   Now I perceive the devil understands Welsh,
And 'tis no marvel he is so humorous.   230
By'r lady, he is a good musician.

Lady P.   Then should you be nothing but musical,
for you are altogether govern'd by humors. Lie still,
ye thief, and hear the lady sing in Welsh.

Hot.   I had rather hear Lady, my brach, howl in
Irish.   236

Lady P.   Wouldst thou have thy head broken?

Hot.   No.

Lady P.   Then be still.

Hot.   Neither, 'tis a woman's fault.   240

Lady P.   Now God help thee!

Hot.   To the Welsh lady's bed.

Lady P.   What's that?

Hot.   Peace, she sings.

Here the lady sings a Welsh song.

Hot.   Come, Kate, I'll have your song too.   245

Lady P.   Not mine, in good sooth.

Hot.   Not yours, in good sooth! Heart, you swear
like a comfit-maker's wife: "Not you, in good sooth,"
and "as true as I live," and "as God shall mend me,"
and "as sure as day";   250
And givest such sarcenet surety for thy oaths

---

164. **profited:** proficient.   165. **concealments:** occult arts.
169. **scope:** freedom of speech.   172. **tempted:** irritated.
175. **willful-blame:** willfully to blame.   179. **blood:** spirit.
180. **dearest grace:** main distinction.   181. **present:** indicate.
182. **government:** self-control.   183. **opinion:** self-conceit.
186. **all parts besides:** all other (good) qualities.
187. **Beguiling:** depriving.   188. **be your speed:** give you success.
190. **spite:** vexation.   193. **she'll to:** she wants to go to.
194. **my aunt Percy:** i.e. Hotspur's wife, who was actually the sister,
not the aunt, of Glendower's son-in-law. See notes to I.i.38, I.iii.80.
196. **She . . . harlotry:** she is hopeless on this point, a willful hussy.
198. **That pretty Welsh:** your language, i.e. your tears.
200. **perfect in:** well acquainted with.
201. **In . . . parley:** i.e. by weeping.
203. **a feeling disputation:** i.e. an exchange of sentiments, not of
language.

208. **division:** embellishment.
211. **wanton:** luxurious, comfortable.   215. **heaviness:** drowsiness.
221. **book:** i.e. the "indentures tripartite" of line 79.
229–30. **Now . . . humorous:** i.e. since the devil understands Welsh
(which is incomprehensible), it's no wonder that he's so whimsical
(*humorous*).   233. **humors:** whims.   235. **brach:** bitch.
240. **Neither . . . fault:** I won't be silent either, for that's a woman's
trait (and I'm a man).   246. **sooth:** truth.
247. **Heart:** by God's (Christ's) heart.
248. **comfit-maker's:** confectioner's.
251. **sarcenet:** i.e. flimsy, insubstantial (from the name of a very
fine, soft material made of silk).

As if thou never walk'st further than Finsbury.
Swear me, Kate, like a lady as thou art,
A good mouth-filling oath, and leave "in sooth,"
And such protest of pepper-gingerbread,   255
To velvet-guards and Sunday-citizens.
Come sing.

Lady P.   I will not sing.

Hot.   'Tis the next way to turn tailor, or be   259
redbreast teacher.   And the indentures be drawn,
I'll away within these two hours, and so come in when
ye will.   *Exit.*

Glend.   Come, come, Lord Mortimer, you are as
    slow
As hot Lord Percy is on fire to go.
By this our book is drawn, we'll but seal,   265
And then to horse immediately.

Mort.   With all my heart.   *Exeunt.*

[SCENE II]

Enter the KING, PRINCE OF WALES, *and others.*

King.   Lords, give us leave, the Prince of Wales
    and I
Must have some private conference, but be near at
    hand,
For we shall presently have need of you.
                                    Exeunt Lords.
I know not whether God will have it so
For some displeasing service I have done,   5
That in his secret doom, out of my blood
He'll breed revengement and a scourge for me;
But thou dost in thy passages of life
Make me believe that thou art only mark'd
For the hot vengeance, and the rod of heaven,   10
To punish my mistreadings.   Tell me else,
Could such inordinate and low desires,
Such poor, such bare, such lewd, such mean attempts,
Such barren pleasures, rude society,
As thou art match'd withal and grafted to,   15
Accompany the greatness of thy blood,
And hold their level with thy princely heart?

Prince.   So please your Majesty, I would I could
Quit all offenses with as clear excuse
As well as I am doubtless I can purge   20
Myself of many I am charg'd withal;
Yet such extenuation let me beg
As in reproof of many tales devis'd,
Which oft the ear of greatness needs must hear

By smiling pick-thanks and base newsmongers,   25
I may for some things true, wherein my youth
Hath faulty wand'red and irregular,
Find pardon on my true submission.

King.   God pardon thee! yet let me wonder, Harry,
At thy affections, which do hold a wing   30
Quite from the flight of all thy ancestors.
Thy place in Council thou hast rudely lost,
Which by thy younger brother is supplied,
And art almost an alien to the hearts
Of all the court and princes of my blood;   35
The hope and expectation of thy time
Is ruin'd, and the soul of every man
Prophetically do forethink thy fall.
Had I so lavish of my presence been,
So common-hackney'd in the eyes of men,   40
So stale and cheap to vulgar company,
Opinion, that did help me to the crown,
Had still kept loyal to possession,
And left me in reputeless banishment,
A fellow of no mark nor likelihood.   45
By being seldom seen, I could not stir
But like a comet I was wond'red at,
That men would tell their children, "This is he";
Others would say, "Where, which is Bullingbrook?"
And then I stole all courtesy from heaven,   50
And dress'd myself in such humility
That I did pluck allegiance from men's hearts,
Loud shouts and salutations from their mouths,
Even in the presence of the crowned King.
Thus did I keep my person fresh and new,   55
My presence, like a robe pontifical,
Ne'er seen but wond'red at, and so my state,
Seldom but sumptuous, show'd like a feast,
And wan by rareness such solemnity.
The skipping King, he ambled up and down,   60
With shallow jesters, and rash bavin wits,
Soon kindled and soon burnt, carded his state,
Mingled his royalty with cap'ring fools,

---

252. **Finsbury:** district much frequented by London citizens and their families. Hotspur implies that his wife's genteel and colorless language makes her sound like a burgher's wife.
255. **such . . . pepper-gingerbread:** i.e. such namby-pamby protestations.
256. **velvet-guards:** velvet trimmings such as citizens' wives wore on their Sunday finery.
259. **next:** quickest.   **tailor.** A trade noted for singing.

III.ii. **Location:** London. The palace.
6. **doom:** judgment.   8. **passages:** actions.
12. **inordinate:** unsuitable (for one of your rank).
13. **lewd:** base, vulgar.   15. **withal:** with.
17. **hold their level:** i.e. maintain their appeal and force.
19. **Quit:** clear myself of.   20. **doubtless:** certain.
23. **reproof:** disproof.

25. **pick-thanks:** busybodies, flatterers. Shakespeare may have got the word from Holinshed (Bullough, IV, 195), who, incidentally, dates the King's reproof of and reconciliation with his wayward son after the battle of Shrewsbury: "Thus were the father and the sonne reconciled, betwixt whom the said pickthanks had sowne division, insomuch that the sonne upon a vehement conceit of unkindnesse sproong in the father, was in the waie to be worne out of favour. Which was the more 'likelie to come to passe, by their informations that privilie charged him with riot and other uncivill demeanor un-seemelie for a prince." **newsmongers:** talebearers.
28. **submission:** confession.
30. **affections:** inclinations.   **hold a wing:** pursue a course.
32–33. **Thy . . . supplied.** An allusion to the apocryphal story—apparently first told by Sir Thomas Elyot in *The Governor* (1531)—of one of the Prince's most flamboyant escapades.   In Holinshed's account (Bullough, IV, 280), "to hie offense of the king his father, he had with his fist striken the cheefe justice [Sir William Gascoigne] for sending one of his minions (upon desert) to prison, when the justice stoutlie commanded himselfe also streict to ward, & he (then prince) obeied.   The king after expelled him out of his privie councell, banish him the court, and made the duke of Clarence (his younger brother) president of councell in his steed." Shakespeare treats the escapade more fully in *2 Henry IV*, V.ii.   **rudely:** by violence.
36. **time:** time of life, i.e. youth.
40. **common-hackney'd:** cheapened, vulgarized. A hackney is a horse kept for hire.   42. **Opinion:** i.e. public opinion.
43. **Had:** would have.   **possession:** the possessor, i.e. Richard II.
57. **state:** i.e. appearance on state occasions.   59. **wan:** won.
61. **bavin:** brushwood, kindling.
62. **carded:** mixed (and so adulterated), a term from cloth-making.
state: royal status.

1 Henry IV
III.ii

Had his great name profaned with their scorns,
And gave his countenance, against his name,   65
To laugh at gibing boys, and stand the push
Of every beardless vain comparative,
Grew a companion to the common streets,
Enfeoff'd himself to popularity,
That, being daily swallowed by men's eyes,   70
They surfeited with honey and began
To loathe the taste of sweetness, whereof a little
More than a little is by much too much.
So when he had occasion to be seen,
He was but as the cuckoo is in June,   75
Heard, not regarded; seen, but with such eyes
As, sick and blunted with community,
Afford no extraordinary gaze,
Such as is bent on sunlike majesty
When it shines seldom in admiring eyes;   80
But rather drows'd and hung their eyelids down,
Slept in his face and rend'red such aspect
As cloudy men use to their adversaries,
Being with his presence glutted, [gorg'd], and full.
And in that very line, Harry, standest thou,   85
For thou hast lost thy princely privilege
With vile participation. Not an eye
But is a-weary of thy common sight,
Save mine, which hath desir'd to see thee more,
Which now doth that I would not have it do,   90
Make blind itself with foolish tenderness.
      Prince. I shall hereafter, my thrice-gracious lord,
Be more myself.
      King.   For all the world
As thou art to this hour was Richard then
When I from France set foot at Ravenspurgh,   95
And even as I was then is Percy now.
Now by my sceptre, and my soul to boot,
He hath more worthy interest to the state
Than thou the shadow of succession.
For of no right, nor color like to right,   100
He doth fill fields with harness in the realm,
Turns head against the lion's armed jaws,
And being no more in debt to years than thou,
Leads ancient lords and reverend bishops on
To bloody battles and to bruising arms.   105
What never-dying honor hath he got
Against renowmed Douglas! whose high deeds,
Whose hot incursions and great name in arms,
Holds from all soldiers chief majority
And military title capital   110
Through all the kingdoms that acknowledge Christ.
Thrice hath this Hotspur, Mars in swathling clothes,

This infant warrior, in his enterprises
Discomfited great Douglas, ta'en him once,
Enlarg'd him and made a friend of him,   115
To fill the mouth of deep defiance up,
And shake the peace and safety of our throne.
And what say you to this? Percy, Northumberland,
The Archbishop's grace of York, Douglas, Mortimer,
Capitulate against us, and are up.   120
But wherefore do I tell these news to thee?
Why, Harry, do I tell thee of my foes,
Which art my nearest and dearest enemy?
Thou that art like enough, through vassal fear,
Base inclination, and the start of spleen,   125
To fight against me under Percy's pay,
To dog his heels and curtsy at his frowns,
To show how much thou art degenerate.
      Prince. Do not think so, you shall not find it so,
And God forgive them that so much have sway'd   130
Your Majesty's good thoughts away from me!
I will redeem all this on Percy's head,
And in the closing of some glorious day
Be bold to tell you that I am your son,
When I will wear a garment all of blood,   135
And stain my favors in a bloody mask,
Which wash'd away shall scour my shame with it.
And that shall be the day, when e'er it lights,
That this same child of honor and renown,
This gallant Hotspur, this all-praised knight,   140
And your unthought-of Harry chance to meet.
For every honor sitting on his helm,
Would they were multitudes, and on my head
My shames redoubled! For the time will come
That I shall make this northren youth exchange   145
His glorious deeds for my indignities.
Percy is but my factor, good my lord,
To engross up glorious deeds on my behalf;
And I will call him to so strict account
That he shall render every glory up,   150
Yea, even the slightest worship of his time,
Or I will tear the reckoning from his heart.
This in the name of God I promise here,
The which if he be pleas'd I shall perform,
I do beseech your Majesty may salve   155
The long-grown wounds of my intemperance.
If not, the end of life cancels all bands,
And I will die a hundred thousand deaths
Ere break the smallest parcel of this vow.
      King. A hundred thousand rebels die in this.   160
Thou shalt have charge and sovereign trust herein.

Enter BLUNT.

How now, good Blunt? thy looks are full of speed.
      Blunt. So hath the business that I come to speak of.

65. **gave . . . name:** lent his authority, to the jeopardy of his kingly
title.
66–67. **stand . . . comparative:** tolerate the impertinent witticisms of
every beardless youth.   69. **Enfeoff'd:** sold, surrendered.
70. **That:** so that.   77. **community:** familiarity.
82. **aspect:** look.   83. **cloudy:** sullen.
87. **participation:** fellowship.   90. **that:** that which.
91. **foolish tenderness:** i.e. tears.
98. **more . . . state:** a better claim to the throne.
99. **shadow:** i.e. because your intrinsic merits are so slight.
100. **color:** pretext.   101. **harness:** (men in) armor.
102. **Turns head:** leads an army.
103. **being . . . thou.** See note to I.i.53.
107. **renowmed:** renowned.   109. **majority:** supremacy.
110. **capital:** pre-eminent.   112. **swathling:** swaddling.

115. **Enlarg'd:** freed.
120. **Capitulate:** combine.   **up:** i.e. in arms.
123. **dearest:** (1) best beloved; (2) direst.
124. **like:** likely.   **vassal:** slavish.
125. **start of spleen:** fit of caprice and ill temper.
136. **favors:** features.   138. **lights:** dawns.
145. **northren:** northern.   147. **factor:** agent.
148. **engross:** gather, amass.
151. **worship:** honor.   **time:** time of life, i.e. youth.
156. **intemperance:** dissolute behavior.
157. **bands:** bonds, debts.   159. **parcel:** part.
161. **charge:** command of troops, i.e. a commission.

Lord Mortimer of Scotland hath sent word
That Douglas and the English rebels met   165
The eleventh of this month at Shrewsbury.
A mighty and a fearful head they are,
If promises be kept on every hand,
As ever off'red foul play in a state.

King. The Earl of Westmerland set forth to-day,
With him my son, Lord John of Lancaster,   171
For this advertisement is five days old.
On Wednesday next, Harry, you shall set forward,
On Thursday we ourselves will march. Our meeting
Is Bridgenorth. And, Harry, you shall march   175
Through Gloucestershire; by which account,
Our business valued, some twelve days hence
Our general forces at Bridgenorth shall meet.
Our hands are full of business, let's away,   179
Advantage feeds him fat while men delay.   *Exeunt.*

[SCENE III]

Enter FALSTAFF *and* BARDOLPH.

Fal. Bardolph, am I not fall'n away vilely since
this last action? do I not bate? do I not dwindle?
Why, my skin hangs about me like an old lady's loose
gown; I am wither'd like an old apple-john. Well,
I'll repent, and that suddenly, while I am in some   5
liking. I shall be out of heart shortly, and then I shall
have no strength to repent. And I have not forgotten
what the inside of a church is made of, I am a pepper-
corn, a brewer's horse. The inside of a church! Company, villainous company, hath been the spoil of me.

Bard. Sir John, you are so fretful you cannot live
long.   12

Fal. Why, there is it. Come sing me a bawdy song,
make me merry. I was as virtuously given as a
gentleman need to be, virtuous enough: swore   15
little, dic'd not above seven times—a week, went to a
bawdy-house not above once in a quarter—of an hour,
paid money that I borrow'd—three or four times,
liv'd well and in good compass, and now I live out of
all order, out of all compass.   20

Bard. Why, you are so fat, Sir John, that you must
needs be out of all compass, out of all reasonable
compass, Sir John.

Fal. Do thou amend thy face, and I'll amend my
life. Thou art our admiral, thou bearest the lan-   25

tern in the poop, but 'tis in the nose of thee. Thou art
the Knight of the Burning Lamp.

Bard. Why, Sir John, my face does you no harm.

Fal. No, I'll be sworn, I make as good use of it as
many a man doth of a death's-head or a *memento*   30
mori. I never see thy face but I think upon hell-fire
and Dives that liv'd in purple; for there he is in his
robes, burning, burning. If thou wert any way given
to virtue, I would swear by thy face; my oath should
be "By this fire, that['s] God's angel." But thou   35
art altogether given over, and wert indeed, but for
the light in thy face, the son of utter darkness. When
thou ran'st up Gadshill in the night to catch my horse,
if I did not think thou hadst been an *ignis fatuus* or a
ball of wildfire, there's no purchase in money. O,   40
thou art a perpetual triumph, an everlasting bonfire
light! Thou hast sav'd me a thousand marks in links
and torches, walking with thee in the night betwixt
tavern and tavern; but the sack that thou hast drunk
me would have bought me lights as good cheap at   45
the dearest chandler's in Europe. I have maintain'd
that salamander of yours with fire any time this two
and thirty years, God reward me for it!

Bard. 'Sblood, I would my face were in your belly!

Fal. God-a-mercy, so should I be sure to be heart-
burnt.   51

Enter HOSTESS.

How now, Dame Partlet the hen? have you inquir'd
yet who pick'd my pocket?

Host. Why, Sir John, what do you think, Sir John?
Do you think I keep thieves in my house? I have   55
search'd, I have inquir'd, so has my husband, man by
man, boy by boy, servant by servant. The [tithe] of a
hair was never lost in my house before.

Fal. Ye lie, hostess, Bardolph was shav'd, and lost
many a hair, and I'll be sworn my pocket was pick'd.
Go to, you are a woman, go.   61

Host. Who, I? No, I defy thee. God's light, I was
never call'd so in mine own house before.

Fal. Go to, I know you well enough.   64

Host. No, Sir John, you do not know me, Sir John.
I know you, Sir John, you owe me money, Sir John,
and now you pick a quarrel to beguile me of it. I
bought you a dozen of shirts to your back.   68

Fal. Dowlas, filthy dowlas. I have given them
away to bakers' wives, they have made bolters of them.

Host. Now as I am a true woman, holland of eight
shillings an ell. You owe money here besides, Sir John,

---

164. **Mortimer of Scotland:** i.e. George Dunbar, the Scottish Earl of the "March," or border, whom Shakespeare confuses with Edmund, Earl of March.   167. **head:** army.
171. **John of Lancaster:** Prince John, third son of Henry IV.
172. **advertisement:** information.
174. **meeting:** meeting place, rendezvous.
175. **Bridgenorth:** town on the Severn River southeast of Shrewsbury.
177. **Our business valued:** the time necessary for our business being considered.
180. **Advantage . . . fat:** i.e. opportunity grows lazy.   **him:** himself.

III.iii. Location: The Boar's Head Tavern.
1. **fall'n away:** shrunk.
2. **this last action:** i.e. the robbery at Gadshill.   **bate:** grow thin.
4. **apple-john:** kind of apple that could be kept a long time and was eaten after its skin had become shrivelled.   5. **suddenly:** at once.
5–6. **in some liking:** (1) in good condition; (2) in the mood.
9. **a brewer's horse:** i.e. decrepit.   14. **given:** inclined.
19. **compass:** moderation.   22. **compass:** circumference, expanse.
25. **admiral:** flagship.

30–31. **memento mori:** reminder of death (e.g. a skull engraved on a seal ring).
32. **Dives:** in Jesus' parable about the beggar Lazarus, "a certain rich man" who went to hell. See Luke 16:19–31.
35. **By . . . angel.** Perhaps an echo of Exodus 3:2.
36. **given over:** i.e. to wickedness.
39. **ignis fatuus:** will-o'-the-wisp.   40. **wildfire:** fireworks.
41. **triumph:** torchlight procession.   42. **links:** torches.
45. **as good cheap:** as cheap.
47. **salamander:** fabulous lizard believed to live in fire.
52. **Dame Partlet:** traditional name for a hen. Falstaff alludes to the Hostess' agitation and flutter.   57. **tithe:** tenth part.
69. **Dowlas:** kind of coarse linen.
70. **bolters:** cloths for sifting flour.   71. **holland:** fine linen.
72. **ell:** a measurement of 45 inches.

1 Henry IV
III.iii

for your diet and by-drinkings, and money lent you, four and twenty pound.

Fal. He had his part of it, let him pay. 75

Host. He? alas, he is poor, he hath nothing.

Fal. How? poor? Look upon his face; what call you rich? Let them coin his nose, let them coin his cheeks. I'll not pay a denier. What, will you make a younker of me? Shall I not take mine ease in mine 80 inn but I shall have my pocket pick'd? I have lost a seal-ring of my grandfather's worth forty mark.

Host. O Jesu, I have heard the Prince tell him, I know not how oft, that that ring was copper! 84

Fal. How? the Prince is a Jack, a sneak-up. 'Sblood, and he were here, I would cudgel him like a dog if he would say so.

Enter the PRINCE *marching,* [*with* PETO,] *and Falstaff meets him playing upon his truncheon like a fife.*

How now, lad? is the wind in that door, i' faith? must we all march?

Bard. Yea, two and two, Newgate fashion. 90

Host. My lord, I pray you hear me.

Prince. What say'st thou, Mistress Quickly? How doth thy husband? I love him well, he is an honest man.

Host. Good my lord, hear me.

Fal. Prithee let her alone, and list to me. 95

Prince. What say'st thou, Jack?

Fal. The other night I fell asleep here behind the arras and had my pocket pick'd. This house is turn'd bawdy-house, they pick pockets.

Prince. What didst thou lose, Jack? 100

Fal. Wilt thou believe me, Hal, three or four bonds of forty pound a-piece, and a seal-ring of my grandfather's.

Prince. A trifle, some eight-penny matter. 104

Host. So I told him, my lord, and I said I heard your Grace say so; and, my lord, he speaks most vilely of you, like a foul-mouth'd man as he is, and said he would cudgel you.

Prince. What, he did not? 109

Host. There's neither faith, truth, nor womanhood in me else.

Fal. There's no more faith in thee than in a stew'd prune, nor no more truth in thee than in a drawn fox, and for womanhood, Maid Marian may be the deputy's wife of the ward to thee. Go, you thing, go. 115

Host. Say, what thing? what thing?

Fal. What thing? why, a thing to thank God on.

Host. I am no thing to thank God on, I would thou shouldst know it. I am an honest man's wife, and 119 setting thy knighthood aside, thou art a knave to call me so.

Fal. Setting thy womanhood aside, thou art a beast to say otherwise.

Host. Say, what beast, thou knave, thou? 124

Fal. What beast? why, an otter.

Prince. An otter, Sir John, why an otter?

Fal. Why? she's neither fish nor flesh, a man knows not where to have her. 128

Host. Thou art an unjust man in saying so. Thou or any man knows where to have me, thou knave, thou!

Prince. Thou say'st true, hostess, and he slanders thee most grossly.

Host. So he doth you, my lord, and said this other day you ought him a thousand pound. 134

Prince. Sirrah, do I owe you a thousand pound?

Fal. A thousand pound, Hal? a million, thy love is worth a million; thou owest me thy love.

Host. Nay, my lord, he call'd you Jack, and said he would cudgel you. 139

Fal. Did I, Bardolph?

Bard. Indeed, Sir John, you said so.

Fal. Yea, if he said my ring was copper.

Prince. I say 'tis copper. Darest thou be as good as thy word now? 144

Fal. Why, Hal! thou knowest, as thou art but man, I dare, but as thou art Prince, I fear thee as I fear the roaring of the lion's whelp.

Prince. And why not as the lion? 148

Fal. The King himself is to be fear'd as the lion. Dost thou think I'll fear thee as I fear thy father? Nay, and I do, I pray God my girdle break.

Prince. O, if it should, how would thy guts fall about thy knees! But, sirrah, there's no room for faith, truth, nor honesty in this bosom of thine; it is all 154 fill'd up with guts and midriff. Charge an honest woman with picking thy pocket! Why, thou whoreson, impudent, emboss'd rascal, if there were any thing in thy pocket but tavern-reckonings, memoran- 158 dums of bawdy-houses, and one poor pennyworth of sugar-candy to make thee long-winded—if thy pocket were enrich'd with any other injuries but these, I am a villain. And yet you will stand to it, you will not pocket up wrong. Art thou not asham'd? 163

Fal. Dost thou hear, Hal? Thou knowest in the state of innocency Adam fell, and what should poor Jack Falstaff do in the days of villainy? Thou seest I have more flesh than another man, and therefore more frailty. You confess then you pick'd my pocket?

Prince. It appears so by the story. 169

Fal. Hostess, I forgive thee. Go make ready breakfast; love thy husband, look to thy servants, cherish thy guesse. Thou shalt find me tractable to any honest reason; thou seest I am pacified still. Nay, prithee be gone. (*Exit Hostess.*) Now, Hal, to 174 the news at court for the robbery, lad, how is that answer'd?

73. **by-drinkings:** drinks between meals.
79. **denier:** French copper coin of little value.
80. **younker:** novice, greenhorn.
85. **Jack:** rascal.   **sneak-up:** sneak.
90. **Newgate:** a London prison.
112–13. **stew'd prune:** i.e. bawd. Stewed prunes were commonly associated with brothels.
113. **drawn:** i.e. out of its hole (and seeking to trick its pursuers).
114–15. **Maid . . . thee:** i.e. compared to you, Maid Marian—a disreputable character in Robin Hood ballads and May-games—was a model of propriety.
120. **setting . . . aside:** disregarding your rank.

128. **where . . . her:** i.e. how to take her. In lines 129–30 the Hostess, repeating the phrase, stumbles on an unflattering double-entendre.
134. **ought:** owed.
157. **emboss'd:** swollen.   **rascal:** lean, inferior deer.
161. **injuries:** things whose loss would be an injury to you (with a play on the phrase *pocket up injuries* = swallow insults).
172. **guesse:** guests.   173. **still:** always.   176. **answer'd:** settled.

Prince. O, my sweet beef, I must still be good angel to thee. The money is paid back again.

Fal. O, I do not like that paying back, 'tis a double labor.   180

Prince. I am good friends with my father and may do any thing.

Fal. Rob me the exchequer the first thing thou doest, and do it with unwash'd hands too.

Bard. Do, my lord.   185

Prince. I have procur'd thee, Jack, a charge of foot.

Fal. I would it had been of horse. Where shall I find one that can steal well? O for a fine thief, of the age of two and twenty or thereabouts! I am hei-   189
nously unprovided. Well, God be thank'd for these rebels, they offend none but the virtuous. I laud them, I praise them.

Prince. Bardolph!

Bard. My lord?

Prince. Go bear this letter to Lord John of
        Lancaster,   195
To my brother John; this to my Lord of Westmerland.
                                                  [*Exit Bardolph.*]
Go, Peto, to horse, to horse, for thou and I
Have thirty miles to ride yet ere dinner-time.
                                                     [*Exit Peto.*]
Jack, meet me to-morrow in the Temple Hall
At two [a'] clock in the afternoon;   200
There shalt thou know thy charge, and there receive
Money and order for their furniture.
The land is burning, Percy stands on high,
And either we or they must lower lie.   [*Exit.*]

Fal. Rare words! brave world! Hostess, my
        breakfast, come!   205
O, I could wish this tavern were my drum!   [*Exit.*]

[ACT IV, SCENE I]

[*Enter* HOTSPUR, WORCESTER, *and* DOUGLAS.]

Hot. Well said, my noble Scot! If speaking truth
In this fine age were not thought flattery,
Such attribution should the Douglas have
As not a soldier of this season's stamp
Should go so general current through the world.   5
By God, I cannot flatter, I do defy
The tongues of soothers, but a braver place
In my heart's love hath no man than yourself.
Nay, task me to my word, approve me, lord.

Doug.   Thou art the king of honor.   10
No man so potent breathes upon the ground
But I will beard him.

184. **with unwash'd hands:** i.e. hastily.
186. **charge of foot:** command of a company of infantry.
190. **unprovided:** ill equipped (for the campaign).
199. **Temple Hall:** hall of the Inner Temple, one of the Inns of Court that housed the legal societies of London.
202. **furniture:** equipment.
206. **I . . . drum.** A disputed passage. Perhaps Falstaff means merely that he would rather continue to take his ease at the inn than go to the wars.

IV.i. **Location:** The rebel camp near Shrewsbury.
3. **attribution:** tribute.   4. **stamp:** coinage.
7. **soothers:** flatterers.   9. **task:** challenge.   **approve:** test.
12. **But . . . him:** but that I will defy him.

Enter one [a MESSENGER] *with letters.*

Hot.   Do so, and 'tis well.—
What letters hast thou there?—I can but thank you.

Mess. These letters come from your father.

Hot. Letters from him! Why comes he not him-
self?   15

Mess. He cannot come, my lord, he is grievous
sick.

Hot. 'Zounds! how has he the leisure to be sick
In such a justling time? Who leads his power?
Under whose government come they along?

Mess. His letters bears his mind, not I, my [lord].

Wor. I prithee tell me, doth he keep his bed?   21

Mess. He did, my lord, four days ere I set forth,
And at the time of my departure thence
He was much fear'd by his physicians.

Wor. I would the state of time had first been whole
Ere he by sickness had been visited,   26
His health was never better worth than now.

Hot. Sick now? droop now? This sickness doth
        infect
The very life-blood of our enterprise,
'Tis catching hither, even to our camp.   30
He writes me here, that inward sickness—
And that his friends by deputation could not
So soon be drawn, nor did he think it meet
To lay so dangerous and dear a trust
On any soul remov'd, but on his own.   35
Yet doth he give us bold advertisement
That with our small conjunction we should on,
To see how fortune is dispos'd to us,
For, as he writes, there is no quailing now,
Because the King is certainly possess'd   40
Of all our purposes. What say you to it?

Wor. Your father's sickness is a maim to us.

Hot. A perilous gash, a very limb lopp'd off—
And yet, in faith, it is not; his present want
Seems more than we shall find it. Were it good   45
To set the exact wealth of all our states
All at one cast? to set so rich a main
On the nice hazard of one doubtful hour?
It were not good, for therein should we read
The very bottom and the soul of hope,   50
The very list, the very utmost bound
Of all our fortunes.

Doug.   Faith, and so we should,
Where now remains a sweet reversion,
We may boldly spend upon the hope of what
[Is] to come in.   55
A comfort of retirement lives in this.

Hot. A rendezvous, a home to fly unto,

18. **justling:** turbulent.   **power:** troops.
19. **government:** command.   24. **fear'd:** feared for.
25. **state of time:** times.   **whole:** sound, healthy.
27. **better worth:** more important.
30. **catching hither:** contagious as far away as this.
32. **by deputation:** through deputies.   33. **drawn:** mustered.
34. **dear:** significant.   35. **remov'd:** i.e. less intimately involved.
36. **advertisement:** advice.   37. **conjunction:** allied force.
40. **possess'd:** informed.   44. **want:** absence.
46. **set . . . states:** i.e. stake the whole of our resources.
47. **main:** stake.   48. **nice:** delicate.   51. **list:** limit.
53. **reversion:** future prospects, expectation.
56. **comfort of retirement:** refuge to fall back on.

1 Henry IV
IV.i

If that the devil and mischance look big
Upon the maidenhead of our affairs.
   Wor. But yet I would your father had been here. 60
The quality and hair of our attempt
Brooks no division. It will be thought
By some that know not why he is away
That wisdom, loyalty, and mere dislike
Of our proceedings kept the Earl from hence, 65
And think how such an apprehension
May turn the tide of fearful faction,
And breed a kind of question in our cause.
For well you know we of the off'ring side
Must keep aloof from strict arbitrement, 70
And stop all sight-holes, every loop from whence
The eye of reason may pry in upon us.
This absence of your father's draws a curtain
That shows the ignorant a kind of fear
Before not dreamt of.
   Hot.   You strain too far. 75
I rather of his absence make this use:
It lends a lustre and more great opinion,
A larger dare to our great enterprise,
Than if the Earl were here, for men must think,
If we without his help can make a head 80
To push against a kingdom, with his help
We shall o'erturn it topsy-turvy down.
Yet all goes well, yet all our joints are whole.
   Doug. As heart can think. There is not such a word
Spoke of in Scotland as this term of fear. 85

       Enter Sir Richard Vernon.

   Hot. My cousin Vernon, welcome, by my soul!
   Ver. Pray God my news be worth a welcome, lord.
The Earl of Westmerland, seven thousand strong,
Is marching hitherwards, with him Prince John.
   Hot. No harm. What more?
   Ver.   And further, I have learn'd,
The King himself in person is set forth, 91
Or hitherwards intended speedily,
With strong and mighty preparation.
   Hot. He shall be welcome too. Where is his son,
The nimble-footed madcap Prince of Wales, 95
And his comrades, that daff'd the world aside
And bid it pass?
   Ver.   All furnish'd, all in arms;
All plum'd like estridges, that with the wind
Bated like eagles having lately bath'd,
Glittering in golden coats like images, 100
As full of spirit as the month of May,
And gorgeous as the sun at midsummer;
Wanton as youthful goats, wild as young bulls.

I saw young Harry with his beaver on,
His cushes on his thighs, gallantly arm'd, 105
Rise from the ground like feathered Mercury,
And vaulted with such ease into his seat
As if an angel [dropp'd] down from the clouds
To turn and wind a fiery Pegasus,
And witch the world with noble horsemanship. 110
   Hot. No more, no more! worse than the sun in March,
This praise doth nourish agues. Let them come!
They come like sacrifices in their trim,
And to the fire-ey'd maid of smoky war
All hot and bleeding will we offer them. 115
The mailed Mars shall on his [altar] sit
Up to the ears in blood. I am on fire
To hear this rich reprisal is so nigh,
And yet not ours. Come let me taste my horse,
Who is to bear me like a thunderbolt 120
Against the bosom of the Prince of Wales.
Harry to Harry shall, hot horse to horse,
Meet and ne'er part till one drop down a corse.
O that Glendower were come!
   Ver.   There is more news:
I learn'd in Worcester, as I rode along, 125
He [cannot] draw his power this fourteen days.
   Doug. That's the worst tidings that I hear of [yet].
   Wor. Ay, by my faith, that bears a frosty sound.
   Hot. What may the King's whole battle reach unto?
   Ver. To thirty thousand.
   Hot.   Forty let it be! 130
My father and Glendower being both away,
The powers of us may serve so great a day.
Come let us take a muster speedily.
Doomsday is near, die all, die merrily.
   Doug. Talk not of dying, I am out of fear 135
Of death or death's hand for this one half year.

                         Exeunt.

              [Scene II]

     Enter Falstaff, Bardolph.

   Fal. Bardolph, get thee before to Coventry; fill me a bottle of sack. Our soldiers shall march through; we'll to Sutton Co'fil' to-night.
   Bard. Will you give me money, captain?
   Fal. Lay out, lay out. 5
   Bard. This bottle makes an angel.
   Fal. And if it do, take it for thy labor, and if it

---

58. **big:** threatening.   59. **maidenhead:** i.e. early phase.
61. **hair:** fiber, nature.   62. **Brooks:** permits.
64. **mere:** outright.   67. **fearful faction:** timorous support.
69. **off'ring:** attacking.
70. **strict arbitrement:** scrupulous inspection.
71. **loop:** loophole.   73. **draws:** draws aside.
77. **opinion:** renown.   80. **make a head:** raise an army.
83. **joints:** limbs.   92. **intended:** i.e. intended to come.
96. **daff'd:** thrust.   97. **furnish'd:** equipped.
98. **estridges:** ostriches.
99. **Bated:** beat their wings (a term from falconry).
103. **Wanton:** frolicsome.

104. **beaver:** helmet.
105. **cushes:** cuisses, armor for the thighs.   107. **seat:** saddle.
109. **wind:** wheel.   **Pegasus:** winged horse of ancient myth.
112. **agues:** fevers (thought to result from vapors drawn by the sun).
113. **trim:** finery.   114. **fire-ey'd maid:** i.e. Bellona, goddess of war.
116. **mailed:** armored.   118. **reprisal:** prize.
119. **taste:** test.   123. **corse:** corpse.
125. **Worcester:** cathedral city on the Severn River south of Shrewsbury.   126. **draw his power:** assemble his troops.
129. **battle:** army.   135. **out of:** free from.

IV.ii. Location: A public road near Coventry.
3. **Sutton Co'fil':** Sutton Coldfield, a town in Warwickshire.
5. **Lay out:** i.e. pay for it yourself.
6. **makes an angel:** i.e. brings your debt to ten shillings. An angel was a gold coin stamped with the figure of the archangel Michael.

make twenty, take them all, I'll answer the coinage.
Bid my lieutenant Peto meet me at town's end.

Bard. I will, captain, farewell.   *Exit.* 10

Fal. If I be not asham'd of my soldiers, I am a
sous'd gurnet. I have misus'd the King's press
damnably. I have got, in exchange of a hundred and
fifty soldiers, three hundred and odd pounds. I press
me none but good householders, [yeomen's] sons, 15
inquire me out contracted bachelors, such as had been
ask'd twice on the banes, such a commodity of warm
slaves, as had as lieve hear the devil as a drum, such as
fear the report of a caliver worse than a struck fowl
or a hurt wild duck. I press'd me none but such 20
toasts-and-butter, with hearts in their bellies no bigger
than pins' heads, and they have bought out their
services; and now my whole charge consists of
ancients, corporals, lieutenants, gentlemen of companies—slaves as ragged as Lazarus in the painted 25
cloth, where the glutton's dogs lick'd his sores, and
such as indeed were never soldiers, but discarded
unjust servingmen, younger sons to younger brothers,
revolted tapsters, and ostlers trade-fall'n, the cankers
of a calm world and a long peace, ten times more 30
dishonorable ragged than an old feaz'd ancient: and
such have I, to fill up the rooms of them as have
bought out their services, that you would think that
I had a hundred and fifty totter'd prodigals lately come
from swine-keeping, from eating draff and husks. 35
A mad fellow met me on the way and told me I had un-
loaded all the gibbets and press'd the dead bodies.
No eye hath seen such scarecrows. I'll not march
through Coventry with them, that's flat. Nay, and
the villains march wide betwixt the legs, as if they 40
had gyves on, for indeed I had the most of them out of
prison. There's not a shirt and a half in all my company, and the half shirt is two napkins tack'd together
and thrown over the shoulders like a herald's coat
without sleeves; and the shirt, to say the truth, 45
stol'n from my host at Saint Albons, or the red-nose
innkeeper of Daventry. But that's all one, they'll find
linen·enough on every hedge.

Enter the PRINCE, LORD OF WESTMERLAND.

Prince. How now, blown Jack? how now, quilt? 49

Fal. What, Hal? how now, mad wag? What a
devil dost thou in Warwickshire? My good Lord of
Westmerland, I cry you mercy! I thought your honor
had already been at Shrewsbury.

West. Faith, Sir John, 'tis more than time that I
were there, and you too, but my powers are there 55
already. The King, I can tell you, looks for us all, we
must away all night.

Fal. Tut, never fear me, I am as vigilant as a cat
to steal cream. 59

Prince. I think, to steal cream indeed, for thy theft
hath already made thee butter. But tell me, Jack,
whose fellows are these that come after?

Fal. Mine, Hal, mine.

Prince. I did never see such pitiful rascals. 64

Fal. Tut, tut, good enough to toss, food for
powder, food for powder; they'll fill a pit as well as
better. Tush, man, mortal men, mortal men.

West. Ay, but, Sir John, methinks they are exceeding poor and bare, too beggarly. 69

Fal. Faith, for their poverty, I know not where
they had that, and for their bareness, I am sure they
never learn'd that of me.

Prince. No, I'll be sworn, unless you call three
fingers in the ribs bare. But, sirrah, make haste, Percy
is already in the field.   *Exit.* 75

Fal. What, is the King encamp'd?

West. He is, Sir John. I fear we shall stay too long.

Fal. Well,
To the latter end of a fray and the beginning of a feast
Fits a dull fighter and a keen guest.   *Exeunt.* 80

[SCENE III]

Enter HOTSPUR, WORCESTER, DOUGLAS, VERNON.

Hot. We'll fight with him to-night.

Wor.   It may not be.

Doug. You give him then advantage.

Ver.   Not a whit.

Hot. Why say you so? Looks he not for supply?

Ver. So do we.

Hot.   His is certain, ours is doubtful.

Wor. Good cousin, be advis'd, stir not to-night. 5

Ver. Do not, my lord.

Doug.   You do not counsel well,
You speak it out of fear and cold heart.

Ver. Do me no slander, Douglas. By my life,
And I dare well maintain it with my life,
If well-respected honor bid me on, 10
I hold as little counsel with weak fear
As you, my lord, or any Scot that this day lives.
Let it be seen to-morrow in the battle
Which of us fears.

1 Henry IV
IV.iii

Doug.   Yea, or to-night.
Ver.   Content.
Hot.   To-night, say I.   15
Ver.   Come, come, it may not be. I wonder much,
Being men of such great leading as you are,
That you foresee not what impediments
Drag back our expedition. Certain horse
Of my cousin Vernon's are not yet come up.   20
Your uncle Worcester's horses came but to-day,
And now their pride and mettle is asleep,
Their courage with hard labor tame and dull,
That not a horse is half the half of himself.
    Hot.   So are the horses of the enemy   25
In general journey-bated and brought low.
The better part of ours are full of rest.
    Wor.   The number of the King exceedeth our.
For God's sake, cousin, stay till all come in.
                              The trumpet sounds a parley.

                Enter Sir Walter Blunt.

    Blunt.   I come with gracious offers from the King,
If you vouchsafe me hearing and respect.   31
    Hot.   Welcome, Sir Walter Blunt; and would to
                    God
You were of our determination!
Some of us love you well, and even those some
Envy your great deservings and good name,   35
Because you are not of our quality,
But stand against us like an enemy.
    Blunt.   And God defend but still I should stand so,
So long as out of limit and true rule
You stand against anointed majesty.   40
But to my charge. The King hath sent to know
The nature of your griefs, and whereupon
You conjure from the breast of civil peace
Such bold hostility, teaching his duteous land
Audacious cruelty. If that the King   45
Have any way your good deserts forgot,
Which he confesseth to be manifold,
He bids you name your griefs, and with all speed
You shall have your desires with interest
And pardon absolute for yourself and these   50
Herein misled by your suggestion.
    Hot.   The King is kind, and well we know the King
Knows at what time to promise, when to pay.
My father and my uncle and myself
Did give him that same royalty he wears,   55
And when he was not six and twenty strong,
Sick in the world's regard, wretched and low,
A poor unminded outlaw sneaking home,
My father gave him welcome to the shore;
And when he heard him swear and vow to God   60
He came but to be Duke of Lancaster,
To sue his livery and beg his peace,

With tears of innocency and terms of zeal,
My father, in kind heart and pity mov'd,
Swore him assistance, and perform'd it too.   65
Now when the lords and barons of the realm
Perceiv'd Northumberland did lean to him,
The more and less came in with cap and knee,
Met him in boroughs, cities, villages,
Attended him on bridges, stood in lanes,   70
Laid gifts before him, proffer'd him their oaths,
Gave him their heirs as pages, followed him
Even at the heels in golden multitudes.
He presently, as greatness knows itself,
Steps me a little higher than his vow   75
Made to my father, while his blood was poor,
Upon the naked shore at Ravenspurgh,
And now forsooth takes on him to reform
Some certain edicts and some strait decrees
That lie too heavy on the commonwealth,   80
Cries out upon abuses, seems to weep
Over his [country's] wrongs, and by this face,
This seeming brow of justice, did he win
The hearts of all that he did angle for;
Proceeded further—cut me off the heads   85
Of all the favorites that the absent King
In deputation left behind him here,
When he was personal in the Irish war.
    Blunt.   Tut, I came not to hear this.
    Hot.   Then to the point.
In short time after, he depos'd the King,   90
Soon after that, depriv'd him of his life,
And in the neck of that, task'd the whole state;
To make that worse, suff'red his kinsman March
(Who is, if every owner were well plac'd,
Indeed his king) to be engag'd in Wales,   95
There without ransom to lie forfeited;
Disgrac'd me in my happy victories,
Sought to entrap me by intelligence,
Rated mine uncle from the Council-board,
In rage dismiss'd my father from the court,   100
Broke oath on oath, committed wrong on wrong,
And in conclusion drove us to seek out
This head of safety, and withal to pry
Into his title, the which we find
Too indirect for long continuance.   105
    Blunt.   Shall I return this answer to the King?
    Hot.   Not so, Sir Walter; we'll withdraw a while.
Go to the King, and let there be impawn'd
Some surety for a safe return again,
And in the morning early shall mine uncle   110
Bring him our purposes. And so farewell.

17. **leading:** leadership.
19. **expedition:** (speedy) progress. **horse:** cavalry.
26. **journey-bated:** weary from travel. 28. **our:** our number.
29. **s.d. parley:** trumpet call sounded to request a conference.
33. **of our determination:** i.e. on our side. 35. **Envy:** begrudge.
36. **quality:** party. 38. **defend:** forbid.
39. **limit . . . rule:** i.e. the bounds of honest conduct.
51. **suggestion:** (evil) prompting.
62. **sue his livery:** claim his inheritance. **beg his peace:** i.e. from King Richard.

63. **terms of zeal:** i.e. declarations of loyalty.
65. **perform'd it:** i.e. fulfilled his oath.
68. **with . . . knee:** with cap in hand and on bended knee, i.e. deferentially. 70. **lanes:** rows. 73. **golden:** resplendent.
74. **knows itself:** comes to recognize its power.
76. **blood:** spirit. 79. **strait:** strict. 82. **face:** pretense.
88. **personal:** personally engaged.
92. **in . . . that:** immediately thereafter. **task'd:** taxed.
94. **if . . . plac'd:** i.e. if everyone occupied his proper station.
95. **engag'd:** held as hostage.
96. **forfeited:** unclaimed, unredeemed.
97. **happy:** fortunate. 98. **intelligence:** espionage.
99. **Rated:** scolded.
103. **head of safety:** army for security. **withal:** moreover.
104. **title:** i.e. to the throne. 108. **impawn'd:** pledged.

Blunt. I would you would accept of grace and love.
Hot. And may be so we shall.
Blunt.   Pray God you do. [Exeunt.]

[Scene IV]

Enter Archbishop of York, Sir Michael.

Arch. Hie, good Sir Michael, bear this sealed brief
With winged haste to the Lord Marshal,
This to my cousin Scroop, and all the rest
To whom they are directed. If you knew
How much they do import, you would make haste. 5
Sir M. My good lord,
I guess their tenor.
Arch.   Like enough you do.
To-morrow, good Sir Michael, is a day
Wherein the fortune of ten thousand men
Must bide the touch; for, sir, at Shrewsbury, 10
As I am truly given to understand,
The King with mighty and quick-raised power
Meets with Lord Harry; and I fear, Sir Michael,
What with the sickness of Northumberland,
Whose power was in the first proportion, 15
And what with Owen Glendower's absence thence,
Who with them was a rated sinew too,
And comes not in, overrul'd by prophecies,
I fear the power of Percy is too weak
To wage an instant trial with the King. 20
Sir M. Why, my good lord, you need not fear,
There is Douglas and Lord Mortimer.
Arch. No, Mortimer is not there.
Sir M. But there is Mordake, Vernon, Lord Harry
        Percy,
And there is my Lord of Worcester, and a head 25
Of gallant warriors, noble gentlemen.
Arch. And so there is; but yet the King hath drawn
The special head of all the land together:
The Prince of Wales, Lord John of Lancaster,
The noble Westmerland, and warlike Blunt, 30
And many moe corrivals and dear men
Of estimation and command in arms.
Sir M. Doubt not, my lord, they shall be well
        oppos'd.
Arch. I hope no less, yet needful 'tis to fear,
And to prevent the worst, Sir Michael, speed; 35
For if Lord Percy thrive not, ere the King
Dismiss his power he means to visit us,
For he hath heard of our confederacy,

And 'tis but wisdom to make strong against him.
Therefore make haste. I must go write again 40
To other friends, and so farewell, Sir Michael.
                    Exeunt.

[ACT V, Scene I]

Enter the King, Prince of Wales, Lord John of
Lancaster, Sir Walter Blunt, Falstaff.

King. How bloodily the sun begins to peer
Above yon bulky hill! the day looks pale
At his distemp'rature.
Prince.   The southren wind
Doth play the trumpet to his purposes,
And by his hollow whistling in the leaves 5
Foretells a tempest and a blust'ring day.
King. Then with the losers let it sympathize,
For nothing can seem foul to those that win.
                    The trumpet sounds.

Enter Worcester [*and* Sir Richard Vernon].

How now, my Lord of Worcester? 'tis not well
That you and I should meet upon such terms 10
As now we meet. You have deceiv'd our trust,
And made us doff our easy robes of peace,
To crush our old limbs in ungentle steel.
This is not well, my lord, this is not well.
What say you to it? Will you again unknit 15
This churlish knot of all-abhorred war?
And move in that obedient orb again
Where you did give a fair and natural light,
And be no more an exhal'd meteor,
A prodigy of fear, and a portent 20
Of broached mischief to the unborn times?
Wor. Hear me, my liege.
For mine own part, I could be well content
To entertain the lag end of my life
With quiet hours; for I protest 25
I have not sought the day of this dislike.
King. You have not sought it, how comes it then?
Fal. Rebellion lay in his way, and he found it.
Prince. Peace, chewet, peace!
Wor. It pleas'd your Majesty to turn your looks
Of favor from myself and all our house, 31
And yet I must remember you, my lord,
We were the first and dearest of your friends.
For you my staff of office did I break
In Richard's time, and posted day and night 35
To meet you on the way, and kiss your hand,
When yet you were in place and in account
Nothing so strong and fortunate as I.
It was myself, my brother, and his son,
That brought you home, and boldly did outdare 40

IV.iv. Location: York. The Archbishop's palace.
o.s.d. **Sir Michael.** Apparently unhistorical.
1. **brief:** letter.
2. **Lord Marshal:** i.e. Thomas Mowbray, third Duke of Nottingham,
son of the Thomas Mowbray of *Richard II* whose quarrel with Bullingbrook led to the exile of both men. He would of course be hostile
to the House of Lancaster.
3. **my cousin Scroop:** perhaps the Scroop (presumably Sir Stephen)
of *Richard II*, III.ii.91 ff.
10. **bide the touch:** withstand the test (as when gold is tested by the
touchstone).
15. **in . . . proportion:** i.e. larger than that of his associates.
17. **rated sinew:** i.e. a force on which they thought they could rely.
20. **wage:** risk. **instant:** immediate. 25. **head:** troop.
31. **moe corrivals:** more associates. **dear:** valued.
35. **prevent:** forestall. 37. **visit:** i.e. attack.

V.i. Location: The King's camp near Shrewsbury.
3. **his distemp'rature:** i.e. the sun's abnormal appearance. **southren:**
southern. 4. **trumpet:** trumpeter. 7. **sympathize:** accord.
17. **obedient orb:** (customary) sphere of obedience.
19. **exhal'd meteor.** It was believed that meteors were formed of
vapors drawn up from the earth (*exhal'd*) by the sun.
20. **prodigy of fear:** terrifying omen. 21. **broached:** set going.
24. **entertain:** pass. 29. **chewet:** jackdaw, i.e. chatterer.
32. **remember:** remind.
34–35. **For . . . time.** See *Richard II*, II.iii.26–28.
38. **Nothing:** by no means.

The dangers of the time. You swore to us,
And you did swear that oath at Doncaster,
That you did nothing purpose 'gainst the state,
Nor claim no further than your new-fall'n right,
The seat of Gaunt, dukedom of Lancaster.   45
To this we swore our aid. But in short space
It rain'd down fortune show'ring on your head,
And such a flood of greatness fell on you,
What with our help, what with the absent King,
What with the injuries of a wanton time,   50
The seeming sufferances that you had borne,
And the contrarious winds that held the King
So long in his unlucky Irish wars
That all in England did repute him dead;
And from this swarm of fair advantages   55
You took occasion to be quickly wooed
To gripe the general sway into your hand,
Forgot your oath to us at Doncaster,
And being fed by us you us'd us so
As that ungentle gull, the cuckoo's bird,   60
Useth the sparrow; did oppress our nest,
Grew by our feeding to so great a bulk
That even our love durst not come near your sight
For fear of swallowing; but with nimble wing
We were enforc'd for safety sake to fly   65
Out of your sight and raise this present head,
Whereby we stand opposed by such means
As you yourself have forg'd against yourself
By unkind usage, dangerous countenance,
And violation of all faith and troth   70
Sworn to us in your younger enterprise.
   King. These things indeed you have articulate,
Proclaim'd at market-crosses, read in churches,
To face the garment of rebellion
With some fine color that may please the eye   75
Of fickle changelings and poor discontents,
Which gape and rub the elbow at the news
Of hurly-burly innovation;
And never yet did insurrection want
Such water-colors to impaint his cause,   80
Nor moody beggars, starving for a time
Of pell-mell havoc and confusion.
   Prince. In both your armies there is many a soul
Shall pay full dearly for this encounter,
If once they join in trial. Tell your nephew   85

The Prince of Wales doth join with all the world
In praise of Henry Percy. By my hopes,
This present enterprise set off his head,
I do not think a braver gentleman,
More active, valiant, or more valiant, young,   90
More daring or more bold, is now alive
To grace this latter age with noble deeds.
For my part, I may speak it to my shame,
I have a truant been to chivalry,
And so I hear he doth account me too;   95
Yet this before my father's Majesty:
I am content that he shall take the odds
Of his great name and estimation,
And will, to save the blood on either side,
Try fortune with him in a single fight.   100
   King. And, Prince of Wales, so dare we venture
            thee,
Albeit considerations infinite
Do make against it. No, good Worcester, no,
We love our people well, even those we love
That are misled upon your cousin's part,   105
And, will they take the offer of our grace,
Both he and they and you, yea, every man
Shall be my friend again, and I'll be his.
So tell your cousin, and bring me word
What he will do. But if he will not yield,   110
Rebuke and dread correction wait on us,
And they shall do their office. So be gone;
We will not now be troubled with reply.
We offer fair, take it advisedly.
            Exit Worcester [with Vernon].
   Prince. It will not be accepted, on my life.   115
The Douglas and the Hotspur both together
Are confident against the world in arms.
   King. Hence therefore, every leader to his charge,
For on their answer will we set on them,
And God befriend us as our cause is just!   120
            Exeunt. Manent Prince, Falstaff.
   Fal. Hal, if thou see me down in the battle and be-
stride me, so; 'tis a point of friendship.
   Prince. Nothing but a Colossus can do thee that
friendship. Say thy prayers, and farewell.   124
   Fal. I would 'twere bed-time, Hal, and all well.
   Prince. Why, thou owest God a death.   [*Exit.*]
   Fal. 'Tis not due yet, I would be loath to pay him
before his day. What need I be so forward with him
that calls not on me? Well, 'tis no matter, honor pricks
me on. Yea, but how if honor prick me off when   130
I come on? how then? Can honor set to a leg? No.
Or an arm? No. Or take away the grief of a wound?
No. Honor hath no skill in surgery then? No. What
is honor? A word. What is in that word honor?
What is that honor? Air. A trim reckoning!   135
Who hath it? He that died a' Wednesday. Doth he
feel it? No. Doth he hear it? No. 'Tis insensible

42. **Doncaster:** town in Yorkshire. According to Holinshed (Bullough, III, 398), when Bullingbrook reached Doncaster, on his march
from Ravenspur, "the earle of Northumberland, and his sonne, sir
Henrie Persie, wardens of the marches against Scotland, with the earle
of Westmerland, came unto him, where he sware unto those lords
that he would demand no more, but the lands that were to him descended by inheritance from his father, and in right of his wife."
44. **new-fall'n:** recently inherited.   50. **injuries:** abuses.
51. **sufferances:** sufferings.   57. **gripe:** seize.
60. **ungentle gull:** rude nestling.
63. **our love:** we who loved you.
64. **swallowing:** i.e. being swallowed.
69. **unkind usage:** unnatural treatment.   **dangerous:** threatening.
70. **troth:** truth.   72. **articulate:** stated in articles.
74. **face:** trim.
76. **changelings:** turncoats.   **discontents:** malcontents.
77. **rub the elbow:** i.e. hug themselves with pleasure.
78. **innovation:** rebellion.
80. **water-colors:** i.e. thin excuses.
81. **moody:** sullen, disaffected.
83. **both:** i.e. the King's and the rebels'.

88. **This . . . head:** not counting his part in this rebellion.
89. **braver:** nobler.   98. **estimation:** renown.
100. **single fight.** The Prince's challenge was apparently Shakespeare's
own invention.   102. **Albeit:** although.   122. **so:** good.
126. **death:** with a homophonic pun on *debt*.   132. **grief:** pain.
135. **trim reckoning:** neat total.
137. **insensible:** imperceptible to the senses.

then? Yea, to the dead. But will['t] not live with the
living? No. Why? Detraction will not suffer it.
Therefore I'll none of it, honor is a mere scutcheon.
And so ends my catechism.   *Exit.*   141

[SCENE II]

Enter WORCESTER, SIR RICHARD VERNON.

Wor.   O no, my nephew must not know, Sir
    Richard,
The liberal and kind offer of the King.
  Ver.   'Twere best he did.
  Wor.   Then are we all [undone];
It is not possible, it cannot be,
The King should keep his word in loving us.   5
He will suspect us still, and find a time
To punish this offense in other faults.
Supposition all our lives shall be stuck full of eyes,
For treason is but trusted like the fox,
Who never so tame, so cherish'd and lock'd up,   10
Will have a wild trick of his ancestors.
Look how we can, or sad or merrily,
Interpretation will misquote our looks,
And we shall feed like oxen at a stall,
The better cherish'd, still the nearer death.   15
My nephew's trespass may be well forgot,
It hath the excuse of youth and heat of blood,
And an adopted name of privilege,
A hare-brain'd Hotspur, govern'd by a spleen.
All his offenses live upon my head   20
And on his father's. We did train him on,
And his corruption being ta'en from us,
We as the spring of all shall pay for all.
Therefore, good cousin, let not Harry know,
In any case, the offer of the King.   25
  Ver.   Deliver what you will, I'll say 'tis so.
Here comes your cousin.

Enter PERCY [HOTSPUR *and* DOUGLAS].

  Hot.   My uncle is return'd,
Deliver up my Lord of Westmerland.
Uncle, what news?
  Wor.   The King will bid you battle presently.   30
  Doug.   Defy him by the Lord of Westmerland.
  Hot.   Lord Douglas, go you and tell him so.
  Doug.   Marry, and shall, and very willingly.
                        Exit Douglas.
  Wor.   There is no seeming mercy in the King.
  Hot.   Did you beg any? God forbid!   35
  Wor.   I told him gently of our grievances,
Of his oath-breaking, which he mended thus,

---

140. **scutcheon:** heraldic device exhibited at funerals, on coaches, etc.

V.ii. Location: A plain near the rebel camp.
6. **still:** always.   8. **Supposition:** suspicion.
10. **never so:** however.
11. **wild trick:** i.e. trace of the characteristic wildness.
18. **adopted . . . privilege:** i.e. a nickname (Hotspur) that sanctions
rash behavior.   19. **spleen:** irrational impulse.
21. **train:** lure (into rebellion).   23. **spring:** source.
26. **Deliver:** report.
28. **Deliver up:** release.   **Westmerland.** The hostage mentioned at
IV.iii.108–9.   30. **presently:** at once.

By now forswearing that he is forsworn.
He calls us rebels, traitors, and will scourge
With haughty arms this hateful name in us.   40

Enter DOUGLAS.

  Doug.   Arm, gentlemen, to arms! for I have thrown
A brave defiance in King Henry's teeth,
And Westmerland, that was engag'd, did bear it,
Which cannot choose but bring him quickly on.
  Wor.   The Prince of Wales stepp'd forth before the
    King,   45
And, nephew, challeng'd you to single fight.
  Hot.   O would the quarrel lay upon our heads,
And that no man might draw short breath to-day
But I and Harry Monmouth! Tell me, tell me,
How show'd his tasking? seem'd it in contempt?   50
  Ver.   No, by my soul, I never in my life
Did hear a challenge urg'd more modestly,
Unless a brother should a brother dare
To gentle exercise and proof of arms.
He gave you all the duties of a man,   55
Trimm'd up your praises with a princely tongue,
Spoke your deservings like a chronicle,
Making you ever better than his praise
By still dispraising praise valued with you,
And which became him like a prince indeed,   60
He made a blushing cital of himself,
And chid his truant youth with such a grace
As if he mast'red there a double spirit
Of teaching and of learning instantly.
There did he pause, but let me tell the world,   65
If he outlive the envy of this day,
England did never owe so sweet a hope,
So much misconstrued in his wantonness.
  Hot.   Cousin, I think thou art enamored
On his follies. Never did I hear   70
Of any prince so wild a liberty.
But be he as he will, yet once ere night
I will embrace him with a soldier's arm
That he shall shrink under my courtesy.
Arm, arm with speed! and, fellows, soldiers, friends,
Better consider what you have to do   76
Than I, that have not well the gift of tongue,
Can lift your blood up with persuasion.

Enter a MESSENGER.

  Mess.   My lord, here are letters for you.
  Hot.   I cannot read them now.   80
O gentlemen, the time of life is short!
To spend that shortness basely were too long
If life did ride upon a dial's point,
Still ending at the arrival of an hour.
And if we live, we live to tread on kings,   85
If die, brave death, when princes die with us!

---

42. **brave:** haughty.
43. **engag'd:** held as hostage.   50. **tasking:** challenge.
52. **urg'd:** presented.   54. **proof:** test.   55. **duties:** due merits.
59. **dispraising:** disparaging, discounting.   **valued:** compared.
61. **cital:** impeachment.   64. **instantly:** simultaneously.
66. **envy:** malice.   67. **owe:** own.
71. **so . . . liberty:** such reckless dissipation.
83. **dial's point:** clock's hand.
84. **Still . . . hour:** i.e. lasting only for an hour.

Now for our consciences, the arms are fair
When the intent of bearing them is just.

Enter another [MESSENGER].

[2.] *Mess.* My lord, prepare, the King comes on
apace.

Hot. I thank him that he cuts me from my tale, 90
For I profess not talking; only this—
Let each man do his best, and here draw I
A sword, whose temper I intend to stain
With the best blood that I can meet withal
In the adventure of this perilous day. 95
Now *Esperance! Percy!* and set on.
Sound all the lofty instruments of war,
And by that music let us all embrace,
For, heaven to earth, some of us never shall
A second time do such a courtesy. 100

Here they embrace [*and exeunt*].

[SCENE III]

The trumpets sound. The KING *enters with his power*
[*and passes over*]. *Alarm to the battle. Then enter*
DOUGLAS *and* SIR WALTER BLUNT.

Blunt. What is thy name, that in battle thus
Thou crossest me? What honor dost thou seek
Upon my head?

Doug.   Know then, my name is Douglas,
And I do haunt thee in the battle thus
Because some tell me that thou art a king. 5

Blunt. They tell thee true.

Doug. The Lord of Stafford dear to-day hath
bought
Thy likeness, for in stead of thee, King Harry,
This sword hath ended him. So shall it thee,
Unless thou yield thee as my prisoner. 10

Blunt. I was not born a yielder, thou proud Scot,
And thou shalt find a king that will revenge
Lord Stafford's death.

They fight. Douglas kills Blunt.

Then enter HOTSPUR.

Hot. O Douglas, hadst thou fought at Holmedon
thus,
I never had triumph'd upon a Scot. 15

Doug. All's done, all's won, here breathless lies
the King.

Hot. Where?

Doug. Here.

Hot. This, Douglas? No, I know this face full
well.

87. **for:** as for.   **fair:** just.
99. **heaven to earth:** heaven wagered against earth.

V.iii. Location: Scene continues.
o.s.d. **power:** army.   **Alarm:** trumpet signal to advance.
10. **yield thee:** surrender yourself.
13. **Lord Stafford's death.** According to Holinshed (Bullough, IV,
190–91), Hotspur and Douglas, intent on killing the King, "gave such
a violent onset upon them that stood about the kings standard, that
slaieing his standard-bearer sir Walter Blunt, and overthrowing the
standard, they made slaughter of all those that stood about it, as the
earle of Stafford, that daie made by the king constable of the realme,
and diverse other."

A gallant knight he was, his name was Blunt, 20
Semblably furnish'd like the King himself.

Doug. [A] fool go with thy soul, whither it goes!
A borrowed title hast thou bought too dear.
Why didst thou tell me that thou wert a king? 24

Hot. The King hath many marching in his coats.

Doug. Now by my sword, I will kill all his coats;
I'll murder all his wardrop, piece by piece,
Until I meet the King.

Hot.   Up and away! 28
Our soldiers stand full fairly for the day. [*Exeunt.*]

Alarm. Enter FALSTAFF *solus*.

Fal. Though I could scape shot-free at London, I
fear the shot here, here's no scoring but upon the pate.
Soft, who are you? Sir Walter Blunt. There's honor
for you! Here's no vanity! I am as hot as molten lead,
and as heavy too. God keep lead out of me! I need no
more weight than mine own bowels. I have led 35
my ragamuffins where they are pepper'd; there's not
three of my hundred and fifty left alive, and they are
for the town's end, to beg during life. But who comes
here?

Enter the PRINCE.

Prince. What, stands thou idle here? Lend me thy
sword. 40
Many a nobleman lies stark and stiff
Under the hoofs of vaunting enemies,
Whose deaths are yet unreveng'd. I prithee lend me
thy sword.

Fal. O Hal, I prithee give me leave to breathe a
while. Turk Gregory never did such deeds in arms 45
as I have done this day. I have paid Percy, I have
made him sure.

Prince. He is indeed, and living to kill thee. I
prithee lend me thy sword. 49

Fal. Nay, before God, Hal, if Percy be alive, thou
gets not my sword, but take my pistol, if thou wilt.

Prince. Give it me. What? is it in the case?

Fal. Ay, Hal, 'tis hot, 'tis hot. There's that will
sack a city. 54

The Prince draws it out, and finds
it to be a bottle of sack.

Prince. What, is it a time to jest and dally now?

He throws the bottle at him. Exit.

Fal. Well, if Percy be alive, I'll pierce him. If he
do come in my way, so; if he do not, if I come in his

21. **Semblably furnish'd:** similarly armed and dressed (to serve as a
decoy).
22. **A fool . . . goes:** i.e. may the opprobrious epithet "fool" be attached to you, wherever you're going.
25. **The King . . . coats.** A common stratagem.
27. **wardrop:** wardrobe.
29. **stand . . . day:** i.e. seem to be upon the point of victory.
30. **shot-free:** i.e. without paying the shot, or tavern bill.
31. **scoring:** cutting (with a pun on scoring one's bill by making
notches on a stick).   33. **vanity:** trifling.
38. **town's end:** i.e. the city gate (where beggars congregated).
45. **Turk:** stock title for a merciless person.   **Gregory:** perhaps
Pope Gregory VII, who was famous for his valor.
46. **paid:** settled with, i.e. killed.
47. **made him sure:** made sure of him.
48. **He is:** i.e. he is sure (to be alive and dangerous).
56. **pierce.** Pronounced *perse*.

willingly, let him make a carbonado of me. I like not
such grinning honor as Sir Walter hath. Give me life,
which if I can save, so; if not, honor comes unlook'd
for, and there's an end.   [*Exit.*] 61

[SCENE IV]

Alarm. Excursions. Enter the KING, *the* PRINCE
[*wounded*], LORD JOHN OF LANCASTER, EARL OF
WESTMERLAND.

King. I prithee,
Harry, withdraw thyself, thou bleedest too much.
Lord John of Lancaster, go you with him.
  Lan. Not I, my lord, unless I did bleed too.
  Prince. I beseech your Majesty make up,   5
Lest your retirement do amaze your friends.
  King. I will do so.
My Lord of Westmerland, lead him to his tent.
  West. Come, my lord, I'll lead you to your tent.
  Prince. Lead me, my lord? I do not need your
      help,   10
And God forbid a shallow scratch should drive
The Prince of Wales from such a field as this,
Where stain'd nobility lies trodden on,
And rebels' arms triumph in massacres!
  Lan. We breathe too long. Come, cousin West-
      merland,   15
Our duty this way lies; for God's sake come.
            [*Exeunt Prince John and Westmerland.*]
  Prince. By God, thou hast deceiv'd me, Lancaster,
I did not think thee lord of such a spirit.
Before, I lov'd thee as a brother, John,
But now I do respect thee as my soul.   20
  King. I saw him hold Lord Percy at the point,
With lustier maintenance than I did look for
Of such an ungrown warrior.
  Prince.   O, this boy
Lends mettle to us all!   *Exit.*

[*Enter* DOUGLAS.]

  Doug. Another king? they grow like Hydra's
      heads.   25
I am the Douglas, fatal to all those
That wear those colors on them. What art thou
That counterfeit'st the person of a king?
  King. The King himself, who, Douglas, grieves at
      heart
So many of his shadows thou hast met   30

And not the very King. I have two boys
Seek Percy and thyself about the field,
But seeing thou fall'st on me so luckily,
I will assay thee, and defend thyself.
  Doug. I fear thou art another counterfeit,   35
And yet in faith thou bearest thee like a king.
But mine I am sure thou art, whoe'er thou be,
And thus I win thee.

They fight; the King being in danger, enter PRINCE OF
WALES.

  Prince. Hold up thy head, vile Scot, or thou art like
Never to hold it up again! The spirits   40
Of valiant Shirley, Stafford, Blunt are in my arms.
It is the Prince of Wales that threatens thee,
Who never promiseth but he means to pay.
                        They fight: Douglas flieth.
Cheerly, my lord, how fares your Grace?
Sir Nicholas Gawsey hath for succor sent,   45
And so hath Clifton. I'll to Clifton straight.
  King. Stay and breathe a while.
Thou hast redeem'd thy lost opinion,
And show'd thou mak'st some tender of my life
In this fair rescue thou hast brought to me.   50
  Prince. O God, they did me too much injury
That ever said I heark'ned for your death.
If it were so, I might have let alone
The insulting hand of Douglas over you,
Which would have been as speedy in your end   55
As all the poisonous potions in the world,
And sav'd the treacherous labor of your son.
  King. Make up to Clifton, I'll to Sir Nicholas
      Gawsey.   *Exit King.*

Enter HOTSPUR.

  Hot. If I mistake not, thou art Harry Monmouth.
  Prince. Thou speak'st as if I would deny my name.
  Hot. My name is Harry Percy.
  Prince.   Why then I see
A very valiant rebel of the name.   62
I am the Prince of Wales, and think not, Percy,
To share with me in glory any more.
Two stars keep not their motion in one sphere,   65
Nor can one England brook a double reign
Of Harry Percy and the Prince of Wales.
  Hot. [Nor] shall it, Harry, for the hour is come
To end the one of us, and would to God
Thy name in arms were now as great as mine!   70
  Prince. I'll make it greater ere I part from thee,
And all the budding honors on thy crest
I'll crop to make a garland for my head.
  Hot. I can no longer brook thy vanities.
                                    They fight.

58. **carbonado:** meat slashed for broiling.

V.iv. Location: Scene continues.
o.s.d. **Excursions:** sallies, sorties.   5. **make up:** advance.
6. **amaze:** dismay.
13. **stain'd:** (1) soiled with battle; (2) disgraced.
15. **breathe:** pause for breath.
22. **lustier maintenance:** more valiant endurance.
25. **Hydra:** in Greek mythology, a many-headed monster that grew
two new heads for each one struck off. Holinshed (Bullough, IV,
191) reports that Douglas "slue sir Walter Blunt, and three other,
apparelled in the kings sute and clothing, saieng: I marvell to see so
many kings thus suddenlie arise one in the necke of an other."
27. **those colors:** i.e. the colors of the King's coat of arms.
30. **shadows:** likenesses.

31. **the very King:** the King himself.   32. **Seek:** who seek.
34. **assay:** challenge.
41, 45, 46. **Shirley, Gawsey, Clifton.** Holinshed (Bullough, IV, 191)
mentions "sir Hugh Shorlie," "sir Nicholas Gausell," and "sir John
Clifton" as notable casualties of the battle of Shrewsbury.
44 s.d. **They . . . flieth.** Holinshed (Bullough, IV, 191) records the
tradition that the King was struck down by Douglas but does not
assign his rescue to the Prince, saying only that the King "was raised."
48. **opinion:** reputation.   49. **mak'st . . . of:** hast some regard for.
54. **insulting:** exulting.   66. **brook:** endure.

1 Henry IV
V.iv

Enter FALSTAFF.

Fal. Well said, Hal! to it, Hal! Nay, you shall find
no boy's play here, I can tell you.   76

Enter DOUGLAS; *he fighteth with Falstaff. He* [Falstaff]
falls down as if he were dead [and exit Douglas]. *The
Prince killeth Percy.*

Hot. O Harry, thou hast robb'd me of my youth!
I better brook the loss of brittle life
Than those proud titles thou hast won of me.
They wound my thoughts worse than thy sword my
          flesh.   80
But thoughts, the slaves of life, and life, time's fool,
And time, that takes survey of all the world,
Must have a stop. O, I could prophesy,
But that the earthy and cold hand of death
Lies on my tongue. No, Percy, thou art dust,   85
And food for—   [*Dies.*]
     Prince. For worms, brave Percy. Fare thee well,
          great heart!
Ill-weav'd ambition, how much art thou shrunk!
When that this body did contain a spirit,
A kingdom for it was too small a bound,   90
But now two paces of the vilest earth
Is room enough. This earth that bears [thee] dead
Bears not alive so stout a gentleman.
If thou wert sensible of courtesy,
I should not make so dear a show of zeal;   95
But let my favors hide thy mangled face,
And even in thy behalf I'll thank myself
For doing these fair rites of tenderness.
Adieu, and take thy praise with thee to heaven!
Thy ignominy sleep with thee in the grave,   100
But not rememb'red in thy epitaph!
               He spieth Falstaff on the ground.
What, old acquaintance! could not all this flesh
Keep in a little life? Poor Jack, farewell!
I could have better spar'd a better man.
O, I should have a heavy miss of thee   105
If I were much in love with vanity!
Death hath not strook so fat a deer to-day,
Though many dearer, in this bloody fray.
Embowell'd will I see thee by and by,
Till then in blood by noble Percy lie.   110
               Exit. Falstaff riseth up.
     Fal. Embowell'd! if thou embowel me to-day, I'll
give you leave to powder me and eat me too to-
morrow. 'Sblood, 'twas time to counterfeit, or that hot
termagant Scot had paid me scot and lot too. Counterfeit? I lie, I am no counterfeit. To die is to be a   115
counterfeit, for he is but the counterfeit of a man who
hath not the life of a man; but to counterfeit dying,

when a man thereby liveth, is to be no counterfeit, but
the true and perfect image of life indeed. The better
part of valor is discretion, in the which better part   120
I have sav'd my life. 'Zounds, I am afraid of this gunpowder Percy though he be dead. How if he should
counterfeit too and rise? By my faith, I am afraid he
would prove the better counterfeit. Therefore I'll
make him sure, yea, and I'll swear I kill'd him.   125
Why may not he rise as well as I? Nothing confutes
me but eyes, and nobody sees me. Therefore, sirrah
[*stabbing him*], with a new wound in your thigh, come
you along with me.   *He takes up Hotspur on his back.*

Enter PRINCE [and] JOHN OF LANCASTER.

     Prince. Come, brother John, full bravely hast thou
          flesh'd   130
Thy maiden sword.
     Lan.   But soft, whom have we here?
Did you not tell me this fat man was dead?
     Prince. I did, I saw him dead,
Breathless and bleeding on the ground. Art thou alive?
Or is it fantasy that plays upon our eyesight?   135
I prithee speak, we will not trust our eyes
Without our ears: thou art not what thou seem'st.
     Fal. No, that's certain, I am not a double man; but
if I be not Jack Falstaff, then am I a Jack. There is
Percy [*throwing the body down*]. If your father will do
me any honor, so; if not, let him kill the next Percy
himself. I look to be either earl or duke, I can assure
you.   143
     Prince. Why, Percy I kill'd myself, and saw thee
          dead.
     Fal. Didst thou? Lord, Lord, how this world is
given to lying! I grant you I was down and out   146
of breath, and so was he, but we rose both at an instant
and fought a long hour by Shrewsbury clock. If I may
be believ'd, so; if not, let them that should reward
valor bear the sin upon their own heads. I'll take it
upon my death, I gave him this wound in the thigh.   151
If the man were alive and would deny it, 'zounds,
I would make him eat a piece of my sword.
     Lan. This is the strangest tale that ever I heard.
     Prince. This is the strangest fellow, brother John.
Come bring your luggage nobly on your back.   156
For my part, if a lie may do thee grace,
I'll gild it with the happiest terms I have.
                    A retrait is sounded.
The trumpet sounds retreat, the day is our.
Come, brother, let us to the highest of the field,   160
To see what friends are living, who are dead.
                    Exeunt [Prince and Lancaster].
     Fal. I'll follow, as they say, for reward. He that
rewards me, God reward him! If I do grow great, I'll
grow less, for I'll purge and leave sack, and live
cleanly as a nobleman should do.   *Exit.* 165

83. **I could prophesy.** Dying men were thought to have the gift of prophecy.
86 s.d. **Dies.** Holinshed (Bullough, IV, 191) does not credit the Prince with Hotspur's death, saying merely that those loyal to the King, "incouraged by his doings, fought valiantlie, and slue the lord Persie, called sir Henrie Hotspurre." 93. **stout:** brave.
95. **make . . . zeal:** i.e. express my admiration so freely.
96. **favors:** scarves, gloves, plumes, or the like (with which the Prince covers Hotspur's "mangled face"). 106. **vanity:** frivolity.
109. **Embowell'd:** disembowelled (for embalming).
112. **powder:** salt.   114. **termagant:** violent.
114. **scot and lot:** completely.

120. **part:** quality.
130. **flesh'd:** initiated (with the first taste of blood).
138. **double man:** (1) spectre; (2) two men.   139. **Jack:** rascal.
157. **grace:** credit.
158 s.d. **retrait:** retreat, trumpet signal to withdraw.
159. **our:** ours.   160. **highest:** highest point.
164. **purge:** (1) take laxatives (to reduce); (2) purge my sins, i.e. repent.

[SCENE V]

The trumpets sound. Enter the KING, PRINCE OF WALES,
LORD JOHN OF LANCASTER, EARL OF WESTMERLAND,
with WORCESTER *and* VERNON *prisoners.*

King.   Thus ever did rebellion find rebuke.
Ill-spirited Worcester, did not we send grace,
Pardon, and terms of love to all of you?
And wouldst thou turn our offers contrary?
Misuse the tenor of thy kinsman's trust?   5
Three knights upon our party slain to-day,
A noble earl, and many a creature else
Had been alive this hour,
If like a Christian thou hadst truly borne
Betwixt our armies true intelligence.   10
    Wor.   What I have done my safety urg'd me to;
And I embrace this fortune patiently,
Since not to be avoided it falls on me.
    King.   Bear Worcester to the death and Vernon
        too.
Other offenders we will pause upon.   15
            [*Exeunt Worcester and Vernon guarded.*]
How goes the field?
    Prince.   The noble Scot, Lord Douglas, when he
        saw
The fortune of the day quite turn'd from him,
The noble Percy slain, and all his men
Upon the foot of fear, fled with the rest,   20

And falling from a hill, he was so bruis'd
That the pursuers took him. At my tent
The Douglas is; and I beseech your Grace
I may dispose of him.
    King.   With all my heart.
    Prince.   Then, brother John of Lancaster, to you
This honorable bounty shall belong.   26
Go to the Douglas, and deliver him
Up to his pleasure, ransomless and free.
His valors shown upon our crests to-day
Have taught us how to cherish such high deeds   30
Even in the bosom of our adversaries.
    Lan.   I thank your Grace for this high courtesy,
Which I shall give away immediately.
    King.   Then this remains, that we divide our
        power.
You, son John, and my cousin Westmerland   35
Towards York shall bend you with your dearest speed,
To meet Northumberland and the prelate Scroop,
Who, as we hear, are busily in arms.
Myself and you, son Harry, will towards Wales,
To fight with Glendower and the Earl of March.   40
Rebellion in this land shall lose his sway,
Meeting the check of such another day,
And since this business so fair is done,
Let us not leave till all our own be won.   *Exeunt.*

V.v. Location: The command post of the King.
2. **grace:** assurance of favor.
3. **terms of love:** expressions of friendship.
5. **Misuse . . . trust:** i.e. abuse Hotspur's confidence in you (as emissaries).   10. **intelligence:** information.
12. **patiently:** tranquilly.   15. **pause upon:** reflect about.
20. **Upon . . . fear:** fleeing in terror.

21–22. **falling . . . him.** According to Holinshed (Bullough, IV, 191), "the earle of Dowglas, for hast, falling from the crag of an hie mounteine, brake one of his cullions [testicles], and was taken, and for his valiantnesse, of the king frankelie and freelie delivered."
24. **dispose of him:** decide what to do with him.
26. **honorable bounty:** gracious assignment.   27. **deliver:** release.
33. **give away:** i.e. inform Douglas of.   34. **power:** army.
36. **dearest:** most zealous.   43. **fair:** successfully.

NOTE ON THE TEXT

The First Part of Henry the Fourth was first published in quarto in 1598. Of this edition (here referred to as Q0) only a single sheet (C) now exists. A second edition, printed in the same year from a copy of Q0, is now generally known as the First Quarto (Q1) and is here used as copy-text, except for I.iii.201–II.ii.111, where Q0 serves as copy-text. Judging by the section of text common to Q0 and Q1, Q1 appears, despite three substantive variants (one, at least, a correction), to be a careful reprint of Q0. Later quartos, each printed from the one immediately preceding, appeared in 1599 (Q2), 1604 (Q3), 1608 (Q4), 1613 (Q5), and 1622 (Q6). After the play had appeared in the First Folio (1623), printed from an edited copy of Q5, two more quarto editions were published, 1632 (Q7) and 1639 (Q8).

The basis of Q0 is believed to be either Shakespeare's "foul papers" or a transcript from them by another hand. The rather pedantic use of uncontracted and generally less colloquial forms, particularly in the prose comic scenes, and the relative scarcity of characteristic Shakespearean spellings would appear to favor the use of a scribal transcript, but no final verdict seems possible on the evidence.

Aside from the errors inherited from its copy-text (Q5), the F1 text offers a number of slight textual variations, especially in the careful deletion or softening of oaths, but it is

not believed that these changes have any dependence on manuscript or prompt-book authority. They suggest rather the hand of a "literary" editor or, apart from the expurgations, the sorts of departures from copy which have come to be associated with Folio Compositor B. All significant variants in F1, and all its additions and omissions, have been recorded in the Textual Notes.

In addition to the early printed texts there exists a manuscript version (called the Dering MS, now in the Folger Shakespeare Library) which telescopes the two parts of *Henry IV* into a single play of roughly 3,390 lines. Precisely when the transcript was made (from a copy of Q5 for *1 Henry IV* and of Q [1600] for *2 Henry IV*) is uncertain, but the most likely date is about 1622. Although it has no independent authority, the textual variants stemming presumably from Sir Edward Dering himself, the manuscript affords occasional helpful stage directions and readings, and a few references to it will be found in the Textual Notes. Absence of citation for the Dering MS must not be interpreted as implying agreement with the lemma.

For further information, see: S. B. Hemingway, ed., New Variorum *1 Henry IV* (Philadelphia, 1936), and G. B. Evans, ed., Supplement to New Variorum *1 Henry IV* (Shakespeare Association of America, 1956); Alice Walker, "The Folio

Text of *1 Henry IV*," *SB*, VI (1954), 45–59; W. W. Greg, *The Shakespeare First Folio* (Oxford, 1955); G. B. Evans, "The 'Dering MS' of Shakespeare's *Henry IV* and Sir Edward Dering," *JEGP*, LIV (1955), 498–503; A. R. Humphreys, ed., New Arden *1 Henry IV* (London, 1960); Charlton Hinman (and W. W. Greg), eds., *Henry IV, Part I* (*1598*), facsimile of Q1 (Oxford, 1966); G. W. Williams and G. B. Evans, eds., *William Shakespeare, "The History of King Henry the Fourth," As Revised by Sir Edward Dering, Bart.* (Folger Facsimiles, 1974).

TEXTUAL NOTES

Title: The First . . . Fourth] The History of Henrie the Fourth; With the battell at Shrewsburie, betweene the King and Lord Henry Percy, surnamed Henrie Hotspur of the North. With the humorous conceits of Sir Iohn Falstalffe. *Q1 (title-page)*; The First Part of Henry the Fourth, with the Life and Death of Henry Sirnamed Hot-Spurre *F1*
Dramatis personae: *subs. as first given by Rowe*
Act-scene division: *none in Q0, Q1–6; from F1, with the following exceptions: V.iii (no scene division in F1); V.iv, v (numbered V.iii, iv in F1); see first note to each scene; present act-scene arrangement as a whole first established by Capell*

I.i

I.i] *F1*
Location: *Capell (after Pope, Theobald)*
o.s.d. **Sir Walter Blunt]** *Capell*
8 **flow'rets]** *F1 (Flowrets)*; flourets *Q1–5*; flowers *Q6*
17 **ill-sheathed]** *hyphen, F2*
22 **levy]** *Q2–6, F1*; leauy *Q1*
32 **Council]** *F1*; counsell *Q1–6*
39 **Herfordshire]** *Q7*; Herdfordshire *Q1–3*; Herdfordshire *Q4–5*; Herefordshire *Q6, F1*
42 **A]** And a *F1*
43 **corpse']** *W. S. Walker conj.*; corpes *Q1, F1*; corps *Q2–6*
52 **Holy-rood]** *Q2–6, F1 (subs.)*; holly rode *Q1*
53 **Archibald]** *Q5–6, F1*; Archibold *Q1–4*
62 **a dear]** *Q5–6, F1*; deere *Q1–4*
69 **blood,]** *Q7*; bloud. *Q1–4*; blood *Q5–6, F1*
70 **plains.]** *F1*; plaines, *Q1–4*; plaines: *Q5*; plaine: *Q6*
73 **Murray]** *Capell*; Murrey *Q1–6*; Murry *F1*
76–7 **West. In . . . of.]** *as in Steevens (after Pope)*; *Q1–6, F1 continue* In . . . is. *to King Henry and begin Westmerland's speech with* A conquest (*in Q1 there is enough space between* not? *and* In *to admit the s.p.* West. *as it appears in the next line*)
87 **night-tripping]** *hyphen, Q2–6, F1*
94 **use he keeps,]** *Q3–6, F1*; vse, he keepes *Q1–2*
104 **so]** and so *F1*

I.ii

I.ii] *F1*
Location: *Sisson (after Theobald)*
4 **after noon]** in the afternoone *F1*
15–6 **"that . . . fair."]** *quotes, Capell*
20 **by my troth]** *om. F1 (oaths are generally om. or softened in F1)*
22 **Come,]** *Theobald*; come *Q1–6, F1*
33 **moon.]** *Q5–6, F1 (subs.)*; moone, *Q1–4*
33 **proof, now:]** *Rowe*; proofe. Now *Q1–6, F1*
39 **By the Lord]** *om. F1*
41 **As]** As is *F1*
58 **apparent—]** *Rowe*, apparant: *Q1–6, F1*
61 **law?]** *F1*; law, *Q1–2*; law: *Q3–6*
64 **By the Lord]** *om. F1*
69 **Hal]** *Q2–5, F1*; Hall *Q1, Q6 (this form appears sporadically throughout the Qq; not hereafter recorded)*
73 **'Sblood]** *om. F1*
79 **similes]** *Q5*; smiles *Q1–4, Q6, F1*
82 **to God]** *om. F1*
88–9 **wisdom . . . and]** *om. F1*
100 **'Zounds]** *om. F1*
106 **Poins! Now]** *Theobald (subs.)*; Poynes now *Q1*; Poynes, now *Q2–3*; *Poines.* Now *Q4–6, F1 (taking* Poines. *as s.p.)*

107 **match]** Watch *F1*
113–4 **Sack . . . Jack,]** *Rowe* (Jack, *from Capell*); Sacke, and Sugar Iacke? *Q1–4*; Sacke and Sugar, Iacke? *Q5–6*; Sacke and Sugar: Iacke? *F1*
130 **night]** *om. F1*
131 **sleep.]** *Q2–6, F1 (subs.)*; sleepe, *Q1*
136 **chops?]** *Q7*; chops. *Q1–6, F1*
138 **Who, I rob?]** *Q2–6, F1*; Who I rob, *Q1*
138 **by my faith]** *om. F1*
146 **By the Lord]** *om. F1*
152–3 **God give thee . . . him]** maist thou haue . . . he *F1*
159 s.d. **Exit Falstaff.]** *F2*
162 **Falstaff]** *Q6, F1*; Falstalffe *Q1–5* (*the most frequent form throughout; not hereafter recorded*)
162 **Bardolph, Peto]** *Theobald*; Haruey, Rossill *Q1–6, F1* (*Dering MS substitutes* Peto *for Rossill and, in l. 163,* Bardolph *for* Gadshill)
190 **lives]** lyes *Q2–6, F1*
204 **holidays]** *F1*; holly-dayes *Q1–3*; holy daies *Q4–6*

I.iii

I.iii] *F1*
Location: *Theobald*
23 **name]** *om. F1*
26, 28 **is]** was *F1*
27 **Either envy, therefore]** Who either through enuy *F1*
42 **bore]** bare *F1*
46 **holiday]** *Q5, F1*; holly-day *Q1*; holy-day *Q2–3*; holy day *Q6*
52 **what—]** *Kittredge*; what *Q1*; what, *Q2–6, F1*
60 **This]** That *F1*
66 **I answered]** Made me to answer *F1*
95 **war;]** *Q2–6, F1 (subs.)*; war, *Q1*
96 **tongue]** *Hanmer*; tongue: *Q1–6, F1*
98 **sedgy]** *F4*; siedgie *Q1–6, F1*
106 **crisp head]** *Johnson*; crispe-head *Q1–6, F1*; Crise-pe head *Dering MS*
108 **bare]** base *F1*
124 s.d. **with . . . Train]** *Capell (subs.)*
128 **Albeit . . . a]** Although it be with *F1*
129 **drunk]** *Q2–6, F1*; dronk *Q1*
131 **'Zounds]** Yes *F1*
133 **Yea . . . part]** In his behalfe *F1*
135 **down-trod]** downfall *F1*
145 **not he]** he not *F1*
159 **starve]** staru'd *F1*
162 **wear]** wore *F1*
194 **good night]** *Q4–6, F1*; god-night *Q1*; good-night *Q2–3*
194 **swim.]** *F1 (subs.)*; swim, *Q1–3*; swime, *Q4*; swimd, *Q5–6*
201] *Beginning with this line and continuing through II.ii.111, the copy-text is Q0 (see "Note on the Text")*
201 s.p. **Hot.]** *Q5–6, F1; lines continued to Northumberland, Q0, Q1–4*
204 **fadom-line]** *hyphen, Q5–6, F1*
208 **half-fac'd]** *hyphen, F1*
211 **a while.]** a-while, / And list to me. *F1*
214 **God]** heauen *F1*
230 **sword-and-buckler]** *hyphens, Pope*
233 **him poisoned]** poyson'd him *F1*
236 **wasp-stung]** waspe-tongue *Q2–6*; Waspe-tongu'd *F1*
239 **whipt]** *Q1–6, F1*; whip *Q0*
244 **kept—]** *Rowe*; kept *Q0, Q1–2*; kept, *Q3–6, F1*
245 **bow'd]** *F1*; bowed *Q0, Q1–6*
247 **'Sblood]** *om. F1*

256 **I]** for I *F1*
258 **i' faith]** insooth *F1*
264 **granted. You]** *Thirlby conj.*; granted you *Q0, Q1, Q4*; granted you, *Q2–3, Q5–6, F1*
264 s.d. **To Northumberland.]** *Thirlby conj.*
281 **ha?]** *Capell*; ha. *Q0, Q1–6, F1*
293 **course.]** *Rowe (subs.)*; course *Q0, Q1–6, F1*

II.i

II.i] *F1*
Location: *Capell (after Theobald)*
4 s.d. **Within.]** *Theobald*
6 **Poor]** the poore *F1*
6 **wrung]** *Q2–6, F1*; wroong *Q0, Q1*
9 **that]** this *F1*
10 **ostler]** the Ostler *F1*
14 **be]** to be *Q5–6*; is *F1*
16 **by the mass]** *om. F1*
17 **christen]** in Christendome *F1*
26 **God's body]** *om. F1*
33 s.p. **1. Car.]** *Hanmer*; Car: *Q0, Q1–6, F1*
36 **by God, soft]** *Q7*; by God soft *Q0, Q1–6*; soft I pray ye *F1*
37 **i' faith]** *om. F1*
39 **when,]** *Q2–6, F1*; when *Q0, Q1*
40 **quoth he!]** *Cowl*; (quoth he) *Q0, Q1–6*; (quoth-a) *F1*
44 **thee.]** *Q2–6, F1*; thee, *Q0, Q1*
46 s.d. **Carriers]** *Rowe*
47 s.d. **Enter Chamberlain.]** *placed as in Kittredge; after l. 46, Q0, Q1–6, F1*
49 **as—]** *Capell*; as *Q0, Q1–6, F1*
55 **franklin]** *Q5–6, F1*; Frankelin *Q0, Q1–4*
64 **Saint]** *Q1–6*; Saine *Q0*; S. *F1*
73 **foot land-rakers]** *Hanmer*; footland rakers *Q0, Q1–3*; foot-landrakers *Q4*; foot-land rakers *Q5–6*; Foot-land-Rakers *F1*
76 **oney'rs]** *M. Spevack (privately)*; Oneyres *Q0, Q1*; Oneyers *Q2–6, F1*
79 **'zounds]** *om. F1*
80 **to]** vnto *F1*
81 **not]** not to *F1*
81 **prey]** *Q5–6, F1*; pray *Q0, Q1–4*
88 **by my faith]** *om. F1*
88 **think]** thinke rather *F1*
89 **than to]** then to the *F1*
92 **purchase]** purpose *F1*
96 **my]** the *F1*
97 s.d. **Exeunt.]** *F1*

II.ii

II.ii] *F1*
Location: *Cambridge (after Pope)*
o.s.d. **Enter . . . behind.]** *Wilson (subs.)*; Enter Prince, Poines, and Peto, &c. *Q0, Q1–6, (om. &c.) F1*
3 s.d. **They retire.]** *Dyce*
4 **hang'd! Poins!]** *Capell*; hangd Poynes. *Q0, Q1–6, F1*
5 s.d. **Coming forward.]** *Dyce*
9 s.d. **Retires.]** *Dyce*
11 **The]** that *F1*
12 **squier]** *Cambridge*; squire *Q0, Q1–6, F1*
13 **afoot]** *Q2*; a foote *Q0, Q1, Q3–6, F1 (not hereafter recorded unless ambiguous)*
16 **two and twenty]** *Dering MS, F1*; xxii: *Q0, Q1–4*; 22. *Q5–6*
21 **Bardolph]** *Dering MS, F1*; Bardol *Q0*; Bardoll *F1 (throughout)*
21 **I'll rob]** I rob *F1*
22 **as drink]** as to drinke *F1*
23 **true man]** *Q3–6*; true-man *Q0, Q1–2, F1*
26 **stony-hearted]** *hyphen, Dering MS, F1*
29 **upon]** light vpon *F1*
29 **me]** *om. F1*
31 s.d. **Coming forward.]** *Dyce*

31 **fat-guts**] hyphen, *Capell*
35 **'Sblood**] *om. F1*
35 **my**] mine *Q1–6, F1*
40 **prince—Hal!—**] *ed.;* prince, Hall, *Q0*; prince, Hal, *Q1–2;* prince Hal, *Q3–6, F1*
46 **poison.**] *Q2–6, F1 (subs.);* poyson, *Q0, Q1*
50 s.d. **Coming . . . Peto.**] *Dyce*
52 **Bard. What news?**] *Johnson conj.;* Bardoll, what newes. *Q0, Q1–6;* Bardolfe, what newes? *F1 (continued to Poins, Q0, Q1–6, F1)*
53 s.p. **Gads.**] *Johnson;* Bar. *Q0, Q1–6, F1*
61 **Poins**] *om. F1*
63 **be there**] be they *Q2–6;* be *F1*
65 **'Zounds**] *om. F1*
67,73 s.p. **Fal.**] *Q1–6 (subs.), F1;* Fast. *Q0*
69 **Well**] *om. F1*
74 s.d. **Aside.**] *Collier*
75 s.d. **Aside.**] *Dyce*
75 s.d. **Exeunt . . . Poins.**] *Malone (after Capell)*
78, 86 s.pp. **1. Trav.**] *Capell;* Trauel. *and* Tra. *Q0, Q1–6, F1*
82 s.p. **Travellers.**] *Dyce;* Trauel. *Q0, Q1–6, F1*
84 **Ah**] *Rowe;* a *Q0, Q1–6*
92 s.d. **in buckram**] *Dyce*
101 s.d. **As . . . them.**] *after l. 103, F1 (om. and Falstaff . . . too,)*
104–10 **Got . . . him.**] *as verse, Pope; as prose, Q0, Q1–6, F1*
110 **Were't**] *Q2–3, F1;* wert *Q0, Q1, Q4–6*
111 **fat**] *om. Q1–6, F1; the fragment of Q0 ends with this line*

II.iii *F1*
Location: *Capell*
14 **so?**] *Rowe;* so, *Q1, Q5–6;* so. *Q2–4;* so: *F1*
16 **lack-brain**] hyphen, *Q2–6, F1*
16 **By the Lord**] I protest *F1*
17 **a good**] as good a *F1*
20 **frosty-spirited**] hyphen, *F1*
22 **'Zounds**] By this hand *F1*
22 **and**] if *F1*
33 **skim-milk**] skim'd Milk *F1*
34 **King**] *Hanmer;* king, *Q1–6;* King *F1*
48 **thee murmur**] *Q2–6, F1;* the murmur, *Q1*
50 **"Courage! . . . field!"**] *Rowe (subs.);* courage to the field. *Q1–6, F1*
51 **retires,**] *Q3–6;* retyres *Q1–2;* Retires; *F1*
51 **of trenches,**] *Q2–3;* of trenches *Q1;* trenches *Q4–6, F1*
59 **late-disturbed**] hyphen, *F1*
65 s.d. **Enter Servant.**] *Dering MS, Rowe*
66 **ago**] agone *F1*
69 **horse?**] *Q3–6, F1;* horse, *Q1–2*
69 **Roan?**] a roane *Q3–5, F1;* roane, *Q6*
70–2 **That . . . park.**] *as verse, Pope; as prose, Q1–6, F1*
71 **O Esperance!**] *Pope;* O Esperance, *Q1–4;* Esperance, *Q5–6, F1 (all three in italics)*
72 s.d. **Exit Servant.**] *Dering MS, Hanmer*
77–83 **Out . . . go—**] *as verse, Pope; as prose, Q1–6, F1*
79 **faith**] sooth *F1*
85–8 **Come . . . true.**] *as verse, Pope; as prose, Q1–6, F1*
87 **In faith**] Indeede *F1*
88 **And**] *om. F1*
88 **all things**] *om. F1*
90 **trifler! Love,**] *ed. (after F1* trifler: Loue,); trifler, loue, *Q1–3;* trifler, loue, *Q4–6*
113 **How!**] *Theobald;* How, *Q1–6;* How *F1*
113 **far?**] *Q2–6, F1;* far. *Q1*

II.iv *F1*
Location: *Theobald (after Pope)*
4 **amongst**] *Q2, Q4–6;* amongst *Q1, Q3*
6 **base-string**] hyphen, *Dering MS, Dyce*
7 **all**] *om. F1*
9 **salvation**] confidence *F1*
11 **and tell**] telling *F1*
12 **mettle**] *F1;* metall *Q1–6*
13 **(by . . . me!)**] *om. F1*
16 **they**] then they *F1*
33 **president**] *F1;* present *Q1–6*
33 s.d. **Exit Poins.**] *Dyce (after Theobald)*

34, 36 s.dd. **Within.**] *Dyce*
36 s.p. **Poins.**] *Q4–6, F1;* Prin. *Q1–3*
43, 51, 56, 63, 77 s.dd. **Within.**] *Capell*
52 **Anon**] Anon, anon *F1*
60 **Lord**] Lord sir *F1*
69 **leathern-jerkin**] hyphen, *Pope*
69–70 **crystal-button**] hyphen, *Pope*
70 **agate-ring**] hyphen, *Dering MS, Rowe*
70 **puke-stocking**] hyphen, *Dering MS, Rowe*
70–1 **caddis-garter**] hyphen, *Dering MS, Rowe*
71 **smooth-tongue**] hyphen, *Theobald*
71 **Spanish-pouch—**] *Capell (hyphen, Pope);* spanish pouch? *Q1–6;* Spanish pouch. *F1*
78 **not**] *om. F1*
81 s.d. **Exit Francis.**] *Johnson (subs.)*
85 s.d. **Exit Vintner.**] *Dering MS, Theobald*
86 s.d. **Within.**] *Neilson*
93 **goodman**] *Q2–5, F1;* good man *Q1, Q6*
95 s.d. **Enter . . . wine.**] *Malone (subs., after Capell); Dering MS has Francis speak from within*
97 s.d. **Exit.**] *Collier*
112 s.d. **Gadshill . . . wine**] *Dyce (Gadshill, Bardolph, and Peto added by Theobald)*
117 **and foot them**] *om. F1*
122 **sun's?**] *Cambridge;* sonnes, *Q1;* sonnes? *Q2;* sunne? *Q3–6, F1*
132 **while!**] *Theobald;* while, *Q1–6, F1*
133–4 **psalms . . . thing**] all manner of songs *F1*
139 **more.**] *F1;* more, *Q1–6*
139 **You,**] *Wilson;* you *Q1–6*
139 **Wales!**] *T. Johnson (in Variorum);* Wales. *Q1–6;* Wales? *F1*
140 **round man**] *Q4–6, F1;* round-man *Q1–3*
144 **'Zounds**] *om. F1*
145 **by the Lord**] *om. F1*
173 s.p. **Prince.**] *F1;* Gad *Q1–6*
174, 176, 180 s.pp. **Gads.**] *F1;* Ross. *Q1–6 (see note on I.ii.162)*
189 **God**] Heauen *F1*
194 **face,**] *F1;* face; *Q1–6*
194 **horse.**] *Q2–6, F1 (horse:);* horse, *Q1*
197 **What,**] *Q2–6, F1;* What *Q1*
200 **afront**] *Q2–4;* a front *Q1, Q5–6;* a-front *F1*
204 **buckrom?**] *Capell;* Buckrom. *Q1–6, F1*
209 **Dost**] *Rowe;* Doest *Q1–6, F1 (so several times, especially in Falstaff's speeches; not hereafter recorded)*
210 **too, Jack**] *Q2–6, F1;* to iacke *Q1*
236 **'Zounds . . . were**] No: were I *F1*
244 **'Sblood**] Away *F1*
244 **eel-skin**] *Hanmer;* elsskin *Q1–2;* elfskin *Q3–6, F1*
257 **here**] *om. F1*
260 **run**] ranne *F1*
263 **starting-hole**] hyphen, *Hanmer*
267 **By the Lord**] *om. F1*
272 **prince.**] *F1 (subs.);* prince, *Q1–6*
275 **by the Lord**] *om. F1*
278 **titles of good**] good Titles of *F1*
283 **Ah**] *Rowe;* A *Q1–6, F1*
284 **O Jesu**] *om. F1*
287 **nobleman**] *Q2–3 (subs.);* noble man *Q1, Q4–6, F1*
303 **Faith**] *om. F1*
320 s.d. **Pointing . . . face.**] *White*
326 **bare-bone**] hyphen, *Q3–6, F1*
329 **knee?**] *F1;* knee, *Q1–6*
340 **O,**] *Q2–5;* O *Q6, F1;* Owen *Dering MS*
349 **mettle**] *Pope;* mettall *Q1–6, F1*
353 **afoot**] *Q2–3;* a foote *Q1, Q4–5, F1;* on foote *Q6*
371 **i' faith**] *om. F1*
390 **O Jesu**] *om. F1*
393 **tristful**] *Dering's emendation in Dering MS, Rowe;* trustfull *Q1–6, F1*
395 **Jesu**] rare *F1*
401 **yet**] *Q3–6, F1;* so *Q1–2*
435 **me?**] *Theobald;* me, *Q1–2, Q5–6;* me; *Q3–4;* me: *F1*
443 **'Sblood**] Yfaith *F1*
444 **i' faith**] *om. F1*
446 **me.**] *F1 (subs.);* me, *Q1–6*
462 **abominable**] *Q2;* abhominable *Q3–6, F1*
470 **God**] Heauen *F1*

473 **lean**] *Q2–6, F1;* lane *Q1*
481 s.d. **A . . . Bardolph.**] *Malone (after Theobald)*
482 **most**] most most *F1*
486 **Jesu**] *om. F1*
492 **made**] mad *F3*
504 s.d. **Exit.**] *F1*
505 s.d. **Exeunt . . . Peto.**] *Collier*
507–8 **First . . . house.**] *as verse, Pope; as prose, Q1–6, F1*
510–1 **One . . . man.**] *as verse, Pope; as prose, Q1–6, F1*
523 **Good**] *Q3–6, F1;* God *Q1–2*
524 **good**] *Q4–6, F1;* god *Q1–3*
525 s.d. **with Carrier**] *Hanmer (subs.)*
526–7 **This . . . forth.**] *as verse, Pope; as prose, Q1–6, F1*
526 **Paul's**] *F4;* Poules *Q1–6, F1*
532 **What**] *Hanmer;* Pr. What *Q1–6, F1 (repeated s.p.)*
535 s.p. **Peto.**] *F1*
535 s.d. **Reads.**] *Capell*
538 **anchoves**] *Q5–6, F1;* anchaues *Q1–4*
540 s.p. **Prince.**] *F1*

III.i
III.i *F1*
Location: *Alexander (after Wilson)*
3–10 **Lord . . . heaven.**] *as verse, F1; as prose, Q1–6*
9 **cheek looks**] Cheekes looke *F1*
11–2 **And . . . of.**] *as verse, Pope; as prose, Q1–6, F1*
17 **Shak'd**] *Q5–6, F1;* Shaked *Q1–4*
17–9 **Why . . . born.**] *as verse, Pope; as prose, Q1–6, F1*
31 **topples**] toples *Q5–6;* tombles *F1*
55–6 **Why . . . devil.**] *as verse, Capell; as prose, Q1–6, F1*
73 **England,**] *F1;* England *Q1–6*
73 **Trent**] *Capell;* Trent, *Q1–6, F1*
99 **cantle**] *F1;* scantle *Q1–6*
100 **damm'd**] *Rowe;* damnd *Q1–6, F1*
105 **wind?**] *Q2–6, F1;* wind *Q1*
106–10 **Yea . . . you.**] *as verse, F1; as prose, Q1–6*
128 **metre**] *F1 (Meeter);* miter *Q1–6*
128 **ballet-mongers**] hyphen, *Q2–6, F1 (F1 reads* Ballad-mongers)
129 **canstick**] Candlestick *F1*
130 **axle-tree**] *Q2–6, F1;* exle tree *Q1*
132 **mincing**] *F1;* minsing *Q1–6*
140 **night.**] *Q2–6, F1 (night:);* night *Q1*
142 **your**] *Q2–6, F1;* your, *Q1*
150 **moulten**] *Q2–6, F1;* molten *Q1*
151 **lion**] *Q2–6, F1;* Leon *Q1*
152 **skimble-skamble**] hyphen, *F1*
160 **windmill**] *Theobald;* Windmil *Q1–6, F1*
170 **come**] doe *F1*
175 **willful-blame**] *Theobald;* wilfullblame *Q1 (?);* wilfull blame *Q2–6, F1*
178 **fault;**] *F1 (fault:);* fault, *Q1–6*
184 **haunting**] *Q5–6, F1;* hanting *Q1–4*
184 **nobleman**] *Q5–6, F1;* noble man *Q1–4*
188 **school'd: good**] *F1;* schoold good *Q1;* schoold, good *Q2–4;* schoold, Good *Q5–6*
195 s.d. **Glendower**] *Q2–6, F1;* Glondower *Q1*
196–7 **She . . . upon.**] *as verse, F1; subs. as prose, Q1–6*
196 **self-will'd**] *Q6, F1;* selfewild *Q1 (?);* selfe wilde *Q2–4;* selfe-wild *Q5*
202 **I**] *Theobald; Mor.* I *Q1–6, F1 (repeated s.p.)*
204 **truant,**] *F1;* truant *Q1–6*
218 **heavenly-harness'd**] hyphen, *Pope*
228 s.p. **Lady P.**] *Malone;* La. *Q1–6, F1 (throughout scene)*
230 **humorous.**] *F1 (humorous:);* humorous, *Q1–6*
232–4 **Then . . . Welsh.**] *as prose, Pope; as verse, Q1–6, F1*
235 **hear Lady, my brach,**] *Q4 (subs.; second comma, Pope after Rowe* i); heare lady my brache *Q1;* hear, lady, my brache *Q2–3;* hear *Lady,* my brach *Q5;* hear Lady, my breech *Q6;* heare (Lady) my Brach *F1*
247 **sooth!**] *Rowe;* sooth. *Q1;* sooth? *Q2–6, F1*

247 Heart] *om. F1*

255 pepper-gingerbread] *F2 (subs.);* pepper ginger bread *Q1–4;* pepper ginger-bread *Q5–6, F1*

256 velvet-guards] *hyphen, F2*

256 Sunday-citizens] *hyphen, F1*

264 hot] *F1;* Hot. *Q1–3;* Hot, *Q4;* Hot *Q5–6*

III.ii

III.ii] *F1*

Location: *Capell*

4, 29 God] Heauen *F1*

32 Council] *F1;* counsell *Q1–6*

40 common-hackney'd] *hyphen, Pope*

58 Seldom] *F1;* Seldome, *Q1–6*

58 sumptuous,] *Q2–6, F1;* sumptuous *Q1*

59 wan] wonne *F1*

63 cap'ring] Carping *F1*

78 gaze,] *F1;* gaze. *Q1–6*

84 gorg'd] *Q3, F1;* gordge *Q1;* gorgde *Q2, Q4–6*

89 desir'd] *F1;* desired *Q1–6*

106 never-dying] *hyphen, F2*

110 capital] *Q2–3;* capitall. *Q1, Q5–6, F1;* capitall, *Q4*

112 Hotspur,] *Warburton;* Hotspur *Q1–6, F1*

130 God] Heauen *F1*

141 unthought-of] *hyphen, F2*

141 meet.] *F1 (subs.);* meet, *Q1–6*

153 God] Heauen *F1*

154 perform,] *Capell;* performe: *Q1–3;* performe *Q4–6; F1 reads the line:* The which, / if I performe, and doe suruiue,

156 intemperance] intemperature *F1*

161 s.d. Enter Blunt.] *placed as in F1; after l. 162, Q1–6*

162 Blunt?] *Q2–6, F1;* blunt *Q1*

176 Gloucestershire;] *F1 (subs.);* Glocestershire, *Q1–6*

177 valued,] *F4;* valued *Q1–6, F1*

III.iii

III.iii] *F1*

Location: *Theobald (after Pope)*

16 times—] *Staunton;* times *Q1–6, F1*

17 quarter—] *Hanmer;* quarter *Q1–6, F1*

18 borrow'd—] *Hanmer (borrowed—);* borrowed *Q1–6;* borrowed, *F1*

35 that's God's angel] *Q3–6;* that Gods Angell *Q1–2; om. F1*

41–2 bonfire light] *Q2* (bon-fire light); bonefire light *Q1, Q3;* bone-fire light *Q4;* Bone-fire-light *Q5–6*

46 chandler's] *Pope;* Chandlers *Q1–6, F1*

48 God] Heauen *F1*

49 'Sblood] *om. F1*

50 God-a-mercy] *om. F1*

51 s.d. Enter Hostess.] *placed as in F1; after* inquir'd *l. 52, Q1–2; after l. 53, Q3–6*

57 tithe] *Theobald;* tight *Q1–6, F1*

62 God's light] *om. F1*

65 John.] *Q2–6, F1 (subs.);* John, *Q1*

70 they] and they *F1*

74 four and twenty] *Dering MS, F1;* xxiiii. *Q1–6*

76 He?] *Q2–6, F1;* He, *Q1*

83 O Jesu] *om. F1*

85 sneak-up] *Vaughan conj.;* sneakeup *Q1–2;* sneak-cup *Q3–6;* sneak-cup *F1*

86 'Sblood] *om. F1*

86 and] and if *F1*

87 s.d. with Peto] *Theobald (subs.)*

88 How] *Dyce;* Falst. How *Q1–6, F1 (repeated s.p.)*

88 i' faith] *om. F1*

92 Quickly] *F1 (in italics);* quickly *Q1–4;* quickly *Q5–6 (in italics)*

94 me.] *Q2–6, F1;* me? *Q1*

107 foul-mouth'd] *hyphen, F1*

109 What,] *F1;* What *Q1–6, F1*

114 womanhood] *Q2–6, F1;* womandood *Q1*

114 Maid Marian] *Q5–6* (Mayd-marian), *F1* (Maid-marian); maid marion *Q1–4*

115 thing] nothing *F1*

117, 118 God] heauen *F1*

118 no thing] *Q5–6, F1;* nothing *Q1–4*

129 an] *om. F1*

146 Prince] a Prince *F1*

---

151 and] if *F1*

151 I pray God] let *F1*

155 fill'd] *Q3, F1;* fild *Q1;* fil'd *Q2;* fillde *Q4;* filde *Q5–6*

160 long-winded] *hyphen, Q5–6, F1*

161–2 these, . . . villain.] *Q2–6, F1 (subs.);* these; . . . villain, *Q1*

172 cherish] and cherish *F1*

172 guesse] *ed.;* ghesse *Q1;* ghests *Q2–6;* Guests *F1*

177 beef] *Q5–6, F1;* beoffe *Q1–4*

188–9 the age of] *om. F1*

189 two and twenty] *Dering MS, F1;* xxii. *Q1–6*

196 s.d. Exit Bardolph.] *Dyce*

198 s.d. Exit Peto.] *Cambridge (after Dyce)*

200 a'] *Q2–6, F1;* of *Q1*

204 s.d. Exit.] *Dyce*

205 world!] *Q2–6, F1 (subs.);* world *Q1*

206 s.d. Exit.] *Capell;* Exeunt. *Q2–6;* Exeunt omnes. *F1*

IV.i

IV.i] *F1*

Location: *Capell (after Pope)*

o.s.d. **Enter . . . Douglas.]** *Q2–6, F1* (Harrie Hotspurre)

1 s.p. Hot.] *Q2–6, F1;* Per. *Q1 (through l. 90)*

5 world] *F1;* world *Q1;* world: *Q2–3, Q5–6;* world, *Q4*

6 God] heauen *F1*

12 s.d. a Messenger] *F1*

17 'Zounds] *om. F1*

17 sick] sicke now *F1*

20 my] his *Q3–6, F1*

20 lord] *Capell;* mind *Q1–6, F1*

29 life-blood] *hyphen, Q2–6, F1*

31 sickness—] *Rowe;* sicknesse, *Q1–6, F1*

55 Is] *F1;* tis *Q1–6*

61 hair] heaire *Q4;* heire *Q5–6, F1*

98 estridges,] *Q2–6, F1;* Estridges *Q1*

99 Bated] *Heath conj.;* Baited *Q1–6, F1*

103 bulls] *F1;* buls, *Q1;* buls: *Q2–6*

108 dropp'd] *Q2–6, F1;* drop *Q1*

116 altar] *Q4–6, F1;* altars *Q1–3*

122 shall, hot] *Johnson;* shal hot *Q1–2;* shall not *Q3–6, F1*

123 ne'er] *Q2–6, F1;* neare *Q1*

124 news:] *F1;* newes, *Q1–6*

126 cannot] *Q5–6, F1;* can *Q1–4*

127 yet] *Q5–6, F1;* it *Q1–4*

134 merrily] *Q2–6, F1;* merely *Q1*

IV.ii

IV.ii] *F1*

Location: *Theobald*

3 Co'fil'] *Cambridge;* cop- / hill *Q1, Q3–4;* cophill *Q2;* -cop- / hill *Q5–6;* -cop-hill *F1*

9 at] at the *F1*

15 yeomen's] *Q2–6, F1;* Yeomans *Q1*

19 fowl] *Rowe;* foule *Q1–3;* foole *Q4–6, F1*

21 toasts-and-butter] *hyphens, Dyce*

29 ostlers] *Q2–6, F1;* Ostlers, *Q1*

31 old feaz'd] *Vaughan conj.;* olde fazd *Q1–4;* old faczde *Q5;* old fac'd *Q6;* old-fac'd *F1*

32 as] that *F1*

46 Albons] *ed.;* Albones *Q1–6, F1*

57 night] to Night *F1*

63 Mine,] *Q2–4, F1;* Mine *Q1, Q5–6*

65 enough] *Q2–6, F1;* inongh *Q1*

78–80 Well . . . guest.] *as verse, Pope; as prose, Q1–6, F1*

IV.iii

IV.iii] *F1*

Location: *Pope, Capell (subs.)*

8 Douglas.] *F1 (subs.);* Douglas, *Q1–6*

10 well-respected] *hyphen, F1*

22 mettle] *F3;* mettall *Q1–6, F1*

26 journey-bated] *hyphen, F3*

38 God] Heauen *F1*

62 peace,] *Q5–6, F1;* peace *Q1–3;* peace. *Q4*

72 heirs as pages] *Singer (after Malone);* heires, as Pages *Q1–6, F1*

82 country's] *Q5–6, F1;* Countrey *Q1–4*

90 after,] *Q2–6, F1;* after *Q1*

92 state;] *Q2–6* (state:); state, *Q1;* State. *F1*

99 Council-board] *F1;* counsell boord *Q1–6*

---

113 God] Heauen *F1*

113 s.d. Exeunt.] *F1*

IV.iv

IV.iv] *F1*

Location: *Theobald*

o.s.d. **Michael]** *Q7;* Mighell *Q1–4 (throughout scene);* Michell *Q5–6, F1 (throughout scene)*

13 Harry; and] *Q2–6, F1 (subs.);* Harry And *Q1*

18 in,] *F1;* in *Q1–6*

31 corrivals] *F1;* coriuals *Q1–6*

36 not,] *Q2–3, F1;* not *Q1, Q4–6*

V.i

V.i] *F1*

Location: *Capell (after Theobald)*

o.s.d. **Lancaster]** *Dering MS, Hanmer;* Lancaster, Earle of Westmerland *Q1–6, F1*

2 bulky] *the 1 in Q1's* bulky *is unclear;* busky *Q2–6, F1*

8 s.d. and . . . Vernon] *Theobald*

9 How] *Capell;* King. How *Q1–6, F1 (repeated s.p.)*

25 I] I do *F1*

37 place] *Q2–3;* place, *Q1, Q4–6, F1*

42 swear] *Q2–6, F1;* sware *Q1*

42, 58 Doncaster] *F1* (Q6, l.58); Dancaster *Q1–6*

44 new-fall'n] *hyphen, Dering MS, F1*

71 your] *om. F1*

72 articulate] articulated *F1*

80 water-colors] *hyphen, F1*

81 time] *F1;* time, *Q1–6*

83 your] our *F1*

85 trial.] *F1;* trial, *Q1–6*

88 off] *F1;* of *Q1–6*

90 valiant,] *ed.;* valiant *Q1–6, F1*

111 wait] *Q2–6, F1;* waight *Q1*

114 s.d. with Vernon] *Theobald (subs.)*

121–4 Hal . . . farewell.] *as prose, Pope; as verse, Q1–6, F1*

122 so;] *F1;* so, *Q1–6*

126 God] heauen *F1*

126 s.d. Exit.] *Hanmer*

130 Yea] *om. F1*

131 then?] *Q2–3, F1;* then *Q1, Q4–6*

131, 132 No.] *Q2–3, F1 (subs.);* no, *Q1, Q4–6*

133 No. . . . No.] *F1;* no, . . . no, *Q1;* No: . . . no: *Q2–3;* no, . . . no: *Q4–6*

135 Air.] *Q2–6, F1 (subs.);* aire, *Q1*

137 No. . . . No.] *F1;* no, . . . no, *Q1;* no: . . . no: *Q2–6*

137 'Tis] Is it *F1*

138 will't] *ed.;* wil *Q1;* will it *Q2–6, F1*

139 No.] *F1;* no, *Q1;* no: *Q2–6*

V.ii

V.ii] *F1*

Location: *Wilson (after Theobald)*

3 are we] we are *F1*

3 undone] *Q5–6, F1;* vnder one *Q1–4*

12 merrily] *Q2–6, F1;* merely *Q1*

15 cherish'd,] *Q2–6, F1;* cherisht *Q1*

19 hare-brain'd] *F2;* hair-braind *Q1–6, F1*

19 spleen.] *Q3, F1 (subs.);* spleene, *Q1–2, Q4–6*

27 s.d. Hotspur] *Q2–6, F1*

27 s.d. and Douglas] *Rowe; s.d. after l. 25, Q1–6; placed as in F1*

50 show'd] *Q3–6, F1;* shewed *Q1–2*

50 tasking] talking *Q2–6, F1*

71 a] at *Q5–6, F1*

88 s.d. Messenger] *F1*

89 s.p. 2. Mess.] *Capell;* Mes. *Q1–6, F1*

89 apace] *Q2–5, F1;* a pace *Q1, Q6*

91 talking;] *F1 (subs.);* talking *Q1;* talking, *Q2–6*

92 draw I] I draw *F1*

93 temper] worthy temper *F1*

94 withal] *Capell;* withall. *Q1;* withall, *Q2–6, F1*

96 Esperance!] *Pope;* esperance *Q1–6;* Esperance *F1*

96 Percy!] *Theobald;* Percy *Q1–6, F1 (in italics, Q5–6, F1)*

100 s.d. and exeunt] *Rowe (subs.)*

V.iii

V.iii] *Capell*
Location: *ed.*
o.s.d. **and passes over**] *White*
16 **won,**] *Q4–6, F1*; won *Q1*; won: *Q2–3*
19 **This,**] *Q2–5*; This *Q1, Q6, F1*
22 **A fool**] *Capell*; Ah foole, *Q1–6*; Ah foole: *F1*
29 s.d. **Exeunt.**] *F1*
34 **God**] heauen *F1*
36 **ragamuffins**] *Capell*; rag of Muffins *Q1–5, F1*; rag of Muffians *Q6*
37 **hundred and fifty**] *Dering MS, Rowe*; 150. *Q1–6, F1*
37 **are**] *om. F1*
41 **nobleman**] *F1*; noble man *Q1–6*
43 **yet**] *om. F1*
48–9 **He . . . sword.**] *as prose, Cambridge; as verse, Q1–6, F1*
50 **before God**] *om. F1*
55 **What,**] *Q2, Q5–6, F1*; What *Q1*; What? *Q3–4*
57 **way,**] *Q5–6, F1*; way *Q1*; way: *Q2–4*
61 s.d. **Exit.**] *F1*

V.iv

V.iv] *Capell*; Scena Tertia. *F1*
Location: *ed.*
o.s.d. **wounded**] *Neilson*
11, 17 **God**] heauen *F1*
16 **God's**] heauens *F1*

16 s.d. **Exeunt . . . Westmerland.**] *Capell*
24 **mettle**] *F3*; mettall *Q1–6, F1*
24 s.d. **Enter Douglas.**] *F1*
25 **king?**] *F1*; king *Q1–6*
34 **and**] so *F1*
48 **redeem'd**] *Q5–6, F1*; redeemed *Q1–4*
51, 69 **God**] heauen *F1*
68 **Nor**] *F1*; Now *Q1–6*
76 s.d. **He**] who *F1*
76 s.d. **and exit Douglas**] *Capell*
81 **thoughts,**] *Neilson-Hill*; thoughts *Q1*; thought's *Q2–6, F1*
81 **and life,**] *F1*; and life *Q1–6*
84 **earthy and**] earth and *Q2–6*; Earth, and the *F1*
86 **for—**] *F1*; for. *Q1–6*
87 **Fare thee well**] Farewell *F1*
88 **shrunk!**] *Q2* (shrunke:); shrunke, *Q1*; shruncke? *Q3–6, F1*
86 s.d. **Dies.**] *Rowe*
87 **heart!**] *F1* (heart:); hart *Q1*; heart, *Q2–6*
88 **Ill-weav'd**] *hyphen, F1*
92 **thee**] *Q7*; the *Q1–6, F1*
95 **dear**] great *Q2–6*
95 **zeal;**] *Q2–6* (subs.); zeale, *Q1*; Zeale. *F1*
98 **rites**] *Q2–6, F1*; rights *Q1*
109, 111 **Embowell'd**] *Q4–6* (Imbowelde *or* Imboweld), *F1* (Imbowell'd); Imboweld *Q1*; Imbowel'd *Q2–3*
111 **embowel**] *Q4–6, F1* (imbowell); inbowel *Q1–3*
113 **'Sblood**] *om. F1*

121 **'Zounds**] *om. F1*
123 **By my faith**] *om. F1*
127 **nobody**] *F1* (no-bodie); no body *Q1–6*
128 s.d. **stabbing him**] *Capell* (subs.)
128 **with**] *om. F1*
129 s.d. **and**] *Q2–6, F1*
140 s.d. **throwing . . . down**] *Capell* (subs.)
144 **Why, Percy,**] *Q2–3, F1*; Why Percy, *Q1, Q6*; Why Percy *Q4–5*
150–1 **take it upon**] take't on *F1*
152 **'zounds**] *om. F1*
159 **The**] *F1*; Prin. The *Q1–6* (repeated s.p.)
159 **our**] ours *Q2–6, F1*
161 s.d. **Prince and Lancaster**] *Capell* (subs.)
163 **God**] heauen *F1*
163 **great**] great again *F1*
165 **nobleman**] *Q4–6, F1*; noble man *Q1–3*

V.v

V.v] *Capell*; Scaena Quarta. *F1*
Location: *Pelican*
1 **rebuke.**] *Q2–3, F1*; rebuke, *Q1, Q4–6*
2 **Ill-spirited**] *hyphen, F1*
2 **not we**] we not *F1*
14 **the**] *om. F1*
15 s.d. **Exeunt . . . Vernon**] *F1*
15 s.d. **guarded**] *Theobald*
32–3 **I . . . immediately.**] *om. Q5–6, F1*
36 **bend**] *Q4–6, F1*; bend, *Q1–3*
41 **lose**] *Q2–3, F1*; loose *Q1, Q4–6*
44 s.d. **Exeunt.**] Exeunt / FINIS. *Q1–6, F1*

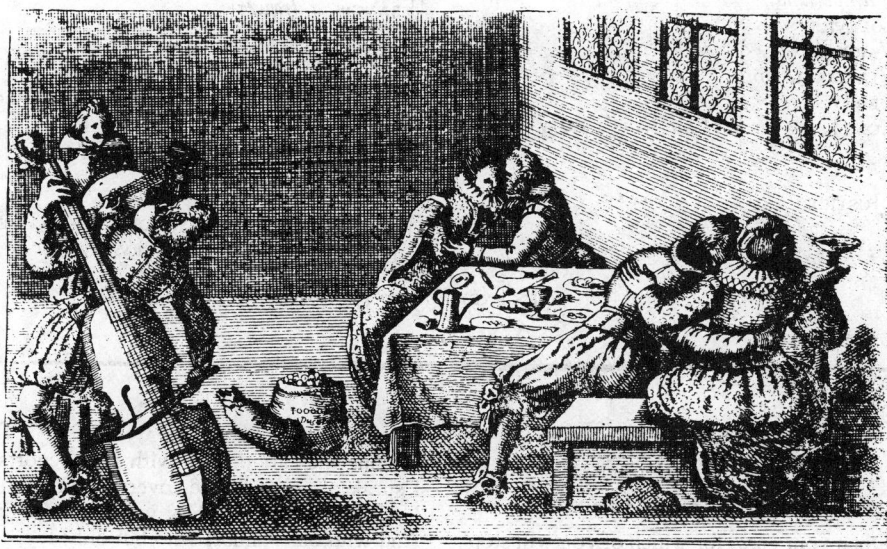

A tavern scene. From *Le Centre de l'Amour* (1630?). In Shakespeare's day, as now, music and food were considered proper precursors to amorous dalliance. It is not clear whether the bag of coins on the floor represents recently acquired booty (such as that taken at Gadshill) or is merely symbolic of the wastefulness of riotous living. One sees here the background of the scenes in Mistress Quickly's Boar's Head Tavern in Eastcheap in both *1 Henry IV* (II.iv) and, particularly, *2 Henry IV* (II.iv). In the latter scene "Sneak's noise" (line 11) is called for to assist the festivities. (*By permission of the Harvard College Library*)

The Second Part of Henry the Fourth

[THE ACTORS' NAMES

RUMOR, *the Presenter*

KING HENRY THE FOURTH

PRINCE HENRY, *afterwards crowned* KING HENRY THE FIFTH

PRINCE JOHN OF LANCASTER ⎱ *sons to Henry the*
HUMPHREY [DUKE] OF ⎰ *Fourth and*
GLOUCESTER *brethren to*
THOMAS [DUKE] OF CLARENCE *Henry V*

[EARL OF] NORTHUMBERLAND
[SCROOP,] *the Archbishop of York*
[LORD] MOWBRAY
[LORD] HASTINGS *opposites against*
LORD BARDOLPH *King Henry*
TRAVERS ⎱ *retainers of North-* *the Fourth*
MORTON ⎰ *umberland*
[SIR JOHN] COLEVILE

[EARL OF] WARWICK
[EARL OF] WESTMERLAND
[EARL OF] SURREY
[SIR JOHN BLUNT] *of the King's party*
GOWER
HARCOURT
LORD CHIEF JUSTICE

POINS
[SIR JOHN] FALSTAFF
BARDOLPH
PISTOL *irregular humorists*
PETO
[*Falstaff's*] PAGE
SHALLOW ⎱ *both country justices*
SILENCE ⎰
DAVY, *servant to Shallow*
FANG *and* SNARE, *two sergeants*
MOULDY
SHADOW
WART *country soldiers*
FEEBLE
BULLCALF
[FRANCIS, *a drawer*]

NORTHUMBERLAND'S WIFE
[LADY PERCY,] *Percy's widow*
HOSTESS QUICKLY [*of the Boar's Head Tavern, Eastcheap*]
DOLL TEARSHEET

EPILOGUE

[LORDS *and* ATTENDANTS; PORTER,] DRAWERS, BEADLE, [OFFICERS, STREWERS, SERVANTS, *etc.*]

[SCENE: *England*]]

[INDUCTION]

Enter RUMOR, *painted full of tongues.*

[*Rum.*] Open your ears; for which of you will stop
The vent of hearing when loud Rumor speaks?
I, from the orient to the drooping west
(Making the wind my post-horse), still unfold
The acts commenced on this ball of earth.   5
Upon my tongues continual slanders ride,
The which in every language I pronounce,
Stuffing the ears of men with false reports.
I speak of peace, while covert enmity
Under the smile of safety wounds the world;   10
And who but Rumor, who but only I,
Make fearful musters and prepar'd defense,
Whiles the big year, swoll'n with some other grief,
Is thought with child by the stern tyrant war,
And no such matter? Rumor is a pipe   15
Blown by surmises, jealousies, conjectures,
And of so easy and so plain a stop
That the blunt monster with uncounted heads,
The still-discordant wav'ring multitude,
Can play upon it. But what need I thus   20
My well-known body to anatomize

Words and passages enclosed in square brackets in the text above are either emendations of the copy-text or additions to it. The Textual Notes immediately following the play cite the earliest authority for every such change or insertion and supply the reading of the copy-text wherever it is emended in this edition.

Ind. o.s.d. **Rumor . . . tongues.** This, like many medieval and Renaissance depictions of Rumor, echoes Virgil's account of *Fama* as a monster covered with eyes, ears, and tongues (*Aeneid*, iv.181–83).
4. **still:** continually.

13. **Whiles:** while.
16. **jealousies:** suspicions. 17. **stop:** i.e. fingering.
18. **blunt:** dull, stupid. 20. **what:** why.
21. **anatomize:** dissect, analyze.

Among my household? Why is Rumor here?
I run before King Harry's victory,
Who in a bloody field by Shrewsbury
Hath beaten down young Hotspur and his troops,   25
Quenching the flame of bold rebellion
Even with the rebels' blood. But what mean I
To speak so true at first? My office is
To noise abroad that Harry Monmouth fell
Under the wrath of noble Hotspur's sword,   30
And that the King before the Douglas' rage
Stoop'd his anointed head as low as death.
This have I rumor'd through the peasant towns
Between that royal field of Shrewsbury
And this worm-eaten [hold] of ragged stone,   35
[Where] Hotspur's father, old Northumberland,
Lies crafty-sick. The posts come tiring on,
And not a man of them brings other news
Than they have learnt of me. From Rumor's tongues
They bring smooth comforts false, worse than true
    wrongs.   *Exit Rumor.*   40

[ACT I, Scene I]

Enter the Lord Bardolph *at one door.*

L. Bard. Who keeps the gate here ho?

[Enter Porter.*]*

                              Where is the Earl?
Port. What shall I say you are?
L. Bard.   Tell thou the Earl
That the Lord Bardolph doth attend him here.
Port. His lordship is walk'd forth into the orchard.
Please it your honor knock but at the gate,   5
And he himself will answer.

Enter the Earl Northumberland *[in a night-cap and supporting himself with a staff].*

L. Bard.   Here comes the Earl. *[Exit Porter.]*
North. What news, Lord Bardolph? Every minute
    now
Should be the father of some stratagem.
The times are wild, contention, like a horse
Full of high feeding, madly hath broke loose,   10
And bears down all before him.
L. Bard.   Noble Earl,
I bring you certain news from Shrewsbury.
North. Good, and God will!
L. Bard.   As good as heart can wish:
The King is almost wounded to the death,

And in the fortune of my lord your son,   15
Prince Harry slain outright, and both the Blunts
Kill'd by the hand of Douglas, young Prince John
And Westmerland and Stafford fled the field,
And Harry Monmouth's brawn, the hulk Sir John,
Is prisoner to your son. O, such a day!   20
So fought, so followed, and so fairly won,
Came not till now to dignify the times,
Since Caesar's fortunes.
North.   How is this deriv'd?
Saw you the field? came you from Shrewsbury?
L. Bard. I spake with one, my lord, that came
    from thence,   25
A gentleman well bred and of good name,
That freely rend'red me these news for true.
North. Here comes my servant Travers, who I sent
On Tuesday last to listen after news.

Enter Travers.

L. Bard. My lord, I overrode him on the way,   30
And he is furnish'd with no certainties
More than he haply may retail from me.
North. Now, Travers, what good tidings comes
    with you?
Tra. My lord, Sir John Umfrevile turn'd me back
With joyful tidings, and being better hors'd,   35
Outrode me. After him came spurring hard
A gentleman, almost forespent with speed,
That stopp'd by me to breathe his bloodied horse.
He ask'd the way to Chester, and of him
I did demand what news from Shrewsbury.   40
He told me that rebellion had bad luck,
And that young Harry Percy's spur was cold.
With that he gave his able horse the head,
And bending forward strook his armed heels
Against the panting sides of his poor jade   45
Up to the rowel-head, and starting so
He seem'd in running to devour the way,
Staying no longer question.
North.   Ha? Again.
Said he young Harry Percy's spur was cold?
Of Hotspur, Coldspur? that rebellion   50
Had met ill luck?
L. Bard.   My lord, I'll tell you what:
If my young lord your son have not the day,
Upon mine honor, for a silken point
I'll give my barony. Never talk of it.
North. Why should that gentleman that rode by
    Travers   55
Give then such instances of loss?

---

22. **household:** i.e. the audience in the theatre.
24. **Shrewsbury:** town in Shropshire, scene of the battle (July 21, 1403) depicted at the end of *1 Henry IV* in which Sir Henry Percy ("young Hotspur") was killed and the rebellion that he—together with his uncle, the Earl of Worcester, and the Earl of Douglas—had led was crushed. 29. **Harry Monmouth:** Prince Henry.
33. **peasant towns:** country villages (whose rustic inhabitants were particularly susceptible to rumor).
35. **hold:** fortress. **ragged:** rough.
37. **crafty-sick:** feigning illness. **The posts . . . on:** the messengers, exhausted by their speed, push on.

I.i. Location: Warworth. Before Northumberland's castle.
3. **attend:** await. 10. **high feeding:** rich food. 13. **and:** if.

16. **both the Blunts.** Only one Blunt—Sir Walter—is killed by the Earl of Douglas in *1 Henry IV* (V.iii).
19. **brawn:** fatted swine. **hulk:** large cargo ship.
20. **day:** day of battle, i.e. combat.
21. **followed:** carried through.
23. **fortunes:** successes. **How . . . deriv'd:** i.e. what's the source of your information. 30. **overrode:** overtook.
34. **Sir John Umfrevile.** Apparently not a historical character. Shakespeare perhaps remembered the Sir Robert Umfrevile whom Holinshed mentions (Bullough, IV, 271) as one loyal to the King.
37. **forespent:** utterly exhausted.
39. **Chester:** important town north of Shrewsbury.
43. **able:** powerful.
46. **Up . . . rowel-head:** i.e. the full depth of the spur.
48. **Staying . . . question:** awaiting no more talk.
53. **point:** lace for tying garments, i.e. a thing of no value.

2 Henry IV
I.i

L. Bard. Who, he?
He was some hilding fellow that had stol'n
The horse he rode on, and, upon my life,
Spoke at a venter. Look, here comes more news.

Enter MORTON.

North. Yea, this man's brow, like to a title-leaf, 60
Foretells the nature of a tragic volume.
So looks the strond whereon the imperious flood
Hath left a witness'd usurpation.
Say, Morton, didst thou come from Shrewsbury?
Mor. I ran from Shrewsbury, my noble lord, 65
Where hateful death put on his ugliest mask
To fright our party.
North. How doth my son and brother?
Thou tremblest, and the whiteness in thy cheek
Is apter than thy tongue to tell thy arrand.
Even such a man, so faint, so spiritless, 70
So dull, so dead in look, so woe-begone,
Drew Priam's curtain in the dead of night,
And would have told him half his Troy was burnt;
But Priam found the fire ere he his tongue,
And I my Percy's death ere thou report'st it. 75
This thou wouldst say, "Your son did thus and thus;
Your brother thus; so fought the noble Douglas"—
Stopping my greedy ear with their bold deeds,
But in the end, to stop my ear indeed,
Thou hast a sigh to blow away this praise, 80
Ending with "Brother, son, and all are dead."
Mor. Douglas is living, and your brother yet,
But for my lord your son—
North. Why, he is dead.
See what a ready tongue suspicion hath!
He that but fears the thing he would not know 85
Hath by instinct knowledge from others' eyes
That what he fear'd is chanced. Yet speak, Morton,
Tell thou an earl his divination lies,
And I will take it as a sweet disgrace
And make thee rich for doing me such wrong. 90
Mor. You are too great to be by me gainsaid,
Your spirit is too true, your fears too certain.
North. Yet for all this, say not that Percy's dead.
I see a strange confession in thine eye.
Thou shak'st thy head, and hold'st it fear or sin 95
To speak a truth. If he be slain, [say so;]
The tongue offends not that reports his death,
And he doth sin that doth belie the dead,
Not he which says the dead is not alive.
Yet the first bringer of unwelcome news 100
Hath but a losing office, and his tongue
Sounds ever after as a sullen bell,
Rememb'red tolling a departing friend.
L. Bard. I cannot think, my lord, your son is dead.
Mor. I am sorry I should force you to believe 105
That which I would to God I had not seen,
But these mine eyes saw him in bloody state,

Rend'ring faint quittance, wearied and outbreath'd,
To Harry Monmouth, whose swift wrath beat down
The never-daunted Percy to the earth, 110
From whence with life he never more sprung up.
In few, his death, whose spirit lent a fire
Even to the dullest peasant in his camp,
Being bruited once, took fire and heat away
From the best-temper'd courage in his troops, 115
For from his metal was his party steeled,
Which once in him abated, all the rest
Turn'd on themselves, like dull and heavy lead.
And as the thing that's heavy in itself
Upon enforcement flies with greatest speed, 120
So did our men, heavy in Hotspur's loss,
Lend to this weight such lightness with their fear
That arrows fled not swifter toward their aim
Than did our soldiers, aiming at their safety,
Fly from the field. Then was that noble Worcester
So soon ta'en prisoner, and that furious Scot, 126
The bloody Douglas, whose well-laboring sword
Had three times slain th' appearance of the King,
Gan vail his stomach and did grace the shame
Of those that turn'd their backs, and in his flight, 130
Stumbling in fear, was took. The sum of all
Is that the King hath won, and hath sent out
A speedy power to encounter you, my lord,
Under the conduct of young Lancaster
And Westmerland. This is the news at full. 135
North. For this I shall have time enough to mourn;
In poison there is physic, and these news,
Having been well, that would have made me sick,
Being sick, have (in some measure) made me well.
And as the wretch whose fever-weak'ned joints, 140
Like strengthless hinges, buckle under life,
Impatient of his fit, breaks like a fire
Out of his keeper's arms, even so my limbs,
Weak'ned with grief, being now enrag'd with grief,
Are thrice themselves. Hence therefore, thou nice
crutch! 145
A scaly gauntlet now with joints of steel
Must glove this hand; and hence, thou sickly coif!
That art a guard too wanton for the head
Which princes, flesh'd with conquest, aim to hit.
Now bind my brows with iron, and approach 150
The ragged'st hour that time and spite dare bring
To frown upon th' enrag'd Northumberland!
Let heaven kiss earth! now let not Nature's hand
Keep the wild flood confin'd! let order die!
And let this world no longer be a stage 155

57. **hilding:** worthless. 59. **venter:** venture.
60. **title-leaf:** title-page. 62. **strond:** strand, shore.
63. **a witness'd usurpation:** i.e. obvious signs of ravage.
72. **Priam:** king of Troy who witnessed the destruction of his city
by the Greeks. 78. **Stopping:** filling. 87. **is chanced:** has happened.
95. **fear:** something to be feared. 98. **belie:** lie about.
101. **losing office:** duty that results in loss or disadvantage.

108. **quittance:** return of blows. **outbreath'd:** out of breath.
112. **In few:** in short. 114. **bruited:** rumored.
115. **best-temper'd:** i.e. like fine steel. The metaphor is expanded
in the next three lines. 117. **abated:** dulled, blunted.
120. **Upon enforcement:** i.e. forced into motion.
123. **aim:** mark, goal.
127–28. **The bloody . . . King.** See *1 Henry IV*, V.iv.25–38, with the
note to line 25.
129. **Gan . . . stomach:** began to lose his courage. **grace:** sanction
(by his own example).
131. **Stumbling . . . took.** See note to *1 Henry IV*, V.v.21–22.
133. **power:** armed force. 134. **conduct:** command.
141. **life:** i.e. the burden of living. 143. **keeper's:** nurse's.
144. **grief . . . grief:** suffering . . . sorrow.
145. **nice:** effeminate, delicate. 146. **scaly:** mailed.
147. **sickly coif:** invalid's cap. 148. **wanton:** luxurious.
149. **flesh'd:** made fierce. 151. **ragged'st:** roughest.

To feed contention in a ling'ring act;
But let one spirit of the first-born Cain
Reign in all bosoms, that each heart being set
On bloody courses, the rude scene may end,
And darkness be the burier of the dead!   160
  [L. Bard.]   This strained passion doth you wrong,
    my lord.
  [Mor.]   Sweet Earl, divorce not wisdom from your
    honor,
The lives of all your loving complices
[Lean] on [your] health, the which, if you give o'er
To stormy passion, must perforce decay.   165
[You cast th' event of war, my noble lord,
And summ'd the accompt of chance before you said,
"Let us make head." It was your presurmise
That in the dole of blows your son might drop.
You knew he walk'd o'er perils, on an edge,   170
More likely to fall in than to get o'er;
You were advis'd his flesh was capable
Of wounds and scars; and that his forward spirit
Would lift him where most trade of danger rang'd;
Yet did you say, "Go forth!" and none of this   175
(Though strongly apprehended) could restrain
The stiff-borne action. What hath then befall'n?
Or what [doth] this bold enterprise bring forth
More than that being which was like to be?]
  L. Bard.   We all that are engaged to this loss   180
Knew that we ventured on such dangerous seas
That if we wrought out life 'twas ten to one,
And yet we ventur'd for the gain propos'd,
Chok'd the respect of likely peril fear'd,
And since we are o'erset, venture again.   185
Come, we will all put forth, body and goods.
  Mor.   'Tis more than time, and, my most noble
    lord,
I hear for certain and dare speak the truth,
[The gentle Archbishop of York is up
With well-appointed pow'rs. He is a man   190
Who with a double surety binds his followers.
My lord your son had only but the corpse',
But shadows and the shows of men, to fight;
For that same word, rebellion, did divide
The action of their bodies from their souls,   195
And they did fight with queasiness, constrain'd
As men drink potions, that their weapons only
Seem'd on our side; but for their spirits and souls,

This word, rebellion, it had froze them up,
As fish are in a pond. But now the Bishop   200
Turns insurrection to religion.
Suppos'd sincere and holy in his thoughts,
He's follow'd both with body and with mind;
And doth enlarge his rising with the blood
Of fair King Richard, scrap'd from Pomfret stones;
Derives from heaven his quarrel and his cause;   206
Tells them he doth bestride a bleeding land,
Gasping for life under great Bullingbrook,
And more and less do flock to follow him.]
  North.   I knew of this before, but to speak truth,
This present grief had wip'd it from my mind.   211
Go in with me, and counsel every man
The aptest way for safety and revenge.
Get posts and letters, and make friends with speed—
Never so few, and never yet more need. *Exeunt.* 215

[SCENE II]

Enter SIR JOHN [FALSTAFF] *alone, with his* PAGE
[*following behind*] *bearing his sword and buckler.*

  Fal.   Sirrah, you giant, what says the doctor to my
water?
  Page.   He said, sir, the water itself was a good
healthy water, but for the party that ow'd it, he might
have moe diseases than he knew for.   5
  Fal.   Men of all sorts take a pride to gird at me.
The brain of this foolish-compounded clay, man, is not
able to invent any thing that intends to laughter more
than I invent or is invented on me: I am not only witty
in myself, but the cause that wit is in other men.   10
I do here walk before thee like a sow that hath overwhelm'd all her litter but one. If the Prince put thee
into my service for any other reason than to set me off,
why then I have no judgment. Thou whoreson mandrake, thou art fitter to be worn in my cap than to   15
wait at my heels. I was never mann'd with an agot
till now, but I will inset you neither in gold nor silver,
but in vile apparel, and send you back again to your
master for a jewel—the juvenal, the Prince your
master, whose chin is not yet fledge. I will sooner   20
have a beard grow in the palm of my hand than he shall
get one [of] his cheek, and yet he will not stick to say
his face is a face royal. God may finish it when he will,
'tis not a hair amiss yet. He may keep it still at a face
royal, for a barber shall never earn sixpence out   25

156. **act:** i.e. act of a play.
157. **spirit . . . Cain:** i.e. spirit of murder.
166. **cast th' event:** calculated the outcome.
167. **accompt:** account.   168. **make head:** raise an army.
169. **dole:** distribution.   172. **advis'd:** aware.
172–73. **capable Of:** susceptible to.
174. **most trade:** the greatest resort.
177. **stiff-borne:** obstinately pursued.
180. **engaged to:** involved in.
182. **if . . . one:** it was ten to one against our coming out of it alive.
184. **Chok'd the respect:** checked consideration.
186. **put forth:** venture.
189–90. **The gentle . . . pow'rs.** Actually Archbishop Scroop's rebellion did not occur until nearly two years after the battle of Shrewsbury. According to Holinshed (Bullough, IV, 269–70), the Earl of
Northumberland, after a few bellicose feints on learning of Hotspur's
death, consented to a friendly meeting with the King, who "gave
him faire words, and suffered him (as saith *Hall*) to depart home,
although after it should seeme, that he was committed for a time
to safe custodie."
190. **well-appointed pow'rs:** well-equipped troops.
192. **corpse':** corpses, i.e. bodies without souls.

204. **enlarge his rising:** extend his rebellion.
205. **Pomfret:** Pontefract Castle, Yorkshire, the scene of Richard II's
murder.   208. **Bullingbrook:** Henry IV.
209. **more and less:** i.e. people of all ranks.
212. **counsel every man:** let every man consider.

I.ii. Location: London. A street.
o.s.d. **buckler:** shield.
1. **Sirrah:** customary form of address to an inferior.   **to my water:**
about my urine.   4. **ow'd:** owned.
5. **moe:** more.   **knew for:** was aware of.
6. **to gird:** in jeering.   8. **intends:** inclines, tends.
14–15. **mandrake:** plant with a forked root thought to resemble a
man.
16. **mann'd:** provided (with a servant).   **agot:** agate, i.e. little figure carved on an agate stone, cameo.   19. **juvenal:** youth.
20. **fledge:** fledged, i.e. covered with down.   22. **of:** on.
23. **royal.** With a pun on *royal* = a coin stamped with the king's
head.   24. **at:** at the value of.

2 Henry IV
I.ii

of it; and yet he'll be crowing as if he had writ man ever since his father was a bachelor. He may keep his own grace, but he's almost out of mine, I can assure him. What said Master Dommelton about the satin for my short cloak and my slops? 30

Page. He said, sir, you should procure him better assurance than Bardolph. He would not take his band and yours, he lik'd not the security.

Fal. Let him be damn'd like the glutton! Pray God his tongue be hotter! A whoreson Achitophel! a 35 [rascally] yea-forsooth knave, to bear a gentleman in hand, and then stand upon security! The whoreson smoothy-pates do now wear nothing but high shoes, and bunches of keys at their girdles, and if a man is through with them in honest taking up, then they 40 must stand upon security. I had as live they would put ratsbane in my mouth as offer to stop it with security. I look'd 'a should have sent me two and twenty yards of satin (as I am a true knight), and he sends me security! Well, he may sleep in security, 45 for he hath the horn of abundance, and the lightness of his wife shines through it; and yet cannot he see, though he have his own lanthorn to light him. Where's Bardolph? 49

Page. He's gone [into] Smithfield to buy your worship a horse.

Fal. I bought him in Paul's, and he'll buy me a horse in Smithfield; and I could get me but a wife in the stews, I were mann'd, hors'd, and wiv'd. 54

Enter LORD CHIEF JUSTICE [*and* SERVANT].

Page. Sir, here comes the nobleman that committed the Prince for striking him about Bardolph.

Fal. Wait close, I will not see him.

Ch. Just. What's he that goes there?

Serv. Falstaff, and't please your lordship. 59

Ch. Just. He that was in question for the robb'ry?

Serv. He, my lord, but he hath since done good service at Shrewsbury, and (as I hear) is now going with some charge to the Lord John of Lancaster.

Ch. Just. What, to York? Call him back again.

---

26. **writ man**: attained manhood.
28. **grace**: (1) title appropriate for a prince; (2) favor.
30. **slops**: baggy breeches.
32. **Bardolph**: a disreputable friend of Falstaff's, not the Lord Bardolph of I.i. **band**: bond.
34. **the glutton**: i.e. Dives, the rich man in the parable of Lazarus (Luke 16:19–31).
35. **hotter**: i.e. than the tongue of Dives, who, in hell, begged that Lazarus would "dip the tip of his finger in water, and cool my tongue." **Achitophel**: Absalom's counsellor (2 Samuel 15–17).
36. **yea-forsooth**: obsequious, flattering (by agreeing emphatically with whatever is said).   36–37. **bear . . . in hand**: lead . . . on.
40. **through**: straightforward.   **taking up**: ordering on credit.
41. **live**: lief.   43. **look'd 'a**: expected that he.
46–48. **horn . . . lanthorn**. A play on *horn* as (1) cornucopia, (2) the sign of the cuckold, and (3) the window of a lantern.
50. **Smithfield**: district north of St. Paul's Cathedral noted for its livestock market.
52. **in Paul's**. Men in search of work congregated in the nave of St. Paul's.
54. **stews**: brothels.   **I . . . wiv'd**. Echoing the proverb that a man who gets a horse at Smithfield, a servant in St. Paul's, and a wife in a brothel is in each instance defrauded.
55–56. **here . . . Bardolph**. Alluding to the Prince's altercation with Sir William Gascoigne; see note to *1 Henry IV*, III.ii.32–33.
55. **committed**: imprisoned.   57. **close**: near.
60. **in question for**: examined in connection with.
63. **charge**: military command.

Serv. Sir John Falstaff! 65

Fal. Boy, tell him I am deaf.

Page. You must speak louder, my master is deaf.

Ch. Just. I am sure he is, to the hearing of any thing good. Go pluck him by the elbow, I must speak with him. 70

Serv. Sir John!

Fal. What? a young knave, and begging? is there not wars? is there not employment? doth not the King lack subjects? do not the rebels need soldiers? Though it be a shame to be on any side but one, 75 it is worse shame to beg than to be on the worst side, were it worse than the name of rebellion can tell how to make it.

Serv. You mistake me, sir. 79

Fal. Why, sir, did I say you were an honest man? Setting my knighthood and my soldiership aside, I had lied in my throat if I had said so.

Serv. I pray you, sir, then set your knighthood and your soldiership aside, and give me leave to tell you you lie in your throat if you say I am any other than an honest man. 86

Fal. I give thee leave to tell me so? I lay aside that which grows to me? If thou get'st any leave of me, hang me; if thou tak'st leave, thou wert better be hang'd. You hunt counter, hence, avaunt! 90

Serv. Sir, my lord would speak with you.

Ch. Just. Sir John Falstaff, a word with you.

Fal. My good lord! God give your lordship good time of day. I am glad to see your lordship abroad. I heard say your lordship was sick, I hope your 95 lordship goes abroad by advice. Your lordship, though not clean past your youth, have yet some smack of an ague in you, some relish of the saltness of time in you, and I most humbly beseech your lordship to have a reverend care of your health. 100

Ch. Just. Sir John, I sent for you before your expedition to Shrewsbury.

Fal. And't please your lordship, I hear his Majesty is return'd with some discomfort from Wales. 104

Ch. Just. I talk not of his Majesty. You would not come when I sent for you.

Fal. And I hear, moreover, his Highness is fall'n into this same whoreson apoplexy.

Ch. Just. Well, God mend him! I pray you let me speak with you. 110

Fal. This apoplexy, as I take it, is a kind of lethargy, and't please your lordship, a kind of sleeping in the blood, a whoreson tingling.

Ch. Just. What tell you me of it? Be it as it is. 114

Fal. It hath it original from much grief, from study, and perturbation of the brain. I have read the cause of his effects in Galen, it is a kind of deafness.

Ch. Just. I think you are fall'n into the disease, for you hear not what I say to you. 119

---

78. **make**: regard, consider.
90. **counter**: in the wrong direction (perhaps with a pun on *Counter* as the name of two ancient London prisons).   **avaunt**: begone.
96. **by advice**: i.e. with your doctor's approval.
103–4. **I . . . Wales**. Falstaff perhaps refers—anachronistically—to an unsuccessful expedition that Henry IV led against Glendower in 1405.   114. **What**: why.   115. **it original**: its origin.
117. **Galen**: Greek medical authority of the second century A.D.

[*Fal.*] Very well, my lord, very well. Rather, and't please you, it is the disease of not list'ning, the malady of not marking, that I am troubled withal.

Ch. Just. To punish you by the heels would amend the attention of your ears, and I care not if I do become your physician. 125

Fal. I am as poor as Job, my lord, but not so patient. Your lordship may minister the potion of imprisonment to me in respect of poverty, but how I should be your patient to follow your prescriptions, the wise may make some dram of a scruple, or indeed a scruple itself. 131

Ch. Just. I sent for you, when there were matters against you for your life, to come speak with me.

Fal. As I was then advis'd by my learned counsel in the laws of this land-service, I did not come. 135

Ch. Just. Well, the truth is, Sir John, you live in great infamy.

Fal. He that buckles himself in my belt cannot live in less. 139

Ch. Just. Your means are very slender, and your waste is great.

Fal. I would it were otherwise, I would my means were greater and my waist [slenderer].

Ch. Just. You have misled the youthful prince. 144

Fal. The young prince hath misled me. I am the fellow with the great belly, and he my dog.

Ch. Just. Well, I am loath to gall a new-heal'd wound. Your day's service at Shrewsbury hath a little gilded over your night's exploit on Gadshill. You may thank th' unquiet time for your quiet o'erposting that action. 151

Fal. My lord?

Ch. Just. But since all is well, keep it so, wake not a sleeping wolf.

Fal. To wake a wolf is as bad as smell a fox. 155

Ch. Just. What, you are as a candle, the better part burnt out.

Fal. A wassail candle, my lord, all tallow; if I did say of wax, my growth would approve the truth. 159

Ch. Just. There is not a white hair in your face but should have his effect of gravity.

Fal. His effect of gravy, gravy, gravy.

Ch. Just. You follow the young prince up and down, like his ill angel. 164

Fal. Not so, my lord. Your ill angel is light, but I hope he that looks upon me will take me without weighing, and yet in some respects I grant I cannot

go. I cannot tell. Virtue is of so little regard in these costermongers' times that true valor is turn'd berrord; pregnancy is made a tapster, and his quick wit 170 wasted in giving reckonings; all the other gifts appertinent to man, as the malice of [this] age shapes [them, are] not worth a gooseberry. You that are old consider not the capacities of us that are young, you do measure the heat of our livers with the bitterness 175 of your galls; and we that are in the vaward of our youth, I must confess, are wags too.

Ch. Just. Do you set down your name in the scroll of youth, that are written down old with all the characters of age? Have you not a moist eye, a 180 dry hand, a yellow cheek, a white beard, a decreasing leg, an increasing belly? Is not your voice broken, your wind short, your chin double, your wit single, and every part about you blasted with antiquity? and will you yet call yourself young? Fie, fie, fie, Sir John! 186

Fal. My lord, I was born about three of the clock in the afternoon, with a white head and something a round belly. For my voice, I have lost it with hallowing and singing of anthems. To approve my youth further, I will not. The truth is, I am only 191 old in judgment and understanding; and he that will caper with me for a thousand marks, let him lend me the money, and have at him! For the box of the year that the Prince gave you, he gave it like a rude prince, and you took it like a sensible lord. I have check'd 196 him for it, and the young lion repents, [*aside*] marry, not in ashes and sackcloth, but in new silk and old sack.

Ch. Just. Well, God send the Prince a better companion! 200

Fal. God send the companion a better prince! I cannot rid my hands of him.

Ch. Just. Well, the King hath sever'd you. I hear you are going with Lord John of Lancaster against the Archbishop and the Earl of Northumberland. 205

Fal. Yea, I thank your pretty sweet wit for it. But look you pray, all you that kiss my Lady Peace at home, that our armies join not in a hot day! for, by the Lord, I take but two shirts out with me, and I mean not to sweat extraordinarily. If it be a hot day, and I brandish any thing but a bottle, I would I might 211 never spit white again. There is not a dangerous action can peep out his head but I am thrust upon it. Well, I cannot last ever, but it was alway yet the trick of our English nation, if they have a good thing, to make it

---

122. **withal:** with.
123. **punish . . . heels:** put you in the stocks (?).
128. **in . . . poverty:** i.e. because I'm too poor to pay a fine.
130. **make . . . scruple:** be reluctant to believe. *Scruple* suggests the use of *dram*, since both words designate small weights used by apothecaries.   132. **matters:** complaints.
133. **for your life:** i.e. of capital offenses.
135. **land-service:** military service.
145–46. **I . . . dog.** Not satisfactorily explained.
147. **gall:** irritate.   149. **your . . . Gadshill.** See *1 Henry IV*, II.ii.
150. **o'erposting:** escaping the consequences of.
155. **smell a fox:** be suspicious.
158. **wassail candle:** large candle for use at feasts.
159. **wax:** (1) beeswax; (2) grow.   **approve:** confirm.
161. **effect:** sign, appearance.
165. **Your . . . light:** i.e. a clipped coin is underweight. An angel was a gold coin bearing the figure of the archangel Michael.

168. **go:** pass (as genuine).
169. **costermongers' times:** i.e. commercial days. A costermonger is a dealer in fruits and vegetables.   **berrord:** bear-ward, keeper of bears.   170. **pregnancy:** intellectual capacity.
175–76. **the heat . . . galls:** the strength of our passions with the bitterness of your bile (rancor).
176. **vaward:** vanguard, advance. Falstaff concedes that he is on the verge of middle age.
180. **characters:** (1) letters; (2) characteristics.
183. **single:** small, trivial.   188–89. **something a:** a somewhat.
190. **hallowing:** shouting to hounds.   **approve:** prove.
193. **caper:** dance.   **mark:** a sum of 13s. 4d.   194. **year:** ear.
196. **check'd:** rebuked.
197. **marry:** indeed (originally the name of the Virgin Mary used as an oath).   198. **sack:** Spanish wine.
212. **spit white.** Not satisfactorily explained. Perhaps Falstaff associates white spittle with deep drinking.   **action:** i.e. military action.
214. **alway:** always.

2 Henry IV
I.ii

too common. If ye will needs say I am an old   216
man, you should give me rest. I would to God my
name were not so terrible to the enemy as it is. I were
better to be eaten to death with a rust than to be
scour'd to nothing with perpetual motion.   220

Ch. Just. Well, be honest, be honest, and God bless
your expedition!

Fal. Will your lordship lend me a thousand pound
to furnish me forth?

Ch. Just. Not a penny, not a penny, you are too
impatient to bear crosses. Fare you well! Commend
me to my cousin Westmerland.   227

[*Exeunt Chief Justice and Servant.*]

Fal. If I do, fillip me with a three-man beetle. A
man can no more separate age and covetousness than 'a
can part young limbs and lechery; but the gout galls the
one, and the pox pinches the other, and so both the
degrees prevent my curses. Boy!   232

Page. Sir?

Fal. What money is in my purse?

Page. Seven groats and two pence.   235

Fal. I can get no remedy against this consumption
of the purse; borrowing only lingers and lingers it out,
but the disease is incurable. Go bear this letter to my
Lord of Lancaster, this to the Prince, this to the Earl of
Westmerland, and this to old Mistress Ursula, whom
I have weekly sworn to marry since I perceiv'd   241
the first white hair of my chin. About it, you know
where to find me. [*Exit Page.*] A pox of this gout! or a
gout of this pox! for the one or the other plays the
rogue with my great toe. 'Tis no matter if I do halt,
I have the wars for my color, and my pension shall   246
seem the more reasonable. A good wit will make use
of any thing. I will turn diseases to commodity.

[*Exit.*]

[SCENE III]

Enter th' ARCHBISHOP [OF YORK], THOMAS MOWBRAY
(*Earl Marshal*), *the* LORD HASTINGS, *and* [LORD]
BARDOLPH.

Arch. Thus have you heard our cause and known
          our means,
And, my most noble friends, I pray you all
Speak plainly your opinions of our hopes.
And first, Lord Marshal, what say you to it?

Mowb. I well allow the occasion of our arms,   5
But gladly would be better satisfied
How in our means we should advance ourselves
To look with forehead bold and big enough
Upon the power and puissance of the King.

Hast. Our present musters grow upon the file   10
To five and twenty thousand men of choice,
And our supplies live largely in the hope
Of great Northumberland, whose bosom burns
With an incensed fire of injuries.

L. Bard. The question then, Lord Hastings,
          standeth thus: 15
Whether our present five and twenty thousand
May hold up head without Northumberland?

Hast. With him, we may.

L. Bard.   Yea, marry, there's the point!
But if without him we be thought too feeble,
My judgment is we should not step too far   20
[Till we had his assistance by the hand.
For in a theme so bloody-fac'd as this,
Conjecture, expectation, and surmise
Of aids incertain should not be admitted.]

Arch. 'Tis very true, Lord Bardolph, for indeed
It was young Hotspur's cause at Shrewsbury.   26

L. Bard. It was, my lord, who lin'd himself with
          hope,
Eating the air, and promise of supply,
Flatt'ring himself in project of a power
Much smaller than the smallest of his thoughts,   30
And so with great imagination,
Proper to madmen, led his powers to death,
And winking, leapt into destruction.

Hast. But by your leave, it never yet did hurt
To lay down likelihoods and forms of hope.   35

L. Bard. [Yes, if this present quality of war—
Indeed the instant action, a cause on foot—
Lives so in hope, as in an early spring
We see th' appearing buds, which to prove fruit
Hope gives not so much warrant, as despair   40
That frosts will bite them. When we mean to build,
We first survey the plot, then draw the model,
And when we see the figure of the house,
Then must we rate the cost of the erection,
Which if we find outweighs ability,   45
What do we then but draw anew the model
In fewer offices, or at least desist
To build at all? Much more, in this great work
(Which is, almost, to pluck a kingdom down
And set another up), should we survey   50
The plot of situation and the model,
Consent upon a sure foundation,
Question surveyors, know our own estate,
How able such a work to undergo,

---

221. **honest:** well behaved.
226. **crosses:** (1) adversities; (2) silver coins stamped with a cross.
228. **fillip:** strike.   **three-man beetle:** heavy sledge or rammer, requiring three men to lift it, for setting paving stones.
231. **pinches:** torments.
232. **degrees:** kinds (of disease).   **prevent:** anticipate.
235. **groats:** coins worth fourpence.   245. **halt:** limp.
246. **color:** excuse, pretext.   248. **commodity:** profit.

I.iii. Location: York. The Archbishop's palace.
4. **Lord Marshal.** See note to *1 Henry IV*, IV.iv.2.
5. **allow ... arms:** concede that war is justified.   7. **in:** with.

---

10. **file:** list.   11. **of choice:** i.e. exceptionally well qualified.
12. **supplies:** reinforcements.   **largely:** bountifully.
17. **hold up head:** i.e. succeed.   22. **theme:** matter.
26. **cause:** situation.   27. **lin'd:** fortified.
28. **Eating the air:** i.e. living on (false) hope.
29. **project:** expectation.   **power:** armed force.
33. **winking:** closing his eyes.
36-41. **Yes ... them.** This difficult passage, which has baffled satisfactory explanation, might be roughly paraphrased as follows: "Yes,
if the present state of affairs—with war not a theme for speculation
but a cruel reality—depended merely on hope, then your optimism
would be justified. But beware of overconfidence, as when the buds
of early spring lead us to ignore the possibility of killing frosts."
42. **plot:** site.   **model:** plan.   43. **figure:** design.
44. **rate:** calculate.   45. **ability:** i.e. our resources.
47. **In fewer offices:** i.e. more modestly.   *Offices* = service quarters.
at least: at worst.   52. **Consent:** agree.
53. **surveyors:** architects.   **estate:** resources.

To weigh against his opposite; or else]   55
We fortify in paper and in figures,
Using the names of men in stead of men,
Like [one] that draws the model of an house
Beyond his power to build it, who, half thorough,
Gives o'er, and leaves his part-created cost   60
A naked subject to the weeping clouds
And waste for churlish winter's tyranny.

   Hast.   Grant that our hopes (yet likely of fair birth)
Should be still-born, and that we now possess'd
The utmost man of expectation,   65
I think we are so [a] body strong enough,
Even as we are, to equal with the King.

   L. Bard.   What, is the King but five and twenty
     thousand?

   Hast.   To us no more, nay, not so much, Lord
     Bardolph,
For his divisions, as the times do brawl,   70
[Are] in three heads: one power against the French,
And one against Glendower; perforce a third
Must take up us. So is the unfirm King
In three divided, and his coffers sound
With hollow poverty and emptiness.   75

   Arch.   That he should draw his several strengths
     together,
And come against us in full puissance,
Need not to be dreaded.

   Hast.   If he should do so,
[To] French and Welsh he leaves his back unarm'd,
They baying him at the heels. Never fear that.   80

   L. Bard.   Who is it like should lead his forces
     hither?

   Hast.   The Duke of Lancaster and Westmerland;
Against the Welsh, himself and Harry Monmouth;
But who is substituted against the French,
I have no certain notice.

   [*Arch.*   Let us on!   85
And publish the occasion of our arms.
The commonwealth is sick of their own choice,
Their over-greedy love hath surfeited.
An habitation giddy and unsure
Hath he that buildeth on the vulgar heart.   90
O thou fond many, with what loud applause
Didst thou beat heaven with blessing Bullingbrook
Before he was what thou wouldst have him be!
And being now trimm'd in thine own desires,
Thou, beastly feeder, art so full of him,   95
That thou provok'st thyself to cast him up.

So, so, thou common dog, didst thou disgorge
Thy glutton bosom of the royal Richard,
And now thou wouldst eat thy dead vomit up,   99
And howl'st to find it. What trust is in these times?
They that, when Richard liv'd, would have him die,
Are now become enamor'd on his grave.
Thou, that threw'st dust upon his goodly head
When through proud London he came sighing on
After th' admired heels of Bullingbrook,   105
Cri'st now, "O earth, yield us that king again,
And take thou this!" O thoughts of men accurs'd!
Past and to come seems best; things present worst.]

   [*Mowb.*] Shall we go draw our numbers and set on?

   Hast.   We are time's subjects, and time bids be
     gone.   *Exeunt.*   110

[ACT II, Scene I]

Enter HOSTESS [QUICKLY] *of the Tavern and an officer
or two* [FANG *and* SNARE, *Snare lagging behind*].

   Host.   Master Fang, have you ent'red the action?

   Fang.   It is ent'red.

   Host.   Where's your yeoman? Is't a lusty yeoman?
Will 'a stand to't?

   Fang.   Sirrah! Where's Snare?   5

   Host.   O Lord, ay! good Master Snare.

   Snare.   Here, here.

   Fang.   Snare, we must arrest Sir John Falstaff.

   Host.   Yea, good Master Snare, I have ent'red him
and all.   10

   Snare.   It may chance cost some of us our lives, for
he will stab.

   Host.   Alas the day, take heed of him! He stabb'd
me in mine own house, most beastly, in good faith. 'A
cares not what mischief he does, if his weapon be   15
out. He will foin like any devil, he will spare neither
man, woman, nor child.

   Fang.   If I can close with him, I care not for his
thrust.

   Host.   No, nor I neither, I'll be at your elbow.   20

   Fang.   And I but fist him once, and 'a come but
within my [vice]—

   Host.   I am undone by his going, I warrant you,
he's an infinitive thing upon my score. Good Master
Fang, hold him sure. Good Master Snare, let him   25
not scape. 'A comes [continuantly] to Pie-corner
(saving your manhoods) to buy a saddle, and he is

---

55. **his opposite:** its adversary.
60. **part-created cost:** expensive half-built house.
62. **churlish:** rough.
65. **The utmost . . . expectation:** i.e. as many men as we could reasonably expect to have.
70. **as . . . brawl:** i.e. made necessary by the disturbed state of affairs.
71. **the French.** Following the battle of Shrewsbury the French
began harassing English shipping in the Channel and English garrisons in France.
72. **Glendower.** According to Holinshed (Bullough, IV, 270), in the
summer of 1403 "the king was minded to have gone into Wales,
against the Welsh rebels, that under their cheefteine Owen Glandouer
ceassed not to doo much mischeefe still against the English subjects."
74. **sound:** resound.   **several:** separate.
81. **Who . . . should:** who is likely to.
84. **substituted:** delegated.   90. **vulgar:** plebeian.
91. **fond many:** foolish multitude.

109. **draw our numbers:** assemble our forces.
110. **time:** present state of affairs.

II.i. Location: London. A street.
1. **ent'red the action:** begun the lawsuit.
3. **yeoman:** assistant.   4. **Will . . . to't:** will he fight bravely.
5. **Sirrah:** customarily a term of address to an inferior, but also
used between equals of low status.
9. **ent'red:** brought suit against.   11. **chance:** perchance.
16. **foin:** thrust (with an indecent equivoque).
18. **close:** grapple.   21. **fist:** grip.   22. **vice:** vise, grasp.
24. **infinitive:** i.e. infinite (one of the Hostess' many malapropisms).
score: books, accounts.
26. **continuantly:** continually.   **Pie-corner:** intersection in London,
so called from its many cooks' shops.
27. **saving:** i.e. no offense intended to. The Hostess apologizes for
mentioning a place so unsavory.

2 Henry IV
II.i

indited to dinner to the Lubber's Head in Lumbert street, to Master Smooth's the silk-man. I pray you, since my exion is ent'red and my case so openly 30 known to the world, let him be brought in to his answer. A hundred mark is a long one for a poor lone woman to bear, and I have borne, and borne, and borne, and have' been fubb'd off, and fubb'd off, and fubb'd off, from this day to that day, that it is a 35 shame to be thought on. There is no honesty in such dealing, unless a woman should be made an ass and a beast, to bear every knave's wrong.

Enter Sir John [Falstaff] *and* Bardolph *and the Boy* [Page].

Yonder he comes, and that arrant malmsey-nose knave, Bardolph, with him. Do your offices, do your 40 offices, Master Fang and Master Snare, do me, do me, do me your offices.

Fal. How now, whose mare's dead? what's the matter? 44

Fang. I arrest you at the suit of Mistress Quickly.

Fal. Away, varlets! Draw, Bardolph, cut me off the villain's head, throw the quean in the channel.

Host. Throw me in the channel? I'll throw thee in the channel. Wilt thou? wilt thou? thou bastardly rogue! Murder, murder! Ah, thou honeysuckle 50 villain! wilt thou kill God's officers and the King's? Ah, thou honeyseed rogue! thou art a honeyseed, a man-queller, and a woman-queller.

Fal. Keep them off, Bardolph.

Officers. A rescue! a rescue! 55

Host. Good people, bring a rescue or two. [*The Page attacks her.*] Thou wo't, wo't thou? thou wo't, wo't ta? Do, do, thou rogue! do, thou hempseed!

Page. Away, you scullion! you rampallian! you fustilarian! I'll tickle your catastrophe. 60

Enter Lord Chief Justice *and his* Men.

Ch. Just. What is the matter? Keep the peace here, ho!

Host. Good my lord, be good to me; I beseech you stand to me.

Ch. Just. How now, Sir John? what are you brawling here? 65
Doth this become your place, your time, and business? You should have been well on your way to York. Stand from him, fellow, wherefore hang'st thou upon him?

Host. O my most worshipful lord, and't please your Grace, I am a poor widow of Eastcheap, and he is arrested at my suit. 71

Ch. Just. For what sum?

Host. It is more than for some, my lord, it is for all I have. He hath eaten me out of house and home, he hath put all my substance into that fat belly of his, 75 but I will have some of it out again, or I will ride thee a' nights like the mare.

Fal. I think I am as like to ride the mare, if I have any vantage of ground to get up. 79

Ch. Just. How comes this, Sir John? What man of good temper would endure this tempest of exclamation? Are you not asham'd to enforce a poor widow to so rough a course to come by her own?

Fal. What is the gross sum that I owe thee? 84

Host. Marry, if thou wert an honest man, thyself and the money too. Thou didst swear to me upon a parcel-gilt goblet, sitting in my Dolphin chamber, at the round table by a sea-coal fire, upon Wednesday in Wheeson week, when the Prince broke thy head for liking his father to a singing-man of Windsor, 90 thou didst swear to me then, as I was washing thy wound, to marry me and make me my lady thy wife. Canst thou deny it? Did not goodwife Keech, the butcher's wife, come in then and call me gossip Quickly? coming in to borrow a mess of vinegar, 95 telling us she had a good dish of prawns, whereby thou didst desire to eat some, whereby I told thee they were ill for a green wound? And didst thou not, when she was gone down stairs, desire me to be no more so familiarity with such poor people, saying that 100 ere long they should call me madam? And didst thou not kiss me, and bid me fetch thee thirty shillings? I put the now to thy book-oath. Deny it if thou canst.

Fal. My lord, this is a poor [mad] soul, and she says up and down the town that her eldest son is like 105 you. She hath been in good case, and the truth is, poverty hath distracted her. But for these foolish officers, I beseech you I may have redress against them.

Ch. Just. Sir John, Sir John, I am well acquainted with your manner of wrenching the true cause 110 the false way. It is not a confident brow, nor the throng of words that come with such more than impudent sauciness from you, can thrust me from a level consideration. You have, as it appears to me, practic'd upon the easy-yielding spirit of this woman, and made her serve your uses both in purse and in person. 116

Host. Yea, in truth, my lord.

Ch. Just. Pray thee peace. Pay her the debt you owe her, and unpay the villainy you have done with her. The one you may do with sterling money, and the other with current repentance. 121

---

28. **indited:** i.e. invited. **Lubber's Head:** an inn.
28–29. **Lumbert street:** Lombard Street, a principal thoroughfare in London. 30. **exion:** i.e. action.
32. **mark.** See note to I.ii.193. 34. **fubb'd:** put.
39. **arrant malmsey-nose:** notorious red-nose. *Malmsey* = a sweet red wine. 40. **offices:** duties.
43. **whose mare's dead:** i.e. what's the commotion.
47. **quean:** slut. **channel:** gutter.
50. **honeysuckle:** blunder for *homicidal.*
52. **honeyseed:** blunder for *homicide.* 53. **man-queller:** man-killer.
58. **hempseed:** gallows-bird.
59. **scullion:** kitchen menial. **rampallian:** ruffian.
60. **fustilarian:** frowsy slut. **catastrophe:** backside.
63. **stand to:** support. 65. **what:** why, for what.

77. **a' nights:** by night. **mare:** nightmare.
79. **get up:** mount (a steed). 84. **gross:** total.
87. **parcel-gilt:** i.e. gilded on the inside (*parcel* = partial). **Dolphin chamber:** a room in the Hostess' tavern.
88. **sea-coal:** mineral coal (as distinguished from charcoal), brought to London by sea. 89. **Wheeson:** Whitsun (Pentecost).
90. **liking:** comparing.
94. **gossip:** familiar term of address for a female friend.
95. **mess:** quantity.
96. **prawns:** shrimps. **whereby:** whereupon. 98. **green:** raw.
101. **call me madam:** i.e. as the wife of a knight.
103. **book-oath:** oath on the Bible.
106. **in good case:** prosperous.
107. **distracted her:** driven her insane. 113. **level:** just.
119. **unpay:** make good. 121. **current:** genuine.

Fal. My lord, I will not undergo this sneap without reply. You call honorable boldness impudent sauciness; if a man will make curtsy and say nothing, he is virtuous. No, my lord, my humble duty remem- 125 b'red, I will not be your suitor. I say to you, I do desire deliverance from these officers, being upon hasty employment in the King's affairs.

Ch. Just. You speak as having power to do wrong, but answer in th' effect of your reputation, and satisfy the poor woman. 131

Fal. Come hither, hostess.

Enter a messenger [MASTER GOWER].

Ch. Just. Now, Master Gower, what news?

Gow. The King, my lord, and Harry Prince of Wales
Are near at hand. The rest the paper tells. 135

Fal. As I am a gentleman!

Host. Faith, you said so before.

Fal. As I am a gentleman! Come, no more words of it. 139

Host. By this heav'nly ground I tread on, I must be fain to pawn both my plate and the tapestry of my dining-chambers.

Fal. Glasses, glasses, is the only drinking, and for thy walls, a pretty slight drollery, or the story of the Prodigal, or the German hunting in waterwork, 145 is worth a thousand of these bed-hangers and these fly-bitten [tapestries]. Let it be ten pound, if thou canst. Come, and 'twere not for thy humors, there's not a better wench in England. Go wash thy face, and draw the action. Come, thou must not be in this humor 150 with me, dost not know me? Come, come, I know thou wast set on to this.

Host. Pray thee, Sir John, let it be but twenty nobles. I' faith, I am loath to pawn my plate, so God save me law! 155

Fal. Let it alone, I'll make other shift. You'll be a fool still.

Host. Well, you shall have it, though I pawn my gown. I hope you'll come to supper. You'll pay me all together? 160

Fal. Will I live? [*To Bardolph.*] Go, with her, with her, hook on, hook on.

Host. Will you have Doll Tearsheet meet you at supper?

Fal. No more words, let's have her. 165

Exeunt Hostess and Sergeant [*Fang, Snare, and Bardolph*].

Ch. Just. I have heard better news.

Fal. What's the news, my lord?

Ch. Just. Where lay the King to-night?

Gow. At [Basingstoke], my lord. 169

Fal. I hope, my lord, all's well. What is the news, my lord?

Ch. Just. Come all his forces back?

Gow. No, fifteen hundred foot, five hundred horse, Are march'd up to my Lord of Lancaster, Against Northumberland and the Archbishop. 175

Fal. Comes the King back from Wales, my noble lord?

Ch. Just. You shall have letters of me presently. Come, go along with me, good Master Gower.

Fal. My lord! 180

Ch. Just. What's the matter?

Fal. Master Gower, shall I entreat you with me to dinner?

Gow. I must wait upon my good lord here, I thank you, good Sir John. 185

Ch. Just. Sir John, you loiter here too long, being you are to take soldiers up in counties as you go.

Fal. Will you sup with me, Master Gower?

Ch. Just. What foolish master taught you these manners, Sir John? 190

Fal. Master Gower, if they become me not, he was a fool that taught them me. This is the right fencing grace, my lord, tap for tap, and so part fair.

Ch. Just. Now the Lord lighten thee! thou art a great fool. [*Exeunt.*] 195

[SCENE II]

Enter the PRINCE [HENRY], POINS, *with other.*

Prince. Before God, I am exceeding weary.

Poins. Is't come to that? I had thought weariness durst not have attach'd one of so high blood.

Prince. Faith, it does me, though it discolors the complexion of my greatness to acknowledge it. Doth it not show vildly in me to desire small beer? 6

Poins. Why, a prince should not be so loosely studied as to remember so weak a composition.

Prince. Belike then my appetite was not princely got, for, by my troth, I do now remember the poor 10 creature, small beer. But indeed these humble considerations make me out of love with my greatness. What a disgrace is it to me to remember thy name, or to know thy face to-morrow, or to take note how many pair of silk stockings thou hast, [viz.,] 15 these, and those that were thy peach-color'd once, or to bear the inventory of thy shirts, as one for superfluity,

---

122. **sneap:** rebuke.
125. **duty:** respect (for one of your position).
130. **in . . . reputation:** suitably to your position.
141. **fain:** content.
143. **Glasses:** i.e. in place of old-fashioned metal tankards.
144. **pretty slight drollery:** comic scene.
145. **hunting in waterwork:** hunting scene in water color.
148. **humors:** whims, moods.
149–50. **draw the action:** withdraw the lawsuit.
154. **nobles:** gold coins worth 6s. 8d.
155. **law:** la (an emphatic interjection).
156. **shift:** i.e. arrangements.   157. **still:** always.
162. **hook on:** i.e. stick close to her (so she won't change her mind about the loan).

---

169. **Basingstoke:** market town west of London.
178. **presently:** at once.   186. **being:** seeing.
187. **take . . . up:** recruit.
193. **grace:** style.   **fair:** i.e. on good terms.
194. **lighten:** (1) illuminate; (2) diminish in weight.

II.ii. Location: London. Prince Henry's house.
3. **attach'd:** seized on.   4–5. **discolors . . . of:** makes blush.
6. **vildly:** vilely, disreputably.   **small:** weak.
8. **studied:** disposed.   10. **got:** begotten.
17. **for superfluity:** as a spare.

2 Henry IV
II.ii

and another for use! But that the tennis-court-keeper knows better than I, for it is a low ebb of linen with thee when thou keepest not racket there; as thou 20 hast not done a great while, because the rest of the low countries have [made a shift to] eat up thy holland. And God knows whether those that [bawl] out the ruins of thy linen shall inherit his kingdom: but the midwives say the children are not in the fault, 25 whereupon the world increases, and kinreds are mightily strengthen'd.

Poins. How ill it follows, after you have labor'd so hard, you should talk so idly! Tell me how many good young princes would do so, their fathers being so sick as yours at this time is. 31

Prince. Shall I tell thee one thing, Poins?

Poins. Yes, faith, and let it be an excellent good thing.

Prince. It shall serve among wits of no higher breeding than thine. 36

Poins. Go to, I stand the push of your one thing that you will tell.

Prince. Marry, I tell thee it is not meet that I should be sad, now my father is sick, albeit I could 40 tell to thee—as to one it pleases me, for fault of a better, to call my friend—I could be sad, and sad indeed too.

Poins. Very hardly, upon such a subject. 44

Prince. By this hand, thou thinkest me as far in the devil's book as thou and Falstaff, for obduracy and persistency. Let the end try the man. But I tell thee, my heart bleeds inwardly that my father is so sick, and keeping such vile company as thou art hath in reason taken from me all ostentation of sorrow. 50

Poins. The reason?

Prince. What wouldst thou think of me if I should weep?

Poins. I would think thee a most princely hypocrite. 55

Prince. It would be every man's thought, and thou art a blessed fellow to think as every man thinks. Never a man's thought in the world keeps the road-way better than thine: every man would think me an 59 hypocrite indeed. And what accites your most worshipful thought to think so?

Poins. Why, because you have been so lewd and so much engraff'd to Falstaff.

Prince. And to thee. 64

Poins. By this light, I am well spoke on, I can hear it with mine own ears. The worst that they can say of me is that I am a second brother, and that I am a proper fellow of my hands, and those two things I confess I cannot help. By the mass, here comes Bardolph. 69

Enter BARDOLPH *and Boy* [PAGE].

Prince. And the boy that I gave Falstaff. 'A had him from me Christian, and look if the fat villain have not transform'd him ape.

Bard. God save your Grace!

Prince. And yours, most noble Bardolph! 74

Poins. Come, you virtuous ass, you bashful fool, must you be blushing? Wherefore blush you now? What a maidenly man-at-arms are you become! Is't such a matter to get a pottle-pot's maidenhead? 78

Page. 'A calls me [e'en now], my lord, through a red lattice, and I could discern no part of his face from the window. At last I spied his eyes, and methought he had made two holes in the ale-wive's petticoat and so peep'd through. 83

Prince. Has not the boy profited?

Bard. Away, you whoreson upright [rabbit], away!

Page. Away, you rascally Althaea's dream, away!

Prince. Instruct us, boy, what dream, boy? 88

Page. Marry, my lord, Althaea dreamt she was deliver'd of a fire-brand, and therefore I call him her dream.

Prince. A crown's worth of good interpretation. There 'tis, boy. 93

Poins. O that this blossom could be kept from cankers! Well, there is sixpence to preserve thee.

Bard. And you do not make him hang'd among you, the gallows shall have wrong.

Prince. And how doth thy master, Bardolph? 98

Bard. Well, my lord. He heard of your Grace's coming to town. There's a letter for you.

Poins. Deliver'd with good respect. And how doth the martlemas, your master?

Bard. In bodily health, sir. 103

Poins. Marry, the immortal part needs a physician, but that moves not him; though that be sick, it dies not.

Prince. I do allow this wen to be as familiar with me as my dog, and he holds his place, for look you how he writes. [*Showing the letter to Poins.*] 108

Poins. [*Reads the superscription.*] "John Falstaff, knight"—Every man must know that, as oft as he has occasion to name himself; even like those that are kin to the King, for they never prick their finger but they say, "There's some of the King's blood spilt." 113 "How comes that?" says he, that takes upon him not to conceive. The answer is as ready as a [borrower's] cap, "I am the King's poor cousin, sir."

Prince. Nay, they will be kin to us, or they will fetch it from Japhet. But the letter: 118 "Sir John Falstaff, knight, to the son of the King

---

18–21. **But . . . while:** i.e. Poins has not played tennis recently because he has no spare shirt to change to after exercising.
21–22. **the low . . . holland:** i.e. the brothels have contrived to strip you naked. *Shift* = contrivance (with pun on the meaning "shirt"); *holland* = fine linen (with pun on *Holland*, suggested by *low countries*).
23–24. **those . . . linen:** i.e. Poins's bastards, who wear his cast-off shirts. 26. **kinreds:** kindreds. 29. **idlely:** idly.
44. **Very hardly:** with difficulty. 46. **obduracy:** persistence in evil.
50. **ostentation:** display. 60. **accites:** prompts. 62. **lewd:** base.
63. **engraff'd:** attached.
67. **second:** younger (and therefore without inheritance).
67–68. **proper . . . hands:** good fighter.

78. **pottle-pot:** two-quart tankard. 80. **discern:** distinguish.
89–90. **Althaea . . . fire-brand.** The page confuses Althaea with Hecuba, who, when pregnant with Paris, dreamed that she would bear a firebrand that would destroy Troy. On Althaea's firebrand see note to *2 Henry VI*, I.i.234–35.
92. **crown:** coin worth five shillings.
95. **cankers:** cankerworms, caterpillars.
101. **with good respect:** in proper form.
102. **martlemas:** fatted ox killed at Martinmas (November 11).
106. **wen:** tumor.
114–15. **takes . . . conceive:** pretends not to understand.
118. **fetch . . . Japhet:** i.e. trace their ancestry back to Japhet, one of Noah's sons.

nearest his father, Harry Prince of Wales, greeting."

Poins. Why, this is a certificate.

Prince. Peace!   122

"I will imitate the honorable Romans in brevity."

Poins. He sure means brevity in breath, short-winded.   125

[*Prince.*] "I commend me to thee, I commend thee, and I leave thee. Be not too familiar with Poins, for he misuses thy favors so much that he swears thou art to marry his sister Nell. Repent at idle times as thou mayst, and so farewell.   130

> Thine, by yea and no, which is as much as to say, as thou usest him, Jack Falstaff with my [familiars], John with my brothers and sisters, and Sir John with all Europe."   134

Poins. My lord, I'll steep this letter in sack and make him eat it.

Prince. That's to make him eat twenty of his words. But do you use me thus, Ned? Must I marry your sister?   139

Poins. God send the wench no worse fortune! but I never said so.

Prince. Well, thus we play the fools with the time, and the spirits of the wise sit in the clouds and mock us. Is your master here in London?

Bard. Yea, my lord.   145

Prince. Where sups he? Doth the old boar feed in the old frank?

Bard. At the old place, my lord, in Eastcheap.

Prince. What company?

Page. Ephesians, my lord, of the old church.   150

Prince. Sup any women with him?

Page. None, my lord, but old Mistress Quickly and Mistress Doll Tearsheet.

Prince. What pagan may that be?

Page. A proper gentlewoman, sir, and a kinswoman of my master's.   156

Prince. Even such kin as the parish heckfers are to the town bull. Shall we steal upon them, Ned, at supper?

Poins. I am your shadow, my lord, I'll follow you.

Prince. Sirrah, you boy, and Bardolph, no word to your master that I am yet come to town. There's for your silence.   162

Bard. I have no tongue, sir.

Page. And for mine, sir, I will govern it.

Prince. Fare you well; go. [*Exeunt Bardolph and Page.*] This Doll Tearsheet should be some road.

Poins. I warrant you, as common as the way between Saint Albons and London.   168

Prince. How might we see Falstaff bestow himself to-night in his true colors, and not ourselves be seen?

Poins. Put on two leathern jerkins and aprons, and wait upon him at his table as drawers.   172

Prince. From a God to a bull? a heavy descension! it was Jove's case. From a prince to a prentice? a low transformation! that shall be mine, for in every thing the purpose must weigh with the folly. Follow me, Ned.   *Exeunt.*   177

[SCENE III]

Enter NORTHUMBERLAND, *his wife* [LADY NORTHUMBERLAND], *and* [LADY PERCY,] *the wife to Harry Percy.*

North. I pray thee, loving wife, and gentle daughter,
Give even way unto my rough affairs;
Put not you on the visage of the times,
And be like them to Percy troublesome.   4

Lady N. I have given over, I will speak no more;
Do what you will, your wisdom be your guide.

North. Alas, sweet wife, my honor is at pawn,
And but my going, nothing can redeem it.

Lady P. O yet for God's sake, go not to these wars!
The time was, father, that you broke your word   10
When you were more [endear'd] to it than now,
When your own Percy, when my heart's dear Harry,
Threw many a northward look to see his father
Bring up his powers; but he did long in vain.
Who then persuaded you to stay at home?   15
There were two honors lost, yours and your son's:
For yours, the God of heaven brighten it!
For his, it stuck upon him as the sun
In the grey vault of heaven, and by his light
Did all the chevalry of England move   20
To do brave acts. He was indeed the glass
Wherein the noble youth did dress themselves:
[He had no legs that practic'd not his gait;
And speaking thick (which nature made his blemish)
Became the accents of the valiant;   25
For those that could speak low and tardily
Would turn their own perfection to abuse
To seem like him; so that in speech, in gait,
In diet, in affections of delight,
In military rules, humors of blood,   30
He was the mark and glass, copy and book,
That fashion'd others. And him, O wondrous him!
O miracle of men! him did you leave,
Second to none, unseconded by you,
To look upon the hideous god of war   35
In disadvantage, to abide a field

---

174. **Jove's case.** To gain Europa's love, Jove transformed himself into a bull.   176. **weigh with:** balance, be equal to.

II.iii. Location: Warkworth. Before Northumberland's castle.
1. **daughter:** i.e. daughter-in-law.
2. **Give even way:** allow free scope.   8. **but:** except for.
10–14. **The time . . . vain.** On Northumberland's failure to come to Hotspur's aid at the battle of Shrewsbury see *1 Henry IV*, IV.i.13–85.
11. **endear'd:** bound.   20. **chevalry:** chivalry.
21. **glass:** mirror.   24. **thick:** hurriedly.
29. **affections of delight:** favorite occupations.
30. **humors of blood:** temperament.
31. **mark:** pattern.   **copy:** example.
36. **In disadvantage:** i.e. against heavy odds.   **abide a field:** sustain a battle.

---

121. **a certificate:** i.e. couched in legal style.
131. **by . . . no.** A common oath with Puritans (Matthew 5:37).
137. **twenty:** i.e. a large number.   147. **frank:** sty.
150. **Ephesians . . . church:** i.e. boon companions of the usual (disreputable) sort.   154. **pagan:** harlot.   157. **heckfers:** heifers.
166. **road:** strumpet.
168. **Saint Albons:** St. Albans, some twenty miles north of London, on the heavily travelled Great North Road.
169. **bestow:** behave.   171. **jerkins:** jackets.
172. **drawers:** tapsters.

2 Henry IV
II.iii

Where nothing but the sound of Hotspur's name
Did seem defensible: so you left him.
Never, O never, do his ghost the wrong
To hold your honor more precise and nice   40
With others than with him! Let them alone.
The Marshal and the Archbishop are strong.
Had my sweet Harry had but half their numbers,
To-day might I, hanging on Hotspur's neck,
Have talk'd of Monmouth's grave.]

North.   Beshrew your heart,
Fair daughter, you do draw my spirits from me   46
With new lamenting ancient oversights,
But I must go and meet with danger there,
Or it will seek me in another place,
And find me worse provided.

Lady N.   O, fly to Scotland, 50
Till that the nobles and the armed commons
Have of their puissance made a little taste.

Lady P. If they get ground and vantage of the
        King,
Then join you with them, like a rib of steel,
To make strength stronger; but, for all our loves, 55
First let them try themselves. So did your son,
He was so suff'red; so came I a widow,
And never shall have length of life enough
To rain upon remembrance with mine eyes,
That it may grow and sprout as high as heaven,   60
For recordation to my noble husband.

North. Come, come, go in with me. 'Tis with my
        mind
As with the tide swell'd up unto his height,
That makes a still-stand, running neither way.
Fain would I go to meet the Archbishop,   65
But many thousand reasons hold me back.
I will resolve for Scotland; there am I,
Till time and vantage crave my company.   *Exeunt.*

[SCENE IV]

Enter a Drawer or two [FRANCIS *and a second* DRAWER].

Fran. What the devil hast thou brought there?
apple-johns? Thou knowest Sir John cannot endure an
apple-john.

[2.] *Draw.* Mass, thou say'st true. The Prince
once set a dish of apple-johns before him, and told   5
him there were five more Sir Johns, and putting off
his hat, said, "I will now take my leave of these six dry,
round, old, wither'd knights." It ang'red him to the
heart, but he hath forgot that.   9

Fran. Why then cover and set them down, and see
if thou canst find out Sneak's noise. Mistress Tearsheet
would fain hear some music.

Enter WILL [*a third* DRAWER].

[3.] *Draw.* Dispatch. The room where they supp'd
is too hot, they'll come in straight.   14

Fran. Sirrah, here will be the Prince and Master
Poins anon, and they will put on two of our jerkins and
aprons, and Sir John must not know of it. Bardolph
hath brought word.

[3.] *Draw.* By the mass, here will be old utis, it
will be an excellent stratagem.   20

[2. *Draw.*] I'll see if I can find out Sneak.

Exit [*with Third Drawer*].

Enter MISTRESS QUICKLY [*the* HOSTESS] *and* DOLL
TEARSHEET.

Host. I' faith, sweet heart, methinks now you are in
an excellent good temperality. Your pulsidge beats as
extraordinarily as heart would desire, and your color,
I warrant you, is as red as any rose, in good truth   25
law! But, i' faith, you have drunk too much canaries,
and that's a marvellous searching wine, and it perfumes
the blood ere one can say, "What's this?" How do
you now?

Doll. Better than I was. Hem!   30

Host. Why, that's well said; a good heart's worth
gold. Lo here comes Sir John.

Enter SIR JOHN [FALSTAFF].

Fal. [*Singing.*] "When Arthur first in court"—
Empty the jordan. [*Exit Francis.*]—[*Singing.*] "And
was a worthy king." How now, Mistress Doll?   35

Host. Sick of a calm, yea, good faith.

Fal. So is all her sect; and they be once in a calm,
they are sick.

Doll. A pox damn you, you muddy rascal, is that all
the comfort you give me?   40

Fal. You make fat rascals, Mistress Doll.

Doll. I make them? Gluttony and diseases make,
I make them not.

Fal. If the cook help to make the gluttony, you help
to make the diseases, Doll. We catch of you, Doll, we
catch of you. Grant that, my poor virtue, grant that.

Doll. Yea, joy, our chains and our jewels.   47

Fal. "Your brooches, pearls, and ouches." For to
serve bravely is to come halting off, you know; to
come off the breach with his pike bent bravely,   50
and to surgery bravely; to venture upon the charg'd
chambers bravely—

---

38. **defensible:** capable of making defense.
40. **nice:** punctilious.
57. **so suff'red:** i.e. permitted to try his own strength.
61. **recordation:** memorial.   65. **Fain:** gladly.
67. **I . . . Scotland.** Actually, as Holinshed makes clear (Bullough, IV, 274), Northumberland—who gave no effective aid to Archbishop Scroop—fled to Scotland *after* the rebels had been seized and executed.

II.iv. Location: London. The Boar's Head Tavern in Eastcheap.
2. **apple-johns:** wrinkled winter apples.   4. **Mass:** by the Mass.
10. **cover:** i.e. spread the cloth.   11. **noise:** band of musicians.

19. **old utis:** great sport (?).
23. **temperality:** i.e. temper.   **pulsidge:** i.e. pulse.
24. **extraordinarily:** i.e. ordinarily.
26. **canaries:** canary, a sweet wine.   27. **searching:** strong.
31. **heart:** disposition.
33. **When . . . court:** fragment of the ballad "Sir Launcelot du Lake."
34. **jordan:** chamber pot.   36. **calm:** blunder for *qualm.*
37. **sect:** sex.   39. **muddy:** dirty.
41. **You . . . rascals.** Using *rascal* in the sense of "lean, inferior deer," Falstaff implies that the term is inappropriate for him.
42. **diseases:** i.e. venereal diseases.
45. **catch of:** become infected by.
46. **poor virtue:** sweet virtuous one.
47. **Yea . . . jewels.** Taking up Falstaff's word *catch,* Doll implies that he has wheedled (or stolen) her trinkets from her.
48. **ouches:** jewels.
48–52. **For . . . bravely.** Like almost all the speeches in this scene, Falstaff's military metaphor is filled with indecent double meanings.

Doll. Hang yourself, you muddy cunger, hang yourself! 54

Host. By my troth, this is the old fashion, you two never meet but you fall to some discord. You are both, i' good truth, as rheumatic as two dry toasts, you cannot one bear with another's confirmities. What the good-year! one must bear, and that must be you, 59 you are the weaker vessel, as they say, the emptier vessel.

Doll. Can a weak empty vessel bear such a huge full hogshead? There's a whole merchant's venture 63 of Burdeaux stuff in him, you have not seen a hulk better stuff'd in the hold. Come, I'll be friends with thee, Jack. Thou art going to the wars, and 66 whether I shall ever see thee again or no, there is nobody cares.

Enter Drawer [FRANCIS].

[*Fran.*] Sir, Ancient Pistol's below, and would speak with you. 70

Doll. Hang him, swaggering rascal! let him not come hither. It is the foul-mouth'd'st rogue in England.

Host. If he swagger, let him not come here. No, by my faith, I must live among my neighbors; 74 I'll no swaggerers, I am in good name and fame with the very best. Shut the door, there comes no swaggerers here; I have not liv'd all this while to have swaggering now. Shut the door, I pray you.

Fal. Dost thou hear, hostess?

Host. Pray ye pacify yourself, Sir John. There comes no swaggerers here. 81

Fal. Dost thou hear? It is mine ancient.

Host. Tilly-fally, Sir John, ne'er tell me; and your ancient [swagger, 'a] comes not in my doors. I was before Master Tisick, the debuty, t' other day, and, as he said to me—'twas no longer ago than Wed'sday last, i' good faith—"Neighbor Quickly," says 87 he—Master Dumbe, our minister, was by then— "Neighbor Quickly," says he, "receive those that are civil, for," said he, "you are in an ill name." Now 'a said so, I can tell whereupon. "For," says he, 91 "you are an honest woman, and well thought on, therefore take heed what guests you receive. Receive," says he, "no swaggering companions." There comes none here. You would bless you to hear what he said. No, I'll no swagg'rers. 96

Fal. He's no swagg'rer, hostess, a tame cheater, i' faith, you may stroke him as gently as a puppy greyhound. He'll not swagger with a Barbary hen, if her feathers turn back in any show of resistance. Call him up, drawer. [*Exit Francis.*] 101

Host. Cheater, call you him? I will bar no honest man my house, nor no cheater, but I do not love swaggering, by my troth. I am the worse when one says swagger. Feel, masters, how I shake, look you, I warrant you. 106

Doll. So you do, hostess.

Host. Do I? yea, in very truth, do I, and 'twere an aspen leaf. I cannot abide swagg'rers.

Enter ANCIENT PISTOL *and* [BARDOLPH *and*] *Boy* [PAGE].

Pist. God save you, Sir John! 110

Fal. Welcome, Ancient Pistol. Here, Pistol, I charge you with a cup of sack, do you discharge upon mine hostess.

Pist. I will discharge upon her, Sir John, with two bullets. 115

Fal. She is pistol-proof, sir; you shall not hardly offend her.

Host. Come, I'll drink no proofs nor no bullets. I'll drink no more than will do me good, for no man's pleasure, I. 120

Pist. Then to you, Mistress Dorothy, I will charge you.

Doll. Charge me? I scorn you, scurvy companion. What, you poor, base, rascally, cheating, lack-linen mate! Away, you mouldy rogue, away! I am meat for your master. 126

Pist. I know you, Mistress Dorothy.

Doll. Away, you cutpurse rascal! you filthy bung, away! By this wine, I'll thrust my knife in your mouldy chaps, and you play the saucy cuttle with me. Away, you bottle-ale rascal! you basket-hilt stale 131 juggler, you! Since when, I pray you, sir? God's light, with two points on your shoulder? Much!

Pist. God let me not live, but I will murther your ruff for this. 135

Fal. No more, Pistol, I would not have you go off here. Discharge yourself of our company, Pistol.

Host. No, good Captain Pistol, not here, sweet captain. 139

Doll. Captain? thou abominable damn'd cheater, art thou not asham'd to be call'd captain? And captains were of my mind, they would truncheon you out for taking their names upon you before you have earn'd them. You a captain! you slave, for what? for tearing a poor whore's ruff in a bawdy-house? He a 145 captain! hang him, rogue! he lives upon mouldy stew'd pruins and dried cakes. A captain! God's light, these villains will make the word as odious as the word "occupy," which was an excellent good word before it was ill sorted; therefore captains had need look to't.

Bard. Pray thee go down, good ancient. 151

Fal. Hark thee hither, Mistress Doll.

---

53. **cunger:** conger eel.   57. **rheumatic:** blunder for *splenetic* (?).
58. **confirmities:** blunder for *infirmities.*
58–59. **What the good-year:** a common expletive, roughly equivalent to "deuce take it."   59. **you:** i.e. Doll.
63–64. **venture . . . stuff:** consignment of Bordeaux wine.
64. **hulk:** cargo ship.   82. **ancient:** ensign, lieutenant.
83. **Tilly-fally:** fiddlesticks.   85. **debuty:** deputy.
94. **companions:** reprobates.
95. **bless you:** count yourself lucky.   97. **cheater:** swindler.
99. **Barbary hen:** guinea hen.
102. **Cheater.** The Hostess perhaps takes the word to mean "escheater," i.e. fiscal officer for the king.

108. **and:** as if.
112. **charge:** salute.   **discharge upon:** toast.
117. **offend:** wound.   125. **mate:** fellow.
128. **bung:** pickpocket.
130. **chaps:** cheeks.   **cuttle:** cutpurse (?) or cutthroat (?).
131. **bottle:** i.e. foamy (?).
131–32. **you . . . juggler:** you sword-bearing impostor (?). *Basket-hilt* = curved hand-guard on a sword.
133. **points:** laces for tying a cuirass to the shoulders.
142. **truncheon:** cudgel.
146–47. **stew'd pruins.** Stewed prunes were commonly associated with brothels.   149. **occupy:** fornicate.   150. **ill sorted:** corrupted.

Pist. Not I. I tell thee what, Corporal Bardolph, I could tear her. I'll be reveng'd of her.

Page. Pray thee go down.   155

Pist. I'll see her damn'd first, to Pluto's damned lake, by this hand, to th' infernal deep, with Erebus and tortures vile also. Hold hook and line, say I. Down, down, dogs! down, faitors! have we not Hiren here?   [*Draws his sword.*]   160

Host. Good Captain Peesel, be quiet, 'tis very late, i' faith. I beseek you now, aggravate your choler.

Pist. These be good humors indeed! Shall pack-horses
And hollow pamper'd jades of Asia,
Which cannot go but thirty mile a day,   165
Compare with Caesars and with Cannibals
And Troiant Greeks? Nay, rather damn them with
King Cerberus, and let the welkin roar.
Shall we fall foul for toys?

Host. By my troth, captain, these are very bitter words.   171

Bard. Be gone, good ancient. This will grow to a brawl anon.

Pist. [Die] men like dogs! give crowns like pins! have we not Hiren here?   175

Host. A' my word, captain, there's none such here. What the good-year, do you think I would deny her? For God's sake be quiet.

Pist. Then feed and be fat, my fair Calipolis. Come give 's some sack.   180
"Si fortune me tormente, sperato me contento."
Fear we broadsides? no, let the fiend give fire.
Give me some sack, and, sweet heart, lie thou there.
[*Laying down his sword.*]
Come we to full points here? and are etceteras no things?

Fal. Pistol, I would be quiet.   185

Pist. Sweet knight, I kiss thy neaf. What! we have seen the seven stars.

Doll. For God's sake thrust him down stairs. I cannot endure such a fustian rascal.

Pist. Thrust him down stairs! Know we not Galloway nags?   191

Fal. Quoit him down, Bardolph, like a shove-groat shilling. Nay, and 'a do nothing but speak nothing, 'a shall be nothing here.

Bard. Come, get you down stairs.   195

Pist. What? shall we have incision? shall we imbrue?   [*Snatching up his sword.*]
Then death rock me asleep, abridge my doleful days!
Why then let grievous, ghastly, gaping wounds
Untwind the Sisters Three! Come, Atropos, I say!

Host. Here's goodly stuff toward!   200

Fal. Give me my rapier, boy.

Doll. I pray thee, Jack, I pray thee do not draw.

Fal. Get you down stairs.
[*Drawing, and driving Pistol out.*]

Host. Here's a goodly tumult! I'll forswear keeping house afore I'll be in these tirrits and frights.   205
So! murder, I warrant now. Alas, alas, put up your naked weapons, put up your naked weapons.
[*Exeunt Pistol and Bardolph.*]

Doll. I pray thee, Jack, be quiet, the rascal's gone. Ah, you whoreson little valiant villain, you!

Host. Are you not hurt i' th' groin? Methought 'a made a shrewd thrust at your belly.   211

[*Enter* Bardolph.]

Fal. Have you turn'd him out a' doors?

Bard. Yea, sir. The rascal's drunk; you have hurt him, sir, i' th' shoulder.

Fal. A rascal! to brave me?   215

Doll. Ah, you sweet little rogue, you! Alas, poor ape, how thou sweat'st! Come let me wipe thy face. Come on, you whoreson chops. Ah, rogue! i' faith, I love thee. Thou art as valorous as Hector of   219
Troy, worth five of Agamemnon, and ten times better than the Nine Worthies. Ah, villain!

Fal. Ah, rascally slave! I will toss the rogue in a blanket.

Doll. Do, and thou dar'st for thy heart. And thou dost, I'll canvass thee between a pair of sheets.   225

Enter Music.

Page. The music is come, sir.

Fal. Let them play. Play, sirs. Sit on my knee, Doll. A rascal bragging slave! The rogue fled from me like quicksilver.   229

Doll. I' faith, and thou follow'dst him like a church. Thou whoreson little tidy Bartholomew boar-pig, when wilt thou leave fighting a' days and foining a' nights, and begin to patch up thine old body for heaven?

156–60. **I'll . . . here.** Pistol's bombast, here and later in the scene, contains echoes of and allusions to various contemporary plays, some of which are identified in the notes that follow.
156. **Pluto:** god of the underworld.
157. **Erebus:** the underworld.
159. **faitors:** swindlers.   **Hiren:** the name that Pistol, following the practice of the heroes of romance, gives to his sword (perhaps with a pun on *iron*). Possibly there is also an allusion to *The Turkish Mahomet and Hiren the Fair Greek*, a lost play by George Peele.
162. **aggravate:** blunder for *moderate*.
163–67. **Shall . . . Greeks:** a mangled quotation from Christopher Marlowe's *Tamburlaine*, Part II, lines 3980–81.
166. **Cannibals:** blunder for *Hannibals* (referring to the famous Carthaginian general).   167. **Troiant:** Trojan.
168. **Cerberus:** three-headed dog at the entrance of the underworld.
169. **fall . . . toys:** fight over trifles.
179. **Then . . . Calipolis:** a garbled quotation from *The Battle of Alcazar* by George Peele.
181. **Si . . . contento:** if fortune torments me, hope contents me. (Pistol's ignorant farrago of Spanish and Italian is perhaps a motto engraved on his sword blade.)   182. **give fire:** shoot.
184. **full points:** stops.   186. **neaf:** fist.
187. **the seven stars:** constellation of the Pleiades.
189. **fustian:** worthless.
191. **Galloway nags:** inferior Irish horses.

192. **Quoit:** throw.   **shove-groat:** game in which coins were aimed at a mark.   196. **imbrue:** shed blood.
199. **Untwind:** untwine.   **Atropos:** one of the Fates ("the Sisters Three").   200. **toward:** forthcoming.   205. **tirrits:** temper tantrums.
211. **shrewd:** sharp.   215. **brave:** defy.   218. **chops:** fat face.
219–20. **Hector, Agamemnon:** leaders of the Trojans and the Greeks respectively in the Trojan war.
221. **the Nine Worthies:** a group of renowned champions (Hector, Alexander, Caesar, et al.).
222–23. **toss . . . blanket.** A punishment for cowards. In the next speech Doll varies the phrase with a different implication.
226 s.d. **Music:** musicians.
231. **Bartholomew boar-pig.** Roast pig was the chief delicacy at the annual fair on St. Bartholomew's Day (August 24) in Smithfield.
232. **foining:** thrusting.

Enter, [*behind,*] Prince [Henry] *and* Poins, [*disguised*].

Fal. Peace, good Doll, do not speak like a death's-head, do not bid me remember mine end.   235

Doll. Sirrah, what humor's the Prince of?

Fal. A good shallow young fellow. 'A would have made a good pantler, 'a would 'a' chipp'd bread well.

Doll. They say Poins has a good wit.   239

Fal. He a good wit? Hang him, baboon! his wit's as thick as Tewksbury mustard, there's no more conceit in him than is in a mallet.

Doll. Why does the Prince love him so then?   243

Fal. Because their legs are both of a bigness, and 'a plays at quoits well, and eats cunger and fennel, and drinks off candles' ends for flap-dragons, and rides the wild-mare with the boys, and jumps upon join'd-stools, and swears with a good grace, and wears his boots   248 very smooth, like unto the sign of the Leg, and breeds no bate with telling of discreet stories; and such other gambol faculties 'a has, that show a weak mind and an able body, for the which the Prince admits him.   252 For the Prince himself is such another, the weight of a hair will turn scales between their haberdepois.

Prince. Would not this nave of a wheel have his ears cut off?   256

Poins. Let's beat him before his whore.

Prince. Look whe'er the wither'd elder hath not his pole claw'd like a parrot.

Poins. Is it not strange that desire should so many years outlive performance?   261

Fal. Kiss me, Doll.

Prince. Saturn and Venus this year in conjunction! What says th' almanac to that?

Poins. And look whether the fiery Trigon, his man, be not lisping to his [master's] old tables, his note-book, his counsel-keeper.   267

Fal. Thou dost give me flattering busses.

Doll. By my troth, I kiss thee with a most constant heart.

Fal. I am old, I am old.   271

Doll. I love thee better than I love e'er a scurvy young boy of them all.

Fal. What stuff wilt have a kirtle of? I shall receive money a' Thursday, shalt have a cap to-morrow.

---

236. **humor:** disposition.
238. **pantler:** servant in the pantry.   **chipp'd:** cut the crusts from.
241. **Tewksbury:** Tewksbury, town in Gloucestershire noted for its mustard balls.   241–42. **conceit:** wit.
245. **cunger and fennel:** conger eels seasoned with the herb fennel.
246. **drinks . . . flap-dragons:** i.e. drinks liquor in which lighted candles are floated.
247. **wild-mare:** seesaw.   **join'd-stools:** stools expertly made by a joiner or carpenter.
248–49. **wears . . . Leg:** i.e. wears well-fitting boots, like those on the sign over a bootmaker's shop.   250. **bate:** discord.
251. **gambol:** sportive.   252. **admits him:** tolerates him (as a friend).
254. **haberdepois:** avoirdupois.
255. **nave:** hub (with a pun on *knave*).
255–56. **have . . . off.** The punishment for slandering royalty.
259. **his . . . parrot.** Doll is scratching Falstaff's head (*pole* = poll).
263. **Saturn and Venus:** planets with strong influence on the aged and on lovers respectively.   Their conjunction is astronomically impossible.
265. **the fiery Trigon.** The zodiac was divided into four "trigons" of three signs, characterized as fiery, airy, watery, and earthy. The "fiery Trigon" (Aries, Leo, and Sagittarius) is in allusion to Bardolph's complexion.
266–67. **lisping . . . counsel-keeper:** i.e. courting the Hostess.   **tables:** account book.   268. **busses:** kisses.   274. **kirtle:** skirt.

A merry song! Come, it grows late, we'll to bed. Thou't forget me when I am gone.   277

Doll. By my troth, thou't set me a-weeping and thou say'st so. Prove that ever I dress myself handsome till thy return—well, hearken a' th' end.

Fal. Some sack, Francis.

Prince, Poins. Anon, anon, sir. [*Coming forward.*]

Fal. Ha? a bastard son of the King's? And art not thou Poins his brother?   284

Prince. Why, thou globe of sinful continents, what a life dost thou lead?

Fal. A better than thou: I am a gentleman, thou art a drawer.

Prince. Very true, sir, and I come to draw you out by the ears.   290

Host. O, the Lord preserve thy Grace! By my troth, welcome to London. Now, the Lord bless that sweet face of thine! O Jesu, are you come from Wales?

Fal. Thou whoreson mad compound of majesty, by this light flesh and corrupt blood, thou art welcome.

Doll. How? you fat fool, I scorn you.   296

Poins. My lord, he will drive you out of your revenge and turn all to a merriment, if you take not the heat.

Prince. You whoreson candle-mine, you, how   300 vildly did you speak of me [even] now before this honest, virtuous, civil gentlewoman!

Host. God's blessing of your good heart! and so she is, by my troth.

Fal. Didst thou hear me?   305

Prince. Yea, and you knew me, as you did when you ran away by Gadshill. You knew I was at your back, and spoke it on purpose to try my patience.

Fal. No, no, no, not so, I did not think thou wast within hearing.   310

Prince. I shall drive you then to confess the willful abuse, and then I know how to handle you.

Fal. No abuse, Hal, a' mine honor, no abuse.

Prince. Not to dispraise me, and call me pantler and bread-chipper, and I know not what?   315

Fal. No abuse, Hal.

Poins. No abuse?

Fal. No abuse, Ned, i' th' world, honest Ned, none. I disprais'd him before the wicked, that   319 the wicked [*turns to the Prince*] might not fall in love with thee; in which doing, I have done the part of a careful friend and a true subject, and thy father is to give me thanks for it. No abuse, Hal; none, Ned, none; no, faith, boys, none.   324

Prince. See now whether pure fear and entire cowardice doth not make thee wrong this virtuous gentlewoman to close with us. Is she of the wicked? is thine hostess here of the wicked? or is thy boy of the

---

280. **hearken . . . end:** i.e. you'll see that I am faithful to you.
283. **bastard.** With punning reference to his assumed role as drawer; *bastard* = a sweet Spanish wine.
285. **globe . . . continents:** (1) terrestrial globe . . . land masses; (2) sphere . . . contents.   285–86. **what a:** what kind of.
295. **this . . . blood:** i.e. Doll.
298–99. **take . . . heat:** i.e. strike . . . when the iron is hot.
300. **candle-mine:** i.e. store of tallow.   301. **vildly:** basely.
306–7. **you . . . Gadshill.** See *1 Henry IV*, II.iv.
325. **entire:** pure.   327. **close with:** pacify.

2 Henry IV
II.iv

wicked? or honest Bardolph, whose zeal burns in his
nose, of the wicked? 330

Poins. Answer, thou dead elm, answer.

Fal. The fiend hath prick'd down Bardolph irre-
coverable, and his face is Lucifer's privy-kitchen,
where he doth nothing but roast malt-worms. 334
For the boy, there is a good angel about him, but the
devil blinds him too.

Prince. For the women?

Fal. For one of them, she's in hell already, and
burns poor souls; for th' other, I owe her money, and
whether she be damn'd for that, I know not. 340

Host. No, I warrant you.

Fal. No, I think thou art not, I think thou art quit
for that. Marry, there is another indictment upon thee,
for suffering flesh to be eaten in thy house, contrary to
the law, for the which I think thou wilt howl. 345

Host. All vict'lers do so. What's a joint of mutton
or two in a whole Lent?

Prince. You, gentlewoman—

Doll. What says your Grace? 349

Fal. His grace says that which his flesh rebels
against. *Peto knocks at door.*

Host. Who knocks so loud at door? Look to th'
door there, Francis.

[*Enter* Peto.]

Prince. Peto, how now, what news? 354

Peto. The King your father is at Westminster,
And there are twenty weak and wearied posts
Come from the north, and as I came along
I met and overtook a dozen captains,
Bare-headed, sweating, knocking at the taverns,
And asking every one for Sir John Falstaff. 360

Prince. By heaven, Poins, I feel me much to blame
So idly to profane the precious time,
When tempest of commotion, like the south
Borne with black vapor, doth begin to melt
And drop upon our bare unarmed heads. 365
Give me my sword and cloak. Falstaff, good night.

Exeunt Prince and Poins, [*Peto and Bardolph*].

Fal. Now comes in the sweetest morsel of the
night, and we must hence and leave it unpick'd.
[*Knocking within.*] More knocking at the door!

[*Enter* Bardolph.]

How now, what's the matter? 370

Bard. You must away to court, sir, presently,
A dozen captains stay at door for you.

Fal. [*To the Page.*] Pay the musicians, sirrah.
Farewell, hostess, farewell, Doll. You see, my 374
good wenches, how men of merit are sought after.
The undeserver may sleep when the man of action is

call'd on. Farewell, good wenches, if I be not sent
away post, I will see you again ere I go.

Doll. I cannot speak. If my heart be not ready to
burst—well, sweet Jack, have a care of thyself. 380

Fal. Farewell, farewell.

Exit [*with Bardolph and Page*].

Host. Well, fare thee well. I have known thee these
twenty-nine years, come peascod-time, but an honester
and truer-hearted man—well, fare thee well.

Bard. [*Within.*] Mistress Tearsheet! 385

Host. What's the matter?

Bard. [*Within.*] Bid Mistress Tearsheet come to
my master.

Host. O, run, Doll, run, run, good Doll. Come.
[*To Bardolph.*] She comes blubber'd.—Yea! will you
come, Doll? *Exeunt.* 391

[ACT III, Scene I]

Enter the King *in his night-gown, alone,* [*followed by a*
Page].

King. Go call the Earls of Surrey and of Warwick;
But, ere they come, bid them o'er-read these letters
And well consider of them. Make good speed.

[*Exit Page.*]

How many thousand of my poorest subjects
Are at this hour asleep! O sleep! O gentle sleep! 5
Nature's soft nurse, how have I frighted thee,
That thou no more wilt weigh my eyelids down,
And steep my senses in forgetfulness?
Why rather, sleep, liest thou in smoky cribs,
Upon uneasy pallets stretching thee, 10
And hush'd with buzzing night-flies to thy slumber,
Than in the perfum'd chambers of the great,
Under the canopies of costly state,
And lull'd with sound of sweetest melody?
O thou dull god, why li'st thou with the vile 15
In loathsome beds, and leavest the kingly couch
A watch-case or a common 'larum-bell?
Wilt thou upon the high and giddy [mast]
Seal up the ship-boy's eyes, and rock his brains
In cradle of the rude imperious surge, 20
And in the visitation of the winds,
Who take the ruffian [billows] by the top,
Curling their monstrous heads and hanging them
With deafing clamor in the slippery clouds,
That with the hurly death itself awakes? 25
Canst thou, O partial sleep, give [then] repose
To the wet [sea-boy] in an hour so rude,
And in the calmest and most stillest night,
With all appliances and means to boot,
Deny it to a king? Then (happy) low, lie down! 30
Uneasy lies the head that wears a crown.

---

332. **prick'd down:** marked.
334. **malt-worms:** beer tipplers.
339. **burns:** i.e. infects with venereal diseases.
342. **quit:** (1) paid; (2) saved.
344. **for . . . house:** i.e. for serving meat during Lent.
346. **vict'lers:** victuallers, purveyors of food.
350–51. **says . . . against:** i.e. in addressing the Hostess and Doll as "gentlewomen."
363. **commotion:** sedition, insurrection. **south:** south wind.
364. **Borne:** laden. 371. **presently:** immediately.
372. **stay:** wait.

378. **post:** in haste.
383. **peascod-time:** i.e. early summer (when peas are in pod).

III.i. Location: Westminster. The palace.
o.s.d. **night-gown:** dressing gown. 9. **cribs:** hovels.
13. **state:** magnificence. 15. **vile:** low in rank.
17. **watch-case:** sentry-box. **'larum-bell:** alarm bell.
25. **That:** so that. **hurly:** tumult.
29. **appliances and means:** comforts and inducements (to sleep).
30. **low:** lowly ones.

Enter WARWICK, SURREY, *and* SIR JOHN BLUNT.

War.   Many good morrows to your Majesty!

King.   Is it good morrow, lords?

War.   'Tis one a' clock, and past.

King.   Why then good morrow to you all, my   35
lords.

Have you read o'er the [letters] that I sent you?

War.   We have, my liege.

King.   Then you perceive the body of our kingdom

How foul it is, what rank diseases grow,

And with what danger, near the heart of it.   40

War.   It is but as a body yet distempered,

Which to his former strength may be restored

With good advice and little medicine.

My Lord Northumberland will soon be cool'd.

King.   O God, that one might read the book of fate,

And see the revolution of the times   46

Make mountains level, and the continent,

Weary of solid firmness, melt itself

Into the sea, and other times to see

The beachy girdle of the ocean   50

Too wide for Neptune's hips; how chance's mocks

And changes fill the cup of alteration

With divers liquors! O, if this were seen,

The happiest youth, viewing his progress through,

What perils past, what crosses to ensue,   55

Would shut the book, and sit him down and die.

'Tis not ten years gone

Since Richard and Northumberland, great friends,

Did feast together, and in two year after

Were they at wars. It is but eight years since   60

This Percy was the man nearest my soul,

Who like a brother toil'd in my affairs,

And laid his love and life under my foot,

Yea, for my sake, even to the eyes of Richard

Gave him defiance. But which of you was by—   65

[*To Warwick.*] You, cousin Nevil, as I may remember—

When Richard, with his eye brimful of tears,

Then check'd and rated by Northumberland,

Did speak these words, now prov'd a prophecy?

"Northumberland, thou ladder by the which   70

My cousin Bullingbrook ascends my throne"

(Though then, God knows, I had no such intent,

But that necessity so bow'd the state

That I and greatness were compell'd to kiss),

"The time shall come," thus did he follow it,   75

"The time will come, that foul sin, gathering head,

Shall break into corruption": so went on,

Foretelling this same time's condition

And the division of our amity.

War.   There is a history in all men's lives,   80

Figuring the natures of the times deceas'd,

The which observ'd, a man may prophesy,

With a near aim, of the main chance of things

As yet not come to life, who in their seeds

And weak beginning lie intreasured.   85

Such things become the hatch and brood of time,

And by the necessary form of this

King Richard might create a perfect guess

That great Northumberland, then false to him,

Would of that seed grow to a greater falseness,   90

Which should not find a ground to root upon

Unless on you.

King.   Are these things then necessities?

Then let us meet them like necessities;

And that same word even now cries out on us.

They say the Bishop and Northumberland   95

Are fifty thousand strong.

War.   It cannot be, my lord.

Rumor doth double, like the voice and echo,

The numbers of the feared. Please it your Grace

To go to bed. Upon my soul, my lord,

The powers that you already have sent forth   100

Shall bring this prize in very easily.

To comfort you the more, I have received

A certain instance that Glendower is dead.

Your Majesty hath been this fortnight ill,

And these unseasoned hours perforce must add   105

Unto your sickness.

King.   I will take your counsel,

And were these inward wars once out of hand,

We would, dear lords, unto the Holy Land. *Exeunt.*

[SCENE II]

Enter JUSTICE SHALLOW *and* JUSTICE SILENCE, [*meeting;*
MOULDY, SHADOW, WART, FEEBLE, BULLCALF, *and*
SERVANTS *behind*].

Shal.   Come on, come on, come on, give me your
hand, sir, give me your hand, sir. An early stirrer, by
the rood! And how doth my good cousin Silence?

Sil.   Good morrow, good cousin Shallow.   4

Shal.   And how doth my cousin, your bedfellow?
and your fairest daughter and mine, my goddaughter
Ellen?

---

33. Is ... morrow: i.e. is it already past midnight.
37. liege: sovereign.   39. rank: festering.
41. distempered: diseased.   47. continent: dry land.
50. beachy: pebbly.
51. Too ... hips. Because the sea, when it recedes, leaves a widened
beach.   55. crosses: adversities.   57. gone: ago.
63. under my foot: i.e. at my absolute disposal.   64. to: before.
66. Nevil. An error. The only Neville to hold the title Earl of Warwick was Richard (1428–71), the famous "Kingmaker" of the reign
of Henry VI. He gained the title through his wife, Anne Beauchamp,
daughter of the Earl of Warwick in the present play.
68. check'd and rated: rebuked and chided.
70–77. Northumberland ... corruption. See *Richard II*, V.i.55–59.
72. then ... intent. Actually, Bullingbrook had already ascended
Richard's throne at the time he imperfectly recalls.

81. Figuring: showing.   deceas'd: departed.
83. aim: probability.   main chance: general probability (a term
from the game of hazard).
87. this: i.e. the principle just enunciated.
94. cries out on: exclaims against.
103. instance: proof.   Glendower is dead. In 1409, reports Holinshed (Bullough, IV, 276), the hard-pressed Glendower "fled into
desert places and solitarie caves, where being destitute of all releefe
and succour, dreading to shew his face to anie creature, and finallie
lacking meat to susteine nature, for meere hunger and lacke of food,
miserablie pined awaie and died." Modern historians place his death
several years later, after the accession of Henry V.
105. unseasoned: unseasonable.
107. inward: civil.   out of hand: concluded.
108. We ... Land. See *Richard II*, V.vi.49–50; *1 Henry IV*, I.i.18–30.

III.ii. Location: Gloucestershire. Before Justice Shallow's house.
3. rood: cross.   5. bedfellow: i.e. wife.

2 Henry IV
III.ii

Sil. Alas, a black woosel, cousin Shallow!

Shal. By yea and no, sir. I dare say my cousin William is become a good scholar. He is at Oxford still, is he not? 11

Sil. Indeed, sir, to my cost.

Shal. 'A must then to the Inns a' Court shortly. I was once of Clement's Inn, where I think they will talk of mad Shallow yet. 15

Sil. You were call'd lusty Shallow then, cousin.

Shal. By the mass, I was call'd any thing, and I would have done any thing indeed too, and roundly too. There was I, and little John Doit of Staffordshire, and black George Barnes, and Francis Pickbone, and 20 Will Squele, a Cotsole man. You had not four such swingebucklers in all the Inns a' Court again; and I may say to you, we knew where the bona [robas] were and had the best of them all at commandement. Then was Jack Falstaff, now Sir John, a boy, and page to Thomas Mowbray, Duke of Norfolk. 26

Sil. This Sir John, cousin, that comes hither anon about soldiers?

Shal. The same Sir John, the very same. I see him break Scoggin's head at the court-gate, when 'a 30 was a crack not thus high; and the very same day did I fight with one Samson Stockfish, a fruiterer, behind Gray's Inn. Jesu, Jesu, the mad days that I have spent! And to see how many of my old acquaintance are dead!

Sil. We shall all follow, cousin. 35

Shal. Certain, 'tis certain, very sure, very sure. Death, as the Psalmist saith, is certain to all, all shall die. How a good yoke of bullocks at [Stamford] fair?

Sil. By my troth, I was not there.

Shal. Death is certain. Is old Double of your town living yet? 41

Sil. Dead, sir.

Shal. Jesu, Jesu, dead! 'A drew a good bow, and dead! 'A shot a fine shoot. John a' Gaunt lov'd him well, and betted much money on his head. Dead! 45 'a would have clapp'd i' th' clout at twelvescore, and carried you a forehand shaft a fourteen and fourteen and a half, that it would have done a man's heart good to see. How a score of ewes now? 49

Sil. Thereafter as they be, a score of good ewes may be worth ten pounds.

Shal. And is old Double dead?

Sil. Here come two of Sir John Falstaff's men, as I think.

---

8. **woosel:** ousel, blackbird.
13. **Inns a' Court:** legal societies of London.
14. **Clement's Inn:** one of the Inns of Chancery, formerly a centre of legal studies preparatory to the Inns of Court.
18. **roundly:** thoroughly.
21. **Cotsole:** Cotswold, referring to a range of hills in Gloucestershire. 22. **swingebucklers:** swashbucklers.
23. **bona robas:** harlots.
24. **at commandement:** at our disposal.
30. **Scoggin.** Shakespeare was perhaps thinking of John Scogan, court jester to Edward IV and hero of a jestbook popular in the later sixteenth century. 31. **crack:** frolicsome boy.
33. **Gray's Inn:** one of the Inns of Court.
38. **How:** i.e. what was the price fetched by. **Stamford:** ancient market town in Lincolnshire.
44. **shoot:** shot (in archery). **John a' Gaunt:** father of Henry IV.
46. **clapp'd ... twelvescore:** hit the target at 240 yards.
47. **forehand shaft:** arrow designed for straightforward shooting (rather than for a curved trajectory).
50. **Thereafter ... be:** depending on their quality.

Enter BARDOLPH *and one with him.*

[*Shal.*] Good morrow, honest gentlemen. 55

Bard. I beseech you, which is Justice Shallow?

Shal. I am Robert Shallow, sir, a poor esquire of this county, and one of the King's justices of the peace. What is your good pleasure with me? 59

Bard. My captain, sir, commends him to you, my captain, Sir John Falstaff, a tall gentleman, by heaven, and a most gallant leader.

Shal. He greets me well, sir. I knew him a good backsword man. How doth the good knight? May I ask how my lady his wife doth? 65

Bard. Sir, pardon, a soldier is better [accommodated] than with a wife.

Shal. It is well said, in faith, sir, and it is well said indeed too. Better accommodated! it is good, yea indeed is it. Good phrases are surely, and ever were, very commendable. Accommodated! it comes of *accommodo,* very good, a good phrase. 72

Bard. Pardon, sir, I have heard the word. Phrase call you it? By this day, I know not the phrase, but I will maintain the word with my sword to be a soldier-like word, and a word of exceeding good command, by heaven. Accommodated: that is, when a man is, as they say, accommodated, or when a man is being whereby 'a may be thought to be accommodated— which is an excellent thing. 80

Enter FALSTAFF.

Shal. It is very just. Look, here comes good Sir John. Give me your good hand, give me your worship's good hand. By my troth, you like well and bear your years very well. Welcome, good Sir John.

Fal. I am glad to see you well, good Master Robert Shallow. Master [Surecard], as I think? 86

Shal. No, Sir John, it is my cousin Silence, in commission with me.

Fal. Good Master Silence, it well befits you should be of the peace. 90

Sil. Your good worship is welcome.

Fal. Fie, this is hot weather, gentlemen. Have you provided me here half a dozen sufficient men?

Shal. Marry, have we, sir. Will you sit?

Fal. Let me see them, I beseech you. 95

Shal. Where's the roll? where's the roll? where's the roll? Let me see, let me see, let me see. So, so, so, so, so, so, so; yea, marry, sir. Rafe Mouldy! Let them appear as I call; let them do so, let them do so. Let me see, where is Mouldy? 100

Moul. Here, and't please you.

Shal. What think you, Sir John? A good-limb'd fellow, young, strong, and of good friends.

Fal. Is thy name Mouldy?

---

61. **tall:** brave.
64. **backsword:** stick with a basket-hilt used in fencing practice.
66–67. **accommodated:** furnished.
68–72. **It ... phrase.** The word *accommodated* was somewhat affected in Shakespeare's time. 70. **phrases:** expressions.
76. **of ... command:** i.e. appropriate to a commander.
81. **just:** true.
83. **troth:** truth. **like well:** are in good condition.
87–88. **in ... me:** i.e. a justice of the peace like me.
93. **sufficient:** fit for service.
103. **of good friends:** well connected.

Moul. Yea, and't please you. 105

Fal. 'Tis the more time thou wert us'd.

Shal. Ha, ha, ha! most excellent, i' faith! Things that are mouldy lack use. Very singular good, in faith, well said, Sir John, very well said.

[*Fal.* Prick him.] 110

Moul. I was prick'd well enough before, and you could have let me alone. My old dame will be undone now for one to do her husbandry and her drudgery. You need not to have prick'd me, there are other men fitter to go out than I. 115

Fal. Go to, peace, Mouldy, you shall go. Mouldy, it is time you were spent.

Moul. Spent?

Shal. Peace, fellow, peace, stand aside, know you where you are? For th' other, Sir John, let me see: Simon Shadow! 121

Fal. Yea, marry, let me have him to sit under, he's like to be a cold soldier.

Shal. Where's Shadow?

Shad. Here, sir. 125

Fal. Shadow, whose son art thou?

Shad. My mother's son, sir.

Fal. Thy mother's son! like enough, and thy father's shadow. So the son of the female is the shadow of the male. It is often so indeed, but much of the father's substance! 131

Shal. Do you like him, Sir John?

Fal. Shadow will serve for summer, prick him, [*aside*] for we have a number of shadows fill up the muster-book. 135

Shal. Thomas Wart!

Fal. Where's he?

Wart. Here, sir.

Fal. Is thy name Wart?

Wart. Yea, sir. 140

Fal. Thou art a very ragged wart.

Shal. Shall I prick him, Sir John?

Fal. It were superfluous, for ['s] apparel is built upon his back, and the whole frame stands upon pins. Prick him no more. 145

Shal. Ha, ha, ha! you can do it, sir, you can do it, I commend you well. Francis Feeble!

Fee. Here, sir.

Shal. What trade art thou, Feeble?

Fee. A woman's tailor, sir. 150

Shal. Shall I prick him, sir?

Fal. You may, but if he had been a man's tailor, he'd 'a' prick'd you. Wilt thou make as many holes in an enemy's battle as thou hast done in a woman's petticoat? 155

Fee. I will do my good will, sir, you can have no more.

Fal. Well said, good woman's tailor! well said, courageous Feeble! Thou wilt be as valiant as the wrathful dove or most magnanimous mouse. Prick the woman's tailor. Well, Master Shallow, deep, Master Shallow. 162

Fee. I would Wart might have gone, sir.

Fal. I would thou wert a man's tailor, that thou mightst mend him and make him fit to go. I cannot put him to a private soldier that is the leader of so many thousands. Let that suffice, most forcible Feeble.

Fee. It shall suffice, sir. 169

Fal. I am bound to thee, reverend Feeble. Who is next?

Shal. Peter Bullcalf o' th' green!

Fal. Yea, marry, let's see Bullcalf.

Bull. Here, sir. 174

Fal. 'Fore God, a likely fellow! Come prick Bullcalf till he roar again.

Bull. O Lord, good my lord captain—

Fal. What, dost thou roar before thou art prick'd?

Bull. O Lord, sir, I am a diseas'd man.

Fal. What disease hast thou? 180

Bull. A whoreson cold, sir, a cough, sir, which I caught with ringing in the King's affairs upon his coronation-day, sir.

Fal. Come, thou shalt go to the wars in a gown. We will have away thy cold, and I will take such 185 order that thy friends shall ring for thee. Is here all?

Shal. Here is two more call'd than your number, you must have but four here, sir. And so I pray you go in with me to dinner. 190

Fal. Come, I will go drink with you, but I cannot tarry dinner. I am glad to see you, by my troth, Master Shallow.

Shal. O Sir John, do you remember since we lay all night in the Windmill in Saint George's Field? 195

Fal. No more of that, Master Shallow, [no more of that].

Shal. Ha, 'twas a merry night. And is Jane Nightwork alive?

Fal. She lives, Master Shallow. 200

Shal. She never could away with me.

Fal. Never, never, she would always say she could not abide Master Shallow.

Shal. By the mass, I could anger her to th' heart. She was then a bona roba. Doth she hold her own well?

Fal. Old, old, Master Shallow. 206

Shal. Nay, she must be old, she cannot choose but be old, certain she's old, and had Robin Nightwork by old Nightwork before I came to Clement's Inn.

Sil. That's fifty-five year ago. 210

---

108. **singular:** singularly.　110. **Prick:** choose.
111. **prick'd:** goaded, i.e. nagged.　112. **old dame:** mother.
113. **husbandry:** farm chores.　117. **spent:** consumed.
120. **other:** others.
123. **cold:** cool (like a shadow), i.e. cowardly.
128–31. **Thy . . . substance.** The wordplay is on *sun* as opposed to *shadow* (image, likeness).
134. **shadows:** i.e. names of fictitious recruits whose pay is pocketed by the officer.
144. **his . . . pins:** i.e. he's held together by pins.
153. **prick'd:** attired.　154. **battle:** line of battle.

167. **thousands:** i.e. of lice.
182. **ringing . . . affairs:** i.e. ringing the church bells in honor of the King.　184. **gown:** dressing gown.　185. **have away:** get rid of.
185–86. **take such order:** make arrangements.
192. **tarry:** stay for.
195. **Windmill:** a brothel.　**Saint George's Field:** open area and place of resort on the south bank of the Thames.
201. **away with:** tolerate.

2 Henry IV
III.ii

Shal. Ha, cousin Silence, that thou hadst seen that that this knight and I have seen! Ha, Sir John, said I well?

Fal. We have heard the chimes at midnight, Master Shallow. 215

Shal. That we have, that we have, that we have, in faith, Sir John, we have. Our watch-word was "Hem, boys!" Come let's to dinner, come let's to dinner. Jesus, the days that we have seen! come, come.

Exeunt [Falstaff and the Justices].

Bull. Good Master Corporate Bardolph, stand my friend, and here's four Harry ten shillings in French crowns for you. In very truth, sir, I had as live 222 be hang'd, sir, as go, and yet for mine own part, sir, I do not care, but rather, because I am unwilling, and for mine own part, have a desire to stay with my friends, else, sir, I did not care for mine own part so much. 227

Bard. Go to, stand aside.

Moul. And, good Master Corporal Captain, for my old dame's sake stand my friend. She has nobody to do any thing about her when I am gone, and she is old, and cannot help herself. You shall have forty, sir. 232

Bard. Go to, stand aside.

Fee. By my troth I care not; a man can die but once, we owe God a death. I'll ne'er bear a base mind. And't be my dest'ny, so; and't be not, so. No man's too good to serve 's prince, and let it go which way it will, he that dies this year is quit for the next. 238

Bard. Well said, th' art a good fellow.

Fee. Faith, I'll bear no base mind.

Enter Falstaff *and the* Justices.

Fal. Come, sir, which men shall I have?

Shal. Four of which you please. 242

Bard. [*To Falstaff.*] Sir, a word with you. [*Aside.*] I have three pound to free Mouldy and Bullcalf.

Fal. Go to, well. 245

Shal. Come, Sir John, which four will you have?

Fal. Do you choose for me.

Shal. Marry, then, Mouldy, Bullcalf, Feeble, and Shadow.

Fal. Mouldy and Bullcalf! for you, Mouldy, stay at home till you are past service; and for your 251 part, Bullcalf, grow till you come unto it. I will none of you.

Shal. Sir John, Sir John, do not yourself wrong. They are your likeliest men, and I would have you serv'd with the best. 256

Fal. Will you tell me, Master Shallow, how to choose a man? Care I for the limb, the thews, the stature, bulk, and big assemblance of a man? Give me the spirit, Master Shallow. Here's Wart, you see

what a ragged appearance it is. 'A shall charge you and discharge you with the motion of a pewterer's hammer, come off and on swifter than he that 263 gibbets on the brewer's bucket. And this same half-fac'd fellow, Shadow, give me this man. He presents no mark to the enemy, the foeman may with as great aim level at the edge of a penknife. And for a retrait, how swiftly will this Feeble the woman's tailor 268 run off! O, give me the spare men, and spare me the great ones. Put me a caliver into Wart's hand, Bardolph. 271

Bard. Hold, Wart, traverse! thas, thas, thas.

Fal. Come manage me your caliver. So—very well, go to, very good, exceeding good. O, give me always a little, lean, old, chopp'd, bald shot. Well said, i' faith, Wart, th' art a good scab. Hold, there's a tester for thee. 277

Shal. He is not his craft's master, he doth not do it right. I remember at Mile-end Green, when I lay at Clement's Inn—I was then Sir Dagonet in Arthur's show—there was a little quiver fellow, and 'a would manage you his piece thus, and 'a would about and about, and come you in and come you in. "Rah, 283 tah, tah," would 'a say, "bounce," would 'a say, and away again would 'a go, and again would 'a come. I shall ne'er see such a fellow.

Fal. These fellows woll do well, Master Shallow. God keep you, Master Silence, I will not use 288 many words with you. Fare you well, gentlemen both, I thank you. I must a dozen mile to-night. Bardolph, give the soldiers coats.

Shal. Sir John, the Lord bless you! God prosper your affairs! God send us peace! At your re- 293 turn visit our house, let our old acquaintance be renew'd. Peradventure I will with ye to the court.

Fal. 'Fore God, would you would.

Shal. Go to, I have spoke at a word. God keep you! 298

Fal. Fare you well, gentle gentlemen. (*Exeunt [Justices].*) On, Bardolph, lead the men away. [*Exeunt Bardolph, recruits, etc.*] As I return, I will fetch off these justices. I do see the bottom of Justice Shallow. Lord, Lord, how subject we old men are to this 303 vice of lying! This same starv'd justice hath done nothing but prate to me of the wildness of his youth, and the feats he hath done about Turnbull Street, and every third word a lie, duer paid to the hearer than the

220. **Corporate:** blunder for *Corporal.*
221. **Harry ten shillings:** coins first minted in the reign of Henry VII (and therefore an anachronism here) that were worth five shillings in Shakespeare's time.
221–22. **French crowns:** coins worth four shillings.
222. **live:** lief.   232. **forty:** i.e. forty shillings.
235. **bear:** harbor, reveal.   238. **quit:** free, clear.
250. **for:** as for.
252. **come unto it:** i.e. attain maturity (with a play on *calf*).
258. **thews:** strength.   259. **assemblance:** appearance (?).

261–62. **charge . . . you:** load and fire his musket.
262–63. **with . . . hammer:** i.e. with a steady rhythm.
264. **gibbets:** hangs (pails of brew).   **bucket:** yoke or beam on a carrier's shoulders.   264–65. **half-fac'd:** thin, meagre.
267. **level:** aim.   **retrait:** retreat.   270. **caliver:** musket.
272. **traverse:** march (?) or take aim (?).   **thas:** thus.
275. **chopp'd:** chapped.   276. **scab:** i.e. wart.
277. **tester:** sixpence.
279. **Mile-end Green:** open area and drill-ground to the east of London.   **lay:** lived.
280–81. **Arthur's show:** annual exhibition at Mile-end Green by a company of London archers (each taking the name of one of King Arthur's knights), in which Sir Dagonet was the fool.
281. **quiver:** nimble.
283. **come you in:** i.e. make a pass or home thrust (a term from fencing).   287. **woll:** will.   290. **must:** must go.
297. **at a word:** in haste, without deliberation.
301. **fetch off:** fleece.   304. **starv'd:** lean, emaciated.
306. **Turnbull Street:** disreputable street in Clerkenwell, one of the lowest districts in London.   307. **duer:** more punctually (?).

Turk's tribute. I do remember him at Clement's 308
Inn, like a man made after supper of a cheese-paring.
When 'a was naked, he was for all the world like a
fork'd redish, with a head fantastically carv'd upon it
with a knife. 'A was so forlorn, that his dimensions to
any thick sight were [invisible]. 'A was the 313
very genius of famine, yet lecherous as a monkey, and
the whores call'd him mandrake. 'A came [ever] in
the rearward of the fashion, and sung those tunes to the
overscutch'd huswives that he heard the carmen
whistle, and sware they were his fancies or his 318
good-nights. And now is this Vice's dagger become a
squire, and talks as familiarly of John a' Gaunt as if he
had been sworn brother to him, and I'll be sworn 'a
ne'er saw him but once in the Tilt-yard, and then he
burst his head for crowding among the marshal's 323
men. I saw it, and told John a' Gaunt he beat his own
name, for you might have thrust him and all his apparel
into an eel-skin. The case of a treble hoboy was a
mansion for him, a court, and now has he land and
beefs! Well, I'll be acquainted with him if I re- 328
turn, and't shall go hard but I'll make him a philosopher's two stones to me. If the young dace be a bait for
the old pike, I see no reason in the law of nature but I
may snap at him: let time shape, and there an end.
                                                    [*Exit.*]

[ACT IV, Scene I]

Enter the Archbishop [*of* York], Mowbray, [Lord]
Bardolph, Hastings, [*and others,*] *within the forest
of Gaultree.*

Arch. What is this forest call'd?
Hast. 'Tis Gaultree forest, and't shall please your
    Grace.
Arch. Here stand, my lords, and send discoverers
    forth
To know the numbers of our enemies.
Hast. We have sent forth already.
Arch.   'Tis well done.
My friends and brethren in these great affairs, 6
I must acquaint you that I have receiv'd
New-dated letters from Northumberland,
Their cold intent, tenure, and substance thus:
Here doth he wish his person, with such powers 10

As might hold sortance with his quality,
The which he could not levy; whereupon
He is retir'd, to ripe his growing fortunes,
To Scotland, and concludes in hearty prayers
That your attempts may overlive the hazard 15
And fearful meeting of their opposite.
    Mowb. Thus do the hopes we have in him touch
        ground
And dash themselves to pieces.

Enter Messenger.

Hast.   Now, what news?
    Mess. West of this forest, scarcely off a mile,
In goodly form comes on the enemy, 20
And by the ground they hide, I judge their number
Upon or near the rate of thirty thousand.
    Mowb. The just proportion that we gave them out.
Let us sway on and face them in the field.
    Arch. What well-appointed leader fronts us here?

Enter Westmerland.

    Mowb. I think it is my Lord of Westmerland. 26
    West. Health and fair greeting from our general,
The Prince, Lord John and Duke of Lancaster.
    Arch. Say on, my Lord of Westmerland, in peace,
What doth concern your coming.
    West.   Then, my lord, 30
Unto your Grace do I in chief address
The substance of my speech. If that rebellion
Came like itself, in base and abject routs,
Led on by bloody youth, guarded with rage,
And countenanc'd by boys and beggary— 35
I say, if damn'd commotion so [appear'd]
In his true, native, and most proper shape,
You, reverend father, and these noble lords
Had not been here to dress the ugly form
Of base and bloody insurrection 40
With your fair honors. You, Lord Archbishop,
Whose see is by a civil peace maintain'd,
Whose beard the silver hand of peace hath touch'd,
Whose learning and good letters peace hath tutor'd,
Whose white investments figure innocence, 45
The dove, and very blessed spirit of peace,
Wherefore do you so ill translate yourself
Out of the speech of peace that bears such grace,
Into the harsh and boist'rous tongue of war?
Turning your books to graves, your ink to blood, 50
Your pens to lances, and your tongue divine
To a loud trumpet and a point of war?

308. **Turk's tribute:** annual exaction collected from merchants by
the sultan.   311. **redish:** radish.   314. **genius:** embodiment.
315. **mandrake:** plant whose roots were thought to resemble a man.
317. **overscutch'd:** battered.   **huswives:** hussies, strumpets.   **carmen:** wagoners.   318. **sware:** swore.
318–19. **fancies, good-nights:** types of songs.
319. **Vice's dagger:** dagger of lath carried by the mischievous comic
character in morality plays.
322. **Tilt-yard:** tournament ground at Westminster.
324–25. **his own name:** i.e. a gaunt person.   326. **hoboy:** oboe.
329–30. **a philosopher's two stones:** i.e. as valuable as two philosopher's stones, which were supposed to change base metals to gold.
330. **dace:** small fish used for live bait.

IV.i. **Location:** Yorkshire. Before the forest of Gaultree (or Galtres,
a royal forest of some 100,000 acres north of York). Holinshed
(Bullough, IV, 271) sets the scene on "a plaine [i.e. Shipton Moor]
within the forrest of Galtree." The date was May 29, 1405.
2. **and:** if.   3. **discoverers:** scouts.   8. **New-dated:** i.e. recent.
9. **tenure:** tenor.   10. **powers:** forces.

11. **hold . . . quality:** be appropriate to his rank.
13. **ripe:** make ripe.
15–16. **overlive . . . opposite:** survive the fearful hazard of meeting
the adversaries.   22. **rate:** estimated total.
23. **just . . . out:** very number that we estimated.
24. **sway on:** advance.   25. **fronts:** confronts.
28. **Duke of Lancaster.** Actually, Prince Henry, John's elder brother,
was Duke of Lancaster at the time.
30. **doth concern:** i.e. is the purpose of.
33. **routs:** disorderly crowds.   34. **guarded:** trimmed, adorned.
35. **countenanc'd:** maintained.   **beggary:** beggars.
36. **commotion:** insurrection.
42. **civil peace:** i.e. established government.
44. **good letters:** scholarship (*literae humaniores*).
45. **investments figure:** vestments symbolize.
47. **translate:** transform.   52. **point:** notes of a trumpet.

2 Henry IV
IV.i

Arch. Wherefore do I this? so the question stands.
Briefly, to this end: we are all diseas'd,
[And with our surfeiting and wanton hours   55
Have brought ourselves into a burning fever,
And we must bleed for it; of which disease
Our late King Richard (being infected) died.
But, my most noble Lord of Westmerland,
I take not on me here as a physician,   60
Nor do I as an enemy to peace
Troop in the throngs of military men;
But rather show a while like fearful war
To diet rank minds sick of happiness,
And purge th' obstructions which begin to stop 65
Our very veins of life. Hear me more plainly.
I have in equal balance justly weigh'd
What wrongs our arms may do, what wrongs we
        suffer,
And find our griefs heavier than our offenses.
We see which way the stream of time doth run,   70
And are enforc'd from our most quiet there
By the rough torrent of occasion,
And have the summary of all our griefs
(When time shall serve) to show in articles;
Which long ere this we offer'd to the King,   75
And might by no suit gain our audience.
When we are wrong'd and would unfold our griefs,
We are denied access unto his person
Even by those men that most have done us wrong.]
The dangers of the days but newly gone,   80
Whose memory is written on the earth
With yet appearing blood, and the examples
Of every minute's instance (present now)
Hath put us in these ill-beseeming arms,
Not to break peace, or any branch of it,   85
But to establish here a peace indeed,
Concurring both in name and quality.
West. When ever yet was your appeal denied?
Wherein have you been galled by the King?
What peer hath been suborn'd to grate on you?   90
That you should seal this lawless bloody book
Of forg'd rebellion with a seal divine.
Arch. My brother general, the commonwealth,
I make my quarrel in particular.
West. There is no need of any such redress,   95
Or if there were, it not belongs to you.
Mowb. Why not to him in part, and to us all

That feel the bruises of the days before,
And suffer the condition of these times
To lay a heavy and unequal hand   100
Upon our honors?
West. [O, my good Lord Mowbray,
Construe the times to their necessities,
And you shall say, indeed, it is the time,
And not the King, that doth you injuries.
Yet, for your part, it not appears to me,   105
Either from the King or in the present time,
That you should have an inch of any ground
To build a grief on. Were you not restor'd
To all the Duke of Norfolk's signories,
Your noble and right well-rememb'red father's? 110
Mowb. What thing, in honor, had my father lost,
That need to be reviv'd and breath'd in me?
The King that lov'd him, as the state stood then,
Was [force] perforce compell'd to banish him;
And then that Henry Bullingbrook and he,   115
Being mounted and both roused in their seats,
Their neighing coursers daring of the spur,
Their armed staves in charge, their beavers down,
Their eyes of fire sparkling through sights of steel,
And the loud trumpet blowing them together;   120
Then, then, when there was nothing could have stay'd
My father from the breast of Bullingbrook,
O, when the King did throw his warder down
(His own life hung upon the staff he threw),
Then threw he down himself and all their lives 125
That by indictment and by dint of sword
Have since miscarried under Bullingbrook.
West. You speak, Lord Mowbray, now you know
        not what.
The Earl of Herford was reputed then
In England the most valiant gentleman.   130
Who knows on whom fortune would then have smil'd?
But if your father had been victor there,
He ne'er had borne it out of Coventry;
For all the country in a general voice
Cried hate upon him; and all their prayers and love
Were set on Herford, whom they doted on   136
And bless'd and grac'd and did, more than the King—]
But this is mere digression from my purpose.
Here come I from our princely general
To know your griefs, to tell you from his Grace 140
That he will give you audience, and wherein
It shall appear that your demands are just,
You shall enjoy them, every thing set off
That might so much as think you enemies.   144
Mowb. But he hath forc'd us to compel this offer,

53–87. **Wherefore . . . quality.** According to Holinshed (Bullough, IV, 272), the Archbishop told Westmorland's emissaries "that he tooke nothing in hand against the kings peace, but that whatsoever he did, tended rather to advance the peace and quiet of the common-wealth, than otherwise; and where he and his companie were in armes, it was for feare of the king, to whom he could have no free accesse, by reason of such a multitude of flatterers as were about him; and therefore he maintained that his purpose to be good & profitable, as well for the king himselfe, as for the realme, if men were willing to understand a truth: & herewith he shewed foorth a scroll, in which the articles were written." 55. **wanton:** self-indulgent.
57. **bleed:** be bled (as a medical treatment).
60. **take . . . as:** do not assume the role of. 63. **show:** appear.
64. **rank:** swollen, surfeited. 69. **griefs:** grievances.
71. **enforc'd . . . there:** i.e. forced from our greatest quiet in the "stream of time." 72. **occasion:** events.
74. **in articles:** i.e. systematically set forth.
83. **Of . . . instance:** presented every minute.
90. **suborn'd . . . on:** instigated to annoy.
93. **My brother general:** i.e. the people of England (whose grievance he makes his own because they are his brothers).

100. **unequal:** unfair. 102. **to:** according to.
106. **Either . . . time:** i.e. whether you blame the King or the dis-ordered times for your supposed grievances. 109. **signories:** estates.
112. **breath'd:** have life breathed into it.
113–27. **The King . . . Bullingbrook.** See *Richard II*, I.i.iii.
114. **force perforce:** against his will. 116. **roused:** lifted.
118. **armed . . . charge:** lances in position. **beavers:** visors.
123. **warder:** staff, mace (which he held as umpire of the trial by combat). 126. **dint:** force. 127. **miscarried:** perished.
129. **Earl of Herford:** Bullingbrook.
133. **it:** i.e. the victor's prize. **Coventry:** site of the abortive en-counter between Bullingbrook and Mowbray.
134. **in . . . voice:** i.e. unanimously. 137. **did:** did for (?).
143. **set off:** disregarded (?) or removed (?).
144. **think you:** suggest that you are.

And it proceeds from policy, not love.

West. Mowbray, you overween to take it so;
This offer comes from mercy, not from fear.
For lo, within a ken our army lies:
Upon mine honor, all too confident   150
To give admittance to a thought of fear.
Our battle is more full of names than yours,
Our men more perfect in the use of arms,
Our armor all as strong, our cause the best;
Then reason will our hearts should be as good.   155
Say you not then our offer is compell'd.

Mowb. Well, by my will we shall admit no parley.

West. That argues but the shame of your offense:
A rotten case abides no handling.

Hast. Hath the Prince John a full commission,   160
In very ample virtue of his father,
To hear and absolutely to determine
Of what conditions we shall stand upon?

West. That is intended in the general's name.
I muse you make so slight a question.   165

Arch. Then take, my Lord of Westmerland, this
schedule,
For this contains our general grievances:
Each several article herein redress'd,
All members of our cause, both here and hence,
That are ensinewed to this action   170
Acquitted by a true substantial form
And present execution of our wills—
To us and [to] our purposes confin'd
We come within our aweful banks again,
And knit our powers to the arm of peace.   175

West. This will I show the general. Please you,
lords,
In sight of both our battles we may meet,
[And] either end in peace, which God so frame!
Or to the place of diff'rence call the swords
Which must decide it.

Arch.   My lord, we will do so.   180
Exit Westmerland.

Mowb. There is a thing within my bosom tells me
That no conditions of our peace can stand.

Hast. Fear you not that; if we can make our peace
Upon such large terms and so absolute
As our conditions shall consist upon,   185
Our peace shall stand as firm as rocky mountains.

Mowb. Yea, but our valuation shall be such
That every slight and false-derived cause,
Yea, every idle, nice, and wanton reason,
Shall to the King taste of this action,   190

That were our royal faiths martyrs in love,
We shall be winnow'd with so rough a wind
That even our corn shall seem as light as chaff,
And good from bad find no partition.

Arch. No, no, my lord, note this: the King is
weary   195
Of dainty and such picking grievances,
For he hath found to end one doubt by death
Revives two greater in the heirs of life;
And therefore will he wipe his tables clean
And keep no tell-tale to his memory   200
That may repeat and history his loss
To new remembrance; for full well he knows
He cannot so precisely weed this land
As his misdoubts present occasion.
His foes are so enrooted with his friends   205
That, plucking to unfix an enemy,
He doth unfasten so and shake a friend,
So that this land, like an offensive wife
That hath enrag'd him on to offer strokes,
As he is striking, holds his infant up   210
And hangs resolv'd correction in the arm
That was uprear'd to execution.

Hast. Besides, the King hath wasted all his rods
On late offenders, that he now doth lack
The very instruments of chastisement,   215
So that his power, like to a fangless lion,
May offer, but not hold.

Arch.   'Tis very true,
And therefore be assur'd, my good Lord Marshal,
If we do now make our atonement well,
Our peace will, like a broken limb united,   220
Grow stronger for the breaking.

Mowb.   Be it so.
Here is return'd my Lord of Westmerland.

Enter WESTMERLAND.

West. The Prince is here at hand. Pleaseth your
lordship
To meet his Grace just distance 'tween our armies.

Mowb. Your Grace of York, in God's name then
set forward.   225

Arch. Before, and greet his Grace.—My lord, we
come.
[*They march about the stage and then move forward
to meet Prince John.*]

[SCENE II]

Enter PRINCE JOHN [OF LANCASTER] *and his army.*

P. John. You are well encount'red here, my cousin
Mowbray,

147. **overween:** presume too much.   149. **ken:** sight.
152. **Our . . . names:** i.e. our army has more illustrious leaders.
155. **reason will:** i.e. it is reasonable that.
157. **by my will:** with my consent.
159. **rotten case:** weak box.   **abides:** permits of.
161. **In . . . virtue of:** with fully delegated power from.
163. **what:** whatever.   **stand:** insist.
164. **intended . . . name:** i.e. indicated by his title.
165. **muse:** am astonished.   166. **schedule:** document.
168. **several:** separate.   170. **ensinewed to:** i.e. involved in.
171. **true substantial form:** formal agreement.
172–73. **present . . . confin'd:** i.e. the immediate satisfaction of our
wishes as regards ourselves and our plans.
174. **aweful banks:** bounds of reverence.   177. **battles:** armies.
178. **frame:** bring to pass.   184. **large:** liberal.
185. **consist:** insist.   187. **valuation:** i.e. reputation with the King.
189. **idle:** foolish.   **nice:** petty.   **wanton:** trivial.

191. **were . . . love:** i.e. though our fidelity to the King were as intense
as the faith of martyrs.   194. **partition:** distinction.
196. **dainty:** minute.   **picking:** trifling.
199. **tables:** tablets, books.   201. **history:** record.
203. **precisely:** entirely.   204. **misdoubts:** suspicions, anxieties.
211. **hangs resolv'd correction:** checks intended punishment.
213. **wasted:** used up.   217. **hold:** grip.
219. **atonement:** reconciliation.
224. **just distance:** i.e. halfway.   226. **Before:** i.e. go first.

IV.ii. Location: Scene continues.
1. **cousin:** here, a title of respect.

2 Henry IV
IV.ii

Good day to you, gentle Lord Archbishop,
And so to you, Lord Hastings, and to all.
My Lord of York, it better show'd with you
When that your flock, assembled by the bell, 5
Encircled you to hear with reverence
Your exposition on the holy text
[Than] now to see you here an iron man, talking,
Cheering a rout of rebels with your drum,
Turning the word to sword and life to death. 10
That man that sits within a monarch's heart
And ripens in the sunshine of his favor,
Would he abuse the countenance of the King,
Alack, what mischiefs might he set abroach
In shadow of such greatness? With you, Lord Bishop,
It is even so. Who hath not heard it spoken 16
How deep you were within the books of God?
To us the speaker in his parliament,
To us th' [imagin'd] voice of God himself,
The very opener and intelligencer 20
Between the grace, the sanctities of heaven,
And our dull workings? O, who shall believe
But you misuse the reverence of your place,
[Employ] the countenance and grace of heav'n,
As a false favorite doth his prince's name, 25
In deeds dishonorable? You have ta'en up,
Under the counterfeited zeal of God,
The subjects of his substitute, my father,
And both against the peace of heaven and him
Have here upswarm'd them.
      Arch.   Good my Lord of Lancaster,
I am not here against your father's peace, 31
But as I told my Lord of Westmerland,
The time misord'red doth, in common sense,
Crowd us and crush us to this monstrous form
To hold our safety up. I sent your Grace 35
The parcels and particulars of our grief,
The which hath been with scorn shov'd from the court,
Whereon this Hydra son of war is born,
Whose dangerous eyes may well be charm'd asleep
With grant of our most just and right desires, 40
And true obedience, of this madness cured,
Stoop tamely to the foot of majesty.
      Mowb. If not, we ready are to try our fortunes
To the last man.
      Hast.   And though we here fall down,
We have supplies to second our attempt; 45
If they miscarry, theirs shall second them,
And so success of mischief shall be born,
And heir from heir shall hold his quarrel up
Whiles England shall have generation.

P. John. You are too shallow, Hastings, much too shallow, 50
To sound the bottom of the after-times.
West. Pleaseth your Grace to answer them directly
How far forth you do like their articles.
P. John. I like them all, and do allow them well,
And swear here, by the honor of my blood, 55
My father's purposes have been mistook,
And some about him have too lavishly
Wrested his meaning and authority.
My lord, these griefs shall be with speed redress'd,
Upon my soul they shall. If this may please you, 60
Discharge your powers unto their several counties,
As we will ours, and here between the armies
Let's drink together friendly and embrace,
That all their eyes may bear those tokens home
Of our restored love and amity. 65
Arch. I take your princely word for these redresses.
[*P. John.*] I give it you, and will maintain my word,
And thereupon I drink unto your Grace.
[*Hast.*] Go, captain, and deliver to the army
This news of peace. Let them have pay, and part. 70
I know it will well please them. Hie thee, captain.
                              [*Exit Officer.*]
Arch. To you, my noble Lord of Westmerland.
West. I pledge your Grace, and if you knew what pains
I have bestowed to breed this present peace,
You would drink freely. But my love to ye 75
Shall show itself more openly hereafter.
Arch. I do not doubt you.
West.   I am glad of it.
Health to my lord, and gentle cousin, Mowbray.
Mowb. You wish me health in very happy season,
For I am on the sudden something ill. 80
Arch. Against ill chances men are ever merry,
But heaviness foreruns the good event.
West. Therefore be merry, coz, since sudden sorrow
Serves to say thus, some good thing comes to-morrow.
Arch. Believe me, I am passing light in spirit. 85
Mowb. So much the worse, if your own rule be
      true.   *Shout* [*within*].
P. John. The word of peace is rend'red. Hark how
      they shout!
Mowb. This had been cheerful after victory.
Arch. A peace is of the nature of a conquest,
For then both parties nobly are subdued, 90
And neither party loser.
P. John.   Go, my lord,
And let our army be discharged too.
                              [*Exit Westmerland.*]
And, good my lord, so please you, let our trains
March by us, that we may peruse the men
We should have cop'd withal.
      Arch.   Go, good Lord Hastings,
And ere they be dismiss'd, let them march by. 96
                              [*Exit Hastings.*]

---

4. **it . . . you:** i.e. you appeared to more advantage.
8. **an iron man.** Holinshed reports (Bullough, IV, 271) that the Archbishop appeared before his followers "clad in armor."
9. **rout:** gang.   10. **word:** i.e. the Scripture.
14. **set abroach:** start flowing.
20. **opener and intelligencer:** interpreter and intermediary.
22. **workings:** mental operations.
24. **countenance and grace:** gracious countenance.
26. **ta'en up:** enlisted.   28. **substitute:** deputy, i.e. the king.
33. **common sense:** ordinary perception.
36. **parcels:** details.   **grief:** grievance.
38. **Hydra:** i.e. many-headed (referring to a monstrous snake destroyed by Hercules).   45. **supplies:** reinforcements.
47. **success:** succession.
49. **Whiles . . . generation:** i.e. so long as Englishmen are born.

57. **lavishly:** arbitrarily, carelessly.   58. **Wrested:** strained.
81. **Against:** in anticipation of.   85. **passing:** exceedingly.
95. **cop'd withal:** fought with.

Enter WESTMERLAND.

P. John.   I trust, lords, we shall lie to-night together.
Now, cousin, wherefore stands our army still?

West.   The leaders, having charge from you to
        stand,
Will not go off until they hear you speak.   100

P. John.   They know their duties.

Enter HASTINGS.

Hast.   My lord, our army is dispers'd already:
Like youthful steers unyok'd, they take their courses
East, west, north, south, or, like a school broke up,
Each hurries toward his home and sporting-place.   105

West.   Good tidings, my Lord Hastings! for the
        which
I do arrest thee, traitor, of high treason,
And you, Lord Archbishop, and you, Lord Mowbray,
Of capital treason I attach you both.

Mowb.   Is this proceeding just and honorable?   110

West.   Is your assembly so?

Arch.   Will you thus break your faith?

P. John.   I pawn'd thee none.
I promis'd you redress of these same grievances
Whereof you did complain, which, by mine honor,
I will perform with a most Christian care.   115
But for you rebels, look to taste the due
Meet for rebellion [and such acts as yours].
Most shallowly did you these arms commence,
Fondly brought here and foolishly sent hence.
Strike up our drums, pursue the scatt'red stray;   120
God, and not we, hath safely fought to-day.
Some guard [these traitors] to the block of death,
Treason's true bed and yielder-up of breath.   [*Exeunt.*]

[SCENE III]

Alarum. Excursions. Enter FALSTAFF [*and* COLEVILE,
meeting].

Fal.   What's your name, sir? Of what condition
are you, and of what place?

Col.   I am a knight, sir, and my name is Colevile of
the Dale.   4

Fal.   Well then, Colevile is your name, a knight is
your degree, and your place the Dale. Colevile shall be
still your name, a traitor your degree, and the dungeon
your place, a place deep enough; so shall you be still
Colevile of the Dale.

Col.   Are not you Sir John Falstaff?   10

Fal.   As good a man as he, sir, whoe'er I am. Do
ye yield, sir? or shall I sweat for you? If I do sweat,
they are the drops of thy lovers, and they weep for thy

death; therefore rouse up fear and trembling, and do
observance to my mercy.   15

Col.   I think you are Sir John Falstaff, and in that
thought yield me.

Fal.   I have a whole school of tongues in this belly
of mine, and not a tongue of them all speaks any other
word but my name. And I had but a belly of any   20
indifferency, I were simply the most active fellow in
Europe. My womb, my womb, my womb undoes me.
Here comes our general.

Enter [PRINCE] JOHN [OF LANCASTER], WESTMERLAND,
[BLUNT,] *and the rest.*

P. John.   The heat is past, follow no further now;
Call in the powers, good cousin Westmerland.   25
                [*Exit Westmerland.*] *Retrait.*
Now, Falstaff, where have you been all this while?
When every thing is ended, then you come.
These tardy tricks of yours will, on my life,
One time or other break some gallows' back.   29

Fal.   I would be sorry, my lord, but it should be
thus. I never knew yet but rebuke and check was the
reward of valor. Do you think me a swallow, an
arrow, or a bullet? Have I, in my poor and old motion,
the expedition of thought? I have speeded hither with
the very extremest inch of possibility; I have   35
found'red ninescore and odd posts, and here, travel-
tainted as I am, have, in my pure and immaculate
valor, taken Sir John Colevile of the Dale, a most
furious knight and valorous enemy. But what of that?
He saw me, and yielded, that I may justly say,   40
with the hook-nos'd fellow of Rome, "There, cousin,
I came, saw, and overcame."

P. John.   It was more of his courtesy than your deserving.   44

Fal.   I know not: here he is, and here I yield him,
and I beseech your Grace let it be book'd with the
rest of this day's deeds, or by the Lord, I will have it
in a particular ballad else, with mine own picture on
the top on't (Colevile kissing my foot), to the which
course if I be enforc'd, if you do not all show like   50
gilt twopences to me, and I in the clear sky of fame
o'ershine you as much as the full moon doth the cinders
of the element (which show like pins' heads to her),
believe not the word of the noble. Therefore let me
have right, and let desert mount.   55

P. John.   Thine's too heavy to mount.

Fal.   Let it shine then.

P. John.   Thine's too thick to shine.

Fal.   Let it do something, my good lord, that may
do me good, and call it what you will.   60

18. **school:** crowd.
21. **indifferency:** i.e. moderate size.   22. **womb:** belly.
24. **heat:** urgency (of pursuit).
25 s.d. **Retrait:** retreat, signal for the withdrawal of forces.
31. **check:** reprimand.
34–35. **with . . . possibility:** i.e. as fast as possible.
36. **found'red:** lamed.   **posts:** post-horses.
37. **tainted:** stained.
41. **with . . . Rome:** i.e. like Julius Caesar.
42. **I . . . overcame:** "*Veni, vidi, vici,*" Caesar's laconic report about
one of his campaigns.
48. **a particular ballad:** i.e. a broadside ballad celebrating this feat.
50. **show:** appear.   51. **to:** compared to.
52–53. **cinders . . . element:** i.e. stars in the sky.

105. **sporting-place:** playground.
109. **attach:** arrest.   112. **pawn'd:** pledged.
118. **shallowly:** i.e. without deliberation.
119. **Fondly:** foolishly.   120. **stray:** stragglers.

IV.iii. Location: Scene continues.
o.s.d. **Alarum:** trumpet call to advance.   **Excursions:** sallies, sorties.   **Colevile.** Holinshed lists (Bullough, IV, 274) "sir John Colle-
vill of the Dale" among those executed by Henry IV as he marched
through Durham in pursuit of the scattered rebels.
1. **condition:** rank.   13. **lovers:** friends.

2 *Henry IV*
IV.iii

P. John. Is thy name Colevile?

Col. It is, my lord.

P. John. A famous rebel art thou, Colevile.

Fal. And a famous true subject took him.

Col. I am, my lord, but as my betters are   65
That led me hither. Had they been rul'd by me,
You should have won them dearer than you have.

Fal. I know not how they sold themselves, but
thou like a kind fellow gavest thyself away gratis,
and I thank thee for thee.   70

Enter WESTMERLAND.

P. John. Now, have you left pursuit?

West. Retrait is made and execution stay'd.

P. John. Send Colevile with his confederates
To York, to present execution.
Blunt, lead him hence, and see you guard him sure.   75
          [*Exeunt Blunt and others with Colevile.*]
And now dispatch we toward the court, my lords,
I hear the King my father is sore sick.
Our news shall go before us to his Majesty,
Which, cousin, you shall bear to comfort him,
And we with sober speed will follow you.   80

Fal. My lord, I beseech you give me leave to go
through Gloucestershire, and when you come to court
stand my good lord in your good report.

P. John. Fare you well, Falstaff. I, in my condition,
Shall better speak of you than you deserve.   85
          [*Exeunt all but Falstaff.*]

Fal. I would you had the wit, 'twere better than
your dukedom. Good faith, this same young sober-
blooded boy doth not love me, nor a man cannot make
him laugh, but that's no marvel, he drinks no wine.
There's never none of these demure boys come   90
to any proof, for thin drink doth so over-cool their
blood, and making many fish-meals, that they fall into
a kind of male green-sickness, and then when they
marry, they get wenches. They are generally fools and
cowards, which some of us should be too, but for   95
inflammation. A good sherris-sack hath a twofold
operation in it. It ascends me into the brain, dries me
there all the foolish and dull and crudy vapors which
environ it, makes it apprehensive, quick, forgetive, full
of nimble, fiery, and delectable shapes, which de-   100
liver'd o'er to the voice, the tongue, which is the birth,
becomes excellent wit. The second property of your
excellent sherris is the warming of the blood, which
before (cold and settled) left the liver white and pale,
which is the badge of pusillanimity and coward-   105
ice; but the sherris warms it, and makes it course from
the inwards to the parts' extremes. It illumineth the
face, which as a beacon gives warning to all the rest of
this little kingdom, man, to arm, and then the vital
commoners and inland petty spirits muster me all   110
to their captain, the heart, who great and puff'd up
with this retinue, doth any deed of courage; and this
valor comes of sherris. So that skill in the weapon is
nothing without sack (for that sets it a-work) and
learning a mere hoard of gold kept by a devil,   115
till sack commences it and sets it in act and use.
Hereof comes it that Prince Harry is valiant, for the
cold blood he did naturally inherit of his father, he
hath, like lean, sterile, and bare land, manur'd, husbanded, and till'd with excellent endeavor of   120
drinking good and good store of fertile sherris, that he
is become very hot and valiant. If I had a thousand
sons, the first humane principle I would teach them
should be, to forswear thin potations and to addict
themselves to sack.   125

Enter BARDOLPH.

How now, Bardolph?

Bard. The army is discharged all and gone.

Fal. Let them go. I'll through Gloucestershire,
and there will I visit Master Robert Shallow, esquire.
I have him already temp'ring between my finger and
my thumb, and shortly will I seal with him. Come
away.   [*Exeunt.*]   132

[SCENE IV]

Enter the KING [*carried in a chair*], WARWICK, THOMAS
DUKE OF CLARENCE, HUMPHREY OF GLOUCESTER,
[*and others*].

King. Now, lords, if God doth give successful end
To this debate that bleedeth at our doors,
We will our youth lead on to higher fields,
And draw no swords but what are sanctified.
Our navy is address'd, our power collected,   5
Our substitutes in absence well invested,
And every thing lies level to our wish.
Only, we want a little personal strength;
And pause us till these rebels, now afoot,
Come underneath the yoke of government.   10

War. Both which we doubt not but your Majesty
Shall soon enjoy.

King.   Humphrey, my son of Gloucester,
Where is the Prince your brother?

Glou. I think he's gone to hunt, my lord, at
Windsor.

72. **stay'd:** stopped.
74. **present:** immediate.   76. **dispatch we:** let us hurry.
83. **stand . . . lord:** i.e. act as my patron.
84. **condition:** official capacity.
90–91. **come . . . proof:** i.e. stand the test.
91. **thin drink:** i.e. beer.
93. **green-sickness:** an anemic condition, supposed to affect unmarried girls.   94. **get wenches:** beget girls.
96. **inflammation:** i.e. through drinking.   **sherris-sack:** sherry.
98. **crudy:** curded.
99. **apprehensive:** perceptive.   **forgetive:** inventive.
102. **wit:** mental capacity.
104. **liver:** i.e. the seat of courage.

116. **commences it:** enables it to use its powers.
123. **humane:** human.   130. **temp'ring:** softening.
131. **seal with:** i.e. make use of.

IV.iv. Location: Westminster. The Jerusalem Chamber. (This hall
adjacent to Westminster Abbey was so called from its inscriptions
concerning Jerusalem.)
2. **debate:** quarrel.   3. **higher fields:** i.e. Palestine.
5–7. **Our . . . wish.** "With sufficient treasure, soldiers, capteins,
vittels, munitions, tall ships, strong gallies, and all things necessarie
for such a royall journie he pretended [intended] to take into the
holie land," says Holinshed (Bullough, IV, 277), Henry had completed preparations for his long-postponed crusade just before his
final illness.   5. **address'd:** prepared.
7. **level to:** in accordance with.   8. **want:** lack.

King. And how accompanied?
Glou.   I do not know, my lord.
King. Is not his brother Thomas of Clarence with
   him?   16
Glou. No, my good lord, he is in presence here.
Clar. What would my lord and father?
King. Nothing but well to thee, Thomas of
   Clarence.
How chance thou art not with the Prince thy brother?
He loves thee, and thou dost neglect him, Thomas. 21
Thou hast a better place in his affection
Than all thy brothers. Cherish it, my boy;
And noble offices thou mayst effect
Of mediation, after I am dead,   25
Between his greatness and thy other brethren.
Therefore omit him not, blunt not his love,
Nor lose the good advantage of his grace
By seeming cold or careless of his will,
For he is gracious if he be observ'd,   30
He hath a tear for pity, and a hand
Open as day for [meting] charity;
Yet notwithstanding, being incens'd, he is flint,
As humorous as winter, and as sudden
As flaws congealed in the spring of day.   35
His temper therefore must be well observ'd.
Chide him for faults, and do it reverently,
When you perceive his blood inclin'd to mirth;
But, being moody, give him time and scope,
Till that his passions, like a whale on ground,   40
Confound themselves with working. Learn this,
      Thomas,
And thou shalt prove a shelter to thy friends,
A hoop of gold to bind thy brothers in,
That the united vessel of their blood,
Mingled with venom of suggestion   45
(As, force perforce, the age will pour it in),
Shall never leak, though it do work as strong
As aconitum or rash gunpowder.
Clar. I shall observe him with all care and love.
King. Why art thou not at Windsor with him,
   Thomas?   50
Clar. He is not there to-day, he dines in London.
King. And how accompanied? [Canst thou tell
   that?]
Clar. With Poins, and other his continual followers.
King. Most subject is the fattest soil to weeds,
And he, the noble image of my youth,   55
Is overspread with them; therefore my grief
Stretches itself beyond the hour of death.
The blood weeps from my heart when I do shape,
In forms imaginary, th' unguided days
And rotten times that you shall look upon,   60
When I am sleeping with my ancestors.
For when his headstrong riot hath no curb,

When rage and hot blood are his counsellors,
When means and lavish manners meet together,
O, with what wings shall his affections fly   65
Towards fronting peril and oppos'd decay!
War. My gracious lord, you look beyond him
   quite:
The Prince but studies his companions
Like a strange tongue, wherein, to gain the language,
'Tis needful that the most immodest word   70
Be look'd upon and learnt, which once attain'd,
Your Highness knows, comes to no further use
But to be known and hated. So, like gross terms,
The Prince will in the perfectness of time
Cast off his followers, and their memory   75
Shall as a pattern or a measure live,
By which his Grace must mete the lives of other,
Turning past evils to advantages.
King. 'Tis seldom when the bee doth leave her
   comb
In the dead carrion.

Enter WESTMERLAND.

                  Who's here? Westmerland?   80
West. Health to my sovereign, and new happiness
Added to that that I am to deliver!
Prince John your son doth kiss your Grace's hand.
Mowbray, the Bishop Scroop, Hastings, and all,
Are brought to the correction of your law.   85
There is not now a rebel's sword unsheath'd,
But Peace puts forth her olive every where.
The manner how this action hath been borne
Here at more leisure may your Highness read,
With every course in his particular.   90
King. O Westmerland, thou art a summer bird,
Which ever in the haunch of winter sings
The lifting up of day.

Enter HARCOURT.

               Look here's more news.
Har. From enemies heavens keep your Majesty,
And, when they stand against you, may they fall   95
As those that I am come to tell you of!
The Earl Northumberland and the Lord Bardolph,
With a great power of English and of Scots,
Are by the shrieve of Yorkshire overthrown.
The manner and true order of the fight   100
This packet, please it you, contains at large.
King. And wherefore should these good news
   make me sick?
Will Fortune never come with both hands full,

17. **in presence:** present at court.   27. **omit:** neglect.
28. **grace:** favor.   30. **observ'd:** shown respectful attention.
32. **meting:** dealing out.   34. **humorous:** subject to shifting moods.
35. **flaws congealed:** snowflakes.   38. **blood:** disposition.
41. **Confound:** spend, exhaust.   **working:** struggling.
45. **venom of suggestion:** i.e. poisonous gossip (of those stirring up
discord).   46. **force perforce:** inevitably.
48. **aconitum:** poison extracted from monkshood.   **rash:** operat-
ing quickly.   54. **fattest:** richest.
58. **shape:** conceive, imagine.

64. **lavish:** unrestrained.
66. **oppos'd decay:** the ruin facing him.
67. **look beyond:** misconstrue.
73. **gross terms:** coarse language.
77. **mete:** appraise.   **other:** others.
79-80. **'Tis . . . carrion:** i.e. having placed her comb in a carcass the
bee seldom leaves her honey.
84-87. **Mowbray . . . every where.** Actually, Henry himself supervised
the execution of the Archbishop and his co-conspirators at York and
then marched north against Northumberland, whose defeat (reported
as already accomplished in lines 97-99) took place three years after
the events in Gaultree forest, and five years before the King's death.
90. **With . . . particular:** i.e. with the details fully set forth.
92. **haunch:** latter end.
99. **shrieve:** sheriff. He was Sir Thomas Rokeby.

2 Henry IV
IV.iv

But [write] her fair words still in foulest terms?
She either gives a stomach and no food—   105
Such are the poor, in health; or else a feast
And takes away the stomach—such are the rich,
That have abundance and enjoy it not.
I should rejoice now at this happy news,
And now my sight fails, and my brain is giddy.   110
O me! come near me, now I am much ill.
    Glou. Comfort, your Majesty!
    Clar.   O my royal father!
    West. My sovereign lord, cheer up yourself, look
up.
    War. Be patient, Princes, you do know these fits
Are with his Highness very ordinary.   115
Stand from him, give him air, he'll straight be well.
    Clar. No, no, he cannot long hold out these pangs.
Th' incessant care and labor of his mind
Hath wrought the mure that should confine it in
So thin that life looks through [and will break out].   120
    Glou. The people fear me, for they do observe
Unfather'd heirs and loathly births of nature.
The seasons change their manners, as the year
Had found some months asleep and leapt them over.
    Clar. The river hath thrice flowed, no ebb between,
And the old folk (time's doting chronicles)   126
Say it did so a little time before
That our great-grandsire, Edward, sick'd and died.
    War. Speak lower, Princes, for the King recovers.
    Glou. This apoplexy will certain be his end.   130
    King. I pray you take me up, and bear me hence
Into some other chamber. [*Softly, pray.*]
        [*The King is carried to one side of the stage
        and placed on a bed.*]

[SCENE V]

[*King.*] Let there be no noise made, my gentle
friends,
Unless some dull and favorable hand
Will whisper music to my weary spirit.
    War. Call for the music in the other room.
    King. Set me the crown upon my pillow here.   5
    Clar. His eye is hollow, and he changes much.
    War. Less noise, less noise!

Enter [PRINCE] HARRY.

    Prince.   Who saw the Duke of Clarence?
    Clar. I am here, brother, full of heaviness.

114–15. **these . . . ordinary.** According to Holinshed (Bullough, IV, 277), Henry's ailment "was not a leprosie, striken by the hand of God . . . as foolish friers imagined; but a verie apoplexie, of the which he languished till his appointed houre."
117. **hold out:** endure.
119. **wrought the mure:** made the wall.   121. **fear:** frighten.
122. **Unfather'd heirs:** i.e. persons thought to be miraculously conceived.   **loathly births:** loathsome or misshapen offspring.
123. **as:** as if.
125. **The river . . . between.** On October 12, 1411, says Holinshed (Bullough, IV, 276), there "were three flouds in the Thames, the one following upon the other, and no ebbing betweene: which thing no man then living could remember the like to be seene."
128. **Edward:** Edward III.   **sick'd:** sickened.

IV.v. Location: Scene continues.
2. **dull:** i.e. making drowsy.   **favorable:** kindly.
6. **changes:** i.e. in complexion.

Prince. How now, rain within doors, and none
abroad?
How doth the King?   10
    Glou. Exceeding ill.
    Prince.   Heard he the good news yet?
Tell it him.
    Glou. He alt'red much upon the hearing it.
    Prince. If he be sick with joy, he'll recover without
physic.   15
    War. Not so much noise, my lords. Sweet Prince,
speak low,
The King your father is dispos'd to sleep.
    Clar. Let us withdraw into the other room.
    War. Will't please your Grace to go along with us?
    Prince. No, I will sit and watch here by the King.
                        [*Exeunt all but the Prince.*]
Why doth the crown lie there upon his pillow,   21
Being so troublesome a bedfellow?
O polish'd perturbation! golden care!
That keep'st the ports of slumber open wide
To many a watchful night, sleep with it now!   25
Yet not so sound, and half so deeply sweet,
As he whose brow with homely biggen bound
Snores out the watch of night. O majesty!
When thou dost pinch thy bearer, thou dost sit
Like a rich armor worn in heat of day,   30
That scald'st with safety. By his gates of breath
There lies a downy feather which stirs not.
Did he suspire, that light and weightless down
Perforce must move. My gracious lord! my father!
This sleep is sound indeed, this is a sleep   35
That from this golden rigol hath divorc'd
So many English kings. Thy due from me
Is tears and heavy sorrows of the blood,
Which nature, love, and filial tenderness
Shall, O dear father, pay thee plenteously.   40
My due from thee is this imperial crown,
Which as immediate from thy place and blood,
Derives itself to me. [*Puts on the crown.*] Lo where
it sits,
Which God shall guard; and put the world's whole
strength
Into one giant arm, it shall not force   45
This lineal honor from me. This from thee
Will I to mine leave, as 'tis left to me.   *Exit.*
    King. Warwick! Gloucester! Clarence!

Enter WARWICK, GLOUCESTER, CLARENCE, [*and the
rest*].

    Clar.   Doth the King call?

9. **rain:** i.e. tears.
17. **The King . . . sleep.** According to Holinshed (Bullough, IV, 277) Henry's seizure was so profound that "he laie as though all his vitall spirits had beene from him departed. Such as were about him, thinking verelie that he had beene departed, covered his face with a linnen cloth."   23. **perturbation:** cause of perturbation.
24. **ports:** gates.
25. **watchful:** sleepless.   **sleep with it:** i.e. may you (i.e. the King) sleep well with it beside you.
26. **Yet not:** i.e. yet even so your sleep will not be.
27. **biggen:** nightcap.   29. **pinch:** torment.
31. **scald'st with safety:** i.e. both protects and burns.
33. **suspire:** breathe.
36. **rigol:** circle, i.e. the crown.   38. **blood:** i.e. heart.
42. **immediate from:** nearest to.   43. **Derives itself:** descends.
46. **lineal:** hereditary.

War. What would your Majesty? [How fares
your Grace?]
King. Why did you leave me here alone, my lords?
Clar. We left the Prince my brother here, my liege,
Who undertook to sit and watch by you.   52
King. The Prince of Wales, where is he? Let me
see him.
He is not here.
War. This door is open, he is gone this way. 55
Glou. He came not through the chamber where we
stay'd.
King. Where is the crown? who took it from my
pillow?
War. When we withdrew, my liege, we left it here.
King. The Prince hath ta'en it hence. Go seek him
out.
Is he so hasty that he doth suppose   60
My sleep my death?
Find him, my Lord of Warwick, chide him hither.
                                 [*Exit Warwick.*]
This part of his conjoins with my disease,
And helps to end me. See, sons, what things you are!
How quickly nature falls into revolt   65
When gold becomes her object!
For this the foolish over-careful fathers
Have broke their sleep with thoughts, their brains with
care,
Their bones with industry;
For this they have engrossed and pil'd up   70
The cank'red heaps of strange-achieved gold;
For this they have been thoughtful to invest
Their sons with arts and martial exercises;
When like the bee tolling from every flower
[The virtuous sweets],   75
Our [thighs] pack'd with wax, our mouths with honey,
We bring it to the hive, and like the bees,
Are murd'red for our pains. This bitter taste
Yields his engrossments to the ending father.

Enter WARWICK.

Now, where is he that will not stay so long   80
Till his friend sickness [have] determin'd me?
War. My lord, I found the Prince in the next room,
Washing with kindly tears his gentle cheeks,
With such a deep demeanor in great sorrow
That tyranny, which never quaff'd but blood,   85
Would, by beholding him, have wash'd his knife
With gentle eye-drops. He is coming hither.
King. But wherefore did he take away the crown?

Enter [PRINCE] HARRY.

Lo where he comes. Come hither to me, Harry.
Depart the chamber, leave us here alone.   90
                        Exeunt [*Warwick and the rest*].

63. **part:** deed.
68. **thoughts:** anxieties.   70. **engrossed:** accumulated.
71. **cank'red:** tarnished.   **strange-achieved:** acquired by crooked
means (?) or by extraordinary exertions (?) or in foreign lands (?).
72. **thoughtful:** careful.   74. **tolling:** gathering.
75. **virtuous:** essential.
78–79. **This...father:** i.e. his accumulations yield the dying father
this bitter taste.   81. **determin'd:** ended.
83. **kindly:** natural.   84. **deep:** heartfelt, intense.

Prince. I never thought to hear you speak again.
King. Thy wish was father, Harry, to that thought:
I stay too long by thee, I weary thee.
Dost thou so hunger for mine empty chair
That thou wilt needs invest thee with my honors   95
Before thy hour be ripe? O foolish youth,
Thou seek'st the greatness that will overwhelm thee.
Stay but a little, for my cloud of dignity
Is held from falling with so weak a wind
That it will quickly drop; my day is dim.   100
Thou hast stol'n that which after some few hours
Were thine without offense, and at my death
Thou hast seal'd up my expectation.
Thy life did manifest thou lov'dst me not,
And thou wilt have me die assur'd of it.   105
Thou hid'st a thousand daggers in thy thoughts,
Whom thou hast whetted on thy stony heart
To stab at half an hour of my life.
What, canst thou not forbear me half an hour?
Then get thee gone, and dig my grave thyself,   110
And bid the merry bells ring to thine ear
That thou art crowned, not that I am dead.
Let all the tears that should bedew my hearse
Be drops of balm to sanctify thy head;
Only compound me with forgotten dust;   115
Give that which gave thee life unto the worms,
Pluck down my officers, break my decrees,
For now a time is come to mock at form.
Harry the Fift is crown'd! Up, vanity!
Down, royal state! All you sage counsellors, hence!
And to the English court assemble now,   121
From every region, apes of idleness!
Now, neighbor confines, purge you of your scum!
Have you a ruffin that will swear, drink, dance,
Revel the night, rob, murder, and commit   125
The oldest sins the newest kind of ways?
Be happy, he will trouble you no more.
England shall double gild his treble guilt,
England shall give him office, honor, might;
For the fift Harry from curb'd license plucks   130
The muzzle of restraint, and the wild dog
Shall flesh his tooth on every innocent.
O my poor kingdom, sick with civil blows!
When that my care could not withhold thy riots,
What wilt thou do when riot is thy care?   135
O, thou wilt be a wilderness again,
Peopled with wolves, thy old inhabitants!
Prince. O, pardon me, my liege! but for my tears,
The moist impediments unto my speech,
I had forestall'd this dear and deep rebuke   140
Ere you with grief had spoke and I had heard
The course of it so far. There is your crown;
And He that wears the crown immortally
Long guard it yours! If I affect it more

94. **chair:** throne.   103. **seal'd up:** confirmed.
113. **hearse:** coffin on a bier.
114. **balm:** oil with which a king is anointed at his coronation.
115. **compound:** mix.   118. **form:** ceremony, decorum.
119. **vanity:** folly.   120. **state:** pomp.
122. **idleness:** frivolity.   123. **confines:** regions.
124. **ruffin:** ruffian.
132. **flesh...on:** plunge his teeth into the flesh of.
134. **care:** i.e. careful discipline.   140. **dear:** grievous.
144. **affect:** love.

2 Henry IV
IV.v

Than as your honor. and as your renown,   145
Let me no more from this obedience rise,   [*Kneels.*]
Which my most inward true and duteous spirit
Teacheth this prostrate and exterior bending.
God witness with me, when I here came in,   149
And found no course of breath within your Majesty,
How cold it strook my heart! If I do feign,
O, let me in my present wildness die,
And never live to show th' incredulous world
The noble change that I have purposed!
Coming to look on you, thinking you dead,   155
And dead almost, my liege, to think you were,
I spake unto this crown as having sense,
And thus upbraided it: "The care on thee depending
Hath fed upon the body of my father;
Therefore thou best of gold art [worst of] gold.   160
Other, less fine in carat, [is] more precious,
Preserving life in med'cine potable;
But thou, most fine, most honor'd, most renown'd,
Hast eat thy bearer up." Thus, my most royal liege,
Accusing it, I put it on my head,   165
To try with it, as with an enemy
That had before my face murdered my father,
The quarrel of a true inheritor.
But if it did infect my blood with joy,
Or swell my thoughts to any strain of pride,   170
If any rebel or vain spirit of mine
Did with the least affection of a welcome
Give entertainment to the might of it,
Let God for ever keep it from my head,
And make me as the poorest vassal is   175
That doth with awe and terror kneel to it!
   King. [O my son,]
God put [it] in thy mind to take it hence,
That thou mightst win the more thy father's love,
Pleading so wisely in excuse of it!   180
Come hither, Harry, sit thou by my bed,
And hear (I think) the very latest counsel
That ever I shall breathe. God knows, my son,
By what by-paths and indirect crook'd ways
I met this crown, and I myself know well   185
How troublesome it sate upon my head.
To thee it shall descend with better quiet,
Better opinion, better confirmation,
For all the soil of the achievement goes
With me into the earth. It seem'd in me   190
But as an honor snatch'd with boist'rous hand,
And I had many living to upbraid
My gain of it by their assistances,
Which daily grew to quarrel and to bloodshed,
Wounding supposed peace. All these bold fears   195

Thou seest with peril I have answered;
For all my reign hath been but as a scene
Acting that argument. And now my death
Changes the mood, for what in me was purchas'd
Falls upon thee in a more fairer sort;   200
So thou the garland wear'st successively.
Yet though thou stand'st more sure than I could do,
Thou art not firm enough, since griefs are green,
And all [my] friends, which thou must make thy
      friends,
Have but their stings and teeth newly ta'en out;   205
By whose fell working I was first advanc'd,
And by whose power I well might lodge a fear
To be again displac'd; which to avoid,
I cut them off, and had a purpose now
To lead out many to the Holy Land,   210
Lest rest and lying still might make them look
Too near unto my state. Therefore, my Harry,
Be it thy course to busy giddy minds
With foreign quarrels, that action, hence borne out,
May waste the memory of the former days.   215
More would I, but my lungs are wasted so
That strength of speech is utterly denied me.
How I came by the crown, O God forgive,
And grant it may with thee in true peace live!
   Prince. [My gracious liege,]   220
You won it, wore it, kept it, gave it me;
Then plain and right must my possession be,
Which I with more than with a common pain
'Gainst all the world will rightfully maintain.

               Enter [PRINCE JOHN OF] LANCASTER.

   King. Look, look, here comes my John of Lan-
      caster.   225
   P. John. Health, peace, and happiness to my royal
      father!
   King. Thou bring'st me happiness and peace, son
      John,
But health, alack, with youthful wings is flown
From this bare wither'd trunk. Upon thy sight
My worldly business makes a period.   230
Where is my Lord of Warwick?
   Prince.   My Lord of Warwick!

                  [*Enter* WARWICK.]

   King. Doth any name particular belong
Unto the lodging where I first did swound?
   War. 'Tis call'd Jerusalem, my noble lord.
   King. Laud be to God! even there my life must
      end.   235

---

146. **obedience:** obeisance.
147. **true:** loyal.   150. **course:** current.
158. **on thee depending:** connected with you.   161. **carat:** value.
162. **potable:** drinkable. Gold in solution (*aurum potabile*) was valued
as a medicine.   166. **try:** ascertain by testing.
170. **strain:** feeling.   172. **affection:** inclination.
182. **latest:** last.
183–85. **God . . . crown.** As Holinshed reports (Bullough, IV, 277–78),
"Well faire sonne (said the king with a great sigh) what right I had
to it [i.e. the crown], God knoweth. Well (said the prince) if you die
king, I will have the garland, and trust to keepe it with the sword
against all mine enimies, as you have doone."
186. **sate:** sat.   188. **opinion:** i.e. support of public opinion.
189. **soil:** moral stain.

198. **argument:** theme.
199. **mood:** mode, i.e. tonality.   **purchas'd:** acquired by exertion.
201. **successively:** by inheritance.
203. **griefs:** grievances.   **green:** fresh.
206. **fell working:** violent exertion.   207. **lodge:** harbor.
211–12. **look . . . state:** inspect my (questionable) regality too closely.
214. **action . . . out:** campaigns conducted abroad.
215. **waste:** consume.   223. **pain:** effort.
229. **Upon thy sight:** seeing you.   230. **period:** end.
233. **swound:** swoon.
235–40. **Laud . . . die.** "Then said the king," reports Holinshed (Bullough, IV, 278), "Lauds be given to the father of heaven, for now I
know that I shall die heere in this chamber, according to the prophesie
of me declared, that I should depart this life in Jerusalem."

It hath been prophesied to me many years,
I should not die but in Jerusalem,
Which vainly I suppos'd the Holy Land.
But bear me to that chamber, there I'll lie,
In that Jerusalem shall Harry die.   [*Exeunt.*]   240

[ACT V, Scene I]

Enter Shallow, Falstaff, *and* Bardolph, [*with* Page].

Shal. By cock and pie, sir, you shall not away to-night. What, Davy, I say!
Fal. You must excuse me, Master Robert Shallow.
Shal. I will not excuse you, you shall not be excus'd, excuses shall not be admitted, there is no excuse shall serve, you shall not be excus'd. Why, Davy!   7

[*Enter* Davy.]

Davy. Here, sir.
Shal. Davy, Davy, Davy, Davy, let me see, Davy, let me see, Davy, let me see. Yea, marry, William cook, bid him come hither. Sir John, you shall not be excus'd.   12
Davy. Marry, sir, thus; those precepts cannot be serv'd; and again, sir, shall we sow the hade land with wheat?   15
Shal. With red wheat, Davy. But for William cook—are there no young pigeons?
Davy. Yes, sir. Here is now the smith's note for shoeing and plough-irons.   19
Shal. Let it be cast and paid. Sir John, you shall not be excus'd.
Davy. Now, sir, a new link to the bucket must needs be had; and, sir, do you mean to stop any of William's wages, about the sack he lost at [Hinckley] fair?   25
Shal. 'A shall answer it. Some pigeons, Davy, a couple of short-legg'd hens, a joint of mutton, and any pretty little tiny kickshaws, tell William cook.
Davy. Doth the man of war stay all night, sir?   29
Shal. Yea, Davy, I will use him well. A friend i' th' court is better than a penny in purse. Use his men well, Davy, for they are arrant knaves, and will backbite.
Davy. No worse than they are backbitten, sir, for they have marvail's foul linen.   35
Shal. Well conceited, Davy. About thy business, Davy.

Davy. I beseech you, sir, to countenance William Visor of Woncote against Clement Perkes a' th' Hill.   39
Shal. There is many complaints, Davy, against that Visor. That Visor is an arrant knave, on my knowledge.
Davy. I grant your worship that he is a knave, sir; but yet God forbid, sir, but a knave should have some countenance at his friend's request. An honest   45 man, sir, is able to speak for himself, when a knave is not. I have serv'd your worship truly, sir, this eight years; and I cannot once or twice in a quarter bear out a knave against an honest man, I have little credit with your worship. The knave is mine honest friend, sir, therefore I beseech you let him be countenanc'd.   51
Shal. Go to, I say, he shall have no wrong. Look about, Davy. [*Exit Davy.*] Where are you, Sir John? Come, come, come, off with your boots. Give me your hand, Master Bardolph.   55
Bard. I am glad to see your worship.
Shal. I thank thee with my heart, kind Master Bardolph, and welcome, my tall fellow [*to the Page*]. Come, Sir John.   59
Fal. I'll follow you, good Master Robert Shallow. [*Exit Shallow.*] Bardolph, look to our horses. [*Exeunt Bardolph and Page.*] If I were saw'd into quantities, I should make four dozen of such bearded hermits' staves as Master Shallow. It is a wonderful thing to see the semblable coherence of his men's spirits   65 and his. They, by observing him, do bear themselves like foolish justices; he, by conversing with them, is turn'd into a justice-like servingman. Their spirits are so married in conjunction with the participation of society that they flock together in consent, like so   70 many wild geese. If I had a suit to Master Shallow, I would humor his men with the imputation of being near their master; if to his men, I would curry with Master Shallow that no man could better command his servants. It is certain that either wise bearing or   75 ignorant carriage is caught, as men take diseases, one of another; therefore let men take heed of their company. I will devise matter enough out of this Shallow to keep Prince Harry in continual laughter the wearing out of six fashions, which is four terms, or two actions,   80 and 'a shall laugh without intervallums. O, it is much that a lie with a slight oath and a jest with a sad brow will do with a fellow that never had the ache in his shoulders! O, you shall see him laugh till his face be like a wet cloak ill laid up.   85
Shal. [*Within.*] Sir John!
Fal. I come, Master Shallow, I come, Master Shallow.   [*Exit.*]

238. **vainly:** foolishly.

V.i. Location: Gloucestershire. Shallow's house.
1. **By . . . pie:** a mild oath of uncertain origin.
13. **precepts:** summonses (that Shallow had issued as a justice of the peace).   14. **hade land:** unploughed strip of land.
18. **note:** bill.   20. **cast:** reckoned, i.e. verified.
24. **Hinckley:** market town in Leicestershire.
26. **answer:** make restitution for.
28. **kickshaws:** fancy dish (French *quelque chose*).
34. **backbitten:** i.e. by lice.   35. **marvail's:** marvellous.
36. **Well conceited:** wittily said.

38. **countenance:** favor, support.
39. **Woncote:** Woodmancote, a town in Gloucestershire.
48. **bear out:** support.   49. **credit:** influence.
62. **quantities:** pieces.   65. **semblable coherence:** similarity.
69–70. **with . . . society:** i.e. through close association.
70. **consent:** agreement.   73. **curry with:** flatter.
80. **four terms:** i.e. twelve months (there being four terms of court in the legal year).   **actions:** lawsuits.
81. **intervallums:** intervals between terms of court.
82. **sad:** serious.
85. **ill laid up:** carelessly packed away (and hence very wrinkled).

2 *Henry IV*
V.ii

[SCENE II]

Enter WARWICK, LORD CHIEF JUSTICE, [*meeting*].

War. How now, my Lord Chief Justice, whither
away?

Ch. Just. How doth the King?

War. Exceeding well, his cares are now all ended.

Ch. Just. I hope, not dead.

War.   He's walk'd the way of nature,
And to our purposes he lives no more.   5

Ch. Just. I would his Majesty had call'd me with
him;
The service that I truly did his life
Hath left me open to all injuries.

War. Indeed I think the young King loves you not.

Ch. Just. I know he doth not, and do arm myself
To welcome the condition of the time,   11
Which cannot look more hideously upon me
Than I have drawn it in my fantasy.

Enter [PRINCE] JOHN [OF LANCASTER], THOMAS [OF
CLARENCE], *and* HUMPHREY [OF GLOUCESTER],
WESTMERLAND, [*and others*].

War. Here come the heavy issue of dead Harry.
O that the living Harry had the temper   15
Of he, the worst of these three gentlemen!
How many nobles then should hold their places,
That must strike sail to spirits of vile sort!

Ch. Just. O God, I fear all will be overturn'd!

P. John. Good morrow, cousin Warwick, good
morrow.   20

Princes [*Glou., Clar.*] *ambo.* Good morrow, cousin.

P. John. We meet like men that had forgot to speak.

War. We do remember, but our argument
Is all too heavy to admit much talk.

P. John. Well, peace be with him that hath made
us heavy!   25

Ch. Just. Peace be with us, lest we be heavier!

Glou. O, good my lord, you have lost a friend
indeed,
And I dare swear you borrow not that face
Of seeming sorrow, it is sure your own.

P. John. Though no man be assur'd what grace to
find,   30
You stand in coldest expectation.
I am the sorrier, would 'twere otherwise!

Clar. Well, you must now speak Sir John Falstaff
fair,
Which swims against your stream of quality.

Ch. Just. Sweet Princes, what I did, I did in honor,
Led by th' impartial conduct of my soul;   36

And never shall you see that I will beg
A ragged and forestall'd remission.
If truth and upright innocency fail me,
I'll to the King my master that is dead,   40
And tell him who hath sent me after him.

War. Here comes the Prince.

Enter the PRINCE *and* BLUNT.

Ch. Just. Good morrow, and God save your
Majesty!

Prince. This new and gorgeous garment, majesty,
Sits not so easy on me as you think.   45
Brothers, you [mix] your sadness with some fear:
This is the English, not the Turkish court,
Not Amurath an Amurath succeeds,
But Harry Harry. Yet be sad, good brothers,
For by my faith it very well becomes you.   50
Sorrow so royally in you appears
That I will deeply put the fashion on
And wear it in my heart. Why then be sad,
But entertain no more of it, good brothers,
Than a joint burden laid upon us all.   55
For me, by heaven (I bid you be assur'd),
I'll be your father and your brother too.
Let me but bear your love, I'll bear your cares.
Yet weep that Harry's dead, and so will I,
But Harry lives, that shall convert those tears   60
By number into hours of happiness.

Princes. We hope no otherwise from your Majesty.

Prince. You all look strangely on me, and you
most.
You are, I think, assur'd I love you not.

Ch. Just. I am assur'd, if I be measur'd rightly,   65
Your Majesty hath no just cause to hate me.

Prince. No?
How might a prince of my great hopes forget
So great indignities you laid upon me?
What, rate, rebuke, and roughly send to prison   70
Th' immediate heir of England! Was this easy?
May this be wash'd in Lethe and forgotten?

Ch. Just. I then did use the person of your father,
The image of his power lay then in me,
And in th' administration of his law,   75
Whiles I was busy for the commonwealth,
Your Highness pleased to forget my place,
The majesty and power of law and justice,
The image of the King whom I presented,
And strook me in my very seat of judgment;   80
Whereon (as an offender to your father)
I gave bold way to my authority,
And did commit you. If the deed were ill,
Be you contented, wearing now the garland,
To have a son set your decrees at nought?   85

V.ii. Location: Westminster. The palace.
7. **truly:** loyally.   13. **fantasy:** imagination.
14. **heavy issue:** sorrowful offspring.
16. **he, the worst:** the worst one.
18. **strike sail:** i.e. be submissive.   21. s.p. **ambo:** both.
23. **argument:** subject.
30. **what . . . find:** what favor he will find (with the new king).
33. **speak . . . fair:** address . . . courteously.
34. **stream of quality:** i.e. natural inclination.
35. **what I did.** On the grounds for the Chief Justice's apprehension
see the note to *1 Henry IV,* III.ii.32–33.

37–38. **I . . . remission:** i.e. like a beggar I will ask a pardon sure to
be refused.
48. **Amurath:** Murad III, Turkish sultan who, on his accession (1574),
strangled his five brothers.
63. **strangely:** coldly, suspiciously.   70. **rate:** upbraid.
71. **easy:** insignificant.
72. **Lethe:** in Greek mythology, the river of oblivion.
73. **use . . . of:** i.e. represent.   74. **image:** symbol.
79. **presented:** represented.   83. **commit:** i.e. to prison.

To pluck down justice from your aweful bench?
To trip the course of law and blunt the sword
That guards the peace and safety of your person?
Nay more, to spurn at your most royal image,
And mock your workings in a second body?　90
Question your royal thoughts, make the case yours:
Be now the father and propose a son,
Hear your own dignity so much profan'd,
See your most dreadful laws so loosely slighted,
Behold yourself so by a son disdained;　95
And then imagine me taking your part,
And in your power soft silencing your son.
After this cold considerance, sentence me,
And as you are a king, speak in your state
What I have done that misbecame my place,　100
My person, or my liege's sovereignty.
　　　Prince.　You are right justice, and you weigh this
　　　　　well,
Therefore still bear the balance and the sword,
And I do wish your honors may increase,
Till you do live to see a son of mine　105
Offend you and obey you, as I did.
So shall I live to speak my father's words:
"Happy am I, that have a man so bold,
That dares do justice on my proper son;
And not less happy, having such a son　110
That would deliver up his greatness so
Into the hands of justice." You did commit me;
For which I do commit into your hand
Th' unstained sword that you have us'd to bear,
With this remembrance, that you use the same　115
With the like bold, just, and impartial spirit
As you have done 'gainst me. There is my hand.
You shall be as a father to my youth,
My voice shall sound as you do prompt mine ear,
And I will stoop and humble my intents　120
To your well-practic'd wise directions.
And, princes all, believe me, I beseech you,
My father is gone wild into his grave;
For in his tomb lie my affections,
And with his spirits sadly I survive,　125
To mock the expectation of the world,
To frustrate prophecies, and to rase out
Rotten opinion, who hath writ me down
After my seeming. The tide of blood in me

86. **aweful:** awesome.　89. **spurn:** kick.
90. **your . . . body:** the actions of your deputy.
92. **propose:** imagine.　97. **soft:** gently.
98. **considerance:** consideration.　99. **state:** royal capacity.
103. **balance:** i.e. scales (symbolizing ideal justice).
109. **proper:** own.　115. **remembrance:** reminder.
122-45. **And . . . day.** "This king even at first appointing with himselfe," says Holinshed (Bullough, IV, 280), "to shew that in his person
princelie honors should change publike manners, he determined to
put on him the shape of a new man. For whereas aforetime he had
made himselfe a companion unto misrulie mates of dissolute order
and life, he now banished them all from his presence (but not un-
rewarded, or else unpreferred) inhibiting them upon a great paine,
not once to approch, lodge, or sojourne within ten miles of his court
or presence: and in their places he chose men of gravitie, wit, and high
policie, by whose wise counsell he might at all times rule to his
honour and dignitie."
123. **My . . . grave:** i.e. my wildness has been buried with my father.
124. **affections:** (unruly) inclinations.　125. **sadly:** soberly.
127. **rase:** erase, blot.
128-29. **who . . . seeming:** which has delineated me as I appeared to
be.　129. **blood:** passion.

Hath proudly flow'd in vanity till now;　130
Now doth it turn and ebb back to the sea,
Where it shall mingle with the state of floods,
And flow henceforth in formal majesty.
Now call we our high court of parliament,
And let us choose such limbs of noble counsel　135
That the great body of our state may go
In equal rank with the best govern'd nation,
That war, or peace, or both at once, may be
As things acquainted and familiar to us,
In which you, father, shall have foremost hand.　140
Our coronation done, we will accite
(As I before remember'd) all our state,
And (God consigning to my good intents)
No prince nor peer shall have just cause to say,　144
God shorten Harry's happy life one day!　　*Exeunt.*

[Scene III]

Enter Sir John [Falstaff], Shallow, Silence,
　Davy, Bardolph, Page.

　　　Shal.　Nay, you shall see my orchard, where, in an
arbor, we will eat a last year's pippin of mine own
graffing, with a dish of caraways, and so forth. Come,
cousin Silence—and then to bed.
　　　Fal.　'Fore God, you have here goodly dwelling
and rich.　6
　　　Shal.　Barren, barren, barren, beggars all, beggars
all, Sir John! Marry, good air. Spread, Davy, spread,
Davy. Well said, Davy.
　　　Fal.　This Davy serves you for good uses, he is your
servingman and your husband.　11
　　　Shal.　A good varlet, a good varlet, a very good
varlet, Sir John. By the mass, I have drunk too much
sack at supper. A good varlet. Now sit down, now sit
down. Come, cousin.　15
　　　Sil.　Ah, sirrah, quoth 'a, we shall
[*Singing.*]
　　　"Do nothing but eat, and make good cheer,
　　　　And praise God for the merry year,
　　　When flesh is cheap and females dear,
　　　　And lusty lads roam here and there　20
　　　　　So merrily,
　　　　And ever among so merrily."
　　　Fal.　There's a merry heart! Good Master Silence,
I'll give you a health for that anon.
　　　Shal.　Give Master Bardolph some wine, Davy.　25
　　　Davy.　Sweet sir, sit, I'll be with you anon, most
sweet sir, sit. Master page, good master page, sit.
Proface! What you want in meat, we'll have in drink,
but you must bear, the heart's all.　　　[*Exit.*]

130. **vanity:** folly.　132. **state of floods:** majesty of the sea.
140. **father:** i.e. the Chief Justice.　141. **accite:** summon.
142. **remember'd:** mentioned.　**state:** dignitaries and peers.
143. **consigning:** assenting.

V.iii. Location: Gloucestershire. Shallow's orchard.
2. **pippin:** kind of apple.
3. **graffing:** grafting.　**caraways.** Caraway seeds were often eaten
with apples.　8. **Spread:** lay the cloth.
11. **husband:** steward.　12. **varlet:** servant.　16. **quoth 'a:** said he.
28. **Proface:** a term of welcome or good wishes to a guest.　**meat:**
food.

2 Henry IV
V.iii

Shal. Be merry, Master Bardolph, and, my little
soldier there, be merry.   31
   Sil. [*Singing.*]
     "Be merry, be merry, my wife has all,
     For women are shrows, both short and tall;
     'Tis merry in hall when beards wags all,
       And welcome merry Shrove-tide.   35
     Be merry, be merry."
   Fal. I did not think Master Silence had been a man
of this mettle.
   Sil. Who, I? I have been merry twice and once
ere now.   40

          Enter Davy.

   Davy. [*To Bardolph.*] There's a dish of leather-
coats for you.
   Shal. Davy!
   Davy. Your worship! I'll be with you straight.
A cup of wine, sir?   45
   Sil. [*Singing.*]
     "A cup of wine that's brisk and fine,
     And drink unto [thee,] leman mine,
     And a merry heart lives long-a."
   Fal. Well said, Master Silence.
   Sil. And we shall be merry, now comes in the
sweet a' th' night.   51
   Fal. Health and long life to you, Master Silence.
   Sil. [*Singing.*]
     "Fill the cup, and let it come,
     I'll pledge you a mile to th' bottom."
   Shal. Honest Bardolph, welcome. If thou want'st
any thing, and wilt not call, beshrew thy heart. 56
Welcome, my little tiny thief [*to the Page*], and wel-
come indeed too. I'll drink to Master Bardolph, and to
all the cabileros about London.
   Davy. I hope to see London once ere I die.   60
   Bard. And I might see you there, Davy!
   Shal. By the mass, you'll crack a quart together,
ha, will you not, Master Bardolph?
   Bard. Yea, sir, in a pottle-pot.   64
   Shal. By God's liggens, I thank thee. The knave
will stick by thee, I can assure thee that 'a will not out,
'a. 'Tis true bred!
   Bard. And I'll stick by him, sir.   68
   Shal. Why, there spoke a king. Lack nothing, be
merry! (*One knocks at door.*) Look who's at door
there ho! Who knocks?   [*Exit Davy.*]
   Fal. [*To Silence, seeing him take off a bumper.*]
Why, now you have done me right.   72
   Sil. [*Singing.*] "Do me right,
       And dub me knight,
          Samingo."   75
Is't not so?

   Fal. 'Tis so.
   Sil. Is't so? Why then an old man can do
somewhat.

          [*Enter* Davy.]

   Davy. And't please your worship, there's one
Pistol come from the court with news.   81
   Fal. From the court? Let him come in.

          Enter Pistol.

How now, Pistol?
   Pist. Sir John, God save you!
   Fal. What wind blew you hither, Pistol?   85
   Pist. Not the ill wind which blows no man to good.
Sweet knight, thou art now one of the greatest men in
this realm.
   Sil. By'r lady, I think 'a be, but goodman Puff of
Barson.   90
   Pist. Puff?
Puff i' thy teeth, most recreant coward base!
Sir John, I am thy Pistol and thy friend,
And helter-skelter have I rode to thee,
And tidings do I bring, and lucky joys,   95
And golden times, and happy news of price.
   Fal. I pray thee now deliver them like a man of
this world.
   Pist. A foutre for the world and worldlings base!
I speak of Africa and golden joys.   100
   Fal. O base Assyrian knight, what is thy news?
Let King Cophetua know the truth thereof.
   Sil. [*Singing.*] "And Robin Hood, Scarlet, and
John."
   Pist. Shall dunghill curs confront the Helicons?
And shall good news be baffled?   105
Then, Pistol, lay thy head in Furies' lap.
   Shal. Honest gentleman, I know not your breeding.
   Pist. Why then lament therefore.
   Shal. Give me pardon, sir. If, sir, you come with
news from the court, I take it there's but two ways,
either to utter them, or conceal them. I am, sir, under
the King, in some authority.   112
   Pist. Under which king, besonian? Speak, or die.
   Shal. Under King Harry.
   Pist.   Harry the Fourth, or Fift?
   Shal. Harry the Fourth.
   Pist.   A foutre for thine office!
Sir John, thy tender lambkin now is king;   116
Harry the Fift's the man. I speak the truth.
When Pistol lies, do this, and fig me like
The bragging Spaniard.
   Fal. What, is the old king dead?   120
   Pist. As nail in door. The things I speak are
    just.

Fal. Away, Bardolph! saddle my horse. Master Robert Shallow, choose what office thou wilt in the land, 'tis thine. Pistol, I will double-charge thee with dignities. 125

Bard. O joyful day! I would not take a [knight-hood] for my fortune.

Pist. What? I do bring good news?

Fal. Carry Master Silence to bed. Master Shallow, my Lord Shallow—be what thou wilt, I am Fortune's steward—get on thy boots. We'll ride all night. 131 O sweet Pistol! Away, Bardolph! [*Exit Bardolph.*] Come, Pistol, utter more to me, and withal devise something to do thyself good. Boot, boot, Master Shallow! I know the young king is sick for me. Let us take any man's horses, the laws of England are at 136 my commandement. Blessed are they that have been my friends, and woe to my Lord Chief Justice!

Pist. Let vultures vile seize on his lungs also! "Where is the life that late I led?" say they. 140 Why, here it is, welcome these pleasant days! *Exeunt.*

[Scene IV]

Enter [Beadle] *and three or four* Officers [*with* Hostess Quickly *and* Doll Tearsheet].

Host. No, thou arrant knave, I would to God that I might die, that I might have thee hang'd. Thou hast drawn my shoulder out of joint.

[*Bead.*] The constables have deliver'd her over to me, and she shall have whipping cheer, I warrant her. There hath been a man or two kill'd about her. 6

Doll. Nuthook, nuthook, you lie. Come on! I'll tell thee what, thou damn'd tripe-visag'd rascal, and the child I go with do miscarry, thou wert better thou hadst strook thy mother, thou paper-fac'd villain! 10

Host. O the Lord, that Sir John were come! I would make this a bloody day to somebody. But I pray God the fruit of her womb miscarry.

[*Bead.*] If it do, you shall have a dozen of cushions again; you have but eleven now. Come, I charge you both go with me, for the man is dead that you and Pistol beat amongst you. 17

Doll. I'll tell you what, you thin man in a censer, I will have you as soundly swing'd for this—you blue-bottle rogue, you filthy famish'd correctioner, if you be not swing'd, I'll forswear half-kirtles. 21

[*Bead.*] Come, come, you she knight-arrant, come.

Host. O God, that right should thus overcome might! Well, of sufferance comes ease. 25

Doll. Come, you rogue, come bring me to a justice.

Host. Ay, come, you starv'd bloodhound.

Doll. Goodman Death, goodman Bones!

Host. Thou atomy, thou!

Doll. Come, you thin thing, come, you rascal. 30

[*Bead.*] Very well. [*Exeunt.*]

[Scene V]

Enter Strewers of rushes.

1. Strewer. More rushes, more rushes.

2. Strewer. The trumpets have sounded twice.

3. Strewer. 'Twill be two a' clock ere they come from the coronation. Dispatch, dispatch. [*Exeunt.*] 4

Trumpets sound, and the King *and his* Train *pass over the stage. After them enter* Falstaff, Shallow, Pistol, Bardolph, *and the* Boy [Page].

Fal. Stand here by me, Master Shallow, I will make the King do you grace. I will leer upon him as 'a comes by, and do but mark the countenance that he will give me.

Pist. God bless thy lungs, good knight. 9

Fal. Come here, Pistol, stand behind me.—O, if I had had time to have made new liveries, I would have bestow'd the thousand pound I borrow'd of you. But 'tis no matter, this poor show doth better, this doth infer the zeal I had to see him.

[*Shal.*] It doth so. 15

Fal. It shows my earnestness of affection—

[*Shal.*] It doth so.

Fal. My devotion—

[*Shal.*] It doth, it doth, it doth.

Fal. As it were, to ride day and night, and not to deliberate, not to remember, not to have patience to shift me— 22

Shal. It is best, certain.

[*Fal.*] But to stand stain'd with travel, and sweating with desire to see him, thinking of nothing else, putting all affairs else in oblivion, as if there were nothing else to be done but to see him. 27

Pist. 'Tis "*semper idem,*" for "*obsque hoc nihil est.*" 'Tis [all] in every part.

Shal. 'Tis so indeed. 30

Pist. My knight, I will inflame thy noble liver,
And make thee rage.
Thy Doll, and Helen of thy noble thoughts,
Is in base durance and contagious prison,
Hal'd thither 35
By most mechanical and dirty hand.
Rouse up revenge from ebon den with fell Alecto's snake,

---

124. **double-charge.** With a pun on Pistol's name.

V.iv. Location: London. A street.
5. **whipping cheer:** i.e. whipping for her supper.
7. **Nuthook:** slang term for an arresting officer; literally, a hooked stick used in nutting. 8. **tripe-visag'd:** flabby-faced.
10. **paper-fac'd:** white-faced.
14–15. **If . . . now.** He accuses Doll of using a pillow to make herself look pregnant. 17. **amongst you:** together.
18. **thin . . . censer:** figure in low relief embossed on the lid of an incense burner. 19. **swing'd:** thrashed (past participle of *swinge*).
19–20. **blue-bottle.** Alluding to the customary blue coats worn by beadles. 21. **half-kirtles:** short skirts. 25. **sufferance:** suffering.

29. **atomy:** the Hostess' confusion of *atom* and *anatomy*, i.e. skeleton.
30. **rascal:** lean, inferior deer.

V.v. Location: Westminster. Near the Abbey.
6. **grace:** honor. **leer:** glance sideways.
12. **bestow'd:** spent. **you:** i.e. Shallow. 14. **infer:** imply.
22. **shift me:** change my clothes.
28–29. **'Tis . . . part:** i.e. it's "always the same," for "without this there is nothing." Integrity is everything. (Pistol paraphrases the Latin tags to express his approval of Falstaff's constancy.)
34. **contagious:** noxious. 36. **mechanical:** menial.
37. **ebon:** black. **Alecto:** one of the Furies.

2 Henry IV
V.v

For Doll is in. Pistol speaks nought but truth.
Fal. I will deliver her.
[*Shouts within. The trumpets sound.*]
Pist. There roar'd the sea, and trumpet-clangor
   sounds.   40

Enter the KING *and his* TRAIN, [*the* LORD CHIEF
JUSTICE *among them*].

Fal. God save thy Grace, King Hal! my royal Hal!
Pist. The heavens thee guard and keep, most royal
   imp of fame!
Fal. God save thee, my sweet boy!
King. My Lord Chief Justice, speak to that vain
   man.
Ch. Just. Have you your wits? know you what 'tis
   you speak?   45
Fal. My King, my Jove! I speak to thee, my heart!
King. I know thee not, old man, fall to thy prayers.
How ill white hairs becomes a fool and jester!
I have long dreamt of such a kind of man,
So surfeit-swell'd, so old, and so profane;   50
But being awak'd, I do despise my dream.
Make less thy body (hence) and more thy grace,
Leave gormandizing, know the grave doth gape
For thee thrice wider than for other men.
Reply not to me with a fool-born jest,   55
Presume not that I am the thing I was,
For God doth know, so shall the world perceive,
That I have turn'd away my former self;
So will I those that kept me company.
When thou dost hear I am as I have been,   60
Approach me, and thou shalt be as thou wast,
The tutor and the feeder of my riots.
Till then I banish thee, on pain of death,
As I have done the rest of my misleaders,
Not to come near our person by ten mile.   65
For competence of life I will allow you,
That lack of means enforce you not to evils,
And as we hear you do reform yourselves,
We will, according to your strengths and qualities,
Give you advancement. Be it your charge, my lord,
To see perform'd the tenure of my word.   71
Set on.   [*Exeunt King and his Train.*]
Fal. Master Shallow, I owe you a thousand pound.
Shal. Yea, marry, Sir John, which I beseech you to
let me have home with me.   75
Fal. That can hardly be, Master Shallow. Do not
you grieve at this, I shall be sent for in private to him.
Look you, he must seem thus to the world. Fear not
your advancements, I will be the man yet that shall
make you great.   80
Shal. I cannot perceive how, unless you give me
your doublet and stuff me out with straw. I beseech
you, good Sir John, let me have five hundred of my
thousand.
Fal. Sir, I will be as good as my word. This that
you heard was but a color.   86

42. **imp:** scion.
44. **vain:** foolish. 50. **surfeit-swell'd:** swollen through gluttony.
52. **hence:** hereafter. **grace:** virtue.
66. **competence of life:** i.e. modest allowance.
69. **qualities:** attainments. 71. **tenure:** tenor.
86. **color:** pretense.

922

Shal. A color that I fear you will die in, Sir John.
Fal. Fear no colors, go with me to dinner. Come,
Lieutenant Pistol, come, Bardolph. I shall be sent for
soon at night.   90

Enter [*the* LORD CHIEF] JUSTICE *and* PRINCE JOHN;
[OFFICERS *with them*].

Ch. Just. Go carry Sir John Falstaff to the Fleet.
Take all his company along with him.
Fal. My lord, my lord—
Ch. Just. I cannot now speak, I will hear you soon.
Take them away.   95
Pist. Si fortuna me tormenta, spero contenta.
Exeunt. [*Manent Prince John and the Chief Justice.*]
P. John. I like this fair proceeding of the King's.
He hath intent his wonted followers
Shall all be very well provided for,
But all are banish'd till their conversations   100
Appear more wise and modest to the world.
Ch. Just. And so they are.
P. John. The King hath call'd his parliament, my
   lord.
Ch. Just. He hath.
P. John. I will lay odds that ere this year expire,
We bear our civil swords and native fire   106
As far as France. I heard a bird so sing,
Whose music, to my thinking, pleas'd the King.
Come, will you hence?   [*Exeunt.*]

EPILOGUE

First my fear, then my cur'sy, last my speech. My
fear, is your displeasure, my cur'sy, my duty, and my
speech, to beg your pardons. If you look for a good
speech now, you undo me, for what I have to say is of
mine own making, and what indeed (I should say)   5
will (I doubt) prove mine own marring. But to the
purpose, and so to the venture. Be it known to you, as
it is very well, I was lately here in the end of a displeasing play, to pray your patience for it and to
promise you a better. I meant indeed to pay you   10
with this, which if like an ill venture it come unluckily
home, I break, and you, my gentle creditors, lose.
Here I promis'd you I would be, and here I commit my
body to your mercies. Bate me some, and I will pay
you some, and (as most debtors do) promise you   15
infinitely; and so I kneel down before you—but,
indeed, to pray for the Queen.
If my tongue cannot entreat you to acquit me, will
you command me to use my legs? And yet that were
but light payment, to dance out of your debt. But a   20

87. **color:** i.e. *collar*, hangman's noose.
88. **colors:** (enemy) flags. 90. **soon at night:** early this evening.
91. **Fleet:** London prison.
96. **Si . . . contenta.** See note to II.iv.181.
100. **conversations:** behavior.
106. **civil . . . fire.** Alluding to the civil broils just ended.

Epi. 1. **cur'sy:** curtsy, bow. 6. **doubt:** fear.
8–9. **a displeasing play.** Not identified.
11. **ill venture:** unsuccessful commercial speculation.
12. **break:** am bankrupt.
14. **Bate me some:** abate me something.

good conscience will make any possible satisfaction, and so would I. All the gentlewomen here have forgiven me; if the gentlemen will not, then the gentlemen do not agree with the gentlewomen, which was never seen in such an assembly. 25

One word more, I beseech you. If you be not too much cloy'd with fat meat, our humble author will con-

tinue the story, with Sir John in it, and make you merry with fair Katherine of France, where (for any thing I know) Falstaff shall die of a sweat, unless 30 already 'a be kill'd with your hard opinions; for Oldcastle died [a] martyr, and this is not the man. My tongue is weary, when my legs are too, I will bid you good night.

27–28. **our . . . story.** Referring to the sequel of this play, *Henry V.*

32. **Oldcastle.** On Shakespeare's use of this name for Falstaff in the original form of the Henry IV plays, see the introduction.

NOTE ON THE TEXT

The Second Part of Henry the Fourth was first published in quarto in 1600 (Q). So far as we know, this was the only printing of the play until its inclusion in the First Folio (1623); nor was there any later seventeenth-century separate edition. Q occurs in two distinct issues. In the first issue, the scene which in F1 (and in the present text) is numbered III.i was accidentally omitted, and the omission was not discovered until a large number of copies had been sold. Sigs. E3 and E4 were then cancelled and replaced by four new leaves which incorporated the missing scene. These two issues are distinguished in the Textual Notes as Qa (first issue) and Qb (second issue).

Q was almost certainly printed from Shakespeare's "foul papers" and here serves as copy-text, except for some 156 lines found only in F1. For III.i, Qb is of necessity the basic copy; for that portion of the text contained in the two cancelled leaves of Qa (II.iv.341–91, III.ii.1–103, ending with the word *young*), the copy-text is of course Qa, but all significant variants in the reset version in Qb are recorded in the Textual Notes.

The evidence for believing that Q was set up from Shakespeare's "foul papers" is very strong. There is considerable inconsistency in the use of speech-prefixes, the most extreme instance being those for Doll Tearsheet, who appears as *Dol.*, *Dorothy*, *Teresh.*, and *Whoore*; a number of the stage directions are authorial in their indefiniteness (see, for example, the Textual Notes at II.i o.s.d., II.iv o.s.d., III.ii.54); the Beadle in V.iv is designated by the actor's name (Sincklo); stage directions list characters who have no part in the play (see I.iii o.s.d., II.ii o.s.d., IV.iv o.s.d.), or in the scene for which they are entered (see III.i, IV.i o.s.d.); at I.i.161 Sir John Umfrevile is assigned a speech, but no such character appears in the scene as it now stands; Falstaff appears once with the speech-prefix *Old.* for Oldcastle (I.ii.120); two lines apparently marked for deletion by Shakespeare are to be found in the uncorrected state of Q at IV.i.92, 93; and several characteristic Shakespearean spellings have survived the compositor, notably *Scilens*, *on* (for *one*), and *mas.* Although the various confusions in Q make it certain that the manuscript from which it was printed could never itself have served as a prompt-book, some connection with the theatre is suggested by the fact that the bulk of the additional lines found only in F1 are clearly original parts of the play and

their absence from Q can only be explained on the supposition that the compositor found them marked as cuts in the manuscript.

The exact provenience of the F1 text is open to question. On one hand, it is argued, most strongly by Alice Walker, that F1 was set from a copy of Q which had been augmented from and corrected against a "fair copy" of Shakespeare's "foul papers" (not against the prompt-book, as W. W. Greg argues), a "fair copy" made by a scribe unfriendly to colloquialisms and contracted or elided forms. On the other hand, M. A. Shaaber argues vigorously that F1 was set from a transcript (possibly by Ralph Crane) of the official prompt-book, a transcript which omitted certain prompt-book notations (such as directions for stage noises), ironed out colloquialisms, and expanded elided forms. The most recent editor of the play, A. R. Humphreys, after carefully weighing the arguments on both sides, declares in favor of a transcript which was either a sophisticated copy made from a theatre manuscript by a scribe who kept one eye on Q, or (as Fredson Bowers had suggested) a scribal copy prepared from a copy of Q considerably augmented, changed, and sophisticated in the process of collation with a theatre manuscript. Of these alternatives Humphreys prefers the first.

F1, apart from the 156 additional lines already noticed, generally tidies up the inconsistencies in Q, adds a number of necessary stage directions, and offers a sizable number of verbal variants. The Textual Notes record all significant variants, and all additions and omissions, in F1. For the Dering MS, to which occasional reference is made, see the "Note on the Text" to *I Henry IV*.

For further information, see: M. A. Shaaber, ed., New Variorum *2 Henry IV* (Philadelphia, 1940); Alice Walker, *Textual Problems of the First Folio* (Cambridge, 1953); Fredson Bowers, "A Definitive Text of Shakespeare," *Studies in Shakespeare* (Univ. of Miami Press, 1953); W. W. Greg, *The Shakespeare First Folio* (Oxford, 1955); M. A. Shaaber, "The Folio Text of *2 Henry IV*," *SQ*, VI (1955), 135–44; W. C. Ferguson, "The Compositors of *Henry IV, Part 2, Much Ado about Nothing, The Shoemakers' Holiday*, and *The First Part of the Contention*," *SB*, XIII (1960), 19–29; A. R. Humphreys, ed., New Arden *2 Henry IV* (London, 1966).

TEXTUAL NOTES

Title: The Second . . . Fourth] The Second part of Henrie the fourth, continuing to his death, and coronation of Henrie the fift. With the humours of sir Iohn Falstaffe, and swaggering Pistoll. As it hath been sundrie

times publikely acted by the right honourable, the Lord Chamberlaine his seruants. Written by William Shakespeare. *Q (title-page)*; The Second Part of Henry the Fourth, Containing his Death: and the

Coronation of King Henry the Fift. *F1* **Dramatis personae:** *as in F1; material in square brackets added by Rowe and later eds.* **Strewers]** *Wilson;* Groomes *F1* **Act-scene division:** *none in Q; from F1, with*

the following exceptions: I.i–iii (numbered
I.ii–iv in F1, which marks the Induction as
I.i); IV.ii, iii (no scene divisions in F1);
IV.iv (numbered IV.ii in F1); IV.v (no scene
division in F1); see first note to each scene;
present act-scene arrangement as a whole
first established by Cambridge

Induction

Induction] F1 (in which this heading is preceded by Actus Primus. Scoena Prima.)
o.s.d. painted . . . tongues] om. F1
1 s.p. Rum.] Capell
6 tongues] Tongue F1
8 men] them F1
8 reports.] F1 (Reports:); reports, Q
13 grief] griefes Q
14–5 war, . . . matter?] F1; Warre? . . .
matter. Q
16 jealousies,] F1; Iealousies Q
21 My well-known body] F1; (My wel knowne
body) Q
21 anatomize] F4; anothomize Q; Anathomize F1
27 rebels'] Theobald; rebels Q, F1
34 that] the F1
35 hold] Theobald; hole Q, F1
36 Where] F1; When Q
37 crafty-sick] hyphen, Pope
40 s.d. Exit Rumor.] Pelican; exit Rumours.
Q; Exit. F1

I.i

I.i] Warburton; Scena Secunda. F1
Location: Capell (subs.)
o.s.d. Bardolph] Rowe; Bardolfe Q, F1
(throughout)
1 s.d. Enter Porter.] Dyce
6 s.d. in . . . staff] ed. (after Dering MS:
Enter Northumberland: alone in his garden
and Night-Cappe: and l. 145 below)
6 s.d. Exit Porter.] Dyce
7 s.p. North.] F1; Earle. Q (throughout
scene)
13 God] heauen F1
23 fortunes] F1; fortuncs Q
28 who] whom F1
29 s.d. Enter Travers.] F1; after l. 25, Q
36 hard] head F1
41 bad] ill Dering MS, F1
44 armed] able F1
48 Again.] F1 (Againe:); againe, Q
53 honor, . . . point] F1; honor . . . point, Q
55 should that] should the F1
59 Spoke . . . venter] Speake at aduenture F1
64 Morton] F1; Mourton Q (and s.p. Mour,
throughout rest of scene)
71 woe-begone] hyphen, F1
79 my] mine F1
83 dead.] F1; dead? Q
86 others'] Capell; others Q, F1
88 an] thy F1
96 say so;] F1
97 tongue] F1; tongne Q
103 tolling] knolling F1
106 God] heauen F1
109 Harry] Henrie F1
126 So] Too F1
127 well-laboring] hyphen, F1
137 these] this F1
143 keeper's] Rowe; keepers Q, F1
144 Weak'ned] F1; Weakened Q
155 this] the F1
161 s.p. L. Bard.] Pope; Vmfr. Q; line om.
F1; a Sir John Umfrevile is mentioned in
l. 34, but he is not present in the scene as we
now have it, though possibly Shakespeare
included him in an earlier draft (see Shaaber,
New Variorum)
162 s.p. Mor.] Daniel conj.; Bard. Q; L. Bar.
F1
163 The] Daniel conj.; Mour. The Q; Mor.
The F1
164 Lean on] F3 (after F1 Leane-on); Leaue
on Q
164 your] F1; you Q
164 which,] Theobald; which Q, F1
164–5 o'er . . . passion,] F1; ore, . . . passion Q

166–79 You . . . be?] F1
170 edge,] Capell; edge F1
178 doth] ed.; hath F1
182 'twas] was F1
186 forth,] Dyce; forth Q; forth; F1
188 dare] do F1
189–209 The gentle . . . him.] F1
192 corpse'] Dyce; Corpes F1
201–2 religion. . . . thoughts,] Rowe (subs.);
Religion, . . . Thoughts: F1
208 Bullingbrook] ed.; Bullingbrooke F1
(throughout)
215 and] nor F1

I.ii

I.ii] Steevens; Scena Tertia. F1
Location: Pope
o.s.d. Sir . . . with] Falstaffe, and F1
o.s.d. following behind] ed. (suggested by Q
Enter sir Iohn alone)
1 s.p. Fal.] F1; Iohn Q (or sir Iohn through
l. 66)
7 foolish-compounded clay, man,] Pope (subs.);
foolish compounded clay-man, Q, F1
14 judgment.] F1; iudgement Q
16 heels.] F1; heels Q
17 inset] Cambridge; in-set Q; sette F1
19 jewel—] Dyce; iewell, Q; Iewell. F1
20 fledge.] Vaughan conj. (after Rowe); fledge,
Q; fledg'd, F1
22 of] Collier conj.; off Q; on F1
22 and] om. F1
23 God] Heauen F1
24 'tis] it is F1 (F1, as in some other plays,
expands contracted forms with considerable
frequency, e.g. he'll (l. 26), he's (l. 28), Is't
(II.i.3), to't (II.i.4), 'twere (II.i.148), there's
(II.i.148), etc.; this type of variant, except
in special cases, is not recorded hereafter)
29 Dommelton] Dombledon F1
30 and my] and F1
31 s.p. Page.] F1; Boy Q (throughout scene)
32 Bardolph] F4; Bardolfe Q (throughout),
F1 (F1 sometimes uses Bardolph)
34 Pray God] may F1
36 rascally . . . knave] F1 (Rascally-yea-
forsooth-knaue); rascall: yea forsooth
knaue Q; rascal! yea forsooth—knave! ed.
conj.
36 gentleman] F1; gentle man Q
38 smoothy-pates] smooth-pates F1
43 'a] hee F1 (a typical F1 sophistication;
not hereafter recorded)
44 an] and Q
45 Well,] F1; well Q
48–9 Where's Bardolph?] placed as in F1;
after l. 47, Q
50 into] F1; in Q
53 and] If F1 (a typical F1 sophistication;
not hereafter recorded)
53 but] om. F1
54 s.d. and Servant] F1
55 nobleman] F1; noble man Q
58 s.p. Ch. Just.] F1; Iustice Q (or Iust.
through l. 163)
72 begging] beg F1
74 need] want F1
80 s.p. Fal.] F1; Iohn Q (through l. 87)
80–1 man? Setting] F1; man, setting Q
87 me so?] F1; me, so Q
88 me? If] F1; me, if Q
90 hunt counter] Hunt-counter F1
93 God] om. F1
94 of] the F1
96 advice.] F3; aduise, Q; aduise. F1
97 have] hath F1
98 an ague] age F1
99 in you] om. F1
101 for] om. F1
103 s.p. Fal.] F1; sir Iohn Q
103 And't] If it F1
103 lordship] F1; lorship Q
109 God] heauen F1
109 you] om. F1
111 as . . . is] Neilson; as I take it? is Q;
is (as I take it) F1
112 and't . . . of] a F1
113 in] of F1

120 s.p. Fal.] F1; Old. Q (i.e. Oldcastle, Falstaff's original name)
124–5 do become] be F1
135 land-service] hyphen, F1
138 himself] him F1
140 are] is F1
141 is] om. F1
143 waist] Hanmer; waste Q
143 slenderer] F1; slender Q
152 lord?] F1; lord. Q
155 smell] to smell F1
156 What,] F1; What Q
160 in] on F1
164 ill] euill F1
168 tell.] F1; tell, Q
169 costermongers'] Theobald; costar-mon-
gers Q; Costor-mongers F1
169 times] om. F1
169 berrord] ed. (cf. Much Ado, II.i.40);
Berod Q; Beare-heard F1
170 and] and hath F1
172 this] his Q
173 them, are] F1; the one Q
174 do] om. F1
178 s.p. Ch. Just.] F1 (Iust.); Lo. Q (or Lord.
throughout rest of scene)
183 your chin double,] om. F1
185 yet] om. F1
187 s.p. Fal.] F1; Iohn Q (throughout rest of
scene)
187–8 about . . . afternoon,] om. F1
194 him! For] F1 (subs.); him for Q
194 the year] th' eare F1
197 s.d. aside] Wilson
199, 201 God] heauen and Heauen F1
203 you.] you and Prince Harry, F1
206 Yea] Yes F1 (a typical F1 sophistication;
not hereafter recorded)
208–9 by the Lord] if F1
211 a] my F1
211 bottle,] F1; bottle. Q
211 I would] would F1
214–20 but . . . motion.] om. F1
221 God] heauen F1
227 s.d. Exeunt . . . Servant.] Capell (subs.);
Exit. F2
228 three-man] hyphen, F1
232 curses. Boy!] F1 (subs.); curses, boy. Q
242 of] on F1
243 s.d. Exit Page.] Capell
248 s.d. Exit.] Capell; Exeunt F1

I.iii

I.iii] Steevens; Scena Quarta. F1
Location: Pope, Theobald
o.s.d. Hastings] F1; Hastings, Fauconbridge
Q (the appearance of Fauconbridge here
follows Holinshed, but he has nothing to say
in the scene and never appears again)
o.s.d. Lord] F1
1 s.p. Arch.] F1; Bishop Q (or Bish. throughout scene)
1 cause and known] causes and kno F1
5 s.p. Mowb.] F1; Marsh. Q
18 Yea] I F1 (a typical F1 sophistication;
not hereafter recorded)
21–4 Till . . . admitted.] F1
26 cause] case F1
27 lin'd] F1; lined Q
28 and] on F1
29 in] with F1
36–55 Yes . . . else] F1
36–7 war— . . . foot—] Knight (subs.);
warre, / Indeed the instant action: a cause
on foot, F1 (a difficult passage for which
many readings have been offered)
38 hope,] Rowe; hope: F1
55 opposite;] Theobald (subs.); Opposite? F1
56 We] F1; Bard. We Q
58 one] F1; on Q
58 an] a F1
59 thorough] through F1
60 part-created] hyphen, F1
66 so a] Kittredge (after Collier conj.); so, Q;
a F1
71 Are] F1; And Q
72 Glendower;] F1 (Glendower:); Glendower
Q

78 to] om. *F1*
78–80 If . . . that.] as verse, *F1*; as prose, *Q*
79 To] Capell (who thus adopts the *F1* arrangement as verse, but the *Q* word order); *F1* arranges ll. 79–80 as follows: He leaues his backe vnarm'd, the French, and Welch / Baying him at the heeles: neuer feare that.
80 heels.] *F1* (heeles:); heeles, *Q*
84 against] 'gainst *F1*
85–108 Arch. Let . . . worst.] *F1*
98 glutton bosom] Theobald; glutton-bosome *F1*
108 Past . . . worst.] in italics, with gnomic quotes, *F1*
109 s.p. Mowb.] *F1*; Bish. *Q*
110 s.d. Exeunt.] Theobald; ex. *Q*

II.i

II.i] *F1*
Location: Pope, Theobald
o.s.d. and . . . Snare] from *Q* and *F1*: and an Officer or two. *Q*; with two Officers, Fang, and Snare. *F1*
o.s.d. Snare lagging behind] ed. (after Capell)
1 Fang] *F1*; Phang *Q* (also in s.pp. throughout scene)
5 Sirrah!] Shaaber; Sirra, *Q*; Sirrah, *F1*
6 O Lord, ay] Theobald; O Lord I *Q*; I, I *F1*
11 for] om. *F1*
14 most . . . 'A] Kittredge; most beastly in good faith, a *Q*; and that most beastly: he *F1*
15 does] doth *F1* (common in *F1*; not hereafter recorded)
16 out.] *F1*; out, *Q*
22 vice—] *F1* (dash, Capell); view. *Q*
23 by] with *F1*
23 going . . . you] going: I warrant *F1*
24 score.] *F1*; score, *Q*
26 continuantly] *F1*; continually *Q*
28–9 Lumbert street] Lombardstreet *F1*
29 silk-man] Capell; silk man *Q*; Silkman *F1*
29 pray you] pra'ye *F1*
34–5 and fubb'd off, from] from *F1*
38 s.d. Enter . . . Page.] placed as *F1* s.d. (Enter Falstaffe and Bardolfe.); after l. 42, *Q*
39 knave] om. *F1*
45 I] Sir Iohn, I *F1*
48–9 in the channel] there *F1*
50, 52 Ah] Cambridge; a *Q*; O *F1*
53 man-queller . . . woman-queller] hyphens, *F1*
55 s.p. Officers.] ed.; Offic. *Q*; Fang. *F1*
56 or two] om. *F1*
56–7 s.d. The . . . her.] Wilson
57–8 Thou . . . ta?] Thou wilt not? thou wilt not? *F1*
59 s.p. Page.] *F1*; Boy. *Q*
60 tickle] tucke *F1*
61 s.p. Ch. Just.] Rowe (after *F1* Iust. and Ch. Iust.); Lord *Q* (or Lo. throughout scene)
61 What is] What's *F1*
68 thou] om. *F1*
73 all] all: all *F1*
80 What] Fy, what a *F1*
85 Marry] *F1*; Mary *Q*
87 parcel-gilt] hyphen, *F4*
88 upon] on *F1*
89 Wheeson] Whitson *F1*
90 liking his father] lik'ning him *F1*
98 thou not] not thou *F1*
99–100 so familiarity] familiar *F1*
103 thou] *F1*; thon *Q*
104 mad] *F1*; made *Q*
114–6 You . . . person.] I know you ha' practis'd vpon the easie-yeelding spirit of this woman. *F1*
115 easy-yielding] hyphen, *F1*
119 with] om. *F1*
124 make] om. *F1*
125 my humble] your humble *F1*
126 do] om. *F1*
132 s.d. Master Gower] *F1*; s.d. after l. 133, *Q*; placed as in *F1*
134 Harry] Henrie *F1*
137 Faith] Nay *F1*

138 gentleman!] ed.; gentleman, *Q*; Gentleman. *F1*
145 German] *F1*; Iarman *Q*
146 bed-hangers] Bed-hangings *F1*
147 tapestries] *F1*; tapestrie *Q*
147 ten pound] *F1*; x.l *Q*
150 the] thy *F1*
151 dost . . . Come,] om. *F1*
154 nobles.] Johnson (subs.); nobles, *Q, F1*
154 I' faith, I am] I *F1*
154–5 so . . . me law] in good earnest la *F1*
158 though] although *F1*
159–60 supper. . . . all together?] *F1* (subs., reading altogether); supper, . . . al together. *Q*
161 s.d. To Bardolph.] Capell
165 s.d. Exeunt . . . Bardolph.] ed. (after Capell; Exeunt Pope); exit hostesse and sergeant. *Q*; om. *F1*
166 better] bitter *F1*
167 lord] good Lord *F1*
168 to-night] last night *F1*
169, 173 s.pp. Gow.] Rowe; Mess. *Q, F1*
169 Basingstoke] *F1*; Billingsgate *Q*
186–7 Sir . . . go.] as prose, *F1*; as verse, *Q*
187 counties] Countries *F1*
195 s.d. Exeunt.] *F1*

II.ii

II.ii] *F1*
Location: Wilson
o.s.d. Enter . . . other.] as Rowe; Enter the Prince, Poynes, sir Iohn Russel, with other. *Q* (Russell appears nowhere else in the play and has no lines in this scene; presumably the same as Rossill in 1 Henry IV, I.ii.162 [see Textual Notes]); Enter Prince Henry, Pointz, Bardolfe, and Page. *F1* (an example of a so-called "massed entry"; Bardolph and Page actually enter at l. 69)
1 Before God] Trust me *F1*
4 Faith, it does] It doth *F1*
10 by my] in *F1*
15 viz.] *F1*; with *Q*
16 once] ones *F1*
18 another] one other *F1*
20 keepest] kept'st *F1*
20 there;] Theobald; there, *Q, F1*
21 the low] thy Low *F1*
22 made . . . to] *F1*
23–7 And . . . strengthen'd.] om. *F1*
23 bawl] Pope; bal *Q*
25 fault,] Pope; fault *Q*
30 being] lying *F1*
31 at this time] om. *F1*
33 faith] om. *F1*
39 Marry] Collier; Mary *Q*; Why *F1*
45 By this hand] om. *F1*
47 persistency.] *F1*; persistancie, *Q*
65 By this light] Nay *F1*
65 spoke on] spoken of *F1*
66 ears.] *F1* (eares:); eares *Q*
69 By the mass] Looke, looke *F1*
69 s.d. and Boy] om. *F1*
71 look] see *F1*
73 God] om. *F1*
75 virtuous] pernitious *F1*
79, 87, etc. s.pp. Page.] *F1*; Boy *Q*
79 'A calls] He call'd *F1*
79 e'en now] Cambridge; enow *Q*; euen now *F1*
82 petticoat] new Petticoat *F1*
83 so] om. *F1*
84 Has] Hath *F1* (common in *F1*; not hereafter recorded)
85 rabbit] *F1*; rabble *Q*
89, 104 Marry] *F1*; Mary *Q*
89 Althaea] *F1*; Althear *Q*
94 blossom] good Blossome *F1*
96 him] him be *F1*
97 have wrong] be wrong'd *F1*
99 lord] good Lord *F1*
107 how] om. *F1*
108 s.d. Showing . . . Poins.] Collier MS (subs.)
109 s.d. Reads the superscription.] ed. (after Wilson); Letter. *F1*

114 that?'' says he,] *F4* (that? (sayes he . . .); that (saies he) *Q, F1*
115 conceive. The] Rowe (subs., after *F4* conceiue the); conceiue the *Q*; conceiue? the *F1*
115 borrower's] Warburton conj.; borowed *Q*; borrowed *F1*
117 or] but *F1*
118 But] But to *F1*
124 He sure] Sure he *F1*
126 s.p. Prince.] Theobald; continued to Poins, *Q, F1*
133 familiars] *F1*; family *Q*
134 sisters] Sister *F1*
135 s.p. Poins.] speech continued to Prince, *F1*
140 God . . . wench] May the Wench haue *F1*
157 heckfers] ed.; Heicfors *Q*; Heyfors *F1*
161 come to] in *F1*
165–6 s.d. Exeunt . . . Page.] Capell
171 leathern] Leather *F1*
172 as] like *F1*
173 bull?] *F1*; bul, *Q*
173 descension] declension *F1*
174 prince] *F1*; pince *Q*
174 prentice?] Theobald; prentise, *Q, F1*
175 every] *F1*; enery *Q*

II.iii

II.iii] *F1*
Location: Capell (subs., after Theobald)
2 even] a euen *F1*
5, 50 s.pp. Lady N.] Rowe; Wife *Q, F1*
5 more;] *F4*; more, *Q, F1*
9, 53 s.pp. Lady P.] Rowe; Kate *Q*; La. and Lady. *F1*
9 God's] heauens *F1*
10 that] when *F1*
11 endear'd] *F1*; endeere *Q*
12 heart's dear Harry] heart-deere-Harry *F1*
17 the . . . heaven] may heauenly glory *F1*
23–45 He . . . grave.] *F1*
32 wondrous him!] Rowe; wondrous! him, *F1*
64 still-stand] hyphen, *F1*

II.iv

II.iv] *F1*
Location: Theobald (after Pope)
o.s.d. Francis . . . Drawer] Ridley (subs., after s.pp. in *Q*); *F1* s.d. reads: Enter two Drawers.
1, 10 s.pp. Fran.] 1. Drawer. *F1*
1 the devil] om. *F1*
1–2 there? apple-johns] *F1*; there apple / Iohns *Q*
4 s.p. 2. Draw.] *F1*; Draw. *Q*
4 Mass] Pope; Mas *Q*; om. *F1*
12 hear] haue *F1*
12 s.d. Enter . . . Drawer.] Alexander (after Ridley conj. and *Q* s.d. Enter Will., following l. 18); om. *F1*
13 s.p. 3. Draw.] Alexander (after Ridley conj.); Dra. *Q*
13–4 Dispatch . . . straight.] om. *F1*
15 s.p. Fran.] 2. Draw. *F1*
19 s.p. 3. Draw.] Alexander; Dra. *Q*; 1. Draw. *F1*
19 By the mass] Malone; By the mas *Q*; Then *F1*
21 s.p. 2. Draw.] *F1*; Francis *Q*
21 s.d. Third Drawer] Alexander
22 s.p. Host.] *F1*; Quickly *Q*
22 I' faith] om. *F1*
22 sweet heart] Sweet-heart *F1*
25–6 in . . . law] om. *F1*
26 i' faith] om. *F1*
28 one] wee *F1*
30, 39, 42 s.pp. Doll.] *F1*; Tere. *Q*
31 that's] that was *F1*
32 Lo] Looke *F1*
33, 34 s.dd. Singing.] Capell (subs.)
33, 34–5] given as quotations from *F1* italics
34 s.d. Exit Francis.] Capell (subs.)
36 good faith] good-sooth *F1*
39 A . . . you,] om. *F1*
42 make,] make them, *F1*
44–5 help to make] make *F1*
47 Yea, joy] I marry *F1*
48 "Your . . . ouches."] quotes, Capell

48 **ouches.**] *F1* (Owches:); ouches *Q*
49 **know;**] *Rowe*; know *Q*; know, *F1*
52 **bravely—**] *Rowe*; brauely. *Q, F1*
53–4 **Hang . . . yourself!**] *om. F1*
55 **By my troth**] Why *F1*
57 **i' good truth**] in good troth *F1*
62 s.p. **Doll.**] *F1*; Dorothy *Q* (but catchword Doll.)
68 s.d. **Francis.**] *Wilson*
69 s.p. **Fran.**] *Wilson*; Dra. *Q*; Drawer. *F1*
73–4 **No . . . faith**] *om. F1*
74 **among**] amongst *F1*
74 **neighbors;**] *Capell*; neighbours, *Q, F1*
80 **ye**] you *F1*
83 **ne'er**] *Cambridge*; nere *Q*; neuer *F1* (*a typical F1 sophistication; not hereafter recorded*)
83 **and**] *om. F1*
84 **swagger, 'a**] *Maxwell (in MLR)*; swagger *Q*; Swaggerer *F1*
85 **debuty, t' other**] Deputie, the other *F1*
86 **Wed'sday**] Wednesday *F1*
87 **i' good faith—** "**Neighbor**"] *Kittredge*; I good faith neighbor *Q*; Neighbour *F1*
90 **said**] sayth *F1*
97, 102, 103, 140 **cheater**] *F1*; cheter *Q*
97–8 **i' faith**] hee *F1*
101 s.d. **Exit Francis.**] *Wilson (after Capell)*
104 **by my troth**] *om. F1*
107 s.p. **Doll.**] *F1*; Teresh. *Q*
109 s.d. **Bardolph.**] *Capell*
109 s.d. **and Boy**] *Kittredge*; Bardolfes boy *Q*; his Boy *F1*
110 **God save**] 'Saue *F1*
116 **pistol-proof, sir;**] *Capell*; pistoll proofe: sir, *Q*; Pistoll-proofe (Sir) *F1*
116 **not**] *om. F1*
123, 128, 140 s.pp. **Doll.**] *F1*; Doro. *Q*
131 **bottle-ale . . . basket-hilt**] *hyphens, F1*
132 **God's light**] what *F1*
134 **God . . . but**] *om. F1*
136–7 **Fal. No . . . Pistol.**] *om. F1*
140 **Captain?**] *F1*; Captain, *Q*
140 **abominable**] *F3*; abhominable *Q, F1*
147 **God's light**] *om. F1*
148–50 **as odious . . . sorted;**] Captaine odious: *F1*
154 **of**] on *F1*
155 s.p. **Page.**] *F1*; Boy *Q*
156 **damned**] *Rowe*; damnd *Q*; damn'd *F1*
157 **by this hand**] *om. F1*
157 **with**] where *F1*
159 **faitors**] *Capell*; faters *Q*; Fates *F1*
160 s.d. **Draws his sword.**] *Wilson (after Capell)*
162 **i' faith**] I pray *F1*
163–9 **These . . . toys?**] *as verse, Pope*; *as prose, Q, F1*
165 **mile**] miles *F1*
167 **Troiant**] Troian *F1*
174 **Die**] *F1*
174 **dogs**] *Dyce*; dogges *Q*; Dogges; *F1*
176 **A'**] On *F1* (*a typical F1 sophistication; not hereafter recorded*)
178 **For God's sake**] I pray *F1*
179–84 **Then . . . things?**] *as verse, Capell (after Pope)*; *as prose, Q, F1*
180 **give 's**] *Capell*; giues *Q*; giue me *F1*
183 **sweet heart**] Sweet-heart *F1*
183 s.d. **Laying . . . sword.**] *Johnson*
184 **no things**] nothing *F1*
188 **For God's sake**] *om. F1*
192 **Quoit**] *F1*; Quaite *Q*
196–9 **What . . . say!**] *as verse, Capell (after Johnson)*; *as prose, Q*
196 **What?**] What *Q*
196 s.d. **Snatching . . . sword.**] *Johnson (after l. 199); placed as in Capell*
198 **grievous**] *F1*; grieuons *Q*
199 **Atropos**] *F1*; Atropose *Q*
200 **goodly**] good *F1*
202 **pray thee . . . pray thee**] prethee . . . prethee *F1*
203 s.d. **Drawing . . . out.**] *Rowe*
205 **afore**] before *F1*
205–6 **frights. So!**] *F1 (subs.)*; frights, so, *Q*
207 s.d. **Exeunt . . . Bardolph.**] *Capell*
208 **pray thee**] prethee *F1*

209 **valiant**] *F1*; vliaunt *Q*
211 s.d. **Enter Bardolph.**] *Capell*
212 **a'**] of *F1* (*a typical F1 sophistication; not hereafter recorded*)
213 **sir.**] *F1* (Sir:); sir, *Q*
215 **rascal!**] *Capell*; rascall *Q, F1*
216, 218, 221 **Ah**] *F1*; A *Q*
218 **i' faith**] *om. F1*
225 s.d. **Enter Music.**] *placed as in F1*; *after l. 226.*
226 s.p. **Page.**] *F1*; Boy *Q*
230 **I' faith**] *om. F1*
230 **church.**] *F1 (subs.)*; church *Q*
233 s.d. **behind**] *Dyce*
233 s.d. **disguised**] *F1*
238 **'a'**] *Kittredge*; a *Q*; haue *F1*
247 **wild-mare**] *hyphen, F1*
248 **boots**] Boot *F1*
253 **a**] an *F1*
254 **scales**] the Scales *F1*
258 **whe'er**] *Neilson*; where *Q*; if *F1*
259 **pole**] *ed.*; poule *Q*; Poll *F1*
266 **master's**] *F1*; master, *Q*
267 **counsel-keeper**] *hyphen, F1*
269 **By my troth**] Nay truely *F1*
274 **wilt**] wilt thou *F1*
275 **shalt**] thou shalt *F1*
276 **song! Come**] *Humphreys*; song, come *Q*; Song, come: *F1*
277, 278 **Thou't**] Thou wilt *F1*
278 **By my troth**] *om. F1*
280 **return—**] *Rowe*; returne, *Q*; returne: *F1*
280 **a' th'**] the *F1*
282 s.d. **Coming forward.**] *Capell*
284 **Poins**] Poines *Q*
291 **Grace**] good Grace *F1*
291–2 **By my troth**] *om. F1*
292 **the Lord**] Heauen *F1*
293 **O Jesu**] what *F1*
295 **light**] *F1*; light, *Q*
301 **even**] *F1*
303 **God's blessing of**] 'Blessing on *F1*
313 **Hal**] *F3*; Hall *Q (throughout rest of scene)*; Hall *F1* (Hal *throughout rest of scene*)
315 **bread-chipper**] Bread-chopper *F1*
320 s.d. **turns . . . Prince**] *Sisson*
321 **thee**] him *F1*
324 **faith**] *om. F1*
328 **thy**] the *F1*
336 **blinds**] outbids *F1*
337 **women**] weomen *Q*
343 **Marry**] *F1*; mary *Q*
346 **vict'lers**] *Kittredge*; vitlors *Q*; Victuallers *F1*
353 s.d. **Enter Peto.**] *F1*
355 **Westminster**] *Qa, F1*; Weminster *Qb*
366 s.d. **Exeunt . . . Bardolph.**] *Capell*; Exeunt Prince and Poynes. *F1*; Exit. *Q*
369 s.d. **Knocking within.**] *Dyce (after Capell)*
369 s.d. **Enter Bardolph.**] *Capell*
373 s.d. **To the Page.**] *Capell*
381 s.d. **Exit . . . Page.**] *Capell (subs.*; Page *from Humphreys)*; exit. *Qb, F1*; *om. Qa*
385, 387 s.dd. **Within.**] *Capell*
389 **Doll. Come.**] *Collier*; Doll, come, *Q*; Dol. *F1*
389–91 **Come . . . Doll?**] *om. F1*
390 s.d. **To Bardolph.**] *Alexander (after Collier)*
390 **Yea!**] *Qb*; yea? *Qa*

III.i

III.i] *F1*
This scene does not appear in Qa
Location: *Dyce, Theobald*
o.s.d. **followed . . . Page**] *ed. (from F1 with a Page)*
1 **Warwick;**] *F1 (subs.)*; War. *Q*
3 s.d. **Exit Page.**] *Rowe*; Exit. *F1*
11 **hush'd . . . night-flies**] huisht with bussing Night, flyes *F1*
14 **sound**] sounds *F1*
18 **mast**] *F1*; masse *Qb*
22 **billows**] *F1*; pillowes *Qb*
24 **deafing clamor**] deaff'ning Clamors *F1*
26 **then**] *ed.*; them *Qb*; thy *F1*
27 **sea-boy**] *F1*; season *Qb*

31 s.d. **and . . . Blunt**] *om. F1 (Blunt has no lines in the scene)*
36 **letters**] *F1*; letter *Qb*
43 **advice**] *F1*; aduise *Qb*
43 **medicine.**] *F1 (subs.)*; medicine, *Qb*
45 **God**] Heauen *F1*
46 **times**] *F1*; times, *Qb*
51 **chance's mocks**] *Wilson*; chances mockes, *Qb*; Chances mocks *F1*
53–6 **O, if . . . die.**] *om. F1*
59 **year**] yeeres *F1*
66 s.d. **To Warwick.**] *Rowe*
66 **Nevil**] *F1*; Neuel *Q*
67 **eye brimful**] *F1 (subs.)*; eye-brimme full *Qb*
71 **Bullingbrook**] *F1* (Bullingbrooke); Bolingbrooke *Qb*
72 **God**] Heauen *F1*
73 **bow'd**] *F1*; bowed *Qb*
78 **Foretelling**] *F1*; Fortelling *Qb*
81 **natures**] *F1*; nature *Q*
84 **who**] which *F1*
85 **beginning**] beginnings *F1*
97 **voice**] *F4*; voice, *Qb, F1*
99 **soul**] Life *F1*
101 **prize**] *F1*; prise *Qb*

III.ii

III.ii] *F1*
Location: *Cambridge (after Theobald)*
o.s.d **meeting**] *Capell*
o.s.d. **Mouldy . . . Bullcalf**] *F1*
o.s.d. **and Servants behind**] *Malone (after Capell)*
1 **on**] *Qa, F1*; on sir *Qb*
8 **woosel**] Ouzell *F1*
9 **no**] nay *F1*
17 **By the mass**] *om. F1*
20 **Barnes**] Bare *F1*
22 **swingebucklers**] *F1 (subs.)*; swinge bucklers *Q*
23 **robas**] *F1*; robes *Q*
27 **This . . . cousin,**] *Qa, F1*; Coosin, this sir Iohn *Qb*
29 **see**] saw *F1*
30 **Scoggin's**] Scoggan's *F1*
33 **Jesu, Jesu**] Oh *F1*
34 **my**] mine *F1*
37 **as . . . saith,**] *om. F1*
38 **Stamford**] *F1*; Samforth *Q*
39 **By my troth**] Truly Cousin *F1*
43 **Jesu, Jesu, dead!**] Dead? See, see: *F1*
47 **a fourteen**] at foureteene *F1*
54 s.d. **with him**] his Boy *F1*
55 s.p. **Shal.**] *F1*; Bardolfe. *Qa (u)*; *om. Qa (c)*, *Qb*
59 **good**] *om. Qb*
61 **by heaven**] *om. F1*
63 **well, sir.**] *Capell (subs.)*; wel, sir, *Q*; well: (Sir) *F1*
66 **accommodated**] *F1*; accommodate *Q*
68 **in faith**] *om. F1*
70–1 **ever were**] euery where *F1*
73 **Pardon**] Pardon me *Qb*
74 **day**] good day *F1*
76–7 **by heaven**] *om. F1*
78 **is**] is, *Qb, F1*
79 **whereby**] *Qb, F1*; whereby, *Qa*
79 **'a may be**] he *F1*
80 s.d. **Falstaff**] sir Iohn Falstaffe *Qb*
82 **good**] *om. F1*
83 **By my troth**] Trust me *F1*
83 **like**] looke *F1*
86 **Surecard**] *F1*; Soccard *Q*
87, 89 **Silence**] *F1*; Scilens *Qa*; Silens *Qb*
93 **dozen**] dozen of *F1*
97 **Let . . . see.**] *repeated only twice, Qb*
98 **so, so, so;**] *Cambridge (subs.)*; so (so, so) *Q*; *om. F1*
98, 173, 248 **marry**] *F1*; mary *Q*
99 **do so . . . do so**] *Qb, F1*; do, so . . . do, so *Qa*
107 **i' faith**] *om. F1*
108–9 **in faith**] *om. F1*
110 **Fal. Prick him.**] *F1*; Iohn prickes him. (*in italics, as s.d., after l. 109*)
116 **go. Mouldy,**] *F1*; go Mouldy *Q*
120 **see:**] *F1*; see *Q*

130 **much**] not *F1*
134 s.d. **aside**] *Wilson*
134 **shadows**] *Ridley*; shadowes, *Q*; shadowes to *F1*
134 **fill**] to fill *F1*
142 **him**] him downe *F1*
143 **for 's**] *ed.*; for *Q*; for his *F1*
153 **he'd 'a'**] *Kittredge*; hee'd a *Q*; he would haue *F1*
169 **sir**] *om. F1*
171 **next**] the next *F1*
175 **'Fore God**] Trust me *F1*
175 **prick**] pricke me *F1*
177, 179 **O Lord**] Oh *F1*
188 **Here**] There *F1*
192 **by my**] in good *F1*
195 **Windmill**] *F1* (Winde-mill); windmil *Q*
196 **Master**] good Master *F1*
196–7 **no . . . that.**] *om. F1*
204 **By the mass**] *om. F1*
204 **could**] *F1*; conld *Q*
210 **year**] yeeres *F1*
211 **Silence**] *F1*; Scilens *Q*
216 **That . . . have**,] *repeated only twice, F1*
218 **Hem, boys**] *Theobald*; Hemboies *Q*; Hem-Boyes *F1*
219 **Jesus**] Oh *F1*
219 s.d. **Falstaff . . . Justices**] *Capell*
234 **By my troth**] *om. F1*
235 **God**] *om. F1*
236 **dest'ny, so;**] *F1* (*subs.*); destny: so, *Q*
237 **serve 's**] serue his *F1*
239 **th' art**] thou art *F1* (*a typical F1 sophistication; not hereafter recorded*)
240 **Faith, I'll**] Nay, I will *F1*
243 s.d. **To Falstaff.**] *Craig*
243 s.d. **Aside.**] *Capell*
249 **Shadow**] *F1*; Sadow *Q*
260 **Here's**] Where's *F1*
264–5 **half-fac'd**] *hyphen, F1*
272 **traverse**] *F1*; trauers *Q*
272 **thas, thas, thas**] thus, thus, thus *F1*
275 **chopp'd, bald**] *F1* (*subs.*); chopt Ballde, *Q*
276 **i' faith**] *om. F1*
279 **Mile-end Green**] *Warburton*; Mile-end-greene *Q*; Mile-end-Greene *F1*
287 **woll**] *ed.*; wooll *Q*; will *F1*
288 **God keep you**] Farewell *F1*
288 **Silence**] *F1*; Scilens *Q*
292–3 **the Lord . . . God . . . God**] Heauen . . . and . . . and *F1*
293 **peace! At your**] *Collier*; peace at your *Q*; Peace. As you *F1*
294 **our**] my *F1*
295 **ye**] you *F1*
296 **'Fore God**] *om. F1*
296 **would you would.**] I would you would, Master Shallow. *F1*
297–8 **God keep you**] Fare you well *F1*
299–300 s.d. **Exeunt Justices.**] *Johnson* (*subs.*); exit *Q* (*apparently referring to Falstaff*), *F1* (*after l. 298*)
300 **On**] *F1*; Shal. On *Q* (*Q thus gives ll. 300–32 to Shallow*)
300–1 s.d. **Exeunt . . . etc.**] *Capell*
303 **Lord, Lord**] *om. F1*
306 **Turnbull Street**] *Cambridge*; Turne-bull street *Q*; Turnball-street *F1*
307 **duer**] *F1*; dewer *Q*
313 **invisible**] *Rowe*; inuincible *Q, F1*
314–5 **yet . . . mandrake**] *om. F1*
315 **ever**] *F1*; ouer *Q*
316–9 **and . . . good-nights**] *om. F1*
326 **eel-skin**] *Q* (*c*), *F1*; eele-shin *Q* (*u*)
328 **beefs**] Beeues *F1*
330 **dace**] *F1*; Dase *Q*
332 **him: let**] *Q* (*u*); him, till *Q* (*c*); him. Let *F1*
332 s.d. **Exit.**] *Capell*; Exeunt. *F1*

IV.i

IV.i] *F1*
Location: *Pope, Q*
o.s.d. **Bardolph**] *om. F1* (*Lord Bardolph has no lines in the scene*)
o.s.d. **Hastings**] Hastings, Westmerland, Coleuile. *F1*
o.s.d. **and others**] *Capell*

o.s.d. **within . . . Gaultree**] *om. F1*
1 s.p. **Arch.**] *Capell*; Bish. *Q, F1* (*or Bishop throughout this scene and the next*)
2 **Gaultree**] Gualtree *F1*
6 **in . . . affairs,**] *Pope*; (in . . . affaires) *Q, F1*
29–30 **peace, . . . coming.**] *Dyce*; peace, . . . comming? *Q*; peace: . . . comming? *F1*
30 **Then, my lord**] *om. Q* (*u*)
35 **beggary—**] *F1* (*subs.*); beggary. *Q*
36 **appear'd**] *Pope*; appeare *Q, F1*
39 **ugly**] *F3*; owgly *Q*; ougly *F1*
42 **see**] *F4*; Sea *Q*
46 **peace,**] *Capell* (*subs.*); peace. *Q, F1*
54 **end:**] *F1*; end *Q*
55–79 **And . . . wrong.**] *F1*
80 **days**] *F1*; daie's *Q*
88 **denied?**] *F1*; denied *Q*
92 *Following this line, Q* (*u*) *reads:* And consecrate commotions bitter edge.; *Q* (*c*) *and F1 om.*
93 *Following this line, Q* (*u*) *reads:* To brother borne an houshold cruelty.; *Q* (*c*) *and F1 om.*
97 **Mowb. Why**] *F1*; Mowbray why *Q*
101–37 **O, my . . . King—**] *F1*
114 **force**] *Theobald*; forc'd, *F1*
129 **Herford**] *ed.*; Hereford *F1*
137 **King—**] *Neilson*; King. *F1*
138 **But**] *West.* But *Q*
167–8 **grievances: . . . redress'd,**] *F1*; grieuances, . . . redrest. *Q*
172–3 **wills . . . confin'd**] *Humphreys*; willes, . . . confinde, *Q, F1*
173 **to**] *F1*
176 **general.**] *F1*; Generall, *Q*
178 **And**] *Thirlby conj.*; At *Q, F1*
178 **God**] Heauen *F1*
180 s.d. **Exit Westmerland.**] *placed as in Rowe*; *after it. l. 180, Q*; *om. F1*
183 **not that;**] *Pope* (*subs., after F2*); not, that *Q, F1*
225 **God's**] heauen's *F1*
225 **set**] *om. F1*
226 **Grace.—My lord**] *Johnson* (*after Theobald*); grace (my lord) *Q, F1*
226 s.d. **They . . . John.**] *ed.*

IV.ii

IV.ii] *Capell*
Location: *ed.* (*after Ridley*)
o.s.d. **Enter . . . army.**] *placed as in F1 s.d.* (Enter Prince Iohn.); *after IV.i.224, Q*
1 s.p. **P. John.**] *Capell*; Iohn *Q, F1*
4 **show'd**] *F1*; shewed *Q*
8 **Than**] *F1*; That *Q*
8 **talking**] *om. F1*
17 **God**] Heauen *F1*
19 **imagin'd**] *Rowe*; imagine *Q, F1*
19 **God himself**] Heauen it selfe *F1*
24 **Employ**] *F1*; Imply *Q* (*possibly correct, either as a variant spelling of* employ *or as meaning "hint at"*)
25–6 **name, . . . dishonorable?**] *F1*; name: . . . dishonorable *Q*
26 **ta'en**] taken *F1*
27 **God**] Heauen *F1*
28 **his**] Heauens *F1*
37 **shov'd**] *F1*; shoued *Q*
38 **Hydra son**] *Hanmer*; Hidra, sonne *Q*; Hydra-Sonne *F1*
48 **his**] this *F1*
50 s.p. **P. John.**] *Capell*; Prince *Q* (or Prin. *throughout rest of scene*); Iohn. *F1*
51 **after-times**] *hyphen, F1*
60 **soul**] Life *F1*
60 **shall.**] *F1*; shal, *Q*
67 s.p. **P. John.**] *F1* (Iohn.); *speech continued to the Archbishop, Q*
69 **Hast.**] *F1*; Prince *Q*
71 s.d. **Exit Officer.**] *Capell*; Exit. *F1*
86 s.d. **within**] *Capell*
92 s.d. **Exit Westmerland.**] *Rowe*; Exit. *F1* (*after l. 94*)
96 s.d. **Exit Hastings.**] *Rowe*; Exit. *F1*
102 **My lord**] *om. F1*
102 **already**] *om. F1*
103 **take their courses**] tooke their course *F1*
105 **toward**] towards *F1*

105 **sporting-place**] *hyphen, Pope*
116 **you rebels,**] you (Rebels) *F1*
117 **and . . . yours.**] *F1*
121 **God . . . hath**] Heauen . . . haue *F1*
122 **these traitors**] *Q*; this traitour *Q*
123 **yielder-up**] *hyphen, Dyce*
123 s.d. **Exeunt.**] *F1*

IV.iii

IV.iii] *Capell*
Location: *ed.* (*after Wilson*)
o.s.d. **Excursions.**] *placed as in Malone* (*after Capell*); *follows Falstaff in Q; om. F1* (*together with Alarum.*)
o.s.d. **and Colevile**] *F1* (Colleuile)
o.s.d. **meeting**] *Capell*
2 **place**] place, I pray? *F1*
6–7 **be still**] still be *F1*
23 s.d. **Blunt**] *Cambridge*
24, 43 s.pp. **P. John.**] *Capell*; Iohn *Q, F1*
24 **further**] farther *F1*
25 s.d. **Exit Westmerland.**] *Rowe*
25 s.d. **Retrait.**] *placed by ed.; after s.d. at l. 23 in Q* (*see l. 72 in the text*); *om. F1*
41–2 **"There, cousin,**] *ed.*; there cosin, *Q* (*catchword their*); *om. F1*
47 **by the Lord**] I sweare *F1*
48 **else**] *om. F1*
56 etc. s.pp. **P. John.**] *Capell*; Prince *Q*; Iohn. *F1*
69 **gratis**] *om. F1*
71 **Now**] *om. F1*
75 s.d. **Exeunt . . . Colevile.**] *Cambridge*; Exit with Colleuile. *F1*
83 **lord**] Lord, 'pray *F1*
84–5 **Fare . . . deserve.**] *as verse, F1; as prose, Q*
85 s.d. **Exeunt . . . Falstaff.**] *Capell*; Exit. *F1*
86 **had**] had but *F1*
90 **none**] any *F1*
92 **fish-meals**] *hyphen, F1*
107 **parts'**] *Wilson*; partes *Q, F1*
107 **illumineth**] illuminateth *F1*
112 **with this**] with his *F1*
113 **sherris.**] *F1*; sherris, *Q*
115 **hoard**] *F1*; whoord *Q*
123 **humane**] *om. F1*
125 s.d. **Enter Bardolph.**] *placed as in F1; after l. 126, Q*
132 s.d. **Exeunt.**] *F1*

IV.iv

IV.iv] *Capell*; Scena Secunda. *F1*
Location: *Cambridge* (*after Theobald*)
o.s.d. **carried . . . chair**] *Sisson*
o.s.d. **Warwick**] *F1*; Warwike, Kent *Q* (*Kent appears in Holinshed, but nowhere in the play except here*)
o.s.d. **and others**] *Capell*
1 **God**] Heauen *F1*
12–3 **Humphrey . . . brother?**] *as verse, Pope; as prose, Q, F1*
14, 50 **Windsor**] *F1*; Winsor *Q*
21 **Thomas.**] *F1*; Thomas, *Q*
32 **meting**] *ed.*; meeting *Q*; melting *F1*
33 **notwithstanding,**] *F1*; notwithstanding *Q*
39 **time**] Line, *F1*
45–6 **Mingled . . . in)**] *Hanmer*; (Mingled . . . in,) *Q, F1*
51, 53 s.pp. **Clar.**] *F1*; Tho. *Q*
52 **Canst . . . that?**] *F1*
69 **wherein . . . language,**] *F1*; wherein . . . language: *Q*
72 **further**] farther *F1*
77 **other**] others *F1*
78 **past evils**] *Dering MS, F3*; past-euils *Q, F1*
80 s.d. **Enter Westmerland**] *placed as in F1; after* Westmerland? *l. 80, Q*
84 **Bishop**] *Theobald*; Bishop, *Q*
93 s.d. **Enter Harcourt.**] *F1*; enter Harcor. *Q* (*after l. 93*)
94 **heavens**] Heauen *F1*
99 **shrieve**] Sherife *F1*
104 **write**] *F1*; wet *Q*
104 **terms**] Letters *F1*
106 **poor,**] *F1*; poore *Q*
112, 121, 130 s.pp. **Glou.**] *Dering MS, F1*; Hum. *Q*
117 **out these pangs.**] out: these pangs, *F1*

120 **and . . . out.**] *F1*
128 **great-grandsire**] *hyphen, Dyce*
132 **Softly, pray.**] *F1*
132 s.d. **The King . . . bed.**] *ed. (after Capell)*

IV.v

IV.v] *Cambridge*
Location: *ed.*
1 s.p. **King.**] *Cambridge; speech continued to the King without any break, Q, F1*
7 s.d. **Prince**] *from F1* Enter Prince Henry.
11, 13, 56 s.pp. **Glou.**] *F1;* Hum. *Q*
16–7 **Not . . . sleep.**] *as verse, F1; as prose, Q*
19 **Will't**] *F1;* Wilt *Q*
20 s.d. **Exeunt . . . Prince.**] *Rowe*
25 **night,**] Night: *F1*
25 **now!**] now, *F1*
31 **safety. By . . . breath**] *F1 (subs.);* safty (by . . . breath) *Q*
32–3 **downy . . . down**] *F4;* dowlny . . . dowlne *Q, F1 (subs.)*
34 **move.**] *F1;* moue *Q*
34 **lord! my father!**] *Rowe;* lord my father: *Q;* Lord, my Father, *F1*
37 **due**] *F1;* deaw *Q*
43 s.d. **Puts . . . crown.**] *Capell (subs.)*
43 **where**] here *F1*
44 **God**] Heauen *F1*
48 s.d. **and the rest**] *Capell; s.d. after l. 47, Q, F1; placed as in Capell*
49 **How . . . Grace?**] *F1*
51–3 **We . . . him.**] *as verse, F1; as prose, Q*
54 **He . . . here.**] *as verse, Capell; as prose, Q; om. F1*
59 **hence. Go**] *F1 (subs.);* hence go *Q*
62 s.d. **Exit Warwick.**] *Capell*
68 **sleep**] sleepes *F1*
70 **pil'd**] *F1;* pilld *Q*
71 **strange-achieved**] *hyphen, F1*
74 **tolling**] culling *F1*
75 **The virtuous sweets,**] *F1*
76 **thighs**] *F1;* thigh, *Q*
79 s.d. **Enter Warwick.**] *placed as in F1; after l. 81, Q*
81 **have**] *Ridley;* hands *Q;* hath *F1*
87 **-drops.**] *F1;* -drops, *Q*
88 s.d. **Prince**] *from F1* Enter Prince Henry.; *s.d. after l. 87, Q; placed as in F1*
90 s.d. **Warwick . . . rest.**] *Capell*
91 s.p. **Prince.**] *F1* (P. Hen.); Harry *Q*
92 **thought:**] *F1;* thought *Q*
94 **mine**] my *F1*
107 **Whom**] Which *F1*
111 **thine**] thy *F1*
114 **head;**] *F1 (subs.);* head, *Q*
115 **compound**] *F1;* compouud *Q*
119 **Harry**] Henry *F1*
124 **ruffin**] Ruffian *F1*
124 **will**] swill *F1*
128 **guilt**] *F1;* gilt *Q*
131 **muzzle**] *F1;* mussel *Q*
132 **on**] in *F1*
139 **moist**] most *F1*
146 s.d. **Kneels.**] *White*
147 **inward true and**] true, and inward *F1*
148–9 **bending. . . . me,**] *F1 (reading* Heauen*);* bending, . . . me. *Q*
149 **God**] Heauen *F1*
157 **this**] the *F1*
160 **worst of**] *F1;* worse then *Q*
161 **fine . . . is**] *F1 (*Charract*);* fine, in karrat *Q*
164 **thy**] the *F1*
164 **most**] *om. F1*
174, 178, 183 **God**] heauen *or* Heauen *F1*
177 **O my son,**] *F1*
178 **it**] *F1*
179 **win**] ioyne *F1*
196 **answered**] *Dering MS, F1;* answerd *Q*
204 **my**] *Tyrwhitt conj.;* thy *Q, F1*
218 **God**] heauen *F1*
220 **My gracious liege,**] *F1*
224 s.d. **Enter . . . Lancaster.**] Enter Lord Iohn of Lancaster. and Warwicke. *F1*
226 s.p. **P. John.**] *Capell;* Lanc. *Q;* Iohn. *F1*
231 s.d. **Enter Warwick.**] *Cambridge (so in MS in Locker-Church-Huntington copy of Q)*
235 **God**] heauen *F1*

240 s.d. **Exeunt.**] *F1*

V.i

V.i] *F1*
Location: *Pope, Theobald*
s.d. **with Page**] *from F1 s.d.:* Enter Shallow, Silence, Falstaffe, Bardolfe, Page, and Dauie.; *Q s.d. in right margin opposite IV.v.239–40*
1 **sir**] *om. F1*
8 s.d. **Enter Davy.**] *Theobald (so in MS in the Locker-Church-Huntington copy of Q)*
9 **Davy, Davy, Davy, Davy**] Dauy, Dauy, Dauy *Q*
10 **see . . . see.**] see: *F1*
10 **Yea, marry,**] *Theobald;* yea mary *Q; om. F1*
11, 16, 28 **cook**] *Capell;* Cooke *Q, F1*
14 **hade land**] head-land *F1*
16–7 **cook—are**] *Theobald;* Cooke are *Q;* Cook: are *F1*
20 **paid**] *F1;* payed *Q*
22 **Now**] *om. F1*
24 **lost**] lost the other day, *F1*
24 **Hinckley**] *F1;* Hunkly *Q*
28 **tiny**] tinie *Q;* tine *F1 (perhaps correctly)*
34 **backbitten**] bitten *F1*
35 **marvail's**] *Kittredge;* maruailes *Q;* maruellous *F1*
40 **is**] are *F1*
44 **God**] heauen *F1*
47 **this**] these *F1*
48 **and**] and if *F1*
49 **have**] haue but a very *F1*
51 **you**] your Worship *F1*
52 **to,**] *F1;* to *Q*
53 s.d. **Exit Davy.**] *Capell*
54 **Come, come, come**] Come *F1*
57 **with**] with all *F1*
58 s.d. **to the Page**] *Rowe*
61 s.d. **Exit Shallow.**] *Capell*
61–2 s.d. **Exeunt . . . Page.**] *Capell*
66 **him**] of him *F1*
81 **without**] with *F1*
86 s.d. **Within.**] *Theobald*
87 s.d. **Exit.**] *Theobald;* Exeunt *F1*

V.ii

V.ii] *F1*
Location: *Capell (subs.)*
o.s.d. **Enter . . . Justice**] *F1* (the Earle of Warwicke, duke Humphrey, L. chiefe Iustice, Thomas / Clarence, Prince Iohn, Westmerland. *Q (c); . . .* Prince, Iohn Westmerland. *Q (u)*
o.s.d. **meeting**] *Capell*
2 s.p. **Ch. Just.**] *F1;* Iust. *Q (throughout scene)*
4 **hope,**] *F1;* hope *Q*
13 s.d. **Westmerland and others**] *Capell (note that Westmerland is included in Q o.s.d.; om. F1)*
16 **he**] him *F1*
19 **O God**] Alas *F1*
20 s.p. **P. John.**] *Capell;* Iohn *Q, F1 (throughout scene)*
21 s.p. **Glou., Clar.**] *F1*
27 s.p. **Glou.**] *F1;* Humph. *Q*
36 **impartial**] Imperiall *F1*
38–9 **remission. . . . me,**] *F1;* remission, . . . me. *Q*
42 s.d. **and Blunt**] *om. F1; s.d. after l. 41, Q; placed as in F1*
43 **God**] heauen *F1*
46 **mix**] *F1;* mixt *Q*
48 **Amurath an Amurath**] Amurah, an Amurah *F1*
50 **by my faith**] to speake truth *F1*
57 **too.**] *F1 (subs.);* too, *Q*
59 **Yet**] But *F1*
62 s.p. **Princes.**] *Staunton;* Bro. *Q;* Iohn, &c. *F1*
62 **otherwise**] other *F1*
72 **Lethe**] *F1;* lethy *Q*
96 **your**] you *F1*
97 s.p. **son.**] *F1 (subs.);* sonne, *Q*
106 **you,**] *F1;* you *Q*
110 **not**] no *F1*

112 **justice." You**] *F1 (subs.);* Iustice you *Q*
127 **rase**] *Pope;* race *Q, F1*
140 **foremost**] *Pope;* formost *Q, F1*
143, 145 **God**] heauen *and* Heauen *F1*
145 s.d. **Exeunt.**] *F1;* exit. *Q*

V.iii

V.iii] *F1*
Location: *Pope, Capell*
o.s.d. **Silence**] *F1;* Scilens *Q (throughout scene in text, except* Silens, *l. 23; and in s.pp., except* Silens, *ll. 73, 78, 89)*
1 **my**] mine *F1*
2 **mine**] my *F1*
5 **'Fore God**] *om. F1*
5–6 **goodly . . . rich**] a goodly . . . a rich *F1*
8 **Marry**] *F1;* mary *Q*
13 **By the mass**] *Pope (subs.);* by the mas *Q; om. F1*
16 **Ah**] *F1;* A *Q*
17, 32, 46, 73 s.dd. **Singing**] *Rowe*
17–22 **"Do . . . merrily."**] *as verse, Malone (after Rowe); as prose, Q, F1*
18 **God**] heauen *F1*
23 s.p. **Fal.**] *F1;* sir Iohn *Q*
23 **heart! . . . Silence,**] *Johnson (subs.);* heart, . . . Silens, *Q, F1 (*Silence*)*
25 **Give Master Bardolph**] Good M. Bardolfe: *F1*
29 **must**] *om. F1*
29 s.d. **Exit.**] *Theobald*
32–6 **"Be . . . merry."**] *as song verse, Capell (after Rowe); as prose, Q; as verse, F1 (but not indicated as a song)*
34 **wags**] wagge *F1*
38 **mettle**] *F1;* mettall *Q*
40 s.d. **Enter Davy.**] *om. F1*
41 s.d. **To Bardolph.**] *Cambridge (after Capell)*
46–8 **"A cup . . . long-a."**] *as song verse, Rowe; as prose, Q, F1*
47 **thee,**] *Wilson;* the *Q, F1*
48 **long-a**] *F1;* long a *Q*
53 s.d. **Singing.**] *Capell*
53–4 **"Fill . . . bottom."**] *as song verse, Capell; as prose, Q, F1*
57 **tiny**] tyne *F1 (perhaps correctly)*
57 s.d. **to the Page**] *Capell*
59 **cabileros**] Cauileroes *F1*
62 **By the mass**] *Malone;* By the mas *Q; om. F1*
65 **By God's liggens**] *om. F1*
66 **that 'a**] that. He *F1*
66–7 **out, 'a. 'Tis**] *Wilson;* out, a tis *Q;* out, he is *F1*
70 s.d. **One . . . door.**] *placed as in Capell; after l. 67, Q; om. F1*
71 s.d. **Exit Davy.**] *Capell*
72 s.d. **To . . . bumper.**] *Capell*
73–5 **"Do . . . Samingo."**] *as song verse, Malone; as prose, Q, F1*
79 s.d. **Enter Davy.**] *Capell*
82 s.d. **Enter Pistol.**] *placed as in F1; after l. 81, Q*
84 **God save you**] 'saue you sir *F1*
86 **no man**] none *F1*
86–7 **good. Sweet knight,**] good, sweet Knight; *F1*
88 **this**] the *F1*
89 **By'r lady**] Indeed *F1*
92–6 **Puff . . . price.**] *as verse, Pope; as prose, Q, F1*
92 **i' thy**] *Neilson;* ith thy *Q;* in thy *F1*
94 **And**] *om. F1*
97 **pray thee**] prethee *F1*
99–102 **A . . . thereof.**] *as verse, F1; as prose, Q*
102 **Cophetua**] *Pope;* Couetua *Q;* Couitha *F1*
103 s.d. **Singing.**] *Johnson*
103 **"And . . . John."**] *quotes, Johnson*
104–6 **Shall . . . lap.**] *as verse, F1; as prose, Q*
106 **Furies'**] *Capell;* Furies *Q, F1*
109 **sir. If**] *F1 (subs.);* sir, if *Q*
111 **or**] or to *F1*
111–2 **sir, . . . King,**] *F1;* sir . . . King *Q*
115–9 **A . . . Spaniard.**] *as verse, F1; as prose, Q*
124 **double-charge**] *hyphen, Capell*

126 **knighthood**] *F1*; Knight *Q*
132 s.d. **Exit Bardolph.**] *Capell*
134 **good.**] *F1*; good, *Q*
137 **Blessed . . . that**] Happie . . . which *F1*
138 **to**] vnto *F1*
139–41 **Let . . . days!**] *as verse, F1; as prose, Q*
140 **"Where . . . led?"**] *quotes, Hanmer*
141 **these**] those *F1*
141 s.d. **Exeunt.**] *F1*; exit. *Q*

V.iv

V.iv] *F1*
Location: *Pope, Theobald*
o.s.d. **Beadle**] *Collier (after Capell);* Sincklo
*Q (Sincklo is the name of the actor who
played the Beadle); F1 s.d. reads:* Enter
Hostesse Quickly, Dol Tearesheete, and
Beadles.
o.s.d. **with . . . Tearsheet**] *from F1 (see
preceding note)*
1 **to God that**] *om. F1*
4, 14, 22, 31 s.pp. **Bead.**] *Rowe;* Sincklo *or*
Sinck. *Q;* Off. *or* Officer. *F1*
5 **cheer**] cheere enough *F1*
6 **two**] two (lately) *F1*
7 s.p. **Doll.**] *F1* (Dol.); Whoore *Q (throughout scene)*
9 **go**] now go *F1*
9 **wert**] had'st *F1*
11 **the Lord**] *om. F1*
11 **I**] hee *F1*
12–3 **pray God**] would *F1*
13 **miscarry**] might miscarry *F1*
17 **amongst**] among *F1*
18 **you . . . you**] thee . . . thou *F1*
18 **censer**] *Theobald;* censor *F1*
19–20 **blue-bottle**] blew-Bottel'd *F1*
22 **she knight-arrant**] *Capell (subs.);* shee-
Knight-arrant *Q, F1*
24 **God**] *om. F1*
24 **overcome**] o'recome *F1*
27 **Ay**] *Capell;* I *Q;* Yes *F1*
29 **atomy**] Anatomy *F1*
31 s.d. **Exeunt.**] *F1*

V.v

V.v] *F1*
Location: *Theobald (subs.)*
o.s.d. **Enter . . . rushes.**] Enter two Groomes.
F1
1, 2, 3 s.pp. **1. Strewer,** etc.] *Wilson;* 1, 2, 3
Q; 1. Groo., 2. Groo., 1. Groo. *F1*
3 **a'**] of the *F1*
4 **Dispatch, dispatch.**] *om. F1*
4 s.d. **Exeunt.**] *F3;* Exit Groo. *F1*
4 s.d. **Trumpets . . . them**] *om. F1*
4 s.d. **Page**] *F1*
5 **Shallow**] Robert Shallow *F1*
9 **God**] *om. F1*
15 s.p. **Shal.**] *F1;* Pist. *Q*
16 **of**] in *F1*
16 **affection—**] *Dyce;* affection. *Q, F1*
17, 19 s.pp. **Shal.**] *Hanmer;* Pist. *Q, F1*
18 **devotion—**] *Dyce;* deuotion. *Q, F1*
22 **me—**] *Dyce;* me. *Q, F1*
23 **best,**] *Cambridge;* best *Q;* most *F1*
24 s.p. **Fal.**] *F1; speech continued to Shallow,
Q*
24 **travel**] *F3;* trauaile *Q, F1*
26 **else**] *om. F1*
29 **all**] *F1*
31–2 **My . . . rage.**] *as verse, Johnson; as
prose, Q, F1*
33–8 **Thy . . . truth.**] *as verse, Capell (after
Pope); as prose, Q, F1*
39 s.d. **Shouts within.**] *Steevens*
39 s.d. **The trumpets sound.**] *F1 (after l. 40);
placed as in Malone*
40 **roar'd**] *F1;* roared *Q*
40 s.d. **the Lord . . . them**] *Capell; F1 s.d.
reads:* Enter King Henrie the Fift, Brothers, Lord Chiefe Iustice.
41 **God**] *om. F1*
41 **Hal . . . Hal**] *Rowe;* Hall . . . Hall *Q, F1*
42 **The . . . fame!**] *as verse, Capell; as prose,
Q, F1*
43 **God save**] 'Saue *F1*
45 s.p. **Ch. Just.**] *F1;* Iust *Q (or* Iustice
throughout scene)

48 **becomes**] become *F1*
51 **awak'd**] awake *F1*
57 **God**] heauen *F1*
67 **evils**] euill *F1*
69 **strengths**] strength *F1*
71 **my**] our *F1*
72 s.d. **Exeunt . . . Train.**] *Capell;* Exit King.
F1
73 s.p. **Fal.**] *F1;* Iohn *Q (throughout rest of
scene, except l. 93)*
74 **marry**] *F1;* mary *Q*
79 **advancements**] aduancement *F1*
81 **cannot**] cannot well *F1*
81 **give**] should giue *F1*
87 **color**] *F1;* collor *Q*
87 **that I fear**] I feare, that *F1*
88–90 **Fear . . . night.**] *as prose, Pope; as
verse, Q, F1*
90 s.d. **Officers with them**] *Capell; s.d. after
Bardolph. l. 89, Q; placed as in Pope;
om. F1*
94–5 **I . . . away.**] *as verse, F1; as prose, Q*
96 **tormenta . . . contenta**] tormento, spera me
contento *Q*
96 s.d. **Exeunt. . . . Justice.**] *F1* (Exit. Manet
Lancaster and Chiefe Iustice.); exeunt.
Q (after l. 95)
97, 103, 105 s.pp. **P. John.**] *Capell;* Iohn *Q,
F1*
107 **heard**] heare *F1*
109 s.d. **Exeunt.**] *F1* (Exeunt / FINIS.)

Epilogue

5 **indeed . . . say**)] (indeed) I should say, *F1*
10 **meant**] did meane *F1*
16–7 **and so . . . Queen.**] *follows l. 34 in F1*
16 **I**] *om. F1*
22 **would**] will *F1*
25 **seen**] seene before *F1*
29 **Katherine**] *F1;* Katharine *Q*
32 **a**] *F1*
34 **night.**] night. / FINIS. *Q;* night; *F1
(see above, ll. 16–7)*

A garden repast. From Didymus Mountain [i.e. Thomas Hill], *The Gardener's Labyrinth*
(1577). (*The Folger Shakespeare Library*)

    Shallow. Nay, you shall see my orchard, where in an arbor we will eat a last year's
pippin of my own graffing, with a dish of caraways, and so forth. (*2 Henry IV*, V.iii.1–3)

Henry V

OF SHAKESPEARE's few actual or alleged allusions to contemporary events—for example, Maria's "new map with the augmentation of the Indies" in *Twelfth Night* and Hamlet's "little eyases"—none has seemed more certain than that in the prologue to Act V of *Henry V*, where the Chorus, "by a lower but by loving likelihood," compares the King's triumphal return from France to that in store for "the general of our gracious Empress" when he comes back from Ireland "bringing rebellion broached on his sword." Although generations of scholars have agreed that the apparent reference to the Earl of Essex's Irish expedition of 1599 fixes the date of the first production of the play between March 27 of that year, when the Queen's young favorite left London to the cheers of its enraptured citizens, and September 28, when he slunk back a failure, Warren D. Smith has argued that the prologues (which were first printed in the Folio of 1623) were probably written by another hand for a performance of the play at court and moreover that "the general of our gracious Empress" was Charles Blount, Lord Mountjoy, who was appointed commander-in-chief in 1600, decisively defeated the Irish rebel Tyrone, and returned victorious in April 1603. Whatever the date and circumstances of the prologues, however, certain borrowings from and allusions to *Henry V* in *Sir John Oldcastle* (a play acted in October 1599 and printed the following year) suggest that the traditional assignment of Shakespeare's work to 1599 is valid. It was the last of his eight plays on English history between Richard II's deposition and the advent of the Tudors, and except for *Henry VIII*—which, like *King John*, lies beyond the limits of this great design—his final contribution to the form that he had made his own.

As usual when he dealt with English history, Shakespeare, although he had his Holinshed at hand, did not tie himself to facts. For example, Henry's show of mercy at Harfleur (III.iii) reveals an unrecorded aspect of that bloody monarch's mind, and the telescoping of events between Agincourt and Troyes does such violence to "their huge and proper life" that the Chorus apologizes in the prologue to Act V for the author's license. Sometimes, however, as when Canterbury "justly and religiously" expounds the Salic law (I.ii.33–95) and when Henry upbraids the conspirators (II.ii.166–81), Shakespeare simply versifies Holinshed's *Third Volume of Chronicles* (1587), errors and all; and sometimes he expands the merest hint into such a telling scene as that about the Dauphin's gift of tennis balls (I.ii.259–97).

But if Holinshed—or Edward Hall, whose text in *The Union of the Two Noble and Illustre Families of Lancaster and York* (1548) Holinshed often reproduces with unabashed fidelity—supplied Shakespeare with the fabric of his play, there are signs of other sources too. For more than a century "the victorious acts of King Henry the Fifth," to use Hall's rubric in the *Union*, had been a favorite English theme, and, as noted in the introduction to the Henry IV plays (pp. 843–44), his short but flashy reign had inspired a stream of biography, propaganda, and legend. Widely if not deeply read in English history, Shakespeare could of course have dipped into this Henrician literature, and so there may be traces, as Dover Wilson thinks, of the *Gesta Henrici Quinti* (by one of Henry's chaplains) in such details as Bardolph's "pax of little price" (III.vi.45) or of Tito Livio's *Vita Henrici Quinti* in the Constable's assertion (IV.ii.61) that he "will the banner from a trumpet take." But it is unlikely that Shakespeare could or would have spent time in working through the various fifteenth-century lives of Henry, most of them in manuscript, when Hall and Holinshed—to say nothing of such things as *A Mirror for Magistrates* and Daniel's *Civil Wars*—were so much more accessible. Equally accessible was *The Famous Victories of Henry V*, or at any rate an early version of that work. In its only extant form —a corrupted text of 1598—*The Famous Victories* is a vulgar and dilapidated relic of what may have been a more substantial play (or perhaps a pair of plays) dating from the 1580's. Although it is of course impossible to itemize Shakespeare's debt to this material in writing *1* and *2 Henry IV* and *Henry V*, there are such striking similarities between *The Famous Victories* and Shakespeare's portrait of the wild young prince transformed into the valiant warrior-king that it is easy to infer at least a common source. In the ordonnance of plot, if nothing else, the early play or plays could have served him as a model.

Whatever its appeal to patriotic Englishmen, *Henry V* has not fared well with critics, partly, no doubt, because not even Shakespeare could convert continued triumph into drama, but mainly because of Henry's unattractive character. Johnson hints at this when, having duly noted the scenes of "high dignity" and "easy merriment," he deplores the final act, which deals with Henry's ursine wooing of the French princess, as a blot upon the play. Moving characteristically from literature to politics, the irascible and republican Hazlitt turns his low opinion of "a very favourite monarch with the English nation" into inspired invective, directed not only toward the hero of the play but also toward the man he represents. The real Henry "was fond of war and low company," says Hazlitt, and of very little else. "He was careless, dissolute and ambitious;—idle, or doing mischief. In private, he seemed to have no idea of the common decencies of life, which he subjected to a kind of regal licence; in public affairs, he seemed to have no idea of any rule or right or wrong, but brute force, glossed over with a little religious hypocrisy and archiepiscopal advice." Although Shakespeare's Henry, like his prototype, is the embodiment of irresponsible power and sleazy success, "we like him in the play," says Hazlitt, because we know he is not real.

> There he is a very amiable monster, a very splendid pageant. As we like to gaze at a panther or a young lion in their cages in the Tower, and catch a pleasing horror from their glistening eyes, their velvet paws, and dreadless roar, so we take a very romantic, heroic, patriotic, and poetical delight in the boasts and feats of our younger Harry, as they appear on the stage and are confined to lines of ten syllables; where no blood follows the stroke that wounds our ears, where no harvest bends beneath horses' hoofs, no city flames, no little child is butchered, no dead men's bodies are found piled on heaps and festering the next morning—in the orchestra!

Many later critics have embellished this indictment. Swinburne, usually so idolatrous, concedes not only that Henry cuts a sorry figure as a suitor but that as a ruler he exemplifies the "commodity" or heartless egotism that Shakespeare elsewhere—in *King John*, for instance—shows to be a moral evil. Yeats, noting the conqueror's "gross vices" and "coarse nerves," concludes that Shakespeare measured him correctly and therefore treated his career with tragic irony. Granville-Barker regrets the fatal absence of "some spiritually significant idea" in a play about success. John Masefield calls Henry "the one commonplace man" in the two tetralogies. E. K. Chambers says that sometimes one can recognize in him "the prototype of the blatant modern imperialist, with his insolent talk of 'little England.'" E. M. W. Tillyard thinks that Shakespeare failed to fuse the princely ironist of *Henry IV* with the strutting king of *Henry V*. Mark Van Doren, in a devastating essay, argues that a certain meretricious splendor does not justify the pumped-up language of the play, its "puerile appeal" to sentimental patriotism, its febrile gaiety as a substitute for passion, and its hero in the guise of "mere good fellow, a hearty undergraduate with enormous initials on his chest." Despite J. Dover Wilson's and J. H. Walter's recent efforts to counter these and similar accusations, *Henry V* seems likely to remain a controversial play.

This critical dissatisfaction must be referred to Henry's almost statutory function as the ideal king; and to understand that function we must recall his complex serial presentation through the so-called second tetralogy. This great cycle of history plays, which treats the main events between Richard II's deposition in 1399 through the "unquiet time" of Henry IV to the summit of Lancastrian success at Troyes in 1420, is a continuing dramatic exploration of the massive, unifying theme of power as exemplified in three monarchs: the ineffectual Richard, who superbly vocalizes, but fails to act upon, his sense of injured merit; the "vile politician" and usurper Bullingbrook, whose ambition and efficiency cannot save him from remorse, or from the mounting troubles that dog him to his grave; and the latter's wayward son, whose long, uneasy preparation for the throne is followed by a reign of unexampled triumph.

Through the course of these four plays Hal (like his antithesis in the first tetralogy, the despot Richard III) is subjected to a most extended treatment. Although he does not appear in *Richard II*, his advent is there announced when Henry IV, even while lamenting his "unthrifty son" as a renegade to duty and a disgrace to the royal line, says he sees in him "some sparks of better hope, which elder years / May happily bring forth" (V.iii.21–22). It is the slow fulfillment of this "better hope" on which the two parts of *Henry IV* are built. Here Hal appears not only as the nimble-footed madcap Prince of Wales whose escapades bring sorrow to his father and danger to the realm but also, when he faces his great test at Shrewsbury, as a paragon of princely virtue. Even after his great show of grace and valor on the field, however, he and his disreputable companions so "play the fools with the time," as he himself admits (*2 Henry IV*, II.ii.142), that his dying father prophesies with dread the reign when "the fift Harry from curb'd license plucks / The muzzle of restraint" and turns England to a wilderness again (IV.v.130 ff.). Although Hal, whose way of using people to his own advantage is perhaps the least attractive aspect of his character, had, early in Part 1, soliloquized upon his plan to indulge in systematic "loose behavior" as a means of underscoring his delayed reform, it is not until his troubled father dies that he baffles expectation, rejects the unimitated and inimitable Falstaff, and briskly rises to his royal station. "The tide of blood in me," he thereupon announces,

> Hath proudly flow'd in vanity till now;
> Now doth it turn and ebb back to the sea,
> Where it shall mingle with the state of floods,
> And flow henceforth in formal majesty.
> (*2 Henry IV*, V.ii.129–33)

This paradox of Hal as wastrel and royal heir is the basic fact of *Henry IV*. Shakespeare's complex presentation of the Prince as he advances toward the fearful, splendid burden of the crown generates and unifies the action of these plays, and it brings into alignment all the foils and mighty opposites—Henry IV, Hotspur, the Lord Chief Justice, even Falstaff—as components of the great design whose centre is Prince Hal. Embracing scenes of politics and battle juxtaposed with vivid genre paintings of the London underworld, this design not only gives to *Henry IV* an unmatched sense of life, it enables us to watch the preparation of a king and to gauge the cost of royal power.

It is the product of this preparation that we see in *Henry V*. Here the self-willed prince whose conduct had led his father to believe him marked "For the hot vengeance, and the rod of heaven, / To punish my mistreadings" (*1 Henry IV*, III.ii.10–11) emerges as a Christian king of such astounding merit that were the age of miracles not past, Canterbury would call the change miraculous.

> The breath no sooner left his father's body,
> But that his wildness, mortified in him,
> Seem'd to die too; yea, at that very moment,
> Consideration like an angel came
> And whipt th' offending Adam out of him,
> Leaving his body as a paradise
> T' envelop and contain celestial spirits.
> Never was such a sudden scholar made;
> Never came reformation in a flood
> With such a heady currance, scouring faults;
> Nor never Hydra-headed willfulness
> So soon did lose his seat (and all at once)
> As in this king.   (I.i.25–37)

When Ely piously responds, "We are blessed in the change," he might have used the word "conversion."

Whatever the process of this change—and one recent editor is inclined to side with Canterbury in regarding it as supernatural—it is presented as an accomplished fact at the very outset of the play, and so it has a vital bearing on the action. For one thing, it disqualifies the King as hero, at least insofar as the heroic function is exemplified in Shakespeare's other plays. With all his very special prowess—moral, military, political, or other—a hero must exhibit struggle and run the danger of defeat, for through struggle he identifies himself with us and so engages and sustains our interest. Not only must he undergo some sort of trial of which the outcome is in doubt—as when Richard meets with Bullingbrook at Flint or Lear confronts the painful knowledge that he is just a foolish fond old man or Romeo defies the angry stars—but he must share the lot of other men, who, whatever their successes, are bound to lose their last encounter. Despite Henry's own assertion (IV.i.106) that he, as king, "is but a man," he seems to be exempt from the condition of humanity: his important struggle —to establish his credentials for the exercise of regal power—is already won, and here, as in the chronicles, the wild young prince of popular tradition becomes the patriotic emblem of success. Despite the hardships he endures, he is not really imperilled, and as we follow his exploits we have merely to await his predetermined triumph. Therefore when he exposes the conspirators, conquers France against such overwhelming odds, and wins the French princess as his bride we are gratified but not astonished at the ease with which these things are done.

We are not astonished, moreover, at a certain hardness in his character, for successful men, especially those whose talents run to war, are rarely noted for their sweetness and compassion. Perhaps, as some have argued, Henry's dreadful talk before Harfleur (III.iii) and his command to kill the prisoners (IV.vi.37–38) were approved procedures in fifteenth-century war, but his bluff, jocose insensitivity would seem to be his own. Brassy, bold, and self-assertive, he lacks, of course, his cousin Richard's need to contemplate his own emotions, as well as his supple, sensuous way with words, but he also lacks his father's humanizing doubts concerning his own motives and behavior. Despite some twinges of remorse (IV.i. 292–305) about the means that Henry IV had used to gain the throne, he shows no burning sense of guilt. He not only exercises royal power with élan but extends it by devices that, however justified by the ecclesiastical politicians of Act I, might well disturb a man of finer moral fibre. Henry IV, mindful not only of his foes but of his ambiguous situation, had unlocked his secret soul when he observed

> how chance's mocks
> And changes fill the cup of alteration
> With divers liquors! O, if this were seen,
> The happiest youth, viewing his progress through,
> What perils past, what crosses to ensue,
> Would shut the book, and sit him down and die.
> (*2 Henry IV*, III.i.51–56)

In a similar situation (*Henry V*, IV.i.230–84), however, his son does not reveal such hard-bought knowledge: he talks not of doubts and ambiguities but of his duties as a king, for it is the royal image that concerns him most and not the promptings of his secret soul. When in II.ii he spreads a net for the conspirators (one of whom had been his special friend) it is as if he took a certain pleasure in the sport, just as he does later in another game with Williams (IV.i.203–21). Although the royal sense of humor, which is very different from the Prince's wit in *Henry IV*, is sometimes flat and coarse (as in V.ii), at other times—when he returns the Dauphin's gift of tennis balls, for instance, or prepares for Agincourt—it shows the pride and gay indifference to mischance essential to a man so self-assured.

> Tell the Constable,
> We are but warriors for the working-day;
> Our gayness and our gilt are all besmirch'd
> With rainy marching in the painful field;
> There's not a piece of feather in our host—
> Good argument I hope we will not fly—
> And time hath worn us into slovenry.
> But by the mass, our hearts are in the trim;
> And my poor soldiers tell me, yet ere night,
> They'll be in fresher robes, or they will pluck
> The gay new coats o'er the French soldiers' heads,
> And turn them out of service.   (IV.iii.108–19)

We see Henry at his best, in fact, when he fulfills his patriotic function. Once resolved about the justice of his cause—for I.ii, however dull to modern critics and producers, is a pivot of the play—he shows a jaunty disregard for adversaries, foreign or domestic, that is his most engaging trait. As he conveys to his bedraggled troops something of his own exhilaration he becomes the ideal man of action and the perfect leader of those "very valiant creatures" who, supplied with beef and iron and steel, "eat like wolves and fight like devils." Although the defiant rhetoric of "Once more unto the breach, dear friends" and "We few, we happy few, we band of brothers" does not disclose the workings of a subtle mind, it serves a more important function: these thunderous and inspiriting declamations, written in the decade of the Grand Armada, epitomize the patriotic zeal that is, in fact, the central subject of the play.

Here as elsewhere in Elizabethan literature the patriotism is presented as an aspect of religion. The convenient and consoling notion, assiduously fostered by the Tudors, that God had England in his special care was a crafty misconstruction of the doctrine of providence (see pp. 588–89) that Shakespeare had employed throughout his early history plays and then, it seems, had put aside with other youthful indiscretions. For if *Henry VI* and *Richard III* explain the horrors of the fifteenth century as a divinely sanctioned preparation for the glad event on Bosworth Field, where Henry VII came to power, *Richard II* and *Henry IV*, shunning *post hoc* rationalization, illuminate the interaction of politics and power. Thus in *3 Henry VI* we are invited to believe that the affairs of state reveal a moral pattern preordained by God; in *Richard II* we are shown that Bullingbrook's grasp of political necessities and realities counts for more than Richard's status as the Lord's anointed. In presenting Henry V's career, however, Shakespeare abandons clear-eyed reappraisal for the religio-political slogans of popular tradition. Not only the clergy in

Act I but Henry too is much given to asserting his distinction as the leader of a chosen people who, while making England great, effects the will of God. "No tyrant, but a Christian king," as he describes himself, he listens to the insults of the French and then announces his intention: he will conquer France, he says, but his plan to do so

> lies all within the will of God,
> To whom I do appeal, and in whose name
> Tell you the Dolphin I am coming on
> To venge me as I may, and to put forth
> My rightful hand in a well-hallow'd cause.
> (I.ii.289–93)

Henry puts himself at God's disposal on the eve of Agincourt (III.vi.169), and since it is the "God of battles" whom he asks to steel his soldiers' hearts and to forget his father's "fault" (IV.i.289 ff.), he looks upon his victory as a sign of special favor. Exeter, learning the details, exclaims "'Tis wonderful!" but Henry, knowing who arranged the outcome of the battle, organizes a religious celebration and orders death for anyone who fails to give God credit for his part in the affair. If we, like Hazlitt, tend to squirm at Henry's strident patriotic piety, we may prefer to think, with Yeats, that Shakespeare treated it ironically. Perhaps he did, but he none the less preserved the icon of "this star of England" that no Elizabethan audience would wish to see defaced.

If Shakespeare's *Henry V* was the product of his reputation and thus a special kind of character, he required a special kind of play. Shakespeare's early histories are a string of helter-skelter episodes selected to present the dynastic struggles of the fifteenth century and thus to illustrate the dangers of dissension. Packed with people and events that cover more than sixty years, the three *Henry VI* plays are crudely stitched together, and despite the presence of a dominating villain in their sequel, *Richard III*, the so-called first tetralogy is mainly rough apprentice work, short on character and construction but long on crime and horror, ghosts and curses, rhetoric and declamation. Although *Richard II*, which inaugurates the second tetralogy, marks a great advance in style and depth of characterization, to say nothing of construction, it partakes almost of ritual in its sombre grace and elevation. With *1* and *2 Henry IV*, however, Shakespeare opens up a new terrain. These are not unwieldy narratives in the style of *Henry VI* or tragic histories in the style of *Richard III* and *Richard II*, but serio-comic treatments of historical events as seen from different levels of perception. Shuttling from verse to prose, from the council-table to the tavern, from Henry's problems as king and father to Hal's as gay young blade and royal heir, they combine a novelistic range of observation with a richly contrapuntal structure that show the full extent of Shakespeare's art.

In writing of a man like Henry V, however, Shakespeare clearly felt the need of something different, for here his subject represents those "king-becoming graces" that Malcolm, in *Macbeth* (IV.iii.92–94), enumerates as

> justice, verity, temp'rance, stableness,
> Bounty, perseverance, mercy, lowliness,
> Devotion, patience, courage, fortitude.

In other words, Shakespeare had in Henry V a hero much too wise and brave and just for real dramatic presentation, and—to make the problem greater—an action almost epic in its scope. He therefore had to try for grandeur—and to settle for the grandiose. The author of the prologues, whether Shakespeare or somebody else, astutely underscores the problem when the Chorus in the prologue to Act I wishes for "a Muse of fire, that would ascend / The brightest heaven of invention" in order to do justice to "so great an object" as Henry's splendid reign. Such choral prologues are employed in Shakespeare's other plays—*Romeo and Juliet* and *2 Henry IV*, for instance—to summarize the action, but here they serve a further function: they proclaim a theme too big for treatment on the stage.

> Can this cockpit hold
> The vasty fields of France? Or may we cram
> Within this wooden O the very casques
> That did affright the air at Agincourt?

This deferential stance is held throughout. The second speech of the Chorus regrets "abuse of distance" in the rapid shifting of the scene; the third suggests we "work" our thoughts to compensate for imperfections in the presentation of a siege; the fourth, which superbly comments on the eve of Agincourt, asks us to "sit and see, / Minding true things by what their mock'ries be"; the fifth, which, as noted earlier, apologizes for the many things omitted from the play, prepares us for the Treaty of Troyes; and the epilogue, in retrospect, concedes that

> with rough and all-unable pen,
> Our bending author hath pursu'd the story,
> In little room confining mighty men,
> Mangling by starts the full course of their glory.

In addition to advancing such apologetic explanations the Chorus also punctuates the action of the play and underscores its structure. *Henry V* reveals no rapid counterpoint like that of *Henry IV*: as befits its hero and its theme it is built of massive, block-like episodes, each with its own curve of action that contributes to the whole. Act I determines Henry's claim to France; Act II brings him through his preparations to his direct challenge to the foe; Act III takes him from Harfleur to Agincourt; Act IV describes his stunning victory; and Act V shows its consequences in the Treaty of Troyes and the union of the royal lovers.

In attempting these effects of size and grandeur Shakespeare has to sacrifice the comic thrust of *Henry IV*. There the comic scenes are contrived not merely to divert us from affairs of state but also to extend the spectrum of the play, for thanks to Falstaff's elemental and protean force they exemplify a mode of action and perception that modifies our own response and endows us with a fresh awareness. We laugh at Falstaff, to be sure, but we also laugh with him, and thus, because we come to share his comic vision, we sharpen and expand our knowledge. In *Henry V*, however, with Falstaff's energizing wit extinguished and with Hal, the subtle ironist, transformed into a pompous king, this comic splendor disappears. What Johnson calls its scenes of "easy merriment" are no longer laced into the fabric of the work, and so they do not cut athwart our stock responses to make us change our stance, nor do they constitute another statement, in a different key, of the "serious" action of the play. Despite his promise in the epilogue to *2 Henry IV* to keep Falstaff alive and let him go to France, Shakespeare really had to kill him off, for Falstaff, with his tonic disrespect and his genius for subversion, would have been a greater threat to Henry V than all the French at Agincourt. Fluellen of course provides a partial compensation; but Nym, Bardolph, and Pistol, deprived of their great chief, are only shabby clowns. Significantly, two of them are hanged and the other slinks away, but in the din of Henry's triumph we hardly hear them go.

Herschel Baker

The Life of Henry the Fifth

[DRAMATIS PERSONAE

CHORUS

KING HENRY THE FIFTH
HUMPHREY DUKE OF GLOUCESTER ⎫
JOHN DUKE OF BEDFORD   ⎬ *brothers to*
DUKE OF CLARENCE   ⎭ *the King*
DUKE OF EXETER, *uncle to the King*
DUKE OF YORK, *cousin to the King*
EARL OF SALISBURY
EARL OF WESTMERLAND
EARL OF WARWICK
ARCHBISHOP OF CANTERBURY
BISHOP OF ELY
EARL OF CAMBRIDGE
LORD SCROOP
SIR THOMAS GREY
SIR THOMAS ERPINGHAM ⎫
GOWER   ⎬ *officers in King*
FLUELLEN   ⎪ *Henry's army*
MACMORRIS   ⎭
JAMY
BATES   ⎫
COURT   ⎬ *soldiers in the same*
WILLIAMS ⎭
PISTOL
NYM

BARDOLPH
BOY
HERALD

CHARLES THE SIXTH, *King of France*
LEWIS, *the Dolphin*
DUKE OF BURGUNDY
DUKE OF ORLEANCE
DUKE OF BOURBON
DUKE OF BRITAIN
DUKE OF BERRI
DUKE OF BEAUMONT
CONSTABLE OF FRANCE
RAMBURES   ⎫
GRANDPRÉ   ⎬ *French lords*
GOVERNOR OF HARFLEUR
MONTJOY, *a French herald*
AMBASSADORS *to the King of England*

ISABEL, *Queen of France*
KATHERINE, *daughter to Charles and Isabel*
ALICE, *a lady attending on her*
HOSTESS *of the Boar's Head Tavern in Eastcheap, formerly Mistress Quickly, and now married to Pistol*

LORDS, LADIES, OFFICERS, SOLDIERS, CITIZENS, MESSENGERS, *and* ATTENDANTS

SCENE: *England; afterwards France*]

Enter PROLOGUE.

O for a Muse of fire, that would ascend
The brightest heaven of invention!
A kingdom for a stage, princes to act,
And monarchs to behold the swelling scene!
Then should the warlike Harry, like himself,   5
Assume the port of Mars, and at his heels
(Leash'd in, like hounds) should famine, sword, and
      fire
Crouch for employment. But pardon, gentles all,
The flat unraised spirits that hath dar'd

Words and passages enclosed in square brackets in the text above are either emendations of the copy-text or additions to it. The Textual Notes immediately following the play cite the earliest authority for every such change or insertion and supply the reading of the copy-text wherever it is emended in this edition.

Pro. 2. **invention:** poetic power (in rhetorical theory, the "finding" of suitable topics). 4. **swelling:** splendid. 6. **port:** demeanor.
7. **Leash'd in:** led in a group of three.

On this unworthy scaffold to bring forth   10
So great an object. Can this cockpit hold
The vasty fields of France? Or may we cram
Within this wooden O the very casques
That did affright the air at Agincourt?
O, pardon! since a crooked figure may   15
Attest in little place a million,
And let us, ciphers to this great accompt,

10. **scaffold:** stage.
11. **cockpit:** i.e. circular theatre (the "wooden O" of line 13, referring either to the Curtain in Shoreditch, where Shakespeare's company acted just before moving to the newly completed Globe in the late summer of 1599, or to the Globe itself).
13. **the very casques:** even the helmets.
14. **Agincourt:** village in northern France, scene of Henry V's greatest victory on October 25, 1415.
15. **crooked figure:** i.e. cipher or zero, which, added to a digit, multiplies its value. 16. **Attest:** represent.
17. **accompt:** (1) story (of King Henry V's career); (2) reckoning (continuing the wordplay on "crooked figure" and "wooden O").

Henry V
Pro.

On your imaginary forces work.
Suppose within the girdle of these walls
Are now confin'd two mighty monarchies,　20
Whose high, upreared, and abutting fronts
The perilous narrow ocean parts asunder.
Piece out our imperfections with your thoughts;
Into a thousand parts divide one man,
And make imaginary puissance;　25
Think, when we talk of horses, that you see them
Printing their proud hoofs i' th' receiving earth;
For 'tis your thoughts that now must deck our kings,
Carry them here and there, jumping o'er times,
Turning th' accomplishment of many years　30
Into an hour-glass: for the which supply,
Admit me Chorus to this history,
Who, Prologue-like, your humble patience pray,
Gently to hear, kindly to judge, our play.　　*Exit.*

ACT I, SCENE I

Enter the two Bishops, [the ARCHBISHOP] OF CANTER-
BURY *and [the* BISHOP OF] ELY.

Cant. My lord, I'll tell you, that self bill is urg'd
Which in th' eleventh year of the last king's reign
Was like, and had indeed against us pass'd,
But that the scambling and unquiet time
Did push it out of farther question.　5
Ely. But how, my lord, shall we resist it now?
Cant. It must be thought on. If it pass against us,
We lose the better half of our possession;
For all the temporal lands, which men devout
By testament have given to the Church,　10
Would they strip from us; being valu'd thus:
As much as would maintain, to the King's honor,
Full fifteen earls and fifteen hundred knights,
Six thousand and two hundred good esquires;
And to relief of lazars, and weak age　15
Of indigent faint souls past corporal toil,
A hundred almshouses right well supplied;
And to the coffers of the King beside,
A thousand pounds by th' year. Thus runs the bill.

Ely. This would drink deep.
Cant.　　　　　'Twould drink the cup and all.
Ely. But what prevention?　21
Cant. The King is full of grace and fair regard.
Ely. And a true lover of the holy Church.
Cant. The courses of his youth promis'd it not.
The breath no sooner left his father's body,　25
But that his wildness, mortified in him,
Seem'd to die too; yea, at that very moment,
Consideration like an angel came
And whipt th' offending Adam out of him,
Leaving his body as a paradise　30
T' envelop and contain celestial spirits.
Never was such a sudden scholar made;
Never came reformation in a flood
With such a heady currance, scouring faults;
Nor never Hydra-headed willfulness　35
So soon did lose his seat (and all at once)
As in this king.
Ely.　　　　We are blessed in the change.
Cant. Hear him but reason in divinity,
And all-admiring, with an inward wish
You would desire the King were made a prelate;　40
Hear him debate of commonwealth affairs,
You would say it hath been all in all his study;
List his discourse of war, and you shall hear
A fearful battle rend'red you in music;
Turn him to any cause of policy,　45
The Gordian knot of it he will unloose,
Familiar as his garter; that, when he speaks,
The air, a charter'd libertine, is still,
And the mute wonder lurketh in men's ears
To steal his sweet and honeyed sentences;　50
So that the art and practic part of life
Must be the mistress to this theoric;
Which is a wonder how his Grace should glean it,
Since his addiction was to courses vain,
His companies unletter'd, rude, and shallow,　55
His hours fill'd up with riots, banquets, sports;
And never noted in him any study,
Any retirement, any sequestration
From open haunts and popularity.　59
Ely. The strawberry grows underneath the nettle,
And wholesome berries thrive and ripen best
Neighbor'd by fruit of baser quality;
And so the Prince obscur'd his contemplation
Under the veil of wildness, which (no doubt)

---

18. **your imaginary forces:** the power of your imagination.
20. **two mighty monarchies:** i.e. France and England.
21. **fronts:** frontiers.　22. **narrow ocean:** i.e. English Channel.
25. **puissance:** troops.
28. **deck our kings:** equip our actors (as kings).
29. **jumping o'er times.** The play deals with events between Henry's preparations to invade France in 1414 and the Treaty of Troyes in 1420.
31. **for . . . supply:** to supply which (i.e. the defects acknowledged).

I.i. Location: London. An antechamber in the King's palace.
1. **self:** same.　2. **in . . . reign:** i.e. in 1410, under Henry IV.
3. **like:** likely (to pass).　**had:** would have.
4. **scambling:** disorderly.　5. **question:** consideration.
7–19. **If . . . bill.** Here as elsewhere in this act Shakespeare follows Holinshed (Bullough, IV, 377) with extraordinary fidelity: "The effect of which supplication was, that the temporall lands devoutlie given, and disordinatlie spent by religious, and other spirituall persons, should be seized into the kings hands, sith the same might suffice to maintaine, to the honor of the king, and defense of the realme, fifteene earles, fifteene hundred knights, six thousand and two hundred esquiers, and a hundred almesse-houses, for reliefe onelie of the poore, impotent, and needie persons, and the king to have cleerelie to his coffers twentie thousand pounds, with manie other provisions and values of religious houses, which I passe over."
9. **temporal lands:** i.e. properties not used for strictly religious purposes.　15. **lazars:** lepers.

22. **grace . . . regard:** favor and kindly interest.
26. **mortified:** killed.　28. **Consideration:** reflection.
29. **th' offending Adam:** i.e. natural depravity.
34. **heady currance:** strong current.　**scouring:** cleansing.
35. **Hydra-headed:** i.e. many-headed (from the name of a monstrous snake with many heads, killed by Hercules).
36. **seat:** i.e. power.　38. **divinity:** theology.
41. **commonwealth affairs:** i.e. politics.
45. **cause of policy:** question of statecraft.
46. **Gordian knot:** an intricate knot, devised by King Gordius of Phrygia, that Alexander the Great cut with his sword; i.e. a problem of great complexity.　47. **Familiar:** as routinely.　**that:** so that.
48. **charter'd libertine:** licensed freeman.
49–50. **the mute . . sentences:** i.e. the effects linger in men's memory and keep them silent to hear more.
51. **art . . . part:** experience and practice.
52. **be:** have been.　**theoric:** theory.
55. **companies:** companions.
59. **open . . . popularity:** places of popular resort and common associates.

Grew like the summer grass, fastest by night,   65
Unseen, yet crescive in his faculty.
　Cant.　It must be so; for miracles are ceas'd;
And therefore we must needs admit the means
How things are perfected.
　Ely.　　　　　　But, my good lord,
How now for mitigation of this bill   70
Urg'd by the commons? Doth his Majesty
Incline to it, or no?
　Cant.　　　　He seems indifferent;
Or rather swaying more upon our part
Than cherishing th' exhibiters against us;
For I have made an offer to his Majesty,   75
Upon our spiritual convocation
And in regard of causes now in hand,
Which I have open'd to his Grace at large,
As touching France, to give a greater sum
Than ever at one time the clergy yet   80
Did to his predecessors part withal.
　Ely.　How did this offer seem receiv'd, my lord?
　Cant.　With good acceptance of his Majesty;
Save that there was not time enough to hear,
As I perceiv'd his Grace would fain have done,   85
The severals and unhidden passages
Of his true titles to some certain dukedoms,
And generally to the crown and seat of France,
Deriv'd from Edward, his great-grandfather.
　Ely.　What was th' impediment that broke this off?
　Cant.　The French embassador upon that instant   91
Crav'd audience; and the hour, I think, is come
To give him hearing. Is it four a' clock?
　Ely.　It is.
　Cant.　Then go we in, to know his embassy;   95
Which I could with a ready guess declare,
Before the Frenchman speak a word of it.
　Ely.　I'll wait upon you, and I long to hear it.
　　　　　　　　　　　　　　　　Exeunt.

[SCENE II]

Enter the KING, *Humphrey* [DUKE OF GLOUCESTER],
BEDFORD, CLARENCE, WARWICK, WESTMERLAND,
and EXETER, [*and other* ATTENDANTS].

　K. Hen.　Where is my gracious Lord of Canterbury?
　Exe.　Not here in presence.
　K. Hen.　　　　　Send for him, good uncle.
　West.　Shall we call in th' ambassador, my liege?
　K. Hen.　Not yet, my cousin. We would be resolv'd,
Before we hear him, of some things of weight   5

66. **crescive . . . faculty:** growing in its natural power.
68. **means:** i.e. natural causes.　72. **indifferent:** i.e. uncommitted.
74. **exhibiters:** sponsors.
76. **Upon . . . convocation:** on behalf of the assembly of clergy.
78. **open'd:** explained.　81. **withal:** with.　85. **fain:** gladly.
86. **severals . . . passages:** details and obvious derivation.
87. **titles:** claims.　88. **seat:** throne.
89. **Edward, his great-grandfather:** i.e. Edward III, whose maternal grandfather was Philip IV of France.
91. **embassador:** ambassador.　**upon that instant:** just then.

I.ii. Location: London. The presence-chamber of the palace.
3. **liege:** sovereign.　4. **cousin:** kinsman.
4–5. **resolv'd . . . of:** clear in our mind . . . about.

That task our thoughts, concerning us and France.

Enter two Bishops, [*the* ARCHBISHOP OF CANTERBURY
　and the BISHOP OF ELY].

　Cant.　God and his angels guard your sacred throne,
And make you long become it!
　K. Hen.　　　　　Sure we thank you.
My learned lord, we pray you to proceed,
And justly and religiously unfold   10
Why the law Salique, that they have in France,
Or should, or should not, bar us in our claim;
And God forbid, my dear and faithful lord,
That you should fashion, wrest, or bow your reading,
Or nicely charge your understanding soul   15
With opening titles miscreate, whose right
Suits not in native colors with the truth;
For God doth know how many now in health
Shall drop their blood in approbation
Of what your reverence shall incite us to.   20
Therefore take heed how you impawn our person,
How you awake our sleeping sword of war—
We charge you, in the name of God, take heed;
For never two such kingdoms did contend
Without much fall of blood, whose guiltless drops   25
Are every one a woe, a sore complaint,
'Gainst him whose wrongs gives edge unto the swords
That makes such waste in brief mortality.
Under this conjuration speak, my lord;
For we will hear, note, and believe in heart,   30
That what you speak is in your conscience wash'd
As pure as sin with baptism.
　Cant.　Then hear me, gracious sovereign, and you
　　peers,
That owe yourselves, your lives, and services
To this imperial throne. There is no bar   35
To make against your Highness' claim to France
But this, which they produce from Pharamond,
"*In terram Salicam mulieres ne* [*succedant*],"
"No woman shall succeed in Salique land";
Which Salique land the French unjustly gloze   40
To be the realm of France, and Pharamond
The founder of this law and female bar.
Yet their own authors faithfully affirm
That the land Salique is in Germany,
Between the floods of Sala and of [Elbe];   45
Where Charles the Great, having subdu'd the Saxons,
There left behind and settled certain French;
Who holding in disdain the German women
For some dishonest manners of their life,
Establish'd then this law: to wit, no female   50
Should be inheritrix in Salique land;
Which Salique, as I said, 'twixt [Elbe] and Sala,

11. **law Salique.** Explained in lines 35 ff.
12. **Or:** either.　**claim:** i.e. to the French throne.
14. **reading:** interpretation.
15. **nicely charge:** foolishly burden.
16. **opening titles miscreate:** expounding spurious claims.
17. **Suits . . . colors:** is naturally incompatible.
19. **approbation:** proof, support.　21. **impawn:** commit.
26. **woe:** grievance.　28. **brief mortality:** i.e. short-lived mortal men.
29. **conjuration:** injunction.
37. **Pharamond:** legendary Frankish king.
39. **Salique:** Salic, Salian, referring to a Frankish tribe that lived on the river Sala, the ancient name for one of the mouths of the Rhine.
40. **gloze:** interpret.　49. **dishonest:** unchaste.

Henry V
I.ii

Is at this day in Germany call'd Meisen.
Then doth it well appear the Salique law
Was not devised for the realm of France;   55
Nor did the French possess the Salique land
Until four hundred one and twenty years
After defunction of King Pharamond,
Idly suppos'd the founder of this law,
Who died within the year of our redemption   60
Four hundred twenty-six; and Charles the Great
Subdu'd the Saxons, and did seat the French
Beyond the river Sala, in the year
Eight hundred five. Besides, their writers say,
King Pepin, which deposed Childeric,   65
Did, as heir general, being descended
Of Blithild, which was daughter to King Clothair,
Make claim and title to the crown of France.
Hugh Capet also, who usurp'd the crown
Of Charles the Duke of Lorraine, sole heir male   70
Of the true line and stock of Charles the Great,
To [fine] his title with some shows of truth,
Though in pure truth it was corrupt and naught,
Convey'd himself as th' heir to th' Lady Lingare,
Daughter to Charlemain, who was the son   75
To Lewis the Emperor, and Lewis the son
Of Charles the Great. Also King Lewis the Tenth,
Who was sole heir to the usurper Capet,
Could not keep quiet in his conscience,
Wearing the crown of France, till satisfied   80
That fair Queen Isabel, his grandmother,
Was lineal of the Lady Ermengare,
Daughter to Charles, the foresaid Duke of Lorraine;
By the which marriage the line of Charles the Great
Was re-united to the crown of France.   85
So that, as clear as is the summer's sun,
King Pepin's title and Hugh Capet's claim,
King Lewis his satisfaction, all appear
To hold in right and title of the female;
So do the kings of France unto this day.   90
Howbeit, they would hold up this Salique law
To bar your Highness claiming from the female,
And rather choose to hide them in a net
Than amply to imbar their crooked titles
Usurp'd from you and your progenitors.   95
     K. Hen. May I with right and conscience make
          this claim?
     Cant. The sin upon my head, dread sovereign!
For in the book of Numbers is it writ,
When the man dies, let the inheritance
Descend unto the daughter. Gracious lord,   100
Stand for your own, unwind your bloody flag,
Look back into your mighty ancestors;
Go, my dread lord, to your great-grandsire's tomb,

From whom you claim; invoke his warlike spirit,
And your great-uncle's, Edward the Black Prince, 105
Who on the French ground play'd a tragedy,
Making defeat on the full power of France,
Whiles his most mighty father on a hill
Stood smiling to behold his lion's whelp
Forage in blood of French nobility.   110
O noble English, that could entertain
With half their forces the full pride of France,
And let another half stand laughing by,
All out of work and cold for action!
     Ely. Awake remembrance of these valiant dead,
And with your puissant arm renew their feats.   116
You are their heir, you sit upon their throne;
The blood and courage that renowned them
Runs in your veins; and my thrice-puissant liege
Is in the very May-morn of his youth,   120
Ripe for exploits and mighty enterprises.
     Exe. Your brother kings and monarchs of the earth
Do all expect that you should rouse yourself,
As did the former lions of your blood.
     West. They know your Grace hath cause, and
          means, and might;   125
So hath your Highness. Never King of England
Had nobles richer and more loyal subjects,
Whose hearts have left their bodies here in England,
And lie pavilion'd in the fields of France.   129
     Cant. O, let their bodies follow, my dear liege,
With [blood] and sword and fire, to win your right;
In aid whereof we of the spirituality
Will raise your Highness such a mighty sum
As never did the clergy at one time
Bring in to any of your ancestors.   135
     K. Hen. We must not only arm t' invade the
          French,
But lay down our proportions to defend
Against the Scot, who will make road upon us
With all advantages.
     Cant. They of those marches, gracious sovereign,
Shall be a wall sufficient to defend   141
Our inland from the pilfering borderers.
     K. Hen. We do not mean the coursing snatchers
          only,
But fear the main intendment of the Scot,
Who hath been still a giddy neighbor to us;   145
For you shall read that my great-grandfather
Never went with his forces into France
But that the Scot on his unfurnish'd kingdom
Came pouring like the tide into a breach,
With ample and brim fullness of his force,   150
Galling the gleaned land with hot assays,

---

57. **four . . . twenty:** actually, 379 years, i.e. four hundred less one and twenty. The source of the error—as of many details and even phrases in this speech—is Holinshed (Bullough, IV, 378–79).
58. **defunction:** death.   59. **Idly:** foolishly.   62. **seat:** establish.
66. **heir general:** i.e. one who inherits through either the male or female parent.   72. **fine:** embellish.
74. **Convey'd:** misrepresented.
75. **Charlemain:** actually, Charles II ("the Bald"). Here and again in line 77, where Louis IX is confused with Louis X, Shakespeare copies Holinshed's mistakes.   82. **lineal of:** descended from.
93. **hide . . . net:** i.e. rely on a tangle of transparent contradictions.
94. **amply to imbar:** frankly to rule out.   **crooked:** fraudulent.
98. **Numbers.** The reference is to 27:8.

106. **tragedy:** i.e. the battle of Crécy (1346), a disaster for the French.
110. **Forage in:** prey on.   111. **entertain:** meet (and overcome).
114. **for:** i.e. for lack of.   118. **renowned:** brought renown to.
120. **youth.** Henry was twenty-seven at the time.
129. **pavilion'd:** tented.   132. **spirituality:** clergy.
137. **lay . . . proportions:** allocate our forces.   138. **road:** inroad.
139. **With all advantages:** i.e. whenever he sees a good chance.
140. **marches:** border regions.
143. **coursing snatchers:** guerrilla raiders.
144. **intendment:** (hostile) intention.
145. **still:** always.   **giddy:** untrustworthy.
148. **unfurnish'd:** unprotected.
151. **Galling . . . assays:** harassing the land depleted of soldiers with strong assaults.

Girding with grievous siege castles and towns;
That England being empty of defense,
Hath shook and trembled at th' ill neighborhood.
   Cant.   She hath been then more fear'd than harm'd,
     my liege;   155
For hear her but exampled by herself:
When all her chevalry hath been in France,
And she a mourning widow of her nobles,
She hath herself not only well defended
But taken and impounded as a stray   160
The King of Scots; whom she did send to France
To fill King Edward's fame with prisoner kings,
And make [her] chronicle as rich with praise
As is the ooze and bottom of the sea
With sunken wrack and sumless treasuries.   165
   Ely.   But there's a saying very old and true,
     "If that you will France win,
       Then with Scotland first begin."
For once the eagle (England) being in prey,
To her unguarded nest the weasel (Scot)   170
Comes sneaking, and so sucks her princely eggs,
Playing the mouse in absence of the cat,
To 'tame and havoc more than she can eat.
   Exe.   It follows then the cat must stay at home,
Yet that is but a crush'd necessity,   175
Since we have locks to safeguard necessaries,
And pretty traps to catch the petty thieves.
While that the armed hand doth fight abroad,
Th' advised head defends itself at home;
For government, though high, and low, and lower,
Put into parts, doth keep in one consent,   181
Congreeing in a full and natural close,
Like music.
   Cant.   Therefore doth heaven divide
The state of man in divers functions,
Setting endeavor in continual motion;   185
To which is fixed, as an aim or butt,
Obedience; for so work the honey-bees,
Creatures that by a rule in nature teach
The act of order to a peopled kingdom.
They have a king, and officers of sorts,   190
Where some, like magistrates, correct at home;
Others, like merchants, venter trade abroad;
Others, like soldiers, armed in their stings,
Make boot upon the summer's velvet buds,
Which pillage they with merry march bring home
To the tent-royal of their emperor;   196
Who busied in his [majesty] surveys
The singing masons building roofs of gold,
The civil citizens kneading up the honey,

The poor mechanic porters crowding in   200
Their heavy burthens at his narrow gate,
The sad-ey'd justice, with his surly hum,
Delivering o'er to executors pale
The lazy yawning drone. I this infer,
That many things, having full reference   205
To one consent, may work contrariously,
As many arrows loosed several ways
Come to one mark; as many ways meet in one town;
As many fresh streams meet in one salt sea;
As many lines close in the dial's centre;   210
So may a thousand actions, once afoot,
[End] in one purpose, and be all well borne
Without defeat. Therefore to France, my liege!
Divide your happy England into four,
Whereof take you one quarter into France,   215
And you withal shall make all Gallia shake.
If we, with thrice such powers left at home,
Cannot defend our own doors from the dog,
Let us be worried, and our nation lose
The name of hardiness and policy.   220
   K. Hen.   Call in the messengers sent from the
     Dolphin.   *[Exeunt some Attendants.]*
Now are we well resolv'd, and by God's help
And yours, the noble sinews of our power,
France being ours, we'll bend it to our awe,
Or break it all to pieces. Or there we'll sit,   225
Ruling in large and ample empery
O'er France and all her (almost) kingly dukedoms,
Or lay these bones in an unworthy urn,
Tombless, with no remembrance over them.
Either our history shall with full mouth   230
Speak freely of our acts, or else our grave,
Like Turkish mute, shall have a tongueless mouth,
Not worshipp'd with a waxen epitaph.

   Enter Ambassadors *of France [attended].*

Now are we well prepar'd to know the pleasure
Of our fair cousin Dolphin; for we hear   235
Your greeting is from him, not from the King.
   [1.] Amb.   May't please your Majesty to give us
     leave
Freely to render what we have in charge?
Or shall we sparingly show you far off
The Dolphin's meaning and our embassy?   240

154. **neighborhood:** neighborliness.   155. **fear'd:** frightened.
156. **exampled by herself:** i.e. instructed by her own example.
157. **chevalry:** chivalry.
159–62. **She . . . kings.** In 1346, when Edward III was waging war in France, David II of Scotland was captured by the English. He was not actually taken to France.   165. **sumless:** incalculable.
169. **in prey:** in search of prey.
173. **'tame:** attame, i.e. pierce, injure.   **havoc:** ravage.
175. **crush'd necessity:** strained conclusion (in view of what follows).
179. **advised:** judicious.   181. **consent:** harmony.
182. **Congreeing:** agreeing.   **close:** cadence.
186. **aim or butt:** i.e. target.   189. **act of order:** orderly action.
190. **sorts:** different kinds.   191. **correct:** dispense justice.
192. **venter:** venture.   194. **boot:** booty.
197. **majesty:** royal office.

200. **mechanic:** menial.   201. **burthens:** burdens.
202. **sad-ey'd:** serious-eyed, grave.   203. **executors:** executioners.
205–6. **having . . . consent:** i.e. united in a common goal.
207. **loosed several ways:** shot from different directions.
208. **mark:** target.   **ways:** roads.
210. **close:** converge.   **dial's:** sundial's.   212. **borne:** conducted.
216. **withal:** therewith.   **Gallia:** France.
219. **worried:** torn to pieces.
220. **name . . . policy:** reputation for valor and statesmanship.
221. **Dolphin:** Dauphin, title of the heir apparent of the French king.
222. **Now . . . resolv'd.** As Holinshed reports (Bullough, IV, 380), "the duke of Excester used such earnest and pithie persuasions, to induce the king and the whole assemblie of the parlement to credit his words, that immediatlie after he had made an end, all the companie began to crie; Warre, warre; France, France. Hereby the bill for dissolving of religious houses was cleerlie set aside, and nothing was thought on but onelie the recovering of France, according as the archbishop had mooved."   224. **our awe:** submission to us.
226. **empery:** imperial power.
229. **Tombless:** i.e. without a monument.   **remembrance:** epitaph.
233. **worshipp'd:** honored.   **with . . . epitaph:** i.e. even with an epitaph written on wax.   238. **render:** report.
239. **sparingly . . . off:** i.e. tactfully suggest.

Henry V
I.ii

K. Hen. We are no tyrant, but a Christian king,
Unto whose grace our passion is as subject
As is our wretches fett'red in our prisons;
Therefore with frank and with uncurbed plainness
Tell us the Dolphin's mind.

[1.] *Amb.*   Thus then in few: 245
Your Highness, lately sending into France,
Did claim some certain dukedoms, in the right
Of your great predecessor, King Edward the Third.
In answer of which claim, the prince our master
Says that you savor too much of your youth,   250
And bids you be advis'd: there's nought in France
That can be with a nimble galliard won;
You cannot revel into dukedoms there.
He therefore sends you, meeter for your spirit,
This tun of treasure; and, in lieu of this,   255
Desires you let the dukedoms that you claim
Hear no more of you. This the Dolphin speaks.

K. Hen. What treasure, uncle?
Exe.   Tennis-balls, my liege.
K. Hen. We are glad the Dolphin is so pleasant
with us,
His present and your pains we thank you for.   260
When we have match'd our rackets to these balls,
We will in France, by God's grace, play a set
Shall strike his father's crown into the hazard.
Tell him he hath made a match with such a wrangler
That all the courts of France will be disturb'd   265
With chaces. And we understand him well,
How he comes o'er us with our wilder days,
Not measuring what use we made of them.
We never valu'd this poor seat of England,
And therefore, living hence, did give ourself   270
To barbarous license; as 'tis ever common
That men are merriest when they are from home.
But tell the Dolphin I will keep my state,
Be like a king, and show my sail of greatness
When I do rouse me in my throne of France.   275
For that I have laid by my majesty,
And plodded like a man for working-days;
But I will rise there with so full a glory
That I will dazzle all the eyes of France,
Yea, strike the Dolphin blind to look on us.   280
And tell the pleasant prince this mock of his
Hath turn'd his balls to gun-stones, and his soul
Shall stand sore charged for the wasteful vengeance
That shall fly with them; for many a thousand widows
Shall this his mock mock out of their dear husbands;
Mock mothers from their sons, mock castles down;
And some are yet ungotten and unborn   287

That shall have cause to curse the Dolphin's scorn.
But this lies all within the will of God,
To whom I do appeal, and in whose name   290
Tell you the Dolphin I am coming on
To venge me as I may, and to put forth
My rightful hand in a well-hallow'd cause.
So get you hence in peace; and tell the Dolphin
His jest will savor but of shallow wit,   295
When thousands weep more than did laugh at it.—
Convey them with safe conduct.—Fare you well.
                    Exeunt Ambassadors.
Exe. This was a merry message.
K. Hen. We hope to make the sender blush at it.
Therefore, my lords, omit no happy hour   300
That may give furth'rance to our expedition;
For we have now no thought in us but France,
Save those to God, that run before our business.
Therefore let our proportions for these wars
Be soon collected, and all things thought upon   305
That may with reasonable swiftness add
More feathers to our wings; for, God before,
We'll chide this Dolphin at his father's door.
Therefore let every man now task his thought,   309
That this fair action may on foot be brought. *Exeunt.*

[ACT II]

Flourish. Enter CHORUS.

Now all the youth of England are on fire,
And silken dalliance in the wardrobe lies;
Now thrive the armorers, and honor's thought
Reigns solely in the breast of every man.
They sell the pasture now to buy the horse,   5
Following the mirror of all Christian kings,
With winged heels, as English Mercuries.
For now sits Expectation in the air,
And hides a sword, from hilts unto the point,
With crowns imperial, crowns and coronets,   10
Promis'd to Harry and his followers.
The French, advis'd by good intelligence
Of this most dreadful preparation,
Shake in their fear, and with pale policy
Seek to divert the English purposes.   15
O England! model to thy inward greatness,
Like little body with a mighty heart,
What mightst thou do, that honor would thee do,
Were all thy children kind and natural!
But see, thy fault France hath in thee found out,   20

---

245. **few:** i.e. few words.
246–58. **Your . . . liege.** There is apparently no historical foundation for this famous episode of the tennis balls.
252. **galliard:** frisky dance.   255. **tun:** barrel.
259. **pleasant:** merry.
263–66. **hazard, wrangler, courts, chaces:** terms of court tennis used punningly. For example, *hazard* means (1) holes or galleries in the walls of a tennis court and (2) jeopardy; **chaces** means (1) missed returns and (2) pursuits.
263. **crown:** (1) coin (staked in a game of chance); (2) the sovereign power of France.   267. **comes o'er:** taunts.   269. **seat:** throne.
272. **from:** away from.
273. **keep my state:** i.e. maintain my royal status.
275. **rouse me in:** mount to.   282. **gun-stones:** cannon balls.
283. **charged:** burdened with the responsibility.   **wasteful:** ruinous.

292. **venge:** avenge. **may:** can.   297. **Convey:** escort.
300. **omit . . . hour:** neglect no favorable opportunity.
304. **proportions:** levies.   307. **God before:** i.e. with God's help.
309. **task:** tax.
II.Cho. o.s.d. **Flourish:** trumpet fanfare.
2. **silken . . . lies:** i.e. gay apparel and frivolous pursuits are laid aside.
7. **Mercuries.** In classical mythology, Mercury was the messenger of the gods.   9. **hilts:** i.e. the pommel, haft, etc. of a sword.
10. **With . . . coronets:** i.e. with crowns appropriate for emperors, kings, and nobles respectively.
12. **advis'd:** informed. **intelligence:** espionage.
14. **pale policy:** frightened intrigue.
16. **model to:** small replica of.   18. **would:** would have.
19. **kind and natural:** i.e. naturally affectionate and loyal.
20. **France:** the King of France.

A nest of hollow bosoms, which he fills
With treacherous crowns; and three corrupted men,
One, Richard Earl of Cambridge, and the second,
Henry Lord Scroop of Masham, and the third,
Sir Thomas Grey, knight, of Northumberland,   25
Have for the gilt of France (O guilt indeed!)
Confirm'd conspiracy with fearful France,
And by their hands this grace of kings must die,
If hell and treason hold their promises,
Ere he take ship for France; and in Southampton.   30
Linger your patience on, and we'll digest
Th' abuse of distance; force a play:
The sum is paid, the traitors are agreed,
The King is set from London, and the scene
Is now transported, gentles, to Southampton;   35
There is the playhouse now, there must you sit,
And thence to France shall we convey you safe,
And bring you back, charming the Narrow Seas
To give you gentle pass; for if we may,
We'll not offend one stomach with our play.   40
But till the King come forth, and not till then,
Unto Southampton do we shift our scene.   *Exit.*

[SCENE I]

Enter CORPORAL NYM *and* LIEUTENANT BARDOLPH.

Bard. Well met, Corporal Nym.
Nym. Good morrow, Lieutenant Bardolph.
Bard. What, are Ancient Pistol and you friends
yet?   4
Nym. For my part, I care not; I say little; but
when time shall serve, there shall be smiles—but that
shall be as it may. I dare not fight, but I will wink and
hold out mine iron. It is a simple one, but what though?
It will toast cheese, and it will endure cold as another
man's sword will; and there's an end.   10
Bard. I will bestow a breakfast to make you
friends, and we'll be all three sworn brothers to
France. Let 't be so, good Corporal Nym.   13
Nym. Faith, I will live so long as I may, that's the
certain of it; and when I cannot live any longer, I will
do as I may: that is my rest, that is the rendezvous of it.
Bard. It is certain, corporal, that he is married to
Nell Quickly, and certainly she did you wrong, for

you were troth-plight to her.   19
Nym. I cannot tell; things must be as they may.
Men may sleep, and they may have their throats about
them at that time, and some say knives have edges. It
must be as it may; though patience be a tir'd [mare],
yet she will plod—there must be conclusions—well,
I cannot tell.   25

Enter PISTOL *and* [HOSTESS] QUICKLY.

Bard. Here comes Ancient Pistol and his wife.
Good corporal, be patient here.
[*Nym.*] How now, mine host Pistol?
Pist. Base tike, call'st thou me host?
Now by [Gadslugs] I swear I scorn the term;   30
Nor shall my Nell keep lodgers.
Host. No, by my troth, not long; for we cannot
lodge and board a dozen or fourteen gentlewomen that
live honestly by the prick of their needles but it will be
thought we keep a bawdy-house straight. [*Nym* 35
and Pistol draw.] O welliday, Lady, if he be not
hewn now, we shall see willful adultery and murther
committed.
Bard. Good lieutenant! good corporal! offer noth-
ing here.   40
Nym. Pish!
Pist. Pish for thee, Iceland dog! thou prick-ear'd
        cur of Iceland!
Host. Good Corporal Nym, show thy valor, and
put up your sword.   44
Nym. Will you shog off? I would have you solus.
Pist. "Solus," egregious dog? O viper vile!
The "solus" in thy most mervailous face,
The "solus" in thy teeth, and in thy throat,
And in thy hateful lungs, yea, in thy maw, perdy;
And which is worse, within thy nasty mouth!   50
I do retort the "solus" in thy bowels,
For I can take, and Pistol's cock is up,
And flashing fire will follow.
Nym. I am not Barbason, you cannot conjure me.
I have an humor to knock you indifferently well.   55
If you grow foul with me, Pistol, I will scour you with
my rapier, as I may, in fair terms. If you would walk
off, I would prick your guts a little in good terms, as I
may, and that's the humor of it.   59
Pist. O braggard vile and damned furious wight!
The grave doth gape, and doting death is near,
Therefore exhale.
Bard. Hear me, hear me what I say. He that
strikes the first stroke, I'll run him up to the hilts, as
I am a soldier.   [*Draws.*] 65
Pist. An oath of mickle might, and fury shall abate.

---

22. **treacherous crowns:** i.e. bribes. 26. **gilt:** gold.
27. **fearful:** timid. 28. **grace of kings:** honor to kingship.
30. **Southampton:** seaport in southern England.
31–32. **digest . . . distance:** i.e. take care of the violation of the unity
of place. 32. **force:** stuff (with incidents). 34. **set:** set forth.
35. **gentles:** ladies and gentlemen.
38. **Narrow Seas:** English Channel.
39. **gentle pass:** smooth voyage.
40. **offend one stomach:** (1) give offense to any spectator; (2) make
anyone seasick.

II.i. Location: London. A street.
o.s.d. **Nym, Bardolph.** The fiery-faced Bardolph, together with the
blustering Pistol and his new wife the Hostess, were among Falstaff's
disreputable companions in *1* and *2 Henry IV*, but Corporal Nym is a
new addition to the gang.
3. **Ancient:** ensign, standard-bearer.
7. **wink:** close both eyes. 8. **iron:** weapon.
12. **sworn brothers:** i.e. band of thieves.
16. **rest:** last stake (a term from gaming). **rendezvous.** By this
word Nym may mean something like "last word on the subject," but
many of his and Pistol's expressions defy explanation.

---

19. **troth-plight:** betrothed. 29. **tike:** cur.
30. **Gadslugs:** corrupt or meaningless oath (?).
36. **Lady:** (by Our) Lady, a mild oath.
37. **adultery.** Possibly the Hostess here perpetrates a double
blunder, intending *assaultery,* her own version of *assault and battery.*
murther: murder. 39–40. **offer nothing:** i.e. don't fight.
42. **Iceland dog:** kind of terrier with long hair and pointed ears.
45. **shog:** jog, move along. **solus:** (1) alone; (2) unmarried.
47. **mervailous:** marvellous.
49. **maw:** stomach. **perdy:** assuredly. 52. **take:** strike.
54. **Barbason:** name of a fiend (?). **conjure:** i.e. frighten by conjurations and big words.
55. **I . . . humor:** I'm in the mood. 56. **foul:** i.e. from firing.
62. **exhale:** i.e. draw your sword. 66. **mickle:** great.

Henry V
II.i

Give me thy fist, thy fore-foot to me give.
Thy spirits are most tall.

　Nym.　I will cut thy throat one time or other in
fair terms, that is the humor of it.　　　　70

　Pist.　*Couple a gorge!*
That is the word.　I [thee defy] again.
O hound of Crete, think'st thou my spouse to get?
No, to the spittle go,
And from the powd'ring-tub of infamy　　　75
Fetch forth the lazar kite of Cressid's kind,
Doll Tearsheet she by name, and her espouse.
I have, and I will hold, the quondam Quickly
For the only she; and—*pauca*, there's enough too!
Go to.　　　　80

Enter the Boy.

　Boy.　Mine host Pistol, you must come to my
master, and your hostess.　He is very sick, and would
to bed.　Good Bardolph, put thy face between his
sheets, and do the office of a warming-pan.　Faith,
he's very ill.　　　　85

　Bard.　Away, you rogue!

　Host.　By my troth, he'll yield the crow a pudding
one of these days.　The King has kill'd his heart.　Good
husband, come home presently.　*Exit [with Boy].*　89

　Bard.　Come, shall I make you two friends?　We
must to France together; why the devil should we keep
knives to cut one another's throats?

　Pist.　Let floods o'erswell, and fiends for food howl
on!

　Nym.　You'll pay me the eight shillings I won of
you at betting?　　　　95

　Pist.　Base is the slave that pays.

　Nym.　That now I will have: that's the humor of it.

　Pist.　As manhood shall compound.　Push home.
　　　　[They] draw.

　Bard.　By this sword, he that makes the first thrust,
I'll kill him; by this sword, I will.　　　*[Draws.]*　100

　Pist.　Sword is an oath, and oaths must have their
course.

　Bard.　Corporal Nym, and thou wilt be friends, be
friends; and thou wilt not, why then be enemies with
me too.　Prithee put up.

　[*Nym.*　I shall have my eight shillings I won of
you at betting?]　　　　106

　Pist.　A noble shalt thou have, and present pay,
And liquor likewise will I give to thee,

And friendship shall combine, and brotherhood.
I'll live by Nym, and Nym shall live by me.　　　110
Is not this just?　For I shall sutler be
Unto the camp, and profits will accrue.
Give me thy hand.

　Nym.　I shall have my noble?

　Pist.　In cash, most justly paid.　　　　115

　Nym.　Well, then that['s] the humor of't.

Enter Hostess.

　Host.　As ever you come of women, come in
quickly to Sir John.　Ah, poor heart! he is so shak'd of
a burning quotidian tertian, that it is most lamentable
to behold.　Sweet men, come to him.　　　　120

　Nym.　The King hath run bad humors on the
knight, that's the even of it.

　Pist.　Nym, thou hast spoke the right.
His heart is fracted and corroborate.　　　　124

　Nym.　The King is a good king, but it must be as it
may; he passes some humors and careers.

　Pist.　Let us condole the knight, for, lambkins, we
will live.　　　*[Exeunt.]*

[SCENE II]

Enter Exeter, Bedford, *and* Westmerland.

　Bed.　'Fore God, his Grace is bold to trust these
traitors.

　Exe.　They shall be apprehended by and by.

　West.　How smooth and even they do bear them-
selves!
As if allegiance in their bosoms sate
Crowned with faith and constant loyalty.　　　5

　Bed.　The King hath note of all that they intend,
By interception which they dream not of.

　Exe.　Nay, but the man that was his bedfellow,
Whom he hath dull'd and cloy'd with gracious favors—
That he should, for a foreign purse, so sell　　　10
His sovereign's life to death and treachery.

Sound trumpets. Enter the King, Scroop, Cambridge,
and Grey, [*with* Attendants].

　K. Hen.　Now sits the wind fair, and we will
aboard.
My Lord of Cambridge, and my kind Lord of Masham,
And you, my gentle knight, give me your thoughts.
Think you not that the pow'rs we bear with us　　　15

---

67. **fist:** hand.　68. **tall:** valiant.
71. **Couple a gorge:** i.e. *couper la gorge*, cut a throat.
74. **spittle:** hospital.
75. **powd'ring-tub:** sort of steam-bath used in treating venereal disease.
76. **lazar . . . kind:** diseased whore like Cressida (the pattern of a depraved woman as depicted in Robert Henryson's *Testament of Cresseid*).
77. **Doll Tearsheet:** another of Falstaff's friends.　At the end of *2 Henry IV* (V.iv) she was sent to prison.　79. **pauca:** few (words).
80 s.d. **Boy:** i.e. the page that Prince Hal had given to Falstaff (*2 Henry IV*, I.ii).
84. **warming-pan.** Alluding to Bardolph's complexion.
87. **he'll . . . pudding:** i.e. crows will peck the page's flesh (when he's hanging on the gallows).
88. **his:** i.e. Falstaff's, alluding to the new king's rejection of his former friend (*2 Henry IV*, V.v).　89. **presently:** immediately.
98. **As . . . compound:** as valor shall determine, i.e. we'll settle it by fighting.　102. **and:** if.
107. **noble:** coin worth 6s. 8d., which is less than Pistol owes but is acceptable because it is in ready cash (*present pay*).

111. **sutler:** seller of provisions.
119. **quotidian tertian:** the Hostess' characteristic confusion of medical terms for two kinds of fever, one occurring daily (*quotidian*) and the other on alternate days (*tertian*).
121. **run . . . on:** shown ill will toward.　122. **even:** truth.
124. **fracted:** broken.　**corroborate:** blunder for *corrupted* (?).
126. **passes . . . careers:** i.e. behaves oddly at times.　*Passes* = lets pass; *careers* = gallops (a term from horsemanship).

II.ii. Location: Southampton. A council-chamber.
2. **apprehended by and by:** arrested shortly.　6. **note:** knowledge.
8. **the man . . . bedfellow.** Of the three traitors, one—Lord Scroop—"was in such favour with the king," says Holinshed (Bullough, IV, 384), "that he admitted him sometime to be his bedfellow, in whose fidelitie the king reposed such trust, that when anie privat or publike councell was in hand, this lord had much in the determination of it."
9. **dull'd:** tired.
10. **foreign purse.** For a more important reason for the conspiracy see note to lines 155–57.　15. **pow'rs:** forces.

Will cut their passage through the force of France,
Doing the execution and the act
For which we have in head assembled them?

  Scroop. No doubt, my liege, if each man do his best.
  K. Hen. I doubt not that, since we are well per-
    suaded   20
We carry not a heart with us from hence
That grows not in a fair consent with ours;
Nor leave not one behind that doth not wish
Success and conquest to attend on us.

  Cam. Never was monarch better fear'd and lov'd
Than is your Majesty. There's not, I think, a subject
That sits in heart-grief and uneasiness   27
Under the sweet shade of your government.

  Grey. True; those that were your father's enemies
Have steep'd their galls in honey, and do serve you
With hearts create of duty and of zeal.   31

  K. Hen. We therefore have great cause of thank-
    fulness,
And shall forget the office of our hand
Sooner than quittance of desert and merit,
According to the weight and worthiness.   35

  Scroop. So service shall with steeled sinews toil,
And labor shall refresh itself with hope
To do your Grace incessant services.

  K. Hen. We judge no less. Uncle of Exeter,
Enlarge the man committed yesterday,   40
That rail'd against our person. We consider
It was excess of wine that set him on,
And on his more advice we pardon him.

  Scroop. That's mercy, but too much security.
Let him be punish'd, sovereign, lest example   45
Breed, by his sufferance, more of such a kind.

  K. Hen. O, let us yet be merciful.
  Cam. So may your Highness, and yet punish too.
  Grey. Sir,
You show great mercy if you give him life   50
After the taste of much correction.

  K. Hen. Alas, your too much love and care of me
Are heavy orisons 'gainst this poor wretch!
If little faults, proceeding on distemper,
Shall not be wink'd at, how shall we stretch our eye
When capital crimes, chew'd, swallow'd, and digested,
Appear before us? We'll yet enlarge that man,   57
Though Cambridge, Scroop, and Grey, in their dear
    care
And tender preservation of our person,
Would have him punish'd. And now to our French
    causes.   60
Who are the late commissioners?

  Cam. I one, my lord.
Your Highness bade me ask for it to-day.

  Scroop. So did you me, my liege.
  Grey. And I, my royal sovereign.   65
  K. Hen. Then, Richard Earl of Cambridge, there
    is yours;
There yours, Lord Scroop of Masham; and, sir knight,
Grey of Northumberland, this same is yours:
Read them, and know I know your worthiness.
My Lord of Westmerland, and uncle Exeter,   70
We will aboard to-night.—Why, how now, gentle-
    men?
What see you in those papers that you lose
So much complexion?—Look ye how they change!
Their cheeks are paper.—Why, what read you there
That have so cowarded and chas'd your blood   75
Out of appearance?

  Cam.   I do confess my fault,
And do submit me to your Highness' mercy.

  Grey, Scroop. To which we all appeal.
  K. Hen. The mercy that was quick in us but late,
By your own counsel is suppress'd and kill'd.   80
You must not dare (for shame) to talk of mercy,
For your own reasons turn into your bosoms,
As dogs upon their masters, worrying you.
See you, my princes and my noble peers,
These English monsters! My Lord of Cambridge here,
You know how apt our love was to accord   86
To furnish [him] with all appertinents
Belonging to his honor; and this man
Hath, for a few light crowns, lightly conspir'd
And sworn unto the practices of France   90
To kill us here in Hampton. To the which
This knight, no less for bounty bound to us
Than Cambridge is, hath likewise sworn. But O,
What shall I say to thee, Lord Scroop, thou cruel,
Ingrateful, savage, and inhuman creature?   95
Thou that didst bear the key of all my counsels,
That knew'st the very bottom of my soul,
That (almost) mightst have coin'd me into gold,
Wouldst thou have practic'd on me, for thy use?
May it be possible that foreign hire   100
Could out of thee extract one spark of evil
That might annoy my finger? 'Tis so strange,
That, though the truth of it stands off as gross
As black and white, my eye will scarcely see it.
Treason and murther ever kept together,   105
As two yoke-devils sworn to either's purpose,
Working so grossly in [a] natural cause
That admiration did not hoop at them;
But thou ('gainst all proportion) didst bring in
Wonder to wait on treason and on murther;   110
And whatsoever cunning fiend it was
That wrought upon thee so preposterously
Hath got the voice in hell for excellence;
And other devils that suggest by treasons

---

18. **head:** aggressive posture.
22. **grows . . . consent:** is not harmonious.
30. **galls:** bitterness, hostility.   31. **create:** composed.
33. **office:** use, function.   34. **quittance:** reward.
39. **Uncle.** Thomas Beaufort, Duke of Exeter, was the youngest son of John of Gaunt by Katherine Swynford.
40. **Enlarge:** set free.   **committed:** imprisoned.
43. **more advice:** thinking better of it.   44. **security:** overconfidence.
46. **his sufferance:** pardoning him.   53. **heavy orisons:** weighty pleas.
54. **proceeding on distemper:** i.e. resulting from drunkenness.
57. **yet:** none the less.   58. **dear:** intense.
61. **late:** recently appointed (to serve during the King's absence).
63. **it:** i.e. document certifying his appointment as commissioner.

76. **appearance:** sight.   79. **quick:** alive.   83. **worrying:** tearing.
86. **accord:** consent.   87. **appertinents:** appurtenances.
90. **practices:** plots.   91. **Hampton:** Southampton.
92. **This knight:** i.e. Grey.
99. **practic'd:** i.e. used your wiles.   **use:** profit.
103. **stands . . . gross:** shows as clear.   107. **grossly:** obviously.
108. **admiration . . . hoop:** astonishment did not whoop, i.e. no cry of astonishment was raised.   109. **proportion:** natural order.
110. **wait on:** consort with.   112. **preposterously:** contrary to nature.
113. **voice:** vote.   114. **suggest:** seduce.

Henry V
II.ii

Do botch and bungle up damnation   115
With patches, colors, and with forms being fetch'd
From glist'ring semblances of piety;
But he that temper'd thee, bade thee stand up,
Gave thee no instance why thou shouldst do treason,
Unless to dub thee with the name of traitor.   120
If that same demon that hath gull'd thee thus
Should with his lion gait walk the whole world,
He might return to vasty Tartar back,
And tell the legions, "I can never win
A soul so easy as that Englishman's."   125
O, how hast thou with jealousy infected
The sweetness of affiance! Show men dutiful?
Why, so didst thou. Seem they grave and learned?
Why, so didst thou. Come they of noble family?
Why, so didst thou. Seem they religious?   130
Why, so didst thou. Or are they spare in diet,
Free from gross passion, or of mirth or anger,
Constant in spirit, not swerving with the blood,
Garnish'd and deck'd in modest complement,
Not working with the eye without the ear,   135
And but in purged judgment trusting neither?
Such and so finely bolted didst thou seem.
And thus thy fall hath left a kind of blot
To [mark the] full-fraught man and best indued
With some suspicion. I will weep for thee;   140
For this revolt of thine, methinks, is like
Another fall of man. Their faults are open,
Arrest them to the answer of the law,
And God acquit them of their practices!
    Exe. I arrest thee of high treason, by the name of
Richard Earl of Cambridge.   146
    I arrest thee of high treason, by the name of [Henry]
Lord Scroop of Masham.
    I arrest thee of high treason, by the name of Thomas
Grey, knight, of Northumberland.   150
    Scroop. Our purposes God justly hath discover'd,
And I repent my fault more than my death,
Which I beseech your Highness to forgive,
Although my body pay the price of it.
    Cam. For me, the gold of France did not seduce,

Although I did admit it as a motive   156
The sooner to effect what I intended.
But God be thanked for prevention,
Which [I] in sufferance heartily will rejoice,
Beseeching God, and you, to pardon me.   160
    Grey. Never did faithful subject more rejoice
At the discovery of most dangerous treason
Than I do at this hour joy o'er myself,
Prevented from a damned enterprise.
My fault, but not my body, pardon, sovereign.   165
    K. Hen. God quit you in his mercy! Hear your
sentence.
You have conspir'd against our royal person,
Join'd with an enemy proclaim'd, and from his
coffers
Receiv'd the golden earnest of our death;
Wherein you would have sold your king to slaughter,
His princes and his peers to servitude,   171
His subjects to oppression and contempt,
And his whole kingdom into desolation.
Touching our person seek we no revenge,
But we our kingdom's safety must so tender,   175
Whose ruin you [have] sought, that to her laws
We do deliver you. Get you therefore hence,
Poor miserable wretches, to your death;
The taste whereof God of his mercy give
You patience to endure, and true repentance   180
Of all your dear offenses! Bear them hence.
    Exeunt [Cambridge, Scroop, and Grey, guarded].
Now, lords, for France; the enterprise whereof
Shall be to you as us, like glorious.
We doubt not of a fair and lucky war,
Since God so graciously hath brought to light   185
This dangerous treason lurking in our way
To hinder our beginnings. We doubt not now
But every rub is smoothed on our way.
Then forth, dear countrymen! Let us deliver
Our puissance into the hand of God,   190
Putting it straight in expedition.
Cheerly to sea! The signs of war advance!
No king of England, if not king of France!
    Flourish. [Exeunt.]

[SCENE III]

Enter PISTOL, NYM, BARDOLPH, BOY, and HOSTESS.

    Host. Prithee, honey-sweet husband, let me bring
thee to Staines.
    Pist. No; for my manly heart doth ern.
Bardolph, be blithe; Nym, rouse thy vaunting veins;
Boy, bristle thy courage up; for Falstaff he is dead,
And we must ern therefore.   6

115–17. botch . . . piety: i.e. clumsily conceal the sin of treason by adorning it with pious motives.
116. colors: pretexts.   fetch'd: derived.
118. temper'd: moulded.   119. instance: reason.
122. lion gait. See 1 Peter 5:8: "your adversary the devil, as a roaring lion, walketh about, seeking whom he may devour."
123. Tartar: Tartarus, in classical mythology the place of torment; i.e. hell.   126. jealousy: suspicion.   127. affiance: trust.
133. blood: passion.   134. complement: appearance.
135. Not . . . ear: i.e. relying on the evidence of neither eye nor ear alone.   136. purged: i.e. impartial.   137. bolted: sifted.
139. full-fraught: i.e. loaded (with good qualities).
142. open: obvious.
155–57. For . . . intended. These lines, hinting at the start of the long struggle between the houses of York and Lancaster for the English throne, are Shakespeare's strangely cryptic introduction to one of the major subjects of his history plays. As a member of the House of York the Earl of Cambridge was eager to replace King Henry with his own brother-in-law Edmund Mortimer, fifth Earl of March, because, as Holinshed points out (Bullough, IV, 386), "after the death of which earle of March, for diverse secret impediments, not able to have issue, the earle of Cambridge was sure that the crowne should come to him by his wife [who was Edmund's sister], and to his children, of hir begotten." On the Mortimers, whose powerful claim to the throne as descendants of Edward III's third son, Lionel, Duke of Clarence, had been recognized by Richard II, see note to 1 Henry IV, I.i.38. The Earl of Cambridge was himself the son of Edward III's fifth son, Edward, Duke of York.

159. in sufferance: though suffering punishment.
166. quit: absolve.   169. earnest: payment to bind a bargain.
175. tender: regard.   181. dear: grievous.   183. like: equally.
188. But: but that.   rub: obstacle (a bowling term).
191. straight in expedition: at once in action.

II.iii. Location: London. Before the Boar's Head Tavern in East-cheap.
1. bring: escort.
2. Staines: town west of London on the road to Southampton.
3. ern: mourn.

Bard. Would I were with him, wheresome'er he is, either in heaven or in hell!

Host. Nay sure, he's not in hell; he's in Arthur's bosom, if ever man went to Arthur's bosom. 'A 10 made a finer end, and went away and it had been any christom child. 'A parted ev'n just between twelve and one, ev'n at the turning o' th' tide; for after I saw him fumble with the sheets, and play with flowers, and smile upon his finger's end, I knew there was but 15 one way; for his nose was as sharp as a pen, and 'a [babbl'd] of green fields. "How now, Sir John?" quoth I, "what, man? be a' good cheer." So 'a cried out, "God, God, God!" three or four times. Now I, to comfort him, bid him 'a should not think of God; 20 I hop'd there was no need to trouble himself with any such thoughts yet. So 'a bade me lay more clothes on his feet. I put my hand into the bed and felt them, and they were as cold as any stone; then I felt to his knees, and so up'ard and up'ard, and all was as cold as any stone. 26

Nym. They say he cried out of sack.

Host. Ay, that 'a did.

Bard. And of women.

Host. Nay, that 'a did not. 30

Boy. Yes, that 'a did, and said they were dev'ls incarnate.

Host. 'A could never abide carnation—'twas a color he never lik'd. 34

Boy. 'A said once, the dev'l would have him about women.

Host. 'A did in some sort, indeed, handle women; but then he was rheumatic, and talk'd of the whore of Babylon. 39

Boy. Do you not remember, 'a saw a flea stick upon Bardolph's nose, and 'a said it was a black soul burning in hell?

Bard. Well, the fuel is gone that maintain'd that fire. That's all the riches I got in his service.

Nym. Shall we shog? the King will be gone from Southampton. 46

Pist. Come, let's away. My love, give me thy lips. Look to my chattels and my moveables. Let senses rule; the [word] is "Pitch and pay"; Trust none; 50 For oaths are straws, men's faiths are wafer-cakes, And Hold-fast is the only dog, my duck; Therefore *Caveto* be thy counsellor. Go, clear thy crystals. Yoke-fellows in arms, Let us to France, like horse-leeches, my boys, 55 To suck, to suck, the very blood to suck!

Boy. And that's but unwholesome food, they say.

Pist. Touch her soft mouth, and march.

Bard. Farewell, hostess. [*Kissing her.*]

Nym. I cannot kiss, that is the humor of it; but adieu. 61

Pist. Let huswifery appear. Keep close, I thee command.

Host. Farewell; adieu. *Exeunt.*

[SCENE IV]

Flourish. Enter the FRENCH KING, *the* DOLPHIN, *the* DUKES OF BERRI *and* BRITAIN, [*the* CONSTABLE, *and others*].

Fr. King. Thus comes the English with full power upon us,
And more than carefully it us concerns
To answer royally in our defenses.
Therefore the Dukes of Berri and of Britain,
Of Brabant and of Orleance, shall make forth, 5
And you, Prince Dolphin, with all swift dispatch,
To line and new repair our towns of war
With men of courage and with means defendant;
For England his approaches makes as fierce
As waters to the sucking of a gulf. 10
It fits us then to be as provident
As fear may teach us out of late examples
Left by the fatal and neglected English
Upon our fields.

Dol.   My most redoubted father,
It is most meet we arm us 'gainst the foe; 15
For peace itself should not so dull a kingdom
(Though war nor no known quarrel were in question)
But that defenses, musters, preparations,
Should be maintain'd, assembled, and collected,
As were a war in expectation. 20
Therefore, I say, 'tis meet we all go forth
To view the sick and feeble parts of France;
And let us do it with no show of fear,
No, with no more than if we heard that England
Were busied with a Whitsun morris-dance; 25
For, my good liege, she is so idly king'd,
Her sceptre so fantastically borne,
By a vain, giddy, shallow, humorous youth,
That fear attends her not.

Con.   O, peace, Prince Dolphin,
You are too much mistaken in this king. 30
Question your Grace the late embassadors,

9–10. **Arthur's bosom.** The Hostess confuses Arthur and Abraham. For Abraham's bosom (i.e. heaven) see Luke 16:22 ff.
12. **christom:** chrisom, i.e. newly christened.
14. **play with flowers:** i.e. pick at the bedclothes.
27. **of sack:** against sack, a Spanish wine of which Falstaff had been very fond.   37. **handle:** talk of.
38. **rheumatic:** blunder for *lunatic*, i.e. delirious (?); perhaps with a pun on *rheum-* and *Rome*, then pronounced similarly (see the following note).
38–39. **whore of Babylon:** common Protestant name for the Roman Catholic Church, regarded as the scarlet woman of Revelation 17:3–6.
49. **Let . . . pay:** i.e. be prudent; your motto (as hostess of a tavern) should be "cash down, no credit."   51. **wafer-cakes:** i.e. fragile.
52. **Hold-fast . . . dog.** Alluding to the proverb "Brag is a good dog, but Holdfast is a better."   53. **Caveto:** beware.
54. **clear thy crystals:** i.e. dry your eyes.

62. **Let . . . close:** i.e. be thrifty and do not run around.

II.iv **Location:** France. The King's palace.
1. **power:** forces.
3. **answer . . . defenses:** i.e. prepare adequate defenses.
4. **Britain:** Brittany.   5. **Orleance:** Orleans.
7. **line:** reinforce, garrison.   **towns of war:** i.e. fortified towns.
8. **means defendant:** i.e. weapons of defense.
9. **England:** the King of England.   10. **gulf:** whirlpool.
12. **late:** recent.
13. **fatal and neglected:** fatally underestimated. The King recalls French defeats at Crécy (1346) and Poitiers (1356) at the hands of Edward III and his son, Edward the Black Prince.   20. **As:** as if.
25. **Whitsun morris-dance:** folk dance celebrating Whitsuntide, a religious festival held in early summer.   26. **idly:** worthlessly.
28. **humorous:** capricious.

Henry V
II.iv

With what great state he heard their embassy,
How well supplied with noble counsellors,
How modest in exception, and withal
How terrible in constant resolution,   35
And you shall find his vanities forespent
Were but the outside of the Roman Brutus,
Covering discretion with a coat of folly,
As gardeners do with ordure hide those roots
That shall first spring and be most delicate.   40
  Dol. Well, 'tis not so, my Lord High Constable;
But though we think it so, it is no matter.
In cases of defense 'tis best to weigh
The enemy more mighty than he seems,
So the proportions of defense are fill'd;   45
Which, of a weak and niggardly projection,
Doth like a miser spoil his coat with scanting
A little cloth.
  Fr. King. Think we King Harry strong;
And, princes, look you strongly arm to meet him.
The kindred of him hath been flesh'd upon us;   50
And he is bred out of that bloody strain
That haunted us in our familiar paths.
Witness our too much memorable shame
When Cressy battle fatally was struck,
And all our princes captiv'd by the hand   55
Of that black name, Edward, Black Prince of Wales;
Whiles that his mountain sire, on mountain standing,
Up in the air, crown'd with the golden sun,
Saw his heroical seed, and smil'd to see him,
Mangle the work of nature, and deface   60
The patterns that by God and by French fathers
Had twenty years been made. This is a stem
Of that victorious stock; and let us fear
The native mightiness and fate of him.

       Enter a MESSENGER.

  Mess. Embassadors from Harry King of England
Do crave admittance to your Majesty.   66
  Fr. King. We'll give them present audience. Go,
    and bring them.
     [*Exeunt Messenger and certain Lords.*]
You see this chase is hotly followed, friends.
  Dol. Turn head, and stop pursuit; for coward dogs
Most spend their mouths when what they seem to
    threaten   70
Runs far before them. Good my sovereign,
Take up the English short, and let them know
Of what a monarchy you are the head.
Self-love, my liege, is not so vile a sin
As self-neglecting.

   Enter [LORDS *with*] EXETER [*and* TRAIN].

Fr. King.   From our brother of England?   75
  Exe. From him, and thus he greets your Majesty:
He wills you, in the name of God Almighty,
That you divest yourself, and lay apart
The borrowed glories that by gift of heaven,
By law of nature and of nations, 'longs   80
To him and to his heirs, namely, the crown,
And all wide-stretched honors that pertain
By custom, and the ordinance of times,
Unto the crown of France. That you may know
'Tis no sinister nor no awkward claim,   85
Pick'd from the worm-holes of long-vanish'd days,
Nor from the dust of old oblivion rak'd,
He sends you this most memorable line,
In every branch truly demonstrative;
            [*Giving a paper.*]
Willing you overlook this pedigree;   90
And when you find him evenly deriv'd
From his most fam'd of famous ancestors,
Edward the Third, he bids you then resign
Your crown and kingdom, indirectly held
From him, the native and true challenger.   95
  Fr. King. Or else what follows?
  Exe. Bloody constraint; for if you hide the crown
Even in your hearts, there will he rake for it.
Therefore in fierce tempest is he coming,
In thunder and in earthquake, like a Jove,   100
That if requiring fail he will compel;
And bids you, in the bowels of the Lord,
Deliver up the crown, and to take mercy
On the poor souls for whom this hungry war
Opens his vasty jaws; and on your head   105
Turning the widows' tears, the orphans' cries,
The dead men's blood, the privy maidens' groans,
For husbands, fathers, and betrothed lovers,
That shall be swallowed in this controversy.
This is his claim, his threat'ning, and my message;
Unless the Dolphin be in presence here,   111
To whom expressly I bring greeting too.
  Fr. King. For us, we will consider of this further.
To-morrow shall you bear our full intent
Back to our brother of England.
  Dol.   For the Dolphin,   115
I stand here for him. What to him from England?
  Exe. Scorn and defiance, slight regard, contempt,
And any thing that may not misbecome
The mighty sender, doth he prize you at.
Thus says my King: and if your father's Highness   120
Do not, in grant of all demands at large,
Sweeten the bitter mock you sent his Majesty,
He'll call you to so hot an answer of it
That caves and womby vaultages of France

---

34. **exception:** raising objections.
36. **vanities forespent:** former follies.
37. **Roman Brutus:** Lucius Junius Brutus, early Roman consul who pretended to be stupid (*brutus*) in order to disarm the suspicions of his uncle, the tyrannical King Tarquin.
45. **So . . . fill'd:** i.e. in order to provide a full defense.
46. **Which:** i.e. defense. **of:** i.e. if it be of. **projection:** scale.
50. **flesh'd upon us:** made fierce by feeding on our flesh.
54. **Cressy:** Crécy; see note to line 13. **struck:** fought.
57. **mountain sire:** imposing father.
64. **native:** hereditary. **fate:** i.e. fortunate lot.
69. **Turn head:** make a stand (a term from hunting). **stop:** put an end to. 70. **Most . . . mouths:** bay the loudest.

78. **lay apart:** set aside, renounce. 80. **'longs:** belongs.
83. **ordinance of times:** ancient law.
85. **sinister:** irregular, illegitimate. **awkward:** indirect.
88. **line:** genealogical table, pedigree. 89. **demonstrative:** decisive.
90. **Willing you overlook:** desiring that you examine.
91. **evenly deriv'd:** truly descended.
94. **indirectly:** unjustly, illegally. 95. **challenger:** claimant.
97. **constraint:** display of force. 101. **requiring:** requests.
102. **bowels:** i.e. compassion.
107. **privy maidens' groans:** maidens' secret laments.
119. **prize:** assess. 121. **grant:** concession.
124. **womby vaultages:** hollow caverns.

Shall chide your trespass and return your mock   125
In second accent of his ordinance.

   Dol. Say: if my father render fair return,
It is against my will; for I desire
Nothing but odds with England. To that end,
As matching to his youth and vanity,   130
I did present him with the Paris balls.

   Exe. He'll make your Paris Louvre shake for it,
Were it the mistress court of mighty Europe;
And, be assur'd, you'll find a difference,
As we his subjects have in wonder found,   135
Between the promise of his greener days
And these he masters now. Now he weighs time
Even to the utmost grain; that you shall read
In your own losses, if he stay in France.

   Fr. King. To-morrow shall you know our mind at
     full.   *Flourish.* 140

   Exe. Dispatch us with all speed, lest that our King
Come here himself to question our delay;
For he is footed in this land already.

   Fr. King. You shall be soon dispatch'd, with fair
     conditions.
A night is but small breath, and little pause,   145
To answer matters of this consequence.   *Exeunt.*

ACT [III]

Flourish. Enter CHORUS.

Thus with imagin'd wing our swift scene flies
In motion of no less celerity
Than that of thought. Suppose that you have seen
The well-appointed king at [Hampton] pier
Embark his royalty; and his brave fleet   5
With silken streamers the young Phoebus [fanning].
Play with your fancies: and in them behold
Upon the hempen tackle ship-boys climbing;
Hear the shrill whistle which doth order give
To sounds confus'd; behold the threaden sails,   10
Borne with th' invisible and creeping wind,
Draw the huge bottoms through the furrowed sea,
Breasting the lofty surge. O, do but think
You stand upon the rivage and behold
A city on th' inconstant billows dancing;   15
For so appears this fleet majestical,

Holding due course to Harflew. Follow, follow!
Grapple your minds to sternage of this navy,
And leave your England as dead midnight, still,
Guarded with grandsires, babies, and old women,   20
Either past or not arriv'd to pith and puissance;
For who is he, whose chin is but enrich'd
With one appearing hair, that will not follow
These cull'd and choice-drawn cavaliers to France?
Work, work your thoughts, and therein see a siege;
Behold the ordinance on their carriages,   26
With fatal mouths gaping on girded Harflew.
Suppose th' embassador from the French comes back,
Tells Harry that the King doth offer him
Katherine his daughter, and with her, to dowry,   30
Some petty and unprofitable dukedoms.
The offer likes not; and the nimble gunner
With linstock now the devilish cannon touches,
     Alarum, and chambers go off.
And down goes all before them. Still be kind,   34
And eche out our performance with your mind.   *Exit.*

[SCENE I]

Enter the KING, EXETER, BEDFORD, *and* GLOUCESTER.
   Alarum. [*Enter Soldiers with*] *scaling-ladders at Harflew.*

   K. Hen. Once more unto the breach, dear friends,
     once more;
Or close the wall up with our English dead.
In peace there's nothing so becomes a man
As modest stillness and humility;
But when the blast of war blows in our ears,   5
Then imitate the action of the tiger;
Stiffen the sinews, [conjure] up the blood,
Disguise fair nature with hard-favor'd rage;
Then lend the eye a terrible aspect;
Let it pry through the portage of the head   10
Like the brass cannon; let the brow o'erwhelm it
As fearfully as doth a galled rock
O'erhang and jutty his confounded base,
Swill'd with the wild and wasteful ocean.
Now set the teeth and stretch the nostril wide,   15
Hold hard the breath, and bend up every spirit
To his full height. On, on, you [noblest] English,
Whose blood is fet from fathers of war-proof!
Fathers that, like so many Alexanders,

---

126. **second accent:** echo. **ordinance:** ordnance, artillery.
127. **fair return:** conciliatory response.
129. **odds with England:** i.e. hostility for the English king.
130. **vanity:** frivolity.   131. **Paris balls:** tennis balls.
132. **Louvre:** palace of the French kings.
133. **mistress:** principal (a term from tennis), perhaps with pun on *lover*, the approximate pronunciation of *Louvre.*
136. **greener:** younger.
138. **grain:** the smallest unit of weight.
143. **footed:** landed. Actually, Henry's invasion of France (August 1415) followed Exeter's embassy by six months.
145. **small breath:** i.e. short time.

III.Cho.1. **imagin'd wing:** wing of imagination.
4. **well-appointed:** well-equipped. 5. **brave:** gallant.
6. **the young Phoebus fanning:** fluttering against the rising sun. Phoebus is the sun-god of Greek mythology.
7. **fancies:** imaginations. 9. **shrill whistle:** i.e. of the ship-master.
10. **threaden:** woven of thread. 12. **bottoms:** ships.
14. **rivage:** shore.
16. **fleet majestical.** Holinshed (Bullough, IV, 386) records "a thousand ships" in Henry's flotilla.

17. **Harflew:** Harfleur, French port near the mouth of the Seine. Actually, Henry put ashore at Caux, a nearby town.
18. **sternage:** the sterns. 21. **pith:** strength.
26. **ordinance:** ordnance. 27. **girded:** encircled, besieged.
30. **Katherine:** Katherine of Valois (1401–37), who married Henry V in 1420 and gave birth to the future Henry VI a year later. Following her husband's death (1422) she may have married Owen Tudor, to whom she bore Edmund Tudor (later Earl of Richmond), father of Henry VII. **to:** as. 32. **likes:** pleases.
33. **linstock:** stick to hold the gunner's match. **touches:** fires. s.d. **Alarum:** call to arms. **chambers:** small cannon. 35. **eche:** eke.

III.i. Location: France. Before Harfleur.
10. **portage:** portholes, i.e. eyes. 11. **o'erwhelm:** overhang.
12. **galled:** worn. 13. **jutty:** jut over. **confounded:** ruined.
14. **Swill'd:** washed. **wasteful:** destructive.
18. **fet:** derived. **of war-proof:** proved in battle.
19. **Alexanders.** Alexander the Great lamented that there were no more worlds for him to conquer.

Henry V
III.i

Have in these parts from morn till even fought,　20
And sheath'd their swords for lack of argument.
Dishonor not your mothers; now attest
That those whom you call'd fathers did beget you.
Be copy now to [men] of grosser blood,
And teach them how to war. And you, good yeomen,
Whose limbs were made in England, show us here　26
The mettle of your pasture; let us swear
That you are worth your breeding, which I doubt not;
For there is none of you so mean and base
That hath not noble lustre in your eyes.　30
I see you stand like greyhounds in the slips,
[Straining] upon the start. The game's afoot!
Follow your spirit; and upon this charge
Cry, "God for Harry, England, and Saint George!"
　　　　[*Exeunt.*]　*Alarum, and chambers go off.*

[SCENE II]

Enter NYM, BARDOLPH, PISTOL, *and* BOY.

Bard. On, on, on, on, on! To the breach, to the
breach!

Nym. Pray thee, corporal, stay. The knocks are
too hot; and for mine own part, I have not a case of
lives. The humor of it is too hot, that is the very
plain-song of it.　6

Pist. The plain-song is most just; for humors do
abound:
　"Knocks go and come; God's vassals drop and die;
　　And sword and shield,
　　　In bloody field,
　　Doth win immortal fame."　10

Boy. Would I were in an alehouse in London,
I would give all my fame for a pot of ale and safety.

Pist. And I:
　"If wishes would prevail with me,　15
　　My purpose should not fail with me,
　　　But thither would I hie."

Boy. "As duly, but not as truly,
　　As bird doth sing on bough."　19

Enter FLUELLEN.

Flu. Up to the breach, you dogs! Avaunt, you
cullions!　　　[*Driving them forward.*]

Pist. Be merciful, great duke, to men of mould.
Abate thy rage, abate thy manly rage,
Abate thy rage, great duke!　24
Good bawcock, bate thy rage; use lenity, sweet chuck!

Nym. These be good humors! your honor wins bad
humors.

　　Exit [*with Bardolph and Pistol; Fluellen steps aside*].

Boy. As young as I am, I have observ'd these three
swashers. I am boy to them all three, but all they three,
though they would serve me, could not be man to　30
me; for indeed three such antics do not amount to a
man. For Bardolph, he is white-liver'd and red-fac'd;
by the means whereof 'a faces it out, but fights not.
For Pistol, he hath a killing tongue and a quiet sword;
by the means whereof 'a breaks words, and keeps　35
whole weapons. For Nym, he hath heard that men of
few words are the best men, and therefore he scorns to
say his prayers, lest 'a should be thought a coward; but
his few bad words are match'd with as few good deeds;
for 'a never broke any man's head but his own,　40
and that was against a post when he was drunk. They
will steal any thing, and call it purchase. Bardolph stole
a lute-case, bore it twelve leagues, and sold it for three
half-pence. Nym and Bardolph are sworn brothers in
filching, and in Callice they stole a fire-shovel.　45
I knew by that piece of service the men would carry
coals. They would have me as familiar with men's
pockets as their gloves or their handkerchers; which
makes much against my manhood, if I should take from
another's pocket to put into mine; for it is plain　50
pocketing up of wrongs. I must leave them, and seek
some better service. Their villainy goes against my
weak stomach, and therefore I must cast it up.　*Exit.*

Enter GOWER. [*Fluellen comes forward.*]

Gow. Captain Fluellen, you must come presently to
the mines; the Duke of Gloucester would speak with
you.　56

Flu. To the mines? Tell you the Duke, it is not so
good to come to the mines; for look you, the mines is
not according to the disciplines of the war; the concavities of it is not sufficient. For look you, th'　60
athversary—you may discuss unto the Duke, look
you—is digt himself four yard under the counter-
mines. By Cheshu, I think 'a will plow up all, if there
is not better directions.　64

Gow. The Duke of Gloucester, to whom the order
of the siege is given, is altogether directed by an Irishman, a very valiant gentleman, i' faith.

Flu. It is Captain Macmorris, is it not?

Gow. I think it be.　69

Flu. By Cheshu, he is an ass, as in the world; I will
verify as much in his beard. He has no more directions
in the true disciplines of the wars, look you, of the
Roman disciplines, than is a puppy-dog.

29. **swashers:** swaggerers.　31. **antics:** buffoons.
32. **white-liver'd:** cowardly.
45. **Callice:** Calais, seaport in France.
46–47. **carry coals:** (1) tolerate affronts; (2) do dirty work.
49. **makes:** i.e. offends.
51. **pocketing . . . wrongs:** (1) submitting to insults; (2) receiving
stolen goods.　55. **mines:** excavations near a besieged fortress.
59. **disciplines . . . war:** military science, tactics.
59–60. **concavities:** i.e. slope, incline.
61. **discuss unto:** inform.　62. **digt:** digged.　63. **plow:** blow.
65–66. **The Duke . . . given.** Holinshed records (Bullough, IV, 387)
that at Harfleur "the duke of Glocecester, to whom the order of the
siege was committed, made three mines under the ground, and
approching to the wals with his engins and ordinance, would not suffer
them within to take anie rest."
71. **verify . . . beard:** tell him so to his face.
73. **Roman disciplines:** i.e. traditional tactics. Fluellen apparently
has small respect for such innovations as gunpowder.

21. **argument:** i.e. something to fight about, adversaries.
24. **copy:** example.　**grosser:** less noble.　27. **mettle:** quality.
31. **slips:** leash.　32. **upon the start:** i.e. to start.
34. **Saint George:** patron saint of England.

III.ii. Location: Scene continues.
4. **case:** set.
5–6. **very plain-song:** i.e. simple truth.　20. **Avaunt:** be off.
21. **cullions:** wretches (Italian *coglioni*, testicles).
22. **men of mould:** men of earth, i.e. mere mortals.
25. **bawcock:** fine fellow (French *beau coq*).

Enter MACMORRIS *and* CAPTAIN JAMY.

Gow. Here 'a comes, and the Scots captain, Captain Jamy, with him.   75

Flu. Captain Jamy is a marvellous falorous gentleman, that is certain, and of great expedition and knowledge in th' aunchiant wars, upon my particular knowledge of his directions. By Cheshu, he will   79
maintain his argument as well as any military man in the world, in the disciplines of the pristine wars of the Romans.

Jamy. I say gud day, Captain Fluellen.

Flu. God-den to your worship, good Captain James.   85

Gow. How now, Captain Macmorris, have you quit the mines? Have the pioners given o'er?

Mac. By Chrish law, 'tish ill done! The work ish give over, the trompet sound the retreat. By my   89
hand I swear, and my father's soul, the work ish ill done; it ish give over. I would have blowed up the town, so Chrish save me law, in an hour! O, 'tish ill done, 'tish ill done; by my hand 'tish ill done!   93

Flu. Captain Macmorris, I beseech you now, will you voutsafe me, look you, a few disputations with you, as partly touching or concerning the disciplines of the war, the Roman wars, in the way of argument, look you, and friendly communication; partly   98
to satisfy my opinion, and partly for the satisfaction, look you, of my mind: as touching the direction of the military discipline, that is the point.

Jamy. It sall be vary gud, gud feith, gud captens bath, and I sall quit you with gud leve, as I may pick occasion; that sall I, mary.   104

Mac. It is no time to discourse, so Chrish save me. The day is hot, and the weather, and the wars, and the King, and the Dukes; it is no time to discourse. The town is beseech'd, and the trumpet call us to the   108
breach, and we talk, and be Chrish, do nothing. 'Tis shame for us all. So God sa' me, 'tis shame to stand still, it is shame, by my hand; and there is throats to be cut, and works to be done, and there ish nothing done, so Christ sa' me law!   113

Jamy. By the mess, ere theise theise eyes of mine take themselves to slomber, ay'll de gud service, or I'll lig i' th' grund for it; ay, or go to death; and I'll pay't as valorously as I may, that sall I suerly do, that is the breff and the long. Mary, I wad full fain heard some question 'tween you tway.   119

Flu. Captain Macmorris, I think, look you, under your correction, there is not many of your nation—

Mac. Of my nation? What ish my nation? Ish a villain, and a basterd, and a knave, and a rascal. What ish my nation? Who talks of my nation?   124

Flu. Look you, if you take the matter otherwise than is meant, Captain Macmorris, peradventure I shall think you do not use me with that affability as in discretion you ought to use me, look you, being as   128
good a man as yourself, both in the disciplines of war, and in the derivation of my birth, and in other particularities.

Mac. I do not know you so good a man as myself. So Chrish save me, I will cut off your head.

Gow. Gentlemen both, you will mistake each other.   135

Jamy. A! that's a foul fault.   *A parley* [*sounded*].

Gow. The town sounds a parley.

Flu. Captain Macmorris, when there is more better opportunity to be required, look you, I will be so bold as to tell you I know the disciplines of war; and there is an end.   *Exeunt.* 141

[SCENE III]

[*Enter some* CITIZENS *on the walls.*] *Enter the* KING *and all his* TRAIN *before the gates.*

K. Hen. How yet resolves the governor of the town?
This is the latest parle we will admit;
Therefore to our best mercy give yourselves,
Or like to men proud of destruction,
Defy us to our worst; for as I am a soldier,   5
A name that in my thoughts becomes me best,
If I begin the batt'ry once again,
I will not leave the half-achieved Harflew
Till in her ashes she lies buried.
The gates of mercy shall be all shut up,   10
And the flesh'd soldier, rough and hard of heart,
In liberty of bloody hand, shall range,
With conscience wide as hell, mowing like grass
Your fresh fair virgins and your flow'ring infants.
What is it then to me, if impious War,   15
Arrayed in flames like to the prince of fiends,
Do with his smirch'd complexion all fell feats
Enlink'd to waste and desolation?
What is't to me, when you yourselves are cause,
If your pure maidens fall into the hand   20
Of hot and forcing violation?
What rein can hold licentious wickedness
When down the hill he holds his fierce career?
We may as bootless spend our vain command
Upon th' enraged soldiers in their spoil,   25
As send precepts to the leviathan
To come ashore. Therefore, you men of Harflew,
Take pity of your town and of your people,
Whiles yet my soldiers are in my command,
Whiles yet the cool and temperate wind of grace   30
O'erblows the filthy and contagious clouds
Of headly murther, spoil, and villainy.

77. **expedition.** Perhaps Fluellen confuses *experience* and *erudition*.
84. **God-den:** good e'en, i.e. afternoon.
87. **pioners given o'er:** sappers and miners stopped working.
88. **law:** la (an emphatic interjection).
89. **retreat:** signal to withdraw forces.   103. **quit:** requite, answer.
104. **mary:** marry, indeed (originally the name of the Virgin Mary used as an oath).   114. **mess:** Mass.   115. **lig:** lie.

136 s.d. **parley:** trumpet signal for negotiations.
139. **required:** found.

III.iii. Location: Before the gates of Harfleur.
2. **latest parle:** last discussion.
4. **proud of destruction:** glorying in their own destruction.
7. **batt'ry:** cannonade.
11. **flesh'd:** enraged. See note to II.iv.50.   12. **liberty:** license.
17. **fell:** cruel.   18. **waste:** destruction.
23. **career:** gallop (a term from horsemanship).
24. **bootless:** unprofitably.
26. **precepts:** written instructions.
31. **O'erblows:** blows away, disperses.   32. **headly:** deadly.

Henry V
III.iii

If not—why, in a moment look to see
The blind and bloody soldier with foul hand
[Defile] the locks of your shrill-shrieking daughters;
Your fathers taken by the silver beards,   36
And their most reverend heads dash'd to the walls;
Your naked infants spitted upon pikes,
Whiles the mad mothers with their howls confus'd
Do break the clouds, as did the wives of Jewry   40
At Herod's bloody-hunting slaughter-men.
What say you? Will you yield, and this avoid?
Or guilty in defense, be thus destroy'd?

Enter Governor [*to the Citizens*].

Gov. Our expectation hath this day an end.
The Dolphin, whom of succors we entreated,   45
Returns us that his powers are yet not ready
To raise so great a siege. Therefore, great King,
We yield our town and lives to thy soft mercy.
Enter our gates, dispose of us and ours,
For we no longer are defensible.   50
K. Hen. Open your gates. Come, uncle Exeter,
Go you and enter Harflew; there remain,
And fortify it strongly 'gainst the French.
Use mercy to them all for us, dear uncle.
The winter coming on, and sickness growing   55
Upon our soldiers, we will retire to Callice.
To-night in Harflew will we be your guest;
To-morrow for the march are we address'd.

Flourish, and enter the town.

[Scene IV]

Enter Katherine *and* [Alice,] *an old gentlewoman.*

Kath. Alice, tu as été en Angleterre, et tu bien
parles le langage.
Alice. Un peu, madame.
Kath. Je te prie, m'enseignez; il faut que j'ap-
prenne à parler. Comment appelez-vous la main en
Anglois?   6
Alice. La main? Elle est appelée de hand.
Kath. De hand. Et les doigts?
[*Alice.*] Les doigts? Ma foi, j'oublie les doigts,

mais je me souviendrai. Les doigts? Je pense qu'ils
sont appelés de fingres, oui, de fingres.   11
[*Kath.*] La main, de hand; les doigts, de fingres.
Je pense que je suis le bon écolier; j'ai gagné deux
mots d'Anglois vitement. Comment appelez-vous les
ongles?   15
Alice. Les ongles? [Nous] les appelons de nailès.
Kath. De nailès. Écoutez, dites-moi si je parle
bien: de hand, de fingres, et de nailès.
Alice. C'est bien dit, madame, il est fort bon
Anglois.   20
Kath. Dites-moi l'Anglois pour le bras.
Alice. De arma, madame.
Kath. Et le coude?
Alice. D' elbow.   24
Kath. D' elbow. Je m'en fais la répétition de tous
les mots que vous m'avez appris dès à présent.
Alice. Il est trop difficile, madame, comme je pense.
Kath. Excusez-moi, Alice; écoutez: d' hand, de
fingre, de nailès, d' arma, de bilbow.
Alice. D' elbow, madame.   30
Kath. O Seigneur Dieu, je m'en oublie d' elbow.
Comment appelez-vous le col?
Alice. De nick, madame.
Kath. De nick. Et le menton?
Alice. De chin.   35
Kath. De sin. Le col, de nick; le menton, de sin.
Alice. Oui. Sauf votre honneur, en vérité, vous
prononcez les mots aussi droit que les natifs d'Angle-
terre.   39
Kath. Je ne doute point d'apprendre, par la grâce
de Dieu, et en peu de temps.
Alice. N'avez vous déjà oublié ce que je vous ai
enseigné?
Kath. Non, je réciterai à vous promptement:
d' hand, de fingre, de mailès—   45
Alice. De nailès, madame.
Kath. De nailès, de arma, de ilbow.
Alice. Sauf votre honneur, d' elbow.
Kath. Ainsi dis-je; d' elbow, de nick, et de sin.
Comment appelez-vous le pied et la robe?   50
Alice. Le foot, madame, et le count.

---

34. **blind:** i.e. with lust.   35. **shriking:** shrieking.
40. **Jewry:** Judea.
41. **Herod's . . . slaughter-men.** See Matthew 2:16–18.
43. **defense:** i.e. not surrendering.
46. **Returns us:** replies.   50. **defensible:** capable of defense.
55–56. **The winter . . . Callice.** Following the fall of Harfleur, says
Holinshed (Bullough, IV, 389), King Henry "determined to have
proceeded further in the winning of other townes and fortresses: but
bicause the dead time of the winter approched, it was determined by
advice of his councell, that he should in all convenient speed set
forward, and march through the countrie towards Calis by land,
least his returne as then homewards shuld of slanderous toongs be
named a running awaie: and yet that journie was adjudged perillous,
by reason that the number of his people was much minished by the
flix and other fevers, which sore vexed and brought to death above
fifteene hundred persons of the armie."   58. **address'd:** prepared.

III.iv. Location: Rouen. The French King's palace.
1–62. *Kath.* Alice, you have been in England, and you know the
language well. *Alice.* A little, madam. *Kath.* I pray you, teach
me; I must learn to speak it. How do you say *la main* in English?
Alice. La main? It is called de hand. *Kath.* De hand. And *les doigts?*
Alice. Les doigts? Dear me, I forget *les doigts,* but it will come to me.
Les doigts. I think they are called de fingres, yes, de fingres. *Kath.
La main,* de hand; *les doigts,* de fingres. I think I am a good pupil;
I have learned two English words quickly. What do you call *les*

ongles? *Alice. Les ongles?* We call them de nailès. *Kath.* De nailès.
Listen, tell me whether I speak correctly: de hand, de fingres, and de
nailès. *Alice.* That is quite correct, madam; it is very good English.
Kath. Tell me the English for *le bras. Alice.* De arma, madam.
Kath. And *le coude? Alice.* D' elbow. *Kath.* D' elbow. I am going
to repeat all the words you have taught me so far. *Alice.* That is
too hard, madam, I'm afraid. *Kath.* Excuse me, Alice; listen:
d' hand, de fingre, de nailès, d' arma, de bilbow. *Alice.* D' elbow,
madam. *Kath.* O Lord, I'm forgetting d' elbow. How do you say
le col? Alice. De nick, madam. *Kath.* De nick. And *le menton?
Alice.* De chin. *Kath.* De sin. *Le col,* de nick; *le menton,* de sin.
Alice. Yes. If I may say so, truly, you pronounce the words as well
as the native English. *Kath.* I'm sure I can learn, by God's grace,
and very quickly. *Alice.* Haven't you already forgotten what I've
taught you? *Kath.* No, I shall recite for you at once: d' hand, de
fingre, de mailès— *Alice.* De nailès, madam. *Kath.* De nailès, de
arma, de ilbow. *Alice.* Pardon me, d' elbow. *Kath.* That's what I
said; d' elbow, de nick, and de sin. What do you call *le pied* and
la robe? Alice. Le foot, madam, and le count. *Kath.* Le foot and
le count! [She mistakes them for indecent French words.] O Lord,
those are bad words, wicked, coarse, and immodest, and not proper
for well-bred ladies to use. I wouldn't utter those words before French
gentlemen for all the world. Foh! le foot and le count! Nevertheless,
I shall recite my whole lesson once more: d' hand, de fingre, de nailès,
d' arma, d' elbow, de nick, de sin, de foot, le count. *Alice.* Excellent,
madam. *Kath.* That's enough for one time; let's go to dinner.

Kath. Le foot et le count! O Seigneur Dieu! ils sont les mots de son mauvais, corruptible, gros, et impudique, et non pour les dames de honneur d'user. 54 Je ne voudrais prononcer ces mots devant les seigneurs de France pour tout le monde. Foh! le foot et le count! Néanmoins, je réciterai une autre fois ma leçon ensemble: d' hand, de fingre, de nailès, d' arma, d' elbow, de nick, de sin, de foot, le count.

Alice. Excellent, madame! 60

Kath. C'est assez pour une fois: allons-nous à dîner.   *Exeunt.*

[SCENE V]

Enter the KING OF FRANCE, *the* DOLPHIN, [*the* DUKE OF BRITAIN,] *the* CONSTABLE OF FRANCE, *and others.*

Fr. King. 'Tis certain he hath pass'd the river
    Somme.
Con. And if he be not fought withal, my lord,
Let us not live in France; let us quit all,
And give our vineyards to a barbarous people.
Dol. O *Dieu vivant!* shall a few sprays of us, 5
The emptying of our fathers' luxury,
Our scions, put in wild and savage stock,
Spirt up so suddenly into the clouds
And overlook their grafters?
Brit. Normans, but bastard Normans, Norman
    bastards! 10
Mort [*Dieu,*] *ma vie!* if they march along
Unfought withal, but I will sell my dukedom,
To buy a slobb'ry and a dirty farm
In that nook-shotten isle of Albion. 14
Con. *Dieu de batailles!* where have they this mettle?
Is not their climate foggy, raw, and dull,
On whom, as in despite, the sun looks pale,
Killing their fruit with frowns? Can sodden water,
A drench for sur-rein'd jades, their barley-broth,
Decoct their cold blood to such valiant heat? 20
And shall our quick blood, spirited with wine,
Seem frosty? O, for honor of our land,
Let us not hang like roping icicles
Upon our houses' thatch, whiles a more frosty people
Sweat drops of gallant youth in our rich fields! 25
Poor we call them in their native lords!
Dol. By faith and honor,
Our madams mock at us, and plainly say
Our mettle is bred out, and they will give
Their bodies to the lust of English youth 30
To new-store France with bastard warriors.
Brit. They bid us to the English dancing-schools,

And teach lavoltas high and swift corantos,
Saying our grace is only in our heels,
And that we are most lofty runaways. 35
Fr. King. Where is Montjoy the herald? Speed
    him hence,
Let him greet England with our sharp defiance.
Up, princes, and, with spirit of honor edged
More sharper than your swords, hie to the field!
Charles Delabreth, High Constable of France, 40
You Dukes of Orleance, Bourbon, and of Berri,
Alanson, Brabant, Bar, and Burgundy,
Jacques Chatillion, Rambures, Vaudemont,
Beaumont, Grandpré, Roussi, and Faulconbridge,
[Foix], Lestrake, Bouciqualt, and Charolois; 45
High dukes, great princes, barons, lords, and [knights],
For your great seats now quit you of great shames.
Bar Harry England, that sweeps through our land
With pennons painted in the blood of Harflew.
Rush on his host, as doth the melted snow 50
Upon the valleys whose low vassal seat
The Alps doth spit and void his rheum upon.
Go down upon him, you have power enough,
And in a captive chariot into Roan
Bring him our prisoner.
Con.   This becomes the great. 55
Sorry am I his numbers are so few,
His soldiers sick and famish'd in their march;
For I am sure, when he shall see our army,
He'll drop his heart into the sink of fear,
And for achievement offer us his ransom. 60
Fr. King. Therefore, Lord Constable, haste on
    Montjoy,
And let him say to England that we send
To know what willing ransom he will give.
Prince Dolphin, you shall stay with us in Roan.
Dol. Not so, I do beseech your Majesty. 65
Fr. King. Be patient, for you shall remain with us.
Now forth, Lord Constable and princes all,
And quickly bring us word of England's fall. *Exeunt.*

[SCENE VI]

Enter Captains, English and Welsh, GOWER *and* FLU-
ELLEN.

Gow. How now, Captain Fluellen, come you from
the bridge?
Flu. I assure you, there is very excellent services
committed at the bridge.
Gow. Is the Duke of Exeter safe? 5

III.v. Location. Rouen. The French King's palace.
1. he . . . Somme: i.e. in retreating to winter quarters at Calais.
2. withal: with.
5. Dieu vivant: living God.   sprays: bastards.
6. fathers' luxury: ancestors' lust.
7. scions: slips for grafting.   put in: grafted upon.
8. Spirt: shoot. 9. overlook: overtop.
11. Mort . . . vie: death of God! my life. 13. slobb'ry: slovenly.
14. nook-shotten: full of nooks, indented.   Albion: England.
15. Dieu de batailles: god of battles.
18. sodden water: boiled water, i.e. ale.
19. drench . . . jades: drink for overworked horses.
20. Decoct: warm.   21. quick: lively.
23. roping: i.e. hanging in rope-like lengths. 32. bid us: bid us go.

33. lavoltas, corantos: kinds of dances.
35. lofty runaways: stylish cowards.
36. Montjoy: title of the chief French herald.
47. seats: fiefs, estates (which were held under the king).   quit you:
redeem yourselves.   51. vassal: base.   52. rheum: i.e. waters.
54. Roan: Rouen, capital city of Normandy.
59. sink: cesspool.   60. for achievement: in place of victory.

III.vi. Location: The English camp in Picardy.
2. bridge. Trying to secure a vital bridge on the road to Calais,
Henry's advance forces found French troops on the point of demolish-
ing it, whereupon, says Holinshed (Bullough, IV, 390), they "assailed
them so vigorouslie, that they discomfited them, and tooke and slue
them; and so the bridge was preserved till the king came, and passed
the river by the same with his whole armie."

Henry V
III.vi

Flu. The Duke of Exeter is as magnanimous as Agamemnon, and a man that I love and honor with my soul, and my heart, and my duty, and my live, and my living, and my uttermost power. He is not—God be praised and blessed!—any hurt in the world, but 10 keeps the bridge most valiantly, with excellent discipline. There is an aunchient lieutenant there at the pridge, I think in my very conscience he is as valiant a man as Mark Antony, and he is a man of no estimation in the world, but I did see him do as gallant service. 16

Gow. What do you call him?

Flu. He is call'd Aunchient Pistol.

Gow. I know him not.

Enter PISTOL.

Flu. Here is the man. 20

Pist. Captain, I thee beseech to do me favors. The Duke of Exeter doth love thee well.

Flu. Ay, I praise God, and I have merited some love at his hands. 24

Pist. Bardolph, a soldier firm and sound of heart,
And of buxom valor, hath by cruel fate,
And giddy Fortune's furious fickle wheel,
That goddess blind,
That stands upon the rolling restless stone— 29

Flu. By your patience, Aunchient Pistol: Fortune is painted blind, with a muffler afore his eyes, to signify to you that Fortune is blind; and she is painted also with a wheel, to signify to you, which is the moral of it, that she is turning, and inconstant, and mutability, and variation; and her foot, look you, is fixed upon 35 a spherical stone, which rolls, and rolls, and rolls. In good truth, the poet makes a most excellent description of it. Fortune is an excellent moral.

Pist. Fortune is Bardolph's foe, and frowns on him;
For he hath stol'n a pax, and hanged must 'a be— 40
A damned death!
Let gallows gape for dog, let man go free,
And let not hemp his windpipe suffocate.
But Exeter hath given the doom of death
For pax of little price. 45
Therefore go speak, the Duke will hear thy voice;
And let not Bardolph's vital thread be cut
With edge of penny cord and vile reproach.
Speak, captain, for his life, and I will thee requite.

Flu. Aunchient Pistol, I do partly understand your meaning. 51

Pist. Why then rejoice therefore.

Flu. Certainly, aunchient, it is not a thing to rejoice at; for if, look you, he were my brother, I would desire the Duke to use his good pleasure, and put him to execution; for discipline ought to be used. 56

Pist. Die and be damn'd! and *figo* for thy friendship!

Flu. It is well.

Pist. The fig of Spain. *Exit.*

Flu. Very good. 60

Gow. Why, this is an arrant counterfeit rascal, I remember him now; a bawd, a cutpurse.

Flu. I'll assure you, 'a utt'red as prave words at the pridge as you shall see in a summer's day. But it is very well; what he has spoke to me, that is well, I warrant you, when time is serve. 66

Gow. Why, 'tis a gull, a fool, a rogue, that now and then goes to the wars, to grace himself at his return into London under the form of a soldier. And such fellows are perfit in the great commanders' 70 names, and they will learn you by rote where services were done—at such and such a sconce, at such a breach, at such a convoy; who came off bravely, who was shot, who disgrac'd, what terms the enemy stood on; and this they con perfitly in the phrase of war, 75 which they trick up with new-tun'd oaths; and what a beard of the general's cut and a horrid suit of the camp will do among foaming bottles and ale-wash'd wits, is wonderful to be thought on. But you must learn to know such slanders of the age, or else you may be marvellously mistook. 81

Flu. I tell you what, Captain Gower: I do perceive he is not the man that he would gladly make show to the world he is. If I find a hole in his coat, I will tell him my mind. [*Drum heard.*] Hark you, the King is coming, and I must speak with him from the pridge. 86

Drum and Colors. Enter the KING *and his poor Soldiers [and* GLOUCESTER].

God pless your Majesty!

K. Hen. How now, Fluellen, cam'st thou from the bridge?

Flu. Ay, so please your Majesty. The Duke of Exeter has very gallantly maintain'd the pridge. 91 The French is gone off, look you, and there is gallant and most prave passages. Marry, th' athversary was have possession of the pridge, but he is enforced to retire, and the Duke of Exeter is master of the pridge. I can tell your Majesty, the Duke is a prave man. 96

K. Hen. What men have you lost, Fluellen?

Flu. The perdition of th' athversary hath been very great, reasonable great. Marry, for my part, I think the Duke hath lost never a man, but one that is like to be executed for robbing a church, one Bardolph, if 101 your Majesty know the man. His face is all bubukles, and whelks, and knobs, and flames a' fire, and his lips blows at his nose, and it is like a coal of fire, sometimes plue and sometimes red, but his nose is executed, and

---

7. **Agamemnon:** Grecian leader in the Trojan war.
12. **aunchient lieutenant:** sub-lieutenant (?). *Ancient* = ensign, standard-bearer.   14. **Mark Antony:** famous Roman general.
14–15. **estimation:** fame.   26. **buxom:** brisk.
33. **moral:** significance.   38. **moral:** symbolic figure, emblem.
40. **pax:** piece of metal with a crucifix stamped on it. Perhaps a mistake for the *pyx* (a box containing the sacramental wafer) that Holinshed reports (Bullough, IV, 389) was stolen by an English soldier who was duly "strangled" for the crime. On landing in France, says Holinshed (Bullough, IV, 386–87), Henry had forbidden "on paine of deathe" any soldier's stealing from churches, molesting priests or other unarmed persons, and brawling.

57. **figo:** contemptuous gesture made by thrusting the thumb between the next two fingers, or between the teeth.
59. **fig of Spain.** Presumably an even greater insult than the *figo* of line 57.   67. **gull:** simpleton.   70. **perfit:** perfect.
72. **sconce:** part of a fortification.   75. **con:** memorize.
77. **horrid . . . camp:** terrifying soldier's garb.
80. **slanders . . . age:** i.e. those who are a scandal of the time.
84. **a hole . . . coat:** i.e. grounds for exposing him.
86 s.d. **Drum and Colors:** drummer and flagbearer.
98. **perdition:** losses.   102. **bubukles:** carbuncles.
103. **whelks:** pimples.
105. **executed:** i.e. slit preparatory to his death on the gallows.

his fire's out.   106

K. Hen. We would have all such offenders so cut off; and we give express charge that in our marches through the country there be nothing compell'd from the villages; nothing taken but paid for; none of the French upbraided or abus'd in disdainful language; 111 for when [lenity] and cruelty play for a kingdom, the gentler gamester is the soonest winner.

Tucket. Enter MONTJOY.

Mont. You know me by my habit.

K. Hen. Well then, I know thee. What shall I know of thee?   115

Mont. My master's mind.

K. Hen. Unfold it.

Mont. Thus says my King: Say thou to Harry of England, Though we seem'd dead, we did but sleep; advantage is a better soldier than rashness. Tell him we could have rebuk'd him at Harflew, but that we 121 thought not good to bruise an injury till it were full ripe. Now we speak upon our cue, and our voice is imperial: England shall repent his folly, see his weakness, and admire our sufferance. Bid him therefore consider of his ransom, which must proportion the 126 losses we have borne, the subjects we have lost, the disgrace we have digested; which in weight to reanswer, his pettiness would bow under. For our losses, his exchequer is too poor; for th' effusion of our blood, the muster of his kingdom too faint a number; and 131 for our disgrace, his own person kneeling at our feet but a weak and worthless satisfaction. To this add defiance; and tell him, for conclusion, he hath betray'd his followers, whose condemnation is pronounc'd. So far my King and master; so much my office. 136

K. Hen. What is thy name? I know thy quality.

Mont. Montjoy.

K. Hen. Thou dost thy office fairly. Turn thee back,
And tell thy King I do not seek him now,   140
But could be willing to march on to Callice
Without impeachment; for to say the sooth,
Though 'tis no wisdom to confess so much
Unto an enemy of craft and vantage,
My people are with sickness much enfeebled,   145
My numbers lessen'd; and those few I have
Almost no better than so many French;
Who when they were in health, I tell thee, herald,
I thought upon one pair of English legs   149
Did march three Frenchmen. Yet forgive me, God,
That I do brag thus! This your air of France
Hath blown that vice in me. I must repent.
Go therefore tell thy master here I am;

My ransom is this frail and worthless trunk;
My army but a weak and sickly guard;   155
Yet, God before, tell him we will come on,
Though France himself and such another neighbor
Stand in our way. There's for thy labor, Montjoy.
Go bid thy master well advise himself.
If we may pass, we will; if we be hind'red,   160
We shall your tawny ground with your red blood
Discolor; and so, Montjoy, fare you well.
The sum of all our answer is but this:
We would not seek a battle as we are,
Nor, as we are, we say we will not shun it.   165
So tell your master.

Mont. I shall deliver so. Thanks to your Highness.
       [*Exit.*]

Glou. I hope they will not come upon us now.

K. Hen. We are in God's hand, brother, not in theirs.
March to the bridge, it now draws toward night;   170
Beyond the river we'll encamp ourselves,
And on to-morrow bid them march away.   *Exeunt.*

[SCENE VII]

Enter the CONSTABLE OF FRANCE, *the* LORD RAMBURES, ORLEANCE, DOLPHIN, *with others.*

Con. Tut, I have the best armor of the world. Would it were day!

Orl. You have an excellent armor; but let my horse have his due.

Con. It is the best horse of Europe.   5

Orl. Will it never be morning?

Dol. My Lord of Orleance, and my Lord High Constable, you talk of horse and armor?

Orl. You are as well provided of both as any prince in the world.   10

Dol. What a long night is this! I will not change my horse with any that treads but on four [pasterns]. *Ça*, ha! he bounds from the earth, as if his entrails were hairs; *le cheval volant*, the Pegasus, *chez les narines de feu!* When I bestride him, I soar, I am a hawk; he 15 trots the air; the earth sings when he touches it; the basest horn of his hoof is more musical than the pipe of Hermes.

Orl. He's of the color of the nutmeg.   19

---

154. **trunk:** i.e. his own body. 156. **God before:** i.e. God leading us.
159–65. **Go . . . it.** "Mine intent is to doo as it pleaseth God," Holinshed reports Henry as replying to Montjoy (Bullough, IV, 390); "I will not seeke your maister at this time; but if he or his seeke me, I will meet with them God willing. If anie of your nation attempt once to stop me in my journie now towards Calis, at their jeopardie be it: and yet wish I not anie of you so unadvised, as to be the occasion that I die your tawnie ground with your red bloud."
159. **well advise himself:** take careful thought.
172. **bid . . . away:** i.e. order the army to proceed toward Calais.

III.vii. Location: The French camp near Agincourt.
12. **pasterns:** hoofs.
13–14. **as . . . hairs:** i.e. like a tennis ball (which was stuffed with hair). 13. **Ça:** that one.
14. **le cheval volant:** the flying horse. **Pegasus:** in Greek mythology, the winged horse ridden by Perseus.
14–15. **chez . . . feu:** with fiery nostrils.
17. **basest horn:** (1) lowest part of the hoof; (2) noise made by the hoofs striking the earth.
18. **Hermes:** in Greek mythology, the messenger of the gods. Ovid tells how with the music of his pipe he lulled to sleep Argus, a monster with a hundred eyes.

---

106. **his:** its. 113 s.d. **Tucket:** trumpet call.
114. **habit:** i.e. herald's costume. 120. **advantage:** circumspection.
122. **bruise an injury:** squeeze a pimple.
123. **upon our cue:** i.e. at the appropriate time.
125. **admire our sufferance:** be astonished at our patience.
126. **proportion:** be proportionate to. 128. **digested:** endured.
128–29. **which . . . under:** i.e. for which he is too puny to make adequate restitution.
131. **muster:** total population. **faint:** small.
137. **quality:** status and calling. 139. **fairly:** admirably.
142. **impeachment:** impediment.
144. **vantage:** i.e. superior resources.
152. **blown:** brought to bloom.

Henry V
III.vii

Dol. And of the heat of the ginger. It is a beast for Perseus. He is pure air and fire; and the dull elements of earth and water never appear in him, but only in patient stillness while his rider mounts him. He is indeed a horse, and all other jades you may call beasts.

Con. Indeed, my lord, it is a most absolute and excellent horse. 26

Dol. It is the prince of palfreys: his neigh is like the bidding of a monarch, and his countenance enforces homage.

Orl. No more, cousin. 30

Dol. Nay, the man hath no wit that cannot, from the rising of the lark to the lodging of the lamb, vary deserv'd praise on my palfrey. It is a theme as fluent as the sea; turn the sands into eloquent tongues, and my horse is argument for them all. 'Tis a subject for a 35 sovereign to reason on, and for a sovereign's sovereign to ride on; and for the world, familiar to us and unknown, to lay apart their particular functions and wonder at him. I once writ a sonnet in his praise and began thus: "Wonder of nature"— 40

Orl. I have heard a sonnet begin so to one's mistress.

Dol. Then did they imitate that which I compos'd to my courser, for my horse is my mistress.

Orl. Your mistress bears well. 45

Dol. Me well, which is the prescript praise and perfection of a good and particular mistress.

Con. Nay, for methought yesterday your mistress shrewdly shook your back.

Dol. So perhaps did yours. 50

Con. Mine was not bridled.

Dol. O then belike she was old and gentle, and you rode like a kern of Ireland, your French hose off, and in your strait strossers.

Con. You have good judgment in horsemanship. 55

Dol. Be warn'd by me then: they that ride so, and ride not warily, fall into foul bogs. I had rather have my horse to my mistress.

Con. I had as live have my mistress a jade.

Dol. I tell thee, Constable, my mistress wears his own hair. 61

Con. I could make as true a boast as that, if I had a sow to my mistress.

Dol. "Le chien est retourné à son propre vomissement, et la [truie] lavée au bourbier." Thou mak'st use of any thing. 66

Con. Yet do I not use my horse for my mistress, or any such proverb so little kin to the purpose.

Ram. My Lord Constable, the armor that I saw in your tent to-night, are those stars or suns upon it? 70

Con. Stars, my lord.

Dol. Some of them will fall to-morrow, I hope.

Con. And yet my sky shall not want.

Dol. That may be, for you bear a many superfluously, and 'twere more honor some were away. 75

Con. Ev'n as your horse bears your praises, who would trot as well, were some of your brags dismounted.

Dol. Would I were able to load him with his desert! Will it never be day? I will trot to-morrow a mile, and my way shall be pav'd with English faces. 81

Con. I will not say so, for fear I should be fac'd out of my way. But I would it were morning, for I would fain be about the ears of the English.

Ram. Who will go to hazard with me for twenty prisoners? 86

Con. You must first go yourself to hazard, ere you have them.

Dol. 'Tis midnight, I'll go arm myself. *Exit.*

Orl. The Dolphin longs for morning. 90

Ram. He longs to eat the English.

Con. I think he will eat all he kills.

Orl. By the white hand of my lady, he's a gallant prince.

Con. Swear by her foot, that she may tread out the oath. 96

Orl. He is simply the most active gentleman of France.

Con. Doing is activity, and he will still be doing.

Orl. He never did harm, that I heard of. 100

Con. Nor will do none to-morrow. He will keep that good name still.

Orl. I know him to be valiant.

Con. I was told that by one that knows him better than you. 105

Orl. What's he?

Con. Marry, he told me so himself, and he said he car'd not who knew it.

Orl. He needs not, it is no hidden virtue in him. 109

Con. By my faith, sir, but it is; never anybody saw it but his lackey. 'Tis a hooded valor, and when it appears, it will bate.

Orl. "Ill will never said well."

Con. I will cap that proverb with "There is flattery in friendship." 115

Orl. And I will take up that with "Give the devil his due."

Con. Well plac'd. There stands your friend for the devil; have at the very eye of that proverb with "A pox of the devil." 120

Orl. You are the better at proverbs, by how much "A fool's bolt is soon shot."

Con. You have shot over.

Orl. 'Tis not the first time you were overshot.

---

24. **jades:** nags.
25. **absolute:** perfect. 27. **palfreys:** saddle horses.
32. **lodging:** lying down. 35. **argument:** subject.
36. **reason:** discourse.
38. **lay apart:** i.e. combine. **particular:** separate.
46. **prescript:** prescribed.
47. **particular:** belonging to only one. 49. **shrewdly:** painfully.
53. **kern:** light-armed Irish soldier. **French hose:** wide breeches.
54. **strait strossers:** tight trousers. 58. **to:** as.
59. **live:** lief. **jade:** (1) nag; (2) loose woman.
64–65. **Le chien . . . bourbier:** "The dog is turned to his own vomit again; and the sow that was washed, to his wallowing in the mire" (2 Peter 2:22).

73. **sky:** i.e. honor. **want:** lack (stars, i.e. honors).
82–83. **fac'd . . . way:** turned aside. 84. **fain:** gladly.
85. **go to hazard:** wager. The French were so certain of success on the eve of Agincourt, says Holinshed (Bullough, IV, 394), that they "made great triumph, for the capteins had determined before, how to divide the spoile, and the soldiers the night before had plaid [i.e. played for] the Englishman at dice." 99. **still:** always.
110–11. **never . . . lackey:** i.e. he is brave only in beating his servant.
111. **hooded.** A hawk was masked or hooded until the prey was sighted. 112. **bate:** (1) flap the wings; (2) be downcast.
123. **shot over:** i.e. missed the mark.
124. **overshot:** i.e. defeated.

Enter a MESSENGER.

Mess. My Lord High Constable, the English lie within fifteen hundred paces of your tents.　126

Con. Who hath measur'd the ground?

Mess. The Lord Grandpré.

Con. A valiant and most expert gentleman. Would it were day! Alas, poor Harry of England! he longs not for the dawning as we do.　131

Orl. What a wretched and peevish fellow is this King of England, to mope with his fat-brain'd followers so far out of his knowledge!

Con. If the English had any apprehension, they would run away.　136

Orl. That they lack; for if their heads had any intellectual armor, they could never wear such heavy head-pieces.

Ram. That island of England breeds very valiant creatures; their mastiffs are of unmatchable courage.　142

Orl. Foolish curs, that run winking into the mouth of a Russian bear and have their heads crush'd like rotten apples! You may as well say, that's a valiant flea that dare eat his breakfast on the lip of a lion.　146

Con. Just, just; and the men do sympathize with the mastiffs in robustious and rough coming on, leaving their wits with their wives; and then give them great meals of beef and iron and steel, they will eat like wolves and fight like devils.　151

Orl. Ay, but these English are shrowdly out of beef.

Con. Then shall we find to-morrow they have only stomachs to eat and none to fight. Now is it time to arm. Come, shall we about it?　155

Orl. It is now two a' clock; but let me see, by ten We shall have each a hundred Englishmen.　*Exeunt.*

ACT [IV]

[*Enter*] CHORUS.

Now entertain conjecture of a time
When creeping murmur and the poring dark
Fills the wide vessel of the universe.
From camp to camp, through the foul womb of night,
The hum of either army stilly sounds,　5
That the fix'd sentinels almost receive
The secret whispers of each other's watch.
Fire answers fire, and through their paly flames
Each battle sees the other's umber'd face.
Steed threatens steed, in high and boastful neighs　10
Piercing the night's dull ear; and from the tents
The armorers, accomplishing the knights,

With busy hammers closing rivets up,
Give dreadful note of preparation.
The country cocks do crow, the clocks do toll,　15
And the third hour of drowsy morning [name].
Proud of their numbers and secure in soul,
The confident and overlusty French
Do the low-rated English play at dice;
And chide the cripple tardy-gaited night,　20
Who like a foul and ugly witch doth limp
So tediously away. The poor condemned English,
Like sacrifices, by their watchful fires
Sit patiently and inly ruminate
The morning's danger; and their gesture sad,　25
Investing lank-lean cheeks and war-worn coats,
Presented them unto the gazing moon
So many horrid ghosts. O now, who will behold
The royal captain of this ruin'd band
Walking from watch to watch, from tent to tent,　30
Let him cry, "Praise and glory on his head!"
For forth he goes, and visits all his host,
Bids them good morrow with a modest smile,
And calls them brothers, friends, and countrymen.
Upon his royal face there is no note　35
How dread an army hath enrounded him;
Nor doth he dedicate one jot of color
Unto the weary and all-watched night;
But freshly looks, and overbears attaint
With cheerful semblance and sweet majesty;　40
That every wretch, pining and pale before,
Beholding him, plucks comfort from his looks.
A largess universal, like the sun,
His liberal eye doth give to every one,
Thawing cold fear, that mean and gentle all　45
Behold, as may unworthiness define,
A little touch of Harry in the night.
And so our scene must to the battle fly;
Where—O for pity!—we shall much disgrace
With four or five most vile and ragged foils　50
(Right ill dispos'd, in brawl ridiculous)
The name of Agincourt. Yet sit and see,
Minding true things by what their mock'ries be.
　　　　　　　　　　　　　　　　　Exit.

[SCENE I]

Enter the KING, BEDFORD, *and* GLOUCESTER.

K. Hen. Gloucester, 'tis true that we are in great
　　danger,
The greater therefore should our courage be.
Good morrow, brother Bedford. God Almighty!
There is some soul of goodness in things evil,
Would men observingly distill it out;　5

Henry V
IV.i

For our bad neighbor makes us early stirrers,
Which is both healthful and good husbandry.
Besides, they are our outward consciences
And preachers to us all, admonishing
That we should dress us fairly for our end.　10
Thus may we gather honey from the weed,
And make a moral of the devil himself.

Enter ERPINGHAM.

Good morrow, old Sir Thomas Erpingham.
A good soft pillow for that good white head
Were better than a churlish turf of France.　15
　　Erp. Not so, my liege, this lodging likes me better,
Since I may say, "Now lie I like a king."
　　K. Hen. 'Tis good for men to love their present
　　　　pains
Upon example; so the spirit is eased;
And when the mind is quick'ned, out of doubt,　20
The organs, though defunct and dead before,
Break up their drowsy grave, and newly move
With casted slough and fresh legerity.
Lend me thy cloak, Sir Thomas. Brothers both,
Commend me to the princes in our camp;　25
Do my good morrow to them, and anon
Desire them all to my pavilion.
　　Glou. We shall, my liege.
　　Erp. Shall I attend your Grace?
　　K. Hen. 　　　　　　　　　No, my good knight;
Go with my brothers to my lords of England.　30
I and my bosom must debate a while,
And then I would no other company.
　　Erp. The Lord in heaven bless thee, noble Harry!
　　　　　　　　　Exeunt [*all but the King*].
　　K. Hen. God-a-mercy, old heart, thou speak'st
　　　　cheerfully.

Enter PISTOL.

　　Pist. *Qui vous là?*　35
　　K. Hen. A friend.
　　Pist. Discuss unto me, art thou officer,
Or art thou base, common, and popular?
　　K. Hen. I am a gentleman of a company.
　　Pist. Trail'st thou the puissant pike?　40
　　K. Hen. Even so. What are you?
　　Pist. As good a gentleman as the Emperor.
　　K. Hen. Then you are a better than the King.
　　Pist. The King's a bawcock, and a heart of gold,
A lad of life, an imp of fame,　45
Of parents good, of fist most valiant.
I kiss his dirty shoe, and from heart-string

I love the lovely bully. What is thy name?
　　K. Hen. Harry le Roy.
　　Pist. Le Roy? a Cornish name. Art thou of Cornish
　　　crew?　50
　　K. Hen. No, I am a Welshman.
　　Pist. Know'st thou Fluellen?
　　K. Hen. Yes.
　　Pist. Tell him I'll knock his leek about his pate
Upon Saint Davy's day.　55
　　K. Hen. Do not you wear your dagger in your cap
that day, lest he knock that about yours.
　　Pist. Art thou his friend?
　　K. Hen. And his kinsman too.
　　Pist. The *figo* for thee then!　60
　　K. Hen. I thank you. God be with you!
　　Pist. My name is Pistol call'd.　　　　　*Exit.*
　　K. Hen. It sorts well with your fierceness.
　　　　　　　　　Manet King [*to one side*].

Enter FLUELLEN *and* GOWER.

　　Gow. Captain Fluellen!　64
　　Flu. So! in the name of Jesu Christ, speak fewer.
It is the greatest admiration in the universal world,
when the true and aunchient prerogatifes and laws of
the wars is not kept. If you would take the pains but
to examine the wars of Pompey the Great, you shall
find, I warrant you, that there is no tiddle taddle　70
nor pibble babble in Pompey's camp. I warrant you,
you shall find the ceremonies of the wars, and the cares
of it, and the forms of it, and the sobriety of it, and the
modesty of it, to be otherwise.
　　Gow. Why, the enemy is loud, you hear him all
night.　76
　　Flu. If the enemy is an ass and a fool, and a prating
coxcomb, is it meet, think you, that we should also,
look you, be an ass and a fool, and a prating coxcomb,
in your own conscience now?　80
　　Gow. I will speak lower.
　　Flu. I pray you, and beseech you, that you will.
　　　　　　　　　　Exit [*with Gower*].
　　K. Hen. Though it appear a little out of fashion,
There is much care and valor in this Welshman.　84

Enter three soldiers, JOHN BATES, ALEXANDER COURT,
and MICHAEL WILLIAMS.

　　Court. Brother John Bates, is not that the morning
which breaks yonder?
　　Bates. I think it be; but we have no great cause to
desire the approach of day.
　　Will. We see yonder the beginning of the day, but
I think we shall never see the end of it. Who goes
there?　91
　　K. Hen. A friend.
　　Will. Under what captain serve you?
　　K. Hen. Under Sir [Thomas] Erpingham.
　　Will. A good old commander and a most kind gen-

---

7. **good husbandry:** i.e. thrifty.
10. **dress us fairly:** i.e. make proper preparation.
15. **churlish:** i.e. sparse. 　16. **likes:** suits.
19. **Upon example:** as an example, i.e. in exemplary fashion.
23. **With casted slough:** i.e. like a snake having shed its old skin.
legerity: nimbleness.
24. **Brothers both:** i.e. Gloucester and Bedford.
25. **Commend me:** present my compliments.
26. **Do . . . morrow:** say good morning for me. 　27. **Desire:** invite.
34. **God-a-mercy:** gramercy, i.e. many thanks.
35. **Qui vous là:** who are you there. 　37. **Discuss unto:** tell.
38. **base . . . popular:** i.e. a common soldier.
39. **gentleman of a company:** i.e. inferior officer.
40. **Trail'st . . . pike:** i.e. do you serve in the infantry.
44. **bawcock.** See note to III.ii.25.
45. **imp of fame:** scion of noble stock.

54–55. **I'll . . . day.** On October 1 the Welsh wore leeks in their caps
to commemorate a victory over the Saxons, as ordered by their
patron saint, David. 　60. **figo.** See note to III.vi.57.
63. **sorts well with:** befits. 　66. **admiration:** wonder.
69. **Pompey the Great:** Roman general.
83. **out of fashion:** eccentric. 　84. **care:** carefulness.

tleman. I pray you, what thinks he of our estate? 96

K. Hen. Even as men wrack'd upon a sand, that look to be wash'd off the next tide.

Bates. He hath not told his thought to the King?

K. Hen. No; nor it is not meet he should. For though I speak it to you, I think the King is but a 101 man, as I am. The violet smells to him as it doth to me; the element shows to him as it doth to me; all his senses have but human conditions. His ceremonies laid by, in his nakedness he appears but a man; 105 and though his affections are higher mounted than ours, yet when they stoop, they stoop with the like wing. Therefore, when he sees reason of fears, as we do, his fears, out of doubt, be of the same relish as ours are; yet in reason, no man should possess him with 110 any appearance of fear, lest he, by showing it, should dishearten his army.

Bates. He may show what outward courage he will; but I believe, as cold a night as 'tis, he could wish himself in Thames up to the neck; and so I would he were, and I by him, at all adventures, so we were quit here. 117

K. Hen. By my troth, I will speak my conscience of the King: I think he would not wish himself any where but where he is. 120

Bates. Then I would he were here alone; so should he be sure to be ransom'd, and a many poor men's lives sav'd.

K. Hen. I dare say you love him not so ill to wish him here alone, howsoever you speak this to 125 feel other men's minds. Methinks I could not die any where so contented as in the King's company, his cause being just and his quarrel honorable.

Will. That's more than we know. 129

Bates. Ay, or more than we should seek after; for we know enough, if we know we are the King's subjects. If his cause be wrong, our obedience to the King wipes the crime of it out of us.

Will. But if the cause be not good, the King himself hath a heavy reckoning to make, when all 135 those legs, and arms, and heads, chopp'd off in a battle, shall join together at the latter day and cry all, "We died at such a place"—some swearing, some crying for a surgeon, some upon their wives left poor behind them, some upon the debts they owe, some upon 140 their children rawly left. I am afeard there are few die well that die in a battle; for how can they charitably dispose of any thing, when blood is their argument? Now, if these men do not die well, it will be a black matter for the King that led them to it; who to disobey were against all proportion of subjection. 146

K. Hen. So, if a son that is by his father sent about merchandise do sinfully miscarry upon the sea, the imputation of his wickedness, by your rule, should be impos'd upon his father that sent him; or if a 150 servant, under his master's command transporting a sum of money, be assail'd by robbers and die in many irreconcil'd iniquities, you may call the business of the master the author of the servant's damnation. But this is not so. The King is not bound to answer 155 the particular endings of his soldiers, the father of his son, nor the master of his servant; for they purpose not their death when they purpose their services. Besides, there is no king, be his cause never so spotless, if it come to the arbitrement of swords, can try it out 160 with all unspotted soldiers. Some, peradventure, have on them the guilt of premeditated and contriv'd murther; some, of beguiling virgins with the broken seals of perjury; some, making the wars their bulwark, that have before gor'd the gentle bosom of peace 165 with pillage and robbery. Now, if these men have defeated the law and outrun native punishment, though they can outstrip men, they have no wings to fly from God. War is his beadle, war is his vengeance; so that here men are punish'd for before-breach of the 170 King's laws in now the King's quarrel. Where they fear'd the death, they have borne life away; and where they would be safe, they perish. Then if they die unprovided, no more is the King guilty of their damnation than he was before guilty of those impieties 175 for the which they are now visited. Every subject's duty is the King's, but every subject's soul is his own. Therefore should every soldier in the wars do as every sick man in his bed, wash every mote out of his conscience; and dying so, death is to him advantage; 180 or not dying, the time was blessedly lost wherein such preparation was gain'd; and in him that escapes, it were not sin to think that making God so free an offer, He let him outlive that day to see His greatness and to teach others how they should prepare. 185

Will. 'Tis certain, every man that dies ill, the ill upon his own head, the King is not to answer it.

Bates. I do not desire he should answer for me, and yet I determine to fight lustily for him.

K. Hen. I myself heard the King say he would not be ransom'd. 191

Will. Ay, he said so, to make us fight cheerfully; but when our throats are cut, he may be ransom'd, and we ne'er the wiser. 194

K. Hen. If I live to see it, I will never trust his word after.

Will. You pay him then. That's a perilous shot out of an elder-gun, that a poor and a private displeasure can do against a monarch! You may as well go about to turn the sun to ice with fanning in his face 200 with a peacock's feather. You'll never trust his word after! come, 'tis a foolish saying.

---

96. **estate:** condition. 103. **element shows:** sky appears.
104. **conditions:** qualities, i.e. limitations. **ceremonies:** robes of state. 106. **affections . . . mounted:** desires mount higher.
107. **stoop:** descend (a term from falconry). **with . . . wing:** similarly. 109. **relish:** taste, i.e. kind.
116. **at all adventures:** whatever the risk.
116–17. **quit here:** i.e. out of this.
118. **conscience:** honest opinion.
141. **rawly left:** i.e. unprovided for.
142. **well:** i.e. as Christians. 143. **argument:** i.e. main concern.
145. **who:** whom.
146. **proportion of subjection:** proper relation of subject to sovereign.

152–53. **in . . . iniquities:** i.e. with his sins upon his head.
160. **arbitrement of:** settlement by. **try it out:** i.e. test its merits.
161. **all unspotted:** completely unblemished.
164. **making . . . bulwark:** i.e. taking advantage of military service to escape punishment. 167. **native:** at home.
169. **beadle:** officer who inflicts punishment.
173–74. **unprovided:** unprepared. 176. **visited:** punished.
186. **dies ill:** dies in sin.
198. **elder-gun:** pop-gun, made by removing the pith from a piece of elder.

Henry V
IV.i

K. Hen. Your reproof is something too round, I should be angry with you, if the time were convenient.

Will. Let it be a quarrel between us, if you live.

K. Hen. I embrace it. 206

Will. How shall I know thee again?

K. Hen. Give me any gage of thine, and I will wear it in my bonnet; then if ever thou dar'st acknowledge it, I will make it my quarrel. 210

Will. Here's my glove; give me another of thine.

K. Hen. There.

Will. This will I also wear in my cap. If ever thou come to me and say, after to-morrow, "This is my glove," by this hand I will take thee a box on the ear. 216

K. Hen. If ever I live to see it, I will challenge it.

Will. Thou dar'st as well be hang'd.

K. Hen. Well, I will do it, though I take thee in the King's company. 220

Will. Keep thy word; fare thee well.

Bates. Be friends, you English fools, be friends, we have French quarrels enow, if you could tell how to reckon. 224

K. Hen. Indeed the French may lay twenty French crowns to one they will beat us, for they bear them on their shoulders; but it is no English treason to cut French crowns, and to-morrow the King himself will be a clipper. *Exeunt Soldiers.*

Upon the King! let us our lives, our souls, 230
Our debts, our careful wives,
Our children, and our sins lay on the King!
We must bear all. O hard condition,
Twin-born with greatness, subject to the breath
Of every fool whose sense no more can feel 235
But his own wringing! What infinite heart's ease
Must kings neglect, that private men enjoy!
And what have kings, that privates have not too,
Save ceremony, save general ceremony?
And what art thou, thou idol Ceremony? 240
What kind of god art thou, that suffer'st more
Of mortal griefs than do thy worshippers?
What are thy rents? what are thy comings-in?
O Ceremony, show me but thy worth!
What is thy soul of [adoration]? 245
Art thou aught else but place, degree, and form,
Creating awe and fear in other men?
Wherein thou art less happy, being fear'd,
Than they in fearing. 249
What drink'st thou oft, in stead of homage sweet,
But poison'd flattery? O, be sick, great greatness,
And bid thy ceremony give thee cure!
Thinks thou the fiery fever will go out
With titles blown from adulation?
Will it give place to flexure and low bending? 255

Canst thou, when thou command'st the beggar's knee,
Command the health of it? No, thou proud dream,
That play'st so subtilly with a king's repose.
I am a king that find thee; and I know
'Tis not the balm, the sceptre, and the ball, 260
The sword, the mace, the crown imperial,
The intertissued robe of gold and pearl,
The farced title running 'fore the king,
The throne he sits on, nor the tide of pomp
That beats upon the high shore of this world— 265
No, not all these, thrice-gorgeous ceremony,
Not all these, laid in bed majestical,
Can sleep so soundly as the wretched slave;
Who, with a body fill'd and vacant mind,
Gets him to rest, cramm'd with distressful bread, 270
Never sees horrid night, the child of hell;
But like a lackey, from the rise to set,
Sweats in the eye of Phoebus, and all night
Sleeps in Elysium; next day after dawn,
Doth rise and help Hyperion to his horse, 275
And follows so the ever-running year
With profitable labor to his grave:
And, but for ceremony, such a wretch,
Winding up days with toil, and nights with sleep,
Had the forehand and vantage of a king. 280
The slave, a member of the country's peace,
Enjoys it; but in gross brain little wots
What watch the King keeps to maintain the peace,
Whose hours the peasant best advantages.

Enter ERPINGHAM.

Erp. My lord, your nobles, jealous of your absence, 285
Seek through your camp to find you.

K. Hen.   Good old knight,
Collect them all together at my tent.
I'll be before thee.

Erp.   I shall do't, my lord. *Exit.*

K. Hen. O God of battles, steel my soldiers' hearts, 289
Possess them not with fear! Take from them now
The sense of reck'ning, [if] th' opposed numbers
Pluck their hearts from them. Not to-day, O Lord,
O, not to-day, think not upon the fault
My father made in compassing the crown!
I Richard's body have interred new, 295
And on it have bestowed more contrite tears,

203. **round:** blunt.   208. **gage:** pledge, token.
215. **take:** give.   223. **enow:** enough.
226. **crowns:** (1) coins; (2) heads.
227. **English treason.** Clipping coins was punished as treason under English law.
228. **cut French crowns:** (1) clip coins; (2) kill Frenchmen.
231. **careful:** burdened by care.   236. **wringing:** stomach ache.
238. **privates:** private men.   243. **rents:** revenues.
245. **thy . . . adoration:** the secret of the admiration paid to you.
246. **place:** rank.   254. **from adulation:** i.e. by flatterers.
255. **flexure:** bowing.

259. **find thee:** discover the truth about you, expose you.
260. **balm:** consecrating oil.   **ball:** globe, a symbol of sovereignty.
263. **farced:** stuffed, inflated.   270. **distressful:** hard-earned.
274. **Elysium:** in Greek mythology, the abode of the blest.
275. **Hyperion:** charioteer of the sun. (In Greek mythology it was his son Helios who was the driver.)   **Winding up:** filling.
280. **Had:** would have.   **forehand:** advantage.
281. **a member of:** i.e. one who shares the benefits of.
282. **wots:** knows.   283. **watch:** wakeful guard.
284. **Whose . . . advantages:** (the King) from whose watchful hours the peasant most benefits.   285. **jealous of:** concerned about.
291. **sense of reck'ning:** ability to count.
293–94. **fault . . . crown:** i.e. the murder of Richard II.
294. **compassing:** obtaining.
295. **I . . . new.** Following his coronation, says Holinshed (Bullough, IV, 281), Henry "caused the bodie of king Richard to be removed with all funerall dignitie convenient for his estate, from Langlie to Westminster, where he was honorablie interred with queene Anne his first wife, in a solemn toome erected and set up at the charges of this king."

Than from it issued forced drops of blood.
Five hundred poor I have in yearly pay,
Who twice a day their wither'd hands hold up   299
Toward heaven, to pardon blood; and I have built
Two chauntries, where the sad and solemn priests
Sing still for Richard's soul. More will I do;
Though all that I can do is nothing worth,
Since that my penitence comes after all,
Imploring pardon.   305

Enter GLOUCESTER.

Glou. My liege!
K. Hen. My brother Gloucester's voice? Ay;
I know thy errand, I will go with thee.
The day, my [friends], and all things stay for me.
Exeunt.

[SCENE II]

Enter the DOLPHIN, ORLEANCE, RAMBURES, *and* BEAU-
MONT.

Orl. The sun doth gild our armor, up, my lords!
Dol. *Montez* [*à*] *cheval!* My horse, varlot lackey!
Ha!
Orl. O brave spirit!
Dol. *Via! les eaux et terre.*
Orl. *Rien puis? l'air et feu?*   5
Dol. [*Cieux*]! cousin Orleance.

Enter CONSTABLE.

Now, my Lord Constable?
Con. Hark how our steeds for present service
neigh!
Dol. Mount them, and make incision in their hides,
That their hot blood may spin in English eyes,   10
And dout them with superfluous courage, ha!
Ram. What, will you have them weep our horses'
blood?
How shall we then behold their natural tears?

Enter MESSENGER.

Mess. The English are embattled, you French
peers.
Con. To horse, you gallant princes! straight to
horse!   15
Do but behold yond poor and starved band,
And your fair show shall suck away their souls,
Leaving them but the shales and husks of men.
There is not work enough for all our hands,
Scarce blood enough in all their sickly veins   20

To give each naked curtle-axe a stain,
That our French gallants shall to-day draw out,
And sheathe for lack of sport. Let us but blow on
them,
The vapor of our valor will o'erturn them.
'Tis positive against all exceptions, lords,   25
That our superfluous lackeys and our peasants,
Who in unnecessary action swarm
About our squares of battle, were enow
To purge this field of such a hilding foe;
Though we upon this mountain's basis by   30
Took stand for idle speculation—
But that our honors must not. What's to say?
A very little little let us do,
And all is done. Then let the trumpets sound
The tucket sonance and the note to mount;   35
For our approach shall so much dare the field,
That England shall couch down in fear, and yield.

Enter GRANDPRÉ.

Grand. Why do you stay so long, my lords of
France?
Yond island carrions, desperate of their bones,
Ill-favoredly become the morning field.   40
Their ragged curtains poorly are let loose,
And our air shakes them passing scornfully.
Big Mars seems bankrout in their beggar'd host,
And faintly through a rusty beaver peeps.
The horsemen sit like fixed candlesticks,   45
With torch-staves in their hand; and their poor jades
Lob down their heads, dropping the hides and hips,
The gum down-roping from their pale-dead eyes,
And in their pale dull mouths the [gimmal'd] bit
Lies foul with chaw'd-grass, still and motionless;   50
And their executors, the knavish crows,
Fly o'er them all, impatient for their hour.
Description cannot suit itself in words
To demonstrate the life of such a battle,
In life so liveless as it shows itself.   55
Con. They have said their prayers, and they stay
for death.
Dol. Shall we go send them dinners and fresh suits,
And give their fasting horses provender,
And after fight with them?
Con. I stay but for my [guidon]; to the field!   60
I will the banner from a trumpet take,
And use it for my haste. Come, come away!
The sun is high, and we outwear the day.   *Exeunt.*

301. **chauntries:** chantries, chapels where masses for the dead were
performed.   **sad:** grave.   302. **still:** continuously.

IV.ii. Location: The French camp.
2. **Montez à cheval:** to horse.   **varlot:** varlet, valet.
4. **Via . . . terre:** away, waters and earth. (The Dauphin imagines
his horse soaring above streams and solid earth—see III.vii.13–18.)
5–6. **Rien . . . Cieux.** Orleans asks whether the horse will not also
soar above the two other elements, air and fire, and the Dolphin
asserts that he will arise to the heavens (*Cieux*) themselves.
8. **present:** immediate.
11. **dout:** put out.   **superfluous courage:** i.e. blood the horses can
spare.   14. **embattled:** drawn up in line of battle.
17. **fair show:** splendid appearance.   18. **shales:** shells.

21. **curtle-axe:** cutlass.
25. **positive . . . exceptions:** i.e. indisputably true.
29. **hilding:** worthless.   30. **basis:** foot.
31. **speculation:** looking-on.   35. **tucket sonance:** trumpet signal.
36. **dare the field:** daze the enemy.
39. **desperate of:** in despair of saving.   41. **curtains:** flags, banners.
43. **Mars:** god of war.   **bankrout:** bankrupt.
44. **beaver:** visor.   47. **Lob:** droop.   49. **gimmal'd:** jointed.
51. **executors:** executioners (?) or executors who will dispose of what
the dead leave behind (i.e. merely their carcasses) (?).
54. **demonstrate . . . of:** i.e. depict realistically.   **battle:** line of battle.
55. **liveless:** lifeless.   56. **stay:** wait.
60–62. **I . . . haste.** The French were so eager for battle, says Holinshed (Bullough, IV, 395), that "some of them would not once staie
for their standards: as amongst other the duke of Brabant, when his
standard was not come, caused a baner to be taken from a trumpet
and fastened to a speare, the which he commanded to be borne before
him in steed of his standard."   60. **guidon:** pennon, standard.
61. **trumpet:** trumpeter.   63. **outwear:** waste.

[SCENE III]

Enter GLOUCESTER, BEDFORD, EXETER, ERPINGHAM
with all his host; SALISBURY *and* WESTMERLAND.

Glou. Where is the King?

Bed. The King himself is rode to view their battle.

West. Of fighting men they have full threescore
    thousand.

Exe. There's five to one; besides, they all are fresh.

Sal. God's arm strike with us! 'tis a fearful odds.
God buy you, princes all; I'll to my charge.   6
If we no more meet till we meet in heaven,
Then joyfully, my noble Lord of Bedford,
My dear Lord Gloucester, and my good Lord Exeter,
And my kind kinsman, warriors all, adieu!   10

Bed. Farewell, good Salisbury, and good luck go
    with thee!

Exe. Farewell, kind lord; fight valiantly to-day!
And yet I do thee wrong to mind thee of it,
For thou art fram'd of the firm truth of valor.

                 [*Exit Salisbury.*]

Bed. He is as full of valor as of kindness,   15
Princely in both.

Enter the KING.

West.   O that we now had here
But one ten thousand of those men in England
That do no work to-day!

K. Hen.   What's he that wishes so?
My cousin Westmerland? No, my fair cousin.
If we are mark'd to die, we are enow   20
To do our country loss; and if to live,
The fewer men, the greater share of honor.
God's will, I pray thee wish not one man more.
By Jove, I am not covetous for gold,
Nor care I who doth feed upon my cost;   25
It yearns me not if men my garments wear;
Such outward things dwell not in my desires.
But if it be a sin to covet honor,
I am the most offending soul alive.
No, faith, my coz, wish not a man from England.   30
God's peace, I would not lose so great an honor
As one man more methinks would share from me,
For the best hope I have. O, do not wish one more!
Rather proclaim it, Westmerland, through my host,
That he which hath no stomach to this fight,   35
Let him depart, his passport shall be made,
And crowns for convoy put into his purse.
We would not die in that man's company
That fears his fellowship to die with us.

This day is call'd the feast of Crispian: 40
He that outlives this day, and comes safe home,
Will stand a' tiptoe when this day is named,
And rouse him at the name of Crispian.
He that shall see this day, and live old age,
Will yearly on the vigil feast his neighbors,   45
And say, "To-morrow is Saint Crispian."
Then will he strip his sleeve and show his scars,
[And say, "These wounds I had on Crispin's day."]
Old men forget; yet all shall be forgot,
But he'll remember with advantages   50
What feats he did that day. Then shall our names,
Familiar in his mouth as household words,
Harry the King, Bedford and Exeter,
Warwick and Talbot, Salisbury and Gloucester,
Be in their flowing cups freshly rememb'red.   55
This story shall the good man teach his son;
And Crispin Crispian shall ne'er go by,
From this day to the ending of the world,
But we in it shall be remembered—
We few, we happy few, we band of brothers;   60
For he to-day that sheds his blood with me
Shall be my brother; be he ne'er so vile,
This day shall gentle his condition;
And gentlemen in England, now a-bed,   64
Shall think themselves accurs'd they were not here;
And hold their manhoods cheap whiles any speaks
That fought with us upon Saint Crispin's day.

Enter SALISBURY.

Sal. My sovereign lord, bestow yourself with
    speed.
The French are bravely in their battles set,
And will with all expedience charge on us.   70

K. Hen. All things are ready, if our minds be so.

West. Perish the man whose mind is backward
    now!

K. Hen. Thou dost not wish more help from
    England, coz?

West. God's will, my liege, would you and I alone,
Without more help, could fight this royal battle!   75

K. Hen. Why, now thou hast unwish'd five thou-
    sand men;
Which likes me better than to wish us one.
You know your places. God be with you all!

Tucket. Enter MONTJOY.

Mont. Once more I come to know of thee, King
    Harry,

IV.iii. Location: The English camp.
6. **buy:** be with.   **charge:** command post.
10. **kinsman:** i.e. Westmorland, whose son had married Salisbury's daughter.   14. **fram'd:** built.
16–67. **O . . . day.** Holinshed reports (Bullough, IV, 394) that when Henry "heard one of the host utter his wish to another thus: I would to God there were with us now so manie good soldiers as are at this houre within England! the king answered: I would not wish a man more here than I have, we are indeed in comparison to the enimies but a few, but if God of his clemencie doo favour us, and our just cause (as I trust he will) we shall speed well inough."
25. **upon my cost:** at my expense.   26. **yearns:** grieves.
30. **coz:** cousin, i.e. kinsman   32. **share from me:** deprive me of.
39. **fears . . . us:** i.e. is unwilling to meet death with me.

40. **feast of Crispian:** i.e. St. Crispin's Day, October 25. Crispin and Crispinian, the patron saints of shoemakers, were early Christian martyrs.   44. **live:** live to see.
45. **vigil:** i.e. the eve of St. Crispin's Day.
50. **advantages:** embellishments.   62. **vile:** lowly.
63. **gentle his condition:** raise him to the rank of gentleman.
68. **bestow yourself:** take your position.
69. **bravely . . . set:** handsomely drawn up.
70. **expedience:** speed.   77. **likes:** pleases.
79–125. **Once . . . Constable.** In their "jolitie" the French, says Holinshed (Bullough, IV, 395), sent a herald to King Henry "to inquire what ransome he would offer. Whereunto he answered, that within two or three houres he hoped it would so happen, that the Frenchmen should be glad to common [confer] rather with the Englishmen for their ransoms, than the English to take thought for their deliverance, promising for his owne part, that his dead carcasse should rather be a prize to the Frenchmen, than that his living bodie should paie anie ransome."

If for thy ransom thou wilt now compound,   80
Before thy most assured overthrow;
For certainly thou art so near the gulf,
Thou needs must be englutted. Besides, in mercy,
The Constable desires thee thou wilt mind
Thy followers of repentance; that their souls   85
May make a peaceful and a sweet retire
From off these fields, where (wretches!) their poor
        bodies
Must lie and fester.

    K. Hen.   Who hath sent thee now?

    Mont. The Constable of France.

    K. Hen. I pray thee bear my former answer back:
Bid them achieve me, and then sell my bones.   91
Good God, why should they mock poor fellows thus?
The man that once did sell the lion's skin
While the beast liv'd, was kill'd with hunting him.
A many of our bodies shall no doubt   95
Find native graves; upon the which, I trust,
Shall witness live in brass of this day's work.
And those that leave their valiant bones in France,
Dying like men, though buried in your dunghills,
They shall be fam'd; for there the sun shall greet them,
And draw their honors reeking up to heaven,   101
Leaving their earthly parts to choke your clime,
The smell whereof shall breed a plague in France.
Mark then abounding valor in our English:
That being dead, like to the bullet's crasing,   105
Break out into a second course of mischief,
Killing in relapse of mortality.
Let me speak proudly: tell the Constable
We are but warriors for the working-day;
Our gayness and our gilt are all besmirch'd   110
With rainy marching in the painful field;
There's not a piece of feather in our host—
Good argument (I hope) we will not fly—
And time hath worn us into slovenry.
But, by the mass, our hearts are in the trim;   115
And my poor soldiers tell me, yet ere night,
They'll be in fresher robes, or they will pluck
The gay new coats o'er the French soldiers' heads
And turn them out of service. If they do this—
As, if God please, they shall—my ransom then   120
Will soon be levied. Herald, save thou thy labor.
Come thou no more for ransom, gentle herald,
They shall have none, I swear, but these my joints;
Which if they have as I will leave 'um them,
Shall yield them little, tell the Constable.   125

    Mont. I shall, King Harry. And so fare thee well;
Thou never shalt hear herald any more.   *Exit.*

    K. Hen. I fear thou wilt once more come again for
a ransom.

Enter YORK.

    York. My lord, most humbly on my knee I beg

The leading of the vaward.   131

    K. Hen. Take it, brave York. Now, soldiers,
    march away,
And how thou pleasest, God, dispose the day!

                  Exeunt.

[SCENE IV]

Alarum. Excursions. Enter PISTOL, FRENCH SOLDIER,
BOY.

    Pist. Yield, cur!

    Fr. Sol. *Je pense que vous êtes le gentilhomme de
bonne qualité.*

    Pist. Qualtitie! [*Calen o] custure me!* Art thou a
gentleman? What is thy name? Discuss.   5

    Fr. Sol. *O Seigneur Dieu!*

    Pist. O Signieur Dew should be a gentleman.
Perpend my words, O Signieur Dew, and mark:
O Signieur Dew, thou diest on point of fox,
Except, O signieur, thou do give to me   10
Egregious ransom.

    Fr. Sol. *O, prenez miséricorde! ayez pitié de moi!*

    Pist. Moy shall not serve, I will have forty moys,
[Or] I will fetch thy rim out at thy throat
In drops of crimson blood.   15

    Fr. Sol. *Est-il impossible d'échapper la force de ton
bras?*

    Pist. Brass, cur?
Thou damned and luxurious mountain goat,
Offer'st me brass?   20

    Fr. Sol. *O, pardonnez moi!*

    Pist. Say'st thou me so? Is that a ton of moys?
Come hither, boy, ask me this slave in French
What is his name.

    Boy. *Écoutez: comment êtes-vous appelé?*   25

    Fr. Sol. *Monsieur le Fer.*

    Boy. He says his name is Master Fer.

    Pist. Master Fer! I'll fer him, and firk him, and
ferret him. Discuss the same in French unto him.

    Boy. I do not know the French for fer, and ferret,
and firk.   31

    Pist. Bid him prepare, for I will cut his throat.

    Fr. Sol. *Que dit-il, monsieur?*

    Boy. *Il me commande à vous dire que vous faites vous
prêt; car ce soldat ici est disposé tout [à cette heure] de
couper votre gorge.*   36

    Pist. Owy, cuppele gorge, permafoy,

---

80. **compound:** make terms.
82. **gulf:** whirlpool. 83. **englutted:** swallowed.
84. **mind:** remind. 91. **achieve:** capture.
93–94. **The man . . . him.** A somewhat altered version of one of
Aesop's fables. 96. **native:** at home.
101. **reeking:** breathing. 105. **crasing:** fatal rebound (?).
109. **We . . . working-day:** i.e. we are here to work.
115. **in the trim:** (1) sprucely attired; (2) in fine condition.
117. **fresher:** i.e. heavenly. 124. **'um:** 'em, i.e. them.

131. **vaward:** vanguard.

IV.iv. Location: The field of battle.
o.s.d. **Excursions:** sallies, sorties.
2–3. **Je . . . qualité:** I think you are a gentleman of good family.
4. **Qualtitie . . . me.** Probably mere nonsense. 5. **Discuss:** declare.
6. **O Seigneur Dieu:** O Lord God. 8. **Perpend:** ponder.
9. **fox:** sword. 12. **O . . . moi:** O have mercy, take pity on me.
13. **Moy.** Pistol takes *moi* (line 12) for the name of a coin. Cf. line
22, and also line 18, where he makes a similar mistake about *bras.*
14. **rim:** diaphragm.
16–17. **Est-il . . . bras:** is it impossible to escape the strength of your
arm. 19. **luxurious:** lascivious.
25. **Écoutez . . . appelé:** listen: what is your name. 28. **firk:** beat.
29. **ferret:** worry (like a ferret).
33. **Que dit-il:** what does he say.
34–36. **Il . . . gorge:** he orders me to tell you to prepare; for this
soldier is disposed to cut your throat at once.
37. **Owy:** Pistol's version of *oui,* "yes." **permafoy:** by my faith.

Henry V
IV.iv

Peasant, unless thou give me crowns, brave crowns;
Or mangled shalt thou be by this my sword.

Fr. Sol.   *O, je vous supplie, pour l'amour de Dieu, me*
pardonner! Je suis le gentilhomme de bonne maison;
gardez ma vie, et je vous donnerai deux cents écus.   42

Pist.   What are his words?

Boy.   He prays you to save his life. He is a gentleman of a good house, and for his ransom he will give
you two hundred crowns.   46

Pist.   Tell him my fury shall abate, and I
The crowns will take.

Fr. Sol.   *Petit monsieur, que dit-il?*   49

Boy.   *Encore qu'il est contre son jurement de pardonner*
aucun prisonnier; néanmoins, pour les écus que vous
[lui] promettez, il est content à vous donner la liberté, le
franchisement.

Fr. Sol.   *Sur mes genoux [je] vous donne mille*
[remerciments]; et je m'estime heureux que je   55
tombe entre les mains d'un chevalier, je pense, le plus brave,
vaillant, et très [distingué] seigneur d'Angleterre.

Pist.   Expound unto me, boy.   58

Boy.   He gives you, upon his knees, a thousand
thanks, and he esteems himself happy that he hath
fall'n into the hands of one (as he thinks) the most
brave, valorous, and thrice-worthy seigneur of
England.

Pist.   As I suck blood, I will some mercy show.
Follow me!   65

Boy.   *Suivez-vous le grand capitaine.* [*Exeunt Pistol
and French Soldier.*] I did never know so full a voice
issue from so empty a heart; but the saying is true,
"The empty vessel makes the greatest sound."
Bardolph and Nym had ten times more valor than   70
this roaring devil i' th' old play, that every one may
pare his nails with a wooden dagger, and they are both
hang'd, and so would this be, if he durst steal any thing
adventurously. I must stay with the lackeys with the
luggage of our camp. The French might have a   75
good prey of us, if he knew of it, for there is none to
guard it but boys.   *Exit.*

[SCENE V]

Enter CONSTABLE, ORLEANCE, BOURBON, DOLPHIN, *and*
RAMBURES.

Con.   *O diable!*

Orl.   *O Seigneur! le jour est perdu, tout est perdu!*

Dol.   *Mort Dieu, ma vie!* all is confounded, all!
Reproach and everlasting shame
Sits mocking in our plumes.   *A short alarum.*
                                    O méchante fortune!   5
Do not run away.

Con.   Why, all our ranks are broke.

Dol.   O perdurable shame! let's stab ourselves.
Be these the wretches that we play'd at dice for?

Orl.   Is this the king we sent to for his ransom?

Bour.   Shame and eternal shame, nothing but shame!
Let us die! In once more! back again!   11
And he that will not follow Bourbon now,
Let him go hence, and with his cap in hand
Like a base pander hold the chamber-door
Whilst [by a] slave, no gentler than my dog,   15
His fairest daughter is contaminated.

Con.   Disorder, that hath spoil'd us, friend us now!
Let us on heaps go offer up our lives.

Orl.   We are enow yet living in the field
To smother up the English in our throngs,   20
If any order might be thought upon.

Bour.   The devil take order now! I'll to the throng:
Let life be short, else shame will be too long.

                                        Exeunt.

[SCENE VI]

Alarum.   *Enter the* KING *and his* TRAIN *with prisoners;*
[EXETER *and others*].

K. Hen.   Well have we done, thrice-valiant countrymen,
But all's not done—yet keep the French the field.

Exe.   The Duke of York commends him to your
Majesty.

K. Hen.   Lives he, good uncle? Thrice within this
hour
I saw him down; thrice up again, and fighting;   5
From helmet to the spur all blood he was.

Exe.   In which array (brave soldier!) doth he lie,
Larding the plain; and by his bloody side
(Yoke-fellow to his honor-owing wounds)
The noble Earl of Suffolk also lies.   10
Suffolk first died, and York, all haggled over,
Comes to him where in gore he lay insteeped,
And takes him by the beard, kisses the gashes
That bloodily did yawn upon his face.
He cries aloud, "Tarry, my cousin Suffolk!   15
My soul shall thine keep company to heaven;
Tarry, sweet soul, for mine, then fly abreast,
As in this glorious and well-foughten field
We kept together in our chivalry!"
Upon these words I came and cheer'd him up.   20
He smil'd me in the face, raught me his hand,
And with a feeble gripe, says, "Dear my lord,
Commend my service to my sovereign."

40–42. **O . . . écus:** O, I beg you to pardon me, for the love of God.
I am a gentleman of good family; preserve my life, and I will give
you two hundred crowns.   45. **house:** family.
49. **Petit . . . dit-il:** little sir, what does he say.
50–53. **Encore . . . franchisement:** once more, that it is contrary to
his oath to pardon any prisoner; nevertheless, for the crowns that
you promise him, he is willing to give you liberty, freedom.
54–57. **Sur . . . d'Angleterre.** These lines are translated almost literally in the Boy's next speech.
64. **suck blood.** Cf. Pistol's words at II.iii.55–56.
66. **Suivez-vous . . . capitaine:** follow the great captain.
71–72. **roaring . . . dagger.** The stock character of the Devil in the
morality plays was often taunted by the mischievous Vice with an
offer to trim his nails with his dagger, made of lath. See the Fool's
song in *Twelfth Night,* IV.ii.120–31.

IV.v. Location: Scene continues.
1. **O diable:** O the devil.
2. **O . . . perdu:** O Lord, the day is lost, all is lost.

3. **Mort . . . vie:** death of God! my life.   **confounded:** lost.
5. **O méchante fortune:** O malicious fate.   7. **perdurable:** lasting.
18. **on:** in.

IV.vi. Location: Scene continues.
8. **Larding:** enriching.
9. **honor-owing:** honor-owning, i.e. honorable.
11. **haggled over:** mangled.   20. **cheer'd him up:** encouraged him.
21. **raught:** reached.   22. **gripe:** grasp.   23. **Commend:** present.

So did he turn and over Suffolk's neck
He threw his wounded arm, and kiss'd his lips,   25
And so espous'd to death, with blood he seal'd
A testament of noble-ending love.
The pretty and sweet manner of it forc'd
Those waters from me which I would have stopp'd,
But I had not so much of man in me,   30
And all my mother came into mine eyes
And gave me up to tears.

K. Hen.   I blame you not,
For hearing this, I must perforce compound
With [mistful] eyes, or they will issue too.   *Alarum.*
But hark, what new alarum is this same?   35
The French have reinforc'd their scatter'd men.
Then every soldier kill his prisoners,
Give the word through.   *Exeunt.*

[SCENE VII]

Enter FLUELLEN *and* GOWER.

Flu. Kill the poys and the luggage! 'Tis expressly
against the law of arms. 'Tis as arrant a piece of
knavery, mark you now, as can be offert; in your
conscience, now, is it not?   4

Gow. 'Tis certain there's not a boy left alive, and
the cowardly rascals that ran from the battle ha' done
this slaughter. Besides, they have burn'd and carried
away all that was in the King's tent; wherefore the
King, most worthily, hath caus'd every soldier to cut
his prisoner's throat. O, 'tis a gallant king!   10

Flu. Ay, he was porn at Monmouth, Captain
Gower. What call you the town's name where
Alexander the Pig was born?

Gow. Alexander the Great.   14

Flu. Why, I pray you, is not "pig" great? The
pig, or the great, or the mighty, or the huge, or the
magnanimous, are all one reckonings, save the phrase
is a little variations.

Gow. I think Alexander the Great was born in
Macedon. His father was called Philip of Macedon,
as I take it.   21

Flu. I think it is in Macedon where Alexander is
porn. I tell you, captain, if you look in the maps of the
orld, I warrant you sall find, in the comparisons between Macedon and Monmouth, that the situa-   25

tions, look you, is both alike. There is a river in
Macedon, and there is also moreover a river at Monmouth. It is call'd Wye at Monmouth; but it is out of
my prains what is the name of the other river; but 'tis
all one, 'tis alike as my fingers is to my fingers,   30
and there is salmons in both. If you mark Alexander's
life well, Harry of Monmouth's life is come after it
indifferent well, for there is figures in all things.
Alexander, God knows, and you know, in his rages,
and his furies, and his wraths, and his cholers, and 35
his moods, and his displeasures, and his indignations,
and also being a little intoxicates in his prains, did, in
his ales and his angers, look you, kill his best friend,
Clytus.   39

Gow. Our King is not like him in that; he never
kill'd any of his friends.

Flu. It is not well done, mark you now, to take the
tales out of my mouth, ere it is made and finished. I
speak but in the figures and comparisons of it: as
Alexander kill'd his friend Clytus, being in his   45
ales and his cups; so also Harry Monmouth, being in
his right wits and his good judgments, turn'd away the
fat knight with the great belly doublet. He was full of
jests, and gipes, and knaveries, and mocks—I have
forgot his name.   50

Gow. Sir John Falstaff.

Flu. That is he. I'll tell you there is good men porn
at Monmouth.

Gow. Here comes his Majesty.   [*Exit.*]   54

Alarum. Enter KING HARRY *and* BOURBON *with* [*other*]
prisoners; [WARWICK, GLOUCESTER, EXETER, HER-
ALDS, *and others*]. *Flourish.*

K. Hen. I was not angry since I came to France
Until this instant. Take a trumpet, herald,
Ride thou unto the horsemen on yond hill.
If they will fight with us, bid them come down,
Or void the field; they do offend our sight.
If they'll do neither, we will come to them,   60
And make them skirr away, as swift as stones
Enforced from the old Assyrian slings;
Besides, we'll cut the throats of those we have,
And not a man of them that we shall take
Shall taste our mercy. Go and tell them so.   65
                                    [*Exit a Herald.*]

Enter MONTJOY.

Exe. Here comes the herald of the French, my
    liege.

Glou. His eyes are humbler than they us'd to be.

---

28. **pretty:** lovely.   33. **perforce compound:** necessarily make terms.
34. **issue:** i.e. weep.
35–38. **But . . . through.** Holinshed reports (Bullough, IV, 397) that
some of the fleeing French cavalry, "either upon a covetous meaning
to gaine by the spoile, or upon a desire to be revenged," circled back
upon King Henry's camp "and there spoiled the hails [shelters],
robbed the tents, brake up chests, and caried awaie caskets, and slue
such servants as they found to make anie resistance." When informed
of this, Henry, fearing that the enemy would regroup their forces and
launch a new attack, "contrarie to his accustomed gentlenes, commanded by sound of trumpet, that everie man (upon paine of death)
should incontinentlie slaie his prisoner. When this dolorous decree,
and pitifull proclamation was pronounced, pitie it was to see how
some Frenchmen were suddenlie sticked with daggers, some were
brained with pollaxes, some slaine with malls, other had their throats
cut, and some their bellies panched, so that in effect, having respect
to the great number, few prisoners were saved."

IV.vii. **Location:** Scene continues.
1. **luggage:** i.e. lackeys left to guard the luggage.
11. **Monmouth:** castle in eastern Monmouthshire.   24. **orld:** world.

32. **is come after:** resembles.
33. **indifferent:** fairly.   **figures:** figurative comparisons, similes.
39. **Clytus:** Cleitus, close friend and associate whom Alexander killed
during a drinking bout.
55–65. **I . . . mercy.** Holinshed reports (Bullough, IV, 397–98) that
to the scattering French Henry sent a herald "commanding them
either to depart out of his sight, or else to come forward at once,
and give battell: promising herewith, that if they did offer to fight
again, not onelie those prisoners which his people alreadie had taken;
but also so manie of them as in this new conflict, which they thus
attempted should fall into his hands, should die the death without
redemption." Appalled by "so terrible a decree," the French "without further delaie parted out of the field."
56. **trumpet:** trumpeter.   59. **void:** abandon.
61. **skirr:** scurry.

Henry V
IV.vii

K. Hen. How now, what means this, herald?
Know'st thou not
That I have fin'd these bones of mine for ransom?
Com'st thou again for ransom?
    Mont.   No, great King;   70
I come to thee for charitable license,
That we may wander o'er this bloody field
To book our dead, and then to bury them;
To sort our nobles from our common men.
For many of our princes (woe the while!)   75
Lie drown'd and soak'd in mercenary blood;
So do our vulgar drench their peasant limbs
In blood of princes, and [their] wounded steeds
Fret fetlock deep in gore, and with wild rage
Yerk out their armed heels at their dead masters,   80
Killing them twice. O, give us leave, great King,
To view the field in safety, and dispose
Of their dead bodies!
    K. Hen.   I tell thee truly, herald,
I know not if the day be ours or no,
For yet a many of your horsemen peer   85
And gallop o'er the field.
    Mont.   The day is yours.
    K. Hen. Praised be God, and not our strength, for
    it!
What is this castle call'd that stands hard by?
    Mont. They call it Agincourt.
    K. Hen. Then call we this the field of Agincourt,
Fought on the day of Crispin Crispianus.   91
    Flu. Your grandfather of famous memory, an't
please your Majesty, and your great-uncle Edward the
Plack Prince of Wales, as I have read in the chronicles,
fought a most prave pattle here in France.   95
    K. Hen. They did, Fluellen.
    Flu. Your Majesty says very true. If your Majes-
ties is rememb'red of it, the Welshmen did good
service in a garden where leeks did grow, wearing leeks
in their Monmouth caps, which, your Majesty   100
know, to this hour is an honorable badge of the service;
and I do believe your Majesty takes no scorn to wear
the leek upon Saint Tavy's day.
    K. Hen. I wear it for a memorable honor;
For I am Welsh, you know, good countryman.   105
    Flu. All the water in Wye cannot wash your
Majesty's Welsh plood out of your pody, I can tell you
that. God pless it, and preserve it, as long as it pleases
his Grace, and his Majesty too!
    K. Hen. Thanks, good my [countryman].   110
    Flu. By Jeshu, I am your Majesty's countryman,
I care not who know it. I will confess it to all the
orld. I need not to be ashamed of your Majesty,
praised be God, so long as your Majesty is an honest
man.   115
    K. Hen. [God] keep me so!

Enter WILLIAMS.

                    Our heralds go with him;
Bring me just notice of the numbers dead
On both our parts. Call yonder fellow hither.
                [*Exeunt Heralds with Montjoy.*]
    Exe. Soldier, you must come to the King.   119
    K. Hen. Soldier, why wear'st thou that glove in
thy cap?
    Will. And't please your Majesty, 'tis the gage of
one that I should fight withal, if he be alive.
    K. Hen. An Englishman?   124
    Will. And't please your Majesty, a rascal that
swagger'd with me last night; who if alive and ever
dare to challenge this glove, I have sworn to take him
a box a' th' ear; or if I can see my glove in his cap,
which he swore, as he was a soldier, he would wear if
alive, I will strike it out soundly.   130
    K. Hen. What think you, Captain Fluellen? is it
fit this soldier keep his oath?
    Flu. He is a craven and a villain else, and't please
your Majesty, in my conscience.   134
    K. Hen. It may be his enemy is a gentleman of
great sort, quite from the answer of his degree.
    Flu. Though he be as good a gentleman as the devil
is, as Lucifer and Belzebub himself, it is necessary,
look your Grace, that he keep his vow and his oath.
If he be perjur'd, see you now, his reputation is   140
as arrant a villain and a Jack sauce, as ever his black
shoe trod upon God's ground and His earth, in my
conscience law!
    K. Hen. Then keep thy vow, sirrah, when thou
meet'st the fellow.   145
    Will. So I will, my liege, as I live.
    K. Hen. Who serv'st thou under?
    Will. Under Captain Gower, my liege.
    Flu. Gower is a good captain, and is good knowl-
edge and literatured in the wars.   150
    K. Hen. Call him hither to me, soldier.
    Will. I will, my liege.   *Exit.*
    K. Hen. Here, Fluellen, wear thou this favor for
me and stick it in thy cap. When Alanson and myself
were down together, I pluck'd this glove from his   155
helm. If any man challenge this, he is a friend to
Alanson, and an enemy to our person. If thou encounter any such, apprehend him, and thou dost me
love.   159
    Flu. Your Grace doo's me as great honors as can be
desir'd in the hearts of his subjects. I would fain see
the man, that has but two legs, that shall find himself
aggrief'd at this glove; that is all. But I would fain see
it once, and please God of his grace that I might see.
    K. Hen. Know'st thou Gower?   165
    Flu. He is my dear friend, and please you.
    K. Hen. Pray thee go seek him, and bring him to
my tent.

---

69. **fin'd:** staked.
71. **license:** permission.   73. **book:** list.
76. **mercenary blood:** i.e. blood of common soldiers, who, unlike the
nobles, fought for pay.   77. **vulgar:** common people.
80. **Yerk:** kick.   **armed:** spiked.   85. **peer:** appear.
92. **grandfather:** i.e. great-grandfather, Edward III.
95. **pattle:** i.e. Crécy.
100. **Monmouth caps:** high-crowned, brimless hats.

117. **just notice:** precise record.   122. **And:** if.   123. **withal:** with.
136. **quite . . . degree:** i.e. too exalted in rank to accept a challenge
from a commoner like Williams.
141. **Jack sauce:** impudent fellow.
144. **sirrah:** form of address to inferiors.
154. **Alanson:** the Duke of Alençon.   158. **apprehend:** arrest.

Flu. I will fetch him.   *Exit.*

K. Hen. My Lord of Warwick, and my brother
Gloucester,   170
Follow Fluellen closely at the heels.
The glove which I have given him for a favor
May haply purchase him a box a' th' ear.
It is the soldier's; I by bargain should
Wear it myself. Follow, good cousin Warwick. 175
If that the soldier strike him, as I judge
By his blunt bearing he will keep his word,
Some sudden mischief may arise of it;
For I do know Fluellen valiant
And touch'd with choler, hot as gunpowder,   180
And quickly will return an injury.
Follow, and see there be no harm between them.
Go you with me, uncle of Exeter.   *Exeunt.*

[SCENE VIII]

Enter GOWER and WILLIAMS.

Will. I warrant it is to knight you, captain.

Enter FLUELLEN.

Flu. God's will, and his pleasure, captain, I beseech
you now, come apace to the King. There is more good
toward you peradventure than is in your knowledge
to dream of.   5

Will. Sir, know you this glove?

Flu. Know the glove? I know the glove is a glove.

Will. I know this, and thus I challenge it.
                                   Strikes him.

Flu. 'Sblud, an arrant traitor as any's in the
universal world, or in France, or in England!   10

Gow. How now, sir? you villain!

Will. Do you think I'll be forsworn?

Flu. Stand away, Captain Gower, I will give
treason his payment into plows, I warrant you.

Will. I am no traitor.   15

Flu. That's a lie in thy throat. I charge you in his
Majesty's name, apprehend him, he's a friend of the
Duke Alanson's.

Enter WARWICK and GLOUCESTER.

War. How now, how now, what's the matter?   19

Flu. My Lord of Warwick, here is—praised be
God for it!—a most contagious treason come to light,
look you, as you shall desire in a summer's day. Here
is his Majesty.

Enter KING and EXETER.

K. Hen. How now, what's the matter?   24

Flu. My liege, here is a villain and a traitor, that,
look your Grace, has strook the glove which your
Majesty is take out of the helmet of Alanson.

Will. My liege, this was my glove, here is the
fellow of it; and he that I gave it to in change promis'd

to wear it in his cap. I promis'd to strike him, if 30
he did. I met this man with my glove in his cap, and I
have been as good as my word.

Flu. Your Majesty hear now, saving your Majesty's manhood, what an arrant, rascally, beggarly, lousy
knave it is. I hope your Majesty is pear me testi-   35
mony and witness, and will avouchment, that this is
the glove of Alanson that your Majesty is give me,
in your conscience now.

K. Hen. Give me thy glove, soldier. Look, here is
the fellow of it.   40
'Twas I indeed thou promisedst to strike,
And thou hast given me most bitter terms.

Flu. And please your Majesty, let his neck answer
for it, if there is any martial law in the world.   44

K. Hen. How canst thou make me satisfaction?

Will. All offenses, my lord, come from the heart.
Never came any from mine that might offend your
Majesty.

K. Hen. It was ourself thou didst abuse.   49

Will. Your Majesty came not like yourself. You
appear'd to me but as a common man; witness the
night, your garments, your lowliness; and what your
Highness suffer'd under that shape, I beseech you take
it for your own fault and not mine; for had you been as
I took you for, I made no offense; therefore I beseech
your Highness pardon me.   56

K. Hen. Here, uncle Exeter, fill this glove with
crowns,
And give it to this fellow. Keep it, fellow,
And wear it for an honor in thy cap
Till I do challenge it. Give him the crowns; 60
And, captain, you must needs be friends with him.

Flu. By this day and this light, the fellow has
mettle enough in his belly. Hold, there is twelvepence
for you, and I pray you to serve God, and keep you out
of prawls and prabbles, and quarrels and dissensions,
and I warrant you it is the better for you.   66

Will. I will none of your money.

Flu. It is with a good will; I can tell you it will
serve you to mend your shoes. Come, wherefore
should you be so pashful? your shoes is not so good.
'Tis a good silling, I warrant you, or I will change
it.   72

Enter [an ENGLISH] HERALD.

K. Hen. Now, herald, are the dead numb'red?

Her. Here is the number of the slaught'red French.
                                   [Gives a paper.]

K. Hen. What prisoners of good sort are taken,
uncle?   75

Exe. Charles Duke of Orleance, nephew to the King,
John Duke of Bourbon, and Lord Bouciqualt:

---

181. **injury:** insult.

IV.viii. **Location:** Before King Henry's pavilion.
9. **'Sblud:** by God's (Christ's) blood (a strong oath).
29. **change:** exchange.

35. **is pear:** will bear.
36. **avouchment:** i.e. testify.   42. **terms:** words.
75. **good sort:** high rank.
76–106. **Charles . . . twenty.** These names and statistics are drawn
with great precision from Holinshed (Bullough, IV, 399), whose figures should be received with caution. He estimates the English before
Agincourt as "onelie two thousand horssemen and thirteene thousand
archers, bilmen, and of all sorts of other footmen" (IV, 389) and the
French as "threescore thousand horssemen, besides footmen, wagoners and other" (IV, 391). Modern historians set the French losses
as perhaps 7,000 and the English as between 400 and 500.

Of other lords and barons, knights and squires,
Full fifteen hundred, besides common men.
 K. Hen. This note doth tell me of ten thousand
  French   80
That in the field lie slain; of princes, in this number,
And nobles bearing banners, there lie dead
One hundred twenty-six; added to these,
Of knights, esquires, and gallant gentlemen,
Eight thousand and four hundred; of the which, 85
Five hundred were but yesterday dubb'd knights.
So that, in these ten thousand they have lost,
There are but sixteen hundred mercenaries;
The rest are princes, barons, lords, knights, squires,
And gentlemen of blood and quality.   90
The names of those their nobles that lie dead:
Charles Delabreth, High Constable of France,
Jacques of Chatillion, Admiral of France,
The master of the cross-bows, Lord Rambures,
Great Master of France, the brave Sir Guichard
 Dolphin,   95
John Duke of Alanson, Anthony Duke of Brabant,
The brother to the Duke of Burgundy,
And Edward Duke of Bar; of lusty earls,
Grandpré and Roussi, Faulconbridge and Foix,
Beaumont and Marle, Vaudemont and Lestrake. 100
Here was a royal fellowship of death!
Where is the number of our English dead?
    [Herald shows him another paper.]
Edward the Duke of York, the Earl of Suffolk,
Sir Richard Ketly, Davy Gam, esquire;
None else of name; and of all other men 105
But five and twenty. O God, thy arm was here;
And not to us, but to thy arm alone,
Ascribe we all! When, without stratagem,
But in plain shock and even play of battle,
Was ever known so great and little loss, 110
On one part and on th' other? Take it, God,
For it is none but thine!
 Exe.   'Tis wonderful!
 K. Hen. Come, go [we] in procession to the village;
And be it death proclaimed through our host
To boast of this, or take that praise from God 115
Which is his only.
 Flu. Is it not lawful, and please your Majesty, to
tell how many is kill'd?
 K. Hen. Yes, captain; but with this acknowledg-
  ment,
That God fought for us.   120
 Flu. Yes, my conscience, he did us great good.
 K. Hen. Do we all holy rites:
Let there be sung *Non nobis* and *Te Deum*,
The dead with charity enclos'd in clay;
And then to Callice, and to England then, 125
Where ne'er from France arriv'd more happy men.
          Exeunt.

ACT V

Enter CHORUS.

Vouchsafe to those that have not read the story,
That I may prompt them; and of such as have,
I humbly pray them to admit th' excuse
Of time, of numbers, and due course of things,
Which cannot in their huge and proper life 5
Be here presented. Now we bear the King
Toward Callice; grant him there; there seen,
Heave him away upon your winged thoughts
Athwart the sea. Behold, the English beach
Pales in the flood with men, wives, and boys, 10
Whose shouts and claps out-voice the deep-mouth'd
 sea,
Which like a mighty whiffler 'fore the King
Seems to prepare his way. So let him land,
And solemnly see him set on to London.
So swift a pace hath thought that even now 15
You may imagine him upon Blackheath;
Where that his lords desire him to have borne
His bruised helmet and his bended sword
Before him through the city. He forbids it,
Being free from vainness and self-glorious pride; 20
Giving full trophy, signal, and ostent
Quite from himself to God. But now behold,
In the quick forge and working-house of thought,
How London doth pour out her citizens!
The Mayor and all his brethren in best sort, 25
Like to the senators of th' antique Rome,
With the plebeians swarming at their heels,
Go forth and fetch their conqu'ring Caesar in;
As by a lower but by loving likelihood,
Were now the general of our gracious Empress, 30
As in good time he may, from Ireland coming,
Bringing rebellion broached on his sword,
How many would the peaceful city quit,
To welcome him! Much more, and much more cause,
Did they this Harry. Now in London place him— 35
As yet the lamentation of the French
Invites the King of England's stay at home;
The Emperor's coming in behalf of France,
To order peace between them—and omit
All the occurrences, what ever chanc'd, 40
Till Harry's back-return again to France.
There must we bring him; and myself have play'd
The interim, by remem'bring you 'tis past.
Then brook abridgment, and your eyes advance,
After your thoughts, straight back again to France. 45
          Exit.

V.Cho.10. **Pales:** fences.
12. **whiffler:** one who clears the way for a procession.
16. **Blackheath:** open space southeast of London.
21. **trophy . . . ostent:** i.e. signs and shows of victory.
25. **sort:** attire.
29. **loving likelihood:** affectionately anticipated possibility.
30. **the general . . . Empress.** On this topical allusion see the introduction. 32. **broached:** spitted.
38–39. **The Emperor . . . them.** Sigismund, the Holy Roman Emperor,
arrived in England with a retinue of 800 knights on May 1, 1416, in a
futile effort to negotiate a peace between France and England.
41. **Harry's . . . France.** Henry returned to France for a second campaign in August 1417, and as Act V opens he has just made a third
invasion—the "back-return" that led to the Treaty of Troyes in 1420,
with which the play concludes. 43. **remem'bring:** reminding.
44. **brook abridgment:** tolerate omissions.

80. **note:** list. 82. **banners:** coats of arms.
88. **mercenaries:** common soldiers.
123. **Non nobis:** Psalm 115, beginning "Not unto us, O Lord, not
unto us, but unto thy name give glory." **Te Deum:** a hymn of
thanksgiving beginning "We praise thee, O God."

[SCENE I]

Enter FLUELLEN *and* GOWER.

Gow. Nay, that's right; but why wear you your leek to-day? Saint Davy's day is past.

Flu. There is occasions and causes why and wherefore in all things. I will tell you asse my friend, Captain Gower: the rascally, scald, beggarly, 5 lousy, pragging knave, Pistol, which you and yourself, and all the world, know to be no petter than a fellow, look you now, of no merits, he is come to me, and prings me pread and salt yesterday, look you, and bid me eat my leek. It was in a place where I could 10 not breed no contention with him; but I will be so bold as to wear it in my cap till I see him once again, and then I will tell him a little piece of my desires.

Enter PISTOL.

Gow. Why, here he comes, swelling like a turkey-cock.

Flu. 'Tis no matter for his swellings nor his 15 turkey-cocks. God pless you, Aunchient Pistol! you scurvy, lousy knave, God pless you!

Pist. Ha, art thou bedlam? Dost thou thirst, base Troyan,
To have me fold up Parca's fatal web? 20
Hence! I am qualmish at the smell of leek.

Flu. I peseech you heartily, scurvy, lousy knave, at my desires, and my requests, and my petitions, to eat, look you, this leek; because, look you, you do not love it, nor your affections, and your appetites, 25 and your disgestions doo's not agree with it, I would desire you to eat it.

Pist. Not for Cadwallader and all his goats.

Flu. There is one goat for you. (*Strikes him.*) Will you be so good, scald knave, as eat it? 30

Pist. Base Troyan, thou shalt die.

Flu. You say very true, scald knave, when God's will is. I will desire you to live in the mean time, and eat your victuals. Come, there is sauce for it. [*Strikes him.*] You call'd me yesterday mountain-squire, 35 but I will make you to-day a squire of low degree. I pray you fall to; if you can mock a leek, you can eat a leek.

Gow. Enough, captain, you have astonish'd him. 39

Flu. I say, I will make him eat some part of my leek, or I will peat his pate four days. Bite, I pray you, it is good for your green wound and your ploody coxcomb.

Pist. Must I bite? 44

Flu. Yes, certainly, and out of doubt and out of question too, and ambiguities.

Pist. By this leek, I will most horribly revenge—I eat and eat—I swear—

Flu. Eat, I pray you. Will you have some more sauce to your leek? There is not enough leek to swear by. 51

Pist. Quiet thy cudgel, thou dost see I eat.

Flu. Much good do you, scald knave, heartily. Nay, pray you throw none away, the skin is good for your broken coxcomb. When you take occasions to see leeks hereafter, I pray you mock at 'em, that is all.

Pist. Good. 57

Flu. Ay, leeks is good. Hold you, there is a groat to heal your pate.

Pist. Me a groat? 60

Flu. Yes, verily, and in truth you shall take it, or I have another leek in my pocket, which you shall eat.

Pist. I take thy groat in earnest of revenge.

Flu. If I owe you any thing, I will pay you in cudgels; you shall be a woodmonger, and buy 65 nothing of me but cudgels. God buy you, and keep you, and heal your pate. *Exit.*

Pist. All hell shall stir for this.

Gow. Go, go, you are a counterfeit cowardly knave. Will you mock at an ancient tradition, 70 [begun] upon an honorable respect, and worn as a memorable trophy of predeceas'd valor, and dare not avouch in your deeds any of your words? I have seen you gleeking and galling at this gentleman twice or thrice. You thought, because he could not speak 75 English in the native garb, he could not therefore handle an English cudgel. You find it otherwise, and henceforth let a Welsh correction teach you a good English condition. Fare ye well. *Exit.*

Pist. Doth Fortune play the huswife with me now?
News have I that my Doll is dead i' th' spittle 81
Of a malady of France,
And there my rendezvous is quite cut off.
Old I do wax, and from my weary limbs
Honor is cudgell'd. Well, bawd I'll turn, 85
And something lean to cutpurse of quick hand.
To England will I steal, and there I'll steal;
And patches will I get unto these cudgell'd scars,
And [swear] I got them in the Gallia wars. *Exit.*

[SCENE II]

Enter, *at one door,* KING HENRY, EXETER, BEDFORD, [GLOUCESTER,] WARWICK, [WESTMERLAND,] *and other* LORDS; *at another,* QUEEN ISABEL, *the* KING [OF FRANCE], *the* DUKE OF BURGUNDY, [KATHERINE, ALICE,] *and other French.*

K. Hen. Peace to this meeting, wherefore we are met!
Unto our brother France, and to our sister,

V.i. Location: France. The English camp.
5. scald: scabby.   9. yesterday: i.e. St. David's Day (March 1).
19. bedlam: mad.   Troyan: rascal.
20. Parca. In Roman mythology, the Parcae were the Three Fates who spun and drew out and cut the thread of destiny.
25. affections: desires.
28. Cadwallader: last of the Welsh kings.
35. mountain-squire: i.e. lord of worthless land.
36. squire . . . degree. Alluding to the title of a popular romance.
39. astonish'd: stunned.   42. green: fresh.

58. groat: fourpence.
63. earnest: payment to bind a transaction.
74. gleeking and galling: sneering and scoffing.
80. huswife: hussy, i.e. fickle betrayer.
81. my Doll. On this name, in place of the expected Nell (II.i. 18, 31), see the "Note on the Text."   82. malady of France: venereal disease.
83. rendezvous: i.e. refuge.   86. something: somewhat.
89. Gallia: French.

V.ii. Location: France. A royal palace.
1. wherefore: for which (i.e. to make peace).
2. brother . . . sister: i.e. Charles VI and his queen.

Henry V
V.ii

Health and fair time of day; joy and good wishes
To our most fair and princely cousin Katherine;
And as a branch and member of this royalty,   5
By whom this great assembly is contriv'd,
We do salute you, Duke of Burgundy,
And, princes French, and peers, health to you all!
    Fr. King.   Right joyous are we to behold your face,
Most worthy brother England, fairly met!   10
So are you, princes English, every one.
    Q. Isa.   So happy be the issue, brother [England],
Of this good day and of this gracious meeting,
As we are now glad to behold your eyes—
Your eyes, which hitherto have borne in them   15
Against the French that met them in their bent
The fatal balls of murthering basilisks.
The venom of such looks we fairly hope
Have lost their quality, and that this day
Shall change all griefs and quarrels into love.   20
    K. Hen.   To cry amen to that, thus we appear.
    Q. Isa.   You English princes all, I do salute you.
    Bur.   My duty to you both, on equal love.
Great Kings of France and England: that I have
    labor'd
With all my wits, my pains, and strong endeavors   25
To bring your most imperial Majesties
Unto this bar and royal interview,
Your mightiness on both parts best can witness.
Since then my office hath so far prevail'd,
That face to face, and royal eye to eye,   30
You have congreeted, let it not disgrace me,
If I demand, before this royal view,
What rub or what impediment there is,
Why that the naked, poor, and mangled Peace,
Dear nurse of arts, plenties, and joyful births,   35
Should not in this best garden of the world,
Our fertile France, put up her lovely visage?
Alas, she hath from France too long been chas'd,
And all her husbandry doth lie on heaps,
Corrupting in it own fertility.   40
Her vine, the merry cheerer of the heart,
Unpruned dies; her hedges even-pleach'd,
Like prisoners wildly overgrown with hair,
Put forth disorder'd twigs; her fallow leas
The darnel, hemlock, and rank femetary   45
Doth root upon, while that the coulter rusts
That should deracinate such savagery;
The even mead, that erst brought sweetly forth
The freckled cowslip, burnet, and green clover,
Wanting the scythe withal, uncorrected, rank,   50
Conceives by idleness, and nothing teems

But hateful docks, rough thistles, kecksies, burs,
Losing both beauty and utility;
And all our vineyards, fallows, meads, and hedges,
Defective in their natures, grow to wildness.   55
Even so our houses, and ourselves, and children,
Have lost, or do not learn for want of time,
The sciences that should become our country,
But grow like savages—as soldiers will
That nothing do but meditate on blood—   60
To swearing and stern looks, defus'd attire,
And every thing that seems unnatural.
Which to reduce into our former favor
You are assembled; and my speech entreats
That I may know the let why gentle Peace   65
Should not expel these inconveniences,
And bless us with her former qualities.
    K. Hen.   If, Duke of Burgundy, you would the
        peace,
Whose want gives growth to th' imperfections
Which you have cited, you must buy that peace   70
With full accord to all our just demands,
Whose tenures and particular effects
You have enschedul'd briefly in your hands.
    Bur.   The King hath heard them; to the which, as
        yet
There is no answer made.
    K. Hen.   Well then: the peace,   75
Which you before so urg'd, lies in his answer.
    Fr. King.   I have but with a [cursitory] eye
O'erglanc'd the articles. Pleaseth your Grace
To appoint some of your Council presently
To sit with us once more, with better heed   80
To re-survey them, we will suddenly
Pass our accept and peremptory answer.
    K. Hen.   Brother, we shall. Go, uncle Exeter,
And brother Clarence, and you, brother Gloucester,
Warwick, and Huntington, go with the King,   85
And take with you free power to ratify,
Augment, or alter, as your wisdoms best
Shall see advantageable for our dignity,
Any thing in or out of our demands,
And we'll consign thereto. Will you, fair sister,   90
Go with the princes, or stay here with us?
    Q. Isa.   Our gracious brother, I will go with them.
Happily a woman's voice may do some good,
When articles too nicely urg'd be stood on.
    K. Hen.   Yet leave our cousin Katherine here with
        us: 95
She is our capital demand, compris'd
Within the fore-rank of our articles.
    Q. Isa.   She hath good leave.
            Exeunt omnes. Manent King [Henry] and
            Katherine [with the gentlewoman Alice].
    K. Hen.   Fair Katherine, and most fair,

---

5. **royalty:** royal family.   12. **issue:** outcome.
16. **bent:** (1) glance; (2) line of fire.
17. **fatal balls:** (1) eyeballs; (2) cannon balls.   **basilisks:** (1) fabulous creatures whose glance was thought to cause death; (2) large cannon.   19. **quality:** (deadly) nature.   23. **on:** deriving from.
24–27. **I . . . interview.** Since 1417 Burgundy had actively supported the various abortive attempts to negotiate a peace between France and England.   27. **bar:** court.   31. **congreeted:** met amicably.
33. **rub:** obstacle.   40. **it:** its.
42. **even-pleach'd:** smoothly interwoven, plaited.
44. **fallow leas:** unplanted fields.
45. **darnel:** a weedy grass.   **femetary:** fumitory, another weed.
46. **coulter:** blade.
47. **deracinate such savagery:** uproot such wildness.
48. **erst:** formerly.   50. **Wanting:** lacking.
51. **Conceives:** i.e. produces weeds.

55. **Defective . . . natures:** i.e. perverted from their natural function, unnatural.   61. **defus'd:** disordered.
63. **reduce . . . favor:** return to our former appearance.
65. **let:** hindrance.   68. **would:** desire.
72. **tenures:** tenors, general principles.
77. **cursitory:** cursory.   78. **Pleaseth:** if it please.
79. **presently:** immediately.
81–82. **suddenly . . . answer:** promptly return our adopted and decisive reply.   93. **Happily:** haply, perhaps.
94. **nicely:** punctiliously.   96. **capital:** chief.

Will you vouchsafe to teach a soldier terms,
Such as will enter at a lady's ear,   100
And plead his love-suit to her gentle heart?

Kath. Your Majesty shall mock at me, I cannot
speak your England.

K. Hen. O fair Katherine, if you will love me
soundly with your French heart, I will be glad to   105
hear you confess it brokenly with your English tongue.
Do you like me, Kate?

Kath. *Pardonnez-moi,* I cannot tell wat is "like me."

K. Hen. An angel is like you, Kate, and you are
like an angel.   110

Kath. *Que dit-il? Que je suis semblable à les anges?*

Alice. *Oui, vraiment, sauf votre grâce, ainsi dit-il.*

K. Hen. I said so, dear Katherine, and I must not
blush to affirm it.

Kath. *O bon Dieu! les langues des hommes sont
pleines de tromperies.*   116

K. Hen. What says she, fair one? That the tongues
of men are full of deceits?

Alice. *Oui, dat de tongeus of de mans is be full of
deceits: dat is de Princess.*   120

K. Hen. The Princess is the better Englishwoman.
I' faith, Kate, my wooing is fit for thy understanding.
I am glad thou canst speak no better English, for if
thou couldst, thou wouldst find me such a plain king
that thou wouldst think I had sold my farm to buy   125
my crown. I know no ways to mince it in love, but
directly to say "I love you"; then if you urge me
farther than to say "Do you in faith?" I wear out my
suit. Give me your answer, i' faith, do, and so clap
hands and a bargain. How say you, lady?   130

Kath. *Sauf votre honneur,* me understand well.

K. Hen. Marry, if you would put me to verses, or
to dance for your sake, Kate, why, you undid me: for
the one, I have neither words nor measure; and for the
other, I have no strength in measure, yet a reason-   135
able measure in strength. If I could win a lady at
leap-frog, or by vauting into my saddle with my armor
on my back, under the correction of bragging be it
spoken, I should quickly leap into a wife. Or if I
might buffet for my love, or bound my horse for   140
her favors, I could lay on like a butcher, and sit like a
jack-an-apes, never off. But, before God, Kate, I
cannot look greenly, nor gasp out my eloquence, nor I
have no cunning in protestation; only downright oaths,
which I never use till urg'd, nor never break for   145
urging. If thou canst love a fellow of this temper,
Kate, whose face is not worth sunburning, that never
looks in his glass for love of any thing he sees there, let
thine eye be thy cook. I speak to thee plain soldier. If
thou canst love me for this, take me! if not, to say   150
to thee that I shall die, is true; but for thy love, by the
Lord, no; yet I love thee too. And while thou liv'st,

dear Kate, take a fellow of plain and uncoin'd constancy, for he perforce must do thee right, because he
hath not the gift to woo in other places; for these   155
fellows of infinite tongue, that can rhyme themselves
into ladies' favors, they do always reason themselves
out again. What? a speaker is but a prater, a rhyme is
but a ballad; a good leg will fall, a straight back will
stoop, a black beard will turn white, a curl'd pate   160
will grow bald, a fair face will wither, a full eye will
wax hollow; but a good heart, Kate, is the sun and the
moon, or rather the sun and not the moon; for it shines
bright and never changes, but keeps his course truly.
If thou would have such a one, take me! and take   165
me, take a soldier; take a soldier, take a king. And
what say'st thou then to my love? Speak, my fair,
and fairly, I pray thee.

Kath. Is it possible dat I sould love de ennemie of
France?   170

K. Hen. No, it is not possible you should love the
enemy of France, Kate; but in loving me, you should
love the friend of France; for I love France so well that
I will not part with a village of it; I will have it all
mine. And, Kate, when France is mine and I am yours,
then yours is France and you are mine.   176

Kath. I cannot tell wat is dat.

K. Hen. No, Kate? I will tell thee in French,
which I am sure will hang upon my tongue like a new-
married wife about her husband's neck, hardly   180
to be shook off. *Je quand sur le possession de France, et
quand vous avez le possession de moi*—let me see, what
then? *Saint Denis be my speed!—donc votre est France
et vous êtes mienne.* It is as easy for me, Kate, to
conquer the kingdom as to speak so much more   185
French. I shall never move thee in French, unless it be
to laugh at me.

Kath. *Sauf votre honneur, le François que vous
parlez, il est [meilleur] que l'Anglois lequel je parle.*   189

K. Hen. No, faith, is't not, Kate; but thy speaking
of my tongue, and I thine, most truly falsely, must
needs be granted to be much at one. But, Kate, dost
thou understand thus much English? Canst thou love
me?

Kath. I cannot tell.   195

K. Hen. Can any of your neighbors tell, Kate?
I'll ask them. Come, I know thou lovest me; and at
night, when you come into your closet, you'll question
this gentlewoman about me; and I know, Kate, you
will to her dispraise those parts in me that you   200
love with your heart. But, good Kate, mock me
mercifully, the rather, gentle Princess, because I love
thee cruelly. If ever thou beest mine, Kate, as I have a
saving faith within me tells me thou shalt, I get thee
with scambling, and thou must therefore needs   205
prove a good soldier-breeder. Shall not thou and I,
between Saint Denis and Saint George, compound a

---

99. **terms:** words.
111–12. **Que . . . dit-il:** What does he say? That I am like the
angels? *Alice.* Yes, truly, save your grace, so he says.
129. **clap:** clasp.
134, 135, 136. **measure:** (1) metre; (2) dancing; (3) amount.
137. **vauting:** vaulting.   140. **buffet:** box.
142. **jack-an-apes:** monkey.   143. **greenly:** bashful.
147. **not worth sunburning:** i.e. because it is already so weather-
beaten.   149. **be thy cook:** i.e. add the garnishing.

153. **uncoin'd:** i.e. like unminted metal, not in common use.
159. **fall:** lose its shape.
181–84. **Je . . . mienne.** A halting translation of the last sentence of
Henry's preceding speech.
183. **Saint Denis:** patron saint of France.   **be my speed:** aid me.
188–89. **Sauf . . . parle.** save your honor, the French you speak is
better than the English I speak.
192. **at one:** (1) alike; (2) united.   198. **closet:** chamber.
200. **parts:** qualities.   205. **scambling:** fighting.

Henry V
V.ii

boy, half French, half English, that shall go to Constantinople and take the Turk by the beard? Shall we not? What say'st thou, my fair flower-de-luce? 210

Kath. I do not know dat.

K. Hen. No; 'tis hereafter to know, but now to promise. Do but now promise, Kate, you will endeavor for your French part of such a boy; and for my English moi'ty, take the word of a king and a 215 bachelor. How answer you, *la plus belle Katherine du monde, mon très cher et devin déesse?*

Kath. Your Majestee ave fausse French enough to deceive de most sage demoiselle dat is en France. 219

K. Hen. Now fie upon my false French! By mine honor, in true English, I love thee, Kate; by which honor I dare not swear thou lovest me, yet my blood begins to flatter me that thou dost—notwithstanding the poor and untempering effect of my visage. Now beshrew my father's ambition! he was thinking of 225 civil wars when he got me; therefore was I created with a stubborn outside, with an aspect of iron, that when I come to woo ladies, I fright them. But in faith, Kate, the elder I wax, the better I shall appear. My comfort is, that old age, that ill layer-up of beauty, 230 can do no more spoil upon my face. Thou hast me, if thou hast me, at the worst; and thou shalt wear me, if thou wear me, better and better; and therefore tell me, most fair Katherine, will you have me? Put off your maiden blushes, avouch the thoughts of your heart 235 with the looks of an empress, take me by the hand, and say, "Harry of England, I am thine"; which word thou shalt no sooner bless mine ear withal, but I will tell thee aloud, "England is thine, Ireland is thine, France is thine, and Henry Plantagenet is thine"; 240 who, though I speak it before his face, if he be not fellow with the best king, thou shalt find the best king of good fellows. Come, your answer in broken music; for thy voice is music and thy English broken; therefore, queen of all, Katherine, break thy mind to me in broken English—wilt thou have me? 246

Kath. Dat is as it shall please de *roi mon père.*

K. Hen. Nay, it will please him well, Kate; it shall please him, Kate.

Kath. Den it sall also content me. 250

K. Hen. Upon that I kiss your hand, and I call you my queen.

Kath. Laissez, *mon seigneur, laissez, laissez, laissez! Ma foi, je ne veux point que vous abaissez votre* [*grandeur*] *en baisant la main d'une* (*Notre Seigneur!*) *indigne serviteur. Excusez-moi, je vous supplie, mon très puissant seigneur.*

K. Hen. Then I will kiss your lips, Kate. 257

Kath. Les dames et demoiselles pour être baisées devant leur noces, il n'est pas la coutume de France.

K. Hen. Madam my interpreter, what says she?

Alice. Dat it is not be de fashon pour les ladies of France—I cannot tell wat is [*baiser*] en Anglish. 262

K. Hen. To kiss.

Alice. Your Majestee *entendre* bettre *que moi.*

K. Hen. It is not a fashion for the maids in France to kiss before they are married, would she say? 266

Alice. Oui, vraiment.

K. Hen. O Kate, nice customs cur'sy to great kings. Dear Kate, you and I cannot be confin'd within the weak list of a country's fashion. We are the 270 makers of manners, Kate; and the liberty that follows our places stops the mouth of all find-faults, as I will do yours, for upholding the nice fashion of your country in denying me a kiss; therefore patiently and yielding. [*Kissing her.*] You have witchcraft in 275 your lips, Kate; there is more eloquence in a sugar touch of them than in the tongues of the French council; and they should sooner persuade Harry of England than a general petition of monarchs. Here comes your father. 280

Enter the FRENCH POWER *and the* ENGLISH LORDS.

Bur. God save your Majesty! My royal cousin, teach you our princess English?

K. Hen. I would have her learn, my fair cousin, how perfectly I love her, and that is good English.

Bur. Is she not apt? 285

K. Hen. Our tongue is rough, coz, and my condition is not smooth; so that having neither the voice nor the heart of flattery about me, I cannot so conjure up the spirit of love in her, that he will appear in his true likeness. 290

Bur. Pardon the frankness of my mirth, if I answer you for that. If you would conjure in her, you must make a circle; if conjure up Love in her in his true likeness, he must appear naked and blind. Can you blame her then, being a maid yet ros'd over 295 with the virgin crimson of modesty, if she deny the appearance of a naked blind boy in her naked seeing self? It were, my lord, a hard condition for a maid to consign to. 299

K. Hen. Yet they do wink and yield, as love is blind and enforces.

Bur. They are then excus'd, my lord, when they see not what they do.

K. Hen. Then, good my lord, teach your cousin to consent winking. 305

Bur. I will wink on her to consent, my lord, if you will teach her to know my meaning; for maids, well summer'd and warm kept, are like flies at Bartholomew-tide, blind, though they have their eyes, and then they will endure handling, which before would not abide looking on. 311

K. Hen. This moral ties me over to time and a hot summer; and so I shall catch the fly, your cousin, in the latter end, and she must be blind too.

Bur. As love is, my lord, before it loves. 315

K. Hen. It is so; and you may, some of you, thank

---

210. **flower-de-luce:** fleur-de-lis, the national emblem of France.
215. **moi'ty:** part.   216. **bachelor:** young knight.
216–17. **la plus . . . déesse:** the most beautiful Katherine in the world, my very dear and divine goddess.   222. **blood:** instinct.
224. **untempering:** uningratiating.   229. **wax:** grow.
230. **layer-up:** preserver.   242. **fellow with:** equal to.
243. **broken music:** music in parts.   245. **break:** open, reveal.
247. **de roi mon père:** the king my father.
253–56. **Laissez . . . seigneur:** Don't, my lord, don't, don't. My faith, I don't want you to lower your dignity by kissing the hand of an (Our Lord!) unworthy servant. Excuse me, I beg you, my most mighty lord.

264. **entendre . . . moi:** understands better than I.
268. **nice:** overrefined.   **cur'sy:** curtsy, i.e. defer, yield.
270. **list:** barrier.   271–72. **follows our places:** befits our rank.
286–87. **condition:** disposition.   300. **wink:** close both eyes.
308. **summer'd:** nurtured.   308–9. **Bartholomew-tide:** August 24.

love for my blindness, who cannot see many a fair
French city for one fair French maid that stands in my
way.   319

Fr. King. Yes, my lord, you see them perspectively: the cities turn'd into a maid; for they are all
girdled with maiden walls that war hath [never]
ent'red.

K. Hen. Shall Kate be my wife?

Fr. King. So please you.   325

K. Hen. I am content, so the maiden cities you talk
of may wait on her; so the maid that stood in the way
for my wish shall show me the way to my will.

Fr. King. We have consented to all terms of
reason.   330

K. Hen. Is't so, my lords of England?

West. The King hath granted every article:
His daughter first; and in sequel, all,
According to their firm proposed natures.

Exe. Only he hath not yet subscribed this: 335
Where your Majesty demands that the King of
France, having any occasion to write for matter of
grant, shall name your Highness in this form, and with
this addition, in French, *Notre très cher fils Henri, Roi
d'Angleterre, Héritier de France;* and thus in Latin,
*Praeclarissimus filius noster Henricus, Rex Angliae, et
Heres Franciae.*   342

Fr. King. Nor this I have not, brother, so denied,
But your request shall make me let it pass.

K. Hen. I pray you then, in love and dear alliance,
Let that one article rank with the rest,   346
And thereupon give me your daughter.

Fr. King. Take her, fair son, and from her blood
        raise up
Issue to me, that the contending kingdoms
Of France and England, whose very shores look pale
With envy of each other's happiness,   351
May cease their hatred; and this dear conjunction
Plant neighborhood and Christian-like accord
In their sweet bosoms, that never war advance
His bleeding sword 'twixt England and fair France.

Lords. Amen!   356

K. Hen. Now welcome, Kate; and bear me wit-
        ness all,
That here I kiss her as my sovereign queen. *Flourish.*

Q. Isa. God, the best maker of all marriages,
Combine your hearts in one, your realms in one!   360
As man and wife, being two, are one in love,
So be there 'twixt your kingdoms such a spousal,
That never may ill office, or fell jealousy,
Which troubles oft the bed of blessed marriage,
Thrust in between the [paction] of these kingdoms,
To make divorce of their incorporate league;   366
That English may as French, French Englishmen,
Receive each other. God speak this Amen!

All. Amen!

K. Hen. Prepare we for our marriage; on which
        day,   370
My Lord of Burgundy, we'll take your oath,
And all the peers', for surety of our leagues.
Then shall I swear to Kate, and you to me,
And may our oaths well kept and prosp'rous be!
                              Sennet. Exeunt.

Enter CHORUS *[as Epilogue].*

Thus far, with rough and all-unable pen,
Our bending author hath pursu'd the story,
In little room confining mighty men,
Mangling by starts the full course of their glory.
Small time; but in that small most greatly lived   5
This star of England. Fortune made his sword;
By which the world's best garden he achieved,
And of it left his son imperial lord.
Henry the Sixt, in infant bands crown'd King
Of France and England, did this king succeed;   10
Whose state so many had the managing,
That they lost France, and made his England bleed;
Which oft our stage hath shown; and for their sake,
In your fair minds let this acceptance take.   *[Exit.]*

320–21. **perspectively:** i.e. as through an optical glass that produces
illusions.   322. **maiden:** i.e. unconquered.
337–38. **for . . . grant:** i.e. in formal documents.
339. **addition:** title.
339–42. **Notre . . . Franciae:** our dear son Henry, King of England
and Heir of France.   343. **so:** i.e. so firmly.
352. **dear conjunction:** solemn union.

363. **ill office:** graceless act.   **fell:** cruel.
365. **paction:** agreement.
370–74. **Prepare . . . be.** The royal wedding, which was solemnized
with great pomp on June 2, 1420, did not bring the peace predicted
here, for the Dauphin, indignant at the concessions that Henry had
exacted from his father, continued his resistance. Consequently
Henry's last two years of life were spent in an unsuccessful effort to
consolidate his gains in France. When he died in 1422, leaving the
throne to his infant son, affairs were in the disordered state described
at the opening of *1 Henry VI.*

Epi. 1–14. These lines form a Shakespearean sonnet.
2. **bending:** bowing (?) or stooped with the labor of composition (?).
13. **Which . . . shown.** Alluding to the great popularity of the Henry
VI plays.   14. **this acceptance take:** this play find favor.

NOTE ON THE TEXT

The First Folio (1623) offers us our only authoritative text
of *Henry the Fifth;* all later texts are basically derived from
that source. There is also, however, a "bad" quarto, a
memorially reconstructed version of the play, published in
1600 (Q1): and two more quartos, each printed from Q1,
were issued in 1602 (Q2) and 1619 (Q3; fraudulently dated
1608). Q3 contains a number of slight variants, some of
which anticipate the F1 text (see below). As the Textual

Notes show, Q1 is useful for occasional stage directions and
for correcting a few errors in the F1 text, but, as a reported
version, it has nothing more than what might be called
"hearsay" authority.

There is general agreement that Shakespeare's "foul
papers" lie somewhere behind the F1 text. The stigmata of
"foul papers" are clearly visible: some inconsistency in
speech-prefixes; occasional indefinite stage directions and

omission of stage directions; the appearance of a ghost character, Beaumont (in IV.ii o.s.d.); and a few characteristic Shakespearean spellings (see Textual Notes, II.iii.31, 35, IV.i.179, IV.ii.11, V.ii.137; and *mervailous*, II.i.47). Until recently it has usually been argued that the F1 text derives directly from the "foul papers." However, A. S. Cairncross, in an article too complex to be discussed in detail here, has argued that F1 was in fact set up from copy composed of pages of Q2 and Q3 corrected and augmented by reference to the "foul papers." That there is some kind of bibliographical link between Q3, at least, and the F1 text seems nearly certain, but, as J. H. Walter points out, printer's copy such as that postulated by Cairncross would have been very cumbersome and hard to follow—even more so, one would suppose, than Shakespeare's "foul papers." The problems here involved suggest an immediate analogy with the textual situation in *2* and *3 Henry VI*, including the possible contamination of the F1 text by a later quarto copy-text (see particularly the "Note on the Text" to *2 Henry VI*). In the case of *Henry V*, however, there is a difference, since the Q3 (Q2)-F1 links are almost entirely limited to single, usually unimportant, words or contractions as compared with the more significant links (in some instances passages) in the two *Henry VI* plays, and this makes it more difficult to accept Greg's suggestion that they arise from someone connected with the printing of Q3 who had heard a recent performance of the play. The problem clearly needs further study. The present text adheres to F1 copy-text, but a record of the most significant agreements between Q3 and F1 against Q1–2 may be consulted in the Textual Notes: II.i.33, II.ii.177, II.iii.31, 42 (an especially tempting reading in Q1–2), II.iv.75, III.ii.44, III.vi.158, III.vii.20, IV.i.284 s.d., IV.iii.4, 65–6 (an important reading), 124, IV.v.19, IV.vi.2, 30, IV.vii.5, 91, 111, 154–5, IV.viii.24, 51, 65, 71, V.i.14, 24, 33, 64, IV.i.171, 340, 341–2. Where only one or two of the three quartos are cited, agreement of the uncited quarto (or quartos) with the lemma may be assumed.

The play as it appears in F1 shows some evidence of revision. It seems likely, for example, that Shakespeare originally intended to include Falstaff among Henry's followers in the French wars and that the scenes connected with his death (II.i, iii) were later additions, a conclusion supported by the feeble extra couplet with which the second Chorus ends. It is even possible that much of Pistol's "business" once belonged to Falstaff, a view that would help to explain the curious reference to Doll Tearsheet (V.i.81), which properly should be to Mistress Quickly, Pistol's wife. Probably, also, the discussion in III.ii between Fluellen, Gower, Macmorris, and Jamy was an afterthought (see the Textual Notes for Fluellen's change of speech-prefix at III.ii.68); neither Macmorris nor Jamy appears again, nor is this part of the scene or these two characters found in Q1–3, where, however, the omission may have been the result of cutting to reduce the number of characters needed for provincial touring. Other evidences of revision have also been noted.

For the treatment of Shakespeare's French in the present text, see the note at the beginning of III.iv below. The editor is indebted to Professor Charles Knudson for advice on sixteenth-century French forms. From Rowe onward there has been much editorial tinkering with Fluellen's "English"; the present text reproduces his speech as it appears in F1.

The Textual Notes generally record the variants in Q1–3 only where they figure in a reading cited in connection with the F1 text. The absence of citation of Q1–3 among the sigla in any entry indicates that the reading of the lemma occurs in a passage which in Q1–3 is either omitted or so differently worded that it offers no recognizable equivalent.

For further information, see: H. T. Price, *The Text of "Henry V"* (Newcastle-under-Lyme, 1920); J. H. Walter, "'With Sir John in It,'" *MLR*, XLVI (1946), 237–45, and ed., New Arden *King Henry V* (London, 1954; rev. ed., 1960); J. D. Wilson, ed., New Cambridge *King Henry V* (Cambridge, 1947); W. W. Greg, *The Shakespeare First Folio* (Oxford, 1955); A. S. Cairncross, "Quarto Copy for Folio *Henry V*," *SB*, VIII (1956), 67–93; Alice Walker, "Some Editorial Principles, with Special Reference to *Henry V*," *SB*, VIII (1956), 95–111; G. I. Duthie, "The Quarto of Shakespeare's *Henry V*," *Papers Mainly Shakespearian*, ed. G. I. Duthie (1964), pp. 106–30.

TEXTUAL NOTES

Title: **The . . . Fifth**] The . . . Fift. *F1*; The Cronicle History of Henry the fift, With his battell fought at Agin Court in France. Togither with Auntient Pistoll. As it hath bene sundry times playd by the Right honorable the Lord Chamberlaine his seruants. *Q1 (title-page)*

Dramatis personae: *subs. as first given in Rowe*

Act-scene division: *none in Q1–3; F1 marks I.i and thereafter acts only, as follows: Acts II and III at the beginning of Acts III and IV, respectively, of the present numbering, Act IV at the present IV.vii, and Act V as in the present text; other act-scene divisions from Pope and later editors (see first note to each scene); present act-scene arrangement as a whole first established by Capell*

Prologue

Prologue and choruses om. Q1–3

I.i

Scene om. Q1–3

Location: *Malone (after Pope, Theobald)*

1 s.p. **Cant.**] *Rowe*; Bish. Cant. *F1*; *(or B. Cant. throughout scene)*

6 s.p. **Ely.**] *Rowe*; Bish. Ely. *F1 (or B. Ely. throughout scene)*

11 **thus:**] *Capell (subs.)*; thus, *F1*

36 **seat . . . once)**] *ed.*; Seat; . . . once; *F1*

66 **crescive**] *F4*; cressiue *F1*

89 **great-grandfather**] *hyphen, Dyce*

I.ii

I.ii] *Pope*

Location: *Theobald (subs.)*

o.s.d. **and other Attendants**] *from Q1–3 s.d.*: Enter King Henry, Exeter, 2. Bishops, Clarence, and other Attendants.

6 s.d. **the Archbishop . . . Ely**] *Rowe*

38 **succedant**] *F2*; succedaul *F1*

45, 52 **Elbe**] *Capell (after Holinshed)*; Elue *F1*; Elme *F1 (om. l. 52)*

53 **call'd**] called *Q1–2*

59 **suppos'd**] supposed *Q1–2*

72 **fine**] *Q1–3*; find *F1*

76 **Lewis**] *Rowe*; Lewes *F1 (throughout; so Holinshed)*

103 **great-grandsire's**] *hyphen, Dyce*

105 **great-uncle's**] *hyphen, Dyce*

115 s.p. **Ely.**] *F3 (subs.)*; Bish. *F1 (Q1–3 om. ll. 115–135)*

131 **blood**] *F3*; Bloods *F1*

138 **Against**] *for Q1, Q3*

146 **great-grandfather**] *hyphen, Dyce*

155 **fear'd:**] feared *Q1–2*

156 **herself:**] *Theobald (subs.)*; her selfe, *F1, Q1–3*

163 **her**] *Johnson conj.*; their *F1*; your *Q1–3*

166 s.p. **Ely.**] Bish. Ely. *F1*; Lord. *Q1–3*

(Holinshed assigns the speech to Westmerland; so also Capell and many later eds.)

168 **begin**] *Q1–3*; begia *F1*

173 **'tame**] *Wilson (after Greg)*; tame *F1*; spoyle *Q1–3*

174 **then**] *Q1–3*; theu *F1*

196 **tent-royal**] tent royall *Q1–2*

197 **majesty**] *Q1–3*; Maiesties *F1*

202 **sad-ey'd**] sad eyde *Q1–3*

208 **many**] many seuerall *Q1–3*

211 **afoot**] *Rowe*; a foote *F1, Q1–3*

212 **End**] *Q1–3*; And *F1*

221 s.d. **Exeunt some Attendants.**] *Capell*

233 s.d. **attended**] *Hudson (after Capell)*

234 **prepar'd**] prepared *Q1–2*

237, 245 s.pp. **1. Amb.**] *Dyce*; Amb. *F1, Q1–3*

240 **meaning**] *F2*; meauing *F1*; pleasure *Q1–3*

269 **valu'd**] valued *Q1–2*

270 **therefore,**] *Theobald*; therefore *F1 (cf. Q1–3's reading of ll. 269–70: We neuer valued [valew'd Q3] this poore seate of England. / And therefore gaue our selues to barbarous licence:)*

276 **that I have**] this haue we *Q1–2*; this we haue *Q3*

277 **working-days**] *hyphen, Capell*

II.Cho.

Act II] *Johnson*

22 **crowns; . . . men,**] *Theobald*; Crownes, . . . men: *F1*

25 **knight,]** *Knight*; Knight *F1*
28 **die,]** *F2*; dye. *F1*

II.i

II.i] *Hanmer*
Location: *Capell*
o.s.d. **Bardolph]** *F4*; Bardolfe *F1*, *Q1–3* (*throughout scene*)
2 **Good morrow]** Godmorrow *Q1*; God morrow *Q2*
22 **time,]** time, and there is [there's *Q3*] the humor of it. *Q1–3*
23 **mare]** *Q1–3*; name *F1*
28 **s.p. Nym.]** *Q1–3*; *speech continued to Bardolph, F1*
29–31 **Base . . . lodgers.]** *as verse, Q1–3*; *as prose, F1*
30 **Gadslugs]** *ed.* (*from Q1, Q3 gads lugges*); this hand *F1*; gads lugge *Q2*
33 **gentlewomen]** honest gentlewomen *Q1–2*
35–6 **s.d. Nym . . . draw.]** *Capell* (*subs.*)
42 **Iceland . . . Iceland]** *Johnson conj.*; Island . . . Island *F1*; *Q1–3 read the line:* What dost thou push, thou prickeard cur of Iseland
46–53 **"Solus," . . . follow.]** *as irregular verse, Q1–3*; *as prose, F1*
65 **s.d. Draws.]** *Malone*; They drawe. *Q1–3* (*after l. 62*)
67–8 **Give . . . tall.]** *as verse, Pope*; *as prose, F1*
71–80 **"Couple . . . to.]** *as irregular verse, Q1–3*; *as prose, F1*
72 **thee defy]** *Q1–3*; defie thee *F1*
79 **and—pauca]** *Capell*; and *Pauca F1*; and Paco *Q1–3*
79–80 **enough . . . to.]** *ed.*; enough to go to. *F1*; inough. *Q1–2*; enough. *Q3*
89 **s.d. with Boy]** *Capell* (*subs.*)
95 **betting]** beating *Q1–2*
98 **s.d. They draw.]** *Q1–3*; Draw *F1*
100 **s.d. Draws.]** *Delius*
102 **Corporal]** *F3*; Coporall *F1*
105–6 **Nym. I . . . betting?]** *Q1–3* (beating *Q1–2*)
107–12 **A . . . accrue.]** *as verse, Q1–3*; *as prose, F1*
116 **that's]** *F2*; that *F1*; theres *Q1–3*
118 **Ah]** *Pope*; A *F1*
123–4 **Nym . . . corroborate.]** *as verse, Capell*; *as prose, F1* (*as single line, Q1–3*)
127 **Let . . . live.]** *as verse, Capell*; *as prose, F1* (*as single line, Q1–3*)
127 **s.d. Exeunt.]** *Q1–3* (Exeunt omnes.)

II.ii

II.ii] *Pope*
Location: *Pope, Malone* (*after Capell*)
11 **s.d. with Attendants]** *Theobald* (*subs.*)
19 **s.p. Scroop.]** Masha. *or* Mash. *Q1–3* (*throughout scene*)
29 **s.p. Grey.]** *Q1–3* (Gray.); Kni. *F1*
56 **digested]** disgested *Q1–2*
67–8 **knight; . . . knight.]** *Q1–3* (Masham. And Sir Thomas Gray [Grey *Q3*] knight); Masham, . . . Knight: Gray *F1*
75 **have]** hath *Q1–3*
87 **him]** *Q1–3* (*in the phrase* to grace him); *F2*
89, 167 **conspir'd]** *Q1, Q3*
95 **inhuman]** *Rowe*; inhumane *F1, Q1–3*
98 **have] a** *Q1*
99 **have] a** *Q1–2*
107 **a]** *F2*; an *F1*
122 **lion gait]** *Capell*; Lyon-gate *F1*
139 **mark the.]** *Theobald*; make thee *F1*
140 **suspicion. . . . thee;]** *Capell* (*after Pope*); suspition, . . . thee. *F1*
147 **Henry]** *Q1–3*; Thomas *F1*
148 **Masham]** *Q1–3*; Marsham *F1*
150 **knight,]** *Dyce*; Knight *F1, Q1–3*
159 **I]** *F2*
175 **must]** *Q1–3*; ɯust *F1*
176 **have]** three *F2*
177 **you]** ye *Q1–2*
181 **s.d. Exeunt . . . guarded.]** *Capell* (*subs.*); Exit. *F1*; Exit three Lords. *Q1–3*
192 **Cheerly]** *Q1–3*; Chearely *F1*
193 **s.d. Exeunt.]** *Q1–3* (Exit omnes.)

II.iii

II.iii] *Pope*
Location: *Theobald* (*subs.*)
1 **honey-sweet]** hyphen, *Theobald*
3–6 **No . . . therefore.]** *as verse, Pope*; *as prose, F1* (*Q1–3 reduce the lines to:* No fur, no fur.)
16–7 **'a babbl'd]** *Theobald* (*after anon. conj.* a' talked): a Table *F1*
22 **on]** at *Q1–2*; om. *Q3*
24 **knees,]** knees, and they were as cold as any stone. *Q1–3*
25 **up'ard and up'ard]** *Wilson*; vp-peer'd, and vpward *F1*; vpward, and vpward *Q1–3*
31 **said]** he sed *Q1–2*
31 **dev'ls]** *ed.*; Deules *F1*; diuels *Q1–3*
33 **s.p. Host.]** *Q1–3*; Woman. *F1*
35 **dev'l]** *ed.*; Deule *F1* (*Q1–3 version of speech assigned to Nim.*)
42 **hell]** hell fire *Q1–2*
47–56 **Come . . . suck!]** *as irregular verse, Q1–3*; *as prose, F1*
49 **word]** *Q1, Q3*; world *F1, Q2*
52 **dog, my duck;]** *pointing from Q1–3* (dog my deare.); Dogge: My Ducke, *F1*
59 **s.d. Kissing her.]** *Capell*
62 **Let . . . command.]** *Q1–3 read:* Keepe fast thy buggle boe.

II.iv

II.iv] *Pope*
Location: *Pope, Theobald*
o.s.d. **the Constable]** *Rowe*
o.s.d. **and others]** *Q1–3*
1 **s.p. Fr. King.]** *Rowe*; King. *F1, Q1–3* (*throughout scene*)
33 **counsellors]** *Q1–3*; Councellors *F1*
67 **s.d. Exeunt . . . Lords.]** *Capell*
74–5 **Self-love . . . self-neglecting]** Selfeloue . . . selfe neglecting *Q1–2* (thing *for* sin)
75 **s.d. Enter . . . Train.]** *Capell* (*subs.*); Enter Exeter. *F1, Q1–3*
75 **of]** om. *Q1–2*
89 **s.d. Giving a paper.]** *Theobald* (*subs.*)
107 **dead men's]** *Q1–3* (mens); dead-mens *F1*
107 **privy]** pining *Q1–3*
112 **too]** *Q1–3*; to *F1*
131 **Paris balls]** *Q1–3*; Paris-Balls *F1*
132 **Louvre]** *Pope*; Louer *F1, Q1–3*; Loouer *F2* (*indicates pronunciation*)
134 **difference]** *Q1–3*; diff'rence *F1*

III.Cho.

Act III] *Pope*; Actus Secundus. *F1*
4 **Hampton]** *Theobald*; Douer *F1*
6 **fanning]** *Rowe*; fayning *F1*

III.i

III.i] *Hanmer*
Scene om. Q1–3
Location: *Theobald* (*after F1 o.s.d.*)
o.s.d. **Enter Soldiers with]** *ed.* (*after Theobald*)
7 **conjure]** *Walter*; commune *F1*
15 **nostril]** *Rowe*; Nosthrill *F1*
17 **noblest]** *F2*; Noblish *F1*
24 **men]** *F4*; me *F1*
32 **Straining]** *Rowe*; Straying *F1*
34 **s.d. Exeunt.]** *Theobald* (*subs.*)

III.ii

III.ii] *Hanmer*
Location: *ed.* (*after Theobald*)
8–11 **"Knocks . . . fame."]** *as verse, Capell* (*after Pope; as fragmentary verse, Q1–3*); *as prose, F1*
15–9 **"If . . . bough."]** *as verse, Capell* (*after Pope; as fragmentary verse, Q1–3*); *as prose, F1*
17 **hie]** *Q1–3*; high *F1*
21 **s.d. Driving them forward.]** *Capell* (*subs., after Q1–3* Enter Flewellen and beates them in.)
22–5 **Be . . . chuck!]** *as verse, Pope* (*omitting l. 25*); *as prose, F1*
27 **s.d. with . . . Pistol]** *Q1–2* (*subs., including the Boy and following his soliloquy*)
27 **s.d. Fluellen steps aside.]** *ed.*
31 **antics]** *Theobald*; Antiques *F1*

43 **lute-case]** Lute case *Q1–2*
44 **half-pence]** hapence *Q1–2*
45 **fire-shovel]** fier shouell *Q1–2*
53 **s.d. Fluellen comes forward.]** *ed.*
63 **Cheshu]** Iesus *Q1–2*; Ieshu *Q3*
66 **Irishman]** *Capell*; Irish man *F1*
68 **s.p. Flu.]** *Rowe*; Welch. *F1* (*throughout scene; note that change of s.p. comes with the introduction of Macmorris and Jamy and that the rest of the scene, after l. 64, is om. in Q1–3*)
68 **Macmorris]** *Pope* (*subs.*); Makmorrice *F1* (*throughout scene*)
83 **s.p. Jamy.]** *Rowe*; Scot. *F1* (*throughout scene*)
88 **s.p. Mac.]** *Rowe*; Irish. *F1* (*throughout scene*)
121 **nation]** *Pope*; Nation. *F1*
136 **A!]** *Cambridge*; Ieshu *F1*
136 **s.d. sounded]** *Rowe*
141 **s.d. Exeunt.]** *Rowe*; Exit. *F1*

III.iii

III.iii] *Hanmer*
Location: *Theobald*
o.s.d. **Enter . . . walls.]** *Walter* (*after Capell*)
o.s.d. **Enter . . . gates.]** Enter the King and his Lords alarum. *Q1–2*, (om. alarum) *Q3*
23 **career]** *F3*; Carriere *F1* (*Q1–3 om. ll. 11–41*)
32 **headly]** heddy *F2*
35 **Defile]** *Rowe*; Desire *F1*
43 **s.d. to the Citizens]** *ed.*

III.iv

III.iv] *Capell* (*scene in italics throughout, F1*)
The French in this and later scenes raises many problems for the editor. The F1 text is very corrupt, and Q1–3 are small help. Editors from Rowe on have done much to make these passages recognizable as French, but that they represent sixteenth-century French has sometimes been forgotten. The present text employs modern spelling forms, but only where they do not represent any significant change in sixteenth-century pronunciation. Useful for III.iv is a contemporary listing in French "Of all the members of a mans bodie" in Claudius Holyband's The French Littleton (*1609 edition, ed. M. St. Clare Byrne, 1953*). *Only the more important emendations are recorded in the notes below.*
Location: *Capell* (*subs., after Theobald*)
o.s.d. **Alice]** *Q3*; Allice *Q1–2*
1–7 *Something of the quality of the French text in the early editions may be judged by comparing the opening lines as they appear in F1 and Q1–3 with the present text.* F1: *Kathe.* Alice, tu as este en Angleterre, & tu bien parlas le Language. / *Alice.* En peu Madame. / *Kath.* Ie te prie m'ensigniez, it faut que ie apprend a parlen: Comient appelle vous le main en Anglois? / *Alice.* Le main il & appelle de Hand. *Q1–3*: *Kate. Allice* venecia, vous aues cates en, / Vou parte fort bon Angloys englatara, / Coman sae palla vou la main en francoy. / *Allice.* La main madam de han.
1 **Alice]** Allice *Q1–2* (*throughout scene*)
8 **Et les]** *Capell*; *Alice.* E le *F1*
9 **s.p. Alice.]** *Theobald*; Kat. *F1*
9 **les doigts]** *Capell* (*after F2* le doyt); e doyt *F1*
12 **s.p. Kath.]** *Theobald*; Alice. *F1*
13 **écolier; j'ai]** *Theobald* (*subs.*); escholier. / *Kath.* I'ay *F1*
16 **Nous]** *Cambridge*
16 **nailès]** *Duthie* (*in Wilson*); Nayles *F1* (*throughout scene*); *Q1–3 do not mention the nails*
22, 47, 58 **arma]** *ed.* (*from Q1–3, in which this form, indicating stage pronunciation, is used throughout; it occurs also in F1 at l. 29*); Arme *F1*
26 **appris]** *Steevens*; apprins *F1*
42 **vous déjà]** *ed.* (déjà *Theobald*); y desia *F1*

52–3 **ils . . . mots**] *Walter (after Wilson);* il
   sont le mots *F1*
52 **foot**] fot *Q1–2*
62 s.d. **Exeunt.**] *F2;* Exit. *F1;* Exit omnes.
   Q1–3

III.v

III.v] *Capell*
Location: *Capell (subs., after Theobald)*
o.s.d. **the Duke of Britain**] *Wilson;* Burbon
   Q1–2; Bourbon *Q3*
5 **O Dieu vivant**] Mordeu ma via *Q1–3 (cf.*
   l. 11)
5 **sprays**] spranes *Q1–3*
7 **scions**] *Malone;* Syens *F1*
11 **Dieu,**] *Alexander (after Wilson and Greg);*
   du *F1 (Q1–3 support Dieu by giving the*
   whole phrase as mor du)
26 **we**] we may *F2*
33 **corantos**] *Johnson;* Carranto's *F1*
39 **hie**] *F4;* high *F1*
42 **Burgundy**] *F3;* Burgonie *F1*
43 **Vaudemont**] *F2;* Vandemont *F1*
45 **Foix**] *Capell;* Loys *F1*
45 **Lestrake**] *Wilson;* Lestrale *F1*
45 **Bouciqualt**] *Theobald;* Bouciquall *F1*
45 **Charolois**] *Capell;* Charaloyes *F1*
46 **knights**] *Theobald conj.;* Kings *F1*

III.vi

III.vi] *Capell*
Location: *Capell (after Theobald)*
14 **Antony**] *Pope;* Anthony *F1, Q3;* Anthonie
   Q1–2
21–2 **Captain . . . well.**] *as verse, Q1–3; as*
   prose, F1
25–9 **Bardolph . . . stone—**] *as irregular*
   verse, Q1–3; as prose, F1
31, 32 **blind**] Plind *Q1–3*
31 **his**] her *Q1–3*
39–49 **Fortune . . . requite.**] *as irregular verse,*
   Q1–3; as prose, F1
48 **penny cord**] *Q1–3;* Penny-Cord *F1*
60 **Very good.**] *following Fluellen's speech,*
   Q1–3 add: Pist. I say the fig within thy
   bowels and thy durty maw. *(having already*
   added: within thy Iawe. *to the end of l. 59)*
   Capell
85 s.d. **Drum heard.**] *Capell*
86 s.d. **and . . . Soldiers**] others *Q1–3*
86 s.d. **Gloucester**] *Malone;* Clarence, Gloster *Q1–3*
87 **God**] *Capell (subs.);* Flu. God *F1 (re-*
   peated s.p.)
99 **my part,**] our own parts, like you now,
   Q1–2; our owne parts *Q3*
111 **upbraided**] abraided *Q1–2*
112 **lenity**] *Q1–3;* Leuitie *F1*
113 s.d. **Montjoy**] *Capell (after Holinshed; so*
   also F1–3 later in the scene); Mountioy
   F1 (throughout scene)
123 **cue**] *Q1–3* (kue); Q. *F1*
151 **air**] heire *Q1–2*
158 **There's**] there is *Q1–2*
167 s.d. **Exit.**] *Rowe*

III.vii

III.vii] *Hanmer*
Location: *Theobald*
o.s.d. **Dolphin**] *In Q1–3 the Dolphin does not*
   appear in this scene or in IV.v (they omit
   IV.ii); this accords with the French King's
   order (III.v.64–6) that the Dolphin remain
   with him in Rouen. Q1–3's characters in
   this scene (in IV.v described as the foure
   French Lords) are: Burbon, Constable,
   Orleance, Gebon.
12 **pasterns**] *F2;* postures *F1*
13 **Ça, ha!**] *Theobald;* ch' ha: *F1*
14 **chez**] *Theobald;* ches *F1*
20 **of the ginger**] a Ginger *Q1–2*
39 **him.**] *F2;* him, *F1*
62 **had**] had had *Q1*
64 **vomissement**] *F3;* vemissement *F1*
65 **et**] *Rowe;* est *F1*
65 **truie**] *Rowe;* leuye *F1*
89 s.d. **Exit.**] *om. Q1–2*
120 **pox**] Iogge *Q1–3*
157 **Englishmen**] *F4;* English men *F1*

IV.Cho.

Act IV] *Pope;* Actus Tertius. *F1*
o.s.d. **Enter**] *Rowe*
15-6 **toll, . . . name.**] *Tyrwhitt conj.;* towle:
   . . . nam'd, *F1*
20 **cripple tardy-gaited**] *Theobald (subs.);*
   creeple-tardy-gated *F1*
46 **define,**] *F2;* define. *F1*
47 **night.**] *Rowe;* night, *F1*

IV.i

IV.i] *Hanmer*
Location: *Theobald*
3 **Good**] *F3;* God *F1*
18–9 **pains Upon example;**] *Pope (reading*
   pain); paines, / Vpon example, *F1*
33 s.d. **all . . . King**] *Cambridge*
35 **Qui**] *Rowe;* Che *F1;* Ke *Q1–3*
35 **vous**] ve *Q1–3*
37–8 **Discuss . . . popular?**] *as verse, Q1–3;*
   as prose, F1
44–8 **The . . . name?**] *as verse, Q1–3; as*
   prose, F1
54–5 **Tell . . . day.**] *as verse, Pope; as prose, F1*
63 s.d. **to one side**] *ed.*
65 **So!**] *Capell;* 'So, *F1*
65 **fewer**] lewer *Q1–2;* lower *Q3*
82 s.d. **with Gower**] *from Q1–3* Exit Gower,
   and Flewellen.
84 s.d. **three . . . Williams**] three Souldiers
   Q1–3 (unnamed, designated as 1. Soul.,
   2. Soul., *and* 3. Soul.)
94 **Thomas**] *Theobald;* Iohn *F1*
104 **human**] *Rowe;* humane *F1*
125 **alone,**] *Collier;* alone: *F1*
126 **minds.**] *Rowe;* minds, *F1*
157 **servant**] seruants *Q1–2*
170 **before-breach**] *hyphen, Capell*
179 **mote**] *Malone;* Moth *F1, Q3;* moath
   Q1–2
197 **You**] Mas youle *Q1–3*
211 **Here's**] Here is *Q1–2*
229 s.d. **Exeunt**] *F2;* Exit *F1, Q1–3; F1 s.d.*
   after l. 224; placed as in Q1–3
236 **heart's ease**] *Steevens;* hearts-ease *F1*
243 **comings-in**] *hyphen, Pope*
245 **What**] *Knight;* What? *F1*
245 **adoration**] *F2;* Odoration *F1*
275 **Hyperion**] *F2;* Hiperio *F1*
284 s.d. **Enter Erpingham.**] *Rowe;* Enter the King
   [to the King *Q3*], Gloster, Epingam, and
   Attendants. *Q1–3 (Q3 thus continues the*
   scene as in F1)
291 **reck'ning, if . . . numbers**] *Tyrwhitt*
   conj.; reckning of . . . numbers: *F1 (cf.*
   Q1–3: rekoning [reckoning *Q3*], / That
   the apposed [opposed *Q2*] multitudes which
   stand before them, / May not appall their
   courage.)
309 **friends**] *Q1–3;* friend *F1*

IV.ii

IV.ii] *Capell*
Scene om. Q1–3
Location: *Theobald*
1 **armor,**] *F2 (subs.);* Armour *F1*
2 **à**] *Steevens*
2 **varlot lackey!**] *ed. (after Dyce);* Verlot
   Lacquay: *F1*
4 **eaux**] *Theobald;* ewes *F1*
5 **l'air**] *Theobald;* le air *F1*
6 **Cieux**] *Wilson conj.;* Cein *F1*
11 **dout**] *Rowe;* doubt *F1*
35 **tucket sonance**] *Johnson;* Tucket Sonuance
   F1
48 **down-roping**] *hyphen, Theobald*
49 **gimmal'd**] *Delius;* Iymold *F1*
60 **guidon;**] *Rann;* Guard: on *F1*

IV.iii

IV.iii] *Capell*
Location: *Theobald*
o.s.d.] *Q1–3 om.* Bedford, Erpingham, and
   Westmerland, *and add* Clarence
4 **There's**] There is *Q1–2*
13–4 **And . . . valor.**] *placed as in Q1–3 (a*
   version of these lines spoken by Clarence);
   after l. 11 as part of Bedford's speech, F1
   (transposition suggested by Thirlby)

14 s.d. **Exit Salisbury.**] *Rowe*
19 **Westmerland?**] *Rowe;* Westmerland. *F1;*
   Warwick? *Q1–3 (Warwick replaces West-*
   merland in Q1–3 in this scene although he
   is not included in the o.s.d.)
48 **And . . . day.**] *Q1–3* (Crispines *Q1–2;*
   Crispins *Q3*)
49 **forgot,**] *Steevens;* forgot: *F1*
53–4 **Harry . . . Gloucester**] *Q1–3 om.* Talbot
   and Salisbury *and add* Clarence and York
59 **remembered**] *Rowe;* remembred *F1, Q1–3*
65–6 **they . . . speaks**] And hold their manhood cheape, / While any speake *Q1–2;*
   They were not there, when any speakes
   Q3
105 **crasing**] *F1, Q1–3;* grasing *F2*
109 **working-day**] *hyphen, Capell*
124 **'um**] am *Q1–2*
133 **pleasest,**] *F3;* pleasest *F1, Q1–3*

IV.iv

IV.iv] *Capell*
Q1–3 reverse the order of Scenes iv and v
Location: *Theobald*
2 s.p. **Fr. Sol.**] *Rowe;* French. *F1, Q1–3*
   (throughout scene)
4 **Calen o**] *Malone conj.;* calmie *F1*
7–11 **O . . . ransom.**] *as verse, Pope; as prose,*
   F1 (Pistol's lines as prose throughout scene
   in F1; arranged as verse largely by Johnson;
   whole scene as irregular verse, Q1–3)
12 **pitié**] *F2 (subs.);* pitez *F1;* petie *Q1–3*
14 **Or**] *Theobald conj.;* for *F1*
35 **à cette heure**] *Theobald;* asture *F1*
38–9 **Peasant . . . sword.**] Vnlesse thou giue
   to me egregions raunsome, dye. / One
   point of a foxe. *Q1–3*
46 **two hundred**] 500. *Q1–3*
52 **lui**] *F2* (luy); layt a *F1*
52 **promettez**] *F2* (promettoz); promets *F1*
54 **je**] *Rowe;* se *F1*
55 **remerciments**] *Rowe (subs.);* remercious *F1*
56 **tombe**] *ed.;* intombe *F1;* ne tombe *F2*
56 **pense**] *F2;* peuse *F1*
57 **distingué**] *Capell;* distinie *F1*
66 **Suivez-vous**] *Rowe (om. vous);* Saaue
   vous *F1*
66 **capitaine.**] *Rowe;* Capitaine? *F1;* Capi-
   tain! *F3*
66–7 s.d. **Exeunt . . . Soldier.**] *Pope*

IV.v

IV.v] *Capell*
Location: *ed. (after Wilson)*
o.s.d. **Bourbon**] *Rowe;* Burbon *F1, Q1–3*
   (throughout scene)
2 **est perdu . . . est perdu!**] *Rowe;* et perdia
   . . . et perdie. *F1*
3 **Mort Dieu,**] *F2 (comma, Alexander);* Mor
   Dieu *F1;* Mor du *Q1, Q3;* Mordu *Q2*
11 **die! In . . . again!**] *ed.;* dye in once more
   backe againe, *F1*
15 **by a**] *Q1–3* (least by a); a base *F1* (base
   repeated from l. 14)
19 **enow**] inough *Q1–2*
23 s.d. **Exeunt.**] *Rowe;* Exit. *F1;* Exit omnes.
   Q1–3

IV.vi

IV.vi] *Capell*
Location: *ed. (after Wilson)*
o.s.d. **Exeter and others**] *Capell*
2 **all's**] all is *Q1–2*
9 **Yoke-fellow**] Yoake fellow *Q1–2*
9 **honor-owing wounds**] *F4;* honour-owing-
   wounds *F1;* honour dying wounds *Q1–2;*
   honour-dying wounds *Q3*
15 **He cries**] And cryde *Q1–3*
18 **well-foughten**] well foughten *Q1–2*
26 **espous'd**] espoused *Q1–2*
27 **noble-ending love**] *Rowe;* Noble-ending-
   loue *F1;* neuer ending loue *Q1–2;* neuer-
   ending loue *Q3*
30 **had not**] not *Q1–3*
34 **mistful**] *Warburton conj.;* mixtfull *F1*
38] *Following this line Q1–3 add:* Pist.
   Couple gorge. *(Pistol is included in Q1–3*
   o.s.d.; cf. IV.iv.37)
38 s.d. **Exeunt**] *Rowe;* Exit *F1;* Exit omnes.
   Q1–3

IV.vii

IV.vii] *Capell;* Actus Quartus. *F1*
Location: *ed. (after Wilson)*
1 **Kill**] Godes plud kil *Q1–3*
3 **offert;**] *pointing from Capell* (offer'd;); offert *F1;* desired, *Q1–2;* desired *Q3*
5 **there's**] there is *Q1–3*
11 **Monmouth**] Monmorth *Q1–2*
15 **not**] nat *Q1–2*
16 **great**] *Q1–3;* grear *F1*
54 s.d. **Exit.**] *Sisson*
54 s.d. **other**] *Theobald*
54 s.d. **Warwick, Gloucester, Exeter**] *Capell*
54 s.d. **Heralds**] *Sisson*
54 s.d. **and others**] *Capell*
65 s.d. **Exit a Herald.**] *Capell* (subs.)
68 **this, herald?**] *Steevens;* this Herald? *F1;* this? *Q1–3*
70 s.p. **Mont.**] *Rowe;* Her. *F1, Q1–3* (*throughout scene*)
78 **their**] *Malone;* with *F1*
91 **Crispin Crispianus**] Cryspin, Cryspin *Q1–2;* Crispin, Crispianus *Q3*
93 **great-uncle**] *hyphen, Capell*
110 **countryman**] *Q1–3;* Countrymen *F1*
111 **Jeshu**] Iesus *Q1–2;* Iesu *Q3*
116 **God**] *Q1–3;* Good *F1*
118 s.d. **Exeunt . . . Montjoy.**] *Theobald;* Exit Heralds. *Q1, Q3;* Exit Herald. *Q2*
137 **gentleman**] *Q1–3;* Ientleman *F1*
143 **law!**] *F2* (law.); law *F1*
154 **Alanson**] Alonson *Q1–2* (*throughout*)
154–5 **myself were**] I was *Q1–2;* I were *Q3*
155 **from his**] off from his *Q1–2;* from's *Q3*
156 **any man**] any do *Q1–2;* any *Q3*

IV.viii

IV.viii] *Capell*
Location: *Theobald*
9 **any's**] *F4;* anyes *F1*
13 **Stand away,**] Gode plut, and his. *Q1–2;* Gods plut, and his *Q3*
24 **what's**] what is *Q1–2*
27 **Majesty**] maiesty in person *Q3*
44 **martial**] *Pope;* Marshall *F1*
51 **but as**] as *Q1–2*
55 **I . . . for**] you seemed *Q1–2;* you seemed then to mee *Q3*
55 **offence**] offence, my gracious Lord *Q3*
65 **prabbles**] brables *Q1–2*
71 **silling**] shilling *Q1–2*
72 s.d. **an English**] *Malone*
74 s.d. **Gives a paper.**] *Capell* (subs.)
77 **Bouciquault**] *Capell;* Bouchiquald *F1;* Bowchquall *Q1;* Bouchquall *Q2–3*
80 s.p. **K. Hen.**] *lines continued to Essex in Q1–3; in Q2–3 given to Henry at l. 101, returned to Essex at l. 103, and given to Henry again beginning* O God *in l. 106*
94 **Rambures**] Ranbieres *Q1–2;* Rambieres *Q3*
99 **Foix**] *Capell;* Foyes *F1;* Foy *Q1–3*
100 **Vaudemont**] *F2;* Vandemont *F1;* Vandemant *Q1–3*
100 **Lestrake**] *Wilson;* Lestrale *F1;* Lestra *Q1–3*
102 s.d. **Herald . . . paper.**] *Capell*
110–1 **loss, . . . other?**] *Pope* (subs.); losse? . . . other, *F1;* losse, on one part and an other. *Q1–2,* (another?) *Q3*
113 **go we**] *F2;* goe me *F1;* let vs go *Q1–3*
122 **rites**] *Pope;* Rights *F1*

V.Cho.

10 **flood**] *Pope;* flood; *F1*
10 **wives**] with Wives *F2*
35–9 **him— . . . them—**] *Theobald;* him. . . . them; *F1*
41 **back-return**] *hyphen, Capell*

V.i

V.i] *Hanmer*
Location: *Theobald*
14 **he**] a *Q1–2*
14–5 **turkey-cock**] Turkecocke *Q1–2*
19–21 **Ha . . . leek.**] *as irregular verse, Q1–3; as prose, F1*
19 **Dost**] *Q1–3;* doest *F1*
25 **appetites**] appetite *Q1–2*
28 **Cadwallader**] Cadwalleder *Q1–2*
29–30 **There . . . it?**] *as prose, Capell; as verse, F1*
33 **in the mean**] meane *Q1–2;* But in the meane *Q3*
34–5 s.d. **Strikes him.**] *Pope*
39 **him.**] him, it is enough. *Q3*
46] *Following this line Q3 inserts s.d.:* He makes Ancient Pistoll bite of the Leeke.
47–8 **revenge— . . . swear—**] *ed. (after Alexander);* reuenge I eate and eate I sweare. *F1*
58 **Hold you, there**] There *Q1–2;* Look you now, there *Q3*
64 **I will**] ile *Q1–2*
66 **God buy you**] And so God be with you *Q3*
71 **begun**] *Capell;* began *F1*
80–7 **Doth . . . steal;**] *as irregular verse, Q1–3; as prose, F1*
80 **Doth**] *Q1–3;* Doeth *F1*
80 **huswife**] huswye *Q1–2*
81 **dead**] sicke *Q1–3*
83–5 **And . . . cudgell'd.**] *om. Q1–3, which substitute:* The warres affordeth nought, home will I trug.
89 **swear**] *Q1–3;* swore *F1*

V.ii

V.ii] *Hanmer*
Location: *Capell* (subs.)
o.s.d. **Gloucester**] *Malone*
o.s.d. **Westmerland**] *Capell*
o.s.d. **of France**] *Q1–3*
o.s.d. **Burgundy**] *Rowe;* Bourgongne *F1;* Burbon *Q1–3*
o.s.d. **Katherine**] *Theobald;* Queene Katherine *Q1–3* (*possibly an error for* Queene, Katherine)
o.s.d. **Alice**] *Capell*
1 s.p. **K. Hen.**] *Rowe;* King. *F1;* Harry. *Q1–3* (*throughout scene*)
7 **Burgundy**] *Q3;* Burgogne *F1;* Burgondie *Q1–2*
9 s.p. **Fr. King.**] *Rowe;* Fra. *F1 (or* France. *throughout scene, except l. 320);* Fran. *Q1–3 (or* France. *throughout scene)*
11 **princes English,**] *Rowe;* Princes (English) *F1;* Princes English *Q1–3*
12 **England**] *F2;* Ireland *F1*
21 s.p. **K. Hen.**] *Rowe;* Eng. *F1 (or* England. *throughout rest of scene, except ll. 98–316, where* King. *is used)*
42 **even-pleach'd**] *hyphen, Hanmer*
50 **scythe withal,**] *ed.;* Sythe, withall *F1;* Sythe, all *Rowe*

68 **Burgundy**] *Q3;* Burgonie *F1;* Burgondy *Q1–2*
77 **cursitory**] *Wilson;* curselarie *F1;* cursenary *Q1–2;* cursory *Q3* (*the reading adopted by most eds. before Wilson, a nonce-word*)
98 s.d. **Exeunt omnes.**] Exit King and the Lords. *Q1–2;* Exit French King and the Lords. *Q3*
98 s.d. **Manent**] *Rowe;* Manet *F1, Q1–3*
98 s.d. **with . . . Alice**] *from Q1–3 s.d. and* the Gentlewoman
98–168] *Q1–3 reduce these lines to:* Hate. [*Kate. Q2; Har. Q3*] Now *Kate*, you haue a blunt wooer here / Left with you. / If I could win thee at leapfrog, / Or with vawting with my armour on my back, / Into my saddle, / Without brag be it spoken, / Ide make compare with any. / But leauing that *Kate*, / If thou takest me now, / Thou shalt haue me at the worst: / And in wearing, thou shalt haue me better and better, [*cf. ll. 231–3*] / Thou shalt haue a face that is not worth sun-burning. / But doost thou thinke, that thou and I, / Betweene Saint *Denis*, / And Saint *George*, shall get a boy, / That shall goe to *Constantinople*, / And take the great Turke by the beard, ha *Kate*? [*cf. ll. 206–10*]
112 s.p. **Alice.**] *Capell;* Lady. *F1* (*throughout scene*); *Q1–3, which om. ll. 98–136* (Fair . . . strength.), *264,* have Lady. *at ll. 261, 267*
116 **pleines**] *Pope;* plein *F1*
137 **vauting**] *ed.;* vawting *F1*
171 **it is**] tis *Q1–2*
178 **tell thee**] tell it you *Q1–2;* tell you *Q3*
189 **meilleur**] *Hanmer (after Rowe);* melieus *F1*
192–3 **But . . . English?**] But *Kate,* / In plaine termes, *Q1–2;* But Kate prethee tell me in plaine tearmes, *Q3*
193 **Canst thou**] do you *Q1–2;* Dost thou *Q3*
243 **good fellows**] *Pope;* Good-fellowes *F1*
247 **de roi**] the King *Q1–2;* de king *Q3*
253 **Laissez . . . laissez, laissez**] *Rowe;* laisse . . . laisse, laisse *F1*
253 **laissez! Ma foi,**] *Theobald* (subs.); Laisse, may foy: *F1*
254 **grandeur**] *F2;* grandeus *F1*
255 **(Notre Seigneur!)**] *ed. (from Knudson);* nostre Seigneur *F1*
255–6 **serviteur. Excusez-moi,**] *Theobald* (subs.); seruiteur excuse moy. *F1*
259 **noces**] *Dyce;* nopcese *F1*
261 **les**] *Theobald;* le *F1*
262 **baiser**] *Hanmer (after Theobald);* buisse *F1;* bassie *Q1–3*
275 s.d. **Kissing her.**] *Rowe*
281 **Majesty! My**] *Pope;* Maiestie, my *F1*
322 **never**] *Rowe*
333 **and in**] and then in *F2*
340 **d'Angleterre**] D'anglaterre *Q1–2*
341–2 **Angliae . . . Franciae**] Anglie . . . Francie *Q1–2*
365 **paction**] *Theobald;* Pation *F1*
372 **peers'**] *Capell;* Peeres *F1*
374 s.d. **Sennet. Exeunt.**] FINIS. *Q1–3*

Epi.

o.s.d. as Epilogue] *Collier MS*
14 s.d. **Exit.**] *Capell;* FINIS. *F1*

Henry VIII

OWING TO A WIDELY NOTED MISHAP early in its history, *Henry VIII* can be dated with precision. At a performance of the play on June 29, 1613, the Globe Theatre, the home of Shakespeare's company since 1599, was destroyed by fire, and this event —which marks for us the ending of a mighty epoch in the history of the English stage but which for contemporary observers was just a lively piece of news— at once became a topic for discussion. Of the various comments on the fire, Sir Henry Wotton's, in a letter written three days later, is the most detailed:

> Now, to let matters of state sleep, I will entertain you at the present with what hath happened this week at the Bank's side. The King's players had a new play called *All Is True*, representing some principal pieces of the reign of Henry 8, which was set forth with many extraordinary circumstances of pomp and majesty, even to the matting of the stage; the Knights of the Order, with their Georges and Garter, the guards with their embroidered coats, and the like: sufficient in truth within a while to make greatness very familiar, if not ridiculous. Now, King Henry making a masque at the Cardinal Wolsey's house, and certain chambers [i.e. short cannon] being shot off at his entry, some of the paper, or other stuff wherewith one of them was stopped, did light on the thatch, where being thought at first but an idle smoke, and their eyes more attentive to the show, it kindled inwardly, and ran round like a train, consuming within less than an hour the whole house to the very grounds.
>
> This was the fatal period of that virtuous fabric; wherein yet nothing did perish but wood and straw, and a few forsaken cloaks; only one man had his breeches set on fire, that would perhaps have broiled him, if he had not by the benefit of a provident wit put it out with bottle ale.

Although Sir Henry's reference to the "new play" by its presumed alternate title *All Is True* and his mention of "the Knights of the Order, with their Georges and Garter" (who do not appear in *Henry VIII*) have occasioned speculation, Thomas Lorkin and Edmund Howes, in their descriptions of the fire, not only give the play its present title but also, with Sir Henry, attribute the disaster to the careless use of "certain chambers" and of "a peal of ordnance," which were clearly those required at I.iv.49. It is rare to find so much converging testimony for any event in Elizabethan or Jacobean drama.

Almost two hundred years ago Edmond Malone, seeking to explain Shakespeare's reversion to a form that he had long since laid aside, suggested that *Henry VIII* may have been rewritten and expanded from a play first acted in the reign of Queen Elizabeth; and early in the present century E. K. Chambers tentatively proposed the anonymous *Buckingham*, which the theatrical entrepreneur Philip Henslowe recorded in his *Diary* in 1593, as a likely early version of our work. Lacking proof for such conjectures, however, most scholars now accept the internal evidence of language, prosody, and theme as decisive for a later date. This evidence is reinforced by the strong possibility that the play was somehow related to the wedding of King James's daughter Elizabeth to the Elector Palatine, a leader of the continental Protestants, which was celebrated with great splendor on February 14, 1613. Although not listed among the "fowerteene severall playes" (six of them by Shakespeare) with which the King's Company had entertained the bridal couple before they left for Germany on April 10, it was perhaps not really "new" the following June, as Sir Henry Wotton called it, for its pageantry and its assertive Protestantism would seem to link it to the many masques and entertainments that were written to adorn the royal nuptials. Whether or not it was the unnamed "stage play" scheduled for a court performance on February 16 and then abruptly cancelled because "greater pleasures were preparing," *Henry VIII* was most likely prompted by, if not commissioned for, the sumptuous wedding celebrations, and therefore it may be plausibly assigned to the early months of 1613. Thus it is the latest of Shakespeare's plays to be included in the Folio of 1623, and, except for his possible contributions to *The Two Noble Kinsmen* and the lost *Cardenio*, his valediction to the stage.

For his final history play, as for almost all the others, Shakespeare—or Shakespeare and a putative collaborator—found his basic source in Holinshed (or in Holinshed's reports of Hall), which he eked out here and there with other things. The details of Cranmer's testing in Act V derive from that bottomless reservoir of Protestant propaganda, Foxe's *Acts and Monuments* (1563 ff.), and there may be traces of John Speed's *History of Great Britain* (1611) in certain lines of Wolsey's farewell speeches (such as the one about the "little wanton boys that swim on bladders" at III.ii.359). Although the alleged debt to Samuel Rowley's *When You See Me You Know Me* (1605, reprinted 1613) is less apparent, Henry's frequent use of the ejaculation "Ha!" may reflect a verbal mannerism of the bluff King Harry in that untidy, boisterous play. Since there is no evidence that Shakespeare had access to George Cavendish's life of Wolsey, any echoes from that splendid biography may be traced through Holinshed to John Stow, who had drawn upon the still unpublished work for his *Summary of English Chronicles* (1565 ff.).

If Shakespeare's forays on the 1587 edition of Holinshed are incessant and direct—ranging from single words like "arrogancy" at II.iv.110 and the guest list at the Princess' christening in V.v to extended passages like Katherine's speech at II.iv.13 ff.—he handles this material with a freedom, or a license, that makes the prologue, with its asseverations of the "truth" to be disclosed, seem something less than candid. In *Henry VIII* as elsewhere in the history plays the authorial distortions are most apparent in chronology. Although the action covers twenty years or more—from the Field of the Cloth of Gold (1520) to Cranmer's deadly peril from Bishop Gardiner (1544?)—events are so depicted that not only time but even sequence is destroyed. Whereas Shakespeare's manipulation of chronology in the other history plays involves little more than telescoping and juxtaposing widely spaced events—for instance, the arrest of Clarence and the death of Edward IV in *Richard III*, or the Battle of Agincourt and the Treaty of Troyes in *Henry V*—his procedure here is one of drastic transposition. Thus Buckingham's arrest and execution

(1521) follow hard upon the monarchs' meeting in the Vale of Andren and coincide with the rebellion of the weavers (1525), Henry's lustful stirrings toward the Lady Anne (1527?), and the arrival of Campeius to look into the "business" of the King's divorce (1530). In similar confusion the royal wedding (1532) precedes Wolsey's fall (1529), and the birth and christening of the Princess Elizabeth (1533) serve to ease the strain of Katherine's death (1536) and Cranmer's close escape (1544?). There is distortion of a different kind in linking Wolsey's fall to a device—the discovery of a secret inventory (III.ii.120 ff.)—that, according to Holinshed, he himself had used to ruin the Bishop of Durham some twenty years before.

Despite the assumption, in what was said above, of Shakespeare's authorship of *Henry VIII*, his part in its production has long been and is likely to remain a matter of dispute. As early as 1758 one Richard Roderick commented on the remarkable stylistic and prosodic variations in the play, and Johnson thought it possible that Ben Jonson had supplied the prologue and epilogue; but apart from Malone's suggestion, in 1778, that the play had been constructed on an earlier work there was no serious attack on the integrity of the text until 1850, when James Spedding published "Who Wrote Shakespeare's *Henry VIII*?" This famous article, first printed in the *Gentleman's Magazine* and reissued, with a different title, in the 1874 *Transactions* of the New Shakspere Society, posed a question for which a hundred years of scholarship has found no certain answer.

Spedding, whose long exertions on behalf of Francis Bacon had certified his learning, begins by appealing to "the individual consciousness of each reader" to testify whether "the effect of this play *as a whole*" is not so "weak and disappointing" that it appears to be an inept collaboration. As dramaturgic evidence he cites, among other things, the slackened tension of Act V (which leaves us "among persons whom we scarcely know, and events for which we do not care"), the questionable morality of King Henry's behavior (which insures "the ultimate triumph of wrong"), and the disjointed, repetitive structure of the work throughout. As more strictly literary evidence—which "a man of first-rate judgment," later identified as Tennyson, had proposed to him—he cites the presence of two styles in *Henry VIII*: one marked by the complex imagery and the "careless felicities" of Shakespeare's later work, and the other, much simpler and more fluent, marked by an inordinate number of run-on lines and of lines with an unaccented eleventh syllable, as in the plays of Fletcher. The cumulative weight of all this evidence led him to the "clear conviction" that two and possibly three hands are evident in the play, but after Samuel Hickson, working independently, had suggested minor changes, he assigned to Shakespeare I.i–ii, II.iii–iv, III.ii.1–203, and V.i, and all the rest he gave to Fletcher. Spedding's inference from this distribution of the scenes was that Shakespeare, having conceived "the idea of a great historical drama on the subject of Henry VIII" which would comprise the divorce of Katherine, the fall of

Wolsey, the rise of Cranmer, the coronation of Anne Boleyn, and "the final separation of the English from the Romish Church," had got as far, perhaps, as the third act when something more appropriate for the royal wedding was required, whereupon he gave his manuscript to Fletcher, whose alterations and additions resulted in the work we have.

Although a few traditionalists, refusing to concede that anyone but Shakespeare could have written Wolsey's great farewell and Katherine's death-scene, protested Spedding's "bold conjecture," for fifty years or so his theory won such wide acceptance that research on *Henry VIII* was directed mainly toward refining his and Hickson's attributions. Thus whereas W. A. Wright (1891) and D. Nichol Smith (1893) and C. K. Pooler (1915), among others, endorsed the claims of Fletcher, A. H. Thorndike (1901) presented new internal evidence (based upon the use of *'em* and *ye* instead of *them* and *you*) in an effort to confirm the attribution. Going even further, Robert Boyle (1885) and H. D. Sykes (1919) rejected Shakespeare altogether and unwisely gave to Massinger all the non-Fletcherian scenes. Despite a more recent swing away from these and similar theories of disintegration, and toward a neo-orthodox defense of Shakespeare's single authorship, the question is by no means settled. Although Peter Alexander (1930) and G. Wilson Knight (1947), arguing from very different grounds, strongly countered any conjecture of dual composition, A. C. Partridge (1949) just as strongly reasserted Fletcher's presence in the work. More recently, R. A. Foakes (1955) and J. C. Maxwell (1962) have toiled through all the evidence only to emerge with conflicting points of view, Foakes regarding Shakespeare as the only author of a play whose theme and language link it firmly to the late romances, and Maxwell—with J. Dover Wilson's warm endorsement—holding that "the case for joint authorship is as fully established as such a case ever can be on purely internal evidence." If these erudite, opposed opinions may be regarded as prophetic, it seems likely that Spedding's question, like the poor, will be with us forever.

Those who think that Shakespeare wrote all, or nearly all, of *Henry VIII* rely on various kinds of evidence. They point to its inclusion in the Folio of 1623, which permits if it does not compel the inference that Heminge and Condell accepted it as genuine, whereas they rejected not only *The Two Noble Kinsmen* (in which Shakespeare's hand is generally conceded) but also such things as *Locrine* and *Edward III* (which were once ascribed to Shakespeare but are now universally held to be apocryphal). They deny or minimize the significance of allegedly Fletcherian traits of style and metrics—feminine endings, run-on lines, frequent parenthetical constructions, forms like *'em* and *ye*, and all the rest—on the ground that they not only appear increasingly in Shakespeare's later plays but are common in the period. They hold that despite the unusual structure of the work its use of sources and its imagery suggest, in Foakes's words, "a single mind at work." And finally they point to its thematic correspondence with such plays as *The Winter's Tale*

and *The Tempest*, where motifs of suffering, restoration, and compassion are serenely fused into the "vision" of romance. Indeed, G. Wilson Knight, noting its progression "from normality and order, through violent conflict to spiritualized music, and thence to concluding ritual," sees *Henry VIII* as the paradigm of Shakespeare's whole career and thus his culminating work.

But such opinions, however strongly held and eloquently expounded, are not to be confused with facts, and since we do not know the facts of Shakespeare's part in *Henry VIII*, those aspects of the play that prompted Spedding's bold conjecture continue to exacerbate the question of its authorship. Even after all the tests are made and all the data are assembled and applied (on one side or the other), it is entirely possible to concede that Shakespeare, with his enormous power of language, could have moved from the virile, packed ellipses of Norfolk's "clinquant" talk or Buckingham's colloquial rage at Wolsey (I.i) to the gently cadenced verse of Katherine's soft laments (III.i) or Wolsey's stately valediction (III.ii). On the other hand it is surely easier to believe that Shakespeare had assistance in the composition of the play than that he, at the summit of his art, would swing awkwardly between widely different styles, or present muddy motives—notably the King's—in a work so "full of state and woe," or skirt the most compelling issues in a play about the English Reformation, or so botch the themes of reconciliation and compassion that they appear as resignation and caprice. Pending the unlikely discovery of some firm external evidence, it would seem that Spedding's main contention, if not his specific attributions, will remain to challenge speculation.

Considered in the light of Shakespeare's other plays on English history—the last of which predated it by fourteen years or so—*Henry VIII* presents some puzzling features. Although there are echoes here and there from the earlier works, in general this play owes little to its predecessors. Even though its episodic structure overlaps the quasi-epic traits of *Henry V*, the polyphonic splendors of *Henry IV*, and the univocal lyricism of *Richard II* to the crude apprentice work of *Henry VI*, it is episodic with a difference; for whereas a younger Shakespeare had made loosely jointed episodes serve at least the purpose of narration, here events are so distorted that the work of exposition must be entrusted to the handy choral gentlemen (II.i, IV.i) who tell us what we need to know. Another curious aspect of the structure is the use of incremental repetition in the depiction of a string of falls. The ancient *de casibus* tradition, which had inspired that perennial best-seller *A Mirror for Magistrates* (1559 ff.) and thereby filtered into many plays, makes an unexpected reappearance here; moreover, its treatment is unusual in that *Henry VIII*, instead of centring on one imposing figure, exhibits three—and almost four—lugubrious *exempla* of fickle Fortune's power. Consequently the play is not only episodic but also repetitious. *Richard III* reveals the same sequential structure, to be sure, but there each sequence, gathering force with repetition, whirls us toward the master-villain's fall; here each sequence, spinning on a single point, tends to block the forward movement of the play.

Some advocates of Shakespeare's single authorship of *Henry VIII* have made a good deal of the fact that Buckingham, Katherine, and Wolsey, who show the uses of adversity seriatim, exemplify the aging Shakespeare's ripest wisdom on the therapeutic role of tribulation. As he goes to his destruction, Buckingham, already "half in heaven," reveals a new (and wholly unexpected) resignation; in a work of ostentatious Protestantism Katherine is more ennobled by her ancient faith than by all the titles she has lost; and Wolsey—the butt of Holinshed's relentless denigration—achieves a moral grandeur in disgrace that almost cancels out his crimes. But although these three great victims of misfortune have the best-loved speeches in the play, their rhetoric serves to sentimentalize and decorate, rather than illuminate, the action. None of them acquires real status as a character, because we are not shown the process of the change they undergo. Drama becomes morally significant only insofar as it explores the necessary connection between what happens to a man and the kind of man he is or grows to be, and this connection is not clear in *Henry VIII*. Buckingham himself, the haughty duke, commends the "justice" of his ruin, and Wolsey's faults are shown to be so gross that he appears a moral monster; but Katherine, a paragon of wifely virtue and "the queen of earthly queens," is put upon a par with them, and since all three suffer similar degradation their suffering makes no sense. To say, as has been said, that they reveal the healing strength of patience, with its balm of reconciliation, is to ignore the fact that they are ruined by a power that neither they nor we can comprehend.

This power is centred in the King, to whom, as God's vice-regent, we are invited to refer the judgments on the Queen, the Cardinal, and the Duke as well as Cranmer's *deus ex machina* salvation. Henry, however, cannot support the thrust of all these moral obligations. Although some critics have described him as a kind of Prospero who beneficently orders all events, and others as the agent of that providence whose workings, Cranmer says, secure the glory of the realm, his conduct does not warrant such interpretations. Now hearty and jocose, now petulant, now regal and assured, but never anything for very long, he is shifty rather than complex. He equivocates so much about the crucial question of divorce, on which the large dynastic implications of the play depend, that his "conscience" is a topic of derision (II.ii.17–19, IV.i.47), and on this—as on other matters—his position is so morally ambiguous that his judgments seem to be the dictates of his will. Therefore he not only fails to exercise the God-like functions that were arrogated to the Tudor kings, he even fails to comprehend a justice commensurate with his power. Remembering Shakespeare's strenuous efforts to define a monarch's rights and obligations in the earlier history plays, one sees Henry as conclusive proof that these efforts now were ended.

However weak in characterization, *Henry VIII* is very strong in pomp and pageantry, and therefore what Johnson called the "splendour" of its spectacle has always been its main attraction. It starts and ends upon a note of triumph, and between the Field of the Cloth of Gold and Cranmer's apocalyptic vision of the bliss in store for England the interpolation of so many big set scenes makes the drama yield often to lavish exhibition. Some of these elaborate display pieces— notably the coronation and the christening—are so frankly theatrical that they do not require the spoken word, but only sights and sounds; and others, even where the focus is dramatic, are so formal in their presentation that they have the weight and texture of tableaux. Consequently the movement of the work suggests a long procession: from the King surrounded by his council (I.ii) to Wolsey's sumptuous ball (I.iv) to Buckingham's farewell (II.i) to Katherine's trial at Blackfriars (II.v) to the fallen cardinal's valediction (III.ii) to the new queen's coronation (IV.i) to the masque-like scene of Katherine's death (IV.ii) to Cranmer's confrontation with his foes (V.iii) to the christening with which the play concludes. From that regrettable performance on June 29, 1613—which in a sense was defeated by its own pretensions—to the present day, it has apparently always been accorded sumptuous presentations.

Herschel Baker

The Famous History of The Life of King Henry the Eighth

[DRAMATIS PERSONAE

KING HENRY THE EIGHTH
CARDINAL WOLSEY
CARDINAL CAMPEIUS
CAPUCHIUS, *ambassador from the Emperor Charles V*
CRANMER, *Archbishop of Canterbury*
DUKE OF NORFOLK
DUKE OF BUCKINGHAM
DUKE OF SUFFOLK
EARL OF SURREY
LORD CHAMBERLAIN
LORD CHANCELLOR
GARDINER, *secretary to the King, afterwards Bishop of Winchester*
BISHOP OF LINCOLN
LORD ABURGAVENNY
LORD SANDS (*called also* SIR WALTER SANDS)
SIR HENRY GUILFORD
SIR THOMAS LOVELL
SIR ANTHONY DENNY
SIR NICHOLAS VAUX
CROMWELL, *servant to Wolsey*
SECRETARIES *to Wolsey*

GRIFFITH, *gentleman usher to Queen Katherine*
Three GENTLEMEN
DOCTOR BUTTS, *physician to the King*
GARTER KING-AT-ARMS
SURVEYOR *to the Duke of Buckingham*
BRANDON, *and a* SERGEANT-AT-ARMS
DOORKEEPER *of the Council-chamber*
PORTER, *and his* MAN
PAGE *to Gardiner*
CRIER

QUEEN KATHERINE, *wife to King Henry, afterwards divorced*
ANNE BULLEN, *her Maid of Honor, afterwards Queen*
OLD LADY, *friend to Anne Bullen*
PATIENCE, *woman to Queen Katherine*

SPIRITS

Several BISHOPS; LORDS *and* LADIES *in the dumb shows;* WOMEN *attending upon the Queen;* SCRIBES, OFFICERS, GUARDS, *and other* ATTENDANTS

SCENE: *London; Westminster; Kimbolton*]

THE PROLOGUE

I come no more to make you laugh; things now
That bear a weighty and a serious brow,
Sad, high, and working, full of state and woe:
Such noble scenes as draw the eye to flow,
We now present. Those that can pity, here   5
May (if they think it well) let fall a tear;
The subject will deserve it. Such as give
Their money out of hope they may believe,
May here find truth too. Those that come to see
Only a show or two, and so agree   10
The play may pass, if they be still and willing,
I'll undertake may see away their shilling

Richly in two short hours. Only they
That come to hear a merry, bawdy play,
A noise of targets, or to see a fellow   15
In a long motley coat guarded with yellow,
Will be deceiv'd. For, gentle hearers, know,
To rank our chosen truth with such a show
As fool and fight is, beside forfeiting
Our own brains and the opinion that we bring   20
To make that only true we now intend,
Will leave us never an understanding friend.
Therefore, for goodness sake, and as you are known
The first and happiest hearers of the town,

Words and passages enclosed in square brackets in the text above are either emendations of the copy-text or additions to it. The Textual Notes immediately following the play cite the earliest authority for every such change or insertion and supply the reading of the copy-text wherever it is emended in this edition.

Pro. 3. **Sad . . . working:** serious, elevated, and moving.   **state:** dignity.   10. **show:** spectacle.

13. **two short hours.** Cf. *Romeo and Juliet*, Prologue, line 12: "the two hours' traffic of our stage."
15. **noise of targets:** clashing of shields.
16. **motley . . . yellow.** The customary garment of a clown.   **guarded:** trimmed.
20–21. **the opinion . . . intend:** i.e. our intention of presenting a veracious account. Here and elsewhere in the Prologue (lines 9, 25 ff.) the emphasis on truth supports the conjecture that when Sir Henry Wotton, in 1613, called the play *All Is True* he was using its subtitle.
24. **happiest:** most discriminating.

Be sad, as we would make ye. Think ye see   25
The very persons of our noble story
As they were living. Think you see them great,
And follow'd with the general throng and sweat
Of thousand friends; then, in a moment, see
How soon this mightiness meets misery;   30
And if you can be merry then, I'll say
A man may weep upon his wedding-day.

ACT I, SCENE I

Enter the DUKE OF NORFOLK *at one door; at the other, the* DUKE OF BUCKINGHAM *and the* LORD ABURGAVENNY.

Buck.   Good morrow, and well met. How have ye done
Since last we saw in France?
Nor.   I thank your Grace:
Healthful, and ever since a fresh admirer
Of what I saw there.
Buck.   An untimely ague
Stay'd me a prisoner in my chamber when   5
Those suns of glory, those two lights of men,
Met in the vale of Andren.
Nor.   'Twixt Guynes and Arde—
I was then present, saw them salute on horseback,
Beheld them when they lighted, how they clung
In their embracement, as they grew together,   10
Which had they, what four thron'd ones could have weigh'd
Such a compounded one?
Buck.   All the whole time
I was my chamber's prisoner.
Nor.   Then you lost
The view of earthly glory. Men might say
Till this time pomp was single, but now married   15
To one above itself. Each following day
Became the next day's master, till the last
Made former wonders its. To-day the French,
All clinquant, all in gold, like heathen gods,
Shone down the English; and, to-morrow, they   20
Made Britain India: every man that stood
Show'd like a mine. Their dwarfish pages were
As cherubins, all gilt; the madams too,
Not us'd to toil, did almost sweat to bear
The pride upon them, that their very labor   25

Was to them as a painting. Now this masque
Was cried incomparable; and th' ensuing night
Made it a fool and beggar. The two kings,
Equal in lustre, were now best, now worst,
As presence did present them: him in eye   30
Still him in praise, and being present both,
'Twas said they saw but one, and no discerner
Durst wag his tongue in censure. When these suns
(For so they phrase 'em) by their heralds challeng'd
The noble spirits to arms, they did perform   35
Beyond thought's compass, that former fabulous story,
Being now seen possible enough, got credit,
That Bevis was believ'd.
Buck.   O, you go far.
Nor.   As I belong to worship and affect
In honor honesty, the tract of ev'ry thing   40
Would by a good discourser lose some life,
Which action's self was tongue to. All was royal;
To the disposing of it nought rebell'd,
Order gave each thing view; the office did
Distinctly his full function.
[*Buck.*]   Who did guide—   45
I mean, who set the body and the limbs
Of this great sport together, as you guess?
Nor.   One, certes, that promises no element
In such a business.
Buck.   I pray you, who, my lord?
Nor.   All this was ord'red by the good discretion   50
Of the right reverend Cardinal of York.
Buck.   The devil speed him! no man's pie is freed
From his ambitious finger. What had he
To do in these fierce vanities? I wonder
That such a keech can with his very bulk   55
Take up the rays o' th' beneficial sun,
And keep it from the earth.
Nor.   Surely, sir,
There's in him stuff that puts him to these ends;
For being not propp'd by ancestry, whose grace
Chalks successors their way, nor call'd upon   60
For high feats done to th' crown, neither allied
To eminent assistants, but spider-like
Out of his self-drawing web, ['a] gives us note
The force of his own merit makes his way—
A gift that heaven gives for him, which buys   65
A place next to the King.
Abur.   I cannot tell

---

25. **sad:** serious.

I.i. Location: London. The palace.
2. **saw in France:** i.e. met at the Field of the Cloth of Gold, scene of a glittering state visit between Henry VIII and Francis I in June 1520.   3. **fresh:** untired.   6. **suns of glory:** i.e. the two monarchs.
7. **vale . . . Arde.** The Vale of Andren, in Picardy, lay between the towns of Guynes and Ardres, which were held respectively by the English and the French.
8–10. **salute . . . together.** "The two kings meeting in the field," reports Holinshed (Bullough, IV, 457), "either saluted other in most loving wise, first on horsebacke, and after alighting on foot eftsoones imbraced with courteous words, to the great rejoising of the beholders."   10. **as:** as if.
11. **Which had they:** i.e. if they had grown together.   **weigh'd:** i.e. weighed as much as.   19. **clinquant:** glittering.
20. **they:** i.e. the English.
21. **Made Britain India:** i.e. made Britain seem as rich as India (the symbol of wealth to the Elizabethans).
23. **cherubins, all gilt:** carved and gilded figures of cherubim in churches (?).   25. **pride:** finery.

25–26. **that . . . painting:** i.e. so that they were flushed, as if with rouge, from their exertion.   30. **presence:** public appearance.
30–31. **him . . . praise:** i.e. whichever one of them was visible was most admired.
33. **censure:** judgment, i.e. in distinguishing the more splendid of the two.
38. **Bevis:** Bevis of Hampton (i.e. Southampton), the hero of a popular romance.   39. **worship:** the nobility.   **affect:** love.
40. **tract:** description.
41–42. **lose . . . to:** i.e. be less impressive than the thing itself.
43–45. **To . . . function:** i.e. there was nothing inappropriate; things were so arranged that everyone could see; each official did his job perfectly.
48. **certes:** surely.   **promises no element:** i.e. would seem to be unsuitable (?).   52. **speed:** prosper.
54. **fierce vanities:** extravagant follies.
55. **keech:** lump of suet (an allusion to Wolsey's being the son of a butcher).   56. **sun:** i.e. King Henry.
58. **stuff . . . ends:** traits that make him do these things.
60. **Chalks . . . way:** marks the path for descendants.
63. **self-drawing:** spun out of his own substance.   **'a . . . note:** he reveals to us.

Henry VIII
I.i

What heaven hath given him—let some graver eye
Pierce into that—but I can see his pride
Peep through each part of him. Whence has he that?
If not from hell, the devil is a niggard,　　　　70
Or has given all before, and he begins
A new hell in himself.

Buck.　　　　　　　Why the devil,
Upon this French going out, took he upon him
(Without the privity o' th' King) t' appoint
Who should attend on him? He makes up the file　75
Of all the gentry; for the most part such
To whom as great a charge as little honor
He meant to lay upon; and his own letter,
The honorable Board of Council out,
Must fetch him in he papers.

Abur.　　　　　　　　I do know　　80
Kinsmen of mine, three at the least, that have
By this so sicken'd their estates, that never
They shall abound as formerly.

Buck.　　　　　　　　　O, many
Have broke their backs with laying manors on 'em
For this great journey. What did this vanity　　85
But minister communication of
A most poor issue?

Nor.　　　　　　Grievingly I think
The peace between the French and us not values
The cost that did conclude it.

Buck.　　　　　　Every man,
After the hideous storm that follow'd, was　　90
A thing inspir'd, and, not consulting, broke
Into a general prophecy: that this tempest,
Dashing the garment of this peace, aboded
The sudden breach on't.

Nor.　　　　　　Which is budded out,
For France hath flaw'd the league, and hath attach'd　95
Our merchants' goods at Burdeaux.

Abur.　　　　　　　Is it therefore
Th' ambassador is silenc'd?

Nor.　　　　　　Marry, is't.

Abur. A proper title of a peace, and purchas'd
At a superfluous rate!

---

73. **going out:** excursion.
74. **privity:** knowledge (of something private).
75. **file:** list.　77. **charge:** expense.
78–80. **his . . . papers:** i.e. his summons alone—the council not consulted—is enough to force the attendance of whomever he lists (*papers*). "The peeres of the realme receiving letters to prepare themselves to attend the king in this journie," says Holinshed (Bullough, IV, 455), "and no apparant necessarie cause expressed, why nor wherefore; seemed to grudge, that such a costlie journie should be taken in hand to their importunate charges and expenses, without consent of the whole boord of the councell."
82. **sicken'd:** depleted.　83. **abound:** be wealthy.
84. **broke . . . 'em:** i.e. ruined themselves by spending their estates on costly clothing.　85. **What . . . vanity:** what good did this folly do.
86. **minister communication:** promote a conference.
87. **poor issue:** inconclusive outcome (with perhaps a pun on the sense "impoverished offspring").　88. **not values:** is not worth.
90. **hideous storm.** Holinshed (Bullough, IV, 458) records such "an hideous storm of wind and weather" on June 18, 1520, "that manie conjectured it did prognosticate trouble and hatred shortlie after to follow betweene princes."　91. **not consulting:** independently.
92. **general:** common, unanimous.　93. **aboded:** foretold.
94. **on't:** of it (the peace).
95. **flaw'd the league:** violated the treaty.　**attach'd:** seized.
96. **Burdeaux:** Bordeaux.　**therefore:** for this reason.
97. **Marry:** indeed (a weakened oath, "By the Virgin Mary").
98–99. **A proper . . . rate:** i.e. what a peace, and achieved at such prodigal expense.

Buck.　　　　　　Why, all this business
Our reverend Cardinal carried.

Nor.　　　　　　Like it your Grace,
The state takes notice of the private difference　101
Betwixt you and the Cardinal. I advise you
(And take it from a heart that wishes towards you
Honor and plenteous safety) that you read
The Cardinal's malice and his potency　　105
Together; to consider further, that
What his high hatred would effect wants not
A minister in his power. You know his nature,
That he's revengeful; and I know his sword
Hath a sharp edge; it's long, and't may be said　110
It reaches far, and where 'twill not extend,
Thither he darts it. Bosom up my counsel,
You'll find it wholesome. Lo, where comes that rock
That I advise your shunning.

Enter Cardinal Wolsey, *the purse borne before him, certain of the* Guard, *and two* Secretaries *with papers. The Cardinal in his passage fixeth his eye on Buckingham, and Buckingham on him, both full of disdain.*

Wol. The Duke of Buckingham's surveyor? ha?
Where's his examination?

[1.] Secr.　　　　Here, so please you.　116

Wol. Is he in person ready?

[1.] Secr.　　　　Ay, please your Grace.

Wol. Well, we shall then know more, and Buckingham
Shall lessen this big look.　　　　119

　　　　　　Exeunt Cardinal and his Train.

Buck. This butcher's cur is venom'd-mouth'd, and I
Have not the power to muzzle him, therefore best
Not wake him in his slumber. A beggar's book
Outworths a noble's blood.

Nor.　　　　What, are you chaf'd?
Ask God for temp'rance, that's th' appliance only
Which your disease requires.

Buck.　　　　　I read in 's looks　125
Matter against me, and his eye revil'd
Me as his abject object; at this instant
He bores me with some trick. He's gone to th' King;
I'll follow and outstare him.

Nor.　　　　　Stay, my lord,
And let your reason with your choler question　130
What 'tis you go about: to climb steep hills
Requires slow pace at first. Anger is like
A full hot horse, who being allow'd his way,

100. **carried:** managed.　**Like it:** if it please.　104. **read:** consider.
107–8. **What . . . power:** i.e. he does not lack the means of doing what his hatred drives him to.　112. **Bosom up:** take to heart.
114 s.d. **purse:** bag containing the Great Seal, one of Wolsey's insignia as chancellor.
115. **surveyor:** overseer of estates. Although Holinshed (Bullough, IV, 458) names Charles Knevet, who was Buckingham's cousin as well as his "surveyor," as the agent of the Duke's downfall, it was probably his chancellor, Robert Gilbert, who betrayed him.
116. **examination:** deposition, testimony given under oath.
120. **butcher's cur.** See note to line 55.
122. **book:** literary attainments, erudition.
123. **blood:** high descent.　**chaf'd:** angry.
124. **appliance:** remedy.　127. **abject:** castoff.
128. **bores:** cheats.　130. **question:** discuss, determine.

Self-mettle tires him. Not a man in England
Can advise me like you; be to yourself   135
As you would to your friend.
     Buck.   I'll to the King,
And from a mouth of honor quite cry down
This Ipswich fellow's insolence; or proclaim
There's difference in no persons.
     Nor.   Be advis'd;
Heat not a furnace for your foe so hot   140
That it do singe yourself. We may outrun
By violent swiftness that which we run at,
And lose by overrunning. Know you not
The fire that mounts the liquor till't run o'er
In seeming to augment it wastes it? Be advis'd;   145
I say again, there is no English soul
More stronger to direct you than yourself,
If with the sap of reason you would quench,
Or but allay, the fire of passion.
     Buck.   Sir,
I am thankful to you, and I'll go along   150
By your prescription; but this top-proud fellow,
Whom from the flow of gall I name not, but
From sincere motions, by intelligence,
And proofs as clear as founts in July when
We see each grain of gravel, I do know   155
To be corrupt and treasonous.
     Nor.   Say not treasonous.
     Buck.   To th' King I'll say't, and make my vouch as
             strong
As shore of rock. Attend. This holy fox,
Or wolf, or both (for he is equal rav'nous
As he is subtile, and as prone to mischief   160
As able to perform't), his mind and place
Infecting one another, yea, reciprocally,
Only to show his pomp as well in France
As here at home, suggests the King our master
To this last costly treaty—th' interview   165
That swallowed so much treasure, and like a glass
Did break i' th' wrenching.
     Nor.   Faith, and so it did.
     Buck.   Pray give me favor, sir: this cunning Car-
             dinal
The articles o' th' combination drew
As himself pleas'd; and they were ratified   170
As he cried, "Thus let be!" to as much end
As give a crutch to th' dead. But our count-cardinal
Has done this, and 'tis well; for worthy Wolsey
(Who cannot err), he did it. Now this follows
(Which, as I take it, is a kind of puppy   175
To th' old dam, treason), Charles the Emperor,

Under pretense to see the Queen his aunt
(For 'twas indeed his color, but he came
To whisper Wolsey), here makes visitation—
His fears were that the interview betwixt   180
England and France might through their amity
Breed him some prejudice; for from this league
Peep'd harms that menac'd him—privily
Deals with our Cardinal, and, as I trow—
Which I do well, for I am sure the Emperor   185
Paid ere he promis'd, whereby his suit was granted
Ere it was ask'd—but when the way was made
And pav'd with gold, the Emperor thus desir'd,
That he would please to alter the King's course,   189
And break the foresaid peace. Let the King know
(As soon he shall by me) that thus the Cardinal
Does buy and sell his honor as he pleases,
And for his own advantage.
     Nor.   I am sorry
To hear this of him; and could wish he were
Something mistaken in't.
     Buck.   No, not a syllable: 195
I do pronounce him in that very shape
He shall appear in proof.

Enter BRANDON, *a* SERGEANT-AT-ARMS *before him, and
     two or three of the* GUARD.

     Bran.   Your office, sergeant; execute it.
     Serg.   Sir,
My lord the Duke of Buckingham and Earl
Of [Herford], Stafford, and Northampton, I   200
Arrest thee of high treason, in the name
Of our most sovereign King.
     Buck.   Lo you, my lord,
The net has fall'n upon me! I shall perish
Under device and practice.
     Bran.   I am sorry
To see you ta'en from liberty, to look on   205
The business present. 'Tis his Highness' pleasure
You shall to th' Tower.
     Buck.   It will help me nothing
To plead mine innocence; for that dye is on me
Which makes my whit'st part black. The will of
             heav'n
Be done in this and all things! I obey.   210
O my Lord Aburga'ny, fare you well!
     Bran.   Nay, he must bear you company. [*To
Aburgavenny.*] The King

134. **Self-mettle:** his own high spirit.
138. **Ipswich:** seaport in Suffolk, Wolsey's birthplace.
139. **difference:** distinction of rank.   **advis'd:** cautious.
144. **mounts:** causes to rise (by boiling).
151. **top-proud:** superlatively proud.
152–53. **Whom . . . motions:** i.e. whom I mention not from spite but
from sincere motives.   153. **intelligence:** secret information.
157. **vouch:** evidence, proof.   161. **place:** (high) office.
164. **suggests:** prompts.
165. **last:** recent.   **interview:** i.e. the Field of the Cloth of Gold.
168. **give me favor:** listen to me.   169. **combination:** treaty.
172. **count-cardinal:** i.e. an ecclesiastic who assumes unwarranted
political functions (?).
176–93. **Charles . . . advantage.** As Emperor of the Holy Roman
Empire, King of Spain, and nephew to Queen Katherine, Charles
had everything to fear from a close alliance between England and

France. Having come to England, says Holinshed (Bullough, IV,
456–57), to warn against a French alliance but finding Henry already
"forward on his journie," he resolved to work through Wolsey. "And
forsomuch as he knew the lord cardinall to be woone with rewards,
as a fish with a bait: he bestowed on him great gifts, and promised him
much more, so that hee would be his friend, and helpe to bring his
purpose to passe. The cardinall not able to susteine the least assault
by force of such rewards as he presentlie received, and of such large
promises as on the emperours behalfe were made to him, promised
to the emperour, that he would so use the matter, as his purpose
should be sped."   178. **color:** pretext.   184. **trow:** believe.
189. **he:** i.e. Wolsey.
195. **Something mistaken:** somewhat misjudged.
197 s.d. **Brandon.** According to Holinshed (Bullough, IV, 459) it was
Sir Henry Marny, captain of the king's guard, who arrested Buckingham. The event occurred in April 1521, almost a year after the meeting of the two kings at the Field of the Cloth of Gold.
204. **device and practice:** schemes and plots.
205. **look on:** witness (?) or (referring to Buckingham, not Brandon)
face (?).

Henry VIII
I.i

Is pleas'd you shall to th' Tower, till you know
How he determines further.
    Abur.   As the Duke said,
The will of heaven be done, and the King's pleasure
By me obey'd!
    Bran.   Here is a warrant from   216
The King t' attach Lord Montacute, and the bodies
Of the Duke's confessor, John de la Car,
One Gilbert [Perk], his [chancellor]—
    Buck.   So, so;
These are the limbs o' th' plot. No more, I hope? 220
    Bran. A monk o' th' Chartreux.
    Buck.   O, [Nicholas] Hopkins?
    Bran.   He.
    Buck. My surveyor is false; the o'er-great Cardinal
Hath show'd him gold; my life is spann'd already.
I am the shadow of poor Buckingham,
Whose figure even this instant cloud puts on 225
By dark'ning my clear sun. My [lord], farewell.
                                   Exeunt.

SCENE II

Cornets. Enter KING HENRY, *leaning on the* CARDINAL's *shoulder, the* NOBLES, *and* SIR THOMAS LOVELL; *the Cardinal places himself under the King's feet on his right side,* [*his* SECRETARY *in attendance*].

    King. My life itself, and the best heart of it,
Thanks you for this great care. I stood i' th' level
Of a full-charg'd confederacy, and give thanks
To you that chok'd it. Let be call'd before us
That gentleman of Buckingham's; in person 5
I'll hear him his confessions justify,
And point by point the treasons of his master
He shall again relate.

A noise within, crying, "Room for the Queen!" [*who is*] *usher'd by the Duke of Norfolk. Enter the* QUEEN [KATHERINE], NORFOLK, *and* SUFFOLK; *she kneels.* [*The*] *King riseth from his state, takes her up, kisses, and placeth her by him.*

    Q. Kath. Nay, we must longer kneel; I am a suitor.
    King. Arise, and take place by us. Half your suit
Never name to us; you have half our power. 11
The other moi'ty ere you ask is given;
Repeat your will and take it.
    Q. Kath.   Thank your Majesty.

That you would love yourself, and in that love
Not unconsidered leave your honor nor   15
The dignity of your office, is the point
Of my petition.
    King.   Lady mine, proceed.
    Q. Kath. I am solicited, not by a few,
And those of true condition, that your subjects
Are in great grievance: there have been commissions
Sent down among 'em, which hath flaw'd the heart 21
Of all their loyalties; wherein, although,
My good Lord Cardinal, they vent reproaches
Most bitterly on you as putter-on
Of these exactions, yet the King our master— 25
Whose honor heaven shield from soil!—even he
    escapes not
Language unmannerly; yea, such which breaks
The sides of loyalty, and almost appears
In loud rebellion.
    Nor.   Not almost appears,
It doth appear; for, upon these taxations, 30
The clothiers all, not able to maintain
The many to them 'longing, have put off
The spinsters, carders, fullers, weavers, who,
Unfit for other life, compell'd by hunger
And lack of other means, in desperate manner 35
Daring th' event to th' teeth, are all in uproar,
And danger serves among them.
    King.   Taxation?
Wherein? and what taxation? My Lord Cardinal,
You that are blam'd for it alike with us,
Know you of this taxation?
    Wol.   Please you, sir, 40
I know but of a single part in aught
Pertains to th' state; and front but in that file
Where others tell steps with me.
    Q. Kath.   No, my lord?
You know no more than others? But you frame
Things that are known alike, which are not whole-
    some 45

216–21. **Here . . . He.** Holinshed (Bullough, IV, 458–59) supplies the names of Buckingham's alleged accomplices. In addition to his son-in-law George Neville, third Baron of Bergavenny, they included "the lord Montacute," "Nicholas Hopkins, a monke of an house of the Chartreux order beside Bristow, called Henton, sometime his [i.e. Buckingham's] confessor," "maister John de la Car *alias* de la Court, the dukes confessor, and sir Gilbert Perke priest, the dukes chancellor." In this play Hopkins is sometimes called by his true name (l. 221 and II.i.22), sometimes Henton (I.ii.147, 148).
217. **attach:** arrest.   221. **Chartreux:** Carthusian order.
223. **spann'd:** measured out.

I.ii. Location: London. The Council-chamber.
o.s.d. **Cornets:** horns (not the modern brass instruments).   **places . . . feet:** i.e. stands below the dais on which the throne is set.
2. **level:** aim.
3. **full-charg'd confederacy:** heavily loaded conspiracy.
6. **justify:** confirm.   8 s.d. **state:** raised throne with a canopy.
12. **moi'ty:** half.   13. **Repeat your will:** state your desire.

18. **solicited:** informed.   19. **true condition:** i.e. loyalty.
20–29. **there . . . rebellion.** Although Holinshed's account of the rebellion of the weavers (Bullough, IV, 464–65)—which occurred in 1525, four years after the fall of Buckingham—makes no mention of Queen Katherine's intercession, it supplies most of the other details for this scene. "The king being determined thus to make wars in France, & to passe the sea himselfe in person, his councell considered that above all things great treasure and plentie of monie must needes be provided. Wherfore, by the cardinall there was devised strange commissions, and sent in the end of March into everie shire, and commissioners appointed, and privie instructions sent to them how they should proceed in their sittings, and order the people to bring them to their purpose: which was, that the sixt part of everie mans substance should be paid in monie or plate to the king without delaie, for the furniture of his war. Hereof followed such cursing, weeping, and exclamation against both king & cardinall, that pitie it was to heare."
20. **commissions:** i.e. (tax) agents with writs of authority.
21. **flaw'd:** cracked.   24. **putter-on:** instigator.
32. **The many . . . 'longing:** i.e. their employees.   **put off:** discharged.
33. **The spinsters . . . weavers.** Holinshed records (Bullough, IV, 464) how the "rich clothiers . . . went about to discharge and put from them their spinsters, carders, fullers, weavers, and other artificers, which they kept in worke afore time." **spinsters:** spinners. **carders:** men who clean and disentangle wool by combing. **fullers:** men who clean and thicken cloth.
36. **event:** outcome. **to th' teeth:** defiantly.
37. **danger serves:** mischief is rife.
42. **front . . . file:** merely march in the front rank.
43. **tell steps:** keep step, i.e. march.
45. **alike:** to all. **wholesome:** i.e. endorsed as beneficial.

To those which would not know them, and yet must
Perforce be their acquaintance. These exactions
(Whereof my sovereign would have note), they are
Most pestilent to th' hearing, and, to bear 'em,
The back is sacrifice to th' load. They say   50
They are devis'd by you, or else you suffer
Too hard an exclamation.

King.   Still exaction!
The nature of it? in what kind, let's know,
Is this exaction?

Q. Kath.   I am much too venturous
In tempting of your patience; but am bold'ned   55
Under your promis'd pardon. The subject's grief
Comes through commissions, which compels from each
The sixt part of his substance, to be levied
Without delay; and the pretense for this
Is nam'd, your wars in France. This makes bold
                              mouths,   60
Tongues spit their duties out, and cold hearts freeze
Allegiance in them; their curses now
Live where their prayers did; and it's come to pass
This tractable obedience is a slave
To each incensed will. I would your Highness   65
Would give it quick consideration, for
There is no primer baseness.

King.   By my life,
This is against our pleasure.

Wol.   And for me,
I have no further gone in this than by
A single voice, and that not pass'd me but   70
By learned approbation of the judges. If I am
Traduc'd by ignorant tongues, which neither know
My faculties nor person, yet will be
The chronicles of my doing, let me say
'Tis but the fate of place, and the rough brake   75
That virtue must go through. We must not stint
Our necessary actions in the fear
To cope malicious censurers, which ever,
As rav'nous fishes, do a vessel follow
That is new trimm'd, but benefit no further   80
Than vainly longing. What we oft do best,
By sick interpreters (once weak ones) is
Not ours, or not allow'd; what worst, as oft,
Hitting a grosser quality, is cried up
For our best act. If we shall stand still,   85
In fear our motion will be mock'd or carp'd at,
We should take root here where we sit, or sit
State-statues only.

King.   Things done well

And with a care exempt themselves from fear;
Things done without example, in their issue   90
Are to be fear'd. Have you a president
Of this commission? I believe, not any.
We must not rend our subjects from our laws,
And stick them in our will. Sixt part of each?
A trembling contribution! Why, we take   95
From every tree, lop, bark, and part o' th' timber;
And, though we leave it with a root, thus hack'd,
The air will drink the sap. To every county
Where this is question'd send our letters, with
Free pardon to each man that has denied   100
The force of this commission. Pray look to't;
I put it to your care.

Wol.   [*Aside to the Secretary.*] A word with you.
Let there be letters writ to every shire,
Of the King's grace and pardon. The grieved commons
Hardly conceive of me; let it be nois'd   105
That through our intercession this revokement
And pardon comes. I shall anon advise you
Further in the proceeding.   *Exit Secretary.*

Enter SURVEYOR.

Q. Kath.   I am sorry that the Duke of Buckingham
Is run in your displeasure.

King.   It grieves many.   110
The gentleman is learn'd, and a most rare speaker,
To nature none more bound; his training such
That he may furnish and instruct great teachers
And never seek for aid out of himself. Yet see,
When these so noble benefits shall prove   115
Not well dispos'd, the mind growing once corrupt,
They turn to vicious forms, ten times more ugly
Than ever they were fair. This man so complete,
Who was enroll'd 'mongst wonders, and when we,
Almost with ravish'd list'ning, could not find   120
His hour of speech a minute—he, my lady,
Hath into monstrous habits put the graces
That once were his, and is become as black
As if besmear'd in hell. Sit by us, you shall hear
(This was his gentleman in trust) of him   125
Things to strike honor sad. Bid him recount
The fore-recited practices, whereof
We cannot feel too little, hear too much.

Wol.   Stand forth, and with bold spirit relate what
                              you,

46. **those:** i.e. members of the council.
47. **their acquaintance:** i.e. known to them.
48. **note:** knowledge.   50. **is sacrifice to:** i.e. bows under.
52. **exclamation:** reproach.
56. **subject's.** *Subject* was frequently used in the collective sense "subjects of the realm."   **grief:** grievance.
64. **a slave:** i.e. subordinate.
67. **primer baseness:** mischief requiring more urgent attention.
69–70. **by . . . voice:** by . . . vote, i.e. as one among many (who concurred in the decision.   73. **faculties:** qualities.
75. **brake:** thicket.   78. **To cope:** of encountering.
80. **new trimm'd:** newly fitted out, seaworthy.
82. **sick interpreters:** envious critics.   **once weak:** in short, unqualified.
83. **Not . . . allow'd:** not credited to us, or else denounced.
84. **Hitting . . . quality:** appealing to coarser natures (?).

90. **example:** precedent.   **issue:** outcome.
91–92. **president Of:** precedent for.
94. **stick . . . will:** subject them to our caprice.
95. **trembling:** accompanied by trembling.   96. **lop:** branches.
98–108. **To . . . proceeding.** Dismayed by rebellion of the weavers, the King, says Holinshed (Bullough, IV, 465), "caused letters to be sent into all shires, that the matter should no further be talked of: & he pardoned all them that had denied the demand openlie or secretlie. The cardinall, to deliver himself of the evill will of the commons, purchased by procuring & advancing of this demand, affirmed, and caused it to be bruted abrode, that through his intercession the king had pardoned and released all things."   101. **force:** validity.
104. **grace:** mercy.   **grieved:** aggrieved.
105. **Hardly conceive:** think harshly.
112. **bound:** obligated (for natural ability).
114. **out of:** beyond.   116. **dispos'd:** used.
118. **complete:** accomplished.   120. **ravish'd:** enchanted.
122. **habits:** (1) garments; (2) moral qualities.
125. **gentleman in trust:** confidential agent.
127. **practices:** contrivances.

Henry VIII   Most like a careful subject, have collected   130
I.ii   Out of the Duke of Buckingham.

   King.   Speak freely.

   Surv.   First, it was usual with him—every day
It would infect his speech—that if the King
Should without issue die, he'll carry it so
To make the sceptre his. These very words   135
I've heard him utter to his son-in-law,
Lord Aburga'ny, to whom by oath he menac'd
Revenge upon the Cardinal.

   Wol.   Please your Highness note
This dangerous conception in this point,
Not friended by his wish, to your high person;   140
His will is most malignant, and it stretches
Beyond you to your friends.

   Q. Kath.   My learn'd Lord Cardinal,
Deliver all with charity.

   King.   Speak on.
How grounded he his title to the crown
Upon our fail? To this point hast thou heard him   145
At any time speak aught?

   Surv.   He was brought to this
By a vain prophecy of Nicholas Henton.

   King. What was that Henton?

   Surv.   Sir, a Chartreux friar,
His confessor, who fed him every minute
With words of sovereignty.

   King.   How know'st thou this?

   Surv.   Not long before your Highness sped to
    France,   151
The Duke being at the Rose, within the parish
Saint Lawrence Poultney, did of me demand
What was the speech among the Londoners
Concerning the French journey. I replied,   155
Men fear the French would prove perfidious,
To the King's danger. Presently the Duke
Said, 'twas the fear indeed, and that he doubted
'Twould prove the verity of certain words
Spoke by a holy monk "that oft," says he,   160
"Hath sent to me, wishing me to permit
John de la Car, my chaplain, a choice hour
To hear from him a matter of some moment;
Whom after under the [confession's] seal
He solemnly had sworn that what he spoke   165
My chaplain to no creature living but
To me should utter, with demure confidence
This pausingly ensu'd: 'Neither the King nor 's heirs
(Tell you the Duke) shall prosper. Bid him strive
To the love o' th' commonalty; the Duke   170
Shall govern England.' "

   Q. Kath.   If I know you well,

You were the Duke's surveyor, and lost your office
On the complaint o' th' tenants. Take good heed
You charge not in your spleen a noble person
And spoil your nobler soul; I say, take heed;   175
Yes, heartily beseech you.

   King.   Let him on.
Go forward.

   Surv.   On my soul, I'll speak but truth.
I told my lord the Duke, by th' devil's illusions
The monk might be deceiv'd, and that 'twas dangerous
    for [him]
To ruminate on this so far, until   180
It forg'd him some design, which being believ'd,
It was much like to do. He answer'd, "Tush,
It can do me no damage"; adding further
That had the King in his last sickness fail'd,
The Cardinal's and Sir Thomas Lovell's heads   185
Should have gone off.

   King.   Ha? what, so rank? Ah ha,
There's mischief in this man. Canst thou say further?

   Surv.   I can, my liege.

   King.   Proceed.

   Surv.   Being at Greenwich,
After your Highness had reprov'd the Duke
About Sir William [Bulmer]—

   King.   I remember   190
Of such a time, being my sworn servant,
The Duke retain'd him his. But on; what hence?

   Surv.   "If," quoth he, "I for this had been com-
    mitted—
As to the Tower, I thought—I would have play'd
The part my father meant to act upon   195
Th' usurper Richard, who, being at Salisbury,
Made suit to come in 's presence; which if granted,
As he made semblance of his duty would
Have put his knife into him."

   King.   A giant traitor!

   Wol. Now, madam, may his Highness live in free-
    dom,   200
And this man out of prison?

   Q. Kath.   God mend all!

   King.   There's something more would out of thee;
    what say'st?

130–31. **collected Out:** gathered from the behavior.
132–209. **First . . . purpose.** The surveyor's evidence against Buckingham is based on Holinshed, much of it being merely versified from
the chronicler's prose (Bullough, IV, 459–60).
132. **it . . . him:** i.e. he habitually said.   134. **carry it so:** contrive.
140. **Not . . . wish:** i.e. disappointed in his hope that you would die
without issue.   143. **Deliver:** relate.
145. **fail:** failure (to have children).
150. **of sovereignty:** i.e. about his prospects for succeeding to the
crown.   152. **the Rose:** manor house in Buckingham's possession.
157. **Presently:** promptly.   158. **doubted:** feared.
162. **choice hour:** appropriate time.   167. **demure:** solemn.
170. **commonalty:** common people.

172–73. **You . . . tenants.** Before accompanying the King to the Field
of the Cloth of Gold, Buckingham, says Holinshed (Bullough, IV,
456), had received "greevous complaints" from "his farmars and tenants against Charles Knevet his surveiour, for such bribing as he had
used there [in Kent] amongst them. Whereupon the duke tooke such
displeasure against him, that he deprived him of his office, not knowing how that in so dooing he procured his owne destruction."
174. **spleen:** spite.
175. **spoil:** destroy.   **nobler:** i.e. than the "noble person" (because
the soul is of more importance than the body).
184. **fail'd:** succumbed.
186. **Ha.** This exclamation, frequently used by the King, no doubt
derives from Samuel Rowley's *When You See Me You Know Me*
(1605), a history play about Henry VIII in which the term is heavily
employed. See III.ii.63.   **rank:** arrogant (?) or seditious (?).
188. **liege:** sovereign.   **Greenwich:** royal residence on the lower
Thames.
190. **Sir William Bulmer:** a functionary who, according to Holinshed
(Bullough, IV, 454, 459), left the King's service for Buckingham's
and thus brought down Henry's wrath on both of them.
195. **my father:** i.e. Henry Stafford (1454?–1483), second Duke of
Buckingham, an adherent of Richard III who turned against his master
and was executed after his abortive insurrection failed. He plays a
conspicuous part in *Richard III*.
198. **made . . . duty:** i.e. made as if to kneel.   200. **may:** can.

Surv. After "the Duke his father," with the "knife,"
He stretch'd him, and with one hand on his dagger,
Another spread on 's breast, mounting his eyes,   205
He did discharge a horrible oath, whose tenor
Was, were he evil us'd, he would outgo
His father by as much as a performance
Does an irresolute purpose.

King.   There's his period,
To sheathe his knife in us. He is attach'd,   210
Call him to present trial. If he may
Find mercy in the law, 'tis his; if none,
Let him not seek't of us. By day and night,
He's traitor to th' height.   *Exeunt.*

SCENE III

Enter LORD CHAMBERLAIN *and* LORD SANDS.

Cham. Is't possible the spells of France should juggle
Men into such strange mysteries?

San.   New customs,
Though they be never so ridiculous
(Nay, let 'em be unmanly), yet are follow'd.

Cham. As far as I see, all the good our English   5
Have got by the late voyage is but merely
A fit or two o' th' face—but they are shrewd ones,
For when they hold 'em, you would swear directly
Their very noses had been councillors
To Pepin or Clotharius, they keep state so.   10

San. They have all new legs, and lame ones. One would take it,
That never see 'em pace before, the spavin
[And] springhalt reign'd among 'em.

Cham.   Death, my lord,
Their clothes are after such a pagan cut to't,
That sure th' have worn out Christendom.

Enter SIR THOMAS LOVELL.

                         How now?   15
What news, Sir Thomas Lovell?

Lov.   Faith, my lord,

I hear of none but the new proclamation
That's clapp'd upon the court gate.

Cham.   What is't for?

Lov. The reformation of our travell'd gallants,
That fill the court with quarrels, talk, and tailors.

Cham. I'm glad 'tis there. Now I would pray our monsieurs   21
To think an English courtier may be wise
And never see the Louvre.

Lov.   They must either
(For so run the conditions) leave those remnants
Of fool and feather that they got in France,   25
With all their honorable points of ignorance
Pertaining thereunto, as fights and fireworks,
Abusing better men than they can be
Out of a foreign wisdom, renouncing clean
The faith they have in tennis and tall stockings,   30
Short blist'red breeches, and those types of travel,
And understand again like honest men,
Or pack to their old playfellows. There, I take it,
They may, *cum privilegio*, ["*oui*"] away
The lag end of their lewdness and be laugh'd at.   35

San. 'Tis time to give 'em physic, their diseases
Are grown so catching.

Cham.   What a loss our ladies
Will have of these trim vanities!

Lov.   Ay, marry,
There will be woe indeed, lords; the sly whoresons
Have got a speeding trick to lay down ladies.   40
A French song and a fiddle has no fellow.

San. The devil fiddle 'em! I am glad they are going,
For sure there's no converting of 'em. Now
An honest country lord, as I am, beaten
A long time out of play, may bring his plain-song   45
And have an hour of hearing, and, by'r lady,
Held current music too.

Cham.   Well said, Lord Sands,
Your colt's tooth is not cast yet?

San.   No, my lord,
Nor shall not while I have a stump.

Cham.   Sir Thomas,
Whither were you a-going?

Lov.   To the Cardinal's.   50
Your lordship is a guest too.

Cham.   O, 'tis true;
This night he makes a supper, and a great one,
To many lords and ladies; there will be
The beauty of this kingdom, I'll assure you.

Lov. That churchman bears a bounteous mind indeed,
                         55
A hand as fruitful as the land that feeds us;
His dews fall every where.

203. **with:** i.e. with mention of.
204. **stretch'd him:** i.e. rose to his full height.
205. **mounting:** lifting up.   209. **period:** end, aim.
210. **attach'd:** arrested.   211. **present:** immediate.
214. **to th' height:** in the highest degree.

I.iii. Location: London. The palace.
o.s.d. **Lord Chamberlain and Lord Sands.** These names present problems. Although this and the following scene—the first perhaps suggested by Holinshed's comments (Bullough, IV, 453) on French fashions at the English court—obviously precede the death of Buckingham in May 1521, the banquet and masque of I.iv occurred, says Holinshed, on January 3, 1527. By that time, Sands (or Sandys)—who, incidentally, was not elevated to the peerage until 1523—was himself Lord Chamberlain. At II.i.53 s.d. he is called a knight.
2. **strange mysteries:** queer behavior.   4. **unmanly:** i.e. effeminate.
6. **the late voyage:** i.e. to the Field of the Cloth of Gold.
7. **A fit . . . face:** a grimace or two.
10. **Pepin, Clotharius:** Frankish kings of the sixth and seventh centuries.
11. **legs:** i.e. ways of walking (perhaps with second sense "bows").
lame ones: i.e. because of an affected gait.
12. **see:** saw (archaic form).
12, 13. **spavin, springhalt:** diseases of animals causing lameness.
14. **to't:** besides.
15. **worn out Christendom:** i.e. run through all the Christian fashions.

27. **fireworks:** i.e. whores.
31. **blist'red:** puffed.   **types:** signs.   33. **pack:** go.
34. **cum privilegio:** with immunity.
34–35. **"oui" . . . lewdness:** i.e. indulge their lechery in aping the French. *Oui* is the French word for "yes."   36. **physic:** medicine.
38. **trim vanities:** finely dressed fools.
40. **speeding:** effective.   **lay down:** i.e. seduce.
43. **converting:** reforming.
45. **play:** i.e. the game of love.   **plain-song:** simple tune.
47. **current:** acceptable.
48. **colt's tooth:** i.e. wanton impulses (especially in old men).   **cast:** lost.   56. **fruitful:** generous.

Cham.   No doubt he's noble;
He had a black mouth that said other of him.
    San.   He may, my lord, h'as wherewithal: in him
Sparing would show a worse sin than ill doctrine.   60
Men of his way should be most liberal,
They are set here for examples.
    Cham.   True, they are so;
But few now give so great ones. My barge stays;
Your lordship shall along. Come, good Sir Thomas,
We shall be late else, which I would not be,   65
For I was spoke to, with Sir Henry Guilford
This night to be comptrollers.
    San.   I am your lordship's. *Exeunt.*

SCENE IV

*Hoboys. A small table under a state for the Cardinal, a
longer table for the guests. Then enter* ANNE BULLEN
and divers other LADIES *and* GENTLEMEN *as guests, at
one door; at another door, enter* SIR HENRY GUILFORD.

    Guil.   Ladies, a general welcome from his Grace
Salutes ye all; this night he dedicates
To fair content and you. None here, he hopes,
In all this noble bevy, has brought with her
One care abroad. He would have all as merry   5
As, first, good company, good wine, good welcome,
Can make good people.

Enter LORD CHAMBERLAIN, LORD SANDS, *and* LOVELL.

                    O my lord, y' are tardy;
The very thought of this fair company
Clapp'd wings to me.
    Cham.   You are young, Sir Harry Guilford.
    San.   Sir Thomas Lovell, had the Cardinal   10
But half my lay-thoughts in him, some of these
Should find a running banket, ere they rested,
I think would better please 'em. By my life,
They are a sweet society of fair ones.
    Lov.   O that your lordship were but now confessor
To one or two of these!
    San.   I would I were,   16
They should find easy penance.
    Lov.   Faith, how easy?
    San.   As easy as a down-bed would afford it.
    Cham.   Sweet ladies, will it please you sit? Sir
      Harry,
Place you that side, I'll take the charge of this.   20
His Grace is ent'ring. Nay, you must not freeze,
Two women plac'd together makes cold weather.
My Lord Sands, you are one will keep 'em waking;
Pray sit between these ladies.
    San.   By my faith,
And thank your lordship. By your leave, sweet ladies.

If I chance to talk a little wild, forgive me;   26
I had it from my father.
    Anne.   Was he mad, sir?
    San.   O, very mad, exceeding mad, in love too;
But he would bite none. Just as I do now,
He would kiss you twenty with a breath.
                                       [*Kisses her.*]
    Cham.   Well said, my lord.
So now y' are fairly seated. Gentlemen,   31
The penance lies on you, if these fair ladies
Pass away frowning.
    San.   For my little cure,
Let me alone.

Hoboys. Enter CARDINAL WOLSEY *and takes his state.*

    Wol.   Y' are welcome, my fair guests. That noble
      lady   35
Or gentleman that is not freely merry
Is not my friend. This, to confirm my welcome,
And to you all good health.   [*Drinks.*]
    San.   Your Grace is noble.
Let me have such a bowl may hold my thanks,
And save me so much talking.
    Wol.   My Lord Sands,   40
I am beholding to you; cheer your neighbors.
Ladies, you are not merry. Gentlemen,
Whose fault is this?
    San.   The red wine first must rise
In their fair cheeks, my lord, then we shall have 'em
Talk us to silence.
    Anne.   You are a merry gamester,   45
My Lord Sands.
    San.   Yes, if I make my play.
Here's to your ladyship, and pledge it, madam,
For 'tis to such a thing—
    Anne.   You cannot show me.
    San.   I told your Grace they would talk anon.
              Drum and trumpet; chambers discharg'd.
    Wol.   What's that?
    Cham.   Look out there, some of ye.
                                       [*Exit a Servant.*]
    Wol.   What warlike voice,
And to what end is this? Nay, ladies, fear not;   51
By all the laws of war y' are privileg'd.

59. **h'as:** he has.   60. **Sparing:** frugality.   **ill doctrine:** i.e. heresy.
61. **way:** i.e. way of life.   63. **stays:** awaits.
66. **spoke to:** requested.   67. **comptrollers:** masters of ceremonies.

I.iv. Location: Westminster. The presence-chamber in York Place.
o.s.d. **Hoboys:** oboes.   **state:** canopy.   4. **bevy:** company.
11. **lay:** i.e. secular (with perhaps a sexual pun).
12. **running banket:** running banquet, i.e. hurried repast (with a
bawdy double meaning).   20. **Place you:** i.e. seat the guests on.
23. **waking:** lively.

30. **twenty . . . breath:** i.e. twenty times without drawing breath.
33. **cure:** (1) charge, parish (carrying on the figure in line 15); (2)
remedy.   34 s.d. **state:** chair of state.
41. **beholding:** beholden, indebted.
46. **make my play:** i.e. win my game (with an implication of amorous
play).
49 s.d. **chambers:** short cannon. It was probably the firing of these
that caused the destruction of the Globe playhouse in 1613.
50–108. Holinshed's account (Bullough, III, 478) of this episode
(to which the play is much indebted) opens thus: "On a time the
king came suddenlie thither [i.e. to Wolsey's palace] in a maske with
a dozen maskers all in garments like sheepheards, made of fine
cloth of gold, and crimosin sattin paned, & caps of the same, with
visards of good physnomie, their haires & beards either of fine
goldwire silke, or blacke silke, having sixteene torch-bearers, besides
their drums and other persons with visards, all clothed in sattin of
the same color. And before his entring into the hall, he came by
water to the water gate without anie noise, where were laid diverse
chambers and guns charged with shot, and at his landing they were
shot off, which made such a rumble in the aire, that it was like
thunder: it made all the noblemen, gentlemen, ladies, and gentlewomen, to muse what it should meane, comming so suddenlie they
sitting quiet at a solemne banket, after this sort."

Enter a SERVANT.

Cham. How now, what is't?

Serv.   A noble troop of strangers,
For so they seem. Th' have left their barge and
landed,
And hither make, as great embassadors   55
From foreign princes.

Wol.   Good Lord Chamberlain,
Go, give 'em welcome: you can speak the French
tongue;
And pray receive 'em nobly and conduct 'em
Into our presence, where this heaven of beauty
Shall shine at full upon them. Some attend him.   60
          [*Exit Chamberlain attended.*] *All
          rise, and tables remov'd.*
You have now a broken banket, but we'll mend it.
A good digestion to you all; and once more
I show'r a welcome on ye. Welcome all!

Hoboys. Enter KING *and others as Maskers, habited
like shepherds, usher'd by the* LORD CHAMBERLAIN.
*They pass directly before the Cardinal and gracefully
salute him.*

A noble company! What are their pleasures?

Cham. Because they speak no English, thus they
pray'd   65
To tell your Grace, that having heard by fame
Of this so noble and so fair assembly
This night to meet here, they could do no less
(Out of the great respect they bear to beauty)
But leave their flocks, and under your fair conduct   70
Crave leave to view these ladies, and entreat
An hour of revels with 'em.

Wol.   Say, Lord Chamberlain,
They have done my poor house grace; for which I
pay 'em
A thousand thanks, and pray 'em take their pleasures.
          Choose ladies; King and Anne Bullen.

King. The fairest hand I ever touch'd! O Beauty,
Till now I never knew thee!   *Music. Dance.*   76

Wol. My lord!

Cham.   Your Grace?

Wol.   Pray tell 'em thus much from me:
There should be one amongst 'em, by his person
More worthy this place than myself, to whom
(If I but knew him) with my love and duty   80
I would surrender it.

Cham.   I will, my lord.
          Whisper [*with the Maskers*].

Wol. What say they?

Cham.   Such a one, they all confess,
There is indeed, which they would have your Grace
Find out, and he will take it.

Wol.   Let me see then,
By all your good leaves, gentlemen; here I'll make
My royal choice.

King.   Ye have found him, Cardinal.   86
          [*Unmasking.*]
You hold a fair assembly; you do well, lord.
You are a churchman, or I'll tell you, Cardinal,
I should judge now unhappily.

Wol.   I am glad   89
Your Grace is grown so pleasant.

King.   My Lord Chamberlain,
Prithee come hither. What fair lady's that?

Cham. An't please your Grace, Sir Thomas
Bullen's daughter—
The Viscount Rochford—one of her Highness' women.

King. By heaven, she is a dainty one. Sweet heart,
I were unmannerly to take you out   95
And not to kiss you. A health, gentlemen!
Let it go round.

Wol. Sir Thomas Lovell, is the banket ready
I' th' privy chamber?

Lov.   Yes, my lord.

Wol.   Your Grace,
I fear, with dancing is a little heated.   100

King. I fear, too much.

Wol.   There's fresher air, my lord,
In the next chamber.

King. Lead in your ladies, ev'ry one. Sweet
partner,
I must not yet forsake you. Let's be merry,
Good my Lord Cardinal: I have half a dozen healths
To drink to these fair ladies, and a measure   106
To lead 'em once again, and then let's dream
Who's best in favor. Let the music knock it.
          Exeunt with Trumpets.

ACT II, SCENE I

Enter two GENTLEMEN *at several doors.*

1. Gent. Whither away so fast?

2. Gent.   O, God save ye!
Ev'n to the hall, to hear what shall become
Of the great Duke of Buckingham.

1. Gent.   I'll save you
That labor, sir. All's now done but the ceremony
Of bringing back the prisoner.

2. Gent.   Were you there?   5

1. Gent. Yes indeed was I.

2. Gent.   Pray speak what has happen'd.

1. Gent. You may guess quickly what.

2. Gent.   Is he found guilty?

1. Gent. Yes, truly is he, and condemn'd upon't.

---

86. Ye . . . him. According to Holinshed (Bullough, IV, 480), Wolsey first offered his place to Sir Edward Neville, whereupon "the king perceiving the cardinall so deceived, could not forbeare laughing, but pulled down his visar and master Nevels also, and dashed out such a pleasant countenance and cheere, that all the noble estates there assembled, perceiving the king to be there among them, rejoised verie much."   89. unhappily: unfavorably.   90. pleasant: merry.
93. her Highness' women: i.e. Queen Katherine's women in waiting.
95. take you out: i.e. into the dance.
106. measure: stately dance.
108. best in favor: handsomest.   knock it: strike up.   s.d. Trumpets: trumpeters.

II.i. Location: Westminster. A street.
o.s.d. several: different.   2. hall: Westminster Hall.

53. strangers: foreigners.   55. embassadors: ambassadors.
61. broken: interrupted.   70. conduct: permission.
74 s.d. Anne Bullen. Henry's meeting Anne Bullen at Wolsey's banquet is not in Holinshed.   79. this place: i.e. the chair of state.
84. it: i.e. Wolsey's "place."

Henry VIII
II.i

2. Gent. I am sorry for't.

1. Gent.　　　　　　　So are a number more.

2. Gent. But pray how pass'd it?　　　　10

1. Gent. I'll tell you in a little. The great Duke
Came to the bar; where to his accusations
He pleaded still not guilty, and alleged
Many sharp reasons to defeat the law.
The King's attorney on the contrary　　　15
Urg'd on the examinations, proofs, confessions
Of divers witnesses, which the Duke desir'd
To him brought *vivâ voce* to his face;
At which appear'd against him his surveyor,
Sir Gilbert [Perk] his chancellor, and John Car,　20
Confessor to him, with that devil monk,
Hopkins, that made this mischief.

2. Gent.　　　　　　　That was he
That fed him with his prophecies?

1. Gent.　　　　　　　The same;
All these accus'd him strongly, which he fain
Would have flung from him; but indeed he could not.
And so his peers upon this evidence　　　26
Have found him guilty of high treason. Much
He spoke, and learnedly, for life; but all
Was either pitied in him or forgotten.

2. Gent. After all this, how did he bear himself?

1. Gent. When he was brought again to th' bar, to
　　hear　　　　　　　31
His knell rung out, his judgment, he was stirr'd
With such an agony he sweat extremely,
And something spoke in choler, ill, and hasty.
But he fell to himself again, and sweetly　35
In all the rest show'd a most noble patience.

2. Gent. I do not think he fears death.

1. Gent.　　　　　　　Sure he does not,
He never was so womanish. The cause
He may a little grieve at.

2. Gent.　　　　　　　Certainly
The Cardinal is the end of this.

1. Gent.　　　　　　　'Tis likely,　40
By all conjectures: first, Kildare's attendure,
Then deputy of Ireland, who remov'd,
Earl Surrey was sent thither, and in haste too,
Lest he should help his father.

2. Gent.　　　　　　　That trick of state
Was a deep envious one.

1. Gent.　　　　　　　At his return　45
No doubt he will requite it. This is noted,
And generally, whoever the King favors,
The Card'nal instantly will find employment,
And far enough from court too.

2. Gent.　　　　　　　All the commons
Hate him perniciously, and, o' my conscience,　50
Wish him ten fadom deep. This duke as much
They love and dote on; call him bounteous Bucking-
　　ham,
The mirror of all courtesy—

Enter BUCKINGHAM *from his arraignment, Tipstaves before him, the axe with the edge towards him, Halberds on each side; accompanied with* SIR THOMAS LOVELL, SIR NICHOLAS VAUX, SIR WALTER SANDS, *and common people, etc.*

1. Gent.　　　　　　　Stay there, sir,
And see the noble ruin'd man you speak of.

2. Gent. Let's stand close and behold him.

Buck.　　　　　　　All good people,
You that thus far have come to pity me,　56
Hear what I say, and then go home and lose me.
I have this day receiv'd a traitor's judgment,
And by that name must die; yet, heaven bear witness,
And if I have a conscience, let it sink me,　60
Even as the axe falls, if I be not faithful!
The law I bear no malice for my death;
'T has done, upon the premises, but justice;
But those that sought it I could wish more Christians.
Be what they will, I heartily forgive 'em;　65
Yet let 'em look they glory not in mischief,
Nor build their evils on the graves of great men,
For then my guiltless blood must cry against 'em.
For further life in this world I ne'er hope,
Nor will I sue, although the King have mercies　70
More than I dare make faults. You few that lov'd me
And dare be bold to weep for Buckingham,
His noble friends and fellows, whom to leave
Is only bitter to him, only dying,
Go with me like good angels to my end,　75
And as the long divorce of steel falls on me,
Make of your prayers one sweet sacrifice,
And lift your soul to heaven. Lead on a' God's name.

Lov. I do beseech your Grace, for charity,
If ever any malice in your heart　　　80
Were hid against me, now to forgive me frankly.

Buck. Sir Thomas Lovell, I as free forgive you
As I would be forgiven. I forgive all.
There cannot be those numberless offenses

---

10. how pass'd it: i.e. what happened at the trial.
11. in a little: in few words.
11–22. The great . . . mischief. These lines follow closely Holinshed's account (Bullough, IV, 461), which begins: "When the lords had taken their place, the duke was brought to the barre, and uppon his arreignement pleaded not guiltie, and put himselfe upon his peeres. Then was his indictment read, which the duke denied to be true, and (as he was an eloquent man) alledged reasons to falsifie the indictment; pleading the matter for his owne justification verie pithilie and earnestlie. The kings attourneie against the dukes reasons alledged the examinations, confessions, and proofes of witnesses."
13–14. alleged . . . defeat: advanced many cogent arguments to overturn.　**16. Urg'd . . . examinations:** dwelt on the depositions.
24. which: i.e. which accusations.　**fain:** gladly.
28–29. all . . . forgotten: i.e. everything he said was either pitied (rather than believed) or ignored.　**34. choler:** anger.
35. fell to: recovered.　**40. end:** ultimate cause.
41–44. Kildare's . . . father. According to Holinshed (Bullough, IV, 456), Wolsey had Gerald Fitzgerald, Earl of Kildare and Lord Lieutenant of Ireland, arrested for maladministration and replaced him with Thomas Howard, Earl of Surrey, "there to remaine rather as an exile, than as lieutenant to the king, even at the cardinals pleasure, as he himself well perceived."　**41. attendure:** attainder.
44. father: i.e. father-in-law. Surrey was married to Buckingham's oldest daughter.

44. trick of state: political stratagem.
45. envious: malicious.　**47. generally:** by everyone.
50. perniciously: so as to desire his death.　**51. fadom:** fathom.
53. mirror: i.e. paragon.　s.d. **Tipstaves:** bailiffs.　**the edge towards him.** Indicating the sentence of death.　**Halberds:** halberdiers, soldiers bearing spears with axe-like heads.　**57. lose:** forget.
60. sink: ruin.　**62. malice:** resentment.
63. premises: evidence (?).
67. evils: hovels (?).　**great men:** noblemen.　**70. sue:** beg.
73–74. whom . . . dying: i.e. dying is bitter only because it means parting from his friends.　**77. sacrifice:** offering.
78. a': in.

'Gainst me, that I cannot take peace with; no black
    envy   85
Shall make my grave. Commend me to his Grace;
And if he speak of Buckingham, pray tell him
You met him half in heaven. My vows and prayers
Yet are the King's; and, till my soul forsake,
Shall cry for blessings on him. May he live   90
Longer than I have time to tell his years;
Ever belov'd and loving may his rule be;
And when old Time shall lead him to his end,
Goodness and he fill up one monument!

    Lov. To th' water side I must conduct your Grace;
Then give my charge up to Sir Nicholas Vaux,   96
Who undertakes you to your end.

    Vaux.   Prepare there,
The Duke is coming. See the barge be ready;
And fit it with such furniture as suits
The greatness of his person.

    Buck.   Nay, Sir Nicholas,   100
Let it alone; my state now will but mock me.
When I came hither, I was Lord High Constable
And Duke of Buckingham; now, poor Edward Bohun.
Yet I am richer than my base accusers,
That never knew what truth meant. I now seal it;   105
And with that blood will make 'em one day groan for't.
My noble father, Henry of Buckingham,
Who first rais'd head against usurping Richard,
Flying for succor to his servant Banister,
Being distress'd, was by that wretch betray'd,   110
And without trial fell; God's peace be with him!
Henry the Seventh succeeding, truly pitying
My father's loss, like a most royal prince
Restor'd me to my honors; and out of ruins
Made my name once more noble. Now his son,   115
Henry the Eight, life, honor, name, and all
That made me happy, at one stroke has taken
For ever from the world. I had my trial,
And must needs say a noble one; which makes me
A little happier than my wretched father.   120
Yet thus far we are one in fortunes: both
Fell by our servants, by those men we lov'd most;
A most unnatural and faithless service.
Heaven has an end in all; yet, you that hear me,
This from a dying man receive as certain: 125
Where you are liberal of your loves and counsels,
Be sure you be not loose; for those you make friends
And give your hearts to, when they once perceive
The least rub in your fortunes, fall away
Like water from ye, never found again   130
But where they mean to sink ye. All good people,
Pray for me! I must now forsake ye. The last hour
Of my long weary life is come upon me.
Farewell!

And when you would say something that is sad,   135
Speak how I fell. I have done; and God forgive me!
                     Exeunt Duke and Train.
    1. Gent. O, this is full of pity! Sir, it calls,
I fear, too many curses on their heads
That were the authors.

    2. Gent.   If the Duke be guiltless,
'Tis full of woe; yet I can give you inkling   140
Of an ensuing evil, if it fall,
Greater than this.

    1. Gent.   Good angels keep it from us!
What may it be? You do not doubt my faith, sir?

    2. Gent. This secret is so weighty, 'twill require
A strong faith to conceal it.

    1. Gent.   Let me have it;   145
I do not talk much.

    2. Gent.   I am confident;
You shall, sir. Did you not of late days hear
A buzzing of a separation
Between the King and Katherine?

    1. Gent.   Yes, but it held not;
For when the King once heard it, out of anger   150
He sent command to the Lord Mayor straight
To stop the rumor, and allay those tongues
That durst disperse it.

    2. Gent.   But that slander, sir,
Is found a truth now; for it grows again
Fresher than e'er it was, and held for certain   155
The King will venture at it. Either the Cardinal,
Or some about him near, have out of malice
To the good Queen possess'd him with a scruple
That will undo her. To confirm this too,
Cardinal Campeius is arriv'd, and lately,   160
As all think, for this business.

    1. Gent.   'Tis the Cardinal;
And merely to revenge him on the Emperor
For not bestowing on him at his asking
The archbishopric of Toledo, this is purpos'd.

    2. Gent. I think you have hit the mark; but is't not
    cruel   165
That she should feel the smart of this? The Cardinal
Will have his will, and she must fall.

    1. Gent.   'Tis woeful.
We are too open here to argue this;
Let's think in private more.   *Exeunt.*

---

85. **envy:** malice.
89. **forsake:** i.e. leave my body.   91. **tell:** count.
94. **monument:** tomb.   97. **undertakes:** conducts.
99. **furniture:** equipment.   101. **state:** rank.
103. **Bohun.** A mistake, copied from Holinshed (Bullough, IV, 462), for Stafford, which was the Duke's family name.
105. **seal it:** i.e. attest to truth.
107–11. **My . . . fell.** See *Richard III*, V.i.
108. **rais'd head:** gathered a military force.   122. **by:** through.
124. **end:** purpose.   127. **loose:** careless.   129. **rub:** check.
133. **long weary life.** Buckingham died at forty-three.

146. **confident:** i.e. of your discretion.   148. **buzzing:** rumor.
149. **held not:** stopped.
150–53. **For . . . disperse it.** Rumors of Henry's divorce and of his projected marriage with Francis I's sister so much offended the King, says Holinshed (Bullough, IV, 465), that he "sent for sir Thomas Seimor mayor of the citie of London, secretlie charging him to see that the people ceassed from such talke."   152. **allay:** silence.
158. **possess'd . . . scruple:** put into his mind a doubt. Katherine and Prince Arthur (eldest son and heir of Henry VII) had been married in 1501, when both were in their early teens. Arthur died the following year, and after prolonged negotiation—including the securing of a papal dispensation—Katherine married her brother-in-law, the newly crowned Henry VIII, in 1509. It was not until 1527, says Holinshed (Bullough, IV, 468–69), that Henry's conscience became "accombred, vexed, and disquieted" by fear that he had sinned through marriage with his brother's widow.
160. **Cardinal . . . lately.** Cardinal Campeggio (or Campeius) reached London in 1528, seven years after Buckingham's execution. See note to II.ii.86–96.
162. **Emperor:** i.e. Charles V, nephew of Queen Katherine.
168. **open:** public.

Henry VIII
II.ii

SCENE II

Enter LORD CHAMBERLAIN *reading this letter.*

[*Cham.*] "My lord, the horses your lordship sent
for, with all the care I had, I saw well chosen, ridden,
and furnish'd. They were young and handsome, and of
the best breed in the north. When they were ready to
set out for London, a man of my Lord Cardinal's,   5
by commission and main power, took 'em from me,
with this reason: his master would be serv'd before a
subject, if not before the King, which stopp'd our
mouths, sir."
I fear he will indeed. Well, let him have them: 10
He will have all, I think.

Enter to the Lord Chamberlain the DUKES OF NORFOLK
and SUFFOLK.

Nor. Well met, my Lord Chamberlain.
Cham. Good day to both your Graces.
Suf. How is the King employ'd?
Cham.   I left him private,
Full of sad thoughts and troubles.
Nor.   What's the cause?   15
Cham. It seems the marriage with his brother's
    wife
Has crept too near his conscience.
Suf.   [*Aside.*] No, his conscience
Has crept too near another lady.
Nor.   'Tis so;
This is the Cardinal's doing. The king-cardinal,
That blind priest, like the eldest son of Fortune,   20
Turns what he list. The King will know him one day.
Suf. Pray God he do, he'll never know himself
    else.
Nor. How holily he works in all his business!
And with what zeal! for now he has crack'd the league
Between us and the Emperor (the Queen's great
    nephew),   25
He dives into the King's soul, and there scatters
Dangers, doubts, wringing of the conscience,
Fears, and despairs, and all these for his marriage.
And out of all these to restore the King,
He counsels a divorce, a loss of her   30
That, like a jewel, has hung twenty years
About his neck, yet never lost her lustre;
Of her that loves him with that excellence
That angels love good men with; even of her
That when the greatest stroke of fortune falls   35
Will bless the King. And is not this course pious?
Cham. Heaven keep me from such counsel! 'Tis
    most true
These news are every where; every tongue speaks 'em,

And every true heart weeps for't. All that dare
Look into these affairs see this main end,   40
The French king's sister. Heaven will one day open
The King's eyes, that so long have slept upon
This bold bad man.
Suf.   And free us from his slavery.
Nor. We had need pray,
And heartily, for our deliverance,   45
Or this imperious man will work us all
From princes into pages. All men's honors
Lie like one lump before him, to be fashion'd
Into what pitch he please.
Suf.   For me, my lords,
I love him not, nor fear him; there's my creed.   50
As I am made without him, so I'll stand,
If the King please; his curses and his blessings
Touch me alike; th' are breath I not believe in.
I knew him, and I know him; so I leave him
To him that made him proud, the Pope.
Nor.   Let's in;   55
And with some other business put the King
From these sad thoughts that work too much upon him.
My lord, you'll bear us company?
Cham.   Excuse me,
The King has sent me otherwhere. Besides,
You'll find a most unfit time to disturb him.   60
Health to your lordships.
Nor.   Thanks, my good Lord Chamberlain.

*Exit Lord Chamberlain; and the King draws
the curtain and sits reading pensively.*

Suf. How sad he looks! Sure he is much afflicted.
King. Who's there? ha?
Nor.   Pray God he be not angry.
King. Who's there, I say? How dare you thrust
    yourselves
Into my private meditations?   65
Who am I? ha?
Nor. A gracious king that pardons all offenses
Malice ne'er meant. Our breach of duty this way
Is business of estate; in which we come
To know your royal pleasure.
King.   Ye are too bold.   70
Go to; I'll make ye know your times of business.
Is this an hour for temporal affairs? ha?

Enter WOLSEY *and* CAMPEIUS *with a commission.*

Who's there? My good Lord Cardinal? O my
    Wolsey,
The quiet of my wounded conscience,
Thou art a cure fit for a king. [*To Campeius.*] You're
    welcome,   75
Most learned reverend sir, into our kingdom,
Use us and it. [*To Wolsey.*] My good lord, have great
    care
I be not found a talker.
Wol.   Sir, you cannot.

II.ii. Location: London. The palace.
2. **ridden:** broken in.   3. **furnish'd:** equipped.
6. **commission:** warrant.   14. **private:** alone.   15. **sad:** serious.
20–21. **blind . . . list.** Alluding to Fortune's blindness and her wheel.
See *Henry V*, III.vi.30–38.
24–28. **he . . . marriage.** "The cardinall verelie was put in most blame
for this scruple now cast into the kings conscience," Holinshed reports (Bullough, IV, 466), "for the hate he bare to the emperor,
bicause he would not grant to him the archbishoprike of Toledo,
for the which he was a suter. And therefore he did not onlie procure
the king of England to joine in freendship with the French king, but
also sought a divorce betwixt the king and the queene, that the king
might have had in marriage the duchesse of Alanson, sister unto the
French king."   35. **greatest stroke:** i.e. worst blow.

42. **slept upon:** been blind to.
49. **pitch:** height (a term from falconry), i.e. degree of dignity. The
figure suggested by *lump* and *fashion'd* (line 48) is not completed.
61 s.d. **draws the curtain.** Presumably at the back of the stage.
68. **this way:** in this respect.   69. **estate:** state.
78. **I . . . talker:** i.e. that you translate my hospitable words into
action.

I would your Grace would give us but an hour
Of private conference.

King.   [*To Norfolk and Suffolk.*] We are
busy; go.   80

Nor. [*Aside to Suffolk.*] This priest has no pride in
him?

Suf.   [*Aside to Norfolk.*] Not to speak of.
I would not be so sick though for his place.
But this cannot continue.

Nor.   [*Aside to Suffolk.*] If it do,
I'll venture one; have at him!

Suf.   [*Aside to Norfolk.*] I another. 84

Exeunt Norfolk and Suffolk.

Wol. Your Grace has given a president of wisdom
Above all princes, in committing freely
Your scruple to the voice of Christendom.
Who can be angry now? What envy reach you?
The Spaniard, tied by blood and favor to her,
Must now confess, if they have any goodness,   90
The trial just and noble. All the clerks
(I mean the learned ones in Christian kingdoms)
Have their free voices. Rome, the nurse of judgment,
Invited by your noble self, hath sent
One general tongue unto us: this good man,   95
This just and learned priest, Card'nal Campeius,
Whom once more I present unto your Highness.

King. And once more in mine arms I bid him
welcome,
And thank the holy conclave for their loves;
They have sent me such a man I would have wish'd for.

Cam. Your Grace must needs deserve all strangers'
loves,   101
You are so noble. To your Highness' hand
I tender my commission; by whose virtue,
The court of Rome commanding, you, my Lord
Cardinal of York, are join'd with me their servant 105
In the unpartial judging of this business.

King. Two equal men. The Queen shall be
acquainted
Forthwith for what you come. Where's Gardiner?

Wol. I know your Majesty has always lov'd her
So dear in heart not to deny her that   110
A woman of less place might ask by law:
Scholars allow'd freely to argue for her.

King. Ay, and the best she shall have; and my
favor
To him that does best, God forbid else. Cardinal,
Prithee call Gardiner to me, my new secretary.   115
I find him a fit fellow.   [*Exit Wolsey.*]

Enter [WOLSEY *with*] GARDINER.

Wol. [*Aside to Gardiner.*] Give me your hand.
Much joy and favor to you;
You are the King's now.

Gard.   [*Aside to Wolsey.*] But to be commanded
For ever by your Grace, whose hand has rais'd me.

King. Come hither, Gardiner.   120

Walks and whispers.

Cam. My Lord of York, was not one Doctor Pace
In this man's place before him?

Wol.   Yes, he was.

Cam. Was he not held a learned man?

Wol.   Yes, surely.

Cam. Believe me, there's an ill opinion spread then,
Even of yourself, Lord Cardinal.

Wol.   How? of me?   125

Cam. They will not stick to say you envied him,
And fearing he would rise (he was so virtuous),
Kept him a foreign man still, which so griev'd him,
That he ran mad, and died.

Wol.   Heav'n's peace be with him!
That's Christian care enough. For living murmurers
There's places of rebuke. He was a fool—   131
For he would needs be virtuous. That good fellow,
If I command him, follows my appointment;
I will have none so near else. Learn this, brother,
We live not to be grip'd by meaner persons.   135

King. Deliver this with modesty to th' Queen.

Exit Gardiner.

The most convenient place that I can think of
For such receipt of learning is Black-Friars;
There ye shall meet about this weighty business.
My Wolsey, see it furnish'd. O my lord,   140
Would it not grieve an able man to leave
So sweet a bedfellow? But conscience, conscience!
O, 'tis a tender place, and I must leave her.   *Exeunt.*

SCENE III

Enter ANNE BULLEN *and an* OLD LADY.

Anne. Not for that neither; here's the pang that
pinches:
His Highness having liv'd so long with her, and she

---

81. **This priest:** i.e. Wolsey.
82. **be . . . place:** i.e. have his place at the cost of being so sick with pride.
84. **one:** i.e. thrust (at Wolsey). **have at him:** A conventional warning that the speaker is about to attack.
85. **president:** precedent, example.
86–96. **in . . . Campeius.** Failing to resolve his doubts about his marriage, Henry, says Holinshed (IV, 466), "sent to all the universities in Italie and France, and to the great clearkes of all christendome, to know their opinions, and desired the court of Rome to send into his realme a legat, which should be indifferent, and of a great and profound judgement, to heare the cause debated. At whose request the whole consistorie of the college of Rome sent thither Laurence Campeius, a preest cardinall, a man of great wit and experience." It was Thomas Cranmer's suggesting this canvass of continental scholars that apparently first brought him to Henry's attention.
87. **voice:** vote.   89. **The Spaniard:** i.e. the Emperor Charles.
91. **clerks:** clerics.
95. **One general tongue:** i.e. a spokesman for the whole Roman Church.   99. **conclave:** i.e. the College of Cardinals.
101. **strangers':** foreigners'.
107. **equal:** impartial.   **acquainted:** informed.
110. **that:** i.e. that which.   111. **less place:** lower rank.

115. **my new secretary.** Stephen Gardiner, who had been secretary to Wolsey, was promoted to the service of the King in July 1529. His diligence about the divorce proceedings earned for him the bishopric of Winchester in 1531.
121. **Doctor Pace:** Richard Pace (1482?–1536), frequently employed by Wolsey in diplomatic missions to the Continent.
126. **stick:** hesitate.
128. **Kept . . . still:** continually sent him abroad on official business.
132. **fellow:** i.e. Gardiner.   133. **appointment:** instructions.
134. **none . . . else:** i.e. no one not under my control so near the King.
135. **grip'd:** grasped (?).   136. **Deliver:** repeat.
138. **such . . . learning:** i.e. the reception of such learned men.   **Black-Friars:** Dominican convent in London.   141. **able:** vigorous.

II.iii. London. The Queen's apartments in the palace.

Henry VIII
II.iii

So good a lady that no tongue could ever
Pronounce dishonor of her—by my life,
She never knew harm-doing—O, now after   5
So many courses of the sun enthroned,
Still growing in a majesty and pomp, the which
To leave a thousandfold more bitter than
'Tis sweet at first t' acquire—after this process,
To give her the avaunt, it is a pity   10
Would move a monster.
    Old L.   Hearts of most hard temper
Melt and lament for her.
    Anne.   O, God's will, much better
She ne'er had known pomp! Though't be temporal,
Yet if that quarrel, fortune, do divorce
It from the bearer, 'tis a sufferance panging   15
As soul and body's severing.
    Old L.   Alas, poor lady!
She's a stranger now again.
    Anne.   So much the more
Must pity drop upon her. Verily,
I swear, 'tis better to be lowly born,
And range with humble livers in content,   20
Than to be perk'd up in a glist'ring grief
And wear a golden sorrow.
    Old L.   Our content
Is our best having.
    Anne.   By my troth and maidenhead,
I would not be a queen.
    Old L.   Beshrew me, I would,
And venture maidenhead for't, and so would you   25
For all this spice of your hypocrisy.
You, that have so fair parts of woman on you,
Have, too, a woman's heart, which ever yet
Affected eminence, wealth, sovereignty;
Which, to say sooth, are blessings; and which gifts
(Saving your mincing) the capacity   31
Of your soft cheveril conscience would receive
If you might please to stretch it.
    Anne.   Nay, good troth.
    Old L. Yes, troth, and troth. You would not be a
        queen?
    Anne. No, not for all the riches under heaven. 35
    Old L. 'Tis strange. A threepence bow'd would
        hire me,
Old as I am, to queen it. But I pray you,
What think you of a duchess? Have you limbs
To bear that load of title?
    Anne.   No, in truth.
    Old L. Then you are weakly made; pluck off a
        little,   40
I would not be a young count in your way

For more than blushing comes to. If your back
Cannot vouchsafe this burthen, 'tis too weak
Ever to get a boy.
    Anne.   How you do talk!
I swear again, I would not be a queen   45
For all the world.
    Old L.   In faith, for little England
You'ld venture an emballing. I myself
Would for Carnarvonshire, although there 'long'd
No more to th' crown but that. Lo, who comes here?

        Enter LORD CHAMBERLAIN.

    Cham. Good morrow, ladies. What were't worth
        to know   50
The secret of your conference?
    Anne.   My good lord,
Not your demand; it values not your asking.
Our mistress' sorrows we were pitying.
    Cham. It was a gentle business, and becoming
The action of good women. There is hope   55
All will be well.
    Anne.   Now I pray God, amen!
    Cham. You bear a gentle mind, and heav'nly
        blessings
Follow such creatures. That you may, fair lady,
Perceive I speak sincerely, and high note's
Ta'en of your many virtues, the King's Majesty   60
Commends his good opinion of you to you, and
Does purpose honor to you no less flowing
Than Marchioness of Pembroke; to which title
A thousand pound a year, annual support,
Out of his grace he adds.
    Anne.   I do not know   65
What kind of my obedience I should tender.
More than my all is nothing: nor my prayers
Are not words duly hallowed, nor my wishes
More worth than empty vanities; yet prayers and
        wishes
Are all I can return. Beseech your lordship,   70
Vouchsafe to speak my thanks and my obedience,
As from a blushing handmaid, to his Highness;
Whose health and royalty I pray for.
    Cham.   Lady,
I shall not fail t' approve the fair conceit
The King hath of you. [Aside.] I have perus'd her
        well;   75
Beauty and honor in her are so mingled
That they have caught the King; and who knows yet
But from this lady may proceed a gem
To lighten all this isle?—I'll to the King,

---

4. **Pronounce:** declare.   7. **Still:** always.
9. **process:** succession of events.
10. **give . . . avaunt:** bid her be gone.
13. **temporal:** worldly (as opposed to heavenly).
14. **quarrel:** quarreller.   15. **sufferance panging:** suffering painful.
17. **stranger:** foreigner.   20. **range:** rank.   **livers:** persons.
21. **perk'd up:** decked out.
23. **having:** possession.   **troth:** truth, faith.
27. **parts:** qualities.   29. **Affected:** loved.   30. **sooth:** truth.
31. **Saving your mincing:** i.e. your affectations notwithstanding.
32. **cheveril:** kid-leather, i.e. elastic, supple.   36. **bow'd:** bent.
37. **queen.** With a pun on *quean*, "strumpet."
40. **pluck . . . little:** i.e. come down a step.
41. **count:** i.e. earl (a rank lower than duke).

43. **vouchsafe this burthen:** (condescendingly) accept this burden.
47. **emballing:** investiture with the ball or orb, the symbol of sovereignty.
48. **Carnarvonshire:** notoriously poor Welsh county.   **'long'd:** belonged.   51. **conference:** conversation.
52. **values not:** is not worth.
58–65. **That . . . adds.** Holinshed records (Bullough, IV, 481) that "on the first of September [1532] being Sundaie, the K. being come to Windsor, created the ladie Anne Bullongne marchionesse of Penbroke, and gave to hir one thousand pounds land by the yeare."
61. **Commends . . . of you:** i.e. presents his compliments.
65. **grace:** favor.   71. **Vouchsafe:** be good enough.
74. **approve . . . conceit:** confirm the good opinion.
79. **lighten:** illuminate.

And say I spoke with you.

Anne.   My honor'd lord.   80
                          Exit Lord Chamberlain.

Old L. Why, this it is! see, see,
I have been begging sixteen years in court
(Am yet a courtier beggarly) nor could
Come pat betwixt too early and too late
For any suit of pounds; and you, O fate!   85
A very fresh fish here—fie, fie, fie upon
This compell'd fortune!—have your mouth fill'd up
Before you open it.

Anne.   This is strange to me.

Old L. How tastes it? Is it bitter? Forty pence, no.
There was a lady once ('tis an old story)   90
That would not be a queen, that would she not,
For all the mud in Egypt. Have you heard it?

Anne. Come, you are pleasant.

Old L.   With your theme, I could
O'ermount the lark. The Marchioness of Pembroke?
A thousand pounds a year for pure respect?   95
No other obligation? By my life,
That promises moe thousands; honor's train
Is longer than his foreskirt. By this time
I know your back will bear a duchess. Say,
Are you not stronger than you were?

Anne.   Good lady,   100
Make yourself mirth with your particular fancy,
And leave me out on't. Would I had no being
If this salute my blood a jot; it faints me
To think what follows.
The Queen is comfortless, and we forgetful   105
In our long absence. Pray do not deliver
What here y' have heard to her.

Old L.   What do you think me?   *Exeunt.*

SCENE IV

Trumpets, sennet, and cornets. Enter two VERGERS,
with short silver wands; next them, two SCRIBES, *in the
habit of doctors; after them, the* [ARCH]BISHOP OF
CANTERBURY *alone; after him, the* BISHOPS OF
LINCOLN, ELY, ROCHESTER, *and* SAINT ASAPH; *next
them, with some small distance, follows a* GENTLEMAN
*bearing the purse, with the great seal, and a cardinal's
hat; then two* PRIESTS *bearing each a silver cross; then
a* GENTLEMAN USHER *bare-headed, accompanied with
a* SERGEANT-AT-ARMS *bearing a silver mace; then two*
GENTLEMEN *bearing two great silver pillars; after
them, side by side, the two* CARDINALS; *two* NOBLE-
MEN *with the sword and mace. The* KING *takes place
under the cloth of state; the two Cardinals sit under him
as judges. The* QUEEN *takes place some distance from
the King. The Bishops place themselves on each side the
court, in manner of a consistory; below them, the Scribes.
The Lords sit next the Bishops. The rest of the Attendants stand in convenient order about the stage.*

Wol. Whilst our commission from Rome is read,
Let silence be commanded.

King.   What's the need?
It hath already publicly been read,
And on all sides th' authority allow'd;
You may then spare that time.

Wol.   Be't so; proceed.   5

Scribe. Say, Henry King of England, come into the
court.

Crier. Henry King of England, etc.

King. Here.

Scribe. Say, Katherine Queen of England, come
into the court.   11

Crier. Katherine Queen of England, etc.

*The Queen makes no answer, rises out of her
chair, goes about the court, comes to the King,
and kneels at his feet; then speaks.*

[*Q. Kath.*] Sir, I desire you do me right and justice,
And to bestow your pity on me; for
I am a most poor woman, and a stranger,   15
Born out of your dominions; having here
No judge indifferent, nor no more assurance
Of equal friendship and proceeding. Alas, sir!
In what have I offended you? What cause
Hath my behavior given to your displeasure,   20
That thus you should proceed to put me off,
And take your good grace from me? Heaven witness,
I have been to you a true and humble wife,
At all times to your will conformable;
Ever in fear to kindle your dislike,   25
Yea, subject to your countenance—glad, or sorry,
As I saw it inclin'd. When was the hour
I ever contradicted your desire?
Or made it not mine too? Or which of your friends
Have I not strove to love, although I knew   30
He were mine enemy? What friend of mine
That had to him deriv'd your anger did I
Continue in my liking? nay, gave notice
He was from thence discharg'd? Sir, call to mind
That I have been your wife in this obedience   35
Upward of twenty years, and have been blest
With many children by you. If, in the course
And process of this time, you can report,
And prove it too, against mine honor aught—
My bond to wedlock or my love and duty,   40
Against your sacred person—in God's name
Turn me away; and let the foul'st contempt

---

83. **beggarly:** i.e. needy and importunate.
85. **suit of pounds:** petition for money.
87. **compell'd:** i.e. thrust upon you.
89. **Forty pence, no:** i.e. I'll wager forty pence (a trivial sum) that it isn't bitter.
93. **pleasant:** facetious. **With your theme:** i.e. if I had your good fortune. 95. **pure:** mere. 97. **moe:** more.
101. **your particular fancy:** your own daydream.
103. **salute:** stir. **faints me:** makes me faint.
II.iv. Location: London. A hall in Blackfriars.
o.s.d. Some of the details of this elaborate stage direction derive from Holinshed's account (Bullough, IV, 477–78) of Wolsey's love of pomp and luxury; others closely follow Holinshed's description (Bullough, IV, 466–67) of the divorce proceedings at Blackfriars on June 18, 1529. **sennet:** fanfare announcing a procession. **habit of**

doctors: i.e. furred gowns and black caps worn by doctors of law.
cloth of state: canopy. 4. **allow'd:** conceded.
13–57. **Sir . . . fulfill'd.** Here as elsewhere in this scene Shakespeare follows Holinshed (Bullough, IV, 467–68) so closely that he often merely versifies the chronicler's prose. 17. **indifferent:** impartial.
18. **equal:** fair. **proceeding:** legal process.
21. **put me off:** reject me. 25. **dislike:** displeasure.
32. **deriv'd:** drawn.

Henry VIII
II.iv

Shut door upon me, and so give me up
To the sharp'st kind of justice. Please you, sir,
The King your father was reputed for　　　　45
A prince most prudent, of an excellent
And unmatch'd wit and judgment; Ferdinand,
My father, King of Spain, was reckon'd one
The wisest prince that there had reign'd by many
A year before. It is not to be question'd　　50
That they had gather'd a wise council to them
Of every realm, that did debate this business,
Who deem'd our marriage lawful; wherefore I humbly
Beseech you, sir, to spare me, till I may
Be by my friends in Spain advis'd, whose counsel　55
I will implore. If not, i' th' name of God,
Your pleasure be fulfill'd!

Wol.　　　　　　　　You have here, lady
(And of your choice), these reverend fathers, men
Of singular integrity and learning,
Yea, the elect o' th' land, who are assembled　　60
To plead your cause. It shall be therefore bootless
That longer you desire the court, as well
For your own quiet, as to rectify
What is unsettled in the King.

Cam.　　　　　　　　　　His Grace
Hath spoken well and justly; therefore, madam,　65
It's fit this royal session do proceed,
And that, without delay, their arguments
Be now produc'd and heard.

Q. Kath.　　　　　　Lord Cardinal,
To you I speak.

Wol.　　Your pleasure, madam?

Q. Kath.　　　　　　　　　Sir,
I am about to weep; but thinking that　　　70
We are a queen (or long have dream'd so), certain
The daughter of a king, my drops of tears
I'll turn to sparks of fire.

Wol.　　　　　　Be patient yet.

Q. Kath. I will, when you are humble; nay, before,
Or God will punish me. I do believe　　　75
(Induc'd by potent circumstances) that
You are mine enemy, and make my challenge
You shall not be my judge; for it is you
Have blown this coal betwixt my lord and me—
Which God's dew quench! Therefore I say again,　80
I utterly abhor, yea, from my soul
Refuse you for my judge, whom, yet once more,
I hold my most malicious foe, and think not
At all a friend to truth.

Wol.　　　　　I do profess
You speak not like yourself, who ever yet　　85
Have stood to charity, and display'd th' effects

Of disposition gentle, and of wisdom
O'ertopping woman's pow'r. Madam, you do me wrong,
I have no spleen against you, nor injustice
For you or any. How far I have proceeded,　　90
Or how far further shall, is warranted
By a commission from the consistory,
Yea, the whole consistory of Rome. You charge me
That I have blown this coal. I do deny it.
The King is present: if it be known to him　　95
That I gainsay my deed, how may he wound,
And worthily, my falsehood! yea, as much
As you have done my truth. If he know
That I am free of your report, he knows
I am not of your wrong. Therefore in him　　100
It lies to cure me, and the cure is to
Remove these thoughts from you; the which before
His Highness shall speak in, I do beseech
You, gracious madam, to unthink your speaking
And to say so no more.

Q. Kath.　　　　　My lord, my lord,　105
I am a simple woman, much too weak
T' oppose your cunning. Y' are meek and humble-mouth'd,
You sign your place and calling, in full seeming,
With meekness and humility; but your heart
Is cramm'd with arrogancy, spleen, and pride.　110
You have, by fortune and his Highness' favors,
Gone slightly o'er low steps and now are mounted
Where pow'rs are your retainers, and your words
(Domestics to you) serve your will as't please
Yourself pronounce their office. I must tell you,　115
You tender more your person's honor than
Your high profession spiritual; that again
I do refuse you for my judge, and here,
Before you all, appeal unto the Pope,
To bring my whole cause 'fore his Holiness,　　120
And to be judg'd by him.

　　　　She curtsies to the King and offers to depart.

Cam.　　　　　　The Queen is obstinate,
Stubborn to justice, apt to accuse it, and
Disdainful to be tried by't: 'tis not well.
She's going away.

King. Call her again.　　　　　　　　125

Crier. Katherine Queen of England, come into the court.

Gent. Ush. Madam, you are call'd back.

Q. Kath. What need you note it? pray you keep your way;　　　　　　　　　129
When you are call'd, return. Now the Lord help!
They vex me past my patience. Pray you pass on.
I will not tarry; no, nor ever more
Upon this business my appearance make

---

47. **wit:** intelligence.　　61. **bootless:** profitless.
62. **desire the court:** i.e. to delay its proceedings.
63–64. **rectify . . . King:** i.e. resolve Henry's doubts about his marriage.　　74. **before:** i.e. because you never will be humble.
75–121. **I . . . by him.** According to Holinshed (Bullough, IV, 469–70), "the queene in presence of the whole court most greevouslie accused the cardinall of untruth, deceit, wickednesse, & malice, which had sowne dissention betwixt hir and the king hir husband; and therefore openlie protested, that she did utterlie abhorre, refuse, and forsake such a judge, as was not onelie a most malicious enimie to hir, but also a manifest adversarie to all right and justice, and there with did she appeale unto the pope, committing hir whole cause to be judged of him."　　77. **challenge:** formal objection.
81. **abhor:** protest (a legal term).　　86. **stood to:** supported.

89. **spleen:** malice.
96. **gainsay my deed:** i.e. deny what I have done.
97. **worthily:** properly.
99. **free . . . report:** innocent of what you charge me with.
100. **am . . . wrong:** have done no wrong to you.　103. **in:** about.
108. **sign:** signalize.　　**in full seeming:** i.e. to all appearances.
112. **slightly:** easily.　　113. **pow'rs:** influential persons.
113–15. **your words . . . office:** i.e. words, like menial servants, are made to serve any function that you choose to give them (?).
116. **tender more:** care more for.　120. **cause:** case.
122. **Stubborn:** stiff.　129. **What:** why.

In any of their courts.

                    Exeunt Queen and her Attendants.
  King.   Go thy ways, Kate.
That man i' th' world who shall report he has   135
A better wife, let him in nought be trusted
For speaking false in that. Thou art alone
(If thy rare qualities, sweet gentleness,
Thy meekness saint-like, wife-like government,
Obeying in commanding, and thy parts   140
Sovereign and pious else, could speak thee out)
The queen of earthly queens. She's noble born;
And like her true nobility she has
Carried herself towards me.
  Wol.   Most gracious sir,
In humblest manner I require your Highness   145
That it shall please you to declare, in hearing
Of all these ears (for, where I am robb'd and bound,
There must I be unloos'd, although not there
At once and fully satisfied), whether ever I
Did broach this business to your Highness, or   150
Laid any scruple in your way which might
Induce you to the question on't? or ever
Have to you, but with thanks to God for such
A royal lady, spake one the least word that might
Be to the prejudice of her present state,   155
Or touch of her good person?
  King.   My Lord Cardinal,
I do excuse you; yea, upon mine honor,
I free you from't. You are not to be taught
That you have many enemies, that know not
Why they are so, but, like to village curs,   160
Bark when their fellows do: by some of these
The Queen is put in anger. Y' are excus'd;
But will you be more justified? You ever
Have wish'd the sleeping of this business, never desir'd
It to be stirr'd; but oft have hind'red, oft,   165
The passages made toward it. On my honor,
I speak my good Lord Card'nal to this point,
And thus far clear him. Now, what mov'd me to't,
I will be bold with time and your attention:
Then mark th' inducement. Thus it came; give heed
  to't: 170
My conscience first receiv'd a tenderness,
Scruple, and prick, on certain speeches utter'd
By th' Bishop of Bayonne, then French embassador,
Who had been hither sent on the debating
[A] marriage 'twixt the Duke of Orleance and   175
Our daughter Mary. I' th' progress of this business,
Ere a determinate resolution, he
(I mean the Bishop) did require a respite,
Wherein he might the King his lord advertise
Whether our daughter were legitimate,   180

Respecting this our marriage with the dowager,
Sometimes our brother's wife. This respite shook
The bosom of my conscience, enter'd me,
Yea, with a spitting power, and made to tremble
The region of my breast, which forc'd such way,   185
That many maz'd considerings did throng
And press'd in with this caution. First, methought
I stood not in the smile of heaven, who had
Commanded nature, that my lady's womb,
If it conceiv'd a male-child by me, should   190
Do no more offices of life to't than
The grave does to th' dead; for her male issue
Or died where they were made, or shortly after
This world had air'd them. Hence I took a thought
This was a judgment on me, that my kingdom   195
(Well worthy the best heir o' th' world) should not
Be gladded in't by me. Then follows, that
I weigh'd the danger which my realms stood in
By this my issue's fail, and that gave to me
Many a groaning throe. Thus hulling in   200
The wild sea of my conscience, I did steer
Toward this remedy, whereupon we are
Now present here together: that's to say,
I meant to rectify my conscience—which
I then did feel full sick, and yet not well—   205
By all the reverend fathers of the land
And doctors learn'd. First I began in private
With you, my Lord of Lincoln. You remember
How under my oppression I did reek
When I first mov'd you.
  Lin.   Very well, my liege.   210
  King. I have spoke long, be pleas'd yourself to say
How far you satisfied me.
  Lin.   So please your Highness,
The question did at first so stagger me,
Bearing a state of mighty moment in't
And consequence of dread, that I committed   215
The daring'st counsel which I had to doubt,
And did entreat your Highness to this course
Which you are running here.
  King.   I then mov'd you,
My Lord of Canterbury, and got your leave
To make this present summons. Unsolicited   220
I left no reverend person in this court;
But by particular consent proceeded
Under your hands and seals. Therefore go on,
For no dislike i' th' world against the person
Of the good Queen, but the sharp thorny points   225
Of my alleged reasons, drives this forward.
Prove but our marriage lawful, by my life
And kingly dignity, we are contented
To wear our mortal state to come with her,
Katherine our queen, before the primest creature   230

---

139. **government**: behavior.
140. **Obeying**: i.e. observing your own moral code (?). **parts**:
qualities. 141. **speak thee out**: describe you fully.
144. **Carried**: behaved. 149. **satisfied**: repaid.
155. **prejudice**: impairment.
156. **touch . . . person**: taint of her good reputation.
157. **excuse**: exonerate. 166. **passages**: proceedings.
167. **I . . . point**: i.e. I speak about the Cardinal's attitude in this
matter.
175. **Duke of Orleance**: son (1519–59) of Francis I; later Henry II,
King of France. 177. **determinate resolution**: final decision.
178. **require**: request. 179. **advertise**: take counsel with.

181. **dowager**: widow. 182. **Sometimes**: formerly.
184. **spitting**: transfixing. 186. **maz'd**: perplexed.
187. **caution**: warning. 193. **Or**: either.
197. **gladded in't**: i.e. made happy with an heir.
200. **hulling**: drifting to and fro. 204. **rectify**: set right.
209. **How . . . reek**: how I sweated in distress.
210. **mov'd**: applied to.
214–15. **Bearing . . . dread**: concerning a matter of great importance
and terrifying consequences.
215–16. **committed . . . doubt**: i.e. doubted my own advice.
230. **primest**: most excellent.

Henry VIII
II.iv

That's paragon'd o' th' world.

Cam. 　　　　　　So please your Highness,
The Queen being absent, 'tis a needful fitness
That we adjourn this court till further day.
Mean while must be an earnest motion
Made to the Queen to call back her appeal　　235
She intends unto his Holiness.

King. 　　　　　　[*Aside.*] I may perceive
These Cardinals trifle with me; I abhor
This dilatory sloth and tricks of Rome.
My learn'd and well-beloved servant, Cranmer,
Prithee return; with thy approach, I know,　　240
My comfort comes along.—Break up the court!
I say, set on. 　　　*Exeunt in manner as they enter'd.*

ACT III, Scene I

Enter Queen *and her* Women *as at work.*

Q. Kath.　Take thy lute, wench, my soul grows sad
　　with troubles.
Sing, and disperse 'em if thou canst. Leave working.

Song

Orpheus with his lute made trees,
And the mountain tops that freeze,
　　Bow themselves when he did sing.　　5
To his music plants and flowers
Ever sprung, as sun and showers
　　There had made a lasting spring.

Every thing that heard him play,
Even the billows of the sea,　　10
　　Hung their heads, and then lay by.
In sweet music is such art,
Killing care and grief of heart
　　Fall asleep, or hearing, die.

Enter a Gentleman.

Q. Kath.　How now?　　15
Gent.　And't please your Grace, the two great
　　Cardinals
Wait in the presence.
Q. Kath.　　　　Would they speak with me?
Gent.　They will'd me say so, madam.
Q. Kath.　　　　　　Pray their Graces
To come near. [*Exit Gentleman.*] What can be their
　　business
With me, a poor weak woman, fall'n from favor?　　20
I do not like their coming. Now I think on't,
They should be good men, their affairs as righteous.
But all hoods make not monks.

Enter the two Cardinals, Wolsey *and* Campeius.

Wol.　　　　　　Peace to your Highness!
Q. Kath.　Your Graces find me here part of a
　　huswife

(I would be all) against the worst may happen.　　25
What are your pleasures with me, reverent lords?
Wol.　May it please you, noble madam, to withdraw
Into your private chamber, we shall give you
The full cause of our coming.
Q. Kath.　　　　　　Speak it here;
There's nothing I have done yet, o' my conscience,　30
Deserves a corner. Would all other women
Could speak this with as free a soul as I do!
My lords, I care not (so much I am happy
Above a number) if my actions
Were tried by ev'ry tongue, ev'ry eye saw 'em,　　35
Envy and base opinion set against 'em,
I know my life so even. If your business
Seek me out, and that way I am wife in,
Out with it boldly: truth loves open dealing.
Wol.　*Tanta est erga te mentis integritas, regina
serenissima—*　　41
Q. Kath.　O, good my lord, no Latin;
I am not such a truant since my coming,
As not to know the language I have liv'd in.
A strange tongue makes my cause more strange,
　　suspicious;　　45
Pray speak in English. Here are some will thank you,
If you speak truth, for their poor mistress' sake;
Believe me, she has had much wrong. Lord Cardinal,
The willing'st sin I ever yet committed
May be absolv'd in English.
Wol.　　　　　　Noble lady,　　50
I am sorry my integrity should breed
(And service to his Majesty and you)
So deep suspicion, where all faith was meant.
We come not by the way of accusation
To taint that honor every good tongue blesses,　　55
Nor to betray you any way to sorrow—
You have too much, good lady; but to know
How you stand minded in the weighty difference
Between the King and you, and to deliver
(Like free and honest men) our just opinions　　60
And comforts to [your] cause.
Cam.　　　　　　Most honor'd madam,
My Lord of York, out of his noble nature,
Zeal and obedience he still bore your Grace,
Forgetting (like a good man) your late censure
Both of his truth and him (which was too far),　　65
Offers, as I do, in a sign of peace,
His service and his counsel.
Q. Kath.　　　　　[*Aside.*] To betray me.—
My lords, I thank you both for your good wills,
Ye speak like honest men (pray God ye prove so!),
But how to make ye suddenly an answer　　70
In such a point of weight, so near mine honor
(More near my life, I fear), with my weak wit,
And to such men of gravity and learning,

---

231. **paragon'd:** regarded as a paragon.　　234. **motion:** request.

III.i. Location: London. The Queen's apartments.
3. **Orpheus:** in Greek mythology, a musician of legendary renown.
7. **as:** as if.　　11. **lay by:** rested.
17. **presence:** presence-chamber.

25. **all:** i.e. entirely given up (to the role of housewife).　　**against:** in
anticipation that.　　31. **corner:** i.e. to hide in.
32. **free:** innocent.　　36. **Envy:** malice.　　37. **even:** consistent.
38. **Seek . . . in:** i.e. concerns me in my capacity as a wife.
41. **Tanta . . . serenissima:** so great is (my) integrity of mind toward
you, most serene queen.　　45. **suspicious:** i.e. even suspicious.
49. **willing'st:** most deliberate.　　59. **deliver:** declare.
60. **free:** frank.　　**honest:** honorable.　　**just:** true.
65. **far:** severe.　　66. **in a sign:** as a token.
70. **suddenly:** extempore.　　72. **wit:** understanding.

In truth I know not. I was set at work
Among my maids, full little, God knows, looking 75
Either for such men or such business.
For her sake that I have been—for I feel
The last fit of my greatness—good your Graces,
Let me have time and counsel for my cause.
Alas, I am a woman, friendless, hopeless!   80
    Wol.   Madam, you wrong the King's love with
        these fears,
Your hopes and friends are infinite.
    Q. Kath.   In England
But little for my profit; can you think, lords,
That any Englishman dare give me counsel?
Or be a known friend, 'gainst his Highness' pleasure 85
(Though he be grown so desperate to be honest),
And live a subject? Nay forsooth, my friends,
They that must weigh out my afflictions,
They that my trust must grow to, live not here.
They are (as all my other comforts) far hence   90
In mine own country, lords.
    Cam.   I would your Grace
Would leave your griefs, and take my counsel.
    Q. Kath.   How, sir?
    Cam.   Put your main cause into the King's pro-
        tection,
He's loving and most gracious. 'Twill be much
Both for your honor better and your cause;   95
For if the trial of the law o'ertake ye,
You'll part away disgrac'd.
    Wol.   He tells you rightly.
    Q. Kath.   Ye tell me what ye wish for both—my
        ruin.
Is this your Christian counsel? Out upon ye!
Heaven is above all yet; there sits a judge   100
That no king can corrupt.
    Cam.   Your rage mistakes us.
    Q. Kath.   The more shame for ye! Holy men I
        thought ye,
Upon my soul, two reverend cardinal virtues;
But cardinal sins and hollow hearts I fear ye.
Mend 'em for shame, my lords! Is this your comfort?
The cordial that ye bring a wretched lady,   106
A woman lost among ye, laugh'd at, scorn'd?
I will not wish ye half my miseries,
I have more charity. But say I warn'd ye;
Take heed, for heaven's sake take heed, lest at once
The burthen of my sorrows fall upon ye.   111

    Wol.   Madam, this is a mere distraction,
You turn the good we offer into envy.
    Q. Kath.   Ye turn me into nothing! Woe upon ye
And all such false professors! Would you have me 115
(If you have any justice, any pity,
If ye be any thing but churchmen's habits)
Put my sick cause into his hands that hates me?
Alas, h'as banish'd me his bed already,
His love, too long ago! I am old, my lords,   120
And all the fellowship I hold now with him
Is only my obedience. What can happen
To me above this wretchedness? All your studies
Make me a curse like this!
    Cam.   Your fears are worse.
    Q. Kath.   Have I liv'd thus long (let me speak
        myself,   125
Since virtue finds no friends) a wife, a true one?
A woman (I dare say without vainglory)
Never yet branded with suspicion?
Have I with all my full affections
Still met the King? lov'd him next heav'n? obey'd him?
Been, out of fondness, superstitious to him?   131
Almost forgot my pray'rs to content him?
And am I thus rewarded? 'Tis not well, lords.
Bring me a constant woman to her husband,
One that ne'er dream'd a joy beyond his pleasure; 135
And to that woman (when she has done most)
Yet will I add an honor—a great patience.
    Wol.   Madam, you wander from the good we aim
        at.
    Q. Kath.   My lord, I dare not make myself so
        guilty
To give up willingly that noble title   140
Your master wed me to. Nothing but death
Shall e'er divorce my dignities.
    Wol.   Pray hear me.
    Q. Kath.   Would I had never trod this English earth,
Or felt the flatteries that grow upon it!
Ye have angels' faces, but heaven knows your hearts.
What will become of me now, wretched lady?   146
I am the most unhappy woman living.
Alas, poor wenches, where are now your fortunes?
Shipwrack'd upon a kingdom, where no pity,
No friends, no hope, no kindred weep for me,   150
Almost no grave allow'd me. Like the lily,
That once was mistress of the field, and flourish'd,
I'll hang my head and perish.
    Wol.   If your Grace
Could but be brought to know our ends are honest,
You'd feel more comfort. Why should we, good lady,
Upon what cause, wrong you? Alas, our places,   156
The way of our profession is against it;
We are to cure such sorrows, not to sow 'em.
For goodness sake, consider what you do,

---

74. **set:** seated. 78. **fit:** phase (of a disease).
82–91. **In . . . lords.** "I need counsell to this case which toucheth me
so neere," Holinshed reports Katherine as saying (Bullough, IV, 471),
"& for anie counsell or freendship that I can find in England, they are
not for my profit. What thinke you my lords, will anie Englishman
counsell me, or be freend to me against the K. pleasure that is his
subject? Naie foresooth. And as for my counsell in whom I will put
my trust, they be not here, they be in Spaine in my owne countrie."
83. **profit:** advantage.
86. **so desperate:** i.e. sufficiently reckless.
88. **weigh out:** counterbalance.   97. **part away:** depart.
101. **mistakes:** misjudges.
103. **cardinal virtues:** i.e. justice, prudence, temperance, and fortitude.
These with the three theological virtues of faith, hope, and charity
constitute the seven virtues corresponding to the seven deadly sins
to which Katherine alludes in the next line.
106. **cordial:** restorative.   110. **at once:** all at once.
111. **burthen:** burden.

112. **mere distraction:** absolute frenzy.
115. **professors:** i.e. those who profess religion.
117. **habits:** robes.   119. **h'as:** he has.
120. **old.** Katherine was forty-three, six years older than her husband.
121. **fellowship:** intercourse.
123–24. **All . . . Make:** i.e. I defy all your exertions to make.
125. **speak:** speak for.   131. **superstitious:** idolatrous.
148. **wenches:** i.e. women in waiting on Queen Katherine.
154. **ends are honest:** purposes are honorable.
156. **places:** offices.

Henry VIII
III.i

How you may hurt yourself—ay, utterly 160
Grow from the King's acquaintance, by this carriage.
The hearts of princes kiss obedience,
So much they love it; but to stubborn spirits
They swell and grow, as terrible as storms.
I know you have a gentle, noble temper, 165
A soul as even as a calm; pray think us
Those we profess, peacemakers, friends, and servants.
   Cam. Madam, you'll find it so. You wrong your
      virtues
With these weak women's fears. A noble spirit
As yours was put into you, ever casts 170
Such doubts, as false coin, from it. The King loves
you,
Beware you lose it not. For us (if you please
To trust us in your business), we are ready
To use our utmost studies in your service.
   Q. Kath. Do what ye will, my lords; and pray
      forgive me; 175
If I have us'd myself unmannerly,
You know I am a woman, lacking wit
To make a seemly answer to such persons.
Pray do my service to his Majesty;
He has my heart yet and shall have my prayers 180
While I shall have my life. Come, reverend fathers,
Bestow your counsels on me. She now begs
That little thought, when she set footing here,
She should have bought her dignities so dear. *Exeunt.*

SCENE II

Enter the DUKE OF NORFOLK, DUKE OF SUFFOLK, LORD
   SURREY, *and* LORD CHAMBERLAIN.

   Nor. If you will now unite in your complaints,
And force them with a constancy, the Cardinal
Cannot stand under them. If you omit
The offer of this time, I cannot promise
But that you shall sustain moe new disgraces 5
With these you bear already.
   Sur.   I am joyful
To meet the least occasion that may give me
Remembrance of my father-in-law, the Duke,
To be reveng'd on him.
   Suf.   Which of the peers
Have uncontemn'd gone by him, or at least 10
Strangely neglected? When did he regard
The stamp of nobleness in any person
Out of himself?
   Cham.   My lords, you speak your pleasures.
What he deserves of you and me I know;
What we can do to him (though now the time 15

161. **from:** away from. **carriage:** behavior.
176. **us'd myself:** behaved.
179. **do my service:** convey my respects.

III.ii. Location: London. The palace.
o.s.d. **Lord Surrey.** Actually, Thomas Howard, the Earl of Surrey
whom Wolsey had sent to Ireland to prevent his aid to his father-
n-law Buckingham (see II.i.4–44 and lines 6–9 below), had succeeded
his father as Duke of Norfolk in 1524.
2. **force:** urge. 3–4. **omit . . . time:** neglect this opportunity.
11. **Strangely neglected:** i.e. not strangely neglected (by extension of
the negative sense of *uncontemn'd*).
13. **Out of:** besides.

Gives way to us) I much fear. If you cannot
Bar his access to th' King, never attempt
Any thing on him; for he hath a witchcraft
Over the King in 's tongue.
   Nor.   O, fear him not,
His spell in that is out. The King hath found 20
Matter against him that for ever mars
The honey of his language. No, he's settled
(Not to come off) in his displeasure.
   Sur.   Sir,
I should be glad to hear such news as this
Once every hour.
   Nor.   Believe it, this is true. 25
In the divorce his contrary proceedings
Are all unfolded; wherein he appears
As I would wish mine enemy.
   Sur.   How came
His practices to light?
   Suf.   Most strangely.
   Sur.   O how? how?
   Suf. The Cardinal's letters to the Pope mis-
carried, 30
And came to th' eye o' th' King, wherein was read
How that the Cardinal did entreat his Holiness
To stay the judgment o' th' divorce; for if
It did take place, "I do," quoth he, "perceive
My king is tangled in affection to 35
A creature of the Queen's, Lady Anne Bullen."
   Sur. Has the King this?
   Suf.   Believe it.
   Sur.   Will this work?
   Cham. The King in this perceives him, how he
      coasts
And hedges his own way. But in this point
All his tricks founder, and he brings his physic 40
After his patient's death. The King already
Hath married the fair lady.
   Sur.   Would he had!
   Suf. May you be happy in your wish, my lord,
For I profess you have it.
   Sur.   Now all my joy
Trace the conjunction!
   Suf.   My amen to't!
   Nor.   All men's! 45
   Suf. There's order given for her coronation.
Marry, this is yet but young, and may be left

16. **Gives way to:** favors.
17–18. **attempt . . . him:** attack him in any way.
20. **spell:** magic. **out:** exhausted. 23. **come off:** escape.
26. **contrary:** contradictory, inconsistent. 29. **practices:** plots.
30–33. **The Cardinal's . . . divorce.** Determined to block the King's
marriage with Anne Bullen, Wolsey, says Holinshed (Bullough, IV,
472), "began with all diligence to disappoint that match, which by
reason of the misliking that he had to the woman, he judged ought
to be avoided more than present death. While the matter stood in
this state, and that the cause of the queene was to be heard and judged
at Rome, by reason of the appeale which by hir was put in: the cardinall required the pope by letters and secret messengers, that in anie
wise he should defer the judgement of the divorse, till he might
frame the kings mind to his purpose."
33. **stay the judgment:** delay the proceedings.
38–39. **coasts And hedges:** i.e. follows indirect courses, as by coasts
and hedgerows.
41–42. **The King . . . lady.** Although Shakespeare thus places Henry's
second marriage before Wolsey's fall (which occurred in 1529), the
secret wedding was actually performed in January 1533, three years
after Wolsey's death.
45. **Trace the conjunction:** follow the union. 47. **young:** recent.

To some ears unrecounted. But, my lords,
She is a gallant creature, and complete
In mind and feature. I persuade me, from her   50
Will fall some blessing to this land, which shall
In it be memoriz'd.
  Sur.   But will the King
Digest this letter of the Cardinal's?
The Lord forbid!
  Nor.   Marry, amen!
  Suf.   No, no;
There be moe wasps that buzz about his nose   55
Will make this sting the sooner. Cardinal Campeius
Is stol'n away to Rome, hath ta'en no leave,
Has left the cause o' th' King unhandled, and
Is posted, as the agent of our Cardinal,
To second all his plot. I do assure you   60
The King cried "Ha!" at this.
  Cham.   Now God incense him,
And let him cry "Ha!" louder!
  Nor.   But, my lord,
When returns Cranmer?
  Suf. He is return'd in his opinions, which
Have satisfied the King for his divorce,   65
Together with all famous colleges
Almost in Christendom. Shortly, I believe,
His second marriage shall be publish'd, and
Her coronation. Katherine no more
Shall be call'd Queen, but Princess Dowager   70
And widow to Prince Arthur.
  Nor.   This same Cranmer's
A worthy fellow, and hath ta'en much pain
In the King's business.
  Suf.   He has, and we shall see him
For it an archbishop.
  Nor.   So I hear.
  Suf.   'Tis so.

        Enter WOLSEY *and* CROMWELL.

The Cardinal!
  Nor.   Observe, observe, he's moody.   75
  Wol. The packet, Cromwell, gave't you the King?
  Crom. To his own hand, in 's bedchamber.
  Wol.   Look'd he
O' th' inside of the paper?
  Crom.   Presently
He did unseal them, and the first he view'd,
He did it with a serious mind; a heed   80

---

49. **complete:** perfect. 52. **memoriz'd:** made memorable.
53. **Digest:** put up with, "swallow."
56–57. **Cardinal . . . leave.** On the contrary, Holinshed reports (Bullough, IV, 471) that after the divorce proceedings had dragged on for several months Campeius "tooke his leave of the king and nobilitie, and returned towards Rome." 58. **unhandled:** i.e. unresolved.
59. **Is posted:** has hastened.
61–62. **The King . . . louder.** See note to I.ii.186.
64. **He . . . opinions:** he has sent his opinions in advance. In January 1530 Cranmer had been sent abroad with the Earl of Wiltshire, ambassador to the court of Charles V. On Henry's canvass of continental scholars, which Cranmer had proposed in 1529, see note to II.ii.86–96.
68. **publish'd:** proclaimed. The marriage "was kept so secret," says Holinshed (Bullough, IV, 482), "that verie few knew it till Easter next insuing [1533], when it was perceived that she was with child."
72. **pain:** pains.
74. **archbishop.** Cranmer succeeded William Warham as Archbishop of Canterbury in March 1533.
78. **paper:** i.e. wrapper. **Presently:** at once.

Was in his countenance. You he bade
Attend him here this morning.
  Wol.   Is he ready
To come abroad?
  Crom.   I think by this he is.
  Wol. Leave me a while.   *Exit Cromwell.*
[*Aside.*] It shall be to the Duchess of Alanson,   85
The French king's sister; he shall marry her.
Anne Bullen? No; I'll no Anne Bullens for him,
There's more in't than fair visage. Bullen?
No, we'll no Bullens. Speedily I wish
To hear from Rome. The Marchioness of Pembroke?
  Nor. He's discontented.
  Suf.   May be he hears the King   91
Does whet his anger to him.
  Sur.   Sharp enough,
Lord, for thy justice!
  Wol. [*Aside.*] The late Queen's gentlewoman? a
    knight's daughter,
To be her mistress' mistress? the Queen's queen?   95
This candle burns not clear, 'tis I must snuff it,
Then out it goes. What though I know her virtuous
And well deserving? yet I know her for
A spleeny Lutheran, and not wholesome to
Our cause, that she should lie i' th' bosom of   100
Our hard-rul'd king. Again, there is sprung up
An heretic, an arch-one, Cranmer; one
Hath crawl'd into the favor of the King,
And is his oracle.
  Nor.   He's vex'd at something.

     Enter KING, *reading of a schedule*, [*and* LOVELL].

  Sur. I would 'twere something that would fret the
    string,   105
The master-cord on 's heart!
  Suf.   The King, the King!
  King. What piles of wealth hath he accumulated
To his own portion! and what expense by th' hour
Seems to flow from him! How, i' th' name of thrift,
Does he rake this together? Now, my lords,   110
Saw you the Cardinal?
  Nor.   My lord, we have
Stood here observing him. Some strange commotion
Is in his brain; he bites his lip, and starts,
Stops on a sudden, looks upon the ground,
Then lays his finger on his temple; straight   115
Springs out into fast gait, then stops again,
Strikes his breast hard, and anon he casts
His eye against the moon. In most strange postures
We have seen him set himself.
  King.   It may well be,
There is a mutiny in 's mind. This morning   120
Papers of state he sent me to peruse,
As I requir'd; and wot you what I found

---

83. **this:** now.
85–86. **It . . . her.** An anachronism; this scheme of Wolsey's is assigned by Holinshed (see note to II.ii.24–28) to 1527, shortly before Margaret, Duchess of Alençon, married King Henry of Navarre.
90. **Marchioness of Pembroke.** See II.iii.63.
94. **late:** recent, former. 99. **spleeny:** ardent.
101. **hard-rul'd:** i.e. difficult to guide. 103. **Hath:** who has.
104 s.d. **schedule:** scroll of paper. 105. **fret:** gnaw through.
106. **on 's:** of his. 115. **straight:** at once.
122. **wot:** know.

Henry VIII
III.ii

There (on my conscience, put unwittingly)?
Forsooth, an inventory, thus importing
The several parcels of his plate, his treasure,   125
Rich stuffs, and ornaments of household, which
I find at such proud rate, that it outspeaks
Possession of a subject.

    Nor.   It's heaven's will!
Some spirit put this paper in the packet,
To bless your eye withal.

    King.   If we did think   130
His contemplation were above the earth,
And fix'd on spiritual object, he should still
Dwell in his musings, but I am afraid
His thinkings are below the moon, not worth
His serious considering.

            King takes his seat; whispers Lovell,
               who goes to the Cardinal.

    Wol.   Heaven forgive me!   135
Ever God bless your Highness!

    King.   Good my lord,
You are full of heavenly stuff, and bear the inventory
Of your best graces in your mind; the which
You were now running o'er. You have scarce time
To steal from spiritual leisure a brief span   140
To keep your earthly audit; sure in that
I deem you an ill husband, and am [glad]
To have you therein my companion.

    Wol.   Sir,
For holy offices I have a time; a time
To think upon the part of business which   145
I bear i' th' state; and Nature does require
Her times of preservation, which perforce
I, her frail son, amongst my brethren mortal,
Must give my tendance to.

    King.   You have said well.

    Wol. And ever may your Highness yoke to-
        gether   150
(As I will lend you cause) my doing well
With my well saying!

    King.   'Tis well said again,
And 'tis a kind of good deed to say well,
And yet words are no deeds. My father lov'd you,
He said he did, and with his deed did crown   155
His word upon you. Since I had my office,
I have kept you next my heart, have not alone
Employ'd you where high profits might come home,
But par'd my present havings, to bestow   159
My bounties upon you.

    Wol.   [*Aside.*] What should this mean?

    Sur. [*Aside.*] The Lord increase this business!

    King.   Have I not made you
The prime man of the state? I pray you tell me,
If what I now pronounce you have found true;
And if you may confess it, say withal

If you are bound to us, or no. What say you?   165

    Wol. My sovereign, I confess your royal graces
Show'r'd on me daily have been more than could
My studied purposes requite, which went
Beyond all man's endeavors. My endeavors
Have ever come too short of my desires,   170
Yet fill'd with my abilities. Mine own ends
Have been mine so, that evermore they pointed
To th' good of your most sacred person and
The profit of the state. For your great graces
Heap'd upon me, poor undeserver, I   175
Can nothing render but allegiant thanks,
My pray'rs to heaven for you, my loyalty,
Which ever has and ever shall be growing,
Till death, that winter, kill it.

    King.   Fairly answer'd.
A loyal and obedient subject is   180
Therein illustrated; the honor of it
Does pay the act of it, as i' th' contrary
The foulness is the punishment. I presume
That, as my hand has open'd bounty to you,   184
My heart dropp'd love, my pow'r rain'd honor, more
On you than any, so your hand and heart,
Your brain, and every function of your power,
Should, notwithstanding that your bond of duty,
As 'twere in love's particular, be more
To me, your friend, than any.

    Wol.   I do profess   190
That for your Highness' good I ever labor'd
More than mine own; that am, have, and will be
(Though all the world should crack their duty to you
And throw it from their soul, though perils did
Abound, as thick as thought could make 'em, and   195
Appear in forms more horrid), yet my duty,
As doth a rock against the chiding flood,
Should the approach of this wild river break,
And stand unshaken yours.

    King.   'Tis nobly spoken.
Take notice, lords, he has a loyal breast,   200
For you have seen him open't. Read o'er this,
                  [*Giving him papers.*]
And after, this, and then to breakfast with
What appetite you have.

       Exit King, frowning upon the Cardinal; the Nobles
         throng after him, smiling and whispering.

    Wol.   What should this mean?
What sudden anger's this? How have I reap'd it?
He parted frowning from me, as if ruin   205
Leap'd from his eyes. So looks the chafed lion
Upon the daring huntsman that has gall'd him;
Then makes him nothing. I must read this paper;
I fear, the story of his anger. 'Tis so!

---

124. **importing:** signifying.
125. **several parcels:** various items.   126. **stuffs:** fabrics.
127. **proud:** high.   **outspeaks:** exceeds (?).
134. **below the moon:** i.e. worldly.
140. **spiritual leisure:** i.e. religious concerns.
142. **ill husband:** bad manager.   149. **tendance:** attention.
154–56. **My . . . you.** In 1507 Henry VII had appointed young Wolsey
his chaplain and two years later named him Dean of Lincoln.
155. **crown:** complete.   159. **havings:** possessions.
162. **prime:** first.

166. **graces:** favors.
171. **fill'd with:** filled out to the capacity of. Most editors emend to
fil'd with = kept pace with.
172. **so:** to this extent.   176. **allegiant:** loyal.
181. **it:** i.e. being loyal to one's sovereign.   182. **pay:** repay.
183. **foulness:** i.e. the moral taint of disloyalty.
188. **that . . . duty:** i.e. your priestly vows.
189. **in love's particular:** in the special case of a person you loved.
192. **have:** have been.   193. **crack:** violate.
198. **break:** stem, check.   206. **chafed:** infuriated.
207. **gall'd:** wounded.

This paper has undone me. 'Tis th' accompt   210
Of all that world of wealth I have drawn together
For mine own ends (indeed to gain the popedom
And fee my friends in Rome). O negligence!
Fit for a fool to fall by. What cross devil
Made me put this main secret in the packet   215
I sent the King? Is there no way to cure this?
No new device to beat this from his brains?
I know 'twill stir him strongly; yet I know
A way, if it take right, in spite of fortune
Will bring me off again. What's this? "To th' Pope"?
The letter, as I live, with all the business   221
I writ to 's Holiness. Nay then, farewell!
I have touch'd the highest point of all my greatness,
And, from that full meridian of my glory,
I haste now to my setting. I shall fall   225
Like a bright exhalation in the evening,
And no man see me more.

Enter to Wolsey the DUKES OF NORFOLK *and* SUFFOLK,
the EARL OF SURREY, *and the* LORD CHAMBERLAIN.

Nor. Hear the King's pleasure, Cardinal, who
    commands you
To render up the great seal presently
Into our hands, and to confine yourself   230
To Asher-house, my Lord of Winchester's,
Till you hear further from his Highness.
    Wol.   Stay!
Where's your commission, lords? Words cannot carry
Authority so weighty.
    Suf.   Who dare cross 'em,   234
Bearing the King's will from his mouth expressly?
    Wol. Till I find more than will or words to do it
(I mean your malice), know, officious lords,
I dare and must deny it. Now I feel
Of what coarse metal ye are moulded, envy,
How eagerly ye follow my disgraces   240
As if it fed ye, and how sleek and wanton
Ye appear in every thing may bring my ruin!
Follow your envious courses, men of malice!

210–13. **'Tis . . . Rome.** One of the charges brought against Wolsey, says Holinshed (Bullough, IV, 474), was "that he had sent innumerable substance to Rome, for the obteining of his dignities, to the great impoverishment of the realme."   210. **accompt:** account.
213. **fee:** pay, bribe.   214. **cross:** perverse.
215. **main:** extremely important.   219. **take right:** succeed.
224. **meridian:** highest point.   226. **exhalation:** meteor.
228–50. **Hear . . . it.** This altercation between Wolsey and the nobles closely follows Holinshed (Bullough, IV, 473): "the seventeenth of November the king sent the two dukes of Norffolke and Suffolke to the cardinals place at Westminster, who went as they were commanded, and finding the cardinall there, they declared that the kings pleasure was that he should surrender up the great seale into their hands, and to depart simplie unto Asher, which was an house situat nigh unto Hampton court, belonging to the bishoprike of Winchester. The cardinall demanded of them their commission that gave them such authoritie, who answered againe, that they were sufficient commissioners, and had authoritie to doo no lesse by the kings mouth. Notwithstanding, he would in no wise agree in that behalfe, without further knowledge of their authoritie, saieng; that the great seale was delivered him by the kings person, to injoy the ministration thereof, with the roome of the chancellor for the terme of his life, whereof for his suertie he had the kings letters patents."
229. **presently:** at once.
231. **Asher-house:** Esher, the Bishop of Winchester's residence near Hampton Court. At the time of his fall Wolsey himself—the most insatiable pluralist of the age—was Bishop of Winchester.
233. **commission:** warrant.   234. **cross:** resist.
236. **do it:** i.e. carry authority.   241. **wanton:** loose, impetuous.

You have Christian warrant for 'em, and no doubt
In time will find their fit rewards. That seal   245
You ask with such a violence, the King
(Mine and your master) with his own hand gave me;
Bade me enjoy it, with the place and honors,
During my life; and, to confirm his goodness,
Tied it by letters-patents. Now, who'll take it?   250
    Sur. The King, that gave it.
    Wol.   It must be himself then.
    Sur. Thou art a proud traitor, priest.
    Wol.   Proud lord, thou liest!
Within these forty hours Surrey durst better
Have burnt that tongue than said so.
    Sur.   Thy ambition,
Thou scarlet sin, robb'd this bewailing land   255
Of noble Buckingham, my father-in-law;
The heads of all thy brother cardinals
(With thee and all thy best parts bound together)
Weigh'd not a hair of his. Plague of your policy!
You sent me deputy for Ireland,   260
Far from his succor, from the King, from all
That might have mercy on the fault thou gav'st him;
Whilst your great goodness, out of holy pity,
Absolv'd him with an axe.
    Wol.   This, and all else
This talking lord can lay upon my credit,   265
I answer is most false. The Duke by law
Found his deserts. How innocent I was
From any private malice in his end,
His noble jury and foul cause can witness.
If I lov'd many words, lord, I should tell you   270
You have as little honesty as honor,
That in the way of loyalty and truth
Toward the King, my ever royal master,
Dare mate a sounder man than Surrey can be,
And all that love his follies.
    Sur.   By my soul,   275
Your long coat, priest, protects you, thou shouldst feel
My sword i' th' life-blood of thee else. My lords,
Can ye endure to hear this arrogance?
And from this fellow? If we live thus tamely,
To be thus jaded by a piece of scarlet,   280
Farewell nobility! Let his Grace go forward,
And dare us with his cap, like larks.
    Wol.   All goodness
Is poison to thy stomach.
    Sur.   Yes, that goodness
Of gleaning all the land's wealth into one,
Into your own hands, Card'nal, by extortion;   285
The goodness of your intercepted packets
You writ to th' Pope against the King. Your goodness,
Since you provoke me, shall be most notorious.
My Lord of Norfolk, as you are truly noble,
As you respect the common good, the state   290

---

244. **Christian warrant:** i.e. an example in the behavior of other (bad) Christians.
250. **letters-patents:** documents openly conferring a right or power.
258. **parts:** qualities.   259. **Weigh'd:** i.e. were worth.
262. **fault . . . him:** offense you charged him with.
265. **lay . . . credit:** i.e. blame me for.   272. **in the way:** as regards.
274. **mate:** match.   280. **jaded:** ridden.
282. **dare . . . larks:** daze us with his cardinal's hat, as larks are netted with the help of a piece of red cloth.

Henry VIII
III.ii

Of our despis'd nobility, our issues
(Whom, if he live, will scarce be gentlemen),
Produce the grand sum of his sins, the articles
Collected from his life. I'll startle you
Worse than the sacring bell, when the brown wench
Lay kissing in your arms, Lord Cardinal.   296
    Wol. How much, methinks, I could despise this man,
But that I am bound in charity against it!
    Nor. Those articles, my lord, are in the King's hand:
But thus much, they are foul ones.
    Wol.   So much fairer
And spotless shall mine innocence arise   301
When the King knows my truth.
    Sur.   This cannot save you.
I thank my memory, I yet remember
Some of these articles, and out they shall.
Now, if you can blush, and cry "Guilty," Cardinal,
You'll show a little honesty.
    Wol.   Speak on, sir,   306
I dare your worst objections. If I blush,
It is to see a nobleman want manners.
    Sur. I had rather want those than my head. Have at you!
First, that without the King's assent or knowledge, 310
You wrought to be a legate, by which power
You maim'd the jurisdiction of all bishops.
    Nor. Then, that in all you writ to Rome, or else
To foreign princes, *"Ego et Rex meus"*   314
Was still inscrib'd; in which you brought the King
To be your servant.
    Suf.   Then, that without the knowledge
Either of King or Council, when you went
Ambassador to the Emperor, you made bold
To carry into Flanders the great seal.
    Sur. *Item*, you sent a large commission   320
To Gregory de Cassado, to conclude,
Without the King's will or the state's allowance,
A league between his Highness and Ferrara.
    Suf. That out of mere ambition, you have caus'd
Your holy hat to be stamp'd on the King's coin.   325
    Sur. Then, that you have sent innumerable substance
(By what means got, I leave to your own conscience)
To furnish Rome, and to prepare the ways
You have for dignities, to the mere undoing
Of all the kingdom. Many more there are,   330
Which since they are of you, and odious,

I will not taint my mouth with.
    Cham.   O my lord,
Press not a falling man too far! 'tis virtue.
His faults lie open to the laws, let them,   334
Not you, correct him. My heart weeps to see him
So little of his great self.
    Sur.   I forgive him.
    Suf. Lord Cardinal, the King's further pleasure is—
Because all those things you have done of late
By your power legative within this kingdom
Fall into th' compass of a *praemunire*—   340
That therefore such a writ be sued against you,
To forfeit all your goods, lands, tenements,
[Chattels], and whatsoever, and to be
Out of the King's protection. This is my charge.
    Nor. And so we'll leave you to your meditations
How to live better. For your stubborn answer   346
About the giving back the great seal to us,
The King shall know it, and, no doubt, shall thank you.
So fare you well, my little good Lord Cardinal.
                                   Exeunt all but Wolsey.
    Wol. So farewell—to the little good you bear me.
Farewell? a long farewell to all my greatness!   351
This is the state of man: to-day he puts forth
The tender leaves of hopes, to-morrow blossoms,
And bears his blushing honors thick upon him;
The third day comes a frost, a killing frost,   355
And when he thinks, good easy man, full surely
His greatness is a-ripening, nips his root,
And then he falls as I do. I have ventur'd,
Like little wanton boys that swim on bladders,
This many summers in a sea of glory,   360
But far beyond my depth. My high-blown pride
At length broke under me, and now has left me,
Weary and old with service, to the mercy
Of a rude stream that must for ever hide me.
Vain pomp and glory of this world, I hate ye!   365
I feel my heart new open'd. O how wretched
Is that poor man that hangs on princes' favors!
There is, betwixt that smile we would aspire to,
That sweet aspect of princes, and their ruin,
More pangs and fears than wars or women have;   370
And when he falls, he falls like Lucifer,
Never to hope again.

                Enter CROMWELL, *standing amazed.*

                              Why, how now, Cromwell?
    Crom. I have no power to speak, sir.
    Wol.   What, amaz'd
At my misfortunes? Can thy spirit wonder   374
A great man should decline? Nay, and you weep
I am fall'n indeed.
    Crom.   How does your Grace?
    Wol.   Why, well;

---

291. **issues:** sons.   293. **articles:** list of charges.
295. **sacring bell:** bell rung at the most solemn moment of the Mass.
299. **hand:** i.e. possession.
300. **thus much:** i.e. this much I can say.
302. **truth:** loyalty.   304. **shall:** i.e. shall come.
307. **objections:** accusations.   308. **want:** lack.
310-32. **First . . . with.** These seven charges against Wolsey are drawn from a list of nine that Holinshed records (Bullough, IV, 474).
311. **wrought:** worked.   **legate:** papal representative.
314. **Ego et Rex meus:** my king and I.
315. **still inscrib'd:** i.e. always prominently displayed.
320. **Item:** further, also.   **large:** having full power to act.
322. **allowance:** assent.   324. **mere:** pure.
325. **holy hat:** i.e. cardinal's hat.
326. **innumerable substance:** measureless wealth. See note to lines 210-13.   329. **mere:** utter.

339. **legative:** pertaining to a legate.
340. **Fall . . . praemunire:** constitute violations of the statute of *praemunire* (which made it illegal to submit to a foreign court—for example, the Roman *curia*—matters pertaining to the king's court).
341. **sued:** issued.   354. **blushing:** glowing.
356. **easy:** easygoing.   359. **wanton:** playful.
364. **rude:** rough.   368. **aspire:** rise.
369. **their ruin:** i.e. the ruin they cause.
372 s.d. **amazed:** astounded.   375. **and:** if.